THE JOHNS HOPKINS
HANDBOOK OF DRUGS

THE JOHNS HOPKINS HANDBOOK OF DRUGS

*For the 100 Major
Medical Disorders of People
Over the Age of 50*

With a Special Expanded
Table of Contents
Organized By Disorder

Medical Editor
Simeon Margolis, M.D., Ph.D.

Prepared by the Editors of
The Johns Hopkins Medical Letter
HEALTH AFTER 50

REBUS • NEW YORK
DISTRIBUTED BY RANDOM HOUSE

THE JOHNS HOPKINS MEDICAL LETTER
HEALTH AFTER 50

THE JOHNS HOPKINS HANDBOOK OF DRUGS *is the companion volume to* THE JOHNS HOPKINS MEDICAL HANDBOOK, *both indispensable home medical reference books from America's leading medical center.*

THE JOHNS HOPKINS MEDICAL LETTER HEALTH AFTER 50, *our monthly, eight-page newsletter, provides the same kind of timely information for everyone concerned with taking control of his or her own health and medical care, using clear, nontechnical language that is easy to understand. And, it comes from the century-old tradition of Johns Hopkins excellence. For information on how to order this unique newsletter, write to Medletter Associates, Inc., Department 1106, 632 Broadway, New York, New York 10012.*

For information about permission to reproduce selections from this book, write to Permissions, Medletter Associates, Inc., 632 Broadway, New York, New York 10012.

Library of Congress Cataloging-in-Publication Data

The Johns Hopkins handbook of drugs: specially edited & organized by disease for people over 50 / medical editor, Simeon Margolis; prepared by the editors of the Johns Hopkins Medical Letter Health after 50.
p. cm. "With full explanations of proper use, drug interactions, side effects, alternative choices; from the complete, up-to-date computer database of the U.S. Pharmacopeia."
Includes index.
ISBN 0-929661-07-9
1. Geriatric pharmacology—Handbooks, manuals, etc.   I. Margolis, Simeon, 1931- . II. Johns Hopkins medical letter health after 50.
RC953.7.J64   1993
615.5'8'0846—dc20   93-7465
                    CIP

Printed in the United States of America
10 9 8 7 6 5 4 3 2
Distributed by Random House, Inc.

The Johns Hopkins Handbook of Drugs

CHARLES L. MEE, JR.
Editorial Director

EVAN HANSEN
Executive Editor

RODNEY FRIEDMAN
Editor and Publisher

BARBARA MAXWELL O'NEILL
Associate Publisher

Johns Hopkins Medical Books
are published under the auspices of
The Johns Hopkins Medical Letter
HEALTH AFTER 50.

RODNEY FRIEDMAN
Editor and Publisher

CHARLES L. MEE, JR.
Editorial Director

MARY CROWLEY
Executive Editor

BETTE PONACK ALBERT, M.D.
Medical Editor

ERIN MICHAEL KELLY
Managing Editor

PATRICE BENNEWARD
Senior Writer

TOM R. DAMRAUER
JANE MARGARETTEN, R.N.
Medical Researchers

BARBARA MAXWELL O'NEILL
Associate Publisher

PREFACE

As we age, our bodies react differently—often with increasing sensitivity—to the medications we take, leaving us more prone to adverse side effects. Furthermore, as we age, we're likely to be taking substantially more medication than ever before. Consider the following:

• Between the ages of 55 and 64, we are given an average of eight separate prescriptions per year.

• People over the age of 65, while comprising only 12% of the population, consume more than 30% of all prescription drugs and 40% of all over-the-counter drugs.

• On any given day, those over the age of 70 take an average of 6.5 medications (including nonprescription drugs).

Since older people are more sensitive to the drugs they take, and are also likely to be taking several drugs at once, the need for a book like this one is abundantly clear. *The Johns Hopkins Handbook of Drugs* provides detailed information (taken from the very source established for doctors and other health care professionals) on the drugs used to treat the more than 100 major medical disorders of people over 50 (discussed at length in this book's companion volume, *The Johns Hopkins Medical Handbook*).

The Handbook of Drugs was specially edited to emphasize the information most important to older people. It can answer crucial questions you may have about the medications you take—such as whether or not to take a drug with meals, what to do if you miss a dose, how your drugs may interact with one another, or if it's safe to drink alcohol while using a certain medication.

How to Use This Book

On the following pages, you will find an expanded table of contents that lists, by chapter, the major medical disorders of people over 50. Beneath each disorder is a list of the drugs (by generic names only) used to treat it, and the page number where information about that drug can be found. This table of contents allows you to see not only the information about the drug you take for a given disorder, but it shows you the alternative drugs used for the same condition. (Note: Drugs administered exclusively in a hospital setting—such as powerful chemotherapy agents used to treat cancer—have been omitted from this volume.)

Perhaps the easiest way to find information about a specific drug is to look it up in the index (page 1083). Here, drugs are listed by both their generic names (or standard chemical names) as well as their more-familiar brand names (the names used by the various pharmaceutical companies that commercially distribute the drugs).

Naturally, the information presented within these pages is not meant to substitute for the advice and expertise of a physician. But since the material in this handbook comes from the very same computer database designed for doctors, we believe that it can foster more meaningful conversations with your physicians or other health care professionals. In this way, we intend *The Johns Hopkins Handbook of Drugs* to serve as yet another useful aid by which you can gain greater personal control over your own health and medical care.

About the USPC

The information in *The Johns Hopkins Handbook of Drugs* was compiled by the United States Pharmacopeial Convention, Inc. (USPC). This organization was established over 170 years ago to set the official standards of strength, quality, purity, packaging, and labeling for medical products used in the United States. USPC is in an independent, not-for-profit corporation consisting of representatives from accredited colleges of medicine and pharmacy, national medical organizations (such as the American Medical Association, American Dental Association, American Nurses Association, and the American Pharmaceutical Association), as well as various departments of the federal government, including the Food and Drug Administration. In addition, four members have been appointed to the USPC specifically to represent the public. The pharmacopeia produced by USPC is the world's oldest regularly revised document of its kind. It is updated each year by the Committee of Revision—a panel of 114 experts elected by USPC, consisting of physicians, pharmacists, dentists, nurses, chemists, microbiologists, and others who are especially qualified to evaluate the drugs available in this country. The committee members serve without pay and are assisted by numerous advisory panels, other outside reviewers, and USPC staff.

—*The Editors*

EXPANDED TABLE OF CONTENTS

Organized by Disorder

This special section is designed to help guide you to information about the drugs that appear in this book as they are classified for use to treat specific disorders. Beneath each major category (for example, the Heart and Blood Vessels), you will find the various disorders (such as hypertension) that belong to that category, followed by a list of the drugs used to treat that disorder, and the page number where information on each drug can be found. (If you want to find information about a particular drug directly, without consulting this section, look up the drug in the general index in the back of the book). In this section, you will find where to turn for entries about the various drugs used for ailments involving the following major categories:

CANCER

THE BLOOD

THE BRAIN AND NERVOUS SYSTEM

HEADACHE, VASCULAR (PROPHYLAXIS)

HEADACHE, VASCULAR (TREATMENT)

THE DIGESTIVE SYSTEM

BOWEL DISEASE, INFLAMMATORY (TREATMENT)

BOWEL SYNDROME, IRRITABLE (TREATMENT)

BOWEL SYNDROME, IRRITABLE (TREATMENT ADJUNCT)

DIARRHEA (TREATMENT)

DIGESTIVE DISORDERS (TREATMENT)

GALLSTONE DISEASE (TREATMENT)

HEPATITIS, CHRONIC, ACTIVE (TREATMENT)

HYPERACIDITY (TREATMENT)

ULCER, DUODENAL (TREATMENT)

ULCER, DUODENAL, HELICOBACTER PYLORI-ASSOCIATED (TREATMENT ADJUNCT)

ULCER, PEPTIC (TREATMENT ADJUNCT)

THE EARS, NOSE, AND THROAT

ALLERGIC DISORDERS, NASAL (TREATMENT)

COLD SYMPTOMS (TREATMENT)—SEE ALSO CONGESTION, NASAL; COUGH (LUNGS AND RESPIRATORY SYSTEM)

CONGESTION, NASAL (TREATMENT)

CONGESTION, SINUS (TREATMENT)

PHARYNGITIS, BACTERIAL (TREATMENT)

RHINITIS, PERENNIAL ALLERGIC (TREATMENT)

RHINITIS, SEASONAL (PROPHYLAXIS)

RHINITIS, SEASONAL (TREATMENT)

RHINITIS, SEASONAL ALLERGIC (PROPHYLAXIS)

RHINITIS, SEASONAL ALLERGIC (TREATMENT)

RHINITIS, VASOMOTOR (PROPHYLAXIS)

RHINITIS, VASOMOTOR (TREATMENT)

RHINORRHEA (TREATMENT)

SINUSITIS (TREATMENT)

THE ENDOCRINE SYSTEM

THE EYES

THE HEART AND BLOOD VESSELS

ANGINA PECTORIS, ACUTE (TREATMENT)

ANGINA PECTORIS, CHRONIC (TREATMENT)

ARRHYTHMIAS, CARDIAC (PROPHYLAXIS)

ARRHYTHMIAS, CARDIAC (TREATMENT)

CONGESTIVE HEART FAILURE (TREATMENT)—SEE ALSO RELATED INDICATIONS, E.G., EDEMA

EDEMA (TREATMENT)

FIBRILLATION, ATRIAL (PROPHYLAXIS)

FIBRILLATION, ATRIAL (TREATMENT)

HYPERTENSION (TREATMENT)

Myocardial reinfarction (prophylaxis)

Tachycardia, atrial, paroxysmal (prophylaxis)

THE KIDNEYS AND URINARY TRACT

GENITOURINARY TRACT INFECTIONS (TREATMENT)—SEE ALSO PELVIC INFECTIONS, FEMALE (HEALTH PROBLEMS OF WOMEN)

GLOMERULONEPHRITIS (TREATMENT)

GONORRHEA (TREATMENT)

RENAL CALCULI, CYSTINE (TREATMENT)

RENAL CALCULI, CYSTINE, RECURRENCE (PROPHYLAXIS)

RENAL CALCULI, PHOSPHATE (PROPHYLAXIS)

RENAL CALCULI, STRUVITE (PROPHYLAXIS)

RENAL CALCULI, URIC ACID (PROPHYLAXIS)

RENAL CALCULI, URIC ACID (TREATMENT)

URINARY TRACT INFECTIONS, BACTERIAL (PROPHYLAXIS)

URINARY TRACT INFECTIONS, BACTERIAL (TREATMENT)

URINARY TRACT INFECTIONS, BACTERIAL (TREATMENT ADJUNCT)— SEE ALSO IRRITATIVE VOIDING, SYMPTOMS OF

URINARY TRACT INFECTIONS, FUNGAL (TREATMENT)

THE LUNGS AND RESPIRATORY SYSTEM

ASTHMA, BRONCHIAL (TREATMENT ADJUNCT)

ASTHMA, BRONCHIAL, CHRONIC (TREATMENT)

BRONCHITIS (TREATMENT)

BRONCHITIS (TREATMENT ADJUNCT)

COUGH (TREATMENT)—SEE ALSO CONGESTION, NASAL (EARS, NOSE, AND THROAT)

INFLUENZA A (TREATMENT)

PNEUMONIA, ANAEROBIC (TREATMENT)

PNEUMONIA, ASPIRATION (TREATMENT)

PNEUMONIA, BACTERIAL (TREATMENT)

THE MUSCLES AND BONES

CALCIUM DEFICIENCY (PROPHYLAXIS)

OSTEOARTHRITIS (TREATMENT)—SEE PAIN (TREATMENT)

OSTEOPOROSIS, POSTMENOPAUSAL (PROPHYLAXIS)

OSTEOPOROSIS, POSTMENOPAUSAL (TREATMENT ADJUNCT)

PAIN (TREATMENT)

THE SKIN

DERMATITIS, SEBORRHEIC (TREATMENT)

DERMATITIS, SEBORRHEIC, OF SCALP (TREATMENT)

OILY SKIN (TREATMENT)

HEALTH PROBLEMS OF MEN

BENIGN PROSTATIC HYPERPLASIA (TREATMENT)

IMPOTENCE (TREATMENT)

IMPOTENCE (TREATMENT ADJUNCT)

HEALTH PROBLEMS OF WOMEN

VAGINITIS, ATROPHIC (TREATMENT)

MENTAL HEALTH

ANXIETY (TREATMENT)

DEPRESSION, MENTAL (TREATMENT)

INSOMNIA (TREATMENT)

PANIC DISORDER (TREATMENT)

PSYCHOTIC DISORDERS (TREATMENT)

ACETAMINOPHEN   Systemic

INN: Paracetamol

Some commonly used *brand names* are:

In the U.S.—

Aceta Elixir
Aceta Tablets
Acetaminophen Uniserts
Actamin
Actamin Extra
Actamin Super‡
Aminofen
Aminofen Max
Anacin-3 Children's Elixir
Anacin-3 Children's Tablets
Anacin-3, Infants'
Anacin-3 Maximum Strength Caplets
Anacin-3 Maximum Strength Tablets
Anacin-3 Regular Strength Tablets
Apacet Capsules
Apacet Elixir
Apacet Extra Strength Caplets
Apacet Extra Strength Tablets
Apacet, Infants'
Apacet Regular Strength Tablets
Arthritis Pain Formula Aspirin Free
Aspirin-Free Excedrin Caplets‡
Banesin
Dapa
Dapa X-S
Datril Extra-Strength
Dolanex
Dorcol Children's Fever and Pain Reducer
Feverall, Children's
Feverall Junior Strength
Feverall Sprinkle Caps, Children's
Feverall Sprinkle Caps Junior Strength
Genapap Children's Elixir
Genapap Children's Tablets
Genapap Extra Strength Caplets
Genapap Extra Strength Tablets
Genapap, Infants'
Genapap Regular Strength Tablets
Genebs Extra Strength Caplets
Genebs Regular Strength Tablets
Genebs X-Tra
Halenol Elixir
Halenol Extra Strength Caplets
Halenol Extra Strength Tablets

Halenol Regular Strength Tablets
Liquiprin Children's Elixir
Liquiprin Infants' Drops
Meda-Cap
Myapap Elixir
Myapap, Infants'
Neopap
Oraphen-PD
Panadol, Children's
Panadol, Infants'
Panadol Junior Strength Caplets
Panadol Maximum Strength Caplets
Panadol Maximum Strength Tablets
Panex
Panex-500
Phenaphen Caplets
Redutemp
Ridenol Caplets
Snaplets-FR
St. Joseph Aspirin-Free Fever Reducer for Children
Summit‡
Suppap-120
Suppap-325
Suppap-650
Tapanol Extra Strength Caplets
Tapanol Extra Strength Tablets
Tempra
Tempra D.S.
Tempra, Infants'
Tempra Syrup
Tenol
Tylenol Children's Elixir
Tylenol Children's Tablets
Tylenol Extra-Strength Adult Liquid Pain Reliever
Tylenol Extra Strength Caplets
Tylenol Extra Strength Gelcaps
Tylenol Extra Strength Tablets
Tylenol, Infants'
Tylenol Junior Strength Caplets
Tylenol Junior Strength Tablets
Tylenol Regular Strength Caplets
Tylenol Regular Strength Tablets
Ty-Pap
Ty-Pap, Infants'
Ty-Pap Syrup

Ty-Tab Caplets
Ty-Tab Capsules
Ty-Tab, Children's
Ty-Tab Tablets

Valadol Liquid
Valadol Tablets
Valorin
Valorin Extra

In Canada—

Abenol
Anacin-3
Anacin-3 Extra Strength
Apo-Acetaminophen
Atasol Caplets
Atasol Drops
Atasol Elixir
Atasol Forte Caplets
Atasol Forte Tablets
Atasol Tablets
Excedrin Caplets‡
Excedrin Extra Strength Caplets‡
Exdol
Exdol Strong
Panadol

Panadol Extra Strength
Robigesic
Rounox
Tempra Caplets
Tempra Chewable Tablets
Tempra Drops
Tempra Syrup
Tylenol Caplets
Tylenol Chewable Tablets
Tylenol Drops
Tylenol Elixir
Tylenol Gelcaps
Tylenol Junior Strength Caplets
Tylenol Tablets

Other commonly used names are APAP and paracetamol.

ORAL

Acetaminophen Capsules USP
   In the U.S.—*Apacet Capsules; Dapa X-S; Meda-Cap; Ty-Tab Capsules;* GENERIC
   In Canada—*Anacin-3; Anacin-3 Extra-Strength; Panadol; Panadol Extra Strength*
Acetaminophen Oral Granules†
   In the U.S.—*Snaplets-FR*
Acetaminophen Oral Powders†
   In the U.S.—*Feverall Sprinkle Caps, Children's; Feverall Sprinkle Caps Junior Strength*
Acetaminophen Oral Solution USP
   In the U.S.—*Aceta Elixir; Anacin-3 Children's Elixir; Anacin-3, Infants'; Apacet Elixir; Apacet, Infants'; Dolanex; Dorcol Children's Fever and Pain Reducer; Genapap Children's Elixir; Genapap, Infants'; Halenol Elixir; Liquiprin Children's Elixir; Myapap Elixir; Myapap, Infants'; Oraphen-PD; Panadol, Children's; Panadol, Infants'; St. Joseph Aspirin-Free Fever Reducer for Children; Tempra, Infants'; Tempra Syrup; Tenol; Tylenol Children's Elixir; Tylenol Extra-Strength Adult Liquid Pain Reliever; Tylenol, Infants'; Ty-Pap, Infants'; Ty-Pap Syrup; Valadol Liquid;* GENERIC
   In Canada—*Atasol Drops; Atasol Elixir; Panadol; Robigesic; Tempra Drops; Tempra Syrup; Tylenol Drops; Tylenol Elixir;* GENERIC
Acetaminophen Oral Suspension USP
   In the U.S.—*Liquiprin Infants' Drops*
Acetaminophen Tablets USP
   In the U.S.—*Aceta Tablets; Actamin; Actamin Extra; Aminofen; Aminofen Max; Anacin-3 Maximum Strength Caplets; Anacin-3 Maximum Strength Tablets; Anacin-3 Regular Strength Tablets; Apacet Extra Strength Caplets; Apacet Extra Strength Tablets; Apacet Regular Strength Tablets; Arthritis Pain Formula Aspirin Free; Banesin; Dapa; Datril Extra-Strength; Genapap Extra Strength Caplets; Genapap Extra Strength Tablets; Genapap Regular Strength Tablets; Genebs Extra Strength Caplets; Genebs Regular Strength Tablets; Genebs X-Tra; Halenol Extra Strength Caplets; Halenol Extra Strength Tablets; Halenol Regular Strength Tablets; Panadol Junior Strength Caplets; Panadol Maximum Strength Caplets; Panadol Maximum Strength Tablets; Panex; Panex-500; Phenaphen Caplets; Redutemp; Ridenol Caplets; Tapanol Extra Strength Caplets;*

Tapanol Extra Strength Tablets; Tenol; Tylenol Extra Strength Caplets; Tylenol Extra Strength Gelcaps; Tylenol Extra Strength Tablets; Tylenol Junior Strength Caplets; Tylenol Regular Strength Caplets; Tylenol Regular Strength Tablets; Ty-Tab Caplets; Ty-Tab Tablets; Valadol Tablets; Valorin; Valorin Extra; GENERIC

In Canada—*Anacin-3; Anacin-3 Extra Strength; Apo-Acetaminophen; Atasol Caplets; Atasol Forte Caplets; Atasol Forte Tablets; Atasol Tablets; Exdol; Exdol Strong; Panadol; Panadol Extra Strength; Robigesic; Rounox; Tempra Caplets; Tylenol Caplets; Tylenol Gelcaps; Tylenol Junior Strength Caplets; Tylenol Tablets;* GENERIC

Acetaminophen Tablets USP (Chewable)

In the U.S.—*Anacin-3 Children's Tablets; Genapap Children's Tablets; Panadol, Children's; St. Joseph Aspirin-Free Fever Reducer for Children; Tempra; Tempra D.S.; Tylenol Children's Tablets; Tylenol Junior Strength Tablets; Ty-Tab, Children's;* GENERIC

In Canada—*Panadol; Tempra Chewable Tablets; Tylenol Chewable Tablets;* GENERIC

Acetaminophen and Caffeine Capsules USP

In the U.S.—*Summit*

Acetaminophen and Caffeine Tablets USP

In the U.S.—*Actamin Super; Aspirin-Free Excedrin Caplets*

In Canada—*Excedrin Caplets; Excedrin Extra Strength Caplets*

Note: In the U.S., *Excedrin* contains aspirin, in addition to acetaminophen and caffeine. See *Acetaminophen and Salicylates (Systemic).* The U.S. product corresponding to the Canadian *Excedrin* formulation is *Aspirin-Free Excedrin.*

RECTAL

Acetaminophen Suppositories

In the U.S.—*Acetaminophen Uniserts; Feverall, Children's; Feverall Junior Strength; Neopap; Suppap-120; Suppap-325; Suppap-650; Ty-Pap;* GENERIC

In Canada—*Abenol*

---

†Not commercially available in Canada.
‡Also contains caffeine.

Category: Analgesic; antipyretic.

Indications

Accepted

Pain (treatment);

Pain, arthritic, mild (treatment); or

Fever (treatment)—Acetaminophen is indicated to relieve mild to moderate pain and reduce fever. It provides symptomatic relief only; additional therapy to treat the cause of the pain or fever should be instituted when necessary.

Acetaminophen has minimal anti-inflammatory activity and does not relieve redness, swelling, or stiffness due to arthritis; it cannot be used in place of aspirin or other salicylates or other nonsteroidal anti-inflammatory agents in the treatment of rheumatoid arthritis. However, it may be used to relieve pain due to mild osteoarthritis.

Acetaminophen may be used when aspirin therapy is contraindicated or inadvisable, i.e., in patients receiving anticoagulants or uricosuric agents, patients with hemophilia or other bleeding problems, and those with upper gastrointestinal disease or intolerance or hypersensitivity to aspirin. However, chronic, high-dose acetaminophen therapy may require adjustment of anticoagulant dosage based on increased monitoring of prothrombin time in patients receiving a coumarin- or indandione-derivative anticoagulant.

Note: The FDA has proposed that caffeine (present as an analgesic adjuvant in some products) be classified as a Category III ingredient (i.e., lacking documentation of efficacy) in OTC analgesic/antipyretic medications.

Pharmacology

Mechanism of action/Effect:

For acetaminophen

Analgesic—The mechanism of analgesic action has not been fully determined. Acetaminophen may act predominantly by inhibiting prostaglandin synthesis in the central nervous system (CNS) and, to a lesser extent, through a peripheral action by blocking pain-impulse generation. The peripheral action may also be due to inhibition of prostaglandin synthesis or to inhibition of the synthesis or actions of other substances that sensitize pain receptors to mechanical or chemical stimulation.

Antipyretic—Acetaminophen probably produces antipyresis by acting centrally on the hypothalamic heat-regulating center to produce peripheral vasodilation resulting in increased blood flow through the skin, sweating, and heat loss. The central action probably involves inhibition of prostaglandin synthesis in the hypothalamus.

For caffeine

Caffeine is a mild CNS stimulant. Caffeine-induced constriction of cerebral blood vessels, which leads to a decrease in cerebral blood flow and in the oxygen tension of the brain, may contribute to relief of some types of headache.

It has been suggested that the addition of caffeine to acetaminophen may provide a more rapid onset of action and/ or enhanced pain relief with lower doses of the analgesic. However, the FDA has determined that studies performed to date have not demonstrated that caffeine is an effective analgesic adjuvant or that it does not interfere with acetaminophen's efficacy as an antipyretic.

Time to peak effect: 1 to 3 hours.

Duration of action: 3 to 4 hours.

Precautions to Consider

Cross-sensitivity and/or related problems

Patients sensitive to aspirin may not be sensitive to acetaminophen; however, mild bronchospastic reactions with acetaminophen have been reported in some aspirin-sensitive asthmatics (less than 5% of those tested).

Geriatrics

Studies performed to date have not demonstrated geriatrics-specific problems that would limit the usefulness of acetaminophen in the elderly.

Drug interactions and/or related problems

The following drug interactions and/or related problems have been selected on the basis of their potential clinical significance (possible mechanism in parentheses where appropriate)—not necessarily inclusive (» = major clinical significance):

Note: Combinations containing any of the following medications, depending on the amount present, may also interact with this medication.

For acetaminophen

» Alcohol, especially chronic abuse of, or

Hepatic enzyme inducers or

Hepatotoxic medications, other

(risk of hepatotoxicity with single toxic doses or prolonged use of high doses of acetaminophen may be increased in alcoholics or in patients regularly taking other hepatotoxic medications or hepatic enzyme inducers)

(chronic use of barbiturates [except butalbital] or primidone has been reported to decrease the therapeutic effects of acetaminophen, probably because of increased metabolism resulting from induction of hepatic microsomal enzyme activity; the possibility should be considered that similar effects may occur with other hepatic enzyme inducers)

Anticoagulants, coumarin- or indandione-derivative
(concurrent chronic, high-dose administration of acetaminophen may increase the anticoagulant effect, possibly by decreasing hepatic synthesis of procoagulant factors; anticoagulant dosage adjustment based on increased monitoring of prothrombin time may be necessary when chronic, high-dose acetaminophen therapy is initiated or discontinued; however, this does not apply to occasional use, or to chronic use of doses below 2 grams per day, of acetaminophen)

Anti-inflammatory drugs, nonsteroidal (NSAIDs), or
Aspirin or other salicylates
(prolonged concurrent use of acetaminophen and a salicylate is not recommended because recent evidence suggests that chronic, high-dose administration of the combined analgesics [1.35 grams daily, or cumulative ingestion of 1 kg annually, for 3 years or longer] significantly increases the risk of analgesic nephropathy, renal papillary necrosis, end-stage renal disease, and cancer of the kidney or urinary bladder; also, it is recommended that for short-term use, the combined dose of acetaminophen plus salicylate not exceed that recommended for acetaminophen or a salicylate given alone)

(prolonged concurrent use of acetaminophen and NSAIDS other than aspirin may also increase the risk of adverse renal effects; it is recommended that patients be under close medical supervision while receiving such combined therapy)

(diflunisal may increase the plasma concentration of acetaminophen by 50%, leading to increased risk of acetaminophen-induced hepatotoxicity)

For formulations containing caffeine (in addition to those interactions listed above)
CNS stimulation-producing medications, other
(concurrent use with caffeine may result in excessive CNS stimulation, leading to unwanted effects such as nervousness, irritability, insomnia, or possibly convulsions or cardiac arrhythmias; close observation is recommended)

Lithium
(caffeine increases urinary excretion of lithium, and may thereby reduce its therapeutic effect)

Monoamine oxidase (MAO) inhibitors, including furazolidone, pargyline, and procarbazine
(the sympathomimetic side effects of caffeine may produce dangerous cardiac arrhythmias or severe hypertension when large doses of caffeine are used concurrently with MAO inhibitors)

Contraindications/Medical problems
The contraindications/medical problems included have been selected on the basis of their potential clinical significance (reasons given in parentheses where appropriate)—not necessarily inclusive (» = major clinical significance).

Risk-benefit should be considered when the following medical problems exist:
» Alcoholism, active, or
» Hepatic disease or
» Viral hepatitis
(increased risk of hepatotoxicity)

Phenylketonuria
(products that contain aspartame, which is metabolized to phenylalanine, may be hazardous to patients with phenylketonuria, especially young children; caution is recommended)

Renal function impairment, severe
(risk of adverse renal effects may be increased with prolonged use of high doses; occasional use is acceptable)

Sensitivity to acetaminophen or aspirin
(increased risk of allergic reaction)

Side/Adverse Effects
The following side/adverse effects have been selected on the basis of their potential clinical significance (possible signs and symptoms in parentheses where appropriate)—not necessarily inclusive:

Those indicating need for medical attention
Incidence rare
Agranulocytosis (unexplained sore throat and fever); *anemia* (unusual tiredness or weakness); *dermatitis, allergic* (skin rash, hives, or itching); *hepatitis* (yellow eyes or skin); *renal colic* (pain, severe and/or sharp, in lower back and/or side)—with prolonged use of high doses in patients with severe renal function impairment; *renal failure* (sudden decrease in amount of urine)—uremia may result, especially with prolonged use of high doses in patients with severe renal function impairment; also, although a causal association has not been established, a retrospective study has suggested that long-term daily use of acetaminophen may be associated with an increased risk of chronic renal disease [analgesic nephropathy] in individuals without pre-existing renal function impairment; *sterile pyuria* (cloudy urine); *thrombocytopenia* (usually asymptomatic; rarely, unusual bleeding or bruising; black, tarry stools; blood in urine or stools; pinpoint red spots on skin)

Signs and symptoms of overdose
Gastrointestinal upset (diarrhea, loss of appetite, nausea or vomiting, stomach cramps or pain); *increased sweating; hepatotoxicity* (pain, tenderness, and/or swelling in upper abdominal area)—may occur 2 to 4 days after the overdose is ingested

Note: Although *gastrointestinal upset* and *increased sweating* often do not occur, they sometimes occur within 6 to 14 hours after ingestion of an overdose and persist for about 24 hours.

The first indications of overdosage may be signs and symptoms of possible *liver damage* and abnormalities in liver function tests, which may not occur until 2 to 4 days after ingestion of the overdose. Maximal changes in liver function tests usually occur 3 to 5 days after ingestion of the overdose.

Overt *hepatic disease or failure* may occur 4 to 6 days after ingestion of the overdose. *Hepatic encephalopathy* (with mental changes, confusion, agitation, or stupor), *convulsions, respiratory depression, coma, cerebral edema, coagulation defects, gastrointestinal bleeding, disseminated intravascular coagulation, hypoglycemia, metabolic acidosis, cardiac arrhythmias, and cardiovascular collapse* may occur.

Renal tubular necrosis leading to *renal failure* (signs may include bloody or cloudy urine and sudden decrease in amount of urine) has also been reported in acetaminophen overdose, usually, but not exclusively, in conjunction with acetaminophen-induced *hepatotoxicity*.

Patient Consultation
In providing consultation, consider emphasizing the following selected information (» = major clinical significance):

Before using this medication
» Conditions affecting use, especially:
Sensitivity to acetaminophen or aspirin
Use in children—Aspartame-containing chewable tablets must be used with caution, if at all, in children with phenylketonuria
Use by athletes—Caffeine (present in some products) is tested for in athletes by the U.S. Olympic Committee (USOC) and the National Collegiate Athletic Association (NCAA); urine concentrations above 12 mcg per mL (61.8 micromoles/L) and 15 mcg per mL (77.25 micromoles/L) are considered unacceptable by the USOC and the NCAA, respectively

Other medical problems, especially phenylketonuria (for products containing aspartame), alcoholism (active), hepatic disease, or viral hepatitis

Proper use of this medication

» Importance of not taking more medication than the amount recommended because acetaminophen may cause kidney or liver damage with long-term use or greater-than-recommended doses
» Unless otherwise directed by physician, children not taking more than 5 doses per day
» Proper administration of:
  Acetaminophen oral granules
  Acetaminophen oral powders
  Acetaminophen suppositories
» Proper storage

Precautions while using this medication

Regular visits to physician to check progress if long-term therapy is prescribed
Checking with physician because additional treatment may be needed:
  —if taking for pain, including arthritic pain, or fever, and pain persists for longer than 10 days for adults or 5 days for children or fever persists for longer than 3 days, condition becomes worse, new symptoms occur, or the painful area is red or swollen
  —if taking for sore throat, and sore throat is severe, persists for longer than 2 days, or occurs together with or is followed by fever, headache, rash, nausea, or vomiting
» Risk of overdose if other medications containing acetaminophen are used
» Avoiding use of alcohol if taking more than an occasional 1 or 2 doses of this medication; increased risk of liver toxicity, especially in alcoholics, with high doses or prolonged use
Not using a salicylate or a nonsteroidal anti-inflammatory drug together with acetaminophen for more than a few days, unless directed by physician
Possible interference with some laboratory tests; preferably discussing use of the medication with physician in charge 3 to 4 days ahead of time; if this is not possible, informing physician in charge if acetaminophen taken within the past 3 or 4 days
Diabetics: Possible false results with blood glucose tests; checking with physician, nurse, or pharmacist if changes in test results noted
Not taking caffeine-containing formulations for at least 4 hours prior to dipyridamole-assisted myocardial perfusion imaging test
» Suspected overdose: Getting emergency help at once even if no symptoms apparent; symptoms of severe overdosage may be delayed, but treatment must be begun as soon as possible; treatment started 24 hours or more after the overdose may be ineffective in preventing liver damage or fatality

Side/adverse effects

Signs and symptoms of potential side effects, especially adverse renal effects, allergic dermatitis, hepatotoxicity, agranulocytosis, and thrombocytopenia

General Dosing Information

The doses are based on the FDA's proposed labeling requirements for over-the-counter (OTC) internal analgesic, antipyretic, and antirheumatic products. The dosage unit of 80 mg (1.23 grains) is used for pediatric doses; the dosage unit of 325 mg (5 grains) is used for adult doses. The conversion factor of 1 grain equal to 65 mg is used. The doses recommended by manufacturers of individual products, and the strengths of individual products, may not conform to the recommended doses.

One retrospective study has suggested that long-term daily use of acetaminophen may be associated with an increased risk of chronic renal disease (analgesic nephropathy). The results of this study are not considered conclusive, and further investigation is required to establish a causal association. However, until more definitive information is available, prolonged daily administration of acetaminophen should probably be limited to patients who are receiving appropriate medical supervision.

Oral Dosage Forms

ACETAMINOPHEN CAPSULES USP

Usual adult and adolescent dose: Oral, 325 to 500 mg every three hours, 325 to 650 mg every four hours, or 650 mg to 1 gram every six hours as needed, while symptoms persist.

Note: For patient self-medication, it is recommended that a physician be consulted if pain is not relieved within ten days, fever within three days, or sore throat within two days.

Usual adult prescribing limits:
For short-term therapy (up to ten days)—Up to 4 grams daily.
For long-term therapy—Up to 2.6 grams daily, unless chronic treatment with higher doses is prescribed and monitored by a physician.

Auxiliary labeling: • Avoid alcoholic beverages.

ACETAMINOPHEN ORAL GRANULES

Usual adult and adolescent dose: See *Acetaminophen Capsules USP.*

ACETAMINOPHEN ORAL POWDERS

Usual adult and adolescent dose: See *Acetaminophen Capsules USP.*

ACETAMINOPHEN ORAL SOLUTION USP

Usual adult and adolescent dose: See *Acetaminophen Capsules USP.*
Usual adult prescribing limits: See *Acetaminophen Capsules USP.*
Auxiliary labeling: • Avoid alcoholic beverages.

ACETAMINOPHEN ORAL SUSPENSION USP

Usual adult and adolescent dose: See *Acetaminophen Capsules USP.*
Auxiliary labeling: • Shake well.

ACETAMINOPHEN TABLETS USP

Usual adult and adolescent dose: See *Acetaminophen Capsules USP.*
Usual adult prescribing limits: See *Acetaminophen Capsules USP.*
Auxiliary labeling: • Avoid alcoholic beverages.

ACETAMINOPHEN TABLETS USP (CHEWABLE)

Usual adult and adolescent dose: See *Acetaminophen Capsules USP.*
Auxiliary labeling:
  • Avoid alcoholic beverages.
  • May be chewed.

ACETAMINOPHEN AND CAFFEINE CAPSULES USP

Usual adult and adolescent dose: See *Acetaminophen Capsules USP.* Dosage is based on acetaminophen only.

Usual adult prescribing limits: See *Acetaminophen Capsules USP.* Dosage is based on acetaminophen only.

Auxiliary labeling: • Avoid alcoholic beverages.

ACETAMINOPHEN AND CAFFEINE TABLETS USP

Usual adult and adolescent dose: See *Acetaminophen Capsules USP.* Dosage is based on acetaminophen only.

Usual adult prescribing limits: See *Acetaminophen Capsules USP.* Dosage is based on acetaminophen only.

Auxiliary labeling: • Avoid alcoholic beverages.

Rectal Dosage Forms

ACETAMINOPHEN SUPPOSITORIES

Usual adult and adolescent dose: Rectal, 325 to 500 mg every three hours, 325 to 650 mg every four hours, or 650 mg to 1 gram every six hours as needed, while symptoms persist.

Note: For patient self-medication, it is recommended that a physician be consulted if pain is not relieved within ten days, fever within three days, or sore throat within two days.

Usual adult prescribing limits:
For short-term therapy (up to ten days)—Up to 4 grams daily.
For long-term therapy—Up to 2.6 grams daily, unless chronic treatment with higher doses is prescribed and monitored by a physician.

Auxiliary labeling: • Avoid alcoholic beverages.

ACETAMINOPHEN AND SALICYLATES   Systemic

INN: Acetaminophen—Paracetamol

Some commonly used *brand names* are:

In the U.S.—

Buffets II [Buffered Acetaminophen, Aspirin, and Caffeine]
Duoprin [Acetaminophen and Salicylamide]
Duradyne [Acetaminophen, Aspirin, and Caffeine]
Excedrin Extra-Strength Caplets [Acetaminophen, Aspirin, and Caffeine]
Excedrin Extra-Strength Tablets [Acetaminophen, Aspirin, and Caffeine]
Gelpirin [Buffered Acetaminophen, Aspirin, and Caffeine]
Gemnisyn [Acetaminophen and Aspirin]
Goody's Extra Strength Tablets [Acetaminophen, Aspirin, and Caffeine]
Goody's Headache Powders [Acetaminophen, Aspirin, and Caffeine]

Presalin [Buffered Acetaminophen, Aspirin, and Salicylamide]
Rid-A-Pain Compound [Acetaminophen, Salicylamide, and Caffeine]
S-A-C [Acetaminophen, Salicylamide, and Caffeine]
Saleto [Acetaminophen, Aspirin, Salicylamide, and Caffeine]
Supac [Buffered Acetaminophen, Aspirin, and Caffeine]
Tri-Pain Caplets [Acetaminophen, Aspirin, Salicylamide, and Caffeine]
Vanquish Caplets [Buffered Acetaminophen, Aspirin, and Caffeine]

ORAL
ACETAMINOPHEN AND ASPIRIN
Acetaminophen and Aspirin Tablets USP
In the U.S.—*Gemnisyn*
Acetaminophen, Aspirin, and Caffeine Oral Powders
In the U.S.—*Goody's Headache Powders*
Acetaminophen, Aspirin, and Caffeine Tablets USP
In the U.S.—*Duradyne; Excedrin Extra-Strength Caplets; Excedrin Extra-Strength Tablets; Goody's Extra Strength Tablets*
Note: In Canada, *Excedrin* contains only acetaminophen and caffeine. See *Acetaminophen (Systemic).*
Buffered Acetaminophen, Aspirin, and Caffeine Tablets
In the U.S.—*Buffets II; Gelpirin; Supac; Vanquish Caplets*
ACETAMINOPHEN, ASPIRIN, AND SALICYLAMIDE
Acetaminophen, Aspirin, Salicylamide, and Caffeine Tablets
In the U.S.—*Saleto; Tri-Pain Caplets*

Buffered Acetaminophen, Aspirin, and Salicylamide Tablets
In the U.S.—*Presalin*
ACETAMINOPHEN AND SALICYLAMIDE
Acetaminophen and Salicylamide Capsules
In the U.S.—*Duoprin*
Acetaminophen, Salicylamide, and Caffeine Capsules
In the U.S.—*Rid-A-Pain Compound*
Acetaminophen, Salicylamide, and Caffeine Tablets
In the U.S.—*S-A-C*

Category: Analgesic; antipyretic.

Indications

Accepted
Pain (treatment);
Pain, arthritic, mild (treatment); or
Fever (treatment)—Acetaminophen and salicylate combinations are indicated to relieve mild to moderate pain and reduce fever. Salicylamide is less effective than acetaminophen or aspirin. These medications provide only symptomatic relief; additional therapy to treat the cause of the pain or fever should be instituted when necessary.

Acetaminophen and salicylate combinations are indicated to provide temporary relief of pain caused by mild inflammation or arthritis. Although acetaminophen may be effective in relieving pain caused by mild osteoarthritis, it has minimal anti-inflammatory activity. Salicylamide also has minimal anti-inflammatory activity. Therefore, efficacy in relieving pain caused by inflammation or arthritis may depend upon the quantity of aspirin present in the individual product.

Note: The FDA has proposed that salicylamide and caffeine be classified as Category III ingredients (i.e., lacking documentation of efficacy) in OTC analgesic/antipyretic products.

Unaccepted
Acetaminophen and salicylate combinations are not recommended for the treatment of severe inflammation or severe arthritic pain, or for long-term treatment of chronic arthritis. Achieving and maintaining therapeutically effective salicylate plasma concentrations may require ingestion of undesirably large daily doses of other ingredients present in these formulations. Also, prolonged high-dose administration of these combinations is not recommended because of the risk of analgesic nephropathy.

Pharmacology

Mechanism of action/Effect:
Analgesic—
   Acetaminophen or
   Salicylates: The mechanism of analgesic action has not been fully determined. Acetaminophen and salicylates may act by inhibiting prostaglandin synthesis in the central nervous system (CNS) and through a peripheral action by blocking pain-impulse generation. The peripheral action may also be due to inhibition of the synthesis of prostaglandins or to inhibition of the synthesis or actions of other substances that sensitize pain receptors to mechanical or chemical stimulation. Acetaminophen may act predominantly in the CNS, whereas salicylates may act predominantly via peripheral actions.
   Caffeine: A mild CNS stimulant. Caffeine-induced constriction of cerebral blood vessels, which leads to a decrease in cerebral blood flow and in the oxygen tension of the brain, may contribute to relief of some types of headache. Also, it has been suggested that the addition of caffeine to acetaminophen and/or aspirin may provide a more rapid onset of action and/or enhanced pain relief with lower doses of analgesics. However, the FDA has determined that studies performed to date have failed to demonstrate that caffeine is an effective analgesic adjuvant or that it does not interfere with the antipyretic efficacy of analgesic/antipyretic medications.
Antipyretic—Acetaminophen and salicylates may produce antipyresis by acting centrally on the hypothalamic heat-regulating center to produce peripheral vasodilation, resulting in increased cutaneous blood flow, sweating, and heat loss. The central action may involve inhibition of prostaglandin synthesis in the hypothalamus. However, there is some evidence that salicylates may also act through other mechanisms to relieve fevers caused by endogenous pyrogens that do not act via a prostaglandin mechanism.

Other actions/effects: Aspirin—
   Also inhibits platelet aggregation.
   Also has anti-inflammatory and antirheumatic actions; however, the required plasma concentrations may not be achievable with the quantities present in these combination medications. The exact mechanisms of anti-inflammatory activity have not been determined, but aspirin may act peripherally in inflamed tissue, probably by inhibiting the synthesis of prostaglandins and possibly by inhibiting the synthesis and/or actions of other mediators of the inflammatory response. Inhibition of leukocyte migration, inhibition of the release and/or actions of lysosomal enzymes, and actions on other cellular and immunological processes in mesenchymal and connective tissues may also be involved. Antirheumatic actions are effected via analgesic and anti-inflammatory mechanisms; the therapeutic effects are not due to pituitary-adrenal stimulation.
   Large doses may decrease hepatic synthesis of procoagulant factors and prolong prothrombin time.

Time to peak effect: Acetaminophen—1 to 3 hours.

Duration of action: Acetaminophen—3 to 4 hours.

Precautions to Consider

Cross-sensitivity and/or related problems

For acetaminophen: Patients sensitive to aspirin may not be sensitive to acetaminophen; however, mild bronchospastic reactions with acetaminophen have been reported in some aspirin-sensitive patients (less than 5% of those tested).

For salicylates: Patients sensitive to one salicylate, including methyl salicylate (oil of wintergreen), may be sensitive to other salicylates also. However, patients sensitive to aspirin may not necessarily be sensitive to salicylamide.

Patients sensitive to other nonsteroidal anti-inflammatory drugs (NSAIDs) also may be sensitive to salicylates, especially aspirin.

Geriatrics

For all acetaminophen and salicylate combinations—Geriatric patients are more likely to have age-related renal function impairment, which may increase susceptibility to the adverse renal effects of combinations containing 2 or more analgesic/antipyretic medications. Geriatric patients should preferably not take these medications for longer than 5 days at a time unless more prolonged therapy is prescribed and monitored by a physician.

For acetaminophen: Studies performed to date have not demonstrated geriatrics-specific problems that would limit the usefulness of acetaminophen in the elderly.

For aspirin: Geriatric patients may be more susceptible to the toxic effects of salicylates.

For caffeine: No information is available on the relationship of age to the effects of caffeine in geriatric patients.

Drug interactions and/or related problems

The following drug interactions and/or related problems have been selected on the basis of their potential clinical significance (possible mechanism in parentheses where appropriate)—not necessarily inclusive (» = major clinical significance):

Note: Combinations containing any of the following medications, depending on the amount present, may also interact with this medication.

In addition to the interactions listed below, the possibility should be considered that additive or multiple effects leading to impaired blood clotting and/or increased risk of bleeding may occur if a salicylate, especially aspirin, is used concurrently with any medication having a significant potential for causing hypoprothrombinemia, thrombocytopenia, or gastrointestinal ulceration or hemorrhage.

For acetaminophen
» Alcohol, especially chronic abuse of, or
   Hepatic enzyme inducers or
   Hepatotoxic medications, other
      (risk of hepatotoxicity with single toxic doses or prolonged use of high doses of acetaminophen may be increased in alcoholics or in patients regularly taking other hepatotoxic medications or hepatic enzyme inducers)

      (chronic use of barbiturates [except butalbital] or primidone has been reported to decrease the therapeutic effects of acetaminophen, probably because of increased metabolism resulting from induction of hepatic microsomal enzyme activity; the possibility should be considered that similar effects may occur with other hepatic enzyme inducers)

   Anticoagulants, coumarin- or indandione-derivative
      (concurrent chronic, high-dose administration of acetaminophen may increase the anticoagulant effect, possibly by decreasing hepatic synthesis of procoagulant factors; anticoagulant dosage adjustment based on increased monitoring of prothrombin time may be necessary when chronic, high-dose acetaminophen therapy is initiated or discontinued; however, this does not apply to occasional use or to chronic use of doses below 2 grams per day of acetaminophen)

   Aspirin or other salicylates or
   Nonsteroidal anti-inflammatory drugs (NSAIDs)
      (prolonged concurrent use of acetaminophen with a salicylate is not recommended because recent evidence suggests that chronic, high-dose administration of the combined analgesics [1.35 grams daily, or cumulative ingestion of 1 kg annually, for 3 years or longer] significantly increases the risk of analgesic nephropathy, renal papillary necrosis, end-stage renal disease, and cancer of the kidney or urinary bladder; also, it is recom-

mended that for short-term use, the combined dose of acetaminophen plus salicylate not exceed that recommended for acetaminophen or a salicylate given alone)

(diflunisal may increase the plasma concentration of acetaminophen by 50%, leading to increased risk of hepatotoxicity)

(prolonged concurrent use of acetaminophen with NSAIDs other than aspirin may also increase the risk of adverse renal effects; it is recommended that patients be under close medical supervision while receiving such combined therapy)

For aspirin
  Acidifiers, urinary, such as:
   Ammonium chloride
   Ascorbic acid
   Potassium or sodium phosphates
    (acidification of the urine by these medications decreases salicylate [from aspirin] excretion, leading to increased salicylate plasma concentrations)

  Adrenocorticoids, glucocorticoid, or
  Alcohol or
  Corticotropin, chronic therapeutic use, or
» Nonsteroidal anti-inflammatory drugs (NSAIDs), other
    (risk of gastrointestinal side effects, including ulceration and gastrointestinal blood loss, may be increased when these agents are used concurrently with aspirin; also, concurrent use of aspirin and other NSAIDs may not provide additional symptomatic relief and is therefore not recommended)

    (aspirin may decrease the bioavailability of many NSAIDs, including diflunisal, fenoprofen, indomethacin, ketoprofen, meclofenamate, piroxicam, and the active sulfide metabolite of sulindac)

» Alkalizers, urinary, such as:
   Carbonic anhydrase inhibitors
   Citrates, or
  Antacids, chronic high-dose use, especially calcium- or magnesium-containing or sodium bicarbonate
    (alkalinization of the urine by these agents increases salicylate [from aspirin] excretion, leading to decreased salicylate plasma concentrations, reduced effectiveness, and shortened duration of analgesic action)

    (carbonic anhydrase inhibitors may also increase the risk of salicylate intoxication in patients receiving large doses of aspirin because metabolic acidosis induced by carbonic anhydrase inhibitors may increase penetration of salicylate into the brain; the increased risk of severe metabolic acidosis and salicylate toxicity must be considered if acetazolamide is used to produce forced alkaline diuresis in the treatment of aspirin overdose)

» Anticoagulants, coumarin- or indandione-derivative, or
» Heparin or
» Thrombolytic agents, such as:
   Alteplase
   Anistreplase
   Streptokinase
   Urokinase
    (aspirin may displace a coumarin- or indandione-derivative anticoagulant from its protein-binding sites and, in high doses, may decrease hepatic synthesis of procoagulant factors, leading to increased anticoagulation and risk of bleeding)

    (concurrent use with combinations containing aspirin is not recommended because aspirin-induced inhibition of platelet function may lead to prolonged bleeding time and hemorrhage in patients receiving anticoagulant or thrombolytic therapy)

    (the potential occurrence of gastrointestinal ulceration or hemorrhage during therapy with aspirin may cause increased risk to patients receiving anticoagulant or thrombolytic therapy)

» Antidiabetic agents, oral, or

Insulin
    (effects of these medications may be increased by large doses of aspirin; dosage adjustments may be necessary; potentiation of oral antidiabetic agents may partially be caused by displacement from serum proteins; glipizide and glyburide, because of their nonionic binding characteristics, may not be affected as much as the other oral agents; however, caution in concurrent use is recommended)

Antiemetics, including antihistamines and phenothiazines
    (antiemetics may mask the symptoms of aspirin-induced ototoxicity, such as dizziness, vertigo, and tinnitus)

Bismuth subsalicylate
    (ingestion of large repeated doses as for traveler's diarrhea may produce substantial plasma salicylate concentrations; concurrent use with large doses of analgesic salicylates may increase the risk of salicylate toxicity)

» Cefamandole or
» Cefoperazone or
» Cefotetan or
» Moxalactam or
» Plicamycin
    (these medications may cause hypoprothrombinemia; in addition, plicamycin may inhibit platelet aggregation, and moxalactam may cause irreversible platelet damage; concurrent use with aspirin may increase the risk of bleeding because of additive interferences with blood clotting and/or the potential occurrence of gastrointestinal ulceration or hemorrhage during aspirin therapy)

Furosemide
    (in addition to an increased risk of ototoxicity, concurrent use of furosemide with high doses of aspirin may lead to salicylate toxicity because of competition for renal excretory sites)

Laxatives, cellulose-containing
    (concurrent use may reduce the salicylate effect because of physical binding or other absorptive hindrance; medications should be administered 2 hours apart)

» Methotrexate
    (aspirin may displace methotrexate from its binding sites and decrease its renal clearance, leading to toxic plasma concentrations of methotrexate; if used concurrently, methotrexate dosage should be decreased, the patient observed for signs of toxicity, and/or methotrexate plasma concentration monitored; also, it is recommended that salicylate therapy be discontinued 24 to 48 hours prior to administration of a high-dose methotrexate infusion, and not resumed until plasma methotrexate concentrations have decreased to a nontoxic level [usually at least 12 hours postinfusion])

Nifedipine or
Verapamil
    (concurrent use with aspirin may result in displacement of either or both medications from protein-binding sites, leading to increased plasma concentrations of the free [unbound] medications and increased risk of toxicity)

Ototoxic medications, other, especially
» Vancomycin
    (concurrent or sequential administration of these medications with aspirin should be avoided because the potential for ototoxicity may be increased; hearing loss may occur and may progress to deafness even after discontinuation of the medication; these effects may be reversible, but usually are permanent)

» Platelet aggregation inhibitors, other
    (concurrent use with combinations containing aspirin is not recommended because of the increased risk of hemorrhage resulting from additive inhibition of platelet aggregation, the potential occurrence of gastrointestinal ulceration or hemorrhage during aspirin therapy, and the hypoprothrombinemic effect of large doses of aspirin)

» Probenecid or
» Sulfinpyrazone
   (uricosuric effects of probenecid or sulfinpyrazone may be decreased by doses of aspirin that produce serum salicylate concentrations above 50 mcg per mL [5 mg per 100 mL; 0.36 mmol/L]; also, probenecid may decrease renal clearance and increase plasma concentrations of salicylate, thereby increasing the risk of toxicity)

   (sulfinpyrazone may decrease salicylate [from aspirin] excretion and/or displace salicylate from its protein binding sites, possibly leading to increased salicylate concentrations and toxicity)

   (concurrent use of sulfinpyrazone with aspirin may increase the risk of gastrointestinal ulceration or hemorrhage; also, concurrent use of sulfinpyrazone with aspirin may increase the risk of bleeding at sites other than the gastrointestinal tract because of additive inhibition of platelet aggregation)

Salicylic acid (topical)
   (concurrent use with aspirin may increase the risk of salicylate toxicity if significant quantities are absorbed)

Vitamin K
   (requirements for this vitamin may be increased in patients receiving high doses of aspirin)

For formulations containing caffeine (in addition to the interactions listed above for acetaminophen or for aspirin)
CNS stimulation-producing medications, other
   (concurrent use with caffeine may result in excessive CNS stimulation, leading to unwanted effects such as nervousness, irritability, insomnia, or possibly convulsions or cardiac arrhythmias; close observation is recommended)

Lithium
   (caffeine increases urinary excretion of lithium, and may thereby reduce its therapeutic effect)

Monoamine oxidase (MAO) inhibitors, including furazolidone and procarbazine
   (the sympathomimetic side effects of caffeine may cause dangerous cardiac arrhythmias or severe hypertension when large amounts of caffeine are used concurrently with MAO inhibitors)

For formulations containing buffering agents (in addition to the interactions listed above for other specific ingredients)
Other medications, oral, especially:
» Ketoconazole
» Tetracyclines
   (antacids present as buffering agents in analgesic products may interfere with the absorption of many other orally administered medications; a buffered analgesic product should be taken at least 3 hours before or after ketoconazole, 3 to 4 hours before or after tetracycline, and at least 1 to 2 hours before or after other orally administered medications)

Contraindications/Medical problems
The contraindications/medical problems included have been selected on the basis of their potential clinical significance (reasons given in parentheses where appropriate)—not necessarily inclusive (» = major clinical significance).

Except under special circumstances, this medication should not be used when the following medical problems exist:

For aspirin
» Angioedema, anaphylaxis, or other severe allergic reaction induced by aspirin or other NSAIDs, history of
   (high risk of recurrence)
» Bleeding ulcers or
» Hemorrhagic states, other active
   (may be exacerbated because of antiplatelet action of aspirin and decreased procoagulant factor synthesis [with high doses])

» Hemophilia or other bleeding problems, including coagulation or platelet function disorders
   (increased risk of hemorrhage)

Risk-benefit should be considered when the following medical problems exist:

For acetaminophen
» Alcoholism (active) or
» Hepatic disease or
» Viral hepatitis
   (increased risk of hepatotoxicity)
Renal function impairment, severe
   (risk of adverse renal effects may be increased with prolonged use of high doses; occasional use is acceptable)
Sensitivity to acetaminophen, history of
   (increased risk of allergic reaction)

For aspirin
Anemia
   (may be exacerbated because of increased gastrointestinal blood loss; also, pseudoanemia may result from peripheral vasodilation)
» Asthma, allergies, and nasal polyps, aspirin-sensitivity induced, or Mild sensitivity reaction to aspirin, history of
   (increased risk of severe allergic reactions)
» Gastritis, erosive, or
» Peptic ulcer
   (may be exacerbated because of ulcerogenic effects; risk of gastrointestinal bleeding is increased)
Gout
   (aspirin may increase serum uric acid concentrations; also, may interfere with efficacy of uricosuric agents)
Hepatic function impairment
   (salicylates metabolized in liver; also, in severe hepatic impairment, inhibition of platelet function by aspirin may increase risk of hemorrhage)
Hypoprothrombinemia or
Vitamin K deficiency
   (increased risk of bleeding because of antiplatelet action of aspirin and decreased procoagulant factor synthesis with high doses)
Renal function impairment
   (salicylates excreted via kidneys)

For formulations containing caffeine (in addition to those listed above for acetaminophen or for aspirin)
Cardiac disease, severe
   (high doses of caffeine may increase risk of tachycardia or extrasystoles, which may lead to heart failure)
Sensitivity to caffeine, history of
   (risk of allergic reaction)

Side/Adverse Effects

Note: Abuse of combinations of analgesic/antipyretic medications (defined as chronic ingestion of 1.35 grams of the medications per day or cumulative ingestion of 1 kg of the medications annually) for 3 years or longer may lead to severe analgesic nephropathy, including renal papillary necrosis and end-stage renal disease, and cancer of the kidney or urinary bladder. Although phenacetin has been suspected of being the causative agent, there is some evidence that the risk of analgesic nephropathy is significantly greater with prolonged concurrent use of 2 or more analgesic/antipyretic medications (including combinations of acetaminophen with aspirin, other salicylates, and possibly nonsteroidal anti-inflammatory drugs other than aspirin) than with use of a single analgesic/antipyretic agent. However, renal tubular necrosis has been reported in severe acetaminophen overdose. Also, although a causal association has not been established, a retrospective study has suggested that long-term daily use of acetaminophen alone may be associated with an increased risk of analgesic nephropathy.

The caffeine in some of the formulations may contribute to analgesic abuse because of its CNS-stimulating effects and because discontinuation of caffeine may lead to withdrawal headache.

Aspirin-induced bronchospasm is most likely to occur in patients with the triad of aspirin-induced asthma, allergies, and nasal polyps. Aspirin-induced angioedema or urticaria may be more likely to occur in patients with a history of recurrent idiopathic angioedema or urticaria.

Gastrointestinal side effects are more likely to occur with aspirin than with other salicylates.

The following side/adverse effects have been selected on the basis of their potential clinical significance (possible signs and symptoms in parentheses where appropriate)—not necessarily inclusive:

Those indicating need for medical attention
Incidence less frequent or rare
  For aspirin
    Anaphylaxis (bluish discoloration or flushing or redness of skin; coughing; difficulty in swallowing; dizziness or feeling faint, severe; skin rash, hives [may include giant urticaria], and/or itching; stuffy nose; swelling of eyelids, face, or lips; tightness in chest, troubled breathing, and/or wheezing, especially in asthmatic patients); **anemia** (unusual tiredness or weakness)—may occur secondary to gastrointestinal microbleeding; **bronchospastic allergic reaction** (shortness of breath, troubled breathing, tightness in chest, and/or wheezing); **dermatitis, allergic** (skin rash, hives, or itching); **gastrointestinal ulceration, possibly with bleeding** (bloody or black, tarry stools; stomach pain, severe; vomiting of blood or material that looks like coffee grounds)
Incidence rare
  For acetaminophen
    Agranulocytosis (unexplained sore throat and fever); **anemia** (unusual tiredness or weakness); **dermatitis, allergic** (skin rash, hives, or itching); **hepatitis** (yellow eyes or skin); **renal colic** (pain, severe and/or sharp, in lower back and/or side)—with prolonged use of high doses in patients with severe renal function impairment; **renal failure** (sudden decrease in amount of urine)—with prolonged use of high doses in patients with renal function impairment; may progress to uremia; **sterile pyuria** (cloudy urine); **thrombocytopenia** (unusual bleeding or bruising)
Signs and symptoms of overdose
  For acetaminophen
    Early signs and symptoms (diarrhea, increased sweating, loss of appetite, nausea or vomiting, stomach cramps or pain)—may occur within 6 to 14 hours after ingestion of the overdose and persist for about 24 hours; **hepatotoxicity** (pain, tenderness, and/or swelling in upper abdominal area)—may occur 2 to 4 days after the overdose is ingested
  Note: Early signs and symptoms often do not occur. The first indications of overdosage may be signs and symptoms of possible *liver damage* and abnormalities in liver function tests, which may not occur until 2 to 4 days after ingestion of the overdose. Maximal changes in liver function tests usually occur 3 to 5 days after ingestion of the overdose.

    Overt *hepatic disease or failure* may occur 4 to 6 days after ingestion of the overdose. *Hepatic encephalopathy* (with mental changes, confusion, agitation, or stupor), *convulsions, respiratory depression, coma, cerebral edema, coagulation defects, gastrointestinal bleeding, disseminated intravascular coagulation, hypoglycemia, metabolic acidosis, renal tubular necrosis leading to renal failure* (signs include bloody or cloudy urine and sudden decrease in amount of urine), *cardiac arrhythmias,* and *cardiovascular collapse* may occur.

  For aspirin
    Mild overdose [salicylism] (continuing ringing or buzzing in ears, or hearing loss; confusion; severe or continuing diarrhea, stomach pain, and/or headache; dizziness or lightheadedness; severe drowsiness; fast or deep breathing; continuing nausea and/or vomiting; uncontrollable flapping movements of the hands, especially in elderly patients; increased thirst; vision problems); **severe overdose** (bloody urine; convulsions; hallucinations; severe nervousness, excitement, or confusion; shortness of breath or troubled breathing; unexplained fever)
  Note: In young children, the only signs of an overdose may be *changes in behavior, severe drowsiness or tiredness,* and/or *fast or deep breathing.*

    Laboratory findings in overdose may indicate encephalographic abnormalities, alterations in acid-base balance (especially respiratory alkalosis and metabolic acidosis), hyperglycemia or hypoglycemia (especially in children), ketonuria, hyponatremia, hypokalemia, and proteinuria.

  For caffeine
    Abdominal or stomach pain; agitation, anxiety, excitement, or restlessness; confusion or delirium; dehydration; fast or irregular heartbeat; fever; frequent urination; headache; increased sensitivity to touch or pain; irritability; muscle trembling or twitching; nausea and vomiting, sometimes with blood; ringing or other sounds in ears; seeing flashes of "zig-zag" lights; seizures, usually tonic-clonic seizures; trouble in sleeping

Those indicating possible analgesic nephropathy and the need for medical attention if they occur during or following long-term high-dose use
Incidence rare
    Renal papillary necrosis leading to renal failure (bloody or cloudy urine; sudden decrease in amount of urine; swelling of face, fingers, feet, or lower legs; weight gain)—may progress to uremia

Those indicating need for medical attention only if they continue or are bothersome
Incidence more frequent
  For aspirin
    Gastrointestinal irritation (mild stomach pain, heartburn or indigestion, nausea with or without vomiting)
Incidence less frequent
  For salicylamide
    Drowsiness
  For caffeine-containing formulations
    CNS stimulation (trouble in sleeping, nervousness, or jitters)

Patient Consultation

In providing consultation, consider emphasizing the following selected information (» = major clinical significance):

Before using this medication
» Conditions affecting use, especially:
    Sensitivity to acetaminophen, aspirin, or nonsteroidal anti-inflammatory drugs (NSAIDs)
    Pregnancy—Not taking aspirin in third trimester unless prescribed by physician; high-dose chronic use or abuse of aspirin in third trimester may be hazardous to the mother as well as the fetus and/or neonate, causing heart problems in fetus or neonate and/or bleeding in mother, fetus, or neonate; high-dose chronic use or abuse may also prolong and complicate labor and delivery
    Use in children—Checking with physician before giving to children with symptoms of acute febrile illness, especially influenza or varicella, because of the risk of Reye's syndrome; also, increased susceptibility to aspirin toxicity in children, especially with fever and dehydration

Use in teenagers—Checking with physician before giving to teenagers with symptoms of acute febrile illness, especially influenza or varicella, because of the risk of Reye's syndrome

Use in elderly—Increased risk of aspirin toxicity and of combination analgesic-induced adverse renal effects

Use by athletes—Caffeine (present in some formulations) is tested for in athletes by the U.S. Olympic Committee (USOC) and the National Collegiate Athletic Association (NCAA); urine concentrations above 12 mcg per mL (61.8 micromoles/L) and 15 mcg per mL (77.25 micromoles/L) are considered unacceptable by the USOC and the NCAA, respectively

Other medications, especially anticoagulants, antidiabetic agents (oral), those cephalosporins that may cause hypoprothrombinemia, methotrexate, moxalactam, NSAIDs, platelet aggregation inhibitors, plicamycin, probenecid, sulfinpyrazone, and urinary alkalizers and, for buffered formulations, ketoconazole and oral tetracyclines

Other medical problems, especially alcoholism (active), coagulation or platelet function disorders, gastrointestinal problems such as ulceration or erosive gastritis (especially a bleeding ulcer), and hepatic disease or viral hepatitis

Proper use of this medication
» Taking with food or a full glass (240 mL) of water to minimize gastrointestinal irritation
» Importance of not taking more medication than recommended on package label, unless otherwise directed by physician, because of risk of acetaminophen-induced liver damage with long-term use or greater-than-recommended doses, gastrointestinal toxicity with salicylates, and acetaminophen or salicylate overdose
» Importance of children not taking more than 5 doses per day unless otherwise directed by physician
» Not taking for chronic or severe inflammatory or rheumatic conditions without first checking with physician because prolonged treatment may be necessary and medication may not be effective unless extremely high doses are taken
» Not taking combinations containing aspirin if a strong vinegar-like odor is present
» Proper storage

Precautions while using this medication
» Regular visits to physician to check progress if long-term or high-dose therapy is prescribed
Checking with physician because additional treatment may be needed:
—if taking for pain or fever, and pain persists for longer than 10 days (5 days for children) or fever persists for longer than 3 days, if condition becomes worse, if new symptoms occur, or if the painful area is red or swollen
—if taking for sore throat, and sore throat is severe, persists for longer than 2 days, or occurs together with or is followed by fever, headache, rash, nausea, or vomiting
Not taking products containing aspirin for 5 days prior to any kind of surgery, unless otherwise directed by physician
» Caution if other medications containing acetaminophen, aspirin, or other salicylates (including diflunisal) are used
» Avoiding alcoholic beverages if taking more than an occasional 1 or 2 doses of these medications; alcohol consumption may increase risk of salicylate-induced gastrointestinal toxicity and acetaminophen-induced liver toxicity
Not using an NSAID together with this medication for more than a few days, unless directed by physician or dentist
Not taking buffered formulations within 3 hours before or after ketoconazole, 3 to 4 hours before or after an oral tetracycline, or 1 to 2 hours before or after other oral medications
Not taking a cellulose-containing laxative within 2 hours of aspirin-containing medications

Possible interference with some laboratory tests; preferably discussing use of the medication with physician in charge 3 to 4 days ahead of time; if this is not possible, informing physician in charge if medication taken within the past 3 or 4 days

Diabetics: Possible false results with blood and urine glucose tests; checking with physician, nurse, or pharmacist if changes in test results noted

Not taking caffeine-containing formulations for at least 4 hours prior to dipyridamole-assisted myocardial perfusion imaging test

» Suspected overdose: Getting emergency help at once

Side/adverse effects
Signs of potential side effects, especially gastrointestinal toxicity, hepatotoxicity, adverse renal effects, agranulocytosis, thrombocytopenia, anaphylaxis, and angioedema

General Dosing Information

Doses are stated in terms of total analgesics present in these combination medications. They are based on USP Advisory Panel recommendations that the total dose of analgesic/antipyretic agents given in combination should be equivalent to the dose recommended for an individual analgesic/antipyretic agent used alone. The stated doses are those proposed by the FDA for over-the-counter (OTC) use of acetaminophen or aspirin given individually. The strengths of individual products, and the doses recommended by manufacturers of individual products, may not conform to the recommended doses.

Medications containing aspirin should be administered with food or a full glass (240 mL) of water to lessen gastric irritation.

Dosage of aspirin should be reduced if fever or illness causes fluid depletion, especially in children.

Because of the possibility of analgesic nephropathy resulting from long-term, high-dose use of analgesic combinations, and possibly even acetaminophen alone, prolonged daily use of these medications should probably be limited to patients who are receiving appropriate medical supervision.

In general, it is recommended that aspirin therapy be discontinued 5 days before surgery to reduce the risk of bleeding problems.

ACETAMINOPHEN AND ASPIRIN

Oral Dosage Forms

ACETAMINOPHEN AND ASPIRIN TABLETS USP

Usual adult and adolescent dose: Oral, up to a total of approximately 650 mg of acetaminophen and aspirin (combined) every four to six hours as needed, while symptoms persist.

Note: For patient self-medication, it is recommended that a physician be consulted if pain is not relieved within ten days, fever within three days, or sore throat within two days.

For geriatric patients, it may be advisable that these medications not be used for longer than five days at a time, because such patients may be more susceptible to adverse renal effects.

Usual adult prescribing limits:
For short-term therapy (up to ten days)—Up to a total of approximately 4 grams of acetaminophen and aspirin (combined) daily.
For long-term therapy—Up to a total of approximately 2.6 grams of acetaminophen and aspirin (combined) daily, unless chronic treatment with higher doses is prescribed and monitored by a physician.

Auxiliary labeling:
- Avoid alcoholic beverages.
- Take with food or a full glass of water.

ACETAMINOPHEN, ASPIRIN, AND CAFFEINE ORAL POWDERS

Usual adult and adolescent dose: See *Acetaminophen and Aspirin Tablets USP*. Dosing is based only on the analgesic ingredients.

Usual adult prescribing limits: See *Acetaminophen and Aspirin Tablets USP*. Dosing is based only on the analgesic ingredients.

Auxiliary labeling:
- Avoid alcoholic beverages.
- Take with a full glass of water or other liquid.

ACETAMINOPHEN, ASPIRIN, AND CAFFEINE TABLETS USP

Usual adult and adolescent dose: See *Acetaminophen and Aspirin Tablets USP*. Dosing is based only on the analgesic ingredients.

Usual adult prescribing limits: See *Acetaminophen and Aspirin Tablets USP*. Dosing is based only on the analgesic ingredients.

Auxiliary labeling:
- Avoid alcoholic beverages.
- Take with food or a full glass of water.

BUFFERED ACETAMINOPHEN, ASPIRIN, AND CAFFEINE TABLETS

Usual adult and adolescent dose: See *Acetaminophen and Aspirin Tablets USP*. Dosing is based only on the analgesic ingredients.

Usual adult prescribing limits: See *Acetaminophen and Aspirin Tablets USP*. Dosing is based only on the analgesic ingredients.

Auxiliary labeling:
- Avoid alcoholic beverages.
- Take with food or a full glass of water.

ACETAMINOPHEN, ASPIRIN, AND SALICYLAMIDE

Oral Dosage Forms

ACETAMINOPHEN, ASPIRIN, SALICYLAMIDE, AND CAFFEINE TABLETS

Usual adult and adolescent dose: Oral, up to a total of approximately 325 to 500 mg of acetaminophen, aspirin, and salicylamide (combined) every three hours, 325 to 650 mg of acetaminophen, aspirin, and salicylamide (combined) every four hours, or 650 mg to 1 gram of acetaminophen, aspirin, and salicylamide (combined) every six hours as needed, while symptoms persist.

Note: For patient self-medication, it is recommended that a physician be consulted if pain is not relieved within ten days, fever within three days, or sore throat within two days.

For geriatric patients, it may be advisable that these medications not be used for longer than five days at a time, because such patients may be more susceptible to adverse renal effects.

Usual adult prescribing limits:
For short-term therapy (up to ten days)—Up to a total of approximately 4 grams of acetaminophen, aspirin, and salicylamide (combined) daily.
For long-term therapy—Up to a total of approximately 2.6 grams of acetaminophen, aspirin, and salicylamide (combined) daily, unless chronic treatment with higher doses is prescribed and monitored by a physician.

Auxiliary labeling:
- Avoid alcoholic beverages.
- Take with food or a full glass of water.
- May cause drowsiness.

BUFFERED ACETAMINOPHEN, ASPIRIN, AND SALICYLAMIDE TABLETS

Usual adult and adolescent dose: See *Acetaminophen, Aspirin, Salicylamide, and Caffeine Tablets*. Dosing is based only on the analgesic ingredients.

Usual adult prescribing limits: See *Acetaminophen, Aspirin, Salicylamide, and Caffeine Tablets*. Dosing is based only on the analgesic ingredients.

Auxiliary labeling:
- Avoid alcoholic beverages.
- Take with food or a full glass of water.
- May cause drowsiness.

ACETAMINOPHEN AND SALICYLAMIDE

Oral Dosage Forms

ACETAMINOPHEN AND SALICYLAMIDE CAPSULES

Usual adult and adolescent dose: Oral, 500 mg of acetaminophen and salicylamide (combined) every four hours, or 1 gram of acetaminophen and salicylamide (combined) every six hours as needed, while symptoms persist.

Note: For patient self-medication, it is recommended that a physician be consulted if pain is not relieved within ten days, fever within three days, or sore throat within two days.

For geriatric patients, it may be advisable that these medications not be used for longer than five days at a time, because such patients may be more susceptible to adverse renal effects.

Usual adult prescribing limits:
For short-term therapy (up to ten days)—Up to a total of approximately 4 grams of acetaminophen and salicylamide (combined) daily.
For long-term therapy—Up to a total of approximately 2.6 grams of acetaminophen and salicylamide (combined) daily, unless chronic treatment with higher doses is prescribed and monitored by a physician.

Auxiliary labeling:
- Avoid alcoholic beverages.
- Take with food or a full glass of water.
- May cause drowsiness.

ACETAMINOPHEN, SALICYLAMIDE, AND CAFFEINE CAPSULES

Usual adult and adolescent dose: See *Acetaminophen and Salicylamide Capsules*. Dosing is based only on the analgesic ingredients.

Usual adult prescribing limits: See *Acetaminophen and Salicylamide Capsules*. Dosing is based only on the analgesic ingredients.

Auxiliary labeling:
- Avoid alcoholic beverages.
- Take with food or a full glass of water.
- May cause drowsiness.

ACETAMINOPHEN, SALICYLAMIDE, AND CAFFEINE TABLETS

Usual adult and adolescent dose: See *Acetaminophen and Salicylamide Capsules*. Dosing is based only on the analgesic ingredients.

Usual adult prescribing limits: See *Acetaminophen and Salicylamide Capsules*. Dosing is based only on the analgesic ingredients.

Auxiliary labeling:
- Avoid alcoholic beverages.
- Take with food or a full glass of water.
- May cause drowsiness.

ACETAMINOPHEN, SALICYLATES, AND CODEINE   Systemic

INN: Acetaminophen—Paracetamol.

Category: Analgesic.

Indications

Accepted

Pain (treatment)—Indicated for the relief of mild pain.

Patient Consultation

In providing consultation, consider emphasizing the following selected information (» = major clinical significance):

Before using this medication
- » Conditions affecting use, especially:
  - Allergic reaction to acetaminophen, aspirin or other salicylates, nonsteroidal anti-inflammatory drugs (NSAIDs), or codeine, history of
  - Pregnancy—Acetaminophen, salicylates, and opioids cross the placenta; regular use of codeine by pregnant women may cause physical dependence in the fetus and withdrawal symptoms in the neonate; high-dose chronic use or abuse of aspirin in the third trimester may be hazardous to the mother as well as the fetus and/or neonate, causing heart problems in fetus or neonate and/or bleeding in mother, fetus, or neonate; high-dose chronic use or abuse may also prolong and complicate labor and delivery; not taking aspirin during third trimester unless prescribed by physician
  - Breast-feeding—Acetaminophen, aspirin, codeine, and caffeine are excreted in breast milk
  - Use in children and teenagers—Checking with physician before giving aspirin to children or teenagers with symptoms of acute viral illness, especially influenza or varicella, because of the risk of Reye's syndrome and because of increased susceptibility to aspirin toxicity in children, especially those with fever and dehydration; also, children up to 2 years of age are more susceptible to the effects of codeine, especially respiratory depression; in addition, children may be more likely to experience codeine-induced paradoxical CNS excitation during therapy
  - Use in the elderly—Geriatric patients are more susceptible to the effects of opioids, especially respiratory depression; also, patients over 60 years of age are more susceptible to the toxic effects of salicylates
  - Use by athletes—Codeine is banned and tested for in athletes by the U.S. Olympic Committee (USOC) and the National Collegiate Athletic Association (NCAA); caffeine is tested for in athletes by the USOC and the NCAA; urine concentrations above 12 mcg per mL (USOC) and 15 mcg per mL (NCAA) are considered unacceptable
  - Other medications, especially alcohol or other CNS depressants, anticoagulants, oral antidiabetic agents, those cephalosporins that may cause hypoprothrombinemia, methotrexate, monoamine oxidase inhibitors, moxalactam, naltrexone, NSAIDs, platelet aggregation inhibitors, plicamycin, probenecid, sulfinpyrazone, and urinary alkalizers
  - Other medical problems, especially alcoholism (active), coagulation or platelet function disorders, diarrhea caused by antibiotics or poisoning, asthma or other respiratory problems, gastrointestinal problems such as ulceration or erosive gastritis (especially a bleeding ulcer) or other severe inflammatory bowel disease, and hepatic disease or viral hepatitis

Proper use of this medication
- » Importance of not taking more medication than the amount prescribed because of risk of acetaminophen-induced liver or kidney damage with long-term use or greater-than-recommended doses, gastrointestinal toxicity with salicylates, habit-forming potential of opioid analgesics, and overdose
- » Not increasing dose if medication seems less effective after a few weeks; checking with physician
- » Taking with food and a full glass (240 mL) of water to minimize gastrointestinal irritation and not lying down for 15 to 30 minutes after taking
- » Not taking medication if a strong vinegar-like odor is present
  - Missed dose (if on scheduled dosing): Taking as soon as possible; not taking if almost time for next dose; not doubling doses
- » Proper storage

Precautions while using this medication
- Regular visits to physician to check progress during long-term or high-dose therapy
- » Caution if other medications containing opioid analgesics, acetaminophen, aspirin, or other salicylates are used
  - Not using an NSAID together with this medication for more than a few days, unless directed by physician or dentist
- » Avoiding use of alcohol or other central nervous system (CNS) depressants during therapy unless prescribed or otherwise approved by physician; alcohol consumption may also increase risk of salicylate-induced gastrointestinal toxicity and acetaminophen-induced liver toxicity
- » Caution if drowsiness, dizziness or lightheadedness, or false sense of well-being occurs
  - Caution when getting up suddenly from a lying or sitting position
  - Lying down if nausea or vomiting, or dizziness or lightheadedness occurs
  - Caution if any kind of surgery or emergency treatment is required
  - Not taking aspirin for 5 days prior to any kind of surgery, unless otherwise directed by physician
  - Not taking a cellulose-containing laxative within 2 hours of salicylate-containing medications
  - Possible dryness of mouth; using sugarless gum or candy, ice, or saliva substitute for relief; checking with dentist if dry mouth continues for more than 2 weeks
  - Diabetics: Medication may cause false blood and urine sugar test results; checking with physician, nurse, or pharmacist if changes in test results noted
  - Possible interference with some laboratory tests; preferably discussing use of the medication with physician in charge 3 to 4 days ahead of time; if this is not possible, informing physician in charge if medication taken within the past 3 or 4 days
  - Not taking caffeine for at least 4 hours prior to dipyridamole-assisted myocardial perfusion imaging test

» Checking with physician before discontinuing medication after prolonged use of high doses; gradual dosage reduction may be necessary to avoid withdrawal symptoms
» Suspected overdose: Getting emergency help at once

Side/adverse effects
Signs of potential side effects, especially respiratory depression or impairment; allergic reactions, especially anaphylaxis and angioedema; confusion, convulsions, hallucinations, mental depression, or other signs of CNS toxicity; gastrointestinal toxicity; hepatotoxicity; hypertension; paradoxical CNS excitation, especially in children; adverse renal effects; agranulocytosis; and thrombocytopenia

Oral Dosage Forms

ACETAMINOPHEN, ASPIRIN, SALICYLAMIDE, CODEINE PHOSPHATE, AND CAFFEINE TABLETS

Usual adult dose: Analgesic—Oral, 1 or 2 tablets every three hours, not to exceed 8 tablets a day.

Auxiliary labeling:
• May cause drowsiness.
• Avoid alcoholic beverages.
• May be habit-forming.
• Take with food and with a full glass of water.

ACETOHYDROXAMIC ACID   Systemic†

A commonly used *brand name* in the U.S. is *Lithostat.*

Category: Antiurolithic (struvite calculi); urinary tract infection treatment adjunct.

Indications

Accepted
Renal calculi, struvite (prophylaxis)—Acetohydroxamic acid is indicated in the prophylaxis of struvite calculi formation that is promoted by urease-producing bacteria such as *Proteus*. Its use may enhance effectiveness of urinary antibacterials, especially following surgical removal of existing stones. Use of acetohydroxamic acid also improves the possibility of reducing the frequency and rate of new stone formation.
Urinary tract infections, bacterial (treatment adjunct)—Acetohydroxamic acid is indicated as an adjunct in the treatment of chronic, urea-splitting urinary tract infections caused by urease-producing bacteria. Its inhibition of urease activity decreases the urinary ammonia and alkalinity produced from the enzyme hydrolysis of urea.

Unaccepted
Acetohydroxamic acid is *not* indicated for dissolution of existing calculi, replacement of indicated surgical treatment, urinary tract infections controllable by culture-specific oral antibacterials, or urinary tract infections caused by nonurease producing organisms.

Pharmacology/Pharmacokinetics

Mechanism of action/Effect: Inhibits the hydrolysis of urea and production of ammonia in urine infected with urea-splitting bacteria, by reversible inhibition of the bacterial enzyme urease, and by the chelation of nickel, an essential component of urease enzymes. Such enzyme inhibition results in reduction of both urine alkalinity and ammonia concentration. The effectiveness of antibacterial medication is then enhanced and the formation of urinary calculi reduced.

Precautions to Consider

Geriatrics
No information is available on the relationship of age to the effects of acetohydroxamic acid in geriatric patients.

Drug interactions and/or related problems
The following drug interactions and/or related problems have been selected on the basis of their potential clinical significance (possible mechanism in parentheses where appropriate)—not necessarily inclusive (» = major clinical significance):

Note: Combinations containing any of the following medications, depending on the amount present, may also interact with this medication.

Alcohol
(concurrent use of alcoholic beverages with acetohydroxamic acid has resulted in a nonpruritic, reddish, macular skin rash about 30 to 45 minutes after ingestion. The rash may be associated with a general feeling of warmth and tingling, and usually disappears spontaneously in 30 to 60 minutes)
» Iron and other heavy metals
(acetohydroxamic acid chelates iron and possibly other heavy metals with concurrent oral administration; this may result in reduced intestinal absorption of both; if iron therapy is indicated, parenteral administration of iron is recommended)

Contraindications/Medical problems
The contraindications/medical problems included have been selected on the basis of their potential clinical significance (reasons given in parentheses where appropriate)—not necessarily inclusive (» = major clinical significance).

Except under special circumstances, this medication should not be used when the following medical problem exists:
» Renal function impairment with creatinine clearance less than 20 mL per minute or serum creatinine concentration greater than 2.5 mg per deciliter
(excessive accumulation of acetohydroxamic acid may result)

Risk-benefit should be considered when the following medical problems exist:
Anemia, hypochromic
(acetohydroxamic acid may make this condition worse)
» Phlebitis, or history of, or
» Phlebothrombosis, or history of, or
» Thrombophlebitis, or history of
(increased risk of recurrence)
Renal function impairment with creatinine clearance not less than 20 mL per minute
(risk of excessive accumulation of acetohydroxamic acid)
Sensitivity to acetohydroxamic acid

Side/Adverse Effects

Note: Acetohydroxamic acid overdose has not been reported. However, if it should occur, concomitant reduction in platelets and/or white blood cells should be anticipated; reticulocyte count is likely to be elevated; and severe hemolysis may occur.

The following side/adverse effects have been selected on the basis of their potential clinical significance (possible signs and symptoms in parentheses where appropriate)—not necessarily inclusive:

Those indicating need for medical attention

Incidence more frequent

Anemia, hemolytic (loss of appetite, nausea or vomiting, unusual tiredness or weakness); *anxiety, confusion, or mental depression; nervousness, shakiness, or tremors; phlebitis or thrombosis* (severe headaches of sudden onset; sudden loss of coordination; pains in chest, groin, or legs, especially calves of legs; sudden onset of shortness of breath for no apparent reason; sudden onset of slurred speech; sudden vision changes)

Those indicating need for medical attention only if they continue or are bothersome

Incidence more frequent

Gastrointestinal effects, specifically anorexia (loss of appetite), *malaise* (general feeling of discomfort or illness), *nausea and vomiting; mild headache*

Incidence less frequent or rare

Hair loss; non-itching skin rash on arms and face

Patient Consultation

In providing consultation, consider emphasizing the following selected information (» = major clinical significance):

Before using this medication

» Conditions affecting use, especially:

Sensitivity to acetohydroxamic acid

Pregnancy—Contraindicated in pregnant patients because animal studies have shown leg deformities, and cardiac, coccygeal, and abdominal-wall anomalies; adequate contraception necessary for women of child-bearing potential

Breast-feeding—Not recommended because of potential adverse effects in infant

Other medications, especially oral iron supplements

Other medical problems, especially severe renal function impairment or history of phlebitis, phlebothrombosis, or thrombophlebitis

Proper use of this medication

» Taking medication on an empty stomach, 1 hour before or 2 hours after meals

» Compliance with therapy; importance of taking medication exactly as directed by physician

» Importance of using an effective method of contraception during therapy in women of child-bearing potential

» Not missing doses; stone formation and growth may recur

Missed dose: Taking as soon as remembered; going back to regular dosing schedule; not doubling doses

» Proper storage

Precautions while using this medication

Regular visits to physician to check progress of therapy

» Not taking oral iron preparations concurrently with acetohydroxamic acid

» Avoiding the use of alcoholic beverages during treatment with acetohydroxamic acid; flushing and skin rash may result

» Stopping medication immediately and checking with doctor if pregnancy occurs

Side/adverse effects

» Stopping medication and notifying physician immediately if symptoms of blood clots occur, such as severe headaches of sudden onset, sudden loss of coordination, pains in chest, groin, or legs, especially calves of legs, sudden onset of shortness of breath for no apparent reason, sudden onset of slurred speech, sudden vision changes

General Dosing Information

Acetohydroxamic acid should not be used in place of surgical treatment when surgery is indicated.

Existing calculi are unlikely to be reduced or dissolved by acetohydroxamic acid therapy.

Diet/Nutrition

Acetohydroxamic acid is administered on an empty stomach.

Dietary iron is chelated and its absorption inhibited by acetohydroxamic acid, possibly leading to hypochromic anemia.

Oral Dosage Forms

ACETOHYDROXAMIC ACID TABLETS USP

Usual adult and adolescent dose: Antiurolithic—Oral, 250 mg three or four times a day at six- to eight-hour intervals.

Note: Dosage must be proportionately reduced and individually adjusted for patients with renal function impairment.

Usual adult prescribing limits: Up to 1.5 grams.

Auxiliary labeling:
• Avoid alcoholic beverages.
• Take 1 hour before or 2 hours after meals.

ACETYLCYSTEINE   Inhalation-Local

Some commonly used *brand names* are:

In the U.S.—*Mucomyst; Mucosil*
In Canada—*Airbron; Mucomyst*

INHALATION

Acetylcysteine Solution USP
In the U.S.—*Mucomyst; Mucosil;* GENERIC
In Canada—*Airbron; Mucomyst*

Category: Mucolytic; diagnostic aid (bronchial studies).

Indications

Note: Bracketed information in the *Indications* section refers to uses not included in U.S. product labeling.

Accepted

Amyloidosis, primary, of lung (treatment adjunct);
Bronchiectasis (treatment adjunct);
Bronchitis (treatment adjunct);
Bronchitis, asthmatic (treatment adjunct);
Cystic fibrosis, pulmonary complications of (treatment adjunct);
Emphysema, pulmonary (treatment adjunct);
[Lung abscess (treatment adjunct)];
Pneumonia (treatment adjunct);
Tracheobronchitis (treatment adjunct);
Tracheostomy care, adjunct; or
Tuberculosis (treatment adjunct)—Acetylcysteine is indicated as adjuvant therapy for abnormal, viscid, or inspissated mucous secretions in acute bronchopulmonary disease (pneumonia, bronchitis, and tracheobronchitis); chronic bronchopulmonary disease (chronic

pulmonary emphysema, emphysema with bronchitis, chronic asthmatic bronchitis, [lung abscess], tuberculosis, bronchiectasis, and primary amyloidosis of the lung); and pulmonary complications of cystic fibrosis. It is also used as an adjunct in tracheostomy care.

Atelectasis due to mucous obstruction (treatment adjunct)—Acetylcysteine is indicated as adjuvant therapy for abnormal, viscid, or inspissated mucous secretions in atelectasis due to mucous obstruction. However, acetylcysteine is of no proven value in atelectasis due to simple hypoventilation, such as postoperative hypoventilation.

Bronchial studies—Acetylcysteine is indicated as a diagnostic aid in bronchial studies, such as bronchograms, bronchospirometry, and bronchial wedge catheterization.

Pharmacology

Mechanism of action/Effect: The viscosity of pulmonary mucous secretions depends on the concentrations of mucoproteins and, to a lesser extent, of deoxyribonucleic acid (DNA). Acetylcysteine decreases the viscosity of pulmonary secretions and facilitates their removal by coughing, postural drainage, or mechanical means. It exerts its mucolytic action through its free sulfhydryl group, which acts directly on the mucoproteins to open the disulfide bonds and lower the viscosity of the mucus. This action increases with increasing pH and is most significant at pH 7 to 9. The mucolytic action of acetylcysteine is not affected by the presence of DNA.

Other actions/effects: Acetylcysteine has no effect on fibrin, blood clots, or living tissue.

Onset of action:
Inhalation—Within 1 minute.
Direct instillation—Immediate.

Time to peak effect: Inhalation—5 to 10 minutes.

Precautions to Consider

Geriatrics
Appropriate studies on the relationship of age to the effects of acetylcysteine inhalation have not been performed in the geriatric population. However, no geriatrics-specific problems have been documented to date.

Contraindications/Medical problems
The contraindications/medical problems included have been selected on the basis of their potential clinical significance (reasons given in parentheses where appropriate)—not necessarily inclusive (» = major clinical significance).

Risk-benefit should be considered when the following medical problems exist:
» Asthma, bronchial, or
» Respiratory insufficiency, severe
 (obstruction of bronchial airways may be increased, especially in debilitated patients; if acetylcysteine is used in these patients, pretreatment with a bronchodilator may be indicated)
 Sensitivity to acetylcysteine

Side/Adverse Effects

The following side/adverse effects have been selected on the basis of their potential clinical significance (possible signs and symptoms in parentheses where appropriate)—not necessarily inclusive:

Those indicating need for medical attention
Incidence less frequent
 Hemoptysis (spitting up blood); *increased airways obstruction* (wheezing, tightness in chest, or difficulty in breathing), especially in asthma patients—more frequent with the 20% solution

Incidence rare
 Sensitization (skin rash or other irritation)—with frequent and prolonged exposure

Those indicating need for medical attention only if they continue or are bothersome
Incidence less frequent
 Clammy skin; fever; increase in bronchial secretions; irritation of throat or lungs; nausea or vomiting; rhinorrhea (runny nose); *stomatitis* (irritation or soreness of mouth)

Those not indicating need for medical attention
Incidence more frequent
 Stickiness on face, after nebulization using a face mask; unpleasant odor during administration, transient

Patient Consultation

In providing consultation, consider emphasizing the following selected information (» = major clinical significance):

Before using this medication
» Conditions affecting use, especially:
 Sensitivity to acetylcysteine
 Other medical problems, especially bronchial asthma or other severe respiratory insufficiency

Proper use of this medication
» Importance of not using more medication than the amount prescribed
 Proper administration: Knowing correct administration technique; checking with physician if necessary
 After using medication, coughing up loosened mucus to prevent excessive accumulation in lungs; mechanical suction may be necessary if cough inadequate to remove mucus
 Missed dose: Using as soon as possible; using any remaining doses for that day at regularly spaced intervals
» Proper storage

Precautions while using this medication
» Checking with physician if condition does not improve or if it becomes worse

Side/adverse effects
 Signs of potential side effects, especially hemoptysis, increased airways obstruction, and sensitization
 Possibility of stickiness on face after nebulization using a face mask; removing by washing with water
 Possibility of acetylcysteine having a transient unpleasant odor during administration

General Dosing Information

The method of acetylcysteine administration depends on the condition being treated. Acetylcysteine, usually as a 10 to 20% solution, may be administered by nebulization, direct instillation, or intratracheal instillation.

Acetylcysteine is usually administered by nebulization, using conventional nebulizers made of plastic or glass. Certain materials used in nebulization equipment react with acetylcysteine, especially iron, copper, and rubber.

When acetylcysteine is administered by nebulization, compressed tank gas (air) or an air compressor should be used to provide pressure for nebulizing the solution. Oxygen may also be used; however, it should be used with the usual precautions in patients with severe respiratory disease and carbon dioxide retention. Acetylcysteine may also be administered by ultrasonic nebulization.

The nebulizer used should be capable of providing optimal quantities of a suitable range of particle sizes. Commercially available nebulizers will produce nebulae of acetylcysteine satisfactory for retention in the respiratory tract, usually providing a high proportion of the acetylcysteine solution as particles of less than 10 microns in diameter.

The nebulized solution may be inhaled directly from the nebulizer or the nebulizer may be attached to a plastic face mask or tent, plastic mouthpiece, conventional plastic oxygen tent, or head tent. Suitable nebulizers may also be fitted for use with the various intermittent positive pressure breathing (IPPB) machines.

Acetylcysteine should not be placed directly into the chamber of a heated (hot pot) nebulizer. A heated nebulizer may be part of the nebulization assembly to provide a warm saturated atmosphere if the acetylcysteine aerosol is introduced by means of a separate unheated nebulizer. The usual precautions for administration of warm saturated nebulae should be followed.

The nebulizing equipment should be cleaned immediately after use because the residues may clog the smaller orifices or corrode metal parts.

Hand bulb nebulizers are not recommended for nebulizing acetylcysteine because their output is generally too small and some of them deliver particles that are larger than optimum for inhalation therapy.

When acetylcysteine is nebulized for a prolonged period of time with a dry gas, the solution may become overconcentrated (due to evaporation) and nebulization may be impaired. After three-fourths of the initial volume of solution has been nebulized, the remaining solution in the nebulizer should be diluted with an approximately equal volume of sterile water for injection.

After administration of acetylcysteine, an increase in volume of liquefied bronchial secretions may occur. This may produce breathing difficulty in patients who have poor ventilatory mechanics and/or poor cough, such as postoperative or trauma patients. When the cough is inadequate to maintain an open airway, mechanical suction or endotracheal aspiration should be used if necessary.

Nebulization with a face mask may leave a sticky residue on the face. This can be removed by washing with water.

When acetylcysteine inhalation is administered to patients with asthma or hyperactive airways disease, a bronchodilator should be administered prior to acetylcysteine to protect against bronchospasm.

Inhalation Dosage Forms

ACETYLCYSTEINE SOLUTION USP

Usual adult and adolescent dose:
    Mucolytic—
       Nebulization via face mask, mouth piece, or tracheostomy: Inhalation, 3 to 5 (range, 1 to 10) mL of a 20% solution or 6 to 10 (range, 2 to 20) mL of a 10% solution three or four times a day (range, every two to six hours).
       Nebulization via tent or croupette: Inhalation, a sufficient volume of a 10 or 20% solution to maintain a very heavy mist in the tent or croupette for the period of time necessary.
         Note: The method of nebulization, via tent or croupette, must be individualized according to the available equipment and the patient's condition. Very large volumes of the solution are required, occasionally as much as 300 mL during a single treatment period.
       Instillation, direct: 1 to 2 mL of a 10 to 20% solution every hour, if necessary.
         For routine care of patients with tracheostomy— Intratracheal, 1 to 2 mL of a 10 to 20% solution every one to four hours.
         For instillation into a particular segment of bronchopulmonary tree via small plastic catheter into trachea— Intratracheal, 2 to 5 mL of a 20% solution instilled by means of a syringe connected to the catheter.
         For instillation via percutaneous intratracheal catheter— Intratracheal, 2 to 4 mL of a 10% solution or 1 to 2 mL of a 20% solution every one to four hours administered by a syringe attached to the catheter.
    Diagnostic aid (bronchial studies)—Inhalation or intratracheal instillation, 1 to 2 mL of a 20% solution or 2 to 4 mL of a 10% solution for two or three doses prior to the procedure.

Usual geriatric dose: See *Usual adult and adolescent dose.*

Auxiliary labeling:
- Store in refrigerator after opening.
- Discard opened vial after 96 hours.

ACYCLOVIR   Systemic

INN: Aciclovir

A commonly used *brand name* in the U.S. and Canada is *Zovirax.* Another commonly used name is acycloguanosine.

ORAL
Acyclovir Capsules†
    In the U.S.—*Zovirax*
Acyclovir Oral Suspension
    In the U.S. and Canada—*Zovirax*
Acyclovir Tablets
    In the U.S. and Canada—*Zovirax*

PARENTERAL
Sterile Acyclovir Sodium
    In the U.S. and Canada—*Zovirax*

†Not commercially available in Canada.

Category: Antiviral (systemic).

Indications

Note: Bracketed information in the *Indications* section refers to uses not included in U.S. product labeling.

Accepted

Herpes genitalis (treatment)—Oral acyclovir is indicated in the treatment of initial episodes and management of recurrent, severe herpes genitalis infections in immunocompromised and nonimmunocompromised patients. Parenteral acyclovir is indicated in the treatment of severe initial herpes genitalis infections in immunocompromised and nonimmunocompromised patients, and in patients who are unable to take (or absorb) oral acyclovir.

Herpes genitalis (prophylaxis)—Oral acyclovir is indicated in the prophylaxis of frequently recurrent (6 episodes per year) herpes genitalis infections in immunocompromised and nonimmunocompromised patients.

Herpes simplex (treatment)—Parenteral [and oral] acyclovir are indicated in the treatment of initial and recurrent mucocutaneous herpes simplex (HSV-1 and HSV-2) infections in immunocompromised patients.

[Herpes simplex (prophylaxis)][1]—Parenteral and oral acyclovir are used in the prophylaxis of herpes simplex virus (HSV) infections in patients who are immunocompromised, including bone marrow and organ transplant patients, HIV-infected patients, and patients receiving chemotherapy.

Herpes simplex encephalitis (treatment)[1]—Parenteral acyclovir is indicated in the treatment of herpes simplex encephalitis.

Herpes zoster (treatment)—Oral acyclovir is indicated in the treatment of zoster infections (shingles) caused by varicella-zoster virus (VZV) in any adult patient with herpes zoster. Therapy is most effective when administered within 48 hours of the onset of rash. Parenteral acyclovir is used in the treatment of zoster infections (shingles) caused by VZV in immunocompromised patients and disseminated zoster in nonimmunocompromised patients.

[Herpes zoster (prophylaxis)][1]—Oral acyclovir is used in the prophylaxis of zoster infections (shingles) caused by VZV, after an initial period of parenteral acyclovir, in any immunocompromised patient, including bone marrow transplant and renal transplant patients, HIV-infected patients, and in patients receiving chemotherapy.

[Herpes zoster ophthalmicus (treatment)][1]—Oral and parenteral acyclovir are used in the treatment of herpes zoster ophthalmicus.

[Herpes simplex virus, disseminated neonatal infection (treatment)][1]—Parenteral acyclovir is used in the treatment of disseminated HSV in neonates.

Varicella (treatment)[1]—Oral acyclovir is indicated in the treatment of varicella infections (chickenpox) in nonimmunocompromised children and adolescents when used within 24 hours of the onset of a typical chickenpox rash. [Parenteral acyclovir is used in the treatment of varicella infections (chickenpox) caused by VZV in immunocompromised patients.]

Reduced sensitivity to acyclovir has been reported to develop with prolonged treatment or repeated therapy in severely immunocompromised patients. However, reduced sensitivity may occasionally develop as quickly as within a few weeks. If lesions due to herpes simplex virus fail to respond to acyclovir therapy, especially with continued viral shedding, viral isolates should be tested for susceptibility to acyclovir.

Unaccepted
Oral acyclovir is not indicated in the suppression of recurrent herpes genitalis in patients with infrequent recurrences.

---

[1]Not included in Canadian product labeling.

Pharmacology

Mechanism of action/Effect: Acyclovir is converted to acyclovir monophosphate, a nucleotide, by the viral thymidine kinases of herpes simplex virus (HSV) and varicella-zoster virus (VZV). Acyclovir monophosphate is converted to the diphosphate by cellular guanylate kinase and to the triphosphate by a number of cellular enzymes. Acyclovir triphosphate interferes with HSV and VZV DNA polymerase and inhibits viral DNA replication. The triphosphate can be incorporated into growing chains of DNA by viral DNA polymerase, resulting in termination of the DNA chain. Acyclovir is therefore selectively converted to the active triphosphate form by HSV- and VZV-infected cells.

Precautions to Consider

Cross-sensitivity and/or related problems
Patients allergic to ganciclovir may also be allergic to acyclovir because of the chemical similarity of the two medications.

Geriatrics
Studies performed to date have not demonstrated geriatric-specific problems that would limit the usefulness of acyclovir in the elderly. However, elderly patients are more likely to have an age-related decrease in renal function, which may require an adjustment of acyclovir dosage or dosing interval.

Drug interactions and/or related problems
The following drug interactions and/or related problems have been selected on the basis of their potential clinical significance (possible mechanism in parentheses where appropriate)—not necessarily inclusive (» = major clinical significance):

Note: Combinations containing any of the following medications, depending on the amount present, may also interact with this medication.

» Nephrotoxic medications, other
(concurrent use with intravenous acyclovir may increase the potential for nephrotoxicity, especially in the presence of renal function impairment)

Probenecid
(may decrease renal tubular secretion of intravenous acyclovir when used concurrently, resulting in increased acyclovir serum and cerebrospinal fluid [CSF] concentrations, prolonged elimination half-life in the serum and CSF, and, potentially, increased toxicity)

Contraindications/Medical problems
The contraindications/medical problems included have been selected on the basis of their potential clinical significance (reasons given in parentheses where appropriate)—not necessarily inclusive (» = major clinical significance):

Risk-benefit should be considered when the following medical problems exist:

» Dehydration or
» Renal function impairment, pre-existing
(intravenous acyclovir may increase the potential for nephrotoxicity; it is recommended that acyclovir be administered in a reduced dosage to patients with impaired renal function)

Hypersensitivity to acyclovir or ganciclovir

Neurological abnormalities or
Prior neurologic reactions to cytotoxic medications
(intravenous acyclovir may increase the potential for neurologic side effects)

Side/Adverse Effects

Note: Acute renal insufficiency may occur due to precipitation of acyclovir in the renal tubules. It is most likely to occur if acyclovir is given by rapid intravenous bolus injection, concurrently with known nephrotoxic medications, to patients who are inadequately hydrated, or to patients with renal dysfunction without appropriate dosage reduction. However, acute renal failure has also been reported in patients receiving oral acyclovir.

Neuropsychiatric toxicity has been associated with high plasma concentrations—which may occur when high doses are used, or when patients with renal dysfunction are not given an appropriately lowered dose. Neuropsychiatric toxicity may also be more likely to occur in immunocompromised patients and geriatric patients.

The following side/adverse effects have been selected on the basis of their potential clinical significance (possible signs and symptoms in parentheses where appropriate)—not necessarily inclusive:

Those indicating need for medical attention
Incidence more frequent
For parenteral acyclovir
Phlebitis or inflammation at the injection site (pain, swelling, or redness)

Incidence less frequent
>   *For parenteral acyclovir—more common with bolus injection*
>   **Acute renal failure** (abdominal pain, decreased frequency of urination or amount of urine, increased thirst, loss of appetite, nausea, vomiting, unusual tiredness or weakness)

Incidence rare
>   *For parenteral acyclovir only*
>   **Encephalopathic changes** (coma, confusion, hallucinations, seizures, tremors)

Those indicating need for medical attention only if they continue or are bothersome

Incidence more frequent—especially with high doses
>   *For parenteral acyclovir*
>   **Gastrointestinal disturbances** (anorexia, nausea or vomiting); *lightheadedness*

Incidence less frequent—with long-term use or high doses
>   *For oral acyclovir*
>   **Gastrointestinal disturbances** (nausea or vomiting, diarrhea, abdominal pain); *headache; lightheadedness*

Patient Consultation

In providing consultation, consider emphasizing the following selected information (» = major clinical significance):

Before using this medication
» Conditions affecting use, especially:
>   Hypersensitivity to acyclovir or ganciclovir
>   Pregnancy—Acyclovir crosses the placenta
>   Breast-feeding—Acyclovir is excreted in breast milk at concentrations from 0.6 to 4.1 times the corresponding plasma concentration
>   In children—Neonates have an age-related decrease in acyclovir clearance
>   Other medications, especially nephrotoxic medications
>   Other medical problems, especially dehydration or pre-existing renal function impairment

Proper use of this medication
>   Supplying patient information about herpes simplex or varicella-zoster infections
>   For treatment of recurrent herpes simplex infections, initiate use of the medication as soon as possible after symptoms of recurrence begin to appear
>   For treatment of chickenpox (varicella), initiate use of oral acyclovir at the earliest sign or symptom; it is most effective when used within 24 hours of the onset of a typical chickenpox rash
>   Capsules, tablets, and oral suspension may be taken with meals
>   Proper administration technique for oral liquids
>   Not using after expiration date
» Compliance with full course of therapy; not using more often or for longer than prescribed
>   Missed dose: Taking as soon as possible; not taking if almost time for next dose; not doubling doses
» Proper storage

Precautions while using this medication
» Women with herpes genitalis may have an increased risk of developing cervical cancer; annual Pap tests may be required
>   Checking with physician if no improvement within a few days
>   Keeping affected areas as clean and dry as possible; wearing loose-fitting clothing to avoid irritation of lesions
» Use of acyclovir has not been shown to prevent the transmission of herpes simplex virus to sexual partners
» Herpes genitalis may be sexually transmitted even if partner is asymptomatic; sexual activity should be avoided if either partner has signs and symptoms of herpes genitalis; use of a condom may help prevent transmission of herpes; however, spermicidal jellies or diaphragms probably will not be adequately protective

Side/adverse effects
>   Signs of potential side effects, especially acute renal failure, phlebitis or inflammation at site of injection, and encephalopathic changes

General Dosing Information

Therapy should be initiated as soon as possible following the onset of signs and symptoms of herpes simplex or varicella zoster infections.

Because it may take longer for lesions to heal in immunocompromised patients (an average of 2 weeks of therapy for herpes simplex infections), the duration of therapy may need to be prolonged beyond the recommended number of days until the lesions are crusted over or epithelialized.

For oral dosage forms only

Acyclovir capsules, tablets, and oral suspension may be taken with meals since absorption has not been shown to be significantly affected by food.

Intermittent short-term treatment of recurrent herpes genitalis infections may be effective for some patients, especially when treatment is patient-initiated during the prodrome or first sign of lesion formation.

For parenteral dosage forms only

Sterile acyclovir sodium should be administered by intravenous infusion only. It should not be administered topically, intramuscularly, orally, subcutaneously, or ophthalmically.

Intravenous infusions of acyclovir should be administered at a constant rate over at least a 1-hour period to avoid renal tubular obstruction. Rapid or bolus injection must be avoided since precipitation of acyclovir crystals in the tubules may occur and may result in renal function impairment in up to 10% of patients receiving intravenous acyclovir.

Obese patients should be dosed based on ideal body weight.

Since maximum urinary concentrations of acyclovir are achieved within 2 hours following intravenous infusions, patients must be adequately hydrated during this period to prevent precipitation of acyclovir in renal tubules.

The dose of acyclovir should be adjusted so that a dose is repeated after hemodialysis since each 6-hour hemodialysis period results in approximately a 60% reduction in acyclovir plasma concentrations.

Oral Dosage Forms

Note: Bracketed uses in the *Dosage Forms* section refer to categories of use and/or indications that are not included in U.S. product labeling.

ACYCLOVIR CAPSULES

Usual adult and adolescent dose:
>   Genital herpes infections—
>   Initial therapy: Oral, 200 mg every four hours while awake, five times a day, for ten days.
>   Recurrent infections, intermittent therapy: Oral, 200 mg every four hours while awake, five times a day, for five days.
>   Recurrent infections, chronic suppressive therapy: Oral, 400 mg twice a day; or 200 mg two to five times a day.
>   Herpes zoster—Oral, 800 mg every four hours while awake, five times a day, for seven to ten days.

Varicella[1]—Oral, 20 mg per kg of body weight, up to 800 mg per dose, four times a day for five days. Treatment should be initiated at the earliest sign or symptom of chickenpox.

[Herpes simplex, mucocutaneous]—Oral, 200 to 400 mg five times a day for ten days in immunocompromised patients.

Note: Adults with acute or chronic renal impairment require a reduction in dose.

The recommended dose for initial therapy and intermittent therapy of genital herpes infections in patients with renal function impairment is:

Creatinine Clearance (mL/min/1.73 M[2]) (mL/sec)	Dose (mg)	Dosing Interval (hr)
Genital herpes: Initial/intermittent therapy		
>10/(0.17)	200	4 (5 times daily)
0–10/(0–0.17)	200	12
Chronic suppressive		
>10/(0.17)	400	12
0–10/(0–0.17)	200	12
Herpes zoster (shingles):		
>25/(0.42)	800	4 (5 times daily)
10–25/(0.17–0.42)	800	8
0–10/(0–0.17)	800	12

Auxiliary labeling: • Continue medicine for full time of treatment.

ACYCLOVIR ORAL SUSPENSION

Usual adult and adolescent dose: See *Acyclovir Capsules.*

Auxiliary labeling:
• Continue medicine for full time of treatment.
• Shake well.
• Take with water.
• Beyond-use date.

Note: When dispensing, include a calibrated liquid-measuring device.

ACYCLOVIR TABLETS

Usual adult and adolescent dose: See *Acyclovir Capsules.*

Auxiliary labeling: • Continue medicine for full time of treatment.

Parenteral Dosage Forms

Note: Bracketed uses in the *Dosage Forms* section refer to categories of use and/or indications that are not included in U.S. product labeling.

The dosing and dosage forms available are expressed in terms of acyclovir base.

STERILE ACYCLOVIR SODIUM

Usual adult and adolescent dose: Intravenous infusion—

Genital herpes infections, severe, initial: 5 mg (base) per kg of body weight every eight hours for five days. Administer at a constant rate over at least a one-hour period.

Herpes simplex (HSV-1 and HSV-2) infections, mucocutaneous, in immunocompromised patients: 5 to 10 mg (base) per kg of body weight every eight hours for seven to ten days. Administer at a constant rate over at least a one-hour period.

Herpes simplex encephalitis[1]: 10 mg (base) per kg of body weight every eight hours for ten days. Administer at a constant rate over at least a one-hour period.

Varicella zoster in immunocompromised patients[1]: 10 mg (base) per kg of body weight every eight hours for seven days. Administer at a constant rate over at least a one-hour period.

Note: Adults with acute or chronic renal impairment require a reduction in dose as follows:

Creatinine Clearance (mL/min/1.73 M[2]) (mL/sec)	Dose (base)	Dosing Interval (hr)
>50/(0.83)	100%	8
25–50/(0.42–0.83)	100%	12
10–25/(0.17–0.42)	100%	24
0–10/(0–0.17)	50%	24

Usual adult prescribing limits: Up to 30 mg (base) per kg of body weight or 1.5 grams per square meter of body surface daily.

†Not included in Canadian product labeling.

ALCOHOL AND ACETONE   Topical†

Some commonly used *brand names* in the U.S. are *Seba-Nil Liquid Cleanser, Tyrosum Liquid*, and *Tyrosum Packets.*

TOPICAL
Alcohol and Acetone Detergent Lotion†
  In the U.S.—*Seba-Nil Liquid Cleanser; Tyrosum Liquid*
Alcohol and Acetone Pledgets†
  In the U.S.—*Tyrosum Packets*

†Not commercially available in Canada.

Category: Antiacne agent (topical); cleansing agent (astringent; defatting).

Indications

Accepted
Acne vulgaris (treatment); or

Oily skin (treatment)—Alcohol and acetone combination is indicated as an aid in the treatment of mild acne vulgaris and oily skin.

Pharmacology

Mechanism of action/Effect: Alcohol and acetone aid in the removal of sebum (oil) from the surface of the skin.

Precautions to Consider

Geriatrics
Appropriate studies on the relationship of age to the effects of alcohol and acetone have not been performed in the geriatric population. However, geriatrics-specific problems that would limit the usefulness of this medication in the elderly are not expected.

Drug interactions and/or related problems
The following drug interactions and/or related problems have been selected on the basis of their potential clinical significance (pos-

sible mechanism in parentheses where appropriate)—not necessarily inclusive (» = major clinical significance):

Note: Combinations containing any of the following medications, depending on the amount present, may also interact with this medication.

Abrasive or medicated soaps or cleansers or
Acne preparations or preparations containing a peeling agent, such as:
  Benzoyl peroxide
  Resorcinol
  Salicylic acid
  Sulfur
  Tretinoin, or
Acne preparations, topical, other, or
Alcohol-containing preparations, topical, such as:
  After-shave lotions
  Astringents
  Perfumed toiletries
  Shaving creams or lotions, or
Cosmetics or soaps with a strong drying effect or
Isotretinoin or
Medicated cosmetics or "cover-ups"
  (concurrent use with alcohol and acetone combination may cause a cumulative irritant or drying effect, especially with the application of peeling, desquamating, or abrasive agents, resulting in excessive irritation of the skin)

Contraindications/Medical problems

The contraindications/medical problems included have been selected on the basis of their potential clinical significance (reasons given in parentheses where appropriate)—not necessarily inclusive (» = major clinical significance).

This medication should not be used when the following medical problems exist:

» Burns or wounds
  (use may cause severe irritation)

Risk-benefit should be considered when the following medical problem exists:

Sensitivity to this medication
  (may cause allergic contact dermatitis, contact urticaria syndrome, sensitive skin [i.e., easily irritated], or subjective irritation [i.e., burning, stinging, and itching without objective signs])

Side/Adverse Effects

The following side/adverse effects have been selected on the basis of their potential clinical significance (possible signs and symptoms in parentheses where appropriate)—not necessarily inclusive:

Those indicating need for medical attention
Hypersensitivity (irritation, pain, redness, or swelling of skin); *skin infection*

Those indicating need for medical attention only if they continue or are bothersome
Burning or stinging of skin

Patient Consultation

In providing consultation, consider emphasizing the following selected information (» = major clinical significance):

Before using this medication
» Conditions affecting use, especially:
    Sensitivity to alcohol or acetone
    Use in children—Not using on children up to 8 years of age
    Other medical problems, especially burns or wounds

Proper use of this medication
» Avoiding contact with the eyes, nostrils, and lips
    Medication is flammable; not using near heat or open flame or while smoking
    Proper administration:
      Applying the lotion by putting a small amount on a gauze pad or cotton ball and wiping or rubbing over face and other affected areas
      Using the pledget by wiping or rubbing over face and other affected areas
      Not rinsing after application
    Missed dose: If on scheduled dosing regimen—Applying as soon as possible
» Proper storage

Precautions while using this medication
» Avoiding simultaneous use with other topical acne preparations or preparations containing peeling agents, other alcohol-containing preparations, abrasive soaps or cleansers, cosmetics or soaps with drying effect, medicated cosmetics, or other topical skin medications, unless otherwise directed by physician

Side/adverse effects
    Signs of potential side effects, especially hypersensitivity or skin infection

Topical Dosage Forms

ALCOHOL AND ACETONE DETERGENT LOTION

Usual adult and adolescent dose: Topical, to the skin, two to four times a day as needed.

Auxiliary labeling:
• For external use only.
• Keep container tightly closed.
• Flammable.

Additional information: The lotion should be applied using a gauze pad or cotton ball.

ALCOHOL AND ACETONE PLEDGETS

Usual adult and adolescent dose: Topical, to the skin, two to four times a day as needed.

Auxiliary labeling:
• For external use only.
• Flammable.

ALCOHOL AND SULFUR   Topical

Some commonly used *brand names* are:

In the U.S.—

Liquimat Creamy Beige	*Liquimat Natural Beige*
Liquimat Dark	*Transact*
Liquimat Light	*Xerac*
Liquimat Medium	

In Canada—
Postacne

TOPICAL

Alcohol and Sulfur Gel
In the U.S.—*Transact; Xerac*
Alcohol and Sulfur Lotion
In the U.S.—*Liquimat Creamy Beige; Liquimat Dark; Liquimat Light; Liquimat Medium; Liquimat Natural Beige*
In Canada—*Postacne*

Category: Antiacne agent (topical); cleansing agent (astringent; defatting)-keratolytic.

Indications

Accepted
Acne vulgaris (treatment); or
Oily skin (treatment)—Indicated as an aid in the treatment of acne vulgaris and oily skin.

Pharmacology

Mechanism of action/Effect:
Alcohol—Aids in the removal of sebum (oil) from the surface of the skin.
Sulfur—Acts as a keratolytic and promotes drying and peeling of the skin. Sulfur also has germicidal action, which results from its conversion to pentathionic acid presumably by epidermal cells or certain microorganisms.

Precautions to Consider

Geriatrics
Appropriate studies on the relationship of age to the effect of alcohol and sulfur have not been performed in the geriatric population. However, geriatrics-specific problems that would limit the usefulness of this medication in the elderly are not expected.

Drug interactions and/or related problems
The following drug interactions and/or related problems have been selected on the basis of their potential clinical significance (possible mechanism in parentheses where appropriate)—not necessarily inclusive (» = major clinical significance):

Note: Combinations containing any of the following medications, depending on the amount present, may also interact with this medication.

Abrasive or medicated soaps or cleansers or
Acne preparations or preparations containing a peeling agent, such as:
Benzoyl peroxide
Resorcinol
Salicylic acid
Tretinoin, or
Acne preparations, topical, other, or
Alcohol-containing preparations, topical, such as:
After-shave lotions
Astringents
Perfumed toiletries

Shaving creams or lotions, or
Cosmetics or soaps with a strong drying effect or
Isotretinoin or
Medicated cosmetics or "cover-ups"
(concurrent use with alcohol and sulfur combination may cause a cumulative irritant or drying effect, especially with the application of peeling, desquamating, or abrasive agents, resulting in excessive irritation of the skin)
Mercury compounds, topical
(concurrent use with sulfur may result in a chemical reaction releasing hydrogen sulfide, which has a foul odor, may be irritating, and may stain the skin black)

Contraindications/Medical problems
The contraindications/medical problems included have been selected on the basis of their potential clinical significance (reasons given in parentheses where appropriate)—not necessarily inclusive (» = major clinical significance).

Risk-benefit should be considered when the following medical problem exists:
Sensitivity to this medication
(may cause allergic contact dermatitis, contact urticaria syndrome, sensitive skin [i.e., easily irritated], or subjective irritation [i.e., burning, stinging, or itching without objective signs])

Side/Adverse Effects

The following side/adverse effects have been selected on the basis of their potential clinical significance (possible signs and symptoms in parentheses where appropriate)—not necessarily inclusive:

Those indicating need for medical attention
Hypersensitivity (skin irritation not present before therapy)

Those indicating need for medical attention only if they continue or are bothersome
Burning or stinging of skin; dryness or peeling of skin—may occur after a few days

Patient Consultation

In providing consultation, consider emphasizing the following selected information (» = major clinical significance):

Before using this medication
» Conditions affecting use, especially:
Sensitivity to alcohol or sulfur
Use in children—Not using on children up to 8 years of age

Proper use of this medication
Proper administration:
Before using, washing or cleansing affected areas thoroughly and patting dry
Applying small amount and rubbing in gently
» Avoiding contact with the eyes, nostrils, and lips
Medication is flammable; not using near heat or open flame or while smoking
» Importance of not using more medication than the amount recommended
Missed dose: Applying as soon as possible
» Proper storage

Precautions while using this medication
» Avoiding simultaneous use with other topical acne preparations or preparations containing peeling agents, other alcohol-containing preparations, abrasive soaps or cleansers, cosmetics or soaps with drying effect, medicated cosmetics, or other topical skin medications, unless prescribed by physician

» Avoiding concurrent use with topical mercury-containing preparations

Side/adverse effects
Signs of potential side effects, especially hypersensitivity

General Dosing Information

Some of the products are tinted a flesh color and can be used as a makeup or cover-up.

Since this medication is an effective drying agent, it should be used sparingly when therapy is initiated, especially for those patients with sensitive skin.

The frequency of applications may be increased gradually up to three times a day as tolerated.

In dry or cold climates, the skin may be more sensitive to this medication, and the frequency of use should be reduced. During warm, humid weather, frequency of use may be increased.

Topical Dosage Forms

ALCOHOL AND SULFUR GEL

Usual adult and adolescent dose: Topical, to the skin, one to three times a day.

Auxiliary labeling: • For external use only.

ALCOHOL AND SULFUR LOTION

Usual adult and adolescent dose: Topical, to the skin, one or two times a day.

Auxiliary labeling:
• Shake well.
• For external use only.

ALLOPURINOL   Systemic

Some commonly used *brand names* are:
In the U.S.—
    Lopurin   *Zyloprim*
In Canada—
    Alloprin   *Purinol*
    Apo-Allopurinol   *Zyloprim*
    Novopurol

ORAL
Allopurinol Tablets USP
    In the U.S.—*Lopurin; Zyloprim;* GENERIC
    In Canada—*Alloprin; Apo-Allopurinol; Novopurol; Purinol; Zyloprim*

Category: Antihyperuricemic; antigout agent; antiurolithic (uric acid calculi; calcium oxalate calculi).

Note: Antihyperuricemic is the basic category; the other categories are specific categories of use.

Indications

Note: Bracketed information in the *Indications* section refers to uses not included in U.S. product labeling.

Accepted
Gouty arthritis, chronic (treatment)—Allopurinol is indicated for the long-term management of hyperuricemia associated with primary or secondary gout.

Allopurinol is not effective in the treatment of acute gout attacks because it has no anti-inflammatory action, and may intensify and prolong inflammation during the acute phase. However, after several months of treatment, allopurinol may prevent acute attacks from occurring.

Hyperuricemia (prophylaxis and treatment)—Allopurinol is indicated to control hyperuricemia secondary to blood dyscrasias, such as polycythemia vera or myeloid metaplasia, or their treatment. It is also indicated to prevent or treat hyperuricemia secondary to tumor lysis induced by cancer chemotherapy with cytotoxic antineoplastic agents or radiation therapy in patients with leukemias, lymphomas, or other neoplastic disease. [Allopurinol is also used to treat hyperuricemia secondary to the neoplastic disease itself.][1] Allopurinol prevents complications of hyperuricemia (e.g., acute uric acid nephropathy or renal calculi, tissue urate deposi-

tion, or gouty arthritis) in these patients. However, allopurinol may increase the toxicity of several antineoplastic agents, and some clinicians have questioned its routine administration during cancer chemotherapy.

[Allopurinol is also used to control hyperuricemia in patients with Lesch-Nyhan syndrome. However, it does not improve neurologic or behavioral abnormalities or affect the course of the disease in these patients.]

Nephropathy, uric acid (prophylaxis and treatment)—Allopurinol is indicated in the treatment of primary or secondary uric acid nephropathy (with or without accompanying symptoms of gout) to prevent progression of the condition. However, allopurinol will not reverse severe renal damage that has already occurred. It is also indicated to prevent uric acid nephropathy in certain patients as described under *Hyperuricemia,* above.

Renal calculi, uric acid (prophylaxis)—Allopurinol is indicated to prevent recurrence of uric acid stone formation in patients with a history of recurrent uric acid calculi. It is also indicated to prevent uric acid calculi in certain other patients as described under *Hyperuricemia,* above.

Renal calculi, calcium oxalate, recurrence (prophylaxis)—Allopurinol is indicated to prevent recurrence of calcium stone formation in patients with a history of recurrent calcium oxalate calculi associated with hyperuricosuria (i.e., uric acid excretion >800 mg per day in males or 750 mg per day in females).

Unaccepted
Allopurinol is not recommended for treatment of asymptomatic hyperuricemia associated with conditions or induced by medications other than those described above.

---

[1]Not included in Canadian product labeling.

Pharmacology

Mechanism of action/Effect: Allopurinol and its metabolite, oxipurinol (alloxanthine), decrease the production of uric acid by inhibiting the action of xanthine oxidase, the enzyme that converts hypoxanthine to xanthine and xanthine to uric acid. Also, allopurinol increases reutilization of hypoxanthine and xanthine for nucleotide and nucleic acid synthesis via an action involving the enzyme hypoxanthine-guanine phosphoribosyltransferase (HGPRTase). The resultant increase in nucleotide concentration leads to feedback inhibition of de novo purine synthesis. Allopurinol thereby decreases uric acid concentrations in both serum and urine.

By lowering both serum and urine concentrations of uric acid below its solubility limits, allopurinol prevents or decreases urate deposition, thereby preventing the occurrence or progression of both gouty arthritis and urate nephropathy. In patients with chronic gout, allopurinol may prevent or decrease tophi formation and chronic joint changes, promote resolution of existing urate crystals and deposits, and, after several months of therapy, reduce the frequency of acute gout attacks. Also, reductions in urine urate concentration prevent or decrease the formation of uric acid or calcium oxalate calculi.

Other actions/effects:

Allopurinol inhibits hepatic microsomal enzyme activity.

Allopurinol increases plasma and urine concentrations of xanthine and hypoxanthine. Although the concentrations of these oxypurines usually remain within their solubility limits, xanthine renal stones have been reported very rarely in patients with HGPRTase deficiency or very high pretreatment uric acid concentrations.

Onset of action: A significant reduction of serum uric acid concentration usually occurs within 2 or 3 days.

Note: In some patients, especially those with severe tophaceous deposits or those who are underexcretors of uric acid, significant reduction of serum and urine uric acid concentrations may be substantially delayed, possibly because of mobilization of urate from existing tissue deposits.

Time to peak effect:

Reduction of serum uric acid concentration to normal range—1 to 3 weeks.

Reduction of frequency of acute gout attacks—Several months of therapy may be required, even though the serum uric acid concentration returns to normal values, possibly because of mobilization and recrystallization of urate as serum concentrations fluctuate.

Duration of action: The serum uric acid concentration usually returns to the pretreatment value 1 to 2 weeks after discontinuation of therapy.

Precautions to Consider

Geriatrics

No information is available on the relationship of age to the effects of allopurinol in geriatric patients. However, elderly patients are more likely to have age-related renal function impairment, which may require adjustment of the dose and/or dosing interval in patients receiving allopurinol.

Drug interactions and/or related problems

The following drug interactions and/or related problems have been selected on the basis of their potential clinical significance (possible mechanism in parentheses where appropriate)—not necessarily inclusive (» = major clinical significance):

Note: Combinations containing any of the following medications, depending on the amount present, may also interact with this medication.

Acidifiers, urinary, such as:

Ammonium chloride

Ascorbic acid

Potassium or sodium phosphate

(urinary acidification by these medications may increase the possibility of allopurinol-induced xanthine kidney stone formation)

Alcohol or

Bumetanide or

Diazoxide or

Ethacrynic acid or

Furosemide or

Mecamylamine or

Pyrazinamide or

Triamterene

(these medications may increase serum uric acid concentrations; dosage adjustment of allopurinol may be necessary to control hyperuricemia and gout)

Amoxicillin or

Ampicillin or

Bacampicillin or

Hetacillin

(concurrent use with allopurinol may significantly increase the possibility of skin rash; however, it has not been established that allopurinol, rather than the presence of hyperuricemia, is responsible for this effect)

» Anticoagulants, coumarin- or indandione-derivative

(allopurinol may inhibit enzymatic metabolism of the anticoagulant, leading to potentiation of the anticoagulant effect; dosage adjustments based on increased monitoring of prothrombin time may be necessary during and after concurrent use)

Antineoplastics

(rapidly cytolytic antineoplastic agents may increase serum uric acid concentrations; prophylactic administration of allopurinol may be indicated to prevent complications associated with antineoplastic agent-induced hyperuricemia; also, patients receiving allopurinol to treat pre-existing hyperuricemia or gout may require allopurinol dosage adjustment during and following concurrent therapy with one of these agents)

(concurrent use of allopurinol with cyclophosphamide and possibly other antineoplastic agents may increase the potential for bone marrow depression; although studies of this possibility have reported conflicting results, it is recommended that patients receiving allopurinol concurrently with antineoplastic agents, especially cyclophosphamide, be carefully monitored)

» Azathioprine or

» Mercaptopurine

(allopurinol-induced inhibition of xanthine oxidase decreases metabolism of these medications and may potentiate therapeutic and toxic effects, especially bone marrow depression; the effect on azathioprine metabolism is especially critical in renal transplant patients because of the high risk of oxipurinol accumulation and consequent azathioprine toxicity if the transplanted kidney is rejected; if concurrent use is essential, it is recommended that azathioprine or mercaptopurine dosage be reduced to one-third to one-fourth of the usual dosage, that the patient be carefully monitored, and that subsequent dosage adjustments be based on patient response and evidence of toxicity)

(mercaptopurine may increase serum uric acid concentration in some patients; patients receiving allopurinol to treat pre-existing hyperuricemia or gout may require allopurinol dosage adjustment when mercaptopurine therapy is initiated or discontinued)

Chlorpropamide

(allopurinol may inhibit renal tubular secretion of chlorpropamide; patients receiving the medications concurrently should be monitored for possible increased hypoglycemic effect)

Dacarbazine

(dacarbazine inhibits xanthine oxidase and may cause additive hypouricemic effects when used concurrently with allopurinol)

Diuretics, thiazide

(these medications may increase serum uric acid concentrations; dosage adjustment of allopurinol may be necessary to control hyperuricemia and gout)

(caution and careful monitoring of the patient are advised when allopurinol and thiazide diuretics are used concurrently, especially in patients with known or possible renal function impairment, because severe hypersensitivity reactions to allopurinol may occur; although it has been suggested that compromised renal function, rather than the combination of medications, may be responsible for the adverse reactions, it has been proposed that thiazide diuretics may increase serum oxipurinol concentrations by decreasing its renal excretion)

Probenecid

(probenecid increases urinary excretion of oxipurinol; however, the antihyperuricemic effects of the two medications are additive, and increased therapeutic benefit has been reported with concurrent use)

Sulfinpyrazone

(the antihyperuricemic effects of allopurinol and sulfinpyrazone are additive; increased therapeutic benefit has been reported with concurrent use)

Vidarabine, systemic

(concurrent use with allopurinol may increase the risk of neurotoxicity and other side effects such as anemia, nausea, pain, and pruritus; caution is recommended if concurrent use is necessary)

Xanthines, such as:
  Aminophylline
  Oxtriphylline
  Theophylline

(concurrent use of large doses [600 mg per day] of allopurinol with the xanthines [except dyphylline] may decrease theophylline clearance, resulting in increased serum theophylline concentrations; when steady-state theophylline concentration is 13 mcg per mL (72.15 micromoles/L) or higher and 600 mg of allopurinol per day is required, serum theophylline concentrations should be monitored and theophylline dosage adjusted if necessary)

Contraindications/Medical problems

The contraindications/medical problems included have been selected on the basis of their potential clinical significance (reasons given in parentheses where appropriate)—not necessarily inclusive (» = major clinical significance).

Risk-benefit should be considered when the following medical problems exist:

Renal function impairment or any illness that may predispose to a change in renal function, such as:
  Diabetes mellitus
  Hypertension

(oxipurinol may accumulate; risk of severe allergic reactions and other adverse effects is increased; a reduction in dosage may be required)

Sensitivity to allopurinol, history of
(increased risk of severe allergic reaction)

Side/Adverse Effects

Note: Following initiation of allopurinol therapy for gouty arthritis, the most commonly encountered adverse effect is a temporary increase in the frequency of acute gout attacks. The occurrence of such reactions may be reduced by initiating therapy with a low dose that is gradually increased until the desired effect is obtained and by administration of prophylactic doses of colchicine or a nonsteroidal anti-inflammatory drug.

In addition to the side/adverse effects listed below, bone marrow depression has been reported to occur from 6 weeks to 6 years after initiation of allopurinol therapy. Anemia, aplastic anemia, and agranulocytosis have been reported. However, a definite causal relationship has not been established.

The following side/adverse effects have been selected on the basis of their potential clinical significance (possible signs and symptoms in parentheses where appropriate)—not necessarily inclusive:

Those indicating need for medical attention
Incidence more frequent
  Dermatitis, allergic (skin rash, hives, or itching)

Note: *Maculopapular skin rash* occurs most often; however, *eczematoid, exfoliative, urticarial, vesicular bullous, or purpuric lesions and lichen planus* have also been reported.

Very rarely, *skin rash* may be followed by more severe allergic reactions, usually in patients with renal function impairment and/or those receiving thiazide diuretics. *Generalized vasculitis, hepatotoxicity, and/or acute renal failure* may occur. Laboratory studies may indicate *eosinophilia and leukopenia or leukocytosis*. Several deaths have been attributed to these reactions.

Incidence rare
  Agranulocytosis (chills, fever, and sore throat); *angiitis [vasculitis], hypersensitivity* (chills, fever, and sore throat; muscle aches, pains, or weakness; shortness of breath, troubled breathing, tightness in chest, or wheezing); *dermatitis, exfoliative* (possible prodrome of chills, fever, sore throat, muscle aches or pains, and/or nausea with or without vomiting; red, thickened, scaly skin); *erythema multiforme* (possible prodrome of chills, fever, sore throat, muscle aches or pains, and/or nausea with or without vomiting; sores, ulcers, or white spots in mouth or on lips; skin rash or sores, hives, and/or itching); *hepatotoxicity* (swelling in upper abdominal area; yellow eyes or skin)—may be hypersensitivity-mediated; hepatic necrosis, granulomatous hepatitis, and cholestatic jaundice have been reported; *hypersensitivity reaction, allopurinol-induced* (initially skin rash immediately preceding or concurrent with chills, fever, and sore throat; muscle aches or pains; and/or nausea with or without vomiting; followed by signs and symptoms of angiitis [vasculitis], hepatotoxicity, and/or acute renal failure); *loosening of fingernails; necrolysis, toxic epidermal* (possible prodrome of chills, fever, sore throat, muscle aches or pains, and/or nausea with or without vomiting; redness, tenderness, itching, burning, or peeling of skin; red or irritated eyes); *neuritis, peripheral* (numbness, tingling, pain, or weakness in hands or feet); *renal calculus, xanthine* (blood in urine, difficult or painful urination, pain in lower back and/or side); *renal failure, acute* (sudden decrease in amount of urine; swelling of face, fingers, feet, and/or lower legs; weight gain, rapid); *Stevens-Johnson syndrome* (possible prodrome of chills, fever, sore throat, muscle aches and pains, and/or nausea with or without vomiting; sores, ulcers, or white spots in mouth or on lips; bleeding sores on lips); *thrombocytopenia* (usually asymptomatic; rarely, unusual bleeding or bruising; black, tarry stools; blood in urine or stools; pinpoint red spots on skin); *unexplained nosebleeds*

Those indicating need for medical attention only if they continue or are bothersome
Incidence less frequent or rare
  Diarrhea; drowsiness; headache; indigestion; nausea or vomiting without symptoms of skin rash, chills or fever, or muscle aches and pains; stomach pain; unusual hair loss

Patient Consultation

In providing consultation, consider emphasizing the following selected information (» = major clinical significance):

Before using this medication
» Conditions affecting use, especially:
    Other medications, especially coumarin- or indandione-derivative anticoagulants, azathioprine, and mercaptopurine

Proper use of this medication
    Taking after meals, if necessary, to minimize gastrointestinal irritation
» Compliance with therapy

Importance of high fluid intake during therapy and compliance with therapy for alkalinization of urine, if prescribed, to help prevent kidney stones

Missed dose: Taking as soon as possible; not taking if almost time for next dose; not doubling doses

For patients taking allopurinol for gout

Several months of continuous therapy may be required for maximum effectiveness

» Medication helps prevent, but does not relieve, acute gout attacks; need to continue taking allopurinol with medication prescribed for gout attacks

» Proper storage

Precautions while using this medication

Regular visits to physician to check progress during therapy; possible need for periodic blood tests to determine efficacy of therapy and/or occurrence of side effects

Avoiding large amounts of alcohol, which may increase uric acid concentrations and reduce effectiveness of medication

Possibility that vitamin C taken in large amounts may increase the potential for kidney stone formation

» Notifying physician immediately if skin rash occurs or if influenza-like symptoms (chills, fever, muscle aches and pains, or nausea or vomiting) occur concurrently with or shortly after skin rash; these symptoms may rarely indicate onset of severe hypersensitivity reaction

» Caution if drowsiness occurs

Side/adverse effects

Signs of potential adverse effects, especially agranulocytosis, hypersensitivity reaction, hepatotoxicity, renal failure, thrombocytopenia, peripheral neuritis, erythema multiforme, Stevens-Johnson syndrome, and toxic epidermal necrolysis

General Dosing Information

Allopurinol may be administered after meals to lessen gastrointestinal irritation.

Allopurinol may increase the frequency of acute attacks of gout during the early months of therapy. The occurrence of such reactions may be reduced by initiating allopurinol therapy with a low dose, then gradually increasing dosage until the desired effect is obtained. Also, prophylactic doses of colchicine or a nonsteroidal anti-inflammatory drug (NSAID) may be administered concurrently during the first 3 to 6 months of allopurinol therapy.

Acute attacks of gout may occur during allopurinol therapy, even with colchicine or NSAID prophylactic therapy. During these acute attacks, allopurinol should be continued at the same dose, with full therapeutic doses of colchicine or an NSAID being administered concurrently for treatment of these attacks.

The total daily dose may be administered in divided doses or as a single dose. Each single dose should not exceed 300 mg. Daily dosage requirements exceeding 300 mg should be administered in divided doses.

Determination of serum uric acid concentrations may be necessary for proper dosing.

To reduce the risk of xanthine calculi formation, and to help prevent renal precipitation of urates in patients receiving concomitant uricosuric agents, a high fluid intake (no less than 2.5 to 3 liters daily) and maintenance of a neutral, or preferably slightly alkaline, urine are recommended.

When uricosuric therapy is being changed to allopurinol therapy, the dose of the uricosuric agent should be reduced gradually over a period of several weeks and the dose of allopurinol increased gradually to the dose required for maintenance of normal serum uric acid concentrations.

It is recommended that allopurinol therapy be discontinued at once if a skin rash or any other sign of adverse reaction occurs. Skin rash may be followed by more severe hypersensitivity reactions. After a severe reaction, therapy should be discontinued permanently. However, after a mild reaction, it may be possible to reinstate therapy at a lower dosage (50 mg per day initially and increased very gradually) after the reaction has subsided. If skin rash recurs, therapy should be discontinued permanently.

Oral Dosage Forms

ALLOPURINOL TABLETS USP

Usual adult and adolescent dose:

Antihyperuricemic—

Antigout agent:

Initial—Oral, 100 mg once a day, to be increased by 100 mg per day at one-week intervals until the desired serum uric acid concentration is attained, not to exceed the maximum recommended dosage of 800 mg per day.

Maintenance—Oral, 100 to 200 mg two or three times a day; or 300 mg as a single dose once a day. The usual maintenance dose is 200 to 300 mg per day in mild gout or 400 to 600 mg per day in moderately severe tophaceous gout.

Neoplastic disease therapy:

Initial—Oral, 600 to 800 mg per day starting twelve hours to three days (preferably two to three days) prior to initiation of chemotherapy or radiation therapy.

Maintenance—Dosage should be based on serum uric acid determinations performed approximately forty-eight hours after initiation of allopurinol therapy and periodically thereafter. Allopurinol should be discontinued following the period of tumor regression.

Antiurolithic (uric acid calculi)—Oral, 100 to 200 mg one to four times a day; or 300 mg as a single dose once a day.

Antiurolithic (calcium oxalate calculi)—Oral, 200 to 300 mg a day as a single dose or in divided doses.

Note: Because oxipurinol is excreted primarily by the kidneys, accumulation may occur in patients with renal failure. Patients receiving dialysis may require usual therapeutic doses of allopurinol; however, in patients not receiving dialysis, it is recommended that the dosage be reduced as follows:

Creatinine Clearance (mL/min)	Dose
10 to 20	200 mg daily
3 to 10	no more than 100 mg daily
< 3	100 mg at intervals of more than 24 hours may be necessary

Some patients with renal function impairment may require even lower doses or longer intervals between doses. In some cases, 300 mg twice a week, or even less, may suffice.

Usual adult prescribing limits: 300 mg per dose or 800 mg per day.

Auxiliary labeling: • Drink large amounts of fluids.

ALPROSTADIL   Intracavernosal

Some commonly used *brand names* are:
In the U.S.—*Prostin VR Pediatric*
In Canada—*Prostin VR*
Other commonly used names are PGE1 and prostaglandin E1.

PARENTERAL
Alprostadil Injection USP
In the U.S.—*Prostin VR Pediatric*
In Canada—*Prostin VR*

Category: Impotence therapy.

Indications

Note: Bracketed information in the *Indications* section refers to uses not included in U.S. product labeling.

Accepted
[Impotence (treatment)][1]—Alprostadil is used by intracavernosal injection to facilitate erections in men with impotence. In general, it is most useful in patients with organic impotence (neurogenic and, to a lesser extent, vascular). It is less useful in patients with impotence due to endocrine problems (hypogonadism, hyper- or hypothyroidism) or medications.

[Impotence (diagnosis)][1]—Alprostadil is used by intracavernosal injection as an aid in the evaluation of penile vasculature, alone or prior to angiography, cavernosography, or cavernosometry.

Unaccepted
Use of alprostadil to enhance erections in men who are not impotent is not recommended because of the risk of priapism and permanent damage to penile tissues.

[1]Not included in Canadian product labeling.

Pharmacology

Mechanism of action/Effect: Alprostadil is one of a family of naturally occurring prostaglandins, which causes vasodilation by means of a direct effect on vascular smooth muscle. It is present naturally in the seminal vesicle and seminal plasma.

When administered by intracavernous injection, it is thought to cause relaxation of the trabecular cavernous smooth muscles and vasodilation of the penile arteries. This results in increased arterial blood flow into the corpus cavernosa, and swelling and elongation of the penis; the glans and corpus spongiosum also swell.

Venous outflow is also reduced, possibly as a result of increased venous resistance.

Onset of action: 5 to 10 minutes.

Time to peak effect: Within 20 minutes.

Duration of action: 1 to 3 hours; dose-related.

Precautions to Consider

Geriatrics
No information is available on the relationship of age to the effects of alprostadil used intracavernosally in geriatric patients. However, elderly patients are more likely to have peripheral vascular disease, which may result in a decreased response to intracavernosal alprostadil; dosage adjustment may be necessary.

Drug interactions and/or related problems
The following drug interactions and/or related problems have been selected on the basis of their potential clinical significance (pos-

sible mechanism in parentheses where appropriate)—not necessarily inclusive (» = major clinical significance):

Note: Combinations containing any of the following medications, depending on the amount present, may also interact with this medication.

Sympathomimetics, alpha-adrenergic, especially metaraminol, epinephrine, and phenylephrine
(reverse the vasodilating effect of alprostadil; may be used to treat priapism or overdose)

Contraindications/Medical problems
The contraindications/medical problems included have been selected on the basis of their potential clinical significance (reasons given in parentheses where appropriate)—not necessarily inclusive (» = major clinical significance).

Risk-benefit should be considered when the following medical problems exist:
» Coagulation defects, severe, or
» Liver disease, severe
(risk of bleeding at injection site; alprostadil inhibits platelet aggregation)
» Priapism, history of, or
» Sickle cell disease
(increased risk of priapism)
Sensitivity to alprostadil

Side/Adverse Effects

The following side/adverse effects have been selected on the basis of their potential clinical significance (possible signs and symptoms in parentheses where appropriate)—not necessarily inclusive:

Those indicating need for medical attention
Incidence rare
Priapism (erection, continuing for more than 4 hours)
Note: Usually due to excessive dosage. Prolonged erection may resolve spontaneously, but in some cases will require treatment.

Those indicating need for medical attention only if they continue or are bothersome
Incidence more frequent
Pain at site of injection; pain during erection (burning or aching)—may be severe
Incidence rare
Superficial hematoma (bruising or bleeding at site of injection)

Patient Consultation

In providing consultation, consider emphasizing the following selected information (» = major clinical significance):

Before using this medication
» Conditions affecting use, especially:
Sensitivity to alprostadil
Other medical problems, especially severe coagulation defects, history of priapism, or sickle cell disease

Proper use of this medication
Proper administration:
»   Cleansing injection site with alcohol; injecting slowly and directly into corpus cavernosum at base or midshaft of penis; avoiding subcutaneous administration; if inadvertently injected subcutaneously (as evidenced by pain at injection site), stopping, withdrawing, and repositioning needle
Putting pressure on injection site for 5 minutes to prevent bruising; massaging penis, as directed by physician, to distribute medication

Effect begins in about 5 to 10 minutes; attempting intercourse within 10 to 30 minutes after administration
Alternating puncture (injection) sites
» Proper storage

Precautions while using this medication
» Compliance with therapy; importance of not exceeding prescribed dosage and frequency of use; risk of priapism, tissue ischemia, and permanent damage with overdose
» Telling physician immediately if erection persists longer than 4 hours or becomes painful
If bleeding occurs at injection site, applying pressure; checking with physician if bleeding persists

Side/adverse effects
Signs of potential side effects, especially excessive dosage or priapism

General Dosing Information

Patients receiving intracavernosal alprostadil should be under supervision of a physician experienced in its use and familiar with proper management of sustained erection and priapism.

Dosage adjustment should be made carefully, based on the degree and duration of tumescence achieved with the previous dose. In general, patients with neurogenic impotence may be more sensitive to the effects of intracavernosal vasodilators and may require lower doses.

Intracavernosal alprostadil may be self-administered by the patient, but only after careful training in the technique to reduce the incidence of inadvertent subcutaneous administration, ecchymosis, and urethral injury.

For treatment of impotence, alprostadil is injected slowly (over 1 to 2 minutes), directly into the the corpus cavernosum at the base or midshaft of the penis. A characteristic give should be noticed as the needle penetrates the tunica albuginea and enters the corpus cavernosum. Proper injection technique is necessary to avoid injury or injection of the urethra or vessels on the dorsal aspect of the penis.

After completion of the injection, pressure is applied to the injection site to prevent bleeding. Then the entire length of the corpus cavernosum should be squeezed firmly to distribute medication to the other side, followed by the same procedure on the other side. The penis should then be pinched transversely in several places to distribute medication to both ends of the corpus cavernosa.

If a sustained erection or pain at the site of injection occurs, the next dose of alprostadil should be reduced.

Intercourse should be attempted within 10 to 30 minutes after administration.

Alternate puncture (injection) sites.

For treatment of prolonged erection or priapism
A sustained erection should be treated if it persists for longer than 4 hours; priapism should be treated promptly. If tumescence is not reversed, interruption of blood flow may result in penile tissue ischemia and permanent damage.

Depending on the severity, treatment may include:
• Aspiration of intracavernous blood.
• Irrigation of the corpus cavernosa with saline to remove clotted blood.
• Intracavernous administration of an alpha-adrenergic agonist, such as metaraminol, epinephrine, or phenylephrine.
• Surgery.

Parenteral Dosage Forms

Note: Bracketed uses in the *Dosage Forms* section refer to categories of use and/or indications that are not included in U.S. product labeling.

ALPROSTADIL INJECTION USP

Usual adult dose: [Impotence therapy][1]—Intracavernosal, 2.5 to 20 mcg (0.0025 to 0.02 mg), the dosage being adjusted according to response.

Note: Patients with neurogenic impotence may require lower doses.

Usual adult prescribing limits: Impotence therapy—Up to 40 mcg (0.04 mg) of alprostadil per dose. The injection should not be given more than three times weekly or two days in succession.

---

[1]Not included in Canadian product labeling.

ALTRETAMINE   Systemic

Some commonly used *brand names* are:
In the U.S.—*Hexalen*
In Canada—*Hexastat*
Another commonly used name is hexamethylmelamine.

ORAL
Altretamine Capsules
In the U.S.—*Hexalen*
In Canada—*Hexastat*

Category: Antineoplastic.

Indications

Accepted
Carcinoma, ovarian (treatment)—Altretamine is indicated for use as a single agent in the palliative treatment of patients with persistent or recurrent ovarian cancer following first-line therapy with a cisplatin- and/or alkylating agent-based combination.

Pharmacology

Note: Pharmacokinetic studies have been done in only a limited number of patients; figures below are based on a study in 11 patients.

Mechanism of action/Effect: The exact mechanism of action is unknown. Although altretamine structurally resembles an alkylating agent, it has not been found to have alkylating activity *in vitro*. There is some evidence that it may inhibit DNA and RNA synthesis.

Precautions to Consider

Geriatrics
Although appropriate studies on the relationship of age to the effects of altretamine have not been performed in the geriatric population, clinical trials have included elderly patients and geriatrics-specific problems that would limit the usefulness of this medication in the elderly are not expected. However, elderly patients are more likely to have age-related renal function impairment, which may require caution in patients receiving altretamine.

Dental

The bone marrow depressant effects of altretamine may result in an increased incidence of microbial infection, delayed healing, and gingival bleeding. Dental work, whenever possible, should be completed prior to initiation of therapy or deferred until blood counts have returned to normal. Patients should be instructed in proper oral hygiene during treatment, including caution in use of regular toothbrushes, dental floss, and toothpicks.

Drug interactions and/or related problems

The following drug interactions and/or related problems have been selected on the basis of their potential clinical significance (possible mechanism in parentheses where appropriate)—not necessarily inclusive (» = major clinical significance):

Note: Combinations containing any of the following medications, depending on the amount present, may also interact with this medication.

Blood dyscrasia-causing medications
(leukopenic and/or thrombocytopenic effects of altretamine may be increased with concurrent or recent therapy if these medications cause the same effects; dosage adjustment of altretamine, if necessary, should be based on blood counts)

» Bone marrow depressants, other, or
Radiation therapy
(additive bone marrow depression may occur; dosage reduction may be required when two or more bone marrow depressants, including radiation, are used concurrently or consecutively)

Cimetidine
(inhibition of the cytochrome-P450 enzyme system by cimetidine would be expected to cause a decrease in the hepatic metabolism of altretamine, which could result in delayed elimination and increased blood concentrations)

» Monoamine oxidase (MAO) inhibitors, including furazolidone, procarbazine, and selegiline
(concurrent use may result in severe orthostatic hypotension)

Vaccines, killed virus
(because normal defense mechanisms may be suppressed by altretamine therapy, the patient's antibody response to the vaccine may be decreased. The interval between discontinuation of medications that cause immunosuppression and restoration of the patient's ability to respond to the vaccine depends on the intensity and type of immunosuppression-causing medication used, the underlying disease, and other factors; estimates vary from 3 months to 1 year)

» Vaccines, live virus
(because normal defense mechanisms may be suppressed by altretamine therapy, concurrent use with a live virus vaccine may potentiate the replication of the vaccine virus, may increase the side/adverse effects of the vaccine virus, and/or may decrease the patient's antibody response to the vaccine; immunization of these patients should be undertaken only with extreme caution after careful review of the patient's hematologic status and only with the knowledge and consent of the physician managing the altretamine therapy. The interval between discontinuation of medications that cause immunosuppression and restoration of the patient's ability to respond to the vaccine depends on the intensity and type of immunosuppression-causing medication used, the underlying disease, and other factors; estimates vary from 3 months to 1 year. Patients with leukemia in remission should not receive live virus vaccine until at least 3 months after their last chemotherapy. In addition, immunization with oral poliovirus vaccine should be postponed in persons in close contact with the patient, especially family members)

Contraindications/Medical problems

The contraindications/medical problems included have been selected on the basis of their potential clinical significance (reasons given in parentheses where appropriate)—not necessarily inclusive (» = major clinical significance).

Risk-benefit should be considered when the following medical problems exist:

» Bone marrow depression
(lower dosage may be necessary)

» Chickenpox, existing or recent (including recent exposure), or
» Herpes zoster
(risk of severe generalized disease)

» Infection
Hepatic function impairment, severe
(reduced activation or metabolism)

» Neurologic toxicity, severe
Renal function impairment
(reduced elimination)

» Sensitivity to altretamine

» Tumor cell infiltration of the bone marrow

» Caution should be used also in patients who have had previous cytotoxic drug therapy or radiation therapy.

Side/Adverse Effects

Note: Many "side effects" of antineoplastic therapy are unavoidable and represent the medication's pharmacologic action. Some of these (for example, leukopenia and thrombocytopenia) are actually used as parameters to aid in individual dosage titration.

Toxicity is dose-related and cumulative.

Altretamine causes mild to moderate myelosuppression and neurotoxicity.

The following side/adverse effects have been selected on the basis of their potential clinical significance (possible signs and symptoms in parentheses where appropriate)—not necessarily inclusive:

Those indicating need for medical attention

Incidence more frequent

Anemia (often asymptomatic; less commonly or rarely, unusual tiredness); *leukopenia* (often asymptomatic; less commonly or rarely, fever or chills, cough or hoarseness, lower back or side pain, painful or difficult urination); *neurotoxicity, including central nervous system (CNS) effects* (anxiety, clumsiness, confusion, dizziness, mental depression, weakness; rarely, seizures) *or peripheral neuropathy* (numbness in arms or legs); *thrombocytopenia* (often asymptomatic; less commonly or rarely, unusual bleeding or bruising; black, tarry stools; blood in urine or stools; pinpoint red spots on skin)

Note: In *leukopenia,* with intermittent dosing (e.g., 8 to 12 mg per kg of body weight [mg/kg] per day for 21 days), the nadir of leukocyte counts occurs at about 3 to 4 weeks, with recovery by 6 weeks; with continuous dosing, the nadir occurs at 6 to 8 weeks (median).

Incidence of *neurotoxicity* is greater with daily high-dose therapy than with intermittent moderate-dose therapy. Neurotoxicity is reversible on withdrawal of altretamine.

In *thrombocytopenia,* with intermittent dosing (e.g., 8 to 12 mg/kg per day for 21 days), the nadir of platelet counts occurs at about 3 to 4 weeks, with recovery by 6 weeks; with continuous dosing, the nadir occurs at 6 to 8 weeks (median).

Incidence rare

Hepatotoxicity (asymptomatic); *skin rash or itching*

Those indicating need for medical attention only if they continue or are bothersome
Incidence more frequent
Nausea and vomiting
Note: *Nausea* and *vomiting* are usually mild to moderate, although they may be dose-limiting. The mechanism of the effect may be central because they usually do not occur until several days after initiation of treatment.
Incidence less frequent
Diarrhea; loss of appetite; stomach cramps

Patient Consultation

In providing consultation, consider emphasizing the following selected information (» = major clinical significance):

Before using this medication
» Conditions affecting use, especially:
   Sensitivity to altretamine
   Pregnancy—Use not recommended because of mutagenic, teratogenic, and carcinogenic potential; advisability of using contraception; telling physician immediately if pregnancy is suspected
   Breast-feeding—Not recommended because of risk of serious side effects
   Other medications, especially other bone marrow depressants, monoamine oxidase (MAO) inhibitors, or other cytotoxic drug or radiation therapy
   Other medical problems, especially chickenpox, herpes zoster, renal function impairment, infection, or severe neurotoxicity

Proper use of this medication
   Frequency of nausea and vomiting; importance of continuing medication despite stomach upset; taking after meals to reduce stomach upset
   Missed dose: Taking as soon as possible; however, if almost time for next dose, not taking missed dose; not doubling doses
» Proper storage

Precautions while using this medication
» Importance of close monitoring by the physician
» Avoiding immunizations unless approved by physician; other persons in patient's household should avoid immunizations with oral poliovirus vaccine; avoiding other persons who have taken oral poliovirus vaccine or wearing a protective mask that covers nose and mouth
   Caution if bone marrow depression occurs:
» Avoiding exposure to persons with bacterial infections, especially during periods of low blood counts; checking with physician immediately if fever or chills, cough or hoarseness, lower back or side pain, or painful or difficult urination occur
» Checking with physician immediately if unusual bleeding or bruising; black, tarry stools; blood in urine or stools; or pinpoint red spots on skin occur
   Caution in use of regular toothbrush, dental floss, or toothpick; physician, dentist, or nurse may suggest alternatives; checking with physician before having dental work done
   Not touching eyes or inside of nose unless hands washed immediately before
   Using caution to avoid accidental cuts with use of sharp objects such as safety razor or fingernail or toenail cutters
   Avoiding contact sports or other situations where bruising or injury could occur

Side/adverse effects
   May cause adverse effects such as blood problems; importance of discussing possible effects with physician

Signs of potential side effects, especially leukopenia, neurotoxicity, and thrombocytopenia
Physician or nurse can help in dealing with side effects

General Dosing Information

Patients receiving altretamine should be under supervision of a physician experienced in cancer chemotherapy.

Dosage must be adjusted to meet the individual requirements of each patient, on the basis of clinical response and degree of bone marrow depression and neurotoxicity.

A variety of dosage schedules and regimens of altretamine, alone or in combination with other antitumor agents, are used. The prescriber may consult the medical literature as well as the manufacturer's literature in choosing a specific dosage.

Altretamine therapy should be temporarily withheld if any of the following occur:
   Gastrointestinal intolerance unresponsive to symptomatic measures
   Leukocyte count less than 2000 per cubic millimeter or granulocyte count less than 1000 per cubic millimeter
   Platelet count less than 75,000 per cubic millimeter
   Progressive neurotoxicity
   After a period of at least 14 days, therapy may be reinitiated at a reduced dose of 200 mg per square meter of body surface per day.

If neurotoxicity continues even after dosage reduction, it is recommended that altretamine be discontinued.

Special precautions are recommended in patients who develop thrombocytopenia as a result of administration of altretamine. These may include extreme care in performing invasive procedures; regular inspection of intravenous sites, skin (including perirectal area), and mucous membrane surfaces for signs of bleeding or bruising; limiting frequency of venipuncture and avoiding intramuscular injections; testing urine, emesis, stool, and secretions for occult blood; care in use of regular toothbrushes, dental floss, toothpicks, safety razors, and fingernail and toenail cutters; avoiding constipation; and using caution to prevent falls and other injuries. Such patients should avoid alcohol and any aspirin intake because of the risk of gastrointestinal bleeding. Platelet transfusions may be required.

Patients who develop leukopenia should be observed carefully for signs of infection. Antibiotic support may be required. In neutropenic patients who develop fever, broad-spectrum antibiotic coverage should be initiated empirically, pending bacterial cultures and appropriate diagnostic tests.

Diet/Nutrition
It is recommended that altretamine be taken after meals to reduce nausea and vomiting.

Oral Dosage Forms

ALTRETAMINE CAPSULES

Usual adult dose: Carcinoma, ovarian—Oral, 260 mg per square meter of body surface per day, in four divided daily doses after meals and at bedtime, for either fourteen or twenty-one consecutive days in a twenty-eight-day cycle.

Note: If excessive nausea and vomiting, leukopenia, thrombocytopenia, or neurotoxicity occur, it is recommended that altretamine be withheld for at least 14 days and then reinstituted at a dose of 200 mg per square meter of body surface per day.

Auxiliary labeling: • Take after meals.

AMANTADINE   Systemic

Some commonly used *brand names* are:
In the U.S.—*Symadine; Symmetrel*
In Canada—*Symmetrel*

ORAL

Amantadine Hydrochloride Capsules USP
In the U.S.—*Symadine; Symmetrel;* GENERIC
In Canada—*Symmetrel*
Amantadine Hydrochloride Syrup USP
In the U.S. and Canada—*Symmetrel*

Category: Antiviral (systemic); antidyskinetic; antifatigue, specifically in multiple sclerosis.

Indications

Note: Bracketed information in the *Indications* section refers to uses not included in U.S. product labeling.

Accepted

Influenza A (prophylaxis and treatment)—Amantadine is indicated as a primary agent in the prophylaxis and treatment of respiratory tract infections caused by influenza A virus strains in high-risk patients (including those with pulmonary or cardiovascular disease, the elderly, and residents of nursing homes and other chronic care facilities who have chronic medical conditions), hospital ward contacts of high-risk patients, immunocompromised patients, those in critical public service positions (e.g., police, firefighters, medical personnel), in high-risk patients for whom the influenza vaccine is contraindicated, and patients with severe influenza A viral infections. It is effective against all strains of influenza A virus that have been tested to date, including Russian, Brazilian, Texan, London, and others. It may be given as chemoprophylaxis concurrently with inactivated influenza A virus vaccine until protective antibodies develop. However, it should be emphasized that vaccination of high-risk persons each year is the single most important measure for reducing the impact of influenza. No well-controlled studies have examined whether amantadine prevents complications of influenza A in high-risk persons.

Resistant strains of influenza A have been reported in patients receiving rimantadine; these resistant strains were also apparently transmitted to household contacts. Rimantadine has a similar chemical structure, spectrum of activity, and mechanism of action to amantadine, and drug-resistant strains of virus have cross-resistance to amantadine and rimantadine.

Extrapyramidal reactions, drug-induced (treatment); or
Parkinsonism (treatment)—Amantadine is indicated in the treatment of idiopathic parkinsonism (paralysis agitans; shaking palsy), postencephalitic parkinsonism, drug-induced extrapyramidal reactions, symptomatic parkinsonism following injury to the nervous system caused by carbon monoxide intoxication, and parkinsonism associated with cerebral arteriosclerosis in the elderly.

[Fatigue, multiple sclerosis-associated (treatment)][1]—Amantadine is used in the management of certain aspects of fatigue associated with multiple sclerosis, including energy level, sense of well-being, perceived attention and memory, and problem solving ability.

Unaccepted

Amantadine is not effective against other respiratory viral infections, including influenza B and parainfluenza.

---

[1]Not included in Canadian product labeling.

Pharmacology

Mechanism of action/Effect:

Antiviral (systemic)—Not completely understood; appears to block the uncoating of influenza A virus and the release of viral nucleic acid into respiratory epithelial cells. May also affect early replicative phase of viruses that have already penetrated cells.

Antidyskinetic—Unknown; causes an increase in dopamine release in the animal brain. Probably increases release of dopamine and norepinephrine from central nerve terminals; also inhibits the reuptake of dopamine and norepinephrine.

Onset of action: Antidyskinetic—Usually within 48 hours.

Precautions to Consider

Geriatrics

Geriatric patients may exhibit increased sensitivity to the anticholinergic-like side effects of amantadine, including confusion. A dosage reduction of 50% (100 mg per day) appears to reduce the frequency of side effects without compromising antiviral prophylactic effectiveness. In addition, elderly patients are more likely to have an age-related decline in renal function. A dosage reduction of greater than 50% may be required in patients receiving amantadine, depending on the extent of renal dysfunction.

Dental

Prolonged use of amantadine may decrease or inhibit salivary flow, thus contributing to the development of caries, periodontal disease, oral candidiasis, and discomfort.

Drug interactions and/or related problems

The following drug interactions and/or related problems have been selected on the basis of their potential clinical significance (possible mechanism in parentheses where appropriate)—not necessarily inclusive (» = major clinical significance):

Note: Combinations containing any of the following medications, depending on the amount present, may also interact with this medication.

» Alcohol
(concurrent use with amantadine is not recommended since this may increase the potential for CNS effects such as dizziness, lightheadedness, orthostatic hypotension, or confusion)

» Anticholinergics, or other medications with anticholinergic activity, or
Antidepressants, tricyclic, or
Antidyskinetics, other, or
Antihistamines or
Phenothiazines
(concurrent use with amantadine may potentiate the anticholinergic-like side effects, especially those of confusion, hallucinations, and nightmares; dosage adjustments of these medications or of amantadine may be necessary; also, patients should be advised to report occurrence of gastrointestinal problems promptly since paralytic ileus may occur with concurrent therapy)

Antidiarrheals, opioid- and anticholinergic-containing
(concurrent use with amantadine may potentiate the anticholinergic-like side effects; although significant interaction is unlikely with usual doses of opioid- and anticholinergic-containing antidiarrheals, significant interaction may occur if these medications are abused)

Carbidopa and levodopa combination or
Levodopa
  (concurrent use with amantadine may result in increased efficacy of carbidopa and levodopa combination, and levodopa;
  however, concurrent use is not recommended if there is a history of psychosis)

» CNS stimulation-producing medications, other
  (concurrent use with amantadine may result in additive CNS
  stimulation to excessive levels, which may cause unwanted
  effects such as nervousness, irritability, or insomnia, and possibly seizures or cardiac arrhythmias; close observation is recommended)

Hydrochlorothiazide and
Triamterene
  (one or both of these drugs may reduce the renal clearance of
  amantadine, resulting in increased plasma concentrations and
  possible amantadine toxicity)

Contraindications/Medical problems

The contraindications/medical problems included have been selected
on the basis of their potential clinical significance (reasons given
in parentheses where appropriate)—not necessarily inclusive (» =
major clinical significance).

*Risk-benefit should be considered when the following medical prob-
lems exist:*

Eczematoid rash, recurrent, history of

» Edema, peripheral, or

» Heart failure, congestive
  (amantadine may cause congestive heart failure and peripheral
  edema; presumed to be due to redistribution of fluid, not a gain
  of body water)

» Epilepsy, history of, or other seizure disorders
  (amantadine may cause increased seizure activity; it may be
  necessary to reduce the dosage by 50% [100 mg per day];
  this appears to reduce the frequency of side effects without
  compromising antiviral prophylactic effectiveness)

Hypersensitivity to amantadine

Psychosis or severe psychoneurosis
  (anticholinergic-like side effects of amantadine may result in
  confusion, hallucinations, and nightmares; it may be necessary
  to reduce the dosage by 50% [100 mg per day]; this appears
  to reduce the frequency of side effects without compromising
  antiviral prophylactic effectiveness)

» Renal function impairment
  (since amantadine is not metabolized and is excreted primarily
  in the urine, toxic concentrations may accumulate in patients
  with impaired renal function; it may be necessary to reduce the
  dosage by 50% [100 mg per day]; this appears to reduce the
  frequency of side effects without compromising antiviral prophylactic effectiveness)

Side/Adverse Effects

Note: In controlled studies, side effects, including nausea, dizziness,
insomnia, nervousness, and impaired concentration, were reported in 5 to 10% of young healthy adults taking the standard
adult dosage of 200 mg per day. Side effects may diminish or
cease after the first week of use. Serious, less frequent central
nervous system (CNS) side effects, such as confusion or seizures, have usually only affected elderly patients, and patients
with renal disease, seizure disorders, or altered mental/behav-
ioral conditions. Reducing the dosage by 50% (100 mg per
day) appears to reduce the frequency of side effects without
compromising antiviral prophylactic effectiveness.

The following side/adverse effects have been selected on the basis of
their potential clinical significance (possible signs and symptoms
in parentheses where appropriate)—not necessarily inclusive:

Those indicating need for medical attention
Incidence less frequent
  Anticholinergic-like effects (blurred vision, confusion, difficult
  urination, hallucinations); *orthostatic hypotension* (fainting)
Incidence rare
  Corneal deposits (irritation and swelling of the eye, decreased
  vision or any change in vision); *CNS toxicity* (impaired coordination, mental depression, seizures); *congestive heart failure* (swelling of feet or lower legs, unexplained shortness of breath)—usually only with chronic therapy; *skin rash*
Symptoms of overdose
  *Arrhythmias; pulmonary edema; status epilepticus; toxic psy-
  chosis* (hallucinations, aggressive and violent behavior)

**Those indicating need for medical attention only if they continue
or are bothersome**
Incidence more frequent
  CNS toxicity (difficulty concentrating, dizziness or lightheadedness,
  headache, insomnia, irritability, nervousness, nightmares); *gastrointestinal disturbances* (loss of appetite, nausea); *livedo
  reticularis* (purplish red, net-like, blotchy spots on skin)—usually
  only with chronic therapy
Incidence less frequent or rare
  Anticholinergic-like effects (constipation; dry mouth, nose, and
  throat)—especially in elderly patients, patients receiving higher
  doses, and patients with renal dysfunction; *vomiting*

Patient Consultation

In providing consultation, consider emphasizing the following selected information (» = major clinical significance):

Before using this medication
» Conditions affecting use, especially:
    Hypersensitivity to amantadine
    Pregnancy—Amantadine crosses the placenta
    Use in the elderly—Geriatric patients may exhibit increased
      sensitivity to the anticholinergic-like side effects of aman-
      tadine
    Other medications, especially alcohol, anticholinergics or other
      medications with anticholinergic activity, or other CNS
      stimulation-producing medications
    Other medical problems, especially congestive heart failure,
      peripheral edema, renal function impairment, seizure disor-
      ders, or a history of epilepsy

Proper use of this medication
» Proper storage
For use as an antiviral
    Receiving a flu shot if have not already done so
» Taking before exposure or as soon as possible after exposure
» Compliance with full course of therapy
» Importance of not missing doses and taking at evenly spaced times
    Missed dose: Taking as soon as possible; not taking if almost time
      for next dose; not doubling doses
    Proper administration technique for oral liquid
For use as an antidyskinetic
» Not taking more medication than the amount prescribed; not miss-
    ing doses
    Missed dose: Taking as soon as possible; not taking if within 4
      hours of next dose; not doubling doses
    May require up to 2 weeks for full benefit

Precautions while using this medication
» Avoiding alcoholic beverages
» Caution if mental acuity or eyesight is impaired

Caution when getting up suddenly from a lying or sitting position

Possible dryness of mouth, nose, and throat; using sugarless candy or gum, ice, or saliva substitute for relief of dry mouth; checking with physician or dentist if dry mouth continues for more than 2 weeks

Possible appearance of livedo reticularis; gradual disappearance within 2 to 12 weeks after stopping medication

For use as an antiviral

Checking with physician if no improvement within a few days

For use as an antidyskinetic

» Resuming physical activities gradually as condition improves

Checking with physician if medication gradually loses its effectiveness

» Checking with physician before discontinuing medication; gradual dosage reduction may be necessary

Side/adverse effects

Signs of potential side effects, especially anticholinergic-like effects, CNS toxicity, congestive heart failure, orthostatic hypotension, corneal deposits, and skin rash

General Dosing Information

In controlled studies, side effects, including nausea, dizziness, insomnia, nervousness, and impaired concentration, were reported in 5 to 10% of young healthy adults taking the standard adult dosage of 200 mg per day. Data suggest that comparable protection may be provided by a daily prophylactic dosage of 100 mg, but with fewer side effects. No studies have been done comparing 100 mg and 200 mg doses for the treatment of influenza A infection.

Patients receiving doses exceeding 200 mg per day should be closely observed for signs of increased incidence of side effects or toxicity. Monitoring of such patients for blood pressure, pulse, respiration, and temperature should be considered, especially for a few days following the increase in dose. Patients with active seizure disorders may be at increased risk for seizures while receiving amantadine.

Changing from once-a-day to twice-a-day administration may eliminate or reduce the severity of side effects such as lightheadedness, insomnia, and nausea.

If possible, plasma concentrations should be monitored in patients with end-stage renal disease since a single dose may provide adequate concentrations for as long as 7 to 10 days.

For use in the prophylaxis and treatment of influenza type A virus infections

Chemoprophylactic administration should be started in anticipation of contact with, or as soon as possible after exposure to, persons having influenza A virus infections. Administration should be continued for at least 10 days following exposure. In influenza epidemics, amantadine should be given daily during the epidemic (usually 6 to 8 weeks in most communities) or until active immunity can be expected from administration of inactivated influenza A virus vaccine. However, rimantadine, chemically similar to amantadine, has been reported to be ineffective when used prophylactically in household members while concurrently treating index cases for influenza A. This was apparently due to transmission of drug-resistant strains of the virus.

If administered concurrently with inactivated influenza A virus vaccine until protective antibodies develop, amantadine should be continued chemoprophylactically for 2 to 3 weeks after the vaccine has been administered. Amantadine may then be discontinued. However, since the vaccine is only 70 to 80% effective, more prolonged administration of amantadine may be beneficial in elderly or high-risk patients. If the vaccine is unavailable or contraindicated, amantadine should be administered for up to 90 days in cases of possible repeated or unknown exposure.

Treatment of the symptoms of influenza A virus infections should be started within 24 to 48 hours after their onset and should be continued for 48 hours after their disappearance. Cough may persist for several weeks.

For use in the treatment of parkinsonism

Patients initially benefiting from the continuous administration of amantadine may experience a decline in effectiveness after a few months. Effectiveness may be restored by increasing the dose to 300 mg daily or temporarily discontinuing amantadine therapy for several weeks, and then resuming it.

Patients who have concurrent serious illnesses or are receiving high doses of other antiparkinsonian medications may be started on 100 mg of amantadine once a day. After one to several weeks, the dose may be increased to 100 mg two times a day, if necessary. If response is still not optimal, patients may benefit from a further increase to 400 mg daily in divided doses.

Concurrent administration of anticholinergic antiparkinsonian medications or levodopa with amantadine may provide additional benefit, including reduction in fluctuations in improvement occurring with levodopa alone. If dosage reductions of levodopa are required because of side effects, the benefit lost by the reduction may be restored by the concurrent administration of amantadine.

If amantadine and carbidopa and levodopa combination, or levodopa are initially being administered concurrently, the dose of amantadine should be maintained at 100 mg one or two times a day while the dose of carbidopa and levodopa combination, or levodopa is gradually increased to provide optimal benefit.

Patients who have drug-induced extrapyramidal reactions may be started on 100 mg of amantadine two times a day. If response is not optimal, dose may be increased to 300 mg daily in divided doses.

When amantadine is to be discontinued, dosage should be reduced gradually in order to prevent a sudden increase in parkinsonian symptoms.

Oral Dosage Forms

Note: Bracketed uses in the *Dosage Forms* section refer to categories of use and/or indications that are not included in U.S. product labeling.

AMANTADINE HYDROCHLORIDE CAPSULES USP

Usual adult and adolescent dose:

Antiviral (systemic)—Oral, 200 mg once a day; or 100 mg every twelve hours.

Antidyskinetic—Oral, 100 mg one or two times a day.

[Antifatigue, multiple sclerosis-associated][1]—Oral, 200 mg once a day; or 100 mg two times a day.

Note: Adults with impaired renal function may require a reduction in dose as noted below. Elderly patients, and patients with seizure disorders, or altered mental/behavioral conditions may require even further dose reductions.

Creatinine Clearance (mL/min/1.73 M^2)	Dose
>50	See *Usual adult and adolescent dose*
30–50	200 mg the first day, then 100 mg once a day
15–29	200 mg the first day, then 100 mg every other day
<15	200 mg once every 7 days
Hemodialysis patients	200 mg once every 7 days

Usual adult prescribing limits:

Antiviral (systemic)—Up to 200 mg daily.

Antidyskinetic—Up to 400 mg daily.

Usual geriatric dose:

Antiviral (systemic)—Oral, 100 mg once a day.

Antidyskinetic—Oral, 100 mg once a day to start, titrating the dose to 100 mg two or three times a day.

Note: A daily dose of amantadine exceeding 100 mg should be used with caution in persons 65 years of age or older for influenza prophylaxis or treatment. If the patient has any renal function impairment, the dose should be reduced further.

Auxiliary labeling:
- May cause dizziness or blurred vision.
- Avoid alcoholic beverages.
- Continue medicine for full time of treatment (antiviral).

AMANTADINE HYDROCHLORIDE SYRUP USP

Usual adult and adolescent dose: See *Amantadine Hydrochloride Capsules USP.*

Usual adult prescribing limits: See *Amantadine Hydrochloride Capsules USP.*

Usual geriatric dose: See *Amantadine Hydrochloride Capsules USP.*

Auxiliary labeling:
- May cause dizziness or blurred vision.
- Avoid alcoholic beverages.
- Continue medicine for full time of treatment (antiviral).

[1]Not included in Canadian product labeling.

AMINOGLUTETHIMIDE   Systemic

A commonly used *brand name* in the U.S. and Canada is *Cytadren.*

ORAL
Aminoglutethimide Tablets USP
    In the U.S. and Canada—*Cytadren*

Category: Antiadrenal; antineoplastic.

Indications

Note: Bracketed information in the *Indications* section refers to uses not included in U.S. product labeling.

Accepted
Cushing's syndrome (treatment)—Aminoglutethimide is indicated for temporary suppression of adrenal function in selected patients with Cushing's syndrome, including that associated with adrenal carcinoma and ectopic adrenocorticotropic hormone (ACTH)-producing tumors or adrenal hyperplasia.

[Carcinoma, breast (treatment)]—Aminoglutethimide is used to produce a "medical adrenalectomy" in the treatment of postmenopausal metastatic breast cancer, especially inoperable or recurrent breast cancer proven to be hormone-dependent.

[Carcinoma, prostatic (treatment)][1]—Aminoglutethimide is used for treatment of prostatic carcinoma unresponsive to hormonal or surgical therapy.

Unaccepted
Aminoglutethimide is no longer used as an anticonvulsant because of its adrenal suppressant effect.

[1]Not included in Canadian product labeling.

Pharmacology

Mechanism of action/Effect: Aminoglutethimide produces suppression of the adrenal cortex by inhibiting enzymatic conversion of cholesterol to pregnenolone, thus blocking synthesis of adrenal steroids; it may also affect other steps in the synthesis and metabolism of these steroids. A compensatory increase in secretion of adrenocorticotropic hormone (ACTH) by the pituitary occurs (except in patients with ACTH-independent adenomas or carcinomas), necessitating glucocorticoid administration to maintain aminoglutethimide's effect. Aminoglutethimide also inhibits estrogen production from androgens in peripheral tissues by blocking the aromatase enzyme. An additional mechanism in breast cancer, involving enhanced metabolism of estrone sulfate, has also been proposed.

Other actions/effects: Hepatic P-450 microsomal enzyme inducer.

Onset of action: Suppression of adrenal function—3 to 5 days.

Duration of action: Recovery of normal adrenal basal secretion and responsiveness to stress usually occurs within 36 to 72 hours after withdrawal of combined aminoglutethimide and hydrocortisone therapy; recovery may take longer after prolonged therapy (e.g., 1 year or longer).

Precautions to Consider

Cross-sensitivity and/or related problems
Patients sensitive to glutethimide may be sensitive to aminoglutethimide also.

Geriatrics
Although appropriate studies have not been performed in the geriatric population, the elderly may be more sensitive to the central nervous system (CNS) effects and more likely to become lethargic with this medication. In addition, elderly patients are more likely to have age-related renal function impairment, which may require caution in patients receiving aminoglutethimide.

Drug interactions and/or related problems
The following drug interactions and/or related problems have been selected on the basis of their potential clinical significance (possible mechanism in parentheses where appropriate)—not necessarily inclusive (» = major clinical significance):

Note: Combinations containing any of the following medications, depending on the amount present, may also interact with this medication.

Adrenocorticoids, mineralocorticoid
    (aminoglutethimide may alter metabolism of mineralocorticoids; dosage adjustments may be required)

Anticoagulants, coumarin-type
    (aminoglutethimide accelerates metabolism of coumarin anticoagulants; dosage adjustments should be based on monitoring of coagulation times)

Corticotropin (ACTH)
    (aminoglutethimide may inhibit the adrenal response to ACTH; this may interfere with the therapeutic response to ACTH)

» Dexamethasone
    (aminoglutethimide accelerates metabolism of dexamethasone, possibly resulting in a two-fold reduction in dexamethasone's half-life; if glucocorticoid therapy is necessary in a patient receiving aminoglutethimide, hydrocortisone is recommended instead)

Digoxin or
Theophylline
(effects may be reduced because of induction of hepatic microsomal enzymes by aminoglutethimide; caution is recommended)

Contraindications/Medical problems

The contraindications/medical problems included have been selected on the basis of their potential clinical significance (reasons given in parentheses where appropriate)—not necessarily inclusive (» = major clinical significance).

Except under special circumstances, this medication should not be used when the following medical problems exist:

» Chickenpox, existing or recent (including recent exposure) or
» Herpes zoster
(risk of severe generalized disease)

Risk-benefit should be considered when the following medical problems exist:

Hepatic function impairment
(reduced biotransformation)
Hypothyroidism
» Infection
(reduced adrenal responsiveness may result in acute adrenocortical insufficiency; additional steroid supplementation may be necessary)
Renal function impairment
(reduced elimination)
Sensitivity to aminoglutethimide or glutethimide

Side/Adverse Effects

Note: Most side effects decrease in incidence and severity after the first 2 to 6 weeks because of accelerated metabolism of the drug with continued use.

The following side/adverse effects have been selected on the basis of their potential clinical significance (possible signs and symptoms in parentheses where appropriate)—not necessarily inclusive:

Those indicating need for medical attention
Incidence less frequent
Adrenocortical insufficiency (fever, darkening of skin, mental depression); *leukopenia or agranulocytosis* (usually asymptomatic; rarely, fever or chills, cough or hoarseness, lower back or side pain, painful or difficult urination); *thrombocytopenia* (usually asymptomatic; rarely, unusual bleeding or bruising; black, tarry stools; blood in urine or stools; pinpoint red spots on skin)
Incidence rare
Hypersensitivity, possible (fever, yellow eyes or skin); *hypothyroidism and goiter* (neck tenderness or swelling)
Note: A rare *hypersensitivity* or drug reaction has been reported, consisting of cholestatic jaundice, fever, skin eruptions, increased aspartate aminotransferase (AST [SGOT]), and possibly eosinophilia.
Hypothyroidism and *goiter* may occur with long-term use because aminoglutethimide blocks iodination of tyrosine.

Those indicating need for medical attention only if they continue or are bothersome
Incidence more frequent
CNS effects—dose-related—*including clumsiness, dizziness, drowsiness, lack of energy, or uncontrolled eye movements; loss of appetite or nausea*—incidence about 12%; *measles-like skin rash or itching on face and/or palms of hands*
Note: *CNS effects* usually are reduced within 2 to 6 weeks with continued treatment, although some may be severe enough to necessitate discontinuing treatment in some patients.

The *measles-like skin rash is* often accompanied by fever. It usually appears within 10 to 15 days after therapy is started and persists for 5 to 7 days; it is recommended that aminoglutethimide be withdrawn if mild to moderate skin rash persists for longer than 5 to 8 days or if skin rash is severe.

Incidence less frequent or rare
Headache; hypotension, orthostatic or persistent, due to suppression of aldosterone production (dizziness or lightheadedness, especially when getting up from a lying or sitting position); *masculinization and hirsutism in females* (deepening of voice, increased hair growth, irregular menstrual periods); *muscle pain; vomiting*

Patient Consultation

In providing consultation, consider emphasizing the following selected information (» = major clinical significance):

Before using this medication
» Conditions affecting use, especially:
Sensitivity to aminoglutethimide or glutethimide
Pregnancy—Teratogenic in humans and animals
Use in children—Rare possibility of precocious sexual development in males and masculinization and hirsutism in females
Use in the elderly—Lethargy may be more frequent
Other medical problems, especially chickenpox, herpes zoster, or infection
Other medications, especially dexamethasone

Proper use of this medication
» Importance of not taking more or less medication than the amount prescribed
» Possible nausea and vomiting; usually lessens with continued therapy; checking with physician before discontinuing medication
Checking with physician if vomiting occurs shortly after dose is taken
Missed dose: Taking as soon as possible if remembered within 2 to 4 hours; not taking if almost time for next dose; not doubling doses
» Proper storage

Precautions while using this medication
» Importance of close monitoring by physician
Carrying medical identification card or wearing bracelet stating that medication is being used
Caution if any kind of surgery (including dental surgery) or emergency treatment is required
» Checking with physician immediately if injury, infection, or other illness occurs, because of the risk of adrenal insufficiency; physician may prescribe steroid supplement
» Caution if drowsiness, dizziness, or hypotension occurs, especially if driving, using machines, or doing other things that require alertness

Side/adverse effects
Signs of potential side effects, especially hypersensitivity, leukopenia or agranulocytosis, and thrombocytopenia

General Dosing Information

Patients receiving aminoglutethimide should be under the supervision of a physician experienced in cancer chemotherapy or a clinical endocrinologist.

Dosage must be adjusted to provide the desired level of adrenal suppression.

Mineralocorticoid replacement (such as fludrocortisone) may be necessary in 20 to 50% of patients because of reduction of aldosterone production caused by aminoglutethimide, which could lead to hyponatremia and orthostatic hypotension.

Patients should be monitored carefully during periods of stress such as surgery, trauma, or acute illness. Additional steroids may be required because adrenal suppression may prevent the normal response to stress. It is recommended that aminoglutethimide be temporarily withdrawn immediately following shock or severe trauma.

It is recommended that dosage be reduced if CNS side effects occur.

It is recommended that aminoglutethimide be withdrawn if mild to moderate skin rash persists for longer than 5 to 8 days or if skin rash is severe. Skin rash may respond to treatment with diphenhydramine. After a mild to moderate rash disappears, aminoglutethimide therapy may be restarted at a dose of 250 mg per day and gradually increased to the therapeutic dose.

For use as an antineoplastic

Inhibition of the adrenal cortex by aminoglutethimide results in a reflex increase in secretion of adrenocorticotropic hormone (ACTH) by the pituitary (except in patients with ACTH-independent adenomas or carcinomas); therefore, replacement with a glucocorticoid (usually hydrocortisone) may be necessary to maintain the desired effect of aminoglutethimide by preventing adrenal cortical hypertrophy and renewed synthesis of steroids.

Replacement glucocorticoid therapy is usually required in patients with metastatic breast cancer.

Because of the rapid return of the adrenal cortex to normal responsiveness following withdrawal of aminoglutethimide and hydrocortisone, dosage tapering is usually not necessary.

Oral Dosage Forms

AMINOGLUTETHIMIDE TABLETS USP

Note: Bracketed uses in the *Dosage Forms* section refer to categories of use and/or indications that are not included in U.S. product labeling.

Usual adult dose:
Antiadrenal—
  Initial: Oral, 250 mg two or three times a day for approximately two weeks (to induce metabolism and minimize CNS side effects).
  Maintenance: Oral, 250 mg four times a day, preferably every six hours.
[Breast cancer]; or
[Prostatic cancer][1]—
  Initial: Oral, 250 mg two or three times a day for approximately two weeks (to induce metabolism and minimize CNS side effects), in combination with 40 mg of hydrocortisone per day (10 mg in the morning and at 5 p.m. and 20 mg at bedtime).
  Maintenance: Oral, 250 mg four times a day, preferably every six hours, in combination with 40 mg of hydrocortisone per day (10 mg in the morning and at 5 p.m. and 20 mg at bedtime).

Usual adult prescribing limits:
Cushing's syndrome—Up to 2 grams per day.
[Breast cancer]; or
[Prostatic cancer][1]—Up to 1 gram per day.

---

[1]Not included in Canadian product labeling.

AMPHETAMINES   Systemic

INN: Included in brackets after individual generic listings, if different from the U.S. generic name.

Some commonly used *brand names* are:
In the U.S.—
  Biphetamine 121/2
    [Amphetamine and Dextroamphetamine Resin Complex]
  Biphetamine 20
    [Amphetamine and Dextroamphetamine Resin Complex]
  Desoxyn
    [Methamphetamine]
In Canada—
  Dexedrine
    [Dextroamphetamine]

  Desoxyn Gradumet
    [Methamphetamine]
  Dexedrine
    [Dextroamphetamine]
  Dexedrine Spansule
    [Dextroamphetamine]
  Oxydess II
    [Dextroamphetamine]
  Spancap No. 1
    [Dextroamphetamine]

  Dexedrine Spansule
    [Dextroamphetamine]

ORAL

AMPHETAMINE [INN: Amfetamine]†
  Amphetamine Sulfate Tablets USP†
    In the U.S.—GENERIC
AMPHETAMINE AND DEXTROAMPHETAMINE RESIN COMPLEX†
  Amphetamine and Dextroamphetamine Resin Complex Capsules†
    In the U.S.—*Biphetamine 121/2; Biphetamine 20*
DEXTROAMPHETAMINE [INN: Dexamfetamine]
  Dextroamphetamine Sulfate Extended-release Capsules
    In the U.S.—*Dexedrine Spansule; Spancap No. 1*
    In Canada—*Dexedrine Spansule*

Dextroamphetamine Sulfate Tablets USP
  In the U.S.—*Dexedrine; Oxydess II;* GENERIC
  In Canada—*Dexedrine*
METHAMPHETAMINE [INN: Metamfetamine]†
  Methamphetamine Hydrochloride Tablets†
    In the U.S.—*Desoxyn*
  Methamphetamine Hydrochloride Extended-release Tablets†
    In the U.S.—*Desoxyn Gradumet*

---

†Not commercially available in Canada.

Category: Central nervous system (CNS) stimulant.

Indications

Note: Bracketed information in the *Indications* section refers to uses not included in U.S. product labeling.

Accepted
Attention-deficit hyperactivity disorder (treatment)—Amphetamines are indicated as an integral part of a total treatment program that includes other remedial measures (psychological, educational, social) for a stabilizing effect in children with attention-deficit hyperactivity disorder, characterized by moderate to severe distractibility, short attention span, hyperactivity, emotional lability, and impulsivity. Nonlocalizing neurological signs, learning disability, and abnormal electroencephalogram (EEG) may also be present. Amphetamines are usually not indicated when the above symptoms are associated with acute stress reactions.

Narcolepsy (treatment)—Amphetamine, dextroamphetamine, and [amphetamine and dextroamphetamine resin complex] are indicated in the treatment of well-established and proven narcolepsy.

Unaccepted
Due to their high potential for abuse, amphetamines are not recommended for use as appetite suppressants.

Amphetamines should not be used to combat fatigue or to replace rest in normal subjects.

Pharmacology

Mechanism of action/Effect: Amphetamines are sympathomimetic amines that increase motor activity and mental alertness, and diminish drowsiness and a sense of fatigue.

In children with attention-deficit hyperactivity disorder, amphetamines decrease motor restlessness and enhance the ability to pay attention.

The exact mechanism of action has not been established. However, in animals, amphetamines facilitate the action of dopamine and norepinephrine by blocking reuptake from the synapse, inhibit the action of monoamine oxidase (MAO), and facilitate the release of catecholamines. Increase in locomotor activity at relatively low doses and increase in stereotypic behavior with a concomitant decrease in activity at higher doses appear to be due to stimulation of mesocorticolimbic and nigrostriatal dopaminergic pathways. Dextroamphetamine may also stimulate inhibitory autoreceptors in the substantia nigra and ventral tegmentum.

Some studies support the theory that amphetamine exerts a dual effect on the striatal dopaminergic nerve terminal, thus explaining the paradoxical effects of amphetamines. Amphetamines may selectively facilitate the dopaminergic transmission by promoting the release of recently synthesized dopamine from a reserpine-resistant pool and, in addition, may inhibit the classical dopaminergic neurotransmission involving the calcium-dependent depolarization-evoked release of dopamine from reserpine-sensitive storage sites.

Other actions/effects: Peripheral actions include elevation of both diastolic and systolic blood pressure, and weak bronchodilator and respiratory stimulant action.

Precautions to Consider

Cross-sensitivity and/or related problems
Patients sensitive to other sympathomimetics (for example, ephedrine, epinephrine, isoproterenol, metaproterenol, norepinephrine, phenylephrine, phenylpropanolamine, pseudoephedrine, terbutaline) may be sensitive to amphetamines also.

Geriatrics
No information is available on the relationship of age to the effects of the amphetamines in geriatric patients.

Drug interactions and/or related problems
The following drug interactions and/or related problems have been selected on the basis of their potential clinical significance (possible mechanism in parentheses where appropriate)—not necessarily inclusive (» = major clinical significance):

Note: Combinations containing any of the following medications, depending on the amount present, may also interact with this medication.

Acidifiers, gastrointestinal, such as:
  Ascorbic acid
  Fruit juices
  Glutamic acid hydrochloride or
Acidifiers, urinary, such as:
  Ammonium chloride

Sodium acid phosphate
  (concurrent use may decrease the effects of amphetamines as a result of decreased absorption and increased elimination)

Alkalizers, urinary, such as:
  Antacids, calcium- and/or magnesium-containing
  Carbonic anhydrase inhibitors
  Citrates
  Sodium bicarbonate
  (concurrent use may increase the effects of amphetamines as a result of decreased elimination caused by alkalinization of urine)

Anesthetics, inhalation
  (halothane and, to a much lesser extent, enflurane, isoflurane, and methoxyflurane, may sensitize the myocardium to the effects of sympathomimetics, including chronic use of amphetamines prior to anesthesia, so that the risk of severe ventricular arrhythmias is increased; sympathomimetics should be used with caution and in substantially reduced dosage in patients receiving these agents)

» Antidepressants, tricyclic
  (although tricyclic antidepressants may be used concurrently with amphetamines for therapeutic effect, concurrent use may potentiate cardiovascular effects due to the release of norepinephrine, possibly resulting in arrhythmias, tachycardia, or severe hypertension or hyperpyrexia; close monitoring is recommended and dosage adjustments may be necessary)

Antidiabetic agents, oral, or
Insulin
  (concurrent use with amphetamines increases the possibility of hyperglycemia; dosage adjustment of either or both medications may be necessary)

Antihypertensives or
Diuretics used as antihypertensives
  (hypotensive effects may be reduced when these medications are used concurrently with amphetamines; the patient should be carefully monitored to confirm that the desired effect is obtained)

» Beta-adrenergic blocking agents, including ophthalmics
  (concurrent use with amphetamines may result in unopposed alpha-adrenergic activity with a risk of hypertension and excessive bradycardia and possible heart block; risk may be less with labetalol because of its alpha-blocking activity)

» CNS stimulation-producing medications, other
  (additive CNS stimulation to excessive levels may result in nervousness, irritability, insomnia, or possibly seizures; close observation is recommended)

  (also, concurrent use of amphetamines with other sympathomimetics may increase cardiovascular effects of either medication)

  (in addition to possibly increasing CNS stimulation, concurrent use of norepinephrine with large doses of amphetamines may enhance the pressor response to norepinephrine; caution may also be warranted in patients receiving usual doses of amphetamines)

» Digitalis glycosides
  (concurrent use with amphetamines may cause additive effects, resulting in cardiac arrhythmias)

Ethosuximide or
Phenobarbital or
Phenytoin
  (concurrent use with amphetamines may cause a delay in the intestinal absorption of ethosuximide, phenobarbital, or phenytoin)

Haloperidol or
Loxapine or
Molindone or
Phenothiazines or

Pimozide or
Thioxanthenes
(central stimulant effects of amphetamines may be inhibited because of alpha-adrenergic blockade by these agents; also, concurrent use with amphetamines may reduce the antipsychotic effects of these agents)

Levodopa
(the risk of cardiac arrhythmias may be increased; dosage reduction of amphetamine is recommended)

Lithium
(central stimulant effects of amphetamines may be antagonized by lithium)

» Meperidine
(the analgesic effects of meperidine may be potentiated by amphetamines; however, concurrent use of meperidine is not recommended, as it may potentially result in hypotension, severe respiratory depression, coma, convulsions, hyperpyrexia, vascular collapse, and death in some patients due to the monoamine oxidase inhibition properties of amphetamines)

Metrizamide
(intrathecal administration of metrizamide may increase the risk of seizures because of lowered seizure threshold; it is recommended that amphetamines be discontinued for at least 48 hours before and 24 hours after myelography)

» Monoamine oxidase (MAO) inhibitors, including furazolidone, procarbazine, and selegiline
(concurrent use may prolong and intensify cardiac stimulant and vasopressor effects [including headache, cardiac arrhythmias, vomiting, sudden and severe hypertensive and hyperpyretic crises] of amphetamines because of the release of catecholamines that accumulate in intraneuronal storage sites during MAO inhibitor therapy; amphetamines should not be administered during or within 14 days following the administration of an MAO inhibitor)

Propoxyphene
(overdosage of propoxyphene may potentiate central stimulant effects of amphetamines; fatal convulsions can occur)

» Thyroid hormones
(the effects of either these medications or amphetamines may be increased; thyroid hormones enhance the risk of coronary insufficiency when amphetamines are administered to patients with coronary artery disease)

Contraindications/Medical problems
The contraindications/medical problems included have been selected on the basis of their potential clinical significance (reasons given in parentheses where appropriate)—not necessarily inclusive (» = major clinical significance).

Risk-benefit should be considered when the following medical problems exist:

» Agitated states or
» Arteriosclerosis, advanced, or
» Cardiovascular disease, symptomatic, or
» Drug abuse or dependence, history of, or
» Glaucoma or
» Hypertension or
» Hyperthyroidism or
Psychoses, especially in children, or
» Tourette's syndrome or other motor or vocal tics
(increased risk of exacerbation)
Sensitivity to amphetamines and other sympathomimetics

Side/Adverse Effects

Note: Psychological dependence and tolerance may occur with amphetamines following prolonged use or high doses.

The following side/adverse effects have been selected on the basis of their potential clinical significance (possible signs and symptoms in parentheses where appropriate)—not necessarily inclusive:

Those indicating need for medical attention
Incidence more frequent
Irregular heartbeat
Incidence rare
Allergic reaction (skin rash or hives); *chest pain; CNS stimulation, severe, or Tourette's syndrome* (uncontrolled movements of the head, neck, arms, and legs); *hyperthermia*
With prolonged use or high doses
Cardiomyopathy (chest discomfort or pain, difficulty in breathing, dizziness or feeling faint, irregular or pounding heartbeat, or unusual tiredness or weakness); *increase in blood pressure; psychotic reactions or toxic psychoses* (mood or mental changes)

Those indicating need for medical attention only if they continue or are bothersome
Incidence more frequent
CNS stimulation (false sense of well-being, irritability, nervousness, restlessness, trouble in sleeping)—drowsiness, fatigue, trembling, or mental depression may follow the stimulant effects
Incidence less frequent
Blurred vision; changes in sexual desire or decreased sexual ability; diarrhea, nausea, vomiting, stomach cramps or pain, constipation, loss of appetite, weight loss; dizziness, lightheadedness, headache; dryness of mouth or unpleasant taste; fast or pounding heartbeat; increased sweating

Those indicating possible withdrawal and the need for medical attention if they occur after medication is discontinued
Mental depression; nausea, vomiting, stomach cramps or pain; trembling; unusual tiredness or weakness

Patient Consultation

In providing consultation, consider emphasizing the following selected information (» = major clinical significance):

Before using this medication
» Conditions affecting use, especially:
Sensitivity to amphetamines and other sympathomimetics
Pregnancy—Increased risk of congenital malformations, especially in cardiovascular system and biliary tract; potential embryotoxic and teratogenic effects in animals given large doses
Breast-feeding—Not recommended since amphetamines excreted in breast milk
Use in children—May inhibit growth; may provoke motor and vocal tics and Tourette's syndrome; may exacerbate behavior problems and thought disorder in psychotic children
Use by athletes—Amphetamines are banned and, in some cases, tested for by the U.S. Olympic Committee (USOC) and the National Collegiate Athletic Association (NCAA)
Other medications, especially tricyclic antidepressants, monoamine oxidase inhibitors, beta-adrenergic blockers, digitalis glycosides, meperidine, other CNS stimulation-producing medications, or thyroid hormones
Other medical problems, especially severe anxiety or tension, advanced arteriosclerosis or symptomatic cardiovascular disease, history of drug dependence, glaucoma, hypertension, hyperthyroidism, or Tourette's syndrome or other tics

Proper use of this medication
Taking the last dose of the day of the regular dosage form at least 6 hours before bedtime and the daily dose of the extended-release dosage form about 10 to 14 hours before bedtime to minimize the possibility of insomnia

Proper administration of extended-release dosage forms:
Swallowing whole
Not breaking, crushing, or chewing
» Importance of not taking more medication than the amount pre-scribed because of habit-forming potential
» Not increasing dose if medication becomes less effective after a few weeks; checking with physician
Missed dose: If dosing schedule is—
Once a day: Taking as soon as possible but not later than stated above; if remembered later, not taking until next day; not doubling doses
Two or three times a day: Taking as soon as possible if remem-bered within an hour or so; not taking if remembered later; not doubling doses
» Proper storage

Precautions while using this medication
Regular visits to physician to check progress during therapy
» Checking with physician before discontinuing medication after prolonged high-dose therapy; gradual dosage reduction may be necessary to avoid possibility of withdrawal symptoms
» Caution if dizziness or euphoria occurs; not driving, using machin-ery, or doing other activities that are potentially hazardous
Caution if any laboratory tests required; possible interference with results of metyrapone test
» Suspected psychological or physical dependence; checking with physician

Side/adverse effects
Signs of potential side effects, especially irregular heartbeat, chest pain, cardiomyopathy, increased blood pressure, psychotic re-actions, tics, or other signs of severe CNS stimulation
Potential unwanted effects during long-term use in children
Possibility of withdrawal effects, especially mental depression, nausea, vomiting, stomach cramps or pain, trembling, or un-usual tiredness or weakness

General Dosing Information

When the regular tablet dosage form of amphetamines is adminis-tered, the first dose should be taken on awakening, followed by 1 or 2 additional doses at intervals of 4 to 6 hours.

To reduce the possibility of insomnia, the last dose of the day of the regular dosage form should be administered at least 6 hours before bedtime, and the daily dose of the extended-release dosage form should be administered approximately 10 to 14 hours before bed-time.

The extended-release dosage form may be used for once-a-day dosing whenever it is feasible.

When symptoms of attention-deficit hyperactivity disorder are con-trolled in children, dosage reduction or interruption in therapy may be possible during the summer months and at other times when the child is under less stress; medication may be given on each of the 5 school days during the week, with medication-free weekends and school holidays.

Prolonged use of amphetamines may result in tolerance, extreme psy-chological dependence, or severe social disability.

When the medication is to be discontinued following prolonged high-dose administration, the dosage should be reduced gradually since abrupt withdrawal may result in extreme fatigue and mental de-pression.

AMPHETAMINE

Oral Dosage Forms

AMPHETAMINE SULFATE TABLETS USP

Usual adult dose: Narcolepsy—Oral, 5 to 20 mg one to three times a day.

Note: Controlled substance in the U.S.

AMPHETAMINE AND DEXTROAMPHETAMINE RESIN COMPLEX

Oral Dosage Forms

Note: Bracketed uses in the *Dosage Forms* section refer to categories of use and/or indications that are not included in U.S. product labeling.

AMPHETAMINE AND DEXTROAMPHETAMINE RESIN COMPLEX CAPSULES

Note: The resin dosage form should not be used for initiation of dosage, nor should it be used until the conventional titrated daily dosage is equal to or greater than the dosage provided in the resin dosage form.

Usual adult dose: [Narcolepsy]—Oral, 6.25 mg of amphetamine and 6.25 mg of dextroamphetamine to 40 mg of amphetamine and 40 mg of dextroamphetamine once a day as a single dose.

Auxiliary labeling: • Swallow capsules whole.

Note: Controlled substance in the U.S.

DEXTROAMPHETAMINE

Oral Dosage Forms

DEXTROAMPHETAMINE SULFATE EXTENDED-RELEASE CAPSULES

Note: The extended-release dosage form should not be used for initia-tion of dosage, nor should it be used until the conventional titrated daily dosage is equal to or greater than the dosage provided in the extended-release dosage form.

Usual adult dose: Narcolepsy—Oral, 5 to 60 mg once a day, or in divided doses.

Auxiliary labeling: • Swallow capsules whole.

Note: Controlled substance in both the U.S. and Canada.

DEXTROAMPHETAMINE SULFATE TABLETS USP

Usual adult dose: Narcolepsy—Oral, 5 to 60 mg a day in divided doses as needed and tolerated.

Note: Controlled substance in both the U.S. and Canada.

METHAMPHETAMINE

Oral Dosage Forms

METHAMPHETAMINE HYDROCHLORIDE TABLETS

Note: Controlled substance in the U.S.

METHAMPHETAMINE HYDROCHLORIDE EXTENDED-RELEASE TABLETS

Note: The extended-release dosage form should not be used for initiation of dosage or until the conventional titrated daily dosage is equal to or greater than the dosage provided in the extended-release dosage form.

Auxiliary labeling:
- Swallow tablets whole.
- Keep container tightly closed.

Note: Controlled substance in the U.S.

AMYL NITRITE   Systemic

INHALATION
  Amyl Nitrite Inhalant USP
    In the U.S. and Canada—GENERIC

Category: Antianginal; antidote (to cyanide poisoning); diagnostic aid (cardiac function).

Indications

Note: Bracketed information in the *Indications* section refers to uses not included in U.S. product labeling.

Accepted
Angina pectoris, acute (treatment)—Amyl nitrite is indicated for treatment of attacks of acute angina pectoris. However, amyl nitrite is seldom used for this indication; its use has generally been replaced by safer, less toxic, and more convenient antianginals such as the nitrates.

[Toxicity, cyanide (treatment)]—Amyl nitrite is used as an antidote in the treatment of cyanide poisoning.

[Cardiac function studies][1]—Amyl nitrite is used as a diagnostic aid for assessment of reserve cardiac function.

Unaccepted
Amyl nitrite is abused to produce euphoria and as a sexual stimulant; these uses are associated with significant risk of toxicity and are not recommended.

---

[1]Not included in Canadian product labeling.

Pharmacology

Mechanism of action/Effect:
  Antianginal—Thought to be the result of a reduction in systemic and pulmonary arterial pressure (afterload) and decreased cardiac output because of peripheral vasodilation, rather than coronary artery dilation.
  Antidote (to cyanide poisoning)—Amyl nitrite promotes formation of methemoglobin, which combines with cyanide to form nontoxic cyanmethemoglobin.

Onset of action: 30 seconds.

Duration of action: 3 to 5 minutes.

Precautions to Consider

Cross-sensitivity and/or related problems
Patients sensitive to nitrates may be sensitive to this medication also, although the reaction is rare.

Geriatrics
Although appropriate studies have not been performed in the geriatric population, orthostatic hypotensive effects may be more likely to occur in the elderly, who are usually more sensitive to the effects of amyl nitrite.

Drug interactions and/or related problems
The following drug interactions and/or related problems have been selected on the basis of their potential clinical significance (possible mechanism in parentheses where appropriate)—not necessarily inclusive (» = major clinical significance).

Note: Combinations containing any of the following medications, depending on the amount present, may also interact with this medication.

Acetylcholine or
Histamine or
Norepinephrine (levarterenol)
  (effects may be decreased when these medicines are used concurrently with amyl nitrite)
» Hypotension-producing medications, other
  (concurrent use may intensify the orthostatic hypotensive effects of amyl nitrite)
Sympathomimetics, such as phenylephrine, ephedrine, or epinephrine
  (concurrent use may reduce the antianginal effects of amyl nitrite; amyl nitrite may block the alpha-adrenergic effects of epinephrine, possibly resulting in severe hypotension and tachycardia)

Contraindications/Medical problems
The contraindications/medical problems included have been selected on the basis of their potential clinical significance (reasons given in parentheses where appropriate)—not necessarily inclusive (» = major clinical significance).

Risk-benefit should be considered when the following medical problems exist:

» Anemia, severe
» Cerebral hemorrhage or
» Head trauma, recent
  (amyl nitrite may increase cerebrospinal fluid pressure)
Glaucoma
  (amyl nitrite may increase intraocular pressure)
» Hyperthyroidism
» Myocardial infarction, recent
  (risk of hypotension and tachycardia with amyl nitrite treatment, which may aggravate ischemia)
Sensitivity to amyl nitrite or nitrates

Side/Adverse Effects

The following side/adverse effects have been selected on the basis of their potential clinical significance (possible signs and symptoms in parentheses where appropriate)—not necessarily inclusive:

Those indicating need for medical attention
Incidence rare
Hemolytic anemia; skin rash

Signs and symptoms of overdose (methemoglobinemia)
Bluish-colored lips, fingernails, or palms of hands; dizziness, extreme, or fainting; feeling of extreme pressure in head; shortness of breath; unusual tiredness or weakness; weak and fast heartbeat

Note: Cyanosis may occur at blood methemoglobin concentrations of 1.5 grams per 100 mL. More pronounced signs occur at concentrations of 20 to 50 grams per 100 mL.

Those indicating need for medical attention only if they continue or are bothersome
Incidence more frequent
Fast pulse; flushing of face and neck; headache, mild; nausea or vomiting; orthostatic hypotension (dizziness or lightheadedness, especially when getting up from a lying or sitting position); *restlessness*

Patient Consultation

In providing consultation, consider emphasizing the following selected information:

Before using this medication
» Conditions affecting use, especially:
  Sensitivity to amyl nitrite or nitrates
  Use in elderly—Increased incidence of orthostatic hypotension
  Other medications, especially other hypotension-producing medications
  Other medical problems, especially severe anemia, cerebral hemorrhage, recent head trauma, hyperthyroidism, or recent myocardial infarction

Proper use of this medication
» Proper administration:
  Crushing capsule between finger and thumb and holding up to nostrils
  Inhaling 1 to 6 times

Remaining seated or lying down during administration because of possible dizziness
Relief usually occurs within 1 to 5 minutes—Dose may be repeated if pain not relieved in 5 minutes; calling physician or going to hospital emergency room if angina pain not relieved by 2 doses in 10 minutes
» Importance of not using more medication than the amount prescribed because of danger of overdose; notifying physician if reduced effect is observed
» Proper storage

Precautions while using this medication
» Flammable: Avoiding exposure to flame or heat
» Caution when getting up suddenly from a lying or sitting position
» Avoiding alcoholic beverages
  Headache as a common effect

Side/adverse effects
Signs of potential side effects, especially skin rash and methemoglobinemia

General Dosing Information

Tolerance of the antianginal effects of amyl nitrite is possible with prolonged use. To reduce development of tolerance, the smallest effective dose should be utilized and amyl nitrite may be alternated with other antianginal agents.

Inhalation Dosage Forms

Note: Bracketed uses in the *Dosage Forms* section refer to categories of use and/or indications that are not included in U.S. product labeling.

AMYL NITRITE INHALANT USP

Usual adult and adolescent dose:
Antianginal—Inhalation, 0.18 or 0.3 mL (1 ampul); may be repeated in three to five minutes if necessary.
[Antidote (to cyanide poisoning)]—Inhalation, as necessary, administered for thirty to sixty seconds every five minutes until the patient is conscious, then repeated at longer intervals for twenty-four hours.

Auxiliary labeling: • For inhalation only.

ANABOLIC STEROIDS   Systemic

Some commonly used *brand names* are:
In the U.S.—

Anabolin [Nandrolone]	*Hybolin Decanoate* [Nandrolone]
Anabolin LA-100 [Nandrolone]	*Hybolin-Improved* [Nandrolone]
Anadrol [Oxymetholone]	*Kabolin* [Nandrolone]
Anavar [Oxandrolone]	*Nandrobolic* [Nandrolone]
Androlone [Nandrolone]	*Nandrobolic L.A.* [Nandrolone]
Androlone 50 [Nandrolone]	*Neo-Durabolic* [Nandrolone]
Androlone D [Nandrolone]	
Deca-Durabolin [Nandrolone]	*Winstrol* [Stanozolol]
Durabolin [Nandrolone]	

In Canada—

Anapolon 50 [Oxymetholone]	*Durabolin* [Nandrolone]
Deca-Durabolin [Nandrolone]	*Winstrol* [Stanozolol]

NANDROLONE
Parenteral
Nandrolone Decanoate Injection USP
  In the U.S.—*Anabolin LA-100; Androlone 50; Androlone D; Deca-Durabolin; Hybolin Decanoate; Kabolin; Nandrobolic L.A.; Neo-Durabolic;* GENERIC
  In Canada—*Deca-Durabolin*
Nandrolone Phenpropionate Injection USP†
  In the U.S.—*Anabolin; Androlone; Durabolin; Hybolin-Improved; Nandrobolic;* GENERIC
  In Canada—*Durabolin*
OXANDROLONE†‡
Oral
Oxandrolone Tablets USP†‡
  In the U.S.—*Anavar*

OXYMETHOLONE
Oral
    Oxymetholone Tablets USP
        In the U.S.—*Anadrol*
        In Canada—*Anapolon 50*
STANOZOLOL
Oral
    Stanozolol Tablets USP
        In the U.S. and Canada—*Winstrol*

---

  †Not commercially available in Canada.
  ‡Product is no longer being manufactured but may still be in circulation.

Category

Note: All anabolic steroids are approximately equal in efficacy. Selection of a particular generic substance or dosage form is dependent upon the incidence of side effects, preferred route of administration, or the duration of action desired. Indications listed for individual generic products included are based on currently marketed product labeling.

Anabolic steroid—Nandrolone; Oxandrolone; Oxymetholone; Stanozolol.
Antianemic—Nandrolone; Oxymetholone; Stanozolol.
Antineoplastic—Nandrolone.
Antiangioedema (hereditary) agent—Oxymetholone; Stanozolol.

Indications

Note: Bracketed information in the *Indications* section refers to uses not included in U.S. product labeling.

Accepted
Catabolic or tissue-depleting processes (treatment)—[Nandrolone decanoate, stanozolol], and oxandrolone are indicated in conditions such as chronic infections, extensive surgery, [corticosteroid-induced myopathy, decubitus ulcers, burns], or severe trauma, which require reversal of catabolic processes or protein-sparing effects. These agents are adjuncts to, and not replacements for, conventional treatment of these disorders.
Anemia (treatment)—
    Nandrolone decanoate[1] is indicated for the treatment of anemia associated with renal insufficiency [and as adjuvant therapy for aplastic and sickle cell anemias]. Adequate iron intake is necessary for maximum therapeutic response.
    [Nandrolone phenpropionate is indicated in the treatment of refractory deficient red cell production anemias. These may include aplastic anemia, myelofibrosis, myelosclerosis, agnogenic myeloid metaplasia, and hypoplastic anemias caused by malignancy or myelotoxic drugs. Anabolic steroid therapy should not replace other supportive measures.]
    Oxymetholone is indicated in the treatment of bone marrow failure anemias and deficient red cell production anemias. Acquired and congenital aplastic anemias, myelofibrosis, and hypoplastic anemias due to myelotoxic medication often respond to oxymetholone. Oxymetholone should not replace other supportive measures such as transfusions; correction of iron, folic acid, vitamin B_{12}, or pyridoxine deficiency; antibacterial therapy; or the use of adrenocorticoids.
    [Stanozolol is effective in raising hemoglobin levels in some cases of aplastic anemia (congenital or idiopathic).]
Carcinoma, breast (treatment)—Anabolic steroids such as [nandrolone decanoate] and nandrolone phenpropionate[1] are indicated as treatment for palliation of inoperable metastatic breast cancer in postmenopausal women. However, anabolic steroids should be considered for use only after inadequate response to newer, less toxic medications such as tamoxifen in hormonally responsive breast cancer. Anabolic steroids have also been used to treat breast cancer in premenopausal women who have undergone oophorectomy and are considered to have a hormone-responsive tumor.
Angioedema, hereditary (prophylaxis)—Stanozolol[1] [and oxymetholone][1] are indicated in the prophylaxis of hereditary angioedema to decrease the frequency and severity of attacks.
[Angioedema, hereditary (treatment)][1]—Stanozolol and oxymetholone are used in the treatment of hereditary angioedema.
[Antithrombin III deficiency (treatment)]; or
[Fibrinogen excess (treatment)]—Stanozolol is indicated in the treatment of conditions associated with decreased fibrinolytic activity due to antithrombin III deficiency or excess fibrinogen. These conditions may include cutaneous vasculitis, scleroderma of Raynaud's disease, vasculitis of Behcet's disease, and complications of deep vein thrombosis such as venous lipodermatosclerosis. Stanozolol is indicated in the prevention of recurrent venous thrombosis associated with antithrombin III deficiency. Stanozolol may be of benefit in patients susceptible to or with a history of thromboembolism for the treatment of vascular disorders associated with these forms of reduced fibrinolytic activity.
[Growth failure (treatment adjunct)]—Anabolic steroids may be used as an adjunct in the treatment of growth failure in children caused by pituitary growth hormone (GH) deficiency (pituitary dwarfism) or if the response to human growth hormone administration is inadequate.
[Turner's syndrome (treatment)]—Oxandrolone is used in the treatment of the short stature that accompanies Turner's syndrome (gonadal dysgenesis in females). Although the therapy is controversial, recent experimental reports seem to indicate that oxandrolone may be as effective as growth hormone and that oxandrolone may increase the efficacy of growth hormone therapy.

Unaccepted
Anabolic steroids have been used for the treatment of symptoms associated with osteoporosis. However, this use has largely been discontinued because the questionable efficacy of these agents for this indication does not justify the risk of serious adverse effects.
Oxandrolone and oxymetholone have been used for the treatment of alcoholic hepatitis with encephalopathy. However, there is currently insufficient evidence to establish the efficacy of these agents for this indication.
Use of anabolic steroids by athletes is not recommended. Objective evidence is conflicting and inconclusive as to whether these medications significantly increase athletic performance by increasing muscle strength. Weight gains reported by athletes are due in part to fluid retention, which is a potentially hazardous side effect of anabolic steroid therapy. The risk of other unwanted effects, such as testicular atrophy and suppression of spermatogenesis in males; menstrual disturbances and virilization, such as deepening of voice, development of acne, and unnatural growth of body hair in females; peliosis hepatis or other hepatotoxicity; and hepatic cancer outweigh any possible benefit received from anabolic steroids and make their use in athletes inappropriate.

---

[1]Not included in Canadian product labeling.

Pharmacology

Mechanism of action/Effect:
    Anabolic steroid—Reverses catabolic processes and negative nitrogen balance by promoting protein anabolism and stimulating appetite if there is concurrently a proper intake of calories and proteins.
    Antianemic—
        Anemias due to bone marrow failure: Increases production of erythropoietin.
        Anemias due to deficient red cell production: Stimulates erythropoietin production and may have a direct action on bone marrow.

Anemias associated with renal disease: Increases hemoglobin and red blood cell volume.

Angioedema (hereditary) prophylactic—Increases serum concentration of C1 esterase inhibitor and, as a result, C2 and C4 concentrations.

Precautions to Consider

Geriatrics
Treatment of geriatric male patients with anabolic steroids may cause increased risk of prostatic hypertrophy or prostatic carcinoma.

Drug interactions and/or related problems
The following drug interactions and/or related problems have been selected on the basis of their potential clinical significance (possible mechanism in parentheses where appropriate)—not necessarily inclusive (» = major clinical significance):

Note: Combinations containing any of the following medications, depending on the amount present, may also interact with this medication.

Adrenocorticoids, glucocorticoid, especially with significant mineralocorticoid activity, or
Adrenocorticoids, mineralocorticoid, or
Corticotropin, especially prolonged therapeutic use, or
Sodium-containing medications or foods
(concurrent use with anabolic steroids may increase the possibility of edema; in addition, concurrent use of glucocorticoids or corticotropin with anabolic steroids may promote development of severe acne)

» Anticoagulants, coumarin- or indandione-derivative, or
Anti-inflammatory analgesics, nonsteroidal, or
Salicylates, in therapeutic doses
(anticoagulant effect may be increased during concurrent use with anabolic steroids, especially 17-alpha-alkylated compounds, because of decreased procoagulant factor concentration caused by alteration of procoagulant factor synthesis or catabolism and increased receptor affinity for the anticoagulant; anticoagulant dosage adjustment based on prothrombin time determinations may be required during and following concurrent use)

Antidiabetic agents, oral, or
Insulin
(anabolic steroids may decrease blood glucose concentration; diabetic patients should be closely monitored for signs of hypoglycemia and dosage of hypoglycemic agent adjusted if necessary)

» Hepatotoxic medications, other
(concurrent use with anabolic steroids may result in an increased incidence of hepatotoxicity; patients, especially those on prolonged administration or those with a history of liver disease, should be carefully monitored)

Somatrem or
Somatropin
(concurrent use of anabolic steroids with somatrem or somatropin may accelerate epiphyseal maturation)

Contraindications/Medical problems
The contraindications/medical problems included have been selected on the basis of their potential clinical significance (reasons given in parentheses where appropriate)—not necessarily inclusive (» = major clinical significance).

Except under special circumstances, these medications should not be used when the following medical problems exist:

» Breast cancer, disseminated, in females with active hypercalcemia
» Breast cancer in males
» Hepatic function impairment, severe
» Hypercalcemia, active or history of
(may be exacerbated or recurrence may result)
» Nephrosis or nephrotic phase of nephritis

» Prostate cancer
(tumor growth may be promoted)

Risk-benefit should be considered when the following medical problems exist:

Cardiac function impairment or
Hepatic function impairment or
Renal function impairment
(use of these medications may cause retention of sodium and water, resulting in edema, with or without congestive heart failure)

» Coronary artery disease, history of, or
» Myocardial infarction, history of
(because of hypercholesterolemic effects of anabolic steroids)

Diabetes mellitus
(anabolic steroids may decrease blood sugar concentrations; insulin or oral hypoglycemic dosage may need to be adjusted)

Intolerance to anabolic steroids or androgens

Prostatic hypertrophy, benign
(further enlargement may occur)

Side/Adverse Effects

Note: Peliosis hepatis and hepatic neoplasms, including hepatocellular carcinoma, have been associated with long-term, high-dose anabolic steroid therapy. These adverse reactions can be life-threatening or fatal.

The following side/adverse effects have been selected on the basis of their potential clinical significance (possible signs and symptoms in parentheses where appropriate)—not necessarily inclusive:

Those indicating need for medical attention
Incidence more frequent
In females only
Virilism (acne or oily skin, enlarging clitoris, hoarseness or deepening of voice, menstrual irregularities, unnatural hair growth or loss)

Note: *Enlarged clitoris, hoarseness* or *deepening of voice, unnatural hair growth,* and *unusual hair loss* usually are not reversible even after prompt discontinuance of therapy. The concurrent use of estrogens will not prevent virilization in females.

In prepubertal males only
Virilism (acne, enlarging penis, increased frequency of erections, unnatural hair growth)

In postpubertal males only
Bladder irritability (frequent urge to urinate); **breast soreness; gynecomastia** (enlargement of breasts); **priapism** (frequent or continuing erections)

Incidence less frequent
In both females and males
Anemia, iron deficiency (loss of appetite, sore tongue); **edema** (swelling of feet or lower legs, rapid weight gain); **gastric irritation** (nausea, vomiting); **hepatic dysfunction** (yellow eyes or skin); **leukemia** (bone pain); **suppression of clotting factors** (unusual bleeding)

In females only
Hypercalcemia (mental depression, nausea, vomiting, unusual tiredness)

In prepubertal males only
Unexplained darkening of skin

In geriatric males only
Prostatic carcinoma or prostatic hypertrophy (difficult or frequent urination)

Incidence rare—with prolonged therapy
In both females and males
Hepatic necrosis (black, tarry stools; continuing feeling of discomfort; continuing headache; continuing unpleasant breath

odor; vomiting of blood); *hepatocellular carcinoma* (abdominal or stomach pain, unexplained weight loss); *peliosis hepatis* (dark-colored urine, hives, light-colored stools, continuing loss of appetite, purple- or red-colored spots on body or inside the mouth or nose, sore throat, fever, nausea, vomiting)

Those indicating need for medical attention only if they continue or are bothersome

Incidence more frequent
>*In males only*
>>*Acne*

Incidence less frequent
>*In both females and males*
>>*Chills; diarrhea; feeling of abdominal or stomach fullness; libido* (decrease or increase); *muscle cramps; trouble in sleeping*
>*In males only*
>>*Decreased sexual ability*

Patient Consultation

In providing consultation, consider emphasizing the following selected information (» = major clinical significance):

Before using this medication
» Conditions affecting use, especially:
> Carcinogencity—Hepatocellular carcinoma associated with long-term, high-dose therapy
> Tumorigenicity—Hepatic neoplasms associated with long-term, high-dose therapy
> Pregnancy—Not recommended during pregnancy because of possible masculinization of fetus
> Use in children—Cautious use because of effects on growth and sexual development (precocious sexual development in males, virilization in females)
> Use in elderly—Increased risk of prostatic hypertrophy or prostatic carcinoma
> Use by athletes—Use of anabolic steroids is banned and tested for by USOC, IOC, and NCAA
> Other medications, especially anticoagulants (coumarin- or indandione-derivatives) or hepatotoxic medications
> Other medical problems, especially breast cancer, hepatic function impairment, hypercalcemia, nephrosis, nephrotic phase of nephritis, prostatic cancer, coronary artery disease, or myocardial infarction

Proper use of this medication
» Importance of not taking more medication than the amount prescribed; to do so may increase chance of side effects
» Importance of diet high in proteins and calories while taking this medication to achieve maximum therapeutic effect
> Missed dose: If dosing schedule is—
>> Once daily: Taking as soon as possible; if not remembered until next day, not taking at all; not doubling doses
>> More than once daily: Taking as soon as possible; not taking if almost time for next dose; not doubling doses
» Proper storage

Precautions while using this medication
> Regular visits to physician to check progress during therapy
> Diabetics: May decrease blood sugar concentrations

Side/adverse effects
> Signs of potential side effects, especially:
>> In females only—Virilism, hypercalcemia
>> In prepubertal males only—Virilism or unexplained darkening of skin
>> In males only—Gynecomastia, priapism, or bladder irritability
>> In geriatric males only—Prostatic carcinoma or hypertrophy
>> In all patients, in addition to those side effects listed above—Leukemia; peliosis hepatis; anemia; edema; clotting factor suppression; and hepatic dysfunction, carcinoma, or necrosis

General Dosing Information

Many of the side/adverse effects of anabolic steroids are dose related; therefore, patients should be placed on the lowest possible effective dose.

A well-balanced diet that provides adequate proteins and calories should accompany all anabolic steroid therapy to achieve a maximum therapeutic effect.

NANDROLONE

Summary of Differences

Category:
> Nandrolone decanoate—Antianemic.
> Nandrolone phenpropionate—Antineoplastic.

Indications:
> Nandrolone decanoate is indicated in the treatment of anemia associated with renal insufficiency.
> Nandrolone phenpropionate is indicated in the treatment of metastatic breast cancer in women.

Additional Dosing Information

See also *General Dosing Information.*

Nandrolone injections should be administered intramuscularly, preferably deep into the gluteal muscle.

When using nandrolone decanoate injection, an adequate iron intake is required for maximum response.

Parenteral Dosage Forms

NANDROLONE DECANOATE INJECTION USP

Usual adult and adolescent dose:
> Females—Intramuscular, 50 to 100 mg given at one- to four-week intervals.
> Males—Intramuscular, 50 to 200 mg given at one- to four-week intervals.

Note: When given at three- to four-week intervals, therapy may be continued for up to 12 weeks. If necessary, cycle may be repeated if second course is preceded by a four-week rest period.

> In the treatment of severe disease states, such as metastatic breast cancer and refractory anemias, a higher dose, based on therapeutic response and the benefit-to-risk ratio, may be required.

NANDROLONE PHENPROPIONATE INJECTION USP

Usual adult dose: Intramuscular, 25 to 100 mg per week.

Note: Therapy may be continued for up to 12 weeks. If necessary, cycle may be repeated if second course is preceded by a four-week rest period.

OXANDROLONE

Summary of Differences

Indications: Indicated in the treatment of catabolic or tissue-depleting processes.

Additional Dosing Information

See also *General Dosing Information.*

In adults, 2 to 4 weeks of therapy are usually adequate. In both adults and children, therapy may be repeated intermittently as needed.

Oral Dosage Forms

Note; Bracketed uses in the *Dosage Forms* section refer to categories of use and/or indications that are not included in U.S. product labeling.

OXANDROLONE TABLETS USP

Usual adult and adolescent dose: Oral, 2.5 mg two to four times a day.

Note: The dosage may range from 2.5 to 20 mg per day.

OXYMETHOLONE

Summary of Differences

Category: Antianemic; angioedema (hereditary) agent.
Indications: Indicated in treatment of bone marrow failure anemias and in deficient red cell production anemias; also used in prophylaxis and treatment of hereditary angioedema.

Additional Dosing Information

See also *General Dosing Information.*

Oxymetholone should be used for a minimum of 3 to 6 months, since a response is not always immediately observed.

Following remission of the anemia, some patients may be maintained without oxymetholone while others may be maintained on a low daily dose. Patients with congenital aplastic anemia usually require continued therapy with an appropriate maintenance dose.

Oral Dosage Forms

OXYMETHOLONE TABLETS USP

Usual adult and adolescent dose: Oral, 1 to 5 mg per kg of body weight per day.

Note: The usual effective dose is 1 to 2 mg per kg of body weight a day, but higher doses may be required in some patients. Treatment of refractory anemias may require 3 to 6 months.

STANOZOLOL

Summary of Differences

Category: Angioedema (hereditary) prophylactic.
Indications: Stanozolol is indicated in the prophylaxis of hereditary angioedema to decrease the frequency and severity of attacks and used in treatment of hereditary angioedema.

Oral Dosage Forms

STANOZOLOL TABLETS USP

Usual adult and adolescent dose: Oral, 2 mg three times a day to 4 mg four times a day for 5 days, initially.

Note: A dose of 2 mg two times a day may be used in young women, who are particularly susceptible to the androgenic effects of stanozolol.

The dosage for continuous treatment of hereditary angioedema should be individualized according to patient response. After a favorable response is obtained, the dose should be decreased at intervals of 1 to 3 months to a maintenance dose of 2 mg a day; some patients may respond to a maintenance dose of 2 mg every other day. During the dose-reduction phase, close monitoring of patient response is indicated, especially if the patient has a history of upper respiratory tract involvement.

ANDROGENS   Systemic

Some commonly used *brand names* are:

In the U.S.—

Andro 100 [Testosterone]	*Andronate 200* [Testosterone]	*Halotestin* [Fluoxymesterone]	*Testoject-LA* [Testosterone]

In the U.S.—

Andro 100 [Testosterone]
Andro-Cyp 100 [Testosterone]
Andro-Cyp 200 [Testosterone]
Android-5 [Methyltestosterone]
Android-10 [Methyltestosterone]
Android-25 [Methyltestosterone]
Android-F [Fluoxymesterone]
Andro L.A. 200 [Testosterone]
Andronaq-50 [Testosterone]
Andronaq-LA [Testosterone]
Andronate 100 [Testosterone]

Andronate 200 [Testosterone]
Andropository 100 [Testosterone]
Andryl 200 [Testosterone]
Delatest [Testosterone]
Delatestryl [Testosterone]
depAndro 100 [Testosterone]
depAndro 200 [Testosterone]
Depotest [Testosterone]
Depo-Testosterone [Testosterone]
Duratest-100 [Testosterone]
Duratest-200 [Testosterone]
Durathate-200 [Testosterone]
Everone [Testosterone]

Halotestin [Fluoxymesterone]
Histerone-50 [Testosterone]
Histerone-100 [Testosterone]
Oreton [Methyltestosterone]
T-Cypionate [Testosterone]
Testa-C [Testosterone]
Testamone 100 [Testosterone]
Testaqua [Testosterone]
Testex [Testosterone]
Testoject-50 [Testosterone]

In Canada—
Delatestryl [Testosterone]
Depo-Testosterone Cypionate [Testosterone]
Halotestin [Fluoxymesterone]

Testoject-LA [Testosterone]
Testone L.A. 100 [Testosterone]
Testone L.A. 200 [Testosterone]
Testred [Methyltestosterone]
Testred Cypionate 200 [Testosterone]
Testrin-P.A. [Testosterone]
Virilon [Methyltestosterone]
Virilon IM [Testosterone]

Malogen [Testosterone]
Malogex [Testosterone]
Metandren [Methyltestosterone]

FLUOXYMESTERONE
Oral
    Fluoxymesterone Tablets USP
        In the U.S.—*Android-F; Halotestin;* GENERIC
        In Canada—*Halotestin*
METHYLTESTOSTERONE
Oral
    Methyltestosterone Capsules USP
        In the U.S.—*Testred; Virilon*
    Methyltestosterone Tablets USP (Buccal)
        In the U.S.—*Android-5; Oreton;* GENERIC
        In Canada—*Metandren*
    Methyltestosterone Tablets USP (Oral)
        In the U.S.—*Android-10; Android-25; Oreton;* GENERIC
        In Canada—*Metandren*
TESTOSTERONE
Parenteral
    Sterile Testosterone Suspension USP
        In the U.S.—*Andro 100; Andronaq-50; Histerone-50; Histerone-100; Testamone 100; Testaqua; Testoject-50;* GENERIC
        In Canada—*Malogen*
    Testosterone Cypionate Injection USP
        In the U.S.—*Andro-Cyp 100; Andro-Cyp 200; Andronaq-LA; Andronate 100; Andronate 200; depAndro 100; depAndro 200; Depotest; Depo-Testosterone; Duratest-100; Duratest-200; T-Cypionate; Testa-C; Testoject-LA; Testred Cypionate 200; Virilon IM;* GENERIC
        In Canada—*Depo-Testosterone Cypionate*
    Testosterone Enanthate Injection USP
        In the U.S.—*Andro L.A. 200; Andropository 100; Andryl 200; Delatest; Delatestryl; Durathate-200; Everone; Testone L.A. 100; Testone L.A. 200; Testrin-P.A.;* GENERIC
        In Canada—*Delatestryl; Malogex*
    Testosterone Propionate Injection USP
        In the U.S.—*Testex;* GENERIC
        In Canada—*Malogen*
Topical
    Testosterone Propionate Ointment*†

*Not commercially available in the U.S.
†Not commercially available in Canada.

Category

Androgen—Fluoxymesterone; Methyltestosterone; Testosterone.
Antineoplastic—Fluoxymesterone; Methyltestosterone; Testosterone.
Antianemic—Fluoxymesterone; Testosterone Cypionate; Testosterone Enanthate.

Indications

Note: Bracketed information in the *Indications* section refers to uses not included in U.S. product labeling.

Accepted

Androgen deficiency (treatment)—Androgens are primarily indicated in males as replacement therapy when endogenous androgen absence or deficiency is associated with primary hypogonadal conditions such as testicular failure due to cryptorchidism, bilateral torsion, orchitis, or vanishing testis syndrome; inborn errors in testosterone biosynthesis; orchidectomy; hypogonadotropic hypogonadism (gonadotropin releasing hormone [GnRH]) deficiency; or pituitary-hypothalamic injury from surgery, tumors, trauma, or radiation. Methyltestosterone, [testosterone cypionate, testosterone enanthate, and fluoxymesterone] are also used as replacement therapy in impotence or for male climacteric symptoms when these conditions are due to a measured or documented androgen deficiency. For long-term therapy, testosterone or a testosterone ester

is preferred over the oral methylated androgens (fluoxymesterone and methyltestosterone), which increase the risk of hepatotoxicity.

Puberty, delayed male (treatment)—Short-term (6 months) therapy with androgens may be used to stimulate puberty when delayed puberty is not secondary to a pathological disorder and is expected to occur spontaneously at a relatively late date, and when the patient does not respond to interval psychological support.

Carcinoma, breast (treatment)—Androgens are indicated as secondary or tertiary hormonal treatment for palliation of metastatic breast cancer in women who have hormone receptor-positive tumors or who have previously demonstrated a response to hormone therapy. Androgens have also been used in the treatment of metastatic breast cancer as a supplement to chemotherapy.

[Anemia (treatment)]—Fluoxymesterone and testosterone cypionate or enanthate have been used to treat certain types of anemia. Fluoxymesterone is indicated in the treatment of refractory deficient red cell production anemias. These may include aplastic anemia, myelofibrosis, myelosclerosis, agnogenic myeloid metaplasia, and hypoplastic anemias caused by malignancy or myelotoxic drugs. However, these agents are rarely used for the treatment of anemia; usually they have been given as a trial in refractory cases of anemia which do not respond well to other less toxic therapy.

[Constitutional delay in growth (treatment)][1]—Androgens are used in the treatment of constitutional delay in growth. However, they are no longer considered the treatment of first choice for all patients.

[Gender change, female-to-male][1]—Testosterone is used for the development and maintenance of secondary sexual characteristics in female-to-male transsexuals.

[Lichen sclerosus (treatment adjunct)][1]—Extemporaneously compounded topical testosterone is used for the treatment of itching resulting from lichen sclerosus.

[Microphallus (treatment)][1]—Intramuscular preparations of testosterone and testosterone esters, and extemporaneously compounded topical testosterone are used in the treatment of microphallus.

Unaccepted

Use of androgens to enhance athletic performance is illegal. Increases in muscle mass and muscle strength can be sufficient to enhance athletic performance. However, the risk of other unwanted effects, such as spermatogenesis suppression, testicular atrophy, menstrual disturbances, virilization in females, peliosis hepatis, hepatotoxicity, potential adverse effects on cardiovascular health, and hepatic cancer counter athletic benefits received from androgens and make their use in athletes inappropriate. Additionally, behavioral disturbances, including aggressive or violent behavior have been reported with supraphysiological self-administered doses in athletes.

The use of androgens for the prevention of postpartum breast engorgement is not recommended. In many patients, postpartum breast engorgement is a benign, self-limited condition that may respond to breast support and mild analgesics, such as acetaminophen and ibuprofen. Evidence supporting the efficacy of androgens for this indication is lacking.

Androgens are not recommended for adjunctive treatment of osteoporosis or in the treatment of vasomotor symptoms of menopause, menorrhagia, or female hypoactive sexual desire disorder.

[1]Not included in Canadian product labeling.

Pharmacology

Mechanism of action/Effect:

Androgen—Androgen secretion is regulated by gonadotropins. Androgens are responsible for stimulation of spermatogenesis, development of male secondary sex characteristics, and stimulation of sexual maturation at puberty. Androgens are highly lipid soluble and enter cells of target tissues by passive diffusion. Within the cells of the target tissues, testosterone is converted by the enzyme 5-alpha reductase to 5 alpha-dihydrotestosterone (DHT). Testosterone and DHT bind to cytosolic receptors, which are loosely bound to sites in the cell nucleus. The steroid receptor complex initiates transcription, resulting in an increase in protein production. Increased serum concentrations of androgens suppress gonadotropin-releasing hormone (GnRH), luteinizing hormone (LH), and follicle-stimulating hormone (FSH) through a negative feedback mechanism involving the hypothalamus and anterior pituitary.

Microphallus: Intramuscular administration of testosterone or testosterone esters or local application of testosterone propionate ointment may result in an increase in circulating serum concentrations of DHT, which is principally responsible for phallic growth.

Lichen sclerosus: The signs and symptoms of lichen sclerosus (vulvar itching, abnormal vulvar skin histology) may be the result of a deficiency of 5-alpha reductase activity and subsequently reduced local DHT concentrations. Local application of testosterone propionate ointment may correct this deficiency in 5-alpha reductase activity. Testosterone may cause a slight increase in local DHT concentrations, which may induce 5-alpha reductase activity, and increase local DHT concentrations.

Antianemic—Stimulates production of red blood cells by enhancing production of erythropoietic stimulating factors.

Duration of action: Testosterone—Dependent upon the ester, dosage form, and route of administration; in order of decreasing duration—enanthate, cypionate, propionate, base.

Precautions to Consider

Geriatrics

Treatment of male patients over the age of approximately 50 years with androgens should be preceded by a thorough examination of the prostate and baseline measurement of prostate-specific antigen serum concentration, since androgens may cause increased risk of prostatic hypertrophy or may stimulate the growth of occult prostatic carcinoma. Periodic evaluation of prostate function should also be performed during the course of therapy.

Drug interactions and/or related problems

The following drug interactions and/or related problems have been selected on the basis of their potential clinical significance (possible mechanism in parentheses where appropriate)—not necessarily inclusive (» = major clinical significance):

Note: Combinations containing any of the following medications, depending on the amount present, may also interact with this medication.

» Anticoagulants, coumarin- or indandione-derivative
(anticoagulant effect may be increased because of decreased procoagulant factor concentration caused by alteration of procoagulant factor synthesis or catabolism and increased receptor affinity for the anticoagulant; anticoagulant dosage adjustment may be required during and following concurrent use)

Antidiabetic agents, oral, or
Insulin
(androgens may decrease blood glucose concentration; diabetic patients should be closely monitored for signs of hypoglycemia and dosage of the hypoglycemic agent adjusted if necessary)

Cyclosporine
(methyltestosterone has been reported to increase plasma concentrations of cyclosporine and may increase the risk of nephrotoxicity; other androgens may have the same effect)

» Hepatotoxic medications, other
(may result in an increased incidence of hepatotoxicity; patients should be carefully monitored, especially those on prolonged administration or those with a history of liver disease)

Human growth hormone (somatrem or somatropin)
(use of excessive doses of androgens in prepubertal males may accelerate epiphyseal maturation, although supplemental use of

androgens may be necessary in patients with androgen deficiency to continue the growth response to human growth hormone)

Contraindications/Medical problems

The contraindications/medical problems included have been selected on the basis of their potential clinical significance (reasons given in parentheses where appropriate)—not necessarily inclusive (» = major clinical significance).

Except under special circumstances, these medications should not be used when the following medical problems exist:

» Breast cancer in males or
» Prostate cancer, known or suspected
(tumor growth may be promoted)

Risk-benefit should be considered when the following medical problems exist:

» Cardiac failure or
Cardiac function impairment or
» Cardio-renal disease, severe, or
Edema or
Hepatic function impairment or
» Nephritis or
» Nephrosis or
Renal function impairment
(may cause fluid retention, resulting in edema with or without congestive heart failure; diuretics may be required before and during therapy)

Coronary artery disease or
» Myocardial infarction, history of
(may be worsened, due to hypercholesterolemic effects of androgens)

Diabetes mellitus
(use may result in loss of control of diabetes, due to an androgen-induced glucose intolerance; routine monitoring of blood glucose concentrations is recommended, especially upon initiation of therapy)

» Hepatic function impairment
(biotransformation of androgens may be impaired, resulting in increased elimination half-life and increase in the incidence of gynecomastia)

» Hypercalcemia
(may be exacerbated in patients with metastatic breast carcinoma)

» Prostatic hypertrophy, benign with urethral obstructive symptoms
(further enlargement may occur)

Sensitivity to anabolic steroids or androgens

Side/Adverse Effects

Note: The side effects of testosterone enanthate and testosterone cypionate cannot be quickly reversed by discontinuing medication because of the long durations of action of these medications.

The following side/adverse effects have been selected on the basis of their potential clinical significance (possible signs and symptoms in parentheses where appropriate)—not necessarily inclusive:

Those indicating need for medical attention
Incidence more frequent
In females only
Amenorrhea or oligomenorrhea (menstrual irregularities); *virilism* (acne, decreased breast size, oily skin, enlarged clitoris, male pattern baldness, hoarseness or deepening of voice, unnatural and excessive hair growth)
Note: *Virilism* may occur with usual systemic doses, as well as with excessive doses of topical testosterone. Virilization has also been reported in the sexual partner of a male patient being treated with topical testosterone. Hoarse-

ness or deepening of voice and enlarged clitoris may not be reversible even after the medication has been discontinued.

In males only

Bladder irritability (frequent urge to urinate); ***breast soreness; gynecomastia*** (enlargement of breasts); ***priapism*** (frequent or continuing erections)—sign of excessive dosage; temporary discontinuance of medication and immediate medical attention are required

In prepubertal males only

Virilism (acne, enlargement of penis, increased frequency of erections, early growth of pubic hair)

Incidence less frequent

In both females and males

Edema (swelling of feet or lower legs, rapid weight gain); ***erythrocytosis*** (dizziness; headache; frequent or continuing; unusual tiredness; flushing or redness of skin; unusual bleeding—in severe cases); ***gastrointestinal irritation*** (nausea, vomiting); ***hepatic dysfunction*** (yellow eyes or skin, itching of skin)—more likely with the oral methylated androgens; ***hypercalcemia*** (confusion, mental depression, unusual tiredness, nausea, polydypsia, polyuria, constipation, vomiting)—in females with breast cancer or immobilized patients

In males only

Nonspecific acute epididymitis (chills, pain in scrotum or groin); ***prostatic carcinoma*** (stimulation of tumor growth) ***or prostatic hypertrophy*** (difficult urination)

Incidence rare—with long-term therapy and/or high doses

In both females and males

Hepatic necrosis (continuing abdominal or stomach pain; black, tarry stools; continuing malaise; continuing headache; continuing unpleasant breath odor; vomiting of blood); ***hepatocellular tumor*** (pain or tenderness in upper abdomen or liver area, swelling of abdomen)—more likely with the oral methylated androgens; may be life-threatening or fatal; ***leukopenia*** (sore throat, fever); ***peliosis hepatis*** (dark-colored urine, hives, light-colored stools, continuing loss of appetite, purple- or red-colored spots on body or inside the mouth or nose, sore throat, fever, nausea, vomiting)—more likely with the oral methylated androgens; may be life-threatening or fatal

Those indicating need for medical attention only if they continue or are bothersome

Incidence less frequent

In both females and males

Mild acne; diarrhea; increase in pubic hair growth; *infection, redness, pain, or other irritation at site of injection*—for intramuscular injection only; ***decrease or increase in libido; stomach pain; stomatitis*—**secondary to buccal administration (irritation or soreness of mouth, watering of mouth); ***trouble in sleeping***

In males only

Impotence; *testicular atrophy* (decrease in testicle size)

Patient Consultation

In providing consultation, consider emphasizing the following selected information (» = major clinical significance):

Before using this medication

» Conditions affecting use, especially:

Sensitivity to androgens or anabolic steroids

Carcinogenicity—Hepatocellular carcinoma associated with long-term, high-dose therapy

Tumorigenicity—Hepatic neoplasms associated with long-term, high-dose therapy

Fertility—May be severely impaired in males

Pregnancy—Contraindicated for use during pregnancy because of possible masculinization of female fetus

Use in children—Cautious use due to effects on growth and sexual development (precocious sexual development in males, virilization in females)

Use in the elderly—Increased risk of prostatic hypertrophy or prostatic carcinoma

Use by athletes—Banned and tested for by IOC, USOC, and NCAA

Other medications, especially anticoagulants (coumarin- or indandione-derivatives) or hepatotoxic medications

Other medical problems, especially male breast cancer, possible prostate cancer, cardiac failure, cardio-renal disease, history of myocardial infarction, hepatic function impairment, hypercalcemia, nephrosis, nephritis, or prostatic hypertrophy

Proper use of this medication

» Importance of not taking more medication than the amount prescribed

Missed dose: Taking as soon as possible; not taking if almost time for next dose; not doubling doses

» Proper storage

For fluoxymesterone, and capsule and oral tablet dosage forms of methyltestosterone

Taking with food to minimize possible stomach upset

For methyltestosterone buccal tablets

» Proper administration

» Importance of not swallowing buccal tablets

Precautions while using this medication

Regular visits to physician to check progress during therapy

Diabetics: May alter blood sugar concentrations

Side/adverse effects

Signs of potential side effects, especially:

In females only—Menstrual irregularities, virilism

In males only—Bladder irritability, breast soreness, gynecomastia, priapism, epididymitis, prostatic carcinoma, prostatic hypertrophy

In prepubertal males only—Virilism

In all patients—Edema, erythrocytosis, gastrointestinal irritation, hepatic necrosis, hepatocellular tumor, hepatic dysfunction, hypercalcemia, leukopenia, peliosis hepatis, or polycythemia

General Dosing Information

The dosage and duration of therapy depends on the patient's age, sex, diagnosis, and response to therapy, and the appearance of adverse effects.

It is usually preferable to begin treatment for anemia and carcinoma with full therapeutic doses and to adjust later to individual requirements.

For treatment of delayed puberty

The dosage used in delayed puberty generally is in the lower range of the usual adult dose for androgen replacement therapy and is given for a limited duration, usually 3 to 6 months. The chronological and skeletal ages should be considered, both in determining the initial dose and in adjusting the dose. After three to six months of therapy, the medication should be discontinued for one to three months and x-rays taken to determine effect on bone growth or maturation.

Various dosage regimens have been used to induce pubertal changes in hypogonadal males. Some physicians prescribe a lower dose initially, gradually increase the dose as puberty progresses, and follow with a maintenance dose which may be decreased.

For treatment of breast cancer

To determine whether there will be an objective response to antineoplastic therapy, treatment should be continued for at least 3 months. A response to therapy is usually apparent within 3 months. Therapy should be discontinued after the disease becomes progressive again. If clinical circumstances allow for an observation period, the patient should be observed for a period of improvement known as "rebound regression."

Women should be checked for signs of virilization during androgen therapy. Some effects, such as voice changes or clitoromegaly, may not be reversible. A decision should be made by patient and physician as to how much virilization will be tolerated as a result of therapy with androgens. Alternatively, the drug should be discontinued or the dosage reduced. If irreversible virilization is to be prevented, drug must be discontinued when mild virilization becomes evident.

Women with metastatic breast cancer should be followed closely because androgen therapy occasionally accelerates the disease. A shorter acting androgen is preferred over one with prolonged activity, especially during the early stages of androgen therapy.

For intramuscular dosage forms
The suspension dosage form is absorbed relatively slowly; therefore, frequent injections may cause overdosage.

Testosterone cypionate or testosterone enanthate should not be used interchangeably with testosterone propionate or testosterone base because of different durations of action.

The intramuscular injections should be administered deeply into the gluteal muscle or the deltoid muscle in larger men. Injections should not be administered intravenously.

FLUOXYMESTERONE

Summary of Differences

Indications: Also used as an antianemic.
Side/adverse effects: Methylated androgens are more likely to predispose patients to jaundice.

Oral Dosage Forms

Note: Bracketed uses in the *Dosage Forms* section refer to categories of use and/or indications that are not included in U.S. product labeling.

FLUOXYMESTERONE TABLETS USP
Usual adult dose:
    Androgen—Replacement therapy: Males—Oral, 5 mg one to four times a day. Replacement therapy is usually started at 10 mg per day, with subsequent adjustments as necessary.
    Antineoplastic—Breast cancer in females: Oral, 20 to 50 mg per day.
    [Antianemic]—Oral, 20 to 50 mg per day, for minimum trial of two to six months.

Auxiliary labeling: • Take with food.

METHYLTESTOSTERONE

Summary of Differences

Indications: Also indicated for androgen replacement in impotence or for male climacteric symptoms.
Pharmacology: Methyltestosterone buccal tablets are nearly twice as potent as the oral preparations.
Side/adverse effects:
    Methylated androgens more likely to predispose patients to jaundice.

Irritation or soreness of mouth or unusual watering of mouth (stomatitis from buccal tablet administration).

Oral Dosage Forms

METHYLTESTOSTERONE CAPSULES USP
Usual adult dose:
    Androgen—
        Replacement therapy: Males—
            Climacteric or impotence or
            Hypogonadism: Oral, 10 to 50 mg per day.
            Cryptorchidism: Oral, 10 mg three times a day.
    Antineoplastic—Breast cancer in females: Oral, 50 mg one to four times a day. After two to four weeks, dose may be decreased to 50 mg two times a day if response occurs.

Auxiliary labeling: • Take with food.

METHYLTESTOSTERONE TABLETS USP (BUCCAL)
Usual adult dose:
    Androgen—
        Replacement therapy: Males—
            Climacteric or impotence or
            Hypogonadism: Buccal, 5 to 25 mg per day.
            Cryptorchidism: Buccal, 5 mg three times a day.
    Antineoplastic—Breast cancer in females: Buccal, 25 mg one to four times a day. After two to four weeks, dose may be decreased to 25 mg two times a day if response occurs.

METHYLTESTOSTERONE TABLETS USP (ORAL)
Usual adult dose:
    Androgen—Replacement therapy: Males—
        Climacteric or impotence or
        Hypogonadism: Oral, 10 to 50 mg per day.
        Postpubertal cryptorchidism: Oral, 10 mg three times a day.
    Antineoplastic—Breast cancer in females: Oral, 50 mg one to four times a day. After two to four weeks, dose may be decreased to 50 mg two times a day if response occurs.

Auxiliary labeling: • Take with food.

TESTOSTERONE

Summary of Differences

Indications: Testosterone enanthate and testosterone cypionate are used as antianemics and in androgen replacement in impotence or for male climacteric symptoms. Testosterone cypionate and testosterone enanthate are also used for female-to-male gender change. Intramuscular testosterone and testosterone esters, and extemporaneously compounded testosterone propionate ointments are used in the treatment of microphallus. Extemporaneously compounded testosterone propionate ointments are used in the treatment of lichen sclerosus.
Side/adverse effects:
    Side effects of the enanthate and cypionate forms cannot be quickly reversed because of the long duration of effect of medication form.
    Hives, infection, redness, pain, or other irritation at site of injection.

Parenteral Dosage Forms

Note: Bracketed uses in the *Dosage Forms* section refers to categories of use and/or indications that are not included in U.S. product labeling.

STERILE TESTOSTERONE SUSPENSION USP

Usual adult dose:
Androgen—
Replacement therapy: Males—Intramuscular, 25 to 50 mg two or three times a week.
Antineoplastic—Breast cancer in females: Intramuscular, 50 to 100 mg three times a week.

Auxiliary labeling: • Shake well.

TESTOSTERONE CYPIONATE INJECTION USP

Usual adult dose:
Androgen—
Replacement therapy: Males—
Climacteric or impotence or
Hypogonadism: Intramuscular, 50 to 400 mg every two to four weeks.
[Gender change][1]: Intramuscular, 200 mg every two weeks. Occasional patients may require a higher dose to cause cessation of menses.
Antineoplastic—Breast cancer in females: Intramuscular, 200 to 400 mg every two to four weeks.

TESTOSTERONE ENANTHATE INJECTION USP

Usual adult dose:
Androgen—
Replacement therapy:
Males—Intramuscular, 50 to 400 mg every two to four weeks.

Antineoplastic: Breast cancer in females: Intramuscular, 200 to 400 mg every two to four weeks.
[Antianemic]: To stimulate erythropoiesis: Intramuscular, 400 mg a day for one week, then 400 mg one or two times a week. The maintenance dose is 200 to 400 mg every 4 weeks.
[Gender change][1]: Intramuscular, 200 mg every two weeks. Occasional patients may require a higher dose to cause cessation of menses.

TESTOSTERONE PROPIONATE INJECTION USP

Usual adult dose:
Androgen—
Replacement therapy: Males—Intramuscular, 25 to 50 mg two or three times a week.
Antineoplastic: Breast cancer in females: Intramuscular, 50 to 100 mg three times a week.

Topical Dosage Forms

TESTOSTERONE PROPIONATE OINTMENT

Usual adult dose: Androgen—Lichen sclerosus: Initial, topical, to the vulva, as a 1 or 2% ointment, two times a day for six weeks or until relief of itching occurs. Dosage should be decreased to minimal effective dose.

ANGIOTENSIN-CONVERTING ENZYME (ACE) INHIBITORS   Systemic

Some commonly used *brand names* are:
In the U.S.—
Accupril [Quinapril]
Altace [Ramipril]
Capoten [Captopril]
Lotensin [Benazepril]
Monopril [Fosinopril]
Prinivil [Lisinopril]
Vasotec [Enalapril]
Zestril [Lisinopril]

In Canada—
Capoten [Captopril]
Prinivil [Lisinopril]
Vasotec [Enalapril]
Zestril [Lisinopril]

BENAZEPRIL†
Oral
Benazepril Hydrochloride Tablets†
In the U.S.—*Lotensin*
CAPTOPRIL
Oral
Captopril Tablets USP
In the U.S. and Canada—*Capoten*
ENALAPRIL
Oral
Enalapril Maleate Tablets USP
In the U.S. and Canada—*Vasotec*
Parenteral
Enalaprilat Injection
In the U.S. and Canada—*Vasotec*
FOSINOPRIL†
Oral
Fosinopril Sodium Tablets†
In the U.S.—*Monopril*
LISINOPRIL
Oral
Lisinopril Tablets
In the U.S. and Canada—*Prinivil; Zestril*

QUINAPRIL†
Oral
Quinapril Hydrochloride Tablets†
In the U.S.—*Accupril*
RAMIPRIL†
Oral
Ramipril Capsules†
In the U.S.—*Altace*

†Not commercially available in Canada.

Category

Antihypertensive—Benazepril; Captopril; Enalapril; Fosinopril; Lisinopril; Quinapril; Ramipril.
Vasodilator, congestive heart failure—Benazepril; Captopril; Enalapril; Lisinopril; Quinapril; Ramipril.

Indications

Note: Bracketed information in the *Indications* section refers to uses not included in U.S. product labeling.

Accepted

Hypertension (treatment)—Angiotensin-converting enzyme (ACE) inhibitors are indicated, alone or in combination with a thiazide diuretic, in the treatment of hypertension.

In the 1988 Report of the Joint National Committee on Detection, Evaluation, and Treatment of High Blood Pressure, a progression in choice of treatments for essential hypertension is recommended:

Nonpharmacologic management (especially sodium restriction, weight reduction and exercise, and moderation of alcohol consumption) is recommended first for some patients, including those with mild hypertension, and is recommended as an adjunct to all pharmacologic hypertensive therapy.

Initial drug therapy usually consists of a diuretic, beta-adrenergic blocking agent, calcium channel blocking agent, or angiotensin-converting enzyme (ACE) inhibitor. If adequate blood pressure control is not achieved and the patient is adherent to the treatment program and not experiencing significant side effects, dosage of the drug may be increased, a drug from another one of these initial classes may be added or substituted, or a second drug from a different class—centrally acting alpha-adrenergic blocking agents (e.g., clonidine, guanabenz, guanfacine, methyldopa), peripheral-acting adrenergic antagonists (e.g., guanadrel, guanethidine, rauwolfia alkaloids), postsynaptic alpha-1 peripheral adrenergic inhibitors (e.g., doxazosin, prazosin, terazosin), or vasodilators (e.g., hydralazine, minoxidil)—may be added or substituted.

If necessary, a drug from another class in the second group may be substituted or added as a third drug. If blood pressure control is still not achieved, a drug from still another class may be substituted or added as a fourth drug, or the patient may need further evaluation and/or referral.

[Captopril is also used for treatment of neonatal hypertension.][1]

ACE inhibitors are also used for [treatment of malignant, refractory, or accelerated hypertension][1], and for treatment of renovascular hypertension (except in patients with bilateral renal artery stenoses or renal artery stenosis in a solitary kidney—See *Medical problems*).

Congestive heart failure (treatment)—Captopril, enalapril, [benazepril], [lisinopril], [quinapril], and [ramipril] are also indicated, in combination with diuretics and digitalis therapy, for treatment of congestive heart failure not responding to other measures.

[Captopril is used for the treatment of congestive heart failure secondary to ventricular left-to-right shunt not responding to standard therapy in infants and neonates.]

[Scleroderma, hypertension in (treatment)][1]; or
[Scleroderma, renal crisis in (treatment)][1]—ACE inhibitors are also used for treatment of hypertension or renal crisis in scleroderma.

---

[1]Not included in Canadian product labeling.

Pharmacology

Mechanism of action/Effect:
Benazepril—Benazeprilat (active metabolite).
Captopril—Not a prodrug.
Enalapril—Enalaprilat (active metabolite).
Fosinopril—Fosinoprilat (active metabolite).
Lisinopril—Not a prodrug.
Quinapril—Quinaprilat (active metabolite).
Ramipril—Ramiprilat (active metabolite).

Antihypertensive—Exact mechanism of antihypertensive action is unknown but is thought to be related to competitive inhibition of angiotensin I-converting enzyme (ACE) activity, resulting in a decreased rate of conversion of angiotensin I to angiotensin II, which is a potent vasoconstrictor. Decreased angiotensin II concentrations result in a secondary increase in plasma renin activity (PRA), through removal of the negative feedback of renin release, and a direct reduction in aldosterone secretion. ACE inhibitors may be less effective in control of blood pressures among hypertensives with low as compared to normal or high renin activity. ACE inhibitors reduce peripheral arterial resistance. In addition, a possible effect on the kallikrein-kinin system (interference with degradation and resulting increased concentrations of bradykinin) and an increase in prostaglandin synthesis have been suggested but not proven.

Vasodilator, congestive heart failure—Decrease in peripheral vascular (afterload) resistance, pulmonary capillary wedge pressure (preload), and pulmonary vascular resistance; and improved cardiac output and exercise tolerance.

Other actions/effects: Captopril may reduce proteinuria in hypertensive patients with diabetic nephropathy. This effect may be due to the beneficial change in intrarenal hemodynamics (renal vasodilatation and reduced filtration pressure) produced by captopril resulting in decreased urinary protein excretion.

Onset of action: Single dose—
Benazepril: Within 1 hour.
Captopril: 15 to 60 minutes.
Enalapril: 1 hour.
Enalaprilat (intravenous): 15 minutes.
Fosinopril: Within 1 hour.
Lisinopril: 1 hour.
Quinapril: Within 1 hour.
Ramipril: Within 1 to 2 hours.

Time to peak effect:
Single dose—
Benazepril: 2 to 4 hours.
Captopril: 60 to 90 minutes.
Enalapril: 4 to 6 hours.
Enalaprilat (intravenous): 1 to 4 hours.
Fosinopril: 2 to 6 hours.
Lisinopril: 6 hours.
Quinapril: 2 to 4 hours.
Ramipril: 4 to 6.5 hours.
Multiple doses—The full therapeutic effect may not be noticed until several weeks after initiation of oral therapy.

Duration of action: Single-dose—
Benazepril: Approximately 24 hours.
Captopril: Approximately 6 to 12 hours; dose related.
Enalapril: Approximately 24 hours.
Enalaprilat (intravenous): Approximately 6 hours.
Fosinopril: Approximately 24 hours.
Lisinopril: Approximately 24 hours.
Quinapril: Up to 24 hours; dose related.
Ramipril: Approximately 24 hours.

Precautions to Consider

Cross-sensitivity and/or related problems
Patients sensitive to one ACE inhibitor may also be sensitive to another.

Geriatrics
ACE inhibitors are thought to be most effective in reducing blood pressure in patients with normal or high plasma renin activity. Since plasma renin activity appears to decline with increasing age, elderly individuals may be less sensitive to the hypotensive effects of ACE inhibitors. However, elevated serum ACE inhibitor concentrations resulting from age-related decline in renal function may compensate for the lower renin dependence. Pharmacokinetic studies with lisinopril, quinapril, and ramipril have revealed higher peak serum concentrations and area under the curve (AUC) in elderly patients given doses similar to those given to younger adults. The net result is that no significant differences in blood pressure response or side/adverse effects have been noted in elderly patients receiving ACE inhibitors. Nevertheless, some elderly patients may be more sensitive to the hypotensive effects of these medications and may require caution when receiving an ACE inhibitor.

Drug interactions and/or related problems
The following drug interactions and/or related problems have been selected on the basis of their potential clinical significance (possible mechanism in parentheses where appropriate)—not necessarily inclusive (» = major clinical significance):

Note: Combinations containing any of the following medications, depending on the amount present, may also interact with this medication.

For all ACE inhibitors

» Alcohol or

» Diuretics or

    Hypotension-producing medications, other

(concurrent use with ACE inhibitors may produce additive hypotensive effects)

(antihypertensive agents that cause renin release or affect sympathetic activity have the greatest additive effect; concurrent use of captopril with beta-adrenergic blocking agents produces an increased but less than fully additive effect; although some antihypertensive and/or diuretic combinations may be used for therapeutic advantage, dosage adjustments may be necessary during concurrent use or when one drug is discontinued)

(if significant systemic absorption of ophthalmic beta-blockers occurs, hypotensive effects of ACE inhibitors may be potentiated)

(sudden and severe hypotension may occur within the first 1 to 5 hours after the initial dose of an ACE inhibitor, particularly in patients who are sodium- and volume-depleted as a result of diuretic therapy. Withdrawal of the diuretic or increase of salt intake approximately 1 week before start of captopril therapy or 2 to 3 days before start of benazepril enalapril, fosinopril, lisinopril, quinapril, or ramipril therapy, or initiating ACE inhibitor therapy in lower doses, will minimize the reaction; this reaction does not usually recur with subsequent doses, although caution in increasing doses is recommended; diuretics may be reinstituted as necessary)

(risk of renal failure may be increased in patients who are sodium- and volume-depleted as a result of diuretic therapy)

(ACE inhibitors may reduce the secondary aldosteronism and hypokalemia caused by diuretics)

Anti-inflammatory drugs, nonsteroidal (NSAIDs), especially indomethacin

(concurrent use of these agents may reduce the antihypertensive effects of ACE inhibitors; indomethacin, and possibly other NSAIDs, may antagonize the antihypertensive effect by inhibiting renal prostaglandin synthesis and/or causing sodium and fluid retention; the patient should be carefully monitored to confirm that the desired effect is being obtained)

Blood from blood bank (may contain up to 30 mEq [mmol] of potassium per liter of plasma or up to 65 mEq [mmol] per liter of whole blood when stored for more than 10 days) or

Cyclosporine or

» Diuretics, potassium-sparing, or

» Low-salt milk (may contain up to 60 mEq [mmol] of potassium per liter) or

» Potassium-containing medications or

» Potassium supplements or substances containing high concentrations of potassium or

» Salt substitutes (most contain substantial amounts of potassium)

(concurrent administration with ACE inhibitors may result in hyperkalemia since reduction of aldosterone production induced by ACE inhibitors may lead to elevation of serum potassium; frequent determination of serum potassium concentrations is recommended if concurrent use of these agents is necessary; concurrent use is not recommended in patients with congestive heart failure)

Bone marrow depressants

(concurrent administration with an ACE inhibitor may result in an increased risk of development of potentially fatal neutropenia and/or agranulocytosis)

Estrogens

(estrogen-induced fluid retention may increase blood pressure; the patient should be carefully monitored to confirm that the desired effect is being obtained)

Lithium

(reversible increases in serum lithium concentrations and toxicity have been reported during concurrent use with ACE inhibitors; frequent monitoring of serum lithium concentrations is recommended during concurrent use)

Sympathomimetics

(concurrent use of these agents may reduce the antihypertensive effects of ACE inhibitors; the patient should be carefully monitored to confirm that the desired effect is being obtained)

For quinapril only

    Tetracyclines or

    Other drugs that interact with magnesium

(concurrent use of these agents with quinapril may reduce their absorption; absorption of tetracycline is reduced by approximately 28 to 37%, possibly due to the high magnesium content in Accupril brand of quinapril tablets)

Contraindications/Medical problems

The contraindications/medical problems included have been selected on the basis of their potential clinical significance (reasons given in parentheses where appropriate)—not necessarily inclusive (» = major clinical significance).

Risk-benefit should be considered when the following medical problems exist:

For all ACE inhibitors

» Angioedema, history of, related to previous ACE inhibitor therapy or

» Hereditary angioedema or

» Idiopathic angioedema

(increased risk for development of ACE inhibitor-related angioedema)

Autoimmune disease, severe, especially systemic lupus erythematosus (SLE) or scleroderma

(increased risk for development of neutropenia or agranulocytosis)

Bone marrow depression

Cerebrovascular insufficiency or

Coronary insufficiency

(ischemia may be aggravated as a result of reduced blood pressure; cerebrovascular accident or myocardial infarction could be precipitated)

Diabetes mellitus

(increased risk of hyperkalemia)

» Hyperkalemia

» Renal artery stenosis, bilateral or in a solitary kidney, or

» Renal transplant

(increased risk of renal function impairment)

» Renal function impairment

(decreased elimination of active ACE inhibitor (except fosinopril), resulting in higher plasma concentrations; increased risk of hyperkalemia, or, for captopril, proteinuria, neutropenia, and agranulocytosis. Patients with impaired renal function may require lower or less frequent doses and smaller increments in dose. However, dosage adjustment may not be necessary with fosinopril since total body drug clearance even in severe renal function impairment is not decreased significantly, possibly due to compensatory hepatobiliary elimination. If a diuretic is also required, a loop diuretic is recommended instead of a thiazide diuretic in patients with severe renal function impairment)

Sensitivity to the ACE inhibitor prescribed, or any other ACE inhibitor

» Caution is required also in patients on severe dietary sodium restriction or dialysis; these patients may be volume-depleted, and sudden reduction by the initial dose of ACE inhibitor in the angiotensin II levels that have been maintaining them at a near-normotensive state may result in sudden and severe hypotension. In addition, the risk of ACE inhibitor-induced renal failure may be increased in patients who are sodium- and volume-depleted, especially those with congestive heart failure.

For benazepril, captopril, enalapril, fosinopril, quinapril, and ramipril (in addition to the above)
Hepatic function impairment
(may reduce metabolism of captopril and may reduce conversion of prodrug to active moiety with benazepril, enalapril, fosinopril, quinapril, and ramipril)

Side/Adverse Effects

Note: Proteinuria has occurred in about 1% of patients receiving greater than 150 mg of captopril per day. This adverse effect is thought to be due to the sulfhydryl moiety of captopril. However, whether this is a true causal relationship is unknown. Proteinuria usually occurs in patients with existing renal function impairment within 8 months of initiation of captopril therapy and usually reverses within 6 months even with continuation of therapy. Membranous glomerulopathy has been reported in some of these patients, especially with doses of captopril greater than 150 mg per day. Proteinuria has also been reported in patients receiving enalapril and lisinopril. Reported incidences range from 0% to 1.4% for enalapril and 0.7% for lisinopril.

There have been reports of reversible renal failure during ACE inhibitor therapy, especially in patients with bilateral renal artery stenoses or renal artery stenosis in a solitary kidney. There is also evidence that renal failure may be related to sodium and volume depletion from previous diuretic therapy or severe sodium restriction, especially in patients with congestive heart failure.

The following side/adverse effects have been selected on the basis of their potential clinical significance (possible signs and symptoms in parentheses where appropriate)—not necessarily inclusive:

Those indicating need for medical attention
Incidence less frequent
Hypotension (dizziness, lightheadedness, or fainting)—especially following the initial dose in sodium- or volume-depleted patients or in patients receiving an ACE inhibitor for congestive heart failure; *skin rash, with or without itching, fever, or joint pain*
Note: Maculopapular or, rarely, urticarial rash usually occurs during the first 4 weeks of the therapy with captopril and usually disappears with dosage reduction or withdrawal, or administration of an antihistamine; between 7 and 10% of these patients may show eosinophilia and/or positive antinuclear antibody (ANA) titers. The reaction may also occur, less frequently, with the other ACE inhibitors.

Rarely, a persistent lichenoid or pemphigoid reaction, possibly with a photosensitive factor, has been reported with captopril.
Incidence rare
Angioedema of the extremities, face, lips, mucous membranes, tongue, glottis, and/or larynx (sudden trouble in swallowing or breathing; swelling of face, mouth, hands, or feet; hoarseness)—especially following the initial dose; *chest pain; hyperkalemia* (confusion; irregular heartbeat; nervousness; numbness or tingling in hands, feet, or lips; shortness of breath or difficult breathing; weakness or heaviness of legs); *neutropenia or agranulocytosis* (fever and chills); *pancreatitis* (abdominal pain, nausea, vomiting, abdominal distention, fever)
Note: *Angioedema* involving the tongue, glottis, or larynx may cause airway obstruction, which could be fatal.

Chest pain is usually associated with severe hypotension.

Incidence of *neutropenia or agranulocytosis* is much higher in patients with renal function impairment (0.2% for captopril) or collagen vascular disease (e.g., SLE or scleroderma) (3.7% for captopril). Neutropenia appears to be dose-related and may begin within 3 months after initiation of therapy, with the nadir of the leukocyte count occurring after 10 to 30 days and persisting about 2 weeks after withdrawal. Deaths from pancytopenia and sepsis have been reported with captopril in patients with and without autoimmune disease.

Those indicating need for medical attention only if they continue or are bothersome
Incidence more frequent
Cough, dry, continuing; headache
Note: *Cough* usually occurs within the first week of therapy (onset varies from 24 hours to several weeks after initiation), persists throughout therapy, and disappears within a few days after withdrawal of the ACE inhibitor. Characteristically the cough begins as a tickling sensation in the back of the throat leading to a dry, nonproductive, persistent cough; may be worse at night or in the supine position; onset can be paroxysmal and course may be episodic or intermittent; may occasionally lead to hoarseness or vomiting.
Incidence less frequent
Diarrhea; dysgeusia (loss of taste); *fatigue* (unusual tiredness); *nausea*
Note: *Loss of taste* is usually reversible after 2 to 3 months, even with continued treatment; may be associated with weight loss.

Patient Consultation

In providing consultation, consider emphasizing the following selected information (» = major clinical significance):

Before using this medication
» Conditions affecting use, especially:
Sensitivity to any ACE inhibitor
Pregnancy—ACE inhibitor-associated fetal hypotension, oliguria, and death reported in humans; fetotoxicity found in animals
Breast-feeding—Benazepril, captopril, and fosinopril are excreted in breast milk
Other medications, especially alcohol, diuretics (particularly potassium-sparing), potassium-containing medications, or potassium supplements
Other medical problems, especially angioedema related to previous ACE inhibitor therapy, hyperkalemia, renal artery stenosis, renal transplant, renal function impairment, or sodium and volume depletion
Use of low-salt milk or salt substitutes

Proper use of this medication
Getting into the habit of taking at same time each day to help increase compliance
Missed dose: Taking as soon as possible; not taking if almost time for next dose; not doubling doses
» Proper storage
For captopril
For best results, taking on an empty stomach 1 hour before meals
For use as an antihypertensive
Possible need for control of weight and diet, especially sodium intake; risks associated with sodium depletion; not taking salt substitutes or using low-salt milk unless approved by physician
» Patient may not experience symptoms of hypertension; importance of taking medication even if feeling well
» Does not cure, but helps control hypertension; possible need for lifelong therapy; checking with physician before discontinuing medication; serious consequences of untreated hypertension

Precautions while using this medication
Regular visits to physician to check progress
Caution when driving or doing other things requiring alertness, because of possible dizziness, especially after initial dose of ACE inhibitor in patients taking diuretics
To prevent dehydration and hypotension, checking with physician if severe nausea, vomiting, or diarrhea occurs and continues

Caution when exercising or during hot weather because of the risk of dehydration and hypotension due to reduced fluid volume

Caution if any kind of surgery (including dental surgery) or emergency treatment is required

For use as an antihypertensive

» Not taking other medications, especially nonprescription sympathomimetics, unless discussed with physician

For captopril and fosinopril

Caution if any laboratory tests required; possible interference with test results

Side/adverse effects

Signs of potential side effects, especially hypotension, skin rash (with or without itching, fever, or joint pain), angioedema, chest pain, neutropenia or agranulocytosis, pancreatitis, and hyperkalemia

General Dosing Information

Dosage must be adjusted to meet the individual requirements of each patient, on the basis of clinical response.

The hypotensive effect of ACE inhibitors is about the same in both standing and supine positions.

Recent evidence suggests that withdrawal of antihypertensive therapy prior to surgery is not necessary, but that the anesthesiologist must be aware of such therapy. If hypotension occurs during surgery, it may be corrected with volume expansion.

If increased blood urea nitrogen (BUN) and creatinine concentrations occur, reduction in dosage of the ACE inhibitor and/or withdrawal of the diuretic may be required. The possibility of renovascular hypertension should also be considered, especially in the presence of a solitary kidney, transplanted kidney, or bilateral renal artery stenosis.

Caution is recommended in initiating ACE inhibitor therapy for congestive heart failure in patients who have been receiving digitalis glycosides and/or diuretics. If the patient is sodium- and water-depleted, a lower initial dosage should be used.

If symptomatic hypotension occurs, dosage reduction of the ACE inhibitor or withdrawal of the ACE inhibitor or diuretic may be necessary.

BENAZEPRIL

Summary of Differences

Precautions: Breast-feeding—Benazepril and benazeprilat are excreted in breast milk.

Additional Dosing Information

See also *General Dosing Information*.

It is recommended that previous diuretic therapy be withdrawn 2 to 3 days before benazepril therapy is initiated, except in patients with accelerated or malignant hypertension or hypertension that is difficult to control. In these patients, benazepril therapy may be initiated immediately at a lower dose under careful medical supervision, and doses increased cautiously.

Benazepril is usually effective in once-daily dosing. However, if the antihypertensive effect is diminished before 24 hours, the total daily dose may be given as 2 divided doses.

Oral Dosage Forms

Note: Bracketed uses in the *Dosage Forms* section refer to categories of use and/or indications that are not included in U.S. product labeling.

The dosing and strengths of the dosage forms available are expressed in terms of benazepril base (not the hydrochloride salt).

BENAZEPRIL HYDROCHLORIDE TABLETS

Usual adult dose:

Antihypertensive—

Initial: Oral, 10 mg (base) once a day.

Maintenance: Oral, 20 to 40 mg (base) once a day as a single dose or in two divided doses.

Note: An initial dose of 5 mg (base) should be used in patients who are sodium- and water-depleted as a result of prior diuretic therapy, patients continuing to receive diuretic therapy, or patients with renal failure (creatinine clearance less than 30 mL per minute per $1.73m^2$). Such patients should be kept under medical supervision for at least two hours after this initial dose (and for an additional hour after blood pressure has stabilized), to watch for excessive hypotension.

[Vasodilator, congestive heart failure]—

Initial: Oral, 5 mg (base) once a day.

Maintenance: Oral, 5 to 10 mg (base) once a day.

Usual adult prescribing limits: Doses above 80 mg per day have not been evaluated.

Auxiliary labeling: • Do not take other medicines without your doctor's advice.

CAPTOPRIL

Summary of Differences

Indications: Captopril is used for the treatment of neonatal hypertension and neonatal and infant congestive heart failure.

Pharmacology:

Mechanism of action/Effect—Captopril is not a prodrug.

Duration of action—Single dose: 6 to 12 hours.

Precautions:

Breast-feeding—Captopril is excreted in breast milk.

Laboratory value alterations—May produce false-positive results in urinary acetone test.

Side/adverse effects: Causes maculopapular or urticarial skin rash, sometimes with fever, joint pain, or elevated antinuclear antibody (ANA) titers.

Additional Dosing Information

See also *General Dosing Information*.

It is recommended that previous antihypertensive therapy be withdrawn 1 week before captopril therapy is initiated, except in patients with accelerated or malignant hypertension or hypertension that is difficult to control. In these patients, captopril therapy may be initiated at the lowest dose immediately after previous therapy (except diuretics) is discontinued, under careful medical supervision, and the dosage increased every 24 hours or less until the medication is effective or the maximum dose is reached.

Oral Dosage Forms

CAPTOPRIL TABLETS USP

Usual adult and adolescent dose:

Antihypertensive—Initial: Oral, 12.5 mg two or three times a day, the dosage being increased if necessary after one or two weeks to 25 mg two or three times a day.

Vasodilator, congestive heart failure—
  Initial: Oral, 12.5 mg two or three times a day, the dosage being increased gradually as necessary on a daily basis up to 50 mg two or three times a day. If further increases in dosage are needed, it is recommended that they be made after an interval of two weeks so that the full effects of captopril will be apparent.
  Maintenance: Oral, 25 to 100 mg two or three times a day.
Note: An initial dose of 6.25 to 12.5 mg two or three times a day should be used in patients who are sodium- and water-depleted as a result of diuretic therapy, in patients continuing to receive diuretic therapy, or in patients with renal function impairment. Such patients should be kept under medical supervision for one hour after this initial dose, to watch for excessive hypotension.

Dosage increases in patients with significant renal function impairment should proceed slowly (one- to two-week intervals), and smaller increments should be used.

Usual adult prescribing limits: Up to 450 mg per day.

Auxiliary labeling:
  • Take on an empty stomach, one hour before meals.
  • Do not take other medicines without your doctor's advice.

ENALAPRIL

Summary of Differences

Pharmacology: Onset of action—
  Enalapril maleate: Oral—Single dose: 1 hour.
  Enalaprilat: Intravenous—Single dose: 15 minutes.

Additional Dosing Information

See also *General Dosing Information.*

It is recommended that previous diuretic therapy be withdrawn 2 to 3 days before enalapril therapy is initiated, except in patients with accelerated or malignant hypertension or hypertension that is difficult to control. In these patients, enalapril therapy may be initiated immediately at a lower dose under careful medical supervision, and increased cautiously.

Enalapril is usually effective in once-daily dosing. However, if the antihypertensive effect is diminished before 24 hours, the total daily dose may be given as 2 divided doses.

Hemodialysis reduces serum enalaprilat concentrations by approximately 35%.

Oral Dosage Forms

ENALAPRIL MALEATE TABLETS USP

Usual adult and adolescent dose:
Antihypertensive—
  Initial: Oral, 5 mg once a day, the dosage being adjusted after one or two weeks according to clinical response.
  Maintenance: Oral, 10 to 40 mg per day, as a single dose or in two divided doses.
    Note: An initial dose of 2.5 mg should be used in patients who are sodium- and water-depleted as a result of prior diuretic therapy, patients continuing to receive diuretic therapy, or patients with renal failure (creatinine clearance less than 30 mL per minute). Such patients should be kept under medical supervision for at least two hours after this initial dose (and for an additional hour after blood pressure has stabilized), to watch for excessive hypotension.

Vasodilator, congestive heart failure—
  Initial: Oral, 2.5 mg once or twice a day, the dosage being adjusted after one or two weeks according to clinical response.
    Note: Patients should be kept under medical supervision for at least two hours and until blood pressure has stabilized for an additional hour after the initial dose.

    In patients with hyponatremia (serum sodium concentration less than 130 mEq per liter) or serum creatinine greater than 1.6 mg per deciliter, an initial dose of 2.5 mg once a day is recommended.

    If possible, the dose of the diuretic should be reduced to decrease the likelihood of hypotension.
  Maintenance: Oral, 5 to 20 mg per day, as a single dose or in two divided doses.

Usual adult prescribing limits: Up to 40 mg per day.

Auxiliary labeling: • Do not take other medicines without your doctor's advice.

Parenteral Dosage Forms

ENALAPRILAT INJECTION

Usual adult and adolescent dose: Antihypertensive—Intravenous (over at least five minutes), 1.25 mg every six hours.

Note: An initial dose of 625 mcg (0.625 mg) should be used in patients who are sodium- and water-depleted as a result of prior diuretic therapy, patients continuing to receive diuretic therapy, or patients with renal failure (creatinine clearance less than or equal to 30 mL per minute). Such patients should be observed for one hour after this initial dose, to watch for excessive hypotension. If the clinical response is inadequate after one hour, the 625-mcg (0.625-mg) dose may be repeated, and therapy continued at a dose of 1.25 mg every six hours.

FOSINOPRIL

Summary of Differences

Precautions:
  Breast-feeding—Fosinoprilat (active metabolite) is excreted in breast milk
  Contraindications/Medical problems—Dosage adjustment is not necessary in renal function impairment.
  Laboratory value alterations—May cause a false low serum digoxin level with the Digi-Tab RIA Kit.

Additional Dosing Information

See also *General Dosing Information.*

It is recommended that previous diuretic therapy be withdrawn 2 to 3 days before fosinopril therapy is initiated, except in patients with accelerated or malignant hypertension or hypertension that is difficult to control. In these patients, fosinopril therapy may be initiated immediately at a lower dose under careful medical supervision (for at least 2 hours and until blood pressure has stabilized for at least an additional hour), and doses increased cautiously.

Fosinopril is usually effective in once-daily dosing. However, if the antihypertensive effect is diminished before 24 hours, the total daily dose may be given as 2 divided doses.

Oral Dosage Forms

FOSINOPRIL SODIUM TABLETS

Usual adult dose: Antihypertensive—

Initial: Oral, 10 mg once a day, the dosage being adjusted according to clinical response.

Maintenance: Oral, 20 to 40 mg once a day.

Note: In patients continuing to receive diuretic therapy, an initial fosinopril dose of 10 mg may be given with careful medical supervision for several hours and until blood pressure is stabilized.

Usual adult prescribing limits: Up to 80 mg per day.

Auxiliary labeling: • Do not take other medicines without your doctor's advice.

LISINOPRIL

Summary of Differences

Pharmacology:

Mechanism of action/Effect—Lisinopril is not a prodrug.

Protein binding—None.

Biotransformation—None.

Additional Dosing Information

See also *General Dosing Information.*

It is recommended that previous diuretic therapy be withdrawn 2 to 3 days before lisinopril therapy is initiated, except in patients with accelerated or malignant hypertension or hypertension that is difficult to control. In these patients, lisinopril therapy may be initiated immediately at a lower dose under careful medical supervision (for at least 2 hours and until blood pressure has stabilized for at least an additional hour), and increased cautiously.

Lisinopril is usually effective in once-daily dosing. However, if the antihypertensive effect is diminished before 24 hours, an increase in dosage may be necessary.

Oral Dosage Forms

Note: Bracketed uses in the *Dosage Forms* section refer to categories of use and/or indications that are not included in U.S. product labeling.

LISINOPRIL TABLETS

Usual adult and adolescent dose:

Antihypertensive—

Initial: Oral, 10 mg once a day, the dosage being adjusted according to clinical response.

Maintenance: Oral, 20 to 40 mg once a day.

Note: An initial dose of 5 mg should be used in patients who are sodium- and water-depleted as a result of prior diuretic therapy, patients continuing to receive diuretic therapy, or patients with renal failure (creatinine clearance less than or equal to 30 mL per minute). An initial dose of 2.5 mg should be used in patients with a creatinine clearance less than 10 mL per minute. Such patients should be kept under medical supervision for at least two hours after this initial dose (and for an additional hour after blood pressure has stabilized), to watch for excessive hypotension.

[Vasodilator, congestive heart failure]—

Initial: Oral, 2.5 to 5 mg per day, the dosage being adjusted according to clinical response.

Maintenance: Oral, 10 to 20 mg per day.

Usual adult prescribing limits: Doses up to 80 mg per day have been used but do not appear to have a greater effect.

Auxiliary labeling: • Do not take other medicines without your doctor's advice.

QUINAPRIL

Summary of Differences

Precautions: Drug interactions and/or related problems—Quinapril may reduce absorption of tetracycline or other drugs that interact with magnesium, since quinapril has a high magnesium content.

Additional Dosing Information

See also *General Dosing Information.*

It is recommended that previous diuretic therapy be withdrawn 2 to 3 days before quinapril therapy is initiated, except in patients with accelerated or malignant hypertension or hypertension that is difficult to control. In these patients, quinapril therapy may be initiated immediately at a lower dose under careful medical supervision (for at least 2 hours and until blood pressure has stabilized for at least an additional hour), and doses increased cautiously.

Quinapril is usually effective in once-daily dosing. However, if the antihypertensive effect is diminished before 24 hours, an increase in dosage may be necessary or the total daily dose may be given as 2 divided doses.

Oral Dosage Forms

Note: Bracketed uses in the *Dosage Forms* section refer to categories of use and/or indications that are not included in U.S. product labeling.

The dosing and strengths of the dosage forms available are expressed in terms of quinapril base (not the hydrochloride salt).

QUINAPRIL HYDROCHLORIDE TABLETS

Usual adult dose:

Antihypertensive—

Initial: Oral, 10 mg (base) once a day, the dosage being adjusted slowly (at 2-week intervals) and according to clinical response.

Maintenance: Oral, 20 to 80 mg (base) once a day or divided into two equal doses.

Note: An initial dose of 5 mg should be used in patients who are sodium- and water-depleted as a result of prior diuretic therapy, patients continuing to receive diuretic therapy, or in patients with a creatinine clearance of 30 to 60 mL per minute. An initial dose of 2.5 mg should be used in patients with a creatinine clearance of 10 to 30 mL per minute. Such patients should be kept under medical supervision for at least two hours after this initial dose (and for an additional hour after blood pressure has stabilized), to watch for excessive hypotension.

There is insufficient data for a dosage recommendation in patients with a creatinine clearance less than 10 mL per minute.

[Vasodilator, congestive heart failure]—

Initial: Oral, 2.5 mg (base) once a day.

Maintenance: Oral, 5 to 40 mg once a day or divided into two equal doses.

Auxiliary labeling: • Do not take other medicines without your doctor's advice.

RAMIPRIL

Additional Dosing Information

See also *General Dosing Information*.

It is recommended that previous diuretic therapy be withdrawn 2 to 3 days before ramipril therapy is initiated, except in patients with accelerated or malignant hypertension or hypertension that is difficult to control. In these patients, ramipril therapy may be initiated immediately at a lower dose under careful medical supervision (for at least 2 hours and until blood pressure has stabilized for at least an additional hour), and doses increased cautiously.

Ramipril is usually effective in once-daily dosing. However, if the antihypertensive effect is diminished before 24 hours, an increase in dosage may be necessary or the total daily dose may be given as 2 divided doses.

Oral Dosage Forms

RAMIPRIL CAPSULES

Usual adult dose: Antihypertensive—
   Initial: Oral, 2.5 mg once a day, the dosage being adjusted according to clinical response.
   Maintenance: Oral, 2.5 to 20 mg once a day or divided into two equal doses.
      Note: An initial dose of 1.25 mg should be used in patients who are sodium- and water-depleted as a result of prior diuretic therapy, patients continuing to receive diuretic therapy, or in patients with a creatinine clearance less than 40 mL per minute per 1.73 m². Such patients should be kept under medical supervision for at least two hours after this initial dose (and for an additional hour after blood pressure has stabilized), to watch for excessive hypotension.

      Dosage may be slowly titrated upward until adequate blood pressure control is achieved or to a maximum total daily dose of 5 mg.

Auxiliary labeling: • Do not take other medicines without your doctor's advice.

ANGIOTENSIN-CONVERTING ENZYME (ACE) INHIBITORS AND HYDROCHLOROTHIAZIDE   Systemic†

Some commonly used *brand names* in the U.S. are:
   Capozide [Captopril and Hydrochlorothiazide]
   Prinzide [Lisinopril and Hydrochlorothiazide]
   Vaseretic [Enalapril and Hydrochlorothiazide]
   Zestoretic [Lisinopril and Hydrochlorothiazide]

ORAL
CAPTOPRIL AND HYDROCHLOROTHIAZIDE†
   Captopril and Hydrochlorothiazide Tablets†
      In the U.S.—*Capozide*
ENALAPRIL AND HYDROCHLOROTHIAZIDE†
   Enalapril Maleate and Hydrochlorothiazide Tablets†
      In the U.S.—*Vaseretic*
LISINOPRIL AND HYDROCHLOROTHIAZIDE†
   Lisinopril and Hydrochlorothiazide Tablets†
      In the U.S.—*Prinzide; Zestoretic*

†Not commercially available in Canada.

Category: Antihypertensive; vasodilator, congestive heart failure.

Indications

Note: Bracketed information in the *Indications* section refers to uses not included in U.S. product labeling.

Accepted
Hypertension (treatment)—The combination of captopril, enalapril, or lisinopril and hydrochlorothiazide is indicated in the treatment of hypertension.

   Fixed-dosage combinations generally are not recommended for initial therapy, but are utilized in maintenance therapy after the required dose is established in order to increase convenience, economy, and patient compliance.

   Nonpharmacologic management (sodium restriction, weight reduction, exercise, and stress reduction) is an integral part of any antihypertensive treatment regimen. Patients requiring antihypertensive medication may be able to reduce their medication dosage and subsequent side effects by following the nonpharmacologic regimen prescribed by their physician.

[Congestive heart failure (treatment)]—Captopril, enalapril, or lisinopril plus a diuretic, such as hydrochlorothiazide, and a digitalis glycoside are also used for treatment of severe congestive heart failure not responding to other measures.

Pharmacology

Mechanism of action/Effect:
ACE inhibitors—
   Activity of enalapril is due to active metabolite, enalaprilat.
   Antihypertensive: Exact mechanism of antihypertensive action is unknown but is thought to be related to competitive inhibition of angiotensin I-converting enzyme (ACE) activity, resulting in a decreased rate of conversion of angiotensin I to angiotensin II, which is a potent vasoconstrictor. Decreased angiotensin II concentrations result in a secondary increase in plasma renin activity (PRA), through removal of the negative feedback of renin release, and a direct reduction in aldosterone secretion. However, ACE inhibitors may also be effective in treating low-renin essential hypertension. ACE inhibitors reduce peripheral arterial resistance. In addition, a possible effect on the kallikrein-kinin system (interference with degradation and resulting increased concentrations of bradykinin) and an increase in prostaglandin synthesis have been suggested but not proven.
   Vasodilator, congestive heart failure: Decrease in peripheral vascular (afterload) resistance, pulmonary capillary wedge pressure (preload), and pulmonary vascular resistance; and improved cardiac output and exercise tolerance.
Thiazide diuretics—
   Diuretic: Thiazide diuretics increase urinary excretion of sodium and water by inhibiting sodium reabsorption in the

early distal tubules. They increase the rate of delivery of tubular fluid and electrolytes to the distal sites of hydrogen and potassium ion secretion, while plasma volume contraction increases aldosterone production. The increased delivery and increase in aldosterone levels promote sodium reabsorption at the distal tubules, thus increasing the loss of potassium and hydrogen ions.

Antihypertensive: Diuretics lower blood pressure initially by reducing plasma and extracellular fluid volume; cardiac output also decreases. Eventually, cardiac output returns to normal. Thiazide diuretics decrease peripheral resistance by a direct peripheral effect on blood vessels.

Onset of action: Single dose—
Captopril: 15 to 60 minutes.
Enalapril: 1 hour.
Lisinopril: 1 hour.

Time to peak effect:
Single dose—
Captopril: 60 to 90 minutes.
Enalapril: 4 to 6 hours.
Lisinopril: 6 hours.
Multiple doses—The full therapeutic effect of ACE inhibitors may not be noticed until several weeks after initiation of oral therapy. The antihypertensive effects of hydrochlorothiazide may be noted after 3 or 4 days of therapy, although up to 3 to 4 weeks may be required for optimal effect.

Duration of action: Single-dose—
Captopril: Approximately 6 to 12 hours; dose related.
Enalapril: Approximately 24 hours.
Hydrochlorothiazide—Antihypertensive effects persist for up to 1 week after withdrawal of therapy.
Lisinopril: Approximately 24 hours.

Precautions to Consider

Cross-sensitivity and/or related problems
Patients sensitive to one ACE inhibitor may also be sensitive to another.
Patients sensitive to other sulfonamide-type medications, bumetanide, furosemide, or carbonic anhydrase inhibitors may be sensitive to hydrochlorothiazide also.

Geriatrics
Captopril, enalapril, and lisinopril—ACE inhibitors are thought to be most effective in reducing blood pressure in patients with normal or high plasma renin activity. Since plasma renin activity appears to decline with increasing age, elderly individuals may be less sensitive to the hypotensive effects of ACE inhibitors. However, elevated serum ACE inhibitor concentrations resulting from age-related decline in renal function may compensate for the lower renin dependence. Pharmacokinetic studies with lisinopril have revealed higher peak serum concentrations and area under the curve (AUC) in elderly patients given doses similar to those given to younger adults. The net result is that no significant differences in blood pressure response or side/adverse effects have been noted in elderly patients receiving ACE inhibitors. Nevertheless, some elderly patients may be more sensitive to the hypotensive effects of these medications and may require caution when receiving an ACE inhibitor.
Hydrochlorothiazide—Although appropriate studies on the relationship of age to the effects of hydrochlorothiazide have not been performed in the geriatric population, the elderly may be more sensitive to the hypotensive and electrolyte effects. In addition, elderly patients are more likely to have age-related renal function impairment, which may require caution in patients receiving hydrochlorothiazide.

Drug interactions and/or related problems
The following drug interactions and/or related problems have been selected on the basis of their potential clinical significance (possible mechanism in parentheses where appropriate)—not necessarily inclusive (» = major clinical significance):
Note: Combinations containing any of the following medications, depending on the amount present, may also interact with this medication.
» Alcohol or
» Diuretics or
Hypotension-producing medications, other
(hypotensive effects may be potentiated when these medications are used concurrently with ACE inhibitors and hydrochlorothiazide; although some antihypertensive and/or diuretic combinations are frequently used for therapeutic advantage, dosage adjustments may be necessary during concurrent use)

(antihypertensive agents that cause renin release or affect sympathetic activity have the greatest additive effect; concurrent use of captopril with beta-adrenergic blocking agents produces an increased but less than fully additive effect; although some antihypertensive and/or diuretic combinations may be used for therapeutic advantage, dosage adjustments may be necessary during concurrent use or when one drug is discontinued)

(if significant systemic absorption of ophthalmic beta-blockers occurs, hypotensive effects of ACE inhibitors may be potentiated)

(sudden and severe hypotension may occur within the first 1 to 5 hours after the initial dose of an ACE inhibitor, particularly in patients who are sodium- and volume-depleted as a result of diuretic therapy. Withdrawal of the diuretic or increase of salt intake approximately 1 week before start of captopril therapy or 2 to 3 days before start of enalapril or lisinopril therapy, or initiating ACE inhibitor therapy in lower doses, will minimize the reaction; this reaction does not usually recur with subsequent doses, although caution in increasing doses is recommended; diuretics may be reinstituted as necessary)

(risk of renal failure may be increased in patients who are sodium- and volume-depleted as a result of diuretic therapy)

(ACE inhibitors may reduce the secondary aldosteronism and hypokalemia caused by diuretics)

Amantadine
(hydrochlorothiazide may reduce the renal clearance of amantadine, resulting in increased plasma concentrations and possible amantadine toxicity)

Amiodarone
(concurrent use of thiazide diuretics with amiodarone may lead to an increased risk of arrhythmias associated with hypokalemia)

Anticoagulants, coumarin- or indandione-derivative
(anticoagulant effects may be decreased when used concurrently with thiazide diuretics as a result of reduction of plasma volume leading to concentration of procoagulant factors in the blood; in addition, diuretic-induced improvement of hepatic congestion may lead to improved hepatic function resulting in increased procoagulant factor synthesis; dosage adjustments may be necessary)

Antidiabetic agents, oral, or
Insulin
(thiazide diuretics may raise blood glucose concentrations; for adult-onset diabetics, dosage adjustment of hypoglycemic medications may be necessary during and after thiazide diuretic therapy; insulin requirements may be increased, decreased, or unchanged)

Anti-inflammatory drugs, nonsteroidal (NSAIDs), especially indomethacin
(concurrent use of these agents may reduce the antihypertensive effects of ACE inhibitors and hydrochlorothiazide; indometha-

cin, and possibly other NSAIDs, may antagonize the antihypertensive effect by inhibiting renal prostaglandin synthesis and/or causing sodium and fluid retention; the patient should be carefully monitored to confirm that the desired effect is being obtained)

(in addition, concurrent use of NSAIDs with a diuretic may increase the risk of renal failure secondary to a decrease in renal blood flow caused by inhibition of renal prostaglandin synthesis)

Blood from blood bank (may contain up to 30 mEq [mmol] of potassium per liter of plasma or up to 65 mEq [mmol] per liter of whole blood when stored for more than 10 days) or
Cyclosporine or
» Diuretics, potassium-sparing, or
» Low-salt milk (may contain up to 60 mEq [mmol] of potassium per liter) or
» Potassium-containing medications or
» Potassium supplements or substances containing high concentrations of potassium or
» Salt substitutes (most contain substantial amounts of potassium)
(concurrent administration with ACE inhibitors may result in hyperkalemia since reduction of aldosterone production induced by ACE inhibitors may lead to elevation of serum potassium; frequent determination of serum potassium concentrations is recommended if concurrent use of these agents is necessary; concurrent use is not recommended in patients with congestive heart failure)

Bone marrow depressants
(concurrent administration with an ACE inhibitor may result in an increased risk of development of potentially fatal neutropenia and/or agranulocytosis)

Calcium-containing medications
(concurrent use of hydrochlorothiazide with large doses of calcium may result in hypercalcemia because of reduced calcium excretion)

» Cholestyramine or
» Colestipol
(may inhibit gastrointestinal absorption of hydrochlorothiazide; administration of hydrochlorothiazide 1 hour before or 4 hours after cholestyramine or colestipol is recommended)

Diazoxide
(concurrent use with thiazide diuretics may enhance hyperglycemic effects; monitoring of blood glucose levels and/or dosage adjustment of one or both agents may be necessary)

Diflunisal
(concurrent use of hydrochlorothiazide with diflunisal produces significantly increased plasma concentrations of hydrochlorothiazide; in addition, the hyperuricemic effect of hydrochlorothiazide is decreased)

» Digitalis glycosides
(concurrent use with hydrochlorothiazide may enhance the possibility of digitalis toxicity associated with hypokalemia)

Dopamine
(concurrent use may increase the diuretic effect of either hydrochlorothiazide or dopamine, as a result of dopamine's direct effect on dopaminergic receptors to produce vasodilation of renal vasculature and increase renal blood flow; dopamine also has a direct natriuretic effect)

Estrogens
(estrogen-induced fluid retention may increase blood pressure; the patient should be carefully monitored to confirm that the desired effect is being obtained)

» Lithium
(concurrent use with hydrochlorothiazide is not recommended, as it may provoke lithium toxicity because of reduced renal clearance; in addition, lithium has nephrotoxic effects)

(reversible increases in serum lithium concentrations and toxicity have been reported during concurrent use with ACE inhibitors; frequent monitoring of serum lithium concentrations is recommended during concurrent use)

Neuromuscular blocking agents, nondepolarizing
(hydrochlorothiazide may induce hypokalemia, which may enhance the blockade of nondepolarizing neuromuscular blocking agents; serum potassium determinations may be necessary prior to administration of nondepolarizing neuromuscular blocking agents; careful postoperative monitoring of the patient may be necessary following concurrent or sequential use, especially if there is a possibility of incomplete reversal of neuromuscular blockade)

Sympathomimetics, such as:
» Cocaine
Dobutamine
Dopamine
Ephedrine
Epinephrine
Mephentermine
Metaraminol
Methoxamine
» Norepinephrine
» Phenylephrine
Phenylpropanolamine
(may antagonize the antihypertensive effect of ACE inhibitors and hydrochlorothiazide; the patient should be carefully monitored to confirm that the desired effect is being obtained; if concurrent use of cocaine, norepinephrine, or phenylephrine is indicated, caution is required, and only very small initial doses should be administered)

Contraindications/Medical problems
The contraindications/medical problems included have been selected on the basis of their potential clinical significance (reasons given in parentheses where appropriate)—not necessarily inclusive (» = major clinical significance).

Risk-benefit should be considered when the following medical problems exist:
» Angioedema, history of, related to previous ACE inhibitor therapy or
» Hereditary angioedema or
» Idiopathic angioedema
(increased risk for development of ACE inhibitor-related angioedema)
» Anuria or severe renal function impairment
(hydrochlorothiazide ineffective; may precipitate azotemia; may produce cumulative effects)
Autoimmune disease, severe, especially systemic lupus erythematosus (SLE) or scleroderma
(increased risk of development of neutropenia or agranulocytosis)
Bone marrow depression—for ACE inhibitors
Cerebrovascular insufficiency or
Coronary insufficiency
(ischemia may be aggravated as a result of reduced blood pressure; cerebrovascular accident or myocardial infarction could be precipitated)
Diabetes mellitus
(increased risk of hyperkalemia with ACE inhibitors; hypoglycemic medication requirements may be altered by hydrochlorothiazide)
Gout, history of, or
Hyperuricemia
(serum uric acid concentrations may be elevated by hydrochlorothiazide)

Hepatic function impairment
>   (reduced breakdown of captopril and reduced conversion of enalapril to enalaprilat)
>   (risk of dehydration with hydrochlorothiazide, which may precipitate hepatic coma and death; plasma half-life is unaltered)

Hypercalcemia—for hydrochlorothiazide

» Hyperkalemia—for ACE inhibitors

Hyponatremia—for hydrochlorothiazide

Lupus erythematosus, history of
>   (exacerbation or activation by thiazide diuretics has been reported)

Pancreatitis—for hydrochlorothiazide

» Renal artery stenosis, bilateral or in a solitary kidney, or

» Renal transplant
>   (increased risk of renal function impairment caused by captopril or enalaprilat)

» Renal function impairment
>   (retention of captopril, enalaprilat, or lisinopril occurs; increased risk of hyperkalemia or, for captopril, proteinuria, neutropenia, and agranulocytosis. Patients with impaired renal function may require lower or less frequent doses and smaller increments in dose. If a diuretic is also required, a loop diuretic is recommended instead of a thiazide diuretic in patients with severe renal function impairment)

Sensitivity to the ACE inhibitor prescribed or to hydrochlorothiazide

Sympathectomy
>   (antihypertensive effects of hydrochlorothiazide may be enhanced)

» Caution is required also in patients on severe dietary sodium restriction or dialysis; these patients may be volume-depleted, and sudden reduction by the initial dose of ACE inhibitor in the angiotensin II levels that have been maintaining them at a near-normotensive state may result in sudden and severe hypotension. In addition, the risk of ACE inhibitor-induced renal failure may be increased in patients who are sodium- and volume-depleted, especially those with congestive heart failure.

» Caution is required also in jaundiced infants because of the risk of hyperbilirubinemia caused by thiazide diuretics.

Side/Adverse Effects

Note: Proteinuria has occurred in about 1% of patients receiving greater than 150 mg of captopril per day. This adverse effect is thought to be due to the sulfhydryl moiety of captopril. However, whether this is a true causal relationship is unknown. Proteinuria usually occurs in patients with existing renal function impairment within 8 months of initiation of captopril therapy and usually reverses within 6 months even with continuation of therapy. Membranous glomerulopathy has been reported in some of these patients, especially with doses of captopril greater than 150 mg per day. Proteinuria has also been reported in patients receiving enalapril and lisinopril. Reported incidences range from 0% to 1.4% for enalapril and 0.7% for lisinopril.

There have been reports of reversible renal failure during ACE inhibitor therapy, especially in patients with bilateral renal artery stenoses or renal artery stenosis in a solitary kidney. There is also evidence that renal failure may be related to sodium and volume depletion from previous diuretic therapy or severe sodium restriction, especially in patients with congestive heart failure.

The following side/adverse effects have been selected on the basis of their potential clinical significance (possible signs and symptoms in parentheses where appropriate)—not necessarily inclusive:

Those indicating need for medical attention
Incidence less frequent
>   *Hypotension* (dizziness, lightheadedness, or fainting)—especially following the initial dose in sodium- or volume-depleted patients or in patients receiving an ACE inhibitor for congestive heart failure; *skin rash, with or without itching, fever, or joint pain*

Note: Maculopapular or, rarely, urticarial rash usually occurs during the first 4 weeks of the therapy with captopril and usually disappears with dosage reduction or withdrawal, or administration of an antihistamine; between 7 and 10% of these patients may show eosinophilia and/or positive antinuclear antibody (ANA) titers. The reaction may also occur, less frequently, with enalapril and lisinopril.

Rarely, a persistent lichenoid or pemphigoid reaction, possibly with a photosensitive factor, has been reported with captopril.

Skin rash or hives may also be a symptom of an allergic reaction to hydrochlorothiazide.

Incidence rare
>   *Angioedema of the extremities, face, lips, mucous membranes, tongue, glottis, and/or larynx* (sudden trouble in swallowing or breathing; swelling of face, mouth, hands, or feet; hoarseness)—especially following the initial dose; *chest pain; cholecystitis or pancreatitis* (severe stomach pain with nausea and vomiting); *hepatic function impairment* (yellow eyes or skin); *hyperuricemia or gout* (joint pain, lower back or side pain); *neutropenia or agranulocytosis* (fever and chills); *thrombocytopenia* (unusual bleeding or bruising)

Note: *Angioedema involving the tongue, glottis, or larynx* may cause airway obstruction, which could be fatal.

Chest pain is usually associated with severe hypotension.

Incidence of *neutropenia or agranulocytosis* is much higher in patients with renal function impairment (0.2% for captopril) or collagen vascular disease (e.g., SLE or scleroderma) (3.7% for captopril). Neutropenia appears to be dose-related and may begin within 3 months after initiation of therapy, with the nadir of the leukocyte count occurring after 10 to 30 days and persisting about 2 weeks after withdrawal. Deaths from pancytopenia and sepsis have been reported with captopril in patients with and without autoimmune disease.

Signs and/or symptoms of electrolyte imbalance
>   *Dryness of mouth; increased thirst; irregular heartbeat; mood or mental changes; muscle cramps or pain; numbness or tingling in hands, feet, or lips; weakness or heaviness of legs; weak pulse*

Those indicating need for medical attention only if they continue or are bothersome
Incidence more frequent
>   *Cough, dry, continuing*

Note: *Continuing dry cough* usually occurs within the first week of therapy (onset varies from 24 hours to several weeks after initiation), persists throughout therapy, and disappears within a few days after withdrawal of the ACE inhibitor. Characteristically, the cough begins as a tickling sensation in the back of the throat leading to a dry, nonproductive, persistent cough; may be worse at night or in the supine position; onset can be paroxysmal and course may be episodic or intermittent; may occasionally lead to hoarseness or vomiting.

Incidence less frequent
>   *Anorexia* (loss of appetite); *diarrhea; headache; photosensitivity* (increased sensitivity of skin to sunlight); *loss of taste; stomach upset; unusual tiredness*

Note: *Loss of taste* is usually reversible after 2 to 3 months, even with continued ACE inhibitor treatment; may be associated with weight loss.

Patient Consultation

In providing consultation, consider emphasizing the following selected information (» = major clinical significance):

Before using this medication
» Conditions affecting use, especially:
  Sensitivity to any ACE inhibitor, thiazide diuretic, carbonic anhydrase inhibitor, or other sulfonamide-type medications
  Pregnancy—ACE inhibitor-associated fetal hypotension, oliguria, and death reported in humans; and fetotoxicity found in animals; hydrochlorothiazide may cause jaundice, thrombocytopenia, hypokalemia in infant
  Breast-feeding—Captopril and hydrochlorothiazide excreted in breast milk
  Use in children—Caution if giving to infants with jaundice
  Use in the elderly—May be more sensitive to hypotensive and electrolyte effects
  Use by athletes—Diuretics are banned and tested for by the U.S. Olympic Committee (USOC), the International Olympic Committee (IOC), and the National Collegiate Athletic Association (NCAA)
  Other medications, especially alcohol, cholestyramine, colestipol, diuretics (particularly potassium-sparing), potassium-containing medications, potassium supplements, low salt milk, salt substitutes, digitalis glycosides, lithium, cocaine, norepinephrine, or phenylephrine
  Other medical problems, especially angioedema related to previous ACE inhibitor therapy, hereditary angioedema, idiopathic angioedema, hyperkalemia, renal artery stenosis, renal transplant, renal function impairment, or sodium and volume depletion

Proper use of this medication
  Getting into the habit of taking at same time each day to help increase compliance
  Diuretic effects of the medication and timing of doses to minimize inconvenience of diuresis
  Missed dose: Taking as soon as possible; not taking if almost time for next dose; not doubling doses
» Proper storage
For captopril and hydrochlorothiazide
  For best results, taking on an empty stomach 1 hour before meals
For use as an antihypertensive
  Possible need for control of weight and diet, especially sodium intake; risks associated with sodium depletion; not taking salt substitutes or using low-salt milk unless approved by physician
» Patient may not experience symptoms of hypertension; importance of taking medication even if feeling well
» Does not cure, but helps control hypertension; possible need for lifelong therapy; checking with physician before discontinuing medication; serious consequences of untreated hypertension

Precautions while using this medication
  Regular visits to physician to check progress
  Caution when driving or doing other things requiring alertness, because of possible dizziness, especially with initial dose
  To prevent dehydration and hypotension, checking with physician if severe nausea, vomiting, or diarrhea occurs and continues
  Caution when exercising or during hot weather because of the risk of dehydration and hypotension due to reduced fluid volume
  Caution if any kind of surgery (including dental surgery) or emergency treatment is required
  Caution in using alcohol
  Diabetics: May increase blood sugar levels
  Possible photosensitivity; avoiding unprotected exposure to sun; using protective clothing and sun block product; avoiding use of sunlamp
  Caution if any laboratory tests required; possible interference with test results

For use as an antihypertensive
» Not taking other medications, especially nonprescription sympathomimetics, unless discussed with physician
Side/adverse effects
  Signs of potential side effects, especially hypotension, skin rash (with or without itching, fever, or joint pain), angioedema, chest pain, neutropenia or agranulocytosis, hyperuricemia or gout, cholecystitis or pancreatitis, thrombocytopenia, hepatic function impairment, and electrolyte imbalance

General Dosing Information

Dosage must be adjusted to meet the individual requirements of each patient, on the basis of clinical response.

Fixed-dosage combinations generally are not recommended for initial therapy, but are utilized in maintenance therapy after the required dose is established in order to increase convenience, economy, and patient compliance.

The hypotensive effect of ACE inhibitors is the same in both standing and supine positions.

The lowest effective dosage of thiazide diuretics should be utilized to minimize potential electrolyte imbalance and the reflex increase in renin and aldosterone levels.

If increased blood urea nitrogen (BUN) and creatinine concentrations occur, reduction in dosage of the ACE inhibitor and/or withdrawal of the diuretic may be required. The possibility of renovascular hypertension should also be considered, especially in the presence of a solitary kidney, transplanted kidney, or bilateral renal artery stenosis.

Caution is recommended in initiating ACE inhibitor therapy for congestive heart failure in patients who have been receiving digitalis glycosides and/or diuretics. If the patient is sodium- and water-depleted, a lower initial dosage should be used.

Concurrent administration of potassium supplements or potassium-sparing diuretics may be indicated in patients considered to be at higher risk for developing hypokalemia. Caution in administering potassium supplements is recommended, however, since loss of potassium caused by thiazide diuretics is not clinically significant in most patients and ACE inhibitors reduce diuretic-induced hypokalemia; supplementation leads to a risk of development of hyperkalemia.

Recent evidence suggests that withdrawal of antihypertensive therapy prior to surgery is not necessary, but that the anesthesiologist must be aware of such therapy. If hypotension occurs during surgery, it may be corrected with volume expansion.

If symptomatic hypotension occurs, dosage reduction or withdrawal of the ACE inhibitor or diuretic may be necessary.

CAPTOPRIL AND HYDROCHLOROTHIAZIDE

Summary of Differences

For captopril
Pharmacology:
  Absorption—Reduced by 30 to 40% in presence of food.
  Half-life—Less than 3 hours (3.5-32 hours in renal failure).
  Duration of action—Single dose: 6 to 12 hours.
Precautions: Laboratory value alterations—May produce false-positive results in urinary acetone test.
Side/adverse effects: Causes maculopapular or urticarial skin rash, sometimes with fever, joint pain, or elevated antinuclear antibody (ANA) titers.

Oral Dosage Forms

Note: Bracketed uses in the *Dosage Forms* section refer to categories of use and/or indications that are not included in U.S. product labeling.

CAPTOPRIL AND HYDROCHLOROTHIAZIDE TABLETS

Usual adult and adolescent dose:
Antihypertensive; or
[Vasodilator, congestive heart failure]—Oral, 1 tablet two or three times a day, as determined by individual titration with the component agents.

Note: Geriatric patients may be more sensitive to the effects of the usual adult dose.

Auxiliary labeling:
- Take on an empty stomach, 1 hour before meals.
- Avoid too much sun or use of sunlamp.
- Do not take other medicines without your doctor's advice.

ENALAPRIL AND HYDROCHLOROTHIAZIDE

Summary of Differences

For enalapril
Pharmacology:
Mechanism of action/effect—Activity due to active metabolite, enalaprilat.
Absorption—Not affected by presence of food.
Half-life—11 hours (increased in renal failure).
Duration of action—Single dose: Approximately 24 hours.

Oral Dosage Forms

Note: Bracketed uses in the *Dosage Forms* section refer to categories of use and/or indications that are not included in U.S. product labeling.

ENALAPRIL MALEATE AND HYDROCHLOROTHIAZIDE TABLETS

Usual adult and adolescent dose:
Antihypertensive; or

[Vasodilator, congestive heart failure]—Oral, 1 tablet per day, as determined by individual titration with the component agents.

Note: Geriatric patients may be more sensitive to the effects of the usual adult dose.

Auxiliary labeling:
- Avoid too much sun or use of sunlamp.
- Do not take other medicines without your doctor's advice.

LISINOPRIL AND HYDROCHLOROTHIAZIDE

Summary of Differences

For lisinopril
Pharmacology:
Absorption—Not affected by presence of food.
Protein-binding—None.
Half-life—12 hours.
Duration of action—Approximately 24 hours.

Oral Dosage Forms

Note: Bracketed uses in the *Dosage Forms* section refer to categories of use and/or indications that are not included in U.S. product labeling.

LISINOPRIL AND HYDROCHLOROTHIAZIDE TABLETS

Usual adult and adolescent dose:
Antihypertensive or
[Vasodilator, congestive heart failure]—Oral, 1 or 2 tablets once a day, as determined by individual titration with the component agents.

Note: Geriatric patients may be more sensitive to the effects of the usual adult dose.

Auxiliary labeling:
- Avoid too much sun or use of sunlamp.
- Do not take other medicines without your doctor's advice.

ANTACIDS Oral-Local

ORAL
Aluminum-containing
ALUMINUM CARBONATE, BASIC†
Basic Aluminum Carbonate Gel USP (Oral Suspension)†
In the U.S.—*Basaljel*
Dried Basic Aluminum Carbonate Gel Capsules USP†
In the U.S.—*Basaljel*
Dried Basic Aluminum Carbonate Gel Tablets USP†
In the U.S.—*Basaljel*
ALUMINUM HYDROXIDE
Aluminum Hydroxide Gel USP (Oral Suspension)
In the U.S.—*AlternaGEL; Amphojel; Nephrox;* GENERIC
In Canada—*Amphojel; Gaviscon;* GENERIC
Dried Aluminum Hydroxide Gel Capsules USP
In the U.S.—*Alu-Cap; Dialume*
In Canada—*Basaljel*

Dried Aluminum Hydroxide Gel Tablets USP
In the U.S. and Canada—*Alu-Tab; Amphojel;* GENERIC
DIHYDROXYALUMINUM AMINOACETATE*
Dihydroxyaluminum Aminoacetate Tablets USP
In Canada—*Robalate*
DIHYDROXYALUMINUM SODIUM CARBONATE†
Dihydroxyaluminum Sodium Carbonate Chewable Tablets†
In the U.S.—*Rolaids*

Aluminum-, Calcium-, and Magnesium-containing
ALUMINA, MAGNESIA, AND CALCIUM CARBONATE†
Alumina, Magnesia, and Calcium Carbonate Oral Suspension USP†
In the U.S.—*Camalox*
Alumina, Magnesia, and Calcium Carbonate Chewable Tablets†
In the U.S.—*Camalox*

SIMETHICONE, ALUMINA, CALCIUM CARBONATE, AND MAGNESIA†
  Simethicone, Alumina, Calcium Carbonate, and Magnesia Chewable Tablets†
    In the U.S.—*Tempo*

Aluminum- and Magnesium-containing
ALUMINA AND MAGNESIA
  Alumina and Magnesia Oral Suspension USP
    In the U.S.—*Alamag; Gelamal; Maalox; Maalox TC; Maalox Whip; Mintox; Rulox; WinGel*
    In Canada—*Amphojel 500; Diovol; Diovol Ex; Gelusil; Gelusil Extra Strength; Maalox; Maalox TC; Mylanta-2 Plain; Neutralca-S; Univol*
  Alumina and Magnesia Tablets USP*
    In Canada—*Diovol; Diovol Ex; Univol*
  Alumina and Magnesia Tablets USP (Chewable)
    In the U.S.—*Creamalin; Maalox; Maalox Extra Strength; Maalox TC; Mintox; Rulox No. 1; Rulox No. 2; WinGel*
    In Canada—*Gelusil; Gelusil Extra Strength; Maalox; Maalox TC; Neutralca-S*
ALUMINA, MAGNESIA, AND SIMETHICONE
  Alumina, Magnesia, and Simethicone Oral Suspension USP
    In the U.S.—*Almacone; Almacone II; Alma-Mag Improved; Aludrox; AntaGel; AntaGel-II; Di-Gel; Gelusil; Gelusil-II; Kudrox Double Strength; Maalox Plus, Extra Strength; Mi-Acid; Mintox Plus; Mygel; Mygel II; Mylanta; Mylanta-II; Simaal Gel; Simaal 2 Gel*
    In Canada—*Amphojel Plus; Diovol Plus; Maalox Plus; Mylanta-2 Extra Strength*
  Alumina, Magnesia, and Simethicone Tablets USP (Chewable)
    In the U.S.—*Almacone; Alma-Mag #4 Improved; Gelusil; Gelusil-II; Maalox Plus, Extra Strength; Mylanta; Mylanta-II*
    In Canada—*Maalox Plus; Mylanta-2*
ALUMINA AND MAGNESIUM CARBONATE
  Alumina and Magnesium Carbonate Oral Suspension USP
    In the U.S.—*Algenic Alka; Gaviscon; Magnagel*
    In Canada—*Algicon*
  Alumina and Magnesium Carbonate Tablets USP (Chewable)
    In the U.S.—*Algicon (not USP); Gaviscon Extra Strength Relief Formula; Magnagel*
    In Canada—*Algicon*
ALUMINA AND MAGNESIUM TRISILICATE
  Alumina and Magnesium Trisilicate Chewable Tablets
    In the U.S.—*Foamicon; Gaviscon; Gaviscon-2; Genaton*
    In Canada—*Gaviscon*
MAGNESIUM TRISILICATE, ALUMINA, AND MAGNESIA†
  Magnesium Trisilicate, Alumina, and Magnesia Oral Suspension†
    In the U.S.—*Magnatril*
  Magnesium Trisilicate, Alumina, and Magnesia Chewable Tablets†
    In the U.S.—*Magnatril*
SIMETHICONE, ALUMINA, MAGNESIUM CARBONATE, AND MAGNESIA
  Simethicone, Alumina, Magnesium Carbonate, and Magnesia Chewable Tablets
    In the U.S.—*Di-Gel*
    In Canada—*Amphojel Plus; Diovol Plus*

Aluminum-, Magnesium-, and Sodium Bicarbonate-containing
ALUMINA, MAGNESIUM TRISILICATE, AND SODIUM BICARBONATE†
  Alumina, Magnesium Trisilicate, and Sodium Bicarbonate Chewable Tablets†
    In the U.S.—*Gas-is-gon; Triconsil*

Calcium Carbonate-containing
CALCIUM CARBONATE†‡
  Calcium Carbonate Chewing Gum†
    In the U.S.—*Chooz*
  Calcium Carbonate Oral Suspension USP†
    In the U.S.—*Titralac; Tums Liquid Extra Strength*

Calcium Carbonate Tablets USP†
  In the U.S.—*Calcilac; Glycate;* GENERIC
Calcium Carbonate Tablets USP (Chewable)†
  In the U.S.—*Alka-Mints; Amitone; Calglycine; Dicarbosil; Equilet; Genalac; Mallamint; Rolaids Calcium Rich; Titracid; Titralac; Titralac Extra Strength; Tums; Tums E-X;* GENERIC
CALCIUM CARBONATE AND SIMETHICONE†
  Calcium Carbonate and Simethicone Oral Suspension†
    In the U.S.—*Titralac Plus; Tums Liquid Extra Strength with Simethicone*
  Calcium Carbonate and Simethicone Chewable Tablets†
    In the U.S.—*Titralac Plus*

Calcium- and Magnesium-containing
CALCIUM CARBONATE AND MAGNESIA†
  Calcium Carbonate and Magnesia Chewable Tablets†
    In the U.S.—*Bisodol; Rolaids Sodium Free*
CALCIUM CARBONATE, MAGNESIA, AND SIMETHICONE†
  Calcium Carbonate, Magnesia, and Simethicone Tablets†
    In the U.S.—*Advanced Formula Di-Gel*
CALCIUM AND MAGNESIUM CARBONATES†
  Calcium and Magnesium Carbonates Oral Suspension†
    In the U.S.—*Marblen*
  Calcium and Magnesium Carbonates Tablets USP†
    In the U.S.—*Marblen*
  Calcium and Magnesium Carbonates Tablets USP (Chewable)†
    In the U.S.—*Noralac; Spastosed*
CALCIUM AND MAGNESIUM CARBONATES AND MAGNESIUM OXIDE†
  Calcium and Magnesium Carbonates and Magnesium Oxide Tablets†
    In the U.S.—*Alkets*

Magaldrate-containing
MAGALDRATE
  Magaldrate Oral Suspension USP
    In the U.S.—*Lowsium; Riopan;* GENERIC
    In Canada—*Riopan; Riopan Extra Strength*
  Magaldrate Tablets USP†
    In the U.S.—*Riopan*
  Magaldrate Tablets USP (Chewable)
    In the U.S.—*Lowsium; Riopan*
    In Canada—*Antiflux; Riopan; Riopan Extra Strength*
MAGALDRATE AND SIMETHICONE
  Magaldrate and Simethicone Oral Suspension USP
    In the U.S.—*Losotron Plus; Lowsium Plus; Riopan Plus; Riopan Plus 2;* GENERIC
    In Canada—*Riopan Plus; Riopan Plus Extra Strength*
  Magaldrate and Simethicone Tablets USP (Chewable)
    In the U.S.—*Lowsium Plus; Riopan Plus; Riopan Plus 2*
    In Canada—*Riopan Plus; Riopan Plus Extra Strength*

Magnesium-containing
MAGNESIUM HYDROXIDE§
  Magnesia Tablets USP
    In the U.S. and Canada—GENERIC
  Magnesia Tablets USP (Chewable)
    In the U.S. and Canada—*Phillips' Milk of Magnesia*
  Milk of Magnesia USP
    In the U.S. and Canada—*Phillips' Milk of Magnesia;* GENERIC
MAGNESIUM OXIDE†§
  Magnesium Oxide Capsules USP†
    In the U.S.—*Uro-Mag*
  Magnesium Oxide Tablets USP†
    In the U.S.—*Mag-Ox 400; Maox*

Magnesium- and Sodium Bicarbonate-containing
MAGNESIUM CARBONATE AND SODIUM BICARBONATE†
  Magnesium Carbonate and Sodium Bicarbonate for Oral Suspension USP†
    In the U.S.—*Bisodol*

Sodium Bicarbonate-containing—See *Sodium Bicarbonate (Systemic)*.

---

*Not commercially available in the U.S.
†Not commercially available in Canada.
‡See *Calcium Supplements (Systemic)* for systemic use of calcium carbonate in hypocalcemia.
§See *Laxatives (Local)* for laxative use of magnesium hydroxide and magnesium oxide.

Category

Antacid—All drugs included in this monograph are used as antacids.
Antiurolithic (phosphate calculi)—Aluminum Carbonate; Aluminum Hydroxide.
Laxative, hyperosmotic, saline—Magnesium Hydroxide; Magnesium Oxide (see *Magnesium Hydroxide* and *Magnesium Oxide, Laxatives (Local)*).
Antihyperphosphatemic—Aluminum Carbonate; Aluminum Hydroxide; Calcium Carbonate (see *Calcium Carbonate, Calcium Supplements (Systemic)*.
Antihypocalcemic—Calcium Carbonate (see *Calcium Carbonate, Calcium Supplements (Systemic)*).
Antiurolithic (calcium calculi)—Magnesium Hydroxide.

Indications

Note: Bracketed information in the *Indications* section refers to uses not included in U.S. product labeling.

Accepted
Hyperacidity (treatment);
Ulcer, duodenal (treatment); or
Ulcer, gastric (treatment)—Antacids are indicated for symptomatic relief of upset stomach associated with hyperacidity (heartburn, acid indigestion, and sour stomach). In addition, antacids are used in hyperacidity associated with gastric and duodenal ulcers. However, there have been reports of increased gastrin levels and increased gastric secretion (acid rebound) associated with the use of antacids.
Some of the antacid combinations contain other ingredients which have no antacid properties. Simethicone, an antiflatulent, has been added as an aid in those conditions in which the retention of gas may be a problem; however, in the treatment of peptic ulcer diseases, the advantage of using antacid and simethicone combinations rather than antacids alone has not been clearly established.
Hypersecretory conditions, gastric (treatment adjunct);
Zollinger-Ellison syndrome (treatment adjunct);
Mastocytosis, systemic (treatment adjunct); or
Adenoma, multiple endocrine (treatment adjunct)—Antacids are indicated in conjunction with histamine H2-receptor antagonists in the treatment of pathological gastric hypersecretion associated with Zollinger-Ellison syndrome (alone or as part of multiple endocrine neoplasia Type-I), systemic mastocytosis, and multiple endocrine adenoma.
Reflux, gastroesophageal (treatment)—Antacids are indicated in the symptomatic treatment of gastroesophageal reflux disease.
Stress-related mucosal damage (prophylaxis and treatment)—Antacids are indicated to prevent and treat upper gastrointestinal, stress-induced ulceration and bleeding, especially in intensive care patients.
Renal calculi (prophylaxis)—Aluminum carbonate and aluminum hydroxide are indicated in conjunction with a low-phosphate diet to prevent formation of phosphatic (struvite) urinary stones. [Magnesium hydroxide is used to prevent recurrence of calcium stones.][1]
Hyperphosphatemia (treatment)—Aluminum carbonate and aluminum hydroxide may be indicated in conjunction with a low-phosphate diet to reduce elevated phosphate levels and demineralization of bones in patients with renal insufficiency.
Hypocalcemia (treatment)—See *Calcium Carbonate, Calcium Supplements (Systemic)*.
[Aluminum hydroxide has been used in the treatment of neonatal hypocalcemia and diarrhea; however, it generally has been replaced by other agents. Use of aluminum-containing antacids in young children and premature infants may lead to aluminum toxicity, especially in those patients with renal failure.][1]

Unaccepted
Antacids have been used in patients undergoing anesthesia or during labor to lessen the danger from aspiration of gastric contents. However, the use of antacids to prevent acid aspiration has generally been replaced by the equally or more effective histamine H2-receptor antagonists or citrate solutions.

---

[1]Not included in Canadian product labeling.

Pharmacology

Mechanism of action/Effect:
Antacid—These medications react chemically to neutralize or buffer existing quantities of stomach acid but have no direct effect on its output. This action results in increased pH value of stomach contents, thus providing relief of hyperacidity symptoms. Also, these medications reduce acid concentration within the lumen of the esophagus, thus causing an increase in intra-esophageal pH and a decrease in pepsin activity, which aids in the control of gastroesophageal reflux.
Antiurolithic—Aluminum carbonate and aluminum hydroxide bind phosphate ions in the intestine to form insoluble aluminum phosphate, which is excreted in the feces. They thereby reduce phosphates in the urine and prevent formation of phosphatic (struvite) urinary stones. Magnesium hydroxide inhibits the precipitation of calcium oxalate and calcium phosphate, thus preventing the formation of calcium stones.
Antihyperphosphatemic—Aluminum carbonate and aluminum hydroxide reduce serum phosphate levels by binding with phosphate ions in the intestine to form insoluble aluminum phosphate, which passes through the intestinal tract unabsorbed.
Antihypocalcemic—Aluminum hydroxide may increase the alimentary absorption of calcium as a result of the decreased serum phosphate levels.
Antidiarrheal—Aluminum hydroxide's astringent and adsorbent properties help decrease the fluidity of stools.

Other actions/effects: Antacids may increase lower esophageal sphincter (LES) pressure. Aluminum-containing antacids have a cytoprotective effect on the gastric mucosa that may be associated with the stimulation of prostaglandin secretion, thus providing protection against mucosal necrosis and hemorrhage caused by corrosive agents, such as aspirin and ethanol.

Onset and duration of action:
Onset of action is dependent upon the ability of the antacid to solubilize in the stomach and react with the hydrochloric acid. The poorly soluble antacids (e.g., magnesium trisilicate) will thus react more slowly with hydrochloric acid than with the more soluble ones. In most cases, with slow-acting antacids, the onset of action is delayed and may not take place if gastric emptying is rapid.
Duration of action is determined primarily by gastric emptying time. Depending on the kind of antacid used, the duration of action in fasting patients may range from 20 to 60 minutes. However, when the antacid is given 1 hour after meals, the acid-neutralizing effect may be prolonged up to 3 hours.
The table that follows indicates a relative comparison among the different antacids regarding their onset of action and duration of action.

Antacid	Onset of action	Duration of action
Aluminum Carbonate	Slow	Short
Aluminum Hydroxide	Slow	Prolonged*
Aluminum Phosphate	Slow	Short
Calcium Carbonate	Fast	Prolonged
Dihydroxyaluminum Sodium Carbonate	Fast	Moderate
Magaldrate	Intermediate	Prolonged
Magnesium Carbonate	Intermediate	Short
Magnesium Hydroxide	Fast	Short
Magnesium Oxide	Fast	Short
Magnesium Trisilicate	Slow	Prolonged†
Sodium Bicarbonate	Fast	Short

*Absorptive properties of the gel prolong its duration of action.
†If gastric emptying is rapid, stomach may empty before much of the acid is neutralized.

Precautions to Consider

Geriatrics
Metabolic bone disease commonly seen in the elderly may be aggravated by the phosphorus depletion, hypercalciuria, and inhibition of absorption of intestinal fluoride caused by the chronic use of aluminum-containing antacids.

Although it is not known whether high intake of aluminum leads to Alzheimer's disease, the use of aluminum-containing antacids in Alzheimer's patients is not generally recommended. Research suggests that aluminum may contribute to the disease's development since it has been found to concentrate in neurofibrillary tangles in brain tissue.

Drug interactions and/or related problems
See *Table 1*, page 65.

Contraindications/Medical problems
See *Table 2*, page 68.

Side/Adverse Effects
See *Table 3*, page 70.

Patient Consultation
See *Table 4*, page 71.

General Dosing Information

For antacid use
The dose of antacid needed to neutralize gastric acid varies among patients, depending on the amount of acid secreted and the buffering capacity of the particular preparation.

It is estimated that 99% of the gastric acid will be neutralized when a gastric pH of 3.3 is achieved.

The amount (in mEq) of 0.1 N hydrochloric acid that can be titrated to pH 3.3 by a certain dose of antacid is referred to as the neutralizing capacity of the antacid. Approximately 15 to 20 mEq of an alumi-num- and magnesium-containing antacid are required to neutralize 1 mEq of gastric hydrochloric acid.

Patients with hypersecretory disorders (e.g., duodenal ulcer, Zollinger-Ellison syndrome, multiple endocrine adenomas, and systemic mastocytosis) may require 80 to 160 mEq of buffer at each dose; this is approximately 30 to 60 mL of most antacids. Only half of this dose is needed for patients with normal acid secretion.

The liquid and powder dosage forms of antacids are considered to be more effective than the solid dosage forms. In most cases, tablets must be thoroughly chewed before being swallowed; otherwise, they may not dissolve completely in the stomach before entering the small intestine.

The maximum recommended dosage should not be taken for more than 2 weeks, except under the advice or supervision of a physician.

Overuse of antacids may inhibit digestive enzyme activity of pepsin, which is ineffective when the stomach contents reach a pH of 4.0 and above.

Combinations of antacids containing aluminum and/or calcium compounds with magnesium salts offer the advantage of balancing the constipating qualities of aluminum and/or calcium and the laxative qualities of magnesium.

For use in peptic ulcer
In the treatment of peptic ulcer disease, to achieve adequate antacid effect in the stomach at the optimum time, most antacids are administered 1 and 3 hours after meals for prolonged acid-neutralizing effect and at bedtime; however, when taken at bedtime, their effect is not prolonged, because of rapid gastric emptying. Additional doses of antacids may be administered to relieve the pain that may occur between the regularly scheduled doses.

Antacid therapy should be continued for at least 4 to 6 weeks after all symptoms have disappeared, since there is no correlation between disappearance of symptoms and actual healing of the ulcer.

Aluminum hydroxide
In the treatment of peptic ulcer, 960 mg to 3.6 grams are given orally every one or two hours during waking hours, the dosage being adjusted as needed. For extremely severe symptoms of peptic ulcer (hospitalized patients), 2.6 to 4.8 grams diluted with two to three parts of milk or water are given intragastrically every thirty minutes for periods of twelve or more hours a day.

For antihyperphosphatemic use
Aluminum hydroxide
In conjunction with dietary phosphate restriction, 1.9 to 4.8 grams of aluminum hydroxide are given orally three or four times a day.

For antiurolithic use
Aluminum carbonate
In the prevention of phosphate stones the equivalent of 1 to 3 grams of aluminum hydroxide is given four times a day, one hour after meals and at bedtime.

Table 1. Drug Interactions and/or Related Problems

The following drug interactions and/or related problems have been selected on the basis of their potential clinical significance (possible mechanism in parentheses where appropriate)—not necessarily inclusive: (» = major clinical significance)

Note: Combinations containing any of the following medications, depending on the amount present, may also interact with this medication.

Only specific interactions between antacids and other oral medications have been identified in this monograph. However, because of antacids' ability to change gastric or urinary pH and to adsorb or form complexes with other drugs, the rate and/or extent of absorption of other medications may be increased or reduced when the medication is used concurrently with antacids. In general, patients should be advised not to take any other oral medications within 1 to 2 hours of antacids.

Legend:
I = Aluminum-containing
II = Calcium-containing
III = Magaldrate
IV = Magnesium-containing
V = Sodium Bicarbonate–containing

	I	II	III	IV	V

Acidifiers, urinary, such as:
  Ammonium chloride
  Ascorbic acid
  Potassium or sodium phosphates
    (antacids may alkalinize the urine and counteract the effect of urinary acidfiers; frequent use of antacids, especially in high doses, is best avoided by patients receiving therapy to acidify the urine)
	✔	✔	✔	✔	✔

Amphetamines or Quinidine (urinary excretion may be inhibited when these medications are used concurrently with antacids in doses that cause the urine to become alkaline, possibly resulting in toxicity; dosage adjustment may be needed when therapy with these antacids is initiated or discontinued or if dosage is changed)	✔	✔	✔	✔	✔
Anticholinergics or other medications with anticholinergic activity (concurrent use with antacids may decrease absorption, reducing the effectiveness of anticholinergics; doses of these medications should be spaced 1 hour apart from doses of antacids)	✔	✔	✔	✔	✔
(urinary excretion may be delayed by alkalinization of the urine, thus potentiating the side effects of the anticholinergic)	✔	✔	✔	✔	✔
Calcitonin or Etidronate (concurrent use with calcium carbonate may antagonize the effect of calcitonin or etidronate in the treatment of hypercalcemia)		✔			
Calcium-containing preparations (concurrent and prolonged use with sodium bicarbonate may result in the milk-alkali syndrome)					✔
» Cellulose sodium phosphate (concurrent use with calcium-containing antacids may decrease effectiveness of cellulose sodium phosphate in preventing hypercalciuria)		✔			
(concurrent use with magnesium-containing antacids may result in binding of magnesium; patients should be advised not to take these medications within 1 hour of cellulose sodium phosphate)				✔	
Chenodiol (concurrent use with aluminum-containing antacids may result in binding of chenodiol, thus decreasing its absorption)	✔			✔	
Ciprofloxacin or Norfloxacin or Ofloxacin (alkalinization of the urine may reduce the solubility of ciprofloxacin, norfloxacin, or ofloxacin in the urine; if antacids and ciprofloxacin, norfloxacin, or ofloxacin are used concurrently, patients should be observed for signs of crystalluria and nephrotoxicity)	✔	✔	✔	✔	✔
(aluminum- and magnesium-containing antacids may reduce absorption of ciprofloxacin, norfloxacin, or ofloxacin resulting in lower serum and urine concentrations of ciprofloxacin, norfloxacin, or ofloxacin; therefore, concurrent use is not recommended; however, if aluminum- and magnesium-containing antacids must be used concurrently with these medicines, the patients should be advised to take antacids at least 4 hours before or 2 hours after ciprofloxacin, norfloxacin, or ofloxacin)	✔			✔	✔
Citrates (concurrent use with antacids containing aluminum, calcium carbonates, or sodium bicarbonate may result in systemic alkalosis)	✔	✔			✔
(concurrent use of sodium citrate with sodium bicarbonate may promote the development of calcium stones in patients with uric acid stones, due to sodium ion opposition to the hypocalciuric effect of the alkaline load; may also cause hypernatremia)					✔
(concurrent use of aluminum-containing antacids with citrate salts can increase aluminum absorption, possibly resulting in acute aluminum toxicity, especially in patients with renal insufficiency)	✔				

Table 1. Drug Interactions and/or Related Problems *(continued)*

	I	II	III	IV	V
Legend: **I** = Aluminum-containing **II** = Calcium-containing **III** = Magaldrate **IV** = Magnesium-containing **V** = Sodium Bicarbonate– containing					
Digitalis glycosides (concurrent use with aluminum- and magnesium-containing antacids may inhibit absorption, possibly decreasing plasma concentrations of digitalis glycosides; although actual clinical importance of this interaction has not been established it is recommended that doses of antacids and digitalis glycosides be separated by several hours)	✔		✔	✔	
Diuretics, potassium-depleting, such as bumetanide, ethacrynic acid, furosemide, indapamide, thiazide diuretics (concurrent use of thiazide diuretics with large doses of calcium carbonate may result in hypercalcemia)		✔			
Enteric-coated medications, such as bisacodyl (concurrent administration of antacids with enteric-coated medications may cause the enteric coating to dissolve too rapidly, resulting in gastric or duodenal irritation)	✔	✔	✔	✔	✔
Ephedrine (urine alkalinization induced by sodium bicarbonate may increase the half-life of ephedrine and prolong its duration of action, especially if the urine remains alkaline for several days or longer; dosage adjustment of ephedrine may be necessary)					✔
Folic acid (prolonged use of aluminum and/or magnesium-containing antacids may decrease folic acid absorption by lowering the pH of the small intestine; patients should be advised to take antacids at least 2 hours after folic acid)	✔		✔	✔	
Histamine H$_2$-receptor antagonists (concurrent use with antacids may be indicated in the treatment of peptic ulcer to relieve pain; however, simultaneous administration of medium to high doses [80 mmol to 150 mmol] of antacids is not recommended since absorption of histamine H$_2$-receptor antagonists may be decreased; patients should be advised not to take any antacids within $^1/_2$ to 1 hour of histamine H$_2$-receptor antagonists)	✔	✔	✔	✔	✔
Iron preparations, oral (absorption may be decreased when these preparations are used concurrently with magnesium trisilicate or antacids containing carbonate; spacing the doses of the iron preparation as far as possible from doses of the antacid is recommended)	✔	✔		✔	✔
» **Isoniazid, oral** (concurrent use with aluminum-containing antacids may delay and decrease absorption of oral isoniazid; concurrent use should be avoided or the patient should be advised to take oral isoniazid at least 1 hour before the antacid)	✔		✔		
» **Ketoconazole** (antacids may cause increased gastrointestinal pH; concurrent administration with antacids may result in a marked reduction in absorption of ketoconazole; patients should be advised to take antacids at least 3 hours after ketoconazole)	✔	✔	✔	✔	✔
Lithium (sodium bicarbonate enhances lithium excretion, possibly resulting in decreased efficacy; this may be partly due to the sodium content)					✔
Mexiletine (marked alkalinization of the urine caused by sodium bicarbonate may slow renal excretion of mexiletine)					✔
» **Mecamylamine** (alkalinization of the urine may slow excretion and prolong the effects of mecamylamine; concurrent use is not recommended)	✔	✔	✔	✔	✔

Table 1. Drug Interactions and/or Related Problems *(continued)*

	Legend: I = Aluminum-containing; II = Calcium-containing; III = Magaldrate; IV = Magnesium-containing; V = Sodium Bicarbonate–containing				
	I	**II**	**III**	**IV**	**V**
» Methenamine (concurrent use with antacids that cause the urine to become alkaline may reduce the effectiveness of methenamine by inhibiting its conversion to formaldehyde; concurrent use is not recommended)	✔	✔	✔	✔	✔
Milk or milk products (concurrent and prolonged use with calcium carbonate or sodium bicarbonate may result in the milk-alkali syndrome)	✔			✔	
Misoprostol (concurrent use with magnesium-containing antacids may aggravate misoprostol-induced diarrhea)				✔	
Pancrelipase (concurrent administration of antacids may be required to prevent inactivation of pancrelipase by gastric pepsin and acid pH; however, calcium carbonate- and/or magnesium-containing antacids are not recommended since they may decrease the effectiveness of pancrelipase)		✔	✔	✔	
Penicillamine (absorption may be reduced when penicillamine is administered concurrently with aluminum- or magnesium-containing antacids; although more studies are needed to establish the significance of this interaction, it is recommended that doses of antacids and penicillamine be separated by 2 hours)	✔			✔	
Phenothiazines, especially chlorpromazine, oral (absorption may be inhibited when these medications are used concurrently with aluminum- or magnesium-containing antacids; although more studies are needed to establish the significance of this interaction, simultaneous administration should be avoided)	✔		✔	✔	
Phenytoin (concurrent use with aluminum-, magnesium-, and/or calcium carbonate-containing antacids may decrease absorption of phenytoin, thus reducing serum phenytoin concentrations; although more studies are needed to establish the significance of this interaction, it is recommended that doses of antacids and phenytoin be separated by about 2 to 3 hours)	✔	✔	✔	✔	
Phosphates, oral (concurrent use with aluminum- or magnesium-containing antacids may bind the phosphate and prevent its absorption)	✔		✔	✔	
(concurrent use with calcium-containing antacids may increase potential of deposition of calcium in soft tissues if serum-ionized calcium is high)		✔			
Salicylates (alkalinization of the urine may increase renal salicylate excretion and lower serum salicylate levels; dosage adjustments of salicylates may be necessary when chronic high-dose antacid therapy is started or stopped, especially in patients receiving large doses of the salicylate, such as patients with rheumatoid arthritis and rheumatic fever)	✔	✔	✔	✔	✔
Sodium bicarbonate or Vitamin D (concurrent and prolonged use with calcium carbonate may result in the milk-alkali syndrome)		✔			
Sodium fluoride (concurrent use with aluminum hydroxide may decrease absorption and increase fecal excretion of fluoride)	✔			✔	
(calcium ions may complex with and inhibit absorption of fluoride)		✔			
» Sodium polystyrene sulfonate resin (SPSR) (neutralization of gastric acid may be impaired when SPSR is used concurrently with calcium- or magnesium-containing antacids, possibly resulting in systemic alkalosis; concurrent use is not recommended)		✔	✔	✔	

Table 1. Drug Interactions and/or Related Problems *(continued)*

	Legend: **I** = Aluminum-containing **II** = Calcium-containing **III** = Magaldrate **IV** = Magnesium-containing **V** = Sodium Bicarbonate– containing				
	I	**II**	**III**	**IV**	**V**
Sucralfate (concurrent use with antacids may be indicated in the treatment of duodenal ulcer to relieve pain; however, simultaneous administration is not recommended since antacids may interfere with binding of sucralfate to the mucosa; patients should be advised not to take any antacids within 1/2 hour before or after sucralfate; concurrent use with aluminum-containing antacids may cause aluminum toxicity in patients with chronic renal failure)	✔	✔	✔	✔	✔
» Tetracyclines, oral (absorption may be decreased when oral tetracyclines are used concurrently with antacids because of possible formation of nonabsorbable complexes and/or increase in intragastric pH; patients should be advised not to take antacids within 3 to 4 hours of tetracyclines)	✔	✔	✔	✔	✔
Vitamin D, including calcifediol and calcitriol (concurrent use with magnesium-containing antacids may result in hypermagnesemia, especially in patients with chronic renal failure)				✔	✔
(concurrent use with calcium-containing antacids may result in hypercalcemia)		✔			

Table 2. Contraindications/Medical problems

Note: A blank space usually signifies lack of information; it is not necessarily an indication that a given medical problem is of no concern. However, the pharmacologic similarity of these agents may suggest that if caution is required in particular medical problems for one agent, then it may be required for the others as well.

	Legend: **I** = Aluminum-containing **II** = Calcium-containing **III** = Magaldrate **IV** = Magnesium-containing **V** = Sodium Bicarbonate– containing				
The contraindications/medical problems included have been selected on the basis of their potential clinical significance (reasons given in parentheses where appropriate)—not necessarily inclusive (» = major clinical significance).	**I**	**II**	**III**	**IV**	**V**
Except under special circumstances, these medications should not be used when the following medical problems exist:					
» Hypercalcemia (increased risk of exacerbation)		✔			
» Renal function impairment, severe (increased risk of hypermagnesemia)				✔	✔
Risk-benefit should be considered when the following medical problems exist:					
» Alzheimer's disease (may be exacerbated)	✔				
» Appendicitis, or symptoms of (may complicate existing condition; laxative or constipating effects may increase danger of perforation or rupture)	✔	✔	✔	✔	✔
Bleeding, gastrointestinal or rectal, undiagnosed (condition may be exacerbated)	✔	✔	✔	✔	✔

Table 2. Contraindications/Medical problems *(continued)*

Legend:
I = Aluminum-containing
II = Calcium-containing
III = Magaldrate
IV = Magnesium-containing
V = Sodium Bicarbonate–containing

	I	II	III	IV	V
Bone fractures	*		*		
» Cirrhosis of liver or	†	†			✔
» Congestive heart failure or	†	†			✔
» Edema or	†	†			✔
» Toxemia of pregnancy (fluid retention may be increased; low-sodium antacids should be used)	†	†			✔
Colitis, ulcerative (may be aggravated by laxative effect of magnesium-containing antacids)			✔	✔	
Colostomy or Diverticulitis or » Ileostomy (increased risk of fluid or electrolyte imbalance)			✔ ✔ ✔	✔ ✔ ✔	
» Constipation or » Fecal impaction (may be exacerbated)	✔ ✔	✔ ✔			
Diarrhea, chronic (possible increased danger of phosphate depletion with aluminum-containing antacids)	✔		✔		
(possible increased laxative effect with magnesium-containing antacids)				✔	
» Gastric outlet obstruction	✔		✔		
» Hemorrhoids (may be aggravated)	✔	✔			
» Hypoparathyroidism (calcium excretion may be decreased)		✔			
» Hypophosphatemia	*				
» Intestinal obstruction	✔	✔	✔	✔	✔
» Renal function impairment (possible increased risk of aluminum toxicity to brain tissue, bone, and parathyroid glands; possible onset of the neurological syndrome—dialysis dementia—in dialysis patients with long-term use of aluminum-containing antacids)	✔		✔		
(possible increased danger of milk-alkali syndrome and hypercalcemia with calcium-containing antacids)		✔			
(possible increased danger of hypermagnesemia)				‡	
(may cause metabolic alkalosis)					✔
» Sarcoidosis (increased risk of hypercalcemia or renal disease)		✔			
Sensitivity to aluminum-, calcium-, magnesium-, simethicone-, or sodium bicarbonate-containing medications	✔	✔	✔	✔	✔

*Aluminum hydroxide has the ability to form the insoluble complex of aluminum phosphate, which is excreted in the feces. This may lead to lowered serum phosphate concentrations and phosphorus mobilization from the bone. If phosphate depletion (e.g., malabsorption syndrome) is already present, osteomalacia, osteoporosis, and fracture may result, especially in patients with other bone disease. In such patients predisposed to phosphate depletion, other aluminum-containing antacids (except aluminum phosphate) will be of concern only in relation to their ability to form an aluminum phosphate complex.

†Antacids containing more than 5 mEq (115 mg) of sodium per total daily dose should not be used without first checking with physician. The usual amount of sodium allowed in restricted diets is 3 grams or less per day.

‡In patients with renal function impairment, use of antacids containing more than 50 mEq (608 mg) of magnesium per total daily dose should be carefully considered.

Table 3. Side/Adverse Effects*

The following side/adverse effects have been selected on the basis of their potential clinical significance (possible signs and symptoms in parentheses where appropriate)—not necessarily inclusive:	Legend: **I** = Aluminum-containing **II** = Calcium-containing **III** = Magaldrate **IV** = Magnesium-containing **V** = Sodium Bicarbonate–containing				
	I	**II**	**III**	**IV**	**V**
Medical attention needed With long-term use in chronic renal failure in dialysis patients *Neurotoxicity* (mood or mental changes)	✔		✔		

With large doses
    Fecal impaction (continuing severe constipation)
    Swelling of feet or lower legs
	✔	✔			✔

With large doses or in renal insufficiency *Metabolic alkalosis* (mood or mental changes; muscle pain or twitching; nervousness or restlessness; slow breathing; unpleasant taste; unusual tiredness or weakness)		✔			✔

With long-term or prolonged use
    Hypercalcemia associated with milk-alkali syndrome (frequent urge to urinate; continuing headache; continuing loss of appetite; nausea or vomiting; unusual tiredness or weakness)†
    Osteomalacia and osteoporosis due to phosphate depletion (bone pain; swelling of wrists or ankles)
	✔	✔	‡		✔

With overuse or prolonged use *Renal calculi* (difficult or painful urination)		✔		§	
With prolonged use or large doses *Phosphorous depletion syndrome* (continuing feeling of discomfort; continuing loss of appetite; muscle weakness; unusual weight loss)	✔		✔		
With prolonged use or large doses and/or in renal disease *Hypermagnesemia or other electrolyte imbalance* (dizziness or lightheadedness; irregular heartbeat; mood or mental changes; unusual tiredness or weakness)			✔	✔	
Medical attention needed only if continuing or bothersome *Chalky taste*	M	M	M	M	U
Constipation, mild	M	L	U	U	U
Diarrhea or laxative effect—with overdose	U	U	U	M	U
Increased thirst	U	U	U	U	L
Nausea or vomiting	L	U	U	L	U
Speckling or whitish discoloration of stools (concretions of fatty acid-salts of aluminum)	L	U	U	U	U
Stomach cramps	M	U	U	L	L

*Differences in frequency of occurrence may reflect either lack of clinical-use data or actual pharmacologic distinctions among agents (although their pharmacologic similarity suggests that side effects occurring with one may occur with the others). M = more frequent; L = less frequent; R = rare; U = unknown.

†May also occur with large doses and/or in chronic renal failure with calcium carbonate.

‡Osteomalacia and osteoporosis have been reported after chronic ingestion of large doses of aluminum hydroxide-containing antacids. Since magaldrate is converted to aluminum and magnesium hydroxides in vivo, it is likely that osteomalacia and osteoporosis may occur with excessive use of magaldrate.

§Chronic administration of magnesium trisilicate may infrequently produce silica renal stones.

Table 4. Patient Consultation

Legend:
I = Aluminum-containing
II = Calcium-containing
III = Magaldrate
IV = Magnesium-containing
V = Sodium Bicarbonate–containing

In providing consultation, consider emphasizing the following selected information (» = major clinical significance):	I	II	III	IV	V
Before using this medication					
» Conditions affecting use, especially:					
Sensitivity to aluminum-, calcium-, magnesium-, simethicone-, or sodium bicarbonate-containing medication	✔	✔	✔	✔	✔
Pregnancy—Concern for fetus or neonate only with chronic high doses; sodium intake may cause edema and weight gain (for sodium-containing)	✔	✔	✔	✔	✔
Use in children—Not recommended for children up to 6 years of age; proper diagnosis required to avoid medical complications	✔	✔	✔	✔	✔
Use in the elderly—					
Possible aggravation of metabolic bone disease	✔				
Possible exacerbation of Alzheimer's disease	✔				
Other medications, especially:					
Cellulose sodium phosphate		✔	✔	✔	
Isoniazid, oral	✔		✔		
Ketoconazole	✔		✔	✔	✔
Mecamylamine		✔	✔	✔	✔
Methenamine		✔	✔	✔	✔
Sodium polystyrene sulfonate resin		✔	✔	✔	✔
Tetracyclines, oral	✔	✔	✔	✔	✔
Other medical problems, especially:					
Alzheimer's disease	✔				
Appendicitis, symptoms of	✔	✔	✔	✔	✔
Constipation or fecal impaction or intestinal obstruction	✔	✔			
Edematous conditions	✔	✔			
Hemorrhoids	✔	✔			
Hypercalcemia		✔			
Hypophosphatenia	✔				
Ileostomy				✔	✔
Renal function impairment				✔	✔
Sarcoidosis		✔			
Proper use of this medication					
Following physician's or manufacturer's instructions	✔	✔	✔	✔	✔
Missed dose: If on regular dosing schedule—Taking as soon as possible; not taking if almost time for next dose; not doubling doses	✔	✔	✔	✔	✔
» Proper storage	✔	✔	✔	✔	✔
For chewable tablet dosage form					
Chewing tablets well before swallowing for faster results and maximum effectiveness	✔	✔	✔	✔	
For use in treatment of ulcers					
» Compliance with therapy	✔	✔	✔	✔	✔
Taking 1 and 3 hours after meals and at bedtime for maximum effectiveness	✔	✔	✔	✔	✔
For aluminum carbonate or aluminum hydroxide as an antiurolithic					
Drinking plenty of fluids for best results	✔				
For aluminum carbonate or aluminum hydroxide as an antihyperphosphatemic					
Possible need for low-phosphate diet	✔				
Precautions while using this medication					
Regular visits to physician to check progress of therapy if:					
—taking large doses		✔			
—taking regularly for long period of time	✔	✔	✔	✔	✔
Possible interference with gastric acid secretion tests; need to inform physician of use of medication	✔	✔	✔	✔	✔

Table 4. Patient Consultation *(continued)*

	I	II	III	IV	V
Legend: **I** = Aluminum-containing **II** = Calcium-containing **III** = Magaldrate **IV** = Magnesium-containing **V** = Sodium Bicarbonate–containing					
» Not taking this medication:					
—if symptoms of appendicitis are present; checking with physician for proper diagnosis	✔	✔	✔	✔	✔
—if symptoms of inflamed bowel are present				✔	
—within 1 to 2 hours of other oral medication	✔	✔	✔	✔	✔
—with large amounts of milk or milk products		✔			✔
Possible need for sodium restriction	✔	✔		✔	✔
Possible interference with test using radiopharmaceutical; need to inform physician of using aluminum-containing antacid	✔		✔		
For antacid use » Not taking this medication for more than 2 weeks or if problem is recurring, unless otherwise directed by physician	✔	✔	✔	✔	✔
Alerting patients to laxative effect when taken too often or in large doses				✔	✔
Side/adverse effects Signs of potential side effects, especially:					
Fecal impaction	✔	✔			
Hypercalcemia		✔			✔
Hypermagnesemia			✔	✔	
Metabolic alkalosis		✔			✔
Neurotoxicity	✔		✔		
Osteomalacia	✔				
Phosphorous depletion	✔		✔		

ANTICHOLINERGICS/ANTISPASMODICS　Systemic

INN: Included in brackets after individual generic listings, if different from the U.S. generic name.

Some commonly used *brand names* are:

In the U.S.—

Anaspaz [Hyoscyamine]
Antispas [Dicyclomine]
A-Spas [Dicyclomine]
Banthine [Methantheline]
Bentyl [Dicyclomine]
Cantil [Mepenzolate]
Cystospaz [Hyoscyamine]
Cystospaz-M
　[Hyoscyamine]
Darbid [Isopropamide]
Daricon
　[Oxyphencyclimine]
Di-Spaz [Dicyclomine]
Gastrosed [Hyoscyamine]
Homapin [Homatropine]
Levsin [Hyoscyamine]
Levsinex Timecaps
　[Hyoscyamine]

Levsin S/L [Hyoscyamine]
Neoquess [Dicyclomine;
　Hyoscyamine]
Norpanth [Propantheline]
Or-Tyl [Dicyclomine]
Pamine
　[Methscopolamine]
Pathilon [Tridihexethyl]
Pro-Banthine
　[Propantheline]
Quarzan [Clidinium]
Robinul [Glycopyrrolate]
Robinul Forte
　[Glycopyrrolate]
Spasmoject [Dicyclomine]
Transderm-Scōp
　[Scopolamine]
Valpin 50 [Anisotropine]

In Canada—

Bentylol [Dicyclomine]
Buscopan [Scopolamine]
Formulex [Dicyclomine]
Gastrozepin [Pirenzepine]
Levsin [Hyoscyamine]
Lomine [Dicyclomine]
Pro-Banthine
　[Propantheline]

Propanthel [Propantheline]
Robinul [Glycopyrrolate]
Robinul Forte
　[Glycopyrrolate]
Spasmoban [Dicyclomine]
Transderm-V
　[Scopolamine]

Other commonly used names are:

Dicycloverine
　[Dicyclomine]
Glycopyrronium bromide
　[Glycopyrrolate]
Hyoscine hydrobromide
　[Scopolamine]

Hyoscine methobromide
　[Methscopolamine]
Methanthelinium
　[Methantheline]
Octatropine [Anisotropine]

ANISOTROPINE [INN: Octatropine]†
Oral
　Anisotropine Methylbromide Tablets†
　　In the U.S.—*Valpin 50*; GENERIC
ATROPINE
Oral
　Atropine Sulfate Tablets USP†
　　In the U.S.—GENERIC
　Atropine Sulfate Soluble Tablets†
　　In the U.S.—GENERIC
Parenteral
　Atropine Sulfate Injection USP
　　In the U.S. and Canada—GENERIC
BELLADONNA†
Oral
　Belladonna Tincture USP†
　　In the U.S.—GENERIC
CLIDINIUM†
Oral
　Clidinium Bromide Capsules USP†
　　In the U.S.—*Quarzan*
DICYCLOMINE [INN: Dicycloverine]
Oral
　Dicyclomine Hydrochloride Capsules USP
　　In the U.S.—*Bentyl; Di-Spaz;* GENERIC
　　In Canada—*Bentylol; Formulex; Lomine*

Dicyclomine Hydrochloride Syrup USP
　In the U.S.—*Bentyl;* GENERIC
　In Canada—*Bentylol*
Dicyclomine Hydrochloride Tablets USP
　In the U.S.—*Bentyl;* GENERIC
　In Canada—*Bentylol; Spasmoban*
Dicyclomine Hydrochloride Extended-release Tablets*
　In Canada—*Bentylol*
Parenteral
　Dicyclomine Hydrochloride Injection USP
　　In the U.S.—*Antispas; A-Spas; Bentyl; Di-Spaz; Neoquess; Or-Tyl; Spasmoject;* GENERIC
　　In Canada—*Bentylol*
GLYCOPYRROLATE [INN: Glycopyrronium Bromide]
Oral
　Glycopyrrolate Tablets USP
　　In the U.S.—*Robinul; Robinul Forte;* GENERIC
　　In Canada—*Robinul; Robinul Forte*
Parenteral
　Glycopyrrolate Injection USP
　　In the U.S. and Canada—*Robinul*
HOMATROPINE†
Oral
　Homatropine Methylbromide Tablets USP†
　　In the U.S.—*Homapin*
HYOSCYAMINE
Oral
　Hyoscyamine Tablets USP†
　　In the U.S.—*Cystospaz*
　Hyoscyamine Sulfate Extended-release Capsules†
　　In the U.S.—*Cystospaz-M; Levsinex Timecaps*
　Hyoscyamine Sulfate Elixir USP†
　　In the U.S.—*Levsin*
　Hyoscyamine Sulfate Oral Solution USP
　　In the U.S.—*Gastrosed; Levsin*
　　In Canada—*Levsin*
　Hyoscyamine Sulfate Tablets USP
　　In the U.S.—*Anaspaz; Gastrosed; Levsin; Levsin S/L; Neoquess;* GENERIC
　　In Canada—*Levsin*
Parenteral
　Hyoscyamine Sulfate Injection USP
　　In the U.S. and Canada—*Levsin*
HYOSCYAMINE AND SCOPOLAMINE†
Oral
　Hyoscyamine and Scopolamine Tablets†
　　In the U.S.—*Bellafoline*
ISOPROPAMIDE†
Oral
　Isopropamide Iodide Tablets USP†
　　In the U.S.—*Darbid*
MEPENZOLATE†
Oral
　Mepenzolate Bromide Tablets USP†
　　In the U.S.—*Cantil*
METHANTHELINE [INN: Methanthelinium]†
Oral
　Methantheline Bromide Tablets USP†
　　In the U.S.—*Banthine*
METHSCOPOLAMINE [INN: Hyoscine Methobromide]†
Oral
　Methscopolamine Bromide Tablets USP†
　　In the U.S.—*Pamine*
OXYPHENCYCLIMINE†
Oral
　Oxyphencyclimine Hydrochloride Tablets USP†
　　In the U.S.—*Daricon*

PIRENZEPINE*
Oral
    Pirenzepine Hydrochloride Tablets*
        In Canada—*Gastrozepin*
PROPANTHELINE
Oral
    Propantheline Bromide Tablets USP
        In the U.S.—*Norpanth; Pro-Banthine;* GENERIC
        In Canada—*Pro-Banthine; Propanthel*
SCOPOLAMINE
Oral
    Scopolamine Butylbromide Tablets*
        In Canada—*Buscopan*
Parenteral
    Scopolamine Butylbromide Injection*
        In Canada—*Buscopan*
    Scopolamine Hydrobromide Injection USP [INN: Hyoscine Hydro-
    bromide]†
        In the U.S.—GENERIC
Rectal
    Scopolamine Butylbromide Suppositories*
        In Canada—*Buscopan*
Transdermal
    Scopolamine Transdermal System
        In the U.S.—*Transderm-Scōp*
        In Canada—*Transderm-V*
TRIDIHEXETHYL†
Oral
    Tridihexethyl Chloride Tablets USP†
        In the U.S.—*Pathilon*

---

*Not commercially available in the U.S.
†Not commercially available in Canada.

Category

Note: All of these medications have anticholinergic and, to some extent, antispasmodic actions; however, the labeled indications for specific agents may vary because of minor differences in potency and/or receptor selectivity. **In general, there is a lack of specific testing and/or clinical-use data to support the indication of anticholinergics/antispasmodics in most conditions.**

Anticholinergic—Anisotropine; Atropine; Belladonna; Clidinium; Dicyclomine; Glycopyrrolate; Homatropine; Hyoscyamine; Isopropamide; Mepenzolate; Methantheline; Methscopolamine; Oxyphencyclimine; Pirenzepine; Propantheline; Scopolamine; Tridihexethyl.

Antispasmodic, gastrointestinal—Dicyclomine; Oxyphencyclimine; Scopolamine Butylbromide.

Antidysmenorrheal—Belladonna; Scopolamine Butylbromide.

Antiarrhythmic—Atropine (parenteral only); Glycopyrrolate (parenteral only); Hyoscyamine (parenteral only); Scopolamine (parenteral only).

Antidote (to cholinesterase inhibitors)—Atropine; Hyoscyamine (parenteral only).

Antidote (to muscarine)—Atropine; Hyoscyamine (parenteral only).

Antidote (to organophosphate pesticides)—Atropine.

Antispasmodic, urinary—Atropine; Scoplamine

Cholinergic adjunct (curariform block)—Atropine (parenteral only); Glycopyrrolate (parenteral only); Hyoscyamine (parenteral only).

Anesthesia adjunct—Scopolamine (parenteral only).

Antiemetic—Scopolamine.

Antivertigo agent—Belladonna; Scopolamine.

Antidiarrheal—Glycopyrrolate.

Indications

Note: Bracketed information in the *Indications* section refers to uses not included in U.S. product labeling.

Accepted

Ulcer, peptic (treatment adjunct)—All anticholinergics included in this monograph, except dicyclomine and scopolamine hydrobromide, are indicated in conjunction with antacids or histamine H2-receptor antagonists in the treatment of peptic ulcer, to reduce further gastric acid secretion and delay gastric emptying. However, results usually are inconsistent and transient and require high doses, which result in significant side effects. Intravenous use of hyoscyamine may be indicated for prompt relief of pain in both the moderately severe and the severe peptic ulcer.

Bowel syndrome, irritable (treatment)—Atropine, belladonna, dicyclomine, homatropine, and hyoscyamine are indicated and [anisotropine], [clidinium], [glycopyrrolate], [isopropamide], [mepenzolate], [methantheline], [methscopolamine], [oxyphencyclimine], [pirenzepine], [propantheline], [scopolamine], and [tridihexethyl] are used in the treatment of irritable bowel syndrome, mainly in patients in whom other therapy, such as sedation and/or change in diet, has failed. In patients with spastic colon, these medications may provide relief of symptoms such as pain and/or constipation. However, results usually are inconsistent and transient and require high doses, which result in significant side effects.

Biliary tract disorders, spastic (treatment adjunct)—Atropine, hyoscyamine, and scopolamine butylbromide may be indicated for concomitant use with morphine in the treatment of spastic disorders of the biliary tract, such as biliary colic. However, results usually are inconsistent and transient and require high doses which result in significant side effects.

Urologic disorders, symptoms of (treatment)—Atropine and scopolamine butylbromide may be indicated in the treatment of ureteral and renal colic to relax smooth muscle spasm in the genitourinary tract. Oral hyoscyamine is indicated to control hypermotility in cystitis. However, results of anticholinergic treatment usually are inconsistent and transient and require high doses, which result in significant side effects.

Radiography, gastrointestinal, adjunct—In hypotonic duodenography or contrast examination of the colon, parenteral atropine and parenteral hyoscyamine are indicated to relax the upper gastrointestinal tract and colon.

Urinary incontinence (treatment)—Atropine and methantheline are indicated and [propantheline][1] is used in the treatment of uninhibited hypertonic neurogenic bladder to increase bladder capacity by reducing amplitude and frequency of bladder contractions.

Dysmenorrhea (treatment); or

Enuresis, nocturnal (treatment)—Belladonna and scopolamine butylbromide are indicated as spasmolytics in the treatment of dysmenorrhea and nocturnal enuresis.

Hypersecretory conditions, gastric, in anesthesia (prophylaxis)—Parenteral glycopyrrolate is indicated as an antisialagogue preanesthetic medication to reduce gastric acid secretion.

Salivation and respiratory tract secretions, excessive, in anesthesia (prophylaxis)—Atropine and the parenteral forms of glycopyrrolate, hyoscyamine, and scopolamine[1] are indicated as antisialagogue preanesthetic medications to prevent or reduce salivation and respiratory tract secretions.

Arrhythmias, succinylcholine-induced (prophylaxis); or

Arrhythmias, surgical procedure-induced (prophylaxis)—The parenteral forms of atropine and scopolamine[1] are indicated as adjuncts to anesthesia to prevent reflex bradycardia, sinus arrest, and hypotension induced by succinylcholine during intubation of the trachea or produced by certain surgical manipulations.

Arrhythmias, cardiac (treatment); or

Bradycardia, sinus (treatment)—Parenteral atropine and parenteral hyoscyamine are indicated to reduce severe sinus bradycardia and syncope associated with hyperactive carotid sinus reflex; and to lessen the degree of atrioventricular heart block in Type I atrioventricular (AV) conduction deficits. Also, parenteral atropine is indicated as an antidote for sinus bradycardia resulting from the improper administration of a choline ester medication.

Arrhythmias, in anesthesia (treatment); or

Arrhythmias, in surgery (treatment)—The parenteral forms of atropine, hyoscyamine, and scopolamine[1] are indicated to restore cardiac rate and arterial pressure when increased vagal activity has reduced pulse rate and cardiac action. Parenteral glycopyrrolate is indicated to block cardiac vagal inhibitory reflexes during induction of anesthesia and intubation. Parenteral glycopyrrolate is also indicated intraoperatively to counteract drug-induced or vagal traction reflexes with the associated arrhythmias.

Toxicity, cholinesterase inhibitor (prophylaxis)—The parenteral forms of atropine, glycopyrrolate, and hyoscyamine are indicated for administration prior to or concurrently with neostigmine or pyridostigmine during treatment of nondepolarizing neuromuscular blockade to protect against the muscarinic effects of these drugs, such as bradycardia and excessive secretions.

Toxicity, cholinesterase inhibitor (treatment);

Toxicity, muscarine (treatment); or

Toxicity, organophosphate pesticide (treatment)—Atropine and parenteral hyoscyamine are indicated in the treatment of poisoning from cholinesterase inhibitors such as neostigmine, pilocarpine, physostigmine, and methacholine, and in the treatment of the rapid type of mushroom (muscarine) poisoning. Atropine is also indicated in the treatment of poisoning caused by pesticides that are organophosphate cholinesterase inhibitors, chemical warfare, and "nerve" gases.

Anesthesia, general, adjunct—Parenteral administration of scopolamine[1], in combination with morphine or meperidine, is indicated in preanesthesia to reduce excitement and produce amnesia. Parenteral scopolamine[1] is also indicated in conjunction with analgesics in cardiopulmonary bypass patients who cannot be deeply anesthetized because of the risk of severe hypotension or circulatory collapse.

Motion sickness (prophylaxis and treatment)—Oral[1] and transdermal scopolamine are also indicated for this use; however, because of the higher incidence of adverse effects when scopolamine is given orally, transdermal administration is preferred. Parenteral scopolamine[1] is indicated to control nausea and vomiting associated with motion sickness.

Pneumonitis, aspiration (prophylaxis)—Parenteral glycopyrrolate may provide some protection against aspiration of gastric contents during anesthesia.

Rhinitis, allergic, severe (treatment)—In acute rhinitis, oral hyoscyamine is indicated as a "drying agent."

[Salivation, excessive, post-surgical (prophylaxis)][1]; or

[Salivation, excessive, medical condition-related (prophylaxis)][1]—Transdermal scopolamine is used for short-term control of drooling in post-surgical patients and in patients with goiter or other medical conditions in whom excessive salivation becomes a social problem.

[Salivation, excessive, in dental procedures (prophylaxis)][1]—The oral forms of atropine and belladonna are used to control excessive salivation that interferes with dental procedures.

[Diarrhea (treatment)][1]—Glycopyrrolate, in individually titrated doses, has been used for severe abdominal cramping and diarrhea.

Unaccepted

Hyoscyamine elixir and oral solution have been used in the treatment of infant colic. However, there is no conclusive evidence of effectiveness for this use.

In parkinsonism, atropine and parenteral hyoscyamine have been used to reduce rigidity and tremors, and control associated sialorrhea and hyperhidrosis. The hyoscyamine and scopolamine combination and large doses of belladonna may also produce symptomatic relief in the treatment of parkinsonism. In addition, oral scopolamine has been used in the symptomatic treatment of postencephalitic parkinsonism and paralysis agitans, and spastic states. However, belladonna alkaloids have generally been replaced by more effective agents for these uses.

---

[1]Not included in Canadian product labeling.

Pharmacology

Mechanism of action/Effect:

Anticholinergic—The naturally occurring belladonna alkaloids, semisynthetic derivatives, quaternary ammonium compounds, and, to a lesser extent, the synthetic tertiary amines inhibit the muscarinic actions of acetylcholine on structures innervated by postganglionic cholinergic nerves as well as on smooth muscles that respond to acetylcholine but lack cholinergic innervation. These postganglionic receptor sites are present in the autonomic effector cells of the smooth muscle, cardiac muscle, sinoatrial and atrioventricular nodes, and exocrine glands. Depending on the dose, anticholinergics may reduce the motility and secretory activity of the gastrointestinal system, and the tone of the ureter and urinary bladder and may have a slight relaxant action on the bile ducts and gallbladder. In general, the smaller doses of anticholinergics inhibit salivary and bronchial secretions, sweating, and accommodation; cause dilatation of the pupil; and increase the heart rate. Larger doses are required to decrease motility of the gastrointestinal and urinary tracts and to inhibit gastric acid secretion.

Antispasmodic, gastrointestinal—Unproven. A local and direct action on smooth muscle, to reduce tone and motility of the gastrointestinal tract, has been suggested to explain the apparent gastrointestinal antispasmodic effect of the synthetic tertiary amine compounds.

Antidysmenorrheal—Effectiveness in relieving dysmenorrhea is due to spasmolytic action.

Antiarrhythmic—Inhibition of muscarinic actions of acetylcholine at postganglionic receptor sites present in the autonomic effector cells of the cardiac muscle, and sinoatrial and atrioventricular nodes.

Antidote (to cholinesterase inhibitors; to muscarine; to organophosphate pesticides)—Atropine and hyoscyamine antagonize the actions of cholinesterase inhibitors at muscarinic receptor sites, including increased tracheobronchial and salivary secretion, bronchoconstriction, autonomic ganglionic stimulation, and, to a moderate extent, central actions.

Cholinergic adjunct (curariform block)—Atropine and hyoscyamine antagonize the actions, such as vagal and secretory enhancing effects, of cholinesterase inhibitors used in the treatment of nondepolarizing neuromuscular blockade.

Anesthesia adjunct—Scopolamine depresses the cerebral cortex; in large doses and in conjunction with analgesics, produces loss of memory.

Antiemetic—Belladonna and scopolamine act primarily by reducing the excitability of the labyrinthine receptors and by depressing conduction in the vestibular cerebellar pathway.

Antivertigo—The exact mechanism by which belladonna and scopolamine exert their antimotion sickness and antivertigo effects is unknown; however, they probably act either on the cortex or more peripherally on the maculae of the utricle and saccule.

Antidiarrheal—Glycopyrrolate may reduce the activity of the gastrocolic reflex and the excessive peristaltic activity of both the small and large bowels.

Other actions/effects:

Natural tertiary amines—

Atropine: Stimulates or depresses the central nervous system (CNS), depending on the dose; and has a more prolonged and potent action than the other belladonna alkaloids on the heart, intestine, and bronchial muscle.

Belladonna alkaloids: In parkinsonism, selectively depress certain central motor mechanisms in the CNS, controlling muscle tone and movement.

Hyoscyamine: Has actions similar to those of atropine, but is more potent in both its central and peripheral effects.

Scopolamine: Has peripheral action similar to that of atropine but, in contrast to atropine, is depressant to the CNS at therapeutic doses; it does not stimulate the medullary centers and therefore does not increase respiration or elevate blood pressure. Scopolamine has a more potent action than atropine on the sphincter muscle of the iris and the ciliary muscle of the lens, and on the secretory glands such as salivary, bronchial, and sweat glands.

Quaternary ammonium compounds, semisynthetic and synthetic— In contrast to atropine and scopolamine, effects of these medications on the CNS are negligible. These medications are also less likely to affect the pupil or ciliary muscle of the eye. Ganglionic blockade is attributed to some increased effects of the high dosage range, and toxic doses produce neuromuscular blockade.

Synthetic tertiary amines—These medications produce less prominent CNS effects than do the natural tertiary amines.

Time to peak effect: Glycopyrrolate—Intramuscular: 30 to 45 minutes.

Drug	Onset of Action	Duration of Action	Elimination (% excreted unchanged)
Anisotropine methylbromide			*
Atropine		Oral: 4–6 hr Parenteral: Brief	Renal (30–50)
Belladonna	1–2 hr	4 hr	Renal (30–50 of atropine and 1 of scopolamine)
Clidinium bromide	1 hr	Up to 3 hr	*
Dicyclomine hydrochloride			*
Glycopyrrolate	IM or SC: 15–30 min IV: 1 min	Antisialagogue: Up to 7 hr Vagal blocking effect: 2–3 hr	Renal
Homatropine			*
Hyoscyamine sulfate	Oral: 20–30 min Parenteral: 2–3 min	4–6 hr	Renal (majority)
Isopropamide iodide		10–12 hr	*
Mepenzolate bromide			Renal (3–22)
Methantheline bromide			*
Methscopolamine bromide	1 hr	6–8 hr	*
Oxyphencyclimine hydrochloride	1–2 hr	>12 hr	*
Pirenzepine hydrochloride			Renal/hepatic (80–90)
Propantheline bromide		6 hr	Renal (<6)
Scopolamine		Transdermal: Up to 72 hr	Renal
Scopolamine hydrobromide	Antisialagogue— Oral: 30–60 min Parenteral: 30 min	Oral: 4–6 hr Parenteral: 4 hr	Renal (1 of oral dose) (3.4 of SC dose)
Tridihexethyl			*

*Assumed to be renal/fecal.

Precautions to Consider

Cross-sensitivity and/or related problems

For all anticholinergics—Patients sensitive to one belladonna alkaloid or derivative may be sensitive to the other belladonna alkaloids or derivatives also.

For isopropamide—Patients sensitive to inorganic iodides or iodine may be sensitive to this medication also.

Geriatrics

Geriatric patients may respond to usual doses of anticholinergics with excitement, agitation, drowsiness, or confusion.

Geriatric patients are especially susceptible to the anticholinergic side effects, such as constipation, dryness of mouth, and urinary retention (especially in males). If these side effects occur and continue or are severe, medication should probably be discontinued.

Caution is also recommended when anticholinergics are given to geriatric patients, because of the danger of precipitating undiagnosed glaucoma.

Memory may become severely impaired in geriatric patients, especially those who already have memory problems, with the continued use of anticholinergics since these drugs block the actions of acetylcholine, which is responsible for many functions of the brain, including memory functions.

Dental

Prolonged use of anticholinergics may decrease or inhibit salivary flow, thus contributing to the development of caries, periodontal disease, oral candidiasis, and discomfort.

Drug interactions and/or related problems

The following drug interactions and/or related problems have been selected on the basis of their potential clinical significance (possible mechanism in parentheses where appropriate)—not necessarily inclusive (» = major clinical significance):

Note: Combinations containing any of the following medications, depending on the amount present, may also interact with this medication.

Only specific interactions between anticholinergics and other oral medications have been identified in this monograph. However, because of decreased gastrointestinal motility and delayed gastric emptying, absorption of other oral medications may be decreased during concurrent use with anticholinergics.

For all anticholinergics

Alkalizers, urinary, such as:
Antacids, calcium- and/or magnesium-containing
Carbonic anhydrase inhibitors
Citrates
Sodium bicarbonate
(urinary excretion of anticholinergics may be delayed by alkalinization of the urine, thus potentiating the anticholinergics' therapeutic and/or side effects)

» Antacids or
» Antidiarrheals, adsorbent
(simultaneous use of these medications may reduce absorption of anticholinergics, resulting in decreased therapeutic effectiveness; doses of these medications should be spaced 2 or 3 hours apart from doses of anticholinergics)
» Anticholinergics or other medications with anticholinergic activity, other
(concurrent use with anticholinergics may intensify anticholinergic effects; patients should be advised to report occurrence of gastrointestinal problems promptly since paralytic ileus may occur with concurrent therapy)
Antimyasthenics
(concurrent use with anticholinergics may further reduce intestinal motility; therefore, caution is recommended; although atropine may be used to reduce or prevent the muscarinic effects of antimyasthenics, routine concurrent use is not recommended since the muscarinic effects may be the first signs of antimyasthenic overdose, and masking such effects with atropine may prevent early recognition of cholinergic crisis)
» Cyclopropane
(concurrent intravenous administration of anticholinergics with cyclopropane anesthesia may result in ventricular arrhythmias; however, if the anticholinergic used is glycopyrrolate, the risk is reduced if glycopyrrolate is given in increments of 100 mcg [0.1 mg] or less)
Haloperidol
(antipsychotic effectiveness of haloperidol may be decreased in schizophrenic patients)
» Ketoconazole
(anticholinergics may increase gastrointestinal pH, possibly resulting in a marked reduction in ketoconazole absorption during concurrent use with anticholinergics; patients should be advised to take these medications at least 2 hours after ketoconazole)
Metoclopramide
(concurrent use with anticholinergics may antagonize metoclopramide's effects on gastrointestinal motility)
Opioid (narcotic) analgesics
(concurrent use with anticholinergics may result in increased risk of severe constipation, which may lead to paralytic ileus, and/or urinary retention)
» Potassium chloride, especially wax-matrix preparations
(concurrent use with anticholinergics may increase severity of potassium chloride-induced gastrointestinal lesions)
For scopolamine (in addition to interactions listed above)
» CNS depression-producing medications, other
(concurrent use may potentiate the effects of either these medications or scopolamine, resulting in additive sedation)
Lorazepam, parenteral
(concurrent use of scopolamine and parenteral lorazepam is reported to have no added beneficial effect and their combined effect may increase the incidence of sedation, hallucination, and irritational behavior)

Contraindications/Medical problems

The contraindications/medical problems included have been selected on the basis of their potential clinical significance (reasons given in parentheses where appropriate)—not necessarily inclusive (» = major clinical significance).

Risk-benefit should be considered when the following medical problems exist:

Brain damage, in children
(CNS effects may be exacerbated)
» Cardiac disease, especially cardiac arrhythmias, congestive heart failure, coronary artery disease, and mitral stenosis
(increase in heart rate may be undesirable)

Down's syndrome (mongolism)
(abnormal increase in pupillary dilation and acceleration of heart rate may occur)
» Esophagitis, reflux
(decrease in esophageal and gastric motility and relaxation of lower esophageal sphincter may promote gastric retention by delaying gastric emptying and may increase gastroesophageal reflux through an incompetent sphincter)
Fever
(may be increased through suppression of sweat gland activity)
» Gastrointestinal tract obstructive disease as in achalasia and pyloroduodenal stenosis
(decrease in motility and tone may occur, resulting in obstruction and gastric retention)
» Glaucoma, angle-closure, or predisposition to
(mydriatic effect resulting in increased intraocular pressure may precipitate an acute attack of angle-closure glaucoma)
» Glaucoma, open-angle
(mydriatic effect may cause a slight increase in intraocular pressure; glaucoma therapy may need to be adjusted)
» Hemorrhage, acute, with unstable cardiovascular status
(increase in heart rate may be undesirable)
Hepatic function impairment
(decreased metabolism of anticholinergic)
» Hernia, hiatal, associated with reflux esophagitis
(anticholinergics may aggravate condition)
Hypertension
(may be aggravated)
Hyperthyroidism
(characterized by tachycardia, which may be increased)
» Intestinal atony in the elderly or debilitated patient or
» Paralytic ileus
(anticholinergic use may result in obstruction)
Lung disease, chronic, especially in infants, small children, and debilitated patients
(reduction in bronchial secretion can lead to inspissation and formation of bronchial plugs)
» Myasthenia gravis
(condition may be aggravated because of inhibition of acetylcholine action)
Neuropathy, autonomic
(urinary retention and cycloplegia may be aggravated)
» Prostatic hypertrophy, nonobstructive, or
» Urinary retention, or predisposition to, or
» Uropathy, obstructive, such as bladder neck obstruction due to prostatic hypertrophy
(urinary retention may be precipitated or aggravated)
» Pyloric obstruction
(may be aggravated)
Renal function impairment
(decreased excretion may increase the risk of side effects)
Sensitivity to any belladonna alkaloids or derivatives
Spastic paralysis, in children
(response to anticholinergics may be increased)
» Tachycardia
(may be increased)
Toxemia of pregnancy
(hypertension may be aggravated)
» Ulcerative colitis
(large anticholinergic doses may suppress intestinal motility, possibly causing paralytic ileus; also, use may precipitate or aggravate the serious complication, toxic megacolon)
Xerostomia
(prolonged use may further reduce limited salivary flow)

Caution in use is also recommended in patients over 40 years of age because of the danger of precipitating undiagnosed glaucoma.

Side/Adverse Effects

Note: When anticholinergics are given to patients, especially children, where the environmental temperature is high, there is risk of a rapid increase in body temperature because of suppression of sweat gland activity.

Infants, patients with Down's syndrome, and children with spastic paralysis or brain damage may show an increased response to anticholinergics, thus increasing the potential for side effects.

Geriatric or debilitated patients may respond to usual doses of anticholinergics with excitement, agitation, drowsiness, or confusion.

Following use of the transdermal disk of scopolamine, a dilated and fixed pupil has been reported on the side where the disk was worn. This condition usually resolves spontaneously within a few days, but may persist for up to 2 weeks after the disk has been removed and thus may be mistaken for a sign of intracranial neoplasm, subdural hematoma, or aneurysm. To avoid extensive neuroradiological tests, instillation of 1% pilocarpine solution is recommended as an aid in the diagnosis of nonneurogenic dilation of the pupil.

See also *Table 1*, page 85.

Patient Consultation

In providing consultation, consider emphasizing the following selected information (» = major clinical significance):

Before using this medication
» Conditions affecting use, especially:
   Sensitivity to any of the belladonna alkaloids or derivatives; sensitivity to iodine (with isopropamide only)
   Breast-feeding—Excreted in breast milk (except for quaternary ammonium compounds); possible inhibition of lactation
   Use in children—Increased susceptibility to toxic effects of anticholinergics; increased response in infants and children with spastic paralysis or brain damage; risk of increased body temperature in hot weather; hyperexcitability (paradoxical reaction) with large doses; increased risk of respiratory depression and collapse (with dicyclomine)
   Use in the elderly—Increased susceptibility to mental and other toxic effects of anticholinergics; danger of precipitating undiagnosed glaucoma; possible impairment of memory
   Use by athletes—Antiemetics, including scopolamine, are banned and, in some cases, tested for in competitors in biathlon and modern pentathlon events by the U.S. Olympic Committee (USOC)
   Dental—Possible development of dental problems because of decreased salivary flow
   Other medications, especially other anticholinergics, antacids, antidiarrheals, cyclopropane, ketoconazole, CNS depressants (with scopolamine), and potassium chloride
   Other medical problems, especially cardiac disease, glaucoma, hemorrhage, hiatal hernia, intestinal atony or paralytic ileus, myasthenia gravis, obstruction in gastrointestinal or urinary tract, prostatic hypertrophy, reflux esophagitis, tachycardia, and ulcerative colitis

Proper use of this medication
» Importance of not taking more medication than the amount prescribed
   Missed dose: Taking as soon as possible; not taking if almost time for next dose; not doubling doses
» Proper storage

For oral dosage forms
   Taking medication 30 minutes to 1 hour before meals
For rectal dosage forms
   Proper administration technique
For transdermal scopolamine
   Reading patient directions
   Washing and drying hands thoroughly before and after application
   Applying to hairless, intact area of skin behind ear; not applying over cuts or irritations

Precautions while using this medication
» Suspected overdose: Getting emergency help at once
» Caution during exercise or hot weather; overheating may result in heat stroke
» Possible increased sensitivity of eyes to light
   Caution about abrupt withdrawal
» Caution if blurred vision occurs
» Possible dizziness or drowsiness; caution when driving or doing things requiring alertness
   Possible dizziness or lightheadedness; caution when getting up suddenly from a lying or sitting position
   Possible dryness of mouth; using sugarless candy or gum, ice or saliva substitute for relief; checking with physician or dentist if dry mouth continues for more than 2 weeks
For isopropamide
   Possible interference with thyroid tests
For scopolamine
» Avoiding use of alcohol or other CNS depressants
For oral dosage forms
   Avoiding use of antacids and antidiarrheal medications within 2 or 3 hours of taking this medication

Side/adverse effects
   Signs of potential side effects, especially allergic reaction, confusion, increased intraocular pressure, orthostatic hypotension (especially with high doses of quaternary ammonium compounds)

General Dosing Information

Tolerance to some of the adverse reactions may develop following continued use and/or smaller doses of anticholinergics, but effectiveness may also be reduced.

Dosage adjustments are often required for infants, patients with Down's syndrome, children with brain damage or spasticity, since an increased responsiveness to anticholinergics has been reported in these patients.

Geriatric and debilitated patients may respond to usual doses with excitement, agitation, drowsiness, or confusion; lower doses may be required in these patients.

Anticholinergics should not be withdrawn abruptly since withdrawal-like symptoms may occur. Vomiting, malaise, sweating, transient dizziness, and salivation have been reported after sudden withdrawal of large doses of scopolamine.

If scopolamine is used as antisialagogue preanesthetic medication in minor surgical procedures that do not require more than a few hours' stay in the hospital, the patient should be alerted at time of discharge about scopolamine's lingering detrimental effects on memory and motor tasks.

High dosage of quaternary ammonium compounds should not be given continuously for prolonged periods, since ganglionic and skeletal neuromuscular transmission may be blocked. Stimulation of the CNS and a curare-like action may result.

For oral dosage forms only
Administration of anticholinergics 30 minutes to 1 hour before meals is recommended to maximize absorption.

For parenteral dosage forms only
Atropine, hyoscyamine, and scopolamine may be administered by intramuscular, subcutaneous, or intravenous injection.

Glycopyrrolate may be administered by intramuscular or intravenous injection.

After parenteral administration a temporary feeling of lightheadedness and local irritation may occur.

For transdermal dosage forms only

Transdermal application delivers reduced doses of scopolamine, which are large enough to be effective but small enough to eliminate most of the adverse effects, except drowsiness and cycloplegia.

ANISOTROPINE

Oral Dosage Forms

ANISOTROPINE METHYLBROMIDE TABLETS

Usual adult and adolescent dose: Anticholinergic—Oral, 50 mg three times a day, the dosage being adjusted as needed and tolerated.

Note: Geriatric patients may be more sensitive to the effects of the usual adult dose.

Auxiliary labeling: • May cause blurred vision.

ATROPINE

Summary of Differences

Category: Also an antidote (to cholinesterase inhibitors; to organophosphate pesticides; to muscarine) and a urinary antispasmodic. Parenteral atropine is used as an antiarrhythmic and cholinergic adjunct (curariform block).

Indications: Also indicated for biliary tract disorders and duodenography. In preanesthesia and dental anesthesia, indicated as antisialagogue.

Pharmacology:
   Protein binding—Moderate.
   Half-life (elimination)—2.5 hours.
   Duration of action—Oral, 4 to 6 hours; parenteral, brief.
   Elimination—Renal; 30 to 50% excreted unchanged.

Precautions:
   Pregnancy—Intravenous administration may produce tachycardia in fetus.
   Laboratory value alterations—May decrease excretion of phenolsulfonphthalein (PSP) during PSP excretion test.

Additional Dosing Information

See also *General Dosing Information.*

Doses of 0.5 to 1 mg of atropine are mildly stimulating to the CNS. Larger doses may produce mental disturbances; very large doses have depressant effect.

The fatal dose of atropine in children may be as low as 10 mg.

Oral Dosage Forms

ATROPINE SULFATE TABLETS USP

Usual adult and adolescent dose: Anticholinergic—Oral, 300 mcg (0.3 mg) to 1.2 mg every four to six hours.
   Prophylaxis of excessive salivation and respiratory tract secretions, in anesthesia: Oral, 2 mg.

Note: Geriatric patients may be more sensitive to the effects of the usual adult dose.

Auxiliary labeling: • May cause blurred vision.

ATROPINE SULFATE SOLUBLE TABLETS

Usual adult and adolescent dose: Anticholinergic—Oral, 300 mcg (0.3 mg) to 1.2 mg every four to six hours.
   Prophylaxis of excessive salivation and respiratory tract secretions, in anesthesia: Oral, 2 mg.

Note: Geriatric patients may be more sensitive to the effects of the usual adult dose.

Auxiliary labeling: • May cause blurred vision.

Parenteral Dosage Forms

ATROPINE SULFATE INJECTION USP

Usual adult and adolescent dose:
   Anticholinergic—Intramuscular, intravenous, or subcutaneous, 400 to 600 mcg (0.4 to 0.6 mg) every four to six hours.
   Gastrointestinal radiography: Intramuscular, 1 mg.
   Prophylaxis of excessive salivation and respiratory tract secretions, in anesthesia: Intramuscular, 200 to 600 mcg (0.2 to 0.6 mg) one-half to one hour before surgery.
   Antiarrhythmic—Intravenous, 400 mcg (0.4 mg) to 1 mg every one to two hours as needed, up to a maximum of 2 mg.
   Cholinergic adjunct (curariform block)—Intravenous, 600 mcg (0.6 mg) to 1.2 mg administered a few minutes before or concurrently with 500 mcg (0.5 mg) to 2 mg of neostigmine methylsulfate, using separate syringes.
   Antidote (to cholinesterase inhibitors)—Intravenous, 2 to 4 mg initially, then 2 mg repeated every five to ten minutes until muscarinic symptoms disappear or signs of atropine toxicity appear.
   Antidote (to muscarine in mushroom poisoning)—Intramuscular or intravenous, 1 to 2 mg every hour until respiratory effects subside.
   Antidote (to organophosphate pesticides)—Intramuscular or intravenous, 1 to 2 mg, repeated in twenty to thirty minutes as soon as cyanosis has cleared. Continue dosage until definite improvement occurs and is maintained, sometimes for two days or more.

Note: Geriatric patients may be more sensitive to the effects of the usual adult dose.

Additional information: The intravenous injection of atropine should be administered *slowly.*

BELLADONNA

Summary of Differences

Category: Also an antidysmenorrheal and antivertigo agent.

Indications: Also indicated in nocturnal enuresis. In dental procedures, may be used as antisialagogue.

Pharmacology:
   Onset of action—1 to 2 hours.
   Duration of action—4 hours.
   Elimination—Renal; 30 to 50% of atropine and 1% of scopolamine excreted unchanged.

Oral Dosage Forms

BELLADONNA TINCTURE USP

Usual adult and adolescent dose: Anticholinergic—Oral, 180 to 300 mcg (0.18 to 0.3 mg) three or four times a day, thirty minutes to one hour before meals and at bedtime, the dosage being adjusted as needed and tolerated.

Note: Geriatric patients may be more sensitive to the effects of the usual adult dose.

Auxiliary labeling:
- May cause blurred vision.
- Keep container tightly closed.

CLIDINIUM

Summary of Differences

Pharmacology:
 Onset of action—1 hour.
 Duration of action—Up to 3 hours.

Oral Dosage Forms

CLIDINIUM BROMIDE CAPSULES USP

Usual adult and adolescent dose: Anticholinergic—Oral, 2.5 to 5 mg three or four times a day, before meals and at bedtime, the dosage being adjusted as needed and tolerated.

Note: Geriatric or debilitated patients—Oral, 2.5 mg three times a day before meals.

Auxiliary labeling: • May cause blurred vision.

DICYCLOMINE

Summary of Differences

Category: Also gastrointestinal antispasmodic.
Indications: Not indicated for peptic ulcer.
Pharmacology: Half-life (elimination)—1.8 hours (initial phase) and 9 to 10 hours (secondary phase).
Precautions: Pediatrics—Respiratory symptoms, seizures, syncope, asphyxia, pulse rate fluctuations, muscular hypotonia, and coma reported with the use of the syrup in some infants 3 months old and under.

Oral Dosage Forms

DICYCLOMINE HYDROCHLORIDE CAPSULES USP

Usual adult and adolescent dose: Antispasmodic, gastrointestinal—Irritable bowel syndrome: Oral, 10 to 20 mg three or four times a day, the dosage being adjusted as needed and tolerated.

Note: Geriatric patients may be more sensitive to the effects of the usual adult dose.

Usual adult prescribing limits: Up to 160 mg daily.

Auxiliary labeling: • May cause blurred vision.

DICYCLOMINE HYDROCHLORIDE SYRUP USP

Usual adult and adolescent dose: Antispasmodic, gastrointestinal—Irritable bowel syndrome: Oral, 10 to 20 mg three or four times a day, the dosage being adjusted as needed and tolerated.

Note: Geriatric patients may be more sensitive to the effects of the usual adult dose.

Usual adult prescribing limits: Up to 160 mg daily.

Auxiliary labeling: • May cause blurred vision.

DICYCLOMINE HYDROCHLORIDE TABLETS USP

Usual adult and adolescent dose: Antispasmodic, gastrointestinal—Irritable bowel syndrome: Oral, 10 to 20 mg three or four times a day, the dosage being adjusted as needed and tolerated.

Note: Geriatric patients may be more sensitive to the effects of the usual adult dose.

Usual adult prescribing limits: Up to 160 mg daily.

Auxiliary labeling: • May cause blurred vision.

DICYCLOMINE HYDROCHLORIDE EXTENDED-RELEASE TABLETS

Usual adult and adolescent dose: Antispasmodic, gastrointestinal—Oral, 30 mg two times a day.

Note: Geriatric patients may be more sensitive to the effects of the usual adult dose.

Auxiliary labeling: • May cause blurred vision.

Parenteral Dosage Forms

DICYCLOMINE HYDROCHLORIDE INJECTION USP

Usual adult and adolescent dose: Antispasmodic, gastrointestinal—Irritable bowel syndrome: Intramuscular, 20 mg every four to six hours, the dosage being adjusted as needed and tolerated.

Note: Not for intravenous use.
 Geriatric patients may be more sensitive to the effects of the usual adult dose.

GLYCOPYRROLATE

Summary of Differences

Category: Also, an [antidiarrheal]. Parenteral glycopyrrolate is used as an antiarrhythmic and cholinergic adjunct (curariform block).
Indications: Indicated as antisialagogue in preanesthesia. Also, indicated as antiarrhythmic in preanesthesia, anesthesia, and surgery. In addition, indicated to prevent aspiration pneumonitis during anesthesia. May be used as antidiarrheal and for cholinesterase inhibitor toxicity.
Pharmacology:
 Half-life (elimination)—1.7 hours (range 0.6-4.6 hours).
 Onset of action—15 to 30 minutes with intramuscular or subcutaneous administration; 1 minute with intravenous administration.
 Duration of action—Antisialagogue effect up to 7 hours; vagal blocking effect 2 to 3 hours.
Precautions:
 Pregnancy—Rates of conception and survival at weaning decreased in studies with rats.
 Laboratory value alterations—Serum uric acid may be decreased in patients with hyperuricemia or gout.

Oral Dosage Forms

GLYCOPYRROLATE TABLETS USP

Usual adult and adolescent dose: Anticholinergic—Peptic ulcer: Oral, initially 1 to 2 mg two or three times a day and occasionally 2 mg at bedtime, then 1 mg two times a day, the dosage being adjusted as needed and tolerated.

Note: Geriatric patients may be more sensitive to the effects of the usual adult dose.

Usual adult prescribing limits: Up to 8 mg daily.

Auxiliary labeling: • May cause blurred vision.

Parenteral Dosage Forms

GLYCOPYRROLATE INJECTION USP

Usual adult and adolescent dose:
Anticholinergic—
Peptic ulcer: Intramuscular or intravenous, 100 to 200 mcg (0.1 to 0.2 mg), the dosage being repeated, if necessary, at four-hour intervals up to a maximum of four times a day.
Prophylaxis of excessive salivation and respiratory tract secretions, in anesthesia; and
Prophylaxis of gastric hypersecretory conditions, in anesthesia: Intramuscular, 4.4 mcg (0.0044 mg) per kg of body weight one-half to one hour before induction of anesthesia or at the time the preanesthetic narcotic and/or sedative are administered.
Antiarrhythmic, in anesthesia; or
Antiarrhythmic, in surgery—Intravenous, 100 mcg (0.1 mg), the dosage being repeated if necessary at two- to three-minute intervals.
Cholinergic adjunct (curariform block)—Intravenous, 200 mcg (0.2 mg) for each 1 mg of neostigmine or 5 mg of pyridostigmine given simultaneously; may be mixed in the same syringe.

Note: Geriatric patients may be more sensitive to the effects of the usual adult dose.

HOMATROPINE

Oral Dosage Forms

HOMATROPINE METHYLBROMIDE TABLETS USP

Usual adult and adolescent dose: Anticholinergic—Oral, 5 to 10 mg three or four times a day, the dosage being adjusted as needed and tolerated.

Note: Geriatric patients may be more sensitive to the effects of the usual adult dose.

Auxiliary labeling: • May cause blurred vision.

HYOSCYAMINE

Summary of Differences

Category: Parenteral hyoscyamine is also an antiarrhythmic, antidote (to cholinesterase inhibitors and to muscarine), and a cholinergic adjunct (curariform block).
Indications: Also indicated for biliary disorders, cystitis, duodenography, and acute rhinitis. In preanesthesia, indicated as antisialagogue and also as antiarrhythmic during anesthesia and surgery.
Pharmacology:
Protein binding—Moderate.
Half-life (elimination)—3.5 hours.
Onset of action—20 to 30 minutes with oral administration of hyoscyamine sulfate; 2 to 3 minutes with parenteral administration.
Duration of action—4 to 6 hours.
Elimination—Renal; majority of drug excreted unchanged.
Precautions: Pregnancy—Intravenous administration may produce tachycardia in fetus.
Side/adverse effects: Constipation has been reported less often with hyoscyamine.

Additional Dosing Information

See also *General Dosing Information.*
Hyoscyamine is effective at half the dosage of atropine.
In dehydrated patients, such as those with diarrhea and vomiting, treatment with hyoscyamine should be initiated at a lower dosage.

Oral Dosage Forms

HYOSCYAMINE TABLETS USP

Usual adult and adolescent dose: Anticholinergic—Oral, 125 to 500 mcg (0.125 to 0.5 mg) three or four times a day, thirty minutes to one hour before meals and at bedtime, the dosage being adjusted as needed and tolerated.

Note: Geriatric patients may be more sensitive to the effects of the usual adult dose.

Auxiliary labeling: • May cause blurred vision.

HYOSCYAMINE SULFATE EXTENDED-RELEASE CAPSULES

Usual adult and adolescent dose: Anticholinergic—Oral, 375 mcg (0.375 mg) two times a day, in the morning and at bedtime, the dosage being increased, if necessary, to obtain the desired response.

Note: Geriatric patients may be more sensitive to the effects of the usual adult dose.

Auxiliary labeling:
• Swallow capsules whole.
• May cause blurred vision.

HYOSCYAMINE SULFATE ELIXIR USP

Usual adult and adolescent dose: Anticholinergic—Oral, 125 to 250 mcg (0.125 to 0.25 mg) every four to six hours, the dosage being adjusted as needed and tolerated.

Note: Geriatric patients may be more sensitive to the effects of the usual adult dose.

Auxiliary labeling:
• May cause blurred vision.
• Keep container tightly closed.

HYOSCYAMINE SULFATE ORAL SOLUTION USP

Usual adult and adolescent dose: Anticholinergic—Oral, 125 to 250 mcg (0.125 to 0.25 mg) every four to six hours, the dosage being adjusted as needed and tolerated.

Note: Geriatric patients may be more sensitive to the effects of the usual adult dose.

Auxiliary labeling:
• May cause blurred vision.
• Keep container tightly closed.

Note: Dispense in dropper bottle.

HYOSCYAMINE SULFATE TABLETS USP

Usual adult and adolescent dose: Anticholinergic—Oral or sublingual, 125 to 500 mcg (0.125 to 0.5 mg) three or four times a day, thirty minutes to one hour before meals and at bedtime, the dosage being adjusted as needed and tolerated.

Note: Geriatric patients may be more sensitive to the effects of the usual adult dose.

Auxiliary labeling:
• May be chewed, swallowed whole, or allowed to dissolve under the tongue.
• May cause blurred vision.

Parenteral Dosage Forms

HYOSCYAMINE SULFATE INJECTION USP

Usual adult and adolescent dose:

Anticholinergic—Intramuscular, intravenous, or subcutaneous, 250 to 500 mcg (0.25 to 0.5 mg) every four to six hours.

Gastrointestinal radiography: Intramuscular, intravenous, or subcutaneous, 250 to 500 mcg (0.25 to 0.5 mg) five to ten minutes prior to the diagnostic procedure.

Peptic ulcer:
Initial—Intravenous, 250 to 500 mcg (0.25 to 0.5 mg).
Maintenance—Intramuscular or subcutaneous, 250 to 500 mcg (0.25 to 0.5 mg) every six hours until all pain has ceased.

Prophylaxis of excessive salivation and respiratory tract secretions, in anesthesia: Intramuscular, intravenous, or subcutaneous, 500 mcg (0.5 mg); or 5 mcg (0.005 mg) per kg of body weight thirty to sixty minutes before induction of anesthesia.

Antiarrhythmic—Intravenous, 125 mcg (0.125 mg), repeated as needed.

Cholinergic adjunct (curariform block)—Intravenous, 200 mcg (0.2 mg) for each 1 mg of neostigmine or the equivalent dose of physostigmine or pyridostigmine.

Note: Geriatric patients may be more sensitive to the effects of the usual adult dose.

ISOPROPAMIDE

Summary of Differences

Pharmacology: Duration of action—10 to 12 hours.
Cross-sensitivity and/or related problems: Sensitivity to inorganic iodides or iodine.
Precautions: Laboratory value alterations—May alter results of thyroid function tests; should be discontinued one week prior to test.

Oral Dosage Forms

ISOPROPAMIDE IODIDE TABLETS USP

Usual adult and adolescent dose: Anticholinergic—Oral, 5 mg (base) two times a day, the dosage being increased to 10 mg two times a day if needed and tolerated.

Note: Geriatric patients may be more sensitive to the effects of the usual adult dose.

Auxiliary labeling: • May cause blurred vision.

MEPENZOLATE

Summary of Differences

Pharmacology: Elimination—Renal; 3 to 22% excreted unchanged.
Precautions: Pregnancy—Reproduction studies in rats and rabbits have not shown adverse effects on fetus.

Oral Dosage Forms

MEPENZOLATE BROMIDE TABLETS USP

Usual adult and adolescent dose: Anticholinergic—Oral, 25 to 50 mg four times a day with meals and at bedtime, the dosage being adjusted as needed and tolerated.

Note: Geriatric patients may be more sensitive to the effects of the usual adult dose.

Auxiliary labeling: • May cause blurred vision.

METHANTHELINE

Summary of Differences

Indications: Also indicated for urinary incontinence.

Oral Dosage Forms

METHANTHELINE BROMIDE TABLETS USP

Usual adult and adolescent dose: Anticholinergic—Oral, 50 to 100 mg every six hours, the dosage being adjusted as needed and tolerated.

Note: Geriatric patients may be more sensitive to the effects of the usual adult dose.

Auxiliary labeling: • May cause blurred vision.

METHSCOPOLAMINE

Summary of Differences

Pharmacology:
Onset of action—1 hour.
Duration of action—6 to 8 hours.

Oral Dosage Forms

METHSCOPOLAMINE BROMIDE TABLETS USP

Usual adult and adolescent dose: Anticholinergic—Oral, 2.5 mg four times a day, one-half hour before meals and 2.5 to 5 mg at bedtime.

For severe symptoms: Oral, initially 5 mg four times a day, one-half hour before meals and at bedtime, the dosage being increased, if necessary, to obtain the desired response.

Note: Geriatric patients may be more sensitive to the effects of the usual adult dose.

Auxiliary labeling: • May cause blurred vision.

OXYPHENCYCLIMINE

Summary of Differences

Category: Also an antispasmodic.
Pharmacology:
Onset of action—1 to 2 hours.
Duration of action—Greater than 12 hours.

Oral Dosage Forms

OXYPHENCYCLIMINE HYDROCHLORIDE TABLETS USP

Usual adult and adolescent dose: Anticholinergic—Oral, 5 to 10 mg two or three times a day, in the morning and at bedtime, the dosage being adjusted as needed.

Note: Geriatric patients may be more sensitive to the effects of the usual adult dose.

Auxiliary labeling: • May cause blurred vision.

PIRENZEPINE

Summary of Differences

Pharmacology:
Half-life (elimination)—10 to 12 hours.
Elimination—Renal and hepatic; 80 to 90% of drug excreted unchanged.

Oral Dosage Forms

PIRENZEPINE HYDROCHLORIDE TABLETS

Usual adult and adolescent dose: Anticholinergic—Oral, 50 mg two times a day, in the morning and at bedtime, the dosage being increased to three times a day, if needed and tolerated.

Note: Geriatric patients may be more sensitive to the effects of the usual adult dose.

Auxiliary labeling: • May cause blurred vision.

PROPANTHELINE

Summary of Differences

Indications: Also used for duodenography and urinary incontinence.
Pharmacology:
Half-life (elimination)—1.6 (mean) hours.
Duration of action—6 hours.
Elimination—Renal; less than 6% of drug excreted unchanged.

Oral Dosage Forms

PROPANTHELINE BROMIDE TABLETS USP

Usual adult and adolescent dose: Anticholinergic—Oral, 15 mg three times a day, one-half hour before meals, and 30 mg at bedtime, the dosage being adjusted as needed and tolerated.

Note: Patients of less than average body weight may require only 7.5 mg three or four times a day.

Usual adult prescribing limits: Up to 120 mg daily.

Usual geriatric dose: Oral, 7.5 mg three or four times a day.

Auxiliary labeling: • May cause blurred vision.

SCOPOLAMINE

Summary of Differences

Category: Also a gastrointestinal antispasmodic, antidysmenorrheal, urinary antispasmodic, antiemetic, and antivertigo agent. Parenteral scopolamine is used as an antiarrhythmic and anesthesia adjunct.
Indications: Indicated in preanesthesia as antisialagogue. Also indicated for biliary tract disorders, nocturnal enuresis, and excessive salivation. Not indicated for peptic ulcer.
Pharmacology:
Protein binding—Scopolamine hydrobromide: Low.
Half-life (elimination)—8 hours.

Onset of action—
Oral scopolamine hydrobromide: 30 to 60 minutes (antisialagogue effect).
Parenteral scopolamine hydrobromide: 30 minutes (antisialagogue effect).
Duration of action—
Scopolamine hydrobromide:
Oral—4 to 6 hours.
Parenteral—4 hours.
Scopolamine: Transdermal—Up to 72 hours.
Elimination—Renal; 1% of oral dose excreted unchanged, and 3.4% of subcutaneous dose excreted unchanged.
Precautions:
Pregnancy—Parenteral administration before onset of labor may cause CNS depression and hemorrhage in neonate.
Drug interactions and/or related problems—Additive sedation with other CNS depressants.
Laboratory value alterations—Residual cycloplegia and mydriasis with transdermal dosage form may affect results of neuro-radiological tests for intracranial neoplasm, subdural hematoma, or cerebral aneurysm.
Side/adverse effects: Scopolamine has been reported to cause paradoxical reaction (trouble in sleeping). Anxiety, irritability, nightmares, and trouble in sleeping may indicate rebound reduction in rapid eye movement (REM) time. Drowsiness and a false sense of well being are more common also.

Additional Dosing Information

See also *General Dosing Information.*

In the presence of pain, scopolamine may act as a stimulant, often producing delirium, if used without morphine or meperidine.

Cardiac rate is much slower with low doses of scopolamine (0.1 to 0.2 mg) than with average clinical doses of atropine. With higher doses, a short-lived cardioacceleration occurs followed within 30 minutes by a return to the normal rate.

Oral Dosage Forms

SCOPOLAMINE BUTYLBROMIDE TABLETS

Usual adult and adolescent dose:
Anticholinergic; or
Antispasmodic, gastrointestinal; or
Antidysmenorrheal—Oral, 10 to 20 mg three or four times a day, the dosage being adjusted as needed and tolerated.

Note: Geriatric patients may be more sensitive to the effects of the usual adult dose.

Auxiliary labeling:
• May cause drowsiness or blurred vision.
• Avoid alcoholic beverages.

Parenteral Dosage Forms

SCOPOLAMINE BUTYLBROMIDE INJECTION

Usual adult and adolescent dose:
Anticholinergic; or
Antispasmodic, gastrointestinal—Intramuscular, intravenous, or subcutaneous, 10 to 20 mg three or four times a day, the dosage being adjusted as needed and tolerated.

SCOPOLAMINE HYDROBROMIDE INJECTION USP

Usual adult and adolescent dose:
Anticholinergic—Intramuscular, intravenous, or subcutaneous, 300 to 600 mcg (0.3 to 0.6 mg) as a single dose.
Prophylaxis of excessive salivation and respiratory tract secretions, in anesthesia: Intramuscular, 200 to 600 mcg (0.2 to 0.6 mg) one-half to one hour before induction of anesthesia.

Antiemetic—Intramuscular, intravenous, or subcutaneous, 300 to 600 mcg (0.3 to 0.6 mg) as a single dose.

Anesthesia adjunct—

Sedation-hypnosis: Intramuscular, intravenous, or subcutaneous, 600 mcg (0.6 mg) three or four times a day.

Amnesia: Intramuscular, intravenous, or subcutaneous, 320 to 650 mcg (0.32 to 0.65 mg).

Note: Geriatric patients may be more sensitive to the effects of the usual adult dose.

Rectal Dosage Forms

SCOPOLAMINE BUTYLBROMIDE SUPPOSITORIES

Usual adult and adolescent dose:

Anticholinergic; or

Antispasmodic, gastrointestinal; or

Antidysmenorrheal—Rectal, 10 mg three or four times a day, the dosage being adjusted as needed and tolerated.

Note: Geriatric patients may be more sensitive to the effects of the usual adult dose.

Auxiliary labeling: • May cause drowsiness or blurred vision.

Transdermal Dosage Forms

SCOPOLAMINE TRANSDERMAL SYSTEM

Usual adult and adolescent dose:

Antiemetic; or

Antivertigo agent—Topical, to the postauricular skin, 1 transdermal system delivering 500 mcg (0.5 mg) over a period of three days, applied at least four hours before antiemetic effect is required.

Note: Canadian brand product delivers 1.0 mg over a period of three days and should be applied approximately twelve hours before the antiemetic effect is required.

Geriatric patients may be more sensitive to the effects of the usual adult dose.

Auxiliary labeling: • May cause drowsiness or blurred vision.

TRIDIHEXETHYL

Oral Dosage Forms

TRIDIHEXETHYL CHLORIDE TABLETS USP

Usual adult and adolescent dose: Anticholinergic—Oral, 25 to 50 mg three or four times a day, before meals and at bedtime, the dosage being adjusted as needed and tolerated. The usual bedtime dose is 50 mg.

Note: Geriatric patients may be more sensitive to the effects of the usual adult dose.

Auxiliary labeling: • May cause blurred vision.

Table 1. Side/Adverse Effects*

Legend:
I = Anisotropine
II = Atropine
III = Belladonna
IV = Clidinium
V = Dicyclomine
VI = Glycopyrrolate
VII = Homatropine
VIII = Hyoscyamine
IX = Isopropamide
X = Mepenzolate
XI = Methantheline
XII = Methscopolamine
XIII = Oxyphencyclimine
XIV = Pirenzepine
XV = Propantheline
XVI = Scopolamine
XVII = Tridihexethyl

The following side/adverse effects have been selected on the basis of their potential clinical significance (possible signs and symptoms in parentheses where appropriate)—not necessarily inclusive:

Side/Adverse Effect	I	II	III	IV	V	VI	VII	VIII	IX	X	XI	XII	XIII	XIV	XV	XVI	XVII
Medical attention needed																	
Symptoms of overdose																	
Blurred vision, continuing, or changes in near vision†	✓	✓	✓	✓	✓	✓	✓	✓	✓	✓	✓	✓	✓	✓	✓	✓	✓
Clumsiness or unsteadiness†																	
Confusion†																	
Difficulty in breathing‡																	
Dizziness																	
Drowsiness†, severe																	
Dryness of mouth, nose, or throat, severe																	
Fast heartbeat																	
Fever																	
Hallucinations†																	
Muscle weakness‡, severe																	
Seizures†																	
Slurred speech																	
Tiredness‡, severe																	
Unusual excitement, nervousness, restlessness, or irritability†																	
Unusual warmth, dryness, and flushing of skin																	
Allergic reaction (skin rash or hives)	R	R	R	R	R	R	R	R	R	R	R	R	R	R	R	R	R
Confusion#	R	R	R	R	R	R	R	R	R	R	R	R	R	R	R	R	R
Increased intraocular pressure (eye pain)†	R	R	R	R	R	R	R	R	R	R	R	R	R	R	R	R	R
Orthostatic hypotension (dizziness, feeling faint, or continuing lightheadedness)	§	R	R	§	R	§	R	R	§	§	§	§	R	R	§	R	§
Medical attention needed only if continuing or bothersome																	
Bloated feeling	R	R	R	R	R	R	R	L	R	R	R	R	R	R	R	R	R
Constipation	M	M	M	M	M	M	M	M	M	M	M	M	M	M	M	M	M

* Differences in frequency of occurrence may reflect either lack of clinical-use data or actual pharmacologic distinctions among agents (although their pharmacologic similarity suggests that side effects occurring with one may occur with the others). M=more frequent; L=less frequent; R=rare; U=unknown.

† Quaternary ammonium compounds are fully ionized in the pH range of body fluids and possess reduced lipid solubility. Therefore, they penetrate cellular barriers less effectively and only pass across the blood-brain barrier or into the eye with difficulty. Central and ocular effects are negligible and/or less likely to occur with quaternary ammonium compounds.

‡ With quaternary ammonium compounds, difficulty in breathing, severe muscle weakness, and severe tiredness may occur because of the compounds' curare-like effects; these effects may lead to respiratory paralysis.

§ Orthostatic hypotension, due to ganglion-blocking activity, is more likely to occur with high doses of quaternary ammonium compounds.

Confusion may occur more frequently in geriatric patients.

** Difficult urination is more likely to occur in older men and may require medical attention in patients with symptoms of prostatism.

†† More frequent with high doses of anticholinergics, but a common side effect with therapeutic doses of oral or parenteral scopolamine.

‡‡ Scopolamine, administered parenterally as preanesthetic medication and/or given in large doses, may have a temporary but detrimental effect on memory. In geriatric patients, especially those who already have memory problems, the continued use of any anticholinergic may severely impair memory.

§§ May indicate rebound reduction in rapid eye movement (REM) time.

Table 1. Side/Adverse Effects* *(continued)*

Legend:
I = Anisotropine
II = Atropine
III = Belladonna
IV = Clidinium
V = Dicyclomine
VI = Glycopyrrolate
VII = Homatropine
VIII = Hyoscyamine
IX = Isopropamide
X = Mepenzolate
XI = Methantheline
XII = Methscopolamine
XIII = Oxyphencyclimine
XIV = Pirenzepine
XV = Propantheline
XVI = Scopolamine
XVII = Tridihexethyl

	I	II	III	IV	V	VI	VII	VIII	IX	X	XI	XII	XIII	XIV	XV	XVI	XVII
Decreased flow of breast milk	L	L	L	L	L	L	L	L	L	L	L	L	L	L	L	L	L
Decreased salivary secretion (difficulty in swallowing)	L	L	L	L	L	L	L	L	L	L	L	L	L	L	L	L	L
Decreased sweating	M	M	M	M	M	M	M	M	M	M	M	M	M	M	M	M	M
*Difficult urination***	R	R	R	R	R	R	R	R	R	R	R	R	R	R	R	R	R
Difficulty in accommodation of the eye (blurred vision)†	R	L	L	R	L	R	R	L	R	R	R	R	L	L	R	L	R
Drowsiness††	R	R	R	R	R	R	R	R	R	R	R	R	R	R	R	M	R
Dryness of mouth, nose, throat, or skin	M	M	M	M	M	M	M	M	M	M	M	M	M	M	M	M	M
False sense of well-being	U	U	U	U	R	U	U	U	U	U	U	U	U	U	U	R	U
Headache	R	R	R	R	R	R	R	R	R	R	R	R	R	R	R	R	R
Lightheadedness, temporary—with parenteral administration	U	U	U	U	R	R	U	R	U	U	U	U	U	U	U	R	U
Loss of memory‡‡	R	R	R	R	R	R	R	R	R	R	R	R	R	R	R	M	R
Mydriatic effect (increased sensitivity of eyes to light)†	R	L	L	R	L	R	R	L	R	R	R	R	L	L	R	L	R
Nausea or vomiting	R	R	R	R	R	R	R	R	R	R	R	R	R	R	R	R	R
Paradoxical reaction (trouble in sleeping)	U	U	U	U	U	U	U	U	U	U	U	U	U	U	U	U	U
Redness or other signs of irritation at injection site	U	M	U	U	M	M	U	M	U	U	U	U	U	U	U	M	U
Unusual tiredness or weakness	R	R	R	R	R	R	R	R	R	R	R	R	R	R	R	R	R

Table 1. Side/Adverse Effects* *(continued)*

Legend:
I = Anisotropine
II = Atropine
III = Belladonna
IV = Clidinium
V = Dicyclomine
VI = Glycopyrrolate
VII = Homatropine
VIII = Hyoscyamine
IX = Isopropamide
X = Mepenzolate
XI = Methantheline
XII = Methscopolamine
XIII = Oxyphencyclimine
XIV = Pirenzepine
XV = Propantheline
XVI = Scopolamine
XVII = Tridihexethyl

	I	II	III	IV	V	VI	VII	VIII	IX	X	XI	XII	XIII	XIV	XV	XVI	XVII
Medical attention needed if they occur after scopolamine is discontinued																	
Anxiety	U	U	U	U	U	U	U	U	U	U	U	U	U	U	U	§§	U
Irritability	U	U	U	U	U	U	U	U	U	U	U	U	U	U	U	§§	U
Nightmares	U	U	U	U	U	U	U	U	U	U	U	U	U	U	U	§§	U
Trouble in sleeping	U	U	U	U	U	U	U	U	U	U	U	U	U	U	U	§§	U

* Differences in frequency of occurrence may reflect either lack of clinical-use data or actual pharmacologic distinctions among agents (although their pharmacologic similarity suggests that side effects occurring with one may occur with the others). M=more frequent; L=less frequent; R=rare; U=unknown.

† Quaternary ammonium compounds are fully ionized in the pH range of body fluids and possess reduced lipid solubility. Therefore, they penetrate cellular barriers less effectively and only pass across the blood-brain barrier or into the eye with difficulty. Central and ocular effects are negligible and/or less likely to occur with quaternary ammonium compounds.

‡ With quaternary ammonium compounds, difficulty in breathing, severe muscle weakness, and severe tiredness may occur because of the compounds' curare-like effects; these effects may lead to respiratory paralysis.

§ Orthostatic hypotension, due to ganglion-blocking activity, is more likely to occur with high doses of quaternary ammonium compounds.

Confusion may occur more frequently in geriatric patients.

** Difficult urination is more likely to occur in older men and may require medical attention in patients with symptoms of prostatism.

†† More frequent with high doses of anticholinergics, but a common side effect with therapeutic doses of oral or parenteral scopolamine.

‡‡ Scopolamine, administered parenterally as preanesthetic medication and/or given in large doses, may have a temporary but detrimental effect on memory. In geriatric patients, especially those who already have memory problems, the continued use of any anticholinergic may severely impair memory.

§§ May indicate rebound reduction in rapid eye movement (REM) time.

ANTICOAGULANTS   Systemic

INN: Included in brackets after individual generic listings, if different from U.S. generic names.

Some commonly used *brand names* are:

In the U.S.—
    Coumadin [Warfarin]   *Panwarfin* [Warfarin]
    Miradon [Anisindione]   *Sofarin* [Warfarin]
In Canada—
    Coumadin [Warfarin]
    Warfilone [Warfarin]

ANISINDIONE
Oral
    Anisindione Tablets
        In the U.S.—*Miradon*
DICUMAROL [INN: Dicoumarol]
Oral
    Dicumarol Tablets USP
        In the U.S.—GENERIC
HEPARIN—See Heparin (Systemic).
WARFARIN
Oral
    Warfarin Sodium Tablets USP
        In the U.S.—*Coumadin; Panwarfin; Sofarin;* GENERIC
        In Canada—*Coumadin; Warfilone*
Parenteral
    Warfarin Sodium for Injection USP
        In the U.S.—*Coumadin*

Category: Anticoagulant.

Indications

Note: Bracketed information in the *Indications* section refers to uses not included in U.S. product labeling.

Several of the indications for coumarin- or indandione-derivative anticoagulant therapy are identical to those for thrombolytic (alteplase [tissue-type plasminogen activator, recombinant; tPA], anistreplase [anisoylated plasminogen-streptokinase activator complex; APSAC] streptokinase, or urokinase) and/or heparin therapy. Thrombolytic agents are used primarily to lyse obstructive thrombi and restore blood flow in a recently occluded blood vessel, whereas anticoagulants are used primarily to prevent thrombus formation and extension of existing thrombi. For treatment of acute deep venous thrombosis and acute pulmonary embolism, a thrombolytic agent may be the treatment of choice; however, the selection of thrombolytic therapy or anticoagulant therapy as opposed to other forms of treatment, including vascular surgery, must be based on determination of the severity of thrombotic disease and assessment of patient condition and history.

Because the therapeutic effects of coumarin- or indandione-derivative anticoagulants may not occur until after several days of therapy, heparin is the agent of choice when an immediate anticoagulant effect is required. A coumarin or indandione derivative is usually administered when an immediate anticoagulant effect is not necessary or when long-term anticoagulation is required following initial thrombolytic and/or heparin therapy.

Accepted
Thrombosis, deep venous (prophylaxis and treatment); or
Thromboembolism, pulmonary (prophylaxis and treatment)—Anticoagulants are indicated in the treatment of patients with recent deep vein thrombosis or thrombophlebitis to prevent extension and embolization of the thrombus and to reduce the risk of pulmonary embolism or recurrent thrombus formation. In acute pulmonary embolism or venous thrombosis, anticoagulants are indicated fol-

lowing initial thrombolytic and/or heparin therapy to decrease the risk of extension, recurrence, or death.

Anticoagulants are indicated for prophylaxis of venous thrombosis and pulmonary embolism postoperatively or in high-risk patients, such as those with a history of thromboembolism or those requiring prolonged immobilization. However, subcutaneous administration of low-dose heparin is more commonly used to prevent postsurgical thromboembolic complications.

Thromboembolism (prophylaxis)—Anticoagulants are indicated [or used] for prophylaxis of thromboembolism associated with:

Chronic atrial fibrillation—Anticoagulants may prevent the formation of mural thrombi in the heart, which may lead to systemic thromboembolism in patients with chronic atrial fibrillation, especially those with rheumatic mitral stenosis, prosthetic heart valves, left atrial enlargement, or cardiomyopathy. In these patients, anticoagulants may decrease the risk of arterial embolism, pulmonary embolism, or subsequent stroke.

Myocardial infarction—Anticoagulants are indicated as adjunctive therapy to reduce the risk of systemic thromboembolic complications following acute myocardial infarction (especially an anterior wall myocardial infarction or a large apical infarction), primarily in high-risk patients such as those with shock, congestive heart failure, prolonged arrhythmias (especially atrial fibrillation), previous myocardial infarction, or history of thromboembolism.

[Cardioversion of chronic atrial fibrillation, electric or pharmacologic—Anticoagulants are used to reduce the risk of postconversion emboli.]

[Prosthetic heart valves—Anticoagulants are used to reduce the risk of thromboembolic complications in patients with certain types of prosthetic heart valves. The effectiveness of these agents may be increased by concurrent use of a platelet aggregation inhibitor such as dipyridamole. Aspirin is also sometimes used concurrently with anticoagulants for this purpose; however, the risk of hemorrhage is increased.]

[Thromboembolism, cerebral, recurrence (prophylaxis)]—Anticoagulants are used to reduce the risk of recurrence of cerebral embolism in patients with recent cerebral embolism, especially when the source of the embolism is thought to be the heart. The possibility that cerebral hemorrhage may be present must be ruled out before anticoagulant therapy is initiated. Although administration of an anticoagulant too soon after a cerebral embolism may increase the risk of cerebral hemorrhage, recent studies have indicated that the risk of early recurrence may be greater than the risk of anticoagulant therapy.

[Myocardial reinfarction (prophylaxis)]—Long-term use of anticoagulants following myocardial infarction to prevent reinfarction remains controversial; many clinicians report that recurrence of acute attacks and/or risk of death may not be reduced by such therapy. A few studies have indicated that long-term anticoagulation may reduce the risk of recurrent myocardial infarction and of nonhemorrhagic cerebrovascular accidents in patients older than 60 years of age. However, aspirin is also effective, and is more commonly used, for this purpose.

[Ischemic attacks, transient, in females and males (treatment)]—Warfarin has been used as an adjunct in the treatment of patients with transient ischemic attacks. It may reduce the incidence of repeat attacks and/or subsequent stroke, especially during the first few months of therapy. However, the risk of death may not be decreased. FDA has classified warfarin as being possibly effective for this indication; this classification requires the submission of adequate and well-controlled studies in order to provide substantial evidence of effectiveness. Platelet aggregation inhibitors (especially aspirin) are more commonly being used for this indication.

[Anticoagulants have also been used to reduce the risk of thrombosis and/or occlusion of the aortocoronary bypass following coronary bypass surgery. However, their efficacy has not been proven and platelet aggregation inhibitors are now being administered for this purpose.]

Pharmacology

Mechanism of action/Effect: Both coumarin and indandione derivatives are indirect-acting anticoagulants (act only *in vivo*); they prevent the formation of active procoagulation factors II, VII, IX, and X in the liver by inhibiting the vitamin K-mediated gamma-carboxylation of precursor proteins. Full therapeutic action is delayed until circulating coagulation factors are removed by normal catabolism, which occurs at different rates for each factor. Although prothrombin time (PT) may be prolonged when factor VII (which has the shortest half-life) is depleted, it is believed that peak antithrombotic effects are not achieved until all four factors are removed. These agents have no direct thrombolytic effect, although they may limit extension of existing thrombi.

Precautions to Consider

Geriatrics

Geriatric patients may be more susceptible to the effects of anticoagulants, resulting in increased risk of hemorrhage, possibly because of the presence of advanced vascular disease resulting in altered homeostatic mechanisms, hepatic function impairment resulting in decreased procoagulant factor synthesis or anticoagulant metabolism, or renal function impairment. Lower maintenance doses than those usually recommended for adults may be required for these patients.

Dental

Bleeding from gingival tissue may be a sign of anticoagulant overdose.

Anticoagulant therapy increases the risk of localized hemorrhage during and following oral surgical procedures. Consultation with the prescribing physician may be advisable prior to oral surgery, to determine whether a temporary dosage reduction or withdrawal of anticoagulant therapy is feasible. Also, local measures to minimize bleeding should be used at the time of surgery.

Drug interactions and/or related problems

See also *Table 1*, page 95.

All interactions between coumarin or indandione derivatives and other medications have not been identified. Also, several medications may interact with anticoagulant therapy by more than one mechanism; in several cases, both increased anticoagulation and decreased anticoagulation have been reported for the same interacting medication. Therefore, the net effect of some concurrently used medications on anticoagulant therapy may be unpredictable. In addition, control of anticoagulant therapy may be more difficult to achieve if an interacting medication is used intermittently rather than chronically.

Because of the possible serious consequences of interference with anticoagulant therapy, increased monitoring of the prothrombin time (PT) is recommended when *any* medication is added to or withdrawn from the regimen of a patient stabilized on a coumarin or indandione derivative, or if the dosage of a concurrently used medication is changed. Anticoagulant dosage must be adjusted as necessary to prevent hemorrhage or loss of effect. Also, substantial alteration of initial anticoagulant dosage may be necessary when anticoagulant therapy is initiated in a patient receiving a medication known to cause significant alteration of anticoagulant effect.

Contraindications/Medical problems

The contraindications/medical problems included have been selected on the basis of their potential clinical significance (reasons given in parentheses where appropriate)—not necessarily inclusive (» = major clinical significance).

Except under special circumstances, these medications should not be used when the following medical problems exist:

- » Abortion, threatened or incomplete, or
- » Aneurysm, cerebral or dissecting aorta, or
- » Bleeding, active, or
- » Cerebrovascular hemorrhage, confirmed or suspected, or
- » Neurosurgery, recent or contemplated, or
- » Ophthalmic surgery, recent or contemplated, or
- » Surgery, major, other, especially if resulting in large open surfaces (increased risk of uncontrollable hemorrhage)

  Note: Although anticoagulants are generally contraindicated following major surgery, they may be required following orthopedic (hip) surgery to reduce the risk of thromboembolism.

- » Blood dyscrasias, hemorrhagic, such as thrombocytopenia, or
- » Hemophilia or
- » Hemorrhagic tendency, other (increased risk of hemorrhage)
- » Hypertension, severe uncontrolled (increased risk of cerebral hemorrhage)
- » Pericardial effusion or
- » Pericarditis (increased risk of severe hemorrhagic pericardial effusions and pericardial tamponade)

Risk-benefit should be considered when the following medical problems exist:

Allergic or anaphylactic disorders, severe

Any condition in which increased risk of hemorrhage is present, such as:

- » Childbirth, recent
- » Diabetes, severe

  Gastrointestinal ulceration, history of

  Intrauterine contraceptive device, use of

  Radiation therapy, recent

  Renal function impairment, mild to moderate
- » Renal function impairment, severe
- » Trauma, severe, especially to the central nervous system (CNS)

  Tuberculosis, active
- » Ulceration or other lesions of the gastrointestinal, respiratory, or urinary tract, active
- » Vasculitis, severe

Any condition that may reduce the effectiveness of the anticoagulant, such as:

Edema

Hypercholesterolemia

Hyperlipidemia

Hypothyroidism

Any condition that may directly or indirectly increase the patient's response to the anticoagulant leading to increased risk of bleeding, such as:

Biliary obstruction
- » Carcinoma, visceral

  Collagen disease

  Congestive heart failure

  Diarrhea, prolonged

  Dietary insufficiency, prolonged

  Fever

  Hepatic function impairment, mild to moderate
- » Hepatic function impairment, severe, or cirrhosis

  Hepatitis, infectious

  Hyperthyroidism

  Pancreatic disorders

  Sprue

Steatorrhea
» Vitamin C deficiency
» Vitamin K deficiency
Any condition that may result in reduced compliance by unsupervised outpatients, such as:
Alcoholism (active)
Emotional instability
Psychosis
Senility
Uncooperative patient
Any medical or dental procedure or condition in which the risk of bleeding or hemorrhage is present, such as:
» Anesthesia, regional or lumbar block
Catheters, indwelling
Drainage tubes in any orifice or wound
» Spinal puncture
» Endocarditis, subacute bacterial
(increased risk of hemorrhage into infarcted area)
Hypertension, mild to moderate
» Polyarthritis
Protein C deficiency, known or suspected, or any other condition predisposing to tissue necrosis
(increased risk of anticoagulant-induced tissue necrosis, although patients with protein C deficiency may require long-term anticoagulant therapy to prevent recurrent thrombus formation; administration of heparin during the first 5 to 7 days of coumarin or indandione anticoagulant therapy may reduce the risk of tissue necrosis)
Sensitivity to the anticoagulant prescribed, history of
Caution in use is also recommended in geriatric or very young patients, and in severely debilitated patients, who may be more sensitive to the effects of anticoagulants.

Side/Adverse Effects

Note: The occurrence of gastrointestinal hemorrhage during anticoagulant therapy, especially if the prothrombin time (PT) is within the therapeutic range, may indicate the presence of an underlying occult lesion such as a tumor or ulcer.

Hemorrhagic necrosis (bleeding into the skin and subcutaneous tissue with resultant necrosis, vasculitis, and thrombosis) has been reported to occur rarely during anticoagulant therapy. This complication occurs more frequently in females than in males; the fatty tissues of the abdomen, breasts, buttocks, and thighs are most often affected. Tissue necrosis may be more likely to occur in patients with protein C deficiency. Concurrent use of heparin during the first 5 to 7 days of anticoagulant therapy may decrease the risk of tissue necrosis.

Adrenal hemorrhage resulting in acute adrenal insufficiency has been reported to occur rarely during anticoagulant therapy. Diagnosis may be difficult because the initial symptoms (abdominal pain, apprehension, diarrhea, dizziness or fainting, headache, loss of appetite, nausea or vomiting, and weakness) are nonspecific and variable. If acute adrenal insufficiency is suspected, anticoagulant therapy must be discontinued and high-dose adrenocorticoid therapy (preferably with hydrocortisone, since other glucocorticoids may not provide sufficient sodium retention) instituted immediately. Delay of treatment while laboratory confirmation of the diagnosis is awaited may prove fatal for the patient. It has been proposed that abdominal computerized axial tomographic (CAT) scanning may be of use in diagnosing this condition more rapidly.

The following side/adverse effects have been selected on the basis of their potential clinical significance (possible signs and symptoms in parentheses where appropriate)— not necessarily inclusive:*	Legend: I=Anisindione II=Dicumarol III=Warfarin		
	I	**II**	**III**
Medical attention needed			
Adrenal insufficiency, acute (diarrhea, nausea with or without vomiting, stomach cramps or pain)	R	R	R
Agranulocytosis or Leukopenia (chills, fever, sore throat, unusual tiredness or weakness)	U†	R	R
	U†	L	L
Dermatitis, allergic (skin rash, hives, and/or itching)	L	R	R
Diarrhea	U†	M	L
Hepatotoxicity (dark urine, yellow eyes or skin)	U†	R	R
Nausea or vomiting	U†	L	L
"Purple toes" syndrome (blue or purple toes, pain in toes)	U	R	R
Renal damage with resultant edema and proteinuria (bloody or cloudy urine; difficult or painful urination; sudden decrease in amount of urine; swelling of face, feet and/or lower legs)	U†	R	R
Sores, ulcers, or white spots in mouth or throat	U†	R	R
Stomach cramps or pain	U†	L	L
Medical attention needed only if continuing or bothersome			
Bloated stomach or gas	U	M	U
Loss of appetite	U	L	U
Paralysis of accommodation (blurred vision or other vision problems)	U†	U	U
Unusual hair loss	U†	L	L

*Differences in frequency of occurrence may reflect either lack of clinical-use data or actual pharmacologic distinctions among agents. M=more frequent; L=less frequent; R=rare; U=unknown.

†Although not documented with anisindione, these effects have been reported with phenindione, an indandione derivative that is no longer commercially available. Other adverse effects or abnormalities reported with phenindione include aplastic anemia, eosinophilia, leukocytosis, thrombocytopenia, atypical mononuclear cells, red cell aplasia, presence of leukocyte agglutinins, and exfoliative dermatitis. Because anisindione is chemically related to phenindione, these side effects should be considered potential side effects of anisindione also.

Signs and symptoms of overdose or internal bleeding indicating need for medical attention
Early signs of overdose
Bleeding from gums when brushing teeth; unexplained bruising or purplish areas on skin; unexplained nosebleeds; unusually heavy bleeding or oozing from cuts or wounds; unusually heavy or unexpected menstrual bleeding

Note: With anisindione, the possibility exists that unusual bruising or bleeding may also indicate thrombocytopenia.

Signs and symptoms of internal bleeding
> *Abdominal pain or swelling; back pain or backaches; blood in urine; bloody or black tarry stools; constipation caused by hemorrhage-induced paralytic ileus or intestinal obstruction; coughing up blood; dizziness; headache, severe or continuing; joint pain, stiffness, or swelling; vomiting blood or material that looks like coffee grounds*

Patient Consultation

In providing consultation, consider emphasizing the following selected information (» = major clinical significance):

Before using this medication
» Conditions affecting use, especially:
   Sensitivity to the anticoagulant considered for therapy
   Pregnancy—Not becoming pregnant during therapy without first discussing plans with physician, or informing physician immediately if any suspicion of pregnancy; these medications should not be used during the first trimester because of their teratogenic effects or after the 37th week of pregnancy because of the risk of fetal and neonatal bleeding
   Use in children—Infants, especially neonates, are especially sensitive to effects because of vitamin K deficiency
   Use in the elderly—Increased risk of bleeding
   Other medications
   Other medical problems, especially bleeding or clotting defects, or history of; recent surgery or childbirth; diabetes mellitus; severe renal or hepatic function impairment; active gastrointestinal, respiratory, or urinary tract ulceration; malignancy; recent spinal puncture; subacute bacterial endocarditis; or polyarthritis

Proper use of this medication
» Taking medication only as directed
» Regular prothrombin-time tests and regular visits to physician or clinic to check progress
» Missed dose: Taking as soon as possible; not taking if not remembered until next day; not doubling doses; keeping a record of doses taken to avoid mistakes; keeping record of missed doses to give physician
» Proper storage

Precautions while using this medication
» Need for patient to inform all physicians, dentists, and pharmacists that this medication is being used
» Not taking or discontinuing any other medication, including salicylates or any other over-the-counter (OTC) medications, without physician's permission
» Carrying identification indicating use of an anticoagulant
   Not engaging in activities that may lead to injuries
   Using care in activities that may cause a cut or bleeding (such as shaving)
   Minimizing alcohol consumption; i.e., not consuming more than an occasional drink or two
   Eating a normal, balanced diet; not changing dietary habits, taking vitamins, or using nutritional supplements without first seeking professional advice because of possible alteration of anticoagulant effect by substantial changes in intake of Vitamin K (present in some multiple vitamins and nutritional supplements as well as foods, including green, leafy vegetables [such as broccoli, cabbage, collard greens, kale, lettuce, spinach], and, to a lesser extent, meats and dairy products)
   Checking with physician if unable to eat for several days or if continuing gastric upset, diarrhea, or fever occurs
   Caution following cessation of therapy while body is recovering blood-clotting abilities

Side/adverse effects
» Checking with physician immediately if any symptoms of bleeding occur
   Checking with physician if anisindione turns urine orange
   Signs and symptoms of potential side effects, especially bleeding, agranulocytosis, renal damage, hepatotoxicity, and "purple toes" syndrome

General Dosing Information

Patient compliance is essential to the safe use of these medications. The patient must be responsible and willing to carry out the demands that accompany the use of anticoagulants.

Dosage of anticoagulants must be individualized and adjusted according to prothrombin-time (PT) determinations. Determinations of clotting time, bleeding time, or anticoagulant plasma concentration are not effective measures for monitoring anticoagulant therapy. It is recommended that PT determinations be performed prior to initiation of therapy, at 24-hour intervals while maintenance dosage is being established, then once or twice weekly for the following 3 to 4 weeks, then at 1- to 4-week intervals for the duration of treatment.

PT is often reported by listing the value in seconds along with the control value in seconds. Alternately, PT may be reported as the ratio of the prolonged (therapeutic) value to the control value. In the past, the therapeutic value was considered to be $1^1/_2$ to $2^1/_2$ times the control value. Because the tissue thromboplastins currently used in the U.S. for PT determinations are less sensitive than those previously used, the therapeutic value for most patients is now considered to be 1.3 to 1.5 times the control value. However, when an especially high risk of thromboembolism exists (e.g., in patients with a history of recurrent systemic embolism or patients with mechanical heart valves), maintaining the PT at 1.5 to 2 times the control value may be necessary. Tissue thromboplastins currently used in North America for PT determinations are not identical to, and are less sensitive than, thromboplastins used in other countries. In 1983, the World Health Organization introduced a standardized system of reporting PT values that provides a common basis for communicating PT results and interpreting therapeutic ranges. This system is based on the determination of an International Normalized Ratio (INR), which is derived from calibrations of commercial thromboplastin reagents against the International Reference Preparation, a sensitive human brain thromboplastin. With the rabbit brain thromboplastins currently commercially available in North America, PT values of 1.3 to 1.5 times the control value are equivalent to INR values of 2 to 3 times the control value and PT values of 1.5 to 2 times the control value are equivalent to INR values of 3 to 4.5 times the control value. For other thromboplastins, the INR can be calculated using the International Sensitivity Index (available from the manufacturer) as a calibration factor.

Levels of anticoagulation (in terms of the desired PT and INR) that are recommended for specific indications by a panel assembled for the Second American College of Chest Physicians Conference on Antithrombotic Therapy are:

For prevention of venous thromboembolism and pulmonary embolism in high-risk surgical patients when low-dose heparin is ineffective (e.g., surgery for fractured hip, other [elective] hip surgery, or knee reconstruction) or when heparin is contraindicated for any reason—
   Surgery for fractured hip: PT 1.3 to 1.5 (INR 2.0 to 3.0) times the control value.
   Elective hip surgery: PT 1.3 to 1.5 (INR 2.0 to 3.0) times the control value.

For treatment of acute deep venous thrombosis of the popliteal and more proximal vessels or pulmonary embolism (following initial thrombolytic and/or heparin therapy)—PT 1.3 to 1.5 (INR 2.0 to 3.0) times the control value. The oral anticoagulant should be administered concurrently with heparin for at least four to five days, after which heparin can be discontinued (provided that prothrombin time determinations indicate an adequate response to the oral anticoagulant). Treatment with the oral anticoagulant should be continued for at least three months (indefinitely if recurrent venous thrombosis or continuing risk factors [e.g., antithrombin III deficiency, protein C or protein S deficiency, malignancy] exist).

For treatment of isolated symptomatic calf-vein thrombosis—PT 1.3 to 1.5 (INR 2.0 to 3.0) times the control value. Therapy should be continued for three months.

For prevention of cardiogenic systemic or cerebral embolism (either a first episode or a recurrence) in patients with the following risk factors—

Mitral valve disease with documented systemic embolism: PT 1.5 to 2.0 (INR 3.0 to 4.5) times the control value. If embolism recurs, dipyridamole (225 to 400 mg per day) should be considered for addition to the regimen. Therapy should be continued at that level of anticoagulation for at least one year after an embolism occurs, after which dosage may be reduced to provide a PT of 1.3 to 1.5 (INR 2.0 to 3.0) times the control value. Long-term therapy is recommended.

Mitral valve disease and associated chronic or paroxysmal atrial fibrillation: PT 1.3 to 1.5 (INR 2.0 to 3.0) times the control value. Long-term therapy is recommended.

Mitral valve disease, when the left atrial diameter is >5.5 cm (but normal sinus rhythm is present): PT 1.3 to 1.5 (INR 2.0 to 3.0) times the control value. Long-term therapy is recommended.

Mitral valve prolapse associated with documented, unexplained transient ischemic attacks unresponsive to a sufficient trial of aspirin therapy: PT 1.3 to 1.5 (INR 2.0 to 3.0) times the control value. Long-term therapy is recommended.

Mitral valve prolapse and documented systemic embolism: PT 1.5 to 2.0 (INR 3.0 to 4.5) times the control value. Therapy should be continued at that level of anticoagulation for at least one year after an embolism occurs, after which dosage may be reduced to provide a PT of 1.3 to 1.5 (INR 2.0 to 3.0) times the control value. Long-term therapy is recommended.

Mitral valve prolapse associated with chronic or paroxysmal atrial fibrillation: PT 1.3 to 1.5 (INR 2.0 to 3.0) times the control value. Long-term therapy is recommended.

Mitral annular calcification complicated by systemic thromboembolism: PT 1.5 to 2.0 (INR 3.0 to 4.5) times the control value. Therapy should be continued at that level of anticoagulation for at least one year after an embolism occurs, after which dosage may be reduced to provide a PT of 1.3 to 1.5 (INR 2.0 to 3.0) times the control value. Long-term therapy is recommended.

Mitral annular calcification associated with atrial fibrillation: PT 1.3 to 1.5 (INR 2.0 to 3.0) times the control value. Long-term therapy is recommended.

Mechanical prosthetic heart valves: PT 1.5 to 2.0 (INR 3.0 to 4.5) times the control value. Dipyridamole (400 mg per day) may be added to the regimen (optional, although it is strongly recommended if an embolism occurs despite adequate anticoagulation). If the recommended level of anticoagulation is contraindicated or not tolerated, a lower dose that provides a PT of 1.3 to 1.5 (INR 2.0 to 3.0) times control should be administered concurrently with dipyridamole (400 mg per day). Long-term therapy is recommended.

Bioprosthetic mitral heart valves: PT 1.3 to 1.5 (INR 2.0 to 3.0) times the control value for three months following insertion. However, if there is a history of systemic embolism, evidence of a left atrial thrombus, or atrial fibrillation, dosage sufficient to prolong the PT to 1.5 to 2.0 (INR 3.0 to 4.5) times the control value should be administered for three months, followed by long-term therapy at a reduced dosage that provides a PT of 1.3 to 1.5 (INR 2.0 to 3.0) times the control value.

Atrial fibrillation and systemic embolism: PT 1.5 to 2 (INR 3.0 to 4.5) times the control value. Therapy should be continued at that level of anticoagulation for one year after an embolism occurs, after which dosage may be reduced to provide a PT of 1.3 to 1.5 (INR 2.0 to 3.0) times the control value. Long-term therapy is recommended.

Atrial fibrillation associated with dilated and hypertrophic cardiomyopathy: PT 1.3 to 1.5 (INR 2.0 to 3.0) times the control value. Long-term therapy is recommended.

Atrial fibrillation associated with congestive heart failure: Long-term anticoagulation providing a PT of 1.3 to 1.5 (INR 2.0 to 3.0) times the control value should be considered.

Atrial fibrillation associated with coronary artery disease, hypertension, congenital heart disease, or other forms of nonvalvular heart disease: Although conclusive evidence indicating that anticoagulation is required in these circumstances is lacking, anticoagulation (PT 1.3 to 1.5 [INR 2.0 to 3.0] times the control value) should be considered for young patients who are not at increased risk of hemorrhagic complications.

Atrial fibrillation associated with thyrotoxic heart disease: PT 1.3 to 1.5 (INR 2.0 to 3.0) times the control value. Treatment should be continued for four weeks after sinus rhythm and a euthyroid state have been restored.

Atrial fibrillation, idiopathic: Long-term anticoagulation is not needed for young patients. However, for patients 60 years of age or older, long-term anticoagulation (PT 1.3 to 1.5 [INR 2.0 to 3.0] times the control value) should be considered on an individual basis.

Cardioversion (elective) of atrial fibrillation: PT 1.3 to 1.5 (INR 2.0 to 3.0) times the control value. Therapy should be started three weeks before elective cardioversion and continued until normal sinus rhythm has been maintained for at least four weeks. Anticoagulation is not needed for cardioversion of atrial fibrillation of only one or two days' duration, or for cardioversion of atrial flutter or supraventricular tachycardia, unless other risk factors for systemic embolism exist.

Anterior transmural myocardial infarction (following initial thrombolytic and/or heparin therapy): PT 1.3 to 1.5 (INR 2.0 to 3.0) times the control value. Therapy is generally continued for three months.

Acute myocardial infarction with atrial fibrillation, history of previous systemic or pulmonary embolism or venous thromboembolism, persistently decreased left ventricular function, or chronic congestive heart failure (following initial thrombolytic and/or heparin therapy): PT 1.3 to 1.5 (INR 2.0 to 3.0) times the control value for at least three months. Long-term anticoagulation may not reduce the risk of recurrent acute myocardial infarction, but is recommended if a risk factor for systemic or pulmonary embolism is still present after three months of therapy.

For prevention of recurrent cardiogenic brain emboli (following initial heparin therapy)—Anticoagulant therapy should be initiated only if the patient is not hypertensive and a computerized tomographic (CT) scan performed 24 hours or longer following the onset of the stroke shows no evidence of hemorrhagic transformation. If severe hypertension is present, or the embolic stroke is large, there is a risk of late hemorrhagic transformation; anticoagulant therapy should be delayed for several days. If hemorrhagic transformation is documented, anticoagulant therapy should be postponed for at least 8 to 10 days. Initially, the oral anticoagulant should be administered in dosage sufficient to provide a PT of 1.5 to 2.0 (INR 3.0 to 4.5) times the control value. Therapy should be continued at that level of anticoagulation for one year after the embolism, after which dosage may be reduced to provide a PT of 1.3 to 1.5 (INR 2.0 to 3.0) times the control value. Long-term therapy is recommended.

For prevention of recurrent arterial thrombi or emboli—PT 1.5 to 2.0 (INR 3.0 to 4.5) times the control value. If no thrombus or embolism has recurred after one year of therapy, dosage may be reduced to provide a PT of 1.3 to 1.5 (INR 2.0 to 3.0) times the control value.

Increased monitoring of the PT is recommended when any new medication, including nonprescription medication, is added to or withdrawn from the regimen of a patient stabilized on a coumarin or indandione derivative, or when the dosage of a concurrently used medication is changed. Anticoagulant dosage must be adjusted as necessary to prevent hemorrhage or loss of effect. Also, substantial alteration of initial anticoagulant dosage may be necessary when anticoagulant therapy is initiated in a patient receiving a medication known to cause significant alteration of anticoagulant effect.

Lower doses may be required for geriatric patients because enhanced anticoagulant effect may occur.

Decreased sensitivity to the effects of anticoagulants may be evident during initiation of therapy in patients with edema, hyperlipidemia, hypercholesterolemia, or hypothyroidism. Loss of anticoagulant effect may occur if any of these conditions develop during therapy. Correction of these problems will increase or restore the effectiveness of the anticoagulant.

Some patients also exhibit resistance to anticoagulant therapy because of genetic variations in the vitamin K receptor site or because of an increased rate of anticoagulant metabolism and excretion. Doses much higher than those usually recommended may be required to achieve successful anticoagulation in these patients. Some patients resistant to therapy with a coumarin derivative may respond to the indandione derivative anisindione.

Increased anticoagulant effect may occur in a previously stabilized patient if prolonged fever occurs during therapy.

When anticoagulant therapy is initiated with heparin and continued with a coumarin or indandione derivative, it is recommended that both agents be given concurrently until PT determinations indicate an adequate response to the coumarin or indandione derivative. However, the fact that heparin may prolong the PT must be kept in mind. Full therapeutic doses given by subcutaneous administration or as a single intravenous injection may prolong the PT considerably because of the high concentrations of heparin in the blood, whereas therapeutic doses of heparin given by continuous intravenous infusion or low (prophylactic) doses of heparin administered subcutaneously usually do not increase the PT by more than a few seconds. To minimize problems in interpreting PT test results, draw blood for the PT test just prior to, or at least 5 hours after, a single intravenous dose or 24 hours following subcutaneous administration of a full therapeutic dose of heparin. Also, the fact that reduction in PT may reflect early depletion of factor VII rather than peak antithrombotic effects of coumarin or indandione derivatives must be kept in mind. Some clinicians recommend continuation of heparin therapy for up to 5 to 7 days after initiation of therapy with a coumarin or indandione derivative to ensure that peak antithrombogenic activity has been reached.

Manufacturers' dosage recommendations may include administration of an initial loading dose that is to be gradually reduced to the maintenance dose indicated by PT determinations. Many clinicians recommend that large loading doses of these medications be avoided because of the increased risk of hemorrhage and because a more rapid anticoagulant effect can be achieved with heparin.

It is recommended that therapy with these medications be discontinued if there is any suspicion that anticoagulant-induced tissue necrosis is developing. Anticoagulant therapy may be continued with heparin, if necessary.

Diet/Nutrition

Loss of anticoagulant effect may occur in a previously stabilized patient if intake of vitamin K from dietary sources (green leafy vegetables such as broccoli, cabbage, collard greens, kale, lettuce, or spinach and, to a lesser extent, dairy products or meats) or vitamin K-containing multiple vitamins or nutritional supplements is increased during therapy.

Increased anticoagulant effect may occur in a previously stabilized patient if prolonged malnutrition or vitamin C deficiency develops, or if diarrhea, other illness, or changes in diet resulting in decreased intake or absorption of vitamin K occur during therapy.

ANISINDIONE

Summary of Differences

Physicochemical characteristics: Indandione-derivative anticoagulant.
Pharmacology: See *Pharmacology.*
Precautions:
　Drug interactions and/or related problems—Concurrent use with heparin does not lead to severe factor IX deficiency.
　Laboratory value alterations—Alkaline urine may turn orange.
　Patient monitoring—Monitoring of hematopoietic function, hepatic function, renal function, and urine protein may also be necessary.
Side/adverse effects: See *Side/Adverse Effects.*

Oral Dosage Forms

ANISINDIONE TABLETS

Usual adult and adolescent dose: Oral, 25 to 250 mg a day, as indicated by prothrombin-time determinations.

Auxiliary labeling: • Do not take other medicines without advice from your doctor.

DICUMAROL

Summary of Differences

Pharmacology:
　Physicochemical characteristics—Coumarin-derivative anticoagulant.
　Pharmacology—See *Pharmacology.*
Side/adverse effects: See *Side/Adverse Effects.*

Oral Dosage Forms

DICUMAROL TABLETS USP

Usual adult and adolescent dose: Oral, 25 to 200 mg a day, as indicated by prothrombin-time determinations.

Auxiliary labeling: • Do not take other medicines without advice from your doctor.

WARFARIN

Summary of Differences

Indications: Also used for treatment of transient ischemic attacks in females and males.

Pharmacology:

Physicochemical characteristics—Coumarin-derivative anticoagulant.

Pharmacology—See *Pharmacology*.

Side/adverse effects: See *Side/Adverse Effects*.

Oral Dosage Forms

WARFARIN SODIUM TABLETS USP

Usual adult and adolescent dose: Anticoagulant—Oral, 10 to 15 mg a day for two to four days, then 2 to 10 mg a day, as indicated by prothrombin-time determinations.

Auxiliary labeling: • Do not take other medicines without advice from your doctor.

Parenteral Dosage Forms

WARFARIN SODIUM FOR INJECTION USP

Usual adult and adolescent dose: Intramuscular or intravenous, 10 to 15 mg a day for two to four days, then 2 to 10 mg a day, as indicated by prothrombin-time determinations.

Table 1. Drug Interactions and/or Related Problems

The following drug interactions and/or related problems have been selected on the basis of their potential clinical significance (possible mechanism in parentheses where appropriate)—not necessarily inclusive:

Note: In addition to the listed interactions, the possibility should be considered that the risk of hemorrhage may be increased by concurrent use of any medication that may inhibit platelet aggregation or cause hypoprothrombinemia, thrombocytopenia, or gastrointestinal ulceration.

Combinations containing any of the following medications, depending on the amount present, may also interact with this medication.

Drug	Effect on Anticoagulant Activity	Mechanism*	Other Effects†	Additional Information
Acetaminophen (chronic high-dose usage)	Increase	A		Does not apply to occasional use or chronic use of less than 2 grams per day of acetaminophen
Alcohol (acute intoxication)	Increase	B		Other acute effects of alcohol on the liver may also be involved
(chronic abuse)	Decrease	C		However, increased activity possible in advanced hepatic cirrhosis
» Allopurinol	Increase	B		
Aminosalicylates	Increase	A		
» Amiodarone	Increase	B		Potentiation reported to occur in 4 to 6 days after initiation of amiodarone therapy and to persist up to 4 months following discontinuation of amiodarone
» Anabolic steroids	Increase	D, E		Especially with 17-alpha-alkylated compounds
» Androgens	Increase	D, E		
Anesthetics, inhalation‡	Increase	Unknown		
Antacids	Decrease	F		May be avoided if medications given several hours apart
Antibiotics‡	Increase	G		Significant potentiation very rare if dietary intake of vitamin K adequate
				See also separate table entries for azlocillin, carbenicillin, cefamandole, cefoperazone, chloramphenicol, erythromycins, mezlocillin, moxalactam, piperacillin, rifampin, and ticarcillin
» Antidiabetic agents, oral	Increase	H		Initial effect
	Decrease	I		With continued concurrent use
				Hepatic metabolism of antidiabetic agent may be decreased, leading to increased plasma concentration and half-life, hypoglycemic effect, and risk of toxicity of antidiabetic agent, especially with dicumarol
Ascorbic acid	Decrease			With large doses of ascorbic acid
» Aspirin	Increase	A (with large doses), H	a, b	Decreased platelet aggregation may occur with single doses as low as 40 mg
» Azlocillin			a	

*Mechanisms leading to increase or decrease in anticoagulant activity as shown by measurement of prothrombin time: (A) Decreased hepatic synthesis of procoagulant factors. (B) Inhibition of enzymatic metabolism of anticoagulant. (C) Accelerated metabolism of anticoagulant secondary to stimulation of hepatic microsomal enzyme activity. (D) Alteration of procoagulant factor synthesis or catabolism. (E) Increased receptor affinity for anticoagulant. (F) Decreased absorption of anticoagulant from gastrointestinal tract. (G) Decreased vitamin K synthesis secondary to alterations in intestinal flora. (H) Displacement of anticoagulant from protein-binding sites. (I) Increased metabolism of anticoagulant. (J) Interference with enterohepatic circulation of anticoagulant. (K) Decreased vitamin K absorption or synthesis. (L) Increased hepatic synthesis of procoagulant factors. (M) Reduction of plasma volume leading to concentration of procoagulant factors in the blood; diuretic-induced improvement of hepatic congestion may lead to improved hepatic function resulting in increased procoagulant factor synthesis. (N) Severe factor IX deficiency (with coumarin derivatives only). (O) Increased prothrombin synthesis or activation.

†Effects resulting in increased risk of hemorrhage in patients receiving anticoagulants; cannot be shown by measurement of prothrombin time: (a) Inhibition of platelet aggregation. (b) Potential occurrence of gastrointestinal ulceration or hemorrhage during therapy. (c) Adverse effect on vascular integrity. (d) Interference with platelet formation. (e) Anticoagulant activity of heparin. (f) Thrombolytic activity may lead to hemorrhage.

‡Clinical significance has not been determined.

Table 1. Drug Interactions and/or Related Problems *(continued)*

Drug	Effect on Anticoagulant Activity	Mechanism*	Other Effects†	Additional Information
» Barbiturates	Decrease	C		
Bromelains	Increase	Unknown		
» Carbamazepine	Decrease	C		
» Carbenicillin (parenteral)			a	
» Cefamandole	Increase	D	a	
» Cefoperazone	Increase	D	a	
» Chloral hydrate	Increase	H		Initial effect, usually during first 2 weeks of concurrent use; with continued concurrent use, anticoagulant activity may return to baseline level or be decreased
» Chloramphenicol	Increase	B		
Chlorinated insecticides‡	Decrease	C		
Chlorobutanol‡	Decrease	Unknown		
Cholestyramine	Decrease	F		May be avoided if medications given 6 hours apart
	Decrease	J		Not avoided if medications given 6 hours apart
	Increase	K		
Chymotrypsin‡	Increase	Unknown		
» Cimetidine	Increase	B		
Cinchophen	Increase	Unknown		
» Clofibrate	Increase	D, H		Other mechanisms may also be involved
» Colestipol	Decrease	F		May be avoided if medications given 6 hours apart
	Increase	K		Not avoided if medications given 6 hours apart
» Contraceptives, oral	Decrease	L		
	Increase	Unknown		
Corticotropin	Increase	Unknown	b, c	
	Decrease	Unknown		
Cyclophosphamide	Increase	A	d	
	Decrease	Unknown		
» Danazol	Increase	A		
» Dextran			a	
» Dextrothyroxine	Increase	D, E		Effect may depend on thyroid status of patient
Diazoxide	Increase	H		
» Diflunisal	Increase	H	a, b	Decreased platelet aggregation occurs only with greater-than-recommended daily doses
» Dipyridamole			a	With doses greater than 400 mg per day
Disopyramide‡	Decrease	Unknown		
	Increase	Unknown		
» Disulfiram	Increase	B		May also act in the liver to increase directly the hypoprothrombinemia-inducing activity of coumarin derivatives
Diuretics‡	Decrease	M		See also separate table entry for ethacrynic acid
Divalproex			a	
» Erythromycins	Increase	B		
» Estramustine	Decrease	L		

Table 1. Drug Interactions and/or Related Problems *(continued)*

Drug	Effect on Anticoagulant Activity	Mechanism*	Other Effects†	Additional Information
» Estrogens	Decrease	L		
Ethacrynic acid‡	Increase	H	b	
» Ethchlorvynol	Decrease	C		
» Fenoprofen	Increase	H	a, b	
» Gemfibrozil	Increase	Unknown		
Glucagon‡	Increase	Unknown		Potentiation reported only with doses >25 mg per day for 2 or more days; however, these doses are rarely if ever used
Glucocorticoids	Increase / Decrease	Unknown / Unknown	b, c	
» Glutethimide	Decrease	C		
» Griseofulvin	Decrease	C		
Haloperidol‡	Decrease / Increase	C / Unknown		
Heparin	Increase	N	e	May prolong prothrombin time used to monitor therapy, especially when given as an intravenous bolus or if full therapeutic doses given subcutaneously; to minimize problems, draw blood for test just prior to, or at least 5 hours after, the intravenous bolus dose or 24 hours after subcutaneous injection of a full therapeutic dose
Ibuprofen			a, b	
» Indomethacin	Increase	H	a, b	
Influenza vaccine	Increase	B		
Isoniazid	Increase	B		
Ketoconazole	Increase	Unknown		
Ketoprofen			a, b	
Laxatives, bulk-forming	Decrease	F		May be avoided if medications given several hours apart
Meclofenamate	Increase	H	b	
» Mefenamic acid	Increase	H	b	
Meperidine	Increase	Unknown		
Mercaptopurine	Increase / Decrease	A / O	d	

*Mechanisms leading to increase or decrease in anticoagulant activity as shown by measurement of prothrombin time: (A) Decreased hepatic synthesis of procoagulant factors. (B) Inhibition of enzymatic metabolism of anticoagulant. (C) Accelerated metabolism of anticoagulant secondary to stimulation of hepatic microsomal enzyme activity. (D) Alteration of procoagulant factor synthesis or catabolism. (E) Increased receptor affinity for anticoagulant. (F) Decreased absorption of anticoagulant from gastrointestinal tract. (G) Decreased vitamin K synthesis secondary to alterations in intestinal flora. (H) Displacement of anticoagulant from protein-binding sites. (I) Increased metabolism of anticoagulant. (J) Interference with enterohepatic circulation of anticoagulant. (K) Decreased vitamin K absorption or synthesis. (L) Increased hepatic synthesis of procoagulant factors. (M) Reduction of plasma volume leading to concentration of procoagulant factors in the blood; diuretic-induced improvement of hepatic congestion may lead to improved hepatic function resulting in increased procoagulant factor synthesis. (N) Severe factor IX deficiency (with coumarin derivatives only). (O) Increased prothrombin synthesis or activation.

†Effects resulting in increased risk of hemorrhage in patients receiving anticoagulants; cannot be shown by measurement of prothrombin time: (a) Inhibition of platelet aggregation. (b) Potential occurrence of gastrointestinal ulceration or hemorrhage during therapy. (c) Adverse effect on vascular integrity. (d) Interference with platelet formation. (e) Anticoagulant activity of heparin. (f) Thrombolytic activity may lead to hemorrhage.

‡Clinical significance has not been determined.

Table 1. Drug Interactions and/or Related Problems *(continued)*

Drug	Effect on Anticoagulant Activity	Mechanism*	Other Effects†	Additional Information
» Methimazole	Increase	A		Effect may also depend upon dosage and subsequent thyroid status of patient
Methotrexate	Increase	A	d	
Methyldopa	Increase	Unknown		
Methylphenidate	Increase	B		
» Metronidazole	Increase	B		
» Mezlocillin			a	
Miconazole	Increase	Unknown		
Mineral oil	Decrease	F		May be avoided if medications given 6 hours apart
	Increase	K		Not avoided if medications given 6 hours apart
Monoamine oxidase (MAO) inhibitors‡	Increase	Unknown		
» Moxalactam	Increase	D	a	May also cause irreversible platelet damage
» Nalidixic acid	Increase	H		
Naproxen			a, b	
Nifedipine	Increase	H		Nifedipine may also be displaced from protein-binding sites, leading to increased plasma concentrations of free [unbound] medication and risk of toxicity
» Phenylbutazone	Increase	B, H	a, b	
» Phenytoin, and possibly other hydantoin-type anticonvulsants	Increase	H		Initial effect
	Decrease	C		With continued concurrent use
				Hepatic metabolism of hydantoin anticonvulsants, especially phenytoin, may be decreased, leading to increased anticonvulsant plasma concentration, half-life, and risk of toxicity, especially with dicumarol
» Piperacillin			a	
Piroxicam			a, b	Possibility that anticoagulant activity may be increased because of displacement from protein-binding sites should be considered; however, has not been demonstrated
» Plicamycin	Increase	A	d	
» Primidone	Decrease	C		Effect caused by barbiturate metabolite
Propoxyphene‡	Increase	Unknown		
» Propylthiouracil	Increase	A		Effect may also depend upon dosage and subsequent thyroid status of patient
» Quinidine	Increase	D, E		
Quinine	Increase	A		
Radioactive compounds	Increase	Unknown		
» Rifampin	Decrease	C		

Table 1. Drug Interactions and/or Related Problems *(continued)*

Drug	Effect on Anticoagulant Activity	Mechanism*	Other Effects†	Additional Information
» Salicylates	Increase	A (with large doses), H	b	See also separate table entries for aspirin and diflunisal
» Streptokinase			f	Concurrent use not recommended; however, sequential use may be indicated
» Sulfinpyrazone	Increase	B, H	a, b	Biphasic response, with decreased anticoagulation occurring following initial potentiation, reported in one patient; reason for this unclear since other reports indicate only potentiation of anticoagulant effect
» Sulfonamides	Increase	B, H		
» Sulindac	Increase	H	a, b	
Testolactone	Increase			
» Thyroid hormones	Increase	D, E		Effect may depend upon dosage and subsequent thyroid status of patient
» Ticarcillin			a	
Tobacco smoking	Decrease	C		Thrombogenic potential of tobacco smoking should also be considered
Tolmetin			a, b	
Tricyclic antidepressants‡	Increase	B		Especially with amitriptyline or nortriptyline
» Urokinase			f	Concurrent use not recommended; however, sequential use may be indicated
Valproic acid	Increase	A	a	
Verapamil	Increase	H		Verapamil may also be displaced from protein-binding sites, leading to increased plasma concentrations of free [unbound] medication and risk of toxicity
Vitamin A	Increase	Unknown		With high doses of vitamin
Vitamin E‡	Increase	Unknown		With high doses of vitamin
» Vitamin K	Decrease	L		

*Mechanisms leading to increase or decrease in anticoagulant activity as shown by measurement of prothrombin time: (A) Decreased hepatic synthesis of procoagulant factors. (B) Inhibition of enzymatic metabolism of anticoagulant. (C) Accelerated metabolism of anticoagulant secondary to stimulation of hepatic microsomal enzyme activity. (D) Alteration of procoagulant factor synthesis or catabolism. (E) Increased receptor affinity for anticoagulant. (F) Decreased absorption of anticoagulant from gastrointestinal tract. (G) Decreased vitamin K synthesis secondary to alterations in intestinal flora. (H) Displacement of anticoagulant from protein-binding sites. (I) Increased metabolism of anticoagulant. (J) Interference with enterohepatic circulation of anticoagulant. (K) Decreased vitamin K absorption or synthesis. (L) Increased hepatic synthesis of procoagulant factors. (M) Reduction of plasma volume leading to concentration of procoagulant factors in the blood; diuretic-induced improvement of hepatic congestion may lead to improved hepatic function resulting in increased procoagulant factor synthesis. (N) Severe factor IX deficiency (with coumarin derivatives only). (O) Increased prothrombin synthesis or activation.

†Effects resulting in increased risk of hemorrhage in patients receiving anticoagulants; cannot be shown by measurement of prothrombin time: (a) Inhibition of platelet aggregation. (b) Potential occurrence of gastrointestinal ulceration or hemorrhage during therapy. (c) Adverse effect on vascular integrity. (d) Interference with platelet formation. (e) Anticoagulant activity of heparin. (f) Thrombolytic activity may lead to hemorrhage.

‡Clinical significance has not been determined.

ANTICONVULSANTS, DIONE   Systemic†

Some commonly used *brand names* are:

In the U.S.—
Paradione
[Paramethadione]
Tridione [Trimethadione]
Tridione Dulcets
[Trimethadione]

ORAL

PARAMETHADIONE†
Paramethadione Capsules USP†
In the U.S.—*Paradione*
TRIMETHADIONE†
Trimethadione Capsules USP†
In the U.S.—*Tridione*
Trimethadione Oral Solution USP†
In the U.S.—*Tridione*
Trimethadione Tablets USP†
In the U.S.—*Tridione Dulcets*

†Not commercially available in Canada.

Category: Anticonvulsant.

Indications

Accepted

Epilepsy, absence seizure pattern (treatment)—Paramethadione and trimethadione are indicated in the control of absence (petit mal) seizures that are refractory to treatment with other medications.

Paramethadione and trimethadione should not be used unless other less toxic anticonvulsants have been ineffective in controlling seizures.

Pharmacology

Mechanism of action/Effect: Paramethadione and trimethadione appear to raise the threshold for cortical seizures while not modifying maximal seizure pattern in patients undergoing electroconvulsive therapy. They decrease projection of focal activity and enhance presynaptic inhibition in the spinal cord, but do not affect cortical spread of nerve transmission. Also decreased are the spike and wave patterns seen with absence seizure electroencephalograms. Trimethadione's active metabolite dimethadione appears to block the T-type calcium current in thalamic neurons.

Precautions to Consider

Cross-sensitivity and/or related problems

Patients sensitive to one dione anticonvulsant may be sensitive to the other also.

Geriatrics

No information is available on the relationship of age to the effects of the dione anticonvulsants in geriatric patients.

Dental

The leukopenic and thrombocytopenic effects of dione anticonvulsants may result in an increased incidence of microbial infection, delayed healing, and gingival bleeding. If leukopenia or thrombocytopenia occurs, dental work should be deferred until blood counts have returned to normal. Patients should be instructed in proper oral hygiene during treatment, including caution in use of regular toothbrushes, dental floss, and toothpicks.

Drug interactions and/or related problems

The following drug interactions and/or related problems have been selected on the basis of their potential clinical significance (possible mechanism in parentheses where appropriate)—not necessarily inclusive (» = major clinical significance):

Note: Combinations containing any of the following medications, depending on the amount present, may also interact with this medication.

Acetazolamide
(concurrent use may potentiate acidosis, enhance ophthalmic toxicity, and alter the distribution and excretion of the active metabolite of trimethadione)

» Alcohol and
» Central nervous system (CNS) depression-producing medications, other
(CNS depression may be enhanced)

Antidepressants, tricyclic, or
Haloperidol or
Loxapine or
Maprotiline or
Molindone or
Monoamine oxidase (MAO) inhibitors, including furazolidone, procarbazine, and more than 10 mg a day of selegiline, or
Phenothiazines or
Pimozide or
Thioxanthenes
(concurrent use may lower the convulsive threshold, enhance CNS depression, and decrease the effects of the anticonvulsant medication; dosage adjustments may be necessary)

Phenacemide
(concurrent use with dione anticonvulsants may result in additive toxicity)

Contraindications/Medical problems

The contraindications/medical problems included have been selected on the basis of their potential clinical significance (reasons given in parentheses where appropriate)—not necessarily inclusive (» = major clinical significance).

Risk-benefit should be considered when the following medical problems exist:

» Blood dyscrasias, severe, or
» Hepatic function impairment, severe, or
Optic nerve or retinal disease or
Renal function impairment, severe
(risk of exacerbation of pre-existing conditions)

Porphyria, acute intermittent
(risk of exacerbation with the use of trimethadione)

» Sensitivity to dione anticonvulsants

Side/Adverse Effects

The following side/adverse effects have been selected on the basis of their potential clinical significance (possible signs and symptoms in parentheses where appropriate)—not necessarily inclusive:

Those indicating need for medical attention

Incidence more frequent
Hemeralopia, scotomata, or diplopia (changes in vision, especially glare or snowy image caused by bright light, or double vision)

Incidence rare
Allergic reaction (itching of skin associated with swollen lymph glands; enlarged liver and spleen); ***blood dyscrasias*** (sore throat and fever; unusual bleeding, especially recurring nosebleeds, bleeding gums, or vaginal bleeding; red or purple spots on skin; unusual

tiredness or weakness); *confusion; convulsions, tonic-clonic, precipitation of; hepatitis* (loss of appetite, unusual tiredness, yellow eyes or skin, weight loss, fever, skin rash or itching, dizziness, nausea or vomiting, dark urine, pain in abdomen and joints); *myasthenia gravis-like syndrome* (severe muscle weakness, including drooping eyelids; double vision; difficulty in chewing, swallowing, talking, and breathing; severe tiredness); *nephrosis* (swelling of face, hands, legs, and feet; cloudy urine)—fatalities have occurred; *skin rash or hives; systemic lupus erythematosus (SLE)-like syndrome* (swollen lymph glands)

> Note: If *skin rash* appears, dione anticonvulsant should be withdrawn promptly to prevent exfoliative dermatitis or severe forms of erythema multiforme.

Symptoms of overdose
> *Ataxia* (clumsiness or unsteadiness); *severe dizziness; severe drowsiness; severe nausea*

Those indicating need for medical attention only if they continue or are bothersome

Incidence more frequent
> *Dizziness; drowsiness; headache; irritability; photophobia* (increased sensitivity of eyes to light)

> Note: *Drowsiness* tends to diminish with continued therapy. However, if drowsiness continues, dosage reduction may be necessary. Paramethadione may have a slightly greater sedative action than trimethadione.

Incidence less frequent
> *Abdominal or stomach pain; anorexia* (loss of appetite); *behavior or mood changes; blood pressure changes; hair loss; hiccups; insomnia* (trouble in sleeping); *paresthesias* (tingling, burning, or prickly sensations); *stomach upset; unusual tiredness or weakness; unusual weight loss*

Patient Consultation

In providing consultation, consider emphasizing the following selected information (» = major clinical significance):

Before using this medication
» Conditions affecting use, especially:
>> Sensitivity to dione anticonvulsants
>> Pregnancy and delivery—Risk of congenital malformations in the fetus; women of child-bearing potential advised to use an effective method of birth control during therapy, and to notify physician immediately if pregnancy occurs; bleeding problems may occur in mother during delivery and in baby immediately after delivery.
>> Dental—Risk of bleeding and infections due to dione-induced blood dyscrasias
>> Use by athletes—Dione anticonvulsants are banned and, in some cases, tested for in competitors in biathlon and modern pentathlon events by the U.S. Olympic Committee (USOC)
>> Other medications, especially CNS depressants
>> Other medical problems, especially blood dyscrasias and hepatic function impairment

Proper use of this medication
> Proper administration:
> *For paramethadione capsules*
>> Swallowing whole; not breaking, chewing, or crushing before swallowing
> *For trimethadione tablets*
>> Chewing, or crushing and dissolving in small amount of water, if necessary
> *For all dosage forms*
>> Taking with a small amount of food or milk to reduce gastric irritation

» Compliance with therapy; taking every day as directed by physician
» Proper dosing
>> Missed dose: Taking as soon as possible; not taking if almost time for next scheduled dose; one missed dose may be added at bedtime
» Proper storage

Precautions while using this medication
» Regular visits to physician to check progress of therapy
» Checking with physician before discontinuing medication; gradual dosage reduction is usually needed
> Possible vision changes, especially intolerance to bright light; wearing sunglasses and avoiding bright light; caution when driving at night
» Avoiding use of alcohol and other CNS depressants
» Caution if drowsiness occurs; not driving or doing jobs requiring alertness
» Caution if any kind of surgery, dental treatment, or emergency treatment is required
» Reporting sore throat, fever, and any unusual bleeding or bruising to physician as soon as possible
» Informing physician as soon as possible if pregnancy occurs during therapy

Side/adverse effects
> Signs of potential side effects, especially allergic reaction; blood dyscrasias; confusion; convulsions; hemeralopia, scotomata, or diplopia; hepatitis; myasthenia gravis-like syndrome; nephrosis; skin rash or hives; and SLE-like syndrome

General Dosing Information

When this medication is to be discontinued, dosage should be reduced gradually to prevent possible occurrence of petit mal status.

When used to replace other anticonvulsant therapy, the dosage of this medication should be increased gradually while that of the other medication is gradually decreased, to maintain seizure control.

This medication does not modify the maximal seizure pattern in patients undergoing electroconvulsive therapy.

Diet/Nutrition
Dione anticonvulsants should be taken with a small amount of food or milk to reduce gastric irritation.

PARAMETHADIONE

Summary of Differences

Side/adverse effects: Slightly greater sedative action than trimethadione.

Oral Dosage Forms

PARAMETHADIONE CAPSULES USP

Usual adult and adolescent dose: Anticonvulsant—Oral, initially 300 mg three or four times a day, the dosage being increased by an additional 300 mg a day at one-week intervals until seizure control is obtained or until toxic symptoms appear.

Usual adult prescribing limits: Up to 2.4 grams a day.

Auxiliary labeling:
• May cause drowsiness.
• Do not chew or crush capsule.

Additional information: Capsules contain an oily liquid.

TRIMETHADIONE

Summary of Differences

Side/adverse effects: Slightly less sedative action than paramethadione.

Oral Dosage Forms

TRIMETHADIONE CAPSULES USP

Usual adult and adolescent dose: Anticonvulsant—Oral, initially 300 mg three or four times a day, the dosage being increased by an additional 300 mg a day at one-week intervals until seizure control is obtained or until toxic symptoms appear.

Usual adult prescribing limits: Up to 2.4 grams a day.

Auxiliary labeling: • May cause drowsiness.

TRIMETHADIONE ORAL SOLUTION USP

Usual adult and adolescent dose: See *Trimethadione Capsules USP*.

Auxiliary labeling: • May cause drowsiness.

TRIMETHADIONE TABLETS USP

Usual adult and adolescent dose: See *Trimethadione Capsules USP*.

Auxiliary labeling:
• May chew or crush tablets before swallowing.
• May cause drowsiness.

ANTICONVULSANTS, HYDANTOIN   Systemic

Some commonly used *brand names* are:

In the U.S.—

Dilantin [Phenytoin]	*Dilantin-30 Pediatric*
Dilantin-125 [Phenytoin]	[Phenytoin]
Dilantin Infatabs	*Diphenylan* [Phenytoin]
[Phenytoin]	*Mesantoin* [Mephenytoin]
Dilantin Kapseals	*Peganone* [Ethotoin]
[Phenytoin]	*Phenytex* [Phenytoin]

In Canada—

Dilantin [Phenytoin]	*Dilantin-30* [Phenytoin]
Dilantin Infatabs	*Dilantin-125* [Phenytoin]
[Phenytoin]	*Mesantoin* [Mephenytoin]

Another commonly used name for phenytoin is diphenylhydantoin.

ETHOTOIN†
Oral
    Ethotoin Tablets USP†
        In the U.S.—*Peganone*
MEPHENYTOIN
Oral
    Mephenytoin Tablets USP
        In the U.S. and Canada—*Mesantoin*
PHENYTOIN
Oral
    Phenytoin Oral Suspension USP
        In the U.S.—*Dilantin-125; Dilantin-30 Pediatric*
        In Canada—*Dilantin-30; Dilantin-125*
    Phenytoin Tablets USP (Chewable)
        In the U.S. and Canada—*Dilantin Infatabs*
    Extended Phenytoin Sodium Capsules USP
        In the U.S.—*Dilantin Kapseals; Phenytex;* GENERIC
        In Canada—*Dilantin*
    Prompt Phenytoin Sodium Capsules USP†
        In the U.S.—*Diphenylan;* GENERIC
Parenteral
    Phenytoin Sodium Injection USP
        In the U.S.—*Dilantin;* GENERIC
        In Canada—*Dilantin;* GENERIC

---

†Not commercially available in Canada.

Category

Anticonvulsant—Ethotoin; Mephenytoin; Phenytoin.
Antiarrhythmic—Phenytoin.

Collagenase synthesis/secretion inhibitor—Phenytoin.
Antineuralgic (trigeminal neuralgia)—Phenytoin.
Skeletal muscle relaxant—Phenytoin.

Indications

Note: Bracketed information in the *Indications* section refers to uses not included in U.S. product labeling.

Accepted

Epilepsy (treatment)—Hydantoin anticonvulsants are indicated in the suppression and control of tonic-clonic (grand mal) and simple or complex partial (psychomotor or temporal lobe) seizures.

Ethotoin may be administered as a second-line agent when seizures have not been adequately controlled by the primary anticonvulsants and before proceeding to more toxic anticonvulsants.

Mephenytoin is also used in the treatment of simple partial (focal and Jacksonian) seizures in patients who have not responded to less toxic anticonvulsants.

Status epilepticus (treatment)—Parenteral phenytoin is indicated for the control of tonic-clonic type status epilepticus. Although diazepam is often used initially for rapid control of status epilepticus, phenytoin is indicated for sustained control of seizure activity because of the short duration of diazepam's effect.

Seizures in neurosurgery (prophylaxis and treatment)—Phenytoin is indicated for the prevention and treatment of seizures during and following neurosurgery.

[Arrhythmias, digitalis-induced (treatment)][1]—Phenytoin is used in the correction of atrial and ventricular arrhythmias, especially those caused by digitalis glycoside toxicity.

[Choreoathetosis, paroxysmal (treatment)][1]—Phenytoin may be effective in treating paroxysmal choreoathetosis, especially the kinesigenic type. This condition, which is considered a form of reflex epilepsy, is characterized by tonic, dystonic, or choreoathetoid contortions of the extremities, trunk, or face, which are usually precipitated by the patient's initiation of sudden voluntary movement.

[Epidermolysis bullosa, recessive dystrophic (treatment)][1]—Phenytoin may be effective in the treatment of blistering and erosions of the skin that may result from even minor trauma or injury in patients with recessive dystrophic epidermolysis bullosa.

[Episodic dyscontrol (treatment)][1]—Phenytoin has been used in the treatment of episodic dyscontrol and in some behavior disorders characterized by hyperexcitability, which include anger, anxiety, irritability, and insomnia.

[Neuralgia, trigeminal (treatment)][1]—Phenytoin is used alone or with other anticonvulsants to control paroxysmal pain in some patients with trigeminal neuralgia (tic douloureux). Carbamazepine is considered the first-line agent, effectively relieving pain in about 66% of patients. However, since phenytoin relieves pain during long-term use in approximately 20% of patients, it may be used alone in some patients or added to carbamazepine therapy when symptoms persist.

[Neuromyotonia (treatment)][1];
[Myotonia congenita (treatment)][1]; or
[Myotonic muscular dystrophy (treatment)][1]—Phenytoin is effective in some patients as a muscle relaxant in the treatment of muscle hyperirritability, characterized by delayed relaxation of muscle after voluntary or mechanically induced contraction and by a state of continuous muscle contraction at rest. Neuromyotonia includes continuous muscle fiber activity syndrome, Isaac's syndrome, and "stiff man" syndrome.

[Toxicity, tricyclic antidepressant (treatment adjunct)][1]—Intravenous phenytoin loading is used to treat quinidine-like conduction defects, bradyarrhythmias, or heart block, in tricyclic antidepressant overdose.

Unaccepted

Hydantoin anticonvulsants are *not* indicated in the treatment of absence (petit mal) or as first-line treatment of febrile, hypoglycemic, or other metabolic seizures. When tonic-clonic (grand mal) seizures coexist with absence seizures, combined therapy may be necessary.

---

[1]Not included in Canadian product labeling.

Pharmacology

Mechanism of action/Effect:

Anticonvulsant—The mechanism of action is not completely known, but it is thought to involve stabilization of neuronal membranes at the cell body, axon, and synapse and limitation of the spread of neuronal or seizure activity. In neurons, phenytoin decreases sodium and calcium ion influx by prolonging channel inactivation time during generation of nerve impulses. In glia and non-neuronal cell types, the efflux of sodium and the uptake of potassium may be increased. At the synapse, phenytoin decreases post-tetanic potentiation and repetitive after-discharge. Hydantoin anticonvulsants have an excitatory effect on the cerebellum, activating inhibitory pathways that extend to the cerebral cortex. This effect may also produce a reduction in seizure activity that is associated with an increased cerebellar Purkinje cell discharge.

Antiarrhythmic—Phenytoin may act to normalize influx of sodium and calcium to cardiac Purkinje fibers. Abnormal ventricular automaticity and membrane responsiveness are decreased. Also, phenytoin shortens the refractory period, and therefore shortens the QT interval and the duration of the action potential.

Collagenase synthesis/secretion inhibitor—Phenytoin may act to inhibit the synthesis and/or secretion of collagenase by dermal fibroblasts. It has been shown that immunoreactive collagenase is increased in blistered and nonblistered skin. Studies with fibroblast cultures suggest that increased levels of an abnormal collagenase are produced by skin fibroblasts as a genetically determined trait.

Antineuralgic—Exact mechanism is unknown. Phenytoin may act in the central nervous system (CNS) to decrease synaptic transmission or to decrease summation of temporal stimulation leading to neuronal discharge (antikindling). Phenytoin raises the threshold of facial pain and shortens the duration of attacks by diminishing self-maintenance of excitation and repetitive firing.

Skeletal muscle relaxant—Phenytoin's mechanism of action as a muscle relaxant is thought to be similar to its anticonvulsant action. In movement disorders, the membrane stabilizing effect reduces abnormal sustained repetitive firing and potentiation of nerve and muscle cells.

Other actions/effects: Hydantoins induce production of liver microsomal enzymes, thereby accelerating the metabolism of concomitantly administered drugs.

Precautions to Consider

Cross-sensitivity and/or related problems

Patients sensitive to one hydantoin anticonvulsant may also be sensitive to other hydantoin anticonvulsants.

Geriatrics

Geriatric patients tend to metabolize hydantoins slowly, thereby increasing the possibility of the medication reaching toxic serum concentrations. Also, serum albumin may be low in older patients, causing a decrease in protein binding of phenytoin. Lower dosage and subsequent adjustments may be required. The rate of administration of intravenous dosage should be no more than 25 mg a minute, and possibly as low as 5 to 10 mg per minute.

Dental

Gingival hyperplasia, a common complication of phenytoin or mephenytoin therapy, usually starts during the first 6 months of treatment as gingivitis or gum inflammation. The incidence is higher in patients under 23 years of age than in older patients, and severe gingival hyperplasia is less likely to occur with dosage under 500 mg per day. Anterior tissue overgrowth may be greater than posterior overgrowth, creating esthetic and psychological problems for the young patient. A strictly enforced program of teeth cleaning by a professional, combined with plaque control by the patient, if begun within 10 days of initiation of hydantoin anticonvulsant therapy, will minimize growth rate and severity of gingival enlargement. Periodontal surgery may be indicated, and should be followed by careful plaque control to inhibit recurrence of gum enlargement. If gingival hyperplasia cannot be controlled by standard dental procedures, ethotoin may be substituted for phenytoin, without loss of seizure control, usually at doses of 4 to 6 times greater than those of phenytoin.

In addition, the leukopenic effects of hydantoin anticonvulsants may result in an increased incidence of microbial infection, delayed healing, and gingival bleeding. If leukopenia occurs, dental work should be deferred until blood counts have returned to normal. Patient instruction in proper oral hygiene should include caution in use of regular toothbrushes, dental floss, and toothpicks.

Drug interactions and/or related problems

The following drug interactions and/or related problems have been selected on the basis of their potential clinical significance (possible mechanism in parentheses where appropriate)—not necessarily inclusive (» = major clinical significance):

Note: Combinations containing any of the following medications, depending on the amount present, may also interact with this medication.

Acetaminophen
(risk of hepatotoxicity from a single toxic dose or prolonged use of acetaminophen may be increased and therapeutic efficacy may be decreased in patients regularly taking other hepatic enzyme-inducing agents such as phenytoin)

» Adrenocorticoids, glucocorticoid and mineralocorticoid, or
Anticonvulsants, succinimide, or
Carbamazepine or

» Contraceptives, estrogen-containing, oral, or

» Corticotropin (ACTH) or
Cyclosporine or
Dacarbazine or
Digitalis glycosides or
Disopyramide or
Doxycycline or

» Estrogens or

Furosemide or
Levodopa or
Mexiletine or
Quinidine
(therapeutic effects of these medications may be decreased because of increased metabolism and decreased plasma concentrations, which may result from hydantoin anticonvulsants' induction of hepatic microsomal enzymes; dosage adjustments of these medications may be necessary)

(carbamazepine may also induce metabolism of hydantoin anticonvulsants; monitoring of blood concentrations is recommended as a guide to dosage, especially when either carbamazepine or the hydantoin is added to or withdrawn from an existing regimen)

(in addition, concurrent use of hydantoin anticonvulsants with oral, estrogen-containing contraceptives may result in breakthrough bleeding and contraceptive failure due to the increased rate of hepatic enzyme metabolism of steroids induced by hydantoins; the dose of the estrogenic substance in the oral contraceptive may be increased to diminish bleeding and decrease the risk of conception)

» Alcohol or
» CNS depression-producing medications
(CNS depression may be enhanced)

(chronic use of alcohol may decrease the serum concentrations and effectiveness of hydantoins; concurrent use of hydantoin anticonvulsants with acute alcohol intake may increase serum hydantoin concentrations)

» Amiodarone
(concurrent use with phenytoin and possibly with other hydantoin anticonvulsants may increase plasma concentrations of the hydantoin, resulting in increased effects and/or toxicity)

» Antacids, aluminum-magnesium-containing and calcium carbonate-containing
(concurrent use may decrease the bioavailability of phenytoin; doses of antacids and phenytoin should be separated by about 2 to 3 hours)

» Anticoagulants, coumarin- or indandione-derivative, or
» Chloramphenicol or
» Cimetidine or
» Disulfiram or
Influenza virus vaccine or
Isoniazid or
Methylphenidate or
» Phenylbutazone or
Ranitidine or
Salicylates or
» Sulfonamides
(serum concentrations of hydantoin anticonvulsants may be increased because of decreased metabolism, thereby increasing the hydantoins' effects and/or toxicity; dosage adjustments of the anticonvulsant may be necessary)

(in addition, the anticoagulant effect of coumarin- or indandione-derivative anticoagulants may be increased initially, but decreased with continued concurrent use)

Antidepressants, tricyclic and, possibly, structurally related compounds such as cyclobenzaprine, or
Haloperidol or
Loxapine or
Maprotiline or
Molindone or
Monoamine oxidase (MAO) inhibitors, including furazolidone and procarbazine, or
Phenothiazines or
Pimozide or
Thioxanthenes
(these medications may lower the seizure threshold and decrease the anticonvulsant effects of hydantoin anticonvulsants;

CNS depression may be enhanced; dosage adjustment of the hydantoin anticonvulsant may be necessary)

(in addition, concurrent use of phenytoin with tricyclic antidepressants may lower serum concentrations of the antidepressant; dosage increases of the tricyclic antidepressant may be required to produce improvement of the depressed state)

(also, molindone contains calcium ions, which interfere with the absorption of phenytoin)

(also, concurrent use of phenothiazines may inhibit phenytoin metabolism, leading to phenytoin intoxication)

Antidiabetic agents, oral, or
Insulin
(hydantoin anticonvulsants may increase serum glucose concentrations and the possibility of hyperglycemia; dosage adjustment of either or both medications may be necessary)

Barbiturates or
Primidone
(concurrent use may produce variable and unpredictable effects on hydantoin metabolism; serum hydantoin concentrations should be closely monitored)

» Calcium
(when used as an excipient in phenytoin capsules, calcium sulfate can decrease phenytoin absorption by as much as 20%)

(concurrent use of phenytoin with calcium supplements or any tablets or capsules that contain calcium sulfate as an excipient may result in formation of nonabsorbable complexes, thereby decreasing the bioavailability of both calcium and phenytoin; patients should be advised to take these medications 1 to 3 hours apart)

Carbonic anhydrase inhibitors
(osteopenia induced by hydantoin anticonvulsants may be enhanced; it is recommended that patients receiving concurrent therapy be monitored for early signs of osteopenia and that the carbonic anhydrase inhibitor be discontinued and appropriate treatment initiated if necessary)

» Diazoxide, oral
(concurrent use with hydantoin anticonvulsants may decrease the efficacy of phenytoin and the hyperglycemic effect of diazoxide and is not recommended)

Dopamine
(use of intravenous phenytoin in patients maintained on dopamine may produce sudden hypotension and bradycardia; this reaction is considered to be dose-rate dependent; if anticonvulsant therapy is necessary during administration of dopamine, an alternative to phenytoin should be considered)

Enflurane or
Halothane or
Methoxyflurane
(chronic use of hydantoin anticonvulsants prior to anesthesia may increase metabolism of anesthetic, leading to increased risk of hepatotoxicity, nephrotoxicity [with methoxyflurane only], and hydantoin toxicity)

Enteral feeding solutions
(concurrent use with phenytoin may decrease phenytoin absorption, possibly necessitating an increase in dosage; some clinicians recommend that at least 2 hours should elapse between feeding and phenytoin administration; if phenytoin suspension or capsule contents are administered via nasogastric tubing, flushing the tube with 2 to 4 ounces of water before and after administration has been suggested; phenytoin serum concentrations should be carefully monitored during concurrent therapy)

» Fluconazole or
Ketoconazole or
Miconazole
(concurrent use of fluconazole with phenytoin may decrease the metabolism of phenytoin, resulting in increased plasma

phenytoin concentrations; a 75% increase in the area under the curve [AUC] of phenytoin was found in volunteers given 200 mg of fluconazole per day; phenytoin concentrations must be carefully monitored)

(concurrent use of ketoconazole with phenytoin may result in altered metabolism of either ketoconazole, phenytoin, or both; in addition, time to peak serum concentration of ketoconazole may be delayed; response to both medications should be closely monitored)

(serum concentrations of phenytoin have been reported to be increased by miconazole, another imidazole derivative, resulting in phenytoin toxicity; dosage adjustments may be necessary before and after miconazole therapy)

Folic acid
(although hydantoin anticonvulsants deplete the body of folate stores, supplementation with folic acid may result in lowered serum hydantoin concentrations and possible loss of seizure control; therefore, an increase in hydantoin dosage may be necessary in patients who receive folate supplementation)

Leucovorin
(large doses of leucovorin may counteract the anticonvulsant effects of hydantoin anticonvulsants)

Levothyroxine
(concurrent use with phenytoin may reduce serum protein binding of levothyroxine and reduce total serum T_4 by 15 to 25%; however, most patients remain euthyroid, and dosage of thyroid hormone does not need to be altered)

» Lidocaine or
Propranolol and probably other beta-adrenergic blocking agents
(concurrent use with intravenous phenytoin may produce additive cardiac depressant effects; hydantoin anticonvulsants may also increase hepatic enzyme metabolism of lidocaine, reducing its intravenous concentration)

» Methadone
(chronic use of phenytoin may increase methadone metabolism, probably by induction of hepatic microsomal enzyme activity, and may precipitate withdrawal symptoms in patients being treated for opioid dependence; methadone dosage adjustments may be necessary when phenytoin therapy is initiated or discontinued)

Nifedipine or
Verapamil
(caution is advised when nifedipine or verapamil is used concurrently with hydantoin anticonvulsants, which are highly protein-bound medications, since changes in serum concentrations of the free, unbound medications may occur)

Omeprazole
(inhibition of the cytochrome P-450 enzyme system by omeprazole, especially at higher doses, may cause a decrease in the hepatic metabolism of phenytoin; delayed elimination and increased serum concentrations may result, with considerable interpatient variablity)

» Phenacemide
(risk of additive toxicity when phenacemide is used concurrently with hydantoin anticonvulsants; concurrent use of phenacemide with ethotoin has been reported to cause paranoid symptoms; extreme caution is recommended during concurrent use of these medications)

Rifampin
(concurrent use with phenytoin may stimulate the hepatic metabolism of phenytoin, increasing its elimination and thus counteracting its anticonvulsant effect; careful monitoring of serum hydantoin concentrations and dosage adjustments may be necessary)

» Streptozocin
(phenytoin may protect pancreatic beta cells from the toxic effects of streptozocin, thus reducing streptozocin's therapeutic effects; concurrent use is not recommended)

Sucralfate
(concurrent use of sucralfate may decrease the absorption of hydantoin anticonvulsants)

Sulfinpyrazone
(sulfinpyrazone may displace hydantoin anticonvulsants from plasma protein-binding sites and decrease their metabolism, possibly leading to increased plasma concentrations and elimination half-life; although plasma hydantoin concentration is not consistently increased, it is recommended that patients be monitored for signs of hydantoin toxicity)

Trazodone
(increased plasma hydantoin concentrations have been reported when hydantoin anticonvulsants are used concurrently with trazodone; caution and close monitoring are suggested)

» Valproic acid
(valproic acid may displace phenytoin from protein-binding sites and may inhibit the metabolism of phenytoin; phenytoin, through enzyme induction, may lower valproate levels; there may be an increased risk of liver toxicity, especially in infants; close monitoring of the patient is required since variable serum phenytoin concentrations have resulted; monitoring of free phenytoin concentrations is advised by some clinicians; dosage of phenytoin should be adjusted as required by clinical situation; caution is advised also for use with other hydantoin anticonvulsants)

Vitamin D
(hydantoin anticonvulsants may reduce effect of vitamin D by accelerating metabolism through hepatic microsomal enzyme induction; patients on long-term anticonvulsant therapy may require vitamin D supplementation to prevent osteomalacia, although rickets is rare)

» Xanthines, such as:
Aminophylline
Caffeine
Oxtriphylline
Theophylline
(concurrent use may stimulate hepatic metabolism of the xanthines [except dyphylline], resulting in increased theophylline clearance, especially if plasma phenytoin concentrations are in the usual therapeutic range for at least 5 days; also, simultaneous use with the xanthines may inhibit phenytoin absorption, resulting in decreased serum phenytoin concentrations; serum concentrations of phenytoin and theophylline should be monitored during concurrent therapy; dosage adjustments of both phenytoin and theophylline may be necessary)

Contraindications/Medical problems
The contraindications/medical problems included have been selected on the basis of their potential clinical significance (reasons given in parentheses where appropriate)—not necessarily inclusive (» = major clinical significance).

Except under special circumstances, this medication should not be used when the following medical problems exist:
» Cardiac function impairment, such as Adams-Stokes syndrome, second and third degree AV block, sino-atrial block, and sinus bradycardia
(parenteral phenytoin administration may affect ventricular automaticity and result in ventricular arrhythmias)

Risk-benefit should be considered when the following medical problems exist:
Alcoholism, active
(serum phenytoin concentrations may be decreased)

» Blood dyscrasias
(risk of serious infections may be increased)

Cardiovascular disease
(parenteral phenytoin administration may result in atrial and ventricular conduction depression, ventricular fibrillation, or reduced cardiac output, especially in the elderly or gravely ill

patients; phenytoin should be administered at a rate of no more than 25 mg a minute, and if necessary, at a slow rate of 5 to 10 mg a minute)

Diabetes mellitus
(hyperglycemia may be potentiated)

Fever or febrile illness—temperature >101 °F for more than 24 hours
(serum concentrations of hydantoin anticonvulsants may be decreased because of induction of hepatic oxidative enzymes during fever)

» Hepatic function impairment
(metabolism of hydantoin anticonvulsants may be reduced, thereby increasing the possibility of toxic serum concentrations; protein-binding alterations are also likely, due to a secondary decrease in albumin concentrations)

» Porphyria
(risk of exacerbation)

» Renal function impairment
(excretion and protein binding may be altered)

» Sensitivity to hydantoin anticonvulsants
Systemic lupus erythematosus
(risk of exacerbation)

Thyroid function impairment
(free, circulating thyroxine [FT_4] and total thyroxine [T_4] concentrations are decreased by phenytoin therapy; patients usually remain euthyroid)

Side/Adverse Effects

Note: Although not all of these side effects have been attributed specifically to each hydantoin anticonvulsant, a potential exists for their occurrence during the use of any hydantoin.

The following side/adverse effects have been selected on the basis of their potential clinical significance (possible signs and symptoms in parentheses where appropriate)—not necessarily inclusive:

Those indicating need for medical attention
Incidence more frequent
CNS toxicity (nystagmus [uncontrolled back-and-forth and/or rolling eye movements]; ataxia [clumsiness or unsteadiness]; confusion; mood or mental changes; muscle weakness; increased frequency of seizures; slurred speech or stuttering; trembling of hands; unusual excitement; nervousness; or irritability)—usually with long-term use, but may be dose-related; *gingival hyperplasia* (bleeding, tender, or enlarged gums)—incidence rare with ethotoin; higher incidence in children and young adults; *lupus erythematosus, phenytoin hypersensitivity syndrome, Stevens-Johnson syndrome, or toxic epidermal necrolysis* (fever, muscle pain, skin rash, or sore throat)

Note: *Phenytoin hypersensitivity syndrome* may be manifest in many ways. Fever, rash, and lymphadenopathy frequently occur together, and may be part of more than one hypersensitivity syndrome. Skin rash is the most frequent hypersensitivity reaction; licheniform or maculopapular or morbilliform rash, often pruritic, may present simply or may be prodromal of more serious dermatological reactions such as *Stevens-Johnson syndrome* or *toxic epidermal necrolysis.* Lymphoid syndromes (including lymphoid hyperplasia, pseudolymphomas, and pseudo-pseudolymphomas) occur less commonly and are generally reversible upon discontinuation of phenytoin. Phenytoin-induced hepatitis and hepatic necrosis are another major hypersensitivity reaction, as is eosinophilia, which occurs commonly. Less commonly occurring syndromes include polyarteritis, polymyositis, or systemic *lupus erythematosus;* disseminated intravascular coagulopathy, serum sickness, and renal failure may also occur.

Rash usually appears in the first two weeks of treatment; *hypersensitivity syndrome* usually occurs 3 to 8 weeks after, but may occur as long as 12 weeks after initiation of phenytoin therapy. Syndrome may be life-threatening, but early intervention may prevent renal failure, severe rhabdomyolysis or hepatic necrosis. Other factors, such as a positive family history for phenytoin hypersensitivity reactions or concomitant administration of cranial radiation therapy, may increase the risk of hypersensitivity syndrome occurring.

Incidence rare
Blood dyscrasias, including agranulocytosis (chills, fever, sore throat, unusual tiredness or weakness); *leukopenia* (fever, chills, sore throat); *pancytopenia* (nosebleeds or other unusual bleeding or bruising); *thrombocytopenia* (fever, sore throat, unusual bleeding or bruising); *cholestatic jaundice or hepatitis* (dark urine, light gray-colored stools, loss of appetite and weight, severe stomach pain, yellow eyes or skin, skin rash or itching, dizziness, nausea or vomiting, joint pain, unusual tiredness or weakness); *choreoathetoid movements, transient* (restlessness or agitation; uncontrolled jerking or twisting movements of hands, arms, or legs; uncontrolled movements of lips, tongue, or cheeks); *cognitive impairment* (defects in intelligence, short-term memory, learning ability, and attention); *periarteritis nodosa* (abdominal pain, soreness of muscles, unusual tiredness or weakness, fever with or without chills, headache, loss of appetite and weight); *Peyronie's disease* (pain of penis on erection); *pulmonary infiltrates or fibrosis* (fever; troubled or quick, shallow breathing; unusual tiredness or weakness; loss of appetite and weight; chest discomfort); *vitamin D and/or calcium imbalance* (frequent bone fractures, bone malformations, slowed growth)

Note: Many cases of mephenytoin-induced *blood dyscrasias* occur in patients given mephenytoin for a second time after a period of abstinence.

Choreoatheloid movements may be due to sudden administration of intravenous phenytoin for status epilepticus; effect usually lasts 24 to 48 hours after discontinuation of phenytoin and may resolve spontaneously; effect is unrelated to serum hydantoin toxicity or duration of use.

With chronic use
Peripheral polyneuropathy, predominantly sensory (numbness, tingling, or pain in hands or feet)—with phenytoin

With parenteral use only
Burning pain at injection site, rarely with necrosis and sloughing

Symptoms of overdose
Ataxia (clumsiness or unsteadiness) *or staggering walk; blurred or double vision; severe confusion; severe dizziness or drowsiness; dysarthria* (stuttering) *or slurred speech; hyperreflexia; nausea and vomiting; nystagmus* (continuous, uncontrolled back-and-forth and/or rolling eye movements); *tremor; unusual tiredness or weakness*

Those indicating need for medical attention only if they continue or are bothersome
Incidence more frequent
Constipation; mild dizziness; mild drowsiness; nausea and vomiting

Incidence less frequent
Diarrhea—with ethotoin; *enlargement of facial features, including thickening of lips, widening of nasal tip, and protrusion of jaw; gynecomastia* (swelling of breasts)—in males; *headache; hypertrichosis* (unusual and excessive hair growth on body and face)—primarily with phenytoin; *insomnia* (trouble in sleeping); *muscle twitching*

Patient Consultation

In providing consultation, consider emphasizing the following selected information (» = major clinical significance):

Before using this medication
» Conditions affecting use, especially:
   Sensitivity to hydantoin anticonvulsants
   Pregnancy—Hydantoin anticonvulsants cross placenta; risk-benefit should be considered because of possibility of increased birth defects; seizures may increase during pregnancy with need for dose increase; bleeding problems may occur in mother during delivery and in baby immediately after delivery
   Breast-feeding—Ethotoin and phenytoin excreted in breast milk
   Use in children—Bleeding, tender, and enlarged gums more common in children; unusual and excessive hair growth, more noticeable in young girls; decreased performance in school (cognitive impairment) may occur with long-term use of high doses
   Use in the elderly—Side effects more likely to occur in the elderly; hydantoin anticonvulsants metabolized more slowly in elderly, possibly leading to toxicity
   Use in athletes—Hydantoin anticonvulsants are banned and, in some cases, tested for in competitors in biathlon and modern pentathlon events by the U.S. Olympic Committee (USOC)
   Dental—Gingival hyperplasia may appear; good dental hygiene and visits to dentist every 3 months for cleaning recommended; agranulocytosis or thrombocytopenia may cause gingival bleeding, slowed healing, and infections
   Other medications, especially adrenocorticoids, estrogen-containing oral contraceptives, estrogens, aminophylline, amiodarone, antacids, anticoagulants, caffeine, CNS depressants, alcohol, chloramphenicol, cimetidine, diazoxide, disulfiram, isoniazid, calcium-containing medicine, fluconazole, lidocaine, methadone, oxtriphylline, phenacemide, phenylbutazone, streptozocin, sulfonamides, theophylline, or valproic acid
   Other medical problems, especially blood dyscrasias, cardiac function impairment, hepatic function impairment, history of hydantoin hypersensitivity, porphyria, or renal function impairment

Proper use of this medication
   Proper administration:
   For liquid dosage forms—Shaking well; using an accurate measuring device, such as a specially marked measuring spoon, a plastic syringe, or a small graduated cup
   For chewable tablet dosage form—Chewing or crushing tablets or swallowing them whole
   For capsule dosage form—Swallowing capsule whole
   Taking with food to reduce gastrointestinal irritation
» Compliance with therapy; taking every day exactly as directed
» Missed dose: If dosing schedule is—
   One dose a day: Taking as soon as possible unless next day, then continuing on schedule; not doubling doses
   Several doses a day: Taking as soon as possible unless within 4 hours of next scheduled dose, then continuing on regular schedule; not doubling doses
   Checking with doctor if doses are missed for 2 or more days in a row
» Proper storage

Precautions while using this medication
» Regular visits to physician to check progress of therapy
» Not taking other medication without physician's advice
» Avoiding the use of alcoholic beverages and other CNS depressants while taking this medicine
   Not taking within 2 to 3 hours of taking antacids or medication for diarrhea

Not changing brands or dosage forms of phenytoin without checking with physician or pharmacist
» Checking with physician before discontinuing medication; gradual dosage reduction is usually needed to maintain seizure control
   Carrying medical identification card or bracelet during therapy
   Diabetic patients: Checking blood or urine sugar concentrations
   Caution if any laboratory tests required; possible interference with test results of dexamethasone, metyrapone, or Schilling tests, thyroid function tests, or gallium citrate Ga 67 imaging
» Caution if any kind of surgery, dental treatment, or emergency treatment is required
» Caution when driving, using machines, or doing other jobs requiring alertness
For phenytoin or mephenytoin only
» Maintaining good dental hygiene and seeing dentist every 3 months for teeth cleaning, to prevent tenderness, bleeding, and enlargement of gums

Side/adverse effects
   Increased incidence of gingival hyperplasia in children and young adults taking phenytoin or mephenytoin
   Unusual and excessive hair growth more noticeable in young girls
   Signs of potential side effects, especially blood dyscrasias, CNS toxicity, cholestatic jaundice, cognitive impairment, hepatitis, an increase in seizures, lupus erythematosus, phenytoin hypersensitivity syndrome, periarteritis nodosa, Peyronie's disease, pulmonary infiltrates or fibrosis, Stevens-Johnson syndrome, toxic epidermal necrolysis, transient choreoathetoid movements, or Vitamin D and/or calcium imbalance

General Dosing Information

Dosage must be individualized. Monitoring of serum phenytoin concentrations is recommended because of the great variation of response among patients to the hydantoin anticonvulsants and because of the relatively narrow therapeutic serum concentration range.

Geriatric patients, seriously ill patients, or patients with impaired hepatic function may require lower initial dosage with subsequent adjustments, because of slow hydantoin metabolism or decreased protein binding. If phenytoin is administered intravenously, the rate must be slowed to not more than 25 mg a minute, and possibly to as low as 5 to 10 mg a minute.

When patients are transferred from hydantoins to other anticonvulsant medication or vice versa, there should be a gradual increase in the dosage of the added medication and a gradual decrease in the dosage of the discontinued medication over a period of a few weeks. When an enzyme-inducing medication is added or removed from a regimen, the metabolism of the remaining medications will be altered. In most patients, changes in enzyme induction may occur over a period of weeks.

When single-drug anticonvulsant therapy is to be discontinued in patients with seizure disorders, dosage should be reduced gradually over a period of 6 to 12 months, to prevent possible recurrence of seizures. Abrupt withdrawal may lead to status epilepticus.

The lethal dose of phenytoin in adults is estimated to be 2 to 5 grams. The lethal dose in children is unknown.

Diet/Nutrition

Oral hydantoin anticonvulsants may be taken with or immediately after meals to lessen gastric irritation. However, the medication should always be taken at the same time in relation to meals to ensure consistent absorption.

Patients on long-term hydantoin therapy may have increased folic acid requirements. However, increased hydantoin dosages may be necessary in patients who receive folate supplementation because such supplementation may result in decreased serum hydantoin concentrations and possible loss of seizure control.

ETHOTOIN

Summary of Differences

Pharmacology: Half-life—3 to 9 hours.
Side/adverse effects:
  Diarrhea has been reported.
  Drowsiness and sedation are dose related and quite common.
  Gum hyperplasia is rare; ethotoin is sometimes substituted for phenytoin therapy when gingival hyperplasia is a problem.
  Incidence of ataxia is rare.
  Incidence of hypertrichosis is lower than with other hydantoin anticonvulsants.

Additional Dosing Information

See also *General Dosing Information.*

Ethotoin may be substituted for phenytoin without loss of seizure control for improvement of gum hyperplasia, or other side effects, during anticonvulsant therapy. Ethotoin doses are usually 4 to 6 times greater than those of phenytoin.

Oral Dosage Forms

ETHOTOIN TABLETS USP

Usual adult and adolescent dose: Anticonvulsant—Oral, 500 mg to 1 gram the first day, usually divided into four to six doses, the dosage being gradually increased over several days until seizure control is obtained.

Note: Maintenance dosage of less than 2 grams a day has been found to be ineffective in most adults.
        Geriatric and debilitated patients may require a lower initial dosage.

Usual adult prescribing limits: Up to 3 grams a day.

Auxiliary labeling:
  • May cause drowsiness.
  • Avoid alcoholic beverages.

MEPHENYTOIN

Summary of Differences

Pharmacology: Half-life averages 95 to 144 hours (including active metabolite, nirvanol).
Side/adverse effects:
  Drowsiness and sedation are dose related and quite common.
  Higher incidence of blood dyscrasias than with other hydantoin anticonvulsants.

Additional Dosing Information

See also *General Dosing Information.*

Mephenytoin is usually used only after safer anticonvulsants have been tried and have proven unsatisfactory.

Oral Dosage Forms

MEPHENYTOIN TABLETS USP

Usual adult and adolescent dose: Anticonvulsant—Oral, 50 to 100 mg once a day, the dosage being increased by an additional 50 to 100 mg a day at one-week intervals until seizure control is obtained up to a maximum of 1.2 grams a day.

Note: Geriatric patients and debilitated patients may require a lower initial dosage.

Auxiliary labeling:
  • May cause drowsiness.
  • Avoid alcoholic beverages.

PHENYTOIN

Summary of Differences

Category: Also used as an antiarrhythmic, for ventricular arrhythmias, especially when arrhythmia is digitalis-induced or caused by tricyclic antidepressant toxicity; as a collagenase synthesis inhibitor in epidermolysis bullosa; as an antineuralgic in trigeminal neuralgia; and as a muscle relaxant in certain movement disorders.
Pharmacology: Because phenytoin exhibits saturable or dose-dependent pharmacokinetics, the apparent half-life of phenytoin changes with dose and serum concentration.
Side/adverse effects: Incidence of hypertrichosis is more frequent than with other hydantoin anticonvulsants.

Additional Dosing Information

See also *General Dosing Information.*

For oral dosage forms

The prescribing physician should be consulted before a prescription is changed from one phenytoin dosage form to another because of possible differences in bioavailability, due to varying amounts of calcium sulfate excipient, or amount of phenytoin acid contained in the product. Phenytoin dosage forms based on phenytoin acid (oral suspension and chewable tablets) contain 8% more drug on a mg-per-mg basis than those based on phenytoin sodium. Phenytoin intoxication has been reported following weight for weight substitution of phenytoin acid for phenytoin sodium.

The prescribing physician should be consulted before a product is dispensed that is different from that currently taken by the patient, or from that originally prescribed. Bioavailability may vary enough among oral phenytoin sodium products of different manufacturers to result in either a loss of seizure control or a toxic blood concentration.

Extended Phenytoin Sodium Capsules USP is the only dosage form used for once-a-day dosing, and then, only after patients have been stabilized on a divided dosage, generally 300 to 400 mg a day.

Phenytoin oral suspension is generally not recommended for once-a-day dosing because it is not an extended-release dosage form. The suspension may be adequate for more frequent dosing, if vigorously shaken to avoid inadequate dispersal of phenytoin throughout the vehicle.

For parenteral dosage forms

Intravenous phenytoin sodium should be administered by direct intravenous injection into a large vein through a large-gauge needle or intravenous catheter at a rate not to exceed 50 mg a minute. Faster rates of administration may result in hypotension, cardiovascular collapse, or CNS depression, related to the propylene glycol diluent.

Intravenous administration should be monitored by cardiac function and blood pressure readings.

To minimize local venous irritation from intravenous injection of phenytoin, each dose must be followed by 0.9% sodium chloride injection through the same in-place needle or catheter. Extravasation should be avoided, as phenytoin injection is caustic to tissues because of its high alkalinity (pH=12), and possibly also because of the propylene glycol in the vehicle. Soft tissue injury ranging from irritation to extensive necrosis and sloughing has been reported even when extravasation has not occurred.

Some clinicians suggest that, to prevent serious local inflammatory reactions, intermittent phenytoin infusion may be desirable and that such an infusion can be made feasible if all of the following criteria are met:

- Phenytoin injection is admixed only with no more than 50 mL of 0.9% sodium chloride injection.
- The final concentration of phenytoin is between 1 and 10 mg per mL.
- Admixture is done *immediately* before beginning the infusion.
- Infusion is completed within 1 hour.
- All tubing is flushed with 0.9% sodium chloride injection before and after infusion.
- A 0.45 to 0.22 micron filter is placed on the line.

When phenytoin injection is administered by infusion, the maximum rate of infusion is 50 mg a minute. However, for patients who may develop hypotension, who are on a sympathomimetic medication, who have cardiovascular disease, or who are older than 65 years of age, the maximum rate of infusion should be 25 mg a minute and possibly as low as 5 to 10 mg a minute. Vigilant ECG monitoring of cardiovascular status throughout the duration of infusion is required.

For rapid control of seizures, concomitant administration of an intravenous benzodiazepine or a short-acting barbiturate may be necessary because of the slow rate of administration necessary for phenytoin injection.

Because of the delayed absorption of intramuscularly administered phenytoin and the high degree of local irritation from the alkaline solution, the intramuscular route of administration is not recommended when the intravenous or oral route is available.

Intramuscular administration is not recommended for treatment of status epilepticus since serum concentrations in the therapeutic range cannot be readily achieved for up to 24 hours. Erratic absorption is partly caused by tissue precipitation of phenytoin. Muscle necrosis has also been reported.

Intramuscular administration during neurosurgery, for patients stabilized on oral phenytoin, requires a dose 50% greater than the oral dosage used to maintain serum concentrations. When a patient is returned to the oral route, dosage should be reduced by 50% of the original oral dosage for 1 week to compensate for the sustained release of medication from prior intramuscular injections.

If the need for intramuscular administration continues for more than 1 week, alternative routes such as gastric intubation should be considered.

Oral Dosage Forms

Note: Bracketed uses in the *Dosage Forms* section refer to categories of use and/or indications that are not included in U.S. product labeling.

PHENYTOIN ORAL SUSPENSION USP

Usual adult and adolescent dose: Anticonvulsant—Oral, initially, 125 mg three times a day, the dosage being adjusted at seven- to ten-day intervals as needed and tolerated.

Note: For seriously ill or debilitated patients, or patients with impaired hepatic function, the total dose is often reduced.

Usual geriatric dose: Anticonvulsant—Oral, initially 3 mg per kg of body weight a day, in divided doses, the dosage being adjusted according to serum hydantoin concentrations and the patient's response.

Auxiliary labeling:
- Shake well.
- Protect from freezing.
- Avoid alcoholic beverages.

Additional information: May contain 0.6% alcohol.

PHENYTOIN TABLETS USP (CHEWABLE)

Usual adult and adolescent dose: Anticonvulsant—Oral, initially, 100 to 125 mg three times a day, the dosage being adjusted at seven- to ten-day intervals as needed and tolerated.

Note: For seriously ill or debilitated patients, or patients with impaired hepatic function, the total dose is often reduced.

Usual geriatric dose: Anticonvulsant—Oral, initially 3 mg per kg of body weight a day, in divided doses, the dosage being adjusted according to serum hydantoin concentrations and the patient's response.

Auxiliary labeling:
- May be chewed or crushed.
- Avoid alcoholic beverages.

EXTENDED PHENYTOIN SODIUM CAPSULES USP

Usual adult and adolescent dose:

Anticonvulsant—Oral, initially, 100 mg three times a day, the dosage being adjusted at seven- to ten-day intervals as needed and tolerated. When established, the daily maintenance dosage may be given on a once-a-day basis in accordance with patient tolerance.

Note: An oral loading dose of 1 gram may be given, the dose being divided as follows: Initially 400 mg, then 300 mg after two hours, followed by an additional 300 mg in two hours; normal maintenance dosing is started twenty-four hours after the loading dose. Alternatively, some clinicians recommend an oral loading dose of 20 mg per kg of body weight, divided into 3 to 4 doses and administered at two-hour intervals.

Patients with a history of renal or liver disease should not receive a loading dose. Use of this regimen should be limited to patients in a clinic or hospital setting where phenytoin serum concentrations can be closely monitored.

Once-a-day dosage should be considered only for adult patients whose condition has been stabilized by divided doses of extended phenytoin sodium capsules given as 100 mg three times a day. This single 300-mg daily dosage has the advantage of convenience and improved compliance.

For geriatric or seriously ill patients or for debilitated patients or patients with impaired hepatic function, the total dose is often reduced.

[Collagenase synthesis/secretion inhibitor][1]—Oral, initially, 2 to 3 mg per kg of body weight a day, divided into two doses, the dosage being increased at two- to three-week intervals as needed and tolerated to bring serum concentrations to at least 8 to 10 mcg per mL. (This usually requires a daily dose of 100 to 300 mg a day.)

[Antineuralgic][1]—Oral, 200 to 600 mg a day, in divided doses, the dose being adjusted as needed and tolerated.

[Skeletal muscle relaxant][1]—Oral, up to 300 to 600 mg a day, as needed and tolerated.

Usual geriatric dose: Anticonvulsant—Oral, initial, 3 mg per kg of body weight a day, in divided doses, the dosage being adjusted according to serum hydantoin concentrations and the patient's response.

Auxiliary labeling: • Avoid alcoholic beverages.

Additional information: The sodium content of phenytoin sodium is 0.35 mEq (8 mg) per 100-mg capsule.

PROMPT PHENYTOIN SODIUM CAPSULES USP

Usual adult and adolescent dose:

Anticonvulsant—Oral, 100 mg three times a day, the dosage being adjusted at seven- to ten-day intervals as needed and tolerated.

Note: For geriatric or seriously ill patients or for debilitated patients or patients with impaired hepatic function, the total dose is often reduced.

[Collagenase synthesis/secretion inhibitor][1]—Oral, initially, 2 to 3 mg per kg of body weight a day, divided into two doses, the dosage being increased at two- to three-week intervals as needed and tolerated to bring serum concentrations to at least 8 mcg per mL. (This usually requires a daily dose of 100 to 300 mg a day.)

Usual geriatric dose: Anticonvulsant—Oral, initial, 3 mg per kg of body weight a day, in divided doses, the dosage being adjusted according to serum hydantoin concentrations and the patient's response.

Auxiliary labeling: • Avoid alcoholic beverages.

Note:

Phenytoin sodium capsules labeled "Prompt" are not intended for once-a-day dosage because the phenytoin may be too promptly bioavailable and may cause toxic serum concentrations of phenytoin.

Note that one 100-mg capsule of phenytoin sodium contains 92% phenytoin and is therefore not equivalent to two 50-mg phenytoin chewable tablets containing 100% phenytoin.

Additional information: The sodium content of phenytoin sodium is 0.35 mEq (8 mg) per 100-mg capsule.

Parenteral Dosage Forms

Note: Bracketed uses in the *Dosage Forms* section refer to categories of use and/or indications that are not included in U.S. product labeling.

PHENYTOIN SODIUM INJECTION USP

Usual adult and adolescent dose:
Anticonvulsant in status epilepticus—

Initial: Intravenous, direct, 15 to 20 mg per kg of body weight administered at a rate not to exceed 50 mg a minute.

Note: For obese patients, the loading dose should be calculated on the basis of ideal body weight plus 1.33 times the excess weight over ideal weight, since phenytoin preferentially distributes into fat.

Maintenance: Intravenous, direct, 100 mg every six to eight hours, at a rate not exceeding 50 mg a minute.

Note: Maintenance therapy, intravenously, 100 mg every six to eight hours, or orally, 5 mg per kg a day, divided into two to four doses, should begin about twelve to twenty-four hours after a loading dose is given.

[Antiarrhythmic][1]—Intravenous, direct, 50 to 100 mg every ten to fifteen minutes as needed and tolerated to stop arrhythmia, but not to exceed a total dose of 15 mg per kg of body weight, administered slowly at a rate not exceeding 50 mg a minute.

Note: For geriatric or seriously ill patients or for debilitated patients or patients with impaired hepatic function, the total dose is often reduced and the rate of intravenous administration slowed to 25 mg a minute, possibly as low as 5 to 10 mg a minute, to lessen the possibility of side effects.

Although the manufacturers recommend that phenytoin not be added to intravenous infusions, some clinicians routinely use such infusions. If phenytoin is administered by infusion, the rate of administration should not exceed 50 mg per minute; some investigators have suggested rates of 20 to 40 mg per minute.

Additional information: The sodium content of phenytoin sodium injection is approximately 0.2 mEq (4.5 mg) per mL.

[1]Not included in Canadian product labeling.

ANTICONVULSANTS, SUCCINIMIDE　Systemic

INN: Included in brackets after individual generic listings, if different from the U.S. or Canadian generic name.

Some commonly used *brand names* are:

In the U.S.—
　Celontin [Methsuximide]　　　　*Zarontin* [Ethosuximide]
　Milontin [Phensuximide]

In Canada—
　Celontin [Methsuximide]
　Zarontin [Ethosuximide]

ORAL
ETHOSUXIMIDE
　Ethosuximide Capsules USP
　　In the U.S. and Canada—*Zarontin*
　Ethosuximide Syrup
　　In the U.S. and Canada—*Zarontin*
METHSUXIMIDE [INN: Mesuximide]
　Methsuximide Capsules USP
　　In the U.S. and Canada—*Celontin*
PHENSUXIMIDE†
　Phensuximide Capsules USP†
　　In the U.S.—*Milontin*

---

†Not commercially available in Canada.

Category: Anticonvulsant.

Indications

Note: Bracketed information in the *Indications* section refers to uses not included in U.S. product labeling.

Accepted

Epilepsy, absence seizure pattern (treatment)—Ethosuximide, the drug of choice, and phensuximide are indicated for the control of seizures in absence (petit mal) epilepsy. Methsuximide is indicated for the management of absence seizures refractory to other medication.

[Epilepsy, complex partial seizure pattern (treatment)][1]—Methsuximide may also be used in the treatment of complex partial seizures.

---

[1]Not included in Canadian product labeling.

Pharmacology

Mechanism of action/Effect: Poorly defined; succinimide anticonvulsants are thought to increase the seizure threshold and suppress the paroxysmal three-cycle-per-second spike-and-wave pattern seen with absence (petit mal) seizures. The frequency of attacks is reduced by depression of nerve transmission in the motor cortex.

These effects may be due to direct modification of membrane function in excitable cells and/or alteration of chemically mediated neurotransmission. The specific effect of ethosuximide against absence seizures appears to be due to its ability to block T-type calcium channels at concentrations that do not affect other ion channels.

Precautions to Consider

Cross-sensitivity and/or related problems
Patients sensitive to one succinimide anticonvulsant may be sensitive to the others also.

Geriatrics
Appropriate studies on the relationship of age to the effects of succinimide anticonvulsants have not been performed in the geriatric population. However, no geriatrics-specific problems have been documented to date.

Dental
The blood dyscrasia-causing effects of succinimide anticonvulsants may result in an increased incidence of microbial infection, delayed healing, and gingival bleeding. If leukopenia or thrombocytopenia occurs, dental work should be deferred until blood counts have returned to normal. Patients should be instructed in proper oral hygiene during treatment, including caution in use of regular toothbrushes, dental floss, and toothpicks.

Drug interactions and/or related problems
The following drug interactions and/or related problems have been selected on the basis of their potential clinical significance (possible mechanism in parentheses where appropriate)—not necessarily inclusive (» = major clinical significance):

Note: Combinations containing any of the following medications, depending on the amount present, may also interact with this medication.

Alcohol or
» Central nervous system (CNS) depression-producing medications, other
    (CNS depression may be enhanced)

Antidepressants, tricyclic, or
Loxapine or
Maprotiline or
Molindone or
Monoamine oxidase (MAO) inhibitors or
Phenothiazines or
Pimozide or
Thioxanthenes
    (concurrent use may lower the convulsive threshold, enhance CNS depression, and decrease the effects of the anticonvulsant medication)

Carbamazepine or
Phenobarbital or
Phenytoin or
Primidone
    (induction of hepatic microsomal enzyme activity resulting in increased metabolism and decreased serum concentrations and elimination half-lives of succinimide anticonvulsants and/or these medications may occur during concurrent therapy; monitoring of serum concentrations as a guide to dosage is recommended, especially when any anticonvulsant is added to or withdrawn from an existing regimen)

Folic acid
    (requirements for folic acid may be increased in patients receiving anticonvulsant therapy)

» Haloperidol
    (concurrent use may cause a change in the pattern and/or the frequency of epileptiform seizures; dosage adjustments of the anticonvulsant may be necessary; serum concentrations of haloperidol may be significantly reduced)

Phenacemide
    (concurrent use may result in additive toxicity)

Valproic acid
    (concurrent use of valproic acid has been reported to both increase and decrease ethosuximide concentrations due to changes in metabolism; monitoring of serum concentrations as a guide to dosage is recommended)

Contraindications/Medical problems
The contraindications/medical problems included have been selected on the basis of their potential clinical significance (reasons given in parentheses where appropriate)—not necessarily inclusive (» = major clinical significance).

Risk-benefit should be considered when the following medical problems exist:

Blood dyscrasias

Hepatic function impairment or
Renal function impairment, severe
    (morphological and functional changes may occur in liver or kidneys)

Intermittent porphyria
Sensitivity to succinimide anticonvulsants

Side/Adverse Effects
The following side/adverse effects have been selected on the basis of their potential clinical significance (possible signs and symptoms in parentheses where appropriate)—not necessarily inclusive:

Those indicating need for medical attention
Incidence more frequent
    Stevens-Johnson syndrome or systemic lupus erythematosus (skin rash and itching, swollen glands, sore throat and fever, muscle pain)
Incidence less frequent
    Aggressiveness; difficulty in concentration; mental depression; nightmares
Incidence rare
    Blood dyscrasias, including agranulocytosis (chills, fever, sore throat, unusual tiredness or weakness), *aplastic anemia* (shortness of breath, troubled breathing, wheezing, or tightness in chest; sores, ulcers, or white spots on lips or in mouth; swollen or painful glands; unusual bleeding or bruising), *eosinophilia* (fever), *leukopenia* (fever, chills, sore throat), *pancytopenia* (nosebleeds or other unusual bleeding or bruising); *precipitation of tonic-clonic convulsions; paranoid psychosis* (mood or mental changes); *pruritic erythematous rash* (skin rash and itching)
Symptoms of overdose
    Central nervous system (CNS) depression (severe drowsiness); *severe nausea and vomiting; respiratory depression* (shortness of breath, slow or irregular breathing, troubled breathing)
    Note: Methsuximide poisoning may have a biphasic profile due to the *N*-desmethyl metabolite; therefore it is important to monitor serum concentrations of *N*-desmethylmethsuximide.

Those indicating need for medical attention only if they continue or are bothersome
Incidence more frequent
    Anorexia (loss of appetite); *ataxia* (clumsiness or unsteadiness); *dizziness; drowsiness; headache; hiccups; nausea and vomiting; stomach cramps*
Incidence less frequent
    Irritability; unusual tiredness or weakness

Those not indicating need for medical attention
    Discoloration of urine (pink, red, or red-brown urine)—for phensuximide only

Patient Consultation

In providing consultation, consider emphasizing the following selected information (» = major clinical significance):

Before using this medication

» Conditions affecting use, especially:

    Sensitivity to succinimide anticonvulsants

    Pregnancy—Possible birth defects

    Use by athletes—Succinimide anticonvulsants are banned and, in some cases, tested for in competitors in biathlon and modern pentathlon events by the U.S. Olympic Committee (USOC)

    Other medications, especially CNS depressants or haloperidol

    Other medical problems, especially blood dyscrasias, intermittent porphyria, severe renal function impairment, or hepatic function impairment

Proper use of this medication

» Compliance with therapy; taking daily in regularly spaced doses as ordered

    Taking with food or milk to reduce gastric irritation

    Missed dose: Taking as soon as possible; if remembered within 4 hours of next dose, skipping missed dose and continuing on regular dosing schedule; not doubling doses

» Proper storage

Precautions while using this medication

» Regular visits to physician to check progress of therapy

» Checking with physician before discontinuing this medication; gradual dosage reduction may be necessary

» Not starting or stopping other medication without physician's advice

» Avoiding the use of alcoholic beverages and other CNS depressants while taking this medication

» Possibility of drowsiness; caution if driving or doing jobs requiring alertness

» Caution if any kind of surgery, dental treatment, or emergency treatment is required

    Carrying medical identification card or bracelet

    Not taking methsuximide capsules that are melted or not full; effectiveness may be reduced

Side/adverse effects

    Signs of potential side effects, especially blood dyscrasias, mood or mental changes, nightmares, pruritic erythematous rash, Stevens-Johnson syndrome, systemic lupus erythematosus, or tonic-clonic convulsions

    Phensuximide may cause harmless discoloration of urine (pink, red, or red-brown)

General Dosing Information

When succinimide anticonvulsants are to be discontinued, dosage should be reduced gradually to prevent possible occurrence of petit mal status.

When used to replace other anticonvulsant therapy, the dosage of the succinimide anticonvulsant should be increased gradually while that of the other medication is gradually decreased, to maintain seizure control.

If succinimide anticonvulsants are used to supplement an existing anticonvulsant regimen, their dosage should be gradually increased to the required level.

When succinimide anticonvulsants are used alone in mixed types of epilepsy, the frequency of primary generalized tonic-clonic seizures may be increased in some patients.

ETHOSUXIMIDE

Summary of Differences

Pharmacology:

    Half-life—56 to 60 hours in adults; 30 to 36 hours in children.

    Peak effect—3 to 7 hours.

    Serum concentrations, therapeutic—40 to 100 mcg/mL.

Additional Dosing Information

See also *General Dosing Information.*

Strict supervision by the physician is required if total daily dosage of ethosuximide exceeds 1.5 grams for adults or 1 gram for children up to 6 years of age.

Ethosuximide dosage may be initiated at maintenance level. When this medication is used concurrently with intravenous diazepam in management of absence status epilepticus (petit mal status), higher-than-usual starting doses may be required to rapidly achieve a therapeutic serum level.

Oral Dosage Forms

ETHOSUXIMIDE CAPSULES USP

Usual adult and adolescent dose: Anticonvulsant—Oral, 15 to 30 mg per kg of body weight a day; or initially 250 mg two times a day, the dosage being increased by an additional 250 mg a day at four- to seven-day intervals until seizure control is obtained or until the total daily dose reaches 1.5 grams.

Auxiliary labeling:
- May cause drowsiness.
- Keep container tightly closed.

ETHOSUXIMIDE SYRUP

Usual adult and adolescent dose: See *Ethosuximide Capsules USP.*

Auxiliary labeling: • May cause drowsiness.

METHSUXIMIDE

Summary of Differences

Category: Indicated in absence seizures refractory to other medication.

Pharmacology:

    Half-life—1 to 3 hours (36 to 45 hours for active metabolites).

    Serum concentration, therapeutic—10 to 40 mcg/mL.

Oral Dosage Forms

METHSUXIMIDE CAPSULES USP

Usual adult and adolescent dose: Anticonvulsant—Oral, initially 300 mg once a day, the dosage being increased by 300 mg a day at one-week intervals until seizure control is obtained or until the total daily dose reaches 1.2 grams. Alternatively, some clinicians advocate making dosage increases of 150 to 300 mg at intervals of no less than 14 days to allow plasma concentrations to reach steady-state levels.

Auxiliary labeling: • May cause drowsiness.

PHENSUXIMIDE

Summary of Differences

Pharmacology:
    Half-life—5 to 12 hours.
    Peak effect—1 to 4 hours.
Precautions: Contraindications/Medical problems—Should be used with caution in patients with intermittent porphyria.
Side/adverse effects: Causes harmless pink, red, or red-brown discoloration of urine.

Oral Dosage Forms

PHENSUXIMIDE CAPSULES USP

Usual adult and adolescent dose: Anticonvulsant—Oral, initially 500 mg two or three times a day, the dosage being increased by an additional 500 mg a day at one-week intervals until seizure control is obtained or until the total daily dose reaches 3 grams.

Auxiliary labeling:
• May cause drowsiness.
• May discolor urine.

ANTIDEPRESSANTS, MONOAMINE OXIDASE (MAO) INHIBITOR   Systemic

---

Some commonly used *brand names* are:
    In the U.S. and Canada—
        Marplan [Isocarboxazid]   *Parnate* [Tranylcypromine]
        Nardil [Phenelzine]

ORAL
ISOCARBOXAZID
    Isocarboxazid Tablets USP
        In the U.S. and Canada—*Marplan*
PHENELZINE
    Phenelzine Sulfate Tablets USP
        In the U.S. and Canada—*Nardil*
TRANYLCYPROMINE
    Tranylcypromine Sulfate Tablets USP
        In the U.S. and Canada—*Parnate*

Note: This monograph does not cover other MAO inhibitors, such as furazolidone and procarbazine, which are not used as antidepressants, and selegiline, which has its own monograph.

Category: Antidepressant; antipanic agent; headache (vascular; tension) prophylactic.

Indications

Note: Bracketed information in the *Indications* section refers to uses not included in U.S. product labeling.

Accepted
Depression, mental (treatment)—
    Phenelzine is effective in the treatment of patients with major depression with or without melancholia, or with atypical, nonendogenous depression, or depressive neurosis. These patients often have mixed anxiety and depression and phobic or hypochondriacal features. Phenelzine is more often used as a second-line antidepressant in patients who have failed to respond to other antidepressants. Nevertheless, many clinicians may consider phenelzine the first choice for treatment of certain dysphorias and minor periodic or chronic depressions (dysthymic disorders).
    Tranylcypromine is indicated for treatment of major depression [with or] without melancholia in closely supervised adult patients not responding to or unable to tolerate other antidepressants. [It is also used to treat the depressed phase of bipolar disorder and depressive neurosis of moderate to severe intensity.]
    Isocarboxazid is classified by the Food and Drug Administration (FDA) as being "probably" effective for the treatment of depressed patients who are refractory to tricyclic antidepressants or electroconvulsive therapy or in whom tricyclic antidepres-

sants are contraindicated. This classification requires the submission of adequate and well-controlled studies in order to provide substantial evidence of effectiveness.
[Panic disorder (treatment)][1]—Phenelzine and, to a lesser extent, tranylcypromine are used in conjunction with psychotherapy and behavior therapy in the treatment of panic disorder, with or without agoraphobia.
[Headache, vascular and/or tension (prophylaxis)][1]—Monoamine oxidase inhibitors are used in the prophylaxis of vascular headaches (including migraine), tension-type headaches, and mixed headache syndrome. However, due to potentially severe side effects, these agents are not considered first-line therapy.

---

[1]Not included in Canadian product labeling.

Pharmacology

Mechanism of action/Effect: The exact mechanism of antidepressant effect is unknown; however, it is established that the activity of the enzyme monoamine oxidase (MAO) is inhibited. MAO subtypes A and B are involved in the metabolism of serotonin and catecholamine neurotransmitters such as epinephrine, norepinephrine, and dopamine. Isocarboxazid, phenelzine, and tranylcypromine, as nonselective MAO inhibitors, bind irreversibly to monoamine oxidase-A (MAO-A) and monoamine oxidase-B (MAO-B). The reduced MAO activity results in an increased concentration of these neurotransmitters in storage sites throughout the central nervous system (CNS) and sympathetic nervous system. This increased availability of one or more monoamines has been thought to be the basis for the antidepressant activity of MAO inhibitors. The nonselective MAO inhibitors, phenelzine, tranylcypromine, and isocarboxazid, result in downregulation (desensitization) of alpha$_2$- or beta-adrenergic and serotonin receptors. It is thought that changes in receptor characteristics produced by chronic administration of MAO inhibitors correlate better with antidepressant action than does the increased activity of the neuron secondary to increased neurotransmitter concentrations, and may also account for the delay of 2 to 4 weeks in therapeutic response.

Other actions/effects:
    MAO inhibitors exhibit a hypotensive effect, which varies with the specific agent; the hypotensive mechanism of action is probably mediated through central inhibition of vasomotor centers, or it may be due to chronic accumulation of the false neurotransmitter octopamine in adrenergic terminals.
    MAO inhibitors prevent the inactivation of tyramine by hepatic and gastrointestinal monoamine oxidase. Circulating tyramine releases norepinephrine from the sympathetic nerve terminals and produces a sudden increase in blood pressure.

Onset of action: As early as 7 to 10 days with appropriate dosage in some patients, but may take up to 4 to 8 weeks to achieve full therapeutic effect.

Duration of action: At least 10 days for MAO activity to be recovered because of irreversible binding.

Precautions to Consider

Geriatrics

Experience with the use of MAO inhibitors in the elderly is relatively limited. However, there have been reports that phenelzine is safe and effective in the treatment of elderly depressed patients with a history of atypical depression or depressive neurosis. MAO inhibitors may also be useful for anergic or apathetic retarded depressions. The potential for increased vascular accidents (especially in the event of sudden hypertensive episodes), increased sensitivity to hypotensive effects, and reduced metabolic capacity discourages the first-time use of MAO inhibitors in patients over 60 years of age. When an MAO inhibitor is prescribed for an elderly patient, the patient's history of depression, ability to comply with prescribing instructions, and any potential drug interactions must also be considered.

Drug interactions and/or related problems

The following drug interactions and/or related problems have been selected on the basis of their potential clinical significance (possible mechanism in parentheses where appropriate)—not necessarily inclusive (» = major clinical significance):

Note: Combinations containing any of the following medications, depending on the amount present, may also interact with this medication.

» Alcohol or
» CNS depression-producing medications, other
    (concurrent use with MAO inhibitors may increase CNS depressant effects)

    (also, possible tyramine content in some alcoholic beverages, especially beer, wine, or ale, may induce hypertensive reactions)

    (in addition to additive CNS depressant effects caused by some antihypertensives such as clonidine, guanabenz, methyldopa, metyrosine, and pargyline, postural hypotension may be aggravated)

» Anesthetics, local, with epinephrine or levonordefrin, or
» Cocaine
    (concurrent use with MAO inhibitors may cause severe hypertension due to sympathomimetic effects)

    (cocaine should not be administered during or within 14 days following administration of an MAO inhibitor; phenelzine also inhibits cholinesterase activity and may reduce or slow cocaine metabolism, thereby increasing the risk of cocaine toxicity)

Anesthetics, spinal
    (concurrent use in patients receiving local anesthesics via subarachnoid block may increase the risk of hypotension; discontinuation of MAO inhibitors 10 days before elective surgery may be advisable; however, to avoid interruption of antidepressant therapy, patients receiving long-term MAO inhibition may undergo surgery without discontinuation of the MAO inhibitor; dosages of the anesthetic must be adjusted carefully)

Anticholinergics or other medications with anticholinergic activity or
Antidyskinetic agents or
Antihistamines
    (concurrent use with MAO inhibitors may intensify the anticholinergic effects of these medications because of secondary anticholinergic activities of MAO inhibitors)

    (also, concurrent use with MAO inhibitors may block detoxification of anticholinergics, thus potentiating their action; pa-

tients should be advised to report occurrence of gastrointestinal problems promptly since paralytic ileus may occur with concurrent therapy)

    (concurrent use with MAO inhibitors may also prolong and intensify the CNS depressant and anticholinergic effects of antihistamines; concurrent use is not recommended)

Anticoagulants, coumarin- or indandione-derivative
    (concurrent use may increase anticoagulant activity; although the mechanism of action and clinical significance are unknown, caution is recommended)

Anticonvulsants
    (in addition to increasing CNS depressant effects, concurrent use with MAO inhibitors may cause a change in the pattern of epileptiform seizures; dosage adjustment of anticonvulsant may be necessary)

» Antidepressants, tricyclic or
» Fluoxetine or
» Trazodone
    (a potentially lethal hyperserotonergic state known as the serotonin syndrome may occur as the result of combining serotonergic agents [such as amitriptyline, clomipramine, doxepin, or imipramine; fluoxetine; or trazodone] with MAO inhibitors. The syndrome may be manifest by mental status changes (confusion, hypomania), restlessness, myoclonus, hyperreflexia, diaphoresis, shivering, tremor, diarrhea, incoordination, and/or fever. If recognized early, the syndrome usually resolves quickly upon withdrawal of the offending agents)

    (in addition to increased anticholinergic effects, concurrent use of tricyclic antidepressants with MAO inhibitors has resulted in an increased risk of hyperpyretic episodes, hypertensive crises, severe convulsions, and death; however, recent studies have shown that some tricyclic antidepressants can be used concurrently with MAO inhibitors for refractory depression with no adverse effects if both medications are initiated simultaneously at lower than usual doses and the doses raised gradually, or if the MAO inhibitor is gradually added to the tricyclic also at low doses; tricyclics should not be added to an established MAO inhibitor regimen; clomipramine, desipramine, imipramine, nortriptyline, and protriptyline are not recommended for use in such a regimen; careful monitoring for side effects of either medication is necessary)

    (concurrent use of fluoxetine with MAO inhibitors may result in confusion, agitation, restlessness, and gastrointestinal symptoms, or possibly hyperpyretic episodes, severe convulsions, and hypertensive crises. Based on experience with tricyclic antidepressants, at least 14 days should elapse between discontinuation of an MAO inhibitor and initiation of fluoxetine. However, because of the long half-lives of fluoxetine and its active metabolite, at least 5 weeks [approximately 5 half-lives of norfluoxetine] should elapse between discontinuation of fluoxetine and initiation of therapy with an MAO inhibitor. Administration of an MAO inhibitor within 5 weeks of discontinuation of fluoxetine may increase the risk of serious events. While a causal relationship to fluoxetine has not been established, death has been reported following the initiation of an MAO inhibitor shortly after fluoxetine administration was stopped)

» Antidiabetic agents, oral, or
» Insulin
    (hypoglycemic effects may be enhanced by MAO inhibitors; reduction in dosage of hypoglycemic medication may be necessary during and after concurrent therapy)

Beta-adrenergic blocking agents
    (a few cases of significant bradycardia have been reported in elderly patients receiving a beta-adrenergic blocking agent concurrently with phenelzine; monitoring of pulse rate during concomitant administration has been recommended)

Bromocriptine

(concurrent use may increase serum prolactin concentrations and interfere with effects of bromocriptine; dosage adjustment of bromocriptine may be necessary)

» Buspirone

(concurrent use with monoamine oxidase inhibitors is not recommended because elevation of blood pressure may occur; at least 10 days should elapse between discontinuation of one medication and initiation of the other)

» Caffeine-containing medications

(concurrent use of excessive amounts of caffeine, consumed in coffee, tea, cola, chocolate, or "stay awake" products with MAO inhibitors may produce dangerous cardiac arrhythmias or severe hypertension because of sympathomimetic side effects of caffeine)

» Carbamazepine or
» Cyclobenzaprine or
» Maprotiline or
» Monoamine oxidase (MAO) inhibitors, other, including furazolidone, procarbazine, or selegiline

(concurrent use with MAO inhibitors has resulted in hyperpyretic crises, hypertensive crises, severe convulsions, and death; a medication-free interval of at least 2 weeks should elapse between discontinuation of one medication and initiation of another; for patients switching from one MAO inhibitor to another, an interval of 2 weeks is recommended)

(in addition, MAO inhibitors cause a change in the pattern of epileptiform seizures in patients receiving carbamazepine as an anticonvulsant)

» Dextromethorphan

(concurrent use with MAO inhibitors may cause excitation, hypertension, and hyperpyrexia)

Diuretics

(concurrent use with MAO inhibitors may result in an increased hypotensive effect)

» Doxapram

(concurrent use may increase the pressor effects of either doxapram or the MAO inhibitor)

» Guanadrel or
» Guanethidine or
» Rauwolfia alkaloids

(concurrent use with these agents may result in moderate to severe hypertension due to release of catecholamines; withdrawal of MAO inhibitor at least 1 week prior to initiation of therapy with these agents is recommended)

(when an MAO inhibitor is added to existing therapy with a rauwolfia alkaloid, serious potentiation of CNS depressant effects may result; however, if a rauwolfia alkaloid is added to an MAO inhibitor regimen, CNS excitation and hypertension may result from release of excessive amounts of accumulated norepinephrine and serotonin)

Haloperidol or
Loxapine or
Molindone or
Phenothiazines or
Pimozide or
Thioxanthenes

(concurrent use may prolong and intensify the sedative, hypotensive, and anticholinergic effects of either these medications or MAO inhibitors)

» Levodopa

(concurrent use with MAO inhibitors is not recommended, as the combination may result in sudden moderate to severe hypertensive crisis; it is recommended that MAO inhibitors be discontinued for 2 to 4 weeks prior to initiation of levodopa therapy)

» Meperidine, and possibly other opioid (narcotic) analgesics

(concurrent use with MAO inhibitors may produce immediate excitation, sweating, rigidity, and severe hypertension; in some patients, hypotension, severe respiratory depression, coma, convulsions, hyperpyrexia, vascular collapse, and death may occur; reactions may be due to accumulation of serotonin resulting from MAO inhibition; avoidance of meperidine use within 2 to 3 weeks following MAO inhibition is recommended; other opioid analgesics such as morphine are not likely to cause such severe reactions and may be used cautiously in reduced dosage in patients receiving MAO inhibitors; however, it is recommended that a small test dose [$^1/_4$ of the usual dose] or several small incremental test doses over a period of several hours should first be administered to permit observation of any adverse effects; caution is also recommended in the use of alfentanil, fentanyl, or sufentanil as an adjunct to anesthesia if the patient has received an MAO inhibitor within 14 days; although the risk of a significant interaction has been questioned, the use of a small test dose is advised to detect any possible interaction)

» Methyldopa

(may cause hyperexcitability in patients receiving an MAO inhibitor; also headache, severe hypertension, and hallucinations have been reported with concurrent use)

» Methylphenidate

(concurrent use with MAO inhibitors may potentiate the CNS stimulant effects of methylphenidate, possibly resulting in a hypertensive crisis; methylphenidate should not be administered during or within 14 days following the administration of MAO inhibitors)

Metrizamide

(concurrent use with MAO inhibitors may lower the seizure threshold and increase the risk of seizures; MAO inhibitors should be discontinued at least 48 hours before myelography and should not be resumed for at least 24 hours after procedure)

Phenylephrine, nasal or ophthalmic

(if significant systemic absorption of nasal or ophthalmic phenylephrine occurs, concurrent use with MAO inhibitors may potentiate the pressor effect of phenylephrine; nasal or ophthalmic phenylephrine should not be administered during or within 14 days following the administration of an MAO inhibitor)

Succinylcholine

(concurrent use with phenelzine may decrease plasma concentrations or activity of pseudocholinesterase, the enzyme that metabolizes succinylcholine, thereby enhancing the neuromuscular blockade of succinylcholine and possibly resulting in prolonged respiratory depression or apnea)

» Sympathomimetics

(concurrent use with MAO inhibitors may prolong and intensify cardiac stimulant and vasopressor effects [including headache, cardiac arrhythmias, vomiting, sudden and severe hypertensive and hyperpyretic crises] of these medications because of release of catecholamines that accumulate in intraneuronal storage sites during MAO inhibitor therapy; these medications should not be administered during or within 14 days following the administration of an MAO inhibitor)

» Tryptophan

(concurrent use with MAO inhibitors may cause hyperreflexia, shivering, hyperventilation, hyperthermia, mania or hypomania, and disorientation or confusion; if tryptophan is added to an MAO inhibitor regimen, especially tranylcypromine, it should be started in low dosages and the dose titrated upwards gradually with close monitoring of mental status and blood pressure)

» Tyramine- or other high pressor amine-containing foods and beverages, such as aged cheese; fava or broad bean pods; yeast/protein extracts; smoked or pickled meats, poultry, or fish;

fermented sausage (bologna, pepperoni, salami, summer sausage) or other fermented meat; sauerkraut; any overripe fruit; beer; reduced-alcohol and alcohol-free beer and wine; red and white wines; sherry; and liqueurs.
(concurrent use with MAO inhibitors may cause sudden and severe hypertensive reactions; reactions are usually limited to a few hours and easily treated with rapidly acting hypotensive agents [such as labetolol, nifedipine, or if necessary in severe cases refractory to other agents, phentolamine]; severity depends on amount of tyramine ingested, rate of gastric emptying, and length of interval between dose of MAO inhibitor and ingestion of tyramine; when MAO inhibitors are discontinued, dietary restrictions must continue for at least 2 weeks; other tyramine- or high pressor amine-containing foods, such as yogurt, sour cream, cream cheese, cottage cheese, chocolate, and soy sauce, if eaten when fresh and in moderation, are considered unlikely to cause serious problems)

Contraindications/Medical problems
The contraindications/medical problems included have been selected on the basis of their potential clinical significance (reasons given in parentheses where appropriate)—not necessarily inclusive (» = major clinical significance).

Except under special circumstances, this medication should not be used when the following medical problems exist:
» Alcoholism, active
» Congestive heart failure
» Hepatic function impairment, severe
(hepatic precoma may be precipitated in patients with cirrhosis, who are extremely sensitive to effects of MAO inhibitors)
» Pheochromocytoma
(pressor substances secreted by such tumors may alter blood pressure during therapy with MAO inhibitors)
» Renal function impairment, severe
(cumulative effects of MAO inhibitors may occur because of reduced renal excretion)
Sensitivity to any MAO inhibitor, including furazolidone, procarbazine, or selegiline

Risk-benefit should be considered when the following medical problems exist:
Asthma or bronchitis
(medications used in the treatment of these conditions may interact with MAO inhibitors)
Bipolar disorder
(switch from depressive to manic phase may occur)
» Cardiac arrhythmias
» Cardiovascular disease or coronary insufficiency or
Cerebrovascular disease
(ischemia may be aggravated as a result of reduced blood pressure; in patients with serious heart block or a conduction disturbance, however, an MAO inhibitor may be preferred to a tricyclic antidepressant because of significant slowing of resting pulse [heart rate] or shortening of the PR and QT intervals, and a significant decrease in blood pressure)
Diabetes mellitus
(insulin or oral hypoglycemic requirements may be altered)
Epilepsy
(pattern of epileptiform seizures may be changed)
» Headaches, severe or frequent
(headache as a first sign of hypertensive reaction during therapy may be masked)
» Hepatic function impairment
(hepatic precoma may be precipitated in patients with cirrhosis, who are extremely sensitive to effects of MAO inhibitors)

» Hypertension
(use of MAO inhibitors is not recommended in patients on multiple-drug therapy since hypotensive effects may be potentiated; hypertensive crises resulting from dietary lapses may be more severe in hypertensive patients)
Hyperthyroidism
(sensitivity to pressor amines may be increased)
Parkinson's disease
(may be aggravated)
» Renal function impairment
(cumulative effects may occur)
» Schizophrenia
(MAO inhibitors may aggravate psychosis and/or cause excessive stimulation in schizophrenic patients)
» Suicidal patients
(may continue to exhibit suicidal tendencies because significant improvement may not occur for several weeks after initiation of therapy with MAO inhibitors)
» Caution is required also in patients who have undergone sympathectomy, who may be more sensitive to the hypotensive effects of MAO inhibitors.

Side/Adverse Effects

The following side/adverse effects have been selected on the basis of their potential clinical significance (possible signs and symptoms in parentheses where appropriate)—not necessarily inclusive:

Those indicating need for medical attention
Incidence more frequent
Orthostatic hypotension, severe (dizziness or lightheadedness, especially when getting up from a lying or sitting position)
Note: Falling or fainting may result; occurs in hypertensive as well as normal and hypotensive patients; reduction in dosage of MAO inhibitor may be required to bring blood pressure up to pretreatment levels.
Incidence less frequent
Diarrhea; peripheral edema (swelling of feet and lower legs); *sympathetic stimulation* (fast or pounding heartbeat; unusual excitement or nervousness)
Note: *Edema* may subside spontaneously within a week; however, if persistent, electrolytes should be monitored to rule out syndrome of inappropriate antidiuretic hormone secretion (SIADH).
Incidence rare
Hepatitis (dark urine, skin rash, yellow eyes or skin); *leukopenia* (fever, sore throat); *parkinsonian syndrome* (slurred speech, staggering gait)
Note: A potentially lethal hyperserotonergic state known as the serotonin syndrome may occur, typically as the result of combining serotonergic agents (such as amitriptyline, clomipramine, doxepin, or imipramine; fluoxetine; or trazodone) with MAO inhibitors. The syndrome may be manifest by mental status changes (confusion, hypomania), restlessness, myoclonus, hyperreflexia, diaphoresis, shivering, tremor, diarrhea, incoordination, and fever. If recognized early, the syndrome usually resolves quickly upon withdrawal of the offending agents.
Symptoms of overdose
Severe anxiety; confusion; convulsions; cool, clammy skin; severe dizziness; severe drowsiness; fast and irregular pulse; fever; hallucinations; severe headache; high or low blood pressure; hyperactive reflexes; muscle stiffness; respiratory depression or failure (troubled breathing); *slowed reflexes; sweating; severe trouble in sleeping; unusual irritability*
Note: *Symptoms of overdose* may not be evident until about 12 hours following ingestion and may not reach maximum effect for 24 to 48 hours. Death has resulted.

Symptoms of hypertensive crisis
> *Severe chest pain; enlarged pupils; fast or slow heartbeat; severe headache; increased sensitivity of eyes to light; increased sweating, possibly with fever or cold, clammy skin; nausea or vomiting; stiff or sore neck*

Note: *Intracranial bleeding* (sometimes fatal in outcome) has occurred in association with hypertensive crisis.

Palpitation or frequent headaches may be prodromal signs of a hypertensive reaction.

Those indicating need for medical attention only if they continue or are bothersome

Incidence more frequent
> *Anticholinergic effect or syndrome of inappropriate antidiuretic hormone secretion [SIADH];* (decreased urine output); *blurred vision; CNS stimulation* (muscle twitching during sleep; restlessness or agitation; trouble in sleeping)—more likely with tranylcypromine; *decreased sexual ability; drowsiness*—more likely with phenelzine and isocarboxazid; *mild headache without increase in blood pressure; increased appetite and weight gain, related to carbohydrate craving; increased sweating; orthostatic hypotension, mild* (dizziness or lightheadedness; tiredness and weakness); *shakiness or trembling; weakness*

Note: *Decreased sexual ability* may include anorgasmia in males and females; ejaculatory disorders; and, less commonly, impotence in males.

Incidence less frequent or rare
> *Anorexia* (decreased appetite); *chills; constipation; dryness of mouth*

Patient Consultation

In providing consultation, consider emphasizing the following selected information (» = major clinical significance):

Before using this medication
» Conditions affecting use, especially:
> Sensitivity to any MAO inhibitor, including furazolidone or procarbazine
> Pregnancy—MAO inhibitors cross placenta; no appropriate human studies done; animal studies have shown hyperexcitability and reduced growth rate in neonates
> Breast-feeding—Not known if excreted in human breast milk; animal studies have shown excretion in milk
> Use in children—Not recommended for use in children under 16 years of age
> Use in the elderly—Increased sensitivity to hypotensive effects
> Use by athletes—MAO inhibitors are banned and, in some cases, tested for in competitors in biathlon and modern pentathlon events by the United States Olympic Committee (USOC)
> Other medications, especially CNS depressants, tricyclic antidepressants, oral antidiabetic agents, insulin, buspirone, caffeine in high doses, carbamazepine, cyclobenzaprine, cocaine, maprotiline, dextromethorphan, fluoxetine, guanadrel, guanethidine, rauwolfia alkaloids, levodopa, methyldopa, methylphenidate, sympathomimetics, tryptophan, or foods and beverages containing tyramine
> Other medical problems, especially alcoholism (active), congestive heart failure, hepatic function impairment, pheochromocytoma, renal function impairment, cardiac arrhythmias, cardiovascular disease, coronary insufficiency, severe or frequent headaches, hypertension, schizophrenia, bipolar disorder, suicidal tendencies, or previous sympathectomy

Proper use of this medication
» May require up to 3 or 4 weeks of therapy to obtain signs of improvement; regular visits to physician, especially during first few months of therapy, to check progress of therapy and to check for unwanted effects

» Importance of not taking more medication than the amount prescribed
> Missed dose: Taking as soon as possible within 2 hours of next dose; going back to regular dosing schedule; not doubling doses
» Proper storage

Precautions while using this medication
» Avoiding tyramine-containing foods, alcoholic beverages, and large quantities of caffeine-containing beverages, over-the-counter cold and cough medicines, and other medications, unless prescribed; having list of such for reference
» Checking with hospital emergency room or physician if symptoms of hypertensive crisis develop
» Checking with physician before discontinuing medication; gradual reduction may be needed to prevent withdrawal effects
» Dizziness may occur; caution when getting up suddenly from a lying or sitting position
» Drowsiness may occur; caution when driving or doing things requiring alertness
» Caution if any kind of surgery, dental treatment, or emergency treatment is required
> Carrying medical identification card
» Patients with angina: Not increasing physical activities without consulting physician
> Diabetic patients: Carefully checking urine or blood sugar; results may be lowered by this medication
» Obeying rules of caution for 14 days after discontinuing medication

Side/adverse effects
» Signs of potential side effects, especially symptoms of hypertensive crisis, severe orthostatic hypotension, diarrhea, fluid retention

General Dosing Information

This medication is usually used for closely supervised patients who have not responded to other antidepressant therapy.

Patient response to these agents is variable, and patients not responsive to one MAO inhibitor may be treated successfully with another.

Potentially suicidal patients should not have access to large quantities of this medication since depressed patients, particularly those who use alcohol excessively, may continue to exhibit suicidal tendencies until significant improvement occurs.

It has been recommended that therapy with an MAO inhibitor be withdrawn gradually at least 10 to 14 days prior to surgery; however, to avoid interruption of antidepressant therapy, patients receiving long-term MAO inhibition may undergo surgery without discontinuation of the MAO inhibitor. Reduction of opioid (narcotic) analgesic or other premedication dosage to $1/4$ of the usual dose is recommended, along with careful adjustment of anesthetic dosage. Avoidance of meperidine or cocaine use within 2 to 3 weeks following MAO inhibition is recommended.

Because insomnia or other sleep disturbances may be produced by their psychomotor-stimulating effect, these medications are usually not given in the evening.

After dosage is stopped, the effects of these medications may persist for up to 2 weeks (time required for regeneration of monoamine oxidase). During this period, food and drug contraindications must be observed.

Diet/Nutrition
Foods and beverages containing tyramine or other high pressor amines, such as aged cheese; fava or broad bean pods; yeast/protein extracts; smoked or pickled meats, poultry, or fish; fermented sausage (bologna, pepperoni, salami, summer sausage) or other fermented meat; sauerkraut; any overripe fruit; beer; reduced-alcohol and alcohol-free beer and wine; red and white wines; sherry; and liqueurs, when used concurrently with MAO inhibitors, may cause sudden and severe hypertensive reactions. The reactions are usu-

ally limited to a few hours and are easily treated with rapidly acting hypotensive agents (such as labetalol, nifedipine, or if necessary in severe cases refractory to other agents, phentolamine). The severity depends on the amount of tyramine ingested, rate of gastric emptying, and length of the interval between the dose of MAO inhibitor and ingestion of tyramine. When MAO inhibitors are discontinued, dietary restrictions must continue for at least 2 weeks. Other foods, such as yogurt, sour cream, cream cheese, cottage cheese, chocolate, and soy sauce, if eaten when fresh and in moderation, are considered unlikely to cause serious problems.

For treatment of hypertensive crisis
Recommended treatment includes:
- Discontinuing MAO inhibitor.
- Lowering blood pressure immediately with intravenous administration of 5 mg of phentolamine, with care being taken to inject slowly, to prevent excessive hypotensive effect. Alternatively, some clinicians prefer to use labetalol (intravenously or orally) or nifedipine (a 10-mg capsule usually punctured and administered sublingually), reserving phentolamine for severe or non-responding cases.
- Reducing fever by external cooling.

ISOCARBOXAZID

Additional Dosing Information

See also *General Dosing Information.*

Isocarboxazid has a cumulative effect; therefore, as soon as clinical improvement is observed, dosage should be stabilized and the patient closely followed for clinical effects.

Daily doses greater than 60 mg are not recommended since the frequency and intensity of side effects become greater as the dosage is increased.

If improvement is not seen within 6 weeks, continued administration is unlikely to be beneficial.

Oral Dosage Forms

ISOCARBOXAZID TABLETS USP

Usual adult dose: Antidepressant—
Initial: Oral, 30 mg a day as a single dose or in divided doses until clinical improvement is evident, the dosage then being reduced to maintenance dose.
Maintenance: Oral, 10 to 20 mg a day, the dosage being adjusted as needed and tolerated.

Usual adult prescribing limits: Up to 60 mg a day.

Auxiliary labeling:
- Avoid alcoholic beverages.
- May cause drowsiness.

PHENELZINE

Additional Dosing Information

See also *General Dosing Information.*

The initial dosage should be increased gradually, depending on patient tolerance. Rapid dosage increases can cause early hypotensive effects and may result in patient noncompliance. A more conservative increase usually avoids this. At least 4 weeks at a given dosage may be necessary for some patients to achieve improvement and significant MAO inhibition.

Oral Dosage Forms

PHENELZINE SULFATE TABLETS USP

Usual adult dose:
Antidepressant—
Initial: Oral, 1 mg per kg of body weight a day.
Maintenance: Oral, 45 mg a day.
Antipanic agent—Oral, initially 15 mg every morning for the first four days, the dosage being increased gradually over two weeks as needed and tolerated, up to 15 mg three or four times a day.

Usual adult prescribing limits: Up to 90 mg a day.

Usual geriatric dose: Antidepressant—Oral, initially 0.8 to 1 mg per kg of body weight a day in divided doses, the dosage being gradually increased as needed and tolerated, up to a maximum of 60 mg a day.

Note: Elderly patients are often started on 15 mg in the morning and require a more gradual titration of dose than other adults, to minimize the adverse effects, especially hypotension.

Auxiliary labeling:
- Avoid alcoholic beverages.
- May cause drowsiness.

TRANYLCYPROMINE

Summary of Differences

Side/adverse effects: May produce more CNS stimulation than other MAO inhibitors.

Additional Dosing Information

See also *General Dosing Information.*

Dosage should be individualized. If there are no signs of improvement after up to 2 weeks on the usual effective dosage of 30 mg a day, the dosage may be increased by 10 mg a day at intervals of 1 to 3 weeks, up to a maximum of 60 mg a day.

When electroconvulsive therapy is being administered concurrently, 10 mg twice a day can usually be given during the series, the dose being reduced to 10 mg a day for maintenance therapy.

Gradual withdrawal from tranylcypromine is recommended, to avoid recurrence of original symptoms, which may reappear if medication is withdrawn prematurely.

Oral Dosage Forms

TRANYLCYPROMINE SULFATE TABLETS USP

Usual adult dose:
Antidepressant—
Initial: Oral, 30 mg a day in divided doses. If there are no signs of improvement after two weeks, the dosage may be increased by 10 mg a day at intervals of one to three weeks, up to a maximum of 60 mg a day.
Maintenance: Oral, 10 to 40 mg a day.
Antipanic agent—Oral, initially 10 mg in the morning for the first four days, the dosage being increased gradually over two weeks as needed and tolerated, up to 20 to 30 mg a day.

Usual adult prescribing limits: Up to 60 mg a day.

Usual geriatric dose: Antidepressant—Oral, initially 2.5 to 5 mg a day, the dosage being increased gradually in increments of 2.5 to 5 mg every three to four days, up to a maximum of 45 mg a day.

Auxiliary labeling:
- Avoid alcoholic beverages.
- May cause drowsiness.

ANTIDEPRESSANTS, TRICYCLIC   Systemic

Some commonly used *brand names* are:

In the U.S.—
Anafranil [Clomipramine]
Asendin [Amoxapine]
Aventyl [Nortriptyline]
Elavil [Amitriptyline]
Emitrip [Amitriptyline]
Endep [Amitriptyline]
Enovil [Amitriptyline]
Janimine [Imipramine]
Norfranil [Imipramine]

Norpramin [Desipramine]
Pamelor [Nortriptyline]
Sinequan [Doxepin]
Surmontil [Trimipramine]
Tipramine [Imipramine]
Tofranil [Imipramine]
Tofranil-PM [Imipramine]
Vivactil [Protriptyline]

In Canada—
Anafranil [Clomipramine]
Apo-Amitriptyline [Amitriptyline]
Apo-Imipramine [Imipramine]
Apo-Trimip [Trimipramine]
Asendin [Amoxapine]
Aventyl [Nortriptyline]
Elavil [Amitriptyline]
Impril [Imipramine]
Levate [Amitriptyline]
Norpramin [Desipramine]
Novo-Doxepin [Doxepin]
Novopramine [Imipramine]

Novotriptyn [Amitriptyline]
Pertofrane [Desipramine]
PMS Amitriptyline [Amitriptyline]
PMS Imipramine [Imipramine]
Rhotrimine [Trimipramine]
Sinequan [Doxepin]
Surmontil [Trimipramine]
Tofranil [Imipramine]
Triadapin [Doxepin]
Triptil [Protriptyline]

AMITRIPTYLINE
Oral
Amitriptyline Hydrochloride Tablets USP
In the U.S.—*Elavil; Emitrip; Endep;* GENERIC
In Canada—*Apo-Amitriptyline; Elavil; Levate; Novotriptyn; PMS Amitriptyline;* GENERIC
Amitriptyline Pamoate Syrup*
In Canada—*Elavil*
Parenteral
Amitriptyline Hydrochloride Injection USP†
In the U.S.—*Elavil; Enovil;* GENERIC

AMOXAPINE
Oral
Amoxapine Tablets
In the U.S.—*Asendin;* GENERIC
In Canada—*Asendin*

CLOMIPRAMINE
Oral
Clomipramine Hydrochloride Capsules†
In the U.S.—*Anafranil*
Clomipramine Hydrochloride Tablets*
In Canada—*Anafranil*

DESIPRAMINE
Oral
Desipramine Hydrochloride Tablets USP
In the U.S.—*Norpramin;* GENERIC
In Canada—*Norpramin; Pertofrane*

DOXEPIN
Oral
Doxepin Hydrochloride Capsules USP
In the U.S.—*Sinequan;* GENERIC
In Canada—*Novo-Doxepin; Sinequan; Triadapin*
Doxepin Hydrochloride Oral Solution USP†
In the U.S.—*Sinequan;* GENERIC

IMIPRAMINE
Oral
Imipramine Hydrochloride Tablets USP
In the U.S.—*Janimine; Norfranil; Tipramine; Tofranil;* GENERIC

In Canada—*Apo-Imipramine; Impril; Novopramine; PMS Imipramine; Tofranil;* GENERIC
Imipramine Pamoate Capsules†
In the U.S.—*Tofranil-PM*
Parenteral
Imipramine Hydrochloride Injection USP†
In the U.S.—*Tofranil*

NORTRIPTYLINE
Oral
Nortriptyline Hydrochloride Capsules USP
In the U.S.—*Aventyl; Pamelor*
In Canada—*Aventyl*
Nortriptyline Hydrochloride Oral Solution USP†
In the U.S.—*Aventyl; Pamelor*

PROTRIPTYLINE
Oral
Protriptyline Hydrochloride Tablets USP
In the U.S.—*Vivactil*
In Canada—*Triptil*

TRIMIPRAMINE
Oral
Trimipramine Maleate Capsules
In the U.S.—*Surmontil;* GENERIC
In Canada—*Rhotrimine; Surmontil*
Trimipramine Maleate Tablets*
In Canada—*Apo-Trimip; Rhotrimine; Surmontil*

*Not commercially available in the U.S.
†Not commercially available in Canada.

Category

Note: All of the tricyclic antidepressants have similar pharmacologic actions; however, clinical uses among specific agents may vary because of actual pharmacokinetic differences, availability of specific testing, differences in side effects, and/or availability of clinical-use data.

Antidepressant—Amitriptyline; Amoxapine; Clomipramine; Desipramine; Doxepin; Imipramine; Nortriptyline; Protriptyline; Trimipramine.
Antienuretic—Imipramine Hydrochloride; Amitriptyline.
Antiobsessive-compulsive agent—Clomipramine.
Antipanic agent—Clomipramine; Desipramine; Doxepin; Imipramine; Nortriptyline.
Antineuralgic—Amitriptyline; Clomipramine; Desipramine; Doxepin; Imipramine; Nortriptyline; Trimipramine.
Antiulcer agent—Amitriptyline; Doxepin; Trimipramine.
Antinarcolepsy adjunct—Imipramine; Protriptyline.
Anticataplectic—Clomipramine; Desipramine; Imipramine; Protriptyline.
Antibulimic—Amitriptyline; Clomipramine; Desipramine; Imipramine.
Antipruritic—Doxepin.

Indications

Note: Bracketed information in the *Indications* section refers to uses not included in U.S. product labeling.

Accepted
Depression, mental (treatment)—Amitriptyline, amoxapine, [clomipramine], desipramine, doxepin, imipramine, nortriptyline, protriptyline, and trimipramine are indicated for the relief of symptoms of major depressive episodes; bipolar disorder, depressed type; dysthymia; and atypical depressions. Some conditions associated with or accompanied by depression that are treated with tricyclic antidepressants include alcoholism, organic disease such as stroke or Parkinson's disease, and agitation or anxiety.

Enuresis (treatment adjunct)—Imipramine hydrochloride, but not pamoate, and [amitriptyline] are indicated as an aid in the temporary treatment of nocturnal enuresis in children 6 years of age or older, after possible organic causes have been excluded by appropriate tests.

Obsessive-compulsive disorder (treatment)—Clomipramine is used to relieve symptoms of obsessive-compulsive disorders, independent of concomitant depression.

[Panic disorder (treatment)][1]—Tricyclic antidepressants, especially clomipramine, desipramine, doxepin, imipramine, and nortriptyline are used in conjunction with psychotherapy and behavior therapy to block the recurrence of panic attacks, with or without phobias. Imipramine's antipanic effect does not appear to be correlated with presence of depressive symptoms.

[Pain, neurogenic (treatment)][1]—Tricyclic antidepressants, especially amitriptyline, clomipramine, desipramine, doxepin, imipramine, nortriptyline, and trimipramine are used in patients with normal or depressed mood for the management of chronic, severe pain as in cancer; migraine and chronic, daily muscle-contraction headaches; rheumatic disorders; atypical facial pain; post-herpetic neuralgia; post-traumatic neuropathy; and diabetic or other peripheral neuropathy.

[Attention deficit hyperactivity disorder (treatment)][1]—Desipramine, imipramine, and protriptyline are used to relieve the symptoms of attention deficit hyperactivity disorder in some children over 6 years of age and in young adults. Tricyclic antidepressants may be more useful than stimulants when the patient has become withdrawn and depressed.

[Headache (prophylaxis)][1]—Tricyclic antidepressants are used in the prophylaxis of vascular headache (including migraine) and mixed headache syndrome.

[Ulcer, peptic (treatment)][1]—Although amitriptyline, doxepin, and trimipramine are effective in the treatment of peptic ulcer disease and in relieving nocturnal ulcer pain, their use has been largely supplanted by histamine H_2-receptor antagonists, omeprazole, and sucralfate.

[Narcolepsy/cataplexy syndrome (treatment)][1]; or

[Narcolepsy/cataplexy syndrome (treatment adjunct)][1]—Tricyclic antidepressants, especially clomipramine, desipramine, imipramine, and protriptyline, are used to treat cataplexy associated with narcolepsy, with little or no effect on narcoleptic sleep attacks. Imipramine may be used in combination with amphetamines or methylphenidate when a patient requires treatment for both cataplexy and sleep attacks. Patients with sleep disorders such as hypersomnia or impaired morning arousal may benefit by the use of protriptyline.

[Bulimia nervosa (treatment)][1]—Amitriptyline, clomipramine, desipramine, and imipramine have been shown to be effective in controlling the binge eating and subsequent purging of bulimia nervosa.

[Cocaine withdrawal (treatment)][1]—Desipramine and imipramine are used to reduce craving and/or prevent depression upon withdrawal of cocaine.

[Urinary incontinence (treatment)][1]—Imipramine is used for the treatment of stress and urge incontinence.

[Pruritus (treatment)][1]—Doxepin is used in treatment of pruritus in idiopathic cold urticaria.

---

[1]Not included in Canadian product labeling.

Pharmacology

Mechanism of action/Effect:

Antidepressant—Although the exact mechanism of action in the treatment of depression is unclear, tricyclic antidepressants have been thought to increase the synaptic concentration of norepinephrine (levarterenol; NE) and/or serotonin (5-hydroxytryptamine; 5-HT) in the central nervous system (CNS). One theory suggests that these neurotransmitters are increased through inhibition of their reuptake by the presynaptic neuronal membrane.

Amoxapine, desipramine, trimipramine, nortriptyline, and probably protriptyline mainly inhibit the reuptake of norepinephrine. Amitriptyline and clomipramine appear to be more potent than other tricyclics in blocking serotonin, although, through their metabolites, they become powerful inhibitors of norepinephrine reuptake also. Clomipramine's effectiveness in the treatment of obsessive-compulsive disorder may be related to the inhibition of serotonin reuptake. Imipramine inhibits reuptake of norepinephrine and serotonin equally. Doxepin is a moderate inhibitor of norepinephrine and a weak inhibitor of serotonin.

Recent research has shown that after long-term treatment with antidepressants, changes in postsynaptic beta-adrenergic receptor sensitivity and increased responsiveness of the adrenergic and serotonergic systems to physiologic and environmental stimuli contribute to the mechanism of action. Antidepressants may produce a downregulation (desensitization) of alpha$_2$- or beta-adrenergic and serotonin receptors, equilibrating the noradrenergic system, and thus correcting the dysregulated monoamine output of depressed patients. Receptor changes resulting from chronic administration of tricyclic antidepressants appear to correlate better with antidepressant action than does the synaptic reuptake blockade of neurotransmitters, and may also account for the delay of 2 to 4 weeks in therapeutic response.

Amoxapine, as a metabolite of the neuroleptic, loxapine, also has a potent postsynaptic dopamine-blocking effect. This may account for the extrapyramidal side effects and increases in serum prolactin concentrations seen with amoxapine. Amoxapine is metabolized to 7-hydroxyamoxapine, also a potent dopamine-blocking agent.

Antienuretic—The exact antienuretic action of imipramine hydrochloride has not been established. It is thought to be associated with the anticholinergic action of imipramine.

Antiobsessional agent—The exact antiobsessional action of clomipramine has not been established. It is thought to be associated with clomipramine's inhibition of serotonin reuptake and compensatory down regulation of serotonin receptor subtypes.

Antianxiety agent—In panic disorders, studies suggest an impaired function of the autonomic nervous system that causes an excessive release of norepinephrine from the locus ceruleus. Tricyclic antidepressants are thought to decrease the firing rate of the locus ceruleus by regulating the alpha$_2$- and beta-adrenergic receptor functions and norepinephrine turnover.

Antineuralgic—The exact mechanism by which tricyclic antidepressants relieve chronic pain is also unknown. Some studies support the theory that pain relief results when depression is relieved. However, other studies have found that pain may be ameliorated without a significant change in depression. Analgesic activity may be effected by the changing concentrations of central monoamines, especially serotonin, and by the direct or indirect effect of tricyclic antidepressants on the endogenous opioid systems.

Antiulcer agent—In peptic ulcer disease, tricyclic antidepressants are effective in relieving pain and aid in complete healing because of their histamine$_2$-receptor blocking property on the parietal cells, and their sedative and anticholinergic effects.

Antibulimic—In bulimia nervosa, the mechanism of action is unclear, although it may be similar to that in depression. Evidence shows there is a distinct antibulimic effect in patients without depression and in depressed patients whose bulimia was relieved without a concomitant relief of depression.

Urinary incontinence—The exact mechanism by which imipramine enhances urinary continence has not been established but may include anticholinergic activity, resulting in increased bladder capacity; direct beta-adrenergic stimulation; alpha-adrenergic agonist activity, resulting in increased sphincter tone; and central blockade of serotonin uptake.

Other actions/effects: Tricyclic antidepressants also produce prominent peripheral and central anticholinergic effects due to their potent and high binding affinity for muscarinic receptors; sedative effects due to strong binding affinity for histamine H_1-receptors (although the central actions of histamine are poorly understood, increased cholinoceptive activity in the brain has been associated with clinical depression); and orthostatic hypotension due to alpha blockade. In addition, tricyclic antidepressants are Class 1A antiarrhythmic agents which, like quinidine, moderately slow ventricular conduction in therapeutic doses, and in overdose may cause severe conduction block and occasional ventricular arrhythmia.

Onset of action: Antidepressant—2 to 3 weeks.

Precautions to Consider

Cross-sensitivity and/or related problems
Patients sensitive to one tricyclic antidepressant may be sensitive to other tricyclic antidepressants, and possibly to carbamazepine, maprotiline, and trazodone, also.

Geriatrics
Elderly patients often require lower dosage and more gradual dose increases to avoid toxicity, because of slower metabolic rates and/ or excretion and an increased ratio of fat to lean tissue. The elderly also exhibit increased sensitivity to anticholinergic effects, such as urinary retention (especially in older men with prostatic hypertrophy), anticholinergic delirium, and increased sedative and hypotensive effects. Increased anxiety may result from these adverse effects, possibly leading to unnecessary dose increases. If cardiovascular disease is present, the risk of conduction defects, arrhythmias, tachycardia, stroke, congestive heart failure, or myocardial infarction is increased.

Dental
The peripheral anticholinergic effects of tricyclic antidepressants may decrease or inhibit salivary flow, especially in middle-aged or elderly patients, thus contributing to the development of caries, periodontal disease, oral candidiasis, and discomfort.

The blood dyscrasia-causing effects of tricyclic antidepressants, although rare, may be life-threatening. The result may be an increased incidence of microbial infection, delayed healing, and gingival bleeding. If agranulocytosis, leukopenia, or thrombocytopenia occurs, dental work should be deferred until blood counts have returned to normal. Patient instruction in proper oral hygiene should include caution in use of regular toothbrushes, dental floss, and toothpicks.

Extrapyramidal reactions that may be induced by amoxapine will result in increased motor activity of the head, face, and neck. Occlusal adjustments, bite registrations, and treatment for bruxism may be made less reliable.

Drug interactions and/or related problems
The following drug interactions and/or related problems have been selected on the basis of their potential clinical significance (possible mechanism in parentheses where appropriate)—not necessarily inclusive (» = major clinical significance):

Note: Combinations containing any of the following medications, depending on the amount present, may also interact with this medication.

Although not all of the following interactions have been reported for every tricyclic antidepressant, the potential for their occurrence exists and should be considered.

Adrenocorticoids, glucocorticoid
  (tricyclic antidepressants do not relieve, and may exacerbate, adrenocorticoid-induced mental depression)

» Alcohol or

» CNS depression-producing medications, other
  (concurrent use with tricyclic antidepressants may result in serious potentiation of CNS depression, respiratory depression, and hypotensive effects; caution is recommended, and dosage of one or both agents should be reduced)
  (in addition, tricyclics may increase the effects of alcohol, especially during first few days of tricyclic antidepressant treatment; in patients who use alcohol excessively, tricyclics may increase the danger inherent in any suicide attempt)

Amantadine or
Anticholinergics or other medications with anticholinergic activity or
Antidyskinetics or
Antihistamines
  (concurrent use with tricyclic antidepressants may intensify anticholinergic effects, especially mental confusion, hallucinations, and nightmares, because of secondary anticholinergic activities of tricyclic antidepressants)
  (concurrent use may potentiate the CNS depressant effects of either antihistamines or tricyclic antidepressants)
  (concurrent use with tricyclic antidepressants may block detoxification of atropine and related compounds; patients should be advised to report occurrence of gastrointestinal problems promptly since paralytic ileus may occur with concurrent therapy)

Anticoagulants, coumarin- or indandione-derivative
  (concurrent use with tricyclic antidepressants, especially amitriptyline or nortriptyline, may increase anticoagulant activity, possibly by inhibiting enzymatic metabolism of the anticoagulant)

Anticonvulsants
  (tricyclic antidepressants may enhance CNS depression, lower the seizure threshold when taken in high doses, and decrease the effects of the anticonvulsant medication; dosage adjustment of the anticonvulsant may be necessary to control seizures; monitoring of serum concentrations of both medications may be necessary to detect possible interaction; concurrent use of phenytoin with desipramine may lower serum concentrations of desipramine; dosage increases of desipramine above maximum recommended doses may be required to produce clinical improvement in depression)

» Antithyroid agents
  (concurrent use with tricyclic antidepressants may increase the risk of agranulocytosis)

Barbiturates or
Carbamazepine
  (plasma concentrations and therapeutic effects of tricyclic antidepressants may be decreased during concurrent use with barbiturates, especially phenobarbital, or carbamazepine because of increased metabolism resulting from induction of hepatic microsomal enzymes)

Bupropion or
Clozapine or
Cyclobenzaprine or
Haloperidol or
Loxapine or
Maprotiline or
Molindone or
» Phenothiazines or
Thioxanthenes
  (the sedative and anticholinergic effects of either these medications or tricyclic antidepressants may be prolonged and intensified; these medications may increase the risk of seizures by lowering the seizure threshold and should be added or withdrawn with caution; psychotic depressions respond well to a combination of tricyclic antidepressant and antipsychotic agent, but both medications must be initially administered at lower doses and are increased only as clinically indicated)

(concurrent use of phenothiazines may increase serum concentrations of tricyclic antidepressants, especially desipramine and imipramine, due to inhibition of metabolism; conversely, tricyclics may inhibit phenothiazine metabolism; also, the risk of neuroleptic malignant syndrome [NMS] may be increased)

» Cimetidine
(cimetidine may inhibit tricyclic metabolism and increase plasma concentrations, leading to toxicity; lowering the dose of the tricyclic antidepressant by 20 to 30% may be necessary when cimetidine is given concurrently; patient should be closely observed for sedation, anticholinergic effects, and orthostatic hypotension)

» Clonidine or
» Guanadrel or
» Guanethidine
(concurrent use may decrease the hypotensive effects of these medications)

(concurrent use of clonidine with tricyclic antidepressants may result in potentiation of CNS depressant effects)

Cocaine
(concurrent use with tricyclic antidepressants may increase the risk of cardiac arrhythmias; if use of cocaine is necessary in patients receiving tricyclics, it is recommended that the cocaine be administered with caution, in reduced dosage, and in conjunction with electrocardiographic monitoring)

Contraceptives, oral, estrogen-containing, or
Estramustine or
Estrogens
(concurrent use of imipramine and possibly other tricyclic antidepressants by chronic long-term users of oral contraceptives or estrogens may increase the bioavailability of imipramine because of inhibition of hepatic enzyme metabolism; this may result in toxicity, obscuring therapeutic effects and worsening depression; may be dose-related, with lower doses of estrogens having less effect on enzyme inhibition than larger doses; dosage adjustments of the tricyclic may be necessary)

Disulfiram or
Ethchlorvynol
(concurrent use with tricyclics, especially amitriptyline, may result in transient delirium)

(also, CNS depressant effects may be increased when ethchlorvynol is used concurrently with tricyclic antidepressants)

Electroconvulsive therapy
(although electroconvulsive therapy may be used in conjunction with tricyclic antidepressants, caution should be used as hazards may be increased)

» Extrapyramidal reaction-causing medications, other
(concurrent use with amoxapine and possibly other tricyclic antidepressants may increase the severity and frequency of extrapyramidal effects)

Fluoxetine
(concurrent use with tricyclic antidepressants has produced increased plasma concentrations of the tricyclic antidepressant, possibly due to inhibition of tricyclic antidepressant metabolism; some clinicians recommend dosage reductions for tricyclic antidepressants of about 50% if used concurrently with fluoxetine)

Methylphenidate
(serum concentrations of tricyclic antidepressants, especially desipramine and imipramine, may be increased due to inhibition of metabolism when methylphenidate is used concurrently; also, concurrent use may antagonize the effects of methylphenidate)

» Metrizamide
(administration of intrathecal metrizamide may lower the seizure threshold and increase the risk of seizures in patients taking tricyclic antidepressants; it is recommended that tricyclic antidepressants be discontinued for at least 48 hours before and at least 24 hours after myelography)

» Monoamine oxidase (MAO) inhibitors, including furazolidone, procarbazine, and selegiline
(concurrent use with tricyclic antidepressants has resulted in an increased incidence of hyperpyretic episodes, severe convulsions, hypertensive crises, and death; however, recent studies have shown that concurrent use of some tricyclic antidepressants with MAO inhibitors can be used for refractory depression with no adverse effects if both medications are initiated simultaneously at lower than usual doses, with doses being raised gradually thereafter, or if the MAO inhibitor is gradually added to the tricyclic, also at low doses; a tricyclic should not be added to an existing MAO inhibitor regimen; the tricyclic antidepressants most commonly used in this combined therapy are amitriptyline, doxepin, and trimipramine; imipramine, desipramine, nortriptyline, protriptyline, and clomipramine are not recommended for use in such a regimen because of potential excessive stimulation)

Naphazoline, ophthalmic, or
Oxymetazoline, nasal or ophthalmic, or
Phenylephrine, nasal or ophthalmic, or
Xylometazoline, nasal
(if significant systemic absorption occurs, concurrent use with tricyclic antidepressants may potentiate pressor effects of these medications)

Pimozide
(concurrent use with tricyclic antidepressants may potentiate cardiac arrhythmias, which are seen on ECG as prolongation of the QT interval)

Probucol
(additive QT interval prolongation may increase risk of ventricular tachycardia)

» Sympathomimetics
(concurrent use with tricyclic antidepressants may potentiate cardiovascular effects possibly resulting in arrhythmias, tachycardia, or severe hypertension or hyperpyrexia; phentolamine can control the adverse reaction)

(significant systemic absorption of ophthalmic epinephrine may also potentiate cardiovascular effects; also, local anesthetics with vasoconstrictors should be avoided or a minimal amount of the vasoconstrictor should be used with the local anesthetic)

(concurrent use with tricyclic antidepressants may decrease the pressor effect of ephedrine and mephentermine)

Thyroid hormones
(concurrent use with tricyclic antidepressants may increase the therapeutic and toxic effects of both medications, possibly due to increased receptor sensitivity to catecholamines; toxic effects include cardiac arrhythmias and CNS stimulation)

Contraindications/Medical problems

The contraindications/medical problems included have been selected on the basis of their potential clinical significance (reasons given in parentheses where appropriate)—not necessarily inclusive (» = major clinical significance).

Note: This medication should *not* be used during the acute recovery period following a myocardial infarction.

Risk-benefit should be considered when the following medical problems exist:

» Alcoholism, active
(CNS depression may be potentiated)

» Asthma
(may be aggravated)

» Bipolar disorder
(swing to hypomanic or manic phase may be accelerated and reversible rapid cycling between mania and depression may be induced by antidepressants in some patients; tricyclic antide-

pressant may have to be discontinued and lithium considered for a sustained remission)

» Blood disorders
  (may be potentiated)
» Cardiovascular disorders, especially in children and the elderly
  (increased risk of arrhythmias, heart block, congestive heart failure, myocardial infarction, or stroke)
» Gastrointestinal disorders
  (risk of paralytic ileus)
  Genitourinary disease
  (may be masked by the use of imipramine for enuresis in children)
» Glaucoma, narrow-angle, predisposition to, or
» Increased intraocular pressure
  (may be aggravated)
» Hepatic function impairment
  (metabolism of tricyclic may be altered)
» Hyperthyroidism
  (risk of cardiovascular toxicity)
» Prostatic hypertrophy
  (risk of urinary retention)
» Renal function impairment
  (excretion of tricyclic may be altered)
» Schizophrenia
  (psychosis may be activated)
» Seizure disorders
  (seizure threshold may be lowered)
» Sensitivity to tricyclic antidepressants, carbamazepine, maprotiline, or trazodone
» Urinary retention
  (may be aggravated)

Side/Adverse Effects

Note: Although not all of these side effects have been attributed specifically to each tricyclic antidepressant, a potential exists for their occurrence during the use of any tricyclic antidepressant.

The following side/adverse effects have been selected on the basis of their potential clinical significance (possible signs and symptoms in parentheses where appropriate)—not necessarily inclusive:

Those indicating need for medical attention
Incidence less frequent
  For all tricyclic antidepressants
    Anticholinergic effects (blurred vision; confusion; delirium or hallucinations; constipation, especially in the elderly, possibly resulting in paralytic ileus; difficult urination; eye pain due to aggravation of glaucoma); *fast, slow, or irregular heartbeat; fine-muscle tremors, especially in arms, hands, head, and tongue* (shakiness); *hypotension* (fainting); *nervousness or restlessness; Parkinsonian syndrome* (difficulty in speaking or swallowing; loss of balance control; mask-like face; shuffling walk; slowed movements; stiffness of arms and legs; trembling and shaking of fingers and hands); *sexual function impairment*—more common with amoxapine and clomipramine
  For amoxapine only (in addition to the above)
    Tardive dyskinesia (lip smacking or puckering; puffing of cheeks; rapid or worm-like movements of tongue; uncontrolled chewing movements; uncontrolled movements of the arms or legs)
Incidence rare
  For all tricyclic antidepressants
    Agranulocytosis or other blood dyscrasias (red or brownish spots on skin; sore throat and fever; unusual bleeding or bruising); *allergic reaction* (increased sensitivity to sunlight; skin

rash and itching; swelling of face and tongue); *alopecia* (hair loss); *anxiety; breast enlargement in both males and females*—more common with amoxapine; *cholestatic jaundice* (yellow eyes or skin); *galactorrhea* (inappropriate secretion of milk)—in females; *seizures*—more common with clomipramine; *syndrome of inappropriate secretion of antidiuretic hormone [SIADH]* (irritability; muscle twitching; weakness); *testicular swelling*—more common with amoxapine; *tinnitus* (ringing, buzzing, or other unexplained noises in the ears); *trouble with teeth or gums*—more common with clomipramine
  For amoxapine only (in addition to the above)
    Neuroleptic malignant syndrome (NMS) (convulsions, difficult or fast breathing; fast heartbeat or irregular pulse; fever; high or low [irregular] blood pressure; increased sweating; loss of bladder control; severe muscle stiffness; unusually pale skin; unusual tiredness or weakness)
    Note: May occur after prolonged treatment or after combined treatment with *tricyclic antidepressants* and *neuroleptics*.
Symptoms of acute overdose
  Confusion; convulsions—more severe and refractory with amoxapine; *disturbed concentration; drowsiness, severe; enlarged pupils; fast, slow, or irregular heartbeat; fever; hallucinations; restlessness and agitation; shortness of breath or troubled breathing; unusual tiredness or weakness, severe; vomiting*

Those indicating need for medical attention only if they continue or are bothersome
Incidence more frequent
  Dizziness (orthostatic hypotension); *drowsiness; dryness of mouth; headache; increased appetite* (may include craving for sweets); *nausea; tiredness or weakness, mild; unpleasant taste; weight gain*
Incidence less frequent
  Diarrhea; excessive sweating; heartburn; trouble in sleeping—more common with protriptyline, especially when taken late in the day; *vomiting*

Those indicating possible withdrawal and the need for medical attention if they occur after medication is discontinued
Occurring upon abrupt withdrawal, due to cholinergic rebound
  For all tricyclic antidepressants
    Headache; nausea, vomiting, or diarrhea; trouble in sleeping, with vivid dreams; unusual excitement
Occurring with gradual withdrawal after long-term treatment
  For all tricyclic antidepressants
    Irritability; restlessness; trouble in sleeping, with vivid dreams
  For amoxapine only (in addition to the above)
    Tardive dyskinesia, withdrawal-emergent (lip smacking or puckering; puffing of cheeks; rapid or worm-like movements of tongue; uncontrolled chewing movements; uncontrolled movements of the arms and legs)

Patient Consultation

In providing consultation, consider emphasizing the following selected information (» = major clinical significance):

Before using this medication
» Conditions affecting use, especially:
    Sensitivity to tricyclic antidepressants, maprotiline, or trazodone
    Pregnancy—Clinical reports of fetal malformations with imipramine; animal studies have shown some tricyclics to cause embryotoxic or fetotoxic effects, and decreased rate of conception; when tricyclics taken by mother immediately before delivery, clinical reports of newborns suffering from muscle spasms, and heart, breathing, and urinary problems
    Breast-feeding—Pass into breast milk and may cause drowsiness in nursing baby

Use in children—Children and adolescents more sensitive to effects, requiring lower doses; may cause nervousness, sleeping problems, tiredness, mild stomach upset; generally not recommended for depression in children

Use in elderly—Elderly more sensitive to effects; lower doses and more gradual increases required

Use by athletes—Tricyclic antidepressants are banned and, in some cases, tested for in competitors in biathlon and modern pentathlon events by the U.S. Olympic Committee (USOC)

Dental—Decreased salivary flow contributes to caries, periodontal disease, candidiasis, and discomfort; blood dyscrasias may cause increased infections, delayed healing, and gingival bleeding; increased extrapyramidal motor activity of head, face, and neck with amoxapine may cause difficulty with occlusal and other procedures

Other medications, especially CNS depressants, antithyroid agents, cimetidine, clonidine, guanadrel, guanethidine, phenothiazines, extrapyramidal reaction; encasing medications, MAO inhibitors, metrimazide, or sympathomimetics

Other medical problems, especially alcoholism (active), asthma, bipolar disorder, blood disorders, cardiovascular disorders, gastrointestinal disorders, glaucoma or increased intraocular pressure, hepatic function impairment, renal function impairment, hyperthyroidism, prostatic hypertrophy, schizophrenia, seizure disorders, or urinary retention

Proper use of this medication

Taking with food to reduce gastrointestinal irritation

» Compliance with therapy; not taking more or less medicine than prescribed

» May require from 1 to 6 weeks of therapy to obtain antidepressant effects

Proper administration of doxepin oral solution

Using dropper provided by manufacturer for accurate measurement

Diluting medication in one-half glass of recommended beverage (water, milk, or fruit juice, but not grape juice or carbonated beverages) immediately before use

Not preparing or storing bulk solutions

Missed dose: If dosing schedule is—

More than one dose a day: Taking as soon as possible unless almost time for next dose; not doubling doses

One dose at bedtime: Not taking in morning because of side effects; checking with physician

» Proper storage

Precautions while using this medication

Regular visits to physician to check progress of therapy

» Avoiding the use of alcoholic beverages; not taking other medication unless prescribed by physician

» Possible drowsiness; caution when driving or doing things requiring alertness

» Possible dizziness or lightheadedness; caution when getting up suddenly from a lying or sitting position

» Possible dryness of mouth; using sugarless gum or candy, ice, or saliva substitute for relief; checking with physician or dentist if dry mouth continues for more than 2 weeks

» Possible skin photosensitivity; avoiding unprotected exposure to sun; using protective clothing; using a sun block product that includes protection against both UVA-caused photosensitivity reactions and UVB-caused sunburn reactions; avoiding use of sunlamp, tanning bed, or tanning booth

Caution if any laboratory tests required; possible interference with results of metyrapone test.

» Caution if any kind of surgery, dental treatment, or emergency treatment is required

» Checking with physician before discontinuing medicine; gradual dosage reduction may be needed to avoid worsening of condition or withdrawal symptoms

» Observing precautions for 3 to 7 days after stopping medication

For protriptyline

Possibility of sleep interference if taken late in the day

Side/adverse effects

Signs of potential side effects, especially anticholinergic effects; hypotension; fast, slow, or irregular heartbeat; Parkinsonian syndrome; nervousness or restlessness; sexual function impairment; shakiness or tremors; neuroleptic malignant syndrome (NMS) or tardive dyskinesia (with amoxapine only); anxiety; breast enlargement in males and females; galactorrhea; testicular swelling; alopecia; allergic reactions; blood dyscrasias; cholestatic jaundice; seizures; SIADH; tinnitus; or trouble with teeth or gums

General Dosing Information

Dosage of tricyclic antidepressants must be individualized for each patient by titration.

Plasma concentrations of tricyclic antidepressants, in general, vary greatly among patients. However, nortriptyline appears to have a well-defined "therapeutic window" at 50 to 150 nanograms per mL of plasma. Other therapeutic plasma concentration ranges which are generally accepted include desipramine, 150 to 250 nanograms per mL, and imipramine, 200 to 250 nanograms per mL.

Although a sedative action may occur following the initial dose (with the possible exception of protriptyline), 1 to 6 weeks of therapy may be required before the desired antidepressant response is obtained.

Maintenance therapy of the sedating tricyclic antidepressants is usually given as a single dose at bedtime. A divided dose may be preferred, however, for protriptyline, and for all tricyclic antidepressants in geriatric or cardiovascular patients, or in adolescents or children. Maintenance is often continued for 6 months to 1 year. Recent data suggest that some patients with recurrent depression may benefit from prolonged maintenance treatment at the full (acute treatment) daily dose.

A trial of four to six weeks at the upper therapeutic dose range may be considered an adequate antidepressant trial, after which alternate therapy should be considered.

The single daily dose at bedtime is useful when side effects such as excessive drowsiness or dizziness might be bothersome or dangerous during working hours. An exception to bedtime dosage is protriptyline, which if taken late in the day may cause insomnia or nightmares in some patients. Therefore, protriptyline is often given in divided doses with the last daily dose in the afternoon.

Withdrawal symptoms, such as headache, malaise, nausea or vomiting, and vivid dreams, may occur if high or prolonged dosage is abruptly discontinued. Also, patients with a history of only unipolar depression may experience a fast-cycling bipolar disorder (manic-depressive illness) with mania or hypomania. Although this has not been reported with all of the tricyclics, a gradual reduction in dosage over a 1- to 2-month period is recommended when any of these medications is to be discontinued.

Potentially suicidal patients should not have access to large quantities of these medications since depressed patients, particularly those who may use alcohol excessively, may continue to exhibit suicidal tendencies until significant improvement occurs. Some clinicians recommend that not more than the equivalent of 1 gram of amitriptyline be dispensed to such patients at any one time. However, most clinicians agree that the judgment must be made according to each patient's individual condition.

The condition of depressed patients with bipolar disorder may sometimes change to the manic phase during tricyclic antidepressant therapy, although such change has not been reported with every tricyclic antidepressant.

Diet/Nutrition

Oral doses may be taken with or immediately after food to lessen gastric irritation.

The requirements for riboflavin may be increased in patients receiving amitriptyline or imipramine.

AMITRIPTYLINE

Summary of Differences

Indications: Also used to manage some types of chronic, severe, neurogenic pain, and to treat bulimia and peptic ulcer disease.
Pharmacology: Effects—
    Anticholinergic: High.
    Sedative: High.
    Orthostatic hypotension—Moderate to high.

Oral Dosage Forms

Note: Bracketed uses in the *Dosage Forms* section refer to categories of use and/or indications that are not included in U.S. product labeling.

AMITRIPTYLINE HYDROCHLORIDE TABLETS USP

Usual adult dose: Antidepressant—Oral, initially 25 mg two to four times a day, the dosage being adjusted gradually as needed and tolerated.

Usual adult prescribing limits:
    Outpatients—Up to 150 mg a day.
    Hospitalized patients—Up to 300 mg a day.
    Geriatric patients—Up to 100 mg a day.

Usual geriatric dose: Antidepressant—Oral, initially 25 mg at bedtime, the dosage being adjusted as needed and tolerated, up to 10 mg three times a day and 20 mg at bedtime.

Auxiliary labeling:
• May cause drowsiness.
• Avoid alcoholic beverages.

AMITRIPTYLINE PAMOATE SYRUP

Usual adult dose: Antidepressant—Oral, initially 25 mg (base) two to four times a day, the dosage being adjusted gradually as needed and tolerated.

Usual geriatric dose: Antidepressant—Oral, initially 10 mg three times a day and 20 mg at bedtime, the dosage being adjusted as needed and tolerated, up to a maximum of 100 mg a day, in divided doses or as a single dose at bedtime.

Auxiliary labeling:
• May cause drowsiness.
• Avoid alcoholic beverages.

Parenteral Dosage Forms

AMITRIPTYLINE HYDROCHLORIDE INJECTION USP

Usual adult dose: Antidepressant—Intramuscular, 20 to 30 mg four times a day.

AMOXAPINE

Summary of Differences

Pharmacology:
    Effects—
        Anticholinergic: Moderate.
        Sedative: Low to moderate.
        Orthostatic hypotension—Low.
    Onset of action—Antidepressant: Within 1 to 2 weeks.
Side/adverse effects: Neuroleptic malignant syndrome, parkinsonian reactions and tardive dyskinesia may occur. Sexual function impairment, breast enlargement in both males and females, testicular swelling, and severe, refractory seizures on acute overdose are all more frequent with amoxapine than with other tricyclic antidepressants.

Oral Dosage Forms

AMOXAPINE TABLETS

Usual adult dose: Antidepressant—Oral, initially 50 mg two or three times a day, the dosage being increased to 100 mg two or three times a day within the first week of treatment as needed and tolerated.

Note: Increases above 300 mg a day should be made with caution and only if 300 mg a day has been ineffective during a trial period of at least two weeks.

Usual adult prescribing limits: Hospitalized patients—Up to 600 mg a day in divided doses.

Usual geriatric dose: Antidepressant—Oral, initially 25 mg two or three times a day, the dosage being increased, if tolerated, to 50 mg two or three times a day within the first week.

Auxiliary labeling:
• May cause drowsiness.
• Avoid alcoholic beverages.

CLOMIPRAMINE

Summary of Differences

Indications: Also used to treat obsessive-compulsive disorder, panic, disorder, bulimia nervosa, cataplexy associated with narcolepsy, and to manage some types of chronic, severe, neurogenic pain.
Pharmacology: Effects—
    Anticholinergic: High.
    Sedative: Moderate.
    Orthostatic hypotension—Moderate.
Precautions: Drug interactions and/or related problems—Not recommended for concurrent use with monoamine oxidase inhibitors.
Side/adverse effects: Sexual function impairment, seizures, and nausea and vomiting may occur more frequently with clomipramine than with other tricyclic antidepressants.

Additional Dosing Information

See also *General Dosing Information.*

Clomipramine should be given in divided doses with meals during initial titration to minimize gastrointestinal side effects; after titration, the total daily dose may be given at bedtime to minimize daytime sedation.

Oral Dosage Forms

Note: Bracketed uses in the *Dosage Forms* section refer to categories of use and/or indications that are not included in U.S. product labeling.

CLOMIPRAMINE HYDROCHLORIDE CAPSULES

Usual adult dose:
[Antidepressant]—Oral, initially 25 mg three times a day, the dosage being adjusted as needed and tolerated.

Antiobsessional agent—Oral, initially 25 mg once a day, the dosage being gradually increased to 100 mg during the first two weeks. The dosage may be further increased over the next several weeks, up to a maximum of 250 mg a day.

Usual adult prescribing limits:
Outpatients—Up to 250 mg a day.
Hospitalized patients—Up to 300 mg a day.

Usual geriatric dose: Oral, 20 to 30 mg a day, the dosage being increased as needed and tolerated.

Note: The strengths of the specific products may not conform to the recommended geriatric doses.

Auxiliary labeling:
• May cause drowsiness.
• Avoid alcoholic beverages.

CLOMIPRAMINE HYDROCHLORIDE TABLETS

Usual adult dose: See *Clomipramine Hydrochloride Capsules.*

Usual adult prescribing limits: See *Clomipramine Hydrochloride Capsules.*

Usual geriatric dose: See *Clomipramine Hydrochloride Capsules.*

Auxiliary labeling:
• May cause drowsiness.
• Avoid alcoholic beverages.

DESIPRAMINE

Summary of Differences

Indications: Also used to manage some types of chronic, severe, neurogenic pain; to reduce craving and/or prevent depression upon withdrawal of cocaine; to control binge eating and purging in bulimia; and to treat cataplexy associated with narcolepsy and is being used to relieve the symptoms of attention deficit hyperactivity disorder in children over 6 years of age and in adolescents.

Pharmacology: Effects—
Anticholinergic: Low.
Sedative: Low.
Orthostatic hypotension—Moderate.

Precautions: Drug interactions and/or related problems—
Not recommended for concurrent use with monoamine oxidase inhibitors.
Concurrent use of phenytoin with desipramine may lower serum concentrations of desipramine; dosage increases above maximum recommended doses of desipramine may be necessary for clinical improvement of depression.

Oral Dosage Forms

DESIPRAMINE HYDROCHLORIDE TABLETS USP

Usual adult dose: Antidepressant—Oral, 100 to 200 mg a day in divided doses or as a single dose, the dosage being adjusted as needed and tolerated.

Usual adult prescribing limits: Up to 300 mg a day.

Note: Geriatric patients—Up to 150 mg a day.

Usual geriatric dose: Antidepressant—Oral, 25 to 50 mg a day in divided doses, the dosage being adjusted as needed and tolerated, up to a maximum of 150 mg a day.

Auxiliary labeling:
• May cause drowsiness.
• Avoid alcoholic beverages.

DOXEPIN

Summary of Differences

Indications: Also used in treatment of some types of chronic, severe neurogenic pain; peptic ulcer disease; and pruritus in idiopathic cold urticaria.

Pharmacology: Effects—
Anticholinergic: High.
Sedative: High.
Orthostatic hypotension—High.

Additional Dosing Information

See also *General Dosing Information.*

Patients with mild symptomology or emotional symptoms accompanying organic disease may be controlled on doses as low as 25 to 50 mg a day.

The once-a-day dosage maximum is 150 mg, which may be given at bedtime.

Oral Dosage Forms

DOXEPIN HYDROCHLORIDE CAPSULES USP

Usual adult dose:
Antidepressant—Oral, initially 25 mg (base) three times a day, the dosage being adjusted gradually as needed and tolerated.

Antipruritic—Oral, initially 10 mg (base) at bedtime, the dosage being increased gradually up to 25 mg, as needed and tolerated.

Usual adult prescribing limits:
Outpatients—Up to 150 mg (base) a day.
Hospitalized patients—Up to 300 mg (base) a day.

Usual geriatric dose: Antidepressant—Oral, initially 25 to 50 mg (base) a day, the dosage being adjusted gradually as needed and tolerated.

Auxiliary labeling:
• May cause drowsiness.
• Avoid alcoholic beverages.

DOXEPIN HYDROCHLORIDE ORAL SOLUTION USP

Usual adult dose: See *Doxepin Hydrochloride Capsules USP.*

Usual adult prescribing limits: See *Doxepin Hydrochloride Capsules USP.*

Auxiliary labeling:
• May cause drowsiness.
• Avoid alcoholic beverages.
• Must be diluted before taking.

IMIPRAMINE

Summary of Differences

Indications:

Imipramine hydrochloride (but not pamoate) is indicated in treatment of childhood enuresis.

Imipramine is also used to manage some types of chronic, severe, neurogenic pain; to reduce craving and/or prevent depression upon cocaine withdrawal; to relieve symptoms of attention deficit hyperactivity disorder in children over 6 years of age and in adolescents; as a treatment adjunct with amphetamines or methylphenidate in cataplexy associated with narcolepsy; to block the recurrence of panic attacks, with or without phobias; in the treatment of stress and urge incontinence; and to control binge eating and purging in bulimia.

Pharmacology: Effects—

Anticholinergic: Moderate.

Sedative: Moderate.

Orthostatic hypotension—High.

Precautions: Drug interactions and/or related problems—Not recommended for concurrent use with monoamine oxidase inhibitors.

Additional Dosing Information

See also *General Dosing Information.*

For oral dosage forms only

In enuretic children, a daily dose exceeding 75 mg does not normally increase results. The usual pediatric prescribing limits are 2.5 mg per kg of body weight (mg/kg) a day.

For early-night bedwetters, the dosage may be more effective when one-half of the dose is given at mid-afternoon and one-half at bedtime.

A gradual decrease in dosage is less likely to cause relapse than an abrupt discontinuation.

Younger children should not be allowed to self-administer imipramine because of their increased sensitivity to side effects, especially cardiovascular effects and acute overdosage (plasma concentrations over 225 nanograms per mL), which are potentially fatal.

A medication-free interval after adequate therapeutic trial should be considered for children. However, dosage should be decreased gradually to prevent relapse. Children who have relapsed may not respond when treatment is reinitiated.

For parenteral dosage forms only

Used only for initiating therapy in patients who are not able or are unwilling to take oral medication. Oral dosage forms should replace the parenteral as soon as possible.

Oral Dosage Forms

IMIPRAMINE HYDROCHLORIDE TABLETS USP

Usual adult dose:

Antidepressant—Oral, 25 to 50 mg three or four times a day, the dosage being adjusted as needed and tolerated.

[Urinary incontinence][1]—Oral, 10 to 50 mg a day, the dosage being adjusted as needed and tolerated, to a maximum of 150 mg a day.

Usual adult prescribing limits:

Outpatients—Up to 200 mg a day.

Hospitalized patients—Up to 300 mg a day.

Geriatric patients—Up to 100 mg a day.

Usual geriatric dose: Antidepressant—Oral, initially 25 mg at bedtime, the dosage being adjusted as needed and tolerated, up to 100 mg a day in divided doses.

Auxiliary labeling:
- May cause drowsiness.
- Avoid alcoholic beverages.

IMIPRAMINE PAMOATE CAPSULES

Usual adult dose: Antidepressant—Oral, initially 75 mg a day, usually given at bedtime, the dosage being adjusted as needed and tolerated.

Note: The dose level at which optimum response is usually obtained is 150 mg a day, usually given at bedtime.

Usual adult prescribing limits:

Outpatients—Up to 200 mg a day.

Hospitalized patients—Up to 300 mg a day.

Auxiliary labeling:
- May cause drowsiness.
- Avoid alcoholic beverages.

Parenteral Dosage Forms

IMIPRAMINE HYDROCHLORIDE INJECTION USP

Usual adult dose: Antidepressant—Intramuscular, up to 100 mg a day in divided doses.

Usual adult prescribing limits: Up to 300 mg a day.

Auxiliary labeling: • For intramuscular use only.

---

[1]Not included in Canadian product labeling.

NORTRIPTYLINE

Summary of Differences

Indications: Also used to manage some types of chronic, severe, neurogenic pain and in the treatment of panic disorder.

Pharmacology: Effects—

Anticholinergic: Low.

Sedative: Moderate.

Orthostatic hypotension—Low.

Oral Dosage Forms

NORTRIPTYLINE HYDROCHLORIDE CAPSULES USP

Usual adult dose: Antidepressant—Oral, 25 mg (base) three or four times a day, the dosage being adjusted as needed and tolerated.

Usual adult prescribing limits: Up to 150 mg (base) a day.

Usual geriatric dose: Oral, 30 to 50 mg a day in divided doses, the dosage being adjusted as needed and tolerated.

Auxiliary labeling:
- May cause drowsiness.
- Avoid alcoholic beverages.

NORTRIPTYLINE HYDROCHLORIDE ORAL SOLUTION USP

Usual adult dose: See *Nortriptyline Hydrochloride Capsules USP.*

Auxiliary labeling:
- May cause drowsiness.
- Avoid alcoholic beverages.

PROTRIPTYLINE

Summary of Differences

Indications: Also used in the treatment of narcolepsy, as an adjunct with amphetamines or methylphenidate in the treatment of cataplexy associated with narcolepsy, in sleep disorders such as hypersomnia or impaired morning arousal, and may be used to relieve symptoms of attention deficit hyperactivity disorder in some children over 6 years of age and in adolescents.
Pharmacology: Effects—
    Anticholinergic: Moderate.
    Sedative: Very low.
    Orthostatic hypotension—Low.

Additional Dosing Information

See also *General Dosing Information.*

When dosage increases of protriptyline are indicated, the increase should be made in the morning. This drug often has a psychic-energizing action and usually not the sedative action exhibited by other tricyclics, although it may intensify the sedative effect of other medications.

Protriptyline is often given in divided doses with the last daily dose in the afternoon to avoid insomnia or nightmares when given to some patients before bedtime.

When protriptyline is used in narcolepsy, 15 to 20 mg given in a single daily dose at bedtime may relieve symptoms of arousal difficulty and daytime sleepiness.

Oral Dosage Forms

Note: Bracketed uses in the *Dosage Forms* section refer to categories of use and/or indications that are not included in U.S. product labeling.

PROTRIPTYLINE HYDROCHLORIDE TABLETS USP

Usual adult dose:
    Antidepressant—Oral, initially 5 to 10 mg three or four times a day, the dosage being adjusted as needed and tolerated.
    [Anticataplectic][1]—Oral, 15 to 20 mg a day at bedtime.

Usual adult prescribing limits: Up to 60 mg a day.

Usual geriatric dose: Antidepressant—Oral, initially 5 mg three times a day, the dosage being adjusted as needed and tolerated.

Note: When the daily dose for geriatric patients exceeds 20 mg, the cardiovascular response should be closely monitored.

Auxiliary labeling:
• May cause drowsiness.
• Avoid alcoholic beverages.

---

[1]Not included in Canadian product labeling.

TRIMIPRAMINE

Summary of Differences

Indications: Also used in treatment of peptic ulcer disease and in the management of some types of chronic, severe, neurogenic pain.
Pharmacology: Effects—
    Anticholinergic: High.
    Sedative: High.
    Orthostatic hypotension—Moderate.

Additional Dosing Information

See also *General Dosing Information.*

For patient compliance and convenience of therapy for outpatients, the total daily dosage may be given at bedtime.

Following remission, maintenance therapy should continue for about 3 months at the lowest dose necessary to maintain remission.

In resistant cases of depression in adults in which dosage exceeds 2.5 mg per kg of body weight (mg/kg) a day, the ECG should be monitored during initiation of therapy and at appropriate intervals during stabilization of dose.

Oral Dosage Forms

Note: The dosing and strengths of the dosage forms available are expressed in terms of trimipramine base (not the maleate).

TRIMIPRAMINE MALEATE CAPSULES

Usual adult dose: Antidepressant—
    Outpatients:
        Initial—Oral, 75 mg (base) a day in divided doses, the dosage being adjusted gradually to 150 mg a day as needed and tolerated, up to a maximum of 200 mg a day.
        Maintenance—Oral, 50 to 150 mg (base) a day.
    Hospitalized patients: Oral, initially 100 mg (base) a day in divided doses, the dosage being increased gradually in a few days to 200 mg a day, up to 250 to 300 mg a day in two to three weeks.

Usual geriatric dose: Oral, initially 50 mg (base) a day in divided doses, the dosage being adjusted as needed and tolerated, up to a maximum of 100 mg a day.

Auxiliary labeling:
• May cause drowsiness.
• Avoid alcoholic beverages.

TRIMIPRAMINE MALEATE TABLETS

Usual adult dose: See *Trimipramine Maleate Capsules.*

Usual geriatric dose: Antidepressant—Oral, initially 25 to 50 mg (base) a day in divided doses, the dosage being increased by 25 mg a week, up to a maximum of 150 mg a day.

Auxiliary labeling:
• May cause drowsiness.
• Avoid alcoholic beverages.

ANTIDIABETIC AGENTS, ORAL   Systemic

INN: Included in brackets after individual generic listings, if different from the U.S. generic name.

Some commonly used *brand names* are:

In the U.S.—

DiaBeta [Glyburide]	*Micronase* [Glyburide]
Diabinese [Chlorpropamide]	*Oramide* [Tolbutamide]
Dymelor [Acetohexamide]	*Orinase* [Tolbutamide]
Glucamide [Chlorpropamide]	*Tolamide* [Tolazamide]
Glucotrol [Glipizide]	*Tolinase* [Tolazamide]

In Canada—

Apo-Chlorpropamide [Chlorpropamide]	*Euglucon* [Glyburide]
Apo-Tolbutamide [Tolbutamide]	*Mobenol* [Tolbutamide]
DiaBeta [Glyburide]	*Novobutamide* [Tolbutamide]
Diabenese [Chlorpropamide]	*Novopropamide* [Chlorpropamide]
Dimelor [Acetohexamide]	*Orinase* [Tolbutamide]

Another commonly used name for glyburide is glibenclamide.

ORAL

ACETOHEXAMIDE
　Acetohexamide Tablets USP
　　In the U.S.—*Dymelor;* GENERIC
　　In Canada—*Dimelor*
CHLORPROPAMIDE
　Chlorpropamide Tablets USP
　　In the U.S.—*Diabinese; Glucamide;* GENERIC
　　In Canada—*Apo-Chlorpropamide; Diabinese; Novopropamide;* GENERIC
GLIPIZIDE
　Glipizide Tablets
　　In the U.S.—*Glucotrol*
GLYBURIDE [INN: Glibenclamide]
　Glyburide Tablets
　　In the U.S.—*DiaBeta; Micronase*
　　In Canada—*DiaBeta; Euglucon*
TOLAZAMIDE
　Tolazamide Tablets USP
　　In the U.S.—*Tolamide; Tolinase;* GENERIC
TOLBUTAMIDE
　Tolbutamide Tablets USP
　　In the U.S.—*Oramide; Orinase;* GENERIC
　　In Canada—*Apo-Tolbutamide; Mobenol; Novobutamide; Orinase;* GENERIC

Category

Antidiabetic—Acetohexamide; Chlorpropamide; Glipizide; Glyburide; Tolazamide; Tolbutamide.
Antidiuretic—Chlorpropamide.

Indications

Note: Bracketed information in the *Indications* section refers to uses not included in U.S. product labeling.

Accepted

Diabetes mellitus, non-insulin-dependent (treatment)—Oral antidiabetic medicines are indicated in the treatment and control of uncomplicated diabetes mellitus of the stable, mild or moderately severe, non-ketotic, maturity-onset type (NIDDM; type II), which cannot be completely controlled by diet alone. Control of diabetes by changes in diet should be tried first. Those patients not responding adequately to diet alone or those patients requiring diet plus insulin, especially if they require 20 Units or less of insulin a day, may be candidates for therapy with oral antidiabetic agents.

[Diabetes insipidus, central, partial (treatment)][1]—Chlorpropamide is also used as secondary therapy in selected patients to treat partial central diabetes insipidus. In about 50% of patients treated with chlorpropamide for central diabetes insipidus (partial), the drug has been successful as an antidiuretic in reducing polyuria. Chlorpropamide may be used alone or in combination with another agent such as carbamazepine or clofibrate so that the dose of both can be reduced and side effects minimized. Nasal or subcutaneous desmopressin is considered the primary treatment for diabetes insipidus.

Use of oral antidiabetic agents in conjunction with insulin in the treatment of insulin-dependent diabetes mellitus (Type I) is controversial. Many studies indicate that oral antidiabetic agents are not effective in the treatment of Type I diabetes mellitus.

Unaccepted

Oral antidiabetic agents are not effective in the treatment of insulin-dependent (juvenile-onset; type I) diabetes.

Chlorpropamide is not effective in the treatment of nephrogenic diabetes insipidus.

---

[1]Not included in Canadian product labeling.

Pharmacology

Mechanism of action/Effect:

　Antidiabetic—Promote release of insulin from the beta cells of pancreatic islet tissue by an unknown process. Insulin production is not increased. Hepatic glycogenolysis and gluconeogenesis are decreased. Insulin sensitivity is increased at peripheral target sites. Therefore, sulfonylureas are effective only in patients whose pancreata are capable of producing insulin.

　Antidiuretic—Chlorpropamide seems to potentiate the effect of minimal levels of antidiuretic hormone present in patients with partial central diabetes insipidus.

Precautions to Consider

Cross-sensitivity and/or related problems

Patients sensitive to one of the oral antidiabetic agents may be sensitive to the others also; cross-sensitivity to other sulfonamide- or thiazide-type medications may also occur.

Geriatrics

Geriatric patients and patients with renal insufficiency may be more sensitive to the effects of this medication because of reduced metabolism and excretion. Dosage should therefore be initiated at a lower level and adjusted cautiously.

Geriatric patients may be more likely to develop SIADH (syndrome of inappropriate diuretic hormone) from the use chlorpropamide.

In the elderly, hypoglycemia may be more difficult to recognize and may cause more neurological symptoms. These symptoms include anxiety, confusion, difficulty in concentrating, drowsiness, nervousness, or unusual tiredness.

Use of oral antidiabetic agents with prolonged duration of action should be avoided in the geriatric patient. However, if they are used, particular caution should be exercised.

Dental

The leukopenic and thrombocytopenic effects of sulfonylureas may result in an increased incidence of microbial infection, delayed healing, and gingival bleeding. If leukopenia or cytopenia occurs, dental work should be deferred until blood counts have returned to normal. Patients should be instructed in the proper oral hygiene required during this period. This includes cautious use of regular toothbrushes, dental floss, and toothpicks.

Drug interactions and/or related problems

The following drug interactions and/or related problems have been selected on the basis of their potential clinical significance (possible mechanism in parentheses where appropriate)—not necessarily inclusive:

Note: Combinations containing any of the following medications, depending on the amount present, may also interact with this medication.

Adrenocorticoids, glucocorticoid effects, systemic, or
Amphetamines or
Anticonvulsants, hydantoin, or
Asparaginase or
Baclofen or
Bumetanide or
Calcium channel blocking agents or
Carbonic anhydrase inhibitors, especially acetazolamide, or
Chlorthalidone or
Contraceptives, oral, estrogen-containing, or
Corticotropin (ACTH), especially chronic therapeutic use, or
Danazol or
Dextrothyroxine or
Epinephrine or
Ethacrynic acid or
Furosemide or
Glucagon or
Molindone, high doses, or
Salicylates, in large overdoses, or
Thiazide diuretics or
Thyroid hormones or
Triamterene

(blood glucose concentrations may be increased; dosage adjustments may be necessary for either or both medications; dosage readjustment of the oral antidiabetic agent may also be required when therapy with the above medications is discontinued)

» Alcohol
(disulfiram-like reaction may occur [abdominal cramps, nausea, vomiting, headaches, flushing, and hypoglycemia]; may occur with any of the sulfonylureas; risk higher with chlorpropamide than with glipizide or glyburide)
(increased risk of hypoglycemia)

Allopurinol
(increased risk of hypoglycemia due to inhibition of renal tubular secretion of chlorpropamide; closer monitoring required)

Anabolic steroids or
Androgens
(increased risk of hypoglycemia; dosage adjustment of antidiabetic agent may be required)

» Anticoagulants, coumarin- or indandione-derivative
(increased plasma concentrations of both the anticoagulant and sulfonylurea may occur initially; with continued therapy, decreased anticoagulant plasma concentrations and increased hepatic metabolism of the sulfonylurea may occur; dosage adjustments of one or both medications may be required)

Anti-inflammatory drugs, nonsteroidal (NSAIDs), or
» Chloramphenicol or
Clofibrate or
» Guanethidine or
» Monoamine oxidase (MAO) inhibitors, including furazolidone, pargyline, and procarbazine, or
Probenecid or
» Salicylates, in therapeutic amounts, or
» Sulfonamides
(increased risk of hypoglycemia due to displacement of sulfonylurea from serum proteins; dosage adjustment may be required; less likely with glipizide and glyburide, due to their non-ionic binding characteristics, though cautious use is recommended)

(NSAIDs and salicylates may increase risk of hypoglycemia because prostaglandins are directly involved in regulatory mechanisms of glucose)

Antithyroid agents
(increased risk of sulfonylurea-induced agranulocytosis)

Appetite suppressants
(when appetite suppressants and a concurrent dietary regimen are used, blood glucose concentrations may be altered in diabetic patients; dosage adjustment of antidiabetic agent may be necessary during and after therapy)

» Beta-adrenergic blocking agents, including ophthalmics, if significant absorption occurs
(nonselective beta-adrenergic blocking agents impair glycogenolysis and the hyperglycemic response to endogenous epinephrine, leading to persistence of hypoglycemia; beta-blockers, especially nonselective agents, decrease the release of insulin in response to hyperglycemia; dosage adjustment of antidiabetic agent may be required to avoid severe hypoglycemic reaction)
(beta-blockers may complicate patient monitoring by masking symptoms of hypoglycemia caused by epinephrine, such as increased heart rate and increased blood pressure; dizziness and sweating are generally unaffected)
(labetalol and selective or relatively selective beta-blockers, such as acebutolol, atenolol, or metoprolol, usually cause fewer problems with blood glucose levels, especially when used in lower doses, although they may still mask symptoms of hypoglycemia)

Bone marrow depressants
(increased risk of sulfonylurea-induced leukopenia or thrombocytopenia; frequent monitoring should be considered)

Carbamazepine or
Clofibrate or
Desmopressin or
Lypressin or
Posterior pituitary or
Vasopressin
(antidiuretic effect may be potentiated by chlorpropamide)

Diazoxide, parenteral
(hyperglycemic action of diazoxide is diminished; dosage adjustment of antidiabetic agent may be required)

Disopyramide
(rarely, risk of hypoglycemia may be increased; patients susceptible to hypoglycemia should be closely monitored)

Hemolytics, other
(increased risk of sulfonylurea-induced hemolysis)

» Insulin
(hypoglycemic effect may be enhanced; although the combination has been used to treat a select group of diabetic patients whose condition is not well-controlled with either agent alone, many studies have shown there is generally no additional benefit from using oral agents for the treatment of type I diabetes)

Ketoconazole or
Miconazole or
Sulfinpyrazone
(miconazole decreases metabolism of sulfonylureas, which has resulted in severe hypoglycemia; use of chemically similar ketoconazole also is not recommended)
(metabolism of sulfonylureas may be decreased by sulfinpyrazone; dosage adjustments may be required during and after sulfinpyrazone therapy)

Rifampin
(metabolism of sulfonylureas may be increased due to stimulation of hepatic microsomal enzymes; dosage adjustments may be necessary during and after rifampin therapy)

Contraindications/Medical problems

The contraindications/medical problems included have been selected on the basis of their potential clinical significance (reasons given

in parentheses where appropriate)—not necessarily inclusive (» = major clinical significance).

Except under special circumstances, this medication should not be used when the following medical problems exist:

For all oral antidiabetic agents
» Acidosis, significant, or
» Burns, severe, or
» Diabetic coma (ketoacidotic, nonketotic hyperosmolar, or associated with hypoglycemia) or
» Infection, severe, or
» Ketoacidosis or
» Ketosis, significant, or
» Surgery, major, or
» Trauma, severe
    (fluctuations in blood glucose levels associated with certain disease states are more closely controlled by titration of insulin dosing, rather than with oral antidiabetic agents)

Risk-benefit should be considered when the following medical problems exist:

For all oral antidiabetic agents
» Adrenal insufficiency, untreated, or
» Pituitary insufficiency, untreated
    (patients prone to hypoglycemia)
» Fever, high
» Nausea and vomiting, prolonged
» Thyroid function impairment
» Debilitated physical condition or
» Hepatic function impairment or
» Malnourishment or
» Renal function impairment
    (hypoglycemia more likely to occur; lower initial dose may be required)
    Sensitivity to oral antidiabetic agents, sulfonamides, or thiazide-type diuretics

For chlorpropamide only
» Cardiac function impairment
    (fluid retention may result in hyponatremia and precipitate congestive heart failure)
» Fluid retention
    (syndrome of inappropriate secretion of antidiuretic hormone [SIADH])

Side/Adverse Effects

Note: Elderly, debilitated, or malnourished patients, and those with untreated adrenal or pituitary insufficiency or renal or hepatic function impairment are particularly susceptible to the hypoglycemic action of antidiabetic agents.

Hypoglycemia may be more likely to occur when the patient skips or delays meals, exercises much more than usual, cannot eat because of nausea and vomiting, or consumes a significant amount of alcohol.

Special warning on increased risk of cardiovascular mortality—The administration of oral hypoglycemic agents has been reported to be associated with increased cardiovascular mortality as compared with treatment with diet alone or diet plus insulin. This warning is based on the study conducted by the University Group Diabetes Program (UGDP), a long-term prospective clinical trial designed to evaluate the effectiveness of glucose-lowering medications in preventing or delaying vascular complications in patients with non-insulin-dependent diabetes.

The UGDP study involved 823 patients who were randomly assigned to one of four treatment groups (*Diabetes,* 19 [Suppl. 2]:747–830, 1970). UGDP reported that patients treated for 5 to 8 years with diet plus a fixed dose of tolbutamide (1.5 grams per day) had a rate of cardiovascular mortality approximately

$2^1/_2$ times that of patients treated with diet alone. A significant increase in total mortality was not observed, but the use of tolbutamide was discontinued based on the increase in cardiovascular mortality, thus limiting the opportunity for the study to show an increase in overall mortality.

Other studies have not reached a similar conclusion and have in fact suggested that control of elevated blood sugars with oral agents may lessen the danger of cardiovascular disease and mortality. Despite questions regarding the interpretation of the results and the adequacy of the experimental design, the findings of the UGDP study provide an adequate basis for caution. The patient should be informed of the potential risks and advantages of oral antidiabetic agents and of alternative modes of therapy. Although only tolbutamide was included in the study, it is prudent to consider that this warning may also apply to all sulfonylurea-type oral antidiabetic agents, in view of their close similarities in mode of action and chemical structure.

The following side/adverse effects have been selected on the basis of their potential clinical significance (possible signs and symptoms in parentheses where appropriate)—not necessarily inclusive:

Those indicating need for medical attention
Incidence less frequent
    For chlorpropamide only
        Antidiuretic effect (SIADH) (drowsiness; muscle cramps; seizures; swelling or puffiness of face, hands, or ankles; unconsciousness; weakness); ***congestive heart failure*** (difficulty in breathing, shortness of breath)—in patients with pre-existing cardiac disease
Incidence rare
    Agranulocytosis or infection (sore throat, fever); ***anemia, aplastic*** (continuing and unexplained tiredness or weakness, headache, shortness of breath brought on by exercise); ***anemia, hemolytic*** (weakness, fever); ***bone marrow depression*** (fatigue); ***eosinophilia*** (chills, increased sweating, general feeling of ill-health, increased production of sputum, shortness of breath, chest pain, blood in sputum); ***cholestatic jaundice, hepatitis, porphyria cutanea tarda, or hepatic function impairment*** (dark urine, itching of the skin, light-colored stools, yellow eyes or skin); ***thrombocytopenia*** (unusual bleeding or bruising)
Symptoms of overdose
    Hypoglycemia (anxiety; continuing chills; cold sweats; coma; confusion; cool, pale skin; difficulty in concentrating; drowsiness; excessive hunger; continuing headache; mild stomach or abdominal pain; continuing nausea; nervousness; fast heartbeat; seizures; shakiness; unsteady gait; unusual tiredness or weakness; vision changes; continuing vomiting)

Those indicating need for medical attention only if they continue or are bothersome
Incidence more frequent
    Changes in sensation of taste—for tolbutamide only; ***constipation; diarrhea; dizziness; mild drowsiness; headache; heartburn; increase in appetite; loss of appetite; nausea; vomiting; stomach pain, fullness, or discomfort***
Incidence less frequent or rare
    Hives; photosensitivity; skin redness, itching, or rash

Patient Consultation

In providing consultation, consider emphasizing the following selected information (» = major clinical significance):

Before using this medication
» Conditions affecting use, especially:
        Sensitivity to oral antidiabetic agents, sulfonamides, or thiazides
        Pregnancy—Should not be used during pregnancy
        Breast-feeding—Because chlorpropamide is excreted in breast milk, its use while breast-feeding is not recommended
        Use in the elderly—May be more susceptible to hypoglycemia and neurological effects associated with hypoglycemia

Dental—Caution advised in dental care if leukopenia or thrombocytopenia occurs

Other medications, especially coumarin- or indandione-derivative anticoagulants; chloramphenicol; guanethidine; MAO inhibitors including furazolidone, pargyline, and procarbazine; salicylates; sulfonamides; or beta-adrenergic blocking agents, including ophthalmics

Other medical problems, especially acute medical conditions requiring use of insulin, adrenal insufficiency, high fever, nausea, vomiting, pituitary insufficiency, thyroid function impairment, or conditions in which increased susceptibility to hypoglycemia occurs; in addition, for chlorpropamide only—cardiac function impairment or fluid retention

Proper use of this medication

» Importance of following prescribed diet; necessary to allow medicine to work properly

» Compliance with therapy; not taking more or less medicine than directed; taking at same time each day

Missed dose: Taking as soon as possible; not taking if almost time for next dose; not doubling doses

» Proper storage

Precautions while using this medication

Regular visits to physician to check progress

Testing for sugar in blood or urine as ordered by physician

» Avoiding use of other medication unless prescribed or approved by physician

» Possible disulfiram-like reactions may occur when alcohol is ingested (less likely with glipizide and glyburide)

Possibility of photosensitivity

» Taking sugar and notifying physician if symptoms of hypoglycemia occur; also caution patients taking chlorpropamide for diabetes insipidus

Caution if any kind of surgery, dental treatment, or emergency treatment is required

Carrying medical identification card or bracelet

Side/adverse effects

Signs of potential side effects, especially aplastic anemia, eosinophilia, porphyria cutanea tarda, hepatic function impairment, bone marrow depression, agranulocytosis, infection, thrombocytopenia, or hemolytic anemia; in addition, for chlorpropamide only—antidiuretic effect and congestive heart failure

General Dosing Information

Secondary failure of oral antidiabetic therapy may occur in certain patients. This may be due to increasing severity of diabetes or to diminished responsiveness to the medication.

Diet/Nutrition

Adherence to a diet low in refined carbohydrates and providing for a prescribed distribution of caloric intake in meals and snacks is the cornerstone of the treatment of diabetes. Compliance with a diabetic diet is critical; without adherence to the recommended diet, oral antidiabetic agents may be only temporarily effective or may be completely ineffective. Patients weighing 20% or more above their ideal body weight also may not respond to oral antidiabetic agents. For this reason a physician-supervised weight reduction diet may be necessary in obese patients.

Absorption of glipizide may be delayed by up to 40 minutes if the medication is ingested with food.

ACETOHEXAMIDE

Summary of Differences

Pharmacology:
Serum half-life—Parent 1.3 hours; metabolite 6 hours.

Duration of action—12 to 24 hours.
Active metabolite.
Precautions: Laboratory value alterations—Reduces serum uric acid concentration.

Additional Dosing Information

See also *General Dosing Information.*

When patients are transferred to acetohexamide from another oral antidiabetic medication (with the exception of chlorpropamide), no conversion period is required. When transferring patients from chlorpropamide, caution should be exercised during the first 1 to 2 weeks because of the prolonged retention of chlorpropamide in the body.

During conversion from insulin therapy to acetohexamide therapy, no gradual dosage adjustment usually is required for patients using less than 20 Units of insulin daily. For patients using 20 or more Units daily, a 25 to 30% reduction in insulin every day or every second day with gradual dosage adjustment is advisable. Hospitalization for some patients on a higher insulin dosage may be required for uneventful conversion.

Oral Dosage Forms

ACETOHEXAMIDE TABLETS USP

Usual adult dose: Oral, initially, 250 mg once a day, the dosage being adjusted gradually until diabetic control is obtained.

Note: For patients requiring 1 gram or more per day, divided doses are administered, usually before the morning and evening meals. This regimen improves gastrointestinal tolerance and control of hyperglycemia in some patients.

Lower initial doses may be required in patients with medical problems that make them more sensitive to the effects of acetohexamide.

Usual adult prescribing limits: Up to 1.5 grams daily.

Usual geriatric dose: Oral, initially, 125 to 250 mg once a day, the dosage being adjusted gradually until diabetic control is obtained.

Note: Lower initial doses may be required in patients with medical problems that make them more sensitive to the effects of acetohexamide.

Auxiliary labeling:
• Avoid alcoholic beverages.
• Do not take other medicines without advice from your doctor.

CHLORPROPAMIDE

Summary of Differences

Category: [Antidiuretic][1].
Indications: [Diabetes insipidus, central, partial (treatment)][1].
Pharmacology: Half-life—36 hours.
Precautions:
Drug interactions and/or related problems—Disulfiram-like reaction with alcohol may be more likely with chlorpropamide than with other antidiabetics.
Contraindications/medical problems—Patients susceptible to fluid retention or with pre-existing cardiac function impairment require frequent monitoring.
Side/adverse effects: Signs of antidiuretic effects or congestive heart failure should be reported to physician.

Additional Dosing Information

See also *General Dosing Information.*

When patients are transferred to chlorpropamide from another oral antidiabetic medication, no conversion period is required.

During conversion from insulin therapy to chlorpropamide therapy, no gradual dosage adjustment usually is required for patients using less than 40 Units of insulin daily. For patients using 40 Units or more daily, a 50% reduction in insulin the first few days is advisable. Hospitalization for some patients on a higher insulin dosage may be required for uneventful conversion.

Oral Dosage Forms

Note: Bracketed uses in the *Dosage Forms* section refer to categories of use and/or indications that are not included in U.S. product labeling.

CHLORPROPAMIDE TABLETS USP

Usual adult dose:
Antidiabetic—Oral, initially, 250 mg once a day, the dosage being increased by 50 to 125 mg at three- to five-day intervals until diabetic control is obtained.

[Antidiuretic][1]—Oral, 100 to 250 mg as a single dose daily, the dosage being adjusted at two- or three-day intervals as needed and tolerated.

Note: Divided doses are administered, usually twice a day before the morning and evening meals, to improve gastrointestinal tolerance and to improve the control of hyperglycemia in some patients.

Lower initial doses such as 100 to 125 mg per day may be required in patients with medical problems that make them more sensitive to the effects of chlorpropamide.

Usual adult prescribing limits:
Antidiabetic—Oral, up to 750 mg per day.
Antidiuretic—Oral, up to 500 mg per day.

Usual geriatric dose: Oral, initially, 100 to 125 mg once a day, the dosage being increased by 50 to 125 mg at three- to five-day intervals until diabetic control is obtained.

Note: Lower initial doses may also be required in patients with medical problems that make them more sensitive to the effects of chlorpropamide.

Auxiliary labeling:
• Avoid alcoholic beverages.
• Do not take other medicines without advice from your doctor.

[1]Not included in Canadian product labeling.

GLIPIZIDE

Summary of Differences

Pharmacology:
Serum half-life—2 to 4 hours.
Duration of action—12 to 24 hours.
Precautions: Drug interactions and/or related problems—Disulfiram-type reaction with concurrent alcohol use less of a problem than with other oral antidiabetic agents.

Additional Dosing Information

See also *General Dosing Information*.

When patients are transferred to glipizide from another oral antidiabetic medication (with the exception of chlorpropamide), no conversion period is required. When transferring patients from chlorpropamide, caution should be exercised during the first one to two weeks because of the prolonged retention of chlorpropamide in the body.

During conversion from insulin therapy to glipizide therapy, no gradual dosage adjustment usually is required for patients using less than 20 Units of insulin daily. For patients using 20 or more Units daily, a 50% reduction of insulin the first day, with gradual dosage adjustments of glipizide as needed, is desirable. Hospitalization for some patients on a higher insulin dosage may be required for uneventful conversion.

Oral Dosage Forms

GLIPIZIDE TABLETS

Usual adult dose: Oral, initially, 5 mg once a day, the dosage being adjusted in increments of 2.5 to 5 mg at weekly intervals until diabetic control is obtained.

Note: Therapy in patients who may be more sensitive to glipizide should be initiated at 2.5 mg once a day.

In patients on a maintenance schedule of 15 mg or more per day, the recommendation is for divided dosage, two times a day, usually before the morning and evening meals.

Usual adult prescribing limits: Oral, up to 40 mg daily.

Usual geriatric dose: Oral, initially, 2.5 mg per day.

Note: This dose should also be used in patients with medical problems that make them more sensitive to the effects of glipizide.

Auxiliary labeling:
• Avoid alcoholic beverages.
• Do not take other medicines without advice from your doctor.
• Take this medication on an empty stomach, 30 minutes before meals.

GLYBURIDE

Summary of Differences

Pharmacology:
Half-life—10 hours.
Duration of action—24 hours.
Elimination—
Biliary: 50%.
Renal: 50%.
Precautions: Drug interactions and/or related problems—Disulfiram-type reaction with concurrent alcohol use less likely with glyburide than with other antidiabetics.

Additional Dosing Information

See also *General Dosing Information*.

When patients are transferred to glyburide from another oral antidiabetic medication (with the exception of chlorpropamide), no conversion period is required. When transferring patients from chlorpropamide, caution should be exercised during the first one to two weeks because of the prolonged retention of chlorpropamide in the body.

During conversion from insulin therapy to glyburide therapy, no gradual dosage adjustment usually is required for patients using less than 40 Units of insulin daily. For patients requiring more than 40 Units daily, a 50% reduction of insulin the first day, with gradual dosage adjustments of glyburide as needed, is advisable. Hospitalization for some patients on a higher insulin dosage may be required for uneventful conversion.

Oral Dosage Forms

GLYBURIDE TABLETS

Usual adult dose: Oral, initially, 2.5 to 5 mg once a day, the dosage being adjusted in increments of no more than 2.5 mg at weekly intervals until diabetic control is obtained.

Note: Therapy in patients who may be more sensitive to glyburide should be initiated at 1.25 mg once a day.

In patients on a maintenance schedule of 10 mg or more per day, administration in divided doses, two times a day (usually before the morning and evening meals), may improve the control of hyperglycemia in some patients.

Usual adult prescribing limits: Oral, up to 20 mg daily.

Usual geriatric dose: Oral, initially, 1.25 to 2.5 mg per day.

Note: This dose should also be used in patients with medical problems that make them more sensitive to the effects of glyburide.

Auxiliary labeling:
- Avoid alcoholic beverages.
- Do not take other medicines without advice from your doctor.

TOLAZAMIDE

Summary of Differences

Pharmacology:
Serum half-life—7 hours.
Duration of action—10 hours.

Additional Dosing Information

See also *General Dosing Information*.

When patients are transferred to tolazamide from another oral antidiabetic medication (with the exception of chlorpropamide), no conversion period is required. When transferring patients from chlorpropamide, caution should be exercised during the first one to two weeks because of the prolonged retention of chlorpropamide in the body.

During conversion from insulin therapy to tolazamide therapy, no gradual dosage adjustment usually is required for patients using less than 40 Units of insulin daily. For patients requiring 40 or more Units daily, a 50% reduction of insulin the first few days with gradual dosage adjustment of tolazamide as needed is advisable. Hospitalization for some patients on a higher insulin dosage may be required for uneventful conversion.

Oral Dosage Forms

TOLAZAMIDE TABLETS USP

Usual adult dose: Oral, initially, 100 to 250 mg once a day in the morning, the dosage being adjusted gradually until diabetic control is obtained.

Note: When more than 500 mg a day is required, divided doses are administered, usually before the morning and evening meals, to improve gastrointestinal tolerance and to improve the control of hyperglycemia in some patients.

Lower initial doses may also be required in patients with medical problems that make them more sensitive to the effects of tolazamide.

Usual adult prescribing limits: Oral, up to 1 gram daily.

Usual geriatric dose: Oral, 100 mg once a day in the morning, the dosage being adjusted gradually until diabetic control is obtained.

Note: Lower initial doses may also be required in patients with medical problems that make them more sensitive to the effects of tolazamide.

Auxiliary labeling:
- Avoid alcoholic beverages.
- Do not take other medicines without advice from your doctor.

TOLBUTAMIDE

Summary of Differences

Pharmacology:
Serum half-life—4.5 to 6.5 hours.
Duration of action—6 to 12 hours.

Additional Dosing Information

See also *General Dosing Information*.

When patients are transferred to tolbutamide from another oral antidiabetic medication (with the exception of chlorpropamide), no conversion period is required. When transferring patients from chlorpropamide, caution should be exercised during the first one to two weeks because of the prolonged retention of chlorpropamide in the body.

During conversion from insulin therapy to tolbutamide therapy, no gradual dosage adjustment usually is required for patients using less than 20 Units of insulin daily. For patients using 20 to 40 Units daily, a 30 to 50% reduction in insulin the first day with gradual dosage adjustment is advisable. For patients requiring more than 40 Units daily, a 20% reduction of insulin the first day with gradual dosage adjustment of tolbutamide as needed is advisable. Hospitalization for some patients on a higher insulin dosage may be required for uneventful conversion.

Oral Dosage Forms

TOLBUTAMIDE TABLETS USP

Usual adult dose: Oral, initially, 500 mg to 2 grams a day in divided doses, the dosage being adjusted gradually until diabetic control is obtained.

Generally, maintenance doses range from 250 mg to 3 grams daily.

Note: Divided doses are administered, usually before the morning and evening meals, to improve gastrointestinal tolerance and to improve the control of hyperglycemia in some patients.

Lower initial doses may also be required in patients with medical problems that make them more sensitive to the effects of tolbutamide.

Usual adult prescribing limits: Oral, up to 3 grams daily.

Usual geriatric dose: Lower initial dose may be required.

Note: Lower initial doses may also be required in patients with medical problems that make them more sensitive to the effects of tolbutamide.

Auxiliary labeling:
- Avoid alcoholic beverages.
- Do not take other medicines without advice from your doctor.

ANTIDYSKINETICS Systemic

INN: Included in brackets after individual generic listings, if different from U.S. generic names.

Some commonly used *brand names* are:

In the U.S.—
Akineton [Biperiden]
Artane [Trihexyphenidyl]
Artane Sequels
    [Trihexyphenidyl]
Cogentin [Benztropine]

Kemadrin [Procyclidine]
Parsidol [Ethopropazine]
Trihexane
    [Trihexyphenidyl]
Trihexy [Trihexyphenidyl]

In Canada—
Akineton [Biperiden]
Aparkane
    [Trihexyphenidyl]
Apo-Benztropine
    [Benztropine]
Apo-Trihex
    [Trihexyphenidyl]
Artane [Trihexyphenidyl]
Artane Sequels
    [Trihexyphenidyl]
Bensylate [Benztropine]
Cogentin [Benztropine]

Kemadrin [Procyclidine]
Novohexidyl
    [Trihexyphenidyl]
Parsitan [Ethopropazine]
PMS Benztropine
    [Benztropine]
PMS Procyclidine
    [Procyclidine]
PMS Trihexyphenidyl
    [Trihexyphenidyl]
Procyclid [Procyclidine]

AMANTADINE—See Amantadine (Systemic).
BENZTROPINE [INN: Benzatropine]
Oral
   Benztropine Mesylate Tablets USP
      In the U.S.—*Cogentin;* GENERIC
      In Canada—*Apo-Benztropine; Bensylate; Cogentin; PMS Benztropine;* GENERIC
Parenteral
   Benztropine Mesylate Injection USP
      In the U.S.—*Cogentin*
      In Canada—*Cogentin;* GENERIC
BIPERIDEN
Oral
   Biperiden Hydrochloride Tablets USP
      In the U.S. and Canada—*Akineton*
Parenteral
   Biperiden Lactate Injection USP†
      In the U.S.—*Akineton*
CARBIDOPA AND LEVODOPA—See Carbidopa and Levodopa (Systemic).
DIPHENHYDRAMINE—See Antihistamines (Systemic).
ETHOPROPAZINE [INN: Profenamine]
Oral
   Ethopropazine Hydrochloride Tablets USP
      In the U.S.—*Parsidol*
      In Canada—*Parsitan*
HALOPERIDOL—See Haloperidol (Systemic).
LEVODOPA—See Levodopa (Systemic).
PROCYCLIDINE
Oral
   Procyclidine Hydrochloride Elixir*
      In Canada—*Kemadrin; PMS Procyclidine; Procyclid*
   Procyclidine Hydrochloride Tablets USP
      In the U.S.—*Kemadrin*
      In Canada—*Kemadrin; PMS Procyclidine; Procyclid*
TRIHEXYPHENIDYL
Oral
   Trihexyphenidyl Hydrochloride Extended-release Capsules USP
      In the U.S. and Canada—*Artane Sequels*
   Trihexyphenidyl Hydrochloride Elixir USP
      In the U.S. and Canada—*Artane*

Trihexyphenidyl Hydrochloride Tablets USP
   In the U.S.—*Artane; Trihexane; Trihexy;* GENERIC
   In Canada—*Aparkane; Apo-Trihex; Artane; Novohexidyl; PMS Trihexyphenidyl*

*Not commercially available in the U.S.
†Not commercially available in Canada.

Category: Antidyskinetic.

Indications

Note: Bracketed information in the *Indications* section refers to uses not included in U.S. product labeling.

Accepted
Parkinsonism (treatment)—Antidyskinetics are indicated in the treatment of mild cases of postencephalitic, arteriosclerotic, or idiopathic parkinsonism (paralysis agitans) in patients in whom anticholinergic therapy is not contraindicated. Antidyskinetics are also indicated as adjuncts to more potent medications to maximize improvement of symptoms. Procyclidine usually produces a more beneficial effect in conditions of rigidity than in those of tremor.

Extrapyramidal reactions, drug-induced (treatment)—Antidyskinetics are indicated in the control of extrapyramidal disorders (except tardive dyskinesia) due to central nervous system (CNS) drugs such as reserpine, phenothiazines, dibenzoxazepines, thioxanthenes, and butyrophenones. However, concomitant therapy with antipsychotics is not recommended beyond 3 months because extrapyramidal symptoms resulting from antipsychotic therapy usually resolve in 3 to 6 months and because prolonged, routine use of antidyskinetics with antipsychotics may predispose patients to the more serious neurological condition, tardive dyskinesia.

[Athetosis, congenital (treatment)][1]; or
[Degeneration, hepatolenticular (treatment)][1]—Ethopropazine is used for the symptomatic treatment of hepatolenticular degeneration and congenital athetosis.

[1]Not included in Canadian product labeling.

Pharmacology

Mechanism of action/Effect: Specific mode of action is unknown, but it is thought that these agents partially block central (striatal) cholinergic receptors, thereby helping to balance cholinergic and dopaminergic activity in the basal ganglia; salivation may be decreased and smooth muscle may be relaxed. Drug-induced extrapyramidal symptoms and those due to parkinsonism may be relieved, but tardive dyskinesia is not alleviated and may be aggravated by anticholinergic effects.

Other actions/effects: Benztropine and ethopropazine also have a slight antihistaminic and local anesthetic effect. Biperiden may have a slight effect on the cardiovascular and respiratory systems. Procyclidine and trihexyphenidyl have a direct antispasmodic effect on smooth muscle. In small doses trihexyphenidyl depresses the CNS, but larger doses may cause cerebral excitation.

Onset of action:
   Benztropine—
      Oral: 1 to 2 hours.
      Intramuscular or intravenous: Within a few minutes.
   Biperiden—
      Intramuscular: Average of 10 to 30 minutes
      Intravenous: Within a few minutes.
   Trihexyphenidyl—Oral: 1 hour.

Duration of action:
Benztropine—Oral, intramuscular, or intravenous: 24 hours.
Biperiden—Intravenous: 1 to 8 hours.
Ethopropazine—Oral: 4 hours.
Procyclidine—Oral: 4 hours.
Trihexyphenidyl—Oral: 6 to 12 hours.

Precautions to Consider

Geriatrics
Chronic use of antidyskinetics may predispose geriatric patients to glaucoma.

Geriatric patients, especially those with arteriosclerotic changes, may respond to the usual doses of antidyskinetics, ethopropazine and procyclidine in particular, with mental confusion, disorientation, agitation, hallucinations, and psychotic-like symptoms.

Memory may become severely impaired in geriatric patients, especially those who already have memory problems, with the continued use of antidyskinetics since these drugs block the action of acetylcholine, which is responsible for many functions of the brain, including memory functions.

Dental
Prolonged use of antidyskinetics may decrease or inhibit salivary flow, thus contributing to the development of caries, periodontal disease, oral candidiasis, and discomfort.

Drug interactions and/or related problems
The following drug interactions and/or related problems have been selected on the basis of their potential clinical significance (possible mechanism in parentheses where appropriate)—not necessarily inclusive (» = major clinical significance):

Note: Combinations containing any of the following medications, depending on the amount present, may also interact with this medication.

» Alcohol or
» CNS depression-producing medications
(concurrent use with antidyskinetics may cause increased sedative effects)

Amantadine or
» Anticholinergics or other medications with anticholinergic action or
Monoamine oxidase (MAO) inhibitors, including furazolidone, pargyline, and procarbazine
(concurrent use may intensify anticholinergic effects of antidyskinetics because of the secondary anticholinergic activities of these medications; patients should be advised to report occurrence of gastrointestinal problems, fever, or heat intolerance promptly since paralytic ileus, hyperthermia, or heat stroke may occur with concurrent therapy)

» Antacids or
Antidiarrheals, adsorbent
(simultaneous administration may reduce therapeutic effects of antidyskinetics because of particle adsorption; to avoid this effect, patients should be advised to allow at least 1 or 2 hours between doses of the different medications)

Carbidopa and levodopa or
Levodopa
(concurrent use of these medications with benztropine, procyclidine, or trihexyphenidyl may result in increased efficacy of levodopa; however, concurrent use is not recommended if there is a history of psychosis)

Chlorpromazine
(concurrent use of chlorpromazine with antidyskinetics may increase metabolism of chlorpromazine, resulting in decreased plasma concentration because of reduction in gastrointestinal motility)

Contraindications/Medical problems
The contraindications/medical problems included have been selected on the basis of their potential clinical significance (reasons given in parentheses where appropriate)—not necessarily inclusive (» = major clinical significance).

Risk-benefit should be considered when the following medical problems exist:
Cardiac arrhythmias
(increased risk of tachycardia)
» Cardiovascular instability
(increased risk of cardiac arrhythmias)
» Dyskinesia, tardive
(may be aggravated)
Extrapyramidal reactions, such as those resulting from phenothiazines or reserpine, in patients with mental disorders
(mental symptoms may be intensified, precipitating toxic psychosis)
» Glaucoma, angle-closure, or predisposition to
(mydriatic effect resulting in increased intraocular pressure may precipitate an acute attack of angle-closure glaucoma)
» Glaucoma, open-angle
(mydriatic effect may cause a slight increase in intraocular pressure; glaucoma therapy may need to be adjusted)
Hepatic function impairment
Hypertension
(may be aggravated)
» Intestinal obstruction, complete, partial, or history of
(decreased motility and tone may aggravate or precipitate obstruction)
» Myasthenia gravis
(condition may be aggravated because of inhibition of acetylcholine action)
Prostatic hypertrophy, moderate to severe, or
» Urinary retention
(anticholinergic effect of antidyskinetics may precipitate or aggravate urinary retention)
Renal function impairment
(decreased elimination may increase risk of side effects)
Sensitivity to antidyskinetics (history of)

Side/Adverse Effects

Note: Anticholinergic side effects that may occur with antidyskinetics are rarely severe and either disappear as therapy is continued, or diminish when the dose is reduced.

Anhydrosis and subsequent hyperthermia may occur with antidyskinetics when patients, especially geriatric, chronically ill, and alcoholic, are exposed to high environmental temperatures.

Ethopropazine is a phenothiazine derivative. Although the likelihood of ethopropazine causing such side effects as changes in vision, jaundice, rare hematologic reactions, and electrocardiogram (ECG) abnormalities associated with phenothiazines seems to be minimal, the possibility exists.

The following side/adverse effects have been selected on the basis of their potential clinical significance (possible signs and symptoms in parentheses where appropriate)—not necessarily inclusive:

Those indicating need for medical attention
Incidence rare
Allergic reaction (skin rash); *confusion*—more frequent in the elderly or with high doses; *increased intraocular pressure* (eye pain)
Symptoms of overdose
Anticholinergic effects, severe (clumsiness or unsteadiness; severe drowsiness; severe dryness of mouth, nose, or throat; fast

heartbeat; shortness of breath or troubled breathing; warmth, dryness, and flushing of skin); *CNS depression* (severe drowsiness); *CNS stimulation* (hallucinations, seizures, trouble in sleeping); *toxic psychoses*—especially in patients with mental illness being treated with neuroleptic drugs (mood or mental changes)

Those indicating need for medical attention only if they continue or are bothersome
Incidence more frequent
　Anticholinergic effects, mild (blurred vision; constipation; decreased sweating; difficult or painful urination, especially in older men; drowsiness; dryness of mouth, nose, or throat; increased sensitivity of eyes to light; nausea or vomiting)
Incidence less frequent or rare
　False sense of well-being—especially in the elderly or with high doses; *headache; loss of memory, especially in the elderly; muscle cramps; nervousness; numbness or weakness in hands or feet; orthostatic hypotension* (dizziness or lightheadedness when getting up from a lying or sitting position); *soreness of mouth and tongue; stomach upset or pain; unusual excitement*—more frequent with high doses of trihexyphenidyl

Those indicating possible withdrawal symptoms and the need for medical attention if they occur after discontinuation of long-term therapy
　Anxiety; extrapyramidal symptoms, recurrence or worsening of—especially after abrupt withdrawal of antidyskinetic medication; may require reinstatement of the antidyskinetic (difficulty in speaking or swallowing; loss of balance control; mask-like face; muscle spasms, especially of face, neck, and back; restlessness or desire to keep moving; shuffling walk; stiffness of arms or legs; trembling and shaking of hands and fingers; twisting movements of body); *fast heartbeat; orthostatic hypotension* (dizziness or lightheadedness when getting up from a lying or sitting position); *trouble in sleeping*

Patient Consultation

In providing consultation, consider emphasizing the following selected information (» = major clinical significance):

Before using this medication
» Conditions affecting use, especially:
　　Sensitivity to antidyskinetics (history of)
　　Breast-feeding—May inhibit lactation
　　Use in children—Increased susceptibility to anticholinergic effects
　　Use in the elderly—Predisposition to glaucoma with chronic use; increased risk of mental confusion and other psychotic-like symptoms; impairment of memory
　　Dental problems—Decrease or inhibition of salivary flow
　　Other medications, especially antacids, other anticholinergics, and CNS depresssants
　　Other medical problems, especially cardiovascular instability, glaucoma, intestinal obstruction, urinary retention

Proper use of this medication
» Importance of not taking more medication than the amount prescribed
　Taking with food to relieve gastric irritation
　Missed dose: Taking as soon as possible; not taking if within 2 hours of next dose; not doubling doses
» Proper storage

Precautions while using this medication
　Regular visits to physician to check progress during prolonged therapy; eye examination may also be needed
» Checking with physician before discontinuing medication; gradual dosage reduction may be necessary
» Avoiding use of alcohol or other CNS depressants
　Avoiding use of antacids or antidiarrheal medications within 1 hour of taking this medication
　Suspected overdose: Getting emergency help at once

Possible increased eye sensitivity to bright light
» Caution if drowsiness or blurred vision occurs
　Caution when getting up suddenly from a lying or sitting position
» Caution during exercise and hot weather
　Possible dryness of mouth; using sugarless gum or candy, ice, or saliva substitute for relief; checking with physician or dentist if dry mouth continues for more than 2 weeks
Side/adverse effects
　Signs of potential side effects, especially allergic reaction, confusion, increased intraocular pressure, anticholinergic effects, or CNS depression or stimulation

General Dosing Information

For oral dosage forms only
Therapy should be initiated with a low dose because of cumulative action, and dosage should be increased gradually at 5- or 6-day intervals.
Titrated dosage is necessary to achieve the individual required therapeutic level, especially for geriatric patients, who tend to be more sensitive to anticholinergic effects, and patients receiving other medications.
During therapy, necessary dosage adjustments of antidyskinetic or other medication used concurrently should be made gradually to maintain proper control of the patient's condition.
Postencephalitic and younger parkinsonism patients often require and tolerate higher dosages than idiopathic, arteriosclerotic, or geriatric parkinsonism patients.
A drug-abuse potential exists with these medications as they may cause euphoria and hallucinations at higher dosages.
When an antidyskinetic is to be discontinued, dosage should be reduced gradually to prevent a sudden increase in adverse symptoms.

Diet/Nutrition
Antidyskinetics may be taken with or immediately after meals to lessen gastric irritation.

BENZTROPINE

Summary of Differences

Pharmacology:
　Other actions/effects—Has slight antihistaminic and local anesthetic effect.
　Onset of action—
　　Oral: 1 to 2 hours.
　　Intramuscular or intravenous: Within a few minutes.
　Duration of action—Oral, intramuscular, or intravenous—24 hours.
Precautions: Drug interactions and/or related problems—May increase efficacy of levodopa if used concurrently; however, concurrent use not recommended if there is history of psychosis.

Additional Dosing Information

A single daily oral dose of benztropine at bedtime often provides maximum benefit for the patient because of the long duration of effect.

Oral Dosage Forms

BENZTROPINE MESYLATE TABLETS USP
Usual adult and adolescent dose:
　Parkinsonism—Oral, 1 to 2 mg a day, the dosage being adjusted as needed and tolerated.

Note: Idiopathic parkinsonism—Therapy may be initiated in some patients with a single oral daily dose of 500 mcg (0.5 mg) to 1 mg at bedtime.

Postencephalitic parkinsonism—Therapy may be initiated in most patients with 2 mg a day, in one or more divided doses.

Drug-induced extrapyramidal reactions—Oral, 1 to 4 mg one or two times a day. Or, 1 to 2 mg two or three times a day if drug-induced extrapyramidal reactions develop soon after initiation of treatment with neuroleptic drugs.

Usual adult prescribing limits: Up to 6 mg daily.

Usual geriatric dose: See *Usual adult and adolescent dose.*

Note: Geriatric patients may be more sensitive to the effects of the usual adult dose.

Auxiliary labeling:
- May cause drowsiness.
- Avoid alcoholic beverages.

Parenteral Dosage Forms

BENZTROPINE MESYLATE INJECTION USP

Usual adult and adolescent dose:
Parkinsonism—Intramuscular or intravenous, 1 to 2 mg a day, the dosage being adjusted as needed and tolerated.
Drug-induced extrapyramidal reactions—Intramuscular or intravenous, 1 to 4 mg one or two times a day.

Usual adult prescribing limits: Up to 6 mg daily.

Usual geriatric dose: See *Usual adult and adolescent dose.*

Note: Geriatric patients may be more sensitive to the effects of the usual adult dose.

BIPERIDEN

Summary of Differences

Pharmacology: Other actions/effects—Slight cardiovascular and respiratory effects.
Side/adverse effects: Has slight effect on cardiovascular and respiratory systems.

Oral Dosage Forms

BIPERIDEN HYDROCHLORIDE TABLETS USP

Usual adult and adolescent dose:
Parkinsonism—Oral, 2 mg three or four times a day, the dosage being adjusted as needed and tolerated.
Drug-induced extrapyramidal reactions—Oral, 2 mg one to three times a day.

Usual adult prescribing limits: Parkinsonism—Up to 16 mg daily.

Usual geriatric dose: See *Usual adult and adolescent dose.*

Note: Geriatric patients may be more sensitive to the effects of the usual adult dose.

Auxiliary labeling:
- May cause drowsiness.
- Avoid alcoholic beverages.
- Keep container tightly closed.

Parenteral Dosage Forms

BIPERIDEN LACTATE INJECTION USP

Note: Biperiden lactate injection is not commercially available in Canada.

Usual adult and adolescent dose: Drug-induced extrapyramidal reactions—Intramuscular or slow intravenous, 2 mg repeated at half-hour intervals as needed and tolerated up to a total of four doses a day.

Usual geriatric dose: See *Usual adult and adolescent dose.*

Note: Geriatric patients may be more sensitive to the effects of the usual adult dose.

ETHOPROPAZINE

Summary of Differences

Indications: Also used for the symptomatic treatment of hepatolenticular degeneration and congenital athetosis.
Pharmacology:
Other actions/effects—Has slight antihistaminic and local anesthetic effect.
Duration of action—Oral: 4 hours.
Side/adverse effects: May possess phenothiazine side effects, especially in high dosages.

Oral Dosage Forms

ETHOPROPAZINE HYDROCHLORIDE TABLETS USP

Usual adult and adolescent dose:
Parkinsonism and
Drug-induced extrapyramidal reactions—Oral, 50 mg one or two times a day, the dosage being increased as needed and tolerated. In severe cases, the dose may be gradually increased to a total of 500 to 600 mg a day.

Usual geriatric dose: See *Usual adult and adolescent dose.*

Note: Geriatric patients may be more sensitive to the effects of the usual adult dose.

Auxiliary labeling:
- May cause drowsiness.
- Avoid alcoholic beverages.

PROCYCLIDINE

Summary of Differences

Pharmacology:
Other actions/effects—Direct antispasmodic effect on smooth muscle.
Duration of action—Oral: 4 hours.
Precautions:
Drug interactions and/or related problems—May increase efficacy of levodopa if used concurrently; however, concurrent use not recommended if there is history of psychosis.
General dosing information: Provides more beneficial effect in conditions of rigidity than in those of tremor.

Oral Dosage Forms

PROCYCLIDINE HYDROCHLORIDE ELIXIR

Note: Procyclidine hydrochloride elixir is not currently commercially available in the U.S.

Usual adult and adolescent dose:

Parkinsonism—Oral, initially 2.5 mg three times a day after meals. If tolerated, the dosage may be gradually increased to 5 mg three times a day and, occasionally, 5 mg at bedtime.

Note: For patients being transferred from other therapy, 2.5 mg three times a day may be substituted for all or part of the original medication. The dose of procyclidine may be increased while the original medication is decreased until a level of maximum benefit is reached.

Drug-induced extrapyramidal reactions—Oral, initially 2.5 mg three times a day, the dosage being increased in 2.5-mg increments per day as needed and tolerated.

Usual geriatric dose: See *Usual adult and adolescent dose.*

Note: Geriatric patients may be more sensitive to the effects of the usual adult dose.

Auxiliary labeling:
- May cause drowsiness.
- Avoid alcoholic beverages.
- Keep container tightly closed.

PROCYCLIDINE HYDROCHLORIDE TABLETS USP

Usual adult and adolescent dose:

Parkinsonism—Oral, initially 2.5 mg three times a day after meals. If tolerated, the dosage may be gradually increased to 5 mg three times a day and, occasionally, 5 mg at bedtime.

Note: For patients being transferred from other therapy, 2.5 mg three times a day may be substituted for all or part of the original medication. The dose of procyclidine may be increased while the original medication is decreased until a level of maximum benefit is reached.

Drug-induced extrapyramidal reactions—Oral, initially 2.5 mg three times a day, the dosage being increased in 2.5-mg increments per day as needed and tolerated.

Usual geriatric dose: See *Usual adult and adolescent dose.*

Note: Geriatric patients may be more sensitive to the effects of the usual adult dose.

Auxiliary labeling:
- May cause drowsiness.
- Avoid alcoholic beverages.
- Keep container tightly closed.

TRIHEXYPHENIDYL

Summary of Differences

Pharmacology:
Other actions/effects—Direct antispasmodic effect on smooth muscle; small doses depress CNS; larger doses may cause cerebral excitation.
Onset of action—Oral: 1 hour.
Duration of action—Oral: 6 to 12 hours.
Precautions: Drug interactions and/or related problems—May increase efficacy of levodopa if used concurrently; however, concurrent use not recommended if there is history of psychosis.
Side/adverse effects: Unusual excitement (with high doses).

Oral Dosage Forms

TRIHEXYPHENIDYL HYDROCHLORIDE EXTENDED-RELEASE CAPSULES USP

Usual adult and adolescent dose: Parkinsonism—Oral, 5 mg a day after breakfast with an additional 5 mg taken twelve hours later as needed.

Note: This dosage form is usually utilized only after the patient has been stabilized on the conventional dosage forms.

Usual adult prescribing limits: Up to 15 mg daily.

Usual geriatric dose: See *Usual adult and adolescent dose.*

Note: Geriatric patients may be more sensitive to the effects of the usual adult dose.

Auxiliary labeling:
- May cause drowsiness.
- Avoid alcoholic beverages.

TRIHEXYPHENIDYL HYDROCHLORIDE ELIXIR USP

Usual adult and adolescent dose:

Parkinsonism—Oral, 1 to 2 mg the first day, the dosage being increased by an additional 2 mg at three- to five-day intervals until the desired response is obtained or until the total dose per day reaches 6 to 10 mg, usually divided into three doses taken at mealtimes.

Note: Postencephalitic parkinsonism—A total dose of 12 to 15 mg per day may be required.

Drug-induced extrapyramidal reactions—Oral, initially 1 mg a day, the dosage increased as needed and tolerated or until the total daily dose reaches 5 to 15 mg.

Usual adult prescribing limits: Up to 15 mg daily.

Usual geriatric dose: See *Usual adult and adolescent dose.*

Note: Geriatric patients may be more sensitive to the effects of the usual adult dose.

Auxiliary labeling:
- May cause drowsiness.
- Avoid alcoholic beverages.
- Keep container tightly closed.

TRIHEXYPHENIDYL HYDROCHLORIDE TABLETS USP

Usual adult and adolescent dose:

Parkinsonism—Oral, 1 to 2 mg the first day, the dosage being increased by an additional 2 mg at three- to five-day intervals until the desired response is obtained or until the total dose per day reaches 6 to 10 mg, usually divided into three doses taken at mealtimes.

Note: Postencephalitic parkinsonism—A total dose of 12 to 15 mg per day may be required.

Drug-induced extrapyramidal reactions—Oral, initially 1 mg a day, the dosage increased as needed and tolerated or until the total daily dose reaches 5 to 15 mg.

Usual adult prescribing limits: Up to 15 mg daily.

Usual geriatric dose: See *Usual adult and adolescent dose.*

Note: Geriatric patients may be more sensitive to the effects of the usual adult dose.

Auxiliary labeling:
- May cause drowsiness.
- Avoid alcoholic beverages.
- Keep container tightly closed.

ANTIFUNGALS, AZOLE   Vaginal

Some commonly used *brand names* are:

In the U.S.—

Femstat [Butoconazole]	*Mycelex-G* [Clotrimazole]
Gyne-Lotrimin [Clotrimazole]	*Terazol 3* [Terconazole]
	Terazol 7 [Terconazole]
Monistat 3 [Miconazole]	*Vagistat* [Tioconazole]
Monistat 7 [Miconazole]	

In Canada—

Canesten [Clotrimazole]	*Monistat* [Miconazole]
Canesten 1 [Clotrimazole]	*Monistat 3* [Miconazole]
Canesten 3 [Clotrimazole]	*Monistat 5* [Miconazole]
Canesten 10% [Clotrimazole]	*Monistat 7* [Miconazole]
	Myclo [Clotrimazole]
Ecostatin [Econazole]	*Terazol 3* [Terconazole]
Femstat [Butoconazole]	*Terazol 7* [Terconazole]
Gyno-Trosyd [Tioconazole]	

VAGINAL

BUTOCONAZOLE

Butoconazole Nitrate Cream USP (Vaginal)
In the U.S. and Canada—*Femstat*
Butoconazole Nitrate Vaginal Suppositories*
In Canada—*Femstat*

CLOTRIMAZOLE

Clotrimazole Cream USP (Vaginal)
In the U.S.—*Gyne-Lotrimin; Mycelex-G*
In Canada—*Canesten; Canesten 3; Canesten 10%; Myclo*
Clotrimazole Vaginal Tablets USP
In the U.S.—*Gyne-Lotrimin; Mycelex-G*
In Canada—*Canesten; Canesten 1; Canesten 3; Myclo*

ECONAZOLE*

Econazole Nitrate Vaginal Suppositories*
In Canada—*Ecostatin*

MICONAZOLE

Miconazole Nitrate Vaginal Cream
In the U.S.—*Monistat 7*
In Canada—*Monistat; Monistat 7*
Miconazole Nitrate Vaginal Suppositories USP
In the U.S. and Canada—*Monistat 3; Monistat 7*
Miconazole Nitrate Vaginal Tampons*
In Canada—*Monistat 5*

TERCONAZOLE

Terconazole Vaginal Cream
In the U.S. and Canada—*Terazol 7*
Terconazole Vaginal Suppositories†
In the U.S. and Canada—*Terazol 3*

TIOCONAZOLE

Tioconazole Vaginal Ointment
In the U.S.—*Vagistat*
In Canada—*Gyno-Trosyd*
Tioconazole Vaginal Suppositories*
In Canada—*Gyno-Trosyd*

*Not commercially available in the U.S.

Category: Antifungal (vaginal).

Indications

Accepted

Candidiasis, vulvovaginal (treatment)—Vaginal azoles are indicated in the local treatment of vulvovaginal candidiasis caused by *Candida albicans* and other species of *Candida* in pregnant (second and third trimesters only) and nonpregnant women.

Not all species or strains of a particular organism may be susceptible to a specific vaginal azole.

Unaccepted

Vaginal azoles are not effective in the treatment of vulvovaginitis caused by other common pathogens such as *Trichomonas vaginalis*.

The three-day regimen of clotrimazole vaginal tablets is not effective in pregnant women.

Pharmacology

Mechanism of action/Effect: Fungistatic; may be fungicidal, depending on concentration; exact mechanism of action unknown. Azoles inhibit biosynthesis of ergosterol or other sterols, damaging the fungal cell membrane and altering its permeability. As a result, loss of essential intracellular elements may occur.

Azoles also inhibit biosynthesis of triglycerides and phospholipids by fungi. In addition, azoles inhibit oxidative and peroxidative enzyme activity, resulting in intracellular buildup of toxic concentrations of hydrogen peroxide, which may contribute to deterioration of subcellular organelles and cellular necrosis. In *Candida albicans*, azoles inhibit transformation of blastospores into invasive mycelial form.

For terconazole—Triazoles are more slowly metabolized than imidazoles. Triazoles also affect sterol synthesis to a lesser degree.

Precautions to Consider

Geriatrics

Appropriate studies on the relationship of age to the effects of vaginal azoles have not been performed in the geriatric population. However, no geriatrics-specific problems have been documented to date.

Contraindications/Medical problems

The contraindications/medical problems included have been selected on the basis of their potential clinical significance (reasons given in parentheses where appropriate)—not necessarily inclusive (» = major clinical significance).

Risk-benefit should be considered when the following medical problem exists:

Allergy to azoles

Side/Adverse Effects

The following side/adverse effects have been selected on the basis of their potential clinical significance (possible signs and symptoms in parentheses where appropriate)—not necessarily inclusive:

Those indicating need for medical attention
Incidence less frequent
Vaginal burning, itching, discharge, or other irritation not present before therapy
Incidence rare
Hypersensitivity (skin rash or hives)

Those indicating need for medical attention only if they continue or are bothersome
Incidence less frequent or rare
Abdominal or stomach cramps or pain; burning or irritation of penis of sexual partner; headache

Patient Consultation

In providing consultation, consider emphasizing the following selected information (» = major clinical significance):

Before using this medication
» Conditions affecting use, especially:
   Allergy to azoles
   Pregnancy—Some animal studies have shown that vaginal azoles may be embryotoxic or fetotoxic, however, problems have not been documented in humans
   Labor—Vaginal azoles have been shown to cause dystocia in some studies when given through labor

Proper use of this medication
   Reading patient instructions before using medication
   Using at bedtime, unless otherwise directed by physician; retaining miconazole vaginal tampons overnight and removing them the following morning
   Checking with physician before using applicator if pregnant
» Compliance with full course of therapy, even if menstruation begins
   Missed dose: Inserting as soon as possible; not inserting if almost time for next dose
» Proper storage

Precautions while using this medication
   Checking with physician if no improvement within a few days
   Protecting clothing because of possible soiling with vaginal azoles; avoiding the use of unmedicated tampons
» Using hygienic measures to cure infection and prevent reinfection
   Wearing cotton panties instead of synthetic underclothes
   Wearing only freshly washed underclothes
» Use of condom by partner to prevent reinfection; possible need for concurrent treatment of male partner; continuing medication if intercourse occurs during treatment
» Using douche prior to next dose; not overfilling vagina with douche solution; avoiding use of a douche during pregnancy

Side/adverse effects
   Signs of potential side effects, especially hypersensitivity, and vaginal burning, itching, or other irritation not present before therapy

General Dosing Information

If there is no response to therapy, the course of therapy may be repeated after other pathogens have been ruled out by potassium hydroxide (KOH) smears and cultures.

If sensitization or irritation occurs, treatment with vaginal azoles should be discontinued.

The vehicles for some vaginal azole products contain lipid-based components. It is not known whether these products affect the performance of latex contraceptive devices, such as cervical caps, condoms, or diaphragms.

BUTOCONAZOLE

Vaginal Dosage Forms

BUTOCONAZOLE NITRATE CREAM USP (VAGINAL)

Usual adult and adolescent dose: Antifungal, vaginal—
   Nonpregnant patients: Intravaginal, 100 mg (1 applicatorful of a 2% cream) once a day at bedtime for three days. May be repeated for an additional three days if needed.

Pregnant patients (second and third trimesters only): Intravaginal, 100 mg (1 applicatorful of a 2% cream) once a day at bedtime for six days.

Auxiliary labeling:
• For vaginal use only.
• Continue medicine for full time of treatment.

BUTOCONAZOLE NITRATE VAGINAL SUPPOSITORIES

Usual adult and adolescent dose: Antifungal, vaginal—Nonpregnant patients: Intravaginal, 100 mg once a day at bedtime for three days. May be repeated for an additional three days if needed.

Auxiliary labeling:
• For vaginal use only.
• Continue medicine for full time of treatment.

CLOTRIMAZOLE

Vaginal Dosage Forms

CLOTRIMAZOLE CREAM USP (VAGINAL)

Usual adult and adolescent dose:
   Intravaginal, 50 mg (1 applicatorful of a 1% vaginal cream), once a day, preferably at bedtime, for six to fourteen consecutive days; or
   Intravaginal, 100 mg (1 applicatorful of a 2% vaginal cream), once a day, preferably at bedtime, for three days; or
   Intravaginal, 500 mg (1 applicatorful of a 10% vaginal cream), as a single dose, preferably at bedtime.

Auxiliary labeling:
• For vaginal use only.
• Continue medicine for full time of treatment.

CLOTRIMAZOLE VAGINAL TABLETS USP

Usual adult and adolescent dose:
   Nonpregnant patients—Intravaginal, 500 mg as a single dose, preferably at bedtime; 200 mg once a day, preferably at bedtime, for three consecutive days; or 100 mg once a day, preferably at bedtime, for six or seven consecutive days.
   Pregnant patients—Intravaginal, 100 mg once a day, preferably at bedtime, for seven consecutive days.
Note: The three-day regimen is not effective in pregnant women.
   In severe vulvovaginal candidiasis, single-dose treatment with clotrimazole 500-mg vaginal tablets may not be effective. Longer treatment with the 100- or 200-mg vaginal tablets or vaginal cream is recommended.

Auxiliary labeling:
• For vaginal use only.
• Continue medicine for full time of treatment.

ECONAZOLE

Vaginal Dosage Forms

ECONAZOLE NITRATE VAGINAL SUPPOSITORIES

Usual adult and adolescent dose: Antifungal (vaginal)—Intravaginal, 150 mg once a day at bedtime for three days. May be repeated if needed.

Auxiliary labeling:
- For vaginal use only.
- Continue medicine for full time of treatment.

MICONAZOLE

Vaginal Dosage Forms

MICONAZOLE NITRATE VAGINAL CREAM

Usual adult and adolescent dose: Intravaginal, one applicatorful once a day at bedtime for seven or fourteen days. May be repeated if needed.

Auxiliary labeling:
- For vaginal use only.
- Continue medicine for full time of treatment.

MICONAZOLE NITRATE VAGINAL SUPPOSITORIES USP

Usual adult and adolescent dose:
Intravaginal, 100 mg once a day at bedtime for seven days. May be repeated for seven days if needed; or
Intravaginal, 200 or 400 mg once a day at bedtime for three days. May be repeated if needed.

Auxiliary labeling:
- For vaginal use only.
- Continue medicine for full time of treatment.

MICONAZOLE NITRATE VAGINAL TAMPONS

Usual adult and adolescent dose: Antifungal (vaginal)—Intravaginal, 100 mg (1 tampon) once a day at bedtime for five consecutive days; retain vaginally overnight and remove tampon the following morning.

Auxiliary labeling:
- For vaginal use only.
- Continue medicine for full time of treatment.

TERCONAZOLE

Vaginal Dosage Forms

TERCONAZOLE VAGINAL CREAM

Usual adult and adolescent dose: Antifungal (vaginal)—
Intravaginal, 20 mg (1 applicatorful of a 0.4% cream) once a day at bedtime for seven days; or

Intravaginal, 40 mg (1 applicatorful of a 0.8% cream) once a day at bedtime for three days.

Auxiliary labeling:
- For vaginal use only.
- Continue medicine for full time of treatment.

TERCONAZOLE VAGINAL SUPPOSITORIES

Usual adult and adolescent dose: Antifungal (vaginal)—Intravaginal, 80 mg once a day at bedtime for three days.

Auxiliary labeling:
- For vaginal use only.
- Continue medicine for full time of treatment.

TIOCONAZOLE

Vaginal Dosage Forms

TIOCONAZOLE VAGINAL OINTMENT

Usual adult and adolescent dose: Antifungal (vaginal)—Intravaginal, 300 mg (1 applicatorful of a 6.5% vaginal ointment), as a single dose, preferably at bedtime.

Note: Limited data suggest that a second dose, 1 to 2 weeks later, may be effective for those patients with residual symptoms after one dose.

Auxiliary labeling: • For vaginal use only.

TIOCONAZOLE VAGINAL SUPPOSITORIES

Usual adult and adolescent dose: Antifungal (vaginal)—Intravaginal, 300 mg, as a single dose, preferably at bedtime.

Note: Limited data suggest that a second dose, 1 to 2 weeks later, may be effective for those patients with residual symptoms after one dose.

Auxiliary labeling: • For vaginal use only.

ANTIGLAUCOMA AGENTS, CHOLINERGIC, LONG-ACTING   Ophthalmic

INN: Included in brackets after individual generic listings, if different from the U.S. generic name.

Some commonly used *brand names* are:

In the U.S.—
  Floropryl [Isoflurophate]   *Phospholine Iodide*
  Humorsol [Demecarium]   [Echothiophate]

In Canada—
  Phospholine Iodide
    [Echothiophate]

Other commonly used names for isoflurophate are DFP, difluorophate, and dyflos.

OPHTHALMIC
DEMECARIUM
  Demecarium Bromide Ophthalmic Solution USP
    In the U.S.—*Humorsol*
ECHOTHIOPHATE [INN: Ecothiopate Iodide]
  Echothiophate Iodide for Ophthalmic Solution USP
    In the U.S. and Canada—*Phospholine Iodide*
ISOFLUROPHATE
  Isoflurophate Ophthalmic Ointment USP
    In the U.S.—*Floropryl*

Category: Antiglaucoma agent (ophthalmic); cyclostimulant (accommodative esotropia); diagnostic aid (accommodative esotropia).

Indications

Accepted
Glaucoma (treatment)—Demecarium, echothiophate, and isoflurophate, which are long-acting cholinesterase inhibitors, are potent miotics. Because of their toxicity, they should be reserved for use in patients with open-angle glaucoma or other chronic glaucomas not satisfactorily controlled with the short-acting miotics and other agents.

Glaucoma, open-angle (treatment): Demecarium, echothiophate, and isoflurophate are indicated in the treatment of chronic open-angle glaucoma.

Glaucoma, angle-closure, *after* iridectomy (treatment): Demecarium, echothiophate, and isoflurophate are indicated in the treatment of subacute or chronic angle-closure glaucoma following iridectomy if continued drug therapy is required and short-acting miotics and other agents are inadequate. Long-acting cholinesterase inhibitors are usually not recommended for use in angle-closure glaucoma *prior* to iridectomy, because they may increase the pupillary block. However, echothiophate may be indicated in subacute or chronic angle-closure glaucoma when surgery is refused or contraindicated in the informed patient who understands the increased risk of pupillary block.

Glaucoma, secondary (treatment): Echothiophate is indicated in the treatment of certain nonuveitic secondary types of glaucoma, especially glaucoma following cataract surgery.

Esotropia, accommodative (diagnosis); or
Esotropia, accommodative (treatment)—Demecarium, echothiophate, and isoflurophate are indicated in the diagnosis of accommodative esotropia. Demecarium and isoflurophate are indicated in the treatment of accommodative esotropia uncomplicated by anisometropia. Echothiophate may be indicated in the treatment of concomitant esotropias with a significant accommodative component.

Pharmacology

Mechanism of action/Effect: Demecarium, echothiophate, and isoflurophate are indirect-acting parasympathomimetic agents, which are also known as cholinesterase inhibitors and anticholinesterases. Cholinesterase inhibitors prolong the effect of acetylcholine, which is released at the neuroeffector junction of parasympathetic postganglion nerves, by inactivating the cholinesterases that break it down. Echothiophate and isoflurophate primarily inactivate pseudocholinesterase and incompletely inactivate acetylcholinesterase, whereas demecarium inactivates both pseudocholinesterase and acetylcholinesterase. In the eye, this causes constriction of the iris sphincter muscle (causing miosis) and the ciliary muscle (affecting the accommodation reflex and causing a spasm of the focus to near vision). The outflow of the aqueous humor is facilitated, which leads to a reduction in intraocular pressure. Of the 2 actions, the effect on the accommodation reflex is the more transient and generally disappears before termination of the miosis.

Antiglaucoma agent (ophthalmic)—Cholinesterase inhibitors reduce intraocular pressure in both types of primary glaucoma (i.e., angle-closure glaucoma and open-angle glaucoma) primarily by lowering the resistance to the outflow of the aqueous humor. In angle-closure glaucoma, the abnormal contact between the peripheral iris and the peripheral cornea blocks the access of the anterior chamber of aqueous humor to the trabecular meshwork. In open-angle glaucoma, the block is between the trabecular meshwork and the canal of Schlemm. Effects on the volumes of the various intraocular vascular beds (e.g., those of the iris and the ciliary body) and on the rate of secretion of the aqueous humor into the posterior chamber may contribute secondarily to the lowering of pressure. Contraction of the ciliary muscle may act to increase tone and alignment of the trabecular meshwork, which improves outflow of aqueous humor through the meshwork to the canal of Schlemm. The longitudinal ciliary muscle is the major component; the iris sphincter is not relevant in open-angle glaucoma, but contraction of it may improve (or worsen) angle closure glaucoma. In angle-closure glaucoma, the outflow of the aqueous humor is facilitated by the drug-induced contraction of the iris sphincter muscle. This contraction prevents the iris from blocking the entrance to the trabecular space at the canal of Schlemm by lessening pupillary block. However, extreme miosis may actually increase pupillary block, thus worsening angle closure glaucoma prior to iridectomy. In open-angle glaucoma, although there is no physical obstruction at the entrance to the trabecular space, the trabeculae, which are a meshwork of small-diameter pores, increase their resistance and lose their permeability.

Cyclostimulant (accommodative esotropia)—Cholinesterase inhibitors reduce the amount of convergence associated with a given amount of accommodation, thereby reducing the degree of esotropia.

Diagnostic aid (accommodative esotropia)—See *Cyclostimulant (accommodative esotropia)* above. An accommodative factor is demonstrated if the eyes become better aligned.

Onset of action:
  Miosis—Less than 1 hour.
  Reduction in intraocular pressure—Within 4 hours.

Time to peak effect:
  Miosis—Within 2 hours.
  Reduction in intraocular pressure—Within 24 hours.

Duration of action:
  Miosis—Up to 1 month.
  Reduction in intraocular pressure—Up to 1 month, but usually 24 to 48 hours.

Precautions to Consider

Geriatrics

No information is available on whether the risk of adverse effects from long-acting cholinergic antiglaucoma agents is increased in the elderly. However, because of the toxicity of these medications, they should be used with caution, after less toxic alternatives have been considered and/or found ineffective. Recommended doses should not be exceeded, and the patient should be carefully monitored during therapy.

Drug interactions and/or related problems

The following drug interactions and/or related problems have been selected on the basis of their potential clinical significance (possible mechanism in parentheses where appropriate)—not necessarily inclusive (» = major clinical significance):

Note: Combinations containing any of the following medications, depending on the amount present, may also interact with this medication.

For echothiophate or isoflurophate only

Physostigmine, ophthalmic

(use of this medication prior to echothiophate or isoflurophate may partially block the effects of the latter medications and shorten their duration of action. Echothiophate and isoflurophate primarily inactivate pseudocholinesterase and incompletely inactivate acetylcholinesterase, whereas physostigmine and demecarium inactivate both pseudocholinesterase and acetylcholinesterase. Prior use of physostigmine inactivates the available acetylcholinesterase, thereby rendering it inaccessible to the incomplete inactivation by echothiophate or isoflurophate. This effect does not occur when physostigmine is given prior to demecarium, because both medications inactivate acetylcholinesterase, thereby producing an additive effect)

For demecarium, echothiophate, or isoflurophate

Adrenocorticoids, ophthalmic

(chronic or intensive use of ophthalmic adrenocorticoids may increase intraocular pressure and decrease the efficacy of the antiglaucoma agents)

Anesthetics, mucosal-local, ester-derivative, such as benzocaine, butacaine, butamben, and tetracaine, or

Anesthetics, parenteral-local, ester-derivative, such as chloroprocaine, procaine, propoxycaine, and tetracaine

(concurrent use with demecarium, echothiophate, or isoflurophate may inhibit the metabolism of these anesthetics leading to prolonged anesthetic effect and increased risk of toxicity)

» Anticholinergics or other medications with anticholinergic activity or

» Antimyasthenics or

» Cholinesterase inhibitors, other, possibly including topical malathion

(concurrent use of these medications with demecarium, echothiophate, or isoflurophate is not recommended except under strict medical supervision, because of the possibility of additive toxicity; caution may also be warranted with topical application of malathion if excessive quantities of it are used)

Belladonna alkaloids, ophthalmic, or

Cyclopentolate or

Tropicamide

(concurrent use of these parasympatholytics may antagonize the antiglaucoma and miotic actions of demecarium, echothiophate, or isoflurophate; however, tropicamide is expected to have little effect, since it is so short acting)

Carbamate- or organophosphate-type insecticides or pesticides

(exposure of patients using demecarium, echothiophate, or isoflurophate to these preparations may increase the possibility of systemic effects due to absorption of the insecticide or pesticide through the respiratory tract or skin; patients should be advised to protect themselves from contact with such insecticides or pesticides during therapy with demecarium, echothiophate, or isoflurophate)

Cocaine

(inhibition of cholinesterase activity by demecarium, echothiophate, or isoflurophate reduces or slows cocaine metabolism, thereby increasing and/or prolonging cocaine's effects and increasing the risk of toxicity; cholinesterase inhibition may persist for weeks or months after demecarium, echothiophate, or isoflurophate has been discontinued)

Edrophonium

(caution is recommended in administering edrophonium to patients with symptoms of myasthenic weakness who are also using demecarium, echothiophate, or isoflurophate; symptoms of cholinergic crisis [overdosage] may be similar to those occurring with myasthenic crisis [underdosage] and the patient's condition may be worsened by use of edrophonium)

» Succinylcholine

(demecarium, echothiophate, or isoflurophate may decrease plasma concentrations or activity of pseudocholinesterase, the enzyme that metabolizes succinylcholine, thereby enhancing the neuromuscular blockade of succinylcholine when it is used concurrently; cardiovascular collapse may occur; in addition, increased or prolonged respiratory depression or paralysis [apnea] may occur, which is of minor clinical significance while the patient is being mechanically ventilated; however, caution and careful monitoring of the patient are recommended during and following concurrent or sequential use, especially if there is a possibility of incomplete reversal of neuromuscular blockade postoperatively; the effects of this interaction may persist for several weeks or months after demecarium, echothiophate, or isoflurophate has been discontinued)

Contraindications/Medical problems

The contraindications/medical problems included have been selected on the basis of their potential clinical significance (reasons given in parentheses where appropriate)—not necessarily inclusive (» = major clinical significance).

Risk-benefit should be considered when the following medical problems exist:

Asthma, bronchial

(systemic absorption of medication may precipitate an attack)

Bradycardia and hypotension, pronounced

Down's syndrome (mongolism)

(echothiophate, and possibly demecarium or isoflurophate, may cause hyperactivity in these children)

Epilepsy

Gastrointestinal disturbances, spastic

Glaucoma, angle-closure, or predisposition to

(medication may increase the narrowing of the angle)

» Glaucoma associated with iridocyclitis

(medication may aggravate the inflammatory process and lead to the development of posterior synechiae)

Hypertension, systemic

Hyperthyroidism

Iritis, quiescent or history of

(medication may aggravate the inflammatory process)

Myasthenia gravis

Myocardial infarction, recent

Parkinsonism

Peptic ulcer

» Retinal detachment, predisposition to or history of

(may result from drug-induced spasm of accommodation)

Sensitivity to the long-acting cholinergic antiglaucoma agent prescribed

Surgery, intraocular

(intraocular surgery performed during the action of these medications may be complicated by severe uveitis that is very difficult to manage; it is recommended that elective intraocular surgery not be performed until the full duration of action of these medications has elapsed)

Urinary tract obstruction

» Uveitis, active, or
Uveitis, quiescent or history of
(medication may predispose the patient to the development of posterior synechiae)

Vagotonia, marked

Side/Adverse Effects

Note: Lens opacities and cataracts may occur following prolonged use of echothiophate, isoflurophate, and possibly demecarium. While there is strong evidence implicating the phosphorylating medications, echothiophate and isoflurophate, there is little or no similar evidence implicating the carbamylating medication, demecarium. If lens opacities occur, they may regress if therapy is discontinued early in their development; however, once cataracts are established, they often continue developing despite cessation of therapy. The incidence of cataracts appears to be directly related to the age of the patient and the concentration, frequency, and duration of the medication.

Retinal detachment has been reported in a few patients during the use of ophthalmic long-acting cholinergic antiglaucoma agents, such as demecarium, echothiophate, or isoflurophate.

Repeated administration of demecarium, echothiophate, or isoflurophate may cause depression of the concentration of cholinesterase in the serum and erythrocytes, resulting in systemic effects.

Iris cysts, conjunctival thickening, and obstruction of nasolacrimal canals may occur following prolonged use of demecarium, echothiophate, or isoflurophate. If iris cysts occur and treatment with demecarium, echothiophate, or isoflurophate is continued, the cysts may enlarge and obscure the vision. In addition, rarely, the cysts may rupture or break free of the iris into the aqueous humor. The cysts usually decrease in size following discontinuation of the medication.

Activation of latent iritis or uveitis may occur following use of demecarium, echothiophate, or isoflurophate.

A paradoxical increase in intraocular pressure may occur following use of demecarium, echothiophate, or isoflurophate. This may be alleviated by the use of a sympathomimetic, such as phenylephrine.

The following side/adverse effects have been selected on the basis of their potential clinical significance (possible signs and symptoms in parentheses where appropriate)—not necessarily inclusive:

Those indicating need for medical attention
Incidence rare
Retinal detachment (veil or curtain appearing across part of vision)

Symptoms of systemic absorption
Bradycardia (slow or irregular heartbeat); *bronchospasm* (shortness of breath, tightness in chest, or wheezing); *hypotension, severe* (unusual tiredness or weakness); *increased sweating; loss of bladder control; muscle weakness; nausea, vomiting, diarrhea, or stomach cramps or pain; watering of mouth*

Note: The most common systemic effects, especially in children, are nausea, vomiting, diarrhea, and stomach cramps or pain.

Systemic absorption is rare with isoflurophate because systemic absorption from ointment bases is minimal and the isoflurophate that is absorbed is hydrolyzed in the circulation almost immediately.

Those indicating need for medical attention only if they continue or are bothersome
Accommodative myopia (blurred vision or change in near or distant vision); *browache; burning, redness, stinging, or other irritation of eyes; eye pain; headache; miosis* (difficulty in seeing at night or in dim light); *twitching of eyelids; watering of eyes*

Patient Consultation

In providing consultation, consider emphasizing the following selected information (» = major clinical significance):

Before using this medication
» Conditions affecting use, especially:
Sensitivity to demecarium, echothiophate, or isoflurophate
Recent exposure to pesticides or insecticides
Pregnancy—Because of the toxicity of cholinesterase inhibitors in general, these medications are not recommended during pregnancy
Breast-feeding—Medications may be absorbed into the body and are not recommended during breast-feeding, since they may cause adverse effects in nursing infants; a decision should be made whether to discontinue nursing or discontinue the medication
Use in children—The iris cysts that may occur following prolonged use of these medications occur frequently in children.
Other medications, especially antimyasthenics; anticholinergics or other medications with anticholinergic activity; or other cholinesterase inhibitors, possibly including topical malathion
Other medical problems, especially glaucoma associated with iridocyclitis, predisposition to or history of retinal detachment, or active uveitis

Proper use of this medication
Proper administration technique
Washing hands immediately after application to avoid possible systemic absorption
Preventing contamination:
Not touching applicator tip to any surface
Keeping container tightly closed
Wiping tip of ointment tube with clean tissue
» Importance of not using more medication than the amount prescribed
Missed dose: If dosing schedule is—
Every other day: Applying as soon as possible if remembered same day; if not remembered until the next day, applying it at that time, then skipping a day; not doubling doses
Once a day: Applying as soon as possible; if not remembered until next day, skipping missed dose and going back to regular dosing schedule; not doubling doses
More than once a day: Applying as soon as possible; if almost time for next dose, skipping missed dose and going back to regular dosing schedule; not doubling doses
» Proper storage
For solution dosage forms only
Removing excess solution around eye with clean tissue, being careful not to touch eye
For ointment dosage form only
Not washing tip of ointment tube or allowing to touch moist surface; medication loses efficacy when exposed to moisture
Applying at bedtime, since ointment causes blurred vision after administration

Precautions while using this medication
Regular visits to physician during therapy to check eye pressure and, for patients on prolonged therapy, to examine eyes
Carrying medical identification card during therapy
» Caution if any kind of surgery is required
» Caution in exposure to carbamate- or organophosphate-type insecticides or pesticides during therapy
» Caution because of decreased night vision if driving or doing other things at night or in dim light
» Caution if blurred vision or change in near or distant vision occurs

Side/adverse effects
Signs of potential side effects, especially symptoms of systemic absorption and retinal detachment

General Dosing Information

To reduce the inconvenience of post-medication miosis, the daily dose or one of the daily doses of the medication may be administered at bedtime.

A stronger concentration may be required to produce adequate miosis and reduction in intraocular pressure in eyes with hazel or brown irides than in eyes with blue or light-colored irides because miotics are less effective in heavily pigmented eyes.

To reduce the incidence of iris cyst formation, the frequency of administration should be minimal in all patients, especially in children. In addition, the simultaneous administration of 2.5 to 10% ophthalmic phenylephrine with demecarium, echothiophate, or isoflurophate may prevent iris cyst formation. However, phenylephrine will not prevent iris cysts if the phenylephrine is administered several hours before or after demecarium, echothiophate, or isoflurophate. The 2.5% concentration of phenylephrine appears to be as effective as the 10% concentration and causes less burning upon administration.

Concurrent use of demecarium, echothiophate, or isoflurophate with epinephrine, a beta-adrenergic blocking agent, and/or a carbonic anhydrase inhibitor results in additive effects, thereby providing better control of glaucoma. A reduced dose of demecarium, echothiophate, or isoflurophate may be possible. A dosage reduction of the miotic medication (i.e., demecarium, echothiophate, or isoflurophate) results in the patient experiencing less miosis and/or accommodative block. In addition, concomitant administration of 2.5 to 10% ophthalmic phenylephrine or 1 to 2% ophthalmic epinephrine may improve the visual acuity of some patients by dilating the miotic eye without increasing the intraocular pressure.

Tolerance to demecarium, echothiophate, or isoflurophate may develop with prolonged use. Effectiveness may be restored by changing to another miotic for a short time and then resuming the original medication.

Following long-term use of these medications, dilation of blood vessels and resulting greater permeability will increase postoperative inflammation and may increase the risk of hyphema during ophthalmic surgery; therefore, demecarium, echothiophate, or isoflurophate should be discontinued 2 to 3 weeks before eye surgery.

For the solution dosage forms only

Although some manufacturers recommend a dose of 2 drops of an ophthalmic solution at appropriate intervals, the conjunctival sac will usually hold only 1 drop. In addition, because of the potency of these medications and the possibility of systemic absorption, the smallest dose possible should be administered.

To avoid excessive systemic absorption, patient should press finger to the lacrimal sac during and for 1 or 2 minutes following instillation of medication.

DEMECARIUM

Summary of Differences

Precautions: Drug interactions and/or related problems—Physostigmine not listed as a precaution.

Ophthalmic Dosage Forms

DEMECARIUM BROMIDE OPHTHALMIC SOLUTION USP

Usual adult and adolescent dose:

Antiglaucoma agent (ophthalmic)—Topical, to the conjunctiva, 1 drop of a 0.125 or 0.25% solution one or two times a day.

Cyclostimulant (accommodative esotropia)—Topical, to the conjunctiva, 1 drop of a 0.125 or 0.25% solution once a day for two to three weeks, then 1 drop every two days for three to four weeks, at which time the patient's status should be reevaluated. Thereafter, 1 drop one or two times a week to once every two days, depending on the patient's condition.

Note: In the treatment of esotropia uncomplicated by anisometropia, the patient's condition should be evaluated every 4 to 12 weeks. It is recommended that therapy be discontinued after four months if a dosage of 1 drop every two days is still required to control condition.

Diagnostic aid (accommodative esotropia)—Topical, to the conjunctiva, 1 drop of a 0.125 or 0.25% solution once a day for two weeks, then 1 drop every two days for two to three weeks.

Auxiliary labeling:
- For the eye.
- Keep container tightly closed.

ECHOTHIOPHATE

Ophthalmic Dosage Forms

ECHOTHIOPHATE IODIDE FOR OPHTHALMIC SOLUTION USP

Usual adult and adolescent dose:

Antiglaucoma agent (ophthalmic)—Topical, to the conjunctiva, 1 drop of a 0.03 to 0.25% solution one or two times a day.

Cyclostimulant (accommodative esotropia)—Topical, to the conjunctiva, 1 drop of a 0.03 to 0.125% solution once a day or every two days.

Diagnostic aid (accommodative esotropia)—Topical, to the conjunctiva, 1 drop of a 0.125% solution once a day at bedtime for two to three weeks.

Auxiliary labeling:
- For the eye.
- Beyond-use date.
- Keep container tightly closed.

ISOFLUROPHATE

Ophthalmic Dosage Forms

ISOFLUROPHATE OPHTHALMIC OINTMENT USP

Usual adult and adolescent dose:

Antiglaucoma agent (ophthalmic)—Topical, to the conjunctiva, a thin strip (approximately 0.5 cm) of a 0.025% ointment once every three days to three times a day.

Cyclostimulant (accommodative esotropia)—Topical, to the conjunctiva, a thin strip (approximately 0.5 cm) of a 0.025% ointment once a day at bedtime for two weeks, then once a week to once every two days, depending on the patient's condition, for two months.

Note: In the treatment of esotropia uncomplicated by anisometropia, it is recommended that therapy be discontinued if the patient's condition cannot be maintained on a dosage interval of at least every two days.

Diagnostic aid (accommodative esotropia)—Topical, to the conjunctiva, a thin strip (approximately 0.5 cm) of a 0.025% ointment once a day at bedtime for two weeks.

Auxiliary labeling:
- For the eye.
- Keep container tightly closed.

ANTIHISTAMINES   Systemic

Note: Products listed in this monograph contain single-entity antihistamines. For products containing antihistamines in combination with other medications, refer to *Antihistamines and Decongestants (Systemic)*, *Antihistamines, Decongestants, and Analgesics (Systemic)*, and *Cough/Cold Combinations (Systemic)*.

INN: Included in brackets after individual generic listings, if different from the U.S. generic names.

Some commonly used *brand names* are:

In the U.S.—

Actidil [Triprolidine]
Alleract [Triprolidine]
Aller-Chlor [Chlorpheniramine]
AllerMax Caplets [Diphenhydramine]
Aller-med [Diphenhydramine]
Anxanil [Hydroxyzine]
Atarax [Hydroxyzine]
Banophen [Diphenhydramine]
Banophen Caplets [Diphenhydramine]
Beldin [Diphenhydramine]
Belix [Diphenhydramine]
Bena-D 10 [Diphenhydramine]
Bena-D 50 [Diphenhydramine]
Benadryl [Diphenhydramine]
Benadryl 25 [Diphenhydramine]
Benadryl Kapseals [Diphenhydramine]
Benahist 10 [Diphenhydramine]
Benahist 50 [Diphenhydramine]
Ben-Allergin-50 [Diphenhydramine]
Benoject-10 [Diphenhydramine]
Benoject-50 [Diphenhydramine]
Benylin Cough [Diphenhydramine]
Bromphen [Brompheniramine]
Bydramine Cough [Diphenhydramine]
Calm X [Dimenhydrinate]
Chlo-Amine [Chlorpheniramine]
Chlor-100 [Chlorpheniramine]
Chlorate [Chlorpheniramine]
Chlor-Niramine [Chlorpheniramine]
Chlorphed [Brompheniramine]
Chlor-Pro [Chlorpheniramine]

Chlor-Pro 10 [Chlorpheniramine]
Chlorspan-12 [Chlorpheniramine]
Chlortab-4 [Chlorpheniramine]
Chlortab-8 [Chlorpheniramine]
Chlor-Trimeton [Chlorpheniramine]
Chlor-Trimeton Repetabs [Chlorpheniramine]
Codimal-A [Brompheniramine]
Compoz [Diphenhydramine]
Conjec-B [Brompheniramine]
Cophene-B [Brompheniramine]
Dehist [Brompheniramine]
Dexchlor [Dexchlorpheniramine]
Diamine T.D. [Brompheniramine]
Dimetabs [Dimenhydrinate]
Dimetane [Brompheniramine]
Dimetane Extentabs [Brompheniramine]
Dinate [Dimenhydrinate]
Diphenacen-50 [Diphenhydramine]
Diphenadryl [Diphenhydramine]
Diphen Cough [Diphenhydramine]
Diphenhist [Diphenhydramine]
Diphenhist Captabs [Diphenhydramine]
Dommanate [Dimenhydrinate]
Dormarex 2 [Diphenhydramine]
Dramamine [Dimenhydrinate]
Dramamine Chewable [Dimenhydrinate]
Dramamine Liquid [Dimenhydrinate]
Dramanate [Dimenhydrinate]
Dramocen [Dimenhydrinate]

Dramoject [Dimenhydrinate]
Dymenate [Dimenhydrinate]
E-Vista [Hydroxyzine]
Fynex [Diphenhydramine]
Genahist [Diphenhydramine]
Genallerate [Chlorpheniramine]
Gen-D-phen [Diphenhydramine]
Hismanal [Astemizole]
Histaject Modified [Brompheniramine]
Hydramine [Diphenhydramine]
Hydramine Cough [Diphenhydramine]
Hydramyn [Diphenhydramine]
Hydrate [Dimenhydrinate]
Hydril [Diphenhydramine]
Hydroxacen [Hydroxyzine]
Hyrexin-50 [Diphenhydramine]
Hyzine-50 [Hydroxyzine]
Marmine [Dimenhydrinate]
Myidil [Triprolidine]
Nasahist B [Brompheniramine]
ND-Stat Revised [Brompheniramine]
Nervine Nighttime Sleep-Aid [Diphenhydramine]
Nico-Vert [Dimenhydrinate]
Nidryl [Diphenhydramine]
Nisaval [Pyrilamine]
Nolahist [Phenindamine]
Noradryl [Diphenhydramine]
Nordryl [Diphenhydramine]
Nordryl Cough [Diphenhydramine]
Nytol Maximum Strength [Diphenhydramine]
Nytol with DPH [Diphenhydramine]
Optimine [Azatadine]
Oraminic II [Brompheniramine]
PBZ [Tripelennamine]
PBZ-SR [Tripelennamine]
PediaCare Allergy Formula [Chlorpheniramine]

In Canada—

Allerdryl [Diphenhydramine]
Apo-Dimenhydrinate [Dimenhydrinate]
Apo-Hydroxyzine [Hydroxyzine]
Atarax [Hydroxyzine]
Benadryl [Diphenhydramine]

Pelamine [Tripelennamine]
Periactin [Cyproheptadine]
Pfeiffer's Allergy [Chlorpheniramine]
Phendry [Diphenhydramine]
Phendry Children's Allergy Medicine [Diphenhydramine]
Phenetron [Chlorpheniramine]
Phenetron Lanacaps [Chlorpheniramine]
Poladex T.D. [Dexchlorpheniramine]
Polaramine [Dexchlorpheniramine]
Polaramine Repetabs [Dexchlorpheniramine]
Quiess [Hydroxyzine]
Seldane [Terfenadine]
Sleep-Eze 3 [Diphenhydramine]
Sominex Formula 2 [Diphenhydramine]
Tavist [Clemastine]
Tavist-1 [Clemastine]
Tega-Vert [Dimenhydrinate]
Telachlor [Chlorpheniramine]
Teldrin [Chlorpheniramine]
Triptone Caplets [Dimenhydrinate]
Trymegen [Chlorpheniramine]
Tusstat [Diphenhydramine]
Twilite Caplets [Diphenhydramine]
Uni-Bent Cough [Diphenhydramine]
Unisom Nighttime Sleep Aid [Doxylamine]
Veltane [Brompheniramine]
Vertab [Dimenhydrinate]
Vistaject-25 [Hydroxyzine]
Vistaject-50 [Hydroxyzine]
Vistaril [Hydroxyzine]
Vistazine 50 [Hydroxyzine]
Wehdryl-10 [Diphenhydramine]
Wehdryl-50 [Diphenhydramine]

Chlor-Tripolon [Chlorpheniramine]
Claritin [Loratadine]
Dimetane [Brompheniramine]
Dimetane Extentabs [Brompheniramine]
Gravol [Dimenhydrinate]

Gravol L/A
[Dimenhydrate]
Hismanal [Astemizole]
Insomnal
[Diphenhydramine]
Multipax [Hydroxyzine]
Nauseatol
[Dimenhydrate]
Novodimenate
[Dimenhydrate]
Novohydroxyzin
[Hydroxyzine]
Novopheniram
[Chlorpheniramine]
Optimine [Azatadine]
Periactin [Cyproheptadine]

PMS-Dimenhydrate
[Dimenhydrate]
Polaramine
[Dexchlorpheniramine]
Polaramine Repetabs
[Dexchlorpheniramine]
Pyribenzamine
[Tripelennamine]
Reactine [Cetirizine]
Seldane [Terfenadine]
Seldane Caplets
[Terfenadine]
Tavist [Clemastine]
Travamine
[Dimenhydrate]

ASTEMIZOLE
Oral
    Astemizole Oral Suspension*
        In Canada—*Hismanal*
    Astemizole Tablets
        In the U.S. and Canada—*Hismanal*
AZATADINE
Oral
    Azatadine Maleate Tablets USP
        In the U.S. and Canada—*Optimine*
BROMODIPHENHYDRAMINE [INN: Bromazine]‡
BROMPHENIRAMINE
Oral
    Brompheniramine Maleate Elixir USP
        In the U.S.—*Bromphen; Dimetane;* GENERIC
        In Canada—*Dimetane*
    Brompheniramine Maleate Tablets USP
        In the U.S.—*Dimetane; Veltane;* GENERIC
        In Canada—*Dimetane*
    Brompheniramine Maleate Extended-release Tablets
        In the U.S.—*Diamine T.D.; Dimetane Extentabs;* GENERIC
        In Canada—*Dimetane Extentabs*
Parenteral
    Brompheniramine Maleate Injection USP†
        In the U.S.—*Chlorphed; Codimal-A; Conjec-B; Cophene-B; Dehist; Histaject Modified; Nasahist B; ND-Stat Revised; Oraminic II*
CARBINOXAMINE‡
CETIRIZINE*
Oral
    Cetirizine Hydrochloride Tablets*
        In Canada—*Reactine*
CHLORPHENIRAMINE [INN: Chlorphenamine]
Oral
    Chlorpheniramine Maleate Extended-release Capsules USP†
        In the U.S.—*Chlorspan-12; Phenetron Lanacaps; Telachlor; Teldrin;* GENERIC
    Chlorpheniramine Maleate Syrup USP
        In the U.S.—*Aller-Chlor; Chlor-Trimeton; PediaCare Allergy Formula; Phenetron;* GENERIC
        In Canada—*Chlor-Tripolon*
    Chlorpheniramine Maleate Tablets USP
        In the U.S.—*Aller-Chlor; Chlorate; Chlor-Niramine; Chlortab-4; Chlor-Trimeton; Genallerate; Pfeiffer's Allergy; Phenetron; Trymegen;* GENERIC
        In Canada—*Chlor-Tripolon; Novopheniram*
    Chlorpheniramine Maleate Tablets USP (Chewable)†
        In the U.S.—*Chlo-Amine*
    Chlorpheniramine Maleate Extended-release Tablets
        In the U.S.—*Chlortab-8; Chlor-Trimeton Repetabs; Phenetron;* GENERIC
        In Canada—*Chlor-Tripolon*

Parenteral
    Chlorpheniramine Maleate Injection USP
        In the U.S.—*Chlor-100; Chlor-Pro; Chlor-Pro 10; Chlor-Trimeton;* GENERIC
        In Canada—*Chlor-Tripolon*
CLEMASTINE
Oral
    Clemastine Fumarate Syrup
        In the U.S. and Canada—*Tavist*
    Clemastine Fumarate Tablets USP
        In the U.S.—*Tavist; Tavist-1*
        In Canada—*Tavist*
CYPROHEPTADINE
Oral
    Cyproheptadine Hydrochloride Syrup USP
        In the U.S.—*Periactin;* GENERIC
        In Canada—*Periactin*
    Cyproheptadine Hydrochloride Tablets USP
        In the U.S.—*Periactin;* GENERIC
        In Canada—*Periactin*
DEXCHLORPHENIRAMINE
Oral
    Dexchlorpheniramine Maleate Syrup USP
        In the U.S. and Canada—*Polaramine*
    Dexchlorpheniramine Maleate Tablets USP
        In the U.S. and Canada—*Polaramine*
    Dexchlorpheniramine Maleate Extended-release Tablets
        In the U.S.—*Dexchlor; Poladex T.D.; Polaramine Repetabs;* GENERIC
        In Canada—*Polaramine Repetabs*
DIMENHYDRINATE
Oral
    Dimenhydrinate Capsules†
        In the U.S.—*Nico-Vert; Tega-Vert; Vertab*
    Dimenhydrinate Extended-release Capsules*
        In Canada—*Gravol L/A*
    Dimenhydrinate Elixir*
        In Canada—*Gravol*
    Dimenhydrinate Syrup USP†
        In the U.S.—*Dramamine Liquid;* GENERIC
    Dimenhydrinate Tablets USP
        In the U.S.—*Calm X; Dimetabs; Dramamine; Marmine; Triptone Caplets;* GENERIC
        In Canada—*Apo-Dimenhydrinate; Gravol; Nauseatol; Novodimenate; PMS-Dimenhydrate; Travamine*
    Dimenhydrinate Tablets USP (Chewable)†
        In the U.S.—*Dramamine Chewable*
Parenteral
    Dimenhydrinate Injection USP
        In the U.S.—*Dinate; Dommanate; Dramamine; Dramanate; Dramocen; Dramoject; Dymenate; Hydrate; Marmine;* GENERIC
        In Canada—*Gravol;* GENERIC
Rectal
    Dimenhydrinate Suppositories*
        In Canada—*Gravol; Nauseatol*
DIPHENHYDRAMINE
Oral
    Diphenhydramine Hydrochloride Capsules USP
        In the U.S.—*Banophen; Benadryl; Benadryl 25; Benadryl Kapseals; Genahist; Nordryl;* GENERIC
        In Canada—*Allerdryl; Benadryl; Insomnal*
    Diphenhydramine Hydrochloride Elixir USP
        In the U.S.—*Belix; Benadryl; Diphenhist; Fynex; Genahist; Hydramine; Hydril; Nidryl; Noradryl; Nordryl; Phendry; Phendry Children's Allergy Medicine; Sominex Formula 2;* GENERIC
        In Canada—*Benadryl*

Diphenhydramine Hydrochloride Syrup†
 In the U.S.—*Beldin; Benylin Cough; Bydramine Cough; Diphenadryl; Diphen Cough; Gen-D-phen; Hydramine Cough; Hydramyn; Noradryl; Nordryl Cough; Tusstat; Uni-Bent Cough;* GENERIC
Diphenhydramine Hydrochloride Tablets†
 In the U.S.—*AllerMax Caplets; Aller-med; Banophen Caplets; Benadryl 25; Compoz; Diphenhist Captabs; Dormarex 2; Genahist; Nervine Nighttime Sleep-Aid; Nytol Maximum Strength; Nytol with DPH; Sleep-Eze 3; Sominex Formula 2; Twilite Caplets;* GENERIC
Parenteral
 Diphenhydramine Hydrochloride Injection USP
 In the U.S.—*Bena-D 10; Bena-D 50; Benadryl; Benahist 10; Benahist 50; Ben-Allergin-50; Benoject-10; Benoject-50; Diphenacen-50; Hyrexin-50; Nordryl; Wehdryl-10; Wehdryl-50;* GENERIC
 In Canada—*Benadryl;* GENERIC
DIPHENYLPYRALINE**
DOXYLAMINE§
Oral
 Doxylamine Succinate Tablets USP†
 In the U.S.—*Unisom Nighttime Sleep Aid*
HYDROXYZINE
Oral
 Hydroxyzine Hydrochloride Capsules*
 In Canada—*Apo-Hydroxyzine; Atarax; Multipax; Novohydroxyzin*
 Hydroxyzine Hydrochloride Syrup USP
 In the U.S.—*Atarax;* GENERIC
 In Canada—*Atarax*
 Hydroxyzine Hydrochloride Tablets USP†
 In the U.S.—*Anxanil; Atarax;* GENERIC
 Hydroxyzine Pamoate Capsules USP†
 In the U.S.—*Vistaril;* GENERIC
 Hydroxyzine Pamoate Oral Suspension USP†
 In the U.S.—*Vistaril*
Parenteral
 Hydroxyzine Hydrochloride Injection USP
 In the U.S.—*E-Vista; Hydroxacen; Hyzine-50; Quiess; Vistaject-25; Vistaject-50; Vistaril; Vistazine 50;* GENERIC
 In Canada—*Atarax;* GENERIC
LORATADINE*
Oral
 Loratadine Tablets*
 In Canada—*Claritin*
METHDILAZINE—See Antihistamines, Phenothiazine-derivative (Systemic).
PROMETHAZINE—See Antihistamines, Phenothiazine-derivative (Systemic).
PHENINDAMINE†
Oral
 Phenindamine Tartrate Tablets†
 In the U.S.—*Nolahist*
PYRILAMINE [INN: Mepyramine]†
Oral
 Pyrilamine Maleate Tablets USP†
 In the U.S.—*Nisaval;* GENERIC
TERFENADINE
Oral
 Terfenadine Oral Suspension*
 In Canada—*Seldane*
 Terfenadine Tablets USP
 In the U.S.—*Seldane*
 In Canada—*Seldane; Seldane Caplets*
TRIMEPRAZINE—See Antihistamines, Phenothiazine-derivative (Systemic).

TRIPELENNAMINE
Oral
 Tripelennamine Citrate Elixir USP†
 In the U.S.—*PBZ*
 Tripelennamine Hydrochloride Tablets USP
 In the U.S.—*PBZ; Pelamine;* GENERIC
 In Canada—*Pyribenzamine*
 Tripelennamine Hydrochloride Extended-release Tablets†
 In the U.S.—*PBZ-SR*
TRIPROLIDINE§
Oral
 Triprolidine Hydrochloride Syrup USP†
 In the U.S.—*Actidil; Myidil;* GENERIC
 Triprolidine Hydrochloride Tablets USP†
 In the U.S.—*Actidil; Alleract*

---

*Not commercially available in the U.S.
†Not commercially available in Canada.
‡Not available in the U.S. or Canada as a single entity; however, it is available in cough/cold combination products.
§Not available in Canada as a single entity; however, it is available in cough/cold combination products.
**Not available in the U.S. or Canada as a single entity; however, it is available in Canada in cough/cold combination products.

Category

Antihistaminic (H_1-receptor)—Astemizole; Azatadine; Bromodiphenhydramine; Brompheniramine; Carbinoxamine; Cetirizine; Chlorpheniramine; Clemastine; Cyproheptadine; Dexchlorpheniramine; Dimenhydrinate; Diphenhydramine; Diphenylpyraline; Doxylamine; Hydroxyzine; Loratadine; Phenindamine; Pyrilamine; Terfenadine; Tripelennamine; Triprolidine.
Antianxiety agent—Hydroxyzine.
Antidyskinetic—Diphenhydramine.
Antiemetic—Dimenhydrinate; Diphenhydramine; Hydroxyzine (parenteral).
Antitussive—Diphenhydramine Syrup.
Antivertigo agent—Dimenhydrinate; Diphenhydramine.
Sedative-hypnotic—Diphenhydramine; Doxylamine.
Appetite stimulant—Cyproheptadine.
Vascular headache suppressant—Cyproheptadine.
Antiasthmatic—Astemizole; Cetirizine; Loratadine; Terfenadine.

Indications

Note: Bracketed information in the *Indications* section refers to uses not included in U.S. product labeling.

Accepted
Rhinitis, perennial and seasonal allergic or vasomotor (prophylaxis and treatment); or
Conjunctivitis, allergic (prophylaxis and treatment)—Antihistamines are indicated in the prophylactic and symptomatic treatment of perennial and seasonal allergic rhinitis, vasomotor rhinitis, and allergic conjunctivitis due to inhalant allergens and foods. Astemizole is considered useful mostly for prophylactic treatment of seasonal allergies rather than treatment of acute allergic reactions, due to its delayed onset of action (several days, unless loading doses are used).

Pruritus (treatment);
Urticaria (treatment);
Angioedema (treatment);
Dermatographism (treatment); or
Transfusion reactions, urticarial (treatment)—Antihistamines are indicated for the symptomatic treatment of pruritus associated with allergic reactions and of mild, uncomplicated allergic skin manifestations of urticaria and angioedema, in dermatographism, and in urticaria associated with transfusions. Cyproheptadine is also indicated for cold urticaria. [Antihistamines are also used in the treatment of pruritus associated with pityriasis rosea.][1]

Sneezing (treatment); or

Rhinorrhea (treatment)—Antihistamines are indicated for the relief of sneezing and rhinorrhea associated with the common cold. However, controlled clinical studies have not demonstrated that antihistamines are significantly more effective than placebo in relieving cold symptoms.

Anaphylactic or anaphylactoid reactions (treatment adjunct)—Antihistamines are indicated as adjunctive therapy to epinephrine and other standard measures for anaphylactic reactions after the acute manifestations have been controlled, and to ameliorate the allergic reactions to blood or plasma.

Anxiety (treatment); and

Tension, psychosis-related (treatment)—Hydroxyzine is indicated for the relief of anxiety and tension associated with psychoneurosis and as an adjunct in organic disease states in which anxiety is manifested. The effectiveness of hydroxyzine as an antianxiety agent for long-term use (for example, more than 4 months) has not been assessed by systematic clinical studies.

Alcohol withdrawal (treatment)—Parenteral hydroxyzine is indicated in the acute or chronic alcoholic with anxiety withdrawal symptoms.

Parkinsonism (treatment)[1]; or

Extrapyramidal reactions, drug-induced (treatment)[1]—Diphenhydramine is indicated for the symptomatic treatment of parkinsonism and drug-induced extrapyramidal reactions in elderly patients unable to tolerate more potent antidyskinetic medications, for mild cases of parkinsonism in other age groups and, in combination with centrally acting anticholinergic agents, for other cases of parkinsonism.

Cough (treatment)—Diphenhydramine hydrochloride syrup is currently indicated as a non-narcotic cough suppressant for control of cough due to colds or allergy.

Motion sickness (prophylaxis and treatment); or

Vertigo (treatment)—Dimenhydrinate and diphenhydramine are indicated for the prevention and treatment of the nausea, vomiting, dizziness, or vertigo of motion sickness.

Nausea or vomiting (prophylaxis and treatment)—Parenteral hydroxyzine is indicated for the control of nausea and vomiting, excluding nausea and vomiting of pregnancy.

Sedation—Diphenhydramine and hydroxyzine are indicated for their sedative and hypnotic effects and as preoperative medications.

Insomnia (treatment)—Diphenhydramine and doxylamine are indicated as nighttime sleep aids to help reduce the time to fall asleep in patients having difficulty falling asleep.

Analgesia adjunct, during surgery;

Anesthesia, general, adjunct; or

Anesthesia, local, adjunct—Parenteral hydroxyzine is useful as pre- and postoperative, and pre- and postpartum adjunctive medication to allow reduction in narcotic dosage, and to control anxiety and emesis.

[Appetite, lack of (treatment)]—Cyproheptadine is used as an appetite stimulant, in adults and children.

[Headache, vascular (treatment)]—Cyproheptadine is used for treatment of vascular headaches, such as migraine and histamine cephalalgia.

[Asthma, bronchial (treatment adjunct)][1]—Astemizole, cetirizine, loratadine, and terfenadine are used as adjunctive treatment to asthma medications to reduce symptoms and improve bronchodilation in patients with mild atopic asthma.

Unaccepted

Cyproheptadine has been used in the treatment of Cushing's disease because of its pronounced antiserotonin properties, which may decrease corticotropin release. Cyproheptadine may also provide antidiarrheal action against intestinal hypermotility associated with the excessive production of serotonin in patients with carcinoid tumors, and in some other conditions involving the release of

serotonin. However, there is no conclusive evidence of effectiveness for these uses.

---

[1]Not included in Canadian product labeling.

Pharmacology

Mechanism of action/Effect:

Antihistaminic (H_1-receptor)—Antihistamines used in the treatment of allergy act by competing with histamine for H_1-receptor sites on effector cells. They thereby prevent, but do not reverse, responses mediated by histamine alone. Antihistamines do not block histamine release, but they antagonize in varying degrees, most of the pharmacological effects of histamine, including urticaria and pruritus. Also, the anticholinergic actions of most antihistamines provide a drying effect on the nasal mucosa.

Antianxiety agent—Hydroxyzine's sedative action may be due to a suppression of activity in certain key regions of the subcortical area of the central nervous system (CNS). It is not a cortical depressant.

Antidyskinetic—The actions of diphenhydramine in parkinsonism and in drug-induced dyskinesias appear to be related to a central inhibition of the actions of acetylcholine, which are mediated via muscarinic receptors (anticholinergic action), and to its sedative effects.

Antiemetic; antivertigo—The mechanism by which some antihistamines exert their antiemetic, anti-motion sickness, and antivertigo effects is not precisely known but may be related to their central anticholinergic actions. They diminish vestibular stimulation and depress labyrinthine function. An action on the medullary chemoreceptive trigger zone may also be involved in the antiemetic effect.

Antitussive—Diphenhydramine suppresses the cough reflex by a direct effect on the cough center in the medulla of the brain.

Sedative-hypnotic—Most antihistamines cross the blood-brain barrier and produce sedation due to inhibition of histamine N-methyltransferase and blockage of central histaminergic receptors. Antagonism of other central nervous system receptor sites, such as those for serotonin, acetylcholine, and alpha-adrenergic stimulation may also be involved. Central depression is not significant with astemizole, cetirizine, loratadine, and terfenadine because they do not readily cross the blood-brain barrier. Also, they bind preferentially to peripheral H_1-receptors rather than to central nervous system H_1-receptors.

Appetite stimulant—Cyproheptadine, and to a lesser extent astemizole, compete with serotonin for receptor sites, thus blocking the responses to serotonin in vascular, intestinal, and other smooth muscles. It is possible that by altering serotonin activity in the appetite center of the hypothalamus, these medications stimulate appetite.

Vascular headache suppressant—Probably due to cyproheptadine's antiserotonin action.

Other actions/effects:

Anticholinergic—Antihistamines prevent responses to acetylcholine that are mediated via muscarinic receptors. The ethanolamine derivatives may show greater anticholinergic activity than the other classes of antihistamines. Astemizole, cetirizine, loratadine, and terfenadine have no significant anticholinergic activity.

Bronchodilator—Astemizole, cetirizine, loratadine, and terfenadine have been shown to cause mild bronchodilation and also to block histamine-induced bronchoconstriction in asthmatic patients. Also, they have been shown to diminish exercise-induced bronchospasm and hyperventilation-induced bronchospasm.

Anesthetic, local, dental—Antihistamines are structurally related to local anesthetics and have local anesthetic activity. Local anesthetics prevent the initiation and transmission of nerve impulses by decreasing the permeability of the nerve cell membrane to sodium ions. This action decreases the rate of depolarization of the membrane and prevents the generation of the action potential.

Onset of action:
Oral—15 to 60 minutes.
Astemizole: 2 to 3 days.
Loratadine: 27 minutes.
Terfenadine: 72 minutes.
Parenteral—Dimenhydrinate: Intramuscular, 20 to 30 minutes.
Rectal—Dimenhydrinate: 30 to 45 minutes.

Time to peak effect: Oral—
Astemizole: 9 to 12 days.
Brompheniramine: 3 to 9 hours.
Chlorpheniramine: 6 hours.
Clemastine: 5 to 7 hours.
Loratadine: 4 to 6 hours.
Terfenadine: 3 to 4 hours.
Triprolidine: 2 to 3 hours.

Duration of action:
Ethanolamine derivatives—6 to 8 hours.
Clemastine: 12 hours.
Dimenhydrinate: 3 to 6 hours.
Ethylenediamine derivatives—
Pyrilamine: 8 hours.
Tripelennamine: 4 to 6 hours.
Piperazine derivative—4 to 6 hours.
Piperidine derivatives—
Azatadine: 12 hours.
Cyproheptadine: 8 hours.
Diphenylpyraline: 12 hours.
Phenindamine: 4 to 6 hours.
Propylamine derivatives—4 to 8 hours.
Miscellaneous—
Astemizole: Depending on the length of therapy, the duration of action may last for several weeks after discontinuation of astemizole.
Loratadine: At least 24 hours.
Terfenadine: Over 12 hours.

Precautions to Consider

Cross-sensitivity and/or related problems
Patients sensitive to one of the antihistamines may be sensitive to others.

Geriatrics
Dizziness, sedation, confusion, and hypotension may be more likely to occur in geriatric patients taking antihistamines.
A paradoxical reaction characterized by hyperexcitability may occur in geriatric patients taking antihistamines.
Geriatric patients are especially susceptible to the anticholinergic side effects, such as dryness of mouth and urinary retention (especially in males), of the antihistamines. If these side effects occur and continue or are severe, medication should probably be discontinued.

For astemizole, cetirizine, loratadine, and terfenadine—Although adequate and well-controlled studies have not been done in the geriatric population, astemizole, cetirizine, loratadine, or terfenadine is not likely to cause anticholinergic or significant CNS effects in geriatric patients.

Dental
Prolonged use of antihistamines (except astemizole, cetirizine, loratadine, or terfenadine) may decrease or inhibit salivary flow, thus contributing to the development of caries, periodontal disease, oral candidiasis, and discomfort.

Drug interactions and/or related problems
The following drug interactions and/or related problems have been selected on the basis of their potential clinical significance (pos-

sible mechanism in parentheses where appropriate)—not necessarily inclusive (» = major clinical significance):

Note: It is not likely that astemizole, cetirizine, loratadine, or terfenadine will interact with the following medications because they lack significant anticholinergic and CNS actions.

Combinations containing any of the following medications, depending on the amount present, may also interact with this medication.

» Alcohol or
» CNS depression-producing medications, other
(concurrent use may potentiate the CNS depressant effects of either these medications or antihistamines; also, concurrent use of maprotiline or tricyclic antidepressants may potentiate the anticholinergic effects of either antihistamines or these medications)

» Anticholinergics or other medications with anticholinergic activity
(anticholinergic effects may be potentiated when these medications are used concurrently with antihistamines; patients should be advised to report occurrence of gastrointestinal problems promptly since paralytic ileus may occur with concurrent therapy)

Apomorphine
(prior administration of dimenhydrinate, diphenhydramine, doxylamine, or hydroxyzine may decrease the emetic response to apomorphine in the treatment of poisoning)

» Erythromycin
(concurrent use with terfenadine has been reported to increase the risk of cardiotoxic effects)

» Ketoconazole
(concurrent use has been reported to increase plasma levels of terfenadine, and possibly astemizole and loratadine, because of inhibition of the P-450 metabolic pathways by ketoconazole; increased plasma levels of these antihistamines may result in cardiotoxic effects)

» Monoamine oxidase (MAO) inhibitors, including furazolidone and procarbazine
(concurrent use of MAO inhibitors with antihistamines may prolong and intensify the anticholinergic and CNS depressant effects of antihistamines; concurrent use is not recommended)

Ototoxic medications
(concurrent use with antihistamines may mask the symptoms of ototoxicity such as tinnitus, dizziness, or vertigo)

Photosensitizing medications, other
(concurrent use of these medications with antihistamines may cause additive photosensitizing effects)

Contraindications/Medical problems
The contraindications/medical problems included have been selected on the basis of their potential clinical significance (reasons given in parentheses where appropriate)—not necessarily inclusive (» = major clinical significance).

Except under special circumstances, this medication should not be used when the following medical problem exists:

» Hepatic function impairment
(increased plasma concentrations of astemizole or terfenadine may result, increasing the risk of cardiac arrhythmias or QT prolongation)

Risk-benefit should be considered when the following medical problems exist:

» Bladder neck obstruction or
» Prostatic hypertrophy, symptomatic, or
» Urinary retention, predisposition to
(anticholinergic effects may precipitate or aggravate urinary retention)

» Glaucoma, angle-closure, or predisposition to
(anticholinergic mydriatic effect resulting in increased intraocular pressure may precipitate an attack of angle-closure glaucoma)

Glaucoma, open-angle
(anticholinergic mydriatic effect may cause a slight increase in intraocular pressure; glaucoma therapy may need to be adjusted)

Sensitivity to the antihistamine used

Caution is recommended when dimenhydrinate, diphenhydramine, or hydroxyzine is used, since their antiemetic action may impede diagnosis of such conditions as appendicitis and obscure signs of toxicity from overdosage of other drugs.

Side/Adverse Effects

The following side/adverse effects have been selected on the basis of their potential clinical significance (possible signs and symptoms in parentheses where appropriate)—not necessarily inclusive:

Those indicating need for medical attention

Incidence less frequent or rare

Blood dyscrasias (sore throat and fever, unusual bleeding or bruising, unusual tiredness or weakness); *cardiac arrhythmias* (fast or irregular heartbeat)—with high doses of astemizole or terfenadine

Note: *Prolonged QT intervals* and *ventricular arrhythmias* (Torsades de pointes or fibrillation), accompanied by syncope and cardiac arrest, have been reported in association with high doses and/or overdose of astemizole and terfenadine. Severe ventricular arrhythmias have been reported with ingestion of 900 mg or more of terfenadine, and with overdoses greater than 200 mg of astemizole, although there have been rare cases of this effect occurring with doses as low as 20 to 30 mg of astemizole a day. Prolongation of the QT interval may occur at overdoses of 600 mg of terfenadine a day.

Symptoms of overdose

Anticholinergic effects (clumsiness or unsteadiness; severe drowsiness; severe dryness of mouth, nose, or throat; flushing or redness of face; shortness of breath or troubled breathing); *cardiac arrhythmias* (fast or irregular heartbeat)—especially with astemizole or terfenadine; *CNS depression* (severe drowsiness); *CNS stimulation* (hallucinations, seizures, trouble in sleeping); *hypotension* (feeling faint)

Note: *Anticholinergic* and *CNS stimulant* effects are more likely to occur in children with overdose. *Hypotension* may also occur in the elderly at usual doses.

Anticholinergic and CNS effects are not clinically significant with astemizole, cetirizine, loratadine, or terfenadine.

Those indicating need for medical attention only if they continue or are bothersome

Incidence more frequent—rare with astemizole, loratadine, and terfenadine; less frequent with cetirizine

Drowsiness; thickening of mucus

Note: In general, sedative effects are more pronounced with the ethanolamine derivatives (except clemastine) and less pronounced with the propylamine (alkylamine) derivatives.

Tolerance to central effects may develop quickly with some antihistamines, so that sedation is no longer troublesome after a few days.

Incidence of sedation may increase when the recommended doses of astemizole, loratadine, and terfenadine are exceeded.

Incidence less frequent or rare

Blurred vision or any change in vision; confusion; difficult or painful urination; dizziness; dryness of mouth, nose, or throat; fast heartbeat; increased appetite or weight gain—with astemizole and cyproheptadine only; *increased sensitivity of skin to sun; increased sweating; loss of appetite*—except with astemizole and cyproheptadine; *paradoxical reaction* (nightmares; unusual excitement, nervousness, restlessness, or irritability); *ringing or buzzing in ears; skin rash; stomach upset or pain*—more frequent with the ethylenediamine derivatives

Note: Confusion; difficult or painful urination; drowsiness; dizziness; and dryness of mouth, nose, or throat are more likely to occur in the elderly.

Nightmares, unusual excitement, nervousness, restlessness, or irritability are more likely to occur in children and elderly patients.

Patient Consultation

In providing consultation, consider emphasizing the following selected information (» = major clinical significance):

Before using this medication

» Conditions affecting use of most antihistamines (to a lesser extent with astemizole, loratadine, and terfenadine), especially:
Sensitivity to any antihistamine
Pregnancy—Not taking during early months of pregnancy because of fetal abnormalities in studies in animals (for hydroxyzine only); risk-benefit should be considered because of fetal abnormalities in studies in animals with doses above the human therapeutic range (for astemizole and terfenadine only)
Breast-feeding—Use not recommended; may cause unusual excitement or irritability in nursing infant
Use in children—Increased susceptibility to anticholinergic side effects in newborn or premature infants; hyperexcitability (paradoxical reaction) may occur in older children
Use in geriatric patients—Increased susceptibility to anticholinergic side effects; hyperexcitability (paradoxical reaction) may occur
Dental—Increased risk of dental problems because of decrease or inhibition of salivary flow
Other medications, especially alcohol or other CNS depressants, anticholinergics, erythromycin or ketoconazole (with terfenadine only), or MAO inhibitors
Other medical problems, especially angle-closure glaucoma, hepatic function impairment (with astemizole or terfenadine only), prostatic hypertrophy, or urinary retention

Proper use of this medication

» Importance of not taking more medication than the amount recommended
Missed dose: If on scheduled dosing regimen—Using as soon as possible; not using if almost time for next dose; not doubling doses
» Proper storage
For oral dosage forms
Taking with food, water, or milk to minimize gastric irritation
Swallowing extended-release dosage forms whole
For injection dosage forms
Knowing correct administration technique for self-administration; checking with physician if necessary
For rectal dosage forms
Proper administration technique
For dimenhydrinate and diphenhydramine when used as antivertigo agent
Taking at least 30 minutes (preferably 1 to 2 hours) before traveling

Precautions while using this medication

Possible interference with skin tests using allergens; need to inform physician if using medication
May mask ototoxic effects of large doses of salicylates
» Avoiding use of alcohol or other CNS depressants
» Caution if drowsiness occurs
Possible dryness of mouth; using sugarless gum or candy, ice, or saliva substitute for relief; checking with physician or dentist if dry mouth continues for more than 2 weeks
For dimenhydrinate, diphenhydramine, or hydroxyzine
Need to inform physician of use: Possible interference with diagnosis of appendicitis; may mask signs of toxicity from overdosage of other drugs

For diphenhydramine and doxylamine when used in the treatment of insomnia
» Not using concurrently with other sedatives or tranquilizers

Side/adverse effects
Signs of potential side effects, especially blood dyscrasias and cardiac arrhythmias (with astemizole and terfenadine only)

General Dosing Information

For oral dosage forms only
Most antihistamines may be taken with food, water, or milk to lessen gastric irritation.

For parenteral dosage forms only
Intramuscular injections should be administered deeply into the muscle.

Intravenous injections should be administered slowly, preferably with the patient in a recumbent position.

For hydroxyzine
Administration should be by deep intramuscular injection into a large muscle mass, preferably the upper outer quadrant of the buttock or the mid-lateral thigh.

Intramuscular injections should not be made into the lower or mid-third of the upper arm.

When used preoperatively or prepartum, narcotic requirements may be decreased as much as 50%.

ASTEMIZOLE

Summary of Differences

Indications: Used as treatment adjunct in asthma.
Pharmacology:
    Other actions/effects—No significant anticholinergic activity. Mild bronchodilator.
    Protein binding—96%.
    Half-life—1.6 ± 0.7 (mean) days.
    Onset of action—2 to 3 days.
    Time to peak concentration—1 to 4 hours.
    Time to peak effect—9 to 12 days.
    Duration of action—Up to several weeks.
    Elimination—Primarily fecal.
Precautions:
    Dental—No dental precaution.
    Drug interactions and/or related problems—Possible cardiotoxic effects with ketoconazole.
    Contraindications/medical problems—Possible cardiotoxic effects with hepatic function impairment.
Side/adverse effects: Sedative and anticholinergic effects not likely. Cardiac arrhythmias with high doses or overdose. May cause increased appetite and weight gain.

Oral Dosage Forms

ASTEMIZOLE ORAL SUSPENSION

Usual adult and adolescent dose: Antihistaminic (H$_1$-receptor)—Oral, 10 mg once a day.

Usual geriatric dose: See *Usual adult and adolescent dose.*

Note: Geriatric patients may be more sensitive to the effects of the usual adult dose.

Auxiliary labeling: • Shake well.

ASTEMIZOLE TABLETS

Usual adult and adolescent dose: Antihistaminic (H$_1$-receptor)—Oral, 10 mg once a day.

Usual geriatric dose: See *Usual adult and adolescent dose.*
Note: Geriatric patients may be more sensitive to the effects of the usual adult dose.

AZATADINE

Summary of Differences

Pharmacology:
    Chemical group—Piperidine derivative.
    pKa—9.3.
    Half-life—12 hours.
    Time to peak concentration—4 hours.
    Duration of action—12 hours.

Oral Dosage Forms

AZATADINE MALEATE TABLETS USP

Usual adult and adolescent dose: Antihistaminic (H$_1$-receptor)—Oral, 1 to 2 mg every eight to twelve hours as needed.

Usual geriatric dose: See *Usual adult and adolescent dose.*

Note: Geriatric patients may be more sensitive to the effects of the usual adult dose.

Auxiliary labeling:
• May cause drowsiness.
• Avoid alcoholic beverages.

BROMPHENIRAMINE

Summary of Differences

Pharmacology:
    Chemical group—Propylamine derivative.
    pKa—3.59 and 9.12.
    Half-life—25 hours.
    Time to peak concentration—2 to 5 hours.
    Time to peak effect—3 to 9 hours.
    Duration of action—4 to 25 hours.
Side/adverse effects: Sedative effects less pronounced.

Oral Dosage Forms

BROMPHENIRAMINE MALEATE ELIXIR USP

Usual adult and adolescent dose: Antihistaminic (H$_1$-receptor)—Oral, 4 mg every four to six hours as needed.

Usual adult prescribing limits: Up to 24 mg daily.

Usual geriatric dose: See *Usual adult and adolescent dose.*

Note: Geriatric patients may be more sensitive to the effects of the usual adult dose.

Auxiliary labeling:
• May cause drowsiness.
• Avoid alcoholic beverages.
• Keep container tightly closed.

BROMPHENIRAMINE MALEATE TABLETS USP

Usual adult and adolescent dose: Antihistaminic (H$_1$-receptor)—Oral, 4 mg every four to six hours as needed.

Usual geriatric dose: See *Usual adult and adolescent dose.*

Note: Geriatric patients may be more sensitive to the effects of the usual adult dose.

Auxiliary labeling:
- May cause drowsiness.
- Avoid alcoholic beverages.

BROMPHENIRAMINE MALEATE EXTENDED-RELEASE TABLETS

Usual adult and adolescent dose: Antihistaminic (H_1-receptor)—Oral, 8 mg every eight or twelve hours or 12 mg every twelve hours as needed.

Usual geriatric dose: See *Usual adult and adolescent dose*.

Note: Geriatric patients may be more sensitive to the effects of the usual adult dose.

Auxiliary labeling:
- Swallow tablets whole.
- May cause drowsiness.
- Avoid alcoholic beverages.

Parenteral Dosage Forms

BROMPHENIRAMINE MALEATE INJECTION USP

Usual adult and adolescent dose: Antihistaminic (H_1-receptor)—Intramuscular, intravenous, or subcutaneous, 10 mg every eight to twelve hours as needed.

Usual adult prescribing limits: Up to 40 mg daily.

Usual geriatric dose: See *Usual adult and adolescent dose*.

Note: Geriatric patients may be more sensitive to the effects of the usual adult dose.

Additional information:
The period of protection provided by a single dose ranges from three to twelve hours.
The concentrated solution (100 mg per mL) is not recommended for intravenous use.

CETIRIZINE

Summary of Differences

Pharmacology:
Chemical group—Hydroxyzine metabolite.
Protein-binding—93%.
Half-life—8 hours.
Time to peak concentration—1 hour.
Precautions:
Dental—No dental precaution.
Side/adverse effects: Anticholinergic effects not likely; low incidence of sedation.

Oral Dosage Forms

CETIRIZINE HYDROCHLORIDE TABLETS

Usual adult and adolescent dose: Antihistaminic (H_1-receptor)—Oral, 5 to 10 mg once a day.

Note: In patients with reduced creatinine clearance, a starting dose of 5 mg is recommended.

Usual geriatric dose: See *Usual adult and adolescent dose*.

Auxiliary labeling:
- May cause drowsiness.
- Avoid alcoholic beverages.

CHLORPHENIRAMINE

Summary of Differences

Pharmacology:
Chemical group—Propylamine derivative.
pKa—9.2.
Protein-binding—72%.
Half-life—14 to 25 hours.
Time to peak concentration—2 to 6 hours.
Time to peak effect—6 hours.
Duration of action—4 to 8 hours.
Side/adverse effects: Sedative effects less pronounced.

Oral Dosage Forms

CHLORPHENIRAMINE MALEATE EXTENDED-RELEASE CAPSULES USP

Usual adult and adolescent dose: Antihistaminic (H_1-receptor)—Oral, 8 or 12 mg every eight to twelve hours as needed.

Usual geriatric dose: See *Usual adult and adolescent dose*.

Note: Geriatric patients may be more sensitive to the effects of the usual adult dose.

Auxiliary labeling:
- Swallow capsules whole.
- May cause drowsiness.
- Avoid alcoholic beverages.

CHLORPHENIRAMINE MALEATE SYRUP USP

Usual adult and adolescent dose: Antihistaminic (H_1-receptor)—Oral, 4 mg every four to six hours as needed.

Usual adult prescribing limits: Up to 24 mg daily.

Usual geriatric dose: See *Usual adult and adolescent dose*.

Note: Geriatric patients may be more sensitive to the effects of the usual adult dose.

Auxiliary labeling:
- May cause drowsiness.
- Avoid alcoholic beverages.

CHLORPHENIRAMINE MALEATE TABLETS USP

Usual adult and adolescent dose: Antihistaminic (H_1-receptor)—Oral, 4 mg every four to six hours as needed.

Usual geriatric dose: See *Usual adult and adolescent dose*.

Note: Geriatric patients may be more sensitive to the effects of the usual adult dose.

Auxiliary labeling:
- May cause drowsiness.
- Avoid alcoholic beverages.

CHLORPHENIRAMINE MALEATE TABLETS USP (CHEWABLE)

Usual adult and adolescent dose: Antihistaminic (H_1-receptor)—Oral, 4 mg every four to six hours as needed.

Usual geriatric dose: See *Usual adult and adolescent dose*.

Note: Geriatric patients may be more sensitive to the effects of the usual adult dose.

Auxiliary labeling:
- Chew before swallowing.
- May cause drowsiness.
- Avoid alcoholic beverages.

CHLORPHENIRAMINE MALEATE EXTENDED-RELEASE TABLETS

Usual adult and adolescent dose: Antihistaminic (H_1-receptor)—Oral, 8 or 12 mg every eight to twelve hours as needed.

Usual geriatric dose: See *Usual adult and adolescent dose*.

Note: Geriatric patients may be more sensitive to the effects of the usual adult dose.

Auxiliary labeling:
- Swallow tablets whole.
- May cause drowsiness.
- Avoid alcoholic beverages.

Parenteral Dosage Forms

CHLORPHENIRAMINE MALEATE INJECTION USP

Usual adult and adolescent dose: Antihistaminic (H_1-receptor)—Intramuscular, intravenous, or subcutaneous, 5 to 40 mg administered as a single dose as needed.

Usual adult prescribing limits: Up to 40 mg daily.

Usual geriatric dose: See *Usual adult and adolescent dose*.

Note: Geriatric patients may be more sensitive to the effects of the usual adult dose.

Additional information: The 10-mg-per-mL solution may be administered intravenously, intramuscularly, or subcutaneously. The 100-mg-per-mL solution is intended for intramuscular or subcutaneous administration only.

CLEMASTINE

Summary of Differences

Pharmacology:
Chemical group—Ethanolamine derivative.
Other actions/effects—Greater anticholinergic activity.
Time to peak concentration—2 to 4 hours.
Time to peak effect—5 to 7 hours.
Duration of action—12 hours.
Side/adverse effects: Sedative effects not as pronounced.

Oral Dosage Forms

CLEMASTINE FUMARATE SYRUP

Usual adult and adolescent dose: Antihistaminic (H_1-receptor)—Oral, 1.34 mg two times a day or 2.68 mg one to three times a day as needed.

Note: Clemastine is indicated for dermatologic conditions at the 2.68-mg dosage level only.

Usual adult prescribing limits: Up to 8.04 mg daily.

Usual geriatric dose: See *Usual adult and adolescent dose*.

Note: Geriatric patients may be more sensitive to the effects of the usual adult dose.

Auxiliary labeling:
- May cause drowsiness.
- Avoid alcoholic beverages.

CLEMASTINE FUMARATE TABLETS USP

Usual adult and adolescent dose: Antihistaminic (H_1-receptor)—Oral, 1.34 mg two times a day or 2.68 mg one to three times a day as needed.

Note: Clemastine is indicated for dermatologic conditions at the 2.68-mg dosage level only.

Usual geriatric dose: See *Usual adult and adolescent dose*.

Note: Geriatric patients may be more sensitive to the effects of the usual adult dose.

Auxiliary labeling:
- May cause drowsiness.
- Avoid alcoholic beverages.

CYPROHEPTADINE

Summary of Differences

Indications: Also indicated in cold urticaria and used as an appetite stimulant in adults and children.
Pharmacology:
Chemical group—Piperidine derivative.
pKa—9.3.
Other actions/effects—Serotonin antagonist.
Duration of action—8 hours.
Precautions: Laboratory value alterations—May increase serum amylase and serum prolactin concentrations when administered with thyrotropin-releasing hormone.
Side/adverse effects: May cause increased appetite and weight gain.

Oral Dosage Forms

Note: Bracketed uses in the *Dosage Forms* section refer to categories of use and/or indications that are not included in U.S. product labeling.

CYPROHEPTADINE HYDROCHLORIDE SYRUP USP

Usual adult and adolescent dose:
Antihistaminic (H_1-receptor)—Oral, initially 4 mg every eight hours, the dosage being increased as needed. For most patients the therapeutic range is 4 to 20 mg a day. However, doses up to 32 mg a day have been used occasionally.
[Appetite stimulant]—Oral, 4 mg three times a day with meals.
Note: Treatment period to promote weight gain should not exceed six months.
[Vascular headache suppressant]—
Initial: Oral, 4 mg at the start of the attack, repeated after thirty minutes if necessary.
Maintenance: Oral, 4 mg every four to six hours.

Usual adult prescribing limits: Up to 500 mcg (0.5 mg) per kg of body weight daily.

Usual geriatric dose: See *Usual adult and adolescent dose*.

Note: Geriatric patients may be more sensitive to the effects of the usual adult dose.

Auxiliary labeling:
- May cause drowsiness.
- Avoid alcoholic beverages.

CYPROHEPTADINE HYDROCHLORIDE TABLETS USP

Usual adult and adolescent dose:
Antihistaminic (H_1-receptor)—Oral, initially 4 mg every eight hours, the dosage being increased as needed. For most patients the therapeutic range is 4 to 20 mg a day. However, doses up to 32 mg a day have been used occasionally.
[Appetite stimulant]—Oral, 4 mg three times a day with meals.
Note: Treatment period to promote weight gain should not exceed six months.
[Vascular headache suppressant]—
Initial: Oral, 4 mg at the start of the attack, repeated after thirty minutes if necessary.
Maintenance: Oral, 4 mg every four to six hours.

Usual adult prescribing limits: Up to 500 mcg (0.5 mg) per kg of body weight daily.

Usual geriatric dose: See *Usual adult and adolescent dose.*

Note: Geriatric patients may be more sensitive to the effects of the usual adult dose.

Auxiliary labeling:
- May cause drowsiness.
- Avoid alcoholic beverages.

DEXCHLORPHENIRAMINE

Summary of Differences

Pharmacology:
  Chemical group—Propylamine derivative.
  Duration of action—4 to 8 hours.
Side/adverse effects: Sedative effects less pronounced.

Oral Dosage Forms

DEXCHLORPHENIRAMINE MALEATE SYRUP USP

Usual adult and adolescent dose: Antihistaminic (H$_1$-receptor)— Oral, 2 mg every four to six hours as needed.

Usual geriatric dose: See *Usual adult and adolescent dose.*

Note: Geriatric patients may be more sensitive to the effects of the usual adult dose.

Auxiliary labeling:
- May cause drowsiness.
- Avoid alcoholic beverages.

DEXCHLORPHENIRAMINE MALEATE TABLETS USP

Usual adult and adolescent dose: Antihistaminic (H$_1$-receptor)— Oral, 2 mg every four to six hours as needed.

Usual geriatric dose: See *Usual adult and adolescent dose.*

Note: Geriatric patients may be more sensitive to the effects of the usual adult dose.

Auxiliary labeling:
- May cause drowsiness.
- Avoid alcoholic beverages.

DEXCHLORPHENIRAMINE MALEATE EXTENDED-RELEASE TABLETS

Usual adult and adolescent dose: Antihistaminic (H$_1$-receptor)— Oral, 4 or 6 mg every eight to twelve hours as needed.

Usual geriatric dose: See *Usual adult and adolescent dose.*

Note: Geriatric patients may be more sensitive to the effects of the usual adult dose.

Auxiliary labeling:
- Swallow tablets whole.
- May cause drowsiness.
- Avoid alcoholic beverages.

DIMENHYDRINATE

Summary of Differences

Category: Also indicated as an antiemetic and antivertigo agent.
Pharmacology:
  Chemical group—Ethanolamine derivative.

Other actions/effects—Greater anticholinergic activity.
  Duration of action—3 to 6 hours.
Precautions: Contraindications/Medical problems—May impede diagnosis of appendicitis; may obscure signs of overdose.
Side/adverse effects: Sedative effects more pronounced.

Additional Dosing Information

See also *General Dosing Information.*

When dimenhydrinate is used for prophylaxis of motion sickness, it should be taken at least 30 minutes, and preferably 1 or 2 hours, before exposure to conditions that may precipitate motion sickness.

For parenteral dosage form only:
- Do not administer intra-arterially.

Oral Dosage Forms

DIMENHYDRINATE CAPSULES

Usual adult and adolescent dose:
  Antiemetic; or
  Antivertigo agent—Oral, 50 to 100 mg every four hours as needed.

Usual adult prescribing limits: Up to 400 mg daily.

Usual geriatric dose: See *Usual adult and adolescent dose.*

Note: Geriatric patients may be more sensitive to the effects of the usual adult dose.

Auxiliary labeling:
- May cause drowsiness.
- Avoid alcoholic beverages.

DIMENHYDRINATE EXTENDED-RELEASE CAPSULES

Usual adult and adolescent dose:
  Antiemetic; or
  Antivertigo agent—Oral, 1 capsule every twelve hours.

Usual geriatric dose: See *Usual adult and adolescent dose.*

Note: Geriatric patients may be more sensitive to the effects of the usual adult dose.

Auxiliary labeling:
- May cause drowsiness.
- Avoid alcoholic beverages.

DIMENHYDRINATE ELIXIR

Usual adult and adolescent dose:
  Antiemetic; or
  Antivertigo agent—Oral, 50 to 100 mg every four hours as needed.

Usual adult prescribing limits: Up to 400 mg daily.

Usual geriatric dose: See *Usual adult and adolescent dose.*

Note: Geriatric patients may be more sensitive to the effects of the usual adult dose.

Auxiliary labeling:
- May cause drowsiness.
- Avoid alcoholic beverages.
- Keep container tightly closed.

DIMENHYDRINATE SYRUP USP

Usual adult and adolescent dose:
  Antiemetic; or
  Antivertigo agent—Oral, 50 to 100 mg every four hours as needed.

Usual geriatric dose: See *Usual adult and adolescent dose.*

Note: Geriatric patients may be more sensitive to the effects of the usual adult dose.

Auxiliary labeling:
- May cause drowsiness.
- Avoid alcoholic beverages.

DIMENHYDRINATE TABLETS USP

Usual adult and adolescent dose:
Antiemetic; or
Antivertigo agent—Oral, 50 to 100 mg every four hours as needed.

Usual geriatric dose: See *Usual adult and adolescent dose.*

Note: Geriatric patients may be more sensitive to the effects of the usual adult dose.

Auxiliary labeling:
- May cause drowsiness.
- Avoid alcoholic beverages.

DIMENHYDRINATE TABLETS USP (CHEWABLE)

Usual adult and adolescent dose:
Antiemetic; or
Antivertigo agent—Oral, 50 to 100 mg every four hours as needed.

Usual geriatric dose: See *Usual adult and adolescent dose.*

Note: Geriatric patients may be more sensitive to the effects of the usual adult dose.

Auxiliary labeling:
- May cause drowsiness.
- Avoid alcoholic beverages.

Parenteral Dosage Forms

DIMENHYDRINATE INJECTION USP

Usual adult and adolescent dose:
Antiemetic; or
Antivertigo agent—
Intramuscular, 50 mg repeated every four hours as needed.
Intravenous, 50 mg in 10 mL of 0.9% sodium chloride injection, administered slowly over a period of at least two minutes, repeated every four hours as needed.

Usual geriatric dose: See *Usual adult and adolescent dose.*

Note: Geriatric patients may be more sensitive to the effects of the usual adult dose.

Rectal Dosage Forms

DIMENHYDRINATE SUPPOSITORIES

Usual adult and adolescent dose:
Antiemetic; or
Antivertigo agent—Rectal, 50 to 100 mg every six to eight hours as needed.

Usual geriatric dose: See *Usual adult and adolescent dose.*

Note: Geriatric patients may be more sensitive to the effects of the usual adult dose.

Auxiliary labeling:
- May cause drowsiness.
- Avoid alcoholic beverages.

DIPHENHYDRAMINE

Summary of Differences

Category: Also indicated as an antidyskinetic, antiemetic, antitussive (syrup only), antivertigo agent, and a sedative-hypnotic.

Pharmacology:
Chemical group—Ethanolamine derivative.
pKa—9.
Other actions/effects—Greater anticholinergic activity.
Protein binding—98 to 99%.
Half-life—1 to 4 hours.
Time to peak concentration—1 to 4 hours.
Duration of action—6 to 8 hours.
Precautions: Contraindications/Medical problems—May impede diagnosis of appendicitis; may obscure signs of overdose.
Side/adverse effects: Sedative effects more pronounced.

Additional Dosing Information

See also *General Dosing Information.*

When diphenhydramine is used for prophylaxis of motion sickness, it should be taken at least 30 minutes, and preferably 1 or 2 hours, before exposure to conditions that may precipitate motion sickness.

Oral Dosage Forms

DIPHENHYDRAMINE HYDROCHLORIDE CAPSULES USP

Usual adult and adolescent dose:
Antihistaminic (H_1-receptor)—Oral, 25 to 50 mg every four to six hours as needed.
Antidyskinetic[1]—For idiopathic and postencephalitic parkinsonism: Oral, 50 to 150 mg a day, 25 mg three times a day initially, the dose then being increased to 50 mg four times a day.
Antiemetic; or
Antivertigo agent—Oral, 25 to 50 mg every four to six hours as needed.
Sedative-hypnotic—Oral, 50 mg twenty to thirty minutes before bedtime if needed.

Usual adult prescribing limits: Up to 300 mg daily.

Usual geriatric dose: See *Usual adult and adolescent dose.*

Note: Geriatric patients may be more sensitive to the effects of the usual adult dose.

Auxiliary labeling:
- May cause drowsiness.
- Avoid alcoholic beverages.

DIPHENHYDRAMINE HYDROCHLORIDE ELIXIR USP

Usual adult and adolescent dose:
Antihistaminic (H_1-receptor)—Oral, 25 to 50 mg every four to six hours as needed.
Antidyskinetic[1]—For idiopathic and postencephalitic parkinsonism: Oral, 50 to 150 mg a day, 25 mg three times a day initially, the dose then being increased to 50 mg four times a day.
Antiemetic; or
Antivertigo agent—Oral, 25 to 50 mg every four to six hours as needed.
Sedative-hypnotic—Oral, 50 mg twenty to thirty minutes before bedtime if needed.

Usual adult prescribing limits: Up to 300 mg daily.

Usual geriatric dose: See *Usual adult and adolescent dose.*

Note: Geriatric patients may be more sensitive to the effects of the usual adult dose.

Auxiliary labeling:
- May cause drowsiness.
- Avoid alcoholic beverages.
- Keep container tightly closed.

DIPHENHYDRAMINE HYDROCHLORIDE SYRUP

Usual adult and adolescent dose:
  Antihistaminic (H_1-receptor)—Oral, 25 to 50 mg every four to six hours as needed.
  Antidyskinetic[1]—For idiopathic and postencephalitic parkinsonism: Oral, 50 to 150 mg a day, 25 mg three times a day initially, the dose then being increased to 50 mg four times a day.
  Antiemetic; or
  Antivertigo agent—Oral, 25 to 50 mg every four to six hours as needed.
  Sedative-hypnotic—Oral, 50 mg twenty to thirty minutes before bedtime if needed.
  Antitussive—Oral, 25 mg every four to six hours.

Usual adult prescribing limits: Up to 300 mg daily.

Usual geriatric dose: See *Usual adult and adolescent dose.*

Note: Geriatric patients may be more sensitive to the effects of the usual adult dose.

Auxiliary labeling:
  • May cause drowsiness.
  • Avoid alcoholic beverages.

DIPHENHYDRAMINE HYDROCHLORIDE TABLETS

Usual adult and adolescent dose:
  Antihistaminic (H_1-receptor)—Oral, 25 to 50 mg every four to six hours as needed.
  Antidyskinetic[1]—For idiopathic and postencephalitic parkinsonism: Oral, 50 to 150 mg a day, 25 mg three times a day initially, the dose then being increased to 50 mg four times a day.
  Antiemetic; or
  Antivertigo agent—Oral, 25 to 50 mg every four to six hours as needed.
  Sedative-hypnotic—Oral, 50 mg twenty to thirty minutes before bedtime if needed.

Usual adult prescribing limits: Up to 300 mg daily.

Usual geriatric dose: See *Usual adult and adolescent dose.*

Note: Geriatric patients may be more sensitive to the effects of the usual adult dose.

Auxiliary labeling:
  • May cause drowsiness.
  • Avoid alcoholic beverages.

Parenteral Dosage Forms

Note: Bracketed uses in the *Dosage Forms* section refer to categories of use and/or indications that are not included in U.S. product labeling.

DIPHENHYDRAMINE HYDROCHLORIDE INJECTION USP

Usual adult and adolescent dose:
  Antihistaminic (H_1-receptor); or
  Antidyskinetic[1]—Intramuscular or intravenous, 10 to 50 mg.
  Antiemetic; or
  Antivertigo agent—Intramuscular or intravenous, 10 mg initially, may be increased to 20 to 50 mg every two to three hours.

Usual adult prescribing limits: Up to 100 mg per dose or 400 mg daily.

Usual geriatric dose: See *Usual adult and adolescent dose.*

Note: Geriatric patients may be more sensitive to the effects of the usual adult dose.

DOXYLAMINE

Summary of Differences

Category: Also indicated as a sedative-hypnotic.
Pharmacology:
  Chemical group—Ethanolamine derivative.
  pKa—5.8 and 9.3.
  Other actions/effects—Greater anticholinergic activity.
  Duration of action—6 to 8 hours.
Side/adverse effects: Sedative effects more pronounced.

Oral Dosage Forms

DOXYLAMINE SUCCINATE TABLETS USP

Usual adult and adolescent dose:
  Antihistaminic (H_1-receptor)—Oral, 12.5 to 25 mg every four to six hours as needed.
  Sedative-hypnotic—Oral, 25 mg thirty minutes before bedtime if needed.

Usual adult prescribing limits: Up to 150 mg daily.

Usual geriatric dose: See *Usual adult and adolescent dose.*

Note: Geriatric patients may be more sensitive to the effects of the usual adult dose.

Auxiliary labeling:
  • May cause drowsiness.
  • Avoid alcoholic beverages.

HYDROXYZINE

Summary of Differences

Category: Also indicated in the treatment of anxiety and psychosis-related tension; antiemetic and antivertigo agent.
Pharmacology:
  Chemical group—Piperazine derivative.
  pKa—Hydroxyzine hydrochloride: 2.6 and 7.
  Half-life (elimination)—20 to 25 hours.
  Duration of action—4 to 6 hours.
Precautions:
  Laboratory value alterations—False increases in urine 17-hydroxycorticosteroid determinations.
  Contraindications/Medical problems—May impede diagnosis of appendicitis; may obscure signs of overdose.

Oral Dosage Forms

HYDROXYZINE HYDROCHLORIDE CAPSULES

Usual adult and adolescent dose:
  Antianxiety agent; or
  Sedative-hypnotic—Oral, 50 to 100 mg as a single dose.
  Antihistaminic (H_1-receptor); or
  Antiemetic—Oral, 25 to 100 mg three or four times a day as needed.

Usual geriatric dose: See *Usual adult and adolescent dose.*

Note: Geriatric patients may be more sensitive to the effects of the usual adult dose.

Auxiliary labeling:
  • May cause drowsiness.
  • Avoid alcoholic beverages.

HYDROXYZINE HYDROCHLORIDE SYRUP USP

Usual adult and adolescent dose:
Antianxiety agent; or
Sedative-hypnotic—Oral, 50 to 100 mg as a single dose.

Antihistaminic (H₁-receptor); or
Antiemetic—Oral, 25 to 100 mg three or four times a day as needed.

Usual geriatric dose: See *Usual adult and adolescent dose.*

Note: Geriatric patients may be more sensitive to the effects of the usual adult dose.

Auxiliary labeling:
• May cause drowsiness.
• Avoid alcoholic beverages.

HYDROXYZINE HYDROCHLORIDE TABLETS USP

Usual adult and adolescent dose:
Antianxiety agent; or
Sedative-hypnotic—Oral, 50 to 100 mg as a single dose.

Antihistaminic (H₁-receptor); or
Antiemetic—Oral, 25 to 100 mg three to four times a day as needed.

Usual geriatric dose: See *Usual adult and adolescent dose.*

Note: Geriatric patients may be more sensitive to the effects of the usual adult dose.

Auxiliary labeling:
• May cause drowsiness.
• Avoid alcoholic beverages.

HYDROXYZINE PAMOATE CAPSULES USP

Usual adult and adolescent dose:
Antianxiety agent; or
Sedative-hypnotic—Oral, 50 to 100 mg as a single dose.

Antihistaminic (H₁-receptor); or
Antiemetic—Oral, 25 to 100 mg three to four times a day as needed.

Usual geriatric dose: See *Usual adult and adolescent dose.*

Note: Geriatric patients may be more sensitive to the effects of the usual adult dose.

Auxiliary labeling:
• May cause drowsiness.
• Avoid alcoholic beverages.

HYDROXYZINE PAMOATE ORAL SUSPENSION USP

Usual adult and adolescent dose:
Antianxiety agent; or
Sedative-hypnotic—Oral, 50 to 100 mg as a single dose.

Antihistaminic (H₁-receptor); or
Antiemetic—Oral, 25 to 100 mg three to four times a day as needed.

Usual geriatric dose: See *Usual adult and adolescent dose.*

Note: Geriatric patients may be more sensitive to the effects of the usual adult dose.

Auxiliary labeling:
• Shake well.
• May cause drowsiness.
• Avoid alcoholic beverages.

Parenteral Dosage Forms

HYDROXYZINE HYDROCHLORIDE INJECTION USP

Usual adult and adolescent dose:
Antianxiety agent—Intramuscular, 50 to 100 mg, repeated as needed every four to six hours.

Sedative-hypnotic—Intramuscular, 50 mg as a single dose.
  Adjunct to narcotic medication: Intramuscular, 25 to 100 mg.
Antiemetic—Intramuscular, 25 to 100 mg.

Usual geriatric dose: See *Usual adult and adolescent dose.*

Note: Geriatric patients may be more sensitive to the effects of the usual adult dose.

LORATADINE

Summary of Differences

Indications: Used as treatment adjunct in asthma.
Pharmacology:
  Other actions/effects—No significant anticholinergic activity. Mild bronchodilator.
  Half-life—7.8 to 11 hours.
  Onset of action—27 minutes.
  Time to peak concentration—1 to 2 hours.
  Time to peak effect—4 to 6 hours.
  Duration of action—At least 24 hours.
Precautions:
  Dental—No dental precaution.
  Drug interactions and/or related problems—Possible cardiotoxic effects with ketoconazole.
Side/adverse effects: Sedative and anticholinergic effects not likely.

Oral Dosage Forms

LORATADINE TABLETS

Usual adult and adolescent dose: Antihistaminic (H₁-receptor)— Oral, 10 mg once a day.

Usual geriatric dose: See *Usual adult and adolescent dose.*

Note: Geriatric patients may be more sensitive to the effects of the usual adult dose.

PHENINDAMINE

Summary of Differences

Pharmacology:
  Chemical group—Piperidine derivative.
  Duration of action—4 to 6 hours.

Oral Dosage Forms

PHENINDAMINE TARTRATE TABLETS

Usual adult and adolescent dose: Antihistaminic (H₁-receptor)— Oral, 25 mg every four to six hours as needed.

Usual adult prescribing limits: Up to 150 mg daily.

Usual geriatric dose: See *Usual adult and adolescent dose.*

Note: Geriatric patients may be more sensitive to the effects of the usual adult dose.

Auxiliary labeling:
• May cause drowsiness.
• Avoid alcoholic beverages.

PYRILAMINE

Summary of Differences

Pharmacology:
   Chemistry group—Ethylenediamine derivative.
   Duration of action—8 hours.
Side/adverse effects: Gastrointestinal effects more pronounced.

Oral Dosage Forms

PYRILAMINE MALEATE TABLETS USP

Usual adult and adolescent dose: Antihistaminic (H_1-receptor)—Oral, 25 to 50 mg every eight hours as needed.

Usual adult prescribing limits: Up to 200 mg daily.

Usual geriatric dose: See *Usual adult and adolescent dose*.

Note: Geriatric patients may be more sensitive to the effects of the usual adult dose.

Auxiliary labeling:
• May cause drowsiness.
• Avoid alcoholic beverages.

TERFENADINE

Summary of Differences

Indications: Used as treatment adjunct in asthma.
Pharmacology:
   Chemical group—Butyrophenone derivative.
   Other actions/effects—No significant anticholinergic activity. Mild bronchodilator.
   Protein binding—97%.
   Half-life—20.3 hours.
   Onset of action: 72 minutes.
   Time to peak concentration: 2 hours.
   Time to peak effect—3 to 4 hours.
   Duration of action—Over 12 hours.
   Elimination—Primarily fecal.
Precautions:
   Dental—No dental precaution.
   Drug interactions and/or related problems—Possible cardiotoxic effects with erythromycin or ketoconazole.
   Contraindications/medical problems—Possible cardiotoxic effects with hepatic function impairment.
Side/adverse effects: Sedative and anticholinergic side effects not likely. Cardiac arrhythmias with high doses or overdose.

Oral Dosage Forms

TERFENADINE ORAL SUSPENSION

Usual adult and adolescent dose: Antihistaminic (H_1-receptor)—Oral, 60 mg every eight to twelve hours, or 120 mg once a day, as needed.

Usual geriatric dose: See *Usual adult and adolescent dose*.

Note: Geriatric patients may be more sensitive to the effects of the usual adult dose.

Auxiliary labeling:
• Shake well.

TERFENADINE TABLETS USP

Usual adult and adolescent dose: Antihistaminic (H_1-receptor)—Oral, 60 mg every eight to twelve hours, or 120 mg once a day, as needed.

Usual geriatric dose: See *Usual adult and adolescent dose*.

Note: Geriatric patients may be more sensitive to the effects of the usual adult dose.

TRIPELENNAMINE

Summary of Differences

Pharmacology:
   Chemical group—Ethylenediamine derivative.
   pKa—3.9 and 9.0.
   Duration of action—4 to 6 hours.
Side/adverse effects: Gastrointestinal effects more pronounced.

Oral Dosage Forms

TRIPELENNAMINE CITRATE ELIXIR USP

Usual adult and adolescent dose: Antihistaminic (H_1-receptor)—Oral, the equivalent of tripelennamine hydrochloride: 25 to 50 mg every four to six hours as needed.

Usual adult prescribing limits: Up to the equivalent of 600 mg of tripelennamine hydrochloride daily.

Usual geriatric dose: See *Usual adult and adolescent dose*.

Note: Geriatric patients may be more sensitive to the effects of the usual adult dose.

Auxiliary labeling:
• May cause drowsiness.
• Avoid alcoholic beverages.
• Keep container tightly closed.

TRIPELENNAMINE HYDROCHLORIDE TABLETS USP

Usual adult and adolescent dose: Antihistaminic (H_1-receptor)—Oral, 25 to 50 mg every four to six hours as needed.

Usual adult prescribing limits: Up to 600 mg daily.

Usual geriatric dose: See *Usual adult and adolescent dose*.

Note: Geriatric patients may be more sensitive to the effects of the usual adult dose.

Auxiliary labeling:
• May cause drowsiness.
• Avoid alcoholic beverages.

TRIPELENNAMINE HYDROCHLORIDE EXTENDED-RELEASE TABLETS

Usual adult and adolescent dose: Antihistaminic (H_1-receptor)—Oral, 100 mg every eight to twelve hours as needed.

Usual adult prescribing limits: Up to 600 mg daily.

Usual geriatric dose: See *Usual adult and adolescent dose*.

Note: Geriatric patients may be more sensitive to the effects of the usual adult dose.

Auxiliary labeling:
• Swallow tablets whole.
• May cause drowsiness.
• Avoid alcoholic beverages.

TRIPROLIDINE

Summary of Differences

Pharmacology:
    Chemical group—Propylamine derivative.
    pKa—3.6 and 9.3.
    Half-life—3 to 3.3 hours.
    Time to peak concentration—2 hours.
    Time to peak effect—2 to 3 hours.
    Duration of action—4 to 8 hours.
Side/adverse effects: Sedative effects less pronounced.

Oral Dosage Forms

TRIPROLIDINE HYDROCHLORIDE SYRUP USP

Usual adult and adolescent dose: Antihistaminic (H_1-receptor)—Oral, 2.5 mg every four to six hours as needed.

Usual adult prescribing limits: Up to 10 mg daily.

Usual geriatric dose: See *Usual adult and adolescent dose.*

Note: Geriatric patients may be more sensitive to the effects of the usual adult dose.

Auxiliary labeling:
- May cause drowsiness.
- Avoid alcoholic beverages.

TRIPROLIDINE HYDROCHLORIDE TABLETS USP

Usual adult and adolescent dose: Antihistaminic (H_1-receptor)—Oral, 2.5 mg every four to six hours as needed.

Usual adult prescribing limits: Up to 10 mg daily.

Usual geriatric dose: See *Usual adult and adolescent dose.*

Note: Geriatric patients may be more sensitive to the effects of the usual adult dose.

Auxiliary labeling:
- May cause drowsiness.
- Avoid alcoholic beverages.

ANTIHISTAMINES AND DECONGESTANTS Systemic

INN: Included in brackets after individual generic listings, if different from U.S. generic names.

Category: Antihistaminic (H_1-receptor)-decongestant.

Indications

Accepted
Congestion, nasal (treatment);
Sneezing (treatment); and
Rhinorrhea (treatment)—Antihistamine and decongestant combinations are indicated for the temporary relief of nasal and sinus congestion, sneezing, and rhinorrhea associated with the common cold and allergic rhinitis.

The therapeutic effectiveness of oral phenylephrine as a nasal decongestant has been questioned, especially at the usual oral dose.

Patient Consultation

In providing consultation, consider emphasizing the following selected information (» = major clinical significance):

Before using this medication
» Conditions affecting use, especially:
    Sensitivity to any of the antihistamines or sympathomimetic amines
    Pregnancy—Concern for the fetus and/or newborn infant only with high doses and long-term therapy; psychiatric disorders more likely with use of phenylpropanolamine in postpartum women
    Breast-feeding—Antihistamines may cause excitement or irritability in nursing infants; high risk for infants from sympathomimetic amines
    Use in children—Increased susceptibility to anticholinergic effects of antihistamines and to vasopressor effects of sympathomimetic amines; psychiatric disorders more likely with use of phenylpropanolamine in children under 6 years of age; hyperexcitability (paradoxical reaction) may occur
    Use in athletes—Stimulants (sympathomimetic amines) are banned and tested for by the U.S. Olympic Committee (USOC) and the National Collegiate Athletic Association (NCAA)
    Use in the elderly—Anticholinergic and CNS stimulant effects more likely to occur
    Other medications, especially anticholinergics, erythromycin or ketoconazole (with terfenadine-containing combination only), medicine for high blood pressure or depression, or CNS depressants or stimulants
    Other medical problems, especially cardiovascular disease, diabetes, hepatic function impairment (with terfenadine-containing combination only), hypertension, hyperthyroidism, or prostatic hypertrophy

Proper use of this medication
» Importance of not taking more medication than the amount recommended
    Taking with food, water, or milk to minimize gastric irritation
    Swallowing extended-release dosage form whole
    Missed dose: If on scheduled dosing regimen—Taking as soon as possible; not taking if almost time for next dose; not doubling doses
» Proper storage

Precautions while using this medication
    Caution if skin tests using allergens required; possible interference with test results
    May mask ototoxic effects of large doses of salicylates
» Avoiding use of alcohol or other CNS depressants
» Caution if drowsiness or dizziness occurs
» Caution if taking phenylpropanolamine-containing appetite suppressants
» Possible insomnia; taking the medication a few hours before bedtime
    Possible dryness of mouth; using sugarless gum or candy, ice, or saliva substitute for relief; checking with dentist if dry mouth continues for more than 2 weeks.

For promethazine
    Possible interference with diagnosis of intestinal obstruction, brain tumor, or overdosage of toxic drugs; need to inform physician of use

Side/adverse effects
    Signs of potential side effects, especially blood dyscrasias, cardiac arrhythmias, psychotic episodes, and tightness in chest

ANTIHISTAMINES, DECONGESTANTS, AND ANALGESICS   Systemic

Category: Antihistaminic (H_1-receptor)-decongestant-analgesic.

Indications

Accepted
Cold symptoms (treatment);
Congestion, nasal (treatment); and
Congestion, sinus (treatment)—Antihistamine, decongestant, and analgesic combinations are indicated for the temporary relief of nasal and sinus congestion and headaches, pains, and general discomfort due to colds, flu, or allergies. The antihistamine in these combinations may provide added relief of nasal congestion, rhinorrhea, and sneezing. It may also serve as an adjunct because of its anticholinergic drying effects.

The therapeutic effectiveness of oral phenylephrine as a nasal decongestant has been questioned, especially at the usual oral dose.

Patient Consultation

In providing consultation, consider emphasizing the following selected information (» = major clinical significance):

Before using this medication
» Conditions affecting use, especially:
    Sensitivity to any of the medications in the combination being taken
    Pregnancy—Concern for the fetus and/or newborn infant only with high doses and long-term therapy; psychiatric disorders more likely with use of phenylpropanolamine in postpartum women; use of aspirin-containing combinations not recommended during third trimester
    Breast-feeding—Antihistamines may cause excitement or irritability in nursing infant; high risk for infants from sympathomimetic amines; also, concern with high doses and chronic use because of high salicylate intake by infant
    Use in children—Increased susceptibility to anticholinergic effects of antihistamines and to vasopressor effects of sympathomimetic amines; psychiatric disorders more likely with use of phenylpropanolamine in children under 6 years of age; hyperexcitability (paradoxical reaction) may occur; also, increased susceptibility to toxic effects of salicylates, especially if fever and dehydration present; possible association between aspirin usage and Reye's syndrome
    Use in adolescents—Possible association between aspirin usage and Reye's syndrome
    Use by athletes—Stimulants (e.g., caffeine and sympathomimetic amines) are banned and tested for by the U.S. Olympic Committee (USOC) and the National Collegiate Athletic Association (NCAA)
    Use in the elderly—Anticholinergic and CNS stimulant effects more likely to occur; increased susceptibility to toxic effects of salicylates
    Other medications, especially anticholinergics, medicine for high blood pressure or depression, or CNS depressants or stimulants

    Other medical problems, especially alcoholism, cardiovascular disease, diabetes, gastritis or peptic ulcer (with salicylate-containing), hypertension, hyperthyroidism, or prostatic hypertrophy

Proper use of this medication
» Importance of not taking more medication than the amount recommended
    Taking with food, water, or milk to minimize gastric irritation
    Swallowing extended-release dosage form whole
» Not taking combinations containing aspirin if a strong vinegar-like odor is present
    Missed dose: If on scheduled dosing regimen—Taking as soon as possible; not taking if almost time for next dose; not doubling doses
» Proper storage

Precautions while using this medication
    Caution if skin tests using allergens required; possible interference with test results
    Checking with physician if symptoms persist or become worse, or if high fever is present
» Caution if drowsiness or dizziness occurs
» Possible insomnia; taking the medication a few hours before bedtime
» Caution if taking phenylpropanolamine-containing appetite suppressants
    Need to inform physician or dentist of use of medication if any kind of surgery (including dental surgery or emergency treatment) is required
    Possible dryness of mouth; using sugarless gum or candy, ice, or saliva substitute for relief; checking with dentist if dry mouth continues for more than 2 weeks
» Caution if other medications containing acetaminophen, aspirin, or other salicylates (including diflunisal) are used
» Avoiding alcoholic beverages or other CNS depressants while taking these medications; also, alcohol consumption may increase risk of salicylate-induced gastrointestinal toxicity and acetaminophen-induced liver toxicity
» Suspected overdose: Getting emergency help at once
    Not taking products containing aspirin for 5 days prior to any kind of surgery, unless otherwise directed by physician
    Diabetics: Aspirin present in some combination formulations may cause false urine sugar test results with prolonged use of 8 or more 325-mg (5-grain) doses per day

Side/adverse effects
    Signs of potential side effects, especially allergic reactions, anticholinergic effects, blood dyscrasias, jaundice (with acetaminophen-containing), and signs of gastrointestinal irritation or bleeding (with salicylate-containing)

ANTIHISTAMINES, PHENOTHIAZINE-DERIVATIVE   Systemic

INN: Included in brackets after individual generic listings, if different from the U.S. generic name.

Some commonly used *brand names* are:

In the U.S.—

Anergan 25 [Promethazine]	*Pro-50* [Promethazine]
Anergan 50 [Promethazine]	*Prometh-25*
Pentazine [Promethazine]	[Promethazine]
Phenameth [Promethazine]	*Prometh-50*
Phenazine 25	[Promethazine]
[Promethazine]	*Promethegan*
Phenazine 50	[Promethazine]
[Promethazine]	*Prorex-25* [Promethazine]
Phencen-50 [Promethazine]	*Prorex-50* [Promethazine]
Phenergan [Promethazine]	*Prothazine* [Promethazine]
Phenergan Fortis	*Prothazine Plain*
[Promethazine]	[Promethazine]
Phenergan Plain	*Tacaryl* [Methdilazine]
[Promethazine]	*Temaril* [Trimeprazine]
Phenoject-50	*V-Gan-25* [Promethazine]
[Promethazine]	*V-Gan-50* [Promethazine]

In Canada—

Histantil [Promethazine]	*PMS Promethazine*
Panectyl [Trimeprazine]	[Promethazine]
Phenergan [Promethazine]	

METHDILAZINE†
Oral
   Methdilazine Hydrochloride Syrup USP†
      In the U.S.—*Tacaryl*
   Methdilazine Hydrochloride Tablets USP†
      In the U.S.—*Tacaryl*
   Methdilazine Hydrochloride Tablets USP (Chewable)†
      In the U.S.—*Tacaryl*
PROMETHAZINE
Oral
   Promethazine Hydrochloride Syrup USP
      In the U.S.—*Phenergan Fortis; Phenergan Plain; Prothazine Plain;* GENERIC
      In Canada—*Phenergan; PMS Promethazine*
   Promethazine Hydrochloride Tablets USP
      In the U.S.—*Phenameth; Phenergan;* GENERIC
      In Canada—*Histantil; Phenergan*
Parenteral
   Promethazine Hydrochloride Injection USP
      In the U.S.—*Anergan 25; Anergan 50; Pentazine; Phenazine 25; Phenazine 50; Phencen-50; Phenergan; Phenoject-50; Pro-50; Prometh-25; Prometh-50; Prorex-25; Prorex-50; Prothazine; V-Gan-25; V-Gan-50;* GENERIC
      In Canada—*Phenergan;* GENERIC
Rectal
   Promethazine Hydrochloride Suppositories USP†
      In the U.S.—*Phenergan; Promethegan;* GENERIC
TRIMEPRAZINE [INN: Alimemazine]
Oral
   Trimeprazine Tartrate Extended-release Capsules†
      In the U.S.—*Temaril*
   Trimeprazine Tartrate Syrup USP
      In the U.S.—*Temaril;* GENERIC
      In Canada—*Panectyl*
   Trimeprazine Tartrate Tablets USP
      In the U.S.—*Temaril*
      In Canada—*Panectyl*

---

†Not commercially available in Canada.

Category

Antihistaminic (H_1-receptor)—Methdilazine; Promethazine; Trimeprazine.
Antiemetic—Promethazine.
Antivertigo agent—Promethazine.
Sedative-hypnotic—Promethazine; Trimeprazine.

Indications

Note: Bracketed information in the *Indications* section refers to uses not included in U.S. product labeling.

Accepted
Rhinitis, perennial and seasonal allergic or vasomotor (treatment); or
Conjunctivitis, allergic (treatment)—Antihistamines are indicated in the symptomatic treatment of perennial and seasonal allergic rhinitis, vasomotor rhinitis, and allergic conjunctivitis due to inhalant allergens and foods.

Pruritus (treatment);
Urticaria (treatment);
Angioedema (treatment);
Dermatographism (treatment); or
Transfusion reactions, urticarial (treatment)—Antihistamines are indicated for the symptomatic treatment of pruritus associated with allergic reactions and of mild, uncomplicated allergic skin manifestations of urticaria and angioedema, in dermatographism, and in urticaria associated with transfusions. [Antihistamines are also used in the treatment of pruritus associated with pityriasis rosea.][1]

Sneezing (treatment); or
Rhinorrhea (treatment)—Antihistamines are indicated for the relief of sneezing and rhinorrhea associated with the common cold. However, controlled clinical studies have not demonstrated that antihistamines are significantly more effective than placebo in relieving cold symptoms.

Anaphylactic or anaphylactoid reactions (treatment adjunct)—Antihistamines are indicated as adjunctive therapy to epinephrine and other standard measures for anaphylactic reactions after the acute manifestations have been controlled, and to ameliorate the allergic reactions to blood or plasma.

Motion sickness (prophylaxis and treatment); or
Vertigo (treatment)—Promethazine is indicated for the prevention and treatment of the nausea, vomiting, dizziness, or vertigo of motion sickness.

Nausea or vomiting (prophylaxis and treatment)—Promethazine is indicated in the control of nausea and vomiting associated with certain types of anesthesia and surgery.

Sedation—Promethazine and [trimeprazine][1] are indicated for their sedative and hypnotic effects and as adjuncts to preoperative and postoperative medication.

Pain, postoperative (treatment adjunct)—Promethazine is indicated as an adjunct to analgesics for control of postoperative pain.

Analgesia adjunct, during surgery;
Anesthesia, general, adjunct; or
Anesthesia, local, adjunct—Intravenous administration of promethazine is indicated in special surgical situations (such as repeated bronchoscopy, ophthalmic surgery, and poor-risk patients) in combination with reduced amounts of meperidine or other narcotic analgesics as an adjunct to anesthesia and analgesia.

---

[1]Not included in Canadian product labeling.

Pharmacology

Mechanism of action/Effect:

Antihistaminic (H_1-receptor)—Antihistamines used in the treatment of allergy act by competing with histamine for H_1-receptor sites on effector cells. They thereby prevent, but do not reverse, responses mediated by histamine alone. Antihistamines do not block histamine release, but they antagonize in varying degrees, most of the pharmacological effects of histamine, including urticaria and pruritus. Also, the anticholinergic actions of most antihistamines provide a drying effect on the nasal mucosa.

Antiemetic; antivertigo—The mechanism by which some antihistamines exert their antiemetic, anti-motion sickness, and antivertigo effects is not precisely known but may be related to their central anticholinergic actions. They diminish vestibular stimulation and depress labyrinthine function. An action on the medullary chemoreceptive trigger zone may also be involved in the antiemetic effect.

Sedative-hypnotic—Most antihistamines cross the blood-brain barrier and produce sedation due to inhibition of histamine N-methyltransferase and blockage of central histaminergic receptors. Antagonism of other central nervous system receptor sites, such as those for serotonin, acetylcholine, and alpha-adrenergic stimulation, may also be involved. Phenothiazines are thought to cause indirect reduction of stimuli to the brain stem reticular system.

Other actions/effects:

Anticholinergic—Antihistamines prevent responses to acetylcholine that are mediated via muscarinic receptors.

Antiemetic—Methdilazine and trimeprazine possess also antiemetic action. However, only promethazine is labeled for this indication.

Onset of action:

Oral—15 to 60 minutes.
Parenteral—Promethazine:
  Intramuscular—20 minutes.
  Intravenous—3 to 5 minutes.
Rectal—Promethazine: 20 minutes.

Duration of action:

Methdilazine—6 to 12 hours.
Promethazine—
  Antihistaminic: 6 to 12 hours.
  Sedative: 2 to 8 hours.
Trimeprazine—3 to 6 hours.

Precautions to Consider

Cross-sensitivity and/or related problems

Patients sensitive to other phenothiazines may be sensitive to methdilazine, promethazine, and trimeprazine also.

Geriatrics

Dizziness, sedation, confusion, and hypotension may be more likely to occur in geriatric patients taking antihistamines.

A paradoxical reaction characterized by hyperexcitability may occur in geriatric patients taking antihistamines.

Geriatric patients are especially susceptible to the anticholinergic side effects, such as dryness of mouth and urinary retention (especially in males), of the antihistamines. If these side effects occur and continue or are severe, medication should probably be discontinued.

Extrapyramidal signs, especially parkinsonism, akathisia, and persistent dyskinesia, may also be more likely to occur in geriatric patients, especially at the higher doses or with parenteral administration.

Dental

Prolonged use of antihistamines may decrease or inhibit salivary flow, thus contributing to the development of caries, periodontal disease, oral candidiasis, and discomfort.

Involuntary orofacial muscle movement may result from extrapyramidal effects.

Drug interactions and/or related problems

The following drug interactions and/or related problems have been selected on the basis of their potential clinical significance (possible mechanism in parentheses where appropriate)—not necessarily inclusive (» = major clinical significance):

Note: Combinations containing any of the following medications, depending on the amount present, may also interact with this medication.

» Alcohol or
» CNS depression-producing medications, other
  (concurrent use may potentiate the CNS depressant effects of either these medications or antihistamines; also, concurrent use of maprotiline or tricyclic antidepressants may potentiate the anticholinergic effects of either antihistamines or these medications)

Amphetamines
  (concurrent use may decrease stimulant effects of amphetamines since phenothiazine derivatives produce alpha-adrenergic blockade)

» Anticholinergics or other medications with anticholinergic activity
  (anticholinergic effects may be potentiated when these medications are used concurrently with antihistamines; patients should be advised to report occurrence of gastrointestinal problems promptly since paralytic ileus may occur with concurrent therapy)

Anticonvulsants, including barbiturates
  (phenothiazine derivatives may lower the convulsion threshold; dosage adjustment of anticonvulsant medications may be necessary; potentiation of anticonvulsant effects does not occur)

» Antithyroid agents
  (concurrent use with phenothiazine derivatives may increase the risk of agranulocytosis)

Appetite suppressants
  (concurrent use with phenothiazine derivatives may antagonize the anorectic effect of appetite suppressants)

Beta-adrenergic blocking agents, especially propranolol
  (concurrent use with phenothiazine derivatives may result in increased plasma concentration of each medication because of inhibition of metabolism; this may result in additive hypotensive effects, irreversible retinopathy, cardiac arrhythmias, and tardive dyskinesia)

Bromocriptine
  (concurrent use may increase serum prolactin concentrations and interfere with effects of bromocriptine; dosage adjustments may be necessary)

Dopamine
  (concurrent use may antagonize peripheral vasoconstriction produced by high doses of dopamine because of the alpha-adrenergic blocking action of phenothiazine derivatives)

Ephedrine
  (alpha-adrenergic blocking action of phenothiazine derivatives may decrease the pressor response to ephedrine when used concurrently)

» Epinephrine
  (alpha-adrenergic effects of epinephrine may be blocked when it is used concurrently with phenothiazine derivatives, possibly resulting in severe hypotension and tachycardia)

» Extrapyramidal reaction-causing medications, other
(concurrent use with phenothiazine derivatives may increase the severity and frequency of extrapyramidal effects)

Guanadrel or
Guanethidine
(neuronal uptake of these medications may be inhibited when they are used concurrently with phenothiazine derivatives, causing a decrease of their antihypertensive effect)

Hepatotoxic medications, other
(concurrent use of phenothiazine derivatives with other hepatotoxic medications may increase the potential for hepatotoxicity; patients, especially those on prolonged administration or with a history of liver disease, should be carefully monitored)

Hypotension-producing medications, other
(concurrent use with phenothiazine derivatives may produce additive hypotensive effects)

» Levodopa
(antiparkinsonian effects of levodopa may be inhibited when used concurrently with phenothiazine derivatives because of blockade of dopamine receptors in brain; levodopa has not been shown to be effective in phenothiazine-induced parkinsonism)

Metaraminol
(concurrent use with phenothiazine derivatives may decrease the pressor response to metaraminol because of the alpha-adrenergic blocking action of phenothiazines)

Methoxamine
(prior administration of phenothiazine derivatives may decrease the pressor effect and shorten the duration of action of methoxamine because of the alpha-adrenergic blocking action of phenothiazines)

» Metrizamide, intrathecal
(concurrent use with phenothiazine derivatives may lower the seizure threshold; these medications should be discontinued at least 48 hours before, and not resumed for at least 24 hours following, myelography)

» Monoamine oxidase (MAO) inhibitors, including furazolidone and procarbazine
(concurrent use of MAO inhibitors with antihistamines in general may prolong and intensify the anticholinergic and CNS depressant effects of antihistamines; concurrent use of MAO inhibitors with phenothiazine-derivative antihistamines may increase the risk of hypotension and extrapyramidal reactions; concurrent use is not recommended)

Ototoxic medications
(concurrent use with antihistamines may mask the symptoms of ototoxicity such as tinnitus, dizziness, or vertigo)

Quinidine
(concurrent use with phenothiazine-derivative antihistamines may result in additive cardiac effects)

Riboflavin
(requirements for riboflavin may be increased in patients receiving phenothiazine-derivative antihistamines)

Contraindications/Medical problems

The contraindications/medical problems included have been selected on the basis of their potential clinical significance (reasons given in parentheses where appropriate)—not necessarily inclusive (» = major clinical significance).

Risk-benefit should be considered when the following medical problems exist:

Asthma, acute
(although antihistamines may decrease allergen-induced bronchoconstriction, their anticholinergic "drying" effects may cause thickening of secretions and impair expectoration during an acute episode of asthma)

» Bladder neck obstruction or
» Prostatic hypertrophy, symptomatic, or
» Urinary retention, predisposition to
(anticholinergic effects may precipitate or aggravate urinary retention)

Bone marrow depression
(increased risk of leukopenia and agranulocytosis)

Cardiovascular disease
(increased risk of transient hypotension)

» Coma
(may be exacerbated)

Epilepsy
(parenteral administration of promethazine may increase severity of seizures)

» Glaucoma, angle-closure, or predisposition to
(mydriatic effect resulting in increased intraocular pressure may precipitate an attack of angle-closure glaucoma)

Glaucoma, open-angle
(mydriatic effect may cause a slight increase in intraocular pressure; glaucoma therapy may need to be adjusted)

Hepatic function impairment
(metabolism may be decreased; higher serum concentrations may increase sensitivity to CNS effects)

» Jaundice
(may be exacerbated with parenteral administration of promethazine)

Reye's syndrome
(extrapyramidal symptoms that may be produced by parenteral administration of promethazine may be confused with CNS signs of Reye's syndrome)

Sensitivity to the antihistamine used

Caution is recommended when phenothiazine-derivative antihistamines are used, since their antiemetic action may impede diagnosis of such conditions as appendicitis and obscure signs of toxicity from overdosage of other drugs.

Side/Adverse Effects

The following side/adverse effects have been selected on the basis of their potential clinical significance (possible signs and symptoms in parentheses where appropriate)—not necessarily inclusive:

Those indicating need for medical attention
Incidence less frequent or rare
Blood dyscrasias (sore throat and fever, unusual bleeding or bruising, unusual tiredness or weakness)

Symptoms of overdose
Anticholinergic effects (clumsiness or unsteadiness; severe drowsiness; severe dryness of mouth, nose, or throat; flushing or redness of face; shortness of breath or troubled breathing); *CNS depression* (severe drowsiness); *CNS stimulation* (hallucinations, seizures, trouble in sleeping); *extrapyramidal effects* (muscle spasms, especially of neck and back; restlessness; shuffling walk; tic-like [jerky] movements of head and face; trembling and shaking of hands); *hypotension, severe* (feeling faint)

Note: *Anticholinergic* and *CNS stimulant* effects are more likely to occur in children with overdose. *Hypotension* may also occur in the elderly at usual doses.

Those indicating need for medical attention only if they continue or are bothersome
Incidence more frequent
Drowsiness; thickening of mucus

Note: Sedative effects are more pronounced with promethazine and less pronounced with trimeprazine and methdilazine, in that order.

Incidence less frequent or rare
> ***Blurred vision or any change in vision; burning or stinging of rectum***—for promethazine rectal dosage form only; ***confusion; difficult or painful urination; dizziness; dryness of mouth, nose, or throat; fast heartbeat; hypotension*** (feeling faint); ***increased sensitivity of skin to sun; increased sweating; loss of appetite; paradoxical reaction*** (nightmares; unusual excitement, nervousness, restlessness, or irritability); ***ringing or buzzing in ears; skin rash***
>
> Note: *Confusion; difficult or painful urination; drowsiness; dizziness; and dryness of mouth, nose, or throat* are more likely to occur in the elderly.
>
> *Nightmares, unusual excitement, nervousness, restlessness, or irritability* are more likely to occur in children and elderly patients.

Patient Consultation

In providing consultation, consider emphasizing the following selected information (» = major clinical significance):

Before using this medication
» Conditions affecting use of most antihistamines, especially:
  Sensitivity to the antihistamine used or to phenothiazine medications
  Pregnancy—Not taking during the 2 weeks before delivery, to avoid possible platelet aggregation in newborn; also, jaundice and extrapyramidal effects may occur in infant
  Breast-feeding—Use not recommended; may cause unusual excitement or irritability in nursing infant; possible association with sudden infant death syndrome (SIDS) and sleep apnea
  Use in children—Increased susceptibility to anticholinergic side effects in newborn or premature infants; hyperexcitability (paradoxical reaction) may occur in older children; possible association with sudden infant death syndrome (SIDS) and sleep apnea; diagnosis of Reye's syndrome may be obscured if extrapyramidal effects occur
  Use in adolescents—Diagnosis of Reye's syndrome may be obscured if extrapyramidal effects occur
  Use in the elderly—Increased susceptibility to CNS and anticholinergic side effects; hyperexcitability (paradoxical reaction) may occur; extrapyramidal symptoms more likely to occur
  Dental—Increased risk of dental problems with prolonged use because of decrease or inhibition of salivary flow; involuntary orofacial muscle movements may result from extrapyramidal effects
  Other medications, especially alcohol or other CNS depressants, anticholinergics, antithyroid agents, epinephrine, extrapyramidal reaction-causing medications, levodopa, MAO inhibitors, or metrizamide (intrathecal)
  Other medical problems, especially angle-closure glaucoma (or predisposition to), bladder neck obstruction, prostatic hypertrophy, or urinary retention; jaundice (for parenteral promethazine)

Proper use of this medication
» Importance of not taking more medication than the amount recommended
  Missed dose: If on scheduled dosing regimen—Using as soon as possible; not using if almost time for next dose; not doubling doses
» Proper storage
For oral dosage forms
  Taking with food, water, or milk to minimize gastric irritation
  Swallowing extended-release dosage forms whole
For injection dosage forms
  Knowing correct administration technique for self-administration; checking with physician if necessary

For rectal dosage forms
  Proper administration technique
For promethazine when used as an antivertigo agent
  Taking 30 minutes to 1 hour before traveling

Precautions while using this medication
  Possible interference with skin tests using allergens; need to inform physician of using medication
  May mask ototoxic effects of large doses of salicylates
» Avoiding use of alcohol or other CNS depressants
» Caution if drowsiness occurs
  Possible dryness of mouth; using sugarless gum or candy, ice, or saliva substitute for relief; checking with physician or dentist if dry mouth continues for more than 2 weeks
  Need to inform physician of use: Possible interference with diagnosis of appendicitis; may mask signs of toxicity from overdosage of other drugs

Side/adverse effects
  Signs of potential side effects, especially blood dyscrasias

General Dosing Information

For oral dosage forms only
Most antihistamines may be taken with food, water, or milk to lessen gastric irritation.

For parenteral dosage forms only
For promethazine
The preferred route of administration is by deep intramuscular injection. Although intravenous administration is well tolerated, promethazine should not be administered in concentrations greater than 25 mg per mL and at a rate in excess of 25 mg per minute. Rapid intravenous administration of promethazine may produce a transient fall in blood pressure.

Intra-arterial administration is not recommended because of the possibility of severe arteriospasm and resultant gangrene; also, subcutaneous administration is not recommended, since chemical irritation has been noted and necrotic lesions have resulted on rare occasions.

METHDILAZINE

Summary of Differences

Pharmacology: Duration of action—6 to 12 hours.
Side/adverse effects: Least sedative effects.

Oral Dosage Forms

METHDILAZINE HYDROCHLORIDE SYRUP USP

Usual adult and adolescent dose: Antihistaminic (H$_1$-receptor)—Oral, 8 mg every six to twelve hours as needed.

Usual geriatric dose: See *Usual adult and adolescent dose.*

Note: Geriatric patients may be more sensitive to the effects of the usual adult dose.

Auxiliary labeling:
• May cause drowsiness.
• Avoid alcoholic beverages.

METHDILAZINE HYDROCHLORIDE TABLETS USP

Usual adult and adolescent dose: Antihistaminic (H$_1$-receptor)—Oral, 8 mg every six to twelve hours as needed.

Usual geriatric dose: See *Usual adult and adolescent dose.*

Note: Geriatric patients may be more sensitive to the effects of the usual adult dose.

Auxiliary labeling:
- May cause drowsiness.
- Avoid alcoholic beverages.

METHDILAZINE HYDROCHLORIDE TABLETS USP (CHEWABLE)

Usual adult and adolescent dose: Antihistaminic (H_1-receptor)—Oral, 8 mg every six to twelve hours as needed.

Usual geriatric dose: See *Usual adult and adolescent dose.*

Note: Geriatric patients may be more sensitive to the effects of the usual adult dose.

Auxiliary labeling:
- May cause drowsiness.
- Avoid alcoholic beverages.

PROMETHAZINE

Summary of Differences

Pharmacology: Duration of action—
   Antihistaminic: 6 to 12 hours.
   Sedative: 2 to 8 hours.
Precautions: Contraindications/Medical problems—Caution needed in jaundice (with parenteral administration).
Side/adverse effects: Most pronounced sedative effects.

Oral Dosage Forms

PROMETHAZINE HYDROCHLORIDE SYRUP USP

Usual adult and adolescent dose:
   Antihistaminic (H_1-receptor)—Oral, 10 to 12.5 mg four times a day before meals and at bedtime; or 25 mg at bedtime as needed.
   Antiemetic—Oral, 25 mg initially, then 10 to 25 mg every four to six hours as needed.
   Antivertigo agent—Oral, 25 mg two times a day as needed.
   Note: For motion sickness, the initial 25-mg dose should be taken one-half to one hour before travel, and the dose repeated 8 to 12 hours later, if necessary.
   Sedative-hypnotic—Oral, 25 to 50 mg for nighttime, presurgical, postsurgical, or obstetrical sedation.
   Note: A 50-mg dose (with an equal amount of meperidine and an appropriate dose of an atropine-like drug) is used the night before surgery to relieve apprehension and produce sleep.

Usual adult prescribing limits: Up to 150 mg daily.

Usual geriatric dose: See *Usual adult and adolescent dose.*

Note: Geriatric patients may be more sensitive to the effects of the usual adult dose.

Auxiliary labeling:
- May cause drowsiness.
- Avoid alcoholic beverages.

PROMETHAZINE HYDROCHLORIDE TABLETS USP

Usual adult and adolescent dose:
   Antihistaminic (H_1-receptor)—Oral, 10 to 12.5 mg four times a day before meals and at bedtime; or 25 mg at bedtime as needed.
   Antiemetic—Oral, 25 mg initially, then 10 to 25 mg every four to six hours as needed.

Antivertigo agent—Oral, 25 mg two times a day as needed.
   Note: For motion sickness, the initial 25-mg dose should be taken one-half to one hour before travel, and the dose repeated 8 to 12 hours later, if necessary.
   Sedative-hypnotic—Oral, 25 to 50 mg for nighttime, presurgical, postsurgical, or obstetrical sedation.
   Note: A 50-mg dose (with an equal amount of meperidine and an appropriate dose of an atropine-like drug) is used the night before surgery to relieve apprehension and produce sleep.

Usual adult prescribing limits: Up to 150 mg daily.

Usual geriatric dose: See *Usual adult and adolescent dose.*

Note: Geriatric patients may be more sensitive to the effects of the usual adult dose.

Auxiliary labeling:
- May cause drowsiness.
- Avoid alcoholic beverages.

Parenteral Dosage Forms

PROMETHAZINE HYDROCHLORIDE INJECTION USP

Usual adult and adolescent dose:
   Antihistaminic (H_1-receptor)—Intramuscular or intravenous, 25 mg; may be repeated within two hours if necessary.
   Antiemetic—Intramuscular or intravenous, 12.5 to 25 mg every four hours as needed.
   Sedative-hypnotic—Intramuscular or intravenous, 25 to 50 mg for nighttime, presurgical, postsurgical, or obstetrical sedation.
   Note: For preoperative and postoperative sedation, 25 to 50 mg of promethazine may be combined with appropriately reduced doses of analgesics and anticholinergics.

   For obstetrical sedation, in the early stages of labor, 50 mg of promethazine will provide sedation and relief of apprehension. After labor is definitely established, 25 to 75 mg of promethazine may be administered with an appropriately reduced dose of a narcotic, and may be repeated once or twice every four hours during the course of a normal labor.

Usual adult prescribing limits: Up to 150 mg daily.

Usual geriatric dose: See *Usual adult and adolescent dose.*

Note: Geriatric patients may be more sensitive to the effects of the usual adult dose.

Rectal Dosage Forms

PROMETHAZINE HYDROCHLORIDE SUPPOSITORIES USP

Usual adult and adolescent dose:
   Antihistaminic (H_1-receptor)—Rectal, 25 mg; may be repeated in two hours if necessary.
   Antiemetic—Rectal, 25 mg initially, then 12.5 to 25 mg every four to six hours as needed.
   Antivertigo agent—Rectal, 25 mg two times a day as needed.
   Sedative-hypnotic—Rectal, 25 to 50 mg for nighttime, presurgical, postsurgical, or obstetrical sedation.
   Note: A 50-mg dose (with an equal amount of meperidine and an appropriate dose of an atropine-like drug) is used the night before surgery to relieve apprehension and produce sleep.

Usual adult prescribing limits: Up to 150 mg daily.

Usual geriatric dose: See *Usual adult and adolescent dose.*

Note: Geriatric patients may be more sensitive to the effects of the usual adult dose.

Auxiliary labeling:
- May cause drowsiness.
- Avoid alcoholic beverages.

TRIMEPRAZINE

Summary of Differences

Pharmacology: Duration of action—3 to 6 hours.

Oral Dosage Forms

Note: The dosing and strengths of the dosage forms available are expressed in terms of trimeprazine base (not the tartrate salt).

TRIMEPRAZINE TARTRATE EXTENDED-RELEASE CAPSULES

Usual adult and adolescent dose: Antihistaminic (H$_1$-receptor)— Oral, 5 mg (base) every twelve hours as needed.

Usual geriatric dose: See *Usual adult and adolescent dose.*

Note: Geriatric patients may be more sensitive to the effects of the usual adult dose.

Auxiliary labeling:
- May cause drowsiness.
- Avoid alcoholic beverages.

TRIMEPRAZINE TARTRATE SYRUP USP

Usual adult and adolescent dose: Antihistaminic (H$_1$-receptor)— Oral, 2.5 mg (base) four times a day as needed.

Usual geriatric dose: See *Usual adult and adolescent dose.*

Note: Geriatric patients may be more sensitive to the effects of the usual adult dose.

Auxiliary labeling:
- May cause drowsiness.
- Avoid alcoholic beverages.

TRIMEPRAZINE TARTRATE TABLETS USP

Usual adult and adolescent dose: Antihistaminic (H$_1$-receptor)— Oral, 2.5 mg (base) four times a day as needed.

Usual geriatric dose: See *Usual adult and adolescent dose.*

Note: Geriatric patients may be more sensitive to the effects of the usual adult dose.

Auxiliary labeling:
- May cause drowsiness.
- Avoid alcoholic beverages.

ANTI-INFLAMMATORY ANALGESICS, NONSTEROIDAL   Systemic

INN: Indomethacin—indometacin.

Some commonly used *brand names* are:

In the U.S.—

Aches-N-Pain [Ibuprofen]
Advil [Ibuprofen]
Advil Caplets [Ibuprofen]
Anaprox [Naproxen]
Anaprox DS [Naproxen]
Ansaid [Flurbiprofen]
Butatab [Phenylbutazone]
Butazolidin [Phenylbutazone]
Butazone [Phenylbutazone]
Children's Advil [Ibuprofen]
Clinoril [Sulindac]
Dolgesic [Ibuprofen]
Dolobid [Diflunisal]
Feldene [Piroxicam]
Genpril [Ibuprofen]
Genpril Caplets [Ibuprofen]
Haltran [Ibuprofen]
Ibren [Ibuprofen]
Ibumed [Ibuprofen]
Ibuprin [Ibuprofen]
Ibupro-600 [Ibuprofen]
Ibuprohm [Ibuprofen]
Ibuprohm Caplets [Ibuprofen]
Ibu-Tab [Ibuprofen]
Ibutex [Ibuprofen]
Ifen [Ibuprofen]
Indameth [Indomethacin]
Indocin [Indomethacin]

Indocin SR [Indomethacin]
Meclofen [Meclofenamate]
Meclomen [Meclofenamate]
Medipren [Ibuprofen]
Medipren Caplets [Ibuprofen]
Midol 200 Caplets [Ibuprofen]
Motrin [Ibuprofen]
Motrin-IB [Ibuprofen]
Motrin-IB Caplets [Ibuprofen]
Nalfon [Fenoprofen]
Nalfon 200 [Fenoprofen]
Naprosyn [Naproxen]
Nuprin [Ibuprofen]
Nuprin Caplets [Ibuprofen]
Orudis [Ketoprofen]
Pamprin-IB [Ibuprofen]
PediaProfen [Ibuprofen]
Ponstel [Mefenamic acid]
Profen [Ibuprofen]
Ro-Profen [Ibuprofen]
Rufen [Ibuprofen]
Tolectin 200 [Tolmetin]
Tolectin 600 [Tolmetin]
Tolectin DS [Tolmetin]
Trendar [Ibuprofen]
Voltaren [Diclofenac]

In Canada—

Actiprofen Caplets [Ibuprofen]
Advil [Ibuprofen]
Advil Caplets [Ibuprofen]
Alka-Butazolidin [Phenylbutazone, Buffered]
Alkabutazone [Phenylbutazone, Buffered]
Alka-Phenylbutazone [Phenylbutazone, Buffered]
Amersol [Ibuprofen]
Anaprox [Naproxen]
Ansaid [Flurbiprofen]
Apo-Ibuprofen [Ibuprofen]
Apo-Indomethacin [Indomethacin]
Apo-Napro-Na [Naproxen]
Apo-Naproxen [Naproxen]
Apo-Phenylbutazone [Phenylbutazone]
Apo-Piroxicam [Piroxicam]
Apo-Sulin [Sulindac]
Butazolidin [Phenylbutazone]
Clinoril [Sulindac]
Dolobid [Diflunisal]
Feldene [Piroxicam]
Froben [Flurbiprofen]
Idarac [Floctafenine]
Indocid [Indomethacin]
Indocid SR [Indomethacin]

Intrabutazone [Phenylbutazone]
Medipren [Ibuprofen]
Medipren Caplets [Ibuprofen]
Motrin [Ibuprofen]
Motrin-IB Caplets [Ibuprofen]
Nalfon [Fenoprofen]
Naprosyn [Naproxen]
Naprosyn-SR [Naproxen]
Naxen [Naproxen]
Novobutazone [Phenylbutazone]
Novomethacin [Indomethacin]
Novonaprox [Naproxen]
Novonaprox Sodium [Naproxen]
Novopirocam [Piroxicam]
Novoprofen [Ibuprofen]
Novo-Sundac [Sulindac]
Nuprin [Ibuprofen]
Orudis [Ketoprofen]
Orudis-E [Ketoprofen]
Orudis-SR [Ketoprofen]
Phenylone Plus [Phenylbutazone, Buffered]
Ponstan [Mefenamic acid]
Rhodis [Ketoprofen]
Rhodis-E [Ketoprofen]
Surgam [Tiaprofenic acid]
Synflex [Naproxen]

Tolectin 200 [Tolmetin]   *Voltaren* [Diclofenac]
Tolectin 400 [Tolmetin]   *Voltaren SR* [Diclofenac]
Tolectin 600 [Tolmetin]

ASPIRIN—See Salicylates (Systemic).
ASPIRIN, BUFFERED—See Salicylates (Systemic).
CHOLINE SALICYLATE—See Salicylates (Systemic).
CHOLINE AND MAGNESIUM SALICYLATES—See Salicylates (Systemic).
DICLOFENAC
Oral
  Diclofenac Sodium Delayed-release Tablets
      In the U.S. and Canada—*Voltaren*
  Diclofenac Sodium Extended-release Tablets*
      In Canada—*Voltaren SR*
Rectal
  Diclofenac Sodium Suppositories*
      In Canada—*Voltaren*
DIFLUNISAL
Oral
  Diflunisal Tablets USP
      In the U.S. and Canada—*Dolobid*
ETODOLAC—See Etodolac (Systemic).
FENOPROFEN
Oral
  Fenoprofen Calcium Capsules USP
      In the U.S.—*Nalfon; Nalfon 200;* GENERIC
      In Canada—*Nalfon*
  Fenoprofen Calcium Tablets USP
      In the U.S.—*Nalfon;* GENERIC
      In Canada—*Nalfon*
FLOCTAFENINE*
Oral
  Floctafenine Tablets*
      In Canada—*Idarac*
FLURBIPROFEN
Oral
  Flurbiprofen Tablets
      In the U.S.—*Ansaid*
      In Canada—*Ansaid; Froben;* GENERIC
IBUPROFEN
Oral
  Ibuprofen Capsules*
      In Canada—*Amersol*
  Ibuprofen Oral Suspension†
      In the U.S.—*Children's Advil; PediaProfen*
  Ibuprofen Tablets USP
      In the U.S.—*Aches-N-Pain; Advil; Advil Caplets; Dolgesic; Genpril; Genpril Caplets; Haltran; Ibren; Ibumed; Ibuprin; Ibupro-600; Ibuprohm; Ibuprohm Caplets; Ibu-Tab; Ibutex; Ifen; Medipren; Medipren Caplets; Midol 200 Caplets; Motrin; Motrin-IB; Motrin-IB Caplets; Nuprin; Nuprin Caplets; Pamprin-IB; Profen; Ro-Profen; Rufen; Trendar;* GENERIC
      In Canada—*Actiprofen Caplets; Advil; Advil Caplets; Apo-Ibuprofen; Medipren; Medipren Caplets; Motrin; Motrin-IB Caplets; Novoprofen; Nuprin;* GENERIC
INDOMETHACIN
Note: See also *Indomethacin (Systemic—for Patent Ductus Arteriosus).*
Oral
  Indomethacin Capsules USP
      In the U.S.—*Indameth; Indocin;* GENERIC
      In Canada—*Apo-Indomethacin; Indocid; Novomethacin*
  Indomethacin Extended-release Capsules USP
      In the U.S.—*Indameth; Indocin SR;* GENERIC
      In Canada—*Indocid SR*
  Indomethacin Oral Suspension USP†
      In the U.S.—*Indocin;* GENERIC

Rectal
  Indomethacin Suppositories USP
      In the U.S.—*Indocin*
      In Canada—*Indocid*
KETOPROFEN
Oral
  Ketoprofen Capsules
      In the U.S.—*Orudis*
      In Canada—*Orudis; Rhodis*
  Ketoprofen Delayed-release Tablets*
      In Canada—*Orudis-E; Rhodis-E*
  Ketoprofen Extended-release Tablets*
      In Canada—*Orudis-SR*
Rectal
  Ketoprofen Suppositories*
      In Canada—*Orudis; Rhodis*
KETOROLAC TROMETHAMINE—See Ketorolac (Systemic).
MAGNESIUM SALICYLATE—See Salicylates (Systemic).
MECLOFENAMATE†
Oral
  Meclofenamate Sodium Capsules USP†
      In the U.S.—*Meclofen; Meclomen;* GENERIC
MEFENAMIC ACID
Oral
  Mefenamic Acid Capsules USP
      In the U.S.—*Ponstel;* GENERIC
      In Canada—*Ponstan*
NAPROXEN
Oral
  Naproxen Oral Suspension
      In the U.S. and Canada—*Naprosyn*
  Naproxen Tablets USP
      In the U.S.—*Naprosyn*
      In Canada—*Apo-Naproxen; Naprosyn; Naxen; Novonaprox*
  Naproxen Extended-release Tablets*
      In Canada—*Naprosyn-SR*
  Naproxen Sodium Tablets USP
      In the U.S.—*Anaprox; Anaprox DS*
      In Canada—*Anaprox; Apo-Napro-Na; Novonaprox Sodium; Synflex*
Rectal
  Naproxen Suppositories*
      In Canada—*Naprosyn; Naxen*
PHENYLBUTAZONE
Oral
  Phenylbutazone Capsules USP†
      In the U.S.—*Butazolidin;* GENERIC
  Phenylbutazone Tablets USP
      In the U.S.—*Butatab; Butazolidin; Butazone;* GENERIC
      In Canada—*Apo-Phenylbutazone; Butazolidin; Novobutazone;* GENERIC
  Phenylbutazone Delayed-release Tablets*
      In Canada—*Intrabutazone*
  Phenylbutazone Tablets, Buffered*
      In Canada—*Alka-Butazolidin; Alkabutazone; Alka-Phenylbutazone; Phenylone Plus*
PIROXICAM
Oral
  Piroxicam Capsules USP
      In the U.S.—*Feldene*
      In Canada—*Apo-Piroxicam; Feldene; Novopirocam*
Rectal
  Piroxicam Suppositories*
      In Canada—*Feldene*
SALSALATE—See Salicylates (Systemic).
SODIUM SALICYLATE—See Salicylates (Systemic).
SULINDAC

Oral
    Sulindac Tablets USP
        In the U.S.—*Clinoril;* GENERIC
        In Canada—*Apo-Sulin; Clinoril; Novo-Sundac*
TIAPROFENIC ACID*
Oral
    Tiaprofenic Acid Tablets*
        In Canada—*Surgam*
TOLMETIN
Oral
    Tolmetin Sodium Capsules USP
        In the U.S.—*Tolectin DS*
        In Canada—*Tolectin 400*
    Tolmetin Sodium Tablets USP
        In the U.S.—*Tolectin 200; Tolectin 600*
        In Canada—*Tolectin 200; Tolectin 600*

---

*Not commercially available in the U.S.
†Not commercially available in Canada.

Category

Note: All of these medications have analgesic, antipyretic, and anti-inflammatory actions; however, indications for specific agents may vary because of lack of specific testing and/or clinical-use data as well as the toxicity of the individual nonsteroidal anti-inflammatory drug (NSAID). **Clinically, most of these agents are used to treat a variety of painful and/or inflammatory conditions, both rheumatic and nonrheumatic, even though the specific uses are not listed in U.S. or Canadian product labeling.**

Antirheumatic (nonsteroidal anti-inflammatory)—Diclofenac; Diflunisal; Fenoprofen; Flurbiprofen; Ibuprofen; Indomethacin; Ketoprofen; Meclofenamate; Naproxen; Phenylbutazone; Piroxicam; Sulindac; Tiaprofenic Acid; Tolmetin.
Analgesic—Diflunisal; Fenoprofen; Floctafenine; Ibuprofen; Ketoprofen; Meclofenamate; Mefenamic Acid; Naproxen.
Antigout agent—Fenoprofen; Ibuprofen; Indomethacin; Ketoprofen; Naproxen; Phenylbutazone; Piroxicam; Sulindac.
Anti-inflammatory (nonsteroidal)—Indomethacin; Naproxen; Sulindac.
Antipyretic—Ibuprofen; Indomethacin.
Antidysmenorrheal—Diclofenac; Flurbiprofen; Ibuprofen; Indomethacin; Ketoprofen; Mefenamic Acid; Naproxen.
Vascular headache prophylactic—Fenoprofen; Ibuprofen; Indomethacin; Mefenamic Acid; Naproxen.
Vascular headache suppressant—Diflunisal; Fenoprofen; Floctafenine; Ibuprofen; Indomethacin; Ketoprofen; Meclofenamate; Mefenamic Acid; Naproxen.
Prostaglandin synthesis inhibitor, renal (Bartter's syndrome)—Indomethacin.

Indications

Note: Bracketed information in the *Indications* section refers to uses not included in U.S. product labeling.

Accepted
Rheumatic disease (treatment), such as:
    Arthritis, rheumatoid—Diclofenac, diflunisal[1], fenoprofen, flurbiprofen, ibuprofen, indomethacin, ketoprofen, meclofenamate, naproxen, phenylbutazone[1], piroxicam, sulindac, tiaprofenic acid, and tolmetin are indicated for the treatment of acute or chronic rheumatoid arthritis.
    Osteoarthritis—Diclofenac, diflunisal, fenoprofen, flurbiprofen, ibuprofen, indomethacin, ketoprofen, meclofenamate, naproxen, phenylbutazone[1], piroxicam, sulindac, tiaprofenic acid, and tolmetin are indicated for relief of acute or chronic osteoarthritis.
    Ankylosing spondylitis—Diclofenac[1], [diflunisal][1], [fenoprofen][1], flurbiprofen, [ibuprofen][1], indomethacin, [ketoprofen], naproxen,

phenylbutazone, [piroxicam], sulindac, and [tolmetin] are indicated for relief of acute or chronic ankylosing spondylitis.
    Arthritis, juvenile—Ibuprofen, indomethacin[1], naproxen, and tolmetin are indicated for relief of acute or chronic juvenile arthritis.
    [Arthritis, psoriatic][1]—Diflunisal, fenoprofen, ibuprofen, indomethacin, ketoprofen, meclofenamate, phenylbutazone, and tolmetin are used in the treatment of psoriatic arthritis.
    [Reiter's disease][1]—Indomethacin is used in the treatment of Reiter's disease.
    [Rheumatic complications associated with Paget's disease of bone][1]—Indomethacin is used in the treatment of this condition.
    Although NSAIDs may be required for relief of [rheumatic complications occurring in association with systemic lupus erythematosus (SLE)][1], extreme caution is recommended because patients with SLE may be predisposed toward NSAID-induced central nervous system (CNS) and/or renal toxicity. Ibuprofen, sulindac, and tolmetin have been shown to cause serious adverse effects, including aseptic meningitis, in patients with SLE. In addition, ibuprofen (although a causal relationship has not been established), meclofenamate, and phenylbutazone have rarely been reported to cause an SLE-like syndrome and/or to exacerbate pre-existing SLE.
    NSAIDs do not affect the progressive course of arthritic disease.
    Concurrent treatment with an adrenocorticoid or a disease-modifying antirheumatic agent may be necessary, depending on the condition being treated and patient response.
Pain (treatment)—Diflunisal, fenoprofen[1], floctafenine, ibuprofen, ketoprofen[1], meclofenamate, mefenamic acid, and naproxen are indicated for relief of mild to moderate pain, especially when anti-inflammatory actions may also be desired, e.g., following dental, obstetric, or orthopedic surgery, and for relief of musculoskeletal pain due to soft tissue athletic injuries (strains or sprains).
    Mefenamic acid is indicated for relief of mild to moderate pain when therapy will not exceed 1 week.
    Those NSAIDs indicated for relief of pain are also recommended for relief of mild to moderate bone pain caused by metastatic neoplastic disease. However, careful patient selection is necessary, especially in patients receiving chemotherapy, because of the potential gastrointestinal or renal toxicity and the platelet aggregation-inhibiting actions of these medications.
Gouty arthritis, acute (treatment); or
[Calcium pyrophosphate deposition disease, acute (treatment)][1]—[Fenoprofen][1], [ibuprofen][1], indomethacin, [ketoprofen][1], naproxen[1], phenylbutazone, [piroxicam][1], and sulindac are indicated [or used] for relief of the pain and inflammation of acute gouty arthritis and [acute calcium pyrophosphate deposition disease (pseudogout; chondrocalcinosis articularis; synovitis, crystal-induced)][1].
    [Long-term prophylactic use of an NSAID may decrease the incidence or severity of recurrent acute gout attacks, especially during the early months of antihyperuricemic therapy. The NSAIDs do not correct hyperuricemia (although diclofenac, diflunisal, and phenylbutazone have some uricosuric activity) and do not eliminate the need for administration of an antihyperuricemic agent for the long-term management of chronic gout. However, phenylbutazone, because of its toxicity, is not recommended for long-term use as prophylaxis against recurrent acute gout attacks.]
Inflammation, nonrheumatic (treatment)—Most of the NSAIDs are indicated [or used] in the treatment of painful nonrheumatic inflammatory conditions, such as:
Athletic injuries;
Bursitis;
Capsulitis;
Synovitis;
Tendinitis; or
Tenosynovitis—Indomethacin[1] and sulindac are indicated for treatment of bursitis and/or tendinitis of the shoulder. Naproxen is indicated for treatment of bursitis and/or tendinitis of any joint. [Other NSAIDs, especially those approved by U.S. and/or Ca-

nadian regulatory agencies for relief of pain, are also used in the treatment of these and other painful inflammatory conditions.][1]

Fever (treatment)—Ibuprofen is indicated for reduction of fever.

[Fever, due to malignancy (treatment)][1]—Indomethacin (rapidly acting dosage forms only) is used to reduce fever in patients with Hodgkin's disease, other lymphomas, and hepatic metastases of solid tumors. Indomethacin should be used only after aspirin and acetaminophen have proven ineffective. If antipyretic therapy at an adequate dosage is not effective within 48 hours, indomethacin should be discontinued.

Dysmenorrhea (treatment)—[Diclofenac][1], [flurbiprofen], ibuprofen, [indomethacin][1], ketoprofen[1], mefenamic acid, and naproxen are indicated for relief of the pain and other symptoms of primary dysmenorrhea. [Other NSAIDs that have been approved by U.S. and/or Canadian regulatory agencies for relief of pain are also used to relieve dysmenorrhea.]

[Because of the high incidence of adverse effects with effective doses of indomethacin, it is recommended that indomethacin be used only for severe primary dysmenorrhea unresponsive to other, less toxic, NSAIDs.]

[In secondary dysmenorrhea due to an intrauterine device, NSAIDs may decrease excessive menstrual blood loss in addition to relieving other symptoms.]

[Headache, vascular (prophylaxis)][1]; or
[Headache, vascular (treatment)][1]—Diflunisal, fenoprofen, floctafenine, ibuprofen, indomethacin, ketoprofen, meclofenamate, mefenamic acid, and naproxen are used to relieve (when taken at the first sign of onset) migraine headache or other vascular headaches. Fenoprofen, ibuprofen, indomethacin, and naproxen are also used chronically to prevent recurrence of such headaches. Fenoprofen, ibuprofen, indomethacin, mefenamic acid, and naproxen may also be taken prior to and during menstruation to prevent migraine associated with menstruation.

[Bartter's syndrome (treatment)][1]—Indomethacin is used in the treatment of Bartter's syndrome. However, its use in this condition has been associated with adverse effects, including pseudotumor cerebri. Because long-term therapy is required, it has been suggested that other, less toxic NSAIDs may be suitable alternatives to indomethacin.

[Pericarditis][1]—Indomethacin (rapidly acting dosage forms only) is used to relieve pain, fever, and inflammation associated with pericarditis.

Unaccepted

Except in the treatment of ankylosing spondylitis, for which it is a treatment of choice, and Bartter's syndrome, indomethacin is not recommended as initial therapy because of its potential for causing severe side effects. Also, although indomethacin, like other NSAIDs, has analgesic and antipyretic activity, it should not be used indiscriminately (because of its toxicity) to relieve pain or reduce fever.

Phenylbutazone is not recommended as initial therapy for any indication. Because of its potential for causing severe side effects, including agranulocytosis and aplastic anemia, it should be used only after less toxic treatments (including other, less toxic NSAIDs) have been found ineffective. In many countries, phenylbutazone is approved only for treatment of severe ankylosing spondylitis unresponsive to other NSAIDs. Use of phenylbutazone to relieve the pain and inflammation of acute painful shoulder (i.e., peritendinitis, capsulitis, or bursitis of that joint) is no longer FDA-approved. It is strongly recommended that use of phenylbutazone be restricted to treatment of severe arthritic disease, gout, or calcium pyrophosphate deposition disease.

Extended-release dosage forms are not recommended for treatment of conditions requiring a rapid onset of action and short-term therapy, e.g., acute gout, acute pain, dysmenorrhea, and calcium pyrophosphate deposition disease.

[1]Not included in Canadian product labeling.

Pharmacology

Mechanism of action/Effect: Nonsteroidal anti-inflammatory drugs (NSAIDs) inhibit the activity of the enzyme cyclo-oxygenase, resulting in decreased formation of precursors of prostaglandins and thromboxanes from arachidonic acid. Also, meclofenamate and mefenamic acid have been shown to inhibit competitively the actions of prostaglandins. Although the resultant decrease in prostaglandin synthesis and activity in various tissues may be responsible for many of the therapeutic (and adverse) effects of NSAIDs, other actions may also contribute significantly to the therapeutic effects of these medications.

Antirheumatic (nonsteroidal anti-inflammatory)—Act via analgesic and anti-inflammatory mechanisms; the therapeutic effects are not due to pituitary-adrenal stimulation. These medications do not affect the progressive course of rheumatoid arthritis.

Analgesic—May block pain impulse generation via a peripheral action that may involve reduction of the activity of prostaglandins, and possibly inhibition of the synthesis or actions of other substances that sensitize pain receptors to mechanical or chemical stimulation. The antibradykinin activity of ketoprofen may also be involved in relief of pain, because bradykinin has been shown to act together with prostaglandins to cause pain.

Antigout agent—Act via analgesic and anti-inflammatory mechanisms; do not correct hyperuricemia.

Anti-inflammatory (nonsteroidal)—Exact mechanisms have not been determined. NSAIDs may act peripherally in inflamed tissue, probably by reducing prostaglandin activity in these tissues and possibly by inhibiting the synthesis and/or actions of other local mediators of the inflammatory response. Inhibition of leukocyte migration, inhibition of the release and/or actions of lysosomal enzymes, and actions on other cellular and immunological processes in mesenchymal and connective tissue may be involved. Indomethacin has been shown to inhibit phosphodiesterase, with a resultant increase in intracellular cyclic adenosine monophosphate (cAMP) concentration. Ketoprofen has been shown to inhibit leukotriene synthesis, inhibit bradykinin activity, and stabilize lysosomal membranes.

Antipyretic—Probably produce antipyresis by acting centrally on the hypothalamic heat-regulating center to produce peripheral vasodilation, resulting in increased blood flow through the skin, sweating, and heat loss. The central action probably involves reduction of prostaglandin activity in the hypothalamus.

Antidysmenorrheal—By inhibiting the synthesis and activity of intrauterine prostaglandins (which are thought to be responsible for the pain and other symptoms of primary dysmenorrhea), NSAIDs decrease uterine contractility and uterine pressure, increase uterine perfusion, and relieve ischemic as well as spasmodic pain. The antibradykinin activity of ketoprofen may also be involved in relief of dysmenorrhea, because bradykinin has been shown to induce uterine contractions and to act together with prostaglandins to cause pain. Also, NSAIDs may relieve to some extent extrauterine symptoms (such as headache, nausea, and vomiting) that may be associated with excessive prostaglandin production.

Vascular headache prophylactic and suppressant—Analgesic actions may be involved in relief of headache. Also, by reducing prostaglandin activity, NSAIDs may directly prevent or relieve certain types of headache thought to be caused by prostaglandin-induced dilation or constriction of cerebral blood vessels.

Prostaglandin synthesis inhibitor, renal—Inhibition of renal prostaglandin synthesis probably is responsible for indomethacin's beneficial effect in patients with Bartter's syndrome, which is thought to be caused by excessive production of renal prostaglandins.

Other actions/effects:

NSAIDs inhibit platelet aggregation. However, their antiplatelet effect, unlike that of aspirin, is reversible. Single doses of 4 to

10 mg of flurbiprofen inhibit platelet aggregation. With diflunisal, the effect is clinically significant only with greater-than-recommended daily doses. Also, usual doses of meclofenamate or mefenamic acid may not significantly alter platelet aggregability. Recovery of platelet function may occur within 1 day after discontinuation of diclofenac, diflunisal, flurbiprofen, ibuprofen, indomethacin, or sulindac; 2 days after discontinuation of tolmetin; 4 days after discontinuation of naproxen; or 2 weeks following discontinuation of piroxicam.

Diclofenac, diflunisal, and phenylbutazone also have uricosuric activity.

Studies have demonstrated that IgM rheumatoid factor production (which may be partially mediated by prostaglandins) may be decreased (but not totally inhibited) during NSAID therapy. However, because these medications do not affect the progressive course of rheumatoid arthritis, the clinical significance of this effect has not been determined.

It has been proposed that the gastrointestinal toxicity of NSAIDs may be caused primarily by reduction of the synthesis and activity of prostaglandins (which exert a protective effect on the gastrointestinal mucosa) because upper gastrointestinal toxicity has been reported following rectal or parenteral administration of some of these medications. However, when administered orally, some of these acidic medications probably also exert a direct irritant or erosive effect on the mucosa.

The renal toxicity associated with NSAIDs (i.e., decreased renal perfusion, sodium and fluid retention, and decreased renal function) may be caused by inhibition of renal prostaglandins, which are directly involved in the maintenance of renal hemodynamics and sodium and fluid balance. Renal prostaglandins are especially important in maintaining renal function in the presence of generalized vasoconstriction or volume depletion.

Sulindac is a prodrug; its sulfide metabolite is the active substance. Because this active metabolite is not excreted via the kidneys, renal toxicity may be less likely with sulindac than with other NSAIDs. However, there have been reports of renal toxicity associated with sulindac therapy.

The analgesic, antipyretic, and anti-inflammatory effects of NSAIDs may mask symptoms of the onset and/or progression of an infection.

Therapeutic effect: When these medications are used in the treatment of arthritis, their analgesic actions may produce some relief of pain within the first day or two. Significant relief of other symptoms of inflammation usually occurs within a few days to one week; however, in severe cases, two weeks or more of continuous use may be required.

Drug and Indication	Onset of Action	Peak Effect	Duration of Action
Diflunisal Pain	1 hr	2–3 hr	8–12 hr
Ibuprofen Pain	0.5 hr		4–6 hr
Indomethacin Gout Heat, tenderness Swelling	2–4 hr	2–3 days 3–5 days	
Naproxen Pain	1 hr	2–4 hr	Up to 7 hr
Piroxicam Gout	2–4 hr	3–5 days	24 hr

Precautions to Consider

Cross-sensitivity and/or related problems

Patients sensitive to one of the nonsteroidal anti-inflammatory drugs (NSAIDs), including aspirin, ketorolac, and NSAIDs no longer commercially available (such as oxyphenbutazone, suprofen, and zomepirac) may be sensitive to any of the other NSAIDs also.

NSAIDs may cause bronchoconstriction or anaphylaxis in aspirin-sensitive asthmatics, especially those with aspirin-induced nasal polyps, asthma, and other allergic reactions (the "aspirin triad").

Patients with bronchospastic reactions to aspirin may be desensitized to this effect by administration of initially small and gradually increasing doses of aspirin. Desensitization must be carried out by physicians who are experienced with the technique, in a facility having personnel, equipment, and medications immediately available for treatment of any adverse reaction to the medication (especially anaphylaxis or severe bronchospasm). Desensitization to aspirin also desensitizes the patient to other NSAIDs. However, unless aspirin or another NSAID is then administered on a daily basis, sensitivity to these medications redevelops within a few days.

Geriatrics

For all NSAIDs: Whether geriatric patients are at increased risk of serious gastrointestinal toxicity during NSAID therapy has not been established. However, NSAID-induced gastrointestinal ulceration and/or bleeding may be more likely to cause serious consequences, including fatalities, in geriatric patients than in younger adults. In addition, elderly patients are more likely to have age-related renal function impairment, which may increase the risk of NSAID-induced hepatic or renal toxicity and may also require dosage reduction to prevent accumulation of the medication. Some clinicians recommend that geriatric patients, especially those 70 years of age or older, be given one-half of the usual adult dose initially. Also, careful monitoring of the patient is recommended.

For flurbiprofen: Studies have shown that the peak plasma concentration of flurbiprofen may be increased in females 74 to 94 years of age, but not in males 66 to 90 years of age.

For indomethacin: In addition to the increased risks of therapy with any NSAID as described above, geriatric patients are more likely to develop adverse CNS effects, especially confusion, while taking indomethacin.

For ketoprofen: Studies have shown that protein binding and clearance of ketoprofen may be reduced, leading to increased and prolonged serum concentration and elimination half-life.

For naproxen: Studies have shown that the unbound (free) fraction of naproxen, but not the total plasma concentration, may be increased in geriatric patients. The steady-state concentration of unbound naproxen may be almost doubled in geriatric patients as compared with younger adults.

For phenylbutazone: In patients 60 years of age and over, therapy should be limited to short periods (not to exceed 1 week if possible) because of the high risk of severe, possibly fatal, toxic reactions. Specifically, the risk of aplastic anemia and agranulocytosis is increased in elderly patients.

For piroxicam: Studies in geriatric patients have shown a tendency toward increased elimination half-life and steady-state plasma concentration in these patients, especially elderly females.

Dental

NSAIDs may cause soreness, irritation, or ulceration of the oral mucosa.

Most of the NSAIDs may rarely cause leukopenia and/or thrombocytopenia, which may result in an increased incidence of microbial infection, delayed healing, and gingival bleeding. If leukopenia or thrombocytopenia occurs, dental work should be deferred until blood counts have returned to normal, and patients should be instructed in proper oral hygiene, including caution in use of regular toothbrushes, dental floss, and toothpicks.

Drug interactions and/or related problems

See *Table 1*, page 185.

Contraindications/Medical problems

The contraindications/medical problems included have been selected on the basis of their potential clinical significance (reasons given in parentheses where appropriate)—not necessarily inclusive (» = major clinical significance).

See also *Table 2*, page 195.

» Caution is recommended in geriatric patients, who may be more likely to develop adverse hepatic or renal effects with these medications and in whom gastrointestinal ulceration or bleeding is more likely to cause serious consequences, including fatalities.

Caution is also recommended when an NSAID, especially fenoprofen, is used in patients who developed genitourinary tract problems such as dysuria, cystitis, hematuria, nephritis, or nephrotic syndrome during treatment with another NSAID.

The sodium content of diclofenac sodium, meclofenamate sodium, naproxen sodium, naproxen oral suspension, and tolmetin sodium should be considered when selecting an NSAID for patients who must restrict their sodium intake.

Side/Adverse Effects

See also *Table 3*, page 199.

Note: *Hypersensitivity reactions* with these medications may be similar to those reported for aspirin, i.e., *rhinosinusitis/asthma* or *angioedema/urticaria. Anaphylaxis* has also been reported, both in aspirin-sensitive patients and in those without known hypersensitivity to any of these agents. The risk of anaphylaxis, characterized by respiratory distress, circulatory collapse, and angioedema and/or urticaria with or without pruritus, may be increased when previously discontinued therapy with one of these medications is reinstituted. Although anaphylaxis occurs rarely with these agents, several reports have indicated a higher incidence of anaphylactic reactions with tolmetin than with the others.

Other *hypersensitivity reactions* affecting multiple body systems have also been reported with several of the NSAIDs. A hypersensitivity syndrome consisting of fever and chills, skin rashes or other cutaneous manifestations, hepatotoxicity, renal toxicity (including renal failure), leukopenia, thrombocytopenia, eosinophilia, inflamed glands or lymph nodes, and arthralgias has been reported rarely with diflunisal and with sulindac. Fever, skin rashes, and arthralgias have also preceded fenoprofen-induced renal toxicity. In addition, a syndrome of fever and chills, nausea, vomiting, and abdominal pain has been reported with ibuprofen, and a serum sickness- or influenza-like syndrome that may consist of troubled breathing, arthralgias, fever and chills, fatigue, pruritus, and/or skin rash or other cutaneous manifestations, has been reported with ibuprofen (although a positive causal relationship has not been established), meclofenamate, phenylbutazone, piroxicam, and tolmetin.

The antipyretic, analgesic, and anti-inflammatory actions of NSAIDs may mask symptoms of the occurrence or worsening of infections. *Reactivation of latent pulmonary tuberculosis* has been reported in a few patients receiving indomethacin.

Two cases of *biliary obstruction* associated with sulindac therapy have been reported. The obstruction was caused in each case by the presence in the common bile duct of a "sludge" of crystals containing a sulindac metabolite.

Metabolic acidosis and *respiratory alkalosis* have also been reported rarely (incidences <1%) with phenylbutazone.

Patients 40 years of age and older may be more susceptible to the toxic effects of phenylbutazone. In patients 60 years of age and older, there is an increased risk of severe, possibly fatal, toxic reactions.

Phenylbutazone-induced *agranulocytosis* may occur with a rapid onset, especially in relatively young patients. *Aplastic anemia* may occur more frequently in patients receiving prolonged therapy, especially older female patients. Both *agranulocytosis* and *aplastic anemia* are more likely to occur in geriatric patients.

Because diflunisal is a salicylic acid derivative, the possibility that it may be associated with the development of *Reye's syndrome* in children, teenagers, or young adults with acute febrile illnesses, especially influenza or varicella, should be kept in mind.

The following side/adverse effects have been selected on the basis of their potential clinical significance (possible signs and symptoms in parentheses where appropriate)—not necessarily inclusive:

Those indicating need for cessation of therapy and immediate medical attention

Signs and symptoms of overdose

For phenylbutazone

Bluish color of fingernails, lips, or skin; convulsions, especially in children; difficulty in hearing or ringing or buzzing in the ears; dizziness or lightheadedness; hallucinations; headache, severe and continuing; increase or decrease in blood pressure; mood or mental changes; nausea, vomiting, or stomach pain, severe; periorbital edema (swelling around the eyes); **shortness of breath, troubled breathing, or unusually slow, fast, or irregular breathing; swelling of face, hands, feet, or lower legs**

Note: The lowest fatal doses reported for phenylbutazone are 14 grams (in an adult) and 2 grams (in a 3-year-old child). The highest doses reported to have been survived are 40 grams (in a young adult) and 5 grams (in a 3-year-old child).

Laboratory findings in overdose may reveal respiratory or metabolic acidosis or alkalosis, other electrolyte disturbances, impaired hepatic or renal function, and abnormalities of formed blood elements.

Late manifestations of massive overdosage may occur 2 to 7 days following ingestion and may include hepatomegaly, jaundice, electrocardiographic abnormalities, blood dyscrasias, and ulceration of the buccal or gastrointestinal mucosa.

For other NSAIDs

Note: The symptoms of overdose of most of the other NSAIDs have not been described as completely as for phenylbutazone. Reported symptoms have generally reflected the gastrointestinal, renal, and CNS toxicities of these medications. Following overdosage with a propionic acid derivative or indomethacin, patients may remain asymptomatic or experience only relatively mild *CNS effects* (e.g., lethargy, drowsiness) or *gastrointestinal symptoms* (e.g., abdominal pain, nausea, vomiting). However, more serious effects, such as *gastrointestinal hemorrhage, acute renal failure, convulsions, and coma* have been reported with these, as well as other, NSAIDs. *Convulsions* may be especially likely to occur following mefenamic acid overdose. Also, *hypoprothrombinemia* has been reported following overdose of several NSAIDs.

Patient Consultation

See *Table 4*, page 207.

General Dosing Information

The sodium content of diclofenac sodium, meclofenamate sodium, naproxen sodium, naproxen oral suspension, and tolmetin sodium should be considered when selecting a nonsteroidal anti-inflammatory drug (NSAID) for patients who must restrict their sodium intake. Also, the sucrose content of ibuprofen and naproxen suspensions must be considered when selecting an NSAID for patients who must restrict their sucrose intake.

Patients who do not respond to one NSAID may respond to another. In responsive patients, partial symptomatic relief of arthritic symptoms usually occurs within 1 or 2 weeks, although maximum effectiveness may occur only after several weeks of therapy.

A reduction of initial dosage, possibly to as low as one-half the usual adult dose, is recommended for geriatric patients, especially those 70 years of age or older. However, if the reduced dose fails to produce an adequate clinical response and the medication is well-tolerated, dosage may be increased as required and tolerated.

A reduction of dosage may also be required to prevent accumulation of NSAIDs and/or their metabolites (some of which may be unstable and may be hydrolyzed to the parent compound when their excretion is delayed) in patients with renal function impairment.

Long-term use of NSAIDs in doses that approach or exceed maximum dosage recommendations should be considered only if the clinical benefit is increased sufficiently to offset the higher risk of gastrointestinal toxicity or other adverse effects.

Mefenamic acid, indomethacin, phenylbutazone, and piroxicam should be administered immediately after meals or with food or antacids to reduce gastrointestinal irritation. The other NSAIDs (except for enteric-coated dosage forms) are also preferably taken after meals or with food or antacids to reduce gastrointestinal irritation, especially during chronic use; however, for faster absorption when a rapid initial effect is required (as for analgesic or antipyretic use), the first few doses may be taken 30 minutes before meals or at least 2 hours after meals. If an antacid is taken concurrently, an aluminum and magnesium-containing formulation may be preferred, since studies have shown that this formulation does not adversely affect absorption of most NSAIDs.

It is recommended that solid oral dosage forms of NSAIDs be taken with a full glass (240 mL) of water and that the patient remain in an upright position for 15 to 30 minutes after administration. These measures may reduce the risk of tablets or capsules becoming lodged in the esophagus, which has been reported to cause prolonged esophageal irritation and difficulty in swallowing in some patients receiving these medications.

In the treatment of primary dysmenorrhea, maximum benefit is achieved by initiating NSAID therapy as rapidly as possible after the onset of menses. Prophylactic therapy (i.e., starting NSAID administration a few days prior to the expected onset of the menstrual period) has not been found to provide additional therapeutic benefit.

Concurrent use of an NSAID with an opioid analgesic provides additive analgesia and may permit lower doses of the opioid analgesic to be utilized.

The analgesic activity of non-opioid analgesics is subject to a ceiling effect. Therefore, administration of an NSAID in higher-than-recommended analgesic doses may not provide additional therapeutic benefit in the treatment of pain not associated with inflammation.

In the treatment of arthritis, most of these agents have been shown to provide additional symptomatic relief when administered concurrently with gold compounds or glucocorticoids. NSAIDs may permit reduction of glucocorticoid dosage; however, reductions of glucocorticoid dosage, especially following long-term use, should be gradual to avoid symptoms associated with adrenal insufficiency or other manifestations of too-sudden withdrawal.

DICLOFENAC

Summary of Differences

Indications: See *Indications*.
Pharmacology:
  Physicochemical characteristics—Chemical group—A phenylacetic acid derivative.

Precautions:
  Pregnancy/reproduction—
    Crosses the placenta.
    Embryotoxicity and other adverse effects, but not teratogenicity, demonstrated in animal studies.
  Drug interactions and/or related problems—See *Table 1, page 185.*
  Contraindications/Medical problems—
    Caution in patients who must restrict their sodium intake. See also *Table 2, page 195.*
  Patient monitoring—Routine liver function tests recommended.
Side/adverse effects: See *Table 3, page 199.*

Additional Dosing Information

See also *General Dosing Information.*

Diclofenac therapy should be discontinued if gastrointestinal bleeding or ulceration occurs.

For oral dosage forms only
The delayed-release tablets and the extended-release tablets are to be swallowed whole, not crushed or chewed.

Oral Dosage Forms

DICLOFENAC SODIUM DELAYED-RELEASE TABLETS

Usual adult dose: Antirheumatic (nonsteroidal anti-inflammatory)—
  Rheumatoid arthritis: Oral, 150 to 200 mg a day in two to four divided doses, initially. After a satisfactory response has been obtained, dosage should be reduced to the minimum dose that provides continuing control of symptoms, usually 75 to 100 mg a day in three divided doses.
  Osteoarthritis: Oral, 100 to 150 mg a day in two or three divided doses, initially. After a satisfactory response has been obtained, dosage should be reduced to the minimum dose that provides continuing control of symptoms.
  Ankylosing spondylitis[1]: Oral, 100 to 125 mg a day in four or five divided doses, initially. After a satisfactory response has been obtained, dosage should be reduced to the minimum dose that provides continuing control of symptoms.

Auxiliary labeling:
  • Swallow tablets whole.
  • Take with a full glass of water.
  • Avoid alcoholic beverages.

DICLOFENAC SODIUM EXTENDED-RELEASE TABLETS

Note: Diclofenac sodium extended-release tablets are not commercially available in the U.S.

Usual adult dose: Antirheumatic (nonsteroidal anti-inflammatory)—
  Oral, 100 mg a day, in the morning or evening.

Note: The extended-release tablets are not intended for initial therapy; they are to be administered only after the daily maintenance dose has been determined (using the delayed-release tablets) to be 100 mg.

Auxiliary labeling:
  • Swallow tablets whole.
  • Take with a full glass of water.
  • Avoid alcoholic beverages.

Rectal Dosage Forms

DICLOFENAC SODIUM SUPPOSITORIES

Note: Diclofenac sodium suppositories are not commercially available in the U.S.

Usual adult dose: Antirheumatic (nonsteroidal anti-inflammatory)—
  Rectal, 50 or 100 mg, as a substitute for the last oral dose of the day.

Usual adult prescribing limits: Total daily dosage (oral and rectal) should not exceed 150 mg.

Auxiliary labeling:
- Avoid alcoholic beverages.
- For rectal use.

DIFLUNISAL

Summary of Differences

Indications: See *Indications*.
Pharmacology: Physicochemical characteristics—
   Chemical group: A salicylate derivative, although not metabolized to salicylate *in vivo*.
   pKa: 3.3.
Precautions:
   Pregnancy/reproduction—Embryotoxic and teratogenic effects demonstrated in studies in rabbits.
   Drug interactions and/or related problems—See *Table 1*, page 185.
   Contraindications/Medical problems—See *Table 2*, page 195.
Side/adverse effects: See *Table 3*, page 199.

Additional Dosing Information

See also *General Dosing Information*.

Administration of a 1-gram initial loading dose is recommended to provide faster onset of analgesic action, shorter time to peak analgesic effect, and greater peak analgesic action. For long-term use, the initial loading dose decreases the time needed to reach steady-state plasma concentrations; if a loading dose is not administered, 2 to 3 days may be required to evaluate changes in treatment regimens.

In patients with impaired renal function, especially if renal function is decreased to $1/2$ the normal value or below, a reduction in dosage and/or an increase in the dosing interval may be necessary to prevent diflunisal accumulation.

Tablets are to be swallowed whole, not crushed or chewed.

Because diflunisal is not hydrolyzed to salicylic acid *in vivo,* serum salicylate concentration cannot be used as a guide to dosage or potential toxicity during therapy.

Oral Dosage Forms

DIFLUNISAL TABLETS USP

Usual adult dose:
   Antirheumatic (nonsteroidal anti-inflammatory)—
     Rheumatoid arthritis[1] or
     Osteoarthritis: Oral, 250 to 500 mg two times a day; dosage may be increased or decreased according to patient response.
   Analgesic—Oral, 1 gram initially, followed by 500 mg every eight to twelve hours as needed.
     Note: For some patients, 500 mg initially followed by 250 mg every eight to twelve hours may be appropriate, depending on the severity of pain or the age, weight, or response of the patient.

Usual adult prescribing limits: Up to 1.5 grams daily.

Auxiliary labeling:
- Swallow tablets whole.
- Take with a full glass of water.
- Avoid alcoholic beverages.

[1]Not included in Canadian product labeling.

FENOPROFEN

Summary of Differences

Indications: See *Indications*.
Pharmacology: Physicochemical characteristics—
   Chemical group: A propionic acid derivative.
   pKa: 4.5.
Precautions:
   Pregnancy/reproduction—No teratogenic or other adverse effects demonstrated in animal studies.
   Drug interactions and/or related problems—See *Table 1*, page 185.
   Contraindications/Medical problems—See *Table 2*, page 195.
Side/adverse effects: See *Table 3*, page 199.

Additional Dosing Information

See also *General Dosing Information.*

In the treatment of arthritis, improvement in condition may occur within a few days, but 2 to 3 weeks of continuous use on a regular basis may be required for maximum effectiveness.

Oral Dosage Forms

Note: Bracketed uses in the *Dosage Forms* section refer to categories of use and/or indications that are not included in U.S. product labeling.

FENOPROFEN CALCIUM CAPSULES USP

Usual adult dose:
   Antirheumatic (nonsteroidal anti-inflammatory)—Oral, 300 to 600 mg of fenoprofen (free acid), depending on the severity of the symptoms, three or four times a day.
     Note: Higher doses generally are required in rheumatoid arthritis than in osteoarthritis.
   Analgesic (mild to moderate pain or [dysmenorrhea])[1]—Oral, 200 mg of fenoprofen (free acid) every four to six hours as needed.

Usual adult prescribing limits: Antirheumatic (nonsteroidal anti-inflammatory)—Up to 3.2 grams of fenoprofen (free acid) daily.

Auxiliary labeling:
- Take with a full glass of water.
- May cause drowsiness.
- Avoid alcoholic beverages.

FENOPROFEN CALCIUM TABLETS USP

Usual adult dose:
   Antirheumatic (nonsteroidal anti-inflammatory)—Oral, 300 to 600 mg of fenoprofen (free acid), depending on the severity of the symptoms, three or four times a day.
     Note: Higher doses generally are required in rheumatoid arthritis than in osteoarthritis.
   Analgesic (mild to moderate pain or [dysmenorrhea])[1]—Oral, 200 mg of fenoprofen (free acid) every four to six hours as needed.

Usual adult prescribing limits: Antirheumatic (nonsteroidal anti-inflammatory)—Up to 3.2 grams of fenoprofen (free acid) daily.

Auxiliary labeling:
- Take with a full glass of water.
- May cause drowsiness.
- Avoid alcoholic beverages.

[1]Not included in Canadian product labeling.

FLOCTAFENINE

Summary of Differences

Indications: See *Indications*.
Precautions:
  Pregnancy/reproduction—Embryotoxicity but not teratogenicity demonstrated in animal studies.
  Drug interactions and/or related problems—See *Table 1*, page 185.
  Contraindications/Medical problems—See *Table 2*, page 195.
Side/adverse effects: See *Table 3*, page 199.

Additional Dosing Information

See also *General Dosing Information*.

Because the safety and efficacy of floctafenine for long-term administration has not been established, this medication is recommended for short-term use only.

Oral Dosage Forms

FLOCTAFENINE TABLETS

Note: Floctafenine tablets are not commercially available in the U.S.

Usual adult dose: Analgesic—Oral, 200 to 400 mg every six to eight hours, as needed.

Usual adult prescribing limits: Dosage should not exceed 1.2 grams per day.

Auxiliary labeling:
  • Take with a full glass of water.
  • May cause drowsiness.
  • Avoid alcoholic beverages.

FLURBIPROFEN

Summary of Differences

Indications: See *Indications*.
Pharmacology:
  Physicochemical characteristics—
    Chemical group: A propionic acid derivative.
    pKa: 4.22.
Precautions:
  Pregnancy/reproduction—Embryocidal and fetotoxic, but not teratogenic, effects demonstrated in animal studies.
  Drug interactions and/or related problems—See *Table 1*, page 185.
  Contraindications/Medical problems—See *Table 2*, page 195.
Side/adverse effects: See *Table 3*, page 199.

Oral Dosage Forms

Note: Bracketed uses in the *Dosage Forms* section refer to categories of use and/or indications that are not included in U.S. product labeling.

FLURBIPROFEN TABLETS

Usual adult dose:
  Antirheumatic (nonsteroidal anti-inflammatory)—
    Rheumatoid arthritis or

Osteoarthritis: Oral, 200 to 300 mg a day in two to four divided doses, initially. Dosage may then be individualized according to the severity of the disease and patient response.
Ankylosing spondylitis: Oral, 200 mg a day in four divided doses, initially, although some patients may require 250 to 300 mg a day.
[Antidysmenorrheal]—Oral, 50 mg four times a day.

Usual adult prescribing limits: The maximum recommended single dose is 100 mg. Total daily dosage should not exceed 300 mg. This maximum dose is recommended for short-term use only, i.e., for initiation of therapy or for treating acute exacerbations of symptoms; it should not be used as a maintenance dose.

Auxiliary labeling:
  • Take with a full glass of water.
  • Avoid alcoholic beverages.

IBUPROFEN

Summary of Differences

Indications: See *Indications*.
Pharmacology:
  Physicochemical characteristics—
    Chemical group: A propionic acid derivative.
    pKa: 4.43.
Precautions:
  Pregnancy/reproduction—Teratogenic effects in animals have not been shown.
  Drug interactions and/or related problems—See *Table 1*, page 185.
  Contraindications/Medical problems—See *Table 2*, page 195.
Side/adverse effects: See *Table 3*, page 199.

Additional Dosing Information

See also *General Dosing Information*.

In the treatment of arthritis, improvement in condition may occur within 7 days, but 1 to 2 weeks of continuous use on a regular basis may be required for maximum effectiveness.

Oral Dosage Forms

IBUPROFEN CAPSULES

Note: Ibuprofen capsules are not commercially available in the U.S.

Usual adult and adolescent dose: Antirheumatic (nonsteroidal anti-inflammatory)—Oral, 1.2 to 3.2 grams a day in three or four divided doses. After a satisfactory response has been obtained, dosage should be reduced to the lowest maintenance dose that provides continuing control of symptoms.

  Note: Higher doses generally are required in rheumatoid arthritis than in osteoarthritis.

Analgesic (mild to moderate pain);
Antipyretic; or
Antidysmenorrheal—Oral, 200 to 400 mg every four to six hours as needed.

Usual adult prescribing limits: Up to 3.2 grams daily. The maximum dosage should be used only if the clinical benefit is increased sufficiently to offset the higher risk of adverse effects.

Note: Some clinicians prescribe up to 3.6 grams daily.

Auxiliary labeling:
  • Take with a full glass of water.
  • May cause drowsiness.
  • Avoid alcoholic beverages.

IBUPROFEN ORAL SUSPENSION

Note: Ibuprofen oral suspension is not commercially available in Canada.

Usual adult and adolescent dose:

Antirheumatic (nonsteroidal anti-inflammatory)—Oral, 1.2 to 3.2 grams a day in three or four divided doses. After a satisfactory response has been obtained, dosage should be reduced to the lowest maintenance dose that provides continuing control of symptoms.

Note: Higher doses generally are required in rheumatoid arthritis than in osteoarthritis.

Analgesic (mild to moderate pain);

Antipyretic; or

Antidysmenorrheal—Oral, 200 to 400 mg every four to six hours as needed.

Usual adult prescribing limits: Antirheumatic—Up to 3.2 grams daily. The maximum dosage should be used only if the clinical benefit is increased sufficiently to offset the higher risk of adverse effects.

Note: Some clinicians prescribe up to 3.6 grams daily.

Auxiliary labeling:
- Shake well.
- Take with food or antacids.
- Avoid alcoholic beverages.

IBUPROFEN TABLETS USP

Usual adult and adolescent dose:

Antirheumatic (nonsteroidal anti-inflammatory)—Oral, 1.2 to 3.2 grams a day in three or four divided doses. After a satisfactory response has been obtained, dosage should be reduced to the lowest maintenance dose that provides continuing control of symptoms.

Note: Higher doses generally are required in rheumatoid arthritis than in osteoarthritis.

Analgesic (mild to moderate pain);

Antipyretic; or

Antidysmenorrheal—Oral, 200 to 400 mg every four to six hours as needed.

Usual adult prescribing limits: Antirheumatic—Up to 3.2 grams daily. The maximum dosage should be used only if the clinical benefit is increased sufficiently to offset the higher risk of adverse effects.

Note: Some clinicians prescribe up to 3.6 grams daily.

For patient self-medication (200-mg tablets)—Up to 6 tablets in twenty-four hours.

Auxiliary labeling:
- Take with a full glass of water.
- May cause drowsiness.
- Avoid alcoholic beverages.

INDOMETHACIN

Summary of Differences

Indications:

Drug of first choice in ankylosing spondylitis; for other indications (except Bartter's syndrome), recommended only for patients unresponsive to less toxic nonsteroidal anti-inflammatory agents. See also *Indications*.

Pharmacology:

Physicochemical characteristics—

Chemical group: An indoleacetic acid derivative.

pKa: 4.5.

Precautions:

Pregnancy/reproduction—

Crosses the placenta.

Fetotoxic, teratogenic, and other adverse effects demonstrated in animal studies.

Breast-feeding—Excreted in breast milk; one report of convulsions in a breast-fed infant exposed to the medication.

Geriatrics—Also, increased risk of adverse CNS effects, especially confusion.

Drug interactions and/or related problems—See *Table 1*, page 185.

Contraindications/Medical problems—See *Table 2*, page 195.

Patient monitoring—Routine monitoring of liver function and periodic stool tests for occult blood loss recommended.

Side/adverse effects: See *Table 3*, page 199.

Additional Dosing Information

See also *General Dosing Information*.

Indomethacin should be administered in the lowest dose that provides symptomatic relief. Doses greater than 150 to 200 mg per day may increase the risk of adverse effects without providing additional clinical benefit. If therapy is to be continued after the acute phase of the disease has been controlled, periodic attempts should be made to reduce the dose to the lowest dose providing continuing control of symptoms.

If minor adverse effects occur, dosage should be reduced and the patient carefully monitored. If severe side effects occur, therapy should be discontinued.

For oral dosage forms only

Oral dosage forms of indomethacin should always be administered after meals or with food or an antacid to reduce gastrointestinal irritation. However, the oral suspension should not be mixed with an antacid or other liquid prior to use.

To facilitate dosage adjustment and assessment of patient tolerance of the medication, it is recommended that an immediate-release, rather than the extended-release, dosage form be used for initiation of therapy or to increase the daily dose. If the extended-release dosage form is used for initial therapy, or to increase the daily dose, careful observation of the patient is recommended.

For rectal dosage form only

To ensure maximum absorption, the suppository should be retained for at least one full hour after insertion.

Oral Dosage Forms

Note: Bracketed uses in the *Dosage Forms* section refer to categories of use and/or indications that are not included in U.S. product labeling.

INDOMETHACIN CAPSULES USP

Usual adult dose:

Antirheumatic (nonsteroidal anti-inflammatory)—Oral, initially 25 or 50 mg two to four times a day; if well tolerated, the dosage per day may be increased by 25 or 50 mg at weekly intervals until a satisfactory response is obtained or up to a maximum dose of 200 mg per day.

Note: In acute flare-ups of rheumatoid arthritis, dosage may be increased by 25 or 50 mg daily, as needed and tolerated.

For those arthritic patients who have persistent night pain and/or morning stiffness, up to 100 mg of the total daily dose may be given at bedtime. Lower bedtime doses may not provide adequate symptomatic relief.

A daily dose of less than 75 mg may not be effective in active inflammatory disease.

A daily dose of more than 150 to 200 mg may increase the risk of adverse effects without providing additional clinical benefit.

Antigout agent—Oral, 100 mg initially, then 50 mg three times a day until pain is relieved, with the dosage then being reduced until medication is discontinued.

Anti-inflammatory (nonsteroidal)[1]—75 to 150 mg per day in 3 or 4 divided doses.

Note: When used to treat conditions not requiring chronic therapy, such as acute bursitis or tendinitis of the shoulder, indomethacin should be discontinued when symptoms of inflammation have been controlled for several days. The usual length of treatment is 7 to 14 days.

[Antipyretic][1]—Oral, 25 or 50 mg three or four times a day.

Usual adult prescribing limits: Oral, 200 mg a day.

Auxiliary labeling:
- Take with food or antacids.
- Take with a full glass of water.
- Avoid alcoholic beverages.

INDOMETHACIN EXTENDED-RELEASE CAPSULES USP

Usual adult dose: Antirheumatic, nonsteroidal anti-inflammatory—Oral, 75 mg once a day, in the morning or at bedtime; may be increased to 75 mg two times a day if necessary.

Note: After the effective and tolerated dose of indomethacin has been established with the capsule dosage form, the extended-release capsules may be substituted. One extended-release capsule daily is equivalent to 25 mg of indomethacin capsules three times a day; one extended-release capsule twice a day is equivalent to 50 mg of indomethacin capsules three times a day.

Careful observation of the patient for signs of intolerance is recommended if the extended-release capsule is used for initiating indomethacin therapy or for increasing the daily dose. Initiation of therapy with one extended-release capsule daily provides the maximum initial dose recommended by the manufacturer. Use of the extended-release capsule to increase the dose provides a greater-than-recommended increase in daily dosage.

Auxiliary labeling:
- Take with food or antacids.
- Take with a full glass of water.
- Avoid alcoholic beverages.

Additional information: The extended-release capsules are designed to release 25 mg of indomethacin immediately and the remaining 50 mg over a 12-hour period.

INDOMETHACIN ORAL SUSPENSION USP

Note: Indomethacin oral suspension is not commercially available in Canada.

Usual adult dose:
Antirheumatic (nonsteroidal anti-inflammatory)—Oral, initially 25 or 50 mg two to four times a day; if well tolerated, the dosage per day may be increased by 25 or 50 mg at weekly intervals until a satisfactory response is obtained or up to a maximum dose of 200 mg per day.

Note: In acute flare-ups of rheumatoid arthritis, dosage may be increased by 25 or 50 mg daily, as needed and tolerated.

For those arthritic patients who have persistent night pain and/or morning stiffness, up to 100 mg of the total daily dose may be given at bedtime. Lower bedtime doses may not provide adequate symptomatic relief.

A daily dose of less than 75 mg may not be effective in active inflammatory disease.

A daily dose of more than 150 to 200 mg may increase the risk of adverse effects without providing additional clinical benefit.

Antigout agent—Oral, 100 mg initially, then 50 mg three times a day until pain is relieved, with the dosage then being reduced until medication is discontinued.

Anti-inflammatory (nonsteroidal)—75 to 150 mg per day in 3 or 4 divided doses.

Note: When used to treat conditions not requiring chronic therapy, such as acute bursitis or tendinitis of the shoulder, indomethacin should be discontinued when symptoms of inflammation have been controlled for several days. The usual length of treatment is 7 to 14 days.

[Antipyretic]—Oral, 25 or 50 mg three or four times a day.

Usual adult prescribing limits: Oral, 200 mg a day.

Auxiliary labeling:
- Shake well.
- Take with food or antacids.
- Avoid alcoholic beverages.

Rectal Dosage Forms

INDOMETHACIN SUPPOSITORIES USP

Usual adult dose:
Antirheumatic, nonsteroidal anti-inflammatory;
Anti-inflammatory, nonsteroidal[1];
Antigout agent; or
[Antipyretic][1]—Rectal, 50 mg up to four times a day.

Note: A daily dose of less than 75 mg may not be effective in active inflammatory disease.

A daily dose of more than 150 to 200 mg may increase the risk of adverse effects without providing additional clinical benefit.

Auxiliary labeling:
- For rectal use.
- Avoid alcoholic beverages.

---

[1]Not included in Canadian product labeling.

KETOPROFEN

Summary of Differences

Indications: See *Indications*.
Pharmacology:
Physicochemical characteristics—Chemical group—A propionic acid derivative.
Precautions:
Pregnancy/reproduction—No teratogenicity demonstrated in animal studies; in rabbits, maternally toxic doses shown to be embryotoxic.
Drug interactions and/or related problems—See *Table 1*, page 185.
Contraindications/Medical problems—See *Table 2*, page 195.
Side/adverse effects: See *Table 3*, page 199.

Oral Dosage Forms

KETOPROFEN CAPSULES

Usual adult dose:
Antirheumatic (nonsteroidal anti-inflammatory)—Oral, 150 to 300 mg a day in three or four divided doses, usually 75 mg three times a day or 50 mg four times a day, initially, then adjusted according to patient response.

Analgesic[1] or

Antidysmenorrheal[1]—Oral, 50 mg every six to eight hours as needed. Dosage may be increased if necessary, but single doses higher than 75 mg have not been shown to provide additional benefit. In the treatment of dysmenorrhea, 75-mg doses may be more effective than lower doses.

Note: In patients with renal function impairment, a 33 to 50% reduction of dosage is recommended.

Usual adult prescribing limits: Oral, 300 mg a day in three or four divided doses.

Note: Risk/benefit must be considered when the maximum dose is prescribed because the incidence of gastrointestinal effects and headache is increased with administration of 300 mg per day (as compared with 200 mg per day).

Auxiliary labeling:
- Take with a full glass of water.
- Avoid alcoholic beverages.

KETOPROFEN DELAYED-RELEASE TABLETS

Note: Ketoprofen delayed-release tablets are not commercially available in the U.S.

Usual adult dose: Antirheumatic (nonsteriodal anti-inflammatory)— Oral, 150 to 300 mg a day in three or four divided doses, usually 75 mg three times a day or 50 mg four times a day, initially, then adjusted according to patient response.

Usual adult prescribing limits: Oral, 300 mg a day in three or four divided doses.

Note: Risk/benefit must be considered when the maximum dose is prescribed because the incidence of gastrointestinal effects and headache is increased with administration of 300 mg per day (as compared with 200 mg per day).

Auxiliary labeling:
- Take with a full glass of water.
- Swallow tablets whole.
- Avoid alcoholic beverages.

KETOPROFEN EXTENDED-RELEASE TABLETS

Note: Ketoprofen extended-release tablets are not commercially available in the U.S.

Usual adult dose: Antirheumatic (nonsteriodal anti-inflammatory)— Oral, 200 mg once a day, in the morning or evening.

Note The extended-release tablets are not intended for initial therapy; they are to be administered only after the daily maintenance dose has been determined (using the capsules or delayed-release tablets) to be 200 mg.

Auxiliary labeling:
- Take with a full glass of water.
- Swallow tablets whole.
- Avoid alcoholic beverages.

Rectal Dosage Forms

KETOPROFEN SUPPOSITORIES

Note: Ketoprofen suppositories are not commercially available in the U.S.

Usual adult dose: Antirheumatic (nonsteroidal anti-inflammatory)— Rectal, 100 mg two times a day, in the morning and evening; or 100 mg in the evening in conjunction with oral administration during the day.

Usual adult prescribing limits: Rectal or combined oral and rectal, 200 mg a day.

Auxiliary labeling:
- For rectal use.
- Avoid alcoholic beverages.

---

[1]Not included in Canadian product labeling.

MECLOFENAMATE

Summary of Differences

Indications: See *Indications*.

Pharmacology:

 Physicochemical characteristics—Chemical group—A fenamate derivative.

Precautions:

 Pregnancy/reproduction—Fetotoxicity and developmental abnormalities have been demonstrated in animals.

 Breast-feeding—Use not recommended because animal studies have shown this agent to interfere with normal development of the young before weaning.

 Drug interactions and/or related problems—See *Table 1*, page 185.

 Contraindications/Medical problems—

  Caution in patients on a sodium-restricted diet.

  See also *Table 2*, page 195.

Side/adverse effects: See *Table 3*, page 199.

Additional Dosing Information

See also *General Dosing Information*.

Improvement in condition may occur within a few days, but 2 to 3 weeks of continuous use on a regular basis may be required for maximum effectiveness.

Gastrointestinal side effects may respond to a reduction in dosage; however, if severe adverse reactions occur, therapy should be discontinued.

Oral Dosage Forms

MECLOFENAMATE SODIUM CAPSULES USP

Note: Meclofenamate sodium capsules are not commercially available in Canada.

Usual adult dose:

 Antirheumatic (nonsteroidal anti-inflammatory)—Oral, 200 mg of meclofenamic acid a day, in three or four divided doses, initially. Dosage may be increased to up to 400 mg a day if necessary. After a satisfactory response has been obtained, dosage should be reduced to the lowest maintenance dose that provides continuing control of symptoms.

 Analgesic—Oral, 50 mg every four to six hours. If necessary, dosage may be increased to 100 mg every four to six hours.

Usual adult prescribing limits: Antirheumatic (nonsteroidal anti-inflammatory) and analgesic—Up to 400 mg daily.

Auxiliary labeling:
- Take with a full glass of water.
- Avoid alcoholic beverages.

MEFENAMIC ACID

Summary of Differences

Indications: See *Indications.*
Pharmacology:
Physicochemical characteristics—
Chemical group:A fenamate derivative.
pKa: 4.2.
Precautions:
Pregnancy/reproduction—Decreased fertility, increased number of resorptions, and decreased survival to weaning demonstrated in rodents.
Drug interactions and/or related problems—See *Table 1,* page 185.
Contraindications/Medical problems—See *Table 2,* page 195.
Side/adverse effects: See *Table 3,* page 199.

Additional Dosing Information

See also *General Dosing Information.*

It is recommended that mefenamic acid therapy be discontinued promptly if diarrhea or a skin rash develops. Patients who develop diarrhea during mefenamic acid therapy are usually unable to tolerate the drug thereafter.

Mefenamic acid should not be used for more than 7 days at a time.

Oral Dosage Forms

MEFENAMIC ACID CAPSULES USP

Usual adult dose:
Analgesic or
Antidysmenorrheal—Oral, 500 mg initially, followed by 250 mg every six hours as needed.
Note: It is recommended that mefenamic acid be used for no longer than 7 days at a time.

Auxiliary labeling:
• Take with food.
• Take with a full glass of water.
• May cause drowsiness.
• Avoid alcoholic beverages.

NAPROXEN

Summary of Differences

Indications: See *Indications.*
Pharmacology:
Physicochemical characteristics—
Chemical group: A propionic acid derivative.
pKa: 4.2.
Precautions:
Pregnancy/reproduction—Teratogenic effects in animals have not been shown.
Pediatrics—Higher risk of skin rash and increases in bleeding time than in adults receiving the medication.
Drug interactions and/or related problems—See *Table 1,* page 185.

Contraindications/Medical problems—
Caution with naproxen sodium and naproxen oral suspension for patients who must restrict their sodium intake.
See also *Table 2,* page 195.
Side/adverse effects: See *Table 3,* page 199.

Additional Dosing Information

See also *General Dosing Information.*

In arthritis, improvement in condition may occur within 2 weeks, but 2 to 4 weeks of continuous use on a regular basis may be required for maximum effectiveness.

Naproxen should be administered in the lowest effective dose to geriatric patients, patients with hepatic function impairment, or patients with renal function impairment (especially if creatinine clearance is <20 mL per minute).

Oral Dosage Forms

NAPROXEN ORAL SUSPENSION

Usual adult dose: Antirheumatic (nonsteroidal anti-inflammatory)—
Oral, 250, 375, or 500 mg two times a day, morning and evening.
Note: During long-term administration, dosage may be adjusted according to patient response; lower doses may suffice.

For acute exacerbations of rheumatic disease, dosage may be increased to up to 1.5 grams per day for limited periods. Use of this high dose requires that the clinical benefit be increased sufficiently to offset the potential increased risk of adverse effects.

Analgesic (mild to moderate pain)—Oral, 500 mg initially, then 250 mg every six to eight hours as needed.
Antigout agent[1]—Oral, 750 mg initially, then 250 mg every eight hours until the attack has subsided.
Antidysmenorrheal—Oral, 500 mg initially, then 250 mg every six to eight hours as needed.

Usual adult prescribing limits: For mild to moderate pain and dysmenorrhea—Up to a total dose of 1.25 grams daily.

Auxiliary labeling:
• Shake well.
• Avoid alcoholic beverages.

NAPROXEN TABLETS USP

Usual adult dose:
Antirheumatic (nonsteroidal anti-inflammatory)—Oral, 250, 375, or 500 mg two times a day, morning and evening.
Note: During long-term administration, dosage may be adjusted according to patient response; lower doses may suffice.

For acute exacerbations of rheumatic disease, dosage may be increased to up to 1.5 grams per day for limited periods. Use of this high dose requires that the clinical benefit be increased sufficiently to offset the potential increased risk of adverse effects.

Analgesic (mild to moderate pain)—Oral, 500 mg initially, then 250 mg every six to eight hours as needed.
Antigout agent[1]—Oral, 750 mg initially, then 250 mg every eight hours until the attack has subsided.
Antidysmenorrheal—Oral, 500 mg initially, then 250 mg every six to eight hours as needed.

Usual adult prescribing limits: For mild to moderate pain and dysmenorrhea—Up to a total dose of 1.25 grams daily.

Auxiliary labeling:
- Take with a full glass of water.
- May cause drowsiness.
- Avoid alcoholic beverages.

NAPROXEN EXTENDED-RELEASE TABLETS

Note: Naproxen extended-release tablets are not commercially available in the U.S.

Usual adult dose: Antirheumatic (nonsteroidal anti-inflammatory)—Oral, 750 or 1000 mg once a day in the morning or evening.

Note: The extended-release tablets are not intended for initial therapy; they are to be administered only after the daily maintenance dose has been determined (using an immediate-release dosage form) to be 750 or 1000 mg.

Auxiliary labeling:
- Take with a full glass of water.
- Swallow tablets whole.
- May cause drowsiness.
- Avoid alcoholic beverages.

NAPROXEN SODIUM TABLETS USP

Usual adult dose:
Antirheumatic (nonsteroidal anti-inflammatory)—Oral, 275 mg two times a day, morning and evening; or 275 mg in the morning and 550 mg in the evening.
> Note: During long-term administration, dosage may be adjusted according to patient response; lower doses may suffice.
>
> Doses exceeding 1.1 grams per day have not been studied.

Analgesic (mild to moderate pain)—Oral, 550 mg initially, then 275 mg every six to eight hours as needed.

Antigout agent[1]—Oral, 825 mg initially, then 275 mg every eight hours until the attack has subsided.

Antidysmenorrheal—Oral, 550 mg initially, then 275 mg every six to eight hours as needed.

Usual adult prescribing limits: For mild to moderate pain and dysmenorrhea—Up to a total dose of 1.375 grams daily.

Auxiliary labeling:
- Take with a full glass of water.
- May cause drowsiness.
- Avoid alcoholic beverages.

Rectal Dosage Forms

NAPROXEN SUPPOSITORIES

Note: Naproxen suppositories are not commercially available in the U.S.

Usual adult dose: Antirheumatic (nonsteroidal anti-inflammatory)—Rectal, 500 mg at bedtime, administered in conjunction with oral administration during the day.

Usual adult prescribing limits: Total daily dose administered orally and rectally should not exceed 1.5 grams a day. The 1.5-gram daily dose is recommended only for short-term administration during acute exacerbations of rheumatic disease. Also, use of this high dose requires that the additional clinical benefit be sufficient to offset the potential increased risk of adverse effects.

Auxiliary labeling:
- For rectal use.
- Avoid alcoholic beverages.

---

[1]Not included in Canadian product labeling.

PHENYLBUTAZONE

Summary of Differences

Indications:
> Recommended only for severe arthritic conditions or gout in patients unresponsive to less toxic nonsteroidal anti-inflammatory agents.
> See also *Indications*.

Pharmacology:
> Physicochemical characteristics—Chemical group—A pyrazone derivative.

Precautions:
> Pregnancy/reproduction—Fetotoxicity, but not teratogenicity, demonstrated in animal studies.
> Breast-feeding—Excreted in breast milk; may cause blood dyscrasias or other adverse effects in nursing infants.
> Pediatrics—Use in children up to 15 years of age not recommended.
> Geriatrics—Also, increased risk of blood dyscrasias.
> Drug interactions and/or related problems—See *Table 1*, page 185.
> Contraindications/Medical problems—See *Table 2*, page 195.
> Patient monitoring—Complete physical examinations, including urinalyses, and hematologic examinations recommended at regular intervals.

Side/adverse effects:
> Increased risk of blood dyscrasias in geriatric patients.
> Blood dyscrasias may occur days or weeks after medication is discontinued.
> See also *Table 3*, page 199.

Additional Dosing Information

See also *General Dosing Information.*

Because of its toxicity, phenylbutazone should be used in the minimum effective dosage and for the shortest possible time.

In geriatric patients, therapy should be limited to short periods, preferably not to exceed 1 week, because of the high risk of severe, possibly fatal, toxic reactions.

Phenylbutazone is generally better tolerated when administered with food to lessen gastric irritation.

If therapy is not effective within 1 week, the medication should be discontinued.

Edema may be dose-related and may be prevented in some patients by reducing the dosage.

Oral Dosage Forms

Note: Bracketed uses in the *Dosage Forms* section refer to categories of use and/or indications that are not included in U.S. product labeling.

PHENYLBUTAZONE CAPSULES USP

Note: Phenylbutazone capsules are not commercially available in Canada.

Usual adult dose:
Antirheumatic (nonsteroidal anti-inflammatory)—
> Rheumatoid arthritis[1] or
> Osteoarthritis, acute attacks[1] or
> Ankylosing spondylitis or
> [Psoriatic arthritis]:
>> Initial—Oral, 300 to 600 mg a day in three or four divided doses.
>> Maintenance—Oral, 100 mg one to four times a day.

Antigout agent—Oral, initially 400 mg as a single dose; then 100 mg every four hours for approximately four days or until a satisfactory response is obtained, with the duration of therapy not exceeding one week.

Note: Some clinicians use a dose of 200 mg every four hours for approximately four days or until a satisfactory response is obtained, with the duration of therapy not exceeding two weeks.

Usual adult prescribing limits: Antirheumatic (nonsteroidal anti-inflammatory)—Maintenance: 400 mg a day.

Auxiliary labeling:
- Take with food.
- Take with a full glass of water.
- Avoid alcoholic beverages.

PHENYLBUTAZONE TABLETS USP

Usual adult dose:
Antirheumatic (nonsteroidal anti-inflammatory)—
Rheumatoid arthritis[1] or
Osteoarthritis, acute attacks[1] or
Ankylosing spondylitis or
[Psoriatic arthritis][1]:
Initial—Oral, 300 to 600 mg a day in three or four divided doses.
Maintenance—Oral, 100 mg one to four times a day.
Antigout agent—Oral, initially 400 mg as a single dose; then 100 mg every four hours for approximately four days or until a satisfactory response is obtained, with the duration of therapy not exceeding one week.

Note: Some clinicians use a dose of 200 mg every four hours for approximately four days or until a satisfactory response is obtained, with the duration of therapy not exceeding two weeks.

Usual adult prescribing limits: Antirheumatic (nonsteroidal anti-inflammatory)—Maintenance: Oral, 400 mg a day.

Auxiliary labeling:
- Take with food.
- Swallow tablets whole.
- Take with a full glass of water.
- Avoid alcoholic beverages.

PHENYLBUTAZONE DELAYED-RELEASE TABLETS

Note: Phenylbutazone delayed-release tablets are not commercially available in the U.S.

Usual adult dose:
Antirheumatic (nonsteroidal anti-inflammatory)—
Rheumatoid arthritis[1] or
Osteoarthritis, acute attacks[1] or
Ankylosing spondylitis or
Psoriatic arthritis[1]:
Initial—Oral, 300 to 600 mg a day in three or four divided doses.
Maintenance—Oral, 100 mg one to four times a day.
Antigout agent—Oral, initially 400 mg as a single dose; then 100 mg every four hours for approximately four days or until a satisfactory response is obtained, with the duration of therapy not exceeding one week.

Note: Some clinicians use a dose of 200 mg every four hours for approximately four days or until a satisfactory response is obtained, with the duration of therapy not exceeding two weeks.

Usual adult prescribing limits: Antirheumatic (nonsteroidal anti-inflammatory)—Maintenance: Oral, 400 mg a day.

Auxiliary labeling:
- Take with a full glass of water.
- Swallow tablets whole.
- Avoid alcoholic beverages.

PHENYLBUTAZONE TABLETS, BUFFERED

Note: Buffered phenylbutazone tablets are not commercially available in the U.S.

Usual adult dose:
Antirheumatic (nonsteroidal anti-inflammatory)—
Rheumatoid arthritis[1] or
Osteoarthritis, acute attacks[1] or
Ankylosing spondylitis or
Psoriatic arthritis[1]:
Initial—Oral, 300 to 600 mg a day in three or four divided doses.
Maintenance—Oral, 100 mg one to four times a day.
Antigout agent—Oral, initially 400 mg as a single dose; then 100 mg every four hours for approximately four days or until a satisfactory response is obtained, with the duration of therapy not exceeding one week.

Note: Some clinicians use a dose of 200 mg every four hours for approximately four days or until a satisfactory response is obtained, with the duration of therapy not exceeding two weeks.

Usual adult prescribing limits: Antirheumatic (nonsteroidal anti-inflammatory)—Maintenance: Oral, 400 mg a day.

Auxiliary labeling:
- Swallow tablets whole.
- Take with a full glass of water.
- Avoid alcoholic beverages.

---

[1]Not included in Canadian product labeling.

PIROXICAM

Summary of Differences

Indications: See *Indications*.
Pharmacology:
Physicochemical characteristics—
Chemical group: An oxicam derivative.
pKa: 1.8 and 5.1.
Precautions:
Pregnancy/reproduction—Teratogenic effects not demonstrated in animal studies.
Breast-feeding—Excreted in breast milk; use by breast-feeding mothers not recommended because piroxicam inhibits lactation in animals.
Drug interactions and/or related problems—See *Table 1*, page 185.
Contraindications/Medical problems—See *Table 2*, page 195.
Side/adverse effects: See *Table 3*, page 199.

Additional Dosing Information

See also *General Dosing Information*.

Because steady-state plasma concentrations are not reached for 7 to 12 days following initiation of therapy, the effectiveness of therapy with piroxicam should not be assessed for 2 weeks.

Oral Dosage Forms

PIROXICAM CAPSULES USP

Usual adult dose: Antirheumatic (nonsteroidal anti-inflammatory)—
Oral, 20 mg a once a day or 10 mg two times a day.

Auxiliary labeling:
- Take after meals.
- Take with a full glass of water.
- Avoid alcoholic beverages.

Rectal Dosage Forms

PIROXICAM SUPPOSITORIES

Note: Piroxicam suppositories are not commercially available in the U.S.

Usual adult dose: Antirheumatic (nonsteroidal anti-inflammatory)—
Rectal, 20 mg once a day or 10 mg two times a day.

Usual adult prescribing limits: Rectal or combined oral and rectal—
20 mg a day.

Auxiliary labeling:
- For rectal use.
- Avoid alcoholic beverages.

SULINDAC

Summary of Differences

Indications: See *Indications.*
Pharmacology:
 Physicochemical characteristics—Chemical group—A pyrroleacetic acid derivative.
 Pharmacology—
  A prodrug; sulfide metabolite is active agent.
  Some indication that may be less toxic to the kidneys than other NSAIDs.
Precautions:
 Pregnancy/reproduction—Fetotoxicity, and, in some studies, a low incidence of teratogenicity, have been demonstrated in animals.
 Drug interactions and/or related problems—See *Table 1*, page 185.
 Contraindications/Medical problems—See *Table 2*, page 195.
Side/adverse effects: See *Table 3*, page 199.

Additional Dosing Information

See also *General Dosing Information.*

In the treatment of arthritis, improvement in condition may occur within 7 days, but 2 to 3 weeks of continuous use on a regular basis may be required for maximum effectiveness.

Patients with impaired renal function may require lower doses.

Therapy for 7 days in acute gouty arthritis and for 7 to 14 days in acute painful shoulder is usually sufficient.

Oral Dosage Forms

SULINDAC TABLETS USP

Usual adult dose:
 Antirheumatic (nonsteroidal anti-inflammatory)—Oral, 150 or 200 mg two times a day; may be increased or decreased, depending on patient response.

Note: Although some patients have received doses higher than 400 mg per day, such doses have not been fully evaluated and are not recommended.

Antigout agent—Oral, 200 mg two times a day; dosage to be decreased according to patient response.

Anti-inflammatory (acute painful shoulder)—Oral, 200 mg two times a day; dosage to be decreased according to patient response.

Auxiliary labeling:
- Take with a full glass of water.
- Avoid alcoholic beverages.

TIAPROFENIC ACID

Summary of Differences

Indications: See *Indications.*
Pharmacology:
 Physicochemical characteristics—
  Chemical group: A propionic acid derivative.
  pKa: 3.0.
Precautions:
 Pregnancy/reproduction—
  Crosses the placenta.
  Fetotoxicity, but not teratogenicity, demonstrated in animal studies.
 Drug interactions and/or related problems—See *Table 1*, page 185.
 Contraindications/Medical problems—See *Table 2*, page 195.
Side/adverse effects: See *Table 3*, page 199.

Oral Dosage Forms

TIAPROFENIC ACID TABLETS

Note: Tiaprofenic acid tablets are not commercially available in the U.S.

Usual adult dose: Antirheumatic (nonsteroidal anti-inflammatory)—
 Rheumatoid arthritis: Oral, 600 mg a day in two or three divided doses.
 Osteoarthritis: Oral, 600 mg a day in two or three divided doses, initially. After a satisfactory response has been obtained, dosage may be reduced. Some patients may be maintained on 300 mg a day in divided doses.

Usual adult prescribing limits: 600 mg a day.

Auxiliary labeling:
- Take with a full glass of water.
- Avoid alcoholic beverages.

TOLMETIN

Summary of Differences

Indications: See *Indications.*
Pharmacology:
 Physicochemical characteristics—
  Chemical group: A pyrroleacetic acid derivative.
  pKa: 3.5.
Precautions:
 Pregnancy/reproduction—No teratogenicity demonstrated in animal studies.

Drug interactions and/or related problems—See *Table 1*, page 185.
Contraindications/Medical problems—
    Caution in patients who must restrict their sodium intake.
    See also *Table 2*, page 195.
Side/adverse effects:
    Higher incidence of anaphylactic reactions than with other NSAIDs.
    See also *Table 3*, page 199.

Additional Dosing Information

See also *General Dosing Information.*

Improvement in condition may occur within 7 days, but 1 to 2 weeks of continuous use on a regular basis may be required for maximum effectiveness.

Oral Dosage Forms

TOLMETIN SODIUM CAPSULES USP

Usual adult dose: Antirheumatic (nonsteroidal anti-inflammatory)—
    Initial: Oral, 400 mg (free acid) three times a day, preferably including a dose in the morning and a dose at bedtime.
    Maintenance:
        Rheumatoid arthritis—Oral, 600 mg to 1.8 grams (free acid) a day in 3 or 4 divided doses.
        Osteoarthritis—Oral, 600 mg to 1.6 grams (free acid) a day in 3 or 4 divided doses.

Usual adult prescribing limits: Up to 2 grams (free acid) daily for rheumatoid arthritis or 1.6 grams (free acid) daily for osteoarthritis.

Auxiliary labeling:
- Take with a full glass of water.
- Avoid alcoholic beverages.

TOLMETIN SODIUM TABLETS USP

Usual adult dose: Antirheumatic (nonsteroidal anti-inflammatory)—
    Initial: Oral, 400 mg (free acid) three times a day, preferably including a dose in the morning and a dose at bedtime.
    Maintenance:
        Rheumatoid arthritis—Oral, 600 mg to 1.8 grams (free acid) a day in 3 or 4 divided doses.
        Osteoarthritis—Oral, 600 mg to 1.6 grams (free acid) a day in 3 or 4 divided doses.

Usual adult prescribing limits: Up to 2 grams (free acid) daily for rheumatoid arthritis or 1.6 grams (free acid) daily for osteoarthritis.

Auxiliary labeling:
- Take with a full glass of water.
- Avoid alcoholic beverages.

Table 1. Drug Interactions and/or Related Problems

Note: In addition to the interactions listed below, the possibility should be considered that additive or multiple effects leading to impaired blood clotting and/or increased risk of bleeding may occur if a nonsteroidal anti-inflammatory drug (NSAID) is used concurrently with any medication having a significant potential for causing hypoprothrombinemia, thrombocytopenia, or gastrointestinal ulceration or hemorrhage.

The following drug interactions and/or related problems have been selected on the basis of their potential clinical significance (possible mechanism in parentheses where appropriate)—not necessarily inclusive (» = major clinical significance):

Note: Combinations containing any of the following medications, depending on the amount present, may also interact with this medication.

Legend:
- I=Diclofenac
- II=Diflunisal
- III=Fenoprofen
- IV=Floctafenine
- V=Flurbiprofen
- VI=Ibuprofen
- VII=Indomethacin
- VIII=Ketoprofen
- IX=Meclofenamate
- X=Mefenamic Acid
- XI=Naproxen
- XII=Phenylbutazone*
- XIII=Piroxicam
- XIV=Sulindac
- XV=Tiaprofenic Acid
- XVI=Tolmetin

Interaction	I	II	III	IV	V	VI	VII	VIII	IX	X	XI	XII	XIII	XIV	XV	XVI
Acetaminophen	✓	✓	✓	✓	✓	✓	✓	✓	✓	✓	✓	✓	✓	✓	✓	✓
Adrenocorticoids, glucocorticoid, or / Alcohol or / Corticotropin or / Potassium supplements	✓	✓	✓	✓	✓	✓	✓	✓	✓	✓	✓	✓✓	✓	✓	✓	✓
Aminoglycosides or / Digitalis glycosides	✓					✓	✓									
Antacids		✓	✓											✓		

Acetaminophen
(prolonged concurrent use of acetaminophen with an NSAID may increase the risk of adverse renal effects; it is recommended that patients be under close medical supervision while receiving such combined therapy)

(concurrent use of acetaminophen with diflunisal may increase the acetaminophen plasma concentration by 50%, leading to increased risk of acetaminophen-induced hepatotoxicity)

Adrenocorticoids, glucocorticoid, or
Alcohol or
Corticotropin (chronic therapeutic use) or
Potassium supplements
(concurrent use may increase the risk of gastrointestinal side effects, including ulceration or hemorrhage; however, concurrent use with glucocorticoids or corticotropin in the treatment of arthritis may provide additional therapeutic benefit and permit reduction of glucocorticoid or corticotropin dosage)

(concurrent use of alcohol with phenylbutazone may also increase the potential for impairment of psychomotor skills)

Aminoglycosides or
Digitalis glycosides
(administration of indomethacin [for treatment of a patent ductus arteriosus] to neonates receiving these medications has resulted in decreased renal clearance and increased plasma concentration of the aminoglycoside or digitalis glycoside; although not documented, the possibility should be considered that similar effects may occur in adults, leading to increased risk of toxicity; adjustment of aminoglycoside or digitalis glycoside dosage may be required)

(diclofenac and ibuprofen have been shown to increase serum digoxin concentrations; adjustment of digoxin dosage may be necessary during and following concurrent use)

Antacids
(concurrent chronic use with diflunisal, fenoprofen, or sulindac may significantly decrease the plasma concentration of the NSAID)

*Phenylbutazone induces hepatic microsomal enzymes and has been shown to increase the metabolism of several medications that are metabolized by these enzymes. However, phenylbutazone has also been reported to inhibit the metabolism of other medications that are metabolized by hepatic microsomal enzymes. Although not documented, it has been proposed that, in some cases, phenylbutazone (which is also metabolized via these enzymes) may compete with other medications for the enzymes.

Table 1. Drug Interactions and/or Related Problems *(continued)*

Legend:
I=Diclofenac
II=Diflunisal
III=Fenoprofen
IV=Floctafenine
V=Flurbiprofen
VI=Ibuprofen
VII=Indomethacin
VIII=Ketoprofen
IX=Meclofenamate
X=Mefenamic Acid
XI=Naproxen
XII=Phenylbutazone*
XIII=Piroxicam
XIV=Sulindac
XV=Tiaprofenic Acid
XVI=Tolmetin

Drug Interactions and/or Related Problems	I	II	III	IV	V	VI	VII	VIII	IX	X	XI	XII	XIII	XIV	XV	XVI
» Anticoagulants, coumarin- or indandione-derivative, or Heparin or Thrombolytic agents, such as: Alteplase (tissue-type plasminogen activator, recombinant); Anistreplase (anisoylated plasminogen-streptokinase activator complex); Streptokinase; Urokinase																
(effects of coumarin- or indandione-derivative anticoagulants may be potentiated when they are used concurrently with the indicated NSAIDs, possibly because of displacement of the anticoagulant from protein-binding sites; although *in vitro* studies have not shown that piroxicam displaces dicumarol from protein-binding sites, piroxicam has been reported to potentiate the effects of warfarin; coagulation tests should be monitored and anticoagulant dosage adjustments made if necessary when NSAID therapy is initiated or discontinued)	✓	✓	✓	✓	✓	✓	✓	✓	✓	✓	✓	✓	✓	✓	✓	✓
(inhibition of platelet aggregation by NSAIDs may be hazardous to patients receiving anticoagulant or thrombolytic therapy; however, with usual doses, diflunisal, meclofenamate, and mefenamic acid may be less likely than other NSAIDs to significantly alter platelet aggregability)	✓	✓	✓	✓	✓	✓	✓	✓	✓	✓	✓	✓	✓	✓	✓	✓
(phenylbutazone may inhibit the metabolism of coumarin or indandione derivatives as well as displacing the anticoagulants from their protein-binding sites, leading to an increase in the anticoagulant effect; concurrent use is not recommended)												✓				
(floctafenine may also increase the effects of coumarin or indandione derivatives; however, this effect [as shown by coagulation test results] becomes apparent only after 2 weeks of concurrent use)				✓												
(the potential occurrence of gastrointestinal ulceration or hemorrhage during NSAID therapy may cause increased risk to patients receiving anticoagulant or thrombolytic therapy)	✓	✓	✓	✓	✓	✓	✓	✓	✓	✓	✓	✓	✓	✓	✓	✓
» Anticonvulsants, hydantoin, especially Phenytoin																
(phenylbutazone and triaprofenic acid may displace hydantoin anticonvulsants from their protein-binding sites, and phenylbutazone may also inhibit their metabolism, possibly leading to increased elimination half-life and toxicity; hydantoin dosage adjustment based on monitoring of plasma concentration and/or observed signs of toxicity may be required)												✓			✓	

Table 1. Drug Interactions and/or Related Problems (*continued*)

Legend:
I=Diclofenac
II=Diflunisal
III=Fenoprofen
IV=Floctafenine
V=Flurbiprofen
VI=Ibuprofen
VII=Indomethacin
VIII=Ketoprofen
IX=Meclofenamate
X=Mefenamic Acid
XI=Naproxen
XII=Phenylbutazone*
XIII=Piroxicam
XIV=Sulindac
XV=Tiaprofenic Acid
XVI=Tolmetin

	I	II	III	IV	V	VI	VII	VIII	IX	X	XI	XII	XIII	XIV	XV	XVI
Antidiabetic agents, oral, or Insulin (NSAIDs may increase the hypoglycemic effect of these medications because prostaglandins are directly involved in regulatory mechanisms of glucose metabolism and possibly because of displacement of the oral antidiabetics from serum proteins; dosage adjustments of the antidiabetic agent may be necessary; glipizide and glyburide, due to their nonionic binding characteristics, may not be affected as much as the other oral antidiabetic agents; however, caution with concurrent use is recommended)		✓		✓	✓	✓	✓	✓	✓	✓	✓	✓	✓	✓	✓	✓
(diclofenac has also been reported to decrease the effects of these medications, leading to hyperglycemia)	✓															
Antihypertensives or Diuretics, especially Triamterene (increased monitoring of the response to any antihypertensive agent may be advisable when an NSAID is used concurrently because indomethacin reduces or reverses the effects of many antihypertensives, possibly by inhibiting renal prostaglandin synthesis and/or by causing sodium and fluid retention; ibuprofen, naproxen, and piroxicam have also been shown to interfere with antihypertensive therapy)	✓	✓		✓	✓	✓	✓	✓	✓	✓	✓	✓	✓	✓	✓	✓
(concurrent use with an NSAID may decrease the diuretic, natriuretic, and antihypertensive effects of diuretics, probably by inhibiting renal prostaglandin synthesis; however, diflunisal does not decrease the diuretic effect of furosemide)		✓		✓	✓	✓	✓	✓	✓	✓	✓	✓	✓	✓	✓	✓
(diflunisal significantly increases the plasma concentration of hydrochlorothiazide and decreases the hyperuricemic effect of hydrochlorothiazide or furosemide)		✓														
(concurrent use of an NSAID and a diuretic may also increase the risk of renal failure secondary to a decrease in renal blood flow caused by inhibition of renal prostaglandin synthesis; specifically, concurrent use of triamterene and indomethacin has caused renal function impairment as indicated by azotemia and reduced creatinine clearance; a few cases of acute renal failure requiring hemodialysis have been reported; concurrent use of indomethacin with triamterene is not recommended)	✓	✓					✓									✓

*Phenylbutazone induces hepatic microsomal enzymes and has been shown to increase the metabolism of several medications that are metabolized by these enzymes. However, phenylbutazone has also been reported to inhibit the metabolism of other medications that are metabolized by hepatic microsomal enzymes. Although not documented, it has been proposed that, in some cases, phenylbutazone (which is also metabolized via these enzymes) may compete with other medications for the enzymes.

Table 1. Drug Interactions and/or Related Problems *(continued)*

Legend:
I=Diclofenac
II=Diflunisal
III=Fenoprofen
IV=Floctafenine
V=Flurbiprofen
VI=Ibuprofen
VII=Indomethacin
VIII=Ketoprofen
IX=Meclofenamate
X=Mefenamic Acid
XI=Naproxen
XII=Phenylbutazone*
XIII=Piroxicam
XIV=Sulindac
XV=Tiaprofenic Acid
XVI=Tolmetin

Interaction and/or Related Problem	I	II	III	IV	V	VI	VII	VIII	IX	X	XI	XII	XIII	XIV	XV	XVI
» **Triamterene** *(continued)*																
(concurrent use of potassium-sparing diuretics with indomethacin or diclofenac may increase the risk of hyperkalemia)	✓						✓									
(indomethacin may block the increase in plasma renin activity [PRA] induced by bumetanide, furosemide, or indapamide)							✓									
» **Anti-inflammatory drugs, two or more concurrently, especially Diflunisal and indomethacin concurrently, or Salicylates, especially Aspirin**																
(concurrent use of two or more NSAIDs [including aspirin] may increase the incidence of gastrointestinal side effects, including ulceration or hemorrhage, without providing additional symptomatic relief, and is therefore not recommended)	✓	✓	✓	✓	✓	✓	✓	✓		✓	✓	✓		✓	✓	✓
(concurrent use of diflunisal and indomethacin has resulted in fatal gastrointestinal hemorrhage and is not recommended; diflunisal has been shown to decrease the renal clearance of indomethacin, resulting in significantly increased indomethacin plasma concentration)		✓					✓									
(concurrent use with aspirin may also increase the risk of bleeding at sites other than the gastrointestinal tract because of additive inhibition of platelet aggregation)	✓	✓	✓	✓	✓	✓	✓	✓		✓	✓	✓	✓	✓	✓	✓
(concurrent use of aspirin with ketoprofen is not recommended because aspirin decreases ketoprofen protein binding, increases ketoprofen plasma clearance, and decreases the formation and excretion of ketoprofen conjugates)								✓								
(aspirin has been shown to decrease the bioavailability of diclofenac, fenoprofen, flurbiprofen [by 50%], indomethacin [plasma concentration decreased by 20%], meclofenamate, piroxicam [plasma concentration decreased 20%], and the active sulfide metabolite of sulindac)	✓		✓		✓		✓		✓				✓	✓		
(diflunisal has been shown to decrease the concentration of the active sulfide metabolite of sulindac by 33%)		✓												✓		
Barbiturates or Cortisone																
(phenylbutazone may decrease the efficacy of these medications by inducing hepatic microsomal enzymes and increasing their metabolism; the possibility should be considered that adrenocorticoids other than cortisone may be similarly affected)												✓				

Table 1. Drug Interactions and/or Related Problems *(continued)*

Legend:
I=Diclofenac
II=Diflunisal
III=Fenoprofen
IV=Floctafenine
V=Flurbiprofen
VI=Ibuprofen
VII=Indomethacin
VIII=Ketoprofen
IX=Meclofenamate
X=Mefenamic Acid
XI=Naproxen
XII=Phenylbutazone*
XIII=Piroxicam
XIV=Sulindac
XV=Tiaprofenic Acid
XVI=Tolmetin

Drug Interactions and/or Related Problems	I	II	III	IV	V	VI	VII	VIII	IX	X	XI	XII	XIII	XIV	XV	XVI
» Blood dyscrasia-causing medications, other, or » Bone marrow depressants or » Radiation therapy (concurrent use with phenylbutazone may increase the potential for agranulocytosis or other serious hematologic adverse effects) (concurrent use of bone marrow depressants or radiation therapy with other NSAIDs may also increase the risk of serious hematologic adverse effects)	✓	✓		✓	✓	✓	✓	✓	✓	✓	✓	✓	✓	✓	✓	✓
» Cefamandole or » Cefoperazone or » Cefotetan or » Moxalactam or » Plicamycin (these medications may cause hypoprothrombinemia; in addition, plicamycin may inhibit platelet aggregation, and moxalactam may cause irreversible platelet damage; concurrent use with an NSAID may increase the risk of bleeding because of additive interferences with blood clotting and/or the potential occurrence of gastrointestinal ulceration or hemorrhage during NSAID therapy)	✓	✓	✓	✓	✓	✓	✓	✓	✓	✓	✓	✓	✓	✓	✓	✓
Cholestyramine (cholestyramine may decrease absorption of phenylbutazone; the possibility of impaired absorption, and the risk of toxicity due to sudden increases in absorption and serum concentration of phenylbutazone if cholestyramine therapy is discontinued, may be decreased if phenylbutazone is administered 1 hour before or 4 to 6 hours after cholestyramine)												✓				
Colchicine (concurrent use with phenylbutazone may increase the risk of adverse hematologic effects, and concurrent use with any NSAID may increase the risk of gastrointestinal ulceration or hemorrhage; in addition, inhibition of platelet aggregation by NSAIDs, added to colchicine's effects on blood clotting mechanisms [colchicine may cause thrombocytopenia with chronic use and clotting defects, including disseminated intravascular coagulation, with overdose], may increase the risk of bleeding at sites other than the gastrointestinal tract)	✓	✓	✓	✓	✓	✓	✓	✓	✓	✓	✓	✓	✓	✓	✓	✓

*Phenylbutazone induces hepatic microsomal enzymes and has been shown to increase the metabolism of several medications that are metabolized by these enzymes. However, phenylbutazone has also been reported to inhibit the metabolism of other medications that are metabolized by hepatic microsomal enzymes. Although not documented, it has been proposed that, in some cases, phenylbutazone (which is also metabolized via these enzymes) may compete with other medications for the enzymes.

Table 1. Drug Interactions and/or Related Problems (continued)

Legend:
I=Diclofenac
II=Diflunisal
III=Fenoprofen
IV=Floctafenine
V=Flurbiprofen
VI=Ibuprofen
VII=Indomethacin
VIII=Ketoprofen
IX=Meclofenamate
X=Mefenamic Acid
XI=Naproxen
XII=Phenylbutazone*
XIII=Piroxicam
XIV=Sulindac
XV=Tiaprofenic Acid
XVI=Tolmetin

Drug Interactions and/or Related Problems	I	II	III	IV	V	VI	VII	VIII	IX	X	XI	XII	XIII	XIV	XV	XVI
Contraceptives, estrogen-containing, oral (concurrent long-term use with phenylbutazone may result in reduced contraceptive reliability and increased incidence of breakthrough bleeding)												✓				
Dermatitis-causing medications, especially chloroquine and hydroxychloroquine (concurrent use with phenylbutazone may increase the possibility of severe dermatologic reactions)												✓				
» Digitalis glycosides, with the possible exception of digoxin (phenylbutazone may decrease digitalis serum concentrations, possibly because of enhanced metabolism caused by induction of hepatic microsomal enzymes; digitalis glycoside dosage adjustment may be necessary during and following concurrent use)												✓				
Dimethyl sulfoxide (DMSO) (topical application of DMSO to arthritic joints [not recommended because safety and efficacy are unproven] by patients receiving sulindac has been reported to decrease the plasma concentration of sulindac's active metabolite, thereby decreasing its efficacy, and to cause peripheral neuropathy)							✓							✓		
Gold compounds (although NSAIDs are commonly used concurrently with gold compounds in the treatment of arthritis, the possibility should be considered that concurrent use may increase the risk of adverse renal effects)	✓	✓	✓	✓	✓	✓	✓	✓	✓	✓	✓	✓	✓	✓	✓	✓
Hepatic enzyme inducers, other (hepatic enzyme inducers may increase phenylbutazone metabolism and decrease its half-life)												✓				
» Lithium (indomethacin may decrease lithium renal clearance, resulting in increased serum lithium concentration [steady-state lithium concentration may be increased by up to 50%] and/or toxicity; patient should be carefully observed for signs of lithium toxicity, and an increase in frequency of monitoring serum lithium concentration is recommended during initial concurrent therapy) (diclofenac, naproxen, and piroxicam have also been reported to increase steady-state plasma lithium concentration; possibility must be considered that other NSAIDs may have a similar effect; monitoring of lithium plasma concentration is recommended during and following concurrent use)	✓	✓	✓	✓	✓	✓	✓	✓	✓	✓	✓	✓	✓	✓	✓	✓

Table 1. Drug Interactions and/or Related Problems *(continued)*

Legend:
I=Diclofenac
II=Diflunisal
III=Fenoprofen
IV=Floctafenine
V=Flurbiprofen
VI=Ibuprofen
VII=Indomethacin
VIII=Ketoprofen
IX=Meclofenamate
X=Mefenamic Acid
XI=Naproxen
XII=Phenylbutazone*
XIII=Piroxicam
XIV=Sulindac
XV=Tiaprofenic Acid
XVI=Tolmetin

	I	II	III	IV	V	VI	VII	VIII	IX	X	XI	XII	XIII	XIV	XV	XVI
Methotrexate (concurrent use of phenylbutazone with methotrexate may increase the risk of agranulocytosis or bone marrow depression and is not recommended; also, phenylbutazone may displace methotrexate from its protein-binding sites and decrease its renal clearance, leading to increased methotrexate plasma concentration and risk of toxicity, especially during high-dose methotrexate infusion therapy. If concurrent use with phenylbutazone cannot be avoided, especially careful monitoring of the patient for signs of methotrexate toxicity and/or adequacy of renal function is recommended; also, phenylbutazone therapy should be discontinued for 7 to 12 days prior to, and for at least 12 hours [or until the methotrexate plasma concentration has decreased to a nontoxic level] following, administration of a high-dose methotrexate infusion)												✔				
(administration of high-dose methotrexate infusions to patients receiving diclofenac or ketoprofen has resulted in severe and [with ketoprofen] sometimes fatal methotrexate toxicity; a few fatalities have also occurred in patients receiving intermediate-dose methotrexate infusions concurrently with indomethacin, possibly because of decreased methotrexate excretion leading to increased and prolonged methotrexate plasma concentration; however, severe methotrexate toxicity did not occur when ketoprofen was administered 12 hours following completion of the methotrexate infusion. It is recommended that NSAID therapy be discontinued for 24 to 48 hours [for diflunisal] or 12 to 24 hours [for ketoprofen] prior to, and for at least 12 hours [or until the methotrexate plasma concentration has decreased to a nontoxic level] following, a high-dose methotrexate infusion and that indomethacin be discontinued for 24 to 48 hours prior to, and for at least 12 hours [or until the methotrexate plasma concentration has decreased to a nontoxic level] following, administration of an intermediate- or high-dose methotrexate infusion)	✔						✔	✔								

*Phenylbutazone induces hepatic microsomal enzymes and has been shown to increase the metabolism of several medications that are metabolized by these enzymes. However, phenylbutazone has also been reported to inhibit the metabolism of other medications that are metabolized by hepatic microsomal enzymes. Although not documented, it has been proposed that, in some cases, phenylbutazone (which is also metabolized via these enzymes) may compete with other medications for the enzymes.

Table 1. Drug Interactions and/or Related Problems (continued)

Legend:
I=Diclofenac
II=Diflunisal
III=Fenoprofen
IV=Floctafenine
V=Flurbiprofen
VI=Ibuprofen
VII=Indomethacin
VIII=Ketoprofen
IX=Meclofenamate
X=Mefenamic Acid
XI=Naproxen
XII=Phenylbutazone*
XIII=Piroxicam
XIV=Sulindac
XV=Tiaprofenic Acid
XVI=Tolmetin

Drug Interactions and/or Related Problems	I	II	III	IV	V	VI	VII	VIII	IX	X	XI	XII	XIII	XIV	XV	XVI
» Methotrexate (continued) — (although not well documented, the possibility exists that other NSAIDs may also decrease methotrexate excretion and increase its plasma concentration to potentially toxic levels; it is recommended that NSAID therapy be discontinued for 12 to 24 hours [for NSAIDs with a short elimination half-life] to up to 10 days [for piroxicam] prior to, and for at least 12 hours [or until the methotrexate plasma concentration has decreased to a nontoxic level] following, administration of a high-dose methotrexate infusion)	✓	✓	✓	✓	✓	✓			✓	✓			✓	✓	✓	✓
(severe, sometimes fatal, methotrexate toxicity has also been reported with low to moderate doses of methotrexate used in the treatment of rheumatoid arthritis or psoriasis in patients receiving diclofenac, indomethacin, naproxen, or phenylbutazone; it is recommended that concurrent use of any of the NSAIDs with low to moderate doses of methotrexate be undertaken with caution, with methotrexate dosage being adjusted as determined by monitoring plasma methotrexate concentration and/or adequacy of the patient's renal function)	✓	✓	✓	✓	✓		✓	✓	✓	✓	✓	✓	✓	✓	✓	✓
Methylphenidate (methylphenidate may inhibit the metabolism of phenylbutazone, leading to increased plasma concentrations and toxicity; dosage adjustments may be necessary)												✓				
Nephrotoxic medications, other (concurrent use with NSAIDs, especially indomethacin, may increase the risk and/or severity of renal adverse effects)	✓	✓	✓	✓	✓	✓	✓	✓	✓	✓	✓	✓	✓	✓	✓	✓
Nifedipine or Verapamil (caution in concurrent use with an NSAID is recommended because of possible displacement of either or both medications from protein-binding sites, leading to increased plasma concentrations of the free [unbound] medications and increased risk of toxicity)	✓	✓	✓	✓	✓	✓	✓	✓	✓	✓	✓	✓	✓	✓	✓	✓
» Penicillamine (concurrent use with phenylbutazone may increase the risk of serious hematologic and/or renal adverse effects)												✓				

Table 1. Drug Interactions and/or Related Problems *(continued)*

Legend:
I=Diclofenac
II=Diflunisal
III=Fenoprofen
IV=Floctafenine
V=Flurbiprofen
VI=Ibuprofen
VII=Indomethacin
VIII=Ketoprofen
IX=Meclofenamate
X=Mefenamic Acid
XI=Naproxen
XII=Phenylbutazone*
XIII=Piroxicam
XIV=Sulindac
XV=Tiaprofenic Acid
XVI=Tolmetin

Drug Interactions and/or Related Problems	I	II	III	IV	V	VI	VII	VIII	IX	X	XI	XII	XIII	XIV	XV	XVI
Phenobarbital (phenobarbital may decrease the elimination half-life of fenoprofen, possibly because of increased metabolism resulting from induction of hepatic microsomal enzyme activity; fenoprofen dosage adjustment may be required)			✓													
Photosensitizing medications, other (concurrent use with photosensitizing NSAIDs may cause additive photosensitizing effects)		✓											✓	✓	✓	
Platelet aggregation inhibitors, other (concurrent use of any of these medications with NSAIDs may increase the risk of bleeding because of additive inhibition of platelet aggregation as well as the potential occurrence of gastrointestinal ulceration or hemorrhage during NSAID therapy)	✓	✓	✓	✓	✓	✓	✓	✓	✓	✓	✓	✓	✓	✓	✓	✓
(concurrent use of sulfinpyrazone with NSAIDs may also increase the risk of gastrointestinal ulceration or hemorrhage)	✓	✓	✓	✓	✓	✓	✓	✓	✓	✓	✓	✓	✓	✓	✓	✓
Probenecid (concurrent use of probenecid with ketoprofen is not recommended because probenecid decreases the renal clearance of ketoprofen [by approximately 66%], ketoprofen protein binding [by 28%], and formation and renal clearance of ketoprofen conjugates, leading to greatly increased ketoprofen plasma concentration and risk of toxicity) (probenecid has also been shown to decrease renal and biliary clearance of indomethacin, and to increase plasma concentrations of indomethacin and naproxen, leading to increased risk of toxicity and possibly to increased effectiveness of the NSAID; if concurrent use is necessary, it is recommended that these NSAIDs be administered in reduced dosage and that increases in dosage be made slowly and in small increments) (probenecid may also decrease excretion and increase the serum concentration of other NSAIDs, possibly enhancing effectiveness and/or increasing the potential for toxicity; a decrease in dosage of the NSAID may be necessary if adverse effects occur)	✓	✓	✓	✓	✓	✓	✓	✓	✓		✓	✓	✓	✓	✓	✓

*Phenylbutazone induces hepatic microsomal enzymes and has been shown to increase the metabolism of several medications that are metabolized by these enzymes. However, phenylbutazone has also been reported to inhibit the metabolism of other medications that are metabolized by hepatic microsomal enzymes. Although not documented, it has been proposed that, in some cases, phenylbutazone (which is also metabolized via these enzymes) may compete with other medications for the enzymes.

Table 1. Drug Interactions and/or Related Problems *(continued)*

Legend:
I=Diclofenac
II=Diflunisal
III=Fenoprofen
IV=Floctafenine
V=Flurbiprofen
VI=Ibuprofen
VII=Indomethacin
VIII=Ketoprofen
IX=Meclofenamate
X=Mefenamic Acid
XI=Naproxen
XII=Phenylbutazone*
XIII=Piroxicam
XIV=Sulindac
XV=Tiaprofenic Acid
XVI=Tolmetin

	I	II	III	IV	V	VI	VII	VIII	IX	X	XI	XII	XIII	XIV	XV	XVI
» Probenecid *(continued)* (probenecid may increase the plasma concentration of sulindac and its sulfone metabolite, and slightly decrease the plasma concentration of the active sulfide metabolite)														✓		
Sulfonamides (concurrent use with phenylbutazone may potentiate phenylbutazone's effects because of displacement from plasma protein binding sites; phenylbutazone has also been reported to potentiate the effects of sulfonamides)												✓				
» Tetracyclines (antacids present in buffered phenylbutazone formulations may decrease absorption of oral tetracyclines by causing formation of nonabsorbable complexes and/or increasing intragastric pH; the medications should be taken 1 to 3 hours apart).												✓				
» Zidovudine (indomethacin may competitively inhibit the hepatic glucuronidation and decrease the clearance of zidovudine, leading to potentiation of zidovudine toxicity; also, the possibility must be considered that indomethacin toxicity may also be increased; concurrent use of the two medications should be avoided)							✓									

*Phenylbutazone induces hepatic microsomal enzymes and has been shown to increase the metabolism of several medications that are metabolized by these enzymes. However, phenylbutazone has also been reported to inhibit the metabolism of other medications that are metabolized by hepatic microsomal enzymes. Although not documented, it has been proposed that, in some cases, phenylbutazone (which is also metabolized via these enzymes) may compete with other medications for the enzymes.

Table 2. Contraindications/Medical Problems

Legend:
I=Diclofenac
II=Diflunisal
III=Fenoprofen
IV=Floctafenine
V=Flurbiprofen
VI=Ibuprofen
VII=Indomethacin
VIII=Ketoprofen
IX=Meclofenamate
X=Mefenamic Acid
XI=Naproxen
XII=Phenylbutazone
XIII=Piroxicam
XIV=Sulindac
XV=Tiaprofenic Acid
XVI=Tolmetin

The contraindications/medical problems included have been selected on the basis of their potential clinical significance (reasons given in parentheses where appropriate)—not necessarily inclusive (» = major clinical significance).

Medical Problem	I	II	III	IV	V	VI	VII	VIII	IX	X	XI	XII	XIII	XIV	XV	XVI
Except under special circumstances, this medication should not be used when the following medical problems exist:																
» Blood dyscrasias, active or history of, or																
» Bone marrow depression (may be induced or exacerbated)	√											√				
» Cardiac disease, severe, or																
» Cardiac failure, incipient, or																
» Cardiopulmonary disease, severe (sodium and fluid retention caused by phenylbutazone may increase the risk of edema, increased plasma volume, acute pulmonary edema, and cardiac decompensation)												√				
» Hepatic disease, severe, or																
» Renal disease, severe (increased phenylbutazone blood concentrations and potential for toxicity may result from decreased clearance; also, potential for adverse renal effects may be increased in the presence of pre-existing severe renal disease)												√				
» Peptic ulcer disease, active (may be exacerbated; increased risk of perforation and/or bleeding)												√				
» Symptoms of nasal polyps associated with bronchospasm, or angioedema, anaphylaxis, or other severe allergic reactions induced by aspirin or other NSAIDs (high risk of severe allergic reactions because of cross-sensitivity)	√	√	√	√	√	√	√	√√	√	√	√	√	√	√	√	√
Risk-benefit should be considered when the following medical problems exist:																
Anemia or Asthma (may be exacerbated)	√	√	√	√	√	√	√	√	√	√	√	√	√	√	√	√

Table 2. Contraindications/Medical Problems (*continued*)

Legend:
I=Diclofenac
II=Diflunisal
III=Fenoprofen
IV=Floctafenine
V=Flurbiprofen
VI=Ibuprofen
VII=Indomethacin
VIII=Ketoprofen
IX=Meclofenamate
X=Mefenamic Acid
XI=Naproxen
XII=Phenylbutazone
XIII=Piroxicam
XIV=Sulindac
XV=Tiaprofenic Acid
XVI=Tolmetin

Contraindications/Medical Problems	I	II	III	IV	V	VI	VII	VIII	IX	X	XI	XII	XIII	XIV	XV	XVI
Conditions predisposing to gastrointestinal toxicity, such as: Alcoholism, active; or » Peptic ulcer, ulcerative colitis, or upper gastrointestinal disease, active or history of; or Tobacco use, or recent history of (NSAIDs should preferably not be given to patients with active peptic ulcer disease or gastrointestinal bleeding; if NSAID therapy is unavoidable, an antiulcer regimen should be administered concurrently) (caution and close supervision are also recommended for other patients in whom there is a significant risk of gastrointestinal toxicity; misoprostol or sucralfate should be considered as prophylaxis for those at high risk)	✓	✓	✓	✓	✓	✓	✓	✓	✓	✓	✓	✓	✓	✓	✓	✓
Conditions predisposing to fluid retention, such as: Compromised cardiac function; or Hypertension (NSAIDs may cause fluid retention and edema; hypertension may be exacerbated)	✓	✓	✓	✓	✓	✓	✓	✓	✓	✓	✓	✓	✓	✓	✓	✓
Congestive heart failure or Diabetes mellitus or Edema, pre-existing, or Extracellular volume depletion or Sepsis (increased risk of renal failure)	✓	✓	✓	✓	✓	✓	✓	✓	✓	✓	✓	✓	✓	✓	✓	✓
Epilepsy or » Mental depression or other psychiatric disturbances or Parkinsonism (may be aggravated by indomethacin)							✓									
» Hemophilia or other bleeding problems including coagulation or platelet function disorders (increased risk of bleeding because NSAIDs inhibit platelet aggregation and may cause gastrointestinal ulceration or hemorrhage)	✓	✓	✓	✓	✓	✓	✓	✓	✓	✓	✓	✓	✓	✓	✓	✓
Hepatic cirrhosis, especially chronic alcoholic (concentration of free [unbound] ketoprofen or naproxen may be increased [even though] total plasma naproxen concentration may be decreased]; the lowest effective dose should be administered and the patient carefully monitored)								✓			✓					

Table 2. Contraindications/Medical Problems *(continued)*

Legend:
I=Diclofenac
II=Diflunisal
III=Fenoprofen
IV=Floctafenine
V=Flurbiprofen
VI=Ibuprofen
VII=Indomethacin
VIII=Ketoprofen
IX=Meclofenamate
X=Mefenamic Acid
XI=Naproxen
XII=Phenylbutazone
XIII=Piroxicam
XIV=Sulindac
XV=Tiaprofenic Acid
XVI=Tolmetin

Contraindications/Medical Problems	I	II	III	IV	V	VI	VII	VIII	IX	X	XI	XII	XIII	XIV	XV	XVI
Hepatic function impairment (most NSAIDs known to be metabolized hepatically; also, increased risk of renal failure)	✓	✓	✓	✓	✓	✓	✓	✓	✓	✓	✓	✓	✓	✓	✓	✓
(metabolism of sulindac to the active sulfide metabolite is slowed; however, biliary elimination of the metabolite is greatly decreased, leading to increased and prolonged plasma concentrations and increased risk of toxicity; the patient should be carefully monitored and dosage adjusted as necessary)														✓		
» Hypoprothrombinemia, when prothrombin activity is 10 to 20% of normal										✓						
» Polymyalgia rheumatica or » Temporal arteritis (may be aggravated by phenylbutazone)												✓				
» Porphyria, hepatic (diclofenac may precipitate an acute attack)	✓															
» Renal calculus or history of (renal calculi containing sulindac metabolites have occurred, rarely, in patients receiving sulindac; it is recommended that the medication be used with caution, and in conjunction with adequate fluid intake, in patients who may be predisposed to calculus formation)														✓		
Renal function impairment (NSAIDs and/or their metabolites are excreted primarily via the kidneys; a reduction in dosage may be required to prevent accumulation) (increased risk of adverse renal effects, including acute renal failure; patient should be carefully monitored)	✓		✓	✓	✓	✓	✓	✓	✓	✓	✓		✓	✓	✓	✓
(in end-stage renal disease, conversion of sulindac to its active metabolite is decreased)														✓		
» Renal function impairment or history of (NSAIDs and/or their metabolites are excreted primarily via the kidneys; a reduction in dosage may be required to prevent accumulation) (increased risk of adverse renal effects, including acute renal failure; patient should be carefully monitored)		✓											✓	✓		
» Stomatitis (may be induced by NSAIDs; one symptom of possible NSAID-induced blood dyscrasias may be masked)	✓	✓					✓	✓	✓	✓	✓	✓		✓	✓	✓

Table 2. Contraindications/Medical Problems *(continued)*

Legend:
I=Diclofenac
II=Diflunisal
III=Fenoprofen
IV=Floctafenine
V=Flurbiprofen
VI=Ibuprofen
VII=Indomethacin
VIII=Ketoprofen
IX=Meclofenamate
X=Mefenamic Acid
XI=Naproxen
XII=Phenylbutazone
XIII=Piroxicam
XIV=Sulindac
XV=Tiaprofenic Acid
XVI=Tolmetin

Contraindications/Medical Problems	I	II	III	IV	V	VI	VII	VIII	IX	X	XI	XII	XIII	XIV	XV	XVI
» Symptoms of bronchospasm, allergic rhinitis, or urticaria, mild, induced by aspirin or other NSAIDs (possibility of cross-sensitivity)	✓	✓	✓	✓	✓	✓	✓	✓	✓	✓	✓	✓	✓	✓	✓	✓
Systemic lupus erythematosus (SLE) (patient predisposed to NSAID-induced central nervous system and/or renal adverse effects)	✓		✓	✓	✓	✓	✓	✓	✓	✓	✓	✓	✓	✓	✓	✓
For rectal dosage forms only » Bleeding, rectal or anal, active or recent history of, or » Hemorrhoids or » Lesions, inflammatory, of anus or rectum, or » Proctitis or recent history of (may be exacerbated [active cases] or reactivated)	✓						✓	✓			✓		✓			

Table 3. Side/Adverse Effects*

The following side/adverse effects have been selected on the basis of their potential clinical significance (possible signs and symptoms in parentheses where appropriate)—not necessarily inclusive:

Legend:
I=Diclofenac, II=Diflunisal, III=Fenoprofen
IV=Floctafenine, V=Flurbiprofen, VI=Ibuprofen
VII=Indomethacin, VIII=Ketoprofen, IX=Meclofenamate
X=Mefenamic Acid, XI=Naproxen, XII=Phenylbutazone, XIII=Piroxicam
XIV=Sulindac, XV=Tiaprofenic Acid, XVI=Tolmetin

Medical attention needed
Cardiovascular effects
Note: Many of these cardiovascular effects may occur secondary to NSAID-induced renal function impairment

	I	II	III	IV	V	VI	VII	VIII	IX	X	XI	XII	XIII	XIV	XV	XVI
Angina pectoris or exacerbation of (chest pain)	L	U	U	U	R†	U	U	U	U	U	U	U	R	U	R	U
Chest pain	R†	R†	U	U	R	R	R	U	U	U	U	U	U	U	R	L
Congestive heart failure or exacerbation of (chest pain; shortness of breath, troubled breathing, tightness in chest, and/or wheezing; decrease in amount of urine; swelling of face, fingers, feet, or lower legs; unusual tiredness; weight gain)	R	U	U	U	R	R	R	R	R	U	R	R	R	R		R
Edema, pulmonary (shortness of breath, troubled breathing, tightness in chest, and/or wheezing)	U	U	R†	U	U	U	R	U	U	U	U	U	R	U	U	U
Increased blood pressure—may reach hypertensive levels	R	U	U	U	R	R	R	R	U	U	U	R	R	R	U	M
Irregular heartbeat	L	U	R†	U	R†	R†	R	R†	U	U	U	U	U	R†	U	U
Nosebleeds, unexplained	R	U	U	U	R	R†	R	R	R	R	R	R	R	R	L	R†
Pericarditis (chest pain; fever with or without chills; shortness of breath, troubled breathing, and/or tightness in chest)	U	U	U	U	U	U	U	U	U	R	U	R	U	U	U	U
Central nervous system effects																
Confusion	U	R	L	L	R	R	R	R	R	R	R	R	R†	U	U	U
Convulsions	R†	U	R†	R†	R†	U	U	U	U	U	U	U	U	R	U	U
Feeling of depersonalization or muzziness	U	U	U	U	U	U	R	U	U	U	U	U	U	U	U	U
Forgetfulness	R†	U	U	U	U	U	R	R	R	R	U	U	R†	R	L	U
Hallucinations	U	R	U	U	U	R†	R†	R†	U	U	U	U	R†	U	U	U

*Differences in frequency of occurrence may reflect either lack of clinical-use data or actual pharmacologic distinctions among agents (although their pharmacologic similarity suggests that side effects occurring with one may occur with the others). M=more frequent (3–9%); L=less frequent (1–3%); R=rare (<1%); U=unknown; unless otherwise specified.
†Has been reported, but a causal relationship has not been established.
‡Has been reported, but actual frequency of occurrence unknown.
§Serious gastrointestinal adverse effects, including ulceration, perforation and/or bleeding, may occur at any time, with or without warning signs and/or symptoms, during chronic therapy with nonsteroidal anti-inflammatory drugs (NSAIDs). The risk of NSAID-induced gastrointestinal toxicity may increase with the duration of therapy as well as with dosage; in clinical trials, upper gastrointestinal tract ulceration, bleeding, or perforation occurred in approximately 1% of patients treated for 3 to 6 months and in approximately 2 to 4% of those treated for 1 year. Risk factors that may increase the risk of NSAID-induced gastrointestinal toxicity, other than those associated with an increased risk of peptic ulcer disease in any patient, have not been identified.
#Frequency of occurrence 10% or higher.
**Diarrhea occurring with mefenamic acid therapy requires medical attention.
††Paralytic ileus has been reported (incidence <1%), but a causal relationship has not been established.

Table 3. Side/Adverse Effects* *(continued)*

Legend:
I=Diclofenac
II=Diflunisal
III=Fenoprofen
IV=Floctafenine
V=Flurbiprofen
VI=Ibuprofen
VII=Indomethacin
VIII=Ketoprofen
IX=Meclofenamate
X=Mefenamic Acid
XI=Naproxen
XII=Phenylbutazone
XIII=Piroxicam
XIV=Sulindac
XV=Tiaprofenic Acid
XVI=Tolmetin

	I	II	III	IV	V	VI	VII	VIII	IX	X	XI	XII	XIII	XIV	XV	XVI
Headache, severe, especially in the morning	U	U	U	U	U	U	M#	U	U	U	U	U	U	U	U	U
Meningitis, aseptic (headache, severe, with fever and stiff neck)	R	R	R†	U	U	R	U	U	R†	U	R	R	R	R	U	R
Mental depression or other mood or mental changes	L	R	M	L	L	R	L	L	M	L	M	R	L	R	L	L
Migraine (headache, severe and throbbing)	U	U	U	U	U	U	R	R	R†	U	U	U	U	U	U	U
Neuropathy, peripheral (numbness, tingling, pain, or weakness in hands or feet)	R†	R†	U	U	U	R†	R	R	R†	U	R†	R	R†	R	R	U
Syncope (fainting)	U	R†	U	U	U	U	R	U	U	U	U	U	U	R	U	U
Dermatologic effects *Dermatitis, allergic*																
(skin rash)	L	M	M	L	R	M	R	L	M	L	M	L	L	M	M	L
(hives)	R	R	L	R	R	R	R	R	L	‡	R†	R	R	U	U	R
(itching)	L	R	M	L	R	L	R	R	L	‡	M	R	L	L	M	L
Dermatitis, exfoliative (fever with or without chills; red, thickened, or scaly skin; swollen and/or painful glands; unusual bruising)	R†	R	R†	U	R	U	R	R	R	U	R	R	R	R	U	U
Erythema multiforme (fever with or without chills; muscle cramps or pain; skin rash; sores, ulcers, or white spots on lips or in mouth)	R	R	U	U	U	U	R	U	R	U	R†	R	R	R	R	R
Erythema nodosum (fever with or without chills; skin rash)	R	R	U	U	U	U	R	U	R	U	U	R	R	R	U	R
Necrolysis, toxic epidermal (redness, tenderness, itching, burning, or peeling of skin; sore throat; fever with or without chills)	U	R	R†	U	R	R†	R	U	U	U	R†	R	R	R	R	R
Stevens-Johnson syndrome (bleeding or crusting sores on lips; chest pain; fever with or without chills; muscle cramps or pain; skin rash; sores, ulcers, or white spots in mouth; sore throat)	R	R	R†	U	R	R	R		R	U	R†	R	R	R	U	R
Gastrointestinal effects *Bleeding from rectum*—with suppository dosage forms	‡	—	—	U	—	—	R	M	—	—	R	—	‡	—	—	U
Esophagitis or Gastritis (burning feeling in throat, chest, or stomach)	U	U	U	U	R	U	R	U	U	U	U	U	U	U	U	U
	U	R	R	U	R	R	U	R	U	U	U	R	U	R	U	L

Table 3. Side/Adverse Effects* (continued)

Legend:
I=Diclofenac
II=Diflunisal
III=Fenoprofen
IV=Floctafenine
V=Flurbiprofen
VI=Ibuprofen
VII=Indomethacin
VIII=Ketoprofen
IX=Meclofenamate
X=Mefenamic Acid
XI=Naproxen
XII=Phenylbutazone
XIII=Piroxicam
XIV=Sulindac
XV=Tiaprofenic Acid
XVI=Tolmetin

	I	II	III	IV	V	VI	VII	VIII	IX	X	XI	XII	XIII	XIV	XV	XVI
Gastrointestinal ulceration, possibly with perforation and/or bleeding (abdominal pain, cramping, or burning, severe; bloody or black tarry stools; vomiting of blood or material that looks like coffee grounds; nausea, heartburn, and/or indigestion, severe and continuing) — in addition to peptic ulceration, may include colitis, regional enteritis, and perforation and hemorrhage of the esophagus or existing sigmoid lesions [diverticula or carcinoma]; intestinal ulceration may also lead to stenosis and obstruction§	L	R	R	M	R	R	R	R	R	R	R	R	R	R	R	R
Genitourinary effects																
Bleeding from vagina, unexplained, unexpected, and/or unusually heavy menstrual	R†	U	U	U	R	R†	R	R		U	U	U	U	R	R	U
Crystalluria, renal calculi, or ureteral obstruction (blood in urine; difficult, burning, or painful urination; severe pain in lower back, side, or abdomen)—with phenylbutazone, may be composed of uric acid crystals because phenylbutazone has uricosuric activity; with sulindac, may be composed of sulindac metabolites	U		U	U	U	U	U	U			U	R	U	R	U	U
Cystitis or other lower urinary tract irritation or Urinary tract infection (bloody or cloudy urine; difficult, burning, or painful urination; frequent urge to urinate)	R†	R	R	M	R	R	R†	L		R	U	U	R†	U	U	R
Incontinence (loss of bladder control)	U	U	U	U	M	U	U	U		U	U	U	U	U	R	U
Hematologic effects																
Agranulocytosis (fever with or without chills; sores, ulcers, or white spots on lips or in mouth; sore throat)	R	R	R	U	R	R	R	R	R	R	R	R	U	R	U	R
Anemia (unusual tiredness and/or weakness)—may be associated with gastrointestinal bleeding or microbleeding	R	U	U	U	R	R	R	R	R	R	U	R	L	L	U	L

*Differences in frequency of occurrence may reflect either lack of clinical-use data or actual pharmacologic distinctions among agents (although their pharmacologic similarity suggests that side effects occurring with one may occur with the others). M=more frequent (3–9%); L=less frequent (1–3%); R=rare (<1%); U=unknown; unless otherwise specified.

†Has been reported, but a causal relationship has not been established.

‡Has been reported, but actual frequency of occurrence unknown.

§Serious gastrointestinal adverse effects, including ulceration, perforation and/or bleeding, may occur at any time, with or without warning signs and/or symptoms, during chronic therapy with nonsteroidal anti-inflammatory drugs (NSAIDs). The risk of NSAID-induced gastrointestinal toxicity may increase with the duration of therapy as well as with dosage; in clinical trials, upper gastrointestinal tract ulceration, bleeding, or perforation occurred in approximately 1% of patients treated for 3 to 6 months and in approximately 2 to 4% of those treated for 1 year. Risk factors that may increase the risk of NSAID-induced gastrointestinal toxicity, other than those associated with an increased risk of peptic ulcer disease in any patient, have not been identified.

#Frequency of occurrence 10% or higher.

**Diarrhea occurring with mefenamic acid therapy requires medical attention.

††Paralytic ileus has been reported (incidence <1%), but a causal relationship has not been established.

Table 3. Side/Adverse Effects* (continued)

Legend:
I=Diclofenac
II=Diflunisal
III=Fenoprofen
IV=Floctafenine
V=Flurbiprofen
VI=Ibuprofen
VII=Indomethacin
VIII=Ketoprofen
IX=Meclofenamate
X=Mefenamic Acid
XI=Naproxen
XII=Phenylbutazone
XIII=Piroxicam
XIV=Sulindac
XV=Tiaprofenic Acid
XVI=Tolmetin

Side/Adverse Effect	I	II	III	IV	V	VI	VII	VIII	IX	X	XI	XII	XIII	XIV	XV	XVI
Anemia, aplastic [pancytopenia] (shortness of breath, troubled breathing, tightness in chest, and/or wheezing; sores, ulcers, or white spots on lips or in mouth; swollen and/or painful glands; unusual bleeding or bruising; unusual tiredness or weakness)	R	U	R	U	R	R	R	U	U	R	R†	R	R	R	U	U
Anemia, hemolytic (troubled breathing, exertional; unusual tiredness or weakness)	U	R	R	U	R	R	R	R	R	R	R†	R	R†	R	U	R
Bone marrow depression—signs and symptoms are listed under individual entries for *Anemia, aplastic* and *Thrombocytopenia*	U	U	U	U	U	U	U	U	U	U	U	R	R	R	U	U
Leukopenia [neutropenia] (usually asymptomatic; rarely, fever or chills, cough or hoarseness, lower back or side pain, painful or difficult urination)	R	U	U	U	R	R	R	U	R	R	R	R	L	R	R	U
Thrombocytopenia with or without purpura (usually asymptomatic; rarely, unusual bleeding or bruising; black, tarry stools; blood in urine or stools; pinpoint red spots on skin)	R	R	R	U	R	R	R	R	U	R	R	R	R	R	U	R
Hepatitis (fever with or without chills, skin rash, swelling and/or tenderness in upper abdominal or stomach area, swollen and/or painful glands, unusual bleeding or bruising, unusual tiredness or weakness, yellow eyes or skin)	R	R	R	U	R	R	R	R	U	R	R	R	R	R	U	R
Hypersensitivity reactions See also *Dermatologic effects*																
Anaphylaxis (changes in facial skin color; skin rash, hives, and/or itching; fast or irregular breathing; puffiness or swelling of the eyelids or around the eyes; shortness of breath, troubled breathing, tightness in chest, and/or wheezing)—may include anaphylactic shock with sudden, severe decrease in blood pressure and collapse	R	R	R	U	R	R	R	R	U	U	R	R	R	R	U	R
Angiitis [vasculitis] (muscle pain, cramps, and/or weakness; shortness of breath, troubled breathing, tightness in chest, and/or wheezing; skin rash; spitting blood; unusual tiredness or weakness)	U	R	U	U	U	R†	R	U	U	U	R†	R	R	R	U	R
Angioedema (hive-like swellings, large, on face, eyelids, mouth, lips, and/or tongue)	R	R	R†	U	R	R†	R	U	U	U	R†	R	R	R	U	U
Bronchospastic allergic reaction (shortness of breath, troubled breathing, tightness in chest, and/or wheezing)	R	U	U	U	U	R	R	R	U	U	U	R	R	R	U	U
Edema, laryngeal (shortness of breath or troubled breathing)	U	U	U	U	U	U	U	R	U	U	U	U	U	U	U	U
Fever with or without chills	U	U	R†	U	R	U	R	U	U	U	R	R	R†	R	U	R

Table 3. Side/Adverse Effects* *(continued)*

Legend:
I=Diclofenac
II=Diflunisal
III=Fenoprofen
IV=Floctafenine
V=Flurbiprofen
VI=Ibuprofen
VII=Indomethacin
VIII=Ketoprofen
IX=Meclofenamate
X=Mefenamic Acid
XI=Naproxen
XII=Phenylbutazone
XIII=Piroxicam
XIV=Sulindac
XV=Tiaprofenic Acid
XVI=Tolmetin

Side/Adverse Effect	I	II	III	IV	V	VI	VII	VIII	IX	X	XI	XII	XIII	XIV	XV	XVI
Hypersensitivity syndrome, multisystemic, diflunisal-induced (sudden decrease in amount of urine; swelling of face, fingers, feet, or lower legs; swollen and/or painful glands; unusual bleeding or bruising; unusual tiredness or weakness; weight gain, rapid; yellow eyes or skin)	—	R	—	—						—	—	—	—		—	—
Hypersensitivity syndrome, multisystemic, sulindac-induced (chest pain; fever with or without chills; sudden decrease in amount of urine; swelling of face, fingers, feet, or lower legs; swollen and/or painful glands; unusual bleeding or bruising; unusual tiredness or weakness; weight gain, rapid; yellow eyes or skin)	—	—	—	—		—				—	—	—	—	R	—	—
Loeffler syndrome [eosinophilic pneumonitis] (chest pain; fever with or without chills; shortness of breath, troubled breathing, tightness in chest, and/or wheezing; unusual weakness)	U	U	R†	U	U	U	U	U		U	R	U	U	U	U	U
Rhinitis, allergic (unexplained runny nose or sneezing)	U	U	U	U	L	R	U	R	U	U	U	U	U	U	R	R
Serum sickness-like reaction (fever with or without chills; muscle cramps, pain, and/or weakness; skin rash, hives, and/or itching; shortness of breath, troubled breathing, tightness in chest, and/or wheezing; swollen and/or painful glands)	U	U	U	U	U	R†	U	U	R	U	U	R	R	U	U	R
Systemic lupus erythematosus [SLE]-like syndrome (bloody or cloudy urine; chest pain; fever with or without chills; shortness of breath, troubled breathing, tightness in chest, and/or wheezing; skin rash, hives, and/or itching; sudden decrease in amount of urine; swelling of face, fingers, feet, and/or lower legs; swollen and/or painful glands; unusual weakness; weight gain, rapid)	U	U	U	U	U	R†	U	R	R	U	U	U	U	U	U	U
Loosening or splitting of fingernails	U	U	U	U	U	U	U	R	U	U	U	U	R†	U	R	U
Muscle cramps or pain	U	R†	M	U	U	U	R	R	U	U	R	R	U	U	U	M

*Differences in frequency of occurrence may reflect either lack of clinical-use data or actual pharmacologic distinctions among agents (although their pharmacologic similarity suggests that side effects occurring with one may occur with the others). M=more frequent (3–9%); L=less frequent (1–3%); R=rare (<1%); U=unknown; unless otherwise specified.

†Has been reported, but a causal relationship has not been established.

‡Has been reported, but actual frequency of occurrence unknown.

§Serious gastrointestinal adverse effects, including ulceration, perforation and/or bleeding, may occur at any time, with or without warning signs and/or symptoms, during chronic therapy with nonsteroidal anti-inflammatory drugs (NSAIDs). The risk of NSAID-induced gastrointestinal toxicity may increase with the duration of therapy as well as with dosage; in clinical trials, upper gastrointestinal tract ulceration, bleeding, or perforation occurred in approximately 1% of patients treated for 3 to 6 months and in approximately 2 to 4% of those treated for 1 year. Risk factors that may increase the risk of NSAID-induced gastrointestinal toxicity, other than those associated with an increased risk of peptic ulcer disease in any patient, have not been identified.

#Frequency of occurrence 10% or higher.

**Diarrhea occurring with mefenamic acid therapy requires medical attention.

††Paralytic ileus has been reported (incidence <1%), but a causal relationship has not been established.

Table 3. Side/Adverse Effects* *(continued)*

Legend:
I=Diclofenac
II=Diflunisal
III=Fenoprofen
IV=Floctafenine
V=Flurbiprofen
VI=Ibuprofen
VII=Indomethacin
VIII=Ketoprofen
IX=Meclofenamate
X=Mefenamic Acid
XI=Naproxen
XII=Phenylbutazone
XIII=Piroxicam
XIV=Sulindac
XV=Tiaprofenic Acid
XVI=Tolmetin

	I	II	III	IV	V	VI	VII	VIII	IX	X	XI	XII	XIII	XIV	XV	XVI
Ocular effects																
Amblyopia, toxic (blurred vision or any change in vision)	R†	U	U	U	U	R	U	U	U	U	U	R†	U	U	U	U
Blurred vision or any change in vision	R	R	L	L	R	R	R	L	R	‡	L	R†	R	R	R	L
Conjunctivitis (eye pain, redness, irritation, and/or swelling)	U	U	U	U	R	R†	U	R	R†	U	U	U	U	U	R	U
Corneal opacity (blurred vision or any change in vision)	U	U	U	U	U	U	U	U	U	U	U	U	U	U	U	U
Dry, irritated, or swollen eyes	U	U	U	U	R	R	R	R	R†	‡	U	U	R	U	R	U
Eye pain	U	U	U	U	U	U	R	U	U	U	U	U	U	U	U	U
Retinal or macular disturbances (blurred vision or any change in vision)—with prolonged use	U	U	U	U	U	U	R	U	R†	U	U	U	U	R†	U	R†
Retinal hemorrhage (red eyes)	U	U	U	U	U	U	U	R	U	U	U	R†	U	U	U	U
Scotomata (change in vision)	R	U	U	U	U	U	U	U	U	U	U	R†	U	U	U	U
Otic effects																
Decreased hearing or any change in hearing	R	U	L	U	R†	R	R	R	U	U	L	R	R†	R	U	U
Ringing or buzzing in ears	L	L	L	L	L	L	L	L	U	U	M	R	L	L	R	L
Pancreatitis, acute (abdominal pain, fever with or without chills, swelling and/or tenderness in upper abdominal or stomach area)	U	U	R†	U	U	R	R	U	U	R	U	R†	R†	R	U	U
Renal effects																
Fluid retention (increased blood pressure; decrease in amount of urine; swelling of face, fingers, feet, and/or lower legs; weight gain, rapid)	M	R					L	M	L		M	M	L	L	U	M
Nephritis, interstitial (bloody or cloudy urine; increased blood pressure; sudden decrease in amount of urine; swelling of face, fingers, feet, and/or lower legs; weight gain, rapid)—may be hypersensitivity-mediated	R	R	R	U	R	U	R	R		U	R	R	R	R	U	U
Nephrosis (sudden decrease in amount of urine; swelling of face, fingers, feet, and/or lower legs; weight gain, rapid)	U	U	R	U	R	U	U	U	U	U	U	U	U	U	U	U
Nephrotic syndrome (cloudy urine, swelling of face)	R	R†	R	U	U	U	R	R	R	U	R	R	U	R	R	R
Polyuria (large increase in frequency and quantity of urination, sudden)	U	U	U	M	U	R	U	U	U	U	U	U	U	R	R	U

Table 3. Side/Adverse Effects* *(continued)*

Legend:
I=Diclofenac
II=Diflunisal
III=Fenoprofen
IV=Floctafenine
V=Flurbiprofen
VI=Ibuprofen
VII=Indomethacin
VIII=Ketoprofen
IX=Meclofenamate
X=Mefenamic Acid
XI=Naproxen
XII=Phenylbutazone
XIII=Piroxicam
XIV=Sulindac
XV=Tiaprofenic Acid
XVI=Tolmetin

	I	II	III	IV	V	VI	VII	VIII	IX	X	XI	XII	XIII	XIV	XV	XVI
Renal impairment or failure (increased blood pressure; shortness of breath, troubled breathing, tightness in chest, and/or wheezing; sudden decrease in amount of urine; swelling of face, fingers, feet, and/or lower legs; thirst, continuing; unusual tiredness or weakness; weight gain)	R	R	R	U	R	R	R	R	R	R	R	R	R	R	U	R
Shortness of breath, troubled breathing, tightness in chest, and/or wheezing	R	R†	L	U	R	R	R	R	U	‡	M	R	R†	R	R	R
Stomatitis, aphthous (sores, ulcers, or white spots on lips or in mouth)	R	R	R†	U	R	R	R	L	L	U	L	R	L	R	U	R
Thirst, continuing	U	U	U	L	U	U	U	R	U	U	L	L	U	U	U	U
Medical attention needed only if continuing or bothersome																
Cardiovascular effects																
Fast heartbeat	R†	U	L	L	L	R†	R	R	R	U	U	U	U	U	U	U
Flushing or hot flushes	R†	U	U	L	L	R	R	U	U	U	U	U	U	U	L	U
Increased sweating	R†	R	L	L	R	U	L	L	U	‡	L	U	R	U	R	U
Pounding heartbeat	R†	R†	M	U	R	R	R	R	R†	R	L	U	R†	R	R	U
Central nervous system effects																
Dizziness or lightheadedness	L	L	M	M	L	M	M	L	M	‡	M	U	U	M	M	M
Drowsiness	R	L	M	M	M	R	R	L	U	‡	M	R	L	R	L	L
Headache, mild to moderate	M	M	M	M	M	L	M#	M	M	‡	M	R	L	M	M	M
Nervousness or irritability	R	R	M	M	L	L	R	M	U	‡	U	R	R	L	L	L
Trembling	R†	U	L	L	L	U	U	U	U	U	U	L	U	U	L	U

*Differences in frequency of occurrence may reflect either lack of clinical-use data or actual pharmacologic distinctions among agents (although their pharmacologic similarity suggests that side effects occurring with one may occur with the others). M=more frequent (3–9%); L=less frequent (1–3%); R=rare (<1%); U=unknown; unless otherwise specified.

†Has been reported, but a causal relationship has not been established.

‡Has been reported, but actual frequency of occurrence unknown.

§Serious gastrointestinal adverse effects, including ulceration, perforation and/or bleeding, may occur at any time, with or without warning signs and/or symptoms, during chronic therapy with nonsteroidal anti-inflammatory drugs (NSAIDs). The risk of NSAID-induced gastrointestinal toxicity may increase with the duration of therapy as well as with dosage; in clinical trials, upper gastrointestinal tract ulceration, bleeding, or perforation occurred in approximately 1% of patients treated for 3 to 6 months and in approximately 2 to 4% of those treated for 1 year. Risk factors that may increase the risk of NSAID-induced gastrointestinal toxicity, other than those associated with an increased risk of peptic ulcer disease in any patient, have not been identified.

#Frequency of occurrence 10% or higher.

**Diarrhea occurring with mefenamic acid therapy requires medical attention.

††Paralytic ileus has been reported (incidence <1%), but a causal relationship has not been established.

Table 3. Side/Adverse Effects* *(continued)*

Legend:
I=Diclofenac
II=Diflunisal
III=Fenoprofen
IV=Floctafenine
V=Flurbiprofen
VI=Ibuprofen
VII=Indomethacin
VIII=Ketoprofen
IX=Meclofenamate
X=Mefenamic Acid
XI=Naproxen
XII=Phenylbutazone
XIII=Piroxicam
XIV=Sulindac
XV=Tiaprofenic Acid
XVI=Tolmetin

	I	II	III	IV	V	VI	VII	VIII	IX	X	XI	XII	XIII	XIV	XV	XVI
Trouble in sleeping	R	L	L	M	L	R	R	U	R†	‡	R	U	R	R	R	L
Unusual tiredness or weakness with no other signs or symptoms	R	L	M	L	U	U	U	U	R†	U	U	R	R†	R	R	M
Dermatologic effects																
Photosensitive or photoallergic dermatologic reaction (severe sunburn; skin rash, redness, itching, and/or discoloration after exposure to sunlight)	R	R	U	U	R	R†	R	R	U	U	R	R	R	R	U	U
Gastrointestinal effects																
Abdominal or stomach cramps, pain, or discomfort, mild to moderate	M	M	L	M	M	M	M	M	M	M	M	M	M	M#	M	M
Bitter taste or other taste change	R	U	R†	L	R	U	U	U	R	U	U	U	U	R	U	U
Bloated feeling or gas	L	L	L	L	L	L	R	M	M	L	M	R	L	L	L	M
Constipation	M	L	M	M	M	L	L	M	M	L	M	R	L	M	L	L
Decreased appetite or loss of appetite	R	R	L	L	L	L	R	L	L	‡	U	U	L	L	R	R
Diarrhea	M	M	L	M	M	L	L	M	M#	M††	L	R	L	M	L	M
Heartburn or indigestion	M	M	M	M	M	M	M	M#	M	M	M	L	M	M	M#	M
Nausea	M	M	M	M	M	M	M	M	M#	M	M	M	M	M	M#	M#
Rectal irritation—with rectal dosage forms	‡	-	-	-	-	-	R	M	-	-	M	-	‡	-	-	-
Vomiting	R	L	L	U	L	L	L	L	R†	U	R	R	R	R	M	M
General feeling of discomfort or illness	R	U	L	U	U	U	L	U	R†	U	R	R	L	L	U	L
Irritation, dryness, or soreness of mouth	R	L	L	L	R	R	R	U	L	U	L	U	R	R	L	R
Weight loss, unexplained	R†	U	U	U	U	U	U	U	R	U	U	U	U	U	U	M

*Differences in frequency of occurrence may reflect either lack of clinical-use data or actual pharmacologic distinctions among agents (although their pharmacologic similarity suggests that side effects occurring with one may occur with the others). M=more frequent (3–9%); L=less frequent (1–3%); R=rare (<1%); U=unknown; unless otherwise specified.

†Has been reported, but a causal relationship has not been established.

‡Has been reported, but actual frequency of occurrence unknown.

§Serious gastrointestinal adverse effects, including ulceration, perforation and/or bleeding, may occur at any time, with or without warning signs and/or symptoms, during chronic therapy with nonsteroidal anti-inflammatory drugs (NSAIDs). The risk of NSAID-induced gastrointestinal toxicity may increase with the duration of therapy as well as with dosage; in clinical trials, upper gastrointestinal tract ulceration, bleeding, or perforation occurred in approximately 1% of patients treated for 3 to 6 months and in approximately 2 to 4% of those treated for 1 year. Risk factors that may increase the risk of NSAID-induced gastrointestinal toxicity, other than those associated with an increased risk of peptic ulcer disease in any patient, have not been identified.

#Frequency of occurrence 10% or higher.

**Diarrhea occurring with mefenamic acid therapy requires medical attention.

††Paralytic ileus has been reported (incidence <1%), but a causal relationship has not been established.

Table 4. Patient Consultation

Legend:
I=Diclofenac
II=Diflunisal
III=Fenoprofen
IV=Floctafenine
V=Flurbiprofen
VI=Ibuprofen
VII=Indomethacin
VIII=Ketoprofen
IX=Meclofenamate
X=Mefenamic Acid
XI=Naproxen
XII=Phenylbutazone
XIII=Piroxicam
XIV=Sulindac
XV=Tiaprofenic Acid
XVI=Tolmetin

In providing consultation, consider emphasizing the following selected information (» = major clinical significance):

	I	II	III	IV	V	VI	VII	VIII	IX	X	XI	XII	XIII	XIV	XV	XVI
Before using this medication																
» Conditions affecting use, especially:																
Allergies to aspirin or any of the nonsteroidal anti-inflammatory drugs (NSAIDs)	✓	✓	✓	✓	✓	✓	✓	✓	✓	✓	✓	✓	✓	✓	✓	✓
Pregnancy—Use during second half of pregnancy not recommended because of potential adverse effect on fetal blood flow and possible prolongation of pregnancy, dystocia, and delayed delivery	✓	✓	✓	✓	✓	✓	✓	✓	✓	✓	✓	✓	✓	✓	✓	✓
Breast-feeding—Caution recommended with indomethacin, which has caused convulsions in a nursing infant; phenylbutazone, which may cause blood dyscrasias or other adverse effects in the infant; and with meclofenamate and piroxicam, which have caused adverse effects in animal studies							✓		✓			✓	✓			
Use in children—Because of toxicity, phenylbutazone not recommended in children <15 years of age and indomethacin should be used with caution and only in patients unresponsive to less toxic NSAIA's; also, naproxen-induced skin rash more common in pediatric patients							✓				✓	✓				
Use in the elderly—Increased risk of toxicity; initial dosage should be reduced and patients carefully monitored	✓	✓	✓	✓	✓	✓	✓	✓	✓	✓	✓	✓	✓	✓	✓	✓
Other medications, especially oral anticoagulants, hypoprothrombinemia-producing cephalosporins, moxalactam, plicamycin, triamterene, phenytoin (for piroxicam and tiaprofenic acid only), aspirin, blood-dyscrasia-causing medications, bone marrow depressants, digitalis (for phenylbutazone only), lithium, methotrexate, penicillamine, probenecid, and tetracycline (for buffered phenylbutazone only)	✓	✓	✓	✓	✓	✓	✓	✓	✓	✓	✓	✓	✓	✓	✓	✓
Other medical problems, especially blood dyscrasias, bone marrow depression, cardiac or cardiopulmonary disease or predisposition to, hepatic disease, renal disease or predisposition to, peptic ulcer or other gastrointestinal tract disease or predisposition to, clotting defects, mental depression (for indomethacin only), stomatitis, and rectal lesions or bleeding	✓	✓	✓	✓	✓	✓	✓	✓	✓	✓	✓	✓	✓	✓	✓	✓

*Suspension dosage form should not be mixed with antacid or other liquid prior to use.

Table 4. Patient Consultation (*continued*)

Legend:
I=Diclofenac
II=Diflunisal
III=Fenoprofen
IV=Floctafenine
V=Flurbiprofen
VI=Ibuprofen
VII=Indomethacin
VIII=Ketoprofen
IX=Meclofenamate
X=Mefenamic Acid
XI=Naproxen
XII=Phenylbutazone
XIII=Piroxicam
XIV=Sulindac
XV=Tiaprofenic Acid
XVI=Tolmetin

	I	II	III	IV	V	VI	VII	VIII	IX	X	XI	XII	XIII	XIV	XV	XVI
Proper use of this medication																
Taking oral dosage forms:																
—on empty stomach for better absorption (acute use) or with food or antacids (a magnesium- and aluminum-containing antacid may be preferred) to reduce gastrointestinal irritation (chronic use), except for delayed-release (enteric-coated) tablets	✓					✓*			✓		✓*					
—with meals or antacids (a magnesium- and aluminum-containing antacid may be preferred) to reduce gastrointestinal irritation		✓	✓	✓	✓	✓	✓*	✓	✓	✓		✓	✓	✓	✓	✓
—with a full glass of water and not lying down for 15 to 30 minutes after taking		✓										✓				
Proper administration:																
Swallowing whole—Diflunisal tablets; delayed-release (enteric-coated) or extended-release tablet dosage forms; all phenylbutazone tablet formulations		✓										✓				
Suppository dosage forms—																
Proper administration technique							✓					✓				
Retaining indomethacin suppository in rectum for 1 full hour to ensure maximum absorption							✓									
» Not taking more medication than prescribed or recommended on ibuprofen OTC package label	✓		✓	✓	✓	✓	✓	✓	✓	✓		✓	✓	✓		✓
» Taking for prescribed indications only; not taking to relieve other aches and pains	✓						✓									
» Not taking longer than 7 days at a time unless otherwise directed by physician	✓					✓				✓						
» Compliance with therapy (when used for arthritis)	✓	✓	✓	✓	✓	✓	✓	✓	✓	✓	✓	✓	✓	✓	✓	✓
» In arthritis, noticeable improvement in condition may require:																
A few days to 1 week	✓	✓	✓		✓	✓		✓			✓		✓		✓	✓
Up to 2 weeks (for some types of arthritis)							✓				✓					
» In arthritis, maximum effectiveness may require:																
1 to 2 weeks	✓						✓									✓
2 to 3 weeks													✓			
Up to 4 weeks (for some types of arthritis)														✓		
Up to 12 weeks (for some types of arthritis)											✓					
Missed dose (scheduled dosing): Taking as soon as possible; not taking if almost time for next dose; not doubling doses	✓	✓	✓	✓	✓	✓	✓	✓	✓	✓	✓	✓	✓	✓	✓	✓
» Proper storage	✓	✓	✓	✓	✓	✓	✓	✓	✓	✓	✓	✓	✓	✓	✓	✓

Table 4. Patient Consultation (continued)

Legend:
I=Diclofenac
II=Diflunisal
III=Fenoprofen
IV=Floctafenine
V=Flurbiprofen
VI=Ibuprofen
VII=Indomethacin
VIII=Ketoprofen
IX=Meclofenamate
X=Mefenamic Acid
XI=Naproxen
XII=Phenylbutazone
XIII=Piroxicam
XIV=Sulindac
XV=Tiaprofenic Acid
XVI=Tolmetin

Precautions while using this medication	I	II	III	IV	V	VI	VII	VIII	IX	X	XI	XII	XIII	XIV	XV	XVI
» Regular visits to physician during prolonged therapy	✓	✓	✓	✓	✓	✓	✓	✓		✓	✓	✓	✓	✓	✓	✓
» Possibility that use of alcohol or chronic concurrent use of 2 or more anti-inflammatory analgesics, including aspirin, may increase the risk of ulceration or other adverse effects	✓	✓	✓	✓	✓	✓	✓	✓	✓	✓	✓	✓	✓	✓	✓	✓
Not using acetaminophen concurrently for longer than a few days, unless directed by physician or dentist	✓	✓	✓	✓	✓	✓	✓	✓		✓	✓	✓	✓	✓	✓	✓
» Not taking buffered phenylbutazone within 1 to 3 hours of oral tetracyclines												✓				
Caution if any surgery is required because of possible enhanced bleeding	✓	✓	✓	✓	✓	✓	✓	✓		✓	✓	✓	✓	✓	✓	✓
» Caution if any of the following occur:																
Confusion		✓	✓	✓	✓		✓	✓	✓	✓	✓	✓	✓	✓	✓	✓
Diarrhea		✓	✓	✓	✓		✓	✓	✓	✓	✓	✓	✓	✓	✓	✓
Dizziness or lightheadedness		✓	✓	✓	✓	✓		✓	✓	✓	✓	✓	✓			
Drowsiness						✓				✓						
Vision problems						✓										
» Possibility of photosensitivity	✓	✓	✓	✓	✓	✓	✓	✓		✓	✓	✓	✓	✓	✓	✓
Possibility of gastrointestinal ulceration and bleeding	✓	✓	✓	✓	✓	✓	✓	✓	✓	✓	✓	✓	✓	✓	✓	✓
» Notifying physician immediately if influenza-like symptoms (chills, fever, or muscle aches and pains) occur shortly prior to or together with a skin rash; rarely, these symptoms may indicate a serious reaction to the medication	✓	✓	✓	✓	✓	✓	✓	✓		✓	✓	✓	✓	✓	✓	✓
Possibility of anaphylaxis	✓	✓	✓	✓	✓	✓	✓	✓	✓	✓	✓	✓	✓	✓	✓	✓
For self-medication (ibuprofen 200 mg) only																
Checking with physician or dentist if:																
Symptoms do not improve or if they worsen						✓										
Using for fever and fever lasts more than 3 days or returns						✓										
Painful area becomes red or swollen						✓										

*Suspension dosage form should not be mixed with antacid or other liquid prior to use.

Table 4. Patient Consultation *(continued)*

Legend:
I=Diclofenac
II=Diflunisal
III=Fenoprofen
IV=Floctafenine
V=Flurbiprofen
VI=Ibuprofen
VII=Indomethacin
VIII=Ketoprofen
IX=Meclofenamate
X=Mefenamic Acid
XI=Naproxen
XII=Phenylbutazone
XIII=Piroxicam
XIV=Sulindac
XV=Tiaprofenic Acid
XVI=Tolmetin

	I	II	III	IV	V	VI	VII	VIII	IX	X	XI	XII	XIII	XIV	XV	XVI
Side/adverse effects																
» Stopping medication and checking with physician immediately if symptoms of the following occur:																
Bronchospasm	√	√	√	√	√	√	√	√	√	√	√	√	√	√	√	√
Blood dyscrasias	√	√	√	√	√	√	√	√	√	√	√	√	√	√	√	√
Gastrointestinal ulceration	√	√	√	√	√	√	√	√	√	√	√	√	√	√	√	√
Edema												√				
Possibility that blood dyscrasias may occur many days or weeks after discontinuation of medication																
Signs and symptoms of other side effects, especially allergic or hypersensitivity reactions, cutaneous adverse effects, renal impairment, hallucinations, and hepatitis	√	√	√	√	√	√	√	√	√	√	√	√	√	√	√	√

*Suspension dosage form should not be mixed with antacid or other liquid prior to use.

ANTITHYROID AGENTS   Systemic

INN: Included in brackets after individual generic listings, if different from U.S. generic names.

Some commonly used *brand names* are:

In the U.S.—
Tapazole [Methimazole]

In Canada—
Propyl-Thyracil [Propylthiouracil]
Tapazole [Methimazole]

METHIMAZOLE [INN: Thiamazole]
Oral
Methimazole Tablets USP
In the U.S. and Canada—*Tapazole*
Rectal
Methimazole Suppositories*†
PROPYLTHIOURACIL
Oral
Propylthiouracil Tablets USP
In the U.S.—GENERIC
In Canada—*Propyl-Thyracil*
Rectal
Propylthiouracil Enema*†
Propylthiouracil Suppositories*†

---

*Not commercially available in the U.S.
†Not commercially available in Canada.

Category: Antihyperthyroid agent.

Indications

Accepted

Hyperthyroidism (treatment)—Methimazole and propylthiouracil are indicated in the treatment of hyperthyroidism, including prior to surgery or radiotherapy, and as adjuncts in the treatment of thyrotoxicosis or thyroid storm. Propylthiouracil may be preferred over methimazole for use in thyroid storm, since propylthiouracil inhibits peripheral conversion of thyroxine [T_4] to triiodothyronine [T_3].

Further studies are needed to establish the safety and efficacy of using propylthiouracil for the treatment of alcoholic liver disease.

Unaccepted

Efficacy of antithyroid medications has been inconsistent in the treatment of angina pectoris. These agents are probably useful for this purpose only in hyperthyroid patients with angina pectoris.

Antithyroid medications are not effective in the treatment of thyrotoxicosis resulting from exogenous thyroid hormone overdosage.

Pharmacology

Mechanism of action/Effect: Inhibit synthesis of thyroid hormone within the thyroid gland by serving as substrates for thyroid peroxidase, which catalyzes the incorporation of oxidized iodide into tyrosine residues in thyroglobulin molecules and couples iodotyrosines. This diverts iodine from the synthesis of thyroid hormones. Antithyroid agents do not interfere with the actions of exogenous thyroid hormone or inhibit the release of thyroid hormones. Therefore, stores of thyroid hormones must be depleted before clinical effects will be apparent. Antithyroid agents may also have moderating effects on the underlying immunologic abnormalities in hyperthyroidism due to Graves' disease (toxic diffuse goiter), but evidence on this point reported to date is inconclusive.

Propylthiouracil—Additionally, inhibits peripheral conversion of T_4 to T_3, which may theoretically make it more effective in the treatment of thyroid storm.

Onset of action: Methimazole—In one study, substantial reductions in mean serum thyroxine and triiodothyronine concentrations were seen after 5 days of methimazole therapy at 40 mg per day.

Time to peak effect:
Methimazole—7 weeks (average) to normalize serum T_3 and T_4 concentrations with use of 30 mg per day. In one study, 4 weeks (approximate) to normalize serum T_3 and T_4 concentrations with use of 40 mg per day.
Propylthiouracil—17 weeks (average) to normalize serum T_3 and T_4 concentrations with use of 300 mg per day.

Precautions to Consider

Cross-sensitivity and/or related problems

Cross-sensitivity may occur frequently (in about 50% of patients) between antithyroid thioamide medications.

If a persistent or severe reaction necessitates withdrawal of one agent, therapy may be switched to the other, although there is a risk of cross-reactivity occurring. However, if agranulocytosis, thrombocytopenia, or hepatic dysfunction occurs, substitution with another thioamide is not recommended.

Geriatrics

One study showed that agranulocytosis is more likely to occur in patients older than 40 years of age or in patients taking more than 40 mg of methimazole per day.

In one pharmacokinetic study, no significant differences were found for geriatric patients in certain pharmacokinetic parameters (e.g., Vd, Vd beta, Vd at steady state, area under the curve, and clearance). Rate of absorption was decreased (approximately one-third that of younger subjects) though there are no data regarding the clinical significance of this finding.

Geriatric patients with severe cardiac disease should be given antithyroid agents and/or beta-adrenergic blocking agents, such as propranolol, for 4 to 6 weeks prior to treatment with radioiodine to help reduce possible exacerbation of heart disease by radiation-induced thyroiditis. Antithyroid drugs must be discontinued at least 3 to 4 days prior to radioiodine treatment and should not be readministered until 1 week after treatment. However, a beta-adrenergic blocking agent may be used throughout the treatment period if needed.

Dental

The bone marrow depressant effects of antithyroid agents may result in an increased incidence of microbial infection, delayed healing, and gingival bleeding. If leukopenia or thrombocytopenia occurs, dental work should be deferred until blood counts have returned to normal, and patients should be instructed in proper oral hygiene, including caution in use of regular toothbrushes, dental floss, and toothpicks.

Drug interactions and/or related problems

The following drug interactions and/or related problems have been selected on the basis of their potential clinical significance (possible mechanism in parentheses where appropriate)—not necessarily inclusive (» = major clinical significance):

Note: Combinations containing any of the following medications, depending on the amount present, may also interact with this medication.

Aminophylline or
Oxtriphylline or

Theophylline
(hyperthyroid patients have exhibited increased metabolic clearance of aminophylline and theophylline, which returned to normal as the patients became euthyroid; decreased dose of aminophylline, oxtriphylline, or theophylline may be necessary as patients become euthyroid)
» Amiodarone or
» Iodinated glycerol or
» Iodine or
» Potassium iodide
(iodide or iodine excess may decrease response to antithyroid agents, requiring an increase in dosage or longer duration of therapy with antithyroid agents; amiodarone contains 37% iodine by weight, and therefore its use significantly increases iodine intake; iodine deficiency may increase response to antithyroid agents, requiring an decrease in dosage or shorter duration of therapy with antithyroid agents)
» Anticoagulants, coumarin- or indandione-derivative
(as thyroid and metabolic status of patient decreases toward normal, response to oral anticoagulants may decrease; however, if thioamide-induced hypoprothrombinemia occurs, anticoagulant effect may be enhanced; adjustment of oral anticoagulant dosage on the basis of prothrombin time is recommended)
» Digitalis glycosides
(serum concentrations of digoxin and digitoxin have been reported to increase as the thyroid and metabolic status of patients taking antithyroid agents decreased; reduction in dosage of any digitalis glycoside may be necessary as patients become euthyroid)
» Sodium iodide I 131
(antithyroid agents may decrease thyroidal uptake of I 131; a rebound increase in uptake may occur up to 5 days after sudden withdrawal of the antithyroid agent)

Contraindications/Medical problems
The contraindications/medical problems included have been selected on the basis of their potential clinical significance (reasons given in parentheses where appropriate)—not necessarily inclusive (» = major clinical significance).

Except under special circumstances, this medication should not be used when the following medical problems exist:
» Severe adverse reaction or severe allergic reaction to either methimazole or propylthiouracil, or history of

Risk-benefit should be considered when the following medical problem exists:
» Hepatic function impairment
(elimination half-life may be prolonged, in proportion to the degree of hepatic insufficiency)

Side/Adverse Effects

Note: Incidence of most adverse reactions is dose-related; most side effects occur within the first 4 to 8 weeks.

The following side/adverse effects have been selected on the basis of their potential clinical significance (possible signs and symptoms in parentheses where appropriate)—not necessarily inclusive:

Those indicating need for medical attention
Incidence more frequent—
Fever, mild and transient; leukopenia (usually asymptomatic; continuing or severe fever or chills, throat infection, cough, mouth sores, or hoarseness); *skin rash or itching*
Note: Mild *leukopenias* occur more frequently in patients (12% of adults and 25% of children) treated with antithyroid agents. Also, approximately 10% of untreated hyperthyroid patients have leukocyte levels below 4000 per cubic millimeter.

Incidence of *skin rash or itching* is 3 to 5%. Usually consists of maculopapular eruptions. An allergic reaction occurs less frequently and may disappear spontaneously with continued treatment; appears to be dose-related. Skin rash may also be a sign of vasculitis.

Incidence less frequent
Agranulocytosis (continuing or severe fever or chills, throat infection, cough, mouth sores, or hoarseness); *arthralgias or arthritis or vasculitis*—usually with propylthiouracil (pain, swelling, or redness in joints); *lupus-like syndrome* (fever or chills, general feeling of discomfort or illness or weakness)—usually with propylthiouracil; *peripheral neuropathy* (numbness or tingling of fingers, toes, or face)
Note: *Agranulocytosis* (incidence 0.4%) usually occurs during the first 3 months of therapy. May occur less predictably and with lower doses of propylthiouracil. Deaths due to agranulocytosis have been reported.

Incidence rare
Aplastic anemia (continuing or severe fever or chills, throat infection, cough, mouth sores, or hoarseness); *hypoprothrombinemia*—for propylthiouracil, *or thrombocytopenia* (usually asymptomatic; rarely, increase in bleeding or bruising; black, tarry stools; blood in urine or stools; pinpoint red spots on skin); *cholestatic jaundice*—for methimazole, *or hepatic necrosis*—primarily with propylthiouracil (yellow eyes or skin); *interstitial pneumonitis* (cough or shortness of breath)—with propylthiouracil; *lymphadenopathy* (swollen lymph nodes); *sialadenopathy* (swollen salivary glands); *nephritis*—for methimazole, *or renal vasculitis*—usually with propylthiouracil (backache, increase or decrease in urination, swelling of feet or lower legs)
Note: *Jaundice* may persist for up to 10 weeks after drug discontinuance. Fatal hepatic necrosis has been reported with both agents.

Signs and symptoms of overdosage (hypothyroidism)
Changes in menstrual periods; coldness; constipation; dry, puffy skin; goiter (swelling in the front of the neck); *headache; listlessness or sleepiness; muscle aches; nausea or vomiting, severe; unusual tiredness or weakness; weight gain, unusual*
Note: *Hypothyroidism* may be an unavoidable long-term sequela to hyperthyroidism.

Those indicating need for medical attention only if they continue or are bothersome
Incidence less frequent
Dizziness; loss of taste—for methimazole; *nausea or vomiting; stomach pain*

Patient Consultation

In providing consultation, consider emphasizing the following selected information (» = major clinical significance):

Before using this medication
» Conditions affecting use, especially:
Allergies to any thioamide
Pregnancy—May be used but careful monitoring is necessary
Breast-feeding—Excreted in breast milk, although propylthiouracil is excreted in much lesser amounts; may continue breast-feeding with low doses and monitoring of infant
Other medications, especially iodides, coumarin- or indandione-derivative anticoagulants, amiodarone, or digitalis glycosides
Other medical problems, especially hepatic function impairment

Proper use of this medication
» Importance of not taking more or less medication than the amount prescribed

» Importance of not missing doses and, if taking more than one dose per day, of taking at evenly spaced intervals

Taking methimazole at same time in relation to meals every day

Missed dose: Taking as soon as possible; taking both doses together if almost time for next dose; checking with physician if more than one dose is missed

» Proper storage

Precautions while using this medication

» Importance of close monitoring by the physician
» Checking with physician before discontinuing medication
» Caution if any kind of surgery (including dental surgery) or emergency treatment is required, because of the risk of thyroid storm
» Checking with physician immediately if injury, infection, or other illness occurs, because of the risk of thyroid storm

Caution if any laboratory tests required; possible interference with test results

Side/adverse effects

Signs of potential side effects, especially fever, skin rash or itching, bone marrow depression, hepatic dysfunction, lupus-like syndrome, arthralgias, arthritis, nephritis (for methimazole), vasculitis, pneumonitis, lymphadenopathy, sialadenopathy, hypoprothrombinemia (for propylthiouracil), or peripheral neuropathy

General Dosing Information

Dosage must be adjusted to meet the individual requirements of each patient, on the basis of clinical response and results of thyroid function tests.

In some patients, once- or twice-a-day therapy may be associated with a decreased incidence of side effects and improved compliance, although divided daily doses may be more effective. If divided daily doses are given, they should be administered at evenly spaced intervals throughout the day. Methimazole has a longer duration of action and therefore may frequently be more effective than propylthiouracil in once-daily dosing.

Confirmation of remission may be by sensitive TSH assay, trial withdrawal of the medication, protirelin test, thyroid suppression test, or thyroid-stimulating immunogloglubin (TSI) titer.

Duration of treatment necessary to produce a prolonged remission varies from 6 months to several years, with an average duration of 1 to 2 years. Control of hyperthyroidism with medication is sometimes followed by a spontaneous remission. Premature withdrawal may result in exacerbation of hyperthyroidism, although some clinicians feel that treatment may be withdrawn as soon as a euthyroid state is obtained (usually within 4 to 5 months), with no problems of rebound.

Iodide is usually added to thioamide antithyroid therapy for 7 to 10 days prior to surgery to reduce the vascularity of the thyroid gland, thereby decreasing subsequent blood loss during surgery.

If an antithyroid agent is being used in severely hyperthyroid patients to improve their thyroid state prior to radioactive iodine therapy, the antithyroid medication must be discontinued 2 to 4 days before treatment to prevent impairment of radioactive iodine uptake. Antithyroid treatment may be resumed, if desired, 3 to 7 days after radioactive iodine treatment to hasten return to euthyroidism, until effects of the iodine are apparent.

Diet/Nutrition

Food may inconsistently alter the bioavailability of methimazole. It is recommended that methimazole be taken at the same time in relation to meals every day.

METHIMAZOLE

Summary of Differences

General dosing information: May be more suitable for once-daily administration.

Oral Dosage Forms

METHIMAZOLE TABLETS USP

Usual adult and adolescent dose: Hyperthyroidism—

Initial:

Mild hyperthyroidism—Oral, 15 mg a day as one daily dose or as two divided daily doses for six to eight weeks until the patient becomes euthyroid.

Moderately severe hyperthyroidism—Oral, 30 to 40 mg a day as one daily dose or as two divided daily doses for six to eight weeks until the patient becomes euthyroid.

Severe hyperthyroidism—Oral, 60 mg a day as one daily dose or as two divided daily doses for six to eight weeks until the patient becomes euthyroid.

Maintenance: Oral, 5 to 30 mg a day in one daily dose or as two divided daily doses.

Thyrotoxic crisis: Oral, 15 to 20 mg every four hours during the first day, as an adjunct to other measures.

Auxiliary labeling: • Take at the same time in relation to meals every day.

Rectal Dosage Forms

METHIMAZOLE SUPPOSITORIES

Usual adult and adolescent dose: Hyperthyroidism—Initial: Thyrotoxic crisis—Rectal, 15 to 20 mg every four hours during the first day, as an adjunct to other measures, with the dosage being adjusted according to patient response.

Note: Use of methimazole suppositories is generally reserved for treatment of thyrotoxic emergencies, in patients who are unable to tolerate oral medications. The efficacy of chronic rectal dosing with extemporaneously compounded formulations has not been established.

Auxiliary labeling:
• Refrigerate.
• For rectal use only.

PROPYLTHIOURACIL

Summary of Differences

Precautions:

Pregnancy—May be preferred to methimazole, due to lower rate of placental transfer.

Breast-feeding—May be preferred to methimazole, due to lower rate of excretion into breast milk.

Side/adverse effects: Agranulocytosis may be less predictable, because it is usually not dose-related.

Oral Dosage Forms

PROPYLTHIOURACIL TABLETS USP

Usual adult and adolescent dose: Hyperthyroidism—

Initial: Oral, 300 to 900 mg a day as one to four divided daily doses until the patient becomes euthyroid.

Note: Patients with severe hyperthyroidism may occasionally require up to 1.2 grams a day.

Maintenance: Oral, 50 to 600 mg a day as one to four divided daily doses.

Thyrotoxic crisis: Oral, 200 to 400 mg every four hours during the first day, as an adjunct to other measures, the dosage then being decreased as the crisis subsides.

Auxiliary labeling: • Take at the same time in relation to meals every day.

Rectal Dosage Forms

PROPYLTHIOURACIL ENEMA

Usual adult and adolescent dose: Hyperthyroidism—Initial: Thyrotoxic crisis—Rectal, 200 to 400 mg every four hours during the first day, as an adjunct to other measures, with the dosage being adjusted according to patient response.

Note: Use of propylthiouracil enema is generally reserved for treatment of thyrotoxic emergencies, in patients who are unable to tolerate oral medications. The efficacy of chronic rectal dosing with extemporaneously compounded formulations has not been established.

Auxiliary labeling: • For rectal use only.

PROPYLTHIOURACIL SUPPOSITORIES

Usual adult and adolescent dose: Hyperthyroidism—Initial: Thyrotoxic crisis—Rectal, 200 to 400 mg every four hours during the first day, as an adjunct to other measures, with the dosage being adjusted according to patient response.

Note: Use of propylthiouracil suppositories is generally reserved for treatment of thyrotoxic emergencies, in patients who are unable to tolerate oral medications. The efficacy of chronic rectal dosing with extemporaneously compounded formulations has not been established.

Auxiliary labeling: • For rectal use only.

APRACLONIDINE   Ophthalmic†

A commonly used *brand name* in the U.S. is *Iopidine*.
Other commonly used names are aplonidine and p-aminoclonidine.

OPHTHALMIC
Apraclonidine Hydrochloride Ophthalmic Solution†
    In the U.S.—*Iopidine*

---

†Not commercially available in Canada.

Category: Antihypertensive, ocular.

Indications

Accepted
Hypertension, ocular (prophylaxis and treatment)—Apraclonidine is indicated to control or prevent postsurgical elevations in intraocular pressure that occur in patients after argon laser trabeculoplasty, argon laser iridotomy, or Nd YAG laser posterior capsulotomy.

Pharmacology

Mechanism of action/Effect: Apraclonidine is a relatively selective alpha$_2$ adrenergic agonist. When instilled into the eye, apraclonidine ophthalmic solution reduces intraocular pressure. The precise mechanism of this ocular hypotensive action has not been established; however, aqueous fluorophotometry studies in humans suggest that the predominant action of ophthalmic apraclonidine may be related to a reduction in the formation of aqueous humor.

Other actions/effects: Apraclonidine does not have significant membrane stabilizing (local anesthetic) activity. In addition, ophthalmic apraclonidine has minimal effect on cardiovascular parameters.

Onset of action: Usually within one hour.

Time to peak effect: Usually three to five hours after application of a single dose.

Precautions to Consider

Cross-sensitivity and/or related problems
Patients sensitive to clonidine may be sensitive to apraclonidine also.

Geriatrics
No information is available on the relationship of age to the effects of this medication in geriatric patients.

Drug interactions and/or related problems
The following drug interactions and/or related problems have been selected on the basis of their potential clinical significance (possible mechanism in parentheses where appropriate)—not necessarily inclusive (» = major clinical significance):

Note: Combinations containing any of the following medications, depending on the amount present, may also interact with this medication.

Monoamine oxidase (MAO) inhibitors, including furazolidone, procarbazine, and selegiline
(some clinicians believe that apraclonidine should not be used during or within 14 days following administration of MAO inhibitors, because the antihypertensive effects of either apraclonidine or the MAO inhibitor may be potentiated by concurrent use; however, this is controversial)

Contraindications/Medical problems
The contraindications/medical problems included have been selected on the basis of their potential clinical significance (reasons given in parentheses where appropriate)—not necessarily inclusive (» = major clinical significance).

Risk-benefit should be considered when the following medical problems exist:

Cardiovascular disease, severe, including hypertension
(in clinical studies, the total usual adult dose of 2 drops of 1% [base] ophthalmic apraclonidine had minimal effect on heart rate and blood pressure. However, since there is a possibility of systemic absorption and because apraclonidine is a potent medication, caution should be used in treating patients with severe cardiovascular disease, including hypertension)

Exaggerated response to medications that reduce intraocular pressure
(patients who exhibit an exaggerated response to medications that reduce intraocular pressure should be closely monitored during treatment with apraclonidine, since apraclonidine is a potent depressor of intraocular pressure)

Sensitivity to apraclonidine

Vasovagal attack, history of
(the possibility of a vasovagal attack occurring during laser surgery should be considered; caution should be used in patients with a history of this medical problem)

Side/Adverse Effects

Note: In investigational non-laser studies using ophthalmic apraclonidine once or twice a day for up to 28 days, ophthalmic apraclonidine was systemically absorbed and caused some potentially serious side/adverse effects.

The side/adverse effects listed below were reported with the use of apraclonidine in laser surgery.

The following side/adverse effects have been selected on the basis of their potential clinical significance (possible signs and symptoms in parentheses where appropriate)—not necessarily inclusive:

Those indicating need for medical attention
Incidence less frequent or rare
Arrhythmia (irregular heartbeat)

Those indicating need for medical attention only if they continue or are bothersome
Incidence more frequent
Conjunctival blanching (paleness of eye and inner lining of eyelid); *mydriasis* (increase in size of pupil of eye); *raising of upper eyelid*

Incidence less frequent or rare
Allergic reaction (swelling of eyelid, watering of eye, redness of eye or inner lining of eyelid); *ocular inflammation* (redness of eye)

Patient Consultation

In providing consultation, consider emphasizing the following selected information (» = major clinical significance):

Before using this medication
» Conditions affecting use, especially:
Sensitivity to apraclonidine or clonidine
Breast-feeding—It may be necessary to stop breast-feeding during the day of surgery

Ophthalmic Dosage Forms

APRACLONIDINE HYDROCHLORIDE OPHTHALMIC SOLUTION

Usual adult and adolescent dose: Topical, to the conjunctiva, 1 drop in the affected eye one hour before initiating anterior segment laser surgery and 1 drop in the same eye immediately upon completion of the laser surgical procedure.

Note: There is 0.25 mL apraclonidine HCl in each single-dose dispenser; a separate dispenser should be used for each single-drop application.

Usual geriatric dose: See *Usual adult and adolescent dose.*

ASPIRIN, SODIUM BICARBONATE, AND CITRIC ACID   Systemic

A commonly used *brand name* in the U.S. and Canada is *Alka-Seltzer Effervescent Pain Reliever and Antacid.*

ORAL
Aspirin Effervescent Tablets for Oral Solution USP
In the U.S. and Canada—*Alka-Seltzer Effervescent Pain Reliever and Antacid*
Note: *Aspirin* is a brand name in Canada; acetylsalicylic acid is the generic name. ASA, a commonly used designation for aspirin (or acetylsalicylic acid) in both the U.S. and Canada, is the term used in Canadian product labeling.

Category: Analgesic-antacid; platelet aggregation inhibitor.

Indications

Note: Bracketed information in the *Indications* section refers to uses not included in U.S. product labeling.

Accepted
Pain and upset stomach (treatment)—Aspirin, sodium bicarbonate, and citric acid combination is indicated to relieve pain, especially when an upset stomach is also present. However, this medication is not recommended for long-term, high-dose use because of the high sodium bicarbonate content.

Platelet aggregation (prophylaxis)[1]—Aspirin, sodium bicarbonate, and citric acid combination is indicated to provide the platelet aggregation-inhibiting action of aspirin in the following:
Ischemic attacks, transient, in males (prophylaxis);
Thromboembolism, cerebral (prophylaxis); or

[Thromboembolism, cerebral, recurrence (prophylaxis)]—
Aspirin is indicated in the treatment of men who have had transient brain ischemia due to fibrin platelet emboli, to reduce the recurrence of transient ischemic attacks (TIAs) and the risk of stroke and death.

[Aspirin is also used in the treatment of women with transient brain ischemia due to fibrin platelet emboli. However, its efficacy in preventing stroke and death in female patients has not been established.]

[Aspirin is also indicated in the treatment of patients with documented, unexplained TIAs associated with mitral valve prolapse. However, if TIAs continue to occur after an adequate trial of aspirin therapy, aspirin should be discontinued and an oral anticoagulant administered instead.]

[Aspirin is also indicated to prevent initial or recurrent cerebrovascular embolism, TIAs, and stroke following carotid endarterectomy.]

[Aspirin is indicated in the treatment of patients who have had a completed thrombotic stroke, to prevent a recurrence.]

Myocardial infarction (prophylaxis); or
Myocardial reinfarction (prophylaxis)—Aspirin is indicated to prevent myocardial infarction in patients with unstable angina pectoris and to prevent recurrence of myocardial infarction in patients with a history of myocardial infarction.

In one study, aspirin significantly reduced the rate of reocclusion, reinfarction, stroke, and death when a single dose was administered within a few hours after the onset of symptoms of acute myocardial infarction and daily thereafter. The benefit of early treatment with aspirin was additive to that of streptokinase.

Therefore, it is recommended that aspirin therapy be initiated as soon as possible after the onset of symptoms, even if the patient is receiving thrombolytic therapy.

[One study has shown that aspirin may also prevent myocardial infarction in individuals who have no history of unstable angina pectoris or myocardial infarction. However, an increased incidence of hemorrhagic stroke was reported in subjects receiving aspirin. Also, the incidence of myocardial infarction, although higher in the placebo group than in the aspirin group, was low in both groups. Therefore, use of aspirin for this purpose remains controversial; whether aspirin's benefit outweighs its risk in apparently healthy individuals has not been established. However, aspirin may be indicated for prevention of an initial myocardial infarction in selected patients, especially those who may be at risk because of the presence of chronic stable coronary artery disease (as shown by exertional or episodic angina pectoris, abnormal coronary arteriogram, or positive stress test) and/or other risk factors.]

[Thromboembolism (prophylaxis)]—

Aspirin is used in low doses to decrease the risk of thromboembolism following orthopedic (hip) surgery (especially total hip replacement) and in patients with arteriovenous shunts.

Platelet aggregation inhibitors, although not as consistently effective as an anticoagulant or an anticoagulant plus dipyridamole, may provide some protection against the development of thromboembolic complications in patients with mechanical prosthetic heart valves. Therefore, administration of aspirin, alone or in combination with dipyridamole, may be considered if anticoagulant therapy is contraindicated for these patients. Patients with bioprosthetic cardiac valves who are in normal sinus rhythm generally do not require prolonged antithrombotic therapy, but long-term aspirin administration may be considered on an individual basis.

Aspirin is also indicated, alone or in combination with dipyridamole, to reduce the risk of thrombosis and/or reocclusion of saphenous vein aortocoronary bypass grafts following coronary bypass surgery.

Aspirin is also indicated, alone or in combination with dipyridamole, to reduce the risk of thrombosis and/or reocclusion of prosthetic or saphenous vein femoral popliteal bypass grafts.

Because the patient may be at risk for thromboembolic complications, including myocardial infarction and stroke, long-term aspirin therapy may also be indicated for maintaining patency following coronary or peripheral vascular angioplasty and for treating patients with peripheral vascular insufficiency caused by arteriosclerosis.

Prolonged antithrombotic therapy is generally not needed to maintain vessel patency following vascular reconstruction procedures in high-flow, low-resistance arteries larger than 6 mm in diameter. However, long-term aspirin therapy may be indicated, because patients requiring such procedures may be at risk for other thrombotic complications.

---

[1]Not included in Canadian product labeling for this formulation. However, other specific products that contain acetylsalicylic acid (ASA) are approved in Canada for some of the listed indications.

Patient Consultation

In providing consultation, consider emphasizing the following selected information (» = major clinical significance):

Before using this medication
» Conditions affecting use, especially:
    Sensitivity to aspirin, nonsteroidal anti-inflammatory drugs (NSAIDs), or sodium bicarbonate
    Pregnancy—Not taking aspirin in third trimester unless prescribed by physician; high-dose, chronic use or abuse of aspirin in third trimester may be hazardous to the mother as well as the fetus and/or neonate, causing heart problems in fetus or neonate and/or bleeding in mother, fetus, or neonate; high-dose, chronic use or abuse may also prolong and complicate labor and delivery; sodium may cause edema and weight gain
    Use in children—Checking with physician before giving to children with symptoms of acute febrile illness, especially influenza or varicella, because of the risk of Reye's syndrome; also, increased susceptibility to aspirin toxicity in children, especially with fever and dehydration
    Use in teenagers—Checking with physician before giving to teenagers with symptoms of acute febrile illness, especially influenza or varicella, because of the risk of Reye's syndrome
    Use in the elderly—Increased risk of aspirin toxicity; also, because of the very high sodium content, use should preferably be limited to 5 days at a time, unless more prolonged therapy is prescribed and monitored by a physician
    Other medications, especially anticoagulants, oral antidiabetic agents, ketoconazole, mecamylamine, methenamine, methotrexate, NSAIDs, platelet aggregation inhibitors, those cephalosporins that may cause hypoprothrombinemia, probenecid, sulfinpyrazone, and oral tetracyclines
    Other medical problems, especially symptoms of appendicitis, coagulation or platelet function disorders, conditions in which sodium may be detrimental, gastrointestinal problems such as ulceration or erosive gastritis (especially a bleeding ulcer) or gastrointestinal obstruction, and renal function impairment

Proper use of this medication
» Importance of not taking more medication than recommended on package label, unless otherwise directed by physician, because of risk of aspirin- or sodium bicarbonate-induced adverse effects
    Proper administration:
        Taking in liquid form only; not ingesting tablets or tablet fragments
        Preparing liquid: Placing 1 or 2 tablets in glass, then adding $\frac{1}{2}$ glass (120 mL) cool water
        Checking for complete tablet dissolution before drinking; drinking while solution is still effervescing, or after it has settled
        Drinking entire amount, then rinsing glass with a little more water and drinking that, to ensure receiving full dosage
    Missed dose (if on scheduled dosing): Taking as soon as possible; not taking if almost time for next dose; not doubling doses
» Proper storage

Precautions while using this medication
» Regular visits to physician to check progress if long-term or high-dose therapy is prescribed
    Checking with physician if symptoms persist for longer than 10 days for adults or 5 days for children, condition becomes worse, new symptoms occur, or the painful area is red or swollen
» Not taking this medication:
    —Within 3 hours of taking ketoconazole
    —Within 3 to 4 hours of taking an oral tetracycline
    —Within 1 or 2 hours of taking any other oral medication
    Not taking a cellulose-containing laxative within 2 hours of taking aspirin
» Possibility of overdose if other medications containing aspirin or other salicylates (including diflunisal) or significant quantities of sodium are used
    Not taking aspirin for 5 days prior to any kind of surgery, unless otherwise directed by physician
» If taking aspirin as a platelet aggregation inhibitor:
    Taking only the amount prescribed; checking with physician to determine whether an alternative medication, rather than additional aspirin, should be used to relieve pain, fever, arthritis

Not discontinuing therapy without first checking with the prescriber

Not using an NSAID together with this medication for more than a few days, unless otherwise directed by physician

If taking more than an occasional 1 or 2 doses of this medication:

»   Avoiding alcoholic beverages, because of the increased risk of aspirin-induced gastrointestinal toxicity

»   Avoiding large amounts of milk or milk products

Possible need for sodium restriction

Caution if any laboratory tests required; possible interference with test results

Diabetics: Aspirin may cause false urine sugar test results with prolonged use of 8 or more 325-mg (5-grain) doses per day

»   Suspected overdose: Getting emergency help at once

Side/adverse effects

Signs of potential side effects, especially allergic dermatitis, anaphylaxis, anemia, bronchospastic allergic reaction, edema, gastrointestinal ulceration or bleeding, hypercalcemia associated with milk-alkali syndrome, increased blood pressure, and metabolic alkalosis

Oral Dosage Forms

ASPIRIN EFFERVESCENT TABLETS FOR ORAL SOLUTION USP

Usual adult and adolescent dose:

Analgesic/antacid—Oral, 324 to 500 mg of aspirin every three hours, 324 to 650 mg of aspirin every four hours, or 650 mg to 1 gram of aspirin every six hours as needed, while symptoms persist.

Note: It is recommended that the total daily dose of aspirin not exceed 4 grams, and that a physician be consulted if symptoms are not relieved within ten days.

Platelet aggregation inhibitor[1]—Oral, 324 mg of aspirin a day.

Note: Optimal dosage has not been established. Doses lower than 324 mg of aspirin a day are often utilized, since there is evidence that 160 mg of aspirin every twenty-four hours may effectively inhibit platelet aggregation while minimizing the risk of aspirin-induced side effects. Doses higher than 324 mg of aspirin a day are also recommended for specific indications responsive to platelet aggregation inhibition. However, because of its high sodium bicarbonate content, this formulation is not recommended for long-term therapy with doses higher than 324 mg of aspirin a day.

Usual adult prescribing limits:

Geriatric patients—Oral, up to 4 regular-strength or extra-strength tablets a day. Limiting the duration of treatment to five days may be advisable, unless longer treatment is prescribed and monitored by a physician.

Nongeriatric adults—Oral, up to 8 regular-strength or extra-strength tablets a day. A physician should be consulted if symptoms are not relieved within ten days.

Auxiliary labeling: • Keep container tightly closed.

ATTAPULGITE   Oral-Local

Some commonly used *brand names* are:

In the U.S.—

Diar-Aid	*Kaopectate Maximum*
Diasorb	*Strength*
Kaopectate	*Rheaban*
Kaopectate Advanced	*St. Joseph*
Formula	*Antidiarrheal*

In Canada—

Fowler's Diarrhea	*Kaopectate*
Tablets	

ORAL-LOCAL

Attapulgite Oral Suspension

In the U.S.—*Diasorb; Kaopectate Advanced Formula; St. Joseph Antidiarrheal*

In Canada—*Kaopectate*

Attapulgite Tablets

In the U.S.—*Diar-Aid; Diasorb; Kaopectate Maximum Strength; Rheaban*

In Canada—*Fowler's Diarrhea Tablets; Kaopectate*

Attapulgite Chewable Tablets

In the U.S.—*Kaopectate*

In Canada—*Kaopectate*

Category: Antidiarrheal (adsorbent).

Indications

Accepted

Diarrhea (treatment)—Attapulgite may be indicated as an adjunct to rest, fluids, and an appropriate diet in the symptomatic treatment of mild to moderately acute diarrhea. Use is recommended in chronic diarrhea only as temporary symptomatic treatment until the etiology is determined.

Pharmacology

Mechanism of action/Effect: Adsorbent and protectant. Attapulgite is a hydrated magnesium aluminum silicate that supposedly adsorbs large numbers of bacteria and toxins and reduces water loss. Activated attapulgite (contained in most of the products commercially available) is attapulgite that has been carefully heated to increase its adsorptive capacity. Results of animal studies with adsorbent antidiarrheals suggest that the fluidity of the stool is decreased but total water loss appears to be unchanged and sodium and potassium loss may be exacerbated.

Precautions to Consider

Geriatrics

In geriatric patients with diarrhea, caution is recommended because of the risk of fluid and electrolyte loss; these patients should be referred to a physician.

Drug interactions and/or related problems

The following drug interactions and/or related problems have been selected on the basis of their potential clinical significance (possible mechanism in parentheses where appropriate)—not necessarily inclusive (» = major clinical significance):

Note: Combinations containing any of the following medications, depending on the amount present, may also interact with this medication.

Anticholinergics or other medications with anticholinergic activity
or
Antidyskinetics or
Digitalis glycosides or
Lincomycins or
Loxapine or
Phenothiazines or
Thioxanthenes or
Xanthines, such as:
  Aminophylline
  Caffeine
  Dyphylline
  Oxtriphylline
  Theophylline
    (concurrent use with attapulgite may impair absorption of these
    medications when they are administered orally, resulting in
    decreased therapeutic effectiveness; it is recommended that
    attapulgite be administered not less than 2 hours before or 3 to
    4 hours after oral lincomycins; patients on digitalis should be
    monitored closely for evidence of altered effect)
Oral medications, other
    (prolonged use of adsorbents may interfere with absorption of
    other oral agents administered concurrently; it is recommended
    that attapulgite be administered at least 2 to 3 hours before or
    after other oral medications)

Contraindications/Medical problems
The contraindications/medical problems included have been selected
    on the basis of their potential clinical significance (reasons given
    in parentheses where appropriate)—not necessarily inclusive (» =
    major clinical significance).

Risk-benefit should be considered when the following medical prob-
lems exist:
» Dehydration
    (although adsorbent antidiarrheals may increase the consistency
    of feces and decrease the frequency of evacuation, they do not
    reduce the amount of fluid loss, but only mask its extent;
    rehydration therapy is essential if signs of dehydration, such as
    dry mouth, excessive thirst, wrinkled skin, decreased urination,
    and dizziness or lightheadedness, are present; fluid loss may
    have serious consequences, such as circulatory collapse and
    renal failure, especially in young children and the elderly)
Diarrhea, parasite-associated, suspected
    (use of adsorbent antidiarrheals may make recognition of para-
    sitic causes of diarrhea more difficult; if parasitic agents are
    suspected pathogens, appropriate stool analyses should be per-
    formed prior to therapy with adsorbents)
» Dysentery, acute, characterized by bloody stools and elevated tem-
    perature
    (sole treatment with adsorbent antidiarrheals may be inadequate;
    antibiotic therapy may be required)
Obstruction of the bowel, suspected
    (condition may be aggravated)

Side/Adverse Effects
The following side/adverse effects have been selected on the basis of
    their potential clinical significance (possible signs and symptoms
    in parentheses where appropriate)—not necessarily inclusive:

Those indicating need for medical attention only if they continue
or are bothersome
Incidence dose-related
    Constipation—usually mild and transient, but may rarely lead to
    fecal impaction

Patient Consultation
In providing consultation, consider emphasizing the following se-
    lected information (» = major clinical significance):

Before using this medication
» Conditions affecting use, especially:
        Use in children—Risk of dehydration associated with diarrhea
        Use in the elderly—Risk of dehydration associated with diar-
        rhea
        Other medications; spacing doses of other oral medications 2
        to 3 hours before or after doses of attapulgite is recom-
        mended
        Other medical problems, especially dehydration and acute dys-
        entery

Proper use of this medication
    Taking after each loose bowel movement until diarrhea is con-
    trolled
» Importance of maintaining adequate hydration and proper diet
» Proper storage

Precautions while using this medication
» Checking with physician if diarrhea is not controlled within 48
    hours and/or fever develops

Oral-Local Dosage Forms

ATTAPULGITE ORAL SUSPENSION

Usual adult and adolescent dose: Oral, 1.2 to 1.5 grams after each
    loose bowel movement, not to exceed 9.0 grams in twenty-four
    hours.

Auxiliary labeling: • Shake well.

ATTAPULGITE TABLETS

Usual adult and adolescent dose: Oral, 1.2 to 1.5 grams after each
    loose bowel movement, not to exceed 9.0 grams in twenty-four
    hours.

Auxiliary labeling: • Do not chew.

ATTAPULGITE CHEWABLE TABLETS

Usual adult and adolescent dose: Oral, 1.2 grams after each loose
    bowel movement, not to exceed 8.4 grams in twenty-four hours.

Auxiliary labeling: • May be chewed.

AZATHIOPRINE　Systemic

A commonly used *brand name* in the U.S. and Canada is *Imuran.*

ORAL
Azathioprine Tablets USP
　In the U.S. and Canada—*Imuran*

PARENTERAL
Azathioprine Sodium for Injection USP
　In the U.S.—*Imuran;* GENERIC
　In Canada—*Imuran*

Category: Immunosuppressant; antirheumatic (disease-modifying); bowel disease (inflammatory) suppressant; lupus erythematosus suppressant.

Indications

Note: Bracketed information in the *Indications* section refers to uses not included in U.S. product labeling.

Accepted
Transplant rejection, organ (prophylaxis)—Azathioprine is indicated as an adjunct for prevention of rejection in renal homotransplantation. [It is also used in the prevention of rejection in cardiac, hepatic, and pancreatic transplantation.]

Arthritis, rheumatoid (treatment)—Azathioprine is indicated for the management of severe, active rheumatoid arthritis unresponsive to rest or conventional medications.

[Bowel disease, inflammatory (treatment)][1];
[Hepatitis, chronic active (treatment)][1];
[Cirrhosis, biliary (treatment)][1];
[Lupus erythematosus, systemic (treatment)][1];
[Glomerulonephritis (treatment)][1];
[Nephrotic syndrome (treatment)][1];
[Myopathy, inflammatory (treatment)][1];
[Myasthenia gravis (treatment)][1];
[Dermatomyositis, systemic (treatment)][1];
[Pemphigoid (treatment)][1]; or
[Pemphigus (treatment)][1]—Azathioprine is also used in the treatment of other immunologic diseases including regional and ulcerative colitis, chronic active hepatitis and biliary cirrhosis, systemic lupus erythematosus (SLE), glomerulonephritis, nephrotic syndrome, inflammatory myopathy, myasthenia gravis, systemic dermatomyositis (polymyositis), pemphigus, and pemphigoid.

[1]Not included in Canadian product labeling.

Pharmacology

Mechanism of action/Effect: The exact mechanism of immunosuppressive action is unknown since the exact mechanism of the immune response itself is complex and not completely understood. The immunosuppressive effects of azathioprine involve a greater suppression of delayed hypersensitivity and cellular cytotoxicity tests than of antibody responses. Azathioprine antagonizes purine metabolism and may inhibit synthesis of DNA, RNA, and proteins; it may also interfere with cellular metabolism and inhibit mitosis.

The mechanism of action of azathioprine in rheumatoid arthritis and other immunologic diseases is unknown but may be related to immunosuppression. Azathioprine has a steroid-sparing effect, which allows a reduction in steroid dose when the two are combined in chronic inflammatory diseases.

Onset of action:
　In rheumatoid arthritis—6 to 8 weeks.
　In other inflammatory disorders—4 to 8 weeks.

Duration of action: Immunosuppressant—Clinical effects may persist for long periods after the medication is eliminated.

Precautions to Consider

Geriatrics
Although appropriate studies with azathioprine have not been performed in the geriatric population, geriatrics-specific problems that would limit the usefulness of this medication in the elderly are not expected. However, elderly patients are more likely to have age-related renal function impairment, which may require reduced dosage in patients receiving azathioprine.

Dental
The bone marrow depressant effects of azathioprine may result in an increased incidence of microbial infection, delayed healing, and gingival bleeding. Dental work, whenever possible, should be completed prior to initiation of therapy or deferred until blood counts have returned to normal. Patients should be instructed in proper oral hygiene during treatment, including caution in use of regular toothbrushes, dental floss, and toothpicks.

In addition, azathioprine rarely causes sores in the mouth and on the lips.

Drug interactions and/or related problems
The following drug interactions and/or related problems have been selected on the basis of their potential clinical significance (possible mechanism in parentheses where appropriate)—not necessarily inclusive (» = major clinical significance):

Note: Combinations containing any of the following medications, depending on the amount present, may also interact with this medication.

» Allopurinol
　(allopurinol-induced inhibition of xanthine oxidase-mediated metabolism may result in greatly increased azathioprine activity and toxicity; concurrent use should be avoided if possible, especially in renal transplant patients, because of the high risk of 6-mercaptopurine [azathioprine metabolite] accumulation and consequent azathioprine toxicity if the transplanted kidney is rejected; if concurrent use is essential, it is recommended that azathioprine dosage be reduced to one-quarter to one-third of the usual dosage, the patient be carefully monitored, and subsequent dosage adjustments be based on patient response and evidence of toxicity)

Blood dyscrasia-causing medications
　(leukopenic and/or thrombocytopenic effects of azathioprine may be increased with concurrent or recent therapy if these medications cause the same effects; dosage adjustment of azathioprine, if necessary, should be based on blood counts)

Bone marrow depressants, other, or
Radiation therapy
　(concurrent use with azathioprine may increase the bone marrow depressant effects of these medications and radiation therapy; dosage reduction may be required; use prior to azathioprine therapy may be associated with an increased risk of development of neoplasms)

» Immunosuppressants, other, such as:
　Adrenocorticoids, glucocorticoid
　Chlorambucil
　Cyclophosphamide

Cyclosporine
Mercaptopurine
Muromonab-CD3
(concurrent use with azathioprine may increase the risk of infection and development of neoplasms)

Vaccines, killed virus
(because normal defense mechanisms may be suppressed by
azathioprine therapy, the patient's antibody response to the
vaccine may be decreased. The interval between discontinuation
of medications that cause immunosuppression and restoration
of the patient's ability to respond to the vaccine depends on the
intensity and type of immunosuppression-causing medication
used, the underlying disease, and other factors; estimates vary
from 3 months to 1 year)

» Vaccines, live virus
(because normal defense mechanisms may be suppressed by
azathioprine therapy, concurrent use with a live virus vaccine
may potentiate the replication of the vaccine virus, may increase the side/adverse effects of the vaccine virus, and/or may
decrease the patient's antibody response to the vaccine; immunization of these patients should be undertaken only with extreme caution after careful review of the patient's hematologic
status and only with the knowledge and consent of the physician managing the azathioprine therapy. The interval between
discontinuation of medications that cause immunosuppression
and restoration of the patient's ability to respond to the vaccine
depends on the intensity and type of immunosuppression-causing medication used, the underlying disease, and other factors;
estimates vary from 3 months to 1 year. Patients with leukemia
in remission should not receive live virus vaccine until at least
3 months after their last chemotherapy. In addition, immunization with oral poliovirus vaccine should be postponed in
persons in close contact with the patient, especially family
members)

Contraindications/Medical problems
The contraindications/medical problems included have been selected
on the basis of their potential clinical significance (reasons given
in parentheses where appropriate)—not necessarily inclusive (» =
major clinical significance).

*Risk-benefit should be considered when the following medical prob-
lems exist:*

» Chickenpox, existing or recent (including recent exposure), or
» Herpes zoster
(risk of severe generalized disease)
» Gout
(because of interaction with allopurinol)
» Hepatic function impairment
» Infection
Pancreatitis
» Renal function impairment
(increased risk of hematologic toxicity; a lower dosage of
azathioprine is recommended for patients with impaired renal
function)
Sensitivity to azathioprine
» Xanthine oxidase deficiency, severe
(reduced metabolism may result in increased azathioprine ac-
tivity and toxicity)
» Caution should be used also in patients who have had previous
cytotoxic drug therapy and radiation therapy.

Side/Adverse Effects
Note: The risk of hematologic and neoplastic toxicity appears to be
lower in rheumatoid arthritis patients because of the lower doses
used.

The following side/adverse effects have been selected on the basis of
their potential clinical significance (possible signs and symptoms
in parentheses where appropriate)—not necessarily inclusive:

Those indicating need for medical attention
Incidence more frequent
Leukopenia or infection (leukopenia is usually asymptomatic; less
frequently, fever or chills, cough or hoarseness, lower back or side
pain, painful or difficult urination); *megaloblastic anemia* (unusual tiredness or weakness)
Note: *Leukopenia or infection* may be severe or delayed and is
dose-related. Not correlated with therapeutic effect.

Incidence less frequent—dose-related
Hepatitis or biliary stasis (yellow eyes or skin); *thrombocytopenia*
(usually asymptomatic; rarely, unusual bleeding or bruising; black,
tarry stools; blood in urine or stools; pinpoint red spots on skin)
Note: *Hepatotoxicity* usually occurs within 6 months of transplantation and is reversible on withdrawal of azathioprine. It is
uncommon in rheumatoid arthritis patients. Hepatotoxicity
occurs more frequently at dosages above 2.5 mg per kg of
body weight (mg/kg) per day.
Thrombocytopenia may be severe or delayed and is dose-
related.

Incidence rare
Hepatic veno-occlusive disease—potentially fatal (stomach pain,
swelling of feet or lower legs); *hypersensitivity* (fast heartbeat,
sudden fever, muscle or joint pain, redness or blisters on skin; may
also be associated with severe nausea, vomiting, and diarrhea);
pancreatitis, hypersensitivity (severe stomach pain with nausea
and vomiting); *pneumonitis* (cough, shortness of breath); *sores in
mouth and on lips*
Note: *Hypersensitivity* reactions usually occur after at least 1 week
of therapy, and are reversible on withdrawal. The reaction
may be more severe on rechallenge and can be fatal.

**Those indicating need for medical attention only if they continue
or are bothersome**
Incidence more frequent
Loss of appetite; nausea or vomiting
Incidence less frequent
Skin rash

**Those indicating possible delayed bone marrow depression and
the need for medical attention if they occur after medication is
discontinued**
*Black, tarry stools; blood in urine; cough or hoarseness; fever or
chills; lower back or side pain; painful or difficult urination;
pinpoint red spots on skin; unusual bleeding or bruising*

Patient Consultation

In providing consultation, consider emphasizing the following selected information (» = major clinical significance):

Before using this medication
» Conditions affecting use, especially:
Sensitivity to azathioprine
Pregnancy—Use not recommended because of mutagenic or
teratogenic potential
Breast-feeding—Not recommended because of risk of serious
side effects
Other medical problems, especially chickenpox, herpes zoster,
gout, hepatic function impairment, infection, or renal function impairment
Other medications, especially allopurinol, other immunosuppressants, or previous cytotoxic drug therapy or radiation
therapy

Proper use of this medication
» Importance of not taking more or less medication than the amount
prescribed

Caution with combination therapy; taking each medication at the right time
» Checking with physician before discontinuing medication
Possible nausea or vomiting; taking after meals or at bedtime to reduce stomach upset
Checking with physician if vomiting occurs shortly after dose is taken
Missed dose: If dosing schedule is—
　Once a day: Not taking missed dose and not doubling next one
　Several times a day: Taking as soon as possible or doubling next dose; checking with physician if more than one dose is missed
» Proper storage

Precautions while using this medication
» Importance of close monitoring by physician
» Avoiding immunizations unless approved by physician; other persons in patient's household should avoid immunizations with oral poliovirus vaccine; avoiding other persons who have taken oral poliovirus vaccine or wearing a protective mask that covers nose and mouth
Caution if bone marrow depression occurs:
　» Avoiding exposure to persons with bacterial or viral infections, especially during periods of low blood counts; checking with physician immediately if fever or chills, cough or hoarseness, lower back or side pain, or painful or difficult urination occurs
　» Checking with physician immediately if unusual bleeding or bruising; black, tarry stools; blood in urine or stools; or pinpoint red spots on skin occur
　Caution in use of regular toothbrush, dental floss, or toothpick; physician, dentist, or nurse may suggest alternatives; checking with physician before having dental work done
　Not touching eyes or inside of nose unless hands washed immediately before
　Using caution to avoid accidental cuts with use of sharp objects such as safety razor or fingernail or toenail cutters
　Avoiding contact sports or other situations where bruising or injury could occur

Side/adverse effects
May cause adverse effects such as blood problems and cancer; importance of discussing possible effects with physician
Signs of potential side effects, especially leukopenia, infection, megaloblastic anemia, hepatitis, biliary stasis, thrombocytopenia, hypersensitivity, pancreatitis, pneumonitis, and sores in mouth and on lips

General Dosing Information

Patients receiving azathioprine should be under supervision of a physician experienced in immunosuppressive therapy.

A variety of dosage schedules and regimens of azathioprine, alone or in combination with other immunosuppressive agents, are used. The prescriber may consult the medical literature as well as the manufacturer's literature in choosing a specific dosage.

Dosage must be adjusted to meet the individual requirements of each patient, on the basis of clinical response and appearance or severity of toxicity.

Cadaveric kidneys frequently develop a tubular necrosis with delayed onset of adequate function, necessitating a reduction in azathioprine dosage. If persistent negative nitrogen balance occurs, dosage should be reduced.

Because of the delayed action of azathioprine, dosage should be reduced or the medication withdrawn at the first sign of an abnormally large or persistent decrease in leukocyte count (to less than 3000 per cubic millimeter) or platelet count (to less than 100,000 per cubic millimeter). Therapy may be reinstituted at a lower dos-

age when leukocyte and platelet counts return to acceptable levels, usually after 7 to 10 days.

Special precautions are recommended in patients who develop thrombocytopenia as a result of administration of azathioprine. These may include extreme care in performing invasive procedures; regular inspection of intravenous sites, skin (including perirectal area), and mucous membrane surfaces for signs of bleeding or bruising; limiting frequency of venipuncture and avoiding intramuscular injections; testing urine, emesis, stool, and secretions for occult blood; care in use of regular toothbrushes, dental floss, toothpicks, safety razors, and fingernail and toenail cutters; avoiding constipation; and using caution to prevent falls and other injuries. Such patients should avoid alcohol and any aspirin intake because of the risk of gastrointestinal bleeding. Platelet transfusions may be required.

Patients who develop leukopenia should be observed carefully for signs of infection. Antibiotic support may be required. In neutropenic patients who develop fever, broad-spectrum antibiotic coverage should be initiated empirically, pending bacterial cultures and appropriate diagnostic tests.

If an infection develops, it must be treated promptly; reduction of azathioprine dosage may be necessary.

If symptoms of toxic hepatitis or biliary stasis appear, azathioprine therapy may have to be withdrawn. Patients with existing hepatic function impairment should be monitored carefully and treated with conservative doses (some clinicians recommend an initial dose of two-thirds the usual dose). If hepatic veno-occlusive disease is clinically suspected, it is recommended that azathioprine be permanently withdrawn.

If signs of homograft rejection occur, a larger dose may be necessary. Other therapy should be considered if signs persist.

Safety considerations for handling this medication
There is limited but increasing evidence and concern that personnel involved in preparation and administration of parenteral antineoplastics and immunosuppressants may be at some risk because of the potential mutagenicity, teratogenicity, and/or carcinogenicity of these agents, although the actual risk is unknown. USP advisory panels recommend cautious handling both in preparation and disposal of antineoplastic and immunosuppressant agents. Precautions that have been suggested include:

• Use of a biological containment cabinet during reconstitution and dilution of parenteral medications and wearing of disposable surgical gloves and masks.

• Use of proper technique to prevent contamination of the medication, work area, and operator during transfer between containers (including proper training of personnel in this technique).

• Cautious and proper disposal of needles, syringes, vials, ampuls, and unused medication.

A number of medical centers have developed detailed guidelines for handling of antineoplastic and immunosuppressant agents.

For parenteral dosage forms
Azathioprine may be administered by intravenous push or infusion. Time for infusion is usually 30 to 60 minutes, but may range from 5 minutes to 8 hours.

Diet/Nutrition
Gastrointestinal upset may be reduced by giving oral azathioprine in divided doses or after meals.

Oral Dosage Forms

Note: Bracketed uses in the *Dosage Forms* section refer to categories of use and/or indications that are not included in U.S. product labeling.

AZATHIOPRINE TABLETS USP

Usual adult and adolescent dose:

Immunosuppressant—

Transplant rejection, organ (prophylaxis):

Initial—Oral, 3 to 5 mg per kg of body weight or 120 mg per square meter of body surface a day, one to three days before or at the time of surgery, the dosage being adjusted to maintain the homograft without causing toxicity.

Maintenance—Oral, 1 to 2 mg per kg of body weight or 45 mg per square meter of body surface a day.

[Bowel disease, inflammatory][1]; or
[Hepatitis, chronic active][1]; or
[Cirrhosis, biliary][1]; or
[Glomerulonephritis][1]; or
[Nephrotic syndrome][1]; or
[Myopathy, inflammatory][1]; or
[Myasthenia gravis][1]; or
[Dermatomyositis, systemic][1]; or
[Pemphigoid][1]; or
[Pemphigus][1]:

Initial—Oral, 1 mg per kg of body weight per day, the dosage being increased in increments of 500 mcg (0.5 mg) per kg of body weight per day after six to eight weeks, then every four weeks as necessary up to a maximum dose of 2.5 mg per kg of body weight per day.

Maintenance—Oral, the dosage being reduced to the minimum effective dose in decrements of 500 mcg (0.5 mg) per kg of body weight per day every four to eight weeks.

Antirheumatic (disease-modifying)—Rheumatoid arthritis; or
[Lupus erythematosus suppressant—Lupus erythematosus, systemic][1]:

Initial—Oral, 1 mg per kg of body weight per day, the dosage increased in increments of 500 mcg (0.5 mg) per kg of body weight per day after six to eight weeks, then every four weeks as necessary up to a maximum dose of 2.5 mg per kg of body weight per day.

Maintenance—Oral, the dosage being reduced to the minimum effective dose in decrements of 500 mcg (0.5 mg) per kg of body weight per day every four to eight weeks.

Parenteral Dosage Forms

AZATHIOPRINE SODIUM FOR INJECTION USP

Usual adult and adolescent dose: Immunosuppressant—Transplant rejection, organ (prophylaxis):

Initial—Intravenous 3 to 5 mg (base) per kg of body weight a day prior to, during, or soon after surgery, the dosage being adjusted to maintain the homograft without causing toxicity.

Maintenance—Intravenous, 1 to 2 mg (base) per kg of body weight a day.

BARBITURATES　Systemic

Some commonly used *brand names* are:

In the U.S.—

Alurate [Aprobarbital]	*Mebaral* [Mephobarbital]
Amytal [Amobarbital]	*Nembutal* [Pentobarbital]
Barbita [Phenobarbital]	*Sarisol No. 2*
Busodium [Butabarbital]	[Butabarbital]
Butalan [Butabarbital]	*Seconal* [Secobarbital]
Butisol [Butabarbital]	*Solfoton* [Phenobarbital]
Luminal [Phenobarbital]	*Tuinal* [Secobarbital and
	Amobarbital]

In Canada—

Amytal [Amobarbital]	*Novopentobarb*
Ancalixir [Phenobarbital]	[Pentobarbital]
Butisol [Butabarbital]	*Novosecobarb*
Mebaral [Mephobarbital]	[Secobarbital]
Nembutal [Pentobarbital]	*Seconal* [Secobarbital]
Nova Rectal [Pentobarbital]	*Tuinal* [Secobarbital and
	Amobarbital]

Other—
　Gemonil [Metharbital]

AMOBARBITAL
Oral
　Amobarbital Tablets USP
　　In the U.S. and Canada—*Amytal*
　Amobarbital Sodium Capsules USP
　　In the U.S.—*Amytal;* GENERIC
　　In Canada—*Amytal*
Parenteral
　Sterile Amobarbital Sodium USP
　　In the U.S. and Canada—*Amytal*
APROBARBITAL†
Oral
　Aprobarbital Elixir†
　　In the U.S.—*Alurate*
BUTABARBITAL
Oral
　Butabarbital Sodium Elixir USP†
　　In the U.S.—*Busodium; Butalan; Butisol;* GENERIC
　Butabarbital Sodium Tablets USP
　　In the U.S.—*Busodium; Butisol; Sarisol No. 2;* GENERIC
　　In Canada—*Butisol*
MEPHOBARBITAL
Oral
　Mephobarbital Tablets USP
　　In the U.S. and Canada—*Mebaral*
METHARBITAL*†
Oral
　Metharbital Tablets USP*†
　　In other countries—*Gemonil*
PENTOBARBITAL
Oral
　Pentobarbital Elixir USP†
　　In the U.S.—*Nembutal*
　Pentobarbital Sodium Capsules USP
　　In the U.S.—*Nembutal;* GENERIC
　　In Canada—*Nembutal; Novopentobarb*
Parenteral
　Pentobarbital Sodium Injection USP
　　In the U.S.—*Nembutal;* GENERIC
　　In Canada—*Nembutal*
Rectal
　Pentobarbital Sodium Suppositories
　　In the U.S.—*Nembutal*
　　In Canada—*Nova Rectal*

PHENOBARBITAL
Oral
　Phenobarbital Capsules†
　　In the U.S.—*Solfoton*
　Phenobarbital Elixir USP
　　In the U.S.—GENERIC
　　In Canada—*Ancalixir*
　Phenobarbital Tablets USP
　　In the U.S.—*Barbita; Solfoton;* GENERIC
　　In Canada—GENERIC
Parenteral
　Phenobarbital Sodium Injection USP
　　In the U.S.—*Luminal;* GENERIC
　　In Canada—GENERIC
　Sterile Phenobarbital Sodium USP†
　　In the U.S.—GENERIC
SECOBARBITAL
Oral
　Secobarbital Sodium Capsules USP
　　In the U.S.—*Seconal;* GENERIC
　　In Canada—*Novosecobarb; Seconal*
Parenteral
　Secobarbital Sodium Injection USP†
　　In the U.S.—GENERIC
SECOBARBITAL AND AMOBARBITAL
Oral
　Secobarbital Sodium and Amobarbital Sodium Capsules USP
　　In the U.S. and Canada—*Tuinal*

---

*Not commercially available in the U.S.
†Not commercially available in Canada.

Category

Sedative-hypnotic—Amobarbital; Aprobarbital; Butabarbital; Pentobarbital; Phenobarbital (parenteral only); Secobarbital.

Anticonvulsant—Amobarbital (parenteral only); Mephobarbital; Metharbital; Pentobarbital (parenteral only); Phenobarbital; Secobarbital (parenteral only).

Antihyperbilirubinemic—Phenobarbital.

Indications

Note: Bracketed information in the *Indications* section refers to uses not included in U.S. product labeling.

Accepted

Anesthesia, adjunct—Amobarbital, butabarbital, pentobarbital, phenobarbital (parenteral), and secobarbital are indicated for use as preoperative medication to help reduce anxiety and facilitate induction of anesthesia.

Narcoanalysis—Amobarbital (parenteral) may be indicated in narcoanalysis.

Epilepsy, tonic-clonic seizure pattern (treatment); or

Epilepsy, simple partial seizure pattern (treatment)—Phenobarbital, a long-acting barbiturate, is indicated as long-term anticonvulsant therapy for the treatment of generalized tonic-clonic and simple partial (cortical focal) seizures; mephobarbital and metharbital, also long-acting barbiturates, may be indicated as alternatives to phenobarbital.

Convulsions (treatment);

Seizures (prophylaxis and treatment);

Status epilepticus (treatment); or

Tetanus (treatment adjunct)—Parenteral barbiturates, especially phenobarbital, are indicated in the emergency treatment of certain acute convulsive episodes such as those associated with status epilepticus, eclampsia, meningitis, and toxic reactions to strychnine. They are also indicated as adjunctive treatment for acute convulsive episodes associated with tetanus.

Phenobarbital is used in the prophylaxis and treatment of febrile seizures.[1]

[Hyperbilirubinemia (prophylaxis and treatment)][1]—Phenobarbital (oral and parenteral) is used in the prevention and treatment of hyperbilirubinemia in neonates. It is used also to lower bilirubin concentrations in patients with congenital nonhemolytic unconjugated hyperbilirubinemia or chronic intrahepatic cholestasis.

[Ischemia, cerebral (treatment)][1]; or

[Hypertension, cerebral (treatment)][1]—Pentobarbital (parenteral) is used for induction of coma to protect the brain from various states, including ischemia and increased intracranial pressure that follow stroke and head trauma; however, this use is controversial and further studies are needed.

Amobarbital, aprobarbital, butabarbital, pentobarbital, phenobarbital, secobarbital, and secobarbital and amobarbital have been used for the short-term treatment of insomnia; however, they generally *have been replaced* by benzodiazepines. If barbiturates are used, they are not recommended for long-term use since they appear to lose their effectiveness in sleep induction and maintenance after 2 weeks or less.

Amobarbital, aprobarbital, butabarbital, mephobarbital, pentobarbital, phenobarbital, and secobarbital have also been used for routine sedation to relieve anxiety, tension, and apprehension; however, barbiturates generally *have been replaced* by benzodiazepines for daytime sedation.

Unaccepted

Amobarbital (parenteral) has been used as a diagnostic aid in schizophrenia but it generally has been replaced by other agents.

Amobarbital (parenteral) has also been used in the management of catatonic and negativistic reactions; however, phenothiazines generally are more appropriate therapy for catatonic reactions. It has also been used in the management of manic reactions, although benzodiazepines and lithium are usually preferred.

[Phenobarbital (oral and parenteral) has been used in the treatment of familial, senile, or essential action tremors; however, it generally has been replaced by other agents, such as benzodiazepines and beta-adrenergic blockers.]

---

[1]Not included in Canadian product labeling.

Pharmacology

Mechanism of action/Effect: Barbiturates act as nonselective depressants of the central nervous system (CNS), capable of producing all levels of CNS mood alteration from excitation to mild sedation, hypnosis, and deep coma. In sufficiently high therapeutic doses, barbiturates induce anesthesia. Recent studies have suggested that the sedative-hypnotic and anticonvulsant effects of barbiturates may be related to their ability to enhance and/or mimic the inhibitory synaptic action of gamma-aminobutyric acid (GABA).

Sedative-hypnotic—Barbiturates depress the sensory cortex, decrease motor activity, alter cerebral function, and produce drowsiness, sedation, and hypnosis. Although the mechanism of action has not been completely established, the barbiturates appear to have a particular effect at the level of the thalamus where they inhibit ascending conduction in the reticular formation, thus interfering with the transmission of impulses to the cortex.

The mechanism of action of pentobarbital in protecting the brain from ischemia and intracranial pressure is not completely understood; however, it is related to pentobarbital's anesthetic action (produced by sufficiently high dosage) and possibly to the depression of neuronal activity and metabolism.

Anticonvulsant—Barbiturates are believed to act by depressing monosynaptic and polysynaptic transmission in the CNS. They also increase the threshold for electrical stimulation of the motor cortex.

Antihyperbilirubinemic—Phenobarbital lowers serum bilirubin concentrations probably by induction of glucuronyl transferase, the enzyme which conjugates bilirubin.

Other actions/effects:

Barbiturates have little analgesic action at subanesthetic doses and may increase reaction to painful stimuli.

Although phenobarbital, mephobarbital, and metharbital are the only barbiturates effective as anticonvulsants in subhypnotic doses, all of the barbiturates exhibit anticonvulsant activity in anesthetic doses.

Barbiturates are respiratory depressants; the degree of respiratory depression is dose-dependent.

Barbiturates have been shown to reduce the rapid eye movement (REM) phase of sleep or dreaming stage. Also, Stages III and IV sleep (slow-wave sleep, SWS) are decreased.

Animal studies have shown that barbiturates cause reduction in the tone and contractility of the uterus, ureters, and urinary bladder; however, concentrations required to produce this effect in humans are not attained with sedative-hypnotic doses.

Barbiturates have been shown to induce liver microsomal enzymes, thereby increasing and altering the metabolism of other medications or compounds.

Onset of action:

Oral or rectal—Varies from 20 to 60 minutes.

Intramuscular—Slightly faster than for oral or rectal.

Intravenous—Ranges from almost immediately for pentobarbital sodium to 5 minutes for phenobarbital sodium.

Time to peak effect: Phenobarbital—Maximal CNS depression may not occur for 15 minutes or more after intravenous administration of phenobarbital sodium.

Precautions to Consider

Cross-sensitivity and/or related problems

Patients sensitive to one of the barbiturates may be sensitive to other barbiturates also.

Geriatrics

Geriatric patients may react to usual doses of barbiturates with excitement, confusion, or mental depression.

The risk of barbiturate-induced hypothermia may be increased in elderly patients, especially with high doses or in acute overdose of barbiturates.

In addition, elderly patients are more likely to have age-related hepatic or renal function impairment, which may require a reduction of dosage in patients receiving a barbiturate.

Drug interactions and/or related problems

The following drug interactions and/or related problems have been selected on the basis of their potential clinical significance (possible mechanism in parentheses where appropriate)—not necessarily inclusive (» = major clinical significance):

Note: Combinations containing any of the following medications, depending on the amount present, may also interact with this medication.

Acetaminophen

(therapeutic effects of acetaminophen may be decreased when the medication is used concurrently in patients receiving chronic barbiturate therapy because of increased metabolism resulting from induction of hepatic microsomal enzymes; also, risk of hepatotoxicity with single toxic doses or prolonged use of high doses of acetaminophen may be increased in alcoholics or in patients regularly using hepatic enzyme inducers such as barbiturates)

Addictive medications, other, especially CNS depressants with habituating potential
(prolonged concurrent use may increase the risk of habituation; caution is recommended)

» Adrenocorticoids, glucocorticoid and mineralocorticoid, or Chloramphenicol or
» Corticotropin or
Cyclosporine or
Dacarbazine or
Digitalis glycosides or
Metronidazole or
Quinidine
(effects may be decreased when these medications are used concurrently with barbiturates, especially phenobarbital, because of enhanced metabolism resulting from induction of hepatic microsomal enzymes; dosage adjustment of these medications, with the exception of digoxin, may be necessary)

» Alcohol or
» CNS depression-producing medications, other
(concurrent use may increase the CNS depressant effects of either these medications or barbiturates; caution is recommended and dosage of one or both agents should be reduced)

Amphetamines
(concurrent use may cause a delay in the intestinal absorption of phenobarbital)

Anesthetics, halogenated hydrocarbon
(chronic use of barbiturates prior to enflurane, halothane, or methoxyflurane anesthesia may increase anesthetic metabolism leading to increased risk of hepatotoxicity)
(chronic use of barbiturates prior to methoxyflurane anesthesia may increase formation of nephrotoxic metabolites leading to increased risk of nephrotoxicity)

» Anticoagulants, coumarin- or indandione-derivative
(effects may be decreased when these medications are used concurrently with barbiturates because of increased metabolism resulting from induction of hepatic microsomal enzymes; also, bleeding may result when the barbiturate is discontinued; periodic prothrombin-time determinations may be required to determine if dosage adjustments of anticoagulants are necessary)

Anticonvulsants, hydantoin
(concurrent use with barbiturates appears to produce variable and unpredictable effects on the metabolism of hydantoin anticonvulsants; blood concentrations of hydantoin anticonvulsants should be closely monitored when these medications are used concurrently)

Anticonvulsants, succinimide, or
» Carbamazepine
(concurrent use with barbiturates may result in increased metabolism, leading to decreased serum concentrations and reduced elimination half-lives of carbamazepine or succinimide anticonvulsants because of induction of hepatic microsomal enzyme activity; monitoring of serum concentrations as a guide to dosage is recommended, especially when carbamazepine or a succinimide anticonvulsant is added to or withdrawn from an existing regimen)

Antidepressants, tricyclic
(effects of tricyclic antidepressants may be decreased when these medications are used concurrently with barbiturates, especially phenobarbital, because of increased metabolism resulting from induction of hepatic microsomal enzymes)

Calcium channel blocking agents
(caution is advised during titration of calcium channel blocker dosage for those patients taking medication known to promote hypotension, such as barbiturate preanesthetics, since the combination may result in excessive hypotension)

Carbonic anhydrase inhibitors
(osteopenia induced by barbiturates, especially phenobarbital, may be enhanced when carbonic anhydrase inhibitors are used concurrently; it is recommended that patients receiving concurrent therapy be monitored for early signs of osteopenia and that the carbonic anhydrase inhibitor be discontinued and appropriate treatment initiated if necessary)

» Contraceptives, estrogen-containing, oral
(concurrent use with barbiturates, especially phenobarbital, may result in reduced contraceptive reliability because of accelerated estrogen metabolism caused by induction of hepatic microsomal enzymes; use of a nonhormonal method of birth control or a progestin-only oral contraceptive may be necessary)

Cyclophosphamide
(concurrent use with barbiturates, especially phenobarbital, may induce microsomal metabolism to increase formation of alkylating metabolites of cyclophosphamide, thereby reducing the half-life and increasing the leukopenic activity of cyclophosphamide)

Disopyramide
(concurrent use with barbiturates, especially phenobarbital, may reduce serum disopyramide to ineffective concentrations; therefore, monitoring of its serum concentrations is necessary during concurrent therapy)

» Divalproex sodium or
» Valproic acid
(concurrent use may decrease the metabolism of barbiturates, resulting in increased serum concentrations, which may lead to increased CNS depression and neurological toxicity; barbiturate serum concentrations should be monitored to determine if dosage adjustment is necessary when these medications are used concurrently; also, the half-life of valproic acid may be decreased and dosage adjustment may be necessary)
(in addition, phenobarbital may enhance valproic acid hepatotoxicity, presumably through the formation of hepatotoxic valproate metabolites)

Doxycycline
(half-life of doxycycline may be shortened when this medication is used concurrently with barbiturates, especially phenobarbital, probably because of increased metabolism resulting from induction of hepatic microsomal enzymes; this effect may continue for up to 2 weeks after barbiturate therapy is discontinued; adjustment of doxycycline dosage during and after therapy or substitution of another tetracycline may be necessary)

Fenoprofen
(concurrent use with phenobarbital may decrease the elimination half-life of fenoprofen, possibly because of increased metabolism resulting from induction of hepatic microsomal enzyme activity; fenoprofen dosage adjustment may be required)

Griseofulvin
(absorption may be decreased when this medication is used concurrently with barbiturates, especially phenobarbital, resulting in decreased serum concentrations; although the effect of decreased serum concentrations on therapeutic response has not been established, concurrent use preferably should be avoided)

Guanadrel or
Guanethidine
(concurrent use with barbiturates may aggravate orthostatic hypotension)

Haloperidol
(concurrent use with barbiturate anticonvulsants may cause a change in the pattern and/or frequency of epileptiform seizures; dosage adjustments of anticonvulsants may be necessary; serum concentrations of haloperidol may be significantly reduced)

Hypothermia-producing medications, other
(concurrent use with barbiturates in high doses or acute overdose may increase the risk of hypothermia)

Ketamine
(concurrent use of ketamine, especially in high doses or when rapidly administered, with barbiturate preanesthetics may increase the risk of hypotension and/or respiratory depression)

Leucovorin
(large doses may counteract the anticonvulsant effects of barbiturate anticonvulsants)

Levothyroxine
(concurrent use of barbiturates may increase hepatic degradation of levothyroxine, which may result in increased requirements; dosage adjustment may be necessary)

Loxapine or
Phenothiazines or
Thioxanthenes
(may lower the seizure threshold; dosage adjustment of barbiturate anticonvulsants may be necessary)

(concurrent use of chlorpromazine with phenobarbital has been shown to increase the metabolism of chlorpromazine; therefore, phenobarbital may decrease serum concentrations of phenothiazines when used concurrently)

Maprotiline
(in addition to possibly enhancing CNS depressant effects, concurrent use of maprotiline may lower the convulsive threshold, at high doses, and decrease the effects of barbiturate anticonvulsants)

Methylphenidate
(concurrent use may increase serum concentrations of barbiturate anticonvulsants, especially phenobarbital, because of metabolism inhibition, possibly resulting in toxicity; dosage adjustment of the barbiturate anticonvulsant may be necessary)

Mexiletine
(concurrent use with barbiturates may accelerate metabolism and result in decreased plasma concentrations of mexiletine; plasma concentrations of mexiletine should be monitored during concurrent use to ensure efficacy is maintained)

Monoamine oxidase (MAO) inhibitors, including furazolidone, pargyline, and procarbazine
(concurrent use may prolong the CNS depressant effects of barbiturates, probably because metabolism of the barbiturate is inhibited)

(concurrent use with barbiturate anticonvulsants may cause a change in the pattern of epileptiform seizures; dosage adjustment of the barbiturate anticonvulsant may be necessary)

Phenylbutazone
(concurrent use may decrease the efficacy of barbiturates by inducing hepatic microsomal enzymes and increasing their metabolism; also, hepatic enzyme inducers such as barbiturates may increase phenylbutazone metabolism and decrease its half-life)

Posterior pituitary
(concurrent use with barbiturates may increase the risk of cardiac arrhythmias and coronary insufficiency)

Primidone
(although concurrent use with barbiturate anticonvulsants is rarely indicated, since primidone is metabolized to phenobarbital, it may cause a change in the pattern of epileptiform seizures because of altered medication metabolism and also

increase the sedative effect of either primidone or the barbiturate anticonvulsant; decreases in primidone dosage may be necessary)

Rifampin
(concurrent use with rifampin may enhance the metabolism of hexobarbital by induction of hepatic microsomal enzymes, resulting in lower serum concentrations; there are conflicting data on rifampin's effect on phenobarbital; dosage adjustment may be required)

Vitamin D
(effects may be reduced by barbiturates, especially phenobarbital, because of accelerated metabolism by hepatic microsomal enzyme induction; vitamin D supplementation may be required in patients on long-term barbiturate anticonvulsant therapy to prevent osteomalacia, although rickets is rare)

Xanthines, such as:
  Aminophylline
  Caffeine
  Oxtriphylline
  Theophylline
(concurrent use with barbiturates, especially phenobarbital, may increase metabolism of the xanthines [except dyphylline] by induction of hepatic microsomal enzymes, resulting in increased theophylline clearance; also, concurrent use may antagonize hypnotic effects of barbiturates)

Contraindications/Medical problems
The contraindications/medical problems included have been selected on the basis of their potential clinical significance (reasons given in parentheses where appropriate)—not necessarily inclusive (» = major clinical significance).

Except under special circumstances, this medication should not be used when the following medical problem exists:

» Porphyria, acute intermittent or variegata, or history of
(barbiturates may aggravate symptoms by inducing enzymes responsible for porphyrin synthesis)

Risk-benefit should be considered when the following medical problems exist:

Anemia, severe
(may be complicated by barbiturate-induced respiratory depression, especially with phenobarbital)

Asthma, history of
(hypersensitivity reactions such as bronchospasm more likely to occur in these patients)

Diabetes mellitus, especially with phenobarbital

» Drug abuse or dependence, history of
(predisposition of patient to habituation and dependence)

» Hepatic coma, premonitory signs of, or
Hepatic function impairment
(barbiturates metabolized in liver; medication should be administered with caution and, initially, in reduced dosage)

Hyperkinesis
(condition may be exacerbated)

Hyperthyroidism
(symptoms may be exacerbated because barbiturates displace thyroxine from plasma proteins)

Hypoadrenalism, borderline
(systemic effects of exogenous hydrocortisone and endogenous cortisol may be diminished by barbiturates)

Mental depression and/or
Suicidal tendencies
(condition may be exacerbated, especially in elderly patients)

» Pain, acute or chronic
(paradoxical excitement may be induced or important symptoms may be masked)

Renal function impairment, especially with intermediate- and long-acting barbiturates
   (barbiturates excreted primarily by kidneys; dosage reduction may be necessary)

» Respiratory disease involving dyspnea or obstruction, particularly status asthmaticus
   (serious ventilatory depression may occur)

» Sensitivity to barbiturate prescribed
   (in patients sensitive to barbiturates, severe hepatic damage can occur from ordinary doses and is usually associated with dermatitis and involvement of parenchymatous organs)

Caution should be used also in debilitated patients because they may react to usual doses with marked excitement, mental depression, and confusion.

For parenteral dosage forms only
Cardiac disease
   (adverse circulatory reactions may occur with intravenous administration, especially with too-rapid administration)

Hypertension
   (hypotension may occur with intravenous administration, especially in these patients; slow administration usually prevents this occurrence)

Side/Adverse Effects

Note: Exfoliative dermatitis and Stevens-Johnson syndrome, possibly fatal, may occur rarely as hypersensitivity reactions to barbiturates. If dermatologic reactions occur, the barbiturate should be discontinued.

Severe respiratory depression, apnea, laryngospasm, bronchospasm, or hypertension may occur with intravenous administration of barbiturates, especially if administered too rapidly.

Prolonged barbiturate therapy may result in osteopenia or rickets.

Barbiturate dependence may occur, especially following prolonged use of high doses. The characteristics of dependence include: a strong desire or need to continue taking the barbiturate; a tendency to increase the dose; a psychological dependence on the effects of the medication; and a physical dependence on the effects of the medication requiring its presence for maintenance of homeostasis and resulting in an abstinence syndrome when the barbiturate is discontinued. Symptoms of withdrawal are related to the pharmacokinetics of the specific barbiturate and can be severe and may even cause death.

In acute barbiturate overdosage, CNS and respiratory depression may progress to Cheyne-Stokes respiration, areflexia, slight constriction of the pupils (in severe toxicity, pupils may be dilated), oliguria, tachycardia, lowered body temperature, and coma. Typical shock syndrome (apnea, circulatory collapse, respiratory arrest, and death) may occur.

In extreme barbiturate overdosage, all electrical activity in the brain may cease. In this case an electroencephalogram (EEG) may be "flat," but this does not necessarily indicate clinical death since, unless hypoxic damage occurs, this effect is fully reversible.

Complications in barbiturate overdosage such as pneumonia, pulmonary edema, cardiac arrhythmias, congestive heart failure, and renal failure may occur.

The following side/adverse effects have been selected on the basis of their potential clinical significance (possible signs and symptoms in parentheses where appropriate)—not necessarily inclusive:

Those indicating need for medical attention
Incidence less frequent
   Sensitivity to barbiturates (confusion)—especially in geriatric or debilitated patients; *mental depression*—especially in geriatric or debilitated patients; *paradoxical reaction* (unusual excitement)—especially in children or geriatric or debilitated patients

Incidence rare
   Agranulocytosis (sore throat and/or fever); *allergic reaction* (skin rash or hives; swelling of eyelids, face, or lips; wheezing or tightness in chest)—especially in patients who have asthma, urticaria, angioedema, and similar conditions; *exfoliative dermatitis* (fever; red, thickened, or scaly skin); *hallucinations; hypotension or megaloblastic anemia* (unusual tiredness or weakness)—with chronic barbiturate use; *Stevens-Johnson syndrome* (bleeding sores on lips; chest pain; muscle or joint pain; painful sores, ulcers, or white spots in mouth; skin rash or hives; sore throat or fever); *thrombocytopenia* (unusual bleeding or bruising); *thrombophlebitis* (soreness, redness, swelling, or pain at injection site)—for parenteral dosage forms only

With prolonged or chronic use
   Hepatic damage (yellow eyes or skin); *osteopenia or rickets* (bone pain, tenderness, or aching; loss of appetite; muscle weakness; unusual weight loss)

Symptoms of acute toxicity
   Confusion, severe; decrease in or loss of reflexes; drowsiness, severe; fever; hypothermia (low body temperature); *shortness of breath or slow or troubled breathing; slow heartbeat; slurred speech; staggering; unusual movements of the eyes; weakness, severe*

Symptoms of chronic toxicity
   Confusion, severe; irritability, continuing; poor judgment; trouble in sleeping

Those indicating need for medical attention only if they continue or are bothersome
Incidence more frequent
   Clumsiness or unsteadiness; dizziness or lightheadedness; drowsiness; "hangover" effect
Incidence less frequent
   Anxiety or nervousness; constipation; feeling faint; headache; irritability; nausea or vomiting; nightmares or trouble in sleeping

Those indicating possible barbiturate withdrawal and need for medical attention if they occur after medication is discontinued
Minor symptoms—may occur within 8 to 12 hours and usually occur in the following sequence:
   Anxiety or restlessness; muscle twitching; trembling of hands; weakness; dizziness; vision problems; nausea; vomiting; trouble in sleeping, increased dreaming, or nightmares; orthostatic hypotension (feeling faint, lightheadedness)
Major symptoms—may occur within 16 hours and last up to 5 days
   Convulsions; hallucinations

Note: Intensity of withdrawal symptoms gradually declines over a period of approximately 15 days.

Patient Consultation

In providing consultation, consider emphasizing the following selected information (» = major clinical significance):

Before using this medication
» Conditions affecting use, especially:
   Sensitivity to barbiturates
   Pregnancy—Barbiturates readily cross placenta; increase in incidence of fetal abnormalities (FDA Pregnancy Category D); use during third trimester of pregnancy may cause physical dependence with resulting withdrawal symptoms in neonate; long-acting barbiturates associated with neonatal coagulation defect that may cause bleeding during early neonatal period; use during labor may cause respiratory depression in neonate
   Breast-feeding—Barbiturates excreted in breast milk; use by nursing mothers may cause CNS depression in infant
   Use in children—Children may react to barbiturates with paradoxical excitement

Use in the elderly—Elderly patients may react to usual doses of barbiturates with excitement, confusion, or mental depression; risk of barbiturate-induced hypothermia may be increased in elderly patients; elderly patients more likely to have age-related hepatic or renal function impairment, which may require a dosage reduction of barbiturates

Use by athletes—Barbiturates are banned and, in some cases, tested for by the U.S. Olympic Committee (USOC) and the National Collegiate Athletic Association (NCAA)

Other medications, especially alcohol, adrenocorticoids, corticotropin, other CNS depression-producing medications, coumarin- or indandione-derivative anticoagulants, carbamazepine, divalproex sodium, estrogen-containing contraceptives, or valproic acid

Other medical problems, especially history of drug abuse or dependence, premonitory signs of hepatic coma, acute or chronic pain, or respiratory disease involving dyspnea or obstruction (particularly status asthmaticus)

Caution if any laboratory tests required; possible interference with results of metyrapone test.

Proper use of this medication
» Importance of not using more medication than the amount prescribed because of habit-forming potential
» Not increasing dose if medication appears less effective after a few weeks; checking with physician
» For anticonvulsant use: Compliance with therapy; not missing any doses

Missed dose: If on scheduled dosing regimen—Taking as soon as possible; not taking if almost time for next dose; not doubling doses

Proper administration:

For extended-release dosage form
Swallowing capsule or tablet whole
Not breaking, crushing, or chewing

For suppository dosage form
Proper administration technique
» Proper storage

Precautions while using this medication
Regular visits to physician to check progress during prolonged therapy

Checking with physician before discontinuing medication after prolonged use; gradual dosage reduction may be necessary to avoid the possibility of withdrawal symptoms
» Avoiding use of alcohol or other CNS depressants
» Suspected psychological or physical dependence: Checking with physician
» Suspected overdose: Getting emergency help at once
» Caution if dizziness, lightheadedness, or drowsiness occurs
» Use of another or additional method of contraception if taking estrogen-containing oral contraceptives concurrently

Side/adverse effects
Signs of potential side effects, especially allergic reaction or intolerance to barbiturate, blood dyscrasias, exfoliative dermatitis, hallucinations, hepatic damage (with prolonged or chronic use), mental depression, paradoxical reaction, osteopenia or rickets (with prolonged or chronic use), or Stevens-Johnson syndrome

Unusual excitement may be more likely to occur in children and in elderly or very ill patients

Confusion and mental depression may be more likely to occur in elderly or very ill patients

General Dosing Information
Dosage of the barbiturates must be individualized, based on the patient's age, weight, and condition.

In patients with impaired hepatic function, lower doses should be used initially. Lower doses may be required also in patients with impaired renal function.

Patients on dialysis may require an increase in dosage.

Tolerance may occur with repeated administration of the barbiturates, especially of the long-acting ones and with large doses of the shorter-acting ones.

Prolonged administration of barbiturates as hypnotics generally is not recommended because they have not been shown to be effective for a period of more than 2 weeks.

Prolonged uninterrupted use of barbiturates, particularly the short-acting ones, may result in psychic or physical dependence.

Chronic use of barbiturates at doses 3 to 4 times the therapeutic concentration will usually produce physical dependence in about 75% of patients.

Daily administration in excess of 400 mg of pentobarbital or secobarbital for approximately 90 days is likely to produce some degree of physical dependence; a dosage of 600 to 800 mg taken for at least 35 days is sufficient to produce withdrawal seizures. The average daily dose for the barbiturate addict generally is about 1.5 grams.

Barbiturates should be withdrawn gradually in order to avoid the possibility of precipitating withdrawal symptoms.

To minimize the possibility of acute or chronic overdosage, the least possible quantity of a barbiturate should be prescribed and dispensed at any one time.

The toxic dose of barbiturates varies but generally an oral dose of 1 gram of most barbiturates produces serious poisoning in an adult. Death commonly occurs after 2 to 10 grams of ingested barbiturate.

Diet/Nutrition
Patients on long-term anticonvulsant therapy with phenobarbital and possibly mephobarbital may have increased folic acid requirements. In addition, patients on long-term therapy may require supplements of Vitamin D to prevent osteomalacia.

For parenteral dosage forms only
Prior to administration, parenteral solutions should be inspected visually for particulate matter and discoloration, if possible.

For intravenous injections, it is preferable to use the larger veins to minimize the risk of irritation and the possibility of resulting thrombosis. Administration into varicose veins is not recommended because of poor circulation in these veins.

Intravenous injections should be administered slowly and patients should be carefully monitored during administration. This requires maintenance of blood pressure, respiration, and cardiac function and recording of vital signs. Equipment for resuscitation and artificial ventilation should be readily available.

Intramuscular injections should be administered deeply into large muscles, such as the gluteus maximus or vastus lateralis because superficial intramuscular injection may be painful and may produce sterile abscesses or sloughs.

No more than 5 mL, regardless of drug concentration, should be injected intramuscularly at any one site because of possible tissue irritation.

Parenteral solutions of barbiturate salts are highly alkaline; therefore, caution should be used to avoid perivascular extravasation or intra-arterial injection, since extravasation may cause local tissue damage with subsequent necrosis and intra-arterial injection may cause spasm, severe pain, and possibly gangrene.

For rectal dosage forms only
Barbiturates may be administered rectally when oral or parenteral administration may be undesirable. If the rectal dosage form is not available, the soluble sodium salt of the barbiturate may be incorporated in a retention enema.

To assure accuracy in dosage, suppositories should not be divided.

Rectal administration of barbiturates is not recommended for status epilepticus; intravenous injection is the preferred route of administration for this condition.

For treatment of dependence
Treatment of dependence consists of the following:
- Gradual withdrawal of the barbiturate.
- An example of the different withdrawal regimens used (all of which require an extended period of time) involves substituting a 30-mg dose of phenobarbital for each 100- to 200-mg dose of the barbiturate that the patient has been taking. The total daily amount of phenobarbital then is administered as a single dose or in 3 or 4 divided doses, not to exceed 600 mg per day. If signs of withdrawal occur on the first day of treatment, a loading dose of 100 to 200 mg of phenobarbital may be administered intramuscularly in addition to the oral dose. After stabilization on phenobarbital, the total daily dose is decreased by 30 mg a day as long as withdrawal is proceeding smoothly. This regimen may be modified by initiating treatment at the patient's regular dosage level and decreasing the daily dosage by 10% if tolerated by the patient.
- For infants physically dependent on barbiturates, initially a dose of 3 to 10 mg of phenobarbital per kg of body weight per day may be given. After withdrawal symptoms (hyperactivity, disturbed sleep, tremors, hyperreflexia) are relieved, the dosage of phenobarbital should be gradually decreased and completely withdrawn over a 2-week period.
- Also, barbiturate withdrawal may be accomplished with benzodiazepines, such as diazepam.

AMOBARBITAL

Summary of Differences

Category: Parenteral amobarbital also may be indicated as an anticonvulsant.
Indications: Parenteral amobarbital also may be indicated in narcoanalysis; and has been used in diagnosis of schizophrenia and for catatonic, negativistic, and manic reactions, but generally has been replaced by other agents.
Pharmacology:
    Long-acting barbiturate—
        Onset of action: 60 minutes or longer.
        Duration of action: 10 to 12 hours.
    Protein binding—Moderate.

Additional Dosing Information

See also *General Dosing Information.*

For parenteral dosage forms only
The rate of intravenous injection should not exceed 100 mg per minute for adults or 60 mg per square meter of body surface per minute for children. Faster rates of administration may cause serious respiratory depression.
Superficial intramuscular or subcutaneous injections may be painful and may produce sterile abscesses or sloughs.

Oral Dosage Forms

AMOBARBITAL TABLETS USP

Usual adult dose: Sedative-hypnotic—
    Hypnotic: Oral, 65 to 200 mg at bedtime.
    Sedative: Daytime—Oral, 50 to 300 mg a day in divided doses.
Note: Geriatric and debilitated patients may react to usual doses with excitement, confusion, or mental depression. Lower doses may be required in these patients.

Auxiliary labeling:
- Avoid alcoholic beverages.
- May cause drowsiness.

AMOBARBITAL SODIUM CAPSULES USP

Usual adult dose: Sedative-hypnotic—
    Hypnotic: Oral, 65 to 200 mg at bedtime.
    Sedative:
        Daytime—Oral, 50 to 300 mg a day in divided doses.
        During labor—Oral, 200 to 400 mg, repeated every one to three hours, if necessary, up to a total dose of 1 gram.
        Preoperative—Oral, 200 mg one to two hours before surgery.
Note: Geriatric and debilitated patients may react to usual doses with excitement, confusion, or mental depression. Lower doses may be required in these patients.

Auxiliary labeling:
- Avoid alcoholic beverages.
- May cause drowsiness.

Parenteral Dosage Forms

STERILE AMOBARBITAL SODIUM USP

Usual adult dose:
    Sedative-hypnotic—
        Hypnotic: Intramuscular or intravenous, 65 to 200 mg.
        Sedative: Intramuscular or intravenous, 30 to 50 mg two or three times a day.
    Anticonvulsant—Intravenous, 65 to 500 mg.
Note: Geriatric and debilitated patients may react to usual doses with excitement, confusion, or mental depression. Lower doses may be required in these patients.

Usual adult prescribing limits:
    Intramuscular, up to 500 mg per dose.
    Intravenous, up to 1 gram per dose.

APROBARBITAL

Summary of Differences

Pharmacology:
    Intermediate-acting barbiturate—
        Onset of action: 45 to 60 minutes.
        Duration of action: 6 to 8 hours.
    Protein binding—Low.

Oral Dosage Forms

APROBARBITAL ELIXIR

Usual adult dose: Sedative-hypnotic—
    Hypnotic: Oral, 40 to 160 mg at bedtime.
    Sedative: Daytime—Oral, 40 mg three times a day.
Note: Geriatric and debilitated patients may react to usual doses with excitement, confusion, or mental depression. Lower doses may be required in these patients.

Auxiliary labeling:
- Avoid alcoholic beverages.
- May cause drowsiness.
- Keep container tightly closed.

BUTABARBITAL

Summary of Differences

Pharmacology:
Intermediate-acting barbiturate—
Onset of action: 45 to 60 minutes.
Duration of action: 6 to 8 hours.
Protein binding—Low.

Oral Dosage Forms

BUTABARBITAL SODIUM ELIXIR USP

Usual adult dose: Sedative-hypnotic—
Hypnotic: Oral, 50 to 100 mg at bedtime.
Sedative:
Daytime—Oral, 15 to 30 mg three or four times a day.
Preoperative—Oral, 50 to 100 mg sixty to ninety minutes before surgery.
Note: Geriatric and debilitated patients may react to usual doses with excitement, confusion, or mental depression. Lower doses may be required in these patients.

Auxiliary labeling:
• Avoid alcoholic beverages.
• May cause drowsiness.
• Keep container tightly closed.

BUTABARBITAL SODIUM TABLETS USP

Usual adult dose: See *Butabarbital Sodium Elixir USP.*

Auxiliary labeling:
• Avoid alcoholic beverages.
• May cause drowsiness.

MEPHOBARBITAL

Summary of Differences

Category: Indicated only as an anticonvulsant.
Pharmacology:
Biotransformation—About 75% of a single dose metabolized to phenobarbital in 24 hours.
Long-acting barbiturate—
Onset of action: 60 minutes or longer.
Duration of action: 10 to 12 hours.
Patient consultation: Compliance with therapy when used as an anticonvulsant.

Additional Dosing Information

See also *General Dosing Information.*
In epilepsy:
• Therapy with mephobarbital should begin with small doses, the dosage being gradually increased over a period of 4 to 5 days until the optimum dosage is determined.
• When used to replace another anticonvulsant, the dosage of mephobarbital should be gradually increased while the dosage of the other medication is maintained initially and then gradually decreased in order to maintain seizure control.
• Mephobarbital may be alternated with phenobarbital therapy.
• When used in conjunction with phenytoin, the dose of phenytoin may need to be reduced, but the full dose of mephobarbital may be given.
• Mephobarbital should be withdrawn slowly in order to avoid precipitating seizures or status epilepticus. When the dosage is to be reduced to a maintenance level or discontinued, the amount should be reduced over a period of 4 to 5 days or possibly longer.

Oral Dosage Forms

MEPHOBARBITAL TABLETS USP

Usual adult dose:
Anticonvulsant—Oral, 200 mg at bedtime to 600 mg a day in divided doses.
Sedative-hypnotic—
Sedative: Daytime—Oral, 32 to 100 mg three or four times a day.
Note: Geriatric and debilitated patients may react to usual doses with excitement, confusion, or mental depression. Lower doses may be required in these patients.

Auxiliary labeling:
• Avoid alcoholic beverages.
• May cause drowsiness.

METHARBITAL

Summary of Differences

Category: Indicated only as an anticonvulsant.
Pharmacology:
Biotransformation—Metabolized to barbital.
Long-acting barbiturate—
Onset of action: 60 minutes or longer.
Duration of action: 10 to 12 hours.
Patient consultation: Compliance with therapy.

Additional Dosing Information

See also *General Dosing Information.*
Metharbital should be withdrawn gradually in order to avoid the possibility of precipitating seizures or status epilepticus.

When used to replace or supplement other anticonvulsant therapy, the dosage of metharbital should be gradually increased while the dosage of the other medication is maintained initially and then gradually decreased in order to maintain seizure control.

Oral Dosage Forms

METHARBITAL TABLETS USP

Usual adult dose: Anticonvulsant—Oral, initially 100 mg one to three times a day, the dosage being increased up to 800 mg per day, if necessary.
Note: Geriatric and debilitated patients may react to usual doses with excitement, confusion, or mental depression. Lower doses may be required in these patients.

Auxiliary labeling:
• Avoid alcoholic beverages.
• May cause drowsiness.

PENTOBARBITAL

Summary of Differences

Category: Parenteral pentobarbital also may be indicated as an anticonvulsant.
Indications: Parenteral pentobarbital also used to protect brain from ischemia and increased intracranial pressure that follow stroke and head trauma.

Pharmacology:
Short-acting barbiturate—
Onset of action: 10 to 15 minutes.
Duration of action: 3 to 4 hours.
Protein binding—Moderate to high.

Additional Dosing Information

See also *General Dosing Information.*

When administered during labor, doses greater than 200 mg may cause respiratory depression in the newborn.

For parenteral dosage forms only

The injection is for intramuscular or intravenous use only; it is not recommended for subcutaneous administration.

Intravenous injections should be made slowly, not to exceed 50 mg per minute, to avoid adverse respiratory and circulatory reactions.

Oral Dosage Forms

PENTOBARBITAL ELIXIR USP

Usual adult dose: Sedative-hypnotic—
Hypnotic: Oral, 100 mg (pentobarbital sodium) at bedtime.
Sedative: Daytime—Oral, 20 mg (pentobarbital sodium) three or four times a day.

Note: Geriatric and debilitated patients may react to usual doses with excitement, confusion, or mental depression. Lower doses may be required in these patients.

Auxiliary labeling:
• Avoid alcoholic beverages.
• May cause drowsiness.
• Keep container tightly closed.

PENTOBARBITAL SODIUM CAPSULES USP

Usual adult dose: Sedative-hypnotic—
Hypnotic: Oral, 100 mg at bedtime.
Sedative: Preoperative—Oral, 100 mg.

Note: Geriatric and debilitated patients may react to usual doses with excitement, confusion, or mental depression. Lower doses may be required in these patients.

Auxiliary labeling:
• Avoid alcoholic beverages.
• May cause drowsiness.

Parenteral Dosage Forms

PENTOBARBITAL SODIUM INJECTION USP

Usual adult dose:
Sedative-hypnotic—
Hypnotic:
Intramuscular, 150 to 200 mg.
Intravenous, 100 mg initially; after one minute, additional small doses may be administered at one-minute intervals, if necessary, up to a total of 500 mg.
Sedative: Preoperative—Intramuscular, 150 to 200 mg.
Anticonvulsant—Intravenous, 100 mg initially; after one minute, additional small doses may be administered at one-minute intervals, if necessary, up to a total of 500 mg.

Note: Geriatric and debilitated patients may react to usual doses with excitement, confusion, or mental depression. Lower doses may be required in these patients.

Rectal Dosage Forms

PENTOBARBITAL SODIUM SUPPOSITORIES

Usual adult dose: Sedative-hypnotic—
Hypnotic: Rectal, 120 to 200 mg at bedtime.
Sedative: Daytime—Rectal, 30 mg two to four times a day.

Note: Geriatric and debilitated patients may react to usual doses with excitement, confusion, or mental depression. Lower doses may be required in these patients.

Auxiliary labeling:
• For rectal use only.
• Avoid alcoholic beverages.
• May cause drowsiness.
• Refrigerate.

PHENOBARBITAL

Summary of Differences

Category:
Also indicated as an anticonvulsant.
Oral and parenteral phenobarbital also used as an antihyperbilirubinemic; and has been used as an antitremor agent, although generally has been replaced by benzodiazepines and beta-adrenergic blockers.
Pharmacology:
Distribution—Distributed less rapidly than other barbiturates because it has lowest lipid solubility.
Time to peak effect—Maximal CNS depression may not occur for 15 minutes or more after intravenous administration.
Long-acting barbiturate—
Onset of action: 60 minutes or longer.
Duration of action: 10 to 12 hours.
Protein binding—Low to moderate.
Patient consultation: Compliance with therapy when used as an anticonvulsant.

Additional Dosing Information

See also *General Dosing Information.*

In epilepsy:
• In children, higher-per-kg dosage of phenobarbital and most other anticonvulsants generally are required to achieve blood concentrations considered therapeutic.
• Several weeks of phenobarbital therapy may be required to achieve maximum antiepilepsy effects.
• Phenobarbital should be withdrawn slowly in order to avoid precipitating seizures or status epilepticus.
• When phenobarbital is replaced by another anticonvulsant, the dosage of phenobarbital should be maintained initially and then reduced gradually while, at the same time, the dosage of the replacement medication is increased gradually in order to maintain seizure control.
• When administered intravenously, phenobarbital sodium may require 15 minutes or more to attain peak concentrations in the brain; therefore, it is important to use the minimal dosage required and to wait for the anticonvulsant effect to develop before administering a second dose, in order to avoid the possibility of severe barbiturate-induced depression.

For parenteral dosage forms only

Sterile phenobarbital sodium may be administered subcutaneously after reconstitution, but phenobarbital sodium injection is not recommended for subcutaneous use.

The rate of the intravenous injection should not exceed 60 mg per minute. Faster rates of administration may cause serious respiratory depression.

Following intravenous administration, up to 30 minutes may be required for maximum effect.

Oral Dosage Forms

Note: Bracketed uses in the *Dosage Forms* section refer to categories of use and/or indications that are not included in U.S. product labeling.

PHENOBARBITAL CAPSULES

Usual adult dose:
Anticonvulsant—Oral, 60 to 250 mg (base) per day, as a single dose or in divided doses.
Sedative-hypnotic—
Hypnotic: Oral, 100 to 320 mg (base) at bedtime.
Sedative: Daytime—Oral, 30 to 120 mg (base) in two or three divided doses a day.
[Antihyperbilirubinemic][1]—Oral, 30 to 60 mg (base) three times a day.

Note: Geriatric and debilitated patients may react to usual doses with excitement, confusion, or mental depression. Lower doses may be required in these patients.

Auxiliary labeling:
• Avoid alcoholic beverages.
• May cause drowsiness.

PHENOBARBITAL ELIXIR USP

Usual adult dose: See *Phenobarbital Capsules.*

Auxiliary labeling:
• Avoid alcoholic beverages.
• May cause drowsiness.
• Keep container tightly closed.

PHENOBARBITAL TABLETS USP

Usual adult dose: See *Phenobarbital Capsules.*

Auxiliary labeling:
• Avoid alcoholic beverages.
• May cause drowsiness.

Parenteral Dosage Forms

Note: Bracketed uses in the *Dosage Forms* section refer to categories of use and/or indications that are not included in U.S. product labeling.

PHENOBARBITAL SODIUM INJECTION USP

Usual adult dose:
Anticonvulsant—Intravenous, 100 to 320 mg, repeated if necessary up to a total dose of 600 mg during a twenty-four-hour period.
Status epilepticus: Intravenous (slow), 10 to 20 mg per kg of body weight, repeated if necessary.
Sedative-hypnotic—
Hypnotic: Intramuscular or intravenous, 100 to 325 mg.
Sedative:
Daytime—Intramuscular or intravenous, 30 to 120 mg a day in two or three divided doses.
Preoperative—Intramuscular, 130 to 200 mg sixty to ninety minutes before surgery.

Note: Geriatric and debilitated patients may react to usual doses with excitement, confusion, or mental depression. Lower doses may be required in these patients.

STERILE PHENOBARBITAL SODIUM USP

Usual adult dose:
Anticonvulsant—Intravenous, 100 to 320 mg, repeated if necessary up to a total dose of 600 mg during a twenty-four-hour period.
Status epilepticus: Intravenous (slow), 10 to 20 mg per kg of body weight, repeated if necessary.
Sedative-hypnotic—
Hypnotic: Intramuscular, intravenous, or subcutaneous, 100 to 325 mg.
Sedative:
Daytime—Intramuscular, intravenous, or subcutaneous, 30 to 120 mg a day in two or three divided doses.
Preoperative—Intramuscular, 130 to 200 mg sixty to ninety minutes before surgery.

Note: Geriatric and debilitated patients may react to usual doses of barbiturates with excitement, confusion, or mental depression. Lower doses may be required in these patients.

---

[1]Not included in Canadian product labeling.

SECOBARBITAL

Summary of Differences

Category: Parenteral secobarbital also may be indicated as an anticonvulsant (in tetanus).
Pharmacology:
Distribution—Distributed more rapidly than other barbiturates because it has highest lipid solubility.
Short-acting barbiturate—
Onset of action: 10 to 15 minutes.
Duration of action: 3 to 4 hours.
Protein binding—Moderate to high.

Additional Dosing Information

See also *General Dosing Information.*

For parenteral dosage forms only
The rate of the intravenous injection should not exceed 50 mg per 15-second period. Faster rates of administration may cause respiratory depression or apnea, laryngospasm, or vasodilation with fall in blood pressure.

For rectal dosage forms only
To prepare a solution for rectal administration, dilute the commercially available 5% secobarbital sodium injection with lukewarm tap water to a concentration of 10 to 15 mg per mL (1 to 1.5%).

Oral Dosage Forms

SECOBARBITAL SODIUM CAPSULES USP

Usual adult dose: Sedative-hypnotic—
Hypnotic: Oral, 100 mg at bedtime.
Sedative:
Daytime—Oral, 30 to 50 mg three or four times a day.
Preoperative—Oral, 200 to 300 mg one to two hours before surgery.

Note: Geriatric and debilitated patients may react to usual doses with excitement, confusion, or mental depression. Lower doses may be required in these patients.

Auxiliary labeling:
- Avoid alcoholic beverages.
- May cause drowsiness.

Parenteral Dosage Forms

SECOBARBITAL SODIUM INJECTION USP

Usual adult dose:
Sedative-hypnotic—
> Hypnotic:
>> Intramuscular, 100 to 200 mg.
>> Intravenous, 50 to 250 mg.
> Sedative: Dentistry—Intramuscular, 1.1 to 2.2 mg per kg of body weight ten to fifteen minutes before procedure. Nerve block—Intravenous, 100 to 150 mg.
> Anticonvulsant (in tetanus)—Intramuscular or intravenous, 5.5 mg per kg of body weight, repeated every three to four hours as needed.

Note: Geriatric and debilitated patients may react to usual doses of barbiturates with excitement, confusion, or mental depression. Lower doses may be required in these patients.

SECOBARBITAL AND AMOBARBITAL

Oral Dosage Forms

SECOBARBITAL SODIUM AND AMOBARBITAL SODIUM CAPSULES USP

Usual adult dose: Sedative-hypnotic—Oral, 1 capsule at bedtime or one hour preoperatively.

Note: Geriatric and debilitated patients may react to usual doses with excitement, confusion, or mental depression. Lower doses may be required in these patients.

Auxiliary labeling:
- Avoid alcoholic beverages.
- May cause drowsiness.

BARBITURATES AND ANALGESICS   Systemic

INN: Acetaminophen—Paracetamol

Some commonly used *brand names* are:

In the U.S.—

Amaphen [Butalbital and Acetaminophen]
Anolor-300 [Butalbital and Acetaminophen]
Anoquan [Butalbital and Acetaminophen]
Arcet [Butalbital and Acetaminophen]
Ascomp with Codeine No.3 [Butalbital, Aspirin, Codeine, and Caffeine]
Axotal [Butalbital and Aspirin]
Bancap [Butalbital and Acetaminophen]
Bucet [Butalbital and Acetaminophen]
Butace [Butalbital and Acetaminophen]
Butalbital Compound with Codeine [Butalbital, Aspirin, Codeine, and Caffeine]
Butalgen [Butalbital and Aspirin]
Butinal with Codeine No.3 [Butalbital, Aspirin, Codeine, and Caffeine]
Conten [Butalbital and Acetaminophen]
Dolmar [Butalbital and Acetaminophen]
Endolor [Butalbital and Acetaminophen]
Esgic [Butalbital and Acetaminophen]

Esgic-Plus [Butalbital and Acetaminophen]
Ezol [Butalbital and Acetaminophen]
Femcet [Butalbital and Acetaminophen]
Fiorgen [Butalbital and Aspirin]
Fioricet [Butalbital and Acetaminophen]
Fiorinal [Butalbital and Aspirin]
Fiorinal with Codeine No.3 [Butalbital, Aspirin, Codeine, and Caffeine]
Fiormor [Butalbital and Aspirin]
Fortabs [Butalbital and Aspirin]
Idenal with Codeine [Butalbital, Aspirin, Codeine, and Caffeine]
Isobutal [Butalbital and Aspirin]
Isobutyl [Butalbital and Aspirin]
Isocet [Butalbital and Acetaminophen]
Isolin [Butalbital and Aspirin]
Isollyl [Butalbital and Aspirin]
Isollyl with Codeine [Butalbital, Aspirin, Codeine, and Caffeine]

Isopap [Butalbital and Acetaminophen]
Laniroif [Butalbital and Aspirin]
Lanorinal [Butalbital and Aspirin]
Marnal [Butalbital and Aspirin]
Medigesic [Butalbital and Acetaminophen]
Pacaps [Butalbital and Acetaminophen]
Pharmagesic [Butalbital and Acetaminophen]
Phrenilin [Butalbital and Acetaminophen]
Phrenilin Forte [Butalbital and Acetaminophen]

Repan [Butalbital and Acetaminophen]
Sedapap [Butalbital and Acetaminophen]
Tencet [Butalbital and Acetaminophen]
Tencon [Butalbital and Acetaminophen]
Triad [Butalbital and Acetaminophen]
Triaprin [Butalbital and Acetaminophen]
Two-Dyne [Butalbital and Acetaminophen]
Vibutal [Butalbital and Aspirin]

In Canada—

Fiorinal [Butalbital and ASA‡]
Fiorinal-C¹/₄ [Butalbital, ASA‡, Codeine, and Caffeine]
Fiorinal-C¹/₂ [Butalbital, ASA‡, Codeine, and Caffeine]
Phenaphen with Codeine No.2 [Phenobarbital, ASA‡, and Codeine]
Phenaphen with Codeine No.3 [Phenobarbital, ASA‡, and Codeine]

Phenaphen with Codeine No.4 [Phenobarbital, ASA‡, and Codeine]
Tecnal [Butalbital and ASA‡]
Tecnal-C¹/₄ [Butalbital, ASA‡, Codeine, and Caffeine]
Tecnal-C¹/₂ [Butalbital, ASA‡, Codeine, and Caffeine]

Other commonly used names for butalbital and aspirin combination are butalbital-AC and butalbital compound.

ORAL

BUTALBITAL AND ACETAMINOPHEN
  Butalbital and Acetaminophen Capsules†
    In the U.S.—*Bancap; Bucet; Conten; Phrenilin Forte; Tencon; Triaprin*
  Butalbital and Acetaminophen Tablets†
    In the U.S.—*Phrenilin; Sedapap;* GENERIC
  Butalbital, Acetaminophen, and Caffeine Capsules†
    In the U.S.—*Amaphen; Anolor-300; Anoquan; Butace; Dolmar; Endolor; Esgic; Ezol; Femcet; Isopap; Medigesic; Pacaps; Repan; Tencet; Triad; Two-Dyne*
  Butalbital, Acetaminophen, and Caffeine Tablets USP†
    In the U.S.—*Arcet; Dolmar; Esgic; Esgic-Plus; Fioricet; Isocet; Medigesic; Pharmagesic; Repan;* GENERIC
BUTALBITAL AND ASPIRIN
  Butalbital and Aspirin Tablets USP†
    In the U.S.—*Axotal*
  Butalbital, Aspirin‡, and Caffeine Capsules
    In the U.S.—*Butalgen; Fiorinal; Isobutal; Isollyl; Laniroif; Lanorinal; Marnal;* GENERIC
    In Canada—*Fiorinal; Tecnal*
  Butalbital, Aspirin‡, and Caffeine Tablets
    In the U.S.—*Butalgen; Fiorgen; Fiorinal; Fiormor; Fortabs; Isobutal; Isobutyl; Isolin; Isollyl; Laniroif; Lanorinal; Marnal; Vibutal;* GENERIC
    In Canada—*Fiorinal; Tecnal*
BUTALBITAL, ASPIRIN‡, CODEINE, AND CAFFEINE
  Butalbital, Aspirin‡, Codeine Phosphate, and Caffeine Capsules
    In the U.S.—*Ascomp with Codeine No.3; Butalbital Compound with Codeine; Butinal with Codeine No.3; Fiorinal with Codeine No.3; Idenal with Codeine; Isollyl with Codeine;* GENERIC
    In Canada—*Fiorinal-C ¹/₄; Fiorinal-C ¹/₂; Tecnal-C ¹/₄; Tecnal-C ¹/₂*
  Butalbital, Aspirin‡, Codeine Phosphate, and Caffeine Tablets†
    In the U.S.—*Idenal with Codeine;* GENERIC
PHENOBARBITAL, ASA‡, AND CODEINE*
  Phenobarbital, ASA‡, and Codeine Phosphate Capsules*
    In Canada—*Phenaphen with Codeine No.2; Phenaphen with Codeine No.3; Phenaphen with Codeine No.4*
  Note: In the U.S., *Phenaphen with Codeine* contains acetaminophen and codeine phosphate. See *Opioid (Narcotic) Analgesics and Acetaminophen (Systemic).*

*Not commercially available in the U.S.
†Not commercially available in Canada.
‡In Canada, *Aspirin* is a brand name; acetylsalicylic acid is the generic name. ASA, a commonly used designation for aspirin (or acetylsalicylic acid) in both the U.S. and Canada, is the term used in Canadian product labeling.

Category: Analgesic.

Indications

Note: Bracketed information in the *Indications* section refers to uses not included in U.S. product labeling.

Accepted
Headache, tension-type (treatment)—Barbiturate and analgesic combinations are indicated for relief of the symptoms of occasional tension-type (muscle contraction) headache.
[Headache, migraine (treatment)—Barbiturate and analgesic combinations are indicated to relieve occasional migraine¹ and coexisting migraine and tension-type headaches ("mixed" headache syndrome).]
Note: Because of the risk of habituation, barbiturate and analgesic combinations are not recommended for treatment of frequent, especially daily, headaches.

To reduce analgesic use, underlying problems that may contribute to tension-type headaches, such as inflammation or structural abnormalities in the cervical or temporomandibular areas, should be identified and treated. In some patients, application of heat, muscle relaxants, and/or physical therapy may be helpful. Other medications having the potential to cause habituation (e.g., benzodiazepines) should be used as infrequently as possible.

Chronic tension-type headaches and severe migraines that occur more frequently than twice a month may require additional prophylactic treatment to reduce the frequency, severity, and/or duration of the headaches. The prophylactic agents most commonly used for tension-type headaches are tricyclic antidepressants, especially amitriptyline, and/or beta-adrenergic blocking agents, especially propranolol. For migraines, beta-adrenergic blocking agents, calcium channel blocking agents, tricyclic antidepressants, monoamine oxidase inhibitors, methysergide, pizotyline (not commercially available in the U.S.), and sometimes cyproheptadine (especially in children) are used for prophylaxis. The combination of amitriptyline plus propranolol has been found superior to either agent used alone in preventing "mixed" headaches.

Identification and avoidance of precipitating factors is also important in the overall management of the patient with migraine headaches. Relaxation and/or biofeedback techniques may also be helpful in controlling migraine headaches, and may reduce the need for medication.

[Pain (treatment)]—Barbiturate and analgesic combinations are also indicated for relief of pain other than headache, especially when an antianxiety or relaxant effect is desired.

¹Not included in Canadian product labeling.

Pharmacology

Mechanism of action/Effect:
  Butalbital or
  Phenobarbital—Butalbital is a short- to intermediate-acting barbiturate; phenobarbital is a long-acting barbiturate. Barbiturates are nonselective depressants of the central nervous system (CNS). They are used in analgesic combinations for their antianxiety and relaxant effects.
  Acetaminophen or
  Aspirin—The mechanism of analgesic action has not been fully determined. Acetaminophen and aspirin may act by inhibiting prostaglandin synthesis in the CNS and through a peripheral action by blocking pain-impulse generation. The peripheral action may also be due to inhibition of the synthesis of prostaglandins or to inhibition of the synthesis or actions of other substances that sensitize pain receptors to mechanical or chemical stimulation. Acetaminophen may act predominantly in the CNS, whereas aspirin may produce analgesia predominantly via peripheral actions.
  Codeine—Opioid analgesics bind with stereospecific receptors at many sites within the CNS to alter processes affecting both the perception of pain and the emotional response to pain. Precise sites and mechanisms of action have not been fully determined. It has been proposed that there are multiple subtypes of opioid receptors, each mediating various therapeutic and/or side effects of opioids. The actions of an opioid analgesic may therefore depend upon its binding affinity for each type of receptor and whether it acts as a full agonist or a partial agonist or is inactive at each type of receptor. At least two of these types of receptors (mu and kappa) mediate analgesia. Codeine probably produces its effects via agonist actions at the mu receptor.
  Caffeine—Caffeine-induced constriction of cerebral blood vessels, which leads to a decrease in cerebral blood flow and in the oxygen tension of the brain, may contribute to relief of some types of headache. Also, it has been suggested that the addition

of caffeine to acetaminophen and/or aspirin may provide a more rapid onset of action and/or enhanced pain relief with lower doses of analgesics. However, the FDA has not accepted caffeine as an effective analgesic adjuvant.

Other actions/Effects:
Butalbital or
Phenobarbital—Barbiturates have dose-dependent respiratory depressant effects.

Phenobarbital is a potent inducer of the activity of the hepatic p-450 microsomal enzyme system and may alter the metabolism and efficacy of many other medications that are metabolized via this enzyme system. Butalbital may also have some enzyme-inducing activity.

Phenobarbital also has anticonvulsant activity.

Acetaminophen—Has antipyretic activity.

Aspirin—Has antipyretic, anti-inflammatory, and platelet aggregation-inhibiting actions.

Codeine—Has CNS depressant, respiratory depressant, antidiarrheal, and antitussive actions.

Caffeine—Has CNS stimulating activity and may therefore inhibit sleep. Because sleep contributes to relief of migraine headaches, this action may be detrimental to the patient.

Onset of action:
Phenobarbital—1 hour or longer.
Codeine—30 to 45 minutes.

Time to peak effect:
Acetaminophen—1 to 3 hours.
Codeine—1 to 2 hours.

Duration of action:
Phenobarbital—10 to 12 hours.
Acetaminophen—3 to 4 hours.
Codeine—4 hours.

Precautions to Consider

Note: Information regarding precautions applying to the use of the individual ingredients in these combination medications is limited to brief summaries of the major precautions that may apply to occasional use of recommended doses. For more complete information that may apply, especially if these agents are ingested frequently or in higher-than-recommended doses, see—

Butalbital: *Barbiturates (Systemic)*. Although butalbital is not specifically mentioned in that monograph, general precautions applying to all barbiturates may apply to butalbital also.

Phenobarbital: *Barbiturates (Systemic)*.
Acetaminophen: *Acetaminophen (Systemic)*.
Aspirin: *Salicylates (Systemic)*.
Codeine: *Opioid (Narcotic) Analgesics (Systemic)*.
Caffeine: *Caffeine (Systemic)*.

Cross-sensitivity and/or related problems
Butalbital and
Phenobarbital—Patients sensitive to other barbiturates may be sensitive to butalbital and phenobarbital also.
Acetaminophen—Patients sensitive to aspirin are usually not sensitive to acetaminophen; however, mild bronchospastic reactions with acetaminophen have been reported in some aspirin-sensitive patients (fewer than 5% of those tested).
Aspirin—Patients sensitive to one salicylate, including methyl salicylate (oil of wintergreen), may be sensitive to aspirin also. However, patients sensitive to aspirin may not necessarily be sensitive to salicylamide.
Patients sensitive to other nonsteroidal anti-inflammatory drugs (NSAIDs) may be sensitive to aspirin also.

Adolescents
Aspirin—Aspirin usage may be associated with the development of Reye's syndrome in adolescents with acute febrile illnesses, especially influenza and varicella. It is recommended that aspirin not be administered to febrile adolescent patients until after the presence of such an illness has been ruled out.

Geriatrics
Butalbital and
Phenobarbital—Geriatric patients may react to usual doses of barbiturates with excitement, confusion, or depression. Also, elderly patients are more likely to have age-related renal function impairment, which may require caution in patients receiving barbiturates.
Acetaminophen—Studies performed to date have not demonstrated geriatrics-specific problems that would limit the usefulness of acetaminophen in the elderly.
Aspirin—Geriatric patients may be more susceptible to the toxic effects of salicylates. Also, elderly patients may be more likely to have age-related renal function impairment, which may require caution in patients receiving aspirin.
Codeine—Geriatric patients may be more susceptible to the effects, especially the respiratory depressant effects, of opioid analgesics such as codeine. Elderly patients tend to eliminate opioid analgesics more slowly than younger adults. Lower doses and/or longer intervals between doses may be required, and are usually effective, for these patients. Also, elderly patients are more likely to have age-related renal function impairment and/or prostatic hypertrophy or obstruction; opioid-induced urinary retention may be detrimental to these patients.
Caffeine—No information is available on the relationship of age to the effects of caffeine in geriatric patients.

Drug interactions and/or related problems
The following drug interactions and/or related problems have been selected on the basis of their potential clinical significance (possible mechanism in parentheses where appropriate)—not necessarily inclusive (» = major clinical significance):

Note: Combinations containing any of the following medications, depending on the amount present, may also interact with this medication.

For barbiturates
Addictive medications, other, especially CNS depressants with habituating potential
(caution in concurrent use is recommended because of the increased risk of habituation)

Any medication that may be rendered less effective, because of accelerated metabolism, by hepatic enzyme induction, especially:
» Adrenocorticoids, glucocorticoid and mineralocorticoid
» Anticoagulants, coumarin- or indandione-derivative
» Carbamazepine
» Contraceptives, estrogen-containing, oral
» Corticotropin
(caution in concurrent use is recommended, especially with phenobarbital)
» Alcohol or
» CNS depression-producing medications, other
(concurrent use with a barbiturate may cause additive CNS depression; caution is recommended and dosage reduction of either or both medications may be needed)
» Divalproex sodium or
» Valproic acid
(these agents may decrease barbiturate metabolism, possibly leading to increased barbiturate serum concentrations and risk of toxicity)
(concurrent use with a barbiturate may also increase the half-life and risk of hepatotoxicity of valproic acid)

For acetaminophen
» Alcohol, especially chronic abuse of, or

Hepatic enzyme inducers or
Hepatotoxic medications, other
   (risk of hepatotoxicity with single toxic doses of acetaminophen may be increased in alcoholics or in patients regularly taking other hepatotoxic medications or hepatic enzyme inducers)

   (chronic use of barbiturates or primidone has been reported to decrease the therapeutic effects of acetaminophen, probably because of increased metabolism resulting from induction of hepatic microsomal enzyme activity; the possibility should be considered that similar effects may occur with other hepatic enzyme inducers; however, such problems have not been reported with occasional use of combination formulations containing butalbital and acetaminophen)

For aspirin
Acidifiers, urinary, such as:
   Ammonium chloride
   Ascorbic acid
   Potassium or sodium phosphates
   (acidification of the urine by these medications decreases salicylate [from aspirin] excretion, leading to increased salicylate plasma concentrations)
» Alkalizers, urinary, such as:
   Carbonic anhydrase inhibitors
   Citrates, or
   Antacids, chronic high-dose use, especially calcium- or magnesium-containing or sodium bicarbonate
   (alkalinization of the urine by these agents increases salicylate [from aspirin] excretion, leading to decreased salicylate plasma concentrations, reduced effectiveness, and shortened duration of analgesic action)

   (carbonic anhydrase inhibitors may also increase the risk of salicylate intoxication in patients receiving large doses of aspirin because metabolic acidosis induced by carbonic anhydrase inhibitors may increase penetration of salicylate into the brain; the increased risk of severe metabolic acidosis and salicylate toxicity must be considered if acetazolamide is used to produce forced alkaline diuresis in the treatment of aspirin overdose)
» Anticoagulants, coumarin- or indandione-derivative, or
» Heparin or
» Thrombolytic agents, such as:
   Alteplase
   Anistreplase
   Streptokinase
   Urokinase
   (because aspirin inhibits platelet aggregation and may induce gastrointestinal ulceration and/or bleeding, which may be hazardous to patients receiving anticoagulant or thrombolytic therapy, it is recommended that aspirin not be administered to patients receiving these agents except as part of a prescribed and monitored antithrombotic regimen)

Furosemide
   (in addition to an increased risk of ototoxicity, concurrent use of furosemide with high doses of aspirin may lead to salicylate toxicity because of competition for renal excretory sites)

Laxatives, cellulose-containing
   (concurrent use may reduce the salicylate effect because of physical binding or other absorptive hindrance; medications should be administered 2 hours apart)
» Methotrexate
   (aspirin may displace methotrexate from its binding sites and decrease its renal clearance, leading to toxic plasma concentrations of methotrexate; if used concurrently, methotrexate dosage should be decreased, the patient observed for signs of toxicity, and/or methotrexate plasma concentration monitored; also, it is recommended that aspirin not be administered for 24 to 48 hours prior to administration of a high-dose methotrexate infusion, or until plasma methotrexate concentrations have decreased to a nontoxic level following the infusion [usually at least 12 hours])

Ototoxic medications, other, especially
» Vancomycin
   (concurrent or sequential administration of these medications with aspirin should be avoided because the potential for ototoxicity may be increased; hearing loss may occur and may progress to deafness even after discontinuation of the medication; these effects may be reversible, but usually are permanent)
» Probenecid or
» Sulfinpyrazone
   (uricosuric effects of probenecid or sulfinpyrazone may be decreased by doses of aspirin that produce serum salicylate concentrations above 50 mcg/mL [5 mg per 100 mL; 0.36 mmol/L]; also, probenecid may decrease renal clearance and increase plasma concentrations of salicylate, thereby increasing the risk of toxicity)

   (sulfinpyrazone may decrease salicylate [from aspirin] excretion and/or displace salicylate from its protein binding sites, possibly leading to increased salicylate concentrations and toxicity)

For codeine
Addictive medications, other, especially CNS depressants with habituating potential
   (increased risk of habituation)
» Alcohol or
» CNS depression-producing medications, other, including other opioid analgesics
   (concurrent use with codeine may lead to additive CNS depression; caution is recommended and dosage reduction of either or both medications may be needed)

Anticholinergics, especially atropine and related compounds
   (concurrent use with codeine may result in increased risk of severe constipation, possibly leading to paralytic ileus, and/or urinary retention)

Antidiarrheals, antiperistaltic
   (risk of constipation, which may lead to paralytic ileus, as well as the risk of CNS and/or respiratory depression, may be increased)

Antihypertensives, especially ganglionic blocking agents such as guanadrel, guanethidine, and mecamylamine, or
Diuretics or
Hypotension-producing medications, other
   (codeine may potentiate the hypotensive effects of these medications, leading to an increased risk of orthostatic hypotension)

Metoclopramide
   (codeine may antagonize the effects of metoclopramide on gastrointestinal motility)

Monoamine oxidase inhibitors, including furazolidone, procarbazine, and selegiline
   (concurrent use with codeine should be undertaken with caution because concurrent use with meperidine has resulted in unpredictable, severe, and sometimes fatal reactions, including immediate excitation, sweating, rigidity, and severe hypertension or, in some patients, hypotension, severe respiratory depression, coma, seizures, hyperpyrexia, and cardiovascular collapse; it is recommended that codeine be administered in reduced dosage to patients receiving an MAO inhibitor)

Naloxone
   (antagonizes the analgesic, CNS, and respiratory depressant effects of codeine and may precipitate withdrawal symptoms in physically dependent patients; dosage of the antagonist should be carefully titrated when used to treat codeine overdose in dependent patients)
» Naltrexone
   (codeine should not be administered as an analgesic to patients receiving naltrexone, which blocks the therapeutic effects of opioids; also, naltrexone therapy should not be initiated in patients receiving codeine for therapeutic purposes)

(administration of naltrexone to a patient physically dependent on codeine will precipitate withdrawal symptoms; symptoms may appear within 5 minutes of naltrexone administration, persist for up to 48 hours, and be difficult to reverse)

Opioid analgesics, other
(concurrent use with codeine may result in additive CNS depressant, respiratory depressant, and hypotensive effects)

(opioid agonist/antagonist analgesics [butorphanol, nalbuphine, or pentazocine] may partially antagonize the therapeutic and CNS depressant effects of codeine; also, nalbuphine and pentazocine may precipitate withdrawal symptoms in patients who are physically dependent on codeine)

For caffeine
CNS stimulation-producing medications, other
(concurrent use with caffeine may result in excessive CNS stimulation, leading to unwanted effects such as nervousness, irritability, insomnia, or possibly convulsions or cardiac arrhythmias; close observation is recommended)

Lithium
(caffeine increases urinary excretion of lithium, and may thereby reduce its therapeutic effect)

Monoamine oxidase (MAO) inhibitors, including furazolidone, procarbazine, and selegiline
(the sympathomimetic side effects of caffeine may lead to cardiac arrhythmias or severe hypertension when large amounts of caffeine are used concurrently with MAO inhibitors; even small doses may cause tachycardia and a slight increase in blood pressure)

Contraindications/Medical problems
The contraindications/medical problems included have been selected on the basis of their potential clinical significance (reasons given in parentheses where appropriate)—not necessarily inclusive (» = major clinical significance).

Except under special circumstances, this medication should not be used when the following medical conditions exist:

For barbiturates
» Porphyria, acute intermittent or variegata, or history of
(barbiturates may aggravate symptoms by inducing enzymes responsible for porphyrin synthesis)

For aspirin
» Angioedema, anaphylaxis, or other severe allergic reaction induced by aspirin or other NSAIDs, history of
(high risk of recurrence)

» Bleeding ulcers or
» Hemorrhagic states, other active
(may be exacerbated)

» Hemophilia or other bleeding problems, including coagulation or platelet function disorders
(increased risk of hemorrhage)

» Nasal polyps associated with aspirin-induced asthma or other allergies
(high risk of severe allergic reactions)

For codeine
» Diarrhea caused by poisoning or antibiotic therapy, until toxic material has been eliminated from the gastrointestinal tract
(codeine may slow elimination of toxic material)

» Respiratory depression, acute
(may be exacerbated)

Risk-benefit should be considered when the following medical problems exist:

For barbiturates
» Allergic reaction to a barbiturate, history of
Asthma, history of
(increased risk of bronchospastic allergic reactions)

Diabetes mellitus, especially with phenobarbital

» Drug abuse or dependence, history of
(patient predisposed to habituation and dependence)

» Hepatic coma, premonitory signs of, or
Hepatic function impairment
(barbiturates metabolized in liver; caution and a reduction in barbiturate dosage is recommended)

Hyperkinesis
(increased risk of barbiturate-induced paradoxical excitement)

Hyperthyroidism
(symptoms may be exacerbated because barbiturates displace thyroxine from plasma proteins)

Mental depression or
Suicidal tendencies
(condition may be exacerbated, especially in elderly patients)

Renal function impairment
(barbiturates excreted via kidneys; reduction in barbiturate dosage may be necessary)

» Respiratory disease involving dyspnea or obstruction, particularly status asthmaticus
(serious ventilatory depression may occur)

Caution is also recommended in geriatric or debilitated patients, who may be more sensitive to the effects of barbiturates and may react to usual doses of a barbiturate with excitement, depression, and confusion and in pediatric patients, who are especially susceptible to paradoxical excitement during barbiturate therapy.

For acetaminophen
» Alcohol abuse, current, or
» Hepatic disease or
» Viral hepatitis
(increased risk of hepatotoxicity)

Renal function impairment, severe
(risk of adverse renal effects may be increased with prolonged use of high doses; occasional use is acceptable)

Sensitivity to acetaminophen, history of
(increased risk of allergic reaction)

For aspirin
» Asthma
(increased risk of bronchospastic allergic reactions)

» Gastritis, erosive, or
» Peptic ulcer
(may be exacerbated because of ulcerogenic effects; risk of gastrointestinal bleeding is increased)

Gout
(aspirin may increase serum uric acid concentrations; also, may interfere with efficacy of uricosuric agents)

Hepatic function impairment
(salicylates metabolized in liver; also, in severe hepatic impairment, inhibition of platelet function by aspirin may increase risk of hemorrhage)

Hypoprothrombinemia or
Vitamin K deficiency
(increased risk of bleeding because of antiplatelet action of aspirin)

Mild sensitivity reaction to aspirin, history of
(increased risk of severe allergic reactions)

Renal function impairment
(salicylates excreted via kidneys)

For codeine
Allergic reaction to codeine, history of
» Asthma, acute attack, or
» Respiratory impairment or disease, chronic
(codeine may decrease respiratory drive and increase airway resistance)

Cardiac arrhythmias or

Convulsions, history of
(may be induced or exacerbated)
Drug abuse or dependence, history of, or
Emotional instability or
Suicidal ideation or attempts
(increased risk of abuse)
Gallbladder disease or gallstones
(codeine may cause biliary tract spasm)
Head injury or
Increased intracranial pressure, pre-existing, or
Intracranial lesions
(risk of respiratory depression and further elevation of cerebrospinal fluid is increased; also, codeine may cause sedation and pupillary changes which may obscure clinical course of head injury)
Hepatic function impairment
(codeine metabolized in liver; may accumulate)
Hypothyroidism
(increased risk of respiratory depression and prolonged CNS depression)
» Inflammatory bowel disease, severe
(risk of toxic megacolon may be increased, especially with repeated dosing)
Prostatic hypertrophy or obstruction or
Urethral stricture
(codeine may cause urinary retention)
Renal function impairment
(codeine excreted primarily via kidneys; also, may cause urinary retention)
Caution is also advised in administration to very young, elderly, or very ill or debilitated patients, who may be more sensitive to the effects, especially the respiratory depressant effects, of codeine.

For caffeine
Cardiac disease, severe
(high doses of caffeine may increase risk of tachycardia or extrasystoles, which may lead to heart failure)
Sensitivity to caffeine, history of
(risk of allergic reaction)

Side/Adverse Effects

Note: Barbiturates and codeine may cause dependence, especially following prolonged use of high doses, in any patient. The characteristics of dependence include: a strong desire or need to continue taking the medication; a tendency to increase the dose; a psychological dependence on the effects of the medication; and a physical dependence on the effects of the medication requiring its presence for maintenance of homeostasis and resulting in an abstinence syndrome when the medication is discontinued. With codeine, the severity of withdrawal symptoms depends upon the abruptness of withdrawal and the extent to which dependence has developed. However, codeine has lower dependence liability and potential for abuse than most other opioid agonists because of its relatively weak agonist activity with usual analgesic doses.

Frequent use of any analgesic for treatment of headaches (including analgesics that do not contain a barbiturate or an opioid) may lead to tolerance, an increased dosage requirement, dependence, withdrawal (rebound) headaches, and further use of the medication. Eventually, chronic (daily or near-daily) headaches may occur. This type of dependence may occur only in headache-prone patients; withdrawal headaches have not been reported in patients who take analgesics frequently for other types of pain. Chronic daily use of caffeine may also result in the development of physical dependence, leading to withdrawal headaches and medication abuse.

Aspirin-induced bronchospasm is most likely to occur in patients with the triad of aspirin-induced asthma, allergies, and nasal polyps. Aspirin-induced angioedema or urticaria may be more likely to occur in patients with a history of recurrent idiopathic angioedema or urticaria.

The side/adverse effects listed below are those that may occur with occasional use of recommended doses of these combination medications (including those that may result from an allergic or idiosyncratic response to individual ingredients in the formulations) or with an acute overdose. For additional information on side/adverse effects that may occur with individual ingredients in these medications, especially if these agents are ingested frequently or in higher-than-recommended doses, see—

For butalbital: *Barbiturates (Systemic)*. Although butalbital is not specifically mentioned in that monograph, side effects that are likely to occur with other barbiturates may occur with butalbital also.

For phenobarbital: *Barbiturates (Systemic)*.
For acetaminophen: *Acetaminophen (Systemic)*.
For aspirin: *Salicylates (Systemic)*.
For codeine: *Opioid (Narcotic) Analgesics (Systemic)*.
For caffeine: *Caffeine (Systemic)*.

The following side/adverse effects have been selected on the basis of their potential clinical significance (possible signs and symptoms in parentheses where appropriate)—not necessarily inclusive:

Those indicating need for medical attention
Incidence less frequent or rare
For barbiturates
Agranulocytosis (fever with or without chills; sores, ulcers, or white spots on lips or in mouth; sore throat); **angioedema** (large, hive-like swellings on eyelids, face, lips, and/or tongue); **bronchospastic allergic reaction** (shortness of breath, troubled breathing, tightness in chest, wheezing); **CNS effects** (confusion; hallucinations; mental depression; unusual tiredness or weakness)—confusion or mental depression especially likely to occur in geriatric or debilitated patients; **CNS stimulation, paradoxical** (unusual excitement)—especially likely to occur in pediatric, geriatric, or debilitated patients; **dermatitis, allergic** (skin rash or hives); **dermatitis, exfoliative** (fever with or without chills; red, thickened, or scaly skin; swollen and/or painful glands; unusual bruising); **erythema multiforme** (fever with or without chills; muscle cramps or pain; skin rash; sores, ulcers, or white spots on lips or in mouth); **hypotension** (decreased blood pressure)—usually asymptomatic, but may lead to tiredness or weakness if severe; **Stevens-Johnson syndrome** (bleeding or crusting sores on lips; chest pain; fever with or without chills; muscle cramps or pain; skin rash; sores, ulcers, or white spots in mouth; sore throat); **thrombocytopenia** (usually asymptomatic; rarely, unusual bleeding or bruising; black, tarry stools; blood in urine or stools; pinpoint red spots on skin)

For acetaminophen
Agranulocytosis (fever with or without chills; sores, ulcers, or white spots on lips or in mouth; sore throat); **dermatitis, allergic** (skin rash, hives, or itching); **thrombocytopenia** (usually asymptomatic; rarely, unusual bleeding or bruising; black, tarry stools; blood in urine or stools; pinpoint red spots on skin)

For aspirin
Anaphylaxis (bluish discoloration or flushing or redness of skin; coughing; difficulty in swallowing; dizziness or feeling faint, severe; skin rash, hives [may include giant urticaria], and/or itching; stuffy nose; large, hive-like swellings on eyelids, face, lips, and/or tongue; tightness in chest, troubled breathing, and/or wheezing, especially in asthmatic patients); **bronchospastic allergic reaction** (shortness of breath, troubled breathing, tightness in chest, and/or wheezing); **dermatitis, allergic** (skin rash, hives, or itching); **necrolysis, toxic epidermal** (redness, tenderness, itching, burning, or peeling of skin; sore throat; fever with or without chills)

For codeine

Angioedema (large, hive-like swellings on face, eyelids, mouth, lips, and/or tongue); **bronchoconstriction, laryngeal edema, or laryngospasm, allergic** (shortness of breath, troubled breathing, tightness in chest, or wheezing); **CNS toxicity** (convulsions, hallucinations, trembling, and/or uncontrolled muscle movements; mental depression); **dermatitis, allergic** (skin rash, itching, or hives)

Signs and symptoms of overdose

For barbiturates

Acute toxicity (confusion, severe drowsiness or weakness, shortness of breath or unusually slow or troubled breathing, slow heartbeat, slurred speech, staggering, unusual movements of the eyes)

Note: In acute barbiturate overdosage, *CNS and respiratory depression* may lead to *Cheyne-Stokes respiration, areflexia,* slight *pupillary constriction* (in severe toxicity, pupils may be dilated), *oliguria, tachycardia, lowered body temperature,* and *coma.* Typical *shock syndrome* (apnea, circulatory collapse, respiratory arrest, and death) may occur.

In extreme barbiturate overdosage, all electrical activity in the brain may cease. In this case an electroencephalogram (EEG) may be "flat," but this does not necessarily indicate clinical death since, unless hypoxic damage occurs, this effect is fully reversible.

Complications in barbiturate overdosage such as *pneumonia, pulmonary edema, cardiac arrhythmias, congestive heart failure,* and *renal failure* may occur.

For acetaminophen

Early signs and symptoms of overdose (diarrhea, increased sweating, loss of appetite, nausea or vomiting, stomach cramps or pain)—may occur within 6 to 14 hours after ingestion of the overdose and persist for about 24 hours; **hepatotoxicity** (pain, tenderness, and/or swelling in upper abdominal area)—may occur 2 to 4 days after the overdose is ingested

Note: Early signs and symptoms often do not occur. The first indications of overdosage may be signs and symptoms of possible *liver damage* and abnormalities in liver function tests, which may not occur until 2 to 4 days after ingestion of the overdose. Maximal changes in liver function tests usually occur 3 to 5 days after ingestion of the overdose.

Overt *hepatic disease or failure* may occur 4 to 6 days after ingestion of the overdose. *Hepatic encephalopathy* (with mental changes, confusion, agitation, or stupor), *convulsions, respiratory depression, coma, cerebral edema, coagulation defects, gastrointestinal bleeding, disseminated intravascular coagulation, hypoglycemia, metabolic acidosis, renal tubular necrosis leading to renal failure* (signs include bloody or cloudy urine and sudden decrease in amount of urine), *cardiac arrhythmias,* and *cardiovascular collapse* may occur.

For aspirin

Mild overdose [salicylism] (continuing ringing or buzzing in ears, or hearing loss; confusion; severe or continuing diarrhea, stomach pain, and/or headache; dizziness or lightheadedness; severe drowsiness; fast or deep breathing; continuing nausea and/or vomiting; uncontrollable flapping movements of the hands, especially in elderly patients; increased thirst; vision problems); **severe overdose** (bloody urine; convulsions; hallucinations; severe nervousness, excitement, or confusion; shortness of breath or troubled breathing; unexplained fever)

Note: In young children, the only signs of an overdose may be *changes in behavior, severe drowsiness or tiredness,* and/or *fast or deep breathing.*

Laboratory findings in overdose may indicate encephalographic abnormalities; alterations in acid-base balance, especially *respiratory alkalosis* and *metabolic acidosis; hyper-*

glycemia or hypoglycemia, especially in children; *ketonuria; hyponatremia; hypokalemia;* and *proteinuria.*

For codeine

CNS toxicity (confusion, convulsions, severe dizziness, severe drowsiness, severe nervousness or restlessness, unconsciousness, severe weakness); **cold, clammy skin; low blood pressure; pinpoint pupils of eyes; respiratory depression** (shortness of breath or unusually slow or troubled breathing); **slow heartbeat**

For caffeine

CNS toxicity (agitation, anxiety, excitement, or restlessness; confusion or delirium; increased sensitivity to touch or pain; irritability; ringing or other sounds in ears; seeing flashes of "zig-zag" lights; seizures, usually tonic-clonic; trouble in sleeping); **dehydration; fast or irregular heartbeat; fever; frequent urination; gastrointestinal effects** (abdominal or stomach pain; nausea and vomiting, sometimes with blood); **headache; muscle trembling or twitching**

Those indicating need for medical attention only if they continue or are bothersome

Incidence more frequent

For all barbiturate and analgesic combinations

CNS effects (dizziness, drowsiness, or lightheadedness, mild); **gastrointestinal irritation** (bloated or "gassy" feeling, mild stomach pain, heartburn or indigestion, nausea with or without vomiting)—especially likely with formulations containing aspirin.

Patient Consultation

See *Table 1,* page 243.

General Dosing Information

When used for relief of headache, especially a migraine headache, a barbiturate and analgesic combination will be most effective if administered when the first symptoms appear (during the prodrome, for migraine with aura).

After the first dose has been administered, it is recommended that the patient lie down and relax in a quiet, darkened room, because this contributes to relief of headaches.

A reduction in dosage may be required for elderly or debilitated patients, who may react to usual doses of barbiturates with excitement, confusion, or depression. This is particularly important for the codeine-containing combinations, because these patients are also more sensitive to the respiratory depressant effects of codeine.

Tolerance may occur with repeated administration of large doses of barbiturates or codeine. Also, patients who are tolerant to the effects of other opioids may be at least partially cross-tolerant to the effects of codeine, and vice versa.

Prolonged uninterrupted use of codeine or barbiturates may result in psychic or physical dependence; in patients taking these medications for relief of pain other than headache pain, gradual withdrawal may be required to reduce the risk of precipitating withdrawal symptoms.

In headache-prone individuals, frequent use of analgesics may cause physical dependence, leading to both analgesic abuse and chronic (daily or near-daily) headaches. Chronic daily use of caffeine may also result in the development of physical dependence, leading to withdrawal (rebound) headaches when the medication is stopped and to further ingestion of caffeine-containing analgesics. Patients who experience frequent headaches may be dependent on a variety of medications, including opioid analgesics, nonopioid analgesics such as acetaminophen or aspirin, ergotamine-containing headache suppressants, and antianxiety agents or sedatives, as well as barbiturate and analgesic combinations.

Chronic headaches resulting from overmedication may be difficult to relieve, especially if the patient continues to take ergotamine-containing headache suppressants and/or analgesics. If such headaches occur, it is recommended that these medications be discontinued. In-patient treatment may be necessary during detoxification. Naproxen, alone or together with amitriptyline, may reduce the severity of the headaches. Repetitive intravenous administration of dihydroergotamine (in conjunction with metoclopramide [to control dihydroergotamine-induced nausea and vomiting]) is recommended by some headache specialists to relieve this type of headache. Appropriate treatment for symptoms of withdrawal from other substances frequently used or abused by chronic headache patients may also be needed. In addition, appropriate prophylactic treatment should be initiated or adjusted to reduce the frequency and severity of future headaches.

BUTALBITAL AND ACETAMINOPHEN

Summary of Differences

Pharmacology:

Mechanism of action/effect—Butalbital: A short- to intermediate-acting barbiturate.

Biotransformation—Acetaminophen: An intermediate metabolite is hepatotoxic and possibly nephrotoxic.

Precautions:

Cross-sensitivity and/or related problems—Acetaminophen: Low risk of cross-sensitivity with aspirin.

Drug interactions and/or related problems—

Butalbital: May be less likely than phenobarbital to cause significant interference with medications adversely affected by hepatic enzyme induction.

Acetaminophen: Caution required with hepatic enzyme inducers and with other hepatotoxic medications.

Laboratory value alterations—Acetaminophen: Interferes with blood glucose determinations, blood 5-hydroxyindoleacetic acid determinations, pancreatic function determinations using bentiromide, serum uric acid determinations. Hepatic function studies may indicate hepatotoxicity.

Contraindications/medical problems—Acetaminophen: Increased risk of hepatotoxicity in alcoholics and patients with hepatic disease or viral hepatitis.

Oral Dosage Forms

BUTALBITAL AND ACETAMINOPHEN CAPSULES

Usual adult and adolescent dose: Analgesic—

Oral, 1 or 2 capsules containing 50 mg of butalbital and 325 mg of acetaminophen every four hours as needed, not to exceed 6 capsules a day; or

Oral, 1 capsule containing 50 mg of butalbital and 650 mg of acetaminophen every four hours as needed, not to exceed 4 capsules a day.

Auxiliary labeling:
- May cause drowsiness.
- Avoid alcoholic beverages.
- May be habit-forming.

BUTALBITAL AND ACETAMINOPHEN TABLETS

Usual adult and adolescent dose: Analgesic—

Oral, 1 or 2 tablets containing 50 mg of butalbital and 325 mg of acetaminophen every four hours as needed, not to exceed 6 tablets a day; or

Oral, 1 tablet containing 50 mg of butalbital and 650 mg of acetaminophen every four hours as needed, not to exceed 4 tablets a day.

Auxiliary labeling:
- May cause drowsiness.
- Avoid alcoholic beverages.
- May be habit-forming.

BUTALBITAL, ACETAMINOPHEN, AND CAFFEINE CAPSULES

Usual adult and adolescent dose: Analgesic—Oral, 1 or 2 capsules every four hours as needed, not to exceed 6 capsules a day.

Auxiliary labeling:
- May cause drowsiness.
- Avoid alcoholic beverages.
- May be habit-forming.

BUTALBITAL, ACETAMINOPHEN, AND CAFFEINE TABLETS USP

Usual adult and adolescent dose: Analgesic—

Oral, 1 or 2 tablets containing 50 mg of butalbital and 325 mg of acetaminophen every four hours as needed, not to exceed 6 tablets a day; or

Oral, 1 tablet containing 50 mg of butalbital and 500 mg of acetaminophen every four hours as needed, not to exceed 6 tablets a day.

Auxiliary labeling:
- May cause drowsiness.
- Avoid alcoholic beverages.
- May be habit-forming.

BUTALBITAL AND ASPIRIN

Summary of Differences

Pharmacology:

Mechanism of action/effect—Butalbital: A short- to intermediate-acting barbiturate.

Other actions/effects—Aspirin: Also has platelet aggregation-inhibiting actions.

Precautions:

Cross-sensitivity and/or related problems—Aspirin: Risk of cross-sensitivity with other nonsteroidal anti-inflammatory drugs (NSAIDs); slight risk of cross-sensitivity with acetaminophen.

Pregnancy/reproduction—Aspirin:

First trimester—Reports of possible birth defects in humans, but teratogenicity not found in controlled studies with usual therapeutic doses.

Third trimester—Use not recommended; chronic, high-dose use has caused complications (including stillbirth or neonatal death) associated with prolonged gestation, premature closure of the fetal ductus arteriosus, prolonged labor, complicated deliveries, and maternal, fetal or neonatal bleeding.

Pediatrics—Aspirin: Risk of Reye's syndrome in children with acute febrile illness, especially influenza and varicella; febrile, dehydrated patients also more susceptible to other forms of salicylate toxicity.

Adolescents—Aspirin: Risk of Reye's syndrome in adolescents with acute febrile illness, especially influenza and varicella.

Geriatrics—Aspirin: Increased susceptibility to salicylate toxicity.

Drug interactions and/or related problems—

Butalbital: May be less likely than phenobarbital to cause significant interference with medications adversely affected by hepatic enzyme induction.

Aspirin: Caution also required with urinary acidifiers or alkalizers; anticoagulants; methotrexate; ototoxic medications; probenecid; sulfinpyrazone; and thrombolytic agents.

Laboratory value alterations—Aspirin: Interferes with determinations of urine aceto-acetic acid (Gerhard test), urine glucose (copper sulfate or enzymatic tests), urine 5-hydroxyindoleacetic acid, renal function test (phenolsulfonphthalein), thyroid imaging (radionuclide), thyroid-stimulating hormone release (protirelin-stimulated), vanillylmandelic acid. May also prolong bleeding time, decrease serum potassium concentrations, and cause dose-dependent increase or decrease in serum uric acid concentration.

Contraindications/medical problems—Aspirin: Should not be used in patients with severe allergic or asthmatic reaction to aspirin or other NSAIDs (history of), bleeding ulcers or other active bleeding states, or hemophilia or other coagulation or platelet function defects. Caution also required in patients with gastrointestinal ulceration, gout, hypoprothrombinemia, and vitamin K deficiency.

Side/adverse effects: Aspirin—May also cause anaphylaxis and toxic epidermal necrolysis.

Additional Dosing Information

See also *General Dosing Information.*

Medications containing aspirin should be administered with food or a full glass (240 mL) of water to lessen gastric irritation.

Dosage of aspirin should be reduced if fever or illness causes fluid depletion, especially in children.

In general, it is recommended that aspirin therapy be discontinued 5 days before surgery to reduce the risk of bleeding problems.

Oral Dosage Forms

BUTALBITAL AND ASPIRIN TABLETS USP

Usual adult and adolescent dose: Analgesic—Oral, 1 tablet every four hours as needed, not to exceed 6 tablets a day.

Auxiliary labeling:
• Avoid alcoholic beverages.
• May cause drowsiness.
• Take with food or with a full glass of water.

BUTALBITAL, ASPIRIN, AND CAFFEINE CAPSULES

Usual adult and adolescent dose: Analgesic—Oral, 1 or 2 capsules every four hours as needed, not to exceed 6 capsules a day.

Auxiliary labeling:
• Avoid alcoholic beverages.
• May cause drowsiness.
• Take with food or with a full glass of water.

BUTALBITAL, ASPIRIN, AND CAFFEINE TABLETS

Usual adult and adolescent dose: Analgesic—Oral, 1 or 2 tablets containing 50 mg of butalbital, 325 mg of aspirin, and 40 mg of caffeine every four hours as needed, not to exceed 6 tablets a day.

Auxiliary labeling:
• Avoid alcoholic beverages.
• May cause drowsiness.
• Take with food or with a full glass of water.

BUTALBITAL, ASPIRIN, CODEINE, AND CAFFEINE

Summary of Differences

Pharmacology:
Mechanism of action/effect—Butalbital: A short- to intermediate-acting barbiturate.
Other actions/effects—
Aspirin: Also has platelet aggregation-inhibiting actions.
Codeine: Also has antidiarrheal and antitussive actions.
Precautions:
Cross-sensitivity and/or related problems—Aspirin: Risk of cross-sensitivity with other nonsteroidal anti-inflammatory drugs (NSAIDs); slight risk of cross-sensitivity with acetaminophen.

Pregnancy/reproduction—
First trimester: Aspirin—Reports of possible birth defects in humans, but teratogenicity not found in controlled studies with usual therapeutic doses.
Third trimester:
Aspirin—Use not recommended; chronic, high-dose use has caused complications (including stillbirth or neonatal death) associated with prolonged gestation, premature closure of the fetal ductus arteriosus, prolonged labor, complicated deliveries, and maternal, fetal or neonatal bleeding.
Codeine—Ingestion shortly prior to delivery may cause neonatal respiratory depression, especially in premature neonates.
Pediatrics—Aspirin: Risk of Reye's syndrome in children with acute febrile illness, especially influenza and varicella; febrile, dehydrated patients also more susceptible to other forms of salicylate toxicity.
Adolescents—Aspirin: Risk of Reye's syndrome in adolescents with acute febrile illness, especially influenza and varicella.
Geriatrics—
Aspirin: Increased susceptiblity to salicylate toxicity.
Codeine: Increased susceptibility to respiratory depressant effects.
Drug interactions and/or related problems—
Butalbital: May be less likely than phenobarbital to cause significant interference with medications adversely affected by hepatic enzyme induction.
Aspirin: Caution also required with urinary acidifiers or alkalizers; anticoagulants; methotrexate; ototoxic medications; probenecid; sulfinpyrazone; and thrombolytic agents.
Codeine: Caution also required with anticholinergics, antiperistaltic antidiarrheals, agents that may reduce blood pressure, metoclopramide, monoamine oxidase inhibitors, naloxone, naltrexone, and other opioid analgesics.
Laboratory value alterations—
Aspirin: Interferes with determinations of urine aceto-acetic acid (Gerhard test), urine glucose (copper sulfate or enzymatic tests), urine 5-hydroxyindoleacetic acid, renal function test (phenolsulfonphthalein), thyroid imaging (radionuclide), thyroid-stimulating hormone release (protirelin-stimulated), vanillylmandelic acid. May also prolong bleeding time, decrease serum potassium concentrations, and cause dose-dependent increase or decrease in serum uric acid concentration.
Codeine: Interferes with gastric emptying studies and hepatobiliary imaging (radionuclide). Also, may increase plasma amylase and/or lipase concentrations.
Contraindications/medical problems—
Aspirin: Should not be used in patients with severe allergic or asthmatic reaction to aspirin or other NSAIDs (history of), bleeding ulcers or other active bleeding states (current), or hemophilia or other coagulation or platelet function defects. Caution also required in patients with gastrointestinal ulceration, gout, hypoprothrombinemia, and vitamin K deficiency.
Codeine: Should not be used if the patient has diarrhea caused by poisoning or by antibiotic therapy, or in the presence of acute respiratory depression. Caution also required in patients with asthma, chronic respiratory disease, and severe inflammatory bowel disease.
Side/adverse effects:
Aspirin—May also cause anaphylaxis and toxic epidermal necrolysis.
Codeine—May also cause laryngospasm or laryngeal edema.

Additional Dosing Information

See also *General Dosing Information.*

Medications containing aspirin should be administered with food or a full glass (240 mL) of water to lessen gastric irritation.

Dosage of aspirin should be reduced if fever or illness causes fluid depletion, especially in children.

In general, it is recommended that aspirin therapy be discontinued 5 days before surgery to reduce the risk of bleeding problems.

Oral Dosage Forms

BUTALBITAL, ASPIRIN, CODEINE PHOSPHATE, AND CAFFEINE CAPSULES

Usual adult and adolescent dose: Analgesic—Oral, 1 or 2 capsules every four hours as needed, not to exceed 6 capsules a day.

Auxiliary labeling:
- Avoid alcoholic beverages.
- May cause drowsiness.
- Take with food or with a full glass of water.
- May be habit-forming.

BUTALBITAL, ASPIRIN, CODEINE PHOSPHATE, AND CAFFEINE TABLETS

Usual adult and adolescent dose: See *Butalbital, Aspirin, Codeine Phosphate, and Caffeine Capsules.*

Auxiliary labeling:
- Avoid alcoholic beverages.
- May cause drowsiness.
- Take with food or with a full glass of water.
- May be habit-forming.

PHENOBARBITAL, ASA, AND CODEINE

Summary of Differences

Pharmacology:
> Mechanism of action/effect—Phenobarbital: A long-acting barbiturate.

Other actions/effects—
> Phenobarbital: Also has anticonvulsant activity.
> Aspirin: Also has platelet aggregation-inhibiting actions.
> Codeine: Also has antidiarrheal and antitussive actions.

Precautions:
> Cross-sensitivity and/or related problems—Aspirin: Risk of cross-sensitivity with other nonsteroidal anti-inflammatory drugs (NSAIDs); slight risk of cross-sensitivity with acetaminophen.

> Pregnancy/reproduction—
>> First trimester: Aspirin—Reports of possible birth defects in humans, but teratogenicity not found in controlled studies with usual therapeutic doses.
>> Third trimester: Aspirin—Use not recommended; chronic, high-dose use has caused complications (including stillbirth or neonatal death) associated with prolonged gestation, premature closure of the fetal ductus arteriosus, prolonged labor, complicated deliveries, and maternal, fetal or neonatal bleeding.

> Pediatrics—Aspirin: Risk of Reye's syndrome in children with acute febrile illness, especially influenza and varicella; febrile, dehydrated patients also more susceptible to other forms of salicylate toxicity.

> Adolescents—Aspirin: Risk of Reye's syndrome in adolescents with acute febrile illness, especially influenza and varicella.

> Geriatrics—
>> Aspirin: Increased susceptiblity to salicylate toxicity.
>> Codeine: Increased susceptibility to respiratory depressant effects.

Drug interactions and/or related problems—
> Phenobarbital: More likely than butalbital to cause significant interference with medications adversely affected by hepatic enzyme induction.
> Aspirin: Caution also required with urinary acidifiers or alkalizers; anticoagulants; methotrexate; ototoxic medications; probenecid; sulfinpyrazone; and thrombolytic agents.
> Codeine: Caution also required with anticholinergics, antiperistaltic antidiarrheals, agents that may reduce blood pressure, metoclopramide, monoamine oxidase inhibitors, naloxone, naltrexone, and other opioid analgesics.

Laboratory value alterations—
> Aspirin: Interferes with determinations of urine aceto-acetic acid (Gerhard test), urine glucose (copper sulfate or enzymatic tests), urine 5-hydroxyindoleacetic acid, renal function test (phenolsulfonphthalein), thyroid imaging (radionuclide), thyroid-stimulating hormone release (protirelin-stimulated), vanillylmandelic acid. May also prolong bleeding time, decrease serum potassium concentrations, and cause dose-dependent increase or decrease in serum uric acid concentration.
> Codeine: Interferes with gastric emptying studies and hepatobiliary imaging (radionuclide). Also, may increase plasma amylase and/or lipase concentrations.

Contraindications/medical problems—
> Aspirin: Should not be used in patients with severe allergic or asthmatic reaction to aspirin or other NSAIDs (history of), bleeding ulcers or other active bleeding states (current), or hemophilia or other coagulation or platelet function defects. Caution also required in patients with gastrointestinal ulceration, gout, hypoprothrombinemia, and vitamin K deficiency.
> Codeine: Should not be used if the patient has diarrhea caused by poisoning or by antibiotic therapy, or in the presence of acute respiratory depression. Caution also required in patients with asthma, chronic respiratory disease, and severe inflammatory bowel disease.

Side/adverse effects:
> Aspirin—May also cause anaphylaxis and toxic epidermal necrolysis.
> Codeine—May also cause laryngospasm or laryngeal edema.

Additional Dosing Information

See also *General Dosing Information.*

Medications containing aspirin should be administered with food or a full glass (240 mL) of water to lessen gastric irritation.

Dosage of aspirin should be reduced if fever or illness causes fluid depletion, especially in children.

In general, it is recommended that aspirin therapy be discontinued 5 days before surgery to reduce the risk of bleeding problems.

Oral Dosage Forms

PHENOBARBITAL, ASA, AND CODEINE PHOSPHATE CAPSULES

Usual adult and adolescent dose: Analgesic—
Oral, 1 or 2 capsules containing 16.2 mg of phenobarbital, 325 mg of ASA, and 16.2 or 32.4 mg of codeine phosphate every three or four hours; or
Oral, 1 capsule containing 16.2 mg of phenobarbital, 325 mg of ASA, and 64.8 mg of codeine phosphate every three or four hours.

Auxiliary labeling:
- Avoid alcoholic beverages.
- May cause drowsiness.
- Take with food or with a full glass of water.

Table 1. Patient Consultation

In providing consultation, consider emphasizing the following selected information (» = major clinical significance):	Legend: I = Butalbital and Acetaminophen; II = Butalbital, Acetaminophen, and Caffeine; III = Butalbital and Aspirin			IV = Butalbital, Aspirin, and Caffeine; V = Butalbital, Aspirin, Codeine, and Caffeine; VI = Phenobarbital, Aspirin, and Codeine		
	I	**II**	**III**	**IV**	**V**	**VI**
Before using this medication						
» Conditions affecting use, especially:						
Sensitivity to—						
Butalbital, phenobarbital, or other barbiturates	✔	✔	✔	✔	✔	✔
Acetaminophen	✔	✔				
Aspirin or other nonsteroidal anti-inflammatory drugs (NSAIDs)			✔	✔	✔	✔
Codeine					✔	✔
Caffeine		✔		✔	✔	
Pregnancy—						
Barbiturates cross the placenta; may cause fetal abnormalities and/or an increased risk of brain tumors in the neonate; may also cause breathing problems in the neonate if taken shortly before delivery	✔	✔	✔	✔	✔	✔
Aspirin crosses the placenta; should not be taken during third trimester unless prescribed by physician; chronic, high-dose use may cause adverse effects on the circulation in fetus or neonate, bleeding in fetus and/or mother, prolonged gestation, and complicated deliveries			✔	✔	✔	✔
Codeine crosses the placenta; may cause breathing problems in the neonate if taken just before delivery					✔	✔
Caffeine crosses the placenta; total daily intake should be limited because of risk of fetal arrhythmias		✔		✔	✔	
Breast-feeding—						
Barbiturates distributed into breast milk; may cause CNS depression in the infant	✔	✔	✔	✔	✔	✔
Caffeine distributed into breast milk; total daily intake should be limited because of risk of CNS stimulation in the infant		✔		✔	✔	
Use in children—						
Possibility of barbiturate-induced paradoxical excitement	✔	✔	✔	✔	✔	✔
Not giving aspirin to children with symptoms of viral illness (especially influenza or varicella) without physician's permission because of risk of Reye's syndrome; children without a viral illness are also more susceptible to aspirin-induced toxicity			✔	✔	✔	✔
Possibility of codeine-induced paradoxical excitement					✔	✔
Use in teenagers—Checking with physician before giving to teenagers with symptoms of acute febrile illness, especially influenza or varicella, because of the risk of Reye's syndrome				✔	✔	✔
Use in the elderly—						
Increased sensitivity to barbiturates; may react to usual doses with confusion, depression, or excitement	✔	✔	✔	✔	✔	✔
Increased susceptibility to toxic effects of aspirin			✔	✔	✔	✔
Increased susceptibility to respiratory depressant and other adverse effects of opioid analgesics					✔	✔
Use by athletes—						
Barbiturates banned in competitors in biathlon and modern pentathlon events by the United States Olympic Committee (USOC)	✔	✔	✔	✔	✔	✔
Codeine banned and tested for by the International Olympic Committee (IOC) and the USOC					✔	✔
Caffeine tested for in athletes by the IOC, USOC, and National Collegiate Athletic Association (NCAA); an athlete can be disqualified if urine concentrations are higher than the acceptable limits set by these organizations		✔		✔	✔	

Table 1. Patient Consultation *(continued)*

Legend:
I = Butalbital and Acetaminophen
II = Butalbital, Acetaminophen, and Caffeine
III = Butalbital and Aspirin
IV = Butalbital, Aspirin, and Caffeine
V = Butalbital, Aspirin, Codeine, and Caffeine
VI = Phenobarbital, Aspirin, and Codeine

	I	II	III	IV	V	VI
Other medications, especially:						
Adrenocorticoids, glucocorticoid and mineralocorticoid	✓	✓	✓	✓	✓	✓
Alcohol	✓	✓	✓	✓	✓	✓
Alkalizers, urinary			✓	✓	✓	✓
Anticoagulants, coumarin or indandione derivative	✓	✓	✓	✓	✓	✓
Carbamazepine	✓	✓	✓	✓	✓	✓
Contraceptives, estrogen-containing, oral	✓	✓	✓	✓	✓	✓
Corticotropin	✓	✓	✓	✓	✓	✓
CNS depressants	✓	✓	✓	✓	✓	✓
Divalproex sodium	✓	✓	✓	✓	✓	✓
Heparin			✓	✓	✓	✓
Methotrexate			✓	✓	✓	✓
Naltrexone					✓	✓
Probenecid			✓	✓	✓	✓
Sulfinpyrazone			✓	✓	✓	✓
Valproic acid	✓	✓	✓	✓	✓	✓
Vancomycin			✓	✓	✓	✓
Other medical problems, especially:						
Alcohol abuse	✓	✓				
Asthma	✓	✓	✓	✓	✓	✓
Bleeding ulcers, or other bleeding problems or coagulation defects			✓	✓	✓	✓
Diarrhea caused by antibiotics or poisoning					✓	✓
Drug abuse or history of	✓	✓	✓	✓	✓	✓
Gastritis (erosive) or peptic ulcer, history of			✓	✓	✓	✓
Inflammatory bowel disease, severe					✓	✓
Liver disease	✓	✓	✓	✓	✓	✓
Porphyria	✓	✓	✓	✓	✓	✓
Respiratory disease	✓	✓	✓	✓	✓	✓
Viral hepatitis	✓	✓				
Proper use of this medication						
» Taking with food or a full glass (240 mL) of water to minimize stomach irritation				✓	✓	✓
» Not taking medication if it has a strong vinegar-like odor				✓	✓	✓
» Importance of not taking more medication than the amount prescribed because of danger of:						
Habituation	✓	✓	✓	✓	✓	✓
Hepatotoxicity	✓	✓				
Overdose	✓	✓	✓	✓	✓	✓
» For relief of headache:						
Most effective when taken as soon as headache appears or at first sign of migraine attack (prodromal stage)	✓	✓	✓	✓	✓	✓
Lying down in a quiet, dark room for a while after taking	✓	✓	✓	✓	✓	✓
Compliance with prophylactic therapy, if prescribed	✓	✓	✓	✓	✓	✓
Missed dose (if on scheduled dosing regimen): Taking as soon as possible; not taking if almost time for next dose; not doubling doses	✓	✓	✓	✓	✓	✓
» Proper storage	✓	✓	✓	✓	✓	✓
Precautions while using this medication						
» Checking with physician if effectiveness of medication decreases and/or frequency of headaches increases; possibility that tolerance to or physical dependence on the medication, leading to withdrawal headaches, has developed	✓	✓	✓	✓	✓	✓

Table 1. Patient Consultation *(continued)*

Legend:
I = Butalbital and Acetaminophen
II = Butalbital, Acetaminophen, and Caffeine
III = Butalbital and Aspirin
IV = Butalbital, Aspirin, and Caffeine
V = Butalbital, Aspirin, Codeine, and Caffeine
VI = Phenobarbital, Aspirin, and Codeine

	I	II	III	IV	V	VI
» Risk of overdose if taking other medications containing:						
Barbiturates	✓	✓	✓	✓	✓	✓
Acetaminophen	✓	✓				
Aspirin or other salicylates			✓	✓	✓	✓
Codeine or other opioids					✓	✓
» Avoiding alcohol or other CNS depressants unless prescribed or otherwise approved by physician	✓	✓	✓	✓	✓	✓
Alcohol consumption may increase probability of stomach problems			✓	✓	✓	✓
Alcohol consumption may increase risk of hepatotoxicity, with high doses or prolonged use	✓	✓				
» Caution if dizziness, lightheadedness, drowsiness, or a false sense of well-being occurs	✓	✓	✓	✓	✓	✓
Caution when getting up suddenly from a lying or sitting position					✓	✓
Lying down if nausea or vomiting, or dizziness or lightheadedness occurs					✓	✓
Need to inform physician or dentist of use of medication if any kind of surgery (including dental surgery) or emergency treatment is required	✓	✓	✓	✓	✓	✓
Caution if any kind of surgery is required; aspirin should be discontinued 5 days prior to surgery unless otherwise directed by physician			✓	✓	✓	✓
Diabetics: May cause false urine sugar test results with prolonged use of 8 or more capsules or tablets per day			✓	✓	✓	✓
Caution if any laboratory tests required						
Possible interference with laboratory test results	✓	✓	✓	✓	✓	✓
Not taking caffeine for 8 to 12 hours prior to dipyridamole-assisted myocardial perfusion studies		✓		✓	✓	
» Checking with physician before discontinuing medication following prolonged use; gradual reduction in dosage may be required to reduce risk of withdrawal symptoms	✓	✓	✓	✓	✓	✓
» Suspected overdose: Getting emergency help at once	✓	✓	✓	✓	✓	✓
Side/adverse effects						
Signs and symptoms of potential side effects, especially:						
Agranulocytosis	✓	✓	✓	✓	✓	✓
Anaphylaxis			✓	✓	✓	✓
Angioedema	✓	✓	✓	✓	✓	✓
Bronchospastic allergic reaction	✓	✓	✓	✓	✓	✓
CNS adverse effects	✓	✓	✓	✓	✓	✓
CNS stimulation (paradoxical)	✓	✓	✓	✓	✓	✓
Dermatitis, allergic	✓	✓	✓	✓	✓	✓
Dermatitis, exfoliative	✓	✓	✓	✓	✓	✓
Erythema multiforme	✓	✓	✓	✓	✓	✓
Laryngospasm, allergic					✓	✓
Laryngeal edema, allergic					✓	✓
Stevens-Johnson syndrome	✓	✓	✓	✓	✓	✓
Thrombocytopenia	✓	✓	✓	✓	✓	✓
Toxic epidermal necrolysis			✓	✓	✓	✓

BELLADONNA ALKALOIDS AND BARBITURATES   Systemic

Some commonly used *brand names* are:

In the U.S.—

Antrocol [Atropine and Phenobarbital]

Barbidonna [Atropine, Hyoscyamine, Scopolamine, and Phenobarbital]

Barbidonna No. 2 [Atropine, Hyoscyamine, Scopolamine, and Phenobarbital]

Barophen [Atropine, Hyoscyamine, Scopolamine, and Phenobarbital]

Bellalphen [Atropine, Hyoscyamine, Scopolamine, and Phenobarbital]

Butibel [Belladonna and Butabarbital]

Chardonna-2 [Belladonna and Phenobarbital]

Donnamor [Atropine, Hyoscyamine, Scopolamine, and Phenobarbital]

Donnapine [Atropine, Hyoscyamine, Scopolamine, and Phenobarbital]

Donnatal [Atropine, Hyoscyamine, Scopolamine, and Phenobarbital]

Donnatal Extentabs [Atropine, Hyoscyamine, Scopolamine, and Phenobarbital]

Donnatal No. 2 [Atropine, Hyoscyamine, Scopolamine, and Phenobarbital]

Donphen [Atropine, Hyoscyamine, Scopolamine, and Phenobarbital]

Hyosophen [Atropine, Hyoscyamine, Scopolamine, and Phenobarbital]

Kinesed [Atropine, Hyoscyamine, Scopolamine, and Phenobarbital]

Levsin-PB [Hyoscyamine and Phenobarbital]

Levsin with Phenobarbital [Hyoscyamine and Phenobarbital]

Malatal [Atropine, Hyoscyamine, Scopolamine, and Phenobarbital]

Relaxadon [Atropine, Hyoscyamine, Scopolamine, and Phenobarbital]

Spaslin [Atropine, Hyoscyamine, Scopolamine, and Phenobarbital]

Spasmolin [Atropine, Hyoscyamine, Scopolamine, and Phenobarbital]

Spasmophen [Atropine, Hyoscyamine, Scopolamine, and Phenobarbital]

Spasquid [Atropine, Hyoscyamine, Scopolamine, and Phenobarbital]

Susano [Atropine, Hyoscyamine, Scopolamine, and Phenobarbital]

In Canada—

Donnatal [Atropine, Hyoscyamine, Scopolamine, and Phenobarbital]

Donnatal Extentabs [Atropine, Hyoscyamine, Scopolamine, and Phenobarbital]

ORAL

ATROPINE, HYOSCYAMINE, SCOPOLAMINE, AND PHENO-BARBITAL

Atropine Sulfate, Hyoscyamine Sulfate (or Hyoscyamine Hydrobromide), Scopolamine Hydrobromide, and Phenobarbital Capsules†

In the U.S.— *Donnatal; Hyosophen*

Atropine Sulfate, Hyoscyamine Sulfate (or Hyoscyamine Hydrobromide), Scopolamine Hydrobromide, and Phenobarbital Elixir

In the U.S.—*Barbidonna; Barophen; Donnamor; Donnapine; Donnatal; Hyosophen; Spasmophen; Spasquid; Susano*

In Canada—*Donnatal*

Atropine Sulfate, Hyoscyamine Sulfate (or Hyoscyamine Hydrobromide), Scopolamine Hydrobromide, and Phenobarbital Tablets

In the U.S.—*Barbidonna; Barbidonna No. 2; Bellalphen; Donnapine; Donnatal; Donnatal No. 2; Donphen; Malatal; Relaxadon; Spaslin; Spasmolin; Spasmophen; Susano;* GENERIC

In Canada—*Donnatal*

Atropine Sulfate, Hyoscyamine Sulfate, Scopolamine Hydrobromide, and Phenobarbital Chewable Tablets†

In the U.S.—*Kinesed*

Atropine Sulfate, Hyoscyamine Sulfate, Scopolamine Hydrobromide, and Phenobarbital Extended-release Tablets

In the U.S. and Canada—*Donnatal Extentabs*

ATROPINE AND PHENOBARBITAL†

Atropine Sulfate and Phenobarbital Capsules†

In the U.S.—*Antrocol*

Atropine Sulfate and Phenobarbital Elixir†

In the U.S.—*Antrocol*

Atropine Sulfate and Phenobarbital Tablets†

In the U.S.—*Antrocol*

BELLADONNA AND BUTABARBITAL†

Belladonna Extract and Butabarbital Sodium Elixir†

In the U.S.—*Butibel*

Belladonna Extract and Butabarbital Sodium Tablets†

In the U.S.—*Butibel*

BELLADONNA AND PHENOBARBITAL†

Belladonna Extract and Phenobarbital Tablets†

In the U.S.—*Chardonna-2*

HYOSCYAMINE AND PHENOBARBITAL†

Hyoscyamine Sulfate and Phenobarbital Elixir†

In the U.S.—*Levsin with Phenobarbital*

Hyoscyamine Sulfate and Phenobarbital Oral Solution†

In the U.S.—*Levsin-PB*

Hyoscyamine Sulfate and Phenobarbital Tablets†

In the U.S.—*Levsin with Phenobarbital*

---

†Not commercially available in Canada.

Category: Anticholinergic-sedative.

Indications

Accepted

Ulcer, peptic (treatment adjunct); or

Bowel syndrome, irritable (treatment adjunct)—FDA has classified these medications as possibly effective for use as adjunctive therapy in the treatment of peptic ulcer and irritable bowel syndrome (irritable colon, spastic colon, mucous colitis).

Note: Less than effective classification requires the submission of adequate and well-controlled studies in order to provide substantial evidence of effectiveness. In the past, FDA has notified manufacturers of the possible withdrawal from the market of products containing a combination of an anticholinergic and a sedative because their efficacy as fixed combinations had not been proven in adequately designed clinical trials. To date, no final action has been taken.

Unaccepted

Anticholinergic and sedative combinations have been used as adjuncts in the treatment of acute enterocolitis; however, their use for this condition is controversial since they cause a reduction in gastrointestinal motility resulting in retention of the causative organism or toxin and the consequent prolongation of symptoms.

Pharmacology

Mechanism of action/Effect:

Anticholinergic—Atropine, hyoscyamine, and scopolamine, the principal belladonna alkaloids, produce an anticholinergic effect by the competitive inhibition of acetylcholine at the parasympathetic neuro-effector junction.

Sedative—Although the mechanism of action has not been completely established, the barbiturates produce a sedative effect probably as a result of their inhibition of synaptic neurotransmitters in the central nervous system (CNS).

Precautions to Consider

Cross-sensitivity and/or related problems

Patients sensitive to any of the belladonna alkaloids or barbiturates may be sensitive to this medication also.

Geriatrics

Geriatric patients may respond to usual doses of belladonna alkaloids or barbiturates with excitement, agitation, drowsiness, or confusion.

Geriatric patients are especially susceptible to the anticholinergic side effects, such as constipation, dryness of mouth, and urinary retention (especially in males), of the belladonna alkaloids. If these side effects occur and continue or are severe, medication should probably be discontinued.

Caution is also recommended when belladonna alkaloids are given to geriatric patients because of the danger of precipitating undiagnosed glaucoma.

Memory may become severely impaired in geriatric patients, especially those who already have memory problems, with the continued use of belladonna alkaloids since these drugs block the action of acetylcholine, which is responsible for many functions of the brain, including memory functions.

Dental

Prolonged use of belladonna alkaloids may decrease or inhibit salivary flow, thus contributing to the development of caries, periodontal disease, oral candidiasis, and discomfort.

Drug interactions and/or related problems

The following drug interactions and/or related problems have been selected on the basis of their potential clinical significance (possible mechanism in parentheses where appropriate)—not necessarily inclusive (» = major clinical significance):

Note: Combinations containing any of the following medications, depending on the amount present, may also interact with this medication.

Only specific interactions between belladonna alkaloids and other oral medications have been identified in this monograph. However, because of decreased gastrointestinal motility and delayed gastric emptying, absorption of other oral medications may be decreased during concurrent use with belladonna alkaloids.

Acetaminophen or
» Anticoagulants, coumarin- or indandione-derivative, or
Digitalis glycosides or
Doxycycline or
Quinidine

(effects may be decreased when these medications are used concurrently with barbiturates, especially phenobarbital, because of increased metabolism resulting from induction of hepatic microsomal enzymes; dosage adjustment of these medications, with the possible exception of digoxin, may be necessary)

» Adrenocorticoids, glucocorticoid, or
» Corticotropin (ACTH)

(concurrent long-term therapy with belladonna alkaloids may increase intraocular pressure)

(effects may be decreased when these medications are used concurrently with barbiturates because of increased metabolism resulting from induction of hepatic microsomal enzymes)

» Alcohol or
» CNS depression-producing medications, other

(concurrent use may increase the CNS depressant effects of either these medications or barbiturates)

Alkalizers, urinary, such as:
Antacids, calcium- and/or magnesium-containing
Carbonic anhydrase inhibitors
Citrates
Sodium bicarbonate

(urinary excretion of belladonna alkaloids may be delayed by alkalinization of urine, thus potentiating side effects)

» Anticholinergics or other medications with anticholinergic activity, other

(anticholinergic effects may be intensified when these medications are used concurrently with belladonna alkaloids)

» Antacids or
» Antidiarrheals, adsorbent

(administration within 1 hour of these medications will tend to reduce therapeutic effects of belladonna alkaloids and barbiturates because of particle adsorption)

Antidepressants, tricyclic

(concurrent use with belladonna alkaloids may intensify anticholinergic effects; concurrent use with barbiturates may decrease the effect of the antidepressant as a result of hepatic microsomal enzyme induction; dosage adjustments may be necessary during and after concurrent therapy with belladonna alkaloids and barbiturates)

Apomorphine

(prior administration of scopolamine-containing medications may decrease the emetic response to apomorphine in the treatment of poisoning; also, the CNS depressant effects of scopolamine and barbiturates are additive to those of apomorphine)

Griseofulvin

(absorption may be decreased when griseofulvin is used concurrently with barbiturates, especially phenobarbital, resulting in decreased blood concentrations; although the effect of decreased blood concentrations on therapeutic response has not been established, concurrent use should be avoided)

» Ketoconazole

(belladonna alkaloids may increase gastrointestinal pH; concurrent administration with belladonna alkaloids may result in a marked reduction in absorption of ketoconazole; patients should be advised to take these medications at least 2 hours after ketoconazole)

Metoclopramide

(concurrent use with belladonna alkaloids may antagonize metoclopramide's effects on gastrointestinal motility)

(concurrent use with barbiturates may increase the sedative effects of either these medications or metoclopramide)

» Monoamine oxidase (MAO) inhibitors, including furazolidone, procarbazine, and selegiline

(concurrent use with barbiturates may potentiate the CNS depressant effects of either medication; dosage adjustments may be necessary)

Opioid (narcotic) analgesics

(concurrent use with belladonna alkaloids may result in increased risk of severe constipation, which may lead to paralytic ileus, and/or urinary retention)

(concurrent use may potentiate the CNS effects of either these medications or the barbiturates, resulting in additive sedation)

Phenytoin, and possibly other hydantoin anticonvulsants
(concurrent use with barbiturates may produce variable and unpredictable effects on phenytoin; serum phenytoin concentrations should be monitored)

» Potassium chloride, especially wax-matrix preparations
(concurrent use with belladonna alkaloids may increase severity of potassium chloride-induced gastrointestinal lesions)

Valproic acid
(concurrent use with barbiturates may cause higher serum concentrations of barbiturates, leading to increased CNS depression and neurological toxicity because of protein binding displacement of the barbiturate and reduced barbiturate metabolism; half-life of valproic acid is decreased; dosage adjustment of barbiturates may be necessary)

Contraindications/Medical problems

The contraindications/medical problems included have been selected on the basis of their potential clinical significance (reasons given in parentheses where appropriate)—not necessarily inclusive (» = major clinical significance).

Risk-benefit should be considered when the following medical problems exist:

Brain damage, in children
(CNS effects of belladonna alkaloids may be exacerbated; dosage adjustment may be required)

Cardiac disease, including cardiac arrhythmias, congestive heart failure, coronary heart disease, and mitral stenosis
(increase in heart rate that may be caused by belladonna alkaloids may be undesirable)

Down's syndrome (mongolism)
(use of belladonna alkaloids may produce abnormal increase in pupillary dilation and acceleration of heart rate; dosage adjustment may be required)

» Gastrointestinal tract obstructive disease as in achalasia and pyloro-duodenal stenosis
(decrease in motility and tone may occur with the use of belladonna alkaloids, resulting in obstruction and gastric retention)

» Glaucoma, angle-closure, or predisposition to
(mydriatic effect of belladonna alkaloids resulting in increased intraocular pressure may precipitate an acute attack of angle-closure glaucoma)

» Glaucoma, open angle
(mydriatic effect of belladonna alkaloids may cause a slight increase in intraocular pressure; glaucoma therapy may need to be adjusted)

» Hepatic function impairment
(decreased metabolism of belladonna alkaloids and barbiturates)

Hyperkinesis, in children
(may be exacerbated by the use of barbiturates)

Prostatic hypertrophy or
» Urinary retention
(anticholinergic effects may precipitate or aggravate urinary retention)

» Renal function impairment
(decreased excretion may increase the risk of side effects)

Respiratory disease involving dyspnea or obstruction, particularly status asthmaticus
(anticholinergic "drying" effects may cause thickening of secretions and impair expectoration; serious ventilatory depression may occur with the use of barbiturates)

Sensitivity to belladonna alkaloids and/or barbiturates

Spastic paralysis, in children
(response to belladonna alkaloids may be increased; dosage adjustment may be required)

Xerostomia
(prolonged use of belladonna alkaloids may further reduce limited salivary flow)

Caution in use is also recommended in patients over 40 years of age because of the danger of precipitating undiagnosed glaucoma.

Side/Adverse Effects

Note: When belladonna alkaloids are given to patients, especially children, where the environmental temperature is high, there is risk of a rapid increase in body temperature because of suppression of sweat gland activity.

Infants, patients with Down's syndrome, and children with spastic paralysis or brain damage may show an increased response to belladonna alkaloids, thus increasing the potential for side effects; dosage adjustments may be required in these patients.

Geriatric or debilitated patients may respond to usual doses of belladonna alkaloids and barbiturates with excitement, agitation, drowsiness, or confusion; lower doses may be required in these patients.

The following side/adverse effects have been selected on the basis of their potential clinical significance (possible signs and symptoms in parentheses where appropriate)—not necessarily inclusive:

Those indicating need for medical attention
Incidence rare
Agranulocytosis (sore throat and fever); *allergic reaction* (skin rash or hives); *hepatitis; jaundice* (yellow eyes or skin); *increased intraocular pressure* (eye pain); *thrombocytopenia* (unusual bleeding or bruising)

Symptoms of overdose
Blurred vision, continuing, or changes in near vision; clumsiness or unsteadiness; confusion; dizziness, continuing; drowsiness, severe; dryness of mouth, nose, or throat, severe; fast heartbeat; fever; hallucinations; paradoxical reaction (unusual excitement, nervousness, restlessness, or irritability); *respiratory depression* (shortness of breath or troubled breathing); *seizures; slurred speech; unusual warmth, dryness, and flushing of skin* (particularly in blush area because of dilation of cutaneous blood vessels)

Those indicating need for medical attention only if they continue or are bothersome
Incidence more frequent
Constipation; decreased sweating; dizziness; drowsiness; dryness of mouth, nose, throat, or skin

Incidence less frequent or rare
Bloated feeling; decreased flow of breast milk; decreased saliva secretion (difficulty in swallowing); *difficult urination; difficulty in eye accommodation* (blurred vision); *headache; loss of memory, especially in elderly patients; mydriatic effect* (increased sensitivity of eyes to sunlight); *nausea or vomiting; unusual tiredness or weakness*

Note: *Difficult urination* is more likely to occur in older men and may require medical attention in patients with symptoms of prostatism.

Patient Consultation

In providing consultation, consider emphasizing the following selected information (» = major clinical significance):

Before using this medication
» Conditions affecting use, especially:
Sensitivity to any of the belladonna alkaloids or barbiturates
Pregnancy—Use not recommended because belladonna alkaloids and barbiturates cross placenta; barbiturates may cause

fetal abnormalities; phenobarbital may cause neonatal hemorrhage

Breast-feeding—Excreted in breast milk; possible inhibition of lactation

Use in children—Increased susceptibility to toxic effects of anticholinergics; increased response in infants and children with spastic paralysis or brain damage; risk of increased body temperature in hot weather; hyperexcitability (paradoxical reaction); hyperkinesis may be induced in hypersensitive children

Use in the elderly—Increased susceptibility to mental and other toxic effects of anticholinergics and barbiturates; danger of precipitating undiagnosed glaucoma; possible impairment of memory

Use by athletes—Antiemetics, including scopolamine, are banned and, in some cases, tested for in competitors in biathlon and modern pentathlon events by the U.S. Olympic Committee (USOC)

Dental—Possible development of dental problems because of decreased salivary flow

Other medications, especially adrenocorticoids or corticotropin, other anticholinergics, antacids, anticoagulants, antidiarrheals, ketoconazole, CNS depressants, MAO inhibitors, or potassium chloride

Other medical problems, especially gastrointestinal obstructive disease, glaucoma, hepatic function impairment, renal function impairment, or urinary retention

Proper use of this medication

Taking dose 30 to 60 minutes before meals unless otherwise directed by physician

» Importance of not taking more medication than the amount prescribed

Missed dose: Taking as soon as possible; not taking if almost time for next dose; not doubling doses

» Proper storage

Precautions while using this medication

» Avoiding use of alcohol or other CNS depressants

Not taking antacids and antidiarrheal medications within 1 hour of taking this medication

» Caution during exercise and hot weather; overheating may result in heat stroke

Possible increased sensitivity of eyes to light

» Caution if drowsiness or blurred vision occurs

Possible dryness of mouth, nose, and throat; using sugarless candy or gum, ice, or saliva substitute for relief; checking with physician or dentist if dry mouth continues for more than 2 weeks

Side/adverse effects

Signs of potential side effects, especially agranulocytosis, allergic reaction, hepatitis, increased intraocular pressure, and thrombocytopenia

General Dosing Information

Administration of belladonna alkaloids and barbiturates combination 30 to 60 minutes before meals is recommended to maximize absorption, and, when used for reducing stomach acid formation, to allow its effect to coincide better with antacid administration following the meal.

Prolonged uninterrupted use of barbiturates has the potential of producing psychic or physical dependence, especially in the higher dose range.

ATROPINE, HYOSCYAMINE, SCOPOLAMINE, AND PHENOBARBITAL

Oral Dosage Forms

ATROPINE SULFATE, HYOSCYAMINE SULFATE (OR HYOSCYAMINE HYDROBROMIDE), SCOPOLAMINE HYDROBROMIDE, AND PHENOBARBITAL CAPSULES

Usual adult and adolescent dose: Anticholinergic-sedative—Oral, 1 or 2 capsules two to four times a day, the dosage being adjusted as needed and tolerated.

Usual geriatric dose: See *Usual adult and adolescent dose.*

Note: Geriatric patients may be more sensitive to the effects of the usual adult dose.

Auxiliary labeling:
- May cause drowsiness.
- Avoid alcoholic beverages.

ATROPINE SULFATE, HYOSCYAMINE SULFATE (OR HYOSCYAMINE HYDROBROMIDE), SCOPOLAMINE HYDROBROMIDE, AND PHENOBARBITAL ELIXIR

Usual adult and adolescent dose: Anticholinergic-sedative—Oral, 5 to 10 mL three or four times a day, the dosage being adjusted as needed and tolerated.

Usual geriatric dose: See *Usual adult and adolescent dose.*

Note: Geriatric patients may be more sensitive to the effects of the usual adult dose.

Auxiliary labeling:
- May cause drowsiness.
- Avoid alcoholic beverages.
- Keep container tightly closed.

ATROPINE SULFATE, HYOSCYAMINE SULFATE (OR HYOSCYAMINE HYDROBROMIDE), SCOPOLAMINE HYDROBROMIDE, AND PHENOBARBITAL TABLETS

Usual adult and adolescent dose: Anticholinergic-sedative—Oral, 1 or 2 tablets two to four times a day, the dosage being adjusted as needed and tolerated.

Usual geriatric dose: See *Usual adult and adolescent dose.*

Note: Geriatric patients may be more sensitive to the effects of the usual adult dose.

Auxiliary labeling:
- May cause drowsiness.
- Avoid alcoholic beverages.

ATROPINE SULFATE, HYOSCYAMINE SULFATE, SCOPOLAMINE HYDROBROMIDE, AND PHENOBARBITAL CHEWABLE TABLETS

Usual adult and adolescent dose: Anticholinergic-sedative—Oral, 1 or 2 tablets three or four times a day, the dosage being adjusted as needed and tolerated.

Usual geriatric dose: See *Usual adult and adolescent dose.*

Note: Geriatric patients may be more sensitive to the effects of the usual adult dose.

Auxiliary labeling:
- May be chewed or swallowed with liquids.
- May cause drowsiness.
- Avoid alcoholic beverages.

ATROPINE SULFATE, HYOSCYAMINE SULFATE, SCOPOLAMINE HYDROBROMIDE, AND PHENOBARBITAL EXTENDED-RELEASE TABLETS

Usual adult and adolescent dose: Anticholinergic-sedative—Oral, 1 tablet every eight to twelve hours, the dosage being adjusted as needed and tolerated.

Usual geriatric dose: See *Usual adult and adolescent dose.*

Note: Geriatric patients may be more sensitive to the effects of the usual adult dose.

Auxiliary labeling:
- Swallow tablets whole.
- May cause drowsiness.
- Avoid alcoholic beverages.

ATROPINE AND PHENOBARBITAL

Oral Dosage Forms

ATROPINE SULFATE AND PHENOBARBITAL CAPSULES

Usual adult and adolescent dose: Anticholinergic-sedative—Oral, 1 or 2 capsules two to four times a day, the dosage being adjusted as needed and tolerated.

Usual geriatric dose: See *Usual adult and adolescent dose.*

Note: Geriatric patients may be more sensitive to the effects of the usual adult dose.

Auxiliary labeling:
- May cause drowsiness.
- Avoid alcoholic beverages.

ATROPINE SULFATE AND PHENOBARBITAL ELIXIR

Usual adult and adolescent dose: Anticholinergic-sedative—Oral, 5 to 10 mL three or four times a day, the dosage being adjusted as needed and tolerated.

Usual geriatric dose: See *Usual adult and adolescent dose.*

Note: Geriatric patients may be more sensitive to the effects of the usual adult dose.

Auxiliary labeling:
- May cause drowsiness.
- Avoid alcoholic beverages.
- Keep container tightly closed.

ATROPINE SULFATE AND PHENOBARBITAL TABLETS

Usual adult and adolescent dose: Anticholinergic-sedative—Oral, 1 or 2 tablets three or four times a day, the dosage being adjusted as needed and tolerated.

Usual geriatric dose: See *Usual adult and adolescent dose.*

Note: Geriatric patients may be more sensitive to the effects of the usual adult dose.

Auxiliary labeling:
- May cause drowsiness.
- Avoid alcoholic beverages.

BELLADONNA AND BUTABARBITAL

Oral Dosage Forms

BELLADONNA EXTRACT AND BUTABARBITAL SODIUM ELIXIR

Usual adult and adolescent dose: Anticholinergic-sedative—Oral, 5 to 10 mL three or four times a day, the dosage being adjusted as needed and tolerated.

Usual geriatric dose: See *Usual adult and adolescent dose.*

Note: Geriatric patients may be more sensitive to the effects of the usual adult dose.

Auxiliary labeling:
- May cause drowsiness.
- Avoid alcoholic beverages.
- Keep container tightly closed.

BELLADONNA EXTRACT AND BUTABARBITAL SODIUM TABLETS

Usual adult and adolescent dose: Anticholinergic-sedative—Oral, 1 or 2 tablets three or four times a day, the dosage being adjusted as needed and tolerated.

Usual geriatric dose: See *Usual adult and adolescent dose.*

Note: Geriatric patients may be more sensitive to the effects of the usual adult dose.

Auxiliary labeling:
- May cause drowsiness.
- Avoid alcoholic beverages.

BELLADONNA AND PHENOBARBITAL

Oral Dosage Forms

BELLADONNA EXTRACT AND PHENOBARBITAL TABLETS

Usual adult and adolescent dose: Anticholinergic-sedative—Oral, 1 or 2 tablets two to four times a day, the dosage being adjusted as needed and tolerated.

Usual geriatric dose: See *Usual adult and adolescent dose.*

Note: Geriatric patients may be more sensitive to the effects of the usual adult dose.

Auxiliary labeling:
- May cause drowsiness.
- Avoid alcoholic beverages.

HYOSCYAMINE AND PHENOBARBITAL

Oral Dosage Forms

HYOSCYAMINE SULFATE AND PHENOBARBITAL ELIXIR

Usual adult and adolescent dose: Anticholinergic-sedative—Oral, 5 to 10 mL every four hours, the dosage being adjusted as needed and tolerated.

Usual geriatric dose: See *Usual adult and adolescent dose.*

Note: Geriatric patients may be more sensitive to the effects of the usual adult dose.

Auxiliary labeling:
- May cause drowsiness.
- Avoid alcoholic beverages.

HYOSCYAMINE SULFATE AND PHENOBARBITAL ORAL SOLUTION

Usual adult and adolescent dose: Anticholinergic-sedative—Oral, 1 to 2 mL every four hours, the dosage being adjusted as needed and tolerated.

Usual geriatric dose: See *Usual adult and adolescent dose.*

Note: Geriatric patients may be more sensitive to the effects of the usual adult dose.

Auxiliary labeling:
- May cause drowsiness.
- Avoid alcoholic beverages.

HYOSCYAMINE SULFATE AND PHENOBARBITAL TABLETS

Usual adult and adolescent dose: Anticholinergic-sedative—Oral, 1 to 2 tablets three or four times a day, the dosage being adjusted as needed and tolerated.

Usual geriatric dose: See *Usual adult and adolescent dose.*

Note: Geriatric patients may be more sensitive to the effects of the usual adult dose.

Auxiliary labeling:
- May cause drowsiness.
- Avoid alcoholic beverages.

BENZODIAZEPINES　Systemic

Some commonly used *brand names* are:

In the U.S.—

Alzapam [Lorazepam]	Lorazepam Intensol [Lorazepam]
Ativan [Lorazepam]	Paxipam [Halazepam]
Centrax [Prazepam]	ProSom [Estazolam]
Dalmane [Flurazepam]	Razepam [Temazepam]
Diazepam Intensol [Diazepam]	Restoril [Temazepam]
Doral [Quazepam]	Serax [Oxazepam]
Durapam [Flurazepam]	T-Quil [Diazepam]
Gen-XENE [Clorazepate]	Tranxene-SD [Clorazepate]
Halcion [Triazolam]	Tranxene T-Tab [Clorazepate]
Klonopin [Clonazepam]	Valium [Diazepam]
Libritabs [Chlordiazepoxide]	Valrelease [Diazepam]
Librium [Chlordiazepoxide]	Vazepam [Diazepam]
Lipoxide [Chlordiazepoxide]	Xanax [Alprazolam]
	Zetran [Diazepam]

In Canada—

Apo-Alpraz [Alprazolam]	Novoclopate [Clorazepate]
Apo-Chlordiazepoxide [Chlordiazepoxide]	Novodipam [Diazepam]
Apo-Clorazepate [Clorazepate]	Novoflupam [Flurazepam]
Apo-Diazepam [Diazepam]	Novolorazem [Lorazepam]
Apo-Flurazepam [Flurazepam]	Novopoxide [Chlordiazepoxide]
Apo-Lorazepam [Lorazepam]	Novotriolam [Triazolam]
Apo-Oxazepam [Oxazepam]	Novoxapam [Oxazepam]
Apo-Triazo [Triazolam]	Nu-Alpraz [Alprazolam]
Ativan [Lorazepam]	Nu-Loraz [Lorazepam]
Dalmane [Flurazepam]	Nu-Triazo [Triazolam]
Diazemuls [Diazepam]	PMS Diazepam [Diazepam]
Halcion [Triazolam]	Restoril [Temazepam]
Lectopam [Bromazepam]	Rivotril [Clonazepam]
Librium [Chlordiazepoxide]	Serax [Oxazepam]
Loftran [Ketazolam]	Solium [Chlordiazepoxide]
Mogadon [Nitrazepam]	Somnol [Flurazepam]
Novo-Alprazol [Alprazolam]	Tranxene [Clorazepate]
	Valium [Diazepam]
	Vivol [Diazepam]
	Xanax [Alprazolam]
	Zapex [Oxazepam]

ALPRAZOLAM
Oral
    Alprazolam Tablets USP
        In the U.S. —*Xanax*
        In Canada—*Apo-Alpraz; Novo-Alprazol; Nu-Alpraz; Xanax*
BROMAZEPAM*
Oral
    Bromazepam Tablets*
        In Canada—*Lectopam*
CHLORDIAZEPOXIDE
Oral
    Chlordiazepoxide Tablets USP†
        In the U.S.—*Libritabs*
    Chlordiazepoxide Hydrochloride Capsules USP
        In the U.S.—*Librium; Lipoxide;* GENERIC
        In Canada—*Apo-Chlordiazepoxide; Librium; Novopoxide; Solium*
Parenteral
    Sterile Chlordiazepoxide Hydrochloride USP
        In the U.S. and Canada—*Librium*
CLONAZEPAM
Oral
    Clonazepam Tablets USP
        In the U.S.—*Klonopin*
        In Canada—*Rivotril*
CLORAZEPATE
Oral
    Clorazepate Dipotassium Capsules
        In the U.S.—GENERIC
        In Canada—*Apo-Clorazepate; Novoclopate; Tranxene*
    Clorazepate Dipotassium Tablets†
        In the U.S.—*Gen-XENE; Tranxene-SD; Tranxene T-Tab;* GENERIC
DIAZEPAM
Oral
    Diazepam Extended-release Capsules USP†
        In the U.S.—*Valrelease*
    Diazepam Oral Solution†
        In the U.S.—*Diazepam Intensol;* GENERIC
    Diazepam Tablets USP
        In the U.S.—*Valium; Vazepam;* GENERIC
        In Canada—*Apo-Diazepam; Novodipam; PMS Diazepam; Valium; Vivol*

Parenteral
    Diazepam Injection USP
        In the U.S.—*T-Quil; Valium; Zetran;* GENERIC
        In Canada—*Valium;* GENERIC
    Sterile Diazepam Emulsion*
        In Canada—*Diazemuls*
Rectal
    Diazepam for Rectal Solution*†
    Note: In the U.S. and Canada, Diazepam Injection USP [*T-Quil; Valium; Zetran;* GENERIC] is the dosage form being used.
ESTAZOLAM†
Oral
    Estazolam Tablets†
        In the U.S.—*ProSom*
FLURAZEPAM
Oral
    Flurazepam Hydrochloride Capsules USP
        In the U.S.—*Dalmane; Durapam;* GENERIC
        In Canada—*Apo-Flurazepam; Dalmane; Novoflupam*
    Flurazepam Monohydrochloride Tablets*
        In Canada—*Somnol*
HALAZEPAM†
Oral
    Halazepam Tablets USP†
        In the U.S.—*Paxipam*
KETAZOLAM*
Oral
    Ketazolam Capsules*
        In Canada—*Loftran*
LORAZEPAM
Oral
    Lorazepam Oral Solution
        In the U.S.—*Lorazepam Intensol*
    Lorazepam Tablets USP
        In the U.S.—*Alzapam; Ativan;* GENERIC
        In Canada—*Apo-Lorazepam; Ativan; Novolorazem; Nu-Loraz*
    Lorazepam Sublingual Tablets*
        In Canada—*Ativan*
Parenteral
    Lorazepam Injection USP
        In the U.S. and Canada—*Ativan*
MIDAZOLAM—See Midazolam (Systemic).
NITRAZEPAM*
Oral
    Nitrazepam Tablets*
        In Canada—*Mogadon*
OXAZEPAM
Oral
    Oxazepam Capsules USP†
        In the U.S.—*Serax;* GENERIC
    Oxazepam Tablets USP
        In the U.S.—*Serax;* GENERIC
        In Canada—*Apo-Oxazepam; Novoxapam; Serax; Zapex*
PRAZEPAM†
Oral
    Prazepam Capsules USP†
        In the U.S.—*Centrax;* GENERIC
    Prazepam Tablets USP†
        In the U.S.—*Centrax;* GENERIC
QUAZEPAM†
Oral
    Quazepam Tablets†
        In the U.S.—*Doral*
TEMAZEPAM
Oral
    Temazepam Capsules
        In the U.S.—*Razepam; Restoril;* GENERIC
        In Canada—*Restoril*

Temazepam Tablets†
    In the U.S.—GENERIC
TRIAZOLAM
Oral
    Triazolam Tablets USP
        In the U.S.—*Halcion*
        In Canada—*Apo-Triazo; Halcion; Novotriolam; Nu-Triazo;* GENERIC

*Not commercially available in the U.S.
†Not commercially available in Canada.

Category

Note: **All of the benzodiazepines have similar pharmacologic actions; however, clinical uses among specific agents may vary because of actual pharmacokinetic differences, availability of specific testing, and/or availability of clinical-use data.**

Antianxiety agent—Alprazolam; Bromazepam; Chlordiazepoxide; Clorazepate; Diazepam; Halazepam; Ketazolam; Lorazepam; Oxazepam; Prazepam.
Sedative-hypnotic—Alprazolam; Bromazepam; Chlordiazepoxide; Clorazepate; Diazepam; Estazolam; Flurazepam; Halazepam; Ketazolam; Lorazepam; Nitrazepam; Oxazepam; Prazepam; Quazepam; Temazepam; Triazolam.
Amnestic—Diazepam (parenteral only); Lorazepam (parenteral only).
Anticonvulsant—Clonazepam; Clorazepate; Diazepam; Lorazepam (parenteral only); Nitrazepam.
Antipanic agent—Alprazolam; Chlordiazepoxide (parenteral only); Clonazepam; Diazepam; Lorazepam.
Skeletal muscle relaxant adjunct—Diazepam; Lorazepam.
Antitremor agent—Chlordiazepoxide (oral only); Diazepam (oral only); Lorazepam (oral only).
Antiemetic, in cancer chemotherapy—Lorazepam (parenteral only).

Indications

Note: Bracketed information in the *Indications* section refers to uses not included in U.S. product labeling.

Accepted
Anxiety (treatment)—Alprazolam, bromazepam, chlordiazepoxide, clorazepate, diazepam, halazepam, ketazolam, lorazepam, oxazepam, and prazepam are indicated for the management of anxiety disorders or for the short-term relief of the symptoms of anxiety. Oral chlordiazepoxide, [oral diazepam][1], and sublingual or intramuscular lorazepam are indicated for treatment of preoperative apprehension and anxiety.

Benzodiazepines are not indicated for the treatment of anxiety or tension associated with the stress of everyday life. Effectiveness of these medications for long-term management of anxiety has not been assessed by systematic clinical studies. The medication's efficacy should be reassessed at periodic intervals.

Anxiety associated with mental depression (treatment adjunct)[1]—Alprazolam, lorazepam (oral), and oxazepam are also indicated for the adjunctive management of anxiety associated with mental depression.

Alcohol withdrawal (treatment)—Chlordiazepoxide, clorazepate, diazepam (except the extended-release dosage form), [lorazepam][1], and oxazepam are indicated for the relief of acute alcohol withdrawal symptoms such as acute agitation, tremor, impending or acute delirium tremens, and hallucinosis.

Anesthesia, adjunct—Parenteral chlordiazepoxide and parenteral diazepam are indicated for preoperative procedures to relieve anxiety and tension. Also, parenteral lorazepam is indicated in adults as preanesthetic medication to produce sedation, relief of anxiety, and anterograde amnesia.

Amnesia, in cardioversion;

Amnesia, in endoscopic procedures;

Anxiety, in cardioversion (treatment); or

Anxiety, in endoscopic procedures (treatment adjunct)—Parenteral diazepam and [parenteral lorazepam][1] are indicated as adjuncts prior to endoscopic procedures if apprehension, anxiety, or acute stress reactions are present and to diminish patient's recall of the procedure.

Parenteral diazepam is also indicated for intravenous administration prior to cardioversion to relieve anxiety and tension and to produce anterograde amnesia.

[Sedation, conscious][1]—Parenteral diazepam is used in dentistry to relieve anxiety and produce amnesia in prolonged or difficult dental procedures. It is used frequently with a local anesthetic.

Insomnia (treatment)—Estazolam, flurazepam, nitrazepam, quazepam, temazepam, and triazolam are indicated for the short-term treatment of insomnia characterized by difficulty in falling asleep, frequent nocturnal awakenings, and/or early morning awakenings. Lorazepam[1] is indicated for insomnia due to anxiety or transient situational stress. Other benzodiazepines, such as [alprazolam][1], bromazepam[1], diazepam, ketazolam[1], [halazepam], and [prazepam], are also used in the treatment of insomnia. Failure of insomnia to remit after 7 to 10 days of treatment may indicate the presence of a primary psychiatric or medical illness. Worsening of insomnia or the emergence of new abnormalities of thinking or behavior may be the consequence of an unrecognized psychiatric or physical disorder.

[Short- and intermediate-acting benzodiazepine hypnotics may be useful in the prevention or treatment (short-term) of transient insomnia associated with a sudden sleep schedule change, such as occurs in trans-meridian travel and shift-work rotation.][1]

Seizures (treatment); or

Status epilepticus (treatment)—Diazepam injection (not the sterile emulsion) or [diazepam for rectal solution] is indicated as an adjunct in status epilepticus and severe recurrent convulsive seizures. It is not recommended for maintenance anticonvulsant therapy; therefore, once seizures are controlled, appropriate maintenance anticonvulsant therapy should be instituted. [Parenteral lorazepam also is used for the treatment of status epilepticus.]

Convulsions (treatment adjunct); or

Seizures (treatment adjunct)—Oral diazepam[1] (except the extended-release dosage form) is indicated as short-term (7 to 14 days) adjunctive therapy in convulsive disorders. It is not useful as sole therapy in convulsive disorders. [Clonazepam may be effective as an adjunct in convulsive disorders such as eclamptic convulsions, infantile spasms, reading epilepsy, and startle-induced seizures.][1]

Epilepsy, Lennox-Gastaut syndrome (treatment);

Epilepsy, akinetic seizure pattern (treatment); or

Epilepsy, myoclonic seizure pattern (treatment)—Clonazepam is indicated for use alone or, more frequently, as an adjunct in the treatment of the Lennox-Gastaut syndrome (petit mal variant), akinetic, and myoclonic seizures.

Nitrazepam also is indicated for the treatment of myoclonic seizures.

[Epilepsy, myoclonic seizure pattern (treatment adjunct)][1]—Oral diazepam is used as adjunctive therapy in myoclonus. It is not useful as sole therapy in this condition.

Epilepsy, absence seizure pattern (treatment)—Clonazepam may be useful in the treatment of absence (petit mal) seizures refractory to the succinimide anticonvulsants or valproic acid.

Epilepsy, simple partial seizure pattern (treatment adjunct)[1]; or

Epilepsy, complex partial seizure pattern (treatment adjunct)[1]— Clorazepate may be indicated as adjunctive therapy in the management of partial seizures.

[Epilepsy, simple partial seizure pattern (treatment)][1]; or

[Epilepsy, complex partial seizure pattern (treatment)][1]—Clonazepam may be effective in refractory seizures such as complex partial (psychomotor, temporal lobe) or elementary partial (focal) seizures.

[Epilepsy, tonic-clonic seizure pattern (treatment)][1]—Clonazepam may be effective in tonic-clonic (grand mal) seizures. However, when clonazepam is used in patients in whom several types of seizure disorders coexist, it may increase the incidence or rarely precipitate the onset of generalized tonic-clonic (grand mal) seizures; addition of another anticonvulsant and/or an increase in dosage may be required.

Panic disorders (treatment)—Alprazolam[1], [chlordiazepoxide (parenteral)], [clonazepam][1], [diazepam][1], and [lorazepam][1] are used in the treatment of panic disorders.

Spasm, skeletal muscle (treatment adjunct)—Diazepam and [lorazepam][1] are indicated as adjunctive therapy for the relief of skeletal muscle spasm due to reflex spasm of local pathology (such as inflammation of the muscles or joints, or secondary to trauma); spasticity caused by upper motor neuron disorders (such as cerebral palsy and paraplegia); athetosis; stiff-man syndrome; and tetanus. [Diazepam is also used to relieve spasms of facial muscles associated with problems of occlusion and temporomandibular joint disorders.][1]

[Nausea and vomiting, cancer chemotherapy-induced (prophylaxis)][1]— Lorazepam injection, alone or in combination with other agents, reduces the severity and duration of nausea and vomiting associated with emetogenic cancer chemotherapy. In addition, lorazepam-induced amnesia can reduce anticipatory anxiety, nausea, and vomiting.

[Headache, tension (treatment)]—Chlordiazepoxide, diazepam[1], lorazepam[1], and possibly other benzodiazepines[1] are used in the treatment of tension headache.

[Tremors (treatment)][1]—Oral alprazolam, chlordiazepoxide, diazepam, and lorazepam are also used in the treatment of familial, senile, or essential action tremors.

---

[1]Not included in Canadian product labeling.

Pharmacology

Mechanism of action/Effect: In general, benzodiazepines act as depressants of the central nervous system (CNS), producing all levels of CNS depression from mild sedation to hypnosis to coma depending on dose.

The precise sites and mechanisms of action have not been completely established. Although various mechanisms of action have been proposed, it is believed that benzodiazepines enhance or facilitate the inhibitory neurotransmitter action of gamma-aminobutyric acid (GABA), which is one of the major inhibitory neurotransmitters in the brain and mediates both pre- and post-synaptic inhibition in all regions of the CNS, following interaction between the benzodiazepine and a specific neuronal membrane receptor.

Benzodiazepines reportedly act as agonists at the benzodiazepine receptors, which have been shown to form a component of a functional supramolecular unit known as the benzodiazepine-GABA receptor-chloride ionophore complex. The receptor complex, believed to reside on neuronal membranes that regulate cell firing, functions mainly in the gating of the chloride channel. Activation of the GABA receptor results in the opening of the chloride channel, allowing the flow of chloride ions through the neuronal membrane. Usually this results in hyperpolarization of the post-synaptic neuron, which inhibits firing of that neuron. That inhibition translates into decreased neuronal excitability, thus attenuating subsequent depolarizing excitatory transmitters. Benzodiazepines reportedly increase the frequency of the chloride channel opening, probably by enhancing the binding of GABA to its receptor or by facilitating the link of the GABA receptors to the chloride ion channels. Benzodiazepines also appear to act at GABA-independent receptors.

Antianxiety agent; sedative-hypnotic—Believed to stimulate GABA receptors in the ascending reticular activating system. Since GABA is inhibitory, receptor stimulation increases inhibition and blocks both cortical and limbic arousal following stimulation of the brain stem reticular formation.

Amnestic—Mechanism of action has not been determined. However, as may occur with all sedative-hypnotic medications, preanesthetic doses of diazepam and lorazepam impair recent memory and interfere with the establishment of the memory trace, thus producing anterograde amnesia for events occurring while therapeutic concentrations of the benzodiazepine are present.

Anticonvulsant—Appear to act, at least partially, by enhancing presynaptic inhibition. Suppress the spread of seizure activity produced by epileptogenic foci in the cortex, thalamus, and limbic structures but do not abolish the abnormal discharge of the focus.

Skeletal muscle relaxant adjunct—The exact mechanism of action of benzodiazepines has not been completely established but these medications appear to produce skeletal muscle relaxation primarily by inhibiting spinal polysynaptic afferent pathways; however, monosynaptic afferent pathways may also be inhibited. Benzodiazepines may also directly depress motor nerve and muscle function.

Onset of action: After single oral doses, onset of action depends largely upon absorption rate. After multiple doses, effects depend partly upon rate and extent of drug accumulation, which in turn relate to elimination half-life and clearance.

Duration of action: After single oral doses, duration of action depends upon rate and extent of drug distribution, as well as rate of elimination once distribution is complete. After multiple doses, effects depend partly upon rate and extent of drug accumulation, which in turn relate to elimination half-life and clearance. The duration of clinical effects of the benzodiazepines is not always predictable from the elimination half-life.

Precautions to Consider

Cross-sensitivity and/or related problems
Patients hypersensitive to one of the benzodiazepines may be hypersensitive to the other benzodiazepines also.

Geriatrics
Geriatric patients are usually more sensitive to the CNS effects of benzodiazepines. It is recommended that dosage be limited to the smallest effective dose and increased gradually, if necessary, to decrease the possibility of development of ataxia, dizziness, and oversedation. A retrospective case-control study has shown that elderly patients receiving long-acting benzodiazepines are more likely than those receiving short-acting benzodiazepines to suffer falls and fall-related fractures. However, both groups had an increased risk of these sequelae as compared to older patients who did not receive benzodiazepines or who received other short-acting sedative-hypnotics.

Parenteral administration of benzodiazepines may be more likely to cause apnea, hypotension, bradycardia, or cardiac arrest in geriatric patients.

Drug interactions and/or related problems
The following drug interactions and/or related problems have been selected on the basis of their potential clinical significance (possible mechanism in parentheses where appropriate)—not necessarily inclusive (» = major clinical significance):

Note: Combinations containing any of the following medications, depending on the amount present, may also interact with this medication.

  Addictive medications, other, especially CNS depressants with habituating potential
  (prolonged concurrent use may increase the risk of habituation; caution is recommended)

» Alcohol or
» CNS depression-producing medications, other
  (concurrent use may increase the CNS depressant effects of either these medications or benzodiazepines; caution is recommended and dosage of one or both agents should be reduced; when a benzodiazepine is used concurrently with an opioid analgesic, the dosage of the opioid analgesic should be reduced by at least one-third and administered in small increments)

Antacids
  (concurrent use may delay, but not reduce, the absorption of chlordiazepoxide and diazepam; whether this effect applies to other benzodiazepines has not been determined)

  (concurrent use with clorazepate may decrease the rate of conversion of clorazepate to desmethyldiazepam, but does not affect the degree of absorption)

Antidepressants, tricyclic
  (in addition to possibly increasing CNS depressant effects, concurrent use with alprazolam in doses of up to 4 mg per day has been reported to increase steady-state plasma concentrations of imipramine and desipramine by an average of 31% and 20%, respectively; however, the clinical significance of these changes is unknown)

Carbamazepine
  (concurrent use with benzodiazepines metabolized via the hepatic enzyme system, especially clonazepam, may result in increased metabolism, leading to decreased serum concentrations and reduced elimination half-lives of benzodiazepines because of induction of hepatic microsomal enzyme activity; monitoring of carbamazepine blood concentrations as a guide to dosage is recommended, especially when carbamazepine is added to or withdrawn from existing benzodiazepine therapy)

Cimetidine or
Contraceptives, estrogen-containing, oral, or
Disulfiram or
Erythromycin
  (concurrent use may inhibit the hepatic metabolism of benzodiazepines that are metabolized by oxidation, especially chlordiazepoxide and diazepam, resulting in delayed elimination and increased plasma concentrations; however, the hepatic metabolism of benzodiazepines such as lorazepam, oxazepam, and temazepam is probably not affected, possibly because these medications do not appear to affect glucuronide conjugation of these benzodiazepines)

  (concurrent use of cimetidine or oral estrogen-containing contraceptives may inhibit the hepatic metabolism of benzodiazepines, such as nitrazepam, that are metabolized primarily by nitro-reduction, possibly resulting in delayed elimination and prolonged elimination half-life; also, during long-term use, serum concentrations may be increased)

  (concurrent use of cimetidine or erythromycin may inhibit the hepatic metabolism of triazolam, resulting in increased plasma concentrations and delayed clearance of triazolam; dosage reductions may be necessary)

Clozapine
  (collapse, sometimes accompanied by respiratory depression or arrest, has been reported in a few patients receiving clozapine concurrently with benzodiazepines. Caution is advised when clozapine is administered concomitantly with any agent that may depress respiration, and the dosage of clozapine should be titrated upwards slowly. Some clinicians have recommended that benzodiazepines be discontinued at least 1 week prior to initiation of therapy with clozapine)

Fentanyl derivatives
  (premedication with diazepam or lorazepam may decrease the dose of a fentanyl derivative required for induction of anesthesia and decrease the time to loss of consciousness with induction doses; also, administration of diazepam or lorazepam prior to or during surgery may decrease risk of patient recall of

surgical events postoperatively; however, these potential benefits must be weighed against the potential risks of concurrent use, such as an increased risk of severe hypotension associated with decreases in systemic vascular resistance, increased risk of respiratory depression, and delayed recovery time, especially when the benzodiazepine is administered intravenously)

Hypotension-producing medications, other
(concurrent use may potentiate the hypotensive effects of benzodiazepine preanesthetics used in surgery; dosage adjustments may be necessary)

(concurrent use of mecamylamine or trimethaphan with benzodiazepine preanesthetics used in surgery may potentiate the hypotensive response, with increased risk of severe hypotension, shock, and cardiovascular collapse during surgery)

(caution is advised during titration of calcium channel blocker dosage for those patients taking medication known to promote hypotension, such as benzodiazepine preanesthetics, since the combination may result in excessive hypotension)

Isoniazid
(concurrent use may inhibit the elimination of diazepam and triazolam, resulting in increased plasma concentrations; whether this effect applies to other benzodiazepines has not been determined; dosage adjustment may be necessary)

Levodopa
(concurrent use with benzodiazepines may decrease the therapeutic effects of levodopa)

Omeprazole
(concurrent use of omeprazole may prolong the elimination of diazepam)

Probenecid
(concurrent use may impair glucuronide conjugation of lorazepam, oxazepam, or temazepam, resulting in increased effects and possibly excessive sedation)

Rifampin
(concurrent use may enhance the elimination of diazepam, resulting in decreased plasma concentrations; whether this effect applies to other benzodiazepines has not been determined; dosage adjustment may be necessary)

Scopolamine, systemic
(concurrent use of scopolamine with parenteral lorazepam is reported to have no added beneficial effect and their combined effect may increase the incidence of sedation, hallucination, and irrational behavior)

Zidovudine
(concurrent use with benzodiazepines may, in theory, competitively inhibit hepatic glucuronidation and decrease the clearance of zidovudine; the toxicity of zidovudine potentially could be increased)

Contraindications/Medical problems

The contraindications/medical problems included have been selected on the basis of their potential clinical significance (reasons given in parentheses where appropriate)—not necessarily inclusive (» = major clinical significance).

Risk-benefit should be considered when the following medical problems exist:

Alcohol intoxication, acute, with depressed vital signs
(additive CNS depression)

Coma or
Shock
(hypnotic or hypotensive effects may be prolonged or intensified by benzodiazepines administered parenterally)

Drug abuse or dependence, history of
(patients predisposed to habituation and dependence)

Epilepsy or

Seizures, history of
(initiation or abrupt withdrawal of clonazepam or diazepam therapy may increase frequency and/or severity of tonic-clonic [grand mal] seizures; use of intravenous diazepam for absence [petit mal] status or Lennox-Gastaut syndrome [petit mal variant] status may precipitate tonic status epilepticus)

(abrupt withdrawal of clonazepam or diazepam used to treat these disorders may precipitate seizures or status epilepticus)

» Glaucoma, angle-closure, acute or predisposition to
(benzodiazepines may have anticholinergic effect)

Hepatic function impairment
(elimination half-life may be prolonged; minimal effect with oxazepam, lorazepam, and temazepam)

Hyperkinesis
(paradoxical reactions may occur)

Hypoalbuminemia
(may predispose patient to higher incidence of sedative side effects, especially with chlordiazepoxide and diazepam)

Mental depression, severe
(suicidal tendencies may be present; protective measures may be necessary; also benzodiazepines, when used alone, may increase depression; episodes of hypomania and mania reported with use of alprazolam in patients with mental depression)

» Myasthenia gravis
(condition may be exacerbated)

Organic brain disorders
(patients may be more prone to disinhibition and CNS depressant effects of benzodiazepines)

Porphyria
(condition may be exacerbated with the use of chlordiazepoxide)

Psychoses
(benzodiazepines are rarely effective as primary treatment for psychosis; also, paradoxical reactions may occur)

» Pulmonary disease, severe chronic obstructive
(ventilatory failure may be exacerbated)

Renal function impairment
(elimination may be prolonged)

Sensitivity to benzodiazepines

Sleep apnea, established or suspected
(condition may be exacerbated)

Swallowing abnormality, in children
(condition may be exacerbated because drooling and aspiration induced by benzodiazepines, such as nitrazepam, may delay cricopharyngeal relaxation; patient should be closely monitored)

Caution should also be used in surgical or nonambulatory patients because of the cough-suppressant effects of clonazepam.

Side/Adverse Effects

Note: Although not all of these side effects have been attributed specifically to each benzodiazepine, a potential exists for their occurrence during the use of any benzodiazepine.

Geriatric and debilitated patients, children (especially the very young), and patients with liver disease or low serum albumin are usually more sensitive to the CNS effects of benzodiazepines.

Parenteral administration of benzodiazepines may cause apnea, hypotension, bradycardia, or cardiac arrest, especially in geriatric or severely ill patients and in patients with limited pulmonary reserve or unstable cardiovascular status or if intravenous administration of medication is too rapid.

Parenteral benzodiazepines have produced hypotension or muscular weakness in some patients, especially when used concurrently with narcotics, barbiturates, or alcohol.

Coughing, depressed respiration, dyspnea, hyperventilation, laryngospasm, and pain in throat and chest have been reported when parenteral diazepam was administered in peroral endoscopic procedures.

The following side/adverse effects have been selected on the basis of their potential clinical significance (possible signs and symptoms in parentheses where appropriate)—not necessarily inclusive:

Those indicating need for medical attention
Incidence less frequent
Intolerance to benzodiazepines (confusion); *mental depression*
Incidence rare
Allergic reaction (skin rash or itching); *behavior problems* (including difficulty in concentrating and outbursts of anger); *blood dyscrasias, including agranulocytosis* (chills, fever, sore throat, unusual tiredness or weakness), *anemia* (unusual tiredness or weakness), *or leukopenia* (chills, fever, sore throat), *neutropenia* (chills, fever, and/or sore throat; ulcers or sores in mouth or throat, continuing; unusual tiredness or weakness), *thrombocytopenia* (unusual bleeding or bruising); *extrapyramidal effects, dystonic* (uncontrolled movements of body, including the eyes); *hepatic dysfunction* (yellow eyes or skin); *hypotension* (low blood pressure); *memory impairment; muscle weakness; paradoxical reactions* (including hallucinations; insomnia; unusual excitement, nervousness, or irritability); *phlebitis or venous thrombosis* (redness, swelling, or pain at injection site)—for parenteral dosage forms only; *seizures*

Note: *Behavioral disturbances* associated with clonazepam are more likely to occur in children or in patients with preexisting brain damage and/or mental retardation or a history of behavioral or psychiatric disturbances; if these effects occur, the medication should be discontinued.

Anterograde amnesia may occur at a higher rate with triazolam.

An increase in daytime *anxiety* has been reported for triazolam after as few as 10 days of continuous use. If this effect occurs, the medications should be discontinued.

Incidence of *phlebitis* or *venous thrombosis* is more common with diazepam, less common with lorazepam, and rare with chlordiazepoxide.

There may be an increased incidence and severity of *seizures*, especially on initiation or abrupt withdrawal of clonazepam and diazepam in patients with epilepsy or history of seizures.

Symptoms of overdose indicating need for medical attention
Confusion, continuing; decreased reflexes; drowsiness, severe; shakiness; slow heartbeat, shortness of breath, or troubled breathing; slurred speech, continuing; staggering; weakness, severe

Those indicating need for medical attention only if they continue or are bothersome
Incidence more frequent
Ataxia (clumsiness or unsteadiness)—especially in elderly or debilitated patients; *dizziness or lightheadedness; drowsiness, including residual daytime drowsiness when used as a hypnotic*—especially in elderly or debilitated patients; *slurred speech*

Note: *Ataxia* and *drowsiness* are dose-related and are most severe during initial therapy. They may decrease in severity or disappear with continued or long-term therapy.

Daytime drowsiness may be dose-related.

Incidence less frequent or rare
Abdominal or stomach cramps or pain; blurred vision or other changes in vision; changes in libido (changes in sexual drive or performance); *constipation; diarrhea; dryness of mouth or increased thirst; euphoria* (false sense of well-being); *headache; increased bronchial secretions or watering of mouth; muscle spasm; nausea or vomiting; problems with urination; tachycardia/palpitations* (fast or pounding heartbeat); *trembling; unusual tiredness or weakness*

Those indicating possible withdrawal and the need for medical attention if they occur (usually within 2 to 3 days with short to intermediate half-life benzodiazepines and 10 to 20 days with long half-life benzodiazepines) after medication is abruptly discontinued
Incidence more frequent
Irritability; nervousness; trouble in sleeping
Incidence less frequent
Abdominal or stomach cramps; confusion; depersonalization (loss of sense of reality); *increased sweating; mental depression; muscle cramps; nausea or vomiting; perceptual disturbances, including hyperacusis* (increased sense of hearing), *hypersensitivity to touch and pain, parasthesias* (tingling, burning, or prickly sensations), *or photophobia* (sensitivity of eyes to light); *tachycardia* (fast or pounding heartbeat); *trembling*
Incidence rare
Convulsions; delirium (confusion as to time, place, or person); *hallucinations; paranoid symptoms* (feelings of suspicion and distrust)

Note: *Withdrawal symptoms,* especially the more serious ones, are usually more common in patients who have received excessive doses over a prolonged period of time. However, symptoms have occurred following abrupt discontinuation of benzodiazepines that have been taken continuously, at therapeutic concentrations, for as few as 1 to 2 weeks. In some patients, withdrawal symptoms have occurred during gradual discontinuation or tapering of benzodiazepines. Withdrawal symptoms may be more likely to occur following the use of short-acting benzodiazepines than with long-acting benzodiazepines. There is no apparent correlation between the severity of withdrawal symptoms and previous benzodiazepine dose or plasma concentrations at the time the benzodiazepine was discontinued.

Rebound insomnia has occurred following withdrawal of single nightly doses of most benzodiazepines. It may occur sooner and be more frequent and severe following withdrawal of short half-life benzodiazepines. Since desmethyldiazepam (an active metabolite of chlordiazepoxide, clorazepate, diazepam, halazepam, ketazolam, and prazepam) and desalkylflurazepam (an active metabolite of flurazepam and quazepam) may persist in the blood for days or weeks, rebound insomnia may not occur for 10 to 20 days, if at all, after withdrawal of these long half-life benzodiazepines.

Patient Consultation

In providing consultation, consider emphasizing the following selected information (» = major clinical significance):

Before using this medication
» Conditions affecting use, especially:
Sensitivity to benzodiazepines
Pregnancy—Benzodiazepines reported to increase risk of congenital malformations when used during first trimester of pregnancy; chronic use may cause physical dependence in the neonate with resulting withdrawal symptoms; use during last weeks of pregnancy may cause neonatal CNS depression; use just prior to or during labor may cause neonatal flaccidity
Breast-feeding—Some benzodiazepines and their metabolites excreted in breast milk and others may be excreted in breast milk; use by nursing mothers may cause sedation, and possibly feeding difficulties and weight loss in the infant
Use in children—Children, especially the very young, usually more sensitive to CNS effects of benzodiazepines
Use in the elderly—Elderly patients usually more sensitive to CNS effects of benzodiazepines
Use by athletes—Benzodiazepines are banned and, in some cases, tested for in competitors in biathlon and modern pentathlon events by the U.S. Olympic Committee (USOC)

Other medications, especially other CNS depression-producing medications

Other medical problems, especially acute angle-closure glaucoma, myasthenia gravis, or severe chronic obstructive pulmonary disease

Proper use of this medication

Proper administration:

For extended-release dosage form of diazepam

Swallowing capsule whole

Not crushing, breaking, or chewing

For oral solution dosage form of lorazepam

Dose may be diluted with liquid or semisolid food such as water, soda or soda-like beverages, applesauce, or pudding

For sublingual tablet dosage form of lorazepam

Not chewing or swallowing tablet whole

Dissolving slowly under tongue; not swallowing for at least 2 minutes to allow sufficient absorption

» Importance of not taking more medication than the amount prescribed because of habit-forming potential

» Not increasing dose if medication is less effective after a few weeks; checking with physician

Missed dose: If on scheduled dosing regimen (e.g., for epilepsy)—Taking right away if remembered within an hour or so; if remembered later, not taking at all; not doubling doses

» Proper storage

For anticonvulsant use of clonazepam, clorazepate, diazepam, or nitrazepam

» Compliance with therapy; not missing any doses

For flurazepam only

» Maximum effectiveness of medication may not occur for 2 or 3 nights after initiation of therapy

Precautions while using this medication

Regular visits to physician to check progress during prolonged therapy (and during initial therapy with clonazepam)

Checking with physician before discontinuing medication after prolonged use; gradual dosage reduction may be necessary to avoid the possibility of withdrawal symptoms and, in patients with epilepsy or history of seizures, the possibility of precipitating seizures

» Avoiding use of alcohol or other CNS depressants during therapy

» Suspected overdose: Getting emergency help at once

Caution if any laboratory tests required; possible interference with results of metyrapone test

» Caution if drowsiness, dizziness, lightheadedness, or clumsiness or unsteadiness occurs, especially in the elderly

For anticonvulsant use of clonazepam, clorazepate, diazepam, or nitrazepam

Carrying medical identification card or bracelet during therapy

Side/adverse effects

Signs of potential side effects, especially allergic reaction, blood dyscrasias, CNS effects, extrapyramidal symptoms, hepatic dysfunction, muscle weakness, and paradoxical reaction

Most of side/adverse effects more likely to occur in children, especially the very young, and in elderly patients; these patients are usually more sensitive to effects of benzodiazepines

For patients receiving chlordiazepoxide, diazepam, or lorazepam injection: Checking with physician if redness, swelling, or pain at injection site occurs

General Dosing Information

Geriatric or debilitated patients, children, or patients with hepatic or renal function impairment or low serum albumin should receive decreased initial dosage since elimination of benzodiazepines, especially those with long half-lives, may be decreased in these patients, resulting in increased CNS side effects such as oversedation, dizziness, or impaired coordination.

Benzodiazepines may suppress respiration, especially in the elderly, the very ill, the very young, and patients with limited pulmonary reserve. Lower doses may be required for these patients.

Optimal dosage of benzodiazepines varies with diagnosis and patient response. Individual dosage adjustments are important. The minimum effective dose should be used for the shortest period, with the need for continuing therapy with benzodiazepines reviewed regularly.

Prolonged use and/or larger than usual therapeutic doses of benzodiazepines may result in psychological or physical dependence. The risk of dependence among panic disorder patients taking higher doses of alprazolam (> 4 mg a day) may be greater than among patients taking lower doses for less severe anxiety. Similarly, rebound and withdrawal symptoms may also be more likely to occur in patients taking alprazolam at higher doses and for longer periods (> 8 to 12 weeks).

Following prolonged administration, benzodiazepines should be withdrawn gradually to lessen the possibility of precipitating withdrawal symptoms.

Depressed patients with suicidal tendencies, particularly those who use alcohol excessively, should not have access to large quantities of benzodiazepines.

For parenteral dosage forms only

Following administration of parenteral dosage forms, patients should be kept under observation for a period of 3 to 8 hours or longer, based on the patient's clinical response and rate of recovery.

Too rapid intravenous administration may result in apnea, hypotension, bradycardia, or cardiac or respiratory arrest.

Inadvertent intra-arterial injection of benzodiazepines may produce arteriospasm, resulting in gangrene.

When parenteral benzodiazepines are to be administered intravenously, equipment necessary to maintain a patent airway should be immediately available.

For treatment of dependence

There are no comparative studies to date documenting superiority of any one withdrawal schedule. Some clinicians substitute a long-acting benzodiazepine for short-acting agents before withdrawal is attempted.

Benzodiazepines should be tapered gradually. Withdrawal schedules ranging from 4 to 16 weeks are usually suggested; however, some practitioners believe withdrawal should be completed within 2 weeks, thus exposing patients to withdrawal symptoms for a shorter length of time.

ALPRAZOLAM

Summary of Differences

Category: In addition to being indicated as an antianxiety agent, used as an antipanic agent.

Indications: Also indicated for adjunctive management of anxiety associated with mental depression.

Pharmacology:

Short to intermediate half-life benzodiazepine.

Accumulation is minimal during repeated dosing.

Steady-state plasma concentration usually attained within a few (2 to 3) days.

Elimination rapid following discontinuation of therapy.

Precautions:

Drug interactions and/or related problems—Elevation of steady-state plasma concentrations of imipramine and desipramine reported with concurrent use of alprazolam.

Contraindications/Medical problems—Episodes of hypomania and mania reported with use of alprazolam in patients with mental depression.

Additional Dosing Information

See also *General Dosing Information*.

Dosage should be reduced gradually when therapy is discontinued or the daily dosage is decreased. It is suggested that the daily dosage be decreased by no more than 500 mcg (0.5 mg) every 3 days. However, some patients may need a slower reduction in dosage.

The occurrence of early morning anxiety or the emergence of anxiety symptoms between doses of alprazolam in panic disorder patients may reflect the development of tolerance, or a time interval between doses that exceeds the duration of clinical action of the administered dose. The manufacturer states that when these effects occur, the prescribed dose is presumed to be insufficient to maintain plasma levels above those needed to prevent relapse, rebound, or withdrawal symptoms over the course of the interdosing interval; they recommend that the same total daily dose be administered in more frequently divided doses.

Oral Dosage Forms

ALPRAZOLAM TABLETS USP

Usual adult dose:

Antianxiety agent—Oral, initially 250 to 500 mcg (0.25 to 0.5 mg) three times a day, the dosage being titrated to the needs of the patient up to a maximum total dose of 4 mg per day.

Antipanic agent[1]—Oral, 500 mcg (0.5 mg) three times a day initially, the dosage being increased as needed and tolerated up to a maximum of 10 mg per day.

Note: Debilitated patients—Antianxiety agent: Oral, initially 250 mcg (0.25 mg) two or three times a day, the dosage being increased as needed and tolerated.

Usual geriatric dose: Antianxiety agent—Oral, initially 250 mcg (0.25 mg) two or three times a day, the dosage being increased as needed and tolerated.

Auxiliary labeling:
- Avoid alcoholic beverages.
- May cause drowsiness.

---

[1]Not included in Canadian product labeling.

BROMAZEPAM

Summary of Differences

Category: Indicated only as an antianxiety agent.
Pharmacology:
Short to intermediate half-life benzodiazepine.
Accumulation is minimal during repeated dosing.
Steady-state plasma concentration usually attained within a few (2 to 3) days.
Elimination rapid following discontinuation of therapy.

Oral Dosage Forms

BROMAZEPAM TABLETS

Usual adult dose: Antianxiety agent—Oral, 6 to 30 mg per day in divided doses.

Note: Doses up to 60 mg may be used in severe cases.
Debilitated patients—Initial daily dose should not exceed 3 mg in divided doses, the dosage being carefully adjusted as needed and tolerated.

Usual geriatric dose: Antianxiety agent—Oral, up to 3 mg initially, the dosage being carefully adjusted as needed and tolerated.

Auxiliary labeling:
- Avoid alcoholic beverages.
- May cause drowsiness.

CHLORDIAZEPOXIDE

Summary of Differences

Category: In addition to being indicated as an antianxiety agent and a sedative-hypnotic, oral chlordiazepoxide is used as an antitremor agent and parenteral chlordiazepoxide is used as an antipanic agent.
Indications:
Also indicated for relief of acute alcohol withdrawal symptoms and as a preoperative medication.
Also used in treatment of tension headache.
Pharmacology:
Absorption of intramuscular chlordiazepoxide may be slow and erratic.
Long half-life benzodiazepine.
Accumulation of chlordiazepoxide and its active metabolites is significant during repeated dosing.
Steady-state plasma concentration usually attained in 5 days to 2 weeks.
Elimination slow since metabolites remain in blood for several days or even weeks.
Precautions:
Drug interactions and/or related problems—
Antacids may delay the rate of but not reduce the extent of absorption of chlordiazepoxide.
Contraindications/Medical problems—
Hypoalbuminemia may predispose patient to an increased incidence of sedative side effects.
Porphyria may be exacerbated by use of chlordiazepoxide.
Side/adverse effects: Intravenous chlordiazepoxide less likely to cause phlebitis or venous thrombosis than diazepam or lorazepam.

Additional Dosing Information

See also *General Dosing Information*.

For parenteral dosage forms only:
- Intravenous administration of chlordiazepoxide is usually preferred, since absorption may be slow and erratic following intramuscular administration.
- If intramuscular injections are used, they should be administered deeply into the muscle.
- Intravenous administration of the intramuscular preparation is not recommended by the manufacturer because of the air bubbles that may form when the intramuscular diluent is added to the chlordiazepoxide hydrochloride powder.
- Intravenous injections should be administered slowly over a 1-minute period.
- The chlordiazepoxide hydrochloride solution prepared with 0.9% sodium chloride injection or sterile water for injection should not be administered intramuscularly because of pain on injection.

Oral Dosage Forms

CHLORDIAZEPOXIDE TABLETS USP

Usual adult dose:

Antianxiety agent—Oral, 5 to 25 mg three or four times a day.
Sedative-hypnotic—Alcohol withdrawal: Oral, 50 to 100 mg initially, repeated as needed, up to 400 mg per day, the dosage then reduced to maintenance levels.

Note: Debilitated patients—Antianxiety agent: Oral, 5 mg two to four times a day, the dosage being increased gradually as needed and tolerated.

Usual geriatric dose: Antianxiety agent—Oral, 5 mg two to four times a day, the dosage being increased gradually as needed and tolerated.

Auxiliary labeling:
- Avoid alcoholic beverages.
- May cause drowsiness.

CHLORDIAZEPOXIDE HYDROCHLORIDE CAPSULES USP

Usual adult dose:
Antianxiety agent—Oral, 5 to 25 mg three or four times a day.
Sedative-hypnotic—Alcohol withdrawal: Oral, 50 to 100 mg initially, repeated as needed, up to 400 mg per day, the dosage then reduced to maintenance levels.
Note: Debilitated patients—Antianxiety agent: Oral, 5 mg two to four times a day, the dosage being increased gradually as needed and tolerated.

Usual geriatric dose: Antianxiety agent—Oral, 5 mg two to four times a day, the dosage being increased gradually as needed and tolerated.

Auxiliary labeling:
- Avoid alcoholic beverages.
- May cause drowsiness.

Parenteral Dosage Forms

Note: Bracketed uses in the *Dosage Forms* section refer to categories of use and/or indications that are not included in U.S. product labeling.

STERILE CHLORDIAZEPOXIDE HYDROCHLORIDE USP

Usual adult dose:
Antianxiety agent—Intramuscular or intravenous, 50 to 100 mg initially, then 25 to 50 mg three or four times a day, if necessary.
Preoperative: Intramuscular, 50 to 100 mg one hour prior to surgery.
Sedative-hypnotic—Alcohol withdrawal: Intramuscular or intravenous, 50 to 100 mg initially, repeated in two to four hours, if necessary.
[Antipanic agent]—Intramuscular or intravenous, 50 to 100 mg initially, repeated in four to six hours if necessary.
Note: Debilitated patients—Intramuscular or intravenous, 25 to 50 mg per dose.

Usual adult prescribing limits: Up to 300 mg daily.

Usual geriatric dose: Antianxiety agent; sedative-hypnotic—Intramuscular or intravenous, 25 to 50 mg per dose.

CLONAZEPAM

Summary of Differences

Category: In addition to being indicated as an anticonvulsant, used as an antipanic agent.
Pharmacology:
Intermediate half-life benzodiazepine.
Precautions:
Pregnancy—Increased incidence of congenital abnormalities in children whose mothers used anticonvulsants during pregnancy; studies in animals have shown that clonazepam caused a non-dose-related incidence of cleft palates, open eyelids, fused sternebrae, and limb defects; withdrawal of clonazepam prior to or during pregnancy should be considered only when seizures mild and infrequent in absence of medication and the possibility of status epilepticus and withdrawal symptoms considered low.
Pediatrics—Long-term use of clonazepam may cause possible adverse effects on physical or mental development which may not become apparent for many years.
Containdications/Medical problems—
Initiation or abrupt withdrawal of clonazepam in patients with epilepsy or a history of seizures may precipitate seizures or status epilepticus.
Caution should be used in surgical or non-ambulatory patients because of cough suppressant effects of clonazepam.

Additional Dosing Information

See also *General Dosing Information.*

Dosage must be adjusted to meet the individual requirements of each patient, based on clinical response.

Since tolerance to clonazepam may develop after a few (often within 3) months of therapy, dosage adjustment may be necessary to restore efficacy of clonazepam.

In order to maintain seizure control, when clonazepam is used to replace other anticonvulsant therapy, the dosage of clonazepam should be gradually increased while the dosage of the other medication is gradually decreased; when clonazepam is used to supplement other anticonvulsant therapy, the dosage of clonazepam should be gradually increased until seizure activity is adequately controlled and then the dosage of the other medication may be gradually decreased if necessary.

Also, clonazepam should be withdrawn gradually, especially in those patients on long-term, high-dose therapy, since abrupt withdrawal may precipitate seizures or status epilepticus. During withdrawal of clonazepam, the simultaneous administration of another anticonvulsant may be indicated.

Oral Dosage Forms

CLONAZEPAM TABLETS USP

Usual adult dose: Anticonvulsant—Oral, initially 500 mcg (0.5 mg) three times a day, the dosage being increased in increments of 500 mcg (0.5 mg) to 1 mg every three days until seizures are controlled or until side effects prevent any further increase.
Note: Maintenance dose must be individualized, depending on patient's response.

Usual adult prescribing limits: Up to 20 mg daily.

Auxiliary labeling:
- Avoid alcoholic beverages.
- May cause drowsiness.

CLORAZEPATE

Summary of Differences

Category: In addition to being indicated as an antianxiety agent and a sedative-hypnotic, indicated as an anticonvulsant.
Indications: Also indicated for relief of acute alcohol withdrawal symptoms.
Pharmacology:
Orally, one of most rapidly absorbed benzodiazepines.
Long half-life benzodiazepine.
Accumulation of active metabolites is significant during repeated dosing.
Steady-state plasma concentration usually attained in 5 days to 2 weeks.

Elimination slow since metabolites remain in blood for several days or even weeks.

Precautions: Drug interactions and/or related problems—Antacids may decrease rate of conversion to desmethyldiazepam but do not affect degree of absorption.

Additional Dosing Information

See also *General Dosing Information*.

When used for alcohol withdrawal, excessive reductions in the total amount of medication administered on successive days should be avoided.

Oral Dosage Forms

CLORAZEPATE DIPOTASSIUM CAPSULES

Usual adult and adolescent dose:
Antianxiety agent—Oral, 7.5 to 15 mg two to four times a day; or 15 mg initially, as a single dose at bedtime, the dosage being adjusted as needed and tolerated.

Sedative-hypnotic—Alcohol withdrawal: Oral, 30 mg initially, followed by 15 mg two to four times a day the first day; 15 mg three to six times a day the second day; 7.5 to 15 mg three times a day the third day; 7.5 mg two to four times a day the fourth day; and thereafter, 3.75 mg two to four times a day.

Anticonvulsant[1]—Oral, initially up to 7.5 mg three times a day, the dosage being increased by no more than 7.5 mg per week, not to exceed 90 mg per day.

Note: Debilitated patients—Antianxiety agent: Oral, initially, 3.75 to 15 mg per day, the dosage being increased gradually as needed and tolerated.

Usual adult prescribing limits: Up to 90 mg daily.

Usual geriatric dose: Antianxiety agent—Oral, initially, 3.75 to 15 mg per day, the dosage being increased gradually as needed and tolerated.

Auxiliary labeling:
• Avoid alcoholic beverages.
• May cause drowsiness.

CLORAZEPATE DIPOTASSIUM TABLETS

Usual adult and adolescent dose:
Antianxiety agent—Oral, 7.5 to 15 mg two to four times a day; or 15 mg initially, as a single dose at bedtime, the dosage being adjusted as needed and tolerated; or 11.25 to 22.5 mg as a single dose every twenty-four hours.

Sedative-hypnotic—Alcohol withdrawal: Oral, 30 mg initially, followed by 15 mg two to four times a day the first day; 15 mg three to six times a day the second day; 7.5 to 15 mg three times a day the third day; 7.5 mg two to four times a day the fourth day; and thereafter, 3.75 mg two to four times a day.

Anticonvulsant—Oral, initially up to 7.5 mg three times a day, the dosage being increased by no more than 7.5 mg per week, not to exceed 90 mg per day.

Note: Debilitated patients—Antianxiety agent: Oral, initially, 3.75 to 15 mg per day, the dosage being increased gradually as needed and tolerated.

Usual adult prescribing limits: See *Clorazepate Dipotassium Capsules*.

Usual geriatric dose: See *Clorazepate Dipotassium Capsules*.

Auxiliary labeling:
• Avoid alcoholic beverages.
• May cause drowsiness.

[1]Not included in Canadian product labeling.

DIAZEPAM

Summary of Differences

Category:
In addition to being indicated as an antianxiety agent and a sedative-hypnotic, indicated as an anticonvulsant and a skeletal muscle relaxant adjunct and used as an antipanic agent.
Parenteral diazepam also indicated as an amnestic.
Oral diazepam also used as an antitremor agent.

Indications:
Also indicated for relief of acute alcohol withdrawal symptoms, for the treatment of status epilepticus, and as a preoperative medication.
Parenteral diazepam also indicated as an adjunct prior to endoscopic procedures; indicated prior to cardioversion; and used in dentistry to produce conscious sedation.
Also used to relieve spasms of facial muscles associated with problems of occlusion and temporomandibular joint disorders, and for the treatment of tension headache.

Pharmacology:
Orally, the most rapidly absorbed benzodiazepine.
Absorption of intramuscular diazepam may be slow and erratic, depending upon administration site; usually rapid and complete when injected into the deltoid muscle.
Absorption of rectal diazepam solution is rapid.
Long half-life benzodiazepine.
Accumulation of diazepam and its active metabolites is significant during repeated dosing.
Steady-state plasma concentration usually attained in 5 days to 2 weeks.
Elimination slow since metabolites remain in blood for several days or even weeks.

Precautions:
Pregnancy—Administration (especially intramuscular or intravenous) in doses of more than 30 mg within 15 hours before delivery may cause apnea, hypotonia, hypothermia, a reluctance to feed, and impaired metabolic response to cold stress in the neonate.
Drug interactions and/or related problems—
Antacids may delay but not reduce the absorption of diazepam.
Premedication with diazepam may decrease dose of a fentanyl derivative required for induction of anesthesia and decrease time to loss of consciousness with induction doses.
Isoniazid may inhibit elimination of diazepam, resulting in increased plasma concentrations.
Rifampin may enhance elimination of diazepam, resulting in decreased plasma concentrations.
Contraindications/Medical problems—
Initiation or abrupt withdrawal of diazepam in patients with epilepsy or a history of seizures may precipitate seizures or status epilepticus. Use of intravenous diazepam for absence status or Lennox-Gastaut syndrome status may precipitate tonic status epilepticus.
Hypoalbuminemia may predispose patient to increased incidence of sedative side effects.

Side/adverse effects: Intravenous diazepam more likely to cause phlebitis or venous thrombosis than chlordiazepoxide and lorazepam.

Additional Dosing Information

See also *General Dosing Information*.

For oral dosage forms only:
• When diazepam is used as an adjunct in treating convulsive disorders, the possibility of an increase in the frequency and/or severity of generalized tonic-clonic (grand mal) seizures may require an increase in dosage of standard anticonvulsant medication. Also, abrupt withdrawal of diazepam may result in a temporary increase in the frequency and/or severity of seizures.

For parenteral dosage forms only:

- Intravenous administration of diazepam is usually preferred, since absorption may be slow and erratic following intramuscular administration depending upon site of injection.
- If intramuscular injections of diazepam (with the exception of sterile diazepam emulsion) are used, they should be administered deeply into the deltoid muscle.
- For intravenous injections of diazepam (with the exception of sterile diazepam emulsion), small veins such as those on the back of the hand or wrist should not be used. Care should be taken with all parenteral forms of diazepam to avoid intra-arterial administration or extravasation in order to reduce the possibility of venous thrombosis, phlebitis, local irritation, swelling, and, rarely, vascular impairment.
- For intravenous injections, the solutions should be injected slowly, into a large vein, at least one minute being taken for each 5 mg (1 mL) of medication given.
- When subsequent doses are administered within 1 to 4 hours, consideration should be given to the possibility that active metabolites may still be present from the initial dose.
- Continuous intravenous infusion of diazepam is not recommended because of the possibility of precipitation of diazepam in intravenous fluids and adsorption of the medication to the plastic of infusion bags and tubing.
- If diazepam cannot be administered by direct intravenous injection, it may be injected slowly through an infusion tubing as close as possible to the insertion point.
- When parenteral diazepam is used for peroral endoscopic procedures, the use of a topical anesthetic and availability of necessary countermeasures are recommended since an increase in cough reflex and laryngospasm may occur.

Oral Dosage Forms

DIAZEPAM EXTENDED-RELEASE CAPSULES USP

Usual adult dose:
　Antianxiety agent—Oral, 15 or 30 mg once a day.
　Skeletal muscle relaxant adjunct—Oral, 15 or 30 mg once a day.

Note: Geriatric or debilitated patients—Use is recommended only when it has been determined that 5 mg of diazepam three times a day is the optimal daily dose; then, one 15-mg capsule per day may be used.

Auxiliary labeling:
- Swallow capsules whole.
- Avoid alcoholic beverages.
- May cause drowsiness.

DIAZEPAM ORAL SOLUTION

Usual adult dose:
　Antianxiety agent—Oral, 2 to 10 mg two to four times a day.
　Sedative-hypnotic—Alcohol withdrawal: Oral, 10 mg three or four times a day during the first twenty-four hours, the dosage being decreased to 5 mg three or four times a day as needed.
　Anticonvulsant—Oral, 2 to 10 mg two to four times a day.
　Skeletal muscle relaxant adjunct—Oral, 2 to 10 mg three or four times a day.

Note: Debilitated patients—Oral, 2 to 2.5 mg one or two times a day, the dosage being increased gradually as needed and tolerated.

Usual geriatric dose: Antianxiety agent; sedative-hypnotic; anticonvulsant; skeletal muscle relaxant adjunct—Oral, 2 to 2.5 mg one or two times a day, the dosage being increased gradually as needed and tolerated.

Auxiliary labeling:
- Avoid alcoholic beverages.
- May cause drowsiness.

DIAZEPAM TABLETS USP

Usual adult dose:
　See *Diazepam Oral Solution.*

Usual geriatric dose: See *Diazepam Oral Solution.*

Auxiliary labeling:
- Avoid alcoholic beverages.
- May cause drowsiness.

Parenteral Dosage Forms

DIAZEPAM INJECTION USP

Usual adult dose:
　Antianxiety agent—
　　Preoperative medication: Dosage must be individualized; however, as a general guideline—Intramuscular or intravenous, 5 to 10 mg prior to surgery.
　　Psychoneurotic reactions: Intramuscular or intravenous, 2 to 10 mg, the dosage being repeated in three or four hours, if necessary.
　Sedative-hypnotic—Alcohol withdrawal: Intramuscular or intravenous, 10 mg initially, followed by 5 to 10 mg in three or four hours, if necessary.
　Amnestic—
　　Cardioversion: Intravenous, 5 to 15 mg five to ten minutes prior to the procedure.
　　Endoscopic procedures:
　　　Intravenous (preferred route), up to 20 mg, the dosage being titrated to give the desired sedative response and administered immediately prior to the procedure.
　　　Intramuscular, 5 to 10 mg approximately thirty minutes prior to the procedure.
　Anticonvulsant—Status epilepticus and severe recurrent convulsive seizures: Intravenous, 5 to 10 mg initially, the dosage being repeated, if necessary, at ten- to fifteen-minute intervals up to a maximum dose of 30 mg. If necessary, therapy may be repeated in two to four hours.

Note: The intravenous route of administration is preferred; however, if intravenous administration is impossible, the intramuscular route of administration may be used.

Some clinicians have used continuous intravenous infusions of diazepam in the treatment of selected patients with status epilepticus refractory to initial treatment. However, this method of administration is problematic due to inherent adsorption problems with plastic infusion bags and tubing.

　Skeletal muscle relaxant adjunct—Muscle spasm: Intramuscular or intravenous, 5 to 10 mg initially, the dosage being repeated in three or four hours, if necessary. For tetanus, larger doses may be required.

Note: Debilitated patients—Intramuscular or intravenous, initially 2 to 5 mg per dose, the dosage being increased gradually as needed and tolerated.

Usual geriatric dose: Antianxiety agent; sedative-hypnotic; amnestic; anticonvulsant; skeletal muscle relaxant adjunct—Intramuscular or intravenous, initially 2 to 5 mg per dose, the dosage being increased gradually as needed and tolerated.

STERILE DIAZEPAM EMULSION

Usual adult dose:
　Antianxiety agent—
　　Preoperative medication: Dosage must be individualized; however, as a general guideline—Intramuscular or intravenous, 10 mg one to two hours prior to surgery.
　　Psychoneurotic reactions: Intramuscular or intravenous, 2 to 10 mg, the dosage being repeated in three or four hours, if necessary.

Sedative-hypnotic—Alcohol withdrawal: Intramuscular or intravenous, 10 mg initially, followed by 5 to 10 mg in three or four hours, if necessary.

Amnestic—
  Cardioversion: Intravenous, 5 to 15 mg ten to twenty minutes prior to the procedure.
  Endoscopic procedures: Intramuscular or intravenous, 5 to 10 mg about thirty minutes prior to procedure.

Skeletal muscle relaxant adjunct—Muscle spasm: Intramuscular or intravenous, 5 to 10 mg initially, the dosage being repeated in three or four hours, if necessary.

Note: Debilitated patients—Intramuscular or intravenous, initially 2 to 5 mg per dose, the dosage being increased gradually as needed and tolerated.

Usual geriatric dose: Antianxiety agent; sedative-hypnotic; amnestic; skeletal muscle relaxant adjunct—Intramuscular or intravenous, initially 2 to 5 mg per dose, the dosage being increased gradually as needed and tolerated.

Additional information: For administration of sterile diazepam emulsion, polyethylene-lined or glass infusion sets and polyethylene/polypropylene plastic syringes are recommended; infusion sets containing polyvinyl chloride should not be used.

Rectal Dosage Forms

DIAZEPAM FOR RECTAL SOLUTION

Usual adult and adolescent dose: Anticonvulsant—Status epilepticus and severe recurrent convulsive seizures: Rectal, 150 to 500 mcg (0.15 to 0.5 mg) of diazepam per kg of body weight, up to a maximum of 20 mg per dose.

Usual geriatric dose: Rectal, 200 to 300 mcg (0.2 to 0.3 mg) of diazepam per kg of body weight.

ESTAZOLAM

Summary of Differences

Category: Indicated only as a sedative-hypnotic.
Indications: May be useful in prevention or treatment of transient insomnia associated with sudden sleep schedule changes.
Pharmacology:
  Intermediate half-life benzodiazepine.
  Small degree of accumulation during repeated dosing.
  Steady-state plasma concentration usually attained within a few days.
  Intermediate rate of elimination following discontinuation of therapy.

Oral Dosage Forms

ESTAZOLAM TABLETS

Usual adult dose: Sedative-hypnotic—Oral, 1 mg.

Note: A dose of 2 mg may be necessary in some patients.

Usual geriatric dose: Sedative-hypnotic—Oral, 1 mg.

Note: Small or debilitated older patients may be started at 0.5 mg initially.

Auxiliary labeling:
• Avoid alcoholic beverages.
• May cause daytime drowsiness.

FLURAZEPAM

Summary of Differences

Category: Indicated only as a sedative-hypnotic.
Pharmacology:
  Long half-life benzodiazepine.
  Accumulation of active metabolites is significant during repeated dosing.
  Steady-state plasma concentration usually attained in 7 to 10 days.
  Elimination slow since metabolites remain in blood for several days.

Additional Dosing Information

Flurazepam is increasingly effective on the second or third night of consecutive use, and for one or two nights after medication is discontinued both sleep latency and total wake time may still be decreased.

Oral Dosage Forms

FLURAZEPAM HYDROCHLORIDE CAPSULES USP

Usual adult dose: Sedative-hypnotic—Oral, 15 or 30 mg.

Note: Debilitated patients—Oral, 15 mg initially, the dosage being increased to 30 mg as needed and tolerated.

Usual geriatric dose: Sedative-hypnotic—Oral, 15 mg initially, the dosage being increased to 30 mg as needed and tolerated.

Auxiliary labeling:
• Avoid alcoholic beverages.
• May cause daytime drowsiness.

FLURAZEPAM MONOHYDROCHLORIDE TABLETS

Usual adult dose: Sedative-hypnotic—Oral, 15 or 30 mg (dihydrochloride).

Note: Debilitated patients—Oral, 15 mg (dihydrochloride) initially, the dosage being increased as needed and tolerated.

Usual geriatric dose: Sedative-hypnotic—Oral, 15 mg (dihydrochloride) initially, the dosage being increased as needed and tolerated.

Auxiliary labeling:
• Avoid alcoholic beverages.
• May cause daytime drowsiness.

HALAZEPAM

Summary of Differences

Category: Indicated only as an antianxiety agent.
Pharmacology:
  Long half-life benzodiazepine.
  Accumulation of active metabolite is significant during repeated dosing.
  Steady-state plasma concentration usually attained in 5 days to 2 weeks.
  Elimination slow since metabolite remains in blood for several days or even weeks.

Oral Dosage Forms

HALAZEPAM TABLETS USP

Usual adult dose: Antianxiety agent—Oral, 20 to 40 mg three or four times a day.

Note: Debilitated patients—Oral, 20 mg one or two times a day, the dosage being adjusted as needed and tolerated.

Usual geriatric dose: Antianxiety agent—Oral, 20 mg one or two times a day, the dosage being adjusted as needed and tolerated.

Auxiliary labeling:
- Avoid alcoholic beverages.
- May cause drowsiness.

KETAZOLAM

Summary of Differences

Category: Indicated only as an antianxiety agent.
Pharmacology:
Long half-life benzodiazepine.
Accumulation of active metabolites is significant during repeated dosing.
Steady-state plasma concentration usually attained in 7 to 10 days.
Elimination slow since metabolites remain in blood for several days.

Oral Dosage Forms

KETAZOLAM CAPSULES

Usual adult dose: Antianxiety agent—Oral, 15 mg one or two times a day, the dosage being increased in 15-mg increments as needed and tolerated.

Note: Debilitated patients—The recommended initial dose is one-half the lowest recommended initial adult dosage.

Usual geriatric dose: Antianxiety agent—Oral, 15 mg once a day, the dosage being increased in 15-mg increments as needed and tolerated.

Auxiliary labeling:
- Avoid alcoholic beverages.
- May cause drowsiness.

LORAZEPAM

Summary of Differences

Category: In addition to being indicated as an antianxiety agent and a sedative-hypnotic, lorazepam is indicated as an amnestic and used as an anticonvulsant (parenteral only), an antiemetic in cancer chemotherapy (parenteral only), an antitremor agent (oral only), and a skeletal muscle relaxant adjunct.
Indications:
Oral lorazepam also indicated for adjunctive management of anxiety associated with mental depression.
Parenteral lorazepam also indicated as a preanesthetic medication; and used as an adjunct prior to endoscopic procedures, and for the treatment of status epilepticus.
Oral and parenteral lorazepam also used for relief of acute alcohol withdrawal symptoms and for treatment of tension headache.
Pharmacology:
Absorption of intramuscular lorazepam is rapid and complete.
Short to intermediate half-life benzodiazepine.
Accumulation is minimal during repeated dosing.
Steady-state plasma concentration usually attained within a few (2 to 3) days.
Elimination rapid following discontinuation of therapy.
Precautions:
Drug interactions and/or related problems—
Cimetidine, oral estrogen-containing contraceptives, disulfiram, and erythromycin, which inhibit the oxidative metabolism of benzodiazepines, are less likely to affect lorazepam, which undergoes glucuronide conjugation.
Premedication with lorazepam may decrease dose of a fentanyl derivative required for induction of anesthesia and reduce time to loss of consciousness with induction doses.
Probenecid may impair glucuronide conjugation of lorazepam, resulting in increased effects and possibly excessive sedation.
Contraindications/Medical problems—Prolongation of elimination half-life due to hepatic function impairment may be minimal with lorazepam.
Side/adverse effects: Intravenous lorazepam more likely than chlordiazepoxide but less likely than diazepam to cause phlebitis or venous thrombosis.

Additional Dosing Information

See also *General Dosing Information.*

For sublingual tablets only:
- Do not swallow for at least 2 minutes to allow sufficient time for absorption.

For parenteral dosage forms only:
- Immediately prior to intravenous use, lorazepam must be diluted with an equal amount of a compatible diluent such as sterile water for injection, 0.9% sodium chloride injection, or 5% dextrose injection.
- Following proper dilution, the medication may be injected directly into the vein or into the tubing of an intravenous infusion.
- Intravenous injection should be made slowly and with repeated aspiration.
- The rate of the intravenous injection should not exceed 2 mg per minute.
- Intra-arterial injection and perivascular extravasation should be avoided. Intra-arterial injection may produce arteriospasm, possibly resulting in gangrene.
- When administered intramuscularly, the injection (undiluted) should be injected deeply into the muscle mass.
- When parenteral lorazepam is used for peroral endoscopic procedures, the use of topical or regional anesthesia is recommended to minimize the reflex activity associated with such procedures.
- When lorazepam is administered intravenously as premedication prior to regional or local anesthesia, potential excessive sleepiness or drowsiness may interfere with patient cooperation in determining levels of anesthesia. This is more likely to occur when doses greater than 0.05 mg per kg of body weight (mg/kg) are given and narcotic analgesics are used concomitantly with recommended doses.

Oral Dosage Forms

LORAZEPAM ORAL SOLUTION

Usual adult and adolescent dose:
Antianxiety agent—Oral, 1 to 3 mg two or three times a day.
Sedative-hypnotic—Oral, 2 to 4 mg as a single dose at bedtime.

Note: Debilitated patients—Oral, initially 1 to 2 mg per day in divided doses, the dosage being increased gradually as needed and tolerated.

Usual adult prescribing limits: Up to 10 mg per day.

Auxiliary labeling:
- Avoid alcoholic beverages.
- May cause drowsiness.

LORAZEPAM TABLETS USP

Usual adult and adolescent dose:
    Antianxiety agent—Oral, 1 to 3 mg two or three times a day.
    Sedative-hypnotic[1]—Oral, 2 to 4 mg as a single dose at bedtime.

Note: Debilitated patients—Oral, initially 500 mcg (0.5 mg) to 2 mg per day in divided doses, the dosage being increased gradually as needed and tolerated.

Usual geriatric dose: Antianxiety agent; sedative-hypnotic[1]—Oral, initially 500 mcg (0.5 mg) to 2 mg per day in divided doses, the dosage being increased gradually as needed and tolerated.

Auxiliary labeling:
- Avoid alcoholic beverages.
- May cause drowsiness.

LORAZEPAM SUBLINGUAL TABLETS

Usual adult dose: Antianxiety agent—Sublingual, 2 to 3 mg per day in divided doses, the dosage being adjusted as needed, usually not exceeding 6 mg per day.

    Note: Debilitated patients—Sublingual, initially 500 mcg (0.5 mg) per day, the dosage being gradually adjusted as necessary.

Preoperative: Sublingual, 50 mcg (0.05 mg) per kg of body weight, up to a maximum of 4 mg, one to two hours before surgery.

Usual geriatric dose: Antianxiety agent—Sublingual, initially 500 mcg (0.5 mg) per day, the dosage being gradually adjusted as necessary.

Auxiliary labeling:
- Dissolve tablets under tongue.
- Avoid alcoholic beverages.
- May cause drowsiness.

Parenteral Dosage Forms

Note: Bracketed uses in the *Dosage Forms* section refer to categories of use and/or indications that are not included in U.S. product labeling.

LORAZEPAM INJECTION USP

Usual adult dose:
    Antianxiety agent; sedative-hypnotic; amnestic—
        Intramuscular, 50 mcg (0.05 mg) per kg of body weight, up to a maximum of 4 mg. Dose should be administered at least two hours prior to surgery for optimum amnestic effect.
        Intravenous, initially 44 mcg (0.044 mg) per kg of body weight or a total dose of 2 mg, whichever is less. For greater amnestic effect, up to 50 mcg (0.05 mg) per kg of body weight, not to exceed a maximum of 4 mg, may be administered. Dose should be administered fifteen to twenty minutes prior to surgery for optimum amnestic effect.
    [Antiemetic, in cancer chemotherapy][1]—Intravenous, initially 2 mg thirty minutes before initiation of chemotherapy, followed by 2 mg every four hours as needed.
    [Status epilepticus]—Intravenous, initially 0.05 mg per kg of body weight up to a maximum of 4 mg, administered slowly. If seizures continue or recur after a ten to fifteen minute observation period, an additional dose of 0.05 mg per kg may be administered. If seizure control is not evident after another ten to fifteen minutes, other measures to control status epilepticus should be used. The total maximum dose should not exceed 8 mg of lorazepam in a twelve-hour period.

---

[1]Not included in Canadian product labeling.

NITRAZEPAM

Summary of Differences

Category: Also indicated as an anticonvulsant.
Pharmacology:
    Absorption of nitrazepam is rapid.
    Short to intermediate half-life benzodiazepine.
    Accumulation is minimal during repeated dosing.
    Steady-state plasma concentration usually attained within a few (2 to 3) days.
    Elimination rapid following discontinuation of therapy.
Precautions:
    Drug interactions and/or related problems—Cimetidine or oral estrogen-containing contraceptives may inhibit the nitro-reduction of nitrazepam, resulting in delayed elimination and prolonged elimination half-life; serum concentrations may also be increased during long-term use.
    Contraindications/Medical problems—Nitrazepam may delay cricopharyngeal relaxation, exacerbating swallowing abnormalities in children.

Oral Dosage Forms

NITRAZEPAM TABLETS

Usual adult dose: Sedative-hypnotic—Oral, 5 or 10 mg before retiring.

Note: Debilitated patients—Oral, initially 2.5 mg, the dosage being increased as needed and tolerated up to 5 mg.

Usual geriatric dose: Sedative-hypnotic—Oral, initially 2.5 mg, the dosage being increased as needed and tolerated up to 5 mg.

Auxiliary labeling:
- Avoid alcoholic beverages.
- May cause drowsiness.

OXAZEPAM

Summary of Differences

Indications: Also indicated for adjunctive management of anxiety associated with mental depression and relief of acute alcohol withdrawal symptoms.
Pharmacology:
    Orally, one of least rapidly absorbed benzodiazepines.
    Short to intermediate half-life benzodiazepine.
    Accumulation is minimal during repeated dosing.
    Steady-state plasma concentration usually attained within a few days.
    Elimination rapid following discontinuation of therapy.
Precautions:
    Drug interactions and/or related problems—
        Cimetidine, oral estrogen-containing contraceptives, disulfiram, and erythromycin, which inhibit the oxidative metabolism of benzodiazepines, are less likely to affect oxazepam, which undergoes glucuronide conjugation.
        Probenecid may impair glucuronide conjugation of oxazepam, resulting in increased effects and possibly excessive sedation.
    Contraindications/Medical problems—Prolongation of elimination half-life due to hepatic function impairment may be minimal with oxazepam.

Oral Dosage Forms

OXAZEPAM CAPSULES USP

Usual adult dose:
Antianxiety agent—Oral, 10 to 30 mg three or four times a day.
Sedative-hypnotic—Alcohol withdrawal: Oral, 15 or 30 mg three or four times a day.

Usual geriatric dose: Antianxiety agent—Oral, initially 10 mg three times a day, the dosage being increased as needed and tolerated to 15 mg three or four times a day. Alternatively, a dose of 5 mg one or two times a day has been recommended.

Auxiliary labeling:
- Avoid alcoholic beverages.
- May cause drowsiness.

OXAZEPAM TABLETS USP

Usual adult dose:
See *Oxazepam Capsules USP.*

Usual geriatric dose: See *Oxazepam Capsules USP.*

Auxiliary labeling:
- Avoid alcoholic beverages.
- May cause drowsiness.

PRAZEPAM

Summary of Differences

Category: Indicated only as an antianxiety agent.
Pharmacology:
Orally, one of least rapidly absorbed benzodiazepines.
Long half-life benzodiazepine.
Accumulation of active metabolites is significant during repeated dosing.
Steady-state plasma concentration usually attained in 5 days to 2 weeks.
Elimination slow since metabolites remain in blood for several days.

Oral Dosage Forms

PRAZEPAM CAPSULES USP

Usual adult dose: Antianxiety agent—Oral, 10 mg three times a day (range, 20 to 60 mg per day); or 20 to 40 mg at bedtime.

Note: Debilitated patients—Oral, initially 10 to 15 mg per day in divided doses, the dosage being increased gradually as needed and tolerated.

Usual geriatric dose: Antianxiety agent—Oral, initially 10 to 15 mg per day in divided doses, the dosage being increased gradually as needed and tolerated.

Auxiliary labeling:
- Avoid alcoholic beverages.
- May cause drowsiness.

PRAZEPAM TABLETS USP

Usual adult dose: See *Prazepam Capsules USP.*

Usual geriatric dose: See *Prazepam Capsules USP.*

Auxiliary labeling:
- Avoid alcoholic beverages.
- May cause drowsiness.

QUAZEPAM

Summary of Differences

Category: Indicated only as a sedative-hypnotic.
Pharmacology:
Long half-life benzodiazepine.
Accumulation of active metabolites may occur during repeated dosing.
Steady-state plasma concentrations usually attained within 7 to 13 days.
Elimination slow since metabolites remain in blood for several days.

Oral Dosage Forms

QUAZEPAM TABLETS

Usual adult dose: Sedative-hypnotic—Oral, 15 mg initially, the dose being reduced to 7.5 mg as needed.

Note: Debilitated patients—Because of increased sensitivity to benzodiazepines, it is suggested that the nightly dose be reduced after 1 or 2 nights of treatment.

Usual geriatric dose: Sedative-hypnotic—Oral, 15 mg initially, the dose being reduced to 7.5 mg after one or two nights.

Auxiliary labeling:
- Avoid alcoholic beverages.
- May cause daytime drowsiness.

TEMAZEPAM

Summary of Differences

Category: Indicated only as a sedative-hypnotic.
Indications: May be useful in prevention or treatment of transient insomnia associated with sudden sleep schedule changes.
Pharmacology:
Short to intermediate half-life benzodiazepine.
Accumulation is minimal during repeated dosing.
Steady-state plasma concentration usually attained within a few (about 3) days.
Elimination rapid following discontinuation of therapy.
Precautions:
Drug interactions and/or related problems—
Cimetidine, oral estrogen-containing contraceptives, disulfiram, and erythromycin, which inhibit the oxidative metabolism of the benzodiazepines, are less likely to affect temazepam, which undergoes glucuronide conjugation.
Probenecid may impair glucuronide conjugation of temazepam, resulting in increased effects and possibly excessive sedation.
Contraindications/Medical problems—Prolongation of elimination half-life due to hepatic function impairment may be minimal with temazepam.

Oral Dosage Forms

TEMAZEPAM CAPSULES

Usual adult dose: Sedative-hypnotic—Oral, 15 mg.

Note: In transient insomnia, 7.5 mg may be sufficient to improve sleep latency.

Debilitated patients—Oral, 7.5 mg initially, the dosage being adjusted as needed and tolerated.

Usual geriatric dose: Sedative-hypnotic—Oral, 7.5 mg initially, the dosage being adjusted as needed and tolerated.

Auxiliary labeling:
- Avoid alcoholic beverages.
- May cause daytime drowsiness.

TEMAZEPAM TABLETS

Usual adult dose: See *Temazepam Capsules.*

Usual geriatric dose: See *Temazepam Capsules.*

Auxiliary labeling:
- Avoid alcoholic beverages.
- May cause daytime drowsiness.

TRIAZOLAM

Summary of Differences

Category: Indicated only as a sedative-hypnotic.

Indications: May be useful in prevention or treatment of transient insomnia associated with sudden sleep schedule change.

Pharmacology:
Short half-life benzodiazepine.
Accumulation is minimal during repeated dosing.
Elimination rapid following discontinuation of therapy.

Precautions: Drug interactions and/or related problems—
Cimetidine and erythromycin may inhibit the hepatic metabolism of triazolam, resulting in increased plasma concentrations and delayed clearance of triazolam; dosage reductions may be necessary

Isoniazid may inhibit the elimination of triazolam, resulting in increased plasma concentrations.

Side/adverse effects: Anterograde amnesia may be more likely to occur with triazolam than with most other benzodiazepines.

Oral Dosage Forms

TRIAZOLAM TABLETS USP

Usual adult dose: Sedative-hypnotic—Oral, 125 to 250 mcg (0.125 to 0.25 mg).

Note: A dose of 500 mcg (0.5 mg) may be necessary in some patients. However, this dose should be reserved for patients who do not respond adequately to lower doses, since the risk of side effects increases with dosage increases.

Debilitated patients—Oral, 125 mcg (0.125 mg) initially, the dosage being increased as needed and tolerated.

Usual geriatric dose: Sedative-hypnotic—Oral, 125 mcg (0.125 mg) initially, the dosage being increased as needed and tolerated.

Auxiliary labeling:
- Avoid alcoholic beverages.
- May cause daytime drowsiness.

BENZONATATE   Systemic†

A commonly used *brand name* in the U.S. is *Tessalon*.

ORAL
Benzonatate Capsules USP†
In the U.S.—*Tessalon*

†Not commercially available in Canada.

Category: Antitussive.

Indications

Accepted
Cough (treatment)—Benzonatate is indicated for the symptomatic relief of nonproductive cough. It is used to provide relief of acute cough due to minor throat and bronchial irritation occurring with colds or inhaled irritants; and the cough associated with chronic diseases, such as pulmonary emphysema, bronchial asthma, pulmonary tumor, and tuberculosis.

Pharmacology

Mechanism of action/Effect: Suppresses cough through a peripheral action, anesthetizing the stretch or cough receptors of vagal afferent fibers, which are located in the respiratory passages, lungs, and pleura; also, suppresses transmission of the cough reflex by a central mechanism, at the level of the medulla.

Other actions: Local anesthetic activity when applied topically to the mucosa.

Onset of action: Usually within 15 to 20 minutes.

Duration of action: Up to 8 hours.

Precautions to Consider

Cross-sensitivity and/or related problems
Patients sensitive to tetracaine or other ester-type local anesthetics may also be sensitive to benzonatate.

Geriatrics
No information is available on the relationship of age to the effects of benzonatate in geriatric patients.

Drug interactions and/or related problems
The following drug interactions and/or related problems have been selected on the basis of their potential clinical significance (possible mechanism in parentheses where appropriate)—not necessarily inclusive:

Note: Combinations containing any of the following medications, depending on the amount present, may also interact with this medication.

Central nervous system (CNS) depression-producing medications, other
(concurrent use may potentiate the CNS depressant effects of these medications or benzonatate)

Contraindications/Medical problems
The contraindications/medical problems included have been selected on the basis of their potential clinical significance (reasons given in parentheses where appropriate)—not necessarily inclusive (» = major clinical significance).

Risk-benefit should be considered when the following medical problem exists:

Sensitivity to benzonatate

Side/Adverse Effects

The following side/adverse effects have been selected on the basis of their potential clinical significance (possible signs and symptoms in parentheses where appropriate)—not necessarily inclusive:

Those indicating need for medical attention
Symptoms of overdose
CNS stimulation (convulsions, restlessness, trembling)
Note: *CNS stimulation* may be followed by profound CNS depression.

Those indicating need for medical attention only if they continue or are bothersome
Incidence less frequent or rare
Constipation; dizziness, mild; drowsiness, mild; nausea or vomiting; skin rash; stuffy nose

Patient Consultation

In providing consultation, consider emphasizing the following selected information:

Before using this medication
» Conditions affecting use, especially:
Sensitivity to benzonatate or topical anesthetics
Use in children—Children may chew capsule resulting in numbness of mouth, tongue, and pharynx, and choking may occur

Proper use of this medication
Not chewing capsules; swallowing whole to avoid local anesthetic effect and choking
Missed dose: Taking as soon as possible; not taking if almost time for next dose; not doubling doses
» Proper storage

Precautions while using this medication
Checking with physician if cough persists after medication has been used for 7 days or if high fever, skin rash, or continuing headache is present with cough

General Dosing Information

It is recommended that the capsules not be chewed before they are swallowed. Release of benzonatate from the capsule may produce temporary local anesthesia of the oral mucosa and choking may occur.

Oral Dosage Forms

BENZONATATE CAPSULES USP

Usual adult and adolescent dose: Oral, 100 mg three times a day, as needed.

Usual adult prescribing limits: Up to 600 mg per day.

Usual geriatric dose: See *Usual adult and adolescent dose.*

Auxiliary labeling: • Do not chew.

BETA-ADRENERGIC BLOCKING AGENTS   Systemic

Some commonly used *brand names* are:

In the U.S.—
Blocadren [Timolol]
Cartrol [Carteolol]
Corgard [Nadolol]
Inderal [Propranolol]
Inderal LA [Propranolol]
Kerlone [Betaxolol]
Levatol [Penbutolol]

Lopressor [Metoprolol]
Normodyne [Labetalol]
Sectral [Acebutolol]
Tenormin [Atenolol]
Trandate [Labetalol]
Visken [Pindolol]

In Canada—
Apo-Atenolol [Atenolol]
Apo-Metoprolol
  [Metoprolol]
Apo-Metoprolol (Type L)
  [Metoprolol]
Apo-Propranolol
  [Propranolol]
Apo-Timol [Timolol]
Betaloc [Metoprolol]
Betaloc Durules
  [Metoprolol]
Blocadren [Timolol]
Corgard [Nadolol]
Detensol [Propranolol]
Inderal [Propranolol]
Inderal LA [Propranolol]
Lopresor [Metoprolol]

Lopresor SR [Metoprolol]
Monitan [Acebutolol]
Novometoprol
  [Metoprolol]
Novopranol [Propranolol]
pms Propranolol
  [Propranolol]
Sectral [Acebutolol]
Slow-Trasicor
  [Oxprenolol]
Sotacor [Sotalol]
Syn-Nadolol [Nadolol]
Syn-Pindolol [Pindolol]
Tenormin [Atenolol]
Trandate [Labetalol]
Trasicor [Oxprenolol]
Visken [Pindolol]

ACEBUTOLOL
Oral
  Acebutolol Hydrochloride Capsules†
    In the U.S.—*Sectral*
  Acebutolol Hydrochloride Tablets*
    In Canada—*Monitan; Sectral*

ATENOLOL
Oral
  Atenolol Tablets
    In the U.S.—*Tenormin*
    In Canada—*Apo-Atenolol; Tenormin*
Parenteral
  Atenolol Injection†
    In the U.S.—*Tenormin*
BETAXOLOL†
Oral
  Betaxolol Hydrochloride Tablets†
    In the U.S.—*Kerlone*
CARTEOLOL†
Oral
  Carteolol Hydrochloride Tablets†
    In the U.S.—*Cartrol*
ESMOLOL—See Esmolol (Systemic).
LABETALOL
Oral
  Labetalol Hydrochloride Tablets USP
    In the U.S.—*Normodyne; Trandate*
    In Canada—*Trandate*
Parenteral
  Labetalol Hydrochloride Injection USP
    In the U.S.—*Normodyne; Trandate*
    In Canada—*Trandate*
METOPROLOL
Oral
  Metoprolol Tartrate Tablets USP
    In the U.S.—*Lopressor*
    In Canada—*Apo-Metoprolol; Apo-Metoprolol (Type L); Betaloc; Lopresor; Novometoprol;* GENERIC
  Metoprolol Tartrate Extended-release Tablets*
    In Canada—*Betaloc Durules; Lopresor SR*

Parenteral
Metoprolol Tartrate Injection USP
In the U.S.—*Lopressor*
In Canada—*Lopresor; Betaloc*
NADOLOL
Oral
Nadolol Tablets USP
In the U.S.—*Corgard*
In Canada—*Corgard; Syn-Nadolol;* GENERIC
OXPRENOLOL*
Oral
Oxprenolol Tablets USP*
In Canada—*Trasicor*
Oxprenolol Extended-release Tablets USP*
In Canada—*Slow-Trasicor*
PENBUTOLOL†
Oral
Penbutolol Sulfate Tablets†
In the U.S.—*Levatol*
PINDOLOL
Oral
Pindolol Tablets USP
In the U.S.—*Visken*
In Canada—*Syn-Pindolol; Visken*
PROPRANOLOL
Oral
Propranolol Hydrochloride Extended-release Capsules USP
In the U.S.—*Inderal LA;* GENERIC
In Canada—*Inderal LA*
Propranolol Hydrochloride Oral Solution†
In the U.S.—GENERIC
Propranolol Hydrochloride Tablets USP
In the U.S.—*Inderal;* GENERIC
In Canada—*Apo-Propranolol; Detensol; Inderal; Novopranol; pms Propranolol;* GENERIC
Parenteral
Propranolol Hydrochloride Injection USP
In the U.S.—*Inderal;* GENERIC
In Canada—*Inderal*
SOTALOL*
Oral
Sotalol Hydrochloride Tablets*
In Canada—*Sotacor*
TIMOLOL
Oral
Timolol Maleate Tablets USP
In the U.S.—*Blocadren;* GENERIC
In Canada—*Apo-Timol; Blocadren*

---

*Not commercially available in the U.S.
†Not commercially available in Canada.

Category

Note: All of the beta-blockers have similar pharmacologic actions; however, clinical uses among specific agents may vary because of pharmacologic or pharmacokinetic differences, availability of specific testing, and/or availability of clinical-use data.

Antiadrenergic—Acebutolol; Atenolol; Betaxolol; Carteolol; Labetalol; Metoprolol; Nadolol; Oxprenolol; Penbutolol; Pindolol; Propranolol; Sotalol; Timolol.

Antianginal—Acebutolol; Atenolol; Carteolol; Labetalol; Metoprolol; Nadolol; Oxprenolol; Penbutolol; Pindolol; Propranolol; Sotalol; Timolol.

Antiarrhythmic—Acebutolol; Atenolol; Metoprolol; Nadolol; Oxprenolol; Propranolol; Sotalol; Timolol.

Antihypertensive—Acebutolol; Atenolol; Betaxolol; Carteolol; Labetalol; Metoprolol; Nadolol; Oxprenolol; Penbutolol; Pindolol; Propranolol; Sotalol; Timolol.

Hypertrophic cardiomyopathy therapy adjunct—Acebutolol; Atenolol; Metoprolol; Nadolol; Oxprenolol; Pindolol; Propranolol; Sotalol; Timolol.

Myocardial reinfarction prophylactic—Acebutolol; Atenolol; Metoprolol; Nadolol; Oxprenolol; Propranolol; Sotalol; Timolol.

Pheochromocytoma therapy adjunct—Acebutolol; Atenolol; Labetalol; Metoprolol; Nadolol; Oxprenolol; Propranolol; Sotalol; Timolol.

Vascular headache prophylactic—Atenolol; Metoprolol; Nadolol; Propranolol; Timolol.

Antitremor agent—Acebutolol; Atenolol; Metoprolol; Nadolol; Oxprenolol; Pindolol; Propranolol; Sotalol; Timolol.

Antianxiety therapy adjunct—Acebutolol; Metoprolol; Oxprenolol; Propranolol; Sotalol; Timolol.

Thyrotoxicosis therapy adjunct—Acebutolol; Atenolol; Metoprolol; Nadolol; Oxprenolol; Propranolol; Sotalol; Timolol.

Antiglaucoma agent—Timolol.

Indications

Note: Bracketed information in the *Indications* section refers to uses not included in U.S. product labeling.

See also *Table 1*, page 279.

Accepted

Angina pectoris, chronic (treatment)—[Acebutolol], atenolol, [carteolol], [labetalol][1], metoprolol, nadolol, oxprenolol[1], [penbutolol], [pindolol], propranolol, sotalol, and [timolol] are indicated in the treatment of classic angina pectoris, also referred to as "effort-associated angina."

Arrhythmias, cardiac (prophylaxis and treatment)—Propranolol is indicated in the control and correction of supraventricular arrhythmias, ventricular tachycardias, digitalis-induced tachyarrhythmias, and catecholamine-induced tachyarrhythmias during anesthesia (with extreme caution because of possible additive myocardial depression with general anesthesia). Propranolol for intravenous injection is recommended only in the treatment of cardiac arrhythmias that occur while the patient is unable to receive oral medication, or when a rapid and observable effect is desired. [Acebutolol][1], [atenolol][1], [metoprolol][1], [nadolol][1], oxprenolol[1], sotalol[1], and [timolol][1] are also used for their antiarrhythmic effects, especially in supraventricular arrhythmias and ventricular tachycardias. Acebutolol is indicated in the control and correction of premature ventricular contractions.[1]

Hypertension (treatment)—Acebutolol, atenolol, betaxolol, carteolol, labetalol, metoprolol, nadolol, oxprenolol, penbutolol, pindolol, propranolol, sotalol, and timolol are indicated in the treatment of hypertension when used alone or in combination with other antihypertensive medication.

In the 1988 Report of the Joint National Committee on Detection, Evaluation, and Treatment of High Blood Pressure, a step-like progression in choice of treatments for essential hypertension is recommended:

Nonpharmacologic management (especially sodium restriction, weight reduction and exercise, and moderation of alcohol consumption) is recommended first for some patients, including those with mild hypertension, and is recommended as an adjunct to all pharmacologic hypertensive therapy.

Initial drug therapy usually consists of a diuretic, beta-adrenergic blocking agent, calcium channel blocker, or angiotensin-converting enzyme (ACE) inhibitor. If adequate blood pressure control is not achieved and the patient is adherent to the treatment program and not experiencing significant side effects, dosage of the drug may be increased, a drug from another one of these initial classes may be added or substituted, or a second drug from a different class—centrally acting alpha-adrenergic blockers (e.g., clonidine, guanabenz, guanfacine, methyldopa), peripheral-acting adrenergic antagonists (e.g., guanadrel, guanethidine, rauwolfia alkaloids), post-synaptic alpha-1 peripheral adrenergic inhibitors (e.g., prazosin, terazosin), or vasodilators (e.g., hydralazine, minoxidil)—may be added or substituted.

If necessary, a drug from another class in the second group may be substituted or added as a third drug. If blood pressure control is still not achieved, a drug from still another class may be substituted or added as a fourth drug, or the patient may need further evaluation and/or referral.

Parenteral labetalol is indicated for treatment of severe hypertension. Intravenous metoprolol or propranolol is not recommended for the management of hypertensive emergencies. Intravenous propranolol has proven useful, however, in controlling hypertension during anesthesia and surgery.

Cardiomyopathy, hypertrophic (treatment)—[Acebutolol][1], [atenolol][1], [metoprolol][1], [nadolol][1], oxprenolol[1], [pindolol][1], propranolol, sotalol[1], and [timolol][1] are indicated in the management of angina, palpitations, and syncope associated with hypertrophic subaortic stenosis.

Myocardial reinfarction (prophylaxis)—[Acebutolol][1], atenolol[1], metoprolol, [nadolol][1], oxprenolol[1], propranolol, sotalol[1], and timolol are indicated in clinically stable patients recovering from an initial definite or suspected acute myocardial infarction in order to reduce cardiac mortality and to decrease incidence of reinfarction.

Pheochromocytoma (treatment adjunct)—Propranolol is indicated in the management of symptoms of tachycardia due to excessive beta-receptor stimulation in pheochromocytoma only after primary treatment with an alpha-adrenergic blocking agent (since use without concomitant alpha-blockade could lead to serious blood pressure elevation). [Acebutolol][1], [atenolol][1], [labetalol (with caution)][1], [metoprolol][1], [nadolol][1], oxprenolol[1], sotalol[1], and [timolol][1] may also be used.

Headache, vascular (prophylaxis)—Propranolol and timolol are indicated for reducing frequency and severity of migraine headaches, but are not recommended for treatment of acute attacks. [Atenolol][1], [metoprolol][1], and [nadolol][1] are also useful for prophylaxis of migraine. A beta-blocker is the drug of choice for vascular headache prophylaxis.

Tremors (treatment)—Propranolol is indicated in the treatment of movement tremors such as those classed as essential, familial, and senile. This beta-adrenergic blocking agent has also been used to reduce the agitation and tremors of alcohol withdrawal. [Acebutolol][1], [atenolol][1], [metoprolol][1], [nadolol][1], oxprenolol[1], [pindolol][1], sotalol[1], and [timolol][1] may also be used to treat tremors. Propranolol is the drug of choice for treatment of essential tremor.

Anxiety (treatment adjunct)—[Propranolol][1] is used to control the physical manifestations of anxiety such as tachycardia and tremor. It is not particularly useful for chronic anxiety or panic attacks but is most useful for reducing anxiety and improving performance in specific stressful situations. [Acebutolol][1], [metoprolol][1], oxprenolol[1], sotalol[1], and [timolol][1] have also been used.

Thyrotoxicosis (treatment adjunct)—[Propranolol][1] has been effective in the short-term preoperative management of thyrotoxic crises (until thioamide therapy is effective) by reducing symptoms such as fever, tachycardia, and hyperkinesia. There is no effect on the hormone production of the thyroid. Abrupt withdrawal of beta-blocker treatment may provoke "thyroid storm." [Acebutolol][1], [atenolol][1], [metoprolol][1], [nadolol][1], oxprenolol[1], sotalol[1], and [timolol][1] are also used for thyrotoxicosis.

Mitral valve prolapse syndrome (treatment)—[Acebutolol][1], [atenolol][1], [metoprolol][1], [nadolol][1], oxprenolol[1], [pindolol][1], [propranolol][1], sotalol[1], and [timolol][1] are used in the treatment of mitral valve prolapse syndrome.

[Hypotension, controlled][1]—Parenteral labetalol is used to produce controlled hypotension during surgery to reduce bleeding into the surgical field.

[Glaucoma, open-angle (treatment)][1]—Timolol is used to lower intraocular pressure in the treatment of open-angle glaucoma.

---

[1]Not included in Canadian product labeling.

Pharmacology

See also *Table 2*, page $.

Mechanism of action/Effect: Beta-adrenergic blocking agents block the agonistic effect of the sympathetic neurotransmitters by competing for receptor binding sites. When they predominantly block the beta-1 receptors in cardiac tissue, they are said to be cardioselective. When they block both beta-1 receptors and beta-2 receptors (primarily located in tissues other than cardiac), they are said to be nonselective. In general, so-called cardioselective betablockers are relatively cardioselective—at lower doses they block beta-1 receptors only but begin to block beta-2 receptors as the dose increases.

Intrinsic sympathomimetic activity (ISA or partial agonist activity) is the ability of a beta-blocker to cause weak stimulation of beta-adrenergic receptors simultaneously with beta-blockade; however, the significance of this property has not been established. Possession of ISA may theoretically result in fewer adverse effects related to unopposed beta blockade (e.g., bradycardia, heart block, bronchoconstriction, peripheral vascular constriction), but studies have not proven clinical benefit. Pindolol exhibits the most ISA of the beta-adrenergic blocking agents currently available; carteolol, oxprenolol, and penbutolol have moderate ISA; acebutolol has mild to moderate ISA; and the other members of the group have little, if any, such activity.

Propranolol possesses moderate membrane-stabilizing (quinidine-like) activity; acebutolol, betaxolol, metoprolol, and oxprenolol have slight activity. The other beta-blockers of this group show little, if any, such activity. At one time membrane-stabilizing activity was thought to be related to the antiarrhythmic effect, but it is no longer considered to be significant because it occurs only at very high (much greater than therapeutic) doses.

Antianginal—Probably due to reduced myocardial oxygen requirements.

Antiarrhythmic—Blockade of adrenergic stimulation of cardiac pacemaker potentials. In the Vaughan Williams classification of antiarrhythmics, beta-blockers are considered to be class II agents.

Antihypertensive—Not known but possibilities include reduced cardiac output, decreased sympathetic outflow to peripheral vasculature, and inhibition of renin release by the kidneys; with labetalol, may be related to reduced peripheral vascular resistance as a result of alpha-adrenergic blockade.

Hypertrophic cardiomyopathy therapy adjunct—Reduction of elevated outflow pressure gradient, which is exacerbated by beta-receptor stimulation.

Myocardial reinfarction prophylactic—Possible reduction in severity of myocardial ischemia by decrease of myocardial oxygen requirements; postinfarction mortality may also be reduced through an antiarrhythmic action.

Vascular headache prophylactic—Unknown.

Antitremor agent—Unknown.

Antianxiety therapy adjunct—Unknown, but probably related to beta-blockade.

Thyrotoxicosis therapy adjunct—Unknown, but probably related to reduction of symptoms such as tremor, tachycardia, and elevated blood pressure caused by increased sensitivity to catecholamines.

Other actions/effects: Labetalol also has selective alpha-1-adrenergic blocking effects, which lead to vasodilation, reduced peripheral vascular resistance, and postural hypotension.

Precautions to Consider

Note: In general, because of the similarity of effect and because the cardioselectivity of beta-1 blockers is relative, the same precautions, especially drug interactions and medical problems, apply to all beta-adrenergic blocking agents.

Geriatrics

Although appropriate studies with most beta-blockers have not been performed in the geriatric population, the elderly may be less sensitive to some of the effects (especially antihypertensive effects) of beta-blockers. However, reduced metabolic and excretory capabilities in many elderly patients may lead to increased myocardial depression and require dosage reduction of beta-blockers, with the possible exception of oxprenolol; studies with betaxolol found an increased incidence of bradycardia in patients 65 years of age and older. The net effect is uncertain; dosage adjustment should be based on clinical response.

In addition, elderly patients are more likely to have age-related peripheral vascular disease, which may require caution in patients receiving beta-blockers.

The risk of beta-blocker-induced hypothermia may be increased in elderly patients.

Drug interactions and/or related problems

The following drug interactions and/or related problems have been selected on the basis of their potential clinical significance (possible mechanisms in parentheses where appropriate)—not necessarily inclusive (» = major clinical significance):

Note: Combinations containing any of the following medications, depending on the amount present, may also interact with this medication.

Information concerning interactions between beta-blockers and other medications is still limited. Therefore, some of the following potential interactions are stated for cautionary reference until additional information is available.

Anesthetics, hydrocarbon inhalation, such as:
Chloroform
Cyclopropane
Enflurane
Halothane (especially)
Isoflurane
Methoxyflurane
Trichloroethylene
(concurrent use with beta-blockers may increase the risk of myocardial depression and hypotension because beta-blockade reduces the ability of the heart to respond to beta-adrenergically mediated sympathetic reflex stimuli; if necessary to reverse the effects of beta-blockers during surgery, agonists such as dobutamine, dopamine, isoproterenol, or norepinephrine may be used but should be administered with caution. In patients scheduled for major surgery, most practitioners believe the danger of precipitating myocardial infarction by too abruptly discontinuing dosage prior to surgery exceeds that of continuing therapy and compensating for medication effects by anesthetic techniques)

(high concentrations of halothane [3% or above] or other halogenated hydrocarbon anesthetics should not be used when labetalol is used to produce controlled hypotension during anesthesia because of the risk of excessive hypotension, large reduction in cardiac output, and increase in central venous pressure)

» Antidiabetic agents, oral, or
» Insulin
(concurrent use with beta-blockers may increase risk of hypoglycemia or hyperglycemia. Beta-blockers may mask certain symptoms of developing hypoglycemia such as increases in pulse rate and blood pressure, thus complicating patient monitoring. In addition, beta-blockers may prolong the period of hypoglycemia by blocking gluconeogenesis. Dosage adjustment of hypoglycemic medication may be necessary during concurrent therapy to avoid excessive hypoglycemia. Labetalol and selective or relatively selective beta-blockers, such as acebutolol, atenolol, betaxolol, or metoprolol, usually cause fewer problems with blood glucose levels, especially at lower dosages, although they may still mask the symptoms)

Anti-inflammatory drugs, nonsteroidal (NSAIDs), especially indomethacin
(antihypertensive effects of beta-blockers may be reduced when they are used concurrently with NSAIDs, possibly as a result of inhibition of renal prostaglandin synthesis and sodium and fluid retention caused by NSAIDs)

Beta-adrenergic blocking agents, ophthalmic
(if significant systemic absorption of the ophthalmic beta-blocker occurs, concurrent use may result in an additive effect either on intraocular pressure or on systemic effects of beta-blockade)

» Calcium channel blocking agents or
» Clonidine or
Diazoxide or
» Guanabenz or
Reserpine or
Hypotension-producing medications, other with the exception of monoamine oxidase (MAO) inhibitors
(antihypertensive effects may be potentiated when these medications are used concurrently with beta-blockers; although some antihypertensive and/or diuretic combinations are frequently used for therapeutic advantage, when any hypotension-producing medication is used concurrently dosage adjustments may be necessary)

(concurrent use of oral diltiazem or verapamil with oral beta-blockers has resulted in no serious additive or adverse effects in patients free of abnormal AV conduction and depressed left ventricular function, but caution is advised when high dosages of either or both medications are used. Concurrent use of nifedipine, although usually well tolerated, may produce excessive hypotension and in rare cases may increase the possibility of congestive heart failure)

(when therapy is discontinued in patients receiving a beta-blocker and clonidine or guanabenz concurrently, the beta-blocker should be gradually discontinued several days before the clonidine or guanabenz is gradually discontinued in order to avoid clonidine- or guanabenz-withdrawal hypertensive crisis; blood pressure control may also be impaired when the two are combined)

(concurrent use of beta-blockers prevents the tachycardia produced by diazoxide but may also increase the hypotensive effects)

(concurrent use of reserpine with beta-blockers may result in additive and possibly excessive beta-adrenergic blockade; close observation is recommended since bradycardia and hypotension may occur)

Cimetidine
(concurrent use with hepatically metabolized beta-blockers increases the beta-blocker effect because of increased blood concentration resulting from inhibition of hepatic enzymes and reduced hepatic blood flow)

» Cocaine
(cocaine may inhibit the therapeutic effects of beta-adrenergic blocking agents)

(although beta-adrenergic blocking agents are recommended to reduce tachycardia, myocardial ischemia, and/or arrhythmias induced by cocaine, concurrent use of a beta-adrenergic blocking agent with cocaine may increase the risk of hypertension, excessive bradycardia, and possibly heart block, because beta-blockade may leave cocaine's alpha-adrenergic activity unopposed; the risk of these adverse effects may be decreased with labetalol because labetalol also has some alpha-adrenergic blocking activity, although its beta-adrenergic blocking activity predominates)

Estrogens
(concurrent use may decrease the antihypertensive effect of beta-blockers because estrogen-induced fluid retention may lead to increased blood pressure)

Fentanyl derivatives
(preoperative chronic use of systemic beta-adrenergic blocking agents may decrease the frequency and/or severity of hypertensive responses to surgery, especially during sternotomy and sternal spread in cardiac or coronary artery surgery; however, chronic preoperative use of systemic beta-adrenergic blocking agents may also increase the risk of initial bradycardia following induction doses of a fentanyl derivative)

Gallamine or
Metocurine or
Pancuronium or
Tubocurarine
(beta-blockers may potentiate and prolong the action of nondepolarizing neuromuscular blocking agents when used concurrently; careful postoperative monitoring of the patient may be necessary following concurrent or sequential use, especially if there is a possibility of incomplete reversal of neuromuscular blockade)

Lidocaine
(concurrent use may slow hepatic metabolism and increase the risk of lidocaine toxicity because of reduced hepatic blood flow; lidocaine dosage should be adjusted on the basis of serum lidocaine concentrations)

Molindone
(concurrent use may increase the effects of some beta-blockers by decreasing first-pass metabolism; reduction in beta-blocker dosage may be required)

» Monoamine oxidase (MAO) inhibitors, including furazolidone, pargyline, and procarbazine
(possible significant hypertension may theoretically occur up to 14 days following discontinuation of the MAO inhibitor; although sufficient clinical reports are lacking, concurrent use with beta-blockers is not recommended)

Nicotine chewing gum or
Smoking deterrents, other, or
Smoking, tobacco, cessation of
(smoking cessation may increase therapeutic effects of propranolol by decreasing metabolism, thereby increasing serum concentrations; dosage adjustments may be necessary)

Nitroglycerin
(labetalol reduces the reflex tachycardia caused by nitroglycerin and may increase the antihypertensive effect)

Phenothiazines
(concurrent use with beta-blockers results in an increased plasma concentration of each medication)

Phenytoin
(concurrent use of propranolol, and probably other beta-blockers, with intravenous phenytoin may produce additive cardiac depressant effects)

Phenoxybenzamine or
Phentolamine
(concurrent use with labetalol may result in additive alpha-adrenergic blocking effects)

» Sympathomimetics
(concurrent use of beta-blockers with sympathomimetic amines having beta-adrenergic stimulant activity may result in mutual inhibition of therapeutic effects)

(for sympathomimetic agents with both alpha- and beta-adrenergic effects [amphetamines, ephedrine, epinephrine, metaraminol, norepinephrine, phenylephrine, pseudoephedrine], beta-blockade may result in unopposed alpha-adrenergic activity with a risk of hypertension and excessive bradycardia and possible heart block; risk should be less with labetalol because of its alpha-blocking activity; beta-blockade also antagonizes the bronchodilating effect of ephedrine and epinephrine)

(for sympathomimetic agents with beta-adrenergic effects, beta-blockade may antagonize beta-1-adrenergic cardiac effects

[dobutamine, dopamine] or the beta-2-adrenergic bronchodilating effect [albuterol, ethylnorepinephrine, isoetharine, isoproterenol, metaproterenol, terbutaline] or both [isoproterenol]; use of a cardioselective beta-1-adrenergic blocker [atenolol, betaxolol, or metoprolol] or labetalol [because of its alpha-blocking activity] at low doses may prevent antagonism of the bronchodilating effect)

» Xanthines, especially aminophylline or theophylline
(concurrent use with beta-blockers may result in mutual inhibition of therapeutic effects; in addition, concurrent use of beta-blockers with the xanthines [except dyphylline] may decrease theophylline clearance, especially in patients with increased theophylline clearance induced by smoking; concurrent use requires careful monitoring)

Contraindications/Medical problems

The contraindications/medical problems included have been selected on the basis of their potential clinical significance (reasons given in parentheses where appropriate)—not necessarily inclusive (» = major clinical significance).

Note: In general, because of the similarity of effect and because the cardioselectivity of beta-1 blockers is relative, the same precautions apply to all beta-adrenergic blocking agents.

Except under special circumstances, this medication should not be used when the following medical problems exist:

For all indications
» Cardiac failure, overt, or
» Cardiogenic shock or
» Heart block, 2nd- or 3rd-degree atrioventricular (AV) block, or
» Sinus bradycardia (heart rate less than 45 beats per minute)
(risk of further myocardial depression; risk may be less with carteolol, labetalol, oxprenolol, penbutolol, and pindolol; beta-blockers may be used with extreme caution in some patients with cardiac failure [e.g., high output failure associated with thyrotoxicosis])

For use in myocardial infarction
» Hypotension—systolic blood pressure less than 100 mm Hg

Risk-benefit should be considered when the following medical problems exist:

For all beta-blockers
» Allergy, history of, or
» Asthma, bronchial, or
» Emphysema or nonallergenic bronchitis
(beta-blockers may promote bronchospasm and block the bronchodilating effect of epinephrine; cardioselective agents such as acebutolol, atenolol, betaxolol, metoprolol, or agents with ISA such as carteolol, oxprenolol, penbutolol, or pindolol are theoretically less likely to cause such effects when used at lower doses; labetalol may also have less risk of bronchoconstriction; however, caution is necessary with all beta-blockers)

(severity and duration of anaphylactic reactions to allergens and allergen immunotherapy may be increased in some patients being treated with beta-blockers; if possible, another medication should be substituted for a beta-blocker in patients on allergen immunotherapy, or allergen immunotherapy for conditions that are not life-threatening should be avoided in patients who cannot discontinue beta-blocker therapy; caution is also recommended during skin testing in patients on beta-blockers)

» Congestive heart failure
(risk of further depression of myocardial contractility; labetalol and agents with ISA such as carteolol, oxprenolol, penbutolol, pindolol, and possibly acebutolol may theoretically be associated with less risk and may be used with caution in patients who are well-compensated)

Coronary artery disease
(risk of exacerbation of angina, myocardial infarction, and dysrhythmias if therapy discontinued abruptly)

» Diabetes mellitus
(all beta-blockers may mask tachycardia associated with hypoglycemia, but not dizziness and sweating; nonselective beta-blockers promote hypoglycemia and impair peripheral circulation, while the risk is less with labetalol and cardioselective agents)

Hepatic function impairment
(relative bioavailability of beta-blockers that undergo extensive hepatic biotransformation may be increased because of decreased metabolism. Patients with impaired hepatic function may require lower doses of beta-blockers [exceptions are atenolol, betaxolol, carteolol, metoprolol (except in severe impairment), and nadolol, which require no dosage adjustment]; such reduction in dosage frequently applies to geriatric patients, many of whom have reduced hepatic function)

» Hyperthyroidism
(abrupt withdrawal of beta-blockers may intensify symptoms; beta-blockers may mask tachycardic symptoms)

» Mental depression, or history of
(may be exacerbated)

Myasthenia gravis
(beta-blockers may potentiate muscle weakness)

Pheochromocytoma
(although labetalol is used to lower blood pressure, higher-than-usual doses may be required; paradoxical hypertensive responses have been reported in a few patients; with other beta-blockers, risk of hypertension if effective alpha-blockade not achieved first)

Psoriasis
(may be exacerbated)

Renal function impairment
(impaired clearance; risk of reduced renal blood flow. Patients with impaired renal function may require reduced doses of beta-blockers [exceptions are labetalol, metoprolol, oxprenolol, penbutolol, pindolol (unless impairment is severe), propranolol, and timolol, which require no dosage adjustment]; such reduction in dosage frequently applies to geriatric patients, many of whom have reduced renal function. Specific dosage recommendations, where available, are included in the *Dosage Forms* section for the particular agent)

Sensitivity to the beta-blocker prescribed

For all beta-blockers except labetalol
Raynaud's syndrome and other peripheral vascular diseases
(beta-blockers may reduce peripheral circulation; cardioselective agents such as acebutolol, atenolol, betaxolol, metoprolol, or agents with ISA such as acebutolol, carteolol, oxprenolol, penbutolol, or pindolol are theoretically less likely to produce adverse effect)

Side/Adverse Effects

See *Table 2*, page 280.

Patient Consultation

In providing consultation, consider emphasizing the following selected information (» = major clinical significance):

Before using this medication

» Conditions affecting use, especially:
Sensitivity to the beta-blocker prescribed
Pregnancy—Risk of hypoglycemia, respiratory depression, bradycardia, and hypotension
Breast-feeding—Pass into breast milk
Use in the elderly—Increased sensitivity to effects; increased risk of beta-blocker-induced hypothermia
Use by athletes—Beta-blockers are banned and tested for in athletes by the U.S. Olympic Committee (USOC) and National Collegiate Athletic Association (NCAA)

Other medications, especially oral antidiabetic agents, insulin, calcium channel blockers, clonidine, guanabenz, cocaine, MAO inhibitors, symphathomimetics, or xanthines
Other medical problems, especially overt cardiac failure, cardiogenic shock, 2nd or 3rd degree AV block, sinus bradycardia, hypotension (when used in myocardial infarction), history of allergy, bronchial asthma, emphysema or non-allergenic bronchitis, congestive heart failure, diabetes mellitus, hyperthyroidism, or mental depression

Proper use of this medication

Proper administration of extended-release dosage forms: Swallowing whole without crushing, breaking, or chewing
Proper use of concentrated oral propranolol solution:
Measuring with calibrated dropper
Mixing with liquid or semi-solid food such as water, juices, soda or soda-like beverages, applesauce, and puddings; making sure entire dose is taken
Not storing after mixing
Checking pulse as directed (checking with physician if less than 50 beats per minute)
Getting into habit of taking at same time each day to help increase compliance

» Importance of not missing doses, especially with schedules of one dose per day
Missed dose: Taking as soon as possible; not taking at all if within 4 hours of next scheduled dose (8 hours for atenolol, betaxolol, carteolol, labetalol, nadolol, penbutolol, sotalol, or extended-release oxprenolol or propranolol); not doubling doses

» Proper storage

For use as an antihypertensive
Importance of diet; possible need for sodium restriction and/or weight reduction

» Compliance with therapy; patient may not experience symptoms of hypertension; importance of taking medication only as directed and keeping appointments with physician, even if feeling well

» Does not cure, but helps control hypertension; possible need for lifelong therapy; checking with physician before discontinuing medication; serious consequences of untreated hypertension

Precautions while using this medication

Regular visits to physician to check progress
» Checking with physician before discontinuing medication; gradual dosage reduction may be necessary
Having enough medication on hand to get through weekends, holidays, and vacations; possibly carrying second written prescription for emergency use
Carrying medical identification card during therapy
» Caution if any kind of surgery (including dental surgery) or emergency treatment is required
» Diabetics: May mask signs and symptoms of hypoglycemia or may cause decreased or sometimes increased blood glucose concentrations
» Caution when driving or doing things requiring alertness because of possible drowsiness, dizziness, or lightheadedness
Caution during exposure to cold weather because of possible increased sensitivity to cold
» Caution against overexertion in response to decreased chest pain
Caution if any laboratory tests required; possible interference with test results
Patients with allergies to foods, medications, or stinging insect venom: Possible increase in severity of allergic reactions; checking with physician immediately if severe allergic reaction occurs

For use as an antihypertensive
» Not taking other medications, especially nonprescription symphatomimetics, unless discussed with physician

For oral labetalol only

» Caution when getting up suddenly from a lying or sitting position, especially during initiation of therapy or when dosage is increased

» Caution in using alcohol, while standing for long periods or exercising, and during hot weather because of enhanced orthostatic hypotensive effects

For parenteral labetalol only

» Lying down during injection and for up to 3 hours after getting injection, then getting up gradually

Side/adverse effects

Signs of potential side effects, especially allergic reaction, back pain or joint pain, bradycardia, breathing difficulty and/or wheezing, chest pain, confusion, congestive heart failure, hallucinations, hepatotoxicity, irregular heartbeat, leukopenia, mental depression, psoriasiform eruption, reduced peripheral circulation, thrombocytopenia, and withdrawal reaction

For labetalol: Transient scalp tingling may occur, usually at beginning of treatment

General Dosing Information

Although plasma concentrations of beta-blockers can be ascertained, there is not always a predictable relationship between plasma concentration and pharmacological effects. Pharmacological effects have been observed when plasma concentrations were not discernible. Therefore, titration of dosage with measurement of heart rate and blood pressure is used to guide therapy.

In some patients, once-daily dosing is effective.

In patients scheduled for major surgery, most practitioners believe the danger of precipitating myocardial infarction by too abruptly discontinuing dosage prior to surgery exceeds that of continuing therapy and compensating for medication effects by anesthetic techniques.

Patients receiving beta-blockers who display symptoms of cardiac failure should be digitalized and/or receive a diuretic. If cardiac failure persists after adequate digitalis-diuretic therapy, the beta-blocker should be discontinued gradually.

For oral dosage forms only

When a beta-blocker must be withdrawn from established therapy (especially that of angina patients), it is recommended that the dosage be gradually reduced over a minimum of 3 days and preferably over a period of 2 weeks (for betaxolol and nadolol—usually over 2 weeks because of the long half-life). During this time the patient should avoid vigorous physical activity in order to minimize the danger of infarction or arrhythmias. If signs of withdrawal (e.g., angina) occur, beta-blocker therapy should be reinstated temporarily and then carefully withdrawn after the patient has stabilized.

It is recommended that beta-blocker therapy be withdrawn if drug-induced mental depression occurs.

Diet/Nutrition

Oral beta-blockers may be given either with food or on an empty stomach. Studies indicate that bioavailability of labetalol, propranolol, and possibly metoprolol may be enhanced by administration with food, which may slow the hepatic metabolism of the medication. Atenolol and nadolol are not affected since they do not undergo significant hepatic metabolism. Penbutolol and pindolol do not undergo significant first-pass effect and are not affected by concurrent food intake. Neither acebutolol nor oxprenolol bioavailability is affected by food intake. Betaxolol and timolol are subject to only moderate first-pass metabolism and are not affected by concurrent food intake. Concurrent food intake may slow carteolol absorption, but does not affect bioavailability.

ACEBUTOLOL

Summary of Differences

Pharmacology: Mild to moderate intrinsic sympathomimetic activity (ISA); relatively cardioselective; bioavailability significantly reduced by first-pass metabolism but effect not reduced because of active metabolite; removable by hemodialysis; low lipid solubility.

Precautions: Contraindications/medical problems—See Side/adverse effects.

Side/adverse effects: Theoretical reduced risk of bronchospasm, hypoglycemia, and peripheral vasoconstriction because of cardioselectivity. Dosage reduction necessary in hepatic function and renal function impairment.

Oral Dosage Forms

ACEBUTOLOL HYDROCHLORIDE CAPSULES

Note: Acebutolol hydrochloride capsules are not commercially available in Canada.

Usual adult dose:

Antiarrhythmic—Oral, 200 mg two times a day, the dosage being adjusted according to response.

Antihypertensive—Oral, initially 400 mg per day as a single dose or in two divided daily doses, the dosage being adjusted according to response.

Note: It is recommended that the dosage of acebutolol be reduced in patients with renal function impairment as follows:

Creatinine clearance (mL/min/1.73m^2)	% of normal dose to be given
<50	50
<25	25

Geriatric patients may have increased or decreased sensitivity to the effects of the usual adult dose.

Usual adult prescribing limits: In geriatric patients, daily doses should not exceed a total of 800 mg.

Auxiliary labeling: • Do not take other medicine without your doctor's advice.

ACEBUTOLOL HYDROCHLORIDE TABLETS

Note: Acebutolol hydrochloride tablets are not commercially available in the U.S.

Usual adult dose:

Antianginal—Oral, initially 200 mg two times a day, the dosage being adjusted according to response.

Antihypertensive—Oral, initially 400 mg per day as a single dose or in two divided daily doses, the dosage being adjusted according to response.

Antiarrhythmic—Oral, 200 mg two times a day, the dosage being adjusted according to response.

Auxiliary labeling: • Do not take other medicines without your doctor's advice.

---

[1]Not included in Canadian product labeling.

ATENOLOL

Summary of Differences

Pharmacology: Relatively cardioselective (beta-1); minimal hepatic metabolism; removable by hemodialysis; very low lipid solubility.

Precautions: Contraindications/medical problems—See Side/adverse effects.

Side/adverse effects: Theoretical reduced risk of bronchospasm, hypoglycemia, and peripheral vasoconstriction when daily dosage is in the lower range, because of cardioselectivity. Dosage reduction necessary in renal function impairment but not necessary in hepatic function impairment.

Oral Dosage Forms

ATENOLOL TABLETS

Usual adult dose:

Antianginal—Oral, initially 50 mg once a day, the dosage being increased gradually to 100 mg after one week if necessary and tolerated. Some patients may require up to 200 mg per day.

Antihypertensive—Oral, initially 25 to 50 mg once a day, the dosage being increased to 50 to 100 mg a day after two weeks if necessary and tolerated.

Myocardial reinfarction prophylactic—Oral, in patients who tolerate the full intravenous dose, initially 50 mg ten minutes after the last intravenous dose, followed by another 50 mg twelve hours later. A dose of 100 mg once a day or 50 mg two times a day may then be given for six to nine days or until discharge from the hospital.

Note: For patients with severe renal function impairment, the following maximum doses are recommended:

Creatinine clearance (mL/min/1.73m²)	Maximum dose
15–35	50 mg per day
<15	50 mg every second day

Geriatric patients may have increased or decreased sensitivity to the effects of the usual adult dose.

Auxiliary labeling: • Do not take other medicine without your doctor's advice.

Parenteral Dosage Forms

ATENOLOL INJECTION

Note: Atenolol injection is not commercially available in Canada.

Usual adult dose: Myocardial reinfarction prophylactic—Early treatment: Intravenous, 5 mg (over five minutes), the dose being repeated ten minutes later.

Note: For patients with severe renal function impairment, the following maximum doses are recommended:

Creatinine clearance (mL/min/1.73m²)	Maximum dose
15–35	50 mg per day
<15	50 mg every second day

Geriatric patients have increased or decreased sensitivity to the effects of the usual adult dose.

In patients who tolerate the full intravenous dose (10 mg), oral atenolol treatment should be initiated ten minutes after the last intravenous dose.

BETAXOLOL

Summary of Differences

Pharmacology: Relatively cardioselective; bioavailability not reduced in hepatic function impairment; not removable by hemodialysis; moderate lipid solubility.

Precautions: Contraindications/medical problems—Dosage reduction may be recommended in renal function impairment; dosage reduction not necessary in hepatic function impairment.

Oral Dosage Forms

BETAXOLOL TABLETS

Usual adult dose: Antihypertensive—Oral, 10 mg once a day initially, the dosage being doubled, if necessary, after seven to fourteen days.

Note: Geriatric patients may have increased or decreased sensitivity to the effects of the usual adult dose. An initial dose of 5 mg should be considered for elderly patients.

For patients with renal function impairment who are undergoing hemodialysis, an initial dose of 5 mg once a day is recommended, with increments of 5 mg per day every fourteen days up to a maximum daily dose of 20 mg as necessary.

Auxiliary labeling: • Do not take other medicine without your doctor's advice.

CARTEOLOL

Summary of Differences

Pharmacology: Moderate intrinsic sympathomimetic activity (ISA); nonselective; minimal hepatic metabolism (one active metabolite); low lipid solubility.

Precautions: Contraindications/medical problems—See Side/adverse effects.

Side/adverse effects: Theoretical reduced risk of bronchospasm, heart failure, and peripheral vasoconstriction because of ISA. Dosage reduction necessary in renal function impairment but not necessary in hepatic function impairment.

Oral Dosage Forms

CARTEOLOL HYDROCHLORIDE TABLETS

Note: Carteolol hydrochloride tablets are not commercially available in Canada.

Usual adult dose: Antihypertensive—Oral, initially 2.5 mg once a day, the dosage being adjusted according to response.

Note: It is recommended that the dosage interval be increased in patients with renal function impairment as follows:

Creatinine clearance (mL/min)	Dosage interval (hrs)
>60	24
20–60	48
<20	72

Geriatric patients may have increased or decreased sensitivity to the effects of the usual adult dose.

Usual adult prescribing limits: Up to 10 mg per day.

Auxiliary labeling: • Do not take other medicine without your doctor's advice.

LABETALOL

Summary of Differences

Pharmacology: Also has selective alpha-1-adrenergic blocking effects; nonselective beta-blocker; bioavailability significantly reduced by first-pass metabolism and enhanced by concurrent administration with food; not removable by hemodialysis; low lipid solubility.

Precautions: Contraindications/medical problems—See Side/adverse effects.

Side/adverse effects: Possible reduced risk of bradycardia, broncho-constriction, cardiac failure, hypoglycemia, and peripheral vasoconstriction, and increased incidence of postural hypotension. Dosage reduction necessary in hepatic function impairment but not necessary in renal function impairment.

Additional Dosing Information

See also *General Dosing Information*.

The hypotensive effect of labetalol may be especially pronounced when the patient is standing. If feasible, blood pressure readings should be taken in the supine position, after standing for 10 minutes, and immediately after exercise. Dosage increases should be made only if there has been no decrease in the standing blood pressure from previous levels.

Hospitalized patients should not be discharged until the effect of labetalol on their standing blood pressure has been determined.

Dosage reduction is indicated if the patient has excessive orthostatic fall in pressure and/or normal supine pressure.

Appropriate laboratory testing is recommended at the first sign and/or symptom of hepatotoxicity; if there is laboratory evidence of hepatotoxicity, it is recommended that labetalol be permanently withdrawn.

For parenteral dosage form

Labetalol hydrochloride injection may be administered as a direct intravenous injection (over a 2-minute period) or by continuous intravenous infusion.

When administered by continuous intravenous infusion, it is recommended that labetalol be administered by means of an infusion pump, a micro-drip regulator, or a similar device to allow precise adjustment of the flow rate.

To reduce the chance of postural hypotension, patients should remain supine for up to 3 hours after receiving parenteral labetalol. Ambulation should not be permitted until the ability of the patient to tolerate the upright position has been determined.

Oral Dosage Forms

LABETALOL HYDROCHLORIDE TABLETS USP

Usual adult dose: Antihypertensive—
Initial: Oral, 100 mg two times a day, the dosage being adjusted in increments of 100 mg two times a day every two or three days until the desired response is achieved.
Maintenance: Oral, 200 to 400 mg two times a day.

Note: Labetalol may be administered in three divided daily doses if necessary because of side effects such as nausea or dizziness.

In severe hypertension, doses of 1.2 to 2.4 grams per day, in two or three divided doses, may be needed.

Geriatric patients may have increased or decreased sensitivity to the effects of the usual adult dose.

Auxiliary labeling: • Do not take other medicines without your doctor's advice.

Parenteral Dosage Forms

LABETALOL HYDROCHLORIDE INJECTION USP

Usual adult dose: Antihypertensive—
Intravenous, 20 mg (0.25 mg per kg of body weight for an 80-kg patient) injected slowly over a two-minute period; additional injections of 40 mg and 80 mg may be given at ten-minute intervals until the desired blood pressure is achieved or a total of 300 mg has been given; or

Intravenous infusion, administered at a rate of 2 mg per minute, the dosage being adjusted according to response; the total dose necessary may range from 50 to 300 mg.

Note: Geriatric patients have increased or decreased sensitivity to the effects of the usual adult dose.

METOPROLOL

Summary of Differences

Pharmacology: Relatively cardioselective (beta-1); bioavailability significantly reduced by first-pass metabolism; not removable by hemodialysis; moderate lipid solubility.

Precautions: Contraindications/medical problems—See Side/adverse effects.

Side/adverse effects: Theoretical reduced risk of bronchospasm, hypoglycemia, and peripheral vasoconstriction when daily dosage does not exceed 200 mg, because of cardioselectivity; increased risk of central nervous system (CNS) side effects because of lipid solubility and relative ease of penetration into CNS. No dosage reduction necessary in hepatic (unless severe) or renal function impairment.

Oral Dosage Forms

Note: Bracketed uses in the *Dosage Forms* section refer to categories of use and/or indications that are not included in U.S. product labeling.

METOPROLOL TARTRATE TABLETS USP

Usual adult dose:
Antianginal; or
Antihypertensive—Oral, initially 100 mg a day in single or divided doses, the dosage being increased at one-week intervals as needed and tolerated up to a total of 450 mg a day if necessary.

Note: To maintain satisfactory blood pressure control, some patients may require division of the total daily dose into three separate doses.

Myocardial reinfarction prophylactic—
Early treatment: Oral, 50 mg every six hours starting fifteen minutes after the last intravenous dose or as soon as clinical condition allows, for patients who tolerate the full intravenous dose (a dose of 25 to 50 mg may be used for patients who do not). This dosage is continued for forty-eight hours, followed by:
Late treatment: Oral, 100 mg two times a day for at least three months and possibly for as long as one to three years.
[Vascular headache prophylactic][1]—Oral, 50 to 100 mg two to four times per day.

Note: Geriatric patients may have increased or decreased sensitivity to the effects of the usual adult dose.

Auxiliary labeling: • Do not take other medicine without your doctor's advice.

METOPROLOL TARTRATE EXTENDED-RELEASE TABLETS

Note: Metoprolol tartrate extended-release tablets are not commercially available in the U.S.

Usual adult dose:
Antianginal; or
Antihypertensive—Oral, 100 to 400 mg administered once a day for maintenance of established dosage requirements.

Note: Geriatric patients may have increased or decreased sensitivity to the effects of the usual adult dose.

Auxiliary labeling: • Do not take other medicine without your doctor's advice.

Parenteral Dosage Forms

METOPROLOL TARTRATE INJECTION USP

Usual adult dose: Myocardial reinfarction prophylactic—Early treatment: Intravenous (rapid), 5 mg every two minutes for three doses.

Note: Geriatric patients may have increased or decreased sensitivity to the effects of the usual adult dose.

NADOLOL

Summary of Differences

Pharmacology: Nonselective; not hepatically metabolized; removable by hemodialysis; low lipid solubility.

Precautions: Contraindications/medical problems—Dosage reduction or increased dosing intervals recommended in renal function impairment; dosage reduction not necessary in hepatic function impairment.

Oral Dosage Forms

Note: Bracketed uses in the *Dosage Forms* section refer to categories of use and/or indications that are not included in U.S. product labeling.

NADOLOL TABLETS USP

Usual adult dose:

Antianginal—Oral, 40 mg once a day initially, the dosage being increased by 40 to 80 mg at three- to seven-day intervals as needed and tolerated up to a total of 240 mg a day if necessary.

Antihypertensive—Oral, 40 mg once a day initially, the dosage being increased in increments of 40 to 80 mg at one-week intervals as needed and tolerated up to a total of 320 mg a day if necessary.

[Vascular headache prophylactic][1]—Oral, 20 to 40 mg once a day initially, the dosage being gradually increased as tolerated up to 120 mg per day if necessary.

Note: Because of the long half-life, once-a-day dosage is sufficient to provide stable plasma concentrations; however, such concentrations may not be achieved for up to 5 days following initiation of therapy or change of dose.

For patients with renal function impairment, the following dosage adjustments are recommended:

Creatinine clearance (mL/min/1.73m²)	Dosage interval (hours)
>50	24
31–50	24–36
10–30	24–48
<10	40–60

Geriatric patients may have increased or decreased sensitivity to the effects of the usual adult dose.

Auxiliary labeling: • Do not take other medicine without your doctor's advice.

---

[1]Not included in Canadian product labeling.

OXPRENOLOL

Summary of Differences

Pharmacology: Moderate intrinsic sympathomimetic activity (ISA); nonselective; bioavailability significantly reduced by first-pass metabolism; moderate lipid solubility.

Precautions: Contraindications/medical problems—See Side/adverse effects.

Side/adverse effects: Theoretical reduced risk of bronchospasm, heart failure, and peripheral vasoconstriction because of ISA. Dosage reduction necessary in hepatic function impairment but not necessary in renal function impairment.

Oral Dosage Forms

OXPRENOLOL TABLETS USP

Note: Oxprenolol tablets are not commercially available in the U.S.

Usual adult dose: Antihypertensive—Oral, 20 mg three times a day initially, the dosage being increased in increments of 60 mg per day every one to two weeks until the desired response is achieved.

Note: Once the optimal daily dose has been reached, twice-daily dosing may be used.

Geriatric patients may have increased or decreased sensitivity to the effects of the usual adult dose.

Usual adult prescribing limits: Up to 480 mg per day.

Auxiliary labeling: • Do not take other medicine without your doctor's advice.

OXPRENOLOL EXTENDED-RELEASE TABLETS USP

Note: Oxprenolol extended-release tablets are not commercially available in the U.S.

Usual adult dose: Antihypertensive—Oral, 80 or 160 mg administered once a day in the morning for maintenance of established dosage requirements.

Note: Geriatric patients may have increased or decreased sensitivity to the effects of the usual adult dose.

Auxiliary labeling: • Do not take other medicine without your doctor's advice.

PENBUTOLOL

Summary of Differences

Pharmacology: Moderate intrinsic sympathomimetic activity (ISA); nonselective; although hepatically metabolized, penbutolol undergoes no significant first-pass effect; not removable by hemodialysis; high lipid solubility.

Precautions: Contraindications/medical problems—See Side/adverse effects.

Side/adverse effects: Theoretical reduced risk of bronchospasm, heart failure, and peripheral vasoconstriction because of ISA. Dosage reduction necessary in hepatic function impairment but not necessary in renal function impairment.

PENBUTOLOL SULFATE TABLETS

Note: Penbutolol sulfate tablets are not commercially available in Canada.

Usual adult dose: Antihypertensive—Oral, 20 mg once a day.

Note: Geriatric patients may have increased or decreased sensitivity to the effects of the usual adult dose.

Auxiliary labeling: • Do not take other medicine without your doctor's advice.

PINDOLOL

Summary of Differences

Pharmacology: Exhibits the most intrinsic sympathomimetic activity (ISA) of beta-blockers currently available; nonselective; although hepatically metabolized, pindolol undergoes no significant first-pass effect; moderate lipid solubility.

Precautions: Contraindications/medical problems—See Side/adverse effects.

Side/adverse effects: Theoretical reduced risk of bronchospasm, heart failure, and peripheral vasoconstriction because of ISA; overdose may produce tachycardia and hypertension. Dosage reduction necessary in hepatic function and severe renal function impairment.

Oral Dosage Forms

PINDOLOL TABLETS USP

Usual adult dose: Antihypertensive—Oral, initially 5 mg two times a day, the dosage being increased in increments of 10 mg per day at two- or three-week intervals as needed and tolerated.

Note: Many hypertensive patients require a maintenance dose of only 5 mg of pindolol two times a day to provide an adequate reduction in blood pressure.

Once the optimal daily dose has been reached, once-daily dosing may be used.

Geriatric patients may have increased or decreased sensitivity to the effects of the usual adult dose.

Usual adult prescribing limits: Up to 60 mg daily.

Auxiliary labeling: • Do not take other medicine without your doctor's advice.

PROPRANOLOL

Summary of Differences

Pharmacology: Nonselective; bioavailability significantly reduced by first-pass metabolism; not removable by hemodialysis; high lipid solubility.

Precautions: Contraindications/medical problems—See Side/adverse effects.

Side/adverse effects: Increased risk of CNS side effects because of high lipid solubility and ease of penetration into CNS. Dosage reduction necessary in hepatic function impairment but not necessary in renal function impairment.

Oral Dosage Forms

Note: Bracketed uses in the *Dosage Forms* section refer to categories of use and/or indications that are not included in U.S. product labeling.

PROPRANOLOL HYDROCHLORIDE EXTENDED-RELEASE CAPSULES USP

Usual adult dose: Oral, 60 to 160 mg administered once a day for maintenance of established dosage requirements.

Note: Geriatric patients have increased or decreased sensitivity to the effects of the usual adult dose.

Auxiliary labeling: • Do not take other medicine without your doctor's advice.

PROPRANOLOL HYDROCHLORIDE ORAL SOLUTION

Note: Propranolol hydrochloride oral solution is not commercially available in Canada.

Usual adult dose:

Antianginal—Oral, 10 to 20 mg three or four times a day, the dosage being increased gradually every three to seven days up to a total of 320 mg a day if necessary (a daily dose of up to 1 gram has been used by some clinicians).

Antiarrhythmic—Oral, 10 to 30 mg three or four times a day, the dosage being adjusted as needed and tolerated.

Antihypertensive—Oral, 40 mg two times a day, the dosage being increased gradually as needed and tolerated up to a total of 640 mg a day if necessary (a total daily dose of 1 gram has been used by some clinicians).

Hypertrophic cardiomyopathy therapy adjunct—Oral, 20 to 40 mg three or four times a day, the dosage being adjusted as needed and tolerated.

Myocardial reinfarction prophylactic—Oral, 180 to 240 mg per day in divided doses.

Pheochromocytoma therapy adjunct—Oral, 20 mg three times a day to 40 mg three or four times a day (as necessary for sufficient beta-blockade) for three days prior to surgery, concomitantly with alpha-adrenergic blocking medication (should *never* be started until alpha-adrenergic blockade is at least partially established). Doses of 30 to 160 mg per day in divided daily doses have been used for management of inoperable tumor.

Vascular headache prophylactic—Oral, 20 mg four times a day initially, the dosage being increased gradually as needed and tolerated up to a total of 240 mg a day if necessary.

Antitremor agent—Oral, 40 mg three or four times a day, the dosage being adjusted as needed and tolerated.

[Antianxiety therapy adjunct][1]—Oral, 10 to 80 mg thirty to ninety minutes prior to the anxiety-provoking activity.

[Thyrotoxicosis therapy adjunct][1]—Oral, 10 to 40 mg three or four times a day, the dosage being adjusted as needed and tolerated.

Note: Twice-daily or, in some patients, once-daily dosing may be effective for use as an antianginal, antihypertensive, or myocardial infarction prophylactic.

Geriatric patients may have increased or decreased sensitivity to the effects of the usual adult dose.

Auxiliary labeling: • Do not take other medicine without your doctor's advice.

PROPRANOLOL HYDROCHLORIDE TABLETS USP

Usual adult dose:

Antianginal—Oral, 10 to 20 mg three or four times a day, the dosage being increased gradually every three to seven days up to a total of 320 mg a day if necessary (a daily dose of up to 1 gram has been used by some clinicians).

Antiarrhythmic—Oral, 10 to 30 mg three or four times a day, the dosage being adjusted as needed and tolerated.

Antihypertensive—Oral, 40 mg two times a day, the dosage being increased gradually as needed and tolerated up to a total of 640 mg a day if necessary (a total daily dose of 1 gram has been used by some clinicians).

Hypertrophic cardiomyopathy therapy adjunct—Oral, 20 to 40 mg three or four times a day, the dosage being adjusted as needed and tolerated.

Myocardial reinfarction prophylactic—Oral, 180 to 240 mg per day in divided doses.

Pheochromocytoma therapy adjunct—Oral, 20 mg three times a day to 40 mg three or four times a day (as necessary for sufficient beta-blockade) for three days prior to surgery, concomitantly with alpha-adrenergic blocking medication (should *never* be started until alpha-adrenergic blockade is at least partially established). Doses of 30 to 160 mg per day in divided daily doses have been used for management of inoperable tumor.

Vascular headache prophylactic—Oral, 20 mg four times a day initially, the dosage being increased gradually as needed and tolerated up to a total of 240 mg a day if necessary.

Antitremor agent—Oral, 40 mg three or four times a day, the dosage being adjusted as needed and tolerated.

[Antianxiety therapy adjunct][1]—Oral, 10 to 80 mg thirty to ninety minutes prior to the anxiety-provoking activity.

[Thyrotoxicosis therapy adjunct][1]—Oral, 10 to 40 mg three or four times a day, the dosage being adjusted as needed and tolerated.

Note: Twice-daily or, in some patients, once-daily dosing may be effective for use as an antianginal, antihypertensive, or myocardial infarction prophylactic.

Geriatric patients may have increased or decreased sensitivity to the effects of the usual adult dose.

Auxiliary labeling: • Do not take other medicine without your doctor's advice.

Parenteral Dosage Forms

PROPRANOLOL HYDROCHLORIDE INJECTION USP

Usual adult dose: Antiarrhythmic—Intravenous, 1 to 3 mg administered at a rate not to exceed 1 mg per minute, repeated after two minutes and again after four hours if necessary.

Note: An intravenous dose of one-tenth the oral dose may be used during surgery to temporarily replace oral dosing.

Geriatric patients may have increased or decreased sensitivity to the effects of the usual adult dose.

SOTALOL

Summary of Differences

Pharmacology: Nonselective; no intrinsic sympathomimetic activity (ISA) or membrane-stabilizing activity; low lipid solubility.

Oral Dosage Forms

SOTALOL HYDROCHLORIDE TABLETS

Note: Sotalol hydrochloride tablets are not commercially available in the U.S.

Usual adult dose:
Antianginal; or
Antihypertensive—
   Initial: Oral, 80 mg two times a day, the dosage being increased in increments of 80 mg two times a day at weekly intervals as needed and tolerated.

Maintenance: Oral, 160 mg two times a day.

Note: Once-daily dosing may be effective in patients taking a total daily maintenance dose of 320 mg or less.

Geriatric patients may have increased or decreased sensitivity to the effects of the usual adult dose.

Usual adult prescribing limits: Up to 480 mg per day.

Auxiliary labeling: • Do not take other medicines without your doctor's advice.

TIMOLOL

Summary of Differences

Pharmacology: Nonselective; no significant intrinsic sympathomimetic activity (ISA); bioavailability significantly reduced by first-pass metabolism; not removable by hemodialysis; moderate lipid solubility.

Precautions: Contraindications/medical problems—Dosage reduction necessary in hepatic function impairment but not necessary in renal function impairment.

Oral Dosage Forms

Note: Bracketed uses in the *Dosage Forms* section refer to categories of use and/or indications that are not included in U.S. product labeling.

TIMOLOL MALEATE TABLETS USP

Usual adult dose:
Antihypertensive; or
[Antianginal]—
   Initial: Oral, 10 mg two times a day initially, the dosage being increased at one-week intervals as needed and tolerated.
   Maintenance: Oral, 20 to 80 mg per day in two to four divided doses (up to 30 mg two times a day, if necessary).

Myocardial reinfarction prophylactic—Oral, 10 mg two times a day prophylactically against reinfarction in clinically stable patients. Treatment is initiated one to four weeks following initial infarction.

Vascular headache prophylactic—Oral, 10 mg two times a day initially; maintenance, 20 mg a day (may be given as a single daily dose); maximum dose is 30 mg per day (10 mg in the morning and 20 mg at night).

Note: Geriatric patients may have increased or decreased sensitivity to the effects of the usual adult dose.

Auxiliary labeling: • Do not take other medicine without your doctor's advice.

Table 1. Indications

Note: Bracketed information in the *Indications* section refers to uses that are not included in U.S. product labeling.

Legend:
I = Acebutolol
II = Atenolol
III = Betaxolol
IV = Carteolol
V = Labetalol
VI = Metoprolol
VII = Nadolol
VIII = Oxprenolol
IX = Penbutolol
X = Pindolol
XI = Propranolol
XII = Sotalol
XIII = Timolol

	I	II	III	IV	V	VI	VII	VIII	IX	X	XI	XII	XIII
Angina pectoris, chronic (treatment)	[✔]	✔		[✔]	[✔]¹	✔	✔	✔¹	[✔]	[✔]	✔	✔	[✔]
Cardiac arrhythmias (prophylaxis and treatment)	[✔]¹	[✔]¹				[✔]¹	[✔]¹	✔¹			✔	✔¹	[✔]¹
Hypertension (treatment)	✔	✔	✔	✔	✔	✔	✔	✔	✔	✔	✔	✔	✔
Cardiomyopathy, hypertrophic (treatment)	[✔]¹	[✔]¹				[✔]¹	[✔]¹	✔¹		[✔]¹	✔	✔¹	[✔]¹
Myocardial reinfarction (prophylaxis)	[✔]¹	✔¹				✔	[✔]¹	✔¹			✔	✔¹	✔
Pheochromocytoma (treatment adjunct)	[✔]¹	[✔]¹			[✔]¹	[✔]¹	[✔]¹	✔¹			✔	✔¹	[✔]¹
Headache, vascular (prophylaxis)		[✔]¹				[✔]¹	[✔]¹				✔		✔
Tremors (treatment)	[✔]¹	[✔]¹				[✔]¹	[✔]¹	✔¹		[✔]¹	✔	✔¹	[✔]¹
Anxiety (treatment adjunct)	[✔]¹					[✔]¹		✔¹		[✔]¹	✔¹	✔¹	[✔]¹
Thyrotoxicosis (treatment adjunct)	[✔]¹	[✔]¹				[✔]¹	[✔]¹	✔¹		[✔]¹	✔	✔¹	[✔]¹
Mitral valve prolapse syndrome (treatment)	[✔]¹	[✔]¹				[✔]¹	[✔]¹	✔¹		[✔]¹	[✔]¹	✔¹	[✔]¹
Hypotension, controlled					[✔]¹								
Glaucoma, open-angle (treatment)													[✔]¹

¹Not included in Canadian product labeling.

Table 2. Side/Adverse Effects*

Note: Because of their greater ability to penetrate into the nervous system, metoprolol, oxprenolol, penbutolol, pindolol, and propranolol are thought to be more often associated with side effects involving the central nervous system (CNS), although this has not been conclusively proven.

Signs and symptoms of overdose may include sudden bradycardia, hypotension, bronchospasm, cardiac failure, peripheral cyanosis, and seizures; hypoglycemia may occur rarely. In contrast, carteolol, oxprenolol, penbutolol, or pindolol overdose may result in tachycardia and hypertension because of intrinsic sympathomimetic activity (ISA). Signs of overdose usually occur within 1 to 2 hours of ingestion.

If severe hypertension is reduced too rapidly with parenteral labetalol, there is a risk of cerebral infarction, optic nerve infarction, and ischemic changes in the electrocardiogram (ECG).

Beta-blocking agents, when taken over an extended period of time, have produced cardiac failure in some patients who had no history of cardiac failure.

As shown with propranolol, the abrupt withdrawal of a beta-blocker that has been given in high dosage to angina patients and patients with atherosclerotic heart disease may result in severe adverse effects including myocardial infarction, angina, and ventricular tachycardia. Intensified symptoms of hyperthyroidism in patients with a pre-existing condition may result from abrupt discontinuation of beta-blockers.

The following side/adverse effects have been selected on the basis of their potential clinical significance (possible signs and symptoms in parentheses where appropriate)—not necessarily inclusive:

Legend:
I = Acebutolol　　IV = Carteolol　　VII = Nadolol　　X = Pindolol
II = Atenolol　　V = Labetalol　　VIII = Oxprenolol　　XI = Propranolol
III = Betaxolol　　VI = Metoprolol　　IX = Penbutolol　　XII = Sotalol
　　　　　　　　　　　　　　　　　　　　　　　　　　XIII = Timolol

	I	II	III	IV	V	VI	VII	VIII	IX	X	XI	XII	XIII
Medical attention needed													
Allergic reaction (skin rash)	L	R	L	L	R	R	L	L	U	L	L	R	R
Back pain or joint pain—may rarely be associated with elevated antinuclear antibody (ANA) titers	R	U	L	L	R	U	U	U	U	M	U	U	U
Bradycardia (slow heartbeat—especially less than 50 beats per minute)	L	L	L	R	R	L	M	L	R	R	M	M	L
Breathing difficulty and/or wheezing, especially in patients with predisposition to bronchospasm—risk theoretically reduced with acebutolol, atenolol, carteolol, labetalol, metoprolol, oxprenolol, penbutolol, or pindolol	L	L	L	L	L	L	L	L	L	L	L	L	L
Chest pain	R	R	R	R	R	R	R	R	R	R	R	R	R
Confusion, especially in elderly	U	U	U	U	U	R	U	U	U	R	L	U	U
Congestive heart failure (swelling of ankles, feet, and/or lower legs)	L	L	L	L	L	L	R	L	L	L	L	L	R
Hallucinations	U	U	R	U	U	R	R	L	U	L	L	U	R
Hepatotoxicity (usually detected on laboratory tests; rarely, dark urine, yellow eyes or skin) Note: Usually reversible, but hepatic necrosis and death have been reported with labetalol.	R	U	U	U	R	U	U	U	U	U	U	U	U
Irregular heartbeat	U	U	L	L	L	L	U	L	U	L	U	L	L

Table 2. Side/Adverse Effects* *(continued)*

Legend:
I = Acebutolol   IV = Carteolol   VII = Nadolol   X = Pindolol
II = Atenolol   V = Labetalol   VIII = Oxprenolol   XI = Propranolol
III = Betaxolol   VI = Metoprolol   IX = Penbutolol   XII = Sotalol
XIII = Timolol

	I	II	III	IV	V	VI	VII	VIII	IX	X	XI	XII	XIII
Leukopenia (fever and sore throat)	U	U	U	U	R	U	U	R	U	U	R	U	U
Mental depression—usually reversible and mild but may progress to catatonia	L	L	R	L	L	M	L	L	U	R	M	L	R
Psoriasiform eruption (red, scaling, or crusted skin)	U	U	U	U	U	U	U	U	U	U	R	U	U
Reduced peripheral circulation (cold hands and feet; theoretically reduced possibility with acebutolol, atenolol, carteolol, metoprolol, oxprenolol, penbutolol, or pindolol)	L	L	L	L	U	L	L	L	L	L	L	L	L
Thrombocytopenia (unusual bleeding and bruising)	U	U	R	U	U	U	U	R	U	U	R	U	U
Slow heartbeat or	✔	✔	✔	✔	✔	✔	✔	✔	✔	✔	✔	✔	✔
Dizziness, severe, or fainting or	✔	✔	✔	✔	✔	✔	✔	✔	✔	✔	✔	✔	✔
Fast or irregular heartbeat or								✔	✔				
Difficulty in breathing or	✔	✔	✔	✔	✔	✔	✔	✔	✔	✔	✔	✔	✔
Bluish-colored fingernails or palms of hands or	✔	✔	✔	✔		✔	✔	✔	✔		✔	✔	✔
Seizures	✔	✔		✔	✔	✔	✔	✔	✔	✔	✔	✔	✔
(signs and symptoms of overdose, listed in order of occurrence)	✔			✔	✔	✔	✔	✔		✔	✔	✔	✔
Medical attention needed only if continuing or bothersome													
Anxiety and/or nervousness	L	U	R	L	U	U	U	L	U	M	L	L	R
Changes in taste	U	U	U	U	L	U	U	U	U	U	U	U	U
Constipation	L	U	R	L	R	R	L	L	U	U	L	L	U
Decreased sexual ability	M	M	M	M	M	M	M	M	M	M	M	M	M
Diarrhea	L	L	L	L	R	L	R	L	L	L	M	L	R
Dizziness	L	L	L	L	L	M	L	M	L	M	M	L	L
Drowsiness, slight—with high doses	U	R	U	L	L	U	R	M	U	U	M	L	U
Dry, sore eyes	U	U	R	R	R	U	R	R	U	R	R	U	R
Frequent urination	L	U	U	L	U	U	U	U	U	U	U	U	U
Itching of skin	R	U	R	U	L	R	R	L	U	L	U	L	L
Nausea or vomiting	L	L	L	L	L	R	R	L	L	L	M	L	R

*Differences in frequency of occurrence may reflect either lack of clinical-use data or actual pharmacologic distinctions among agents (although their pharmacologic similarity suggests that side effects occurring with one may occur with the others). M = more frequent; L = less frequent; R = rare; U = unknown; ✔ = may occur.

Table 2. Side/Adverse Effects* *(continued)*

	Legend: I = Acebutolol, II = Atenolol, III = Betaxolol			IV = Carteolol, V = Labetalol, VI = Metoprolol			VII = Nadolol, VIII = Oxprenolol, IX = Penbutolol			X = Pindolol, XI = Propranolol, XII = Sotalol, XIII = Timolol			
	I	II	III	IV	V	VI	VII	VIII	IX	X	XI	XII	XIII
Nightmares and vivid dreams	L	R	L	R	R	R	R	L	R	L	L	L	R
Numbness and/or tingling of fingers and/or toes	U	U	R	L	U	U	R	L	U	L	M	U	R
Numbness and/or tingling of skin, especially on scalp	U	U	U	U	L	U	U	U	U	U	U	U	U
Orthostatic hypotension (dizziness or light-headedness, especially when getting up from a lying or sitting position)	U	U	R	U	L	U	R	U	U	U	U	U	U
Stomach discomfort	L	U	L	L	L	R	R	L	L	L	L	L	R
Stuffy nose	R	U	L	L	L	U	R	R	U	U	U	U	U
Trouble in sleeping	L	U	L	L	U	R	U	M	L	M	M	L	U
Unusual tiredness or weakness	M	L	L	L	L	M	L	M	L	M	M	L	L
Medical attention needed if occurring after medication abruptly discontinued (possible withdrawal) *Chest pain*	✔	✔	✔	✔	✔	✔	✔	✔	✔	✔	✔	✔	✔
Fast or irregular heartbeat	✔	✔	✔	✔	✔	✔	✔	✔	✔	✔	✔	✔	✔
General feeling of discomfort or illness or weakness	✔	✔	✔	✔	✔	✔	✔	✔	✔	✔	✔	✔	✔
Headache	✔	✔	✔	✔	✔	✔	✔	✔	✔	✔	✔	✔	✔
Shortness of breath, sudden	✔	✔	✔	✔	✔	✔	✔	✔	✔	✔	✔	✔	✔
Sweating	✔	✔	✔	✔	✔	✔	✔	✔	✔	✔	✔	✔	✔
Trembling	✔	✔	✔	✔	✔	✔	✔	✔	✔	✔	✔	✔	✔

*Differences in frequency of occurrence may reflect either lack of clinical-use data or actual pharmacologic distinctions among agents (although their pharmacologic similarity suggests that side effects occurring with one may occur with the others). M = more frequent; L = less frequent; R = rare; U = unknown; ✔ = may occur.

BETA-ADRENERGIC BLOCKING AGENTS AND THIAZIDE DIURETICS   Systemic

Category: Antihypertensive—Atenolol and Chlorthalidone; Labetalol and Hydrochlorothiazide; Metoprolol and Hydrochlorothiazide; Nadolol and Bendroflumethiazide; Pindolol and Hydrochlorothiazide; Propranolol and Hydrochlorothiazide; Timolol and Hydrochlorothiazide.

Indications

Accepted

Hypertension (treatment)—The above combinations of beta-adrenergic blocking agents (beta-blockers) with thiazide diuretics are indicated in the management of hypertension.

Fixed-dosage combinations generally are not recommended for initial therapy, but are utilized in maintenance therapy after the required dose is established in order to increase convenience, economy, and patient compliance.

Nonpharmacologic management (especially sodium restriction, weight reduction and exercise, and moderation of alcohol consumption) is recommended first for some patients, including those with mild hypertension, and is recommended as an adjunct to all pharmacologic hypertensive therapy.

Patient Consultation

In providing consultation, consider emphasizing the following selected information (» = major clinical significance):

Before using this medication
» Conditions affecting use, especially:
    Sensitivity to the beta-blocker prescribed, or to any thiazide diuretic or other sulfonamide-type medications
    Pregnancy—Risk of hypoglycemia, respiratory depression, bradycardia, and hypotension with beta-blockers; thiazide diuretics may cause jaundice, thrombocytopenia, hypokalemia in infant
    Breast-feeding—Pass into breast milk
    Use in the elderly—Increased sensitivity to effects; increased risk of beta-blocker-induced hypothermia
    Use by athletes—Beta-blockers and thiazide diuretics are banned and tested for in athletes by the U.S. Olympic Committee (USOC) and National Collegiate Athletic Association (NCAA)
    Other medications, especially adrenocorticoids, oral antidiabetic agents, insulin, calcium channel blockers, clonidine, digitalis glycosides, guanabenz, cocaine, lithium, methenamine, MAO inhibitors, synmpathomimetics, or xanthines
    Other medical problems, especially overt cardiac failure, cardiogenic shock, 2nd or 3rd degree AV block, sinus bradycardia, hypotension, history of allergy, bronchial asthma, emphysema or nonallergenic bronchitis, congestive heart failure, diabetes mellitus, hyperthyroidism, mental depression, or renal function impairment

Proper use of this medication
    Importance of diet; possible need for sodium restriction and/or weight reduction
» Compliance with therapy; patient may not experience symptoms of hypertension; importance of taking medication only as directed and keeping appointments with physician, even if feeling well
» Does not cure, but helps control hypertension; possible need for lifelong therapy; checking with physician before discontinuing medication; serious consequences of untreated hypertension
    Proper administration of extended-release dosage forms: Swallowing whole without crushing, breaking, or chewing

    Getting into habit of taking at same time each day to help increase compliance
    Checking pulse as directed (checking with physician if less than 50 beats per minute)
    Diuretic effects of the medication and timing of doses to minimize inconvenience of diuresis
» Importance of not missing doses, especially with schedules of one dose per day
    Missed dose: Taking as soon as possible; not taking at all if within 4 hours of next scheduled dose (8 hours for atenolol and chlorthalidone, labetalol and hydrochlorothiazide, nadolol and bendroflumethiazide, or extended-release propranolol and hydrochlorothiazide); not doubling doses
» Proper storage

Precautions while using this medication
    Regular visits to physician to check progress
» Checking with physician before discontinuing medication; gradual dosage reduction may be necessary
    Having enough medication on hand to get through weekends, holidays, and vacations; possibly carrying second written prescription for emergency use
    Carrying medical identification card during therapy
» Not taking other medications, especially nonprescription sympathomimetics, unless discussed with physician
» Caution if any kind of surgery (including dental surgery) or emergency treatment is required
» Diabetics: May mask signs and symptoms of hypoglycemia or cause increased or decreased blood glucose concentrations
» Possibility of hypokalemia; possible need for additional potassium in diet; not changing diet without first checking with physician
    To prevent dehydration, checking with physician if severe nausea, vomiting, or diarrhea occurs and continues
» Caution when driving or doing things requiring alertness, because of possible drowsiness, dizziness, or lightheadedness
    Caution during exposure to cold weather because of possible increased sensitivity to cold
    Possible skin photosensitivity; avoiding unprotected exposure to sun; using protective clothing and sun block product; avoiding use of sunlamp, tanning bed, or tanning booth
    Caution if any laboratory tests required; possible interference with test results
    Patients with allergies to foods, medications, or stinging insect venom: Possible increase in severity of allergic reactions; checking with physician immediately if severe allergic reaction occurs

Side/adverse effects
    Signs of potential side effects, especially breathing difficulty and/or wheezing, reduced peripheral circulation, confusion (especially in elderly), hallucinations, hepatotoxicity, irregular heartbeat, mental depression, bradycardia, chest pain, leukopenia, agranulocytosis, hyperuricemia, gout, psoriasiform eruption, allergic reaction, cholecystitis, pancreatitis, congestive heart failure, thrombocytopenia, hepatic function impairment, and hypokalemia

Oral Dosage Forms

ATENOLOL AND CHLORTHALIDONE TABLETS

Usual adult dose: Antihypertensive—Oral, 1 or 2 tablets per day, as a single dose or in divided daily doses, as determined by individual titration with the component agents.

Note: Geriatric patients may have increased or decreased sensitivity to the effects of the usual adult dose.

Auxiliary labeling: • Do not take other medicines without your doctor's advice.

Oral Dosage Forms

LABETALOL HYDROCHLORIDE AND HYDROCHLOROTHIAZIDE TABLETS

Note: Labetalol hydrochloride and hydrochlorothiazide tablets are not commercially available in Canada.

Usual adult dose: Antihypertensive—Oral, 1 tablet two times a day, as determined by individual titration with the component agents.

Note: Geriatric patients may have increased or decreased sensitivity to the effects of the usual adult dose.

Auxiliary labeling: • Do not take other medicines without your doctor's advice.

METOPROLOL AND HYDROCHLOROTHIAZIDE

Oral Dosage Forms

METOPROLOL TARTRATE AND HYDROCHLOROTHIAZIDE TABLETS USP

Note: Metoprolol tartrate and hydrochlorothiazide tablets are not commercially available in Canada.

Usual adult dose: Antihypertensive—Oral, 1 or 2 tablets per day, as a single dose or in divided daily doses, as determined by individual titration with the component agents.

Note: Geriatric patients may have increased or decreased sensitivity to the effects of the usual adult dose.

Auxiliary labeling: • Do not take other medicines without your doctor's advice.

Oral Dosage Forms

NADOLOL AND BENDROFLUMETHIAZIDE TABLETS USP

Usual adult dose: Antihypertensive—Oral, 1 tablet once a day, as determined by individual titration with the component agents.

Note: Geriatric patients may have increased or decreased sensitivity to the effects of the usual adult dose.

Auxiliary labeling: • Do not take other medicines without your doctor's advice.

Oral Dosage Forms

PINDOLOL AND HYDROCHLOROTHIAZIDE TABLETS

Note: Pindolol and hydrochlorothiazide tablets are not commercially available in the U.S.

Usual adult dose: Antihypertensive—Oral, 1 or 2 tablets per day, as a single dose or in divided daily doses, as determined by individual titration with the component agents.

Note: Geriatric patients may have increased or decreased sensitivity to the effects of the usual adult dose.

Auxiliary labeling: • Do not take other medicines without your doctor's advice.

Oral Dosage Forms

PROPRANOLOL HYDROCHLORIDE AND HYDROCHLOROTHIAZIDE EXTENDED-RELEASE CAPSULES USP

Note: Propranolol hydrochloride and hydrochlorothiazide extended-release capsules are not commercially available in Canada.

Usual adult dose: Antihypertensive—Oral, 1 capsule per day, as determined by individual titration with the component agents.

Note: Geriatric patients may have increased or decreased sensitivity to the effects of the usual adult dose.

Auxiliary labeling: • Do not take other medicines without your doctor's advice.

PROPRANOLOL HYDROCHLORIDE AND HYDROCHLOROTHIAZIDE TABLETS USP

Usual adult dose: Antihypertensive—Oral, 1 or 2 tablets two times a day, as determined by individual titration with the component agents.

Note: Geriatric patients may have increased or decreased sensitivity to the effects of the usual adult dose.

Auxiliary labeling: • Do not take other medicines without your doctor's advice.

Oral Dosage Forms

TIMOLOL MALEATE AND HYDROCHLOROTHIAZIDE TABLETS USP

Usual adult dose: Antihypertensive—Oral, 1 tablet two times a day, as determined by individual titration with the component agents.

Note: Geriatric patients may have increased or decreased sensitivity to the effects of the usual adult dose.

Auxiliary labeling: • Do not take other medicine without your doctor's advice.

BETAXOLOL Ophthalmic

Some commonly used *brand names* are:
  In the U.S.—*Betoptic; Betoptic S*
  In Canada—*Betoptic*

OPHTHALMIC
Betaxolol Hydrochloride Ophthalmic Solution
  In the U.S. and Canada—*Betoptic*
Betaxolol Hydrochloride Ophthalmic Suspension
  In the U.S.—*Betoptic S*

Category: Antiglaucoma agent (ophthalmic).

Indications

Note: Bracketed information in the *Indications* section refers to uses not included in U.S. product labeling.

Accepted
Glaucoma, open-angle (treatment);
[Glaucoma, in aphakic eyes (treatment)][1];
[Glaucoma, secondary (treatment)][1]; or
Hypertension, ocular (treatment)—Betaxolol lowers intraocular pressure and is indicated in the treatment of ocular hypertension and chronic open-angle glaucoma. It may be used alone or in combination with other antiglaucoma agents. In addition, betaxolol may be used in patients with glaucoma in aphakic eyes and in some patients with secondary glaucoma.

[Glaucoma, angle-closure (treatment adjunct)][1]—Betaxolol may be used in conjunction with miotics to reduce intraocular pressure in acute and chronic angle-closure glaucoma. However, betaxolol's action alone is unlikely to terminate an acute attack of angle-closure glaucoma, because betaxolol produces little or no constriction of the pupil, which is necessary to pull the iris away from the trabeculum to relieve blockage of the trabecular meshwork.

[Glaucoma, angle-closure, *during* or *after* iridectomy (treatment)][1]; or
[Glaucoma, malignant (treatment)][1]—Betaxolol is used to lower intraocular pressure in the treatment of angle-closure glaucoma *during* or *after* iridectomy and in the treatment of malignant glaucoma.

Ophthalmic betaxolol may be especially useful in patients with pulmonary disease because it is a selective beta-1-adrenergic antagonist and appears to have a minimal effect on pulmonary function.

---

[1]Not included in Canadian product labeling.

Pharmacology

Mechanism of action/Effect: Betaxolol is a cardioselective (beta-1-adrenergic) receptor blocking agent. The exact mechanism of its ocular hypotensive action has not been established. However, betaxolol appears to lower intraocular pressure by reducing aqueous humor production as shown by tonography and aqueous humor fluorophotometry.

Other actions/effects:
  Betaxolol 1% solution, when compared to a placebo, was not shown to have a significant effect on pulmonary function as measured by forced expiratory volume in 1 second (FEV1), forced vital capacity (FVC), and FEV1/VC.
  Also, betaxolol has not been shown to significantly decrease the heart rate.
  The magnitude and duration of the ocular hypotensive effect of the 0.5% ophthalmic solution and the 0.25% ophthalmic suspension were found to be clinically equivalent.

Onset of action: Within 30 minutes for either the ophthalmic solution or suspension.

Time to peak effect: 2 hours for either the ophthalmic solution or suspension.

Duration of action: 12 hours, following a single dose of either the ophthalmic solution or suspension.

Precautions to Consider

Cross-sensitivity and/or related problems
Patients sensitive to other beta-adrenergic blockers, either systemic or ophthalmic, (such as acebutolol, atenolol, carteolol, labetalol, levobunolol, metipranolol, metoprolol, nadolol, oxprenolol, penbutolol, pindolol, propranolol, sotalol, or timolol) may be sensitive to betaxolol also.

Geriatrics
Although appropriate studies on the relationship of age to the effects of this medicine have not been performed in the geriatric population, no geriatrics-specific problems have been documented to date. However, if significant systemic absorption of ophthalmic beta-blockers occurs, the same geriatrics-related problems may occur that are possible with the systemic beta-blockers. These include increased myocardial depression because of reduced metabolic and excretory capabilities in many elderly patients and the increased risk of beta-blocker-induced hypothermia in elderly patients.
In addition, elderly patients are more likely to have age-related peripheral vascular disease, which may require caution in patients receiving beta-blockers.

Drug interactions and/or related problems
The following drug interactions and/or related problems have been selected on the basis of their potential clinical significance (possible mechanism in parentheses where appropriate)—not necessarily inclusive (» = major clinical significance):

Note: Combinations containing any of the following medications, depending on the amount present, may also interact with this medication.

  Information concerning interactions between ophthalmic betaxolol and other medications is still limited. Some of the following potential interactions apply to beta-adrenergic blocking agents in general and are stated for cautionary reference until additional information specific for betaxolol is available.

Amphetamines
  (if significant systemic absorption of the ophthalmic beta-adrenergic blocking agents, betaxolol, levobunolol, and timolol, occurs, concurrent use of amphetamines may result in unopposed alpha-adrenergic activity with a risk of hypertension and excessive bradycardia and possible heart block)

Anesthetics, hydrocarbon inhalation, such as:
  Chloroform
  Cyclopropane
  Enflurane
  Halothane
  Isoflurane
  Methoxyflurane
  Trichloroethylene
  (if significant systemic absorption of the ophthalmic beta-adrenergic blocking agents, betaxolol, levobunolol, and timolol, occurs, concurrent use of hydrocarbon inhalation anesthetics may result in prolonged severe hypotension because the beta-adrenergic blockade reduces the ability of the heart to respond to beta-adrenergically mediated sympathetic reflex stimuli; if necessary to reverse the effects of beta-adrenergic blocking agents during surgery, agonists, such as dobutamine, dopamine, isoproterenol, or norepinephrine, may be used but should be administered with caution, especially in patients receiving halothane. Some clinicians recommend gradual withdrawal of

beta-adrenergic blocking agents 48 hours prior to elective surgery; however, this recommendation is controversial)

Antidiabetic agents, oral, or
Insulin
(systemic beta-adrenergic blocking agents may affect diabetes mellitus therapy. This may also occur with the ophthalmic beta-adrenergic blocking agents, betaxolol, levobunolol, and timolol, if there is significant systemic absorption. Nonselective beta-adrenergic blocking agents impair glycogenolysis and the hyperglycemic response to endogenous epinephrine, leading to persistence of hypoglycemia. Also, beta-adrenergic blocking agents, especially nonselective agents, decrease the release of insulin in response to hyperglycemia. Dosage adjustment of the antidiabetic agent may be required to avoid severe hypoglycemic reaction. In addition, beta-adrenergic blocking agents may complicate patient monitoring by masking symptoms of hypoglycemia caused by epinephrine, such as increased heart rate and increased blood pressure, but not dizziness and sweating. Although selective or relatively selective beta-adrenergic blocking agents usually cause fewer problems with blood glucose levels, they may still mask symptoms of hypoglycemia)

Beta-adrenergic blocking agents, systemic
(if significant systemic absorption of the ophthalmic beta-adrenergic blocking agents, betaxolol, levobunolol, and timolol, occurs, concurrent use of these medications may result in an additive effect either on intraocular pressure or on systemic effects of beta-blockade)

Calcium channel blocking agents
(if significant systemic absorption of the ophthalmic beta-adrenergic blocking agents, betaxolol, levobunolol, and timolol, occurs, concurrent use of calcium channel blocking agents, such as diltiazem, nicardipine, nifedipine, nimodipine, and verapamil, may result in atrioventricular conduction disturbances, left ventricular failure, and hypotension; in some patients, if a calcium antagonist is necessary, nicardipine or nifedipine may be preferred because it has less effect on heart rate and conduction, although it may also cause greater hypotension; concurrent use of calcium channel blockers and ophthalmic beta-adrenergic blocking agents should be used with care in patients with impaired cardiac function)

Catecholamine-depleting medications, such as the rauwolfia alkaloids:
Alseroxylon
Deserpidine
Rauwolfia serpentina
Reserpine
(if significant systemic absorption of the ophthalmic beta-adrenergic blocking agents, betaxolol, levobunolol, and timolol, occurs, concurrent use of catecholamine-depleting medications may result in additive and possibly excessive beta-adrenergic blockade; although this effect is largely theoretical, close observation is recommended, since bradycardia and marked hypotension may occur)

Cocaine
(cocaine may inhibit the therapeutic effects of systemic beta-adrenergic blocking agents, and may also have this effect on ophthalmic betaxolol, levobunolol, or timolol)
(concurrent use of a systemic beta-adrenergic blocking agent with cocaine may increase the risk of hypertension, excessive bradycardia, and possibly heart block because beta-blockade may leave cocaine's alpha-adrenergic activity unopposed. This may also occur with the ophthalmic beta-adrenergic blocking agents, betaxolol, levobunolol, or timolol, if significant systemic absorption of the ophthalmic beta-blocker occurs)

Diazoxide
(if significant systemic absorption of the ophthalmic beta-adrenergic blocking agents, levobunolol, timolol, and possibly betaxolol, occurs, concurrent use may prevent the diazoxide-induced tachycardia; however, the risk of hypotension may be increased)

Dipivefrin or
Epinephrine, ophthalmic
(concurrent use of dipivefrin or ophthalmic epinephrine with the ophthalmic beta-adrenergic blocking agents, betaxolol, levobunolol, and timolol, may provide a beneficial additive effect in lowering intraocular pressure in some patients)

Fentanyl derivatives
(chronic preoperative use of ophthalmic beta-adrenergic blocking agents [especially levobunolol, timolol, and possibly betaxolol] may increase the risk of initial bradycardia following induction doses of a fentanyl derivative)

Flecainide
(if significant systemic absorption of the ophthalmic beta-adrenergic blocking agents, betaxolol, levobunolol, and timolol, occurs, concurrent use may result in additive negative cardiac inotropic effects)

Hypotension-producing medications, other
(if significant systemic absorption of the ophthalmic beta-adrenergic blocking agents, levobunolol, timolol, and possibly betaxolol, occurs, concurrent use may potentiate the hypotensive effects of these medications)

Phenothiazines
(if significant systemic absorption of the ophthalmic beta-adrenergic blocking agents, betaxolol, levobunolol, and timolol, occurs, concurrent use may result in an increased plasma concentration of either the phenothiazine or the ophthalmic beta-adrenergic blocking agent because of inhibition of metabolism. This may result in additive hypotensive effects, irreversible retinopathy, cardiac arrhythmias, or tardive dyskinesia)

Sympathomimetics with beta-1-adrenergic stimulant effect, such as:
Dobutamine
Dopamine
Ephedrine
Epinephrine
Isoproterenol
Metaraminol
Norepinephrine
(if significant systemic absorption of ophthalmic betaxolol occurs, beta-adrenergic blockade may antagonize the beta-1-adrenergic cardiac effects of these medications; in addition, beta-adrenergic blockade may result in unopposed alpha-adrenergic activity with a risk of hypertension and excessive bradycardia with possible heart block)

Xanthines, such as:
Aminophylline
Caffeine
Dyphylline
Oxtriphylline
Theophylline
(if significant systemic absorption of the ophthalmic beta-adrenergic blocking agents, levobunolol, timolol, and possibly betaxolol, occurs, concurrent use may result in inhibition of therapeutic effects of xanthines; in addition, concurrent use of xanthines [except dyphylline] with the ophthalmic beta-adrenergic blocking agents, levobunolol, timolol, and possibly betaxolol, may decrease theophylline clearance, especially in patients with increased theophylline clearance induced by smoking; concurrent use requires careful monitoring)

(in addition, concurrent use with caffeine may enhance the cardiac inotropic effects of the ophthalmic beta-adrenergic blocking agents, levobunolol, timolol, and possibly betaxolol, if significant systemic absorption occurs)

Contraindications/Medical problems
The contraindications/medical problems included have been selected on the basis of their potential clinical significance (reasons given

in parentheses where appropriate)—not necessarily inclusive (» = major clinical significance).

Except under special circumstances, this medication should not be used when the following medical problems exist:

» Cardiac failure, overt, or
» Heart block, 2nd- or 3rd-degree atrioventricular (AV) block, or
» Shock, cardiogenic, or
» Sinus bradycardia
    (possible risk of further myocardial depression)
» Previous allergic reaction to betaxolol

Risk-benefit should be considered when the following medical problems exist:

» Cardiac failure, history of, or
   Heart block, history of,
    (possible risk of myocardial depression; treatment should be discontinued at first signs of cardiac failure)
» Diabetes mellitus, especially labile diabetes
    (betaxolol may mask some signs and symptoms of hypoglycemia, such as tachycardia and tremor, but not dizziness and sweating)
» Hyperthyroidism
    (may mask certain signs and symptoms of hyperthyroidism, such as tachycardia; abrupt withdrawal may precipitate a thyroid storm)
   Myasthenia gravis
    (beta-adrenergic blockade has been reported to potentiate muscle weakness, such as diplopia, ptosis, and generalized weakness)
   Pulmonary function impairment
    (although effects of betaxolol have been shown to be minimal in patients with reactive airway disease, the potential for bronchoconstriction exists)

Side/Adverse Effects

Note: Available data suggest that there may be less potential for systemic side/adverse effects with ophthalmic betaxolol than with ophthalmic nonselective beta-adrenergic blocking agents because of betaxolol's relatively selective beta-1-adrenergic receptor inhibition.

The ophthalmic suspension dosage form appears to be less irritating to the eye than the ophthalmic solution dosage form, although eye irritation occurs more frequently than other side effects with both dosage forms.

The following side/adverse effects have been selected on the basis of their potential clinical significance (possible signs and symptoms in parentheses where appropriate)—not necessarily inclusive:

Those indicating need for medical attention
Incidence rare
   Glossitis (redness or irritation of the tongue); *headache; hives; keratitis* (severe irritation or inflammation of eye or eyelid); *toxic epidermal necrolysis* (raw or red areas of the skin); *vertigo* (dizziness)
Symptoms of systemic absorption
   Confusion or mental depression; slow heartbeat; trouble in sleeping; unusual tiredness or weakness; wheezing or troubled breathing, especially in patients with predisposition to bronchoconstriction

Those indicating need for medical attention only if they continue or are bothersome
Incidence more frequent
   Stinging of eye or other eye irritation, transient upon administration of medication
Incidence less frequent or rare
   Blurred vision or other vision problems—with suspension; *crusting of eye lashes*—with suspension; *dryness of eye*—with suspen-

sion; *hair loss; increased sensitivity of eye to light; redness, itching, or watering of eye*

Patient Consultation

In providing consultation, consider emphasizing the following selected information (» = major clinical significance):

Before using this medication
» Conditions affecting use, especially:
   Sensitivity to betaxolol or other beta blockers (such as acebutolol, atenolol, carteolol, labetalol, levobunolol, metipranolol, metoprolol, nadolol, oxprenolol, penbutolol, pindolol, propranolol, sotalol, or timolol)
   Pregnancy—Ophthalmic betaxolol may be absorbed into the body. Some studies in animals have shown that betaxolol increases the chance of death in the animal fetus
   Use in children—Infants may be especially sensitive to the effects of betaxolol, thus increasing the risk of side effects
   Use in the elderly—If significant systemic absorption of ophthalmic beta-blockers occurs, the chance of side effects during treatment may be increased, since elderly people are especially sensitive to the effects of these medications
   Use by athletes—Beta-blockers are banned and tested for in athletes; because ophthalmic betaxolol may be absorbed into the body, the medication may appear in the urine; if the agent is found in the urine, the athlete will be disqualified
   Other medical problems, especially overt cardiac failure; 2nd- or 3rd-degree atrioventricular (AV) heart block; cardiogenic shock; sinus bradycardia; history of cardiac failure; diabetes mellitus, especially labile diabetes; or hyperthyroidism

Proper use of this medication
» Proper administration technique; using nasolacrimal occlusion is especially important in infants and children
   Preventing contamination: Not touching applicator tip to any surface; keeping container tightly closed
» Importance of not using more medication than the amount prescribed
   Missed dose: Applying as soon as possible; not applying if almost time for next dose; applying next dose at regularly scheduled time
» Proper storage

Precautions while using this medication
   Regular visits to physician to check eye pressure during therapy
» Caution if any kind of surgery (including dental surgery) or emergency treatment is required
» Diabetics: May mask some signs of hypoglycemia, such as increased pulse rate and trembling, but not dizziness and sweating
   Possible photophobia: Wearing sunglasses and avoiding too much exposure to bright light

Side/adverse effects
   Signs of potential side effects, especially glossitis, headache, hives, keratitis, toxic epidermal necrolysis, vertigo, or symptoms of systemic absorption

General Dosing Information

Although some manufacturers recommend a dose of 2 drops of an ophthalmic solution at appropriate intervals, the conjunctival sac will usually hold only 1 drop.

When betaxolol is used to replace another ophthalmic beta-adrenergic blocking agent, the other beta-blocker should be discontinued simultaneously with initiation of therapy with betaxolol.

When betaxolol is used to replace a single antiglaucoma agent other than another ophthalmic beta-blocker, the other antiglaucoma agent may be continued on the first day that betaxolol is used but should be discontinued on the second day.

When betaxolol is used to replace several concomitantly administered antiglaucoma agents, the patient's dosage should be individualized as required. If any of the other antiglaucoma agents used is a beta-blocker, it should be discontinued before betaxolol is added to the regimen. The other antiglaucoma agents being used may be continued on the first day that betaxolol is used but one of the agents should be discontinued on the second day. Then the remaining antiglaucoma agents may be decreased or discontinued according to patient's response. Additional adjustments usually should involve only one agent at a time and should be made at intervals of not less than one week.

Betaxolol may be used concurrently with direct and indirect muscarinic agonists (e.g., pilocarpine, echothiophate, carbachol), beta-agonists (e.g., ophthalmic epinephrine or dipivefrin), or systemic carbonic anhydrase inhibitors (such as acetazolamide), if necessary to control intraocular pressure.

In patients scheduled for major surgery, some practitioners recommend that beta-adrenergic blocking agents be gradually withdrawn 48 hours prior to surgery because beta-adrenergic receptor blockade impairs the ability of the heart to respond to beta-adrenergically mediated reflex stimuli. This recommendation is controversial. However, since ophthalmic betaxolol may be absorbed systemically, gradual withdrawal of the medication should be considered for patients undergoing elective surgery because prolonged severe hypotension during anesthesia has occurred in some pa-tients receiving systemic beta-adrenergic blocking agents. If necessary during surgery, the effects of beta-adrenergic blocking agents may be reversed by sufficient doses of agonists, such as isoproter-enol, dopamine, dobutamine, or norepinephrine.

Ophthalmic Dosage Forms

BETAXOLOL HYDROCHLORIDE OPHTHALMIC SOLUTION

Usual adult and adolescent dose: Topical, to the conjunctiva, 1 drop of a 0.5% solution of betaxolol (base) two times a day.

Auxiliary labeling:
- For the eye.
- Keep container tightly closed.

BETAXOLOL HYDROCHLORIDE OPHTHALMIC SUSPENSION

Usual adult and adolescent dose: Topical, to the conjunctiva, 1 drop of a 0.25% suspension of betaxolol (base) two times a day.

Auxiliary labeling:
- Shake well.
- For the eye.
- Keep container tightly closed.

BISMUTH SUBSALICYLATE   Oral-Local

A commonly used *brand name* in the U.S. and Canada is *Pepto-Bismol*.

ORAL
Bismuth Subsalicylate Oral Suspension
    In the U.S. and Canada—*Pepto-Bismol*
Bismuth Subsalicylate Chewable Tablets
    In the U.S. and Canada—*Pepto-Bismol*

Category: Antidiarrheal (antisecretory); antacid; antiulcer agent.

Indications

Note: Bracketed information in the *Indications* section refers to uses not included in U.S. product labeling.

Accepted
Diarrhea (treatment)—Bismuth subsalicylate is indicated for the symptomatic treatment of nonspecific diarrhea.

Gastric distress (treatment)—Bismuth subsalicylate is indicated for the symptomatic relief of upset stomach, including heartburn, acid indigestion, and nausea.

[Traveler's diarrhea (prophylaxis)][1]—Bismuth subsalicylate is used for the prevention of secretory diarrhea produced by enterotoxigenic *Escherichia coli* (traveler's diarrhea) and viral infections.

[Ulcer, duodenal, *Helicobacter pylori*-associated (treatment adjunct)][1]; or

[Gastritis, *Helicobacter pylori*-associated (treatment adjunct)][1]—Bismuth subsalicylate is used, in combination with oral antibiotic therapy, in the treatment of *Helicobacter pylori*-associated gastritis and duodenal ulcer.

[1]Not included in Canadian product labeling.

Pharmacology

Mechanism of action/Effect:
Antidiarrheal—Exact mechanism has not been determined. Bismuth subsalicylate may exert its antidiarrheal action not only by stimulating absorption of fluid and electrolytes across the intestinal wall (antisecretory action) but also, when hydrolyzed to salicylic acid, by inhibiting synthesis of a prostaglandin responsible for intestinal inflammation and hypermotility. In addition, bismuth subsalicylate binds toxins produced by *Escherichia coli*. Both bismuth subsalicylate and the intestinal reaction products, bismuth oxychloride and bismuth hydroxide, are believed to have bactericidal action.
Antacid—Bismuth has weak antacid properties.

Precautions to Consider

Cross-sensitivity and/or related problems
Patients sensitive to salicylates including methyl salicylate (oil of wintergreen), or to other nonsteroidal anti-inflammatory drugs (NSAIDs), may be sensitive to bismuth subsalicylate also.

Geriatrics
In geriatric patients with diarrhea, caution is recommended because of the risk of fluid and electrolyte loss; these patients should be referred to a physician.
Also, elderly patients are more likely to have age-related renal function impairment, which may increase the risk of salicylate toxicity. Dosage reduction may be required to prevent accumulation of the medication.
Bismuth is more likely to cause impaction in elderly patients.

Drug interactions and/or related problems

The following drug interactions and/or related problems have been selected on the basis of their potential clinical significance (possible mechanism in parentheses where appropriate)—not necessarily inclusive (» = major clinical significance):

Note: Although significant interactions are unlikely with usual doses of bismuth subsalicylate in the treatment of diarrhea and for occasional relief of gastric distress, the higher doses and the longer therapy used in the prophylaxis of traveler's diarrhea increase the potential for significant drug interactions.

Combinations containing any of the following medications, depending on the amount present, may also interact with this medication.

» Anticoagulants, coumarin- or indandione-derivative, or
» Heparin or
» Thrombolytic agents, such as:
Alteplase (tissue-type plasminogen activator, recombinant)
Anistreplase
Streptokinase
Urokinase
(increased risk of bleeding may occur when these medications are used concurrently with salicylates)

» Antidiabetic agents, oral, or
Insulin
(large doses of salicylate may enhance the hypoglycemic effect of these medications; dosage adjustment may be necessary)

» Probenecid or
» Sulfinpyrazone
(concurrent use of salicylates is not recommended when these medications are used to treat hyperuricemia or gout because uricosuric effects of these medications may be decreased by doses of salicylates that produce serum salicylate concentrations above 50 mcg per mL)

(probenecid may decrease renal clearance and increase plasma concentrations and toxicity of salicylates)

» Salicylates, other
(ingestion of large repeated doses of bismuth subsalicylate, as for traveler's diarrhea, may produce substantial plasma salicylate concentrations thus increasing the risk of salicylate toxicity during concurrent use with other salicylates)

» Tetracyclines, oral
(calcium carbonate contained in the tablet dosage form may decrease gastrointestinal absorption and bioavailability of tetracyclines; patients should be advised not to take bismuth subsalicylate tablets within 1 to 3 hours of oral tetracyclines)

Contraindications/Medical problems

The contraindications/medical problems included have been selected on the basis of their potential clinical significance (reasons given in parentheses where appropriate)—not necessarily inclusive (» = major clinical significance).

Risk-benefit should be considered when the following medical problems exist:

» Bleeding ulcers or
» Hemorrhagic states, other active
(may be exacerbated by the salicylate)

» Dehydration
(rehydration therapy is essential if signs of dehydration, such as dry mouth, excessive thirst, wrinkled skin, decreased urination, dizziness or lightheadedness, are present with the diarrhea; fluid loss may have serious consequences, such as circulatory collapse and renal failure, especially in young children)

» Dysentery, acute, characterized by bloody stools and elevated temperature
(sole treatment with bismuth subsalicylate may be inadequate; antibiotic therapy may be required)

Gout
(salicylates may have variable dose-dependent effects on serum uric acid concentrations; also, salicylates may interfere with efficacy of uricosuric antigout agents)

» Hemophilia
(salicylate may increase risk of hemorrhage)

Renal function impairment
(increased risk of bismuth and salicylate toxicity because of decreased excretion)

Sensitivity to bismuth subsalicylate

Side/Adverse Effects

The following side/adverse effects have been selected on the basis of their potential clinical significance (possible signs and symptoms in parentheses where appropriate)—not necessarily inclusive:

Those indicating need for medical attention

Incidence rare—reported with higher-than-recommended doses and/or chronic dosing; may also be signs of overdose

Bismuth encephalopathy (anxiety; confusion; difficulty in speaking or slurred speech; severe and/or continuing headache; mental depression; muscle spasms, especially of face, neck, and back; muscle weakness; trembling; uncontrolled body movements); *constipation, severe; salicylism, symptoms of* (any loss of hearing; confusion; severe or continuing diarrhea; dizziness or lightheadedness; severe drowsiness; fast or deep breathing; severe or continuing headache; increased sweating; increased thirst; severe or continuing nausea or vomiting; continuing ringing or buzzing in ears; severe or continuing stomach pain; uncontrollable flapping movements of the hands, especially in elderly patients; vision problems)

Those not indicating need for medical attention

Incidence more frequent

Discoloration produced by bismuth (darkening of tongue or grayish black stools)

Patient Consultation

In providing consultation, consider emphasizing the following selected information (» = major clinical significance):

Before using this medication

» Conditions affecting use, especially:
Allergies to salicylates or other nonsteroidal anti-inflammatory drugs
Pregnancy—Salicylates cross the placenta; concern only with high doses and long-term therapy because of salicylate effects
Breast-feeding—Concern only with high doses and chronic use because of salicylate intake by infant
Use in children—Risk of fluid and electrolyte loss due to diarrhea; increased susceptibility to toxic effects of salicylates if fever and dehydration present; risk of impaction due to bismuth
Use in the elderly—Risk of fluid and electrolyte loss due to diarrhea; increased susceptibility to toxic effects of salicylates possibly due to decreased renal function; risk of impaction due to bismuth
Other medications, especially anticoagulants, heparin, or thrombolytic agents; antidiabetic agents; probenecid or sulfinpyrazone; other salicylates; or oral tetracyclines (for tablet dosage form)
Other medical problems, especially bleeding ulcers or other active hemorrhagic states, acute dysentery, dehydration, or hemophilia

Proper use of this medication

Following physician's or manufacturer's instructions
» Not giving to children with symptoms of influenza or varicella without first checking with physician

Missed dose: If on a regular schedule—Taking as soon as possible; not taking if almost time for next dose; not doubling doses
» For use in treatment of diarrhea—Importance of maintaining adequate hydration and proper diet
» Proper storage

Precautions while using this medication
» Caution if other medications containing aspirin or other salicylates are used
Diabetics:
   Possibility of false urine sugar test results with prolonged use
   Checking with physician, nurse, or pharmacist, if changes in urine sugar test results occur, or if any other questions, especially if diabetes is not well-controlled
» Suspected overdose: Getting emergency help immediately
For antidiarrheal use
   Checking with physician if—
      Symptoms do not improve within 2 days or become worse
      Diarrhea is accompanied by high fever

Side/adverse effects
   May cause encephalopathy, severe constipation, and/or salicylism with higher-than-recommended doses and/or chronic use
   Dark tongue or grayish black stools may be alarming to patient although medically insignificant

General Dosing Information

Each 262-mg tablet of bismuth subsalicylate contains 102 mg of salicylate, and a tablespoon of the regular strength (262 mg per 15 mL) oral suspension contains 130 mg of salicylate. When the maximum daily dose (240 mL) of the regular strength oral suspension is used, the total amount of salicylate ingested is 2.1 grams, which may result in serum salicylate concentrations equivalent to those reached with the intake of 8 aspirin tablets.

Oral Dosage Forms

Note: Bracketed uses in the *Dosage Forms* section refer to categories of use and/or indications that are not included in U.S. product labeling.

BISMUTH SUBSALICYLATE ORAL SUSPENSION

Usual adult and adolescent dose:
   Diarrhea (treatment); or
   Gastric distress (treatment)—Oral, 525 mg every half-hour to one hour or 1050 mg every hour if needed.
   [Traveler's diarrhea (prophylaxis)][1]—Oral, 525 mg four times a day, starting one day prior to departure and continuing for two

days after returning, but not to exceed three weeks of continued use.
   [Ulcer, duodenal, *Helicobacter pylori*-associated (treatment adjunct)][1]; or
   [Gastritis, *Helicobacter pylori*-associated (treatment adjunct)][1]—Dosage has not been established. However, in one study, 525 mg was administered orally three times a day one hour before meals, in conjunction with 500 mg of amoxicillin and 500 mg of metronidazole administered three times a day after meals, for one to two weeks.

Note: The recommended maximum daily dose is 4.2 grams.

Usual geriatric dose: See *Usual adult and adolescent dose.*

Note: Geriatric patients with reduced renal function may be more sensitive to the effects of the usual adult dose and may require lower doses.

Auxiliary labeling:
• Shake well.
• May cause darkening of tongue and/or stools.

BISMUTH SUBSALICYLATE CHEWABLE TABLETS

Usual adult and adolescent dose:
   Diarrhea (treatment); or
   Gastric distress (treatment)—Oral, 525 mg every half-hour to one hour or 1050 mg every hour if needed.
   [Traveler's diarrhea (prophylaxis)][1]—Oral, 525 mg four times a day, starting one day prior to departure and continuing for two days after returning, but not to exceed three weeks of continued use.
   [Ulcer, duodenal, *Helicobacter pylori*-associated (treatment adjunct)][1]; or
   [Gastritis, *Helicobacter pylori*-associated (treatment adjunct)][1]—Dosage has not been established. However, in one study, 525 mg was administered orally three times a day one hour before meals, in conjunction with 500 mg of amoxicillin and 500 mg of metronidazole administered three times a day after meals, for one to two weeks.

Usual geriatric dose: See *Usual adult and adolescent dose.*

Note: Geriatric patients with reduced renal function may be more sensitive to the effects of the usual adult dose and may require lower doses.

Auxiliary labeling:
• Chew or allow to disintegrate in mouth before swallowing.
• May cause darkening of tongue and/or stools.

---

[1]Not included in Canadian product labeling.

BROMOCRIPTINE   Systemic

A commonly used *brand name* in the U.S. and Canada is *Parlodel.*

ORAL
Bromocriptine Mesylate Capsules
   In the U.S. and Canada—*Parlodel*
Bromocriptine Mesylate Tablets USP
   In the U.S. and Canada—*Parlodel*

Category: Dopamine agonist; antihyperprolactinemic; infertility therapy adjunct; lactation inhibitor; antidyskinetic; growth hormone suppressant (acromegaly); neuroleptic malignant syndrome therapy.

Indications

Note: Bracketed information in the *Indications* section refers to uses not included in U.S. product labeling.

Accepted
Prolactinomas, pituitary (treatment)—Bromocriptine is indicated in the treatment of prolactin-secreting pituitary tumors in men and women. Bromocriptine is usually considered to be the treatment of choice for microadenomas and by many clinicians for macroadenomas as well. However, surgery may be required to treat macroadenomas in those patients who either cannot take bromocriptine or who exhibit a poor therapeutic response to bromocriptine. Bromocriptine may also be used as an adjunct to radiotherapy when the tumor is inoperable.

[Bromocriptine is used by some clinicians in the treatment of visual field defects that develop during pregnancy. Visual field defects that respond to bromocriptine are secondary to pituitary adenoma enlargement. Bromocriptine therapy should be reserved for those adenomas without suprasellar extensions.][1]

Amenorrhea (treatment);

Galactorrhea (treatment); or

Infertility, female (treatment)—Bromocriptine is indicated for short-term symptomatic treatment of amenorrhea and/or galactorrhea or female infertility associated with hyperprolactinemia. Usefulness in normoprolactinemic amenorrhea or anovulation is controversial.

Lactation, after second- or third-trimester pregnancy loss (prophylaxis)—Bromocriptine can be used in selected individuals for the prevention of physiological lactation and breast engorgement after stillbirth, neonatal death, or abortion. However, in many patients, breast engorgement is a benign, self-limited condition, which may respond to breast support and mild analgesics, such as acetaminophen and ibuprofen. With the use of bromocriptine, a high rate of rebound symptoms occurs. Also, the relative risk of all of the rare, severe or life-threatening side effects, which have included strokes, seizures, and myocardial infarction, has yet to be determined.

[Infertility, male (treatment)]—Bromocriptine is indicated for treatment of prolactin-dependent male hypogonadism.

Parkinsonism (treatment)—Bromocriptine is indicated, usually as an adjunct to levodopa/carbidopa therapy, for treatment of the signs and symptoms of idiopathic or postencephalic parkinsonism.

Acromegaly (treatment)—Bromocriptine is indicated in the treatment of some cases of acromegaly, usually as an adjunct to surgery or radiotherapy. There are some reports that patients who respond may have elevated prolactin as well as elevated growth hormone concentrations.

[Neuroleptic malignant syndrome (treatment)][1]—Although controlled clinical trials have not been conducted, bromocriptine is widely used as adjunctive therapy in the treatment of neuroleptic malignant syndrome. Individual case reports and the known pharmacological activity of bromocriptine indicate that it may have some utility in the treatment of this disorder, as well as a lower incidence of side effects, as compared with other modes of therapy for this condition.

Unaccepted

The routine use of bromocriptine for elective suppression of postpartum lactation is not recommended.

---

[1]Not included in Canadian product labeling.

Pharmacology

Mechanism of action/Effect: Dopamine agonist—

Antihyperprolactinemic;

Infertility therapy adjunct; and

Lactation inhibitor: Amenorrhea and/or galactorrhea or infertility—Reduction of serum prolactin concentrations by direct inhibition of release of prolactin from the anterior pituitary gland through binding to dopamine type 2 (D_2) receptors, resulting in restoration of testicular or ovarian function and suppression of lactation.

Antidyskinetic: Parkinsonism—In high doses, stimulation of postsynaptic dopamine type 2 (D_2) receptors in the neostriatum of the central nervous system (CNS); may also decrease dopamine turnover. At low doses, bromocriptine may worsen dyskinesia by stimulating pre-synaptic dopamine receptors. Is most effective when used concurrently with levodopa, as stimulation of D_1 receptors by levodopa enhances the antidyskinetic effects of postsynaptic D_2 receptor stimulation by bromocriptine.

Growth hormone suppressant (acromegaly): Suppression of secretion and reduction of elevated growth hormone serum concentrations.

Neuroleptic malignant syndrome (NMS): Some evidence exists that NMS may result from depletion of dopamine or blockade of dopamine receptors in the nigrostriatal, hypothalamic, and mesolimbic cortical pathways.

Onset of action: Single dose—

Serum prolactin-lowering effect: 2 hours.

Antiparkinsonism effect: 30 to 90 minutes.

Growth hormone-lowering effect: 1 to 2 hours.

Time to peak effect:

Serum prolactin-lowering effect—8 hours (after a single dose).

Note: The maximum obtainable reduction in serum prolactin occurs after approximately 4 weeks of continuous therapy. The average duration of therapy required to reinitiate menses is 6 to 8 weeks. In the treatment of galactorrhea, a significant reduction in lactation usually occurs within 6 to 7 weeks, with cessation of lactation occurring by 12 to 13 weeks. Suppression of postpartum lactation requires 2 to 3 weeks of therapy; some clinicians believe that 3 weeks of therapy is necessary to prevent rebound lactation.

Antiparkinsonism effect—2 hours (after a single dose).

Growth hormone-lowering effect—A clinical response occurs within 4 to 8 weeks with continuous therapy.

Duration of action:

Serum prolactin-lowering effect—Approximately 24 hours (after a single dose).

Note: Serum prolactin concentrations usually return to pretreatment levels within 2 months after bromocriptine is discontinued.

Growth hormone-lowering effect—4 to 8 hours.

Precautions to Consider

Cross-sensitivity and/or related problems

Patients sensitive to other ergot derivatives may be sensitive to this medication also.

Adolescents

Appropriate studies performed to date have not demonstrated adolescent-specific problems that would limit the use of bromocriptine in adolescents.

Geriatrics

Appropriate studies on the relationship of age to the effects of bromocriptine have not been performed in the geriatric population. However, clinical experience with the use of bromocriptine has shown that CNS effects may occur more frequently in the elderly.

Dental

Use of large doses of bromocriptine (for example, in the treatment of acromegaly or parkinsonism) may decrease or inhibit salivary flow, thus contributing to the development of caries, periodontal disease, oral candidiasis, and discomfort.

Drug interactions and/or related problems

The following drug interactions and/or related problems have been selected on the basis of their potential clinical significance (possible mechanism in parentheses where appropriate)—not necessarily inclusive (» = major clinical significance):

Note: Combinations containing any of the following medications, depending on the amount present, may also interact with this medication.

» Alcohol

(disulfiram-like reaction may occur, including chest pain, confusion, fast or pounding heartbeat, flushing or redness of face, sweating, nausea, vomiting, throbbing headache, blurred vision, and severe weakness)

» Contraceptives, oral, or

» Estrogens or

» Progestins
(both estrogens and progestins may cause amenorrhea and/or galactorrhea, interfering with effects of bromocriptine; concurrent use in patients being treated for amenorrhea or galactorrhea is not recommended)

» Ergot alkaloids, other
(although there is no conclusive evidence of a drug interaction, rarely occurring cases of hypertension associated with the use of bromocriptine may be aggravated with use of ergot alkaloids)

Haloperidol or
Loxapine or
Methyldopa or
Metoclopramide or
Molindone or
Monoamine oxidase (MAO) inhibitors, including furazolidone and pargyline, or
Phenothiazines or
Reserpine or
Thioxanthenes
(may increase serum prolactin concentrations and interfere with effects of bromocriptine; dosage adjustment of bromocriptine may be necessary)

Hypotension-producing medications, other
(concurrent use may result in additive hypotensive effects; antihypertensive dosage adjustment may be necessary)

Levodopa
(bromocriptine may produce additive effects, allowing reduction in levodopa dosage)

Contraindications/Medical problems

The contraindications/medical problems included have been selected on the basis of their potential clinical significance (reasons given in parentheses where appropriate)—not necessarily inclusive (» = major clinical significance).

Except under special circumstances, this medication should not be used when the following medical problems exist:

» Hypertension, or history of, or
» Hypertension, pregnancy-induced, history of
(may be aggravated)

Risk-benefit should be considered when the following medical problems exist:

Hepatic function impairment
(metabolism may be reduced; dosage reduction may be required)
Psychiatric disorders
(may be exacerbated)
Sensitivity to bromocriptine or other ergot alkaloids

Side/Adverse Effects

Note: The most common side effects occur on initiation of therapy. Most side effects occurring with continuous therapy are dose-related.

Long-term treatment (6 to 36 months) with bromocriptine mesylate has rarely been associated with pulmonary infiltrates, pleural effusion, and thickening of the pleura. These occurred in a few patients taking doses ranging from 20 to 100 mg per day. When bromocriptine was discontinued, the changes slowly reversed towards normal.

The following side/adverse effects have been selected on the basis of their potential clinical significance (possible signs and symptoms in parentheses where appropriate)—not necessarily inclusive:

Those indicating need for medical attention
Incidence less frequent
Confusion or dyskinesia (uncontrolled movements of the body, such as the face, tongue, arms, hands, head, and upper body) *or hallucinations*

Note: *Confusion, dyskinesia, or hallucinations* are usually associated with use of high doses but may occur in 20 to 25% of patients being treated for parkinsonism, even at low doses, and may persist for a week or more after bromocriptine is withdrawn.

Incidence rare
Myocardial infarction (severe chest pain, fainting, fast heartbeat, increased sweating, continuing or severe nausea and vomiting, nervousness, unexplained shortness of breath, weakness); *seizures or strokes* (atypical headache; vision changes, such as blurred vision or temporary blindness; sudden weakness)

Note: There have been a few reports of *myocardial infarction* occurring in patients treated with bromocriptine, including patients being treated with bromocriptine to suppress lactation, although a direct causal relationship has not been established.

There have been a number of reports of *postpartum hypertension, seizures, and strokes* as well as reports of fatalities occurring in patients treated with bromocriptine to suppress lactation; however, further studies are being conducted to determine if a causal relationship exists between the incidence of hypertension, strokes, and seizures and the use of bromocriptine for suppression of lactation. Mean onset of the reactions was 9 days postpartum. The cases of cerebrovascular accident were all associated with hypertension. Use of bromocriptine should be discontinued in those patients who experience atypical headaches.

With high doses
Cerebrospinal fluid rhinorrhea (continuing runny nose)—in patients treated for pituitary macroadenomas; *fainting*—has also occurred with lower doses used in postpartum patients; *gastrointestinal hemorrhage or peptic ulcer* (black, tarry stools; blood in vomit; severe or continuing stomach pain); *retroperitoneal fibrosis* (continuing or severe abdominal or stomach pain, increased frequency of urination, continuing loss of appetite, lower back pain, continuing or severe nausea and vomiting, weakness)—with long-term use

Those indicating need for medical attention only if they continue or are bothersome
Incidence more frequent
Hypotension (dizziness or lightheadedness, especially when getting up from a lying or sitting position); *nausea*

Note: *Hypotension* occurs frequently, but is symptomatic only in 1 to 5% of patients (8% of postpartum patients). Rarely, hypotension may be severe. A "first-dose phenomenon" has been reported.

Incidence less frequent—more frequent with high doses (for example, when used for acromegaly or parkinsonism)
Constipation; diarrhea; drowsiness or tiredness; dry mouth; leg cramps at night; loss of appetite; mental depression; Raynaud's phenomenon (tingling or pain in fingers or toes when exposed to cold); *stomach pain; stuffy nose; vomiting*

Patient Consultation

In providing consultation, consider emphasizing the following selected information (» = major clinical significance):

Before using this medication
» Conditions affecting use, especially:
Sensitivity to bromocriptine or other ergot alkaloids
Pregnancy—Use is not generally recommended
Breast-feeding—Will prevent lactation in mothers who intend to breast-feed
Use in the elderly—CNS effects may occur more frequently
Dental—Reduced salivary flow caused by large doses may contribute to dental disorders
Other medications, especially alcohol, oral contraceptives, estrogens, progestins, or other ergot alkaloids

Other medical problems, especially history of hypertension or pregnancy-induced hypertension

Proper use of this medication

Taking first dose vaginally

Taking with meals or milk to reduce gastrointestinal irritation; taking dose at bedtime to better tolerate nausea

Missed dose: Taking if remembered within 4 hours; otherwise not taking at all; not doubling doses

» Proper storage

Precautions while using this medication

Regular visits to physician to check progress

» Caution when driving or doing jobs requiring alertness because of possible drowsiness or dizziness

Dizziness may be more likely to occur after initial dose; taking first dose at bedtime or lying down; getting up slowly from sitting or lying position; taking first dose vaginally

» Possible dryness of mouth; using sugarless gum or candy, ice, or saliva substitute for relief; checking with physician or dentist if dry mouth continues for more than 2 weeks

Checking with physician before reducing dosage or discontinuing medication

» Possibility of disulfiram-like reaction with alcohol

For treatment of amenorrhea, galactorrhea, acromegaly, or pituitary prolactinomas in females of child-bearing potential

Advisability of using nonhormonal contraception during therapy; patients desiring pregnancy should discuss with physician proper time to discontinue use of contraception; telling physician immediately if pregnancy is suspected

» Telling physician right away if symptoms of enlargement of pituitary tumor (blurred vision, sudden headache, severe nausea and vomiting) occur

For treatment of female infertility

Advisability of using nonhormonal contraception until normal menstrual cycle is established; discussing with physician proper time to discontinue use of contraception; telling physician immediately if pregnancy is suspected

» Telling physician right away if symptoms of enlargement of pituitary tumor (blurred vision, sudden headache, severe nausea and vomiting) occur

Side/adverse effects

Signs of potential side effects, especially CNS effects, myocardial infarction, seizures, retroperitoneal fibrosis, gastrointestinal hemorrhage, peptic ulcer, strokes, and rhinorrhea

General Dosing Information

Incidence and severity of side effects (especially nausea) may be reduced by initiating therapy at a low dose (for example, 1.25 mg at bedtime) and increasing gradually (increments of 2.5 mg every 14 to 28 days for parkinsonism and 3 to 7 days for other indications) to the minimum effective dose, and by administration of bromocriptine with food. Also, dizziness and nausea may be better tolerated by administering some or all of the dose at bedtime or by administering the initial dose intravaginally.

Because of the risk of significant hypotension when bromocriptine is used to treat postpartum lactation, it is recommended that the medication not be given until vital signs have stabilized, and not for at least 4 hours after delivery.

Treatment of hyperprolactinemia with bromocriptine may be symptomatic rather than curative. Following withdrawal, rebound amenorrhea usually occurs within 4 to 24 weeks and galactorrhea within 2 to 12 weeks. Pituitary adenoma regrowth and increase in serum prolactin concentrations may occur after withdrawal of bromocriptine. Elevated growth hormone concentrations will also return when the medication is withdrawn if the cause of acromegaly is not eliminated.

Oral Dosage Forms

Note: Bracketed uses in the *Dosage Forms* section refer to categories of use and/or indications that are not included in U.S. product labeling.

BROMOCRIPTINE MESYLATE CAPSULES

Usual adult and adolescent dose: For doses less than 5 mg, see *Bromocriptine Mesylate Tablets USP*.

Pituitary prolactinomas—Oral, 5.0 to 20 mg (base or mesylate) per day. Occasionally, higher doses may be required.

Antidyskinetic—Parkinsonism:

Maintenance—Oral, 5 to 100 mg (base or mesylate) a day in divided doses, adjusted according to response; up to 300 mg a day has been used.

Growth hormone suppressant (acromegaly)—

Maintenance: Oral, 10 to 30 mg (base or mesylate) a day in divided doses. Up to 100 mg per day has been used.

[Neuroleptic malignant syndrome][1]—Oral, initially 5 mg (base or mesylate) once a day, with the dosage being titrated according to patient response.

Doses of up to 20 mg four times a day have been used.

Note: To reduce incidence of side effects, it is recommended that dosage increments be made at 14- to 28-day intervals for parkinsonism and at 3- to 7-day intervals for other indications.

Auxiliary labeling:

• Avoid alcoholic beverages.
• Take with meals or milk.
• May cause drowsiness.

BROMOCRIPTINE MESYLATE TABLETS USP

Usual adult and adolescent dose:

Antihyperprolactinemic or

Infertility therapy adjunct—

Amenorrhea and/or galactorrhea or

Infertility, [male] or female:

Initial—Oral, 1.25 to 2.5 mg (base or mesylate) once a day.

Maintenance—Oral, 2.5 mg (base or mesylate) two or three times a day.

Prolactinomas, pituitary: Oral, 1.25 to 20 mg (usually 5.0 to 7.5 mg) (base or mesylate) per day. Occasionally, higher doses may be required.

Antidyskinetic—Parkinsonism:

Initial—Oral, 1.25 to 2.5 mg (base or mesylate) once a day.

Maintenance—Oral, 2.5 to 100 mg (base or mesylate) a day in divided doses, adjusted according to response; up to 300 mg a day has been used.

Growth hormone suppressant (acromegaly)—

Initial: Oral, 1.25 to 2.5 mg (base or mesylate) once a day, increased gradually to the effective dose.

Maintenance: Oral, 10 to 30 mg (base or mesylate) a day in divided doses. Up to 100 mg per day has been used.

[Neuroleptic malignant syndrome][1]—Oral, initially 5 mg (base or mesylate) once a day, with the dosage being titrated according to patient response.

Doses of up to 20 mg four times a day have been used.

Note: To reduce incidence of side effects, it is recommended that dosage increments be made at 14- to 28-day intervals for parkinsonism and at 3- to 7-day intervals for other indications.

Auxiliary labeling:

• Avoid alcoholic beverages.
• Take with meals or milk.
• May cause drowsiness.

BRONCHODILATORS, ADRENERGIC   Systemic

INN: Included in brackets after individual generic listings, if different from the U.S. generic name.

Some commonly used *brand names* are:

In the U.S.—

Adrenalin [Epinephrine]
Aerolone [Isoproterenol]
Alupent [Metaproterenol]
Arm-a-Med Isoetharine [Isoetharine]
Arm-a-Med Metaproterenol [Metaproterenol]
AsthmaHaler [Epinephrine]
AsthmaNefrin [Racepinephrine]
Brethaire [Terbutaline]
Brethine [Terbutaline]
Bricanyl [Terbutaline]
Bronitin Mist [Epinephrine]
Bronkaid Mist [Epinephrine]
Bronkaid Mist Suspension [Epinephrine]
Bronkephrine [Ethylnorepinephrine]
Bronkometer [Isoetharine]
Bronkosol [Isoetharine]
Dey-Dose Isoetharine [Isoetharine]
Dey-Dose Isoetharine S/F [Isoetharine]
Dey-Dose Isoproterenol [Isoproterenol]
Dey-Dose Metaproterenol [Metaproterenol]
Dey-Dose Racepinephrine [Racepinephrine]
Dey-Lute Isoetharine [Isoetharine]
Dey-Lute Isoetharine S/F [Isoetharine]
Dey-Lute Metaproterenol [Metaproterenol]

Dispos-a-Med Isoetharine [Isoetharine]
Dispos-a-Med Isoproterenol [Isoproterenol]
Ephed II [Ephedrine]
EpiPen Auto-Injector [Epinephrine]
EpiPen Jr. Auto-Injector [Epinephrine]
Isuprel [Isoproterenol]
Isuprel Glossets [Isoproterenol]
Isuprel Mistometer [Isoproterenol]
Maxair [Pirbuterol]
Medihaler-Epi [Epinephrine]
Medihaler-Iso [Isoproterenol]
Metaprel [Metaproterenol]
Norisodrine Aerotrol [Isoproterenol]
Primatene Mist [Epinephrine]
Primatene Mist Suspension [Epinephrine]
Proventil [Albuterol]
Proventil Repetabs [Albuterol]
Sus-Phrine [Epinephrine]
Tornalate [Bitolterol]
Vapo-Iso [Isoproterenol]
Vaponefrin [Racepinephrine]
Ventolin [Albuterol]
Ventolin Rotacaps [Albuterol]

In Canada—

Adrenalin [Epinephrine]
Alupent [Metaproterenol]
Berotec [Fenoterol]
Bricanyl [Terbutaline]
Bronkaid Mistometer [Epinephrine]
EpiPen Auto-Injector [Epinephrine]
EpiPen Jr. Auto-Injector [Epinephrine]
Isuprel [Isoproterenol]
Isuprel Mistometer [Isoproterenol]

Medihaler-Epi [Epinephrine]
Medihaler-Iso [Isoproterenol]
Novosalmol [Albuterol]
Pro-Air [Procaterol]
Vaponefrin [Racepinephrine]
Ventolin [Albuterol]
Ventolin Rotacaps [Albuterol]

Another commonly used name for albuterol is salbutamol.

ALBUTEROL [INN: Salbutamol]
Inhalation
   Albuterol Inhalation Aerosol
      In the U.S.—*Proventil; Ventolin;* GENERIC
      In Canada—*Ventolin*

Albuterol Sulfate Inhalation Solution
   In the U.S.—*Proventil; Ventolin*
   In Canada—*Ventolin*
Albuterol Sulfate for Inhalation
   In the U.S. and Canada—*Ventolin Rotacaps*
Oral
   Albuterol Sulfate Oral Solution*
      In Canada—*Ventolin*
   Albuterol Sulfate Syrup
      In the U.S.—*Proventil; Ventolin*
   Albuterol Sulfate Tablets
      In the U.S.—*Proventil; Ventolin;* GENERIC
      In Canada—*Novosalmol; Ventolin*
   Albuterol Sulfate Extended-release Tablets
      In the U.S.—*Proventil Repetabs*
Parenteral
   Albuterol Sulfate Injection*
      In Canada—*Ventolin*
BITOLTEROL
Inhalation
   Bitolterol Mesylate Inhalation Aerosol
      In the U.S.—*Tornalate*
EPHEDRINE
Oral
   Ephedrine Sulfate Capsules USP
      In the U.S.—*Ephed II;* GENERIC
   Ephedrine Sulfate Syrup USP
      In the U.S.—GENERIC
Parenteral
   Ephedrine Sulfate Injection USP
      In the U.S. and Canada—GENERIC
EPINEPHRINE
Inhalation
   Epinephrine Inhalation Aerosol USP
      In the U.S.—*Bronkaid Mist; Primatene Mist;* GENERIC
      In Canada—*Bronkaid Mistometer*
   Epinephrine Inhalation Solution USP
      In the U.S.—*Adrenalin*
   Epinephrine Bitartrate Inhalation Aerosol USP
      In the U.S.—*AsthmaHaler; Bronitin Mist; Bronkaid Mist Suspension; Medihaler-Epi; Primatene Mist Suspension*
      In Canada—*Medihaler-Epi*
   Racepinephrine Inhalation Solution USP
      In the U.S.—*AsthmaNefrin; Dey-Dose Racepinephrine; Vaponefrin*
      In Canada—*Vaponefrin*
Parenteral
   Epinephrine Injection USP
      In the U.S. and Canada—*Adrenalin; EpiPen Auto-Injector; EpiPen Jr. Auto-Injector;* GENERIC
   Sterile Epinephrine Suspension
      In the U.S.—*Sus-Phrine*
ETHYLNOREPINEPHRINE
Parenteral
   Ethylnorepinephrine Hydrochloride Injection USP
      In the U.S.—*Bronkephrine*
FENOTEROL*
Inhalation
   Fenoterol Hydrobromide Inhalation Aerosol*
      In Canada—*Berotec*
   Fenoterol Hydrobromide Inhalation Solution*
      In Canada—*Berotec*

Oral
  Fenoterol Hydrobromide Tablets*
    In Canada—*Berotec*
ISOETHARINE
Inhalation
  Isoetharine Inhalation Solution USP
    In the U.S.—*Arm-a-Med Isoetharine; Bronkosol; Dey-Dose Isoetharine; Dey-Dose Isoetharine S/F; Dey-Lute Isoetharine; Dey-Lute Isoetharine S/F; Dispos-a-Med Isoetharine;* GENERIC
  Isoetharine Mesylate Inhalation Aerosol USP
    In the U.S.—*Bronkometer;* GENERIC
ISOPROTERENOL
Inhalation
  Isoproterenol Inhalation Solution USP
    In the U.S.—*Aerolone; Dey-Dose Isoproterenol; Dispos-a-Med Isoproterenol; Isuprel; Vapo-Iso;* GENERIC
    In Canada—*Isuprel*
  Isoproterenol Hydrochloride Inhalation Aerosol USP
    In the U.S.—*Isuprel Mistometer; Norisodrine Aerotrol*
    In Canada—*Isuprel Mistometer*
  Isoproterenol Sulfate Inhalation Aerosol USP
    In the U.S. and Canada—*Medihaler-Iso*
Oral
  Isoproterenol Hydrochloride Tablets USP
    In the U.S.—*Isuprel Glossets*
    In Canada—*Isuprel*
Parenteral
  Isoproterenol Hydrochloride Injection USP
    In the U.S. and Canada—*Isuprel;* GENERIC
METAPROTERENOL
Inhalation
  Metaproterenol Sulfate Inhalation Aerosol USP
    In the U.S.—*Alupent; Metaprel*
    In Canada—*Alupent*
  Metaproterenol Sulfate Inhalation Solution USP
    In the U.S.—*Alupent; Arm-a-Med Metaproterenol; Dey-Dose Metaproterenol; Dey-Lute Metaproterenol; Metaprel;* GENERIC
    In Canada—*Alupent*
Oral
  Metaproterenol Sulfate Syrup USP
    In the U.S.—*Alupent; Metaprel;* GENERIC
    In Canada—*Alupent*
  Metaproterenol Sulfate Tablets USP
    In the U.S.—*Alupent; Metaprel;* GENERIC
    In Canada—*Alupent*
PIRBUTEROL
Inhalation
  Pirbuterol Acetate Inhalation Aerosol
    In the U.S.—*Maxair*
PROCATEROL*
Inhalation
  Procaterol Hydrochloride Hemihydrate Inhalation Aerosol*
    In Canada—*Pro-Air*
TERBUTALINE
Inhalation
  Terbutaline Sulfate Inhalation Aerosol
    In the U.S.—*Brethaire*
    In Canada—*Bricanyl*
Oral
  Terbutaline Sulfate Tablets USP
    In the U.S.—*Brethine; Bricanyl*
    In Canada—*Bricanyl*
Parenteral
  Terbutaline Sulfate Injection USP
    In the U.S.—*Brethine; Bricanyl*

*Not commercially available in the U.S.

Category

Bronchodilator—Albuterol; Bitolterol; Ephedrine; Epinephrine; Ethylnorepinephrine; Fenoterol; Isoetharine; Isoproterenol; Metaproterenol; Pirbuterol; Procaterol; Terbutaline.
Asthma prophylactic—Albuterol Inhalation Aerosol; Albuterol Inhalation Solution; Bitolterol; Epinephrine (Inhalation); Isoetharine; Metaproterenol (Inhalation); Pirbuterol; Procaterol; Terbutaline (Inhalation).
Vasopressor—Ephedrine (Parenteral); Epinephrine Injection.
Cardiac stimulant—Epinephrine Injection; Isoproterenol (Oral and Parenteral).
Anesthetic (local) adjunct—Epinephrine Injection.
Antiallergic (systemic)—Epinephrine Injection.
Surgical aid (antihemorrhagic; decongestant; mydriatic)—Epinephrine Injection.
Antihemorrhagic (topical)—Epinephrine Injection.
Decongestant, nasal (systemic)—Ephedrine (Oral).
Central nervous system (CNS) stimulant—Ephedrine (Oral).
Labor (premature) inhibitor—Terbutaline (Oral and Parenteral).
Urticaria therapy adjunct—Ephedrine.
Priapism reversal agent—Epinephrine Injection.

Indications

Note: Bracketed information in the *Indications* section refers to uses not included in U.S. product labeling.

Accepted
Asthma, bronchial (treatment);
Bronchitis (treatment);
Bronchospasm (treatment);
Emphysema, pulmonary (treatment);
Bronchiectasis (treatment); or
Pulmonary disease, obstructive, other (treatment)—Albuterol, bitolterol, epinephrine, ethylnorepinephrine, fenoterol, isoetharine, isoproterenol inhalation, metaproterenol, pirbuterol, procaterol, and terbutaline are indicated for the symptomatic treatment of bronchial asthma. These medications are also indicated for the treatment of reversible bronchospasm associated with bronchitis, pulmonary emphysema, bronchiectasis, and other obstructive pulmonary diseases.

Also, ephedrine may be indicated for the symptomatic treatment of bronchial asthma and reversible bronchospasm associated with other obstructive pulmonary diseases; however, agents with less beta-1-adrenergic effects and more selective beta-2-adrenergic effects are generally preferred. In the treatment of acute bronchospasm, parenteral ephedrine is usually less effective than epinephrine.

Isoproterenol sublingual tablets may be used for the treatment of bronchial asthma and in the management of obstructive pulmonary disease, but isoproterenol inhalation is preferred because absorption after sublingual administration may be erratic and unpredictable.

Asthma, bronchial (prophylaxis); or
Bronchospasm (prophylaxis)—Albuterol inhalation aerosol[1], bitolterol, and pirbuterol are indicated for the prophylaxis of bronchial asthma and reversible bronchospasm. [Other adrenergic bronchodilators, albuterol inhalation solution, epinephrine inhalation, isoetharine, metaproterenol inhalation, procaterol, and terbutaline inhalation, are also used for the prophylaxis of bronchial asthma and reversible bronchospasm.][1]

Albuterol inhalation[1] and procaterol inhalation are indicated for the prevention of exercise-induced bronchospasm. [Other inhaled adrenergic bronchodilators are also used in the prevention of exercise-induced bronchospasm.][1]

Bronchospasm, during anesthesia (treatment)—Parenteral isoproterenol may be indicated in the management of bronchospasm during anesthesia. [Parenteral epinephrine and terbutaline may also be useful in the management of bronchospasm during anesthesia.]

Allergic reactions, drug-induced (treatment);
Anaphylactic reactions (treatment);
Angioedema (treatment);
Anaphylactic shock (treatment adjunct);
Bites or stings, insect (treatment);
Laryngeal edema, acute noninfectious (treatment); or
Transfusion reactions, urticarial (treatment)—Epinephrine injection is indicated in the emergency treatment of severe allergic reactions, including anaphylactic shock, to drugs, foods, sera, insect stings, or other allergens. It relieves symptoms such as bronchospasm, urticaria, pruritus, hives, angioedema, and swelling of lips, eyelids, tongue, and nasal mucosa. Epinephrine injection is also used in the treatment of acute noninfectious laryngeal edema.

Croup (treatment)—Racepinephrine inhalation is indicated in the treatment of postintubation and infectious croup.

Hypotension, acute (treatment)—Parenteral ephedrine is indicated primarily to counteract the hypotensive effects of spinal or other types of nontopical conduction anesthesia. It may also be used in hypotensive states following sympathectomy, or following overdosage with ganglionic-blocking agents, antiadrenergic agents, or other agents used for lowering blood pressure in the treatment of arterial hypertension. Epinephrine injection may be useful in the treatment of acute hypotension, especially after cardiopulmonary bypass.

Cardiac arrest (treatment)—Epinephrine injection and isoproterenol injection are indicated in the treatment of cardiac standstill or arrest. Epinephrine injection may be used for resuscitation in cardiac arrest following anesthetic accidents; however, it should be used with great caution in patients receiving cyclopropane or halogenated hydrocarbon general anesthetics because these anesthetics sensitize the myocardium and cardiac arrhythmias may be induced.

In acute attacks of ventricular standstill, physical measures should be used prior to administration of epinephrine. However, if external cardiac compression and attempts to restore circulation by electrical defibrillation or use of a pacemaker fail, intravenous injection of epinephrine into a major vein may be effective.

Adams-Stokes syndrome (treatment);
Heart block (treatment); or
Syncope, due to complete heart block (treatment)—Isoproterenol injection is indicated in the treatment of Adams-Stokes syndrome or atrioventricular (AV) heart block. Epinephrine injection may be indicated for the treatment of attacks of transitory AV heart block with syncopal seizures (Adams-Stokes syndrome), but isoproterenol injection is generally preferred. Also, sublingual or rectal administration of isoproterenol may be indicated in the treatment of Adams-Stokes syndrome and AV heart block.

Epinephrine injection is also indicated in the treatment of syncope due to complete heart block.

In symptomatic heart block, electrical pacing is the preferred treatment for maintenance of an adequate ventricular rate and isoproterenol is used only for temporary support when electrical pacing is unavailable.

Arrhythmias, cardiac, including ventricular arrhythmias (treatment);
Carotid sinus hypersensitivity (treatment); or
Syncope, due to carotid sinus hypersensitivity (treatment)—Parenteral isoproterenol is indicated in the treatment of carotid sinus hypersensitivity, and ventricular tachycardia and ventricular arrhythmias that require increased inotropic activity for therapy. Epinephrine injection is used in the treatment of syncope due to carotid sinus hypersensitivity. In ventricular arrhythmias, especially certain types of ventricular tachycardia and fibrillation, electroshock therapy may be necessary and is usually the preferred treatment.

Cardiac output, low (treatment)—Epinephrine injection may be used in the treatment of low cardiac output following extracorporeal cardiopulmonary bypass, usually given in low doses or with a peripheral vasodilator such as phentolamine. Isoproterenol injection may be used when bradycardia is present or when systemic vascular resistance is contraindicated.

Shock, hypoperfusion syndrome (treatment adjunct)—Parenteral isoproterenol may be indicated as an adjunct in the management of shock (hypoperfusion syndrome); however, the use of isoproterenol for the treatment of shock is controversial. It should be used only as an adjunct to fluid volume replacement and other measures appropriate in the management of shock. If evidence of hypoperfusion persists after adequate volume replacement, isoproterenol may be administered. Isoproterenol is not generally recommended for use in shock caused by myocardial infarction.

Anesthesia, local, adjunct—Epinephrine injection is indicated for concurrent use with some local anesthetics to decrease the rate of vascular absorption and thereby localize anesthesia, prolong the duration of action, and decrease the risk of toxicity due to the local anesthetic. Epinephrine injection should be used cautiously and in carefully circumscribed quantities, if at all, with local anesthetics for anesthetizing areas with end arteries (such as the fingers, toes, or penis) or otherwise compromised blood supply because ischemia leading to gangrene may result.

Hemorrhage, superficial, in ocular surgery (treatment);
Congestion, conjunctival, during surgery (treatment);
Mydriasis, during surgery; or
Hypertension, ocular, during surgery (treatment)—Epinephrine may be injected intracamerally or subconjunctivally to control hemorrhage, produce conjunctival decongestion and mydriasis, and reduce intraocular pressure during ocular surgery.

Hemorrhage, superficial (treatment)—Epinephrine injection may be applied topically to control superficial bleeding from arterioles and capillaries in the skin, mucous membranes, or other tissues. However, only small doses should be used because topically applied epinephrine can be systemically absorbed.

Congestion, nasal (treatment); or
Congestion, sinus (treatment)—Oral ephedrine may be indicated for the local treatment of nasal congestion in acute coryza, vasomotor rhinitis, acute sinusitis, and hay fever. It may also be used in the treatment of sinus congestion.

Narcolepsy (treatment); or
Depression, mental (treatment)—Oral ephedrine may be indicated as a CNS stimulant in the treatment of narcolepsy and depressive states.

Status asthmaticus (treatment)—Parenteral albuterol is used for the treatment of status asthmaticus.

[Labor, premature (prophylaxis and treatment)][1]—Terbutaline (oral and parenteral) is used for prophylaxis and treatment of preterm labor.

[Urticaria (treatment adjunct)][1]—Ephedrine may be useful as an adjunct in the treatment of acute and chronic urticaria.

[Hemorrhage, gingival (treatment adjunct)][1]; or
[Hemorrhage, pulpal (treatment)][1]—Epinephrine injection is used topically as an adjunct in the treatment of gingival hemorrhage. It is also used in the treatment of pulpal hemorrhage.

[Priapism (treatment)][1]—Epinephrine injection, administered intracavernosally, has been reported to be effective in the treatment of priapism resulting from use of intracavernosal papaverine or phentolamine or from other causes. However, epinephrine should be used with caution because hypertension and ischemic electrocardiographic changes can occur.

Unaccepted
Oral ephedrine has been used in the treatment of enuresis and myasthenia gravis but it has been replaced by more effective agents.

Parenteral ephedrine has been used in Adams-Stokes syndrome with complete heart block; however, it has been replaced by more effective agents.

Epinephrine injection has been used to correct hypoglycemia in insulin shock; however, it generally has been replaced by more effective antihypoglycemics.

---

[1]Not included in Canadian product labeling.

Pharmacology

See also *Table 1*, page 306.

Mechanism of action/Effect:

Bronchodilator—Adrenergic bronchodilators act by stimulating beta-2-adrenergic receptors in the lungs to relax bronchial smooth muscle, thereby relieving bronchospasm, increasing vital capacity, decreasing residual volume, and reducing airway resistance. This action is believed to result from increased production of cyclic adenosine $3',5'$-monophosphate (cyclic $3',5'$-AMP or c-AMP) caused by activation of the enzyme adenyl cyclase, the enzyme that catalyzes the conversion of adenosine triphosphate (ATP) to c-AMP. Increased c-AMP concentrations, in addition to relaxing bronchial smooth muscle, inhibit release of mediators of immediate hypersensitivity from cells, especially from mast cells. Also, epinephrine acts by stimulating alpha-adrenergic receptors to constrict bronchial arterioles.

Epinephrine also inhibits antigen-induced release of histamine and the slow-reacting substance of anaphylaxis and directly antagonizes histamine-induced bronchiolar constriction, vasodilation, and edema. Ephedrine, isoetharine, and metaproterenol may also inhibit antigen-induced release of histamine, and isoproterenol may inhibit antigen-induced release of histamine and the slow-reacting substance of anaphylaxis.

Vasopressor—Ephedrine acts on beta-1-adrenergic receptors in the heart, producing an increase in force of contraction via a positive inotropic effect on the myocardium. This action increases cardiac output, resulting in an increase in systolic and, usually, diastolic blood pressure. Ephedrine may also act on alpha-adrenergic receptors in the skeletal muscle vasculature to produce vasoconstriction, which increases peripheral resistance, possibly contributing to the pressor effects.

Epinephrine, in low doses, produces a moderate elevation of systolic blood pressure, primarily via cardiostimulation-induced increases in cardiac output. However, in low doses, epinephrine acts on beta-2-adrenergic receptors in the skeletal muscle vasculature, producing vasodilation, which decreases peripheral resistance, so that diastolic pressure may be decreased. In higher doses, epinephrine acts on alpha-adrenergic receptors in the skeletal muscle vasculature to produce vasoconstriction, which increases peripheral resistance, resulting in an increase in both systolic and diastolic blood pressure.

Cardiac stimulant—Epinephrine and isoproterenol act on beta-1-adrenergic receptors in the heart, producing an increase in heart rate via a positive chronotropic effect through the sino-atrial node and an increase in force of contraction via a positive inotropic effect on the myocardium. Isoproterenol also increases conduction velocity and shortens the refractory period of the atrioventricular node.

Isoproterenol also dilates peripheral blood vessels by an action on beta-2-adrenergic receptors. This action, along with the medication's cardiostimulating actions, may provide beneficial effects in shock due to low cardiac output and intensive vasoconstriction that persist after adequate fluid replacement.

Anesthetic (local) adjunct—Epinephrine acts on alpha-adrenergic receptors in the skin, mucous membranes, and viscera to produce vasoconstriction. This action decreases the rate of vascular absorption of the local anesthetic used with epinephrine, thereby localizing anesthesia, prolonging the duration of action, and decreasing the risk of toxicity due to the anesthetic.

Surgical aid (antihemorrhagic; decongestant; mydriatic)—Epinephrine acts on alpha-adrenergic receptors in the conjunctiva to produce vasoconstriction and hemostasis in bleeding from small vessels; also, conjunctival congestion is decreased. Epinephrine contracts the dilator muscle of the pupil by acting on alpha-adrenergic receptors, resulting in dilation of the pupil (mydriasis).

Antihemorrhagic (topical)—Epinephrine acts on alpha-adrenergic receptors in the skin, mucous membranes, and viscera to produce vasoconstriction and hemostasis in bleeding from small vessels.

Decongestant, nasal (systemic)—Ephedrine acts on alpha-adrenergic receptors of blood vessels in the nasal mucosa, producing vasoconstriction, which may result in nasal decongestion.

CNS stimulant—Ephedrine stimulates the cerebral cortex and subcortical centers to produce its effects in narcolepsy and depressive states.

Labor (premature) inhibitor—Terbutaline acts primarily as a beta-adrenergic stimulant to relax the uterine muscle, thereby inhibiting uterine contractions.

Urticaria therapy adjunct—Ephedrine acts on alpha-adrenergic receptors of blood vessels in the skin to produce vasoconstriction, which may help to reverse cutaneous vasodilation and thereby reduce the increased vascular permeability that results in localized edema in urticaria.

Other actions/effects: Other adrenergic effects include alpha-receptor-mediated contraction of gastrointestinal and urinary sphincters; beta-1-receptor-mediated lipolysis; and beta-2-receptor-mediated decrease in gastrointestinal tone, and increases in uterine relaxation, renin secretion, hepatic glycogenolysis/gluconeogenesis, and pancreatic beta cell secretion.

Precautions to Consider

Geriatrics

For albuterol, bitolterol, epinephrine, ethylnorepinephrine, fenoterol, isoproterenol, metaproterenol, pirbuterol, procaterol, and terbutaline—No published geriatrics-specific information is available.

For ephedrine—Although appropriate studies with ephedrine have not been performed in the geriatric population, no geriatrics-specific problems have been documented to date. However, elderly patients are more likely to have age-related prostatic hypertrophy and caution should be used in patients receiving ephedrine.

Dental

For epinephrine—Epinephrine is used in gingival retraction cords. Systemic absorption of epinephrine can occur from application of retraction cords, especially to abraded surfaces. Epinephrine retraction cords should be used with caution in patients with cardiovascular problems, since the amount of epinephrine absorbed systemically cannot be predicted.

Contraindications/Medical problems

See *Table 2*, page 307.

Side/Adverse Effects

Note: Supraventricular and ventricular ectopic beats have occurred with beta-adrenergic agonist inhalations.

Hypokalemia may be induced by higher-than-recommended doses of beta-agonists, especially in those patients receiving digitalis glycosides or diuretics or who are prone to cardiac dysrhythmias.

See also *Table 3*, page 308.

Patient Consultation

See *Table 4*, page 311.

General Dosing Information

Patients taking this medication for bronchial asthma, bronchitis, emphysema, or other obstructive pulmonary disease should be advised to contact their physician if they do not respond to the usual dose of this medication, since this may be a sign of seriously worsening asthma or bronchospasm that requires reassessment of therapy.

Following administration of an adrenergic bronchodilator, a sufficient interval of time should elapse before administration of another sympathomimetic agent.

For inhalation aerosol dosage forms only
When an adrenergic bronchodilator inhalation aerosol is used in conjunction with an adrenocorticoid or ipratropium oral inhalation aerosol, the adrenergic bronchodilator inhalation aerosol should be administered 5 minutes prior to the adrenocorticoid or ipratropium inhalation aerosol. This interval allows for bronchodilation to occur and increased deposition of the adrenocorticoid or ipratropium within the bronchi.

Repeated excessive use may result in paradoxical bronchospasm. If this occurs, the adrenergic bronchodilator should be discontinued immediately and alternative therapy instituted.

ALBUTEROL

Summary of Differences

Indications: Parenteral albuterol also used in treatment of status asthmaticus.
Pharmacology:
  Half-life—
    Elimination: 3.8 hours.
    Plasma: 2.7 to 5 hours.
  Onset of action—
    Inhalation: 5 to 15 minutes.
    Oral: 15 to 30 minutes.
  Time to peak effect—
    Inhalation: 1 to 1.5 hours after 2 inhalations.
    Oral: 2 to 3 hours.
  Duration of action—
    Inhalation: 3 to 6 hours.
    Oral: 8 hours or more (12 hours for extended-release tablets).
  Elimination—Secondary route of elimination is fecal.
Precautions:
  Pregnancy/reproduction—Labor: Albuterol administered intravenously or orally reportedly inhibits uterine contractions.
  Contraindications/medical problems—Caution also needed in ketoacidosis when large parenteral doses of albuterol are administered.
Side/adverse effects: Difficult or painful urination, drowsiness, flushing or redness of face or skin, heartburn, loss of appetite, muscle cramps or twitching, unusual paleness, or unusual taste may occur.

Additional Dosing Information

See also *General Dosing Information.*

For parenteral dosage forms only
Parenteral albuterol is preferably administered by continuous intravenous infusion. However, if a rapid response is required, it may be administered by direct intravenous injection, followed by a continuous intravenous infusion. Albuterol injection may also be administered by intramuscular injection, if necessary.

Inhalation Dosage Forms

ALBUTEROL INHALATION AEROSOL

Usual adult and adolescent dose: Bronchodilator—
  Bronchospasm in obstructive pulmonary disease (prophylaxis[1] and treatment): Oral inhalation, 180 or 200 mcg (0.18 or 0.2 mg—2 inhalations) every four to six hours.
    Note: For some patients, a dose of 90 or 100 mcg (0.09 or 0.1 mg—1 inhalation) every four hours may be sufficient.

Bronchospasm, exercise-induced (prophylaxis): Oral inhalation, 180 or 200 mcg (0.18 or 0.2 mg—2 inhalations) fifteen minutes prior to exercise.

Auxiliary labeling:
• For oral inhalation only.
• Shake well.
• Store away from heat and direct sunlight.

ALBUTEROL SULFATE INHALATION SOLUTION

Usual adult and adolescent dose: Bronchodilator—Oral inhalation, administered by nebulization or intermittent positive pressure breathing (IPPB), 1.25 to 5 mg (base) in 2 to 5 mL or more of sterile 0.9% sodium chloride solution or sterile water for inhalation, depending on product, repeated three or four times a day every four to six hours if necessary.

Note: When albuterol inhalation solution is administered through a nebulizer, a mouthpiece or face mask may be used. The nebulizer should be used with compressed air or oxygen and the gas flow should be about 6 to 10 liters per minute. With an average volume of 3 mL, a single treatment lasts about 10 (range, 5 to 15) minutes.

When administered through IPPB, the inspiratory pressure is usually 10 to 20 cm H_2O and the duration of administration varies from 5 to 20 minutes, depending on the patient and the control of the apparatus.

Auxiliary labeling:
• For oral inhalation only.
• Refrigerate.

ALBUTEROL SULFATE FOR INHALATION

Usual adult and adolescent dose: Bronchodilator—
  Bronchospasm in obstructive pulmonary disease (treatment): Oral inhalation, 200 or 400 mcg (0.2 or 0.4 mg, respectively) every four to six hours.
  Bronchospasm, exercise-induced (prophylaxis): Oral inhalation, 200 mcg (0.2 mg), fifteen minutes before exercise.

Auxiliary labeling: • For oral inhalation only.

Oral Dosage Forms

ALBUTEROL SULFATE ORAL SOLUTION

Note: Albuterol sulfate oral solution is not commercially available in the U.S.

Usual adult dose: Bronchodilator—Oral, 2 to 4 mg (base) three or four times a day.

ALBUTEROL SULFATE SYRUP

Usual adult and adolescent dose: Bronchodilator—Bronchospasm in obstructive pulmonary disease (treatment): Oral, 2 to 6 mg (base) three or four times a day initially, the dosage being increased as needed and tolerated up to a maximum of 8 mg four times a day.

Note: Patients sensitive to beta-adrenergic stimulants—Oral, 2 mg (base) three or four times a day initially, the dosage being increased as needed and tolerated up to a maximum of 8 mg three or four times a day.

Usual geriatric dose: Bronchodilator—Oral, 2 mg (base) three or four times a day initially, the dosage being increased as needed and tolerated up to a maximum of 8 mg three or four times a day.

ALBUTEROL SULFATE TABLETS

Usual adult and adolescent dose: Bronchodilator—Bronchospasm in obstructive pulmonary disease (treatment): Oral, 2 to 6 mg (base) three or four times a day initially, the dosage being increased as needed and tolerated up to a maximum of 8 mg four times a day.

Note: Patients sensitive to beta-adrenergic stimulants—Oral, 2 mg (base) three or four times a day initially, the dosage being increased as needed and tolerated up to a maximum of 8 mg three or four times a day.

Usual geriatric dose: Bronchodilator—Oral, 2 mg (base) three or four times a day initially, the dosage being increased as needed and tolerated up to a maximum of 8 mg three or four times a day.

ALBUTEROL SULFATE EXTENDED-RELEASE TABLETS

Usual adult and adolescent dose: Bronchodilator—Bronchospasm in obstructive pulmonary disease (treatment): Oral, 4 or 8 mg (base) every twelve hours.

Usual adult prescribing limits: Up to 32 mg (base) per day.

Auxiliary labeling: • Swallow tablets whole.

Parenteral Dosage Forms

ALBUTEROL SULFATE INJECTION

Note: Albuterol sulfate injection is not commercially available in the U.S.

Usual adult dose: Bronchodilator—
Intramuscular, 500 mcg (0.5 mg) (base), or 8 mcg (0.008 mg) per kg of body weight, repeated every four hours as required up to a maximum dose of 2 mg per day.
Intravenous, 250 mcg (0.25 mg) (base), or 4 mcg (0.004 mg) per kg of body weight, administered over a period of two to five minutes, the dosage being repeated after fifteen minutes, if necessary, up to a maximum dose of 1 mg per day.
Intravenous infusion, administered at a rate of 5 mcg (0.005 mg) (base) per minute, the dosage being increased to 10 mcg (0.01 mg) per minute and then 20 mcg (0.02 mg) per minute at fifteen-to-thirty minute intervals, if necessary.

BITOLTEROL

Summary of Differences

Pharmacology:
Biotransformation—A prodrug hydrolyzed by esterases in tissue and blood to the active compound colterol.
Onset of action—3 to 4 minutes.
Time to peak effect—0.5 to 1 hour.
Duration of action—5 to 8 hours.
Precautions: Contraindications/medical problems—Caution also needed in convulsive disorders.
Side/adverse effects: Irregular heartbeat, flushing or redness of face or skin, or unpleasant taste may occur.

Additional Dosing Information

See also *General Dosing Information.*

Although dosing studies showed bitolterol to be effective throughout a 3-month period of treatment in the majority of the patients, there was some decreased effectiveness in steroid-dependent asthmatic patients.

Inhalation Dosage Forms

BITOLTEROL MESYLATE INHALATION AEROSOL

Usual adult and adolescent dose: Bronchodilator—
Prophylaxis: Oral inhalation, 740 mcg (0.74 mg—2 inhalations) every eight hours.

Treatment: Oral inhalation, 740 mcg (0.74 mg—2 inhalations), the 2 inhalations being separated by an interval of at least one to three minutes, followed by an additional 370 mcg (0.37 mg—1 inhalation) if needed. Dosage per day should not exceed 740 mcg (0.74 mg—2 inhalations) every four hours or 1.11 mg (3 inhalations) every six hours.

Auxiliary labeling:
• For oral inhalation only.
• Store away from heat and direct sunlight.

EPHEDRINE

Summary of Differences

Category:
Parenteral ephedrine also indicated as a vasopressor.
Oral ephedrine also indicated as a nasal decongestant and CNS stimulant.
Oral and parenteral ephedrine also used as an urticaria therapy adjunct.
Indications:
Oral ephedrine has been used in treatment of enuresis and myasthenia gravis, but has been replaced by more effective agents.
Parenteral ephedrine has been used in Adams-Stokes syndrome with complete heart block, but has been replaced by more effective agents.
Pharmacology:
Ephedrine also has alpha- and beta-1-adrenergic receptor action.
Half-life—Elimination:
At urine pH 5—About 3 hours.
At urine pH 6.3—About 6 hours.
Onset of action—
Oral: 15 to 60 minutes.
Intramuscular: 10 to 20 minutes.
Duration of action—
Oral: 3 to 5 hours.
Intramuscular or subcutaneous: 0.5 to 1 hour after 25 to 50 mg dose.
Elimination—Mostly excreted unchanged; dependent on urinary pH; increased in acidic urine.
Precautions:
Pregnancy/reproduction—Delivery: Parenteral administration of ephedrine to maintain blood pressure during spinal anesthesia for delivery can cause acceleration of fetal heart rate and should not be used when maternal blood pressure exceeds 130/80.
Breast-feeding—Ephedrine excreted in breast milk; use by nursing mothers not recommended because of higher than usual risks for infants.
Drug interactions and/or related problems—Caution also needed with glucocorticoid adrenocorticoids, corticotropin, urinary alkalizers, alpha-adrenergic blocking agents, diatrizoates, iothalamate, ioxaglate, ergot alkaloids, methysergide, oxytocin, doxapram, guanadrel, guanethidine, mazindol, mecamylamine, methyldopa, trimethaphan, methylphenidate, and rauwolfia alkaloids.
Contraindications/medical problems—Caution also needed in angle-closure glaucoma (or predisposition to) and prostatic hypertrophy.
Side/adverse effects: Hallucinations or mood or mental changes may occur rarely with high doses of ephedrine; also, difficult or painful urination, loss of appetite, or unusual paleness may occur.

Additional Dosing Information

See also *General Dosing Information.*

Tolerance to ephedrine may develop with prolonged or excessive use. Discontinuation of the medication for a few days and subsequent readministration may restore its effectiveness.

For oral dosage forms only

To minimize the possibility of insomnia, the last dose of ephedrine for each day should be administered a few hours before bedtime.

For parenteral dosage forms only

When ephedrine is administered intravenously, the injection should be given slowly.

Oral Dosage Forms

EPHEDRINE SULFATE CAPSULES USP

Usual adult dose: Bronchodilator; decongestant, nasal (systemic); or CNS stimulant—Oral, 25 to 50 mg every three or four hours, if necessary.

Note: Ephedrine has been used in the treatment of enuresis and myasthenia gravis. For enuresis, 25 to 50 mg once a day at bedtime; for myasthenia gravis, 25 mg three or four times a day.

EPHEDRINE SULFATE SYRUP USP

Usual adult dose: Bronchodilator; decongestant, nasal (systemic); or CNS stimulant—Oral, 25 to 50 mg every three or four hours, if necessary.

Note: Ephedrine has been used in the treatment of enuresis and myasthenia gravis. For enuresis, 25 to 50 mg once a day at bedtime; for myasthenia gravis, 25 mg three or four times a day.

Parenteral Dosage Forms

EPHEDRINE SULFATE INJECTION USP

Usual adult dose:

Bronchodilator—Intramuscular, intravenous, or subcutaneous, 12.5 to 25 mg; subsequent dosage to be determined by patient response.

Vasopressor—

Intramuscular or subcutaneous, 25 to 50 mg, repeated if necessary.

Intravenous, 5 to 25 mg administered slowly, repeated in five to ten minutes if necessary.

Usual adult prescribing limits: Up to 150 mg per twenty-four hours.

EPINEPHRINE

Summary of Differences

Category: Epinephrine injection also indicated as a vasopressor, cardiac stimulant, local anesthetic adjunct, surgical aid (antihemorrhagic; decongestant; mydriatic), and topical antihemorrhagic.

Indications:

Epinephrine injection also indicated in treatment of anaphylactic reactions; and may be used in management of bronchospasm during anesthesia.

Racepinephrine inhalation also indicated in treatment of postintubation and infectious croup.

Epinephrine injection has been used to correct hypoglycemia in insulin shock but generally has been replaced by more effective antihypoglycemics.

Pharmacology:

Epinephrine also has alpha- and beta-1-adrenergic receptor action.

Biotransformation—Also metabolized in sympathetic nerve endings and other tissues.

Onset of action—

Inhalation: 3 to 5 minutes.

Intramuscular: Variable.

Subcutaneous: 6 to 15 minutes.

Time to peak effect—Subcutaneous: 0.3 hours.

Duration of action—

Inhalation: 1 to 3 hours.

Intramuscular or subcutaneous: <1 to 4 hours.

Elimination—Very small amount excreted unchanged.

Precautions:

Pregnancy/reproduction—Epinephrine crosses placenta; use during pregnancy may cause anoxia in fetus; not recommended for use during labor since it may delay second stage; high doses, sufficient to reduce uterine contraction, may cause prolonged uterine atony with hemorrhage; parenteral administration of epinephrine to maintain blood pressure during spinal anesthesia for delivery can cause acceleration of fetal heart rate and should not be used when maternal blood pressure exceeds 130/80.

Breast-feeding—Epinephrine excreted in breast milk; use by nursing mothers may cause serious adverse reactions in infant.

Pediatrics—Syncope has occurred following administration of epinephrine to asthmatic children.

Drug interactions and/or related problems—Caution also needed with alpha-adrenergic blocking agents, parenteral-local anesthetics, oral antidiabetic agents, insulin, diatrizoates, iothalamate, ioxaglate, ergot alkaloids, methysergide, oxytocin, doxapram, guanadrel, guanethidine, mazindol, mecamylamine, methyldopa, trimethaphan, methylphenidate, and rauwolfia alkaloids.

Contraindications/medical problems—Caution also needed in phenothiazine-induced circulatory collapse or hypotension; angle-closure glaucoma (or predisposition to); Parkinson's disease; prostatic hypertrophy; and cardiogenic, traumatic, or hemorrhagic shock.

Side/adverse effects: Hallucinations may occur with high doses of epinephrine; also, flushing or redness of face or skin may occur.

Additional Dosing Information

See also *General Dosing Information.*

Tolerance to epinephrine may develop with prolonged or excessive use. Discontinuation of the medication for a few days and subsequent readministration may restore its effectiveness.

For inhalation dosage forms only

When using epinephrine inhalation solution, approximately 10 drops of a 1% (base) solution should be placed in the reservoir of the nebulizer.

When racepinephrine inhalation solution is used for topical pulmonary chemotherapy in the combination nebulizer/respirator, the 2.25% solution must be diluted.

For epinephrine inhalation aerosol, epinephrine inhalation solution, or epinephrine bitartrate inhalation aerosol, an interval of 1 to 2 minutes should elapse between the first and second inhalations to make certain a second inhalation is necessary.

If difficulty in breathing persists or relief does not occur within 20 minutes of inhalation, or if condition becomes worse, the medication should be discontinued and physician contacted immediately.

Epinephrine, isoproterenol, and other beta-adrenergic agents may be used interchangeably, but not concurrently. An interval of 4 hours is recommended before changing from one medication to another.

For parenteral dosage forms only

The 1:1000 (1 mg/mL) concentration of epinephrine injection must be diluted before administering intracardially or intravenously.

If epinephrine injection is to be administered by intracardiac injection, it should be administered only by personnel well trained in the technique.

If the patient has been intubated, epinephrine can be injected via the endotracheal tube directly into the bronchial tree at the same dosage as for intravenous injection.

Intra-arterial administration of epinephrine injection is not recommended since marked vasoconstriction may result in gangrene.

It is recommended that sterile epinephrine suspension be administered with a tuberculin syringe and a 26-gauge, $1/2$-inch needle.

After withdrawing a dose of sterile epinephrine suspension into the syringe, prompt injection is recommended to avoid settling of the suspension.

A single dose of sterile epinephrine suspension may be effective for up to 10 hours.

Repeated local injections may result in necrosis at the site of injection because of vascular constriction. Sites of injection should be rotated.

Intramuscular injection of epinephrine injection into the buttocks should be avoided since the vasoconstriction produced by the epinephrine reduces the oxygen tension of the tissues, enabling any anaerobic *Clostridium welchii* that may be present on the buttocks to multiply and possibly cause gas gangrene.

When epinephrine injection is used in anaphylactic shock, volume replacement is an essential concomitant treatment, since effective intravascular volume may have been depleted by increased vascular permeability in anaphylaxis.

Inhalation Dosage Forms

EPINEPHRINE INHALATION AEROSOL USP

Usual adult and adolescent dose: Bronchodilator—Oral inhalation, 200 to 275 mcg (0.2 to 0.275 mg—1 inhalation), repeated after one to two minutes, if necessary; subsequent dose(s) should not be administered for at least three hours.

Auxiliary labeling:
- For oral inhalation only.
- Store away from heat and direct sunlight.

EPINEPHRINE INHALATION SOLUTION USP

Usual adult and adolescent dose: Bronchodilator—Oral inhalation, 1 inhalation of a 1% solution of epinephrine (base), repeated if necessary after one or two minutes, as needed.

Auxiliary labeling: • For oral inhalation only.

EPINEPHRINE BITARTRATE INHALATION AEROSOL USP

Usual adult and adolescent dose: Bronchodilator—Oral inhalation, 160 mcg (0.16 mg—1 inhalation) (base), repeated after one minute, if necessary; subsequent dose(s) should not be administered for at least three hours.

Auxiliary labeling:
- For oral inhalation only.
- Shake well.
- Store away from heat and direct sunlight.

RACEPINEPHRINE INHALATION SOLUTION USP

Usual adult and adolescent dose: Bronchodilator—

Hand nebulizer: Oral inhalation, 2 or 3 inhalations of a 2.25% (epinephrine) solution, followed in five minutes by two or three additional inhalations if necessary, four to six times a day.

Nebulization via respirator: Oral inhalation, 5 mL of a 0.1% solution in a combination nebulizer/respirator for a period of fifteen minutes every three to four hours.

Auxiliary labeling: • For oral inhalation only.

Parenteral Dosage Forms

EPINEPHRINE INJECTION USP

Usual adult and adolescent dose:

Bronchodilator—Subcutaneous, initially 200 to 500 mcg (0.2 to 0.5 mg) (base), repeated every twenty minutes to four hours as needed, the dosage being increased up to a maximum of 1 mg per dose, if necessary.

Anaphylactic reactions—Intramuscular or subcutaneous, initially 200 to 500 mcg (0.2 to 0.5 mg) (base), repeated every ten to fifteen minutes as needed, the dosage being increased up to a maximum of 1 mg per dose if necessary.

Vasopressor (anaphylactic shock)—

Intramuscular or subcutaneous, initially 500 mcg (0.5 mg) (base), repeated every five minutes if necessary; may be followed by intravenous administration of 25 to 50 mcg (0.025 to 0.05 mg) every five to fifteen minutes as needed, if inadequate response to intramuscular or subcutaneous administration. Or;

Intravenous, 100 to 250 mcg (0.1 to 0.25 mg) (base) administered slowly. May be repeated every five to fifteen minutes as needed or followed by an intravenous infusion at an initial rate of 1 mcg (0.001 mg) per minute, the rate being increased to 4 mcg (0.004 mg) per minute if necessary.

Cardiac stimulant—Intracardiac or intravenous, 100 mcg (0.1 mg) to 1 mg (base), repeated every five minutes, if necessary.

Note: Instillation via endotracheal tube in cardiac resuscitation, 1 mg (base).

Anesthetic (local) adjunct—

For use with local anesthetics, 100 to 200 mcg (0.1 to 0.2 mg) (base) in a 1:200,000 to 1:20,000 solution.

For use with intraspinal anesthetics, 200 to 400 mcg (0.2 to 0.4 mg) (base) added to the anesthetic spinal fluid mixture.

Surgical aid (antihemorrhagic; decongestant; mydriatic)—Intracameral or subconjunctival, a 0.01 to 0.1% (1:10,000 to 1:1000) (base) solution.

Antihemorrhagic (topical)—Topical, a 0.002 to 0.1% (1:50,000 to 1:1000) (base) solution.

STERILE EPINEPHRINE SUSPENSION

Usual adult dose: Bronchodilator—Subcutaneous, 500 mcg (0.5 mg) initially, then 500 mcg (0.5 mg) to 1.5 mg not more often than every six hours as needed.

Auxiliary labeling:
- Shake well.
- Refrigerate.

ETHYLNOREPINEPHRINE

Summary of Differences

Pharmacology:

Ethylnorepinephrine also has beta-1-adrenergic receptor action. Onset of action—Intramuscular or subcutaneous: 6 to 12 minutes. Duration of action—Intramuscular or subcutaneous: 1 to 2 hours.

Additional Dosing Information

See also *General Dosing Information*.

Intraneural or intravascular injection of ethylnorepinephrine should be avoided.

Parenteral Dosage Forms

ETHYLNOREPINEPHRINE HYDROCHLORIDE INJECTION USP

Usual adult dose: Bronchodilator—Intramuscular or subcutaneous, 1 to 2 mg.

Note: Smaller doses of 600 mcg (0.6 mg) to 1 mg may be sufficient, depending on the severity of the asthmatic attack.

FENOTEROL

Summary of Differences

Pharmacology:
Onset of action—
Inhalation: 5 minutes.
Oral: 30 to 60 minutes.
Time to peak effect—
Inhalation: 0.5 to 1 hour.
Oral: 2 to 3 hours.
Duration of action—
Inhalation: 2 to 3 hours.
Oral: 6 to 8 hours.
Precautions: Contraindications/medical problems—Caution also needed in angle-closure glaucoma (or predisposition to).
Side/adverse effects: Heartburn, muscle cramps or twitching, or unpleasant taste (with inhalation dosage form only) may occur.

Inhalation Dosage Forms

FENOTEROL HYDROBROMIDE INHALATION AEROSOL

Note: Fenoterol hydrobromide inhalation aerosol is not commercially available in the U.S.

Usual adult and adolescent dose: Bronchodilator—Oral inhalation, 200 or 400 mcg (0.2 or 0.4 mg—1 or 2 inhalations), repeated up to four times a day, if necessary, but not to be administered more often than every four hours.

Auxiliary labeling:
• For oral inhalation only.
• Store away from heat and direct sunlight.

FENOTEROL HYDROBROMIDE INHALATION SOLUTION

Note: Fenoterol hydrobromide inhalation solution is not commercially available in the U.S.

Usual adult and adolescent dose: Bronchodilator—Oral inhalation, administered via nebulization or intermittent positive-pressure breathing (IPPB), 500 mcg (0.5 mg) to 1 mg (up to 2.5 mg in some cases) as a 0.1% solution, diluted to 5 mL with 0.9% sodium chloride solution, the total volume nebulized over a period of ten to fifteen minutes. Dosage may be repeated every six hours, if necessary.

Note: When administered by IPPB, the inspiratory pressure should be set at 10 to 20 cm H2O.

When administered by nebulization, motorized, compressed air, or ultrasonic nebulizers (which generate low pressure, low velocity aerosols) are recommended.

Auxiliary labeling: • For oral inhalation only.

Oral Dosage Forms

FENOTEROL HYDROBROMIDE TABLETS

Note: Fenoterol hydrobromide tablets are not commercially available in the U.S.

Usual adult and adolescent dose: Bronchodilator—Oral, 2.5 mg two times a day initially, the dosage being increased up to a maximum of 5 mg three times a day, if necessary, but not to be administered more often than every six hours.

ISOETHARINE

Summary of Differences

Pharmacology:
Biotransformation—Also metabolized in the lungs, gastrointestinal tract, and other tissues.
Onset of action—1 to 6 minutes.
Time to peak effect—0.25 to 1 hour.
Duration of action—1 to 4 hours.
Elimination—About 10% isoetharine excreted unchanged.

Additional Dosing Information

See also *General Dosing Information.*

Excessive use may result in loss of effectiveness. If this occurs, discontinuation of the medication and use of alternative therapy such as epinephrine or another sympathomimetic are recommended.

Inhalation Dosage Forms

ISOETHARINE INHALATION SOLUTION USP

Usual adult dose: Bronchodilator—Isoetharine inhalation solution may be administered by hand-bulb nebulizer, intermittent positive-pressure breathing (IPPB), or oxygen aerosolization, usually not more often than every four hours, as follows:

Method of Administration	Strength(s) of Solution (%)	Usual Dose		Usual Dose Range	Usual Dilution
Hand-bulb nebulizer	0.5	4 inhalations			Undiluted
	1	4 inhalations		3–7 inhalations	Undiluted
IPPB	0.062	4	mL		Undiluted
	0.08	3.0	mL		Undiluted
	0.1	2.5	mL	2.5–10 mL	Undiluted
	0.125	4	mL	2–8 mL	Undiluted
	0.14	3.5	mL		Undiluted
	0.167	3.0	mL		Undiluted
	0.2	2.5	mL	1.25–5 mL	Undiluted
	0.25	2	mL		Undiluted
	0.5	1	mL		1:3*
	0.5	0.5	mL		1:3*
	1	0.5	mL	0.25–1 mL	1:3*
Oxygen aerosolization	0.062	4	mL		Undiluted
	0.08	3.0	mL		Undiluted
	0.1	2.5	mL	2.5–5 mL	Undiluted
	0.125	4	mL	2–4 mL	Undiluted
	0.14	3.5	mL		Undiluted
	0.167	3.0	mL		Undiluted
	0.2	2.5	mL	1.25–2.5 mL	Undiluted
	0.25	2	mL		Undiluted
	0.5	1	mL		1:3*
	0.5	0.5	mL		1:3*
	1	0.5	mL	0.25–0.5 mL	1:3*

*With sterile purified water, sterile water, or 0.45 or 0.9% sodium chloride sterile solution.

Note: When administered by oxygen aerosolization, the oxygen flow is adjusted to 4 to 6 liters per minute over a period of 15 to 20 minutes.

When administered by IPPB, an inspiratory flow rate of 15 liters per minute at a cycling pressure of 15 cm of water is recommended. Depending on the patient and type of IPPB apparatus, it may be necessary to adjust the flow rate to 6 to 30 liters per minute and the cycling pressure to 10 to 15 cm of water, and to dilute further.

Auxiliary labeling • For oral inhalation only.

ISOETHARINE MESYLATE INHALATION AEROSOL USP

Usual adult dose: Bronchodilator—Oral inhalation, 340 mcg (0.34 mg—1 inhalation), repeated after one to two minutes, if necessary. Dosage may be repeated every four hours as needed.

Auxiliary labeling:
• For oral inhalation only.
• Store away from heat and direct sunlight.

ISOPROTERENOL

Summary of Differences

Category: Oral and parenteral isoproterenol also indicated as a cardiac stimulant.
Pharmacology:
Isoproterenol also has beta-1-adrenergic receptor action.
Absorption of sublingual tablets may be erratic and unpredictable.
Biotransformation—Also metabolized in the lungs and other tissues.
Onset of action—
Inhalation: 2 to 5 minutes.
Intravenous: Immediate.
Rectal: Within 30 minutes.
Sublingual: 15 to 30 minutes.
Duration of action—
Inhalation: 0.5 to 2 hours.
Intravenous: <1 hour.
Rectal: 2 to 4 hours.
Sublingual: 1 to 2 hours.
Elimination—
Intravenous: About 40 to 50% excreted unchanged.
Oral or inhalation: About 5 to 15% excreted unchanged.
Side/adverse effects: Irregular heartbeat, pinkish to red coloration of saliva (for inhalation and sublingual dosage forms only), and flushing or redness of face or skin may occur.

Additional Dosing Information

See also *General Dosing Information.*

For inhalation dosage forms only

Isoproterenol inhalation solution may be administered by hand-bulb nebulizer (all glass or plastic), nebulization by compressed air or oxygen, or intermittent positive-pressure breathing (IPPB). See manufacturer's package insert for instructions.

When used for bronchospasm in chronic obstructive lung disease, the treatment should not be repeated at less than 3- to 4-hour intervals.

When 0.25% isoproterenol inhalation solution is used and relief is not noticeable after 3 treatments of 6 to 12 inhalations at 15-minute intervals, the patient should immediately consult a physician.

Patients requiring more than 3 aerosol treatments within 24 hours should be under close medical supervision.

If 3 to 5 treatments within 6 to 12 hours provide minimal or no relief, further therapy with the aerosol alone is not recommended.

Excessive use may result in loss of effectiveness. If this occurs, discontinuation of the medication and use of alternative therapy are recommended.

For parenteral dosage forms only

When isoproterenol is used for the treatment of shock (hypoperfusion syndrome), hypovolemia should be corrected by suitable volume expanders prior to treatment with isoproterenol.

Inhalation Dosage Forms

ISOPROTERENOL INHALATION SOLUTION USP

Usual adult dose: Bronchodilator—Oral inhalation, 6 to 12 inhalations of a 0.25% nebulized solution, repeated at fifteen-minute intervals, if necessary, for three doses, not to exceed eight treatments per twenty-four hours; or
Acute bronchial asthma: Oral inhalation, 5 to 15 deep inhalations of a 0.5% nebulized solution or 3 to 7 deep inhalations of a 1% nebulized solution, repeated once, if necessary, after five to ten minutes; subsequent doses may be administered up to five times a day, if necessary.
Bronchospasm in chronic obstructive lung disease:
Hand-bulb nebulizer—Oral inhalation, 5 to 15 deep inhalations of a 0.5% solution or 3 to 7 deep inhalations of a 1% solution, not more often than every three to four hours.
Intermittent positive-pressure breathing (IPPB)—Oral inhalation, 2 mL of a 0.125% solution or 2.5 mL of a 0.1% solution, administered over a period of ten to twenty minutes; treatment may be repeated up to five times a day, if necessary.
Nebulization by compressed air or oxygen—Oral inhalation, 2 mL of a 0.125% solution or 2.5 mL of a 0.1% solution, administered over a period of fifteen to twenty minutes; treatment may be repeated up to five times a day, if necessary.

Auxiliary labeling: • For oral inhalation only.

ISOPROTERENOL HYDROCHLORIDE INHALATION AEROSOL USP

Usual adult and adolescent dose: Bronchodilator—
Acute bronchial asthma: Oral inhalation, 120 to 131 mcg (0.12 to 0.131 mg—1 inhalation), repeated after one to five minutes if necessary, four to six times a day.
Bronchospasm in chronic obstructive lung disease: Oral inhalation, 120 to 131 mcg (0.12 to 0.131 mg—1 inhalation), not more often than every three to four hours.

Auxiliary labeling:
• For oral inhalation only.
• Store away from heat and direct sunlight.

ISOPROTERENOL SULFATE INHALATION AEROSOL USP

Usual adult and adolescent dose: Bronchodilator—Oral inhalation, 75 or 80 mcg (0.075 or 0.08 mg—1 inhalation), repeated after two to five minutes if necessary, four to six times a day.

Auxiliary labeling:
• For oral inhalation only.
• Shake well.
• Store away from heat and direct sunlight.

Oral Dosage Forms

ISOPROTERENOL HYDROCHLORIDE TABLETS USP

Usual adult dose:
Bronchodilator—Sublingual, 10 to 15 mg three or four times a day.
Cardiac stimulant—
Heart block: Sublingual, 10 mg initially, followed by 5 to 50 mg as required.
Prevention of heart block in carotid sinus hypersensitivity: Sublingual, 10 to 30 mg four to six times a day.
Note: In the treatment of heart block, the sublingual tablet may be administered rectally in a dose of 5 mg initially, followed by 5 to 15 mg as required.

Auxiliary labeling:
- Dissolve tablets under tongue.
- Keep container tightly closed.

Parenteral Dosage Forms

ISOPROTERENOL HYDROCHLORIDE INJECTION USP

Usual adult dose:
Bronchodilator (bronchospasm during anesthesia)—Intravenous, 10 to 20 mcg (0.01 to 0.02 mg), repeated as needed.
Cardiac stimulant—
Cardiac arrhythmias and cardiac standstill:
Intracardiac, 20 mcg (0.02 mg); subsequent dosage, if necessary, should be adjusted according to patient response.
Intramuscular, 200 mcg (0.2 mg) initially, then 20 mcg (0.02 mg) to 1 mg as needed.
Intravenous, 20 to 60 mcg (0.02 to 0.06 mg) initially, then 10 to 200 mcg (0.01 to 0.2 mg) as needed.
Intravenous infusion, 2 mg in 500 mL of 5% dextrose injection, administered at a rate of 5 mcg (0.005 mg) per minute or adjusted according to patient response.
Subcutaneous, 200 mcg (0.2 mg) initially, then 150 to 200 mcg (0.15 to 0.2 mg) as needed.
Shock (hypoperfusion syndrome): Intravenous infusion, 1 mg in 500 mL of 5% dextrose injection, administered at a rate of 0.5 to 5 mcg (0.0005 to 0.005 mg) per minute or adjusted according to patient response.
Note: Infusion rates greater than 30 mcg (0.03 mg) per minute have been used in the advanced stages of shock.

METAPROTERENOL

Summary of Differences

Pharmacology:
Onset of action—
Inhalation aerosol: Within 1 minute.
Inhalation by hand-bulb nebulizer or intermittent positive-pressure breathing (IPPB): 5 to 30 minutes.
Oral: Within 15 to 30 minutes.
Time to peak effect—
Inhalation aerosol: About 1 hour.
Oral: Within 1 hour.
Duration of action—
Inhalation aerosol: 1 to 5 hours after single dose; 1 to 2.5 hours after repeated doses.
Inhalation by hand-bulb nebulizer or intermittent positive-pressure breathing (IPPB): 2 to 6 hours after single dose; 4 to 6 hours after repeated doses.
Oral: Up to 4 hours.
Elimination—Primarily excreted as glucuronic acid conjugates.
Precautions: Contraindications/medical problems—Caution also needed in convulsive disorders.
Side/adverse effects: Muscle cramps or twitching or unpleasant taste may occur.

Inhalation Dosage Forms

METAPROTERENOL SULFATE INHALATION AEROSOL USP

Usual adult and adolescent dose: Bronchodilator—Oral inhalation, 1.3 to 2.25 mg (2 or 3 inhalations) every three to four hours, not to exceed 9 mg (12 inhalations) per day.

Auxiliary labeling:
- For oral inhalation only.
- Shake well.
- Store away from heat and direct sunlight.

Note: Include patient instructions when dispensing.

METAPROTERENOL SULFATE INHALATION SOLUTION USP

Usual adult and adolescent dose: Bronchodilator—Oral inhalation, administered by using a hand-bulb nebulizer or intermittent positive-pressure breathing (IPPB), usually not more often than every four hours to relieve acute attacks of bronchospasm and three or four times a day in chronic bronchospastic pulmonary diseases, as follows:

Method of Administration	Usual Dose	Usual Dose Range	Usual Dilution
Hand-bulb nebulizer	10 inhalations	5–15 inhalations	Undiluted
IPPB	0.3 mL	0.2–0.3 mL	*

*Diluted in approximately 2.5 mL of saline solution or other diluent. The 0.4% unit dose vial contains the equivalent of 0.2 mL of a 5% solution diluted to 2.5 mL with normal saline. The 0.6% unit dose vial contains the equivalent of 0.3 mL of a 5% solution diluted to 2.5 mL with normal saline.

Auxiliary labeling: • For oral inhalation only.

Oral Dosage Forms

METAPROTERENOL SULFATE SYRUP USP

Usual adult and adolescent dose: Bronchodilator—Oral, 20 mg three or four times a day.

METAPROTERENOL SULFATE TABLETS USP

Usual adult and adolescent dose: Bronchodilator—Oral, 20 mg three or four times a day.

PIRBUTEROL

Summary of Differences

Pharmacology:
Biotransformation—Metabolized primarily by sulfate conjugation; not metabolized by catechol-O-methyltransferase.
Half-life—2 hours.
Onset of action—Within 5 minutes.
Time to peak effect—0.5 to 1 hour.
Duration of action—5 hours.
Elimination—51% of inhaled dose excreted as pirbuterol plus sulfate conjugate.
Side/adverse effects: Irregular heartbeat, mood or mental changes, numbness in hands or feet, unusual bruising, loss of appetite, or smell or taste changes may occur.

Additional Dosing Information

See also *General Dosing Information*.

Pirbuterol may be administered concurrently with adrenocorticoid and/or theophylline therapy.

With chronic dosing of pirbuterol, tolerance to the bronchodilator effect has occurred in some patients.

Inhalation Dosage Forms

PIRBUTEROL ACETATE INHALATION AEROSOL

Usual adult and adolescent dose: Bronchodilator—Oral inhalation, 200 or 400 mcg (0.2 or 0.4 mg—1 or 2 inhalations) every four to six hours, not to exceed a total dose of 2.4 mg (12 inhalations) per day.

Auxiliary labeling:
- For oral inhalation only.
- Shake well.
- Store away from heat and direct sunlight.

PROCATEROL

Summary of Differences

Pharmacology:
    Onset of action—Within 5 minutes.
    Time to peak effect—About 1.5 hours.
    Duration of action—6 to 8 hours.

Inhalation Dosage Forms

PROCATEROL HYDROCHLORIDE HEMIHYDRATE INHALATION AEROSOL

Note: Procaterol hydrochloride hemihydrate inhalation aerosol is not commercially available in the U.S.

Usual adult and adolescent dose: Bronchodilator—Oral inhalation, 20 mcg (0.02 mg—2 inhalations) three times a day.

    Bronchospasm, exercise-induced (prophylaxis): Oral inhalation, 20 mcg (0.02 mg—2 inhalations) at least fifteen minutes before exertion.

Auxiliary labeling:
- For oral inhalation only.
- Shake well.
- Store away from heat and direct sunlight.

TERBUTALINE

Summary of Differences

Category: Oral and parenteral terbutaline also used as a labor (premature) inhibitor; and parenteral terbutaline may be used in management of bronchospasm during anesthesia.
Pharmacology:
    Biotransformation—Metabolized primarily to inactive sulfate conjugate.
    Onset of action—
        Inhalation: 5 to 30 minutes.
        Oral: Within 60 to 120 minutes.
        Parenteral: Within 15 minutes.
    Time to peak effect—
        Inhalation: 1 to 2 hours.
        Oral: Within 2 to 3 hours.
        Parenteral: Within 0.5 to 1 hour.
    Duration of action—
        Inhalation: 3 to 6 hours.
        Oral: 4 to 8 hours.
        Parenteral: 1.5 to 4 hours.
Precautions:
    Pregnancy/reproduction—
        Pregnancy: Parenteral administration during pregnancy reported to cause fetal tachycardia.

    Labor and delivery: Inhibits uterine activity during the second and third trimesters of pregnancy and may inhibit labor; when administered during labor, reported to cause serious adverse reactions such as transient hypokalemia, pulmonary edema, and hypoglycemia in the mother and hypoglycemia in neonates of mothers treated with parenteral terbutaline.
Contraindications/medical problems—Caution also needed in ketoacidosis when large parenteral doses of terbutaline are administered and in patients with history of seizures.
Side/adverse effects: Irregular heartbeat, drowsiness, muscle cramps or twitching, or unusual taste may occur.

Additional Dosing Information

See also *General Dosing Information*.

For parenteral dosage forms only
The subcutaneous injection is usually injected into the lateral deltoid area.

Inhalation Dosage Forms

TERBUTALINE SULFATE INHALATION AEROSOL

Usual adult and adolescent dose: Bronchodilator—Oral inhalation, 200 to 500 mcg (0.2 to 0.5 mg—1 or 2 inhalations, 2 inhalations being separated by a sixty-second interval) every four to six hours.

Auxiliary labeling:
- For oral inhalation only.
- Shake well.

Oral Dosage Forms

Note: Bracketed uses in the *Dosage Forms* section refer to categories of use and/or indications that are not included in U.S. product labeling.

TERBUTALINE SULFATE TABLETS USP

Usual adult dose:
    Bronchodilator—Oral, 2.5 to 5 mg three times a day, administered at approximately six-hour intervals.
    [Labor (premature) inhibitor][1]—Maintenance: Oral, 2.5 mg every four to six hours until term.

Usual adult prescribing limits: Up to 15 mg per twenty-four hours.

Parenteral Dosage Forms

Note: Bracketed uses in the *Dosage Forms* section refer to categories of use and/or indications that are not included in U.S. product labeling.

TERBUTALINE SULFATE INJECTION USP

Usual adult dose:
    Bronchodilator—Subcutaneous, 250 mcg (0.25 mg), repeated after fifteen to thirty minutes if necessary; a total dose of 500 mcg (0.5 mg) should not be exceeded within a four-hour period.
    [Labor (premature) inhibitor][1]—
        Intravenous infusion, administered at a rate of 10 mcg (0.01 mg) per minute initially, the rate being increased by 5 mcg (0.005 mg) per minute every ten minutes until contractions cease or up to a maximum dose of 80 mcg (0.08 mg) per minute. After contractions cease for thirty minutes to one hour, the rate of administration is decreased by 5 mcg (0.005 mg) per minute to the lowest effective dose. The minimum effective dosage should be continued for four to eight hours after contractions cease.
        Subcutaneous, 250 mcg (0.25 mg) every hour until contractions cease.

---

[1]Not included in Canadian product labeling.

Table 1. Pharmacology

Drug	Onset of Action (min)	Time to Peak Effect (hr)	Duration of Action (hr)
Albuterol			
Inhalation	5–15	1–1.5 after 2 inhalations	3–6
Oral	15–30	2–3	8 or more (12 for extended-release tablets)
Bitolterol			
Inhalation	3–4	0.5–1	5–8
Ephedrine			
Oral	15–60	—	3–5
Intramuscular	10–20	—	0.5–1 after 25–50 mg dose
Subcutaneous	—	—	0.5–1 after 25–50 mg dose
Epinephrine			
Inhalation	3–5	—	1–3
Intramuscular	Variable	—	<1–4
Subcutaneous	6–15	0.3	<1–4
Ethylnorepinephrine			
Intramuscular	6–12	—	1–2
Subcutaneous	6–12	—	1–2
Fenoterol			
Inhalation	5	0.5–1	2–3
Oral	30–60	2–3	6–8
Isoetharine			
Inhalation	1–6	0.25–1	1–4
Isoproterenol			
Inhalation	2–5	—	0.5–2
Intravenous	Immediate	—	<1
Rectal	Within 30	—	2–4
Sublingual	15–30	—	1–2
Metaproterenol			
Inhalation aerosol	Within 1	About 1	1–5 after single dose 1–2.5 after repeated doses
Inhalation by hand-bulb nebulizer or intermittent positive-pressure breathing (IPPB)	5–30	—	2–6 after single dose; 4–6 after repeated doses
Oral	Within 15–30	Within 1	Up to 4
Pirbuterol			
Inhalation	Within 5	0.5–1	5
Procaterol			
Inhalation	Within 5	About 1.5	6–8
Terbutaline			
Inhalation	5–30	1–2	3–6
Oral	Within 60–120	Within 2–3	4–8
Parenteral	Within 15	Within 0.5–1	1.5–4

Table 2. Contraindications/Medical problems

Note: A blank space usually signifies lack of information; it is not necessarily an indication that a given medical problem is of no concern. However, the pharmacologic similarity of these agents may suggest that if caution is required in particular medical problems for one agent, then it may be required for the others as well.

The contraindications/medical problems included have been selected on the basis of their potential clinical significance (reasons given in parentheses where appropriate)—not necessarily inclusive (» = major clinical significance).

Legend:
I = Albuterol
II = Bitolterol
III = Ephedrine
IV = Epinephrine
V = Ethylnorepinephrine
VI = Fenoterol
VII = Isoetharine
VIII = Isoproterenol
IX = Metaproterenol
X = Pirbuterol
XI = Procaterol
XII = Terbutaline

Risk-benefit should be considered when the following medical problems exist:

	I	II	III	IV	V	VI	VII	VIII	IX	X	XI	XII
» Brain damage, organic				✔								
» Cardiovascular disease, including: Angina pectoris			✔	✔				✔				
Cardiac arrhythmias	✔	✔	✔	✔					✔	✔	✔	✔
Cardiac arrhythmias associated with tachycardia						✔		✔	✔		✔	
Cardiac asthma							✔					
Cardiac dilatation				✔								
Cerebral arteriosclerosis				✔								
Congestive heart failure				✔		✔			✔		✔	
Coronary artery disease				✔	✔	✔	✔	✔	✔			
Coronary insufficiency	✔		✔	✔				✔			✔	✔
Degenerative heart disease				✔				✔				
Hypertension	✔	✔	✔	✔	✔	✔	✔	✔	✔	✔	✔	✔
Idiopathic hypertrophic subvalvular aortic stenosis						✔					✔	
Ischemic heart disease	✔	✔		✔					✔	✔		
Limited cardiac reserve						✔						
Organic heart disease				✔				✔				
Stroke, history of				✔								
Tachycardia caused by digitalis intoxication (condition may be exacerbated due to drug-induced cardiovascular effects)								✔				
Circulatory collapse or hypotension, phenothiazine-induced (pressor effect of epinephrine may be reversed by the phenothiazine, resulting in further lowering of blood pressure)				✔								
Convulsive disorders		✔							✔	✔		
Diabetes mellitus (potential drug-induced hyperglycemia may result in loss of diabetic control; dosage of insulin or hypoglycemic agents may need to be increased, especially with epinephrine)	✔	✔	✔	✔		✔		✔	✔	✔	✔	✔
Glaucoma, angle-closure, or predisposition to			✔	✔		✔						
Hyperthyroidism (adverse reactions more likely to occur)	✔	✔	✔	✔	✔	✔	✔	✔	✔	✔	✔	✔
Ketoacidosis (large parenteral doses of albuterol or terbutaline may aggravate condition)	✔											✔

Table 2. Contraindications/Medical problems *(continued)*

Legend:
I = Albuterol   II = Bitolterol   III = Ephedrine   IV = Epinephrine
V = Ethylnorepinephrine   VI = Fenoterol   VII = Isoetharine   VIII = Isoproterenol
IX = Metaproterenol   X = Pirbuterol   XI = Procaterol   XII = Terbutaline

	I	II	III	IV	V	VI	VII	VIII	IX	X	XI	XII
Parkinson's disease (rigidity and tremor may be increased temporarily)				✔								
Pheochromocytoma, diagnosed or suspected	✔	✔	✔	✔	✔	✔	✔	✔	✔			✔
Prostatic hypertrophy			✔									
Psychoneurotic disorders (worsening of symptoms)				✔								
Seizures, history of												✔
Sensitivity to sympathomimetics	✔	✔	✔	✔	✔	✔	✔	✔	✔	✔	✔	✔
» Shock, cardiogenic, traumatic, or hemorrhagic (increases myocardial oxygen demand in cardiogenic shock)				✔								

Table 3. Side/Adverse Effects*

Note: Fatalities have been reported in association with excessive use of inhaled sympathomimetics. The exact cause of death is unknown; however, cardiac arrest following unexpected development of a severe acute asthmatic crisis and subsequent hypoxia is suspected.

Parenteral albuterol may induce reversible metabolic changes, including hyperglycemia and hypokalemia, which are more pronounced during intravenous infusion.

If high arterial blood pressure is inadvertently induced by parenteral epinephrine, it may result in angina pectoris, aortic rupture, or cerebral hemorrhage.

Legend:
I = Albuterol   II = Bitolterol   III = Ephedrine   IV = Epinephrine
V = Ethylnorepinephrine   VI = Fenoterol   VII = Isoetharine   VIII = Isoproterenol
IX = Metaproterenol   X = Pirbuterol   XI = Procaterol   XII = Terbutaline

The following side/adverse effects have been selected on the basis of their potential clinical significance (possible signs and symptoms in parentheses where appropriate)—not necessarily inclusive:

	I	II	III	IV	V	VI	VII	VIII	IX	X	XI	XII
Medical attention needed												
Chest discomfort or pain, continuing or severe, or	✔	✔	✔	✔	✔	✔	✔	✔	✔	✔	✔	✔
Chills or fever or			✔	✔	✔							
Convulsions or			✔	✔	✔							
Dizziness or lightheadedness, continuing or severe, or	✔	✔	✔	✔	✔	✔	✔	✔	✔	✔	✔	✔
Fast heartbeat, continuing, or	✔	✔	✔	✔	✔	✔	✔	✔	✔	✔	✔	✔
Hallucinations or			✔									
Headache, continuing or severe, or	✔	✔	✔	✔	✔	✔	✔	✔	✔	✔	✔	✔
Increase in blood pressure, severe, or	✔	✔	✔†	✔†	✔	✔	✔	✔	✔	✔	✔	✔
Irregular heartbeat, continuing or severe, or				✔	✔	✔		✔	✔	✔	✔	✔
Mood or mental changes or			✔									
Muscle cramps, severe, or											✔	✔
Nausea or vomiting, continuing or severe, or	✔		✔	✔	✔	✔			✔	✔	✔	✔
Pounding heartbeat, continuing or severe, or	✔	✔	✔	✔	✔	✔	✔	✔	✔	✔	✔	✔
Shortness of breath or troubled breathing, severe, or			✔	✔								
Slow heartbeat or				✔	✔							
Trembling, severe, or	✔	✔	✔	✔	✔	✔	✔	✔	✔	✔	✔	✔
Unusual anxiety, nervousness, or restlessness or	✔	✔	✔	✔	✔	✔	✔	✔	✔	✔	✔	✔
Unusually large pupils or blurred vision or			✔	✔	✔							

Table 3. Side/Adverse Effects* *(continued)*

Legend: **I** = Albuterol **II** = Bitolterol **III** = Ephedrine **IV** = Epinephrine				**V** = Ethylnorepinephrine **VI** = Fenoterol **VII** = Isoetharine **VIII** = Isoproterenol				**IX** = Metaproterenol **X** = Pirbuterol **XI** = Procaterol **XII** = Terbutaline			
	I	**II**	**III**	**IV**	**V**	**VI**	**VII**	**VIII**	**IX**	**X**	**XI**	**XII**
Unusual paleness and coldness of skin or Weakness, severe (signs of overdose)			✔	✔	✔	✔	✔	✔	✔	✔		✔
Chest discomfort or pain	R	R (1%)	R	R‡	U	U	U	R	U	R	R§	R
Hallucinations	U	U	§	§	U	U	U	U	U	U	U	U
Irregular heartbeat	U	R	R	R‡	U	U	U	R	U	R	U	R
Mood or mental changes	U	U	§	U	U	U	U	U	U	R	U	U
Numbness in hands or feet	U	U	U	U	U	U	U	U	U	R	U	U
Paradoxical bronchospasm (increase in wheezing or difficulty in breathing)	R	R (<1%)	R	R	R	R	R	R	R	R	R	R
Unusual bruising	U	U	U	U	U	U	U	U	U	R	U	U
For preparations containing sulfites **Allergic reaction to sulfites** (bluish coloration of skin; dizziness, severe, or feeling faint; flushing or redness of skin, continuing; skin rash, hives, or itching; swelling of face, lips, or eyelids; wheezing or difficulty in breathing)			✔	✔	✔	✔	✔	✔				
Medical attention needed only if continuing or bothersome *Coughing or other bronchial irritation#*	L	L (4%)	—	§	—	L	U	L	L	L	U	U
Difficult or painful urination	L	U	L	U	U	U	U	U	U	U	U	U
Dizziness or lightheadedness	L	L (3%)	L	L**	L	L	L	L	L	L	L	L
Drowsiness	L	U	U	U	U	U	U	U	U	U	U	L
Dryness or irritation of mouth or throat#	L	L (5%)	L	R	—	L	L	M	U	R	R	L
Fast heartbeat	M	R (<1%)	L	M‡‡	L	L	L	L	L	L	L	L
Flushing or redness of face or skin	L	L	U	L**	U	U	U	L	U	R	U	U
Headache	L	L (4%)	L	L**	L	L	L	L	L	L	M	L
Heartburn	L	U	U	U	—	L	U	U	U	U	U	U
Increased sweating	L	U	L	L**	U	L	U	L	L	U	U	L

  * Differences in frequency of occurrence may reflect either lack of clinical-use data or actual pharmacologic distinctions among agents (although the agents' pharmacologic similarity suggests that side effects occurring with one may occur with the others). M=more frequent; L=less frequent; R=rare; U=unknown.

  † Or possibly a severe decrease in blood pressure.
  ‡ More frequent with high doses.
  § With high doses.
  # With inhalation dosage forms only.
  ** Less frequent with injection; rare with recommended doses of inhalation.
  †† Or possibly a decrease in blood pressure.
  ‡‡ More frequent with injection; rare with recommended doses of inhalation.
  §§ For inhalation and sublingual dosage forms of isoproterenol only.

Table 3. Side/Adverse Effects* *(continued)*

	Legend: **I** = Albuterol **II** = Bitolterol **III** = Ephedrine **IV** = Epinephrine				**V** = Ethylnorepinephrine **VI** = Fenoterol **VII** = Isoetharine **VIII** = Isoproterenol				**IX** = Metaproterenol **X** = Pirbuterol **XI** = Procaterol **XII** = Terbutaline			
	I	**II**	**III**	**IV**	**V**	**VI**	**VII**	**VIII**	**IX**	**X**	**XI**	**XII**
Increase in blood pressure	L††	L	L	L	L††	U	L††	L††	L	R	U	L
Loss of appetite	R	U	L	U	U	U	U	U	U	R	U	U
Muscle cramps or twitching	L	U	U	U	U	L	U	U	L	U	U	L
Nausea	M	L (3%)	L	L**	L	L	L	L	L	L	L	L
Nervousness or restlessness	M	L (5%)	M	M‡‡	U	M	L	M	M	M	L	M
Pain or stinging at intramuscular injection site	L	—	U	U	U	—	—	U	—	—	—	—
Pounding heartbeat	M	L (3%)	L	M‡‡	L	L	L	L	L	L	L	L
Trembling	M	M (14%)	L	L**	L	M	L	L	L	M	M	M
Trouble in sleeping	L	R (<1%)	M	L**	U	L	L	M	U	R	U	L
Unusual paleness	R	U	L	L**	U	U	U	U	U	U	U	U
Vomiting	L	U	L	L**	U	L	L	L	L	L	U	L
Weakness	L	U	L	L**	L	L	L	L	L	R	U	L
Medical attention *not* needed *Pinkish to red coloration of saliva*	—	—	—	—	—	—	—	M§§	—	—	—	—
Smell or taste changes	U	U	U	U	—	U	U	U	U	L	U	U
Unpleasant taste	U	L	U	U	—	L#	U	U	L	U	U	U
Unusual taste	L	U	U	U	—	U	U	U	U	U	U	L

  * Differences in frequency of occurrence may reflect either lack of clinical-use data or actual pharmacologic distinctions among agents (although the agents' pharmacologic similarity suggests that side effects occurring with one may occur with the others). M=more frequent; L=less frequent; R=rare; U=unknown.

  † Or possibly a severe decrease in blood pressure.
  ‡ More frequent with high doses.
  § With high doses.
  # With inhalation dosage forms only.
  ** Less frequent with injection; rare with recommended doses of inhalation.
  †† Or possibly a decrease in blood pressure.
  ‡‡ More frequent with injection; rare with recommended doses of inhalation.
  §§ For inhalation and sublingual dosage forms of isoproterenol only.

Table 4. Patient Consultation

In providing consultation, consider emphasizing the following selected information (» = major clinical signficance):	Legend: I = Albuterol II = Bitolterol III = Ephedrine IV = Epinephrine				V = Ethylnorepinephrine VI = Fenoterol VII = Isoetharine VIII = Isoproterenol				IX = Metaproterenol X = Pirbuterol XI = Procaterol XII = Terbutaline			
	I	**II**	**III**	**IV**	**V**	**VI**	**VII**	**VIII**	**IX**	**X**	**XI**	**XII**
Before using this medication												
» Conditions affecting use, especially:												
Sensitivity to sympathomimetics	✔	✔	✔	✔	✔	✔	✔	✔	✔	✔	✔	✔
Allergies to sulfites present in some preparations			✔	✔	✔	✔	✔	✔				
Pregnancy—												
Studies in animals have shown albuterol, bitolterol, epinephrine, and metaproterenol to cause teratogenic effects when medication given in doses many times human dose	✔	✔		✔					✔			
Use of epinephrine during pregnancy may cause anoxia in fetus				✔								
Studies in animals have shown pirbuterol at high doses to cause abortions and fetal mortality										✔		
Parenteral administration of terbutaline during pregnancy reported to cause fetal tachycardia												✔
Labor and/or delivery—												
Albuterol given intravenously or orally reportedly inhibits uterine contractions	✔											
Epinephrine is not recommended for use during labor because it may delay second stage; also may cause prolonged uterine atony with hemorrhage when given in sufficient dosage to reduce uterine contractions				✔								
Parenteral administration of ephedrine or epinephrine to maintain blood pressure during low or other spinal anesthesia for delivery can cause acceleration of fetal heart rate			✔	✔								
Terbutaline inhibits uterine activity during second and third trimesters of pregnancy and may inhibit labor: when administered during labor; terbutaline reported to cause serious adverse reactions (e.g., transient hypokalemia, pulmonary edema, hypoglycemia) in mother and hypoglycemia in neonates of mothers treated with parenteral terbutaline												✔
Breast-feeding—												
Not known if albuterol is excreted in breast milk; however, some animal studies have shown albuterol to be potentially tumorigenic	✔											
Epinephrine excreted in breast milk; use by nursing mothers may cause serious adverse reactions in infant				✔								
Terbutaline excreted in breast milk; some animal studies have shown terbutaline to be potentially tumorigenic												✔
Use in children—Epinephrine should be used with caution in infants and children, since syncope has occurred following administration of epinephrine in asthmatic children				✔								

*USOC permits use of inhalation beta-2 agonists.
†For inhalation dosage forms.
‡With high doses.

Table 4. Patient Consultation *(continued)*

Legend:
I = Albuterol   V = Ethylnorepinephrine   IX = Metaproterenol
II = Bitolterol   VI = Fenoterol   X = Pirbuterol
III = Ephedrine   VII = Isoetharine   XI = Procaterol
IV = Epinephrine   VIII = Isoproterenol   XII = Terbutaline

	I	II	III	IV	V	VI	VII	VIII	IX	X	XI	XII
Dental—Epinephrine present in gingival retraction cords; systemic absorption of epinephrine from retraction cords may occur; epinephrine retraction cords should be used with caution in patients with cardiovascular problems				✔								
Use by athletes—Stimulants, including sympathomimetic amines and related substances, are banned and tested for in athletes by the U.S. Olympic Committee (USOC)	✔*	*	✔	✔	✔	✔	✔	✔	✔*	*	*	✔*
Other medications, especially—												
Beta-adrenergic blocking agents	✔	✔	✔	✔	✔	✔	✔	✔	✔	✔	✔	✔
Cocaine, mucosal-local	✔	✔	✔	✔	✔	✔	✔	✔	✔	✔	✔	✔
Digitalis glycosides	✔	✔	✔	✔	✔	✔	✔	✔	✔	✔	✔	✔
Ergoloid mesylates			✔	✔								
Ergotamine			✔	✔								
Maprotiline	✔		✔	✔				✔		✔	✔	✔
Monoamine oxidase (MAO) inhibitors	✔		✔	✔		✔		✔	✔	✔	✔	✔
Tricyclic antidepressants	✔		✔	✔				✔		✔	✔	✔
Other medical problems, especially—												
Brain damage, organic				✔								
Cardiovascular disease	✔	✔	✔	✔	✔	✔	✔	✔	✔	✔	✔	✔
Proper use of this medication												
Not using if solution or suspension is pinkish to brownish in color or if solution contains a precipitate				✔			✔	✔				
» Not using inhalation dosage form of epinephrine without a physician's prescription unless medical problem is diagnosed as asthma				✔								
» Importance of not using more medication than the amount recommended	✔	✔	✔	✔	✔	✔	✔	✔	✔	✔	✔	✔
» Taking the medication a few hours before bedtime to minimize the possibility of insomnia			✔									
Missed dose: If on scheduled dosing regimen, using as soon as possible; using any remaining doses for the day at regularly spaced intervals; not doubling doses	✔	✔	✔	✔		✔	✔	✔	✔	✔	✔	✔
For all inhalation dosage forms												
Proper administration:												
Reading patient instructions carefully before using	✔	✔		✔			✔	✔	✔	✔	✔	✔
Knowing correct administration technique if using in a nebulizer or a combination nebulizer and respirator; checking with physician, nurse, or pharmacist if necessary	✔			✔			✔	✔	✔			
For inhalation aerosols	✔	✔		✔			✔	✔	✔	✔	✔	✔
» Avoiding contact with the eyes												
» Taking no more than 2 inhalations at one time with interval of 1 to 2 minutes between inhalations												
Saving applicator; refill units may be available												
For extended-release tablet dosage form												
Swallowing tablet whole; not crushing, breaking, or chewing	✔											

Table 4. Patient Consultation *(continued)*

	Legend: I = Albuterol II = Bitolterol III = Ephedrine IV = Epinephrine				V = Ethylnorepinephrine VI = Fenoterol VII = Isoetharine VIII = Isoproterenol				IX = Metaproterenol X = Pirbuterol XI = Procaterol XII = Terbutaline			
	I	**II**	**III**	**IV**	**V**	**VI**	**VII**	**VIII**	**IX**	**X**	**XI**	**XII**
For sublingual tablet dosage form Not chewing or swallowing tablet whole, but dissolving slowly under tongue; not swallowing until tablet completely dissolved								✔				
For injection dosage forms » Using only for conditions as prescribed by physician				✔	✔							
Keeping ready for use at all times; also keeping telephone numbers for physician and nearest hospital emergency room readily available				✔	✔							
Checking expiration date routinely; replacing medication before it expires				✔	✔							
Knowing correct administration technique for self-administration; checking with physician if necessary				✔	✔							
For emergency use in allergic reaction— » Using medication immediately Notifying physician immediately or going to nearest hospital emergency room If stung by an insect, removing insect's stinger; applying ice packs or sodium bicarbonate soaks, if available, to area stung For auto-injector use: Importance of not removing safety cap on auto-injector before ready to use Reading patient instructions carefully before need to use medication Procedures for using— Removing gray safety cap Placing black tip on thigh at right angle to leg Pressing hard into thigh until auto-injector functions; holding in place several seconds; removing and properly discarding Massaging injection area for 10 seconds				✔								
» Proper storage	✔	✔	✔	✔	✔	✔	✔	✔	✔	✔	✔	✔
Precautions while using this medication » Checking with physician immediately if difficulty in breathing persists after use of medication or if condition becomes worse	✔	✔		✔†		✔	✔	✔	✔	✔	✔	✔
Diabetics: May increase blood glucose concentrations				✔								
» Possibility of allergic reaction to sulfites contained in some preparations; checking with physician immediately if signs of allergic reaction occur			✔	✔	✔	✔	✔	✔				
For inhalation dosage forms Possible dryness of mouth and throat; rinsing mouth with water after each dose to help prevent dryness	✔	✔		✔			✔	✔		✔	✔	✔

*USOC permits use of inhalation beta-2 agonists.
†For inhalation dosage forms.
‡With high doses.

Table 4. Patient Consultation *(continued)*

Legend:
I = Albuterol   V = Ethylnorepinephrine   IX = Metaproterenol
II = Bitolterol   VI = Fenoterol   X = Pirbuterol
III = Ephedrine   VII = Isoetharine   XI = Procaterol
IV = Epinephrine   VIII = Isoproterenol   XII = Terbutaline

	I	II	III	IV	V	VI	VII	VIII	IX	X	XI	XII
For inhalation aerosol dosage forms												
» For patients also using an adrenocorticoid or ipratropium inhalation aerosol: Using adrenergic bronchodilator inhalation aerosol 5 minutes prior to the adrenocorticoid or ipratropium inhalation aerosol, unless otherwise directed by physician	✔	✔		✔		✔	✔	✔	✔	✔	✔	✔
Checking with physician if contents of one canister used in less than 2 weeks	✔											
Side/adverse effects												
Signs of potential side effects, especially:												
Allergic reaction to sulfites present in some preparations			✔	✔	✔	✔	✔	✔				
Chest discomfort or pain	✔	✔	✔	✔				✔		✔	✔‡	✔
Hallucinations, with high doses			✔	✔								
Irregular heartbeat		✔	✔	✔				✔		✔		✔
Mood or mental changes			✔							✔		
Numbness in feet or hands										✔		
Paradoxical bronchospasm	✔	✔	✔	✔	✔	✔	✔	✔	✔	✔	✔	✔
Unusual bruising										✔		
In some animal studies, albuterol caused increased incidence of benign leiomyomas of mesovarium when administered at doses many times the maximum human inhalation or oral dose	✔											
Some studies in animals have shown that terbutaline caused increased incidence of leiomyomas of mesovarium, ovarian cysts, and hyperplasia of mesovarium when administered at oral doses many times the recommended daily adult dose												✔
Pinkish to red coloration of saliva caused by oxidation of isoproterenol in mouth may be alarming to patient although medically insignificant								✔				
Unusual or bad taste may occur	✔					✔			✔			✔
Changes in smell or taste may occur										✔		

*USOC permits use of inhalation beta-2 agonists.
†For inhalation dosage forms.
‡With high doses.

BRONCHODILATORS, XANTHINE-DERIVATIVE   Systemic

Some commonly used *brand names* are:

In the U.S.—

Accurbron [Theophylline]
Aerolate [Theophylline]
Aerolate III [Theophylline]
Aerolate Jr. [Theophylline]
Aerolate Sr. [Theophylline]
Aminophyllin
  [Aminophylline]
Aquaphyllin [Theophylline]
Asmalix [Theophylline]
Bronkodyl [Theophylline]
Choledyl [Oxtriphylline]
Choledyl Delayed-release
  [Oxtriphylline]
Choledyl SA [Oxtriphylline]
Constant-T [Theophylline]
Dilor [Dyphylline]
Dilor-400 [Dyphylline]
Duraphyl [Theophylline]
Dyflex [Dyphylline]
Dyflex 400 [Dyphylline]
Elixicon [Theophylline]
Elixomin [Theophylline]
Elixophyllin [Theophylline]
Elixophyllin SR
  [Theophylline]
Lanophyllin [Theophylline]
Lixolin [Theophylline]
Lufyllin [Dyphylline]
Lufyllin-400 [Dyphylline]
Neothylline [Dyphylline]
Phyllocontin
  [Aminophylline]
Quibron-T Dividose
  [Theophylline]
Quibron-T/SR Dividose
  [Theophylline]
Respbid [Theophylline]
Slo-bid Gyrocaps
  [Theophylline]
Slo-Phyllin [Theophylline]
Slo-Phyllin Gyrocaps
  [Theophylline]
Solu-Phyllin [Theophylline]
Somophyllin
  [Aminophylline]
Somophyllin-CRT
  [Theophylline]

Somophyllin-DF
  [Aminophylline]
Somophyllin-T
  [Theophylline]
Sustaire [Theophylline]
Synophylate
  [Theophylline]
Theo-24 [Theophylline]
Theo 250 [Theophylline]
Theobid Duracaps
  [Theophylline]
Theobid Jr. Duracaps
  [Theophylline]
Theochron [Theophylline]
Theoclear-80
  [Theophylline]
Theoclear L.A.-130
  Cenules
  [Theophylline]
Theoclear L.A.-260
  Cenules
  [Theophylline]
Theocot [Theophylline]
Theo-Dur [Theophylline]
Theo-Dur Sprinkle
  [Theophylline]
Theolair [Theophylline]
Theolair-SR
  [Theophylline]
Theomar [Theophylline]
Theon [Theophylline]
Theophylline SR
  [Theophylline]
Theospan-SR
  [Theophylline]
Theostat 80 [Theophylline]
Theo-Time [Theophylline]
Theovent Long-Acting
  [Theophylline]
Thylline [Dyphylline]
T-Phyl [Theophylline]
Truphylline
  [Aminophylline]
Truxophyllin
  [Theophylline]
Uniphyl [Theophylline]

In Canada—

Apo-Oxtriphylline
  [Oxtriphylline]
Choledyl [Oxtriphylline]
Choledyl SA [Oxtriphylline]
Corophyllin
  [Aminophylline]
Elixophyllin [Theophylline]
Novotriphyl [Oxtriphylline]
Palaron [Aminophylline]
Phyllocontin
  [Aminophylline]
Phyllocontin-350
  [Aminophylline]
PMS Theophylline
  [Theophylline]
Protophylline [Dyphylline]

Pulmophylline
  [Theophylline]
Quibron-T [Theophylline]
Quibron-T/SR
  [Theophylline]
Slo-Bid [Theophylline]
Somophyllin-12
  [Theophylline]
Somophyllin-T
  [Theophylline]
Theochron [Theophylline]
Theo-Dur [Theophylline]
Theolair [Theophylline]
Theolair-SR
  [Theophylline]
Theo-SR [Theophylline]
Uniphyl [Theophylline]

AMINOPHYLLINE
Oral
  Aminophylline Oral Solution USP
    In the U.S.—*Somophyllin; Somophyllin-DF;* GENERIC
    In Canada—*Palaron*
  Aminophylline Tablets USP
    In the U.S.—*Aminophyllin;* GENERIC
    In Canada—GENERIC
  Aminophylline Tablets USP (Enteric-coated)
    In the U.S.—GENERIC
  Aminophylline Extended-release Tablets
    In the U.S.—*Phyllocontin*
    In Canada—*Phyllocontin; Phyllocontin-350*
Parenteral
  Aminophylline Injection USP
    In the U.S.—*Aminophyllin;* GENERIC
    In Canada—GENERIC
  Aminophylline and Sodium Chloride Injection
    In the U.S.—GENERIC
Rectal
  Aminophylline Enema USP
    In the U.S.—*Somophyllin*
  Aminophylline Suppositories USP
    In the U.S.—*Truphylline;* GENERIC
    In Canada—*Corophyllin*
DYPHYLLINE
Oral
  Dyphylline Elixir USP
    In the U.S.—*Dilor; Lufyllin*
    In Canada—*Protophylline*
  Dyphylline Oral Solution
    In Canada—*Protophylline*
  Dyphylline Tablets USP
    In the U.S.—*Dilor; Dilor-400; Dyflex; Dyflex 400; Lufyllin; Lufyllin-400; Neothylline; Thylline;* GENERIC
    In Canada—*Protophylline*
Parenteral
  Dyphylline Injection USP
    In the U.S.—*Dilor; Lufyllin; Neothylline;* GENERIC
OXTRIPHYLLINE
Oral
  Oxtriphylline Oral Solution USP
    In the U.S.—*Choledyl;* GENERIC
    In Canada—*Choledyl*
  Oxtriphylline Syrup
    In the U.S.—*Choledyl;* GENERIC
    In Canada—*Choledyl*
  Oxtriphylline Tablets
    In the U.S.—GENERIC
    In Canada—*Apo-Oxtriphylline; Choledyl; Novotriphyl*
  Oxtriphylline Delayed-release Tablets USP
    In the U.S.—*Choledyl Delayed-release;* GENERIC
  Oxtriphylline Extended-release Tablets USP
    In the U.S. and Canada—*Choledyl SA*
THEOPHYLLINE
Oral
  Theophylline Capsules USP
    In the U.S.—*Bronkodyl; Elixophyllin; Somophyllin-T;* GENERIC
    In Canada—*Elixophyllin; Somophyllin-T*
  Theophylline Extended-release Capsules
    In the U.S.—*Aerolate III; Aerolate Jr.; Aerolate Sr.; Elixophyllin SR; Slo-bid Gyrocaps; Slo-Phyllin Gyrocaps; Somophyllin-CRT; Theo-24; Theo 250; Theobid Duracaps; Theobid Jr. Duracaps; Theoclear L.A.-130 Cenules; Theoclear L.A.-260 Cenules; Theocot; Theo-Dur Sprinkle; Theospan-SR; Theovent Long-Acting;* GENERIC
    In Canada—*Slo-Bid; Somophyllin-12*

Theophylline Elixir
   In the U.S.—*Accurbron; Asmalix; Elixomin; Elixophyllin; Lanophyllin; Lixolin; Truxophyllin;* GENERIC
   In Canada—*Elixophyllin; PMS Theophylline; Pulmophylline*
Theophylline Oral Solution
   In the U.S.—*Aerolate; Theolair;* GENERIC
   In Canada—*Quibron-T; Theolair*
Theophylline Oral Suspension
   In the U.S.—*Elixicon*
Theophylline Syrup
   In the U.S.—*Accurbron; Aquaphyllin; Slo-Phyllin; Solu-Phyllin; Theoclear-80; Theomar; Theon; Theostat 80*
Theophylline Tablets USP
   In the U.S.—*Quibron-T Dividose; Slo-Phyllin; Theolair;* GENERIC
   In Canada—*Theolair*
Theophylline Extended-release Tablets
   In the U.S.—*Constant-T; Duraphyl; Quibron-T/SR Dividose; Respbid; Sustaire; Theochron; Theo-Dur; Theolair-SR; Theophylline SR; Theo-Time; T-Phyl; Uniphyl;* GENERIC
   In Canada—*Quibron-T/SR; Theochron; Theo-Dur; Theolair-SR; Theo-SR; Uniphyl*
Theophylline Sodium Glycinate Elixir USP
   In the U.S.—*Synophylate*
Parenteral
Theophylline in Dextrose Injection USP
   In the U.S. and Canada—GENERIC

Category

Bronchodilator—Aminophylline; Aminophylline and Sodium Chloride; Dyphylline; Oxtriphylline; Theophylline; Theophylline Sodium Glycinate; Theophylline in Dextrose.
Asthma prophylactic—Aminophylline (oral); Oxtriphylline; Theophylline (oral); Theophylline Sodium Glycinate.
Stimulant, respiratory—Aminophylline (injection, oral solution, and enema); Aminophylline and Sodium Chloride Injection; Theophylline (oral liquids); Theophylline Sodium Glycinate Elixir; Theophylline in Dextrose Injection.

Indications

Note: Bracketed information in the *Indications* section refers to uses not included in U.S. product labeling.

Accepted

Asthma, bronchial (prophylaxis and treatment)—Xanthine-derivative bronchodilators are indicated for the symptomatic relief of bronchial asthma. They relieve shortness of breath, wheezing, and dyspnea associated with asthma and improve pulmonary function. Oral aminophylline, oxtriphylline, and theophylline are also used to prevent exercise-induced asthma and symptoms of bronchial asthma. Although subcutaneous epinephrine or an inhaled beta-2 agonist is the preferred initial medication in the treatment of moderate to severe acute asthma attacks, intravenous xanthines may be indicated in asthma refractory to these medications.
Bronchitis (treatment);
Emphysema, pulmonary (treatment); or
Pulmonary disease, chronic obstructive, other (treatment)—Xanthine-derivative bronchodilators may be indicated for the treatment of reversible airway obstruction associated with chronic bronchitis, emphysema, or other chronic obstructive pulmonary disease.
Although theophylline, theophylline salts, and dyphylline are indicated in bronchial asthma, chronic bronchitis, and emphysema, theophylline or one of its salts is preferred because dyphylline has only about one-tenth the bronchodilator effect of theophylline and

has a very short half-life. In addition, dyphylline's therapeutic serum concentration has not been defined.
[Apnea, neonatal (treatment adjunct)][1]—Aminophylline (injection, oral solution, enema) and theophylline (oral liquids, injection) are used in the treatment of neonatal apnea, especially primary apnea of prematurity that is characterized by periodic breathing and apneic episodes of more than 15 seconds accompanied by cyanosis and bradycardia. However, these xanthines should be considered only as adjuncts to nondrug measures such as decreased ambient temperature and ambient humidity, administration of oxygen, sensory stimulation, and, if necessary, mechanical support of ventilation. Xanthine therapy in the management of apnea is usually required for only a few weeks and rarely for more than a few months.
[Cheyne-Stokes respiration (treatment)][1]—Parenteral aminophylline and theophylline are used in the treatment of Cheyne-Stokes respiration to relieve the periodic apnea and increase arterial blood pH.

Unaccepted

Parenteral aminophylline has been used as an antispasmodic (in acute biliary colic), a cardiac stimulant, and a diuretic, but generally it has been replaced by more effective agents.
[Parenteral aminophylline has been used as an adjunct in the treatment of congestive heart failure and pulmonary edema but it has been replaced by more effective agents for these conditions.][1]

---

[1]Not included in Canadian product labeling.

Pharmacology

Mechanism of action/Effect:
   Bronchodilator; asthma prophylactic—
      Theophylline directly relaxes smooth muscle of the bronchial airways and pulmonary blood vessels to relieve bronchospasm and increase flow rates and vital capacity. This action is believed to be primarily due to increased intracellular cyclic 3′,5′-adenosine monophosphate (cyclic AMP) following inhibition of phosphodiesterase, the enzyme that degrades cyclic AMP; however, this proposed mechanism of action is controversial since it is based on *in vitro* studies that used concentrations that would be toxic *in vivo*. Other proposed mechanisms of action for theophylline include alteration in smooth muscle calcium ion concentration, inhibition of the effects of prostaglandins on smooth muscle, blockade of adenosine receptors, and inhibition of the release of histamine and leukotrienes from mast cells.
      It is presumed that dyphylline (when administered in therapeutic dosage) has the same mechanism of action as theophylline, although this has not been proven. Dyphylline has only about one-tenth the bronchodilator effect of theophylline.
   Respiratory stimulant—The exact mechanism of action has not been completely established. However, theophylline is believed to act primarily through stimulation of the medullary respiratory center. It appears to increase the sensitivity of the respiratory center to the stimulatory actions of carbon dioxide and to increase alveolar ventilation, thereby reducing the severity and frequency of apneic episodes.

Other actions/effects: The xanthines exert other actions such as coronary vasodilation; diuresis; and cardiac, cerebral, and skeletal muscle stimulation. They also relax smooth muscle of the biliary and gastrointestinal tracts, stimulate gastric secretion, inhibit uterine contractions, and, in patients with chronic obstructive pulmonary disease, may increase biventricular performance. In addition, at toxic, and possibly at therapeutic, serum concentrations, the xanthines may decrease the seizure threshold.

Precautions to Consider

Geriatrics

Caution should be used in patients over 55 years of age because of possible decreased plasma clearance and increased potential for toxicity.

Drug interactions and/or related problems

The following drug interactions and/or related problems have been selected on the basis of their potential clinical significance (possible mechanism in parentheses where appropriate)—not necessarily inclusive (» = major clinical significance):

Note: Combinations containing any of the following medications, depending on the amount present, may also interact with this medication.

» Adrenocorticoids, glucocorticoid and mineralocorticoid
(concurrent use with aminophylline and sodium chloride injection may result in hypernatremia)

Allopurinol
(concurrent use of large doses [600 mg per day] of allopurinol with the xanthines [except dyphylline] may decrease theophylline clearance, resulting in increased serum theophylline concentrations; when steady-state theophylline concentration is 13 mcg per mL or higher and 600 mg of allopurinol per day is required, serum theophylline concentrations should be monitored and theophylline dosage adjusted if necessary)

Anesthetics, hydrocarbon inhalation, especially halothane
(concurrent use with the xanthines may increase the risk of cardiac arrhythmias)

Antidiarrheals, adsorbent
(concurrent use may impair absorption of the oral xanthines, resulting in decreased therapeutic effectiveness)

Barbiturates, especially phenobarbital, or
Carbamazepine or
» Phenytoin or
Primidone or
Rifampin
(concurrent use may stimulate hepatic metabolism of the xanthines [except dyphylline], resulting in increased theophylline clearance; for phenytoin, this effect is more likely to occur if phenytoin plasma concentrations are in the usual therapeutic range for at least 5 days)

(also, simultaneous use of phenytoin with the xanthines may inhibit phenytoin absorption, resulting in decreased serum phenytoin concentrations; serum concentrations of phenytoin and theophylline should be monitored during concurrent therapy; dosage adjustments of both phenytoin and theophylline may be necessary)

» Beta-adrenergic blocking agents, systemic, or
Levobunolol, ophthalmic, or
Timolol, ophthalmic
(concurrent use of beta-blockers, including ophthalmic levobunolol and timolol [significant systemic absorption possible], with the xanthines may result in mutual inhibition of therapeutic effects; in addition, concurrent use with the xanthines [except dyphylline] may decrease theophylline clearance, especially in patients with increased theophylline clearance induced by smoking; concurrent use requires careful monitoring)

Bronchodilators, adrenergic
(concurrent use with the xanthines may result in additive toxicity)

Charcoal-broiled foods
(a high polycyclic hydrocarbons content in these foods may accelerate hepatic metabolism of the xanthines [except dyphyl-line], resulting in increased theophylline clearance and decreased serum theophylline concentrations)

» Cimetidine or
» Erythromycin or
» Ranitidine or
» Troleandomycin
(concurrent use with the xanthines [except dyphylline] may decrease theophylline hepatic clearance, resulting in increased serum theophylline concentrations and/or toxicity [effect occurs to a lesser extent with ranitidine]; erythromycin in doses of 1 gram per day slows clearance an average of 25%, with interpatient variability; the magnitude of theophylline clearance reduction is proportional to the peak serum erythromycin concentrations; troleandomycin in doses of 1 gram per day slows clearance an average of 50%; dosage adjustment of the xanthines may be necessary during and after therapy with these medications)

Central nervous system (CNS) stimulation-producing medications, other
(concurrent use with xanthines may result in additive CNS stimulation to excessive levels, which may cause unwanted effects such as nervousness, irritability, insomnia, or possibly seizures or cardiac arrhythmias; close observation is recommended)

» Ciprofloxacin or
» Norfloxacin
(concurrent use reduces the hepatic clearance of theophylline, probably by competitive inhibition at the cytochrome P-450 binding sites, resulting in prolonged elimination half-life, increased theophylline serum concentrations, and increased risk of theophylline-related CNS toxicity; nausea, vomiting, tremors, restlessness, agitation, and palpitations may occur; serum theophylline concentrations should be monitored and dosage adjustments may be required)

Contraceptives, estrogen-containing, oral
(concurrent use with xanthines [except dyphylline] may alter the effectiveness of these medications)

Diltiazem or
Verapamil
(concurrent use may inhibit cytochrome P-450 metabolism of theophylline, resulting in increased concentrations and toxicity)

High-protein, low-carbohydrate diet
(concurrent use may enhance metabolism of the xanthines [except dyphylline], resulting in increased theophylline clearance [averages about 25%] and decreased serum theophylline concentrations)

Influenza vaccine
(although there are conflicting reports as to whether theophylline elimination is decreased following vaccination against influenza, monitoring of serum theophylline concentrations may be required for at least 48 hours following influenza vaccination in patients on xanthine [except dyphylline] therapy with serum theophylline concentrations in the upper therapeutic range; dosage reduction of theophylline may be necessary)

Lithium
(therapeutic effect may be decreased when lithium is used concurrently with the xanthines because renal excretion of lithium may be increased)

Low-protein, high-carbohydrate diet
(concurrent use may inhibit metabolism of the xanthines [except dyphylline], resulting in decreased theophylline clearance [averages about 25%] and increased serum theophylline concentrations)

Mexiletine
(concurrent use may decrease theophylline clearance, resulting in prolonged elimination half-life, increased serum theophylline concentrations, and increased risk of theophylline-related CNS toxicity; serum theophylline concentrations should be monitored and dosage adjustments may be required)

» Nicotine chewing gum or
Smoking deterrents, other, or
Smoking, tobacco, cessation of
(smoking cessation may increase therapeutic effects of the xanthines [except dyphylline] by decreasing metabolism, thereby increasing serum concentration; however, after cessation of smoking, normalization of theophylline's pharmacokinetics may not occur for 3 months to 2 years; dosage adjustments may be necessary)

Probenecid
(concurrent use may increase the half-life of dyphylline, possibly permitting less frequent dyphylline dosing)

» Smoking, tobacco or marijuana
(concurrent use induces hepatic metabolism of the xanthines [except dyphylline], resulting in increased theophylline clearance and decreased serum theophylline concentrations; smokers may require a 50 to 100% increase in dosage)

Xanthines, other, such as caffeine
(concurrent use of one xanthine with another xanthine may increase the potential for toxic side effects)

Contraindications/Medical problems
The contraindications/medical problems included have been selected on the basis of their potential clinical significance (reasons given in parentheses where appropriate)—not necessarily inclusive (» = major clinical significance).

Risk-benefit should be considered when the following medical problems exist:
For all xanthines
Arrhythmias, pre-existing, or
Hypertension
(condition may be exacerbated)

Cardiac disease, severe, or
Congestive heart failure
(xanthines are potentially cardiotoxic; in patients receiving theophylline, plasma clearance may be decreased, resulting in prolonged plasma half-life)

Diarrhea
(absorption of xanthines, especially the extended-release forms, may be incomplete)

Fibrocystic breast disease
(symptoms may be increased)

» Gastritis, active, or
» Peptic ulcer, active or history of
(condition may be exacerbated; xanthines may act centrally to stimulate gastric acid secretion and as a local irritant on gastric mucosa)

Myocardial injury, acute
(myocardial stimulation produced by the xanthines may be harmful)

Prostatic enlargement
(urinary retention may occur)

Sensitivity to xanthines or to ethylenediamine

For aminophylline, oxtriphylline, and theophylline only
Alcoholism, active, or
Cor pulmonale or
Fever, prolonged, or
Hypoxemia, severe, or
Respiratory infections, febrile viral
(plasma clearance may be decreased, resulting in prolonged plasma half-life)

Hepatic disease
(theophylline metabolized in liver; hepatic clearance may be decreased, resulting in prolonged plasma half-life)

Hyperthyroidism
(plasma clearance may be increased, resulting in decreased serum theophylline concentration)

For aminophylline rectal enema only
» Irritation or infection of rectum or lower colon
(condition may be exacerbated since rectal administration may be irritating)

For aminophylline and sodium chloride injection only
» Congestive heart failure or
» Renal function impairment, especially severe renal insufficiency, or
» Other edematous conditions or conditions promoting sodium retention
(potential increase in sodium retention)

For dyphylline
Renal disease
(plasma clearance may be decreased, resulting in prolonged plasma half-life)

Side/Adverse Effects

Note: Gastrointestinal side effects are probably mediated by a central effect (usually when serum theophylline concentrations are greater than 20 mcg per mL but occasionally at lower doses) and a direct irritant effect on the gastric mucosa.

Gastrointestinal and CNS side effects may be avoided if dosage is titrated over a period of 1 week.

Therapeutic doses of xanthines have been shown to induce gastroesophageal reflux when the patient is asleep or recumbent, thereby increasing the potential for aspiration which can aggravate bronchospasm; infants less than 2 years of age and elderly, debilitated, and stuporous patients with feeble gag and cough reflexes are especially susceptible to this effect.

Toxicity may occur at serum concentrations between 15 and 20 mcg per mL, especially during initiation of therapy. The incidence of serious theophylline toxicity increases at serum concentrations greater than 20 mcg per mL.

The early and less severe signs of toxicity do not always precede the more serious ones; tachycardia, ventricular arrhythmias, or seizures may be the first signs of toxicity.

The following side/adverse effects have been selected on the basis of their potential clinical significance (possible signs and symptoms in parentheses where appropriate)—not necessarily inclusive:

Note: Although not all of these side effects have been attributed specifically to dyphylline (possibly due to use of ineffective dosage) as they have to the other xanthines, a potential exists for their occurrence during the use of any xanthine.

Those indicating need for medical attention
Incidence less frequent
Gastroesophageal reflux (heartburn and/or vomiting)
Incidence rare
Allergic reaction to ethylenediamine in aminophylline (skin rash or hives)
Note: *Allergic reaction to ethylenediamine in aminophylline* may not occur for 12 to 24 hours after initial administration.

For parenteral aminophylline and theophylline—with too rapid intravenous administration
Chest pain; decrease in blood pressure; dizziness; fast breathing; flushing; headache; pounding heartbeat; reaction to solution or administration technique (chills; fever; pain, redness, or swelling at site of injection)

Symptoms of toxicity
> *Confusion or change in behavior; convulsions; diarrhea; dizziness or lightheadedness; fast breathing; fast, pounding, or irregular heartbeat; flushing or redness of face; gastrointestinal bleeding* (bloody or black, tarry stools); *headache; increased urination; irritability; loss of appetite; muscle twitching; nausea, continuing or severe, or vomiting; stomach cramps or pain; trembling; trouble in sleeping; unusual tiredness or weakness; vomiting blood or material that looks like coffee grounds*

Those indicating need for medical attention only if they continue or are bothersome
Incidence more frequent
> *Nausea; nervousness or restlessness*

Incidence less frequent
> *Burning or irritation of rectum*—for rectal dosage form only

Patient Consultation

In providing consultation, consider emphasizing the following selected information (» = major clinical significance):

Before using this medication
» Conditions affecting use, especially:
  Sensitivity to xanthines or to ethylenediamine in aminophylline
  Mutagenicity—Theophylline reported to cause chromosomal breakage in human cells in culture at concentrations up to 50 times maximum therapeutic serum concentration
  Pregnancy—Studies in mice have shown theophylline to cause teratogenic effects when given in doses 30 times the human dose (FDA Pregnancy Category C); use during pregnancy may result in potentially dangerous serum theophylline and caffeine concentrations in neonates; tachycardia, jitteriness, irritability, gagging, and vomiting reported in some neonates; neonates of mothers taking theophylline during pregnancy should be monitored for signs of theophylline toxicity
  Breast-feeding—Theophylline and dyphylline excreted in breast milk; use of aminophylline, oxtriphylline, or theophylline by nursing mothers may cause irritability, fretfulness, or insomnia in infants
  Use in children—Possible decreased plasma clearance and increased serum concentrations and/or toxicity in neonates, especially premature neonates; repeated doses should not be given if heart rate greater than 80 beats per minute
  Use in the elderly—Possible decreased plasma clearance and increased potential for toxicity in patients over 55 years of age
  Other medications, especially adrenocorticoids, beta-adrenergic blocking agents, cimetidine, ciprofloxacin, erythromycin, phenytoin, nicotine chewing gum, norfloxacin, ranitidine, troleandomycin, or smoking tobacco or marijuana
  Other medical problems, especially active gastritis, active or history of peptic ulcer, congestive heart failure (for aminophylline and sodium chloride only), irritation or infection of rectum or lower colon (for rectal enema only), or renal function impairment (for aminophylline and sodium chloride and dyphylline only)

Proper use of this medication
» Importance of not using more medication than the amount prescribed
» Compliance with therapy; not missing any doses
  Missed dose: Taking as soon as possible; not taking if almost time for next dose; not doubling doses
  Proper administration:
  For enteric-coated or delayed-release tablet dosage form
    Swallowing tablets whole
    Not breaking, crushing, or chewing
  For extended-release dosage forms
    Swallowing capsules or tablets whole

  Not breaking (unless tablet dosage form is scored for breaking), crushing, or chewing
  For enema dosage form
    Reading patient directions carefully before use
    Possible crystal formation in aminophylline enema; dissolving crystals by placing closed container of solution in warm water; not using medication if crystals do not dissolve
» Proper storage
For oral liquid, immediate-release capsule or tablet, or extended-release (not including once-a-day) capsule or tablet dosage forms
» Taking on empty stomach with a glass of water for faster absorption or, if necessary, taking with meals or immediately after meals to lessen gastrointestinal irritation, unless otherwise directed
For once-a-day capsule or tablet dosage forms
» Taking once a day each morning after fasting overnight and at least 1 hour before eating or taking each morning or evening with or without food, depending on product; trying to take at same time each day

Precautions while using this medication
  Regular visits to physician to check progress during initial period of therapy
» Not changing brands or dosage forms without first checking with physician
» Caution in eating or drinking large amounts of xanthine-containing foods or beverages during therapy with this medication
For aminophylline, oxtriphylline, and theophylline only
  Not eating charcoal-broiled foods daily because of possible decrease in effects of medication
» Notifying physician immediately if symptoms of influenza, a fever, or diarrhea occur because of possible need to alter dosage
For enema dosage form
  Checking with physician if burning or other irritation of rectal area occurs and continues or becomes worse

Side/adverse effects
  Signs of potential side effects, especially gastroesophageal reflux, allergic reaction to ethylenediamine in aminophylline, and reaction to too-rapid intravenous administration or to solution or administration technique (parenteral dosage forms only)

General Dosing Information

The bronchodilator action of the xanthines, except for dyphylline, depends upon their theophylline content. The various xanthine preparations contain the following amounts of anhydrous theophylline:

Drug	Anhydrous Theophylline Approx. (%)
Aminophylline anhydrous	86
Aminophylline dihydrate	79
Dyphylline	None
Oxtriphylline	64
Theophylline monohydrate	91
Theophylline sodium glycinate	49

Tolerance to the bronchodilator effect does not appear to occur during long-term use of the xanthines.

Parenteral or rapidly acting dosage forms of the xanthines may be required in severe attacks of bronchospasm to achieve rapid therapeutic serum concentrations.

If an oral or parenteral dosage form is administered within 12 hours after rectal administration of an aminophylline preparation, caution is recommended since absorption of the rectal preparations, especially the suppository, is variable and may be delayed.

If any signs of toxicity occur or if dosage is not tolerated, the medication should be temporarily discontinued. If therapy is resumed, it should be at a lower dosage after all signs of toxicity have disappeared.

In patients not rapidly responsive to bronchodilators, additional medication including corticosteroids is generally required for optimal therapy.

For aminophylline, oxtriphylline, and theophylline only

Dosage must be individualized. Monitoring of serum theophylline concentrations is recommended, especially with prolonged use or higher-than-usual dosage, because of the variation among patients in dosage required to achieve a therapeutic serum concentration and because of the relatively narrow therapeutic serum concentration range.

Measurement of serum theophylline concentrations is used to titrate dosage, manage dosage during acute asthmatic attacks, clarify maximal endpoint for a dosage regimen, identify toxicity, and detect noncompliance. The trough serum concentration (time point before the next dose) measurement is used for evaluating serum concentration-time profiles. It is more consistent from dosing interval to dosing interval than the peak serum concentration. The peak serum concentration measurement is used for identifying theophylline toxicity. Time to peak serum concentration is a function of both the absorption rate and the elimination rate. It is most useful in patients with rapid theophylline clearance. The serum samples for measurement of peak and trough concentrations should be obtained under steady-state conditions.

All dosages should be calculated from lean (ideal) body weight since theophylline does not distribute into fatty tissue.

In treatment of the acute attack in patients not currently receiving a theophylline preparation, an initial loading dose based on the mean volume of distribution is required to rapidly obtain maximum bronchodilation.

Although the intravenous route of administration provides the most rapid effect in treatment of the acute attack, rapidly absorbed dosage forms such as oral liquids, uncoated or chewable tablets, and the rectal enema may also be used.

When changing from a continuous intravenous infusion to an oral immediate-release dosage form, an interval of 4 to 6 hours should elapse before the first oral dose is administered; however, when changing to an extended-release dosage form, the first dose should be administered at the time the intravenous infusion is discontinued, especially in children.

When rapidly absorbed dosage forms (such as liquids or uncoated tablets) are used, dosing to maintain serum concentrations usually requires administration every 6 hours, especially in children and smoking adults; however, dosing intervals of up to 8 hours may be satisfactory in nonsmoking adults, elderly or debilitated patients, and neonates because their clearance rate is slower. In premature neonates and patients with hepatic cirrhosis, dosing every 12 hours with an oral rapid-release or intravenous formulation will usually provide relatively constant serum concentrations. Patients requiring higher-than-usual doses (those having rapid clearance rates) may benefit and be more effectively controlled during chronic therapy when given extended-release preparations since these provide longer dosing intervals and/or less fluctuation in serum concentration.

Generally, extended-release dosage forms for once-a-day administration are more appropriate for patients who metabolize theophylline at a normal or slow rate. Patients who metabolize theophylline rapidly (e.g., children and adult smokers) and who have symptoms repeatedly at the end of a dosing interval usually require either increased once-a-day dosage or a twice-a-day dosage regimen with the extended-release preparation.

In determination of theophylline dosage for chronic therapy, the dosage should be titrated up to the maximum dose recommended without measurement of serum concentration or to a lower but maximum tolerated dose. To guide final dosage adjustment, a peak serum measurement should be obtained during steady-state conditions (for example, no doses missed or added during the previous 48 to 96 hours [depending on the specific product used], approximately equal intervals between doses, and no other medications that may transiently alter clearance). The serum sample should be obtained at the time of peak absorption (1 to 2 hours after administration for immediate-release dosage forms and about 4 to 12 hours [depending on the specific product used] after dosing for most extended-release dosage forms).

For once-a-day dosage forms, the peak and trough serum theophylline concentrations may vary from those produced by the previous product and/or dosage regimen used. Serum concentrations should be determined for peak concentration at the approximate time of the expected peak concentration (about 9 to 12 hours after the morning dose or about 12 hours after the evening dose) of once-a-day dosage forms. Serum concentrations should be determined for trough concentration just prior to administration of the next dose (24 hours after the morning dose or after the evening dose) of once-a-day dosage forms.

For final dosage adjustment in chronic therapy after serum theophylline measurement, the following dosage adjustments are recommended:

Peak Serum Theophylline Concentration (mcg/mL)	Adjustment in Dose
5–7.5	About 25% increase to nearest dose increment; recheck serum theophylline concentration for guidance in further dosage adjustment
7.5–10	About 25% increase*; recheck serum theophylline concentration at 6- to 12-month intervals†‡
10–20	Maintain dosage if tolerated; recheck serum theophylline concentration at 6- to 12-month intervals†
20–25	About 10% decrease; recheck serum theophylline concentration at 6- to 12-month intervals†‡
25–30	Omit next dose; about 25% decrease in subsequent doses‡
>30	Omit next 2 doses; 50% decrease in subsequent doses; recheck serum theophylline concentration‡

*Dividing daily dose of an extended-release dosage form into 3 doses administered at 8-hour intervals or, for once-a-day dosage forms, 2 doses administered at 12-hour intervals may be indicated if symptoms occur repeatedly at the end of a dosing interval.

†Finer adjustments in dosage may be required for some patients.

‡For the once-a-day dosage forms, serum theophylline concentration should be rechecked after 3 days.

Geriatric patients, neonates, or patients with congestive heart failure, chronic obstructive pulmonary disease, cor pulmonale, febrile viral respiratory infections, or hepatic function impairment may require lower doses since theophylline clearance is usually decreased in these patients. Also, high fever for prolonged periods of time may decrease theophylline elimination.

Patients who smoke may require higher doses since metabolism of theophylline is usually increased in these patients.

For oral dosage forms only

Alcohol-free liquid dosage forms are generally preferred to the elixir dosage form because of the high alcohol content in elixirs.

There are marked differences in the rate and extent of absorption among the various brands of extended-release dosage forms; therefore, these preparations are not bioequivalent and one brand should not be substituted for another unless otherwise directed by the patient's physician.

Extended-release dosage forms should not be used when rapid attainment of therapeutic serum theophylline concentrations is required; they should be used only after therapy has been initiated and daily dosage requirements have been established.

For patients who have difficulty in swallowing the extended-release capsule, the contents may be mixed with or sprinkled on a teaspoonful of jam, jelly, or applesauce and taken without chewing.

When oral liquid dosage forms of aminophylline or theophylline are used in the treatment of neonatal apnea, the less concentrated (e.g., 5 mg per mL) liquids are preferred in order to minimize dosage errors due to small volume. The parenteral dosage form used orally may be preferred.

For parenteral dosage forms only

Parenteral preparations should be visually inspected for particulate matter and discoloration prior to administration, if possible.

It is recommended that the intravenous administration apparatus be replaced at least once every 24 hours.

Diet/Nutrition

Preferably, the liquid, immediate-release capsule or tablet, or extended-release (not including once-a-day) capsule or tablet dosage forms should be taken with a glass of water on an empty stomach (either 30 minutes to 1 hour before meals or 2 hours after meals) for faster absorption; however, these dosage forms may be taken with meals or immediately after meals to lessen local gastrointestinal irritation.

Patients taking once-a-day dosage forms should take the medication either in the morning after fasting overnight and at least 1 hour before eating or in the evening with or without food, depending on the product. It is important that the medication whenever dosed be dosed consistently with or without food. The medication should be taken at approximately the same time each day.

Administration of once-a-day dosage forms of theophylline with food may increase the extent of absorption and increase peak serum concentrations as compared with administration in the fasting state, especially when high serum theophylline concentrations are being maintained and/or when large single doses (greater than 13 mg per kg of body weight (mg/kg) or 900 mg) of an extended-release preparation are administered. Therefore, theophylline taken in once-daily doses of 900 mg or more with food may increase serum theophylline concentrations above 20 mcg per mL, possibly resulting in toxicity.

Large amounts of caffeine-containing foods or beverages should be avoided, since they may increase the CNS stimulant effects of xanthine-derivative bronchodilators.

A high-protein, low-carbohydrate diet may increase the metabolism of theophylline, resulting in decreased serum theophylline concentrations. A low-protein, high-carbohydrate diet may inhibit the metabolism of theophylline, resulting in increased serum theophylline concentrations.

High intake of charcoal-broiled foods, which contain a large amount of polycyclic hydrocarbons, may increase metabolism of theophylline, resulting in decreased serum theophylline concentrations.

AMINOPHYLLINE

Summary of Differences

Category: Aminophylline (injection, oral solution, enema) is also used as a respiratory stimulant in neonatal apnea; in addition, aminophylline injection is used as a respiratory stimulant in Cheyne-Stokes respiration.

Indications: Parenteral aminophylline has been used as an antispasmodic (in acute biliary colic), a cardiac stimulant, a diuretic, and as an adjunct in treatment of congestive heart failure and pulmonary edema, but it has been replaced by more effective agents.

Pharmacology:

Aminophylline is the ethylenediamine salt of theophylline.

Aminophylline releases free theophylline *in vivo*.

Precautions:

Drug interactions and/or related problems—Caution needed when parenteral aminophylline and sodium chloride is used concurrently with adrenocorticoids.

Contraindications/medical problems—Caution needed in edematous conditions or conditions promoting sodium retention when parenteral aminophylline and sodium chloride is used.

Side/adverse effects: Ethylenediamine in aminophylline may cause urticaria or exfoliative dermatitis.

General dosing information:

Aminophylline anhydrous contains about 86% of anhydrous theophylline.

Aminophylline dihydrate contains about 79% of anhydrous theophylline.

Additional Dosing Information

See also *General Dosing Information.*

When aminophylline is used in the treatment of neonatal apnea, the oral or intravenous route of administration is preferred to the rectal enema.

For parenteral dosage forms only

Intramuscular administration of aminophylline injection is not recommended since severe, persistent local pain may occur at the site of injection.

For intravenous administration of aminophylline injection, only the 25-mg-per-mL injection is to be used. This solution should be further diluted with intravenous fluids.

Since rapid intravenous administration may cause transient lowering of blood pressure or peripheral circulatory collapse, it is recommended that aminophylline be administered slowly at a rate of approximately 25 mg per minute. If the 25-mg-per-mL strength is used, it preferably should be diluted.

The intravenous administration of aminophylline and sodium chloride injection may cause fluid and/or solute overloading, resulting in dilution of serum electrolyte concentrations, overhydration, congested states, or pulmonary edema.

For rectal dosage forms only

USP DI Advisory Panels do not recommend the use of aminophylline suppositories because of the potential for slow and unreliable absorption, especially if the suppository base is composed of hydrogenated vegetable oils. The suppositories may also cause local irritation.

The retention enema gives rapid and reliable absorption, if retained; however, it should be used only when the patient is unable to take an oral preparation, such as in the presence of vomiting from causes other than theophylline toxicity or when fasting before surgery. Rectal enema administration should not exceed 24 to 36 hours to avoid local irritation caused by the alkaline solution.

Generally, doses should not be repeated at less than 6-hour, preferably 8-hour, intervals.

Oral Dosage Forms

Note: Bracketed uses in the *Dosage Forms* section refer to categories of use and/or indications that are not included in U.S. product labeling.

AMINOPHYLLINE ORAL SOLUTION USP

Usual adult dose: Bronchodilator—

Acute attack:

Loading dose—

For patients *not* currently receiving theophylline preparations: Oral, the equivalent of 5 to 6 mg of anhydrous theophylline per kg of body weight.

For patients currently receiving theophylline preparations: A serum theophylline measurement should be obtained immediately, if possible. The loading dose for theophylline is based on the principle that each 0.5 mg of theophylline per kg of lean (ideal) body weight will result in a 1 (range, 0.5 to 1.6) mcg per mL increase in serum theophylline concentration. If a serum theophylline measurement cannot be obtained rapidly and the patient's condition requires immediate therapy, a single dose of the equivalent of 2.5 mg of anhydrous theophylline per kg of body weight may be administered if there are no symptoms of theophylline toxicity.

Maintenance (in acute attack)—

Young adult smokers: Oral, the equivalent of anhydrous theophylline—4 mg per kg of body weight every six hours.

Otherwise healthy nonsmoking adults: Oral, the equivalent of anhydrous theophylline—3 mg per kg of body weight every eight hours.

Older patients and patients with cor pulmonale: Oral, the equivalent of anhydrous theophylline—2 mg per kg of body weight every eight hours.

Patients with congestive heart failure or liver failure: Oral, the equivalent of anhydrous theophylline—2 mg per kg of body weight every twelve hours.

Note: **To achieve optimal therapeutic theophylline dosage, and minimize the risk of toxicity, monitoring of serum theophylline concentration and patient response is recommended.**

In patients with cor pulmonale, congestive heart failure, or liver failure, dosage should not exceed the equivalent of 400 mg of anhydrous theophylline per day unless serum theophylline concentrations can be monitored at twenty-four-hour intervals.

Chronic therapy: Oral, the equivalent of anhydrous theophylline—Initially, 6 to 8 mg per kg of body weight, up to a maximum of 400 mg, per day in three or four divided doses at six- to eight-hour intervals. The dosage may be increased, if tolerated, in approximately 25% increments at two- to three-day intervals, up to a maximum dose of 13 mg per kg of body weight or 900 mg per day, whichever is less, without measurement of serum concentration.

Note: If the above maximum dose in chronic therapy is to be maintained or exceeded, serum theophylline measurement is recommended. Final dosage adjustment is based on subsequent serum theophylline measurements and patient response.

AMINOPHYLLINE TABLETS USP

Usual adult dose: Bronchodilator—

Acute attack:

Loading dose—

For patients *not* currently receiving theophylline preparations: Oral, the equivalent of 5 to 6 mg of anhydrous theophylline per kg of body weight.

For patients currently receiving theophylline preparations: A serum theophylline measurement should be obtained immediately, if possible. The loading dose for theophylline is based on the principle that each 0.5 mg of theophylline per kg of lean (ideal) body weight will result in a 1 (range, 0.5 to 1.6) mcg per mL increase in serum theophylline concentration. If a serum theophylline measurement cannot be obtained rapidly and the patient's condition requires immediate therapy, a single dose of the equivalent of 2.5 mg of anhydrous theophylline per kg of body weight may be administered if there are no symptoms of theophylline toxicity.

Maintenance (in acute attack)—

Young adult smokers: Oral, the equivalent of anhydrous theophylline—4 mg per kg of body weight every six hours.

Otherwise healthy nonsmoking adults: Oral, the equivalent of anhydrous theophylline—3 mg per kg of body weight every eight hours.

Older patients and patients with cor pulmonale: Oral, the equivalent of anhydrous theophylline—2 mg per kg of body weight every eight hours.

Patients with congestive heart failure or liver failure: Oral, the equivalent of anhydrous theophylline—2 mg per kg of body weight every twelve hours.

Note: **To achieve optimal therapeutic theophylline dosage, and minimize the risk of toxicity, monitoring of serum theophylline concentration and patient response is recommended.**

In patients with cor pulmonale, congestive heart failure, or liver failure, dosage should not exceed the equivalent of 400 mg of anhydrous theophylline per day unless serum theophylline concentrations can be monitored at twenty-four-hour intervals.

Chronic therapy: Oral, the equivalent of anhydrous theophylline—Initially, 6 to 8 mg per kg of body weight, up to a maximum of 400 mg, per day in three or four divided doses at six- to eight-hour intervals. The dosage may be increased, if tolerated, in approximately 25% increments at two- to three-day intervals, up to a maximum dose of 13 mg per kg of body weight or 900 mg per day, whichever is less, without measurement of serum concentration.

Note: If the above maximum dose in chronic therapy is to be maintained or exceeded, serum theophylline measurement is recommended. Final dosage adjustment is based on subsequent serum theophylline measurements and patient response.

AMINOPHYLLINE TABLETS USP (ENTERIC-COATED)

Note: Aminophylline enteric-coated tablets may be slowly and incompletely absorbed.

Usual adult dose: Bronchodilator—Chronic therapy: Oral, the equivalent of anhydrous theophylline—Initially, 6 to 8 mg per kg of body weight, up to a maximum of 400 mg, per day in three or four divided doses at six- to eight-hour intervals. The dosage may be increased, if tolerated, in approximately 25% increments at two- to three-day intervals, up to a maximum dose of 13 mg per kg of body weight or 900 mg per day, whichever is less, without measurement of serum concentration.

Note: If the above maximum dose in chronic therapy is to be maintained or exceeded, serum theophylline measurement is recommended. Final dosage adjustment is based on subsequent serum theophylline measurements and patient response.

Auxiliary labeling: • Swallow tablets whole.

AMINOPHYLLINE EXTENDED-RELEASE TABLETS

Usual adult dose: Bronchodilator—Chronic therapy: Oral, the equivalent of anhydrous theophylline—Initially, 4 mg per kg of body weight every eight to twelve hours. The dosage may be increased, if tolerated, by 2 to 3 mg per kg of body weight per day at three-day intervals, up to a maximum dose of 13 mg per kg of body weight or 900 mg per day, whichever is less, without measurement of serum concentration.

Note: If the above maximum dose in chronic therapy is to be maintained or exceeded, serum theophylline measurement is recommended. Final dosage adjustment is based on subsequent serum theophylline measurements and patient response.

Auxiliary labeling: • Swallow tablets whole.

Parenteral Dosage Forms

Note: Bracketed uses in the *Dosage Forms* section refer to categories of use and/or indications that are not included in U.S. product labeling.

AMINOPHYLLINE INJECTION USP

Usual adult dose: Bronchodilator—Acute attack:

Loading dose—

For patients *not* currently receiving theophylline preparations: Intravenous infusion, the equivalent of 5 mg of anhydrous theophylline per kg of body weight administered over a period of twenty minutes.

For patients currently receiving theophylline preparations: A serum theophylline measurement should be obtained immediately, if possible. The loading dose for theophylline is based on the principle that each 0.5 mg of theophylline per kg of lean (ideal) body weight will result in a 1 (range, 0.5 to 1.6) mcg per mL increase in serum theophylline concentration. If a serum theophylline measurement cannot be obtained rapidly and the patient's condition requires immediate therapy, a single dose of the equivalent of 2.5 mg of anhydrous theophylline per kg of body weight may be administered if there are no symptoms of theophylline toxicity.

Maintenance (in acute attack)—

Young adult smokers: Intravenous infusion, the equivalent of anhydrous theophylline—700 mcg (0.7 mg) per kg of body weight per hour.

Otherwise healthy nonsmoking adults: Intravenous infusion, the equivalent of anhydrous theophylline—430 mcg (0.43 mg) per kg of body weight per hour.

Older patients and patients with cor pulmonale: Intravenous infusion, the equivalent of anhydrous theophylline—260 mcg (0.26 mg) per kg of body weight per hour.

Patients with congestive heart failure or liver failure: Intravenous infusion, the equivalent of anhydrous theophylline—200 mcg (0.2 mg) per kg of body weight per hour.

Note: **To achieve optimal therapeutic theophylline dosage, and minimize the risk of toxicity, monitoring of serum theophylline concentration and patient response is recommended.**

AMINOPHYLLINE AND SODIUM CHLORIDE INJECTION

Usual adult dose: Bronchodilator—Acute attack:

Loading dose—

For patients *not* currently receiving theophylline preparations: Intravenous infusion, the equivalent of 5 mg of anhydrous theophylline per kg of body weight administered over a period of twenty minutes.

For patients currently receiving theophylline preparations: A serum theophylline measurement should be obtained immediately, if possible. The loading dose for theophylline is based on the principle that each 0.5 mg of theophylline per kg of lean (ideal) body weight will result in a 1 (range, 0.5 to 1.6) mcg per mL increase in serum theophylline concentration. If a serum theophylline measurement cannot be obtained rapidly and the patient's condition requires immediate therapy, a single dose of the equivalent of 2.5 mg of anhydrous theophylline per kg of body weight may be administered if there are no symptoms of theophylline toxicity.

Maintenance (in acute attack)—

Young adult smokers: Intravenous infusion, the equivalent of anhydrous theophylline—700 mcg (0.7 mg) per kg of body weight per hour.

Otherwise healthy nonsmoking adults: Intravenous infusion, the equivalent of anhydrous theophylline—430 mcg (0.43 mg) per kg of body weight per hour.

Older patients and patients with cor pulmonale: Intravenous infusion, the equivalent of anhydrous theophylline—260 mcg (0.26 mg) per kg of body weight per hour.

Patients with congestive heart failure or liver failure: Intravenous infusion, the equivalent of anhydrous theophylline—200 mcg (0.2 mg) per kg of body weight per hour.

Note: **To achieve optimal therapeutic theophylline dosage, and minimize the risk of toxicity, monitoring of serum theophylline concentration and patient response is recommended.**

Rectal Dosage Forms

Note: Bracketed uses in the *Dosage Forms* section refer to categories of use and/or indications that are not included in U.S. product labeling.

AMINOPHYLLINE ENEMA USP

Usual adult dose: Bronchodilator—Acute attack:

Loading dose—

For patients *not* currently receiving theophylline preparations: Rectal, the equivalent of 5 to 6 mg of anhydrous theophylline per kg of body weight.

For patients currently receiving theophylline preparations: A serum theophylline measurement should be obtained immediately, if possible. The loading dose for theophylline is based on the principle that each 0.5 mg of theophylline per kg of lean (ideal) body weight will result in a 1 (range, 0.5 to 1.6) mcg per mL increase in serum theophylline concentration. If a serum theophylline measurement cannot be obtained rapidly and the patient's condition requires immediate therapy, a single dose of the equivalent of 2.5 mg of anhydrous theophylline per kg of body weight may be administered if there are no symptoms of theophylline toxicity.

Maintenance (in acute attack)—

Young adult smokers: Rectal, the equivalent of anhydrous theophylline—4 mg per kg of body weight every six hours.

Otherwise healthy nonsmoking adults: Rectal, the equivalent of anhydrous theophylline—3 mg per kg of body weight every eight hours.

Older patients and patients with cor pulmonale: Rectal, the equivalent of anhydrous theophylline—2 mg per kg of body weight every eight hours.

Patients with congestive heart failure or liver failure: Rectal, the equivalent of anhydrous theophylline—2 mg per kg of body weight every twelve hours.

Note: **To achieve optimal therapeutic theophylline dosage, and minimize the risk of toxicity, monitoring of serum theophylline concentration and patient response is recommended.**

In patients with cor pulmonale, congestive heart failure, or liver failure, the dosage should not exceed the equivalent of 400 mg of anhydrous theophylline per day unless serum theophylline concentrations can be monitored at twenty-four-hour intervals.

Auxiliary labeling: • For rectal use only.

AMINOPHYLLINE SUPPOSITORIES USP

Note: **USP DI Advisory Panels do not recommend the use of Aminophylline Suppositories USP because of the potential for slow and unreliable absorption, especially if the suppository base is composed of hydrogenated vegetable oils.**

DYPHYLLINE

Note: Because dyphylline has only about one-tenth the bronchodilator effect of theophylline and has a very short half-life, and because its therapeutic serum concentration has not been defined, theophylline or one of its salts is preferred in the treatment of asthma and reversible airway obstruction.

Summary of Differences

Pharmacology:
Dyphylline is a derivative of theophylline, not a theophylline salt as are aminophylline and oxtriphylline.
Has only about one-tenth the bronchodilator effect of theophylline.
Not metabolized to theophylline.
Amount of dyphylline protein bound is unknown.
Therapeutic range of serum concentration not defined.
Half-life is 2 to 2.5 hours.
Excreted primarily as unchanged drug in the urine.
Precautions:
Pregnancy—Studies have not been done in either animals or humans.
Drug interactions and/or related problems—
Caution needed with probenecid.
Because dyphylline is not hepatically metabolized, its clearance is not affected by concurrent use of allopurinol; barbiturates; carbamazepine; charcoal-broiled foods; cimetidine; ciprofloxacin; diltiazem; erythromycin; high-protein, low carbohydrate or low-protein, high carbohydrate diet; influenza vaccine; nicotine chewing gum or other smoking deterrents; norfloxacin; phenytoin; primidone; rifampin; smoking; troleandomycin; or verapamil.
Contraindications/medical problems—
Caution needed in renal function impairment.
Caution probably not needed in alcoholism, hepatic disease, fever (prolonged), cor pulmonale, febrile viral respiratory infections, hyperthyroidism, or severe hypoxemia because dyphylline is not hepatically metabolized and, therefore, its clearance is not affected by these conditions.
Laboratory value alterations—Serum dyphylline concentrations not falsely increased by coffee, tea, cola beverages, chocolate, acetaminophen, caffeine, some cephalosporins, and sulfa medications.
Patient monitoring—Serum concentration should be determined by specific assay method for dyphylline; assay methods used for measuring serum theophylline concentrations should not be used since they will give a zero concentration in patients taking dyphylline.

Additional Dosing Information

See also *General Dosing Information.*

Although dyphylline is 70% theophylline by molecular weight ratio, the amount of dyphylline equivalent to a given amount of theophylline is not known.

Dosage must be individualized by titration according to the condition and the response of the patient, since the therapeutic range of serum concentrations has not been defined.

Geriatric patients or patients with renal function impairment may require lower doses since plasma clearance may be decreased in these patients.

For parenteral dosage forms only
Dyphylline injection is recommended for intramuscular use only.

Oral Dosage Forms

DYPHYLLINE ELIXIR USP

Usual adult dose: Bronchodilator—Oral, 15 mg per kg of body weight every six hours, up to four times a day.

Auxiliary labeling: • Keep container tightly closed.

DYPHYLLINE ORAL SOLUTION

Note: Dyphylline oral solution is not commercially available in the U.S.

Usual adult dose: Bronchodilator—Oral, 15 mg per kg of body weight every six hours, up to four times a day.

DYPHYLLINE TABLETS USP

Usual adult dose: Bronchodilator—Oral, 15 mg per kg of body weight every six hours, up to four times a day.

Parenteral Dosage Forms

DYPHYLLINE INJECTION USP

Usual adult dose: Bronchodilator—Intramuscular, 500 mg initially, followed by 250 to 500 mg every two to six hours as indicated by patient's response.

Usual adult prescribing limits: Up to 15 mg per kg of body weight every six hours.

OXTRIPHYLLINE

Summary of Differences

Pharmacology:
Oxtriphylline is the choline salt of theophylline.
Oxtriphylline releases free theophylline *in vivo.*
General dosing information: Oxtriphylline contains about 64% of anhydrous theophylline.

Oral Dosage Forms

OXTRIPHYLLINE ORAL SOLUTION USP

Usual adult dose: Bronchodilator—
Acute attack:
Loading dose—
For patients *not* currently receiving theophylline preparations: Oral, the equivalent of 5 to 6 mg of anhydrous theophylline per kg of body weight.
For patients currently receiving theophylline preparations: A serum theophylline measurement should be obtained immediately, if possible. The loading dose for theophylline is based on the principle that each 0.5 mg of theophylline per kg of lean (ideal) body weight will result in a 1 (range, 0.5 to 1.6) mcg per mL increase in serum theophylline concentration. If a serum theophylline measurement cannot be obtained rapidly and the patient's condition requires immediate therapy, a single dose of the equivalent of 2.5 mg of anhydrous theophylline per kg of body weight may be administered if there are no symptoms of theophylline toxicity.
Maintenance (in acute attack)—
Young adult smokers: Oral, the equivalent of anhydrous theophylline—4 mg per kg of body weight every six hours.
Otherwise healthy nonsmoking adults: Oral, the equivalent of anhydrous theophylline—3 mg per kg of body weight every eight hours.

Older patients and patients with cor pulmonale: Oral, the equivalent of anhydrous theophylline—2 mg per kg of body weight every eight hours.

Patients with congestive heart failure or liver failure: Oral, the equivalent of anhydrous theophylline—2 mg per kg of body weight every twelve hours.

Note: To achieve optimal therapeutic theophylline dosage, and minimize the risk of toxicity, monitoring of serum theophylline concentration and patient response is recommended.

In patients with cor pulmonale, congestive heart failure, or liver failure, dosage should not exceed the equivalent of 400 mg of anhydrous theophylline per day unless serum theophylline concentrations can be monitored at twenty-four-hour intervals.

Chronic therapy: Oral, the equivalent of anhydrous theophylline—Initially, 6 to 8 mg per kg of body weight, up to a maximum of 400 mg, per day in three or four divided doses at six- to eight-hour intervals. The dosage may be increased, if tolerated, in approximately 25% increments at two- to three-day intervals, up to a maximum dose of 13 mg per kg of body weight or 900 mg per day, whichever is less, without measurement of serum concentration.

Note: If the above maximum dose in chronic therapy is to be maintained or exceeded, serum theophylline measurement is recommended. Final dosage adjustment is based on subsequent serum theophylline measurements and patient response.

Auxiliary labeling: • Keep container tightly closed.

OXTRIPHYLLINE SYRUP

Usual adult dose: Bronchodilator—
Acute attack:
Loading dose—
For patients *not* currently receiving theophylline preparations: Oral, the equivalent of 5 to 6 mg of anhydrous theophylline per kg of body weight.

For patients currently receiving theophylline preparations: A serum theophylline measurement should be obtained immediately, if possible. The loading dose for theophylline is based on the principle that each 0.5 mg of theophylline per kg of lean (ideal) body weight will result in a 1 (range, 0.5 to 1.6) mcg per mL increase in serum theophylline concentration. If a serum theophylline measurement cannot be obtained rapidly and the patient's condition requires immediate therapy, a single dose of the equivalent of 2.5 mg of anhydrous theophylline per kg of body weight may be administered if there are no symptoms of theophylline toxicity.

Maintenance (in acute attack)—
Young adult smokers: Oral, the equivalent of anhydrous theophylline—4 mg per kg of body weight every six hours.

Otherwise healthy nonsmoking adults: Oral, the equivalent of anhydrous theophylline—3 mg per kg of body weight every eight hours.

Older patients and patients with cor pulmonale: Oral, the equivalent of anhydrous theophylline—2 mg per kg of body weight every eight hours.

Patients with congestive heart failure or liver failure: Oral, the equivalent of anhydrous theophylline—2 mg per kg of body weight every twelve hours.

Note: To achieve optimal therapeutic theophylline dosage, and minimize the risk of toxicity, monitoring of serum theophylline concentration and patient response is recommended.

In patients with cor pulmonale, congestive heart failure, or liver failure, dosage should not exceed the equivalent

of 400 mg of anhydrous theophylline per day unless serum theophylline concentrations can be monitored at twenty-four-hour intervals.

Chronic therapy: Oral, the equivalent of anhydrous theophylline—Initially, 6 to 8 mg per kg of body weight, up to a maximum of 400 mg, per day in three or four divided doses at six- to eight-hour intervals. The dosage may be increased, if tolerated, in approximately 25% increments at two- to three-day intervals, up to a maximum dose of 13 mg per kg of body weight or 900 mg per day, whichever is less, without measurement of serum concentration.

Note: If the above maximum dose in chronic therapy is to be maintained or exceeded, serum theophylline measurement is recommended. Final dosage adjustment is based on subsequent serum theophylline measurements and patient response.

OXTRIPHYLLINE TABLETS

Usual adult dose: Bronchodilator—
Acute attack:
Loading dose—
For patients *not* currently receiving theophylline preparations: Oral, the equivalent of 5 to 6 mg of anhydrous theophylline per kg of body weight.

For patients currently receiving theophylline preparations: A serum theophylline measurement should be obtained immediately, if possible. The loading dose for theophylline is based on the principle that each 0.5 mg of theophylline per kg of lean (ideal) body weight will result in a 1 (range, 0.5 to 1.6) mcg per mL increase in serum theophylline concentration. If a serum theophylline measurement cannot be obtained rapidly and the patient's condition requires immediate therapy, a single dose of the equivalent of 2.5 mg of anhydrous theophylline per kg of body weight may be administered if there are no symptoms of theophylline toxicity.

Maintenance (in acute attack)—
Young adult smokers: Oral, the equivalent of anhydrous theophylline—4 mg per kg of body weight every six hours.

Otherwise healthy nonsmoking adults: Oral, the equivalent of anhydrous theophylline—3 mg per kg of body weight every eight hours.

Older patients and patients with cor pulmonale: Oral, the equivalent of anhydrous theophylline—2 mg per kg of body weight every eight hours.

Patients with congestive heart failure or liver failure: Oral, the equivalent of anhydrous theophylline—2 mg per kg of body weight every twelve hours.

Note: To achieve optimal therapeutic theophylline dosage, and minimize the risk of toxicity, monitoring of serum theophylline concentration and patient response is recommended.

In patients with cor pulmonale, congestive heart failure, or liver failure, dosage should not exceed the equivalent of 400 mg of anhydrous theophylline per day unless serum theophylline concentrations can be monitored at twenty-four-hour intervals.

Chronic therapy: Oral, the equivalent of anhydrous theophylline—Initially, 6 to 8 mg per kg of body weight, up to a maximum of 400 mg, per day in three or four divided doses at six- to eight-hour intervals. The dosage may be increased, if tolerated, in approximately 25% increments at two- to three-day intervals, up to a maximum dose of 13 mg per kg of body weight or 900 mg per day, whichever is less, without measurement of serum concentration.

Note: If the above maximum dose in chronic therapy is to be maintained or exceeded, serum theophylline measurement is recommended. Final dosage adjustment is based on subsequent serum theophylline measurements and patient response.

OXTRIPHYLLINE DELAYED-RELEASE TABLETS USP

Usual adult dose: Bronchodilator—Chronic therapy: Oral, the equivalent of anhydrous theophylline—Initially, 6 to 8 mg per kg of body weight, up to a maximum of 400 mg, per day in three or four divided doses at six- to eight-hour intervals. The dosage may be increased, if tolerated, in approximately 25% increments at two- to three-day intervals, up to a maximum dose of 13 mg per kg of body weight or 900 mg per day, whichever is less, without measurement of serum concentration.

Note: If the above maximum dose in chronic therapy is to be maintained or exceeded, serum theophylline measurement is recommended. Final dosage adjustment is based on subsequent serum theophylline measurements and patient response.

OXTRIPHYLLINE EXTENDED-RELEASE TABLETS USP

Usual adult dose: Bronchodilator—Chronic therapy: Oral, the equivalent of anhydrous theophylline—Initially, 4 mg per kg of body weight every eight to twelve hours. The dosage may be increased, if tolerated, by 2 to 3 mg per kg of body weight per day at three-day intervals, up to a maximum dose of 13 mg per kg of body weight or 900 mg per day, whichever is less, without measurement of serum concentration.

Note: If the above maximum dose in chronic therapy is to be maintained or exceeded, serum theophylline measurement is recommended. Final dosage adjustment is based on subsequent serum theophylline measurements and patient response.

Auxiliary labeling: • Swallow tablets whole.

THEOPHYLLINE

Summary of Differences

Category: Theophylline (oral liquids) is also used as a respiratory stimulant in neonatal apnea; theophylline and dextrose injection is also used as a respiratory stimulant in neonatal apnea and Cheyne-Stokes respiration.

Pharmacology:
Theophylline sodium glycinate is an equimolar mixture of theophylline sodium and aminoacetic acid (glycine).
Theophylline sodium glycinate releases free theophylline *in vivo*.
General dosing information: Theophylline sodium glycinate contains about 49% of anhydrous theophylline.

Additional Dosing Information

See also *General Dosing Information*.

For parenteral dosage forms only
Both the loading and maintenance dosage of theophylline may be given intravenously via either intermittent or, preferably, continuous infusion.

The rate of administration of theophylline and dextrose injection should not exceed 25 mg per minute.

No additives should be made to theophylline and dextrose injection because dosages are titrated to response.

The intravenous infusion should be discontinued if adverse reactions occur.

The intravenous administration of theophylline and dextrose injection may cause fluid overloading, resulting in dilution of serum electro-

lyte concentrations, overhydration, congested states, or pulmonary edema.

Oral Dosage Forms

Note: Bracketed uses in the *Dosage Forms* section refer to categories of use and/or indications that are not included in U.S. product labeling.

THEOPHYLLINE CAPSULES USP

Usual adult dose: Bronchodilator—
Acute attack:
Loading dose—
For patients *not* currently receiving theophylline preparations: Oral, the equivalent of 5 to 6 mg of anhydrous theophylline per kg of body weight.
For patients currently receiving theophylline preparations: A serum theophylline measurement should be obtained immediately, if possible. The loading dose for theophylline is based on the principle that each 0.5 mg of theophylline per kg of lean (ideal) body weight will result in a 1 (range, 0.5 to 1.6) mcg per mL increase in serum theophylline concentration. If a serum theophylline measurement cannot be obtained rapidly and the patient's condition requires immediate therapy, a single dose of the equivalent of 2.5 mg of anhydrous theophylline per kg of body weight may be administered if there are no symptoms of theophylline toxicity.
Maintenance (in acute attack)—
Young adult smokers: Oral, the equivalent of anhydrous theophylline—4 mg per kg of body weight every six hours.
Otherwise healthy nonsmoking adults: Oral, the equivalent of anhydrous theophylline—3 mg per kg of body weight every eight hours.
Older patients and patients with cor pulmonale: Oral, the equivalent of anhydrous theophylline—2 mg per kg of body weight every eight hours.
Patients with congestive heart failure or liver failure: Oral, the equivalent of anhydrous theophylline—2 mg per kg of body weight every twelve hours.

Note: To achieve optimal therapeutic theophylline dosage, and minimize the risk of toxicity, monitoring of serum theophylline concentration and patient response is recommended.

In patients with cor pulmonale, congestive heart failure, or liver failure, dosage should not exceed the equivalent of 400 mg of anhydrous theophylline per day unless serum theophylline concentrations can be monitored at twenty-four-hour intervals.

Chronic therapy: Oral, the equivalent of anhydrous theophylline—Initially, 6 to 8 mg per kg of body weight, up to a maximum of 400 mg, per day in three or four divided doses at six- to eight-hour intervals. The dosage may be increased, if tolerated, in approximately 25% increments at two- to three-day intervals, up to a maximum dose of 13 mg per kg of body weight or 900 mg per day, whichever is less, without measurement of serum concentration.

Note: If the above maximum dose in chronic therapy is to be maintained or exceeded, serum theophylline measurement is recommended. Final dosage adjustment is based on subsequent serum theophylline measurements and patient response.

THEOPHYLLINE EXTENDED-RELEASE CAPSULES USP

Usual adult dose: Bronchodilator—Chronic therapy: Oral, the equivalent of anhydrous theophylline—Initially, 4 mg per kg of body weight every eight to twelve hours; or, for once-a-day dosage forms, 400 mg as a single dose every twenty-four hours, administered in the morning. The dosage may be increased, if tolerated, by 2 to 3 mg per kg of body weight per day at three-day intervals, up to a maximum dose of 13 mg per kg of body weight or 900 mg per day, whichever is less, without measurement of serum concentration.

Note: If the above maximum dose in chronic therapy is to be maintained or exceeded, serum theophylline measurement is recommended. Final dosage adjustment is based on subsequent serum theophylline measurements and patient response.

THEOPHYLLINE ELIXIR

Usual adult dose: Bronchodilator—
Acute attack:
Loading dose—
For patients *not* currently receiving theophylline preparations: Oral, the equivalent of 5 to 6 mg of anhydrous theophylline per kg of body weight.
For patients currently receiving theophylline preparations: A serum theophylline measurement should be obtained immediately, if possible. The loading dose for theophylline is based on the principle that each 0.5 mg of theophylline per kg of lean (ideal) body weight will result in a 1 (range, 0.5 to 1.6) mcg per mL increase in serum theophylline concentration. If a serum theophylline measurement cannot be obtained rapidly and the patient's condition requires immediate therapy, a single dose of the equivalent of 2.5 mg of anhydrous theophylline per kg of body weight may be administered if there are no symptoms of theophylline toxicity.
Maintenance (in acute attack)—
Young adult smokers: Oral, the equivalent of anhydrous theophylline—4 mg per kg of body weight every six hours.
Otherwise healthy nonsmoking adults: Oral, the equivalent of anhydrous theophylline—3 mg per kg of body weight every eight hours.
Older patients and patients with cor pulmonale: Oral, the equivalent of anhydrous theophylline—2 mg per kg of body weight every eight hours.
Patients with congestive heart failure or liver failure: Oral, the equivalent of anhydrous theophylline—2 mg per kg of body weight every twelve hours.
Note: To achieve optimal therapeutic theophylline dosage, and minimize the risk of toxicity, monitoring of serum theophylline concentration and patient response is recommended.
In patients with cor pulmonale, congestive heart failure, or liver failure, dosage should not exceed the equivalent of 400 mg of anhydrous theophylline per day unless serum theophylline concentrations can be monitored at twenty-four-hour intervals.
Chronic therapy: Oral, the equivalent of anhydrous theophylline— Initially, 6 to 8 mg per kg of body weight, up to a maximum of 400 mg, per day in three or four divided doses at six- to eight-hour intervals. The dosage may be increased, if tolerated, in approximately 25% increments at two- to three-day intervals, up to a maximum dose of 13 mg per kg of body weight or 900 mg per day, whichever is less, without measurement of serum concentration.
Note: If the above maximum dose in chronic therapy is to be maintained or exceeded, serum theophylline measurement is recommended. Final dosage adjustment is based on subsequent serum theophylline measurements and patient response.

Auxiliary labeling:
• Keep container tightly closed.
• Do not refrigerate.

THEOPHYLLINE ORAL SOLUTION

Usual adult dose: Bronchodilator—
Acute attack:
Loading dose—
For patients *not* currently receiving theophylline preparations: Oral, the equivalent of 5 to 6 mg of anhydrous theophylline per kg of body weight.
For patients currently receiving theophylline preparations: A serum theophylline measurement should be obtained immediately, if possible. The loading dose for theophylline is based on the principle that each 0.5 mg of theophylline per kg of lean (ideal) body weight will result in a 1 (range, 0.5 to 1.6) mcg per mL increase in serum theophylline concentration. If a serum theophylline measurement cannot be obtained rapidly and the patient's condition requires immediate therapy, a single dose of the equivalent of 2.5 mg of anhydrous theophylline per kg of body weight may be administered if there are no symptoms of theophylline toxicity.
Maintenance (in acute attack)—
Young adult smokers: Oral, the equivalent of anhydrous theophylline—4 mg per kg of body weight every six hours.
Otherwise healthy nonsmoking adults: Oral, the equivalent of anhydrous theophylline—3 mg per kg of body weight every eight hours.
Older patients and patients with cor pulmonale: Oral, the equivalent of anhydrous theophylline—2 mg per kg of body weight every eight hours.
Patients with congestive heart failure or liver failure: Oral, the equivalent of anhydrous theophylline—2 mg per kg of body weight every twelve hours.
Note: To achieve optimal therapeutic theophylline dosage, and minimize the risk of toxicity, monitoring of serum theophylline concentration and patient response is recommended.
In patients with cor pulmonale, congestive heart failure, or liver failure, dosage should not exceed the equivalent of 400 mg of anhydrous theophylline per day unless serum theophylline concentrations can be monitored at twenty-four-hour intervals.
Chronic therapy: Oral, the equivalent of anhydrous theophylline— Initially, 6 to 8 mg per kg of body weight, up to a maximum of 400 mg, per day in three or four divided doses at six- to eight-hour intervals. The dosage may be increased, if tolerated, in approximately 25% increments at two- to three-day intervals, up to a maximum dose of 13 mg per kg of body weight or 900 mg per day, whichever is less, without measurement of serum concentration.
Note: If the above maximum dose in chronic therapy is to be maintained or exceeded, serum theophylline measurement is recommended. Final dosage adjustment is based on subsequent serum theophylline measurements and patient response.

Auxiliary labeling: • Do not refrigerate.

THEOPHYLLINE ORAL SUSPENSION

Usual adult dose: Bronchodilator—
Acute attack:
Loading dose—
For patients *not* currently receiving theophylline preparations: Oral, the equivalent of 5 to 6 mg of anhydrous theophylline per kg of body weight.

For patients currently receiving theophylline preparations: A serum theophylline measurement should be obtained immediately, if possible. The loading dose for theophylline is based on the principle that each 0.5 mg of theophylline per kg of lean (ideal) body weight will result in a 1 (range, 0.5 to 1.6) mcg per mL increase in serum theophylline concentration. If a serum theophylline measurement cannot be obtained rapidly and the patient's condition requires immediate therapy, a single dose of the equivalent of 2.5 mg of anhydrous theophylline per kg of body weight may be administered if there are no symptoms of theophylline toxicity.

Maintenance (in acute attack)—

Young adult smokers: Oral, the equivalent of anhydrous theophylline—4 mg per kg of body weight every six hours.

Otherwise healthy nonsmoking adults: Oral, the equivalent of anhydrous theophylline—3 mg per kg of body weight every eight hours.

Older patients and patients with cor pulmonale: Oral, the equivalent of anhydrous theophylline—2 mg per kg of body weight every eight hours.

Patients with congestive heart failure or liver failure: Oral, the equivalent of anhydrous theophylline—2 mg per kg of body weight every twelve hours.

Note: To achieve optimal therapeutic theophylline dosage, and minimize the risk of toxicity, monitoring of serum theophylline concentration and patient response is recommended.

In patients with cor pulmonale, congestive heart failure, or liver failure, dosage should not exceed the equivalent of 400 mg of anhydrous theophylline per day unless serum theophylline concentrations can be monitored at twenty-four-hour intervals.

Chronic therapy: Oral, the equivalent of anhydrous theophylline—Initially, 6 to 8 mg per kg of body weight, up to a maximum of 400 mg, per day in three or four divided doses at six- to eight-hour intervals. The dosage may be increased, if tolerated, in approximately 25% increments at two- to three-day intervals, up to a maximum dose of 13 mg per kg of body weight or 900 mg per day, whichever is less, without measurement of serum concentration.

Note: If the above maximum dose in chronic therapy is to be maintained or exceeded, serum theophylline measurement is recommended. Final dosage adjustment is based on subsequent serum theophylline measurements and patient response.

Auxiliary labeling:
• Shake well.
• Do not refrigerate.

THEOPHYLLINE SYRUP

Usual adult dose: Bronchodilator—

Acute attack:

Loading dose—

For patients *not* currently receiving theophylline preparations: Oral, the equivalent of 5 to 6 mg of anhydrous theophylline per kg of body weight.

For patients currently receiving theophylline preparations: A serum theophylline measurement should be obtained immediately, if possible. The loading dose for theophylline is based on the principle that each 0.5 mg of theophylline per kg of lean (ideal) body weight will result in a 1 (range, 0.5 to 1.6) mcg per mL increase in serum theophylline concentration. If a serum theophylline measurement cannot be obtained rapidly and the patient's

condition requires immediate therapy, a single dose of the equivalent of 2.5 mg of anhydrous theophylline per kg of body weight may be administered if there are no symptoms of theophylline toxicity.

Maintenance (in acute attack)—

Young adult smokers: Oral, the equivalent of anhydrous theophylline—4 mg per kg of body weight every six hours.

Otherwise healthy nonsmoking adults: Oral, the equivalent of anhydrous theophylline—3 mg per kg of body weight every eight hours.

Older patients and patients with cor pulmonale: Oral, the equivalent of anhydrous theophylline—2 mg per kg of body weight every eight hours.

Patients with congestive heart failure or liver failure: Oral, the equivalent of anhydrous theophylline—2 mg per kg of body weight every twelve hours.

Note: To achieve optimal therapeutic theophylline dosage, and minimize the risk of toxicity, monitoring of serum theophylline concentration and patient response is recommended.

In patients with cor pulmonale, congestive heart failure, or liver failure, dosage should not exceed the equivalent of 400 mg of anhydrous theophylline per day unless serum theophylline concentrations can be monitored at twenty-four-hour intervals.

Chronic therapy: Oral, the equivalent of anhydrous theophylline—Initially, 6 to 8 mg per kg of body weight, up to a maximum of 400 mg, per day in three or four divided doses at six- to eight-hour intervals. The dosage may be increased, if tolerated, in approximately 25% increments at two- to three-day intervals, up to a maximum dose of 13 mg per kg of body weight or 900 mg per day, whichever is less, without measurement of serum concentration.

Note: If the above maximum dose in chronic therapy is to be maintained or exceeded, serum theophylline measurement is recommended. Final dosage adjustment is based on subsequent serum theophylline measurements and patient response.

Auxiliary labeling: • Do not refrigerate.

THEOPHYLLINE TABLETS USP

Usual adult dose: Bronchodilator—

Acute attack:

Loading dose—

For patients *not* currently receiving theophylline preparations: Oral, the equivalent of 5 to 6 mg of anhydrous theophylline per kg of body weight.

For patients currently receiving theophylline preparations: A serum theophylline measurement should be obtained immediately, if possible. The loading dose for theophylline is based on the principle that each 0.5 mg of theophylline per kg of lean (ideal) body weight will result in a 1 (range, 0.5 to 1.6) mcg per mL increase in serum theophylline concentration. If a serum theophylline measurement cannot be obtained rapidly and the patient's condition requires immediate therapy, a single dose of the equivalent of 2.5 mg of anhydrous theophylline per kg of body weight may be administered if there are no symptoms of theophylline toxicity.

Maintenance (in acute attack)—

Young adult smokers: Oral, the equivalent of anhydrous theophylline—4 mg per kg of body weight every six hours.

Otherwise healthy nonsmoking adults: Oral, the equivalent of anhydrous theophylline—3 mg per kg of body weight every eight hours.

Older patients and patients with cor pulmonale: Oral, the equivalent of anhydrous theophylline—2 mg per kg of body weight every eight hours.

Patients with congestive heart failure or liver failure: Oral, the equivalent of anhydrous theophylline—2 mg per kg of body weight every twelve hours.

Note: **To achieve optimal therapeutic theophylline dosage, and minimize the risk of toxicity, monitoring of serum theophylline concentration and patient response is recommended.**

In patients with cor pulmonale, congestive heart failure, or liver failure, dosage should not exceed the equivalent of 400 mg of anhydrous theophylline per day unless serum theophylline concentrations can be monitored at twenty-four-hour intervals.

Chronic therapy: Oral, the equivalent of anhydrous theophylline—Initially, 6 to 8 mg per kg of body weight, up to a maximum of 400 mg, per day in three or four divided doses at six- to eight-hour intervals. The dosage may be increased, if tolerated, in approximately 25% increments at two- to three-day intervals, up to a maximum dose of 13 mg per kg of body weight or 900 mg per day, whichever is less, without measurement of serum concentration.

Note: If the above maximum dose in chronic therapy is to be maintained or exceeded, serum theophylline measurement is recommended. Final dosage adjustment is based on subsequent serum theophylline measurements and patient response.

THEOPHYLLINE EXTENDED-RELEASE TABLETS

Usual adult dose: Bronchodilator—Chronic therapy: Oral, the equivalent of anhydrous theophylline—Initially, 4 mg per kg of body weight every eight to twelve hours; or, for once-a-day dosage forms, 400 mg as a single dose every twenty-four hours, administered in the morning or evening (depending on the product). The dosage may be increased, if tolerated, by 2 to 3 mg per kg of body weight per day at three-day intervals, up to a maximum dose of 13 mg per kg of body weight or 900 mg per day, whichever is less, without measurement of serum concentration.

Note: If the above maximum dose in chronic therapy is to be maintained or exceeded, serum theophylline measurement is recommended. Final dosage adjustment is based on subsequent serum theophylline measurements and patient response.

Once-a-day dosage forms administered in the evening are limited to those patients whose total daily dose is 800 mg or less until further data are available.

Auxiliary labeling: • Swallow tablets whole, unless otherwise directed.

THEOPHYLLINE SODIUM GLYCINATE ELIXIR USP

Usual adult dose: Bronchodilator—

Acute attack:

Loading dose—

For patients *not* currently receiving theophylline preparations: Oral, the equivalent of 5 to 6 mg of anhydrous theophylline per kg of body weight.

For patients currently receiving theophylline preparations: A serum theophylline measurement should be obtained immediately, if possible. The loading dose for theophylline is based on the principle that each 0.5 mg of theophylline per kg of lean (ideal) body weight will result in a 1 (range, 0.5 to 1.6) mcg per mL increase in serum theophylline concentration. If a serum theophylline measurement cannot be obtained rapidly and the patient's condition requires immediate therapy, a single dose of the equivalent of 2.5 mg of anhydrous theophylline per

kg of body weight may be administered if there are no symptoms of theophylline toxicity.

Maintenance (in acute attack)—

Young adult smokers: Oral, the equivalent of anhydrous theophylline—4 mg per kg of body weight every six hours.

Otherwise healthy nonsmoking adults: Oral, the equivalent of anhydrous theophylline—3 mg per kg of body weight every eight hours.

Older patients and patients with cor pulmonale: Oral, the equivalent of anhydrous theophylline—2 mg per kg of body weight every eight hours.

Patients with congestive heart failure or liver failure: Oral, the equivalent of anhydrous theophylline—2 mg per kg of body weight every twelve hours.

Note: **To achieve optimal therapeutic theophylline dosage, and minimize the risk of toxicity, monitoring of serum theophylline concentration and patient response is recommended.**

In patients with cor pulmonale, congestive heart failure, or liver failure, dosage should not exceed the equivalent of 400 mg of anhydrous theophylline per day unless serum theophylline concentrations can be monitored at twenty-four-hour intervals.

Chronic therapy: Oral, the equivalent of anhydrous theophylline—Initially, 6 to 8 mg per kg of body weight, up to a maximum of 400 mg, per day in three or four divided doses at six- to eight-hour intervals. The dosage may be increased, if tolerated, in approximately 25% increments at two- to three-day intervals, up to a maximum dose of 13 mg per kg of body weight or 900 mg per day, whichever is less, without measurement of serum concentration.

Note: If the above maximum dose in chronic therapy is to be maintained or exceeded, serum theophylline measurement is recommended. Final dosage adjustment is based on subsequent serum theophylline measurements and patient response.

Auxiliary labeling: • Keep container tightly closed.

Parenteral Dosage Forms

Note: Bracketed uses in the *Dosage Forms* section refer to categories of use and/or indications that are not included in U.S. product labeling.

THEOPHYLLINE IN DEXTROSE INJECTION USP

Usual adult dose: Bronchodilator—Acute attack:

Loading dose—

For patients *not* currently receiving theophylline preparations: Intravenous infusion, the equivalent of 5 mg of anhydrous theophylline per kg of body weight administered over a period of twenty minutes.

For patients currently receiving theophylline preparations: A serum theophylline measurement should be obtained immediately, if possible. The loading dose for theophylline is based on the principle that each 0.5 mg of theophylline per kg of lean (ideal) body weight will result in a 1 (range, 0.5 to 1.6) mcg per mL increase in serum theophylline concentration. If a serum theophylline measurement cannot be obtained rapidly and the patient's condition requires immediate therapy, a single dose of the equivalent of 2.5 mg of anhydrous theophylline per kg of body weight may be administered if there are no symptoms of theophylline toxicity.

Maintenance (in acute attack)—

Young adult smokers: Intravenous infusion, the equivalent of anhydrous theophylline—700 mcg (0.7 mg) per kg of body weight per hour.

Otherwise healthy nonsmoking adults: Intravenous infusion, the equivalent of anhydrous theophylline—430 mcg (0.43 mg) per kg of body weight per hour.

Older patients and patients with cor pulmonale: Intravenous infusion, the equivalent of anhydrous theophylline—260 mcg (0.26 mg) per kg of body weight per hour.

Patients with congestive heart failure or liver failure: Intravenous infusion, the equivalent of anhydrous theophylline—200 mcg (0.2 mg) per kg of body weight per hour.

Note: To achieve optimal therapeutic theophylline dosage, and minimize the risk of toxicity, monitoring of serum theophylline concentration and patient response is recommended.

BUPRENORPHINE   Systemic

A commonly used *brand name* in the U.S. is *Buprenex.*

PARENTERAL
Buprenorphine Hydrochloride Injection
   In the U.S.—*Buprenex*

Category: Analgesic; anesthesia adjunct.
Note: Buprenorphine is an opioid agonist/antagonist analgesic.

Indications

Note: Bracketed information in the *Indications* section refers to uses not included in U.S. product labeling.

Accepted
Pain (treatment)—Indicated for the treatment of moderate to severe pain.

[Anesthesia, general, adjunct]; or
[Anesthesia, local, adjunct]—Buprenorphine is used as an opioid analgesic adjunct to general and local anesthesia.

Prior to administration of buprenorphine, its antagonist activity and its high affinity for, and slow rate of dissociation from, receptor binding sites must be considered. Buprenorphine may precipitate withdrawal symptoms if administered to a patient physically dependent on an opioid analgesic. Also, buprenorphine may temporarily reduce or block the effects of subsequently administered opioid analgesics. In addition, buprenorphine-induced respiratory depression or other adverse effects may be difficult to reverse.

Buprenorphine (unlike pentazocine, which has cardiovascular effects that tend to increase cardiac work) may be administered to patients with angina pectoris or compromised cardiac function, following cardiac or cardiovascular surgery, and to relieve pain due to acute myocardial infarction.

Pharmacology

Mechanism of action/Effect:

Analgesic—Opioid analgesics bind with stereospecific receptors at many sites within the central nervous system (CNS) to alter processes affecting both the perception of pain and the emotional response to pain. Precise sites and mechanisms of action have not been fully determined, but may partially involve alterations in release of various neurotransmitters from afferent nerves sensitive to painful stimuli.

It has been proposed that there are multiple subtypes of opioid receptors, each mediating various therapeutic and/or side effects of opioid drugs. The actions of an opioid analgesic may therefore depend upon its binding affinity for each type of receptor and whether it acts as a full agonist or a partial agonist or is inactive at each type of receptor. At least two of these types of receptors (mu and kappa) mediate analgesia. Mu receptors are widely distributed throughout the CNS, especially in the limbic system (frontal cortex, temporal cortex, amygdala, and hippocampus), thalamus, striatum, hypothalamus, and midbrain as well as laminae I, II, IV, and V of the dorsal horn in the spinal cord. Kappa receptors are localized primarily in the spinal cord and in the cerebral cortex. A third type of receptor (sigma) may not mediate analgesia; actions at this receptor may produce the subjective and psychotomimetic effects characteristic of most opioids having mixed agonist/antagonist activity. Buprenorphine may act primarily as a partial agonist at the mu receptor; it may also have some agonist activity at the kappa receptor. Buprenorphine has little if any activity at the sigma receptor.

Antagonist—Buprenorphine may displace mu-receptor opioid agonists from their receptor binding sites and competitively inhibit their actions. Because buprenorphine has high affinity for the mu receptor, but less intrinsic activity at this receptor than morphine or other potent mu-receptor agonists, it may precipitate withdrawal symptoms in physically dependent patients who are chronically receiving these agonists. However, because of its partial agonist activity, buprenorphine may attenuate spontaneous withdrawal symptoms caused by abrupt discontinuation of opioid agonists. Also, buprenorphine dissociates from the mu receptor very slowly and may reduce or block the effects of subsequently administered mu-receptor agonists. In some animal studies, the antagonist activity of buprenorphine was comparable to that of naloxone. One study indicates that buprenorphine may also have some antagonist activity at the kappa receptor.

Other actions/effects:

Buprenorphine shares the CNS depressant, respiratory depressant, and hypotensive effects of opioid analgesics.

Buprenorphine may have less potential for causing habituation or abuse than other strong opioid analgesics. Studies in animals have indicated that it has less reinforcing efficacy than other opioids. Also, its slow rate of dissociation from the mu receptor reduces the risk that a severe abstinence syndrome will occur following abrupt withdrawal. Studies in opioid addicts have shown that withdrawal effects may not reach maximum intensity for up to 15 days following abrupt discontinuation. Withdrawal effects are morphine-like, mild to moderate, and may persist for 1 to 2 weeks. Despite the relatively low risk of habituation, abuse has been reported; further experience with this medication is necessary before its true abuse potential can be assessed.

Although studies in humans have not been done, animal studies have indicated that buprenorphine has potent, prolonged antitussive activity.

Onset of action:
Analgesic—
   Intramuscular: About 15 minutes.
   Intravenous: More rapid than with intramuscular administration.

Antagonist—When used to antagonize effects of fentanyl or sufentanil used in conjunction with nitrous oxide for anesthesia: 15 minutes.

Respiratory depressant—1 to 3 hours following intramuscular administration.

Note: Pharmacokinetic studies have demonstrated no apparent relationship between the onset of buprenorphine's activity and its plasma concentration.

Time to peak effect:

Analgesic—

Intramuscular: 1 hour.

Intravenous: Somewhat less than with intramuscular injection.

Antagonist—When used to antagonize effects of fentanyl or sufentanil used in conjunction with nitrous oxide for anesthesia: 1.5 to 2 hours.

Duration of action:

Analgesia—Up to 6 hours in most patients, but 10 hours or longer in some studies.

Epidural: 12 hours following a 0.3-mg dose; 6 hours following a 0.15-mg dose.

Antagonist—

When used to antagonize effects of fentanyl or sufentanil used in conjunction with nitrous oxide for anesthesia: 4 hours.

Following chronic administration of large doses of buprenorphine: In one study in opioid addicts receiving chronic administration of 8 mg per day of buprenorphine subcutaneously, the effects of large doses (up to 120 mg) of subsequently administered morphine were blocked for more than 30 hours following the last dose of buprenorphine.

Respiratory depression—May persist significantly longer than morphine-induced respiratory depression.

Note: Pharmacokinetic studies have demonstrated no apparent relationship between the duration of buprenorphine's activity and its plasma concentration. The medication's prolonged duration of action is more likely related to its slow rate of dissociation from receptor binding sites.

Precautions to Consider

Geriatrics

Geriatric patients may be more sensitive to the effects, especially the respiratory depressant effects, of opioid analgesics, including buprenorphine. Also, elderly patients are more likely to have age-related renal function impairment, which may require caution and dosage adjustment in patients receiving buprenorphine. It is recommended that initial dosage for these patients be reduced by one-half. However, geriatric patients may also be more sensitive to the analgesic effects of the medication so that lower doses and/or a longer interval between doses may provide sufficient analgesia.

Drug interactions and/or related problems

The following drug interactions and/or related problems have been selected on the basis of their potential clinical significance (possible mechanism in parentheses where appropriate)—not necessarily inclusive (» = major clinical significance):

Note: Combinations containing any of the following medications, depending on the amount present, may also interact with this medication.

Other interactions applying to opioid analgesics may apply to buprenorphine also, although documentation is currently not available.

» CNS depression-producing medications, other, or

Monoamine oxidase (MAO) inhibitors, including furazolidone, pargyline, and procarbazine

(concurrent use may increase the CNS depressant, respiratory depressant, and hypotensive effects of these medications and/or buprenorphine; caution is recommended; it is recommended

that dosage of buprenorphine be reduced by one-half; a reduction in dosage of the other agent may also be required)

Naltrexone

(although not documented, the possibility must be considered that usual doses of buprenorphine will be ineffective if administered to a patient receiving naltrexone therapy [because naltrexone blocks the therapeutic effects of other potent opioids] and that administration of increased doses of buprenorphine to override naltrexone-induced blockade of opioid receptors may increase the risk of adverse effects)

» Opioid analgesics, other

(if administered prior to another opioid analgesic, buprenorphine may reduce the therapeutic effects of the other opioid; in one study in opioid addicts receiving chronic administration of 8 mg per day of buprenorphine, the effects of large doses [up to 120 mg] of morphine were blocked during buprenorphine therapy and for at least 30 hours following the last dose of buprenorphine)

(buprenorphine antagonizes the respiratory depressant effects of large doses of previously administered opioids; however, additive respiratory depression may occur if buprenorphine is administered in conjunction with low doses of other opioids)

(when administered following fentanyl derivative-assisted anesthesia, buprenorphine may reverse the respiratory depressant effects of fentanyl or its derivatives [alfentanil and sufentanil] while providing adequate postoperative analgesia; however, in one study, administration of 0.3 or 0.45 mg of buprenorphine intramuscularly every 6 hours following opioid-assisted anesthesia with total doses of 0.2 or 0.3 mg of fentanyl or 1.75 or 4 mg of phenoperidine [not available in the U.S.] caused a higher incidence of hypotension, respiratory depression, and CNS depression than equianalgesic doses [10 or 15 mg] of morphine intramuscularly every 6 hours)

(buprenorphine may precipitate withdrawal symptoms in physically dependent patients who are chronically receiving potent mu-receptor agonists such as morphine; however, because of its partial agonist activity, buprenorphine may partially suppress spontaneous withdrawal symptoms caused by abrupt discontinuation of opioid agonists)

Contraindications/Medical problems

The contraindications/medical problems included have been selected on the basis of their potential clinical significance (reasons given in parentheses where appropriate)—not necessarily inclusive (» = major clinical significance).

Except under special circumstances, this medication should not be used when the following medical problems exist:

» Diarrhea caused by poisoning, until toxic material has been eliminated from gastrointestinal tract

(may slow elimination of toxic material)

» Respiratory depression, acute

(may be exacerbated)

Risk-benefit should be considered when the following medical problems exist:

Abdominal conditions, acute

(diagnosis or clinical course may be obscured)

» Asthma, acute attack, or

» Respiratory impairment or disease, chronic

(opioids may decrease respiratory drive and increase airway resistance in these patients; it is recommended that dosage be reduced by one-half, unless the patient is being mechanically ventilated)

Cardiac arrhythmias or

Seizures, history of

(may be induced or exacerbated by opioids)

Dependence on opioid analgesics, current
(buprenorphine may precipitate withdrawal symptoms if patient is currently receiving other opioids)

Drug abuse or dependence, history of, including acute alcoholism, or

Emotional instability or

Suicidal ideation or attempts
(increased risk of opioid abuse)

Gallbladder disease or gallstones
(opioids may cause biliary colic)

Gastrointestinal tract surgery, recent
(opioids may alter gastrointestinal motility)

Head injury or

Increased intracranial pressure, pre-existing, or

Intracranial lesions
(risk of respiratory depression and further elevation of cerebrospinal fluid pressure is increased; also, opioids may cause sedation and pupillary changes that may obscure clinical course of head injury)

Hepatic function impairment
(opioids metabolized in liver)

Hypothyroidism
(risk of respiratory depression and prolonged CNS depression is greatly increased)

» Inflammatory bowel disease, severe
(risk of toxic megacolon may be increased, especially with repeated dosing)

Prostatic hypertrophy or obstruction or

Urethral stricture or

Urinary tract surgery, recent
(opioids may cause urinary retention)

Renal function impairment
(buprenorphine metabolites excreted via kidneys; also, may cause urinary retention)

Sensitivity to buprenorphine, history of

Caution is also advised in administration to geriatric or very ill or debilitated patients, who may be more sensitive to the effects, especially the respiratory depressant effects, of buprenorphine.

Side/Adverse Effects

Note: Buprenorphine appears less likely than other opioid agonist/antagonist analgesics to cause the subjective and psychotomimetic effects characteristic of this class of drugs. These effects may include several or all of the following, occurring as a group: confusion, delusions, feelings of depersonalization or unreality, hallucinations (usually visual), dysphoria, nightmares, and nervousness or anxiety. However, several of these effects have been reported individually (incidence <1%) in patients receiving buprenorphine.

Buprenorphine may have less dependence or abuse liability than other potent opioid analgesics. However, abuse has been reported.

In some studies, the incidence and/or severity of nausea and vomiting occurring with buprenorphine was greater than that induced by meperidine or morphine.

Epidural administration of buprenorphine may be associated with a lower incidence of adverse effects, such as late respiratory depression, pruritus, and urinary retention, than has been reported with epidural morphine. However, early respiratory depression resistant to naloxone therapy has been reported. Also, signs of shock (pallor, cold skin, low blood pressure, and tachycardia) have been reported in a few patients following epidural buprenorphine. Although these signs eventually abated spontaneously, naloxone and other treatments were not effective in reversing them.

The following side/adverse effects have been selected on the basis of their potential clinical significance (possible signs and symptoms in parentheses where appropriate)—not necessarily inclusive:

Those indicating need for medical attention
Incidence 1 to 5%
Decreased blood pressure; respiratory depression, mild (unusually slow breathing)

Note: Whether buprenorphine's respiratory depressant activity is subject to the same ceiling effect (i.e., the depth of respiratory depression is not increased with higher doses) reported for other opioid agonist/antagonist drugs has not been established in humans. Studies in animals indicate that such a ceiling effect may occur, but at higher dosage levels than with other opioid agonist/antagonist drugs.

Incidence <1%
CNS effects (confusion, hallucinations, mental depression or other mood or mental changes, ringing or buzzing in ears); *conjunctivitis* (red and/or irritated eyes); *dermatitis, allergic* (skin rash, hives, or itching); *increased blood presssure; increased or decreased heart rate; paresthesia* (pain, numbness, tingling, or burning feeling in hands or feet); *respiratory depression, severe* (blue color of face, lips, or fingernails; difficult or troubled breathing); *urinary retention* (decrease in amount of urine; swelling of face, fingers, hands, feet, or lower legs; weight gain)

Symptoms of overdose
Cold, clammy skin; confusion; convulsions; dizziness, severe; drowsiness, severe; low blood pressure; nervousness or restlessness, severe; pinpoint pupils of eyes; slow heartbeat; slow or troubled breathing; unconsciousness; weakness (severe)

Those indicating need for medical attention only if they continue or are bothersome
Incidence up to 66%
Drowsiness

Incidence 5 to 10%
Dizziness or lightheadedness; nausea—especially in ambulatory patients

Incidence 1 to 5%
Headache; increased sweating; vomiting—especially in ambulatory patients

Incidence <1%
Blurred vision or any change in vision; false sense of well-being; general feeling of discomfort or illness; pain, redness, or swelling at place of injection; slurred speech; trembling; unusual nervousness; unusual tiredness; unusual weakness

Those indicating possible withdrawal and the need for medical attention if they occur within 15 days after medication is discontinued
Body aches; diarrhea; fast heartbeat; gooseflesh; increased sweating; loss of appetite; nausea or vomiting; nervousness, restlessness, or irritability; runny nose; shivering or trembling; sneezing; stomach cramps; trouble in sleeping; unexplained fever; unusually large pupils of eyes; weakness; yawning

Patient Consultation

In providing consultation, consider emphasizing the following selected information (» = major clinical significance):

Before using this medication
» Conditions affecting use, especially:
Allergic reaction to buprenorphine, history of
Breast-feeding—Buprenorphine has inhibited milk production in animal studies
Use in the elderly—Lower doses recommended because of increased sensitivity to opioids
Use by athletes—Opioid analgesics are banned and tested for by the U.S. Olympic Committee (USOC)

Other medications, especially other CNS depression-producing medications and other opioids

Medical problems, especially diarrhea caused by poisoning, respiratory depression or disease (including asthma), and severe inflammatory bowel disease

Proper use of this medication

Proper administration technique (if dispensed for home use)

» Importance of not taking more medication than the amount prescribed because of danger of overdose and habit-forming potential

» Not increasing dose if medication is less effective after a few weeks; checking with physician

» Missed dose (if on scheduled dosing): Using as soon as possible; not using if almost time for next dose; not doubling doses

» Proper storage

Precautions while using this medication

Regular visits to physician to check progress during long-term therapy

» Avoiding alcohol or other CNS depressants during therapy

» Caution if dizziness, drowsiness, lightheadedness, or false sense of well-being occurs

Caution when getting up suddenly from a lying or sitting position

Lying down if nausea, vomiting, dizziness, or lightheadedness occurs

Caution if any kind of surgery (including dental surgery) or emergency treatment is required

» Checking with physician before discontinuing medication after prolonged use of high doses; gradual dosage reduction may be necessary to avoid withdrawal symptoms

» Suspected overdose: Getting emergency help at once

Side/adverse effects

Signs and symptoms of potential side effects, especially respiratory and/or CNS depression, allergic dermatitis, hallucinations, and overdose

General Dosing Information

Intramuscular administration of 300 mcg (0.3 mg) of buprenorphine provides analgesia equivalent to that produced by intramuscular administration of 10 mg of morphine.

Buprenorphine may suppress respiration, especially in geriatric, very ill, or debilitated patients and patients with respiratory problems. It is recommended that dosage for these patients be reduced by one-half initially, then adjusted as required and tolerated. However, geriatric patients may also be more sensitive to the analgesic effects of the medication so that lower doses and/or a longer interval between doses may be sufficient to provide effective analgesia.

Dosage and dosing intervals should be individualized on the basis of the severity of pain, the condition of the patient, other medications given concurrently, and patient response.

Some clinicians recommend that patients in chronic pain due to neoplastic disease receive opioid analgesics on a fixed dosage schedule in order that they remain free of pain rather than on an as needed basis after pain recurs.

Concurrent administration of a non-opioid analgesic (such as aspirin or other salicylates, other nonsteroidal anti-inflammatory analgesics, or acetaminophen) with opioid analgesics provides additive analgesia and may permit lower doses of the opioid analgesic to be utilized.

Although buprenorphine may have less potential for causing habituation or abuse than other opioid analgesics, psychological and physical dependence may occur with chronic administration. An abstinence syndrome may be precipitated when the medication is abruptly discontinued. Although withdrawal symptoms may not reach maximum intensity for up to 15 days following discontinuation, if they occur they may persist for 1 to 2 weeks. Also, abuse has been reported.

Rapid intravenous injection of most opioid analgesics has caused anaphylactoid reactions, severe respiratory depression, hypotension, peripheral circulatory collapse, and cardiac arrest. Although these effects have not been documented with buprenorphine, the same precautions applying to other opioid analgesics may apply, i.e., administering the medication slowly, with an opioid antagonist and equipment for artificial ventilation available. It is recommended that intravenous injections of buprenorphine be administered over at least 2 minutes.

Frequent monitoring of the patient's respiratory status is recommended during buprenorphine therapy because of the risk of respiratory depression.

When an opioid analgesic is administered parenterally, the patient usually should be lying down and should remain recumbent for a period of time to minimize side effects such as hypotension, dizziness, lightheadedness, nausea, and vomiting. If these side effects occur in an ambulatory patient, they may be relieved if the patient lies down.

In patients with shock, impaired perfusion may prevent complete absorption following intramuscular injection. Repeated administration may result in overdose due to an excessive amount suddenly being absorbed when circulation is restored.

Tolerance to buprenorphine requiring increased dosage to maintain adequate analgesia has not occurred in long-term studies in cancer patients. However, tolerance has been demonstrated in studies with opioid addicts.

Parenteral Dosage Forms

BUPRENORPHINE HYDROCHLORIDE INJECTION

Usual adult and adolescent dose: Intramuscular or slow intravenous, 300 mcg (0.3 mg) of buprenorphine (base) every six or more hours as needed. An additional dose of up to 300 mcg (0.3 mg) may be administered thirty to sixty minutes following the initial dose, if necessary.

Note: Dosage may be increased to 600 mcg (0.6 mg) of buprenorphine (base), or the frequency of administration may be increased to every four hours if necessary, depending upon the severity of pain and patient response. Although doses exceeding 600 mcg (0.6 mg) have been administered in some studies, long-term use of such doses is not recommended because of insufficient data.

Auxiliary labeling:
• May cause drowsiness.
• Avoid alcoholic beverages.
• May be habit-forming.

BUPROPION   Systemic†

INN: Amfebutamone

A commonly used *brand name* in the U.S. is *Wellbutrin*.

ORAL
Bupropion Hydrochloride Tablets†
  In the U.S.—*Wellbutrin*

---

  †Not commercially available in Canada.

Category: Antidepressant.

Indications

Accepted
Depression, mental (treatment)—Bupropion is indicated for the treatment of major depression.

Pharmacology

Mechanism of action/Effect:
  Although the exact mechanism of antidepressant action is unclear, one *in vivo* effect of bupropion on biogenic amine systems appears to be its weak blockade of dopamine reuptake; however, this inhibition occurs at doses higher than those required for its antidepressant effects. Recent animal studies have suggested that bupropion's antidepressant activity may be mediated through noradrenergic pathways involving the locus ceruleus.
  Bupropion is also a weak blocker of the neuronal reuptake of serotonin and norepinephrine, and it does *not* inhibit monoamine oxidase.

Other actions/effects:
  May be an inducer of hepatic microsomal enzymes.
  May produce dose-related central nervous system (CNS) stimulation.

Onset of action: 1 to 3 weeks.

Precautions to Consider

Geriatrics
Studies performed in patients 60 years of age and older have not demonstrated geriatrics-specific problems that would limit the usefulness of bupropion in the elderly. However, older patients are known to be more sensitive to the anticholinergic, sedative, and cardiovascular side effects of antidepressants. In addition, elderly patients are more likely to have age-related renal or hepatic function impairment, which may require dosage adjustment in patients receiving bupropion.

Drug interactions and/or related problems
The following drug interactions and/or related problems have been selected on the basis of their potential clinical significance (possible mechanism in parentheses where appropriate)—not necessarily inclusive (» = major clinical significance):

Note: Combinations containing any of the following medications, depending on the amount present, may also interact with this medication.

» Alcohol
    (concurrent use or the cessation of chronic alcohol use during therapy may lower the seizure threshold and increase the risk of seizures; patients should be advised to minimize alcohol consumption or avoid the use of alcohol completely)

» Antidepressants, tricyclic, or
» Clozapine or
» Fluoxetine or
» Haloperidol or
» Lithium or
» Loxapine or
» Maprotiline or
» Molindone or
» Phenothiazines or
» Thioxanthenes or
» Trazodone
    (concurrent use of these medications with bupropion may lower the seizure threshold and increase the risk of major motor seizures; in addition, changes in treatment regimen, such as abrupt discontinuation of a benzodiazepine, may precipitate a seizure)

Hepatic enzyme inducers, other
    (concurrent use with bupropion may increase the metabolism of these agents or bupropion)

Hepatic enzyme inhibitors
    (these medications may inhibit hepatic microsomal enzymes, thereby decreasing metabolism and increasing serum concentrations of bupropion, thus increasing the risk of seizures)

Levodopa
    (concurrent use with bupropion may result in a greater incidence of adverse effects; small initial doses of bupropion and small gradual dose increases are recommended during concurrent therapy)

» Monoamine oxidase (MAO) inhibitors, including furazolidone, procarbazine, and selegiline
    (concurrent use of bupropion with these medications may increase the risk of acute toxicity of bupropion and is contraindicated; a medication-free interval of at least 2 weeks should elapse between discontinuation of the MAO inhibitor and initiation of bupropion therapy)

Contraindications/Medical problems
The contraindications/medical problems included have been selected on the basis of their potential clinical significance (reasons given in parentheses where appropriate)—not necessarily inclusive (» = major clinical significance).

Except under special circumstances, this medication should not be used when the following medical problems exist:
» Anorexia nervosa or
» Bulimia
    (increased risk of seizures in patients with current or prior diagnosis of these conditions)
» Seizure disorders
    (increased risk of major motor seizures)

Risk-benefit should be considered when the following medical problems exist:
Bipolar disorder
    (mania may be precipitated during the depressed phase in patients with manic-depressive illness)
» CNS tumor or
» Head trauma or
» Spontaneous seizures, history of
    (increased risk of major motor seizures)
Drug abuse
    (patients with a history of amphetamine or stimulant abuse may be attracted to bupropion because of its mild amphetamine-like activity, especially at higher doses; however, risk of seizures has prevented adequate testing)

» Hepatic function impairment or
» Renal function impairment
(metabolism or excretion may be altered)
» Myocardial infarction, recent history of, or
Heart disease, unstable .
Psychosis, especially schizoaffective disorder, depressed
(latent psychosis or mania may be activated in susceptible patients)
Sensitivity to bupropion

Side/Adverse Effects

The following side/adverse effects have been selected on the basis of their potential clinical significance (possible signs and symptoms in parentheses where appropriate)—not necessarily inclusive:

Those indicating need for medical attention
Incidence more frequent
CNS stimulation (agitation or excitement, anxiety, restlessness, insomnia, confusion); *fast or irregular heartbeat; headache, severe*
Incidence less frequent
Hallucinations; skin rash
Incidence rare
Fainting; seizures, especially with higher doses
Note: The risk of *seizures* with bupropion may be greater than with other antidepressants, approximately 0.4% (4/1000 patients) at doses up to 450 mg of bupropion a day. At doses above 450 mg, the risk increases almost tenfold.

Those indicating need for medical attention only if they continue or are bothersome
Incidence more frequent
Constipation; decrease in appetite; dizziness; dryness of mouth; increased sweating; nausea or vomiting; tremor; weight loss, unusual
Incidence less frequent or rare
Blurred vision; difficulty in concentration; drowsiness; fever or chills; hostility or anger; sleep disturbances; tiredness; unusual feeling of well-being

Patient Consultation

In providing consultation, consider emphasizing the following selected information (» = major clinical significance):

Before using this medication
» Conditions affecting use, especially:
Sensitivity to bupropion
Pregnancy—Crosses placenta
Breast-feeding—Excreted in breast milk
Use by athletes—Bupropion is banned and, in some cases, tested for in competitors in biathlon and modern pentathlon events by the U.S. Olympic Committee (USOC)
Other medications, especially alcohol, tricyclic antidepressants, antipsychotic medications, clozapine, fluoxetine, maprotiline, trazodone, lithium, or MAO inhibitors
Other medical problems, especially seizure disorders, anorexia nervosa, bulimia, head trauma, CNS tumor, recent myocardial infarction, or hepatic or renal function impairment

Proper use of this medication
» Compliance with therapy; not taking more or less medication than prescribed
Taking with food if needed to lessen gastrointestinal irritation
May require up to 4 weeks or longer for optimal antidepressant effects

Missed dose: Taking as soon as possible; taking any remaining doses for that day at regularly spaced intervals; not doubling doses
» Proper storage

Precautions while using this medication
Regular visits to physician to check progress during therapy
» Checking with physician before discontinuing medication; gradual dosage reduction may be necessary to prevent adverse effects
» Minimizing consumption of or avoiding use of alcoholic beverages to prevent possible seizures
» Possible dizziness, drowsiness, or euphoria; caution when driving, using machinery, or doing other things requiring alertness and judgment

Side/adverse effects
Signs of potential side effects, especially CNS stimulation, anxiety, confusion, severe headache, seizures, fast or irregular heartbeat, skin rash, or fainting

General Dosing Information

To reduce the risk of agitation, motor restlessness, or insomnia, which are more frequent at initiation of therapy, increases in dosage must be made gradually.

Seizures occur more frequently at higher doses, the incidence being approximately 0.4% (4/1000 patients) at doses up to 450 mg a day and increasing almost tenfold at doses between 450 mg and 600 mg a day.

Equally divided doses taken three or four times a day at 4- to 6-hour intervals will avoid high peak concentrations of bupropion or its metabolites.

Full antidepressant action may not be evident for 4 weeks or longer.

Potentially suicidal patients should not have access to large quantities of this medication since depressed patients, particularly those who use alcohol excessively, may continue to exhibit suicidal tendencies until significant improvement occurs.

Diet/Nutrition
Bupropion may be taken with food to lessen gastrointestinal irritation.

For prevention of seizures
The risk of seizures may be reduced if:
• The total daily dose does not exceed 450 mg and is administered in divided doses.
• Each single dose does not exceed 150 mg.
• The dosage is increased gradually
• Caution is used in patients with a history of seizures or cranial trauma; during concurrent use with other medications that may lower the seizure threshold; or when changes in treatment regimens occur.

Oral Dosage Forms

BUPROPION HYDROCHLORIDE TABLETS

Usual adult dose: Oral, initially 100 mg two times a day, the dosage being increased gradually, no sooner than three days after beginning therapy, to 100 mg three times a day as needed and tolerated.
Note: Dosing intervals must be at least every four hours.

Usual adult prescribing limits: 450 mg a day, with no single dose exceeding 150 mg.

Auxiliary labeling:
• May cause drowsiness.
• Avoid alcoholic beverages.

BUSPIRONE   Systemic

A commonly used *brand name* in the U.S. and Canada is *BuSpar*.

ORAL
Buspirone Hydrochloride Tablets
  In the U.S. and Canada—*BuSpar*

Category: Antianxiety agent.

Indications

Accepted
Anxiety (treatment)—Buspirone is indicated for the management of anxiety disorders or the short-term relief of the symptoms of anxiety. However, buspirone is usually not indicated for the treatment of anxiety or tension associated with the stress of everyday life.

The efficacy of buspirone in the treatment of anxiety has been shown to be comparable to that of benzodiazepines, such as diazepam, clorazepate, alprazolam, and lorazepam.

Buspirone has been shown to cause less sedation than other antianxiety agents, especially at lower doses. Therefore, it may be a useful alternative to other antianxiety agents in the treatment of generalized anxiety, particularly in patients hypersensitive to the sedative effects of the other agents.

In controlled studies, buspirone has not been shown to be effective for long-term (more than 3 to 4 weeks) management of anxiety. However, buspirone has not been shown to cause adverse effects when used for several months. If buspirone is used for extended periods of time, efficacy of the medication should be reassessed at periodic intervals.

Pharmacology

Note: Buspirone is not pharmacologically related to benzodiazepines, barbiturates, or other sedative/antianxiety agents.

Mechanism of action/Effect: The site and mechanism of action of buspirone have not been determined. The medication is believed to have a unique anxioselective action, since it has no anticonvulsant or muscle relaxant activity and does not appear to cause physical dependence or significant sedation. Buspirone has been shown to have a high affinity for serotonin (5-HT_{1A}) receptors in the dorsal raphe neurons and a moderate affinity for brain D_2-dopamine receptors. It has no significant affinity for benzodiazepine receptors and does not affect gamma-aminobutyric acid (GABA) binding. Some studies have suggested that buspirone may have indirect effects on other neurotransmitter systems.

In contrast to the benzodiazepines, the spontaneous firing rate of noradrenergic cells in the locus ceruleus is increased rather than decreased by buspirone. Differences in dependence and tolerance between benzodiazepines and buspirone are due to these site-specific differences.

Onset of therapeutic effect: May require 1 to 2 weeks. Because buspirone does not cause muscle relaxation or significant sedation, patient may not immediately notice effects of medication.

Precautions to Consider

Geriatrics
Although buspirone has not been systematically evaluated in older patients, clinical studies performed in several hundred elderly patients have not demonstrated geriatrics-specific problems that would limit the usefulness of buspirone in the elderly. However, elderly patients are more likely to have age-related renal function impairment, which may require reduction of dosage in patients receiving buspirone.

Drug interactions and/or related problems
The following drug interactions and/or related problems have been selected on the basis of their potential clinical significance (possible mechanism in parentheses where appropriate)—not necessarily inclusive (» = major clinical significance):

Note: Combinations containing any of the following medications, depending on the amount present, may also interact with this medication.

Alcohol or
Central nervous system (CNS) depression-producing medications, other
  (although studies have shown that buspirone does not increase alcohol-induced impairment in mental and motor performance, caution is recommended with the concurrent use of buspirone and alcohol or other CNS depressants, since buspirone may cause sedation, especially at doses greater than 30 mg per day, and its CNS effects in an individual patient may not be predictable)

Digoxin
  (may be displaced from serum protein binding when used concurrently with buspirone)

» Monoamine oxidase (MAO) inhibitors, including furazolidone, pargyline, and procarbazine
  (concurrent use with buspirone is not recommended because an elevation in blood pressure may occur)

Contraindications/Medical problems
The contraindications/medical problems included have been selected on the basis of their potential clinical significance (reasons given in parentheses where appropriate)—not necessarily inclusive (» = major clinical significance).

Risk-benefit should be considered when the following medical problems exist:

Drug abuse or dependence, history of
  (potential misuse or abuse of buspirone; patients should be observed closely for development of tolerance, incrementation of dose, and drug-seeking behavior)

Hepatic function impairment
  (buspirone metabolized by liver)

Renal function impairment
  (buspirone excreted via kidneys)

Sensitivity to buspirone

Side/Adverse Effects

Note: Buspirone appears to have little potential for physical dependence or abuse. Although it does not produce euphoria, and usually does not produce sedation, at usual doses of 20 mg per day, it has been shown to cause dysphoria and sedation at doses greater than 30 mg per day.

Studies have shown that buspirone causes less sedation than other antianxiety agents (about one-third of that occurring with benzodiazepines) and does not produce significant functional impairment. However, the CNS effects of buspirone in any individual patient may not be predictable.

If side/adverse effects occur, they usually appear at the beginning of buspirone therapy and subside during continued therapy, with or without dosage reduction.

Withdrawal symptoms or rebound anxiety have not been reported when the medication was abruptly discontinued.

The following side/adverse effects have been selected on the basis of their potential clinical significance (possible signs and symptoms in parentheses where appropriate)—not necessarily inclusive:

Those indicating need for medical attention
Incidence rare
> *Chest pain; confusion or mental depression; fast or pounding heartbeat; neurological effects* (muscle weakness; numbness, tingling, pain, or weakness in hands or feet; uncontrolled movements of the body); *sore throat or fever*

Symptoms of overdose
> *Dizziness, severe; drowsiness, severe; stomach upset, including severe nausea or vomiting; unusually small pupils*

Those indicating need for medical attention only if they continue or are bothersome
Incidence more frequent
> *Dizziness or lightheadedness; headache; nausea; syndrome of restlessness* (restlessness, nervousness, or unusual excitement)
> Note: May occur shortly after buspirone therapy is initiated and may be due to increased central noradrenergic activity or to dopaminergic effects.

Incidence less frequent or rare
> *Blurred vision; decreased concentration; drowsiness*—more frequent with doses >20 mg per day; *dryness of mouth; musculoskeletal effects* (muscle pain, spasms, cramps, or stiffness); *ringing in the ears; stomach upset; trouble in sleeping, nightmares, or vivid dreams; unusual tiredness or weakness*

Patient Consultation

In providing consultation, consider emphasizing the following selected information (» = major clinical significance):

Before using this medication
> » Conditions affecting use, especially:
>> Sensitivity to buspirone
>> Use by athletes—Buspirone is banned and, in some cases, tested for in competitors in certain events by the U.S. Olympic Committee (USOC) and the National Collegiate Athletic Association (NCAA)
>> Other medications, especially monoamine oxidase (MAO) inhibitors

Proper use of this medication
> » Importance of not using more medication than the amount prescribed
> One to two weeks of therapy may be required before antianxiety effect is noticeable

Missed dose: If on scheduled dosing regimen—Taking as soon as possible; not taking if almost time for next dose; not doubling doses
> » Proper storage

Precautions while using this medication
> Regular visits to physician to check progress during prolonged therapy
> Caution in taking alcohol or other CNS depressants during therapy
> » Caution if dizziness or drowsiness occurs
> » Suspected overdose: Getting emergency help at once

Side/adverse effects
> Signs of potential side effects, especially chest pain, confusion, fast or pounding heartbeat, mental depression, neurological effects, and sore throat or fever

General Dosing Information

Although buspirone does not appear to cause tolerance or physical or psychological dependence, patients with a history of drug abuse or dependence should be observed closely for development of tolerance or dependence on the medication.

Since buspirone does not exhibit cross-tolerance with benzodiazepines and other common sedative/hypnotic agents, the medication will not block the withdrawal syndrome associated with discontinuation of therapy with these agents. Therefore, prior to initiating therapy with buspirone, these agents should be withdrawn gradually, especially in patients who have been chronically using these CNS depressants.

One to two weeks of therapy may be required before the antianxiety effect of buspirone is noticeable, as compared to the immediate effect of benzodiazepines.

Oral Dosage Forms

BUSPIRONE HYDROCHLORIDE TABLETS

Usual adult dose: Oral, initially 5 mg three times a day, the dosage being increased by 5 mg per day at two- to three-day intervals until the desired response is obtained.

Usual adult prescribing limits: Up to 60 mg per day.

Auxiliary labeling:
- Avoid alcoholic beverages.
- May cause dizziness or drowsiness.

BUSULFAN   Systemic

A commonly used *brand name* in the U.S. and Canada is *Myleran*.

ORAL
Busulfan Tablets USP
   In the U.S. and Canada—*Myleran*

Category: Antineoplastic.

Indications

Note: Bracketed information in the *Indications* section refers to uses not included in U.S. product labeling.

Accepted
Leukemia, chronic myelocytic (treatment)—Busulfan is indicated for palliative treatment of chronic myelocytic leukemia. It is not useful in the "blastic crisis" phase.

[Leukemia, acute myelocytic (treatment)][1]— Busulfan is used for treatment of acute myelocytic leukemia.

---

[1]Not included in Canadian product labeling.

Pharmacology

Mechanism of action/Effect: Busulfan is a bifunctional alkylating agent of the alkylsulfonate type and is cell cycle-phase nonspecific. Its mechanism of action is not clear but is thought to consist of alkylation and cross-linking of strands of DNA and myelosuppression.

Onset of action: A clinical response usually begins within 1 to 2 weeks after initiation of therapy.

Precautions to Consider

Geriatrics
Appropriate studies on the relationship of age to the effects of busulfan have not been performed in the geriatric population. However, geriatrics-specific problems that would limit the usefulness of this medication in the elderly are not expected.

Dental
The bone marrow depressant effects of busulfan may result in an increased incidence of microbial infection, delayed healing, and gingival bleeding. Dental work, whenever possible, should be completed prior to initiation of therapy or deferred until blood counts have returned to normal. Patients should be instructed in proper oral hygiene during treatment, including caution in use of regular toothbrushes, dental floss, and toothpicks.

Busulfan may also cause stomatitis associated with considerable discomfort.

Drug interactions and/or related problems
The following drug interactions and/or related problems have been selected on the basis of their potential clinical significance (possible mechanism in parentheses where appropriate)—not necessarily inclusive (» = major clinical significance):

Note: Combinations containing any of the following medications, depending on the amount present, may also interact with this medication.

Allopurinol or
Colchicine or
» Probenecid or
» Sulfinpyrazone
   (busulfan may raise the concentration of blood uric acid; dosage adjustment of antigout agents may be necessary to control hyperuricemia and gout; allopurinol may be preferred to prevent or reverse busulfan-induced hyperuricemia because of risk of uric acid nephropathy with uricosuric antigout agents)

Blood dyscrasia-causing medications
   (leukopenic and/or thrombocytopenic effects of busulfan may be increased with concurrent or recent therapy if these medications cause the same effects; dosage adjustment of busulfan, if necessary, should be based on blood counts)
» Bone marrow depressants, other, or
» Radiation therapy
   (additive bone marrow depression may occur; dosage reduction may be required when two or more bone marrow depressants, including radiation, are used concurrently or consecutively)

Vaccines, killed virus
   (because normal defense mechanisms may be suppressed by busulfan therapy, the patient's antibody response to the vaccine may be decreased. The interval between discontinuation of medications that cause immunosuppression and restoration of the patient's ability to respond to the vaccine depends on the intensity and type of immunosuppression-causing medication used, the underlying disease, and other factors; estimates vary from 3 months to 1 year)

» Vaccines, live virus
   (because normal defense mechanisms may be suppressed by busulfan therapy, concurrent use with a live virus vaccine may potentiate the replication of the vaccine virus, may increase the side/adverse effects of the vaccine virus, and/or may decrease the patient's antibody response to the vaccine; immunization of these patients should be undertaken only with extreme caution after careful review of the patient's hematologic status and only with the knowledge and consent of the physician managing the busulfan therapy. The interval between discontinuation of medications that cause immunosuppression and restoration of the patient's ability to respond to the vaccine depends on the intensity and type of immunosuppression-causing medication used, the underlying disease, and other factors; estimates vary from 3 months to 1 year. Patients with leukemia in remission should not receive live virus vaccine until at least 3 months after their last chemotherapy. In addition, immunization with oral poliovirus vaccine should be postponed in persons in close contact with the patient, especially family members)

Contraindications/Medical problems
The contraindications/medical problems included have been selected on the basis of their potential clinical significance (reasons given in parentheses where appropriate)—not necessarily inclusive (» = major clinical significance).

Risk-benefit should be considered when the following medical problems exist:

» Bone marrow depression

» Chickenpox, existing or recent (including recent exposure), or
» Herpes zoster
   (risk of severe generalized disease)

Gout, history of, or
Urate renal stones, history of
   (risk of hyperuricemia)

» Infection

Sensitivity to busulfan

Caution is necessary when using very high doses of busulfan in patients with head trauma or a history of seizure disorder; some clinicians use prophylactic anticonvulsant therapy.

» Caution should be used also in patients who have had previous cytotoxic drug therapy or radiation therapy or who have evidence of myelofibrosis.

Side/Adverse Effects

Note: Many "side effects" of antineoplastic therapy are unavoidable and represent the medication's pharmacologic action. Some of these (for example, leukopenia and thrombocytopenia) are actually used as parameters to aid in individual dosage titration.

Busulfan can cause cellular dysplasia in many tissues, including lungs, lymph nodes, pancreas, thyroid, adrenal gland, liver, bone marrow, bladder, breast, and uterine cervix.

Seizures have been reported in 2 of 130 patients receiving very high investigational doses (1 mg per kg of body weight [mg/kg] four times a day for four days, total dose 16 mg/kg).

Hepatic veno-occlusive disease has been reported following investigational use of very high doses of busulfan in combination with other chemotherapy prior to bone marrow transplantation.

Continuous treatment with a combination of busulfan and thioguanine in approximately 330 patients was associated with esophageal varices along with abnormal hepatic function tests and evidence of nodular regenerative hyperplasia on liver biopsy in 12 patients after six to forty-five months of therapy. No hepatic toxicity was found in the busulfan alone arm of the study.

The following side/adverse effects have been selected on the basis of their potential clinical significance (possible signs and symptoms in parentheses where appropriate)—not necessarily inclusive:

Those indicating need for medical attention
Incidence more frequent
   Anemia; leukopenia or infection (usually asymptomatic; less frequently, fever or chills, cough or hoarseness, lower back or side pain, painful or difficult urination); *thrombocytopenia* (unusual bleeding or bruising; black, tarry stools; blood in urine or stools; pinpoint red spots on skin)

Note: Onset of *leukopenia* is usually 10 to 15 days after initiation of therapy (leukocyte counts usually increase transiently before this), with nadir of white cell count at 11 to 30 days; white cell counts may continue to fall for more than 1 month after withdrawal but usually recover within 12 to 20 weeks.

Bone marrow depression may be severe and progressive, leading to pancytopenia. Recovery from pancytopenia after withdrawal of busulfan may take 1 month to 2 years.

Symptoms of *bone marrow depression* may also indicate transformation of chronic myelocytic leukemia into the acute blastic form.

Incidence less frequent—occurring with long-term use or high dosage
Bronchopulmonary dysplasia with pulmonary fibrosis (fever, cough, shortness of breath); *hyperuricemia or uric acid nephropathy* (joint pain, lower back or side pain, swelling of feet or lower legs); *stomatitis* (sores in mouth and on lips)

Note: *Bronchopulmonary dysplasia with pulmonary fibrosis* usually occurs 8 months to 10 years (average 4 years) after initiation of therapy and is usually fatal within 6 months after diagnosis. Associated with decreased diffusion capacity and pulmonary compliance. Histologically resembles changes following pulmonary irradiation. Lung biopsy may be necessary to establish the diagnosis.

Hyperuricemia or uric acid nephropathy occur most commonly during initial treatment of patients with leukemia or lymphoma, as a result of rapid cell breakdown which leads to elevated serum uric acid concentrations.

Incidence rare
Cataracts (blurred vision)—occur after prolonged administration

Those indicating need for medical attention only if they continue or are bothersome
Incidence more frequent
Amenorrhea and ovarian suppression (missed or irregular menstrual periods); *darkening of skin*—5 to 10%

Incidence less frequent—occurring with long-term use
Confusion; diarrhea; hypotension (dizziness); *loss of appetite; nausea and vomiting; unusual tiredness or weakness; sudden weight loss*

Note: All of the above, as well as darkening of skin, may occur after prolonged therapy and may resemble adrenocortical insufficiency, although adrenocortical function is not suppressed in most patients. Symptoms are sometimes reversible on withdrawal of busulfan. Adrenal responsiveness to exogenous adrenocorticotropic hormone (ACTH) is usually normal, but pituitary function testing with metyrapone has shown blunted urinary 17-hydroxycorticosteroid excretion in some patients that returned to normal when busulfan was discontinued.

Those indicating the need for medical attention if they occur after medication is discontinued
Bone marrow depression, thrombocytopenia, or pancytopenia (unusual bleeding or bruising; black, tarry stools; blood in urine or stools; pinpoint red spots on skin; fever or chills; cough or hoarseness; lower back or side pain; painful or difficult urination); *pulmonary fibrosis* (fever, cough, shortness of breath)

Patient Consultation

In providing consultation, consider emphasizing the following selected information (» = major clinical significance):

Before using this medication
» Conditions affecting use, especially:
   Sensitivity to busulfan
   Pregnancy—Use not recommended because of mutagenic, teratogenic, and carcinogenic potential; advisability of using

contraception; telling physician immediately if pregnancy is suspected
   Breast-feeding—Not recommended because of risk of serious side effects
   Other medications, especially probenecid, sulfinpyrazone, other bone marrow depressants, or previous cytotoxic drug therapy or radiation therapy
   Other medical problems, especially chickenpox, herpes zoster, or infection

Proper use of this medication
» Importance of not taking more or less medication than the amount prescribed
   Taking each dose at the same time each day to ensure uniform effect
   Importance of ample fluid intake and subsequent increase in urine output to aid in excretion of uric acid
» Possible nausea and vomiting; importance of continuing medication despite stomach upset
   Checking with physician if vomiting occurs shortly after dose is taken
   Missed dose: Not taking at all; not doubling doses
» Proper storage

Precautions while using this medication
» Importance of close monitoring by the physician
» Avoiding immunizations unless approved by physician; other persons in patient's household should avoid immunizations with oral poliovirus vaccine; avoiding other persons who have taken oral poliovirus vaccine or wearing a protective mask that covers nose and mouth

   Caution if bone marrow depression occurs:
» Avoiding exposure to persons with bacterial infections, especially during periods of low blood counts; checking with physician immediately if fever or chills, cough or hoarseness, lower back or side pain, or painful or difficult urination occurs
» Checking with physician immediately if unusual bleeding or bruising; black, tarry stools; blood in urine or stools; or pinpoint red spots on skin occur
   Caution in use of regular toothbrush, dental floss, or toothpick; physician, dentist, or nurse may suggest alternatives; checking with physician before having dental work done
   Not touching eyes or inside of nose unless hands washed immediately before
   Using caution to avoid accidental cuts with use of sharp objects such as safety razor or fingernail or toenail cutters
   Avoiding contact sports or other situations where bruising or injury might occur
   Caution if any laboratory tests required; possible interference with tissue study results

Side/adverse effects
   May cause adverse effects such as lung or blood problems; importance of discussing possible effects with physician
   Signs of potential side effects, especially anemia, leukopenia, infection, thrombocytopenia, bronchopulmonary dysplasia with pulmonary fibrosis, hyperuricemia, uric acid nephropathy, stomatitis, and cataracts
   Physician or nurse can help in dealing with side effects

General Dosing Information

Patients receiving busulfan should be under supervision of a physician experienced in cancer chemotherapy.

Dosage must be adjusted to meet the individual requirements of each patient, based on clinical response and degree of bone marrow depression.

Development of uric acid nephropathy in patients with leukemia or lymphoma may be prevented by adequate oral hydration and, in some cases, administration of allopurinol. Alkalinization of urine may be necessary if serum uric acid concentrations are elevated.

Busulfan therapy should be discontinued at the first sign of interstitial pulmonary fibrosis.

Because of the delayed effect, it is recommended that busulfan therapy be discontinued or dosage reduced at the first sign of a sudden large decrease in leukocyte (particularly granulocyte) count to prevent irreversible bone marrow depression.

Special precautions are recommended in patients who develop thrombocytopenia as a result of administration of busulfan. These may include extreme care in performing invasive procedures; regular inspection of intravenous sites, skin (including perirectal area), and mucous membrane surfaces for signs of bleeding or bruising; limiting frequency of venipuncture and avoiding intramuscular injections; testing urine, emesis, stool, and secretions for occult blood; care in use of regular toothbrushes, dental floss, toothpicks, safety razors, and fingernail and toenail cutters; avoiding constipation; and using caution to prevent falls and other injuries. Such patients should avoid alcohol and any aspirin intake because of the risk of gastrointestinal bleeding. Platelet transfusions may be required.

Patients who develop leukopenia should be observed carefully for signs of infection. Antibiotic support may be required. In neutropenic patients who develop fever, broad-spectrum antibiotic coverage should be initiated empirically, pending bacterial cultures and appropriate diagnostic tests.

Oral Dosage Forms

BUSULFAN TABLETS USP

Usual adult dose: Chronic myelocytic leukemia—

Induction: Oral, 1.8 mg per square meter of body surface or 60 mcg (0.06 mg) per kg of body weight a day until the white cell count falls below 15,000 cells per cubic millimeter. Usual dosage range is 4 to 8 mg per day but may range from 1 to 12 mg per day. During remission, treatment is resumed when a monthly white cell count reaches 50,000 cells per cubic millimeter.

Note: Some patients may be unusually sensitive to busulfan and develop myelosuppression more rapidly than usual. Therefore, frequent and careful monitoring of blood counts is necessary. The total leukocyte count decreases exponentially at a constant busulfan dose, so a weekly plot of leukocyte count on semi-logarithmic paper can aid in predicting when leukocyte counts will reach 15,000 and busulfan should be discontinued.

Maintenance: Oral, 1 to 3 mg per day.

Note: Maintenance therapy with busulfan is recommended only when a remission is shorter than 3 months.

CALCITONIN   Systemic

Some commonly used *brand names* are:
   In the U.S.—*Calcimar; Cibacalcin; Miacalcin*
   In Canada—*Calcimar*

PARENTERAL
CALCITONIN-HUMAN†
Calcitonin-Human for Injection†
   In the U.S.—*Cibacalcin*
CALCITONIN-SALMON
Calcitonin-Salmon Injection
   In the U.S.—*Calcimar; Miacalcin*
   In Canada—*Calcimar*

†Not commercially available in Canada.

Category: Bone resorption inhibitor; osteoporosis therapy adjunct; antihypercalcemic therapy adjunct.

Indications

Note: Bracketed information in the *Indications* section refers to uses not included in U.S. product labeling.

Accepted
Paget's disease of bone (treatment)—Calcitonin-salmon and calcitonin-human are indicated in the treatment of moderate to severe symptomatic Paget's disease (osteitis deformans), characterized by abnormal and accelerated bone metabolism in one or more bones. Signs and symptoms may include bone pain, deformity, and/or fractures; increased concentrations of serum alkaline phosphatase and/or urinary hydroxyproline; neurologic disorders associated with skull lesions and spinal deformities; and elevated cardiac output and other vascular disorders associated with increased vascularity of bones. Calcitonin-human may be effective for treatment of patients who have developed resistance to calcitonin-salmon.

Osteoporosis, postmenopausal (treatment adjunct)—Calcitonin-salmon[1] is indicated [and calcitonin-human is used] for the treatment of osteoporosis in postmenopausal women in conjunction with an adequate intake of calcium (1.5 grams of elemental calcium per day) and vitamin D (400 IU per day) to aid in the prevention of the progressive loss of bone mass. An adequate diet is also essential.

Although calcitonin may increase bone mass or help slow the loss of bone mass in some patients, questions still remain as to whether treatment with calcitonin will actually decrease the incidence of compression fractures in postmenopausal women with osteoporosis.

Hypercalcemia (treatment adjunct)—Calcitonin-salmon is indicated [and calcitonin-human is used] with intravenous saline and other appropriate hypocalcemic agents in the treatment of hypercalcemic emergencies. Calcitonin has been shown to effectively lower serum calcium concentrations in patients with carcinoma, multiple myeloma, or, to a lesser degree, primary hyperparathyroidism. Calcitonin-salmon may be added to existing therapeutic regimens for the treatment of hypercalcemia, such as intravenous fluids, furosemide, oral phosphates, or adrenocorticoids.

[Osteoporosis, secondary (treatment adjunct)][1]—Calcitonin-human and calcitonin-salmon are used in conjunction with an adequate intake of calcium and vitamin D for the treatment of osteoporosis secondary to hormonal disturbances, drug therapy, immobilization, and other causes. Calcitonin therapy is initiated when treatment of the underlying etiology is not feasible.

[1]Not included in Canadian product labeling.

Pharmacology

Mechanism of action/Effect:
   Paget's disease—Calcitonin reduces the rate of bone turnover, possibly by an initial blocking of bone resorption, resulting in decreases in serum alkaline phosphatase (reflecting decreased bone formation) and decreases in urinary hydroxyproline excretion (reflecting decreased bone resorption, i.e., breakdown of collagen).
   Osteoporosis; or
   Hypercalcemia—Calcitonin lowers serum calcium concentration primarily by a direct inhibition of bone resorption. The number and/or function of osteoclasts is reduced and a decrease in osteocytic resorption may also be involved. These effects may be mediated in part by a drug-induced increase in cyclic adenosine monophosphate concentration in bone cells and subsequent alteration of calcium and/or phosphate transport across the plasma membrane of the osteoclast.

Other actions/effects:
   Calcitonin also has a direct effect on the kidneys, increasing the excretion of calcium, phosphate, and sodium by inhibiting their tubular reabsorption. These effects are also mediated in part by cyclic adenosine monophosphate. However, in some patients, calcitonin-induced inhibition of bone resorption has a greater effect on calcium excretion than does the drug's direct renal action, so that urinary calcium is decreased rather than increased.
   Short-term administration of calcitonin results in decreases in the volume and acidity of gastric juice, and in trypsin and amylase content and volume of pancreatic juice.

Onset of therapeutic action: Calcitonin-human and calcitonin-salmon—Maximum reductions of serum alkaline phosphatase and urinary hydroxyproline excretion in Paget's disease may take 6 to 24 months of continuous treatment.

Time to peak effect: Cacitonin-salmon—Hypercalcemia: 2 hours.

Duration of effect: Calcitonin-salmon—Hypercalcemia: 6 to 8 hours.

Precautions to Consider

Cross-sensitivity and/or related problems
Patients who are allergic to proteins may be allergic to calcitonin, since calcitonin is a protein. Its use is not recommended in patients with suspected sensitivity who show a positive response to skin testing prior to initiating therapy. Since calcitonin-salmon is a foreign protein, it may induce antibodies with continued use. In short-term treatment (2 years or less), antibody titers appear in 30 to 60% of treated patients, but only 5 to 15% become resistant to treatment as a result. Long-term treatment may be possible in patients who are not limited by antibody formation. Because synthetic human calcitonin is identical to naturally occurring human calcitonin, antibody formation is rare, allowing longer term treatment that is not limited by antibody-mediated resistance.

Geriatrics
Appropriate studies on the relationship of age to the effects of calcitonin have not been performed in the geriatric population. However, no geriatrics-specific problems have been documented to date.

Drug interactions and/or related problems
The following drug interactions and/or related problems have been selected on the basis of their potential clinical significance (possible mechanism in parentheses where appropriate)—not necessarily inclusive (» = major clinical significance):

Note: Combinations containing any of the following medications, depending on the amount present, may also interact with this medication.

Calcium-containing preparations or
Vitamin D, including calcifediol and calcitriol
(in the treatment of hypercalcemia, concurrent use may antagonize the effect of calcitonin; in the treatment of other conditions, calcium-containing preparations may be given 4 hours after calcitonin)

Contraindications/Medical problems

The contraindications/medical problems included have been selected on the basis of their potential clinical significance (reasons given in parentheses where appropriate)—not necessarily inclusive (» = major clinical significance).

Risk-benefit should be considered when the following medical problems exist):

» Allergy to proteins (or history of) or
» Sensitivity to calcitonin
(possibility of systemic allergic reaction, especially in patients with a history of severe allergy, even with a negative skin test reaction to calcitonin, because of the protein nature of calcitonin; allergic reaction is more likely with calcitonin-salmon)

Side/Adverse Effects

The following side/adverse effects have been selected on the basis of their potential clinical significance (possible signs and symptoms in parentheses where appropriate)—not necessarily inclusive:

Those indicating need for medical attention
Incidence rare
Allergic reactions, specifically skin rash and urticaria (hives)

Those indicating need for medical attention only if they continue or are bothersome
Incidence more frequent
Flushing, redness, or tingling of face, ears, hands, or feet; gastrointestinal effects, specifically diarrhea, loss of appetite, nausea or vomiting, and stomach pain; redness, soreness, or swelling at injection site
Incidence less frequent
Increased frequency of urination
Incidence rare
Chills; dizziness; headache; pressure in chest; stuffy nose; tenderness or tingling of hands or feet; trouble in breathing; weakness

Patient Consultation

In providing consultation, consider emphasizing the following selected information (» = major clinical significance):

Before using this medication
» Conditions affecting use, especially:
Allergies (history of) or sensitivity to calcitonin or other proteins
Breast-feeding—Excreted in breast milk; lactation inhibited in animal studies

Proper use of this medication
Proper administration: Using aseptic technique; subcutaneous injection preferred for self-administration
Importance of using reconstituted solution of calcitonin-human within 6 hours
Importance of inspecting solution for particles or discoloration before administering
» Importance of not using more medication than the amount prescribed
Missed dose: If dosage schedule is:
Two doses a day—Taking missed dose, if remembered within 2 hours, and continuing on schedule; if remembered later, skipping missed dose, not doubling doses, and continuing on schedule

One dose a day—Taking as soon as possible unless remembered the next day; then skipping missed dose and continuing on schedule, but not doubling doses
One dose every other day—Taking as soon as possible if on scheduled day; taking if remembered on alternate day, but skipping the following day and restarting schedule
One dose three times a week (Monday-Wednesday-Friday)—Taking missed dose the next day; setting each injection back a day and resuming regular schedule the following week
» Proper storage

Precautions while using this medication
Regular visits to physician to check progress during therapy
Possible need for calcium and vitamin D restriction, including calcifediol and calcitriol, in patients with hypercalcemia

Side/adverse effects
Signs of potential side effects, especially allergic reaction

General Dosing Information

For use in Paget's disease of bone
Clinical or biochemical improvement (decreased serum alkaline phosphatase) usually occurs within the first few months of therapy if calcitonin is effective. A longer period of therapy, often more than a year, may be required for maximum improvement.

Dosage adjustments depend on clinical and radiologic evidence, changes in serum alkaline phosphatase and urinary hydroxyproline excretion, and severity of nausea or flushing.

Bedtime administration may help to reduce the severity of nausea or flushing. Reduction in dosage may also be helpful.

After at least 6 months of treatment for Paget's disease, if symptoms have been relieved, therapy may be reduced for 6 months, monitoring biochemical and clinical responses, before being discontinued. Since biochemical indexes will relapse after cessation of treatment, they cannot be relied on to indicate a need for restarting therapy.

CALCITONIN-HUMAN

Summary of Differences

Cross-sensitivity and/or related problems: May be used for longer term treatment with less antibody formation or protein hypersensitivity than calcitonin-salmon.

Additional Dosing Information

See also *General Dosing Information.*

More severe cases of Paget's disease of bone (evidence of weak bones with osteolytic lesions) may require doses of up to 1 mg a day, given in divided doses.

Parenteral Dosage Forms

CALCITONIN-HUMAN FOR INJECTION

Usual adult dose: Paget's disease of bone—Subcutaneous, initially 500 mcg (0.5 mg) a day, the dosage being reduced for some patients to 500 mcg (0.5 mg) two or three times a week, or 250 mcg (0.25 mg) a day.

Note: To diminish side effects, some clinicians recommend starting with a low dose and gradually increasing dosage over 2 weeks.

Additional information: One chamber of the dual syringe contains 0.5 mg of calcitonin-human for injection and mannitol (20 mg) in sterile, lyophilized form. The other chamber contains mannitol (30 mg) in 1 mL of water for injection.

CALCITONIN-SALMON

Summary of Differences

Cross-sensitivity and/or related problems: Risk of protein hypersensitivity and antibody-mediated resistance greater than with calcitonin-human.

Additional Dosing Information

See also *General Dosing Information.*

This medicine is for intramuscular or subcutaneous injection. The subcutaneous route of administration is usually preferred for patient self-administration.

If the volume to be injected exceeds 2 mL, the intramuscular route of administration is usually preferred and multiple sites of injection should be used to minimize local inflammatory reactions.

Skin testing should be considered prior to treatment of patients with suspected sensitivity to calcitonin-salmon. The manufacturer's recommendation for preparing the solution for skin testing is as follows:

• Prepare a dilution of 10 IU per mL by withdrawing 0.05 mL into a tuberculin syringe (an insulin syringe with no "dead space" may be preferred for a more accurate dilution).

• Fill to 1 mL with 0.9% sodium chloride injection. Mix well.

• Discard 0.9 mL and inject 0.1 mL intracutaneously on the inner forearm.

• Observe injection site 15 minutes after injection.

• A positive response is considered to be the appearance of a more than mild erythema or wheal.

In any patient who has an acceptable initial response but later relapses, either clinically or biochemically, there is the possibility of antibody formation. Testing the patient for high antibody titer by an appropriate specialized test or by critical clinical evaluation should be considered. Alternatively, a trial of therapy with calcitonin-human may be considered. Patient compliance should also be assessed in the event of relapse.

In patients who have relapsed, a dosage increase above 100 IU per day does not appear to improve patient response.

Parenteral Dosage Forms

CALCITONIN-SALMON INJECTION

Usual adult dose:

Paget's disease of bone—Intramuscular or subcutaneous, initially 100 IU a day, the dosage being decreased to 50 IU once a day, once every other day, or three times a week, in patients without serious deformity or bone involvement.

Hypercalcemia—Intramuscular or subcutaneous, initially 4 IU per kg of body weight every twelve hours, the dosage being increased, if necessary for a more satisfactory response, to 8 IU per kg of body weight every twelve hours, up to a maximum of 8 IU per kg of body weight every six hours.

Postmenopausal osteoporosis[1]—Intramuscular or subcutaneous, 100 IU once a day, once every other day, or three times a week.

Note: To diminish side effects, some clinicians recommend starting with a low dose and gradually increasing dosage over 2 weeks.

Auxiliary labeling: • Refrigerate.

Additional information:

May also contain 5 mg of phenol per mL, as a preservative.

The activity of calcitonin-salmon is stated in terms of International Units (IU), which are equal to Medical Research Council Units (MRC).

---

[1]Not included in Canadian product labeling.

CALCIUM CHANNEL BLOCKING AGENTS   Systemic

Some commonly used *brand names* are:

In the U.S.—

Adalat [Nifedipine]	*Isoptin* [Verapamil]
Bepadin [Bepridil]	*Isoptin SR* [Verapamil]
Calan [Verapamil]	*Nimotop* [Nimodipine]
Calan SR [Verapamil]	*Plendil* [Felodipine]
Cardene [Nicardipine]	*Procardia* [Nifedipine]
Cardizem [Diltiazem]	*Procardia XL* [Nifedipine]
Cardizem CD [Diltiazem]	*Vascor* [Bepridil]
Cardizem SR [Diltiazem]	*Verelan* [Verapamil]
DynaCirc [Isradipine]	

In Canada—

Adalat [Nifedipine]	*Nimotop* [Nimodipine]
Adalat FT [Nifedipine]	*Novo-Diltazem* [Diltiazem]
Adalat P.A. [Nifedipine]	*Novo-Nifedin* [Nifedipine]
Apo-Diltiaz [Diltiazem]	*Novo-Veramil* [Verapamil]
Apo-Nifed [Nifedipine]	*Nu-Diltiaz* [Diltiazem]
Apo-Verap [Verapamil]	*Nu-Nifed* [Nifedipine]
Cardene [Nicardipine]	*Nu-Verap* [Verapamil]
Cardizem [Diltiazem]	*Plendil* [Felodipine]
Cardizem SR [Diltiazem]	*Renedil* [Felodipine]
Isoptin [Verapamil]	*Sibelium* [Flunarizine]
Isoptin SR [Verapamil]	*Syn-Diltiazem* [Diltiazem]

BEPRIDIL†
Oral
Bepridil Hydrochloride Tablets†
In the U.S.—*Bepadin; Vascor*
DILTIAZEM
Oral
Diltiazem Hydrochloride Extended-release Capsules
In the U.S.—*Cardizem CD; Cardizem SR*
In Canada—*Cardizem SR*
Diltiazem Tablets USP
In the U.S.—*Cardizem*
In Canada—*Apo-Diltiaz; Cardizem; Novo-Diltazem; Nu-Diltiaz; Syn-Diltiazem;* GENERIC
Parenteral
Diltiazem Hydrochloride Injection†
In the U.S.—*Cardizem*
FELODIPINE
Oral
Felodipine Extended-release Tablets
In the U.S.—*Plendil*
In Canada—*Plendil; Renedil*

FLUNARIZINE*
Oral
    Flunarizine Hydrochloride Capsules*
        In Canada—*Sibelium*
ISRADIPINE†
Oral
    Isradipine Capsules†
        In the U.S.—*DynaCirc*
NICARDIPINE
Oral
    Nicardipine Hydrochloride Capsules
        In the U.S. and Canada—*Cardene*
NIFEDIPINE
Oral
    Nifedipine Capsules USP
        In the U.S.—*Adalat; Procardia;* GENERIC
        In Canada—*Adalat; Apo-Nifed; Novo-Nifedin; Nu-Nifed*
    Nifedipine Tablets*
        In Canada—*Adalat FT*
    Nifedipine Extended-release Tablets
        In the U.S.—*Procardia XL*
        In Canada—*Adalat P.A.*
NIMODIPINE
Oral
    Nimodipine Capsules
        In the U.S. and Canada—*Nimotop*
VERAPAMIL
Oral
    Verapamil Tablets USP
        In the U.S.—*Calan; Isoptin;* GENERIC
        In Canada—*Apo-Verap; Isoptin; Novo-Veramil; Nu-Verap;* GENERIC
    Verapamil Hydrochloride Extended-release Capsules†
        In the U.S.—*Verelan*
    Verapamil Hydrochloride Extended-release Tablets
        In the U.S.—*Calan SR; Isoptin SR*
        In Canada—*Isoptin SR*
Parenteral
    Verapamil Injection USP
        In the U.S.—*Isoptin;* GENERIC
        In Canada—*Isoptin*

---

*Not commercially available in the U.S.
†Not commercially available in Canada.

Category

Antianginal—Bepridil; Diltiazem; Felodipine; Isradipine; Nicardipine; Nifedipine; Verapamil.
Antiarrhythmic—Diltiazem; Verapamil.
Antihypertensive—Diltiazem; Felodipine; Isradipine; Nicardipine; Nifedipine; Verapamil.
Hypertrophic cardiomyopathy therapy adjunct—Verapamil.
Subarachnoid hemorrhage therapy—Flunarizine; Nicardipine; Nimodipine.
Vascular headache prophylactic—Flunarizine; Verapamil.

Indications

Note: Bracketed information in the *Indications* section refers to uses not included in U.S. product labeling.

Accepted
Angina pectoris, chronic (treatment)—Bepridil, diltiazem, [felodipine], [isradipine], nicardipine, nifedipine, and verapamil are indicated in the management of classic angina (chronic stable angina or effort-associated angina) with no evidence of vasospasm. Nicardipine [and other calcium channel blockers] may be used alone or in combination, with caution, with beta-adrenergic blocking agents.

Diltiazem, [felodipine], [isradipine], [nicardipine], nifedipine, and verapamil are also indicated in the management of vasospastic angina (Prinzmetal's variant, or at-rest angina) or unstable angina in patients who are unable to tolerate or whose symptoms are not relieved by adequate doses of beta-adrenergic blocking agents or organic nitrates. They are generally indicated when vasospastic angina is confirmed by: (a) the classical pattern accompanied by elevation of ST segment; (b) ergonovine-induced angina or coronary artery spasm; or (c) coronary artery spasm demonstrated by angiography, although they may also be used when a vasospastic component is indicated but not confirmed (e.g., where pain has a variable threshold on exertion or in unstable angina where electrocardiographic findings are compatible with intermittent vasospasm).

Tachycardia, supraventricular (treatment and prophylaxis)—Verapamil and parenteral diltiazem are indicated in the treatment of supraventricular tachyarrhythmias. Diltiazem and verapamil produce rapid conversion to sinus rhythm of paroxysmal supraventricular tachycardia (including those associated with accessory bypass tracts, such as Wolff-Parkinson-White [W-P-W] or Lown-Ganong-Levine [L-G-L] syndrome) in patients who do not respond to vagal maneuvers when the atrioventricular (AV) node is required for reentry to sustain tachycardia. Parenteral diltiazem and verapamil also produce temporary control of rapid ventricular rate in atrial flutter or atrial fibrillation. Oral verapamil is indicated, alone or in association with digitalis, for control of ventricular rate at rest and during stress in patients with chronic atrial flutter and/or atrial fibrillation (not otherwise controllable with digitalis), and for prophylaxis of repetitive paroxysmal supraventricular tachycardia. Diltiazem and verapamil do not produce class I, II, or III antiarrhythmic effects.

Hypertension (treatment)—Diltiazem, felodipine, isradipine, nicardipine, nifedipine, and verapamil are indicated, alone or in combination with other agents, for treatment of hypertension.

In the 1988 Report of the Joint National Committee on Detection, Evaluation, and Treatment of High Blood Pressure, a progression in choice of treatments for essential hypertension is recommended:

    Nonpharmacologic management (especially sodium restriction, weight reduction and exercise, and moderation of alcohol consumption) is recommended first for some patients, including those with mild hypertension, and is recommended as an adjunct to all pharmacologic hypertensive therapy.

    Initial drug therapy usually consists of a diuretic, beta-adrenergic blocking agent, calcium channel blocker, or angiotensin-converting enzyme (ACE) inhibitor. If adequate blood pressure control is not achieved and the patient is adherent to the treatment program and not experiencing significant side effects, dosage of the drug may be increased, a drug from another one of these initial classes may be added or substituted, or a second drug from a different class—centrally acting alpha-adrenergic blockers (e.g., clonidine, guanabenz, guanfacine, methyldopa), peripheral-acting adrenergic antagonists (e.g., guanadrel, guanethidine, rauwolfia alkaloids), post-synaptic alpha-1 peripheral adrenergic inhibitors (e.g., doxazosin, prazosin, terazosin), or vasodilators (e.g., hydralazine, minoxidil)—may be added or substituted.

    If necessary, a drug from another class in the second group may be substituted or added as a third drug. If blood pressure control is still not achieved, a drug from still another class may be substituted or added as a fourth drug, or the patient may need further evaluation and/or referral.

[Nifedipine capsules, punctured and administered sublingually, are being used for treatment of hypertensive crisis, including that associated with MAO inhibitors and autonomic dysreflexia.]

[Cardiomyopathy, hypertrophic (treatment adjunct)]—Verapamil is used in the treatment of hypertrophic cardiomyopathy to relieve ventricular outflow obstruction. However, extreme caution is recommended when hypertrophic cardiomyopathy is complicated by left ventricular obstruction, high pulmonary wedge pressure, paroxysmal nocturnal dyspnea or orthopnea, sinoatrial (SA) nodal function impairment, or severe heart block.

Raynaud's phenomenon (treatment)—[Felodipine], [isradipine], [nicardipine], and [nifedipine][1] are used for symptomatic treatment of Raynaud's phenomenon.

Subarachnoid hemorrhage-associated neurologic deficits (treatment)—Nimodipine is indicated for improvement of neurological outcome by reducing the incidence and severity of ischemic deficits in patients with subarachnoid hemorrhage from ruptured congenital intracranial aneurysms who are in good neurological condition post-ictus (e.g., Hunt and Hess Grades I-III). [Flunarizine] and [nicardipine] are also used for this indication.

Headache, vascular (prophylaxis)—Flunarizine and [verapamil] are indicated for reducing frequency and severity of vascular headaches, but are not recommended for treatment of acute attacks.

---

[1]Not included in Canadian product labeling.

Pharmacology

Mechanism of action/Effect: These agents are calcium-ion influx inhibitors (slow-channel blocking agents). Although their mechanism is not completely understood, they are thought to inhibit calcium ion entry through select voltage-sensitive areas termed "slow channels" across cell membranes. By reducing intracellular calcium concentration in cardiac and vascular smooth muscle cells, they dilate coronary arteries and peripheral arteries and arterioles, and may reduce heart rate, decrease myocardial contractility (negative inotropic effect), and slow atrioventricular (AV) nodal conduction. Serum calcium concentrations are unchanged, although there is some evidence that elevated serum calcium concentrations may alter the therapeutic effect of verapamil.

Calcium channel blockers may be classified into subgroups according to structure:
Bepridil.
Benzothiazepine (diltiazem).
Diphenylpiperazine (flunarizine).
Dihydropyridine (felodipine, isradipine, nicardipine, nifedipine, nimodipine).
Diphenylalkylamine (verapamil).
Effects within each subgroup are generally the same:
Bepridil is a nonselective calcium channel blocker that affects both cardiac and smooth muscle. It also inhibits the fast sodium inward current in myocardial and vascular smooth muscle.
Piperazine derivatives act on vascular smooth muscle, with few or no direct myocardial effects.
Dihydropyridines are selective for vascular smooth muscle compared with myocardium and therefore act primarily as vasodilators. Hypotensive effects are accompanied by reflex tachycardia.
Diltiazem (a benzothiazepine) and verapamil (a diphenylalkylamine) are less selective vasodilators that also have direct effects on the myocardium, including depression of sinoatrial (SA) and atrioventricular (AV) nodal conduction.

See *Table 1*, page $ for a summary of the hemodynamic effects of each agent.

Antianginal—Dilation of the peripheral vasculature reduces systemic pressure or cardiac afterload, which results in lessened myocardial wall tension and reduced oxygen requirements of the myocardial tissues. In vasospastic angina, a relaxation of coronary arteries and arterioles and inhibition of coronary artery spasm improves blood flow and oxygen supply to myocardial tissues. May also be related to enhanced left ventricular diastolic relaxation and decreased wall stiffness (improved diastolic compliance).

Antiarrhythmic—The inhibited influx of calcium ions in cardiac tissues prolongs the effective refractory period and results in slowed AV nodal conduction. Normal sinus rhythm is usually not affected, except in some elderly or patients with sick sinus syndrome, in whom calcium channel blockade may interfere with sinus-node impulse generation and may induce sinus or sinoatrial block. Normal atrial action potential or intraventricular conduction are not altered, but in depressed atrial fibers amplitude, velocity of depolarization, and conduction velocity are decreased. The antegrade effective refractory period of the accessory bypass tract may be shortened.

Antihypertensive—Reduction of total peripheral vascular resistance as a result of vasodilation.

Hypertrophic cardiomyopathy therapy adjunct—Improvement of left ventricular outflow. May also be related to enhanced left ventricular diastolic relaxation and decreased wall stiffness.

Subarachnoid hemorrhage therapy—Theoretically, nimodipine may prevent cerebral arterial spasm following subarachnoid hemorrhage, but that has not been confirmed by arteriography. Its exact mechanism of action in treatment of neurologic deficits caused by subarachnoid hemorrhage is not known.

Vascular headache prophylactic—By inhibiting the vasoconstriction that occurs in the prodrome phase, calcium channel blockade may relieve or prevent reactive vasodilation.

Other actions/effects: Inhibition of platelet aggregation. Decrease in esophageal contraction amplitude. Diltiazem and verapamil may inhibit cytochrome P450 metabolism, thereby inhibiting the metabolism of other medications or compounds. Flunarizine has antihistaminic effects. Isradipine has diuretic effects. Verapamil decreases gastrointestinal transit time.

Onset of action:
Diltiazem—
Oral:
Extended-release capsules—2 to 3 hours.
Tablets—30 to 60 minutes.
Parenteral: Rapid intravenous injection—Reduction in heart rate or conversion of paroxysmal supraventricular tachycardia to sinus rhythm: Within 3 minutes.
Felodipine—Within 2 to 5 hours.
Isradipine—2 to 3 hours.
Nifedipine—Oral: Capsules and tablets—20 minutes.
Verapamil—
Oral: 1 to 2 hours.
Intravenous:
Antiarrhythmic—Within 1 to 5 minutes and usually less than 2 minutes.
Hemodynamic—Within 3 to 5 minutes.

Time to peak effect:
Bepridil—Time to steady-state plasma concentration: 8 days.
Diltiazem—
Antihypertensive: Multiple doses—Within 2 weeks.
Antiarrhythmic: Rapid intravenous injection—Hypotension or reduction in heart rate: Within 2 to 7 minutes.
Flunarizine—Multiple doses: Several weeks.
Isradipine—Antihypertensive: Multiple doses—2 to 4 weeks.
Nicardipine—Single dose: 1 to 2 hours.
Verapamil—
Oral: About 30 to 90 minutes. The maximum effects from oral dosage are usually evident sometime during the first 24 to 48 hours of therapy (for some patients the time may be slightly extended because the half-life of verapamil tends to increase during this period).
Intravenous: Within 3 to 5 minutes after completion of injection.

Duration of action:
Bepridil—24 hours.

Diltiazem—
 Oral:
  Extended-release capsules—
   Cardizem CD: 24 hours.
   Cardizem SR: 12 hours.
  Tablets—4 to 8 hours.
 Parenteral:
  Rapid intavenous injection—Hypotension or reduction in heart rate: 1 to 3 hours.
  Continuous intravenous infusion—Hypotension or reduction in heart rate: 0.5 to more than 10 hours (median 7 hours).
Felodipine—24 hours.
Isradipine—More than 12 hours.
Nicardipine—8 hours.
Nifedipine—
 Capsules and tablets: 4 to 8 hours.
 Extended-release tablets:
  Adalat P.A.: 12 hours.
  Procardia XL: 24 hours.
Verapamil—
 Oral:
  Extended-release capsules: 24 hours.
  Tablets—8 to 10 hours.
  Extended-release tablets—24 hours.
 Intravenous:
  Antiarrhythmic—About 2 hours.
  Hemodynamic—10 to 20 minutes.

Precautions to Consider

Geriatrics

For diltiazem, nimodipine, verapamil, and possibly other calcium channel blockers—Half-life of calcium channel blockers may be increased in the elderly as a result of decreased clearance.

  For felodipine only: Plasma concentrations increase with age. Mean clearance at mean age of 76 was found to be only 45% of that at mean age of 26.

  For isradipine only: Bioavailability may be increased in patients over 65 years of age.

  For nicardipine only: Studies in patients 65 years of age and older found no difference in half-life or protein binding from that in young normal volunteers.

  For nimodipine only: Risk of hypotension may be increased.

For all calcium channel blockers—Elderly patients are more likely to have age-related renal function impairment, which may require caution in patients receiving calcium channel blockers.

Dental

Gingival hyperplasia is a rare side effect that has been reported with diltiazem, felodipine, nifedipine, and verapamil. It usually starts as gingivitis or gum inflammation in the first 1 to 9 months of treatment. A strictly enforced program of teeth cleaning by a professional combined with plaque control by the patient will minimize growth rate and severity of gingival enlargement. Periodontal surgery may be indicated in some cases, and should be followed by careful plaque control to inhibit recurrence of gum enlargement.

Drug interactions and/or related problems

The following drug interactions and/or related problems have been selected on the basis of their potential clinical significance (possible mechanism in parentheses where appropriate)—not necessarily inclusive (» = major clinical significance):

Note: Information concerning interactions between calcium channel blockers and other medications is still limited. Therefore, some of the following potential interactions are stated for cautionary reference until additional information is available.

Combinations containing any of the following medications, depending on the amount present, may also interact with these medications.

Anesthetics, hydrocarbon inhalation
 (concurrent use with calcium channel blockers may produce additive hypotension; although calcium channel blockers may be useful to prevent supraventricular tachycardias, hypertension, or coronary spasm during surgery, caution is recommended during use)

Anti-inflammatory drugs, nonsteroidal (NSAIDs), especially indomethacin
 (indomethacin, and possibly other NSAIDs, may antagonize the antihypertensive effect of calcium channel blockers by inhibiting renal prostaglandin synthesis and/or by causing sodium and fluid retention; the patient should be carefully monitorep firm that the desired effect is being obtained)

» Beta-adrenergic blocking agents, systemic or ophthalmic
 (concurrent use of oral dosage forms with oral bepridil, diltiazem, or verapamil or intravenous verapamil usually results in no serious negative inotropic, chronotropic, or dromotropic effects. However, caution and careful monitoring are necessary since the additive effect may prolong sinoatrial [SA] and atrioventricular [AV] conduction [which may lead to severe hypotension, bradycardia, and cardiac failure], especially in patients with impaired ventricular function or abnormal cardiac conduction or sinus node depression. When verapamil and beta-adrenergic blocking agents are to be given intravenously, they should be administered at least a few hours apart since they may have additive depressant effects on myocardial contractility or SA or AV conduction, and asystole has been reported with concurrent use)

 (in a single small study, diltiazem was reported to significantly increase the bioavailability of propranolol; in other studies, verapamil was found to decrease clearance of both metoprolol and propranolol, with a variable effect on atenolol)

 (concurrent use with dihydropyridines, although usually well tolerated, may produce excessive hypotension, and in rare cases may increase the possibility of congestive heart failure. Occasionally, angina has occurred upon initiation of nicardipine or nifedipine therapy, especially after recent abrupt discontinuation of beta-adrenergic blocking agent therapy. If possible, it is recommended that beta-adrenergic blocking agent dosage be discontinued gradually, but especially before nicardipine or nifedipine therapy is begun. However, if concurrent use is necessary, nicardipine or nifedipine may be preferred over other calcium channel blockers in some patients because it has less effect on heart rate and conduction)

 (if significant systemic absorption of an ophthalmic beta-blocker occurs, concurrent use of calcium channel blocking agents may result in atrioventricular conduction disturbances, left ventricular failure, and hypotension; in some patients, if a calcium antagonist is necessary, nicardipine or nifedipine may be preferred because it has less effect on heart rate and conduction, although it may also cause greater hypotension; concurrent use of calcium channel blockers and ophthalmic beta-blockers should be avoided in patients with impaired cardiac function)

Calcium supplements
 (concurrent use in quantities sufficient to elevate serum calcium concentrations above normal may reduce the response to verapamil and probably other calcium channel blockers)

» Carbamazepine or
» Cyclosporine or
» Quinidine or
 Theophylline or
 Valproate
  (diltiazem or verapamil may inhibit cytochrome P450 metabolism, resulting in increased concentrations and toxicity of these medications)

(an idiosyncratic reaction has been reported in which concurrent use of nifedipine and quinidine resulted in significantly reduced serum quinidine concentrations; caution is recommended when nifedipine therapy is initiated or discontinued in a patient stabilized on quinidine)

Cimetidine
(concurrent use may result in accumulation of calcium channel blockers as a result of inhibition of first-pass metabolism; caution and careful titration of calcium channel blocker dose is recommended on initiation of therapy in patients receiving cimetidine; ranitidine and famotidine do not appear to significantly affect calcium channel blocker metabolism)

» Digitalis glycosides
(concurrent use of digoxin with some calcium channel blocking agents [especially verapamil and, to a lesser extent, bepridil, diltiazem, and nifedipine] has been reported to increase the serum concentration of digoxin; the effect of verapamil on digoxin kinetics is enhanced in patients with hepatic function impairment; felodipine significantly increased peak plasma concentrations of digoxin, although there was no significant change in the area under the curve [AUC], isradipine and nicardipine do not appear to have a significant effect. Digoxin serum concentrations should be monitored and dosage may need to be altered when concurrent dosage of the calcium channel blocking agent is initiated, changed, or discontinued. Concurrent use of oral digitalis preparations with oral diltiazem or verapamil or intravenous verapamil has resulted in no serious adverse effects when patients were closely monitored; however, both groups of medications slow AV conduction. Patients receiving them concurrently should be monitored for AV block or excessive bradycardia, especially during the first week of concurrent dosage. To avoid toxicity, dosage reduction of digitalis glycoside may be necessary)

» Disopyramide or
Flecainide
(disopyramide should not be administered within 48 hours before or 24 hours following verapamil administration since both medications possess negative inotropic properties; deaths have been reported; caution is also recommended when disopyramide is used concurrently with diltiazem, nicardipine, or nifedipine; caution is also recommended when flecainide is used concurrently with a calcium channel blocker)

Estrogens
(estrogen-induced fluid retention tends to increase blood pressure; the patient should be carefully monitored to confirm that the desired effect is being obtained)

Highly protein-bound medications, such as:
Anticoagulants, coumarin- and indandione-derivative
Anticonvulsants, hydantoin
Anti-inflammatory drugs, nonsteroidal
Quinine
Salicylates
Sulfinpyrazone
(caution is advised when these medications are used concurrently with nifedipine or verapamil since changes in serum concentrations of the free, unbound medications may occur)

» Hypokalemia-producing medications, such as:
Amphotericin B, parenteral
Carbonic anhydrase inhibitors
Corticosteroids, glucocorticoid, especially those with significant mineralocorticoid activity
Corticosteroids, mineralocorticoid
Corticotropin (ACTH)
Diuretics, potassium-depleting (such as bumetanide, ethacrynic acid, furosemide, indapamide, mannitol, or thiazides)
Sodium phosphates
(risk of bepridil-induced arrhythmias may be increased)

Hypotension-producing medications, other
(antihypertensive effects may be potentiated when these medications are used concurrently with hypotension-producing calcium channel blockers; although some antihypertensive and/or diuretic combinations are frequently used for therapeutic advantage, when any hypotension-producing medication is used concurrently dosage adjustments may be necessary)

Lithium
(concurrent use with calcium channel blockers may result in neurotoxicity in the form of nausea, vomiting, diarrhea, ataxia, tremors, and/or tinnitus; caution is recommended)

Neuromuscular blocking agents
(verapamil may potentiate the activity of curare-like and depolarizing neuromuscular blocking agents; dosage reduction of either or both medications may be necessary during concurrent use)

Phenobarbital
(may increase clearance of verapamil)

Prazosin, and possibly other alpha-adrenergic blocking agents
(concurrent use with calcium channel blockers may produce an increased hypotensive effect, possibly related to impairment of compensatory responses by alpha-blockade and/or inhibition of prazosin metabolism by calcium channel blockers; caution is recommended)

» Procainamide or
» Quinidine or
» Other medications causing QT interval prolongation
(risk of increased QT interval prolongation)

(caution is recommended when procainamide or quinidine is used with a calcium channel blocker since both groups of medications possess negative inotropic properties)

Rifampin, and possibly other hepatic enzyme inducers
(rifampin may reduce the bioavailability of oral verapamil by induction of first-pass metabolism; other calcium channel blockers may also be affected, depending on the extent of first-pass metabolism)

Sympathomimetics
(concurrent use may reduce antihypertensive effects of calcium channel blockers; the patient should be carefully monitored to confirm that the desired effect is being obtained)

Contraindications/Medical problems
See *Table 1*, page 353.

Side/Adverse Effects

See *Table 2*, page 355.

Patient Consultation

In providing consultation, consider emphasizing the following selected information (» = major clinical significance):

Before using this medication
» Conditions affecting use, especially:
Sensitivity to the calcium channel blocker prescribed
Pregnancy—High doses in animals cause birth defects, prolonged pregnancy, poor bone development, and stillbirth
Use in the elderly—Elderly patients may be more sensitive to effects
Other medications, especially parenteral amphotericin B (for bepridil), beta-blockers, carbamazepine, carbonic anhydrase inhibitors, corticosteroids (for bepridil), cyclosporine, digitalis glycosides, disopyramide, potassium-depleting diuretics (for bepridil), procainamide, or quinidine
Other medical problems, especially arrhythmias (for bepridil), other cardiovascular problems, or hypokalemia (for bepridil)

Proper use of this medication

» Compliance with therapy; importance of not taking more medication than amount prescribed

Missed dose: Taking as soon as possible; not taking if almost time for next scheduled dose; not doubling doses

» Proper storage

For bepridil

If nausea occurs, may be taken with meals or at bedtime

For extended-release diltiazem capsules

Swallowing capsules whole without crushing or chewing

» Caution if switching brands; one is for once-daily dosing and one is for twice-daily dosing

For extended-release nifedipine or verapamil capsules

Swallowing capsules whole without crushing or chewing

For regular nifedipine or extended-release felodipine or nifedipine tablets

Swallowing tablets whole, without breaking, crushing, or chewing

For *Procardia XL*—Patient may notice empty shell in stool left over after medication is absorbed

For extended-release verapamil tablets

Swallowing tablets whole, without crushing or chewing; may be broken in half on instructions from physician

Taking with food or milk

For use as an antihypertensive

Importance of diet; possible need for sodium restriction and/or weight reduction

» Patient may not experience symptoms of hypertension; importance of taking medication even if feeling well

» Does not cure, but helps control hypertension; possible need for lifelong therapy; serious consequences of untreated hypertension

Precautions while using this medication

Regular visits to physician to check progress during therapy

Checking with physician before discontinuing medication; gradual dosage reduction may be necessary

» Discussing exercise or physical exertion limits with physician; reduced occurrence of chest pain may tempt patient to be overactive

Possible headache; checking with physician if continuing or severe

» Maintaining good dental hygiene and seeing dentist frequently for teeth cleaning to prevent tenderness, bleeding, and gum enlargement

For use as an antihypertensive

» Not taking other medications, especially nonprescription sympathomimetics, unless discussed with physician

For patients taking bepridil, diltiazem, or verapamil

» Checking pulse as directed; checking with physician if less than 50 beats per minute

For patients taking flunarizine

Caution when driving or doing other things requiring alertness because of risk of drowsiness

Side/adverse effects

Signs of potential side effects, especially angina, congestive heart failure or pulmonary edema, extrapyramidal effects (for flunarizine), galactorrhea (for flunarizine), peripheral edema, tachycardia, bradycardia, excessive hypotension, gingival hyperplasia, allergic reaction, mental depression (for flunarizine), arthritis (for nifedipine), and transient blindness (for nifedipine)

General Dosing Information

For oral dosage forms only

Oral dosage must be titrated for each patient as needed and tolerated.

Concurrent administration of nitroglycerin sublingually or long-acting nitrates with calcium channel blocking agents may produce an additive antianginal effect. Nitroglycerin may be used sublingually as required to abort acute angina attacks during calcium channel blocking agent therapy. Nitrate medication may be used during calcium channel blocking agent therapy for angina prophylaxis.

Although no "rebound effect" has been reported upon discontinuation of calcium channel blockers, a gradual decrease of dosage with physician supervision is recommended.

BEPRIDIL

Summary of Differences

Pharmacology:

Nonselective calcium channel blocker; also affects fast sodium inward current.

Depresses sinoatrial (SA) and atrioventricular (AV) nodes; negative inotropic effect; causes bradycardia.

Precautions:

Laboratory value alterations—Increases QT interval and alters T-wave morphology.

Contraindications/medical problems—Contraindicated in patients with history of serious ventricular arrhythmias or QT interval prolongation. Also, contraindicated in patients with 2nd or 3rd degree atrioventricular (AV) block or sinoatrial (SA) nodal function impairment, except in patients with a functioning artificial ventricular pacemaker. Extreme caution necessary in patients with hypokalemia.

Side/adverse effects: Differences in frequencies are due to differences in pharmacological effects. Also causes agranulocytosis (rare); arrhythmias, including torsades de pointes (less common).

Oral Dosage Forms

BEPRIDIL HYDROCHLORIDE TABLETS

Usual adult dose: Antianginal—Oral, initially 200 mg once a day, the dosage being increased after ten days, if necessary, to 300 mg once a day.

Usual geriatric dose: See *Usual adult dose*.

Usual adult prescribing limits: Up to 400 mg daily.

DILTIAZEM

Summary of Differences

Pharmacology:

Benzothiazepine structure.

Depresses sinoatrial (SA) and atrioventricular (AV) nodes; little or no negative inotropic effect; usually does not significantly alter heart rate, but may cause slight bradycardia.

Precautions:

Laboratory value alterations—Increases PR interval.

Contraindications/medical problems—Contraindicated in patients with 2nd or 3rd degree atrioventricular (AV) block, sinoatrial (SA) nodal function impairment, or Wolff-Parkinson-White or Lown-Ganong-Levine syndrome accompanied by atrial flutter or fibrillation, except in patients with a functioning artificial ventricular pacemaker.

Side/adverse effects: Differences in frequencies are due to differences in pharmacological effects.

Additional Dosing Information

See also *General Dosing Information.*

Dermatologic side effects usually disappear even with continued use. However, if skin eruptions persist, it is recommended that diltiazem therapy be withdrawn, since progression to erythema multiform and/or exfoliative dermatitis or Stevens-Johnson syndrome have been reported rarely.

Oral Dosage Forms

Note: Bracketed uses in the *Dosage Forms* section refer to categories of use and/or indications that are not included in U.S. product labeling.

DILTIAZEM HYDROCHLORIDE EXTENDED-RELEASE CAPSULES

Usual adult and adolescent dose: Antihypertensive—

Cardiazem CD—Oral, 180 to 240 mg once a day, the dosage being adjusted after fourteen days as needed and tolerated.

　Note: The total daily dose usually ranges from 240 to 360 mg.

Cardizem SR—Oral, initially 60 to 120 mg two times a day, the dosage being adjusted after fourteen days as needed and tolerated.

Note: Geriatric patients may be more sensitive to the effects of the usual adult dose.

Usual adult prescribing limits: Up to 360 mg daily.

Auxiliary labeling: • Do not take other medicines without physician's advice.

DILTIAZEM TABLETS USP

Note: The dosing and strengths of diltiazem are expressed in terms of hydrochloride salt.

Usual adult and adolescent dose:

Antianginal; or

[Antihypertensive][1]—Oral, initially 30 mg (HCl) three or four times a day, the dosage being increased gradually at one- or two-day intervals as needed and tolerated.

Note: Geriatric patients may be more sensitive to the effects of the usual adult dose.

Usual adult prescribing limits: Up to 360 mg (HCl) daily.

Auxiliary labeling: • Do not take other medicines without physician's advice.

---

[1]Not included in Canadian product labeling.

Parenteral Dosage Forms

DILTIAZEM HYDROCHLORIDE INJECTION

Usual adult and adolescent dose: Antiarrythmic—

Intravenous (rapid), 250 mcg (0.25 mg) per kg of actual body weight administered slowly over a two-minute period with continuous ECG and blood pressure monitoring. If response is not adequate, 350 mcg (0.35 mg) per kg of actual body weight may be administered fifteen minutes after completion of initial dose. Subsequent doses should be individualized.

　Note: Some patients may respond to an initial dose of 150 mcg (0.15 mg) per kg of actual body weight, although the duration of action may be shorter.

Intravenous infusion, continuous (for continued reduction of heart rate [up to twenty-four hours] in patients with atrial fibrillation or atrial flutter), initially 10 mg per hour beginning immediately after the last rapid intravenous dose. The rate of infusion may be increased in increments of 5 mg per hour as needed, up to a maximum rate of 15 mg per hour.

Note: Some patients may respond to an initial rate of 5 mg per hour.

FELODIPINE

Summary of Differences

Pharmacology:

Dihydropyridine structure.

Potent peripheral vasodilator; does not depress sinoatrial (SA) or atrioventricular (AV) node; reflex increase in heart rate in response to vasodilation masks negative inotropic effect.

Precautions: Contraindications/medical problems—No caution necessary in renal function impairment.

Side/adverse effects: Differences in frequencies are due to differences in pharmacological effects.

Oral Dosage Forms

FELODIPINE EXTENDED-RELEASE TABLETS

Usual adult dose:

Antihypertensive—

Initial: Oral, 5 mg once a day, the dosage being adjusted as needed, usually at intervals of not less than two weeks.

Maintenance: Oral, 5 to 10 mg once a day.

Antianginal—Oral, 10 mg once a day.

Note: Geriatric patients may be more sensitive to the effects of the usual adult dose.

Usual adult prescribing limits: Up to 20 mg once a day.

Auxiliary labeling: • Do not take other medicines without physician's advice.

FLUNARIZINE

Summary of Differences

Indications: Indicated for prophylaxis of migraine.

Pharmacology:

Diphenylpiperazine structure.

Does not depress sinoatrial (SA) or atrioventricular (AV) node; no negative inotropic effect; no reflex increase in heart rate; no antihypertensive effect.

Cerebroselective.

Precautions: Contraindications/medical problems—Caution required in patients with history of mental depression or with Parkinson's syndrome or other extrapyramidal disorders.

Side/adverse effects: Differences in frequencies are due to differences in pharmacological effects. Also causes parkinsonian extrapyramidal effects (less common), galactorrhea (rare), mental depression (less common), drowsiness (more common), dryness of mouth (less common), increased appetite and/or weight gain (more common).

Oral Dosage Forms

FLUNARIZINE HYDROCHLORIDE CAPSULES

Usual adult dose: Vascular headache prophylactic—Oral, 10 mg once a day in the evening.

Note: Geriatric patients may be more sensitive to the effects of the usual adult dose.

ISRADIPINE

Summary of Differences

Pharmacology:

Dihydropyridine structure.

Potent peripheral vasodilator; does not depress sinoatrial (SA) or atrioventricular (AV) node; reflex increase in heart rate in response to vasodilation masks negative inotropic effect.

Side/adverse effects: Differences in frequencies are due to differences in pharmacological effects.

Oral Dosage Forms

ISRADIPINE CAPSULES

Usual adult dose: Antihypertensive—Oral, initially 2.5 mg two times a day, alone or in combination with a thiazide diuretic, the dosage being increased, if necessary, in increments of 5 mg per day at two- to four-week intervals.

Note: Geriatric patients may be more sensitive to the effects of the usual adult dose.

Usual adult prescribing limits: Up to 10 mg two times a day.

Auxiliary labeling: • Do not take other medicines without physician's advice.

NICARDIPINE

Summary of Differences

Pharmacology:

Dihydropyridine structure.

Potent peripheral vasodilator; does not depress sinoatrial (SA) or atrioventricular (AV) node; reflex increase in heart rate in response to vasodilation masks negative inotropic effect.

Precautions:

Geriatrics—No change in half-life or protein binding.

Contraindications/medical problems—Caution necessary in patients with acute cerebral infarction or hemorrhage.

Side/adverse effects: Differences in frequencies are due to differences in pharmacological effects.

Oral Dosage Forms

NICARDIPINE HYDROCHLORIDE CAPSULES

Usual adult and adolescent dose:

Antianginal; or

Antihypertensive—Oral, initially 20 mg three times a day, the dosage being adjusted as needed and tolerated.

Auxiliary labeling: • Do not take other medicines without physician's advice.

NIFEDIPINE

Summary of Differences

Pharmacology:

Dihydropyridine structure.

Potent peripheral vasodilator; does not depress sinoatrial (SA) or atrioventricular (AV) node; reflex increase in heart rate in response to vasodilation masks negative inotropic effect.

Side/adverse effects: Differences in frequencies are due to differences in pharmacological effects. Also causes arthritis associated with elevated antinuclear antibody (ANA) titers (rare), transient blindness at peak plasma concentrations (rare).

Additional Dosing Information

See also *General Dosing Information.*

In solution, degradation of nifedipine occurs more rapidly at 25 °C (77 °F) than at 4 °C (39 °F). However, when nifedipine solutions are protected from light and refrigerated, concentrations of nifedipine decline to approximately 90% of the original concentrations within 6 hours of preparation. It is recommended that extemporaneous preparations be made immediately before use.

Oral Dosage Forms

Note: Bracketed uses in the *Dosage Forms* section refer to categories of use and/or indications that are not included in U.S. product labeling.

NIFEDIPINE CAPSULES USP

Usual adult and adolescent dose:

Antianginal; or

[Antihypertensive][1]—Essential hypertension: Oral, initially 10 mg three times a day, the dosage being gradually increased over a seven- to fourteen-day period as needed and tolerated.

Note: For hospitalized patients under close supervision, dosage may be increased by 10-mg increments over four- to six-hour periods until symptoms are controlled.

When justified by symptom frequency and/or severity, dosage titration may be accomplished over a three-day period (medication given three times a day and increased stepwise from 10 mg to 20 mg, then to 30 mg per dose as needed and tolerated), but only if the patient is monitored frequently.

Geriatric patients may be more sensitive to the effects of the usual adult dose.

In some cases, nifedipine capsules are bitten or punctured and administered buccally or sublingually in patients who are unable for various reasons to swallow the capsules. Capsules may also be bitten before being swallowed. Bioavailability is not significantly different however the capsules are administered, although peak plasma concentrations may be achieved slightly earlier when they are bitten or punctured before being swallowed.

[Antihypertensive][1]—Hypertension associated with autonomic dysreflexia: Oral or sublingual (after capsule is bitten or punctured), 10 mg, repeated if necessary after fifteen minutes.

Usual adult prescribing limits: Single dose, up to 30 mg; total daily dose, up to 180 mg (a total daily dose greater than 120 mg is rarely required).

Auxiliary labeling: • Do not take other medicines without physician's advice.

NIFEDIPINE TABLETS

Usual adult and adolescent dose:

Antianginal; or

Antihypertensive[1]—Oral, initially 10 mg three times a day, the dosage being gradually increased over a seven- to fourteen-day period as needed and tolerated.

Note: For hospitalized patients under close supervision, dosage may be increased by 10-mg increments over four- to six-hour periods until symptoms are controlled.

When justified by symptom frequency and/or severity, dosage titration may be accomplished over a three-day period (medication given three times a day and increased stepwise from 10 mg to 20 mg, then to 30 mg per dose as needed and tolerated), but only if the patient is monitored frequently.

Geriatric patients may be more sensitive to the effects of the usual adult dose.

Usual adult prescribing limits: Single dose, up to 30 mg; total daily dose, up to 180 mg (a total daily dose greater than 120 mg is rarely required).

Auxiliary labeling: • Do not take other medicines without physician's advice.

NIFEDIPINE EXTENDED-RELEASE TABLETS

Usual adult and adolescent dose:

Procardia XL—
Antianginal; or
Antihypertensive: Oral, 30 or 60 mg once a day, the dosage being gradually adjusted over a seven- to fourteen-day period as needed and tolerated.

Adalat P.A.—
Antianginal[1]; or
Antihypertensive: Oral, initially 20 mg two times a day, the dosage being gradually increased as needed and tolerated.

Note: Geriatric patients may be more sensitive to the effects of the usual adult dose.

Usual adult prescribing limits: Up to 80 mg (*Adalat P.A.*), or 90 mg (antianginal) or 120 mg (antihypertensive) (*Procardia XL*) per day.

Auxiliary labeling: • Do not take other medicines without physician's advice.

---

[1]Not included in Canadian product labeling.

NIMODIPINE

Summary of Differences

Indications: Indicated for treatment of subarachnoid hemorrhage-associated neurologic deficits.
Pharmacology:
Dihydropyridine structure.
Potent peripheral vasodilator; does not depress sinoatrial (SA) or atrioventricular (AV) node; no negative inotropic effect; reflex increase in heart rate in response to vasodilation occurs.
Cerebroselective.
Side/adverse effects: Differences in frequencies are due to differences in pharmacological effects. Also causes thrombocytopenia (rare).

Oral Dosage Forms

NIMODIPINE CAPSULES

Usual adult dose: Oral, 60 mg every four hours, beginning within ninety-six hours after the subarachnoid hemorrhage and continuing for twenty-one days.

Note: In patients with hepatic function impairment, dosage should be reduced to 30 mg every four hours, with close monitoring of blood pressure and heart rate.

Geriatric patients may be more sensitive to the effects of the usual adult dose.

VERAPAMIL

Summary of Differences

Indications:
Indicated for treatment of supraventricular tachyarrhythmias; oral dosage form indicated for prophylaxis.
Also used to treat hypertrophic cardiomyopathy.
Pharmacology:
Diphenylalkylamine structure.
Depresses sinoatrial (SA) and atrioventricular (AV) nodes; usually does not significantly alter heart rate but may cause bradycardia; negative inotropic effect countered by reduction in afterload.
Precautions:
Pediatrics—In rare instances, severe adverse hemodynamic effects have occurred after intravenous administration of verapamil in neonates and infants.
Laboratory value alterations—Prolongs PR interval in serum concentrations greater than 30 nanograms per mL.
Contraindications/medical problems—Contraindicated in patients with 2nd or 3rd degree atrioventricular (AV) block, sinoatrial (SA) nodal function impairment, or Wolff-Parkinson-White or Lown-Ganong-Levine syndrome accompanied by atrial flutter or fibrillation, except in patients with a functioning artificial ventricular pacemaker. Caution necessary in patients with neuromuscular transmission deficiency, and wide-complex ventricular tachycardia (with intravenous use).
Side/adverse effects: Differences in frequencies are due to differences in pharmacological effects.

Additional Dosing Information

See also *General Dosing Information.*

Dermatologic side effects usually disappear even with continued use. However, if skin eruptions persist, it is recommended that verapamil therapy be withdrawn, since progression to erythema multiform has been reported rarely.

For parenteral dosage forms only

Parenteral dosage is indicated in the management of cardiac arrhythmias with close monitoring. Emergency equipment and medications should be readily available.

Oral Dosage Forms

Note: Bracketed uses in the *Dosage Forms* section refer to categories of use and/or indications that are not included in U.S. product labeling.

VERAPAMIL TABLETS USP

Note: The dosing and strengths of verapamil are expressed in terms of hydrochloride salt.

Usual adult and adolescent dose:
Antianginal; or
Antiarrhythmic; or
Antihypertensive[1]; or
[Hypertrophic cardiomyopathy therapy adjunct]—Oral, initially 80 to 120 (HCl) three times a day, the dosage being increased at daily or weekly intervals as needed and tolerated.

Note: An initial dose of 40 mg (HCl) three times a day is recommended in patients who may have an increased response to verapamil (e.g., those with hepatic function impairment, elderly patients, patients with poor left ventricular function).

The total daily dose usually ranges from 240 to 480 mg.

Because of prolongation of the half-life with repeated dosing, decreased frequency of dosing may be possible; dosage should be individualized.

Geriatric patients may be more sensitive to the effects of the usual adult dose.

Usual adult prescribing limits: Up to 480 mg (HCl) daily in divided doses; has been used in doses up to 720 mg per day in the treatment of hypertrophic cardiomyopathy.

Usual geriatric dose: Oral, initially 40 mg (HCl) three times a day, the dosage being adjusted as needed and tolerated.

Auxiliary labeling: • Do not take other medicines without physician's advice.

VERAPAMIL HYDROCHLORIDE EXTENDED-RELEASE CAPSULES

Usual adult and adolescent dose: Antihypertensive—Oral, initially 240 mg once a day, the dosage being increased in increments of 120 mg per day at daily or weekly intervals as needed and tolerated.

Note: An initial dose of 120 mg per day is recommended in patients who may have an increased response to verapamil (e.g., elderly, small people, etc.).

The total daily dose usually ranges from 240 to 480 mg.

Geriatric patients may be more sensitive to the effects of the usual adult dose.

Auxiliary labeling: • Do not take other medicines without physician's advice.

VERAPAMIL HYDROCHLORIDE EXTENDED-RELEASE TABLETS

Usual adult and adolescent dose: Antihypertensive—Oral, initially 180 mg once a day in the morning with food, the dosage being increased at daily or weekly intervals as needed and tolerated in the following order: 240 mg once a day in the morning; 180 mg every twelve hours or 240 mg in the morning and 120 mg in the evening; 240 mg every twelve hours.

Note: Lower initial doses (e.g., 120 mg per day) may be necessary in patients with a potential increased response to verapamil.

Tablets may be broken in half, but should not be crushed or chewed.

Geriatric patients may be more sensitive to the effects of the usual adult dose.

Auxiliary labeling:
  • Take with meals or milk.
  • Do not take other medicines without physician's advice.

Parenteral Dosage Forms

VERAPAMIL INJECTION USP

Note: The dosing and strengths of verapamil are expressed in terms of hydrochloride salt.

Usual adult dose: Intravenous, initially 5 to 10 mg (HCl) (or 75 to 150 mcg [0.075 to 0.15 mg] per kg of body weight) administered slowly over a two-minute period with continuous ECG and blood pressure monitoring. If response is not adequate, 10 mg (or 150 mcg [0.15 mg] per kg of body weight) may be administered thirty minutes after completion of initial dose.

Note: In geriatric patients, the intravenous dose should be administered slowly over a three-minute period to minimize undesired effects.

---

[1]Not included in Canadian product labeling.

Table 1. Contraindications/Medical Problems

The contraindications/medical problems included have been selected on the basis of their potential clinical significance (reasons given in parentheses where appropriate)—not necessarily inclusive (» = major clinical significance).	Legend: **I** = Bepridil **II** = Diltiazem **III** = Felodipine **IV** = Flunarizine **V** = Isradipine					**VI** = Nicardipine **VII** = Nifedipine **VIII** = Nimodipine **IX** = Verapamil			
	I	**II**	**III**	**IV**	**V**	**VI**	**VII**	**VIII**	**IX**
Except under special circumstances, this medication should not be used when the following medical problems exist:									
» Arrhythmias, ventricular, serious, history of or » QT interval prolongation, history of (increased risk of bepridil-induced arrhythmias)	✔								
» Heart block—2nd or 3rd degree atrioventricular (AV) block, except in patients with a functioning artificial ventricular pacemaker (use of calcium channel blocker may lead to excessive bradycardia)	✔	✔							✔
» Hypotension, severe	✔	✔	✔		✔	✔	✔	✔	✔
» Sinoatrial (SA) nodal function impairment (sick sinus syndrome) except in patients with functioning artificial ventricular pacemaker (use of calcium channel blocker may lead to severe hypotension, bradycardia, and asystole)	✔	✔							✔
» Wolff-Parkinson-White or Lown-Ganong-Levine syndrome accompanied by atrial flutter or fibrillation, except in patients with a functioning artificial ventricular pacemaker (use of calcium channel blocker for treatment of atrial fibrillation or flutter may precipitate severe ventricular arrhythmias)	✔								✔
Risk-benefit should be considered when the following medical problems exist: Aortic stenosis, severe (increased risk of heart failure when calcium channel blocker initiated, because of fixed impedance to flow across aortic valve)		✔				✔	✔		✔
» Bradycardia, extreme, or » Heart failure (reduced sinus node and AV node activity may be worsened) Note: When not severe or rate-related, heart failure should be controlled with digitalization and diuretics before administration of a calcium channel blocker. Heart failure, severe or moderately severe (pulmonary wedge pressure above 20 mm of mercury, ejection fraction less than 30%), may be acutely worsened by administration of a calcium channel blocker.	✔	✔							✔
Bradycardia, extreme, or Heart failure (because these agents have a slight negative inotropic effect, caution is recommended)				✔		✔	✔	✔	
» Cardiogenic shock	✔	✔	✔		✔	✔	✔	✔	✔
Cerebral infarction or hemorrhage, acute						✔			
Hepatic function impairment (clearance and duration of effect may be prolonged; clearance of felodipine is reduced to about 60%; half-life of nicardipine may be increased to 19 hours in patients with severe hepatic function impairment; half-life of verapamil may be increased to 14 to 16 hours and plasma clearance reduced to about 30% of normal; dosage reduction may be necessary)	✔	✔	✔	✔	✔	✔	✔	✔	✔
» Hypokalemia (risk of bepridil-induced arrhythmias may be increased)	✔								
Hypotension, mild to moderate (tendency to hypotension is augmented by the peripheral vasodilating effect of the calcium channel blocker)		✔	✔		✔	✔	✔	✔	✔

Table 1. Contraindications/Medical Problems *(continued)*

	I	II	III	IV	V	VI	VII	VIII	IX
Legend: **I** = Bepridil **II** = Diltiazem **III** = Felodipine **IV** = Flunarizine **V** = Isradipine **VI** = Nicardipine **VII** = Nifedipine **VIII** = Nimodipine **IX** = Verapamil									
Mental depression, history of (flunarizine may precipitate mental depression)				✔					
» Myocardial infarction, acute, with pulmonary congestion documented by x-ray on admission (associated heart failure may be acutely worsened by administration of a calcium channel blocker)	✔	✔							✔
Myocardial infarction, acute, with pulmonary congestion documented by x-ray on admission (because these agents have a slight negative inotropic effect, there is a possibility that associated heart failure may be acutely worsened)				✔		✔	✔	✔	✔
Narrowing of the gastrointestinal tract, pathologic or iatrogenic, severe (passage of the nondeformable extended-release nifedipine system [*Procardia XL*] may be impaired; obstructive symptoms may occur)							✔		
Neuromuscular transmission deficiency (verapamil has been reported to decrease neuromuscular transmission in patients with Duchenne's muscular dystrophy, and to prolong recovery from the neuromuscular blocking agent vecuronium; dosage reduction may be required)									✔
Parkinson's syndrome or Extrapyramidal disorders, other (flunarizine may produce parkinsonian extrapyramidal symptoms not responsive to parkinsonian medications)				✔					
Renal function impairment (possible reduced clearance of the calcium channel blocker or metabolites, although half-life is only slightly increased; dosage adjustment may be necessary) (plasma concentrations of felodipine are unchanged; although reduced excretion results in increased concentrations of metabolites, they are inactive)	✔	✔		✔		✔	✔	✔	✔
» Sensitivity to the calcium channel blocker prescribed	✔	✔	✔	✔	✔	✔	✔	✔	✔
Ventricular tachycardia, wide-complex (risk of ventricular fibrillation if intravenous diltiazem or verapamil administered)		✔							✔

Table 2. Side/Adverse Effects

Note: Side/adverse effects tend to be dose-related and occur most frequently during periods of dosage titration.

Although not reported to occur in humans, lenticular changes and cataracts have developed during chronic dosage with verapamil in beagles. These effects resulted from daily dosage of 30 mg and more per kg of body weight and are considered likely to be species-specific.

A possible hyperglycemic effect has been reported with nicardipine (at a daily dose of 40 mg) and nifedipine therapy (when the daily dosage exceeds 60 mg). No significant effect on fasting serum glucose has been seen with felodipine.

Depression of atrioventricular (AV) and sinoatrial (SA) nodal conduction by bepridil, diltiazem, and verapamil may result in asymptomatic 1st degree block and transient sinus bradycardia, sometimes accompanied by nodal escape rhythms.

Use of verapamil for hypertrophic cardiomyopathy, especially in patients with pre-existing risk factors, has resulted in serious side effects (including pulmonary edema, sinus bradycardia, severe hypotension, 2nd degree AV block, and sudden death).

Legend:
I = Bepridil VI = Nicardipine
II = Diltiazem VII = Nifedipine
III = Felodipine VIII = Nimodipine
IV = Flunarizine IX = Verapamil
V = Isradipine

The following side/adverse effects have been selected on the basis of their potential clinical significance (possible signs and symptoms in parentheses where appropriate)—not necessarily inclusive:*

	I	II	III	IV	V	VI	VII	VIII	IX
Medical attention needed									
Agranulocytosis (not symptomatic)	R	U	U	U	U	U	U	U	U
Allergic reaction (skin rash)	R	L	L	R	L	R	R	R	L
Note: May disappear, even with continued diltiazem use. Rarely, may progress to erythema multiform (diltiazem, verapamil), exfoliative dermatitis (diltiazem), or Stevens-Johnson syndrome (diltiazem, verapamil).									
Angina (chest pain)—may occur about 30 minutes after administration	U	R	L	U	L	L	R	U	R
Note: Rarely, especially in patients with severe obstructive coronary artery disease, increased frequency, duration, and/or severity of angina or acute myocardial infarction have occurred when therapy is initiated or dosage increased.									
Arrhythmias, including torsades de pointes (usually asymptomatic)	L	U	U	U	U	U	U	U	U
Arthritis (painful, swollen joints)—associated with elevated ANA titres	U	U	U	U	U	U	R	U	U
Blindness, transient, at peak plasma concentration	U	U	U	U	U	U	R	U	U
Bradycardia less than 50 per minute; rarely, 2nd or 3rd degree AV block, with a few patients progressing to asystole (slow heartbeat)	L	R	X	U	X	X	X	X	L
Congestive heart failure or pulmonary edema, possible (breathing difficulty, coughing, or wheezing)	L	L	U	U	R	R	L	R	L
Extrapyramidal effects, parkinsonian (loss of balance control, mask-like face, shuffling walk, stiffness of arms or legs, trembling and shaking of hands and fingers, trouble in speaking or swallowing)	U	R	U	L	U	U	U	U	U
Note: Symptoms are not responsive to antiparkinsonian medications, but are reversible on withdrawal of flunarizine.									
Galactorrhea (unusual secretion of milk)	U	U	U	R	U	U	U	U	R
Gingival hyperplasia (bleeding, tender, or swollen gums)	U	R	R	U	U	U	R	U	R
Hypotension (usually not symptomatic; not orthostatic)	R	L	R	U	L	L	L	L	L
Hypotension, excessive (fainting)	R	R	R	U	R	R	R	R	R
Mental depression	U	R	R	L	U	U	U	U	U
Peripheral edema (swelling of ankles, feet, or lower legs)	R	L	M	U	L	L	M	L	L

*Differences in frequency of occurrence may reflect either lack of clinical-use data or actual pharmacologic distinctions among agents (although their pharmacologic similarity suggests that side effects occurring with one may occur with the others). M = more frequent; L = less frequent; R = rare; U = unknown; X = does not occur.

Table 2. Side/Adverse Effects *(continued)*

	Legend: **I** = Bepridil **II** = Diltiazem **III** = Felodipine **IV** = Flunarizine **V** = Isradipine					**VI** = Nicardipine **VII** = Nifedipine **VIII** = Nimodipine **IX** = Verapamil			
	I	**II**	**III**	**IV**	**V**	**VI**	**VII**	**VIII**	**IX**
Tachycardia (irregular or fast, pounding heartbeat) Note: In patients receiving verapamil, rapid ventricular rate may occur in patients with atrial flutter/fibrillation and an accessory AV pathway as with Wolff-Parkinson-White, or Lown-Ganong-Levine syndrome; in patients receiving felodipine, isradipine, nicardipine, nifedipine, or nimodipine, reflex tachycardia may occur because of its hypotensive effect)	X	R	L	U	L	L	L	R	R
Thrombocytopenia (not symptomatic)	U	R	U	U	U	U	U	R	U
Medical attention needed only if continuing or bothersome *Constipation*	L	L	L	U	R	R	L	U	L
Diarrhea	M	L	L	U	L	R	U	L	U
Dizziness or lightheadedness	M	L	L	L	L	L	M	L	L
Drowsiness	U	R	U	M	U	R	U	U	U
Dryness of mouth	U	R	R	L	U	R	U	U	U
Flushing and feeling of warmth	U	L	L	U	L	M	M	R	R
Headache	L	L	M	U	M	L	M	L	L
Increased appetite and/or weight gain	U	U	U	M	U	U	U	U	U
Nausea	M	L	L	L	L	L	M	L	L
Unusual tiredness or weakness	L	L	L	L	L	L	L	U	L

*Differences in frequency of occurrence may reflect either lack of clinical-use data or actual pharmacologic distinctions among agents (although their pharmacologic similarity suggests that side effects occurring with one may occur with the others). M = more frequent; L = less frequent; R = rare; U = unknown; X = does not occur.

CALCIUM SUPPLEMENTS   Systemic

INN: Included in brackets after individual generic listings, if different
from the U.S. generic name.

Some commonly used *brand names* are:

In the U.S.—

BioCal [Calcium
Carbonate]
Calcarb 600 [Calcium
Carbonate]
Calci-Chew [Calcium
Carbonate]
Calciday 667 [Calcium
Carbonate]
Calcilac [Calcium
Carbonate]
Calcium 600 [Calcium
Carbonate]
Calglycine [Calcium
Carbonate]
Calphosan [Calcium
Glycerophosphate and
Calcium Lactate]
Caltrate 600 [Calcium
Carbonate]
Chooz [Calcium Carbonate]
Citracal [Calcium Citrate]
Citracal Liquitabs [Calcium
Citrate]
Dicarbosil [Calcium
Carbonate]
Gencalc [Calcium
Carbonate]
Kalcinate [Calcium
Gluconate]

Mallamint [Calcium
Carbonate]
Neo-Calglucon [Calcium
Glubionate]
Nephro-Calci [Calcium
Carbonate]
Os-Cal 500 [Calcium
Carbonate]
Oysco [Calcium
Carbonate]
Oysco 500 Chewable
[Calcium Carbonate]
Oyst-Cal 500 [Calcium
Carbonate]
Oyst-Cal 500 Chewable
[Calcium Carbonate]
Oystercal 500 [Calcium
Carbonate]
Posture [Tribasic Calcium
Phosphate]
Rolaids Calcium Rich
[Calcium Carbonate]
Super Calcium 1200
[Calcium Carbonate]
Tums [Calcium Carbonate]
Tums E-X [Calcium
Carbonate]
Titralac [Calcium
Carbonate]

In Canada—

Apo-Cal [Calcium
Carbonate]
Calciject [Calcium
Chloride]
Calcite 500 [Calcium
Carbonate]
Calcium 500 [Calcium
Carbonate]
Calcium-Sandoz [Calcium
Glubionate]
Calcium-Sandoz Forte
[Calcium Lactate-
Gluconate and Calcium
Carbonate]
Calcium Stanley [Calcium
Gluceptate and Calcium
Gluconate]
Calsan [Calcium
Carbonate]

Caltrate 300 [Calcium
Carbonate]
Caltrate 600 [Calcium
Carbonate]
Caltrate Chewable
[Calcium Carbonate]
Gramcal [Calcium Lactate-
Gluconate and Calcium
Carbonate]
Mega-Cal [Calcium
Carbonate]
Nu-Cal [Calcium
Carbonate]
Os-Cal [Calcium
Carbonate]
Os-Cal Chewable
[Calcium Carbonate]

CALCIUM CARBONATE
Oral
  Calcium Carbonate Capsules
    In the U.S.—*Super Calcium 1200*
    In Canada—*Calsan*
  Calcium Carbonate Oral Suspension USP†
    In the U.S.— *Titralac;* GENERIC
  Calcium Carbonate Tablets USP
    In the U.S.—*BioCal; Calcarb 600; Calciday 667; Calcium
      600; Caltrate 600; Gencalc; Nephro-Calci;* GENERIC
    In Canada—*Apo-Cal; Calcite 500; Calcium 500; Caltrate 300;
      Caltrate 600; Nu-Cal;* GENERIC

  Calcium Carbonate Tablets USP (Chewable)
    In the U.S.—*BioCal; Calci-Chew; Calcilac; Calglycine; Chooz;
      Dicarbosil; Mallamint; Rolaids Calcium Rich‡; Titralac;
      Tums‡; Tums E-X‡*
    In Canada—*Calsan; Caltrate Chewable; Mega-Cal*
  Calcium Carbonate (Oyster-Shell Derived) Tablets
    In the U.S.—*Os-Cal 500; Oysco; Oyst-Cal 500; Oystercal
      500;* GENERIC
    In Canada—*Os-Cal*
  Calcium Carbonate (Oyster-Shell Derived) Tablets (Chewable)
    In the U.S.—*Oysco 500 Chewable; Oyst-Cal 500 Chewable*
    In Canada—*Os-Cal Chewable*
CALCIUM CHLORIDE
Parenteral
  Calcium Chloride Injection USP
    In the U.S.—GENERIC
    In Canada—*Calciject;* GENERIC
CALCIUM CITRATE†
Oral
  Calcium Citrate Tablets†
    In the U.S.—*Citracal*
  Calcium Citrate Effervescent Tablets†
    In the U.S.—*Citracal Liquitabs*
CALCIUM GLUBIONATE‡
Oral
  Calcium Glubionate Syrup USP‡
    In the U.S.—*Neo-Calglucon*
    In Canada—*Calcium-Sandoz§*
Parenteral
  Calcium Glubionate Injection*
    In Canada—*Calcium-Sandoz§*
CALCIUM GLUCEPTATE [INN: Calcium Glucoheptonate]†
Parenteral
  Calcium Gluceptate Injection USP†
    In the U.S.—GENERIC
**CALCIUM GLUCEPTATE [INN: Calcium Glucoheptonate] AND
CALCIUM GLUCONATE***
Oral
  Calcium Gluceptate and Calcium Gluconate Oral Solution*
    In Canada—*Calcium Stanley*
CALCIUM GLUCONATE
Oral
  Calcium Gluconate Tablets USP (Chewable)
    In the U.S. and Canada—GENERIC
Parenteral
  Calcium Gluconate Injection USP
    In the U.S.—*Kalcinate;* GENERIC
    In Canada—GENERIC
CALCIUM GLYCEROPHOSPHATE AND CALCIUM LACTATE†
Parenteral
  Calcium Glycerophosphate and Calcium Lactate Injection†
    In the U.S.—*Calphosan*
CALCIUM LACTATE
Oral
  Calcium Lactate Tablets USP
    In the U.S. and Canada—GENERIC
**CALCIUM LACTATE-GLUCONATE AND CALCIUM CARBON-
ATE***
Oral
  Calcium Lactate-Gluconate and Calcium Carbonate Effervescent
    Tablets*
    In Canada—*Calcium-Sandoz Forte; Gramcal*
DIBASIC CALCIUM PHOSPHATE†
Oral
  Dibasic Calcium Phosphate Tablets USP†
    In the U.S.—GENERIC

TRIBASIC CALCIUM PHOSPHATE†
Oral

Tribasic Calcium Phosphate Tablets†
    In the U.S.—*Posture*

---

*Not commercially available in the U.S.
†Not commercially available in Canada.
‡Antacid product commonly recommended as calcium supplement.
§In Canada, calcium glubionate is known as calcium glucono-galacto gluconate.

Category

Antihypocalcemic—Calcium Carbonate; Calcium Chloride; Calcium Citrate; Calcium Glubionate; Calcium Gluceptate; Calcium Gluconate; Calcium Glycerophosphate and Calcium Lactate; Calcium Lactate; Calcium Lactate-Gluconate and Calcium Carbonate; Dibasic Calcium Phosphate; Tribasic Calcium Phosphate.

Electrolyte replenisher—Calcium Chloride; Calcium Glubionate Injection; Calcium Gluceptate; Calcium Gluconate Injection.

Cardiotonic—Calcium Chloride; Calcium Glubionate Injection; Calcium Gluconate Injection.

Antihyperkalemic—Calcium Chloride; Calcium Glubionate Injection; Calcium Gluconate Injection.

Antihypermagnesemic—Calcium Chloride; Calcium Glubionate Injection; Calcium Gluceptate; Calcium Gluconate Injection.

Antacid—Calcium Carbonate.

Nutritional supplement (mineral)—Calcium Carbonate; Calcium Citrate; Calcium Glubionate, Oral; Calcium Gluceptate and Calcium Gluconate; Calcium Gluconate, Oral; Calcium Lactate; Calcium Lactate-Gluconate and Calcium Carbonate; Dibasic Calcium Phosphate; Tribasic Calcium Phosphate.

Antihyperphosphatemic—Calcium Carbonate; Calcium Citrate.

Indications

Note: Bracketed information in the *Indications* section refers to uses not included in U.S. product labeling.

Accepted

Hypocalcemia, acute (treatment)—Parenteral calcium salts (i.e., chloride, glubionate, gluceptate, and gluconate) are indicated in the treatment of hypocalcemia in conditions that require a rapid increase in serum calcium-ion concentration, such as in neonatal hypocalcemic tetany; tetany due to parathyroid deficiency; hypocalcemia due to "hungry bones" syndrome (remineralization hypocalcemia) following surgery for hyperparathyroidism; vitamin D deficiency; and alkalosis. Calcium salts have been used as adjunctive therapy for insect bites or stings, such as Black Widow Spider bites, and sensitivity reactions, especially when characterized by urticaria; and as an aid in the management of acute symptoms of lead colic. Parenteral calcium gluconate and calcium gluceptate are also used for the prevention of hypocalcemia during exchange transfusions.

Electrolyte depletion (treatment)—Parenteral calcium chloride, calcium gluconate, calcium glubionate, and calcium gluceptate are used in conditions that require an increase in calcium ions for electrolyte adjustment.

Cardiac arrest (treatment adjunct)—Parenteral calcium chloride, calcium glubionate, [or calcium gluconate] may be used also as an adjunct in cardiac resuscitation, particularly after open heart surgery, to strengthen myocardial contractions, such as following defibrillation or when there is an inadequate response to catecholamines.

Hyperkalemia (treatment)—Calcium chloride, parenteral calcium gluconate, and parenteral calcium glubionate are used to decrease or reverse the cardiac depressant effects of hyperkalemia on electrocardiographic (ECG) function.

Hypermagnesemia (treatment adjunct)—Calcium chloride, calcium glubionate, [calcium gluceptate], and [calcium gluconate] injections have also been used as an aid in the treatment of central nervous system (CNS) depression due to overdosage of magnesium sulfate.

Hypocalcemia, chronic (treatment)—Oral calcium supplements provide a source of calcium ion for treating calcium depletion occurring in conditions such as chronic hypoparathyroidism, pseudohypoparathyroidism, osteomalacia, rickets, chronic renal failure, and hypocalcemia secondary to the administration of anticonvulsant medications. When chronic hypocalcemia is due to vitamin D deficiency, oral calcium salts may be administered concomitantly with vitamin D analogs. However, calcium phosphate should *not* be used in patients with hypoparathyroidism or renal failure, since phosphate levels may be too high and giving more phosphate would exacerbate the condition. Calcium supplements should not be used in hyperparathyroidism, unless the need for a calcium supplement is high and the patient is carefully monitored.

Calcium deficiency (prophylaxis)—Oral calcium salts are used as dietary supplemental therapy for persons who may not get enough calcium in their regular diet. Due to increased needs, children and pregnant women are at greatest risk. Pre- and postmenopausal women; adolescents, especially girls and the elderly may not receive adequate calcium in their diets. However, studies have shown that supplemental calcium in postmenopausal women without functioning ovaries does not lead to increases in bone density, even in the presence of supplemental vitamin D. Calcium supplements are used as part of the prevention and treatment of osteoporosis in patients with an inadequate calcium intake. The use of calcium citrate may reduce the risk of kidney stones in susceptible patients. The use of water-soluble salts of calcium (i.e., citrate, gluconate, and lactate) may be preferable to acid-soluble salts (i.e., carbonate and phosphate) for patients with reduced stomach acid or patients taking acid-inhibiting medication, such as the histamine H_2-receptor antagonists.

Some unusual diets (e.g., reducing diets that drastically restrict food selection) may not supply minimum daily requirements of calcium. Supplementation is necessary in patients receiving total parenteral nutrition (TPN) or undergoing rapid weight loss or in those with malnutrition, because of inadequate dietary intake.

Requirements for all vitamins and most minerals are increased during pregnancy; however, they should be provided by an adequate diet. Many physicians recommend that pregnant women receive multivitamin and mineral supplements, especially those pregnant women who do not consume an adequate diet and those in high-risk categories (i.e., women carrying more than one fetus, heavy cigarette smokers, and alcohol and drug abusers). Taking excessive amounts of a multivitamin and mineral supplement may be harmful to the mother and/or fetus and should be avoided.

Requirements for all vitamins and most minerals are increased during breast-feeding.

Hyperacidity (treatment)—See Calcium Carbonate, *Antacids (Oral-Local)*.

[Hyperphosphatemia (treatment)]—Calcium carbonate is used in patients with end-stage renal failure (renal osteodystrophy) to lower serum phosphate concentrations. However, it should be used with caution in patients on chronic hemodialysis. Calcium citrate is also used in renal failure as a phosphate binder.

Pharmacology

Mechanism of action/Effect: Calcium is essential for the functional integrity of the nervous, muscular, and skeletal systems. It plays a role in normal cardiac function, renal function, respiration, blood coagulation, and cell membrane and capillary permeability. Also, calcium helps to regulate the release and storage of neurotransmitters and hormones, the uptake and binding of amino acids, absorption of vitamin B_{12}, and gastrin secretion. The major fraction (99%) of calcium is in the skeletal structure primarily as hydroxyapatite, $Ca_{10}(PO_4)_6(OH)_2$; small amounts of calcium carbonate and amorphous calcium phosphates are also present. The calcium of bone is in a constant exchange with the calcium of plasma. Since the metabolic functions of calcium are essential for life, when there is a disturbance in the calcium balance because of dietary deficiency or other causes, the stores of calcium in bone may be depleted to fill the body's more acute needs. Therefore, on a chronic basis, normal mineralization of bone depends on adequate amounts of total body calcium.

Precautions to Consider

Geriatrics

With advancing age, intestinal calcium absorption decreases. Therefore, calcium requirements are increased in the elderly, and dosages of oral supplements may need to be adjusted accordingly. Impaired absorption may be due to low levels of active vitamin D metabolites.

Drug interactions and/or related problems

The following drug interactions and/or related problems have been selected on the basis of their potential clinical significance (possible mechanism in parentheses where appropriate)—not necessarily inclusive (» = major clinical significance):

Note: Combinations containing any of the following medications, depending on the amount present, may also interact with this medication.

Not all interactions between calcium supplements and other oral medications have been identified in this monograph. Because the rate and/or extent of absorption of other oral medications may vary when used concurrently with calcium supplements, especially calcium carbonate, patients should be advised not to take any other oral medications within 1 to 2 hours of calcium supplements.

Alcohol or
Caffeine, usually more than 8 cups of coffee a day, or
Tobacco
(concurrent use of excessive amounts of these substances has been reported to decrease calcium absorption)

Antacids containing aluminum
(concurrent use with calcium citrate may enhance aluminum absorption)

Calcitonin
(concurrent use with calcium supplements may antagonize the effect of calcitonin in the treatment of hypercalcemia; however, when calcitonin is prescribed for osteoporosis or Paget's disease of the bone, calcium intake should be generous to prevent hypocalcemia which might generate secondary hyperparathyroidism)

Calcium-channel blocking agents
(concurrent use of these medications with calcium supplements in quantities sufficient to raise serum calcium concentrations above normal may reduce the response to verapamil and probably other calcium-channel blockers)

» Calcium-containing medications, other, or
Magnesium-containing medications, oral
(concurrent use with calcium supplements may increase serum calcium or magnesium concentrations in susceptible patients, mainly patients with impaired renal function, leading to hypercalcemia or hypermagnesemia, respectively)

» Cellulose sodium phosphate
(concurrent use with calcium supplements may decrease effectiveness of cellulose sodium phosphate in preventing hypercalciuria)

Ciprofloxacin or
Norfloxacin or

Ofloxacin
(concurrent use with calcium carbonate may reduce absorption by chelation of ciprofloxacin, norfloxacin, or ofloxacin, resulting in lower serum and urine concentrations of ciprofloxacin, norfloxacin, or ofloxacin; therefore, concurrent use is not recommended)

Contraceptives, estrogen-containing, oral, or
Estrogens
(concurrent use with calcium supplements may increase calcium absorption, which is used to therapeutic advantage when estrogens are prescribed for the treatment of postmenopausal osteoporosis)

» Digitalis glycosides
(concurrent use of parenteral calcium salts with digitalis glycosides may increase the risk of cardiac arrhythmias; therefore, when the parenteral administration of calcium salts to digitalized patients is deemed necessary, caution and close electrocardiographic [ECG] monitoring are recommended)

Diuretics, thiazide
(concurrent use with large doses of calcium supplements may result in hypercalcemia because of reduced calcium excretion)

» Etidronate
(concurrent use with calcium supplements may prevent absorption of etidronate; patients should be advised not to take etidronate within 2 hours of calcium supplements)

Fiber, found in bran, whole-grain breads and cereals, or
Phytates, found in bran and whole-grain breads and cereals
(concurrent use of large amounts of fiber or phytates, especially in patients being treated for hypocalcemia, with calcium supplements may reduce calcium absorption by formation of nonabsorbable complexes)

» Gallium nitrate
(concurrent use with calcium supplements may antagonize the effect of gallium nitrate)

Iron supplements
(concurrent use with calcium carbonate and calcium phosphate will decrease the absorption of iron; iron supplements should not be taken within 1 or 2 hours of calcium carbonate or phosphate; however, when iron and calcium carbonate are present in multivitamin-with-minerals formulations, the absorption of iron is not significantly changed, possibly because the ascorbic acid in the formulation maintains the iron in the ferrous state, thus increasing its solubility and absorption)

» Magnesium sulfate, parenteral
(parenteral calcium salts may neutralize effects of parenteral magnesium sulfate and should be readily available to counteract the potentially serious risk of magnesium intoxication; also, calcium sulfate may precipitate when a calcium salt is admixed with magnesium sulfate in the same intravenous solution, although commercial nutritional solutions are formulated to avoid precipitation; calcium and magnesium should be administered through separate intravenous lines if required in post-parathyroidectomy "hungry bones" syndrome or tetany associated with hypocalcemia and hypomagnesemia)

Milk or milk products
(concurrent and prolonged use with calcium supplements may result in the milk-alkali syndrome)

Neuromuscular blocking agents, except succinylcholine
(concurrent use with parenteral calcium salts usually reverses the effects of nondepolarizing neuromuscular blocking agents)
(also, concurrent use with calcium salts has been reported to enhance or prolong the neuromuscular blocking action of tubocurarine)

» Phenytoin
(concurrent use decreases the bioavailability of both phenytoin and calcium because of possible formation of a nonabsorbable complex; patients should be advised not to take calcium supple-

ments within 1 to 3 hours of taking phenytoin; also, enteral feeding solutions containing calcium should not be administered through a nasogastric feeding tube together with phenytoin oral suspension; a 2-hour interval should elapse between the administration of the feeding solution and of the phenytoin)

Potassium phosphates or
Potassium and sodium phosphates
(concurrent use with calcium supplements may increase potential for deposition of calcium in soft tissues if serum ionized calcium is high; also, calcium phosphate may precipitate when a calcium salt is admixed with phosphates in the same intravenous solution)

Sodium bicarbonate
(concurrent and prolonged use with calcium supplements may result in milk-alkali syndrome)

Sodium fluoride
(concurrent use with calcium supplements may cause the calcium ions to complex with fluoride and inhibit absorption of both fluoride and calcium; however, if sodium fluoride is used with calcium supplements to treat osteoporosis, a one- to two-hour interval should elapse between doses)

» Tetracyclines, oral
(concurrent use with calcium supplements may decrease absorption of tetracyclines because of possible formation of non-absorbable complexes and increase in intragastric pH; patients should be advised not to take calcium supplements within 1 to 3 hours of taking tetracyclines)

Vitamin A
(excessive intake, more than 5000 IU per day, of vitamin A may stimulate bone loss and counteract the effects of calcium supplementation and may cause hypercalcemia)

Vitamin D, especially calcifediol and calcitriol
(concurrent use of large doses of vitamin D with calcium supplements may excessively increase intestinal absorption of calcium, increasing risk of chronic hypercalcemia in susceptible patients; however, it may be therapeutically advantageous in elderly and high-risk groups when it is necessary to prescribe vitamin D or its derivatives with calcium; careful monitoring of serum calcium concentrations is essential during long-term therapy)

Contraindications/Medical problems

The contraindications/medical problems included have been selected on the basis of their potential clinical significance (reasons given in parentheses where appropriate)—not necessarily inclusive (» = major clinical significance).

Except under special circumstances, these medications should not be used when the following medical problems exist:

For all calcium supplements
» Hypercalcemia, primary or secondary or
» Hypercalciuria or
» Renal calculi, calcium
(risk of exacerbation)
» Sarcoidosis
(may potentiate hypercalcemia)

For calcium phosphate, dibasic or tribasic, only
» Hypoparathyroidism or
» Renal insufficiency
(may increase risk of hyperphosphatemia)

For parenteral calcium salts only
» Digitalis toxicity
(increased risk of arrhythmias)

Risk-benefit should be considered when the following medical problems exist:

For all calcium supplements
» Dehydration or

Electrolyte imbalance, other
(may increase risk of hypercalcemia)
Diarrhea or
Malabsorption, gastrointestinal, chronic
(fecal excretion of calcium may be increased, although patients with chronic diarrhea or malabsorption commonly need calcium supplements)
» Renal calculi, history of
(risk of recurrent stone formation)
» Renal function impairment, chronic
(may increase risk of hypercalcemia; however, calcium carbonate or calcium citrate may be used as a phosphate binder in renal failure; also, some patients with renal failure have symptomatic hypocalcemia and need cautious treatment with calcium salts)

For calcium carbonate and calcium phosphate only
Achlorhydria or hypochlorhydria
(calcium absorption may be decreased unless the calcium carbonate or phosphate is taken with meals)

For parenteral calcium salts only
» Cardiac function impairment
» Ventricular fibrillation during cardiac resuscitation
(increased risk of arrhythmias; however, calcium may increase strength of myocardial contraction, make fibrillation coarser, and help in electrical defibrillation, especially with concomitant hyperkalemia)

Side/Adverse Effects

Note: Side/adverse effects may be more likely to occur if oral calcium supplements are taken in much larger doses than recommended (greater than 2000 to 2500 mg a day), if they are taken for a longer period of time, or if they are taken by patients with renal function impairment or milk-alkali syndrome.

The following side/adverse effects have been selected on the basis of their potential clinical significance (possible signs and symptoms in parentheses where appropriate)—not necessarily inclusive:

Those indicating need for medical attention
Incidence more frequent
With parenteral dosage forms only
Hypotension (dizziness); *flushing and/or sensation of warmth or heat; irregular heartbeat; nausea or vomiting; skin redness, rash, pain, or burning at injection site; sweating; tingling sensation; decrease in blood pressure, moderate*—with calcium chloride only

Note: *Tingling sensation* may result when intravenous injection is too rapid; *skin redness, rash, pain,* or *burning* may indicate extravasation and can precede sloughing or necrosis of skin.

Incidence rare
Hypercalcemic syndrome, acute (drowsiness, continuing nausea and vomiting, weakness); ***renal calculi, calcific*** (difficult or painful urination)—with oral dosage forms

Early symptoms of hypercalcemia
Constipation, severe; dryness of mouth; headache, continuing; increased thirst; irritability; loss of appetite; mental depression; metallic taste; unusual tiredness or weakness

Late symptoms of hypercalcemia
Confusion; drowsiness; high blood pressure; increased sensitivity of eyes or skin to light, especially in hemodialysis patients; irregular, fast, or slow heartbeat; nausea and vomiting; unusually large amount of urine or increased frequency of urination

Note: In severe *hypercalcemia,* ECG changes consisting of shortened Q-T intervals are also seen.

Patient Consultation

In providing consultation, consider emphasizing the following selected information (» = major clinical significance):

Importance of diet

Food sources may be preferable to supplements for intake of recommended dietary allowances (RDA) of calcium

Supplement may be needed because of inadequate dietary intake or increased requirements

List of daily RDA for various age groups

Importance of adequate weight-bearing exercise, especially during younger years, for building and maintaining dense bones to prevent osteoporosis in later life

Calcium content of selected foods

Importance of adequate amounts of vitamin D or exposure to sunlight for enhancement of calcium absorption; avoiding too much vitamin D

Not exceeding recommended amounts if self-medicating

Importance of not using bonemeal or dolomite as a source of calcium because of potential lead contamination

Calcium content per tablet of supplements

Before using this dietary supplement

» Conditions affecting use, especially:

Use in children—Use of injectable calcium preparations may cause extreme irritation and possible tissue necrosis and sloughing

Use in the elderly—Absorption is decreased; dosage adjustments may be necessary

Other medications, especially cellulose sodium phosphate, digitalis glycosides (for parenteral calcium salts only), etidronate, gallium nitrate, parenteral magnesium sulfate (for parenteral calcium salts only), phenytoin, oral tetracyclines, or other calcium-containing medications

Other medical problems, especially hypercalcemia, hypercalciuria, calcium renal calculi, sarcoidosis, hypoparathyroidism (for calcium phosphate only), dehydration, diarrhea or malabsorption, hyperparathyroidism, renal function impairment, or achlorhydria or hypochlorhydria (for calcium carbonate and calcium phosphates only)

Proper use of this dietary supplement

Drinking full glass (8 ounces) of water or juice with all oral dosage forms, except when taking calcium carbonate as a phosphate binder in renal dialysis

» Proper administration of calcium carbonate or phosphate: Taking tablets 1 to $1^{1}/_{2}$ hours after meals, unless otherwise directed by physician

Proper administration of chewable tablet: Chewing tablets well before swallowing

Proper administration of syrup: Taking calcium glubionate syrup *before* meals; diluting syrup in water or fruit juice, if desired, for infants or children

Missed dose: If on scheduled dosing regimen—Taking as soon as possible; then going back to regular schedule

» Proper storage

Precautions while using this dietary supplement

Regular visits to physician to check progress if taking dietary supplement in large doses or if taking regularly for long period of time

» Not taking within 1 or 2 hours of other oral medication, if possible

» Avoiding concurrent use with other medications containing significant amounts of calcium, phosphates, magnesium, or vitamin D, unless otherwise directed or approved by physician

» Avoiding concomitant use with certain fiber-containing foods such as bran and whole-grain breads and cereals; not eating these foods within 1 or 2 hours of taking calcium supplements

» Avoiding excessive use of alcoholic beverages, tobacco, or caffeine-containing beverages

» Importance of using calcium carbonate products labeled "USP," to avoid differences in bioavailability

Side/adverse effects

Signs of potential side effects, especially calcium renal calculi or hypercalcemia

General Dosing Information

The action of calcium supplements depends upon their content of calcium ion. The various calcium salts contain the following amounts of elemental calcium:

Calcium salt	Calcium (mg/gram)	Calcium (mEq/gram)	% Calcium
Calcium carbonate	400	20	40
Calcium chloride	272	13.6	27.2
Calcium citrate	211	10.5	21.1
Calcium glubionate	65	3.2	6.5
Calcium gluceptate	82	4.1	8.2
Calcium gluconate	90	4.5	9
Calcium lactate	130	6.5	13
Calcium phosphate			
Dibasic	230	11.5	23
Tribasic	380	19	38

The following table includes the number of tablets of each calcium salt required to provide 1000 mg of elemental calcium:

Calcium supplement	Amount of salt in tablet (in milligrams)	Amount of calcium per tablet (in milligrams)	Number of tablets to provide 1000 milligrams of calcium
Calcium carbonate	625	250	4
	650	260	4
	750	300	4
	835	334	3
	1250	500	2
	1500	600	2
Calcium citrate	950	200	5
Calcium gluconate	500	45	22
	650	58	17
	1000	90	11
Calcium lactate	325	42	24
	650	84	12
Calcium phosphate, dibasic	500	115	9
Calcium phosphate tribasic	800	304	4
	1600	608	2

Administration of calcium supplements should not preclude the use of other measures intended to correct the underlying cause of calcium depletion.

In the prevention of osteoporosis, postmenopausal women are sometimes also given estrogens to prevent bone resorption and/or small doses of vitamin D (usually 400 IU per day) to enhance calcium absorption. If estrogens are prescribed, either cyclically or continuously for women who have not undergone a hysterectomy, it is recommended that a progestin such as medroxyprogesterone acetate also be given to reduce or prevent the possibility of adverse endometrial changes from occurring.

The Food and Drug Administration has issued warnings that bonemeal and dolomite (sometimes used as sources of calcium) may contain lead in sufficient quantities to be dangerous.

For parenteral dosage forms only

The injection should be warmed to body temperature prior to administration, unless precluded by an emergency situation. Following
injection, the patient should remain recumbent for a short period of
time to prevent dizziness.

Parenteral calcium salts are administered by *slow* intravenous injection (excepting calcium glycerophosphate and calcium lactate combination which is given by intramuscular injection) to prevent a
high concentration of calcium from reaching the heart and causing
cardiac syncope.

Side effects experienced by the conscious patient are often the result
of too rapid a rate of intravenous administration of calcium salts.
Administration should be temporarily discontinued with the appearance of abnormal electrocardiogram (ECG) readings or with
patient complaints of discomfort; administration may be resumed
when the abnormal reading or the discomfort has disappeared.

Severe necrosis, requiring skin grafting, and calcification can occur at
the site of infiltration after intravenous injection, especially after
push injection.

Transient increases in blood pressure, especially in the elderly or
patients with hypertension, may occur during intravenous administration of calcium salts.

Diet/Nutrition

Oral calcium supplements are best taken 1 to 1½ hours after meals in
3 to 4 daily doses. However, calcium glubionate syrup should be
administered before meals to enhance absorption.

In the elderly, who may be more prone than younger patients to
impaired stomach acid production, calcium absorption may be
increased by the use of a more soluble calcium salt, such as calcium citrate, gluconate, or lactate. The poor solubility of carbonate
and phosphate salts makes them less desirable as antihypocalcemic
agents in patients with known achlorhydria or hypochlorhydria.

The recommended dietary allowances (RDA) of calcium a day are as
follows:

Infants and children—
    Birth to 6 months: 400 mg.
    6 months to 1 year: 600 mg.
    1 to 10 years: 800 mg.
Adolescent and adult males—
    11 to 24 years: 1200 mg.
    24 years and over: 800 mg.
Adolescent and adult females—
    11 to 24 years: 1200 mg.
    24 years and over: 800 mg.
Pregnant women—1200 mg.
Breast-feeding women—1200 mg.

The following table indicates the calcium content of selected foods:

Food (amount)	Milligrams of calcium
Nonfat dry milk, reconstituted (1 cup)	375
Lowfat, skim, or whole milk (1 cup)	290 to 300
Yogurt (1 cup)	275 to 400
Sardines with bones (3 ounces)	370
Ricotta cheese, part skim (½ cup)	340
Salmon, canned, with bones (3 ounces)	285
Cheese, Swiss (1 ounce)	272
Cheese, cheddar (1 ounce)	204
Cheese, American (1 ounce)	174
Cottage cheese, lowfat (1 cup)	154
Tofu (4 ounces)	154
Shrimp (1 cup)	147
Ice milk (¾ cup)	132

CALCIUM CARBONATE

Summary of Differences

Category: Also used as an antihyperphosphatemic and as an antacid
(see *Calcium Carbonate, Antacids [Oral-Local]*).

Precautions:

Drug interactions and/or related problems—Concurrent use with
ciprofloxacin those medicines may decrease the absorption of
ciprofloxacin, norfloxacin, or ofloxacin, resulting in lower serum and urine concentrations of ciprofloxacin, norfloxacin, or
ofloxacin.

Contraindications/Medical problems—Calcium absorption may be
decreased in patients with achlorhydria or hypochlorhydria,
unless the supplement is taken with meals.

Additional Dosing Information

See also *General Dosing Information.*

Calcium carbonate contains the equivalent of 400 mg of calcium ion
per gram.

Oral Dosage Forms

Note: Bracketed uses in the *Dosage Forms* section refer to categories
of use and/or indications that are not included in U.S. product
labeling.

CALCIUM CARBONATE CAPSULES

Usual adult dose:

Antihypocalcemic or

Nutritional supplement (mineral)—Oral, 1.25 to 1.5 grams (500 to
600 mg of calcium ion) one to three times a day with or after
meals.

Antacid—See *Calcium Carbonate, Antacids (Oral-Local).*

[Antihyperphosphatemic]—Oral, 5 to 13 grams (2 to 5.2 grams of
calcium ion) a day, in divided doses with meals.

Note: Careful titration is recommended to prevent hypercalcemia, which has been reported with doses above 2 grams
of calcium ion a day.

Auxiliary labeling: • Drink a full glass of water.

CALCIUM CARBONATE ORAL SUSPENSION USP

Usual adult dose:

Antihypocalcemic or

Nutritional supplement (mineral)—Oral, 1.25 grams (500 mg of
calcium ion) one to three times a day with or after meals.

Antacid—See *Calcium Carbonate, Antacids (Oral-Local).*

[Antihyperphosphatemic]—Oral, 5 to 13 grams (2 to 5.2 grams of
calcium ion) a day, in divided doses with meals.

Note: Careful titration is recommended to prevent hypercalcemia, which has been reported with doses above 2 grams
of calcium ion a day.

Auxiliary labeling:
• Shake well before using.
• Drink a full glass of water.

CALCIUM CARBONATE TABLETS USP

Usual adult dose:

Antihypocalcemic or

Nutritional supplement (mineral)—Oral, 1.25 gram (500 mg of
calcium ion) one to three times a day with or after meals.

Antacid—See *Calcium Carbonate, Antacids (Oral-Local).*

[Antihyperphosphatemic]—Oral, 5 to 13 grams (2 to 5.2 grams of
calcium ion) a day, in divided doses with meals.

Note: Careful titration is recommended to prevent hypercalcemia, which has been reported with doses above 2 grams of calcium ion a day.

Auxiliary labeling: • Drink a full glass of water.

CALCIUM CARBONATE TABLETS USP (CHEWABLE)

Usual adult dose:

Antihypocalcemic or

Nutritional supplement (mineral)—Oral, 1.25 grams (500 mg of calcium ion) one to three times a day with or after meals.

Antacid—See *Calcium Carbonate, Antacids (Oral-Local).*

[Antihyperphosphatemic]—Oral, 5 to 13 grams (2 to 5.2 grams of calcium ion) a day, in divided doses with meals.

Note: Careful titration is recommended to prevent hypercalcemia, which has been reported with doses above 2 grams of calcium ion a day.

Auxiliary labeling:
• Chew tablets before swallowing.
• Drink a full glass of water.

CALCIUM CARBONATE (OYSTER-SHELL DERIVED) TABLETS

Usual adult dose:

Antihypocalcemic or

Nutritional supplement (mineral)—Oral, 1.25 gram (500 mg of calcium ion) one to three times a day with or after meals.

Antacid—See *Calcium Carbonate, Antacids (Oral-Local).*

[Antihyperphosphatemic]—Oral, 5 to 13 grams (2 to 5.2 grams of calcium ion) a day, in divided doses with meals.

Note: Careful titration is recommended to prevent hypercalcemia, which has been reported with doses above 2 grams of calcium ion a day.

Auxiliary labeling: • Drink a full glass of water.

CALCIUM CARBONATE (OYSTER-SHELL DERIVED) TABLETS (CHEWABLE)

Usual adult dose:

Antihypocalcemic or

Nutritional supplement (mineral)—Oral, 1.25 grams (500 mg of calcium ion) one to three times a day with or after meals.

Antacid—See *Calcium Carbonate, Antacids (Oral-Local).*

[Antihyperphosphatemic]—Oral, 5 to 13 grams (2 to 5.2 grams of calcium ion) a day, in divided doses with meals.

Note: Careful titration is recommended to prevent hypercalcemia, which has been reported with doses above 2 grams of calcium ion a day.

Auxiliary labeling:
• Chew tablets before swallowing.
• Drink a full glass of water.

CALCIUM CHLORIDE

Summary of Differences

Category: Also used as an electrolyte replenisher, a cardiotonic, an antihyperkalemic, and an antihypermagnesemic.

Precautions:

Pediatrics—Parenteral calcium chloride use is usually restricted in pediatric patients due to possibility of irritation in small vasculature.

Side/adverse effects: Causes peripheral vasodilation with moderate decrease in blood pressure.

General dosing information: Has three times as much calcium per mL as calcium gluconate injection.

Additional Dosing Information

See also *General Dosing Information.*

For intravenous use only; not to be administered intramuscularly, intramyocardially, subcutaneously, or permitted to extravasate into any body tissue; may cause severe tissue necrosis and/or sloughing and abscess formation.

Injected through a small-bore needle inserted into a large vein to minimize irritation.

Calcium chloride contains 272 mg of calcium ion per gram.

Parenteral Dosage Forms

CALCIUM CHLORIDE INJECTION USP

Usual adult dose:

Antihypocalcemic or

Electrolyte replenisher—Intravenous, 500 mg to 1 gram (136 to 272 mg of calcium ion) administered slowly at a rate not to exceed 0.5 mL (13.6 mg of calcium ion) to 1 mL (27.2 mg of calcium ion) a minute, the dosage being repeated at intervals of one to three days as indicated by patient response and serum calcium concentrations.

Note: For use in cases such as hungry bones syndrome, some clinicians recommend that calcium chloride be diluted in saline or dextrose and given by continuous intravenous infusion at a dosage of 0.5 to 1 mg per minute (up to 2 or more mg per minute). The rate and/or concentration can be adjusted until oral calcium supplements can be given.

Cardiotonic—

Intravenous, 500 mg to 1 gram (136 to 272 mg of calcium ion) administered at a rate not to exceed 1 mL (27.2 mg of calcium ion) a minute.

Intraventricular, 200 to 800 mg (54.4 mg to 217.6 mg of calcium ion) administered directly into cavity as a single dose.

Note: Injection into the cardiac muscle must be avoided.

Antihyperkalemic—Dosage must be titrated by constant monitoring of ECG changes during administration.

Antihypermagnesemic—Intravenous, initially 500 mg (136 mg of calcium ion) repeated as indicated by patient response.

CALCIUM CITRATE

Summary of Differences

Indications:

May reduce risk of kidney stones in susceptible patients.

Also used to treat hyperphosphatenia in renal osteodystrophy

Additional Dosing Information

See also *General Dosing Information.*

Calcium citrate contains 211 mg of calcium ion per gram.

Oral Dosage Forms

CALCIUM CITRATE TABLETS

Usual adult and adolescent dose:

Antihypocalcemic—Oral, 950 mg to 1.9 grams (200 to 400 mg of calcium ion, respectively) two to four times a day after meals.

Nutritional supplement (mineral)—Oral, 3.8 to 7.1 grams (800 to 1500 mg of calcium ion, respectively) a day in three or four divided doses.

Auxiliary labeling: • Drink a full glass of water.

CALCIUM CITRATE EFFERVESCENT TABLETS

Usual adult and adolescent dose:
Antihypocalcemic—Oral, 2.38 grams (500 mg of calcium ion) two to four times a day after meals.
Nutritional supplement (mineral)—Oral, 2.38 to 7.10 grams (500 to 1500 mg of calcium ion) a day in three or four divided doses.

Auxiliary labeling: • Take dissolved in glass of water.

CALCIUM GLUBIONATE

Summary of Differences

Category: Injection also used as an electrolyte replenisher, a cardiotonic, an antihyperkalemic, and an antihypermagnesemic.

Oral Dosage Forms

CALCIUM GLUBIONATE SYRUP USP

Usual adult and adolescent dose: Antihypocalcemic—Oral, 5.4 grams (345 mg of calcium ion) three to four times a day before meals.

Parenteral Dosage Form

CALCIUM GLUBIONATE INJECTION USP

Usual adult and adolescent dose:
Antihypocalcemic or
Electrolyte replenisher—
Intramuscular, 1.375 grams (90 mg of calcium ion) administered by deep injection, one to three times a day.
Note: Injections should be given in the gluteus minimus muscle.
Intravenous, 1.375 grams (90 mg of calcium ion) administered slowly over three minutes, one to three times a day.
Note: In emergencies, up to 2.75 grams (180 mg calcium ion) may be given once daily.
Cardiotonic—Intracardiac (intraventricular), 412.5 to 687.5 mg (27 to 45 mg of calcium ion); may be repeated at short intervals if necessary.

CALCIUM GLUCEPTATE

Summary of Differences

Category: Also used as an electrolyte replenisher and as an antihypermagnesemic.
Precautions: Pediatrics—Administered intramuscularly to infants and children only in emergencies when intravenous route is technically impossible.

Additional Dosing Information

See also *General Dosing Information*.
Calcium gluceptate contains 82 mg of calcium ion per gram.
May also be administered intramuscularly to adults.

Parenteral Dosage Forms

Note: Bracketed uses in the *Dosage Forms* section refer to categories of use and/or indications that are not included in U.S. product labeling.

CALCIUM GLUCEPTATE INJECTION USP

Usual adult dose:
Antihypocalcemic or
Electrolyte replenisher—
Intramuscular, 440 mg to 1.1 gram (36 to 90 mg of calcium ion).
Note: When a dose of 5 mL (90 mg of calcium ion) or more is administered, injection should be in the gluteal region.
Intravenous, 1.1 to 4.4 grams (90 to 360 mg of calcium ion) administered slowly at a rate not to exceed 2 mL (36 mg of calcium ion) a minute.
[Antihypermagnesemic]—Intravenous, initially 1.2 to 2.4 grams (98 to 196 mg of calcium ion) administered slowly at a rate not to exceed 2 mL (36 mg of calcium ion) a minute.

CALCIUM GLUCEPTATE AND CALCIUM GLUCONATE

Oral Dosage Forms

CALCIUM GLUCEPTATE AND CALCIUM GLUCONATE ORAL SOLUTION

Usual adult and adolescent dose:
Nutritional deficiency—Oral, 2.64 grams calcium gluceptate and, 2.24 grams calcium gluconate (total of 400 mg calcium ion), three to four times a day.
Nutritional supplement—Oral, 1.32 grams calcium gluceptate and, 1.12 grams calcium gluconate (total of 200 mg of calcium ion), one to three times a day.

CALCIUM GLUCONATE

Summary of Differences

Category: Injection may also be used as an electrolyte replenisher, a cardiotonic, an antihyperkalemic, and an antihypermagnesemic.

Additional Dosing Information

See also *General Dosing Information*.
Calcium gluconate injection is for intravenous use only; it is not to be administered intramuscularly, intramyocardially, subcutaneously, or permitted to extravasate into any body tissue; may cause severe tissue necrosis and/or sloughing, and abscess formation.
Calcium gluconate contains 90 mg of calcium ion per gram.

Oral Dosage Forms

CALCIUM GLUCONATE TABLETS USP (CHEWABLE)

Usual adult dose:
Antihypocalcemic or
Nutritional supplement—Oral, 8.8 to 16.5 grams (800 to 1500 mg of calcium ion) a day, in divided doses.

Auxiliary labeling:
- Chew tablets before swallowing.
- Drink a full glass of water.

Parenteral Dosage Forms

Note: Bracketed uses in the *Dosage Forms* section refer to categories of use and/or indications that are not included in U.S. product labeling.

CALCIUM GLUCONATE INJECTION USP

Usual adult dose:
Antihypocalcemic or
Electrolyte replenisher—Intravenous, 970 mg (94.7 mg of calcium ion), administered slowly at a rate not to exceed 5 mL (47.5 mg of calcium ion) a minute. The dosage may be repeated, if necessary, until tetany is controlled.

Note: For use in cases such as hungry bones syndrome, some clinicians recommend that calcium gluconate be diluted in isotonic solution and given by continuous intravenous infusion at a dosage of 0.5 to 1 mg per minute (up to 2 or more mg per minute). The rate and/or concentration can be adjusted until oral calcium supplements can be given.

Antihyperkalemic—Intravenous, 1 to 2 grams (94.7 to 189 mg of calcium ion), administered slowly at a rate not to exceed 5 mL (47.5 mg of calcium ion) a minute, the dosage being titrated and adjusted by constant monitoring of ECG changes during administration.

[Antihypermagnesemic]—Intravenous, 1 to 2 grams (94.7 to 189 mg of calcium ion), administered at a rate not to exceed 5 mL (47.5 mg of calcium ion) a minute.

Usual adult prescribing limits: 15 grams (1.42 gram of calcium ion) a day.

Additional information: Injection also contains 3.5 mg of calcium d-saccharate tetrahydrate per mL for stabilization.

CALCIUM GLYCEROPHOSPHATE AND CALCIUM LACTATE

Additional Dosing Information

See also *General Dosing Information.*
Intramuscular administration does not produce inflammation or sloughing at site of injection.

Parenteral Dosage Forms

CALCIUM GLYCEROPHOSPHATE AND CALCIUM LACTATE INJECTION

Usual adult and adolescent dose: Antihypocalcemic—Intramuscular, initially 10 mL one or two times a week for four to five weeks, the dosage being repeated as needed to raise serum calcium concentrations.

Note: May also be administered intravenously or subcutaneously because of neutral pH (approximately 7).

Additional information: Contains phenol 0.25% as a preservative.

CALCIUM LACTATE

Additional Dosing Information

See also *General Dosing Information.*
Calcium lactate contains 130 mg of calcium ion per gram.

Oral Dosage Forms

CALCIUM LACTATE TABLETS USP

Usual adult and adolescent dose: Antihypocalcemic—Oral, 7.7 grams (1 gram of calcium ion) a day, in divided doses.

Auxiliary labeling: • Drink a full glass of water.

CALCIUM LACTATE-GLUCONATE AND CALCIUM CARBONATE

Oral Dosage Forms

CALCIUM LACTATE-GLUCONATE AND CALCIUM CARBONATE EFFERVESCENT TABLETS

Usual adult and adolescent dose:
Nutritional deficiency—Oral, 5.88 grams calcium lactate-gluconate, and 600 mg calcium carbonate (total of 1 gram of calcium ion) two times a day.
Nutritional supplement—Oral, 2.94 grams calcium lactate-gluconate, and 300 mg calcium carbonate (total of 500 mg of calcium ion) to 5.88 grams calcium lactate-gluconate, and 600 mg calcium carbonate (total of 1 gram of calcium ion) a day.

DIBASIC CALCIUM PHOSPHATE

Summary of Differences

Contraindications/Medical problems:
Calcium absorption may be decreased in patients with achlorhydria or hypochlorhydria, unless the supplement is taken with meals.
Risk of hyperphosphatemia may be increased in patients with hypoparathyroidism or renal insufficiency.

Additional Dosing Information

See also *General Dosing Information.*
Dibasic calcium phosphate contains 230 mg of calcium ion per gram.

Oral Dosage Forms

DIBASIC CALCIUM PHOSPHATE TABLETS USP

Usual adult and adolescent dose: Antihypocalcemic—Oral, 4.4 grams (1 gram of calcium ion) a day with or after meals, in divided doses.

Auxiliary labeling: • Drink a full glass of water.

TRIBASIC CALCIUM PHOSPHATE

Summary of Differences

Contraindications/Medical problems:

Calcium absorption may be decreased in patients with achlorhydria or hypochlorhydria, unless the supplement is taken with meals.

Risk of hyperphosphatemia may be increased in patients with hypoparathyroidism or renal insufficiency.

Additional Dosing Information

See also *General Dosing Information.*

Tribasic calcium phosphate contains 380 mg of calcium ion per gram.

Oral Dosage Forms

TRIBASIC CALCIUM PHOSPHATE TABLETS

Usual adult dose: Antihypocalcemic—Oral, 1.6 grams (600 mg of calcium ion) two times a day with or after meals.

Auxiliary labeling: • Drink a full glass of water.

CAPSAICIN   Topical

Some commonly used *brand names* are:

In the U.S.—*Zostrix; Zostrix-HP*

In Canada—*Axsain; Zostrix*

TOPICAL

Capsaicin Cream

In the U.S.—*Zostrix; Zostrix-HP*

In Canada—*Axsain; Zostrix*

Category: Antineuralgic, specific pain syndromes (topical); analgesic, specific pain syndromes (topical).

Indications

Note: Bracketed information in the *Indications* section refers to uses not included in U.S. product labeling.

Accepted

Neuralgia (treatment)—Capsaicin is indicated for the treatment of neuralgias, such as the pain following herpes zoster (shingles) and painful diabetic neuropathy.

Osteoarthritis (treatment); or

Rheumatoid arthritis (treatment)—Capsaicin is indicated for the treatment of pain from osteoarthritis and rheumatoid arthritis.

[Pain, neurogenic, other (treatment)]—Capsaicin is used to treat the pain associated with postmastectomy pain syndrome (PMPS) and reflex sympathetic dystrophy syndrome (RSDS, causalgia).

Pharmacology

Mechanism of action/Effect: The precise mechanism of action has not been fully elucidated. Capsaicin is a neuropeptide-active agent that affects the synthesis, storage, transport, and release of substance P. Substance P is thought to be the principal chemical mediator of pain impulses from the periphery to the central nervous system. In addition, substance P has been shown to be released into joint tissues where it activates inflammatory intermediates that are involved with the development of rheumatoid arthritis. Capsaicin renders skin and joints insensitive to pain by depleting and preventing reaccumulation of substance P in peripheral sensory neurons. With the depletion of substance P in the nerve endings, local pain impulses cannot be transmitted to the brain.

Note: Capsaicin is not a local anesthetic, since it only blocks the conduction of painful impulses carried by the type-C fibers, whereas local anesthetics block the conduction of impulses in all afferent neurons, which impairs all sensations including touch, pressure, heat, and vibration.

Capsaicin is not a traditional counterirritant, since it does not produce vasodilation.

Precautions to Consider

Geriatrics

Appropriate studies on the relationship of age to the effects of capsaicin have not been performed in the geriatric population. However, geriatrics-specific problems that would limit the usefulness of this medication in the elderly are not expected.

Contraindications/Medical problems

The contraindications/medical problems included have been selected on the basis of their potential clinical significance (reasons given in parentheses where appropriate)—not necessarily inclusive (» = major clinical significance).

Except under special circumstances, this medication should not be used when the following medical problem exists:

» Broken or irritated skin on area to be treated
  (will cause pain and further irritation of skin)

Risk-benefit should be considered when the following medical problem exists:

Sensitivity to capsaicin or to the fruits of capsicum plants (e.g., hot peppers)

Side/Adverse Effects

Note: Capsaicin has no known systemic side effects.

Patients may experience a warm, stinging, or burning sensation at the site of application, especially during the initial few days of use. Although this sensation frequently disappears after the first several days of treatment, it may persist for 2 to 4 weeks or longer. This effect is related to the initial excitatory effect of capsaicin on type-C fibers and their release of substance P. The burning usually decreases in frequency and intensity with continued administration of capsaicin. However, application schedules of capsaicin of less than 3 or 4 times daily may prolong the the burning sensation while not providing optimum pain relief. Environmental factors, such as heat or humidity; wrappings, such as clothing or bandages; bathing in warm water; or sweating may intensify the sensation. The incidence of the burning sensation has been variable in different studies. This may be related to the etiology and pathogenesis of the pain syndrome in different persons. For example, patients with arthritis generally experience less intense burning than do patients with peripheral neuropathies.

Removal of clothing or bedsheets that have covered the area of topical capsaicin application has been associated rarely with respiratory irritation, such as coughing, in the patient and by-standers who were present at the time. This has been attributed to the inhalation of the residue of the dried cream.

There is some concern that capsaicin may be potentially neuro-toxic, although animal and clinical studies with topical capsaicin have not shown this to occur. Capsaicin is thought to be capable of elevating the heat-pain threshold in the treated skin areas, especially in patients with diabetic neuropathy; these patients often already have an elevated threshold for heat and pain.

The following side/adverse effects have been selected on the basis of their potential clinical significance (possible signs and symptoms in parentheses where appropriate)—not necessarily inclusive:

Those indicating need for medical attention only if they continue or are bothersome
Incidence more frequent
Warm, stinging, or burning sensation at the site of application

Patient Consultation

In providing consultation, consider emphasizing the following se-lected information (» = major clinical significance):

Before using this medication
» Conditions affecting use, especially:
     Sensitivity to capsaicin or to the fruits of capsicum plants (e.g., hot peppers)
     Use in children—Not recommended in infants and children up to 2 years of age, except under the direction of a physician
     Other medical problems, especially broken or irritated skin on area to be treated

Proper use of this medication
     If using capsaicin for treatment of neuralgia due to herpes zoster, not applying medicine until after zoster sores have healed
     Washing areas to be treated will not cause harm, but is not neces-sary
     Rubbing cream into the affected area well so that little or no cream is left on surface of skin
     Washing hands with soap and water after applying capsaicin to avoid getting medicine in eyes or on other sensitive areas of body; however, if medication used on arthritic hands, not wash-ing hands for at least 30 minutes after application
     If bandage is being used, not applying tightly
     Warm, stinging, or burning sensation may occur and is related to the action of capsaicin on the skin; usually disappears after first several days of treatment, however, may last 2 to 4 weeks or longer; heat, humidity, clothing, bathing in warm water, or sweating may increase sensation; sensation usually lessens in frequency and intensity the longer medication is used; reducing number of daily doses of capsaicin will not lessen sensation, and may prolong period of time that sensation occurs; reducing number of doses also will reduce amount of pain relief ob-tained
     Relief from pain may not occur right away; also, time it takes for capsaicin to work differs depending on type of pain; with ar-thritis, pain relief usually begins within 1 or 2 weeks; with neuralgia, pain relief usually begins within 2 to 4 weeks; with head and neck neuralgias, pain relief may take 4 to 6 weeks

     Using capsaicin 3 or 4 times a day or as directed by doctor; pain relief will last only as long as capsaicin is used regularly; if medicine is discontinued and pain recurs, capsaicin treatment may be restarted
» Proper dosage
     Missed dose: Using as soon as possible; if almost time for next dose, skipping missed dose and returning to regular dosing schedule; not doubling doses
» Proper storage

Precautions while using this medication
     If capsaicin gets into eyes, flushing with water; if capsaicin gets on other sensitive areas of body, washing with warm (not hot) soapy water
     If condition worsens, or does not improve after 1 month, discon-tinuing use and checking with physician

General Dosing Information

The cream should be applied sparingly and rubbed well into the af-fected area so that little or no cream is left on the surface of the skin.

During the first 1 or 2 weeks of treatment, application of a topical lidocaine product before capsaicin application may reduce initial discomfort.

A therapeutic pain response is usually achieved within 14 to 28 days. Most patients with arthritis notice an initial response within 1 or 2 weeks. Most patients with neuralgia pain begin to respond within 2 to 4 weeks, although patients with pain from head and neck neural-gias may take 4 to 6 weeks to respond.

Continued application of capsaicin 3 or 4 times daily is necessary to sustain pain relief. If the medicine is discontinued and pain recurs, capsaicin treatment may be restarted.

Persons using capsaicin to treat arthritis in their hands should avoid washing their hands for at least 30 minutes after application.

When capsaicin is used for the treatment of neuralgia due to herpes zoster, it should not be applied to the skin until after the zoster lesions have healed.

If a bandage is being used on the treated area, it should not be applied tightly.

Topical Dosage Forms

CAPSAICIN CREAM

Usual adult and adolescent dose: Topical, to the affected area, three or four times a day.

Auxiliary labeling:
- For external use only.
- Avoid contact with eyes.

CARBACHOL   Ophthalmic

Some commonly used *brand names* in the U.S. and Canada are *Isopto Carbachol* and *Miostat.*

Another commonly used name is carbamylcholine.

OPHTHALMIC
Carbachol Intraocular Solution USP
  In the U.S. and Canada—*Miostat*
Carbachol Ophthalmic Solution USP
  In the U.S. and Canada—*Isopto Carbachol*

Category

Antiglaucoma agent (ophthalmic)—Carbachol Ophthalmic Solution USP.
Miotic—Carbachol Intraocular Solution USP; Carbachol Ophthalmic Solution USP.

Indications

Note: Bracketed information in the *Indications* section refers to uses not included in U.S. product labeling.

Accepted
Miosis induction, during surgery—Carbachol intraocular solution is indicated to produce pupillary miosis during surgery.

Glaucoma, open-angle (treatment)—Carbachol ophthalmic solution is indicated for lowering intraocular pressure in the treatment of chronic open-angle glaucoma. It is especially useful as a replacement drug, particularly in eyes that have become intolerant of, or resistant to, pilocarpine.

[Glaucoma, angle-closure (treatment)][1]—Carbachol ophthalmic solution is used for emergency treatment of angle-closure glaucoma; however, pilocarpine is usually preferred.

[Glaucoma, angle-closure, *during* or *after* iridectomy (treatment)][1]—Carbachol ophthalmic solution is used in the treatment of angle-closure glaucoma during or after iridectomy.

[Glaucoma, secondary (treatment)][1]—Carbachol ophthalmic solution is used in the treatment of secondary glaucoma if there is no active intraocular inflammation present.

[1]Not included in Canadian product labeling.

Pharmacology

Mechanism of action/Effect:
Carbachol is a parasympathomimetic that directly stimulates cholinergic receptors. It may also act indirectly by promoting release of acetylcholine and by a weak anticholinesterase action. Carbachol produces contraction of the iris sphincter muscle resulting in pupillary constriction (miosis), constriction of the ciliary muscle resulting in increased accommodation, and a reduction in intraocular pressure associated with decreased resistance to aqueous humor outflow.

In chronic open-angle glaucoma, the exact mechanism by which carbachol lowers intraocular pressure is not precisely known; however, contraction of the ciliary muscle apparently opens the intertrabecular spaces and facilitates aqueous humor outflow.

In angle-closure glaucoma, constriction of the pupil apparently pulls the iris away from the trabeculum, thereby relieving blockage of the trabecular meshwork.

Onset of action: Ophthalmic solution—Miosis: Within 10 to 20 minutes.

Time to peak effect:
Intraocular solution—Miosis: Within 2 to 5 minutes.
Ophthalmic solution—Reduction in intraocular pressure: Within 4 hours.

Duration of action:
Intraocular solution—Miosis: About 24 hours.
Ophthalmic solution—
  Miosis: About 4 to 8 hours.
  Reduction in intraocular pressure: About 8 hours.

Precautions to Consider

Geriatrics
Appropriate studies on the relationship of age to the effects of carbachol have not been performed in the geriatric population. However, no geriatrics-specific problems have been documented to date.

Drug interactions and/or related problems
The following drug interactions and/or related problems have been selected on the basis of their potential clinical significance (possible mechanism in parentheses where appropriate)—not necessarily inclusive (» = major clinical significance):

Note: Combinations containing any of the following medications, depending on the amount present, may also interact with this medication.

Belladonna alkaloids, ophthalmic, or
Cyclopentolate
    (concurrent use of these medications may interfere with the antiglaucoma action of carbachol. Also, concurrent use with carbachol counteracts the mydriatic effects of these medications; this counteraction may be used to therapeutic advantage)

Flurbiprofen, ophthalmic
    (ophthalmic carbachol may be ineffective when administered following ophthalmic flurbiprofen; the pharmacologic basis for this interference is not known)

Contraindications/Medical problems
The contraindications/medical problems included have been selected on the basis of their potential clinical significance (reasons given in parentheses where appropriate)—not necessarily inclusive (» = major clinical significance).

Risk-benefit should be considered when the following medical problems exist:

Asthma, bronchial

Cardiac failure, acute

Corneal abrasion or injury
    (possible excessive absorption of medication, which can produce systemic toxicity)

Gastrointestinal spasm

Hyperthyroidism

» Iritis, acute, or other conditions in which pupillary constriction is undesirable

Parkinson's disease

Peptic ulcer, active

Sensitivity to carbachol

Urinary tract obstruction

Side/Adverse Effects

The following side/adverse effects have been selected on the basis of their potential clinical significance (possible signs and symptoms in parentheses where appropriate)—not necessarily inclusive:

Note: The following side effects have not been reported following the use of Carbachol Intraocular Solution USP.

Those indicating need for medical attention

Symptoms of systemic absorption

Asthma (shortness of breath, wheezing, or tightness in chest); *diarrhea, stomach cramps or pain, or vomiting; flushing or redness of face; frequent urge to urinate; increased sweating; watering of mouth*

Those indicating need for medical attention only if they continue or are bothersome

Incidence more frequent

Blurred vision or change in near or distant vision; eye pain

Incidence less frequent

Headache; irritation of eyes; twitching of eyelids

Patient Consultation

In providing consultation, consider emphasizing the following selected information (» = major clinical significance):

Before using this medication

» Conditions affecting use, especially:
  Sensitivity to carbachol
  Other medical problems, especially acute iritis or other conditions in which pupillary constriction is undesirable

Proper use of this medication

For the ophthalmic solution

» Importance of not using more medication than the amount prescribed
  Proper administration technique
  Washing hands immediately after applying eye drops
  Preventing contamination: Not touching applicator tip to any surface; keeping container tightly closed
  Missed dose: Applying as soon as possible; not applying if almost time for next dose; applying next dose at regularly scheduled time
» Proper storage

Precautions while using this medication

For the ophthalmic solution

  Regular visits to physician to check eye pressure during therapy
» Caution if driving or doing anything else at night or in dim light

» Caution if blurred vision or change in near or distant vision occurs

Side/adverse effects

  Signs of potential side effects, especially symptoms of systemic absorption

General Dosing Information

For ophthalmic solution

Although some manufacturers recommend a dose of 2 drops of an ophthalmic solution at appropriate intervals, the conjunctival sac will usually hold only 1 drop.

More frequent instillation or use of a stronger solution may be required to produce an adequate reduction in intraocular pressure in eyes with hazel or brown irides than is needed in eyes with blue or light-colored irides.

To avoid excessive systemic absorption, patient should press finger to the lacrimal sac during and for 1 or 2 minutes following instillation of medication.

Tolerance to carbachol may develop with prolonged use. Effectiveness may be restored by changing to another miotic for a short time and then resuming the original medication.

Ophthalmic Dosage Forms

CARBACHOL INTRAOCULAR SOLUTION USP

Usual adult and adolescent dose: Miotic—Intraocular irrigation, no more than 0.5 mL of a 0.01% solution instilled into the anterior chamber.

Usual geriatric dose: See *Usual adult and adolescent dose.*

Auxiliary labeling:
• For single-dose intraocular use only.
• Discard unused portion.

CARBACHOL OPHTHALMIC SOLUTION USP

Usual adult and adolescent dose: Antiglaucoma agent (ophthalmic)—Topical, to the conjunctiva, 1 drop of a 0.75 to 3% solution one to three times a day.

Usual geriatric dose: See *Usual adult and adolescent dose.*

Auxiliary labeling:
• For the eye.
• Keep container tightly closed.

CARBAMAZEPINE   Systemic

Some commonly used *brand names* are:

In the U.S.—
  Epitol
  Tegretol

In Canada—
  Apo-Carbamazepine   *Tegretol*
  Mazepine   *Tegretol Chewtabs*
  Novocarbamaz   *Tegretol CR*
  PMS Carbamazepine

ORAL
Carbamazepine Oral Suspension†
  In the U.S.—*Tegretol*

Carbamazepine Tablets USP
  In the U.S.—*Epitol; Tegretol;* GENERIC
  In Canada—*Apo-Carbamazepine; Mazepine; Novocarbamaz; PMS Carbamazepine; Tegretol*
Carbamazepine Tablets USP (Chewable)
  In the U.S.—*Tegretol;* GENERIC
  In Canada—*Tegretol Chewtabs*
Carbamazepine Extended-release Tablets*
  In Canada—*Tegretol CR*

---

*Not commercially available in the U.S.
†Not commercially available in Canada.

Category: Anticonvulsant; antineuralgic (specific pain syndromes); antimanic; antidiuretic; antipsychotic.

Indications

Note: Bracketed information in the *Indications* section refers to uses not included in U.S. product labeling.

Accepted

Epilepsy (treatment)—Carbamazepine is indicated for the treatment of partial seizures with simple or complex symptomatology (psychomotor, temporal lobe); generalized tonic-clonic seizures (grand mal); mixed seizure patterns that include the above; or other partial or generalized seizures.

Carbamazepine is a first-choice anticonvulsant because of its relatively low behavioral and psychological toxicity and the rarity of serious adverse effects.

Neuralgia, trigeminal (treatment)—Carbamazepine is indicated for relief of pain due to true trigeminal neuralgia (tic douloureux) and glossopharyngeal neuralgia.

[Pain, neurogenic, other (treatment)][1]—Carbamazepine may also be used in some patients to relieve the lightning pains of tabes dorsalis; neuralgic pain associated with multiple sclerosis, acute idiopathic neuritis (Guillain-Barré syndrome), peripheral diabetic neuropathy, phantom limb, restless leg syndrome (Ekbom's syndrome), and hemifacial spasm; post-traumatic neuropathy or neuralgia; and postherpetic neuralgia.

[Bipolar disorder (prophylaxis and treatment)][1]—Carbamazepine is used alone or in combination with lithium and/or antidepressants or antipsychotics to treat patients with manic-depressive illness who are unresponsive to, or cannot tolerate, lithium or neuroleptics alone.

[Diabetes insipidus, central partial (treatment)][1]—Carbamazepine is used alone or with other agents such as clofibrate or chlorpropamide in the treatment of partial central diabetes insipidus.

[Alcohol withdrawal (treatment)][1]—Carbamazepine is used for the detoxification of alcoholics. It has been found to be effective in rapidly relieving anxiety and distress of acute alcohol withdrawal and for such symptoms as seizures, hyperexcitability, and sleep disturbances.

[Psychotic disorders (treatment)][1]—Carbamazepine has been shown to be effective in certain psychiatric disorders including schizoaffective illness, resistant schizophrenia, and dyscontrol syndrome, associated with limbic system dysfunction.

Unaccepted

Carbamazepine is not a simple analgesic and should not be used to relieve general aches or pains.

Carbamazepine is *not* indicated for atypical or generalized absence seizures (petit mal) or myoclonic or atonic seizures.

Although carbamazepine has also been reported to relieve dystonic attacks in children, reduce migraine attacks, and relieve intractable hiccups in some patients, its therapeutic efficacy in such cases has not been established.

Carbamazepine should not be used prophylactically during long periods of remission in trigeminal neuralgia.

---

[1]Not included in Canadian product labeling.

Pharmacology

Mechanism of action/Effect:

Anticonvulsant—Exact mechanism unknown; may act postsynaptically by limiting the ability of neurons to sustain high frequency repetitive firing of action potentials through enhancement of sodium channel inactivation; in addition to altering neuronal excitability, may act presynaptically to block the release of neurotransmitter by blocking presynaptic sodium channels and the firing of action potentials, which in turn decreases synaptic transmission.

Antineuralgic—Exact mechanism unknown; may involve gamma-aminobutyric acid (GABAB) receptors, which may be linked to calcium channels.

Antidiuretic—Exact mechanism unknown; may exert a hypothalamic effect on the osmoreceptors mediated via secretion of antidiuretic hormone (ADH), or may have a direct effect on the renal tubule.

Antimanic; antipsychotic—Exact mechanism unknown; may be related to either the anticonvulsant or the antineuralgic effects of carbamazepine, or to its effects on neurotransmitter modulator systems.

Other actions/effects: Anticholinergic, antidepressant, neuromuscular transmission-inhibiting, and antiarrhythmic actions have been reported.

Onset of action:

Anticonvulsant effect—Varies from hours to days, depending on individual patient. A stable therapeutic concentration may require a month to achieve due to autoinduction of metabolism.

Relief of pain of trigeminal neuralgia—8 to 72 hours.

Antimanic response—Usually 7 to 10 days.

Precautions to Consider

Cross-sensitivity and/or related problems

Patients who are sensitive to tricyclic antidepressants may be sensitive to carbamazepine also. Carbamazepine should be given with caution, if at all, to such patients.

Geriatrics

Geriatric patients may be more susceptible to carbamazepine-induced confusion or agitation, atrioventricular (AV) heart block, syndrome of inappropriate antidiuretic hormone (SIADH) and bradycardia than younger patients.

Dental

The leukopenic and thrombocytopenic effects of carbamazepine may result in an increased incidence of microbial infection, delayed healing, and gingival bleeding. If leukopenia or thrombocytopenia occurs, dental work should be deferred until blood counts have returned to normal. Patient instruction in proper oral hygiene should include caution in use of regular toothbrushes, dental floss, and toothpicks.

Drug interactions and/or related problems

The following drug interactions and/or related problems have been selected on the basis of their potential clinical significance (possible mechanism in parentheses where appropriate)—not necessarily inclusive (» = major clinical significance):

Note: Combinations containing any of the following medications, depending on the amount present, may also interact with this medication.

Acetaminophen
(risk of hepatotoxicity with single toxic doses or prolonged use of high doses of acetaminophen may be increased, and therapeutic effects of acetaminophen may be decreased, in patients taking hepatic enzyme-inducing agents such as carbamazepine)

» Adrenocorticoids, glucocorticoid and mineralocorticoid
(concurrent use may decrease the adrenocorticoid effect because of increased adrenocorticoid metabolism resulting from induction of hepatic microsomal enzymes)

Aminophylline or
Oxtriphylline or
Theophylline
(concurrent use with carbamazepine may stimulate hepatic metabolism of the xanthines [except dyphylline], resulting in increased theophylline clearance)

» Anticoagulants, coumarin- or indandione-derivative

(anticoagulant effects may be decreased because of induction of hepatic microsomal enzyme activity, resulting in increased anticoagulant metabolism leading to decreased anticoagulant serum concentration and elimination half-life; dosage adjustments based on monitoring of prothrombin time may be necessary during and after carbamazepine therapy)

» Anticonvulsants, hydantoin, or
» Anticonvulsants, succinimide, or
» Barbiturates or
» Benzodiazepines metabolized via hepatic microsomal enzymes, especially clonazepam, or
» Primidone or
» Valproic acid

(concurrent use with carbamazepine may result in increased metabolism, leading to decreased serum concentrations and reduced elimination half-lives of these medications because of induction of hepatic microsomal enzyme activity; monitoring of blood concentrations as a guide to dosage is recommended, especially when any of these medications or carbamazepine is added to or withdrawn from an existing regimen)

(valproic acid may prolong the half-life and reduce the protein-binding of carbamazepine; the concentration of the active 10,11-epoxide metabolite may be increased)

(in addition, use of carbamazepine in combination with other anticonvulsants has been reported to be associated with an increased risk of congenital defects)

» Antidepressants, tricyclic, or
Haloperidol or
Loxapine or
Maprotiline or
Molindone or
Phenothiazines or
Pimozide or
Thioxanthenes

(concurrent use of these agents with carbamazepine may enhance the CNS depressant effects of carbamazepine, lower the seizure threshold, and decrease the anticonvulsant effects of carbamazepine; dosage adjustments may be necessary to control seizures; anticholinergic effects may be potentiated, leading to confusion and delirium)

(also, concurrent use of haloperidol, and possibly other neuroleptics, with carbamazepine may decrease plasma concentrations of the neuroleptic by about 60% with or without adverse clinical effects; close observation of patient for clinical signs of ineffectiveness of the neuroleptic is recommended; dosage adjustment may be necessary)

Carbonic anhydrase inhibitors

(concurrent use may increase the risk of carbamazepine-induced osteopenia; it is recommended that patients receiving concurrent therapy be monitored for early signs of osteopenia and that the carbonic anhydrase inhibitor be discontinued and appropriate treatment initiated if necessary)

Chlorpropamide or
Clofibrate or
Desmopressin or
Lypressin or
Posterior pituitary or
Thiazide diuretics, when used for their paradoxical antidiuretic activity in the treatment of diabetes insipidus, or
Vasopressin

(concurrent use with carbamazepine may potentiate the antidiuretic effect, leading to a lower sodium concentration and causing adverse effects that include increased seizure activity; a reduction in dosage of either or both medications may be necessary for optimal therapeutic effect in the treatment of diabetes insipidus)

» Cimetidine

(concurrent use may result in increased plasma concentration of carbamazepine by delaying its clearance, leading to carbamazepine toxicity)

» Contraceptives, estrogen-containing, oral, or
Cyclosporine or
Dacarbazine or
Digitalis glycosides, with the possible exception of digoxin, or
Disopyramide or
» Estrogens, including estramustine, or
Levothyroxine or
Mexiletine or
» Quinidine

(concurrent use may decrease the effects of these medications because of increased metabolism resulting from induction of hepatic microsomal enzyme activity; dosage adjustments may be necessary)

(in addition, concurrent use of oral, estrogen-containing contraceptives with carbamazepine may result in breakthrough bleeding and contraceptive failure due to the increased rate of hepatic enzyme metabolism of steroids induced by carbamazepine; the dose of the estrogenic substance in the oral contraceptive may be increased to diminish bleeding and decrease the risk of conception; parenteral medroxyprogesterone or nonhormonal methods of birth control may be considered as alternatives)

Danazol or
» Diltiazem or
» Verapamil

(concurrent use of these agents with carbamazepine may inhibit carbamazepine metabolism, resulting in increased plasma concentrations and toxicity)

(carbamazepine toxicity may be delayed for several weeks after initiation of danazol therapy; carbamazepine dosage may need to be reduced)

(it is recommended that nifedipine be used as an alternative to verapamil or diltiazem)

Doxycycline

(concurrent use may decrease plasma concentration and elimination half-life of doxycycline because of induction of hepatic microsomal enzyme activity; if concurrent use cannot be avoided, doxycycline plasma concentrations or the therapeutic response to doxycycline should be closely monitored and dosage adjustments made as necessary)

Enflurane or
Halothane or
Methoxyflurane

(chronic use of a hepatic enzyme-inducing agent such as carbamazepine prior to anesthesia may increase the metabolism of these anesthetics, leading to an increased risk of hepatotoxicity)

(formation of nephrotoxic metabolites of methoxyflurane may be increased by chronic use of a hepatic enzyme-inducing agent such as carbamazepine prior to anesthesia, leading to increased risk of nephrotoxicity)

(in addition, cardiac arrhythmias may occur, possibly due to sensitization of the myocardium resulting from increased concentrations of norepinephrine)

» Erythromycin or
Troleandomycin

(concurrent use of these agents with carbamazepine may inhibit carbamazepine metabolism, resulting in increased plasma concentrations and toxicity; it is recommended that an alternate antibiotic to erythromycin or troleandomycin be used)

Folic acid

(requirements for folic acid may be increased in patients receiving anticonvulsant therapy)

Influenza virus vaccine
(concurrent use with carbamazepine may inhibit carbamazepine metabolism, resulting in increased plasma concentrations and toxicity; carbamazepine serum concentrations may be increased on days 7 to 14 after influenza virus vaccination; dosage adjustments of carbamazepine based on the patient's clinical status and serum carbamazepine concentrations may be necessary)

» Isoniazid
(carbamazepine may induce microsomal metabolism of isoniazid, increasing formation of a reactive intermediate and leading to hepatotoxicity; also, isoniazid administration may result in elevated plasma concentrations of carbamazepine and possible toxicity)

Lithium
(concurrent use may decrease the antidiuretic effect of carbamazepine and increase the neurotoxic side effects even at nontoxic blood concentrations of both lithium and carbamazepine; however, the concurrent use of lithium with carbamazepine may be synergistic in the treatment of patients with manic-depressive illness who fail to respond to either drug alone)

Mebendazole
(in patients receiving high oral doses of mebendazole for treatment of tissue-dwelling organisms such as *Echinococcus multolocularis* or *granulosus* [Hydatid disease], carbamazepine has been shown to lower plasma mebendazole concentrations by induction of hepatic microsomal enzymes and to impair the therapeutic response; if carbamazepine is being used for seizures, replacement with another anticonvulsant is recommended; treatment of intestinal helminths such as whipworms or hookworms does not appear to be affected by the rate of hepatic metabolism of mebendazole)

» Monoamine oxidase (MAO) inhibitors, including furazolidone and procarbazine
(concurrent use with carbamazepine has resulted in hyperpyretic crises, hypertensive crises, severe convulsions, and death; a medication-free interval of at least 14 days is recommended between discontinuation of MAO inhibitor therapy and initiation of carbamazepine therapy, or vice versa)

(MAO inhibitors may also cause a change in the pattern of epileptiform seizures in patients receiving carbamazepine as an anticonvulsant)

» Propoxyphene
(concurrent use with carbamazepine may inhibit carbamazepine metabolism, resulting in increased plasma concentrations and toxicity; an analgesic other than propoxyphene should be used)

Contraindications/Medical problems
The contraindications/medical problems included have been selected on the basis of their potential clinical significance (reasons given in parentheses where appropriate)—not necessarily inclusive (» = major clinical significance).

Except under special circumstances, this medication should not be used when the following medical problems exist:

» Absence seizures, atypical or generalized, or
» Atonic seizures or
» Myoclonic seizures
(increased risk of generalized seizures)
» Atrioventricular (AV) heart block or
» Blood disorders characterized by serious abnormalities in blood count, platelets, or serum iron
» Bone marrow depression, history of
(increased risk of exacerbation)

Risk-benefit should be considered when the following medical problems exist:

Alcoholism, active
(CNS depression may be potentiated; in addition, the metabolism of carbamazepine may be accelerated)

Behavioral disorders
(latent psychosis may be activated, or agitation or confusion may be produced in elderly patients, especially when carbamazepine is used concurrently with other medications)

Cardiac damage, including organic heart disease and congestive heart disease

Coronary artery disease

Diabetes mellitus

Glaucoma or
Increased intraocular pressure
(may be exacerbated because of mild anticholinergic effects of carbamazepine)

Hematologic reactions, adverse, to other medications, history of
(patients may be especially at risk for carbamazepine-induced bone marrow depression)

Hepatic function impairment
(increased risk of liver damage)

Hyponatremia, dilutional, caused by syndrome of inappropriate antidiuretic hormone (SIADH) secretion or other conditions such as hypopituitarism, hypothyroidism, or adrenocortical insufficiency, or

Urinary retention
(may be exacerbated)

Renal function impairment

Sensitivity to carbamazepine or to tricyclic antidepressants

Caution is also advised in administration to patients who have had interrupted courses of therapy with carbamazepine.

Side/Adverse Effects

Note: Carbamazepine-induced stimulation of antidiuretic hormone (ADH) release may cause water retention resulting in significant volume expansion and dilutional hyponatremia (syndrome of inappropriate secretion of antidiuretic hormone). Patients reporting lethargy, weakness, nausea, vomiting, confusion or hostility, neurological abnormalities, stupor, or increased seizure frequency should be suspected of being hyponatremic, although many of these symptoms may also be associated with other carbamazepine-induced side effects.

A case of aseptic meningitis accompanied by myoclonus and peripheral eosinophilia has been reported in a patient taking carbamazepine in conjunction with other medications; rechallenge with carbamazepine resulted in recurrence of meningitis.

The following side/adverse effects have been selected on the basis of their potential clinical significance (possible signs and symptoms in parentheses where appropriate)—not necessarily inclusive:

Those indicating need for medical attention
Incidence more frequent
CNS toxicity (blurred or double vision, nystagmus [continuous back-and-forth eye movements])

Incidence less frequent
Allergic reaction, Stevens-Johnson syndrome, or toxic epidermal necrolysis (skin rash, hives, or itching); *behavioral changes, especially in children; diarrhea, severe; hyponatremia, dilutional, or water intoxication (SIADH)* (confusion, agitation, or hostility, especially in the elderly; continuing headache; increase in seizure frequency; severe nausea and vomiting; unusual drowsiness; weakness); *systemic lupus erythematosus (SLE)-like syndrome* (skin rash, hives, or itching; fever; sore throat; bone or joint pain; unusual tiredness or weakness)

Note: The risk of *hyponatremia* and *SIADH* appears to increase with patient age and serum concentration of carbamazepine; *hyponatremia* seemingly does not occur in children.

Incidence rare

Adenopathy or lymphadenopathy (swollen glands); *blood dyscrasias, including aplastic anemia* (shortness of breath, troubled breathing, wheezing, or tightness in chest; sores, ulcers, or white spots on lips or in mouth; swollen or painful glands; unusual bleeding or bruising), *agranulocytosis* (chills, fever, sore throat, unusual tiredness or weakness), *eosinophilia* (fever), *leukopenia* (usually asymptomatic; rarely, fever or chills, cough or hoarseness, lower back or side pain, painful or difficult urination), *pancytopenia* (nosebleeds or other unusual bleeding or bruising), *thrombocytopenia* (usually asymptomatic; rarely, unusual bleeding or bruising; black, tarry stools; blood in urine or stools; pinpoint red spots on skin); *bone marrow depression* (chills, fever, sore throat, unusual bleeding or bruising); *cardiovascular effects, including arrhythmias* (fast, slow, or irregular heartbeat), *atrioventricular (AV) heart block* (unusual weakness, pounding heartbeat, troubled breathing, fainting), *bradycardia* (slow heartbeat), *congestive heart failure* (chest pain, troubled breathing, swelling of feet or lower legs, rapid weight gain), *edema* (swelling of face, hands, feet, or lower legs), *hypertension, increased* (high blood pressure), *hypotension* (low blood pressure), *syncope* (fainting); *CNS toxicity* (difficulty in speaking or slurred speech; mental depression with restlessness and nervousness; rigidity; ringing, buzzing, or other unexplained sounds in the ears; trembling; uncontrolled body movements; visual hallucinations); *hypersensitivity hepatitis* (darkening of urine, pale stools, yellow eyes or skin); *hypocalcemia* (increase in seizure frequency, muscle or abdominal cramps); *hypersensitivity, renal toxicity, renal failure, acute, or water intoxication (SIADH)* (frequent urination, sudden decrease in amount of urine, swelling of feet or lower legs); *paresthesias or peripheral neuritis* (numbness, tingling, pain, or weakness in hands and feet); *porphyria, acute intermittent* (darkening of urine); *pulmonary hypersensitivity* (fever, troubled breathing, cough, shortness of breath, tightness in chest, wheezing); *thrombophlebitis* (pain, tenderness, bluish color, or swelling of leg or foot)

Note: Geriatric patients and those with a defective conduction system may be especially susceptible to *AV heart block* or *bradycardia* with carbamazepine.

Hypocalcemia may lead to osteopenia as a direct effect of carbamazepine on bone metabolism.

Symptoms of overdose

Anuria, oliguria, or urinary retention (sudden decrease in amount of urine); *cardiovascular effects, including conduction disorders or tachycardia* (fast or irregular heartbeat), *hypertension or hypotension* (high or low blood pressure), *shock* (fainting); *nausea or vomiting, severe; neurological effects, including ataxia* (clumsiness or unsteadiness), *athetoid movements or ballism* (abnormal body movements), *convulsions*—especially in small children, *dizziness, severe, drowsiness, severe, dysmetria* (poor control in body movements—for example, when reaching or stepping), *hyperreflexia, followed by hyporeflexia* (overactive reflexes, followed by underactive reflexes), *motor restlessness, muscular twitching, mydriasis* (large pupils), *opisthotonus* (body spasm in which head and heels are bent backward and body bowed forward), *tremor; respiratory depression* (irregular, slow, or shallow breathing)

Note: Signs and symptoms of acute toxicity may occur 1 to 3 hours following ingestion of an overdose. Neurological and neuromuscular symptoms predominate, followed by cardiovascular toxicity. Symptoms resemble those observed following overdose with tricyclic antidepressants. Cardiotoxic effects are more likely to occur in elderly and cardiopathic patients.

Laboratory findings in overdosage may indicate leukocytosis, reduced leukocyte count, glycosuria, acetonuria, and electroencephalogram (EEG) dysrhythmias.

Those indicating need for medical attention only if they continue or are bothersome

Incidence more frequent, especially during initiation of therapy

Clumsiness or unsteadiness; confusion; dizziness, mild, or lightheadedness; drowsiness, mild; nausea or vomiting, mild

Incidence less frequent or rare

Aching joints or muscles or leg cramps; alopecia (loss of hair); *anorexia* (loss of appetite); *constipation; diaphoresis* (increased sweating); *diarrhea; dryness of mouth; glossitis or stomatitis* (irritation or soreness of tongue or mouth); *headache; increased sensitivity of skin to sunlight; sexual problems in males; stomach pain or discomfort; unusual tiredness or weakness*

Patient Consultation

In providing consultation, consider emphasizing the following selected information (» = major clinical significance):

Before using this medication

» Conditions affecting use, especially:

Sensitivity to tricyclic antidepressants or carbamazepine

Pregnancy—Crosses placenta; babies reportedly born with small head circumference, low birth weight, craniofacial defects, fingernail hypoplasia, and developmental delays; animal studies have shown rib anomalies, cleft palate, foot deformities, or anophthalmos with doses 10 to 25 times the human dose

Breast-feeding—Excreted in breast milk; animal studies have shown lack of weight gain and unkempt appearance of young at high doses

Use in children—Appropriate studies have not been done in children up to 6 years of age; behavior changes more likely to occur in children

Use in elderly—Elderly more likely to have confusion or agitation, AV heart block, SIADH, or bradycardia than are younger people

Use by athletes—Carbamazepine is banned and tested for in competitors in biathlon and pentathlon events by the U.S. Olympic Committee (USOC)

Dental—Increased incidence of blood dyscrasias that cause infection, delayed healing, or gingival bleeding; proper oral hygiene necessary

Other medications, especially adrenocorticoids, anticoagulants, other anticonvulsants, tricyclic antidepressants, barbiturates, benzodiazepines metabolized via hepatic microsomal enzymes (especially clonazepam), cimetidine, oral estrogen-containing contraceptives, diltiazem, erythromycin, estrogens, isoniazid, MAO inhibitors, propoxyphene, quinidine, or verapamil

Other medical problems, especially absence, atonic, or myoclonic seizures; AV heart block; blood disorders; or bone marrow depression

Proper use of this medication

» Taking with food to lessen gastrointestinal irritation

» Not using medication for minor aches and pains

» Compliance with therapy; not taking more or less medication than prescribed

Missed dose: Taking as soon as possible; not taking if almost time for next dose; not doubling doses; calling physician if more than one dose a day is missed

» Proper storage; not storing tablet dosage forms in bathroom or other high-moisture areas due to loss of potency and effectiveness

For use in epilepsy

» Checking with physician before discontinuing medication; gradual dosage reduction may be necessary to prevent seizures or status epilepticus

Precautions while using this medication

» Regular visits to physician to check progress of therapy

» Avoiding the use of alcoholic beverages and other CNS depressants while taking this medicine

» Possible drowsiness, dizziness, lightheadedness, blurred or double vision, weakness, or muscular incoordination; caution when driving or using machinery, or doing jobs requiring alertness and coordination

» Possible skin photosensitivity; avoiding unprotected exposure to sun; using protective clothing; using a sun block product that includes protection against both UVA-caused photosensitivity reactions and UVB-caused sunburn reactions; avoiding use of sunlamp, tanning bed, or tanning booth

Diabetic patients: May increase urine sugar concentrations

Caution if any laboratory tests required; possible interference with results of metyrapone or pregnancy tests

» Caution if any kind of surgery, dental treatment, or emergency treatment is needed

Carrying medical identification card or bracelet during therapy

Side/adverse effects

Signs of potential side effects, especially adenopathies, allergic reaction, behavioral changes, blood dyscrasias, bone marrow depression, cardiovascular effects, CNS toxicity, dilutional hyponatremia, hepatitis, hypocalcemia, hypersensitivity, paresthesias, peripheral neuritis, porphyria, pulmonary hypersensitivity, renal toxicity or failure, severe diarrhea, Stevens-Johnson syndrome, SIADH, SLE-like syndrome, thrombophlebitis, or toxic epidermal necrolysis

General Dosing Information

Side effects may be minimized by initiating therapy with low doses, which should be increased gradually at weekly intervals until an adequate response is obtained; administering carbamazepine with meals, and giving the total daily dosage in 3 or 4 divided doses may also minimize side effects.

When carbamazepine is added to existing anticonvulsant therapy, it should be added gradually while the other anticonvulsants are maintained or gradually decreased, except for phenytoin, which may have to be increased.

The maintenance dosage of carbamazepine may need to be increased progressively over the first few weeks of treatment to avoid low plasma carbamazepine concentrations caused by autoinduction.

Abrupt discontinuation in a responsive epileptic patient may result in convulsions and possibly status epilepticus; gradual withdrawal is recommended.

Therapy should be discontinued if cardiovascular reactions or skin rashes occur.

When carbamazepine is used as an antineuralgic in specific pain syndromes, *an attempt should be made at least once every few months to reduce dosage or discontinue therapy* if the patient is totally free of pain.

Since administration of the suspension results in higher peak serum concentrations than does the same dose administered as tablets, it is recommended that doses of the suspension be initially lower and be increased more slowly than doses of the tablets to avoid side effects.

If carbamazepine suspension is administered through a nasogastric feeding tube, it should be mixed with an equal volume of diluent before administration.

Diet/Nutrition

Carbamazepine should be taken with food to lessen gastrointestinal irritation.

Oral Dosage Forms

Note: Bracketed uses in the *Dosage Forms* section refer to categories of use and/or indications that are not included in U.S. product labeling.

CARBAMAZEPINE ORAL SUSPENSION

Note: Carbamazepine oral suspension is not commercially available in Canada.

Usual adult and adolescent dose:

Anticonvulsant—

Initial: Oral, 100 mg four times a day on the first day, the dosage being increased by up to 200 mg a day at weekly intervals. Some clinicians recommend initiating therapy at 100 mg a day and increasing to full therapeutic dosage slowly at weekly intervals to avoid side effects and potential noncompliance.

Maintenance: Oral, usually 800 mg to 1.2 grams a day.

Antineuralgic—

Initial: Oral, 50 mg four times a day on the first day, the dosage being increased by up to 200 mg a day, using increments of 50 mg four times a day only as needed until pain is relieved.

Maintenance: Oral, 200 mg to 1.2 grams a day (average 400 to 800 mg a day) in divided doses.

[Antidiuretic]—Oral, 300 to 600 mg a day if used as sole therapy; or 200 to 400 mg a day if used concurrently with other antidiuretic agents.

[Antimanic] or

[Antipsychotic]—Oral, initially 200 to 400 mg a day in divided doses, the dosage being gradually increased at weekly intervals up to a maximum of 1.6 grams a day as needed and tolerated according to clinical response.

Note: Whenever possible, total daily dosage should be given in 3 or 4 divided doses.

Usual adult and adolescent prescribing limits:

Anticonvulsant—

Patients 12 to 15 years of age: Dosage should generally not exceed 1 gram a day.

Patients 15 years of age and over: Dosage should generally not exceed 1.2 grams a day. In rare instances, doses up to 1.6 grams a day have been used in adults.

Antineuralgic—Dosage should not exceed 1.2 grams a day.

Auxiliary labeling:

• Shake well before using.
• May cause drowsiness.
• Take with meals.

CARBAMAZEPINE TABLETS USP

Usual adult and adolescent dose:

Anticonvulsant—

Initial: Oral, 200 mg two times a day on the first day, the dosage being increased by up to 200 mg a day at weekly intervals until the best response is obtained. Some clinicians recommend initiating therapy at 100 mg a day and increasing to full therapeutic dosage slowly at weekly intervals to avoid side effects and potential noncompliance.

Maintenance: Oral, adjusted to the minimum effective dosage, usually 600 mg to 1.6 grams a day.

Antineuralgic—

Initial: Oral, 100 mg two times a day on the first day, the dosage being increased by up to 200 mg a day, using increments of 100 mg every twelve hours only as needed until pain is relieved.

Maintenance: Oral, 200 mg to 1.2 grams a day (average 400 to 800 mg a day) in divided doses.

[Antidiuretic][1]—Oral, 300 to 600 mg a day if used as sole therapy; or 200 to 400 mg a day if used concurrently with other antidiuretic agents.

[Antimanic][1] or

[Antipsychotic][1]—Oral, initially 200 to 400 mg a day in divided doses, the dosage being gradually increased at weekly intervals up to a maximum of 1.6 grams a day as needed and tolerated according to clinical response.

Note: Whenever possible, total daily dosage should be given in 3 or 4 divided doses.

Usual adult and adolescent prescribing limits:
Anticonvulsant—
Patients 12 to 15 years of age: Dosage should generally not exceed 1 gram a day.
Patients 15 years of age and over: Dosage should generally not exceed 1.2 grams a day. In rare instances, doses up to 1.6 grams a day have been used in adults.
Antineuralgic—Dosage should not exceed 1.2 grams a day.

Auxiliary labeling:
• May cause drowsiness.
• Take with meals.
• Store in a dry place.
• Protect from moisture.

CARBAMAZEPINE TABLETS USP (CHEWABLE)

Usual adult and adolescent dose:
Anticonvulsant—
Initial: Oral, 200 mg two times a day on the first day, the dosage being increased by up to 200 mg a day at weekly intervals until the best response is obtained. Some clinicians recommend initiating therapy at 100 mg a day and increasing to full therapeutic dosage slowly at weekly intervals to avoid side effects and potential noncompliance.
Maintenance: Oral, adjusted to the minimum effective dosage, usually 600 mg to 1.6 grams a day.
Antineuralgic—
Initial: Oral, 100 mg two times a day on the first day, the dosage being increased by up to 200 mg a day, using increments of 100 mg every twelve hours only as needed until pain is relieved.
Maintenance: Oral, 200 mg to 1.2 grams a day (average 400 to 800 mg a day) in divided doses.
[Antidiuretic][1]—Oral, 300 to 600 mg a day if used as sole therapy; or 200 to 400 mg a day if used concurrently with other antidiuretic agents.
[Antimanic][1] or
[Antipsychotic][1]—Oral, initially 200 to 400 mg a day in divided doses, the dosage being gradually increased at weekly intervals up to a maximum of 1.6 grams a day as needed and tolerated according to clinical response.
Note: Whenever possible, total daily dosage should be given in 3 or 4 divided doses.

Usual adult and adolescent prescribing limits:
Anticonvulsant—
Patients 12 to 15 years of age: Dosage should generally not exceed 1 gram a day.

Patients 15 years of age and over: Dosage should generally not exceed 1.2 grams a day. In rare instances, doses up to 1.6 grams a day have been used in adults.
Antineuralgic—Dosage should not exceed 1.2 grams a day.

Auxiliary labeling:
• May cause drowsiness.
• Take with meals.
• May be chewed.
• Store in a dry place.
• Protect from moisture.

CARBAMAZEPINE EXTENDED-RELEASE TABLETS
Note: Carbamazepine extended-release tablets are not commercially available in the U.S.

Usual adult and adolescent dose:
Anticonvulsant—
Initial: Oral, 100 to 200 mg one or two times a day with meals, the dosage being increased gradually as needed and tolerated. Some clinicians recommend initiating therapy at 100 mg a day and increasing to full therapeutic dosage slowly at weekly intervals to avoid side effects and potential noncompliance.
Maintenance: Oral, adjusted to the minimum effective dosage, usually 800 to 1200 mg a day.
Antineuralgic—Oral, initially 100 mg two times a day on the first day, the dosage being increased by 200 mg a day only as needed and tolerated until pain is relieved.
Note: As soon as pain relief is maintained, the dosage should be reduced to the minimum effective dose.
Attempts should be made at intervals of not more than 3 months to reduce or discontinue use.

Usual adult and adolescent prescribing limits:
Anticonvulsant—
Patients 12 to 15 years of age: Dosage should generally not exceed 1 gram a day.
Patients 15 years of age and over: Dosage should generally not exceed 1.2 grams a day. In rare instances, doses up to 1.6 grams a day have been used in adults.
Antineuralgic—Dosage should not exceed 1.2 grams a day.

Auxiliary labeling:
• May cause drowsiness.
• Take with meals.
• Do not chew.

---

[1]Not included in Canadian product labeling.

CARBIDOPA AND LEVODOPA   Systemic

Pharmacy Equivalent Name (PEN): Co-Careldopa

Some commonly used *brand names* in the U.S. and Canada are *Sinemet* and *Sinemet CR*.

ORAL
Carbidopa and Levodopa Tablets USP
In the U.S. and Canada—*Sinemet*
Carbidopa and Levodopa Extended-release Tablets
In the U.S. and Canada—*Sinemet CR*

Category: Antidyskinetic.

Indications

Accepted
Parkinsonism (treatment)—Carbidopa and levodopa combination is indicated in the treatment of idiopathic Parkinson's disease (paralysis agitans), postencephalitic parkinsonism, or symptomatic parkinsonism, which may follow injury to the nervous system by carbon monoxide intoxication or manganese intoxication, to permit achievement of symptomatic relief with a lower dosage of levodopa than with levodopa alone. Also, it permits a smoother and more rapid dosage titration, reduces nausea and vomiting, and allows concurrent administration of pyridoxine when necessary.

Pharmacology

See also *Levodopa (Systemic).*

Mechanism of action/Effect: Carbidopa—Inhibits the peripheral decarboxylation of levodopa, thus slowing its conversion to dopamine in extracerebral tissues. This results in an increased availability of levodopa for transport to the brain where it undergoes decarboxylation to dopamine.

Precautions to Consider

Geriatrics

Smaller doses may be required in geriatric patients since they may have reduced tolerance to the effects of levodopa. Also, peripheral dopa decarboxylase, the enzyme responsible for decarboxylation, decreases with age, thus making large doses unnecessary.

Geriatric patients, especially those with osteoporosis, responsive to antiparkinsonian therapy should resume normal activity gradually and with caution because increased mobility may increase risk of fractures.

Psychic side effects, such as anxiety, confusion, or nervousness, are more common in geriatric patients receiving other antiparkinsonian medications, especially anticholinergics.

Dental

Involuntary movements of jaws may result in poor retention of full dentures; dosage reduction may be required.

Drug interactions and/or related problems

The following drug interactions and/or related problems have been selected on the basis of their potential clinical significance (possible mechanism in parentheses where appropriate)—not necessarily inclusive:

Note: Combinations containing any of the following medications, depending on the amount present, may also interact with this medication.

Amantadine or
Benztropine or
Procyclidine or
Trihexyphenidyl
  (concurrent use may result in increased efficacy of levodopa; however, concurrent use is not recommended if there is a history of psychosis)

» Anesthetics, hydrocarbon inhalation
  (administration prior to anesthesia with these agents may result in cardiac arrhythmias because of increased endogenous dopamine concentration; carbidopa and levodopa combination should be discontinued 6 to 8 hours before the administration of these anesthetics, especially halothane)

» Anticonvulsants, hydantoin, or
Benzodiazepines or
Droperidol or
» Haloperidol or
Loxapine or
Metyrosine or
Papaverine or
» Phenothiazines or
Rauwolfia alkaloids or
Thioxanthenes
  (concurrent use may decrease the therapeutic effects of levodopa; hydantoin anticonvulsants increase the metabolism of levodopa, thus decreasing its therapeutic effects; since droperidol, haloperidol, loxapine, papaverine, phenothiazines, and the thioxanthenes block the dopamine receptors in the brain, they may induce extrapyramidal symptoms, thus aggravating parkinsonism and antagonizing the effects of levodopa; the rauwolfia alkaloids cause dopamine depletion in the brain, thus opposing the effects of levodopa)

Bromocriptine
  (may produce additive effects, allowing reduction in levodopa dosage)

» Cocaine
  (concurrent use with levodopa may increase the risk of cardiac arrhythmias; if use of cocaine is necessary in patients receiving levodopa, it is recommended that cocaine be administered with caution, in reduced dosage, and in conjunction with electrocardiographic monitoring)

Foods, especially high-protein
  (concurrent or previous ingestion of food may decrease the absorption of levodopa from the gastrointestinal tract, consequently delaying its effect; in addition, proteins in food may be degraded into the amino acids that compete with levodopa for transport to the brain, thus decreasing and/or making erratic the response to levodopa; however, rather than cutting down on daily protein intake to avoid this effect on levodopa, it is recommended that the intake of proteins be distributed equally throughout the day)

Hypotension-producing medications, other
  (concurrent use with levodopa may result in an increased hypotensive effect)

Methyldopa
  (concurrent use with levodopa may alter the antiparkinsonian effects of levodopa and may also produce additive toxic CNS effects such as psychosis)

Metoclopramide
  (gastric emptying of levodopa may be accelerated with concurrent use of metoclopramide, thus possibly increasing levodopa's rate and extent of absorption from the small intestine; the clinical significance of this interaction has not been determined)

Molindone
  (concurrent use may inhibit antiparkinsonian effects of levodopa by blocking dopamine receptor in the brain; also, levodopa may counteract the antipsychotic effects of molindone)

» Monoamine oxidase (MAO) inhibitors, including furazolidone and procarbazine
  (although high doses [300 to 400 mg a day] of carbidopa in combination with levodopa may help suppress the hypertensive reactions caused by concurrent use with MAO inhibitors, it is recommended that MAO inhibitors be discontinued for 2 to 4 weeks prior to initiation of carbidopa and levodopa combination therapy)

» Selegiline
  (although sometimes used in conjunction with carbidopa and levodopa combination, selegiline may enhance levodopa-induced dyskinesias, nausea, orthostatic hypotension, confusion, and hallucinations; levodopa dosage should be reduced within 2 to 3 days after the initiation of selegiline therapy)

Contraindications/Medical problems

The contraindications/medical problems included have been selected on the basis of their potential clinical significance (reasons given in parentheses where appropriate)—not necessarily inclusive (» = major clinical significance).

Risk-benefit should be considered when the following medical problems exist:

» Bronchial asthma, emphysema, and other severe pulmonary diseases
  (respiratory effects of levodopa may aggravate condition)

» Cardiovascular disease, severe
  (increased risk of cardiac arrhythmias)

Convulsive disorders, history of
  (use of levodopa may precipitate seizures)

Diabetes mellitus
  (use of levodopa may adversely affect control of glucose in blood)

Endocrine diseases
> (use of levodopa may adversely affect hypothalamus or pituitary function)
» Glaucoma, angle-closure, or predisposition to
> (mydriatic effect resulting in increased intraocular pressure may precipitate an acute attack of angle closure glaucoma)

Glaucoma, open-angle, chronic
> (mydriatic effect may cause a slight increase in intraocular pressure; glaucoma therapy may need to be adjusted)

Hepatic function impairment
» Melanoma, history of or suspected
> (use of levodopa may activate a malignant melanoma)
» Myocardial infarction, history of, with residual arrhythmias
> (use of levodopa may precipitate or aggravate condition)
» Peptic ulcer, history of
> (increased risk of upper gastrointestinal hemorrhage)
» Psychotic states
> (increased risk of developing depression and suicidal tendencies)
» Renal function impairment
> (use of levodopa may lead to urinary retention)

Sensitivity to carbidopa and/or levodopa
» Urinary retention
> (use of levodopa may precipitate or aggravate condition)

Side/Adverse Effects

Note: Carbidopa, in doses used to inhibit peripheral decarboxylation of levodopa, has no significant ability to produce side effects. However, it allows certain CNS side effects of levodopa, such as dyskinesias and mental effects, to develop sooner and at lower levodopa doses because of the resultant greater efficiency per dose of levodopa.

Patients receiving carbidopa and levodopa combination for one to several years may experience sudden, unexpected akinesia, tremor, and rigidity, such as the "on-off" phenomenon. Emotional stress may precipitate akinesia paradoxica or "start hesitation" in these patients.

A syndrome resembling neuroleptic malignant syndrome, which includes intermittent dystonia alternating with substantial agitation, hyperthermia and mental changes, has been reported after the abrupt discontinuation of levodopa therapy.

Convulsions have been reported but a causal relationship to the use of levodopa or carbidopa and levodopa combination has not been established.

The following side/adverse effects have been selected on the basis of their potential clinical significance (possible signs and symptoms in parentheses where appropriate)—not necessarily inclusive:

Those indicating need for medical attention
Incidence more frequent
  Mental depression; mood or mental changes, such as aggressive behavior; uncontrolled movements of the body, including the face, tongue, arms, hands, head, and upper body—may indicate excessive concentration of dopamine in the corpus striatum
  Note: *Mental depression, mood or mental changes, and uncontrolled movements of the body* tend to appear earlier during therapy with carbidopa and levodopa than with levodopa alone.
    Choreiform and other involuntary movements occur in 50 to 80% of patients and are usually dose-related.
Incidence less frequent
  Difficult urination; irregular heartbeat; nausea or vomiting, severe or continuing; orthostatic hypotension (dizziness or lightheadedness when getting up from a lying or sitting position); *spasm or closing of eyelids*—possible early sign of overdose

Note: *Nausea and vomiting* may occur frequently in early carbidopa and levodopa therapy with tolerance being gradually achieved during continued use. The concurrent use of carbidopa with levodopa often reduces the frequency and severity of nausea and vomiting, although approximately 15% of patients continue to experience these side effects.
Incidence rare
  Duodenal ulcer (stomach pain); *hemolytic anemia* (unusual tiredness or weakness); *hypertension* (high blood pressure)

Those indicating need for medical attention only if they continue or are bothersome
Incidence more frequent
  Anxiety, confusion, or nervousness—especially in elderly patients receiving other antiparkinsonian medication
Incidence less frequent
  Anorexia (loss of appetite); *blurred vision; constipation; diarrhea; dryness of mouth; flushing of skin; headache; insomnia* (trouble in sleeping); *muscle twitching; nightmares; unusual tiredness or weakness*

Those not indicating need for medical attention
Incidence less frequent
  Darkening in color of urine or sweat

Patient Consultation

In providing consultation, consider emphasizing the following selected information (» = major clinical significance):

Before using this medication
» Conditions affecting use, especially:
    Sensitivity to carbidopa and/or levodopa
    Pregnancy—No studies in humans; depressed growth and malformations in animal studies
    Breast-feeding—Levodopa is excreted in breast milk; may inhibit lactation
    Use in the elderly—Reduced tolerance to effects of levodopa; caution in resuming normal activity, especially in patients with osteoporosis; psychic effects more common with concurrent use of anticholinergics
    Dental—Possible difficulty in retention of full dentures
    Other medications, especially haloperidol, hydantoin anticonvulsants, hydrocarbon inhalation anesthetics, phenothiazines, cocaine, MAO inhibitors, and selegiline
    Other medical problems, especially severe cardiovascular disease, severe pulmonary diseases, glaucoma, melanoma (history of or suspected), peptic ulcer (history of), psychosis, renal function impairment, or urinary retention

Proper use of this medication
» Taking food shortly after taking medication to relieve gastric irritation; taking food before or concurrently may retard levodopa's effect
» Compliance with therapy; taking medication only as directed; not stopping medication unless ordered by physician
» Maximum effectiveness of medication may not occur for several weeks or months after therapy is initiated
    Missed dose: Taking as soon as possible; skipping dose if next scheduled dose is within 2 hours; not doubling doses
» Proper storage

Precautions while using this medication
    Caution if any kind of surgery (including dental surgery) or emergency treatment is required
    For diabetic patients—May interfere with urine tests for sugar and ketones
» Caution if drowsiness occurs
» Caution when getting up suddenly from lying or sitting position; dizziness and fainting may occur
    Possibility of "on-off" phenomenon

Side/adverse effects

Occasional darkening of urine or sweat may be alarming to patient although medically insignificant

Signs of potential side effects, especially difficult urination, duodenal ulcer, hemolytic anemia, hypertension, irregular heartbeat, mental depression, mood or mental changes, severe nausea or vomiting, orthostatic hypotension, spasm or closing of eyelids, or uncontrolled movements of body

General Dosing Information

Titrated dosage is necessary to achieve the individual therapeutic blood concentration requirements and to avoid side effects. This is especially important for geriatric patients and patients receiving other medications.

Postencephalitic and geriatric patients often require and tolerate lower dosage levels than other parkinsonism patients.

Levodopa must be discontinued at least 8 hours before the carbidopa and levodopa combination dosage is begun. Levodopa may be discontinued in the evening and the carbidopa and levodopa combination started the following morning.

The concurrent administration of carbidopa may permit the dose of levodopa to be reduced by up to 75% with no decrease in therapeutic results. Carbidopa also reduces the adverse effect of pyridoxine on levodopa.

Because carbidopa and levodopa extended-release tablets are 25 to 30% less systemically bioavailable than Carbidopa and Levodopa Tablets USP, increased daily doses of the extended-release tablets may be required to achieve the same level of symptomatic relief.

Amantadine or anticholinergic medications are often used concurrently with carbidopa and levodopa in the more advanced cases of parkinsonism or when response to carbidopa and levodopa decreases. However, gradual dosage reduction of these medications is recommended during initiation of therapy with carbidopa and levodopa and after optimum dosage is reached to maintain proper control of patient's condition.

When carbidopa and levodopa combination is to be discontinued, dosage should be reduced gradually to prevent the occurrence of a syndrome that resembles the neuroleptic malignant syndrome. Careful patient monitoring after withdrawal of carbidopa and levodopa will allow early diagnosis and treatment of neuroleptic malignant-like syndrome.

Diet/Nutrition

Food should be eaten shortly after carbidopa and levodopa combination is taken to relieve gastric irritation; taking food before or concurrently may retard levodopa's effects.

High protein diets should be avoided, because amino acid degradation products compete with levodopa for transport to the brain, resulting in a decreased or erratic response to levodopa. It is recommended that intake of normal amounts of protein be distributed equally throughout the day.

Oral Dosage Forms

CARBIDOPA AND LEVODOPA TABLETS USP

Usual adult dose: Antidyskinetic—

For patients not being converted from levodopa therapy: Oral, initially, 10 mg of carbidopa and 100 mg of levodopa three or four times a day or 25 mg of carbidopa and 100 mg of levodopa three times a day, the dosage per day being increased gradually at one- or two-day intervals as needed and tolerated.

For patients being converted from levodopa therapy (levodopa must be discontinued for at least eight hours prior to conversion to carbidopa and levodopa therapy):

Patients who require less than 1.5 grams of levodopa per day—Oral, 10 mg of carbidopa and 100 mg of levodopa or 25 mg of carbidopa and 100 mg of levodopa three or four times a

day initially, the dosage per day being increased gradually at one- or two-day intervals as needed and tolerated.

Patients who require more than 1.5 grams of levodopa per day—Oral, 25 mg of carbidopa and 250 mg of levodopa three or four times a day initially, the dosage per day being increased gradually at one- or two-day intervals as needed and tolerated.

Note: Postencephalitic patients may be more sensitive to the effects of the usual adult dose.

For patients being converted from levodopa therapy, the initial dose of carbidopa and levodopa per day should provide approximately 25% of the total dosage of levodopa per day previously required.

Usual adult prescribing limits: Up to 200 mg of carbidopa and 2 grams of levodopa in combination daily.

Note: Additional levodopa may be administered alone if it is required and tolerated.

Usual geriatric dose: See *Usual adult dose.*

Note: Geriatric patients may be more sensitive to the effects of the usual adult dose.

Auxiliary labeling: • May darken urine or sweat.

CARBIDOPA AND LEVODOPA EXTENDED-RELEASE TABLETS

Usual adult dose: Antidyskinetic—

Initial dosage:

For patients not receiving levodopa therapy—Mild to moderate disease: Oral, initially, 1 tablet twice a day, at intervals of at least 6 hours.

For patients currently treated with conventional carbidopa-levodopa preparations—Dosage with the extended-release tablets should be substituted at an amount that provides approximately 10% more levodopa per day, although this may need to be increased to 30% more levodopa per day based on clinical response. The interval between doses of the extended-release tablets should be 4 to 8 hours during the waking day, although a few patients may require more frequent dosing.

Guidelines for initial conversion from Carbidopa and Levodopa Tablets USP to carbidopa and levodopa extended-release tablets:

Total daily dose of levodopa (mg)	Suggested dosage regimen of carbidopa and levodopa extended-release tablets
300–400	1 tablet twice a day
500–600	1½ tablets twice a day or 1 tablet three times a day
700–800	A total of 4 tablets in 3 or more divided doses (e.g., 1½ tablets a.m., 1½ tablets early p.m., and 1 tablet later p.m.)
900–1000	A total of 5 tablets in 3 or more divided doses (e.g., 2 tablets a.m., 2 tablets early p.m., and 1 tablet later p.m.)

For patients currently treated with levodopa without a decarboxylase inhibitor—Levodopa must be discontinued at least 8 hours before initiating therapy with carbidopa and levodopa extended-release tablets. The extended-release tablets should be substituted at a dosage of approximately 25% of the previous levodopa dosage.

Mild to moderate disease: Oral, initially, 1 tablet twice a day.

Maintenance dosing:
> Depending upon therapeutic response, doses and dosing intervals may be increased or decreased following initiation of therapy. An interval of at least 3 days between dosage adjustments is recommended. Most patients have been adequately treated with 2 to 8 tablets per day, administered as divided doses at intervals ranging from 4 to 8 hours. A few patients may require higher doses (12 or more tablets per day) and shorter intervals (less than 4 hours).
> When the extended-release tablets are given at less than 4-hour intervals, and/or if the divided doses are not equal, the smaller doses should be given at the end of the day.

Carbidopa and Levodopa Tablets USP may be added to the dosage regimen in selected patients with advanced disease who need additional levodopa for a brief time during daytime hours. Usually one-half or one tablet of carbidopa 10 mg and levodopa 100 mg or carbidopa 25 mg and levodopa 100 mg is added.

Usual geriatric dose: See *Usual adult dose.*

Auxiliary labeling:
- May darken urine or sweat.
- Do not chew or crush tablets.

CARBOHYDRATES AND ELECTROLYTES   Systemic

Some commonly used *brand names* are:

In the U.S.—
- *Naturalyte* [Dextrose and Electrolytes Solution]
- *Pedialyte* [Dextrose and Electrolytes Solution]
- *Rehydralyte* [Dextrose and Electrolytes Solution]
- *Resol* [Dextrose and Electrolytes Solution]
- *Ricelyte* [Rice Syrup Solids and Electrolytes Solution]

In Canada—
- *Gastrolyte* [Oral Rehydration Salts]
- *Lytren* [Dextrose and Electrolytes Solution]
- *Pedialyte* [Dextrose and Electrolytes Solution]
- *Rapolyte* [Oral Rehydration Salts]

Other commonly used names are oral rehydration salts, ORS-bicarbonate, and ORS-citrate.§

ORAL

DEXTROSE AND ELECTROLYTES
> Dextrose and Electrolytes Solution
>> In the U.S.—*Naturalyte; Pedialyte; Rehydralyte; Resol‡*
>> In Canada—*Lytren; Pedialyte*

ORAL REHYDRATION SALTS*§
> Oral Rehydration Salts USP (for Oral Solution)*§
>> In Canada—*Gastrolyte; Rapolyte*
>> Other—GENERIC§

RICE SYRUP SOLIDS AND ELECTROLYTES†
> Rice Syrup Solids and Electrolytes Solution†
>> In the U.S.—*Ricelyte*

---

*Not commercially available in the U.S.
†Not commercially available in Canada.
‡*Resol* is available to hospitals only.
§Distributed by the World Health Organization (WHO).

Category: Electrolyte replenisher.

Indications

Accepted

Diarrhea (treatment); and

Electrolyte depletion (prophylaxis and treatment)—Carbohydrate and electrolytes solutions are indicated for oral replacement of fluids and electrolytes (especially sodium and potassium) in the treatment of clinically evident dehydration caused by diarrhea; to prevent severe dehydration by replacing losses early in the course of diarrhea; and to maintain hydration in the presence of continuing fluid loss. Oral rehydration therapy (ORT) consists of rehydration (the expansion of intravascular volume and deficit replacement); replacement of ongoing abnormal losses of fluids and electrolyte salts from continuing diarrhea and vomiting and normal water losses through skin and respiration; and the maintenance of fluids and electrolytes in the body until adequate nutrition can be restored. Acute diarrhea is not immediately terminated by oral rehydration therapy, but it is usually self-limiting. Some carbohydrate and electrolytes solutions are also used for maintenance of water and electrolytes when food and liquid intake has been discontinued after surgery, and some are indicated for maintenance of hydration only, rather than for rehydration.

ORT is recommended by the World Health Organization (WHO) Diarrheal Disease Control Program and United Nations Children's Fund (UNICEF) as a fundamental treatment for acute diarrheal disease in infants and children and provides the basis for all national programs of diarrhea control. The WHO formulations of ORS-bicarbonate or ORS-citrate rehydration salts, consisting of preweighed sodium chloride, potassium chloride, sodium citrate or sodium bicarbonate, and dextrose, are distributed in aluminum foil or polyethylene packets to be prepared at home and given at the onset of diarrhea. The solutions are simple to prepare (i.e., the contents of each packet are dissolved in one liter of potable water) and are very effective, inexpensive, and therapeutically appropriate for routine use in prevention and treatment of dehydration from diarrhea of any cause in all age groups. These powders are not widely used or commercially available in the U.S.

Some commercial carbohydrate and electrolytes solutions available in the U.S. and Canada have a lower sodium content than the recommended WHO formulas. This reflects the concern that the higher sodium content of the WHO solution may cause hypernatremia, especially in developed countries, due to the use of high solute diets and the lower incidence of malnutrition in young children. However, there is no evidence that the WHO solution causes hypernatremia when used as directed. Carbohydrate and electrolytes solutions with a lower sodium content have been found to be as effective as the WHO formulas.

Intravenous replacement of fluids and electrolytes is not used routinely in treatment of diarrhea, but it may be necessary to treat severe dehydration (fluid loss of 10% or more of body weight) or impending shock.

Pharmacology

Mechanism of action/Effect: During normal digestion, about 9 liters of fluid a day in adults and about 3 to 6 liters a day in infants and children pass through the duodenum where most of the dietary sugars, fats, and amino acids are absorbed. The fluid, containing ingested food and liquids and digestive secretions, reaches the ileum mainly as an isotonic salt solution that is similar to plasma in its ionic sodium and potassium content. The ileum absorbs most of this isotonic solution by various active transport mechanisms, but about 1 liter a day is emptied into the colon where all but about 100 mL is absorbed. The rest is excreted into the feces to prevent desiccation. In addition, cells in the small intestine both absorb and secrete water and electrolytes, but less secretion occurs than absorption, so that the net effect of small bowel transport is absorption. In acute diarrheal states, various infectious agents produce alterations in the intestinal mucosa, inhibiting absorption or stimulating secretion. The large volume of secretions thus produced cannot be fully absorbed by the colon and are expelled as watery diarrhea. Essential water and salts are lost in stools and vomitus, and dehydration results when blood volume is decreased because of fluid loss from the extracellular fluid compartment. Thirst is the first sign of dehydration when fluid loss is less than 5% of the body weight. Tachycardia, decreased skin elasticity, sunken eyes, hypotension, irritability, oliguria or anuria, severe thirst, and stupor or coma develop rapidly when fluid loss is greater than 5% of the body weight. Shock occurs when the deficit equals about 10% of body weight, and death is caused by greater losses of fluids.

Preservation of the facilitated glucose-sodium cotransport system in the small-bowel mucosa is the rationale of oral rehydration therapy. Glucose is actively absorbed in the normal intestine and carries sodium with it in about an equimolar ratio. Therefore, there is a greater net absorption of an isotonic salt solution with glucose than of one without it. During acute diarrhea, the absorption of sodium is impaired and an isotonic salt solution without glucose can increase stool volume by passing through the intestine unabsorbed. Since the glucose absorption system usually remains intact during diarrheal illnesses, the net absorption of water and electrolytes from an isotonic dextrose-salt or a hypotonic rice-salt solution can equal or exceed diarrheal stool volume, even if the loss is rapid. Sucrose (ordinary sugar) may be substituted for dextrose in the dextrose-based oral rehydration solutions, but twice the amount of sugar is needed for near equal efficacy. However, excessive use of dextrose or sucrose to increase palatability of the solution or to increase nutritive value for small children may exacerbate diarrhea, because of the osmotic effect of unabsorbed glucose. A solution with 2 to 2.5% dextrose in the dextrose-based oral rehydration solutions is optimal for promoting coupled absorption of sodium from the intestine.

Rice-based oral rehydration solutions use starch rather than dextrose as a base. The ingested starch gradually releases glucose which along with sodium preserves the glucose-sodium transport system in the manner described above. The rice-based formula has the advantage of a lower osmotic effect and provides a few more calories than the dextrose-based electrolytes solution. This formula has also been found to be more effective in reducing stool output and shortening the duration of diarrhea.

Potassium replacement during acute diarrhea prevents below-normal serum concentrations of potassium, especially in children, in whom stool potassium losses are higher than in adults.

When added to oral rehydration solutions, bicarbonate and citrate are equally effective in correcting the metabolic acidosis caused by diarrhea and dehydration. However, citrate is used instead of the bicarbonate in the WHO formulation, to prevent the occurrence of bicarbonate-induced discoloration and decomposition of the dextrose in the packets.

Treatment started early in the course of diarrhea minimizes vomiting, anorexia, lethargy, or coma, which interfere with continued feeding; allows the homeostatic mechanisms of thirst and renal function to remain intact; and avoids the risk of death from severe dehydration. Thirst determines the amount of rehydration required, and normal renal function allows the excretion of any excess water and salts.

Time to peak effect: 8 to 12 hours.

Precautions to Consider

Geriatrics
Carbohydrate and electrolytes solutions are well tolerated by elderly patients.

Contraindications/Medical problems
The contraindications/medical problems included have been selected on the basis of their potential clinical significance (reasons given in parentheses where appropriate)—not necessarily inclusive (» = major clinical significance).

Except under special circumstances, this medication should not be used when the following medical problems exist:

» Anuria or
» Oliguria
   (since normal renal function is required to allow the excretion of any excess water or salt, patients with prolonged anuria or oliguria usually require precise parenteral administration of water and electrolytes; however, transient oliguria is a feature of dehydration due to diarrhea and is not a contraindication for oral rehydration therapy)

» Dehydration, severe, with symptoms of shock
   (oral rehydration is too slow; rapid intravenous therapy is necessary; symptoms of severe dehydration include severe thirst, rapid heartbeat, decreased skin turgor, hypotension, oliguria or anuria, sunken eyes, loss of body weight, convulsions, stupor, and coma; if symptoms of severe dehydration appear after oral therapy has been attempted, rehydration must be achieved with parenteral therapy)

» Diarrhea, severe
   (when amounts of diarrhea exceed 30 mL per kg of body weight per hour, patient may be unable to drink enough fluids to replace continuing loss)

» Glucose malabsorption
   (diarrhea is exacerbated and dehydration worsened when oral rehydration solutions are given to patients with this problem; volume of stool greatly increases and contains large amounts of glucose; rehydration therapy should be discontinued)

» Inability to drink or
» Vomiting, severe and sustained
   (parenteral therapy is required for patients unable to drink because of extreme fatigue, stupor, coma, or uncontrollable vomiting)

» Intestinal obstruction or
» Paralytic ileus or
» Perforated bowel
   (delayed passage of carbohydrate and electrolytes solutions through the gastrointestinal tract may increase risk of gastrointestinal irritation)

Side/Adverse Effects

The following side/adverse effects have been selected on the basis of their potential clinical significance (possible signs and symptoms in parentheses where appropriate)—not necessarily inclusive:

Those indicating need for medical attention
Incidence rare
   Hypernatremia (dizziness, fast heartbeat, high blood pressure, irritability, muscle twitching, restlessness, seizures, swelling of feet or lower legs, or weakness)

Symptoms of overhydration
   Puffy eyelids
   Note: Therapy may need to be discontinued temporarily.

Those indicating need for medical attention only if they continue or are bothersome
Incidence more frequent
   Vomiting, mild

Note: *Mild vomiting* may occur when oral therapy is begun, but therapy should be continued with frequent, small amounts of solution administered slowly.

Patient Consultation

In providing consultation, consider emphasizing the following selected information (» = major clinical significance):

Before using this medication
» Conditions affecting use, especially:
   Other medical problems, especially renal function impairment, severe dehydration, severe and continuing diarrhea, glucose malabsorption, inability to drink, severe and continuing vomiting, intestinal obstruction, paralytic ileus, or perforated bowel

Proper use of this medication
   Importance of helping infants and small children to drink solution slowly and frequently in small amounts, given with a spoon
   Importance of not taking for a longer time than recommended by physician
» Proper storage
For patients using the commercial powder form
   Adding recommended amount of boiled, cooled drinking water to contents of packet; stirring or shaking container for 2 or 3 minutes to dissolve completely
   Not adding more water to the solution after it is mixed
   Not boiling solution
   Making and using fresh solution each day
For patients using the powder form distributed by the World Health Organization (WHO)
   Adding powder to recommended amount of drinking water; shaking container for 2 or 3 minutes to dissolve completely
   Not adding more water to the solution after it is mixed
   Not boiling solution
   Making and using fresh solution each day

Precautions while using this medication
   Eating soft foods, such as cereals, bananas, cooked peas and beans, and potatoes, to maintain nutrition
   Giving breast milk to breast-fed infants between doses of solution
   Checking with physician if diarrhea does not improve in a day or 2 or becomes worse during treatment with this medication
   Checking with physician as soon as possible if signs of severe dehydration occur, including doughy skin (decreased skin turgor), sunken eyes, dizziness or lightheadedness, weakness or tiredness, irritability, and weight loss
For patients taking ORS-citrate or ORS-bicarbonate
   Drinking water between doses of rehydration solution (except breast-fed infants)
For patients taking the premixed liquid form
   Avoiding other electrolyte-containing foods or liquids, such as fruit juices or foods with added salt, until rehydration solutions are discontinued, to prevent excessive electrolyte ingestion or osmotic diarrhea

Side/adverse effects
   Signs of potential side effects, especially hypernatremia

General Dosing Information

Infants and young children should be given small, frequent, and slowly administered amounts of oral rehydration fluid. Infants who finish 150 mL of solution per kg of body weight in less than 24 hours should be encouraged to drink plain water to prevent hypernatremia and to quench thirst.

The commercially prepared solutions do not require additional water intake because of the generally lower sodium content.

Rehydration solutions must not be diluted with water, because dilution decreases the absorptive properties of the glucose-sodium cotransport system.

Acute watery diarrhea, dysentery, and persistent diarrhea in children can also result in tissue catabolism, which may in turn lead to malnutrition. This can be further aggravated by the common practice of withholding fluids and nutrition during diarrhea. Although early feeding may result in slightly increased stool volume, nutrient absorption is increased and weight loss is lessened. Therefore, continued feeding (including breast milk) of infants and children and supplementation with plain drinking water during the maintenance phase of oral rehydration therapy are important for maintaining hydration and nutrition in the management of diarrhea.

The oral rehydration solution should be taken alternately with soft foods, such as rice cereal, bananas, cooked legumes, potatoes, or other non-lactose-containing, carbohydrate-rich food. Older children and adults should resume their normal diets as soon as the appetite returns. Other electrolyte-containing foods or liquids such as fruit juices or foods with added salt should be withheld until oral rehydration solutions are discontinued, to prevent excessive electrolyte ingestion or osmotic diarrhea.

Cow's milk should be discontinued only if diarrhea worsens considerably after feeding and the stool becomes acidic and contains reducing substances. This reflects a depression of lactase activity, which may occur when the brush borders of jejunal mucosal cells are damaged. Soy formulas without lactose are given alternately with carbohydrate and electrolytes solutions for the first 24 to 48 hours.

If the initial dehydration is severe, rehydration must be achieved by intravenous administration of an appropriate isotonic electrolyte solution, after which the oral solution may be used for maintenance when tolerance to oral intake has been established.

Parenteral rehydration therapy should be started if symptoms of dehydration reappear after aggressive oral replacement of fluids and electrolytes has been attempted.

DEXTROSE AND ELECTROLYTES

Oral Dosage Forms

DEXTROSE AND ELECTROLYTES SOLUTION

Usual adult and adolescent dose:
   Rehydration—
      Mild dehydration: Oral, initially 50 mL of solution per kg of body weight over four to six hours, the amounts and rates being adjusted as needed and tolerated, depending on thirst and response to therapy.
      Moderate dehydration: Oral, initially 100 mL of solution per kg of body weight over six hours, the amounts and rates being adjusted as needed and tolerated, depending on thirst and response to therapy.
      Note: Severe dehydration must be treated with intravenous electrolyte solutions.
   Maintenance of hydration—
      Mild continuing diarrhea: Oral, 100 to 200 mL of solution per kg of body weight over twenty-four hours until diarrhea stops.
      Severe continuing diarrhea: Oral, 15 mL of solution per kg of body weight every hour until diarrhea stops.

Usual adult prescribing limits: Up to 1000 mL per hour.

ORAL REHYDRATION SALTS

Oral Dosage Forms

ORAL REHYDRATION SALTS USP (FOR ORAL SOLUTION)

Usual adult and adolescent dose:
Rehydration—
Mild dehydration: Oral, initially 50 mL of solution per kg of body weight over four to six hours, the amounts and rates being adjusted as needed and tolerated, depending on thirst and response to therapy.
Moderate dehydration: Oral, initially 100 mL of solution per kg of body weight over six hours, the amounts and rates being adjusted as needed and tolerated, depending on thirst and response to therapy.
Note: Severe dehydration must be treated with intravenous electrolyte solutions.

Maintenance of hydration—
Mild continuing diarrhea: Oral, 100 to 200 mL of solution per kg of body weight over twenty-four hours until diarrhea stops.
Severe continuing diarrhea: Oral, 15 mL of solution per kg of body weight every hour until diarrhea stops.

Usual adult prescribing limits: Up to 1000 mL per hour.

Additional information: The WHO oral rehydration solution contains sodium chloride 3.5 grams, potassium chloride 1.5 grams, sodium bicarbonate 2.5 grams or sodium citrate (dihydrate) 2.9 grams, and dextrose 20.0 grams, per liter of water.

RICE SYRUP SOLIDS AND ELECTROLYTES

Oral Dosage Forms

RICE SYRUP SOLIDS AND ELECTROLYTES SOLUTION

Usual adult and adolescent dose: See *Dextrose and Electrolytes Solution.*

CARBONIC ANHYDRASE INHIBITORS   Systemic

INN: Included in brackets after individual generic listings, if different from the U.S. generic name.

Some commonly used *brand names* are:
In the U.S.—
Ak-Zol [Acetazolamide]   *Daranide*
Dazamide [Acetazolamide]   [Dichlorphenamide]
Diamox [Acetazolamide]   *Neptazane*
Diamox Sequels   [Methazolamide]
   [Acetazolamide]
In Canada—
Acetazolam   *Diamox Sequels*
   [Acetazolamide]   [Acetazolamide]
Apo-Acetazolamide   *Neptazane*
   [Acetazolamide]   [Methazolamide]
Diamox [Acetazolamide]

ACETAZOLAMIDE
Oral
Acetazolamide Extended-release Capsules
In the U.S. and Canada— *Diamox Sequels*
Acetazolamide Tablets USP
In the U.S.—*Ak-Zol; Dazamide; Diamox;* GENERIC
In Canada—*Acetazolam; Apo-Acetazolamide; Diamox*
Parenteral
Sterile Acetazolamide Sodium USP
In the U.S.—*Diamox;* GENERIC
In Canada—*Diamox*
DICHLORPHENAMIDE [INN: Diclofenamide]
Oral
Dichlorphenamide Tablets USP
In the U.S.—*Daranide*
METHAZOLAMIDE
Oral
Methazolamide Tablets USP
In the U.S. and Canada—*Neptazane*

Category

Antiglaucoma agent—Acetazolamide, Dichlorphenamide, Methazolamide.
Anticonvulsant—Acetazolamide (tablets and injection).
Altitude sickness (acute) agent—Acetazolamide.
Antiparalytic (familial periodic paralysis)—Acetazolamide.
Diuretic, urinary alkalinizing—Acetazolamide (parenteral).
Antiurolithic (uric acid calculi; cystine calculi)—Acetazolamide Tablets USP.

Indications

Note: Bracketed information in the *Indications* section refers to uses not included in U.S. product labeling.

Accepted
Glaucoma, open-angle (treatment);
Glaucoma, secondary (treatment);
Glaucoma, angle-closure (treatment); or
[Glaucoma, malignant (treatment)]—Carbonic anhydrase inhibitors are indicated primarily as adjuncts to other agents in the treatment of open-angle (chronic simple) glaucoma and secondary glaucoma, and to lower intraocular pressure prior to surgery for some types of glaucoma.

These medications should not be used for long-term therapy in noncongestive angle-closure (closed-angle) glaucoma; organic closure of the angle may occur while the worsening condition is masked by the lowered intraocular pressure.

[Acetazolamide is used also to lower intraocular pressure in the treatment of malignant (ciliary block) glaucoma, which may occur after inflammation, surgery, trauma, or use of miotics.]

Epilepsy, absence seizure pattern (treatment);
Epilepsy, tonic-clonic seizure pattern (treatment);
Epilepsy, mixed seizure pattern (treatment);
Epilepsy, simple partial seizure pattern (treatment); or

Epilepsy, myoclonic seizure pattern (treatment)—Acetazolamide is indicated as an adjunct to other anticonvulsants in the management of absence seizures (petit mal), generalized tonic-clonic seizures (grand mal), mixed seizure patterns, simple partial seizure patterns, and myoclonic seizure patterns. It may be especially useful for intermittent therapy in females who experience increased seizure activity at the time of menstruation.

Altitude sickness (prophylaxis)[1]; or

Altitude sickness (treatment)[1]—Oral acetazolamide is indicated to decrease the incidence and/or severity of symptoms (such as headache, nausea, shortness of breath, dizziness, drowsiness, and fatigue) associated with acute altitude sickness in mountain climbers who are attempting rapid ascent and in those who are very susceptible to altitude sickness despite gradual ascent. Gradual ascent is desirable for prevention of acute altitude sickness even when acetazolamide is used. However, prompt descent may still be necessary if severe manifestations of acute altitude sickness, such as pulmonary edema or cerebral edema, occur.

[Paralysis, familial periodic (treatment)[1]—Acetazolamide is used to treat both the hypokalemic and hyperkalemic forms of familial periodic paralysis. It terminates the acute attacks and, with chronic use, prevents their recurrence. It may be the drug of choice in the hypokalemic form of the condition.]

[Toxicity, weakly acidic medications (treatment)—Parenteral acetazolamide is used to produce a forced alkaline diuresis as a method of increasing the elimination of certain weakly acidic medications.]

[Renal calculi, uric acid (prophylaxis)][1]; or

[Renal calculi, cystine (prophylaxis)[1]—Oral acetazolamide is used to alkalinize the urine as a means of preventing the occurrence or recurrence of uric acid renal stones, especially in patients receiving uricosuric antigout agents, or of cystine renal stones.]

Unaccepted

Acetazolamide has also been used to prevent or counteract metabolic alkalosis, including that which may occur following open-heart surgery; however, it is no longer used for these indications.

Acetazolamide has also been used as a diuretic in the treatment of edema due to congestive heart disease and drug-induced edema. However, it has been replaced by newer diuretics for these indications.

---

[1]Not included in Canadian product labeling.

Pharmacology

Mechanism of action/Effect: Nonbacteriostatic sulfonamide derivatives. Inhibition of the enzyme carbonic anhydrase decreases formation of hydrogen and bicarbonate ions from carbon dioxide and water and reduces the availability of these ions for active transport. These agents reduce plasma bicarbonate concentration and increase plasma chloride concentration, producing systemic metabolic acidosis. Although all of these medications may produce diuresis with acute or intermittent administration, loss of diuretic effect occurs with chronic administration. Therefore, dichlorphenamide and methazolamide are not used as diuretics, and acetazolamide is now being used only to produce alkaline diuresis in certain cases of drug overdose. Methazolamide has less diuretic effect and less influence on urinary bicarbonate than do other carbonic anhydrase inhibitors with doses used in glaucoma.

Antiglaucoma agent—Lower intraocular pressure by decreasing the production of aqueous humor by 50 to 60%. The mechanism is not completely understood but probably involves a decrease of the bicarbonate ion concentration in ocular fluids. These agents have no effect on the facility of aqueous outflow. The ocular action is independent of any diuretic action.

For acetazolamide

Anticonvulsant—Mechanism of action has not been fully determined. Inhibition of carbonic anhydrase in the central nervous

system (CNS) may increase carbon dioxide tension, resulting in a retardation of neuronal conduction. The production of systemic metabolic acidosis may also be involved. This action is independent of any diuretic action.

Altitude sickness, acute, agent—May act by producing metabolic acidosis resulting in increased respiratory drive and arterial oxygen tension and/or by causing diuresis.

In clinical trials, pulmonary function, such as minute ventilation, expired vital capacity, and peak flow, was greater in climbers treated with acetazolamide, whether they had acute altitude sickness or were asymptomatic. Acetazolamide-treated climbers also had less difficulty sleeping.

Antiparalytic (for familial periodic paralysis)—May stabilize muscle membranes against abnormal fluxes of potassium ions. Alternatively, may produce metabolic acidosis resulting in prevention of the intracellular shift of potassium.

Diuretic, urinary alkalinizing—Induces alkaline diuresis by lowering hydrogen ion concentration in the renal tubule and increasing excretion of bicarbonate, sodium, potassium, and water. This increases the solubility in urine of weakly acidic drugs and promotes their excretion.

Antiurolithic—Alkalinization of the urine increases the solubility in urine of uric acid and cystine, thereby reducing the formation of uric acid- or cystine-containing renal stones.

Effects on intraocular pressure:

Drug	Onset of Action	Peak Effect	Duration of Action (hr)
Acetazolamide Extended-release			
capsules	2 hr	8–12 hr	18–24
Tablets	1–1.5 hr	2–4 hr	8–12
Intravenous	2 min	15 min	4–5
Dichlorphenamide Tablets	0.5–1 hr	2–4 hr	6–12
Methazolamide Tablets	2–4 hr	6–8 hr	10–18

Precautions to Consider

Cross-sensitivity and/or related problems

Patients sensitive to antibacterial sulfonamides, thiazide diuretics, or other sulfonamide-derivative diuretics may be sensitive to carbonic anhydrase inhibitors also.

Geriatrics

Although appropriate studies with carbonic anhydrase inhibitors have not been performed in the geriatric population, no geriatrics-specific problems have been documented to date. However, elderly patients are more likely to have age-related renal problems, which may require caution in patients receiving these medications.

Dental

Acetazolamide may cause facial paresthesia, such as numbness, tingling, or burning feeling of the mouth, tongue, or lips. Other carbonic anhydrase inhibitors may cause similar side effects.

Drug interactions and/or related problems

The following drug interactions and/or related problems have been selected on the basis of their potential clinical significance (possible mechanism in parentheses where appropriate)—not necessarily inclusive (» = major clinical significance):

Note: Combinations containing any of the following medications, depending on the amount present, may also interact with this medication.

Adrenocorticoids, glucocorticoid, especially with significant mineralocorticoid activity, or

Adrenocorticoids, mineralocorticoid, or
Amphotericin B, parenteral, or
Corticotropin, especially prolonged therapeutic use
  (concurrent use with carbonic anhydrase inhibitors may result in severe hypokalemia and should be undertaken with caution; serum potassium concentrations and cardiac function should be monitored during concurrent use)

  (concurrent use of adrenocorticoids or corticotropin with acetazolamide sodium may increase the risk of hypernatremia and/or edema because these medications cause sodium and fluid retention; the risk with adrenocorticoids or corticotropin may depend on the patient's sodium requirement as determined by the condition being treated)

  (the possibility should be considered that concurrent chronic use of adrenocorticoids or corticotropin with carbonic anhydrase inhibitors may increase the risk of hypocalcemia and osteoporosis because these medications increase calcium excretion)

» Amphetamines or
Anticholinergics, especially atropine and related compounds, or
» Mecamylamine or
» Quinidine
  (therapeutic and/or side effects may be enhanced or prolonged when these medications are used concurrently with carbonic anhydrase inhibitors, especially acetazolamide, as a result of decreased excretion caused by alkalinization of urine; concurrent use with mecamylamine is not recommended; dosage adjustments of the other medications may be needed when carbonic anhydrase inhibitor therapy is initiated or discontinued or if the dosage is changed)

Antidiabetic agents, oral, or
Insulin
  (hypoglycemic response may be decreased during concurrent use because carbonic anhydrase inhibitors may cause hyperglycemia and glycosuria in diabetic patients; dosage adjustments may be required)

Barbiturates, especially phenobarbital, or
Carbamazepine or
Phenytoin or other hydantoin anticonvulsants or
Primidone
  (osteopenia induced by these agents may be enhanced; it is recommended that patients receiving concurrent therapy be monitored for early signs of osteopenia and that the carbonic anhydrase inhibitor be discontinued and appropriate treatment initiated if necessary)

Ciprofloxacin
  (urinary alkalizers, such as carbonic anhydrase inhibitors, may reduce the solubility of ciprofloxacin in the urine; patients should be observed for signs of crystalluria and nephrotoxicity)

Digitalis glycosides
  (concurrent use with carbonic anhydrase inhibitors may enhance the possibility of digitalis toxicity associated with hypokalemia)

Diuretics, other
  (diuretic effects may be enhanced during concurrent therapy; however, the hypokalemic and hyperuricemic effects of many diuretics may also be enhanced during concurrent therapy)

Ephedrine
  (urine alkalinization induced by carbonic anhydrase inhibitors may increase the half-life of ephedrine and prolong its duration of action, especially if the urine remains alkaline for several days or longer; dosage adjustment of ephedrine may be necessary)

Lithium
  (carbonic anhydrase inhibitors may increase lithium excretion; single doses of intravenous acetazolamide may be useful in the management of lithium toxicity)

Mannitol or
Urea
  (concurrent use with carbonic anhydrase inhibitors may lead to increased reduction of intraocular pressure as well as increased diuresis)

» Methenamine
  (efficacy may be reduced because alkaline urine produced by carbonic anhydrase inhibitors inhibits methenamine conversion to formaldehyde, which is the active bacteriostatic derivative of methenamine; concurrent use is not recommended)

Mexiletine
  (marked alkalinization of urine by carbonic anhydrase inhibitors may retard renal excretion of mexiletine)

Neuromuscular blocking agents, nondepolarizing
  (hypokalemia induced by carbonic anhydrase inhibitors may enhance the blockade of nondepolarizing neuromuscular blocking agents, possibly leading to increased or prolonged respiratory depression or paralysis [apnea]; serum potassium concentration determinations may be necessary prior to administration of a nondepolarizing neuromuscular blocking agent)

Salicylates
  (the risk of salicylate intoxication in patients receiving large doses of salicylates may be increased during concurrent therapy because metabolic acidosis induced by carbonic anhydrase inhibitors may increase penetration of salicylate into the brain; on the other hand, alkalinization of the urine results in increased salicylate excretion and decreased salicylate plasma concentrations; nevertheless, the increased risk of severe metabolic acidosis and salicylate toxicity must be considered if acetazolamide is used to produce forced alkaline diuresis in the treatment of salicylate overdose)

Contraindications/Medical problems
The contraindications/medical problems included have been selected on the basis of their potential clinical significance (reasons given in parentheses where appropriate)—not necessarily inclusive (» = major clinical significance).

Risk-benefit should be considered when the following medical problems exist:
» Adrenal gland failure or adrenocortical insufficiency (Addison's disease)
  (patients more susceptible to electrolyte imbalances)

Diabetes mellitus
  (may increase blood and urine sugar concentrations)

Gout, except when used to prevent uric acid calculi in patients receiving uricosuric antigout agents, or
» Hyperchloremic acidosis or
» Hypokalemia, hyponatremia, or other electrolyte imbalance, or
Respiratory acidosis
  (may be exacerbated)

» Hepatic disease, including cirrhosis, or impairment
  (patients more susceptible to electrolyte imbalances; increased risk of hepatic coma and hepatotoxicity)

Impaired alveolar ventilation due to pulmonary disease, edema, infection, or obstruction
  (respiratory acidosis may be induced or increased)

» Renal failure, disease, or impairment
  (excessively high plasma concentrations may result and the acidosis of renal failure may be aggravated)

» Renal calculi, calcium-containing, or history of
  (may be exacerbated or induced during therapy)

Sensitivity to carbonic anhydrase inhibitors

Side/Adverse Effects

Note: Serious side/adverse effects occur infrequently; many of the serious adverse effects are those that are common to all sulfonamide derivatives. Many side effects are dose-related and may respond to a reduction of dosage.

Hypokalemia may occur if diuresis is brisk and may be especially likely to occur if hepatic cirrhosis is present, if potassium intake is inadequate, or if other potassium-wasting drugs are used concurrently. Potassium supplementation may be necessary in some patients.

Severe metabolic acidosis or acidotic coma may occur rarely during long-term carbonic anhydrase inhibitor therapy and may be corrected by administration of bicarbonate.

The following side/adverse effects have been selected on the basis of their potential clinical significance (possible signs and symptoms in parentheses where appropriate)—not necessarily inclusive:*	Legend: **I** = Acetazolamide **II** = Dichlorphenamide **III** = Methazolamide		
	I	**II**	**III**
Medical attention needed			
Acidosis (shortness of breath, troubled breathing)#	R	R	R
Blood dyscrasias (fever and sore throat, unusual bruising or bleeding)†	R	R	R
Bloody or black, tarry stools	R	R	R
Cholestatic jaundice (darkening of urine, pale stools, yellow eyes or skin)	R	U	U
Clumsiness or unsteadiness	R	R	R
Confusion	R	R	R
Convulsions	R	R	R
Crystalluria, renal calculus, or sulfonamide-like nephrotoxicity (blood in urine, difficult urination, pain in lower back, pain or burning while urinating, sudden decrease in amount of urine)†	L	L	L
Hypersensitivity (fever, hives, itching, skin rash or sores)	R	R	R
Hypokalemia (dryness of mouth, increased thirst, irregular heartbeats, mood or mental changes, muscle cramps or pain, nausea or vomiting, unusual tiredness or weakness, weak pulse)‡	R	R	R
Mental depression	L	L	L
Nearsightedness§	R	R	R
Ringing or buzzing in ears	R	R	R
Severe muscle weakness or trembling	R	R	R
*Unusual tiredness or weakness**	M	M	M
Medical attention needed only if continuing or bothersome			
Constipation	U	R	U
Diarrhea	M	M	M
Dizziness or lightheadedness	U	L	L
Drowsiness	L	L	L
Feeling of choking or lump in throat	U	R	U
General feeling of discomfort or illness	M	M	M
Headache	R	R	R

	Legend: **I** = Acetazolamide **II** = Dichlorphenamide **III** = Methazolamide		
	I	**II**	**III**
Increase in frequency of urination or amount of urine	M	M	R
Increased sensitivity of eyes to sunlight	R	U	R
Loss of appetite	M	M	M
Loss of taste and smell	R	R	R
Metallic taste in mouth	M	M	M
Nausea or vomiting	M	M	M
Nervousness or irritability	U	R	U
Numbness, tingling, or burning in hands, fingers, feet, toes, mouth, tongue, lips, or anus†	M	M	M
Weight loss	M	M	M

*Acetazolamide is the most widely used carbonic anhibitor; most of the data concerning side effects have been reported for that medication. The comparatively infrequent reports of side effects with other agents of this group may reflect their less frequent usage rather than actual reduced incidence. The pharmacologic similarity of these medications suggests that side effects occurring with one may potentially occur with the others. However, many side effects may not occur with the same severity or frequency with all carbonic anhydrase inhibitors, and patients unable to tolerate one of these medications may be able to tolerate another. Frequency of side effects (generalized): M = more frequent; L = less frequent; R = rare; U = unknown.

†May be more likely to occur with acetazolamide and least likely to occur with methazolamide.

‡May be more likely to occur with dichlorphenamide.

§Transient myopia may occur when therapy is initiated and usually responds to a reduction in dosage or withdrawal of therapy. This may not recur if therapy is restarted.

#May be less likely to occur with dichlorphenamide.

**Usually part of a general feeling of malaise induced by these agents but should be evaluated because rarely may indicate acidosis, blood dyscrasias, or hypokalemia.

Patient Consultation

In providing consultation, consider emphasizing the following selected information (» = major clinical significance):

Before using this medication
» Conditions affecting use, especially:
   Sensitivity to carbonic anhydrase inhibitors, antibacterial sulfonamides, thiazide diuretics, or other sulfonamide-derivative diuretics
   Pregnancy—Studies in animals have shown teratogenic (skeletal anomalies) and embryocidal effects
   Use by athletes—Acetazolamide, dichlorphenamide, and methazolamide are banned in athletes by the U.S. Olympic Committee (USOC) and the National Collegiate Athletic Association (NCAA)
   Other medications, especially amphetamines, mecamylamine, methenamine, or quinidine
   Other medical problems, especially adrenal gland failure or adrenocortical insufficiency; hyperchloremic acidosis; hypokalemia, hyponatremia, or other electrolyte imbalance; hepatic disease, including cirrhosis or impairment; renal failure, disease, or impairment; or calcium-containing renal calculi or history of

Proper use of this medication
» Importance of not taking more medication than the amount prescribed

Taking medication with meals to lessen gastrointestinal upset

How to minimize inconvenience of unwanted diuresis

Missed dose: Taking as soon as possible; not taking if almost time for next dose; not doubling doses
» Proper storage

Precautions while using this medication
» Caution if drowsiness, dizziness, lightheadedness, or tiredness occurs

Regular visits to physician to check progress during therapy
» Possibility of hypokalemia

Diabetics: May increase blood and urine glucose concentrations

Importance of adequate fluid intake during therapy to help prevent kidney stones

Checking with physician before discontinuing acetazolamide (when used as anticonvulsant); gradual dosage reduction may be desirable

Side/adverse effects
Signs of potential side effects, especially crystalluria, renal calculus, sulfonamide-like nephrotoxicity, cholestatic jaundice, hypokalemia, blood dyscrasias, hypersensitivity, or acidosis

General Dosing Information

Carbonic anhydrase inhibitors are usually used concurrently with other antiglaucoma agents including miotics, mydriatics, and osmotic agents.

Dosage should be adjusted according to the requirements and response of the individual patient as indicated by measurement of ocular tension and symptomatology.

Carbonic anhydrase inhibitors may be given with meals to minimize gastrointestinal upset.

Maintenance of a high fluid intake may be advisable, especially in patients with hypercalciuria or gout, to reduce the risk of renal calculi.

Patients unable to tolerate one carbonic anhydrase inhibitor because of side effects may be able to tolerate another.

If a satisfactory lowering of intraocular pressure is not achieved or maintained with one carbonic anhydrase inhibitor, one of the other agents in this group may provide a beneficial effect.

It is recommended that various brands of acetazolamide marketed by different manufacturers not be used interchangeably unless data indicating therapeutic equivalence are available; bioequivalence problems have been reported.

It is recommended that carbonic anhydrase inhibitor therapy be discontinued if hematopoietic reactions, fever, skin rash, or renal problems occur.

If potassium supplementation is needed in a patient receiving a carbonic anhydrase inhibitor, the fact that plasma chloride concentration may be elevated should be kept in mind and a potassium preparation chosen that does not contain chloride.

ACETAZOLAMIDE

Summary of Differences

Indications: Also indicated as an anticonvulsant, to prevent or reduce severity of symptoms of acute altitude sickness, to treat toxicity caused by weakly acidic medications, to treat familial periodic paralysis, and to prevent uric acid or cystine renal calculi.

Side effects: See *Side/Adverse Effects*.

Additional Dosing Information

See also *General Dosing Information*.

When acetazolamide is added to existing anticonvulsant therapy, an initial daily dose of 4 to 5 mg per kg of body weight per day in addition to existing medication is recommended. Dosage may be increased as necessary. Changes from other anticonvulsants to acetazolamide or withdrawal of acetazolamide therapy should be gradual to prevent increased seizure activity and possible status epilepticus.

Tolerance to the anticonvulsant effect of acetazolamide develops rapidly, over weeks or months in some patients.

For oral dosage forms only:
• Both the acetazolamide tablets and extended-release capsules are indicated for use in glaucoma and for prophylaxis and treatment of acute altitude sickness. Although the extended release capsules may be better tolerated than the acetazolamide tablets or the tablets of the other carbonic anhydrase inhibitors, they may be less effective in some patients.

For parenteral dosage forms only:
• Direct intravenous administration is preferred; intramuscular injection may be employed but is painful.

• Parenteral administration is usually used when the patient cannot take oral medication or when a rapid initial intraocular pressure-lowering action is necessary. Therapy is usually continued with oral acetazolamide, depending on the patient's condition and response.

Oral Dosage Forms

Note: Bracketed uses in the *Dosage Forms* section refer to categories of use and/or indications that are not included in U.S. product labeling.

ACETAZOLAMIDE EXTENDED-RELEASE CAPSULES

Usual adult and adolescent dose:
Antiglaucoma agent—Oral, 500 mg two times a day, in the morning and evening.

Note: In the treatment of glaucoma, dosage greater than 1 gram per day usually does not produce an increased effect.

Altitude sickness, acute, agent[1]—Oral, 500 mg one or two times a day.

Note: During rapid ascent, such as in rescue or military operations, 1,000 mg a day is recommended. Therapy should preferably be initiated 24 to 48 hours before ascent and, while at high altitude, continued for 48 hours or longer as necessary to control symptoms.

The use of acetazolamide for rapid ascent does not obviate the need for prompt descent if severe forms of high altitude sickness, such as high altitude pulmonary edema (HAPE) or high altitude cerebral edema, occur.

Auxiliary labeling: • May cause drowsiness.

ACETAZOLAMIDE TABLETS USP

Usual adult and adolescent dose:
Antiglaucoma agent—
Open-angle glaucoma:
Initial—Oral, 250 mg one to four times a day.
Maintenance—To be titrated according to patient response; lower doses may be sufficient.
Secondary glaucoma and preoperative lowering of intraocular pressure: Oral, 250 mg every four hours. Some patients may respond to 250 mg two times a day. In some acute cases, an initial dose of 500 mg followed by 125 or 250 mg every four hours may be preferable.

Malignant (ciliary block) glaucoma: Oral, 250 mg four times a day to reduce intraocular pressure.

Anticonvulsant—Oral, 4 to 30 mg (usually 10 mg initially) per kg of body weight a day in up to 4 divided doses; usually 375 mg to 1 gram a day.

Altitude sickness, acute, agent[1]—Oral, 250 mg two to four times a day.

Note: During rapid ascent, such as in rescue or military operations, 1,000 mg a day is recommended. Therapy should preferably be initiated 24 to 48 hours before ascent and, while at high altitude, continued for 48 hours or longer as necessary to control symptoms.

The use of acetazolamide for rapid ascent does not obviate the need for prompt descent if severe forms of high altitude sickness, such as high altitude pulmonary edema (HAPE) or high altitude cerebral edema, occur.

[Antiparalytic][1]—Oral, 250 mg to 1.5 grams a day in divided doses.

[Antiurolithic][1]—Oral, 250 mg daily at bedtime.

Note: For use as an anticonvulsant or in open-angle glaucoma, dosage greater than 1 gram per day usually does not produce an increased effect.

Auxiliary labeling: • May cause drowsiness.

---

[1]Not included in Canadian product labeling.

Parenteral Dosage Forms

Note: Bracketed uses in the *Dosage Forms* section refer to categories of use and/or indications that are not included in U.S. product labeling.

STERILE ACETAZOLAMIDE SODIUM USP

Usual adult and adolescent dose:

Antiglaucoma agent—For rapid initial lowering of intraocular pressure: Intravenous (preferred) or intramuscular, the equivalent of acetazolamide—500 mg. Alternatively, 250 mg intravenously plus 250 mg intramuscularly may be given.

Note: Parenteral administration may be repeated in two to four hours in some acute cases but therapy is usually continued with oral acetazolamide, depending on the patient's response.

[Diuretic (urinary alkalinizing)]—Intravenous, 5 mg per kg of body weight or as required to achieve and maintain a forced alkaline diuresis.

Note: For other uses or when the patient is unable to take oral medication, acetazolamide may be given parenterally in dosages equivalent to those recommended for the oral tablets. (See *Acetazolamide Tablets USP*.)

DICHLORPHENAMIDE

Summary of Differences

Side effects: See *Side/Adverse Effects*.

Oral Dosage Forms

DICHLORPHENAMIDE TABLETS USP

Usual adult and adolescent dose: Antiglaucoma agent—
Initial: 100 to 200 mg for the first dose followed by 100 mg every twelve hours until the desired response is obtained.
Maintenance: 25 to 50 mg one to three times a day.

Auxiliary labeling: • May cause drowsiness.

METHAZOLAMIDE

Summary of Differences

Side effects: See *Side/Adverse Effects*.

Oral Dosage Forms

METHAZOLAMIDE TABLETS USP

Usual adult and adolescent dose: Antiglaucoma agent—Oral, 25 to 100 mg two to three times a day.

Auxiliary labeling: • May cause drowsiness.

CELLULOSE SODIUM PHOSPHATE   Systemic†

A commonly used *brand name* in the U.S. is *Calcibind*.

ORAL
Cellulose Sodium Phosphate USP (for Oral Suspension)†
In the U.S.—*Calcibind*.

---

†Not commercially available in Canada.

Category: Antiurolithic (calcium calculi).

Indications

Accepted
Renal calculi, calcium (prophylaxis)—Cellulose sodium phosphate is indicated for reducing the incidence of new renal stone formation in patients with absorptive hypercalciuria Type I (characterized by recurrent formation or passage of calcium oxalate and/or calcium phosphate renal calculi; evidence of high intestinal calcium ab-

sorption, i.e., urinary calcium concentration >0.2 mg per mg creatinine after oral load of 1 gram of calcium; hypercalciuria, i.e., 24-hour urinary calcium >200 mg per day on a diet of 400 mg calcium and 100 mEq sodium per day; normal fasting urinary calcium; no evidence of bone disease; normal serum calcium and phosphorus; normal parathyroid function; and lack of excessive skeletal mobilization of calcium, or renal leak).

Although some clinicians recommend the use of cellulose sodium phosphate as the primary agent for treatment of absorptive hypercalciuria Type I, others prefer to use dietary restriction of calcium and oxalate, thiazide diuretics, and increased fluid intake as the primary method of treatment.

Minimal diagnostic tests for different causes of hypercalciuria include serum calcium, phosphorus, and parathyroid hormone (PTH) determinations obtained on an empty stomach; 24-hour urinary calcium on a diet restricted for at least 10 days in calcium and sodium; and a determination of urinary excretion of calcium while fasting for 12 hours.

Unaccepted

Cellulose sodium phosphate is *not* indicated for causes of hypercalciuria other than hyperabsorption. This medication may be used on a temporary basis for absorptive hypercalciuria Type II (identical to Type I, but the hypercalciuria can usually be eliminated by a calcium-restricted diet alone). Cellulose sodium phosphate should not be used for absorptive hypophosphatemic hypercalciuria Type III because hypercalciuria may result, in part, from an increased skeletal mobilization of calcium.

Pharmacology

Mechanism of action/Effect: Binds dietary and secreted calcium, preventing intestinal calcium absorption. Thus, decreased urinary saturation of calcium, with only slightly increased urinary oxalate and phosphorus, may prevent the spontaneous nucleation of calcium oxalate and calcium phosphate to form stones.

Other actions/effects: Also binds dietary magnesium and decreases urinary magnesium concentration. Increases urinary oxalate by binding divalent cations, making them unavailable to oxalate, thus increasing oxalate absorption. Increases urinary phosphorus, reflecting hydrolysis of 7 to 30% of cellulose sodium phosphate in the intestinal tract and absorption of released phosphorus.

Precautions to Consider

Geriatrics

No information is available on the relationship of age to the effects of cellulose sodium phosphate in geriatric patients.

Drug interactions and/or related problems

The following drug interactions and/or related problems have been selected on the basis of their potential clinical significance (possible mechanism in parentheses where appropriate)—not necessarily inclusive (» = major clinical significance):

Note: Combinations containing any of the following medications, depending on the amount present, may also interact with this medication.

Ascorbic acid
(concurrent use with cellulose sodium phosphate may result in metabolism of ascorbic acid to oxalate)

» Calcium-containing medications, including calcium supplements, or

» Milk or other dairy products
(concurrent use may decrease effectiveness of cellulose sodium phosphate in preventing hypercalciuria)

Foods high in oxalate content, such as spinach (and similar dark greens), chocolate, brewed tea, and rhubarb
(concurrent use with cellulose sodium phosphate may lead to hyperoxaluria, negating the beneficial effect of hypocalciuria)

» Magnesium-containing medications, including magnesium supplements
(simultaneous use with cellulose sodium phosphate may result in binding of magnesium; patients should be advised not to take these medications within 1 hour of cellulose sodium phosphate)

Contraindications/Medical problems

The contraindications/medical problems included have been selected on the basis of their potential clinical significance (reasons given in parentheses where appropriate)—not necessarily inclusive (» = major clinical significance).

Except under special circumstances, this medication should not be used when the following medical problems exist:

» Bone disease, such as osteitis, osteomalacia, and osteoporosis
(may further deplete calcium needed to prevent loss of bone mass)

» High fasting urinary calcium, unless a high skeletal mobilization of calcium can be excluded, or

» Hypophosphatemia
(may indicate presence of hyperparathyroidism or renal tubular defects; stimulation of parathyroid hormone (PTH) by drug-induced hypocalcemia may further deplete phosphorus and lead to muscle weakness and osteomalacia)

» Hyperoxaluria, enteric
(increases propensity of oxalate stone formation)

» Hyperparathyroidism, primary or secondary
(increases risk of parathyroid bone disease)

» Hypocalcemic states, such as hypoparathyroidism and intestinal malabsorption
(further depletion of calcium may lead to osteomalacia)

» Hypomagnesemic states—serum magnesium <1.5 mg per deciliter
(further depletion of magnesium may lead to generalized tonic-clonic seizures)

» Normal or low intestinal absorption and renal excretion of calcium
(may cause excessive PTH secretion and possible parathyroid bone disease)

Risk-benefit should be considered when the following medical problems exist:

Ascites or
Congestive heart failure or
Nephrotic syndrome
(sodium content of cellulose sodium phosphate may increase fluid retention)

Sensitivity to cellulose sodium phosphate

Side/Adverse Effects

The following side/adverse effects have been selected on the basis of their potential clinical significance (possible signs and symptoms in parentheses where appropriate)—not necessarily inclusive:

Those indicating need for medical attention

With long-term use
Hypomagnesemia (drowsiness, loss of appetite, mood or mental changes, muscle spasms [tetany] or twitching, nausea or vomiting, seizures, trembling, unusual tiredness or weakness)

Those indicating need for medical attention only if they continue or are bothersome

Incidence more frequent
Abdominal or stomach discomfort; loose bowel movements or diarrhea

Patient Consultation

In providing consultation, consider emphasizing the following selected information (» = major clinical significance):

Before using this medication

» Conditions affecting use, especially
Sensitivity to cellulose sodium phosphate
Pregnancy—Use not recommended during pregnancy because of increased need for calcium in pregnant women, unless clearly needed
Use in children—Use not recommended in children up to 16 years of age because of increased need for calcium in growing children
Other medications, especially calcium- or magnesium-containing medications
Other medical problems, especially bone disease, high fasting urinary calcium, hypophosphatemia, enteric hyperoxaluria, hypoparathyroidism, hypocalcemia, hypomagnesemia, or normal or low intestinal absorption and renal excretion of calcium

Proper use of this medication

» Taking powder mixed with a full glass (240 mL) of water, soft drink, or fruit juice; rinsing glass and drinking all of liquid to get full dose
» Taking with a meal for optimum calcium binding
» Importance of not taking more medication than the amount prescribed
» Importance of high fluid intake (240 mL hourly while awake) during therapy to dilute urine and help prevent kidney stones
  Missed dose: Skipping missed dose; not doubling doses
» Proper storage

Precautions while using this medication

» Regular visits to physician to check progress during therapy
  Avoiding simultaneous use of magnesium-containing medications; taking at least 1 hour before or after cellulose sodium phosphate
  Avoiding concurrent use with vitamin C or high oxalate foods such as spinach (and similar dark greens), chocolate, brewed tea, and rhubarb
  Avoiding concurrent use with milk or other dairy products
  Avoiding salty foods and use of extra salt to help achieve an intake of <150 mEq of sodium a day
  Patients on a sodium-restricted diet: Medication contains sodium

Side/adverse effects

Signs of potential side effects, especially hypomagnesemia

General Dosing Information

Both the initial and maintenance doses of cellulose sodium phosphate are based on measurements of 24-hour urinary calcium excretion.

If there is an inadequate hypocalciuric response (reduction of urinary calcium <30 mg per 5 grams of cellulose sodium phosphate) to treatment while patient is maintained on moderate calcium and sodium restriction, the treatment may be considered ineffective and should be stopped.

Cellulose sodium phosphate is usually administered concomitantly with magnesium supplements to replace dietary magnesium. However, supplemental magnesium should be taken at least 1 hour before or after cellulose sodium phosphate to avoid binding of magnesium.

The dose of oral magnesium supplements, given as magnesium gluconate, depends on the dose of cellulose sodium phosphate. Patients receiving 15 grams of cellulose sodium phosphate a day

should take 1.5 grams of magnesium gluconate twice a day. Those taking 10 grams of cellulose sodium phosphate a day should take 1 gram of magnesium gluconate twice a day.

Diet/Nutrition

Cellulose sodium phosphate should be taken with meals because the amount of calcium that is bound is reduced considerably when the medication is administered more than one hour after a meal. The amount of bound calcium depends on actual mixing of medication with food.

High fluid intake (240 mL hourly while awake) should be encouraged to achieve a urinary output of 2 liters a day. This keeps urine diluted and prevents stone formation.

Avoiding the use of salty foods or extra salt will help limit sodium intake to <150 mEq a day.

Ingestion of foods high in oxalate content, such as spinach or similar dark greens, chocolate, brewed tea, and rhubarb, may lead to hyperoxaluria, negating the beneficial effect of hypocalciuria.

Vitamin C supplementation may result in metabolism of ascorbic acid to oxalate.

Milk or other dairy products may decrease the effectiveness of cellulose sodium phosphate by adding more calcium to the diet.

Oral Dosage Forms

CELLULOSE SODIUM PHOSPHATE USP (FOR ORAL SUSPENSION)

Usual adult dose: Renal calculi—
  Patients with urinary calcium >300 mg a day: Oral, initially, 15 grams a day (5 grams three times a day with meals), the dosage being decreased to 10 grams a day (5 grams with main meal, 2.5 grams with each of other two meals) when urinary calcium concentration declines to <200 mg a day.
  Patients with controlled urinary calcium (<300 mg but >200 mg a day): Oral, initially, 10 grams a day with meals, the continuing dosage being determined by the physician.

Auxiliary labeling:
• Take with meals.
• Drink large amounts of fluids.

Additional information: Cellulose sodium phosphate contains 25 to 50 mEq of exchangeable sodium per 15 grams.

CEPHALOSPORINS   Systemic

Some commonly used *brand names* are:

In the U.S.—

Ancef [Cefazolin]	*C-Lexin* [Cephalexin]
Anspor [Cephradine]	*Duricef* [Cefadroxil]
Ceclor [Cefaclor]	*Fortaz* [Ceftazidime]
Cefadyl [Cephapirin]	*Keflet* [Cephalexin]
Cefanex [Cephalexin]	*Keflex* [Cephalexin]
Cefizox [Ceftizoxime]	*Keflin* [Cephalothin]
Cefobid [Cefoperazone]	*Keftab* [Cephalexin]
Cefotan [Cefotetan]	*Kefurox* [Cefuroxime]
Ceftin [Cefuroxime]	*Kefzol* [Cefazolin]
Cefzil [Cefprozil]	*Mandol* [Cefamandole]
Ceptaz [Ceftazidime]	*Mefoxin* [Cefoxitin]
Claforan [Cefotaxime]	*Monocid* [Cefonicid]

Moxam [Moxalactam]	*Ultracef* [Cefadroxil]
Precef [Ceforanide]	*Velosef* [Cephradine]
Rocephin [Ceftriaxone]	*Zefazone* [Cefmetazole]
Suprax [Cefixime]	*Zinacef* [Cefuroxime]
Tazicef [Ceftazidime]	*Zolicef* [Cefazolin]
Tazidime [Ceftazidime]	

In Canada—

Ancef [Cefazolin]	
Apo-Cephalex [Cephalexin]	*Ceporacin* [Cephalothin]
Ceclor [Cefaclor]	*Ceporex* [Cephalexin]
Cefadyl [Cephapirin]	*Ceptaz* [Ceftazidime]
Cefizox [Ceftizoxime]	*Claforan* [Cefotaxime]
Cefobid [Cefoperazone]	*Duricef* [Cefadroxil]
Cefotan [Cefotetan]	*Fortaz* [Ceftazidime]
	Keflex [Cephalexin]

Keflin [Cephalothin]
Kefzol [Cefazolin]
Mandol [Cefamandole]
Mefoxin [Cefoxitin]
Monocid [Cefonicid]
Novolexin [Cephalexin]

Nu-Cephalex [Cephalexin]
Rocephin [Ceftriaxone]
Suprax [Cefixime]
Velosef [Cephradine]
Zinacef [Cefuroxime]

CEFACLOR
Oral
    Cefaclor Capsules USP
        In the U.S. and Canada—*Ceclor*
    Cefaclor for Oral Suspension USP
        In the U.S. and Canada—*Ceclor*

CEFADROXIL
Oral
    Cefadroxil Capsules USP
        In the U.S.—*Duricef; Ultracef;* GENERIC
        In Canada—*Duricef*
    Cefadroxil for Oral Suspension USP
        In the U.S.—*Duricef; Ultracef;* GENERIC
        In Canada—*Duricef*
    Cefadroxil Tablets USP
        In the U.S.—*Duricef; Ultracef;* GENERIC
        In Canada—*Duricef*

CEFAMANDOLE
Parenteral
    Cefamandole Nafate for Injection USP
        In the U.S. and Canada—*Mandol*

CEFAZOLIN
Parenteral
    Cefazolin Sodium Injection USP†
        In the U.S.—*Ancef;* GENERIC
    Sterile Cefazolin Sodium USP
        In the U.S.—*Ancef; Kefzol; Zolicef;* GENERIC
        In Canada—*Ancef; Kefzol*

CEFIXIME
Oral
    Cefixime for Oral Suspension
        In the U.S. and Canada—*Suprax*
    Cefixime Tablets
        In the U.S. and Canada—*Suprax*

CEFMETAZOLE†
Parenteral
    Cefmetazole Sodium for Injection†
        In the U.S.—*Zefazone*

CEFONICID
Parenteral
    Sterile Cefonicid Sodium USP
        In the U.S. and Canada—*Monocid*

CEFOPERAZONE
Parenteral
    Cefoperazone Sodium Injection USP†
        In the U.S.—*Cefobid*
    Sterile Cefoperazone Sodium USP
        In the U.S. and Canada—*Cefobid*

CEFORANIDE†
Parenteral
    Ceforanide for Injection USP†
        In the U.S.—*Precef*

CEFOTAXIME
Parenteral
    Cefotaxime Sodium Injection USP†
        In the U.S.—*Claforan*
    Sterile Cefotaxime Sodium USP
        In the U.S. and Canada—*Claforan*

CEFOTETAN
Parenteral
    Sterile Cefotetan Disodium USP
        In the U.S. and Canada—*Cefotan*

CEFOXITIN
Parenteral
    Cefoxitin Sodium Injection USP†
        In the U.S.—*Mefoxin*
    Sterile Cefoxitin Sodium USP
        In the U.S. and Canada—*Mefoxin*

CEFPROZIL†
Oral
    Cefprozil for Oral Suspension†
        In the U.S.—*Cefzil*
    Cefprozil Tablets†
        In the U.S.—*Cefzil*

CEFTAZIDIME
Parenteral
    Ceftazidime Injection†
        In the U.S.—*Fortaz*
    Ceftazidime for Injection USP
        In the U.S.—*Ceptaz; Fortaz; Tazicef; Tazidime*
        In Canada—*Ceptaz; Fortaz*

CEFTIZOXIME
Parenteral
    Ceftizoxime Sodium Injection USP†
        In the U.S.—*Cefizox*
    Sterile Ceftizoxime Sodium USP
        In the U.S. and Canada—*Cefizox*

CEFTRIAXONE
Parenteral
    Ceftriaxone Sodium Injection†
        In the U.S.—*Rocephin*
    Sterile Ceftriaxone Sodium USP
        In the U.S. and Canada—*Rocephin*

CEFUROXIME
Oral
    Cefuroxime Axetil Tablets USP†
        In the U.S.— *Ceftin*
Parenteral
    Cefuroxime Sodium Injection†
        In the U.S.—*Zinacef*
    Sterile Cefuroxime Sodium USP
        In the U.S.—*Kefurox; Zinacef*
        In Canada—*Zinacef*

CEPHALEXIN
Oral
    Cephalexin Capsules USP
        In the U.S.—*Cefanex; C-Lexin; Keflex;* GENERIC
        In Canada—*Ceporex; Novolexin*
    Cephalexin for Oral Suspension USP
        In the U.S.—*C-Lexin; Keflex;* GENERIC
        In Canada—*Ceporex; Keflex; Novolexin*
    Cephalexin Tablets USP
        In the U.S.—*Keflet;* GENERIC
        In Canada—*Apo-Cephalex; Keflex; Novolexin; Nu-Cephalex*
    Cephalexin Hydrochloride Tablets†
        In the U.S.—*Keftab*

CEPHALOTHIN
Parenteral
    Cephalothin Sodium Injection USP†
        In the U.S.—*Keflin;* GENERIC
    Cephalothin Sodium for Injection USP
        In the U.S.—*Keflin;* GENERIC
        In Canada—*Ceporacin; Keflin*

CEPHAPIRIN
Parenteral
    Sterile Cephapirin Sodium USP
        In the U.S.—*Cefadyl;* GENERIC
        In Canada—*Cefadyl*

CEPHRADINE
Oral
    Cephradine Capsules USP
        In the U.S.—*Anspor; Velosef;* GENERIC
        In Canada—*Velosef*
    Cephradine for Oral Suspension USP†
        In the U.S.—*Anspor; Velosef;* GENERIC
Parenteral
    Cephradine for Injection USP†
        In the U.S.—*Velosef*
MOXALACTAM†
Parenteral
    Moxalactam Disodium for Injection USP†
        In the U.S.—*Moxam*

†Not commercially available in Canada.

Category: Antibacterial (systemic).

Indications

Accepted

Note: All of the indications listed in this section are approved in the U.S. and Canada for at least one of the organisms within the spectrum of activity of that generation of cephalosporin. Exceptions to this, documented by bracketed information and superscript "1", identify indications not included in the product labeling in the U.S. and Canada, respectively.

Cephalosporins have been classified by "generation" based on their spectrum of antibacterial activity, providing a useful, although somewhat arbitrary, means of grouping the many cephalosporins available.

First-generation cephalosporins include cefadroxil, cefazolin, cephalexin, cephalothin, cephapirin, and cephradine.

Second-generation cephalosporins include cefaclor, cefamandole, cefmetazole, cefonicid, ceforanide, cefotetan, cefoxitin, cefprozil, and cefuroxime.

Third-generation cephalosporins include cefixime, cefoperazone, cefotaxime, ceftazidime, ceftizoxime, ceftriaxone, and moxalactam.

Cephalosporins are broad-spectrum, beta-lactam antibiotics indicated in the treatment of a wide range of infections. Cefamandole, cefazolin, cefmetazole, cefonicid, ceforanide, cefotaxime, cefotetan, cefoxitin, ceftriaxone, cefuroxime, cephalothin, and cephapirin are also indicated in the prophylaxis of perioperative infections. A few cephalosporins (e.g., cefazolin, cefotetan, cefoxitin, cefuroxime) may be preferred agents in the prophylaxis of perioperative infections because of their pharmacokinetic properties and spectrum of antibacterial activity.

The decision of which cephalosporin to use is usually based on the organism(s) that are present or most likely to be present, site(s) of infection, resistance patterns, and the side effects, cost, and pharmacokinetic properties of the cephalosporin. (See also *Table 1*, page $, and *Table 2*, page $.)

First-generation cephalosporins have the highest degree of activity against most gram-positive bacteria, including beta-lactamase-producing *Staphylococcus aureus* and most streptococci; exceptions include methicillin-resistant staphylococci, and penicillin-resistant *Streptococcus pneumoniae*. No cephalosporin is effective against *Enterococcus faecalis* infections. Gram-negative bacteria coverage is generally limited to *Escherichia coli, Klebsiella* species, and *Proteus mirabilis*. Cephalothin and cefazolin have similar spectrums of activity *in vitro*, but cefazolin is more active against *E. coli* and *Klebsiella* species. Cefazolin may also be less stable against staphylococcal penicillinases than is cephalothin. Cephalexin, cefadroxil, and cephradine all have very similar activity *in vitro* and are available in an oral dosage form.

First-generation cephalosporins are used to treat septicemia, bone and joint infections, otitis media, pneumonia, skin and soft tissue infections, including burn wound infections, and urinary tract infections caused by susceptible bacterial organisms. They are not effective in treating meningitis. These medications are possible alternatives to the penicillins for staphylococcal and nonenterococcal streptococcal infections, including pneumonias, bone and joint infections, and bacterial endocarditis. Cefazolin is the preferred agent for use in perioperative prophylaxis because of its longer half-life. Because first-generation cephalosporins provide inconsistent coverage against gram-negative bacilli, their empiric use as monotherapy is not recommended.

Second-generation cephalosporins have enhanced activity against *Escherichia coli, Klebsiella* species, and *Proteus mirabilis*; in addition, they have greater activity *in vitro* against a larger number of gram-negative bacteria, including *Haemophilus influenzae*, indole-positive *Proteus, Neisseria meningitidis, N. gonorrhoeae*, and some strains of *Serratia* and *Enterobacter* species. *Serratia* and *Enterobacter* species may induce beta-lactamases that inactivate the drug after a period of exposure to the cephalosporin, producing a resistance that may be expressed late. These cephalosporins also have slightly less or variable activity against most gram-positive cocci. None of the second-generation cephalosporins have activity against *Pseudomonas aeruginosa*. Cefaclor and cephalexin have comparable activity *in vitro* against most gram-positive cocci; however, cefaclor has better activity than cephalexin against *H. influenzae, E. coli*, and *P. mirabilis*. Cefamandole, cefonicid, ceforanide, and cefuroxime all have similar activity *in vitro*. However, cefuroxime may be more stable against certain beta-lactamases (e.g., TEM-1) than is cefamandole, and cefonicid and ceforanide have less activity *in vitro* against *S. aureus*. Cefuroxime is the only second-generation cephalosporin to adequately penetrate into the cerebral spinal fluid (CSF). Cefprozil has *in vitro* activity that covers a broader range of organisms, including many gram-positive and gram-negative organisms that are typically considered to be first-generation, as well as *H. influenzae, Moraxella (Branhamella) catarrhalis, Citrobacter diversus*, and penicillinase-producing strains of *N. gonorrhoeae*.

Second-generation cephalosporins are used in the treatment of septicemia, bone and joint infections, gram-negative pneumonia, skin and soft tissue infections, including burn wound infections, and urinary tract infections caused by susceptible bacterial organisms. Cefuroxime is commonly used to treat community-acquired pneumonias because of its activity against *S. pneumoniae, S. aureus, and H. influenzae*. It has also been used to treat meningitis caused by *S. pneumoniae, H. influenzae, and N. meningitidis*, although some third-generation cephalosporins have better penetration into the CSF. Because cefaclor has good activity against many strains of *H. influenzae*, it is used in the treatment of amoxicillin-resistant otitis media and sinusitis. Cefuroxime axetil, an oral prodrug of cefuroxime that is hydrolyzed to cefuroxime after absorption, has been used to treat mild to moderate bronchitis, otitis media, skin and soft tissue infections, uncomplicated gonococcal urethritis, and urinary tract infections. Cefprozil is also used to treat bronchitis, otitis media, and skin and soft tissue infections, as well as pharyngitis and tonsillitis.

Most third-generation cephalosporins have a high degree of stability in the presence of beta-lactamases (penicillinases and cephalosporinases), and, therefore, they have excellent activity against a wider spectrum of gram-negative bacteria, including penicillinase-producing strains of *N. gonorrhoeae* and most Enterobacteriaceae (*E. coli, Citrobacter, Enterobacter, Klebsiella, Morganella, Proteus, Providencia, and Serratia* species). Cefoperazone tends to have slightly less activity against Enterobacteriaceae than the other third-generation cephalosporins because of its greater susceptibility to certain beta-lactamases (e.g., TEM-1, TEM-2). Strains of *Pseudomonas aeruginosa, Serratia* and *Enterobacter* species may induce beta-lactamases after a period of exposure to the cephalosporin, producing a resistance that may be expressed late. These medications are generally not as active against gram-positive cocci as are the first- and second-generation cephalosporins. Cefotaxime, ceftizoxime, and ceftriaxone all have similar activity *in vitro*. Cefixime, the only oral third-generation cephalosporin, has the most activity of all oral cephalosporins against *S. pyogenes, S. pneumoniae*, and all gram-negative bacilli, including beta-lactamase-producing strains of *H. influenzae, Branhamella catarrhalis*, and *N. gonorrhoeae*. Cefixime has little activity against staphylococci, and no activity against *Pseudomonas aeruginosa*.

Ceftazidime has the greatest activity of the third-generation cephalosporins against *Pseudomonas aeruginosa*. Cefoperazone also has some *P. aeruginosa* coverage. The other third-generation cephalosporins tend to have variable activity against this pathogen. Cefoperazone achieves higher biliary concentrations than the other third-generation cephalosporins, but has poor CSF penetration. Moxalactam has moderate to poor activity against *P. aeruginosa* and the least activity of the third-generation cephalosporins against gram-positive cocci.

Third-generation cephalosporins and aminoglycosides (amikacin, gentamicin, netilmicin, or tobramycin) are synergistic *in vitro* against certain susceptible and resistant strains of *P. aeruginosa, S. marcescens*, and other Enterobacteriaceae, including *Enterobacter cloacae, E. coli, K. pneumoniae*, and *P. mirabilis*.

Third-generation cephalosporins are used in the treatment of serious gram-negative bacterial infections, including septicemia, bone and joint infections, female pelvic infections, intra-abdominal infections, gram-negative pneumonia, skin and soft tissue infections, including burn wound infections, and complicated urinary tract infections caused by susceptible organisms. Cefotaxime, ceftriaxone, and ceftazidime are used to treat meningitis in both children and adults. Single-dose ceftriaxone has been found to be effective in the treatment of uncomplicated gonorrhea; and [ceftriaxone and cefotaxime have also been used in the treatment of the later stages of Lyme disease][1].

Cefoxitin, cefotetan, cefmetazole, and moxalactam have the greatest activity of the cephalosporins against anaerobes, particularly the *Bacteroides fragilis* group. Cefoxitin has the greatest stability in the presence of beta-lactamases produced by the *Bacteroides fragilis* group. Cefotetan has similar activity against *B. fragilis*, but cefotetan has greater activity than cefmetazole, which has greater activity than cefoxitin, against aerobic gram-negative bacilli. Most strains of *Bacteroides distasonis, B. ovatus*, and *B. thetaiotaomicron* are resistant to cefotetan. Many of the second- and third-generation cephalosporins that are active against anaerobic organisms are not effective against resistant strains of the *Bacteroides fragilis* group.

Cefoxitin, cefotetan, and cefmetazole are primarily used in the treatment of mixed aerobic-anaerobic bacterial infections, including aspiration pneumonia, diabetic foot infections, intra-abdominal and female pelvic infections. They are also used prophylactically to help prevent perioperative infections that may result from colorectal surgery and appendectomies, and in the treatment of penicillin-resistant strains of gonorrhea.

Unaccepted

None of the cephalosporins is considered to be effective against enterococci, *Listeria* species, chlamydia, *Clostridium difficile*, or methicillin-resistant *Staphylococcus epidermidis* or *S. aureus*.

---

[1]Not included in Canadian product labeling.

Pharmacology

Mechanism of action/Effect: Bactericidal; action depends on ability to reach and bind penicillin-binding proteins located in bacterial cytoplasmic membranes; cephalosporins inhibit bacterial septum and cell wall synthesis, probably by acylation of membrane-bound transpeptidase enzymes. This prevents cross-linkage of peptidoglycan chains, which is necessary for bacterial cell wall strength and rigidity. Also, cell division and growth are inhibited, and lysis and elongation of susceptible bacteria frequently occur. Rapidly dividing bacteria are those most susceptible to the action of cephalosporins.

Precautions to Consider

Cross-sensitivity and/or related problems

Patients allergic to one cephalosporin or cephamycin may be allergic to other cephalosporins or cephamycins also.

Patients allergic to penicillins, penicillin derivatives, or penicillamine may be allergic to cephalosporins or cephamycins also. Cephalosporin cross-reactivity is approximately 3 to 7% in patients with a documented history of penicillin allergy. Although cephalosporins have been administered without incident to some patients with rash-type penicillin allergy, caution is recommended when cephalosporins are administered to patients with a history of penicillin anaphylaxis since anaphylaxis may also occur after cephalosporin administration.

Geriatrics

Cephalosporins have been used in the geriatric population, and no geriatrics-specific problems have been documented to date. However, elderly patients are more likely to have an age-related decrease in renal function, which may require an adjustment of dosage and/or dosing interval in patients receiving cephalosporins.

Dental

Long-term therapy with cephalosporins may allow for the overgrowth of *Candida albicans*, resulting in oral candidiasis.

Drug interactions and/or related problems

The following drug interactions and/or related problems have been selected on the basis of their potential clinical significance (possible mechanism in parentheses where appropriate)—not necessarily inclusive (» = major clinical significance):

Note: Combinations containing any of the following medications, depending on the amount present, may also interact with this medication.

» Alcohol

(concurrent use of alcohol with cefamandole, cefmetazole, cefoperazone, cefotetan, or moxalactam is not recommended since these cephalosporins, due to their *N*-methylthiotetrazole side chain, may inhibit the enzyme acetaldehyde dehydrogenase, resulting in accumulation of acetaldehyde in the blood)

(disulfiram-like effects such as abdominal or stomach cramps, nausea, vomiting, headache, hypotension, palpitations, shortness of breath, tachycardia, sweating, or facial flushing may occur following ingestion of alcohol or administration of intravenous alcohol-containing solutions; these effects usually occur within 15 to 30 minutes following ingestion of alcohol and usually subside spontaneously over several hours; no problems have been documented when alcohol was consumed prior to or concurrently with the first dose of moxalactam)

(patients should be advised not to drink alcoholic beverages, take alcohol-containing medications, or receive intravenous alcohol-containing solutions while receiving these cephalosporins and for several days after discontinuing them)

» Anticoagulants, coumarin- or indandione-derivative, or
» Heparin or
» Thrombolytic agents

(concurrent use of these medications with cefamandole, cefmetazole, cefoperazone, cefotetan, or moxalactam may potentially increase the risk of bleeding because of the *N*-methylthiotetrazole (NMTT) side chain on these medications. However, critical illness, poor nutritional status, and the presence of liver disease may be more important risk factors for hypoprothrombinemia and bleeding. All cephalosporins can inhibit vitamin K synthesis by suppressing gut flora. Prophylactic vitamin K therapy is recommended when any of these medications are used for prolonged periods in malnourished or seriously ill patients. In addition, moxalactam causes irreversible platelet damage; dosage adjustments of anticoagulants may be necessary during and after therapy with cefamandole, cefmetazole, cefoperazone, cefotetan, or moxalactam; concurrent use of these 5 cephalosporins with thrombolytic agents may increase the risk of severe hemorrhage and is not recommended)

Nephrotoxic medications
(cephalothin has been associated with an increased incidence of nephrotoxicity when used concurrently with aminoglycosides; this effect has rarely been seen with other commercially available cephalosporins used at appropriate doses; the potential for increased nephrotoxicity exists when cephalosporins are used with other nephrotoxic medications, such as loop diuretics, especially in patients with pre-existing renal function impairment)

» Platelet aggregation inhibitors, other
(concurrent use of these medications with high-dose moxalactam may increase the risk of hemorrhage because of additive inhibition of platelet function; in addition, hypoprothrombinemia induced by large doses of salicylates and/or cephalosporins, and the gastrointestinal ulcerative or hemorrhagic potential of nonsteroidal anti-inflammatory drugs (NSAIDs), salicylates, or sulfinpyrazone may also increase the risk of hemorrhage)

» Probenecid
(probenecid decreases renal tubular secretion of those cephalosporins excreted by this mechanism, resulting in increased and prolonged cephalosporin serum concentrations, prolonged elimination half-life, and increased risk of toxicity; probenecid has no effect on the excretion of cefoperazone, ceforanide, ceftazidime, ceftriaxone, or moxalactam; however, other cephalosporins and probenecid might be used concurrently in the treatment of infections, such as sexually transmitted diseases [STDs] or other infections, in which high and/or prolonged antibiotic serum and tissue concentrations are required)

Contraindications/Medical problems

The contraindications/medical problems included have been selected on the basis of their potential clinical significance (reasons given in parentheses where appropriate)—not necessarily inclusive (» = major clinical significance).

Except under special circumstances, this medication should not be used when the following medical problem exists:

» Previous allergic reaction (anaphylaxis) to penicillins, penicillin derivatives, penicillamine, or cephalosporins

Risk-benefit should be considered when the following medical problems exist:

» Bleeding disorders, history of
(cefamandole, cefmetazole, cefoperazone, cefotetan, and moxalactam, which contain the NMTT side chain, have been associated with an increased risk of bleeding; however, all cephalosporins may cause hypoprothrombinemia and, potentially, bleeding)

» Gastrointestinal disease, history of, especially ulcerative colitis, regional enteritis, or antibiotic-associated colitis
(cephalosporins may cause pseudomembranous colitis)

» Hepatic function impairment
(cefoperazone is primarily excreted in bile; may also cause elevated AST [SGOT], ALT [SGPT], and alkaline phosphatase; it is recommended that patients with both severe liver disease and significant renal disease receive a reduced dosage of cefoperazone)

Phenylketonuria
(cefprozil for oral suspension contains 28 mg of phenylalanine per 5 mL)

» Renal function impairment
(many cephalosporins are excreted renally; a reduced dosage is recommended in patients with renal function impairment receiving cefadroxil, cefamandole, cefazolin, cefixime, cefmetazole, cefonicid, ceforanide, cefotaxime, cefotetan, cefoxitin, cefprozil, ceftazidime, ceftizoxime, cefuroxime, cephalexin, cephalothin, cephradine, and moxalactam)

Side/Adverse Effects

The following side/adverse effects have been selected on the basis of their potential clinical significance (possible signs and symptoms in parentheses where appropriate)—not necessarily inclusive:

Those indicating need for medical attention
Incidence less frequent or rare
For all cephalosporins—may be more frequent for cefamandole, cefmetazole, cefoperazone, cefotetan, and moxalactam
Hypoprothrombinemia (unusual bleeding or bruising)—may be more frequent for cefamandole, cefmetazole, cefoperazone, cefotetan, and moxalactam; *pseudomembranous colitis* (severe abdominal or stomach cramps and pain; abdominal tenderness; watery and severe diarrhea, which may also be bloody; fever)
For moxalactam only
Platelet dysfunction (unusual bleeding or bruising)
Incidence rare
For all cephalosporins
Allergic reactions, specifically anaphylaxis (bronchospasm, hypotension), **erythema multiforme, or Stevens-Johnson syndrome** (blistering, peeling, or loosening of skin and mucous membranes; may involve the eyes or other organ systems); **renal dysfunction** (decrease in urine output or decrease in urine concentrating ability); **serum sickness-like reactions** (skin rash, joint pain, fever)—may be more frequent with cefaclor; **hypersensitivity** (fever, skin rash, itching, redness, or swelling); **seizures**—especially with high doses and in patients with renal function impairment; **thrombophlebitis** (pain, redness, and swelling at site of injection)
For ceftriaxone only
Biliary "sludge" or pseudolithiasis (epigastric pain, anorexia, nausea and vomiting)—more likely when administered by intravenous bolus over 3 to 5 minutes

Those indicating need for medical attention only if they continue or are bothersome
Incidence more frequent—less frequent with some cephalosporins
Oral candidiasis (sore mouth or tongue); **gastrointestinal reactions** (mild diarrhea, abdominal cramps, nausea or vomiting)
Incidence less frequent or rare
Vaginitis (vaginal itching and discharge)

Those indicating possible pseudomembranous colitis and the need for medical attention if they occur after medication is discontinued
Severe abdominal or stomach cramps and pain; abdominal tenderness; watery and severe diarrhea, which may also be bloody; fever

Patient Consultation

In providing consultation, consider emphasizing the following selected information (» = major clinical significance):

Before using this medication
» Conditions affecting use, especially:
Allergies to penicillins, penicillin derivatives, penicillamine, or cephalosporins
Pregnancy—Cephalosporins cross the placenta
Breast-feeding—Cephalosporins are excreted in breast-milk, although it is not known for cefixime and ceforanide; no problems in humans have been documented

Use in children—Accumulation of cephalosporins, with resulting prolonged half-life, has been reported in newborn infants. Cefoxitin and ceftizoxime have been associated with an increased incidence of eosinophilia and elevated aspartate aminotransferase (AST [SGOT]). Ceftizoxime has also been associated with elevated alanine aminotransferase (ALT [SGPT]) and creatine kinase (CK). Ceftriaxone should be used with caution in hyperbilirubinemic neonates since it may be more likely than other cephalosporins to displace bilirubin from serum albumin

Other medications, especially alcohol, anticoagulants, heparin, thrombolytic agents, platelet aggregation inhibitors, or probenecid

Other medical problems, especially a history of bleeding disorders; a history of gastrointestinal disease, such as colitis; hepatic function impairment; or renal function impairment

Proper use of this medication

Taking on a full or empty stomach, or with food if gastrointestinal irritation occurs; absorption of cefuroxime axetil is enhanced when it is administered with food

Proper administration technique for oral liquids and/or pediatric drops; not using after expiration date

» Compliance with full course of therapy, especially in streptococcal infections

» Importance of not missing doses and taking at evenly spaced times Missed dose: Taking as soon as possible; not taking if almost time for next dose; not doubling doses

» Proper storage

For patients unable to swallow cefuroxime axetil tablets whole

Crushing tablets and mixing with food to mask the strong, persistent bitter taste

Precautions while using this medication

Checking with physician if no improvement within a few days

» Diabetics: False-positive reactions with copper sulfate urine glucose tests may occur

» For severe diarrhea, checking with physician before taking any antidiarrheals; for mild diarrhea, kaolin- or attapulgite-containing, but not other, antidiarrheals may be tried; checking with physician or pharmacist if mild diarrhea continues or worsens

» Avoiding alcoholic beverages or other alcohol-containing preparations while receiving and for several days after discontinuing cefamandole, cefmetazole, cefoperazone, cefotetan, or moxalactam

Side/adverse effects

Signs of potential side effects, especially pseudomembranous colitis, allergic reactions, hypoprothrombinemia, oral candidiasis, seizures, hypersensitivity reactions, gastrointestinal reactions, serum sickness-like reactions, vaginitis, thrombophlebitis, biliary "sludge," and pseudolithiasis

General Dosing Information

Therapy should be continued for at least 10 days in group A beta-hemolytic streptococcal infections to help prevent the occurrence of acute rheumatic fever or glomerulonephritis.

Patients with renal dysfunction will require a reduction in dose for many of the cephalosporins. Creatinine clearance (mL per min) may be calculated as follows:

Adult males: Creatinine clearance

$$= \frac{(140 - age) \times (ideal\ body\ weight\ in\ kg)}{72 \times patient's\ serum\ creatinine\ concentration}$$

Adult females: Creatinine clearance

$$= \frac{(140 - age) \times (ideal\ body\ weight\ in\ kg)}{72 \times patient's\ serum\ creatinine\ concentration} \times 0.85$$

Creatinine clearance may also be calculated in SI units (as mL per second) as follows:

Adult males: Creatinine clearance

$$= \frac{(140 - age) \times (ideal\ body\ weight\ in\ kg)}{50 \times serum\ creatinine\ (micromoles\ per\ L)}$$

Adult females: Creatinine clearance

$$= \frac{(140 - age) \times (ideal\ body\ weight\ in\ kg)}{50 \times serum\ creatinine\ (micromoles\ per\ L)} \times 0.85$$

For oral dosage forms only

Cephalosporins may be taken on a full or empty stomach. Taking them with food may help if gastrointestinal irritation occurs. Absorption of cefuroxime axetil is enhanced when it is administered with food.

For parenteral dosage forms only

Perioperative (preoperative, intraoperative, and postoperative) prophylactic administration of parenteral cephalosporins should usually be discontinued within 24 hours following surgery.

CEFACLOR

Summary of Differences

Category:
Second-generation cephalosporin.
One of two oral second-generation cephalosporins.
Indications: Good activity against *Haemophilus influenzae*.
Side/adverse effects: Serum sickness-like reactions more common.

Oral Dosage Forms

CEFACLOR CAPSULES USP

Usual adult and adolescent dose: Oral, 250 to 500 mg every eight hours.

Usual adult prescribing limits: Up to 4 grams daily.

Auxiliary labeling: • Continue medicine for full time of treatment.

CEFACLOR FOR ORAL SUSPENSION USP

Usual adult and adolescent dose: See *Cefaclor Capsules USP.*

Usual adult prescribing limits: See *Cefaclor Capsules USP.*

Auxiliary labeling:
• Refrigerate.
• Shake well.
• Continue medicine for full time of treatment.
• Beyond-use date.

CEFADROXIL

Summary of Differences

Category: First-generation cephalosporin.

Oral Dosage Forms

CEFADROXIL CAPSULES USP

Usual adult and adolescent dose: Oral—
Group A beta-hemolytic streptococcal pharyngitis (including tonsillitis): 500 mg every twelve hours; or 1 gram once a day for ten days.

Skin and soft tissue infections: 500 mg every twelve hours; or 1 gram once a day.

Urinary tract infections: 500 mg to 1 gram every twelve hours; or 1 to 2 grams once a day.

Note: After an initial loading dose of 1 gram, adults with impaired renal function may require a reduction in dose as follows:

Creatinine Clearance (mL/min)/(mL/sec)	Dose
>50/(0.83)	See *Usual adult and adolescent dose*
25–50/(0.42–0.83)	500 mg every 12 hours
10–25/(0.17–0.42)	500 mg every 24 hours
0–10/(0–0.17)	500 mg every 36 hours

Usual adult prescribing limits: Up to 4 grams daily.

Auxiliary labeling: • Continue medicine for full time of treatment.

CEFADROXIL FOR ORAL SUSPENSION USP

Usual adult and adolescent dose: See *Cefadroxil Capsules USP*.

Usual adult prescribing limits: See *Cefadroxil Capsules USP*.

Auxiliary labeling:
• Refrigerate.
• Shake well.
• Continue medicine for full time of treatment.
• Beyond-use date.

Note: When dispensing, include a calibrated liquid-measuring device.

CEFADROXIL TABLETS USP

Usual adult and adolescent dose: See *Cefadroxil Capsules USP*.

Usual adult prescribing limits: See *Cefadroxil Capsules USP*.

Auxiliary labeling: • Continue medicine for full time of treatment.

CEFAMANDOLE

Summary of Differences

Category: Second-generation cephalosporin.
Pharmacology: Contains *N*-methylthiotetrazole (NMTT) side chain.
Precautions:
    Drug interactions and/or related problems—Interacts with alcohol (disulfiram-like reaction), oral anticoagulants, and other medications that affect blood clotting.
    Laboratory value alterations—May produce false-positive tests for proteinuria with acid and denaturization-precipitation tests.
    Contraindications/medical problems—Caution also required in patients with history of bleeding problems.
    Patient monitoring—PT determinations may be required.
Side/adverse effects: May also cause unusual bleeding or bruising.

Parenteral Dosage Forms

CEFAMANDOLE NAFATE FOR INJECTION USP

Usual adult and adolescent dose: Intramuscular or intravenous—
    Pneumonia (uncomplicated) and skin and soft tissue infections: 500 mg (base) every six hours.
    Urinary tract infections: 500 mg to 1 gram (base) every eight hours.
    Other infections: 500 mg to 2 grams (base) every four to six hours.

Note: Perioperative prophylaxis[1]—Intramuscular or intravenous, 1 to 2 grams (base) one-half to one hour prior to the start of surgery; and 1 to 2 grams every six hours following surgery for up to twenty-four hours.

    After an initial loading dose of 1 to 2 grams (base), adults with impaired renal function may require a reduction in dose as follows:

Creatinine Clearance (mL/min)/(mL/sec)	Dose (base) Severe Infections	Life-threatening Infections (maximum)
>80/(1.33)	1–2 grams every 6 hours	2 grams every 4 hours
50–80/(0.83–1.33)	750 mg–1.5 grams every 6 hours	1.5 grams every 4 hours; or 2 grams every 6 hours
25–50/(0.42–0.83)	750 mg–1.5 grams every 8 hours	1.5 grams every 6 hours; or 2 grams every 8 hours
10–25/(0.17–0.42)	500 mg–1 gram every 8 hours	1 gram every 6 hours; or 1.25 grams every 8 hours
2–10/(0.03–0.17)	500–750 mg every 12 hours	670 mg every 8 hours; or 1 gram every 12 hours
<2/(0.03)	250–500 mg every 12 hours	500 mg every 8 hours; or 750 mg every 12 hours

Usual adult prescribing limits: Up to 12 grams (base) daily.

Note: Doses up to 16 grams (base) daily have been used.

Additional information:
    Cefamandole nafate is rapidly hydrolyzed to cefamandole after initial dilution.
    A solution containing 1 gram in 22 mL of sterile water for injection is isotonic.

---

[1]Not included in Canadian product labeling.

CEFAZOLIN

Summary of Differences

Category: First-generation cephalosporin.

Parenteral Dosage Forms

CEFAZOLIN SODIUM INJECTION USP

Usual adult and adolescent dose: Intravenous infusion, 250 mg to 1.5 grams (base) every six to eight hours.

Note: Perioperative prophylaxis—Intravenous infusion, 1 gram (base) one-half to one hour prior to the start of surgery; 500 mg to 1 gram during surgery; and 500 mg to 1 gram every eight hours following surgery for up to twenty-four hours.

    Pneumococcal pneumonia—Intravenous infusion, 500 mg (base) every eight to twelve hours.

    Urinary tract infections (acute, uncomplicated)—Intravenous infusion, 1 gram (base) every twelve hours.

After an initial loading dose of 500 mg (base), adults with impaired renal function may require a reduction in dose as follows:

Creatinine Clearance (mL/min)/(mL/sec)	Dose (base)
55/(0.92)	See *Usual adult and adolescent dose*
35–54/(0.58–0.90)	Full dose every 8 hours or less frequently
11–34/(0.18–0.57)	¹/₂ usual dose every 12 hours
10/(0.17)	¹/₂ usual dose every 18–24 hours

Usual adult prescribing limits: Up to 6 grams (base) daily; however, doses up to 12 grams daily have been used in rare instances.

STERILE CEFAZOLIN SODIUM USP

Usual adult and adolescent dose: See *Cefazolin Sodium Injection USP.*

Usual adult prescribing limits: See *Cefazolin Sodium Injection USP.*

CEFIXIME

Summary of Differences

Category:
    Third-generation cephalosporin.
    Only oral third-generation cephalosporin.

Additional Dosing Information

See also *General Dosing Information.*

Patients with impaired renal function may require a reduction in dose as follows:

Creatinine Clearance (mL/min)/(mL/sec)	Dose
>60/(1.00)	See *Usual adult and adolescent dose*
21–60/(0.35–1.00) or hemodialysis patients	75% of standard dosage at standard dosing interval
<20/(0.33) or CAPD patients	50% of standard dosage at standard dosing interval

Oral Dosage Forms

CEFIXIME FOR ORAL SUSPENSION

Usual adult and adolescent dose: Oral, 200 mg every twelve hours; or 400 mg once a day.

Auxiliary labeling:
• Does not require refrigeration.
• Shake well.
• Continue medicine for full time of treatment.
• Beyond-use date.

CEFIXIME TABLETS

Usual adult and adolescent dose: See *Cefixime for Oral Suspension.*

Auxiliary labeling: • Continue medicine for full time of treatment.

CEFMETAZOLE

Summary of Differences

Category: Cephamycin; second-generation cephalosporin.
Indications: Good activity against anaerobic organisms.
Pharmacology: Contains *N*-methylthiotetrazole (NMTT) side chain.
Precautions:
    Drug interactions and/or related problems—Interacts with alcohol (disulfiram-like reaction), oral anticoagulants, and other medications that affect blood clotting.
    Contraindications/medical problems—Caution also required in patients with history of bleeding problems.
    Patient monitoring—PT determinations may be required.
Side/adverse effects: May also cause unusual bleeding or bruising.

Parenteral Dosage Forms

CEFMETAZOLE SODIUM FOR INJECTION

Usual adult dose: Intravenous, 2 grams (base) every six to twelve hours for five to fourteen days.

Note: Perioperative prophylaxis—Cesarean-section patients: Intravenous, 2 grams (base) as soon as the umbilical cord is clamped; or 1 gram as soon as the umbilical cord is clamped, and repeat in eight and sixteen hours.

Perioperative prophylaxis—Other patients: Intravenous, 2 grams (base) thirty to ninety minutes prior to the start of surgery; or 1 to 2 grams thirty to ninety minutes prior to the start of surgery, and repeat in eight and sixteen hours.

Adults with impaired renal function may require a reduction in dose as follows:

Creatinine Clearance (mL/min)/(mL/sec)	Dose (base)
>90/(1.5)	See *Usual adult dose*
50–90/(0.83–1.5)	1 or 2 grams every 12 hours
30–49/(0.50–0.82)	1 or 2 grams every 16 hours
10–29/(0.17–0.48)	1 or 2 grams every 24 hours
<10/(0.17)	1 or 2 grams every 48 hours

CEFONICID

Summary of Differences

Category: Second-generation cephalosporin.

Additional Dosing Information

See also *General Dosing Information.*

Intramuscular doses of 2 grams should be administered as divided doses in different sites.

Parenteral Dosage Forms

STERILE CEFONICID SODIUM USP

Usual adult dose:
Intramuscular or intravenous, 500 mg (base) to 1 gram every twenty-four hours.

For severe or life-threatening infections—Intramuscular or intravenous, 2 grams (base) every twenty-four hours.

Note: Perioperative prophylaxis—Cesarean-section patients: Intravenous, 1 gram (base) as soon as the umbilical cord is clamped.

Perioperative prophylaxis—Other surgical patients: Intravenous, 1 gram (base) one hour prior to the start of surgery.

After an initial loading dose of 7.5 mg (base) per kg of body weight, adults with impaired renal function may require a reduction in dose as follows:

Creatinine Clearance (mL/min)/(mL/sec)	Dose (base)	
	Mild to Moderate Infections	Severe Infections
80/(1.33)	See *Usual adult dose*	See *Usual adult dose*
60–79/(1.00–1.31)	10 mg/kg every 24 hours	25 mg/kg every 24 hours
40–59/(0.67–0.98)	8 mg/kg every 24 hours	20 mg/kg every 24 hours
20–39/(0.33–0.65)	4 mg/kg every 24 hours	15 mg/kg every 24 hours
10–19/(0.17–0.32)	4 mg/kg every 48 hours	15 mg/kg every 48 hours
5–9/(0.08–0.15)	4 mg/kg every 3 to 5 days	15 mg/kg every 3 to 5 days
<5/(0.08)	3 mg/kg every 3 to 5 days	4 mg/kg every 3 to 5 days

Additional information: A solution containing 1 gram in 18 mL of sterile water for injection is isotonic.

CEFOPERAZONE

Summary of Differences

Category: Third-generation cephalosporin.
Pharmacology:
Achieves high biliary concentrations.
Contains *N*-methylthiotetrazole (NMTT) side chain.
Precautions:
Drug interactions and/or related problems—
Interacts with alcohol (disulfiram-like reaction), oral anticoagulants, and other medications that affect blood clotting.
Does not interact with probenecid.
Contraindications/medical problems—Caution required in patients with history of bleeding problems, and in patients with both severe hepatic function impairment and renal dysfunction.
Patient monitoring—PT determinations may be required.
Side/adverse effects: May also cause unusual bleeding or bruising.

Additional Dosing Information

See also *General Dosing Information.*

Cefoperazone should be administered intermittently by intravenous infusion over a 15- to 30-minute period or by continuous intravenous infusion. Rapid bolus injection is not recommended.

Patients with impaired renal function do not generally require a reduction in dose since cefoperazone is excreted primarily in the bile. Also, patients with impaired hepatic function or biliary obstruction who are not receiving maximum doses do not generally require a reduction in dose since a corresponding increase in renal excretion (up to 90% or more) usually compensates, to a large degree, for reduced biliary excretion.

Patients with combined renal and hepatic function impairment require a reduction in dose since cefoperazone is not significantly metabolized and toxic serum concentrations may occur.

Parenteral Dosage Forms

CEFOPERAZONE SODIUM INJECTION USP

Usual adult dose: Intravenous infusion—
Mild to moderate infections: 1 to 2 grams (base) every twelve hours.
Severe infections: 2 to 4 grams (base) every eight hours; or 3 to 6 grams every twelve hours.

Note: Adults with impaired hepatic function and/or biliary obstruction should not receive more than 4 grams (base) daily.

Adults with combined hepatic and renal function impairment should not receive more than 1 to 2 grams (base) daily.

In patients who are receiving hemodialysis treatments, a dose should be scheduled to follow hemodialysis.

Usual adult prescribing limits: Up to 12 grams (base) daily. However, up to 16 grams daily have been given by continuous infusion in severely immunocompromised patients without adverse effect.

Additional information: Cefoperazone sodium injection is an isoosmotic solution (approximately 300 mOsmol per L) containing approximately 3.6% dextrose.

STERILE CEFOPERAZONE SODIUM USP

Usual adult dose: See *Cefoperazone Sodium Injection USP.*

Usual adult prescribing limits: See *Cefoperazone Sodium Injection USP.*

CEFORANIDE

Summary of Differences

Category: Second-generation cephalosporin.
Precautions:
Drug interactions and/or related problems—Does not interact with probenecid.
Laboratory value alterations—May falsely elevate serum and urine creatinine concentrations when the Jaffe method is used.

Parenteral Dosage Forms

CEFORANIDE FOR INJECTION USP

Usual adult and adolescent dose: Intramuscular or intravenous, 500 mg to 1 gram every twelve hours.

Note: Perioperative prophylaxis—Intramuscular or intravenous, 500 mg to 1 gram one hour prior to the start of surgery.

Adults with impaired renal function may require a reduction in dose as follows:

Creatinine Clearance (mL/min)/(mL/sec)	Dose
60/(1.00)	See *Usual adult and adolescent dose*
20–59/(0.33–0.98)	500 mg to 1 gram every 24 hours
5–19/(0.08–0.32)	500 mg to 1 gram every 48 hours
<5/(0.08)	500 mg to 1 gram every 48–72 hours

Additional information: Ceforanide for injection is a mixture of ceforanide and lysine and forms the lysine salt when reconstituted. It is sodium-free.

CEFOTAXIME

Summary of Differences

Category: Third-generation cephalosporin.

Additional Information

Intramuscular doses of 2 grams should be administered as divided doses in different sites.

Parenteral Dosage Forms

CEFOTAXIME SODIUM INJECTION USP

Usual adult and adolescent dose: Intravenous infusion, 1 to 2 grams (base) every four to twelve hours.

Note: Uncomplicated infections—Intravenous infusion, 1 gram (base) every twelve hours.

Moderate to severe infections—Intravenous infusion, 1 to 2 grams (base) every six to eight hours.

Life-threatening infections—Intravenous infusion, 2 grams (base) every four hours.

Adults with impaired renal function (creatinine clearance <20 mL/min or 0.33 mL/sec)—One-half the *Usual adult and adolescent dose.*

Usual adult prescribing limits: Up to 12 grams (base) daily.

STERILE CEFOTAXIME SODIUM USP

Usual adult and adolescent dose: See *Cefotaxime Sodium Injection USP.*

Usual adult prescribing limits: See *Cefotaxime Sodium Injection USP.*

Additional information: A solution containing 1 gram in 14 mL of sterile water for injection is isotonic.

CEFOTETAN

Summary of Differences

Category: Cephamycin; second-generation cephalosporin.
Indications: Good activity against anaerobic organisms.
Pharmacology: Contains *N*-methylthiotetrazole (NMTT) side chain.

Precautions:
Drug interactions and/or related problems—Interacts with alcohol (disulfiram-like reaction), oral anticoagulants, and other medications that affect blood clotting.
Laboratory value alterations—May falsely elevate serum and urine creatinine concentrations when the Jaffe method is used.
Contraindications/medical problems—Caution also required in patients with history of bleeding problems.
Patient monitoring—PT determinations may be required.
Side/adverse effects: May also cause unusual bleeding or bruising.

Parenteral Dosage Forms

STERILE CEFOTETAN DISODIUM USP

Usual adult dose:
Mild to moderate infections—Intramuscular or intravenous, 1 to 2 grams (base) every twelve hours for five to ten days.
Severe infections—Intravenous, 2 grams (base) every twelve hours.
Life-threatening infections—Intravenous, 3 grams (base) every twelve hours.

Note: Perioperative prophylaxis—Cesarean-section patients: Intravenous, 1 to 2 grams (base) as soon as the umbilical cord is clamped.

Perioperative prophylaxis—Other patients: Intravenous, 1 to 2 grams (base) one-half to one hour prior to the start of surgery.

Urinary tract infections—Intramuscular or intravenous, 500 mg to 2 grams (base) every twelve hours; or 1 to 2 grams every twenty-four hours.

Adults with impaired renal function may require a reduction in dose as follows:

Creatinine Clearance (mL/min)/(mL/sec)	Dose (base)
>30/(0.50)	See *Usual adult dose*
10–30/(0.17–0.50)	Usual adult dose every 24 hours; or one-half the usual adult dose every 12 hours
<10/(0.17)	Usual adult dose every 48 hours; or one-fourth the usual adult dose every 12 hours
Hemodialysis patients	One-fourth the usual adult dose every 24 hours on the days between hemodialysis sessions; and one-half the usual adult dose on the day of hemodialysis

Usual adult prescribing limits: Up to a maximum of 6 grams (base) daily.

CEFOXITIN

Summary of Differences

Category: Cephamycin; second-generation cephalosporin.
Indications: Good activity against anaerobic organisms.
Precautions:
Pediatrics—Higher doses associated with increased incidence of eosinophilia and elevated AST (SGOT).
Laboratory value alterations—May falsely elevate serum and urine creatinine concentrations when the Jaffe method is used.

Parenteral Dosage Forms

CEFOXITIN SODIUM INJECTION USP

Usual adult and adolescent dose:

Mild or uncomplicated infections—Intravenous, 1 gram (base) every six to eight hours.

Moderately severe or severe infections—Intravenous, 1 gram (base) every four hours; or 2 grams every six to eight hours.

Life-threatening infections—Intravenous, 2 grams (base) every four hours; or 3 grams every six hours.

Note: Perioperative prophylaxis—Cesarean-section patients: Intravenous, 2 grams (base) as soon as the umbilical cord is clamped; followed by 2 grams, intramuscularly or intravenously, four and eight hours after the first dose.

Perioperative prophylaxis—Other surgical patients: Intravenous, 2 grams (base) one-half to one hour prior to the start of surgery; and 2 grams every six hours following surgery for up to twenty-four hours.

After an initial loading dose of 1 to 2 grams (base), adults with impaired renal function may require a reduction in dose as follows:

Creatinine Clearance (mL/min)/(mL/sec)	Dose (base)
>50/(0.83)	See *Usual adult and adolescent dose*
30–50/(0.50–0.83)	1–2 grams every 8–12 hours
10–29/(0.17–0.48)	1–2 grams every 12–24 hours
5–9/(0.08–0.15)	500 mg–1 gram every 12–24 hours
<5/(0.08)	500 mg–1 gram every 24–48 hours

Usual adult prescribing limits: Up to 12 grams (base) daily.

STERILE CEFOXITIN SODIUM USP

Usual adult and adolescent dose:

Mild or uncomplicated infections—See *Cefoxitin Sodium Injection USP*.

Moderately severe or severe infections—See *Cefoxitin Sodium Injection USP*.

Life-threatening infections—See *Cefoxitin Sodium Injection USP*.

Note: Gonorrhea (uncomplicated)—Intramuscular, 2 grams (base) and 1 gram of probenecid orally, administered approximately thirty minutes prior to cefoxitin or simultaneously as a single dose.

Perioperative prophylaxis—Cesarean-section patients: See *Cefoxitin Sodium Injection USP*.

Perioperative prophylaxis—Other surgical patients: See *Cefoxitin Sodium Injection USP*.

After an initial loading dose of 1 to 2 grams (base), adults with impaired renal function may require a reduction in dose as follows:

Creatinine Clearance (mL/min)/(mL/sec)	Dose (base)
>50/(0.83)	See *Usual adult and adolescent dose*
30–50/(0.50–0.83)	1–2 grams every 8–12 hours
10–29/(0.17–0.48)	1–2 grams every 12–24 hours
5–9/(0.08–0.15)	500 mg–1 gram every 12–24 hours
<5/(0.08)	500 mg–1 gram every 24–48 hours

Usual adult prescribing limits: See *Cefoxitin Sodium Injection USP*.

CEFPROZIL

Summary of Differences

Category: Second-generation cephalosporin, with broad *in vitro* activity.

Precautions: Contraindications/medical problems—Patients with phenylketonuria should be aware that cefprozil for oral solution contains 28 mg of phenylalanine per 5 mL.

Oral Dosage Forms

CEFPROZIL FOR ORAL SUSPENSION

Usual adult and adolescent dose:

Bronchitis, bacterial exacerbations—Oral, 500 mg every twelve hours for ten days.

Pharyngitis, bacterial—Oral, 500 mg every twenty-four hours for ten days.

Skin and soft tissue infections—Oral, 250 to 500 mg every twelve hours for ten days; or 500 mg every twenty-four hours for ten days.

Note: Patients with renal function impairment may require a reduction in dose as follows:

Creatinine Clearance) (mL/min)/(mL/sec	% of Usual Dose
30/(0.50)	100%
0–30/(0–0.50)	50%
Hemodialysis	100% after hemodialysis

Auxiliary labeling:
- Refrigerate.
- Shake well.
- Continue medicine for full time of treatment.
- Beyond-use date.

CEFPROZIL TABLETS

Usual adult and adolescent dose: See *Cefprozil for Oral Suspension.*

Auxiliary labeling: • Continue medicine for full time of treatment.

CEFTAZIDIME

Summary of Differences

Category: Third-generation cephalosporin.

Indications: Good activity against *Pseudomonas aeruginosa*.

Precautions: Drug interactions and/or related problems—Does not interact with probenecid.

Additional Dosing Information

See also *General Dosing Information.*

Patients with impaired hepatic function do not generally require a reduction in dose, unless renal function is also impaired.

Parenteral Dosage Forms

CEFTAZIDIME INJECTION

Usual adult and adolescent dose: Intravenous infusion, 500 mg to 2 grams every eight to twelve hours.

Note: Urinary tract infections (uncomplicated)—Intravenous infusion, 250 mg every twelve hours.

Urinary tract infections (complicated)—Intravenous infusion, 500 mg every eight to twelve hours.

Pneumonia (uncomplicated), and skin structure infections—Intravenous, 500 mg to 1 gram every eight hours.

Bone and joint infections—Intravenous, 2 grams every twelve hours.

Severe or life-threatening infections—Intravenous, 2 grams every eight hours.

After an initial loading dose of 1 gram, adults (including dialysis patients) with impaired renal function may require a reduction in dose as follows:

Creatinine Clearance (mL/min)/(mL/sec)	Dose
>50/(0.83)	See *Usual adult and adolescent dose*
31–50/(0.52–0.83)	1 gram every 12 hours
16–30/(0.27–0.50)	1 gram every 24 hours
6–15/(0.10–0.25)	500 mg every 24 hours
<5/(0.08)	500 mg every 48 hours
Hemodialysis patients	1 gram after each hemodialysis period
Peritoneal dialysis patients	500 mg every 24 hours

CEFTAZIDIME FOR INJECTION USP

Usual adult and adolescent dose: See *Ceftazidime Injection.*

CEFTIZOXIME

Summary of Differences

Category: Third-generation cephalosporin.
Precautions: Pediatrics—Associated with transient elevation in eosinophils, ALT (SGOT), AST (SGPT), and CK.

Additional Dosing Information

See also *General Dosing Information.*

Intramuscular doses of 2 grams should be administered as divided doses in different sites.

Parenteral Dosage Forms

CEFTIZOXIME SODIUM INJECTION USP

Usual adult and adolescent dose:
Mild to moderate infections—Intravenous, 1 gram (base) every eight to twelve hours.
Severe infections—Intravenous, 1 to 2 grams (base) every eight to twelve hours.
Life-threatening infections—Intravenous, 3 to 4 grams (base) every eight hours.
Note: Urinary tract infections (uncomplicated)—Intravenous, 500 mg (base) every twelve hours.

After an initial loading dose of 500 mg (base) to 1 gram, adults with impaired renal function may require a reduction in dose as follows:

Creatinine Clearance (mL/min)/(mL/sec)	Dose (base)	
	Less Severe Infections	Life-threatening Infections
80/(1.33)	See *Usual adult and adolescent dose*	See *Usual adult and adolescent dose*
50–79/(0.83–1.32)	500 mg every 8 hours	750 mg to 1.5 grams every 8 hours
5–49/(0.08–0.82)	250 to 500 mg every 12 hours	500 mg to 1 gram every 12 hours
0–4 /(0–0.07)	500 mg every 48 hours; or 250 mg every 24 hours	500 mg to 1 gram every 48 hours; or 500 mg every 24 hours

STERILE CEFTIZOXIME SODIUM USP

Usual adult and adolescent dose:
Mild to moderate infections—See *Ceftizoxime Sodium Injection USP.*
Severe infections—See *Ceftizoxime Sodium Injection USP.*
Life-threatening infections—See *Ceftizoxime Sodium Injection USP.*
Note: Gonorrhea (uncomplicated)—Intramuscular, 1 gram (base) as a single dose.

Urinary tract infections (uncomplicated)—See *Ceftizoxime Sodium Injection USP.*

After an initial loading dose of 500 mg to 1 gram (base), adults with impaired renal function may require a reduction in dose as follows:

Creatinine Clearance (mL/min)/(mL/sec)	Dose (base)	
	Less Severe Infections	Life-threatening Infections
80/(1.33)	See *Usual adult and adolescent dose*	See *Usual adult and adolescent dose*
50–79/(0.83–1.32)	500 mg every 8 hours	750 mg to 1.5 grams
5–49/(0.08–0.82)	250 to 500 mg every 12 hours	500 mg to 1 gram every 12 hours
0–4 /(0–0.07)	500 mg every 48 hours; or 250 mg every 24 hours	500 mg to 1 gram every 48 hours; or 500 mg every 24 hours

Additional information: A solution containing 1 gram in 13 mL of sterile water for injection is isotonic.

CEFTRIAXONE

Summary of Differences

Category: Third-generation cephalosporin.
Pharmacology: Long half-life; may be dosed once a day.
Precautions: Drug interactions and/or related problems—Does not interact with probenecid.
Side/adverse effects: Associated with "biliary sludge" or pseudolithiasis.

Additional Dosing Information

See also *General Dosing Information*.

Patients with impaired hepatic function do not generally require a reduction in dose. However, in patients with both impaired hepatic and renal function, the daily dose should not exceed 2 grams.

Parenteral Dosage Forms

CEFTRIAXONE SODIUM INJECTION

Usual adult and adolescent dose: Intravenous, 1 to 2 grams (base) every twenty-four hours; or 500 mg to 1 gram every twelve hours.

Usual adult and adolescent prescribing limits: Up to 4 grams (base) daily.

STERILE CEFTRIAXONE SODIUM USP

Usual adult and adolescent dose: See *Ceftriaxone Sodium Injection*.

Note: Gonococcal infections (uncomplicated cervical, urethral, rectal, and pharyngeal)—Intramuscular, 250 mg (base) as a single dose.

Usual adult prescribing limits: See *Ceftriaxone Sodium Injection*.

CEFUROXIME

Summary of Differences

Category:
   Second-generation cephalosporin.
   One of two oral second-generation cephalosporins.
Pharmacology: Parenteral cefuroxime is the only second-generation cephalosporin to adequately penetrate into the CSF.
Precautions: Laboratory value alteration—May give false-negative test result with ferricyanide blood glucose test.

Additional Dosing Information

See also *General Dosing Information*.

For oral dosage forms only:
   • Cefuroxime axetil may be given without regard to meals; however, absorption is enhanced when it is given with food.
   • For patients who cannot swallow whole tablets, cefuroxime axetil tablets may be crushed and mixed with food to mask the strong, persistent, bitter taste. It has been found to be stable when mixed in apple juice, orange juice, grape juice, and chocolate milk.
   • Because of the strong, bitter taste of this medication, the physician and parent should ascertain whether the child can reliably ingest cefuroxime axetil, preferably before leaving the doctor's office.

Oral Dosage Forms

CEFUROXIME AXETIL TABLETS USP

Usual adult and adolescent dose: Oral, 250 to 500 mg (base) every twelve hours.

Note: Urinary tract infections (uncomplicated)—Oral, 125 to 250 mg (base) every twelve hours.
   Gonorrhea (uncomplicated cervical and urethral)—Oral, 1 gram (base) as a single dose.

Auxiliary labeling: • Continue medicine for full time of treatment.

Parenteral Dosage Forms

Note: The dosing and dosage forms available are expressed in terms of cefuroxime base.

CEFUROXIME SODIUM INJECTION

Usual adult and adolescent dose: Intramuscular or intravenous, 750 mg to 1.5 grams (base) every eight hours.

Note: Gonococcal infections (uncomplicated)—Intramuscular, 1.5 grams (base), divided into two doses and administered at two separate sites, and 1 gram of probenecid orally, administered simultaneously as a single dose.
   Meningitis, bacterial—Intravenous, up to 3 grams (base) every eight hours.
   Perioperative prophylaxis—Open-heart surgical patients: Intravenous, 1.5 grams (base) at the induction of anesthesia and every twelve hours thereafter for up to twenty-four hours.
   Perioperative prophylaxis—Other surgical patients: Intravenous, 1.5 grams (base) one-half to one hour prior to the start of surgery; and 750 mg intravenously or intramuscularly every eight hours if the surgical procedure is prolonged, for up to twenty-four hours.

Adults with impaired renal function may require a reduction in dose as follows:

Creatinine Clearance (mL/min)/(mL/sec)	Dose
>20/(0.33)	750 mg to 1.5 grams every 8 hours
10–20/(0.17–0.33)	750 mg every 12 hours
<10/(0.17)	750 mg every 24 hours
Hemodialysis patients	750 mg at the end of each dialysis period

STERILE CEFUROXIME SODIUM USP

Usual adult and adolescent dose: See *Cefuroxime Sodium Injection*.

CEPHALEXIN

Summary of Differences

Category: First-generation cephalosporin.

Additional Dosing Information

See also *General Dosing Information*.

When daily doses greater than 4 grams are required, parenteral cephalosporins should be considered.

Oral Dosage Forms

CEPHALEXIN CAPSULES USP

Usual adult and adolescent dose: Oral, 250 to 500 mg every six hours.

Note: Cystitis (uncomplicated), skin and soft tissue infections, and streptococcal pharyngitis—Oral, 500 mg every twelve hours.

Usual adult prescribing limits: Up to 4 grams daily.

Auxiliary labeling: • Continue medicine for full time of treatment.

CEPHALEXIN FOR ORAL SUSPENSION USP

Usual adult and adolescent dose: See *Cephalexin Capsules*.

Usual adult prescribing limits: See *Cephalexin Capsules*.

Auxiliary labeling:
- Refrigerate.
- Shake well.
- Continue medicine for full time of treatment.
- Beyond-use date.
- For oral use only (pediatric drops).

CEPHALEXIN TABLETS USP

Usual adult and adolescent dose: See *Cephalexin Capsules USP.*

Usual adult prescribing limits: See *Cephalexin Capsules USP.*

Auxiliary labeling: • Continue medicine for full time of treatment.

CEPHALEXIN HYDROCHLORIDE TABLETS

Usual adult dose: See *Cephalexin Capsules USP.*

Usual adult prescribing limits: See *Cephalexin Capsules USP.*

Auxiliary labeling: • Continue medicine for full time of treatment.

CEPHALOTHIN

Summary of Differences

Category: First-generation cephalosporin.
Precautions:
Drug interactions and/or related problems—May be more likely to interact with nephrotoxic medications.
Laboratory value alterations—May falsely elevate serum and urine creatinine concentrations when the Jaffe method is used.

Additional Dosing Information

See also *General Dosing Information.*

Since pain, induration, tenderness, and elevated temperature may occur on intramuscular administration, cephalothin sodium for injection should be administered by deep intramuscular injection or by intravenous injection.

When intravenous doses greater than 6 grams daily are given for more than 3 days, thrombophlebitis may occur. To help minimize the incidence of thrombophlebitis, larger veins may be used, 10 to 25 mg of hydrocortisone may be added to intravenous infusions containing 4 to 6 grams, or more dilute solutions may be given.

Parenteral Dosage Forms

CEPHALOTHIN SODIUM INJECTION USP

Usual adult and adolescent dose: Intravenous infusion, 500 mg to 2 grams (base) every four to six hours.

Note: Perioperative prophylaxis—Intravenous infusion, 1 to 2 grams (base) one-half to one hour prior to the start of surgery; 1 to 2 grams during surgery; and 1 to 2 grams every six hours following surgery for up to twenty-four hours.

Pneumonia (uncomplicated), furunculosis (with cellulitis), and urinary tract infections—Intravenous infusion, 500 mg (base) every six hours.

After an initial loading dose of 1 to 2 grams (base), adults with impaired renal function may require a reduction in dose as follows:

Creatinine Clearance (mL/min)/(mL/sec)	Dose (base)
>80/(1.33)	See *Usual adult and adolescent dose*
50–80/(0.83–1.33)	Up to 2 grams every 6 hours
25–50/(0.42–0.83)	Up to 1.5 grams every 6 hours
10–25/(0.17–0.42)	Up to 1 gram every 6 hours
2–10/(0.03–0.17)	Up to 500 mg every 6 hours
<2/(0.03)	Up to 500 mg every 8 hours

Usual adult prescribing limits: Up to 12 grams (base) daily.

Additional information: The vehicles are 0.9% sodium chloride injection and 5% dextrose injection.

CEPHALOTHIN SODIUM FOR INJECTION USP

Usual adult and adolescent dose: See *Cephalothin Sodium Injection USP.*

Usual adult prescribing limits: See *Cephalothin Sodium Injection USP.*

CEPHAPIRIN

Summary of Differences

Category: First-generation cephalosporin.

Additional Dosing Information

See also *General Dosing Information.*

Cephapirin sodium should be administered by deep intramuscular injection or by intravenous injection only.

Parenteral Dosage Forms

STERILE CEPHAPIRIN SODIUM USP

Usual adult and adolescent dose: Intramuscular or intravenous, 500 mg to 1 gram (base) every four to six hours.

Note: Perioperative prophylaxis[1]—Intramuscular or intravenous, 1 to 2 grams (base) one-half to one hour prior to the start of surgery; 1 to 2 grams during surgery; and 1 to 2 grams every six hours following surgery for up to twenty-four hours.

Patients with impaired renal function (moderately severe oliguria or serum creatinine above 5 mg per 100 mL)—7.5 to 15 mg (base) per kg of body weight every twelve hours.

Usual adult prescribing limits: Up to 12 grams (base) daily.

---

[1]Not included in Canadian product labeling.

CEPHRADINE

Summary of Differences

Category: First-generation cephalosporin.

Additional Dosing Information

See also *General Dosing Information.*

Adults with impaired renal function may require a reduction in dose as follows:

Creatinine Clearance (mL/min)/(mL/sec)	Dose
>20/(0.33)	500 mg every 6 hours
5–20/(0.08–0.33)	250 mg every 6 hours
<5/(0.08)	250 mg every 12 hours

For parenteral dosage forms only:
- A solution containing 30 mg per mL is approximately isotonic.
- Since sterile abscesses may occur following subcutaneous injection, cephradine for injection should be administered by deep intramuscular injection or by intravenous injection only.

Oral Dosage Forms

CEPHRADINE CAPSULES USP

Usual adult and adolescent dose: Oral, 250 to 500 mg every six hours; or 500 mg to 1 gram every twelve hours.

Usual adult prescribing limits: Up to 4 grams daily.

Auxiliary labeling: • Continue medicine for full time of treatment.

CEPHRADINE FOR ORAL SUSPENSION USP

Usual adult and adolescent dose: See *Cephradine Capsules USP.*

Usual adult prescribing limits: See *Cephradine Capsules USP.*

Auxiliary labeling:
- Refrigerate.
- Shake well.
- Continue medicine for full time of treatment.
- Beyond-use date.

Parenteral Dosage Forms

CEPHRADINE FOR INJECTION USP

Usual adult and adolescent dose: Intramuscular or intravenous, 500 mg to 1 gram every six hours.

Note: Perioperative prophylaxis—Cesarean-section patients: Intravenous, 1 gram as soon as the umbilical cord is clamped; and 1 gram intramuscularly or intravenously six and twelve hours after the first dose.

Perioperative prophylaxis—Other surgical patients: Intramuscular or intravenous, 1 gram one-half to one and one-half hours prior to the start of surgery; and 1 gram every four to six hours for up to twenty-four hours.

Usual adult prescribing limits: Up to 8 grams daily.

MOXALACTAM

Summary of Differences

Category: Oxacephem, chemically related to third-generation cephalosporins.

Pharmacology: Contains *N*-methylthiotetrazole (NMTT) side chain.

Precautions:
Drug interactions and/or related problems—
Interacts with alcohol (disulfiram-like reaction) and other medications that affect blood clotting.
Does not interact with probenecid.
Contraindications/medical problems—Caution also required in patients with history of bleeding problems.
Patient monitoring—Bleeding time and PT determinations may be required.
Side/adverse effects: May cause platelet dysfunction, resulting in unusual bleeding or bruising.

Additional Dosing Information

See also *General Dosing Information.*

Serum determinations are recommended in patients with impaired renal function.

In patients with end-stage renal disease, maintenance doses should be repeated following regular hemodialysis.

Parenteral Dosage Forms

MOXALACTAM DISODIUM FOR INJECTION USP

Usual adult and adolescent dose: Intramuscular or intravenous, 667 mg to 1.33 grams (base) every eight hours; or 1 to 2 grams every twelve hours for five to fourteen days.

Note: Mild to moderate infections—Intramuscular or intravenous, 500 mg to 2 grams (base) every twelve hours.

Skin and soft tissue infections (mild) and uncomplicated pneumonia—Intramuscular or intravenous, 500 mg (base) every eight hours.

Urinary tract infections—Intramuscular or intravenous, 250 to 500 mg (base) every eight to twelve hours.

After an initial loading dose of 1 to 2 grams (base), adults with impaired renal function may require a reduction in dose as follows. Bleeding time should be monitored in patients with significantly impaired renal function.

Creatinine Clearance (mL/min)/(mL/sec)	Dose (base)	
	Less Severe Infections	Life-threatening Infections (maximum)
>80/(1.33)	500 mg–2 grams every 8–12 hours	4 grams every 8 hours
50–80/(0.83–1.33)	500 mg–1 gram every 8 hours	3 grams every 8 hours
25–50/(0.42–0.83)	250 mg–1 gram every 12 hours	2 grams every 8 hours; or 3 grams every 12 hours
2–25/(0.03–0.42)	250–500 mg every 8 hours	1 gram every 8 hours; or 1.25 grams every 12 hours
<2/(0.03)	250–500 mg every 12 hours	1 gram every 24 hours

Usual adult prescribing limits: Up to 4 grams (base) daily because of bleeding problems.

CHARCOAL, ACTIVATED   Oral-Local

Some commonly used *brand names* are:

In the U.S.—

Actidose-Aqua [Activated Charcoal]

Actidose with Sorbitol [Activated Charcoal and Sorbitol]

Charcoaid [Activated Charcoal and Sorbitol]

Charcocaps [Activated Charcoal]

Insta-Char [Activated Charcoal]

Insta-Char Aqueous Suspension [Activated Charcoal]

Liqui-Char [Activated Charcoal]

In Canada—

Aqueous Charcodote [Activated Charcoal]

Charac-50 [Activated Charcoal]

Charac-tol 50 [Activated Charcoal and Sorbitol]

Charcodote [Activated Charcoal and Sorbitol]

Charcodote TFS [Activated Charcoal and Sorbitol]

Insta-Char Aqueous Suspension [Activated Charcoal]

Pediatric Aqueous Charcodote [Activated Charcoal]

Pediatric Charcodote [Activated Charcoal and Sorbitol]

ORAL-LOCAL

ACTIVATED CHARCOAL

Activated Charcoal USP

In the U.S.—*Insta-Char;* GENERIC

In Canada—GENERIC

Activated Charcoal Capsules

In the U.S.—*Charcocaps;* GENERIC

In Canada—GENERIC

Activated Charcoal Oral Suspension

In the U.S.—*Actidose-Aqua; Insta-Char Aqueous Suspension; Liqui-Char;* GENERIC

In Canada—*Aqueous Charcodote; Charac-50; Insta-Char Aqueous Suspension; Pediatric Aqueous Charcodote*

Activated Charcoal Tablets†

In the U.S.—GENERIC

ACTIVATED CHARCOAL AND SORBITOL

Activated Charcoal and Sorbitol Oral Suspension

In the U.S.—*Actidose with Sorbitol; Charcoaid*

In Canada—*Charac-tol 50; Charcodote; Charcodote TFS; Pediatric Charcodote*

---

†Not commercially available in Canada.

Category

Antidote (adsorbent)—Activated Charcoal USP; Activated Charcoal Oral Suspension.

Antidote (adsorbent)-laxative—Activated Charcoal and Sorbitol Oral Suspension.

Antidiarrheal (adsorbent)—Activated Charcoal Capsules.

Antiflatulent—Activated Charcoal Capsules; Activated Charcoal Tablets.

Indications

Accepted

Toxicity, nonspecific (treatment)—Activated charcoal powder (prepared as an aqueous slurry) and oral suspension and activated charcoal and sorbitol oral suspension are indicated for use as an emergency antidote in the treatment of poisoning by most drugs and chemicals. However, activated charcoal is relatively ineffective in adsorbing caustic alkalis, boric acid, lithium, petroleum distillates (e.g., kerosene, gasoline, coal oil, fuel oil, paint thinner, cleaning fluid), ethanol, methanol, iron salts, and mineral acids.

Diarrhea (treatment); or

Gas, intestinal (treatment)—Activated charcoal capsules and tablets are indicated in the treatment of diarrhea and as a temporary aid in the adsorption of intestinal gas causing flatulence; however, enough studies have not been done to confirm its efficacy for these uses.

Pharmacology

Mechanism of action/Effect:

Activated charcoal—

Antidote (adsorbent): Adsorbs the toxic substance ingested, thus inhibiting gastrointestinal absorption.

Antidiarrheal (adsorbent): Adsorbs many toxic irritants that cause diarrhea and gastrointestinal discomfort.

Antiflatulent: Adsorbs intestinal gas to relieve discomfort.

Sorbitol—

Laxative, hyperosmotic: Hygroscopic action results in increased water in the large intestine and increased intraluminal pressure, thus stimulating catharsis.

Flavoring agent: Provides a sweet vehicle to enhance palatability.

Precautions to Consider

Geriatrics

For use as an antidote

Although adequate and well-controlled studies have not been done in the geriatric population, caution is recommended when using preparations of activated charcoal with sorbitol because of the increased risk of catharsis, which may result in fluid and electrolyte loss in geriatric patients.

For antidiarrheal use (preparations without sorbitol only)

In geriatric patients with diarrhea, caution is recommended because of the risk of fluid and electrolyte loss; these patients should be referred to a physician.

Drug interactions and/or related problems

The following drug interactions and/or related problems have been selected on the basis of their potential clinical significance (possible mechanism in parentheses where appropriate)—not necessarily inclusive (» = major clinical significance):

» Acetylcysteine, oral

(effectiveness of orally administered acetylcysteine as antidote in acetaminophen overdose may be decreased because of adsorption by activated charcoal; activated charcoal is recommended if ingestion of other substances [in addition to acetaminophen] is confirmed or suspected, but its removal by gastric lavage may be advisable prior to acetylcysteine administration)

Chocolate syrup or

Ice cream or sherbet

(should not be used as vehicles for the administration of activated charcoal since they will decrease the adsorptive capacity of the activated charcoal)

Ipecac

(if both ipecac and activated charcoal are to be used in the treatment for oral poisoning, it is generally recommended that the charcoal be administered only after vomiting has been induced and completed; however, in some clinical trials in which activated charcoal was administered pre-emesis 10 minutes after high doses of ipecac, the emetic properties of ipecac were not inhibited)

Oral medications, other
(the effectiveness of other concurrently used medications may be decreased because of adsorption and increased elimination by the activated charcoal; patients should be advised not to take any other medication within 2 hours of the activated charcoal)

Contraindications/Medical problems
The contraindications/medical problems included have been selected on the basis of their potential clinical significance (reasons given in parentheses where appropriate)—not necessarily inclusive (» = major clinical significance).

Risk-benefit should be considered when the following medical problems exist:
» Bowel sounds, absence of
(increased risk of gastrointestinal complications, such as gastrointestinal obstruction)

For antidiarrheal use only (preparations without sorbitol only)
» Dehydration
(rehydration therapy is essential if signs of dehydration, such as dry mouth, excessive thirst, wrinkled skin, decreased urination, dizziness or lightheadedness, are present; fluid loss may have serious consequences, such as circulatory collapse and renal failure, especially in young children and the elderly)

Diarrhea, parasite-associated, suspected
(use of adsorbent antidiarrheals may make recognition of parasitic causes of diarrhea more difficult; if parasitic agents are suspected pathogens, appropriate stool analyses should be performed prior to therapy with adsorbents)
» Dysentery, acute, characterized by bloody stools and elevated temperature
(sole treatment with adsorbent antidiarrheals may be inadequate; antibiotic therapy may be required)

Side/Adverse Effects
The following side/adverse effects have been selected on the basis of their potential clinical significance (possible signs and symptoms in parentheses where appropriate)—not necessarily inclusive:

Note: Dehydration, cardiac arrest, and brain damage occurred as a result of sorbitol overdose in a 3-year-old child who was being treated with activated charcoal and sorbitol combination for an overdose of a drug used to treat asthma.

Those indicating need for medical attention
Incidence less frequent or rare
Swelling of abdomen or pain

Those indicating need for medical attention only if they continue
Incidence more frequent—with sorbitol-containing preparations
Diarrhea or vomiting
Note: *Diarrhea or vomiting* may persist for several hours; precautions should be taken against possible fluid and electrolyte loss.

Those not indicating need for medical attention
Incidence more frequent
Black stools

Patient Consultation
In providing consultation, consider emphasizing the following selected information (» = major clinical significance):

Before using this medication
» Conditions affecting use, especially:
Use in children—Preparations with sorbitol are not recommended for children up to 1 year of age and should be used only under a physician's supervision in older children because of risk of excessive catharsis; prolonged use of activated charcoal as an antidiarrheal/antiflatulent in children

under 3 years of age may interfere with nutrition; risk of dehydration associated with diarrhea (for antidiarrheal use)
Use in the elderly—Risk of fluid and electrolyte loss with preparations containing sorbitol; risk of dehydration associated with diarrhea (for antidiarrheal use)
Other medical problems, especially absence of bowel sounds (for antidote use); dehydration and acute dysentery (for antidiarrheal/antiflatulent use)

Proper use of this medication
» Importance of not taking medication mixed with chocolate syrup, ice cream, or sherbet
» Proper storage
When used as an antidote only
» Calling poison control center, physician, or emergency room before taking medication
» Importance of shaking the oral liquid dosage form well; taking full dose
» Taking medication only after vomiting has been induced and completed if ipecac syrup is used also
When used as an antidiarrheal/antiflatulent only
Taking doses of other oral medications at least 2 hours before or after doses of activated charcoal
When used as an antidiarrheal only
» Importance of maintaining adequate hydration and proper diet

Precautions while using this medication
When used as an antidiarrheal/antiflatulent only
Checking with physician if condition has not improved after 7 days (when used as an antiflatulent only)
Checking with physician if diarrhea continues after medication has been used for 2 days or if fever is present with diarrhea

Side/adverse effects
Signs of potential side effects, especially continuing diarrhea or vomiting (for sorbitol-containing preparations)
Medication will color stools black, which may be alarming to patient although medically insignificant

General Dosing Information

For use as an antidote only
Activated charcoal is most effective when it is administered early in acute poisoning, preferably within 30 minutes following ingestion of the poison.

When the amount of toxic substance ingested is known, the dose of activated charcoal recommended is usually 5 to 10 times the amount of toxic substance ingested; however, a dose of 50 grams is considered the minimum adult dose by many clinicians.

Tablets or granules of activated charcoal are less effective than the powder form of the medication and should not be used in the treatment of poisoning.

The administration of activated charcoal as an aqueous slurry is generally preferred. However, to improve the palatability of activated charcoal, it has been administered in combination with suspending agents such as bentonite or carboxymethylcellulose. Also, a flavoring agent such as chocolate syrup has been added to the combination at the time of administration. However, some studies have shown that these agents, especially the flavoring agents, decrease the adsorptive capacity of activated charcoal and should not be used.

Following administration of activated charcoal, it is recommended that a cathartic be administered to enhance removal of the drug/charcoal complex since failure to excrete the drug/charcoal complex promptly may result in enhanced toxicity. However, administration of a cathartic may not be necessary when an activated charcoal product containing sorbitol is used.

Multiple-dose activated charcoal therapy may be useful in severe poisonings to prevent desorption from the charcoal; to hasten elimination of chronically used medications by the gastrointestinal tract (gastrointestinal dialysis); also, to increase clearance of certain drugs or substances that undergo enterohepatic circulation, to prevent their reabsorption. Some substances for which multiple-dose activated charcoal therapy has been demonstrated to be effective are amitriptyline, carbamazepine, diazepam, digoxin, doxepin, meprobamate, methotrexate, nortriptyline, phenobarbital, piroxicam, salicylates, and theophylline.

When multiple doses of activated charcoal are required, preparations that contain sorbitol should not be used in each dose of the multiple-dose regimen since they may produce excessive catharsis, which may result in dehydration and hypotension. Instead, doses of activated charcoal preparations without sorbitol should be alternated with the sorbitol-containing products.

The presence of normal bowel sounds is necessary to determine whether to continue multiple-dose activated charcoal therapy. If bowel sounds are absent or hypoactive, continuing multiple dosing of activated charcoal with or without sorbitol is not recommended, because of the possibility of constipation (or aggravation of) and the possibility of pooling of fluids in the colon if sorbitol continues to be administered with the activated charcoal.

If catharsis does not occur, within four to eight hours after use of an activated charcoal preparation containing sorbitol, an additional dose of sorbitol (1.5 grams per kg of body weight) or a saline laxative, such as magnesium citrate, may be administered.

ACTIVATED CHARCOAL

Oral-Local Dosage Forms

ACTIVATED CHARCOAL USP

Usual adult and adolescent dose: Antidote (adsorbent)—Oral, 25 to 100 grams, as a slurry in water.

Usual geriatric dose: Antidote (adsorbent)—Oral, 25 to 100 grams, as a slurry in water.

Note: If this medication is to be used as an antidote for emergency use in poisoning, consider providing on the label the telephone number for physician, poison control center, or emergency room.

ACTIVATED CHARCOAL CAPSULES

Usual adult and adolescent dose:
Antidiarrheal (adsorbent)—Oral, 520 mg, repeated every thirty minutes to one hour as needed up to 4.16 grams per day.
Antiflatulent—Oral, 1.04 to 3.9 grams three times a day after meals.

Note: Activated charcoal capsules are not to be used as an antidote for emergency use in poisoning.

Usual geriatric dose:
Antidiarrheal (adsorbent)—Oral, 520 mg, repeated every thirty minutes to one hour as needed up to 4.16 grams per day.
Antiflatulent—Oral, 1.04 to 3.9 grams three times a day after meals.

ACTIVATED CHARCOAL ORAL SUSPENSION

Usual adult and adolescent dose: Antidote (adsorbent)—Oral, 25 to 100 grams as a single dose.

Note: For multiple-dose therapy—Oral, 25 to 50 grams every four to six hours.

Usual geriatric dose: Antidote (adsorbent)—Oral, 25 to 100 grams as a single dose.

Note: For multiple-dose therapy—Oral, 25 to 50 grams every four to six hours.

Auxiliary labeling: • Shake well.

ACTIVATED CHARCOAL TABLETS

Usual adult and adolescent dose: Antiflatulent—Oral, 975 mg to 3.9 grams three times a day after meals.

Note: Activated charcoal tablets are not to be used as an antidote for emergency use in poisoning.

Usual geriatric dose: Antiflatulent—Oral, 975 mg to 3.9 grams three times a day after meals.

Note: Activated charcoal tablets are not to be used as an antidote for emergency use in poisoning.

ACTIVATED CHARCOAL AND SORBITOL

Oral-Local Dosage Forms

ACTIVATED CHARCOAL AND SORBITOL ORAL SUSPENSION

Usual adult and adolescent dose: Antidote (adsorbent)—Oral, 50 grams of activated charcoal as a single dose.

Note: For multiple-dose therapy—Use is not recommended because of excessive catharsis, unless repeat doses are alternated with activated charcoal preparations that contain no sorbitol.

Sorbitol content is different among the different preparations available. Product label should be consulted to determine the amount of sorbitol. For adults, the usual dose of sorbitol 70% (70 Grams per mL) is 50 to 150 mL.

Usual geriatric dose: Antidote (adsorbent)—Oral, 50 grams of activated charcoal as a single dose.

Note: For multiple-dose therapy—Use is not recommended, because of excessive catharsis, unless repeat doses are alternated with activated charcoal preparations that contain no sorbitol.

Sorbitol content is different among the different preparations available. Product label should be consulted to determine the amount of sorbitol. For adults, the usual dose of sorbitol 70% (70 Grams per mL) is 50 to 150 mL.

Auxiliary labeling: • Shake well.

CHENODIOL   Systemic†

INN: Chenodeoxycholic acid

A commonly used *brand name* in the U.S. is *Chenix.*

ORAL
Chenodiol Tablets†
 In the U.S.—*Chenix*

---

†Not commercially available in Canada.

Category: Anticholelithic.

Indications

Accepted
Gallstone disease (treatment)—Chenodiol is indicated for oral dissolution of cholesterol gallstones in selected patients with uncomplicated radiolucent gallstone disease and functioning gallbladder.

 Chenodiol therapy is more likely to be effective if the stones are
 small and of the floatable type.

 Body weight and dietary factors may influence gallstone formation
 and/or dissolution rate. A high-fiber and low-fat diet and maintenance of reduced body weight are recommended as adjunctive
 measures to increase response to therapy.

Unaccepted
Chenodiol is *not* indicated when there is a confirmed nonvisualizing
 gallbladder, radiopaque stones (calcium-containing), or when surgery is clearly indicated.

Pharmacology

Mechanism of action/Effect: Although the exact mechanism of
 chenodiol's anticholelithic action is not completely understood,
 chenodiol given orally in pharmacological doses contributes to
 desaturation of the bile by increasing the ratio of bile acids to
 cholesterol. The reduced cholesterol saturation allows for the gradual
 solubilization of cholesterol from gallstones, resulting in their eventual dissolution.

Other actions/effects: Chenodiol may increase secretion of bile acids. Chenodiol also increases low-density lipoprotein (LDL) fraction of cholesterol (by about 10%); inhibits colonic fluid absorption and may induce fluid secretion.

Precautions to Consider

Cross-sensitivity and/or related problems
Patients sensitive to other bile acid products may be sensitive to
 chenodiol also.

Geriatrics
Appropriate studies on the relationship of age to the effects of chenodiol
 have not been performed in the geriatric population. However,
 geriatrics-specific problems that would limit the usefulness of this
 medication in the elderly are not expected.

Drug interactions and/or related problems
The following drug interactions and/or related problems have been
 selected on the basis of their potential clinical significance (possible mechanism in parentheses where appropriate)—not necessarily inclusive (» = major clinical significance):

Note: Combinations containing any of the following medications, depending on the amount present, may also interact with this
 medication.

Antacids, aluminum-containing, or
Cholestyramine or
Colestipol
 (concurrent use may result in binding of chenodiol, thus de-
 creasing its absorption)
Antihyperlipidemics, especially clofibrate, or
Estrogens or
Neomycin or
Progestins
 (concurrent use of these medications with chenodiol may de-
 crease the effect of chenodiol since they tend to increase cho-
 lesterol saturation of bile)

Contraindications/Medical problems
The contraindications/medical problems included have been selected
 on the basis of their potential clinical significance (reasons given
 in parentheses where appropriate)—not necessarily inclusive (» =
 major clinical significance).

*Risk-benefit should be considered when the following medical prob-
 lems exist:*

Atherosclerosis
 (condition may be aggravated because of increase in the low-
 density lipoprotein [LDL] fraction of cholesterol)
» Bile duct abnormalities, such as:
 Biliary cirrhosis, primary
 Cholangitis, sclerosing
 Cholestasis, intrahepatic, or
» Gallstone complications, such as:
 Biliary gastrointestinal fistula
 Biliary obstruction
 Cholangitis
 Cholecystitis
 Pancreatitis
 (medical treatment with chenodiol would be too lengthy; sur-
 gery may be indicated)
» Hepatic function impairment
 (impaired bile acid metabolism may be further aggravated)

Side/Adverse Effects

Note: Although serious liver damage has not been observed in humans, hepatotoxicity has occurred in animal species unable to
 sulfate lithocholic acid. Also, mild, transient hypertransamin-
 asaemia has occurred in some patients.

The following side/adverse effects have been selected on the basis of
 their potential clinical significance (possible signs and symptoms
 in parentheses where appropriate)—not necessarily inclusive:

Those indicating need for medical attention
Incidence less frequent or rare
 Diarrhea, severe—may indicate overdose

**Those indicating need for medical attention only if they continue
or are bothersome**
Incidence more frequent
 Diarrhea, mild and transient—dose related; may also occur at
 initiation of therapy
Incidence less frequent or rare
 *Constipation; frequent urge for bowel movement; gas or indiges-
 tion*—usually disappears within 2 to 4 weeks after initiation of
 treatment; *loss of appetite; nausea or vomiting; stomach cramps
 or pain*

Patient Consultation

In providing consultation, consider emphasizing the following selected information (» = major clinical significance):

Before using this medication
» Conditions affecting use, especially:
     Sensitivity to bile acid products
     Pregnancy—Contraindicated in pregnancy because studies in
       animals have shown hepatic, renal, and adrenal damage to
       fetus
     Breast-feeding—Not known if excreted in breast milk
     Other medical problems, especially bile duct abnormalities,
       gallstone complications, or hepatic function impairment

Proper use of this medication
     Taking with food or milk for optimal therapeutic effect
» Compliance with full course of therapy
     Missed dose: Taking as soon as possible; not taking if almost time
       for next dose; not doubling doses
» Proper storage

Precautions while using this medication
     Avoiding aluminum-containing antacids; may interfere with ab-
       sorption of chenodiol
» Regular visits to physician to check progress; laboratory tests re-
     quired during therapy
» Notifying physician immediately if symptoms of acute cholecysti-
     tis develop

Side/adverse effects
     Signs of potential side effects, especially severe diarrhea

General Dosing Information

Chenodiol should preferably be taken with food or milk since it dis-
     solves more rapidly when bile and pancreatic juice are present in
     the intestinal chyme.

Gallstone dissolution may require 3 months to 2 years depending on
     the size and composition of the stone(s). Response should be moni-
     tored by oral cholecystograms or ultrasonograms performed at 6-
     to 9-month intervals. Therapy may be discontinued if dissolution
     has been confirmed by a second cholecystogram 1 to 3 months
     later.

Chenodiol therapy is unlikely to be effective if partial dissolution has
     not occurred after 9 to 12 months of treatment. If there are still no
     signs of response to therapy after 18 months, treatment with
     chenodiol should be discontinued.

Dosage of chenodiol should be reduced by one-half if diarrhea is
     persistent during dosage buildup or later in treatment. Antidiar-
     rheal agents may also be used during this period. The dose may be
     increased gradually to the original level after diarrhea subsides.

Overweight patients are often less responsive to chenodiol therapy,
     because of greater cholesterol secretion into bile, and may require
     a higher dose on a body weight basis.

Oral Dosage Forms

CHENODIOL TABLETS

Usual adult and adolescent dose: Oral, 13 to 16 mg per kg of body
     weight a day, divided into two doses, taken in the morning and at
     night with food or milk.

Note: An initial dose of 250 mg per day is recommended for the first
     two weeks of treatment, the dose being increased each week
     thereafter by 250 mg a day until the recommended or maxi-
     mum tolerated dose is reached.

     Overweight patients may require up to 20 mg per kg of body
     weight a day.

Usual geriatric dose: See *Usual adult and adolescent dose.*

Auxiliary labeling:
     • Continue medicine for full time of treatment.
     • Take with food.

CHLOPHEDIANOL   Systemic*

A commonly used *brand name* in Canada is *Ulone.*

ORAL
Chlophedianol Hydrochloride Syrup*
     In Canada—*Ulone*

*Not commercially available in the U.S.

Category: Antitussive.

Indications

Accepted
Cough (treatment)—Indicated for the symptomatic relief of nonpro-
     ductive cough.

Pharmacology

Mechanism of action/Effect: Suppresses the cough reflex by a direct
     effect on the cough center in the medulla of the brain.

Other actions/effects: It may also possess moderate local anesthetic
     effect and some anticholinergic action.

Time to peak effect: Slower than narcotic antitussives.

Duration of action: Longer than narcotic antitussives.

Precautions to Consider

Geriatrics
No information is available on the relationship of age to the effects of
     chlophedianol in geriatric patients.

Drug interactions and/or related problems
The following drug interactions and/or related problems have been
     selected on the basis of their potential clinical significance (pos-
     sible mechanism in parentheses where appropriate)—not necessar-
     ily inclusive (» = major clinical significance):

Note: Combinations containing any of the following medications, de-
     pending on the amount present, may also interact with this
     medication.

     Central nervous system (CNS) depression-producing medications
       or
     Monoamine oxidase (MAO) inhibitors, including furazolidone and
       procarbazine
       (concurrent use may potentiate CNS depressant effects of ei-
         ther these medications or chlophedianol)

CNS stimulation-producing medications
(concurrent use may potentiate CNS stimulant effects of chlophedianol)

Contraindications/Medical problems

The contraindications/medical problems included have been selected on the basis of their potential clinical significance (reasons given in parentheses where appropriate)—not necessarily inclusive (» = major clinical significance).

Except under special circumstances, this medication should not be used when the following medical problems exist:

» Cough, productive
(inhibition of cough reflex may lead to retention of secretions)
Sensitivity to chlophedianol

Side/Adverse Effects

The following side/adverse effects have been selected on the basis of their potential clinical significance (possible signs and symptoms in parentheses where appropriate)—not necessarily inclusive:

Those indicating need for medical attention
Incidence rare
CNS stimulant effects (hallucinations, nightmares, or unusual excitement or irritability); *hypersensitivity* (skin rash or hives)
With large doses
Anticholinergic effects (blurred vision, drowsiness or dizziness, dryness of the mouth, nausea or vomiting)

Patient Consultation

In providing consultation, consider emphasizing the following selected information (» = major clinical significance):

Before using this medication
» Conditions affecting use, especially:
Sensitivity to chlophedianol
Other medical problems, especially a productive cough

Proper use of this medication
Not taking liquids immediately after taking medication
» Importance of not taking more medication than the amount prescribed
Missed dose (if on regular dosing schedule): Taking as soon as possible; not taking if almost time for next dose; not doubling doses
» Proper storage

Precautions while using this medication
Checking with physician if cough persists after medication has been used for 7 days or if high fever, skin rash, or continuing headache is present with cough
» Avoiding use of alcohol or other CNS depressants
» Caution in taking appetite suppressants or drinking large amounts of xanthine-containing beverages during therapy
» Caution if drowsiness occurs

Side/adverse effects
Signs of potential side effects, especially CNS stimulant effects, hypersensitivity, or anticholinergic effects (with large dose)

General Dosing Information

Liquids should not be taken immediately after the syrup is taken because soothing effects will be decreased.

Reduced dosage may be necessary in sedated or debilitated patients since excessive depression of the cough reflex might be undesirable in these patients.

Oral Dosage Forms

CHLOPHEDIANOL HYDROCHLORIDE SYRUP

Usual adult and adolescent dose: Antitussive—Oral, 25 mg every six to eight hours as needed.

Usual geriatric dose: See *Usual adult and adolescent dose.*

Auxiliary labeling:
• May cause drowsiness.
• Avoid alcoholic beverages.

CHLORAMBUCIL   Systemic

A commonly used *brand name* in the U.S. and Canada is *Leukeran.*

ORAL
Chlorambucil Tablets USP
In the U.S. and Canada—*Leukeran*

Category: Antineoplastic; immunosuppressant.

Indications

Note: Bracketed information in the *Indications* section refers to uses not included in U.S. product labeling.

Accepted
Leukemia, chronic lymphocytic (treatment)—Chlorambucil is indicated for palliative treatment of chronic lymphocytic leukemia.

Lymphomas, Hodgkin's (treatment); or
Lymphomas, non-Hodgkin's (treatment)—Chlorambucil is indicated for palliative treatment of Hodgkin's disease and other malignant lymphomas including lymphosarcoma and giant follicular lymphoma.

[Carcinoma, ovarian (treatment)][1]; or
[Carcinoma, testicular (treatment)][1]—Chlorambucil is used for treatment of ovarian and testicular carcinoma.

[Leukemia, hairy cell (treatment)][1]—Chlorambucil is used in the treatment of hairy cell leukemia.

[Polycythemia vera (treatment)][1]—Chlorambucil is used for treatment of polycythemia vera.

[Nephrotic syndrome (treatment)][1]—Chlorambucil has been used as an immunosuppressant, in combination with prednisone, in the treatment of steroid-resistant or frequently relapsing steroid-sensitive minimal-change nephrotic syndrome in children and adults, although there are significant risks associated with its use. The most common dose-limiting short-term toxicity is bone marrow depression. Because of potential long-term toxicity (male sterility, leukemia), use of chlorambucil is recommended only for patients unresponsive to or seriously intolerant of steroid treatment.

Extreme caution is recommended in use of chlorambucil for non-neoplastic conditions because of potential carcinogenicity with long-term use of this agent.

[1]Not included in Canadian product labeling.

Pharmacology

Mechanism of action/Effect: Chlorambucil is a bifunctional alkylating agent of the nitrogen mustard type. Chlorambucil is cell cycle-phase nonspecific, although it is also cytotoxic to nonproliferating cells. Activity occurs as a result of formation of an unstable ethylenimmonium ion, which alkylates or binds with many intracellular molecular structures, including nucleic acids. Its cytotoxic action is primarily due to cross-linking of strands of DNA and RNA, as well as inhibition of protein synthesis.

Other actions/effects: Also has immunosuppressant activity.

Onset of action: Clinical effects usually occur within 3 to 4 weeks.

Precautions to Consider

Cross-sensitivity and/or related problems
Patients sensitive to other alkylating agents (i.e., those who experience skin rash) may also be sensitive to chlorambucil.

Geriatrics
No information is available on the relationship of age to the effects of chlorambucil in geriatric patients.

Dental
The bone marrow depressant effects of chlorambucil may result in an increased incidence of microbial infection, delayed healing, and gingival bleeding. Dental work, whenever possible, should be completed prior to initiation of therapy or deferred until blood counts have returned to normal. Patients should be instructed in proper oral hygiene during treatment, including caution in use of regular toothbrushes, dental floss, and toothpicks.

Chlorambucil may also cause stomatitis associated with considerable discomfort.

Drug interactions and/or related problems
The following drug interactions and/or related problems have been selected on the basis of their potential clinical significance (possible mechanism in parentheses where appropriate)—not necessarily inclusive (» = major clinical significance):

Note: Combinations containing any of the following medications, depending on the amount present, may also interact with this medication.

Allopurinol or
Colchicine or
» Probenecid or
» Sulfinpyrazone
(chlorambucil may raise the concentration of blood uric acid; dosage adjustment of antigout agents may be necessary to control hyperuricemia and gout; allopurinol may be preferred to prevent or reverse chlorambucil-induced hyperuricemia because of risk of uric acid nephropathy with uricosuric antigout agents)

Antidepressants, tricyclic and possibly, structurally related compounds such as cyclobenzaprine, or
Haloperidol or
Loxapine or
Maprotiline or
Molindone or
Monoamine oxidase (MAO) inhibitors, including furazolidone, procarbazine, and selegiline, or
Phenothiazines or
Pimozide or
Thioxanthenes
(these medications may lower the seizure threshold and increase the risk of chlorambucil-induced seizures)

Blood dyscrasia-causing medications
(leukopenic and/or thrombocytopenic effects of chlorambucil may be increased with concurrent or recent therapy if these medications cause the same effects; dosage adjustment of chlorambucil, if necessary, should be based on blood counts)
» Bone marrow depressants, other, or
» Radiation therapy
(additive bone marrow depression may occur; dosage reduction may be required when two or more bone marrow depres-

sants, including radiation, are used concurrently or consecutively)
» Immunosuppressants, other, such as:
Azathioprine
Corticosteroids, glucocorticoid
Corticotropin (ACTH)
Cyclophosphamide
Cyclosporine
Mercaptopurine
Muromonab-CD3
(concurrent use with chlorambucil may increase the risk of infection and development of neoplasms)
Lovastatin
(concurrent use in cardiac transplant patients may be associated with an increased risk of rhabdomyolysis and acute renal failure)
Vaccines, killed virus
(because normal defense mechanisms may be suppressed by chlorambucil therapy, the patient's antibody response to the vaccine may be decreased. The interval between discontinuation of medications that cause immunosuppression and restoration of the patient's ability to respond to the vaccine depends on the intensity and type of immunosuppression-causing medication used, the underlying disease, and other factors; estimates vary from 3 months to 1 year)
» Vaccines, live virus
(because normal defense mechanisms may be suppressed by chlorambucil therapy, concurrent use with a live virus vaccine may potentiate the replication of the vaccine virus, may increase the side/adverse effects of the vaccine virus, and/or may decrease the patient's antibody response to the vaccine; immunization of these patients should be undertaken only with extreme caution after careful review of the patient's hematologic status and only with the knowledge and consent of the physician managing the chlorambucil therapy. The interval between discontinuation of medications that cause immunosuppression and restoration of the patient's ability to respond to the vaccine depends on the intensity and type of immunosuppression-causing medication used, the underlying disease, and other factors; estimates vary from 3 months to 1 year. Patients with leukemia in remission should not receive live virus vaccine until at least 3 months after their last chemotherapy. In addition, immunization with oral poliovirus vaccine should be postponed in persons in close contact with the patient, especially family members)

Contraindications/Medical problems
The contraindications/medical problems included have been selected on the basis of their potential clinical significance (reasons given in parentheses where appropriate)—not necessarily inclusive (» = major clinical significance).

Risk-benefit should be considered when the following medical problems exist:

» Bone marrow depression
» Chickenpox, existing or recent (including recent exposure), or
» Herpes zoster
(risk of severe generalized disease)
Gout, history of, or
Urate renal stones, history of
(risk of hyperuricemia)
Head trauma or
Seizure disorder, history of
(increased risk of seizures)
» Infection
Sensitivity to chlorambucil
» Tumor cell infiltration of bone marrow

» Caution should be used also in patients who have had previous cytotoxic drug therapy or radiation therapy.

Side/Adverse Effects

Note: Many "side effects" of antineoplastic therapy are unavoidable and represent the medication's pharmacologic action. Some of these (for example, leukopenia and thrombocytopenia) are actually used as parameters to aid in individual dosage titration.

The following side/adverse effects have been selected on the basis of their potential clinical significance (possible signs and symptoms in parentheses where appropriate)—not necessarily inclusive:

Those indicating need for medical attention
Incidence more frequent—dose-related
Lymphopenia, leukopenia, neutropenia, immunosuppression, or infection (usually asymptomatic; less frequently, fever or chills, cough or hoarseness, lower back or side pain, painful or difficult urination); *thrombocytopenia* (usually asymptomatic; less frequently, unusual bleeding or bruising; black, tarry stools; blood in urine or stools; pinpoint red spots on skin)

Note: With a short course of therapy, *leukopenia* and *thrombocytopenia* may not occur until the third week of treatment and usually persist for 1 to 2 weeks (or sometimes up to 3 to 4 weeks) after withdrawal of chlorambucil. The neutrophil count may continue to decrease for up to 10 days after the last dose. After a single high dose of chlorambucil, the nadir of the leukocyte and platelet counts occurs after 7 to 14 days, with recovery in 2 to 3 weeks.

In general, short intermittent courses are thought to cause less risk of serious *bone marrow depression* than continuous therapy, by allowing bone marrow regeneration between courses. Excessive doses or prolonged therapy (a total dose of 6.5 mg per kg of body weight [mg/kg] in a single course) may result in pancytopenia and irreversible bone marrow damage.

Incidence less frequent
Allergic reaction (skin rash); *hyperuricemia or uric acid nephropathy* (joint pain, lower back or side pain, swelling of feet or lower legs); *stomatitis* (sores in mouth and on lips)

Note: *Hyperuricemia* or *uric acid nephropathy* occurs most commonly during initial treatment of patients with leukemia or lymphoma, as a result of rapid cell breakdown which leads to elevated serum uric acid concentrations.

Stomatitis may be associated with neutropenia.

Incidence rare
Drug fever; hepatotoxicity, hepatic necrosis, or cirrhosis (yellow eyes or skin); *neurotoxicity* (agitation, confusion, hallucinations, muscle twitching, seizures, severe weakness or paralysis, tremors, trouble in walking); *pulmonary fibrosis*—occurs after long-term use (cough, shortness of breath)

Note: Rare, focal and/or generalized seizures have been reported in both children and adults at therapeutic daily doses, and in pulse dosing regimens and acute overdose. However, the risk may be increased in children with nephrotic syndrome (seizures may occur 6 to 90 days after initiation of treatment) and in patients receiving high pulse doses. *Neurotoxicity* is usually reversible on withdrawal of chlorambucil.

Pulmonary fibrosis is usually reversible after chlorambucil is withdrawn, but fatalities have been reported.

Those indicating need for medical attention only if they continue or are bothersome
Incidence less frequent or rare
Changes in menstrual period; dermatitis (itching of skin); *nausea and vomiting*

Note: *Nausea and vomiting* are associated with single oral doses of 20 mg or more, usually last less than 24 hours, and become less frequent with continued therapy; may persist up to 7 days after a single high dose.

Those indicating need for medical attention if they occur after medication is discontinued
Bone marrow damage, possibly irreversible (fever or chills; cough or hoarseness; lower back or side pain; painful or difficult urination; unusual bleeding or bruising; black, tarry stools; blood in urine or stools; pinpoint red spots on skin); *pulmonary toxicity* (cough, shortness of breath)

Patient Consultation

In providing consultation, consider emphasizing the following selected information (» = major clinical significance):

Before using this medication
» Conditions affecting use, especially:
Sensitivity to chlorambucil or other alkylating agents
Pregnancy—Use not recommended because of mutagenic, teratogenic, and carcinogenic potential; advisability of using contraception; telling physician immediately if pregnancy is suspected
Breast-feeding—Not recommended because of risk of serious side effects
Other medications, especially probenecid, sulfinpyrazone, other bone marrow depressants, or previous cytotoxic drug or radiation therapy
Other medical problems, especially chickenpox, herpes zoster, or infection

Proper use of this medication
» Importance of not taking more or less medication than the amount prescribed
Caution in taking combination therapy; taking each medication at the right time
Importance of ample fluid intake and subsequent increase in urine output to aid in excretion of uric acid
» Possible nausea and vomiting; importance of continuing medication despite stomach upset
Checking with physician if vomiting occurs shortly after dose is taken
Missed dose: If dosing schedule is—
Once a day: Taking as soon as possible if remembered same day; if not remembered until next day, skipping missed dose and taking next regularly scheduled dose
Several times a day: Taking as soon as possible; however, if almost time for next dose, not taking missed dose; not doubling doses
» Proper storage

Precautions while using this medication
» Importance of close monitoring by the physician
» Avoiding immunizations unless approved by physician; other persons in patient's household should avoid immunizations with oral poliovirus vaccine; avoiding other persons who have taken oral poliovirus vaccine or wearing a protective mask that covers nose and mouth
Caution if bone marrow depression occurs:
» Avoiding exposure to persons with bacterial infections, especially during periods of low blood counts; checking with physician immediately if fever or chills, cough or hoarseness, lower back or side pain, or painful or difficult urination occur
» Checking with physician immediately if unusual bleeding or bruising; black, tarry stools; blood in urine or stools; or pinpoint red spots on skin occur

Caution in use of regular toothbrush, dental floss, or toothpick; physician, dentist, or nurse may suggest alternatives; checking with physician before having dental work done

Not touching eyes or inside of nose unless hands washed immediately before

Using caution to avoid accidental cuts with use of sharp objects such as safety razor or fingernail or toenail cutters

Avoiding contact sports or other situations where bruising or injury might occur

Side/adverse effects

May cause adverse effects such as blood problems and cancer

Signs of potential side effects, especially lymphopenia, leukopenia, neutropenia, immunosuppression, infection, thrombocytopenia, allergic reaction, hyperuricemia, uric acid nephropathy, stomatitis, drug fever, hepatotoxicity, hepatic necrosis, cirrhosis, neurotoxicity, and pulmonary fibrosis

Physician or nurse can help in dealing with side effects

General Dosing Information

Patients receiving chlorambucil should be under supervision of a physician experienced in use of alkylating agents.

A variety of dosage schedules and regimens of chlorambucil, alone or in combination with other antitumor agents, are used. The prescriber may consult the medical literature as well as the manufacturer's literature in choosing a specific dosage.

Dosage must be adjusted to meet the individual requirements of each patient, based on clinical response and degree of bone marrow depression.

Development of uric acid nephropathy in patients with leukemia or lymphoma may be prevented by adequate oral hydration and, in some cases, administration of allopurinol. Alkalinization of urine may be necessary if serum uric acid concentrations are elevated.

It is recommended that chlorambucil be withdrawn if signs of pulmonary toxicity occur.

Because of the risk of enhanced bone marrow toxicity, use of chlorambucil is not recommended within 4 to 6 weeks of radiation therapy or chemotherapy with drugs that depress bone marrow function.

Because the decrease in neutrophil count may continue for 10 days after the last dose of chlorambucil, caution is necessary as the total dose approaches 65 mg per kg of body weight (mg/kg) because of the risk of pancytopenia.

If the white blood cell count (particularly granulocyte count) falls suddenly, a reduction in dosage or withdrawal of therapy plus continued monitoring is required until leukocyte and platelet levels become adequate. Persistence of low neutrophil and platelet counts or presence of peripheral lymphocytosis may indicate bone marrow infiltration; if that is confirmed by bone marrow examination, the daily dosage of chlorambucil should not exceed 100 mcg (0.1 mg) per kg of body weight.

Special precautions are recommended in patients who develop thrombocytopenia as a result of administration of chlorambucil. These may include extreme care in performing invasive procedures; regular inspection of intravenous sites, skin (including perirectal area), and mucous membrane surfaces for signs of bleeding or bruising; limiting frequency of venipuncture and avoiding intramuscular injections; testing urine, emesis, stool, and secretions for occult blood; care in use of regular toothbrushes, dental floss, toothpicks, safety razors, and fingernail and toenail cutters; avoiding constipation; and using caution to prevent falls and other injuries. Such patients should avoid alcohol and any aspirin intake because of the risk of gastrointestinal bleeding. Platelet transfusions may be required.

Patients who develop leukopenia should be observed carefully for signs of infection. Antibiotic support may be required. In neutropenic patients who develop fever, broad-spectrum antibiotic coverage should be initiated empirically, pending bacterial cultures and appropriate diagnostic tests.

Combination chemotherapy

Although chlorambucil is usually used alone, it may be used in combination with other agents in various regimens. As a result, incidence and/or severity of side effects may be altered and different dosages (usually reduced) may be used. For example, chlorambucil is part of the following chemotherapeutic combination (a commonly used acronym is in parentheses):

—chlorambucil and prednisone (CHL + PRED).

For specific dosages and schedules, consult the literature. For information regarding each agent, consult the individual monographs.

Oral Dosage Forms

Note: Bracketed uses in the *Dosage Forms* section refer to categories of use and/or indications that are not included in U.S. product labeling.

CHLORAMBUCIL TABLETS USP

Usual adult dose:

Leukemia, chronic lymphocytic; or

Lymphomas, Hodgkin's; or

Lymphomas, non-Hodgkin's—Initiation or short course: Oral, 100 to 200 mcg (0.1 to 0.2 mg) per kg of body weight a day or 3 to 6 mg per square meter of body surface, usually 4 to 10 mg, a day, as a single dose or in divided doses.

Note: An intermittent biweekly course of therapy may produce less hematologic toxicity; an initial dose of 400 mcg (0.4 mg) per kg of body weight or 12 mg per square meter of body surface is increased by 100 mcg (0.1 mg) per kg or 3 mg per square meter of body surface every two weeks until an effective or toxic dose is reached, then adjusted as necessary.

[Immunosuppressant—Nephrotic syndrome][1]: Oral, 100 to 200 mcg (0.1 to 0.2 mg) per kg of body weight per day, in a single dose, for 8 to 12 weeks.

Note: The maximum recommended cumulative dose is 14 mg per kg of body weight or a maximum duration of treatment of 12 weeks; some clinicians recommend a maximum cumulative dose of 8.2 mg per kg of body weight or a maximum of 6 weeks of treatment.

Usual adult prescribing limits: Presence of lymphocytic infiltration of bone marrow or hypoplastic bone marrow—Up to 100 mcg (0.1 mg) per kg of body weight per day.

---

[1]Not included in Canadian product labeling.

CHLORDIAZEPOXIDE AND CLIDINIUM   Systemic

Category: Anticholinergic-sedative.

Indications

Accepted

Ulcer, peptic (treatment adjunct); or

Bowel syndrome, irritable (treatment)—FDA has classified chlordiazepoxide and clidinium combination as possibly effective as adjunctive therapy in the treatment of peptic ulcer and irritable bowel syndrome.

Note: The less-than-effective classifications require submission of adequate and well-controlled studies to provide substantial evidence of effectiveness. FDA has notified manufacturers of the possible withdrawal from the market of products containing a combination of an anticholinergic and a sedative because their efficacy as fixed combinations have not been proven in adequately designed clinical trials. To date, no final action has been taken.

Unaccepted

Anticholinergic and sedative combinations have been used as adjuncts in the treatment of acute enterocolitis; however, their use for this condition is controversial since they cause a reduction in gastrointestinal motility, resulting in retention of the causative organism or toxin and the consequent prolongation of symptoms.

Patient Consultation

In providing consultation, consider emphasizing the following selected information (» = major clinical significance):

Before using this medication

» Conditions affecting use, especially:

Sensitivity to clidinium and chlordiazepoxide or to other benzodiazepines or any of the belladonna alkaloids

Pregnancy—Use is not recommended; chronic use of chlordiazepoxide may cause physical dependence and withdrawal symptoms in the neonate; chlordiazepoxide increases risk of congenital malformations in first trimester

Breast-feeding—Chlordiazepoxide excreted in breast milk; clidinium may cause inhibition of lactation

Use in children—Increased susceptibility to anticholinergic effects of clidinium and to CNS effects of chlordiazepoxide

Use in the elderly—Increased susceptibility to mental and other anticholinergic effects of clidinium and to CNS effects of chlordiazepoxide; danger of precipitating undiagnosed glaucoma; possible impairment of memory

Dental—Possible development of dental problems because of decreased salivary flow

Other medications, especially other anticholinergics, antacids, antidiarrheals, CNS depressants, ketoconazole, or potassium chloride

Other medical problems, especially cardiac disease, glaucoma, hepatic disease, hiatal hernia with reflux esophagitis, intestinal atony, myasthenia gravis, obstruction in gastrointestinal or urinary tract, ulcerative colitis, or urinary retention

Proper use of this medication

Taking dose 30 to 60 minutes before meals unless told otherwise by physician

» Taking medication only as directed

Missed dose: Taking as soon as possible; not taking if almost time for next dose; not doubling doses

» Proper storage

Precautions while using this medication

Regular visits to physician to check progress of therapy if used for extended period of time

Avoiding medicine for diarrhea within 1 to 2 hours of taking this medication

» Caution if dizziness, lightheadedness, drowsiness, or blurred vision occurs

» Avoiding use of alcohol or other CNS depressants during and for a few days following therapy

» Caution during exercise and hot weather; overheating may result in heat stroke

Possible dryness of mouth, nose, and throat; using sugarless gum or candy, ice, or saliva substitute for relief; checking with dentist if mouth continues to feel dry for more than 2 weeks

» Checking with physician if constipation occurs

Checking with physician before discontinuing medication after prolonged use; gradual dosage reduction may be necessary to avoid the possibility of withdrawal symptoms

Side/adverse effects

Signs of potential side effects, especially agranulocytosis, granulocytopenia, or leukopenia; allergic reaction; CNS depression; increased intraocular pressure; jaundice; and paradoxical reaction

Oral Dosage Forms

CHLORDIAZEPOXIDE HYDROCHLORIDE AND CLIDINIUM BROMIDE CAPSULES

Usual adult dose: Oral, 1 or 2 capsules one to four times a day, thirty to sixty minutes before meals or food, the dosage then being adjusted as needed and tolerated.

Note: Debilitated patients—See *Usual geriatric dose.*

Usual adult prescribing limits: Up to a total of 8 capsules daily (40 mg of chlordiazepoxide hydrochloride and 20 mg of clidinium bromide).

Usual geriatric dose: Oral, initially no more than 1 capsule two times a day, the dosage then being adjusted as needed and tolerated.

Auxiliary labeling:

- Take before meals.
- Avoid alcoholic beverages.
- May cause drowsiness.

CHLORMEZANONE   Systemic

Some commonly used *brand names* are:
    In the U.S.—*Trancopal Caplets*
    In Canada—*Trancopal*

ORAL
Chlormezanone Tablets
    In the U.S.—*Trancopal Caplets*
    In Canada—*Trancopal*

Category: Antianxiety agent.

Indications

Accepted
Anxiety (treatment)—Chlormezanone may be useful for the treatment of mild anxiety and tension states. However, this medication generally has been replaced by more effective antianxiety agents. Chlormezanone should not be used for the stress of everyday life.

Effectiveness of chlormezanone for long-term (more than 4 months) management of anxiety has not been assessed by systematic clinical studies. The medication's efficacy should be reassessed at periodic intervals.

Pharmacology

Mechanism of action/Effect: The exact mechanism of action of chlormezanone as an antianxiety agent is not known; however, studies in animals have shown that chlormezanone acts on subcortical levels of the central nervous system (CNS). The CNS depressant actions of chlormezanone are similar to those of meprobamate.

Onset of action: 15 to 30 minutes.

Duration of action: Up to 6 hours or longer.

Precautions to Consider

Geriatrics
Although appropriate studies with chlormezanone have not been performed in the geriatric population, no geriatrics-specific problems have been documented to date. However, elderly patients are more likely to have age-related hepatic function impairment and renal function impairment, which may require reduction of dosage in patients receiving chlormezanone.

Drug interactions and/or related problems
The following drug interactions and/or related problems have been selected on the basis of their potential clinical significance (possible mechanism in parentheses where appropriate)—not necessarily inclusive (» = major clinical significance):

Note: Combinations containing any of the following medications, depending on the amount present, may also interact with this medication.

» Alcohol or
» CNS depression-producing medications
    (concurrent use may increase the CNS depressant effects of either these medications or chlormezanone)

Contraindications/Medical problems
The contraindications/medical problems included have been selected on the basis of their potential clinical significance (reasons given in parentheses where appropriate)—not necessarily inclusive (» = major clinical significance).

Risk-benefit should be considered when the following medical problems exist:
    Drug abuse or dependence, history of
        (predisposition of patients to habituation and dependence)
    Hepatic function impairment
        (chlormezanone metabolized in liver)
    Renal function impairment
        (chlormezanone excreted via kidneys)
    Sensitivity to chlormezanone

Side/Adverse Effects

Note: Withdrawal symptoms have been reported rarely when chlormezanone was suddenly discontinued in patients who received the medication daily for weeks or months.

The following side/adverse effects have been selected on the basis of their potential clinical significance (possible signs and symptoms in parentheses where appropriate)—not necessarily inclusive:

Those indicating need for medical attention
Incidence less frequent
    Confusion; mental depression
Incidence rare
    Allergic reaction (skin rash); *cholestatic jaundice* (abdominal or stomach pains, aching muscles and joints, fever and chills, severe skin itching, skin rash, yellow eyes or skin)—reversible on discontinuation of medication; *swelling of the feet or lower legs; unusual excitement*
Signs and/or symptoms of overdose
    Confusion, severe; drowsiness, severe; loss of reflexes; unusual tiredness or weakness, continuing

Those indicating need for medical attention only if they continue or are bothersome
Incidence more frequent
    Drowsiness
Incidence less frequent
    Clumsiness or unsteadiness; difficult urination; dizziness; flushing or redness of skin; headache; nausea; trembling; weakness

Patient Consultation

In providing consultation, consider emphasizing the following selected information (» = major clinical significance):

Before using this medication
» Conditions affecting use, especially:
        Sensitivity to chlormezanone
        Use by athletes—Chlormezanone is banned and, in some cases, tested for in shooters by the U.S. Olympic Committee (USOC) and the National Collegiate Athletic Association (NCAA)
        Other medications, especially alcohol or other CNS depression-producing medications

Proper use of this medication
» Importance of not using more medication than the amount prescribed because of habit-forming potential and possible increase in side effects
    Missed dose: Taking right away if remembered within an hour or so; not taking if remembered later; not doubling doses
» Proper storage

Precautions while using this medication
    Regular visits to physician to check progress during prolonged therapy

Checking with physician before discontinuing medication after prolonged use; gradual dosage reduction may be necessary to avoid possibility of withdrawal symptoms
» Avoiding use of alcohol or other CNS depressants
» Suspected overdose: Getting emergency help at once
» Caution if dizziness or drowsiness occurs

Side/adverse effects
Signs of potential side effects, especially allergic reaction, cholestatic jaundice, confusion, edema, mental depression, and unusual excitement

General Dosing Information

Dosage must be individualized. The smallest effective dosage should be used to avoid oversedation.

Following prolonged administration, chlormezanone should be withdrawn gradually to avoid the precipitation of withdrawal symptoms.

Oral Dosage Forms

CHLORMEZANONE TABLETS

Usual adult dose: Oral, 100 to 200 mg three or four times a day.

Auxiliary labeling:
• Avoid alcoholic beverages.
• May cause drowsiness.

CHLOROQUINE   Systemic

Some commonly used *brand names* are:
In the U.S.—*Aralen; Aralen HCl*
In Canada—*Aralen*

ORAL
Chloroquine Phosphate Tablets USP
In the U.S.—*Aralen;* GENERIC
In Canada—*Aralen*

PARENTERAL
Chloroquine Hydrochloride Injection USP†
In the U.S.—*Aralen HCl*

†Not commercially available in Canada.

Category

Antiprotozoal—Chloroquine.
Antihypercalcemic—Chloroquine (Oral).
Antirheumatic (disease-modifying)—Chloroquine (Oral).
Lupus erythematosus suppressant—Chloroquine (Oral).
Polymorphous light eruption suppressant—Chloroquine (Oral).
Porphyria cutanea tarda suppressant—Chloroquine (Oral).

Indications

Note: Bracketed information in the *Indications* section refers to uses not included in U.S. product labeling.

Accepted
Malaria (prophylaxis and treatment)—Chloroquine is indicated in the suppressive treatment and the treatment of acute attacks of malaria caused by *Plasmodium vivax, P. malariae, P. ovale,* and chloroquine-susceptible strains of *P. falciparum.* The radical cure of *P. vivax* and *P. ovale* malaria requires the concurrent or subsequent administration of primaquine. However, there have been reports of chloroquine-resistant *P. vivax* in patients who have traveled to Papua New Guinea and Indonesia.
Liver abscess, amebic (treatment)—Chloroquine is indicated in the treatment of amebic liver abscess, usually in combination with an effective intestinal amebicide. However, it is not considered a primary drug.
[Arthritis, juvenile (treatment)][1]—Chloroquine (oral) is used in the treatment of juvenile arthritis.
[Arthritis, rheumatoid (treatment)][1]—Chloroquine (oral) is indicated in the treatment of acute and chronic rheumatoid arthritis in pa-

tients who do not respond adequately to other less toxic antirheumatics. Chloroquine may be used in addition to nonsteroidal anti-inflammatory agents.
[Hypercalcemia, sarcoid-associated (treatment)][1]—Chloroquine (oral) is used to reduce urinary calcium excretion and the levels of 1,25-dihydroxyvitamin D in the serum of sarcoid patients who are unable to take corticosteroids.
[Lupus erythematosus, discoid (treatment)][1]; or
[Lupus erythematosus, systemic (treatment)][1]—Chloroquine (oral) is used as a suppressant for chronic discoid and systemic lupus erythematosus.
[Polymorphous light eruption (treatment)][1]—Chloroquine (oral) is used as a suppressant for polymorphous light eruption.
[Porphyria cutanea tarda (treatment)][1]—Chloroquine (oral) is used in the treatment of porphyria cutanea tarda.
[Urticaria, solar (treatment)][1]; or
[Vasculitis, chronic cutaneous (treatment)][1]—Chloroquine is also used in the treatment of solar urticaria and chronic cutaneous vasculitis unresponsive to other therapy.
Chloroquine-resistant strains of *P. falciparum,* originally seen only in Southeast Asia and South America, are now documented in all malarious areas except Central America west of the Canal Zone, the Middle East, and the Caribbean. Chloroquine is still the drug of choice for the treatment of susceptible strains of *P. falciparum* and the other 3 malarial species; however, chloroquine-resistant *P. vivax* has recently been reported.

Unaccepted
Chloroquine does not prevent relapses in patients with *P. vivax* or *P. ovale* malaria since it is not effective against exo-erythrocytic forms of the parasite. In these species, "hypnozoites," which remain dormant in the liver, are responsible for relapses.
Chloroquine is not indicated in the treatment of acute amebic dysentery or asymptomatic carriers.

[1]Not included in Canadian product labeling.

Pharmacology

Note: Because chloroquine concentrates in the cellular fraction of blood, chloroquine concentrations measured in the blood are higher than those measured in the plasma, with concentration ratios between blood and plasma ranging from 1 to 25.

Mechanism of action/Effect:

Antiprotozoal—Malaria: Unknown, but may be based on ability of chloroquine to bind to and alter the properties of DNA. Chloroquine is also taken up into the acidic food vacuoles of the parasite in the erythrocyte. It increases the pH of the acid vesicles, interfering with vesicle functions and possibly inhibiting phospholipid metabolism. In suppressive treatment, chloroquine inhibits the erythrocytic stage of development of plasmodia. In acute attacks of malaria, chloroquine interrupts erythrocytic schizogony of the parasite. Its ability to concentrate in parasitized erythrocytes may account for its selective toxicity against the erythrocytic stages of plasmodial infection.

Antirheumatic—Chloroquine is thought to act as a mild immunosuppressant, inhibiting the production of rheumatoid factor and acute phase reactants. It also accumulates in white blood cells, stabilizing lysosomal membranes and inhibiting the activity of many enzymes, including collagenase and the proteases that cause cartilage breakdown.

Precautions to Consider

Cross-sensitivity and/or related problems

Patients hypersensitive to hydroxychloroquine may also be hypersensitive to chloroquine, a structurally similar 4-aminoquinoline compound.

Geriatrics

No information is available on the relationship of age to the effects of chloroquine in geriatric patients.

Drug interactions and/or related problems

The following drug interactions and/or related problems have been selected on the basis of their potential clinical significance (possible mechanism in parentheses where appropriate)—not necessarily inclusive (» = major clinical significance):

Note: Combinations containing any of the following medications, depending on the amount present, may also interact with this medication.

Penicillamine
(concurrent use of penicillamine with chloroquine may increase penicillamine plasma concentrations, increasing the potential for serious hematologic and/or renal adverse reactions, as well as the possibility of severe skin reactions)

Contraindications/Medical problems

The contraindications/medical problems included have been selected on the basis of their potential clinical significance (reasons given in parentheses where appropriate)—not necessarily inclusive (» = major clinical significance).

Risk-benefit should be considered when the following medical problems exist:

» Blood disorders, severe
(chloroquine may cause blood dyscrasias, including agranulocytosis, aplastic anemia, neutropenia, or thrombocytopenia)

Gastrointestinal disorders, severe
(chloroquine may cause gastrointestinal irritation)

Glucose-6-phosphate dehydrogenase (G6PD) deficiency
(chloroquine may cause hemolytic anemia in G6PD-deficient patients, although this is unlikely when chloroquine is given in therapeutic doses)

» Hepatic function impairment
(because chloroquine is metabolized in the liver, hepatic function impairment may increase blood concentrations of chloroquine, increasing the risk of side effects)

Hypersensitivity to chloroquine or hydroxychloroquine

» Neurological disorders, severe
(chloroquine may cause polyneuritis, ototoxicity, seizures, or neuromyopathy)

Porphyria
(chloroquine may cause exacerbation of porphyria)

Psoriasis
(chloroquine may precipitate severe attacks of psoriasis)

» Retinal or visual field changes, presence of
(chloroquine may cause corneal opacities, keratopathy, or retinopathy)

Side/Adverse Effects

Note: Side/adverse effects of chloroquine are usually dose-related. When chloroquine is used for the short-term treatment of malaria or other parasitic diseases, side/adverse effects are usually mild and reversible. However, following prolonged use and/or high-dose therapy such as in the treatment of rheumatoid arthritis, lupus erythematosus, or polymorphous light eruption, side/adverse effects may be serious and sometimes irreversible.

Irreversible retinal damage may be more likely to occur when the daily dosage equals or exceeds the equivalent of 150 mg (base), or 2.4 mg (base) per kg per day of chloroquine.

The following side/adverse effects have been selected on the basis of their potential clinical significance (possible signs and symptoms in parentheses where appropriate)—not necessarily inclusive:

Those indicating need for medical attention
Incidence less frequent
Ocular toxicity (corneal opacities [blurred vision or any other change in vision]; keratopathy [blurred vision or any other change in vision]; retinopathy [blurred vision or any other change in vision])
Incidence rare
Blood dyscrasias (agranulocytosis [sore throat and fever]; aplastic anemia [weakness, fatigue]; neutropenia [sore throat and fever]; thrombocytopenia [bleeding, bruising]); *cardiovascular toxicity* (hypotension [feeling faint or lightheaded]; prolonged QRS interval); *emotional changes or psychosis* (mood or other mental changes); *neuromyopathy* (increased muscle weakness); *ototoxicity* (any loss of hearing, ringing or buzzing in ears)—usually in patients with pre-existing auditory damage; *seizures*
Symptoms of overdose
Cardiovascular toxicities (conduction disturbances; hypotension); *neurotoxicity* (drowsiness; headache; hyperexcitability; seizures; coma); *respiratory and cardiac arrest; visual disturbances* (blurred vision)

Those indicating need for medical attention only if they continue or are bothersome
Incidence more frequent
Ciliary muscle dysfunction (difficulty in reading); *gastrointestinal irritation* (diarrhea, loss of appetite, nausea, stomach cramps or pain, vomiting); *headache; itching* (especially in black patients)—not an indication for discontinuation of therapy in black patients
Incidence less frequent
Bleaching of hair or increased hair loss; blue-black discoloration of skin, fingernails, or inside of mouth—with prolonged oral therapy; *skin rash or itching*

Those indicating possible retinal changes or visual disturbances and the need for medical attention if they occur or progress after medication is discontinued
Blurred vision or any other change in vision

Patient Consultation

In providing consultation, consider emphasizing the following selected information (» = major clinical significance):

Before using this medication
» Conditions affecting use, especially:
Hypersensitivity to chloroquine or hydroxychloroquine

Pregnancy—May cause toxicity to the fetus when given to mother in therapeutic doses; however, chloroquine has not been shown to cause adverse effects in the fetus when used as a prophylactic agent against malaria

Use in children—Infants and children are especially sensitive to effects of chloroquine

Other medical problems, especially impaired hepatic function, severe blood disorders, severe neurologic disorders, or presence of retinal or visual field changes

Proper use of this medication

» Taking with meals or milk to minimize possible gastrointestinal irritation

» Keeping medication out of reach of children; fatalities reported with as little as 300 mg of chloroquine base (1 tablet) in a 12 month old

» Importance of not taking more medication than the amount prescribed

» Compliance with full course of therapy

» Importance of not missing doses and taking medication on regular schedule

Missed dose: If dosing schedule is—

Every 7 days: Taking as soon as possible

Once a day: Taking as soon as possible; not taking if not remembered until next day; not doubling doses

More than once a day: Taking right away if remembered within an hour or so; not taking if not remembered until later; not doubling doses

» Proper storage

For prevention of malaria

Starting medication 1 to 2 weeks before entering malarious area to ascertain patient response and allow time to substitute another medication if reactions occur

» Continuing medication while staying in area and for 4 weeks after leaving area; checking with physician immediately if fever develops while traveling or within 2 months after departure from endemic area

For arthritis and lupus erythematosus

Importance of taking medication on regular schedule

May require up to 6 months for full benefit

Precautions while using this medication

» Regular visits to physician to check for blood problems, muscle weakness, and ophthalmologic examinations during or after long-term therapy

Checking with physician if no improvement within a few days (or a few weeks or months for arthritis)

» Caution if blurred vision, difficulty in reading, or other change in vision occurs

Mosquito-control measures to reduce the chance of getting malaria:

Sleeping under mosquito netting

Wearing long-sleeved shirts or blouses and long trousers to protect arms and legs between dusk and dawn

Applying mosquito repellent to uncovered areas of skin between dusk and dawn

Side/adverse effects

Signs of potential side effects, especially ocular toxicity, cardiovascular toxicity, neuromyopathy, emotional or psychological changes, ototoxicity, seizures, and blood dyscrasias

General Dosing Information

Long-term and/or high-dosage therapy may cause irreversible retinal damage and/or neurosensorial deafness.

Chloroquine should be discontinued if any of the following problems occur: any abnormality in visual acuity, visual fields, retinal macular changes, or any visual symptoms; muscle weakness; or severe blood disorders.

Malaria-suppressive therapy should be started 1 to 2 weeks before the patient enters a malarious area and should be continued for 4 weeks after patient leaves the area. Starting the medication in advance will help to determine the patient's tolerance to the medication and allow time to substitute other antimalarials if the patient develops allergies to the medication or other adverse effects.

For oral dosage form only

Chloroquine should be taken with meals or milk to minimize the possibility of gastrointestinal irritation.

When chloroquine is used in the treatment of rheumatoid arthritis, up to 6 months of therapy may be required for it to reach its maximum effectiveness.

For parenteral dosage forms only

If chloroquine hydrochloride injection is given intravenously in pediatric patients, it should be diluted and administered very slowly.

Oral Dosage Forms

Note: Bracketed uses in the *Dosage Forms* section refer to categories of use and/or indications that are not included in U.S. product labeling.

CHLOROQUINE PHOSPHATE TABLETS USP

Usual adult and adolescent dose:

Antiprotozoal—

Malaria:

Suppressive—Oral, 500 mg (300 mg base) once every seven days.

Therapeutic—Oral, 1 gram (600 mg base) initially, followed by 500 mg (300 mg base) in six to eight hours, and 500 mg (300 mg base) once a day on the second and third days.

Liver abscess, amebic: In combination with other "tissue-acting" antiprotozoals—Oral, 250 mg (150 mg base) four times a day for two days, followed by 250 mg (150 mg base) two times a day for at least two to three weeks.

Note: The dosage schedule may be revised up or down, if necessary, or the course of therapy may be repeated.

[Antirheumatic (disease-modifying)][1]—Oral, up to 4 mg (2.4 mg base) per kg of lean body weight daily.

[Lupus erythematosus suppressant][1]—Oral, up to 4 mg (2.4 mg base) per kg of lean body weight daily.

[Polymorphous light eruption suppressant][1]—Oral, 250 mg (150 mg base) two times a day for two weeks, then 250 mg (150 mg base) once a day.

Auxiliary labeling:

• Continue medicine for full time of treatment.

• Keep out of reach of children.

• Take with food or milk.

Parenteral Dosage Forms

CHLOROQUINE HYDROCHLORIDE INJECTION USP

Usual adult and adolescent dose: Antiprotozoal—

Malaria: Intramuscular, initially 200 to 250 mg (160 to 200 mg base), repeated in six hours if necessary, not to exceed 1 gram (800 mg base) in the first twenty-four hours.

Liver abscess, amebic: Intramuscular, 200 to 250 mg (160 to 200 mg base) per day for ten to twelve days.

Note: Slow intravenous infusion, over at least four hours, has not been associated with any increase in side effects compared with oral administration.

CHLOROXINE   Topical

A commonly used *brand name* in the U.S. is *Capitrol*.

TOPICAL
Chloroxine Lotion Shampoo
    In the U.S.—*Capitrol*

Category: Antiseborrheic.

Indications

Accepted
Dandruff (treatment); or
Dermatitis, seborrheic, of scalp (treatment)—Chloroxine is indicated in the treatment of dandruff and mild to moderately severe seborrheic dermatitis of the scalp.

Pharmacology

Mechanism of action/Effect: Although the mechanism of action is not understood, chloroxine may slow down mitotic activity in the epidermis, thereby reducing excessive scaling in dandruff or seborrheic dermatitis of the scalp.

Other actions/effects:
    Chloroxine has an antibacterial action, inhibiting the growth of gram-positive as well as some gram-negative organisms.
    Also, chloroxine has shown some antifungal activity against certain dermatophytes and yeasts.

Onset of action: Improvement in condition is usually noticeable after 14 days of therapy.

Precautions to Consider

Cross-sensitivity and/or related problems
Patients sensitive to hydroxyquinolines (for example, clioquinol [iodochlorhydroxyquin] or iodoquinol [diiodohydroxyquin]) or edetate disodium may be sensitive to this medication also.

Geriatrics
Appropriate studies on the relationship of age to the effects of this medicine have not been performed in the geriatric population. However, no geriatrics-specific problems have been documented to date.

Contraindications/Medical problems
The contraindications/medical problems included have been selected on the basis of their potential clinical significance (reasons given in parentheses where appropriate)—not necessarily inclusive (» = major clinical significance).

Risk-benefit should be considered when the following medical problems exist:
» Acutely inflamed or exudative lesions of scalp
    Sensitivity to chloroxine

Side/Adverse Effects

The following side/adverse effects have been selected on the basis of their potential clinical significance (possible signs and symptoms in parentheses where appropriate)—not necessarily inclusive:

Those indicating need for medical attention
    Allergic reaction (skin rash); *irritation or burning of scalp not present before therapy*

Those indicating need for medical attention only if they continue or are bothersome
    Chemical conjunctivitis (eye irritation)—may occur if this medication enters the eyes; *dryness or increased itching of scalp*

Patient Consultation

In providing consultation, consider emphasizing the following selected information (» = major clinical significance):

Before using this medication
» Conditions affecting use, especially:
        Allergy to hydroxyquinolines, such as iodoquinol or clioquinol, or to edetate disodium or chloroxine
        Other medical problems, especially acutely inflamed or exudative lesions of scalp

Proper use of this medication
» Not using medication if blistered, raw, or oozing areas are present on scalp
» Avoiding contact with the eyes; if contact occurs, thoroughly flushing eyes with cool water
    Proper administration:
        Wetting hair and scalp with lukewarm water
        Applying enough medication to scalp to work up lather; rubbing in well
        Allowing lather to remain on scalp for 3 minutes, then rinsing
        Applying medication again and rinsing thoroughly
        Using twice a week or as directed by physician
» Proper storage

Precautions while using this medication
    Medication may slightly discolor light-colored hair

Side/adverse effects
    Signs of potential side effects, especially irritation or burning of scalp not present before therapy and allergic reaction

General Dosing Information

Chloroxine should be massaged thoroughly onto the wet scalp. The lather should remain on the scalp for approximately 3 minutes; then the hair and scalp should be rinsed. The application should be repeated; then the hair and scalp should be rinsed thoroughly. Two treatments per week are usually sufficient.

Topical Dosage Forms

CHLOROXINE LOTION SHAMPOO

Usual adult and adolescent dose: Topical, to the scalp, two times a week.

Auxiliary labeling: • For external use only.

CHOLESTYRAMINE   Oral-Local

Some commonly used *brand names* are:
   In the U.S.—*Cholybar; Questran; Questran Light*
   In Canada—*Questran; Questran Light*

ORAL
Cholestyramine Chewable Bar†
   In the U.S.—*Cholybar*
Cholestyramine for Oral Suspension USP
   In the U.S. and Canada—*Questran; Questran Light*

†Not commercially available in Canada.

Category: Antihyperlipidemic; antipruritic (cholestasis); antidiarrheal (postoperative colonic bile acids); antidote (anion-exchange resin); antihyperoxaluric.

Indications

Note: Bracketed information in the *Indications* section refers to uses not included in U.S. product labeling.

Accepted
Hyperlipidemia (treatment)—Cholestyramine is indicated for use in patients with primary hypercholesterolemia (type IIa hyperlipidemia) and a significant risk of coronary artery disease who have not responded to diet or other measures alone. Cholestyramine reduces plasma cholesterol concentrations, but causes no change or a slight increase in serum triglyceride concentrations, and so is not useful in patients with elevated triglyceride concentrations alone. Its use is limited in other types of hyperlipidemia (including type IIb) because it may cause further elevation of triglycerides.

In the 1988 Report of the National Cholesterol Education Program Expert Panel on Detection, Evaluation, and Treatment of High Blood Cholesterol in Adults, the following guidelines for the treatment of high blood cholesterol are recommended:

   Nonpharmacologic management (especially reduction in dietary intake of saturated fatty acids and cholesterol, weight reduction and exercise, and quitting smoking) is recommended first for all patients and as an adjunct to all pharmacologic cholesterol therapy.

   If, after six months of diet therapy, adequate low density lipoprotein (LDL)-cholesterol reduction is not achieved, then medication therapy is recommended to be added to diet therapy.

   Initial medication therapy usually consists of a bile acid sequestrant (e.g., cholestyramine, colestipol) or niacin. A 3-hydroxy-3-methylglutanyl coenzyme A (HMG-CoA) reductase inhibitor (e.g., lovastatin) should be considered after the bile acid sequestrants and niacin. Other lipid-lowering agents, including fibric acid derivatives (e.g., gemfibrozil and clofibrate) and probucol, are not as effective in lowering LDL cholesterol as the above mentioned medications. Two other agents, neomycin (not approved by FDA as a lipid-lowering agent) and dextrothyroxine are not recommended for general use because other medications are available that have a more favorable benefit/risk ratio.

   If adequate LDL-cholesterol control is not achieved with initial medication therapy, it is recommended that the patient be switched to another medication or a combination of two medications with synergistic mechanisms of action. Although experience with such drug combinations is somewhat limited, preliminary studies indicate that the bile acid sequestrants given with either niacin, lovastatin, probucol, or gemfibrozil are useful in controlling LDL cholesterol. Lovastatin in combination with either niacin or gemfibrozil needs further study because of the potential increased risk of side effects.

   If effective control of LDL cholesterol is not obtained after use of primary medications and medication combinations, then referral to a lipid specialist may be necessary.

Studies have suggested that control of elevated cholesterol and triglycerides may not lessen the danger of cardiovascular disease and mortality, although incidence of nonfatal myocardial infarctions may be decreased.

Cholestyramine is indicated to reduce the risks of atherosclerotic heart disease and myocardial infarctions.

Pruritus, associated with partial biliary obstruction (treatment)—Cholestyramine is indicated for the relief of pruritus associated with partial biliary obstruction (including primary biliary cirrhosis and various other forms of bile stasis). It is not useful in patients with complete biliary obstruction or with pruritus due to other causes.

[Diarrhea, due to bile acids (treatment)]—Cholestyramine has also been used to treat diarrhea caused by increased bile acids in the colon after surgery, although the risk of steatorrhea is increased.

[Hyperoxaluria (treatment)][1]—Cholestyramine is also being used in the treatment of hyperoxaluria.

[Cholestyramine has been used in the treatment of digitalis glycoside overdose; however, it generally has been replaced by other agents such as digoxin immune fab.]

[1]Not included in Canadian product labeling.

Pharmacology

Mechanism of action/Effect: Cholestyramine binds with bile acids in the intestine, preventing their reabsorption and producing an insoluble complex, which is excreted in the feces.

   Antihyperlipidemic—Cholestyramine binds with bile acids in the intestine, causing an increase in hepatic synthesis of bile acids from cholesterol. This depletion of hepatic cholesterol increases hepatic low-density lipoprotein (LDL) receptor activity, which removes LDL cholesterol from the plasma. Cholestyramine may also increase hepatic very low-density lipoprotein (VLDL) production, thereby increasing the plasma concentration of triglycerides, especially in patients with hypertriglyceridemia.

   Antipruritic (cholestasis)—Reduction of serum bile acids and subsequent reduction of excess bile acids, which are deposited in dermal tissue, may lead to reduced pruritus.

   Antidiarrheal (postoperative colonic bile acids)—Cholestyramine binds with and removes bile acids.

   Antidote (anion-exchange resin)—Because it is an anion-exchange resin, cholestyramine is capable of binding negatively charged medications as well as some others, causing a decreased effect or shortened half-life.

Onset of action:
   Reduction of plasma cholesterol concentrations—Generally reduced within 24 to 48 hours after initiation of cholestyramine therapy, but may continue to fall for up to 1 year. In some patients, after the initial decrease, serum cholesterol concentrations return to or exceed baseline levels with continued therapy.
   Relief of pruritus associated with biliary stasis—Usually occurs within 1 to 3 weeks after initiation of therapy.
   Relief of diarrhea associated with bile acids—Within 24 hours.

Duration of action:
   Reduction of plasma cholesterol concentrations—After withdrawal of cholestyramine, cholesterol concentrations return to baseline in about 2 to 4 weeks.
   Relief of pruritus associated with biliary stasis—Pruritus returns within 1 to 2 weeks when the medication is withdrawn.

Precautions to Consider

Geriatrics

Appropriate studies on the relationship of age to the effects of cholestyramine have not been performed in the geriatric population. However, patients over 60 years of age may be more likely to experience gastrointestinal side effects, as well as adverse nutritional
effects.

Drug interactions and/or related problems

The following drug interactions and/or related problems have been
selected on the basis of their potential clinical significance (possible mechanism in parentheses where appropriate)—not necessarily inclusive (» = major clinical significance):

Note: Combinations containing any of the following medications, depending on the amount present, may also interact with this
medication.

» Anticoagulants, coumarin- or indandione-derivative
(concurrent use may significantly increase the anticoagulant
effect as a result of depletion of vitamin K, but cholestyramine
may also bind with oral anticoagulants in the gastrointestinal
tract and reduce their effects; administration at least 6 hours
before cholestyramine and adjustment of anticoagulant dosage
based on frequent prothrombin-time determinations are recommended)

Chenodiol or
Ursodiol
(effect may be decreased when chenodiol or ursodiol is used
concurrently with cholestyramine, which binds these medications and decreases their absorption and also tends to increase
cholesterol saturation of bile)

» Digitalis glycosides, especially digitoxin
(cholestyramine may reduce the half-life of these medications
by decreasing intestinal reabsorption and enterohepatic circulation; caution is recommended, especially when cholestyramine
is withdrawn from a patient who was stabilized on the digitalis
glycoside while receiving cholestyramine, because of the potential for serious toxicity; some clinicians recommend administration of cholestyramine approximately 8 hours after the
digitalis glycoside)

» Diuretics, thiazide, oral, or
» Penicillin G, oral, or
» Phenylbutazone or
» Propranolol, oral, or
» Tetracyclines, oral
(concurrent use with cholestyramine may result in binding of
these medications, thus decreasing their absorption; an interval
of several hours between administration of cholestyramine and
any of these medications is recommended)

Folic acid
(concurrent use with cholestyramine may interfere with absorption of folic acid; folic acid supplementation recommended
in patients receiving cholestyramine for prolonged periods)

» Thyroid hormones, including dextrothyroxine
(concurrent use with cholestyramine may decrease the effects
of thyroid hormones by binding and delaying or preventing
absorption; an interval of 4 to 5 hours between administration
of the two medications and regular monitoring of thyroid function tests are recommended)

» Vancomycin, oral
(cholestyramine has been shown to bind oral vancomycin significantly when used concurrently, resulting in decreased stool
concentrations and marked reduction in antibacterial activity of
vancomycin; concurrent use is not recommended; patients
should be advised to take oral vancomycin and cholestyramine
several hours apart)

Vitamins, fat-soluble
(cholestyramine may interfere with absorption of fat-soluble
vitamins as a result of its interference with fat absorption;
supplemental vitamin A and D in water-miscible or parenteral
form are recommended in patients receiving cholestyramine
for prolonged periods; supplemental vitamin K may be required in some patients who develop bleeding tendencies)

Medications, other
(cholestyramine may delay or reduce absorption of other medications administered concurrently because of its anion-binding
activity; administration of other medications 1 to 2 hours before or 4 to 6 hours after cholestyramine is recommended,
although absorption of some medications is impaired even then;
caution is recommended when cholestyramine is withdrawn
because of the risk of toxicity when suddenly increased absorption of the other medication leads to higher serum concentrations)

Contraindications/Medical problems

The contraindications/medical problems included have been selected
on the basis of their potential clinical significance (reasons given
in parentheses where appropriate)—not necessarily inclusive (» =
major clinical significance).

*Risk-benefit should be considered when the following medical prob-
lems exist:*

Bleeding disorders or
Gallstones or
Gastrointestinal function impairment or
Hypothyroidism or
Malabsorption states, especially steatorrhea, or
Peptic ulcer
(these conditions may be exacerbated)

» Complete biliary obstruction or complete atresia
(no bile acids in gastrointestinal tract for cholestyramine to
bind)

» Constipation
(risk of fecal impaction)

Coronary artery disease and
Hemorrhoids
(because of the risks associated with severe constipation)

» Phenylketonuria
(sensitivity to phenylalanine in aspartame, which is included in
sugar-free preparation)

Renal function impairment
(increased risk of development of hyperchloremic acidosis)

Sensitivity to cholestyramine

Side/Adverse Effects

Note: Side effects are more likely to occur with high doses and in
patients over 60 years of age.

Less frequently, osteoporosis has been reported as a result of
chronic long-term cholestyramine use.

The following side/adverse effects have been selected on the basis of
their potential clinical significance (possible signs and symptoms
in parentheses where appropriate)—not necessarily inclusive:

Those indicating need for medical attention

Incidence more frequent
Constipation—usually mild and transient, but may be severe and
lead to fecal impaction

Incidence rare
Gallstones or pancreatitis (severe stomach pain with nausea and
vomiting); *gastrointestinal bleeding or peptic ulcer* (black, tarry
stools); *steatorrhea or malabsorption syndrome* (sudden loss of
weight)

Those indicating need for medical attention only if they continue or are bothersome

Incidence more frequent
Heartburn or indigestion; nausea or vomiting; stomach pain

Incidence less frequent
Belching; bloating; diarrhea; dizziness; headache

Patient Consultation

In providing consultation, consider emphasizing the following selected information (» = major clinical significance):

Before using this medication
» Conditions affecting use, especially:
Sensitivity to cholestyramine
Use in children—Not recommended since cholesterol is required for normal development
Use in the elderly—Increased incidence of gastrointestinal side effects and adverse nutritional effects in patients over 60 years of age
Other oral medications, especially anticoagulants, digitalis glycosides, penicillin G, tetracyclines, phenylbutazone, propranolol, thyroid hormones, thiazide diuretics, or vancomycin
Other medical problems, especially complete biliary obstruction or complete atresia, constipation, malabsorption states, or phenylketonuria

Proper use of this medication
» Importance of not taking more or less medication than the amount prescribed
Missed dose: Taking as soon as possible; not taking if almost time for next dose; not doubling doses
» Proper storage
For oral suspension dosage form
» Importance of mixing with fluids before taking; instructions for measuring and mixing—Placing in 2 ounces of any beverage and stirring vigorously, then adding 2 to 4 ounces of beverage and shaking vigorously (does not dissolve); rinsing glass and drinking to make sure all medication is taken; may also be mixed with milk in cereals, thin soups, or pulpy fruits
For resin bar dosage form
Chewing bar thoroughly
For use as an antihyperlipidemic
» Diet as preferred therapy; importance of following prescribed diet
This medication does not cure the condition but rather helps control it

Precautions while using this medication
» Importance of close monitoring by the physician
» Not taking any other medication unless discussed with physician
For use as an antihyperlipidemic
» Checking with physician before discontinuing medication; blood lipid concentrations may increase significantly

Side/adverse effects
Signs of potential side effects, especially constipation, gallstones, pancreatitis, gastrointestinal bleeding, peptic ulcer, and steatorrhea or malabsorption syndrome

General Dosing Information

To prevent accidental inhalation or esophageal distress with the dry form, it is recommended that cholestyramine for suspension be mixed with at least 120 to 180 mL of water or other fluids before being ingested. It may also be taken in soups or with cereals or pulpy fruits.

Reduction in cholestyramine dosage or withdrawal of the medication may be necessary in some patients if constipation occurs or worsens, to prevent impaction. Administration of a laxative or stool softener or increased fluid intake may be helpful.

For use as an antihyperlipidemic
If a paradoxical increase in plasma cholesterol concentrations occurs, it is recommended that cholestyramine therapy be withdrawn.

If response is inadequate after 1 to 3 months of treatment, cholestyramine therapy should be withdrawn, except in the case of xanthoma tuberosum, which may require up to 1 year of treatment as long as reduction in size and/or number of xanthomata occurs.

For use as an antipruritic
Dosage may be reduced when relief of pruritus occurs.

Oral Dosage Forms

Note: Bracketed uses in the *Dosage Forms* section refer to categories of use and/or indications that are not included in U.S. product labeling.

CHOLESTYRAMINE CHEWABLE BAR

Usual adult and adolescent dose:
Antihyperlipidemic; or
Antipruritic (cholestasis); or
[Antidiarrheal, postoperative colonic bile acids]—
Initial: Oral, 4 grams (anhydrous cholestyramine) one to six times a day before meals, adjusted according to response.
Maintenance: Oral, 4 grams (anhydrous cholestyramine) one to six times a day before meals and at bedtime.

Note: A single daily dose or two divided daily doses are equally effective, but three or more divided daily doses may be more convenient for the patient, especially with the larger doses.

Usual adult prescribing limits:
Antihyperlipidemic—Up to 32 grams (anhydrous cholestyramine) a day; some clinicians recommend a maximum of 24 grams a day because of the risk of steatorrhea.
Antipruritic (cholestasis)—Up to 16 grams (anhydrous cholestyramine) a day.

CHOLESTYRAMINE FOR ORAL SUSPENSION USP

Usual adult and adolescent dose:
Antihyperlipidemic; or
Antipruritic (cholestasis); or
[Antidiarrheal, postoperative colonic bile acids]—
Initial: Oral, 4 grams (anhydrous cholestyramine) one to six times a day before meals, adjusted according to response.
Maintenance: Oral, 4 grams (anhydrous cholestyramine) one to six times a day before meals and at bedtime.

Note: A single daily dose or two divided daily doses are equally effective, but three or more divided daily doses may be more convenient for the patient, especially with the larger doses.

Usual adult prescribing limits:
Antihyperlipidemic—Up to 32 grams (anhydrous cholestyramine) a day; some clinicians recommend a maximum of 24 grams a day because of the risk of steatorrhea.
Antipruritic (cholestasis)—Up to 16 grams (anhydrous cholestyramine) a day.

Auxiliary labeling: • Take mixed in cold water or juice.

CINOXACIN   Systemic†

A commonly used *brand name* in the U.S. is *Cinobac*.

ORAL
Cinoxacin Capsules USP†
In the U.S.—*Cinobac*

---

†Not commercially available in Canada.

Category: Antibacterial (systemic).
Note: Cinoxacin is a synthetic antibacterial similar in bacterial spectrum to nalidixic acid.

Indications

Note: Bracketed information in the *Indications* section refers to uses not included in U.S. product labeling.

Accepted
Urinary tract infections, bacterial (prophylaxis)—Cinoxacin is indicated in the prophylaxis of urinary tract infections in women with a history of recurrent urinary tract infections.

Urinary tract infections, bacterial (treatment)—Cinoxacin is indicated in the treatment of initial and recurrent urinary tract infections in adults caused by *Escherichia coli, Klebsiella pneumoniae* and other *Klebsiella* species, *Enterobacter* species (including *E. aerogenes, and E. cloacae*), *Proteus mirabilis, P. vulgaris,* and [*Morganella morganii* and some strains of *Serratia* and *Citrobacter*].

Urea-splitting organisms (e.g., *Proteus mirabilis*) may cause an increase in urine pH and thereby decrease the effectiveness of cinoxacin.

Not all species or strains of a particular organism may be susceptible to cinoxacin.

Unaccepted
Cinoxacin is not effective against *Pseudomonas* species, *Enterococcus faecalis*, or staphylococci.

Pharmacology

Mechanism of action/Effect: Bactericidal in the urine and acts by inhibition of bacterial DNA replication.

Precautions to Consider

Cross-sensitivity and/or related problems
Since cinoxacin is closely related chemically to other quinolone derivatives (e.g., ciprofloxacin, nalidixic acid, norfloxacin, ofloxacin), patients allergic to other quinolones may be allergic to this medication also.

Geriatrics
No information is available on the relationship of age to the effects of cinoxacin in geriatric patients. However, elderly patients are more likely to have an age-related decrease in renal function, which may require an adjustment of dosage in patients receiving cinoxacin.

Contraindications/Medical problems
The contraindications/medical problems included have been selected on the basis of their potential clinical significance (reasons given in parentheses where appropriate)—not necessarily inclusive (» = major clinical significance).

Except under special circumstances, this medication should not be used when the following medical problem exists:
» Previous allergic reaction to cinoxacin or other quinolones

Risk-benefit should be considered when the following medical problem exists:
» Renal function impairment
    (cinoxacin is primarily excreted renally; it is recommended that cinoxacin be administered in a reduced dose in patients with impaired renal function)

Side/Adverse Effects

The following side/adverse effects have been selected on the basis of their potential clinical significance (possible signs and symptoms in parentheses where appropriate)—not necessarily inclusive:

Those indicating need for medical attention
Incidence 3% or less
    Hypersensitivity (skin rash, itching, redness, or swelling)
Incidence 1% or less
    Central nervous system toxicity (dizziness, headache)

Those indicating need for medical attention only if they continue or are bothersome
Incidence 3% or less
    Gastrointestinal reactions (anorexia, diarrhea, nausea, stomach cramps, vomiting)

Patient Consultation

In providing consultation, consider emphasizing the following selected information (» = major clinical significance):

Before using this medication
» Conditions affecting use, especially:
    Allergies to cinoxacin or other quinolone derivatives
    Pregnancy—Cinoxacin crosses the placenta. Cinoxacin is not recommended for use during pregnancy because it has been shown to cause arthropathy in immature animals
    Breast-feeding—Not recommended since cinoxacin has been shown to cause arthropathy in immature animals
    Use in children—Cinoxacin is not recommended for use in infants and prepubertal children since it has been shown to cause arthropathy in immature animals
    Other medical problems, especially renal function impairment

Proper use of this medication
    Taking with food, unless otherwise directed by physician
» Not giving to infants, children under 12 years of age, or pregnant women; may cause arthropathy in immature animals
» Compliance with full course of therapy
» Importance of not missing doses and taking at evenly spaced times
    Missed dose: Taking as soon as possible; if almost time for next dose and dosing schedule is—
       2 doses a day: Spacing missed dose and next dose 5 to 6 hours apart
       3 or more doses a day: Spacing missed dose and next dose 2 to 4 hours apart
» Proper storage

Precautions while using this medication
    Checking with physician if no improvement within a few days
» Caution if dizziness occurs

Side/adverse effects
    Signs of potential side effects, especially central nervous system toxicity and hypersensitivity

General Dosing Information

Cinoxacin may be taken with food.

Patients with impaired renal function may require a reduction in dosage based on creatinine clearance. Creatinine clearance (in mL per minute) may be calculated as follows:

Adult males: Creatinine clearance

$$= \frac{(140 - age) \times (body\ weight\ in\ kg)}{72 \times patient's\ serum\ creatinine\ concentration}$$

Adult females: Creatinine clearance

$$= \frac{(140 - age) \times (body\ weight\ in\ kg)}{72 \times patient's\ serum\ creatinine\ concentration} \times 0.85$$

Creatinine clearance may also be calculated in SI units (as mL per second) as follows:

Adult males: Creatinine clearance

$$= \frac{(140 - age) \times (ideal\ body\ weight\ in\ kg)}{50 \times serum\ creatinine\ (micromoles\ per\ L)}$$

Adult females: Creatinine clearance

$$= \frac{(140 - age) \times (ideal\ body\ weight\ in\ kg)}{50 \times serum\ creatinine\ (micromoles\ per\ L)} \times 0.85$$

Oral Dosage Forms

CINOXACIN CAPSULES USP

Usual adult dose:

Prophylaxis—Oral, 250 mg at bedtime for up to five months.

Treatment—Oral, 250 mg every six hours; or 500 mg every twelve hours for seven to fourteen days.

Note: After an initial loading dose of 500 mg, adults with impaired renal function may require a reduction in dose as follows:

Creatinine Clearance (mL/min/1.73 M^2)/ (mL/sec)	Dose
>80/(1.33)	See *Usual adult dose*
50–80/(0.83–1.33)	250 mg every 8 hours
20–50/(0.33–0.83)	250 mg every 12 to 24 hours
<20/(0.33)	Use is not recommended

Auxiliary labeling:
- Continue medicine for full time of treatment.
- May cause dizziness.

CIPROFLOXACIN   Systemic

Some commonly used *brand names* in the U.S. and Canada are *Cipro* and *Cipro IV.*

ORAL
Ciprofloxacin Hydrochloride Tablets USP
In the U.S. and Canada—*Cipro*

PARENTERAL
Ciprofloxacin Injection†
In the U.S.—*Cipro IV*
Ciprofloxacin for Injection†
In the U.S.—*Cipro IV*

†Not commercially available in Canada.

Category: Antibacterial (systemic).

Indications

Note: Bracketed information in the *Indications* section refers to uses not included in U.S. product labeling.

Accepted
Ciprofloxacin is a broad-spectrum anti-infective, active against a wide range of aerobic gram-positive and gram-negative organisms. It is active *in vitro* against most Enterobacteriaceae, including *Escherichia coli, Klebsiella pneumoniae, Enterobacter cloacae, Citrobacter freundii, Proteus mirabilis,* indole-positive *Proteus* species, *Morganella morganii, Providencia* species, and *Serratia marcescens.* Other organisms that ciprofloxacin is generally active against *in vitro* include *Haemophilus influenzae* (including beta-lactamase-producing strains), *Neisseria gonorrhoeae* (including penicillin-resistant strains), *Staphylococcus aureus* (including methicillin-resistant strains), *S. epidermidis, H. ducreyi, Pseudomonas aeruginosa,* and *N. meningitidis.* Ciprofloxacin is only moderately active against other species of pseudomonas and streptococcus, including enterococcus and *S. pneumoniae, Chlamydia trachomatis,*

and *Mycobacterium tuberculosis.* Other organisms with good *in vitro* susceptibility to ciprofloxacin include *Salmonella* and *Shigella* species, and *Campylobacter jejuni.* Ciprofloxacin is generally not active against most anaerobic bacteria, including *Bacteroides* sp. and *Clostridium* sp., and *Candida albicans.* Resistance has been reported to develop in strains of *Pseudomonas aeruginosa, Serratia marcescens* and methicillin-resistant *Staphylococcus aureus.*

Ciprofloxacin is used for the treatment of the following infections caused by susceptible organisms:

Bone and joint infections
Diarrhea, bacterial
Pneumonia, gram-negative, bacterial
Skin and soft tissue infections
Urinary tract infections, bacterial
[Chancroid][1]
[Prostatitis][1]
[Urethritis, gonococcal][1]

Note: Caution should be used in treating streptococcal and pneumococcal pneumonia with quinolones. Although they have been effective in limited trials, treatment failures have been reported; quinolones should not be considered the drug of first choice in the treatment of presumed or confirmed pneumococcal pneumonia.

Not all species or strains of a particular organism may be susceptible to ciprofloxacin.

Unaccepted
Ciprofloxacin is not generally effective against most strains of *Ps. cepacia,* some strains of *Ps. maltophilia,* and most anaerobic bacteria (including *Bacteroides fragilis* and *Clostridium difficile*).
Ciprofloxacin is only moderately effective against most strains of streptococci (including *Enterococcus faecalis*), *Mycobacterium tuberculosis,* and *Chlamydia trachomatis.*

[1]Not included in Canadian product labeling.

Pharmacology

Mechanism of action/Effect: Bactericidal; exact mechanism unknown; ciprofloxacin acts intracellularly by inhibiting DNA gyrase, a type II topoisomerase essential for ATP-dependent coiling and supercoiling of bacterial DNA, enabling it to be replicated and repacked in both daughter cells; inhibits relaxation of supercoiled DNA; and promotes double-stranded DNA breakage.

Precautions to Consider

Cross-sensitivity and/or related problems

Since ciprofloxacin is closely related chemically to other quinolone derivatives (e.g., cinoxacin, nalidixic acid, norfloxacin, ofloxacin), patients allergic to other quinolones may be allergic to this medication also.

Geriatrics

Studies performed to date have not demonstrated geriatrics-specific problems that would limit the usefulness of ciprofloxacin in the elderly. However, elderly patients are more likely to have an age-related decrease in renal function, which may require an adjustment of dosage in patients receiving ciprofloxacin.

Dental

Ciprofloxacin may cause oral candidiasis, resulting in painful oral mucosa.

Drug interactions and/or related problems

The following drug interactions and/or related problems have been selected on the basis of their potential clinical significance (possible mechanism in parentheses where appropriate)—not necessarily inclusive (» = major clinical significance):

Note: Combinations containing any of the following medications, depending on the amount present, may also interact with this medication.

Alkalizers, urinary, such as:
Carbonic anhydrase inhibitors
Citrates
Sodium bicarbonate
(urinary alkalizers may reduce the solubility of ciprofloxacin in the urine; patients should be observed for signs of crystalluria and nephrotoxicity, although the incidence is rare)

» Antacids, aluminum-, calcium-, and magnesium-containing or
» Ferrous sulfate or
Laxatives, magnesium-containing or
» Sucralfate or
Zinc
(antacids, ferrous sulfate, zinc, and sucralfate may reduce absorption by chelation of ciprofloxacin, resulting in lower serum and urine concentrations of ciprofloxacin; therefore, concurrent use is not recommended)

Caffeine
(concurrent use with ciprofloxacin reduces the hepatic metabolism and clearance of caffeine, increasing its half-life and the risk of caffeine-related CNS stimulation)

Probenecid
(decreases renal tubular secretion of ciprofloxacin by approximately 50% when used concurrently, resulting in decreased urinary excretion of ciprofloxacin, increased serum concentrations, prolonged elimination half-life, and increased risk of toxicity)

» Theophylline
(concurrent use with ciprofloxacin reduces the hepatic metabolism and clearance of theophylline by approximately 30%, probably by competitive inhibition at the cytochrome P-450 binding sites, resulting in prolonged elimination half-life, increased theophylline serum concentrations, and increased risk of theophylline-related toxicity; nausea, vomiting, tremors, restlessness, agitation, seizures, and palpitations may occur; serum theophylline concentrations should be monitored and dosage adjustments may be required)

» Warfarin
(concurrent use with ciprofloxacin has been reported to increase the anticoagulant effect of warfarin, increasing the chance of bleeding; the prothrombin time [PT] of patients receiving warfarin should be carefully monitored)

Contraindications/Medical problems

The contraindications/medical problems included have been selected on the basis of their potential clinical significance (reasons given in parentheses where appropriate)—not necessarily inclusive (» = major clinical significance).

Except under special circumstances, this medication should not be used when the following medical problem exists:

» Allergy to ciprofloxacin or other quinolones

Risk-benefit should be considered when the following medical problems exist:

CNS disorders, including cerebral arteriosclerosis or epilepsy (ciprofloxacin may cause CNS toxicity)

Hepatic function impairment
(patients with *both* hepatic and renal function impairment may require a dosage reduction)

» Renal function impairment
(ciprofloxacin elimination is primarily renal; it is recommended that ciprofloxacin dosage be reduced in patients with impaired renal function)

Side/Adverse Effects

Note: The relative insolubility of ciprofloxacin at an alkaline pH has resulted in crystalluria, usually when the urinary pH exceeds 7.0. Because normal urinary pH is acidic, approximately 5-6, crystalluria is very unlikely to occur unless the patient's urine has become alkalinized.

Seizures have been reported very rarely with ciprofloxacin therapy; however, the patients who did have seizures either had a previous seizure history, were alcoholic, or were taking ciprofloxacin concurrently with theophylline.

The following side/adverse effects have been selected on the basis of their potential clinical significance (possible signs and symptoms in parentheses where appropriate)—not necessarily inclusive:

Those indicating need for medical attention

Incidence rare
Central nervous system (CNS) stimulation (agitation, confusion, hallucinations, tremors); *hypersensitivity reactions* (skin rash, itching, or redness, swelling of face or neck); *interstitial nephritis* (rash, fever, azotemia, eosinophilia, eosinophiluria, hematuria, proteinuria); *phlebitis* (pain at site of injection); *photosensitivity* (increased sensitivity of skin to sunlight)

Those indicating need for medical attention only if they continue or are bothersome

Incidence more frequent
CNS toxicity (dizziness or lightheadedness, headache, nervousness, drowsiness, insomnia); *gastrointestinal reactions* (abdominal or stomach pain or discomfort, diarrhea, nausea or vomiting)

Patient Consultation

In providing consultation, consider emphasizing the following selected information (» = major clinical significance):

Before using this medication

» Conditions affecting use, especially:
Allergies to ciprofloxacin or other quinolone derivatives

Pregnancy—Ciprofloxacin is not recommended for use during pregnancy because it has been shown to cause arthropathy in immature animals

Breast-feeding—Not recommended since ciprofloxacin has been shown to cause arthropathy in immature animals

Use in children—Use of ciprofloxacin is not recommended in infants, children, and adolescents since it has been shown to cause arthropathy in immature animals

Dental—May cause oral candidiasis

Other medications, especially aluminum- and magnesium-containing antacids, sucralfate, theophylline, or warfarin

Other medical problems, especially renal function impairment

Proper use of this medication

» Not giving to infants, children, adolescents, or pregnant women; has been shown to cause arthropathy in immature animals

» Taking with full glass (240 mL) of water; maintaining adequate fluid intake

» Taking with meals or on an empty stomach

» Compliance with full course of therapy

» Importance of not missing doses and taking at evenly spaced times
Missed dose: Taking as soon as possible; not taking if almost time for next dose; not doubling doses

» Proper storage

Precautions while using this medication

Checking with physician if no improvement within a few days

» Avoiding concurrent use of antacids or sucralfate and ciprofloxacin; taking antacids or sucralfate at least 4 hours before or 2 hours after administration of ciprofloxacin

» Possible photosensitivity reactions

» Caution if blurred vision or other vision problems, dizziness, lightheadedness, or drowsiness occurs

Side/adverse effects

Signs of potential side effects, especially CNS stimulation, hypersensitivity reactions, interstitial nephritis, phlebitis, and photosensitivity

General Dosing Information

The presence of food in the stomach may delay absorption of ciprofloxacin; however, the overall absorption is not affected. Therefore, ciprofloxacin may be taken with meals or on an empty stomach. Ciprofloxacin should be taken with a full glass (240 mL) of water.

Crystalluria has been reported, especially in patients with alkaline urine (pH 7 or above). Therefore, alkalinization of the urine should be avoided. Although crystalluria has been reported only rarely in humans, fluid intake should be sufficient to maintain urine output of at least 1200 to 1500 mL per day in adults.

Intravenous ciprofloxacin should be administered over at least 60 minutes to minimize patient discomfort and reduce the risk of venous irritation.

Patients with renal function impairment may need an adjustment in dosage, based on creatinine clearance. Creatinine clearance (in mL per minute) may be calculated as follows:

Adult males: Creatinine clearance
$$= \frac{(140 - age) \times (body\ weight\ in\ kg)}{72 \times patient's\ serum\ creatinine\ concentration}$$

Adult females: Creatinine clearance
$$= \frac{(140 - age) \times (body\ weight\ in\ kg)}{72 \times patient's\ serum\ creatinine\ concentration} \times 0.85$$

Creatinine clearance may also be calculated in SI units (as mL per second) as follows:

Adult males: Creatinine clearance
$$= \frac{(140 - age) \times (ideal\ body\ weight\ in\ kg)}{50 \times serum\ creatinine\ (micromoles\ per\ L)}$$

Adult females: Creatinine clearance
$$= \frac{(140 - age) \times (ideal\ body\ weight\ in\ kg)}{50 \times serum\ creatinine\ (micromoles\ per\ L)} \times 0.85$$

Oral Dosage Forms

Note: Bracketed uses in the *Dosage Forms* section refer to categories of use and/or indications that are not included in U.S. product labeling.

CIPROFLOXACIN HYDROCHLORIDE TABLETS USP

Usual adult dose:

Bone and joint infections;

Pneumonia, gram-negative, bacterial; or

Skin and soft tissue infections—Oral, 500 to 750 mg (base) every twelve hours for seven to fourteen days. Severe or complicated infections may require prolonged therapy.

Diarrhea, bacterial—Oral, 500 mg (base) every twelve hours for five to seven days.

[Urethritis, gonococcal][1]—Oral, 250 to 500 mg (base) as a single dose.

Urinary tract infections, bacterial—Oral, 250 to 500 mg (base) every twelve hours for seven to fourteen days. Severe or complicated infections may require prolonged therapy.

Note: Bone infections may require treatment for four to six weeks or longer.

Adults with impaired renal function may require a reduction in dose as follows:

Creatinine Clearance (mL/min)/(mL/sec)	Dose (base)
>50/(0.83)	See *Usual adult dose*
30–50/(0.50–0.83)	250–500 mg every 12 hours
5–29/(0.08–0.48)	250–500 mg every 18 hours
Hemodialysis or Peritoneal dialysis patients	250–500 mg every 24 hours after dialysis

Usual adult prescribing limits: Up to 1.5 grams (base) daily.

Auxiliary labeling:

• Take with a full glass of water.

• May cause dizziness, or lightheadedness.

• Continue medicine for full time of treatment.

• Avoid too much sun or use of sunlamp.

• Do not take antacids, or iron preparations within 4 hours of this medicine.

[1]Not included in Canadian product labeling.

Parenteral Dosage Forms

CIPROFLOXACIN INJECTION

Usual adult dose:

Bone and joint infections;

Pneumonia, gram-negative, bacterial; or

Skin and soft tissue infections—Intravenous injection, 400 mg every twelve hours. Administer over at least 60 minutes. Severe or complicated infections may require prolonged therapy.

Urinary tract infections, bacterial—Oral, 200 to 400 mg every twelve hours for seven to fourteen days. Severe or complicated infections may require prolonged therapy.

Note: Bone infections may require treatment for four to six weeks or longer.

Adults with impaired renal function may require a reduction in dose as follows:

Creatinine Clearance (mL/min)/(mL/sec)	Dose (base)
30/(0.50)	See *Usual adult dose*
5–29/(0.08–0.48)	200–400 mg every 18 to 24 hours

CIPROFLOXACIN FOR INJECTION

Usual adult dose:

Bone and joint infections;
Pneumonia, gram-negative, bacterial; or

Skin and soft tissue infections—Intravenous injection, 400 mg every twelve hours for seven to fourteen days. Administer over at least 60 minutes. Severe or complicated infections may require prolonged therapy.

Urinary tract infections, bacterial—Oral, 200 to 400 mg every twelve hours for seven to fourteen days. Severe or complicated infections may require prolonged therapy.

Note: Bone infections may require treatment for four to six weeks or longer.

Adults with impaired renal function may require a reduction in dose as follows:

Creatinine Clearance (mL/min)/(mL/sec)	Dose (base)
30/(0.50)	See *Usual adult dose*
5–29/(0.08–0.48)	200–400 mg every 18 to 24 hours

CITRATES   Systemic

Some commonly used *brand names* are:

In the U.S.—

Bicitra [Sodium Citrate and Citric Acid]
Citrolith [Potassium Citrate and Sodium Citrate]
Oracit [Sodium Citrate and Citric Acid]
Polycitra-K [Potassium Citrate and Citric Acid]

Polycitra-K Crystals [Potassium Citrate and Citric Acid]
Polycitra-LC [Tricitrates]
Polycitra Syrup [Tricitrates]
Urocit-K [Potassium Citrate]

In Canada—

Oracit [Sodium Citrate and Citric Acid]

Other commonly used names for sodium citrate and citric acid are Albright's solution and modified Shohl's solution.

CALCIUM CITRATE—See Calcium Supplements (Systemic).
MAGNESIUM CITRATE—See Laxatives (Local).
POTASSIUM CITRATE
Oral
    Potassium Citrate Tablets
        In the U.S.—*Urocit-K*
POTASSIUM CITRATE AND CITRIC ACID
Oral
    Potassium Citrate and Citric Acid Oral Solution USP
        In the U.S.—*Polycitra-K*
    Potassium Citrate and Citric Acid for Oral Solution
        In the U.S.—*Polycitra-K Crystals*
POTASSIUM CITRATE AND SODIUM CITRATE
Oral
    Potassium Citrate and Sodium Citrate Tablets
        In the U.S.—*Citrolith*
SODIUM CITRATE AND CITRIC ACID
Oral
    Sodium Citrate and Citric Acid Oral Solution USP
        In the U.S.—*Bicitra; Oracit* (not USP)
        In Canada—*Oracit*
TRICITRATES
Oral
    Tricitrates Oral Solution USP (Potassium Citrate, Sodium Citrate, and Citric Acid)
        In the U.S.—*Polycitra-LC; Polycitra Syrup*

Category

Antiurolithic, uric acid calculi—Potassium Citrate; Potassium Citrate and Citric Acid; Potassium Citrate and Sodium Citrate; Sodium Citrate and Citric Acid; Tricitrates.
Antiurolithic, cystine calculi—Potassium Citrate; Potassium Citrate and Citric Acid; Potassium Citrate and Sodium Citrate; Sodium Citrate and Citric Acid; Tricitrates.
Antiurolithic, calcium oxalate calculi—Potassium Citrate; Potassium Citrate and Citric Acid.
Antiurolithic, calcium phosphate calculi—Potassium Citrate; Potassium Citrate and Citric Acid.
Alkalizer, systemic—Potassium Citrate and Citric Acid; Sodium Citrate and Citric Acid; Tricitrates.
Alkalizer, urinary—Potassium Citrate; Potassium Citrate and Citric Acid; Potassium Citrate and Sodium Citrate; Sodium Citrate and Citric Acid; Tricitrates.
Buffer, neutralizing—Sodium Citrate and Citric Acid; Tricitrates.

Indications

Accepted

Renal calculi, cystine (prophylaxis and treatment); or
Renal calculi, uric acid (prophylaxis and treatment)—Citrates are indicated as urinary alkalizers in the prevention and treatment of uric acid or cystine lithiasis. They are often used in gout therapy as urinary alkalizers to prevent crystallization of urates.

Renal calculi, calcium (prophylaxis and treatment); or
Hypocitraturia (prophylaxis and treatment)—Potassium citrate and potassium citrate and citric acid are also indicated to increase urinary citrate in the prevention and treatment of calcium phosphate, calcium oxalate, or uric acid kidney stones in such conditions as renal tubular acidosis with calcium stones, hypocitraturic calcium oxalate nephrolithiasis of any etiology, and uric acid or cystine lithiasis with or without calcium stones.

Acidosis, in renal tubular disorders (treatment)—Potassium citrate and citric acid, sodium citrate and citric acid, and tricitrates are also used in the treatment of chronic metabolic acidosis resulting from chronic renal insufficiency or the syndrome of renal tubular acidosis. Sodium citrate is especially useful when the administration of potassium salts is undesirable or contraindicated.

Pneumonitis, aspiration (prophylaxis)—Sodium citrate and citric acid and tricitrates are used in preanesthesia medication as nonparticulate acid-neutralizing buffers of gastric acid to lessen the danger from acid-aspiration pneumonitis in patients at risk. Citrates have generally been replaced by the equally or more effective H_2-receptor antagonists in the prevention of acid aspiration in elective surgery. However, citrates and other antacids have a more rapid onset of action than H_2-receptor antagonists and may be more useful in emergency situations.

Pharmacology

Mechanism of action/Effect:

Alkalizer, urinary; or

Antiurolithic, uric acid calculi; or

Antiurolithic, cystine calculi—Sodium citrate and potassium citrate are metabolized to bicarbonates, which increase urinary pH by increasing the excretion of free bicarbonate ions, without producing systemic alkalosis when administered in recommended doses. A rise in urinary pH increases the solubility of cystine in the urine and the ionization of uric acid to more soluble urate ion. By maintaining an alkaline urine, the actual dissolution of uric acid stones may be accomplished.

Antiurolithic, calcium calculi—Metabolism of absorbed potassium citrate produces an alkaline load, raising urinary pH and increasing urinary citrate by augmenting citrate clearance. Thus, potassium citrate therapy appears to increase urinary citrate mainly by changing the renal handling of citrate, and, to a smaller extent, by increasing the filterable load of citrate. Increased urinary citrate and pH decreases calcium ion activity by increasing calcium complexation to dissociated anions and thus decreasing the saturation of calcium oxalate.

Potassium citrate also inhibits the crystallization and spontaneous nucleation of calcium oxalate and calcium phosphate in hypocitraturic calcium nephrolithiasis. However, potassium citrate does not alter the urinary saturation of calcium phosphate, because the effect of increased citrate complexation of calcium is antagonized by the rise in pH-dependent dissociation of phosphate. Calcium phosphate stones are more stable in alkaline urine.

Alkalizer, systemic—Increases the plasma bicarbonate, buffers excess hydrogen ion concentration, and raises blood pH, thereby reversing the clinical manifestations of acidosis.

Neutralizing buffer—Reacts chemically to neutralize or buffer existing quantities of gastric hydrochloric acid but has no direct effect on its output.

Onset of action: Potassium citrate—Single dose: Within 1 hour.

Duration of action:

Potassium citrate tablets—

    Single dose: Up to 12 hours.

    Multiple doses: 3 days.

Potassium citrate and citric acid oral solution—Up to 24 hours at dosage of:

    10 to 15 mL four times a day: Maintains a urine pH of 6.5 to 7.4.

    15 to 20 mL four times a day: Maintains a urine pH of 7.0 to 7.6.

Tricitrates oral solution—Up to 24 hours at dosage of:

    10 to 15 mL four times a day—Maintains a urine pH of 6.5 to 7.4.

    15 to 20 mL four times a day—Maintains a urine pH of 7.0 to 7.6.

Precautions to Consider

Geriatrics

No information is available on the relationship of age to the effects of citrates in geriatric patients.

Drug interactions and/or related problems

The following drug interactions and/or related problems have been selected on the basis of their potential clinical significance (possible mechanism in parentheses where appropriate)—not necessarily inclusive (» = major clinical significance):

Note: Combinations containing any of the following medications, depending on the amount present, may also interact with this medication.

    Amphetamines or

    Ephedrine or

    Pseudoephedrine or

»   Quinidine

    (concurrent use with citrates may inhibit urinary excretion and prolong the duration of action of these medications)

»   Antacids, especially those containing aluminum or sodium bicarbonate

    (concurrent use with citrates may result in systemic alkalosis)

    (concurrent use of sodium citrate with sodium bicarbonate may promote the development of calcium stones in patients with uric acid stones, due to sodium ion opposition to the hypocalciuric effect of the alkaline load; may also cause hypernatremia)

    (concurrent use of aluminum-containing antacids with citrate salts can increase aluminum absorption, possibly resulting in acute aluminum toxicity, especially in patients with renal insufficiency)

    Anticholinergics or other medications with anticholinergic activity

    (concurrent use with potassium citrate may increase risk of gastrointestinal irritation because of slowed gastrointestinal transit time; patients should be carefully monitored endoscopically for evidence of lesions)

»   Angiotensin-converting enzyme (ACE) inhibitors or

»   Anti-inflammatory drugs, nonsteroidal (NSAIDs) or Cyclosporine or

»   Diuretics, potassium-sparing, or

»   Heparin or

»   Low-salt milk or

»   Potassium-containing medications, other, or

»   Salt substitutes

    (concurrent use with potassium citrate may increase serum potassium concentrations, which may cause severe hyperkalemia and lead to cardiac arrest, especially in renal insufficiency; low-salt milk may contain up to 60 mEq of potassium per liter and most salt substitutes contain substantial amounts of potassium)

    Ciprofloxacin or

    Norfloxacin or

    Ofloxacin

    (citrates may reduce the solubility of ciprofloxacin, norfloxacin, or ofloxacin in the urine; patients should be observed for signs of crystalluria and nephrotoxicity)

»   Digitalis glycosides

    (concurrent use with potassium citrate may increase risk of hyperkalemia in digitalized patients; careful monitoring of serum potassium concentrations during concurrent use is recommended)

    Laxatives

    (concurrent administration with citrates may have an additive effect since sodium or potassium citrate may act as a saline laxative; however, these medications may be used concurrently as a preoperative for therapeutic advantage)

    Lithium

    (concurrent use with sodium citrate may increase the urinary excretion of lithium and reduce its therapeutic effects, possibly due to the sodium content of the citrate and/or the effect of urinary alkalinization)

» Methenamine
(concurrent use with citrates is not recommended because alkalinizing the urine may inhibit the effects of methenamine)

Salicylates
(concurrent use with citrates may increase the urinary excretion and decrease the therapeutic effects of salicylates due to alkalinization of the urine)

Sodium-containing medications
(concurrent use with sodium citrate may increase the risk of hypernatremia, especially in patients with renal disease)

Contraindications/Medical problems
The contraindications/medical problems included have been selected on the basis of their potential clinical significance (reasons given in parentheses where appropriate)—not necessarily inclusive (» = major clinical significance).

Except under special circumstances, this medication should not be used when the following medical problems exist:

For potassium citrate- and/or sodium citrate-containing
» Aluminum toxicity
(citrate salts have been found to increase aluminum absorption and may exacerbate the condition, especially in renal insufficiency)

» Heart failure or
» Myocardial damage, severe
(because of impaired mechanisms for excreting potassium, potentially fatal asymptomatic hyperkalemia can develop, rapidly leading to cardiovascular failure and cardiac arrest)
(sodium retention may result when patients with congestive heart failure are administered sodium citrate)

» Renal impairment, severe, with azotemia or oliguria, or
» Renal insufficiency, when glomerular filtration rate (GFR) is less than 0.7 mL per kg per minute
(danger of soft tissue calcification; increased risk of hyperkalemia or alkalosis)
(sodium retention may occur with use of sodium citrate)

» Urinary tract infection, active, with urea-splitting or other organisms, in association with calcium or struvite stones
(bacterial enzymatic degradation of citrate may occur, preventing it from increasing urinary citrate; also, the rise in urinary pH may promote further bacterial growth)

For potassium citrate-containing only (in addition to those listed above)
» Hyperkalemia, or conditions predisposing to hyperkalemia such as:
Adrenal insufficiency
Dehydration, acute
Diabetes mellitus, uncontrolled
Physical exercise, strenuous, in unconditioned persons
Renal failure, chronic
Tissue breakdown, extensive
(increased serum potassium concentrations leading to cardiac arrest may occur; exercise-induced hyperkalemia is transient and is a problem only in patients with renal insufficiency from dehydration or those taking medications that increase serum potassium)

» Peptic ulcer
(increased risk of gastrointestinal lesions with potassium citrate, especially with tablets)

For potassium citrate tablets only (in addition to those listed above)
» Gastric emptying, delayed, or
» Esophageal compression or
» Intestinal obstruction or stricture
(delayed passage of tablets through gastrointestinal tract may increase risk of gastrointestinal irritation)

Risk-benefit should be considered when the following medical problems exist:

For potassium citrate- and sodium citrate-containing
» Acidosis, renal tubular, severe, or
Diarrheal syndromes, chronic, such as ulcerative colitis, regional enteritis, or jejuno-ileal bypass surgery
(when urinary citrate in these conditions is very low [below 100 mg per day], citrates may be relatively ineffective in raising urinary citrate; higher doses may be required to produce the desired citraturic response; when urinary pH is high in renal tubular acidosis, citrates may produce only a small rise in pH; rapid transit time associated with diarrheal syndromes may prevent proper breakdown of tablets [especially wax matrix], liquid preparations should be used in diarrheal syndromes)

For sodium citrate-containing only (in addition to those listed above)
Edema, peripheral or pulmonary, or
Hypertension or
Toxemia of pregnancy
(sodium salts should be used cautiously in patients with these conditions to prevent exacerbation; also, patients on sodium restricted diets should not take sodium citrate)

Side/Adverse Effects
The following side/adverse effects have been selected on the basis of their potential clinical significance (possible signs and symptoms in parentheses where appropriate)—not necessarily inclusive:

Those indicating need for medical attention
Incidence rare
For potassium citrate- and sodium citrate-containing
Metabolic alkalosis (mood or mental changes, muscle pain or twitching, nervousness or restlessness, slow breathing, unpleasant taste, unusual tiredness or weakness)

For potassium citrate-containing only (in addition to those listed above)
Bowel obstruction or bowel perforation (abdominal or stomach cramps or pain; black, tarry stools; severe vomiting, sometimes with blood)—for tablet dosage form only; **hyperkalemia** (confusion; irregular heartbeat; numbness or tingling in hands, feet, or lips; shortness of breath or difficult breathing; unexplained anxiety; unusual tiredness or weakness; weakness or heaviness of legs)

Note: *Bowel obstruction* or *bowel perforation* caused by high concentration of potassium ions in region of dissolving tablets. Because the wax matrix is not an enteric coating, improper release of some of the potassium ions from the wax matrix into the stomach may cause upper gastrointestinal bleeding with the same frequency as other wax-matrix potassium products; if these adverse effects occur, potassium citrate should be discontinued immediately.

Hyperkalemia may often be asymptomatic or manifested only by characteristic ECG changes. Late signs may include muscle paralysis and cardiac arrest. When citrates are used at recommended doses, hyperkalemia is rare in patients without predisposing conditions.

For sodium citrate-containing only (in addition to those listed for potassium citrate- or sodium citrate-containing)
Hypernatremia (dizziness, fast heartbeat, high blood pressure, irritability, muscle twitching, restlessness, seizures, swelling of feet or lower legs, weakness)—occurs very rarely

Those indicating need for medical attention only if they continue or are bothersome
Incidence less frequent
For potassium citrate- and sodium citrate-containing
Laxative effect (diarrhea or loose bowel movements)

For potassium citrate only (in addition to those listed above)
   Irritation, contact (mild abdominal or stomach soreness or pain, nausea or vomiting)—for tablet dosage form only
   Note: *Contact irritation* may be due to possible contact with ulcerous areas or high concentration of potassium ions in one area resulting from improper release of potassium ions from wax-matrix dosage form or delayed passage of dosage form through alimentary tract.

Patient Consultation

In providing consultation, consider emphasizing the following selected information (» = major clinical significance):

Before using this medication
» Conditions affecting use, especially:
   Other medications, especially—
      For all citrates: Quinidine, calcium-containing medications, methenamine, antacids
      For potassium citrate-containing only: Angiotensin-converting enzyme (ACE) inhibitors, digitalis glycosides, heparin, nonsteroidal anti-inflammatory drugs (NSAIDs), potassium-sparing diuretics, other potassium-containing medications
   Other medical problems, especially—
      For potassium citrate- and/or sodium citrate-containing: Aluminum toxicity, heart failure, severe myocardial damage, severe renal function impairment with azotemia or oliguria, renal insufficiency, or urinary tract infection
      For potassium citrate-containing only: Hyperkalemia or conditions predisposing to hyperkalemia, peptic ulcer, or severe renal tubular acidosis
      For potassium citrate tablets only: Delayed gastric emptying, esophageal compression, or intestinal obstruction or stricture

Proper use of this medication
   Proper administration:
   For tablet dosage form
      Swallowing tablet whole; not crushing, chewing, or sucking
      Taking with a full glass (240 mL) of water or juice
»   Checking with physician at once if trouble in swallowing tablets or if tablets seem to stick in the throat
   For oral liquid dosage form
      Diluting with 6 ounces of water or juice before swallowing; after swallowing, following with additional water, if desired
      Chilling, but *not* freezing, before swallowing to enhance palatability
   For crystals dosage form
      Adding contents of one packet to at least 6 ounces of cool water or juice; stirring well to dissolve completely
      Following with additional water after swallowing mixture, if desired
» Taking each dose immediately after a meal or within 30 minutes after a meal or bedtime snack to lessen gastrointestinal pain or saline laxative effect
» Importance of high fluid intake (at least 3 liters per day) to prevent supersaturation of urine and to assure a minimum urine volume of 2.5 liters per day
   Compliance with therapy, especially when taking with diuretics and digitalis
» Proper dosing
   Missed dose: Taking as soon as possible if remembered within 2 hours; not taking if almost time for next dose; not doubling doses
» Proper storage

Precautions while using this medication
   Regular visits to physician to check progress of therapy
   Checking with physician before starting strenuous physical exercise if out of condition, to prevent possible hyperkalemia
      For potassium citrate-containing only
         Not taking salt substitutes or drinking low-salt milk unless prescribed by physician
      For sodium citrate-containing only
         Avoiding salty foods and use of extra table salt
» Checking with physician at once if black, tarry stools or other signs of gastrointestinal bleeding are observed
   Not being alarmed at appearance of "whole" tablet in stools; checking with physician

Side/adverse effects
   Signs of potential side effects, especially:
      For potassium citrate- or sodium citrate-containing—Metabolic alkalosis or diarrhea or loose bowel movements
      For potassium citrate-containing only—Hyperkalemia
      For potassium citrate tablets only—Bowel perforation or obstruction, or contact irritation resulting from improper release from wax matrix of tablets
      For sodium citrate-containing only—Hypernatremia

General Dosing Information

For patients on sodium-restricted diets, potassium citrate preparations may be preferable as urinary alkalizers; conversely, sodium citrate may be used when potassium citrate is contraindicated.

The goal of therapy with potassium citrate tablets or potassium citrate and citric acid solution is to increase the urinary citrate to normal (greater than 320 mg a day) and as close to the normal mean (640 mg a day) as possible, and to increase urinary pH to 6.0 to 7.0.

The rise in urinary citrate is directly dependent on the dosage of potassium citrate tablets or potassium citrate and citric acid oral solution. After long-term treatment, a dosage of 6.5 grams of potassium citrate (60 mEq of potassium ion) a day raises urinary citrate by approximately 400 mg a day and increases urinary pH by approximately 0.7 units. When treatment is withdrawn, urinary citrate begins to fall toward the pretreatment level of the first day.

Potassium citrate tablets and potassium citrate and citric acid oral solution are equally efficacious in raising urinary pH and citrate excretion.

Diet/Nutrition
Each dose should be taken immediately after a meal or within 30 minutes after a meal or bedtime snack, to lessen gastrointestinal pain or the saline laxative effect.

High fluid intake (at least 3 liters a day) is important to prevent supersaturation of urine and to assure a minimum urine volume of 2.5 liters a day.

Low-salt milk may contain up to 60 mEq of potassium per liter, and salt substitutes may contain substantial amounts of potassium. Both should be avoided if a patient is taking a potassium citrate-containing product, to prevent hyperkalemia.

POTASSIUM CITRATE

Summary of Differences

Indications: Also used to prevent or treat hypocitraturia in patients with calcium renal calculi.
Precautions: Contraindications/Medical problems—May increase risk of gastrointestinal lesions in peptic ulcer disease; may increase risk of gastrointestinal irritation in delayed gastric emptying, esophageal compression, or intestinal obstruction.

Side/adverse effects: Tablets may cause severe abdominal or stomach pain; black, tarry stools; or severe vomiting, sometimes with blood.

Additional Dosing Information

May be used as a urinary alkalizer when sodium citrate is contraindicated.

Oral Dosage Forms

POTASSIUM CITRATE TABLETS

Usual adult dose:
Antiurolithic or
Alkalizer, urinary—
  Mild to moderate hypocitraturia (more than 150 mg of urinary citrate a day): Oral, initially 1.08 grams (10 mEq of potassium ion) three times a day with meals.
  Severe hypocitraturia (less than 150 mg of urinary citrate a day): Oral, initially, 2.16 grams (20 mEq of potassium ion) three times a day, with meals or within thirty minutes after a meal or bedtime snack; or 1.62 grams (15 mEq of potassium ion) four times a day, with meals or within thirty minutes after a meal or bedtime snack.
  Note: Dosage should be adjusted as determined by 24-hour fasting urinary citrate and/or urinary pH measurements.

Usual adult prescribing limits: 10.8 grams of potassium citrate (100 mEq of potassium ion) a day.

Auxiliary labeling:
• Swallow tablets whole
• Take with a full glass of water.
• Take with meals or snack.

Additional information: Intact wax matrix may appear in the feces.

POTASSIUM CITRATE AND CITRIC ACID

Summary of Differences

Indications: Also used to prevent or treat hypocitraturia in patients with calcium renal calculi.

Additional Dosing Information

May be used as a urinary alkalizer when sodium citrate is contraindicated.

Oral Dosage Forms

POTASSIUM CITRATE AND CITRIC ACID ORAL SOLUTION USP

Usual adult dose:
Antiurolithic or
Alkalizer, systemic, or
Alkalizer, urinary—Oral, initially 10 to 15 mL (2.2 to 3.3 grams of potassium citrate [20 to 30 mEq of potassium ion]) four times a day, after meals and at bedtime, the dosage being adjusted as needed and tolerated.
  Note: Dosage should be adjusted as determined by 24-hour fasting urinary citrate and/or urinary pH measurements.

Auxiliary labeling:
• Dilute with water or juice.
• Take with meals or snack.

Additional information: Citric acid is present as a temporary buffer with only a transient effect on the systemic acid-base balance.

POTASSIUM CITRATE AND CITRIC ACID FOR ORAL SOLUTION

Usual adult dose:
Antiurolithic or
Alkalizer, systemic, or
Alkalizer, urinary—Oral, initially 3.3 grams of potassium citrate (30 mEq of potassium ion) four times a day, after meals and at bedtime, the dosage being adjusted as needed and tolerated.
  Note: Dosage should be adjusted as determined by 24-hour fasting urinary citrate and/or urinary pH measurements.

Auxiliary labeling:
• Dilute with water or juice.
• Take with meals or snack.

Additional information:
  Each packet provides the same amounts of potassium citrate and citric acid as 15 mL of potassium citrate and citric acid oral solution.
  Citric acid is present as a temporary buffer with only a transient effect on the systemic acid-base balance.

POTASSIUM CITRATE AND SODIUM CITRATE

Summary of Differences

Indications: Used as a urinary alkalizing agent only, in patients with uric acid or cystine calculi.

Oral Dosage Forms

POTASSIUM CITRATE AND SODIUM CITRATE TABLETS

Usual adult dose:
Antiurolithic or
Alkalizer, urinary—Oral, initially, 1 to 4 tablets (50 to 200 mg of potassium citrate [0.45 to 1.8 mEq of potassium ion] and 950 mg to 3.8 grams of sodium citrate [9.5 to 38 mEq of sodium ion]) after meals and at bedtime.

Auxiliary labeling:
• Swallow tablets whole.
• Take with a full glass of water.
• Take with meals or snack.

SODIUM CITRATE AND CITRIC ACID

Summary of Differences

Indications: Also used to prevent acid-aspiration pneumonitis.

Additional Dosing Information

May be used when potassium citrate is contraindicated.

Oral Dosage Forms

SODIUM CITRATE AND CITRIC ACID ORAL SOLUTION USP

Usual adult dose:
Antiurolithic or
Alkalizer, systemic, or

Alkalizer, urinary—Oral, initially 10 to 30 mL (1 to 3 grams of sodium citrate [10 to 30 mEq of sodium ion]) four times a day, after meals and at bedtime, diluted in 30 to 90 mL of water, the dosage being adjusted as needed.

Note: Dosage should be adjusted as determined by urinary pH measurements.

Neutralizing buffer—Oral, 15 to 30 mL (1.5 to 3 grams of sodium citrate [15 to 30 mEq of sodium ion]), as a single dose, or diluted in 15 to 30 mL of water.

Usual adult prescribing limits: Up to 150 mL (15 grams of sodium citrate [150 mEq of sodium ion]) a day.

Auxiliary labeling:
- Dilute with water or juice.
- Take with meals or snack.

Additional information: Citric acid is a temporary buffer with only a transient effect on systemic acid-base balance.

TRICITRATES

Summary of Differences

Indications: Also used to treat chronic metabolic acidosis and to prevent acid-aspiration pneumonitis.

Oral Dosage Forms

TRICITRATES ORAL SOLUTION USP

Usual adult dose:
Antiurolithic or
Alkalizer, systemic, or
Alkalizer, urinary—Oral, initially 15 to 30 mL (1.6 to 3.3 grams of potassium citrate [15 to 30 mEq of potassium ion] and 1.5 to 3 grams of sodium citrate [15 to 30 mEq of sodium ion]) four times a day after meals and at bedtime, the dosage being adjusted as needed.

Note: Dosage should be adjusted as determined by urinary pH measurements.

Neutralizing buffer—Oral, 15 mL (1.65 grams of potassium citrate [15 mEq of potassium ion] and 1.5 grams of sodium citrate [15 mEq of sodium ion]), as a single dose, diluted in 15 mL of water.

Auxiliary labeling:
- Dilute with water or juice.
- Take with meals or snack.

Additional information: Citric acid is a temporary buffer with only a transient effect on the systemic acid-base balance.

CLARITHROMYCIN   Systemic†

A commonly used *brand name* in the U.S. is *Biaxin*.

ORAL
Clarithromycin Tablets†
  In the U.S.—*Biaxin*

---

†Not commercially available in Canada.

Category: Antibacterial (systemic).

Indications

Note: Bracketed information in the *Indications* section refers to uses not included in U.S. product labeling.

Accepted
Clarithromycin is a macrolide antibiotic with *in vitro* activity against many gram-positive and gram-negative aerobic and anaerobic organisms. The minimum inhibitory concentrations (MICs) of clarithromycin are generally 2- to 4-fold lower than those of erythromycin against gram-positive bacteria, such as methicillin-sensitive *Staphylococcus aureus* and most *Streptococcus* species. Clarithromycin is bactericidal against *S. pyogenes* and *S. pneumoniae*.

The activity of erythromycin is twice that of clarithromycin against *Haemophilus influenzae*; however, clarithromycin's active metabolite, 14-hydroxyclarithromycin, is as active as erythromycin. When clarithromycin and 14-hydroxyclarithromycin are combined, their MIC is 2- to 4-fold lower than that of erythromycin, suggesting additive or synergistic *in vitro* activity against *H. influenzae*.

Clarithromycin has been found to have greater *in vitro* activity than erythromycin against *Legionella pneumophilia*, *Moraxella (Branhamella) catarrhalis*, *Chlamydia trachomatis*, and *Ureaplasma urealyticum*. Its activity is similar to that of erythromycin against *Neisseria gonorrhoeae*, anaerobic gram-positive cocci, and *Bacteroides* sp.

Clarithromycin displays *in vitro* activity against *Mycobacterium avium* complex (MAC), being 8- to 32-fold more active than erythromycin. High intracellular concentrations are achieved with clarithromycin, and it has been found to be effective against MAC in human macrophages. Clarithromycin may act synergistically with other agents used to treat MAC. It is also very active against *M. kansasii*, *M. xenopi*, and most strains of *M. fortuitum*. *In vitro* and *in vivo* activity against *M. leprae* have also been demonstrated.

Bronchitis, bacterial exacerbations, and
Pharyngitis, streptococcal, and
Pneumonia, mycoplasma, and
Pneumonia, streptococcal, and
Sinusitis, acute maxillary, and
Skin and soft tissue infections (treatment)—Clarithroymcin is indicated in the treatment of these disease states when caused by susceptible organsims.

[Legionnaires' disease (treatment)]—Clarithromycin has been used in the treatment of Legionnaires' disease, caused by *Legionella pneumophila*.

[*Mycobacterium avium* complex (treatment)]—Clarithromycin has been used, in combination with other antimycobacterials, in the treatment of *Mycobacterium avium* complex in patients with acquired immunodeficiency syndrome (AIDS).

Pharmacology

Mechanism of action/Effect: Clarithromycin binds to the 50S ribosomal subunit of the 70S ribosome of susceptible organisms, thereby inhibiting bacterial RNA-dependent protein synthesis.

Precautions to Consider

Cross-sensitivity and/or related problems

Patients who are hypersensitive to erythromycin or other macrolides may also be hypersensitive to clarithromycin.

Geriatrics

One study performed in healthy, elderly subjects found increased peak steady-state concentrations of clarithromycin and 14-hydroxy-clarithromycin; this was thought to be due to an age-related decrease in renal function. There was no increase in side effects compared to younger subjects. Elderly patients with severe renal function impairment may require a decrease in dose.

Drug interactions and/or related problems

The following drug interactions and/or related problems have been selected on the basis of their potential clinical significance (possible mechanism in parentheses where appropriate)—not necessarily inclusive (» = major clinical significance):

Note: Combinations containing any of the following medications, depending on the amount present, may also interact with this medication.

Carbamazepine

(single-dose administration of carbamazepine with clarithromycin has been shown to significantly increase the area under the concentration-time curve [AUC] of carbamazepine; monitoring of carbamazepine serum levels should be considered)

» Theophylline

(concurrent administration with clarithromycin has been shown to increase the AUC of theophylline by 17%; monitoring of theophylline serum levels is recommended in patients receiving high doses of theophylline or patients with theophylline serum levels in the upper therapeutic range)

» Zidovudine

(initial results of a dose escalation study in HIV-infected patients found that concurrent use of zidovudine and clarithromycin resulted in a lower peak serum concentration [Cmax], lower AUC, and delayed time to peak concentration [Tmax] of zidovudine)

Contraindications/Medical problems

The contraindications/medical problems included have been selected on the basis of their potential clinical significance (reasons given in parentheses where appropriate)—not necessarily inclusive (» = major clinical significance).

Risk-benefit should be considered when the following medical problems exist:

Hypersensitivity to erythromycins or other macrolides

Renal function impairment, severe

(the elimination of clarithromycin is reduced in patients with renal function impairment, especially those with a creatinine clearance of <30 mL/min; an adjustment in dose may be necessary in patients with a creatinine clearance of <30 mL/min)

(liver function impairment alters the pharmacokinetics of clarithromycin by decreasing the amount of metabolites formed and increasing the renal clearance of the parent drug; however, steady-state concentrations in patients with mild to severe hepatic function impairment does not differ from those in patients with normal hepatic function, unless there is also concurrent severe renal function impairment)

Side/Adverse Effects

The following side/adverse effects have been selected on the basis of their potential clinical significance (possible signs and symptoms in parentheses where appropriate)—not necessarily inclusive:

Those indicating need for medical attention only if they continue or are bothersome
Incidence less frequent
   Abnormal taste—3%; *gastrointestinal disturbances* (abdominal discomfort or pain, diarrhea, nausea)—2 to 3%; *headache*—2%

Patient Consultation

In providing consultation, consider emphasizing the following selected information (» = major clinical significance):

Before using this medication
» Conditions affecting use, especially:
   Hypersensitivity to erythromycins or other macrolides
   Pregnancy—Clarithromycin has produced embryotoxicity and fetal toxicity in animals
   Other medications, especially theophylline and zidovudine

Proper use of this medication
   May be taken with food or milk or on an empty stomach
   Missed dose: Taking as soon as possible; not taking if almost time for next dose; not doubling doses
   Compliance with full course of therapy
» Proper storage

Precautions while using this medication
   Checking with physician if no improvement within a few days

General Dosing Information

Patients with renal function impairment need an adjustment in dosage, based on creatinine clearance. Creatinine clearance (in mL per minute) may be calculated as follows:

Adult males: Creatinine clearance

$$= \frac{(140 - age) \times (body\ weight\ in\ kg)}{72 \times patient's\ serum\ creatinine\ concentration}$$

Adult females: Creatinine clearance

$$= \frac{(140 - age) \times (body\ weight\ in\ kg)}{72 \times patient's\ serum\ creatinine\ concentration} \times 0.85$$

Creatinine clearance may also be calculated in SI units (as mL per second) as follows:

Adult males: Creatinine clearance

$$= \frac{(140 - age) \times (ideal\ body\ weight\ in\ kg)}{50 \times serum\ creatinine\ (micromoles\ per\ L)}$$

Adult females: Creatinine clearance

$$= \frac{(140 - age) \times (ideal\ body\ weight\ in\ kg)}{50 \times serum\ creatinine\ (micromoles\ per\ L)} \times 0.85$$

Diet/Nutrition

Clarithromycin tablets may be taken with meals or on an empty stomach.

Oral Dosage Forms

CLARITHROMYCIN TABLETS

Usual adult and adolescent dose:
   Bronchitis, bacterial exacerbations due to *H. influenzae*—Oral, 500 mg every twelve hours for seven to fourteen days.

Bronchitis, bacterial exacerbations due to other organisms—Oral, 250 mg every twelve hours for seven to fourteen days.

Pharyngitis, streptococcal—Oral, 250 mg every twelve hours for ten days.

Pneumonia, due to *S. pneumoniae* or *M. pneumoniae*—Oral, 250 mg every twelve hours for seven to fourteen days.

Sinusitis, acute maxillary—Oral, 500 mg every twelve hours for fourteen days.

Skin and soft tissue infections—Oral, 250 mg every twelve hours for seven to fourteen days.

The dose of clarithromycin needs to be adjusted in patients with severe renal function impairment (creatinine clearance [CrCl] <30 mL/min or 0.50 mL/sec). The following dosing guidelines are suggested:

Dose for CrCl of >30 mL/min (0.50 mL/sec)	Adjusted dose for CrCl of <30 mL/min (0.50 mL/sec)
500 mg twice a day	500 mg loading dose, then 250 mg twice a day
250 mg twice a day	250 mg once a day

Auxiliary labeling: • Continue medicine for full time of treatment.

CLINDAMYCIN   Systemic

Some commonly used *brand names* are:

In the U.S.—*Cleocin; Cleocin Pediatric*
In Canada—*Dalacin C; Dalacin C Palmitate; Dalacin C Phosphate*

ORAL

Clindamycin Hydrochloride Capsules USP
In the U.S.—*Cleocin;* GENERIC
In Canada—*Dalacin C*
Clindamycin Palmitate Hydrochloride for Oral Solution USP
In the U.S.—*Cleocin Pediatric*
In Canada—*Dalacin C Palmitate*

PARENTERAL

Clindamycin Phosphate Injection USP
In the U.S.—*Cleocin;* GENERIC
In Canada—*Dalacin C Phosphate*

Category: Antibacterial (systemic); antiprotozoal.

Indications

Accepted

Bone and joint infections (treatment)—Parenteral clindamycin is indicated in the adjunctive surgical treatment of chronic bone and joint infections, and acute hematogenous osteomyelitis caused by staphylococci.

Pelvic infections, female (treatment)—Clindamycin is indicated in the treatment of female pelvic infections, including endometritis, nongonococcal tubo-ovarian abscess, pelvic cellulitis, and postsurgical vaginal cuff infections caused by anaerobes.

Intra-abdominal infections (treatment)—Clindamycin is indicated in the treatment of intra-abdominal infections (such as peritonitis and abscesses) caused by anaerobes.

Pneumonia, anaerobic (treatment);
Pneumonia, pneumococcal (treatment);
Pneumonia, staphylococcal (treatment); or
Pneumonia, streptococcal (treatment)—Clindamycin is indicated as a primary agent in the treatment of pneumonia, including serious respiratory tract infections (such as empyema, pneumonitis, and lung abscess) caused by anaerobes. Clindamycin is indicated as a secondary agent in the treatment of pneumonia caused by susceptible strains of pneumococci, staphylococci, and streptococci.

Septicemia, bacterial (treatment)—Oral and parenteral clindamycin are indicated in the treatment of septicemia caused by anaerobes.

In addition, parenteral clindamycin is indicated in the treatment of septicemia caused by streptococci and staphylococci.

Skin and soft tissue infections (treatment)—Clindamycin is indicated in the treatment of serious skin and soft tissue infections caused by anaerobes, streptococci, and staphylococci.

[Actinomycosis (treatment)][1]—Clindamycin is used in the treatment of actinomycosis.

[Babesiosis (treatment)][1]—Clindamycin is used concurrently with quinine in the treatment of severe babesiosis caused by *Babesia microti*.

[Erysipelas (treatment)][1]—Clindamycin is used in the treatment of erysipelas.

[Malaria (treatment)][1]—Clindamycin is used in combination with quinine in the treatment of chloroquine-resistant malaria caused by *Plasmodium falciparum* in patients for whom standard therapy is contraindicated (e.g., children, pregnant women, sulfa allergy).

[Otitis media, chronic suppurative (treatment)][1]—Clindamycin is used in the treatment of chronic suppurative otitis media.

[Pneumonia, *Pneumocystis carinii* (treatment)][1]—Clindamycin is used in combination with primaquine in the treatment of *Pneumocystis carinii* pneumonia (PCP) in patients unresponsive or intolerant to standard therapy.

[Sinusitis (treatment)][1]—Clindamycin is used in the treatment of sinusitis.

[Toxoplasmosis, central nervous system (CNS) (treatment)][1]—Clindamycin is used in combination with pyrimethamine in the treatment of CNS toxoplasmosis in patients who are unresponsive or intolerant to standard therapy.

Not all species or strains of a particular organism may be susceptible to clindamycin.

Unaccepted

Clindamycin is not indicated in the treatment of meningitis since it penetrates poorly into cerebrospinal fluid (CSF), even in the presence of inflamed meninges.

[1]Not included in Canadian product labeling.

Pharmacology

Mechanism of action/Effect: Antibacterial (systemic)—The lincomycins inhibit protein synthesis in susceptible bacteria by binding to the 50 S subunits of bacterial ribosomes and preventing peptide bond formation. They are usually considered bacteriostatic, but may be bactericidal in high concentrations or when used against highly susceptible organisms.

Precautions to Consider

Cross-sensitivity and/or related problems

Patients hypersensitive to lincomycin may be hypersensitive to clindamycin also. There is also a report of a possible cross-sensitivity between clindamycin and doxorubicin.

Geriatrics

No information is available on the relationship of age to the effects of clindamycin in geriatric patients.

Drug interactions and/or related problems

The following drug interactions and/or related problems have been selected on the basis of their potential clinical significance (possible mechanism in parentheses where appropriate)—not necessarily inclusive (» = major clinical significance):

Note: Combinations containing any of the following medications, depending on the amount present, may also interact with this medication.

» Anesthetics, hydrocarbon inhalation, or
» Neuromuscular blocking agents
(concurrent use of these medications with clindamycin, if necessary, should be carefully monitored since neuromuscular blockade may be enhanced, resulting in skeletal muscle weakness and respiratory depression or paralysis [apnea]; caution is also recommended when these medications are used concurrently with clindamycin during surgery or in the postoperative period; treatment with anticholinesterase agents or calcium salts may help reverse the blockade)

» Antidiarrheals, adsorbent
(concurrent use of kaolin- or attapulgite-containing antidiarrheals with oral clindamycin may significantly delay the absorption of oral clindamycin; concurrent use should be avoided or patients should be advised to take adsorbent antidiarrheals not less than 2 hours before or 3 to 4 hours after oral lincomycins)

Antimyasthenics
(concurrent use of medications with neuromuscular blocking action may antagonize the effect of antimyasthenics on skeletal muscle; temporary dosage adjustments of antimyasthenics may be necessary to control symptoms of myasthenia gravis during and following concurrent use)

» Chloramphenicol or
» Erythromycins
(may displace clindamycin from or prevent its binding to 50 S subunits of bacterial ribosomes, thus antagonizing the effects of clindamycin; concurrent use is not recommended)

Opioid (narcotic) analgesics
(respiratory depressant effects of drugs with neuromuscular blocking activity may be additive to central respiratory depressant effects of opioid analgesics, possibly leading to increased or prolonged respiratory depression or paralysis [apnea]; caution and careful monitoring of the patient are recommended)

Contraindications/Medical problems

The contraindications/medical problems included have been selected on the basis of their potential clinical significance (reasons given in parentheses where appropriate)—not necessarily inclusive (» = major clinical significance).

Risk-benefit should be considered when the following medical problems exist:

» Gastrointestinal disease, history of, especially ulcerative colitis, regional enteritis, or antibiotic-associated colitis
(clindamycin may cause pseudomembranous colitis)

» Hepatic function impairment, severe
(the half-life of clindamycin is prolonged in patients with severe hepatic function impairment; this may require an adjustment in dosage)

Hypersensitivity to lincomycins or doxorubicin

Renal function impairment, severe
(patients with impaired renal function do not generally require a reduction in dose unless the impairment is severe; however, patients receiving clindamycin with very severe renal impairment and/or very severe hepatic impairment accompanied by severe metabolic abnormalities may require a reduction in dosage)

Side/Adverse Effects

The following side/adverse effects have been selected on the basis of their potential clinical significance (possible signs and symptoms in parentheses where appropriate)—not necessarily inclusive:

Those indicating need for medical attention

Incidence more frequent
Pseudomembranous colitis (severe abdominal or stomach cramps and pain; abdominal tenderness; diarrhea, watery and severe, which may also be bloody; fever)

Incidence less frequent
Hypersensitivity (skin rash, redness, and itching); *neutropenia* (sore throat and fever); *thrombocytopenia* (unusual bleeding or bruising)

Those indicating need for medical attention only if they continue or are bothersome

Incidence more frequent
Gastrointestinal disturbances (abdominal pain, diarrhea, nausea and vomiting)

Incidence less frequent
Fungal overgrowth (itching of rectal or genital areas)

Those indicating possible pseudomembranous colitis and the need for medical attention if they occur after medication is discontinued

Severe abdominal or stomach cramps and pain; abdominal tenderness; watery and severe diarrhea, which may also be bloody; fever

Patient Consultation

In providing consultation, consider emphasizing the following selected information (» = major clinical significance):

Before using this medication

» Conditions affecting use, especially:
Hypersensitivity to clindamycin, lincomycin, or doxorubicin
Pregnancy—Clindamycin crosses the placenta
Breast-feeding—Clindamycin is excreted in breast milk
Use in children—Clindamycin should be used cautiously in infants up to 1 month of age; clindamycin injection contains benzyl alcohol, which has been associated with a fatal gasping syndrome in infants
Other medications, especially hydrocarbon inhalation anesthetics, neuromuscular blocking agents, adsorbent antidiarrheals, chloramphenicol, or erythromycins
Other medical problems, especially a history of gastrointestinal disease, particularly ulcerative colitis, or severe hepatic function impairment

Proper use of this medication

» Taking clindamycin capsules with a full glass of water or meals to avoid esophageal ulceration
Proper administration technique for clindamycin oral solution; not using after expiration date

» Compliance with full course of therapy, especially in streptococcal infections

» Importance of not missing doses and taking at evenly spaced times
Missed dose: Taking as soon as possible; not taking if almost time for next dose; not doubling doses

» Proper storage

Precautions while using this medication
Regular visits to physician to check progress
Checking with physician if no improvement within a few days
» For severe diarrhea, checking with physician before taking any antidiarrheals; for mild diarrhea, taking attapulgite-containing antidiarrheals at least 2 hours before or 3 to 4 hours after taking oral clindamycin; other antidiarrheals may worsen or prolong the diarrhea; checking with physician or pharmacist if mild diarrhea continues or worsens
Caution if surgery with general anesthesia is required

Side/adverse effects
Signs of potential side effects, especially pseudomembranous colitis, hypersensitivity, neutropenia, and thrombocytopenia

General Dosing Information

Therapy should be continued for at least 10 days in group A beta-hemolytic streptococcal infections to help prevent the occurrence of acute rheumatic fever.
For oral dosage forms only:
• The capsule dosage form should be taken with food or a full glass (240 mL) of water to avoid esophageal irritation.

Oral Dosage Forms

Note: Bracketed uses in the *Dosage Forms* section refer to categories of use and/or indications that are not included in U.S. product labeling.

CLINDAMYCIN HYDROCHLORIDE CAPSULES USP

Usual adult and adolescent dose:
Antibacterial—Oral, 150 to 300 mg (base) every six hours.
[Malaria (treatment)][1]—Oral, 900 mg (base) three times a day for three days.
[Pneumonia, *Pneumocystis carinii* (treatment)][1]—Oral, 1200 to 1800 mg (base) per day in divided doses in combination with 15 to 30 mg of primaquine daily.
[Toxoplasmosis, central nervous system (CNS) (treatment)][1]—Oral, 1200 to 2400 mg (base) per day in divided doses in combination with 50 to 100 mg of pyrimethamine daily.

Auxiliary labeling:
• Take with food or water.
• Continue medicine for full time of treatment.

CLINDAMYCIN PALMITATE HYDROCHLORIDE FOR ORAL SOLUTION USP

Usual adult and adolescent dose: See *Clindamycin Hydrochloride Capsules USP.*

Auxiliary labeling:
• Do not refrigerate.
• Shake well.
• Continue medicine for full time of treatment.
• Beyond-use date.

Parenteral Dosage Forms

Note: Bracketed uses in the *Dosage Forms* section refer to categories of use and/or indications that are not included in U.S. product labeling.

CLINDAMYCIN PHOSPHATE INJECTION USP

Usual adult and adolescent dose:
Antibacterial—Intramuscular or intravenous, 300 to 600 mg (base) every six to eight hours; or 900 mg every eight hours.
[Babesiosis (treatment)][1]—Intravenous, 300 to 600 mg clindamycin (base) four times a day with concurrent oral administration of 650 mg of quinine, three or four times a day for seven to ten days.
[Pneumonia, *Pneumocystis carinii* (treatment)][1]—Oral, 2400 to 2700 mg (base) per day in divided doses in combination with 15 to 30 mg of primaquine daily.
[Toxoplasmosis, central nervous system (CNS) (treatment)][1]—Oral, 1200 to 4800 mg (base) per day in divided doses in combination with 50 to 100 mg of pyrimethamine daily.

Usual adult prescribing limits: Up to 2.7 grams (base) daily.

Note: Doses up to 4.8 grams daily have been used. However, some medical experts recommend a maximum dose of 2.7 grams daily.

Additional information: Clindamycin phosphate may also be administered as a single rapid infusion (initial dose) followed by continuous intravenous infusion as follows:

Clindamycin Serum Concentrations (desired maintenance—mcg/mL)	Infusion Rate and Duration (initial)		Infusion Rate (continuous—mg/min)
	Rate (mg/min)	Duration (min)	
>4	10	30	0.75
>5	15	30	1.00
>6	20	30	1.25

[1]Not included in Canadian product labeling.

CLOFIBRATE   Systemic

Some commonly used *brand names* are:
In the U.S.—*Abitrate; Atromid-S*
In Canada—*Atromid-S; Claripex; Novofibrate*

ORAL
Clofibrate Capsules USP
In the U.S.—*Abitrate; Atromid-S;* GENERIC
In Canada—*Atromid-S; Claripex; Novofibrate*

Category: Antihyperlipidemic; antidiuretic (central diabetes insipidus).

Indications

Note: Bracketed information in the *Indications* section refers to uses not included in U.S. product labeling.

Accepted
Hyperlipidemia (treatment)—Clofibrate is indicated in the treatment of hyperlipidemia. Because of risks associated with its use (see *Side/Adverse Effects*), clofibrate is recommended for use as an adjunct only in patients with severe primary hyperlipidemia (type III hyperlipidemia) and a significant risk of coronary artery disease who have not responded to diet or other measures alone. Clofibrate

reduces plasma triglyceride concentrations to a greater extent than plasma cholesterol concentrations, and so is not useful in patients with elevated cholesterol concentrations alone. Its use is limited in type II hyperlipidemia because of its variable effect on cholesterol concentrations. Clofibrate is not recommended for community-wide prevention of ischemic heart disease.

In the 1988 Report of the National Cholesterol Education Program Expert Panel on Detection, Evaluation, and Treatment of High Blood Cholesterol in Adults, the following guidelines for the treatment of high blood cholesterol are recommended:

Nonpharmacologic management (especially reduction in dietary intake of saturated fatty acids and cholesterol, weight reduction and exercise, and quitting smoking) is recommended first for all patients and as an adjunct to all pharmacologic cholesterol therapy.

If, after six months of diet therapy, adequate low density lipoprotein (LDL)-cholesterol reduction is not achieved, then medication therapy is recommended to be added to diet therapy.

Initial medication therapy usually consists of a bile acid sequestrant (e.g., cholestyramine, colestipol) or niacin. A 3-hydroxy-3-methylglutaryl coenzyme A (HMG-CoA) reductase inhibitor (e.g., lovastatin) should be considered after the bile acid sequestrants and niacin. Other lipid-lowering agents, including fibric acid derivatives (e.g., gemfibrozil and clofibrate) and probucol, are not as effective in lowering LDL cholesterol as the above mentioned medications. Two other agents, neomycin (not approved by FDA as a lipid-lowering agent) and dextrothyroxine are not recommended for general use because other medications are available that have a more favorable benefit/risk ratio.

If adequate LDL-cholesterol control is not achieved with initial medication therapy, it is recommended that the patient be switched to another medication or a combination of two medications with synergistic mechanisms of action. Although experience with such drug combinations is somewhat limited, preliminary studies indicate that the bile acid sequestrants given with either niacin, lovastatin, probucol, or gemfibrozil are useful in controlling LDL cholesterol. Lovastatin in combination with either niacin or gemfibrozil needs further study because of the potential increased risk of side effects.

If effective control of LDL cholesterol is not obtained after use of primary medications and medication combinations, then referral to a lipid specialist may be necessary.

Studies have suggested that control of elevated cholesterol and triglycerides may not lessen the danger of cardiovascular disease and mortality, although incidence of nonfatal myocardial infarctions may be decreased.

[Clofibrate has been used in the treatment of partial central diabetes insipidus in patients with some residual posterior pituitary function; however, it generally has been replaced by other agents.][1]

Unaccepted

Although clofibrate alters platelet function (decreases platelet adhesiveness), it has not shown significant efficacy as an antiplatelet drug.

[1]Not included in Canadian product labeling.

Pharmacology

Mechanism of action/Effect:

Antihyperlipidemic—Not completely understood, but may involve inhibition of biosynthesis of cholesterol before mevalonate formation, increased secretion and fecal excretion of neutral sterols, enhanced catabolism of very low-density lipoproteins (VLDL) due to increased lipoprotein lipase activity in extrahepatic tissues, and/or increased clearance of triglycerides (VLDL) from the circulation.

Antidiuretic—May stimulate release of antidiuretic hormone (ADH) from the posterior pituitary.

Onset of action: Plasma VLDL concentrations are reduced within 2 to 5 days.

Time to peak effect: 3 weeks (with continued use).

Duration of action: Return to pretreatment VLDL concentrations occurs within 3 weeks after clofibrate is withdrawn.

Precautions to Consider

Geriatrics

Although appropriate studies on the relationship of age to the effects of clofibrate have not been performed in the geriatric population, geriatrics-specific problems that would limit the usefulness of this medication in the elderly are not expected. However, elderly patients are more likely to have age-related renal function impairment, which may require dosage adjustment in patients receiving clofibrate.

Drug interactions and/or related problems

The following drug interactions and/or related problems have been selected on the basis of their potential clinical significance (possible mechanism in parentheses where appropriate)—not necessarily inclusive (» = major clinical significance):

Note: Combinations containing any of the following medications, depending on the amount present, may also interact with this medication.

» Anticoagulants, coumarin- or indandione-derivative (concurrent use with clofibrate may significantly increase the anticoagulant effect; adjustment of anticoagulant dosage based on frequent prothrombin-time determinations is recommended; some clinicians recommend reduction of the anticoagulant dosage by one-half)

Antidiabetic agents, oral, especially tolbutamide (concurrent use of clofibrate with oral antidiabetic agents may enhance the hypoglycemic effect through displacement from serum proteins; dosage adjustments may be necessary. Glipizide and glyburide, due to their non-ionic binding characteristics, may not be affected as much as the other oral agents; however, caution with concurrent use is recommended)

Chenodiol or
Ursodiol (effect may be decreased when chenodiol or ursodiol is used concurrently with clofibrate since clofibrate tends to increase cholesterol saturation of bile)

HMG-CoA reductase inhibitors (concurrent use with clofibrate may increase the risk of rhabdomyolysis; cases of rhabdomyolysis have not been reported with concurrent use of clofibrate and HMG-CoA reductase inhibitors; however, there have been reported cases of rhabdomyolysis with concurrent use of another fibrate, gemfibrozil, and lovastatin)

Oral contraceptives (concurrent use may alter the effectiveness of clofibrate)

Probenecid (concurrent use of probenecid may decrease renal and metabolic clearances and alter the protein binding of clofibrate, increasing the therapeutic and toxic effects of clofibrate)

Rifampin (concurrent use with clofibrate may enhance the metabolism of clofibrate by induction of hepatic microsomal enzymes, resulting in significantly lower serum clofibrate concentrations)

Contraindications/Medical problems

The contraindications/medical problems included have been selected on the basis of their potential clinical significance (reasons given

in parentheses where appropriate)—not necessarily inclusive (» = major clinical significance).

Except under special circumstances, this medication should not be used when the following medical problem exists:

» Primary biliary cirrhosis
(use of clofibrate may further raise the cholesterol)

Risk-benefit should be considered when the following medical problems exist:

Cardiovascular disease
(condition may be exacerbated)

Gallstones
(increased risk of biliary complications)

» Hepatic function impairment
(protein binding of clofibrate is reduced but half-life is not altered. It is recommended that patients with impaired hepatic function receive a reduced dose of clofibrate; some clinicians recommend reduction of dosage by one-half in patients with cirrhosis)

Hypothyroidism
(may predispose to clofibrate-induced myopathy)

Peptic ulcer
(reactivation has been reported)

» Renal function impairment
(reduced protein binding and clearance of clofibrate leads to increased incidence of side effects, especially myopathy and rhabdomyolysis. It is recommended that clofibrate be administered in reduced dosage to patients with impaired renal function. However, dosage reduction is not necessary in nephrotic syndrome when renal function is not impaired, since steady-state concentration of unbound drug is unchanged in spite of markedly reduced protein binding and half-life)

Sensitivity to clofibrate

Side/Adverse Effects

Note: The suggestion that long-term use of clofibrate may increase the risk of death from noncardiovascular causes (malignancy, postcholecystectomy complications, pancreatitis) was made after results first published in 1978 of a large prospective study (the WHO study). This suggestion has been controversial, in part because other studies (for example, the Coronary Drug Project report published in 1975) have not reached a similar conclusion, although both major studies agree that the risk of cholelithiasis and cholecystitis requiring surgery is greatly increased in clofibrate users. Clofibrate has been found to increase the risk of development of peripheral vascular disease, pulmonary embolism, thrombophlebitis, angina pectoris, arrhythmias, and intermittent claudication. Clofibrate, in doses 5 to 8 times the human dose, has been found to increase the incidence of malignant hepatic tumors in rodents.

Rhabdomyolysis and severe hyperkalemia have been reported in patients with pre-existing renal function impairment.

The following side/adverse effects have been selected on the basis of their potential clinical significance (possible signs and symptoms in parentheses where appropriate)—not necessarily inclusive:

Those indicating need for medical attention
Incidence rare
Anemia or leukopenia (fever or chills, cough or hoarseness, lower back or side pain, painful or difficult urination); *angina* (chest pain, shortness of breath); *cardiac arrhythmias* (irregular heartbeat); *gallstones or pancreatitis* (severe stomach pain with nausea and vomiting); *renal toxicity* (blood in urine, decrease in urination, painful urination, swelling of feet and lower legs)

Note: Increased creatine kinase (CK) and serum transaminase concentrations may be caused by clofibrate rather than by myocardial infarction.

Those indicating need for medical attention only if they continue or are bothersome
Incidence more frequent
Diarrhea; nausea
Incidence less frequent or rare
Decreased sexual ability; flu-like syndrome or myositis (muscle aches or cramps, unusual tiredness or weakness); *headache; increased appetite or weight gain, slight; stomach pain, gas, or heartburn; stomatitis* (sores in mouth and on lips); *vomiting*

Note: *Flu-like syndrome* or *myositis* occurs more frequently in patients with existing renal disease, and usually is accompanied by increased CK and serum transaminases.

Patient Consultation

In providing consultation, consider emphasizing the following selected information (» = major clinical significance):

Before using this medication
Potential serious toxicity; WHO study controversy
Diet as preferred therapy
» Conditions affecting use, especially:
Sensitivity to clofibrate
Pregnancy—May cross placenta; enzyme system required for excretion may not be developed in fetus; withdrawal of clofibrate therapy several months before conception is recommended if pregnancy is planned
Breast-feeding—Use not recommended while nursing because of potentially serious adverse effects on nursing infants
Use in children—Not recommended in children less than 2 years of age since cholesterol is required for normal development
Other medications, especially anticoagulants
Other medical problems, especially primary biliary cirrhosis, hepatic function impairment, or renal function impairment

Proper use of this medication
» Importance of not taking more or less medication than the amount prescribed
» Compliance with prescribed diet
Taking with meals to prevent possible gastric irritation
Missed dose: Taking as soon as possible; not taking if almost time for next dose; not doubling doses
» Proper storage

Precautions while using this medication
» Importance of close monitoring by the physician
» Checking with physician before discontinuing medication; blood lipid concentrations may increase significantly

Side/adverse effects
Signs of potential side effects, especially angina, cardiac arrhythmias, leukopenia, anemia, pancreatitis, gallstones, and renal toxicity

General Dosing Information

If response is inadequate after 3 months of treatment, clofibrate therapy should be withdrawn, except in the case of xanthoma tuberosum, which may require up to 1 year of treatment as long as reduction in size and/or number of xanthomata occurs.

If results of hepatic function tests rise significantly or show significant abnormalities, it is recommended that clofibrate therapy be withdrawn and not resumed; laboratory abnormalities are usually reversible.

If an increase in serum amylase concentrations or a paradoxical increase in plasma cholesterol or plasma LDL concentrations occurs, it is recommended that clofibrate therapy be withdrawn.

When clofibrate is discontinued, an appropriate hypolipidemic diet and monitoring of serum lipids are recommended until the patient stabilizes, since a rise in serum cholesterol and triglyceride concentrations to or above the original base may occur.

Diet/Nutrition

It is recommended that clofibrate be taken with food to minimize gastrointestinal upset.

Oral Dosage Forms

CLOFIBRATE CAPSULES USP

Usual adult dose: Antihyperlipidemic—Oral, 1.5 to 2 grams per day in two to four divided doses.

> Note: Clofibrate has been used in the treatment of diabetes insipidus at an oral dose of 6 to 8 grams per day in two or four divided doses.

Usual adult prescribing limits: Antihyperlipidemic—2 grams daily.

Auxiliary labeling: • Take with meals.

CLONIDINE   Systemic

Some commonly used *brand names* are:

> In the U.S.—*Catapres; Catapres-TTS*
> In Canada—*Catapres; Dixarit*

ORAL
Clonidine Hydrochloride Tablets USP
> In the U.S.—*Catapres;* GENERIC
> In Canada—*Catapres; Dixarit*

TOPICAL
Clonidine Transdermal System†
> In the U.S.—*Catapres-TTS*

---

†Not commercially available in Canada.

Category: Antihypertensive; menopausal syndrome therapy adjunct; vascular headache prophylactic; antidysmenorrheal; opioid withdrawal syndrome suppressant.

Indications

Note: Bracketed information in the *Indications* section refers to uses not included in U.S. product labeling.

Accepted
Hypertension (treatment)—Oral and transdermal dosage forms of clonidine are indicated in the treatment of hypertension. Because it causes only mild postural hypotension, clonidine may be useful as a substitute for guanethidine or other adrenergic blockers in patients who cannot tolerate these agents because of severe orthostatic hypotension.

In the 1988 Report of the Joint National Committee on Detection, Evaluation, and Treatment of High Blood Pressure, a step-like progression in choice of treatments for essential hypertension is recommended:

> Nonpharmacologic management (especially sodium restriction, weight reduction and exercise, and moderation of alcohol consumption) is recommended first for some patients, including those with mild hypertension, and is recommended as an adjunct to all pharmacologic hypertensive therapy.

> Initial drug therapy usually consists of a diuretic, beta-adrenergic blocking agent, calcium channel blocker, or angiotensin-converting enzyme (ACE) inhibitor. If adequate blood pressure control is not achieved and the patient is adherent to the treatment program and not experiencing significant side effects, dosage of the drug may be increased, a drug from another one

of these initial classes may be added or substituted, or a second drug from a different class—centrally acting alpha-adrenergic blockers (e.g., clonidine, guanabenz, guanfacine, methyldopa), peripheral-acting adrenergic antagonists (e.g., guanadrel, guanethidine, rauwolfia alkaloids), post-synaptic alpha-1 peripheral adrenergic inhibitors (e.g., prazosin, terazosin), or vasodilators (e.g., hydralazine, minoxidil)—may be added or substituted.

If necessary, a drug from another class in the second group may be substituted or added as a third drug. If blood pressure control is still not achieved, a drug from still another class may be substituted or added as a fourth drug, or the patient may need further evaluation and/or referral.

[Oral clonidine is also used in the urgent treatment of hypertensive emergencies.][1]

[Pheochromocytoma (diagnosis)][1]—A clonidine suppression test is used in the diagnosis of pheochromocytoma.

[Headache, vascular (prophylaxis)][1]—Clonidine has been used orally in the prevention of migraine.

[Dysmenorrhea (treatment)][1]; or

[Menopause, vasomotor symptoms of (treatment)]—Clonidine is used orally as an adjunct in the treatment of dysmenorrhea and menopausal flushing.

[Opioid (narcotic) abstinence syndrome (treatment)][1]—Clonidine is also used to control symptoms and aid in rapid detoxification in the treatment of opioid withdrawal.

[Nicotine dependence (treatment adjunct)][1]—Clonidine is used as an adjunct in the treatment of nicotine withdrawal.

[Gilles de la Tourette's syndrome (treatment)][1]—Clonidine is used in the treatment of Gilles de la Tourette's syndrome.

---

[1]Not included in Canadian product labeling.

Pharmacology

Mechanism of action/Effect: Alpha-adrenergic agonist; also has some alpha-adrenergic antagonist effects.

> Antihypertensive—Thought to be due to central alpha$_2$-adrenergic stimulation, which results in a decreased sympathetic outflow to the heart, kidneys, and peripheral vasculature and thus decreased peripheral vascular resistance, decreased systolic and diastolic blood pressure, and decreased heart rate.

> Vascular headache prophylactic—May block central vasomotor reflexes.

Dysmenorrhea therapy adjunct; or

Menopausal syndrome therapy adjunct—Unknown, although may act as peripheral vascular stabilizer to reduce menopausal flushing.

Opioid withdrawal syndrome suppressant—May be result of alpha-adrenergic inhibiting activity in areas of the brain such as the locus ceruleus.

Other actions/effects: Stimulates growth hormone release acutely, but not chronically.

Onset of effect: Antihypertensive—

Oral: 30 to 60 minutes.

Transdermal: 2 to 3 days.

Time for peak effect: Antihypertensive—Oral: 2 to 4 hours.

Duration of effect: Antihypertensive—

Oral: Up to 8 hours (24 to 36 hours in some patients).

Transdermal: About 7 days with the system in place; about 8 hours after removal.

Precautions to Consider

Cross-sensitivity and/or related problems

Patients sensitive to clonidine may be sensitive to ophthalmic apraclonidine also.

Geriatrics

The elderly may be more sensitive to the hypotensive effects. In addition, elderly patients are more likely to have age-related renal function impairment, which may require reduction of dosage in patients receiving clonidine.

Dental

Use of clonidine may decrease or inhibit salivary flow, thus contributing to the development of caries, periodontal disease, oral candidiasis, and discomfort.

Drug interactions and/or related problems

The following drug interactions and/or related problems have been selected on the basis of their potential clinical significance (possible mechanism in parentheses where appropriate)—not necessarily inclusive (» = major clinical significance):

Note: Combinations containing any of the following medications, depending on the amount present, may also interact with this medication.

Alcohol or

Central nervous system (CNS) depression-producing medications (concurrent use may enhance the CNS depressant effects of either these medications or clonidine)

» Antidepressants, tricyclic, or

Appetite suppressants, with the exception of fenfluramine (concurrent use may decrease the hypotensive effects of clonidine)

Anti-inflammatory analgesics, nonsteroidal (NSAIAs), especially indomethacin

(concurrent use may reduce antihypertensive effects of clonidine; indomethacin, and possibly other NSAIAs, may antagonize the antihypertensive effect by inhibiting renal prostaglandin synthesis and/or by causing sodium and fluid retention; the patient should be carefully monitored to confirm that the desired effect is being obtained)

» Beta-adrenergic blocking agents (systemic)

(discontinuation of therapy during concurrent use may increase the risk of clonidine-withdrawal hypertensive crisis; ideally, beta-adrenergic blocking agents should be discontinued several days before clonidine is discontinued; blood pressure control may also be impaired when the two are combined)

Estrogens

(estrogen-induced fluid retention may increase blood pressure)

Fenfluramine

(concurrent use may increase the hypotensive effects of clonidine)

Hypotension-producing medications, other with the exception of systemic beta-adrenergic blocking agents and tricyclic antidepressants

(concurrent use may potentiate antihypertensive effects; although some antihypertensive and/or diuretic combinations are frequently used for therapeutic advantage, dosage adjustments may be necessary during concurrent use)

Sympathomimetics

(concurrent use may reduce the antihypertensive effects of clonidine; the patient should be carefully monitored to confirm that the desired effect is being obtained)

Contraindications/Medical problems

The contraindications/medical problems included have been selected on the basis of their potential clinical significance (reasons given in parentheses where appropriate)—not necessarily inclusive (» = major clinical significance).

Risk-benefit should be considered when the following medical problems exist:

Atrioventricular (AV) node function impairment (vagal effect of clonidine)

Cerebrovascular disease

Coronary insufficiency

Mental depression, history of

Myocardial infarction, recent

Raynaud's syndrome

Renal function impairment, chronic

(slowed elimination of clonidine; increased risk of toxicity; dosage reduction may be necessary)

Sensitivity to clonidine

Sinus node function impairment

(function may be further impaired)

Thromboangiitis obliterans

For transdermal dosage form only (in addition to above)

Polyarteritis nodosa or

Scleroderma or

Systemic lupus erythematosus (SLE)

(absorption may be decreased; placement of patches on affected areas should be avoided)

Skin irritation or abrasion

(absorption may be increased; placement of patches on irritated or abraded areas should be avoided)

Side/Adverse Effects

Note: Incidence and severity of adverse systemic effects may be reduced with the transdermal dosage form, possibly because of the maintenance of lower peak blood concentrations and less fluctuation in blood concentration than occur with oral administration.

Administration of clonidine for 6 months or longer to albino rats has resulted in a dose-related increase in the incidence and severity of spontaneously occurring retinal degeneration. These effects have not been observed in humans.

The following side/adverse effects have been selected on the basis of their potential clinical significance (possible signs and symptoms in parentheses where appropriate)—not necessarily inclusive:

Those indicating need for medical attention

Incidence more frequent—about 15 to 20%, with transdermal systems only
> *Itching or redness of skin*

Note: Patients who develop either a localized or extended allergic reaction to the transdermal system may also experience a generalized allergic skin rash if oral clonidine is substituted.

Incidence less frequent
> *Mental depression; sodium and water retention or edema* (swelling of feet and lower legs)

Incidence rare
> *Raynaud's phenomenon* (paleness or cold feeling in fingertips and toes); *vivid dreams or nightmares*

Signs and symptoms of overdose
> *Difficulty in breathing; dizziness, extreme, or faintness; pinpoint pupils of eyes; slow heartbeat; unusual tiredness or weakness, extreme*

Note: Massive overdose may result in hypertension.
> Toxicity may occur with ingestion of 100 mcg (0.1 mg) in children.

Those indicating need for medical attention only if they continue or are bothersome

Incidence more frequent
> *Constipation*—about 10%; *dizziness*—about 16% with oral use; *drowsiness*—about 33% with oral use; *dry mouth*—about 40% with oral use; *unusual tiredness or weakness*—about 10%

Incidence less frequent—1 to 5%
> *Darkening of skin*—with transdermal systems only; *decreased sexual ability; dizziness, lightheadedness, or fainting, especially when getting up from a lying or sitting position; dry, itching, or burning eyes; loss of appetite; nausea or vomiting; nervousness*

Those indicating possible rebound hypertension and need for medical attention if they occur after medication is abruptly discontinued
> *Anxiety or tenseness; chest pain; fast or irregular heartbeat; headache; increased salivation; nausea; nervousness; restlessness; shaking or trembling of hands and fingers; stomach cramps; sweating; trouble in sleeping; vomiting*

Note: Rebound hypertension may occur but is symptomatic in only 5 to 20% of patients. It is more likely to occur after abrupt withdrawal of clonidine in patients who had been receiving doses exceeding 1.2 mg per day or if clonidine therapy is discontinued before or at the same time as concurrent beta-blocker therapy.

Patient Consultation

In providing consultation, consider emphasizing the following selected information (» = major clinical significance):

Before using this medication
> » Conditions affecting use, especially:
>> Sensitivity to clonidine or to ophthalmic apraclonidine
>> Pregnancy—Increased resorptions in rats and mice
>> Breast-feeding—Excreted in breast milk
>> Use in the elderly—Hypotensive effects may be more likely
>> Other medications, especially tricyclic antidepressants or beta-blockers

Proper use of this medication
> Proper administration of the transdermal dosage form:
> » Compliance with therapy; reading patient instructions carefully
>> Not trimming or cutting patch
>> Applying to clean, dry skin area on upper arm or torso free of hair, scars, cuts, or irritation
>> Should remain in place even during showering, bathing, or swimming; applying adhesive overlay to loose systems; replacing systems that have loosened excessively or fallen off
>> Alternating application sites
>> Folding used patches in half with adhesive sides together; disposing of patch carefully, out of reach of children
> Getting into the habit of taking or using at same time each day or week to help increase compliance
> » Missed dose: Taking or using as soon as possible; checking with physician if two or more oral doses in a row are missed or if the transdermal system is late in being changed by three or more days; possible severe reaction if stopped abruptly
> » Proper storage

For use as an antihypertensive
> Importance of diet; possible need for sodium restriction and/or weight reduction
> » Patient may not experience symptoms of hypertension; importance of taking medication even if feeling well
> » Does not cure, but helps control hypertension; possible need for lifelong therapy; serious consequences of untreated hypertension

Precautions while using this medication
> Regular visits to physician to check progress
> » Checking with physician before discontinuing medication; gradual dosage reduction may be necessary to avoid serious rebound hypertension
> » Having enough medication on hand to get through weekends, holidays, and vacations; possibly carrying second prescription for emergency use
> » Caution in taking alcohol or other CNS depressants
> » Caution when driving or doing things requiring alertness, because of possible drowsiness
> » Caution if any kind of surgery or emergency treatment is required
> Caution when getting up suddenly from a lying or sitting position
> Caution in using alcohol, while standing for long periods or exercising, and during hot weather, because of enhanced orthostatic hypotensive effects
> Possible dryness of mouth; using sugarless candy or gum, ice, or saliva substitute for relief; checking with physician or dentist if dry mouth continues for more than 2 weeks

For use as an antihypertensive
> » Not taking other medications, especially nonprescription sympathomimetics, unless discussed with physician

Side/adverse effects
> Signs of potential side effects, especially itching or redness of skin (transdermal), mental depression, sodium and water retention, edema, Raynaud's phenomenon, vivid dreams or nightmares, and withdrawal reaction

General Dosing Information

With continued use, apparent tolerance to the antihypertensive effects of clonidine may develop as a result of fluid retention and expanded plasma volume. Concurrent administration of a diuretic may decrease this likelihood and will enhance the antihypertensive effects of clonidine. Other antihypertensives have also been used concurrently with clonidine. If combination therapy is indicated, individual titration is required to ensure the lowest possible therapeutic dose of each drug.

The abrupt interruption of clonidine therapy, including several consecutive missed doses, may result in rebound hypertension, which may be severe (acute post-treatment syndrome) or, in rare cases, overshoot hypertension, occurring within 12 to 48 hours and lasting several days. Some patients may experience associated symptoms such as nervousness, agitation, and headache. At cessation of therapy, dosage should be gradually reduced (in the case of the transdermal system, by reducing patch strength and, if necessary, administering oral clonidine) over a 2- to 4-day period. Alternative therapy should be considered for unreliable or noncompliant patients. An excessive rise in blood pressure may be treated by resumption of oral clonidine therapy or by intravenous administration of diazoxide or an alpha-adrenergic blocking agent.

It is recommended that this medication be discontinued if mental depression occurs.

For oral dosage form only

It is recommended that the last daily dose be taken at bedtime to ensure overnight control of blood pressure and reduce daytime drowsiness.

If clonidine therapy must be interrupted for surgery, it is recommended that the last dose be given no later than 4 to 6 hours prior to surgery, that parenteral hypotensive medication be administered throughout the procedure, and that clonidine therapy be reinstituted as soon as possible afterwards.

Clonidine has been used investigationally for rapid detoxification in the treatment of opioid withdrawal. One protocol used consists of a test dose of 5 to 6 mcg (0.005 to 0.006 mg) of clonidine hydrochloride per kg of body weight on the first day. Patients showing a positive response then receive 17 mcg (0.017 mg) of clonidine hydrochloride per kg of body weight in divided daily doses for 9 or 10 days (adjusted to avoid hypotension and oversedation), followed by a reduction to 50% of the dose on Days 11, 12, and 13, and no medication on Day 14. Dosage must be individualized according to each patient's tolerance.

For transdermal dosage form only

Because the onset of action of transdermal clonidine is 2 to 3 days, when a patient is being switched from oral to transdermal therapy, the dose of oral clonidine should be gradually reduced over 2 to 3 days after transdermal therapy is begun, to avoid a withdrawal reaction.

Application should preferably be made at the same time of day each week to areas of clean, dry, hairless skin on the upper arm or torso. Skin areas with extensive scarring, calluses, or irritation should be avoided. Application sites should be alternated to avoid causing skin irritation.

The transdermal units *should not* be cut or trimmed in an attempt to adjust dosage.

If the transdermal system begins to loosen, the adhesive overlay provided by the manufacturer should be applied over the unit to hold it in place. A new dosage unit should be applied if the first becomes overly loosened or falls off.

If local skin irritation occurs before the system has been in place for 7 days, the system may be removed and a new one placed on a different site. If contact sensitization persists, withdrawal of transdermal therapy may be necessary.

Oral Dosage Forms

Note: Bracketed uses in the *Dosage Forms* section refer to categories of use and/or indications that are not included in U.S. product labeling.

CLONIDINE HYDROCHLORIDE TABLETS USP

Usual adult dose:

Antihypertensive—

Initial: Oral, 100 mcg (0.1 mg) two times a day, the dosage being increased by 100 or 200 mcg (0.1 or 0.2 mg, respectively) per day every two to four days if necessary for control of blood pressure.

Maintenance: Oral, 200 to 600 mcg (0.2 to 0.6 mg) per day, in divided doses.

Severe hypertension in the urgent but not emergency situation (loading dose): Oral, 200 mcg (0.2 mg), followed by 100 mcg (0.1 mg) every hour until diastolic blood pressure is controlled or a total of 800 mcg (0.8 mg) has been given; the patient is then controlled on a normal maintenance dose.

[Vascular headache prophylactic][1]—Oral, 25 mcg (0.025 mg) two to four times a day up to 50 mcg (0.05 mg) three times a day.

[Antidysmenorrheal][1]—Severe dysmenorrhea: Oral, 25 mcg (0.025 mg) two times a day for fourteen days before and during menses.

[Menopausal syndrome therapy adjunct]—Oral, 25 to 75 mcg (0.025 to 0.075 mg) two times a day.

Note: Geriatric patients may be more sensitive to the effects of the usual adult dose.

Usual adult prescribing limits: Antihypertensive—Up to 2.4 mg daily.

Auxiliary labeling:
- Avoid alcoholic beverages.
- Do not miss doses.
- Do not take other medicines without your doctor's advice.

Topical Dosage Forms

CLONIDINE TRANSDERMAL SYSTEM

Note: Clonidine transdermal systems are not commercially available in Canada.

Usual adult dose: Antihypertensive—Topical, to the intact skin, 1 transdermal dosage system, beginning with the system delivering 100 mcg (0.1 mg) per day, once a week. Dosage adjustments may be made every one or two weeks by changing to the next larger dosage system or a combination of systems.

Auxiliary labeling:
- Avoid alcoholic beverages.
- For external use only.
- Do not miss doses.
- Do not take other medicines without your doctor's advice.

---

[1]Not included in Canadian product labeling.

CLONIDINE AND CHLORTHALIDONE   Systemic

Category: Antihypertensive.

Indications

Accepted

Hypertension (treatment)—The combination of clonidine and chlorthalidone is indicated for treatment of hypertension.

Fixed-dosage combinations are generally not recommended for initial therapy and are useful for subsequent therapy only when the proportion of the component agents corresponds to the dose of the individual agents, as determined by titration.

Nonpharmacologic management (especially sodium restriction, weight reduction and exercise, and moderation of alcohol consumption) is recommended first for some patients, including those with mild hypertension, and is recommended as an adjunct to all pharmacologic hypertensive therapy.

Patient Consultation

In providing consultation, consider emphasizing the following selected information (» = major clinical significance):

Before using this medication
» Conditions affecting use, especially:
  Sensitivity to clonidine or to ophthalmic apraclonidine, or to sulfonamide-type medications
  Pregnancy—
    Clonidine: Causes resorption in animals
    Chlorthalidone: Risk of jaundice, thrombocytopenia, hypokalemia in infant
  Breast-feeding—Excreted in breast milk
  Use in the elderly—Hypotensive and hypokalemic effects may be more likely
  Other medications, especially tricyclic antidepressants, beta-blockers, adrenocorticoids, digitalis glycosides, lithium, or methenamine
  Other medication problems, especially severe renal function impairment

Proper use of this medication
  Diuretic effects of the medication and timing of doses to minimize inconvenience of diuresis
  Importance of diet; possible need for sodium restriction and/or weight reduction
» Patient may not experience symptoms of hypertension; importance of taking medication even if feeling well
» Does not cure, but helps control hypertension; possible need for lifelong therapy; serious consequences of untreated hypertension
  Getting into habit of taking at same time each day to help increase compliance
» Missed dose: Taking as soon as remembered; checking with physician if two or more doses in a row are missed
» Proper storage

Precautions while using this medication
  Regular visits to physician to check progress
» Checking with physician before discontinuing medication; gradual dosage reduction may be necessary to avoid serious rebound hypertension

» Having enough medication on hand to get through weekends, holidays, and vacations; possibly carrying second prescription for emergency use
» Caution if any kind of surgery or emergency treatment is required
» Not taking other medications, especially nonprescription sympathomimetics, unless discussed with physician
» Caution in taking alcohol or other central nervous system (CNS) depressants
» Caution when driving or doing things requiring alertness, because of possible drowsiness
  Caution when getting up suddenly from a lying or sitting position
  Caution in using alcohol, while standing for long periods or exercising, and during hot weather because of enhanced orthostatic hypotensive effects
» Possibility of hypokalemia; possible need for additional potassium in diet; not changing diet without first checking with physician
  To prevent dehydration, checking with physician if severe nausea, vomiting, or diarrhea occurs and continues
  Diabetics: May increase blood sugar levels
  Possible photosensitivity; avoiding unprotected exposure to sun; using protective clothing and sun block product; avoiding use of sunlamp, tanning bed, or tanning booth
  Possible dryness of mouth; using sugarless candy or gum, ice, or saliva substitute for relief; checking with physician or dentist if dry mouth continues for more than 2 weeks

Side/adverse effects
  Signs of potential side effects, especially electrolyte imbalance, hyperuricemia or gout, Raynaud's phenomenon, skin rash or hives, agranulocytosis, cholecystitis or pancreatitis, thrombocytopenia, vivid dreams or nightmares, hepatic function impairment, and withdrawal reaction

Oral Dosage Forms

CLONIDINE HYDROCHLORIDE AND CHLORTHALIDONE TABLETS USP

Usual adult dose: Oral, 1 or 2 tablets two to four times a day, as determined by individual titration with the component agents.

Note: Geriatric patients may be more sensitive to the effects of the usual adult dose.

Usual adult prescribing limits: Up to 2.4 mg of clonidine hydrochloride daily.

Auxiliary labeling:
- Avoid alcoholic beverages.
- Do not miss doses.
- Do not take other medicines without your doctor's advice.

COAL TAR   Topical

Some commonly used *brand names* are:

In the U.S.—
Alphosyl
Aquatar
Balnetar Therapeutic Tar
Bath
Cutar Water Dispersible
Emollient Tar
Denorex Extra Strength
Medicated Shampoo
Denorex Extra Strength
Medicated Shampoo with
Conditioners
Denorex Medicated
Shampoo
Denorex Medicated
Shampoo and
Conditioner
Denorex Mountain Fresh
Herbal Scent Medicated
Shampoo
DHS Tar Gel Shampoo
DHS Tar Shampoo
Doak Oil Forte Therapeutic
Bath Treatment
Doak Oil Therapeutic Bath
Treatment For All-Over
Body Care
Doak Tar Lotion
Doak Tar Shampoo
Doctar Hair & Scalp
Shampoo and
Conditioner
Doctar Shampoo
Estar
Fototar
Ionil T Plus
Lavatar
Medotar

Pentrax Anti-Dandruff Tar
Shampoo
Psorigel
PsoriNail Topical Solution
Taraphilic
Tarbonis
Tarpaste 'Doak'
T/Derm Tar Emollient
Tegrin Lotion for Psoriasis
Tegrin Medicated Cream
Shampoo
Tegrin Medicated
Shampoo Concentrated
Gel
Tegrin Medicated
Shampoo Extra
Conditioning Formula
Tegrin Medicated
Shampoo Herbal
Formula
Tegrin Medicated
Shampoo Original
Formula
Tegrin Medicated Soap for
Psoriasis
Tegrin Skin Cream for
Psoriasis
Tersa-Tar Soapless Tar
Shampoo
T/Gel Therapeutic
Conditioner
T/Gel Therapeutic
Shampoo
Theraplex T Shampoo
Zetar Emulsion
Zetar Medicated
Antiseborrheic Shampoo

In Canada—
Alphosyl
Balnetar
Denorex
Doak Oil
Doak Oil Forte
Estar
Lavatar
Liquor Carbonis Detergens
Pentrax Extra-Strength
Therapeutic Tar
Shampoo
Psorigel

Tar Doak
Tarpaste
Tersa-Tar Mild
Therapeutic Shampoo
with Protein and
Conditioner
Tersa-Tar Therapeutic
Shampoo
T-Gel
Zetar Emulsion
Zetar Shampoo

TOPICAL
Coal Tar Cleansing Bar
In the U.S.—*Tegrin Medicated Soap for Psoriasis*
Coal Tar Cream
In the U.S.—*Alphosyl; Fototar; Tarbonis; Tegrin Skin Cream for Psoriasis*
In Canada—*Alphosyl*
Coal Tar Gel
In the U.S.—*Aquatar; Estar; Psorigel*
In Canada—*Estar; Psorigel*

Coal Tar Lotion
In the U.S.—*Alphosyl; Cutar Water Dispersible Emollient Tar; Doak Tar Lotion; T/Derm Tar Emollient; Tegrin Lotion for Psoriasis; T/Gel Therapeutic Conditioner*
In Canada—*Alphosyl; Tar Doak*
Coal Tar Ointment USP
In the U.S.—*Medotar; Taraphilic; Tarpaste 'Doak'*
In Canada—*Tarpaste*
Coal Tar Shampoo
In the U.S.—*Denorex Extra Strength Medicated Shampoo; Denorex Extra Strength Medicated Shampoo with Conditioners; Denorex Medicated Shampoo; Denorex Medicated Shampoo and Conditioner; Denorex Mountain Fresh Herbal Scent Medicated Shampoo; DHS Tar Gel Shampoo; DHS Tar Shampoo; Doak Tar Shampoo; Doctar Hair & Scalp Shampoo and Conditioner; Doctar Shampoo; Ionil T Plus; Pentrax Anti-Dandruff Tar Shampoo; Tegrin Medicated Cream Shampoo; Tegrin Medicated Shampoo Concentrated Gel; Tegrin Medicated Shampoo Extra Conditioning Formula; Tegrin Medicated Shampoo Herbal Formula; Tegrin Medicated Shampoo Original Formula; Tersa-Tar Soapless Tar Shampoo; T/Gel Therapeutic Shampoo; Theraplex T Shampoo; Zetar Medicated Antiseborrheic Shampoo*
In Canada—*Pentrax Extra-Strength Therapeutic Tar Shampoo; Tersa-Tar Mild Therapeutic Shampoo with Protein and Conditioner; Tersa-Tar Therapeutic Shampoo; T-Gel; Zetar Shampoo*
Coal Tar Topical Solution USP
In the U.S.—*Balnetar Therapeutic Tar Bath; Doak Oil Forte Therapeutic Bath Treatment; Doak Oil Therapeutic Bath Treatment For All-Over Body Care; Lavatar; PsoriNail Topical Solution*
In Canada—*Balnetar; Denorex; Doak Oil; Doak Oil Forte; Lavatar; Liquor Carbonis Detergens*
Coal Tar Topical Suspension
In the U.S. and Canada—*Zetar Emulsion*

Category: Keratolytic (topical); antipsoriatic (topical); antiseborrheic.

Indications

Accepted
Dandruff (treatment);
Dermatitis, seborrheic (treatment);
Dermatitis, atopic (treatment);
Eczema (treatment); or
Psoriasis (treatment)—Indicated for the relief of itching, burning, and other symptoms associated with generalized persistent dermatoses, such as psoriasis, eczema, atopic dermatitis, and seborrheic dermatitis, and for the control of dandruff.

Coal tar preparations are also used in conjunction with ultraviolet (UV) light or sunlight, under the supervision of a physician, in the treatment of psoriasis or other conditions responding to this combined therapy.

Pharmacology

Mechanism of action/Effect: Coal tar suppresses the hyperplastic skin in some proliferative disorders. Although there is no confirmed evidence as to its pharmacologic effects, its actions in humans have been reported as antiseptic, antipruritic, antiparasitic, antifungal, antibacterial, keratoplastic, and antiacantholic. Vasoconstrictive activity has also been reported.

Precautions to Consider

Cross-sensitivity and/or related problems
Patients sensitive to any of the tars may be sensitive to coal tar also.

Geriatrics
Appropriate studies on the relationship of age to the effects of this medicine have not been performed in the geriatric population. However, no geriatrics-specific problems have been documented to date.

Drug interactions and/or related problems
The following drug interactions and/or related problems have been selected on the basis of their potential clinical significance (possible mechanism in parentheses where appropriate)—not necessarily inclusive (» = major clinical significance):

Note: Combinations containing any of the following medications, depending on the amount present, may also interact with this medication.

Photosensitizing medications, other
  (concurrent use of coal tar with these medications may cause additive photosensitizing effects; concurrent use of coal tar with systemic or topical methoxsalen or trioxsalen is not recommended)

Contraindications/Medical problems
The contraindications/medical problems included have been selected on the basis of their potential clinical significance (reasons given in parentheses where appropriate)—not necessarily inclusive (» = major clinical significance).

Risk-benefit should be considered when the following medical problems exist:
» Acute inflammation, open wounds, or infection of skin
   Sensitivity to coal tar

Side/Adverse Effects
The following side/adverse effects have been selected on the basis of their potential clinical significance (possible signs and symptoms in parentheses where appropriate)—not necessarily inclusive:

Those indicating need for medical attention
Incidence rare
  Allergic or irritant contact dermatitis, folliculitis, or pustular or keratocystic response (skin rash); *skin irritation not present before therapy*

Those indicating need for medical attention only if they continue or are bothersome
Incidence more frequent
  Stinging, mild—especially for gel and solution dosage forms

Patient Consultation
In providing consultation, consider emphasizing the following selected information (» = major clinical significance):

Before using this medication
» Conditions affecting use, especially:
   Allergy to coal tar or any of the other tars
   Use in children—Coal tar products should not be used on infants, unless under close supervision of physician
   Other medical problems, especially acute inflammation, open wounds, or infection of skin

Proper use of this medication
» Importance of not using more medication than the amount recommended
» Protecting treated area from direct sunlight for 72 hours following application of medication, unless otherwise directed by physician

» Not applying medication to infected, blistered, raw, or oozing areas of skin
» Avoiding contact with the eyes
   Missed dose: Applying as soon as possible; not applying if almost time for next dose; not doubling doses
   Proper administration:
   For cream and ointment dosage forms
      Applying enough to cover affected area and rubbing in gently
   For gel dosage form
      Applying enough to cover affected area and rubbing in gently
      Allowing to remain on affected area for 5 minutes, then removing excess by patting with clean tissue
   For shampoo dosage form
      Wetting scalp and hair with lukewarm water
      Applying generous amount and rubbing into scalp, then rinsing
      Applying again, working up lather, and allowing to remain on scalp for 5 minutes, then rinsing thoroughly
   For nonshampoo liquid dosage forms
      Applying directly to dry or wet skin or adding to lukewarm bath water, depending on product
      If applying directly to skin, applying enough to cover affected area and rubbing in gently
      Possibly flammable; not using near heat, open flame, or while smoking
» Proper storage

Precautions while using this medication
   Medication may temporarily discolor blond, bleached, or tinted hair
» Medication may stain skin or clothing

Side/adverse effects
   Signs of potential side effects, especially folliculitis, allergic or irritant contact dermatitis, pustular or keratocystic response, or skin irritation not present before therapy

General Dosing Information
After using this medication, patient should avoid exposure of treated areas to sunlamps or direct sunlight for 72 hours unless otherwise directed by physician, since a photosensitivity reaction may occur. Before subsequent exposure to direct sunlight or sunlamps, all coal tar should be removed from patient's skin.

If coal tar is used in conjunction with ultraviolet (UV) light or sunlight, exposure to light may be undertaken 2 to 72 hours after coal tar is applied. A determination of the minimal erythemal dosage (MED) should be made for each patient and the initial irradiation should not exceed the MED.

For cleansing bar dosage form
For best results on hard scales, soak in a warm bath first, then lather with the cleansing bar.

For gel dosage form
If dryness occurs, an emollient may be applied 1 hour after the gel is applied and between applications as needed.

For lotion dosage form
This medication may be applied directly to dry or wet skin or added to lukewarm bath water, depending on the product.

For shampoo dosage form
The scalp should be moistened with lukewarm water, and a liberal amount of shampoo massaged into the scalp, then rinsed. Application is to be repeated and the shampoo allowed to remain on the scalp for 5 minutes, then rinsed thoroughly. The shampoo may be reapplied as necessary or as directed by the physician.

For solution dosage form
The solution may be used full strength or diluted with 3 parts of water and applied to a cotton or gauze pad and then massaged gently on the affected area.

A coal tar solution bath may be prepared by adding 4 to 6 tablespoonfuls of the solution to a tubful of lukewarm water.

Topical Dosage Forms

COAL TAR CLEANSING BAR

Usual adult and adolescent dose: Topical, to the skin, one or two times a day or as directed.

Auxiliary labeling: • For external use only.

COAL TAR CREAM

Usual adult and adolescent dose: Topical, to the skin, up to four times a day.

Auxiliary labeling: • For external use only.

COAL TAR GEL

Usual adult and adolescent dose: Topical, to the skin, one or two times a day.

Auxiliary labeling: • For external use only.

COAL TAR LOTION

Usual adult and adolescent dose: Topical, to the skin, as a direct application, as a bath, as a hand or foot soak, or as a hair rinse, depending on the product.

Auxiliary labeling:
• Shake well (depending on the product).
• For external use only.

COAL TAR OINTMENT USP

Usual adult and adolescent dose: Topical, to the skin, two or three times a day.

Auxiliary labeling: • For external use only.

COAL TAR SHAMPOO

Usual adult and adolescent dose: Topical, to the scalp, once a week to once a day or as directed.

Auxiliary labeling:
• Shake well (depending on the product).
• For external use only.

COAL TAR TOPICAL SOLUTION USP

Usual adult and adolescent dose: Topical, to the skin, as a direct application to wet skin or scalp or as a bath, depending on the product.

Auxiliary labeling:
• Shake well (depending on the product).
• For external use only.

COAL TAR TOPICAL SUSPENSION

Usual adult and adolescent dose: Topical, to the skin, as a bath.

Auxiliary labeling:
• Shake well.
• For external use only.

COLESTIPOL   Oral-Local

A commonly used *brand name* in the U.S. and Canada is *Colestid*.

ORAL
Colestipol Hydrochloride for Oral Suspension USP
  In the U.S. and Canada—*Colestid*

Category: Antihyperlipidemic; antipruritic (cholestasis); antidiarrheal (postoperative colonic bile acids).

Indications

Note: Bracketed information in the *Indications* section refers to uses not included in U.S. product labeling.

Accepted
Hyperlipidemia (treatment)—Colestipol is indicated for use as an adjunct only in patients with primary hypercholesterolemia (type IIa hyperlipidemia) and a significant risk of coronary artery disease who have not responded to diet or other measures alone. Colestipol reduces plasma cholesterol concentrations but causes no change or a slight increase in serum triglyceride concentrations, and so is not useful in patients with elevated triglyceride concentrations alone. Its use is limited in other types of hyperlipidemia (including type IIb) because it may cause further elevation of triglycerides.

In the 1988 Report of the National Cholesterol Education Program Expert Panel on Detection, Evaluation, and Treatment of High Blood Cholesterol in Adults, the following guidelines for the treatment of high blood cholesterol are recommended:

Nonpharmacologic management (especially reduction in dietary intake of saturated fatty acids and cholesterol, weight reduction and exercise, and quitting smoking) is recommended first for all patients and as an adjunct to all pharmacologic cholesterol therapy.

If, after six months of diet therapy, adequate low density lipoprotein (LDL)-cholesterol reduction is not achieved, then medication therapy is recommended to be added to diet therapy.

Initial medication therapy usually consists of a bile acid sequestrant (e.g., cholestyramine, colestipol) or niacin. A 3-hydroxy-3-methylglutanyl coenzyme A (HMG-CoA) reductase inhibitor (e.g., lovastatin) should be considered after the bile acid sequestrants and niacin. Other lipid-lowering agents, including fibric acid derivatives (e.g., gemfibrozil and clofibrate) and probucol, are not as effective in lowering LDL cholesterol as the above mentioned medications. Two other agents, neomycin (not approved by FDA as a lipid-lowering agent) and dextrothyroxine are not recommended for general use because other medications are available that have a more favorable benefit/risk ratio.

If adequate LDL-cholesterol control is not achieved with initial medication therapy, it is recommended that the patient be switched to another medication or a combination of two medications with synergistic mechanisms of action. Although experience with such drug combinations is somewhat limited, preliminary studies indicate that the bile acid sequestrants given with either niacin, lovastatin, probucol, or gemfibrozil are useful in controlling LDL cholesterol. Lovastatin in combination with either niacin or gemfibrozil needs further study because of the potential increased risk of side effects.

If effective control of LDL cholesterol is not obtained after use of primary medications and medication combinations, then referral to a lipid specialist may be necessary.

Studies have suggested that control of elevated cholesterol and triglycerides may not lessen the danger of cardiovascular disease and mortality, although incidence of nonfatal myocardial infarctions may be decreased.

[Pruritus, associated with partial biliary obstruction (treatment)][1]—Colestipol is also used for the relief of pruritus associated with partial biliary obstruction (including primary biliary cirrhosis and various other forms of bile stasis). It is not useful in patients with complete biliary obstruction or with pruritus due to other causes.

[Diarrhea, due to bile acids (treatment)][1]—Colestipol may also be used to treat diarrhea caused by increased bile acids in the colon after surgery, although the risk of steatorrhea is increased.

[Colestipol has been used in the treatment of digitalis glycoside overdose and hyperoxaluria; however, it generally has been replaced by more effective agents.][1]

[1]Not included in Canadian product labeling.

Pharmacology

Mechanism of action/Effect: Colestipol binds with bile acids in the intestine, preventing their reabsorption and producing an insoluble complex, which is excreted in the feces.

Antihyperlipidemic—Colestipol binds with bile acids in the intestine, causing an increase in hepatic synthesis of bile acids from cholesterol. This depletion of hepatic cholesterol increases hepatic low-density lipoprotein (LDL) receptor activity, which removes LDL cholesterol from the plasma. Colestipol may also increase hepatic very low-density lipoprotein (VLDL) production, thereby increasing plasma concentration of triglycerides, especially in patients with hypertriglyceridemia.

Antipruritic (cholestasis)—Reduction of serum bile acids and subsequent reduction of excess bile acids, which are deposited in dermal tissue, may lead to reduced pruritus.

Antidiarrheal (postoperative colonic bile acids)—Colestipol binds with and removes bile acids.

Other actions: Because it is an anion-exchange resin, colestipol is capable of binding negatively charged medications as well as some others, causing a decreased effect or shortened half-life.

Onset of action: Plasma cholesterol concentrations are generally reduced within 24 to 48 hours after initiation of colestipol therapy.

Time to peak effect: Within 1 month. In some patients, after the initial decrease, serum cholesterol concentrations return to or exceed baseline levels with continued therapy.

Duration of action: After withdrawal of colestipol, cholesterol concentrations return to baseline in about 1 month.

Precautions to Consider

Geriatrics

Appropriate studies on the relationship of age to the effects of colestipol have not been performed in the geriatric population. However, patients over 60 years of age may be more likely to experience gastrointestinal side effects, as well as adverse nutritional effects.

Drug interactions and/or related problems

The following drug interactions and/or related problems have been selected on the basis of their potential clinical significance (possible mechanism in parentheses where appropriate)—not necessarily inclusive (» = major clinical significance):

Note: Combinations containing any of the following medications, depending on the amount present, may also interact with this medication.

» Anticoagulants, coumarin- or indandione-derivative
(concurrent use may significantly increase the anticoagulant effect as a result of depletion of vitamin K, but colestipol may also bind with oral anticoagulants in the gastrointestinal tract and reduce their effects; administration at least 6 hours before colestipol and adjustment of anticoagulant dosage based on frequent prothrombin-time determinations are recommended)

Chenodiol or
Ursodiol
(effect may be decreased when chenodiol or ursodiol is used concurrently with colestipol, which binds the medication and decreases its absorption and also tends to increase cholesterol saturation of bile)

» Digitalis glycosides
(colestipol may reduce the half-life of these medications by decreasing intestinal reabsorption and enterohepatic circulation; caution is recommended, especially when colestipol is withdrawn from a patient who was stabilized on the digitalis glycoside while receiving colestipol, because of the potential for serious toxicity; some clinicians recommend administration of colestipol approximately 8 hours after the digitalis glycoside)

» Diuretics, thiazide, oral, or
» Penicillin G, oral, or
» Propranolol, oral, or
» Tetracyclines, oral
(concurrent administration with colestipol has been found to impair absorption of these medications; an interval of several hours between administration of colestipol and any of these medications is recommended; effects on absorption of other beta-blockers has not been determined)

» Thyroid hormones, including dextrothyroxine
(concurrent use with colestipol may decrease the effects of thyroid hormones by binding and delaying or preventing absorption; an interval of 4 to 5 hours between administration of the 2 medications and regular monitoring of thyroid function tests are recommended)

» Vancomycin, oral
(colestipol has been shown to bind oral vancomycin significantly when used concurrently, resulting in decreased stool concentrations and marked reduction in antibacterial activity of vancomycin; concurrent use is not recommended; patients should be advised to take oral vancomycin and colestipol several hours apart)

Vitamins, fat-soluble
(colestipol may interfere with absorption of fat-soluble vitamins as a result of its interference with fat absorption; supplemental vitamin A and D in water-miscible or parenteral form are recommended in patients receiving colestipol for prolonged periods; supplemental vitamin K may be required in some patients who develop bleeding tendencies)

Medications, other
(colestipol may delay or reduce absorption of other medications administered concurrently because of its anion-binding activity; administration of other medications 1 to 2 hours before or 4 hours after colestipol is recommended, although absorption of some medications is impaired even then; caution is recommended when colestipol is withdrawn because of the risk of toxicity when suddenly increased absorption of the other medication leads to higher serum concentrations)

Contraindications/Medical problems

The contraindications/medical problems included have been selected on the basis of their potential clinical significance (reasons given in parentheses where appropriate)—not necessarily inclusive (» = major clinical significance).

Except under special circumstances, this medication should not be used when the following medical problem exists:

» Primary biliary cirrhosis
   (may further raise the cholesterol concentration)

Risk-benefit should be considered when the following medical problems exist:

Bleeding disorders and
Gallstones and
Gastrointestinal dysfunction and
Hypothyroidism and
Malabsorption states, especially steatorrhea, and
Peptic ulcer
   (these conditions may be exacerbated)

» Complete biliary obstruction or complete atresia
   (no bile acids in gastrointestinal tract for colestipol to bind)

» Constipation
   (risk of fecal impaction)

Coronary artery disease and
Hemorrhoids
   (because of the risks associated with severe constipation)

Renal function impairment
   (increased risk of development of hyperchloremic acidosis)

Sensitivity to colestipol

Side/Adverse Effects

The following side/adverse effects have been selected on the basis of their potential clinical significance (possible signs and symptoms in parentheses where appropriate)—not necessarily inclusive:

Those indicating need for medical attention

Incidence more frequent—about 10%
   Constipation—usually mild and transient, but may be severe and lead to fecal impaction

Incidence rare
   Gallstones (severe stomach pain with nausea and vomiting); *gastrointestinal bleeding or peptic ulcer* (black, tarry stools); *steatorrhea or malabsorption syndrome, especially with doses greater than 30 grams a day* (sudden loss of weight)

Those indicating need for medical attention only if they continue or are bothersome

Incidence less frequent
   Belching; bloating; diarrhea; dizziness; headache; nausea or vomiting; stomach pain

Patient Consultation

In providing consultation, consider emphasizing the following selected information (» = major clinical significance):

Before using this medication

Diet as preferred therapy; importance of following prescribed diet
This medication does not cure the condition but rather helps control it

» Conditions affecting use, especially:
   Sensitivity to colestipol
   Use in children—Not recommended in children under 2 years of age since cholesterol is required for normal development
   Use in the elderly—Increased incidence of gastrointestinal side effects and adverse nutritional effects in patients over 60 years of age

Other medications, especially anticoagulants, digitalis glycosides, oral penicillin G, oral tetracyclines, oral propranolol, thyroid hormones, thiazide diuretics, or oral vancomycin

Other medical problems, especially primary biliary cirrhosis, complete biliary obstruction or complete atresia, or constipation

Proper use of this medication

» Importance of not taking more or less medication than the amount prescribed

» Compliance with prescribed diet

» Importance of mixing with fluids before taking; instructions for mixing: Stirring until completely mixed (does not dissolve); rinsing glass and drinking to make sure all medication is taken; may also be mixed with milk in cereals, thin soups, or pulpy fruits

Missed dose: Taking as soon as possible; not taking if almost time for next dose; not doubling doses

» Proper storage

Precautions while using this medication

» Importance of close monitoring by the physician

» Checking with physician before discontinuing medication; blood lipid concentrations may increase significantly

» Not taking any other medication unless discussed with physician

Side/adverse effects

Signs of potential side effects, especially constipation, gallstones, gastrointestinal bleeding, peptic ulcer, and steatorrhea or malabsorption syndrome

General Dosing Information

To prevent accidental inhalation or esophageal distress with the dry form, it is recommended that colestipol be mixed with at least 90 mL of water or other fluids (i.e., carbonated beverages, flavored drinks, juices, or milk) before being ingested. It may also be taken in soups or with cereals or pulpy fruits.

Reduction in colestipol dosage or withdrawal of the medication may be necessary in some patients if constipation occurs or worsens, to prevent impaction. Administration of a laxative or stool softener or increased fluid intake may be helpful.

For use as an antihyperlipidemic

If a paradoxical increase in plasma cholesterol levels occurs, it is recommended that colestipol therapy be withdrawn.

If response is inadequate after 3 months of treatment, colestipol therapy should be withdrawn, except in the case of xanthoma tuberosum, which may require up to 1 year of treatment as long as reduction in size and/or number of xanthomata occurs.

Oral Dosage Forms

COLESTIPOL HYDROCHLORIDE FOR ORAL SUSPENSION USP

Usual adult dose: Antihyperlipidemic—Oral, 15 to 30 grams a day before meals in two to four divided doses.

Note: Colestipol has been used to treat digitalis glycoside toxicity at an oral dose of 10 grams, followed by 5 grams every six to eight hours.

Auxiliary labeling: • Take mixed in cold water or juice.

CORTICOSTEROIDS   Inhalation-Local

INN: Included in brackets after generic listings, if different from U.S. generic names.

Some commonly used *brand names* are:

In the U.S.—

AeroBid [Flunisolide]	*Decadron Respihaler*
Azmacort [Triamcinolone]	[Dexamethasone]
Beclovent	*Vanceril* [Beclomethasone]
[Beclomethasone]	

In Canada—

Azmacort [Triamcinolone]	*Bronalide* [Flunisolide]
Beclovent	*Vanceril* [Beclomethasone]
[Beclomethasone]	
Beclovent Rotacaps	
[Beclomethasone]	

Another commonly used name for beclomethasone is beclometasone.

INHALATION-LOCAL

BECLOMETHASONE [INN: Beclometasone]
    Beclomethasone Dipropionate Inhalation Aerosol
        In the U.S. and Canada—*Beclovent; Vanceril*
    Beclomethasone Dipropionate for Inhalation (capsules)*
        In Canada—*Beclovent Rotacaps*
DEXAMETHASONE†
    Dexamethasone Sodium Phosphate Inhalation Aerosol USP†
        In the U.S.—*Decadron Respihaler*
FLUNISOLIDE
    Flunisolide Inhalation Aerosol
        In the U.S.—*AeroBid*
        In Canada—*Bronalide*
TRIAMCINOLONE
    Triamcinolone Acetonide Inhalation Aerosol
        In the U.S. and Canada—*Azmacort*

---

*Not commercially available in the U.S.
†Not commercially available in Canada.

Category: Adrenocorticoid (inhalation-local); antiasthmatic.

Indications

Accepted

Asthma, bronchial, chronic (treatment)—Adrenocorticoid inhalation aerosol therapy is considered a primary therapy for patients who require continuing treatment with adrenocorticoids or other medications for control of symptoms of chronic bronchial asthma. In many patients, orally inhaled adrenocorticoids are preferable to theophylline as primary therapy for chronic treatment of asthma.

Dexamethasone inhalation is less frequently used because it has demonstrated a significantly higher incidence of adverse effects with no additional benefit over other inhaled adrenocorticoids.

Unaccepted

Adrenocorticoid inhalation therapy does not relieve acute bronchospasm and is not indicated for the primary treatment of status asthmaticus or other acute asthmatic episodes requiring more intensive treatment measures.

Adrenocorticoid inhalation aerosol therapy is not indicated in the treatment of nonasthmatic bronchitis.

Pharmacology

Mechanism of action/Effect:
In the treatment of chronic bronchial asthma, orally inhaled adrenocortioids have many probable sites of action. They are especially potent in reducing experimentally induced late-phase allergic reactions, peaking at 4 to 8 hours after antigen inhalation. There is evidence that inhaled adrenocorticoids, but not systemic adrenocorticoids, also decrease the immediate allergic reaction. Specific points of action of adrenocorticoids include reduced IgE synthesis, increased beta-adrenergic receptors on leukocytes, and reduced arachidonic acid metabolism with decreased release of prostaglandins and leukotrienes. The gross changes observed during chronic bronchial asthma include increased peribronchial edema and mucus secretion, which are retarded by adrenocorticoids. The immediate allergic reaction is triggered by allergen bridging of IgE antibodies on the surface of mast cells with release of vasoactive and chemotactic substances. These cells in turn release additional chemotactic factors, and peptides and high-energy oxygen radicals that are directly damaging to the mucosa. Inflammation of the bronchial tissue contributes to the airway hyperresponsiveness characteristic of asthma. Influx of these inflammatory cells as well as their activation are markedly reduced by adrenocorticoids.

Onset of action: Improved pulmonary function (in patients not receiving systemic adrenocorticoids when inhalation therapy is instituted)—
    Beclomethasone: Although some improvement may occur in less than 1 week, significant improvement may require 1 to 4 weeks.
    Flunisolide: Usually 1 to 4 weeks.
    Triamcinolone: Usually 1 to 2 weeks.

Precautions to Consider

Cross-sensitivity and/or related problems
Patients intolerant of fluorocarbon propellants may be intolerant of the fluorocarbon propellants in these preparations.

Geriatrics
Appropriate studies with inhalation adrenocorticoids have not been performed in the geriatric population. However, geriatrics-specific problems that would limit the usefulness of this medication in the elderly are not expected.

Drug interactions and/or related problems
The following drug interactions and/or related problems have been selected on the basis of their potential clinical significance (possible mechanism in parentheses where appropriate)—not necessarily inclusive (» = major clinical significance):

Note: Combinations containing any of the following medications, depending on the amount present, may also interact with this medication.

    Interactions listed below as applying to dexamethasone and triamcinolone inhalations apply to usual inhalation doses of the medications, unless otherwise specified. However, these interactions may also occur with chronic inhalation of greater-than-recommended doses of other adrenocorticoids.

For dexamethasone and triamcinolone inhalation aerosols only
    Alcohol or
    Anti-inflammatory medications, other steroidal or nonsteroidal
        (may increase risk of gastrointestinal side effects, such as ulceration and hemorrhage)

Amphotericin B, parenteral, or
Carbonic anhydrase inhibitors or
Diuretics or
Potassium supplements
  (natriuretic and diuretic activity may be decreased if excessive amounts of adrenocorticoid are absorbed)

  (risk of hypokalemia may be increased if excessive amounts of adrenocorticoid are absorbed during concurrent use of parenteral amphotericin B, carbonic anhydrase inhibitors, or potassium-depleting diuretics)

  (desired effects of potassium supplements and potassium-sparing diuretics on serum potassium may be decreased if excessive amounts of adrenocorticoid are absorbed)

  (risk of carbonic anhydrase inhibitor-induced hypocalcemia may be increased if excessive amounts of adrenocorticoid are absorbed)

  (monitoring of serum electrolytes may be advisable in patients receiving very high doses of dexamethasone or triamcinolone inhalation concurrently with any of these medications)

Anticoagulants, coumarin- or indandione-derivative, or
Heparin or
Streptokinase or
Urokinase
  (effects of coumarin- or indandione-derivative anticoagulants are usually decreased but may be increased in some patients; anticoagulant dosage adjustments may be necessary during and after adrenocorticoid aerosol therapy)

  (risk of gastrointestinal ulceration or hemorrhage and adverse effects on vascular integrity may be increased)

» Antidiabetic agents, oral, or
» Insulin
  (blood glucose concentrations may be increased; dosage adjustments of either or both medications may be required during therapy; dosage readjustment of hypoglycemic agent may be required if adrenocorticoid is discontinued)

Digitalis glycosides
  (risk of arrhythmias or digitalis toxicity associated with hypokalemia may be increased)

Salicylates
  (increased doses of salicylates may be required during therapy; dosage should be decreased when adrenocorticoid therapy is discontinued)

Somatrem or
Somatropin
  (response to somatrem or somatropin may be decreased; usual aerosol doses are not likely to produce this effect; the possible additive effect of the inhalation should be considered if the patient is also receiving a systemic adrenocorticoid)

Streptozocin
  (risk of hyperglycemia may be increased)

Contraindications/Medical problems
The contraindications/medical problems included have been selected on the basis of their potential clinical significance (reasons given in parentheses where appropriate)—not necessarily inclusive (» = major clinical significance).

Except under special circumstances, these medications should not be used when the following medical problem exists:
» Bronchiectasis, moderate to severe

Risk-benefit should be considered when the following medical problems exist:
For all adrenocorticoid inhalation aerosols
  Bacterial, fungal, or viral infection of the mouth, throat, or lungs, active, untreated
    (symptoms may be masked or recovery impaired)
  Intolerance to adrenocorticoids
For chronic use of usual inhalation doses of dexamethasone and triamcinolone inhalation aerosols or greater-than-recommended daily doses of other inhalation aerosols
  Amebiasis, latent
    (may be activated)
» Cardiac disease or
  Congestive heart failure or
  Hypertension
    (may be exacerbated by sodium- and fluid-retaining effects of adrenocorticoids)
» Diabetes mellitus
    (may be exacerbated)
  Diverticulitis or
» Peptic ulcer or
  Gastritis or
  Esophagitis or
  Ulcerative colitis, in presence of infection or possible perforation
    (may be exacerbated; also, symptoms of progression may be masked)
» Fungal infections, systemic
    (may be exacerbated)
  Glaucoma, open-angle
    (may be exacerbated)
  Hepatic function impairment
» Herpes simplex, ocular
    (possible corneal perforation)
  Hyperlipidemia
    (serum cholesterol concentrations may be increased)
  Hypothyroidism
    (adrenocorticoid effects may be enhanced)
» Myasthenia gravis, especially with respiratory involvement
    (respiratory weakness may occur)
» Myocardial infarction, recent
    (occurrence of left ventricular free wall rupture has been reported with use of aerosol adrenocorticoids; extreme caution advised)
  Osteoporosis
    (may be exacerbated)
  Renal function impairment or stones
    (may be exacerbated)
  Tuberculosis, latent
    (may be reactivated during prolonged dexamethasone therapy unless chemoprophylaxis is administered concurrently; potential effects of prolonged therapy with other adrenocorticoids have not been determined)

Side/Adverse Effects
See also *Table 1*, page 453.
Note: Pulmonary infiltrates with eosinophilia have been reported in a few patients receiving beclomethasone or flunisolide inhalation aerosol. Although it has been proposed that these effects may have become apparent following withdrawal of systemic adrenocorticoids, the possible causative role of the adrenocorticoid and/or other ingredients in the formulations has not been ruled out.

If absorbed in sufficient quantities, inhalation adrenocorticoids may produce hypothalamic-pituitary-adrenal (HPA) axis suppression or other systemic glucocorticoid effects. HPA axis suppression may occur with usual inhalation doses of dexamethasone or triamcinolone, but only with greater-than-recommended doses of beclomethasone (may occur within 28 days with doses of 1.6 mg or more per day) or flunisolide. None of these agents has significant mineralocorticoid activity.

Patient Consultation

In providing consultation, consider emphasizing the following selected information (» = major clinical significance):

Before using this medication
» Conditions affecting use, especially:
  Allergies to adrenocorticoids
  Carcinogenicity—Flunisolide has caused certain types of lung and breast cancers in some animal studies
  Tumorigenicity—Triamcinolone has demonstrated tumorigenicity in animal studies
  Pregnancy—Risk-benefit should be considered because systemic adrenocorticoids have demonstrated embryotoxicity, fetotoxicity, and teratogenicity in animals; beclomethasone inhalation study in humans has shown no adverse effects on fetus; infants born to mothers who received substantial doses of adrenocorticoids during pregnancy should be observed for hypoadrenalism
  Breast-feeding—Use of dexamethasone or triamcinolone is not recommended because dexamethasone is excreted in breast milk and triamcinolone has demonstrated tumorigenicity in animals
  Use in children—Significant effect on growth by beclomethasone, flunisolide, or triamcinolone has not been documented; importance of monitoring of growth and development with prolonged or high-dose therapy
  Other medications, especially oral antidiabetic agents or insulin
  Other medical problems, especially bronchiectasis, cardiac disease, diabetes mellitus, peptic ulcer, gastritis, esophagitis, systemic fungal infections, ocular herpes simplex, myasthenia gravis, or recent myocardial infarction

Proper use of this medication
» Proper administration technique: Reading patient instructions carefully
» Not using more medication than the amount prescribed
» Compliance with therapy; patients not taking systemic adrenocorticoids when inhalation therapy started may require up to 4 weeks for full benefit
» Not using to relieve acute asthma attack; continuing use even if using other medication for asthma attack
  Cleaning oral inhaler daily as described in patient instructions
  Gargling and rinsing mouth with water after each dose; not swallowing rinse water
  Missed dose: Using as soon as possible; not using if almost time for next dose; not doubling doses
  Checking with pharmacist to determine availability of refills; saving inhaler if refills available
» Proper storage
  Proper dose may not be delivered if aerosol canister is cold

Precautions while using this medication
» Checking with physician if:
  —unusual stress occurs
  —asthma attack not responsive to bronchodilator occurs
  —any sign indicating possible infection occurs
  —symptoms do not improve
  —condition becomes worse

» Checking with physician at once if signs of systemic adrenocorticoid withdrawal occur (such as abdominal or back pain, depression, dizziness or fainting, fever, muscle or joint pain, nausea or vomiting, prolonged loss of appetite, shortness of breath, unusual tiredness or weakness, or unusual weight loss)
  Carrying medical identification card stating that supplemental systemic adrenocorticoid therapy may be required in emergency situations, periods of unusual stress, or acute asthma attack
» Caution if any kind of surgery or emergency treatment is required; informing physician or dentist in charge that inhalation adrenocorticoid is being used
  Using bronchodilator aerosol 5 minutes prior to the adrenocorticoid aerosol, unless otherwise directed by physician

For patients receiving systemic adrenocorticoid therapy
» Importance of not discontinuing systemic adrenocorticoid therapy without physician's advice; carefully reducing dose or discontinuing treatment if so directed
» Importance of regular visits to physician during time that systemic adrenocorticoid therapy is being withdrawn; obtaining physician's instructions to follow if severe asthma attack occurs, medical or surgical treatment needed, or symptoms of adrenocorticoid withdrawal occur

Side/adverse effects
  Signs of potential side effects, especially local, respiratory, immunologic, neurologic, musculoskeletal, hematologic, gastrointestinal, or endocrine effects

General Dosing Information

These medications are adrenocorticoids with the same actions, side effects, and adverse reactions as exist with systemic adrenocorticoids. However, with proper use of inhalation adrenocorticoids, the incidence of adverse effects is generally slight and primarily limited to local effects. The incidence of systemic side effects associated with the use of orally inhaled adrenocorticoids is significantly lower than that associated with the use of systemic adrenocorticoids. However, significant systemic effects may occur with beclomethasone or flunisolide inhalation if the recommended prescribing limits are exceeded. Adrenal suppression has been documented with usual inhalation doses of dexamethasone or triamcinolone.

When used in conjunction with a bronchodilator inhalation aerosol, the aerosol bronchodilator should be used 5 minutes prior to the adrenocorticoid. This interval allows for bronchodilation to occur and increases deposition of adrenocorticoid within the bronchi.

Gargling and rinsing the mouth with water after each dose is recommended to help prevent hoarseness, throat irritation, and oral candidiasis. Rinse water should not be swallowed. The use of a spacing device may also greatly decrease the incidence of these local adverse effects. Use of a spacer eliminates the need for proper timing of patient inhalation with activation of the inhaler. Therefore the inhaled adrenocorticoid tends to be deposited less in the mouth and throat and more in the respiratory tract. If laryngeal or pharyngeal candidiasis develops, treatment should be discontinued and antifungal therapy such as topical nystatin suspension instituted.

When excessive mucous is present in the bronchioles, infection is present, or severe asthma attack is underway, the inhaled adrenocorticoid may not reach the site of action. If no response is seen after 7 to 10 days of use, use of expectorants and/or a short course of systemic adrenocorticoid therapy may be required before continuing inhalation therapy.

For patients receiving systemic adrenocorticoid therapy

Before instituting inhalation adrenocorticoid therapy, the patient's asthma should be relatively stable.

Caution is required when transferring patients from systemic adrenocorticoids to inhalation adrenocorticoids. Deaths due to adrenal insufficiency have occurred in asthmatic patients during and after transfer.

Full maintenance dosage of systemic adrenocorticoids should be continued initially when inhalation therapy is instituted. After 1 to 2 weeks of inhalation therapy, systemic steroid dosage may be reduced gradually at 1- or 2-week intervals, depending on patient response. *Dosage reductions must be made very slowly and in small increments* (not more than 2.5 mg of prednisone or the equivalent).

During reduction of systemic adrenocorticoid dosage, the patient should be carefully monitored for signs of adrenal insufficiency, and systemic dosage increased to the previous dose for approximately one week if necessary. Subsequent reductions in systemic dosage should proceed even more slowly.

Continued monitoring of the patient for signs of adrenal insufficiency is recommended following complete withdrawal of systemic adrenocorticoid therapy. Recovery of adrenal function may require up to 12 months in some patients, depending on the dosage and duration of systemic therapy.

Reinstitution or supplementation of systemic therapy may be required if a severe asthma attack occurs, during periods of stress or infection, or if surgery is required.

Some patients may not be able to discontinue use of systemic adrenocorticoids. A minimum oral maintenance dose may be required when they begin inhalation adrenocorticoid therapy, along with the inhaled adrenocorticoid.

BECLOMETHASONE

Summary of Differences

Pharmacology:

Other actions/effects—HPA axis suppression likely only with greater-than-recommended doses; may occur within 28 days at doses from 1 mg to 4 mg per day.

Onset of action—Improved pulmonary function may require 1 to 4 weeks in patients not receiving systemic adrenocorticoids.

Elimination—Fecal 35 to 65%; 10 to 15% renal.

Precautions:

Carcinogenicity—No carcinogenicity demonstrated in rats.

Pregnancy/reproduction—Increased resorptions and birth defects shown in animal studies. No problems reported in one inhalation study in humans.

Breast-feeding—Not known if excreted in breast milk.

Drug interactions and/or related problems—Cautions applying to systemic adrenocorticoids do not apply to usual inhalation doses.

Laboratory value alterations—Interferences reported for systemic adrenocorticoids do not apply to usual inhalation doses.

Contraindications/medical problems—Precautions applying to systemic adrenocorticoids do not apply to usual inhalation doses.

Side/adverse effects: See *Table 1*, page 453.

Inhalation Dosage Forms

BECLOMETHASONE DIPROPIONATE INHALATION AEROSOL

Usual adult dose: Oral inhalation, 84 mcg to 100 mcg (0.084 to 0.1 mg—2 metered sprays) three or four times a day.

Alternate regimen: Oral inhalation, 168 to 200 mcg (0.168 to 0.2 mg—4 metered sprays) two times a day.

For severe asthma—Initially, 504 to 672 mcg or 600 to 800 mcg (0.504 to 0.672 mg or 0.6 to 0.8 mg—12 to 16 metered sprays) a day. Dosage should then be decreased according to patient response.

Usual adult prescribing limits: Oral inhalation, 840 mcg (0.84 mg—20 metered sprays) or 1 mg (20 metered sprays) per day.

Auxiliary labeling: • Shake well.

BECLOMETHASONE DIPROPIONATE FOR INHALATION

Note: Beclomethasone dipropionate for inhalation is not commercially available in the U.S.

Usual adult dose: Oral inhalation, 200 mcg (0.2 mg) three or four times a day. Dosage should then be decreased according to patient response; many patients may be maintained on 400 mcg (0.4 mg) a day.

Usual adult prescribing limits: Oral inhalation, up to 1 mg per day.

DEXAMETHASONE

Summary of Differences

Indications: Less frequently used due to significantly increased incidence of adverse effects.

Pharmacology:

Other actions/effects—HPA axis suppression or other glucocorticoid effects may occur with usual inhalation doses.

Absorption—30 to 50% of an inhaled dose absorbed; patients receiving 12 inhalations per day may absorb 400 to 600 mcg (0.4 to 0.6 mg) of dexamethasone.

Elimination—Renal.

Precautions:

Breast-feeding—Excreted in breast milk; nursing by mothers receiving pharmacologic doses not recommended.

Drug interactions and/or related problems—Cautions applying to systemic adrenocorticoids may apply with usual inhalation doses.

Laboratory value alterations—Interferences reported for systemic adrenocorticoids may apply to usual inhalation doses.

Contraindications/medical problems—Precautions applying to systemic adrenocorticoids apply to usual inhalation doses.

Side/adverse effects: See *Table 1*, page 453.

Inhalation Dosage Forms

DEXAMETHASONE SODIUM PHOSPHATE INHALATION AEROSOL USP

Note: Dexamethasone sodium phosphate inhalation aerosol is not commercially available in Canada.

Usual adult dose: Oral inhalation—
    Initial: 300 mcg (0.3 mg—3 metered sprays) of dexamethasone phosphate three or four times a day.
    Maintenance: Dosage to be decreased according to patient response; 200 mcg (0.2 mg or two metered sprays) of dexamethasone phosphate two times a day may be sufficient in some patients.

Usual adult prescribing limits: Oral inhalation, 300 mcg (0.3 mg—3 metered sprays) of dexamethasone phosphate per single dose, or 1.2 mg (12 metered sprays) per day.

Auxiliary labeling: • Shake well.

FLUNISOLIDE

Summary of Differences

Pharmacology:
    Other actions/effects—HPA axis suppression likely only with greater-than-recommended daily doses.
    Absorption—40% of an inhaled dose absorbed.
    Elimination—53% renal; 42% fecal.
Precautions:
    Pregnancy/reproduction—
        Fertility: Impaired fertility demonstrated in rats receiving large doses.
        Pregnancy: Fetotoxic and teratogenic in animal studies (FDA Pregnancy Category C).
    Breast-feeding—Not known if excreted in breast milk.
    Drug interactions and/or related problems—Cautions applying to systemic adrenocorticoids do not apply to usual inhalation doses.
    Laboratory value alterations—Interferences reported for systemic adrenocorticoids do not apply to usual inhalation doses.
    Contraindications/medical problems—Precautions applying to systemic adrenocorticoids may not apply to usual inhalation doses.
Side/adverse effects: See *Table 1*, page 453.

Inhalation Dosage Forms

FLUNISOLIDE INHALATION AEROSOL

Usual adult dose: Oral inhalation, 500 mcg (0.5 mg—2 metered sprays) two times a day, morning and evening.

Usual adult prescribing limits: Oral inhalation, 2 mg per day (four metered sprays twice a day).

Auxiliary labeling: • Shake well.

TRIAMCINOLONE

Summary of Differences

Pharmacology:
    Other actions/effects—HPA axis suppression reported with usual doses.
    Onset of action—Improved pulmonary function usually occurs within 1 to 2 weeks in patients not receiving systemic adrenocorticoids.
    Elimination—Primarily fecal.
Precautions:
    Tumorigenicity—Tumorigenic action demonstrated in animals.
    Pregnancy/reproduction—Embryotoxic, fetotoxic, and teratogenic actions shown in animal studies (FDA Pregnancy Category D).
    Breast-feeding—Not known if excreted in breast milk; nursing not recommended because of tumorigenicity in animals.
    Drug interactions and/or related problems—Cautions applying to systemic adrenocorticoids may apply to usual inhalation doses.
    Laboratory value alterations—Interferences reported for systemic glucocorticoids may apply to usual inhalation doses.
    Contraindications/medical problems—Precautions applying to systemic adrenocorticoids apply to usual inhalation doses.
Side/adverse effects: See *Table 1*, page 453.

Inhalation Dosage Forms

TRIAMCINOLONE ACETONIDE INHALATION AEROSOL

Usual adult dose:
    Initial—Oral inhalation, 200 mcg (0.2 mg—2 metered sprays) three or four times a day.
        For severe asthma: Oral inhalation, 1.2 to 1.6 mg (12 to 16 metered sprays) per day.
    Maintenance—Dosage to be decreased according to patient response; maintenance may be achieved in some patients by administering the total daily dose in two divided doses.

Usual adult prescribing limits: Oral inhalation, 1.6 mg (16 metered sprays) per day.

Auxiliary labeling: • Shake well.

Table 1. Side/Adverse Effects*

The following side/adverse effects have been selected on the basis of their potential clinical significance (possible signs and symptoms in parentheses where appropriate)—not necessarily inclusive:	Legend: **I** = Beclomethasone **II** = Dexamethasone		**III** = Flunisolide **IV** = Triamcinolone	
	I	**II**	**III**	**IV**
Medical attention needed *Acne or other skin problems*†	U	L	L	U
Allergic reaction (hives)	U	U	L	U
(itching of skin)	U	U	M	U
(skin rash)	R	R	M	R
Bronchitis, chest congestion, fluid in lungs, or pneumonia (shortness of breath or troubled breathing, tightness in chest, or wheezing)	U	U	M‡	U
Bronchospasm	R	R	R‡	R
Cataracts (decreased or blurred vision)†	U	L	L	U
Cushing's syndrome, symptom of chronic overdose (fullness or rounding out of the face)†	U	L	U	U
Diabetes mellitus (frequent urination, increased thirst, decreased or blurred vision)†	U	L	U	U
Edema (increase in blood pressure)	U	R	L	U
(swelling of face)	U	U	U	R
(swelling of feet or lower legs)	U	R	L	U
(unusual weight gain)	U	R	L	U
Endocrine imbalance (menstrual problems)†	U	L	M	U
Eye infection (eye pain, redness, tearing)	U	U	L	U
Fast or pounding heartbeat	U	U	M	U
Gastrointestinal bleeding (bloody or black, tarry stools)†	U	L	U	U
Gastrointestinal irritation (nausea or vomiting)	U	L	M (25%)	U
Increased susceptibility to infections	U	M	M	U
Monilial esophagitis (difficulty in swallowing)	R	R	U	R
Oral candidiasis (creamy white, curd-like patches inside mouth)	M	M	M	M
Osteoporosis (back or rib pain)†	U	L	U	U
Peptic ulcer or pancreatitis (stomach pain or burning, severe and continuing; nausea; vomiting)†	U	R	U	U
Potassium loss (irregular heartbeat, muscle cramps or pain, unusual tiredness or weakness)†	U	R	U	U
Psychic changes (mental depression, mood or mental changes)	U	R	L	U
Steroid myopathy (muscle weakness)†	U	R	U	U
Upper respiratory tract infection such as influenza, common cold, and sinusitis (chest pain, chills, cough, ear congestion or pain, fever, head congestion, hoarseness or other voice changes, nasal congestion, runny nose, sneezing, sore throat)	U	U	M (up to 25%)	U
Wounds that will not heal†	U	R	U	U
Medical attention needed only if continuing or bothersome *Cough without symptoms of infection*	M	L/R	M‡	L/R
Decreased appetite	U	U	M	U

*Frequency of occurrence: For beclomethasone, dexamethasone, and triamcinolone—M=more frequent; L=less frequent; L/R=less frequent or rare; R=rare; U=unknown. For flunisolide—M=3–9%; L=1–3%; R=<1%; U=unknown; unless otherwise specified.

†Primarily with long-term use.

‡Side effect may be related to vehicle in flunisolide preparation.

Table 1. Side/Adverse Effects* *(continued)*

	Legend: **I** = Beclomethasone **II** = Dexamethasone		**III** = Flunisolide **IV** = Triamcinolone	
	I	**II**	**III**	**IV**
Dizziness or lightheadedness	U	U	M	U
Dry or irritated nose, mouth, tongue, or throat	L/R	L/R	L	L/R
False sense of well-being	U	L	U	U
Gastrointestinal irritation (abdominal pain, mild; bloated feeling or gas; constipation; diarrhea; heartburn or indigestion)	U	M	M	U
General feeling of discomfort, illness, shakiness, or faintness	U	U	L	U
Headache	U	U	M (25%)	U
Hoarseness or other voice changes without symptoms of infection	M	L/R	M	L/R
Increase in appetite	U	L	L	U
Increased sweating	U	U	L	U
Loss of smell or taste sense	U	U	M	U
Nervousness or restlessness	U	L	M	U
Trouble in sleeping	U	L	L	U
Unexplained nosebleeds	U	U	L	U
Unpleasant taste	U	U	M (10%)	U

*Frequency of occurrence: For beclomethasone, dexamethasone, and triamcinolone—M=more frequent; L=less frequent; L/R=less frequent or rare; R=rare; U=unknown. For flunisolide—M=3–9%; L=1–3%; R=<1%; U=unknown; unless otherwise specified.
†Primarily with long-term use.
‡Side effect may be related to vehicle in flunisolide preparation.

CORTICOSTEROIDS   Nasal

INN: Included in brackets after dosage form for individual generic listings, if different from U.S. generic names.

Some commonly used *brand names* are:

In the U.S.—
    Beconase [Beclomethasone]   *Nasalide* [Flunisolide]
    Beconase AQ   *Vancenase*
      [Beclomethasone]   [Beclomethasone]
    Decadron Turbinaire   *Vancenase AQ*
      [Dexamethasone]   [Beclomethasone]

In Canada—
    Beconase [Beclomethasone]   *Rhinalar* [Flunisolide]
    Beconase AQ   *Vancenase*
      [Beclomethasone]   [Beclomethasone]

Another commonly used name for beclomethasone is beclometasone.

NASAL

BECLOMETHASONE [INN: Beclometasone]
  Beclomethasone Dipropionate Nasal Aerosol
    In the U.S. and Canada—*Beconase; Vancenase*
  Beclomethasone Dipropionate Monohydrate Nasal Spray
    In the U.S.—*Beconase AQ; Vancenase AQ*
    In Canada—*Beconase AQ*
DEXAMETHASONE†
  Dexamethasone Sodium Phosphate Nasal Aerosol†
    In the U.S.—*Decadron Turbinaire*
FLUNISOLIDE
  Flunisolide Nasal Solution USP
    In the U.S.—*Nasalide*
    In Canada—*Rhinalar*

---

†Not commercially available in Canada.

Category: Adrenocorticoid (nasal); anti-inflammatory (steroidal), nasal.

Indications

Note: Bracketed information in the *Indications* section refers to uses not included in U.S. product labeling.

Accepted
Rhinitis, perennial (treatment);
Rhinitis, seasonal (treatment); or
[Rhinitis, seasonal (prophylaxis)]—Nasal adrenocorticoids are indicated in the treatment of seasonal or perennial rhinitis in patients who have exhibited significant side effects from or have developed tolerance to other therapy, such as antihistamines and decongestants, or who have exhibited poor response to other therapy. Antihistamines, decongestants, and nasal cromolyn are generally considered primary therapies for these disorders. However, some clinicians consider nasal adrenocorticoids primary therapy for perennial or seasonal rhinitis because they are more effective and the incidence of side effects appears to be lower as compared to antihistamines and decongestants.

[Nasal adrenocorticoids are used in some patients for prophylaxis of seasonal rhinitis. This form of therapy is generally reserved for patients who have chronically demonstrated a need for nasal adrenocorticoids to control seasonal rhinitis symptoms. Antihistamines, decongestants, and nasal cromolyn are considered primary therapies for this disorder.]

Dexamethasone nasal aerosol is less frequently used because it has demonstrated a significantly higher incidence of systemic adverse effects with no additional benefit over other nasal adrenocorticoids.

Allergic disorders, nasal (treatment);

Inflammatory conditions, noninfectious, nasal (treatment); or
Polyps, nasal (treatment)—Nasal adrenocorticoids are indicated in the treatment of allergic or inflammatory nasal conditions and nasal polyps.

Polyps, nasal, postsurgical recurrence of (prophylaxis)—Beclomethasone is indicated [and dexamethasone and flunisolide are used] for the prevention of recurrence of nasal polyps following their surgical removal and sufficient mucosal healing.

Pharmacology

Mechanism of action/Effect: In the treatment of nasal symptoms, the primary action of nasally applied adrenocorticoids is anti-inflammatory. Nasal adrenocorticoids inhibit the IgE- and mast cell-mediated early-phase allergic reaction. They also inhibit the migration of inflammatory cells into the nasal tissue (the late-phase or late-onset allergic reaction), which may play a significant role in the pathology of chronic rhinitis.

During the late-phase allergic reaction, eosinophils, neutrophils, basophils, and mononuclear cells produce inflammatory mediators, which cause a reappearance of nasal symptoms. Nasal adrenocorticoids inhibit the release of prostaglandins from neutrophils. These prostaglandins are vasodilators and increase capillary permeability. Within the neutrophil, adrenocorticoids increase the formation of lipocortin. Lipocortin, in turn, inhibits phospholipase A_2, resulting in decreased amounts of arachidonic acid available for the formation of leukotrienes and prostaglandins. Nasal adrenocorticoids also inhibit the release of histamine and kinins from basophils. Histamine release causes sneezing, itching, and rhinorrhea. Bradykinin release results in nasal obstruction and rhinorrhea.

Onset of action: For beclomethasone and flunisolide—Usually 5 to 7 days; however, may rarely be as long as 2 to 3 weeks in some patients.

Time to maximum benefit: For beclomethasone and flunisolide—Up to 3 weeks in some patients.

Precautions to Consider

Cross-sensitivity and/or related problems
Patients intolerant of benzalkonium chloride, disodium edetate, or phenylethanol may be intolerant of some nasal adrenocorticoid preparations since they may contain these substances as preservatives.
Beclomethasone and dexamethasone aerosols also contain fluorocarbon propellants; beclomethasone monohydrate and flunisolide dosage forms contain no fluorocarbon propellants.
Flunisolide solution contains propylene glycol and polyethylene glycols.

Geriatrics
Appropriate studies with nasal adrenocorticoids have not been performed in the geriatric population. However, geriatrics-specific problems that would limit the usefulness of this medication in the elderly are not expected.

Contraindications/Medical problems
The contraindications/medical problems included have been selected on the basis of their potential clinical significance (reasons given in parentheses where appropriate)—not necessarily inclusive (» = major clinical significance).

Risk-benefit should be considered when the following medical problems exist:

  Glaucoma
    (may increase intraocular pressure)

Hepatic function impairment

Herpes simplex, ocular

Hypothyroidism

» Infections, fungal, bacterial, or systemic viral

Intolerance to adrenocorticoids

Nasal septal ulcers, recent, or

Nasal surgery, recent, or

Nasal trauma, recent
(adrenocorticoids inhibit wound healing)

Tuberculosis, latent or active, of respiratory tract

Side/Adverse Effects

Note: The risk of systemic effects is minimal with usual doses of nasal beclomethasone and flunisolide. Side effects from usual doses of beclomethasone are generally limited to local effects.

Systemic effects including hypothalamic-pituitary-adrenal (HPA) axis suppression may occur with usual doses of nasal dexamethasone or greater-than-recommended doses of beclomethasone or flunisolide. If the patient is particularly sensitive or has recently used systemic adrenocorticoids prior to using nasal adrenocorticoids, the patient may also be predisposed to hypercorticism.

The following side/adverse effects have been selected on the basis of their potential clinical significance (possible signs and symptoms in parentheses where appropriate)—not necessarily inclusive:

Those indicating need for medical attention
Incidence less frequent
For all nasal adrenocorticoids
Crusting inside nose or epistaxis—especially if spray is improperly aimed toward nasal septum, rather than onto the turbinates; **sore throat; ulceration of nasal mucosa**

For dexamethasone
Allergic reaction or bronchial asthma (shortness of breath, troubled breathing, tightness in chest, hives, or wheezing)

For beclomethasone (monohydrate), dexamethasone, and flunisolide
Cough; dizziness; headache; hoarseness; lethargy; lightheadedness; loss of sense of taste or smell—for dexamethasone and flunisolide only; **nausea or vomiting; rhinorrhea, stuffy nose, or watery eyes, continuing; stomach pains**

Incidence rare
For all nasal adrenocorticoids
Nasal candidiasis (white patches on nasal membranes); **nasal septal perforation; ocular hypertension** (eye pain, nausea, vomiting, gradual loss of vision); **pharyngeal candidiasis** (white patches in throat)

For beclomethasone
Hypersensitivity reaction, delayed or immediate (hives, rash, bronchospasm, angioedema); **rhinitis, atrophic** (nasal odor, dryness or obstruction of nose, headache behind eye sockets)

Symptoms of chronic overdose
Acneiform lesions; Cushing's syndrome (fullness or rounding of the face); **menstrual changes**

Those indicating need for medical attention only if they continue or are bothersome
Incidence more frequent
Burning, dryness, or other irritation inside the nose, mild and transient

For beclomethasone and flunisolide
Irritation of throat—possibly due to vehicle in nasal spray; **sneezing attacks**—may be more common in children using beclomethasone aerosol or flunisolide spray

Patient Consultation

In providing consultation, consider emphasizing the following selected information (» = major clinical significance):

Before using this medication
» Conditions affecting use, especially:
Allergies to adrenocorticoids
Pregnancy—Risk-benefit must be considered since systemic adrenocorticoids cross the placenta and have demonstrated embryotoxicity, fetotoxicity, and teratogenicity in animals; beclomethasone oral inhalation study in humans has shown no adverse effects on fetus; infants born to mothers who received substantial doses of adrenocorticoids during pregnancy should be observed for hypoadrenalism
Breast-feeding—Use of dexamethasone is not recommended since dexamethasone is excreted in breast milk
Use in children—Significant effect on growth by beclomethasone or flunisolide has not been documented; importance of monitoring growth and development with prolonged or high-dose therapy
Other medical problems, especially infections

Proper use of this medication
» Proper administration technique; reading patient directions carefully before use
» Compliance with therapy; may require up to 3 weeks for full benefit
» Importance of not using more medication than the amount prescribed because of potential enhanced absorption and side effects
» Checking with physician before using medication for other nasal problems
Saving beclomethasone or dexamethasone special inhaler; refills may be available
Missed dose: Using as soon as possible if remembered within an hour or so; if remembered later, not using at all; not doubling doses
Efficacy may be decreased if aerosol canister is cold
Discarding unused portion of beclomethasone monohydrate or flunisolide inhalation 3 months after opening package
» Proper storage

Precautions while using this medication
Regular visits to physician to check progress during prolonged therapy
» Checking with physician if:
—signs of infection of nose, throat, or sinuses occur
—no improvement within 7 days (for dexamethasone)
—no improvement within 3 weeks (for beclomethasone or flunisolide)
—condition becomes worse

Side/adverse effects
Signs of potential side effects, especially local effects, hypersensitivity reactions, infections, throat and respiratory effects, Cushing's syndrome, or epistaxis

General Dosing Information

In patients with blocked nasal passages, a topical decongestant may be used just prior to use of the nasal adrenocorticoid. However, because prolonged use of topical nasal decongestants may cause congestive rebound, they should preferably be used for a maximum of 3 to 5 days. An oral decongestant is recommended for chronic nasal congestion.

The smallest dose required to control symptoms should be used as a maintenance dose after the desired clinical response is achieved.

BECLOMETHASONE

Summary of Differences

Pharmacology: See *Pharmacology*.
Precautions: Cross-sensitivity and/or related problems—Nasal spray dosage form contains no fluorocarbon propellants.
Side/adverse effects: Systemic adverse effects may occur if the recommended prescribing limits are exceeded.

Additional Dosing Information

Regular use is required to obtain full therapeutic benefit. Medication should be discontinued if improvement is not evident after 3 weeks.

Nasal Dosage Forms

BECLOMETHASONE DIPROPIONATE NASAL AEROSOL

Usual adult dose: Nasal, 42 or 50 mcg (0.042 or 0.05 mg—1 metered spray) in each nostril two to four times a day (total daily dose, 168 to 400 mcg [0.168 to 0.4 mg]).
Note: Some patients may be maintained on 42 or 50 mcg (0.042 or 0.05 mg—1 metered spray) in each nostril three times a day (total daily dose, 252 or 300 mcg [0.252 or 0.3 mg]).
Usual adult prescribing limits: Nasal, 840 mcg (0.84 mg) or 1 mg (20 metered sprays) per day.
Note: If orally inhaled beclomethasone is used concurrently, usual adult prescribing limit is 420 or 500 mcg (0.42 or 0.5 mg—10 metered sprays) per day.
Usual pediatric prescribing limits: Nasal, 420 or 500 mcg (0.42 or 0.5 mg—10 metered sprays) per day. If orally inhaled beclomethasone is used concurrently, usual pediatric prescribing limits are 210 or 250 mcg (0.21 to 0.25 mg—5 metered sprays) per day.

Auxiliary labeling:
- For the nose.
- Shake well.

BECLOMETHASONE DIPROPIONATE MONOHYDRATE NASAL SPRAY

Usual adult dose: Nasal, 42 or 50 mcg (0.042 or 0.05 mg—1 metered spray) or 84 or 100 mcg (0.084 or 0.1 mg—2 metered sprays) in each nostril two times a day (total daily dose 168 to 400 mcg [0.168 to 0.4 mg]).
Usual adult prescribing limits: Nasal, 504 or 600 mcg (0.504 or 0.6 mg—12 metered sprays) per day.
Note: If orally inhaled beclomethasone is used concurrently, the combined daily dose should not exceed 840 mcg (0.84 mg) or 1 mg (20 metered sprays), the usual adult prescribing limits for beclomethasone dipropionate.

Auxiliary labeling:
- For the nose.
- Shake well.

DEXAMETHASONE

Summary of Differences

Indications: Less frequently used due to significantly increased incidence of adverse effects.
Pharmacology: See *Pharmacology*.
Precautions: Laboratory value alterations—False-negative results may occur with nitroblue tetrazolium test for bacterial infections.
Side/adverse effects:
HPA axis suppression or other systemic adrenocorticoid effects may occur with usual nasal inhalation doses.
See also *Side/Adverse Effects*.

Additional Dosing Information

When medication is to be discontinued, dosage usually should be reduced gradually depending on the dose, frequency, and duration of therapy.
Use of dexamethasone should be limited to a maximum of 2 weeks.

Nasal Dosage Forms

DEXAMETHASONE SODIUM PHOSPHATE NASAL AEROSOL

Note: Dexamethasone sodium phosphate nasal aerosol is not commercially available in Canada.
Usual adult dose: Nasal, initially 200 mcg (0.2 mg—2 metered sprays) of dexamethasone phosphate in each nostril two or three times a day (total daily dose, 800 mcg [0.8 mg] to 1.2 mg of dexamethasone phosphate), the dosage then being decreased according to patient response.
Note: Some patients may be maintained on 100 mcg (0.1 mg—1 metered spray) of dexamethasone phosphate in each nostril two times a day.
Usual adult prescribing limits: Up to 1.2 mg (12 metered sprays) of dexamethasone phosphate per day.

Auxiliary labeling:
- For the nose.
- Shake well.

FLUNISOLIDE

Summary of Differences

Pharmacology: See *Pharmacology*.
Precautions: Cross-sensitivity and/or related problems—Dosage form contains no fluorocarbon propellants.
Side/adverse effects: Systemic adverse effects may occur if the recommended prescribing limits are exceeded.

Additional Dosing Information

Regular use is required to obtain full therapeutic benefits. Discontinue medication if improvement is not evident after 3 weeks.

Nasal Dosage Forms

FLUNISOLIDE NASAL SOLUTION USP

Usual adult dose:
Initial—Nasal, 50 mcg (0.05 mg—2 metered sprays) in each nostril two times a day (total daily dose, 200 mcg [0.2 mg]); if necessary, dosing frequency may be increased to three times a day (total daily dose, 300 mcg [0.3 mg]).
Maintenance—Nasal, 25 mcg (0.025 mg—1 metered spray) in each nostril once a day (total daily dose, 50 mcg [0.05 mg]).
Usual adult prescribing limits: Up to 200 mcg (0.2 mg—8 metered sprays) in each nostril per day (total daily dose, 400 mcg [0.4 mg]).

Auxiliary labeling: • For the nose.

CORTICOSTEROIDS   Topical

INN: Included in brackets after individual generic listings, if different from U.S. generic names.

Some commonly used *brand names* are:

In the U.S.—

Aclovate [Alclometasone]

Acticort 100 [Hydrocortisone]

Aeroseb-Dex [Dexamethasone]

Aeroseb-HC [Hydrocortisone]

Ala-Cort [Hydrocortisone]

Ala-Scalp HP [Hydrocortisone]

Allercort [Hydrocortisone]

Alphaderm [Hydrocortisone]

Alphatrex [Betamethasone]

Anucort-HC [Hydrocortisone]

Anusol-HC [Hydrocortisone]

Aristocort [Triamcinolone]

Aristocort A [Triamcinolone]

Bactine [Hydrocortisone]

Beta-HC [Hydrocortisone]

Betatrex [Betamethasone]

Beta-Val [Betamethasone]

Bio-Syn [Fluocinolone]

CaldeCORT Anti-Itch [Hydrocortisone]

CaldeCORT Light [Hydrocortisone]

Carmol-HC [Hydrocortisone]

Cetacort [Hydrocortisone]

Cloderm [Clocortolone]

Cordran [Flurandrenolide]

Cordran SP [Flurandrenolide]

Cortaid [Hydrocortisone]

Cort-Dome [Hydrocortisone]

Cort-Dome High Potency [Hydrocortisone]

Cortef Feminine Itch [Hydrocortisone]

Corticaine [Hydrocortisone]

Cortifair [Hydrocortisone]

Cortril [Hydrocortisone]

Cutivate [Fluticasone]

Cyclocort [Amcinonide]

Decaderm [Dexamethasone]

Decadron [Dexamethasone]

Decaspray [Dexamethasone]

Delacort [Hydrocortisone]

Delta-Tritex [Triamcinolone]

Dermabet [Betamethasone]

Dermacort [Hydrocortisone]

Dermarest DriCort [Hydrocortisone]

DermiCort [Hydrocortisone]

Dermtex HC [Hydrocortisone]

DesOwen [Desonide]

Diprolene [Betamethasone]

Diprolene AF [Betamethasone]

Diprosone [Betamethasone]

Elocon [Mometasone]

Epifoam [Hydrocortisone]

Florone [Diflorasone]

Florone E [Diflorasone]

Fluocet [Fluocinolone]

Fluocin [Fluocinonide]

Fluonid [Fluocinolone]

Flurosyn [Fluocinolone]

Flutex [Triamcinolone]

FoilleCort [Hydrocortisone]

Gly-Cort [Hydrocortisone]

Gynecort [Hydrocortisone]

Gynecort 10 [Hydrocortisone]

Halog [Halcinonide]

Halog-E [Halcinonide]

Hemril-HC [Hydrocortisone]

Hi-Cor 1.0 [Hydrocortisone]

Hi-Cor 2.5 [Hydrocortisone]

Hydro-Tex [Hydrocortisone]

Hytone [Hydrocortisone]

Kenac [Triamcinolone]

Kenalog [Triamcinolone]

Kenalog-H [Triamcinolone]

Kenalog in Orabase [Triamcinolone]

Kenonel [Triamcinolone]

LactiCare-HC [Hydrocortisone]

Lanacort [Hydrocortisone]

Lanacort 10 [Hydrocortisone]

Lemoderm [Hydrocortisone]

Licon [Fluocinonide]

Lidex [Fluocinonide]

Lidex-E [Fluocinonide]

Locoid [Hydrocortisone]

Maxiflor [Diflorasone]

Maximum Strength Cortaid [Hydrocortisone]

Maxivate [Betamethasone]

MyCort [Hydrocortisone]

9-1-1 [Hydrocortisone]

Nutracort [Hydrocortisone]

Orabase-HCA [Hydrocortisone]

Oracort [Triamcinolone]

Oralone [Triamcinolone]

Penecort [Hydrocortisone]

Pentacort [Hydrocortisone]

Pharma-Cort [Hydrocortisone]

Proctocort [Hydrocortisone]

Psorcon [Diflorasone]

Rederm [Hydrocortisone]

Rhulicort [Hydrocortisone]

S-T Cort [Hydrocortisone]

Synacort [Hydrocortisone]

Synalar [Fluocinolone]

Synalar-HP [Fluocinolone]

Synemol [Fluocinolone]

In Canada—

Aristocort C [Triamcinolone]

Aristocort D [Triamcinolone]

Aristocort R [Triamcinolone]

Barriere-HC [Hydrocortisone]

Beben [Betamethasone]

Betacort Scalp Lotion [Betamethasone]

Betaderm [Betamethasone]

Betaderm Scalp Lotion [Betamethasone]

Betnovate [Betamethasone]

Betnovate-1/2 [Betamethasone]

Celestoderm-V [Betamethasone]

Celestoderm-V/2 [Betamethasone]

Cortacet [Hydrocortisone]

Cortate [Hydrocortisone]

Cortef [Hydrocortisone]

Corticreme [Hydrocortisone]

Cortiment-10 [Hydrocortisone]

Cortiment-40 [Hydrocortisone]

Cortoderm [Hydrocortisone]

Cyclocort [Amcinonide]

Dermovate [Clobetasol]

Dermovate Scalp Lotion [Clobetasol]

Diprolene [Betamethasone]

Diprosone [Betamethasone]

Drenison [Flurandrenolide]

Drenison-1/4 [Flurandrenolide]

Ectosone Mild [Betamethasone]

Ectosone Regular [Betamethasone]

Ectosone Scalp Lotion [Betamethasone]

Teladar [Betamethasone]

Temovate [Clobetasol]

Temovate Scalp Application [Clobetasol]

Texacort [Hydrocortisone]

Topicort [Desoximetasone]

Topicort LP [Desoximetasone]

Triacet [Triamcinolone]

Triderm [Triamcinolone]

Tridesilon [Desonide]

Ultravate [Halobetasol]

Uticort [Betamethasone]

Valisone [Betamethasone]

Valisone Reduced Strength [Betamethasone]

Valnac [Betamethasone]

Westcort [Hydrocortisone]

Elocom [Mometasone]

Emo-Cort [Hydrocortisone]

Emo-Cort Scalp Solution [Hydrocortisone]

Eumovate [Clobetasone]

Florone [Diflorasone]

Fluoderm [Fluocinolone]

Fluolar [Fluocinolone]

Fluonide [Fluocinolone]

Halog [Halcinonide]

Hyderm [Hydrocortisone]

Kenalog [Triamcinolone]

Kenalog in Orabase [Triamcinolone]

Lidemol [Fluocinonide]

Lidex [Fluocinonide]

Locacorten [Flumethasone]

Lyderm [Fluocinonide]

Metaderm Mild [Betamethasone]

Metaderm Regular [Betamethasone]

Nerisone [Diflucortolone]

Nerisone Oily [Diflucortolone]

Novobetamet [Betamethasone]

Novohydrocort [Hydrocortisone]

Prevex B [Betamethasone]

Prevex HC [Hydrocortisone]

Propaderm [Beclomethasone]

Rectocort [Hydrocortisone]

Sarna HC 1.0% [Hydrocortisone]

Sential [Hydrocortisone]

Synalar [Fluocinolone]

Synamol [Fluocinolone]

Topicort [Desoximetasone]

Topicort Mild [Desoximetasone]

Topilene [Betamethasone]

Topisone [Betamethasone]

Topsyn [Fluocinonide]

Triaderm [Triamcinolone]

Trianide Mild [Triamcinolone]

Trianide Regular
  [Triamcinolone]
Tridesilon [Desonide]
Unicort [Hydrocortisone]

Valisone Scalp Lotion
  [Betamethasone]
Westcort [Hydrocortisone]

Other commonly used names are:

Beclometasone
  [Beclomethasone]
Cortisol [Hydrocortisone]

Fludroxycortide
  [Flurandrenolide]
Flumetasone
  [Flumethasone]

ALCLOMETASONE (DE200)†
Topical
  Alclometasone Dipropionate Cream USP†
    In the U.S.—*Aclovate*
  Alclometasone Dipropionate Ointment USP†
    In the U.S.—*Aclovate*

AMCINONIDE (DE200)
Topical
  Amcinonide Cream USP
    In the U.S. and Canada—*Cyclocort*
  Amcinonide Lotion
    In the U.S. and Canada—*Cyclocort*
  Amcinonide Ointment USP
    In the U.S. and Canada—*Cyclocort*

BECLOMETHASONE (DE200) [INN: Beclometasone]*
Topical
  Beclomethasone Dipropionate Cream*
    In Canada—*Propaderm*
  Beclomethasone Dipropionate Lotion*
    In Canada—*Propaderm*
  Beclomethasone Dipropionate Ointment*
    In Canada—*Propaderm*

BETAMETHASONE
Topical (DE200)
  Betamethasone Benzoate Cream
    In the U.S.—*Uticort*
  Betamethasone Benzoate Gel USP
    In the U.S.—*Uticort*
    In Canada—*Beben*
  Betamethasone Benzoate Lotion
    In the U.S.—*Uticort*
  Betamethasone Dipropionate Cream (Augmented)
    In the U.S.—*Diprolene AF*
    In Canada—*Diprolene*
  Betamethasone Dipropionate Cream USP
    In the U.S.—*Alphatrex; Diprosone; Maxivate; Teladar;* GENERIC
    In Canada—*Diprosone; Topilene; Topisone*
  Betamethasone Dipropionate Gel†
    In the U.S.—*Diprolene*
  Betamethasone Dipropionate Lotion (Augmented)†
    In the U.S.—*Diprolene*
  Betamethasone Dipropionate Lotion USP
    In the U.S.—*Alphatrex; Diprosone; Maxivate;* GENERIC
    In Canada—*Diprosone; Topisone*
  Betamethasone Dipropionate Ointment (Augmented)
    In the U.S. and Canada—*Diprolene*
  Betamethasone Dipropionate Ointment USP
    In the U.S.—*Alphatrex Diprosone; Maxivate;* GENERIC
    In Canada—*Diprosone; Topilene; Topisone*
  Betamethasone Dipropionate Topical Aerosol
    In the U.S.—*Diprosone*
  Betamethasone Valerate Cream USP
    In the U.S.—*Betatrex; Beta-Val; Dermabet; Valisone; Valisone Reduced Strength; Valnac;* GENERIC
    In Canada—*Betaderm; Betnovate; Betnovate-¹/₂; Celestoderm-V; Celestoderm-V/2; Ectosone Mild; Ectosone Regular; Metaderm Mild; Metaderm Regular; Novobetamet; Prevex B*

Betamethasone Valerate Lotion USP
  In the U.S.—*Betatrex; Beta-Val; Valisone;* GENERIC
  In Canada—*Betacort Scalp Lotion; Betaderm Scalp Lotion; Betnovate; Betnovate-¹/₂; Ectosone Mild; Ectosone Regular; Ectosone Scalp Lotion; Valisone Scalp Lotion*
Betamethasone Valerate Ointment USP
  In the U.S.—*Betatrex; Beta-Val; Valisone; Valnac;* GENERIC
  In Canada—*Betaderm; Betnovate; Betnovate-¹/₂; Celestoderm-V; Celestoderm-V/2; Metaderm Mild; Metaderm Regular*

CLOBETASOL (DE200)
Topical
  Clobetasol Propionate Cream
    In the U.S.—*Temovate*
    In Canada—*Dermovate*
  Clobetasol Propionate Solution
    In the U.S.—*Temovate Scalp Application*
    In Canada—*Dermovate Scalp Lotion*
  Clobetasol Propionate Ointment
    In the U.S.—*Temovate*
    In Canada—*Dermovate*

CLOBETASONE (DE200)*
Topical
  Clobetasone Butyrate Cream*
    In Canada—*Eumovate*
  Clobetasone Butyrate Ointment*
    In Canada—*Eumovate*

CLOCORTOLONE (DE200)†
Topical
  Clocortolone Pivalate Cream USP†
    In the U.S.—*Cloderm*

DESONIDE (DE200)
Topical
  Desonide Cream
    In the U.S.—*DesOwen; Tridesilon;* GENERIC
    In Canada—*Tridesilon*
  Desonide Lotion†
    In the U.S.—*DesOwen*
  Desonide Ointment
    In the U.S.—*DesOwen; Tridesilon*
    In Canada—*Tridesilon*

DESOXIMETASONE (DE200)
Topical
  Desoximetasone Cream USP
    In the U.S.—*Topicort; Topicort LP;* GENERIC
    In Canada—*Topicort; Topicort Mild*
  Desoximetasone Gel USP
    In the U.S. and Canada—*Topicort*
  Desoximetasone Ointment USP†
    In the U.S.—*Topicort*

DEXAMETHASONE (DE200)†
Topical
  Dexamethasone Gel USP†
    In the U.S.—*Decaderm*
  Dexamethasone Topical Aerosol USP (Solution)†
    In the U.S.—*Aeroseb-Dex; Decaspray*
  Dexamethasone Sodium Phosphate Cream USP†
    In the U.S.—*Decadron*

DIFLORASONE (DE200)
Topical
  Diflorasone Diacetate Cream USP
    In the U.S.—*Florone; Florone E; Maxiflor*
    In Canada—*Florone*
  Diflorasone Diacetate Ointment USP
    In the U.S.—*Florone; Maxiflor; Psorcon*
    In Canada—*Florone*

DIFLUCORTOLONE (DE200)*
Topical
  Diflucortolone Valerate Cream*
    In Canada—*Nerisone; Nerisone Oily*

Diflucortolone Valerate Ointment*
  In Canada—*Nerisone*
FLUMETHASONE (DE200) [INN: Flumetasone]*
Topical
  Flumethasone Pivalate Cream USP*
    In Canada—*Locacorten*
  Flumethasone Pivalate Ointment*
    In Canada—*Locacorten*
FLUOCINOLONE (DE200)
Topical
  Fluocinolone Acetonide Cream USP
    In the U.S.—*Bio-Syn; Fluocet; Flurosyn; Synalar; Synalar-HP; Synemol;* GENERIC
    In Canada—*Fluoderm; Fluolar; Fluonide; Synalar; Synamol*
  Fluocinolone Acetonide Ointment USP
    In the U.S.—*Flurosyn; Synalar;* GENERIC
    In Canada—*Fluoderm; Synalar*
  Fluocinolone Acetonide Topical Solution USP
    In the U.S.—*Fluonid; Synalar;* GENERIC
    In Canada—*Synalar*
FLUOCINONIDE (DE200)
Topical
  Fluocinonide Cream USP
    In the U.S.—*Fluocin; Licon; Lidex; Lidex-E;* GENERIC
    In Canada—*Lidemol; Lidex; Lyderm*
  Fluocinonide Gel USP
    In the U.S.—*Lidex;* GENERIC
    In Canada—*Topsyn*
  Fluocinonide Ointment USP
    In the U.S.—*Lidex;* GENERIC
    In Canada—*Lidex*
  Fluocinonide Topical Solution USP
    In the U.S.—*Lidex;* GENERIC
    In Canada—*Lidex*
FLURANDRENOLIDE (DE200) [INN: Fludroxycortide]
Topical
  Flurandrenolide Cream USP
    In the U.S.—*Cordran SP*
    In Canada—*Drenison; Drenison-¹/₄*
  Flurandrenolide Lotion USP†
    In the U.S.—*Cordran;* GENERIC
  Flurandrenolide Ointment USP
    In the U.S.—*Cordran*
    In Canada—*Drenison; Drenison-¹/₄*
  Flurandrenolide Tape USP
    In the U.S.—*Cordran*
    In Canada—*Drenison*
FLUTICASONE (DE200)†
Topical
  Fluticasone Propionate Cream†
    In the U.S.—*Cutivate*
  Fluticasone Propionate Ointment†
    In the U.S.—*Cutivate*
HALCINONIDE (DE200)
Topical
  Halcinonide Cream USP
    In the U.S.—*Halog; Halog-E*
    In Canada—*Halog*
  Halcinonide Ointment USP
    In the U.S. and Canada—*Halog*
  Halcinonide Topical Solution USP
    In the U.S. and Canada—*Halog*
HALOBETASOL (DE200) [INN: Ulobetasol]†
  Halobetasol Propionate Cream†
    In the U.S.—*Ultravate*
  Halobetasol Propionate Ointment†
    In the U.S.—*Ultravate*

HYDROCORTISONE [INN: Cortisol]
Dental (OR900)
  Hydrocortisone Acetate Dental Paste†
    In the U.S.—*Orabase-HCA*
Rectal (RS100)
  Hydrocortisone Cream USP†
    In the U.S.—*Proctocort*
  Hydrocortisone Rectal Ointment*
    In Canada—*Rectocort*
  Hydrocortisone Suppositories*
    In Canada—*Rectocort*
  Hydrocortisone Acetate Cream USP†
    In the U.S.—*Anusol-HC; Corticaine*
  Hydrocortisone Acetate Suppositories
    In the U.S.—*Anucort-HC; Anusol-HC; Cort-Dome High Potency; Hemril-HC;* GENERIC
    In Canada—*Cortiment-10; Cortiment-40*
Topical (DE200)
  Hydrocortisone Cream USP
    In the U.S.—*Ala-Cort; Allercort; Alphaderm; Anusol-HC; Bactine; Cort-Dome; Cortifair; Dermacort; DermiCort; Dermtex HC; Hi-Cor 1.0; Hi-Cor 2.5; Hydro-Tex; Hytone; Lemoderm; Nutracort; Penecort; Synacort;* GENERIC
    In Canada—*Barriere-HC; Cortate; Emo-Cort; Prevex HC; Sential; Unicort*
  Hydrocortisone Lotion USP
    In the U.S.—*Acticort 100; Ala-Cort; Ala-Scalp HP; Allercort; Beta-HC; Cetacort; Cort-Dome; Delacort; Dermacort; Gly-Cort; Hytone; LactiCare-HC; Lemoderm; MyCort; Nutra-cort; Pentacort; Rederm; S-T Cort;* GENERIC
    In Canada—*Cortate; Emo-Cort; Sarna HC 1.0%*
  Hydrocortisone Ointment USP
    In the U.S.—*Allercort; Cortril; Hytone; Lemoderm;* GENERIC
    In Canada—*Cortate; Cortef*
  Hydrocortisone Topical Solution
    In the U.S.—*Aeroseb-HC; CaldeCORT Anti-Itch; Cortaid; Maximum Strength Cortaid; Penecort; Texacort;* GENERIC
    In Canada—*Emo-Cort Scalp Solution*
  Hydrocortisone Acetate Cream USP
    In the U.S.—*Anusol-HC; CaldeCORT Light; Carmol-HC; Cortaid; Cortef Feminine Itch; Corticaine; Dermarest DriCort; FoilleCort; Gynecort; Gynecort 10; Lanacort; Lanacort 10; Maximum Strength Cortaid; 9-1-1; Pharma-Cort;* GENERIC
    In Canada—*Cortacet; Corticreme; Hyderm; Novohydrocort*
  Hydrocortisone Acetate Topical Aerosol Foam†
    In the U.S.—*Epifoam*
  Hydrocortisone Acetate Lotion USP†
    In the U.S.—*Cortaid; Rhulicort*
  Hydrocortisone Acetate Ointment USP
    In the U.S.—*Cortaid; Lanacort; Maximum Strength Cortaid;* GENERIC
    In Canada—*Cortef; Cortoderm; Novohydrocort*
  Hydrocortisone Butyrate Cream USP†
    In the U.S.—*Locoid*
  Hydrocortisone Butyrate Ointment†
    In the U.S.—*Locoid*
  Hydrocortisone Valerate Cream USP
    In the U.S. and Canada—*Westcort*
  Hydrocortisone Valerate Ointment
    In the U.S. and Canada—*Westcort*
MOMETASONE (DE200)
Topical
  Mometasone Furoate Cream
    In the U.S.—*Elocon*
    In Canada—*Elocom*
  Mometasone Furoate Lotion
    In the U.S.—*Elocon*
    In Canada—*Elocom*

Mometasone Furoate Ointment
    In the U.S.—*Elocon*
    In Canada—*Elocom*
TRIAMCINOLONE
Dental (OR900)
    Triamcinolone Acetonide Dental Paste USP
        In the U.S.—*Kenalog in Orabase; Oracort; Oralone*
        In Canada—*Kenalog in Orabase*
Topical (DE200)
    Triamcinolone Acetonide Cream USP
        In the U.S.—*Aristocort; Aristocort A; Delta-Tritex; Flutex; Kenac; Kenalog; Kenalog-H; Kenonel; Triacet; Triderm;* GENERIC
        In Canada—*Aristocort C; Aristocort D; Aristocort R; Kenalog; Triaderm; Trianide Mild; Trianide Regular*
    Triamcinolone Acetonide Lotion USP†
        In the U.S.—*Kenalog; Kenonel;* GENERIC
    Triamcinolone Acetonide Ointment USP
        In the U.S.—*Aristocort; Aristocort A; Flutex; Kenac; Kenalog; Kenonel;* GENERIC
        In Canada—*Aristocort D; Aristocort R; Kenalog; Triaderm*
    Triamcinolone Acetonide Topical Aerosol USP†
        In the U.S.—*Kenalog*

---

*Not commercially available in the U.S.
†Not commercially available in Canada.

Category: Corticosteroid (topical); anti-inflammatory, steroidal (topical).

Note: Beclomethasone, Clobetasone, Diflucortolone, and Flumethasone are not commercially available in the U.S. Therefore, there is no U.S. product labeling identifying approved indications for these medications.

Indications

Note: Bracketed information in the *Indications* section refers to uses not included in U.S. product labeling.

Accepted

Skin disorders (treatment)—Topical corticosteroids are indicated to provide symptomatic relief of inflammation and/or pruritus associated with acute and chronic corticosteroid-responsive disorders.

The location of the skin lesion to be treated should be considered in selecting a formulation. In areas with thinner skin, such as facial, eye, and intertriginous areas, low-potency corticosteroid preparations are preferred for long-term therapy. Low- to medium-potency products may be used on the ears, trunk, arms, legs, and scalp. Medium- to very high-potency formulations may be required for treatment of dermatologic disorders in areas with thicker skin, such as the palms and soles. Lotion, aerosol, and gel formulations are cosmetically better suited for hairy areas.

The type of lesion to be treated should also be considered in product selection. For dry, scaly, cracked, thickened, or hardened skin, ointments of medium potency are often used. Medium-potency lotions, aerosols, or creams are preferred in treating moister, weeping lesions or areas or in treating conditions with intense inflammation. High- to very high-potency ointments may be required to treat hyperkeratotic or thick skin lesions.

Topical corticosteroids of low to medium potency are used in the treatment of the following dermatologic disorders. Occlusive dressings may also be required for chronic or severe cases of lichen simplex chronicus, psoriasis, eczema, atopic dermatitis, or chronic hand eczema. The more potent topical corticosteroids and/or occlusive dressings may be required for conditions such as discoid lupus erythematosus, lichen planus, granuloma annulare, psoriatic plaques, and psoriasis affecting the palms, soles, elbows, or knees.

Dermatitis, atopic, mild to moderate;
Dermatitis, contact;
Dermatitis, nummular, mild;
Dermatitis, seborrheic, facial and intertriginous areas;
Dermatoses, inflammatory, other, mild to moderate;
Dermatitis, other forms of, mild to moderate;
Intertrigo;
Lichen planus, facial and intertriginous areas;
Lupus erythematosus, discoid, facial and intertriginous areas;
Polymorphous light eruption;
Pruritus, anogenital;
Pruritus senilis;
Psoriasis, facial and intertriginous areas; or
Xerosis, inflammatory phase

Topical corticosteroids of medium to very high potency are used in the treatment of the following dermatologic disorders. Systemic therapy with, or intralesional injection of, a corticosteroid may be required for some of the disorders, as determined by the type and severity of the condition or inadequate response to topical therapy. Occlusive dressings may also be required for conditions such as discoid lupus erythematosus; bullous disorders; lichen planus; granuloma annulare; psoriatic plaques; and psoriasis affecting the palms, soles, elbows, or knees.

Alopecia areata;
Dermatitis, atopic, moderate to severe;
Dermatitis, exfoliative, generalized;
Dermatitis, nummular, moderate to severe;
Dermatoses, inflammatory, other, moderate to severe;
Dermatitis, other forms of, moderate to severe;
Granuloma annulare;
Keloids, reduction of associated itching;
Lichen planus;
Lichen simplex chronicus;
Lichen striatus;
Lupus erythematosus, discoid and subacute cutaneous;
Myxedema, pretibial;
Necrobiosis lipoidica diabeticorum;
Pemphigoid;
Pemphigus;
Pityriasis rosea;
Psoriasis;
Sarcoidosis; or
Sunburn

Rectal disorders (treatment)—
    Hydrocortisone rectal suppositories are indicated as adjuvants in the treatment of ulcerative colitis of the rectum.
    Hydrocortisone rectal ointment and suppositories are indicated in the treatment of inflammatory rectal disorders, such as cryptitis, inflamed hemorrhoids, and postirradiation or factitial proctitis.
    Hydrocortisone rectal dosage forms are indicated in the treatment of anogenital pruritus.

Oral lesions, inflammatory or ulcerative (treatment)—
    Hydrocortisone acetate and triamcinolone acetonide dental pastes are indicated for adjunctive treatment and temporary relief of symptoms associated with nonherpetic oral inflammatory and ulcerative lesions, including recurrent aphthous stomatitis. [Formulations of high potency gels and very high potency ointments are also used in the treatment of aphthous stomatitis.][1]
    [These agents are also used to treat other gingival disorders, such as desquamative gingivitis and oral lichen planus when the diagnosis has been confirmed by biopsy testing. Gel formulations of high potency corticosteroids and dental triamcinolone are used in the treatment of lichen planus of the mucous membranes.][1]
    [Other topical corticosteroids are also used to treat gingival disorders.][1]

Unaccepted

Medium to very high potency topical corticosteroids should not be used in the treatment of rosacea and perioral dermatitis. Although topical corticosteroids may initially reduce the burning and pustulation associated with rosacea, a severe rebound flare-up may occur upon discontinuance of the steroid.

Topical corticosteroids should not be used in the treatment of acne.

Topical corticosteroids are not indicated for routine gingivitis, which should be treated by the removal of local causative factors and an improvement in oral hygiene.

---

[1]Not included in Canadian product labeling.

Pharmacology

Mechanism of action/Effect: Corticosteroids diffuse across cell membranes and complex with specific cytoplasmic receptors. These complexes then enter the cell nucleus, bind to DNA (chromatin), and stimulate transcription of messenger RNA (mRNA) and subsequent protein synthesis of various inhibitory enzymes responsible for anti-inflammatory effects of topical corticosteroids. These anti-inflammatory effects include inhibition of early processes such as edema, fibrin deposition, capillary dilatation, movement of phagocytes into the area, and phagocytic activities. Later processes, such as capillary production, collagen deposition, and keloid formation, are also inhibited by corticosteroids. The overall actions of topical corticosteroids are catabolic.

Factors that increase the clinical efficacy and potential for adverse effects of topical corticosteroids include enhancement of pharmacologic activity of the compound by altering molecular structure, increasing stratum corneum penetration of the compound, and increasing bioavailability of the compound from the vehicle.

The pharmacologic activity of topical corticosteroids is increased by several changes in molecular structure. Addition of a 9-alpha-fluorine atom increases the anti-inflammatory glucocorticoid activity, but simultaneously increases undesired mineralocorticoid activity. Mineralocorticoid activity is diminished by addition of a 16-hydroxy or 16-methyl group. Substitution or masking of 16- or 17-hydroxy groups with longer side chains such as acetonide, propionate, or valerate increases lipophilicity and subsequently stratum corneum penetration.

Dental paste in dental dosage forms acts as an adhesive vehicle for application of corticosteroids to oral mucosa. The vehicle also reduces pain by serving as a protective covering.

Precautions to Consider

Geriatrics

Although appropriate studies with topical corticosteroids have not been performed in the geriatric population, geriatrics-specific problems are not expected to limit the usefulness of topical corticosteroids in the elderly. However, elderly patients may be more likely to have pre-existing skin atrophy secondary to aging. Purpura and skin lacerations that may raise the skin and subcutaneous tissue from deep fascia may be more likely to occur with the use of topical corticosteroids in geriatric patients. Therefore, topical corticosteroids should be used infrequently, for brief periods, or under close medical supervision in patients with evidence of pre-existing skin atrophy. Use of lower potency topical corticosteroids may also be necessary in some patients.

Contraindications/Medical problems

The contraindications/medical problems included have been selected on the basis of their potential clinical significance (reasons given in parentheses where appropriate)—not necessarily inclusive (» = major clinical significance).

Risk-benefit should be considered when the following medical problems exist:

Allergy to corticosteroids

Infection at treatment site
(may be exacerbated if no appropriate antimicrobial agent is used concurrently)

Skin atrophy, pre-existing
(may be exacerbated due to atrophigenic properties of corticosteroids)

For use in the oral cavity

Herpes simplex at treatment site
(may be transmitted to other sites, including the eye)

With long-term use of more potent formulations or if substantial absorption occurs

Cataracts
(corticosteroids may promote progression of cataracts, especially with the use of high- to very high-potency products in periorbital area)

Diabetes mellitus
(loss of control of diabetes may occur due to possible elevations in blood glucose)

Glaucoma
(intraocular pressure may be increased, especially with the use of high- to very high-potency products in periorbital area)

Tuberculosis
(may be exacerbated or reactivated; appropriate antitubercular chemotherapy or prophylaxis should be administered concurrently)

Side/Adverse Effects

Note: Generally, local or systemic adverse effects do not often occur with the use of low-potency topical corticosteroids. However, as with all topical corticosteroids, the incidence and severity of local or systemic side effects increase with factors that increase percutaneous absorption.

Percutaneous absorption of topical corticosteroids has resulted in systemic side effects such as hyperglycemia, glycosuria, and hypothalamic-pituitary-adrenal (HPA) axis suppression. HPA axis suppression has resulted from use of low doses of very high-potency products. HPA axis suppression has also resulted from use of less potent topical steroid preparations when occlusive dressings or excessive quantities were used. In all cases of HPA axis suppression, the effect was reversible upon discontinuation of therapy.

The following side/adverse effects have been selected on the basis of their potential clinical significance (possible signs and symptoms in parentheses where appropriate)—not necessarily inclusive:

Those indicating the need for medical attention
Incidence less frequent or rare

Allergic contact dermatitis (burning and itching of skin, apparent chronic therapeutic failure)—may also be caused by vehicle ingredients; *folliculitis, furunculosis, pustules, pyoderma, or vesiculation* (painful, red or itchy, pus-containing blisters in hair follicles)—more frequent with occlusion or use of ointments in intertriginous areas; *hyperesthesia* (increased skin sensitivity); *numbness in fingers; purpura* (blood-containing blisters on skin); *rectal irritation* (rectal bleeding, pain, burning, itching, or blistering not present before therapy)—for rectal dosage forms; *skin atrophy* (thinning of skin with easy bruising, especially when used on facial or intertriginous areas); *skin infection, secondary*—more frequent with occlusion; *stripping of epidermal layer*—for tape dosage forms; *telangiectasia* (raised, dark red, wart-like spots on skin, especially when used on the face)

Incidence rare—with prolonged use or other factors that increase absorption

> *Acneiform eruptions* (acne or oily skin, especially when used on the face); *cataracts, posterior subcapsular* (gradual blurring or loss of vision)—reported with use of systemic corticosteroids; caution advised with use of high- and very high-potency topical corticosteroids in periorbital area; *Cushing's syndrome* (filling or rounding out of the face, unusual tiredness or weakness, backache, irritability, mental depression, menstrual irregularities; in men—unusual decrease in sexual desire or ability); *dermatitis, perioral* (irritation of skin around mouth); *ecchymosis; edema* (increased blood pressure, swelling of feet or lower legs, rapid weight gain); *gastric ulcer* (stomach bloating, pain, cramping, or burning; loss of appetite; weight loss; nausea; vomiting); *glaucoma, secondary* (eye pain, gradual decrease in vision, nausea, vomiting)—with use of high- and very high-potency topical corticosteroids in periorbital area; *hirsutism or hypertrichosis* (unusual increase in hair growth, especially on the face); *hypertension; hypokalemic syndrome* (severe weakness of extremities and trunk, loss of appetite, nausea, vomiting, irregular heartbeat, muscle cramps or pain); *hypopigmentation* (lightened skin color) *or skin pigmentation changes, other; infection, aggravation of; miliaria rubra* (burning and itching of skin with pinhead-sized red blisters); *protein depletion* (muscle weakness); *skin laceration* (tearing of skin); *skin maceration* (softening of skin); *striae* (reddish purple lines on arms, face, legs, trunk, or groin); *subcutaneous tissue atrophy; unusual loss of hair*—especially on the scalp

Those indicating need for medical attention only if they continue or are bothersome

Incidence less frequent or rare

> *Burning, dryness, irritation, itching, or redness of skin, mild and transient; increased redness or scaling of skin lesions, mild and transient; skin rash, minor and transient*

Patient Consultation

In providing consultation, consider emphasizing the following selected information (» = major clinical significance):

Before using this medication

» Conditions affecting use, especially:

　Allergies to corticosteroids

　Pregnancy—Use restricted because of possible fetal abnormalities

　Breast-feeding—Should not be applied to the breasts prior to nursing

　Use in children—Adrenal suppression, Cushing's syndrome, intracranial hypertension, growth retardation possible with improper use

　Use in the elderly—Caution recommended because purpura, skin lacerations may be more likely

Proper use of this medication

Proper administration technique:

For all topical corticosteroids

　Keeping away from eyes

» Not bandaging or otherwise wrapping the treated skin area unless directed to do so by physician

　Proper use of occlusive dressing, if prescribed

For dental paste dosage forms

　Applying with cotton applicator; pressing, not rubbing, paste on lesion

　Applying at bedtime and after meals for maximum effect

For aerosol dosage forms

　Reading and following patient directions carefully

　Avoiding breathing vapors of spray

　Avoiding getting vapors of spray in eyes

　Not smoking while using aerosols

　Not using aerosols near open flame

For flurandrenolide tape

　Reading and following patient directions carefully

For rectal cream or ointment dosage forms

　Reading and following patient directions carefully

For rectal suppository dosage forms

　Proper insertion technique

» Importance of not using more medication than the amount prescribed or recommended on package

» Checking with physician before using medication for other dental, skin, or rectal problems

　Missed dose: Using as soon as possible; not using if almost time for next dose

» Proper storage

Precautions while using this medication

» Checking with physician or dentist if symptoms do not improve within 1 week or condition becomes worse

For topical dosage forms

　Not using tight-fitting diapers or plastic pants on a child if the diaper area is being treated with this medication

Side/adverse effects

　Possible stinging when gel, lotion, solution, or aerosol form of medication is applied

　Signs of potential side effects, especially development of additional dermatologic problems, or rectal irritation (for rectal dosage forms)

General Dosing Information

For rectal and topical dosage forms

To minimize the possibility of significant systemic absorption of corticosteroids during long term therapy, treatment may be interrupted periodically, small amounts of the preparation may be applied, or one area of the body may be treated at a time.

Occlusion, whether by oleaginous ointment, a thin film of polyethylene, dermatological patch, or tape, promotes increased hydration of the stratum corneum and increased absorption. Rarely, body temperature may be elevated if large areas are covered with an occlusive dressing; occlusive dressings should not be used if body temperature is elevated. Use of intermittent, rather than continuous, occlusion may decrease the risk of side effects. Generally, occlusive dressings should be changed every 24 hours or more frequently. Very high-potency topical corticosteroid formulations should not be used with occlusive dressings.

Rarely, gradual withdrawal of therapy or supplemental systemic corticosteroid therapy may be required to avoid symptoms of steroid withdrawal. Gradual withdrawal of therapy by decreasing frequency of application or by using products of decreasing potency may be necessary also to avoid a rebound flare-up of certain conditions such as psoriasis. Tachyphylaxis may also result from continual usage.

Certain topical corticosteroids may be used as adjunctive therapy to antimicrobial agents for controlling inflammation, erythema, and pruritus associated with bacterial or fungal skin infections. If symptomatic relief is not noted within a few days to one week, the topical corticosteroid should be discontinued until the infection is controlled.

For dental dosage forms only

Applying the paste with a cotton applicator will help to eliminate any possible absorption from contact with the skin.

The paste should be pressed, not rubbed, on the lesion. Rubbing the paste on the lesion will result in a granular, gritty sensation and cause the medication to crumble. A smooth, slippery film forms after application.

If significant repair or regeneration of oral tissues has not occurred in 7 days, the etiology of the lesion should be reinvestigated.

ALCLOMETASONE

Summary of Differences

Pharmacology:
 Substituted; non-fluorinated.
 Potency ranking—Low.

Topical Dosage Forms

ALCLOMETASONE DIPROPIONATE CREAM USP

Usual adult dose: Topical, to the skin, as a 0.05% cream two or three times a day.

Auxiliary labeling:
 • For external use only.
 • Do not use in or around the eye.

ALCLOMETASONE DIPROPIONATE OINTMENT USP

Usual adult dose: Topical, to the skin, as a 0.05% ointment two or three times a day.

Auxiliary labeling:
 • For external use only.
 • Do not use in or around the eye.

AMCINONIDE

Summary of Differences

Pharmacology:
 Substituted; fluorinated.
 Potency ranking—High.

Topical Dosage Forms

AMCINONIDE CREAM USP

Usual adult dose: Topical, to the skin, as a 0.1% cream two or three times a day.

Auxiliary labeling:
 • For external use only.
 • Do not use in or around the eye.

AMCINONIDE LOTION

Usual adult dose: Topical, to the skin, as a 0.1% lotion two or three times a day.

Auxiliary labeling:
 • For external use only.
 • Do not use in or around the eye.

AMCINONIDE OINTMENT USP

Usual adult dose: Topical, to the skin, as a 0.1% ointment two times a day.

Auxiliary labeling:
 • For external use only.
 • Do not use in or around the eye.

BECLOMETHASONE

Summary of Differences

Pharmacology:
 Substituted; non-fluorinated.
 Potency ranking—Medium.

Topical Dosage Forms

BECLOMETHASONE DIPROPIONATE CREAM

Usual adult dose: Topical, to the skin, as a 0.025% cream one or two times a day.

Auxiliary labeling:
 • For external use only.
 • Do not use in or around the eye.

BECLOMETHASONE DIPROPIONATE LOTION

Usual adult dose: Topical, to the skin, as a 0.025% lotion one or two times a day.

Auxiliary labeling:
 • For external use only.
 • Do not use in or around the eye.

BECLOMETHASONE DIPROPIONATE OINTMENT

Usual adult dose: Topical, to the skin, as a 0.025% ointment one or two times a day.

Auxiliary labeling:
 • For external use only.
 • Do not use in or around the eye.

BETAMETHASONE

Summary of Differences

Pharmacology:
 Substituted (benzoate, dipropionate, valerate); fluorinated (base, benzoate, dipropionate, valerate).
 Potency ranking—
  Betamethasone benzoate, Medium.
  Betamethasone dipropionate (except for *Diprolene* and *Diprolene AF* products), High.
  Diprolene and *Diprolene AF* products, Very high.
  Betamethasone valerate, Medium.

Topical Dosage Forms

BETAMETHASONE BENZOATE CREAM

Usual adult dose: Topical, to the skin, as a 0.025% cream two to four times a day.

Auxiliary labeling:
 • For external use only.
 • Do not use in or around the eye.

BETAMETHASONE BENZOATE GEL USP

Usual adult dose: Topical, to the skin, as a 0.025% gel two to four times a day.

Auxiliary labeling:
 • For external use only.
 • Do not use in or around the eye.

BETAMETHASONE BENZOATE LOTION

Usual adult dose: Topical, to the skin, as a 0.025% lotion two to four times a day.

Auxiliary labeling:
- For external use only.
- Do not use in or around the eye.
- Shake well.

BETAMETHASONE DIPROPIONATE CREAM (AUGMENTED)

Note: The dosing and strengths of betamethasone dipropionate cream (augmented) are expressed in terms of betamethasone base.

Usual adult dose: Topical, to the skin, as a 0.05% (base) cream one or two times a day. Augmented betamethasone dipropionate cream may be used for only a short duration of therapy and on small surface areas. Occlusive dressings should not be used.

Auxiliary labeling:
- For external use only.
- Do not use in or around the eye.

BETAMETHASONE DIPROPIONATE CREAM USP

Note: The dosing and strengths of betamethasone dipropionate cream are expressed in terms of betamethasone base.

Usual adult dose: Topical, to the skin, as a 0.05% (base) cream one or two times a day.

Auxiliary labeling:
- For external use only.
- Do not use in or around the eye.

BETAMETHASONE DIPROPIONATE GEL

Note: The dosing and strengths of betamethasone dipropionate gel are expressed in terms of betamethasone base.

Usual adult dose: Topical, to the skin, as a 0.05% (base) gel one or two times a day. Betamethasone dipropionate gel may be used for only a short duration of therapy and on small surface areas. Occlusive dressings should not be used.

Auxiliary labeling:
- For external use only.
- Do not use in or around the eye.

BETAMETHASONE DIPROPIONATE LOTION (AUGMENTED)

Note: The dosing and strengths of betamethasone dipropionate lotion (augmented) are expressed in terms of betamethasone base.

Usual adult dose: Topical, to the skin, as a 0.05% (base) lotion two times a day. Augmented betamethasone dipropionate lotion may be used for only a short duration of therapy and on small surface areas. Occlusive dressings should not be used.

Auxiliary labeling:
- For external use only.
- Do not use in or around the eye.
- Shake well.

BETAMETHASONE DIPROPIONATE LOTION USP

Note: The dosing and strengths of betamethasone dipropionate lotion are expressed in terms of betamethasone base.

Usual adult dose: Topical, to the skin, as a 0.05% (base) lotion two times a day.

Auxiliary labeling:
- For external use only.
- Do not use in or around the eye.
- Shake well.

BETAMETHASONE DIPROPIONATE OINTMENT (AUGMENTED)

Note: The dosing and strengths of betamethasone dipropionate ointment (augmented) are expressed in terms of betamethasone base.

Usual adult dose: Topical, to the skin, as a 0.05% (base) ointment one or two times a day. Augmented betamethasone dipropionate ointment may be used for only a short duration of therapy and on small surface areas. Occlusive dressings should not be used.

Auxiliary labeling:
- For external use only.
- Do not use in or around the eye.

BETAMETHASONE DIPROPIONATE OINTMENT USP

Note: The dosing and strengths of betamethasone dipropionate ointment are expressed in terms of betamethasone base.

Usual adult dose: Topical, to the skin, as a 0.05% (base) ointment one or two times a day.

Auxiliary labeling:
- For external use only.
- Do not use in or around the eye.

BETAMETHASONE DIPROPIONATE TOPICAL AEROSOL

Note: The dosing and strengths of betamethasone dipropionate topical aerosol are expressed in terms of betamethasone base.

Usual adult dose: Topical, to the skin, a three-second spray of a 0.1% (base) aerosol three times a day.

Auxiliary labeling:
- For external use only.
- Do not use in or around the eye.

BETAMETHASONE VALERATE CREAM USP

Note: The dosing and strengths of betamethasone valerate cream are expressed in terms of betamethasone base.

Usual adult dose: Topical, to the skin, as a 0.01 or 0.1% (base) cream one to three times a day.

Auxiliary labeling:
- For external use only.
- Do not use in or around the eye.

BETAMETHASONE VALERATE LOTION USP

Note: The dosing and strengths of betamethasone valerate lotion are expressed in terms of betamethasone base.

Usual adult dose: Topical, to the skin, as a 0.1% (base) lotion one or two times a day.

Auxiliary labeling:
- For external use only.
- Do not use in or around the eye.
- Shake well.

BETAMETHASONE VALERATE OINTMENT USP

Note: The dosing and strengths of betamethasone valerate ointment are expressed in terms of betamethasone base.

Usual adult dose: Topical, to the skin, as a 0.1% (base) ointment one to three times a day.

Auxiliary labeling:
- For external use only.
- Do not use in or around the eye.

CLOBETASOL

Summary of Differences

Pharmacology—
   Substituted; fluorinated.
   Potency rating: Very high.

Topical Dosage Forms

CLOBETASOL PROPIONATE CREAM

Usual adult dose: Topical, to the skin, as a 0.05% cream two or three times a day. Clobetasol propionate cream may be used for only a short duration of therapy and on small surface areas. Occlusive dressings should not be used.

Auxiliary labeling:
   • For external use only.
   • Do not use in or around the eye.

CLOBETASOL PROPIONATE SOLUTION

Usual adult dose: Topical, to the scalp, as a 0.05% solution two times a day. Clobetasol propionate solution may be used for only a short duration of therapy and on small surface areas. Occlusive dressings should not be used.

Auxiliary labeling:
   • For external use only.
   • Do not use in or around the eye.

CLOBETASOL PROPIONATE OINTMENT

Usual adult dose: Topical, to the skin, as a 0.05% ointment two or three times a day. Clobetasol propionate ointment may be used for only a short duration of therapy and on small surface areas. Occlusive dressings should not be used.

Auxiliary labeling:
   • For external use only.
   • Do not use in or around the eye.

CLOBETASONE

Summary of Differences

Pharmacology:
   Substituted; fluorinated.
   Potency rating—Medium.

Topical Dosage Forms

CLOBETASONE BUTYRATE CREAM

Usual adult dose: Topical, to the skin, as a 0.05% cream two or three times a day.

Usual adult prescribing limits: Topical, to the skin, up to 100 grams per week.

Auxiliary labeling:
   • For external use only.
   • Do not use in or around the eye.

CLOBETASONE BUTYRATE OINTMENT

Usual adult dose: Topical, to the skin, as a 0.05% ointment two or three times a day.

Usual adult prescribing limits: Topical, to the skin, up to 100 grams per week.

Auxiliary labeling:
   • For external use only.
   • Do not use in or around the eye.

CLOCORTOLONE

Summary of Differences

Pharmacology:
   Substituted; fluorinated.
   Potency rating—Low.

Topical Dosage Forms

CLOCORTOLONE PIVALATE CREAM USP

Usual adult dose: Topical, to the skin, as a 0.1% cream three times a day.

Auxiliary labeling:
   • For external use only.
   • Do not use in or around the eye.

DESONIDE

Summary of Differences

Pharmacology:
   Substituted; non-fluorinated.
   Potency rating—Low.

Topical Dosage Forms

DESONIDE CREAM

Usual adult dose: Topical, to the skin, as a 0.05% cream two to four times a day.

Auxiliary labeling:
   • For external use only.
   • Do not use in or around the eye.

DESONIDE LOTION

Usual adult dose: Topical, to the skin, as a 0.05% lotion two to four times a day.

Auxiliary labeling:
   • For external use only.
   • Shake well before using.
   • Do not use in or around the eye.

DESONIDE OINTMENT

Usual adult dose: Topical, to the skin, as a 0.05% ointment two to four times a day.

Auxiliary labeling:
   • For external use only.
   • Do not use in or around the eye.

DESOXIMETASONE

Summary of Differences

Pharmacology:
  Substituted (17-H); fluorinated.
  Potency rating—High (except cream 0.05%).
    Cream 0.05%, Medium.

Topical Dosage Forms

DESOXIMETASONE CREAM USP

Usual adult dose: Topical, to the skin, as a 0.05 or 0.25% cream two times a day.

Auxiliary labeling:
  • For external use only.
  • Do not use in or around the eye.

DESOXIMETASONE GEL USP

Usual adult dose: Topical, to the skin, as a 0.05% gel two times a day.

Auxiliary labeling:
  • For external use only.
  • Do not use in or around the eye.

DESOXIMETASONE OINTMENT USP

Usual adult dose: Topical, to the skin, as a 0.25% ointment two times a day.

Auxiliary labeling:
  • For external use only.
  • Do not use in or around the eye.

DEXAMETHASONE

Summary of Differences

Pharmacology:
  Unsubstituted; fluorinated.
  Potency rating—Low.

Topical Dosage Forms

DEXAMETHASONE GEL USP

Usual adult dose: Topical, to the skin, as a 0.1% gel three or four times a day.

Auxiliary labeling:
  • For external use only.
  • Do not use in or around the eye.

DEXAMETHASONE TOPICAL AEROSOL USP (SOLUTION)

Usual adult dose: Topical, to the skin, as a 0.01 or 0.04% aerosol two to four times a day.

Auxiliary labeling:
  • For external use only.
  • Do not use in or around the eye.
  • Shake gently.

DEXAMETHASONE SODIUM PHOSPHATE CREAM USP

Usual adult dose: Topical, to the skin, as a 0.1% (phosphate) cream three or four times a day.

Auxiliary labeling:
  • For external use only.
  • Do not use in or around the eye.

DIFLORASONE

Summary of Differences

Pharmacology:
  Substituted; fluorinated.
  Potency rating—High (except *Psorcon* ointment).
    Psorcon ointment, Very high.

Topical Dosage Forms

DIFLORASONE DIACETATE CREAM USP

Usual adult dose: Topical, to the skin, as a 0.05% cream one to four times a day.

Note: Some patients may be maintained with once daily applications after the initial acute symptoms subside. Once daily dosage may also be used to taper therapy before discontinuance.

Auxiliary labeling:
  • For external use only.
  • Do not use in or around the eye.

DIFLORASONE DIACETATE OINTMENT USP

Usual adult dose: Topical, to the skin, as a 0.05% ointment one to four times a day.

Note: Some patients may be maintained with once daily applications after the initial acute symptoms subside. Once daily dosage may also be used to taper therapy before discontinuance.

  Psorcon may be used for only a short duration of therapy and on small surface areas. Occlusive dressings should not be used with *Psorcon*.

Auxiliary labeling:
  • For external use only.
  • Do not use in or around the eye.

DIFLUCORTOLONE

Summary of Differences

Pharmacology:
  Unsubstituted; fluorinated.
  Potency rating—Medium.

Topical Dosage Forms

DIFLUCORTOLONE VALERATE CREAM

Usual adult dose: Topical, to the skin, as a 0.1% cream one to three times a day.

Note: Some patients may be maintained with once daily applications after the initial acute symptoms subside. Once daily dosage may also be used to taper therapy before discontinuance.

Usual adult prescribing limits: Topical, to the skin, up to 100 grams per week.

Auxiliary labeling:
  • For external use only.
  • Do not use in or around the eye.

DIFLUCORTOLONE VALERATE OINTMENT

Usual adult dose: Topical, to the skin, as a 0.1% ointment one to three times a day.

Note: Some patients may be maintained with once daily applications after the initial acute symptoms subside. Once daily dosage may also be used to taper therapy before discontinuance.

Usual adult prescribing limits: Topical, to the skin, up to 100 grams per week.

Auxiliary labeling:
- For external use only.
- Do not use in or around the eye.

FLUMETHASONE

Summary of Differences

Pharmacology:
Unsubstituted; fluorinated.
Potency rating—Low.

Topical Dosage Forms

FLUMETHASONE PIVALATE CREAM USP

Usual adult dose: Topical, to the skin, as a 0.03% cream one to three times a day.

Auxiliary labeling:
- For external use only.
- Do not use in or around the eye.

FLUMETHASONE PIVALATE OINTMENT

Usual adult dose: Topical, to the skin, as a 0.03% ointment one to three times a day.

Auxiliary labeling:
- For external use only.
- Do not use in or around the eye.

FLUOCINOLONE

Summary of Differences

Pharmacology:
Substituted; fluorinated.
Potency rating—Medium (except cream 0.2%).
Cream 0.2%, High.

Topical Dosage Forms

FLUOCINOLONE ACETONIDE CREAM USP

Usual adult dose: Topical, to the skin, as a 0.01 to 0.2% cream two to four times a day.

Auxiliary labeling:
- For external use only.
- Do not use in or around the eye.

FLUOCINOLONE ACETONIDE OINTMENT USP

Usual adult dose: Topical, to the skin, as a 0.025% ointment two to four times a day.

Auxiliary labeling:
- For external use only.
- Do not use in or around the eye.

FLUOCINOLONE ACETONIDE TOPICAL SOLUTION USP

Usual adult dose: Topical, to the skin, as a 0.01% solution two to four times a day.

Auxiliary labeling:
- For external use only.
- Do not use in or around the eye.

FLUOCINONIDE

Summary of Differences

Pharmacology:
Substituted; fluorinated.
Potency rating—High.

Topical Dosage Forms

FLUOCINONIDE CREAM USP

Usual adult dose: Topical, to the skin, as a 0.05% cream two to four times a day.

Auxiliary labeling:
- For external use only.
- Do not use in or around the eye.

FLUOCINONIDE GEL USP

Usual adult dose: Topical, to the skin, as a 0.05% gel two to four times a day.

Auxiliary labeling:
- For external use only.
- Do not use in or around the eye.

FLUOCINONIDE OINTMENT USP

Usual adult dose: Topical, to the skin, as a 0.05% ointment two to four times a day.

Auxiliary labeling:
- For external use only.
- Do not use in or around the eye.

FLUOCINONIDE TOPICAL SOLUTION USP

Usual adult dose: Topical, to the skin, as a 0.05% solution two to four times a day.

Auxiliary labeling:
- For external use only.
- Do not use in or around the eye.

FLURANDRENOLIDE

Summary of Differences

Pharmacology:
Substituted; fluorinated.
Potency ranking—Medium (except cream and ointment 0.0125%).
Cream and ointment 0.0125%, Low.

Topical Dosage Forms

FLURANDRENOLIDE CREAM USP

Usual adult dose: Topical, to the skin, as a 0.025 or 0.05% cream two or three times a day.

Auxiliary labeling:
- For external use only.
- Do not use in or around the eye.

FLURANDRENOLIDE LOTION USP

Usual adult dose: Topical, to the skin, as a 0.05% lotion two or three times a day.

Auxiliary labeling:
- For external use only.
- Do not use in or around the eye.
- Shake well.

FLURANDRENOLIDE OINTMENT USP

Usual adult dose: Topical, to the skin, as a 0.025 or 0.05% ointment two or three times a day.

Auxiliary labeling:
- For external use only.
- Do not use in or around the eye.

FLURANDRENOLIDE TAPE USP

Usual adult dose: Topical, to the skin, as a tape containing 4 mcg (0.004 mg) of flurandrenolide per square centimeter, to be replaced every twelve to twenty-four hours.

Auxiliary labeling: • For external use only.

Additional information: Tape of flexible polyethylene film impregnated with flurandrenolide in the acrylic adhesive serves as an occlusive dressing, and should not be used in intertriginous areas or applied to lesions exuding serum.

FLUTICASONE

Summary of Differences

Pharmacology:
  Substituted; fluorinated.
  Potency ranking—Medium.

Topical Dosage Forms

FLUTICASONE PROPIONATE CREAM

Usual adult dose: Topical, to the skin, as a 0.05% cream two times a day.

Auxiliary labeling:
- For external use only.
- Do not use in or around the eye.

FLUTICASONE PROPIONATE OINTMENT

Usual adult dose: Topical, to the skin, as a 0.005% ointment two times a day.

Auxiliary labeling:
- For external use only.
- Do not use in or around the eye.

HALCINONIDE

Summary of Differences

Pharmacology:
  Substituted; fluorinated.
  Potency ranking—High.

Topical Dosage Forms

HALCINONIDE CREAM USP

Usual adult dose: Topical, to the skin, as a 0.025 or 0.1% cream one to three times a day.

Auxiliary labeling:
- For external use only.
- Do not use in or around the eye.

HALCINONIDE OINTMENT USP

Usual adult dose: Topical, to the skin, as a 0.1% ointment two or three times a day.

Auxiliary labeling:
- For external use only.
- Do not use in or around the eye.

HALCINONIDE TOPICAL SOLUTION USP

Usual adult dose: Topical, to the skin, as a 0.1% solution two or three times a day.

Auxiliary labeling:
- For external use only.
- Do not use in or around the eye.

HALOBETASOL

Summary of Differences

Pharmacology:
  Substituted; fluorinated.
  Potency ranking—Very high.

Topical Dosage Forms

HALOBETASOL PROPIONATE CREAM

Usual adult dose: Topical, to the skin, as a 0.05% cream one or two times a day. Halobetasol propionate cream may be used for only a short duration of therapy and on small surface areas. Occlusive dressings should not be used.

Auxiliary labeling:
- For external use only.
- Do not use in or around the eye.

HALOBETASOL PROPIONATE OINTMENT

Usual adult dose: Topical, to the skin, as a 0.05% ointment one or two times a day. Halobetasol propionate ointment may be used for only a short duration of therapy and on small surface areas. Occlusive dressings should not be used.

Auxiliary labeling:
- For external use only.
- Do not use in or around the eye.

HYDROCORTISONE

Summary of Differences

Pharmacology:
  Substituted (butyrate, valerate); non-fluorinated.
  Potency ranking—Low (acetate and base); Medium (butyrate and valerate).

Dental Dosage Forms

HYDROCORTISONE ACETATE DENTAL PASTE

Usual adult dose: Topical, to the oral mucous membranes, as a 0.5% paste two or three times a day after meals and at bedtime.

Auxiliary labeling: • For use in the mouth only.

Rectal Dosage Forms

HYDROCORTISONE CREAM USP

Usual adult dose: Topical, to the anorectal area, as a 1% cream three or four times a day.

Auxiliary labeling: • For external use only.

HYDROCORTISONE RECTAL OINTMENT

Usual adult dose: Topical, to the anorectal area, as a 0.5 to 0.75% ointment one to four times a day.

Auxiliary labeling: • For external use only.

HYDROCORTISONE SUPPOSITORIES

Usual adult dose: Rectal, 20 to 30 mg a day.

Auxiliary labeling:
  • Store in a cool place.
  • May be refrigerated.
  • For rectal use only.

HYDROCORTISONE ACETATE CREAM USP

Usual adult dose: Topical, to the anorectal area, as a 0.5 or 1% cream one to four times a day.

Auxiliary labeling:
  • For external use only.
  • Do not use in or around the eye.

HYDROCORTISONE ACETATE SUPPOSITORIES

Usual adult dose: Rectal, up to 100 mg per day, in one to three divided doses.

Auxiliary labeling:
  • Store in a cool place.
  • May be refrigerated.
  • For rectal use only.

Topical Dosage Forms

HYDROCORTISONE CREAM USP

Usual adult dose: Topical, to the skin, as a 0.25 to 2.5% cream one to four times a day.

Auxiliary labeling:
  • For external use only.
  • Do not use in or around the eye.

HYDROCORTISONE LOTION USP

Usual adult dose: Topical, to the skin, as a 0.25 to 2.5% lotion one to four times a day.

Auxiliary labeling:
  • For external use only.
  • Do not use in or around the eye.
  • Shake well.

HYDROCORTISONE OINTMENT USP

Usual adult dose: Topical, to the skin, as a 0.5 to 2.5% ointment one to four times a day.

Auxiliary labeling:
  • For external use only.
  • Do not use in or around the eye.

HYDROCORTISONE TOPICAL SOLUTION

Usual adult dose: Topical, to the skin, as a 2.5% solution one to four times a day.

Auxiliary labeling:
  • For external use only.
  • Do not use in or around the eye.

HYDROCORTISONE ACETATE CREAM USP

Usual adult dose: Topical, to the skin, as a 0.1 to 1% cream one to four times a day.

Auxiliary labeling:
  • For external use only.
  • Do not use in or around the eye.

HYDROCORTISONE ACETATE TOPICAL AEROSOL FOAM

Usual adult dose: Topical, to the skin, as a 1% foam one to four times a day.

Auxiliary labeling:
  • Shake well.
  • For external use only.
  • Do not use in or around the eye.

HYDROCORTISONE ACETATE LOTION USP

Usual adult dose: Topical, to the skin, as a 0.5% lotion one to four times a day.

Auxiliary labeling:
  • For external use only.
  • Do not use in or around the eye.
  • Shake well.

HYDROCORTISONE ACETATE OINTMENT USP

Usual adult dose: Topical, to the skin, as a 0.5 to 2.5% ointment one to four times a day.

Auxiliary labeling:
  • For external use only.
  • Do not use in or around the eye.

HYDROCORTISONE BUTYRATE CREAM USP

Usual adult dose: Topical, to the skin, as a 0.1% cream two or three times a day.

Auxiliary labeling:
  • For external use only.
  • Do not use in or around the eye.

HYDROCORTISONE BUTYRATE OINTMENT

Usual adult dose: Topical, to the skin, as a 0.1% ointment two or three times a day.

Auxiliary labeling:
- For external use only.
- Do not use in or around the eye.

HYDROCORTISONE VALERATE CREAM USP

Usual adult dose: Topical, to the skin, as a 0.2% cream two or three times a day.

Auxiliary labeling:
- For external use only.
- Do not use in or around the eye.

HYDROCORTISONE VALERATE OINTMENT

Usual adult dose: Topical, to the skin, as a 0.2% ointment two or three times a day.

Auxiliary labeling:
- For external use only.
- Do not use in or around the eye.

MOMETASONE

Summary of Differences

Pharmacology:
　Substituted; non-fluorinated.
　Potency ranking—Medium.

Topical Dosage Forms

MOMETASONE FUROATE CREAM

Usual adult dose: Topical, to the skin, as a 0.1% cream once a day.

Auxiliary labeling:
- For external use only.
- Do not use in or around the eye.

MOMETASONE FUROATE LOTION

Usual adult dose: Topical, to the skin, as a 0.1% lotion once a day.

Auxiliary labeling:
- For external use only.
- Do not use in or around the eye.

MOMETASONE FUROATE OINTMENT

Usual adult dose: Topical, to the skin, as a 0.1% ointment once a day.

Auxiliary labeling:
- For external use only.
- Do not use in or around the eye.

TRIAMCINOLONE

Summary of Differences

Pharmacology:
　Substituted; fluorinated.
　Potency ranking—Medium (except cream and ointment 0.5%).
　　Cream and ointment 0.5%, High.

Dental Dosage Forms

TRIAMCINOLONE ACETONIDE DENTAL PASTE USP

Usual adult dose: Topical, to the oral mucous membranes, as a 0.1% paste two or three times a day after meals and at bedtime.

Auxiliary labeling: • For use in the mouth only.

Topical Dosage Forms

TRIAMCINOLONE ACETONIDE CREAM USP

Usual adult dose: Topical, to the skin, as a 0.025 to 0.5% cream two to four times a day.

Auxiliary labeling:
- For external use only.
- Do not use in or around the eye.

TRIAMCINOLONE ACETONIDE LOTION USP

Usual adult dose: Topical, to the skin, as a 0.025 or 0.1% lotion two to four times a day.

Auxiliary labeling:
- For external use only.
- Do not use in or around the eye.
- Shake well.

TRIAMCINOLONE ACETONIDE OINTMENT USP

Usual adult dose: Topical, to the skin, as a 0.025 to 0.5% ointment two to four times a day.

Auxiliary labeling:
- For external use only.
- Do not use in or around the eye.

TRIAMCINOLONE ACETONIDE TOPICAL AEROSOL USP

Usual adult dose: Topical, to the skin, as a 0.015% aerosol spray three or four times a day.

Auxiliary labeling:
- For external use only.
- Do not use in or around the eye.

CORTICOSTEROIDS/CORTICOTROPIN—Glucocorticoid Effects   Systemic

Some commonly used *brand names* are:

In the U.S.—

Acthar [Corticotropin]
A-hydroCort
　[Hydrocortisone]
AK-Dex [Dexamethasone]
Amcort [Triamcinolone]
A-methaPred
　[Methylprednisolone]
Aristocort [Triamcinolone]
Aristocort Forte
　[Triamcinolone]
Aristocort Intralesional
　[Triamcinolone]
Aristospan Intra-articular
　[Triamcinolone]
Aristospan Intralesional
　[Triamcinolone]
Articulose-50
　[Prednisolone]
Articulose-L.A.
　[Triamcinolone]
Celestone [Betamethasone]
Celestone Phosphate
　[Betamethasone]
Celestone Soluspan
　[Betamethasone]
Cenocort A-40
　[Triamcinolone]
Cenocort Forte
　[Triamcinolone]
Cinalone 40
　[Triamcinolone]
Cinonide 40
　[Triamcinolone]
Cortef [Hydrocortisone]
Cortenema
　[Hydrocortisone]
Cortifoam [Hydrocortisone]
Cortone Acetate [Cortisone]
Cortrophin-Zinc
　[Corticotropin]
Dalalone [Dexamethasone]
Dalalone D.P.
　[Dexamethasone]
Dalalone L.A.
　[Dexamethasone]
Decadrol [Dexamethasone]
Decadron [Dexamethasone]
Decadron-LA
　[Dexamethasone]
Decadron Phosphate
　[Dexamethasone]
Decaject [Dexamethasone]
Decaject-L.A.
　[Dexamethasone]
Delta-Cortef [Prednisolone]
Deltasone [Prednisone]
depMedalone 40
　[Methylprednisolone]
depMedalone 80
　[Methylprednisolone]
Depoject-40
　[Methylprednisolone]
Depoject-80
　[Methylprednisolone]

Depo-Medrol
　[Methylprednisolone]
Depopred-40
　[Methylprednisolone]
Depopred-80
　[Methylprednisolone]
Depo-Predate 40
　[Methylprednisolone]
Depo-Predate 80
　[Methylprednisolone]
Dexacen-4
　[Dexamethasone]
Dexacen LA-8
　[Dexamethasone]
Dexamethasone Intensol
　[Dexamethasone]
Dexasone
　[Dexamethasone]
Dexasone-LA
　[Dexamethasone]
Dexone [Dexamethasone]
Dexone 0.5
　[Dexamethasone]
Dexone 0.75
　[Dexamethasone]
Dexone 1.5
　[Dexamethasone]
Dexone 4
　[Dexamethasone]
Dexone LA
　[Dexamethasone]
Duralone-40
　[Methylprednisolone]
Duralone-80
　[Methylprednisolone]
Haldrone [Paramethasone]
Hexadrol [Dexamethasone]
Hexadrol Phosphate
　[Dexamethasone]
H.P. Acthar Gel
　[Corticotropin]
Hydeltrasol [Prednisolone]
Hydeltra T.B.A.
　[Prednisolone]
Hydrocortone
　[Hydrocortisone]
Hydrocortone Acetate
　[Hydrocortisone]
Hydrocortone Phosphate
　[Hydrocortisone]
Kenacort [Triamcinolone]
Kenacort Diacetate
　[Triamcinolone]
Kenaject-40
　[Triamcinolone]
Kenalog-10
　[Triamcinolone]
Kenalog-40
　[Triamcinolone]
Key-Pred 25
　[Prednisolone]
Key-Pred 50
　[Prednisolone]

Key-Pred SP [Prednisolone]
Liquid Pred [Prednisone]
Medralone-40
　[Methylprednisolone]
Medralone-80
　[Methylprednisolone]
Medrol
　[Methylprednisolone]
Medrol Enpak
　[Methylprednisolone]
Meprolone
　[Methylprednisolone]
Meticorten [Prednisone]
Mymethasone
　[Dexamethasone]
Nor-Pred T.B.A.
　[Prednisolone]
Orasone 1 [Prednisone]
Orasone 5 [Prednisone]
Orasone 10 [Prednisone]
Orasone 20 [Prednisone]
Orasone 50 [Prednisone]
Pediapred [Prednisolone]
Predaject-50 [Prednisolone]
Predalone 50
　[Prednisolone]
Predalone T.B.A.
　[Prednisolone]
Predate 50 [Prednisolone]
Predate S [Prednisolone]
Predate TBA [Prednisolone]
Predcor-25 [Prednisolone]
Predcor-50 [Prednisolone]
Predcor-TBA
　[Prednisolone]

In Canada—

Acthar [Corticotropin]
Acthar Gel (H.P.)
　[Corticotropin]
Apo-Prednisone
　[Prednisone]
Aristocort [Triamcinolone]
Aristocort Forte
　[Triamcinolone]
Aristocort Intralesional
　[Triamcinolone]
Aristospan Intra-articular
　[Triamcinolone]
Betnelan [Betamethasone]
Betnesol [Betamethasone]
Celestone [Betamethasone]
Celestone Soluspan
　[Betamethasone]
Cortef [Hydrocortisone]
Cortenema
　[Hydrocortisone]
Cortifoam [Hydrocortisone]
Cortone [Cortisone]

Other commonly used names are:
ACTH [Corticotropin]

BETAMETHASONE
Oral
　Betamethasone Syrup USP
　　In the U.S.—*Celestone*

Predicort-50
　[Prednisolone]
Predicort-RP
　[Prednisolone]
Prednicen-M [Prednisone]
Prednisone Intensol
　[Prednisone]
Prelone [Prednisolone]
Rep-Pred 40
　[Methylprednisolone]
Rep-Pred 80
　[Methylprednisolone]
Selestoject
　[Betamethasone]
Solu-Cortef
　[Hydrocortisone]
Solu-Medrol
　[Methylprednisolone]
Solurex [Dexamethasone]
Solurex-LA
　[Dexamethasone]
Sterapred [Prednisone]
Sterapred DS [Prednisone]
Tac-3 [Triamcinolone]
Triam-A [Triamcinolone]
Triam-Forte
　[Triamcinolone]
Triamolone 40
　[Triamcinolone]
Triamonide 40
　[Triamcinolone]
Tri-Kort [Triamcinolone]
Trilog [Triamcinolone]
Trilone [Triamcinolone]
Tristoject [Triamcinolone]

Decadron
　[Dexamethasone]
Deltasone [Prednisone]
Depo-Medrol
　[Methylprednisolone]
Deronil [Dexamethasone]
Dexasone
　[Dexamethasone]
Hexadrol [Dexamethasone]
Kenacort [Triamcinolone]
Kenalog-10
　[Triamcinolone]
Kenalog-40
　[Triamcinolone]
Medrol
　[Methylprednisolone]
Oradexon
　[Dexamethasone]
Solu-Cortef
　[Hydrocortisone]
Solu-Medrol
　[Methylprednisolone]
Winpred [Prednisone]

Cortisol [Hydrocortisone]

Betamethasone Tablets USP
In the U.S.—*Celestone*
In Canada—*Betnelan; Celestone*
Betamethasone Effervescent Tablets*
In Canada—*Betnesol*
Betamethasone Sodium Phosphate Extended-release Tablets*
In Canada—*Celestone*
Parenteral
Betamethasone Sodium Phosphate Injection USP
In the U.S.—*Celestone Phosphate; Selestoject;* GENERIC
Sterile Betamethasone Sodium Phosphate and Betamethasone Acetate Suspension USP
In the U.S. and Canada—*Celestone Soluspan*
Rectal
Betamethasone Disodium Phosphate Enema*
In Canada—*Betnesol*
CORTICOTROPIN
Parenteral
Corticotropin for Injection USP
In the U.S.—*Acthar;* GENERIC
In Canada—*Acthar*
Repository Corticotropin Injection USP
In the U.S.—*H.P. Acthar Gel;* GENERIC
In Canada—*Acthar Gel (H.P.)*
Sterile Corticotropin Zinc Hydroxide Suspension USP
In the U.S.—*Cortrophin-Zinc*
CORTISONE
Oral
Cortisone Acetate Tablets USP
In the U.S.—*Cortone Acetate;* GENERIC
In Canada—*Cortone;* GENERIC
Parenteral
Sterile Cortisone Acetate Suspension USP
In the U.S.—*Cortone Acetate;* GENERIC
In Canada—*Cortone*
COSYNTROPIN—See Cosyntropin (Systemic).
DEXAMETHASONE
Oral
Dexamethasone Elixir USP
In the U.S.—*Decadron; Hexadrol; Mymethasone;* GENERIC
Dexamethasone Oral Solution
In the U.S.—*Dexamethasone Intensol;* GENERIC
Dexamethasone Tablets USP
In the U.S.—*Decadron; Dexone 0.5; Dexone 0.75; Dexone 1.5; Dexone 4; Hexadrol;* GENERIC
In Canada—*Deronil; Dexasone; Hexadrol; Oradexon*
Parenteral
Sterile Dexamethasone Acetate Suspension USP
In the U.S.—*Dalalone D.P.; Dalalone L.A.; Decadron-LA; Decaject-L.A.; Dexacen LA-8; Dexasone-LA; Dexone LA; Solurex-LA;* GENERIC
Dexamethasone Sodium Phosphate Injection USP
In the U.S.—*AK-Dex; Dalalone; Decadrol; Decadron Phosphate; Decaject; Dexacen-4; Dexone; Hexadrol Phosphate; Solurex;* GENERIC
In Canada—*Decadron;* GENERIC
HYDROCORTISONE
Oral
Hydrocortisone Tablets USP
In the U.S.—*Cortef; Hydrocortone;* GENERIC
In Canada—*Cortef*
Hydrocortisone Cypionate Oral Suspension USP
In the U.S.—*Cortef*
Parenteral
Sterile Hydrocortisone Suspension USP
In the U.S.—GENERIC
Sterile Hydrocortisone Acetate Suspension USP
In the U.S.—*Hydrocortone Acetate;* GENERIC
Hydrocortisone Sodium Phosphate Injection USP
In the U.S.—*Hydrocortone Phosphate;* GENERIC

Hydrocortisone Sodium Succinate for Injection USP
In the U.S.—*A-hydroCort; Solu-Cortef;* GENERIC
In Canada—*Solu-Cortef*
Rectal
Hydrocortisone Enema USP
In the U.S. and Canada—*Cortenema*
Hydrocortisone Acetate Rectal Aerosol (Foam)
In the U.S. and Canada—*Cortifoam*
METHYLPREDNISOLONE
Oral
Methylprednisolone Tablets USP
In the U.S.—*Medrol; Meprolone;* GENERIC
In Canada—*Medrol*
Parenteral
Sterile Methylprednisolone Acetate Suspension USP
In the U.S.—*depMedalone 40; depMedalone 80; Depoject-40; Depoject-80; Depo-Medrol; Depopred-40; Depopred-80; Depo-Predate 40; Depo-Predate 80; Duralone-40; Duralone-80; Medralone-40; Medralone-80; Rep-Pred 40; Rep-Pred 80;* GENERIC
In Canada—*Depo-Medrol*
Methylprednisolone Sodium Succinate for Injection USP
In the U.S.—*A-methaPred; Solu-Medrol;* GENERIC
In Canada—*Solu-Medrol*
Rectal
Methylprednisolone Acetate for Enema USP
In the U.S.—*Medrol Enpak*
PARAMETHASONE
Oral
Paramethasone Acetate Tablets USP
In the U.S.—*Haldrone*
PREDNISOLONE
Oral
Prednisolone Syrup USP
In the U.S.—*Prelone*
Prednisolone Tablets USP
In the U.S.—*Delta-Cortef;* GENERIC
Prednisolone Sodium Phosphate Oral Solution
In the U.S.—*Pediapred*
Parenteral
Sterile Prednisolone Acetate Suspension USP
In the U.S.—*Articulose-50; Key-Pred 25; Key-Pred 50; Predaject-50; Predalone 50; Predate 50; Predcor-25; Predcor-50; Predicort-50;* GENERIC
Sterile Prednisolone Acetate and Prednisolone Sodium Phosphate Suspension
In the U.S.—GENERIC
Prednisolone Sodium Phosphate Injection USP
In the U.S.—*Hydeltrasol; Key-Pred SP; Predate S; Predicort-RP;* GENERIC
Sterile Prednisolone Tebutate Suspension USP
In the U.S.—*Hydeltra T.B.A.; Nor-Pred T.B.A.; Predalone T.B.A.; Predate TBA; Predcor-TBA;* GENERIC
PREDNISONE
Oral
Prednisone Oral Solution USP
In the U.S.—*Prednisone Intensol;* GENERIC
Prednisone Syrup USP
In the U.S.—*Liquid Pred*
Prednisone Tablets USP
In the U.S.—*Deltasone; Meticorten; Orasone 1; Orasone 5; Orasone 10; Orasone 20; Orasone 50; Prednicen-M; Sterapred; Sterapred DS;* GENERIC
In Canada—*Apo-Prednisone; Deltasone; Winpred;* GENERIC
TRIAMCINOLONE
Oral
Triamcinolone Tablets USP
In the U.S.—*Aristocort; Kenacort;* GENERIC
In Canada—*Aristocort; Kenacort*

Triamcinolone Diacetate Syrup USP
    In the U.S.—*Aristocort; Kenacort Diacetate*
    In Canada—*Aristocort*
Parenteral
    Sterile Triamcinolone Acetonide Suspension USP
        In the U.S.—*Cenocort A-40; Cinonide 40; Kenaject-40; Kenalog-10; Kenalog-40; Tac-3; Triam-A; Triamonide 40; Tri-Kort; Trilog;* GENERIC
        In Canada—*Kenalog-10; Kenalog-40*
    Sterile Triamcinolone Diacetate Suspension USP
        In the U.S.—*Amcort; Aristocort Forte; Aristocort Intralesional; Articulose-L.A.; Cenocort Forte; Cinalone 40; Triam-Forte; Triamolone 40; Trilone; Tristoject;* GENERIC
        In Canada—*Aristocort Forte; Aristocort Intralesional;* GENERIC
    Sterile Triamcinolone Hexacetonide Suspension USP
        In the U.S.—*Aristospan Intra-articular; Aristospan Intralesional*
        In Canada—*Aristospan Intra-articular*

---

*Not commercially available in the U.S.

Category

Adrenocorticoid—Betamethasone; Cortisone; Dexamethasone; Hydrocortisone; Methylprednisolone; Paramethasone; Prednisolone; Prednisone; Triamcinolone.
Adrenocorticotropic hormone—Corticotropin.
Anti-inflammatory (steroidal)—Betamethasone; Cortisone; Dexamethasone; Hydrocortisone; Methylprednisolone; Paramethasone; Prednisolone; Prednisone; Triamcinolone.
Diagnostic aid (adrenocortical function)—Corticotropin for Injection USP.
Diagnostic aid (Cushing's syndrome)—Dexamethasone Elixir USP; Dexamethasone Oral Solution; Dexamethasone Tablets USP; Dexamethasone Sodium Phosphate Injection USP.
Immunosuppressant—Betamethasone; Corticotropin; Cortisone; Dexamethasone; Hydrocortisone; Methylprednisolone; Paramethasone; Prednisolone; Prednisone; Triamcinolone.
Pituitary (anterior) hormone—Corticotropin.
Anticonvulsant (specific in infantile myoclonic seizures)—Corticotropin for Injection USP.
Antiemetic, in cancer chemotherapy—Corticotropin; Dexamethasone Elixir USP; Dexamethasone Tablets USP; Dexamethasone Sodium Phosphate Injection USP; Hydrocortisone (oral and parenteral); Prednisone.
Diagnostic aid (endogenous depression)—Dexamethasone (oral dosage forms).

Indications

Note: Bracketed information in the *Indications* section refers to uses not included in U.S. product labeling.

Accepted
Adrenocorticoids are indicated (in physiologic doses) as replacement therapy in the treatment of adrenal insufficiency states.
In patients with known or suspected adrenal insufficiency, intravenous or intramuscular administration of a rapidly acting adrenocorticoid is indicated prior to surgery, including dental surgery, or if shock, severe trauma, illness, or other stress conditions occur. Patients already receiving replacement therapy require supplemental pharmacologic doses.
Glucocorticoids are indicated for their anti-inflammatory and immunosuppressant effects in the treatment of many disorders. Agents having minimal mineralocorticoid activity are preferred. For most indications, glucocorticoid administration provides symptomatic relief but has no effect on the underlying disease processes. Use of these medications does not eliminate the need for other therapies that may be required.

Adrenocorticoid therapy for conditions other than adrenocortical insufficiency, adrenogenital syndrome, or severe or life-threatening conditions is generally instituted only after less toxic therapies have proven ineffective.

Unaccepted
Although corticotropin may be useful in treating secondary adrenocortical insufficiency (i.e., that caused by adrenocorticotropic hormone [ACTH] deficiency), adrenocorticoid therapy is preferred.
Corticotropin is ineffective, and (except for diagnostic purposes) should not be used for any indication, in patients with primary adrenocortical insufficiency. Although corticotropin is FDA-approved for treatment of many conditions responsive to adrenocorticoid therapy as shown in *Table 1, corticotropin should not be used in emergencies or other situations requiring an immediate effect.* Also, corticotropin is of limited value in the treatment of adrenocorticoid-responsive diseases and is rarely used; adrenocorticoid therapy is preferred.

Pharmacology

See also *Table 1,* page 487.

Mechanism of action/Effect:
Corticotropin—Corticotropin is not an adrenocorticoid. However, it shares many actions and precautions of the adrenocorticoids, due to its ability to increase endogenous adrenocorticoid synthesis. Corticotropin combines with a specific receptor in the adrenal cell plasma membrane; in patients with normal adrenocortical function, stimulates the initial reaction involved in the synthesis of adrenal steroids (including cortisol, cortisone, weak androgenic substances, and a limited quantity of aldosterone) from cholesterol by increasing the quantity of the substrate within the mitochondria. Corticotropin does *not* significantly increase serum cortisol concentrations in patients with primary adrenocortical insufficiency. In patients with adrenocortical insufficiency secondary to corticotropin deficiency, corticotropin administration corrects the deficiency. In the treatment of other adrenocorticoid-responsive conditions, the effects of corticotropin are due to the actions of the generated endogenous corticosteroids.
Adrenocorticoids—Diffuse across cell membranes and complex with specific cytoplasmic receptors. These complexes then enter the cell nucleus, bind to DNA, and stimulate transcription of messenger RNA (mRNA) and subsequent protein synthesis of various enzymes thought to be ultimately responsible for two categories of effects of systemic adrenocorticoids. However, these agents may suppress transcription of mRNA in some cells (e.g., lymphocytes).

For glucocorticoid effects
Anti-inflammatory (steroidal)—Glucocorticoids decrease or prevent tissue responses to inflammatory processes, thereby reducing development of symptoms of inflammation without affecting the underlying cause. Glucocorticoids inhibit accumulation of inflammatory cells, including macrophages and leukocytes, at sites of inflammation. They also inhibit phagocytosis, lysosomal enzyme release, and synthesis and/or release of several chemical mediators of inflammation. Although the exact mechanisms are not completely understood, actions that may contribute significantly to these effects include blockade of the action of macrophage inhibitory factor (MIF), leading to inhibition of macrophage localization; reduction of dilatation and permeability of inflamed capillaries and reduction of leukocyte adherence to the capillary endothelium, leading to inhibition of both leukocyte migration and edema formation; and increased synthesis of lipomodulin (macrocortin), an inhibitor of phospholipase A_2-mediated arachidonic acid release from membrane phospholipids, with subsequent inhibition of the synthesis of arachidonic acid-derived mediators of inflammation (prostaglandins, thromboxanes, and leukotrienes). Immu-

nosuppressant actions may also contribute significantly to the anti-inflammatory effect.

Immunosuppressant—Mechanisms of immunosuppressant action are not completely understood but may involve prevention or suppression of cell-mediated (delayed hypersensitivity) immune reactions as well as more specific actions affecting the immune response. Glucocorticoids reduce the concentration of thymus-dependent lymphocytes (T-lymphocytes), monocytes, and eosinophils. They also decrease binding of immunoglobulin to cell surface receptors and inhibit the synthesis and/or release of interleukins, thereby decreasing T-lymphocyte blastogenesis and reducing expansion of the primary immune response. Glucocorticoids may also decrease passage of immune complexes through basement membranes and decrease concentrations of complement components and immunoglobulins.

For mineralocorticoid effects

Water and electrolyte balance—Sodium reabsorption, and potassium and hydrogen excretion, along with subsequent water retention, are mediated through an action of mineralocorticoids on the renal distal tubule that facilitates sodium transport. Cation transport in other secretory cells is similarly affected; excretion of water and electrolytes by the large intestine and by salivary and sweat glands is also altered, but to a lesser extent. Only cortisone and hydrocortisone have clinically useful mineralocorticoid activity.

For specific indications

Adrenogenital syndrome—Glucocorticoids inhibit corticotropin (adrenocorticotropin or ACTH) secretion, leading to suppression of adrenal hypersecretion of androgens responsible for the androgenism associated with various enzyme deficiencies.

Hypercalcemia—Glucocorticoids reduce plasma calcium concentration by decreasing gastrointestinal absorption of calcium, probably by interfering with intestinal calcium transport (by decreasing the effect of vitamin D), and increasing calcium excretion.

Respiratory distress syndrome prophylaxis—Glucocorticoids may induce enzymes which accelerate or increase production of lung surfactant by type 2 pneumonocytes.

Other actions/effects:

Pharmacologic (supraphysiologic) doses of exogenous adrenocorticoids produce hypothalamic-pituitary-adrenal (HPA) axis suppression via a negative feedback mechanism, i.e., they inhibit pituitary ACTH secretion, thereby reducing ACTH-mediated production of corticosteroids and androgens in the adrenal cortex. The development of adrenocortical insufficiency and the time required for recovery of adrenal function depend primarily on the duration of adrenocorticoid therapy and, to a lesser extent, on dosage, timing, and frequency of administration, as well as on the potency and biologic (tissue) half-life of the specific agent. Adrenal insufficiency may occur in approximately 5 to 7 days with daily administration of doses equivalent to 20 to 30 mg of prednisone or in up to 30 days with lower doses. Following discontinuation of short-term (up to 5 days) high-dose use, adrenal recovery may occur within 1 week. Following prolonged high-dose use, complete recovery of adrenal function may require up to 1 year and, in some patients, may never occur.

Glucocorticoids stimulate protein catabolism and induce enzymes responsible for metabolism of amino acids. They decrease synthesis and increase degradation of protein in lymphoid tissue, connective tissue, muscle, and skin. With prolonged use, atrophy of these tissues may occur.

Glucocorticoids increase glucose availability by inducing hepatic enzymes involved in gluconeogenesis, stimulating protein catabolism (which increases hepatic concentrations of amino acids required for gluconeogenesis), and decreasing peripheral utilization of glucose. These actions lead to increased hepatic glycogen storage, increased blood glucose concentrations, and insulin resistance.

Glucocorticoids increase lipolysis and mobilize fatty acids from adipose tissues, leading to increased plasma fatty acid concentrations. With prolonged use, an abnormal redistribution of fat may occur.

Glucocorticoids decrease bone formation and increase bone resorption. They reduce plasma calcium concentration, leading to secondary hyperparathyroidism and subsequent stimulation of osteoclasts, and directly inhibit osteoblasts. These actions, together with a decrease in the protein matrix of bone secondary to increased protein catabolism, may lead to inhibition of bone growth in children and adolescents and the development of osteoporosis at any age.

Duration of action: Duration of action depends upon the route/site of administration, solubility of the dosage form, dose administered, and the condition being treated. Following oral or intravenous administration, the duration of action depends upon the biological (tissue) half-life. Following intramuscular administration, the duration of action depends upon the solubility of the dosage form as well as the biological (tissue) half-life. Following local injections, the duration of action depends upon the solubility of the dosage form and the specific route/site of administration.

Precautions to Consider

Geriatrics

Geriatric patients may be more likely to develop hypertension during adrenocorticoid or corticotropin therapy. Geriatric patients, especially postmenopausal women, may also be more likely to develop glucocorticoid-induced osteoporosis.

Drug interactions and/or related problems

The following drug interactions and/or related problems have been selected on the basis of their potential clinical significance (possible mechanism in parentheses where appropriate)—not necessarily inclusive (» = major clinical significance):

Note: Combinations containing any of the following medications, depending on the amount present, may also interact with this medication.

Interactions listed below involving alterations in serum potassium concentration and/or changes in sodium or fluid balance are especially likely to occur with corticotropin and with adrenocorticoids having significant mineralocorticoid activity. However, these interactions may also occur with other adrenocorticoids, depending on dosage and patient predisposition.

Acetaminophen
(induction of hepatic enzymes by adrenocorticoids may increase the formation of a hepatotoxic acetaminophen metabolite, thereby increasing the risk of hepatotoxicity, when they are used concurrently with chronic or high-dose acetaminophen therapy)

Alcohol or
Anti-inflammatory drugs, nonsteroidal (NSAIDs)
(risk of gastrointestinal ulceration or hemorrhage may be increased when these substances are used concurrently with glucocorticoids; however, concurrent use of NSAIDs in the treatment of arthritis may provide additive therapeutic benefit and permit glucocorticoid dosage reduction)

» Aminoglutethimide
(therapeutic use of corticotropin is not recommended during aminoglutethimide administration because aminoglutethimide decreases adrenal responsiveness to corticotropin)

(aminoglutethimide suppresses adrenal function so that glucocorticoid supplementation may be required; however, aminoglutethimide accelerates the metabolism of dexamethasone so that dexamethasone half-life may be reduced two-fold; hydrocortisone is recommended instead because its metabolism is not known to be altered by aminoglutethimide and because its mineralocorticoid activity may also be required)

» Amphotericin B, parenteral, or
Carbonic anhydrase inhibitors
    (concurrent use with adrenocorticoids may result in severe hypokalemia and should be undertaken with caution; serum potassium concentrations and cardiac function should be monitored during concurrent use)

    (the use of hydrocortisone to control adverse reactions to amphotericin B has resulted in cases of cardiac enlargement and congestive heart failure)

    (amphotericin B also decreases adrenal responsiveness to corticotropin)

    (concurrent use of adrenocorticoids or corticotropin with acetazolamide sodium may increase the risk of hypernatremia and/or edema because adrenocorticoids/corticotropin cause sodium and fluid retention; the risk with adrenocorticoids or corticotropin may depend on the patient's sodium requirement as determined by the condition being treated)

    (the possibility should be considered that concurrent chronic use of both carbonic anhydrase inhibitors and adrenocorticoids may increase the risk of hypocalcemia and osteoporosis because carbonic anhydrase inhibitors also increase calcium excretion)

Anabolic steroids or
Androgens
    (concurrent use with glucocorticoids may increase the risk of edema; also, concurrent use may promote the development of severe acne)

» Antacids
    (concurrent chronic use with prednisone or dexamethasone may decrease absorption of these glucocorticoids; efficacy may be decreased sufficiently to require dosage adjustment in patients receiving small doses, but probably not in those receiving large doses, of the adrenocorticoid)

Anticholinergics, especially atropine and related compounds
    (concurrent long-term use with glucocorticoids may increase intraocular pressure)

Anticoagulants, coumarin- or indandione-derivative, or
Heparin or
Streptokinase or
Urokinase
    (effects of coumarin or indandione derivatives are usually decreased [but may be increased in some patients] when these medications are used concurrently with glucocorticoids; dosage adjustments based on prothrombin time determinations may be necessary during and after glucocorticoid therapy)

    (the potential occurrence of gastrointestinal ulceration or hemorrhage during glucocorticoid therapy, and the effects of glucocorticoids on vascular integrity, may cause increased risk to patients receiving anticoagulant or thrombolytic therapy)

Antidepressants, tricyclic
    (these medications do not relieve, and may exacerbate, adrenocorticoid-induced mental disturbances; they should not be used for treatment of these adverse effects)

» Antidiabetic agents, oral, or
» Insulin
    (glucocorticoids may increase blood glucose concentration; dosage adjustment of one or both agents may be necessary during concurrent use; dosage readjustment of the hypoglycemic agent may also be required when glucocorticoid therapy is discontinued)

Antithyroid agents or
Thyroid hormones
    (changes in the thyroid status of the patient that may occur as a result of administration, changes in dosage, or discontinuation of thyroid hormones or antithyroid agents may necessitate adjustment of adrenocorticoid dosage because metabolic clearance of adrenocorticoids is decreased in hypothyroid patients and increased in hyperthyroid patients. Dosage adjustment should be based on results of thyroid function tests)

Asparaginase
    (glucocorticoids, especially prednisone, may increase the hyperglycemic effect of asparaginase and the risk of neuropathy and disturbances in erythropoiesis; the toxicity appears to be less pronounced when asparaginase is administered following, rather than before or with, these medications)

Contraceptives, oral, estrogen-containing, or
Estrogens
    (estrogens may alter the metabolism and protein binding of glucocorticoids, leading to decreased clearance, increased elimination half-life, and increased therapeutic and toxic effects of the glucocorticoid; glucocorticoid dosage adjustment may be required during and following concurrent use)

    (concurrent chronic use of estrogens may also potentiate the anti-inflammatory effects of corticotropin)

» Digitalis glycosides
    (concurrent use with glucocorticoids may increase the possibility of arrhythmias or digitalis toxicity associated with hypokalemia)

» Diuretics
    (natriuretic and diuretic effects of these medications may be decreased by sodium- and fluid-retaining actions of adrenocorticoids, and vice versa)

    (concurrent use of potassium-depleting diuretics with adrenocorticoids may result in severe hypokalemia; monitoring of serum potassium concentration and cardiac function is recommended)

    (effects of potassium-sparing diuretics and/or adrenocorticoids on serum potassium concentration may be decreased during concurrent use; monitoring of serum potassium concentration is recommended)

Ephedrine
    (ephedrine may increase the metabolic clearance of adrenocorticoids; adrenocorticoid dosage adjustment may be required during and following concurrent use)

Folic acid
    (requirements may be increased in patients receiving long-term adrenocorticoid therapy)

» Hepatic enzyme-inducing agents
    (concurrent use may decrease the adrenocorticoid effect because of increased adrenocorticoid metabolism resulting from induction of hepatic microsomal enzymes)

Immunosuppressant agents, other
    (concurrent use with immunosuppressant doses of glucocorticoids may increase the risk of infection and possibly the development of lymphomas or other lymphoproliferative disorders; these neoplasms may be associated with Epstein-Barr virus infections; a few studies in organ transplant patients receiving immunosuppressant therapy indicate that progression of the neoplasm may be reversed after immunosuppressant dosage is decreased or therapy is discontinued)

Iophendylate or
Metrizamide
    (concurrent intrathecal administration of metrizamide or iophendylate with intrathecal administration of glucocorticoids may increase the risk of arachnoiditis)

Isoniazid
    (glucocorticoids, especially prednisolone, may increase hepatic metabolism and/or excretion of isoniazid, leading to decreased plasma concentration and effectiveness of isoniazid, especially in patients who are rapid acetylators; isoniazid dosage adjustment may be required during and following concurrent use)

Mexiletine
(concurrent use with glucocorticoids may accelerate mexiletine metabolism, leading to decreased mexiletine plasma concentration)

» Mitotane
(therapeutic use of corticotropin is not recommended during mitotane therapy because mitotane reduces adrenal responsiveness to corticotropin)

(mitotane suppresses adrenocortical function; glucocorticoid supplementation is usually required during mitotane administration, but higher doses than those generally used for replacement therapy may be required because mitotane alters glucocorticoid metabolism)

Neuromuscular blocking agents, nondepolarizing
(hypokalemia induced by glucocorticoids may enhance the blockade of nondepolarizing neuromuscular blocking agents, possibly leading to increased or prolonged respiratory depression or paralysis [apnea]; serum potassium determinations may be necessary prior to administration of these agents)

(hydrocortisone and prednisone have also been reported to decrease the efficacy of pancuronium by an unknown mechanism; increased dosage of pancuronium or use of an alternate neuromuscular blocking agent may be necessary)

» Potassium supplements
(effects of these medications and/or adrenocorticoids on serum potassium concentration may be decreased when these medications are used concurrently; monitoring of serum potassium concentration is recommended)

» Ritodrine
(concurrent use may cause pulmonary edema in the mother; maternal death has been reported; both medications should be discontinued at the first sign of pulmonary edema)

Salicylates
(although concurrent use with glucocorticoids in the treatment of arthritis may provide additive therapeutic benefit and permit glucocorticoid dosage reduction, glucocorticoids may increase salicylate excretion and reduce salicylate plasma concentrations so that the salicylate dosage requirement may be increased; salicylism may occur when glucocorticoid dosage is subsequently decreased or discontinued, especially in patients receiving large [antirheumatic] doses of salicylates; also, the risk of gastrointestinal ulceration or hemorrhage may be increased during concurrent use)

» Sodium-containing medications or foods
(concurrent use with pharmacologic doses of glucocorticoids or with corticotropin may result in edema and increased blood pressure, possibly to hypertensive levels)

(although patients receiving replacement doses of glucocorticoids may require sodium supplementation, adjustment of dietary sodium intake may be required when a medication having a high sodium content is also administered concurrently)

» Somatrem or
» Somatropin
(inhibition of the growth response to somatrem or somatropin may occur with chronic therapeutic use of corticotropin or with daily doses [per square meter of body surface] in excess of:

	Oral	Parenteral
Betamethasone	300–450 mcg	150–225 mcg
Cortisone	12.5–18.8 mg	6.25–9.4 mg
Dexamethasone	375–563 mcg	187.5–281.5 mcg
Hydrocortisone	10–15 mg	5–7.5 mg
Methylprednisolone	2–3 mg	1–1.5 mg
Paramethasone	1–1.5 mg	
Prednisolone	2.5–3.75 mg	1.25–1.88 mg
Prednisone	2.5–3.75 mg	
Triamcinolone	2–3 mg	1–1.5 mg

It is recommended that these doses not be exceeded during somatrem or somatropin therapy; if larger doses are required, administration of somatrem or somatropin should be postponed; also, concurrent use with corticotropin is not recommended)

Streptozocin
(concurrent use with glucocorticoids may increase the risk of hyperglycemia)

Troleandomycin
(troleandomycin may decrease metabolism of methylprednisolone and possibly other glucocorticoids, leading to increased plasma concentration, elimination half-life, and therapeutic and toxic effects; glucocorticoid dosage adjustment may be required during and following concurrent use)

» Vaccines, live virus, or other immunizations
(administration of live virus vaccines to patients receiving pharmacologic [immunosuppressant] doses of glucocorticoids may potentiate replication of the vaccine virus, thereby increasing the risk of the patient's developing the viral disease, and/or decrease the patient's antibody response to the vaccine and is not recommended; the patient's immunologic status should be evaluated prior to administration of a live virus vaccine; also, immunization with oral poliovirus vaccine should be postponed in persons in close contact with the patient, especially family members)

(other immunizations are not recommended in patients receiving pharmacologic [immunosuppressant] doses of glucocorticoids because of the increased risk of neurological complications and the possibility of decreased or absent antibody response)

(immunizations may be administered to patients receiving glucocorticoids via routes or in quantities that are not likely to cause immunosuppression, for example, those receiving local injections, short-term [less than 2 weeks] therapy, or physiologic doses)

Contraindications/Medical problems
The contraindications/medical problems included have been selected on the basis of their potential clinical significance (reasons given in parentheses where appropriate)—not necessarily inclusive (» = major clinical significance).

Note: The medical problems listed below apply only to pharmacologic (supraphysiologic) doses of glucocorticoids, unless otherwise stated.

Except under special circumstances, these medications should not be used when the following medical problems exist:

For intra-articular injection
» Arthroplasty of joint, prior
(increased risk of infection)

» Blood clotting disorders
(risk of intra- and extra-articular hemorrhage)

» Fracture, intra-articular
(healing may be retarded)

» Infection, periarticular, current or history of
(may be exacerbated or reactivated)

» Osteoporosis, juxta-articular, non-arthritic
(may be exacerbated)

» Unstable joint

For rectal administration
» Anastomoses, intestinal, recent
» Fistulas and sinus tracts, extensive
» Ileocolostomy, recent
» Infection, abdominal, including peritonitis and intestinal or rectal abscesses
(may be exacerbated)

» Obstruction, intestinal
» Perforation, intestinal

For neonatal respiratory distress syndrome prophylaxis
» Amnionitis
» Bleeding, uterine
» Febrile illness or infection, especially tuberculosis, maternal, or
» Herpes type II infection, active, maternal, or
» Keratitis, viral, maternal
    (may be exacerbated; if adrenocorticoid administration is essential, appropriate antimicrobial therapy must be administered concurrently)
» Placental insufficiency
» Premature membrane rupture
    (increased risk of maternal infection; the glucocorticoid should be administered immediately if this occurs, since the risk of infection increases with time)

For corticotropin
» Congestive heart failure or
» Hypertension
    (will be exacerbated by edema)
» Cushing's syndrome
    (will be exacerbated)
» Herpes simplex, ocular
    (risk of corneal perforation)
» Osteoporosis
» Scleroderma
» Sensitivity to porcine proteins
    (risk of allergic reactions)
» Surgery, recent

Risk-benefit should be considered when the following medical problems exist:

For all indications
» Acquired immunodeficiency syndrome (AIDS) or
» Human immunodeficiency virus (HIV) infection
    (although pharmacologic doses of adrenocorticoids can be effective in the treatment of certain HIV-related diseases, careful medical evaluation of the risks and benefits of this therapy must be done, due to the possible increased risk of severe uncontrollable infections and/or neoplasms; in one study in patients given tapering doses of intravenous methylprednisolone starting with 60 mg every 6 hours for 8 days as an adjunct to antipneumocystis therapy, an increase in frequency or severity of life-threatening opportunistic infections was observed; in a study of similar patients given tapering doses of prednisone starting at 40 mg two times a day for 21 days, no increase in the incidence of Kaposi's sarcoma or life-threatening opportunistic infections was observed, though the incidence of oral candidiasis and mucocutaneous herpes simplex infection did increase)
» Anastomoses, intestinal, recent
» Cardiac disease or
» Congestive heart failure or
    Hypertension or
» Renal function impairment or disease, severe
    (edema may be hazardous, especially with agents having significant mineralocorticoid activity)
    (patients undergoing dialysis may have increased risk of avascular necrosis with long-term adrenocorticoid use)
» Diabetes mellitus or predisposition to
    (may be exacerbated or activated)
    Colitis, ulcerative nonspecific, with possibility of impending perforation, abscess, or other infection, or
    Diverticulitis or
» Esophagitis, gastritis, or peptic ulcer, active or latent
    (symptoms of progression or reactivation may be masked; hemorrhage and/or perforation may occur without warning)

» Fungal infections, systemic
    (may be exacerbated; pharmacologic doses should not be given unless the patient is concurrently receiving an antifungal agent)
    Glaucoma, open-angle
    (intraocular pressure may be increased)
    Hepatic function impairment or disease
    (increased risk of glucocorticoid toxicity, especially if hypoalbuminemia present; possibility of impaired conversion of cortisone or prednisone to their active metabolites, although effect may be offset by decreased protein binding or clearance and/or conversion in other tissues)
» Herpes simplex, ocular
    (possible corneal perforation)
    Herpetic lesions, oral
    Hyperlipidemia
    (concentrations of fatty acids or cholesterol may be increased)
    Hyperthyroidism
    (glucocorticoid effect may be impaired because of accelerated metabolism; may be especially important with physiologic doses or low pharmacologic doses)
    Hypoalbuminemia or conditions predisposing to, including hepatic cirrhosis or nephrotic syndrome
    (increased risk of toxicity because reduced availability of albumin for glucocorticoid binding leads to increased serum concentration of unbound drug; reduction in initial dosage is recommended)
    Hypothyroidism
    (decreased metabolism of adrenocorticoid may result)
    Infections, viral or bacterial, uncontrolled, systemic or at site of local injection
    (may be exacerbated; concurrent antimicrobial therapy required)
    Intolerance to corticotropin, cosyntropin, or adrenocorticoids
» Myasthenia gravis
    (muscle weakness may be increased initially, possibly leading to respiratory distress; patient should be hospitalized, and respiratory support should be immediately available, when glucocorticoid therapy is initiated)
    Osteoporosis
    (may be exacerbated)
    Renal function impairment, mild to moderate, or stones
    (fluid retention may exacerbate these conditions; increased risk of edema, especially with agents having mineralocorticoid activity)
    (patients receiving dialysis may have increased risk of avascular necrosis with long-term adrenocorticoid use)
    Systemic lupus erythematosus (SLE)
    (cautious use is recommended because of an increased risk of aseptic necrosis)
» Tuberculosis—active, positive skin test, latent, or history of
    (may be exacerbated or reactivated; appropriate antitubercular chemotherapy or prophylaxis should be administered concurrently)

Side/Adverse Effects

Note: The risk of adverse effects with pharmacologic doses of adrenocorticoids generally increases with the duration of therapy and frequency of administration and, to a lesser extent, with dosage.

Chronic administration of physiologic replacement doses of adrenocorticoids rarely causes adverse effects.

Administration of glucocorticoids rectally or via local injection reduces the risk of systemic effects. The risk of both systemic and local adverse effects is still present to a degree, however, and increases with the duration of rectal therapy and with the frequency of injections.

Pharmacologic doses of glucocorticoids and chronic therapeutic use of corticotropin lower resistance to infection; the patient may be predisposed to systemic infections during, and for a time following, therapy. Increased susceptibility to infection may occur with short-term high-dose use ("pulse" therapy) as well as with more prolonged use. Also, symptoms of onset or progression of infections may be masked.

The following side/adverse effects have been selected on the basis of their potential clinical significance (possible signs and symptoms in parentheses where appropriate)—not necessarily inclusive:

Those indicating need for medical attention
Incidence less frequent
   Local allergic reaction or rectal irritation (rectal bleeding, blistering, burning, itching, or pain not present before therapy)—with rectal dosage forms; *cataracts* (decreased or blurred vision); *diabetes mellitus* (decreased or blurred vision, frequent urination, increased thirst)
Incidence rare
   Generalized allergic reaction (skin rash or hives); *local allergic reaction or infection at injection site* (redness, swelling, pain, or other signs of infection or allergic reaction); *sudden blindness; burning, numbness, pain, or tingling at or near place of injection; psychic disturbances such as delirium* (confusion, excitement, or restlessness), *disorientation, euphoria* (false sense of well-being), *hallucinations* (seeing, hearing, or feeling things that are not there), *manic-depressive episodes* (sudden, wide mood swings), *mental depression, or paranoia* (mistaken feelings of self-importance or being mistreated)
   Note: *Sudden blindness* following injection into sites in the head or neck area, such as nasal turbinates or scalp, due to possible entry of drug crystals into ocular blood vessels.
   Psychic disturbances are more likely in patients with chronic debilitating illnesses that predispose them to psychic disturbances and in patients receiving higher daily dosages. Psychic disturbances may be related to dose rather than duration of therapy; symptoms may appear within a few days to 2 weeks after initiation of therapy and are usually associated with doses equivalent to 40 mg or more of prednisone per day. Additionally, euphoria or fear of relapse may lead to psychological dependence or abuse of adrenocorticoids.
With rapid intravenous administration of high doses (pulse therapy)
   Generalized anaphylaxis (swelling of face, nasal membranes, and eyelids; hives; shortness of breath; troubled breathing; tightness in chest; or wheezing); *flushing of face or cheeks; irregular or pounding heartbeat; seizures*
   Note: *Rapid intravenous administration of high doses* of adrenocorticoids has been reported to cause convulsions, angioedema and/or anaphylactic reactions, and sudden death associated with cardiac arrhythmias. Monitoring of the electrocardiogram (ECG) is recommended. Equipment, medications, and trained personnel necessary for treating these complications should be immediately available.

Those occurring principally during long-term use indicating need for medical attention
   Acne or other skin problems; avascular necrosis (hip or shoulder pain); *Cushing's syndrome* (filling or rounding out of the face); *edema* (swelling of feet or lower legs, rapid weight gain); *endocrine imbalance* (menstrual irregularities); *gastrointestinal irritation* (nausea, vomiting); *hypokalemic syndrome* (irregular heartbeat, muscle cramps or pain, unusual tiredness or weakness); *osteoporosis or bone fractures*—includes vertebral compression and long bone pathologic fractures (pain in back, ribs, arms, or legs); *pancreatitis* (continuing abdominal or stomach pain or burning, nausea, vomiting); *peptic ulceration or intestinal perforation* (continuing abdominal or stomach pain or burning; bloody or black, tarry stools); *scarring at injection site; steroid myopathy* (muscle weakness); *striae* (reddish purple lines on arms, face, legs, trunk,

or groin); *tendon rupture*—with local injection; *cutaneous or subcutaneous tissue atrophy*—with frequent repository injections (thin, shiny skin; pitting or depression of skin at place of injection); *unusual bruising; wounds that will not heal*

Those indicating need for medical attention only if they continue or are bothersome
Incidence more frequent
   Increased appetite; indigestion; nervousness or restlessness; trouble in sleeping
For triamcinolone
   Loss of appetite
Incidence less frequent or rare
   Changes in skin color or hypopigmentation (darkening or lightening of skin color); *dizziness or lightheadedness; flushing of face or cheeks; headache;*emfollowing intranasal injection; *increased joint pain;*emfollowing intra-articular injection; *increased sweating; nosebleeds*—following intranasal injection; *unusual increase in hair growth on body or face*
   Note: *Hypopigmentation* is more likely at the injection site.
   Flushing of face or cheeks may persist for 24 to 48 hours.
   Increased joint pain may occur within a few hours postinjection and persist for up to 48 hours.

Those occurring principally after medication is discontinued, indicating an adrenocorticoid withdrawal syndrome and the need for medical attention
   Withdrawal syndrome (abdominal or back pain, dizziness, fainting, low-grade fever, prolonged loss of appetite, muscle or joint pain, nausea, vomiting, shortness of breath, frequent or continuing unexplained headaches, unusual tiredness or weakness, rapid weight loss, reappearance of disease symptoms)
   Note: Too-rapid *withdrawal of therapy*, especially after prolonged use, may cause acute, possibly life-threatening, adrenal insufficiency and/or a withdrawal syndrome not related to HPA axis suppression.

Patient Consultation

In providing consultation, consider emphasizing the following selected information (» = major clinical significance):

Before using this medication
» Conditions affecting use, especially:
      Allergies to cosyntropin, corticotropin, or adrenocorticoids
      Pregnancy—Pharmacologic doses in animals show some evidence of increased risk of placental insufficiency, decreased birthweight, or stillbirths; other animal studies show increased incidence of cleft palate, placental insufficiency, spontaneous abortions, or intrauterine growth retardation. Hypoadrenalism may occur in infants if mothers received substantial doses of adrenocorticoids prenatally
      Breast-feeding—Breast-feeding is not recommended during use of higher doses
      Use in children—Close monitoring required since chronic therapy may result in suppression of growth and development; increased risk of osteoporosis, avascular necrosis of femoral heads, and cataracts
      Use in the elderly—Increased risk of osteoporosis (especially in postmenopausal females) or hypertension
      Other medications, especially aminoglutethimide, parenteral amphotericin B, antacids, oral antidiabetic agents, insulin, digitalis glycosides, diuretics, hepatic enzyme-inducing agents, mitotane, potassium supplements, ritodrine, sodium-containing medications, human growth hormone, or immunizations
      Other medical problems, especially:
         For all uses—AIDS, systemic or local infections, gastrointestinal disorders, cardiac disease, congestive heart failure, renal diseases, diabetes, or myasthenia gravis

For intra-articular injection only—Arthroplasty, clotting disorders, fracture, osteoporosis, or unstable joint

For rectal use only—Recent ileocolostomy

For neonatal respiratory distress syndrome prophylaxis only—Amnionitis, uterine bleeding, febrile illness, placental insufficiency, or premature membrane rupture

For corticotropin only—Adrenocortical hyperfunction, congestive heart failure, hypertension, ocular herpes simplex, osteoporosis, scleroderma, porcine protein sensitivity, or recent surgery

Proper use of this medication

For oral dosage forms:

» Taking with food to minimize gastrointestinal irritation

Possibility that alcohol may enhance ulcerogenic effects of medication

For rectal dosage forms:

Proper administration technique; reading patient directions carefully

Saving applicator for methylprednisolone acetate for enema; refill units may be available

» Importance of not using more medication than the amount prescribed

Missed dose: If dosing schedule is—

Every other day: Taking as soon as possible if remembered same morning; if remembered later, not taking until next morning, then skipping a day

Once a day: Taking as soon as possible; not taking if almost time for next dose; not doubling doses

Several times a day: Taking as soon as possible; doubling if time for next dose

» Proper storage

Precautions while using this medication

» Regular visits to physician to check progress during and following therapy

» Checking with physician before discontinuing medication; gradual dosage reduction may be necessary

Checking with physician if symptoms recur or worsen when dose decreased or therapy discontinued

» Possible need for calorie and/or sodium restriction or potassium supplementation during long-term therapy

Possible need for increased protein intake during long-term therapy

Ophthalmologic examinations during long-term therapy

Carrying medical identification card indicating use of medication during long-term therapy

» Caution in receiving skin tests

» Caution if any kind of surgery or emergency treatment is required

» Caution in receiving vaccinations or other immunizations or coming in contact with persons receiving oral poliovirus vaccine

» Caution if serious infections or injuries occur

Diabetics: May increase blood sugar concentrations

For parenteral dosage forms

Restricting use of joint following intra-articular injection

Checking with physician if redness or swelling occurs, and continues or becomes worse, following local injection

For rectal dosage forms

Checking with physician if signs of rectal irritation or infection occur

Side/adverse effects

Signs of potential side effects, especially visual disturbances, diabetes mellitus, local irritation, allergic reactions, local or systemic infection, psychic disturbances, seizures, hypertension, tachycardia, musculoskeletal disorders, Cushing's syndrome, edema, endocrine imbalance, hypokalemic syndrome, gastrointestinal effects, myopathy, striae, tissue atrophy, scarring at injection site, bruising, or delayed wound healing

General Dosing Information

For replacement therapy in chronic adrenocortical insufficiency states, adrenocorticoid therapy must be continued for the life of the patient. It is recommended that dosage of cortisone or hydrocortisone be timed to simulate endogenous corticosteroid secretion, with $^2/_3$ of the daily dose administered in the morning and $^1/_3$ in the evening. Other adrenocorticoids are usually given once a day.

For treatment of adrenogenital syndrome, suppression of corticotropin secretion is required to decrease hypersecretion of adrenal androgens. This is usually achieved by administering $^1/_3$ of the daily dose of cortisone or hydrocortisone in the morning and $^2/_3$ in the evening or giving $^1/_3$ of the daily dose three times a day at evenly spaced intervals. Other adrenocorticoids are usually given once a day.

Except in severe conditions or emergency situations, it is recommended that therapy be instituted with low doses that should be increased as necessary to provide the desired effect. For most conditions, administration in the lowest effective dose for the shortest time possible is recommended. Dosage requirements are variable and should be individualized according to the disease being treated and patient response rather than by age or body weight. Whenever possible, local administration is recommended in order to concentrate the medication at the affected site and reduce the risk of systemic effects. After a favorable response is obtained, the dosage should be decreased gradually to the lowest dose that will maintain an adequate clinical response.

Frequent monitoring of drug effect is required. Situations that may necessitate dosage adjustments include remissions or exacerbations of the disease process and the patient's response to the medication.

Clinically significant hypothalamic-pituitary-adrenal (HPA) axis suppression leading to adrenal insufficiency may occur more readily with multiple daily doses or evening administration than with single doses given every morning or every other morning. Administration of a single daily dose of a short- or intermediate-acting adrenocorticoid prior to 9 a.m. may reduce the risk of HPA axis suppression (because maximum endogenous corticosteroid secretion occurs in the morning) and is recommended for daily administration whenever possible. However, some disease conditions may require multiple daily doses.

Following discontinuation of short-term (up to 5 days) high-dose use, adrenal recovery may occur within 1 week; however, following prolonged high-dose administration, complete recovery of adrenal function may require up to 1 year. Following very prolonged suppression, complete recovery may never occur. During the recovery period, monitoring of adrenal function may be required to assess the patient's ability to respond to stress.

Patients with known or suspected adrenal insufficiency, including those already receiving replacement therapy, require an increase in dosage or reinstitution of therapy prior to, during, and for a time following, exposure to emotional stress or physical stress such as severe infection, surgery (including dental surgery), or injury. Administration of sodium and/or a mineralocorticoid may also be required. Dosage and duration of such therapy are dependent on the severity of the stress.

When medication is to be discontinued, dosage should be reduced gradually. The rate at which dosage can be decreased and the time required for complete withdrawal of therapy are variable, depending on the specific agent used; dose, frequency and route of administration; duration of therapy; condition being treated; and patient response.

For oral dosage forms only

If oral long-term use is required for disease therapy, an alternate-day regimen using an intermediate-acting adrenocorticoid is recommended to minimize HPA axis suppression and possibly other adverse effects. An intermediate-acting adrenocorticoid is one that suppresses HPA axis activity for 12 to 36 hours following a single dose. Administration of longer-acting adrenocorticoids on an alternate-day schedule does not reduce the risk of HPA axis suppression and is not recommended.

Alternate-day therapy utilizes a single dose administered every other morning, usually in a quantity equivalent to, or somewhat higher than, twice the usual or pre-established daily dose. The patient should have a normal or moderately responsive HPA axis.

If treatment has been initiated with daily administration, changes to alternate-day therapy should be made gradually, after the patient's condition has stabilized. However, for some diseases, such as childhood nephrosis, therapy may be initiated with alternate-day dosing.

Alternate-day therapy may not be effective in treating hematologic disorders, malignancies, ulcerative colitis, or severe conditions. Also, some patients, such as those with asthma or rheumatoid arthritis, may experience exacerbation of symptoms on the second day. Administration of (or increasing the dosage of) suitable supplemental therapy on the second day may provide sufficient symptomatic relief to permit alternate-day dosing in some patients.

For parenteral dosage forms only

For acute adrenocortical insufficiency, initiation of adrenocorticoid therapy by intravenous injection followed by slow intravenous infusion or intramuscular administration is recommended. Certain other acute conditions may also require initiation of therapy with intravenous administration or intramuscular administration of a rapidly acting formulation. Administration of corticotropin or intramuscular injection of a repository dosage form is *not* recommended in acute or emergency situations.

In severe or life-threatening conditions, single-dose or short-term intravenous administration of a very high dose ("pulse" therapy) may produce the required therapeutic response with a minimum risk of prolonged HPA axis suppression or other adverse effects. Such therapy has been recommended for treating conditions such as organ transplant rejection reactions, acute nephritis associated with systemic lupus erythematosus, vasculitis, adult respiratory distress syndrome, and shock. However, rapid intravenous administration of high doses of adrenocorticoids has been reported to cause potentially life-threatening side effects and appropriate precautions should be observed.

When the suspension dosage forms are administered intramuscularly, they should be injected deeply into the gluteal muscle to prevent local tissue atrophy. It is recommended that the deltoid muscle not be used because of a higher incidence of local atrophy. In addition, do not inject repeatedly into the same site.

A standard textbook should be consulted for specific techniques and procedures applicable to local injection of adrenocorticoids for various indications.

It is recommended that intra-articular injections be repeated no more often than once every 3 weeks. Frequent repeated injections may cause joint damage.

Following intra-articular injection, the injected joint should not be overused, even if pain is relieved, because of the increased risk of joint damage or deterioration. It is recommended that weight-bearing joints be rested for 24 to 48 hours postinjection.

Administration of a local anesthetic concurrently with intra-articular or soft tissue injection of an adrenocorticoid may reduce the pain of injection and provide immediate relief of symptoms. However, a post-injection flare of pain may occur when the local anesthetic effect subsides.

Dosages for local injections (e.g., intra-articular, intrabursal, intradermal, intralesional) are given as ranges only. The actual dosage depends upon the size of the joint or lesion and the severity of the condition being treated.

Diet/Nutrition

Administration of oral dosage forms with food may relieve indigestion or mild gastrointestinal irritation that may occur.

Patients receiving prolonged therapy with corticotropin or with pharmacologic doses of adrenocorticoids, especially those with significant mineralocorticoid activity, may require sodium restriction and/or potassium supplementation during therapy.

Because adrenocorticoids promote protein catabolism, increased protein intake may be necessary during prolonged therapy.

Administration of calcium and vitamin D and, if the patient's condition permits, exercise or physical therapy may reduce the risk of adrenocorticoid-induced osteoporosis during prolonged therapy.

BETAMETHASONE

Summary of Differences

Pharmacology: See *Table 1*, page 487.
Precautions: Pediatrics—Not recommended for chronic use; especially likely to inhibit growth.

Oral Dosage Forms

BETAMETHASONE SYRUP USP

Usual adult and adolescent dose: Oral, 600 mcg (0.6 mg) to 7.2 mg a day as a single dose or in divided doses.

BETAMETHASONE TABLETS USP

Usual adult and adolescent dose: Oral, 600 mcg (0.6 mg) to 7.2 mg a day as a single dose or in divided doses.

BETAMETHASONE EFFERVESCENT TABLETS

Usual adult and adolescent dose: Oral, 600 mcg (0.6 mg) to 7.2 mg a day as a single dose or in divided doses.

BETAMETHASONE SODIUM PHOSPHATE EXTENDED-RELEASE TABLETS

Usual adult and adolescent dose: Oral, 2 to 6 mg per day initially, then adjusted according to patient response.

Parenteral Dosage Forms

BETAMETHASONE SODIUM PHOSPHATE INJECTION USP

Usual adult and adolescent dose:
Intra-articular, intralesional, or soft-tissue injection, up to 9 mg (base), repeated as needed.
Intramuscular or intravenous, up to 9 mg (base) a day.

STERILE BETAMETHASONE SODIUM PHOSPHATE AND BETAMETHASONE ACETATE SUSPENSION USP

Usual adult and adolescent dose:
Intra-articular, 1.5 to 12 mg, depending upon the size of the affected joint, repeated as needed.
Intrabursal, 6 mg, repeated as needed.
Intradermal or intralesional, 1.2 mg per square centimeter of affected skin up to a total amount of 6 mg, repeated at one-week intervals, if necessary.
Intramuscular, 500 mcg (0.5 mg) to 9 mg a day.

Auxiliary labeling: • Shake well.

Additional dosing information:
For administration of injections, see manufacturer's labeling. Do not administer this medication intravenously.

Rectal Dosage Forms

BETAMETHASONE DISODIUM PHOSPHATE ENEMA

Usual adult and adolescent dose: Rectal, 5 mg (base) as a retention enema each night for fourteen to twenty-eight days initially, then as determined by patient response.

Note: It is recommended that the medication be discontinued, and alternate methods of treatment considered, if a favorable response is not obtained within 4 weeks.

CORTICOTROPIN

Summary of Differences

Category: Adrenocorticotropic hormone; diagnostic aid (adrenocortical function); pituitary (anterior) hormone. Also, antiemetic (in cancer chemotherapy) and anticonvulsant (specific in infantile myoclonic seizures). Corticotropin is *not* an adrenocorticoid, although it shares many indications and precautions common to adrenocorticoids.
Pharmacology: See *Table 1*, page 487.

Additional Dosing Information

See also *General Dosing Information.*

Adrenal responsiveness to corticotropin should be verified, using the intended route of administration, prior to initiation of therapy.

The severity of the disease, plasma and urine corticosteroid concentrations, and the patient's initial response may be used to determine frequency and dose of corticotropin.

Corticotropin for injection is administered intravenously only for diagnostic purposes or for the treatment of idiopathic thrombocytopenic purpura in adults.

Following intramuscular or subcutaneous administration or during intravenous administration, patient should be observed for sensitivity reactions. Such reactions may occur more frequently following subcutaneous administration than with other routes of administration. Also, prolonged therapeutic use increases the risk of such reactions.

Uncontrollable adverse reactions may be associated with chronic administration of more than 40 USP Units per day.

Reduction in dosage may be achieved either by increasing the interval between injections or by decreasing the quantity of corticotropin administered per injection.

Parenteral Dosage Forms

CORTICOTROPIN FOR INJECTION USP

Usual adult and adolescent dose:
Diagnostic aid (adrenal-pituitary function)—Intravenous infusion, 10 to 25 USP Units in 500 mL of 5% Dextrose Injection USP administered over a period of eight hours.
Therapeutic use—Intramuscular (preferred) or subcutaneous, 40 to 80 USP Units per day, with the dose and frequency of administration being individualized according to the disease being treated and the condition and response of the patient.
Acute exacerbations of multiple sclerosis: Intramuscular, 80 to 120 USP Units per day for two to three weeks.

REPOSITORY CORTICOTROPIN INJECTION USP

Usual adult and adolescent dose: Therapeutic use—Intramuscular (preferred) or subcutaneous, 40 to 80 USP Units every twenty-four to seventy-two hours.
Acute exacerbations of multiple sclerosis: Intramuscular, 80 to 120 USP Units per day for two to three weeks.

STERILE CORTICOTROPIN ZINC HYDROXIDE SUSPENSION USP

Usual adult and adolescent dose: Therapeutic use—Intramuscular, 40 USP Units every twelve to twenty-four hours.

Auxiliary labeling: • Shake well.

CORTISONE

Summary of Differences

Pharmacology: See *Table 1*, page 487.

Oral Dosage Forms

CORTISONE ACETATE TABLETS USP

Usual adult and adolescent dose: Oral, 25 to 300 mg a day as a single dose or in divided doses.

Parenteral Dosage Forms

STERILE CORTISONE ACETATE SUSPENSION USP

Usual adult and adolescent dose: Intramuscular, 20 to 300 mg a day.

Auxiliary labeling: • Shake well.

Additional information: Do not administer this medication intravenously.

DEXAMETHASONE

Summary of Differences

Category: Also, diagnostic aid (Cushing's syndrome and endogenous depression) and antiemetic (in cancer chemotherapy).
Pharmacology: See *Table 1*, page 487.
Precautions: Pediatrics—Not recommended for chronic use; especially likely to inhibit growth.

Oral Dosage Forms

DEXAMETHASONE ELIXIR USP

Usual adult and adolescent dose: Oral, 500 mcg (0.5 mg) to 9 mg a day as a single dose or in divided doses.
Dexamethasone suppression test—
Test for Cushing's syndrome: Oral, 1 mg as a single dose at 11:00 p.m. or 500 mcg (0.5 mg) every six hours for forty-eight hours.
Test to distinguish Cushing's syndrome due to pituitary ACTH excess from Cushing's syndrome due to other causes: Oral, 2 mg every six hours for forty-eight hours.
Depression diagnosis: Oral, 1 mg as a single dose at 11:00 p.m.

In cerebral edema associated with recurrent or inoperable brain tumor—Oral, 2 mg two or three times a day, administered as maintenance therapy after cerebral edema has initially been controlled using parenteral dexamethasone sodium phosphate.

Auxiliary labeling: • Keep container tightly closed.

DEXAMETHASONE ORAL SOLUTION

Usual adult and adolescent dose: Oral, 500 mcg (0.5 mg) to 9 mg a day as a single dose or in divided doses.
Dexamethasone suppression test—
Test for Cushing's syndrome: Oral, 1 mg as a single dose at 11:00 p.m. or 500 mcg (0.5 mg) every six hours for forty-eight hours.
Test to distinguish Cushing's syndrome due to pituitary ACTH excess from Cushing's syndrome due to other causes: Oral, 2 mg every six hours for forty-eight hours.
Depression diagnosis: Oral, 1 mg as a single dose at 11:00 p.m.
In cerebral edema associated with recurrent or inoperable brain tumor—Oral, 2 mg two or three times a day, administered as maintenance therapy after cerebral edema has initially been controlled using parenteral dexamethasone sodium phosphate.

DEXAMETHASONE TABLETS USP

Usual adult and adolescent dose: Oral, 500 mcg (0.5 mg) to 9 mg a day as a single dose or in divided doses.
Dexamethasone suppression test—
Test for Cushing's syndrome: Oral, 1 mg as a single dose at 11:00 p.m. or 500 mcg (0.5 mg) every six hours for forty-eight hours.
Test to distinguish Cushing's syndrome due to pituitary ACTH excess from Cushing's syndrome due to other causes: Oral, 2 mg every six hours for forty-eight hours.
Depression diagnosis: Oral, 1 mg as a single dose at 11:00 p.m.
In cerebral edema associated with recurrent or inoperable brain tumor—Oral, 2 mg two or three times a day, administered as maintenance therapy after cerebral edema has initially been controlled using parenteral dexamethasone sodium phosphate.

Parenteral Dosage Forms

STERILE DEXAMETHASONE ACETATE SUSPENSION USP

Usual adult and adolescent dose:
Intra-articular or soft-tissue injection, 4 to 16 mg of dexamethasone (base), repeated at one- to three-week intervals, if necessary.
Intralesional, 800 mcg (0.8 mg) to 1.6 mg of dexamethasone (base) per injection site, repeated as needed.
Intramuscular, 8 to 16 mg of dexamethasone (base), repeated at one- to three-week intervals, if necessary.

Auxiliary labeling: • Shake well.

Additional information:
For administration of injections, see manufacturer's labeling.
Do not administer this medication intravenously.
The suspension containing the equivalent of 16 mg of dexamethasone per mL is not for intralesional use.

DEXAMETHASONE SODIUM PHOSPHATE INJECTION USP

Usual adult and adolescent dose:
Intra-articular, intralesional, or soft-tissue injection, 200 mcg (0.2 mg) to 6 mg of dexamethasone (phosphate), repeated at three-day to three-week intervals, if necessary.
Intramuscular or intravenous, 500 mcg (0.5 mg) to 9 mg of dexamethasone (phosphate) a day.

For cerebral edema—
Initial: Intravenous, 10 mg (phosphate), followed by 4 mg (phosphate) intramuscularly every six hours until symptoms subside. Dosage may be reduced after two to four days and gradually discontinued over a period of five to seven days, unless a brain tumor, which must be treated before dexamethasone can be discontinued, is present.
Maintenance (for recurrent or inoperable brain tumors): Intramuscular, 2 mg (phosphate) two or three times a day initially, then adjusted according to patient response.
For shock—The following regimens have been utilized:
Intravenous, 20 mg (phosphate) as a single dose initially, followed by 3 mg (phosphate) per kg of body weight per 24 hours via continuous intravenous infusion, or
Intravenous, 2 to 6 mg (phosphate) per kg of body weight as a single injection, or
Intravenous, 40 mg (phosphate) as a single dose, administered every two to six hours as needed, or
Intravenous, 1 mg (phosphate) per kg of body weight as a single injection.
Note: Administration of high-dose therapy for shock should be discontinued after the patient's condition has stabilized and is usually continued for no longer than two to three days.

Usual adult prescribing limits: Up to 80 mg daily.

Additional information:
For administration of injections, see manufacturer's labeling.
Dosage forms containing 24 mg (phosphate) per mL are for intravenous use only.

HYDROCORTISONE

Summary of Differences

Pharmacology: See *Table 1*, page 487.

Oral Dosage Forms

HYDROCORTISONE TABLETS USP

Usual adult and adolescent dose: Oral, 20 to 240 mg a day as a single dose or in divided doses.

HYDROCORTISONE CYPIONATE ORAL SUSPENSION USP

Usual adult and adolescent dose: Oral, 20 to 240 mg (base) a day as a single dose or in divided doses.

Auxiliary labeling: • Shake well.

Parenteral Dosage Forms

STERILE HYDROCORTISONE SUSPENSION USP

Usual adult and adolescent dose: Intramuscular, 15 to 240 mg a day.

Auxiliary labeling: • Shake well.

Additional information: Do not administer this medication intravenously.

STERILE HYDROCORTISONE ACETATE SUSPENSION USP

Usual adult and adolescent dose: Intra-articular, intralesional, or soft-tissue injection, 5 to 75 mg, repeated at two- to three-week intervals.

Note: Severe conditions may require doses at one-week intervals.

Auxiliary labeling: • Shake well.

Additional information:
    For administration of injections, see manufacturer's labeling. Do not administer this medication intravenously.

HYDROCORTISONE SODIUM PHOSPHATE INJECTION USP

Usual adult and adolescent dose: Intramuscular, intravenous, or subcutaneous, 100 to 500 mg (base); may be repeated every two to six hours, depending upon patient condition and response.

Additional information: For administration of injections, see manufacturer's labeling.

HYDROCORTISONE SODIUM SUCCINATE FOR INJECTION USP

Usual adult and adolescent dose: Intramuscular or intravenous, 100 to 500 mg (base); may be repeated every two to six hours, depending upon patient condition and response.

Note: Initial intravenous dosage should be administered over a period of thirty seconds (100-mg dose) to ten minutes (doses 500 mg or higher).

    Maintenance dosage (if required) should be no less than 25 mg per day.

Additional information: For preparation and administration of injections, see manufacturer's labeling.

Rectal Dosage Forms

HYDROCORTISONE ENEMA USP

Usual adult and adolescent dose: Rectal, 100 mg as a retention enema each night for twenty-one days, or until clinical and proctological remission is obtained.

Auxiliary labeling:
• Shake well.
• For rectal use only.

Additional information: If the hydrocortisone enema dosage form is to be discontinued after long-term (longer than 21 days) therapy, the dosage should be reduced gradually by decreasing the frequency to once every other night for 2 or 3 weeks.

HYDROCORTISONE ACETATE RECTAL AEROSOL (FOAM)

Usual adult and adolescent dose: Rectal, 90 mg (one applicatorful) one or two times a day for two or three weeks, the frequency being decreased to every other day thereafter.

Auxiliary labeling:
• Shake well.
• For rectal use only.

METHYLPREDNISOLONE

Summary of Differences

Pharmacology: See *Table 1*, page 487.

Oral Dosage Forms

METHYLPREDNISOLONE TABLETS USP

Usual adult and adolescent dose: Oral, 4 to 48 mg a day as a single dose or in divided doses.

    In multiple sclerosis—Oral, 160 mg a day for one week, then 64 mg every other day for one month.

Parenteral Dosage Forms

Note: Bracketed uses in the *Dosage Forms* section refer to categories of use and/or indications that are not included in U.S. product labeling.

STERILE METHYLPREDNISOLONE ACETATE SUSPENSION USP

Usual adult and adolescent dose:
    Intra-articular, intralesional, or soft-tissue injection, 4 to 80 mg, repeated at one- to five-week intervals, if necessary.

    Intramuscular, 40 to 120 mg, repeated at one-day to two-week intervals, if necessary.

       For acute exacerbations of multiple sclerosis—Intramuscular, 177.6 mg per day for one week, then 71 mg every other day for one month.

Auxiliary labeling: • Shake well.

Additional information:
    For preparation and administration of injections, see manufacturer's labeling.

    Do not administer this medication intrathecally or intravenously.

METHYLPREDNISOLONE SODIUM SUCCINATE FOR INJECTION USP

Usual adult and adolescent dose: Intramuscular or intravenous, 10 to 40 mg (base), repeated as needed.

    For high-dose ("pulse" therapy)—Intravenous, 30 mg (base) per kg of body weight administered over at least thirty minutes. This dose may be repeated every four to six hours as needed.

    For acute exacerbations of multiple sclerosis—Intramuscular or intravenous, 160 mg (base) per day for one week, followed by 64 mg every other day for one month.

    [For treatment of acute spinal cord injury][1]—Intravenous, 30 mg (base) per kg of body weight administered over fifteen minutes, followed in forty-five minutes by a continuous infusion of 5.4 mg per kg of body weight per hour, for twenty-three hours.

    [For adjunctive treatment in AIDS-associated *Pneumocystis carinii* pneumonia][1]—Intravenous, 30 mg (base) two times a day on days one through five, 30 mg once a day on days six through ten, and 15 mg once a day on days eleven through twenty-one.

Additional information:
    For preparation and administration of injections, see manufacturer's labeling.

    When used intravenously, Methylprednisolone Sodium Succinate for Injection USP should be administered over a period of 1 to several minutes.

Rectal Dosage Forms

METHYLPREDNISOLONE ACETATE FOR ENEMA USP

Usual adult and adolescent dose: Rectal, 40 mg three to seven times a week for two or more weeks.

Auxiliary labeling:
• For rectal use only.
• Shake well.

Additional information:
The medication may be administered by continuous drip at a rate of 1 or 2 drops per second, or as a retention enema.
The constituted product is a suspension; when administered as continuous drip, shake bottle occasionally during administration.

---

[1]Not included in Canadian product labeling.

PARAMETHASONE

Summary of Differences

Pharmacology: See *Table 1*, page 487.
Precautions: Pediatrics—Not recommended for chronic use; especially likely to inhibit growth.

Oral Dosage Forms

PARAMETHASONE ACETATE TABLETS USP

Usual adult and adolescent dose: Oral, 2 to 24 mg a day as a single dose or in divided doses.

PREDNISOLONE

Summary of Differences

Pharmacology: See *Table 1*, page 487.

Oral Dosage Forms

PREDNISOLONE SYRUP USP

Usual adult and adolescent dose: Oral, 5 to 60 mg a day as a single dose or in divided doses.
For acute exacerbations of multiple sclerosis—Oral, 200 mg per day for one week, followed by 80 mg every other day for one month.

Usual adult prescribing limits: Up to 250 mg daily.

PREDNISOLONE TABLETS USP

Usual adult and adolescent dose: Oral, 5 to 60 mg a day as a single dose or in divided doses.
For acute exacerbations of multiple sclerosis—Oral, 200 mg per day for one week, followed by 80 mg every other day for one month.

Usual adult prescribing limits: Oral, up to 250 mg a day.

PREDNISOLONE SODIUM PHOSPHATE ORAL SOLUTION

Usual adult and adolescent dose: Oral, 5 to 60 mg (base) a day as a single dose or in divided doses.
For acute exacerbations of multiple sclerosis—Oral, 200 mg (base) per day for one week, followed by 80 mg every other day for one month.

Usual adult prescribing limits: Oral, up to 250 mg (base) a day.

Auxiliary labeling: • Keep container tightly closed.

Parenteral Dosage Forms

STERILE PREDNISOLONE ACETATE SUSPENSION USP

Usual adult and adolescent dose:
Intra-articular, intralesional, or soft-tissue injection, 4 to 100 mg, repeated as needed.
Intramuscular, 4 to 60 mg a day.

Auxiliary labeling: • Shake well.

Additional information: Do not administer this medication intravenously.

STERILE PREDNISOLONE ACETATE AND PREDNISOLONE SODIUM PHOSPHATE SUSPENSION

Usual adult and adolescent dose: Intra-articular, intramuscular, or intrasynovial, 20 to 80 mg of prednisolone acetate and 5 to 20 mg of prednisolone sodium phosphate, repeated at three-day to four-week intervals, if necessary.

Auxiliary labeling: • Shake well.

Additional information: Do not administer this medication intravenously.

PREDNISOLONE SODIUM PHOSPHATE INJECTION USP

Usual adult and adolescent dose:
Intra-articular, intralesional, or soft-tissue injection, 2 to 30 mg of prednisolone phosphate, repeated at three-day to three-week intervals, if necessary.
Intramuscular or intravenous, 4 to 60 mg of prednisolone phosphate a day.

Additional information: For preparation and administration of injections, see manufacturer's labeling.

STERILE PREDNISOLONE TEBUTATE SUSPENSION USP

Usual adult and adolescent dose: Intra-articular, intralesional, or soft-tissue injection, 4 to 40 mg, repeated at two- to three-week intervals, if necessary.

Note: Severe conditions may require doses at one-week intervals.

Auxiliary labeling: • Shake well.

Additional information:
For preparation and administration of injections, see manufacturer's labeling.
Do not administer this medication intravenously.

PREDNISONE

Summary of Differences

Pharmacology: See *Table 1*, page 487.

Oral Dosage Forms

Note: Bracketed uses in the *Dosage Forms* section refer to categories of use and/or indications that are not included in U.S. product labeling.

PREDNISONE ORAL SOLUTION USP

Usual adult and adolescent dose: Oral, 5 to 60 mg a day as a single dose or in divided doses.

For acute exacerbations of multiple sclerosis—Oral, 200 mg a day for one week followed by 80 mg every other day for one month.

For adrenogenital syndrome—Oral, 5 to 10 mg a day as a single dose.

[For adjunctive treatment in AIDS-associated *Pneumocystis carinii* pneumonia][1]—Oral, 40 mg two times a day on days one through five, 40 mg once a day on days six through ten, and 20 mg once a day on days eleven through twenty-one.

Usual adult prescribing limits: Up to 250 mg daily.

PREDNISONE SYRUP USP

Usual adult and adolescent dose: Oral, 5 to 60 mg a day as a single dose or in divided doses.

For acute exacerbations of multiple sclerosis—Oral, 200 mg a day for one week followed by 80 mg every other day for one month.

For adrenogenital syndrome—Oral, 5 to 10 mg a day as a single dose.

[For adjunctive treatment in AIDS-associated *Pneumocystis carinii* pneumonia][1]—Oral, 40 mg two times a day on days one through five, 40 mg once a day on days six through ten, and 20 mg once a day on days eleven through twenty-one.

Usual adult prescribing limits: Up to 250 mg daily.

PREDNISONE TABLETS USP

Usual adult and adolescent dose: Oral, 5 to 60 mg a day as a single dose or in divided doses.

For acute exacerbations of multiple sclerosis—Oral, 200 mg per day for one week followed by 80 mg every other day for one month.

For adrenogenital syndrome—Oral, 5 to 10 mg a day as a single dose.

[For adjunctive treatment in AIDS-associated *Pneumocystis carinii* pneumonia][1]—Oral, 40 mg two times a day on days one through five, 40 mg once a day on days six through ten, and 20 mg once a day on days eleven through twenty-one.

Usual adult prescribing limits: Up to 250 mg daily.

TRIAMCINOLONE

Summary of Differences

Indications: See *Table 1*, page $.
Pharmacology: See *Table 1*, page 487, and *Table 3*, page $.
General dosing information: See *Table 4*, page $.

Oral Dosage Forms

TRIAMCINOLONE TABLETS USP

Usual adult and adolescent dose:

Adrenocortical insufficiency—Oral, 4 to 12 mg a day as a single dose or in divided doses.

Other indications—Oral, 4 to 48 mg a day as a single dose or in divided doses.

Note: In some patients (e.g., those with systemic lupus erythematosus, acute rheumatic carditis, or certain hematologic disorders), initial doses as high as 60 mg per day may be required.

TRIAMCINOLONE DIACETATE SYRUP USP

Usual adult and adolescent dose:

Adrenocortical insufficiency—Oral, 4 to 12 mg (base) a day as a single dose or in divided doses.

Other indications—Oral, 4 to 48 mg (base) a day as a single dose or in divided doses.

Note: After an initial response has been attained, this medication may be administered on an intermittent schedule. An example of this schedule is as follows: three or four days of medication followed by three medication-free days.

In some patients (e.g., those with systemic lupus erythematosus, acute rheumatic carditis, or certain hematologic disorders), initial doses as high as 60 mg (base) per day may be required.

Parenteral Dosage Forms

STERILE TRIAMCINOLONE ACETONIDE SUSPENSION USP

Usual adult and adolescent dose:

Intra-articular, intrabursal, or tendon-sheath injection, 2.5 to 15 mg.

Intradermal or intralesional, up to 1 mg per injection site, repeated at one-week or less frequent intervals, if necessary.

Intramuscular, 40 to 80 mg, repeated at four-week intervals, if necessary.

Auxiliary labeling: • Shake well.

Additional information:

For preparation and administration of injections, see manufacturer's labeling.

Do not administer this medication intravenously.

Do not administer the 40-mg-per-mL strength intradermally or intralesionally.

Do not administer the 10-mg-per-mL strength intramuscularly.

STERILE TRIAMCINOLONE DIACETATE SUSPENSION USP

Usual adult and adolescent dose:

Intra-articular, intrasynovial, intralesional, sublesional, or soft-tissue injection, 3 to 48 mg, repeated at one- to eight-week intervals, if necessary.

Intramuscular, 40 mg once a week. Alternatively, a dose equal to four to seven times the predetermined oral daily dose may be administered as a single injection and repeated at four-day to four-week intervals as required.

Auxiliary labeling: • Shake well.

Additional information:

For preparation and administration of injections, see manufacturer's labeling.

Do not administer this medication intravenously.

STERILE TRIAMCINOLONE HEXACETONIDE SUSPENSION USP

Usual adult and adolescent dose:

Intra-articular, 2 to 20 mg, repeated at three- or four-week intervals, if necessary.

Intralesional or sublesional, up to 500 mcg (0.5 mg) per square inch of affected skin, repeated as needed.

Auxiliary labeling: • Shake well.

Additional information:

For preparation and administration of injections, see manufacturer's labeling.

Do not administer this medication intravenously.

The 5-mg-per-mL strength is recommended for intralesional and sublesional injections only.

The 20-mg-per-mL strength is recommended for intra-articular injection only.

Table 1. Pharmacology*

Drug and Route	Onset of Action	Peak Effect	Duration of Action	Drug and Route	Onset of Action	Peak Effect	Duration of Action
Betamethasone				Methylprednisolone			
Oral		1–2 hr	3.25 days	Oral		1–2 hr	1.25–1.5 days
Sodium phosphate				Acetate			
IV	Rapid			IM	Slow 6–48 hr	4–8 days	1–4 wk
IM	Rapid			IA, IL, ST	Very slow	7 days	1–5 wk
Acetate/Sodium phosphate				Sodium succinate			
IM	1–3 hr		1 wk	IV	Rapid		
IA, IS			1–2 wk	IM	Rapid		
IL, ST			1 wk				
Corticotropin				Paramethasone acetate			
Repository				Oral		1–2 hr	2 days
IM			12–24 hr	Prednisolone			
Zinc hydroxide				Oral		1–2 hr	1.25–1.5 days
IM			48 hr	Acetate			
Cortisone acetate				IM	Slow		
Oral	Rapid	2 hr	1.25–1.5 days	Acetate/Sodium phosphate			
IM	Slow	20–48 hr		IM			Up to 4 wk
Dexamethasone				IB, IS, IA, ST			3 days–4 wk
Oral		1–2 hr	2.75 days	Sodium phosphate			
Acetate				IV	Rapid	1 hr	
IM		8 hr	6 days	IM	Rapid	1 hr	
IA, ST, IL			1–3 wk	IA, IL, ST			3 days–3 wk
Sodium phosphate				Tebutate			
IV	Rapid			IA, IL, ST	Slow 1–2 days		1–3 wk
IM	Rapid						
IA, IS, IL, ST			3 days–3 wk	Prednisone			
Hydrocortisone				Oral		1–2 hr	1.25–1.5 days
Oral		1 hr	1.25–1.5 days	Triamcinolone			
IM		4–8 hr		Oral		1–2 hr	2.25 days
Rectal (retention enema)	3–5 days			Acetonide			
Acetate				IM	Slow 24–48 hr		1–6 wk
IA, IS, IB, IL, ST		24–48 hr	3 days–4 wk	IB, IA, IS, IL, ST			Several wk
Rectal (foam)	5–7 days			Diacetate			
Cypionate				Oral		1–2 hr	
Oral	Slower than tablet	1–2 hr		IM	Slow		4 days–4 wk
Sodium phosphate				IL			1–2 wk
IV	Rapid			IA, IS, ST			1–8 wk
IM	Rapid	1 hr		Hexacetonide			
Sodium succinate				IA, IL			3–4 wk
IV	Rapid						
IM	Rapid	1 hr	Variable				

*Abbreviations: IA=intra-articular; IB=intrabursal; IL=intralesional; IM=intramuscular; IS=intrasynovial; ST=soft tissue.

COUGH/COLD COMBINATIONS   Systemic

Antihistaminic (H$_1$-receptor)-decongestant-antitussive—

Brompheniramine, Phenylephrine, Phenylpropanolamine, and Codeine [*Dimetapp with Codeine*]* (RE301)

Brompheniramine, Phenylephrine, Phenylpropanolamine, and Dextromethorphan [*Dimetapp-DM*]* (RE502)

Brompheniramine, Phenylpropanolamine, and Codeine [*Biphetane DC Cough; Bromanate DC Cough; Bromphen DC with Codeine Cough; Dimetane-DC Cough; Myphetane DC Cough; Normatane DC; Poly-Histine-CS*] (RE301)

Brompheniramine, Phenylpropanolamine, and Dextromethorphan [*Dimetapp DM Cough and Cold; Poly-Histine-DM*] (RE502)

Brompheniramine, Pseudoephedrine, and Dextromethorphan [*Bromfed-AT; Bromfed-DM; Brotane DX Cough; Dimetane-DX Cough*] (RE502)

Carbinoxamine, Pseudoephedrine, and Dextromethorphan [*Baydec DM Drops; Carbinoxamine Compound; Carbodec DM Drops; Pseudo-Car DM; Rondec-DM; Rondec-DM Drops; Tussafed*] (RE502)

Chlorpheniramine, Ephedrine, Phenylephrine, and Carbetapentane [*Histatuss Pediatric; Rentamine Pediatric; Rynatuss; Rynatuss Pediatric*] (RE502)

Chlorpheniramine, Phenylephrine, and Dextromethorphan [*Cerose-DM; Dondril; Trimedine Liquid*] (RE502)

Chlorpheniramine, Phenylephrine, and Hydrocodone [*Anamine HD; Chlorgest-HD; Endal-HD; Tussanil DH; Vanex-HD*] (RE301)

Chlorpheniramine, Phenylephrine, Phenylpropanolamine, and Codeine [*T-Koff*] (RE301)

Chlorpheniramine, Phenylephrine, Phenylpropanolamine, and Dextromethorphan [*Tusquelin*] (RE502)

Chlorpheniramine, Phenylephrine, Phenylpropanolamine, and Dihydrocodeine [*Cophene-S*] (RE301)

Chlorpheniramine, Phenylpropanolamine, and Caramiphen [*Tuss-Ornade Spansules*]* (RE502)

Chlorpheniramine, Phenylpropanolamine, and Dextromethorphan [*Bayaminicol; Cheracol Plus; Efficol Cough Whip (Cough Suppressant/Decongestant/Antihistamine); Kophane Cough and Cold Formula; Ornade-DM 10*; Ornade-DM 15*; Ornade-DM 30*; Orthoxicol Cough; Snaplets-Multi; Triaminicol Multi-Symptom Relief; Tricodene Forte; Tricodene NN; Trind DM Liquid*] (RE502)

Chlorpheniramine, Pseudoephedrine, and Codeine [*Alamine-C Liquid; Bayhistine DH; Codehist DH; Dihistine DH; Midahist DH; Myhistine DH; Novahistine DH Liquid; Ryna-C Liquid*] (RE301)

Chlorpheniramine, Pseudoephedrine, and Dextromethorphan [*Children's NyQuil Nighttime Cold Medicine; PediaCare Children's Cold Relief Night Rest Cough-Cold Formula; PediaCare Children's Cough-Cold Formula; Rhinosyn-DM; Triaminic Nite Light; Tussar DM*] (RE502)

Chlorpheniramine, Pseudoephedrine, and Hydrocodone [*Promist HD Liquid*] (RE301)

Diphenylpyraline, Phenylephrine, and Codeine [*Novahistex C*]* (RE301)

Diphenylpyraline, Phenylephrine, and Dextromethorphan [*Novahistex DM*]* (RE502)

Diphenylpyraline, Phenylephrine, and Hydrocodone [*Coristex-DH; Coristine-DH; Novahistex DH; Novahistine DH*]* (RE301)

Pheniramine, Pyrilamine, Phenylephrine, Phenylpropanolamine, and Hydrocodone [*Ru-Tuss with Hydrocodone Liquid*] (RE301)

Pheniramine, Pyrilamine, Phenylpropanolamine, and Codeine [*Tussaminic C Forte; Tussaminic C Pediatric*]* (RE301)

Pheniramine, Pyrilamine, Phenylpropanolamine, and Dextromethorphan [*Triaminicol DM*]* (RE502)

Pheniramine, Pyrilamine, Phenylpropanolamine, and Hydrocodone [*Caldomine-DH Forte; Caldomine-DH Pediatric; Tussaminic DH Forte; Tussaminic DH Pediatric*]* (RE301)

Promethazine, Phenylephrine, and Codeine [*Mallergan-VC with Codeine; Phenameth VC with Codeine; Phenergan VC with Codeine; Pherazine VC with Codeine; Prometh VC with Codeine*] (RE301)

Pyrilamine, Phenylephrine, and Codeine [*Codimal PH*] (RE301)

Pyrilamine, Phenylephrine, and Dextromethorphan [*Codimal DM*] (RE502)

Pyrilamine, Phenylephrine, and Hydrocodone [*Codimal DH*] (RE301)

Triprolidine, Pseudoephedrine, and Codeine [*Actagen-C Cough; Actifed with Codeine Cough; Allerfrin with Codeine; Co-Actifed*; Histafed C; Pseudodine C Cough; Triacin C Cough; Trifed-C Cough*] (RE301)

Triprolidine, Pseudoephedrine, and Dextromethorphan [*Actifed DM*]* (RE502)

Antihistaminic (H$_1$-receptor)-decongestant-expectorant—

Brompheniramine, Phenylephrine, Phenylpropanolamine, and Guaifenesin [*Dimetane Expectorant*]* (RE503)

Carbinoxamine, Pseudoephedrine, and Guaifenesin [*Brexin*] (RE503)

Chlorpheniramine, Ephedrine, and Guaifenesin [*Bronkotuss Expectorant*] (RE503)

Chlorpheniramine, Phenylephrine, and Guaifenesin [*Donatussin Drops*] (RE503)

Chlorpheniramine, Phenylpropanolamine, and Guaifenesin [*Ornade Expectorant*]* (RE503)

Chlorpheniramine, Phenylpropanolamine, Guaifenesin, Sodium Citrate, and Citric Acid [*Lanatuss Expectorant*] (RE503)

Chlorpheniramine, Pseudoephedrine, and Guaifenesin [*Trinex*] (RE503)

Dexchlorpheniramine, Pseudoephedrine, and Guaifenesin [*Polaramine Expectorant*] (RE503)

Pheniramine, Pyrilamine, Phenylpropanolamine, and Guaifenesin [*Triaminic Expectorant*]* (RE503)

Antihistaminic (H$_1$-receptor)-decongestant-antitussive-expectorant—

Brompheniramine, Phenylephrine, Phenylpropanolamine, Codeine, and Guaifenesin [*Dimetane Expectorant-C*]* (RE301)

Brompheniramine, Phenylephrine, Phenylpropanolamine, Hydrocodone, and Guaifenesin [*Dimetane Expectorant-DC*]* (RE301)

Chlorpheniramine, Ephedrine, Phenylephrine, Dextromethorphan, Ammonium Chloride, and Ipecac [*Quelidrine Cough*] (RE504)

Chlorpheniramine, Phenindamine, Pyrilamine, Phenylephrine, Hydrocodone, and Ammonium Chloride [*P-V-Tussin*] (RE301)

Chlorpheniramine, Phenylephrine, Codeine, Ammonium Chloride, Potassium Guaiacolsulfonate, and Sodium Citrate [*Efricon Expectorant Liquid*] (RE301)

Chlorpheniramine, Phenylephrine, Codeine, and Potassium Iodide [*Pediacof Cough*] (RE301)

Chlorpheniramine, Phenylephrine, Dextromethorphan, and Guaifenesin [*Donatussin; Meda Syrup Forte*] (RE504)

Chlorpheniramine, Phenylephrine, Dextromethorphan, Guaifenesin, and Ammonium Chloride [*Father John's Medicine Plus*] (RE504)

Chlorpheniramine, Phenylephrine, Phenylpropanolamine, Carbetapentane, and Potassium Guaiacolsulfonate [*Cophene-X; Cophene-XP*] (RE504)

Chlorpheniramine, Phenylpropanolamine, Dextromethorphan, and Ammonium Chloride [*Kophane*] (RE504)

Chlorpheniramine, Phenyltoloxamine, Ephedrine, Codeine, and Guaiacol Carbonate [*Omni-Tuss*]* (RE301)

Chlorpheniramine, Phenyltoloxamine, Phenylpropanolamine, Dextromethorphan, and Guaifenesin [*Medatussin Plus*] (RE504)

Diphenylpyraline, Phenylephrine, Hydrocodone, and Guaifenesin [*Novahistex DH Expectorant; Novahistine DH Expectorant*]* (RE301)

Pheniramine, Pyrilamine, Phenylpropanolamine, Dextromethorphan, and Ammonium Chloride [*Prominicol Cough*] (RE504)

Pheniramine, Pyrilamine, Phenylpropanolamine, Dextromethorphan, and Guaifenesin [*Triaminic-DM Expectorant*]* (RE504)

Pheniramine, Pyrilamine, Phenylpropanolamine, Hydrocodone, and Guaifenesin [*Triaminic Expectorant DH*]* (RE301)

Pyrilamine, Phenylephrine, Hydrocodone, and Ammonium Chloride [*Hycomine; Hycomine-S Pediatric*]* (RE301)

Pyrilamine, Phenylpropanolamine, Dextromethorphan, Guaifenesin, Potassium Citrate, and Citric Acid [*Phanadex*] (RE504)

Triprolidine, Pseudoephedrine, Codeine, and Guaifenesin [*Co-Actifed Expectorant*]* (RE301)

Antihistaminic (H₁-receptor)-decongestant-antitussive-expectorant-analgesic—

Chlorpheniramine, Phenylephrine, Phenylpropanolamine, Dextromethorphan, Guaifenesin, and Acetaminophen [*Anatuss*] (RE505)

Chlorpheniramine, Phenylpropanolamine, Codeine, Guaifenesin, and Acetaminophen [*Anatuss with Codeine*] (RE301)

Chlorpheniramine, Phenylpropanolamine, Hydrocodone, Guaifenesin, and Salicylamide [*Tussanil DH*] (RE301)

Chlorpheniramine, Pseudoephedrine, Dextromethorphan, Guaifenesin, and Aspirin [*Viro-Med*] (RE505)

Pheniramine, Phenylephrine, Codeine, Sodium Citrate, Sodium Salicylate, and Caffeine [*Tussirex with Codeine Liquid*] (RE301)

Antihistaminic (H₁-receptor)-decongestant-antitussive-analgesic—

Chlorpheniramine, Phenindamine, Phenylephrine, Dextromethorphan, Acetaminophen, Salicylamide, Caffeine, and Ascorbic Acid [*Omnicol*] (RE506)

Chlorpheniramine, Pheniramine, Pyrilamine, Phenylephrine, Hydrocodone, Salicylamide, Caffeine, and Ascorbic Acid [*Citra Forte*] (RE301)

Chlorpheniramine, Phenylephrine, Dextromethorphan, Acetaminophen, and Salicylamide [*Improved Sino-Tuss*] (RE506)

Chlorpheniramine, Phenylephrine, Hydrocodone, Acetaminophen, and Caffeine [*Hycomine Compound*] (RE301)

Chlorpheniramine, Phenylpropanolamine, Dextromethorphan, and Acetaminophen [*Comtrex Multi-Symptom Cold Reliever*] (RE506)

Chlorpheniramine, Phenylpropanolamine, Dextromethorphan, Acetaminophen, and Caffeine [*Kolephrin/DM*] (RE506)

Chlorpheniramine, Pseudoephedrine, Dextromethorphan, and Acetaminophen [*Co-Apap; Comtrex Nighttime; Contac Severe Cold Formula; CoTylenol Cold Medication; Medi-Flu; Medi-Flu Caplets; TheraFlu/Flu, Cold and Cough Medicine; Ty-Cold Cold Formula; Tylenol Cold and Flu; Tylenol Cold Medication*] (RE506)

Diphenhydramine, Pseudoephedrine, Dextromethorphan, and Acetaminophen [*NyQuil Liquicaps; Tylenol Cold Night Time*] (RE506)

Doxylamine, Pseudoephedrine, Dextromethorphan, and Acetaminophen [*Contac Severe Cold Formula Night Strength; NyQuil Nighttime Colds Medicine; Nytime Cold Medicine Liquid; Pertussin PM*] (RE506)

Pheniramine, Pyrilamine, Phenylpropanolamine, Codeine, Acetaminophen, and Caffeine [*Triaminicin with Codeine*]* (RE301)

Pyrilamine, Phenylephrine, Dextromethorphan, and Acetaminophen [*Robitussin Night Relief; Robitussin Night Relief Colds Formula Liquid*] (RE506)

Pyrilamine, Phenylpropanolamine, Dextromethorphan, and Sodium Salicylate [*Kolephrin NN Liquid*] (RE506)

Antihistaminic (H₁-receptor)-antitussive—

Bromodiphenhydramine and Codeine [*Ambay Cough; Ambenyl Cough*] (RE301)

Chlorpheniramine and Dextromethorphan [*Vicks Formula 44 Cough Mixture*] (RE507)

Chlorpheniramine and Hydrocodone [*Tussionex*] (RE301)

Phenyltoloxamine and Hydrocodone [*Tussionex*] *(RE301)

Promethazine and Codeine [*Phenergan with Codeine*]† (RE301)

Promethazine and Dextromethorphan [*Phenergan with Dextromethorphan*] (RE507)

Antihistaminic (H₁-receptor)-antitussive-expectorant—

Bromodiphenhydramine, Diphenhydramine, Codeine, Ammonium Chloride, and Potassium Guaiacolsulfonate [*Ambophen Expectorant*] (RE301)

Chlorpheniramine, Codeine, and Guaifenesin [*Tussar-2; Tussar SF*] (RE301)

Diphenhydramine, Codeine, and Ammonium Chloride [*Benylin with Codeine; Calmylin with Codeine*]* (RE301)

Diphenhydramine, Dextromethorphan, and Ammonium Chloride [*Benylin-DM*]* (RE508)

Phenindamine, Hydrocodone, and Guaifenesin [*P-V-Tussin*] (RE301)

Pheniramine, Codeine, and Guaifenesin [*Robitussin A-C; Robitussin with Codeine*]* (RE301)

Pheniramine, Pyrilamine, Hydrocodone, and Potassium Citrate [*Citra Forte*] (RE301)

Antihistaminic (H₁-receptor)-antitussive-analgesic—

Chlorpheniramine, Codeine, Aspirin, and Caffeine [*Coricidin with Codeine*]* (RE301)

Chlorpheniramine, Dextromethorphan, and Acetaminophen [*Remcol-C*] (RE509)

Antitussive-expectorant—

Codeine and Calcium Iodide [*Calcidrine*] (RE301)

Codeine and Guaifenesin [*Baytussin AC; Cheracol; Glydeine Cough; Guiatuss A.C.; Guiatussin with Codeine Liquid; Mytussin AC; Nortussin with Codeine; Robitussin A-C; Tolu-Sed Cough*] (RE301)

Codeine and Iodinated Glycerol [*Iophen-C Liquid; Iotuss; Par Glycerol C; Tussi-Organidin Liquid*] (RE301)

Dextromethorphan and Guaifenesin [*Anti-Tuss DM Expectorant; Baytussin DM; Benylin Expectorant Cough Formula; Cheracol D Cough; Codistan No. 1; Efficol Cough Whip (Cough Suppressant/Expectorant); Extra Action Cough; 2/G-DM Cough; Glycotuss-dM; Guiamid D.M. Liquid; Guiatuss-DM; Halotussin-DM Expectorant; Kolephrin GG/DM; Mytussin DM; Naldecon Senior DX; Pertussin CS; Queltuss; Rhinosyn-DMX Expectorant; Robitussin-DM; Silexin Cough; Tolu-Sed DM Cough; Tuss-DM; Unproco; Vicks Children's Cough*] (RE302)

Dextromethorphan, Guaifenesin, Potassium Citrate, and Citric Acid [*Medatussin; Phanatuss*] (RE302)

Dextromethorphan and Iodinated Glycerol [*Iotuss-DM; Par Glycerol DM; Tussi-Organidin DM Liquid; Tusso-DM*] (RE302)

Hydrocodone and Guaifenesin [*Adatuss D.C. Expectorant; Codiclear DH; Entuss Expectorant; Hycotuss Expectorant; Kwelcof Liquid*] (RE301)

Hydrocodone and Potassium Guaiacolsulfonate [*Entuss Expectorant*] (RE301)

Hydromorphone and Guaifenesin [*Dilaudid Cough*] (RE301)

Antitussive-anticholinergic—

Hydrocodone and Homatropine [*Baycodan; Codan; Hycodan; Hydropane; Tussigon*]† (RE301)

Decongestant-antitussive—

Phenylephrine and Dextromethorphan [*Conar*] (RE512)

Phenylpropanolamine and Caramiphen [*Rescaps-D S.R.; Tuss-Ade; Tuss Allergine Modified T.D.; Tussogest; Tuss-Ornade Liquid; Tuss-Ornade Spansules*] (RE512)

Phenylpropanolamine and Dextromethorphan [*Efficol Cough Whip (Cough Suppressant/Decongestant); Hold (Children's Formula); Snaplets-DM; Syracol Liquid; Triaminic-DM Cough Formula; Tricodene Pediatric*] (RE512)

Phenylpropanolamine and Hydrocodone [*Baycomine; Baycomine Pediatric; Codamine; Codamine Pediatric; Hycomine; Hycomine Pediatric; Hydromine; Hydromine Pediatric; Hydrophen; Myhydromine; Myhydromine Pediatric*] (RE301)

Pseudoephedrine and Codeine [*Nucochem; Nucofed*] (RE301)

Pseudoephedrine and Dextromethorphan [*Mediquell Decongestant Formula; Sudafed DM**] (RE512)

Pseudoephedrine and Hydrocodone [*BayCotussend Liquid; De-Tuss; Detussin Liquid; Entuss-D; Mycotussin*] (RE301)

Decongestant-antitussive-expectorant—

Phenylephrine, Dextromethorphan, and Guaifenesin [*Conar Expectorant*] (RE513)

Phenylephrine, Hydrocodone, and Guaifenesin [*Donatussin DC*] (RE301)

Phenylpropanolamine, Codeine, and Guaifenesin [*Codegest Expectorant; Conex with Codeine Liquid; Naldecon-CX Adult Liquid; Triaminic Expectorant with Codeine*] (RE301)

Phenylpropanolamine, Dextromethorphan, and Guaifenesin [*Coricidin Cough; Dorcol DM*; Ipsatol Cough Formula for Children; Kiddy Koff; Naldecon-DX Adult Liquid; Naldecon-DX Children's Syrup; Naldecon-DX Pediatric Drops; Robitussin-CF*] (RE513)

Pseudoephedrine, Codeine, and Guaifenesin [*Alamine Expectorant; Bayhistine Expectorant; C-Tussin Expectorant; Deproist Expectorant with Codeine; Isoclor Expectorant; Myhistine Expectorant; Mytussin DAC; Novahistine Expectorant; Nucochem Expectorant; Nucochem Pediatric Expectorant; Nucofed Expectorant; Nucofed Pediatric Expectorant; Phenhist Expectorant; Robitussin-DAC; Ryna-CX Liquid*] (RE301)

Pseudoephedrine, Dextromethorphan, and Guaifenesin [*Ambenyl-D Decongestant Cough Formula; Concentrin; Dimacol; Dorcol Children's Cough; Noratuss II Liquid; Novahistine DMX Liquid; Pertussin AM; Rhinosyn-X; Ru-Tuss Expectorant; Sudafed Cough; Vicks Formula 44D Decongestant Cough Mixture*] (RE513)

Pseudoephedrine, Hydrocodone, and Guaifenesin [*Detussin Expectorant; Entuss-D; Entuss Pediatric Expectorant; SRC Expectorant; Vanex Expectorant*] (RE301)

Decongestant-antitussive-expectorant-analgesic—

Phenylephrine, Dextromethorphan, Guaifenesin, and Acetaminophen [*Conar-A*] (RE514)

Pseudoephedrine, Dextromethorphan, Guaifenesin, and Acetaminophen [*DayCare; Vicks Formula 44M Multi-symptom Cough Mixture*] (RE514)

Decongestant-antitussive-analgesic—

Phenylpropanolamine, Dextromethorphan, and Acetaminophen [*Contac Jr. Children's Cold Medicine; Saleto-CF*] (RE515)

Pseudoephedrine, Dextromethorphan, and Acetaminophen [*Comtrex Daytime Caplets; Comtrex Multi-Symptom Non-Drowsy Caplets; Sudafed Severe Cold Formula Caplets; Tylenol Cold Medication, Non-Drowsy; Tylenol Cough*] (RE515)

Decongestant-expectorant—

Ephedrine and Guaifenesin [*Broncholate*] (RE516)

Ephedrine and Potassium Iodide [*KIE*] (RE516)

Phenylephrine, Phenylpropanolamine, and Guaifenesin [*Banex; Banex Liquid; Entex; Entex Liquid; Respinol-G; Rymed; Rymed Liquid*] (RE516)

Phenylpropanolamine and Guaifenesin [*Ami-Tex LA; Banex-LA; Bayaminic Expectorant; Codimal Expectorant; Conex; Dura-Vent; Entex LA; Gentab-LA; Guaipax; Naldecon-EX; Nolex LA; Phenylfenesin L.A.; Prominic Expectorant; Snaplets-EX; Triaminic Expectorant; Triphenyl Expectorant; Utex-S.R.*] (RE516)

Pseudoephedrine and Guaifenesin [*Congess JR; Congess SR; Entex PSE; Fedahist Expectorant; Fedahist Expectorant Pediatric Drops; Guaifed; Guaifed-PD; Guaitab; Histalet X; Respaire-60 SR; Respaire-120 SR; Robitussin-PE; Ru-Tuss DE; Rymed-TR; Sinufed Timecelles; Sudafed Expectorant*; Tuss-LA; Zephrex; Zephrex-LA*] (RE516)

Decongestant-expectorant-analgesic—

Phenylephrine, Guaifenesin, Acetaminophen, Salicylamide, and Caffeine [*Fendol*] (RE599)

---

*Not commercially available in the U.S.

†Generic name product available in the U.S.

Indications

Accepted

Cough (treatment)—Combination products containing antitussives and/or expectorants may be indicated for the symptomatic relief of cough due to colds and minor upper respiratory infections.

Cough and nasal congestion (treatment)—Combination products containing antitussives and/or expectorants, and nasal decongestants may be indicated for the symptomatic relief of cough and nasal congestion due to the common cold and other respiratory infections. Also, products containing antihistamines may provide relief of the cough, nasal congestion, rhinorrhea, and sneezing associated with allergy and the common cold. However, controlled clinical studies have not demonstrated that antihistamines are significantly more effective than placebo in relieving cold symptoms.

Cold symptoms (treatment)—Combination products containing antihistamines, antitussives or expectorants, nasal decongestants, and analgesics may be indicated for the temporary relief of coughs, nasal congestion, and associated aches, pains, and general discomfort due to colds, flu, or allergy. The antihistamine in these cold combinations may provide relief of nasal congestion, rhinorrhea, and sneezing. It may also serve as an adjunct because of its anticholinergic drying effects. However, in many cough/cold combinations, the dosage level of the antihistamine is below that required to obtain a significant effect. Also, controlled clinical studies have not demonstrated that antihistamines are significantly more effective than placebo in relieving cold symptoms.

Unaccepted

Cough/cold combination products that contain both an antitussive and an expectorant usually do not offer any advantage over products that contain only one of these agents. In some cases, their combination may be detrimental in the treatment of coughs, since antitussives should be used only in the treatment of dry coughs and not for productive coughs.

Some products containing an anticholinergic have been used to help dry excessive nasal secretions associated with the common cold and allergic rhinitis; however, the efficacy of anticholinergics for this use in these combination products has not been established. In most products, the anticholinergic is included in doses below the therapeutic level in an attempt to prevent abuse by deliberate overdosage (e.g., in combinations containing a narcotic antitussive).

Combination products that contain an analgesic are generally not recommended for regular use for the treatment of cold symptoms during the common cold or acute allergic rhinitis since they may mask fever, which may indicate a secondary bacterial infection.

Ammonium chloride, calcium iodide, citric acid, guaiacol carbonate, iodinated glycerol, ipecac, potassium citrate, potassium guaiacolsulfonate, potassium iodide, and sodium citrate are included as expectorants in these combinations; however, the Food and Drug Administration (FDA) has not found them to be useful for this indication. Therefore, FDA has requested manufacturers to reformulate their products to replace these ingredients with guaifenesin.

Pharmacology

Antihistamine-containing—See *Antihistamines (Systemic)*.
Antihistamine- and decongestant-containing—See *Antihistamines and Decongestants (Systemic)*.
Decongestant-containing—See:
　Ephedrine, Bronchodilators, Adrenergic (Systemic).
　Phenylpropanolamine (Systemic).
　Pseudoephedrine (Systemic).
Dextromethorphan-containing—See *Dextromethorphan (Systemic)*.
Opioid (narcotic) antitussive-containing—See *Opioid (Narcotic) Analgesics (Systemic)*.
Expectorant-containing—See:
　Guaifenesin (Systemic).
　Iodinated Glycerol (Systemic).
Analgesic-containing—See:
　Acetaminophen (Systemic).
　Acetaminophen and Salicylates (Systemic).
　Salicylates (Systemic).
Homatropine-containing—See *Anticholinergics/Antispasmodics (Systemic)*.

Precautions to Consider

Antihistamine-containing—See *Antihistamines (Systemic)*.
Antihistamine- and decongestant-containing—See *Antihistamines and Decongestants (Systemic)*.
Decongestant-containing—See:
　Ephedrine, Bronchodilators, Adrenergic (Systemic).
　Phenylpropanolamine (Systemic).
　Pseudoephedrine (Systemic).
Dextromethorphan-containing—See *Dextromethorphan (Systemic)*.
Opioid (narcotic) antitussive-containing—See *Opioid (Narcotic) Analgesics (Systemic)*.
Expectorant-containing—See:
　Guaifenesin (Systemic).
　Iodinated Glycerol (Systemic).

Analgesic-containing—See:
　Acetaminophen (Systemic).
　Acetaminophen and Salicylates (Systemic).
　Salicylates (Systemic).
Homatropine-containing—See *Anticholinergics/Antispasmodics (Systemic)*.

Side/Adverse Effects

Antihistamine-containing—See *Antihistamines (Systemic)*.
Antihistamine- and decongestant-containing—See *Antihistamines and Decongestants (Systemic)*.
Decongestant-containing—See:
　Ephedrine, Bronchodilators, Adrenergic (Systemic).
　Phenylpropanolamine (Systemic).
　Pseudoephedrine (Systemic).
Dextromethorphan-containing—See *Dextromethorphan (Systemic)*.
Opioid (narcotic) antitussive-containing—See *Opioid (Narcotic) Analgesics (Systemic)*.
Expectorant-containing—See:
　Guaifenesin (Systemic).
　Iodinated Glycerol (Systemic).
Analgesic-containing—See:
　Acetaminophen (Systemic).
　Acetaminophen and Salicylates (Systemic).
　Salicylates (Systemic).
Homatropine-containing—See *Anticholinergics/Antispasmodics (Systemic)*.

CROMOLYN   Inhalation-Local

Some commonly used *brand names* are:
　In the U.S.—*Intal*
　In Canada—*Fivent; Intal*
Another commonly used name is sodium cromoglycate.

INHALATION
Cromolyn Sodium Inhalation Aerosol
　In the U.S.—*Intal*
　In Canada—*Fivent*
Cromolyn Sodium for Inhalation USP (Capsules)
　In the U.S. and Canada—*Intal*
Cromolyn Sodium Inhalation USP (Solution)
　In the U.S. and Canada—*Intal*

Category: Mast cell stabilizer; asthma prophylactic; antiallergic (inhalation).

Indications

Accepted
Asthma, bronchial (prophylaxis)—Cromolyn inhalation is indicated as a prophylactic, either alone or as an adjunct, in the management of bronchial asthma in patients who require continuing symptomatic relief. Cromolyn inhalation has no role in the treatment of an acute attack of asthma, especially status asthmaticus, because it has no intrinsic bronchodilating activity.

Bronchospasm (prophylaxis)—Cromolyn inhalation is indicated to prevent bronchospasm induced by exposure to allergens, cold dry air, environmental pollutants, or other known precipitating factors when exposure is either episodic or continuous. In episodic exposure, cromolyn inhalation can be used acutely, prior to anticipated exposure to the precipitating factor.

Cromolyn inhalation is also indicated prior to exercise to prevent exercise-induced bronchospasm.

Pharmacology

Mechanism of action/Effect: Cromolyn inhibits mast cell release of histamine, leukotrienes, and other substances that cause hypersensitivity reactions, probably by interfering with calcium transport across the mast cell membrane.

In vitro and *in vivo* animal studies have shown that cromolyn inhibits the degranulation of sensitized mast cells that occurs after exposure to specific antigens. Some *in vitro* studies have shown that cromolyn inhibits the degranulation of nonsensitized rat mast cells by phospholipase A and the subsequent release of chemical mediators.

Other actions/effects: Cromolyn has no intrinsic bronchodilator, antihistaminic, or anti-inflammatory action.

Precautions to Consider

Geriatrics

Although appropriate studies with cromolyn inhalation have not been performed in the geriatric population, no geriatrics-specific problems have been documented to date. However, elderly patients are more likely to have age-related hepatic function impairment and renal function impairment, which may require reduction of dosage in patients receiving cromolyn.

Drug interactions and/or related problems

The following drug interactions and/or related problems have been selected on the basis of their potential clinical significance (possible mechanism in parentheses where appropriate)—not necessarily inclusive (» = major clinical significance):

Note: Combinations containing any of the following medications, depending on the amount present, may also interact with this medication.

Methacholine, for inhalation
(cromolyn may decrease slightly, but inconsistently, the response to methacholine challenge in the diagnosis of bronchial airway hyperreactivity; however, cromolyn generally does not cause false-negative tests)

Contraindications/Medical problems

The contraindications/medical problems included have been selected on the basis of their potential clinical significance (reasons given in parentheses where appropriate)—not necessarily inclusive (» = major clinical significance):

Risk-benefit should be considered when the following medical problems exist:

Hepatic function impairment, severe
(excretion via biliary route; dosage reduction may be necessary)

Renal function impairment, severe
(excretion via renal route; dosage reduction may be necessary)

Sensitivity to cromolyn

For cromolyn inhalation aerosol only
Cardiac arrhythmias, history of, or
Coronary artery disease
(inhalation aerosol contains propellants)

Side/Adverse Effects

Note: Drowsiness, nasal itching and burning, nosebleed, stomach pain, and serum sickness have been reported with cromolyn inhalation solution; however, no causal relationship has been established.

Anemia, exfoliative dermatitis, nephrosis, periarteritic vasculitis, pericarditis, peripheral neuritis, photodermatitis, polymyositis, and hemoptysis have been reported rarely with cromolyn capsules for inhalation; however, the causal relationship is unknown.

The following side/adverse effects have been selected on the basis of their potential clinical significance (possible signs and symptoms in parentheses where appropriate)—not necessarily inclusive:

Those indicating need for medical attention
Incidence less frequent
Angioedema (swelling of the face, lips, eyelids, hands, feet, or inside of mouth); *bronchospasm, increased* (increased wheezing, tightness in chest, or difficulty in breathing); *dizziness; dysuria* (difficult or painful urination); *frequent urge to urinate; headache, severe or continuing; joint pain or swelling; muscle pain or weakness; nausea or vomiting; skin rash, hives, or itching*

Incidence rare
Anaphylactic reaction (difficulty in swallowing; hives; itching of skin; swelling of face, lips, or eyelids; increased wheezing or difficulty in breathing); *eosinophilic pneumonia* (chest pain, chills, severe difficulty in breathing, sweating, severe wheezing); *laryngeal edema* (difficulty in swallowing)

Those indicating need for medical attention only if they continue or are bothersome
Incidence more frequent
Cough; hoarseness
Incidence less frequent
Dryness of the mouth or throat; sneezing; stuffy nose; throat irritation; watering of the eyes

Those not indicating need for medical attention
Incidence more frequent
Unpleasant taste—with inhalation aerosol

Patient Consultation

In providing consultation, consider emphasizing the following selected information (» = major clinical significance):

Before using this medication
» Conditions affecting use, especially:
   Sensitivity to cromolyn

Proper use of this medication
» Helps prevent, but does not relieve, acute asthma or bronchospasm attacks; if used during acute attack, may cause irritation and worsen attack
» Importance of not using more medication than the amount prescribed
   Proper administration:
   For inhalation aerosol dosage form
      Reading patient instructions carefully before using
      Avoiding contact with the eyes
   For inhalation capsule dosage form
      Using with a special inhaler; reading patient instructions carefully before using
» Not swallowing capsules; medication not effective if swallowed
   For inhalation solution dosage form
      Using in a power-operated nebulizer with an adequate flow rate and equipped with face mask or mouthpiece; hand-operated nebulizers not suitable
» Proper storage
For patients on scheduled dosing regimen
» Compliance with therapy; may require up to 4 weeks for full benefit
   Missed dose: Using as soon as possible; using any remaining doses for that day at regularly spaced intervals; not doubling doses

Precautions while using this medication
» Checking with physician if symptoms do not improve or if condition becomes worse
» Importance of not discontinuing concurrent systemic adrenocorticoid therapy without physician's advice
   Possible dryness of mouth or throat, throat irritation, and hoarseness; gargling and rinsing mouth after each dose to help prevent these effects

Side/adverse effects
   Signs of potential side effects, especially anaphylactic reaction; angioedema; dizziness; eosinophilic pneumonia; severe or continuing headache; increased bronchospasm; joint pain or swelling; laryngeal edema; muscle pain or weakness; nausea or vomiting; problems with urination; and skin rash, hives, or itching
   Cromolyn inhalation aerosol may cause an unpleasant taste

General Dosing Information

A decrease in severity of clinical symptoms or in the need for concomitant therapy is a sign of improvement that will be evident in the first 4 weeks of therapy if patient responds to cromolyn therapy.

After a patient becomes stabilized on cromolyn, the frequency of administration may be slowly decreased to a level of frequency that maintains the patient free from exacerbations of asthma.

In asthmatic patients receiving adrenocorticoids and/or bronchodilators prior to cromolyn, these medications should be continued following initiation of cromolyn therapy. However, an attempt should be made to reduce the dosage of the adrenocorticoid and/or institute an alternate-day regimen. The dosage of the adrenocorticoid should be reduced gradually to avoid an exacerbation of asthma.

If eosinophilic pneumonia occurs during the course of cromolyn inhalation therapy, the medication should be discontinued.

For inhalation solution dosage form only

Cromolyn solution should be administered from a power-operated nebulizer having an adequate flow rate (6 to 8 liters per minute) and equipped with a suitable face mask or mouthpiece. Hand-operated nebulizers are not suitable for administration of cromolyn solution.

Inhalation Dosage Forms

CROMOLYN SODIUM INHALATION AEROSOL

Usual adult and adolescent dose:
Asthma, bronchial (prophylaxis)—Oral inhalation, 1.6 or 2 mg (2 inhalations) four times a day at regular intervals, the dosage being adjusted as needed and tolerated.

Bronchospasm (prophylaxis)—Oral inhalation, 1.6 or 2 mg (2 inhalations) as a single dose ten to fifteen (but not more than sixty) minutes before exposure to the precipitating factor; or, if used chronically, 1.6 or 2 mg (2 inhalations) four times a day at regular intervals, the dosage being adjusted as needed and tolerated.

Usual geriatric dose: See *Usual adult and adolescent dose.*

Auxiliary labeling:
- For oral inhalation only.
- Store away from heat and direct sunlight.

CROMOLYN SODIUM FOR INHALATION USP (CAPSULES)

Usual adult and adolescent dose:
Asthma, bronchial (prophylaxis)—Oral inhalation, 20 mg (1 capsule) four times a day at regular intervals, the dosage being adjusted as needed and tolerated.

Bronchospasm (prophylaxis)—Oral inhalation, 20 mg (1 capsule) as a single dose just prior to exposure to the precipitating factor; or, if used chronically, 20 mg (1 capsule) four times a day at regular intervals, the dosage being adjusted as needed and tolerated.

Usual adult prescribing limits: Up to 160 mg (8 capsules) daily.

Usual geriatric dose: See *Usual adult and adolescent dose.*

Auxiliary labeling: • For inhalation only—Do not swallow capsules.

CROMOLYN SODIUM INHALATION USP (SOLUTION)

Usual adult and adolescent dose:
Asthma, bronchial (prophylaxis)—Oral inhalation, 20 mg four times a day at regular intervals, the dosage being adjusted as needed and tolerated.

Bronchospasm (prophylaxis)—Oral inhalation, 20 mg as a single dose just prior to exposure to the precipitating factor; or, if used chronically, 20 mg four times a day at regular intervals, the dosage being adjusted as needed and tolerated.

Usual adult prescribing limits: Up to 160 mg daily.

Usual geriatric dose: See *Usual adult and adolescent dose.*

Auxiliary labeling: • For inhalation only.

CROMOLYN   Nasal

Some commonly used *brand names* are:
In the U.S.—*Nasalcrom*
In Canada—*Rynacrom*
Another commonly used name is sodium cromoglycate.

NASAL
Cromolyn Sodium for Nasal Insufflation*
In Canada—*Rynacrom*
Cromolyn Sodium Nasal Solution USP
In the U.S.—*Nasalcrom*
In Canada—*Rynacrom*

*Not commercially available in the U.S.

Category: Mast cell stabilizer (nasal); antiallergic (nasal).

Indications

Accepted
Rhinitis, allergic (prophylaxis and treatment)—Cromolyn sodium nasal solution is indicated for the prevention and treatment of the symptoms of perennial and seasonal allergic rhinitis.

Cromolyn sodium for nasal insufflation is indicated for the prophylaxis of seasonal allergic rhinitis.

Pharmacology

Mechanism of action/Effect: Cromolyn inhibits mast cell release of histamine, leukotrienes, and other substances that cause hypersensitivity reactions, probably by interfering with calcium transport across the mast cell membrane.

In vitro and *in vivo* animal studies have shown that cromolyn inhibits the degranulation of sensitized mast cells that occurs after exposure to specific antigens. Some *in vitro* studies have shown that cromolyn inhibits the degranulation of nonsensitized rat mast cells by phospholipase A and the subsequent release of chemical mediators.

Other actions/effects: Cromolyn has no intrinsic bronchodilator, antihistaminic, or anti-inflammatory action.

Onset of therapeutic effect: Seasonal allergic rhinitis—Results are usually noticeable in less than 1 week.

Time to peak effect: Perennial allergic rhinitis—May require up to 4 weeks.

Precautions to Consider

Geriatrics

Although appropriate studies on the relationship of age to the effects of nasal cromolyn have not been performed in the geriatric population, no geriatrics-specific problems have been documented to date. However, elderly patients are more likely to have age-related hepatic function impairment and renal function impairment, which may require reduction of dosage in patients receiving nasal cromolyn.

Drug interactions and/or related problems

The following drug interactions and/or related problems have been selected on the basis of their potential clinical significance (possible mechanism in parentheses where appropriate)—not necessarily inclusive (» = major clinical significance):

Methacholine, for inhalation
    (cromolyn may decrease slightly, but inconsistently, the response to methacholine challenge in the diagnosis of bronchial airway hyperreactivity; however, cromolyn generally does not cause false-negative tests)

Contraindications/Medical problems

The contraindications/medical problems included have been selected on the basis of their potential clinical significance (reasons given in parentheses where appropriate)—not necessarily inclusive (» = major clinical significance).

Risk-benefit should be considered when the following medical problems exist:

Hepatic function impairment, severe
    (excretion via biliary route)

Polyps, nasal
    (medication may not be effective if nasal passage obstruction exists)

Renal function impairment, severe
    (excretion via renal route)

Sensitivity to cromolyn

Side/Adverse Effects

Note: Although not reported for cromolyn nasal solution, some side/adverse effects that have occurred with cromolyn formulations for inhalation include angioedema, joint pain and swelling, and, reported rarely, serum sickness, periarteritic vasculitis, polymyositis, pericarditis, photodermatitis, exfoliative dermatitis, peripheral neuritis, and nephrosis.

The following side/adverse effects have been selected on the basis of their potential clinical significance (possible signs and symptoms in parentheses where appropriate)—not necessarily inclusive:

Those indicating need for medical attention

Incidence rare
    Anaphylactic reaction (coughing; difficulty in swallowing; hives; itching of skin; swelling of face, lips, or eyelids; wheezing or difficulty in breathing); *nosebleed; skin rash*

Those indicating need for medical attention only if they continue or are bothersome

Incidence more frequent
    Burning, stinging, or irritation inside of nose; increase in sneezing
Incidence less frequent
    Headache; postnasal drip; unpleasant taste

Patient Consultation

In providing consultation, consider emphasizing the following selected information (» = major clinical significance):

Before using this medication

»   Conditions affecting use, especially:
        Sensitivity to cromolyn

Proper use of this medication

Proper administration:
    Before using—Reading patient directions carefully; clearing nasal passages
    Using nasal solution with special metered spray device
    Using powder for nasal insufflation with nasal insufflator, supplied separately
    Not cleaning metered spray device; replacing device at 6-month intervals
»   Importance of not using more medication than the amount prescribed
»   Compliance with therapy; in seasonal allergic rhinitis, results are usually noticeable in less than 1 week; in perennial allergic rhinitis, up to 4 weeks may be required for full benefit
    Missed dose: Using as soon as possible; using any remaining doses for that day at regularly spaced intervals; not doubling doses
»   Proper storage

Precautions while using this medication

»   Checking with physician if symptoms do not improve or if condition becomes worse

Side/adverse effects

Signs of potential side effects, especially anaphylactic reaction, nosebleed, and skin rash

General Dosing Information

Prior to administration of cromolyn nasal solution or cromolyn for nasal insufflation, the nasal passages should be cleared. During administration, patient should inhale through the nose.

In the management of seasonal allergic rhinitis (pollinosis) and for the prevention of rhinitis caused by other types of specific inhalant allergens, treatment with nasal cromolyn is more effective if started prior to exposure to the offending allergen. Therapy should be continued throughout the period of exposure (i.e., until the pollen season is over or until the patient is no longer exposed to the offending allergen).

In the management of perennial allergic rhinitis, concurrent use of an antihistamine and/or a nasal decongestant may be necessary during the initial period of treatment; however, the need for these medications should decrease and may be discontinued when the full effect of nasal cromolyn is achieved.

Nasal Dosage Forms

CROMOLYN SODIUM FOR NASAL INSUFFLATION

Usual adult and adolescent dose: Allergic rhinitis, seasonal (prophylaxis)—
    Initial: Nasal insufflation, 10 mg in each nostril four times a day at four- to six-hour intervals.
    Maintenance: Nasal insufflation, 10 mg in each nostril every eight to twelve hours.

Usual geriatric dose: See *Usual adult and adolescent dose.*

Auxiliary labeling: • For the nose.

CROMOLYN SODIUM NASAL SOLUTION USP

Usual adult and adolescent dose: Allergic rhinitis, perennial or seasonal (prophylaxis and treatment)—Intranasal, 2.6 mg in each nostril six times a day; or 5.2 mg in each nostril three or four times a day at regular intervals.

Note: The dosage may be increased to 5.2 mg in each nostril six times a day, if necessary.

Usual geriatric dose: See *Usual adult and adolescent dose.*

Auxiliary labeling: • For the nose.

Additional information: The nasal spray bottle containing 520 mg/13 mL delivers at least 100 sprays.

DAPSONE   Systemic

A commonly used *brand name* in Canada is *Avlosulfon*.

Another commonly used name is DDS.

ORAL
Dapsone Tablets USP
   In the U.S.—GENERIC
   In Canada—*Avlosulfon*

Category: Antibacterial (antileprosy agent); dermatitis herpetiformis suppressant; antiprotozoal; antifungal.

Indications

Note: Bracketed information in the *Indications* section refers to uses not included in U.S. product labeling.

Accepted

Leprosy (treatment)—Dapsone is indicated in combination with other antileprosy agents in the treatment of all types of leprosy (Hansen's disease) caused by *Mycobacterium leprae*.

Dermatitis herpetiformis (treatment)—Dapsone is indicated in the treatment of dermatitis herpetiformis.

[Actinomycotic mycetoma (treatment)]—Dapsone is used in the treatment of actinomycotic mycetoma.

[Cicatricial pemphigoid (treatment)][1]—Dapsone is used in the treatment of desquamative gingival lesions caused by cicatricial pemphigoid.

[Dermatosis, subcorneal pustular (treatment)][1]—Dapsone is used in the treatment of subcorneal pustular dermatosis.

[Granuloma annulare (treatment)][1]—Dapsone is used in the treatment of granuloma annulare.

[Lupus erythematosus, systemic (treatment)][1]—Dapsone is used in the treatment of certain skin lesions of systemic lupus erythematosus, including bullous eruptions and urticarial vasculitis.

[Malaria (prophylaxis)][1]—Dapsone is used in combination with pyrimethamine as secondary agents in the prophylaxis of chloroquine-resistant malaria caused by *Plasmodium falciparum*. Dapsone is also used in combination with pyrimethamine and chloroquine in the prophylaxis of malaria caused by *Plasmodium vivax*.

[Pemphigoid (treatment)][1]—Dapsone is used in the treatment of pemphigoid lesions with oral manifestations.

[Pneumonia, *Pneumocystis carinii* (prophylaxis and treatment)][1]—Dapsone is used in combination with trimethoprim in the treatment of mild to moderate pneumonia caused by *Pneumocystis carinii* (PCP). No difference in efficacy was found in a study comparing the dapsone-trimethoprim combination with oral trimethoprim-sulfamethoxazole. However, studies have shown that dapsone alone appeared to have inferior efficacy for treatment of PCP.

Dapsone has also been used alone in the prophylaxis of PCP.

[Polychondritis, relapsing (treatment)][1]—Dapsone is used in the treatment of relapsing polychondritis.

[Pyoderma gangrenosum (treatment)][1]—Dapsone is used in the treatment of pyoderma gangrenosum.

[1]Not included in Canadian product labeling.

Pharmacology

Mechanism of action/Effect:

Antibacterial (antileprosy agent)—Dapsone, a sulfone, is bacteriostatic and probably acts by a mechanism similar to that of the sulfonamides, interfering with folate synthesis. Both have a similar range of antibacterial activity and are antagonized by para-aminobenzoic acid.

Dermatitis herpetiformis suppressant—Mechanism is unknown, but not due to dapsone's bacteriostatic effect. Dapsone may act as an enzyme inhibitor or oxidizing agent. In addition, it has numerous immunologic effects (e.g., immunosuppression), which most likely account for its suppression of dermatitis herpetiformis.

Precautions to Consider

Cross-sensitivity and/or related problems
Patients allergic to dapsone may be allergic to sulfonamides, although this has not been clearly established.

Geriatrics
No information is available on the relationship of age to the effects of dapsone in geriatric patients.

Drug interactions and/or related problems
The following drug interactions and/or related problems have been selected on the basis of their potential clinical significance (possible mechanism in parentheses where appropriate)—not necessarily inclusive (» = major clinical significance):

Note: Combinations containing any of the following medications, depending on the amount present, may also interact with this medication.

Aminobenzoates (PABA)
(concurrent use in the treatment of leprosy is not recommended since aminobenzoates may be absorbed by bacteria preferentially over sulfones, thereby antagonizing the bacteriostatic effect of sulfones; however, aminobenzoates do not antagonize the effect of dapsone in the treatment of dermatitis herpetiformis)

Blood dyscrasia-causing medications
(dapsone may, on rare occasions, cause an idiosyncratic agranulocytosis, aplastic anemia, or other blood dyscrasias; if concurrent use is required, close observation for myelotoxic effects should be considered)

» Dideoxyinosine (ddI)
(concurrent administration of dapsone with ddI may decrease the absorption of dapsone; ddI must be given with a buffer to neutralize stomach acidity in order to increase its absorption, and dapsone requires an acidic environment for optimal absorption; until studies are completed that confirm this interaction, dapsone should be administered at least 2 hours before or 2 hours after ddI is given)

» Hemolytics, other
(concurrent use with dapsone may increase the potential for toxic side effects)

Rifampin
(concurrent use may stimulate hepatic microsomal enzyme activity, resulting in as much as a 7- to 10-fold decrease in dapsone concentrations; however, dapsone dosage adjustments are not required during concurrent rifampin therapy for leprosy since dapsone concentrations are still higher than the MIC, although they may be required in the treatment of other diseases, such as PCP)

Trimethoprim
(concurrent use with dapsone may increase the plasma concentrations of both dapsone and trimethoprim, possibly due to an inhibition in dapsone metabolism, and/or competition for renal secretion between the 2 medications; increased serum dapsone concentrations may increase the frequency and severity of side effects, especially methemoglobinemia and hemolytic anemia)

Contraindications/Medical problems
The contraindications/medical problems included have been selected on the basis of their potential clinical significance (reasons given

in parentheses where appropriate)—not necessarily inclusive (» = major clinical significance).

Risk-benefit should be considered when the following medical problems exist:

Allergy to dapsone or sulfonamides
» Anemia, severe, or
» Glucose-6-phosphate dehydrogenase (G6PD) deficiency or
» Methemoglobin reductase deficiency
      (hemolytic anemia may occur)
Hepatic function impairment
      (dapsone may cause toxic hepatitis and cholestatic jaundice; alcoholic liver disease may decrease the plasma protein binding of dapsone, increasing the amount of circulating free drug)

Side/Adverse Effects

Note: When dapsone is used in high doses, peripheral motor weakness may occur more frequently.

Fatalities have occurred due to agranulocytosis, aplastic anemia, and other blood dyscrasias. In addition, serious cutaneous reactions, such as exfoliative dermatitis, toxic erythema, erythema multiforme, toxic epidermal necrolysis, morbilliform and scarlatiniform reactions, and erythema nodosum may occur. Dapsone therapy should be promptly discontinued if new or toxic dermatologic reactions occur. However, leprosy reactional states do not require discontinuation of therapy.

A dose-related hemolysis is seen in all patients, with a slight decrease in hemoglobin and an increase in reticulocyte count. Patients with G6PD-deficiency or a decrease in activity in glutathione reductase are more susceptible to hemolysis. A low level of methemoglobinemia also occurs in all patients at recommended doses.

The following side/adverse effects have been selected on the basis of their potential clinical significance (possible signs and symptoms in parentheses where appropriate)—not necessarily inclusive:

Those indicating need for medical attention
Incidence more frequent
   Hemolytic anemia (back, leg, or stomach pains; loss of appetite; pale skin; unusual tiredness or weakness; fever); *hypersensitivity* (skin rash); *methemoglobinemia* (cyanosis—bluish fingernails, lips, or skin; difficult breathing; unusual tiredness or weakness)
Incidence rare
   Blood dyscrasias (fever and sore throat, unusual bleeding or bruising, unusual tiredness and weakness); *exfoliative dermatitis* (itching, dryness, redness, scaling, or peeling of the skin or loss of hair); *hepatic damage* (yellow eyes or skin); *mood or other mental changes; peripheral neuritis* (numbness, tingling, pain, burning, or weakness in hands or feet); *"sulfone syndrome"* (fever, malaise, exfoliative dermatitis, jaundice, lymphadenopathy, methemoglobinemia, anemia)—a hypersensitivity reaction that usually occurs after 6 to 8 weeks of therapy

Those indicating need for medical attention only if they continue or are bothersome
Incidence rare—usually dose-related
   Central nervous system toxicity (headache, insomnia, nervousness); *gastrointestinal disturbances* (anorexia, nausea or vomiting)

Patient Consultation

In providing consultation, consider emphasizing the following selected information (» = major clinical significance):

Before using this medication
» Conditions affecting use, especially:
   Allergy to sulfonamides
   Pregnancy—Dapsone crosses the placenta

Breast-feeding—Dapsone is excreted in breast milk; it may cause hemolytic anemia in G6PD-deficient neonates
Other medications, especially other hemolytics and dideoxyinosine
Other medical problems, especially severe anemia, G6PD deficiency, or methemoglobin reductase deficiency

Proper use of this medication
» Proper storage
For leprosy
» Compliance with full course of therapy, which may take years
» Importance of not missing doses and taking at same time every day
   Missed dose: Taking as soon as possible; not taking if almost time for next dose; not doubling doses
For dermatitis herpetiformis
   Possible need for gluten-free diet
   Missed dose: Taking as soon as possible if symptoms return or worsen; not taking if almost time for next dose; not doubling doses
For Pneumocystis carinii pneumonia
» Compliance with full course of therapy
   Missed dose: Taking as soon as possible; not taking if almost time for next dose; not doubling doses

Precautions while using this medication
Regular visits to physician to check progress
Checking with physician if no improvement within 2 to 3 months (leprosy), within 1 week (PCP), or within a few days (dermatitis herpetiformis)

Side/adverse effects
Signs of potential side effects, especially hemolytic anemia, blood dyscrasias, hypersensitivity reactions, methemoglobinemia, exfoliative dermatitis, peripheral neuropathy, hepatic damage, "sulfone syndrome," and mood and other mental changes

General Dosing Information

Since bacterial resistance may develop when dapsone is administered alone in the treatment of leprosy, for initial treatment, concurrent administration with rifampin is generally recommended. Clofazimine, ethionamide, or prothionamide (investigational) may be used in place of rifampin, but they are considered less effective.

Dapsone therapy should be discontinued promptly if new or toxic dermatologic reactions occur. However, leprosy reactional states do not require discontinuation of therapy. Large doses of adrenocorticoids should be given if severe "reversal" reactions (type 1) or neuritis occurs during treatment of leprosy.

Depending on the drug regimen used, therapy may have to be continued for 6 months to 3 years or more in indeterminate and tuberculoid leprosy, 2 to 10 years in borderline (dimorphous) leprosy, and 2 years to life in lepromatous leprosy.

In the treatment of dermatitis herpetiformis, a gluten-free diet for 6 months may allow a reduction in dose by approximately 50% or discontinuation of dapsone.

Oral Dosage Forms

Note: Bracketed uses in the *Dosage Forms* section refer to categories of use and/or indications that are not included in U.S. product labeling.

DAPSONE TABLETS USP

Usual adult and adolescent dose:
Leprosy (Hansen's disease)—Oral, in combination with one or more other antileprosy agents, 50 to 100 mg of dapsone once a day; or 1.4 mg per kg of body weight once a day.

Dermatitis herpetiformis suppressant—Oral, initially 50 mg daily. Doses may be increased up to 300 mg daily if symptoms are not completely controlled. The dose should then be reduced to the lowest effective maintenance dose as soon as possible.

[Actinomycotic mycetoma]—Oral, 100 mg twice a day for several months after clinical symptoms have disappeared.

[Dermatosis, subcorneal pustular][1]—Oral, initially 100 mg once a day, increasing the dose by 50 mg every one to two weeks until remission occurs. The dose should then be gradually reduced to the lowest effective maintenance dose.

[Granuloma annulare][1]—Oral, 100 mg once a day.

[Malaria (prophylaxis)][1]—Oral, 100 mg of dapsone in combination with 12.5 mg of pyrimethamine once every seven days.

[Pneumonia, *Pneumocystis carinii*][1]—

Treatment: Oral, 100 mg of dapsone once a day in combination with 20 mg per kg of body weight per day of trimethoprim, for twenty-one days.

Prophylaxis: Oral, 50 to 100 mg once a day.

[Polychondritis, relapsing][1]—Oral, 100 mg once or twice a day.

[Pyoderma gangrenosum][1]—Oral, 50 to 100 mg once a day, in combination with other medications.

Usual adult prescribing limits:
Leprosy (Hansen's disease)—Up to 100 mg daily.
Dermatitis herpetiformis suppressant—Up to 300 mg daily.
Polychondritis, relapsing[1]—Up to 200 mg daily.

Auxiliary labeling: • Continue medicine for full time of treatment (for leprosy and PCP).

---

[1]Not included in Canadian product labeling

DECONGESTANTS AND ANALGESICS   Systemic

Category: Decongestant-analgesic.

Indications

Accepted
Congestion, nasal (treatment);
Congestion, sinus (treatment); and
Headache, sinus (treatment)—Decongestant and analgesic combinations are indicated for the temporary relief of nasal and sinus congestion and headache pain caused by sinusitis, common colds, allergy and hay fever.

The therapeutic effectiveness of oral phenylephrine as a nasal decongestant has been questioned, especially at the usual oral dose.

Patient Consultation

In providing consultation, consider emphasizing the following selected information (» = major clinical significance):

Before using this medication
» Conditions affecting use, especially:
   Sensitivity to other sympathomimetic amines, salicylates or other nonsteroidal anti-inflammatory drugs
   Pregnancy—Concern with high doses and long-term therapy because of salicylate effects; use of aspirin-containing combinations not recommended during third trimester; use of ibuprofen-containing combinations during second half of pregnancy not recommended because of potential adverse effect on fetal blood flow
   Breast-feeding—High risk for infants from sympathomimetic amines; also, concern with high doses and chronic use because of high salicylate intake by infant
   Use in children—Increased sensitivity to vasopressor and psychiatric effects of sympathomimetic amines; also, increased susceptibility to toxic effects of salicylates, especially if fever and dehydration present; possible association between aspirin usage and Reye's syndrome

   Use in adolescents—Possible association between aspirin usage and Reye's syndrome
   Use in the elderly—Increased susceptibility to effects of sympathomimetic amines and toxic effects of salicylates; increased risk of toxicity with ibuprofen
   Use by athletes—Decongestants are banned and tested for by the U.S. Olympic Committee (USOC); caffeine is tested for by the USOC and the National Collegiate Athletic Association (NCAA); urine concentrations above 12 mcg per mL (61.8 micromoles/L) are considered unacceptable by the USOC; the NCAA limit is 15 mcg per mL (77.25 micromoles/L)
   Other medications, especially for high blood pressure or depression, CNS depressants or stimulants, and others that may interact with acetaminophen and/or salicylates depending on specific ingredients of combination
   Other medical problems, especially hypertension (for all combinations); alcoholism or hepatitis (for acetaminophen-containing combinations); asthma, gastritis, or peptic ulcer (with salicylate-containing combinations); clotting defects, peptic ulcer or other gastrointestinal tract disease, or stomatitis (for ibuprofen-containing combinations)

Proper use of this medication
» Importance of not taking more medication than the amount recommended
   Missed dose: If on scheduled dosing regimen—Taking as soon as possible; not taking if almost time for next dose; not doubling doses
» Proper storage
For salicylate-containing combinations
   Taking with food or a full glass (240 mL) of water to minimize gastrointestinal irritation
» Not taking combinations containing aspirin if a strong vinegar-like odor is present
For ibuprofen-containing combinations
   Taking with food or antacids (a magnesium- and aluminum-containing antacid may be preferred) to reduce gastrointestinal irritation; not lying down for 15 to 30 minutes after taking

Precautions while using this medication

Checking with physician if symptoms persist or become worse, or if high fever is present

» Caution if taking phenylpropanolamine-containing appetite suppressants

» Possible insomnia; taking the medication a few hours before bedtime

Need to inform physician or dentist of use of medication if any kind of surgery (including dental surgery or emergency treatment is required)

» Caution if other medications containing acetaminophen, aspirin, or other salicylates (including diflunisal) are used

» Avoiding use of alcoholic beverages while taking these medications; alcohol consumption may increase risk of ibuprofen- or salicylate-induced gastrointestinal toxicity and acetaminophen-induced liver toxicity

» Suspected overdose: Getting emergency help at once

Not taking products containing aspirin for 5 days prior to any kind of surgery, unless otherwise directed by physician

Diabetics: Aspirin present in some combination formulations may cause false urine sugar test results with prolonged use of 8 or more 325-mg (5-grain) doses per day

For ibuprofen-containing combinations

» Caution if drowsiness or dizziness occurs

Side/adverse effects

Signs of potential side effects, especially allergic reactions, anemia, cardiac effects, CNS stimulation, psychotic episodes, severe dizziness, severe nervousness or restlessness (for all combinations); blood dyscrasias, hepatitis, hepatotoxicity (for acetaminophen-containing); signs of gastrointestinal irritation or bleeding (for ibuprofen- or salicylate-containing); and cutaneous adverse effects, hepatitis, renal impairment (for ibuprofen-containing)

Oral Dosage Forms

See *Table 1*, page 498.

Table 1. Oral Dosage Forms

Note: Content per capsule, tablet, or 5 mL, unless otherwise stated.

Brand or generic name [availability]	Decongestants*	Analgesics	Usual adult and adolescent dose† (prn)	Auxiliary labeling‡
Allerest No-Drowsiness Tablets (OTC) [U.S.]	Pseudoephedrine HCl 30 mg	Acetaminophen 325 mg	2 tabs q 4–6 hr	
Alpha-Phed Capsules (OTC) [U.S.]	Pseudoephedrine HCl 20 mg	Aspirin 400 mg	2 caps q 6 hr	
BC Cold Powder Non-Drowsy Formula for Oral Solution (OTC) [U.S.]	Phenylpropanolamine HCl 25 mg/packet	Aspirin 650 mg/packet	1 packet dissolved in water q 6 hr	
Beta-Phed Capsules (OTC) [U.S.]	Pseudoephedrine HCl 20 mg	Acetaminophen 500 mg	2 caps q 6 hr	
CoAdvil Caplets Tablets (OTC) [U.S.]	Pseudoephedrine HCl 30 mg	Ibuprofen 200 mg	1 tab q 4–6 hr	
Coldrine Tablets (OTC) [U.S.]	Pseudoephedrine HCl 30 mg	Acetaminophen 325 mg	2 tabs q 6 hr	
Congespirin for Children Cold Tablets Chewable Tablets (OTC) [U.S.]	Phenylephrine HCl 1.25 mg	Acetaminophen 81 mg	Intended for pediatric use	a

Table 1. Oral Dosage Forms *(continued)*

Note: Content per capsule, tablet, or 5 mL, unless otherwise stated.

Brand or generic name [availability]	Decongestants*	Analgesics	Usual adult and adolescent dose† (prn)	Auxiliary labeling‡
Congespirin for Children Liquid Cold Medicine Oral Solution (OTC) [U.S.]	Phenylpropanolamine HCl 6.25 mg	Acetaminophen 130 mg	Intended for pediatric use	
Contac Maximum Strength Sinus Caplets Tablets (OTC) [U.S.]	Pseudoephedrine HCl 30 mg	Acetaminophen 500 mg	2 tabs q 6 hr	
Dilotab Tablets (OTC) [U.S.]	Phenylpropanolamine HCl 12.5 mg	Acetaminophen 325 mg	2 tabs q 4 hr	
Drinophen Capsules (OTC) [U.S.]	Phenylpropanolamine HCl 15 mg	Acetaminophen 200 mg, Aspirin 230 mg	1 cap q 4–6 hr	
Dristan Maximum Strength Caplets Tablets (OTC) [U.S.]	Pseudoephedrine HCl 30 mg	Acetaminophen 500 mg	2 tabs q 6 hr	
Dristan Sinus Caplets Tablets (OTC) [U.S.]	Pseudoephedrine HCl 30 mg	Ibuprofen 200 mg	1 tab q 4–6 hr	
Genex Capsules (OTC) [U.S.]	Phenylpropanolamine HCl 18 mg	Acetaminophen 325 mg	2 caps q 4 hr	
Naldegesic Tablets (OTC) [U.S.]	Pseudoephedrine HCl 15 mg	Acetaminophen 325 mg	2 tabs q 4 hr	
Neo Citran Sinus Medicine for Oral Solution (OTC) [Canada]	Phenylephrine HCl 10 mg/pouch	Acetaminophen 650 mg/pouch	Contents of 1 pouch dissolved in 240 mL hot water	
Ornex No Drowsiness Caplets Tablets (OTC) [U.S.]	Pseudoephedrine HCl 30 mg	Acetaminophen 325 mg	2 tabs q 4 hr	
PhenAPAP No. 2 Tablets (OTC) [U.S.]	Phenylpropanolamine HCl 25 mg	Acetaminophen 325 mg	1 tab q 4 hr	

*Stimulants, such as decongestants, are banned and tested for in athletes by the U.S. Olympic Committee (USOC). Caffeine, another stimulant, is tested for in athletes by the USOC and the National Collegiate Athletic Association (NCAA). Urine concentrations of caffeine greater than 12 mcg per mL (61.8 micromoles/L) are considered to be unacceptable by the USOC; the NCAA limit is 15 mcg per mL (77.25 micromoles/L).

†Geriatric patients may be more sensitive to the effects of usual adult dose.

‡For appropriate *Auxiliary labeling* information refer to designated letters as follows:
Auxiliary labeling: • May be chewed.

Table 1. Oral Dosage Forms *(continued)*

Note: Content per capsule, tablet, or 5 mL, unless otherwise stated.

Brand or generic name [availability]	Decongestants*	Analgesics	Usual adult and adolescent dose† (prn)	Auxiliary labeling‡
Rhinocaps Capsules (OTC) [U.S.]	Phenylpropanolamine HCl 20 mg	Acetaminophen 162 mg, Aspirin 162 mg	2 caps q 4 hr	
Saleto D Capsules (OTC) [U.S.]	Phenylpropanolamine HCl 18 mg	Acetaminophen 240 mg, Salicylamide 120 mg	2 caps q 4 hr	
Sinarest No-Drowsiness Tablets (OTC) [U.S.]	Pseudoephedrine HCl 30 mg	Acetaminophen 500 mg	2 tabs q 6 hr	
Sine-Aid Tablets (OTC) [U.S.]	Pseudoephedrine HCl 30 mg	Acetaminophen 325 mg	2 tabs q 4–6 hr	
Sine-Aid Maximum Strength Tablets (OTC) [U.S.]	Pseudoephedrine HCl 30 mg	Acetaminophen 500 mg	2 tabs q 4–6 hr	
Sine-Aid Maximum Strength Caplets Tablets (OTC) [U.S.]	Pseudoephedrine HCl 30 mg	Acetaminophen 500 mg	2 tabs q 4–6 hr	
Sine-Off Maximum Strength No Drowsiness Formula Caplets Tablets (OTC) [U.S.]	Pseudoephedrine HCl 30 mg	Acetaminophen 500 mg	2 tabs q 6 hr	
Sinus Excedrin No Drowsiness Tablets (OTC) [U.S.]	Pseudoephedrine HCl 30 mg	Acetaminophen 500 mg	2 tabs q 6 hr	
Sinus Excedrin No Drowsiness Caplets Tablets (OTC) [U.S.]	Pseudoephedrine HCl 30 mg	Acetaminophen 500 mg	2 tabs q 6 hr	
Sinutab II Maximum Strength Capsules (OTC) [U.S.]	Pseudoephedrine HCl 30 mg	Acetaminophen 500 mg	2 caps q 6 hr	
Tablets (OTC) [U.S.]	Pseudoephedrine HCl 30 mg	Acetaminophen 500 mg	2 tabs q 6 hr	
Sinutab Maximum Strength Without Drowsiness Tablets (OTC) [U.S.]	Pseudoephedrine HCl 30 mg	Acetaminophen 500 mg	2 tabs q 6 hr	
Sinutab Maximum Strength Without Drowsiness Caplets Tablets (OTC) [U.S.]	Pseudoephedrine HCl 30 mg	Acetaminophen 500 mg	2 tabs q 6 hr	

Table 1. Oral Dosage Forms *(continued)*

Note: Content per capsule, tablet, or 5 mL, unless otherwise stated.

Brand or generic name [availability]	Decongestants*	Analgesics	Usual adult and adolescent dose† (prn)	Auxiliary labeling‡
Sinutab *No Drowsiness* Tablets (OTC) [Canada]	Pseudoephedrine HCl 30 mg	Acetaminophen 325 mg	1–2 tabs q 4–6 hr	
Sinutab *No Drowsiness Extra Strength* Tablets (OTC) [Canada]	Pseudoephedrine HCl 30 mg	Acetaminophen 500 mg	1–2 tabs q 4–6 hr	
St. Joseph Cold *Tablets for Children* Chewable Tablets (OTC) [U.S.]	Phenylpropanolamine HCl 3.125 mg	Acetaminophen 80 mg	Intended for pediatric use	a
Sudafed Sinus Maximum *Strength* Tablets (OTC) [U.S.]	Pseudoephedrine HCl 30 mg	Acetaminophen 500 mg	2 tabs q 6 hr	
Sudafed Sinus Maximum *Strength Caplets* Tablets (OTC) [U.S.]	Pseudoephedrine HCl 30 mg	Acetaminophen 500 mg	2 tabs q 6 hr	
Super-Anahist Tablets (OTC) [U.S.]	Pseudoephedrine HCl 30 mg	Acetaminophen 325 mg	2 tabs q 4 hr	
Tylenol Sinus Maximum *Strength* Tablets (OTC) [U.S.]	Pseudoephedrine HCl 30 mg	Acetaminophen 500 mg	2 tabs q 4–6 hr	
Tylenol Sinus Maximum *Strength Caplets* Tablets (OTC) [U.S.]	Pseudoephedrine HCl 30 mg	Acetaminophen 500 mg	2 tabs q 4–6 hr	
Tylenol Sinus Medication Tablets (OTC) [Canada]	Pseudoephedrine HCl 30 mg	Acetaminophen 325 mg	1–2 tabs q 4 hr	
Tylenol Sinus *Medication Extra* *Strength* Tablets (OTC) [Canada]	Pseudoephedrine HCl 30 mg	Acetaminophen 500 mg	1–2 tabs q 4 hr	
Ursinus Inlay Tablets (OTC) [U.S.]	Pseudoephedrine HCl 30 mg	Aspirin 325 mg	2 tabs q 4 hr	

*Stimulants, such as decongestants, are banned and tested for in athletes by the U.S. Olympic Committee (USOC). Caffeine, another stimulant, is tested for in athletes by the USOC and the National Collegiate Athletic Association (NCAA). Urine concentrations of caffeine greater than 12 mcg per mL (61.8 micromoles/L) are considered to be unacceptable by the USOC; the NCAA limit is 15 mcg per mL (77.25 micromoles/L).

†Geriatric patients may be more sensitive to the effects of usual adult dose.

‡For appropriate *Auxiliary labeling* information refer to designated letters as follows:

    a—Auxiliary labeling: • May be chewed.

DEXTROMETHORPHAN   Systemic

Some commonly used *brand names* are:

In the U.S.—

Benylin DM	*Pertussin ES*
Children's Hold	*Robitussin Pediatric*
Delsym	*St. Joseph for Children*
Hold	*Sucrets Cough Control*
Mediquell	*Formula*
Pertussin Cough	*Trocal*
Suppressant	*Vicks Formula 44*
Pertussin CS	*Pediatric Formula*

In Canada—

Balminil D.M.	*Neo-DM*
Broncho-Grippol-DM	*Ornex•DM 15*
Delsym	*Ornex•DM 30*
DM Syrup	*Robidex*
Koffex	*Sedatuss*

ORAL

Dextromethorphan Hydrobromide Capsules*
In Canada—*Ornex•DM 30*

Dextromethorphan Hydrobromide Lozenges†
In the U.S.—*Children's Hold; Hold; Pertussin Cough Suppressant; Sucrets Cough Control Formula; Trocal*

Dextromethorphan Hydrobromide Syrup USP
In the U.S.—*Benylin DM; Pertussin CS; Pertussin ES; Robitussin Pediatric; St. Joseph for Children; Vicks Formula 44 Pediatric Formula*
In Canada—*Balminil D.M.; Broncho-Grippol-DM; DM Syrup; Koffex; Neo-DM; Ornex•DM 15; Robidex; Sedatuss*

Dextromethorphan Hydrobromide Chewable Tablets†
In the U.S.—*Mediquell*

Dextromethorphan Polistirex Extended-release Oral Suspension
In the U.S. and Canada—*Delsym*

---

*Not commercially available in the U.S.
†Not commercially available in Canada.

Category: Antitussive.

Indications

Accepted
Cough (treatment)—Dextromethorphan is indicated for the symptomatic relief of nonproductive cough due to minor throat and bronchial irritation occurring with colds or inhaled irritants.

Pharmacology

Mechanism of action/Effect: Suppresses the cough reflex by a direct action on the cough center in the medulla of the brain.

Onset of action: Usually within one-half hour.

Duration of action: Up to 6 hours.

Note: The extended-release oral suspension delivers dextromethorphan from an ion-exchange complex over a period of 9 to 12 hours.

Precautions to Consider

Geriatrics
No information is available on the relationship of age to the effects of dextromethorphan in geriatric patients.

Drug interactions and/or related problems
The following drug interactions and/or related problems have been selected on the basis of their potential clinical significance (possible mechanism in parentheses where appropriate)—not necessarily inclusive (» = major clinical significance):

Note: Combinations containing any of the following medications, depending on the amount present, may also interact with this medication.

» Central nervous system (CNS) depression-producing medications, other
(concurrent use may potentiate the CNS depressant effects of these medications or dextromethorphan)

» Monoamine oxidase (MAO) inhibitors, including furazolidone and procarbazine
(concurrent use with dextromethorphan may cause excitation, hypertension, and hyperpyrexia)

Contraindications/Medical problems
The contraindications/medical problems included have been selected on the basis of their potential clinical significance (reasons given in parentheses where appropriate)—not necessarily inclusive (» = major clinical significance).

Risk-benefit should be considered when the following medical problems exist:

» Asthma
(may impair expectoration and thus increase airway resistance)
Hepatic function impairment
(metabolism of dextromethorphan may be impaired)
Sensitivity to dextromethorphan

Side/Adverse Effects

Note: One case of toxic psychosis (hyperactivity, visual and auditory hallucinations) has been reported after ingestion of 300 mg.
Respiratory depression would be expected to occur with very high doses; however, there are no reported cases to date.

The following side/adverse effects have been selected on the basis of their potential clinical significance (possible signs and symptoms in parentheses where appropriate)—not necessarily inclusive:

Those indicating need for medical attention
Symptoms of overdose
Confusion; drowsiness or dizziness; severe nausea or vomiting; severe unusual excitement, nervousness, restlessness, or irritability

Those indicating need for medical attention only if they continue or are bothersome
Incidence less frequent or rare
Mild dizziness; mild drowsiness; nausea or vomiting; stomach pain

Patient Consultation

In providing consultation, consider emphasizing the following selected information (» = major clinical significance):

Before using this medication
» Conditions affecting use, especially:
Sensitivity to dextromethorphan
Other medications, especially other CNS depressants and MAO inhibitors
Other medical problems, especially asthma

Proper use of this medication
Missed dose: If on a scheduled dosing regimen—Taking as soon as possible; not taking if almost time for next dose; not doubling doses
» Proper storage

Precautions while using this medication

Checking with physician if cough persists after medication has been used for 7 days or if high fever, skin rash, or continuing headache is present with cough

Oral Dosage Forms

DEXTROMETHORPHAN HYDROBROMIDE CAPSULES

Usual adult and adolescent dose: Oral, 10 to 20 mg every four hours or 30 mg every six to eight hours, as needed.

Usual adult prescribing limits: Up to 120 mg per day.

Usual geriatric dose: See *Usual adult and adolescent dose.*

DEXTROMETHORPHAN HYDROBROMIDE LOZENGES

Usual adult and adolescent dose: Oral, 10 to 20 mg every four hours or 30 mg every six to eight hours, as needed.

Usual adult prescribing limits: Up to 120 mg per day.

Usual geriatric dose: See *Usual adult and adolescent dose.*

DEXTROMETHORPHAN HYDROBROMIDE SYRUP USP

Usual adult and adolescent dose: Oral, 10 to 20 mg every four hours or 30 mg every six to eight hours, as needed.

Usual adult prescribing limits: Up to 120 mg per day.

Usual geriatric dose: See *Usual adult and adolescent dose.*

DEXTROMETHORPHAN HYDROBROMIDE CHEWABLE TABLETS

Usual adult and adolescent dose: Oral, 10 to 20 mg every four hours or 30 mg every six to eight hours, as needed.

Usual adult prescribing limits: Up to 120 mg per day.

Usual geriatric dose: See *Usual adult and adolescent dose.*

Auxiliary labeling: • Chew well before swallowing.

DEXTROMETHORPHAN POLISTIREX EXTENDED-RELEASE ORAL SUSPENSION

Usual adult and adolescent dose: Oral, 60 mg every twelve hours, as needed.

Usual adult prescribing limits: Up to 120 mg per day.

Usual geriatric dose: See *Usual adult and adolescent dose.*

Auxiliary labeling: • Shake well.

DEXTROTHYROXINE   Systemic

Some commonly used *brand names* are:

In the U.S.—
   Choloxin
In Canada—
   Choloxin
Other—

Biotirmone	*Dynothel*
Debetrol	*Eulipos*
Dethyrona	*Lisolipin*
Dethyrone	*Nadrothyron-D*

ORAL

Dextrothyroxine Sodium Tablets USP
   In the U.S. and Canada—*Choloxin*
   Other—*Biotirmone; Debetrol; Dethyrona; Dethyrone; Dynothel; Eulipos; Lisolipin; Nadrothyron-D*

Category: Antihyperlipidemic.

Note: Dextrothyroxine is a thyroid hormone with only weak thyroid hormone effects, which may be the result of levothyroxine (T4) contamination.

Indications

Accepted

Hyperlipidemia (treatment)—Dextrothyroxine has been used to treat primary hypercholesterolemia (type IIa hyperlipidemia); however, this medication generally *has been replaced* by other antihyperlipidemic agents. Significant cardiovascular risks are associated with the use of dextrothyroxine.

In the 1988 Report of the National Cholesterol Education Program Expert Panel on Detection, Evaluation, and Treatment of High Blood Cholesterol in Adults, the following guidelines for the treatment of high blood cholesterol are recommended:

Nonpharmacologic management (especially reduction in dietary intake of saturated fatty acids and cholesterol, weight reduction and exercise, and quitting smoking) is recommended first for all patients and as an adjunct to all pharmacologic cholesterol therapy.

If, after six months of diet therapy, adequate low density lipoprotein (LDL)-cholesterol reduction is not achieved, then medication therapy is recommended to be added to diet therapy.

Initial medication therapy usually consists of a bile acid sequestrant (e.g., cholestyramine, colestipol) or niacin. A 3-hydroxy-3-methylglutanyl coenzyme A (HMG CoA) reductase inhibitor (e.g., lovastatin) should be considered after the bile acid sequestrants and niacin. Other lipid-lowering agents, including fibric acid derivatives (e.g., gemfibrozil and clofibrate) and probucol, are not as effective in lowering LDL cholesterol as the above mentioned medications. Two other agents, neomycin (not approved by FDA as a lipid-lowering agent) and dextrothyroxine are not recommended for general use because other medications are available that have a more favorable benefit/risk ratio.

If adequate LDL-cholesterol control is not achieved with initial medication therapy, it is recommended that the patient be switched to another medication or a combination of two medications with synergistic mechanisms of action. Although experience with such drug combinations is somewhat limited, preliminary studies indicate that the bile acid sequestrants given with either niacin, lovastatin, probucol, or gemfibrozil are useful in controlling LDL cholesterol. Lovastatin in combination with either niacin or gemfibrozil needs further study because of the potential increased risk of side effects.

If effective control of LDL cholesterol is not obtained after use of primary medications and medication combinations, then referral to a lipid specialist may be necessary.

Studies have suggested that control of elevated cholesterol and triglycerides may not lessen the danger of cardiovascular disease and mortality, although incidence of nonfatal myocardial infarctions may be decreased.

Unaccepted

Dextrothyroxine has also been used for treatment of hypothyroidism in patients with cardiac disease who cannot tolerate other thyroid preparations. However, it is seldom used because of the availability of more effective preparations.

Use of dextrothyroxine, because of its thyroid hormone activity, to treat obesity without laboratory confirmation of contributing hypothyroidism is inappropriate and may cause hyperthyroidism in euthyroid individuals.

Pharmacology

Mechanism of action/Effect: Antihyperlipidemic—Not completely understood, but dextrothyroxine apparently acts in the liver to stimulate formation of low-density lipoprotein (LDL) and, to a much greater extent, to increase catabolism of LDL; this leads to increased excretion of cholesterol and bile acids via the biliary route into the feces, with a resulting reduction in serum cholesterol and LDL. Dextrothyroxine has no significant effect on high-density lipoproteins (HDL).

Other actions/effects: Thyroid hormone—The action of thyroid hormones is not completely understood, but they have both catabolic (calorigenic) and anabolic effects and are therefore involved in normal metabolism, growth, and development, especially the development of the central nervous system (CNS) of infants. A feedback system involving the hypothalamus, anterior pituitary, and thyroid normally regulates circulating thyroid hormone concentrations. Most, if not all, of dextrothyroxine's thyroid hormone effects may be the result of levothyroxine (T_4) contamination. A dose of 4 mg of dextrothyroxine produces about the same metabolic effects as 0.15 mg of levothyroxine.

Time to peak effect: Antihyperlipidemic—1 to 2 months.

Duration of action: Serum lipid concentrations return to pretreatment concentrations within 6 weeks to 3 months after withdrawal.

Precautions to Consider

Geriatrics

Appropriate studies on the relationship of age to the effects of dextrothyroxine have not been performed in the geriatric population. However, the elderly may be more sensitive to the effects of thyroid hormones. In addition, elderly patients are more likely to have age-related renal function impairment, which may require caution in patients receiving dextrothyroxine.

Drug interactions and/or related problems

The following drug interactions and/or related problems have been selected on the basis of their potential clinical significance (possible mechanism in parentheses where appropriate)—not necessarily inclusive (» = major clinical significance):

Note: Combinations containing any of the following medications, depending on the amount present, may also interact with this medication.

» Anticoagulants, coumarin- or indandione-derivative
      (the effects of the oral anticoagulant may be altered, depending on the thyroid status of the patient; effect may consist of alteration of procoagulant synthesis or catabolism or increased receptor affinity for the anticoagulant; administration of dextrothyroxine may necessitate a decrease in anticoagulant dosage; adjustment of anticoagulant dosage on the basis of prothrombin time is recommended)

Antidiabetic agents, oral, or

Insulin
      (thyroid hormones may affect insulin or antidiabetic agent requirements; careful monitoring of diabetic control is recommended, especially when dextrothyroxine therapy is started, changed, or discontinued)

Chenodiol or
Ursodiol
      (effect may be decreased when chenodiol or ursodiol is used concurrently with dextrothyroxine, which tends to increase cholesterol saturation of bile)

» Cholestyramine or
» Colestipol
      (concurrent use may decrease the effects of dextrothyroxine by binding and delaying or preventing absorption; an interval of 4 to 5 hours between administration of the two medications is recommended)

Digitalis glycosides
      (administration of a thyroid hormone to a hypothyroid patient receiving a digitalis glycoside may increase the dosage requirements of the digitalis glycoside)

Sodium iodide I 123 or
Sodium iodide I 131
      (thyroid hormones may decrease thyroidal uptake of I 123 or I 131)

Thyroid hormones, other
      (concurrent use may result in additive metabolic effects)

Contraindications/Medical problems

The contraindications/medical problems included have been selected on the basis of their potential clinical significance (reasons given in parentheses where appropriate)—not necessarily inclusive (» = major clinical significance).

Except under special circumstances, this medication should not be used when the following medical problems exist:

» Cardiovascular disease, including angina pectoris, arteriosclerosis, coronary artery disease, hypertension, myocardial infarction, cardiac arrhythmia or tachycardia (or history of), rheumatic heart disease, congestive heart failure
      (because of the risks associated with increased metabolic demands caused by thyroid hormone administration)

Risk-benefit should be considered when the following medical problems exist:

» Diabetes mellitus
      (possible reduced glucose tolerance and increased insulin or oral antidiabetic agent requirements)

» Hepatic function impairment or
» Hyperthyroidism or iodism, history of
      (conditions may be exacerbated)

Hypothyroidism
      (these patients are more sensitive to dextrothyroxine's thyroid hormone effects than euthyroid individuals)

» Renal function impairment
      (may result in reduced clearance of dextrothyroxine)

Sensitivity to dextrothyroxine

Side/Adverse Effects

Note: Incidence of adverse effects is greatest in patients with hypothyroidism and/or organic heart disease, and with doses greater than 8 mg per day.

Administration of dextrothyroxine has been associated with an increased incidence of both fatal and nonfatal myocardial infarctions and ischemic heart disease. Mortality risk appears to increase with increased duration of treatment.

Side effects may not occur until 1 to 6 weeks after treatment is begun.

The following side/adverse effects have been selected on the basis of their potential clinical significance (possible signs and symptoms in parentheses where appropriate)—not necessarily inclusive:

Those indicating need for medical attention
Incidence rare
Angina (chest pain, fast or irregular heartbeat)—especially with high doses; *gallstones* (severe stomach pain with nausea and vomiting)
Signs and symptoms of hyperthyroidism or overdosage
Changes in menstrual periods; diarrhea; fast or irregular heartbeat; fever; hand tremors; headache; increase in urination; irritability, nervousness, or trouble in sleeping; leg cramps; shortness of breath; skin rash or itching; sweating, flushing, or increased sensitivity to heat; vomiting; weight loss, unusual; or changes in appetite

Patient Consultation

In providing consultation, consider emphasizing the following selected information (» = major clinical significance):

Before using this medication
Diet as preferred therapy; importance of following prescribed diet
» Conditions affecting use, especially:
   Sensitivity to dextrothyroxine
   Pregnancy—Crosses placenta to limited extent
   Breast-feeding—Excreted in breast milk
   Use in children—Not recommended in children under 2 years of age since cholesterol is required for normal development
   Use in the elderly—Elderly patients may be more sensitive to thyroid hormone effects
   Other medications, especially anticoagulants, cholestyramine, or colestipol
   Other medical problems, especially cardiovascular disease, diabetes mellitus, hepatic function impairment, history of hyperthyroidism or iodism, or renal function impairment

Proper use of this medication
» Importance of not taking more medication than the amount prescribed; not missing any doses
   Does not cure the condition but rather helps control it; continue taking as directed in order to lower cholesterol level

» Compliance with prescribed diet
   Missed dose: Taking as soon as possible; not taking if almost time for next dose; not doubling doses
» Proper storage

Precautions while using this medication
» Importance of close monitoring by physician
» Checking with physician before discontinuing medication; blood lipid concentrations may increase significantly
» Caution if any kind of surgery (including dental surgery) or emergency treatment is required

Side/adverse effects
   Signs of potential side effects, especially angina, gallstones, and hyperthyroidism

General Dosing Information

If signs or symptoms of cardiac disease (angina, tachycardia, extrasystoles) develop, dextrothyroxine should be withdrawn.

It is recommended that dextrothyroxine therapy be discontinued 10 to 14 days prior to scheduled surgery, especially in patients with coronary artery disease or if use of anticoagulants is anticipated. In addition, patients treated with thyroid hormones are at increased risk of precipitation of cardiac arrhythmias.

If response is inadequate after 3 months of treatment, dextrothyroxine therapy should be withdrawn, except in the case of xanthoma tuberosum, which may require up to 1 year of treatment as long as reduction in size and/or number of xanthomata occurs.

Dextrothyroxine therapy may be continued as long as cholesterol concentrations are reduced.

Oral Dosage Forms

DEXTROTHYROXINE SODIUM TABLETS USP

Usual adult dose: Antihyperlipidemic—Oral, initially 1 to 2 mg per day, the dosage being increased in increments of no more than 1 to 2 mg at intervals of no less than one month up to the minimum effective dose.

Usual adult prescribing limits: Up to 8 mg per day.

DIAZOXIDE   Oral-Systemic

A commonly used *brand name* in the U.S. and Canada is *Proglycem.*

ORAL
Diazoxide Capsules USP
   In the U.S. and Canada—*Proglycem*
Diazoxide Oral Suspension USP
   In the U.S. and Canada—*Proglycem*

Category: Antihypoglycemic.

Indications

Accepted
Hypoglycemia (treatment)—Diazoxide is indicated orally for the management of hypoglycemia due to hyperinsulinism associated with inoperable islet cell adenoma or carcinoma, or extrapancreatic malignancy; leucine sensitivity; islet cell hyperplasia; nesidioblastosis; or adenomatosis. Diazoxide should only be used in hypoglycemia

that is confirmed to be caused by hyperinsulinism unresponsive to other treatment.

Unaccepted
Although oral diazoxide reduces blood pressure gradually, it is not used in the chronic treatment of hypertension because of its side effects.

Diazoxide is not recommended for use in the treatment of functional hypoglycemia.

Pharmacology

Mechanism of action/Effect: Hyperglycemic effect is due primarily to inhibition of insulin release from the pancreas, as well as an extrapancreatic (catecholamine-induced) effect.

Onset of action: 1 hour.

Duration of action: Normal renal function—8 hours or less.

Precautions to Consider

Cross-sensitivity and/or related problems
Patients sensitive to thiazide diuretics or other sulfonamide-type medications may be sensitive to this medication also.

Geriatrics
No information is available on the relationship of age to the effects of diazoxide in geriatric patients. However, elderly patients are more likely to have age-related renal function impairment, which may require a reduction in dosage and/or a longer dosing interval.

Drug interactions and/or related problems
The following drug interactions and/or related problems have been selected on the basis of their potential clinical significance (possible mechanism in parentheses where appropriate)—not necessarily inclusive (» = major clinical significance):

Note: Combinations containing any of the following medications, depending on the amount present, may also interact with this medication.

Alpha-adrenergic blocking agents, such as:
Labetalol
Phenoxybenzamine
Phentolamine
Prazosin
Tolazoline, or
Other medications with alpha-adrenergic blocking action, such as:
Dihydroergotamine
Ergoloid mesylates
Ergotamine
Haloperidol
Loxapine
Phenothiazines
Thioxanthenes
(concurrent use antagonizes the inhibition of insulin release by diazoxide)

Anticoagulants, coumarin- or indandione-derivative
(increased anticoagulant effects may occur because of displacement of the anticoagulant from protein-binding sites; adjustment of anticoagulant dosage may be necessary)

» Anticonvulsants, hydantoin
(concurrent use is generally not recommended since it may result in decreased efficacy of either medication)

Antigout medications
(diazoxide may raise the concentration of blood uric acid; dosage adjustment of antigout medications may be necessary)

Beta-adrenergic blocking agents, ophthalmic, if significant systemic absorption occurs, or
Beta-adrenergic blocking agents, systemic
(concurrent use prevents diazoxide-induced tachycardia; however, risk of hypotension may be increased)

Diuretics, loop, or
Diuretics, thiazide, or
Indapamide
(may potentiate the antihypertensive, hyperglycemic, and hyperuricemic actions of diazoxide; when used concurrently, adjustment of diazoxide dosage may be necessary)

» Hypotension-producing medications, other or
» Vasodilators, peripheral, for example, cyclandelate, hydralazine, isoxsuprine, nicotinyl alcohol, nylidrin, papaverine
(concurrent use with diazoxide may result in an additive hypotensive effect, which may be severe; dosage adjustments may be necessary, and patients should be continuously observed for excessive fall in blood pressure for several hours after concurrent administration)

Contraindications/Medical problems
The contraindications/medical problems included have been selected on the basis of their potential clinical significance (reasons given in parentheses where appropriate)—not necessarily inclusive (» = major clinical significance).

Risk-benefit should be considered when the following medical problems exist:
» Acute aortic dissection
» Compensatory hypertension, such as that associated with aortic coarctation or arteriovenous shunt
» Coronary or cerebral insufficiency
Gout, history of, or
Hyperuricemia
(may be exacerbated)
Hepatic function impairment
Hypokalemia
(hyperglycemic effects are potentiated)
» Inadequate cardiac reserve, such as uncompensated congestive heart failure
Renal function impairment
(half-life of diazoxide may be prolonged; reduced dosage may be necessary with frequent use)
Sensitivity to diazoxide, sulfonamides, or thiazides

Side/Adverse Effects

The following side/adverse effects have been selected on the basis of their potential clinical significance (possible signs and symptoms in parentheses where appropriate)—not necessarily inclusive:

Those indicating need for medical attention
Incidence more frequent
Edema (decreased urination, rapid weight gain, swelling of feet or lower legs)
Note: *Edema* occurs most commonly in young infants and adults and may lead to congestive heart failure in susceptible patients.
Incidence less frequent
Tachycardia (fast heartbeat)
Incidence rare
Allergic reaction (skin rash, fever); *angina pectoris, myocardial infarction, or myocardial ischemia* (chest pain, most commonly occurring during physical exertion; unexplained shortness of breath); *thrombocytopenia* (unusual bleeding or bruising); *transient focal cerebral ischemic attacks* (confusion, numbness of the hands)
With long-term use
Extrapyramidal effects (stiffness of limbs, trembling and shaking of hands and fingers)
Symptoms of overdose
Hyperglycemia or ketoacidosis (drowsiness; flushed, dry skin; fruit-like breath odor; increased urination; continuing loss of appetite; unusual thirst)—more likely when administered during intercurrent illness

Those indicating need for medical attention only if they continue or are bothersome
Incidence less frequent
Changes in ability to taste; ileus (constipation); *loss of appetite; nausea; stomach pain; vomiting*
With long-term use
Hypertrichosis (increased hair growth on forehead, back, arms, and legs)

Patient Consultation

In providing consultation, consider emphasizing the following selected information (» = major clinical significance):

Before using this medication
» Conditions affecting use, especially:
Sensitivity to diazoxide, thiazide diuretics, or other sulfonamide-type medications

Pregnancy—Studies in animals have demonstrated teratogenicity; effects on infants born to mothers who received diazoxide may include hyperglycemia, hyperbilirubinemia, alopecia, hypertrichosis, and thrombocytopenia

Labor—May inhibit labor

Other medications, especially hydantoin anticonvulsants, other hypotension-producing medications, or peripheral vasodilators

Other medical problems, especially acute aortic dissection, compensatory hypertension, coronary or cerebral insufficiency, or inadequate cardiac reserve

Proper use of this medication

» Not taking more or less medication than the amount prescribed; taking at same time each day

» Importance of diet in helping control condition

» Testing for sugar in urine or blood, and ketones in urine

Missed dose: Taking as soon as possible; not taking if almost time for next dose; not doubling doses

» Proper storage

Precautions while using this medication

» Regular visits to physician to check progress, especially during the first few weeks of treatment

» Caution if any kind of surgery (including dental surgery) or emergency treatment is required

» Not taking other medications, especially OTC sympathomimetics, unless discussed with physician

» Symptoms of hyperglycemia or ketoacidosis

Symptoms of hypoglycemia

Side/adverse effects

Possibility of excessive hair growth, which is reversible in several weeks or months when medication is withdrawn

Signs of potential side effects, especially allergic reaction, angina pectoris, edema, myocardial infarction or ischemia, tachycardia, thrombocytopenia, and transient focal cerebral ischemic attacks

General Dosing Information

Diazoxide is often administered concurrently with a diuretic to prevent congestive heart failure due to fluid retention.

In some patients, the oral suspension dosage form of diazoxide produces higher blood concentrations than the capsule form; caution is recommended when a patient is switched from one dosage form to another.

Hyperglycemia is usually transient after intravenous administration of diazoxide (persisting 24 to 48 hours), but may be more persistent after prolonged oral administration and may rarely progress to ketoacidosis or hyperosmolar coma.

If diazoxide is not effective within 2 to 3 weeks in the treatment of hypoglycemia, it is recommended that therapy with the medication be re-evaluated.

Oral Dosage Forms

DIAZOXIDE CAPSULES USP

Usual adult and adolescent dose: Antihypoglycemic—

Initial: Oral, 1 mg per kg of body weight every eight hours, adjusted according to clinical response.

Maintenance: Oral, 3 to 8 mg per kg of body weight a day, divided into two or three equal doses every twelve or eight hours, respectively.

Usual adult prescribing limits: Oral, up to 15 mg per kg of body weight a day.

DIAZOXIDE ORAL SUSPENSION USP

Usual adult and adolescent dose: See *Diazoxide Capsules USP*.

Auxiliary labeling: • Shake well before using.

DIFENOXIN AND ATROPINE   Systemic†

A commonly used *brand name* in the U.S. is *Motofen*.

ORAL

Difenoxin Hydrochloride and Atropine Sulfate Tablets†

In the U.S.—*Motofen*

---

†Not commercially available in Canada.

Category: Antidiarrheal (antiperistaltic).

Indications

Accepted

Diarrhea (treatment)—Difenoxin and atropine combination is indicated in the symptomatic treatment of acute nonspecific diarrhea and acute exacerbations of chronic functional diarrhea.

Pharmacology

Mechanism of action/Effect:

Difenoxin—Probably acts both locally and centrally to reduce intestinal motility. Antidiarrheal activity is about 5 times that of diphenoxylate.

Atropine—Has anticholinergic activity. However, in this preparation atropine is included in doses below the therapeutic level in an attempt to prevent abuse by deliberate overdosage.

Precautions to Consider

Geriatrics

No geriatrics-specific information is available on the use of difenoxin and atropine. However, geriatric patients may be more susceptible to the respiratory depressant effects of difenoxin.

In geriatric patients with diarrhea, caution is recommended because of the risk of fluid and electrolyte loss.

Drug interactions and/or related problems

The following drug interactions and/or related problems have been selected on the basis of their potential clinical significance (possible mechanism in parentheses where appropriate)—not necessarily inclusive (» = major clinical significance):

Note: Combinations containing any of the following medications, depending on the amount present, may also interact with this medication.

Addictive medications, other, especially central nervous system (CNS) depressants with habituating potential
(concurrent use with difenoxin may increase the risk of habituation; caution is recommended)

» Alcohol or
» CNS depression-producing medications, other
(concurrent use with difenoxin may increase the CNS depressant effects of either difenoxin or these medications; also, when tricyclic antidepressants are used concurrently with atropine, their anticholinergic effects may be intensified; dosage adjustment may be required)

» Anticholinergics or other medications with anticholinergic activity
(these medications may enhance the effects of atropine during concurrent use; significant interaction is unlikely with usual doses of difenoxin and atropine, but may occur with its abuse)

» Monoamine oxidase (MAO) inhibitors, including furazolidone and procarbazine
(concurrent use with difenoxin may precipitate hypertensive crisis; MAO inhibitors may block detoxification of atropine, thus potentiating its action)

» Naltrexone
(administration of naltrexone to a patient physically dependent on opioid drugs, such as difenoxin, will precipitate withdrawal symptoms; symptoms may appear within 5 minutes of naltrexone administration, persist for up to 48 hours, and be difficult to reverse)

(naltrexone blocks the therapeutic effects of opioids [i.e., antidiarrheal]; naltrexone therapy should not be initiated in patients receiving difenoxin; also, patients receiving naltrexone should be advised to use alternative antidiarrheals when necessary)

Opioid (narcotic) analgesics
(concurrent use with difenoxin may result in increased risk of severe constipation and additive CNS depressant effects)

Contraindications/Medical problems

The contraindications/medical problems included have been selected on the basis of their potential clinical significance (reasons given in parentheses where appropriate)—not necessarily inclusive (» = major clinical significance).

Except under special circumstances, this medication should not be used when the following medical problem exists:

» Colitis, severe
(patient may develop toxic megacolon)

» Diarrhea associated with pseudomembranous colitis resulting from treatment with broad-spectrum antibiotics
(inhibition of peristalsis may delay the removal of toxin from the colon, thereby prolonging and/or worsening the diarrhea)

Risk-benefit should be considered when the following medical problems exist:

Alcoholism, active or in remission, or
Drug abuse or dependence, history of
(difenoxin content may increase chances of drug abuse in patient already predisposed to dependence)

Cardiovascular instability
(possible increase in heart rate may be undesirable)

» Dehydration, especially in children
(may predispose to delayed difenoxin intoxication; inhibition of peristalsis may result in fluid retention in colon and may further aggravate dehydration; discontinuation of medication and rehydration therapy is essential if signs of dehydration, such as dry mouth, excessive thirst, wrinkled skin, decreased urination, and dizziness or lightheadedness, are present; fluid loss may have serious consequences, such as circulatory collapse and renal failure, especially in young children)

Diarrhea caused by infectious organisms
(bacterial diarrhea may worsen due to the increased contact time between the mucosa and the penetrating microorganism; however, evidence of this occurring in actual practice is lacking)

» Diarrhea caused by poisoning, until toxic material has been eliminated from gastrointestinal tract

Down's syndrome, in children
(atropine may cause abnormal increase in pupillary dilation and acceleration of heart rate)

» Dysentery, acute, characterized by bloody stools and elevated temperature
(sole treatment with antiperistaltic antidiarrheals may be inadequate; antibiotic therapy may be required)

Gallbladder disease or gallstones
(difenoxin may cause biliary tract spasm)

Glaucoma, angle-closure
(although unlikely with usual doses of this combination, atropine may precipitate an acute attack of angle-closure glaucoma)

» Hepatic function impairment or jaundice
(difenoxin may precipitate hepatic coma; it is recommended that dosage be reduced in patients with impaired hepatic function)

Hiatal hernia associated with reflux esophagitis or
Hypertension
(although unlikely with usual doses of this combination, atropine may aggravate these conditions)

Hyperthyroidism
(characterized by tachycardia, which may be increased by atropine)

Hypothyroidism
(difenoxin may increase risk of respiratory depression)

Intestinal atony in the elderly or debilitated
(although unlikely with usual doses of this combination, use of atropine may result in obstruction)

Myasthenia gravis
(although unlikely with usual doses of this combination, atropine may aggravate condition because of inhibition of acetylcholine action)

Prostatic hypertrophy or
Urethral stricture, acute, or
Urinary retention
(reduction in tone of urinary bladder may aggravate or lead to complete urinary retention)

Renal function impairment
(decreased excretion may increase the risk of side effects)

Respiratory disease or impairment
(increased risk of respiratory depression)

Sensitivity to atropine or difenoxin

Side/Adverse Effects

The following side/adverse effects have been selected on the basis of their potential clinical significance (possible signs and symptoms in parentheses where appropriate)—not necessarily inclusive:

Those indicating need for medical attention
Incidence less frequent or rare
Paralytic ileus or toxic megacolon (bloating, constipation, loss of appetite, severe stomach pain with nausea and vomiting)

Symptoms of overdose
Anticholinergic effects, severe (continuing blurred vision or changes in near vision; severe drowsiness; severe dryness of mouth, nose, and throat; fast heartbeat; unusual warmth, dryness, and flushing of skin); *respiratory depression* (severe shortness of breath or troubled breathing); *unusual excitement, nervousness, restlessness, or irritability, especially in children*

Note: *Respiratory depression* may occur as late as 12 to 30 hours after ingestion.

Those indicating need for medical attention only if they continue, worsen, or are bothersome
Incidence less frequent or rare
Anticholinergic effects, mild (blurred vision, difficult urination, dryness of skin and mouth, fever); *confusion; dizziness or lightheadedness; drowsiness; headache; trouble in sleeping; unusual tiredness or weakness*

Note: Since atropine is present in a subtherapeutic dose, symptoms of *mild anticholinergic effects* probably indicate overdosage, although in children they may occur at therapeutic doses.

Those indicating possible withdrawal and the need for medical attention if they occur after discontinuation of prolonged high-dose therapy
Incidence rare
Increased sweating; muscle cramps; nausea or vomiting; shivering or trembling; stomach cramps

Patient Consultation

In providing consultation, consider emphasizing the following selected information (» = major clinical significance):

Before using this medication
» Conditions affecting use, especially:
   Sensitivity to atropine or difenoxin
   Pregnancy—Studies in rats show increased delivery time and stillbirth at doses 20 times maximum human dose
   Breast-feeding—Difenoxin and atropine excreted in breast milk; potential for serious adverse effects in nursing infant
   Use in children—Increased susceptibility to toxic effects of atropine and respiratory depressant effects of difenoxin; risk of dehydration
   Use in the elderly—Increased risk of respiratory depression; risk of dehydration
   Other medications, especially other anticholinergics, CNS depressants, MAO inhibitors, or naltrexone
   Other medical problems, especially acute dysentery; dehydration; diarrhea caused by antibiotics or poisoning; hepatic function impairment or jaundice; or severe colitis

Proper use of this medication
   Taking with food or meals if gastric irritation occurs
» Importance of not taking more medication than the amount prescribed because of habit-forming potential
» Importance of maintaining adequate hydration and proper diet
   Missed dose: If on scheduled dosing regimen—Taking as soon as possible; not taking if almost time for next dose; not doubling doses
» Proper storage

Precautions while using this medication
   Regular visits to physician to check progress during prolonged therapy
» Consulting physician if diarrhea is not controlled within 48 hours and/or fever develops
» Avoiding use of alcohol or other CNS depressants during therapy
» Suspected overdose: Getting emergency help at once
   Need to inform physician or dentist of use of medication if any kind of surgery (including dental surgery) or emergency treatment is required
» Caution if dizziness or drowsiness occurs

Side/adverse effects
   Signs of potential side effects, especially paralytic ileus or toxic megacolon

General Dosing Information

If clinical improvement is not observed within 48 hours, treatment with difenoxin and atropine should be discontinued.

Inhibition of peristalsis may produce fluid retention in the bowel, which may aggravate dehydration and depletion of electrolytes, especially in young children, and may also increase variability of response to the medication. If dehydration or electrolyte imbalance occurs, difenoxin and atropine therapy should be withheld until appropriate corrective therapy has begun.

To prevent development of toxic megacolon in patients with acute ulcerative colitis, treatment with difenoxin and atropine should be discontinued promptly if abdominal pain or distention or other specific gastrointestinal symptoms such as anorexia, bloating, constipation, nausea, or vomiting occur.

Prolonged use of larger-than-usual therapeutic doses may theoretically result in physical dependence.

Tolerance to the antidiarrheal effects of difenoxin and atropine may develop with prolonged use.

This medication may suppress respiration, especially in children or the elderly, the very ill, and patients with respiratory problems. Lower doses may be required for these patients.

Oral Dosage Forms

DIFENOXIN HYDROCHLORIDE AND ATROPINE SULFATE TABLETS

Note: Difenoxin hydrochloride and atropine sulfate tablets are not commercially available in Canada.

Usual adult and adolescent dose: Antidiarrheal (antiperistaltic)— Oral, the equivalent of difenoxin hydrochloride—2 mg initially, then 1 mg after each loose stool or every three or four hours as needed.

Usual adult prescribing limits: Up to the equivalent of 8 mg of difenoxin hydrochloride daily.

Usual geriatric dose: See *Usual adult and adolescent dose.*

Note: Geriatric patients may be more sensitive to the effects of the usual adult dose.

Auxiliary labeling:
• May cause drowsiness.
• Avoid alcoholic beverages.
• Keep out of reach of children.
• May be habit-forming.

DIGITALIS GLYCOSIDES   Systemic

Some commonly used *brand names* are:

In the U.S.—
    Cedilanid-D [Deslanoside]   *Lanoxicaps* [Digoxin]
    Crystodigin [Digitoxin]   *Lanoxin* [Digoxin]

In Canada—
    Cedilanid [Deslanoside]   *Novodigoxin* [Digoxin]
    Lanoxin [Digoxin]

DESLANOSIDE
Parenteral
    Deslanoside Injection USP
        In the U.S.—*Cedilanid-D*
        In Canada—*Cedilanid*
DIGITOXIN†
Oral
    Digitoxin Tablets USP†
        In the U.S.—*Crystodigin;* GENERIC
DIGOXIN
Oral
    Digoxin Capsules†
        In the U.S.—*Lanoxicaps*
    Digoxin Elixir USP
        In the U.S.—*Lanoxin;* GENERIC
        In Canada—*Lanoxin*
    Digoxin Tablets USP
        In the U.S.—*Lanoxin;* GENERIC
        In Canada—*Lanoxin; Novodigoxin;* GENERIC
Parenteral
    Digoxin Injection USP
        In the U.S. and Canada—*Lanoxin;* GENERIC

---

†Not commercially available in Canada.

Category: Antiarrhythmic; cardiotonic.

Indications

Accepted
Arrhythmias, cardiac (prophylaxis and treatment)—Digitalis glyco-
sides are indicated for the control of the following arrhythmias:
Atrial fibrillation;
Atrial flutter;
Paroxysmal atrial tachycardia.

Congestive heart failure (treatment)—Digitalis glycosides are indicated for the treatment of all degrees of congestive heart failure.
They are generally most effective in "low output" failure associated with depressed left ventricular function and much less effective in "high output" failure (bronchopulmonary insufficiency, arteriovenous fistula, anemia, beriberi, infection, hyperthyroidism).
Their positive inotropic action results in improved cardiac output
and an improvement in the signs and symptoms of hemodynamic
insufficiency such as dyspnea, edema, and/or venous congestion.

Cardiogenic shock (treatment)[1]—Although the value is not established,
digitalis glycosides are frequently used to treat cardiogenic shock,
especially when it is accompanied by pulmonary edema. However,
digitalis may adversely affect shock related to gram-negative septicemia.

Unaccepted
The use of digitalis glycosides in the treatment of obesity has been
determined unwarranted and dangerous, since these drugs may
cause potentially fatal arrhythmias or other adverse effects.

---

[1]Not included in Canadian product labeling.

Pharmacology

See also *Table 1*, page 514.

Mechanism of action/Effect: Two major actions are produced by
therapeutic doses of digitalis glycosides:

(1) Force and velocity of myocardial contraction are increased
(positive inotropic effect). This effect is thought to result from
inhibition of movement of sodium and potassium ions across
myocardial cell membranes by complexing with adenosine triphosphatase. As a result, there is enhancement of calcium influx
and an augmented release of free calcium ions within the myocardial cells to subsequently potentiate the activity of the con-
tractile muscle fibers of the heart.

(2) A decrease in the conduction rate and increase in the effective
refractory period of the atrioventricular (AV) node is predominantly due to an indirect effect caused by enhancement of
parasympathetic tone and decrease in sympathetic tone.

Precautions to Consider

Cross-sensitivity and/or related problems
Allergic reactions to a digitalis glycoside preparation occur rarely.
Such reactions do not necessarily encompass all digitalis glycosides and therefore may not preclude the trial of another digitalis
glycoside.

Geriatrics
Although appropriate studies have not been performed in the geriatric
population, many elderly patients have reduced renal and/or hepatic function, a decreased volume of distribution for digitalis
glycosides, and electrolyte imbalances (e.g., hypokalemia), and
may require lower doses of digitalis glycosides in order to avoid
toxicity. (Digoxin clearance is less affected by hepatic function
impairment, while digitoxin clearance is less affected by renal
function impairment.)

Digoxin-induced loss of appetite is a significant risk in frail elderly
patients.

Dental
An increased gag reflex may increase the difficulty of taking a dental
impression.

Drug interactions and/or related problems
The following drug interactions and/or related problems have been
selected on the basis of their potential clinical significance (possible mechanism in parentheses where appropriate)—not necessarily inclusive (» = major clinical significance):

Note: Combinations containing any of the following medications, depending on the amount present, may also interact with this
medication.

» Adrenocorticoids, glucocorticoid, especially with significant min-
eralocorticoid activity, or
» Adrenocorticoids, mineralocorticoid, or
» Amphotericin B, parenteral, or
   Carbonic anhydrase inhibitors or
» Corticotropin (ACTH) or
» Diuretics, potassium-depleting (such as bumetanide, ethacrynic acid,
furosemide, indapamide, mannitol, or thiazides), or
   Sodium phosphates
      (hypokalemia caused by these medications may enhance the
possibility of digitalis toxicity; frequent potassium determina-
tions are recommended)
» Amiodarone
      (amiodarone increases serum concentrations of digoxin and
probably other digitalis glycosides, possibly to toxic levels;
when amiodarone therapy is initiated, the digitalis glycoside

should be withdrawn or the dose reduced by 50%; if digitalis glycoside therapy is continued, serum concentrations should be carefully monitored; amiodarone and digitalis glycosides may also produce additive effects on sinoatrial [SA] and atrioventricular [AV] nodes)

Antacids
(aluminum- and magnesium-containing antacids may inhibit absorption of digitalis glycosides, resulting in decreased plasma concentrations)

» Antiarrhythmics, other, including other digitalis preparations, or
» Calcium salts, parenteral, or
Cocaine or
Pancuronium or
Rauwolfia alkaloids or
» Succinylcholine or
» Sympathomimetics
(concurrent use with digitalis glycosides may increase the risk of cardiac arrhythmias; caution and close electrocardiographic [ECG] monitoring are very important if concurrent use is necessary)
(concurrent use of amiodarone may result in increased serum digoxin concentrations)

» Antidiarrheal adsorbents (e.g., kaolin and pectin) or
» Cholestyramine or
» Colestipol or
Dietary fiber, such as bran (large quantities), or
Laxatives or
Neomycin, oral, or
Sulfasalazine
(concurrent use may inhibit digitalis glycosides absorption, resulting in decreased therapeutic effect of the glycoside; patients should be monitored closely for evidence of altered digitalis effect)

» Calcium channel blocking agents
(serum digitalis glycoside concentrations may be increased during concurrent use, especially with verapamil and, to a lesser extent, diltiazem; nicardipine and nifedipine do not appear to have a significant effect. Concurrent use of digitalis glycosides with diltiazem and verapamil may result in excessive bradycardia because of additive depression of AV nodal conduction; nicardipine and nifedipine do not produce this effect. Digitalis glycoside dosage may need to be reduced and the patient carefully monitored for digitalis toxicity)

Captopril
(concurrent use may result in increased serum digoxin concentrations; however, digitalis glycoside toxicity is unlikely unless serum concentrations are already elevated)

Edrophonium
(when digitalis glycosides are used concurrently with edrophonium, the additive vagomimetic effects may cause excessive slowing of the heart rate)

Erythromycin
(may increase absorption of digoxin by altering gastrointestinal flora that normally inactivate some digoxin prior to absorption)

Heparin
(digitalis glycosides may partially counteract the anticoagulant effect of heparin; heparin dosage adjustment may be required during and following concurrent use)

Hepatic enzyme inducers
(concurrent use may require dosage adjustment of digitalis glycosides, with the possible exception of digoxin, because of their increased metabolism)

Indomethacin
(when indomethacin is administered concurrently with digitalis glycosides to the premature neonate, renal clearance of the digitalis glycoside may be decreased, leading to increased plasma concentrations, elimination half-lives, and risk of digitalis toxicity; it is recommended that digitalis dosage be reduced by 50% when indomethacin therapy is initiated and that further digitalis dosage adjustment be based on monitoring of ECG and digitalis concentration)
(although not documented, the possibility should be considered that indomethacin may also increase digitalis concentration in adults and that digitalis dosage adjustment may be required)

» Magnesium sulfate, parenteral
(parenteral magnesium sulfate must be administered with extreme caution in digitalized patients, especially if intravenous calcium salts are also employed; cardiac conduction changes and heart block may occur)

Phenylbutazone
(concurrent use may result in reduced plasma concentrations of digitalis glycosides)

» Potassium salts
(not recommended for concurrent use with digitalis glycosides in digitalized patients with severe or complete heart block; however, potassium supplements are often used to prevent or correct hypokalemia, especially when potassium-depleting diuretics such as the thiazides are administered concurrently with digitalis glycosides. Careful monitoring of serum potassium during use of supplemental potassium is extremely important in order to avoid hyperkalemia, which is very dangerous in digitalized patients)

» Quinidine or
Quinine
(concurrent use may result in substantially increased serum concentrations of digoxin; studies with digitoxin indicate a similar change; serum concentrations should be monitored and dosage adjusted as indicated)

» Spironolactone
(spironolactone may increase the half-life of digoxin; dosage reduction or increased dosing intervals of digoxin may be necessary and careful monitoring is recommended)

Succinylcholine
(may cause sudden release of potassium from muscle cells, increasing the risk of digitalis-induced arrhythmias)

Thallous chloride Tl 201
(in animal studies, concurrent use of digitalis glycosides decreased myocardial uptake of thallous chloride Tl 201; human data are not available)

Thyroid hormones
(initial administration of supplemental thyroid hormones to digitalized patients may necessitate a dosage increase of digitalis glycosides to maintain therapeutic concentrations; patients may be stabilized on both medications concurrently with careful dosage adjustments)

Contraindications/Medical problems
The contraindications/medical problems included have been selected on the basis of their potential clinical significance (reasons given in parentheses where appropriate)—not necessarily inclusive (» = major clinical significance).

Except under special circumstances, these medications should not be used when the following medical problems exist:
» Toxic effects present from prior administration of any digitalis preparation
» Ventricular fibrillation

Risk-benefit should be considered when the following medical problems exist:
For all digitalis glycosides
» Atrioventricular (AV) block, incomplete, especially in patients with Stokes-Adams attacks
(may progress to complete block)
» Carotid sinus hypersensitivity
(digitalis glycosides may cause an increase in vagal tone)

» Glomerulonephritis, acute, accompanied by heart failure
(use of a low total daily dose is recommended, administered in divided doses, with constant ECG monitoring; use of antihypertensives and diuretics is also recommended and the digitalis glycoside should be withdrawn as soon as possible)

Hepatic function impairment, especially with digitoxin
(reduced metabolism; dosage reduction may be necessary)

» Hypercalcemia or
» Hyperkalemia
(increased risk of digitalis-induced arrhythmias, primarily heart block)

» Hypocalcemia
(digitalis glycosides may be ineffective; administration of calcium may be necessary)

» Hypokalemia (including that resulting from drugs, dialysis, mechanical suction of gastrointestinal secretions, malnutrition, diarrhea, prolonged vomiting, old age, and long-standing heart failure) or
» Hypomagnesemia
(increased risk of digitalis toxicity)

Hypothyroidism
(dosage requirements may be reduced; administration of thyroid hormones may increase requirements)

» Idiopathic hypertrophic subaortic stenosis
(aggravated left ventricular outflow restrictions)

» Ischemic heart disease or
» Myocardial infarction, acute, or
» Myocarditis, acute, including rheumatic carditis or viral myocarditis, or
» Myxedema or
» Pulmonary disease, severe
(increased sensitivity of the myocardium to the effects of digitalis glycosides and increased risk of digitalis-induced arrhythmias)

Pericarditis, chronic constrictive
(patients may fail to respond to digitalis glycosides, and slowing of the heart rate may further reduce cardiac output)

» Premature ventricular contractions or
» Ventricular tachycardia
(risk of exacerbation; digitalis glycosides should not be used unless congestive heart failure supervenes after a protracted episode not due to digitalis)

Sensitivity to the digitalis glycoside prescribed

» Sick sinus syndrome
(possible worsening of sinus bradycardia or sinoatrial [SA] block)

» Wolff-Parkinson-White syndrome, especially when associated with atrial fibrillation
(possibility of fatal ventricular arrhythmias)

» Caution is also recommended in debilitated patients and patients using electronic cardiac pacemakers; these patients require careful dosage titration, as they may exhibit toxic responses at doses and serum concentrations generally tolerated by other patients.

For all except digitoxin
Renal function impairment
(reduced excretion and potential toxicity; dosage reduction may be required; in addition, time to achieve a new or steady-state concentration is increased; although digitoxin excretion is also reduced, no dosage reduction is necessary because metabolism and half-life are not affected)

Side/Adverse Effects

Note: Some side/adverse affects, including nausea and vomiting and some arrhythmias, may also be symptoms of toxicity. If there is

any doubt about the cause of these symptoms, the digitalis glycoside should be withdrawn until the cause is determined.

The first signs of toxicity in infants and small children are usually cardiac arrhythmias, while in adults and older children, the first symptoms of overdose may be stomach upset, abdominal pain, loss of appetite, or unusually slow heart rate.

In adults, the most common arrhythmia is premature ventricular beats (extrasystoles); paroxysmal and nonparoxysmal nodal rhythms, atrioventricular (AV) (interference) dissociation, and paroxysmal atrial tachycardia with block are also common; increasing AV block may occur; death may occur from ventricular fibrillation. In children, premature ventricular systoles are rare, while nodal and atrial systoles are more frequent; atrial arrhythmias, atrial ectopic rhythms, and paroxysmal atrial tachycardia (particularly with AV block) are more common; ventricular arrhythmias are rare. An increase in PR interval may occur in newborns.

The following side/adverse effects have been selected on the basis of their potential clinical significance (possible signs and symptoms in parentheses where appropriate)—not necessarily inclusive:

Those indicating need for medical attention
Incidence rare
Allergic reaction (skin rash or hives)

Signs and/or symptoms of toxicity or intolerance (in order of occurrence)
Stimulation of medullary centers (loss of appetite, nausea or vomiting); *lower stomach pain; diarrhea; electrolyte imbalance, possible* (unusual tiredness or weakness, extreme); *slow or irregular heartbeat*—may be fast heartbeat in children; *blurred vision or other visual disturbances such as colored halos seen around objects*—"yellow," "green," or "white vision"; *drowsiness; confusion or mental depression; headache; fainting*

Note: Large doses may also have a local irritating emetic action.

Patient Consultation

In providing consultation, consider emphasizing the following selected information (» = major clinical significance):

Before using this medication
» Conditions affecting use, especially:
Sensitivity to the digitalis glycoside prescribed
Pregnancy—Cross placenta
Use in children—Infant responses vary; careful dosage adjustment required
Use in the elderly—Increased sensitivity to effects
Other medications, especially adrenocorticoids, parenteral amphotericin B, potassium-depleting diuretics, amiodarone, other antiarrhythmics, sympathomimetics, antidiarrheal adsorbents, cholestyramine, colestipol, diltiazem, verapamil, potassium-containing medications or supplements, quinidine, or spironolactone
Other medical problems, especially hepatic function impairment, renal function impairment, severe pulmonary disease, recent myocardial infarction, or rheumatic fever

Proper use of this medication
» Compliance with therapy; taking exactly as directed, not taking more or less
Proper administration of elixir: Taking orally; special dropper to be used for accurate measuring
Taking medication at the same time each day to help increase compliance
Checking apical pulse as directed (checking with physician if less than 60 beats per minute)
Missed dose: Taking as soon as remembered if within 12 hours of scheduled dose; not taking if remembered later; not doubling doses; checking with doctor if dose missed for 2 days or more
» Proper storage

Precautions while using this medication

Regular visits to physician to check progress

» Checking with physician before discontinuing medication

» Keeping medication out of reach of children

» Reporting to physician any nausea, vomiting, diarrhea, loss of appetite, or extremely slow pulse as possible signs of overdose

» Caution if medical or dental surgery or emergency treatment is required

Carrying medical identification card

» Avoiding other medications unless prescribed by physician

Caution in using medications of similar appearance

Side/adverse effects

Signs of potential side effects, especially allergic reaction, and signs and symptoms of overdose

General Dosing Information

Recommended doses are averages only; each dose must be adjusted to meet the individual patient's requirements.

Before a loading dose of a digitalis preparation is administered, it is extremely important to determine whether the patient has taken any form of digitalis during the previous 2 or 3 weeks, since some residual effect may require a reduced dosage to avoid toxicity.

Dosage calculations should be based on ideal (lean) body weight, since digitalis glycosides are not taken up by adipose tissue.

Digoxin may be the preferred cardioglycoside in some patients with liver function impairment because it does not undergo extensive hepatic metabolism.

Reduction of digitalis glycoside dosage prior to cardioversion may be desirable to avoid induction of ventricular arrhythmias; however, the benefit must be weighed against the risk of rapid increase in ventricular response to atrial fibrillation if the digitalis glycoside is withheld 1 to 2 days prior to cardioversion. If digitalis glycoside toxicity is suspected, electrical cardioversion of arrhythmias should be delayed, if possible. When it is considered absolutely necessary, use of the lowest possible energy level and/or pretreatment with lidocaine is recommended.

For parenteral dosage forms only

The intravenous route is preferred when parenteral administration is indicated. Intramuscular use involves greater local discomfort, slower effect, and erratic bioavailability. Intravenous injections should be administered over a period of at least 5 minutes.

Intramuscular injections are used only when the oral or intravenous routes cannot be used. The injection should be administered deeply into the muscle and preferably should not exceed 2 mL at any one injection site. Following the injection, each site should be massaged well to reduce painful local reactions.

When a patient is transferred from a parenteral digitalis glycoside to an oral digitalis dosage form, dosage adjustments may be necessary to compensate for the pharmacokinetic differences among the medications. One exception is the transfer from digoxin injection to the liquid-filled, soft capsules of digoxin, because both dosage forms have the same bioavailability.

DESLANOSIDE

Summary of Differences

Pharmacology:
Protein binding—Low.
Half-life—33 to 36 hours.
Onset of action—10 to 30 minutes.
Time to peak effect—1 to 3 hours.
Duration of action—Approximately 2 to 5 days.

Precautions: Contraindications/medical problems—Dosage reduction may be required in renal function impairment.

Parenteral Dosage Forms

DESLANOSIDE INJECTION USP

Usual adult dose: Digitalization—
Intravenous: 1.6 mg administered as a single dose; or 800 mcg (0.8 mg) initially and repeated after four hours.
Intramuscular: 800 mcg (0.8 mg) given at each of two separate injection sites.

Note: The intravenous route is usually preferred for immediate action. Maintenance dosage is accomplished by utilizing an orally effective glycoside within twelve hours.

Patients with impaired renal function, geriatric patients, debilitated patients, and patients using electronic cardiac pacemakers require careful dosage titration, as they may exhibit toxic responses at doses and serum concentrations generally tolerated by other patients.

Usual adult prescribing limits: Up to 2 mg per day.

DIGITOXIN

Summary of Differences

Pharmacology:
Hepatically metabolized; renal excretion of inactive metabolites has little effect on digitoxin action.
Protein binding—Very high.
Half-life—120 to 216 hours.
Onset of action—1 to 4 hours.
Time to peak effect—8 to 14 hours.
Duration of action—Approximately 14 days.
Precautions: Contraindications/medical problems—Dosage reduction not necessary in renal function impairment.

Oral Dosage Forms

DIGITOXIN TABLETS USP

Note: Digitoxin tablets are not commercially available in Canada.

Usual adult dose:
Antiarrhythmic; or
Cardiotonic—
Digitalization:
Rapid—Oral, 600 mcg (0.6 mg) initially, then 400 mcg (0.4 mg) after four to six hours and 200 mcg (0.2 mg) after another four- to six-hour period, followed by a daily maintenance dose as needed and tolerated, or
Slow—Oral, 200 mcg (0.2 mg) twice a day for four days, followed by a daily maintenance dose as needed and tolerated.
Maintenance: Oral, 50 to 300 mcg (0.05 to 0.3 mg) once a day, the dosage being adjusted as needed and tolerated.

Note: Geriatric patients, debilitated patients, and patients using electronic cardiac pacemakers require careful dosage titration, as they may exhibit toxic responses at doses and serum concentrations generally tolerated by other patients.

Usual adult prescribing limits: Digitalization—Up to a total of 1.6 mg over one or two days.

Auxiliary labeling:
• Keep out of reach of children.
• Do not take other medicines without advice from your doctor.

DIGOXIN

Summary of Differences

Pharmacology:

Bioavailability—60 to 80% (tablets), 70 to 85% (oral elixir or intramuscular injection), or 90 to 100% (capsules).

Protein binding—Low.

Biotransformation—Not hepatically metabolized; excretion and half-life determined by renal function.

Half-life—36 to 48 hours.

Onset of action—5 to 30 minutes (intravenous) or 30 minutes to 2 hours (oral).

Time to peak effect—1 to 4 hours (intravenous) or 2 to 6 hours (oral).

Duration of action—Approximately 6 days.

Precautions: Contraindications/medical problems—Dosage reduction may be required in renal function impairment.

Additional Dosing Information

Bioavailability differences exist among dosage forms of digoxin. Changing therapy from one dosage form to another may require dosage adjustments. A 100-mcg (0.1-mg) dose of the injection or of the digoxin-solution capsule is bioequivalent to a 125-mcg (0.125-mg) dose of the tablet or elixir.

Oral Dosage Forms

DIGOXIN CAPSULES

Note: Digoxin capsules are not commercially available in Canada.

Usual adult dose:

Antiarrhythmic; or

Cardiotonic—

Digitalization:

Rapid—Oral, initially, 400 to 600 mcg (0.4 to 0.6 mg) with additional doses of 100 to 300 mcg (0.1 to 0.3 mg) administered every six to eight hours as needed and tolerated until the desired effect is clinically evident.

Slow—Oral, a total of 50 to 350 mcg (0.05 to 0.35 mg) per day *divided* and administered in two doses, the dosage being repeated for seven to 22 days as needed to reach steady-state serum concentrations.

Maintenance: Oral, 50 to 350 mcg (0.05 to 0.35 mg) administered as one or two doses per day as needed and tolerated.

Note: Patients with impaired renal function, geriatric patients, debilitated patients, and patients using electronic cardiac pacemakers require careful dosage titration, as they may exhibit toxic responses at doses and serum concentrations generally tolerated by other patients.

Auxiliary labeling:

• Keep out of reach of children.

• Keep container tightly closed.

• Do not take other medicines without advice from your doctor.

DIGOXIN ELIXIR USP

Usual adult dose:

Digitalization—

Rapid: Oral, a total of 0.75 to 1.25 mg *divided* into two or more doses, each then being administered every six to eight hours.

Slow: Oral, 125 to 500 mcg (0.125 to 0.5 mg) once a day for seven days.

Maintenance—Oral, 125 to 500 mcg (0.125 to 0.5 mg) once a day.

Note: Patients with impaired renal function, geriatric patients, debilitated patients, and patients using electronic cardiac pacemakers require careful dosage titration, as they may exhibit toxic responses at doses and serum concentrations generally tolerated by other patients.

Auxiliary labeling:

• Keep out of reach of children.

• Keep container tightly closed.

• Do not take other medicines without advice from your doctor.

DIGOXIN TABLETS USP

Usual adult dose:

Digitalization—

Rapid: Oral, a total of 0.75 to 1.25 mg *divided* into two or more doses, each then being administered every six to eight hours.

Slow: Oral, 125 to 500 mcg (0.125 to 0.5 mg) once a day for seven days.

Maintenance—Oral, 125 to 500 mcg (0.125 to 0.5 mg) once a day.

Note: Patients with impaired renal function, geriatric patients, debilitated patients, and patients using electronic cardiac pacemakers require careful dosage titration, as they may exhibit toxic responses at doses and serum concentrations generally tolerated by other patients.

Auxiliary labeling:

• Keep out of reach of children.

• Do not take other medicines without advice from your doctor.

Parenteral Dosage Forms

DIGOXIN INJECTION USP

Usual adult dose:

Digitalization—Intravenous, initially, 400 to 600 mcg (0.4 to 0.6 mg) with additional doses of 100 to 300 mcg (0.1 to 0.3 mg) administered every four to eight hours as needed and tolerated until the desired effect is clinically evident.

Maintenance—Intravenous, 125 to 500 mcg (0.125 to 0.5 mg) per day in divided doses or as a single dose.

Note: Patients with impaired renal function, geriatric patients, debilitated patients, and patients using electronic cardiac pacemakers require careful dosage titration, as they may exhibit toxic responses at doses and serum concentrations generally tolerated by other patients.

Table 1. Pharmacology

Drug and Route	Onset of Action	Time to Peak Effect (hr)	Duration of Action (approx. days)
Deslanoside IV	10–30 min	1–3	2–5
Digitoxin Oral	1–4 hr	8–14	14
Digoxin IV Oral	5–30 min 1/2–2 hr	1–4 2–6	6 6

DIPHENIDOL   Systemic

INN: Difenidol

A commonly used *brand name* in the U.S. and Canada is *Vontrol.*

ORAL
Diphenidol Hydrochloride Tablets
  In the U.S. and Canada—*Vontrol*

Category: Antiemetic; antivertigo agent.

Indications

Accepted
Vertigo (prophylaxis and treatment)—Diphenidol is indicated in the prevention and symptomatic treatment of peripheral (labyrinthine) vertigo and associated nausea and vomiting that occur in such conditions as Meniere's disease and surgery of the middle and inner ear.

Nausea and vomiting (prophylaxis and treatment); and

Nausea and vomiting, cancer chemotherapy-induced (prophylaxis and treatment)—Diphenidol is indicated also for the control of nausea and vomiting associated with postoperative states, malignant neoplasms, labyrinthine disturbances, antineoplastic agent therapy, radiation sickness, and infectious diseases.

Unaccepted
Diphenidol has been used in the treatment of ventricular tachyarrhythmias; however, the use of diphenidol as an antiarrhythmic is unwarranted because of the frequency and severity of adverse central nervous system (CNS) effects.

Diphenidol is *not* indicated for use in the nausea and vomiting of pregnancy.

Pharmacology

Mechanism of action/Effect: The mechanism by which diphenidol exerts its antiemetic and antivertigo effects is not precisely known. It is thought to diminish vestibular stimulation and depress labyrinthine function. An action on the medullary chemoreceptive trigger zone may also be involved in the antiemetic effect.

Other actions/effects: Diphenidol has no significant sedative, tranquilizing, or antihistaminic action. It has a weak peripheral anticholinergic effect.

Precautions to Consider

Geriatrics
No published geriatrics-specific information is available.

Drug interactions and/or related problems
The following drug interactions and/or related problems have been selected on the basis of their potential clinical significance (possible mechanism in parentheses where appropriate)—not necessarily inclusive (» = major clinical significance):

Note: Combinations containing any of the following medications, depending on the amount present, may also interact with this medication.

Anticholinergics or other medications with anticholinergic activity
  (anticholinergic effects may be potentiated when these medications are used concurrently with diphenidol)

Apomorphine
  (prior ingestion of diphenidol may decrease the emetic response to apomorphine in the treatment of poisoning)

» CNS depression-producing medications
  (concurrent use may potentiate the effects of either these medications or diphenidol)

Contraindications/Medical problems
The contraindications/medical problems included have been selected on the basis of their potential clinical significance (reasons given in parentheses where appropriate)—not necessarily inclusive (» = major clinical significance).

Except under special circumstances, this medication should not be used when the following medical problem exists:
» Anuria
  (renal shut-down may increase risk of systemic accumulation of diphenidol)

Risk-benefit should be considered when the following medical problems exist:

Gastrointestinal tract obstructive disease, such as stenosing peptic ulcer and pyloric or duodenal obstruction
  (decrease in motility and tone may occur, resulting in obstruction and gastric retention)

Genitourinary tract obstructive disease, such as prostatic hypertrophy
  (use may precipitate urinary retention)

Glaucoma
  (use may increase intraocular pressure)

» Hypotension
  (may be exacerbated)

» Renal function impairment
  (decreased excretion may increase the risk of side effects)

Sensitivity to diphenidol

Caution is recommended when diphenidol is used, since signs of intestinal obstruction, brain tumor, or overdosage of toxic drugs may be obscured by its antiemetic action.

Side/Adverse Effects

Note: Hallucinations, disorientation, and confusion have been reported with usual doses of diphenidol within the first 3 days of therapy. Upon cessation of therapy, symptoms disappeared within 3 days.

The following side/adverse effects have been selected on the basis of their potential clinical significance (possible signs and symptoms in parentheses where appropriate)—not necessarily inclusive:

Those indicating need for medical attention
Incidence rare—less than 0.5%
  Confusion; hallucinations

Symptoms of overdose
  Drowsiness, severe; hypotension (severe unusual tiredness or weakness); *respiratory depression* (shortness of breath or troubled breathing)

Those indicating need for medical attention only if they continue or are bothersome   ·
Incidence more frequent
  Drowsiness
Incidence less frequent or rare
  Blurred vision; dizziness; dryness of mouth; headache; heartburn; nervousness, restlessness, or trouble in sleeping; skin rash; stomach upset or pain; unusual tiredness or weakness

Patient Consultation

In providing consultation, consider emphasizing the following selected information (» = major clinical significance):

Before using this medication

» Conditions affecting use, especially:
   Sensitivity to diphenidol
   Use in children—Not recommended for prophylaxis or treatment of nausea and vomiting in children weighing less than 22.8 kg
   Other medications, especially CNS depressants
   Other medical problems, especially anuria, hypotension, renal function impairment

Proper use of this medication

   Taking with food, water, or milk to minimize gastric irritation
» Importance of not taking more medication than the amount prescribed
   Missed dose: If on a regular dosing schedule—using as soon as possible; if almost time for next dose, not using at all; not doubling doses
» Proper storage

Precautions while using this medication

» Avoiding use of alcohol or other CNS depressants
» Caution if drowsiness or blurred vision occurs

Side/adverse effects

   Signs of potential side effects, especially confusion and hallucinations

General Dosing Information

Because of its potential to cause hallucinations, disorientation, or confusion, use of diphenidol should be limited to patients who are hospitalized or under comparable continuous close professional supervision.

Diet/Nutrition

In the preventive treatment of vertigo and associated nausea and vomiting, diphenidol may be taken with food, water, or milk to minimize gastric irritation. However, if nausea and vomiting are present, the further intake of liquids or food may aggravate the condition.

Oral Dosage Forms

DIPHENIDOL HYDROCHLORIDE TABLETS

Usual adult and adolescent dose:
   Antiemetic and
   Antivertigo—Oral, 25 to 50 mg every four hours as needed.

Usual adult prescribing limits: 300 mg a day.

Auxiliary labeling:
 • May cause drowsiness.
 • Avoid alcoholic beverages.

DIPHENOXYLATE AND ATROPINE   Systemic†

Some commonly used *brand names* are:
   In the U.S.—

Diphenatol	*Lomotil*
Lofene	*Lonox*
Logen	*Lo-Trol*
Lomanate	*Nor-Mil*

ORAL

Diphenoxylate Hydrochloride and Atropine Sulfate Oral Solution USP†
   In the U.S.—*Logen; Lomanate; Lomotil;* GENERIC
Diphenoxylate Hydrochloride and Atropine Sulfate Tablets USP†
   In the U.S.—*Diphenatol; Lofene; Logen; Lomotil; Lonox; Lo-Trol; Nor-Mil;* GENERIC

---

†The combination of diphenoxylate and atropine is not commercially available in Canada; however, diphenoxylate is available as a single entity.

Category: Antidiarrheal (antiperistaltic).

Indications

Accepted

Diarrhea (treatment)—Diphenoxylate and atropine combination is indicated in the symptomatic treatment of acute and chronic diarrhea.

Pharmacology

Mechanism of action/Effect:

   Diphenoxylate—Probably acts both locally and centrally to reduce intestinal motility.

   Atropine—Has anticholinergic activity. However, in this preparation atropine is included in doses below the therapeutic level in an attempt to prevent abuse by deliberate overdosage.

Onset of effect: 45 to 60 minutes.

Duration of effect: 3 to 4 hours.

Precautions to Consider

Geriatrics

No geriatrics-specific information is available on the use of diphenoxylate and atropine. However, geriatric patients may be more susceptible to the respiratory depressant effects of diphenoxylate.
In geriatric patients with diarrhea, caution is recommended because of the risk of fluid and electrolyte loss.

Drug interactions and/or related problems

The following drug interactions and/or related problems have been selected on the basis of their potential clinical significance (possible mechanism in parentheses where appropriate)—not necessarily inclusive (» = major clinical significance):

Note: Combinations containing any of the following medications, depending on the amount present, may also interact with this medication.

   Addictive medications, other, especially central nervous system (CNS) depressants with habituating potential
   (concurrent use with diphenoxylate may increase the risk of habituation; caution is recommended)
» Alcohol or
» CNS depression-producing medications, other
   (concurrent use with diphenoxylate may increase the CNS depressant effects of either diphenoxylate or these medications;

also, when tricyclic antidepressants are used concurrently with atropine, their anticholinergic effects may be intensified; dosage adjustment may be required)

» Anticholinergics or other medications with anticholinergic action
(these medications may enhance the effects of atropine during concurrent use; significant interaction is unlikely with usual doses of diphenoxylate and atropine, but may occur with its abuse)

» Monoamine oxidase (MAO) inhibitors, including furazolidone and procarbazine
(concurrent use with diphenoxylate may precipitate hypertensive crisis; MAO inhibitors may block detoxification of atropine, thus potentiating its action)

» Naltrexone
(administration of naltrexone to a patient physically dependent on opioid drugs, such as diphenoxylate, will precipitate withdrawal symptoms; symptoms may appear within 5 minutes of naltrexone administration, persist for up to 48 hours, and be difficult to reverse)

(naltrexone blocks the therapeutic effects of opioids [e.g., antidiarrheal]; also, patients receiving naltrexone should be advised to use alternative antidiarrheals when necessary)

Opioid (narcotic) analgesics
(concurrent use with diphenoxylate may result in increased risk of severe constipation and additive CNS depressant effects)

Contraindications/Medical problems
The contraindications/medical problems included have been selected on the basis of their potential clinical significance (reasons given in parentheses where appropriate)—not necessarily inclusive (» = major clinical significance).

Except under special circumstances, this medication should not be used when the following medical problems exist:

» Colitis, severe
(patient may develop toxic megacolon)

» Diarrhea associated with pseudomembranous colitis resulting from treatment with broad-spectrum antibiotics
(inhibition of peristalsis may delay the removal of toxins from the colon, thereby prolonging and/or worsening the diarrhea)

Risk-benefit should be considered when the following medical problems exist:

Alcoholism, active or in remission, or
Drug abuse or dependence, history of
(diphenoxylate content may increase chances of drug abuse in patient already predisposed to dependence)

Cardiovascular instability
(possible increase in heart rate may be undesirable)

» Dehydration, especially in children
(may predispose to delayed diphenoxylate intoxication; inhibition of peristalsis may result in fluid retention in colon and may further aggravate dehydration; discontinuation of medication and rehydration therapy is essential if signs of dehydration, such as dry mouth, excessive thirst, wrinkled skin, decreased urination, and dizziness or lightheadedness, are present; fluid loss may have serious consequences, such as circulatory collapse and renal failure, especially in young children)

Diarrhea caused by infectious organisms
(bacterial diarrhea may worsen due to the increased contact time between the mucosa and the penetrating microorganism; however, evidence of this occurring in actual practice is lacking)

» Diarrhea caused by poisoning, until toxic material has been eliminated from gastrointestinal tract

Down's syndrome, in children
(atropine may cause abnormal increase in pupillary dilation and acceleration of heart rate)

» Dysentery, acute, characterized by bloody stools and elevated temperature
(sole treatment with antiperistaltic antidiarrheals may be inadequate; antibiotic therapy may be required)

Gallbladder disease or gallstones
(diphenoxylate may cause biliary tract spasm)

Glaucoma, angle-closure
(although unlikely with usual doses of this combination, atropine may precipitate an acute attack of angle-closure glaucoma)

» Hepatic function impairment or jaundice
(diphenoxylate may precipitate hepatic coma; it is recommended that dosage be reduced in patients with impaired hepatic function)

Hiatal hernia associated with reflux esophagitis
(although unlikely with usual doses of this combination, atropine may aggravate condition)

Hypertension
(although unlikely with usual doses of this combination, atropine may aggravate condition)

Hyperthyroidism
(characterized by tachycardia, which may be increased by atropine)

Hypothyroidism
(diphenoxylate may increase risk of respiratory depression)

Intestinal atony of the elderly or debilitated
(although unlikely with usual doses of this combination, use of atropine may result in obstruction)

Myasthenia gravis
(although unlikely with usual doses of this combination, atropine may aggravate condition because of inhibition of acetylcholine action)

Prostatic hypertrophy or
Urethral stricture, acute, or
Urinary retention
(reduction in tone of urinary bladder may aggravate or lead to complete urinary retention)

Renal function impairment
(decreased excretion may increase the risk of side effects)

Respiratory disease or impairment
(increased risk of respiratory depression)

Sensitivity to atropine or diphenoxylate

Side/Adverse Effects
The following side/adverse effects have been selected on the basis of their potential clinical significance (possible signs and symptoms in parentheses where appropriate)—not necessarily inclusive:

Those indicating need for medical attention
Incidence less frequent or rare
Paralytic ileus or toxic megacolon (bloating, constipation, loss of appetite, severe stomach pain with nausea and vomiting)

Symptoms of overdose
Anticholinergic effects, severe (continuing blurred vision or changes in near vision; severe drowsiness; severe dryness of mouth, nose, and throat; fast heartbeat; unusual warmth, dryness, and flushing of skin); *respiratory depression* (severe shortness of breath or troubled breathing); *unusual excitement, nervousness, restlessness, or irritability, especially in children*

Note: *Respiratory depression* may occur as late as 12 to 30 hours after ingestion.

Those indicating need for medical attention only if they continue, worsen, or are bothersome
Incidence less frequent or rare
Anticholinergic effects, mild (blurred vision, difficult urination, dryness of skin and mouth, fever); *CNS depression* (dizziness or

lightheadedness, drowsiness, mental depression); *headache; numbness of hands or feet; skin rash or itching; swelling of the gums*

Note: Since atropine is present in a subtherapeutic dose, the appearance of these symptoms probably indicates overdosage, although the symptoms may occur at therapeutic doses in children.

Those indicating possible withdrawal and the need for medical attention if they occur after discontinuation of prolonged high-dose therapy
Incidence rare
   Increased sweating; muscle cramps; nausea or vomiting; shivering or trembling; stomach cramps

Patient Consultation

In providing consultation, consider emphasizing the following selected information (» = major clinical significance):

Before using this medication
» Conditions affecting use, especially:
      Sensitivity to atropine or diphenoxylate
      Pregnancy—Studies in rats show decreased fertility and decreased maternal weight gain
      Breast-feeding—Diphenoxylate and atropine excreted in breast milk; potential for serious adverse effects in nursing infant
      Use in children—Increased susceptibility to toxic effects of atropine and respiratory depressant effects of diphenoxylate; risk of dehydration
      Use in the elderly—Increased risk of respiratory depression; risk of dehydration
      Other medications, especially other anticholinergics, CNS depressants, MAO inhibitors, or naltrexone
      Other medical problems, especially acute dysentery; dehydration; diarrhea caused by antibiotics or poisoning; hepatic function impairment or jaundice; or severe colitis

Proper use of this medication
   Taking with food or meals if gastric irritation occurs
» Importance of not taking more medication than the amount prescribed because of habit-forming potential and risk of overdose in children
» Importance of maintaining adequate hydration and proper diet
   Missed dose: If on a scheduled dosing regimen—Taking as soon as possible; not taking if almost time for next dose; not doubling doses
» Proper storage
For liquid dosage form
   Proper administration technique: Measuring amount with dropper and taking by mouth

Precautions while using this medication
   Regular visits to physician to check progress during prolonged therapy
» Consulting physician if diarrhea is not controlled within 48 hours and/or fever develops
» Avoiding use of alcohol or other CNS depressants during therapy
» Suspected overdose: Getting emergency help at once
   Need to inform physician or dentist of use of medication if any kind of surgery (including dental surgery) or emergency treatment is required
» Caution if dizziness or drowsiness occurs

Side/adverse effects
   Signs of potential side effects, especially paralytic ileus or toxic megacolon

General Dosing Information

Treatment with diphenoxylate and atropine should be continued for 24 to 36 hours before it is considered ineffective in acute diarrhea.

Inhibition of peristalsis may produce fluid retention in the bowel, which may aggravate dehydration and depletion of electrolytes, especially in young children, and may also increase variability of response to the medication. If dehydration or electrolyte imbalance occurs, diphenoxylate and atropine therapy should be withheld until appropriate corrective therapy has begun.

To prevent development of toxic megacolon in patients with acute ulcerative colitis, treatment with diphenoxylate and atropine should be discontinued promptly if abdominal distention or other specific gastrointestinal symptoms such as anorexia, bloating, constipation, nausea, vomiting, or abdominal pain occur.

Prolonged use of larger than usual therapeutic doses may theoretically result in physical dependence.

Tolerance to the antidiarrheal effects of diphenoxylate and atropine may develop with prolonged use.

This medication may suppress respiration, especially in children or the elderly, the very ill, and patients with respiratory problems. Lower doses may be required for these patients.

Oral Dosage Forms

DIPHENOXYLATE HYDROCHLORIDE AND ATROPINE SULFATE ORAL SOLUTION USP

Note: Diphenoxylate hydrochloride and atropine sulfate oral solution is not commercially available in Canada.

Usual adult and adolescent dose: Antidiarrheal (antiperistaltic)—
   Initial: Oral, the equivalent of diphenoxylate hydrochloride—2.5 to 5 mg three or four times a day.
   Maintenance: Oral, the equivalent of diphenoxylate hydrochloride—2.5 mg two or three times a day as needed.

Usual geriatric dose: See *Usual adult and adolescent dose.*

Note: Geriatric patients may be more sensitive to the effects of the usual adult dose.

Auxiliary labeling:
 • May cause drowsiness.
 • Avoid alcoholic beverages.
 • Keep out of reach of children.

DIPHENOXYLATE HYDROCHLORIDE AND ATROPINE SULFATE TABLETS USP

Note: Diphenoxylate hydrochloride and atropine sulfate tablets are not commercially available in Canada.

Usual adult and adolescent dose: Antidiarrheal (antiperistaltic)—
   Initial: Oral, the equivalent of diphenoxylate hydrochloride—2.5 to 5 mg three or four times a day.
   Maintenance: Oral, the equivalent of diphenoxylate hydrochloride—2.5 mg two or three times a day as needed.

Usual geriatric dose: See *Usual adult and adolescent dose.*

Note: Geriatric patients may be more sensitive to the effects of the usual adult dose.

Auxiliary labeling:
 • May cause drowsiness.
 • Avoid alcoholic beverages.
 • Keep out of reach of children.
 • May be habit-forming.

DIPIVEFRIN   Ophthalmic

INN: Dipivefrine

Some commonly used *brand names* are:
> In the U.S.—*Propine C Cap B.I.D.*
> In Canada—*Propine C Cap B.I.D; Propine C Cap Q.I.D.*

OPHTHALMIC
Dipivefrin Hydrochloride Ophthalmic Solution USP
> In the U.S.—*Propine C Cap B.I.D.*
> In Canada—*Propine C Cap B.I.D; Propine C Cap Q.I.D.*

Category: Antiglaucoma agent (ophthalmic).

Note: Dipivefrin belongs to a group of drugs known as prodrugs. Prodrugs are usually not active in themselves, but require biotransformation to the parent compound before being therapeutically active. Dipivefrin is a prodrug of epinephrine.

Indications

Note: Bracketed information in the *Indications* section refers to uses not included in U.S. product labeling.

Accepted
Glaucoma, open-angle (treatment)—Indicated as initial therapy for the control of intraocular pressure in chronic open-angle glaucoma. Also, for open-angle glaucoma that is difficult to control, the addition of dipivefrin to other antiglaucoma agents, such as pilocarpine, carbachol, echothiophate, timolol, or acetazolamide, has been shown to be effective.

[Glaucoma, secondary (treatment)][1]—Dipivefrin is used in the treatment of secondary glaucoma.

---

[1]Not included in Canadian product labeling.

Pharmacology

Mechanism of action/Effect: Dipivefrin is converted to epinephrine inside the eye by enzyme hydrolysis. The liberated epinephrine, an adrenergic agonist, appears to exert its action by decreasing aqueous production and enhancing aqueous outflow facility.

Onset of action: About 30 minutes.

Time to peak effect: About 1 hour.

Precautions to Consider

Cross sensitivity and/or related problems
Patients sensitive to epinephrine may be sensitive to dipivefrin also, since ophthalmic dipivefrin is converted to epinephrine inside the eye by enzyme hydrolysis.

Geriatrics
Appropriate studies on the relationship of age to the effects of this medicine have not been performed in the geriatric population. However, no geriatrics-specific problems have been documented to date.

Drug interactions and/or related problems
The following drug interactions and/or related problems have been selected on the basis of their potential clinical significance (possible mechanism in parentheses where appropriate)—not necessarily inclusive (» = major clinical significance):

Note: Combinations containing any of the following medications, depending on the amount present, may also interact with this medication.

Dipivefrin is converted to epinephrine inside the eye by enzyme hydrolysis.
Anesthetics, hydrocarbon inhalation, such as:
> Chloroform
> Cyclopropane
> Enflurane
> Halothane
> Isoflurane
> Methoxyflurane
> Trichloroethylene
> (if significant systemic absorption of ophthalmic epinephrine occurs, concurrent use of cyclopropane, halothane, or possibly chloroform may increase the risk of severe ventricular arrhythmias because these anesthetics greatly sensitize the myocardium to the effects of sympathomimetics; therapy with dipivefrin should be interrupted prior to general anesthesia in patients receiving these anesthetics)

> (enflurane, isoflurane, methoxyflurane, or especially trichloroethylene may also cause some sensitization of the myocardium to the effects of sympathomimetics; caution is recommended during concurrent use with dipivefrin)

Antidepressants, tricyclic, or
Maprotiline or
Nomifensine or
> (if significant systemic absorption of ophthalmic epinephrine occurs, concurrent use of these medications may potentiate the cardiovascular effects of the epinephrine, possibly resulting in arrhythmias, hypertension, or tachycardia)

Beta-adrenergic blocking agents, ophthalmic
> (concurrent use of ophthalmic betaxolol, levobunolol, or timolol with ophthalmic dipivefrin may provide a beneficial additive effect in lowering intraocular pressure)

Digitalis glycosides
> (if significant systemic absorption of ophthalmic epinephrine occurs, concurrent use of digitalis glycosides may increase the risk of cardiac arrhythmias; caution is recommended if concurrent use is necessary)

Sympathomimetics, systemic
> (if significant systemic absorption of ophthalmic epinephrine occurs, concurrent use of systemic sympathomimetics may result in additive toxic effects)

Contraindications/Medical problems
The contraindications/medical problems included have been selected on the basis of their potential clinical significance (reasons given in parentheses where appropriate)—not necessarily inclusive (» = major clinical significance).

Except under special circumstances, this medication should not be used when the following medical problem exists:
» Glaucoma, angle-closure, predisposition to
> (dilation of pupil may predispose patient to an attack of angle-closure glaucoma)

Risk-benefit should be considered when the following medical problems exist):
> Aphakic eyes
> (macular edema may occur)
> Sensitivity to dipivefrin

Side/Adverse Effects

Note: Therapy with epinephrine (or its prodrug dipivefrin) can lead to adrenochrome deposits in the conjunctiva and cornea.

The following side/adverse effects have been selected on the basis of their potential clinical significance (possible signs and symptoms in parentheses where appropriate)—not necessarily inclusive:

Those indicating need for medical attention
Incidence rare
   Systemic absorption (fast or irregular heartbeat or increase in blood pressure)

Those indicating need for medical attention only if they continue or are bothersome
Incidence less frequent
   Burning, stinging, or other eye irritation; increased sensitivity of eyes to light

Patient Consultation

In providing consultation, consider emphasizing the following selected information (» = major clinical significance):

Before using this medication
» Conditions affecting use, especially:
       Sensitivity to dipivefrin or epinephrine
       Use by athletes—Stimulants, such as sympathomimetic amines, are banned and tested for in athletes; because ophthalmic dipivefrin may be absorbed into the body, the medication may appear in the urine; if the agent is found in the urine, the athlete will be disqualified
       Other medical problems, especially predisposition to angle-closure glaucoma

Proper use of this medication
» Importance of not using more medication than the amount prescribed
       Proper administration technique
       Washing hands immediately after applying eye drops
       Preventing contamination: Not touching applicator tip to any surface; keeping container tightly closed

Missed dose: Applying as soon as possible; if almost time for next dose, skipping missed dose and going back to regular dosing schedule; not doubling doses
» Proper storage

Precautions while using this medication
   Regular visits to physician to check eye pressure during therapy

Side/adverse effects
   Signs of potential side effects, especially fast or irregular heartbeat or increase in blood pressure

General Dosing Information

Although some manufacturers recommend a dose of 2 drops of an ophthalmic solution at appropriate intervals, the conjunctival sac will usually hold only 1 drop.

When used to replace epinephrine, the epinephrine should be discontinued when dipivefrin therapy is started.

When used to replace an antiglaucoma agent other than epinephrine, the other antiglaucoma agent should be continued on the first day that dipivefrin is used but discontinued on the second day.

When used in addition to other antiglaucoma agents, dipivefrin should be administered at the usual adult dose.

Ophthalmic Dosage Forms

DIPIVEFRIN HYDROCHLORIDE OPHTHALMIC SOLUTION USP

Usual adult and adolescent dose: Topical, to the conjunctiva, 1 drop of a 0.1% solution every twelve hours.

Usual geriatric dose: See *Usual adult and adolescent dose.*

Auxiliary labeling:
• For the eye.
• Keep container tightly closed.

DISOPYRAMIDE   Systemic

Some commonly used *brand names* are:

   In the U.S.—
       Norpace
       Norpace CR

   In Canada—
       Norpace   *Rythmodan*
       Norpace CR   *Rythmodan-LA*

ORAL
Disopyramide Capsules*
   In Canada—*Rythmodan*
Disopyramide Phosphate Capsules USP
   In the U.S.—*Norpace;* GENERIC
   In Canada—*Norpace*
Disopyramide Phosphate Extended-release Capsules USP†
   In the U.S.—*Norpace CR;* GENERIC
Disopyramide Phosphate Extended-release Tablets*
   In Canada—*Norpace CR; Rythmodan-LA*

---
*Not commercially available in the U.S.
†Not commercially available in Canada.

Category: Antiarrhythmic.

Indications

Note: Bracketed information in the *Indications* section refers to uses not included in U.S. product labeling.

Accepted
Arrhythmias, ventricular (prophylaxis and treatment)—Oral disopyramide is indicated for the suppression and the prevention of recurrence of the following cardiac arrhythmias whether they occur singly or in combination:
   Episodic ventricular tachycardia (information is inadequate for use in treatment of persistent ventricular tachycardia, which is usually treated with D.C. cardioversion)
   Multifocal premature (ectopic) ventricular contractions
   Paired premature ventricular contractions (couplets)
   Unifocal premature (ectopic) ventricular contractions
[Tachycardia, supraventricular (prophylaxis and treatment)][1]—Disopyramide is also being used for prophylaxis and treatment of some supraventricular tachycardias.

---
[1]Not included in Canadian product labeling.

Pharmacology

Mechanism of action/Effect: Disopyramide depresses myocardial responsiveness and the electrophysiological conduction rate with the exception of the atrioventricular (AV) nodal and the His-Purkinje rates, which are essentially unchanged. Diastolic depolarization is slowed in those tissues having augmented automaticity, and the effective refractory period of the atrium and the ventricles is increased. However, conduction in accessory pathways is prolonged. In the Vaughan Williams classification of antiarrhythmics, disopyramide is considered to be a class I agent.

Other actions/effects: Disopyramide has a negative inotropic effect. It possesses anticholinergic activity but no noticeable alpha- or beta-adrenergic effects.

Onset of therapeutic effect: A 300-mg oral loading dose with regular capsules will usually produce a therapeutic effect in 30 minutes to 3.5 hours.

Duration of action: After 300-mg oral dose with regular capsules—1.5 to 8.5 hours.

Precautions to Consider

Geriatrics

Although appropriate studies have not been performed in the geriatric population, the elderly may exhibit increased sensitivity to anticholinergic effects such as urinary retention and dry mouth. In addition, elderly patients are more likely to have age-related renal function impairment, which may require caution and reduction of dosage in patients receiving disopyramide.

Dental

The secondary anticholinergic effects of disopyramide may decrease or inhibit salivary flow, especially in middle-aged or elderly patients, thus contributing to the development of caries, periodontal disease, oral candidiasis, and discomfort.

Drug interactions and/or related problems

The following drug interactions and/or related problems have been selected on the basis of their potential clinical significance (possible mechanism in parentheses where appropriate)—not necessarily inclusive (» = major clinical significance):

Note: Combinations containing any of the following medications, depending on the amount present, may also interact with this medication.

Alcohol
(concurrent use of moderate to excessive quantities with disopyramide may enhance the development of hypoglycemia and/or hypotension because of additive effects)

» Antiarrhythmics, other, especially:
Diltiazem or
Encainide or
Flecainide or
Lidocaine or
Procainamide or
Propranolol and other beta-adrenergic blocking agents or
Quinidine or
Tocainide or
Verapamil
(caution is advised when used concurrently with disopyramide, as such usage may result in excessively prolonged electrocardial conduction with decreased cardiac output)

(close monitoring is essential, as clinical heart failure may worsen during use of disopyramide with beta-adrenergic blocking agents in patients with decreased ventricular performance)

(disopyramide should not be administered within 48 hours before or 24 hours following verapamil; deaths have been reported)

Anticholinergics or other medications with anticholinergic activity
(anticholinergic effects may be intensified when these medications are used concurrently with disopyramide because of secondary anticholinergic activity of disopyramide)

Anticoagulants, coumarin- or indandione-derivative
(concurrent use of warfarin and disopyramide has been reported to increase or decrease the anticoagulant effect; although clinical significance has not been determined, caution is recommended)

Antidiabetic agents, oral, or
Insulin
(hypoglycemic effects may be intensified in rare cases by the concurrent use of disopyramide because of additive hypoglycemic effects; patients prone to hypoglycemia should be closely monitored)

Hepatic enzyme inducers
(concurrent use may reduce serum disopyramide to ineffective concentrations; therefore monitoring of its serum concentrations is necessary during concurrent therapy)

Hypotension-producing medications, other
(concurrent use with disopyramide may increase the hypotensive effects)

» Pimozide
(concurrent use with disopyramide may potentiate cardiac arrhythmias, which are seen on electrocardiogram [ECG] as prolongation of QT interval)

Contraindications/Medical problems

The contraindications/medical problems included have been selected on the basis of their potential clinical significance (reasons given in parentheses where appropriate)—not necessarily inclusive (» = major clinical significance).

Except under special circumstances, this medication should not be used when the following medical problems exist:

» Atrioventricular (AV) block, pre-existing second or third degree without pacemaker
» Cardiogenic shock

Risk-benefit should be considered when the following medical problems exist:

Bladder neck obstruction
(anticholinergic activity of disopyramide may cause urinary retention)
» Cardiac conduction abnormalities, such as sick sinus syndrome, Wolff-Parkinson-White syndrome, or bundle branch block
(disopyramide may produce additive cardiac depression)
» Cardiomyopathies
(risk of congestive heart failure and hypotension with disopyramide; patient should not receive loading dose and dose reduction may be indicated)
» Congestive heart failure, uncompensated or poorly compensated
(possible aggravation and risk of hypotension)
» Diabetes mellitus
(possible hypoglycemia caused by disopyramide)
» Glaucoma, closed-angle, history of
(anticholinergic activity of disopyramide may result in precipitation of acute condition)
» Hepatic function impairment
(possible accumulation of disopyramide; dosage reduction may be required)
» Hyperkalemia
(serious arrhythmias may result)
» Hypokalemia
(reduced efficacy of therapy)
» Myasthenia gravis
(anticholinergic effect of disopyramide may result in myasthenic crisis)

» Prostatic enlargement
    (possible urinary retention; may be exacerbated by anticholinergic effect)
» Renal function impairment
    (accumulation of disopyramide because of reduced excretion; dosage reduction may be required; disopyramide extended-release capsules are not recommended for patients with severe renal insufficiency [creatinine clearance of 40 mL per minute (0.67 mL per Hertz) or less])
    Sensitivity to disopyramide

Side/Adverse Effects

Note: Overdose may lead to apnea, loss of consciousness, cardiac arrhythmias, loss of spontaneous respiration, and death. Toxic plasma concentrations are associated with excessive widening of the QRS complex and QT interval, worsening of congestive heart failure, hypotension, conduction disturbances, bradycardia, and ultimately asystole; obvious anticholinergic effects also occur.

The following side/adverse effects have been selected on the basis of their potential clinical significance (possible signs and symptoms in parentheses where appropriate)—not necessarily inclusive:

Those indicating need for medical attention
Incidence more frequent—10 to 20%
    Anticholinergic effect (difficult urination)
Incidence less frequent—1 to 10%
    Chest pains; confusion; congestive heart failure, possible, or fluid retention (fast or slow heartbeat, unexplained shortness of breath, swelling of feet or lower legs, rapid weight gain); *hypotension* (dizziness, lightheadedness, or fainting); *muscle weakness*
Incidence rare—<1%
    Aggravation of glaucoma, possible (eye pain); *agranulocytosis* (sore throat and fever); *cholestatic jaundice* (yellow eyes or skin); *mental depression; signs and symptoms of hypoglycemia, such as anxious feeling, chills, cold sweats, confusion, cool, pale skin, drowsiness, fast heartbeat, headache, hunger, excessive, nausea, nervousness, shakiness, unsteady walk, or unusual tiredness or weakness*

Those indicating need for medical attention only if they continue or are bothersome
Incidence more frequent—40%
    Anticholinergic effect (dry mouth and throat)
Incidence less frequent—1–10%
    Anticholinergic effect (blurred vision, constipation, dry eyes and nose); *bloating or stomach pain; decreased sexual ability; frequent urge to urinate; loss of appetite*

Patient Consultation

In providing consultation, consider emphasizing the following selected information (» = major clinical significance):

Before using this medication
» Conditions affecting use, especially:
    Sensitivity to disopyramide
    Pregnancy—May initiate uterine contractions
    Breast-feeding—Passes into breast milk
    Use in the elderly—Increased sensitivity to anticholinergic effects
    Other medications, especially other antiarrhythmics or pimozide
    Other medical problems, especially second or third degree atrioventricular (AV) block, cardiogenic shock, cardiac conduction abnormalities, cardiomyopathies, uncompensated or poorly compensated congestive heart failure, diabetes mellitus, history of closed-angle glaucoma, hepatic function impairment, hyperkalemia or hypokalemia, myasthenia gravis, prostatic enlargement, or renal function impairment

Proper use of this medication
» Compliance with therapy; not taking more medication than directed
    Proper administration of extended-release capsules: Swallowing capsule whole, without breaking, crushing, or chewing
    Proper administration of extended-release tablets: Not crushing or chewing
» Importance of not missing doses and taking at evenly spaced intervals
» Missed dose: Taking as soon as possible, unless within 4 hours of next dose; not doubling doses
» Proper storage

Precautions while using this medication
» Regular visits to physician to check progress
» Checking with physician before stopping medication because of adverse cardiac effects with sudden withdrawal
» Caution when driving or doing things requiring alertness because of possible dizziness, lightheadedness, or fainting, especially when getting up suddenly from lying or sitting position
» Avoiding alcoholic beverages
» Notifying physician and taking sugar if symptoms of hypoglycemia occur
» Possible blurred vision; avoiding driving, using machines, or doing other things requiring clear vision if blurred vision occurs
    Possible dryness of eyes, mouth, and nose; using sugarless candy or gum, ice, or saliva substitute for relief; checking with physician or dentist if dry mouth continues for more than 2 weeks
» Caution during exercise or hot weather because of possible reduced sweating and impaired heat tolerance

Side/adverse effects
    Signs of potential side effects, especially difficult urination, chest pains, confusion, congestive heart failure, fluid retention, hypotension, muscle weakness, aggravation of glaucoma, agranulocytosis, cholestatic jaundice, mental depression, and hypoglycemia

General Dosing Information

The dosage for all patients should be individualized within limits of response and tolerance, with required dosage adjustments being made gradually.

Patients of small body size (less than 50 kg body weight) may require reduced dosage.

When a loading dose is used, close monitoring is required for possible development of hypotension and/or congestive heart failure.

Patients receiving quinidine sulfate or procainamide may be changed to disopyramide therapy by starting the regular maintenance dose of disopyramide 6 to 12 hours after the last quinidine sulfate dose or 3 to 6 hours after the last dose of procainamide.

Patients with atrial flutter or fibrillation should be digitalized prior to disopyramide treatment to ensure that drug-induced enhancement of atrioventricular (AV) conduction does not increase the ventricular rate beyond acceptable limits.

Because disopyramide is removed by hemodialysis, additional dosage may be required following dialysis.

If first-degree AV block develops, dosage of disopyramide should be reduced. If block persists or worsens, the medication may have to be withdrawn.

Oral Dosage Forms

DISOPYRAMIDE CAPSULES

Note: Disopyramide (base) capsules are not commercially available in the U.S.

Usual adult dose: Antiarrhythmic—
    Loading dose (for rapid control of ventricular arrhythmia): Oral, 300 mg (200 mg for body weight less than 50 kg).

Maintenance: Oral, 150 mg every six hours (or 100 mg every six hours for body weight less than 50 kg or in patients with cardiomyopathy or possible cardiac decompensation), the dosage being adjusted as needed and tolerated.

Note: Geriatric patients may be more sensitive to the effects of the usual adult dose.

Creatinine clearance is used to determine adjustment of dosing interval in cases of renal insufficiency:

Creatinine Clearance (mL/min)	(mL/s)	Approximate Maintenance Dosing Interval
30–40	0.5–0.67	Every 8 hr
15–30	0.25–0.5	Every 12 hr
<15	<0.25	Every 24 hr

Usual adult prescribing limits: Up to 800 mg daily.

Note: Although total daily doses of up to 1.6 grams have been used in patients with severe refractory ventricular tachycardia, such high doses are restricted to the hospitalized patient.

Auxiliary labeling:
- Avoid alcoholic beverages.
- May cause blurred vision.
- Do not take other medicines without advice from your doctor.

DISOPYRAMIDE PHOSPHATE CAPSULES USP

Usual adult dose: Antiarrhythmic—

Loading dose (for rapid control of ventricular arrhythmia): Oral, 300 mg (base) (200 mg for body weight less than 50 kg).

Maintenance: Oral, 150 mg (base) every six hours (or 100 mg every six hours for body weight less than 50 kg or in patients with cardiomyopathy or possible cardiac decompensation), the dosage being adjusted as needed and tolerated.

Note: Geriatric patients may be more sensitive to the effects of the usual adult dose.

Creatinine clearance is used to determine adjustment of dosing interval in cases of renal insufficiency:

Creatinine Clearance (mL/min)	(mL/s)	Approximate Maintenance Dosing Interval
30–40	0.5–0.67	Every 8 hr
15–30	0.25–0.5	Every 12 hr
<15	<0.25	Every 24 hr

Usual adult prescribing limits: Up to 800 mg (base) daily.

Note: Although total daily doses of up to 1.6 grams (base) have been used in patients with severe refractory ventricular tachycardia, such high doses are restricted to the hospitalized patient.

Auxiliary labeling:
- Avoid alcoholic beverages.
- May cause blurred vision.
- Do not take other medicines without advice from your doctor.

For oral suspension—
- Avoid alcoholic beverages.
- May cause blurred vision.
- Shake well.
- Refrigerate.
- Do not take other medicines without advice from your doctor.

DISOPYRAMIDE PHOSPHATE EXTENDED-RELEASE CAPSULES USP

Note: Disopyramide phosphate extended-release capsules are not commercially available in Canada.

Usual adult dose: Antiarrhythmic—Oral, 300 mg (base) every twelve hours (200 mg every twelve hours for body weight less than 50 kg).

Note: Extended-release dosage form is not recommended for initial dosage, but for maintenance dosage only.

When transferring from the regular oral dosage form, it is recommended that the first dose of the extended-release dosage form be given six hours after the last regular dose.

Usual adult prescribing limits: Up to 800 mg (base) daily.

Note: Although total daily doses of up to 1.6 grams (base) have been used in patients with severe refractory ventricular tachycardia, such high doses are restricted to the hospitalized patient.

Auxiliary labeling:
- Avoid alcoholic beverages.
- May cause blurred vision.
- Do not take other medicines without advice from your doctor.
- Swallow capsule whole.

DISOPYRAMIDE PHOSPHATE EXTENDED-RELEASE TABLETS

Note: Disopyramide phosphate extended-release tablets are not commercially available in the U.S.

Usual adult dose: Antiarrhythmic—Oral, 300 mg (base) every twelve hours (200 mg every twelve hours for body weight less than 50 kg).

Note: Extended-release dosage form is not recommended for initial dosage, but for maintenance dosage only.

When transferring from the regular oral dosage form, it is recommended that the first dose of the extended-release dosage form be given six hours after the last regular dose.

Auxiliary labeling:
- Avoid alcoholic beverages.
- May cause blurred vision.
- Swallow tablet whole.
- Do not take other medicines without advice from your doctor.

DIURETICS, LOOP   Systemic

INN: Included in brackets after individual generic listings, if different from U.S. generic names.

Some commonly used *brand names* are:

In the U.S.—
Bumex [Bumetanide]	*Lasix* [Furosemide]
Edecrin [Ethacrynic Acid]	*Myrosemide* [Furosemide]

In Canada—
Apo-Furosemide [Furosemide]	*Lasix* [Furosemide]
	Lasix Special [Furosemide]
Edecrin [Ethacrynic Acid]	*Novosemide* [Furosemide]
Furoside [Furosemide]	*Uritol* [Furosemide]

BUMETANIDE†
Oral
    Bumetanide Tablets USP†
        In the U.S.—*Bumex*
Parenteral
    Bumetanide Injection USP†
        In the U.S.—*Bumex*
ETHACRYNIC ACID [INN: Etacrynic acid]
Oral
    Ethacrynic Acid Oral Solution*†
    Ethacrynic Acid Tablets USP
        In the U.S. and Canada—*Edecrin*
Parenteral
    Ethacrynate Sodium for Injection USP
        In the U.S. and Canada—*Edecrin*
FUROSEMIDE
Oral
    Furosemide Oral Solution
        In the U.S.—*Lasix; Myrosemide;* GENERIC
        In Canada—*Lasix*
    Furosemide Tablets USP
        In the U.S.—*Lasix;* GENERIC
        In Canada—*Apo-Furosemide; Furoside; Lasix; Lasix Special; Novosemide; Uritol;* GENERIC
Parenteral
    Furosemide Injection USP
        In the U.S.—*Lasix;* GENERIC
        In Canada—*Lasix; Lasix Special;* GENERIC

---

*Not commercially available in the U.S.
†Not commercially available in Canada.

Category

Diagnostic aid adjunct (renal disease)—Furosemide.
Diuretic—Bumetanide; Ethacrynic Acid; Furosemide.
Antihypertensive—Bumetanide; Ethacrynic Acid; Furosemide.
Antihypercalcemic—Bumetanide; Ethacrynic Acid; Furosemide.

Indications

Note: Bracketed information in the *Indications* section refers to uses not included in U.S. product labeling.

Edema (treatment)—Bumetanide, ethacrynic acid, and furosemide are indicated in the treatment of edema associated with congestive heart failure, hepatic cirrhosis, and renal disease (including nephrotic syndrome).

Bumetanide, ethacrynic acid, and furosemide are indicated as adjuncts in the treatment of acute pulmonary edema.

Ethacrynic acid is indicated in the short-term management of ascites due to malignancy, idiopathic edema, and lymphedema; and in the short-term management of hospitalized pediatric patients with congenital heart disease or nephrotic syndrome.

Bumetanide, ethacrynic acid, and furosemide are especially useful in patients refractory to other diuretics or with existing acid-base disorders, congestive heart failure, or renal disease.

Hypertension (treatment)—[Bumetanide], [ethacrynic acid][1], and furosemide are indicated in the treatment of mild to moderate hypertension, usually in combination with other antihypertensive agents, and as adjuncts in the treatment of hypertensive crisis.

Bumetanide, ethacrynic acid, and furosemide are not considered to be primary agents in the treatment of essential hypertension. They may, however, be indicated in combination with other antihypertensives in the treatment of hypertension associated with impaired renal function. In the stepped-care approach to antihypertensive treatment, bumetanide, ethacrynic acid, or furosemide may be substituted for a thiazide diuretic in patients with renal function impairment.

Nonpharmacologic management (especially sodium restriction, weight reduction and exercise, and moderation of alcohol consumption) is recommended first for some patients, including those with mild hypertension, and is recommended as an adjunct to all pharmacologic hypertensive therapy.

Hypercalcemia (treatment)—[Bumetanide], [ethacrynic acid][1], and [furosemide][1] are used in the treatment of hypercalcemia.

[Renography, adjunct][1]; and

[Renal imaging, radionuclide, adjunct][1]—Furosemide augments radionuclide renography and renal scintigraphy by stimulating the flow of urine and thereby aiding in the differentiation of mechanical obstruction versus nonobstructive dilatation in patients with hydroureteronephrosis.

---

[1]Not included in Canadian product labeling.

Pharmacology

Mechanism of action/Effect:

Diuretic—Bumetanide, ethacrynic acid, and furosemide inhibit reabsorption of sodium and water in the ascending limb of the loop of Henle by interfering with the chloride binding site of the $1Na+, 1K+, 2Cl-$ cotransport system. Loop diuretics increase the rate of delivery of tubular fluid and electrolytes to the distal sites of hydrogen and potassium ion secretion, while plasma volume contraction increases aldosterone production. This increased delivery and high aldosterone levels promote sodium reabsorption at the distal tubules, thus increasing the loss of potassium and hydrogen ions. Bumetanide may have a small additional action on sodium reabsorption in the proximal tubule since phosphate reabsorption is reduced.

Antihypertensive—Diuretics lower blood pressure initially by reducing plasma and extracellular fluid volume; cardiac output also decreases. Eventually, cardiac output returns to normal with an accompanying decrease in peripheral resistance.

Antihypercalcemic—Loop diuretics increase the urinary excretion of calcium.

Onset of action: Diuretic—

Bumetanide:
    Oral—30 to 60 minutes.
    Intravenous—Within minutes.

Ethacrynic acid:
Oral—30 minutes.
Intravenous—5 minutes.
Furosemide:
Oral—20 to 60 minutes.
Intravenous—5 minutes.

Time to peak effect: Diuretic—
Bumetanide:
Oral—1 to 2 hours.
Intravenous—15 to 30 minutes.
Ethacrynic acid:
Oral—2 hours.
Intravenous—15 to 30 minutes.
Furosemide:
Oral—1 to 2 hours.
Intravenous—Within 30 minutes.

Note: The maximum antihypertensive effect may not occur until several days after initiation of loop diuretic therapy.

Duration of action: Diuretic—
Bumetanide:
Oral—4 hours with usual doses (1 to 2 mg); 4 to 6 hours with higher doses.
Intravenous—3.5 to 4 hours.
Ethacrynic acid:
Oral—6 to 8 hours.
Intravenous—2 hours.
Furosemide:
Oral—6 to 8 hours.
Intravenous—2 hours.

Precautions to Consider

Cross-sensitivity and/or related problems
Patients sensitive to sulfonamides (including thiazide diuretics) may be sensitive to bumetanide or furosemide also.

Geriatrics
Although appropriate studies on the relationship of age to the effects of loop diuretics have not been performed in the geriatric population, the elderly may be more sensitive to the hypotensive and electrolyte effects. In addition, elderly patients are at greater risk of developing circulatory collapse and thromboembolic episodes. Elderly patients are also more likely to have age-related renal function impairment, which may require adjustment of dosage or dosing interval in patients receiving loop diuretics.

Drug interactions and/or related problems
The following drug interactions and/or related problems have been selected on the basis of their potential clinical significance (possible mechanism in parentheses where appropriate)—not necessarily inclusive (» = major clinical significance):

Note: Combinations containing any of the following medications, depending on the amount present, may also interact with this medication.

Alcohol or
Hypotension-producing medications, other
(hypotensive and/or diuretic effects may be potentiated when these medications are used concurrently with loop diuretics; although some antihypertensive and/or diuretic combinations are frequently used for therapeutic advantage, when used concurrently dosage adjustments may be necessary)

Amiodarone
(concurrent use of loop diuretics with amiodarone may lead to an increased risk of arrhythmias associated with hypokalemia)

» Amphotericin B, parenteral
(concurrent and/or sequential administration should be avoided since the potential for ototoxicity and nephrotoxicity may be increased, especially in the presence of renal function impairment; in addition, concurrent use with loop diuretics may intensify electrolyte imbalance, particularly hypokalemia; frequent electrolyte determinations are recommended and potassium supplementation may be required)

» Anticoagulants, coumarin- or indandione-derivative, or
Heparin or
Streptokinase or
Urokinase
(anticoagulant effects may be decreased when these medications are used concurrently with loop diuretics, as a result of reduction of plasma volume leading to concentration of procoagulant factors in the blood; in addition diuretic-induced improvement of hepatic congestion may lead to improved hepatic function, resulting in increased procoagulant factor synthesis; dosage adjustments may be necessary)

(anticoagulant effects may be potentiated when these medications are used concurrently with ethacrynic acid as a result of displacement of anticoagulant from protein-binding sites; dosage adjustments of the anticoagulant may be necessary during and after ethacrynic acid therapy or, alternatively, use of furosemide is recommended)

(gastrointestinal ulcerative or hemorrhagic potential of ethacrynic acid may increase the risk of hemorrhage in patients receiving anticoagulant or thrombolytic therapy; use of a different diuretic is recommended)

Antidiabetic agents, oral, or
Insulin
(furosemide, and possibly bumetanide or ethacrynic acid, may rarely raise blood glucose concentrations or interfere with the hypoglycemic effects of these agents; for adult-onset diabetics, dosage adjustment of hypoglycemic medications may be necessary during and after therapy)

Anti-inflammatory drugs, nonsteroidal (NSAIDs), especially indomethacin
(may antagonize the natriuresis and increase in plasma renin activity [PRA] caused by loop diuretics; indomethacin, and possibly other NSAIDs with the exception of diflunisal, may also reduce the increase in urine volume caused by loop diuretics, possibly by inhibiting renal prostaglandin synthesis and/or by causing sodium and fluid retention)

(in addition, concurrent use of NSAIDs with a diuretic may increase the risk of renal failure secondary to a decrease in renal blood flow caused by inhibition of renal prostaglandin synthesis)

(in the premature neonate, administration of 1 mg/kg of furosemide immediately following indomethacin has been shown to prevent or reduce indomethacin-induced adverse renal effects without interfering with ductus arteriosus closure)

Captopril or
Enalapril or
Lisinopril
(sudden and severe hypotension may occur within the first 1 to 5 hours after the initial dose of captopril, enalapril, or lisinopril, particularly in patients who are sodium- and volume-depleted as a result of diuretic therapy. Withdrawal of the diuretic or increase of salt intake approximately 1 week before start of captopril therapy or 2 to 3 days before start of enalapril or lisinopril therapy, or initiating ACE inhibitor therapy in lower doses, will minimize the reaction; this reaction does not usually recur with subsequent doses, although caution in increasing doses is recommended; diuretics may be reinstituted as necessary)

(risk of renal failure may be increased in patients who are sodium- and volume-depleted as a result of diuretic therapy)

(captopril, enalapril, or lisinopril may reduce the secondary aldosteronism and hypokalemia caused by diuretics)

Digitalis glycosides
(concurrent use with loop diuretics may enhance the possibility of digitalis toxicity associated with hypokalemia and hypomagnesemia)

» Hypokalemia-causing medications, other
(risk of severe hypokalemia due to other hypokalemia-causing medications may be increased; monitoring of serum potassium concentrations and cardiac function and potassium supplementation may be required)

» Lithium
(concurrent use with loop diuretics may provoke lithium toxicity because of reduced renal clearance and is not recommended unless patient can be closely monitored)

» Nephrotoxic medications, other or
Ototoxic medications, other
(concurrent and/or sequential administration should be avoided since the potential for ototoxicity and nephrotoxicity may be increased, especially in the presence of renal function impairment)

Neuromuscular blocking agents, nondepolarizing
(loop diuretics may induce hypokalemia, which may enhance the blockade of nondepolarizing neuromuscular blocking agents; serum potassium determinations may be necessary prior to administration of nondepolarizing neuromuscular blocking agents; careful postoperative monitoring of the patient may be necessary following concurrent or sequential use, especially if there is a possibility of incomplete reversal of neuromuscular blockade)

Sympathomimetics
(concurrent use may reduce the antihypertensive effects of the loop diuretics; the patient should be carefully monitored to confirm that the desired effect is being obtained)

For furosemide only (in addition to those listed above)
Chloral hydrate
(administration of chloral hydrate followed by intravenous furosemide may result in diaphoresis, hot flashes, and variable blood pressure including hypertension due to a hypermetabolic state caused by displacement of thyroxine from its bound state)

Probenecid
(probenecid has been found to increase serum concentrations of furosemide by inhibiting active renal tubular secretion)

Contraindications/Medical problems
The contraindications/medical problems included have been selected on the basis of their potential clinical significance (reasons given in parentheses where appropriate)—not necessarily inclusive (» = major clinical significance).

Risk-benefit should be considered when the following medical problems exist:

For bumetanide, ethacrynic acid, and furosemide
» Anuria or
» Renal function impairment, severe
(impaired effectiveness and possible delayed excretion with increased risk of toxicity. Although bumetanide, ethacrynic acid, and furosemide are effective diuretics in patients with renal function impairment, reduced clearance may necessitate use of higher doses combined with more prolonged dosing intervals to prevent accumulation and reduce the risk of ototoxicity)

Diabetes mellitus
(loop diuretics cause impaired glucose tolerance)

Gout, history of, or
Hyperuricemia
(loop diuretics may elevate serum uric acid concentrations)

Hearing function impairment

Hepatic function impairment, including cirrhosis and ascites
(risk of dehydration and electrolyte imbalance, which may precipitate hepatic coma and death; hospitalization during initiation of therapy is recommended)

Myocardial infarction, acute
(excessive diuresis should be avoided because of the danger of precipitating shock)

Pancreatitis, or history of
(pancreatitis has been reported with bumetanide, ethacrynic acid, and furosemide)

Sensitivity to loop diuretic prescribed

Caution is recommended also in patients who are at increased risk if hypokalemia occurs, including those taking digitalis and diuretics and those with:
Certain diarrheal states
Congestive heart failure
Hepatic cirrhosis and ascites
History of ventricular arrhythmias
Potassium-losing nephropathy
States of aldosterone excess with normal renal function

For ethacrynic acid and furosemide only (in addition to the above)
Lupus erythematosus, history of
(exacerbation or activation by ethacrynic acid and furosemide has been reported)

Side/Adverse Effects
See *Table 1*, page 530.

Patient Consultation
In providing consultation, consider emphasizing the following selected information (» = major clinical significance):

Before using this medication
» Conditions affecting use, especially:
Sensitivity to the loop diuretic prescribed, or to sulfonamides (for bumetanide and furosemide)
Pregnancy—Not recommended for routine use; reported to cause harmful effects, including birth defects (for ethacrynic acid), in animals
Breast-feeding—Furosemide excreted in breast milk
Use in the elderly—Elderly patients may be more sensitive to hypotensive and electrolyte effects, and may be at greater risk of developing circulatory collapse and thromboembolic episodes
Use by athletes—Diuretics are banned and tested for by the U.S. Olympic Committee (USOC) and the National Collegiate Athletic Association (NCAA)
Other medications, especially adrenocorticoids, parenteral amphotericin B, oral anticoagulants, lithium, or other nephrotoxic medications
Other medical problems, especially severe renal function impairment

Proper use of this medication
Diuretic effects of the medication and timing of doses to minimize inconvenience of diuresis
Getting into habit of taking at same time each day to help increase compliance

Taking with food or milk to reduce gastrointestinal irritation

Missed dose: Taking as soon as possible; not taking if almost time for next dose; not doubling doses

» Proper storage

For use as an antihypertensive

Importance of diet; possible need for sodium restriction and/or weight reduction

» Patient may not experience symptoms of hypertension; importance of taking medication even if feeling well

» Does not cure, but controls hypertension; possible need for life-long therapy; serious consequences of untreated hypertension

For oral solution dosage form of furosemide (in addition to the above)

Taking orally, even if in dropper bottle; importance of accurate measurement

Precautions while using this medication

Regular visits to physician to check progress

» Possibility of hypokalemia; possible need for additional potassium in diet; not changing diet without first checking with physician

To prevent dehydration, notifying physician if severe nausea, vomiting, or diarrhea occurs and continues

Caution if any kind of surgery (including dental surgery) is required

» Caution when getting up suddenly from a lying or sitting position

» Caution in using alcohol, while standing for long periods or exercising, and during hot weather because of enhanced orthostatic hypotensive effects

Diabetics: May increase blood sugar levels

For use as an antihypertensive

» Not taking other medications, especially nonprescription sympathomimetics, unless discussed with physician

For furosemide (in addition to the above)

» Possible skin photosensitivity; avoiding unprotected exposure to sun; using protective clothing; using a sun block product that includes protection against both UVA-caused photosensitivity reactions and UVB-caused sunburn reactions; avoiding use of sunlamp, tanning bed, or tanning booth

Side/adverse effects

Signs of potential side effects, especially allergic reaction, blood in urine, electrolyte imbalance, gastrointestinal bleeding, gout, hepatic dysfunction, leukopenia, agranulocytosis, ototoxicity, pancreatitis, thrombocytopenia, and xanthopsia

General Dosing Information

Dosage must be adjusted to meet the individual requirements of each patient, on the basis of clinical response. The lowest effective dosage should be utilized to minimize potential fluid and electrolyte imbalance.

When used to promote diuresis, intermittent dosage schedules may reduce the possibility of electrolyte imbalance or hyperuricemia resulting from therapy.

Concurrent administration of potassium supplements or potassium-sparing diuretics may be indicated in patients considered to be at higher risk for developing hypokalemia.

If a single daily dose is indicated, it is preferably taken on arising in order to minimize the effect of increased frequency of urination on sleep.

When bumetanide, ethacrynic acid, or furosemide is added to an antihypertensive regimen, the dose of other antihypertensive agents may have to be reduced in order to prevent an excessive drop in blood pressure.

It is recommended that bumetanide, ethacrynic acid, and furosemide be discontinued if oliguria persists for more than 24 hours at maximal dosage.

BUMETANIDE

Summary of Differences

Pharmacology:

Mechanism of action/effect—May have additional action on proximal tubule.

Biotransformation and elimination—Excreted largely unchanged.

Side/adverse effects: Muscle pain may occur with large doses. Chest pain, premature ejaculation, and difficulty in keeping an erection have also been reported.

Additional Dosing Information

See also *General Dosing Information.*

For parenteral dosage forms only

Intravenous administration is generally preferred over intramuscular administration.

Intravenous administration should be at a slow, controlled rate over a 2-minute period.

Oral Dosage Forms

Note: Bracketed uses in the *Dosage Forms* section refer to categories of use and/or indications that are not included in U.S. product labeling.

BUMETANIDE TABLETS USP

Usual adult dose:

[Antihypertensive]; or

Diuretic—Oral, 500 mcg (0.5 mg) to 2 mg per day as a single daily dose. The dose may be increased, if necessary, by addition of a second or third daily dose with intervals of four to five hours between doses. An intermittent dosage schedule (administration on alternate days for three or four days, with one or two days in between) may also be used.

Note: Geriatric patients may be more sensitive to the effects of the usual adult dose.

Usual adult prescribing limits: Up to 10 mg per day.

Auxiliary labeling: • Do not take other medicines without your doctor's advice.

Parenteral Dosage Forms

BUMETANIDE INJECTION USP

Usual adult dose:

[Antihypertensive]; or

Diuretic—Intravenous or intramuscular, 500 mcg (0.5 mg) to 1 mg, repeated at intervals of two to three hours, if necessary.

Usual adult prescribing limits: Up to 10 mg per day.

ETHACRYNIC ACID

Summary of Differences

Indications: Also indicated for short-term management of ascites due to malignancy, idiopathic edema, and lymphedema, and for treatment of hypercalcemia.

Side/adverse effects: Greatest risk of ototoxicity. Gastrointestinal bleeding and blood in urine may occur with parenteral use. Higher incidence of gastrointestinal upset. Confusion, loss of appetite, and nervousness were reported more often than with other loop diuretics.

Additional Dosing Information

See also *General Dosing Information.*

Concurrent administration of ammonium chloride or arginine chloride may be indicated in patients considered to be at higher risk of developing metabolic alkalosis as a result of the chloruretic effect.

Because of the profound effect of ethacrynic acid on sodium excretion, rigid dietary salt restriction is not necessary in most patients and may in fact increase the risk of adverse effects due to hyponatremia.

In patients with renal edema, administration of salt-poor albumin may be helpful in preventing reduced response to ethacrynic acid because of hypoproteinemia.

If severe, watery diarrhea occurs, it is recommended that ethacrynic acid be permanently withdrawn.

For parenteral dosage forms only

Intramuscular or subcutaneous administration is not recommended because of local pain and irritation.

Intravenous administration should be at a slow, controlled rate over a period of about 30 minutes.

If a second injection is required, use of a different injection site is recommended to prevent thrombophlebitis.

Oral Dosage Forms

ETHACRYNIC ACID ORAL SOLUTION

Usual adult dose: Diuretic—
   Initial: Oral, 50 to 100 mg a day, in single or divided daily doses with increments of 25 to 50 mg per day as needed.
   Maintenance: Oral, reduced to meet individual requirements once dry weight is achieved; usually 50 to 200 mg a day.
Note: Geriatric patients may be more sensitive to the effects of the usual adult dose.

Usual adult prescribing limits: Up to 400 mg a day.

Auxiliary labeling:
   • Take with meals or milk.
   • Do not take other medicines without your doctor's advice.

ETHACRYNIC ACID TABLETS USP

Usual adult dose: Diuretic—
   Initial: Oral, 50 to 100 mg a day, in single or divided daily doses with increments of 25 to 50 mg per day as needed.
   Maintenance: Oral, reduced to meet individual requirements once dry weight is achieved; usually 50 to 200 mg a day.
Note: Geriatric patients may be more sensitive to the effects of the usual adult dose.

Usual adult prescribing limits: Up to 400 mg a day.

Auxiliary labeling:
   • Take with meals or milk.
   • Do not take other medicines without your doctor's advice.

Parenteral Dosage Forms

ETHACRYNATE SODIUM FOR INJECTION USP

Usual adult dose: Diuretic—Intravenous, 50 mg (base), or 500 mcg (0.5 mg) to 1 mg per kg of body weight; may be repeated in two to four hours if necessary, then every four to six hours if the patient is responsive. In some emergency situations, the injection may be repeated every hour.
Note: Geriatric patients may be more sensitive to the effects of the usual adult dose.

Usual adult prescribing limits: Up to 100 mg (base).

FUROSEMIDE

Summary of Differences

Category: Furosemide is used as a diagnostic aid adjunct in renal disease.
Precautions:
   Breast-feeding—Excreted in breast milk.
   Pediatrics—Prolonged half-life in neonates.
   Drug interactions and/or related problems—Also interacts with chloral hydrate and probenecid.
Side/adverse effects: Also causes xanthopsia and increased sensitivity of skin to sunlight.

Additional Dosing Information

See also *General Dosing Information.*

When furosemide is used as an antihypercalcemic, body fluid and sodium chloride should be replaced in order to maintain extracellular fluid volume and increase calcium excretion effectively.

For parenteral dosage forms only

Intravenous administration is generally preferred over intramuscular administration.

Intravenous administration should be at a slow, controlled rate over a 1- to 2-minute period.

If high-dose parenteral therapy is indicated, administration should be by controlled intravenous infusion at a rate not exceeding 4 mg per minute.

Oral Dosage Forms

Note: Bracketed uses in the *Dosage Forms* section refer to categories of use and/or indications that are not included in U.S. product labeling.

FUROSEMIDE ORAL SOLUTION

Usual adult dose:
   Diuretic—Oral, initially 20 to 80 mg as a single dose, the dosage then being increased by an additional 20 to 40 mg at six- to eight-hour intervals, until the desired response is obtained. The maintenance dose as determined by titration is then given daily as a single dose or divided into two or three doses, given once a day every other day, or given once a day for two to four consecutive days out of each week.
   Antihypertensive—Oral, initially 40 mg two times a day, the dosage then being adjusted according to patient response.

[Antihypercalcemic][1]—Oral, 120 mg a day as a single dose or divided into two or three doses.

Note: Geriatric patients may be more sensitive to the effects of the usual adult dose.

Usual adult prescribing limits: Up to 600 mg daily.

Note: In chronic renal failure, doses of up to 4 grams daily have been used.

Auxiliary labeling:
- Take by mouth only (when dispensed with graduated dropper).
- Do not take other medicines without your doctor's advice.

FUROSEMIDE TABLETS USP

Usual adult dose:

Diuretic—Oral, initially 20 to 80 mg as a single dose, the dosage then being increased by an additional 20 to 40 mg at six- to eight-hour intervals, until the desired response is obtained. The maintenance dose as determined by titration is then given daily as a single dose or divided into two or three doses, given once a day every other day, or given once a day for two to four consecutive days out of each week.

Antihypertensive—Oral, initially 40 mg two times a day, the dosage then being adjusted according to patient response.

[Antihypercalcemic][1]—Oral, 120 mg a day as a single dose or divided into two or three doses.

Note: Geriatric patients may be more sensitive to the effects of the usual adult dose.

Usual adult prescribing limits: Up to 600 mg daily.

Note: In chronic renal failure, doses of up to 4 grams daily have been used.

Auxiliary labeling: • Do not take other medicines without your doctor's advice.

Parenteral Dosage Forms

Note: Bracketed uses in the *Dosage Forms* section refer to categories of use and/or indications that are not included in U.S. product labeling.

FUROSEMIDE INJECTION USP

Usual adult dose:

Diuretic—Intramuscular or intravenous, initially 20 to 40 mg as a single dose, the dosage then being increased by an additional 20 mg at two-hour intervals until the desired response is obtained. The maintenance dose as determined by titration is then given one or two times a day.

Note: In acute pulmonary edema (not accompanied by hypertensive crisis), the usual initial dose is 40 mg intravenously, repeated as 80 mg in one hour if a satisfactory response is not obtained.

Antihypertensive—

Hypertensive crisis in patients with normal renal function: Intravenous, 40 to 80 mg.

Hypertensive crisis accompanied by pulmonary edema or acute renal failure: Intravenous, 100 to 200 mg.

[Antihypercalcemic][1]—Intramuscular or intravenous, 80 to 100 mg in severe cases, the dosage being repeated if necessary every one to two hours until the desired response is obtained. In less severe cases, smaller doses may be given every two to four hours.

[Diagnostic aid adjunct (renal disease)]—Intravenous, 0.3 to 0.5 mg per kg of body weight to a maximum of 40 mg.

Note: Geriatric patients may be more sensitive to the effects of the usual adult dose.

Usual adult prescribing limits: Although controversial, doses of up to 6 grams daily administered by slow intravenous infusion have been used in acute renal failure by some clinicians.

---

[1]Not included in Canadian product labeling.

Table 1. Side/Adverse Effects*

Note: Nephrocalcinosis or nephrolithiasis may occur with furosemide administration if hypercalciuria is present.

Ethacrynic acid appears to be more likely to cause ototoxicity than bumetanide or furosemide and less likely to cause hyperglycemia than furosemide.

The following side/adverse effects have been selected on the basis of their potential clinical significance (possible signs and symptoms in parentheses where appropriate)—not necessarily inclusive:	Legend **I**=Bumetanide **II**=Ethacrynic acid **III**=Furosemide		
	I	**II**	**III**
Those indicating need for medical attention			
Allergic reaction (skin rash)	R	R	R
Blood in urine—associated with parenteral use	U	R	U
Electrolyte imbalance such as hyponatremia, hypochloremic alkalosis, and hypokalemia—occurs frequently, up to 10 to 15% of patients receiving ethacrynic acid (usually not symptomatic; symptoms include dry mouth, increased thirst, irregular heartbeat, mood or mental changes, muscle cramps or pain, nausea or vomiting, unusual tiredness or weakness, weak pulse)	L	L	L
Gastrointestinal bleeding (black, tarry stools)—associated with parenteral use	U	R	U
Gout (joint pain, lower back or side pain)	R	R	R
Hepatic dysfunction (yellow eyes or skin)	R	R	R
Leukopenia or agranulocytosis (fever or chills, cough or hoarseness, lower back or side pain, painful or difficult urination)	R	R	R
Ototoxicity—more frequent with renal function impairment and in rapid parenteral administration of large doses (ringing or buzzing in ears or any loss of hearing; usually transient, but permanent deafness has occurred, especially in patients receiving other ototoxic drugs)	R	L†	R
Pancreatitis (severe stomach pain with nausea and vomiting)	R	R	R
Thrombocytopenia (unusual bleeding or bruising; black, tarry stools; blood in urine or stools; pinpoint red spots on skin)	R	R	R
Xanthopsia (yellow vision)	U	U	R
Those indicating need for medical attention only if they continue or are bothersome			
Blurred vision	L	L	L
Chest pain	L	U	U
Confusion	U	L	U
Diarrhea	L	M†	L
Headache	L	L	L
Increased sensitivity of skin to sunlight	U	U	L
Local irritation (redness or pain at site of injection)	R	R	R
Loss of appetite	L	M†	L
Nervousness	U	L	U
Orthostatic hypotension as a result of massive diuresis (dizziness or lightheadedness when getting up from a lying or sitting position)	M	M	M
Premature ejaculation or difficulty in keeping an erection	L	U	U
Stomach cramps or pain	L	L	L

*Differences in frequency of occurrence may reflect either lack of clinical-use data or actual pharmacologic distinctions among agents (although their basic pharmacologic similarity suggests that side effects occurring with one may occur with the others). M = more frequent; L = less frequent; R = rare; U = unknown.

†Dose-related.

DIURETICS, POTASSIUM-SPARING   Systemic

Some commonly used *brand names* are:

In the U.S.—
     Aldactone [Spironolactone]   *Midamor* [Amiloride]
     Dyrenium [Triamterene]

In Canada—
     Aldactone [Spironolactone]   *Midamor* [Amiloride]
     Dyrenium [Triamterene]   *Novospiroton*
                              [Spironolactone]

ORAL
AMILORIDE
   Amiloride Hydrochloride Tablets USP
     In the U.S.—*Midamor;* GENERIC
     In Canada—*Midamor*
SPIRONOLACTONE
   Spironolactone Tablets USP
     In the U.S.—*Aldactone;* GENERIC
     In Canada—*Aldactone; Novospiroton*
TRIAMTERENE
   Triamterene Capsules USP†
     In the U.S.—*Dyrenium*
   Triamterene Tablets*
     In Canada—*Dyrenium*

---

*Not commercially available in the U.S.
†Not commercially available in Canada.

Category:

Diuretic—Amiloride; Spironolactone; Triamterene.
Antihypertensive—Amiloride; Spironolactone; Triamterene.
Aldosterone antagonist—Spironolactone.
Diagnostic aid (primary hyperaldosteronism)—Spironolactone.
Antihypokalemic—Amiloride; Spironolactone; Triamterene.

Indications

Note: Bracketed information in the *Indications* section refers to uses
     not included in U.S. product labeling.

Accepted
Edema (treatment)—Amiloride, spironolactone, and triamterene are
     indicated as adjuncts in the management of edematous states, es-
     pecially when a potassium-sparing diuretic effect is desired. These
     may include congestive heart failure, hepatic cirrhosis, and ne-
     phrotic syndrome, which often involve secondary hyperaldoste-
     ronism, as well as idiopathic edema.
Hypertension (treatment adjunct)—Amiloride, spironolactone, and
     [triamterene][1] are indicated as adjuncts in the treatment of hyper-
     tension (for spironolactone, with or without accompanying hyper-
     aldosteronism), especially when a potassium-sparing diuretic ef-
     fect is desired.
     Nonpharmacologic management (especially sodium restriction,
     weight reduction and exercise, and moderation of alcohol con-
     sumption) is recommended first for some patients, including those
     with mild hypertension, and is recommended as an adjunct to all
     pharmacologic hypertensive therapy.
Hyperaldosteronism, primary (diagnosis and treatment)—Spironolac-
     tone is indicated for diagnosis and short- or long-term manage-
     ment of primary hyperaldosteronism.
Hypokalemia (prophylaxis and treatment)—[Amiloride][1], spironolac-
     tone, and [triamterene][1] are indicated for prevention and treatment
     of hypokalemia in patients for whom other measures are inappro-
     priate or inadequate.
[Polycystic ovary syndrome (treatment)][1]—Spironolactone is also used
     with some success in the treatment of polycystic ovary syndrome.

[Hirsutism, female (treatment)][1]—Spironolactone has been used in the
     treatment of female hirsutism.

---

[1]Not included in Canadian product labeling.

Pharmacology

Mechanism of action/Effect:
Diuretic; or
Antihypokalemic—Potassium-sparing diuretics interfere with so-
     dium reabsorption in the distal convoluted tubule, thereby pro-
     moting excretion of sodium and water and retention of potas-
     sium. Amiloride and triamterene have a direct inhibiting effect
     on the entry of sodium into the cells, while spironolactone
     competitively inhibits the action of aldosterone.
Antihypertensive—Diuretics lower blood pressure initially by re-
     ducing plasma and extracellular fluid volume; cardiac output
     also decreases. Eventually, the extracellular fluid volume and
     the cardiac output return to normal with an accompanying de-
     crease in peripheral resistance.
Aldosterone antagonist; or
Diagnostic aid (primary hyperaldosteronism)—Spironolactone is a
     competitive inhibitor of aldosterone; neither amiloride nor tri-
     amterene has this effect.
Hirsutism; or
Polycystic ovary syndrome—May be due to an antiandrogenic
     effect of spironolactone.

Onset of action: Diuretic—
     Amiloride: Single dose—Within 2 hours.
     Triamterene: Single dose—2 to 4 hours.

Time to peak effect: Diuretic—
     Amiloride: Single dose—6 to 10 hours.
     Spironolactone: Multiple doses—2 to 3 days.
     Triamterene: Multiple doses—1 day to several days.

Duration of action: Diuretic—
     Amiloride: Single dose—24 hours.
     Spironolactone: Multiple doses—2 to 3 days.
     Triamterene: Single dose—7 to 9 hours.

Precautions to Consider

Geriatrics
Although appropriate studies on the relationship of age to the effects
     of potassium-sparing diuretics have not been performed in the
     geriatric population, the elderly may be at increased risk of devel-
     oping hyperkalemia. In addition, elderly patients are more likely to
     have age-related renal function impairment, which may require
     caution in patients receiving potassium-sparing diuretics.

Drug interactions and/or related problems
The following drug interactions and/or related problems have been
     selected on the basis of their potential clinical significance (pos-
     sible mechanism in parentheses where appropriate)—not necessar-
     ily inclusive (» = major clinical significance):

Note: Combinations containing any of the following medications, de-
     pending on the amount present, may also interact with this
     medication.

For all potassium-sparing diuretics
   Allopurinol or
   Colchicine or
   Probenecid or
   Sulfinpyrazone
     (triamterene may raise the concentration of blood uric acid, but
     to a lesser extent than thiazide diuretics or ethacrynic acid or

furosemide; dosage adjustment of antigout medications may be necessary to control hyperuricemia and gout)

» Anticoagulants, coumarin- or indandione-derivative, or
» Heparin

(anticoagulant effects may be decreased when these medications are used concurrently with potassium-sparing diuretics, as a result of reduction of plasma volume leading to concentration of procoagulant factors in the blood; in addition, diuretic-induced improvement of hepatic congestion may lead to improved hepatic function, resulting in increased procoagulant factor synthesis; dosage adjustments may be necessary)

Anti-inflammatory drugs, nonsteroidal (NSAIDs), especially indomethacin

(may reduce the antihypertensive effects of the potassium-sparing diuretics; indomethacin may also reduce the natriuretic and diuretic effects of potassium-sparing diuretics, possibly because of renal prostaglandin synthesis inhibition and/or sodium and fluid retention; the patient should be carefully monitored to confirm that the desired effect is being obtained)

(concurrent use of NSAIDs with a diuretic may increase the risk of renal failure secondary to a decrease in renal blood flow caused by inhibition of renal prostaglandin synthesis)

» Angiotensin-converting enzyme (ACE) inhibitors or
Anti-inflammatory drugs, nonsteroidal (NSAIDs), especially indomethacin, or

» Blood from blood bank (may contain up to 30 mEq [mmol] of potassium per liter of plasma or up to 65 mEq [mmol] per liter of whole blood when stored for more than 10 days) or

» Cyclosporine or
» Diuretics, potassium-sparing, other, or
Heparin or

» Low-salt milk (may contain up to 60 mEq [mmol] of potassium per liter) or

» Potassium-containing medications or
» Potassium supplements or substances containing high levels of potassium or

Salt substitutes (most contain substantial amounts of potassium)

(concurrent administration with potassium-sparing diuretics tends to promote serum potassium accumulation; hyperkalemia may result, especially in patients with renal insufficiency)

Exchange resins, sodium cycle (such as sodium polystyrene sulfonate)

(whether administered orally or rectally, these medications reduce serum potassium levels by replacing potassium with sodium; fluid retention may occur in some patients because of the increased sodium intake)

Hypotension-producing medications, other

(antihypertensive and/or diuretic effects may be potentiated when these medications are used concurrently with potassium-sparing diuretics; although some antihypertensive and/or diuretic combinations are frequently used for therapeutic advantage, dosage adjustments may be necessary during concurrent use)

» Lithium

(concurrent use with potassium-sparing diuretics is not recommended, as they may provoke lithium toxicity by reducing renal clearance)

Sympathomimetics

(may reduce the antihypertensive effects of potassium-sparing diuretics; the patient should be carefully monitored to confirm that the desired effect is being obtained)

For spironolactone only (in addition to those listed for all potassium-sparing diuretics)

» Digoxin

(spironolactone may increase the half-life of digoxin; dosage reduction or increased dosing intervals of digoxin may be necessary and careful monitoring is recommended)

For triamterene only (in addition to those listed for all potassium-sparing diuretics)

Amantadine

(triamterene may reduce the renal clearance of amantadine, resulting in increased plasma concentrations and possible amantadine toxicity)

Folic acid

(triamterene may act as a folate antagonist by inhibiting dihydrofolate reductase; most significant with high doses and/or prolonged triamterene use; leucovorin calcium must be used instead of folic acid in patients receiving triamterene)

Contraindications/Medical problems

The contraindications/medical problems included have been selected on the basis of their potential clinical significance (reasons given in parentheses where appropriate)—not necessarily inclusive (» = major clinical significance).

Except under special circumstances, this medication should not be used when the following medical problem exists:

» Hyperkalemia

(potassium-sparing diuretics may further increase serum potassium concentrations)

Risk-benefit should be considered when the following medical problems exist:

For amiloride, spironolactone, and triamterene

» Anuria or
» Renal function impairment

(potassium-sparing diuretics may aggravate electrolyte imbalance; risk of developing hyperkalemia is increased)

Diabetes mellitus, especially in patients with confirmed or suspected renal insufficiency, or

» Diabetic nephropathy

(increased risk of hyperkalemia; potassium-sparing diuretic should be discontinued at least 3 days prior to a glucose tolerance test because of the risk of severe hyperkalemia)

» Hepatic function impairment

(increased sensitivity to electrolyte changes)

Hyponatremia

Metabolic or respiratory acidosis, predisposition to

(acidosis potentiates hyperkalemic effects of potassium-sparing diuretics; potassium-sparing diuretics may potentiate acidosis)

Sensitivity to the potassium-sparing diuretic prescribed

» Caution is also required in severely ill patients and those with relatively small urine volumes, who are at greater risk of developing hyperkalemia

For spironolactone only (in addition to those listed above for all potassium-sparing diuretics)

Menstrual abnormalities or breast enlargement

For triamterene only (in addition to those listed above for all potassium-sparing diuretics)

Hyperuricemia or gout

Nephrolithiasis, history of

(increased risk of forming triamterene stones)

Side/Adverse Effects

See *Table 1*, page 535.

Patient Consultation

In providing consultation, consider emphasizing the following selected information (» = major clinical significance):

Before using this medication

» Conditions affecting use, especially:

Sensitivity to the potassium-sparing diuretic prescribed

Pregnancy—Not recommended for routine use; triamterene crosses placenta; spironolactone may cross placenta

Breast-feeding—All potassium-sparing diuretics may be excreted in breast milk

Use in the elderly—Increased risk of hyperkalemia

Use by athletes—Diuretics are banned and tested for by the U.S. Olympic Committee (USOC), the International Olympic Committee (IOC), and the National Collegiate Athletic Association (NCAA)

Other medications, especially angiotensin-converting enzyme (ACE) inhibitors, cyclosporine, digoxin, other potassium-sparing diuretics, potassium-containing medications or supplements, or lithium

Other medical problems, especially diabetic nephropathy, hyperkalemia, renal function impairment or hepatic function impairment

Proper use of this medication

Diuretic effects of the medication and timing of doses to minimize inconvenience of diuresis

Getting into habit of taking at same time each day to help increase compliance

Taking with meals or milk to reduce gastrointestinal irritation

Missed dose: Taking as soon as possible; not taking if almost time for next dose; not doubling doses

» Proper storage

For use as an antihypertensive (amiloride and spironolactone only)

Possible need for control of weight and diet, especially sodium intake

» Patient may not experience symptoms of hypertension; importance of taking medication even if feeling well

» Does not cure, but helps control hypertension; possible need for lifelong therapy; checking with physician before discontinuing medication; serious consequences of untreated hypertension

Precautions while using this medication

Regular visits to physician to check progress

Avoiding excessive ingestion of foods high in potassium or use of salt substitutes or other potassium supplements

To prevent dehydration, checking with physician if severe nausea, vomiting, or diarrhea occurs and continues

Caution if any kind of surgery or emergency treatment is required

Caution if any laboratory tests required; possible interference with test results

For use as an antihypertensive (amiloride and spironolactone only)

» Not taking other medications, especially nonprescription sympathomimetics, unless discussed with physician

For triamterene only

Possible photosensitivity; avoiding unprotected exposure to sun; using protective clothing and sun block product; avoiding use of sunlamp, tanning bed, or tanning booth

Side/adverse effects

Signs of potential side effects, especially agranulocytosis, allergic reaction, anaphylaxis, and hyperkalemia (for all potassium-sparing diuretics); megaloblastosis, nephrolithiasis, and thrombocytopenia (for triamterene)

For spironolactone only (in addition to the above)

Possibility of enlargement of breasts in males; usually reversible within several months

General Dosing Information

Dosage must be adjusted to meet the individual requirements of each patient, on the basis of clinical response. The lowest effective dose should be utilized to minimize potential electrolyte imbalance.

If a single daily dose is indicated, it is preferably taken on arising in order to minimize the effect of increased frequency of urination on sleep, although the diuretic effect of potassium-sparing diuretics alone is mild.

The normal adult concentration of plasma potassium is 3.5 to 5.0 mEq (mmol) per liter, with 4.5 mEq (mmol) often being used as a reference point. Potassium concentrations exceeding 6 mEq (mmol) per liter are dangerous because of possible initiation of cardiac arrhythmias. Normal potassium concentrations tend to be higher in neonates (7.7 mEq [mmol] per liter) than in adults.

Plasma potassium concentrations do not necessarily indicate the true body potassium concentration. A rise in serum pH may cause a decrease in serum potassium concentration and an increase in the intracellular potassium concentration.

It is recommended that potassium-sparing diuretic therapy be withdrawn if hyperkalemia occurs. If hyperkalemia is associated with ECG changes, prompt additional therapy with intravenous sodium bicarbonate, calcium gluconate, or calcium chloride; with oral or rectal sodium polystyrene sulfonate; or with parenteral glucose and insulin may be indicated. It is important to remember that severe hyperkalemia may occur suddenly and may not be preceded by any warning signs.

Recent evidence suggests that withdrawal of antihypertensive therapy prior to surgery is not necessary, but that the anesthesiologist must be aware of such therapy.

Diet/Nutrition

It is recommended that oral potassium-sparing diuretics be taken with or after meals to minimize stomach upset, and possibly also to enhance bioavailability.

AMILORIDE

Summary of Differences

Pharmacology:
Protein binding—Minimal.
Biotransformation—None; excreted unchanged.
Duration of action—Diuretic: Single dose—24 hours.

Side/adverse effects: No reported cases of agranulocytosis. Amiloride has been reported to cause constipation and muscle cramps.

Oral Dosage Forms

AMILORIDE HYDROCHLORIDE TABLETS USP

Usual adult dose:
Diuretic; or
Antihypertensive—Oral, 5 to 10 mg per day as a single dose.

Note: Geriatric patients may be more sensitive to the effects of the usual adult dose.

Usual adult prescribing limits: Up to 20 mg per day.

Auxiliary labeling:
• Take with meals or milk.
• Do not take other medicines without your doctor's advice.

SPIRONOLACTONE

Summary of Differences

Indications: Diagnosis and treatment of primary hyperaldosteronism. Treatment of polycystic ovary syndrome and female hirsutism.

Pharmacology:
Mechanism of action/effect—Aldosterone antagonist.
Protein binding—Very high (more than 90%).
Biotransformation—Hepatic, extensive, to active metabolite (canrenone).
Duration of action—Diuretic: Multiple doses—2 to 3 days.

Precautions:
   Carcinogenicity—Tumorigenic in rats and possibly associated with breast carcinoma in humans.
   Drug interactions and/or related problems—Use with digoxin may increase digoxin half-life.
   Laboratory value alterations—May falsely increase plasma cortisol determinations by Mattingly (fluorometric) assay. May falsely elevate digoxin radioimmunoassays.
   Contraindications/medical problems—Menstrual abnormalities or breast enlargement.
Side/adverse effects: Endocrine or antiandrogenic effects more common at doses exceeding 100 mg per day. May cause CNS effects and causes more frequent gastrointestinal irritation.

Additional Dosing Information

See also *General Dosing Information.*

To reduce delay in onset of effect, a loading dose of 2 to 3 times the daily dose may be administered on the first day of therapy.

When spironolactone is added to therapy with another diuretic or antihypertensive agent, it is recommended that the dosage of the other drug (especially ganglionic blocking agents) be reduced by at least 50% and then adjusted as required.

It is recommended that spironolactone be discontinued several days prior to adrenal vein catheterization for measurement of aldosterone concentrations, for the purpose of attempting lateralization in primary hyperaldosteronism, and for measurements of plasma renin activity.

When high doses of spironolactone are required for treatment of edema due to hepatic cirrhosis, drug dosage may be reduced prior to completion of diuresis to avoid dehydration and precipitation of hepatic coma, although dry weight may be achieved.

Oral Dosage Forms

Note: Bracketed uses in the *Dosage Forms* section refer to categories of use and/or indications that are not included in U.S. product labeling.

SPIRONOLACTONE TABLETS USP

Usual adult dose:
   Diuretic—Edema due to congestive heart failure, hepatic cirrhosis, or nephrotic syndrome:
      Initial—Oral, 25 to 200 mg a day in two to four divided doses for at least five days.
      Maintenance—Oral, 75 to 400 mg a day in two to four divided doses.
   Antihypertensive—
      Initial: Oral, 50 to 100 mg a day as a single daily dose or in two to four divided doses for at least two weeks, followed by gradual dosage adjustment every two weeks as necessary up to 200 mg a day.
      Maintenance: Oral, adjusted to meet individual requirements.
   Aldosterone antagonist—Primary hyperaldosteronism: Maintenance—Oral, 100 to 400 mg per day in two to four divided daily doses prior to surgery; smaller doses may be used for long-term maintenance in patients unsuitable for surgery.
      [Polycystic ovary disease]—Oral, 100 to 200 mg per day in two divided daily doses.
      [Hirsutism, female]—Oral, 100 mg two times a day.
   Diagnostic aid (primary hyperaldosteronism)—
      Long test: Oral, 400 mg per day in two to four divided daily doses for three to four weeks.
      Short test: Oral, 400 mg per day in two to four divided daily doses for four days.
   Antihypokalemic—Diuretic-induced hypokalemia: Oral, 25 to 100 mg per day as a single daily dose or in two to four divided doses.

Note: Geriatric patients may be more sensitive to the effects of the usual adult dose.

Usual adult prescribing limits: Dose may be increased up to three times the initial dose or up to a maximum of 400 mg a day.

Auxiliary labeling:
   • Take with meals or milk.
   • Do not take other medicines without your doctor's advice.

TRIAMTERENE

Summary of Differences

Pharmacology:
   Biotransformation—Hepatic.
   Duration of action—Diuretic: Single dose—7 to 9 hours.
Precautions:
   Drug interactions and/or related problems—Triamterene may increase blood uric acid and antagonize allopurinol, colchicine, probenecid, or sulfinpyrazone.
   Laboratory value alterations—May interfere with fluorescent measurement of quinidine.
   Contraindications/medical problems—Hyperuricemia or gout; history of nephrolithiasis.
Side/adverse effects: Nephrolithiasis; megaloblastosis; photosensitivity; thrombocytopenia. No decrease in sexual ability reported.

Additional Dosing Infomation

See also *General Dosing Information.*

Since triamterene is a weak folic acid antagonist, it may contribute to development of megaloblastosis in patients who have depleted folic acid stores (e.g., in pregnancy, hepatic cirrhosis).

When triamterene is combined with another diuretic, it is recommended that the initial dosage of each be reduced and then adjusted as required.

Oral Dosage Forms

TRIAMTERENE CAPSULES USP

Usual adult dose: Diuretic—
   Initial: Oral, 25 to 100 mg a day.
   Maintenance: Oral, adjusted to meet individual requirements.

Note: Geriatric patients may be more sensitive to the effects of the usual adult dose.

Usual adult prescribing limits: Up to 300 mg daily.

Auxiliary labeling:
   • Take with meals or milk.
   • Avoid overexposure to sun or use of sunlamp.
   • Do not take other medicines without your doctor's advice.

TRIAMTERENE TABLETS

Usual adult dose: Diuretic—
   Initial: Oral, 25 to 100 mg a day.
   Maintenance: Oral, adjusted to meet individual requirements.

Note: Geriatric patients may be more sensitive to the effects of the usual adult dose.

Usual adult prescribing limits: Up to 300 mg daily.

Auxiliary labeling:
   • Take with meals or milk.
   • Avoid overexposure to sun or use of sunlamp.
   • Do not take other medicines without your doctor's advice.

Table 1. Side/Adverse Effects*

The following side/adverse effects have been selected on the basis of their potential clinical significance (possible signs and symptoms in parentheses where appropriate)—not necessarily inclusive:	Legend: I=Amiloride II=Spironolactone III=Triamterene		
	I	**II**	**III**
Those indicating need for medical attention			
Agranulocytosis (fever or chills, cough or hoarseness, lower back or side pain, painful or difficult urination)	U	R	R
Allergic reaction or anaphylaxis (shortness of breath, skin rash or itching)	R	R	R
Hyperkalemia (confusion; irregular heartbeat; nervousness; numbness or tingling in hands, feet, or lips; shortness of breath or difficult breathing; unusual tiredness or weakness; weakness or heaviness of legs) Note: *Irregular heartbeat* is usually the earliest clinical indication of hyperkalemia and is readily detected by electrocardiogram (ECG).	M†	M†	M†
Megaloblastosis or overdose (burning, inflamed, or bright red tongue or cracked corners of mouth; weakness)	U	U	R
Nephrolithiasis (severe lower back or side pain)	U	U	R
Thrombocytopenia (unusual bleeding or bruising; black, tarry stools; blood in urine or stools; pinpoint red spots on skin)	U	U	R
Those indicating need for medical attention only if they continue or are bothersome			
Antiandrogenic or endocrine effect (breast tenderness in females, deepening of voice in females, enlargement of breasts in males, inability to have or keep an erection, increased hair growth in females, irregular menstrual periods, sweating) Note: *Gynecomastia* occurs frequently after several months of treatment at doses of spironolactone greater than 100 mg per day and rarely may persist even after spironolactone is discontinued.	U	L‡	U
Central nervous system (CNS) effect (clumsiness)	U	L‡	U
CNS effect (headache)	L	L‡	L
Constipation	L	U	U
Decreased sexual ability	L	L	U
Dizziness	L	L	L
Gastrointestinal irritation (nausea or vomiting, stomach cramps and diarrhea)	L	M	L
Hyponatremia (drowsiness, dryness of mouth, increased thirst, lack of energy)	L	L	L
Increased sensitivity of skin to sunlight	U	U	L
Muscle cramps	L	U	U

*Differences in frequency of occurrence may reflect either lack of clinical-use data or actual pharmacologic distinctions among agents. M = more frequent; L= less frequent; R = rare; U= unknown.

†Signs and symptoms of hyperkalemia may occur even when potassium-sparing diuretics are combined with thiazide diuretics. Hyperkalemia occurs in approximately 10% of patients when amiloride is used alone and may occur in up to 26% of patients receiving spironolactone even when combined with thiazide diuretics.

‡Incidence related to dose and/or duration of therapy.

DIURETICS, POTASSIUM-SPARING, AND HYDROCHLOROTHIAZIDE   Systemic

Some commonly used *brand names* are:

In the U.S.—

Aldactazide [Spironolactone and Hydrochlorothiazide]

Dyazide [Triamterene and Hydrochlorothiazide]

Maxzide [Triamterene and Hydrochlorothiazide]

Moduretic [Amiloride and Hydrochlorothiazide]

Spirozide [Spironolactone and Hydrochlorothiazide]

In Canada—

Aldactazide [Spironolactone and Hydrochlorothiazide]

Apo-Triazide [Triamterene and Hydrochlorothiazide]

Dyazide [Triamterene and Hydrochlorothiazide]

Moduret [Amiloride and Hydrochlorothiazide]

Novo-Spirozine [Spironolactone and Hydrochlorothiazide]

Novo-Triamzide [Triamterene and Hydrochlorothiazide]

Another commonly used name is Co-triamterzide [Triamterene and Hydrochlorothiazide]

ORAL

AMILORIDE AND HYDROCHLOROTHIAZIDE

Amiloride Hydrochloride and Hydrochlorothiazide Tablets USP

In the U.S.—*Moduretic;* GENERIC

In Canada—*Moduret*

SPIRONOLACTONE AND HYDROCHLOROTHIAZIDE

Spironolactone and Hydrochlorothiazide Tablets USP

In the U.S.—*Aldactazide; Spirozide;* GENERIC

In Canada—*Aldactazide; Novo-Spirozine*

TRIAMTERENE AND HYDROCHLOROTHIAZIDE

Triamterene and Hydrochlorothiazide Capsules USP†

In the U.S.—*Dyazide;* GENERIC

Triamterene and Hydrochlorothiazide Tablets USP

In the U.S.—*Maxzide;* GENERIC

In Canada—*Apo-Triazide; Dyazide; Novo-Triamzide*

†Not commercially available in Canada.

Category

Diuretic—Amiloride and Hydrochlorothiazide; Spironolactone and Hydrochlorothiazide; Triamterene and Hydrochlorothiazide.

Antihypertensive—Amiloride and Hydrochlorothiazide; Spironolactone and Hydrochlorothiazide; Triamterene and Hydrochlorothiazide.

Antihypokalemic—Amiloride and Hydrochlorothiazide; Spironolactone and Hydrochlorothiazide; Triamterene and Hydrochlorothiazide.

Indications

Note: Bracketed information in the *Indications* section refers to uses not included in U.S. product labeling.

Accepted

Edema (treatment)—These combinations are indicated as adjuncts in the management of edematous states such as congestive heart failure, hepatic cirrhosis, and nephrotic syndrome, as well as in adrenocorticoid- and estrogen-induced edema and idiopathic edema.

Hypertension (treatment)—Spironolactone and hydrochlorothiazide, triamterene and hydrochlorothiazide, and amiloride and hydrochlorothiazide[1] are also indicated in the treatment of hypertension, especially when a potassium-sparing diuretic effect is desired.

Fixed-dosage combinations are generally not recommended in initial therapy and are useful in subsequent therapy only when the proportion of the component agents corresponds to the dose of the individual agents, as determined by titration.

Nonpharmacologic management (especially sodium restriction, weight reduction and exercise, and moderation of alcohol consumption) is recommended first for some patients, including those with mild hypertension, and is recommended as an adjunct to all pharmacologic hypertensive therapy.

Hypokalemia (treatment)—[Amiloride and hydrochlorothiazide][1], [triamterene and hydrochlorothiazide][1], and spironolactone and hydrochlorothiazide[1] combinations are also indicated for treatment of diuretic-induced hypokalemia in hypertensive patients in whom other measures are inappropriate or inadequate.

[1]Not included in Canadian product labeling.

Pharmacology

Amiloride—See *Diuretics, Potassium-sparing (Systemic).*

Hydrochlorothiazide—See *Diuretics, Thiazide (Systemic).*

Spironolactone—See *Diuretics, Potassium-sparing (Systemic).*

Triamterene—See also *Diuretics, Potassium-sparing (Systemic).*

Absorption: Bioavailability of triamterene and hydrochlorothiazide in the tablet dosage form currently available in the U.S. is greater than in the capsule dosage form.

Precautions to Consider

Note: To save space, only information pertaining to actual precautions is included in the Precautions to Consider section of this combination monograph. For the complete text of this section for each of the components of these combinations, see—

Diuretics, Potassium-sparing (Systemic)
Diuretics, Thiazide (Systemic).

Cross-sensitivity and/or related problems

For hydrochlorothiazide—Patients sensitive to other sulfonamide-type medications, bumetanide, furosemide, or carbonic anhydrase inhibitors may be sensitive to hydrochlorothiazide also.

Geriatrics

Although appropriate studies with these medications have not been performed in the geriatric population, the elderly may be more sensitive to the hypotensive and electrolyte effects. In addition, elderly patients are more likely to have age-related renal function impairment, which may require caution in patients receiving these medications.

Drug interactions and/or related problems

The following drug interactions and/or related problems have been selected on the basis of their potential clinical significance (possible mechanism in parentheses where appropriate)—not necessarily inclusive (» = major clinical significance):

Note: Combinations containing any of the following medications, depending on the amount present, may also interact with this medication.

For amiloride

» Adrenocorticoids, glucocorticoid, especially with significant mineralocorticoid activity

» Adrenocorticoids, mineralocorticoid

   Amantadine

   Amphotericin B, parenteral

   Anticoagulants, coumarin- or indandione-derivative

   Anti-inflammatory drugs, nonsteroidal (NSAIDs), especially indomethacin

» Blood from blood banks

» Captopril

   Carbonic anhydrase inhibitors

» Corticotropin (ACTH)

» Cyclosporine
» Diuretics, other potassium-sparing
Dopamine
» Enalapril
Estrogens
Exchange resins, sodium cycle (such as sodium polystyrene sulfonate)
Glucose-insulin infusion
Hypotension-producing medications
Laxatives
» Lisinopril
» Lithium
» Low-salt milk
» Potassium-containing medications
» Potassium supplements or substances containing high levels of potassium
Salt substitutes
Sodium bicarbonate
Sympathomimetics

For hydrochlorothiazide
» Adrenocorticoids, glucocorticoid, especially with significant mineralocorticoid activity
» Adrenocorticoids, mineralocorticoid
Allopurinol
Amphotericin B, parenteral
Anticoagulants, coumarin- or indandione-derivative
Antidiabetic agents, oral
Anti-inflammatory drugs, nonsteroidal (NSAIDs), especially indomethacin
Calcium-containing medications
Carbonic anhydrase inhibitors
Cholestyramine
Colchicine
Colestipol
» Corticotropin (ACTH)
Diflunisal
» Digitalis glycosides
Dopamine
Estrogens
Exchange resins, sodium cycle (such as sodium polystyrene sulfonate)
Glucose-insulin infusion
Hypotension-producing medications
Insulin
» Lithium
» Methenamine
Neuromuscular blocking agents, nondepolarizing
Photosensitizing medications, other
Probenecid
Sodium bicarbonate
Sulfinpyrazone
Sympathomimetics

For spironolactone
» Adrenocorticoids, glucocorticoid, especially with significant mineralocorticoid activity
» Adrenocorticoids, mineralocorticoid
Amantadine
Ammonium chloride
Amphotericin B, parenteral
Anticoagulants, coumarin- or indandione-derivative
Anti-inflammatory drugs, nonsteroidal (NSAIDs), especially indomethacin
» Blood from blood banks
» Captopril
» Carbenoxolone
Carbonic anhydrase inhibitors
» Corticotropin (ACTH)
» Cyclosporine
» Digoxin

» Diuretics, other potassium-sparing
Dopamine
» Enalapril
Estrogens
Exchange resins, sodium cycle (such as sodium polystyrene sulfonate)
Glucose-insulin infusion
Hypotension-producing medications
Laxatives
» Lisinopril
» Lithium
» Low-salt milk
» Potassium-containing medications
» Potassium supplements or substances containing high levels of potassium
Salt substitutes
Sodium bicarbonate
Sympathomimetics

For triamterene
» Adrenocorticoids, glucocorticoid, especially with significant mineralocorticoid activity
» Adrenocorticoids, mineralocorticoid
Allopurinol
Amantadine
Amphotericin B, parenteral
Anticoagulants, coumarin- or indandione-derivative
Antidiabetic agents, oral
Anti-inflammatory drugs, nonsteroidal (NSAIDs), especially indomethacin
» Blood from blood banks
» Captopril
Carbonic anhydrase inhibitors
Colchicine
» Corticotropin (ACTH)
» Cyclosporine
» Diuretics, other potassium-sparing
Dopamine
» Enalapril
Estrogens
Exchange resins, sodium cycle (such as sodium polystyrene sulfonate)
Glucose-insulin infusion
Hypotension-producing medications
Insulin
Laxatives
» Lisinopril
» Lithium
» Low-salt milk
» Potassium-containing medications
» Potassium supplements or substances containing high levels of potassium
Probenecid
Salt substitutes
Sodium bicarbonate
Sulfinpyrazone
Sympathomimetics

Contraindications/Medical problems
The contraindications/medical problems included have been selected on the basis of their potential clinical significance (reasons given in parentheses where appropriate)—not necessarily inclusive (» = major clinical significance).

Except under special circumstances, this medication should not be used when the following medical problem exists:
» Hyperkalemia

Risk-benefit should be considered when the following medical problems exist:
For amiloride
» Anuria or renal function impairment

Congestive heart failure
Diabetes mellitus
» Diabetic nephropathy
» Hepatic function impairment
Hyponatremia
Metabolic or respiratory acidosis, predisposition to
Sensitivity to amiloride

For hydrochlorothiazide
» Anuria or severe renal function impairment
Congestive heart failure
Diabetes mellitus, especially in patients with confirmed or suspected renal insufficiency
Gout, history of
» Hepatic function impairment
Hypercalcemia
Hyperuricemia
Hyponatremia
Lupus erythematosus, history of
Pancreatitis
Sensitivity to thiazide diuretics
Sympathectomy

For spironolactone
» Anuria or renal function impairment
Congestive heart failure
Diabetes mellitus
» Diabetic nephropathy
» Hepatic function impairment
Hyponatremia
Menstrual abnormalities or breast enlargement
Metabolic or respiratory acidosis, predisposition to
Sensitivity to spironolactone

For triamterene
» Anuria or renal function impairment
Congestive heart failure
Diabetes mellitus
» Diabetic nephropathy
Gout, history of
» Hepatic function impairment
Hyperuricemia
Hyponatremia
Metabolic or respiratory acidosis, predisposition to
Nephrolithiasis, history of
Sensitivity to triamterene

Side/Adverse Effects

Note: To save space, only the presenting symptoms are listed in the *Side/Adverse Effects* section of this combination monograph. For the complete text of this section each of the components of this combination, see—

Diuretics, Potassium-sparing (Systemic)
Diuretics, Thiazide (Systemic).

Those indicating need for medical attention
Signs and symptoms of hyperkalemia, hypokalemia, or hyponatremia
Confusion; dryness of mouth; increased thirst; irregular heartbeats; mood or mental changes; muscle cramps or pain; numbness or tingling in hands, feet, or lips; shortness of breath or difficulty breathing; unusual tiredness or weakness; weak pulse; weakness or heaviness of legs
Incidence rare
Black, tarry stools; blood in urine or stools; cough or hoarseness; fever or chills; joint pain; lower back or side pain; painful or difficult urination; pinpoint red spots on skin; skin rash or hives; stomach pain, severe, with nausea and vomiting; unusual bleeding or bruising; yellow eyes or skin
Incidence rare (for triamterene only)
Bright red tongue; burning, inflamed feeling in tongue; cracked corners of mouth

Those indicating need for medical attention only if they continue or are bothersome
Incidence more frequent (less frequent with triamterene)
Loss of appetite; nausea and vomiting; stomach cramps and diarrhea; upset stomach
Incidence less frequent
Decreased sexual ability; dizziness or lightheadedness when getting up from a lying or sitting position; headache—more common with amiloride; *increased sensitivity of skin to sunlight*
Incidence less frequent (for amiloride only)
Constipation
Incidence related to dose and/or duration of therapy (for spironolactone only)
Breast tenderness in females; clumsiness; deepening of voice in females; enlargement of breasts in males; increased hair growth in females; irregular menstrual periods; sweating

Patient Consultation

In providing consultation, consider emphasizing the following selected information (» = major clinical significance):

Before using this medication
» Conditions affecting use, especially:
Sensitivity to the potassium-sparing diuretic prescribed, hydrochlorothiazide or other thiazide diuretics, other sulfonamide-type medications, bumetanide, furosemide, or carbonic anhydrase inhibitors
Pregnancy—Not recommended for routine use; triamterene crosses placenta; spironolactone may cross placenta; hydrochlorothiazide may cause jaundice, thrombocytopenia, hypokalemia in infant
Breast-feeding—Hydrochlorothiazide excreted in breast milk; spironolactone, triamterene may be excreted in breast milk
Use in the elderly—Elderly patients may be more sensitive to hypotensive and electrolyte effects
Use by athletes—Diuretics are banned and tested for by the U.S. Olympic Committee (USOC) and the National Collegiate Athletic Association (NCAA)
Other medications, especially adrenocorticoids, captopril, cyclosporine, digitalis glycosides, enalapril, lisinopril, lithium, methenamine, other potassium-sparing diuretics, or potassium-containing medications or supplements
Other medical problems, especially renal function impairment or hepatic function impairment

Proper use of this medication
Diuretic effects of the medication and timing of doses to minimize inconvenience of diuresis
Getting into habit of taking at same time each day to help increase compliance
Taking with meals or milk to reduce stomach upset
Missed dose: Taking as soon as possible; not taking if almost time for next dose; not doubling doses
» Proper storage
For use an an antihypertensive
Importance of diet; possible need for sodium restriction and/or weight reduction
» Patient may not experience symptoms of hypertension; importance of taking medication even if feeling well
» Does not cure, but helps control hypertension; possible need for lifelong therapy; checking with physician before discontinuing medication; serious consequences of untreated hypertension

Precautions while using this medication
Regular visits to physician to check progress
» Possibility of hypokalemia or hyperkalemia; possible need for monitoring potassium in diet; not changing diet without first checking with physician
To prevent dehydration, checking with physician if severe nausea, vomiting, or diarrhea occurs and continues

Diabetics: May increase blood sugar levels

Possible photosensitivity; avoiding too much sun; using protective clothing and sun block product; avoiding use of sunlamp, tanning bed, or tanning booth

Caution if any kind of surgery or emergency treatment is required

Caution if any laboratory tests required; possible interference with test results

For triamterene and hydrochlorothiazide combination

Not changing brands of triamterene and hydrochlorothiazide combination without checking with physician

For use an an antihypertensive

» Not taking other medications, especially nonprescription sympathomimetics, unless discussed with physician

Side/adverse effects

Signs of potential side effects, especially allergic reaction, agranulocytosis, cholecystitis, pancreatitis, hepatic function impairment, hyperuricemia, nephrolithiasis, thrombocytopenia, hyperkalemia or other electrolyte imbalance, and megaloblastosis (for triamterene)

For spironolactone

Possibility of enlargement of breasts in males; usually reversible within several months

General Dosing Information

Dosage must be adjusted to meet the individual requirements of each patient, based on clinical response. The lowest effective dosage should be utilized to minimize potential electrolyte imbalance.

Fixed-dosage combinations are generally not recommended in initial therapy and are useful in subsequent therapy only when the proportion of the component agents corresponds to the dose of the individual agents, as determined by titration.

If a single daily dose is indicated, it is preferably taken on arising in order to minimize the effect of increased frequency of urination on sleep.

When these medications are used to promote diuresis, intermittent dosage schedules (drug-free days) may reduce the possibility of electrolyte imbalance or hyperuricemia resulting from therapy.

The normal adult concentration of serum potassium is 3.5 to 5.0 mEq (mmoL) per liter with 4.5 mEq (mmoL) often being used as a reference point. Potassium concentrations exceeding 6 mEq (mmoL) per liter are dangerous because of possible precipitation of cardiac arrhythmias. Normal potassium concentrations tend to be higher in neonates (7.7 mEq [mmoL] per liter) than in adults.

Serum potassium concentrations do not necessarily indicate the true body potassium concentration. A rise in plasma pH or an increase in the circulating levels of insulin or epinephrine may cause a decrease in plasma potassium concentration and an increase in the intracellular potassium concentration.

If anuria or signs of progressive hepatic or renal (including azotemia or hyperkalemia) dysfunction occur, it is recommended that treatment with this medication be permanently discontinued. If hyperkalemia is associated with ECG changes, prompt additional therapy with intravenous sodium bicarbonate, calcium gluconate, or calcium chloride or with oral or rectal sodium polystyrene sulfonate, or with parenteral glucose and insulin may be indicated. It is important to remember that severe hyperkalemia may occur suddenly and may not be preceded by any warning signs.

Although concurrent administration of potassium supplements may be indicated in some patients considered to be at high risk for developing hypokalemia, extreme caution in administering potassium supplements is recommended, and close monitoring of serum potassium concentrations is essential. Loss of potassium is not clinically significant in most patients, and supplementation leads to a risk of development of hyperkalemia. Use of potassium supplements is not recommended in patients with renal function impairment.

Recent evidence suggests that withdrawal of antihypertensive therapy prior to surgery is not necessary, but that the anesthesiologist must be aware of such therapy.

Diet/Nutrition

It is recommended that potassium-sparing diuretics be taken with or after meals to minimize stomach upset, and possibly also to enhance bioavailability.

AMILORIDE AND HYDROCHLOROTHIAZIDE

Summary of Differences

For amiloride

Pharmacology:

Biotransformation—None; excreted unchanged.

Onset of action—Diuretic: Single dose—Within 2 hours.

Duration of action—Diuretic: Single dose—24 hours.

Side/adverse effects: Amiloride may cause constipation or muscle cramps. Agranulocytosis has not been reported.

Oral Dosage Forms

AMILORIDE HYDROCHLORIDE AND HYDROCHLOROTHIAZIDE TABLETS USP

Usual adult dose:

Diuretic; or

Antihypertensive[1]—Oral, 1 or 2 tablets per day.

Note: Geriatric patients may be more sensitive to the effects of the usual adult dose.

Auxiliary labeling:

• Take with meals or milk.

• Avoid overexposure to the sun or use of sunlamp.

• Do not take other medicines without your doctor's advice.

---

[1]Not included in Canadian product labeling.

SPIRONOLACTONE AND HYDROCHLOROTHIAZIDE

Summary of Differences

For spironolactone

Pharmacology:

Mechanism of action/effect—Aldosterone antagonist.

Protein-binding—Very high (more than 90%).

Biotransformation—Hepatic, extensive, to active metabolite (canrenone).

Duration of action—Diuretic: Multiple doses—2 to 3 days.

Precautions:

Carcinogenicity—Tumorigenic in rats and possibly associated with breast carcinoma in humans.

Drug interactions and/or related problems—Ammonium chloride (systemic acidosis) and digoxin (increases digoxin half-life).

Laboratory value alterations—May falsely increase plasma cortisol determinations by Mattingly (fluorometric) assay and may falsely elevate digoxin radioimmunoassays.

Contraindications/medical problems—Menstrual abnormalities or breast enlargement.

Side/adverse effects: Endocrine or antiandrogenic effects more common at doses exceeding 100 mg per day. May cause CNS effects and causes more frequent gastrointestinal irritation.

Additional Dosing Information

See also *General Dosing Information.*

When the spironolactone and hydrochlorothiazide combination is added to therapy with another diuretic or antihypertensive agent, it is recommended that the dosage of the other drug (especially ganglionic blocking agents) be reduced by at least 50% and then adjusted as required.

Oral Dosage Forms

SPIRONOLACTONE AND HYDROCHLOROTHIAZIDE TABLETS USP

Usual adult dose:
Diuretic—Edema due to congestive heart failure, hepatic cirrhosis, or nephrotic syndrome: Maintenance—Oral, 1 tablet four times a day (1 to 8 tablets a day).
Antihypertensive—Maintenance: Oral, 2 to 4 tablets a day in divided doses.
Note: Geriatric patients may be more sensitive to the effects of the usual adult dose.

Auxiliary labeling:
• Take with meals or milk.
• Avoid overexposure to the sun or use of sunlamp.
• Do not take other medicines without your doctor's advice.

TRIAMTERENE AND HYDROCHLOROTHIAZIDE

Summary of Differences

For triamterene
Pharmacology:
Biotransformation—Hepatic.
Onset of action—Diuretic: Single dose—2 to 4 hours.
Duration of action—Diuretic: Single dose—7 to 9 hours.
Precautions:
Drug interactions and/or related problems—Use with allopurinol, colchicine, probenecid, or sulfinpyrazone may raise blood uric acid concentrations; use with antidiabetic agents or insulin may raise blood glucose concentrations.
Laboratory value alterations—May interfere with fluorescent measurement of quinidine.
Contraindications/medical problems—Hyperuricemia or gout; history of nephrolithiasis.
Side/adverse effects: Nephrolithiasis; megaloblastosis; photosensitivity; thrombocytopenia. No decrease in sexual ability reported.

Additional Dosing Information

See also *General Dosing Information.*

Since triamterene is a weak folic acid antagonist, it may contribute to development of megaloblastosis in patients who have depleted folic acid stores (e.g., in pregnancy, hepatic cirrhosis).

Oral Dosage Forms

TRIAMTERENE AND HYDROCHLOROTHIAZIDE CAPSULES USP

Note: Triamterene and hydrochlorothiazide capsules are not commercially available in Canada.

Usual adult dose: Oral, 1 or 2 capsules two times a day, as determined by individual titration with the component agents; some patients may be maintained on 1 capsule a day or every other day.

Note: Geriatric patients may be more sensitive to the effects of the usual adult dose.

Usual adult prescribing limits: Up to 4 capsules daily.

Auxiliary labeling:
• Take with meals or milk.
• Avoid overexposure to the sun or use of sunlamp.
• Do not take other medicines without your doctor's advice.

TRIAMTERENE AND HYDROCHLOROTHIAZIDE TABLETS USP

Usual adult dose:
Maxzide—Oral, 1 tablet per day, as determined by individual titration.
Apo-Triazide; Dyazide (Canada); *Novotriamzide*—Oral, 1 or 2 tablets two times a day, as determined by individual titration with the component agents; some patients may be maintained on 1 tablet a day or every other day.
Note: Geriatric patients may be more sensitive to the effects of the usual adult dose.

Auxiliary labeling:
• Take with meals or milk.
• Avoid overexposure to the sun or use of sunlamp.
• Do not take other medicines without your doctor's advice.

DIURETICS, THIAZIDE   Systemic

INN: Included in brackets after individual generic listings, if different
from U.S. generic names.

Some commonly used *brand names* are:

In the U.S.—
Anhydron [Cyclothiazide]
Aquatensen
[Methyclothiazide]
Diucardin
[Hydroflumethiazide]
Diulo [Metolazone]
Diuril [Chlorothiazide]
Enduron [Methyclothiazide]
Esidrix
[Hydrochlorothiazide]
Exna [Benzthiazide]
Hydrex [Benzthiazide]
Hydro-chlor
[Hydrochlorothiazide]
Hydro-D
[Hydrochlorothiazide]
HydroDIURIL
[Hydrochlorothiazide]

In Canada—
Apo-Chlorthalidone
[Chlorthalidone]
Apo-Hydro
[Hydrochlorothiazide]
Diuchlor H
[Hydrochlorothiazide]
Duretic [Methyclothiazide]
HydroDIURIL
[Hydrochlorothiazide]
Hygroton [Chlorthalidone]
Naturetin
[Bendroflumethiazide]

Hydromox [Quinethazone]
Hygroton [Chlorthalidone]
Metahydrin
[Trichlormethiazide]
Mykrox [Metolazone]
Naqua
[Trichlormethiazide]
Naturetin
[Bendroflumethiazide]
Oretic
[Hydrochlorothiazide]
Renese [Polythiazide]
Saluron
[Hydroflumethiazide]
Thalitone [Chlorthalidone]
Trichlorex
[Trichlormethiazide]
Zaroxolyn [Metolazone]

Neo-Codema
[Hydrochlorothiazide]
Novo-Hydrazide
[Hydrochlorothiazide]
Novo-Thalidone
[Chlorthalidone]
Uridon [Chlorthalidone]
Urozide
[Hydrochlorothiazide]
Zaroxolyn [Metolazone]

BENDROFLUMETHIAZIDE
Oral
Bendroflumethiazide Tablets USP
In the U.S. and Canada—*Naturetin*
BENZTHIAZIDE†
Oral
Benzthiazide Tablets USP†
In the U.S.—*Exna; Hydrex;* GENERIC
CHLOROTHIAZIDE†
Oral
Chlorothiazide Oral Suspension USP†
In the U.S.—*Diuril*
Chlorothiazide Tablets USP†
In the U.S.—*Diuril;* GENERIC
Parenteral
Chlorothiazide Sodium for Injection USP†
In the U.S.—*Diuril*
CHLORTHALIDONE [INN: Chlortalidone]
Oral
Chlorthalidone Tablets USP
In the U.S.—*Hygroton; Thalitone;* GENERIC
In Canada—*Apo-Chlorthalidone; Hygroton; Novo-Thalidone;
Uridon;* GENERIC

CYCLOTHIAZIDE†
Oral
Cyclothiazide Tablets USP†
In the U.S.—*Anhydron*
HYDROCHLOROTHIAZIDE
Oral
Hydrochlorothiazide Oral Solution†
In the U.S.—GENERIC
Hydrochlorothiazide Tablets USP
In the U.S.—*Esidrix; Hydro-chlor; Hydro-D; HydroDIURIL;
Oretic;* GENERIC
In Canada—*Apo-Hydro; Diuchlor H; HydroDIURIL; Neo-Co-
dema; Novo-Hydrazide; Urozide;* GENERIC
HYDROFLUMETHIAZIDE†
Oral
Hydroflumethiazide Tablets USP†
In the U.S.—*Diucardin; Saluron;* GENERIC
METHYCLOTHIAZIDE
Oral
Methyclothiazide Tablets USP
In the U.S.—*Aquatensen; Enduron;* GENERIC
In Canada—*Duretic*
METOLAZONE
Oral
Extended Metolazone Tablets
In the U.S.—*Diulo; Zaroxolyn*
In Canada—*Zaroxolyn*
Prompt Metolazone Tablets†
In the U.S.—*Mykrox*
POLYTHIAZIDE†
Oral
Polythiazide Tablets USP†
In the U.S.—*Renese*
QUINETHAZONE†
Oral
Quinethazone Tablets USP†
In the U.S.—*Hydromox*
TRICHLORMETHIAZIDE†
Oral
Trichlormethiazide Tablets USP†
In the U.S.—*Metahydrin; Naqua; Trichlorex;* GENERIC

†Not commercially available in Canada.

Category: Diuretic; antihypertensive; antidiuretic (central and nephrogenic diabetes insipidus); antiurolithic (calcium calculi).

Indications

Note: Bracketed information in the *Indications* section refers to uses
not included in U.S. product labeling.

Accepted

Edema (treatment)—Indications include edema associated with congestive heart failure, hepatic cirrhosis with ascites, adrenocorticoid
and estrogen therapy, and some forms of renal function impairment including nephrotic syndrome, acute glomerulonephritis, and
chronic renal failure. However, prompt metolazone tablets are not
indicated for treatment of edema because a safe and effective
diuretic dosage has not been established.

Hypertension (treatment)—Thiazide diuretics are indicated either alone
or as adjunctive therapy in the treatment of hypertension.

In the 1988 Report of the Joint National Committee on Detection, Evaluation, and Treatment of High Blood Pressure, a step-like progression in choice of treatments for essential hypertension is recommended:

> Nonpharmacologic management (especially sodium restriction, weight reduction and exercise, and moderation of alcohol consumption) is recommended first for some patients, including those with mild hypertension, and is recommended as an adjunct to all pharmacologic hypertensive therapy.

> Initial drug therapy usually consists of a diuretic, beta-adrenergic blocking agent, calcium channel blocking agent, or angiotensin-converting enzyme (ACE) inhibitor. If adequate blood pressure control is not achieved and the patient is adherent to the treatment program and not experiencing significant side effects, dosage of the drug may be increased, a drug from another one of these initial classes may be added or substituted, or a second drug from a different class—centrally acting alpha-adrenergic blocking agents (e.g., clonidine, guanabenz, guanfacine, methyldopa), peripheral-acting adrenergic antagonists (e.g., guanadrel, guanethidine, rauwolfia alkaloids), post-synaptic alpha-1 peripheral adrenergic inhibitors (e.g., prazosin, terazosin), or vasodilators (e.g., hydralazine, minoxidil)—may be added or substituted.

> If necessary, a drug from another class in the second group may be substituted or added as a third drug. If blood pressure control is still not achieved, a drug from still another class may be substituted or added as a fourth drug, or the patient may need further evaluation and/or referral.

[Diabetes insipidus, central or nephrogenic (treatment)][1]—Thiazide diuretics are used in the treatment of central and nephrogenic diabetes insipidus.

[Renal calculi, calcium (prophylaxis)][1]—Thiazide diuretics are also used for prevention of calcium-containing renal stones.

---

[1]Not included in Canadian product labeling.

Pharmacology

Note: Although they are not chemically the same, chlorthalidone, metolazone, and quinethazone have the same actions as the thiazide diuretics.

Mechanism of action/Effect:

Diuretic—Thiazide diuretics increase urinary excretion of sodium and water by inhibiting sodium reabsorption in the early distal tubules. They increase the rate of delivery of tubular fluid and electrolytes to the distal sites of hydrogen and potassium ion secretion, while plasma volume contraction increases aldosterone production. The increased delivery and increase in aldosterone levels promote sodium reabsorption at the distal tubules, thus increasing the loss of potassium and hydrogen ions.

Antihypertensive—Diuretics lower blood pressure initially by reducing plasma and extracellular fluid volume; cardiac output also decreases. Eventually, cardiac output returns to normal. Thiazide diuretics decrease peripheral resistance by a direct peripheral effect on blood vessels.

Antidiuretic—The antidiuretic effect of thiazide diuretics is a result of mild sodium and water depletion leading to increased reabsorption of glomerular filtrate in the proximal renal tubule and reduced delivery of tubular fluid available for excretion.

Antiurolithic (calcium calculi)—Thiazide diuretics decrease urinary calcium excretion by a direct action on the distal tubule, which may prevent recurrence of calcium-containing renal calculi.

Drug	Half-life (hr)	Diuretic Effect (hr)		
		Onset	Peak	Duration
Bendroflumethiazide	8.5	1–2	4	6–12
Benzthiazide		2	4–6	12–18
Chlorothiazide	1–2	2	4	6–12
Chlorthalidone	35 to 50	2	2	48–72
Cyclothiazide		2–4	7–12	18–24
Hydrochlorothiazide	5.6–14.8	2	4	6–12
Hydroflumethiazide	17	1–2	3–4	18–24
Methyclothiazid		2	6	>24
Metolazone	14	1*	2*	12–24*
Polythiazide		2	6	24–48
Quinethazone		2	6	18–24
Trichlormethiazide		2	6	24

*Information on diuretic effect applies to extended metolazone tablets.

Note: In the absence of edema, negative sodium balance induced by thiazide diuretics lasts for 3 days to 4 weeks with chronic administration. Extracellular fluid volumes remain steady thereafter, although at a lower concentration and volume than before initiation of therapy.

The antihypertensive effects of the thiazide diuretics may be noted after 3 to 4 days of therapy, although up to 3 to 4 weeks may be required for optimal effect. Antihypertensive effects persist for up to 1 week after withdrawal of therapy.

Precautions to Consider

Cross-sensitivity and/or related problems

Patients sensitive to other sulfonamide-type medications, bumetanide, furosemide, or carbonic anhydrase inhibitors may be sensitive to this medication also.

Geriatrics

Although appropriate studies on the relationship of age to the effects of thiazide diuretics have not been performed in the geriatric population, the elderly may be more sensitive to the hypotensive and electrolyte effects. In addition, elderly patients are more likely to have age-related renal function impairment, which may require caution in patients receiving thiazide diuretics.

Drug interactions and/or related problems

The following drug interactions and/or related problems have been selected on the basis of their potential clinical significance (possible mechanism in parentheses where appropriate)—not necessarily inclusive (» = major clinical significance):

Note: Combinations containing any of the following medications, depending on the amount present, may also interact with this medication.

Amantadine
(hydrochlorothiazide may reduce the renal clearance of amantadine, resulting in increased plasma concentrations and possible amantadine toxicity)

Amiodarone
(concurrent use of thiazide diuretics with amiodarone may lead to an increased risk of arrhythmias associated with hypokalemia)

Anticoagulants, coumarin- or indandione-derivative
(effects may be decreased when used concurrently with thiazide diuretics as a result of reduction of plasma volume leading to concentration of procoagulant factors in the blood; in addition, diuretic-induced improvement of hepatic congestion may lead to improved hepatic function resulting in increased procoagulant factor synthesis; dosage adjustments may be necessary)

Antidiabetic agents, oral, or
Insulin
(thiazide diuretics may raise blood glucose concentrations; for adult-onset diabetics, dosage adjustment of hypoglycemic medications may be necessary during and after thiazide diuretic therapy; insulin requirements may be increased, decreased, or unchanged)

Anti-inflammatory drugs, nonsteroidal (NSAIDs), especially indomethacin
(may antagonize the natriuresis and increase in plasma renin activity [PRA] caused by thiazide diuretics; they may also reduce the antihypertensive effect and increase in urine volume caused by thiazide diuretics, possibly by inhibiting renal prostaglandin synthesis and/or by causing sodium and fluid retention; the patient should be carefully monitored to confirm that the desired effect is being obtained)

(in addition, concurrent use of NSAIDs with a diuretic may increase the risk of renal failure secondary to a decrease in renal blood flow caused by inhibition of renal prostaglandin synthesis)

Calcium-containing medications
(concurrent use of thiazide diuretics with large doses of calcium may result in hypercalcemia because of reduced calcium excretion)

» Cholestyramine or
» Colestipol
(may inhibit gastrointestinal absorption of the thiazide diuretics; administration of thiazide diuretics 1 hour before or 4 hours after cholestyramine or colestipol is recommended)

Diazoxide
(concurrent use with thiazide diuretics may enhance hyperglycemic effects; monitoring of blood glucose levels and/or dosage adjustment of one or both agents may be necessary)

(in addition, concurrent use with thiazide diuretics may enhance hyperuricemic and antihypertensive effects)

Diflunisal
(concurrent use of hydrochlorothiazide with diflunisal produces significantly increased plasma concentrations of hydrochlorothiazide; in addition, the hyperuricemic effect of hydrochlorothiazide is decreased)

» Digitalis glycosides
(concurrent use with thiazide diuretics may enhance the possibility of digitalis toxicity associated with hypokalemia or hypomagnesemia)

Dopamine
(concurrent use may increase the diuretic effect of either thiazide diuretics or dopamine, as a result of dopamine's direct effect on dopaminergic receptors to produce vasodilation of renal vasculature and increase renal blood flow; dopamine also has a direct natriuretic effect)

Hypokalemia-causing medications, other
(risk of severe hypokalemia due to other hypokalemia-causing medications may be increased; monitoring of serum potassium concentrations and cardiac function and potassium supplementation may be necessary)

Hypotension-producing medications, other
(antihypertensive and/or diuretic effects may be potentiated when these medications are used concurrently with thiazide diuretics; although some antihypertensive and/or diuretic combinations are frequently used for therapeutic advantage, when used concurrently dosage adjustments may be necessary)

» Lithium
(concurrent use with thiazide diuretics is not recommended, as they may provoke lithium toxicity because of reduced renal clearance; in addition, lithium has nephrotoxic effects)

Neuromuscular blocking agents, nondepolarizing
(thiazide diuretics may induce hypokalemia, which may enhance the blockade of nondepolarizing neuromuscular blocking agents; serum potassium determinations may be necessary prior to administration of nondepolarizing neuromuscular blocking agents; careful postoperative monitoring of the patient may be necessary following concurrent or sequential use, especially if there is a possibility of incomplete reversal of neuromuscular blockade)

Sympathomimetics
(may antagonize the antihypertensive effect of the thiazide diuretics; the patient should be carefully monitored to confirm that the desired effect is being obtained)

Contraindications/Medical problems
The contraindications/medical problems included have been selected on the basis of their potential clinical significance (reasons given in parentheses where appropriate)—not necessarily inclusive (» = major clinical significance).

Risk-benefit should be considered when the following medical problems exist:
» Anuria or severe renal function impairment
(ineffective; may precipitate azotemia; may produce cumulative effects)

Diabetes mellitus
(hypoglycemic medication requirements may be altered)

Gout, history of, or
Hyperuricemia
(serum uric acid concentrations may be elevated)

Hepatic function impairment
(risk of dehydration which may precipitate hepatic coma and death; plasma half-life is unaltered)

Hypercalcemia or
Hypercholesterolemia or
Hypertriglyceridemia or
Hyponatremia
(conditions may be exacerbated; onset of hyponatremia can be sudden and life-threatening)

Lupus erythematosus, history of
(exacerbation or activation by thiazide diuretics has been reported)

Pancreatitis

Sensitivity to thiazide diuretics or other sulfonamide-derived medications

Sympathectomy
(antihypertensive effects may be enhanced)

» Caution is required also in jaundiced infants because of the risk of hyperbilirubinemia.

Side/Adverse Effects

Note: Most side effects are dose-related.

The following side/adverse effects have been selected on the basis of their potential clinical significance (possible signs and symptoms in parentheses where appropriate)—not necessarily inclusive:

Those indicating need for medical attention
Incidence more frequent
Electrolyte imbalance such as hyponatremia (confusion, convulsions, decreased mentation, fatigue, irritability, muscle cramps), *hypochloremic alkalosis, and hypokalemia* (dryness of mouth, increased thirst, irregular heartbeat, mood or mental changes, muscle cramps or pain, nausea or vomiting, unusual tiredness or weakness, weak pulse)

Note: *Hyponatremia* as a complication is rare, but constitutes a medical emergency as onset may be rapid.

Incidence rare
>   *Agranulocytosis* (fever or chills, cough or hoarseness, lower back or side pain, painful or difficult urination); ***allergic reaction*** (skin rash or hives); ***cholecystitis or pancreatitis*** (severe stomach pain with nausea and vomiting); ***gout or hyperuricemia*** (joint pain, lower back or side pain); ***hepatic function impairment*** (yellow eyes or skin); ***thrombocytopenia*** (unusual bleeding or bruising; black, tarry stools; blood in urine or stools; pinpoint red spots on skin)

Those indicating need for medical attention only if they continue or are bothersome
Incidence less frequent
>   *Anorexia* (loss of appetite); ***decreased sexual ability; diarrhea; orthostatic hypotension*** (dizziness or lightheadedness when getting up from a lying or sitting position); ***photosensitivity*** (increased sensitivity of skin to sunlight); ***upset stomach***

Patient Consultation

In providing consultation, consider emphasizing the following selected information (» = major clinical significance):

Before using this medication
>   Conditions affecting use, especially:
>   Sensitivity to thiazide diuretics, other sulfonamide-type medications, bumetanide, furosemide, or carbonic anhydrase inhibitors
>   Pregnancy—Not recommended for routine use; may cause jaundice, thrombocytopenia, hypokalemia in infant
>   Breast-feeding—Excreted in breast milk; recommended that nursing mothers avoid thiazides during first month of breast-feeding because of reports of suppression of lactation
>   Pediatrics—Caution if giving to infants with jaundice
>   Use in the elderly—Elderly patients may be more sensitive to hypotensive and electrolyte effects
>   Use by athletes—Diuretics are banned and tested for by the U.S. Olympic Committee (USOC), the International Olympic Committee (IOC), and the National Collegiate Athletic Association (NCAA)
>   Other medications, especially cholestyramine, colestipol, digitalis glycosides, or lithium
>   Other medical problems, especially anuria or severe renal function impairment or infants with jaundice

Proper use of this medication
Diuretic effects of the medication and timing of doses to minimize inconvenience of diuresis (except in diabetes insipidus)
Getting into habit of taking at same time each day to help increase compliance
Proper administration of concentrated oral hydrochlorothiazide solution: Taking orally; special dropper to be used for accurate measuring
Missed dose: Taking as soon as possible; not taking if almost time for next dose; not doubling doses
»   Proper storage
For use as an antihypertensive
Importance of diet; possible need for sodium restriction and/or weight reduction
»   Patient may not experience symptoms of hypertension; importance of taking medication even if feeling well
»   Does not cure, but helps control hypertension; possible need for lifelong therapy; checking with physician before discontinuing medication; serious consequences of untreated hypertension

Precautions while using this medication
Regular visits to physician to check progress
»   Possibility of hypokalemia; possible need for additional potassium in diet; not changing diet without first checking with physician
To prevent dehydration, checking with physician if severe nausea, vomiting, or diarrhea occurs and continues
Diabetics: May increase blood sugar levels

Possible photosensitivity; avoiding unprotected exposure to sun; using protective clothing and sun block product; avoiding use of sunlamp, tanning bed, or tanning booth
For use as an antihypertensive
»   Not taking other medications, especially nonprescription sympathomimetics, unless discussed with physician

Side/adverse effects
Signs of potential side effects, especially electrolyte imbalance, agranulocytosis, allergic reaction, cholecystitis, pancreatitis, hepatic function impairment, hyperuricemia, gout, and thrombocytopenia

General Dosing Information

The lowest effective dosage should be utilized to minimize potential electrolyte imbalance and the reflex increase in renin and aldosterone levels.

A single daily dose is preferably taken on arising in order to minimize the effect of increased frequency of urination on sleep. When used to promote diuresis, intermittent dosage schedules (drug-free days) may reduce the possibility of electrolyte imbalance or hyperuricemia resulting from therapy.

Concurrent administration of potassium supplements or potassium-sparing diuretics may be indicated in patients considered to be at higher risk for developing hypokalemia. Caution in administering potassium supplements is recommended, however, since loss of potassium is not clinically significant in most patients, and supplementation leads to a risk of development of hyperkalemia.

Recent evidence suggests that withdrawal of antihypertensive therapy prior to surgery is not necessary, but that the anesthesiologist must be aware of such therapy.

For hypertension
Low dose thiazide therapy has been found to be effective in the treatment of hypertension.

BENDROFLUMETHIAZIDE

Summary of Differences

Pharmacology:
Protein binding—Very high.
Half-life—Normal: 8.5 hours.
Onset of action—Diuretic: 1 to 2 hours.
Time to peak effect—Diuretic: 4 hours.
Duration of action—Diuretic: 6 to 12 hours.
Laboratory value alterations: May produce false negative results in phentolamine, phenolsulfonphthalein, and tyramine tests.

Oral Dosage Forms

Note: Bracketed uses in the *Dosage Forms* section refer to categories of use and/or indications that are not included in U.S. product labeling.

BENDROFLUMETHIAZIDE TABLETS USP
Usual adult dose:
Diuretic; or
[Antidiuretic (central or nephrogenic diabetes insipidus)][1]—
Initial: Oral, 2.5 to 10 mg one or two times a day, once every other day, or once a day for three to five days a week.
Maintenance: Oral, 2.5 to 5 mg once a day, once every other day, or once a day for three to five days a week.
Antihypertensive—Oral, 2.5 to 20 mg per day, as a single dose or in two divided daily doses, the dosage being adjusted according to response.

Note: Geriatric patients may be more sensitive to the effects of the usual adult dose.

Auxiliary labeling:
- Avoid overexposure to the sun or use of sunlamp.
- Do not take other medicines without your doctor's advice.

---

[1]Not included in Canadian product labeling.

BENZTHIAZIDE

Summary of Differences

Pharmacology:
Onset of action—Diuretic: 2 hours.
Time to peak effect—Diuretic: 4 to 6 hours.
Duration of action—Diuretic: 12 to 18 hours.

Oral Dosage Forms

Note: Bracketed uses in the *Dosage Forms* section refer to categories of use and/or indications that are not included in U.S. product labeling.

BENZTHIAZIDE TABLETS USP

Usual adult dose:
Diuretic; or
[Antidiuretic (central or nephrogenic diabetes insipidus)]—Oral, 25 to 100 mg two times a day, once every other day, or once a day for three to five days a week.
Antihypertensive—Oral, 50 to 100 mg per day, as a single dose or in two divided daily doses, the dosage being adjusted according to response.

Note: Geriatric patients may be more sensitive to the effects of the usual adult dose.

Auxiliary labeling:
- Avoid overexposure to the sun or use of sunlamp.
- Do not take other medicines without your doctor's advice.

CHLOROTHIAZIDE

Summary of Differences

Pharmacology:
Protein binding—Low to high.
Half-life—Normal: 13 hours.
Onset of action—Diuretic: 2 hours.
Time to peak effect—Diuretic: 4 hours.
Duration of action—Diuretic: 6 to 12 hours.

Additional Dosing Information

See also *General Dosing Information.*

For parenteral dosage forms only:
- Care must be taken to avoid extravasation during intravenous administration.
- Chlorothiazide should not be administered intramuscularly or subcutaneously.

Oral Dosage Forms

Note: Bracketed uses in the *Dosage Forms* section refer to categories of use and/or indications that are not included in U.S. product labeling.

CHLOROTHIAZIDE ORAL SUSPENSION USP

Usual adult dose:
Diuretic; or
[Antidiuretic (central or nephrogenic diabetes insipidus)]—Oral, 250 mg every six to twelve hours.
Antihypertensive—Oral, 250 mg to 1 gram per day, as a single dose or in divided daily doses, the dosage being adjusted according to response.

Note: Geriatric patients may be more sensitive to the effects of the usual adult dose.

Auxiliary labeling:
- Shake well.
- Avoid overexposure to the sun or use of sunlamp.
- Do not take other medicines without your doctor's advice.

CHLOROTHIAZIDE TABLETS USP

Usual adult dose:
Diuretic; or
[Antidiuretic (central or nephrogenic diabetes insipidus)]—Oral, 250 mg every six to twelve hours.
Antihypertensive—Oral, 250 mg to 1 gram per day, as a single dose or in divided daily doses, the dosage being adjusted according to response.

Note: Geriatric patients may be more sensitive to the effects of the usual adult dose.

Auxiliary labeling:
- Avoid overexposure to the sun or use of sunlamp.
- Do not take other medicines without your doctor's advice.

Parenteral Dosage Forms

Note: Bracketed uses in the *Dosage Forms* section refer to categories of use and/or indications that are not included in U.S. product labeling.

CHLOROTHIAZIDE SODIUM FOR INJECTION USP

Usual adult dose:
Diuretic; or
[Antidiuretic (central or nephrogenic diabetes insipidus)]—Intravenous, 250 mg (base) every six to twelve hours.
Antihypertensive—Intravenous, 500 mg to 1 gram (base) of chlorothiazide a day, as a single dose or in two divided daily doses.

Note: Geriatric patients may be more sensitive to the effects of the usual adult dose.

Additional information:
Chlorothiazide Sodium for Injection USP is reconstituted for intravenous administration by adding no less than 18 mL of sterile water for injection to the vial and shaking to dissolve, producing a solution containing 25 mg (base) per mL.
Reconstituted solutions may be further diluted with dextrose injection or 0.9% sodium chloride injection for administration by intravenous infusion.

CHLORTHALIDONE

Summary of Differences

Pharmacology:
Although not chemically the same, chlorthalidone has the same actions as the thiazide diuretics.
Protein binding—Very high to carbonic anhydrase in red blood cells.
Half-life—Normal: 35 to 50 hours.

Onset of action—Diuretic: 2 hours.
Time to peak effect—Diuretic: 2 hours.
Duration of action—Diuretic: 48 to 72 hours.

Oral Dosage Forms

CHLORTHALIDONE TABLETS USP

Usual adult dose:
Diuretic—Oral, 25 to 100 mg once a day, or 100 to 200 mg once every other day, or once a day for three days a week.
Antihypertensive—Oral, 25 to 100 mg once a day, the dosage being adjusted according to response.
Note: Geriatric patients may be more sensitive to the effects of the usual adult dose.

Auxiliary labeling:
• Avoid overexposure to the sun or use of sunlamp.
• Do not take other medicines without your doctor's advice.

CYCLOTHIAZIDE

Summary of Differences

Pharmacology:
Onset of action—Diuretic: Less than 6 hours.
Time to peak effect—Diuretic: 7 to 12 hours.
Duration of action—Diuretic: 18 to 24 hours.

Oral Dosage Forms

Note: Bracketed uses in the *Dosage Forms* section refer to categories of use and/or indications that are not included in U.S. product labeling.

CYCLOTHIAZIDE TABLETS USP

Usual adult dose:
Diuretic; or
[Antidiuretic (central or nephrogenic diabetes insipidus)]—Oral, 1 to 2 mg once a day, once every other day, or once a day for two or three days a week.
Antihypertensive—Oral, 2 mg once a day, the dosage being adjusted according to response.
Note: Geriatric patients may be more sensitive to the effects of the usual adult dose.

Usual adult prescribing limits: Up to 6 mg daily in divided doses.

Auxiliary labeling:
• Avoid overexposure to the sun or use of sunlamp.
• Do not take other medicines without your doctor's advice.

HYDROCHLOROTHIAZIDE

Summary of Differences

Pharmacology:
Half-life—Normal: 15 hours.
Onset of action—Diuretic: 2 hours.
Time to peak effect—Diuretic: 4 hours.
Duration of action—Diuretic: 6 to 12 hours.

Oral Dosage Forms

Note: Bracketed uses in the *Dosage Forms* section refer to categories of use and/or indications that are not included in U.S. product labeling.

HYDROCHLOROTHIAZIDE ORAL SOLUTION

Usual adult dose:
Diuretic; or
[Antidiuretic (central or nephrogenic diabetes insipidus)]—Oral, 25 to 100 mg one or two times a day, once every other day, or once a day for three to five days a week.
Antihypertensive—Oral, 25 to 100 mg a day, as a single dose or in two divided daily doses, the dosage being adjusted according to response.
Note: Geriatric patients may be more sensitive to the effects of the usual adult dose.

Auxiliary labeling:
• Avoid overexposure to the sun or use of sunlamp.
• Do not take other medicines without your doctor's advice.

HYDROCHLOROTHIAZIDE TABLETS USP

Usual adult dose:
Diuretic; or
[Antidiuretic (central or nephrogenic diabetes insipidus)][1]—Oral, 25 to 100 mg one or two times a day, once every other day, or once a day for three to five days a week.
Antihypertensive—Oral, 25 to 100 mg a day, as a single dose or in two divided daily doses, the dosage being adjusted according to response.
Note: Geriatric patients may be more sensitive to the effects of the usual adult dose.

Auxiliary labeling:
• Avoid overexposure to the sun or use of sunlamp.
• Do not take other medicines without your doctor's advice.

---

[1]Not included in Canadian product labeling.

HYDROFLUMETHIAZIDE

Summary of Differences

Pharmacology:
Protein binding—High.
Onset of action—Diuretic: 1 to 2 hours.
Time to peak effect—Diuretic: 3 to 4 hours.
Duration of action—Diuretic: 18 to 24 hours.

Oral Dosage Forms

Note: Bracketed uses in the *Dosage Forms* section refer to categories of use and/or indications that are not included in U.S. product labeling.

HYDROFLUMETHIAZIDE TABLETS USP

Usual adult dose:
Diuretic; or
[Antidiuretic (central or nephrogenic diabetes insipidus)]—Oral, 25 to 100 mg one or two times a day, once every other day, or once a day for three to five days a week.
Antihypertensive—Oral, 50 to 100 mg per day, as a single dose or in two divided daily doses, the dosage being adjusted according to response.

Note: Geriatric patients may be more sensitive to the effects of the usual adult dose.

Usual adult prescribing limits: Up to 200 mg per day in divided doses.

Auxiliary labeling:
- Avoid overexposure to the sun or use of sunlamp.
- Do not take other medicines without your doctor's advice.

METHYCLOTHIAZIDE

Summary of Differences

Pharmacology:
    Onset of action—Diuretic: 2 hours.
    Time to peak effect—Diuretic: 6 hours.
    Duration of action—Diuretic: More than 24 hours.

Oral Dosage Forms

Note: Bracketed uses in the *Dosage Forms* section refer to categories of use and/or indications that are not included in U.S. product labeling.

METHYCLOTHIAZIDE TABLETS USP

Usual adult dose:
    Diuretic; or
    [Antidiuretic (central or nephrogenic diabetes insipidus)][1]—Oral, 2.5 to 10 mg once a day, once every other day, or once a day for three to five days a week.
    Antihypertensive—Oral, 2.5 to 5 mg once a day, the dosage being adjusted according to response.
        Note: Doses beyond 5 mg once a day will usually not result in further lowering of blood pressure.
Note: Geriatric patients may be more sensitive to the effects of the usual adult dose.

Auxiliary labeling:
- Avoid overexposure to the sun or use of sunlamp.
- Do not take other medicines without your doctor's advice.

---

[1]Not included in Canadian product labeling.

METOLAZONE

Summary of Differences

Pharmacology:
    Although not chemically the same, metolazone has actions similar to the thiazide diuretics.
    Absorption—More rapid and more complete with prompt metolazone tablets than with extended metolazone tablets.
    Protein binding—Very high (50 to 70% to red blood cells).
    Half-life—Normal: 8 hours.
    Onset of action—Diuretic: 1 hour.
    Time to peak effect—Diuretic: 2 hours.
    Duration of action—Diuretic: 12 to 24 hours.
    Elimination—Metolazone undergoes some enterohepatic recycling, and slightly greater amounts are excreted in the bile.

Additional Dosing Information

Extended metolazone tablets and prompt metolazone tablets should not be substituted for one another because of significant differences in rate of absorption and bioavailability.

Absorption of metolazone after oral administration is reduced in patients with cardiac disease (65% in normal subjects as compared with 40% in cardiac disease patients).

Plasma clearance of metolazone is 20 mL per minute in patients with renal failure as compared with 110 mL per minute in healthy subjects.

Duration of diuretic effect is dose-related.

Metolazone may be more effective as a diuretic than other thiazides in patients with severe renal failure. Because of this, metolazone has been added to furosemide therapy in resistant patients; however, caution is necessary because of the risk of severe electrolyte imbalance.

Oral Dosage Forms

EXTENDED METOLAZONE TABLETS

Usual adult dose:
    Diuretic—Oral, 5 to 20 mg once a day.
    Antihypertensive—Oral, 2.5 to 5 mg once a day, the dosage being adjusted according to response.
Note: Geriatric patients may be more sensitive to the effects of the usual adult dose.

Auxiliary labeling:
- Avoid overexposure to the sun or use of sunlamp.
- Do not take other medicines without your doctor's advice.

PROMPT METOLAZONE TABLETS

Usual adult dose: Antihypertensive—
    Initial: Oral, 500 mcg (0.5 mg) once a day, the dosage being adjusted according to response.
    Maintenance: Oral, 500 mcg (0.5 mg) to 1 mg once a day.

Usual adult prescribing limits: Up to 1 mg per day.

Auxiliary labeling:
- Avoid overexposure to the sun or use of sunlamp.
- Do not take other medicines without your doctor's advice.

POLYTHIAZIDE

Summary of Differences

Pharmacology:
    Protein binding—High.
    Onset of action—Diuretic: 2 hours.
    Time to peak effect—Diuretic: 6 hours.
    Duration of action—Diuretic: 24 to 48 hours.

Oral Dosage Forms

Note: Bracketed uses in the *Dosage Forms* section refer to categories of use and/or indications that are not included in U.S. product labeling.

POLYTHIAZIDE TABLETS USP

Usual adult dose:
    Diuretic; or
    [Antidiuretic (central or nephrogenic diabetes insipidus)]—Oral, 1 to 4 mg once a day, once every other day, or once a day for three to five days a week.

Antihypertensive—Oral, 2 to 4 mg once a day, the dosage being adjusted according to response.

Note: Geriatric patients may be more sensitive to the effects of the usual adult dose.

Auxiliary labeling:
- Avoid overexposure to the sun or use of sunlamp.
- Do not take other medicines without your doctor's advice.

QUINETHAZONE

Summary of Differences

Pharmacology:
Although not chemically the same, quinethazone has the same actions as the thiazide diuretics.
Onset of action—Diuretic: 2 hours.
Time to peak effect—Diuretic: 6 hours.
Duration of action—Diuretic: 18 to 24 hours.

Oral Dosage Forms

QUINETHAZONE TABLETS USP

Usual adult dose:
Diuretic; or
Antihypertensive—Oral, 50 to 200 mg per day, as a single dose or in two divided daily doses, adjusted according to response.

Note: Geriatric patients may be more sensitive to the effects of the usual adult dose.

Usual adult prescribing limits: Up to 200 mg daily in divided doses.

Auxiliary labeling:
- Avoid overexposure to the sun or use of sunlamp.
- Do not take other medicines without your doctor's advice.

TRICHLORMETHIAZIDE

Summary of Differences

Pharmacology:
Onset of action—Diuretic: 2 hours.
Time to peak effect—Diuretic: 6 hours.
Duration of action—Diuretic: Up to 24 hours.
Laboratory value alterations: May produce false negative results in phentolamine, phenolsulfonphthalein, and tyramine tests.

Oral Dosage Forms

Note: Bracketed uses in the *Dosage Forms* section refer to categories of use and/or indications that are not included in U.S. product labeling.

TRICHLORMETHIAZIDE TABLETS USP

Usual adult dose:
Diuretic; or
[Antidiuretic (central or nephrogenic diabetes insipidus)]—Oral, 1 to 4 mg once a day, once every other day, or once a day for three to five days a week.
Antihypertensive—Oral, 2 to 4 mg once a day, the dosage being adjusted according to response.

Note: Geriatric patients may be more sensitive to the effects of the usual adult dose.

Auxiliary labeling:
- Avoid overexposure to the sun or use of sunlamp.
- Do not take other medicines without your doctor's advice.

DOXAZOSIN   Systemic

A commonly used *brand name* in the U.S. and Canada is *Cardura*.

ORAL
Doxazosin Mesylate Tablets
In the U.S. and Canada—*Cardura*

Category: Antihypertensive.

Indications

Note: Bracketed information in the *Indications* section refers to uses not included in U.S. product labeling.

Accepted
Hypertension (treatment)—Doxazosin is indicated in the treatment of hypertension.

In the 1988 Report of the Joint National Committee on Detection, Evaluation, and Treatment of High Blood Pressure, a progression in choice of treatments for essential hypertension is recommended:

Nonpharmacologic management (especially sodium restriction, weight reduction and exercise, and moderation of alcohol consumption) is recommended first for some patients, including those with mild hypertension, and is recommended as an adjunct to all pharmacologic hypertensive therapy.

Initial drug therapy usually consists of a diuretic, beta-adrenergic blocking agent, calcium channel blocking agent, or angiotensin-converting enzyme (ACE) inhibitor. If adequate blood pressure control is not achieved and the patient is adherent to the treatment program and not experiencing significant side effects, dosage of the drug may be increased, a drug from another one of these initial classes may be added or substituted, or a second drug from a different class—centrally acting alpha-adrenergic blocking agents (e.g., clonidine, guanabenz, guanfacine, methyldopa), peripheral-acting adrenergic antagonists (e.g., guanadrel, guanethidine, rauwolfia alkaloids), post-synaptic alpha1 peripheral adrenergic inhibitors (e.g., doxazosin, prazosin, terazosin), or vasodilators (e.g., hydralazine, minoxidil)—may be added or substituted.

If necessary, a drug from another class in the second group may be substituted or added as a third drug. If blood pressure control is still not achieved, a drug from still another class may be substituted or added as a fourth drug, or the patient may need further evaluation and/or referral.

[Benign prostatic hypertrophy (treatment)][1]—Doxazosin may be used for the treatment of urinary symptoms associated with benign prostatic hypertrophy. Although studies with doxazosin for this indication are limited, controlled trials with prazosin have shown beneficial results.

---

[1]Not included in Canadian product labeling.

Pharmacology

Mechanism of action/Effect: Doxazosin has a selective alpha$_1$-adrenergic blocking action, which is thought to account primarily for its effects.

Hypertension—Blockade of alpha$_1$-adrenergic receptors by doxazosin results in peripheral vasodilation, which produces a fall in blood pressure because of decreased peripheral vascular resistance.

Other actions/effects: Doxazosin lowers the levels of total cholesterol, low density lipoprotein (LDL) cholesterol, and triglycerides. In addition, doxazosin increases high density lipoprotein (HDL) cholesterol and the HDL/total cholesterol ratio. These lipid effects appear to be the result of doxazosin's effect on lipid metabolism (i.e., increasing LDL receptor activity, decreasing intracellular LDL cholesterol synthesis, decreasing synthesis and secretion of very low density lipoprotein [VLDL] cholesterol, stimulation of lipoprotein lipase activity, and decreasing the rate of cholesterol absorption). However, the implications of these changes are unclear.

Onset of action: 1 to 2 hours; there is a slight initial fall in blood pressure within the first hour, but the main hypotensive effect is apparent from 2 hours onwards.

Time to peak effect: Single dose—5 to 6 hours.

Duration of action: Single dose—24 hours.

Precautions to Consider

Cross-sensitivity and/or related problems
Patients sensitive to other quinazolines (prazosin, terazosin) may also be sensitive to doxazosin.

Geriatrics
A study performed in approximately 2000 patients older than 65 years of age did not demonstrate geriatrics-specific problems that would limit the usefulness of doxazosin in the elderly. However, the hypotensive effect of doxazosin may be more pronounced in elderly individuals, and lower daily maintenance doses may be required.

Drug interactions and/or related problems
The following drug interactions and/or related problems have been selected on the basis of their potential clinical significance (possible mechanism in parentheses where appropriate)—not necessarily inclusive (» = major clinical significance):

Note: Combinations containing any of the following medications, depending on the amount present, may also interact with this medication.

Anti-inflammatory drugs, nonsteroidal (NSAIDs), especially indomethacin
(antihypertensive effects of doxazosin may be reduced when the medication is used concurrently with these agents; indomethacin, and possibly other NSAIDs, may antagonize the antihypertensive effect by inhibiting renal prostaglandin synthesis and/or by causing sodium and fluid retention; the patient should be carefully monitored to confirm that the desired effect is being obtained)

Estrogens
(estrogen-induced fluid retention tends to increase blood pressure)

Hypotension-producing medications, other
(antihypertensive effects may be potentiated when these medications are used concurrently with doxazosin; although some antihypertensive and/or diuretic combinations are frequently used to therapeutic advantage, dosage adjustments are necessary during concurrent use)

Sympathomimetics
(antihypertensive effects of doxazosin may be reduced when it is used concurrently with these agents; the patient should be carefully monitored to confirm that the desired effect is being obtained)
(concurrent use of doxazosin antagonizes the peripheral vasoconstriction produced by high doses of dopamine)
(concurrent use of doxazosin may decrease the pressor response to ephedrine)
(concurrent use of doxazosin may block the alpha-adrenergic effects of epinephrine, possibly resulting in severe hypotension and tachycardia)
(concurrent use of doxazosin usually decreases, but does not reverse or completely block, the pressor effect of metaraminol)
(prior administration of doxazosin may decrease the pressor effect and shorten the duration of action of methoxamine and phenylephrine)

Contraindications/Medical problems
The contraindications/medical problems included have been selected on the basis of their potential clinical significance (reasons given in parentheses where appropriate)—not necessarily inclusive (» = major clinical significance).

Risk-benefit should be considered when the following medical problems exist:

Hepatic function impairment
(although studies in patients with impaired hepatic function have not been done, doxazosin is primarily metabolized in the liver, and, therefore, increased sensitivity or prolonged doxazosin effect may occur)

Renal function impairment
(small incidence of increased risk of first-dose orthostatic hypotensive reaction and prolonged hypotensive effect)

Sensitivity to doxazosin

Side/Adverse Effects

Note: A "first-dose orthostatic hypotensive reaction" sometimes occurs with the initial dose of doxazosin, especially when the patient is in the upright position. Syncope or other postural symptoms such as dizziness may occur. Subsequent occurrence with dosage increases is also possible. Incidence appears to be dose-related, thus, it is important that therapy be initiated with the 1-mg dose. Patients who are volume-depleted or sodium-restricted may be more sensitive to the orthostatic hypotensive effects of doxazosin, and the effect may be exaggerated after exercise.

Hypotensive side effects are more likely to occur in geriatric patients

The following side/adverse effects have been selected on the basis of their potential clinical significance (possible signs and symptoms in parentheses where appropriate)—not necessarily inclusive:

Those indicating need for medical attention
Incidence more frequent
Dizziness; vertigo (dizziness or lightheadedness)
Incidence less frequent
Arrhythmias (irregular heartbeat); *dyspnea* (shortness of breath); *orthostatic hypotension* (dizziness or lightheadedness when getting up from a lying or sitting position; sudden fainting); *palpitations* (pounding heartbeat); *peripheral edema* (swelling of feet or lower legs); *tachycardia* (fast heartbeat)

Those indicating need for medical attention only if they continue or are bothersome
Incidence more frequent
  Headache; unusual tiredness
Incidence less frequent
  Nausea; nervousness, restlessness, or unusual irritability; rhinitis (runny nose); *somnolence* (sleepiness or unusual drowsiness)

Patient Consultation

In providing consultation, consider emphasizing the following selected information (» = major clinical significance):

Before using this medication
» Conditions affecting use, especially:
    Sensitivity to quinazolines
    Use in the elderly—Increased sensitivity to hypotensive effects
    Other medical problems, especially hepatic function impairment or renal function impariment

Proper use of this medication
  Getting into the habit of taking at same times each day to help increase compliance
  Missed dose: Taking as soon as possible; not taking if almost time for next dose; not doubling doses
» Proper storage
For use as an antihypertensive
  Possible need for control of weight and diet, especially sodium intake
» Patient may not experience symptoms of hypertension; importance of taking medication even if feeling well
» Does not cure, but helps control hypertension; possible need for lifelong therapy; serious consequences of untreated hypertension

Precautions while using this medication
  Regular visits to physician to check progress
» Not taking other medications, especially nonprescription sympathomimetics, unless discussed with physician
» Caution if dizziness, lightheadedness, or sudden fainting occurs, especially after initial dose; taking first dose at bedtime
» Caution when getting up suddenly from a lying or sitting position
» Caution in using alcohol, while standing for long periods or exercising, and during hot weather, because of enhanced orthostatic hypotensive effects
» Possibility of drowsiness
» Caution when driving or doing anything else requiring alertness because of possible drowsiness, dizziness, or lightheadedness

Side/adverse effects
  Signs of potential side effects, especially arrhythmias, dizziness, dyspnea, orthostatic hypotension, palpitations, peripheral edema, tachycardia, and vertigo

General Dosing Information

Dosage of doxazosin should be adjusted to meet the individual requirements of each patient, on the basis of blood pressure response.

Doxazosin may be used alone or in combination with a thiazide diuretic or beta-adrenergic blocking agent, both of which reduce the tendency for sodium and water retention, although they also produce additive hypotension. If combination therapy is indicated, individual titration is required to ensure the lowest possible therapeutic dose of each medication.

In order to minimize the "first-dose orthostatic hypotensive reaction," an initial dose of 1 mg is recommended, with gradual increases in dose every 2 weeks as needed. Administration of the initial dose at bedtime is recommended, as well as the initial dose of each increment.

Increases in dose beyond 4 mg increase the likelihood of excessive postural effects including syncope, postural dizziness/vertigo, and postural hypotension.

When a diuretic or another antihypertensive agent is added to doxazosin therapy, the dose of doxazosin may be reduced, followed by slow dosage titration of the combination. When doxazosin is added to existing diuretic or antihypertensive therapy, the dose of the other agent may be reduced and doxazosin started at a dose of 1 mg once a day.

Oral Dosage Forms

Note: Bracketed uses in the *Dosage Forms* section refer to categories of use and/or indications that are not included in U.S. product labeling.

  The dosing and strengths of the dosage forms available are expressed in terms of doxazosin base (not the mesylate salt).

DOXAZOSIN MESYLATE TABLETS
Usual adult dose:
  Antihypertensive—
    Initial: Oral, 1 mg (base) once a day, at bedtime.
    Maintenance: Oral, the dosage being increased gradually to meet individual requirements; depending on periodic blood pressure measurements, dosage may be increased every two weeks, titrating upwards to 2, 4, 8, and 16 mg (base) once a day as needed and tolerated.
    Note: Increases in dose beyond 4 mg (base) increase the likelihood of excessive postural effects including syncope, postural dizziness/vertigo, and postural hypotension.
  [Benign prostatic hypertrophy][1]—
    Initial: Oral, 1 mg (base) once a day, at bedtime.
    Maintenance: Oral, 2 to 4 mg (base) once a day.
Note: Geriatric patients may be more sensitive to the effects of the usual adult dose.

Usual adult prescribing limits: 16 mg once a day.

Auxiliary labeling:
  • Do not take other medicines without your doctor's advice.
  • May cause dizziness.

[1]Not included in Canadian product labeling.

ENCAINIDE   Systemic†

A commonly used *brand name* in the U.S. is *Enkaid*.

ORAL
Encainide Hydrochloride Capsules†
   In the U.S.—*Enkaid*

---

   †Not commercially available in Canada.

Category: Antiarrhythmic.

Indications

Accepted
Arrhythmias, ventricular (treatment)—Encainide is indicated for suppression of documented life-threatening ventricular arrhythmias, including sustained ventricular tachycardia.

Unaccepted
Use of encainide is no longer accepted for treatment of less severe arrhythmias such as nonsustained ventricular tachycardias or frequent premature ventricular contractions, even if patients are symptomatic, because of results of a trial that found increased mortality in patients with non-life-threatening arrhythmias treated with encainide.

Pharmacology

Mechanism of action/Effect: Decreases excitability, conduction velocity, and automaticity as a result of slowed atrial, atrioventricular (AV) nodal, His-Purkinje, and intraventricular conduction, and causes a slight but significant prolongation of refractory periods in these tissues. The greatest effect is on the His-Purkinje system. Decreases the rate of rise of the action potential without markedly affecting its duration. Electrophysiologic effects are greater in ischemic than in normal myocardial tissue. In the Vaughan Williams classification of antiarrhythmics, encainide is considered to be a class IC agent.

Other actions/effects: Very little negative inotropic effect.

Onset of action: 1 to 3 hours.

Precautions to Consider

Geriatrics
Although appropriate studies with encainide have not been performed in the geriatric population, no geriatrics-specific problems have been documented to date. However, elderly patients are more likely to have age-related renal function impairment, which may require dosage reduction and increase in dosage intervals in patients receiving encainide.

Drug interactions and/or related problems
The following drug interactions and/or related problems have been selected on the basis of their potential clinical significance (possible mechanism in parentheses where appropriate)—not necessarily inclusive (» = major clinical significance):

Antiarrhythmics, other
   (concurrent use with encainide may result in increased cardiac effects)

Cimetidine
   (concurrent use of cimetidine increases plasma concentrations of encainide and its active metabolites; dosage reduction of encainide is recommended if concurrent use with cimetidine is necessary)

Contraindications/Medical problems
The contraindications/medical problems included have been selected on the basis of their potential clinical significance (reasons given in parentheses where appropriate)—not necessarily inclusive (» = major clinical significance).

Except under special circumstances, this medication should not be used when the following medical problems exist:
» Atrioventricular (AV) block, pre-existing second or third degree without pacemaker, or
» Right bundle branch block associated with a left hemiblock (bifascicular block) without pacemaker
   (risk of complete heart block)

Risk-benefit should be considered when the following medical problems exist:
» Cardiogenic shock
   Cardiomyopathy
   Congestive heart failure
   Hepatic function impairment
   (reduced conversion to metabolites O-demethylencainide [ODE] and 3-methoxy-O-demethylencainide [MODE], but concentrations of metabolites are not significantly changed; no specific dosage adjustment recommendations can be made, but dosage should be increased cautiously)
   Hypokalemia or hyperkalemia
   (effects of encainide may be altered; any electrolyte imbalance should be corrected prior to beginning therapy with encainide)
   Myocardial infarction, history of, with associated left ventricular function impairment
   (increased risk of encainide-induced arrhythmias)
   Renal function impairment
   (reduced elimination; in patients with renal function impairment, the interval between dosage increments should be greater than 3 to 5 days, usually at least 7 days, and dosage reduction may be necessary)
   Sensitivity to encainide
» Sick sinus syndrome
   (sinus node recovery time prolonged; sinus bradycardia, sinus pause, or sinus arrest may occur)
   Caution is also recommended in patients with permanent pacemakers or temporary pacing electrodes because encainide may increase endocardial pacing thresholds and may suppress ventricular escape rhythms; use is not recommended in patients with existing poor thresholds or nonprogrammable pacemakers unless suitable pacing rescue is available.

Side/Adverse Effects

Note: In the National Heart Lung and Blood Institute's Cardiac Arrhythmia Suppression Trial (CAST), encainide treatment was found to be associated with excessive mortality or increased nonfatal cardiac arrest rate as compared with placebo in patients with asymptomatic, non-life-threatening arrhythmias who had a recent myocardial infarction.

Adverse cardiac effects reported with encainide administration include new or exacerbated ventricular arrhythmias in about 10% of patients and, in 1% or less of patients, new or exacerbated congestive heart failure, second or third degree atrioventricular (AV) block, sinus bradycardia, sinus pause, or sinus arrest.

Incidence of cardiac and other effects is at least partially dose-related. Proarrhythmic effects are much more frequent at doses exceeding 200 mg per day.

Signs of overdose include excessive QRS widening and QT prolongation, AV dissociation, hypotension, and bradycardia; asystole may develop. Seizures have been reported. Deaths have occurred.

The following side/adverse effects have been selected on the basis of their potential clinical significance (possible signs and symptoms in parentheses where appropriate)—not necessarily inclusive:

Those indicating need for medical attention

Incidence more frequent

Chest pain; ventricular tachyarrhythmias (fast or irregular heartbeat)

Note: *Ventricular tachyarrhythmias* are dose-related and potentially fatal; incidence increased in patients with sustained ventricular tachycardia, cardiomyopathy, congestive heart failure, or history of myocardial infarction with associated left ventricular function impairment. Proarrhythmic effects usually occur during the first week of therapy.

Incidence rare

Central nervous system (CNS) effect (trembling or shaking); *congestive heart failure* (shortness of breath, swelling of feet or lower legs)

Those indicating need for medical attention only if they continue or are bothersome

Incidence less frequent

CNS effects (blurred or double vision, dizziness, headache, unusual tiredness or weakness); *nausea; pain in arms or legs; skin rash*

Patient Consultation

In providing consultation, consider emphasizing the following selected information (» = major clinical significance):

Before using this medication

» Conditions affecting use, especially:

Sensitivity to encainide

Pregnancy—Reduces fertility in rats

Other medical problems, especially second or third degree atrioventricular (AV) block, right bundle branch block associated with a left hemiblock, cardiogenic shock, or sick sinus syndrome

Proper use of this medication

» Compliance with therapy; taking as directed even if feeling well

» Importance of not missing doses and taking at evenly spaced intervals

Missed dose: Taking as soon as possible if remembered within 4 hours; not taking if remembered later; not doubling doses

» Proper storage

Precautions while using this medication

Regular visits to physician to check progress

Carrying medical identification card or bracelet

» Caution if any kind of surgery (including dental surgery) or emergency treatment is required

Caution when driving or doing things requiring alertness because of possible dizziness

Side/adverse effects

Signs of potential side effects, especially chest pain, ventricular tachyarrhythmias, congestive heart failure, and trembling or shaking

General Dosing Information

Because of long half-life of encainide's metabolites and the long half-life of encainide in slow metabolizers, dosage increments should be made no more frequently than every 3 to 5 days.

It is recommended that treatment be initiated in the hospital because of the increased risk of proarrhythmic effects associated with encainide administration. Hospitalization is also recommended for patients requiring doses of 200 mg per day or more.

In general, it is recommended that previous antiarrhythmic therapy be withdrawn 2 to 4 plasma half-lives before initiation of encainide therapy.

In patients with pacemakers, it is recommended that the pacing threshold be determined prior to initiation of therapy, after one week of administration, and then at regular intervals.

Oral Dosage Forms

ENCAINIDE HYDROCHLORIDE CAPSULES

Note: Encainide hydrochloride capsules are not commercially available in Canada.

Usual adult dose: Antiarrhythmic—Oral, initially 25 mg every eight hours, increased, if necessary, after three to five days to 35 mg every eight hours; may be further increased after an additional three to five days, if necessary, to 50 mg every eight hours.

Note: Patients well controlled by doses of 50 mg every eight hours or less may be changed to every-twelve-hour dosing if necessary to aid in compliance. No more than 75 mg should be taken in each dose.

Occasional patients may require doses of 50 mg every six hours or, for life-threatening arrhythmias, 75 mg every six hours.

In patients with severe renal function impairment (serum creatinine greater than 3.5 mg per deciliter or creatinine clearance less than 20 mL per minute), therapy should be initiated at a dose of 25 mg once a day. If necessary, dosage may be increased to 25 mg every twelve hours after at least seven days, followed by 25 mg every eight hours after an additional seven days (up to a maximum of 150 mg per day).

EPINEPHRINE   Ophthalmic

Some commonly used *brand names* are:

In the U.S.—
Ayerst Epitrate [Epinephrine]
Epifrin [Epinephrine]
Epinal [Epinephryl Borate]
Eppy/N [Epinephryl Borate]
Glaucon [Epinephrine]
L-Epinephrine [Epinephrine]

In Canada—
Epifrin [Epinephrine]
Epinal [Epinephryl Borate]
Eppy/N [Epinephryl Borate]
Glaucon [Epinephrine]

OPHTHALMIC
Epinephrine Ophthalmic Solution USP
In the U.S.—*Epifrin; Glaucon; L-Epinephrine;* GENERIC
In Canada—*Epifrin; Glaucon*
Epinephrine Bitartrate Ophthalmic Solution USP
In the U.S.—*Ayerst Epitrate*
Epinephryl Borate Ophthalmic Solution USP
In the U.S. and Canada—*Epinal; Eppy/N*

Category: Antiglaucoma agent (ophthalmic); surgical aid.

Indications

Note: Bracketed information in the *Indications* section refers to uses not included in U.S. product labeling.

Accepted
Glaucoma, open-angle (treatment)—The 0.25 to 2% solution of ophthalmic epinephrine is indicated primarily in the treatment of open-angle (chronic simple) glaucoma, either alone or in combination with miotics, beta-blockers, hyperosmotic agents, or carbonic anhydrase inhibitors.

[Congestion, conjunctival, during surgery (treatment)][1]—Ophthalmic epinephrine is used in the treatment of conjunctival congestion during surgery.

[Glaucoma, secondary (treatment)][1]—Ophthalmic epinephrine is used in the treatment of secondary glaucoma.

Unaccepted
Epinephrine is not an effective mydriatic when used topically in the eye.

[1]Not included in Canadian product labeling.

Pharmacology

Mechanism of action/Effect: Epinephrine is a direct-acting sympathomimetic amine.

Antiglaucoma agent (ophthalmic)—The mechanism by which epinephrine lowers intraocular pressure is not completely known, but appears to involve both a decrease in production of aqueous humor and an increase in aqueous outflow facility.

Surgical aid (antihemorrhagic; mydriatic)—Epinephrine acts on alpha-adrenergic receptors in the conjunctiva to produce vasoconstriction and hemostasis in bleeding from small vessels. It contracts the dilator muscle of the pupil by acting on alpha-adrenergic receptors, resulting in dilation of the pupil (mydriasis).

Onset of action:
Reduction in intraocular pressure—Within 1 hour.
Vasoconstriction—Within 5 minutes.

Time to peak effect: Reduction in intraocular pressure—4 to 8 hours.

Duration of action:
Reduction in intraocular pressure—Up to 24 hours.
Vasoconstriction—Less than 1 hour.

Precautions to Consider

Geriatrics
Appropriate studies on the relationship of age to the effects of this medicine have not been performed in the geriatric population. However, no geriatrics-specific problems have been documented to date.

Dental
Epinephrine is used in gingival retraction cords, and systemic absorption may occur, especially from application of topical cords to abraded surfaces. Concurrent systemic absorption of ophthalmic epinephrine will result in an additive effect.

Drug interactions and/or related problems
The following drug interactions and/or related problems have been selected on the basis of their potential clinical significance (possible mechanism in parentheses where appropriate)—not necessarily inclusive (» = major clinical significance):

Note: Combinations containing any of the following medications, depending on the amount present, may also interact with this medication.

Anesthetics, hydrocarbon inhalation, such as:
Chloroform
Cyclopropane
Enflurane
Halothane
Isoflurane
Methoxyflurane
Trichloroethylene
(if significant systemic absorption of ophthalmic epinephrine occurs, concurrent use of cyclopropane, halothane, or possibly chloroform may increase the risk of severe ventricular arrhythmias because these anesthetics greatly sensitize the myocardium to the effects of sympathomimetics; therapy with ophthalmic epinephrine should be interrupted prior to general anesthesia in patients receiving these anesthetics)

(enflurane, isoflurane, methoxyflurane, or especially trichloroethylene may cause some sensitization of the myocardium to the effects of sympathomimetics; caution is recommended during concurrent use with ophthalmic epinephrine)

Antidepressants, tricyclic, or
Maprotiline or
Nomifensine
(if significant systemic absorption of ophthalmic epinephrine occurs, concurrent use of these medications may potentiate the cardiovascular effects of epinephrine, possibly resulting in arrhythmias, hypertension, or tachycardia)

Beta-adrenergic blocking agents, ophthalmic
(concurrent use of ophthalmic betaxolol, levobunolol, or timolol with ophthalmic epinephrine may provide a beneficial additive effect in lowering intraocular pressure)

Digitalis glycosides
(if significant systemic absorption of ophthalmic epinephrine occurs, concurrent use of digitalis glycosides may increase the risk of cardiac arrhythmias; caution is recommended if concurrent use is necessary)

Monoamine oxidase (MAO) inhibitors, including furazolidone, procarbazine, and selegiline
(if significant systemic absorption of ophthalmic epinephrine occurs, concurrent use of MAO inhibitors may result in exaggerated adrenergic effects; adjustment of the ophthalmic epinephrine dose is required when it is administered concurrently or within 21 days after administration of MAO inhibitors)

Sympathomimetics, systemic or local
(if significant systemic absorption of ophthalmic epinephrine occurs, concurrent use of systemic sympathomimetics may re-

sult in additive toxic effects; in addition, local anesthetics with vasoconstrictors should be avoided or a minimal amount of the vasoconstrictor should be used with the local anesthetic)

Contraindications/Medical problems

The contraindications/medical problems included have been selected on the basis of their potential clinical significance (reasons given in parentheses where appropriate)—not necessarily inclusive (» = major clinical significance).

Risk-benefit should be considered when the following medical problems exist:

Aphakia
    (epinephrine therapy may cause reversible macular edema)
Asthma, bronchial
» Cardiovascular disease
Cerebral arteriosclerosis
Diabetes mellitus
» Glaucoma, angle-closure, or predisposition to
    (may precipitate an acute attack of angle-closure glaucoma)
Hypertension
Hyperthyroidism
Sensitivity to epinephrine or sulfites

Side/Adverse Effects

Note: Pigmentary deposits in the conjunctiva may occur after prolonged use of ophthalmic epinephrine; on rare occasions, deposits in the eyelids or cornea may also occur.

The following side/adverse effects have been selected on the basis of their potential clinical significance (possible signs and symptoms in parentheses where appropriate)—not necessarily inclusive:

Those indicating need for medical attention
Incidence less frequent
    Maculopathy in aphakic eyes (blurred or decreased vision); *systemic absorption* (fast, irregular, or pounding heartbeat; feeling faint; increased sweating; paleness; trembling; increased blood pressure)

Those indicating need for medical attention only if they continue or are bothersome
Incidence more frequent
    Headache or browache; stinging, burning, redness, or other eye irritation; watering of eyes
Incidence less frequent
    Eye pain or ache

Patient Consultation

In providing consultation, consider emphasizing the following selected information (» = major clinical significance):

Before using this medication
» Conditions affecting use, especially:
    Sensitivity to epinephrine or sulfites
    Use by athletes—Stimulants, such as sympathomimetic amines, are banned and tested for in athletes; because ophthalmic epinephrine may be absorbed into the body, the medication may appear in the urine; if the agent is found in the urine, the athlete will be disqualified
    Other medical problems, especially cardiovascular disease, angle-closure glaucoma, or predisposition to angle-closure glaucoma

Proper use of this medication
» Importance of not using more medication than the amount prescribed
    Proper administration technique
    Preventing contamination: Not touching applicator tip to any surface; keeping container tightly closed

Not using if medication becomes discolored or contains a precipitate
Missed dose: Applying as soon as possible; if almost time for next dose, skipping missed dose and returning to regular dosing schedule; not doubling doses
» Proper storage

Precautions while using this medication
Regular visits to physician to check eye pressure during therapy

Side/adverse effects
Signs of potential side effects, especially maculopathy in aphakic eyes or signs of systemic absorption

General Dosing Information

Although some manufacturers recommend a dose of 2 drops of an ophthalmic solution at appropriate intervals, the conjunctival sac will usually hold only 1 drop.

To avoid excessive systemic absorption, patient should press finger to the lacrimal sac during and for 1 or 2 minutes following instillation of medication.

Caution is recommended when epinephrine is used in aphakic eyes, since maculopathy may occur rarely, resulting in decreased visual acuity. In this event, medication should be promptly discontinued.

Although some manufacturers recommend that patients not wear soft contact lenses during treatment with ophthalmic epinephrine, USP medical experts do not believe this precaution is necessary unless the patient has corneal epithelial problems and the medication is to be used more often than once every 1 to 2 hours. No significant problems have been documented with ophthalmic solutions containing 0.03% or less of benzalkonium chloride as a preservative, and used as eyedrops in patients with no significant corneal surface problems.

Ophthalmic Dosage Forms

EPINEPHRINE OPHTHALMIC SOLUTION USP

Usual adult and adolescent dose: Antiglaucoma agent (ophthalmic)— Topical, to the conjunctiva, 1 drop one or two times a day.

Usual geriatric dose: See *Usual adult and adolescent dose.*

Auxiliary labeling:
• For the eye.
• Keep container tightly closed.

EPINEPHRINE BITARTRATE OPHTHALMIC SOLUTION USP

Usual adult and adolescent dose: Antiglaucoma agent (ophthalmic)— Topical, to the conjunctiva, 1 drop up to two times a day.

Usual adult prescribing limits: More frequent administration than four times a day usually does not elicit further improvement in therapeutic response.

Usual geriatric dose: See *Usual adult and adolescent dose.*

Auxiliary labeling:
• For the eye.
• Keep container tightly closed.

EPINEPHRYL BORATE OPHTHALMIC SOLUTION USP

Usual adult and adolescent dose: Antiglaucoma agent (ophthalmic)— Topical, to the conjunctiva, 1 drop one or two times a day.

Usual geriatric dose: See *Usual adult and adolescent dose.*

Auxiliary labeling:
• For the eye.
• Keep container tightly closed.

ERGOTAMINE, BELLADONNA ALKALOIDS, AND PHENOBARBITAL   Systemic

For information on the specific components of this combination, see the *USP DI* monographs for *Vascular Headache Suppressants, Ergot Derivative-containing (Systemic), Anticholinergics/Antispasmodics (Systemic),* and *Barbiturates (Systemic).*

Category: Vascular headache prophylactic.

Indications

Accepted

Headache, vascular (prophylaxis)—This combination is used in the prevention of vascular headaches.

This combination is also used in the treatment of menopausal, cardiovascular, gastrointestinal, and genitourinary disorders because of its autonomic effects.

Patient Consultation

In providing consultation, consider emphasizing the following selected information (» = major clinical significance):

Before using this medication

» Conditions affecting use, especially:

Allergies to ergotamine, belladonna alkaloids, or barbiturates

Pregnancy—Use is not recommended because of ergotamine's oxytocic activity; also, belladonna alkaloids and barbiturates cross placenta; phenobarbital may cause fetal abnormalities and neonatal hemorrhage

Breast-feeding—Ergot alkaloids inhibit lactation; also, they are excreted in breast milk and may cause ergotism in the infant; belladonna alkaloids may also inhibit lactation; phenobarbital is excreted in breast milk and may cause CNS depression in the infant

Use in children—Increased susceptibility to toxic effects of belladonna alkaloids; increased response to belladonna alkaloids in children with spastic paralysis or brain damage; also, risk of paradoxical phenobarbital-induced excitement in hypersensitive children

Use in the elderly—Increased risk of hypothermia and other adverse effects associated with peripheral vasoconstriction; also, increased susceptibility to mental and other toxic effects of anticholinergics and barbiturates; danger of precipitating undiagnosed glaucoma; possible memory impairment

Athletes—Barbiturates are banned and tested for in shooters by the U.S. Olympic Committee and the National Collegiate Athletic Association (NCAA)

Dental—Possible development of dental problems because belladonna alkaloids may decrease salivary flow

Other medications, especially adrenocorticoids or corticotropin, other anticholinergics, antacids, anticoagulants, antidiarrheals, CNS depressants, estrogen- and progestin-containing oral contraceptives, other ergot alkaloids, ketoconazole, monoamine oxidase (MAO) inhibitors, potassium chloride, and other vasoconstrictors (including those present in local anesthetic solutions)

Other medical problems, especially angina pectoris, coronary artery disease, gastrointestinal obstructive disease, glaucoma, hepatic function impairment, hypertension, severe infection, peripheral vascular disease, pruritus, renal function impairment, urinary retention, and recent or contemplated angioplasty or vascular surgery

Proper use of this medication

» Importance of not using more medication than the amount prescribed; risk of ergotism with overdosage; habit-forming potential

Proper administration of extended-release tablets: Swallowing whole without crushing, breaking, or chewing

Missed dose: Not taking missed dose at all; not doubling doses

» Proper storage

Precautions while using this medication

» Checking with physician before discontinuing medication after prolonged use; gradual dosage reduction may be necessary to avoid the possibility of withdrawal symptoms

Avoiding antacids and antidiarrheal medication within 1 hour of taking this medicine

» Avoiding use of alcohol or other central nervous system (CNS) depressants; alcohol also aggravates headache

» Caution when driving or doing jobs requiring alertness because of possible dizziness, lightheadedness, or drowsiness

Avoiding smoking, since nicotine constricts blood vessels

Avoiding exposure to excessive cold, which may aggravate peripheral vasoconstriction

» Caution during exercise and hot weather; overheating may result in heat stroke

Possible increased sensitivity of eyes to light

Notifying physician if infection develops, since infection may cause increased sensitivity to medication

Possible dryness of mouth, nose, and throat; using sugarless candy or gum, ice or saliva substitute for relief; checking with physician or dentist if dry mouth continues for more than 2 weeks

Side/adverse effects

Signs of potential side effects, especially agranulocytosis, allergic reaction, edema, fast or slow heartbeat, gangrene, hepatitis, increased intraocular pressure, cerebral or peripheral ischemia, thrombocytopenia, and coronary or ocular vasospasm

Oral Dosage Forms

ERGOTAMINE TARTRATE, BELLADONNA ALKALOIDS, AND PHENOBARBITAL SODIUM TABLETS

Note: Ergotamine tartrate, belladonna alkaloids, and phenobarbital sodium tablets are not commercially available in the U.S.

Usual adult dose: Vascular headache prophylactic—Oral, 1 tablet in the morning and at noon and 2 tablets at bedtime. In more resistant cases, therapy may begin with 6 tablets per day, the dosage being gradually reduced at weekly intervals to the lowest effective dose.

Note: Geriatric and debilitated patients may react to usual doses of barbiturates with excitement, confusion, or mental depression. Lower doses may be required in these patients.

Auxiliary labeling:
• May cause drowsiness.
• Avoid alcoholic beverages.

ERGOTAMINE TARTRATE, BELLADONNA ALKALOIDS, AND PHENOBARBITAL SODIUM EXTENDED-RELEASE TABLETS

Usual adult dose: Oral, 1 tablet in the morning and 1 tablet in the evening.

Note: Geriatric and debilitated patients may react to usual doses of barbiturates with excitement, confusion, or mental depression. Lower doses may be required in these patients.

Auxiliary labeling:
• May cause drowsiness.
• Avoid alcoholic beverages.
• Swallow whole.

ERYTHROMYCIN   Ophthalmic

A commonly used *brand name* in the U.S. and Canada is *Ilotycin.*

OPHTHALMIC
Erythromycin Ophthalmic Ointment USP
   In the U.S.—*Ilotycin;* GENERIC
   In Canada—*Ilotycin*

Category: Antibacterial (ophthalmic).

Indications

Note: Bracketed information in the *Indications* section refers to uses not included in U.S. product labeling.

Accepted
Conjunctivitis, neonatal (prophylaxis)—Erythromycin is indicated in the topical prophylaxis of neonatal conjunctivitis caused by *Chlamydia trachomatis.*

Ocular infections (treatment)—Erythromycin is indicated in the topical treatment of superficial ocular infections of the conjunctiva and/or cornea caused by susceptible organisms.

Ophthalmia neonatorum (prophylaxis)—Erythromycin is indicated alone in the prophylaxis of ophthalmia neonatorum caused by *Neisseria gonorrhoeae* or *C. trachomatis.* However, in infants born to mothers who have clinically apparent gonorrhea, ophthalmic erythromycin is indicated concurrently with parenteral aqueous penicillin G.

[Blepharitis, bacterial (treatment)][1];
[Blepharoconjunctivitis (treatment)][1];
[Chlamydial infections (treatment)][1];
[Conjunctivitis, bacterial (treatment)][1];
[Keratitis, bacterial (treatment)][1];
[Keratoconjunctivitis, bacterial (treatment)][1];
[Meibomianitis (treatment)][1]; or
[Trachoma (treatment)][1]—Erythromycin is used in the topical treatment of bacterial blepharitis, blepharoconjunctivitis, chlamydial infections, bacterial conjunctivitis, bacterial keratitis, bacterial keratoconjunctivitis, meibomianitis, and trachoma.

Not all species or strains of a particular organism may be susceptible to erythromycin.

[1]Not included in Canadian product labeling.

Pharmacology

Mechanism of action/Effect: Erythromycin is a bacteriostatic macrolide antibiotic. However, it may be bactericidal in high concentrations or when used against highly susceptible organisms. It is thought to penetrate the bacterial cell membrane and to reversibly bind to the 50 S subunit of bacterial ribosomes or near the "P" or donor site so that binding of tRNA (transfer RNA) to the donor site is blocked. Translocation of peptides from the "A" or acceptor site to the "P" or donor site is prevented, and subsequent protein synthesis is inhibited.

Erythromycin is effective only against actively dividing organisms.

Precautions to Consider

Cross-sensitivity and/or related problems
Patients intolerant of one erythromycin may be intolerant of other erythromycins also.

Geriatrics
Appropriate studies on the relationship of age to the effects of this medicine have not been performed in the geriatric population. However, no geriatrics-specific problems have been documented to date.

Contraindications/Medical problems
The contraindications/medical problems included have been selected on the basis of their potential clinical significance (reasons given in parentheses where appropriate)—not necessarily inclusive (» = major clinical significance).

Risk-benefit should be considered when the following medical problem exists:
Intolerance to erythromycin

Side/Adverse Effects

The following side/adverse effects have been selected on the basis of their potential clinical significance (possible signs and symptoms in parentheses where appropriate)—not necessarily inclusive:

Those indicating need for medical attention
Incidence rare
Eye irritation not present before therapy

Patient Consultation

In providing consultation, consider emphasizing the following selected information (» = major clinical significance):

Before using this medication
» Conditions affecting use, especially:
     Allergy to this or any of the other erythromycins

Proper use of this medication
   Proper administration technique for ophthalmic ointment
» Compliance with full course of therapy
   Missed dose: Applying as soon as possible; not applying if almost time for next dose
» Proper storage

Precautions while using this medication
   Checking with physician if no improvement within a few days
   Blurred vision after application of ophthalmic ointments

General Dosing Information

Use of topical antibacterials may lead to skin sensitization, resulting in hypersensitivity reactions with subsequent topical or systemic use of the medication.

In the prophylaxis of ophthalmia neonatorum, erythromycin ophthalmic ointment should not be flushed from the eye following administration. In addition, ophthalmic erythromycin is given concurrently with parenteral aqueous penicillin G in infants born to mothers who have clinically apparent gonorrhea.

Ophthalmic Dosage Forms

ERYTHROMYCIN OPHTHALMIC OINTMENT USP

Usual adult and adolescent dose: Ocular infections—Topical, to the conjunctiva, a thin strip (approximately 1 cm) of ointment once daily or more frequently.

Auxiliary labeling:
• For the eye.
• Continue medicine for full time of treatment.

ERYTHROMYCINS   Systemic

Some commonly used *brand names* are:

In the U.S.—

E.E.S. [Erythromycin Ethylsuccinate]

E-Mycin [Erythromycin Base]

ERYC [Erythromycin Base]

EryPed [Erythromycin Ethylsuccinate]

Ery-Tab [Erythromycin Base]

Erythro [Erythromycin Ethylsuccinate]

Erythrocin [Erythromycin Lactobionate; Erythromycin Stearate]

Erythrocot [Erythromycin Stearate]

Erythrozone [Erythromycin Estolate]

Ilosone [Erythromycin Estolate]

Ilotycin [Erythromycin Gluceptate]

My-E [Erythromycin Stearate]

PCE Dispertab [Erythromcyin Base]

Robimycin [Erythromycin Base]

Wintrocin [Erythromycin Stearate]

Wyamycin-S [Erythromycin Stearate]

In Canada—

Apo-Erythro [Erythromycin Base]

Apo-Erythro-EC [Erythromycin Base]

Apo-Erythro-ES [Erythromycin Ethylsuccinate]

Apo-Erythro-S [Erythromycin Stearate]

E.E.S. [Erythromycin Ethylsuccinate]

E-Mycin [Erythromycin Base]

Erybid [Erythromycin Base]

ERYC-125 [Erythromycin Base]

ERYC-250 [Erythromycin Base]

Erythrocin [Erythromycin Lactobionate; Erythromycin Stearate]

Erythromid [Erythromycin Base]

Ilosone [Erythromycin Estolate]

Ilotycin [Erythromycin Gluceptate]

Novorythro [Erythromycin Base; Erythromycin Estolate; Erythromycin Stearate]

PCE Dispertab [Erythromycin Base]

ERYTHROMYCIN BASE
Oral

Erythromycin Delayed-release Capsules USP

In the U.S.—*ERYC;* GENERIC

In Canada—*Apo-Erythro-EC; ERYC-125; ERYC-250*

Erythromycin Tablets USP

In the U.S.—GENERIC

In Canada—*Apo-Erythro; Erythromid; Novorythro*

Erythromycin Delayed-release Tablets USP

In the U.S.—*E-Mycin; Ery-Tab; PCE Dispertab; Robimycin;* GENERIC

In Canada—*E-Mycin; Erybid; PCE Dispertab;* GENERIC

ERYTHROMYCIN ESTOLATE
Oral

Erythromycin Estolate Capsules USP

In the U.S.—*Ilosone;* GENERIC

In Canada—*Ilosone; Novorythro*

Erythromycin Estolate Oral Suspension USP

In the U.S.—*Erythrozone; Ilosone;* GENERIC

In Canada—*Ilosone; Novorythro*

Erythromycin Estolate Tablets USP

In the U.S.—*Erythrozone; Ilosone;* GENERIC

In Canada—*Ilosone*

Erythromycin Estolate Tablets USP (Chewable)†

In the U.S.—*Ilosone*

ERYTHROMYCIN ETHYLSUCCINATE
Oral

Erythromycin Ethylsuccinate Oral Suspension USP†

In the U.S.—*E.E.S.; Erythro;* GENERIC

Erythromycin Ethylsuccinate for Oral Suspension USP

In the U.S.—*E.E.S.; EryPed;* GENERIC

In Canada—*E.E.S.*

Erythromycin Ethylsuccinate Tablets USP

In the U.S.—*E.E.S.;* GENERIC

In Canada—*Apo-Erythro-ES; E.E.S.*

Erythromycin Ethylsuccinate Tablets USP (Chewable)

In the U.S.—*E.E.S.; EryPed*

In Canada—*E.E.S.*

ERYTHROMYCIN GLUCEPTATE
Parenteral

Sterile Erythromycin Gluceptate USP

In the U.S. and Canada—*Ilotycin*

ERYTHROMYCIN LACTOBIONATE
Parenteral

Erythromycin Lactobionate for Injection USP

In the U.S.—*Erythrocin;* GENERIC

In Canada—*Erythrocin*

ERYTHROMYCIN STEARATE
Oral

Erythromycin Stearate Oral Suspension*

In Canada—*Erythrocin; Novorythro*

Erythromycin Stearate Tablets USP

In the U.S.—*Erythrocin; Erythrocot; My-E; Wintrocin; Wyamycin-S;* GENERIC

In Canada—*Apo-Erythro-S; Erythrocin; Novorythro*

---

*Not commercially available in the U.S.

†Not commercially available in Canada.

Category: Antibacterial (systemic) (oral and parenteral); antiacne agent (systemic) (oral); bowel preparation (preoperative) adjunct (oral).

Indications

Note: Bracketed information in the *Indications* section refers to uses not included in U.S. product labeling.

Accepted

Bowel preparation, preoperative—Enteric-coated erythromycin base is indicated concurrently with oral-local neomycin as part of an adjunctive regimen for the suppression of normal bacterial flora in the preoperative preparation of the bowel.

Conjunctivitis, chlamydial (treatment);

Genitourinary tract infections (treatment); or

Pneumonia, chlamydial (treatment)—Erythromycins are indicated in the treatment of conjunctivitis in newborns, genitourinary tract infections during pregnancy, and pneumonia in infants caused by *Chlamydia trachomatis.*

Diphtheria (treatment)—Erythromycins are indicated in the treatment of diphtheria caused by *Corynebacterium diphtheriae* (as an adjunct to antitoxin).

Endocarditis, bacterial (prophylaxis)—Erythromycins are indicated in the prophylaxis of bacterial endocarditis in penicillin-allergic patients who have congenital heart disease or rheumatic or other acquired valvular heart disease and who undergo dental procedures or surgical procedures of the upper respiratory tract.

Erythrasma (treatment)—Erythromycins are indicated in the treatment of erythrasma caused by *Corynebacterium minutissimum.*

Gonorrhea, endocervical (treatment); or

Gonorrhea, urethral (treatment)—Erythromycins are indicated in the treatment of gonorrhea caused by *Neisseria gonorrhoeae.*

Legionnaires' disease (treatment)—Erythromycins are indicated in the treatment of Legionnaires' disease caused by *Legionella pneumophila.*

Listeriosis (treatment)—Erythromycins are indicated in the treatment of listeriosis caused by *Listeria monocytogenes.*

Otitis media, acute (treatment)—Erythromycins are indicated concurrently with sulfonamides in the treatment of acute otitis media caused by *Haemophilus influenzae* and *Streptococcus pneumoniae.*

Pertussis (treatment)—Erythromycins are indicated in the treatment of pertussis caused by *Bordetella pertussis.*

Pharyngitis, bacterial (treatment); or

Sinusitis (treatment)—Erythromycins are indicated in the treatment of pharyngitis and sinusitis caused by *Streptococcus pyogenes* (group A beta-hemolytic).

Pneumonia, mycoplasmal (treatment); or

Pneumonia, pneumococcal (treatment)—Erythromycins are indicated in the treatment of pneumonia caused by *Mycoplasma pneumoniae* and *Streptococcus pneumoniae.*

Rheumatic fever (prophylaxis)—Erythromycins are indicated in the long-term prophylaxis of rheumatic fever.

Skin and soft tissue infections (treatment)—Erythromycins are indicated in the treatment of skin and soft tissue infections, including burn wound infections, caused by *S. pyogenes* (group A beta-hemolytic).

Syphilis (treatment)—Erythromycins are indicated in the treatment of syphilis caused by *Treponema pallidum* in penicillin-allergic patients.

Urethritis, nongonococcal (treatment)—Erythromycins are indicated in the treatment of nongonococcal urethritis.

[Acne vulgaris (treatment)]—Oral erythromycins are used in the treatment of acne vulgaris.

[Actinomycosis (treatment)];

[Anthrax (treatment)];

[Chancroid (treatment)];

[Diphtheria (prophylaxis)]; or

[Ecthyma (treatment)]—Erythromycins are used in the treatment of actinomycosis, anthrax, chancroid, and ecthyma. They are also used in the prophylaxis of diphtheria.

[Enterocolitis, *Campylobacter* (treatment)]—Erythromycins are used in the treatment of enterocolitis (including diarrhea) caused by *Campylobacter jejuni.*

[Erysipelas (treatment)];

[Erysipeloid (treatment)];

[Granuloma inguinale (treatment)];

[Lymphogranuloma venereum (treatment)]; or

[Relapsing fever (treatment)]—Erythromycins are used in the treatment of erysipelas, erysipeloid, granuloma inguinale, lymphogranuloma venereum, and relapsing fever.

[Gastroparesis (treatment)][1]—Erythromycins have been used in the treatment of gastroparesis, including severe diabetic gastroparesis, gastroparesis associated with progressive systemic sclerosis, and postvagotomy gastroparesis. The data from short-term, controlled studies suggest that erythromycin may be effective in these conditions.

[Trachoma (treatment)]—Erythromycins are used in the treatment of trachoma.

Not all species or strains of a particular organism may be susceptible to erythromycins.

---

[1]Not included in Canadian product labeling.

Pharmacology

Mechanism of action/Effect: Antibacterial (systemic)—Erythromycin is a bacteriostatic macrolide antibiotic. However, it may be bactericidal in high concentrations or when used against highly susceptible organisms. It is thought to penetrate the bacterial cell membrane and to reversibly bind to the 50 S subunit of bacterial ribosomes or near the "P" or donor site so that binding of tRNA (transfer RNA) to the donor site is blocked. Translocation of peptides from the "A" or acceptor site to the "P" or donor site is prevented and subsequent protein synthesis is inhibited.

Erythromycin is effective only against actively dividing organisms.

Precautions to Consider

Cross-sensitivity and/or related problems

Patients intolerant of one erythromycin may be intolerant of other erythromycins also.

Geriatrics

Studies performed to date have not demonstrated geriatrics-specific problems that would limit the usefulness of erythromycin in the elderly.

Dental

Systemic erythromycins may cause oral candidiasis (sore mouth or tongue) in patients undergoing long-term therapy.

Drug interactions and/or related problems

The following drug interactions and/or related problems have been selected on the basis of their potential clinical significance (possible mechanism in parentheses where appropriate)—not necessarily inclusive (» = major clinical significance):

Note: Combinations containing any of the following medications, depending on the amount present, may also interact with this medication.

» Alfentanil

(chronic preoperative or perioperative use of erythromycins, which are hepatic enzyme inhibitors, may decrease the plasma clearance and prolong the duration of action of alfentanil)

» Carbamazepine

(erythromycins may inhibit carbamazepine metabolism, resulting in increased carbamazepine plasma concentrations and toxicity; it is recommended that erythromycins be used with caution if at all in patients receiving carbamazepine)

» Chloramphenicol or

» Lincomycins

(may be displaced from or prevented from binding to 50 S subunits of bacterial ribosomes by erythromycins, thus antagonizing the effects of chloramphenicol and lincomycins; concurrent use is not recommended)

» Cyclosporine

(erythromycin has been reported to increase cyclosporine plasma concentrations and may increase the risk of nephrotoxicity)

Digoxin

(erythromycin may alter gut flora, which prevents inactivation of digoxin, allowing more digoxin to be absorbed; this results in increased digoxin levels)

Ergotamine

(erythromycin inhibits the metabolism of ergotamine and has been reported to increase the vasospasm associated with ergotamines)

» Hepatotoxic medications, other

(concurrent use of other hepatotoxic medications with erythromycins may increase the potential for hepatotoxicity)

Lovastatin

(concurrent use of lovastatin with erythromycin may increase the risk of rhabdomyolysis, which typically occurs after the completion of erythromycin therapy; this is thought to be due to erythromycin's inhibition of lovastatin metabolism, which increases lovastatin serum concentrations; simultaneous administration of erythromycin and lovastatin should be used with caution)

Ototoxic medications, other
(concurrent use of other ototoxic medications with high-dose erythromycin in patients with renal function impairment may increase the potential for ototoxicity)

Penicillins
(since bacteriostatic drugs may interfere with the bactericidal effect of penicillins in the treatment of meningitis or in other situations where a rapid bactericidal effect is necessary, it is best to avoid concurrent therapy)

» Terfenadine
(concurrent use of terfenadine with erythromycins may increase the risk of cardiotoxicity, such as torsades de pointes)

» Warfarin
(concurrent use of erythromycins in patients receiving chronic warfarin therapy may result in excessive prolongation of prothrombin time and increased risk of hemorrhage, especially in elderly patients, because of possible decreased warfarin metabolism and clearance; warfarin dosage adjustments may be necessary during and after therapy with erythromycins, and prothrombin times should be monitored closely)

» Xanthines, such as:
Aminophylline
Caffeine
Oxtriphylline
Theophylline
(concurrent use of the xanthines [except dyphylline] with erythromycins may decrease theophylline hepatic clearance, resulting in increased serum theophylline concentrations and/or toxicity; this effect may be more likely to occur after 6 days of concurrent therapy because the magnitude of theophylline clearance reduction is proportional to the peak serum erythromycin concentrations; dosage adjustment of the xanthines may be necessary during and after therapy with erythromycins)

Contraindications/Medical problems
The contraindications/medical problems included have been selected on the basis of their potential clinical significance (reasons given in parentheses where appropriate)—not necessarily inclusive (» = major clinical significance).

Risk-benefit should be considered when the following medical problems exist:

Cardiac arrhythmias, history of, or QT prolongation
(patients with a history of cardiac arrhythmias or QT prolongation may be at risk for arrhythmias or torsades de pointes while receiving high doses of erythromycin)

» Hepatic function impairment, especially with erythromycin estolate
Hypersensitivity to erythromycins
Loss of hearing

Side/Adverse Effects
The following side/adverse effects have been selected on the basis of their potential clinical significance (possible signs and symptoms in parentheses where appropriate)—not necessarily inclusive:

Those indicating need for medical attention
Incidence less frequent
Hypersensitivity (skin rash, redness, or itching)
Incidence less frequent with erythromycin estolate—rare with other erythromycins
Cholestatic jaundice (dark or amber urine; pale stools; stomach pain, severe; unusual tiredness or weakness; yellow eyes or skin)

Incidence less frequent—parenteral erythromycins only
Inflammation or phlebitis at the injection site
Incidence rare—with hepatic or renal function impairment and high doses
Loss of hearing, reversible; torsades de pointes (recurrent fainting, sudden death)

Those indicating need for medical attention only if they continue or are bothersome
Incidence more frequent
Gastrointestinal disturbances (abdominal or stomach cramping and discomfort, diarrhea, nausea or vomiting)
Incidence less frequent
Oral candidiasis (sore mouth or tongue)

Patient Consultation
In providing consultation, consider emphasizing the following selected information (» = major clinical significance):

Before using this medication
» Conditions affecting use, especially:
Hypersensitivity to erythromycins
Pregnancy—Erythromycins cross the placenta; erythromycin estolate has been associated with an increased risk of reversible, subclinical hepatotoxicity in pregnant women
Breast-feeding—Erythromycins are excreted in breast milk
Dental—Oral candidiasis may occur with long-term therapy
Other medications, especially alfentanil, carbamazepine, chloramphenicol, cyclosporine, other hepatotoxic medications, lincomycins, terfenadine, warfarin, and xanthines
Other medical problems, especially hepatic function impairment

Proper use of this medication
Proper administration technique for oral liquids and/or pediatric drops, chewable tablets, delayed-release capsules and tablets; not using oral liquids and/or pediatric drops after expiration date
» Compliance with full course of therapy, especially in streptococcal infections
» Importance of not missing doses and taking at evenly spaced times
Missed dose: Taking as soon as possible; not taking if almost time for next dose; not doubling dose
» Proper storage

Precautions while using this medication
Checking with physician if no improvement within a few days

Side/adverse effects
Signs of potential side effects, especially cholestatic jaundice, hearing loss, hypersensitivity, inflammation or phlebitis at the injection site, or torsades de pointes

General Dosing Information
Therapy should be continued for at least 10 days in group A beta-hemolytic streptococcal infections to help prevent the occurrence of acute rheumatic fever.

For oral dosage forms only
Erythromycins may be taken with food if gastrointestinal irritation occurs.

ERYTHROMYCIN BASE

Oral Dosage Forms
Note: Bracketed uses in the *Dosage Forms* section refer to categories of use and/or indications that are not included in U.S. product labeling.

ERYTHROMYCIN DELAYED-RELEASE CAPSULES USP

Usual adult and adolescent dose: Antibacterial (systemic)—Oral, 250 mg (base) every six hours; or 500 mg every twelve hours if twice a day dosage is desired.

Note: Endocarditis prophylaxis—In patients with congenital heart disease or rheumatic or other acquired valvular heart disease who undergo dental procedures or surgical procedures of the upper respiratory tract: Oral, 1 gram (base) one hour prior to the procedure; and 500 mg six hours following the procedure.

Genitourinary tract infections, including chlamydial—Oral, 500 mg (base) every six hours for at least seven days. For patients unable to tolerate the higher dosage regimen, the dosage may be halved and given for at least fourteen days.

Legionnaires' disease—Oral, 500 mg (base) to 1 gram every six hours.

Streptococcal prophylaxis—Continuous prophylaxis of streptococcal infections in patients with a history of rheumatic heart disease: Oral, 250 mg (base) every twelve hours.

[Gastroparesis][1]—Oral 150 to 250 mg (base) taken thirty minutes before meals, three times a day.

Usual adult prescribing limits: Antibacterial (systemic)—Up to 4 grams (base) daily.

Auxiliary labeling:
• Continue medicine for full time of treatment.
• Swallow capsules whole.

ERYTHROMYCIN TABLETS USP

Usual adult and adolescent dose: See *Erythromycin Delayed-release Capsules USP.*

Usual adult prescribing limits: See *Erythromycin Delayed-release Capsules USP.*

Auxiliary labeling: • Continue medicine for full time of treatment.

ERYTHROMYCIN DELAYED-RELEASE TABLETS USP

Usual adult and adolescent dose: Antibacterial (systemic)—Oral, 250 mg (base) every six hours; 333 mg every eight hours; or 500 mg every twelve hours if twice a day dosage is desired.

Note: Endocarditis prophylaxis—In patients with congenital heart disease or rheumatic or other acquired valvular heart disease who undergo dental procedures or surgical procedures of the upper respiratory tract: Oral, 1 gram (base) one hour prior to the procedure; and 500 mg six hours following the procedure.

Genitourinary tract infections, including chlamydial—Oral, 500 mg (base) every six hours; or 666 mg every eight hours for at least seven days. For patients unable to tolerate the higher dosage regimen, the dosage may be halved and given for at least fourteen days.

Legionnaires' disease—Oral, 500 mg (base) to 1 gram every six hours.

Streptococcal prophylaxis—Continuous prophylaxis of streptococcal infections in patients with a history of rheumatic heart disease: Oral, 250 mg (base) every twelve hours.

[Gastroparesis][1]—Oral 150 to 250 mg (base) taken thirty minutes before meals, three times a day.

Usual adult prescribing limits: Antibacterial (systemic)—Up to 4 grams (base) daily.

Auxiliary labeling:
• Continue medicine for full time of treatment.
• Swallow tablets whole.

[1]Not included in Canadian product labeling.

ERYTHROMYCIN ESTOLATE

Summary of Differences

Precautions:

Pregnancy—Associated with increased risk of reversible, subclinical hepatotoxicity.

Laboratory value alterations—Serum alkaline phosphatase, bilirubin, AST (SGOT), and ALT (SGPT) concentrations may be increased more frequently than with other erythromycins.

Side/adverse effects: May also cause cholestatic jaundice less frequently (rare with other erythromycins).

Oral Dosage Forms

Note: Bracketed uses in the *Dosage Forms* section refer to categories of use and/or indications that are not included in U.S. product labeling.

ERYTHROMYCIN ESTOLATE CAPSULES USP

Usual adult and adolescent dose: Antibacterial (systemic)—Oral, 250 mg (base) every six hours; or 500 mg every twelve hours if twice a day dosage is desired.

Note: Endocarditis prophylaxis—In patients with congenital heart disease or rheumatic or other acquired valvular heart disease who undergo dental procedures or surgical procedures of the upper respiratory tract: Oral, 1 gram (base) one hour prior to the procedure; and 500 mg six hours following the procedure.

Genitourinary tract infections, including chlamydial—Oral, 500 mg (base) every six hours for at least seven days. For patients unable to tolerate the higher dosage regimen, the dosage may be halved and given for at least fourteen days.

Legionnaires' disease—Oral, 500 mg (base) to 1 gram every six hours.

Streptococcal prophylaxis—Continuous prophylaxis of streptococcal infections in patients with a history of rheumatic heart disease: Oral, 250 mg (base) every twelve hours.

[Gastroparesis][1]—Oral 150 to 250 mg (base) taken thirty minutes before meals, three times a day.

Usual adult prescribing limits: Antibacterial (systemic)—Up to 4 grams (base) daily.

Auxiliary labeling: • Continue medicine for full time of treatment.

ERYTHROMYCIN ESTOLATE ORAL SUSPENSION USP

Usual adult and adolescent dose: See *Erythromycin Estolate Capsules USP.*

Usual adult prescribing limits: See *Erythromycin Estolate Capsules USP.*

Auxiliary labeling:
• Refrigerate.
• Shake well.
• Continue medicine for full time of treatment.
• Take by mouth only (pediatric drops).

ERYTHROMYCIN ESTOLATE TABLETS USP

Usual adult and adolescent dose: See *Erythromycin Estolate Capsules USP.*

Usual adult prescribing limits: See *Erythromycin Estolate Capsules USP.*

Auxiliary labeling: • Continue medicine for full time of treatment.

ERYTHROMYCIN ESTOLATE TABLETS USP (CHEWABLE)

Usual adult and adolescent dose: See *Erythromycin Estolate Capsules USP.*

Usual adult prescribing limits: See *Erythromycin Estolate Capsules USP.*

Auxiliary labeling:
- Chew or crush tablets before swallowing.
- Continue medicine for full time of treatment.

¹Not included in Canadian product labeling.

ERYTHROMYCIN ETHYLSUCCINATE

Summary of Differences

Usual adult dose: Antibacterial (systemic)—400 mg every six hours.

1.6 grams of erythromycin ethylsuccinate produce approximately the same blood levels as 1 gram erythromycin base.

Oral Dosage Forms

Note: Bracketed uses in the *Dosage Forms* section refer to categories of use and/or indications that are not included in U.S. product labeling.

The dosing and dosage forms available are expressed in terms of ethylsuccinate salt. 400 mg of erythromycin ethylsuccinate produces approximately the same blood levels as 250 mg erythromycin base.

ERYTHROMYCIN ETHYLSUCCINATE ORAL SUSPENSION USP

Usual adult and adolescent dose: Antibacterial (systemic)—Oral, 400 mg every six hours; or 800 mg every twelve hours if twice a day dosing is desired.

Note: Endocarditis prophylaxis—In patients with congenital heart disease or rheumatic or other acquired valvular heart disease who undergo dental procedures or surgical procedures of the upper respiratory tract: Oral, 1.6 grams one hour prior to the procedure; and 800 mg six hours following the procedure.

Legionnaires' disease—Oral, 800 mg to 1.6 grams every six hours.

Streptococcal prophylaxis—Continuous prophylaxis of streptococcal infections in patients with a history of rheumatic heart disease: Oral, 400 mg every twelve hours.

Urethritis, nongonococcal (including chlamydial)—Oral, 800 mg every eight hours for seven days.

[Gastroparesis]¹—Oral 240 to 400 mg taken thirty minutes before meals, three times a day.

Usual adult prescribing limits: Antibacterial (systemic)—Up to 4 grams daily.

Auxiliary labeling:
- Shake well.
- Continue medicine for full time of treatment.
- Beyond-use date.

ERYTHROMYCIN ETHYLSUCCINATE FOR ORAL SUSPENSION USP

Usual adult and adolescent dose: See *Erythromycin Ethylsuccinate Oral Suspension USP.*

Usual adult prescribing limits: See *Erythromycin Ethylsuccinate Oral Suspension USP.*

Auxiliary labeling:
- Refrigerate.
- Shake well.
- Continue medicine for full time of treatment.
- Beyond-use date.
- Take by mouth only (pediatric drops).

ERYTHROMYCIN ETHYLSUCCINATE TABLETS USP

Usual adult and adolescent dose: See *Erythromycin Ethylsuccinate Oral Suspension USP.*

Usual adult prescribing limits: See *Erythromycin Ethylsuccinate Oral Suspension USP.*

Auxiliary labeling: • Continue medicine for full time of treatment.

ERYTHROMYCIN ETHYLSUCCINATE TABLETS USP (CHEWABLE)

Usual adult and adolescent dose: See *Erythromycin Ethylsuccinate Oral Suspension USP.*

Usual adult prescribing limits: See *Erythromycin Ethylsuccinate Oral Suspension USP.*

Auxiliary labeling:
- Chew or crush tablets before swallowing.
- Continue medicine for full time of treatment.

¹Not included in Canadian product labeling.

ERYTHROMYCIN GLUCEPTATE

Summary of Differences

Category: Indicated only as an antibacterial.

Parenteral Dosage Forms

STERILE ERYTHROMYCIN GLUCEPTATE USP

Usual adult and adolescent dose: Antibacterial (systemic)—Intravenous infusion, 250 to 500 mg (base) every six hours; or 3.75 to 5 mg per kg of body weight every six hours.

Usual adult prescribing limits: Up to 4 grams (base) daily.

Note: Doses up to 6 grams (base) daily have been used.

Additional information:
Infusions with a pH below 5.5 tend to lose potency rapidly and should be administered completely within 4 hours after dilution.

If administration time is prolonged, infusions should be buffered to neutrality with a suitable buffer and administered completely within 24 hours after dilution.

If administered by intermittent infusion, dose may be diluted in 100 to 250 mL of 0.9% sodium chloride injection or 5% dextrose injection and administered slowly over a 20- to 60-minute period.

ERYTHROMYCIN LACTOBIONATE

Summary of Differences

Category: Indicated only as an antibacterial.

Parenteral Dosage Forms

ERYTHROMYCIN LACTOBIONATE FOR INJECTION USP

Usual adult and adolescent dose: Antibacterial (systemic)—Intravenous infusion, 250 to 500 mg (base) every six hours; or 3.75 to 5 mg per kg of body weight every six hours.

Usual adult prescribing limits: Up to 4 grams (base) daily.

Additional information:

Acidic infusions are unstable and lose potency rapidly. A pH of at least 5.5 is recommended for final dilutions, which should be administered completely within 8 hours after dilution.

If administered by intermittent infusion, dose may be diluted to a maximum concentration of 5 mg/mL with specified diluent and administered slowly over a 20- to 60-minute period.

ERYTHROMYCIN STEARATE

Oral Dosage Forms

Note: Bracketed uses in the *Dosage Forms* section refer to categories of use and/or indications that are not included in U.S. product labeling.

ERYTHROMYCIN STEARATE ORAL SUSPENSION

Usual adult and adolescent dose: Antibacterial (systemic)—Oral, 250 mg (base) every six hours; or 500 mg every twelve hours if twice a day dosage is desired.

Note: Endocarditis prophylaxis—In patients with congenital heart disease or rheumatic or other acquired valvular heart disease who undergo dental procedures or surgical procedures of the upper respiratory tract: Oral, 1 gram (base) one hour prior to the procedure; and 500 mg six hours following the procedure.

Genitourinary tract infections, including chlamydial—Oral, 500 mg (base) every six hours for at least seven days. For patients unable to tolerate the higher dosage regimen, the dosage may be halved and given for at least fourteen days.

Legionnaires' disease—Oral, 500 mg (base) to 1 gram every six hours.

Streptococcal prophylaxis—Continuous prophylaxis of streptococcal infections in patients with a history of rheumatic heart disease: Oral, 250 mg (base) every twelve hours.

[Gastroparesis][1]—Oral 150 to 250 mg (base) taken thirty minutes before meals, three times a day.

Usual adult prescribing limits: Antibacterial (systemic)—Up to 4 grams (base) daily.

Auxiliary labeling:

- Refrigerate.
- Shake well.
- Continue medicine for full time of treatment.
- Beyond-use date.

ERYTHROMYCIN STEARATE TABLETS USP

Usual adult and adolescent dose: See *Erythromycin Stearate Oral Suspension.*

Usual adult prescribing limits: See *Erythromycin Stearate Oral Suspension.*

Auxiliary labeling: • Continue medicine for full time of treatment.

---

[1]Not included in Canadian product labeling.

ERYTHROMYCIN AND SULFISOXAZOLE   Systemic

Some commonly used *brand names* are:

In the U.S.—*Eryzole; Pediazole; Sulfimycin*
In Canada—*Pediazole*

ORAL

Erythromycin Ethylsuccinate and Sulfisoxazole Acetyl for Oral Suspension USP

In the U.S.—*Eryzole; Pediazole; Sulfimycin;* GENERIC
In Canada—*Pediazole*

Category: Antibacterial (systemic).

Indications

Note: Bracketed information in the *Indications* section refers to uses not included in U.S. product labeling.

Accepted

Otitis media, acute (treatment)—Erythromycin and sulfisoxazole combination is indicated in the treatment of acute otitis media caused by *Haemophilus influenzae,* [pneumococci, group A streptococci, and *Branhamella catarrhalis*] in children.

[Sinusitis (treatment)][1]—Erythromycin and sulfisoxazole combination is used in the treatment of acute sinusitis caused by *H. influenzae,* pneumococci, group A streptococci, and *B. catarrhalis* in children.

Not all species or strains of a particular organism may be susceptible to erythromycin and sulfisoxazole combination.

---

[1]Not included in Canadian product labeling.

Pharmacology

Erythromycin—See *Erythromycins (Systemic).*
Sulfisoxazole—See *Sulfonamides (Systemic).*

Precautions to Consider

Erythromycin—See *Erythromycins (Systemic).*
Sulfisoxazole—See *Sulfonamides (Systemic).*

Side/Adverse Effects

Erythromycin—See *Erythromycins (Systemic).*
Sulfisoxazole—See *Sulfonamides (Systemic).*

Patient Consultation

In providing consultation, consider emphasizing the following selected information (» = major clinical significance):

Before using this medication

» Conditions affecting use, especially:

Allergy to erythromycins or sulfonamides; patients allergic to furosemide, thiazide diuretics, sulfonylureas, or carbonic anhydrase inhibitors may also be allergic to this medication

Pregnancy—Erythromycin crosses the placenta; sulfisoxazole also crosses the placenta and should not be used at term because it may cause kernicterus in the infant; it has also been associated with cleft palates and skeletal defects in the offspring of mice and rats

Breast-feeding—Erythromycins are excreted in breast milk in concentrations that may exceed maternal serum concentrations; sulfisoxazole is also excreted in breast-milk and is not recommended in nursing women since sulfonamides may cause kernicterus in nursing infants

Use in children—Sulfonamides should not be used in children up to 2 months of age because they may cause kernicterus

Dental—Systemic erythromycins may cause oral candidiasis; the leukopenic and thrombocytopenic effects of sulfonamides may result in an increased incidence of certain microbial infections, delayed healing, and gingival bleeding

Other medications, especially alfentanil; coumarin- or indandione-derivative anticoagulants; hydantoin anticonvulsants; oral antidiabetic agents; carbamazepine; chloramphenicol; cyclosporine; other hemolytics; other hepatotoxic medications; lincomycins; methenamine; methotrexate; or xanthines, especially theophylline

Other medical problems, especially blood dyscrasias, glucose-6-phosphate dehydrogenase (G6PD) deficiency, hepatic function impairment, porphyria, or renal function impairment

Proper use of this medication

» Maintaining adequate fluid intake; taking with food
» Not giving to infants under 2 months of age

Proper administration technique for oral liquids; not using after expiration date

» Compliance with full course of therapy

» Importance of not missing doses and taking at evenly spaced times

Missed dose: Taking as soon as possible; not taking if almost time for next dose; not doubling dose

» Proper storage

Precautions while using this medication

» Regular visits to physician to check blood counts, especially in long-term therapy

Checking with physician if no improvement within a few days

» Possible photosensitivity reactions

Using caution in use of regular toothbrushes, dental floss, and toothpicks; delaying dental work until blood counts have returned to normal; checking with physician or dentist concerning proper oral hygiene

Side/adverse effects

Signs of potential side effects, especially blood dyscrasias, crystalluria, goiter, hematuria, hepatitis, hypersensitivity reactions, interstitial nephritis, Lyell's syndrome, Stevens-Johnson syndrome, thyroid function disturbance, and tubular necrosis

General Dosing Information

Erythromycin and sulfisoxazole combination may be taken with food.

Because of its relatively high solubility even in acid urine, the risk of crystalluria with sulfisoxazole is low and alkalinization of the urine is usually unnecessary.

Patients with impaired renal function may require a reduction in dose.

Oral Dosage Forms

ERYTHROMYCIN ETHYLSUCCINATE AND SULFISOXAZOLE ACETYL FOR ORAL SUSPENSION USP

Usual adult and adolescent dose: Use is not indicated in adults.

Auxiliary labeling:

- Refrigerate.
- Shake well.
- Take with water.
- Avoid too much sun or use of sunlamp.
- Continue medicine for full time of treatment.
- Beyond-use date.

ESTRAMUSTINE   Systemic

Some commonly used *brand names* are:

In the U.S. and Canada—*Emcyt*
In other countries—*Estracyt*

ORAL

Estramustine Phosphate Sodium Capsules
In the U.S. and Canada—*Emcyt*
Other—*Estracyt*

Category: Antineoplastic.

Indications

Accepted

Carcinoma, prostatic (treatment)—Estramustine is indicated for palliative treatment of metastatic and/or progressive carcinoma of the prostate gland.

Pharmacology

Mechanism of action/Effect: Exact mechanism of antineoplastic action is unknown. Structurally, estramustine is a phosphorylated combination of estradiol and mechlorethamine (nitrogen mustard). However, estramustine has very weak alkylating activity and may be effective in some patients refractory to estrogen therapy. Therefore, its antineoplastic activity may be due to the estrogen component, a direct effect of estramustine or one of its metabolites, other antimitotic activity, or a combination of effects. Prolonged use elevates total plasma estradiol concentrations to within ranges similar to those produced in prostatic carcinoma patients given conventional estradiol therapy. Estrogenic effects (changes in circulating concentrations of steroids and pituitary hormones) are also similar to those produced by estradiol. A suppressive effect on the hypothalamic-hypophyseal-gonadal axis with a resultant reduction in serum testosterone concentrations may also be involved. Estramustine is highly localized in prostatic tissue because of binding to an estramustine-specific protein.

Precautions to Consider

Cross-sensitivity and/or related problems
Patients sensitive to estradiol or mechlorethamine may be sensitive to estramustine also.

Geriatrics
Appropriate studies on the relationship of age to the effects of estramustine have not been performed in the geriatric population. However, elderly patients are more likely to have age-related renal function impairment and/or peripheral vascular disease, which may require caution in patients receiving estrogens.

Drug interactions and/or related problems
The following drug interactions and/or related problems have been selected on the basis of their potential clinical significance (possible mechanism in parentheses where appropriate)—not necessarily inclusive (» = major clinical significance):

Note: Combinations containing any of the following medications, depending on the amount present, may also interact with this medication.

Calcium-containing medications or
Calcium supplements
  (calcium binds with estramustine in the gastrointestinal tract and forms an insoluble calcium phosphate salt, which is not absorbed; simultaneous administration should be avoided)

Corticosteroids, glucocorticoid
  (concurrent use with estrogens may alter the metabolism and protein binding of the glucocorticoids, leading to decreased clearance, increased elimination half-life, and increased therapeutic and toxic effects of the glucocorticoids; glucocorticoid dosage adjustment may be required during and following concurrent use)

Corticotropin (chronic therapeutic use)
  (concurrent use with estrogens may potentiate the anti-inflammatory effects of endogenous cortisol [adrenal secretion of endogenous cortisol is increased by corticotropin])

» Hepatotoxic medications
  (concurrent use of these medications with estrogens may increase the risk of hepatotoxicity)

» Smoking, tobacco
  (not recommended during estrogen therapy because of the increased risk of serious cardiovascular side effects, including cerebrovascular accident, transient ischemic attacks, thrombophlebitis, and pulmonary embolism; risk increases with increasing tobacco usage and with age)

Vaccines, killed virus
  (because normal defense mechanisms may be suppressed by estramustine therapy, the patient's antibody response to the vaccine may be decreased. The interval between discontinuation of medications that cause immunosuppression and restoration of the patient's ability to respond to the vaccine depends on the intensity and type of immunosuppression-causing medication used, the underlying disease, and other factors; estimates vary from 3 months to 1 year)

Vaccines, live virus
  (because normal defense mechanisms may be suppressed by estramustine therapy, concurrent use with a live virus vaccine may potentiate the replication of the vaccine virus, may increase the side/adverse effects of the vaccine virus, and/or may decrease the patient's antibody response to the vaccine; immunization of these patients should be undertaken only with ex-

treme caution after careful review of the patient's hematologic status and only with the knowledge and consent of the physician managing the estramustine therapy. The interval between discontinuation of medications that cause immunosuppression and restoration of the patient's ability to respond to the vaccine depends on the intensity and type of immunosuppression-causing medication used, the underlying disease, and other factors; estimates vary from 3 months to 1 year. Patients with leukemia in remission should not receive live virus vaccine until at least 3 months after their last chemotherapy. In addition, immunization with oral poliovirus vaccine should be postponed in persons in close contact with the patient, especially family members)

Contraindications/Medical problems
The contraindications/medical problems included have been selected on the basis of their potential clinical significance (reasons given in parentheses where appropriate)—not necessarily inclusive (» = major clinical significance).

Except under special circumstances, this medication should not be used when the following medical problems exist:

» Thromboembolic disorders, active, including recent myocardial infarction or stroke, or
» Thrombophlebitis, active
  (may be aggravated by estrogen component; an exception may be made when the actual tumor mass is the cause of the thromboembolic phenomenon)

Risk-benefit should be considered when the following medical problems exist:

Asthma or
Cardiac insufficiency or
Epilepsy or
Mental depression, or history of, or
Migraine headaches or
Renal function impairment
  (fluid retention sometimes caused by estrogen component may aggravate these conditions)

Bone disease, metabolic, associated with hypercalcemia, or
Renal insufficiency
  (estrogens influence metabolism of calcium and phosphorus)

Bone marrow depression, moderate to severe

Cerebrovascular disease or
Coronary artery disease or
» Thrombophlebitis, thrombosis, or thromboembolic disorders, history of, especially if associated with estrogen therapy
  (risk of thromboembolic disorders caused by estrogens)

» Chickenpox, existing or recent (including recent exposure), or
» Herpes zoster
  (risk of severe generalized disease)

Cholestatic jaundice, history of, including previous jaundice that occurred with estrogens or as a reaction to other medication

Diabetes mellitus
  (glucose tolerance may be decreased)

Gallbladder disease, or history of, especially gallstones

Hepatic function impairment
  (reduced metabolism and possible hepatotoxicity)

» Hypercalcemia associated with metastatic breast disease
» Peptic ulcer
» Sensitivity to estramustine

Side/Adverse Effects

The following side/adverse effects have been selected on the basis of their potential clinical significance (possible signs and symptoms in parentheses where appropriate)—not necessarily inclusive:

Those indicating need for medical attention

Incidence more frequent

Sodium and fluid retention (swelling of feet or lower legs)

Incidence rare

Allergic reaction (skin rash or fever); **anemia** (unusual tiredness or weakness); **leukopenia** (usually asymptomatic; rarely, fever or chills, cough or hoarseness, lower back or side pain, painful or difficult urination); **thrombocytopenia** (usually asymptomatic; rarely, unusual bleeding or bruising; black, tarry stools; blood in urine or stools; pinpoint red spots on skin); **thrombosis** (severe or sudden headaches; sudden loss of coordination; pains in chest, groin, or leg, especially calf of leg; sudden and unexplained shortness of breath; sudden slurred speech; sudden vision changes; weakness or numbness in arm or leg)

Those indicating need for medical attention only if they continue or are bothersome

Incidence more frequent

Breast tenderness or enlargement—incidence 20 to 50%; **decreased interest in sex**—occurs in most patients; **diarrhea**—incidence 20 to 50%; **nausea**—incidence 20 to 50%

Incidence less frequent

Trouble in sleeping; vomiting

Note: *Vomiting* is intolerable in approximately 8% of patients.

Patient Consultation

In providing consultation, consider emphasizing the following selected information (» = major clinical significance):

Before using this medication

» Conditions affecting use, especially:

Sensitivity to estramustine, estradiol, or mechlorethamine

Pregnancy—Use not recommended because of mutagenic and teratogenic potential

Other medications, especially hepatotoxic medications

Other medical problems, especially chickenpox, herpes zoster, active or history of thromboembolic disorders (including recent myocardial infarction or stroke), active or history of thrombophlebitis, or peptic ulcer

Smoking

Proper use of this medication

» Importance of not taking more or less medication than the amount prescribed

For best results, taking 1 hour before or 2 hours after meals or milk or milk products

» Frequently causes nausea and sometimes causes vomiting; checking with physician before discontinuing medication

Checking with physician if vomiting occurs shortly after dose is taken

Missed dose: Not taking at all; not doubling doses

» Proper storage

Precautions while using this medication

» Importance of close monitoring by physician

» Avoiding immunizations unless approved by physician; other persons in patient's household should avoid immunizations with oral poliovirus vaccine; avoiding other persons who have taken oral poliovirus vaccine or wearing a protective mask that covers nose and mouth

Side/adverse effects

Signs of potential side effects, especially allergic reaction, anemia, leukopenia, thrombocytopenia, and thrombosis

General Dosing Information

Patients receiving estramustine should be under supervision of a physician experienced in cancer chemotherapy.

A trial period of 30 to 90 days is usually considered adequate for determining whether or not a response will occur.

Estramustine therapy may be continued for as long as a favorable response is maintained.

Nausea and vomiting sometimes responds to treatment with phenothiazines but may be severe enough to necessitate withdrawal of estramustine in some patients.

Diet/Nutrition

It is recommended that estramustine be taken 1 hour before or 2 hours after meals. Milk, milk products, calcium-rich foods, or calcium-containing medications should not be taken simultaneously.

Oral Dosage Forms

ESTRAMUSTINE PHOSPHATE SODIUM CAPSULES

Usual adult dose: Carcinoma, prostatic—Oral, 600 mg (base) per square meter of body surface per day in three divided doses (one hour before or two hours after meals) or 14 mg per kg of body weight (range 10 to 16 mg per kg) per day in three or four divided doses (one hour before or two hours after meals).

Auxiliary labeling:

• Take 1 hour before or 2 hours after meals.

• Avoid milk or milk products.

ESTROGENS   Systemic

Some commonly used *brand names* are:

In the U.S.—

Deladiol-40 [Estradiol]
Delestrogen [Estradiol]
depGynogen [Estradiol]
Depo-Estradiol [Estradiol]
Depogen [Estradiol]
Dioval [Estradiol]
Dioval 40 [Estradiol]
Dioval XX [Estradiol]
Dura-Estrin [Estradiol]
Duragen-10 [Estradiol]
Duragen-20 [Estradiol]
Duragen-40 [Estradiol]
E-Cypionate [Estradiol]
Estinyl [Ethinyl Estradiol]
Estrace [Estradiol]
Estra-D [Estradiol]
Estraderm [Estradiol]
Estradiol L.A. [Estradiol]
Estradiol L.A. 20 [Estradiol]
Estradiol L.A. 40 [Estradiol]
Estra-L 20 [Estradiol]
Estra-L 40 [Estradiol]
Estratab [Esterified Estrogens]
Estraval [Estradiol]
Estro-Cyp [Estradiol]
Estrofem [Estradiol]
Estroject-2 [Estrone]
Estroject-LA [Estradiol]
Estrone '5' [Estrone]
Estrone-A [Estrone]
Estronol [Estrone]

Estronol-LA [Estradiol]
Estrovis [Quinestrol]
Feminone [Ethinyl Estradiol]
Foygen Aqueous [Estrone]
Gynogen [Estrone]
Gynogen L.A. 10 [Estradiol]
Gynogen L.A. 20 [Estradiol]
Gynogen L.A. 40 [Estradiol]
Hormogen Depot [Estradiol]
Kestrin Aqueous [Estrone]
Kestrone-5 [Estrone]
L.A.E. 20 [Estradiol]
Menest [Esterified Estrogens]
Ogen .625 [Estropipate]
Ogen 1.25 [Estropipate]
Ogen 2.5 [Estropipate]
Ogen 5 [Estropipate]
Premarin [Conjugated Estrogens]
Premarin Intravenous [Conjugated Estrogens]
Stilphostrol [Diethylstilbestrol]
TACE [Chlorotrianisene]
Theelin Aqueous [Estrone]
Unigen [Estrone]
Valergen-10 [Estradiol]
Valergen-20 [Estradiol]
Wehgen [Estrone]

In Canada—

C.E.S. [Conjugated Estrogens]
Conjugated Estrogens C.S.D. [Conjugated Estrogens]
Delestrogen [Estradiol]
Estinyl [Ethinyl Estradiol]
Estrace [Estradiol]
Estraderm [Estradiol]
Femogen Forte [Estrone]

Femogex [Estradiol]
Honvol [Diethylstilbestrol]
Neo-Estrone [Esterified Estrogens]
Ogen [Estropipate]
Premarin [Conjugated Estrogens]
Premarin Intravenous [Conjugated Estrogens]
TACE [Chlorotrianisene]

Other commonly used names are:

DES [Diethylstilbestrol]

Piperazine Estrone Sulfate [Estropipate]

CHLOROTRIANISENE
Oral
Chlorotrianisene Capsules USP
In the U.S. and Canada—*TACE*

DIETHYLSTILBESTROL
Oral
Diethylstilbestrol Tablets USP
In the U.S.—GENERIC
Diethylstilbestrol Tablets USP (Enteric-coated)
In the U.S.—GENERIC
Diethylstilbestrol Diphosphate Tablets
In the U.S.—*Stilphostrol*
In Canada—*Honvol*

Parenteral
Diethylstilbestrol Diphosphate Injection USP
In the U.S.—*Stilphostrol*
In Canada—*Honvol*

ESTRADIOL
Oral
Estradiol Tablets USP
In the U.S. and Canada—*Estrace*
Parenteral
Estradiol Cypionate Injection USP
In the U.S.—*depGynogen; Depo-Estradiol; Depogen; Dura-Estrin; E-Cypionate; Estra-D; Estro-Cyp; Estrofem; Estroject-LA; Estronol-LA; Hormogen Depot;* GENERIC
Estradiol Valerate Injection USP
In the U.S.—*Deladiol-40; Delestrogen; Dioval; Dioval 40; Dioval XX; Duragen-10; Duragen-20; Duragen-40; Estradiol L.A.; Estradiol L.A. 20; Estradiol L.A. 40; Estra-L 20; Estra-L 40; Estraval; Gynogen L.A. 10; Gynogen L.A. 20; Gynogen L.A. 40; L.A.E. 20; Valergen-10; Valergen-20;* GENERIC
In Canada—*Delestrogen; Femogex*
Topical
Estradiol Transdermal System
In the U.S. and Canada—*Estraderm*

ESTROGENS, CONJUGATED
Oral
Conjugated Estrogens Tablets USP
In the U.S.—*Premarin*
In Canada—*C.E.S.; Conjugated Estrogens C.S.D.; Premarin*
Parenteral
Conjugated Estrogens for Injection
In the U.S. and Canada—*Premarin Intravenous*

ESTROGENS, ESTERIFIED
Oral
Esterified Estrogens Tablets USP
In the U.S.—*Estratab; Menest*
In Canada—*Neo-Estrone*

ESTRONE
Parenteral
Sterile Estrone Suspension USP
In the U.S.—*Estroject-2; Estrone '5'; Estrone-A; Estronol; Foygen Aqueous; Gynogen; Kestrin Aqueous; Kestrone-5; Theelin Aqueous; Unigen; Wehgen;* GENERIC
In Canada—*Femogen Forte*

ESTROPIPATE
Oral
Estropipate Tablets USP
In the U.S.—*Ogen .625; Ogen 1.25; Ogen 2.5; Ogen 5*
In Canada—*Ogen*

ETHINYL ESTRADIOL
Oral
Ethinyl Estradiol Tablets USP
In the U.S.—*Estinyl; Feminone*
In Canada—*Estinyl*

QUINESTROL
Oral
Quinestrol Tablets USP
In the U.S.—*Estrovis*

Category

Estrogen (systemic)—Chlorotrianisene; Conjugated Estrogens; Diethylstilbestrol; Esterified Estrogens; Estradiol; Estrone; Estropipate; Ethinyl Estradiol; Quinestrol.

Antineoplastic—Chlorotrianisene; Conjugated Estrogens Tablets USP; Diethylstilbestrol; Esterified Estrogens; Estradiol; Estradiol Valerate; Estrone; Ethinyl Estradiol.

Osteoporosis prophylactic—Conjugated Estrogens Tablets USP; Diethylstilbestrol Tablets USP; Diethylstilbestrol Tablets USP (Enteric-coated); Esterified Estrogens; Estradiol Tablets USP; Estradiol Transdermal System; Estropipate; Ethinyl Estradiol.

Indications

Note: Bracketed information in the *Indications* section refers to uses not included in U.S. product labeling.

Accepted

Estrogen deficiency (treatment);

Vaginitis, atrophic (treatment);

Hypogonadism, female (treatment);

Vulvar squamous hyperplasia (treatment);

Ovarian failure, primary (treatment);

Menopause, vasomotor symptoms of (treatment); or

Bleeding, uterine, hormonal imbalance-induced (treatment)—Conjugated estrogens tablets, estradiol, estradiol valerate, esterified estrogens, estrone, estropipate, and quinestrol are indicated as estrogen replacement therapy in the treatment of atrophic vaginitis, female hypogonadism or castration, vulvar squamous hyperplasia, primary ovarian failure, and moderate to severe vasomotor symptoms associated with menopause.

Chlorotrianisene is indicated as estrogen replacement therapy in the treatment of atrophic vaginitis, female hypogonadism, vulvar squamous hyperplasia, and moderate to severe vasomotor symptoms of menopause.

Conjugated estrogens for injection, [estradiol valerate], estrone, and [ethinyl estradiol] are indicated in the treatment of inorganic abnormal uterine bleeding caused by hormonal imbalance.

Estradiol cypionate[1] and ethinyl estradiol[1] are indicated as estrogen replacement therapy in the treatment of female hypogonadism and moderate to severe vasomotor symptoms of menopause.

Carcinoma, breast (treatment)—Conjugated estrogens tablets, diethylstilbestrol tablets and enteric-coated tablets, [estradiol valerate], esterified estrogens[1], estradiol tablets, and [ethinyl estradiol] are indicated for treatment of metastatic breast carcinoma in selected men and postmenopausal women.

Carcinoma, prostatic (treatment)—Chlorotrianisene, conjugated estrogens tablets, diethylstilbestrol, esterified estrogens[1], estradiol, estradiol valerate, estrone, and [ethinyl estradiol] are indicated for treatment of advanced prostatic carcinoma.

Osteoporosis, postmenopausal (prophylaxis)—Conjugated estrogens tablets, diethylstilbestrol tablets[1], diethylstilbestrol enteric-coated tablets[1], esterified estrogens[1], estradiol tablets[1] and transdermal system, ethinyl estradiol[1], and estropipate[1] are indicated in postmenopausal women to retard bone loss and estrogen deficiency-induced osteoporosis. Estrogen replacement therapy can reduce the rate of bone loss and fractures in postmenopausal women. Proper diet, calcium supplementation, and physical activity should also be encouraged along with estrogen replacement therapy.

[Osteoporosis, premenopausal, estrogen deficiency-induced (prophylaxis)][1]—Conjugated estrogens tablets, diethylstilbestrol tablets, diethylstilbestrol enteric-coated tablets, esterified estrogens, estradiol tablets, ethinyl estradiol, and estropipate are also used in premenopausal women who are estrogen-deficient to protect them against bone loss.

[Atherosclerotic disease (prophylaxis)][1]—Estrogens may be effective in the prevention of cardiovascular disease in postmenopausal women.

[Turner's syndrome (treatment)][1]—Ethinyl estradiol is used in the treatment of Turner's syndrome (gonadal dysgenesis).

Chlorotrianisene, estropipate, and quinestrol are infrequently prescribed for estrogen replacement therapy. Also, there is very little use for estrogens administered parenterally.

Unaccepted

The use of estrogens to reduce postpartum breast engorgement is not recommended. In many patients, postpartum breast engorgement is a benign, self-limited condition that may respond to breast support and mild analgesics, such as acetaminophen and ibuprofen. Evidence supporting the efficacy of estrogens for this indication is lacking. Therefore, the questionable benefits of administering the large doses of estrogens required for this indication are outweighed by the risk of increasing the incidence of puerperal thromboembolism.

Ethinyl estradiol, conjugated estrogens, and diethylstilbestrol tablets have been used as postcoital contraceptives (the "morning-after pill"), primarily in emergency care situations, such as the management of rape or incest victims. However, the combination oral contraceptive, norgestrel and ethinyl estradiol, is more commonly prescribed for this indication.

---

[1]Not included in Canadian product labeling.

Pharmacology

Mechanism of action/Effect: At the cellular level, estrogens increase the synthesis of DNA, RNA, and various proteins in target tissues. Pituitary mass is also increased. Estrogens reduce the release of gonadotropin-releasing hormone from the hypothalamus, leading to a reduction in release of follicle-stimulating hormone and luteinizing hormone from the pituitary.

For estrogen replacement—In healthy females, endogenous estrogens maintain genitourinary function and vasomotor stability. Estrogens are used as replacement therapy to alleviate or prevent symptoms caused by the decreased amounts of estrogens produced by the ovaries after natural or surgical menopause or other estrogen-deficiency states.

For prevention of postmenopausal osteoporosis—During periods of estrogen deficiency, the rate of bone resorption by osteoclasts greatly exceeds the rate of bone formation by osteoblasts. Estrogen replacement therapy prevents this accelerated bone loss by inhibiting bone resorption to a level where the near equilibrium between bone resorption and formation is restored. However, estrogens do not replace previously lost bone or significantly increase total bone mass.

For prostatic carcinoma—Inhibition of pituitary secretion of luteinizing hormone and a possible minor, direct effect on the testis, resulting in decreased serum concentrations of testosterone.

Precautions to Consider

Geriatrics

Studies performed to date have not demonstrated geriatrics-specific problems that would limit the usefulness of estrogens in the elderly.

Dental

Estrogens may predispose the patient to bleeding of the gingival tissues. In addition, gingival hyperplasia may occur during estrogen therapy, usually starting as gingivitis or gum inflammation. A strictly enforced program of teeth cleaning by a professional, combined with plaque control by the patient, will minimize growth rate and severity of gingival enlargement.

Drug interactions and/or related problems

The following drug interactions and/or related problems have been selected on the basis of their potential clinical significance (possible mechanism in parentheses where appropriate)—not necessarily inclusive (» = major clinical significance):

Note: Combinations containing any of the following medications, depending on the amount present, may also interact with this medication.

Adrenocorticoids, glucocorticoid

(concurrent use with estrogens may alter the metabolism and protein binding of the glucocorticoids, leading to decreased

clearance, increased elimination half-life, and increased therapeutic and toxic effects of the glucocorticoids; glucocorticoid
dosage adjustment may be required during and following concurrent use)

» Bromocriptine
  (estrogens may cause amenorrhea, interfering with effects of
  bromocriptine; concurrent use is not recommended)

Calcium supplements
  (concurrent use with estrogens may increase calcium absorption; this can be used to therapeutic advantage)

Corticotropin (chronic therapeutic use)
  (concurrent use with estrogens may potentiate the anti-inflammatory effects of endogenous cortisol induced by corticotropin)

» Cyclosporine
  (estrogens have been reported to inhibit cyclosporine metabolism and thereby increase plasma concentrations of cyclosporine,
  possibly increasing the risk of hepatotoxicity and nephrotoxicity; concurrent use is recommended only with great caution
  and frequent monitoring of blood cyclosporine concentrations
  and liver and renal function)

» Hepatotoxic medications, especially dantrolene
  (concurrent use of these medications with estrogens may increase the risk of hepatotoxicity; with use in females over 35
  years of age, prolonged use, or use in patients with a history of
  liver disease, risk may be further increased)

Smoking, tobacco
  (data from studies on tobacco smoking and the use of high-
  dose estrogen oral contraceptives indicate that there is an increased risk of serious cardiovascular side effects, including
  cerebrovascular accident, transient ischemic attacks, thrombophlebitis, and pulmonary embolism; risk increases with increasing tobacco usage and with age, especially in women over
  35 years of age; it is not known whether any elevation of risk
  occurs with tobacco smoking during the use of estrogen replacement therapy)
  (metabolism of estrogens may also be increased by smoking,
  resulting in a decreased estrogenic effect)

Somatrem or
Somatropin
  (in prepubertal patients, concurrent use of estrogens with
  somatrem or somatropin may accelerate epiphyseal maturation)

Tamoxifen
  (concurrent use may interfere with therapeutic effect of
  tamoxifen)

Contraindications/Medical problems
The contraindications/medical problems included have been selected
  on the basis of their potential clinical significance (reasons given
  in parentheses where appropriate)—not necessarily inclusive (» =
  major clinical significance).

*Except under special circumstances, this medication should not be
used when the following medical problems exist:*

» Breast cancer, known or suspected, except in selected patients
  treated for metastatic diseases
  (possible promotion of tumor growth in breast cancer)

» Vaginal bleeding, abnormal and undiagnosed
  (may indicate the presence of endometrial hyperplasia or carcinoma, which may be exacerbated or promoted by the use of
  estrogens)

*Risk-benefit should be considered when the following medical prob-
lems exist:*

Endometriosis
  (endometrial implants may be aggravated by use of estrogens)

Gallbladder disease, or history of, especially gallstones
  (conflicting evidence exists as to whether an increased risk of
  recurrence or exacerbation occurs secondary to estrogen use)

Hepatic dysfunction
  (metabolism of estrogens may be impaired)

» Hypercalcemia associated with metastatic breast disease
  (severe hypercalcemia may occur in patients with breast cancer
  and bone metastases who are treated with estrogens; estrogens
  may aggravate breast cancer-induced hypercalcemia, through
  alterations in the metabolism of calcium and phosphorus; appropriate monitoring is recommended)

Jaundice, or history of during pregnancy
  (estrogens may increase risk of recurrence)

Porphyria, hepatic—acute intermittent or variegate
  (may be exacerbated)

Sensitivity to estrogens

» Thrombophlebitis or thromboembolic disorders, active
  (may be exacerbated)

Uterine fibroids
  (may increase in size during estrogen therapy)

*For all indications, except for the treatment of breast cancer or pros-
tatic cancer*

» Thrombophlebitis, thrombosis, or thromboembolic disorders, estrogen-induced, history of
  (resumption of estrogen therapy may result in recurrence)

*For treatment of male breast cancer or prostatic cancer only (in
addition to those conditions listed above)*

Cerebrovascular disease or
Coronary artery disease or
Thrombophlebitis, active, or
Thromboembolic disorders
  (the large doses of estrogens used in males to treat breast and
  prostate cancer have been associated with an increased risk of
  myocardial infarction, pulmonary embolism, and thrombophlebitis)

Side/Adverse Effects
The following side/adverse effects have been selected on the basis of
  their potential clinical significance (possible signs and symptoms
  in parentheses where appropriate)—not necessarily inclusive:

Those indicating need for medical attention
Incidence more frequent
  Breast pain or tenderness—in females as well as in males treated
  for prostatic cancer; *peripheral edema* (swelling of feet and lower
  legs, rapid weight gain); *enlargement of breasts*—in females; *gynecomastia* (increased breast size)—in males treated for prostatic
  cancer

Incidence less frequent or rare
  Amenorrhea (stopping of menstrual bleeding), *breakthrough bleeding* (heavier vaginal bleeding between regular menses), *menorrhagia* (prolonged or heavier menses), *or spotting* (lighter vaginal
  bleeding between regular menses); *breast tumors* (breast lumps,
  discharge from breast); *chorea* (involuntary jerky muscular movements); *gallbladder obstruction or hepatitis* (yellow eyes or skin;
  pains in stomach, side, or abdomen)

  Note: If persistent or recurring *abnormal vaginal bleeding* occurs,
  malignancy should be ruled out. However, *withdrawal bleeding* will frequently occur in patients placed on cyclic estrogen therapy with a progestin who have not undergone hysterectomy.

*For treatment of male breast cancer or prostatic cancer only (in
addition to those listed above)*
  Thromboembolism or thrombus formation (severe or sudden headache; sudden loss of coordination; pains in chest, groin, or leg,
  especially calf; sudden and unexplained shortness of breath; sudden slurred speech; sudden vision changes; weakness or numbness
  in arm or leg)

  Note: The use of large doses of estrogens in males to treat breast
  and prostate cancer has been associated with an increased

risk of *myocardial infarction, pulmonary embolism,* and *thrombophlebitis.*

Those indicating need for medical attention only if they continue or are bothersome
Incidence more frequent
> *Abdominal cramping or bloating; anorexia* (loss of appetite); *nausea; skin irritation and redness*—with transdermal system

Incidence less frequent
> *Diarrhea, mild; dizziness, mild; headaches, mild; intolerance to contact lenses; libido, decrease*—in males; *libido, increase*—in females; *migraine headaches; vomiting*—primarily of central origin; usually with high doses

Patient Consultation

In providing consultation, consider emphasizing the following selected information (» = major clinical significance):

Before using this medication
» Conditions affecting use, especially:
   Sensitivity to estrogens
   Carcinogenicity—Increased risk of endometrial cancer for patients with intact uteri placed on unopposed estrogen replacement therapy; decreased risk occurs when used with a progestin; male breast cancer has occurred in association with estrogen use; continuous, long-term estrogen use in animal studies increased frequency of cancers of the breast, cervix, and liver
   Pregnancy—Use of some estrogens suggested to be associated with congenital abnormalities
   Breast-feeding—Use is not recommended because estrogens are excreted in breast milk and may have unpredictable effects
   Use in children—Use in children or growing adolescents may slow or stop growth
   Other medications, especially bromocriptine, cyclosporine, or hepatotoxic medications; smoking tobacco may increase risk of cardiovascular side effects and increase metabolism of estrogen
   Other medical problems, especially some types of breast cancer; abnormal and undiagnosed vaginal bleeding; history of estrogen-induced thrombophlebitis, thrombosis, or thromboembolic disorders; or active thrombophlebitis or thromboembolic disorders
» Reading patient package insert carefully

Proper use of this medication
» Proper storage
For oral or parenteral dosage forms
» Compliance with therapy
   Taking with or immediately after food to reduce nausea
   Missed dose: Taking as soon as possible; not taking if almost time for next dose; not doubling doses

For transdermal estradiol
   Reading patient directions
   Washing and drying hands thoroughly before and after application
   Applying to clean, dry, non-oily, hairless, intact area of skin on the abdomen or buttocks; not applying over cuts or irritation
» Not applying to breasts; not applying to waistline or other areas where tight clothes may rub disk loose
   Pressing the disk firmly in place with palm for about 10 seconds; making sure there is good contact, especially around edges
   Reapplying disk if it comes loose, or discarding and applying a new one
   Applying each patch to different area of skin on abdomen or buttocks so at least 1 week elapses before the area is used again to help prevent skin irritation
   Missed dose: Using as soon as possible; not using if almost time for next dose; not doubling doses

Precautions while using this medication
» Regular visits to physician every year, or more often, as determined by physician
   Possibility of dental problems, such as tenderness, swelling, or bleeding of gums; brushing and flossing teeth, massaging gums, and having dentist clean teeth regularly; checking with dentist if there are questions about care of teeth or gums or if tenderness, swelling, or bleeding of gums is noticed
» Stopping medication immediately and checking with physician if pregnancy is suspected
   Importance of not giving medication to anyone else

Side/adverse effects
> Withdrawal bleeding will occur in many postmenopausal patients with an intact uterus who are placed on cyclic estrogen therapy with a progestin
> Signs of potential side effects, especially menstrual irregularities, chorea, breast tumors, peripheral edema, gallbladder obstruction, hepatitis; for treatment of prostatic cancer and male breast cancer only—thromboembolism or thrombus formation

General Dosing Information

As a general rule, unopposed (without a progestin) estrogen therapy should be administered at the lowest effective dosage. When prolonged therapy is necessary, the patient should be re-evaluated at least every year to determine the need for continued therapy.

An estrogen may be administered for the entire period of estrogen deficiency. With chronic administration of estrogens in patients with the uterus in situ, the concurrent use of a progestin during the last 10 to 14 days of the cycle should be considered. Administration of a progestin decreases the risk of occurrence of endometrial hyperplasia and endometrial carcinoma. There is no risk of endometrial hyperplasia or endometrial carcinoma in patients who do not have an intact uterus. In the prevention of conditions such as osteoporosis or atherosclerotic disease, estrogen and progestin therapy may continue for several years or for the remainder of the life of the patient. With prolonged therapy, the patient should be evaluated at least every year.

Estrogens may be administered on a cyclic or continuous regimen when used to treat estrogen deficiency states, for prevention of osteoporosis, and for prevention of atherosclerotic disease. Some patients are placed on a cyclic regimen consisting of three weeks of estrogen therapy, with a progestin being concurrently administered (if indicated) for 10 to 14 days of the three-week period. The fourth and final week of the cycle, no medication is administered. An alternative cyclical schedule consists of the administration of an estrogen for the first 25 days of each calendar month, with no drug being administered for the remainder of the month (3 to 6 days). A progestin may be administered concurrently during the final 10 to 14 days of each estrogen cycle (monthly dates 12 or 16 through 25). Other physicians advocate the use of continuous estrogen dosing with a progestin administered (if indicated) for 10 to 14 days of each month.

Estrogen therapy may cause nausea, especially in the morning, when either oral or parenteral dosage is used. Although this nausea is primarily of central origin, eating solid food often provides some relief.

For parenteral dosage forms only
Intramuscular injections should be administered slowly and deeply into a large muscle area such as the upper outer quadrant of the buttock.

Rapid intravenous injections may cause perineal or vaginal burning.

A dry syringe and needle of at least 21 gauge should be used for the oil-vehicle preparations.

For transdermal dosage forms of estradiol only
Patients who are currently taking oral estrogens should wait 1 week after withdrawal of oral estrogens before the transdermal dosage system is initiated.

Transdermal estradiol is generally administered on a continuous regimen, with a progestin administered (if indicated) for 10 to 14 days of each month.

The adhesive side of the transdermal system should be placed on a clean, dry area of the skin on the trunk of the body. The abdomen is the preferred site, though the patch may also be applied to the buttocks. It should not be applied to the breasts or waistline. The area selected should not be oily or irritated and the skin should not be broken. The application site should be rotated, and no site should be reused until 1 week has passed.

The system should be applied immediately after removal from the pouch and removal of the protective liner. It should not be stored unpouched. The system should be pressed firmly in place with the palm of the hand for about 10 seconds, making sure there is good contact, especially around the edges.

If a transdermal system loosens or falls off, it may be reapplied or a new system may be applied instead. In either case, the patient should continue with the original treatment schedule.

CHLOROTRIANISENE

Oral Dosage Forms

CHLOROTRIANISENE CAPSULES USP

Usual adult dose:
Estrogen (replacement therapy)—
Atrophic vaginitis or
Menopausal symptoms (vasomotor) or
Vulvar squamous hyperplasia: Oral, 12 to 25 mg a day, cyclically or continuously.
Female hypogonadism: Oral, 12 to 25 mg a day, cyclically or continuously.
Antineoplastic—Prostatic carcinoma: Oral, 12 to 25 mg a day.

Note: Chlorotrianisene provides a long-acting effect, which sometimes makes cyclical therapy difficult.

DIETHYLSTILBESTROL

Oral Dosage Forms

DIETHYLSTILBESTROL TABLETS USP

Usual adult dose: Antineoplastic—
Breast carcinoma (inoperable and progressing in selected men and postmenopausal women): Oral, 15 mg a day.
Prostatic carcinoma (inoperable and progressing): Oral, 1 to 3 mg initially and increased as needed in advanced cases, with the dosage later being reduced to 1 mg a day.
Note: The doses in prostatic carcinoma have been found to have a maximal effect in maintenance doses of up to 1 mg a day. Higher doses do not appreciably increase the therapeutic results, but may increase the risk of cardiovascular embolism.

DIETHYLSTILBESTROL TABLETS USP (ENTERIC-COATED)

Usual adult dose:
Antineoplastic—
Breast carcinoma (inoperable and progressing in selected men and postmenopausal women): Oral, 15 mg a day.
Prostatic carcinoma (inoperable and progressing): Oral, 1 to 3 mg initially and increased as needed in advanced cases, with the dosage later being reduced to 1 mg a day.

Note: The doses in prostatic carcinoma have been found to have a maximal effect in maintenance doses of up to 1 mg a day. Higher doses do not appreciably increase the therapeutic results, but may increase the risk of thromboembolism or myocardial toxicity.

Auxiliary labeling: • Do not break, crush, or chew tablets.

DIETHYLSTILBESTROL DIPHOSPHATE TABLETS

Usual adult dose: Antineoplastic—Prostatic carcinoma (inoperable and progressing): Oral, 50 to 166 mg three times a day, the dosage being increased gradually to 200 mg or more, three times a day as needed and tolerated.

Usual adult prescribing limits: Oral, 1 gram a day.

Parenteral Dosage Forms

DIETHYLSTILBESTROL DIPHOSPHATE INJECTION USP

Usual adult dose: Antineoplastic—Prostatic carcinoma (inoperable and progressing):
Induction—Intravenous infusion, initially 500 mg in 250 mL of Sodium Chloride Injection USP or 5% Dextrose Injection USP administered at a rate of 1 mL per minute during the first ten to fifteen minutes, the flow then being adjusted to permit dose completion within one hour. The dosage is increased to 1 gram a day for the subsequent five or more days as needed for relief.
Maintenance—Intravenous infusion, 250 to 500 mg in 250 mL of Sodium Chloride Injection USP or 5% Dextrose Injection USP administered once or twice a week at same rate as during induction.

ESTRADIOL

Oral Dosage Forms

ESTRADIOL TABLETS USP

Usual adult dose:
Estrogen (replacement therapy)—
Atrophic vaginitis or
Female hypogonadism or
Menopausal (vasomotor) symptoms or
Ovariectomy or
Primary ovarian failure or
Vulvar squamous hyperplasia: Oral, 500 mcg (0.5 mg) to 2 mg a day, cyclically or continuously.
Antineoplastic—
Breast carcinoma (inoperable and progressing in selected men and postmenopausal women): Oral, 10 mg three times a day for at least three months.
Prostatic carcinoma (inoperable and progressing): Oral, 1 to 2 mg three times a day.

Parenteral Dosage Forms

Note: Bracketed uses in the *Dosage Forms* section refer to categories of use and/or indications that are not included in U.S. product labeling.

ESTRADIOL CYPIONATE INJECTION USP

Usual adult dose: Estrogen (replacement therapy)—
Female hypogonadism: Intramuscular, 1.5 to 2 mg administered at monthly intervals.
Menopausal (vasomotor) symptoms: Intramuscular, 1 to 5 mg administered at three- to four-week intervals.

ESTRADIOL VALERATE INJECTION USP

Usual adult dose:
Estrogen (replacement therapy)—
Atrophic vaginitis or
Female hypogonadism or
Menopausal (vasomotor) symptoms or
Ovariectomy or
Primary ovarian failure or
Vulvar squamous hyperplasia: Intramuscular, 10 to 20 mg repeated every four weeks as needed.
[Antineoplastic]—Prostatic carcinoma (inoperable and progressing): Intramuscular, 30 mg every one or two weeks, the dose being adjusted as needed.

Topical Dosage Forms

ESTRADIOL TRANSDERMAL SYSTEM

Usual adult dose: Estrogen (replacement therapy)—
Atrophic vaginitis or
Female hypogonadism or
Menopausal (vasomotor) symptoms or
Osteoporosis, postmenopausal (prophylaxis) or
Ovariectomy or
Primary ovarian failure or
Vulvar squamous hyperplasia: Topical, to the skin, one transdermal dosage system delivering per day 50 mcg (0.05 mg) or 100 mcg (0.10 mg), worn continuously and replaced twice a week. Treatment is usually initiated with 50 mcg (0.05 mg), the dosage being adjusted as necessary to control symptoms.

ESTROGENS, CONJUGATED

Oral Dosage Forms

CONJUGATED ESTROGENS TABLETS USP

Usual adult dose:
Estrogen (replacement therapy)—
Atrophic vaginitis or
Vulvar squamous hyperplasia: Oral, 300 mcg (0.3 mg) to 1.25 mg or more a day, cyclically or continuously.
Note: May be used in conjunction with vaginal dosage forms.
Female hypogonadism: Oral, 2.5 to 7.5 mg a day, in divided doses, cyclically or continuously.
Menopausal (vasomotor) symptoms: Oral, 625 mcg (0.625 mg) to 1.25 mg a day, cyclically or continuously.
Ovariectomy or
Primary ovarian failure: Oral, 1.25 mg a day, cyclically or continuously. For maintenance, adjust estrogen dose to lowest level that provides control.
Antineoplastic—
Breast carcinoma (inoperable and progressing in selected men and postmenopausal women): Oral, 10 mg three times a day for at least three months.
Prostatic carcinoma (inoperable and progressing): Oral, 1.25 to 2.5 mg three times a day.
Osteoporosis prophylactic—Oral, 300 mcg (0.3 mg) to 1.25 mg a day, cyclically or continuously.

Parenteral Dosage Forms

CONJUGATED ESTROGENS FOR INJECTION

Usual adult dose: Estrogen—Abnormal uterine bleeding (hormonal imbalance): Intramuscular or intravenous, 25 mg repeated in six to twelve hours if needed.
Note: Intravenous administration is preferred because of the more rapid response obtained. To reduce the possibility of a flushing reaction, the medication should be administered slowly.

ESTROGENS, ESTERIFIED

Oral Dosage Forms

ESTERIFIED ESTROGENS TABLETS USP

Usual adult dose:
Estrogen (replacement therapy)—
Atrophic vaginitis or
Vulvar squamous hyperplasia: Oral, 300 mcg (0.3 mg) to 1.25 mg or more a day, depending on response of patient, cyclically or continuously.
Note: May be used in conjunction with vaginal dosage forms.
Female hypogonadism: Oral, 2.5 to 7.5 mg a day, in divided doses, cyclically or continuously.
Menopausal (vasomotor) symptoms: Oral, 625 mcg (0.625 mg) to 1.25 mg a day, cyclically or continuously.
Ovariectomy or
Primary ovarian failure: Oral, 1.25 mg a day, cyclically or continuously. For maintenance, adjust estrogen dose to lowest level that provides control.
Antineoplastic—
Breast carcinoma (inoperable and progressing in selected men and postmenopausal women): Oral, 10 mg three times a day for at least three months.
Prostatic carcinoma (inoperable and progressing): Oral, 1.25 to 2.5 mg three times a day.
Osteoporosis (prophylaxis)—Oral, 300 mcg (0.3 mg) to 1.25 mg a day, cyclically or continuously.

ESTRONE

Parenteral Dosage Forms

STERILE ESTRONE SUSPENSION USP

Usual adult dose:
Estrogen—Abnormal uterine bleeding (hormonal imbalance): Intramuscular, 2 to 5 mg a day for several days.
Estrogen (replacement therapy)—
Female hypogonadism or
Ovariectomy or
Primary ovarian failure: Intramuscular, 100 mcg (0.1 mg) to 2 mg a week, administered as a single dose or in divided doses, cyclically or continuously.
Atrophic vaginitis or
Menopausal (vasomotor) symptoms or
Vulvar squamous hyperplasia: Intramuscular, 100 to 500 mcg (0.1 to 0.5 mg) two or three times a week, cyclically or continuously.
Antineoplastic—Prostatic carcinoma (inoperable and progressing): Intramuscular, 2 to 4 mg two or three times a week.

ESTROPIPATE

Oral Dosage Forms

ESTROPIPATE TABLETS USP

Usual adult dose: Estrogen (replacement therapy)—
Atrophic vaginitis or
Vulvar squamous hyperplasia: Oral, 750 mcg (0.75 mg) to 6 mg of estropipate a day, cyclically or continuously.
Female hypogonadism: Oral, 1.5 to 9 mg of estropipate a day, cyclically or continuously.
Menopausal (vasomotor) symptoms: Oral, 750 mcg (0.75 mg) to 6 mg of estropipate a day, cyclically or continuously.
Ovariectomy or
Primary ovarian failure: Oral, 1.5 to 9 mg of estropipate a day, cyclically or continuously. For maintenance, adjust dose to lowest level that provides control.

ETHINYL ESTRADIOL

Oral Dosage Forms

ETHINYL ESTRADIOL TABLETS USP

Usual adult dose:
Estrogen (replacement therapy)—
Female hypogonadism: Oral, 50 mcg (0.05 mg) one to three times a day, cyclically or continuously, the dosage being repeated for three to six months to establish a normal menses.

Menopausal (vasomotor) symptoms: Oral, 20 to 50 mcg (0.02 to 0.05 mg) a day, cyclically or continuously.
Antineoplastic—
Breast carcinoma (inoperable and progressing in selected postmenopausal women): Oral, 1 mg three times a day.
Prostatic carcinoma (inoperable and progressing): Oral, 150 mcg (0.15 mg) to 3 mg a day.

QUINESTROL

Oral Dosage Forms

QUINESTROL TABLETS USP

Usual adult dose: Estrogen (replacement therapy)—
Atrophic vaginitis or
Female hypogonadism or
Menopausal (vasomotor) symptoms or
Ovariectomy or
Primary ovarian failure or
Vulvar squamous hyperplasia: Oral, 100 mcg (0.1 mg) a *day* for seven days, followed by one *week* of no medication, after which a maintenance dose of 100 mcg (0.1 mg) once a *week* is taken.

Note: CAUTION patient regarding the unusual dosage: 1 tablet *a day* for induction and then usually 1 tablet *a week* for maintenance.
The weekly maintenance dose may be increased to 200 mcg (0.2 mg) if needed and tolerated.

ESTROGENS   Vaginal

Some commonly used *brand names* are:
In the U.S.—
DV [Dienestrol]
Estrace [Estradiol]
Ogen [Estropipate]
Ortho Dienestrol [Dienestrol]
Premarin [Conjugated Estrogens]
In Canada—
Oestrilin [Estrone]
Ortho Dienestrol [Dienestrol]
Premarin [Conjugated Estrogens]

Another commonly used name for estropipate is piperazine estrone sulfate.

VAGINAL
DIENESTROL
Dienestrol Cream USP
In the U.S.—*DV; Ortho Dienestrol;* GENERIC
In Canada—*Ortho Dienestrol*
ESTRADIOL
Estradiol Vaginal Cream
In the U.S.—*Estrace*
ESTROGENS, CONJUGATED
Conjugated Estrogens Vaginal Cream
In the U.S. and Canada—*Premarin*
ESTRONE*
Estrone Vaginal Cream*
In Canada—*Oestrilin*
Estrone Vaginal Suppositories*
In Canada—*Oestrilin*

ESTROPIPATE
Estropipate Vaginal Cream USP
In the U.S. and Canada—*Ogen*

*Not commercially available in the U.S.

Category: Estrogen (vaginal).

Indications

Accepted
Vaginitis, atrophic (treatment); or
Vulvar squamous hyperplasia (treatment)—Vaginal application of estrogens is indicated in the treatment of atrophic vaginitis or vulvar squamous hyperplasia associated with estrogen deficiency, such as that resulting from menopause or ovariectomy.

Pharmacology

Mechanism of action/Effect: At the cellular level, estrogens increase the cellular synthesis of DNA, RNA, and various proteins in responsive tissues. Estrogens reduce the release of gonadotropin-releasing hormone (GnRH) from the hypothalamus, leading to a reduction in release of follicle-stimulating hormone (FSH) and luteinizing hormone (LH) from the pituitary.

For estrogen replacement—In healthy females, endogenous estrogens maintain genitourinary function and vasomotor stability. Estrogens are used as replacement therapy to alleviate or prevent symptoms caused by the decreased amounts of estrogens produced by the ovaries after natural or surgical menopause or other estrogen-deficiency states.

Precautions to Consider

Note: Recent studies have shown that vaginal estrogen preparations are extensively absorbed. Therefore, some of the same estrogenic effects may be anticipated whether administration is systemic or vaginal.

Geriatrics
Studies performed to date have not demonstrated geriatrics-specific problems that would limit the usefulness of vaginal estrogens in the elderly.

Dental
Estrogens may predispose the patient to bleeding of the gingival tissues. In addition, gingival hyperplasia may occur during estrogen therapy, usually starting as gingivitis or gum inflammation. A strictly enforced program of teeth cleaning by a professional, combined with plaque control by the patient, will minimize growth rate and severity of gingival enlargement.

Drug interactions and/or related problems
The following drug interactions and/or related problems have been selected on the basis of their potential clinical significance (possible mechanism in parentheses where appropriate)—not necessarily inclusive (» = major clinical significance):

Note: Combinations containing any of the following medications, depending on the amount present, may also interact with this medication.

Adrenocorticoids, glucocorticoid
(concurrent use with estrogens may alter the metabolism and protein binding of glucocorticoids, leading to decreased clearance, increased elimination half-life, and increased therapeutic and toxic effects of the glucocorticoids; glucocorticoid dosage adjustment may be required during and following concurrent use)

» Bromocriptine
(estrogens may cause amenorrhea, interfering with effects of bromocriptine; concurrent use is not recommended)

Calcium supplements
(concurrent use with estrogens may increase calcium absorption; this can be used to therapeutic advantage)

Corticotropin (chronic therapeutic use)
(concurrent use with estrogens may potentiate the anti-inflammatory effects of endogenous cortisol induced by corticotropin)

» Cyclosporine
(systemic estrogens have been reported to inhibit cyclosporine metabolism and thereby increase plasma concentrations of cyclosporine, possibly increasing the risk of hepatotoxicity and nephrotoxicity; concurrent use is recommended only with great caution and frequent monitoring of blood cyclosporine concentrations and liver and renal function)

» Hepatotoxic medications, especially dantrolene
(concurrent use of these medications with estrogens may increase the risk of hepatotoxicity; with concurrent use of dantrolene, use in females over 35 years of age, prolonged use, or use in patients with a history of liver disease, risk may be further increased)

Smoking, tobacco
(data from studies on tobacco smoking and the use of high-dose estrogen oral contraceptives indicate that there is an increased risk of serious cardiovascular side effects, including cerebrovascular accident, transient ischemic attacks, thrombo-phlebitis, and pulmonary embolism; risk increases with increasing tobacco usage and with age, especially in women over 35 years of age; it is not known whether any elevation of risk occurs with tobacco smoking during the use of vaginal estrogens for estrogen deficiency)
(metabolism of estrogens may also be increased by smoking, resulting in a decreased estrogenic effect)

Tamoxifen
(concurrent use may interfere with therapeutic effect of tamoxifen)

Contraindications/Medical problems
The contraindications/medical problems included have been selected on the basis of their potential clinical significance (reasons given in parentheses where appropriate)—not necessarily inclusive (» = major clinical significance).

Except under special circumstances, this medication should not be used when the following medical problems exist:

» Breast cancer, known or suspected
(possible promotion of tumor growth in breast cancer)

» Vaginal bleeding, abnormal and undiagnosed
(may indicate the presence of endometrial hyperplasia or carcinoma, which may be exacerbated or promoted by the use of estrogens)

Risk-benefit should be considered when the following medical problems exist:

Endometriosis
(endometrial implants may be aggravated by use of estrogens)

Gallbladder disease, or history of, especially gallstones
(conflicting evidence exists as to whether an increased risk of recurrence or exacerbation occurs secondary to estrogen use)

Hepatic dysfunction
(metabolism of estrogens may be impaired)

Jaundice, or history of during pregnancy
(estrogens may increase risk of recurrence)

Porphyria, hepatic—acute intermittent or variegate
(may be exacerbated)

Sensitivity to estrogens

» Thrombophlebitis or thromboembolic disorders, active
(may be exacerbated)

» Thrombophlebitis, thrombosis, or thromboembolic disorders, estrogen-induced, history of
(resumption of estrogen therapy may result in recurrence)

Uterine fibroids
(may increase in size during estrogen therapy)

Side/Adverse Effects

Note: Recent studies have shown that vaginal estrogen preparations are extensively absorbed. Therefore, some of the same estrogenic effects may be anticipated whether administration is systemic or vaginal.

The following side/adverse effects have been selected on the basis of their potential clinical significance (possible signs and symptoms in parentheses where appropriate)—not necessarily inclusive:

Those indicating need for medical attention
Incidence more frequent
Breast pain or tenderness; enlargement of breasts; peripheral edema (swelling of feet and lower legs, rapid weight gain)

Incidence less frequent or rare
Amenorrhea (stopping of menstrual bleeding), *breakthrough bleeding* (heavier vaginal bleeding between regular menses), *menorrhagia* (prolonged or heavier menses), or *spotting* (lighter vaginal bleeding between regular menses); *breast tumors* (breast lumps, discharge from breast); *chorea* (involuntary jerky muscular move-

ments); ***gallbladder obstruction or hepatitis*** (yellow eyes or skin; pains in stomach, side, or abdomen); ***local irritation, such as swelling, redness, or itching***

Note: If *persistent or recurring abnormal vaginal bleeding* occurs, malignancy should be ruled out. However, withdrawal bleeding will frequently occur in patients placed on cyclic estrogen therapy with a progestin who have not undergone hysterectomy.

Those indicating need for medical attention only if they continue or are bothersome
Incidence more frequent
    Abdominal cramping or bloating; anorexia (loss of appetite)
Incidence less frequent
    Diarrhea, mild; dizziness, mild; headaches, mild; intolerance to contact lenses; libido, increase; migraine headaches

Patient Consultation

In providing consultation, consider emphasizing the following selected information (» = major clinical significance):

Before using this medication
» Conditions affecting use, especially:
    Sensitivity to estrogens
    Carcinogenicity—Increased risk of endometrial cancer for patients with an intact uterus placed on unopposed estrogen replacement therapy; decreased risk occurs when used with a progestin; continuous, long-term estrogen use in animal studies increased frequency of cancers of the breast, cervix, and liver
    Pregnancy—Use of some estrogens suggested to be associated with congenital abnormalities
    Breast-feeding—Use is not recommended because estrogens are excreted in breast milk and may have unpredictable effects
    Other medications, especially bromocriptine, cyclosporine, hepatotoxic medications; smoking tobacco may increase risk of cardiovascular side effects and increase metabolism of estrogen
    Other medical problems, especially some types of breast cancer; abnormal and undiagnosed vaginal bleeding; history of estrogen-induced thrombophlebitis, thrombosis, or thromboembolic disorders; or active thrombophlebitis or thromboembolic disorders
» Reading patient package insert carefully

Proper use of this medication
» Compliance with therapy
    Using medication at bedtime to increase effectiveness; wearing sanitary napkin to protect clothing
    Proper administration technique
    Missed dose: Not using missed dose at all but returning to regular dosing schedule
» Proper storage

Precautions while using this medication
» Regular visits to physician at least every year, or more often, as determined by physician
    Possibility of dental problems, such as tenderness, swelling, or bleeding of gums; brushing and flossing teeth, massaging gums, and having dentist clean teeth regularly; checking with dentist if there are questions about care of teeth or gums or if tenderness, swelling, or bleeding of gums is noticed
» Stopping medication immediately and checking with physician if pregnancy is suspected
    Importance of not giving medication to anyone else

Side/adverse effects
    Withdrawal bleeding will occur in many postmenopausal patients with an intact uterus who are placed on cyclic estrogen therapy with a progestin

Signs of potential side effects, especially menstrual irregularities, chorea, breast tumors, peripheral edema, gallbladder obstruction, or hepatitis

General Dosing Information

Detailed instructions for inserting or applying estrogens vaginally should be furnished to the patient. The manufacturer provides such information on the medication carton or in a patient package insert (PPI).

As a general rule, unopposed estrogen therapy should be administered at the lowest effective dosage. When prolonged therapy is necessary, the patient should be re-evaluated at least every year to determine the need for continued therapy.

In order to avoid overstimulation of estrogen-sensitive tissues, estrogens are applied vaginally each day for 10 days to 3 weeks. During the third and/or fourth weeks of the cycle, the dose is either reduced or the medication discontinued. This schedule is repeated cyclically until improvement of the condition allows a reduced regimen. With chronic use of vaginal estrogens in patients with the uterus in situ, the concurrent use of a progestin during the last 10 to 14 days of the cycle should be considered. Administration of a progestin decreases the risk of occurrence of endometrial hyperplasia and endometrial carcinoma. There is no risk of endometrial hyperplasia or endometrial carcinoma in patients who do not have an intact uterus.

DIENESTROL

Vaginal Dosage Forms

DIENESTROL CREAM USP

Usual adult dose:
    Initial—Intravaginal, one applicatorful one or two times a day for one or two weeks, the dose then being reduced to either one-half to one applicatorful a day or one applicatorful every other day, for an additional one or two weeks.
    Maintenance—Intravaginal, one applicatorful one to three times a week for three weeks with no medication used the fourth week may be used after restoration of vaginal mucosa is achieved.

Auxiliary labeling: • For vaginal use only.

Additional information: One applicatorful holds either 5 grams, containing 500 mcg (0.5 mg), or 6 grams, containing 600 mcg (0.6 mg), of dienestrol, depending on the manufacturer.

ESTRADIOL

Vaginal Dosage Forms

ESTRADIOL VAGINAL CREAM

Usual adult dose:
    Initial—Intravaginal, 2 to 4 grams (containing 200 mcg [0.2 mg] to 400 mcg [0.4 mg] of estradiol) daily for one or two weeks, the dosage then being gradually reduced to one half the initial dosage for one or two weeks.
    Maintenance—Intravaginal, one gram one to three times a week for three weeks with no medication used the fourth week may be used after restoration of vaginal mucosa is achieved.

Auxiliary labeling: • For vaginal use only.

ESTROGENS, CONJUGATED

Vaginal Dosage Forms

CONJUGATED ESTROGENS VAGINAL CREAM

Usual adult dose: Intravaginal or topical, 2 to 4 grams (containing 1.25 to 2.5 mg of conjugated estrogens) daily for three weeks with no medication used the fourth week, the schedule being repeated cyclically as indicated.

Auxiliary labeling: • For vaginal use only.

ESTRONE

Vaginal Dosage Forms

ESTRONE VAGINAL CREAM

Note: Estrone vaginal cream is not commercially available in the U.S.

Usual adult dose: Intravaginal, 2 to 4 grams (containing 2 to 4 mg of estrone) daily.

Auxiliary labeling: • For vaginal use only.

ESTRONE VAGINAL SUPPOSITORIES

Note: Estrone vaginal suppositories are not commercially available in the U.S.

Usual adult dose: Intravaginal, 250 to 500 mcg (0.25 to 0.5 mg) daily.

Auxiliary labeling: • For vaginal use only.

ESTROPIPATE

Vaginal Dosage Forms

ESTROPIPATE VAGINAL CREAM USP

Usual adult dose: Intravaginal, 2 to 4 grams (containing 3 to 6 mg of estropipate) daily for three weeks with no medication used the fourth week, the schedule being repeated cyclically as indicated.

Auxiliary labeling: • For vaginal use only.

ETODOLAC　Systemic†

INN: Etodolic Acid

A commonly used *brand name* in the U.S. is *Lodine*.

Another commonly used name is etodolic acid.

ORAL
Etodolac Capsules†
　In the U.S.—*Lodine*

---

†Not commercially available in Canada.

Category: Antirheumatic (nonsteroidal anti-inflammatory); analgesic; antidysmenorrheal; antigout agent; anti-inflammatory (nonsteroidal); vascular headache suppressant.

Note: Etodolac, like other nonsteroidal anti-inflammatory drugs (NSAIDs), has analgesic, antipyretic, and anti-inflammatory actions. However, indications among NSAIDs may vary because of lack of specific testing and/or clinical-use data.

Indications

Note: Bracketed information in the *Indications* section refers to uses not included in U.S. product labeling.

Accepted
Osteoarthritis (treatment)—Etodolac is indicated for relief of acute or chronic osteoarthritis.

Pain (treatment)—Etodolac is indicated for relief of pain. NSAIDs are especially useful for relieving pain associated with inflammation, e.g., pain following dental, obstetric, or orthopedic surgery, and for relief of musculoskeletal pain due to soft tissue athletic injuries (strains or sprains).

NSAIDs are also recommended for relief of mild to moderate bone pain caused by metastatic neoplastic disease. However, careful patient selection is necessary, especially for patients receiving chemotherapy, because of the potential gastrointestinal or renal toxicity and the platelet aggregation-inhibiting actions of these medications.

NSAIDs that are used to relieve pain are also used in the treatment of the following painful conditions:

[Gouty arthritis, acute (treatment)]; or
[Calcium pyrophosphate deposition disease, acute (treatment)]—NSAIDs are used to relieve the pain and inflammation of acute gouty arthritis and acute calcium pyrophosphate deposition disease (pseudogout, chondrocalcinosis articularis, crystal-induced synovitis).

[Inflammation, nonrheumatic (treatment)]—NSAIDs are used in the treatment of painful nonrheumatic inflammatory conditions, such as athletic injuries, bursitis, capsulitis, synovitis, tendinitis, or tenosynovitis.

[Dysmenorrhea (treatment)]—NSAIDs are used to relieve the pain of primary dysmenorrhea.

[Headache, vascular (treatment)]—NSAIDs are used to relieve pain caused by migraine headache or other vascular headaches.

Pharmacology

Mechanism of action/Effect: NSAIDs inhibit the activity of the enzyme cyclo-oxygenase, resulting in decreased formation of precursors of prostaglandins and thromboxanes from arachidonic acid. Although the resultant decrease in prostaglandin synthesis and activity in various tissues may be responsible for many of the therapeutic (and adverse) effects of NSAIDs, other actions may also contribute significantly to the therapeutic effects of these medications.

Antirheumatic (nonsteroidal anti-inflammatory)—NSAIDs act via analgesic and anti-inflammatory mechanisms; the therapeutic effects are not due to pituitary-adrenal stimulation.

Analgesic—NSAIDs probably block pain impulse generation via a peripheral action that may involve reduction of the activity of prostaglandins, and possibly inhibition of the synthesis or actions of other substances that sensitize pain receptors to mechanical or chemical stimulation.

Antigout agent—NSAIDs act via analgesic and anti-inflammatory mechanisms.

Anti-inflammatory (nonsteroidal)—Exact mechanisms have not been determined. NSAIDs may act peripherally in inflamed tissue, probably by reducing prostaglandin activity in these tissues and possibly by inhibiting the synthesis and/or actions of other local mediators of the inflammatory response. Inhibition of leukocyte migration, inhibition of the release and/or actions of lysosomal enzymes, and actions on other cellular and immunological processes in mesenchymal and connective tissue may be involved.

Antidysmenorrheal—By inhibiting the synthesis and activity of intrauterine prostaglandins (which are thought to be responsible for the pain and other symptoms of primary dysmenorrhea), NSAIDs decrease uterine contractility and uterine pressure, increase uterine perfusion, and relieve ischemic as well as spasmodic pain. Also, NSAIDs may relieve to some extent extrauterine symptoms (e.g., headache, nausea, and vomiting) that may be associated with excessive prostaglandin production.

Vascular headache suppressant—Analgesic actions may be involved in relief of headache. Also, by reducing prostaglandin activity, NSAIDs may directly relieve certain types of headache thought to be caused by prostaglandin-induced dilation or constriction of cerebral blood vessels.

Other actions/effects:

Etodolac inhibits collagen-induced platelet aggregation *in vitro,* but it is not as potent as aspirin.

NSAID-induced gastrointestinal toxicity may be caused by a direct irritant or erosive effect of these acidic medications on the mucosa. Also, it has been proposed that the gastrointestinal toxicity of NSAIDs may be caused by decreased synthesis of prostaglandins (which exert a protective effect on the gastrointestinal mucosa) because upper gastrointestinal toxicity has been reported following rectal or parenteral administration of some of these medications. However, in one study, gastric and duodenal prostaglandin concentrations were not altered by 4 weeks of administration of therapeutic doses of etodolac.

The renal toxicity associated with NSAIDs (i.e., decreased renal perfusion, sodium and fluid retention, and decreased renal function) may be caused by inhibition of renal prostaglandins, which are directly involved in the maintenance of renal hemodynamics and sodium and fluid balance. Renal prostaglandins are especially important in maintaining renal function in the presence of generalized vasoconstriction or volume depletion. In studies of the effects of etodolac on renal function, the medication decreased some measures of renal function, with maximum effects occurring within 1.5 to 2.5 hours after administration of a dose. With administration of up to 500 mg every 12 hours, recovery of renal function occurred prior to the next dose, even in patients with pre-existing mild to moderate renal function impairment (creatinine clearances ranging from 20 to 88 mL per minute). Whether more frequent administration of etodolac may cause cumulative effects on renal function has not been determined.

The analgesic, antipyretic, and anti-inflammatory effects of NSAIDs may mask symptoms of the onset and/or progression of an infection.

Onset of action:

Analgesia—Within 30 minutes following administration of single 200- to 400-mg doses.

Osteoarthritis—Analgesic actions of NSAIDs may produce some pain relief within the first day or two of treatment. Significant relief of other symptoms of inflammation usually occurs within a few days to one week; however, in severe cases, two weeks or more of continuous use may be required.

Time to peak effect: Analgesia—1 to 2 hours following administration of a single dose of 200 or 400 mg.

Duration of action:

Single 200-mg dose—4 to 5 hours.

Single 400-mg dose—5 to 6 hours, although analgesia has persisted for 8 to 12 hours in some patients.

Precautions to Consider

Cross-sensitivity and/or related problems

Patients sensitive to one of the nonsteroidal anti-inflammatory drugs (NSAIDs), including aspirin, ketorolac, and NSAIDs no longer commercially available (such as oxyphenbutazone, suprofen, and zomepirac) may be sensitive to etodolac also.

NSAIDs may cause bronchoconstriction or anaphylaxis in aspirin-sensitive asthmatics, especially those with the "aspirin triad" (nasal polyps, asthma, and other allergic reactions induced by aspirin). Patients with bronchospastic reactions to aspirin may be desensitized to this effect by administration of initially small and gradually increasing doses of aspirin. Desensitization must be carried out by physicians who are experienced with the technique, in a facility having personnel, equipment, and medications immediately available for treatment of any adverse reaction to the medication (especially anaphylaxis or severe bronchospasm). Desensitization to aspirin also desensitizes the patient to other NSAIDs. However, unless aspirin or another NSAID is then administered on a daily basis, sensitivity to these medications redevelops within a few days.

Geriatrics

Studies performed to date with 200 mg of etodolac twice a day have not shown differences in the pharmacokinetics of the medication in geriatric patients compared with younger adults. Also, studies with 600 mg of etodolac per day have not shown differences in the side effects profile of etodolac in geriatric patients compared with younger adults. However, there is some evidence that NSAID-induced side effects, if they occur, may be more hazardous to geriatric patients than to younger adults. Specifically, NSAID-induced gastrointestinal ulceration and/or bleeding may be more likely to cause serious consequences, including fatalities, in geriatric patients. In general, geriatric patients seem to be more susceptible to NSAID-induced hepatic and/or renal function impairment, especially patients with pre-existing renal function impairment. Therefore, caution and careful titration of dosage are recommended, especially when an increase in dosage is required.

Dental

Etodolac rarely causes ulcerative stomatitis.

Etodolac rarely causes thrombocytopenia, which may result in an increased incidence of microbial infection, delayed healing, and gingival bleeding. If thrombocytopenia occurs, dental work should be deferred until blood counts have returned to normal, and patients should be instructed in proper oral hygiene, including caution in use of regular toothbrushes, dental floss, and toothpicks.

Drug interactions and/or related problems

The following drug interactions and/or related problems have been selected on the basis of their potential clinical significance (possible mechanism in parentheses where appropriate)—not necessarily inclusive (» = major clinical significance):

Note: Combinations containing any of the following medications, depending on the amount present, may also interact with this medication.

All of the interactions listed below have not been documented with etodolac. However, they have been reported with other NSAIDs and should be considered potential precautions to the use of etodolac also, especially with chronic administration.

In addition to the interactions listed below, the possibility should be considered that additive or multiple effects leading to impaired blood clotting and/or increased risk of bleeding may occur if any NSAID is used concurrently with any medication having a significant potential for causing hypoprothrombinemia, thrombocytopenia, or gastrointestinal ulceration or hemorrhage.

Acetaminophen
(prolonged concurrent use of acetaminophen with an NSAID may increase the risk of adverse renal effects; it is recommended that patients be under close medical supervision while receiving such combined therapy)

Adrenocorticoids, glucocorticoid, or
Alcohol or
Corticotropin (chronic therapeutic use) or
Potassium supplements
(concurrent use with an NSAID may increase the risk of gastrointestinal side effects, including ulceration or hemorrhage)

» Anticoagulants, coumarin- or indandione-derivative, or
» Heparin or
» Thrombolytic agents, such as:
Alteplase
Anistreplase
Streptokinase
Urokinase
(etodolac decreases the protein-binding of warfarin, but does not increase clearance of free warfarin; concurrent use has not been shown to alter the activity of warfarin as measured via the prothrombin time test; however, inhibition of platelet aggregation by etodolac, and the potential occurrence of gastrointestinal ulceration or bleeding with prolonged etodolac administration, may be hazardous to patients receiving anticoagulant or thrombolytic therapy)

Antidiabetic agents, oral, or
Insulin
(NSAIDs may increase the hypoglycemic effect of these medications because prostaglandins are directly involved in regulatory mechanisms of glucose metabolism and possibly because of displacement of the oral antidiabetics from serum proteins; dosage adjustments of the antidiabetic agent may be necessary; glipizide and glyburide, due to their nonionic binding characteristics, may not be affected as much as the other oral antidiabetic agents; however, caution with concurrent use is recommended)

Antihypertensives or
Diuretics
(increased monitoring of the response to any antihypertensive agent may be advisable when etodolac is used concurrently because several other NSAIDs have been shown to reduce or reverse the effects of many antihypertensives, possibly by inhibiting renal prostaglandin synthesis and/or by causing sodium and fluid retention)

(etodolac has not interfered with the diuretic effect of diuretics in healthy subjects; however, concurrent use of an NSAID and a diuretic may increase the risk of renal failure secondary to a decrease in renal blood flow caused by inhibition of renal prostaglandin synthesis)

» Aspirin or other salicylates or
Other NSAIDs, especially:
» Phenylbutazone
(concurrent use of salicylates or other NSAIDs with etodolac is not recommended because of the potential for additive toxicity)

(aspirin decreases the protein binding of etodolac, but has no effect on etodolac clearance)

(*in vitro*, phenylbutazone has been shown to decrease the protein binding of etodolac, leading to an 80% increase in the concentration of active [unbound] etodolac; studies to determine whether phenylbutazone alters etodolac clearance have not been done)

» Cefamandole or
» Cefoperazone or
» Cefotetan or
» Moxalactam or
» Plicamycin or
» Valproic acid
(these medications may cause hypoprothrombinemia; in addition, plicamycin or valproic acid may inhibit platelet aggregation, and moxalactam may cause irreversible platelet damage; concurrent use with an NSAID may increase the risk of bleeding because of additive interferences with platelet function and/or the potential occurrence of gastrointestinal ulceration or hemorrhage during NSAID therapy)

» Cyclosporine or
Gold compounds or
Nephrotoxic medications, other
(inhibition of renal prostaglandin activity by NSAIDs may increase the plasma concentration of cyclosporine and/or the risk of cyclosporine-induced nephrotoxicity; patients should be carefully monitored during concurrent use)

(concurrent use of other nephrotoxic medications, including a gold compound, with an NSAID may increase the risk of adverse renal effects)

Digoxin or
» Lithium
(NSAIDs may decrease the excretion and increase the serum concentration of digoxin or lithium, leading to an increased risk of toxicity; careful monitoring of the patient is recommended if concurrent use is necessary)

» Methotrexate
(administration of moderate- or high-dose methotrexate infusions to patients receiving an NSAID may result in severe, even fatal, methotrexate toxicity, possibly because of reduced renal function leading to decreased methotrexate excretion; it is recommended that etodolac not be administered for 12 to 24 hours prior to, and for at least 12 hours [or until the methotrexate plasma concentration has decreased to a nontoxic level] following, a high-dose methotrexate infusion)

(severe, sometimes fatal, methotrexate toxicity has also been reported with the relatively low to moderate doses of methotrexate used in the treatment of rheumatoid arthritis or psoriasis when an NSAID was given concurrently; it is recommended that concurrent use of etodolac with low to moderate doses of methotrexate also be undertaken with caution, with methotrexate dosage being adjusted as determined by monitoring plasma methotrexate concentration and/or adequacy of the patient's renal function)

Nifedipine or
Verapamil
(caution in concurrent use with any NSAID is recommended because of possible displacement of either or both medications from protein-binding sites, leading to increased plasma con-

centrations of the free [unbound] medications and increased risk of toxicity)

Platelet aggregation inhibitors, other

(concurrent use of any of these medications with an NSAID may increase the risk of bleeding because of additive inhibition of platelet aggregation as well as the potential occurrence of gastrointestinal ulceration or hemorrhage during NSAID therapy)

» Probenecid

(although the effect of probenecid on the pharmacokinetics of etodolac has not been studied, concurrent use of the 2 medications should be undertaken with caution because probenecid decreases the renal clearance of many other NSAIDs, resulting in increased plasma concentrations and risk of toxicity)

Contraindications/Medical problems

The contraindications/medical problems included have been selected on the basis of their potential clinical significance (reasons given in parentheses where appropriate)—not necessarily inclusive (» = major clinical significance).

Except under special circumstances, this medication should not be used when the following medical problem exists:

» Nasal polyps associated with bronchospasm, aspirin-induced, or angioedema, anaphylaxis, or other severe allergic reaction induced by aspirin, etodolac, or other NSAIDs, history of

(high risk of severe allergic reactions because of cross-sensitivity)

Risk-benefit should be considered when the following medical problems exist:

Allergic reaction, mild, such as allergic rhinitis, urticaria, or skin rash, induced by aspirin, etodolac, or other NSAIDs, history of

(possibility of cross-sensitivity)

Asthma

(may be exacerbated)

Conditions predisposing to gastrointestinal toxicity, such as:

Alcoholism, active

» Peptic ulcer, ulcerative colitis, or upper gastrointestinal disease, active or history of

Tobacco use, or recent history of

(NSAIDs should preferably not be given to patients with active peptic ulcer disease or gastrointestinal bleeding; if etodolac administration is considered essential, an antiulcer regimen should be administered concurrently)

(caution and close supervision are also recommended for other patients in whom there is a significant risk of gastrointestinal toxicity; misoprostol or sucralfate should be considered as prophylaxis for those at high risk)

Conditions predisposing to fluid retention, such as:

Compromised cardiac function

Hypertension

(etodolac may cause fluid retention and edema; hypertension may be exacerbated)

Congestive heart failure or

Diabetes mellitus or

Edema, pre-existing, or

Extracellular volume depletion or

Hepatic function impairment or

Renal function impairment or

Sepsis

(increased risk of renal failure)

(etodolac is metabolized hepatically; although stable hepatic cirrhosis does not alter the clearance of etodolac, the possibility should be considered that unstable hepatic disease or severe hepatic function impairment may do so)

(etodolac has not been shown to increase the risk of renal toxicity, and the pharmacokinetic profile of etodolac is not altered, when up to 500 mg of etodolac is administered every 12 hours to patients with mild to moderate renal function impairment; however, the possibility of renal toxicity associated with a reduction of renal prostaglandin synthesis leading to a decrease in renal blood flow cannot be discounted; caution and monitoring of patients considered to be at risk are recommended)

» Hemophilia or other bleeding problems including coagulation or platelet function disorders

(increased risk of bleeding because etodolac inhibits platelet aggregation and may cause gastrointestinal ulceration or hemorrhage)

Systemic lupus erythematosus (SLE)

(patient may be predisposed to NSAID-induced central nervous system and/or renal adverse effects)

Side/Adverse Effects

Note: Hypersensitivity reactions with nonsteroidal anti-inflammatory drugs (NSAIDs) may be similar to those reported for aspirin, i.e., rhinosinusitis/asthma or angioedema/urticaria. Although anaphylactic reactions have not been reported with etodolac, they have occurred, rarely, with other NSAIDs, both in aspirin-sensitive patients and in those without known hypersensitivity to any of these agents. The risk of anaphylaxis, characterized by respiratory distress, circulatory collapse, and angioedema and/or urticaria with or without pruritus, may be increased when previously discontinued therapy with an NSAID is reinstituted.

One case of etodolac overdose has been reported, in which an estimated 3 to 8.6 grams was ingested. Five hours after ingestion (3 hours after gastric lavage was performed), the plasma concentration was within the range measured following normal therapeutic doses (22 mcg per mL [76.56 micromoles/L]). Laboratory tests showed a prolonged prothrombin time and false-positive urine bilirubin. However, no signs or symptoms of toxicity occurred.

In rats, long-term administration of etodolac has caused renal papillary necrosis and other renal medullary changes similar to those induced by other NSAIDs. Also, although a causal relationship has not been established, renal pelvic transitional epithelial hyperplasia occurred with increased frequency in male rats during a 2-year chronic study.

The following side/adverse effects have been selected on the basis of their potential clinical significance (possible signs and symptoms in parentheses where appropriate)—not necessarily inclusive:

Those indicating need for medical attention

Incidence less frequent (1 to 3%)

Bloody stools; blurred vision; chills and fever; dermatitis, allergic (skin rash or itching); *frequent or painful urination; gastritis* (burning feeling in chest or stomach); *mental depression; ringing or buzzing in ears*

Incidence rare (< 1%)

Cardiovascular effects, specifically congestive heart failure (chest pain; shortness of breath, troubled breathing, tightness in chest, and/or wheezing; decrease in amount of urine; swelling of face, fingers, feet, or lower legs; unusual tiredness; weight gain), *increase in blood pressure*—may reach hypertensive levels, *or syncope* (fainting); *edema* (swelling of face, fingers, feet, and/or lower legs; weight gain; possibly increased blood pressure); *gastrointestinal tract toxicity, specifically peptic ulceration, possibly with perforation and/or bleeding* (abdominal pain, cramping, or burning, severe; bloody or black, tarry stools; vomiting of blood or material that looks like coffee grounds; nausea, heartburn, and/or indigestion, severe and continuing) *or stomatitis, ulcerative* (sores, ulcers, or white spots in mouth or on lips); *hematologic effects, specifically anemia* (unusual tiredness or weakness)—may occur secondary to gastrointestinal microbleeding or to fluid retention-induced hemodilution, *bruising, unexplained, or thrombocytopenia* (usually asymptomatic; rarely, unusual bleeding or bruising; black, tarry stools; blood in urine or stools; pinpoint red spots on skin); *hepatotoxicity [hepatitis and/or jaundice]* (fever with or without chills, skin rash, swelling and/or tenderness in upper abdominal or stomach area, swollen and/or painful glands, unusual bleeding or bruising, unusual tiredness or weakness, yellow eyes or skin); *hypersensitivity reactions, specifically angiitis [vasculitis]*—cutaneous, with purpura, *angioedema* (hive-like swellings, large, on face, eyelids, mouth, lips, and/or tongue), *bronchospasm* (shortness of breath, troubled breathing, tightness in chest, and/or wheezing), *dermatitis, allergic* (hives, vesiculobullous rash), *or Stevens-Johnson syndrome* (bleeding or crusting sores on lips; chest pain; fever with or without chills; muscle cramps or pain; skin rash; sores, ulcers, or white spots in mouth; sore throat); *vision disturbances*

Those indicating need for medical attention only if they continue or are bothersome

Incidence more frequent (> 3%)

CNS effects, specifically dizziness, headache—reported in postmarketing surveillance studies conducted abroad; incidences 4% in a 52-week study and < 1% in a 6-week study *or weakness; gastrointestinal irritation* (indigestion [incidence 10%]; mild abdominal pain, bloated feeling or gas, diarrhea, nausea)

Incidence less frequent (1 to 3%) or rare (< 1%)

Cardiovascular effects (flushing or pounding heartbeat); *CNS effects* (drowsiness, nervousness, or trouble in sleeping); *gastrointestinal effects* (constipation, decrease or loss of appetite, increased thirst, or vomiting); *increased sensitivity of eyes to light*

Note: In addition to the side/adverse effects listed above, the following side effects have been reported (incidence <1%). Although a causal relationship to etodolac therapy has not been established, many of these adverse effects have been reported with other NSAIDs.

Cardiovascular—arrhythmias, myocardial infarction.
CNS—confusion, paresthesia.
Dermatologic—alopecia, maculopapular rash, peeling skin, photosensitivity.
Gastrointestinal—esophagitis (with or without stricture or cardiospasm), colitis.
Hematologic—leukopenia.
Ophthalmic—conjunctivitis.
Otic—deafness.
Renal—cystitis, hematuria, interstitial nephritis, renal calculus.
Respiratory—bronchitis, dyspnea, pharyngitis, rhinitis, sinusitis.
Other—infection, leukorrhea, uterine bleeding abnormalities, weight changes.

Patient Consultation

In providing consultation, consider emphasizing the following selected information (» = major clinical significance):

Before using this medication

» Conditions affecting use, especially:

Hypersensitivity to etodolac, aspirin, or other nonsteroidal anti-inflammatory drugs (NSAIDs)

Pregnancy—Use during second half of pregnancy not recommended, because of potential adverse effect on fetal blood flow and possible prolongation of pregnancy, dystocia, and delayed delivery; also, has caused birth defects in animal studies

Other medications, especially anticoagulants, cyclosporine, hypoprothrombinemia-producing cephalosporins, lithium, moxalactam, methotrexate, NSAIDs (especially aspirin and phenylbutazone), plicamycin, probenecid, and valproic acid

Other medical problems, especially peptic ulcer or other gastrointestinal tract disease (or predisposition to) and clotting defects

Proper use of this medication

Taking with food or an antacid to reduce gastrointestinal irritation, although the first few doses may be taken on an empty stomach for more rapid onset of analgesic action

Taking with a full glass (240 mL) of water; not lying down for 15 to 30 minutes after taking

» Not taking more medication than prescribed

» Compliance with therapy—when taking for osteoarthritis

Missed dose (scheduled dosing): Taking as soon as possible; not taking if almost time for next dose; not doubling doses

» Proper storage

Precautions while using this medication

» Regular visits to physician during prolonged therapy

» Possibility that use of alcohol may increase the risk of gastrointestinal irritation or ulceration

Not using acetaminophen, aspirin, or other NSAIDs concurrently for more than a few days, unless directed by physician or dentist

Caution if any surgery is required, because of possible enhanced bleeding

Caution if drowsiness, dizziness or lightheadedness, or blurred vision occurs

Possible interference with urine bilirubin tests

Diabetics: Possible interference with dipstick-type urine ketone tests

Possibility of photophobia

Possibility of gastrointestinal ulceration and bleeding

Side/adverse effects

Stopping medication and checking with physician immediately if symptoms of angioedema, bronchospasm, gastrointestinal ulceration, or thrombocytopenia occur

Signs and symptoms of other side effects, especially other allergic or hypersensitivity reactions, cardiovascular effects, cutaneous adverse effects, edema, hepatotoxicity, mental depression, stomatitis, and vision disturbances

General Dosing Information

Long-term use of nonsteroidal anti-inflammatory drugs (NSAIDs) in doses that approach or exceed maximum dosage recommendations should be considered only if the clinical benefit is increased sufficiently to offset the higher risk of gastrointestinal toxicity or other adverse effects.

It is recommended that solid oral dosage forms of NSAIDs be taken with a full glass (240 mL) of water and that the patient remain in an upright position for 15 to 30 minutes after administration. These measures may reduce the risk of the capsules becoming lodged in the esophagus, which has been reported to cause prolonged esophageal irritation and difficulty in swallowing in some patients receiving these medications.

In the treatment of primary dysmenorrhea, maximum benefit is achieved by initiating NSAID therapy as rapidly as possible after the onset of menses.

Concurrent use of an NSAID with an opioid analgesic provides additive analgesia and may permit lower doses of the opioid analgesic to be utilized.

The analgesic activity of non-opioid analgesics is subject to a ceiling effect. Therefore, administration of an NSAID in higher-than-recommended analgesic doses may not provide additional therapeutic benefit in the treatment of pain not associated with inflammation.

NSAIDs are preferably taken after meals or with food or antacids to reduce gastrointestinal irritation, especially during chronic use; however, for faster absorption when a rapid initial effect is required (as for analgesic use), the first few doses may be taken 30 minutes before meals or at least 2 hours after meals. Alternatively, antacids have not been shown to adversely affect absorption of etodolac and may be taken concurrently.

Oral Dosage Forms

ETODOLAC CAPSULES

Usual adult dose:

Antirheumatic (nonsteroidal anti-inflammatory)—Oral, 800 mg to 1.2 grams per day in two to four divided doses (400 mg two or three times a day or 300 mg three or four times a day), initially. After a satisfactory response has been obtained, dosage should be individualized according to patient tolerance and response. Most patients are maintained on 600 mg to 1.2 grams per day (400 mg two or three times a day, 300 mg two to four times a day, or 200 mg three or four times a day). However, as little as 200 mg two times a day has been effective in some patients.

Note: Although doses of up to 1 gram per day have been effective when administered in two divided doses (500 mg every twelve hours), administration on a three-dose-a-day schedule may provide greater benefit.

Analgesic—Oral, 400 mg initially, then 200 to 400 mg every six to eight hours as needed. If a 400-mg dose fails to provide eight hours of analgesia, a regimen of 300 mg every six hours may be effective.

Usual adult prescribing limits:

Patients weighing less than 60 kg—20 mg per kg of body weight per day.

Patients weighing 60 kg or more—1.2 grams per day.

Usual geriatric dose: See *Usual adult dose.*

Auxiliary labeling: • Take with a full glass of water.

FINASTERIDE   Systemic

A commonly used *brand name* in the U.S. and Canada is *Proscar.*

Category: 5-Alpha-reductase inhibitor.

Indications

Accepted
Benign prostatic hyperplasia (treatment)—Finasteride is indicated for the treatment of symptomatic benign prostatic hyperplasia (BPH).

Although regression of the enlarged prostate gland occurs in most treated patients, significant increases in urinary flow and improvement in symptoms of BPH are slight and occur in only about one-third of treated patients. The long-term effect on the incidence of surgery, acute urinary obstruction, or other complications of BPH has not been determined.

Because finasteride causes only slight improvement in symptoms, it is probably less useful in patients with severe symptoms than in patients with mild to moderate symptoms.

Prior to initiation of finasteride therapy, infection, prostate cancer, stricture disease, hypotonic bladder, or other neurogenic disorders that might mimic BPH should be ruled out.

Unaccepted
Finasteride is not useful in patients with obstructive uropathy accompanied by urinary retention.

Pharmacology/Pharmacokinetics

Mechanism of action/Effect: Finasteride competitively and specifically inhibits 5-alpha-reductase, an enzyme that metabolizes testosterone to dihydrotestosterone (DHT) in the prostate gland, liver, and skin. Development of the prostate gland is dependent on DHT, which is a potent androgen. After administration of finasteride, 5-alpha-reduced steroid metabolites in blood and and urine are decreased; serum DHT is reduced by approximately 70% by daily dosing. Concentrations of both DHT and prostate specific antigen (PSA) are decreased in prostatic tissue. Finasteride has no affinity for the androgen receptor and the hypothalamic-pituitary-testicular axis does not appear to be affected.

Time to peak effect: Reduction in serum DHT concentration—8 hours after the first dose.

Duration of action:
Single dose—Reduction in serum DHT concentration: 24 hours.
Multiple doses—DHT concentrations return to pretreatment levels within approximately 2 weeks after withdrawal of daily therapy. The prostate returns to pretreatment size in about 4 months.

Precautions to Consider

Geriatrics
The elimination rate of finasteride is decreased in the elderly (70 years of age or older); however, no dosage adjustment is necessary.

Drug interactions and/or related problems
The following drug interactions and/or related problems have been selected on the basis of their potential clinical significance (possible mechanism in parentheses where appropriate)—not necessarily inclusive (» = major clinical significance):

Note: Combinations containing any of the following medications, depending on the amount present, may also interact with this medication.

» Anticholinergics or other medications with anticholinergic activity or
» Bronchodilators, adrenergic, or
» Bronchodilators, xanthine-derivative or
   Sympathomimetic decongestants, especially ephedrine, phenylpropanolamine, and pseudoephedrine
   (may precipitate or aggravate urinary retention, reducing the effectiveness of finasteride in BPH, and should be avoided)

Contraindications/Medical problems
The contraindications/medical problems included have been selected on the basis of their potential clinical significance (reasons given in parentheses where appropriate)—not necessarily inclusive (» = major clinical significance).

Risk-benefit should be considered when the following medical problems exist:
   Hepatic function impairment
      (reduced metabolism)

   Large residual urinary volume or
   Reduced urinary flow
      (because of possible presence of obstructive uropathy, patients with these conditions may not be candidates for finasteride therapy)
» Sensitivity to finasteride

Side/Adverse Effects

Note: Most side/adverse effects are mild and transient.

The following side/adverse effects have been selected on the basis of their potential clinical significance (possible signs and symptoms in parentheses where appropriate)—not necessarily inclusive:

Those indicating need for medical attention only if they continue or are bothersome
Incidence less frequent or rare
   Decreased libido; decreased volume of ejaculate; impotence

Patient Consultation

In providing consultation, consider emphasizing the following selected information (» = major clinical significance):

Before using this medication
» Conditions affecting use, especially:
   Sensitivity to finasteride
   Carcinogenicity—Increased incidence of testicular tumors in mice and rats receiving very high doses
   Pregnancy—When sexual partner is or may become pregnant, patient should either avoid exposure of sexual partner to semen or discontinue finasteride
   Other medications, especially anticholinergics or medications with anticholinergic effects, adrenergic bronchodilators, xanthine bronchodilators, or sympathomimetic decongestants

Proper use of this medication
   Getting into the habit of taking at same time each day to help increase compliance
» Does not cure, but helps control BPH; possible need for lifelong therapy; checking with physician before discontinuing medication
   Tablets may be crushed
   All patients with BPH should avoid drinking fluids, especially coffee or alcohol, in the evening, to reduce nocturia

» Proper dosing
Missed dose: Taking as soon as possible; not taking if almost time for next dose; not doubling doses
» Proper storage

Precautions while using this medication
» Not taking other medications, especially nonprescription sympathomimetics, unless discussed with physician
Women who are or who may become pregnant should not handle crushed tablets

Side/adverse effects
Signs of potential side effects, especially decreased libido, decreased volume of ejaculate, or impotence (these side effects occur less frequently or rarely, and usually do not need medical attention)

General Dosing Information

Diet/Nutrition
Finasteride may be taken with or without food.

Oral Dosage Forms

FINASTERIDE TABLETS

Usual adult dose: Benign prostatic hyperplasia—Oral, 5 mg once a day.

Note: At least six to twelve months of therapy may be required to assess clinical response.

FLAVOXATE   Systemic

A commonly used *brand name* in the U.S. and Canada is *Urispas.*

ORAL
Flavoxate Hydrochloride Tablets
  In the U.S. and Canada—*Urispas*

Category: Antispasmodic (urinary tract).

Indications

Accepted
Urologic disorders, symptoms of (treatment); and
Irritative voiding, symptoms of (treatment)—Flavoxate is indicated for the symptomatic relief, but not the definitive treatment, of dysuria, urgency, nocturia, suprapubic pain, and frequency and incontinence associated with cystitis, prostatitis, urethritis, urethrocystitis, or urethrotrigonitis.

Pharmacology

Mechanism of action/Effect: Exerts direct antispasmodic (relaxant) effect on smooth muscle, mainly of the urinary tract.

Other actions/effects: Also has weak antihistaminic, local anesthetic, and analgesic action. With high doses, flavoxate has weak anticholinergic properties.

Precautions to Consider

Geriatrics
Confusion is more likely to occur in geriatric patients taking flavoxate.

Dental
Prolonged use or use of large doses of flavoxate may decrease or inhibit salivary flow, thus contributing to the development of caries, periodontal disease, oral candidiasis, and discomfort.

Contraindications/Medical problems
The contraindications/medical problems included have been selected on the basis of their potential clinical significance (reasons given in parentheses where appropriate)—not necessarily inclusive (» = major clinical significance).

Risk-benefit should be considered when the following medical problems exist:
» Gastrointestinal tract obstructive disease as in achalasia and pyloroduodenal stenosis

(decrease in motility and tone may occur, resulting in obstruction and gastric retention)
Glaucoma, angle-closure
(mydriatic effect of flavoxate resulting in increased intraocular pressure may precipitate an acute attack of angle-closure glaucoma)
» Hemorrhage, gastrointestinal
(may exacerbate condition)
» Paralytic ileus
(may result in obstruction)
Sensitivity to flavoxate
» Uropathy, obstructive, such as bladder neck obstruction due to prostatic hypertrophy
(urinary retention may be precipitated)

Side/Adverse Effects

Note: Although weak, flavoxate's anticholinergic action should be taken into consideration when it is given to patients where the environmental temperature is high, since there is risk of a rapid increase in body temperature because of suppression of sweat gland activity.

The following side/adverse effects have been selected on the basis of their potential clinical significance (possible signs and symptoms in parentheses where appropriate)—not necessarily inclusive:

Those indicating need for medical attention
Incidence rare
Confusion—especially in the elderly; *hypersensitivity* (skin rash or hives); *increased intraocular pressure* (eye pain); *leukopenia* (sore throat and fever)
Symptoms of overdose
Anticholinergic effects (clumsiness or unsteadiness, severe dizziness, severe drowsiness, fever, flushing or redness of face, hallucinations, shortness of breath or troubled breathing, unusual excitement, nervousness, restlessness, or irritability)

Those indicating need for medical attention only if they continue or are bothersome
Incidence more frequent
Drowsiness; dryness of mouth and throat
Incidence less frequent or rare
Constipation—more frequent with doses of 800 mg or above; *difficult urination; difficulty concentrating; difficulty in eye accommodation* (blurred vision); *dizziness; fast heartbeat; head-*

ache; increased sweating; mydriatic effect (increased sensitivity of eyes to light); *nausea or vomiting; nervousness; stomach pain*

Patient Consultation

In providing consultation, consider emphasizing the following selected information (» = major clinical significance):

Before using this medication
» Conditions affecting use, especially:
  Sensitivity to flavoxate
  Use in the elderly—Confusion more likely
  Dental—Possible development of dental problems because of decreased salivary flow
  Other medical problems, especially gastrointestinal hemorrhage, paralytic ileus, or obstruction in gastrointestinal or urinary tract

Proper use of this medication
  Taking medication on an empty stomach with water, or with food or milk to reduce gastric irritation
» Importance of not taking more medication than the amount prescribed
» Proper dosing
  Missed dose: Taking as soon as possible; if almost time for next dose, not taking at all; not doubling doses
» Proper storage

Precautions while using this medication
  Possible increased sensitivity of eyes to light
» Caution if drowsiness or blurred vision occurs

» Caution during exercise or hot weather; overheating may result in heat stroke
  Possible dryness of mouth and throat; using sugarless gum or candy, ice, or saliva substitute for relief; checking with physician or dentist if dry mouth continues for more than 2 weeks

Side/adverse effects
  Signs of potential side effects, especially hypersensitivity, confusion, increased intraocular pressure, and leukopenia

General Dosing Information

Flavoxate may be taken on an empty stomach with water; however, if gastric irritation occurs it may be taken with food or milk.

If urinary tract infection is present, appropriate antibacterial therapy should be administered.

Oral Dosage Forms

FLAVOXATE HYDROCHLORIDE TABLETS

Usual adult and adolescent dose:
  Urologic disorders or
  Irritative voiding—Oral, 100 to 200 mg three or four times a day, the dosage being adjusted as needed and tolerated.

Usual geriatric dose: See *Usual adult and adolescent dose.*

Auxiliary labeling: • May cause drowsiness or blurred vision.

FLUCYTOSINE   Systemic

Some commonly used *brand names* are:
  In the U.S.—*Ancobon*
  In Canada—*Ancotil*
Other commonly used names are 5-fluorocytosine and 5-FC.

ORAL
Flucytosine Capsules USP
  In the U.S.—*Ancobon*
  In Canada—*Ancotil*

Category: Antifungal (systemic).

Indications

Note: Bracketed information in the *Indications* section refers to uses not included in U.S. product labeling.

Accepted
Endocarditis, fungal (treatment)—Flucytosine is indicated in the treatment of endocarditis caused by *Candida* species.

Meningitis, fungal (treatment)—Flucytosine is indicated in the treatment of meningitis caused by *Cryptococcus* species.

Pneumonia, fungal (treatment);
Septicemia, fungal (treatment); or
Urinary tract infections, fungal (treatment)—Flucytosine is indicated in the treatment of pneumonia, septicemia, and urinary tract infections caused by *Candida* and *Cryptococcus* species.

[Candidiasis, disseminated (treatment)][1];
[Chromomycosis (treatment)][1]; or
[Cryptococcosis (treatment)][1]—Flucytosine is used in the treatment of disseminated candidiasis, chromomycosis, and cryptococcosis.

In the treatment of disseminated fungal disease, flucytosine is usually administered concurrently with parenteral amphotericin B because of rapid development of resistance when flucytosine is administered alone.

Not all species or strains of a particular organism may be susceptible to flucytosine.

---

[1]Not included in Canadian product labeling.

Pharmacology

Mechanism of action/Effect: Flucytosine penetrates into fungal cells and is converted to fluorouracil, an antimetabolite. By interfering with pyrimidine metabolism, flucytosine interrupts nucleic acid and protein synthesis. The cells of the host do not convert large quantities of flucytosine to fluorouracil, accounting for the selective toxicity of the compound against fungi.

Precautions to Consider

Geriatrics
No information is available on the relationship of age to the effects of flucytosine in geriatric patients. However, elderly patients are more likely to have an age-related decrease in renal function, which may require an adjustment of dosage in patients receiving flucytosine.

Dental
The bone marrow-depressant effects of flucytosine may result in an increased incidence of microbial infection, delayed healing, and gingival bleeding. Dental work, whenever possible, should be completed prior to initiation of therapy or deferred until blood counts have returned to normal. Patients should be instructed in proper

oral hygiene during treatment, including caution in use of regular toothbrushes, dental floss, and toothpicks.

Drug interactions and/or related problems

The following drug interactions and/or related problems have been selected on the basis of their potential clinical significance (possible mechanism in parentheses where appropriate)—not necessarily inclusive (» = major clinical significance):

Note: Combinations containing any of the following medications, depending on the amount present, may also interact with this medication.

Amphotericin B, parenteral
(concurrent use of amphotericin B and flucytosine may have additive or slightly synergistic effects; amphotericin B-induced renal dysfunction may increase the bone marrow toxicity of flucytosine. However, 2-drug therapy may allow the total daily dose of amphotericin B to be lowered, decreasing its risk of nephrotoxicity)

Blood dyscrasia-causing medications or
» Bone marrow depressants, other or
» Radiation therapy
(concurrent use with flucytosine may increase the bone marrow-depressant effects of these medications and radiation therapy; dosage reduction may be required)

Cytarabine
(cytarabine has been reported to antagonize the antifungal activity of flucytosine by competitive inhibition)

Contraindications/Medical problems

The contraindications/medical problems included have been selected on the basis of their potential clinical significance (reasons given in parentheses where appropriate)—not necessarily inclusive (» = major clinical significance):

Except under special circumstances, this medication should not be used when the following medical problem exists:

» Allergy to flucytosine

Risk-benefit should be considered when the following medical problems exist:

» Bone marrow depression or
Hematologic disease
(flucytosine may cause bone marrow depression, resulting in anemia, leukopenia, and thrombocytopenia)

Hepatic function impairment
(flucytosine may cause jaundice or hepatic dysfunction, worsening any pre-existing hepatic function impairment)

» Renal function impairment
(because flucytosine is excreted renally, it is recommended that this medication be administered in a reduced dosage to patients with impaired renal function)

» Risk-benefit should be considered in patients who have had previous cytotoxic drug therapy or radiation therapy also.

Side/Adverse Effects

The following side/adverse effects have been selected on the basis of their potential clinical significance (possible signs and symptoms in parentheses where appropriate)—not necessarily inclusive:

Those indicating need for medical attention

Incidence more frequent
Anemia (unusual tiredness or weakness); *hepatitis or jaundice* (yellow eyes or skin); *hypersensitivity* (skin rash, redness, or itching); *leukopenia* (sore throat and fever); *thrombocytopenia* (unusual bleeding or bruising)

Incidence less frequent
Confusion; hallucinations; photosensitivity (increased sensitivity of skin to sunlight)

Those indicating need for medical attention only if they continue or are bothersome

Incidence more frequent
Gastrointestinal disturbances (abdominal pain, diarrhea, loss of appetite, nausea, or vomiting)

Incidence less frequent
CNS effects (dizziness or lightheadedness, drowsiness, headache)

Patient Consultation

In providing consultation, consider emphasizing the following selected information (» = major clinical significance):

Before using this medication

» Conditions affecting use, especially:
Allergy to flucytosine
Pregnancy—Flucytosine crosses the placenta; studies in rats have shown this medication to be teratogenic
Dental—Bone marrow depression effects of flucytosine may result in an increased incidence of microbial infection, delayed healing, and gingival bleeding
Other medication, especially bone marrow depressants or radiation therapy
Other medical problems, especially bone marrow depression or renal function impairment
Previous cytotoxic drug therapy or radiation therapy

Proper use of this medication

Taking multiple dosage units, prescribed as a single dose, over a period of 15 minutes to minimize nausea or vomiting
» Compliance with full course of therapy
Missed dose: Taking as soon as possible; not taking if almost time for next dose; not doubling doses
» Proper storage

Precautions while using this medication

Regular visits to physician to check progress during therapy
Using caution in use of regular toothbrushes, dental floss, and toothpicks; completing dental work prior to initiation of therapy or delaying it until blood counts have returned to normal; checking with physician or dentist concerning proper oral hygiene
» Possible photosensitivity reactions
» Caution if dizziness, lightheadedness, or drowsiness occurs

Side/adverse effects

Signs of potential side effects, especially anemia, confusion, hallucinations, hepatitis, hypersensitivity, jaundice, leukopenia, photosensitivity and thrombocytopenia

General Dosing Information

If multiple dosage units are prescribed as a single dose, administration may be spaced over a period of 15 minutes to prevent or reduce nausea or vomiting.

Since fungal resistance may develop rapidly when flucytosine is administered alone, it is usually administered concurrently with parenteral amphotericin B.

Reduction of dosage is recommended in the presence of renal impairment. Creatinine clearance (in mL per minute) may be calculated as follows:

Adult males: Creatinine clearance

$$= \frac{(140 - \text{age}) \times (\text{body weight in kg})}{72 \times \text{patient's serum creatinine concentration}}$$

Adult females: Creatinine clearance

$$= \frac{(140 - \text{age}) \times (\text{body weight in kg})}{72 \times \text{patient's serum creatinine concentration}} \times 0.85$$

Creatinine clearance may also be calculated in SI units (as mL per second) as follows:

Adult males: Creatinine clearance

$$= \frac{(140 - age) \times (\text{ideal body weight in kg})}{50 \times \text{serum creatinine (micromoles per L)}}$$

Adult females: Creatinine clearance

$$= \frac{(140 - age) \times (\text{ideal body weight in kg})}{50 \times \text{serum creatinine (micromoles per L)}} \times 0.85$$

Dosing intervals may be adjusted according to creatinine clearance as follows:

Creatinine Clearance (mL/min)/(mL/sec)	Dosing Interval (hr)
>40/(0.67)	6
20–40/(0.33–0.67)	12
10–20/(0.17–0.33)	24
<10/(0.17)	>24

Oral Dosage Forms

FLUCYTOSINE CAPSULES USP

Usual adult and adolescent dose: Oral, 12.5 to 37.5 mg per kg of body weight every six hours.

Auxiliary labeling: • Continue medicine for full time of treatment.

FLUOROURACIL   Topical

Some commonly used *brand names* are:
   In the U.S.—*Efudex; Fluoroplex*
   In Canada—*Efudex*
Another commonly used name is 5-FU.

TOPICAL
Fluorouracil Cream USP
   In the U.S.—*Efudex; Fluoroplex*
   In Canada—*Efudex*
Fluorouracil Topical Solution USP†
   In the U.S.—*Efudex; Fluoroplex*

†Not commercially available in Canada.

Category: Antineoplastic, topical.

Indications

Note: Bracketed information in the *Indications* section refers to uses not included in U.S. product labeling.

Accepted
Actinic keratoses, multiple (treatment);
[Actinic cheilitis (treatment)][1];
[Leukoplakia, mucosal (treatment)][1];
[Radiodermatitis (treatment)][1];
[Bowen's disease (treatment)][1]; or
[Erythroplasia of Queyrat (treatment)][1]—Topical fluorouracil is indicated for treatment of precancerous skin conditions including multiple actinic (solar) keratoses, actinic cheilitis, mucosal leukoplakia, radiodermatitis, Bowen's disease, and erythroplasia of Queyrat.

Carcinoma, skin (treatment)—Topical fluorouracil is indicated for treatment of superficial basal cell carcinomas (multiple lesions or difficult access sites), although conventional treatment is preferred whenever possible.

[1]Not included in Canadian product labeling.

Pharmacology

Mechanism of action/Effect: Fluorouracil is an antimetabolite of the pyrimidine analog type. Fluorouracil is considered to be cell cycle-specific for the S phase of cell division. Activity occurs as a result of activation in the tissues and includes inhibition of DNA and RNA synthesis. Topical fluorouracil selectively destroys rapidly proliferating cells.

Onset of action: 2 to 3 days. A treatment period of 2 to 6 weeks is usually required to reach the erosion and necrosis stage, or up to 12 weeks in some patients with superficial basal cell carcinomas. Complete healing may not occur for 1 to 2 months after therapy is stopped.

Precautions to Consider

Geriatrics
Appropriate studies on the relationship of age to the effects of topical fluorouracil have not been performed in the geriatric population. However, geriatrics-specific problems that would limit the usefulness of this medication in elderly patients are not expected.

Contraindications/Medical problems
The contraindications/medical problems included have been selected on the basis of their potential clinical significance (reasons given in parentheses where appropriate)—not necessarily inclusive (» = major clinical significance).

Risk-benefit should be considered when the following medical problems exist:

Hemorrhagic ulcerated tissues
   (significant systemic absorption and toxicity may occur)

Pre-existing dermatoses, especially chloasma and rosacea
   (may be accentuated by the inflammatory response to fluorouracil)

» Sensitivity to fluorouracil

Side/Adverse Effects

The following side/adverse effects have been selected on the basis of their potential clinical significance (possible signs and symptoms in parentheses where appropriate)—not necessarily inclusive:

Those indicating need for medical attention
Incidence more frequent
   Inflammatory response or allergic reaction (redness and swelling of normal skin)

Note: A delayed *hypersensitivity* reaction may occur. Patch testing for hypersensitivity may be inconclusive.

Those indicating need for medical attention only if they continue or are bothersome
Incidence more frequent
  Burning feeling at site of application; contact dermatitis (skin rash); *increased sensitivity of skin to sunlight; itching; oozing; soreness or tenderness of skin*
Incidence less frequent or rare
  Darkening of skin; scaling; watery eyes

Patient Consultation

In providing consultation, consider emphasizing the following selected information (» = major clinical significance):

Before using this medication
» Conditions affecting use, especially:
    Sensitivity to fluorouracil
    Pregnancy—Use not recommended because of teratogenic potential; some systemic absorption occurs
    Breast-feeding—Not recommended because of risk of serious side effects; some systemic systemic absorption occurs

Proper use of this medication
» Compliance with therapy; applying enough medication to cover affected areas
    Washing area to be treated with soap and water and drying thoroughly; using cotton-tipped applicator or fingertips to apply
» Washing hands immediately after application if fingertips are used
    Possible unsightly and uncomfortable reaction during therapy and for several weeks after therapy is completed; possible temporary pink, smooth spot left during healing; checking with physician before discontinuing medication
    Missed dose: Applying as soon as remembered; not applying if not remembered within a few hours; checking with physician if more than one dose is missed
» Proper storage

Precautions while using this medication
» Importance of close monitoring by physician
» Caution in applying medication; avoiding eyes, nose, and mouth
» Possible photosensitivity reactions during therapy and for 1 or 2 months after therapy is completed; avoiding sun; using protective clothing and sun block product; avoiding use of sunlamp, tanning bed, or tanning booth

Side/adverse effects
    Signs of potential side effects, especially inflammatory response or allergic reaction

General Dosing Information

Patients using topical fluorouracil should be under supervision of a physician experienced in use of the medication.

Increased frequency of application may be required on areas other than the head and neck.

Application of fluorouracil to easily irritated areas such as around the eyes, nasolabial folds, and wrinkles is not recommended.

Inflammatory and clinical response to fluorouracil in diseased skin areas after topical application is indicated by the following sequence: erythema, usually followed by vesiculation, tenderness, erosion, necrosis, and epithelialization. Use of the medication is terminated when the reaction reaches the stage of erosion, necrosis, and ulceration.

Application of a topical adrenocorticoid after completion of treatment with fluorouracil may hasten healing.

Responses in areas that appear clinically normal may indicate subclinical solar keratoses or an adverse reaction.

Use of occlusive dressings may result in increased incidence of inflammatory reactions on adjacent normal skin and is not recommended.

It is recommended that treatment with fluorouracil be discontinued if an excessive inflammatory response occurs on normal skin.

Topical Dosage Forms

FLUOROURACIL CREAM USP

Usual adult dose:
    Actinic or solar keratoses—Topical, to the skin, as a 1% cream once or twice a day in a sufficient amount to cover the lesions. Usually the 1% strength is effective on the head, neck, and chest; 2 to 5% may be needed on the hands.
    Superficial basal cell carcinomas—Topical, to the skin, as a 5% cream twice a day in a sufficient amount to cover the lesions, for at least three to six weeks, and possibly up to twelve weeks.

Auxiliary labeling:
• For the skin.
• Continue medicine for full course of treatment.
• Avoid overexposure to sun.

FLUOROURACIL TOPICAL SOLUTION USP

Usual adult dose:
    Actinic or solar keratoses—Topical, to the skin, as a 1 or 2% solution once or twice a day in a sufficient amount to cover the lesions. Usually the 1% strength is effective on the head, neck, and chest; 2 to 5% may be needed on the hands.
    Superficial basal cell carcinomas—Topical, to the skin, as a 5% solution twice a day in a sufficient amount to cover the lesions, for at least three to six weeks, and possibly up to twelve weeks.

Auxiliary labeling:
• For the skin.
• Continue medicine for full course of treatment.
• Avoid overexposure to sun.

FLUOXETINE   Systemic

A commonly used *brand name* in the U.S. and Canada is *Prozac*.

ORAL
Fluoxetine Hydrochloride Capsules
   In the U.S. and Canada—*Prozac*
Fluoxetine Hydrochloride Oral Solution
   In the U.S. and Canada—*Prozac*

Category: Antidepressant; antiobsessional agent.

Indications

Note: Bracketed information in the *Indications* section refers to uses
   not included in U.S. product labeling.

Accepted
Depression, mental (treatment)—Fluoxetine is indicated for the treatment of major depressive disorder.

[Obsessive-compulsive disorder (treatment)]—Fluoxetine is used to
   relieve symptoms of obsessive-compulsive disorder.

Pharmacology

Mechanism of action/Effect: Fluoxetine is a potent and selective
   inhibitor of serotonin (5-HT) uptake, but not of norepinephrine
   uptake, in the central nervous system (CNS). Because uptake inactivates serotonin by removing it from the synaptic cleft, uptake
   inhibition by fluoxetine enhances serotonergic function. As a consequence, the 5-HT_1 receptors are desensitized or downregulated
   after chronic fluoxetine administration. Fluoxetine does not interact directly with serotonergic receptors, muscarinic-cholinergic receptors, histaminergic H_1 receptors, or alpha-adrenergic receptors.
   Fluoxetine, unlike most other antidepressant medications, does not
   appear to cause downregulation of postsynaptic beta-adrenergic
   receptors.

Other actions/effects: Fluoxetine has an anorectic effect and potentially causes weight loss proportional to the degree of initial obesity as measured by the body mass index (BMI).

Onset of action: Between 1 and 4 weeks.

Precautions to Consider

Geriatrics
No geriatrics-related problems have been documented in studies done
   to date that included elderly patients.

Drug interactions and/or related problems
The following drug interactions and/or related problems have been
   selected on the basis of their potential clinical significance (possible mechanism in parentheses where appropriate)—not necessarily inclusive (» = major clinical significance):

Note: Combinations containing any of the following medications, depending on the amount present, may also interact with this
   medication.

» Alcohol or
» CNS depression-producing medications, other
      (concurrent use with fluoxetine may result in potentiation of
      CNS depressant effects)

   Antidepressants, tricyclic, or
   Maprotiline or

Trazodone
      (plasma concentrations of these medications may be doubled
      when fluoxetine is used concurrently; some clinicians recom-
      mend dosage reductions of about 50% in tricyclic antidepres-
      sants if these agents are given concurrently with fluoxetine)
Diazepam
      (concurrent use may prolong the half-life of diazepam in some
      patients but the psychomotor and physiological responses may
      be unaffected)
Electroconvulsive therapy
      (prolonged seizures have been reported in patients on concomi-
      tant fluoxetine therapy)
Haloperidol or
Loxapine or
Molindone or
Phenothiazines or
Pimozide or
Thioxanthenes or
      (caution in concurrent use of other CNS-active medications
      with fluoxetine is recommended because of a potentially in-
      creased risk of side effects)
» Highly protein-bound medications, especially:
   Anticoagulants
   Digitalis or digitoxin
      (caution in concurrent use with fluoxetine is recommended
      because of possible displacement of either medication from
      protein-binding sites, leading to increased plasma concentra-
      tions of the free [unbound] medications and increased risk of
      adverse effects)
Lithium
      (lithium concentrations may be altered, leading to toxicity;
      close monitoring of lithium concentrations is recommended)
» Monoamine oxidase (MAO) inhibitors, including furazolidone,
   procarbazine and selegiline
      (a potentially lethal hyperserotonergic state known as the sero-
      tonin syndrome may occur as the result of combining a sero-
      tonergic agent such as fluoxetine with MAO inhibitors. The
      syndrome may be manifest by mental status changes [confu-
      sion, hypomania], restlessness, myoclonus, hyperreflexia, dia-
      phoresis, shivering, tremor, diarrhea, incoordination, and/or fe-
      ver. If recognized early, the syndrome usually resolves quickly
      upon withdrawal of the offending agents)
      (concurrent use of fluoxetine with MAO inhibitors may result
      in confusion, agitation, restlessness, and gastrointestinal symp-
      toms, or possibly hyperpyretic episodes, severe convulsions,
      and hypertensive crises. Based on experience with tricyclic
      antidepressants, at least 14 days should elapse between discon-
      tinuation of an MAO inhibitor and initiation of fluoxetine.
      However, because of the long half-lives of fluoxetine and its
      active metabolite, at least 5 weeks [approximately 5 half-lives
      of norfluoxetine] should elapse between discontinuation of
      fluoxetine and initiation of therapy with an MAO inhibitor.
      Administration of an MAO inhibitor within 5 weeks of discon-
      tinuation of fluoxetine may increase the risk of serious events.
      While a causal relationship to fluoxetine has not been estab-
      lished, death has been reported following the initiation of an
      MAOI shortly after fluoxetine administration was stopped)
» Tryptophan
      (concurrent use may potentiate agitation, restlessness, and gas-
      trointestinal problems)

Contraindications/Medical problems

The contraindications/medical problems included have been selected on the basis of their potential clinical significance (reasons given in parentheses where appropriate)—not necessarily inclusive (» = major clinical significance).

Risk-benefit should be considered when the following medical problems exist:

   Diabetes mellitus
      (glycemic control may be altered)

» Hepatic function impairment
      (metabolism of fluoxetine is delayed; lower doses or less frequent dosing is recommended in patients with liver disease)

» Renal function impairment
      (excretion of fluoxetine may be delayed; lower doses or less frequent dosing is recommended in patients with renal disease)

   Seizure disorders, history of
      (seizures may be induced by fluoxetine in patients with a history of seizure disorders)

   Sensitivity to fluoxetine

   Caution should also be used in debilitated patients or in patients taking multiple CNS-active medications, who may be more susceptible to fluoxetine-induced seizures.

Side/Adverse Effects

Note: There have been recent anecdotal reports of suicidal ideation occurring in a few patients receiving fluoxetine. However, controversy exists regarding the role of fluoxetine in these episodes, and a causal relationship has not been established.

The following side/adverse effects have been selected on the basis of their potential clinical significance (possible signs and symptoms in parentheses where appropriate)—not necessarily inclusive:

Those indicating need for medical attention
Incidence less frequent
   Chills or fever; joint or muscle pain; skin rash, hives, or itching; trouble in breathing

Incidence rare
   Allergic reaction or serum sickness-like syndrome (skin rash or hives associated with burning or tingling in fingers, hands, or arms [carpal tunnel syndrome], chills or fever, swollen glands, joint or muscle pain, swelling of feet or lower legs, or trouble in breathing); *hypoglycemia* (anxiety, chills, cold sweats, confusion, cool pale skin, difficulty in concentration, drowsiness, excessive hunger, fast heartbeat, headache, nervousness, shakiness, unsteady walk, unusual tiredness or weakness); *hyponatremia*—especially in geriatric or volume-depleted patients (lack of energy); *mania or hypomania* (unusual excitement); *seizures; swollen glands*
   Note: *Allergic reaction* or *serum sickness—like syndrome* may be associated with proteinuria, leukocytosis, and mild transaminase elevation.

Symptoms of overdose
   Agitation and restlessness; hypomania (unusual excitement); *nausea and vomiting, severe; seizures*

Those indicating need for medical attention only if they continue or are bothersome
Incidence more frequent
   Anxiety and nervousness; diarrhea; drowsiness; headache; increased sweating; insomnia (trouble in sleeping); *nausea*

Incidence less frequent
   Abnormal dreams; change in taste; changes in vision; chest pain; constipation; cough; decreased appetite or weight loss; decrease in concentration; decreased sexual drive or ability; dizziness or lightheadedness; dryness of mouth; fast or irregular heartbeat; feeling of warmth or heat; flushing or redness of skin, especially on face and neck; frequent urination; increased appetite; menstrual pain; stomach cramps, gas, or pain; stuffy nose; tiredness or weakness; tremor; vomiting

Patient Consultation

In providing consultation, consider emphasizing the following selected information (» = major clinical significance):

Before using this medication
» Conditions affecting use, especially:
      Recent anecdotal reports of fluoxetine use possibly related to suicidal ideation in a few patients
      Sensitivity to fluoxetine
      Other medications, especially CNS depression-causing medications; highly protein-bound medications such as anticoagulants, digitalis, or digitoxin; monoamine oxidase (MAO) inhibitors; or tryptophan
      Other medical problems, especially hepatic or renal function impairment

Proper use of this medication
» Compliance with therapy; not taking more or less medicine than prescribed
   May be taken with food to lessen possible stomach upset
» May require up to 4 weeks or longer of therapy to obtain antidepressant effects
   Missed dose: Skipping the missed dose and continuing on regular schedule with next dose; not doubling doses
» Proper storage

Precautions while using this medication
   Regular visits to physician to check progress of therapy
» Avoiding use of alcoholic beverages; not taking other CNS depressants unless prescribed by physician
» Stopping fluoxetine and checking with physician as soon as possible if skin rash or hives occurs
» Possible drowsiness, impairment of judgment, thinking, or motor skills; caution when driving or doing jobs requiring alertness
» Possible dizziness or lightheadedness; caution when getting up suddenly from a lying or sitting position
» Possible dryness of mouth; using sugarless gum or candy, ice, or saliva substitute for relief; checking with physician or dentist if dry mouth continues for more than 2 weeks

Side/adverse effects
   Signs of potential side effects, especially chills or fever, swollen glands, joint or muscle pain, skin rash, hives, or itching, trouble in breathing, allergic reaction, serum sickness-like syndrome, convulsions, mania, or hypomania

General Dosing Information

Because of the long elimination half-lives of fluoxetine and norfluoxetine, dosing changes are not reflected in plasma for several weeks. This must be taken into consideration when titrating to a final dose. In addition, it is unlikely that any withdrawal effect would develop upon cessation of therapy, since fluoxetine is essentially self-tapering. However, a gradual return of symptoms of depression may occur after discontinuation.

Potentially suicidal patients should not have access to large quantities of this medication since depressed patients, particularly those who may use alcohol excessively, may continue to exhibit suicidal tendencies until significant improvement occurs. Some clinicians recommend that the patient be supplied with the least amount of medication necessary for satisfactory patient management.

Diet/Nutrition
Fluoxetine may be taken with food to lessen possible stomach upset.

Oral Dosage Forms

FLUOXETINE HYDROCHLORIDE CAPSULES

Usual adult dose: Depression—Oral, initially 20 mg (base) a day as a single morning dose. After several weeks, the dose may be increased by 20 mg a day at weekly intervals, as needed and tolerated.

Note: The manufacturer recommends that doses over 20 mg a day be taken in two divided doses, in the morning and at noon.

Usual adult prescribing limits: 80 mg (base) a day.

Usual geriatric dose: See *Usual adult dose.*

Note: Dosage for elderly patients is often initiated at 10 mg (base) a day and should not exceed 60 mg (base) a day.

Auxiliary labeling:
- May cause drowsiness.
- Avoid alcoholic beverages.

FLUOXETINE HYDROCHLORIDE ORAL SOLUTION

Usual adult dose: See *Fluoxetine Hydrochloride Capsules.*

Usual adult prescribing limits: See *Fluoxetine Hydrochloride Capsules.*

Usual geriatric dose: See *Fluoxetine Hydrochloride Capsules.*

Auxiliary labeling:
- May cause drowsiness.
- Avoid alcoholic beverages.

Additional information: The oral solution is mint-flavored.

FLUTAMIDE   Systemic

Some commonly used *brand names* are:
    In the U.S.—*Eulexin*
    In Canada—*Euflex*

ORAL
Flutamide Capsules†
    In the U.S.—*Eulexin*
Flutamide Tablets*
    In Canada—*Euflex*

---

*Not commercially available in the U.S.
†Not commercially available in Canada.

Category: Antineoplastic.

Indications

Accepted
Carcinoma, prostatic (treatment)—Flutamide is indicated, in combination with luteinizing hormone-releasing hormone (LHRH) analogs such as leuprolide, for treatment of metastatic prostatic carcinoma (stage D_2).

Pharmacology

Mechanism of action/Effect: Flutamide has antiandrogenic effects, including inhibition of androgen uptake and/or inhibition of nuclear binding of androgen in target tissues. Its interference with testosterone at the cellular level complements the medical castration produced by LHRH analogs.

Precautions to Consider

Geriatrics
Half-life is increased in the elderly.

Contraindications/Medical problems
The contraindications/medical problems included have been selected on the basis of their potential clinical significance (reasons given in parentheses where appropriate)—not necessarily inclusive (» = major clinical significance).

Risk-benefit should be considered when the following medical problem exists:
    Sensitivity to flutamide

Side/Adverse Effects

Note: Side/adverse effects listed are for combined flutamide and LHRH analog therapy.

During LHRH analog therapy, some signs and symptoms of prostatic carcinoma, including difficult urination, may worsen transiently. In addition, worsening of neurologic signs and symptoms in patients with vertebral metastases may result in temporary weakness and paresthesias of the lower extremities. There is some evidence that flutamide attenuates these effects of LHRH analogs.

The following side/adverse effects have been selected on the basis of their potential clinical significance (possible signs and symptoms in parentheses where appropriate)—not necessarily inclusive:

Those indicating need for medical attention
Incidence rare
    Hepatitis (yellow eyes or skin); *hypertension* (usually not symptomatic)

Those indicating need for medical attention only if they continue or are bothersome
Incidence more frequent
    Decrease in sexual desire or impotence; diarrhea; hot flashes (sudden sweating and feelings of warmth); *nausea or vomiting*
    Note: Flutamide alone causes little *impairment of sexual function.*
Incidence less frequent
    Gynecomastia (swelling and increased tenderness of breasts); *loss of appetite; numbness or tingling of hands or feet; swelling of feet or lower legs*

Patient Consultation

In providing consultation, consider emphasizing the following selected information (» = major clinical significance):

Before using this medication
» Conditions affecting use, especially:
    Sensitivity to flutamide
    Fertility—Flutamide reduces sperm count and leuprolide causes potentially irreversible impairment of fertility
    Use in the elderly—Half-life increased, but no precautions necessary

Proper use of this medication
» Importance of not using more or less medication than the amount prescribed

» Importance of following physician's instructions for simultaneous use with LHRH analog
» Importance of continuing medication despite side effects
Checking with physician if vomiting occurs shortly after dose is taken
Missed dose: Taking as soon as possible; not taking if almost time for next dose; not doubling doses
» Proper storage

Precautions while using this medication
» Importance of close monitoring by the physician

Side/adverse effects
Signs of potential side effects, especially hepatitis and hypertension

General Dosing Information

Patients taking flutamide should be under supervision of a physician experienced in cancer chemotherapy.

Flutamide therapy should begin simultaneously with LHRH analog therapy.

Oral Dosage Forms

FLUTAMIDE CAPSULES
Note: Flutamide capsules are not commercially available in Canada.

Usual adult dose: Oral, 250 mg every eight hours.

Note: Flutamide should be given simultaneously with LHRH analog (e.g., leuprolide) therapy. The usual dose of leuprolide is 1 mg subcutaneously per day or 7.5 mg intramuscularly once a month.

FLUTAMIDE TABLETS
Note: Flutamide tablets are not commercially available in the U.S.

Usual adult dose: Oral, 250 mg every eight hours.

Note: Flutamide should be given simultaneously with LHRH analog (e.g., leuprolide) therapy. The usual dose of leuprolide is 1 mg subcutaneously per day or 7.5 mg intramuscularly once a month.

FOLIC ACID　Systemic

Some commonly used *brand names* are:
In the U.S.—*Folvite*
In Canada—*Apo-Folic; Folvite; Novo-Folacid*
Another commonly used name is Vitamin B_9.

ORAL
Folic Acid Tablets USP
In the U.S.—*Folvite;* GENERIC
In Canada—*Apo-Folic; Folvite; Novo-Folacid;* GENERIC

PARENTERAL
Folic Acid Injection USP
In the U.S. and Canada—*Folvite;* GENERIC

Category: Nutritional supplement (vitamin); diagnostic aid (folate deficiency).

Note: Folic acid (vitamin B_9) is a water-soluble vitamin.

Indications

Note: Bracketed information in the *Indications* section refers to uses not included in U.S. product labeling.

Accepted
Vitamin deficiency (prophylaxis and treatment)—
Folic acid is indicated for prevention and treatment of folic acid deficiency states. Folic acid deficiency may occur as a result of inadequate nutrition or intestinal malabsorption but does not occur in healthy individuals receiving an adequate balanced diet. Simple nutritional deficiency of individual B vitamins is rare since dietary inadequacy usually results in multiple deficiencies. Dietary improvement is preferred over supplementation whenever possible.
Folic acid should not be given until the diagnosis of pernicious anemia has been ruled out, since it corrects the hematologic manifestations and masks pernicious anemia while allowing neurologic damage to progress.
Deficiency of folic acid may lead to megaloblastic and macrocytic anemias and glossitis.

Requirements may be increased and/or supplementation may be necessary in the following persons or conditions (although clinical deficiencies are usually rare):
Alcoholism
Anemia, hemolytic
Fever, chronic
Gastrectomy
Hemodialysis, chronic
Infants—low-birthweight, breast-fed, or those receiving unfortified formulas such as evaporated milk or goat's milk
Intestinal diseases—celiac disease, tropical sprue, persistent diarrhea
Malabsorption syndromes associated with hepatic-biliary disease—hepatic function impairment, alcoholism with cirrhosis
Stress, prolonged
Some unusual diets (e.g., reducing diets that drastically restrict food selection) may not supply minimum daily requirements of folic acid. Supplementation is necessary in patients receiving total parenteral nutrition (TPN) or undergoing rapid weight loss or in those with malnutrition, because of inadequate dietary intake.
Requirements for all vitamins and most minerals are increased during pregnancy; however, they should be provided by an adequate diet. Many physicians recommend that pregnant women receive multivitamin and mineral supplements, especially those pregnant women who do not consume an adequate diet and those in high-risk categories (i.e., women carrying more than one fetus, heavy cigarette smokers, and alcohol and drug abusers). Taking excessive amounts of a multivitamin and mineral supplement may be harmful to the mother and/or fetus and should be avoided.
Some studies have found that folic acid supplementation alone or in combination with other vitamins given before conception and during early pregnancy may reduce the incidence of neural tube defects in infants.
Requirements for all vitamins and most minerals are increased during breast-feeding.
Requirements may be increased by the following medications: Analgesics (long-term use), anticonvulsants, epoetin, estrogens, sulfasalazine.

[Folate deficiency (diagnosis)][1]—Folic acid is being used in the diagnosis of folate deficiency.

Unaccepted
Folic acid has not been proven effective for prevention of mental disorders or in the treatment of normocytic, refractory, or aplastic anemias.

---

[1]Not included in Canadian product labeling.

Pharmacology

Mechanism of action/Effect: Folic acid, after conversion to tetrahydrofolic acid, is necessary for normal erythropoiesis, synthesis of purine and thymidylates, metabolism of amino acids such as glycine and methionine, and the metabolism of histidine.

Precautions to Consider

Geriatrics
Appropriate studies with folic acid have not been performed in the geriatric population. However, no geriatrics-specific problems have been documented to date.

Drug interactions and/or related problems
The following drug interactions and/or related problems have been selected on the basis of their potential clinical significance (possible mechanism in parentheses where appropriate)—not necessarily inclusive (» = major clinical significance):

Note: Combinations containing any of the following medications, depending on the amount present, may also interact with this medication.

Analgesics, long-term use, or
Anticonvulsants, hydantoin, or
Carbamazepine or
Estrogens or
Oral contraceptives
　(requirements for folic acid may be increased in patients receiving these medications)
　(concurrent use with folic acid may decrease the effects of hydantoin anticonvulsants by antagonism of their central nervous system [CNS] effects; an increase in hydantoin dosage may be necessary for patients who receive folic acid supplementation)

Antacids, aluminum- or magnesium-containing
　(prolonged use of aluminum- and/or magnesium-containing antacids may decrease folic acid absorption by lowering the pH of the small intestine; patients should be advised to take antacids at least 2 hours after folic acid)

Antibiotics
　(may interfere with the microbiologic method of assay for serum and erythrocyte folic acid concentrations and cause falsely low results)

Cholestyramine
　(concurrent use with folic acid may interfere with absorption of folic acid; folic acid supplementation taken at least 1 hour before or 4 to 6 hours after cholestyramine is recommended in patients receiving cholestyramine for prolonged periods)

Methotrexate or
Pyrimethamine or
Triamterene or
Trimethoprim
　(act as folate antagonists by inhibiting dihydrofolate reductase; most significant with high doses and/or prolonged use; leucovorin calcium must be used instead of folic acid in patients receiving these medications)

Sulfonamides, including sulfasalazine
　(inhibit absorption of folate; folic acid requirements may be increased in patients receiving sulfasalazine)

Zinc supplements
　(some studies have found that folate may decrease the absorption of zinc, but not in the presence of excessive zinc; other studies have found no inhibition)

Contraindications/Medical problems
The contraindications/medical problems included have been selected on the basis of their potential clinical significance (reasons given in parentheses where appropriate)—not necessarily inclusive (» = major clinical significance).

Risk-benefit should be considered when the following medical problems exist:
» Pernicious anemia
　(folic acid will correct hematologic abnormalities but neurologic problems will progress irreversibly; doses of folic acid greater than 0.4 mg per day are not recommended until pernicious anemia has been ruled out, except during pregnancy and lactation)
　Sensitivity to folic acid

Side/Adverse Effects

Note: No side effects other than an allergic reaction have been reported with folic acid administration, even at doses of up to 10 times the recommended dietary allowances (RDA) for 1 month.

The following side/adverse effects have been selected on the basis of their potential clinical significance (possible signs and symptoms in parentheses where appropriate)—not necessarily inclusive:

Those indicating need for medical attention
Incidence rare
　Allergic reaction, specifically bronchospasm (shortness of breath, troubled breathing, tightness of chest, or wheezing), *erythema* (reddened skin), *fever, or skin rash or itching*

Patient Consultation

In providing consultation, consider emphasizing the following selected information (» = major clinical significance):

Description of use
　Description should include function in the body, signs of deficiency, and unproven uses

Importance of diet
　Diet as treatment of choice; importance of diet
　Food sources of folic acid; effects of processing
　Not using vitamins as substitute for balanced diet
　Supplement may be needed because of inadequate dietary intake or increased requirements
　Importance of not exceeding recommended dietary allowance (RDA) if self-medicating with vitamin supplements

Before using this dietary supplement
» Conditions affecting use, especially:
　Sensitivity to folic acid
　Other medical problems, especially pernicious anemia

Proper use of this dietary supplement
　Megadoses not recommended without physician's advice
　Missed dose: No cause for concern because of length of time necessary for depletion; remembering to take as directed
» Proper storage

Side/adverse effects:
　Signs of potential side effects, especially allergic reaction

General Dosing Information

Because of the infrequency of single B vitamin deficiencies, combinations are commonly administered. Many commercial combinations of B vitamins are available.

The effectiveness of megadoses (10 times the RDA or more) for treatment of various conditions is unproven and their use should be discouraged until benefit has been proven.

For parenteral dosage forms only

In most cases, parenteral administration is indicated only when oral administration is not acceptable (for example, in nausea, vomiting, preoperative and postoperative conditions) or possible (for example, in malabsorption syndromes or following gastric resection).

Diet/Nutrition

Recommended dietary allowances (RDA) for vitamins are values determined by the Food and Nutrition Board of the National Research Council. Intake of the RDA provides adequate nutrition in most healthy persons under usual environmental stresses; they are not minimum requirements. RDA are not the same as USRDA (United States Recommended Daily Allowances), which are values established by the FDA for labeling purposes.

RDA of folic acid per day:
Infants and children—
    Birth to 6 months: 25 mcg.
    6 months to 1 year: 35 mcg.
    1 to 3 years: 50 mcg.
    4 to 6 years: 75 mcg.
    7 to 10 years: 100 mcg.
Adolescent and adult males—
    11 to 14 years: 150 mcg.
    15 years and over: 200 mcg.
Adolescent and adult females—
    11 to 14 years: 200 mcg.
    15 years and over: 180 mcg.
Pregnant females—400 mcg.
Lactating females—
    First 6 months: 280 mcg.
    Second 6 months: 260 mcg.
These are usually provided by adequate diets.

Best dietary sources of folic acid include vegetables, especially green vegetables; potatoes; cereal and cereal products; fruits; and organ meats (liver, kidney). Heat destroys folic acid (50 to 90%) in foods.

Oral Dosage Forms

Note: Bracketed uses in the *Dosage Forms* section refer to categories of use and/or indications that are not included in U.S. product labeling.

FOLIC ACID TABLETS USP

Usual adult and adolescent dose:
    Nutritional supplement (vitamin)—
        Dietary supplement: Oral, 100 mcg (0.1 mg) a day (up to 1 mg a day in pregnancy). This dose is increased to 500 mcg (0.5 mg) to 1 mg when conditions causing increased requirements are present.
        Note: A dose of 3 to 15 mg a day is used in tropical sprue.
    Treatment of deficiency:
        Initial—Oral, 250 mcg (0.25 mg) to 1 mg a day until a hematologic response occurs.
        Maintenance—Oral, 400 mcg (0.4 mg) a day (800 mcg [0.8 mg] in pregnancy and lactation).
    [Diagnostic aid (folate deficiency)][1]—Oral, 100 to 200 mcg (0.1 to 0.2 mg) a day for ten days plus low dietary folic acid and vitamin B_{12}.

Parenteral Dosage Forms

Note: Bracketed uses in the *Dosage Forms* section refer to categories of use and/or indications that are not included in U.S. product labeling.

FOLIC ACID INJECTION USP

Usual adult and adolescent dose:
    Nutritional supplement (vitamin)—Treatment of deficiency: Intramuscular, intravenous, or deep subcutaneous, 250 mcg (0.25 mg) to 1 mg (base) a day until a hematologic response occurs.
    [Diagnostic aid (folate deficiency)][1]—Intramuscular, 100 to 200 mcg (0.1 to 0.2 mg) (base) a day for ten days plus low dietary folic acid and vitamin B_{12}.

GEMFIBROZIL   Systemic

A commonly used *brand name* in the U.S. and Canada is *Lopid*.

ORAL
Gemfibrozil Capsules USP
   In the U.S. and Canada—*Lopid*
Gemfibrozil Tablets
   In the U.S. and Canada—*Lopid*

Category: Antihyperlipidemic.

Indications

Accepted
Hyperlipidemia (treatment)—Gemfibrozil is indicated in the treatment of hyperlipidemia and to reduce the risk of coronary heart disease.

Gemfibrozil is indicated in those patients with Type IIb hyperlipidemia and a significant risk of coronary artery disease, who have not responded to diet, other measures, or other pharmacologic therapy (bile acid sequestrants and niacin) alone. It is not indicated for treatment of type IIa hyperlipidemia because the potential benefits do not outweigh the risks.

It is also recommended for use in patients with severe primary hyperlipidemia (types IV and V hyperlipidemia) and a significant risk of coronary artery disease, abdominal pain typical of pancreatitis, or pancreatitis, who have not responded to diet or other measures alone. Its use is limited in type III hyperlipidemia because of its limited effect on cholesterol concentrations. It is not useful in the treatment of type I hyperlipidemia.

Caution and close observation are recommended in patients with high triglyceride concentrations, since in some of these patients treatment with gemfibrozil is associated with significant increases in low density lipoprotein (LDL)-cholesterol concentrations.

In the 1988 Report of the National Cholesterol Education Program Expert Panel on Detection, Evaluation, and Treatment of High Blood Cholesterol in Adults, the following guidelines for the treatment of high blood cholesterol are recommended:

Nonpharmacologic management (especially reduction in dietary intake of saturated fatty acids and cholesterol, weight reduction and exercise, and quitting smoking) is recommended first for all patients and as an adjunct to all pharmacologic cholesterol therapy.

If, after six months of diet therapy, adequate LDL-cholesterol reduction is not achieved, then medication therapy is recommended to be added to diet therapy.

Initial medication therapy usually consists of a bile acid sequestrant (e.g., cholestyramine, colestipol) or niacin. A 3-hydroxy-3-methylglutanyl coenzyme A (HMG CoA) reductase inhibitor (e.g., lovastatin) should be considered after the bile acid sequestrants and niacin. Other lipid-lowering agents, including fibric acid derivatives (e.g., gemfibrozil and clofibrate) and probucol, are not as effective in lowering LDL cholesterol as the above mentioned medications. Two other agents, neomycin (not approved by FDA as a lipid-lowering agent) and dextrothyroxine are not recommended for general use because other medications are available that have a more favorable benefit/risk ratio.

If adequate LDL-cholesterol control is not achieved with initial medication therapy, it is recommended that the patient be switched to another medication or a combination of two medications with synergistic mechanisms of action. Although experience with such drug combinations is somewhat limited, preliminary studies indicate that the bile acid sequestrants given with either niacin, lovastatin, probucol, or gemfibrozil are useful in controlling LDL cholesterol. Lovastatin in combination with either niacin or gemfibrozil needs further study because of the potential increased risk of side effects.

If effective control of LDL cholesterol is not obtained after use of primary medications and medication combinations, then referral to a lipid specialist may be necessary.

Gemfibrozil is not recommended for community-wide prevention of ischemic heart disease.

Studies have suggested that control of elevated cholesterol and triglycerides may not lessen the danger of cardiovascular disease and mortality, although incidence of nonfatal myocardial infarctions may be decreased.

Pharmacology

Mechanism of action/Effect: Gemfibrozil reduces plasma triglyceride (very low-density lipoprotein [VLDL]) concentrations and increases high-density lipoprotein (HDL) concentrations. Although gemfibrozil may slightly reduce total and low-density lipoprotein (LDL) cholesterol concentrations, use of gemfibrozil in patients with elevated triglycerides associated with type IV hyperlipidemia often results in significant increases in LDL; LDL concentrations are not significantly affected by gemfibrozil in patients with Type IIb hyperlipidemia (although HDL is significantly increased). The mechanism of this action is not completely understood but may involve inhibition of peripheral lipolysis; reduced hepatic extraction of free fatty acids, which reduces hepatic triglyceride production; inhibition of synthesis and increased clearance of VLDL carrier, apolipoprotein B, which also reduces VLDL production; and, according to animal studies, reduced incorporation of long-chain fatty acids into newly formed triglycerides, accelerated turnover and removal of cholesterol from the liver (stimulates incorporation of cholesterol precursors into liver sterols), and increased excretion of cholesterol in the feces.

Onset of action: Reduction of plasma VLDL concentrations—2 to 5 days.

Time to peak effect: Reduction of plasma VLDL concentrations—4 weeks (major effect; further decreases occur over several months).

Precautions to Consider

Geriatrics
No information is available on the relationship of age to the effects of gemfibrozil in geriatric patients. However, elderly patients are more likely to have age-related renal function impairment, which may require reduction of dosage in patients receiving gemfibrozil.

Drug interactions and/or related problems
The following drug interactions and/or related problems have been selected on the basis of their potential clinical significance (possible mechanism in parentheses where appropriate)—not necessarily inclusive (» = major clinical significance):

» Anticoagulants, coumarin- or indandione-derivative
   (concurrent use with gemfibrozil may significantly increase the anticoagulant effect of these medications; adjustment of anticoagulant dosage based on frequent prothrombin-time determinations is recommended)

Chenodiol or
Ursodiol
   (effect may be decreased when chenodiol or ursodiol is used concurrently with gemfibrozil, which tends to increase cholesterol saturation of bile)

» Lovastatin
(concurrent use with gemfibrozil may be associated with an increased risk of rhabdomyolysis, significant increases in creatine kinase [CK] concentrations, and myoglobinuria that leads to acute renal failure; may be seen as early as 3 weeks or as late as several months after initiation of combined therapy; monitoring of CK has not been shown to prevent severe myopathy or renal damage)

Contraindications/Medical problems

The contraindications/medical problems included have been selected on the basis of their potential clinical significance (reasons given in parentheses where appropriate)—not necessarily inclusive (» = major clinical significance).

Except under special circumstances, this medication should not be used when the following medical problem exists:

» Primary biliary cirrhosis
(use of gemfibrozil may further raise the cholesterol)

Risk-benefit should be considered when the following medical problems exist:

Gallbladder disease or
Gallstones
(increased risk of biliary complications, including possible formation of gallstones)

» Hepatic function impairment
(reduced biotransformation; reduced dosage is recommended)

» Renal function impairment, severe
(reduced clearance leads to increased incidence of side effects; reduced dosage is recommended)

Sensitivity to gemfibrozil

Side/Adverse Effects

Note: Because of the chemical, pharmacologic, and clinical similarity of gemfibrozil to clofibrate, the possibility of similar long-term effects should be kept in mind. Studies with clofibrate have associated long-term use of the medication with an increased incidence of deaths from noncardiovascular causes and have also found a greatly increased incidence of cholelithiasis and cholecystitis requiring surgery in clofibrate users (see *Clofibrate [Systemic]*). In addition, studies have suggested that control of elevated cholesterol and triglycerides may not lessen the danger of cardiovascular disease and mortality, although incidence of nonfatal myocardial infarctions may be decreased.

Subcapsular bilateral cataracts and unilateral cataracts have been reported in 10% and 6.3%, respectively, of male rats given 10 times the human dose.

The following side/adverse effects have been selected on the basis of their potential clinical significance (possible signs and symptoms in parentheses where appropriate)—not necessarily inclusive:

Those indicating need for immediate medical attention

Incidence rare
Anemia or leukopenia (cough or hoarseness, fever or chills, lower back or side pain, painful or difficult urination); *gallstones* (severe stomach pain with nausea and vomiting); *myositis* (muscle pain, unusual tiredness or weakness)

Note: Gemfibrozil may increase cholesterol secretion into the bile.

Those indicating need for medical attention only if they continue or are bothersome

Incidence more frequent
Stomach pain, gas, or heartburn

Incidence less frequent
Diarrhea; nausea or vomiting; skin rash; unusual tiredness

Patient Consultation

In providing consultation, consider emphasizing the following selected information (» = major clinical significance):

Before using this medication

Potential serious toxicity because of similarity to clofibrate
» Diet as preferred therapy
» Conditions affecting use especially:
Sensitivity to gemfibrozil
Pregnancy—High doses in animals cause increase in fetal deaths
Breast-feeding—High doses associated with increased incidence of tumors in rats; consider when deciding whether to breast-feed
Use in children—Not recommended in children under 2 years of age since cholesterol is required for normal development
Other medications, especially lovastatin or oral anticoagulants
Other medical problems, especially primary biliary cirrhosis, hepatic function impairment, or severe renal function impairment

Proper use of this medication

» Importance of not taking more or less medication than the amount prescribed
Taking 30 minutes before morning and evening meal
» Compliance with prescribed diet
Missed dose: Taking as soon as possible; not taking if almost time for next dose; not doubling doses
» Proper storage

Precautions while using this medication

» Importance of close monitoring by physician
» Checking with physician before discontinuing medication; blood lipid concentrations may increase significantly

Side/adverse effects

Signs of potential side effects, especially gallstones, leukopenia, anemia, and myositis

General Dosing Information

If response is inadequate after 3 months of treatment, gemfibrozil therapy should be withdrawn.

When gemfibrozil is discontinued, an appropriate hypolipidemic diet and monitoring of serum lipids are recommended until the patient stabilizes, since a rise in serum triglyceride and cholesterol concentrations to the original base may occur.

If results of hepatic function tests rise significantly or show significant abnormalities, it is recommended that gemfibrozil therapy be withdrawn and not resumed; laboratory abnormalities are usually reversible.

If gallstones are found, gemfibrozil therapy should be withdrawn.

If patients receiving gemfibrozil experience muscle pain or weakness, evaluation for myositis (including serum CK determinations) is recommended. It is recommended that gemfibrozil be withdrawn if myositis is suspected or diagnosed.

Diet/Nutrition

Gemfibrozil should be taken 30 minutes before the morning and evening meals.

Oral Dosage Forms

GEMFIBROZIL CAPSULES USP

Usual adult dose: Oral, 1.2 grams a day in two divided doses thirty minutes before the morning and evening meals.

GEMFIBROZIL TABLETS

Usual adult dose: Oral, 1.2 grams a day in two divided doses thirty minutes before the morning and evening meals.

GENTIAN VIOLET   Vaginal

A commonly used *brand name* in the U.S. is *Genapax.*

VAGINAL
Gentian Violet Vaginal Tampons
    In the U.S.—*Genapax*

Category: Antifungal (vaginal).

Indications

Accepted
Candidiasis, vulvovaginal (treatment)—Vaginal gentian violet is used occasionally for a short duration as second-line therapy in the treatment of vulvovaginal candidiasis caused by *Candida* species. It is used specifically in those patients in whom conventional therapies (such as vaginal imidazoles) have failed.

Not all species or strains of a particular organism may be susceptible to gentian violet.

Pharmacology

Mechanism of action/Effect: Gentian violet possesses antifungal and anthelmintic activity, as well as bactericidal and bacteriostatic activities against gram-positive bacteria.

Precautions to Consider

Geriatrics
Appropriate studies on the relationship of age to the effects of vaginal gentian violet have not been performed in the geriatric population. However, no geriatrics-specific problems have been documented to date.

Side/Adverse Effects

Note: The use of tampons has been associated with toxic shock syndrome (TSS), a rare but serious side effect that may result in death.

The following side/adverse effects have been selected on the basis of their potential clinical significance (possible signs and symptoms in parentheses where appropriate)—not necessarily inclusive:

Those indicating need for medical attention
Vaginal burning, itching, pain, or other sign of irritation not present before therapy

Patient Consultation

In providing consultation, consider emphasizing the following selected information (» = major clinical significance):

Proper use of this medication
Reading patient directions before using medication
After inserting, removing tampon after 3 to 4 hours
»   Compliance with full course of therapy
Not using regular tampons if menstrual period occurs during therapy; use of sanitary napkins instead
Missed dose: Inserting as soon as possible; not inserting if almost time for next dose
»   Proper storage

Precautions while using this medication
»   Checking with physician if no improvement in a few days
Using hygienic measures to control sources of infection or reinfection
Use of condom for partner if patient has intercourse during therapy
Checking with physician about douching
»   Medication will stain the skin and clothing
Protection of clothing because of possible vaginal drainage

Side/adverse effects
Vaginal burning, itching, pain, or other sign of irritation not present before therapy

General Dosing Information

Pregnant patients may require a slightly longer period of treatment.

Treatment with gentian violet tampons may be repeated if infection persists.

Vaginal Dosage Forms

GENTIAN VIOLET VAGINAL TAMPONS

Usual adult and adolescent dose: Antifungal—Intravaginal, 5 mg, retained for three to four hours, one or two times a day for twelve consecutive days.

Note: In resistant cases, an additional tampon may be used overnight.

Auxiliary labeling:
• For vaginal use only.
• Continue medicine for full time of treatment.
• Will stain skin and clothing.

GLUCAGON   Systemic

PARENTERAL
Glucagon for Injection USP
    In the U.S. and Canada—*Glucagon Emergency Kit;* GENERIC

Category: Antihypoglycemic; diagnostic aid adjunct (antispasmodic); antispasmodic; antidote (to beta-adrenergic blocking agents; to calcium channel blocking agents).

Indications

Note: Bracketed information in the *Indications* section refers to uses not included in U.S. product labeling.

Accepted
Hypoglycemia (treatment)—Glucagon is indicated in the correction of severe hypoglycemic conditions. Glucagon is helpful in hypoglycemia only if liver glycogen is available. Glucagon and glucose may be used together without decreasing the effects of either. When glucagon is used for patients in a very deep state of coma (such as Stage IV or Stage V of Himwich), intravenous glucose is given in addition to glucagon for a more immediate response.

Radiography, gastrointestinal, adjunct—Glucagon is indicated in barium radiographic examinations to produce hypotonicity and relaxation of the esophagus, stomach, duodenum, small bowel, and colon. Glucagon is administered to provide relaxation of smooth musculature, and to decrease peristalsis thereby reducing patient discomfort, slowing emptying, and improving the examination quality.

[Abdominal imaging, digital angiographic, adjunct][1]; or
[Abdominal imaging, computed tomographic, adjunct][1]; or
[Abdominal imaging, magnetic resonance, adjunct][1]; or
[Pelvic imaging, magnetic resonance, adjunct][1]—Glucagon is being used to inhibit bowel peristalsis in abdominal digital vascular imaging, abdominal and pelvic magnetic resonance imaging, and in abdominal CT scanning to prevent motion-related artifact.

[Bleeding, gastrointestinal (diagnosis adjunct)][1]—Glucagon may be beneficial as an adjuvant to Tc 99m-labeled red blood cells in the scintigraphic diagnosis of small bowel hemorrhage.

[Hysterosalpingography, adjunct][1]—Glucagon is used rarely by some clinicians to eliminate possible spasm of the fallopian tubes during hysterosalpingography in those patients whose fallopian tubes are not visualized during examination.

[Toxicity, beta-adrenergic blocking agent (treatment)][1]—Glucagon administered in large intravenous doses is used to treat the cardiotoxic effects, specifically bradycardia and hypotension, in overdoses of beta-adrenergic blocking agents. Glucagon may be used with isoproterenol or dobutamine. Supplemental potassium may be necessary for treated patients since glucagon tends to reduce serum potassium.

[Toxicity, calcium channel blocking agent (treatment)][1]—Glucagon may be of use in treating myocardial depression due to calcium channel blocking agents in those patients in whom conventional therapies have been ineffective.

[Esophageal obstruction, foreign body (treatment)][1]—Glucagon is used in the treatment of lower esophageal obstruction due to foreign bodies, including food boluses.

Unaccepted

Glucagon is of little or no help in the treatment of hypoglycemia in conditions where hepatic glycogen stores are depleted, such as starvation, adrenal insufficiency, or chronic hypoglycemia.

Glucagon should not be used to treat birth asphyxia or hypoglycemia in premature infants or in infants who have had intrauterine growth retardation.

Glucagon has been used as an aid in the diagnosis of insulinoma and pheochromocytoma; however, USP advisory panels do not generally recommend this use because of questions about safety.

[1]Not included in Canadian product labeling.

Pharmacology

Mechanism of action/Effect: Promotes hepatic glycogenolysis and gluconeogenesis. Stimulates adenylate cyclase to produce increased cyclic-AMP, which is involved in a series of enzymatic activities. The resultant effects are increased concentrations of plasma glucose, a relaxant effect on smooth musculature, and an inotropic myocardial effect. Hepatic stores of glycogen are necessary for glucagon to elicit an antihypoglycemic effect.

Onset of action:
Hyperglycemic action—
    Intravenous: 5 to 20 minutes.
    Intramuscular: 15 minutes.
    Subcutaneous: 30 to 45 minutes.
Smooth muscle relaxation—
    Intravenous: 0.25 to 2 USP Units—45 seconds.
    Intramuscular:
        1 USP Unit—8 to 10 minutes.
        2 USP Units—4 to 7 minutes.

Duration of action:
Hyperglycemic action—90 minutes.

Smooth muscle relaxation—
    Intravenous:
        0.25 to 0.5 USP Units—9 to 17 minutes.
        2 USP Units—22 to 25 minutes.
    Intramuscular:
        1 USP Unit—12 to 27 minutes.
        2 USP Units—21 to 32 minutes.

Precautions to Consider

Cross-sensitivity and/or related problems
Patients who are allergic to beef or porcine proteins may be allergic to glucagon, since glucagon is either of beef or porcine origin.

Geriatrics
Appropriate studies on the relationship of age to the effects of glucagon have not been performed in the geriatric population. However, geriatrics-specific problems that would limit the usefulness of this medication in the elderly are not expected.

Drug interactions and/or related problems
The following drug interaction has been selected on the basis of its potential clinical significance (possible mechanism in parentheses where appropriate)—not necessarily inclusive (» = major clinical significance):

Anticoagulants, coumarin- or indandione-derivative
    (concurrent use with glucagon may potentiate the anticoagulant effects; enhanced anticoagulant activity has been reported with unusually high doses such as 25 mg or more per day for 2 or more days)

Contraindications/Medical problems
The contraindications/medical problems included have been selected on the basis of their potential clinical significance (reasons given in parentheses where appropriate)—not necessarily inclusive (» = major clinical significance).

Risk-benefit should be considered when the following medical problems exist:

Allergy to beef or porcine proteins, history of
» Diabetes mellitus
    (risk of hyperglycemia when glucagon is used as a diagnostic adjunct; however, glucagon is commonly used by diabetic patients to treat hypoglycemia resulting from overdose of oral antidiabetic agents or insulin)
» Insulinoma, or history of
    (may paradoxically decrease blood glucose concentrations)
» Pheochromocytoma
    (may cause hypertension due to stimulation of the release of catecholamines)
Sensitivity to glucagon

Side/Adverse Effects

The following side/adverse effects have been selected on the basis of their potential clinical significance (possible signs and symptoms in parentheses where appropriate)—not necessarily inclusive:

Those indicating need for medical attention
Incidence less frequent
    Allergic reaction (dizziness, lightheadedness, skin rash, or trouble in breathing)
Symptoms of overdose (in order of usual occurrence)
    Continuing nausea; continuing vomiting; hypokalemic syndrome (severe weakness of extremities and trunk, loss of appetite, nausea, vomiting, irregular heartbeat, muscle cramps or pain)

Those indicating need for medical attention only if they continue or are bothersome

Nausea or vomiting—incidence is generally dependent upon dose and (with intravenous use) the rate of injection; these effects may be diminished by slower intravenous administration

Patient Consultation

In providing consultation, consider emphasizing the following selected information (» = major clinical significance):

Before using this medication

» Conditions affecting use especially:

Sensitivity to glucagon

Other medical problems, especially diabetes mellitus (for diagnostic procedures only), insulinoma or history of, or pheochromocytoma

Proper use of this medication

» Using medication only as directed by physician; need to explain use to family or friend; reviewing use on a regular basis

» Reading directions in glucagon kit before medication is actually needed; knowing how to reconstitute and inject properly

» Knowing which type of syringe to use; keeping sterile syringe and needles always readily available; knowing how to use syringe supplied with some kits

May be reconstituted when emergency occurs or ahead of time, but must be used within 48 hours of reconstitution

» Not keeping after expiration date on vial; checking date regularly; replacing medication before it expires

» Proper dosing

» Proper storage:

Storing unmixed medication at room temperature

Storing mixed solution in refrigerator for no longer than 48 hours and protecting from freezing

Precautions while using this medication

» Importance of knowing symptoms of hypoglycemia: mild abdominal or stomach pain; anxious feeling; continuing chills; cold sweats; confusion; convulsions; cool, pale skin; difficulty in concentrating; drowsiness; fast heartbeat; continuing headache; excessive hunger; continuing nausea or vomiting; nervousness; shakiness; unconsciousness; unsteady walk; vision changes; unusual tiredness or weakness

» Importance of eating some form of sugar (glucose tablets or gel; fruit juice; corn syrup; honey; nondiet soft drinks; sugar cubes or table sugar dissolved in water) if symptoms of hypoglycemia occur

» Steps to be taken after glucagon is injected for hypoglycemia in unconscious patient:

After injection, turning patient on one side to avoid choking if emesis occurs

Contacting an emergency medical service and physician

Monitoring blood glucose concentrations throughout episode, treatment, and for 3 to 4 hours after patient conscious

If patient not conscious in 5 minutes (intravenous use) or 15 minutes (intramuscular use), giving second dose; simultaneously, getting emergency help

When patient conscious enough to swallow, initially giving some form of sugar to take orally then having patient eat crackers and cheese or half a sandwich or drink a glass of milk to prevent hypoglycemia from recurring before the next scheduled meal or snack

If nausea and vomiting prevent a patient from swallowing some form of sugar for an hour after injection, getting medical assistance

» Importance of keeping physician informed of hypoglycemic episodes and use of glucagon

» Replacing supply of glucagon as soon as possible

Side/adverse effects

Signs of potential side effects, especially allergic reaction

General Dosing Information

For use as an antihypoglycemic

For ambulatory-care use of glucagon kits that do not supply the user with a syringe, USP medical advisory panelists generally recommend that a standard 1-mL insulin syringe be used for injection. Using an insulin syringe will ensure availability when needed and reduce the potential for confusion or improper injection. However, the injection should be made at a 90-degree angle rather than the standard subcutaneous approach. Although the standard insulin syringe will not generally allow for a true intramuscular injection, the deeper injection may provide for a more rapid response time than would the subcutaneous route. A different syringe may be considered if the user is able to make such an injection in an appropriate manner and/or if the insulin syringe being used will not hold the appropriate amount of glucagon solution required.

A rapid blood glucose test should be performed to confirm that the patient has low blood sugar. Emergency medical assistance should also be obtained as soon as possible. Blood glucose should also be monitored throughout the hypoglycemic episode, treatment period, and for 3 to 4 hours after the patient regains consciousness.

Patient response usually occurs 5 minutes following intravenous administration or 15 minutes following intramuscular administration. Dose may be repeated if no response is evident within this time. Medical care will be needed if response is not obtained following a second glucagon dose; intravenous glucose will be required if the patient fails to respond to glucagon.

After the patient is sufficiently alert and oriented, oral supplemental sugar (glucose or sucrose) must be given to prevent secondary hypoglycemia. Patients with insulin-dependent diabetes (type I) do not have as great a response in blood glucose levels as do the non-insulin-dependent (type II), stable diabetic patients. Therefore, it is especially important that supplemental carbohydrates be given as soon as possible to patients with type I diabetes. Emergency room evaluation and/or hospital admission should be considered for all patients experiencing a hypoglycemic episode from oral antidiabetic agents (especially chlorpropamide), since hypoglycemia may recur after blood glucose concentrations are normalized.

If nausea and vomiting result from glucagon administration and the patient is unable to ingest some form of sugar for 1 hour, medical assistance should be obtained immediately. Severe hypoglycemia may rapidly recur under these circumstances.

Parenteral Dosage Forms

Note: Bracketed uses in the *Dosage Forms* section refer to categories of use and/or indications that are not included in U.S. product labeling.

GLUCAGON FOR INJECTION USP

Usual adult and adolescent dose:

Antihypoglycemic—Intramuscular, intravenous, or subcutaneous, 0.5 to 1 mg (0.5 to 1 USP Unit), repeated in twenty minutes if necessary.

Diagnostic aid—Radiography, gastrointestinal, or

[Abdominal imaging, computed tomographic or magnetic resonance][1], or

[Pelvic imaging, computed tomographic or magnetic resonance][1] or

[Hysterosalpingography]—Intravenous, 0.25 to 1.0 mg (0.25 to 1 USP Unit).

Note: Doses in the upper range and/or intramuscular dosing may be preferred by some clinicians to achieve hypotonicity during the prolonged scan times associated with magnetic resonance imaging. The duration of action of glucagon is longer with intramuscular dosing.

[Antidote (to beta-adrenergic blocking agents)][1]—Intravenous, initially, 50 to 150 mcg (0.05 to 0.15 USP Unit) per kg of body weight over one minute, to be followed by a 1 to 5 mg-per-hour infusion.

[Antidote (to calcium channel blocking agents)][1]—Intravenous, initially 2 mg (2 USP Units). Maintenance dosing is then titrated according to patient response.

[Antispasmodic (esophageal obstruction due to foreign body)][1]—Intravenous, 0.5 to 2 mg (0.5 to 2 USP Units), repeated in ten to twenty minutes if necessary.

Auxiliary labeling:
- Refrigerate after reconstituting.
- After reconstituting, discard after 48 hours.

GLYCERIN   Systemic

Some commonly used *brand names* in the U.S. are *Glyrol* and *Osmoglyn*.

ORAL
Glycerin Oral Solution USP
   In the U.S.—*Glyrol; Osmoglyn;* GENERIC

Category: Diuretic; antiglaucoma agent (systemic).

Indications

Note: Bracketed information in the *Indications* section refers to uses not included in U.S. product labeling.

Accepted
Glaucoma (treatment)—Glycerin is indicated for short-term reduction of intraocular pressure in treatment of an acute attack of glaucoma or during or after ophthalmic surgery.

[Edema, cerebral (treatment)]—Glycerin is used to reduce elevated intracranial pressure due to a variety of causes.

Pharmacology

Mechanism of action/Effect:
Cerebral edema—Glycerin elevates blood plasma osmolality, resulting in enhanced flow of water from extravascular spaces into plasma. Withdrawal of fluid from the brain and cerebrospinal fluid by osmosis may result in reduction of elevated intracranial pressure and cerebrospinal fluid volume and pressure.

Glaucoma—Glycerin elevates blood plasma osmolality, resulting in enhanced flow of water from the eye into plasma and a consequent reduction in intraocular pressure.

Onset of action: Reduction in intraocular pressure—Within 10 minutes.

Time to peak effect: Reduction in intraocular pressure and vitreous volume—60 to 90 minutes.

Duration of action: Reduction in intraocular pressure—Approximately 5 hours.

Precautions to Consider

Geriatrics
Although appropriate studies on the relationship of age to the effects of oral glycerin have not been performed in the geriatric population, the possibility of dehydration may be increased in elderly patients. In addition, elderly patients are more likely to have age-related renal function impairment, which may require caution in patients receiving glycerin.

Drug interactions and/or related problems
The following drug interactions and/or related problems have been selected on the basis of their potential clinical significance (possible mechanism in parentheses where appropriate)—not necessarily inclusive (» = major clinical significance):

Note: Combinations containing any of the following medications, depending on the amount present, may also interact with this medication.

Diuretics, including carbonic anhydrase inhibitors
   (diuretic and intraocular pressure-reducing effects may be potentiated when used concurrently with glycerin; dosage adjustments may be necessary)

Contraindications/Medical problems
The contraindications/medical problems included have been selected on the basis of their potential clinical significance (reasons given in parentheses where appropriate)—not necessarily inclusive (» = major clinical significance).

Risk-benefit should be considered when the following medical problems exist:
Cardiac disease
   (sudden expansion of extracellular fluid may lead to congestive heart failure)
Confused mental states or
Dehydration, severe or
Hypovolemia
   (conditions may be exacerbated)
Diabetes mellitus
   (patients may already be dehydrated)
Hypervolemia
   (expansion of extracellular fluid may lead to circulatory overload, which may produce congestive symptoms in patients with reduced cardiac function)
Renal disease
   (accumulation may lead to overexpansion of extracellular fluid and circulatory overload)
Sensitivity to glycerin

Side/Adverse Effects

Note: Severe dehydration, cardiac arrhythmias, and hyperosmolar nonketotic coma have been reported and may be fatal.

The following side/adverse effects have been selected on the basis of their potential clinical significance (possible signs and symptoms in parentheses where appropriate)—not necessarily inclusive:

Those indicating need for medical attention
Incidence less frequent
   Confusion
Incidence rare
   Irregular heartbeat

Those indicating need for medical attention only if they continue or are bothersome

Incidence more frequent
Headache; nausea or vomiting

Incidence less frequent
Diarrhea; dizziness; dry mouth or increased thirst

Patient Consultation

In providing consultation, consider emphasizing the following selected information (» = major clinical significance):

Before using this medication
» Conditions affecting use, especially:
 Sensitivity to glycerin
 Use in the elderly—Possibility of dehydration may be increased

Proper use of this medication
» Importance of not taking more medication than the amount prescribed
 May be mixed with unsweetened fruit juice, poured over cracked ice, and sipped through a straw to improve taste
 Missed dose: Taking as soon as possible; not taking if almost time for next dose; not doubling doses
» Proper storage

Precautions while using this medication
 Regular visits to physician to check progress during therapy

Possibility of headache; lying down while and for a short time after taking to minimize this effect

Side/adverse effects
 Signs of potential side effects, especially confusion and irregular heartbeat

General Dosing Information

To improve the taste, the solution may be mixed with a small amount of unsweetened lemon, lime, or orange juice, poured over cracked ice, and sipped through a straw.

When used preoperatively, the dose should be administered 1 to 1½ hours prior to surgery. In addition, precautions should be taken to avoid acute urinary retention.

To help prevent or relieve headache resulting from cerebral dehydration, the patient should lie down during and after administration of glycerin.

Oral Dosage Forms

GLYCERIN ORAL SOLUTION USP

Usual adult dose: Oral, 1.0 to 1.5 grams per kg of body weight as a single dose. Additional doses of 500 mg per kg of body weight may be administered at approximately six-hour intervals, if necessary.

GOLD COMPOUNDS   Systemic

INN: Included in brackets after individual generic listings, if different from U.S. generic names.

Some commonly used *brand names* are:

In the U.S.—
 Myochrysine [Gold Sodium   *Ridaura* [Auranofin]
 Thiomalate]   *Solganal* [Aurothioglucose]

In Canada—
 Myochrysine [Gold Sodium   *Ridaura* [Auranofin]
 Thiomalate]

A commonly used name for gold sodium thiomalate is sodium aurothiomalate.

ORAL
AURANOFIN
 Auranofin Capsules
 In the U.S. and Canada—*Ridaura*

PARENTERAL
AUROTHIOGLUCOSE
 Sterile Aurothioglucose Suspension USP
 In the U.S.—*Solganal*
GOLD SODIUM THIOMALATE [INN: Sodium Aurothiomalate]
 Gold Sodium Thiomalate Injection USP
 In the U.S.—*Myochrysine;* GENERIC
 In Canada—*Myochrysine*

Category: Antirheumatic (disease-modifying).

Indications

Note: Bracketed information in the *Indications* section refers to uses not included in U.S. product labeling.

Accepted
Arthritis, rheumatoid (treatment); or

Arthritis, juvenile (treatment)—Auranofin is indicated in the treatment of adult rheumatoid arthritis and is used in the treatment of [juvenile arthritis][1]. Aurothioglucose and gold sodium thiomalate are indicated in the treatment of adult or juvenile rheumatoid arthritis. These agents are usually used for treating patients who show evidence of continued or additional disease activity despite conservative therapy, e.g., with salicylates (especially aspirin) or other nonsteroidal anti-inflammatory agents, glucocorticoids, etc. Gold compounds may induce remission or suppression of rheumatoid arthritis. In chronic advanced rheumatoid arthritis, they may prevent further damage to affected joints; however, they do not reverse existing damage.

[Arthritis, psoriatic (treatment)][1]; or
[Felty's syndrome (treatment)][1]—Gold compounds are used in the treatment of these rheumatic conditions.

---

[1]Not included in Canadian product labeling.

Pharmacology

Mechanism of action/Effect: The predominant clinical effect of the gold compounds appears to be suppression of the synovitis of the active stage of rheumatoid disease. The precise mechanism of anti-inflammatory effect is unknown, but it has been suggested that these agents alter cellular mechanisms by inhibiting sulfhydryl systems. Other proposed mechanisms for gold compounds' effects in patients with rheumatoid arthritis include alteration or inhibition of various enzyme systems, suppression of the phagocytic activity of macrophages and polymorphonuclear leukocytes, alteration of immune response, and alteration of collagen biosynthesis. *In vitro,* the gold compounds have been shown to inhibit prostaglandin synthesis.

Onset of action:
 Oral—Usually 3 to 4 months but up to 6 months in some patients.
 Parenteral—At least 6 to 8 weeks.

Precautions to Consider

Cross-sensitivity and/or related problems

Patients sensitive to gold or other heavy metals may be sensitive to this medication also.

Patients sensitive to sesame products may also be sensitive to the sesame oil vehicle of parenteral aurothioglucose.

Patients intolerant of parabens may be intolerant of parenteral aurothioglucose, which may contain propylparaben, also.

Geriatrics

Studies performed to date have not demonstrated geriatrics-specific problems that would limit the usefulness of these medications in the elderly. However, elderly patients are more likely to have age-related renal function impairment, which may require caution in patients receiving gold compounds.

Dental

The leukopenic and/or thrombocytopenic effects of gold compounds may result in an increased incidence of microbial infection, delayed healing, and gingival bleeding. If leukopenia or thrombocytopenia occurs, dental work should be deferred until blood counts have returned to normal and patients should be instructed in proper oral hygiene, including caution in use of regular toothbrushes, dental floss, and toothpicks.

Gold compounds may cause glossitis, gingivitis, or stomatitis.

Drug interactions and/or related problems

The following drug interactions and/or related problems have been selected on the basis of their potential clinical significance (possible mechanism in parentheses where appropriate)—not necessarily inclusive (» = major clinical significance):

Bone marrow depressants or
Dermatitis-causing medications, other, or
Hepatotoxic medications, other, or
Nephrotoxic medications, other
  (the possibility of additive toxicity should be considered if these medications are used concurrently with gold compounds)
» Penicillamine
  (concurrent use of penicillamine with gold compounds may be especially likely to increase the risk of serious hematologic and/or renal adverse effects; concurrent use is not recommended)

Contraindications/Medical problems

The contraindications/medical problems included have been selected on the basis of their potential clinical significance (reasons given in parentheses where appropriate)—not necessarily inclusive (» = major clinical significance).

Except under special circumstances, this medication should not be used when the following medical problems exist:

» Serious adverse effects associated with previous gold therapy, such as bone marrow aplasia or other severe hematologic disorders, exfoliative dermatitis, necrotizing enterocolitis, or pulmonary fibrosis, history of
  (high risk of recurrence)

Risk-benefit should be considered when the following medical problems exist:

» Blood dyscrasias or a history of agranulocytosis or hemorrhagic diathesis
  Blood dyscrasias, such as granulocytopenia or anemia caused by drug sensitivity, history of
  Colitis—especially for auranofin
» Debilitation, severe
  Inadequate or compromised cerebral or cardiovascular circulation
  Renal disease, or history of
» Sensitivity to any of the gold compounds, history of
» Sjögren's syndrome in rheumatoid arthritis
  Skin rash
» Systemic lupus erythematosus
» Urticaria or eczema

Side/Adverse Effects

See *Table 1*, page 602.

Patient Consultation

In providing consultation, consider emphasizing the following selected information (» = major clinical significance):

Before using this medication

» Conditions affecting use, especially:
    Sensitivity to gold, other heavy metals, or sesame products
    Pregnancy—Studies in humans have not been done, but gold compounds have caused teratogenic and fetotoxic effects in animal studies
    Breast-feeding—Use is not recommended because of potential adverse effects in the nursing infant; aurothioglucose and gold sodium thiomalate are excreted in human breast milk; it is not known whether auranofin is excreted in human breast milk
    Dental—Risk of adverse effects such as infection, delayed healing, and gingival bleeding associated with blood dyscrasias, as well as gold compound-induced gingivitis, glossitis, and/or stomatitis
    Other medications, especially penicillamine
    Other medical problems, especially serious adverse effects to prior gold therapy, blood dyscrasias (especially hemorrhagic or caused by sensitivity to a medication), severe debilitation, Sjögren's syndrome, systemic lupus erythematosus, eczema, or urticaria

Proper use of this medication

    Compliance with therapy; symptomatic relief may not occur until after three to six months of continuous use

For auranofin (oral dosage form) only

» Not taking more medication than amount prescribed
    Missed dose: If dosing schedule is—
      Once a day: Taking as soon as possible; not taking if not remembered until next day; not doubling doses
      More than once a day: Taking as soon as possible; not taking if almost time for next dose; not doubling doses
» Proper storage

Precautions while using this medication

    Possibility of phototoxicity

For oral dosage form only

    Regular visits to physician to check progress during therapy; blood and urine tests may be required to detect possible adverse effects

For parenteral dosage forms only

    Possibility of nitritoid reactions immediately following injection
    Possibility of joint pain occurring for 1 or 2 days after injection

Side/adverse effects

    Signs and symptoms of potential side effects, especially allergic reactions, blood dyscrasias, central nervous system or neurologic effects, cutaneous or dermatologic effects, difficulty in swallowing, fever, ulcerative enterocolitis, gastrointestinal bleeding, hepatotoxicity, mucous membrane reactions, ocular effects, pulmonary effects, and renal effects
    Possibility of side effects occurring up to many months after discontinuation of medication

General Dosing Information

Concurrent therapy with salicylates or other nonsteroidal anti-inflammatory drugs or glucocorticoids is necessary, especially during the first few months of gold therapy, to provide symptomatic relief.

Following mild adverse reactions, therapy should be discontinued temporarily. After the reactions have cleared, therapy may be resumed using a reduced dosage schedule.

Therapy should not be reinstituted after severe or idiosyncratic reactions.

AURANOFIN

Summary of Differences

Pharmacology:

Protein-binding—Less extensive than with parenteral gold formulations.

Onset of action—Usually 3 to 4 months, but up to 6 months in some patients.

Precautions: Patient monitoring—Hepatic and renal function tests also recommended.

Side/adverse effects:

Nitritoid reactions and temporary joint pain that sometimes occur following injections have not been reported.

Lower incidence of mucous membrane reactions (other than stomatitis) than with injectible gold formulations.

Higher incidence of gastrointestinal irritation (e.g., cramping, indigestion, constipation, diarrhea, nausea) than with injectible gold products.

Additional Dosing Information

See also *General Dosing Information.*

Diarrhea occurring during auranofin therapy may respond to a reduction in dosage.

Oral Dosage Forms

AURANOFIN CAPSULES

Usual adult dose: Oral, 6 mg once a day or 3 mg twice a day.

Note: Initiation of therapy with doses higher than 6 mg per day is associated with an increased incidence of diarrhea and is not recommended.

If an adequate response has not been achieved after six months, the daily dose may be increased to 9 mg, administered in three divided doses. If an adequate response has not been achieved after three months of treatment at the higher dose, therapy should be discontinued.

Usual adult prescribing limits: 9 mg per day.

AUROTHIOGLUCOSE

Summary of Differences

Pharmacology:

Protein-binding—More extensive than with auranofin.

Onset of action—Usually 6 to 8 weeks.

Side/adverse effects:

May cause nitritoid reactions and temporary joint pain after an injection.

Higher incidence of mucous membrane reactions (other than stomatitis) than with auranofin.

Lower incidence of gastrointestinal irritation (e.g., cramping, indigestion, constipation, diarrhea, nausea) than with auranofin.

Additional Dosing Information

See also *General Dosing Information.*

Aurothioglucose is for intramuscular injection only. Injections should be administered deeply into the upper outer quadrant of the gluteal region, using an 18-gauge, 1½-inch (2-inch for obese patients) needle.

Before withdrawing the dose, the vial should be thoroughly shaken to obtain a uniform suspension.

The needle and syringe used to withdraw the dose from the vial must be dry.

To facilitate withdrawing the suspension from the vial, the vial may be heated by immersing in warm water.

Parenteral Dosage Forms

STERILE AUROTHIOGLUCOSE SUSPENSION USP

Usual adult and adolescent dose:

Initial—Intramuscular, 10 mg the first week, 25 mg the second and third weeks, then 25 to 50 mg once a week until a total dose of 800 mg to 1 gram has been given.

Maintenance—Intramuscular, 25 to 50 mg every two weeks for two to twenty weeks, then 25 to 50 mg every three to four weeks.

Usual adult prescribing limits: Up to 50 mg per week.

Auxiliary labeling: • Shake well.

GOLD SODIUM THIOMALATE

Summary of Differences

Pharmacology:

Protein-binding—More extensive than with auranofin.

Onset of action—Usually 6 to 8 weeks.

Side/adverse effects:

May cause nitritoid reactions and temporary joint pain after an injection.

Higher incidence of mucous membrane reactions (other than stomatitis) than with auranofin.

Lower incidence of gastrointestinal irritation (e.g., cramping, indigestion, constipation, diarrhea, nausea) than with auranofin.

Additional Dosing Information

See also *General Dosing Information.*

Gold sodium thiomalate should be administered only by intramuscular injection, preferably intragluteally.

To reinstitute therapy following mild adverse reactions, an initial dose of 5 mg is given. If the medication is well tolerated, the dose may be increased in 5- to 10-mg increments at weekly to monthly intervals until a dose of 25 to 50 mg is reached.

Maintenance treatment at intervals of 1 to 3 weeks may be required for some patients.

Parenteral Dosage Forms

GOLD SODIUM THIOMALATE INJECTION USP

Usual adult and adolescent dose:

Initial—Intramuscular, 10 mg the first week, 25 mg the second week, then 25 to 50 mg once a week until the desired therapeutic response is obtained or until toxicity occurs, up to a total dose of 1 gram.

Maintenance—Intramuscular, 25 to 50 mg every two weeks for two to twenty weeks, then 25 to 50 mg every three or four weeks.

Table 1. Side/Adverse Effects*

The following side/adverse effects have been selected on the basis of their potential clinical significance (possible signs and symptoms in parenthese where appropriate)—not necessarily inclusive:	Legend: **I** = Auranofin **II** = Aurothioglucose **III** = Gold Sodium Thiomalate		
	I	**II**	**III**
Medical attention needed			
Allergic reactions			
Anaphylactic shock (changes in facial skin color; skin rash, hives, and/or itching; fast or irregular breathing; puffiness or swelling of the eyelids or around the eyes; shortness of breath, troubled breathing, tightness in chest, and/or wheezing; sudden, severe decrease in blood pressure and collapse)	U	R	R
Angioedema without other signs and symptoms of nitritoid or allergic reaction (large hive-like swellings on face, eyelids, mouth, lips, and/or tongue)	R	U	U
Nitritoid or allergic reaction, severe (difficulty in breathing or swallowing; fainting; slow heartbeat; large hive-like swellings on face, eyelids, mouth, lips, and/or tongue; thickening of tongue)—may occur up to 10 minutes after injection	†	R	R
Central nervous system (CNS)/Neurologic effects			
Confusion	U	U	R
Convulsions	U	U	R
Encephalitis	U	R	U
Electroencephalographic (EEG) abnormalities	U	R	U
Guillain-Barre syndrome (tingling, numbness, and weakness in arms, trunk, or face; problems with muscle coordination)	U	U	R
Hallucinations	U	U	R
Neuropathy, peripheral (numbness, tingling, pain, or weakness in hands or feet)‡	R	R	R
Cutaneous/dermatologic effects			
Dermatitis, allergic‡			
(hives)	L	U	U
(itching)—may occur first and indicate an impending cutaneous reaction	M (17%)	M	M
(skin rash)—both papular and vesicular dermatitis have been reported with aurothioglucose; in some patients, skin rash may indicate toxicity rather than an allergic reaction; also, skin rash may be caused or aggravated by exposure to sunlight	M (24%)	M	M
Dermatitis, exfoliative (fever with or without chills; red, thickened, or scaly skin; swollen and/or painful glands; unusual bruising)—may lead to alopecia and shedding of nails	U	R	R
Hair loss without symptoms of exfoliative dermatitis	L	U	U
Reddened skin	U	M	U
Difficulty in swallowing without other symptoms of nitritoid or allergic reaction	R	U	U
Fever	U	R	R

Table 1. Side/Adverse Effects* *(continued)*

	Legend: I = Auranofin / II = Aurothioglucose / III = Gold Sodium Thiomalate		
	I	**II**	**III**
Gastrointestinal effects			
Enterocolitis, ulcerative (abdominal pain, cramping, or burning, severe; bloody or black tarry stools; vomiting of blood or material that looks like coffee grounds; nausea, heartburn, and/or indigestion, severe and continuing)	R	R	R
Gastrointestinal bleeding without other signs and symptoms of ulcerative enterocolitis (bloody or black tarry stools)—occult blood in the stool has also been reported with auranofin	R	U	U
Hematologic effects—may occur individually or in combination			
Agranulocytosis (sore throat and fever with or without chills; sores, ulcers, or white spots on lips or in mouth)	R	R	R
Anemia (unusual tiredness or weakness)‡	R	U	U
Anemia, aplastic [anemia, hypoplastic; pancytopenia; red cell aplasia] (shortness of breath, troubled breathing, tightness in chest, and/or wheezing; sores, ulcers, or white spots on lips or in mouth; swollen and/or painful glands; unusual bleeding or bruising; unusual tiredness or weakness)‡	R	R	R
Eosinophilia	L	R	R
Leukopenia [neutropenia] (usually asymptomatic; rarely, fever or chills, cough or hoarseness, lower back or side pain, painful or difficult urination)‡	L	R	U
Thrombocytopenia with or without purpura (usually asymptomatic; rarely, unusual bleeding or bruising; black, tarry stools; blood in urine or stools; pinpoint red spots on skin)‡	L	R	R
Hepatotoxicity (dark urine, pale stools, and/or yellow eyes or skin)—cholestatic hepatitis and toxic hepatitis have both been reported‡	R	R	R
Mucous membrane reactions			
Gingivitis (redness, soreness, swelling, or bleeding of gums)‡	R	M	M
Glossitis (irritation or soreness of tongue)‡	L	M	M
Metallic taste—may indicate impending gingivitis, glossitis, or stomatitis‡	R	M	M
Pharyngitis, tracheitis, or upper respiratory tract inflammation (irritation of nose, throat, and/or upper chest area, possibly with hoarseness and/or coughing)	U	R	U
Stomatitis‡ (ulcers, sores, or white spots in mouth or throat)—indicative of toxicity	M (13%)	M	M
Vaginitis (irritation of vagina)	U	R	U
Ocular effects			
Conjunctivitis (redness, itching, or tearing of eyes; feeling of something in the eye)‡	M	R	R
Corneal ulcers	U	R	R
Iritis (eye pain, tearing, decreased vision)	U	R	R

*Differences in frequency of occurrence may reflect either lack of clinical-use data or actual pharmacologic distinctions among agents (although their pharmacologic similarity suggests that side effects occurring with one may occur with the others).

For auranofin: M=3–9%; L=1–3%; R=<1%; U=unknown; unless otherwise specified.

For aurothioglucose and gold sodium thiomalate (actual percentages not available): M=more frequent; F=less frequent; R=rare; U=unknown.

†Has not been reported with auranofin.

‡May occur during therapy or up to several months after cessation of therapy.

§If severe, may indicate overdose (parenteral dosage forms only).

Table 1. Side/Adverse Effects* *(continued)*

	Legend: **I** = Auranofin **II** = Aurothioglucose **III** = Gold Sodium Thiomalate		
	I	**II**	**III**

Pulmonary effects (coughing, shortness of breath)
    Bronchitis [gold bronchitis], or
    Fibrosis, pulmonary‡, or
    Pneumonitis‡, interstitial
	
	U
	U
	R
		
		R
		R
		R
			
			R
			R
			R

Renal effects‡ *Glomerulitis* (pain in lower back or abdomen; bloody urine; difficulty in breathing; decreased urination; swelling of face and/or legs)	 U	 R	 R
Hematuria without other signs or symptoms of renal toxicity (bloody urine)—may be detected microscopically before bleeding is visually apparent	L	R	R
Nephrotic syndrome (swelling of face, fingers, ankles, lower legs, and/or feet; cloudy urine)	U	R	R
Proteinuria without other signs or symptoms of renal toxicity (cloudy urine)	M	L	L
Medical attention needed only if continuing or bothersome *Allergic reaction* *Nitritoid or allergic reaction, mild* (dizziness, feeling faint, flushing or redness of face, increased sweating, nausea with or without vomiting, weakness)—may occur immediately after injection	 †	 R	 R
Gastrointestinal effects *Abdominal or stomach cramps or pain, mild to moderate‡*	M (14%)	R	R
Bloated feeling, gas, or indigestion, mild to moderate	M	U	U
Constipation	L	U	U
Decrease or loss of appetite	M	R	R
Diarrhea or loose stools‡	M (47%)	R§	R§
Loss of or other change in taste sense	L	U	U
Nausea with or without vomiting, mild to moderate	M (10%)	R§	R§
Joint pain—may occur for 1 or 2 days after injection	—	L	L

*Differences in frequency of occurrence may reflect either lack of clinical-use data or actual pharmacologic distinctions among agents (although their pharmacologic similarity suggests that side effects occurring with one may occur with the others).

For auranofin: M=3–9%; L=1–3%; R=<1%; U=unknown; unless otherwise specified.

For aurothioglucose and gold sodium thiomalate (actual percentages not available): M=more frequent; F=less frequent; R=rare; U=unknown.

†Has not been reported with auranofin.

‡May occur during therapy or up to several months after cessation of therapy.

§If severe, may indicate overdose (parenteral dosage forms only).

GOSERELIN   Systemic

A commonly used *brand name* in the U.S. and Canada is *Zoladex*.

PARENTERAL
Goserelin Acetate Implants
   In the U.S. and Canada—*Zoladex*

Category: Antineoplastic.

Indications

Accepted
Carcinoma, prostatic (treatment)—Goserelin is indicated for the palliative treatment of advanced prostatic carcinoma, especially as an alternative to orchiectomy or estrogen administration.

Pharmacology

Mechanism of action/Effect: Goserelin is a synthetic luteinizing hormone-releasing hormone (LHRH) analog. Like naturally occurring LHRH that is produced by the hypothalamus, initial or intermittent administration of goserelin stimulates release of luteinizing hormone (LH) and follicle-stimulating hormone (FSH) from the anterior pituitary, which in turn transiently increases testosterone concentrations in males. However, continuous daily administration of goserelin in the treatment of prostatic carcinoma suppresses secretion of LH and FSH, with a resultant fall in testosterone concentrations and a "medical castration".

Onset of action: Testosterone concentrations—Transient increase occurs within first week of therapy; a decline to castrate levels occurs within 2 to 4 weeks.

Duration of action: Suppression of testosterone concentrations to castrate levels persists for the duration of therapy.

Precautions to Consider

Geriatrics
Appropriate studies on the relationship of age to the effects of goserelin have not been performed in the geriatric population. However, clinical trials were conducted mainly in older patients and geriatrics-specific problems that would limit the usefulness of this medication in the elderly are not expected.

Contraindications/Medical problems
The contraindications/medical problems included have been selected on the basis of their potential clinical significance (reasons given in parentheses where appropriate)—not necessarily inclusive (» = major clinical significance).

Risk-benefit should be considered when the following medical problems exist:
Obstructive uropathy, history of
   (increased incidence of disease flare during initial goserelin treatment because of the initial increase in serum testosterone concentrations)
Sensitivity to goserelin
Vertebral metastases
   (risk of spinal cord compression as a result of disease flare during initial goserelin treatment)

Side/Adverse Effects

The following side/adverse effects have been selected on the basis of their potential clinical significance (possible signs and symptoms in parentheses where appropriate)—not necessarily inclusive:

Those indicating need for medical attention
Incidence more frequent—approximately 10%
   Possible disease flare (bone pain, numbness or tingling of hands or feet, trouble in urinating, weakness in legs)

   Note: A transient, sometimes severe, increase in bone or tumor pain may occur shortly after initiation of therapy, usually associated with the increase in serum testosterone, but usually subsides with continued goserelin treatment. Analgesics may be required during this time. Other signs and symptoms of prostatic carcinoma, including difficult urination, may also worsen transiently. In addition, worsening of neurologic signs and symptoms in patients with vertebral metastases may result in temporary weakness and paresthesias of the lower extremities.

Incidence less frequent
   Anemia; cardiovascular effects, including arrhythmias (irregular heartbeat), *cerebrovascular accident* (sudden weakness), *hypertension, myocardial infarction* (chest pain, shortness of breath), *or peripheral vascular disorder* (painful or cold hands or feet); *gout* (joint pain); *skin rash*

Those indicating need for medical attention only if they continue or are bothersome
Incidence more frequent
   "Hot flashes" (sudden sweating and feelings of warmth)—incidence about 60%; *impotence or decrease in sexual desire*—incidence about 20%
Incidence less frequent
   Anxiety or mental depression; chronic obstructive pulmonary disease (COPD) or upper respiratory infection (shortness of breath); *congestive heart failure or edema* (swelling of feet or lower legs); *constipation; diarrhea; dizziness; headache; loss of appetite; nausea or vomiting; swelling and increased tenderness of breasts; trouble in sleeping; unusual tiredness or weakness; weight gain*

Patient Consultation

In providing consultation, consider emphasizing the following selected information (» = major clinical significance):

Before using this medication
» Conditions affecting use, especially:
     Sensitivity to goserelin
     Pregnancy/Reproduction—May cause sterility

Proper use of this medication
» Importance of continuing medication despite side effects
     Missed dose: Getting as soon as possible

Precautions while using this medication
» Importance of close monitoring by the physician

Side/adverse effects
   Signs of potential side effects, especially transient disease flare, anemia, cardiovascular effects, gout, and skin rash

General Dosing Information

Patients receiving goserelin should be under supervision of a physician experienced in cancer therapy. Administration of goserelin should be carried out, using sterile technique, under supervision of a physician.

Goserelin has a longer duration of action than naturally occurring luteinizing hormone-releasing hormone.

Parenteral Dosage Forms

GOSERELIN ACETATE IMPLANTS

Usual adult dose: Prostatic carcinoma—Subcutaneous (into upper abdominal wall), 3.6 mg (base) every twenty-eight days.

> Note: If the implant needs to be removed for any reason, it can be located by ultrasound.

GUAIFENESIN   Systemic

Some commonly used *brand names* are:

In the U.S.—

Amonidrin	Humibid L.A.
Anti-Tuss	Humibid Sprinkle
Breonesin	Hytuss
Gee-Gee	Hytuss-2X
Genatuss	Malotuss
GG-CEN	Mytussin
Glyate	Naldecon Senior EX
Glycotuss	Nortussin
Glytuss	Robafen
Guiatuss	Robitussin
Halotussin	Scot-tussin

In Canada—

Balminil Expectorant	Robitussin
Resyl	

Another commonly used name is glyceryl guaiacolate.

ORAL
Guaifenesin Capsules USP†
In the U.S.—*Breonesin; GG-CEN; Hytuss-2X*
Guaifenesin Extended-release Capsules†
In the U.S.—*Humibid Sprinkle*
Guaifenesin Oral Solution†
In the U.S.—*Naldecon Senior EX*
Guaifenesin Syrup USP
In the U.S.—*Anti-Tuss; Genatuss; Glyate; Guiatuss; Halotussin; Malotuss; Mytussin; Nortussin; Robafen; Robitussin; Scot-tussin;* GENERIC
In Canada—*Balminil Expectorant; Robitussin*
Guaifenesin Tablets USP
In the U.S.—*Amonidrin; Gee-Gee; Glycotuss; Glytuss; Hytuss*
In Canada—*Resyl*
Guaifenesin Extended-release Tablets†
In the U.S.—*Humibid L.A.*

---

†Not commercially available in Canada.

Category: Expectorant.

Indications

Accepted
Cough (treatment)—Guaifenesin is indicated as an expectorant for the symptomatic relief of cough due to colds and minor upper respiratory infections.

Pharmacology

Mechanism of action/Effect: Guaifenesin has an expectorant action which increases the output of respiratory tract fluid by reducing adhesiveness and surface tension. The increased flow of less viscid secretions promotes ciliary action and facilitates the removal of mucus. This changes a dry, unproductive cough to a cough that is more productive and less frequent.

Precautions to Consider

Geriatrics
Appropriate studies on the relationship of age to the effects of guaifenesin have not been performed in the geriatric population. However, no geriatrics-specific problems have been documented to date.

Contraindications/Medical problems
The contraindications/medical problems included have been selected on the basis of their potential clinical significance (reasons given in parentheses where appropriate)—not necessarily inclusive (» = major clinical significance).

Risk-benefit should be considered when the following medical problem exists:
Sensitivity to guaifenesin

Side/Adverse Effects

The following side/adverse effects have been selected on the basis of their potential clinical significance (possible signs and symptoms in parentheses where appropriate)—not necessarily inclusive:

Those indicating need for medical attention only if they continue or are bothersome
Less frequent or rare
> *Diarrhea; drowsiness; nausea or vomiting; stomach pain*

Patient Consultation

In providing consultation, consider emphasizing the following selected information (» = major clinical significance):

Before using this medication
» Conditions affecting use, especially:
    Sensitivity to guaifenesin

Proper use of this medication
» Importance of drinking a glass of water after each dose of medication to help loosen mucus in lungs
    Missed dose (if on a scheduled dosing regimen): Taking as soon as possible; not taking if almost time for next dose; not doubling doses
    Swallowing extended-release tablet dosage form whole
» Proper storage

Precautions while using this medication
    Checking with physician if cough persists after medication has been used for 7 days or if high fever, skin rash, or continuing headache, or sore throat is present with cough

General Dosing Information

To help loosen mucus in the lungs, patient should drink a glass of water after each dose of guaifenesin.

Oral Dosage Forms

GUAIFENESIN CAPSULES USP

Usual adult and adolescent dose: Oral, 200 to 400 mg every four hours, not to exceed 2400 mg a day.

Usual geriatric dose: See *Usual adult and adolescent dose.*

GUAIFENESIN EXTENDED-RELEASE CAPSULES

Usual adult and adolescent dose: Oral, 600 to 1200 mg every twelve hours, not to exceed 2400 mg a day.

Usual geriatric dose: See *Usual adult and adolescent dose.*

GUAIFENESIN ORAL SOLUTION

Usual adult and adolescent dose: Oral, 200 to 400 mg every four hours, not to exceed 2400 mg a day.

Usual geriatric dose: See *Usual adult and adolescent dose.*

GUAIFENESIN SYRUP USP

Usual adult and adolescent dose: Oral, 200 to 400 mg every four hours, not to exceed 2400 mg a day.

Usual geriatric dose: See *Usual adult and adolescent dose.*

GUAIFENESIN TABLETS USP

Usual adult and adolescent dose: Oral, 200 to 400 mg every four hours, not to exceed 2400 mg a day.

Usual geriatric dose: See *Usual adult and adolescent dose.*

GUAIFENESIN EXTENDED-RELEASE TABLETS

Usual adult and adolescent dose: Oral, 600 or 1200 mg every twelve hours, not to exceed 2400 mg a day.

Usual geriatric dose: See *Usual adult and adolescent dose.*

Auxiliary labeling: • Swallow tablets whole.

GUANABENZ Systemic†

A commonly used *brand name* in the U.S. is *Wytensin.*

ORAL
Guanabenz Acetate Tablets USP†
In the U.S.—*Wytensin*

---

†Not commercially available in Canada.

Category: Antihypertensive.

Indications

Accepted

Hypertension (treatment)—Guanabenz is indicated for treatment of hypertension. Because it usually does not cause postural hypotension, guanabenz may be useful as a substitute for other central adrenergic blockers in patients who cannot tolerate these agents because of severe orthostatic hypotension.

In the 1988 Report of the Joint National Committee on Detection, Evaluation, and Treatment of High Blood Pressure, a progression in choice of treatments for essential hypertension is recommended:

Nonpharmacologic management (especially sodium restriction, weight reduction and exercise, and moderation of alcohol consumption) is recommended first for some patients, including those with mild hypertension, and is recommended as an adjunct to all pharmacologic hypertensive therapy.

Initial drug therapy usually consists of a diuretic, beta-adrenergic blocking agent, calcium channel blocking agent, or angiotensin-converting enzyme (ACE) inhibitor. If adequate blood pressure control is not achieved and the patient is adherent to the treatment program and not experiencing significant side effects, dosage of the drug may be increased, a drug from another one of these initial classes may be added or substituted, or a second drug from a different class—centrally acting alpha-adrenergic blockers (e.g., clonidine, guanabenz, guanfacine, methyldopa), peripheral-acting adrenergic antagonists (e.g., guanadrel, guanethidine, rauwolfia alkaloids), post-synaptic alpha-1 peripheral adrenergic blocking agents (e.g., doxazosin, prazosin, terazosin), or vasodilators (e.g., hydralazine, minoxidil)—may be added or substituted.

If necessary, a drug from another class in the second group may be substituted or added as a third drug. If blood pressure control is still not achieved, a drug from still another class may be substituted or added as a fourth drug, or the patient may need further evaluation and/or referral.

Pharmacology

Mechanism of action/Effect: Alpha-2 adrenergic agonist. The antihypertensive effect is thought to be due to central alpha-adrenergic stimulation, which results in a decreased sympathetic outflow to the heart, kidneys, and peripheral vasculature; decreased systolic and diastolic blood pressure; and slight slowing of pulse rate. Chronic administration of guanabenz also causes a decrease in peripheral vascular resistance.

Onset of action: Within 60 minutes (after a single dose).

Time to peak effect: 2 to 4 hours.

Duration of action: 12 hours (after a single dose).

Precautions to Consider

Geriatrics

Although appropriate studies on the relationship of age to the effects of guanabenz have not been performed in the geriatric population, no geriatrics-specific problems have been documented to date. However, elderly patients are more likely to have age-related renal function impairment, which may require caution in patients receiving guanabenz. In addition, elderly patients may be more sensitive to the hypotensive and sedative effects of guanabenz.

Dental

Use of guanabenz may decrease or inhibit salivary flow, thus contributing to the development of caries, periodontal disease, oral candidiasis, and discomfort.

Drug interactions and/or related problems

The following drug interactions and/or related problems have been selected on the basis of their potential clinical significance (possible mechanism in parentheses where appropriate)—not necessarily inclusive (» = major clinical significance):

Note: Combinations containing any of the following medications, depending on the amount present, may also interact with this medication.

Alcohol or

Central nervous system (CNS) depression-producing medications
(concurrent use may enhance the CNS depressant effects of either these medications or guanabenz)

Anti-inflammatory drugs, nonsteroidal (NSAIDs), especially indomethacin
(concurrent use may reduce antihypertensive effects of guanabenz; indomethacin, and possibly other NSAIDs, may antagonize the antihypertensive effect by inhibiting renal prostaglandin synthesis and/or by causing sodium and fluid retention; the patient should be carefully monitored to confirm that the desired effect is being obtained)

Beta-adrenergic blocking agents, ophthalmic
(if significant systemic absorption of ophthalmic beta-blockers occurs, concurrent use may increase the hypotensive effect of guanabenz)

» Beta-adrenergic blocking agents, systemic, or
Hypotension-producing medications, other
(antihypertensive effects may be potentiated when these medications are used concurrently with guanabenz; although some antihypertensive and/or diuretic combinations are frequently used for therapeutic advantage, dosage adjustments may be necessary during concurrent use)
(when therapy is discontinued in patients receiving a beta-blocker and guanabenz concurrently, the beta-blocker should be gradually discontinued in order to avoid guanabenz-withdrawal hypertensive crisis; blood pressure control may also be impaired when the two are combined)

Estrogens
(estrogen-induced fluid retention may increase blood pressure)

Sympathomimetics
(concurrent use may reduce the antihypertensive effects of guanabenz; the patient should be carefully monitored to confirm that the desired effect is being obtained)

Contraindications/Medical problems

The contraindications/medical problems included have been selected on the basis of their potential clinical significance (reasons given in parentheses where appropriate)—not necessarily inclusive (» = major clinical significance).

Risk-benefit should be considered when the following medical problems exist:

Cerebrovascular disease or
Coronary insufficiency or
Myocardial infarction, recent
(may be aggravated by reduced blood pressure)

Hepatic function impairment
(plasma concentrations of guanabenz may increase; careful monitoring of blood pressure during dosage titration is recommended)

Renal function impairment
(half-life of guanabenz is increased and clearance is decreased; careful monitoring of blood pressure during dosage titration is recommended)

Sensitivity to guanabenz

Side/Adverse Effects

The following side/adverse effects have been selected on the basis of their potential clinical significance (possible signs and symptoms in parentheses where appropriate)—not necessarily inclusive:

Those indicating need for medical attention
Signs and symptoms of overdose
Dizziness, severe, or faintness; irritability; nervousness; pinpoint pupils; slow heartbeat; unusual tiredness or weakness

Those indicating need for medical attention only if they continue or are bothersome
Incidence more frequent
Dizziness; drowsiness; dryness of mouth; weakness

Note: Incidence of *drowsiness* is dose-related and usually declines with continued administration.

Incidence less frequent or rare
Decreased sexual ability; headache; nausea

Those indicating possible withdrawal and the need for medical attention if they occur after medication is abruptly discontinued
Anxiety or tenseness; chest pain; fast or irregular heartbeat; headache; increased salivation; increase in sweating; nausea or vomiting; nervousness or restlessness; shaking or trembling of hands or fingers; stomach cramps; trouble in sleeping

Note: The above are symptoms of sympathetic overactivity; elevation of blood pressure above baseline levels does not usually occur. The risk appears to be increased in patients receiving doses of greater than 32 mg of guanabenz per day.

Patient Consultation

In providing consultation, consider emphasizing the following selected information (» = major clinical significance):

Before using this medication
» Conditions affecting use, especially:
   Sensitivity to guanabenz
   Pregnancy—High doses in animals cause decreased fertility, birth defects, and fetal death
   Use in the elderly—Increased sensitivity to hypotensive and sedative effects
   Dental—May decrease or inhibit salivary flow
   Other medications, especially systemic beta-adrenergic blocking agents

Proper use of this medication
   Possible need for control of weight and diet, especially sodium intake
» Patient may not experience symptoms of hypertension; importance of taking medication even if feeling well
» Does not cure but helps control hypertension; possible need for lifelong therapy; serious consequences of untreated hypertension
   Getting into the habit of taking at same time each day to help increase compliance
   Missed dose: Taking as soon as possible; not taking if almost time for next dose; checking with physician if two or more doses in a row are missed; possible unpleasant effects if stopped abruptly
» Proper storage

Precautions while using this medication
   Regular visits to physician to check progress
   Checking with physician before discontinuing medication; possible need for gradual dosage reduction
   Caution if any kind of surgery (including dental surgery) or emergency treatment is required
» Not taking other medications, especially nonprescription sympathomimetics, unless discussed with physician

» Caution in taking alcohol or other CNS depressants
» Caution when driving or doing things requiring alertness because of possible dizziness or drowsiness
Possible dryness of mouth; using sugarless candy or gum, ice, or saliva substitute for relief; checking with physician or dentist if dry mouth continues for more than 2 weeks

Side/adverse effects
Signs of potential side effects, especially signs and symptoms of overdose or withdrawal reaction

General Dosing Information

It is recommended that the last daily dose be taken at bedtime to ensure overnight control of blood pressure and reduce daytime drowsiness.

Recent evidence suggests that withdrawal of antihypertensive therapy prior to surgery is not necessary, but that the anesthesiologist must be aware of such therapy.

The possibility of withdrawal syndrome should be kept in mind if guanabenz is discontinued abruptly, although rebound hypertension does not usually occur.

Oral Dosage Forms

GUANABENZ ACETATE TABLETS USP

Usual adult dose: Antihypertensive—Oral, 4 mg two times a day initially, the dosage being increased if necessary in increments of 4 to 8 mg per day every one to two weeks up to the minimum effective dose.

Note: Geriatric patients may be more sensitive to the effects of the usual adult dose.

Usual adult prescribing limits: Up to 32 mg per day.

Auxiliary labeling:
- Do not take other medicines without your doctor's advice.
- May cause dizziness.
- May cause drowsiness.

GUANADREL   Systemic†

A commonly used *brand name* in the U.S. is *Hylorel*.

ORAL
Guanadrel Sulfate Tablets USP†
  In the U.S.—*Hylorel*

  †Not commercially available in Canada.

Category: Antihypertensive.

Indications

Accepted
Hypertension (treatment)—Guanadrel is indicated in the treatment of hypertension.

In the 1988 Report of the Joint National Committee on Detection, Evaluation, and Treatment of High Blood Pressure, a progression in choice of treatments for essential hypertension is recommended:

Nonpharmacologic management (especially sodium restriction, weight reduction and exercise, and moderation of alcohol consumption) is recommended first for some patients, including those with mild hypertension, and is recommended as an adjunct to all pharmacologic hypertensive therapy.

Initial drug therapy usually consists of a diuretic, beta-adrenergic blocking agent, calcium channel blocking agent, or angiotensin-converting enzyme (ACE) inhibitor. If adequate blood pressure control is not achieved and the patient is adherent to the treatment program and not experiencing significant side effects, dosage of the drug may be increased, a drug from another one of these initial classes may be added or substituted, or a second drug from a different class—centrally acting alpha-adrenergic blockers (e.g., clonidine, guanabenz, guanfacine, methyldopa), peripheral-acting adrenergic antagonists (e.g., guanadrel, guanethidine, rauwolfia alkaloids), post-synaptic alpha-1 peripheral adrenergic blocking agents (e.g., doxazosin, prazosin, terazosin), or vasodilators (e.g., hydralazine, minoxidil)—may be added or substituted.

If necessary, a drug from another class in the second group may be substituted or added as a third drug. If blood pressure control is still not achieved, a drug from still another class may

be substituted or added as a fourth drug, or the patient may need further evaluation and/or referral.

Pharmacology

Mechanism of action/Effect: Guanadrel is a postganglionic adrenergic blocking agent. Uptake of guanadrel and storage in sympathetic neurons occurs via the norepinephrine pump; guanadrel slowly displaces norepinephrine from its storage in nerve endings and thereby blocks the release of norepinephrine normally produced by nerve stimulation. The reduction in neurotransmitter release in response to sympathetic nerve stimulation, as a result of catecholamine depletion, leads to reduced arteriolar vasoconstriction, especially the reflex increase in sympathetic tone that occurs with a change in position.

Onset of action: 2 hours (after a single dose).

Time to peak effect: 4 to 6 hours (after a single dose).

Duration of action: Average—9 hours (range 4 to 14 hours) after a single dose.

Precautions to Consider

Geriatrics
Appropriate studies with on the relationship of age to the effects of guanadrel have not been performed in the geriatric population. However, the elderly may be more sensitive to the hypotensive effects of guanadrel.

Drug interactions and/or related problems
The following drug interactions and/or related problems have been selected on the basis of their potential clinical significance (possible mechanism in parentheses where appropriate)—not necessarily inclusive (» = major clinical significance):

Note: Because of the similarity of guanadrel's actions to those of guanethidine, some of the following potential interactions are stated for cautionary reference until additional information is available.

Combinations containing any of the following medications, depending on the amount present, may also interact with this medication.

Alcohol or
Barbiturates or
Opioid (narcotic) analgesics
  (concurrent use with guanadrel will produce additive orthostatic hypotensive effects)
Alpha-adrenergic blocking agents, such as:
  Doxazosin
  Labetalol
  Phenoxybenzamine
  Phentolamine
  Prazosin
  Terazosin
  Tolazoline, or
Other medications with alpha-adrenergic blocking action, such as:
  Dihydroergotamine
  Ergoloid mesylates
  Ergotamine
  Haloperidol
  Loxapine
  Phenothiazines
  Thioxanthenes, or
Beta-adrenergic blocking agents or
Rauwolfia alkaloids
  (concurrent use with guanadrel may cause an increased incidence of orthostatic hypotension or bradycardia)

Amphetamines or
» Antidepressants, tricyclic, or
Appetite suppressants, with the exception of fenfluramine, or
Cyclobenzaprine or
Haloperidol or
» Loxapine or
Maprotiline or
Methylphenidate or
Phenothiazines, especially chlorpromazine, or
» Thioxanthenes or
» Trimeprazine
  (concurrent use may decrease the hypotensive effects of guanadrel because of its displacement from and inhibition of uptake by adrenergic neurons; caution is recommended when these medications are discontinued, especially if discontinued abruptly, because effects of guanadrel might be suddenly increased)
Anticholinergics, especially atropine and related compounds
  (concurrent use with guanadrel may antagonize the inhibitory action of these medications on gastric acid secretion)
Anti-inflammatory drugs, nonsteroidal (NSAIDs), especially indomethacin
  (antihypertensive effects of guanadrel may be reduced when it is used concurrently with these agents; indomethacin, and possibly other NSAIDs, may antagonize the antihypertensive effect by inhibiting renal prostaglandin synthesis and/or by causing sodium and fluid retention; the patient should be carefully monitored to confirm that the desired effect is being obtained)
Estrogens
  (concurrent use may decrease the antihypertensive effect of guanadrel because estrogen-induced fluid retention may lead to increased blood pressure)
Fenfluramine
  (concurrent use with guanadrel may produce additive hypotensive effects, and may result in postural hypotension; dosage adjustments of the antihypertensive may be necessary)
Hypotension-producing medications, other
  (antihypertensive effects may be potentiated when these medications are used concurrently with guanadrel; although some antihypertensive and/or diuretic combinations are frequently used for therapeutic advantage, dosage adjustments may be necessary during concurrent use)

» Monoamine oxidase (MAO) inhibitors, including furazolidone, procarbazine, and selegiline
  (concurrent use with guanadrel may result in moderate to severe hypertension due to release of catecholamines; withdrawal of MAO inhibitors at least 1 week prior to initiation of guanadrel therapy is recommended)
Sympathomimetics, such as:
  Cocaine or
  Dobutamine or
  Dopamine or
  Ephedrine or
  Epinephrine or
» Metaraminol or
  Methoxamine or
  Norepinephrine or
  Phenylephrine or
  Phenylpropanolamine
  (concurrent use of any sympathomimetics with guanadrel may reduce the antihypertensive effects of guanadrel; the patient should be carefully monitored to confirm that the desired effect is being obtained)
  (in addition to possibly decreasing the hypotensive effects of guanadrel, concurrent use of cocaine, dobutamine, dopamine, ephedrine, epinephrine, metaraminol, methoxamine, norepinephrine, phenylephrine, or phenylpropanolamine with guanadrel may potentiate the pressor effect of these medications, as a result of inhibition of sympathomimetic uptake by adrenergic neurons, possibly resulting in hypertension and cardiac arrhythmias)
  (concurrent use of ephedrine or phenylpropanolamine with guanadrel may decrease the hypotensive effects of guanadrel because of its displacement from and inhibition of uptake by adrenergic neurons)
  (concurrent use of metaraminol with guanadrel may cause a hypertensive crisis. When metaraminol is used within 5 days after discontinuation of guanadrel, a hypertensive potential may remain)
  (concurrent use of phenylephrine ophthalmic solution with guanadrel may increase the pupillary response)

Contraindications/Medical problems
The contraindications/medical problems included have been selected on the basis of their potential clinical significance (reasons given in parentheses where appropriate)—not necessarily inclusive (» = major clinical significance).

Risk-benefit should be considered when the following medical problems exist:
Asthma, history of
  (may be aggravated because of hypersensitivity to catecholamine depletion)
Cerebrovascular insufficiency or
Coronary insufficiency or
Myocardial infarction, recent
  (ischemia may be aggravated as a result of reduced blood pressure)
» Congestive heart failure not due to hypertension
  (may be aggravated by fluid retention; in addition, guanadrel may directly depress the myocardium)
Diarrhea
  (may be aggravated)
Fever
  (dosage requirements may be reduced)
Peptic ulcer, history of
  (may be aggravated by relative increase in parasympathetic tone)

» Pheochromocytoma
(release of catecholamines and increased sensitivity to circulating norepinephrine may exacerbate symptoms)

Sensitivity to guanadrel

Sinus bradycardia
(may be aggravated)

Side/Adverse Effects

Note: Side/adverse effects are largely due to selective sympathetic blockade and unopposed parasympathetic activity.

Side/adverse effects are usually reduced after the first 8 weeks of therapy.

The following side/adverse effects have been selected on the basis of their potential clinical significance (possible signs and symptoms in parentheses where appropriate)—not necessarily inclusive:

Those indicating need for medical attention
Incidence more frequent
Edema, peripheral (swelling of feet or lower legs)
Incidence less frequent or rare
Angina (chest pain); *dyspnea* (shortness of breath)
Symptoms of overdose
Blurred vision; dizziness or faintness, severe

Those indicating need for medical attention only if they continue or are bothersome
Incidence more frequent
Difficulty in ejaculating; drowsiness or tiredness; orthostatic hypotension (dizziness, lightheadedness, or fainting, especially when getting up from a lying or sitting position)
Note: Morning *orthostatic hypotension* is less frequent with guanadrel than with guanethidine.
Incidence less frequent or rare
Diarrhea or increase in bowel movements; dryness of mouth; headache; muscle pain or tremors; nocturia (nighttime urination)

Patient Consultation

In providing consultation, consider emphasizing the following selected information (» = major clinical significance):

Before using this medication
» Conditions affecting use, especially:
Sensitivity to guanadrel
Use in the elderly—Increased sensitivity to hypotensive effects
Other medications, especially tricyclic antidepressants, loxapine, thioxanthenes, trimeprazine, or MAO inhibitors
Other medical problems, especially congestive heart failure or pheochromocytoma

Proper use of this medication
Importance of diet; possible need for sodium restriction and/or weight reduction
» Patients may not experience symptoms of hypertension; importance of taking medication even if feeling well
» Does not cure, but helps control hypertension; possible need for lifelong therapy; checking with physician before discontinuing medication; serious consequences of untreated hypertension
Getting into the habit of taking at same time each day to help increase compliance
Missed dose: Taking as soon as possible; not taking if almost time for next dose; not doubling doses
» Proper storage

Precautions while using this medication
Regular visits to physician to check progress
» Caution when getting up suddenly from a lying or sitting position, especially in the morning
» Caution in using alcohol, while standing for long periods or exercising, and during hot weather because of enhanced orthostatic hypotensive effects
» Not taking other medications, especially nonprescription sympathomimetics, unless discussed with physician
Caution if any kind of surgery (including dental surgery) or emergency treatment is required
Reporting fever to physician; dosage adjustment may be required

Side/adverse effects
Signs of potential side effects, especially peripheral edema, dyspnea, and angina

General Dosing Information

Because of wide variation in response to guanadrel, dosage must be adjusted to meet the requirements of each patient on the basis of clinical response.

The hypotensive effect of guanadrel is especially pronounced when the patient is standing. If feasible, blood pressure readings should be taken in the supine position, after standing for 10 minutes, and immediately after exercise. Dosage increases should be made only if there has been no decrease in the standing blood pressure from previous levels.

Hospitalized patients should not be discharged until the effect of guanadrel on their standing blood pressure has been determined.

With continuing use, apparent tolerance to the antihypertensive effects of guanadrel may develop as a result of fluid retention and expanded plasma volume. Concurrent administration of a diuretic is recommended.

Recent evidence suggests that withdrawal of antihypertensive therapy prior to surgery is not necessary, but that the anesthesiologist must be aware of such therapy.

Dosage reduction is indicated if the patient has:
Excessive orthostatic fall in pressure
Normal supine pressure
Severe diarrhea

Oral Dosage Forms

GUANADREL SULFATE TABLETS USP

Usual adult dose: Antihypertensive—
Initial: Oral, 5 mg two times a day, the dosage being increased at daily, weekly, or monthly intervals as necessary to control blood pressure.
Maintenance: Oral, 20 to 75 mg per day in two to four divided doses.
Note: Geriatric patients may be more sensitive to the effects of the usual adult dose.

Auxiliary labeling:
• Avoid alcoholic beverages.
• Do not take other medicines without your doctor's advice.

GUANETHIDINE   Systemic

Some commonly used *brand names* are:
　In the U.S.—*Ismelin*
　In Canada—*Apo-Guanethidine; Ismelin*

ORAL
Guanethidine Monosulfate Tablets USP
　In the U.S.—*Ismelin;* GENERIC
　In Canada—*Apo-Guanethidine; Ismelin*

Category: Antihypertensive.

Indications

Accepted
Hypertension (treatment)—Guanethidine is indicated in the treatment of moderate to severe hypertension.

　In the 1988 Report of the Joint National Committee on Detection, Evaluation, and Treatment of High Blood Pressure, a progression in choice of treatments for essential hypertension is recommended:

　　Nonpharmacologic management (especially sodium restriction, weight reduction and exercise, and moderation of alcohol consumption) is recommended first for some patients, including those with mild hypertension, and is recommended as an adjunct to all pharmacologic hypertensive therapy.

　　Initial drug therapy usually consists of a diuretic, beta-adrenergic blocking agent, calcium channel blocking agent, or angiotensin-converting enzyme (ACE) inhibitor. If adequate blood pressure control is not achieved and the patient is adherent to the treatment program and not experiencing significant side effects, dosage of the drug may be increased, a drug from another one of these initial classes may be added or substituted, or a second drug from a different class—centrally acting alpha-adrenergic blockers (e.g., clonidine, guanabenz, guanfacine, methyldopa), peripheral-acting adrenergic antagonists (e.g., guanadrel, guanethidine, rauwolfia alkaloids), post-synaptic alpha-1 peripheral adrenergic inhibitors (e.g., doxazosin, prazosin, terazosin), or vasodilators (e.g., hydralazine, minoxidil)—may be added or substituted.

　　If necessary, a drug from another class in the second group may be substituted or added as a third drug. If blood pressure control is still not achieved, a drug from still another class may be substituted or added as a fourth drug, or the patient may need further evaluation and/or referral.

Guanethidine is also indicated in the treatment of renal hypertension, including that secondary to pyelonephritis, renal amyloidosis, and renal artery stenosis.

Pharmacology

Mechanism of action/Effect: Guanethidine is a postganglionic adrenergic blocking agent. Uptake of guanethidine and storage in sympathetic neurons occur via the norepinephrine pump; guanethidine slowly displaces norepinephrine from its storage in nerve endings and thereby blocks the release of norepinephrine normally produced by nerve stimulation; catecholamine depletion leads to reduced arteriolar vasoconstriction, especially the reflex increase in sympathetic tone that occurs with a change in position.

Time to peak effect:
Single dose—The peak effect occurs within 8 hours after a single dose.
Multiple doses—The full therapeutic effects may not be noticed until 1 to 3 weeks after initiation of therapy.

Duration of action: Multiple doses—Blood pressure returns gradually to pretreatment levels within 1 to 3 weeks after withdrawal.

Precautions to Consider

Geriatrics
Although appropriate studies on the relationship of age to the effects of guanethidine have not been performed in the geriatric population, the elderly may be more sensitive to the hypotensive effects. In addition, elderly patients are more likely to have age-related renal function impairment, which may require caution in patients receiving guanethidine.

Drug interactions and/or related problems
The following drug interactions and/or related problems have been selected on the basis of their potential clinical significance (possible mechanism in parentheses where appropriate)—not necessarily inclusive (» = major clinical significance):

　Note:　Combinations containing any of the following medications, depending on the amount present, may also interact with this medication.

Alcohol or
Barbiturates or
Methotrimeprazine or
Opioid (narcotic) analgesics
　　(concurrent use with guanethidine will contribute to additive orthostatic hypotensive effects)

Alpha-adrenergic blocking agents, such as:
　Doxazosin
　Labetalol
　Phenoxybenzamine
　Phentolamine
　Prazosin
　Terazosin
　Tolazoline, or
Other medications with alpha-adrenergic blocking action, such as:
　Dihydroergotamine
　Ergoloid mesylates
　Ergotamine
　Haloperidol
　Loxapine
　Phenothiazines
　Thioxanthenes, or
Beta-adrenergic blocking agents or
Rauwolfia alkaloids
　　(concurrent use with guanethidine may cause an increased incidence of orthostatic hypotension or bradycardia)

　　Amphetamines or
»　Antidepressants, tricyclic, or
　　Appetite suppressants, with the exception of fenfluramine, or
　　Cyclobenzaprine or
　　Haloperidol or
»　Loxapine or
　　Maprotiline or
　　Methylphenidate or
　　Phenothiazines, especially chlorpromazine, or
»　Thioxanthenes or
»　Trimeprazine
　　　(concurrent use may decrease the hypotensive effects of guanethidine because of its displacement from and inhibition of uptake by adrenergic neurons)

　　　(however, up to 150 mg of doxepin a day can be given without antagonizing the antihypertensive effect of guanethidine)

Anticholinergics, especially atropine and related compounds
(concurrent use with guanethidine may antagonize the inhibitory action of these medications on gastric acid secretion)

» Antidiabetic agents, oral, or
Insulin
(concurrent use with guanethidine may enhance the hypoglycemic effect, in part through displacement of oral antidiabetic agents from serum proteins; dosage adjustments may be necessary)

Anti-inflammatory drugs, nonsteroidal (NSAIDs), especially indomethacin
(antihypertensive effects of guanethidine may be reduced when it is used concurrently with these agents; indomethacin, and possibly other NSAIDs, may antagonize the antihypertensive effect by inhibiting renal prostaglandin synthesis and/or by causing sodium and fluid retention; the patient should be carefully monitored to confirm that the desired effect is being obtained)

Estrogens
(concurrent use may decrease the antihypertensive effect of guanethidine because estrogen-induced fluid retention may lead to increased blood pressure)

Fenfluramine
(concurrent use with guanethidine may produce additive hypotensive effects, and may result in postural hypotension; dosage adjustments of the antihypertensive may be necessary)

» Minoxidil or
Hypotension-producing medications, other
(antihypertensive effects may be potentiated when these medications are used concurrently with guanethidine; although some antihypertensive and/or diuretic combinations are frequently used for therapeutic advantage, when used concurrently dosage adjustments may be necessary; concurrent use with minoxidil is not recommended)

» Monoamine oxidase (MAO) inhibitors, including furazolidone, procarbazine, and selegiline
(concurrent use with guanethidine may result in moderate to severe hypertension due to release of catecholamines; withdrawal of MAO inhibitors at least 1 week prior to initiation of guanethidine therapy is recommended)

Sympathomimetics, such as:
Cocaine
Dobutamine
Dopamine
Ephedrine
Epinephrine
» Metaraminol
Methoxamine
Norepinephrine
Phenylephrine
Phenylpropanolamine
(antihypertensive effects of guanethidine may be reduced when it is used concurrently with any sympathomimetics; the patient should be carefully monitored to confirm that the desired effect is being obtained)

(in addition to possibly decreasing the hypotensive effects of guanethidine, concurrent use of cocaine, dobutamine, dopamine, epinephrine, metaraminol, methoxamine, norepinephrine, or phenylephrine may potentiate the pressor effect of these medications as a result of inhibition of sympathomimetic uptake by adrenergic neurons, possibly resulting in hypertension and cardiac arrhythmias)

(concurrent use of ephedrine or phenylpropanolamine with guanethidine may decrease the hypotensive effects of guanethidine because of its displacement from and inhibition of uptake by adrenergic neurons)

(concurrent use of metaraminol with guanethidine may cause a hypertensive crisis. When metaraminol is used within 5 days of discontinuation of guanethidine, a hypertensive potential may remain)

(concurrent use of phenylephrine ophthalmic solution with guanethidine may increase the pupillary response)

Contraindications/Medical problems
The contraindications/medical problems included have been selected on the basis of their potential clinical significance (reasons given in parentheses where appropriate)—not necessarily inclusive (» = major clinical significance).

Risk-benefit should be considered when the following medical problems exist:

Asthma, history of
(may be aggravated because of hypersensitivity to catecholamine depletion)

Cerebrovascular insufficiency or
Coronary insufficiency or
Myocardial infarction, recent
(ischemia may be aggravated as a result of reduced blood pressure)

» Congestive heart failure not due to hypertension
(may be aggravated by fluid retention)

Diabetes mellitus
(guanethidine may enhance effects of hypoglycemic medications)

Diarrhea or
Sinus bradycardia
(may be aggravated)

Fever
(dosage requirements may be reduced)

Hepatic function impairment
(reduced metabolism and excessive accumulation of guanethidine may occur; lower doses may be required)

Peptic ulcer, history of
(may be aggravated by relative increase in parasympathetic tone)

» Pheochromocytoma
(release of catecholamines may exacerbate symptoms)

Renal function impairment
(guanethidine further reduces glomerular filtration rate and renal plasma flow; may produce transient urinary retention; severe orthostatic hypotension may occur because of excessive accumulation)

Sensitivity to guanethidine

Side/Adverse Effects

Note: Side effects are largely due to selective sympathetic blockade and unopposed parasympathetic activity.

The following side/adverse effects have been selected on the basis of their potential clinical significance (possible signs and symptoms in parentheses where appropriate)—not necessarily inclusive:

Those indicating need for medical attention
Incidence more frequent
Edema, peripheral (swelling of feet or lower legs)
Incidence less frequent or rare
Angina (chest pain); *edema, pulmonary* (shortness of breath)

Those indicating need for medical attention only if they continue or are bothersome
Incidence more frequent
Bradycardia (slow heartbeat); *diarrhea or increase in bowel movements; difficulty in ejaculating; nasal congestion* (stuffy nose); *orthostatic hypotension* (dizziness, lightheadedness, or fainting, especially when getting up from a lying or sitting position); *unusual tiredness or weakness*

Incidence less frequent or rare
> *Blurred vision; drooping eyelids; dryness of mouth; headache; loss of hair on scalp; muscle pain or tremors; nausea or vomiting; nocturia* (nighttime urination); *skin rash*

Patient Consultation

In providing consultation, consider emphasizing the following selected information (» = major clinical significance):

Before using this medication
» Conditions affecting use, especially:
    Sensitivity to guanethidine
    Fertility—Reversible inhibition of ejaculation
    Breast-feeding—Small quantities excreted in breast milk
    Use in the elderly—Increased sensitivity to hypotensive effects
    Other medications, especially tricyclic antidepressants, loxapine, thioxanthenes, trimeprazine, minoxidil, MAO inhibitors, oral antidiabetic agents, or metaraminol
    Other medical problems, especially congestive heart failure or pheochromocytoma

Proper use of this medication
    Possible need for control of weight and diet, especially sodium intake
» Patient may not experience symptoms of hypertension; importance of taking medication even if feeling well
» Does not cure, but helps control hypertension; possible need for lifelong therapy; checking with physician before discontinuing medication; serious consequences of untreated hypertension
    Getting into the habit of taking at same time each day to help increase compliance
    Missed dose: Taking as soon as possible; not taking if almost time for next dose; not doubling doses
» Proper storage

Precautions while using this medication
    Regular visits to physician to check progress
» Caution when getting up suddenly from a lying or sitting position, especially in the morning
» Caution in using alcohol, while standing for long periods or exercising, and during hot weather because of enhanced orthostatic hypotensive effects
» Not taking other medications, especially nonprescription sympathomimetics, unless discussed with physician
    Caution if any kind of surgery (including dental surgery) or emergency treatment is required
    Reporting fever to physician; dosage adjustment may be required

Side/adverse effects
    Signs of potential side effects, especially peripheral and pulmonary edema and angina

General Dosing Information

Because of wide individual variation in response to guanethidine, dosage must be adjusted to meet the requirements of each patient on the basis of clinical response.

Because of its long half-life, the effects of guanethidine are cumulative over long periods. Initial doses should be small with gradual increases being made if necessary. Unless the patient is hospitalized, dosage increases should not be made more often than every 5 to 7 days.

The hypotensive effect of guanethidine is especially pronounced when the patient is standing. If feasible, blood pressure readings should be taken in the supine position, after standing for 10 minutes, and immediately after exercise. Dosage increases should be made only if there has been no decrease in the standing blood pressure from previous levels.

Hospitalized patients should not be discharged until the effect of guanethidine on their standing blood pressure has been determined.

With continuing use, apparent tolerance to the antihypertensive effects of guanethidine may develop as a result of fluid retention and expanded plasma volume. Concurrent administration of a diuretic is recommended.

Recent evidence suggests that withdrawal of antihypertensive therapy prior to surgery is not necessary, but that the anesthesiologist must be aware of such therapy.

Dosage reduction is indicated if the patient has:
    Excessive orthostatic fall in pressure
    Normal supine pressure
    Severe diarrhea

Oral Dosage Forms

GUANETHIDINE MONOSULFATE TABLETS USP

Usual adult dose: Antihypertensive—
    Ambulatory patients:
        Initial—Oral, 10 or 12.5 mg once a day, the daily dosage being increased by 10 or 12.5 mg at five- to seven-day intervals if necessary for control of blood pressure.
        Maintenance—Oral, 25 to 50 mg once a day.
    Hospitalized patients: Initial—Oral, 25 to 50 mg once a day, the daily dosage being increased by 25 to 50 mg at daily or every-other-day intervals if necessary for control of blood pressure.
    Note: Geriatric patients may be more sensitive to the effects of the usual adult dose.

Auxiliary labeling:
• Avoid alcoholic beverages.
• Do not take other medicines without your doctor's advice.

GUANETHIDINE AND HYDROCHLOROTHIAZIDE   Systemic

Some commonly used *brand names* are:
In the U.S.—*Esimil*
In Canada—*Ismelin-Esidrix*

ORAL
Guanethidine Monosulfate and Hydrochlorothiazide Tablets
    In the U.S.—*Esimil*
    In Canada—*Ismelin-Esidrix*

Category: Antihypertensive.

Indications

Accepted
Hypertension (treatment)—This medication is indicated for treatment of hypertension.

Fixed-dosage combinations are generally not recommended for initial therapy and are useful for subsequent therapy only when the proportion of the component agents corresponds to the dose of the individual agents, as determined by titration.

Nonpharmacologic management (especially sodium restriction, weight reduction and exercise, and moderation of alcohol consumption) is recommended first for some patients, including those with mild hypertension, and is recommended as an adjunct to all pharmacologic hypertensive therapy.

Patient Consultation

In providing consultation, consider emphasizing the following selected information (» = major clinical significance):

Before using this medication
» Conditions affecting use, especially:
  Sensitivity to guanethidine, hydrochlorothiazide, other sulfonamide-type medications, bumetanide, furosemide, or carbonic anhydrase inhibitors
  Pregnancy—Hydrochlorothiazide may cause jaundice, thrombocytopenia, hypokalemia in infant
  Breast-feeding—Hydrochlorothiazide is excreted in breast milk; small quantities of guanethidine are excreted in breast milk
  Pediatrics—Caution if giving to infants with jaundice
  Use in the elderly—Increased sensitivity to hypotensive and electrolyte aeffects
  Use by athletes—Diuretics are banned and tested for by the U.S. Olympic Committee (USOC), the International Olympic Committee (IOC), and the National Collegiate Athletic Association (NCAA)
  Other medications, especially tricyclic antidepressants, loxapine, thioxanthenes, trimeprazine, minoxidil, MAO inhibitors, cholestyramine or colestipol, digitalis glycosides, lithium, or oral antidiabetic agents
  Other medical problems, especially congestive heart failure, pheochromocytoma, or anuria or severe renal function impairment

Proper use of this medication
  Diuretic effects of the medication and timing of doses to minimize inconvenience of diuresis
  Possible need for control of weight and diet, especially sodium intake
» Patient may not experience symptoms of hypertension; importance of taking medication even if feeling well
» Does not cure, but helps control hypertension; possible need for lifelong therapy; checking with physician before discontinuing medication; serious consequences of untreated hypertension
  Getting into the habit of taking at same time each day to help increase compliance

Missed dose: Taking as soon as possible; not taking if almost time for next dose; not doubling doses
» Proper storage

Precautions while using this medication
» Regular visits to physician to check progress
» Not taking other medications, especially nonprescription sympathomimetics, unless discussed with physician
» Possibility of hypokalemia; possible need for additional potassium in diet; not changing diet without first checking with physician
  To prevent dehydration, checking with physician if severe nausea, vomiting, or diarrhea occurs and continues
» Caution when getting up suddenly from a lying or sitting position, especially in the morning
» Caution in using alcohol, while standing for long periods or exercising, and during hot weather because of enhanced orthostatic hypotensive effects
  Diabetics: May increase blood sugar levels
  Possible photosensitivity; avoiding unprotected exposure to sun; using protective clothing and sun block product; avoiding use of sunlamp, tanning bed, or tanning booth
  Reporting fever to physician; dosage adjustment may be required
  Caution if any kind of surgery (including dental surgery) or emergency treatment is required

Side/adverse effects
  Signs of potential side effects, especially electrolyte imbalance, angina, agranulocytosis, allergic reaction, cholecystitis, pancreatitis, hepatic function impairment, hyperuricemia, gout, thrombocytopenia, peripheral and pulmonary edema

Oral Dosage Forms

GUANETHIDINE MONOSULFATE AND HYDROCHLOROTHIAZIDE TABLETS

Usual adult dose: Antihypertensive—Oral, 2 tablets a day as determined by individual titration with the component agents.

Note: Geriatric patients may be more sensitive to the effects of the usual adult dose.

Usual adult prescribing limits: Up to 4 tablets daily.

Auxiliary labeling:
• Avoid alcoholic beverages.
• Do not take other medicines without your doctor's advice.

GUANFACINE   Systemic†

A commonly used *brand name* in the U.S. is *Tenex*.

ORAL
Guanfacine Hydrochloride Tablets†
  In the U.S.—*Tenex*

---

†Not commercially available in Canada.

Category: Antihypertensive.

Indications

Accepted
Hypertension (treatment)—Guanfacine is indicated, usually in combination with a thiazide diuretic, in the treatment of hypertension.

  In the 1988 Report of the Joint National Committee on Detection, Evaluation, and Treatment of High Blood Pressure, a progression in choice of treatments for essential hypertension is recommended:

Nonpharmacologic management (especially sodium restriction, weight reduction and exercise, and moderation of alcohol consumption) is recommended first for some patients, including those with mild hypertension, and is recommended as an adjunct to all pharmacologic hypertensive therapy.

Initial drug therapy usually consists of a diuretic, beta-adrenergic blocking agent, calcium channel blocking agent, or angiotensin-converting enzyme (ACE) inhibitor. If adequate blood pressure control is not achieved and the patient is adherent to the treatment program and not experiencing significant side effects, dosage of the drug may be increased, a drug from another one of these initial classes may be added or substituted, or a second drug from a different class—centrally acting alpha-adrenergic blocking agents (e.g., clonidine, guanabenz, guanfacine, methyldopa), peripheral-acting adrenergic antagonists (e.g., guanadrel, guanethidine, rauwolfia alkaloids), post-synaptic alpha-1 peripheral adrenergic blocking agents (e.g., doxazosin, prazosin, terazosin), or vasodilators (e.g., hydralazine, minoxidil)—may be added or substituted.

If necessary, a drug from another class in the second group may be substituted or added as a third drug. If blood pressure control is still not achieved, a drug from still another class may be substituted or added as a fourth drug, or the patient may need further evaluation and/or referral.

Pharmacology

Mechanism of action/Effect: Thought to be due to central alpha2-adrenergic stimulation, which results in a decreased sympathetic outflow to the heart, kidneys, and peripheral vasculature; decreased systolic and diastolic blood pressure; and slightly decreased heart rate.

Other actions/effects: Growth hormone secretion stimulated by single doses (no effect with long-term use).

Onset of action: Multiple doses—Within 1 week.

Time to peak effect:
Single dose—8 to 12 hours.
Multiple doses—1 to 3 months.

Duration of action: Single dose—24 hours.

Precautions to Consider

Geriatrics

Appropriate studies on the relationship of age to the effects of guanfacine have not been performed in the geriatric population. However, the elderly may be more sensitive to the hypotensive and sedative effects.

Dental

Use of guanfacine may decrease or inhibit salivary flow, thus contributing to the development of caries, periodontal disease, oral candidiasis, and discomfort.

Drug interactions and/or related problems

The following drug interactions and/or related problems have been selected on the basis of their potential clinical significance (possible mechanism in parentheses where appropriate)—not necessarily inclusive (» = major clinical significance):

Note: Combinations containing any of the following medications, depending on the amount present, may also interact with this medication.

Alcohol or
Central nervous system (CNS) depression-producing medications
(concurrent use may enhance the CNS depressant effects of either these medications or guanfacine)

Anti-inflammatory drugs, nonsteroidal (NSAIDs), especially indomethacin
(may reduce antihypertensive effects of guanfacine; indomethacin, and possibly other NSAIDs, may antagonize the antihypertensive effect by inhibiting renal prostaglandin synthesis and/or by causing sodium and fluid retention; the patient should be carefully monitored to confirm that the desired effect is being obtained)

Estrogens
(estrogen-induced fluid retention may increase blood pressure)

Hypotension-producing medications, other
(concurrent use may potentiate antihypertensive effects; although some antihypertensive and/or diuretic combinations are frequently used for therapeutic advantage, dosage adjustments may be necessary during concurrent use)

Sympathomimetics
(may reduce antihypertensive effects of guanfacine; the patient should be carefully monitored to confirm that the desired effect is being obtained)

Contraindications/Medical problems

The contraindications/medical problems included have been selected on the basis of their potential clinical significance (reasons given in parentheses where appropriate)—not necessarily inclusive (» = major clinical significance).

Risk-benefit should be considered when the following medical problems exist:

Cerebrovascular disease or
Coronary insufficiency or
Myocardial infarction, recent
(may be aggravated by reduced blood pressure)

Hepatic function impairment, chronic
(increased sensitivity or prolonged guanfacine effect may occur, since guanfacine undergoes hepatic biotransformation)

Mental depression, history of
(may be aggravated by CNS effects of guanfacine)

Sensitivity to guanfacine

Side/Adverse Effects

Note: Side/adverse effects are dose-related and incidence usually declines with continued administration.

The following side/adverse effects have been selected on the basis of their potential clinical significance (possible signs and symptoms in parentheses where appropriate)—not necessarily inclusive:

Those indicating need for medical attention
Incidence less frequent
Confusion; mental depression
Signs and symptoms of overdose
Difficulty in breathing; dizziness, extreme, or faintness; slow heartbeat; unusual tiredness or weakness, severe

Those indicating need for medical attention only if they continue or are bothersome
Incidence more frequent
Constipation; dizziness; drowsiness; dryness of mouth
Incidence less frequent
Conjunctivitis (dry, itching, or burning eyes); **decreased sexual ability; headache; nausea or vomiting; trouble in sleeping; unusual tiredness or weakness**

Those indicating possible withdrawal and the need for medical attention if they occur after medication is discontinued
Sympathetic overactivity (anxiety or tenseness, chest pain, fast or irregular heartbeat, headache, increased salivation, nausea, nervousness, restlessness, shaking or trembling of hands and fingers, stomach cramps, sweating, trouble in sleeping, vomiting)

Note: *Sympathetic overactivity* is usually infrequent and mild and does not occur until 2 to 7 days after abrupt withdrawal of guanfacine. The risk appears to be increased in patients receiving divided doses totaling more than 4 mg per day. Rebound hypertension occurs less frequently.

Patient Consultation

In providing consultation, consider emphasizing the following selected information (» = major clinical significance):

Before using this medication
» Conditions affecting use, especially:
  Sensitivity to guanfacine
  Pregnancy—Use of extremely high doses in animals caused increased fetal deaths
  Use in the elderly—Increased sensitivity to hypotensive effects

Proper use of this medication
  Possible need for control of weight and diet, especially sodium intake
» Patient may not experience symptoms of hypertension; importance of taking medication even if feeling well
» Does not cure, but helps control hypertension; possible need for lifelong therapy; serious consequences of untreated hypertension
  Taking at bedtime to reduce daytime drowsiness
» Missed dose: Taking as soon as possible; checking with physician if two or more doses in a row are missed; possible reaction if stopped abruptly
» Proper storage

Precautions while using this medication
  Regular visits to physician to check progress
  Checking with physician before discontinuing medication; gradual dosage reduction may be necessary to avoid rebound hypertension
  Having enough medication on hand to get through weekends, holidays, and vacations; possibly carrying second prescription for emergency use
  Caution if any kind of surgery (including dental surgery) or emergency treatment is required
» Not taking other medications, especially nonprescription sympathomimetics, unless discussed with physician
» Avoiding use of alcohol or other CNS depressants
» Caution when driving or doing things requiring alertness because of possible drowsiness
  Possible dryness of mouth; using sugarless gum or candy, ice, or saliva substitute for relief; checking with dentist if dry mouth continues for more than 2 weeks

Side/adverse effects
  Signs of potential side effects, especially confusion, mental depression, and withdrawal reaction

General Dosing Information

It is recommended that the daily dose be taken at bedtime to reduce daytime drowsiness.

Recent evidence suggests that withdrawal of antihypertensive therapy prior to surgery is not necessary, but that the anesthesiologist must be aware of such therapy. In addition, the possibility of withdrawal syndrome should be kept in mind if guanfacine is discontinued abruptly, although the syndrome does not generally occur until the patient has been without the drug for more than 2 days.

Guanfacine therapy should be discontinued if drug-related mental depression occurs.

Oral Dosage Forms

GUANFACINE HYDROCHLORIDE TABLETS
Note: The dosing and strengths of the dosage form available are expressed in terms of guanfacine base.

Usual adult dose: Antihypertensive—Oral, 1 mg (base) once a day at bedtime, the dosage being increased after three to four weeks, if necessary, to 2 mg per day. If necessary, dosage may be further increased after an additional three to four weeks to 3 mg per day.

Note: If reduction in blood pressure is not maintained over 24 hours, divided daily dosing may be more effective, although the incidence of side/adverse effects may be increased.

Auxiliary labeling:
- Avoid alcoholic beverages.
- Keep container tightly closed.

HALOPERIDOL   Systemic

Some commonly used *brand names* are:

In the U.S.—
Haldol
Haldol Decanoate

In Canada—
Apo-Haloperidol   *Novo-Peridol*
Haldol   *Peridol*
Haldol LA   *PMS Haloperidol*

ORAL
Haloperidol Oral Solution USP
In the U.S.—*Haldol;* GENERIC
In Canada—*Apo-Haloperidol; Haldol; Novo-Peridol; Peridol; PMS Haloperidol;* GENERIC
Haloperidol Tablets USP
In the U.S.—*Haldol;* GENERIC
In Canada—*Apo-Haloperidol; Haldol; Novo-Peridol; Peridol;* GENERIC

PARENTERAL
Haloperidol Injection USP
In the U.S. and Canada—*Haldol;* GENERIC
Haloperidol Decanoate Injection
In the U.S.—*Haldol Decanoate*
In Canada—*Haldol LA*

Category: Antipsychotic; antidyskinetic (Gilles de la Tourette's syndrome or Huntington's chorea); antiemetic.

Indications

Note: Bracketed information in the *Indications* section refers to uses not included in U.S. product labeling.

Accepted
Psychotic disorders (treatment)—Haloperidol is indicated for the management of the manifestations of acute and chronic psychotic disorders including schizophrenia, manic states, and drug-induced psychoses, such as steroid psychosis. It may also be useful in the management of aggressive and agitated patients, including patients with organic mental syndrome or mental retardation. Haloperidol decanoate, a long-acting parenteral form, is intended for maintenance use in the management of patients requiring prolonged parenteral therapy, as in chronic schizophrenia.

Behavior problems, severe (treatment)—Haloperidol is effective in the treatment of children with severe behavior problems of apparently unprovoked, combative, explosive hyperexcitability. It is also effective in the *short-term* treatment of hyperactivity in children who show excessive motor activity with accompanying conduct disorders such as aggressiveness, impulsiveness, easy frustration, short attention span, and/or rapid mood fluctuations. In these two groups of children, haloperidol should be tried only in patients who fail to respond to psychotherapy or other nonneuroleptic medication.

Gilles de la Tourette's syndrome (treatment)—Haloperidol is used to control tics and vocalizations of Tourette's syndrome in children and adults.

[Autism, infantile (treatment)][1]—Haloperidol has been used to reduce abnormal behaviors, such as withdrawal, stereotypy, abnormal object relationships, fidgetiness, hyperactivity, negativism, angry affect, and labile affect, and may improve learning, in some patients with autism.

[Chorea, Huntington's (treatment)][1]—Because of its strong extrapyramidal effects, haloperidol is used to reduce disabling choreiform movements in Huntington's disease.

[Nausea and vomiting, cancer chemotherapy-induced (prophylaxis and treatment)][1]—Haloperidol is used as a second-line agent to control nausea and vomiting associated with antineoplastic therapy and surgery.

[1]Not included in Canadian product labeling.

Pharmacology

Note: Pharmacological effects of haloperidol are similar to the effects of piperazine-derivative phenothiazines, which include acetophenazine, fluphenazine, perphenazine, prochlorperazine, and trifluoperazine.

Mechanism of action/Effect: Although the complex mechanism of the therapeutic effect is not clearly established, haloperidol is known to produce a selective effect on the central nervous system (CNS) by competitive blockade of postsynaptic dopamine (D_2) receptors in the mesolimbic dopaminergic system and an increased turnover of brain dopamine to produce its tranquilizing effects. With subchronic therapy, depolarization blockade, or diminished firing rate of the dopamine neuron (decreased release) along with D postsynaptic blockade results in the antipsychotic action.

The long-acting decanoate form acts as a pro-drug, slowly and steadily releasing haloperidol from the vehicle.

Other actions/effects: Blockade of dopamine receptors in the nigrostriatal dopamine pathway produces extrapyramidal motor reactions; blockade of dopamine receptors in the tuberoinfundibular system decreases growth hormone release and increases prolactin release by the pituitary. There is also some blockade of alpha-adrenergic receptors of the autonomic system.

Precautions to Consider

Geriatrics
Geriatric patients tend to develop higher plasma concentrations of haloperidol because of changes in distribution due to decreases in lean body mass, total body water, and albumin, and often an increase in total body fat composition. These patients usually require lower initial dosage and a more gradual titration of dose.

Elderly patients appear to be more prone to orthostatic hypotension and exhibit an increased sensitivity to the anticholinergic and sedative effects of haloperidol. In addition, they are more prone to develop extrapyramidal side effects, such as tardive dyskinesia and parkinsonism. The symptoms of tardive dyskinesia are persistent, difficult to control, and, in some patients, appear to be irreversible. The symptoms may be masked during long-term treatment, but may appear if haloperidol is discontinued. There is no known effective treatment. Careful observation during haloperidol therapy for early signs of tardive dyskinesia and reduction of dosage or discontinuation of medication may prevent a more severe manifestation of the syndrome.

It has been suggested that elderly patients receive half the usual adult dose. Patients with organic brain syndrome or acute confusional states, should initially receive one-third to one-half the usual adult dose, with the dose being increased no more frequently than every 2 or 3 days, and preferably at intervals of 7 to 10 days. A periodic attempt should be made to discontinue medication as soon as the patient improves.

Dental
The peripheral anticholinergic effects of haloperidol may decrease or inhibit salivary flow, especially in middle-aged or elderly patients, thus contributing to the development of caries, periodontal disease, oral candidiasis, and discomfort.

Extrapyramidal reactions induced by haloperidol will result in increased motor activity of the head, face, and neck. Occlusal adjustments, bite registrations, and treatment for bruxism may be made less reliable.

The leukopenic and thrombocytopenic effects of haloperidol may result in an increased incidence of microbial infection, delayed healing, and gingival bleeding. If leukopenia or thrombocytopenia occurs, dental work should be deferred until blood counts have returned to normal. Patients should be instructed in proper oral hygiene, including caution in use of regular toothbrushes, dental floss, and toothpicks.

Drug interactions and/or related problems

The following drug interactions and/or related problems have been selected on the basis of their potential clinical significance (possible mechanism in parentheses where appropriate)—not necessarily inclusive (» = major clinical significance):

Note: Combinations containing any of the following medications, depending on the amount present, may also interact with this medication.

» Alcohol or
» CNS depression-producing medications, other

(concurrent use with haloperidol may result in increased CNS and respiratory depression and increased hypotensive effects)

(concurrent use with haloperidol may potentiate alcohol intoxication)

Amphetamines

(concurrent use may decrease stimulant effects of amphetamines due to alpha-adrenergic blockade by haloperidol; also, the antipsychotic effects of haloperidol may be reduced when amphetamines and haloperidol are used concurrently)

Anticholinergics or other medications with anticholinergic activity or
Antidyskinetic agents or
Antihistamines

(concurrent use with haloperidol may intensify anticholinergic side effects, especially those of confusion, hallucinations, nightmares, and increased intraocular pressure, because of secondary anticholinergic effects of haloperidol; also, patients should be advised to report occurrence of gastrointestinal problems since paralytic ileus may occur with concurrent therapy; in addition, antipsychotic effectiveness of haloperidol may be decreased because of reduced gastrointestinal absorption; dosage adjustments may be necessary)

Anticoagulants, coumarin- or indandione-derivative

(concurrent use with haloperidol may either increase or decrease anticoagulant activity; although the clinical significance has not been determined, caution is recommended)

Anticonvulsants, including barbiturates

(concurrent use with haloperidol may cause a change in the pattern and/or frequency of epileptiform seizures; dosage adjustments of anticonvulsants may be necessary; serum concentrations of haloperidol may be significantly reduced)

Antidepressants, tricyclic, or
Maprotiline or
Monoamine oxidase (MAO) inhibitors, including furazolidone, procarbazine, or selegiline, or
Trazodone

(concurrent use with haloperidol may prolong and intensify the sedative and anticholinergic effects of either these medications or haloperidol)

Bromocriptine

(concurrent use may increase serum prolactin concentrations and interfere with effects of bromocriptine; dosage adjustment of bromocriptine may be necesary)

Bupropion

(concurrent use of bupropion with haloperidol may lower the seizure threshold and increase the risk of major motor seizures)

Diazoxide

(concurrent use antagonizes the inhibition of insulin release by diazoxide)

Dopamine

(concurrent use may antagonize peripheral vasoconstriction produced by high doses of dopamine because of the alpha-adrenergic blocking action of haloperidol)

Ephedrine

(concurrent use may decrease the pressor response to ephedrine)

» Epinephrine

(concurrent use may block the alpha-adrenergic effects of epinephrine, possibly resulting in severe hypotension and tachycardia)

» Extrapyramidal reaction-causing medications, other

(concurrent use with haloperidol may increase the severity and frequency of extrapyramidal effects)

Fluoxetine

(caution in concurrent use of fluoxetine with haloperidol is recommended because of a potentially increased risk of CNS side effects, particularly extrapyramidal reactions)

Guanadrel or
Guanethidine

(concurrent use with haloperidol may decrease the hypotensive effects of these agents because of displacement from and inhibition of uptake into alpha-adrenergic neurons)

» Levodopa or
Pergolide

(concurrent use may decrease the therapeutic effects of these agents because of blockade of dopamine receptors by haloperidol)

» Lithium

(lithium is frequently used concurrently with haloperidol during the first week or two of treatment for acute manic episodes; lithium alone may be adequate thereafter, although some patients may continue to need both; however, concurrent use with haloperidol has been associated with irreversible neurological toxicity and brain damage, especially in patients with organic mental syndrome or other CNS impairment, although this interaction has been reported only with high doses; extrapyramidal symptoms may be increased by enhancement of dopamine blockade by haloperidol; patients should be monitored closely during concurrent use; dosage adjustments or discontinuation of treatment may be necessary)

(admixture of the liquid forms of lithium and haloperidol may result in precipitation of free haloperidol)

Metaraminol

(concurrent use with haloperidol usually decreases, but does not reverse or completely block, the pressor response to metaraminol because of the alpha-adrenergic blocking action of haloperidol)

Methoxamine

(prior administration of haloperidol may decrease the pressor effect and duration of action of methoxamine because of the alpha-adrenergic blocking action of haloperidol)

Methyldopa

(concurrent use with haloperidol may cause unwanted mental effects such as disorientation and slowed or difficult thought processes)

Phenylephrine

(prior administration of haloperidol may decrease the pressor response to phenylephrine because of the alpha-adrenergic blocking action of haloperidol)

Contraindications/Medical problems

The contraindications/medical problems included have been selected on the basis of their potential clinical significance (reasons given in parentheses where appropriate)—not necessarily inclusive (» = major clinical significance).

Except under special circumstances, this medication should not be used when the following medical problems exist:

» CNS depression, toxic, drug-induced, severe
(may be potentiated)

Risk-benefit should be considered when the following medical problems exist:

Alcoholism, active
(CNS depression may be potentiated; risk of heat stroke may be increased)

» Cardiovascular disease, severe, especially angina
(transient hypotension and anginal pain may be provoked)

» Epilepsy
(seizure threshold may be lowered)

Glaucoma or predisposition to
(may be potentiated because of secondary anticholinergic effects of haloperidol)

Hepatic function impairment
(metabolism may be altered)

Hyperthyroidism or thyrotoxicosis
(severe neurotoxicity such as rigidity and inability to walk or talk may result)

» Parkinson's disease
(may be potentiated)

Pulmonary insufficiency, such as asthma, emphysema, or acute pulmonary infections
(potentiation of breathing impairment may possibly lead to "silent pneumonias")

Renal function impairment
(excretion may be altered; more applicable to higher dosage since renal clearance of unchanged drug is relatively low)

» Sensitivity to haloperidol
(patients with known allergies or with a history of allergic reactions to other medications may also be sensitive to haloperidol)

» Urinary retention
(may be potentiated)

Side/Adverse Effects

Note: A few cases of sudden and unexpected death have been reported in patients who were receiving haloperidol therapy. Although the possibility does exist, there is no definite evidence that haloperidol is a causative factor.

Children are highly susceptible to extrapyramidal effects.

Geriatric and debilitated patients are more prone to develop extrapyramidal side effects and orthostatic hypotension and usually require a lower initial dosage and a more gradual titration of dose.

The following side/adverse effects have been selected on the basis of their potential clinical significance (possible signs and symptoms in parentheses where appropriate)—not necessarily inclusive:

Those indicating need for medical attention

Incidence more frequent

Akathisia (restlessness or need to keep moving); *dystonic extrapyramidal effects* (muscle spasms of face, neck, and back; tic-like or twitching movements; twisting movements of body, inability to move eyes; weakness of arms and legs); *parkinsonian extrapyramidal effects* (difficulty in speaking or swallowing, loss of balance control, mask-like face, shuffling walk, stiffness of arms or legs, trembling and shaking of hands and fingers)

Note: *Akathisia* may appear within first 6 hours of dose; often indistinguishable from psychotic agitation; differentiation with benztropine may improve haloperidol-induced akathisia but not psychotic agitation.

Dystonic extrapyramidal effects appear most often in children and young adults and early in treatment; may subside within 24 to 48 hours after drug has been discontinued.

Parkinsonian extrapyramidal effects are more frequent in the elderly; symptoms may be seen in the first few days of treatment or after prolonged treatment, and can recur after even a single dose.

Incidence less frequent

Allergic reaction (red and raised, or acne-like skin rash); *anticholinergic effects* (difficult urination, hallucinations); *CNS effect* (hallucinations); *decreased thirst, or unusual tiredness or weakness; orthostatic hypotension* (dizziness, lightheadedness, or fainting); *persistent tardive dyskinesia* (lip smacking or puckering; puffing of cheeks; rapid or worm-like movements of tongue; uncontrolled chewing movements; uncontrolled movements of the arms and legs)

Note: *Decreased thirst* or *unusual tiredness or weakness* may precede dehydration, hemoconcentration, reduced pulmonary ventilation, and bronchopneumonia; occur most often in elderly or debilitated patients.

Tardive dyskinesia is more frequent in elderly patients, women, and patients with brain damage; initially dose related, but may increase with long-term treatment and total cumulative dose; may persist after discontinuation of haloperidol.

Incidence rare

Agranulocytosis (sore throat and fever, unusual bleeding or bruising); *heat stroke* (hot, dry skin, inability to sweat, muscle weakness, confusion); *obstructive jaundice* (yellow eyes or skin); *neuroleptic malignant syndrome (NMS)* (difficult or unusually fast breathing; fast heartbeat or irregular pulse; high fever; high or low [irregular] blood pressure; increased sweating; loss of bladder control; severe muscle stiffness; seizures; unusual tiredness or weakness; unusually pale skin); *tardive dystonia* (increased blinking or spasms of eyelid; unusual facial expressions or body positions; uncontrolled twisting movements of neck, trunk, arms, or legs)

Note: *Heat stroke,* caused by haloperidol-induced suppression of central and peripheral temperature regulation in the hypothalamus, may occur during environmental conditions of high heat and high humidity. The effectiveness of sweating as a cooling mechanism may be reduced by humid conditions and by the anticholinergic effects of haloperidol or its combination with other anticholinergic medications such as nonprescription cold medications or antihistamines. Adequate interior temperature control (air conditioning) must be maintained for institutionalized patients during hot weather because of the increased risk of heat stroke and NMS. Patients should be advised to avoid exertion, stay in cool areas, and avoid dehydration and other anticholinergic medications.

NMS may occur at any time during neuroleptic therapy, but is more commonly seen soon after start of therapy, or after patient has switched from one neuroleptic to another, during combined therapy with another psychotropic medication, or after a dosage increase. Along with the overt signs of skeletal muscle rigidity, hyperthermia, autonomic dysfunction, and altered consciousness, differential diagnosis may reveal leukocytosis (9500 to 26,000 cells per cubic millimeter), elevated liver function test values, and elevated creatine phosphokinase (CPK).

Symptoms of overdose

Severe breathing difficulty; dizziness; severe drowsiness or comatose state; severe muscle trembling, jerking, stiffness, or uncontrolled movements; severe tiredness or weakness

Those indicating need for medical attention only if they continue or are bothersome

Incidence more frequent
Blurred vision; changes in menstrual period; constipation; dryness of mouth; swelling or soreness in breasts in females; unusual secretion of milk; weight gain

Incidence less frequent
Decreased sexual ability; drowsiness; increased sensitivity of skin to sun; nausea or vomiting

Those indicating the need for medical attention if they occur after the medication is discontinued
Withdrawal emergent dyskinesia (trembling of fingers and hands; uncontrolled, repetitive movements of mouth, tongue, and jaw)—more frequent in elderly patients, women, and patients with brain damage

Patient Consultation

In providing consultation, consider emphasizing the following selected information (» = major clinical significance):

Before using this medication
» Conditions affecting use, especially:
  Sensitivity to haloperidol or other medications
  Pregnancy—Reports of limb malformations with maternal use of haloperidol and other drugs of suspected teratogenicity during first trimester; animal reproduction studies have shown a decrease in fertility, increased incidence of fetal resorption, delayed delivery, and neonatal death with very high doses
  Breast-feeding—Excreted in breast milk; animal studies have shown sedation, impaired motor function in nursing offspring; not recommended for use during breast-feeding
  Use in children—Children are more prone to extrapyramidal symptoms, especially dystonias
  Use in the elderly—Elderly patients are more likely to develop extrapyramidal, anticholinergic, hypotensive, and sedative effects; reduced dosage recommended
  Use by athletes—Haloperidol is banned and, in some cases, tested for in competitors in biathlon and modern pentathlon events by the USOC
  Dental—Haloperidol-induced blood dyscrasias may result in infections, delayed healing, and bleeding; dry mouth may cause caries, candidiasis, periodontal disease, and discomfort; increased motor activity of face, head, and neck may interfere with some dental procedures
  Other medications, especially alcohol, other CNS depression-producing medications, epinephrine, other extrapyramidal reaction-producing medications, levodopa, or lithium
  Other medical problems, especially severe cardiovascular disease, severe CNS depression, Parkinson's disease, allergies, epilepsy, or urinary retention

Proper use of this medication
  Taking with food or milk to reduce gastrointestinal irritation
  Proper administration of oral liquid form:
    Using special dropper
    Not taking in tea or coffee
» Importance of not taking more or less medication than the amount prescribed
» Compliance with therapy; may require several weeks of therapy to obtain desired effects
  Missed dose: Taking as soon as possible; taking any remaining doses for that day at regularly spaced intervals; not doubling doses
» Proper storage

Precautions while using this medication
  Regular visits to physician to check progress of therapy
» Checking with physician before discontinuing medication; gradual dosage reduction may be needed

» Avoiding use of alcoholic beverages or other CNS depressants during therapy
  Avoiding the use of over-the-counter medications for colds or allergies, to prevent increased anticholinergic effects and risk of heat stroke
» Possible drowsiness or dizziness; caution when driving, using machinery, or doing things requiring alertness
  Possible dizziness or lightheadedness: caution when getting up suddenly from a lying or sitting position
» Possible heat stroke: caution during exercise, hot baths, or hot weather
» Caution if any kind of surgery, dental treatment, or emergency treatment is required; telling physician or dentist in charge about taking haloperidol because of possible drug interactions or blood dyscrasias
  Possible skin photosensitivity; avoiding unprotected exposure to sun; using protective clothing; using a sun block product that includes protection against both UVA-caused photosensitivity reactions and UVB-caused sunburn reactions; avoiding use of sunlamp, tanning bed, or tanning booth
  Possible dryness of mouth; using sugarless gum or candy, ice, or saliva substitute for relief; checking with physician or dentist if dry mouth continues for more than 2 weeks
  Observing precautions for up to 6 weeks with long-acting parenteral form

Side/adverse effects
» Stopping medication and notifying physician immediately if symptoms of neuroleptic malignant syndrome (NMS) appear
  Extrapyramidal effects are more likely to occur in children, the elderly, and debilitated patients
  Notifying physician as soon as possible if early symptoms of tardive dyskinesia appear
  Possibility of withdrawal symptoms
  Signs of potential side effects, especially akathisia, dystonias, parkinsonism, tardive dyskinesia or dystonia, allergic reaction, symptoms of dehydration, blood dyscrasias, neuroleptic malignant syndrome (NMS), obstructive jaundice, and heat stroke

General Dosing Information

Dosage must be individualized by titration from the lower dose range. After a favorable response is noted (usually within 3 weeks), the proper maintenance dosage should be determined by gradually decreasing to the lowest level of therapeutic dosage that will maintain an adequate clinical response.

The antiemetic effect of haloperidol may mask signs of drug toxicity or may obscure diagnosis of conditions whose primary symptom is nausea.

When extended therapy is discontinued, a gradual reduction in haloperidol dosage over several weeks is recommended, since abrupt withdrawal may cause some patients on high or long-term dosage to experience withdrawal-emergent neurological symptoms.

For oral dosage forms only
When haloperidol concentrated oral solution is mixed with coffee, tea, or lithium citrate syrup, free haloperidol will precipitate.

The solution should be administered to the patient directly from a premeasured oral syringe without dilution. If this is not desirable, the necessary dosage should be added to at least 60 mL of a suitable diluent just prior to administration to prevent precipitation.

For long-acting dosage form only
Patients being considered for haloperidol decanoate therapy should be first converted to oral haloperidol from any other neuroleptic they may have been taking to prevent unexpected adverse sensitivity to haloperidol.

Variations in patient response may require adjustments of dose and dosing intervals. Each patient must be carefully supervised to determine the optimal dosing interval and lowest effective dose, depending on patient's response, age, physical condition, symptoms, severity of illness, and drug history.

Effects of the extended-action injectable form may last up to 6 weeks in some patients. The side effects information and precautions apply during this period of time.

Diet/Nutrition

Haloperidol may be taken with food or a full glass (240 mL) of water or milk if necessary to lessen gastrointestinal irritation.

Oral Dosage Forms

Note: Bracketed uses in the *Dosage Forms* section refer to categories of use and/or indications that are not included in U.S. product labeling.

HALOPERIDOL ORAL SOLUTION USP

Usual adult and adolescent dose: Oral, 500 mcg (0.5 mg) to 5 mg two or three times a day initially, the dosage being gradually adjusted as needed and tolerated.

Usual adult prescribing limits: 100 mg a day.

Usual geriatric dose: Oral, 500 mcg (0.5 mg) to 2 mg two or three times a day, the dosage being increased gradually as needed and tolerated.

Note: The dose for debilitated patients is the same as the geriatric dose.

Auxiliary labeling:
• May cause drowsiness.
• Avoid alcoholic beverages.

HALOPERIDOL TABLETS USP

Usual adult and adolescent dose: See *Haloperidol Oral Solution USP*.

Usual adult prescribing limits: See *Haloperidol Oral Solution USP*.

Usual geriatric dose: See *Haloperidol Oral Solution USP*.

Auxiliary labeling:
• May cause drowsiness.
• Avoid alcoholic beverages.

Parenteral Dosage Forms

HALOPERIDOL INJECTION USP

Usual adult and adolescent dose: Acute psychosis—Intramuscular 2 to 5 mg initially, the dosage being repeated at one-hour interval if necessary, or at four- to eight-hour intervals if symptoms ar satisfactorily controlled.

Note: For the rapid control of acute psychosis or delirium, halo peridol has also been administered intravenously, in dose of 0.5 to 50 mg at a rate of 5 mg per minute, the dose bein, repeated as needed at 30-minute intervals. Alternatively, th dose of haloperidol can be diluted in 30 to 50 mL of com patible intravenous fluid and administered over 30 minutes

Usual adult prescribing limits: Intramuscular—100 mg daily.

HALOPERIDOL DECANOATE INJECTION

Note: The dosing of haloperidol decanoate injection is expressed i terms of haloperidol base (not the decanoate).

Usual adult and adolescent dose: Chronic psychosis—Intramuscu lar, initially 10 to 15 times the previous daily oral dose of haloperi dol, up to a maximum initial dose of 100 mg (base), at monthly intervals, the dosing interval and dose being adjusted as neede and tolerated.

Note: Administration is by deep intramuscular injection into glutea region using Z-track technique. A 2-inch long, 21-gauge needl is recommended.

The maximum volume per injection site should not exceed ? mL.

Usual adult prescribing limits: 300 mg (base) per month.

Note: Monthly doses as high as 900 mg (base) have been re ported.

Note: Not to be administered intravenously.

---

[1]Not included in Canadian product labeling.

HISTAMINE H$_2$-RECEPTOR ANTAGONISTS   Systemic

Some commonly used *brand names* are:

In the U.S.—
    Axid [Nizatidine]   *Tagamet* [Cimetidine]
    Pepcid [Famotidine]   *Zantac* [Ranitidine]
    Pepcid I.V. [Famotidine]

In Canada—
    Apo-Cimetidine   *Pepcid I.V.* [Famotidine]
      [Cimetidine]   *Peptol* [Cimetidine]
    Apo-Ranitidine [Ranitidine] *Tagamet* [Cimetidine]
    Axid [Nizatidine]   *Zantac* [Ranitidine]
    Novocimetine [Cimetidine]   *Zantac-C* [Ranitidine]
    Pepcid [Famotidine]

CIMETIDINE
Oral
    Cimetidine Tablets USP
        In the U.S.—*Tagamet*
        In Canada—*Apo-Cimetidine; Novocimetine; Peptol; Tagamet*
    Cimetidine Hydrochloride Oral Solution
        In the U.S. and Canada—*Tagamet*
Parenteral
    Cimetidine Hydrochloride Injection
        In the U.S. and Canada—*Tagamet*

FAMOTIDINE
Oral
    Famotidine for Oral Suspension†
        In the U.S.—*Pepcid*
    Famotidine Tablets USP
        In the U.S. and Canada—*Pepcid*
Parenteral
    Famotidine Injection
        In the U.S. and Canada—*Pepcid I.V.*
NIZATIDINE
Oral
    Nizatidine Capsules
        In the U.S. and Canada—*Axid*
RANITIDINE
Oral
    Ranitidine Capsules*
        In Canada—*Zantac-C*
    Ranitidine Tablets USP
        In the U.S.—*Zantac*
        In Canada—*Apo-Ranitidine; Zantac*
    Ranitidine Hydrochloride Syrup
        In the U.S. and Canada—*Zantac*

Parenteral
　Ranitidine Injection USP
　　In the U.S. and Canada—*Zantac*

　　*Not commercially available in the U.S.
　　†Not commercially available in Canada.

Category

Histamine H₂-receptor antagonist—All drugs in this monograph are used as histamine H₂-receptor antagonists.
Antiulcer agent—All drugs in this monograph are used as antiulcer agents.
Gastric acid secretion inhibitor—All drugs in this monograph are used as gastric acid secretion inhibitors.
Urticaria therapy adjunct—Cimetidine.

Indications

Note: Bracketed information in the *Indications* section refers to uses not included in U.S. product labeling.

Accepted

Ulcer, duodenal (prophylaxis and treatment)—Histamine H₂-receptor antagonists are indicated in the short-term treatment of active duodenal ulcer. They are also indicated (at reduced dosage) in the prevention of duodenal ulcer recurrence in selected patients.
Ulcer, gastric (treatment)—Cimetidine, famotidine, [nizatidine], and ranitidine are indicated in the short-term treatment of active benign gastric ulcer.
Hypersecretory conditions, gastric (treatment);
Zollinger-Ellison syndrome (treatment);
Mastocytosis, systemic (treatment); or
Adenoma, multiple endocrine (treatment)—Cimetidine, famotidine, [nizatidine][1], and ranitidine are indicated in the treatment of pathological gastric hypersecretion associated with Zollinger-Ellison syndrome (alone or as part of multiple endocrine neoplasia Type-1), systemic mastocytosis, and multiple endocrine adenoma.
Reflux, gastroesophageal (treatment)—Cimetidine, famotidine, nizatidine[1], and ranitidine are indicated in the treatment of acute gastroesophageal reflux disease, which may or may not cause erosive or ulcerative esophagitis.
[Pancreatic insufficiency (treatment adjunct)][1]—Cimetidine is used to enhance pancreatic replacement by reducing peptic acid deactivation and to enhance the efficacy of orally administered pancreatic enzymes in patients with pancreatic insufficiency by reducing the secretion of hydrochloric acid. However, the efficacy of cimetidine in acute pancreatitis has not been established, and some studies have demonstrated that cimetidine may increase and prolong hyperamylasemia.
Bleeding, upper gastrointestinal (treatment)—[Cimetidine], [famotidine][1], and [ranitidine] are used to treat upper gastrointestinal bleeding secondary to gastric ulcer, duodenal ulcer, or hemorrhagic gastritis.
Stress-related mucosal damage (prophylaxis and treatment)—[Parenteral ranitidine] is used to prevent and treat and parenteral cimetidine is indicated to prevent and used to treat upper gastrointestinal, stress-induced ulceration and bleeding, especially in intensive care patients. However, the efficacy of histamine H₂-receptor antagonists in treating hemorrhage in critically ill patients has not been established.
[Pneumonitis, aspiration (prophylaxis)]—Cimetidine, ranitidine, and famotidine are also used before anesthesia induction for the prophylaxis of aspiration pneumonitis.
Arthritis, rheumatoid (treatment adjunct)—[Cimetidine] and [ranitidine][1] are used for the relief of gastrointestinal symptoms associated with the use of nonsteroidal anti-inflammatory drugs in the treatment of rheumatoid arthritis.

[Urticaria, acute (treatment adjunct)][1]—Cimetidine is used in combination with an antihistamine to treat acute urticaria.

Unaccepted

Histamine H₂-receptor antagonists are not recommended for minor digestive complaints.

　　[1]Not included in Canadian product labeling.

Pharmacology

See also *Table 1,* page 628.

Mechanism of action/Effect: H₂-receptor antagonists inhibit basal and nocturnal gastric acid secretion by competitive inhibition of the action of histamine at the histamine H₂-receptors of the parietal cells. They also inhibit gastric acid secretion stimulated by food, betazole, pentagastrin, caffeine, insulin, and physiological vagal reflex.
　Urticaria therapy adjunct—Cimetidine blocks H₂-receptors, which in part are responsible for the inflammatory response, in the cutaneous blood vessels of humans.

Other actions/effects:
　Cimetidine—Inhibits hepatic cytochrome P-450 and P-448 mixed function oxidase (microsomal enzyme) systems; antagonizes dihydrotestosterone (antiandrogenic action); produces transient and clinically insignificant increases in prolactin concentrations (with intravenous bolus administration only). May enhance gastromucosal defense and healing in acid-related disorders, particularly stress-induced ulceration and bleeding, by increasing production of gastric mucus, content of mucus glycoprotein, mucosal secretion of bicarbonate, gastric mucosal blood flow, endogenous mucosal prostaglandin synthesis, and rate of epithelial cell renewal.
　Famotidine—Weak inhibitor of hepatic cytochrome P-450 mixed function oxidase system.
　Nizatidine—Weak inhibitor of hepatic cytochrome P-450 mixed function oxidase system.
　Ranitidine—Weak inhibitor of hepatic cytochrome P-450 mixed function oxidase system; produces small, transient, and clinically insignificant increases in serum prolactin concentrations (reported with intravenous bolus administration of 100 mg or more).

Onset of action: Famotidine—Oral: 1 hour.

Precautions to Consider

Cross-sensitivity and/or related problems
Patients sensitive to one of the histamine H₂-receptor antagonists may be sensitive to the other histamine H₂-receptor antagonists also.

Geriatrics
For cimetidine, famotidine, and ranitidine—Although appropriate studies on the relationship of age to the effects of these medicines have not been performed in the geriatric population, no geriatrics-specific problems have been documented to date. However, confusion is more likely to occur in elderly patients with impaired hepatic or renal function.
For nizatidine—Studies performed to date have not demonstrated geriatrics-specific problems that would limit the usefulness of nizatidine in the elderly.

Drug interactions and/or related problems
The following drug interactions and/or related problems have been selected on the basis of their potential clinical significance (possible mechanism in parentheses where appropriate)—not necessarily inclusive (» = major clinical significance):

Note: Only specific interactions between histamine H₂-receptor antagonists and other medications have been identified in this monograph. However, histamine H₂-receptor antagonists, by increasing gastric pH, have the potential to affect the bioavailability of those medications and dosage forms (e.g., enteric-coated) whose absorption is pH-dependent. Also, histamine H$_2$-receptor antagonists may prevent the degradation of acid-labile drugs.

In addition, because of cimetidine's documented ability to inhibit hepatic microsomal drug metabolism, elimination of other medications that require hepatic metabolism via the cytochrome (P-450) system or that are highly extracted by the liver, may be decreased during concurrent use with cimetidine. This same possibility should be kept in mind for ranitidine, although ranitidine's ability to inhibit hepatic microsomal drug metabolism is significantly less than that for cimetidine. To date, there is no evidence that famotidine or nizatidine binds to cytochrome P-450 to a significant extent, and interactions with medications metabolized by this system have not been reported; however, clinical experience with famotidine and nizatidine is very limited.

Combinations containing any of the following medications, depending on the amount present, may also interact with this medication.

For all histamine H$_2$-receptor antagonists
Antacids
(concurrent use with histamine H$_2$-receptor antagonists in the treatment of peptic ulcer may be indicated for the relief of pain; however, simultaneous administration of antacids of medium to high potency [80 mmol to 150 mmol HCl] is not recommended since absorption of histamine H$_2$-receptor antagonists may be decreased; patients should be advised not to take any antacids within $^1/_2$ to 1 hour of histamine H$_2$-receptor antagonists)

Bone marrow depressants
(concurrent use with H$_2$-receptor antagonists may increase the risk of neutropenia or other blood dyscrasias)

» Ketoconazole
(histamine H$_2$-receptor antagonists may increase gastrointestinal pH; concurrent administration of ketoconazole with histamine H$_2$-receptor antagonists may result in a marked reduction in absorption of ketoconazole; patients should be advised to take histamine H$_2$-receptor antagonists at least 2 hours after ketoconazole)

Sucralfate
(although a decrease in absorption is only reported in the literature for cimetidine and ranitidine, concurrent use with sucralfate may decrease the absorption of any H$_2$-receptor antagonist; patients should be advised to take an H$_2$-receptor antagonist 2 hours before sucralfate)

For cimetidine
Alcohol
(some studies in humans have found increased blood alcohol levels when oral cimetidine was given in conjunction with alcohol; the clinical significance of this effect is not known)

» Anticoagulants, coumarin- or indandione-derivative, or
» Antidepressants, tricyclic, or
Benzodiazepines, especially chlordiazepoxide, diazepam, and midazolam, or
Glipizide or
Glyburide or
» Metoprolol or
Metronidazole or
» Phenytoin or
» Propranolol or
» Xanthines, such as:
Aminophylline
Caffeine
Oxtriphylline

Theophylline
(inhibition of the cytochrome P-450 enzyme system by cimetidine may cause a decrease in the hepatic metabolism of these medications, which may result in delayed elimination and increased blood concentrations, when these medications are used concurrently with cimetidine)

(monitoring of blood concentrations, or prothrombin time for anticoagulants, as a guide to dosage is recommended since dosage adjustment of these medications may be necessary during and after cimetidine therapy to prevent bleeding due to anticoagulant potentiation)

(concurrent use of phenytoin with cimetidine may increase the risk of ataxia due to increased blood concentrations of phenytoin)

(concurrent use of metoprolol or propranolol with cimetidine may require monitoring of blood pressure)

Calcium channel blocking agents
(concurrent use with cimetidine may result in accumulation of the calcium channel blocking agent as a result of inhibition of first-pass metabolism; caution and careful titration of the calcium channel blocking agent dose is recommended on initiation of therapy in patients receiving cimetidine)

Cyclosporine
(although this effect is rare, cimetidine has been reported to increase plasma concentrations of cyclosporine and may increase the risk of nephrotoxicity)

Lidocaine
(concurrent administration of lidocaine with cimetidine may result in reduced hepatic clearance of lidocaine, possibly resulting in delayed elimination and increased blood concentrations; lower doses of lidocaine may be required)

Procainamide
(renal elimination of procainamide may be decreased due to competition between cimetidine and procainamide for active tubular secretion, resulting in increased blood concentration of procainamide)

Quinine
(concurrent use of quinine with cimetidine may reduce the clearance of quinine)

For ranitidine
Alcohol
(some studies in humans have found increased blood alcohol levels when oral ranitidine was given in conjunction with alcohol; the clinical significance of this effect is not known)

Glipizide or
Glyburide or
Metoprolol or
Midazolam or
Nifedipine or
Phenytoin or
Theophylline or
Warfarin
(ranitidine is a weak inhibitor of hepatic drug metabolism; isolated cases of drug interactions have been reported between ranitidine and glipizide, glyburide, metoprolol, midazolam, nifedipine, phenytoin, theophylline, and warfarin)

(monitoring of blood concentrations or prothrombin time for anticoagulants as a guide to dosage is recommended since dosage adjustment of these medications may be necessary during and after ranitidine therapy to prevent bleeding due to anticoagulant potentiation)

(concurrent use of phenytoin with ranitidine may increase the risk of ataxia due to increased blood concentrations of phenytoin)

Procainamide
　(renal elimination of procainamide may be decreased due to competition between ranitidine and procainamide for active tubular secretion, resulting in increased blood concentration of procainamide)

For ranitidine only (in addition to those listed above for all histamine H$_2$-receptor antagonists)
　Urine protein test
　　(a false-positive reaction may be produced during ranitidine therapy; testing with sulphosalicylic acid is recommended)

With physiology/laboratory test values
For cimetidine
　Creatinine and
　Transaminase
　　(serum concentrations may be increased)
　Parathyroid hormone
　　(concentrations may be decreased, especially when abnormally elevated as in primary hyperparathyroidism)
　Prolactin
　　(serum concentrations may be increased after intravenous bolus administration)
For famotidine
　Transaminase
　　(serum concentrations may be increased)
For nizatidine
　Alanine aminotransferase (ALT [SGPT]) and
　Alkaline phosphatase and
　Aspartate aminotransferase (AST [SGOT])
　　(serum concentrations may be increased)
For ranitidine
　Creatinine and
　Gamma-glutamyl transpeptidase and
　Transaminase
　　(serum concentrations may be increased)

Contraindications/Medical problems

The contraindications/medical problems included have been selected on the basis of their potential clinical significance (reasons given in parentheses where appropriate)—not necessarily inclusive (» = major clinical significance).

Risk-benefit should be considered when the following medical problems exist:

　Cirrhosis, with history of portal systemic encephalopathy, or
　Hepatic function impairment or
» Renal function impairment
　　(decreased hepatic or renal clearance of histamine H$_2$-receptor antagonists may result in increased plasma concentrations thus increasing the risk of side effects, especially CNS effects; dosage reduction of histamine H$_2$-receptor antagonists or longer intervals between doses are recommended with renal function impairment and may be necessary with hepatic function impairment)
　Sensitivity to any of the histamine H$_2$-receptor antagonists

Side/Adverse Effects

See also *Table 2,* page 629.

Note: Rapid intravenous bolus administration (an infusion time of less than 5 minutes) of histamine H$_2$-receptor antagonists may cause significant, transient hypotension. Also, rare instances of cardiac arrhythmias have been reported with intravenous boluses of cimetidine and ranitidine.

Rare cases of hepatitis, with or without jaundice, have been reported in patients using histamine H$_2$-receptor antagonists; however, a direct association with the use of histamine H$_2$-receptor antagonists has not been established.

Experience with overdose in humans is limited. In animals, toxic doses of cimetidine have caused respiratory failure and tachycardia. Toxic doses of famotidine given intravenously to dogs caused emesis, restlessness, pallor of mucous membranes or redness of mouth and ears, hypotension, tachycardia, and collapse. Muscular tremors, vomiting, and rapid respiration have been reported with daily doses in excess of 225 mg of ranitidine per kg of body weight in animals.

Patient Consultation

In providing consultation, consider emphasizing the following selected information (» = major clinical significance):

Before using this medication
» Conditions affecting use, especially:
　　Sensitivity to any of the H$_2$-receptor antagonists
　　Pregnancy—All cross placenta
　　Breast-feeding—Cimetidine, famotidine, nizatidine, and ranitidine excreted in breast milk; nursing not recommended during cimetidine therapy, because of high concentration in breast milk
　　Use in the elderly—Confusion more likely with cimetidine, famotidine, and ranitidine in elderly patients with impaired hepatic or renal function
　　Other medications, especially ketoconazole (with all H$_2$-receptor antagonists); anticoagulants, metoprolol, phenytoin, xanthines (with cimetidine and possibly ranitidine only); propranolol or tricyclic antidepressants (with cimetidine only)
　　Other medical problems, especially renal function impairment

Proper use of this medication
　Dosing schedule:
　　1 dose a day—Taking at bedtime
　　2 doses a day—Taking in the morning and at bedtime
　　Several doses a day—Taking with meals and at bedtime
　Taking antacids for relief of ulcer pain; not taking within $1/2$ to 1 hour of histamine H$_2$-receptor antagonists
» Compliance with full course of therapy
　Missed dose: Taking as soon as possible; not taking if almost time for next dose; not doubling doses
» Proper storage

Precautions while using this medication
　Possible interference with gastric acid secretion tests or skin tests using allergens; need to inform physician of use of medication
　Avoiding use of foods, drinks, or other medication that may cause gastrointestinal irritation
　Discontinuing smoking or at least avoiding smoking after last dose of day
　Avoiding alcoholic beverages
　Checking with physician if condition does not improve or worsens

Side/adverse effects
　Signs of possible side effects, especially allergic reaction, bradycardia or tachycardia, bronchospasm, confusion, fever, and neutropenia or other blood dyscrasias

General Dosing Information

Use of histamine H$_2$-receptor antagonists in the treatment of duodenal ulcer rarely continues beyond 8 weeks, since no long-term, carefully monitored studies have been done with these medications. Also, most patients taking histamine H$_2$-receptor antagonists heal within 6 to 8 weeks.

Although the symptoms of duodenal ulcers may subside within 1 or 2 weeks after initiation of therapy, therapy should be continued for at least 4 to 6 weeks, unless healing has been documented by endoscopic examination or x-rays.

Histamine H$_2$-receptor antagonists may be used, in reduced doses, to prevent ulcer recurrence. However, until consequences of very long term use are fully determined, such use should be limited to patients likely to need surgical treatment, patients with concomitant illnesses in whom surgery would constitute a greater-than-usual risk, and patients with recurrent ulcers.

Initial titration of doses and subsequent dosage adjustment of histamine H$_2$-receptor antagonists is recommended in the long-term treatment of pathological hypersecretory conditions (e.g., Zollinger-Ellison syndrome, systemic mastocytosis, multiple endocrine adenomas). Doses of cimetidine should generally not exceed 2.4 grams per day; however, doses up to 12 grams per day have been used. Up to 160 mg of famotidine every 6 hours and up to 6 grams of ranitidine per day have been administered to some patients with severe Zollinger-Ellison syndrome.

The efficacy of histamine H$_2$-receptor antagonists in inhibiting nocturnal gastric acid secretion may be decreased by cigarette smoking. Patients with peptic ulcer disease should discontinue smoking, or at least avoid smoking after their last dose of the day.

Dosage of histamine H$_2$-receptor antagonists may need to be increased in burn patients to achieve adequate control of gastric pH, because of enhanced clearance of histamine H$_2$-receptor antagonists in these patients. Individualization of dosage should be based on monitoring of gastric pH and/or plasma concentrations of histamine H$_2$-receptor antagonists since their clearance varies in proportion to burn size.

No dosage adjustment of histamine H$_2$-receptor antagonists is necessary for hemodialysis and peritoneal dialysis patients, since only small amounts of the medications are removed.

For oral dosage forms only

In the treatment of peptic ulcer and other hypersecretory conditions, optimal therapeutic effect is obtained when histamine H$_2$-receptor antagonists are taken with meals and at bedtime. By administering histamine H$_2$-receptor antagonists with meals, maximum serum concentrations and antisecretory effects are achieved when the stomach is no longer protected by the buffering capacity of the food. However, more recent information indicates that ulcer healing rates may be greatest with a bedtime only dosage regimen.

If required, antacids of standard neutralizing capacity (e.g., 13 mEq per 15 mL) may be administered concurrently with histamine H$_2$-receptor antagonists for the relief of pain. However, spacing of doses one-half to one hour apart is recommended, especially with antacids of greater neutralizing capacity, since absorption of histamine H$_2$-receptor antagonists may be decreased.

For parenteral dosage forms only

Parenteral administration may be indicated in hospitalized patients with pathological hypersecretory disorders or intractable ulcers, or in patients who are unable to take oral medication.

Rapid intravenous bolus administration of cimetidine, famotidine, or ranitidine is not recommended because it may increase the risk of cardiac arrhythmias and hypotension.

CIMETIDINE

Summary of Differences

Indications: Also used in treatment of pancreatic insufficiency and as a treatment adjunct in acute urticaria.

Pharmacology: Other actions/effects—Inhibits hepatic cytochrome P-450 and P-448 mixed function oxidase (microsomal enzyme) systems; possesses antiandrogenic activity; increases prolactin concentration (with IV bolus injection); enhances gastromucosal defense and healing in stress-induced ulceration and bleeding.

Precautions:

Drug interactions and/or related problems—May interact with alcohol, anticoagulants, tricyclic antidepressants, benzodiazepines,

glipizide, glyburide, metoprolol, metronidazole, phenytoin, propranolol, xanthines, calcium channel blocking agents, cyclosporine, lidocaine, procainamide, sucralfate, quinine.

Laboratory value alterations—May increase serum prolactin concentrations; may decrease parathyroid hormone concentrations.

Side/adverse effects: Constipation has not been reported. Bronchospasms have not been reported as a side/adverse effect with cimetidine.

Oral Dosage Forms

Note: Bracketed uses in the *Dosage Forms* section refer to categories of use and/or indications that are not included in U.S. product labeling.

CIMETIDINE TABLETS USP

Usual adult and adolescent dose:

Duodenal ulcer—

Treatment: Oral, 300 mg four times a day, with meals and at bedtime; 400 or 600 mg two times a day, in the morning and at bedtime; or 800 mg at bedtime.

Note: A 1600-mg dose of cimetidine at bedtime has been found to produce a more rapid healing in some ulcer patients who have an endoscopically demonstrated ulcer larger than 1 cm and are also heavy smokers.

Prophylaxis of recurrent duodenal ulcer: Oral, 300 mg two times a day, in the morning and at bedtime; or 400 mg at bedtime. Patients have been maintained on continued treatment with 400 mg at bedtime for periods of up to five years.

Gastric ulcer, benign, active—Oral, 300 mg four times a day, with meals and at bedtime; or 600 mg two times a day, in the morning and at bedtime; or 800 mg at bedtime.

Gastric hypersecretory conditions (e.g., Zollinger-Ellison syndrome, systemic mastocytosis, multiple endocrine adenomas)—Oral, 300 mg four times a day, with meals and at bedtime, the dosage being adjusted as needed, and therapy continued for as long as clinically indicated.

Gastroesophageal reflux—Oral, 800 to 1600 mg per day in divided doses for 12 weeks.

[Upper gastrointestinal bleeding]—Oral, 300 mg every six hours; or 600 mg two times a day, in the morning and at bedtime.

Note: For patients with impaired renal function—Oral, 300 mg every twelve hours, the dosage being increased to 300 mg every eight hours or more frequently, if necessary. Further reduction in dosage may be required if hepatic function impairment is also present.

Usual adult prescribing limits: Up to 2.4 grams daily; however, doses up to 12 grams per day have been used in the treatment of pathological hypersecretory conditions.

Usual geriatric dose: See *Usual adult and adolescent dose*.

Auxiliary labeling: • Continue medicine for full time of treatment.

CIMETIDINE HYDROCHLORIDE ORAL SOLUTION

Usual adult and adolescent dose: See *Cimetidine Tablets USP*.

Usual adult prescribing limits: See *Cimetidine Tablets USP*.

Usual geriatric dose: See *Usual adult and adolescent dose*.

Auxiliary labeling: • Continue medicine for full time of treatment.

Parenteral Dosage Forms

Note: Bracketed uses in the *Dosage Forms* section refer to categories of use and/or indications that are not included in U.S. product labeling.

CIMETIDINE HYDROCHLORIDE INJECTION

Usual adult and adolescent dose:
Duodenal ulcer;
Gastric ulcer;
Gastric hypersecretory conditions (e.g., Zollinger-Ellison syndrome, systemic mastocytosis, multiple endocrine adenomas); and
[Upper gastrointestinal bleeding]—
Intramuscular, 300 mg (base) every six to eight hours.
Intravenous, 300 mg (base) every six to eight hours, diluted with a compatible intravenous solution and administered over a period of not less than five minutes.
Intravenous infusion, 300 mg (base) every six to eight hours, diluted in a compatible intravenous solution and administered over a fifteen- to twenty-minute period.
Note: If necessary, increases in dosage should be made by more frequent administration of a 300 mg dose.
Continuous intravenous infusion, 37.5 (base) mg per hour (900 mg per day), diluted in a compatible intravenous solution. The infusion rate should be adjusted to individual patient requirements.
Note: For patients requiring a rapid elevation of gastric pH, a loading dose of 150 mg may be administered by intravenous infusion before continuous infusion is begun.
Prophylaxis of stress-related mucosal bleeding—Continuous intravenous infusion, 50 mg (base) per hour, diluted in a compatible intravenous solution for up to 7 days.
Note: Patients with a creatinine clearance less than 30 mL per minute should receive 25 mg per hour.
[Prophylaxis of aspiration pneumonitis]—Intramuscular, 300 mg (base) one hour before induction of anesthesia, and 300 mg (base) given intramuscularly or intravenously every four hours until patient responds to verbal commands.
[Urticaria therapy adjunct]—Intravenous, 300 mg over 15 to 20 minutes.
Note: For patients with impaired renal function—Intravenous, 300 mg (base) every twelve hours, the dosage being increased to 300 mg every eight hours or more frequently, if necessary. Further reduction in dosage may be required if hepatic function impairment is also present.

Usual adult prescribing limits: Up to 2.4 grams (base) daily.

Usual geriatric dose: See *Usual adult and adolescent dose.*

FAMOTIDINE

Summary of Differences

Side/adverse effects: Loss of appetite, dryness of mouth or skin, ringing or buzzing in ears have been reported. A decrease in sexual ability has not been reported with famotidine.

Oral Dosage Forms

FAMOTIDINE FOR ORAL SUSPENSION

Usual adult and adolescent dose:
Duodenal ulcer—
Treatment: Oral, 40 mg once a day at bedtime or 20 mg two times a day.
Prophylaxis of recurrent duodenal ulcer: Oral, 20 mg at bedtime.
Gastric ulcer, benign, active—Oral, 40 mg once a day at bedtime.
Gastric hypersecretory conditions (e.g., Zollinger-Ellison syndrome, systemic mastocytosis, multiple endocrine adenomas)—Oral, 20 mg every six hours, the dosage being adjusted as needed

and therapy continued for as long as clinically indicated. Doses up to 160 mg every six hours have been administered to some patients with severe Zollinger-Ellison syndrome.
Gastroesophageal reflux—Oral, 20 mg two times a day for up to six weeks.
Note: The recommended oral dose for esophagitis due to gastroesopohageal reflux disease is 20 to 40 mg two times a day for up to 12 weeks.
[Prophylaxis of aspiration pneumonitis]—Oral, 40 mg given either the night before or the morning of surgery.
Note: For patients with severely impaired renal function (creatinine clearance less than 10 mL per minute)—Oral, 20 mg at bedtime. Depending on patient's response, the dosing interval may have to be increased to thirty-six to forty-eight hours.

Usual geriatric dose: See *Usual adult and adolescent dose.*

Auxiliary labeling:
- Shake well.
- Continue medicine for full time of treatment.

FAMOTIDINE TABLETS USP

Usual adult and adolescent dose: See *Famotidine for Oral Suspension.*

Usual geriatric dose: See *Usual adult and adolescent dose.*

Auxiliary labeling: • Continue medicine for full time of treatment.

Parenteral Dosage Forms

FAMOTIDINE INJECTION

Usual adult and adolescent dose:
Duodenal ulcer;
Gastric ulcer, benign, active; and
Gastric hypersecretory conditions (e.g., Zollinger-Ellison syndrome, systemic mastocytosis, multiple endocrine adenomas)—
Intravenous, 20 mg every twelve hours, diluted with a compatible intravenous solution and administered over a period of not less than two minutes.
Intravenous infusion, 20 mg every twelve hours, diluted with a compatible intravenous solution and administered over a fifteen- to thirty-minute period.
[Prophylaxis of aspiration pneumonitis]—Intramuscular, 20 mg given either the night before or the morning of surgery.

Usual geriatric dose: See *Usual adult and adolescent dose.*

NIZATIDINE

Summary of Differences

Pharmacology: Nizatidine is moderately protein bound, approximately 35%.
Precautions: Laboratory value alterations—Increases serum aspartate aminotransferase concentrations. May cause false-positive reaction with urine urobilinogen test.
Side/adverse effects: Agranulocytosis, diarrhea, joint or muscle pain, and loss of hair have not been reported with nizatidine. Increase in sweating has been reported.

Oral Dosage Forms

NIZATIDINE CAPSULES

Usual adult and adolescent dose:
Duodenal ulcer—
Treatment: Oral, 300 mg once a day at bedtime or 150 mg two times a day.

For patients with impaired renal function—
   With creatinine clearance less than 20 mL per minute: Oral, 150 mg every other day.
   With creatinine clearance from 20 to 50 mL per minute: Oral, 150 mg every day.
Prophylaxis of recurrent duodenal ulcer: Oral, 150 mg once a day at bedtime.
   For patients with impaired renal function—
      With creatinine clearance less than 20 mL per minute: Oral, 150 mg every three days.
      With creatinine clearance from 20 to 50 mL per minute: Oral, 150 mg every other day.
Gastroesophageal reflux[1]—Oral, 150 mg two times a day.

Usual geriatric dose: See *Usual adult and adolescent dose.*

Auxiliary labeling: • Continue medicine for full time of treatment.

---

[1]Not included in Canadian product labeling.

RANITIDINE

Summary of Differences

Pharmacology: Other actions/effects—Weak inhibitor of P-450 mixed function oxidase (microsomal enzyme) system; produces small, transient increase in prolactin concentration (with IV bolus injection).
Precautions:
   Laboratory value alterations—May increase glutamyl transpeptidase. May cause false-positive reaction with urine protein test.
   Drug interactions and/or related problems—May interact with alcohol, antacids, glipizide, glyburide, metoprolol, midazolam, nifedipine, phenytoin, theophylline, warfarin, procainamide, sucralfate.
Side/adverse effects: Blurred vision has been reported.

Oral Dosage Forms

RANITIDINE CAPSULES

Usual adult and adolescent dose: See *Ranitidine Tablets USP.*

Usual geriatric dose: See *Usual adult and adolescent dose.*

Auxiliary labeling: • Continue medicine for full time of treatment.

RANITIDINE TABLETS USP

Usual adult and adolescent dose:
   Duodenal ulcer—
      Treatment: Oral, 150 mg two times a day or 300 mg at bedtime.
      Prophylaxis of recurrent duodenal ulcer: Oral, 150 mg at bedtime.
   Gastric ulcer, benign, active—Oral, 150 mg two times a day.
   Gastric hypersecretory conditions (e.g., Zollinger-Ellison syndrome, systemic mastocytosis, multiple endocrine adenomas)—Oral, 150 mg two times a day, the dosage being adjusted as needed and therapy continued as long as clinically indicated. Doses up to 6 grams per day have been used in severe cases.
   Gastroesophageal reflux—Oral, 150 mg two times a day.
      Note: The recommended oral dose for erosive esophagitis is 150 mg four times a day.
Note: For patients with impaired renal function (creatinine clearance of less than 50 mL per minute)—Oral, 150 mg every twenty-four hours, the frequency of the dosage being increased to every twelve hours or more frequently, if necessary. Reductions in dosage may also be required if hepatic function impairment is present.

Usual geriatric dose: See *Usual adult and adolescent dose.*

Auxiliary labeling: • Continue medicine for full time of treatment.

RANITIDINE HYDROCHLORIDE SYRUP

Usual adult and adolescent dose: See *Ranitidine Tablets USP.*

Usual geriatric dose: See *Usual adult and adolescent dose.*

Auxiliary labeling: • Continue medicine for full time of treatment.

Parenteral Dosage Forms

Note: Bracketed uses in the *Dosage Forms* section refer to categories of use and/or indications that are not included in U.S. product labeling.

RANITIDINE INJECTION USP

Usual adult and adolescent dose:
   Duodenal ulcer;
   Gastric ulcer;
   Gastric hypersecretory conditions (e.g., Zollinger-Ellison syndrome, systemic mastocytosis, multiple endocrine adenomas); and
   [Prophylaxis of stress-related mucosal bleeding]—
      Intramuscular, 50 mg every six to eight hours.
      Intravenous, 50 mg every six to eight hours, diluted to a total volume of 20 mL with a compatible intravenous solution and administered over a period of not less than five minutes.
      Intravenous infusion, 50 mg every six to eight hours, diluted in 100 mL of a compatible intravenous solution and administered over a fifteen- to twenty-minute period.
      Continuous intravenous infusion, 6.25 mg per hour, diluted in a compatible intravenous solution.
   Note: For gastric hypersecretory conditions, the infusion should be started at 1 mg per kg of body weight per hour and increased by 0.5 mg per kg of body weight per hour increments (if gastric acid output is greater than 10 mEq per hour or patient is symptomatic), up to 2.5 mg per kg of body weight per hour.
   [Prophylaxis of aspiration pneumonitis]—Intramuscular or slow intravenous injection, 50 mg administered forty-five to sixty minutes before induction of general anesthesia.
Note: For patients with impaired renal function (creatinine clearance of less than 50 mL per minute)—Intravenous, 50 mg every eighteen to twenty-four hours, the frequency of the dosage being increased to every twelve hours or more frequently, if necessary. Further reduction in dosage may be required if hepatic function impairment is also present.

Usual adult prescribing limits: Up to 400 mg daily.

Usual geriatric dose: See *Usual adult and adolescent dose.*

Table 1. Pharmacology

Drug	Time to peak effect (hr)	Duration of action (hr)
Cimetidine	Oral: 1–2	Nocturnal: 6–8 Basal: 4–5
Famotidine	Oral: 1–3 Parenteral: 1/2	Nocturnal and basal: 10–12 (oral and IV)
Nizatidine	Oral: 1/2–3	Nocturnal: Up to 12 Basal: Up to 8
Ranitidine	Oral: 1–3	Nocturnal: 13 Basal: 4

Table 2. Side/Adverse Effects*

The following side/adverse effects have been selected on the basis of their potential clinical significance (possible signs and symptoms in parentheses where appropriate)—not necessarily inclusive:

Legend:
I = Cimetidine
II = Famotidine
III = Nizatidine
IV = Ranitidine

	I	II	III	IV
Medical attention needed				
Agranulocytosis (fever, sore throat, or unusual tiredness or weakness)	R§	R§	—	R§
Allergic reaction (burning, redness, skin rash, or swelling)	✔	R	R	✔
Bradycardia (slow heartbeat)	R‡	R	R	R
Bronchospasm (tightness in chest)	—	R	R	R
Confusion	R†	✔	R	R†
Fever	R	R	R	R
Neutropenia (sore throat and fever)	R§	R§	R§	R§
Tachycardia (fast, pounding, or irregular heartbeat)	R	R	R	R
Thrombocytopenia (unusual bleeding or bruising)	R§	R§	R§	R§
Medical attention needed only if continuing or bothersome				
Antiandrogenic effect				
(decreased sexual ability)	R**	—	✔	✔
(swelling of the breasts or breast soreness in females and males)	R††	✔	✔	✔
Blurred vision	—	—	—	✔
Constipation	—	<2%	✔	<2%
Decrease in sexual desire	✔	✔	✔	✔
Diarrhea	<2%	<2%	—	<2%
Dizziness	<2%	<2%	✔	<2%
Drowsiness	<2%	✔	2.4%	<2%
Dryness of mouth or skin	—	✔	—	—
Headache	<3.5%	<5%	✔	2%
Increased sweating	—	—	1%	—
Joint or muscle pain	✔	✔	—	✔
Loss of appetite	—	✔	—	—
Loss of hair	✔	✔	—	✔
Nausea or vomiting	<2%	✔	✔	<2%
Ringing or buzzing in ears	—	✔	—	—
Skin rash	<2%	✔	✔	<2%

*Differences in frequency of occurrence may reflect either lack of clinical-use data or actual pharmacologic distinctions among agents (although their pharmacologic similarity suggests that side effects occurring with one may occur with the others). M = more frequent; L = less frequent; R = rare; — = not reported; ✔ = reported, but percentage of occurrence and/or direct relationship to therapy has not been established.

†More likely to occur in severely ill patients or in patients with impaired hepatic or renal function, particularly elderly patients. Reversible within 3 to 4 days following discontinuation of medication. This side effect may mimic alcohol withdrawal syndrome (delirium tremens) in patients treated for gastrointestinal complications of alcoholism.

‡Cardiac effects after intravenous bolus injection.

§Neutropenia or other blood dyscrasias are more likely to occur in patients with serious concomitant illnesses or in those who also received antimetabolites, alkylating agents, or other medications and/or treatment known to produce neutropenia. Appear to be reversible and tend to occur within the first 30 days of administration.

**Rare; more likely to occur in patients with Zollinger-Ellison syndrome receiving high doses (3 to 10 grams of cimetidine a day) for at least 1 year.

††Rare; more frequent (about 4%) with long-term therapy.

HMG-CoA REDUCTASE INHIBITORS   Systemic

Some commonly used *brand names* are:

In the U.S.—
    Mevacor [Lovastatin]   *Zocor* [Simvastatin]
    Pravachol [Pravastatin]

In Canada—
    Mevacor [Lovastatin]   *Zocor* [Simvastatin]
    Pravachol [Pravastatin]

Other commonly used names are:

    Epistatin [Simvastatin]   Mevinolin [Lovastatin]
    Eptastatin [Pravastatin]   Synvinolin [Simvastatin]

LOVASTATIN
Oral
    Lovastatin Tablets
        In the U.S. and Canada—*Mevacor*

PRAVASTATIN
Oral
    Pravastatin Tablets
        In the U.S. and Canada—*Pravachol*

SIMVASTATIN
Oral
    Simvastatin Tablets
        In the U.S. and Canada—*Zocor*

Category: HMG-CoA reductase inhibitor; antihyperlipidemic.

Indications

Accepted

Hyperlipidemia (treatment)—3-Hydroxy-3-methylglutaryl coenzyme A (HMG-CoA) reductase inhibitors are indicated as adjuncts in the treatment of primary hypercholesterolemia (type IIa and IIb hyperlipoproteinemia) caused by elevated low-density lipoprotein (LDL) cholesterol concentrations in patients with a significant risk of coronary artery disease, who have not responded to diet or other measures alone. The HMG-CoA reductase inhibitors may also be useful for the reduction of elevated LDL cholesterol concentrations in patients with combined hypercholesterolemia and hypertriglyceridemia.

In the 1988 Report of the National Cholesterol Education Program Expert Panel on Detection, Evaluation, and Treatment of High Blood Cholesterol in Adults, the following guidelines for the treatment of high blood cholesterol are recommended:

    Nonpharmacologic management (especially reduction in dietary intake of saturated fatty acids and cholesterol, weight reduction and exercise, and quitting smoking) is recommended first for all patients and as an adjunct to all pharmacologic cholesterol therapy.

    If, after six months of diet therapy, adequate LDL-cholesterol reduction is not achieved, then medication therapy is recommended to be added to diet therapy.

    Initial medication therapy usually consists of a bile acid sequestrant (e.g., cholestyramine, colestipol) or niacin. A 3-hydroxy-3-methylglutaryl coenzyme A (HMG-CoA) reductase inhibitor (e.g., lovastatin; pravastatin; simvastatin) should be considered after the bile acid sequestrants and niacin. Other lipid-lowering agents, including fibric acid derivatives (e.g., gemfibrozil and clofibrate) and probucol, are not as effective in lowering LDL cholesterol as the above mentioned medications. Two other agents, neomycin (not approved by FDA as a lipid-lowering agent) and dextrothyroxine are not recommended for general use because other medications are available that have a more favorable benefit/risk ratio.

If adequate LDL-cholesterol control is not achieved with initial medication therapy, it is recommended that the patient be switched to another medication or a combination of two medications with synergistic mechanisms of action. Although experience with such drug combinations is somewhat limited, preliminary studies indicate that the bile acid sequestrants given with either niacin, lovastatin, pravastatin, simvastatin, probucol, or gemfibrozil are useful in controlling LDL cholesterol. Lovastatin, pravastatin, or simvastatin in combination with either niacin or gemfibrozil needs further study because of the potential increased risk of side effects.

If effective control of LDL cholesterol is not obtained after use of primary medications and medication combinations, then referral to a lipid specialist may be necessary.

Studies have suggested that short-term control of elevated cholesterol and triglycerides may not lessen the danger of mortality, although incidence of cardiovascular disease and nonfatal myocardial infarctions may be decreased.

Pharmacology

Mechanism of action/Effect: Action is at least partly due to the active form, beta-hydroxyacid, which inhibits 3-hydroxy-3-methylglutaryl-coenzyme A (HMG-CoA) reductase. Pravastatin is administered in the active form, while lovastatin and simvastatin must be hydrolyzed to beta-hydroxyacid. Inhibition of HMG-CoA reductase prevents conversion of HMG-CoA to mevalonate, an early step in cholesterol biosynthesis. Depletion of cellular cholesterol content stimulates production of more cell surface receptors that recognize low-density lipoprotein (LDL). The primary site of action of HMG-CoA reductase inhibitors is the liver; the increase in LDL receptors leads to an increase in catabolism of LDL cholesterol. There is also a reduction in LDL synthesis. HMG-CoA reductase inhibitors reduce LDL cholesterol, very low-density lipoprotein (VLDL), and plasma triglyceride concentrations, and slightly increase high-density lipoprotein (HDL) concentrations.

Duration of action: Lovastatin—After withdrawal of continuous therapy—4 to 6 weeks.

Precautions to Consider

Geriatrics

No information is available on the relationship of age to the effects of HMG-CoA reductase inhibitors in geriatric patients.

Drug interactions and/or related problems

The following drug interactions and/or related problems have been selected on the basis of their potential clinical significance (possible mechanism in parentheses where appropriate)—not necessarily inclusive (» = major clinical significance):

Note: Combinations containing any of the following medications, depending on the amount present, may also interact with this medication.

Anticoagulants, coumarin- or indandione-derivative
    (concurrent use with HMG-CoA reductase inhibitors may increase bleeding or prothrombin-time; prothrombin-time should be monitored in patients taking HMG-CoA reductase inhibitors with anticoagulants)

» Cyclosporine or
    Erythromycin or
» Gemfibrozil or
    Immunosuppressants, other, or

» Niacin
(concurrent use with HMG-CoA reductase inhibitors may be associated with an increased risk of rhabdomyolysis and acute renal failure; combined therapy with gemfibrozil, niacin, or immunosuppressants should include careful monitoring for symptoms of myopathy or rhabdomyolysis; although cases have been reported with lovastatin only, the potential also exists with pravastatin and simvastatin)

For simvastatin (in addition to those listed above)
Digoxin
(concurrent use with simvastatin may cause a slight elevation in serum digoxin levels)

Contraindications/Medical problems
The contraindications/medical problems included have been selected on the basis of their potential clinical significance (reasons given in parentheses where appropriate)—not necessarily inclusive (» = major clinical significance).

Except under special circumstances, this medication should not be used when the following medical problem exists:

» Hepatic disease, active
(condition may be exacerbated)

Risk-benefit should be considered when the following medical problems exist:

Alcoholism, active or in remission, or
Hepatic disease, history of
(further increases in liver enzymes may occur)
» Hypotension or
» Infection, severe acute, or
» Metabolic, endocrine, or electrolyte disorders, severe, or
» Seizures, uncontrolled, or
» Surgery, major, or
» Trauma
(increased risk of secondary renal failure if rhabdomyolysis occurs)
» Organ transplant, with immunosuppressant therapy
(increased risk of rhabdomyolysis and renal failure)
Sensitivity to any HMG-CoA reductase inhibitor

Side/Adverse Effects

Note: An increased incidence of opacities noted on slit-lamp ophthalmic examination occurred in one study involving lovastatin but this has not been confirmed in other studies. To date, no increased incidence of lens opacities has been found with pravastatin or simvastatin.

The following side/adverse effects have been selected on the basis of their potential clinical significance (possible signs and symptoms in parentheses where appropriate)—not necessarily inclusive:

Those indicating need for medical attention
Incidence less frequent
For all HMG-CoA reductase inhibitors
Myalgia (fever, muscle aches or cramps, unusual tiredness or weakness)
Note: Rarely, along with markedly elevated creatine kinase (CK) concentrations, *fever, muscle aches or cramps,* or *unusual tiredness or weakness* may be symptoms of myositis or rhabdomyolysis and may progress to renal failure; incidence may be increased in patients treated with immunosuppressants, gemfibrozil, erythromycin, or niacin; may occur weeks to months after initiation of treatment)

For lovastatin and pravastatin (in addition to those listed above)
Blurred vision

Those indicating need for medical attention only if they continue or are bothersome
Incidence more frequent
For all HMG-CoA reductase inhibitors
Constipation, diarrhea, gas, heartburn, or stomach pain; dizziness; headache; nausea; skin rash
For lovastatin (in addition to those listed above)
Impotence (decreased sexual ability); **insomnia** (trouble in sleeping)

Patient Consultation
In providing consultation, consider emphasizing the following selected information (» = major clinical significance):

Before using this medication
Diet as preferred therapy; importance of following prescribed diet
» Conditions affecting use, especially:
Sensitivity to any HMG-CoA reductase inhibitor
Pregnancy—Use not recommended in pregnancy or in a woman who plans to become pregnant because inhibited formation of cholesterol may impair fetal development
Breast-feeding—Use not recommended, because it may cause potentially serious adverse effects in nursing infants
Use in children—Not recommended in children under 2 years of age since cholesterol is required for normal development
Other medications, especially cyclosporine, gemfibrozil, or niacin
Other medical problems, especially uncontrolled seizures; recent major surgery; organ transplant with immunosuppressant therapy; hypotension; severe infection; severe metabolic, endocrine, or electrolyte disorders; major surgery; trauma

Proper use of this medication
For all HMG-CoA reductase inhibitors
» Importance of not taking more or less medication than the amount prescribed
This medication does not cure the condition but instead helps control it
» Compliance with prescribed diet
Missed dose: Taking as soon as possible; not taking if almost time for next dose; not doubling doses
» Proper storage
For lovastatin
Taking with meals, since medication is more effective with food

Precautions while using this medication
» Importance of close monitoring by physician
» Checking with physician before discontinuing medications; blood lipid levels may increase significantly
» Caution if any kind of surgery (including dental surgery) or emergency treatment is required

Side/adverse effects
Signs of potential side effects, especially myalgia, myositis, or rhabdomyolysis (for all HMG-CoA reductase inhibitors); blurred vision (for lovastatin and simvastatin)

General Dosing Information
If serum transaminase concentrations increase to 3 times the upper limit of normal, HMG-CoA reductase inhibitor therapy should be withdrawn.

If creatine kinase (CK) concentrations are markedly increased or myositis occurs, HMG-CoA reductase inhibitor therapy should be withdrawn.

LOVASTATIN

Summary of Differences

Pharmacology:
    Absorption—Reduced by one-third on empty stomach.
    Biotransformation—By hydrolysis to active metabolites.
    Time to peak concentration—2 to 4 hours.
Drug interactions and/or related problems: Has not been shown to interact with digoxin.
Side/adverse effects: Increased incidence of lens opacities; blurred vision, insomnia, and impotence have been reported.

Additional Dosing Information

Diet/Nutrition
Should be taken with meals to maximize absorption.

Oral Dosage Forms

LOVASTATIN TABLETS

Usual adult and adolescent dose: Antihyperlipidemic—
    Initial: Oral, 20 mg per day with the evening meal, the dosage being adjusted at four-week intervals as needed and tolerated. An initial dose of 40 mg per day may be used in patients with severely elevated cholesterol concentrations.
    Maintenance: Oral, 20 to 80 mg per day, as a single dose or in divided doses, with meals.

Usual adult prescribing limits: Up to 80 mg per day.

Auxiliary labeling: • Take with meals.

PRAVASTATIN

Summary of Differences

Pharmacology:
    Biotransformation—Administered in active form.
    Time to peak concentration—1 hour.

Drug interactions and/or related problems: Has not been shown to interact with digoxin.
Side/adverse effects: Blurred vision has been reported; insomnia and impotence have not been reported.

Additional Dosing Information

Diet/Nutrition
Can be taken with meals or on an empty stomach.

Oral Dosage Forms

PRAVASTATIN TABLETS

Usual adult and adolescent dose: Antihyperlipidemic—Oral, 10 to 20 mg per day at bedtime, the dosage being adjusted at four-week intervals as needed and tolerated. An initial dose of 40 mg per day may be used in patients with severely elevated cholesterol concentrations.

SIMVASTATIN

Summary of Differences

Pharmacology:
    Biotransformation—By hydrolysis to active metabolites.
    Time to peak concentration—1.3 to 2.4 hours.
Drug interactions and/or related problems: Elevation of serum digoxin.
Side/adverse effects: Blurred vision, insomnia, or impotence have not been reported.

Additional Dosing Information

Diet/Nutrition
Can be taken with meals or on an empty stomach.

Oral Dosage Forms

SIMVASTATIN TABLETS

Usual adult and adolescent dose: Antihyperlipidemic—Oral, 10 mg per day in the evening, the dosage being adjusted at four-week intervals to a maximum of 40 mg per day.

HYDRALAZINE   Systemic

Some commonly used *brand names* are:
    In the U.S—*Apresoline*
    In Canada—*Apresoline; Novo-Hylazin*

ORAL
Hydralazine Hydrochloride Tablets USP
    In the U.S.—*Apresoline;* GENERIC
    In Canada—*Apresoline; Novo-Hylazin*

PARENTERAL
Hydralazine Hydrochloride Injection USP
    In the U.S.—*Apresoline;* GENERIC
    In Canada—*Apresoline*

Category: Antihypertensive; vasodilator, congestive heart failure.

Indications

Note: Bracketed information in the *Indications* section refers to uses not included in U.S. product labeling.

Accepted
Hypertension (treatment)—Hydralazine is indicated orally in the treatment of moderate and severe hypertension, and as an adjunct in the treatment of malignant or accelerated hypertension or essential hypertension complicated by renal insufficiency or congestive heart failure. It may be used intravenously in the treatment of hypertensive crisis.

In the 1988 Report of the Joint National Committee on Detection, Evaluation, and Treatment of High Blood Pressure, a progression in choice of treatments for essential hypertension is recommended:

    Nonpharmacologic management (especially sodium restriction, weight reduction and exercise, and moderation of alcohol consumption) is recommended first for some patients, including those with mild hypertension, and is recommended as an adjunct to all pharmacologic hypertensive therapy.

Initial drug therapy usually consists of a diuretic, beta-adrenergic blocking agent, calcium channel blocking agent, or angiotensin-converting enzyme (ACE) inhibitor. If adequate blood pressure control is not achieved and the patient is adherent to the treatment program and not experiencing significant side effects, dosage of the drug may be increased, a drug from another one of these initial classes may be added or substituted, or a second drug from a different class—centrally acting alpha-adrenergic blockers (e.g., clonidine, guanabenz, guanfacine, methyldopa), peripheral-acting adrenergic blocking agents (e.g., guanadrel, guanethidine, rauwolfia alkaloids), post-synaptic alpha-1 peripheral adrenergic inhibitors (e.g., doxazosin, prazosin, terazosin), or vasodilators (e.g., hydralazine, minoxidil)—may be added or substituted.

If necessary, a drug from another class in the second group may be substituted or added as a third drug. If blood pressure control is still not achieved, a drug from still another class may be substituted or added as a fourth drug, or the patient may need further evaluation and/or referral.

[Congestive heart failure (treatment)][1]—Hydralazine is also used, usually in combination with nitrates and/or diuretics and/or digitalis glycosides, in the treatment of congestive heart failure.

---

[1]Not included in Canadian product labeling.

Pharmacology

Mechanism of action/Effect:
Antihypertensive—Exact mechanism of antihypertensive action unknown. The predominant effect of hydralazine is direct vasodilation of arterioles with little effect on veins, resulting in a decrease in peripheral resistance and an increase in heart rate, stroke volume, and cardiac output.
Vasodilator, congestive heart failure—Beneficial effects are due to increased cardiac output, decreased systemic resistance, and afterload reduction.

Onset of action:
Oral—45 minutes.
Intravenous—10 to 20 minutes.

Time to peak effect: Intravenous—15 to 30 minutes.

Duration of action: Oral or intravenous—3 to 8 hours.

Precautions to Consider

Cross-sensitivity and/or related problems
Patients sensitive to tartrazine may be sensitive to the tablet dosage form also, since some tablets contain tartrazine.

Geriatrics
Although appropriate studies on the relationship of age to the effects of hydralazine have not been performed in the geriatric population, geriatrics-specific problems are not expected to limit the usefulness of hydralazine in the elderly. However, elderly patients may be more sensitive to the hypotensive effects of hydralazine and are more likely to have age-related renal function impairment, both of which may require dosage reduction.

Drug interactions and/or related problems
The following drug interactions and/or related problems have been selected on the basis of their potential clinical significance (possible mechanism in parentheses where appropriate)—not necessarily inclusive (» = major clinical significance):

Note: Combinations containing any of the following medications, depending on the amount present, may also interact with this medication.

Anti-inflammatory drugs, nonsteroidal (NSAIDs), especially indomethacin
(may reduce antihypertensive effects of hydralazine; indomethacin, and possibly other NSAIDs, may antagonize the antihypertensive effect by inhibiting renal prostaglandin synthesis and/or by causing sodium and fluid retention; the patient should be carefully monitored to confirm that the desired effect is being obtained)
» Diazoxide or
Hypotension-producing medications, other
(antihypertensive effects may be potentiated when these medications are used concurrently with hydralazine; concurrent use of diazoxide or other potent parenteral antihypertensives with hydralazine may result in a severe, additive hypotensive effect; although some antihypertensive and/or diuretic combinations are frequently used for therapeutic advantage, dosage adjustments may be necessary during concurrent use)
(patients should be continuously observed for excessive fall in blood pressure for several hours after concurrent administration of diazoxide or other potent parenteral antihypertensives)
Estrogens
(estrogen-induced fluid retention may increase blood pressure)
Sympathomimetics
(may reduce antihypertensive effects of hydralazine; the patient should be carefully monitored to confirm that the desired effect is being obtained)

Contraindications/Medical problems
The contraindications/medical problems included have been selected on the basis of their potential clinical significance (reasons given in parentheses where appropriate)—not necessarily inclusive (» = major clinical significance).

Risk-benefit should be considered when the following medical problems exist:
Aortic aneurysm
Cerebrovascular disease or accident
(decreased blood pressure may increase cerebral ischemia)
Congestive heart failure
(use of hydralazine alone is not recommended, although it may improve cardiac performance in some patients with intractable left ventricular failure)
» Coronary artery disease
(myocardial stimulation and increased myocardial oxygen demands may cause or aggravate ischemia and angina and reportedly may precipitate myocardial infarction)
Renal function impairment, advanced
(accumulation of hydralazine may occur because of slower acetylation and reduced elimination, although incidence of toxic side effects is not increased; lower dosage may be required)
» Rheumatic heart disease, mitral valvular
(hydralazine may increase pulmonary artery pressure)
Sensitivity to hydralazine
Note: There is no substantial evidence that use of hydralazine in the treatment of hypertension in patients with systemic vasculitis or systemic lupus erythematosus exacerbates the underlying disease process.

Side/Adverse Effects

Note: Side/adverse effects are rare at lower dosages and are generally reversible.
Hepatotoxicity has been reported in a few patients.

The following side/adverse effects have been selected on the basis of their potential clinical significance (possible signs and symptoms in parentheses where appropriate)—not necessarily inclusive:

Those indicating need for medical attention
Incidence less frequent

> *Allergic reaction* (skin rash or itching); *angina pectoris* (chest pain); *cutaneous vasculitis* (blisters on skin); *lymphadenopathy* (swelling of lymph glands); *peripheral neuritis* (numbness, tingling, pain, or weakness in hands or feet); *sodium and water retention and edema* (swelling of feet or lower legs); *systemic lupus erythematosus (SLE)-like syndrome, including glomerulonephritis* (blisters on skin, chest pain, general feeling of discomfort, illness, or weakness, joint pain, skin rash or itching, sore throat and fever)

> Note: The *SLE-like syndrome* is a pharmacologic rather than an allergic effect and occurs more frequently in patients receiving higher doses of hydralazine (especially greater than 200 mg per day), in "slow acetylators," and in patients with impaired renal function. It is rarely seen with doses lower than 200 mg per day.
>
> Rarely, sore throat and fever or general feeling of discomfort, illness, or weakness may be signs or symptoms of blood dyscrasias.

Those indicating need for medical attention only if they continue or are bothersome
Incidence more frequent

> *Diarrhea; palpitations* (pounding heartbeat); *tachycardia* (fast heartbeat); *headache; anorexia* (loss of appetite); *nausea or vomiting*

> Note: In patients with severe heart failure, sympathetic tone is already high and there will be little or no change in heart rate.

Incidence less frequent

> *Constipation; hypotension* (dizziness or lightheadedness); *redness or flushing of face; dyspnea* (shortness of breath); *lacrimation* (watering eyes); *nasal congestion* (stuffy nose)

Patient Consultation

In providing consultation, consider emphasizing the following selected information (» = major clinical significance):

Before using this medication
» Conditions affecting use, especially:
> Sensitivity to hydralazine
> Pregnancy—Blood problems reported in infants of mothers who took hydralazine; causes birth defects in animals
> Use in the elderly—Increased sensitivity to hypotensive effects
> Other medications, especially diazoxide
> Other medical problems, especially coronary artery disease or rheumatic heart disease

Proper use of this medication
> Getting into the habit of taking at same times each day to help increase compliance
> Missed dose: Taking as soon as possible; not taking if almost time for next dose; not doubling doses
» Proper storage

For use as an antihypertensive
> Possible need for control of weight and diet, especially sodium intake
» Patient may not experience symptoms of hypertension; importance of taking medication even if feeling well
» Does not cure, but helps control hypertension; possible need for lifelong therapy; checking with physician before discontinuing medication; serious consequences of untreated hypertension

Precautions while using this medication
> Regular visits to physician to check progress
» Caution when driving or doing things requiring alertness because of possible headache or dizziness

For use as an antihypertensive
» Not taking other medications, especially nonprescription sympathomimetics, unless discussed with physician

Side/adverse effects
> Signs of potential side effects, especially allergic reaction, angina pectoris, cutaneous vasculitis, lymphadenopathy, peripheral neuritis, sodium and water retention, edema, and SLE-like syndrome

General Dosing Information

Apparent tolerance to the antihypertensive effects of hydralazine may develop with chronic administration, as a result of fluid retention and expanded plasma volume and reflex activation of the sympathetic nervous system, which increases heart rate and cardiac output. Concurrent administration of a diuretic may decrease this likelihood and will enhance the antihypertensive effects of hydralazine.

If combination therapy is indicated, individual titration is required to ensure the lowest possible therapeutic dose of each drug.

Incidence and severity of some of the side effects of hydralazine can be minimized if the dosage is increased slowly to its therapeutic level. In addition, some side effects (especially tachycardia, headache, and dizziness) may be less pronounced if beta-adrenergic blocking agents are administered concurrently.

All patients may be divided into 2 groups: slow and fast acetylators of hydralazine. Patients who are slow acetylators may be more prone to development of adverse effects (especially the systemic lupus erythematosus [SLE]-like syndrome) and may require lower-than-usual doses. Eskimo, Oriental, and American Indian populations have the lowest prevalence of slow acetylators, while Egyptian, Israeli, Scandinavian, other Caucasian, and black populations have the highest prevalence of slow acetylators.

Recent evidence suggests that withdrawal of antihypertensive therapy prior to surgery is not necessary, but that the anesthesiologist must be aware of such therapy.

Peripheral neuritis has been observed in some patients on hydralazine therapy. Evidence suggests that this may be due to an antipyridoxine effect. Discontinuation of hydralazine or continuation of hydralazine with supplemental vitamin B_6 (pyridoxine)—100 to 200 mg per day—usually results in remission of the neuritis over a period of 4 to 6 weeks.

It is recommended that hydralazine therapy be discontinued if a systemic lupus erythematosus (SLE)-like syndrome occurs.

To avoid a sudden increase in blood pressure, patients on hydralazine who have shown a significant decrease in blood pressure should have the medication withdrawn gradually at cessation of therapy.

For oral dosage forms
Food may enhance the bioavailability of hydralazine by reducing first-pass metabolism in the gastrointestinal wall. Consistent administration in relation to meals is recommended.

For parenteral dosage forms
Most patients can be transferred to the oral dosage form of hydralazine within 24 to 48 hours after initiation of parenteral therapy.

Oral Dosage Forms

Note: Bracketed uses in the *Dosage Forms* section refer to categories of use and/or indications that are not included in U.S. product labeling.

HYDRALAZINE HYDROCHLORIDE TABLETS USP

Usual adult dose:

Antihypertensive; or

[Vasodilator, congestive heart failure][1]—

Initial: Oral, 10 mg four times a day for the first two to four days, followed by 25 mg four times a day for the balance of the first week.

Maintenance: Oral, 50 mg four times a day for the second and subsequent weeks; dosage should be adjusted to the lowest effective levels.

Note: Geriatric patients may be more sensitive to the effects of the usual adult dose.

Usual adult prescribing limits: Up to 300 mg daily (higher doses have been used in treatment of congestive heart failure).

Auxiliary labeling: • Do not take other medicines without your doctor's advice.

Parenteral Dosage Forms

HYDRALAZINE HYDROCHLORIDE INJECTION USP

Usual adult dose: Antihypertensive—Intramuscular or intravenous, 10 to 40 mg, repeated as needed.

Note: Geriatric patients may be more sensitive to the effects of the usual adult dose.

HYDRALAZINE AND HYDROCHLOROTHIAZIDE   Systemic

Category: Antihypertensive.

Indications

Accepted

Hypertension (treatment)—Hydralazine and hydrochlorothiazide combination is indicated in the treatment of hypertension.

Fixed-dosage combinations are generally not recommended for initial therapy and are useful for subsequent therapy only when the proportion of the component agents corresponds to the dose of the individual agents, as determined by titration.

Nonpharmacologic management (especially sodium restriction, weight reduction and exercise, and moderation of alcohol consumption) is recommended first for some patients, including those with mild hypertension, and is recommended as an adjunct to all pharmacologic hypertensive therapy.

Patient Consultation

In providing consultation, consider emphasizing the following selected information (» = major clinical significance):

Before using this medication

» Conditions affecting use, especially:

Sensitivity to hydralazine, hydrochlorothiazide, sulfonamide-type medications, bumetanide, furosemide, or carbonic anhydrase inhibitors

Pregnancy—Blood problems reported in infants of mothers who took hydralazine and birth defects found in animals; hydrochlorothiazide may cause jaundice, thrombocytopenia, hypokalemia in infant

Breast-feeding—Hydrochlorothiazide is excreted in breast milk

Use in the elderly—Increased sensitivity to hypotensive and electrolyte effects; increased risk of hydralazine-induced hypothermia

Use by athletes—Diuretics are banned and tested for by the U.S. Olympic Committee (USOC), the International Olympic Committee (IOC), and the National Collegiate Athletic Association (NCAA)

Other medications, especially diazoxide, digitalis glycosides, lithium

Other medical problems, especially coronary artery disease, rheumatic heart disease, anuria or severe renal function impairment, or infants with jaundice

Proper use of this medication

Diuretic effects of the medication and timing of doses to minimize inconvenience of diuresis

Possible need for control of weight and diet, especially sodium intake

» Patient may not experience symptoms of hypertension; importance of taking medication even if feeling well

» Does not cure, but helps control hypertension; possible need for lifelong therapy; checking with physician before discontinuing medication; serious consequences of untreated hypertension

Getting into the habit of taking at same times each day to help increase compliance

Missed dose: Taking as soon as possible; not taking if almost time for next dose; not doubling doses

» Proper storage

Precautions while using this medication

Regular visits to physician to check progress

» Not taking other medications, especially nonprescription sympathomimetics, unless discussed with physician

» Caution when driving or doing things requiring alertness because of possible headache or dizziness

» Caution when getting up suddenly from a lying or sitting position

» Caution in using alcohol, while standing for long periods or exercising, and during hot weather because of enhanced orthostatic hypotensive effects

» Possibility of hypokalemia; possible need for additional potassium in diet; not changing diet without first checking with physician

To prevent dehydration, checking with physician if severe nausea, vomiting, or diarrhea occurs and continues

Diabetics: May increase blood sugar levels

Possible photosensitivity; avoiding unprotected exposure to sun; using protective clothing and sun block product; avoiding use of sunlamp, tanning bed, or tanning booth

Side/adverse effects

Signs of potential side effects, especially electrolyte imbalance, agranulocytosis, allergic reaction, angina pectoris, cutaneous vasculitis, lymphadenopathy, peripheral neuritis, SLE-like syndrome, agranulocytosis, cholecystitis, pancreatitis, hepatic function impairment, hyperuricemia, gout, and thrombocytopenia

Oral Dosage Forms

HYDRALAZINE HYDROCHLORIDE AND HYDROCHLOROTHIAZIDE CAPSULES

Usual adult dose: Antihypertensive—Oral, 1 capsule two times a day, as determined by individual titration with the component agents.

Note: Geriatric patients may be more sensitive to the effects of the usual adult dose.

Auxiliary labeling: • Do not take other medicines without your doctor's advice.

HYDRALAZINE HYDROCHLORIDE AND HYDROCHLOROTHIAZIDE TABLETS

Usual adult dose: Antihypertensive—Oral, 1 tablet two times a day, as determined by individual titration with the component agents.

Note: Geriatric patients may be more sensitive to the effects of the usual adult dose.

Auxiliary labeling: • Do not take other medicines without your doctor's advice.

HYDROXYCHLOROQUINE   Systemic

A commonly used *brand name* in the U.S. and Canada is *Plaquenil*.

ORAL
Hydroxychloroquine Sulfate Tablets USP
   In the U.S. and Canada—*Plaquenil*

Category: Antiprotozoal; antirheumatic (disease-modifying); lupus erythematosus suppressant; antihypercalcemic; polymorphous light eruption suppressant; porphyria cutanea tarda suppressant.

Indications

Note: Bracketed information in the *Indications* section refers to uses not included in U.S. product labeling.

Accepted
Malaria (prophylaxis and treatment)—Hydroxychloroquine is indicated in the suppressive treatment and the treatment of acute attacks of malaria caused by *Plasmodium vivax, P. malariae, P. ovale,* and susceptible strains of *P. falciparum*. The radical cure of *P. vivax* and *P. ovale* malaria requires the concurrent or subsequent administration of primaquine.

Arthritis, rheumatoid (treatment)—Hydroxychloroquine is indicated in the treatment of acute and chronic rheumatoid arthritis in patients who do not respond adequately to other less toxic antirheumatics. [It may be used in addition to nonsteroidal anti-inflammatory agents.]

Lupus erythematosus, discoid (treatment); or
Lupus erythematosus, systemic (treatment)—Hydroxychloroquine is indicated as a suppressant for chronic discoid and systemic lupus erythematosus.

[Arthritis, juvenile (treatment)][1]—Hydroxychloroquine is used in the treatment of juvenile arthritis.

[Hypercalcemia, sarcoid-associated (treatment)][1]—Hydroxychloroquine is used to reduce urinary calcium excretion and the levels of 1,25-dihydroxyvitamin D in the serum of sarcoid patients who are unable to take corticosteroids.

[Polymorphous light eruption (treatment)][1]—Hydroxychloroquine is used as a suppressant for polymorphous light eruption.

[Porphyria cutanea tarda (treatment)][1]—Hydroxychloroquine is used in the treatment of porphyria cutanea tarda.

[Urticaria, solar (treatment)][1]; or
[Vasculitis, chronic cutaneous (treatment)][1]—Hydroxychloroquine is used in the treatment of solar urticaria and chronic cutaneous vasculitis unresponsive to other therapy.

Chloroquine-resistant strains of *P. falciparum*, originally seen only in Southeast Asia and South America, are now documented in all malarious areas except Central America west of the Canal Zone, the Middle East, and the Caribbean. Chloroquine is still the drug of choice for the treatment of susceptible strains of *P. falciparum* and the other 3 malarial species; however, chloroquine-resistant *P. vivax* has recently been reported.

Unaccepted
Hydroxychloroquine does not prevent relapses in patients with *P. vivax* or *P. ovale* malaria since it is not effective against exo-erythrocytic forms of the parasite. In these species, "hypnozoites," which remain dormant in the liver, are responsible for relapses.

---

[1]Not included in Canadian product labeling

Pharmacology

Note: Because hydroxychloroquine concentrates in the cellular fraction of blood, hydroxychloroquine concentrations measured in the blood are higher than those measured in the plasma.

Mechanism of action/Effect:
   Antiprotozoal—Malaria: Unknown, but may be based on ability of hydroxychloroquine to bind to and alter the properties of DNA. Also has been found to be taken up into the acidic food vacuoles of the parasite in the erythrocyte. This increases the pH of the acid vesicles, interfering with vesicle functions and possibly inhibiting phospholipid metabolism. In suppressive treatment, hydroxychloroquine inhibits the erythrocytic stage of development of plasmodia. In acute attacks of malaria, it interrupts erythrocytic schizogony of the parasite. Its ability to concentrate in parasitized erythrocytes may account for their selective toxicity against the erythrocytic stages of plasmodial infection.

   Antirheumatic—Hydroxychloroquine is thought to act as a mild immunosuppressant, inhibiting the production of rheumatoid factor and acute phase reactants. It also accumulates in white blood cells, stabilizing lysosomal membranes and inhibiting the activity of many enzymes, including collagenase and the proteases that cause cartilage breakdown.

Precautions to Consider

Cross-sensitivity and/or related problems
Patients hypersensitive to chloroquine, a 4-aminoquinoline compound structurally similar to hydroxychloroquine, may also be hypersensitive to hydroxychloroquine.

Geriatrics

No information is available on the relationship of age to the effects of hydroxychloroquine in geriatric patients.

Drug interactions and/or related problems

The following drug interactions and/or related problems have been selected on the basis of their potential clinical significance (possible mechanism in parentheses where appropriate)—not necessarily inclusive:

Note: Combinations containing any of the following medications, depending on the amount present, may also interact with this medication.

Penicillamine

(concurrent use of penicillamine with hydroxychloroquine may increase penicillamine plasma concentrations, increasing the potential for serious hematologic and/or renal adverse reactions, as well as the possibility of severe skin reactions)

Contraindications/Medical problems

The contraindications/medical problems included have been selected on the basis of their potential clinical significance (reasons given in parentheses where appropriate)—not necessarily inclusive (» = major clinical significance).

Risk-benefit should be considered when the following medical problems exist:

» Blood disorders, severe

(hydroxychloroquine may cause blood dyscrasias, including agranulocytosis, aplastic anemia, neutropenia, or thrombocytopenia)

Gastrointestinal disorders, severe

(hydroxychloroquine may cause gastrointestinal irritation)

Glucose-6-phosphate dehydrogenase (G6PD) deficiency

(hydroxychloroquine may cause hemolytic anemia in G6PD-deficient patients, although this is unlikely when hydroxychloroquine is given in therapeutic doses)

» Hepatic function impairment

(because hydroxychloroquine is metabolized in the liver, hepatic function impairment may increase blood concentrations of hydroxychloroquine, increasing the risk of side effects)

Hypersensitivity to hydroxychloroquine or chloroquine

» Neurological disorders, severe

(hydroxychloroquine may cause polyneuritis, ototoxicity, seizures, or neuromyopathy)

Porphyria

(hydroxychloroquine may cause exacerbation of porphyria)

Psoriasis

(hydroxychloroquine may precipitate severe attacks of psoriasis)

» Retinal or visual field changes, presence of

(hydroxychloroquine may cause corneal opacities, keratopathy, or retinopathy)

Side/Adverse Effects

Note: Side/adverse effects of hydroxychloroquine are usually dose-related. When hydroxychloroquine is used for the short-term treatment of malaria or other parasitic diseases, side/adverse effects are usually mild and reversible. However, following prolonged use and/or high-dose therapy such as in the treatment of rheumatoid arthritis, lupus erythematosus, or polymorphous light eruption, side/adverse effects may be serious and sometimes irreversible.

Irreversible retinal damage may be more likely to occur when the daily dosage equals or exceeds the equivalent of 310 mg (base), or 5 mg (base) per kg daily, of hydroxychloroquine.

The following side/adverse effects have been selected on the basis of their potential clinical significance (possible signs and symptoms in parentheses where appropriate)—not necessarily inclusive:

Those indicating need for medical attention

Incidence less frequent

Ocular toxicity specifically corneal opacities (blurred vision or any other change in vision), *keratopathy* (blurred vision or any other change in vision), *or retinopathy* (blurred vision or any other change in vision)

Incidence rare

Blood dyscrasias, specifically agranulocytosis (sore throat and fever), *aplastic anemia* (fatigue, weakness), *neutropenia* (sore throat and fever), *thrombocytopenia* (unusual bleeding or bruising); *emotional changes or psychosis* (mood or other mental changes); *neuromyopathy* (increased muscle weakness); *ototoxicity* (any loss of hearing, ringing or buzzing in ears)—usually in patients with pre-existing auditory damage; *seizures*

Symptoms of overdose

Cardiovascular toxicities, specifically conduction disturbances or hypotension; neurotoxicity, specifically drowsiness, headache, hyperexcitability, seizures, or coma; respiratory and cardiac arrest; visual disturbances (blurred vision)

Those indicating need for medical attention only if they continue or are bothersome

Incidence more frequent

Ciliary muscle dysfunction (difficulty in reading); *gastrointestinal irritation* (diarrhea, loss of appetite, nausea, stomach cramps or pain, vomiting); *headache*; *itching* (especially in black patients)—not an indication for discontinuation of therapy in black patients

Incidence less frequent

Bleaching of hair or increased hair loss; blue-black discoloration of skin, fingernails, or inside of mouth; dizziness or lightheadedness; nervousness or restlessness; skin rash or itching

Those indicating possible retinal changes, visual disturbances and the need for medical attention if they occur or progress after medication is discontinued

Blurred vision or any other change in vision

Patient Consultation

In providing consultation, consider emphasizing the following selected information (» = major clinical significance):

Before using this medication

» Conditions affecting use, especially:

Hypersensitivity to hydroxychloroquine or chloroquine

Pregnancy—May cause toxicity to the fetus when given to mother in therapeutic doses; however, hydroxychloroquine has not been shown to cause adverse effects in the fetus when used as a prophylactic agent against malaria

Use in children—Infants and children are especially sensitive to effects of hydroxychloroquine

Other medical problems, especially impaired hepatic function, severe blood disorders, severe neurologic disorders, or presence of retinal or visual field changes

Proper use of this medication

» Taking with meals or milk to minimize possible gastrointestinal irritation

» Keeping medication out of reach of children; fatalities reported with as few as 3 or 4 tablets (250-mg strength) of chloroquine phosphate; hydroxychloroquine is assumed to be equally toxic

» Importance of not taking more medication than the amount prescribed

» Compliance with full course of therapy

» Importance of not missing doses and taking medication on regular schedule

Missed dose: Taking as soon as possible; not taking if almost time for next dose; not doubling doses
» Proper storage

For prevention of malaria
Starting medication 1 to 2 weeks before entering malarious area to ascertain patient response and allow time to substitute another medication if reactions occur
» Continuing medication while staying in area and for 4 to 6 weeks after leaving area; checking with physician immediately if fever develops while traveling or within 2 months after departure from endemic area

For arthritis and lupus erythematosus
Importance of taking medication on regular schedule
May require up to 6 months for full benefit

For patients unable to swallow hydroxychloroquine tablets
Crushing tablets and putting each dose in capsules; contents of capsules may be mixed with jam, jelly, or jello

Precautions while using this medication
» Regular visits to physician to check for blood problems, muscle weakness, and ophthalmologic examinations during or after long-term therapy
Checking with physician if no improvement within a few days (or a few weeks or months for arthritis)
» Caution if blurred vision, difficulty in reading, other change in vision, dizziness, or lightheadedness occurs
Mosquito-control measures to reduce the chance of getting malaria:
Sleeping under mosquito netting
Wearing long-sleeved shirts or blouses and long trousers to protect arms and legs between dusk and dawn
Applying mosquito repellent to uncovered areas of skin between dusk and dawn

Side/adverse effects
Signs of potential side effects, especially ocular toxicity, neuro-myopathy, emotional or psychological changes, ototoxicity, seizures, and blood dyscrasias

General Dosing Information

Long-term and/or high-dosage therapy may cause irreversible retinal damage and/or neurosensorial deafness.

Hydroxychloroquine should be discontinued if any of the following problems occur: any abnormality in visual acuity, visual fields, retinal macular changes, or any visual symptoms; muscle weakness; or severe blood disorders.

Malaria-suppressive therapy should be started 1 to 2 weeks before the patient enters a malarious area and should be continued for 4 to 6 weeks after patient leaves the area. Starting the medication in advance will help to determine the patient's tolerance to the medication and allow time to substitute other antimalarials if the patient develops allergies to the medication or develops other adverse effects.

Hydroxychloroquine should be taken with meals or milk to minimize the possibility of gastrointestinal irritation.

Corticosteroids and/or nonsteroidal anti-inflammatory analgesics (including salicylates) may be given concurrently with hydroxychloroquine in the treatment of rheumatoid arthritis. These medications can usually be reduced gradually in dosage or discontinued after hydroxychloroquine has been given for several weeks.

When hydroxychloroquine is used in the treatment of rheumatoid arthritis, several months of therapy may be required for it to reach its maximum effectiveness. If improvement (such as reduced joint swelling and increased mobility) does not occur within 6 months, the medication should be discontinued.

Oral Dosage Forms

Note: Bracketed uses in the *Dosage Forms* section refer to categories of use and/or indications that are not included in U.S. product labeling.

HYDROXYCHLOROQUINE SULFATE TABLETS USP

Usual adult and adolescent dose:
Antiprotozoal—Malaria:
Suppressive—Oral, 400 mg (310 mg base) once every seven days.
Therapeutic—Oral, 800 mg (620 mg base) as a single dose; or 800 mg (620 mg base) initially, followed by 400 mg (310 mg base) in six to eight hours, and 400 mg (310 mg base) once a day on the second and third days.
Antirheumatic (disease-modifying)—Oral, up to 6.5 mg (5 mg base) per kg of lean body weight daily, with meals or a glass of milk.
Note: In a small number of patients who experience side effects with the usual initial dose in the treatment of rheumatoid arthritis, a temporary reduction in the initial dose of hydroxychloroquine may be required. After five to ten days the dose may be gradually increased until the desired response is obtained.

If relapse occurs after withdrawal of hydroxychloroquine, therapy may be resumed or continued on an intermittent schedule if there are no ocular contraindications.

Lupus erythematosus suppressant—Oral, up to 6.5 mg (5 mg base) per kg of lean body weight daily.
[Polymorphous light eruption suppressant][1]—Oral, 200 mg (155 mg base) two or three times a day.

Auxiliary labeling:
• Continue medicine for full time of treatment.
• Keep out of reach of children.
• Take with food or milk.
• May cause dizziness.

---

[1]Not included in Canadian product labeling.

HYDROXYUREA　Systemic

A commonly used *brand name* in the U.S. and Canada is *Hydrea*.

ORAL
Hydroxyurea Capsules USP
　In the U.S. and Canada—*Hydrea*

Category: Antineoplastic.

Indications

Note:　Bracketed information in the *Indications* section refers to uses not included in U.S. product labeling.

Accepted
Carcinoma, head and neck (treatment);
Carcinoma, ovarian (treatment); or
[Carcinoma, cervical (treatment)][1]—Hydroxyurea is indicated, in combination with radiation therapy, for local control of primary squamous cell (epidermoid) carcinomas of the head and neck, excluding the lip. Hydroxyurea is also indicated for treatment of recurrent, metastatic, or inoperable carcinoma of the ovary, and is used for treatment of advanced prostatic carcinoma.

Leukemia, chronic myelocytic (treatment)—Hydroxyurea is indicated for treatment of resistant chronic myelocytic leukemia.

Melanoma, malignant (treatment)—Hydroxyurea is indicated for treatment of melanoma.

[Polycythemia vera (treatment)][1]—Hydroxyurea is used for treatment of polycythemia vera.

---

[1]Not included in Canadian product labeling.

Pharmacology

Mechanism of action/Effect: Hydroxyurea is classified as an antimetabolite. Hydroxyurea is thought to be cell cycle-specific for the S phase of cell division. The exact mechanism of antineoplastic activity is unknown but is thought to involve interference with synthesis of DNA, with no effect on synthesis of RNA or protein.

Precautions to Consider

Cross-sensitivity and/or related problems
Patients sensitive to tartrazine may be sensitive to the capsule dosage form available in Canada also, since the capsules may contain tartrazine.

Geriatrics
Although appropriate studies on the relationship of age to the effects of hydroxyurea have not been performed in the geriatric population, the elderly may be more sensitive to effects of hydroxyurea. In addition, elderly patients are more likely to have age-related renal function impairment, which may require reduction of dosage in patients receiving hydroxyurea.

Dental
The bone marrow depressant effects of hydroxyurea may result in an increased incidence of microbial infection, delayed healing, and gingival bleeding. Dental work, whenever possible, should be completed prior to initiation of therapy or deferred until blood counts have returned to normal. Patients should be instructed in proper oral hygiene during treatment, including caution in use of regular toothbrushes, dental floss, and toothpicks.

Hydroxyurea may also cause stomatitis associated with considerable discomfort.

Drug interactions and/or related problems
The following drug interactions and/or related problems have been selected on the basis of their potential clinical significance (possible mechanism in parentheses where appropriate)—not necessarily inclusive (» = major clinical significance):

Allopurinol or
Colchicine or
» Probenecid or
» Sulfinpyrazone
　(hydroxyurea may raise the concentration of blood uric acid; dosage adjustment of antigout agents may be necessary to control hyperuricemia and gout; allopurinol may be preferred to prevent or reverse hydroxyurea-induced hyperuricemia because of risk of uric acid nephropathy with uricosuric antigout agents)

Blood dyscrasia-causing medications
　(leukopenic and/or thrombocytopenic effects of hydroxyurea may be increased with concurrent or recent therapy if these medications cause the same effects; dosage adjustment of hydroxyurea, if necessary, should be based on blood counts)

» Bone marrow depressants, other or
Radiation therapy
　(additive bone marrow depression may occur; dosage reduction may be required when two or more bone marrow depressants, including radiation, are used concurrently or consecutively)

Vaccines, killed virus
　(because normal defense mechanisms may be suppressed by hydroxyurea therapy, the patient's antibody response to the vaccine may be decreased. The interval between discontinuation of medications that cause immunosuppression and restoration of the patient's ability to respond to the vaccine depends on the intensity and type of immunosuppression-causing medications used, the underlying disease, and other factors; estimates vary from 3 months to 1 year)

» Vaccines, live virus
　(because normal defense mechanisms may be suppressed by hydroxyurea therapy, concurrent use with a live virus vaccine may potentiate the replication of the vaccine virus, may increase the side/adverse effects of the vaccine virus, and/or may decrease the patient's antibody response to the vaccine; immunization of these patients should be undertaken only with extreme caution after careful review of the patient's hematologic status and only with the knowledge and consent of the physician managing the hydroxyurea therapy. The interval between discontinuation of medications that cause immunosuppression and restoration of the patient's ability to respond to the vaccine depends on the intensity and type of immunosuppression-causing medications used, the underlying disease, and other factors; estimates vary from 3 months to 1 year. Patients with leukemia in remission should not receive live virus vaccine until at least 3 months after their last chemotherapy. Immunization with oral poliovirus vaccine should also be postponed in persons in close contact with the patient, especially family members)

Contraindications/Medical problems
The contraindications/medical problems included have been selected on the basis of their potential clinical significance (reasons given in parentheses where appropriate)—not necessarily inclusive (» = major clinical significance).

Risk-benefit should be considered when the following medical problems exist:
» Anemia
　(if severe, must be corrected with whole blood replacement before initiation of hydroxyurea therapy)

» Bone marrow depression
» Chickenpox, existing or recent (including recent exposure), or
» Herpes zoster
      (risk of severe generalized disease)
    Gout, history of, or
    Urate renal stones, history of
      (risk of hyperuricemia)
» Infection
» Renal function impairment
      (reduced elimination; lower dosage is recommended)
    Sensitivity to hydroxyurea
» Caution should be used in patients who have had previous cyto-
    toxic drug therapy and radiation therapy.

Side/Adverse Effects

Note: Many "side effects" of antineoplastic therapy are unavoidable
    and represent the medication's pharmacologic action. Some of
    these (for example, leukopenia and thrombocytopenia) are ac-
    tually used as parameters to aid in individual dosage titration.

    Administration of hydroxyurea to patients with severe renal
    function impairment may produce visual and auditory halluci-
    nations and pronounced hematologic toxicity.

    Skin changes resembling atrophic lichen planus, including atro-
    phy, brittle nails, darkening or redness of skin, and skin ulcers,
    have been reported rarely in patients receiving prolonged (over
    several years) daily treatment with hydroxyurea.

The following side/adverse effects have been selected on the basis of
    their potential clinical significance (possible signs and symptoms
    in parentheses where appropriate)—not necessarily inclusive:

Those indicating need for medical attention
Incidence more frequent
    Anemia or erythrocytic abnormalities; leukopenia (usually asymp-
    tomatic; less frequently, fever or chills, cough or hoarseness, lower
    back or side pain, painful or difficult urination)

    Note: Self-limiting *megaloblastic erythropoiesis* occurs commonly
        early in the course of therapy; morphologic changes re-
        semble pernicious anemia, but are not related to vitamin B_{12}
        or folic acid deficiency. Plasma iron clearance may be de-
        layed and rate of iron utilization by erythrocytes reduced,
        but hydroxyurea does not appear to alter red blood cell
        survival time.

        Onset of *leukopoenia* occurs about 10 days after initiation
        of therapy.

Incidence less frequent
    Stomatitis (sores in mouth and on lips); *thrombocytopenia* (usu-
    ally asymptomatic; rarely, unusual bleeding or bruising; black,
    tarry stools; blood in urine or stools; pinpoint red spots on skin)

Incidence rare
    Hyperuricemia or uric acid nephropathy (joint pain, lower back
    or side pain, swelling of feet or lower legs); *neurotoxicity or
    cerebral metastatic disease* (confusion, convulsions, dizziness, hal-
    lucinations, headache); *renal function impairment*

    Note: *Hyperuricemia* or *uric acid nephropathy* occur most com-
        monly during initial treatment of patients with leukemia or
        lymphoma, as a result of rapid cell breakdown, which leads
        to elevated serum uric acid concentrations.

Those indicating need for medical attention only if they continue or are bothersome
Incidence more frequent—dose-related
    Diarrhea; drowsiness—large doses; *loss of appetite; nausea or
    vomiting*

Incidence less frequent
    Constipation; exacerbation of postirradiation erythema (redness
    of skin); *skin rash and itching*

Those indicating the need for medical attention if they occur after medication is discontinued
    Bone marrow depression (black, tarry stools; blood in urine; cough
    or hoarseness; fever or chills; lower back or side pain; painful or
    difficult urination; pinpoint red spots on skin; unusual bleeding or
    bruising)

Patient Consultation

In providing consultation, consider emphasizing the following selected information (» = major clinical significance):

Before using this medication
» Conditions affecting use, especially:
        Sensitivity to hydroxyurea
        Pregnancy—Use not recommended because of mutagenic, ter-
        atogenic, and carcinogenic potential; advisability of using
        contraception; telling physician immediately if pregnancy
        is suspected
        Breast-feeding—Not recommended because of risk of serious
        side effects
        Use in children—Children may be more sensitive to effects
        Use in the elderly—Elderly patients may be more sensitive to
        effects
        Other medications, especially probenecid, sulfinpyrazone, other
        bone marrow depressants, or previous cytotoxic drug or
        radiation therapy
        Other medical problems, especially chickenpox, herpes zoster,
        anemia, infection, or renal function impairment

Proper use of this medication
» Importance of not taking more or less medication than the amount
    prescribed
    For patients who cannot swallow capsules: Contents of capsules
        may be emptied into glass of water and taken immediately;
        some inert material may not dissolve and may float on surface
    Caution in taking combination chemotherapy; taking each medica-
        tion at the right time
    Importance of ample fluid intake and subsequent increase in urine
        output to aid in excretion of uric acid
» Frequency of nausea, vomiting, and diarrhea; importance of con-
    tinuing medication despite stomach upset
    Checking with physician if vomiting occurs shortly after dose is
        taken
    Missed dose: Not taking at all; not doubling doses
» Proper storage

Precautions while using this medication
» Importance of close monitoring by the physician
» Avoiding immunizations unless approved by physician; other per-
    sons in patient's household should avoid immunizations with
    oral poliovirus vaccine; avoiding other persons who have taken
    oral poliovirus vaccine or wearing a protective mask that cov-
    ers nose and mouth
    Caution if bone marrow depression occurs:
» Avoiding exposure to persons with bacterial infections, espe-
    cially during period of low blood counts; checking with
    physician immediately if fever or chills, cough or hoarse-
    ness, lower back or side pain, or painful or difficult urina-
    tion occur
» Checking with physician immediately if unusual bleeding or
    bruising; black, tarry stools; blood in urine; or pinpoint red
    spots on skin occur

Caution in use of regular toothbrush, dental floss, or toothpick; physician, dentist, or nurse may suggest alternatives; checking with physician before having dental work done

Not touching eyes or inside of nose unless hands washed immediately before

Using caution to avoid accidental cuts with use of sharp objects such as safety razor or fingernail or toenail cutters

Avoiding contact sports or other situations where bruising or injury could occur

Side/adverse effects

May cause adverse effects such as blood problems and cancer; importance of discussing possible effects with physician

Signs of potential side effects, especially leukopenia, stomatitis, thrombocytopenia, neurotoxicity, cerebral metastatic disease, hyperuricemia, and uric acid nephropathy

Physician or nurse can help in dealing with side effects

General Dosing Information

Patients receiving hydroxyurea should be under supervision of a physician experienced in antimetabolite chemotherapy.

Dosage must be adjusted to meet the individual requirements of each patient, based on clinical response and appearance or severity of toxicity.

Dosage reduction may be necessary in children and in the elderly, who may be more sensitive to effects of the drug.

If the patient is unable to swallow capsules, the contents of the capsule may be emptied into a glass of water (some inert material may float on the surface) and taken immediately.

Development of uric acid nephropathy in patients with leukemia or lymphoma may be prevented by adequate oral hydration and, in some cases, administration of allopurinol. Alkalinization of urine may be necessary if serum uric acid concentrations are elevated.

If there is no clinical response after 6 weeks of therapy, the medication should be discontinued; if a response occurs, the medication may be continued indefinitely.

Combination therapy with radiation may be associated with more frequent and severe side effects of the radiation, including gastric distress and inflammation of mucous membranes at the irradiated site. Severe reactions may require temporary withdrawal of hydroxyurea therapy.

It is recommended that hydroxyurea therapy be temporarily withdrawn if marked leukopenia (particularly granulocytopenia) or thrombocytopenia occurs. Therapy may be resumed if, after 3 days, the counts rise significantly towards normal values; counts usually return to normal within 10 to 30 days after discontinuation of hydroxyurea. If anemia occurs, it may be corrected with whole blood replacement, without interruption of hydroxyurea therapy.

Special precautions are recommended in patients who develop thrombocytopenia as a result of administration of hydroxyurea. These may include extreme care in performing invasive procedures; regular inspection of intravenous sites, skin (including perirectal area), and mucous membrane surfaces for signs of bleeding or bruising; limiting frequency of venipuncture and avoiding intramuscular injections; testing urine, emesis, stool, and secretions for occult blood; care in use of regular toothbrushes, dental floss, toothpicks, safety razors, and fingernail and toenail cutters; avoiding constipation; and using caution to prevent falls and other injuries. Such patients should avoid alcohol and any aspirin intake because of the risk of gastrointestinal bleeding. Platelet transfusions may be required.

Patients who develop leukopenia should be observed carefully for signs of infection. Antibiotic support may be required. In neutropenic patients who develop fever, broad-spectrum antibiotic coverage should be initiated empirically, pending bacterial cultures and appropriate diagnostic tests.

Oral Dosage Forms

HYDROXYUREA CAPSULES USP

Usual adult dose:

Carcinoma, head and neck; or

Carcinoma, ovarian; or

Melanoma, malignant—Oral, 60 to 80 mg per kg of body weight or 2000 to 3000 mg per square meter of body surface in a single dose every third day, alone or in combination with radiation therapy, or 20 to 30 mg per kg of body weight per day in a single dose.

Note: Administration of hydroxyurea should begin at least seven days prior to initiation of radiation therapy, and should be continued during radiation therapy and indefinitely afterwards.

Leukemia, chronic myelocytic, resistant—Oral, 20 to 30 mg per kg of body weight a day in a single dose or two divided daily doses.

Note: Although dosages are based on the patient's actual weight, use of estimated lean body mass (dry weight) is recommended in obese patients or those with abnormal fluid retention.

In general, use of intermittent dosage is associated with less risk of serious toxicity than continuous daily dosage.

Auxiliary labeling: • Keep container tightly closed.

INDAPAMIDE   Systemic

Some commonly used *brand names* are:

In the U.S.—*Lozol*
In Canada—*Lozide*

ORAL
Indapamide Tablets
In the U.S.—*Lozol*
In Canada—*Lozide*

Category: Antihypertensive; diuretic.

Indications

Accepted
Hypertension (treatment)—Indapamide is indicated, alone or in combination with other agents, for treatment of hypertension.

In the 1988 Report of the Joint National Committee on Detection, Evaluation, and Treatment of High Blood Pressure, a progression in choice of treatments for essential hypertension is recommended:

Nonpharmacologic management (especially sodium restriction, weight reduction and exercise, and moderation of alcohol consumption) is recommended first for some patients, including those with mild hypertension, and is recommended as an adjunct to all pharmacologic hypertensive therapy.

Initial drug therapy usually consists of a diuretic, beta-adrenergic blocking agent, calcium channel blocking agent, or angiotensin-converting enzyme (ACE) inhibitor. If adequate blood pressure control is not achieved and the patient is adherent to the treatment program and not experiencing significant side effects, dosage of the drug may be increased, a drug from another one of these initial classes may be added or substituted, or a second drug from a different class—centrally acting alpha-adrenergic agonists (e.g., clonidine, guanabenz, guanfacine, methyldopa), peripheral-acting adrenergic antagonists (e.g., guanadrel, guanethidine, rauwolfia alkaloids), post-synaptic alpha-1 peripheral adrenergic blocking agents (e.g., doxazosin, prazosin, terazosin), or vasodilators (e.g., hydralazine, minoxidil)—may be added or substituted.

If necessary, a drug from another class in the second group may be substituted or added as a third drug. If blood pressure control is still not achieved, a drug from still another class may be substituted or added as a fourth drug, or the patient may need further evaluation and/or referral.

Indapamide is effective in treating hypertension in patients with renal function impairment, although its diuretic effect is reduced.

Edema (treatment)—Indapamide is indicated for treatment of salt and fluid retention associated with congestive heart failure.

Pharmacology

Mechanism of action/Effect:
Antihypertensive—Not clearly understood, but may involve both renal and extrarenal effects. The diuretic effect (reduction of extracellular fluid and blood volume) probably contributes only minimally since indapamide decreases blood pressure at a dose well below the effective diuretic dose. The antihypertensive effect is thought to be the result of reduction in peripheral vascular resistance.
Diuretic—Indapamide inhibits reabsorption of water and electrolytes, primarily as a result of action on the cortical diluting segment of the distal tubule.

Onset of action: Antihypertensive—Multiple dose: 1 to 2 weeks.

Time to peak effect: Antihypertensive—
Single dose: Approximately 24 hours.
Multiple doses: 8 to 12 weeks.

Duration of action: Antihypertensive—Multiple doses: Up to 8 weeks.

Precautions to Consider

Cross-sensitivity and/or related problems
Patients sensitive to other sulfonamide-type medications may be sensitive to indapamide also.

Geriatrics
Although appropriate studies on the relationship of age to the effects of indapamide have not been performed in the geriatric population, the elderly may be more sensitive to the hypotensive and electrolyte effects. In addition, elderly patients are more likely to have age-related renal function impairment, which may require caution in patients receiving indapamide.

Drug interactions and/or related problems
The following drug interactions and/or related problems have been selected on the basis of their potential clinical significance (possible mechanism in parentheses where appropriate)—not necessarily inclusive (» = major clinical significance):

Note: Combinations containing any of the following medications, depending on the amount present, may also interact with this medication.

Amiodarone
(concurrent use of indapamide with amiodarone may lead to an increased risk of arrhythmias associated with hypokalemia)

Anticoagulants, coumarin- or indandione-derivative
(effects may be decreased when these medications are used concurrently with indapamide, as a result of reduction of plasma volume leading to concentration of procoagulant factors in the blood; in addition, diuretic-induced improvement of hepatic congestion may lead to improved hepatic function resulting in increased procoagulant factor synthesis; dosage adjustments may be necessary)

» Digitalis glycosides
(concurrent use with indapamide may enhance the possibility of digitalis toxicity associated with hypokalemia)

Hypotension-producing medications, other
(antihypertensive and/or diuretic effects may be increased when these medications are used concurrently with indapamide; although some antihypertensive and/or diuretic combinations are used frequently for therapeutic advantage, dosage adjustment may be necessary during concurrent use)

» Lithium
(concurrent use with indapamide is not recommended, as it may provoke lithium toxicity because of reduced renal clearance; in addition, lithium has nephrotoxic effects)

Neuromuscular blocking agents, nondepolarizing
(indapamide may induce hypokalemia, which may enhance the blockade of nondepolarizing neuromuscular blocking agents; serum potassium determinations may be necessary prior to administration of nondepolarizing neuromuscular blocking agents; careful postoperative monitoring of the patient may be necessary following concurrent or sequential use, especially if there is a possibility of incomplete reversal of neuromuscular blockade)

Sympathomimetics
> (antihypertensive effects of indapamide may be reduced when it is used concurrently with sympathomimetics; the patient should be carefully monitored to confirm that the desired effect is being obtained)
>
> (indapamide may decrease arterial responsiveness to norepinephrine, but does not usually significantly interfere with its clinical effects)

Contraindications/Medical problems

The contraindications/medical problems included have been selected on the basis of their potential clinical significance (reasons given in parentheses where appropriate)—not necessarily inclusive (» = major clinical significance).

Risk-benefit should be considered when the following medical problems exist:

» Anuria or severe renal function impairment
> (diuretic effect reduced; may precipitate azotemia)

Diabetes mellitus
> (possible impaired glucose tolerance)

Gout, history of, or
Hyperuricemia
> (serum uric acid concentrations may be elevated)

Hepatic function impairment
> (risk of dehydration, which may precipitate hepatic coma and death)

Sensitivity to indapamide or other sulfonamide-type medications

Sympathectomy
> (antihypertensive effects may be enhanced)

Side/Adverse Effects

The following side/adverse effects have been selected on the basis of their potential clinical significance (possible signs and symptoms in parentheses where appropriate)—not necessarily inclusive:

Those indicating need for medical attention
Incidence rare
> *Allergic reaction* (skin rash, itching, or hives); *electrolyte imbalance, specifically hyponatremia* (dryness of mouth, increased thirst, unusual tiredness or weakness), *hypochloremic alkalosis, or hypokalemia* (irregular heartbeat, mood or mental changes, muscle cramps or pain, nausea or vomiting, weak pulse)
>
> Note: *Electrolyte imbalance* is dose-related (*hypokalemia* occurs fairly frequently) but is not usually symptomatic.

Those indicating need for medical attention only if they continue or are bothersome
Incidence less frequent or rare
> *Anorexia* (loss of appetite); *diarrhea; headache; orthostatic hypotension as a result of volume depletion* (dizziness or lightheadedness, especially when getting up from a lying or sitting position); *trouble in sleeping; stomach upset*

Patient Consultation

In providing consultation, consider emphasizing the following selected information (» = major clinical significance):

Before using this medication
» Conditions affecting use, especially:
> Sensitivity to indapamide or other sulfonamide-type medications
> Pregnancy—Routine use not recommended
> Use in the elderly—Increased sensitivity to hypotensive and electrolyte effects
> Use by athletes—Diuretics are banned and tested for by the U.S. Olympic Committee (USOC), the International Olympic Committee (IOC), and the National Collegiate Athletic Association (NCAA)

Other medications, especially digitalis glycosides or lithium
Other medical problems, especially anuria or severe renal function impairment

Proper use of this medication
Diuretic effects of the medication and timing of doses to minimize inconvenience of diuresis
Getting into habit of taking at same time each day to help increase compliance
Missed dose: Taking as soon as possible; not taking if almost time for next dose; not doubling doses
» Proper storage

For use as an antihypertensive
Possible need for control of weight and diet, especially sodium intake
» Patients may not experience symptoms of hypertension; importance of taking medication even if feeling well
» Does not cure but helps control hypertension; possible need for lifelong therapy; checking with physician before discontinuing therapy; serious consequences of untreated hypertension

Precautions while using this medication
Regular visits to physician to check progress
» Possibility of hypokalemia; possible need for additional potassium in diet; not changing diet without first checking with physician
To prevent dehydration, checking with physician if severe nausea, vomiting, or diarrhea occurs and continues

For use as an antihypertensive
» Not taking other medications, especially nonprescription sympathomimetics, unless discussed with physician

Side/adverse effects
Signs of potential side effects, especially allergic reaction and electrolyte imbalance

General Dosing Information

The lowest effective dosage should be utilized to minimize potential electrolyte imbalance.

When used to promote diuresis, a single daily dose is preferably taken on arising in order to minimize the effect of increased frequency of urination on sleep. Intermittent dosage schedules (drug-free days) may reduce the possibility of electrolyte imbalance or hyperuricemia resulting from therapy.

Concurrent administration of potassium supplements or potassium-sparing diuretics may be indicated in patients considered to be at higher risk for developing hypokalemia. Caution in administering potassium supplements is recommended, however, since loss of potassium is not clinically significant in most patients, and supplementation leads to a risk of development of hyperkalemia.

Recent evidence suggests that withdrawal of antihypertensive therapy prior to surgery is not necessary, but that the anesthesiologist must be aware of such therapy.

Oral Dosage Forms

INDAPAMIDE TABLETS

Usual adult dose: Diuretic—Oral, 2.5 mg once a day, adjusted according to response after one (for edema) to four (for hypertension) weeks up to 5 mg once a day.

Note: Geriatric patients may be more sensitive to the effects of the usual adult dose.

INSULIN   Systemic

Some commonly used *brand names* or other names are:

Humulin 70/30 [Isophane
   Insulin, Human, and
   Insulin Human
Humulin BR [Buffered
   Insulin Human]
Humulin L [Insulin Zinc,
   Human]
Humulin N [Isophane
   Insulin, Human]
Humulin R [Insulin Human]
Humulin U Ultralente
   [Extended Insulin Zinc,
   Human]
Insulatard NPH [Isophane
   Insulin]
Insulatard NPH Human
   [Isophane Insulin,
   Human]
Lente Iletin I [Insulin Zinc]
Lente Iletin II [Insulin Zinc]
Lente insulin [Insulin Zinc]
Lente Insulin [Insulin Zinc]
Mixtard [Isophane Insulin
   and Insulin]
Mixtard Human 70/30
   [Isophane Insulin,
   Human, and Insulin
   Human]
Novolin 70/30 [Isophane
   Insulin, Human, and
   Insulin Human]
Novolin L [Insulin Zinc,
   Human]
Novolin N [Isophane
   Insulin,Human]
Novolin R [Insulin Human]

NPH Iletin I [Isophane
   Insulin]
NPH Iletin II [Isophane
   Insulin]
NPH insulin [Isophane
   Insulin]
NPH Insulin [Isophane
   Insulin]
Protamine Zinc & Iletin I
   [Protamine Zinc Insulin]
Protamine Zinc & Iletin II
   [Protamine Zinc Insulin]
PZI insulin [Protamine
   Zinc Insulin]
Regular (Concentrated)
   Iletin II, U-500
   [Insulin]
Regular Iletin I [Insulin]
Regular Iletin II [Insulin]
Regular insulin [Insulin]
Regular Insulin [Insulin]
Semilente Iletin I [Prompt
   Insulin Zinc]
Semilente insulin [Prompt
   Insulin Zinc]
Semilente Insulin [Prompt
   Insulin Zinc]
Ultralente Iletin I
   [Extended Insulin Zinc]
Ultralente insulin
   [Extended Insulin Zinc]
Ultralente Insulin
   [Extended Insulin Zinc]
Velosulin [Insulin]
Velosulin Human [Insulin
   Human]

PARENTERAL

Insulin Injection USP [*Regular (Concentrated) Iletin II, U-500; Regular Iletin I; Regular Iletin II; Regular Insulin; Velosulin*]

Insulin Human Injection USP [*Humulin R; Novolin R; Velosulin Human*]

Buffered Insulin Human Injection [*Humulin BR*]

Isophane Insulin Suspension USP [*Insulatard NPH; NPH Iletin I; NPH Iletin II; NPH Insulin*]

Isophane Insulin, Human, Suspension [*Humulin N; Insulatard NPH Human; Novolin N*]

Isophane Insulin Suspension and Insulin Injection [*Mixtard*]

Isophane Insulin, Human, Suspension and Insulin Human Injection [*Humulin 70/30; Mixtard Human 70/30; Novolin 70/30*]

Insulin Zinc Suspension USP [*Lente Iletin I; Lente Iletin II; Lente Insulin*]

Insulin Zinc, Human, Suspension [*Humulin L; Novolin L*]

Extended Insulin Zinc Suspension USP [*Ultralente Iletin I; Ultralente Insulin*]

Extended Insulin Zinc, Human, Suspension [*Humulin U Ultralente*]

Prompt Insulin Zinc Suspension USP [*Semilente Iletin I; Semilente Insulin*]

Protamine Zinc Insulin Suspension USP [*Protamine Zinc & Iletin I; Protamine Zinc & Iletin II*]

Category: Antidiabetic.

Indications

Accepted

Diabetes mellitus, insulin-dependent (treatment)—Insulin is utilized as a replacement for the physiological production of endogenous insulin in patients with insulin-dependent diabetes (IDDM; Type I; ketosis-prone; brittle; or juvenile-onset diabetes).

Diabetes mellitus, non-insulin-dependent (treatment)—Insulin is utilized as a supplement to the physiological production of endogenous insulin in patients with non-insulin-dependent diabetes mellitus (NIDDM; Type II). Insulin is also indicated in otherwise stable non-insulin-dependent diabetics who develop significant acidosis, diabetic coma, fever, severe infection, ketoacidosis, or significant ketosis; experience severe burns, major surgery, or severe trauma; become pregnant; or cannot tolerate oral medications.

Insulin has been added to hyperalimentation solutions in order to facilitate glucose utilization in patients with poor glucose tolerance. However, the addition of insulin to an intravenous hyperalimentation process has been found to provide the patient with significantly less available insulin. A more efficient route of administration when insulin is required during hyperalimentation therapy is either by subcutaneous injection or by a separate intravenous line.

Use of insulin in conjunction with oral antidiabetic agents in the treatment of insulin-dependent diabetes mellitus (type I) is controversial. Many studies indicate that oral antidiabetic agents are not effective in the treatment of Type I diabetes mellitus.

Pharmacology

Mechanism of action/Effect: Insulin is a hormone that controls the storage and metabolism of carbohydrate, protein, and fats. Such activity occurs primarily in liver, muscle, and adipose tissues subsequent to attachment of insulin molecules to receptor sites on cellular plasma membranes. Although the mechanisms of molecular actions in the cellular area are still being explored, it is known that cell membrane transport characteristics, cellular growth, enzyme activation and inhibition, and alterations in protein and fat metabolism are all influenced by insulin.

Precautions to Consider

Cross-sensitivity and/or related problems

Patients intolerant of beef or pork insulins may use the alternative single-source insulin under the direction of their physician. Intolerance of beef insulin is more common than intolerance of pork insulin. Intolerance is often reduced by the use of purified pork insulin, biosynthetic human insulin, or semisynthetic human insulin.

Geriatrics

No geriatrics-specific information is available on the use of insulin in geriatric patients. However, geriatrics-specific problems that would limit the usefulness of this medication in geriatric patients are not expected.

Drug interactions and/or related problems

The following drug interactions and/or related problems have been selected on the basis of their potential clinical significance (possible mechanism in parentheses where appropriate)—not necessarily inclusive (» = major clinical significance):

Note: Combinations containing any of the following medications, depending on the amount present, may also interact with this medication.

» Adrenocorticoids, glucocorticoid, or
   Amphetamines or

Baclofen or
Contraceptives, oral, estrogen-containing, or
Corticotropin (ACTH) or
Danazol or
Dextrothyroxine or
Diuretics, thiazide or thiazide-related, or
Epinephrine or
Estrogens or
Ethacrynic acid or
Furosemide or
Glucagon or
Molindone or
Phenytoin or
Thyroid hormones or
Triamterene
  (these medications may increase blood glucose concentrations and enhance the possibility of hyperglycemia; dosage adjustment of these medications or insulin or both may be necessary)

» Alcohol or
Anabolic steroids or
Androgens or
Disopyramide or
Guanethidine or
Monoamine oxidase (MAO) inhibitors, including furazolidone, pargyline, and procarbazine, or
Salicylates, large doses
  (these medications may enhance the hypoglycemic effect of insulin; dosage adjustment of these medications or insulin or both may be necessary)

Antidiabetic agents, oral
  (hypoglycemic effect may be enhanced; although the combination has been used to treat a select group of diabetic patients whose condition is not well-controlled with either agent alone, many studies have shown there is generally no additional benefit from using oral agents for the treatment of Type I diabetes)

Anti-inflammatory analgesics, nonsteroidal (NSAIAs)
  (concurrent use with insulin may increase the hypoglycemic effect of insulin because prostaglandins are directly involved in regulatory mechanisms of glucose metabolism)

Appetite suppressants
  (blood glucose concentrations may be altered in patients with diabetes mellitus taking appetite suppressants and following the concurrent dietary regimen for the treatment of obesity; dosage adjustment of insulin may be necessary during and after therapy for obesity)

» Beta-adrenergic blocking agents
  (concurrent use with insulin may increase risk of hypoglycemia or hyperglycemia. Beta blockers, possibly including ophthalmic agents, may mask certain symptoms of developing hypoglycemia, such as increases in pulse rate and blood pressure, thus complicating patient monitoring. In addition, beta-blockers may prolong the period of hypoglycemia by blocking gluconeogenesis. Therefore, the insulin dosage may require adjustment in order to avoid hypoglycemia during concurrent use. Labetalol and selective or relatively selective beta-blockers, such as metoprolol or atenolol, usually cause fewer problems with blood glucose levels, especially when used in lower doses. However, they may still mask the symptoms)

Carbonic anhydrase inhibitors, especially acetazolamide
  (hypoglycemic response may be decreased during concurrent therapy because carbonic anhydrase inhibitors may cause hyperglycemia and glycosuria in diabetic patients; dosage adjustments may be necessary)

Diazoxide, parenteral
  (concurrent or consecutive use with insulin reverses the hyperglycemic effects of diazoxide; dosage adjustments of insulin may be necessary if diazoxide is administered to diabetic patients)

Nicotine chewing gum or
Smoking deterrents, other, such as lobeline sulfate and silver acetate, or
Smoking, tobacco, cessation of
  (cessation of smoking and concurrent therapy with nicotine chewing gum or other smoking deterrents may increase the therapeutic effects of insulin by increasing absorption of insulin, thereby increasing serum concentrations; dosage reduction of insulin may be necessary when an insulin-dependent diabetic patient suddenly stops smoking)

Contraindications/Medical problems
The contraindications/medical problems included have been selected on the basis of their potential clinical significance (reasons given in parentheses where appropriate)—not necessarily inclusive (» = major clinical significance).

Risk-benefit should be considered when the following medical problems exist:
» Fever, high, or
» Hyperthyroidism or
» Infections, severe, or
» Ketoacidosis, diabetic, or
» Trauma or surgery
  (insulin requirements may be increased)
» Diarrhea due to malabsorption or
Eating disorders or
Hepatic function impairment or
» Hypothyroidism or
» Nausea or vomiting or
» Renal function impairment
  (insulin requirements may be decreased)

Patient Consultation

Consider advising the patient on the following (» = major clinical significance):

Before using this medication
» Emphasis on diabetic meal plan
  See also *Precautions to Consider.*

Proper use of this medication
» Using correct insulin and syringe
  How insulin syringes are marked
» Proper preparation of medication; gently shaking, inverting, or rolling contents of insulin vial immediately before use; not shaking hard; not using if contents are lumpy or grainy or if they stick to bottle; not using regular insulin that is cloudy or discolored; drawing insulin into syringe
  Mixing types of insulin (only when directed by physician); always drawing in same order; if using regular insulin, drawing it first; knowing whether injection must be given right after mixing; if not using mixed insulins right after mixing, gently shaking or rolling syringe prior to use in order to remix
» Proper administration technique
» Carefully reading patient instruction sheet contained in insulin package
  Use of disposable syringes
  Use of glass syringe and metal needle
  Use of insulin infusion pump; always using clear and colorless insulin; not mixing buffered regular insulin with any other insulin; following pump manufacturer's directions on filling syringe or reservoir; checking tubing and infusion-site dressing frequently for improper infusion
» Compliance with therapy
  Storage and expiration date of insulin

Precautions while using this medication
» Regular visits to physician to check progress, especially during the first few weeks of treatment

» Carefully following special instructions of physician:
  Discussing use of alcohol with physician
  Carefully following diabetic meal plan
  Exercising as directed by physician
  Testing for acetone in urine
  Testing for blood glucose levels
  Carefully selecting and rotating injection sites, following physician's recommendations
» Not taking other medications unless discussed with physician
» Preparing for emergency
» Recognizing symptoms of hypoglycemia and knowing what to do if they occur:
  Anxious feeling
  Cold sweats
  Confusion
  Cool, pale skin
  Difficulty in concentration
  Drowsiness
  Excessive hunger
  Headache
  Nausea
  Nervousness
  Rapid pulse
  Shakiness
  Unusual tiredness or weakness
  Vision changes
  Knowing what to do if nausea, vomiting, or fever develops; continuing use of insulin even if patient cannot eat regular diet; checking with physician if vomiting is severe or if blood sugar levels are not controlled
» Recognizing symptoms of hyperglycemia and ketoacidosis:
  Drowsiness
  Dry mouth
  Flushed, dry skin
  Fruit-like breath odor
  Increased blood sugar concentration
  Increased urination
  Loss of appetite
  Stomach ache, nausea, or vomiting
  Tiredness
  Trouble in breathing (rapid and deep)
  Unusual thirst
» Suggestions when traveling

General Dosing Information

Adherence to a diet low in refined carbohydrates and fat and providing for a prescribed distribution of caloric intake in meals and snacks is the cornerstone of treatment of diabetes.

The dosage and administration of insulin can vary greatly and must therefore be determined for each individual patient by the attending physician. By matching the patient's specific insulin needs over a 24-hour period through the use of short-acting and longer-acting preparations, long-term complications of diabetes mellitus may be decreased.

Patients changing to different formulation types of insulin products should be informed of the possible need for dosage adjustment. Patients should be advised to consult their physician.

Insulin commercially available in the United States is a mixture of beef and pork insulins or is a single-source insulin, which is appropriately marked "beef," "pork," or "human insulin (biosynthetic or semisynthetic)" on the package label.

It is generally not recommended that patients who are well-controlled with animal insulins be automatically switched to human insulins. Human insulins may not offer any significant advantage over the highly purified pork insulins, with the exception of reduced antibody levels, which may be a consideration for some patients, especially children and young adults. Purified pork insulins or the human insulins may be particularly appropriate for non-insulin-dependent patients requiring intermittent or short-term insulin therapy (e.g., during pregnancy, surgery, infections, or total-parenteral-nutrition (TPN) therapy, and possibly during treatment for ketoacidosis); for patients with insulin resistance (using more than 100 to 200 units a day); for patients who experience allergic responses to the less purified animal insulins; or for patients who develop lipoatrophy.

Single-source beef and pork insulins should not be used interchangeably even when type and strength are equivalent, since there is a species difference that may require dosage adjustment.

Regular insulin (Insulin Injection USP and Insulin Human Injection USP) in the 40-Unit or 100-Unit concentration is the only insulin type suitable for intravenous administration. Buffered insulin human injection is the only insulin currently recommended for use in insulin pumps; the phosphate-buffered regular insulins are less likely to crystallize and block insulin pump catheters. Consult individual manufacturer's package inserts.

Dilution of insulin preparations generally should be avoided. However, some pediatric doses may be too small to accurately measure; also, low-dose insulin pump infusions must occasionally be diluted to avoid crystallization of insulin in the catheters. In these rare cases, dilution should be performed aseptically in a laminar flow hood with diluents and mixing vials provided or recommended by the manufacturer. The differences in strength, dosage volume, and expiration date should be clearly labeled by the pharmacist and emphasized to the patient. If insulin needs to be diluted during an emergency and the diluents are not readily available, normal saline injection without preservative may be used for dilution of small insulin doses; however, these solutions are not stable and should be used promptly. Stinging or burning at the site of injection may also occur due to a lower pH of these solutions.

Different types of insulin are sometimes mixed in the syringe in proportions ordered by the physician in order to achieve a more accurate matching of insulin availability to the patient's requirements in a single dose. If insulins are to be mixed, several factors should be considered:

• Each patient should always follow the same sequence of mixing the separate insulin preparations. As a general rule, regular insulin should be drawn first to avoid contamination and clouding of the vial of regular insulin by the other insulin. A mixture of regular insulin and another insulin will have a greater duration of action than that of regular insulin.

• When regular insulin is mixed with NPH or lente insulin, some loss of the characteristics of the individual insulins may occur. The binding of regular insulin by the protamine in NPH (unless the NPH insulin contains no excess of protamine) or by the zinc in lente insulin may result in a loss of free (active) regular insulin. Depending on the specific brand of insulins used, it is generally recommended that the resulting mixture be used immediately after mixing or within 5 minutes of mixing, unless the manufacturer's literature states that mixtures involving its particular brand are stable for longer periods of time. Insulins premixed by the manufacturer are stable until the date stamped on the vial.

• Mixtures of regular insulin and insulin zinc preparations may not give predictable clinical results. The excess zinc in the insulin zinc preparations may result in the formation of an extra zinc insulin complex. The extent of this complex formation depends on the brand of insulin used, the time between mixing and injection, and the temperature. In addition, the phosphate buffers used in certain regular insulin products may precipitate out the zinc in insulin zinc preparations. Therefore, if a short-acting and longer-acting mixture is needed, a mixture of regular insulin and NPH insulin is generally recommended instead of a mixture of regular insulin and an insulin zinc preparation unless the manufacturers of the brands involved have product-specific information that would support the use of such a mixture. If a regular insulin and insulin zinc mixture must be used, injection should be made immediately.

• Lente, semilente, and ultralente insulins may be mixed in any proportion without loss of the characteristics of the individual insulins. Such mixtures are stable for up to 18 months.

• Most brands of regular insulin may be mixed with protamine zinc insulin (PZI), but the excess free protamine content in the PZI combines with the regular insulin to give varying durations of action. In proportions of regular to PZI of less than 1:1, the duration approximates that of unmixed PZI insulin. In proportions of regular to PZI of almost 2:1 the duration approximates that of unmixed NPH insulin. In proportions of regular insulin to PZI of more than 2:1, the activity is much like a mixture of regular insulin and NPH insulin. It must be kept in mind that certain brands of regular insulin, because of their phosphate buffering, will precipitate out the zinc in protamine zinc insulin. Consult the manufacturer's literature.

The patient should always use only one brand or type of syringe. Before changing brands or syringe types, the physician should be consulted. Among different brands or syringe types, the unmeasured volume between needle point and bottom calibration on the syringe barrel ("dead space") may differ enough to cause improper dosage.

The use of a disposable syringe and needle to administer more than one injection is controversial. Although USP medical advisory panels do not recommend this practice, it must be recognized that some patients reuse disposable syringes and needles because of economic constraints. Where this is occurring, it must be emphasized that the syringe and needle be used only for that particular patient, the needle should be wiped with alcohol and the cap replaced after each use, and the syringe and needle should be reused only for a limited number of injections. Disposable syringes and needles should not be reused on a continuing basis.

The bottle of insulin must not be shaken hard before using. Frothing or bubbles can cause an incorrect dose. Contents are mixed well by rolling the bottle slowly between the palms of the hands or by gently tipping the bottle over a few times. Insulin should not be used if it looks lumpy or grainy, or sticks to the bottle. Do not use a regular insulin if it becomes viscous or cloudy; use only if it is clear and colorless.

Parenteral Dosage Forms

INSULIN INJECTION USP (REGULAR INSULIN, CRYSTALLINE ZINC INSULIN)

Usual adult dose:
  Diabetic hyperglycemia—Subcutaneous, as directed by physician, fifteen to thirty minutes before meals up to three or four times a day.
  Diabetic ketoacidosis—Intravenous, approximately 0.1 USP Units per kg of body weight per hour, administered by continuous infusion.
Note: The rate of insulin infusion should be decreased when the plasma glucose concentration reaches 250 mg per dL.
  Large single intravenous doses are not recommended because of the short blood half-life of insulin.
  Treatment requires physician attention and includes fluid and electrolyte replacement in addition to insulin.
  Patients in diabetic coma with ketoacidosis or in nonketotic hyperosmolar coma must be hospitalized as soon as possible.

Auxiliary labeling:
  • Refrigerate.
  • Do not freeze.

INSULIN HUMAN INJECTION USP (REGULAR INSULIN HUMAN)

Usual adult dose: See *Insulin Injection USP.*

Auxiliary labeling:
  • Refrigerate.
  • Do not freeze.

BUFFERED INSULIN HUMAN INJECTION

Usual adult dose: See *Insulin Injection USP.*

Auxiliary labeling:
  • Refrigerate.
  • Do not freeze.
  • Use in insulin pump only.

ISOPHANE INSULIN SUSPENSION USP (NPH INSULIN)

Usual adult dose: Subcutaneous, as directed by physician, once a day, thirty to sixty minutes before breakfast. An additional dose is often necessary about thirty minutes before a meal or at bedtime.

Auxiliary labeling:
  • Shake gently.
  • Refrigerate.
  • Do not freeze.

ISOPHANE INSULIN, HUMAN, SUSPENSION

Usual adult dose: See *Isophane Insulin Suspension USP.*

Auxiliary labeling:
  • Shake gently.
  • Refrigerate.
  • Do not freeze.

ISOPHANE INSULIN SUSPENSION AND INSULIN INJECTION

Usual adult dose: Subcutaneous, as directed by physician, once a day, fifteen to thirty minutes before breakfast, or as otherwise directed.

Auxiliary labeling:
  • Shake gently.
  • Refrigerate.
  • Do not freeze.

ISOPHANE INSULIN, HUMAN, SUSPENSION AND INSULIN HUMAN INJECTION

Usual adult dose: See *Isophane Insulin Suspension and Insulin Injection.*

Auxiliary labeling:
  • Shake gently.
  • Refrigerate.
  • Do not freeze.

INSULIN ZINC SUSPENSION USP (LENTE INSULIN)

Usual adult dose: Subcutaneous, as directed by physician, once a day thirty to sixty minutes before breakfast. An additional dose may be necessary for some patients about thirty minutes before a meal or at bedtime.

Auxiliary labeling:
  • Shake gently.
  • Refrigerate.
  • Do not freeze.

INSULIN ZINC, HUMAN, SUSPENSION

Usual adult dose: See *Insulin Zinc Suspension USP.*

Auxiliary labeling:
  • Shake gently.
  • Refrigerate.
  • Do not freeze.

EXTENDED INSULIN ZINC SUSPENSION USP (ULTRALENTE INSULIN)

Usual adult dose: Subcutaneous, as directed by physician, once a day thirty to sixty minutes before breakfast.

Auxiliary labeling:
- Shake gently.
- Refrigerate.
- Do not freeze.

Note: Extended insulin zinc suspension is sometimes mixed with other insulin types as directed by physician.

EXTENDED INSULIN ZINC, HUMAN, SUSPENSION

Usual adult dose: Subcutaneous, as directed by physician, once a day thirty to sixty minutes before breakfast.

Auxiliary labeling:
- Shake gently.
- Refrigerate.
- Do not freeze.

PROMPT INSULIN ZINC SUSPENSION USP (SEMILENTE INSULIN)

Usual adult dose: Subcutaneous, as directed by physician, once a day thirty to sixty minutes before breakfast. Additional doses may be necessary for some patients about thirty minutes before a meal or at bedtime.

Auxiliary labeling:
- Shake gently.
- Refrigerate.
- Do not freeze.

PROTAMINE ZINC INSULIN SUSPENSION USP (PZI INSULIN)

Usual adult dose: Subcutaneous, as directed by physician, once a day thirty to sixty minutes before breakfast.

Auxiliary labeling:
- Shake gently.
- Refrigerate.
- Do not freeze.

INTERFERONS, ALPHA   Systemic

Some commonly used *brand names* are:

In the U.S.—
 Alferon N [Interferon Alfa-n3]
 Intron A [Interferon Alfa-2b, Recombinant]
 Roferon-A [Interferon Alfa-2a, Recombinant]

In Canada—
 Intron A [Interferon Alfa-2b, Recombinant]
 Roferon-A [Interferon Alfa-2a, Recombinant]
 Wellferon [Interferon Alfa-n1 (lns)]

PARENTERAL
INTERFERON ALFA-2a, RECOMBINANT
 Interferon Alfa-2a, Recombinant, Injection
  In the U.S. and Canada—*Roferon-A*
 Interferon Alfa-2a, Recombinant, for Injection
  In the U.S. and Canada —*Roferon-A*
INTERFERON ALFA-2b, RECOMBINANT
 Interferon Alfa-2b, Recombinant, for Injection
  In the U.S. and Canada—*Intron A*
INTERFERON ALFA-n1 (LNS)*
 Interferon Alfa-n1 (lns) Injection*
  In Canada—*Wellferon*
INTERFERON ALFA-n3†
 Interferon Alfa-n3 Injection†
  In the U.S.—*Alferon N*

---

*Not commercially available in the U.S.
†Not commercially available in Canada.

Category: Biological response modifier; antineoplastic.

Indications

Note: Bracketed information in the *Indications* section refers to uses not included in U.S. product labeling.

Accepted

Leukemia, hairy cell (treatment)—Recombinant interferon alfa-2a, recombinant interferon alfa-2b, and interferon alfa-n1 (lns) are indicated for treatment of hairy cell leukemia, in splenectomized or nonsplenectomized patients. [Interferon alfa-n3] is also used for treatment of hairy cell leukemia.

Condylomata acuminata (treatment)—Recombinant interferon alfa-2b[1], interferon alfa-n1 (lns), and interferon alfa-n3 are indicated by intralesional injection for treatment of refractory or recurrent external condylomata acuminata (genital warts).

Hepatitis, chronic, active (treatment)—[Recombinant interferon alfa-2a][1], recombinant interferon alfa-2b[1], interferon alfa-n1 (lns), and [interferon alfa-n3] are indicated for treatment of non-A, non-B/C hepatitis in patients 18 years of age or older with compensated liver disease who have a history of blood or blood product exposure and/or are HCV (hepatitis C virus) antibody positive . Safety and efficacy have not been established for treatment of patients with decompensated liver disease or for immune suppressed transplant recipients. Use is not recommended in patients with autoimmune hepatitis or a history of autoimmune disease.

Available data indicate that serum transaminase activity and markers of viral activity are reduced during alpha interferon treatment, although abnormalities may recur when treatment is withdrawn. Long-term effects of alpha interferon on development of chronic hepatitis are not established.

Kaposi's sarcoma, AIDS-associated (treatment)—Recombinant interferon alfa-2a and recombinant interferon alfa-2b[1] are used for treatment of AIDS-associated Kaposi's sarcoma in selected patients 18 years of age and older. Interferon alfa-n1 (lns) and [interferon alfa-n3] are also used for this indication.

Carcinoma, bladder (treatment);

Carcinoma, renal (treatment); or

Leukemia, chronic myelocytic (treatment)—[Recombinant interferon alfa-2a][1], [recombinant interferon alfa-2b][1], interferon alfa-n1 (lns), and [interferon alfa-n3] are also used to treat superficial bladder carcinoma (intravesically), renal carcinoma, and chronic myelocytic leukemia.

[Carcinoma, cervical (treatment)][1]—Recombinant interferon alfa-2b is being used for treatment of advanced cervical carcinoma.

Papillomatosis, laryngeal (treatment)—[Recombinant interferon alfa-2b][1], interferon alfa-n1 (lns), and [interferon alfa-n3] are indicated for treatment of laryngeal papillomatosis, including juvenile laryngeal papilloma.

Lymphomas, non-Hodgkin's (treatment);
Malignant melanoma (treatment);
Multiple myeloma (treatment); or
Mycosis fungoides (treatment)—[Recombinant interferon alfa-2a][1], [recombinant interferon alfa-2b][1], interferon alfa-n1 (lns), and [interferon alfa-n3] are used for treatment of non-Hodgkin's lymphomas, especially follicular small cleaved cell lymphoma (nodular poorly differentiated types), malignant melanoma, multiple myeloma, and mycosis fungoides.

Although efficacy of all alpha interferons for various indications appears to be similar, differences in relative efficacy for a particular indication may exist.

---

[1]Not included in Canadian product labeling.

Pharmacology

Mechanism of action/Effect: In general, interferons have antiviral, antiproliferative, and immunomodulatory activities. Antiviral and antiproliferative actions are thought to be related to alterations in synthesis of RNA, DNA, and cellular proteins, including oncogenes. The exact mechanism of antineoplastic activity is unknown, but may be related to any of these three actions.

Antiviral—Inhibit virus replication in virus-infected cells.
Antiproliferative—Suppress cell proliferation.
Immunomodulatory—Enhance phagocytic activity of macrophages and augment specific cytotoxicity of lymphocytes for target cells.

Onset of action:
Hepatitis, chronic, active—Normalization of serum alanine aminotransferase (ALT) concentrations may occur as early as 2 weeks after initiation of treatment, although 6 months of treatment is usually recommended.

Time to peak effect: Condylomata acuminata—4 to 8 weeks after initiation of treatment.

Precautions to Consider

Cross-sensitivity and/or related problems
Patients sensitive to any alpha interferon may also be sensitive to any other alpha interferon.
Patients sensitive to mouse immunoglobulin may also be sensitive to recombinant interferon alfa-2a .
Patients sensitive to mouse immunoglobulin, egg protein, or neomycin may also be sensitive to interferon alfa-n3.

Geriatrics
Although appropriate studies on the relationship of age to the effects of alpha interferons have not been performed in the geriatric population, neurotoxicity and cardiotoxicity may be more likely to occur in the elderly, who may have underlying central nervous system (CNS) and cardiac function impairment. In addition, elderly patients are more likely to have age-related renal function impairment, which may require caution in patients receiving alpha interferons.

Dental
The bone marrow depressant effects of alpha interferons may result in an increased incidence of microbial infection, delayed healing, and gingival bleeding. If leukopenia or thrombocytopenia occurs, dental work should be deferred until blood counts have returned to normal and patients should be instructed in proper oral hygiene, including caution in use of regular toothbrushes, dental floss, and toothpicks.
Interferon alfa-2a and alfa-2b may cause stomatitis and discomfort. Use of interferon alfa-2a or alfa-2b may decrease or inhibit salivary flow, thus contributing to the development of caries, periodontal disease, oral candidiasis, and discomfort.

Drug interactions and/or related problems
The following drug interactions and/or related problems have been selected on the basis of their potential clinical significance (possible mechanism in parentheses where appropriate)—not necessarily inclusive (» = major clinical significance):

Note: Combinations containing any of the following medications, depending on the amount present, may also interact with this medication.

The following information applies to systemic use.

Alcohol or
CNS depression-producing medications
(concurrent use may enhance the CNS depressant effects of either these medications or alpha interferon)

Blood dyscrasia-causing medications
(leukopenic and/or thrombocytopenic effects of interferon may be increased with concurrent or recent therapy if these medications cause the same effects; dosage adjustment of alpha interferon, if necessary, should be based on blood counts)

Bone marrow depressants, other or
Radiation therapy
(additive bone marrow depression may occur; dosage reduction may be required when two or more bone marrow depressants, including radiation, are used concurrently or consecutively)

Contraindications/Medical problems
The contraindications/medical problems included have been selected on the basis of their potential clinical significance (reasons given in parentheses where appropriate)—not necessarily inclusive (» = major clinical significance).

Risk-benefit should be considered when the following medical problems exist:

» Autoimmune disease, history of
(caution is recommended because alpha interferon may increase the activity of the immune system and thereby worsen the condition; use for treatment of non-A, non-B/C hepatitis is not recommended)

Bone marrow depression
(may be exacerbated)

» Cardiac disease, severe, including recent myocardial infarction, or
» Diabetes mellitus prone to ketoacidosis or
» Pulmonary disease
(may be exacerbated as a result of the stress of the fever and chills that occur in most patients receiving alpha interferon)

(the risk of cardiotoxicity of alpha interferon may be increased in patients with a history of cardiac disease; myocardial infarction has been reported rarely)

» Chickenpox, existing or recent, including recent exposure, or
» Herpes zoster
    (risk of severe generalized disease)
» CNS function, compromised, or
» Psychiatric conditions, severe, or history of, or
» Seizure disorders
    (risk of severe CNS side effects)
    Hepatic disease, severe
      (alpha interferons may elevate serum hepatic enzyme concentrations)
    Herpes labialis, history of
      (may be reactivated)
    Renal disease, severe
      (may be exacerbated by fever and dehydration caused by alpha interferon)
» Sensitivity to alpha interferon
    Caution should be used also in patients who have had previous cytotoxic drug therapy or radiation therapy.

For treatment of non-A, non-B/C hepatitis (in addition to the above)
» Thyroid function impairment)
      (recombinant interferon alfa-2b has been reported to cause thyroid function abnormalities; serum thyroid-stimulating hormone [TSH] concentrations must be within normal limits before initiation of treatment)

For recombinant interferon alfa-2b and interferon alfa-n3 only (in addition to the above)
    Coagulation disorders
      (caution is recommended; recombinant interferon alfa-2b may prolong PT and PTT)

Side/Adverse Effects

See *Table 1*, page 653.

Patient Consultation

In providing consultation, consider emphasizing the following selected information (» = major clinical significance):

Before using this medication
» Conditions affecting use, especially:
      Sensitivity to alpha interferons
      Pregnancy—Abortifacient effects found in rhesus monkeys
      Breast-feeding—Possible need to avoid during alpha interferon therapy because of risk of serious adverse effects
      Use in teenagers—Possible effects on menstrual cycle
      Use in the elderly—Risk of cardiotoxic and neurotoxic effects may be increased
      Other medical problems, especially history of autoimmune disease, severe cardiac disease, chicken pox, compromised CNS function, diabetes mellitus, herpes zoster, history of psychiatric disease, pulmonary disease, seizure disorders, and thyroid function impairment

Proper use of this medication
» Compliance with therapy
» Reading patient directions carefully with regard to:
      —Preparation of the injection
      —Use of disposable syringes
      —Proper administration technique
      —Stability of the injection
    Importance of ample fluid intake to reduce risk of hypotension
    Administration at bedtime to minimize inconvenience of fatigue

    Missed dose: Skipping missed dose and going back to regular schedule; not doubling doses; checking with physician
» Proper storage

Precautions while using this medication
» Importance of close monitoring by physician
» Not changing brands of interferon without consulting physician, because of differences in dosage
» Caution in taking alcohol or other CNS depressants during therapy
» Caution when driving or doing anything else requiring alertness because of possible fatigue and dizziness
» Frequency of fever and flu-like symptoms; possible need for acetaminophen before and after a dose is given
    Caution if bone marrow depression occurs:
    » Avoiding exposure to persons with bacterial infections, especially during periods of low blood counts; checking with physician immediately if fever or chills, cough or hoarseness, lower back or side pain, or painful or difficult urination occur
    » Checking with physician immediately if unusual bleeding or bruising; black, tarry stools; blood in urine or stools; or pinpoint red spots on skin occur
    Caution in use of regular toothbrush, dental floss, or toothpick; physician, dentist, or nurse may suggest alternatives; checking with physician before having dental work done
    Not touching eyes or inside of nose unless hands washed immediately before
    Using caution to avoid accidental cuts with use of sharp objects such as safety razor or fingernail or toenail cutters
    Avoiding contact sports or other situations where bruising or injury could occur

Side/adverse effects
    Signs of potential side effects, especially cardiotoxicity, neurotoxicity, peripheral neuropathy, leukopenia, and thrombocytopenia
    Possibility of minor hair loss; hair should return after treatment has ended

General Dosing Information

Strengths and dosages of recombinant interferon alfa-2a and alfa-2b, interferon alfa-n1, and interferon alfa-n3 are expressed in terms of Units. Units are determined by comparison of the antiviral activity of the interferon with the activity of the international reference preparation of human leukocyte interferon established by the World Health Organization (WHO).

Patients receiving alpha interferon should be under supervision of a physician experienced in immunomodulatory and/or cancer chemotherapy.

It is recommended that the patient be premedicated with acetaminophen at the time of alpha interferon dosing and that the acetaminophen be continued as needed to treat fever and headache. Dosage reduction of alpha interferon may be necessary if headache persists.

Patients who develop leukopenia should be observed carefully for signs of infection. Antibiotic support may be required. In neutropenic patients who develop fever, broad-spectrum antibiotic coverage should be initiated empirically, pending bacterial cultures and appropriate diagnostic tests. In some cases, it may be difficult to distinguish fever due to infection from fever associated with the flu-like syndrome.

Special precautions are recommended in patients who develop thrombocytopenia as a result of administration of alpha interferons. These may include extreme care in performing invasive procedures; regular inspection of intravenous sites, skin (including perirectal area), and mucous membrane surfaces for signs of bleeding or bruising; limiting frequency of venipuncture and avoiding intramuscular injections; testing urine, emesis, stool, and secretions for occult blood; care in use of regular toothbrushes, dental floss, toothpicks, safety razors, and fingernail and toenail cutters; avoiding constipation; and using caution to prevent falls and other injuries. Such patients should avoid alcohol and any aspirin intake because of the risk of gastrointestinal bleeding. Platelet transfusions may be required.

For systemic use

The subcutaneous route of administration is recommended for patients with thrombocytopenia or at risk for bleeding.

If severe adverse effects occur, dosage reduction by 50% or temporary withdrawal of alpha interferon is recommended.

It is recommended that patients be well hydrated, especially during initial treatment with alpha interferon, to reduce the risk of hypotension associated with fluid depletion. Hypotension may require supportive treatment, including fluid replacement to maintain intravascular volume.

INTERFERON ALFA-2a, RECOMBINANT

Summary of Differences

Pharmacology:
  Source—Synthetic; produced by a recombinant DNA process. Purification procedure includes affinity chromatography using a murine monoclonal antibody. Single alpha interferon subtype.
  Half-life—
    Intramuscular: 6 to 8 hours.
    Intravenous infusion: 3.7 to 8.5 hours.
  Time to peak concentration—Single dose:
    Intramuscular—3.8 hours.
    Subcutaneous—7.3 hours.

Parenteral Dosage Forms

INTERFERON ALFA-2A, RECOMBINANT, INJECTION

Usual adult dose:
  Hairy cell leukemia—
    Induction: Intramuscular or subcutaneous, 3 million Units per day for sixteen to twenty-four weeks.
    Maintenance: Intramuscular or subcutaneous, 3 million Units three times per week.
  Kaposi's sarcoma, AIDS-associated—
  Induction:
    Intramuscular or subcutaneous, 36 million Units (1 mL) per day for ten to twelve weeks, or
    Intramuscular or subcutaneous, 3 million Units per day on Days 1 to 3, 9 million Units per day on Days 4 to 6, and 18 million Units per day on Days 7 to 9, followed by 36 million Units (1 mL) per day for the remainder of the ten- to twelve-week induction period.
    Maintenance: Intramuscular or subcutaneous, 36 million Units (1 mL) three times per week.

Note: A variety of dosage schedules of interferon have been used for the unlabeled indications. Since these regimens are still largely investigational, the prescriber should consult the medical literature in choosing a specific dosage.

INTERFERON ALFA-2A, RECOMBINANT, FOR INJECTION

Usual adult dose: Hairy cell leukemia—
  Induction: Intramuscular or subcutaneous, 3 million Units per day for sixteen to twenty-four weeks.
  Maintenance: Intramuscular or subcutaneous, 3 million Units three times per week.

Note: A variety of dosage schedules of interferon have been used for the unlabeled indications. Since these regimens are still largely investigational, the prescriber should consult the medical literature in choosing a specific dosage.

INTERFERON ALFA-2b, RECOMBINANT

Summary of Differences

Pharmacology:
  Source—Synthetic; produced by a recombinant DNA process. Purification is done by proprietary methods. Single alpha interferon subtype.
  Half-life—Intramuscular or subcutaneous: 2 to 3 hours.
  Time to peak concentration—Intramuscular or subcutaneous: 3 to 12 hours.
Precautions:
  Laboratory value alterations—
    Nadir of leukocyte and platelet counts is at 3 to 5 days, with recovery within 3 to 5 days after withdrawal.
    Prothrombin time (PT) and partial thromboplastin time (PTT) may be increased.
  Contraindications/medical problems—Caution in coagulation disorders.

Parenteral Dosage Forms

INTERFERON ALFA-2B, RECOMBINANT, FOR INJECTION

Usual adult dose:
  Hairy cell leukemia—Intramuscular or subcutaneous, 2 million Units per square meter of body surface three times per week.
  Condylomata acuminata[1]—Intralesional, 1 million units (using 10 million Units-per-mL strength) per wart (up to five warts) three times a week on alternate days for three weeks. If response is not satisfactory twelve to sixteen weeks after the initial treatment course, a second course may be given. Patients with six to ten warts may be given a second (sequential) course of treatment at the same dose to treat up to five additional warts per course; for patients with more than ten warts, additional courses may be given as needed with up to five additional warts per course.
  Kaposi's sarcoma, AIDS-associated—Intramuscular or subcutaneous, 30 million Units (using 50 million Units-per-mL strength) per square meter of body surface three times a week.
  Hepatitis, chronic, active[1]—Non-A, non-B/C hepatitis: Intramuscular or subcutaneous, 3 million Units three times per week. Patients who relapse may be retreated with the same dose to which they had previously responded.

Note: A variety of dosage schedules of interferon have been used for the unlabeled indications. Since these regimens are still largely investigational, the prescriber should consult the medical literature in choosing a specific dosage.

[1]Not included in Canadian product labeling.

INTERFERON ALFA-n1 (LNS)

Summary of Differences

Pharmacology:
   Source—Obtained from pooled units of human lymphoblastoid cells following induction with Sendai virus. Mixture of natural alpha interferon subtypes, but in different proportions than in human leukocyte interferon.
   Half-life—Intravenous infusion: About 8 hours.

Parenteral Dosage Forms

INTERFERON ALFA-N1 (LNS) INJECTION

Usual adult dose:
   Hairy cell leukemia—
      Induction: Intramuscular or subcutaneous, 3 million Units per day for sixteen to twenty-four weeks.
      Maintenance: Intramuscular or subcutaneous, 3 million Units three times per week.
   Condylomata acuminata—Intramuscular or subcutaneous, 1 to 3 million Units per square meter of body surface five times a week for two weeks, followed by three times a week for four weeks. The same dose is then continued every other day or three times a week for one month.
      Note: As an adjunct to laser surgery or cryosurgery, the dose is 1 million Units per square meter of body surface intramuscularly or subcutaneously per day for seven days prior to and seven days following surgical resection of the lesions.
Note: A variety of dosage schedules of interferon have been used for the unlabeled indications. Since these regimens are still largely investigational, the prescriber should consult the medical literature in choosing a specific dosage.

INTERFERON ALFA-n3

Summary of Differences

Pharmacology:
   Source—Obtained from pooled units of human leukocytes that have been induced to produce interferon alfa-n3. Contains up to 14 natural alpha interferon subtypes. Human leukocyte interferon.
Precautions: Contraindications/medical problems—Caution in coagulation disorders.

Parenteral Dosage Forms

INTERFERON ALFA-N3 INJECTION

Usual adult dose: Condylomata acuminata—Intralesional (at the base of the wart, preferably using a 30 gauge needle), 250,000 Units two times a week for up to eight weeks.
Note: For large warts, it may be injected at several points around the periphery of the wart, using a total dose of 250,000 Units.
   Safety and efficacy of more than one 8-week course have not been established.
   A variety of dosage schedules of interferon have been used for the unlabeled indications. Since these regimens are still largely investigational, the prescriber should consult the medical literature in choosing a specific dosage.

Usual adult prescribing limits: Up to 2.5 million Units per treatment session.

Table 1. Side/Adverse Effects

Note: Most side/adverse effects, except the flu-like syndrome, are dose-related. They are usually mild to moderate at systemic doses less than 10 million Units per day; hematologic and hepatic toxicities tend to be more frequent with doses above 10 million Units, and cardiovascular and neurologic toxicities tend to be more frequent with doses above 30 million Units. However, patient sensitivity varies.

Reduced blood pressure occurs frequently with systemic use but is rarely symptomatic; hypotension may occur during administration or up to two days after therapy, and may require supportive therapy including fluid replacement to maintain intravascular volume; hypertension may occur but is usually mild and transient.

Development of neutralizing antibodies has been reported. Relationship of the presence of neutralizing antibodies to loss of antitumor effects is controversial; a possible correlation with titer of neutralizing antibodies has been suggested but not confirmed. Differences in frequency of antibody formation have been reported among alpha interferons but relative frequency has not been studied prospectively. Differences may be related to the differences in the sensitivity of tests used in antibody detection, as well as to disease state, dose, schedule, and route of administration.

The following side/adverse effects have been selected on the basis of their potential clinical significance (possible signs and symptoms in parentheses where appropriate)—not necessarily inclusive:*	Indication				
	Hairy cell leukemia	Other malignancies	Condylomata acuminata	Kaposi's sarcoma	Hepatitis
Those indicating need for medical attention *Anemia* (usually asymptomatic)	N/A	M	L	M	M
Cardiotoxicity (chest pain, irregular heartbeat) Note: Arrhythmias are usually supraventricular.	R	R	U	R	R
Hepatotoxicity (usually asymptomatic)	L	L	L	M	L
Hyperthyroidism or hypothyroidism (usually asymptomatic)	U	U	U	U	R
Leukopenia (usually asymptomatic; rarely, fever or chills, cough or hoarseness, lower back or side pain, painful or difficult urination)	N/A	M	M	M	M
Neurotoxicity (confusion, mental depression, nervousness, trouble in sleeping, trouble in thinking or concentrating) Note: Usually reversible after withdrawal; in some patients, especially the elderly or those treated with high doses, stupor, obtundation, and coma have occurred.	L	L	L	L	L
Peripheral neuropathy (numbness or tingling of fingers, toes, or face)	L	L	L	L	R
Thrombocytopenia (usually asymptomatic; rarely, unusual bleeding or bruising; black, tarry stools; blood in urine or stools; pinpoint red spots on skin)	N/A	M	L	M	M
Those indicating need for medical attention only if they continue or are bothersome *Blurred vision*	L	L	L	L	L
Change in taste or metallic taste	M	M	R	M	R
Cold sores or stomatitis (sores in mouth and on lips)	L	L	R	R	R
Diarrhea	M	M	L	M	M
Dizziness Note: Dizziness is a CNS effect.	M	M	L	M	L
Dry mouth	M	M	R	M	L
Dry skin or itching	L	L	L	L	L

*Differences in frequency of occurrence may reflect either lack of clinical-use data or actual pharmacologic distinctions among agents (although their pharmacologic similarity suggests that side effects occurring with one may occur with the others). M = more frequent; L = less frequent; R = rare; U = unknown; X = does not occur; N/A = Not applicable.

Table 1. Side/Adverse Effects *(continued)*

	Indication				
	Hairy cell leukemia	Other malignancies	Condylomata acuminata	Kaposi's sarcoma	Hepatitis
Flu-like syndrome (aching muscles, fever and chills, headache, general feeling of discomfort or illness; less frequently, joint pain, back pain) Note: Occurs in most patients; most pronounced in first week of treatment and gradually reduced, as a result of tachyphylaxis, within 2 to 4 weeks with continued treatment.	M	M	M	M	M
Increased sweating	L	L	L	L	L
Leg cramps	L	L	L	U	R
Loss of appetite Note: Loss of appetite tends to become more prominent with continued treatment and may necessitate dosage reduction; usually resolves within 4 weeks after withdrawal of alpha interferon.	M	M	L	M	M
Nausea or vomiting Note: Nausea or vomiting usually resolves within 3 to 5 days after withdrawal of alpha interferon.	M	M	M	M	M
Skin rash	M	M	L	M	L
Unusual tiredness Note: Unusual tiredness tends to become more prominent with continued treatment and may necessitate dosage reduction; usually resolves several weeks after withdrawal of alpha interferon.	M	M	M	M	M
Weight loss	R	R	R	L	R
Those not indicating need for medical attention Incidence less frequent *Loss of hair, partial* Note: Hair growth returns promptly after withdrawal of alpha interferon.	L	L	U	M	M

*Differences in frequency of occurrence may reflect either lack of clinical-use data or actual pharmacologic distinctions among agents (although their pharmacologic similarity suggests that side effects occurring with one may occur with the others). M = more frequent; L = less frequent; R = rare; U = unknown; X = does not occur; N/A = Not applicable.

IPRATROPIUM   Inhalation-Local

A commonly used *brand name* in the U.S. and Canada is *Atrovent*.

INHALATION
Ipratropium Bromide Inhalation Aerosol
    In the U.S. and Canada—*Atrovent*
Ipratropium Bromide Inhalation Solution*
    In Canada—*Atrovent*

*Not commercially available in the U.S.

Category: Bronchodilator.

Indications

Note: Bracketed information in the *Indications* section refers to uses not included in U.S. product labeling.

Accepted
Bronchitis (treatment);
Emphysema, pulmonary (treatment); or
Pulmonary disease, chronic obstructive, other (treatment)—Ipratropium is indicated for maintenance treatment of bronchospasm associated with chronic obstructive pulmonary disease, including chronic bronchitis and pulmonary emphysema.

Ipratropium inhalation solution is indicated for treatment of acute exacerbations of chronic bronchitis.

[Asthma, bronchial (treatment)]—Ipratropium is used for maintenance treatment of bronchial asthma.

Ipratropium inhalation solution, when used in conjunction with a beta-2-adrenergic stimulant solution such as albuterol or fenoterol, is indicated for acute asthmatic attacks. However, ipratropium should not be used alone for the treatment of an acute asthmatic attack because it has a slower onset of action than that of an adrenergic beta-2-agonist inhalation aerosol or solution.[1]

[Ipratropium is useful as adjunctive therapy in bronchial asthma in patients who respond inadequately to beta-agonists or as an alternative to beta-agonists in patients who develop significant side/adverse effects with these medications.][1]

[Ipratropium appears to be at least as effective, and possibly more effective, than the sympathomimetics in the treatment of chronic bronchitis. However, it is less effective than beta-agonists in the treatment of bronchial asthma.][1]

Unaccepted
Ipratropium is not indicated for use alone in the initial treatment of acute attacks of bronchospasm where rapid response is required.

[1]Not included in Canadian product labeling.

Pharmacology

Mechanism of action/Effect: The bronchodilation produced by ipratropium is primarily a local, site-specific effect rather than a systemic effect. Ipratropium appears to produce bronchodilation by competitive inhibition of cholinergic receptors on bronchial smooth muscle. This effect antagonizes the action of acetylcholine at its membrane-bound receptor site and thereby blocks the bronchoconstrictor action of vagal efferent impulses. Ipratropium may also inhibit acetylcholine-enhanced release of chemical mediators by blocking cholinergic receptors at the surface of mast cells.

Although ipratropium was initially thought to exert its bronchodilating effect primarily in large airways, more recent studies suggest that ipratropium's action is generalized throughout the airways.

Onset of action: Within 5 to 15 minutes.

Time to peak effect: 1 to 2 hours.

Duration of action: About 3 to 4 hours in the majority of patients, but up to 6 hours in some patients.

Precautions to Consider

Cross-sensitivity and/or related problems
Patients sensitive to belladonna alkaloids may be sensitive to ipratropium also, since ipratropium is a derivative of atropine.

Geriatrics
No published geriatrics-specific information is available. However, elderly patients are more likely to have age-related prostatic hypertrophy, which may require adjustment of dosage in patients receiving ipratropium.

Dental
Prolonged use of ipratropium inhalation may decrease or inhibit salivary flow, thus contributing to the development of caries, periodontal disease, oral candidiasis, and discomfort.

Drug interactions and/or related problems
The following drug interactions and/or related problems have been selected on the basis of their potential clinical significance (possible mechanism in parentheses where appropriate)—not necessarily inclusive (» = major clinical significance):

Note: Combinations containing any of the following medications, depending on the amount present, may also interact with this medication.

Anticholinergics, other, or other medications with anticholinergic activity
    (concurrent use of other anticholinergics, including ophthalmic preparations, or other medications with anticholinergic action with ipratropium may result in additive effects)

» Cromolyn, inhalation solution
    (the mixing of cromolyn inhalation solution with ipratropium inhalation solution for nebulization is not recommended, because a precipitate will form due to complexation between cromolyn sodium and the benzalkonium chloride in ipratropium inhalation)

Contraindications/Medical problems
The contraindications/medical problems included have been selected on the basis of their potential clinical significance (reasons given in parentheses where appropriate)—not necessarily inclusive (» = major clinical significance).

Risk-benefit should be considered when the following medical problems exist:

Bladder neck obstruction or
Prostatic hypertrophy
    (urinary retention may be precipitated)
Glaucoma, angle-closure
    (an acute attack may be precipitated or condition may be exacerbated)
Sensitivity to ipratropium or belladonna alkaloids
Urinary retention
    (condition may be aggravated)

Side/Adverse Effects

Note: Usual therapeutic doses of ipratropium generally do not cause systemic side/adverse effects because of the low blood concentrations achieved with the inhalation; however, the potential for systemic side/adverse effects exists.

In addition, acute overdose of ipratropium by inhalation is unlikely since the medication is not well absorbed systemically.

The following side/adverse effects have been selected on the basis of their potential clinical significance (possible signs and symptoms in parentheses where appropriate)—not necessarily inclusive:

Those indicating need for medical attention
Incidence rare
Skin rash or hives; stomatitis (ulcers or sores in mouth and on lips)

Those indicating need for medical attention only if they continue or are bothersome
Incidence more frequent
Cough or dryness of mouth or throat; headache or dizziness; nervousness; stomach upset or nausea

Incidence less frequent or rare
Blurred vision or other changes in vision; hypotension (unusual tiredness or weakness); *insomnia* (trouble in sleeping); *metallic or unpleasant taste; palpitations* (pounding heartbeat); *stuffy nose; trembling; urinary retention* (difficult urination)

Patient Consultation

In providing consultation, consider emphasizing the following selected information (» = major clinical significance):

Before using this medication
» Conditions affecting use, especially:
   Sensitivity to ipratropium or belladonna alkaloids
   Pregnancy—In some animal studies, ipratropium at extremely high doses (500 mg to 1 gram per kg of body weight) caused fetal death in some pregnant rats and reduced the birth weight of the animal fetuses
   Dental—Prolonged use of ipratropium may decrease or inhibit salivary flow, which may contribute to the development of caries, periodontal disease, oral candidiasis, and discomfort

Proper use of this medication
Proper administration technique:
   Reading patient instructions carefully before using
   If more than 1 inhalation is required, allowing 1 minute between inhalations for maximum benefit
» Importance of not using more medication than the amount prescribed
» Avoiding contact with the eyes; if accidentally sprayed into the eyes, irritation or temporary blurring of vision may occur
   Missed dose: Using as soon as possible; not using if almost time for next dose; not doubling doses
» Proper storage

Precautions while using this medication
» Checking with physician immediately if symptoms do not improve within 30 minutes after using this medication or if condition becomes worse
   Possible dryness of mouth or throat; using sugarless candy or gum, ice, or saliva substitute for relief; checking with physician or dentist if dry mouth continues for more than 2 weeks

For patients also using a beta-agonist inhalation aerosol
   Using beta-agonist aerosol about 5 minutes prior to the ipratropium aerosol, unless otherwise directed by physician

For patients also using an adrenocorticoid or cromolyn inhalation aerosol
   Using ipratropium aerosol about 5 minutes prior to the adrenocorticoid or cromolyn aerosol, unless otherwise directed by physician

For patients also using cromolyn inhalation solution
» Not mixing cromolyn inhalation solution with ipratropium inhalation solution for use in a nebulizer

Side/adverse effects
   Signs of potential side effects, especially skin rash or hives and stomatitis

General Dosing Information

For nebulization of ipratropium bromide inhalation solution, a gas flow (oxygen or compressed air) of 6 to 10 liters per minute should be used. Nebulizers with either a facemask or mouthpiece have been used.

Patients should be advised to contact their physician immediately if they do not respond to the usual dose of ipratropium because this may be a sign of seriously worsening bronchospasm requiring reassessment of therapy.

Ipratropium may be used concurrently with beta-agonists, theophylline, cromolyn, or other medications used for obstructive pulmonary disease in patients who fail to respond to single-drug therapy.

When used in conjunction with a beta-agonist inhalation aerosol, the beta-agonist aerosol should be administered about 5 minutes prior to the ipratropium aerosol to increase the effectiveness of ipratropium.

When used in conjunction with an adrenocorticoid or cromolyn inhalation aerosol, the ipratropium aerosol should be administered about 5 minutes prior to the adrenocorticoid or cromolyn aerosol. This interval allows for bronchodilation to occur and increases deposition of the adrenocorticoid or cromolyn within the bronchi.

Inhalation Dosage Forms

IPRATROPIUM BROMIDE INHALATION AEROSOL

Usual adult and adolescent dose: Oral inhalation, 18 to 40 mcg (0.018 to 0.04 mg—1 or 2 inhalations) three or four times a day, administered not more often than every four hours.

Note: During initial therapy, some patients may require up to 80 mcg (0.08 mg—4 inhalations) at a time to obtain maximum benefit.
   Geriatric patients may require lower dosage of this medication.

Usual adult prescribing limits: 216 mcg (0.216 mg—12 inhalations) per twenty-four hours.

Auxiliary labeling:
• For oral inhalation only.
• Shake well before using.
• Store away from heat and direct sunlight.

IPRATROPIUM BROMIDE INHALATION SOLUTION

Note: Ipratropium bromide inhalation solution is not commercially available in the U.S.

Usual adult and adolescent dose: Oral inhalation, 250 to 500 mcg (0.25 to 0.5 mg—1 to 2 mL) of a 0.025% solution diluted to three to five mL with preservative-free sterile sodium chloride inhalation solution 0.9% or bacteriostatic sodium chloride injection 0.9%, administered via nebulization over a period of ten to fifteen minutes; treatment may be repeated every four to six hours as necessary.

IRON SUPPLEMENTS   Systemic

Some commonly used *brand names* are:

In the U.S.—

Femiron [Ferrous Fumarate]
Feosol [Ferrous Sulfate]
Feostat [Ferrous Fumarate]
Feostat Drops [Ferrous Fumarate]
Fergon [Ferrous Gluconate]
Fer-In-Sol [Ferrous Sulfate]
Fer-In-Sol Drops [Ferrous Sulfate]
Fer-In-Sol Syrup [Ferrous Sulfate]
Fer-Iron Drops [Ferrous Sulfate]
Fero-Gradumet [Ferrous Sulfate]
Ferospace [Ferrous Sulfate]
Ferralet [Ferrous Gluconate]
Ferralyn Lanacaps [Ferrous Sulfate]
Ferra-TD [Ferrous Sulfate]
Fumasorb [Ferrous Fumarate]

Fumerin [Ferrous Fumarate]
Hemocyte [Ferrous Fumarate]
Hytinic [Iron-Polysaccharide]
InFeD [Iron Dextran]
Ircon [Ferrous Fumarate]
Mol-Iron [Ferrous Sulfate]
Niferex [Iron-Polysaccharide]
Niferex-150 [Iron-Polysaccharide]
Nu-Iron [Iron-Polysaccharide]
Nu-Iron 150 [Iron-Polysaccharide]
Palmiron [Ferrous Fumarate]
Simron [Ferrous Gluconate]
Slow Fe [Ferrous Sulfate]
Span-FF [Ferrous Fumarate]

In Canada—

Apo-Ferrous Gluconate [Ferrous Gluconate]
Apo-Ferrous Sulfate [Ferrous Sulfate]
Fer-In-Sol Drops [Ferrous Sulfate]
Fer-In-Sol Syrup [Ferrous Sulfate]
Fero-Grad [Ferrous Sulfate]
Fertinic [Ferrous Gluconate]
Imferon [Iron Dextran]
Jectofer [Iron Sorbitol]

Neo-Fer [Ferrous Fumarate]
Novoferrogluc [Ferrous Gluconate]
Novoferrosulfa [Ferrous Sulfate]
Novofumar [Ferrous Fumarate]
Palafer [Ferrous Fumarate]
Palafer Pediatric Drops [Ferrous Fumarate]
PMS Ferrous Sulfate [Ferrous Sulfate]
Slow Fe [Ferrous Sulfate]

Another commonly used name for ferrous sulfate is ferrous sulfate exsiccated.

FERROUS FUMARATE
Oral
Ferrous Fumarate Capsules*
  In Canada—*Neo-Fer; Palafer*
Ferrous Fumarate Extended-release Capsules†
  In the U.S.—*Span-FF*
Ferrous Fumarate Oral Solution
  In the U.S.—*Feostat Drops*
  In Canada—*Palafer Pediatric Drops*
Ferrous Fumarate Oral Suspension
  In the U.S.—*Feostat*
  In Canada—*Palafer*
Ferrous Fumarate Tablets USP
  In the U.S.—*Femiron; Fumasorb; Fumerin; Hemocyte; Ircon; Palmiron;* GENERIC
  In Canada—*Novofumar*
Ferrous Fumarate Chewable Tablets†
  In the U.S.—*Feostat*
FERROUS GLUCONATE
Oral
Ferrous Gluconate Capsules USP†
  In the U.S.—*Simron;* GENERIC

Ferrous Gluconate Elixir USP†
  In the U.S.—*Fergon*
Ferrous Gluconate Syrup*
  In Canada—*Fertinic*
Ferrous Gluconate Tablets USP
  In the U.S.—*Fergon; Ferralet;* GENERIC
  In Canada—*Apo-Ferrous Gluconate; Fertinic; Novoferrogluc;* GENERIC
FERROUS SULFATE
Oral
Ferrous Sulfate (Dried) Capsules†
  In the U.S.—*Feosol; Fer-In-Sol*
Ferrous Sulfate Extended-release Capsules
  In the U.S.—*Ferospace; Ferralyn Lanacaps; Ferra-TD;* GENERIC
  In Canada—GENERIC
Ferrous Sulfate Elixir†
  In the U.S.—*Feosol;* GENERIC
Ferrous Sulfate Oral Solution USP
  In the U.S.—*Fer-In-Sol Drops; Fer-In-Sol Syrup; Fer-Iron Drops;* GENERIC
  In Canada—*Fer-In-Sol Drops; Fer-In-Sol Syrup*
Ferrous Sulfate Tablets USP
  In the U.S.—*Mol-Iron;* GENERIC
  In Canada—*PMS Ferrous Sulfate;* GENERIC
Ferrous Sulfate Tablets USP (Dried)†
  In the U.S.—*Feosol*
Ferrous Sulfate Enteric-coated Tablets
  In the U.S.—GENERIC
  In Canada—*Apo-Ferrous Sulfate; Novoferrosulfa;* GENERIC
Ferrous Sulfate Extended-release Tablets
  In the U.S.—*Fero-Gradumet*
  In Canada—*Fero-Grad*
Ferrous Sulfate (Dried) Extended-release Tablets
  In the U.S. and Canada—*Slow Fe*
IRON DEXTRAN
Parenteral
Iron Dextran Injection USP
  In the U.S.—*InFeD*
  In Canada—*Imferon*
IRON-POLYSACCHARIDE†
Oral
Iron-Polysaccharide Capsules†
  In the U.S.—*Hytinic; Niferex-150; Nu-Iron 150*
Iron-Polysaccharide Elixir†
  In the U.S.—*Hytinic; Niferex; Nu-Iron*
Iron-Polysaccharide Tablets†
  In the U.S.—*Niferex*
IRON SORBITOL*
Parenteral
Iron Sorbitol Injection*
  In Canada—*Jectofer*

---

*Not commercially available in the U.S.
†Not commercially available in Canada.

Category: Antianemic.

Indications

Accepted
Iron deficiency anemia (prophylaxis and treatment)—Iron supplements are indicated in the prevention and treatment of iron deficiency anemia resulting from inadequate diet, malabsorption, pregnancy, and/or blood loss.

Iron dextran and iron sorbitol are recommended only for patients in whom iron deficiency has been determined, only after the cause has been corrected, if possible, and only when oral administration has been found unsatisfactory or impossible.

Note: The cause of iron deficiency states should always be determined, as it may relate to a serious condition.

Deficiency of iron may lead to fatigue, shortness of breath, decreased physical performance, impaired learning in children, altered body temperature, and altered immune function.

Requirements may be increased and/or supplementation may be necessary in the following persons or conditions (although clinical deficiencies are usually rare):
Burns
Gastrectomy
Hemodialysis
Hemorrhage
Infants—premature, those receiving unfortified formulas
Intestinal diseases—celiac, Crohn's, diarrhea, sprue, inflammatory bowel disease,

Some unusual diets (e.g., reducing diets that drastically restrict food selection) may not supply minimum daily requirements of iron. Supplementation may be necessary in patients receiving total parenteral nutrition (TPN) or undergoing rapid weight loss or in those with malnutrition, because of inadequate dietary intake.

Requirements for all vitamins and most minerals are increased during pregnancy; however, they should be provided by an adequate diet. Many physicians recommend that pregnant women receive multivitamin and mineral supplements, especially those pregnant women who do not consume an adequate diet and those in high-risk categories (i.e., women carrying more than one fetus, heavy cigarette smokers, and alcohol and drug abusers). However, taking excessive amounts of multivitamin and mineral supplements may be harmful to the mother and/or fetus and should be avoided.

Requirements for all vitamins and most minerals are increased during breast-feeding.

Requirements may be increased by the following medications: Antacids, calcium supplements, epoetin, penicillamine, trientine, zinc supplements, and any medications that cause bleeding from the gastrointestinal tract.

Pharmacology

Mechanism of action/Effect: Iron is an essential component in the physiological formation of hemoglobin, adequate amounts of which are necessary for effective erythropoiesis and the resultant oxygen transport capacity of the blood. A similar function is provided by iron in myoglobin production. Iron also serves as a cofactor of several essential enzymes, including cytochromes that are involved in electron transport. Iron is necessary for catecholamine metabolism and the proper functioning of neutrophils.

When taken orally, in food or as a supplement, iron passes through the mucosal cells in the ferrous state and is bound with the protein transferrin. In this form, iron is transported in the body to bone marrow for red blood cell production.

Iron dextran is absorbed from the injection site into the capillaries and lymphatic system. It is removed from the plasma by cells of the reticuloendothelial system and dissociated into iron and dextran. The released iron is immediately bound to protein moieties to form hemosiderin or ferritin or, to a lesser extent, transferrin. The protein-bound iron eventually replenishes the depleted iron stores and is incorporated into hemoglobin.

Iron sorbitol is absorbed directly into the bloodstream as well as by way of the lymphatic system.

Precautions to Consider

Geriatrics
Some geriatric patients may require a larger than usual daily ingestion of bioavailable iron to correct an iron deficiency, because their ability to absorb iron has been diminished by reduced gastric secretions and achlorhydria.

Drug interactions and/or related problems
The following drug interactions and/or related problems have been selected on the basis of their potential clinical significance (possible mechanism in parentheses where appropriate)—not necessarily inclusive (» = major clinical significance):

Note: Combinations containing any of the following medications, depending on the amount present, may also interact with this medication.

» Acetohydroxamic acid
(iron and possibly other heavy metals, when taken orally, are chelated by acetohydroxamic acid; this may result in reduced intestinal absorption of both acetohydroxamic acid and oral iron supplements; if iron therapy is indicated during therapy with acetohydroxamic acid, parenteral administration of iron is recommended)

Alcohol
(concurrent use with ferric iron for a prolonged period may result in toxicity since absorption and hepatic storage of iron are increased, especially if alcohol usage is high)

Antacids or
Calcium supplements (calcium carbonate or phosphate) or
Coffee or
Eggs or
Foods or medications containing bicarbonates, carbonates, oxalates, or phosphates or
Milk or milk products or
Tea (contains tannic acid) or
Whole-grain breads and cereals (contain phytic acid) and dietary fiber
(concurrent use with iron may decrease iron absorption because of the formation of less soluble or insoluble complexes; iron supplements should not be taken within 1 hour before or 2 hours after ingestion of any of the above)

Cimetidine
(the decrease in gastric acid caused by cimetidine may decrease the absorption of nonheme iron; concurrent use is not recommended)

Ciprofloxacin
(iron may reduce absorption by chelation of ciprofloxacin, resulting in lower serum and urine concentrations of ciprofloxacin; concurrent use is not recommended)

Deferoxamine, and possibly other chelating agents
(deferoxamine chelates iron and is used in the treatment of iron overdose and other iron overload conditions; iron may be necessary in patients receiving other chelating agents; however, it should be given at least 2 hours after the chelating agent)

» Dimercaprol
(concurrent administration of medicinal iron with dimercaprol results in the formation of a toxic complex; if iron deficiency is present, its treatment should be postponed until therapy with dimercaprol has been discontinued for at least 24 hours; severe iron deficiency anemia occurring during dimercaprol therapy should be managed with blood transfusion)

» Etidronate
(concurrent use may prevent absorption of oral etidronate; patients should be advised to avoid using iron supplements within 2 hours of etidronate)

Pancreatin or
Pancrelipase
  (concurrent use of these medications with iron supplements
  may decrease iron absorption)

Penicillamine or
Trientine
  (concurrent use with iron medications may decrease the therapeutic effects of these medications; if necessary, iron may be
  administered in short courses, but a period of 2 hours should
  elapse between administration of penicillamine or trientine and
  iron)

» Tetracyclines, oral
  (concurrent use with iron reduces absorbability and resultant
  therapeutic effects of oral tetracyclines; patients should be advised to take iron supplements 2 hours after tetracycline)

Zinc supplements, oral
  (large doses of iron supplements have been found to inhibit the
  intestinal absorption of zinc; this may be a problem in individuals taking commercial multivitamin-mineral preparations
  or infant formulas that have a high iron-to-zinc ratio; however,
  most firms in the U.S. have reformulated their products; zinc
  supplements should be taken 2 hours after iron supplements)

Contraindications/Medical problems

The contraindications/medical problems included have been selected
  on the basis of their potential clinical significance (reasons given
  in parentheses where appropriate)—not necessarily inclusive (» =
  major clinical significance).

*This medication should not be used when the following medical
  problems exist:*

» Hemochromatosis or
» Hemosiderosis
  (existing iron overload may be increased)

» Other anemic conditions, unless accompanied by iron deficiency
  (some conditions, such as hemolytic anemia or thalassemia,
  may cause excess storage of iron)

*Risk-benefit should be considered when the following medical prob-
  lems exist:*

Alcoholism, active or in remission
  (alcohol may increase absorption and hepatic storage of iron
  and increase iron toxicity)

Allergies or
Asthma
  (increased risk of hypersensitivity reactions with parenteral administration)

Hepatitis or hepatic function impairment or
Kidney disease, acute, infectious
  (may cause an accumulation of iron)

Intestinal tract inflammatory conditions, such as enteritis, colitis,
  diverticulitis, and ulcerative colitis, or
Peptic ulcer
  (may be exacerbated with oral iron dosage forms)

Rheumatoid arthritis
  (acute exacerbation of joint pain and swelling following intravenous administration of parenteral iron)

Sensitivity to iron

» Caution is recommended also in patients receiving repeated blood
  transfusions because the addition of high erythrocytic iron content may produce iron overload.

Side/Adverse Effects

Note: Stools commonly become dark green or black when iron preparations are taken orally. This is caused by the presence of
  unabsorbed iron and is harmless. However, bleeding in the
  gastrointestinal tract may also cause black stools of a sticky
  consistency, often accompanied by other symptoms such as red
  streaks in the stool, cramping, soreness, or sharp pains in the
  stomach or abdominal region. Medical attention is needed for
  proper evaluation of the cause.

The parenteral administration of iron has resulted in anaphylactic reactions that, on rare occasions, have been fatal. Such
  reactions occur within the first several minutes of administration and have been characterized by sudden onset of respiratory
  difficulties and/or cardiovascular collapse. Therefore, adrenalin
  should be kept near the patient in case of emergency.

The following effects have been selected on the basis of their potential
  clinical significance (possible signs and symptoms in parentheses
  where appropriate)—not necessarily inclusive:

Those indicating need for medical attention
Incidence more frequent
  Oral use only
    Abdominal or stomach pain, cramping, or soreness
  Parenteral use only
    Allergic reaction (skin rash or hives, trouble in breathing);
    **backache or muscle pain, chills, dizziness, fever with increased
    sweating, headache, metallic taste, nausea or vomiting, or
    numbness, pain, or tingling of hands or feet; intravenous
    administration, excessive rate of** (chest pain, dizziness or faint-
    ing [hypotension], fast heartbeat, flushing or redness of skin);
    **pain and redness or sores at intramuscular injection site;
    redness at intravenous injection site**

  Note: *Backache or muscle pain, chills, dizziness, fever with
    increased sweating, headache, metallic taste, nausea or
    vomiting, or numbness, pain, or tingling of hands or feet*
    due to delayed reaction, with recommended doses; onset
    may be 24 to 48 hours after administration and sub-
    sides in 3 to 7 days.

Incidence less frequent or rare
  Oral use only
    Contact irritation (chest or throat pain, especially when swal-
    lowing; stools containing fresh or digested blood)

  Note: *Contact irritation* due to contact with ulcerous areas or
    high concentration of iron in one area resulting from
    improper release from dosage form or delayed passage
    of dosage form through alimentary tract.

Early symptoms of acute iron toxicity
  Oral use only
    **Diarrhea, sometimes containing blood; fever; nausea, severe;
    stomach pain or cramping, sharp; vomiting, severe, some-
    times containing blood**

  Note: Early symptoms may not be evident for up to 60 min-
    utes or longer; if overdose is suspected, emergency room
    treatment should not be delayed for evidence of symp-
    toms, but should begin immediately.

    Early signs may also include increased blood glucose
    and leukocytosis.

    A latency period lasting from 2 to about 48 hours after
    ingestion may occur between the 2 symptomatic phases.
    During this time, the patient may appear to improve
    clinically.

Late symptoms of acute iron toxicity
  Oral use only
      ***Bluish-colored lips, fingernails, palms of hands; drowsiness;
      pale, clammy skin; seizures; unusual tiredness or weakness;
      weak and fast heartbeat***
         Note: Late signs may also include metabolic acidosis, hypo-
               tension, hypoglycemia, hepatic injury or failure, cardio-
               vascular collapse, and gastrointestinal scarring.

**Those indicating need for medical attention only if they continue
or are bothersome**
Incidence more frequent
  Oral use only
      Constipation; diarrhea; nausea; vomiting
  Parenteral use only
      Brown discoloration of skin—usually fading within several
      weeks or months
Incidence less frequent
  Oral use only
      Darkened urine (iron sulfide formation following large doses);
      heartburn; staining of teeth—with liquid dosage forms

Patient Consultation

In providing consultation, consider emphasizing the following selected information (» = major clinical significance):

Description of use
    Description should include function in body, signs of deficiency

Importance of diet
    Diet as treatment of choice; importance of diet
    List of daily RDA for various age groups
    Best dietary sources of iron

Before using this dietary supplement
» Conditions affecting use, especially:
        Sensitivity to iron
        Other medications, especially acetohydroxamic acid, dimerca-
        prol, etidronate, or oral tetracyclines
        Other medical problems, especially hemochromatosis, hemo-
        siderosis, or other anemic conditions

Proper use of this dietary supplement
    Taking on empty stomach 1 hour before or 2 hours after meals; or
        with food to lessen possibility of stomach upset
    Taking with water or fruit juice, a full glass (240 mL) for adults, 1/
        2 glass (120 mL) for children
    Following physician's directions if dietary supplement was pre-
        scribed
    Following manufacturer's package directions on nonprescription
        (OTC) iron
    For preventing, reducing, or removing iron stains on teeth:
        Diluting liquid forms in water or fruit juice
        Using drinking tube or straw
        Placing dropper doses well back on tongue
        Brushing teeth with baking soda or hydrogen peroxide 3%
    Missed dose: Skipping missed dose; going back to regular sched-
        ule; not doubling doses
» Proper storage

Precautions while using this dietary supplement
    Taking iron supplements 1 hour before or 2 hours after eating
        dairy products, eggs, coffee, tea, whole-grain breads and cere-
        als, antacids, or calcium supplements

Not taking iron supplements orally if receiving iron by injection
Avoiding regular use of large amounts of iron supplements several
    times daily for more than 6 months unless approved by physi-
    cian
Considering dietary iron as part of total daily intake
Extended-release dosage forms may not release iron properly;
    checking with physician if stools are not black during therapy
Keeping iron preparations out of the reach of children. Keeping
    syrup of ipecac readily available in case ordered for emergency
Keeping telephone numbers of poison control center, nearest hos-
    pital emergency room, and doctor readily available
» Suspected overdose: Immediately contacting physician, poison con-
    trol center, or emergency room; following any instructions given
    on phone; not delaying emergency treatment; taking container
    of iron medicine to emergency room

Side/adverse effects
    Dietary supplement causes black stools which may be alarming to
        patient although medically insignificant; checking with physi-
        cian if black stools occur with other symptoms of internal
        blood loss
    Signs of potential side effects, especially abdominal pain or con-
        tact irritation in alimentary tract

General Dosing Information

The elemental iron content of iron salts is as follows:

Iron Salt		% Elemental Iron
Ferrous fumarate	Ferrous	33
Ferrous gluconate	Ferrous	11.6
Ferrous sulfate	Ferrous	20
Ferrous sulfate, dried	Ferrous	30
Iron dextran	Ferric	*
Iron-polysaccharide	Ferric	*

*Variable, depending on product.

Noncompliance is a major factor in slow therapeutic results, espe-
    cially in patients requiring prolonged treatment.
In healthy adult males, there are approximately 50 mg of iron per kg
    of body weight and a hemoglobin concentration of about 14 to 18
    grams per 100 mL of whole blood.
In healthy adult females, there are approximately 35 mg of iron per kg
    of body weight and a hemoglobin concentration of about 12 to 16
    grams per 100 mL of whole blood.
The hemoglobin concentration of an iron-deficient patient usually
    reaches normal parameters after iron therapy of 1 or 2 months, but
    the plasma iron concentration often requires 3 to 6 months of
    therapy to reflect the normalization of body iron stores.
Normal term infants often receive 1 mg of supplemental iron per kg of
    body weight per day starting at about 3 months of age to meet
    requirements during rapid growth.
Infants of low birth weight may receive up to 2 mg per kg of body
    weight (mg/kg) of supplemental iron per day about 5 to 6 weeks
    after birth; dose then is gradually reduced to 1 mg/kg per day.
Concurrent use of ascorbic acid with iron in proper ratio is thought to
    enhance iron absorption by maintaining ferrous salts in the re-
    duced state and by reducing ferric salts to the more absorbable
    ferrous form; the suggested ratio is over 200 mg of ascorbic acid to
    30 mg of elemental iron.

Diet/Nutrition

Absorption of iron is most effective when the iron is ingested on an empty stomach; taking it with food will lessen absorption but will also lessen the chance of gastrointestinal irritation.

Taking iron supplements 1 hour before or 2 hours after eating dairy products, eggs, coffee, tea, or whole-grain breads and cereals will prevent the formation of less soluble or insoluble complexes, which decrease iron absorption.

The recommended dietary allowances (RDA) per day of iron (elemental) are as follows:

Infants and children—
    Birth to 6 months: 6 mg.
    6 months to 10 years: 10 mg.
Adolescent and adult males—
    11 to 18 years: 12 mg.
    19 years and over: 10 mg.
Adolescent and adult females—
    11 to 50 years: 15 mg.
    51 years and over: 10 mg.
Pregnant females—30 mg.
Lactating females—15 mg.

The best dietary source of iron is lean red meat. Chicken, turkey, and fish are less important sources of iron. Foods rich in vitamin C (e.g., citrus fruits and fresh vegetables) and heme iron-containing foods (such as found in meats) enhance nonheme iron absorption from cereals, beans, and other vegetables. Foods containing phytates, oxalates, fiber, and calcium may inhibit the absorption of nonheme iron. In food preparation, additional iron may be added through cooking in iron pots.

FERROUS FUMARATE

Summary of Differences

General dosing information: Contains 33% elemental ferrous iron.

Oral Dosage Forms

FERROUS FUMARATE CAPSULES

Usual adult and adolescent dose: Iron deficiency anemia—Oral, 300 mg one or two times a day.

Note: Caution patients about toxic effects of accidental overdose, especially in children, and need for immediate medical aid.

Auxiliary labeling: • Keep out of reach of children.

FERROUS FUMARATE EXTENDED-RELEASE CAPSULES

Usual adult and adolescent dose: Iron deficiency anemia—
Prophylactic: Oral, 325 mg a day.
Therapeutic: Oral, 325 mg two times a day.

Note: Caution patients about toxic effects of accidental overdose, especially in children, and need for immediate medical aid.

Auxiliary labeling:
• Swallow capsules whole.
• Keep out of reach of children.

FERROUS FUMARATE ORAL SOLUTION

Usual adult and adolescent dose: Iron deficiency anemia—
Prophylactic: Oral, 200 mg a day.
Therapeutic: Oral, 200 mg three or four times a day, the dosage being adjusted gradually, as needed and tolerated.

Auxiliary labeling:
• Protect from freezing.
• Keep out of reach of children.

FERROUS FUMARATE ORAL SUSPENSION

Usual adult and adolescent dose: Iron deficiency anemia—
Prophylactic: Oral, 200 mg a day.
Therapeutic: Oral, 200 mg three or four times a day, the dosage being adjusted gradually, as needed and tolerated.

Auxiliary labeling:
• Shake well before using.
• Protect from freezing.
• Keep out of reach of children.

FERROUS FUMARATE TABLETS USP

Usual adult and adolescent dose: Iron deficiency anemia—
Prophylactic: Oral, 200 mg a day.
Therapeutic: Oral, 200 mg three or four times a day, the dosage being adjusted gradually, as needed and tolerated.

Note: Caution patients about toxic effects of accidental overdose, especially in children, and need for immediate medical aid.

Auxiliary labeling: • Keep out of reach of children.

FERROUS FUMARATE CHEWABLE TABLETS

Usual adult and adolescent dose: Iron deficiency anemia—
Prophylactic: Oral, 200 mg a day.
Therapeutic: Oral, 200 mg three or four times a day, the dosage being adjusted gradually, as needed and tolerated.

Note: Caution patients about toxic effects of accidental overdose, especially in children, and need for immediate medical aid.

Auxiliary labeling:
• Chew well before swallowing.
• Keep out of reach of children.

FERROUS GLUCONATE

Summary of Differences

General dosing information: Contains 11.6% elemental ferrous iron.

Oral Dosage Forms

FERROUS GLUCONATE CAPSULES USP

Usual adult and adolescent dose: Iron deficiency anemia—
Prophylactic—Oral, 325 mg a day.
Therapeutic—Oral, 325 mg four times a day, the dosage being gradually increased up to 650 mg four times a day, as needed and tolerated.

Auxiliary labeling: • Keep out of reach of children.

FERROUS GLUCONATE ELIXIR USP

Usual adult and adolescent dose: Iron deficiency anemia—
Prophylactic—Oral, 300 mg a day.
Therapeutic—Oral, 300 mg four times a day, the dosage being gradually increased up to 650 mg four times a day, as needed and tolerated.

Auxiliary labeling: • Keep out of reach of children.

FERROUS GLUCONATE SYRUP

Usual adult and adolescent dose: Iron deficiency anemia—
Prophylactic—Oral, 300 mg a day.
Therapeutic—Oral, 300 mg four times a day, the dosage being
gradually increased up to 600 mg four times a day as needed
and tolerated.

Auxiliary labeling: • Keep out of reach of children.

FERROUS GLUCONATE TABLETS USP

Usual adult and adolescent dose: Iron deficiency anemia—
Prophylactic—Oral, 325 mg a day.
Therapeutic—Oral, 325 mg four times a day, the dosage being
gradually increased up to 650 mg four times a day, as needed
and tolerated.

Auxiliary labeling: • Keep out of reach of children.

FERROUS SULFATE

Summary of Differences

Precautions: Laboratory value alterations—Ferrous sulfate may give
false-negative results for glucose oxidase tests.
General dosing information: Contains 20% of elemental ferrous iron
(dried ferrous sulfate contains approximately 32% of elemental
iron).

Oral Dosage Forms

FERROUS SULFATE (DRIED) CAPSULES

Usual adult and adolescent dose: Iron deficiency anemia—
Prophylactic—Oral, 300 mg a day.
Therapeutic—Oral, 300 mg two times a day, the dosage being
gradually increased up to 300 mg four times a day, as needed
and tolerated.

Auxiliary labeling:
• Swallow capsules whole.
• Keep out of reach of children.

FERROUS SULFATE EXTENDED-RELEASE CAPSULES

Usual adult and adolescent dose: Iron deficiency anemia—Oral, 150
to 250 mg one or two times a day.

Auxiliary labeling:
• Swallow capsules whole.
• Keep out of reach of children.

FERROUS SULFATE ELIXIR

Usual adult and adolescent dose: Iron deficiency anemia—
Prophylactic—Oral, 300 mg a day.
Therapeutic—Oral, 300 mg two times a day, the dosage being
gradually increased up to 300 mg four times a day, as needed
and tolerated.

Auxiliary labeling: • Keep out of reach of children.

FERROUS SULFATE ORAL SOLUTION USP

Note: The oral solution is sometimes known as concentrate, drops, or
syrup.

Usual adult and adolescent dose: Iron deficiency anemia—
Prophylactic—Oral, 300 mg a day.
Therapeutic—Oral, 300 mg two times a day, the dosage being
gradually increased up to 300 mg four times a day, as needed
and tolerated.

Auxiliary labeling: • Keep out of reach of children.

FERROUS SULFATE TABLETS USP

Usual adult and adolescent dose: Iron deficiency anemia—
Prophylactic—Oral, 300 mg a day.
Therapeutic—Oral, 300 mg two times a day, the dosage being
gradually increased up to 300 mg four times a day, as needed
and tolerated.

Auxiliary labeling:
• Swallow tablets whole.
• Keep out of reach of children.

FERROUS SULFATE TABLETS USP (DRIED)

Usual adult and adolescent dose: Iron deficiency anemia—
Prophylactic—Oral, 200 mg a day.
Therapeutic—Oral, 200 mg two times a day, the dosage being
gradually increased up to 200 mg four times a day, as needed
and tolerated.

Auxiliary labeling:
• Swallow tablets whole.
• Keep out of reach of children.

FERROUS SULFATE ENTERIC-COATED TABLETS

Usual adult and adolescent dose: Iron deficiency anemia—
Prophylactic—Oral, 300 mg a day.
Therapeutic—Oral, 300 mg two times a day, the dosage being
gradually increased up to 300 mg four times a day as needed
and tolerated.

Auxiliary labeling:
• Swallow tablets whole.
• Keep out of reach of children.

FERROUS SULFATE EXTENDED-RELEASE TABLETS

Usual adult and adolescent dose: Iron deficiency anemia—Oral,
525 mg (of ferrous sulfate, heptahydrate) one or two times a day.

Additional information: Products utilize a plastic matrix that may
appear intact in the stool.

Auxiliary labeling:
• Swallow tablets whole.
• Keep out of reach of children.

FERROUS SULFATE (DRIED) EXTENDED-RELEASE TABLETS

Usual adult and adolescent dose: Iron deficiency anemia—Oral,
160 mg one or two times a day

Note: Caution patients about toxic effects of overdose, especially in
children, and need for immediate medical aid.

Additional information: Products utilize a porous wax matrix that
may appear intact in the stool.

Auxiliary labeling:
• Swallow tablets whole.
• Keep out of reach of children.

IRON DEXTRAN

Summary of Differences

General dosing information: Contains elemental ferric form of iron.

Additional Dosing Information

Oral iron must be discontinued before the administration of parenteral iron.

Epinephrine should be immediately available during injection of iron dextran, especially in patients with allergies or asthma.

Overdose with iron dextran produces no acute toxicity. However, excessive doses beyond the amounts required for restoration of hemoglobin and replenishment of iron stores may result in hemosiderosis. Excess iron may also increase a patient's susceptibility to infection, especially *Yersinia enterocolitica*.

Factors contributing to the formula for determining dosages for patients with iron deficiency include:

Blood volume—7.0% of body weight
Normal hemoglobin (males and females)—
15 kg (33 lb) or less: 12 grams/deciliter (dL)
Over 15 kg (33 lb): 14.8 grams/deciliter (dL)
Iron content of hemoglobin—0.34%
Body weight

For intravenous injection:

Iron dextran is administered undiluted and injected slowly at a rate not exceeding 1 mL per minute. However, some clinicians recommend that the calculated dose of iron dextran for the patient be added to 500 mL of dextrose 5% and infused over 4 to 5 hours, after a test infusion of 10 drops per minute for 10 minutes.

The manufacturer does not recommend that iron dextran be mixed with other medications or added to parenteral nutrition solutions for intravenous infusion; however, iron dextran is added to total parenteral nutrition solutions in current medical practice.

For intramuscular injection:

• Iron dextran should be injected only into the muscle mass of the upper outer quadrant of the buttock. It should *never* be injected into the arm or other exposed areas.
• Deep injection with a 2- to 3-inch, 19- or 20-gauge needle is recommended.
• If the patient is standing during administration of iron dextran, body weight should be on the leg opposite to the injection site.
• If the patient is lying down during administration of iron dextran, he/she should be in a lateral position with injection site uppermost.
• A Z-track technique (displacement of the skin laterally prior to injection) is recommended to avoid injection or leakage into subcutaneous tissue.

Test dose—An intramuscular or intravenous test dose of 25 mg (elemental iron) should be given to all patients before receiving their first therapeutic dose. Although anaphylactic reactions may be evident within the first few minutes after injection, one hour or longer should elapse before the initial therapeutic dose. The intramuscular test dose should be administered in the same injection site and by the same technique as the therapeutic dose.

If no adverse reactions are observed after the test dose, the daily dose of iron dextran may be given according to the following schedule until the total calculated amount has been reached:

For infants up to 5 kg of body weight—25 mg (elemental iron)
For children under 10 kg—50 mg (elemental iron)
Other patients—100 mg (elemental iron)

Parenteral Dosage Forms

IRON DEXTRAN INJECTION USP

Usual adult and adolescent dose: Iron deficiency anemia—

To restore hemoglobin and replenish iron stores: Intravenous or intramuscular, the dosage being determined by the following dosage table:

Patient Weight		Total Iron Dextran Requirement (mL)*							
		Based on Observed Hemoglobin (grams/dL) of:							
lb	kg	3	4	5	6	7	8	9	10
11	5	3	3	3	2	2	2	2	1
22	10	6	6	5	5	4	4	3	3
33	15	9	9	8	7	7	6	5	4
44	20	15	14	13	12	11	10	10	9
55	25	19	18	17	15	14	13	12	11
66	30	23	21	20	19	17	16	14	13
77	35	27	25	23	22	20	18	17	15
88	40	30	29	27	25	23	21	19	17
99	45	34	32	30	28	26	24	21	19
110	50	38	36	33	31	29	26	24	21
121	55	42	39	37	34	31	29	26	24
132	60	46	43	40	37	34	31	29	26
143	65	50	46	43	40	37	34	31	28
154	70	53	50	47	43	40	37	33	30
165	75	56	53	49	45	42	38	35	31
176	80	59	55	51	48	44	40	36	32
187	85	62	58	54	50	46	42	37	33
198	90	65	60	56	52	47	43	39	35
209	95	67	63	58	54	49	45	40	36
220	100	70	65	61	56	51	46	42	37
230	105	73	68	63	58	53	48	43	38
242	110	76	71	65	60	55	50	44	39
253	115	79	73	68	62	57	51	46	40
264	120		81	76	70	64	59	53	47

*Dosage was calculated using the formula: Dose = 0.0476 3 W 3 (Normal H — Observed H) + 1 mL per 5 kg of body weight to a maximum of 14 mL for iron stores.

To calculate the total amount of iron dextran (mL) required to restore hemoglobin and to replenish iron stores in adults and children weighing over 15 kg (33 lb), when W=body weight in kg, and H=hemoglobin in grams per deciliter:

• Iron dextran (mL)=0.0476 3 W 3 (14.8 — H) + iron stores.
• Add 1 mL of iron dextran injection per 5 kg of body weight to provide for the replenishment of iron stores to a maximum of 14 mL.
• For weight in pounds, use the factor 0.0216.
• The dosage table above is *not* to be used for simple iron replacement from periodic blood loss in patients with hemorrhagic diatheses (familial telangiectasia; hemophilia; gastrointestinal bleeding) or patients on renal hemodialysis.

To replace the equivalent amount of iron represented in blood loss (based on the approximation that 1 mL of normocytic, normochromic red cells contains 1 mg of elemental iron)—Intramuscular or intravenous, the total iron requirement to be determined as follows:

- Replacement iron (mg) = Blood loss (mL) 3 hematocrit.
- To calculate dose in mL of iron dextran injection, divide result by 50.

Additional information: Vehicle in iron dextran injection is 0.9% sodium chloride injection.

IRON-POLYSACCHARIDE

Summary of Differences

General dosing information: Contains elemental ferric form of iron.

Additional Dosing Information

Strengths of products expressed in terms of elemental iron content only.

Oral Dosage Forms

IRON-POLYSACCHARIDE CAPSULES

Usual adult and adolescent dose: Iron deficiency anemia—
Prophylactic—Oral, 150 mg (elemental ferric iron) a day.
Therapeutic—Oral, 150 mg (elemental ferric iron) two times a day, the dosage being increased up to 150 mg four times a day as needed and tolerated.

Auxiliary labeling: • Keep out of reach of children.

IRON-POLYSACCHARIDE ELIXIR

Usual adult and adolescent dose: Iron deficiency anemia—
Prophylactic—Oral, 100 mg (elemental ferric iron) a day.
Therapeutic—Oral, 100 mg (elemental ferric iron) two times a day, the dosage being increased up to 100 mg four times a day as needed and tolerated.

Auxiliary labeling: • Keep out of reach of children.

IRON-POLYSACCHARIDE TABLETS

Usual adult and adolescent dose: Iron deficiency anemia—
Prophylactic—Oral, 150 mg (elemental ferric iron) a day.
Therapeutic—Oral, 150 mg (elemental ferric iron) two times a day, the dosage being increased up to 150 mg four times a day as needed and tolerated.

Auxiliary labeling: • Keep out of reach of children.

IRON SORBITOL

Summary of Differences

General dosing information: Contains elemental ferric form of iron.

Additional Dosing Information

Oral iron must be discontinued before the administration of parenteral iron.

For intramuscular injection:

- Iron sorbitol should be injected only into the muscle mass of the upper outer quadrant of the buttock. It should *never* be injected into the arm or other exposed areas.
- Deep injection with a 2- to 3-inch, 19- or 20-gauge needle is recommended.
- If the patient is standing during administration of iron sorbitol, body weight should be on the leg opposite to the injection site.
- If the patient is lying down during administration of iron sorbitol, he/she should be in a lateral position with injection site uppermost.
- A Z-track technique (displacement of the skin laterally prior to injection) is recommended to avoid injection or leakage into subcutaneous tissue.

Parenteral Dosage Form

IRON SORBITOL INJECTION

Usual adult and adolescent dose: Iron deficiency anemia—
To restore hemoglobin and replenish iron stores: Intramuscular, the daily dosage is determined based on 1.5 mg of elemental iron per kg of body weight. The calculated daily dose may be administered daily or every other day until hemoglobin values are normal.

To increase hemoglobin by 1 gram per 100 mL: Intramuscular administration of 200 mg elemental iron for women and 250 mg for men is necessary. To replenish iron stores, an additional 250 to 1000 mg of elemental iron is needed.

Note: Some clinicians recommend that iron sorbitol injection be given in divided doses of 50 mg per week because larger doses are painful to the patient.

Usual adult prescribing limits: 100 mg per day.

ISOMETHEPTENE, DICHLORALPHENAZONE, AND ACETAMINOPHEN   Systemic

INN: Acetaminophen—Paracetamol

Some commonly used *brand names* are:

In the U.S.—
Amidrine	*Migquin*
I.D.A.	*Migratine*
Iso-Acetazone	*Migrazone*
Isocom	*Migrend*
Midchlor	*Migrex*
Midrin	*Mitride*
Migrapap	

ORAL

Isometheptene Mucate, Dichloralphenazone, and Acetaminophen Capsules

In the U.S.—*Amidrine; I.D.A.; Iso-Acetazone; Isocom; Midchlor; Midrin; Migrapap; Migquin; Migratine; Migrazone; Migrend; Migrex; Mitride*

Category: Vascular headache suppressant (migraine).

Note: Some headache specialists question the validity of the term "vascular headache" because a correlation between dilatation of cerebral blood vessels and symptoms of migraine has not been demonstrated conclusively.

Indications

Accepted

Headache, migraine (treatment) and

Headache, tension-type (treatment)—Isometheptene, dichloralphenazone, and acetaminophen combination is indicated to relieve occasional migraine headaches (with or without aura) and coexisting migraine and tension-type headaches ("mixed" headache syndrome). However, the U.S. FDA has classified this combination as being "possibly" effective in the treatment of migraine headaches. This classification requires the submission of adequate and well-controlled studies in order to provide substantial evidence of effectiveness.

Note: Some headache specialists question the value of this formulation in pure tension-type headaches. However, the distinction between vascular, tension-type, and "mixed" headaches is often difficult or uncertain, and the medication may relieve some headaches characterized as tension-type.

Because frequent use of headache-aborting medications by headache-prone individuals may lead to tolerance and dependence, this medication is not recommended for regular use by patients who experience frequent, especially daily, headaches.

To reduce analgesic use, underlying problems that may contribute to tension-type headaches, such as inflammation or structural abnormalities in the cervical or temporomandibular areas, should be identified and treated. In some patients, application of heat, muscle relaxants, and/or physical therapy may be helpful. Other medications having the potential to cause habituation (e.g., benzodiazepines used as muscle relaxants) should be used as infrequently as possible.

Chronic tension-type headaches and severe migraines that occur more frequently than twice a month may require additional prophylactic treatment to reduce the frequency, severity, and/or duration of the headaches. The prophylactic agents most commonly used for tension-type headaches are tricyclic antidepressants, especially amitriptyline, and/or beta-adrenergic blocking agents, especially propranolol. For migraines, beta-adrenergic blocking agents, calcium channel blocking agents, tricyclic antidepressants, monoamine oxidase inhibitors, methysergide, pizotyline (not commercially available in the U.S.), and sometimes cyproheptadine (especially in children) are used as prophylaxis. The combination of amitriptyline plus propranolol has been found superior to either agent used alone as prophylaxis against "mixed" headaches.

Identification and avoidance of precipitating factors is also important in the overall management of the patient with migraine headaches. Relaxation and/or biofeedback techniques may also be helpful in controlling some types of headache, and may reduce the need for medication.

Pharmacology

Mechanism of action/Effects:

Isometheptene—The mechanism of action has not been established. Isometheptene is an indirect-acting sympathomimetic agent with vasoconstricting activity. It has been proposed that constriction of cerebral blood vessels reduces the pulsation in cerebral arteries that may be responsible for the pain of migraine headaches. However, studies have not consistently shown a significant correlation between dilatation of cerebral blood vessels and pain or other symptoms of migraine headaches, or between a vasoconstrictive action and relief of migraine.

Dichloralphenazone—A complex of chloral hydrate and antipyrine (INN: phenazone). It is present in this formulation as a mild sedative and relaxant.

Acetaminophen—The mechanism of analgesic action has not been fully determined. Acetaminophen may act predominantly by inhibiting prostaglandin synthesis in the central nervous system (CNS) and, to a lesser extent, through a peripheral action by blocking pain-impulse generation. The peripheral action may also be due to inhibition of prostaglandin synthesis or to inhibition of the synthesis or actions of other substances that sensitize pain receptors to mechanical or chemical stimulation.

Time to peak effect: Acetaminophen—1 to 3 hours.

Duration of action: Acetaminophen—3 to 4 hours.

Precautions to Consider

Note: The quantity of dichloralphenazone in this combination formulation does not provide full therapeutic doses of its active components chloral hydrate and antipyrine (phenazone). However, the possibility should be considered that precautions applying to chloral hydrate (see *Chloral Hydrate [Systemic]*) and to antipyrine may apply to ingestion of an overdose or to overuse of this combination medication.

Cross-sensitivity and/or related problems

Patients sensitive to aspirin are usually not sensitive to acetaminophen; however, acetaminophen has caused mild bronchospastic reactions in some aspirin-sensitive asthmatics (less than 5% of those tested).

Geriatrics

No published information is available on the relationship of age to the effects of this combination medication in geriatric patients. Geriatric patients are more likely to have peripheral vascular disease, and are therefore more likely to be adversely affected by peripheral vasoconstriction, than are younger adults. However, isometheptene may be safer for elderly patients than the ergot derivatives used to abort acute vascular headaches. Also, elderly patients are more likely to have age-related renal function impairment, which may require caution in patients receiving acetaminophen and isometheptene.

Drug interactions and/or related problems

The following drug interactions and/or related problems have been selected on the basis of their potential clinical significance (possible mechanism in parentheses where appropriate)—not necessarily inclusive (» = major clinical significance):

Note: Combinations containing any of the following medications, depending on the amount present, may also interact with this medication.

Alcohol or
CNS depressants
(concurrent use with dichloralphenazone may cause additive sedation)

Alcohol, especially chronic abuse of, or
Hepatic enzyme inducers or
Hepatotoxic medications, other
(risk of hepatotoxicity with single toxic doses of acetaminophen may be increased in alcoholics or in patients regularly taking other hepatotoxic medications or hepatic enzyme-inducing agents)

(chronic use of barbiturates [except butalbital] or primidone has been reported to decrease the therapeutic effects of acetaminophen, probably because of increased metabolism resulting from induction of hepatic microsomal enzyme activity; the possibility should be considered that similar effects may occur with other hepatic enzyme inducers)

» Monoamine oxidase (MAO) inhibitors
(concurrent use with an indirect-acting sympathomimetic such as isometheptene may cause sudden and severe hypertension and hyperpyrexia, which can reach crisis levels)

Contraindications/Medical problems

The contraindications/medical problems included have been selected on the basis of their potential clinical significance (reasons given in parentheses where appropriate)—not necessarily inclusive (» = major clinical significance).

Risk-benefit should be considered when the following medical problems exist

» Alcoholism, active, or
» Hepatic function impairment or
» Viral hepatitis
(increased risk of acetaminophen-induced hepatotoxicity)

Any condition in which the vasoconstrictive or other sympathomimetic effects of isometheptene may be hazardous, such as:
Cardiovascular or cerebrovascular insufficiency, including recent myocardial infarction or stroke

» Glaucoma, not optimally controlled
» Hypertension, not optimally controlled
» Organic heart disease
Peripheral vascular disease

» Renal function impairment, severe
Sensitivity to acetaminophen or to isometheptene, history of

Side/Adverse Effects

Note: The quantity of dichloralphenazone in this combination formulation does not provide full therapeutic doses of its active metabolites chloral hydrate and antipyrine (phenazone). However, the possibility should be considered that ingestion of an overdose or overuse of this combination medication may induce side effects characteristic of chloral hydrate (see *Chloral Hydrate [Systemic]*) and/or antipyrine.

The following side/adverse effects have been selected on the basis of their potential clinical significance (possible signs and symptoms in parentheses where appropriate)—not necessarily inclusive:

Those indicating need for medical attention
Incidence less frequent
Anemia or methemoglobinemia (unusual tiredness or weakness)

Incidence rare
Agranulocytosis (unexplained sore throat and fever); *anemia* (unusual tiredness or weakness); *dermatitis, allergic* (skin rash, hives, or itching); *hepatitis* (yellow eyes or skin); *thrombocytopenia* (usually asymptomatic; rarely, unusual bleeding or bruising; black, tarry stools; blood in urine or stools; pinpoint red spots on skin)

Symptoms of tolerance and/or dependence—with overuse
Headaches—more frequent, severe, and difficult to treat than previously

Signs and symptoms of acetaminophen overdose
Gastrointestinal upset (diarrhea, loss of appetite, nausea or vomiting, stomach cramps or pain); *increased sweating; hepatotoxicity* (pain, tenderness, and/or swelling in upper abdominal area)

Note: Early signs and symptoms of acetaminophen overdose, i.e., *gastrointestinal upset* and *increased sweating* often do not occur. However, when they do occur, they usually appear within 6 to 14 hours after ingestion of an overdose and persist for about 24 hours.

The first indications of overdosage may be signs and symptoms of possible *liver damage* and abnormalities in liver function tests, which may not occur until 2 to 4 days after ingestion of the overdose. Maximal changes in liver function tests usually occur 3 to 5 days after ingestion of the overdose.

Overt *hepatic disease or failure* may occur 4 to 6 days after ingestion of the overdose. *Hepatic encephalopathy* (with mental changes, confusion, agitation, or stupor), *convulsions, respiratory depression, coma, cerebral edema, coagulation defects, gastrointestinal bleeding, disseminated intravascular coagulation, hypoglycemia, metabolic acidosis, cardiac arrhythmias, and cardiovascular collapse* may occur.

Renal tubular necrosis leading to *renal failure* (signs may include bloody or cloudy urine and sudden decrease in amount of urine) has also been reported in acetaminophen overdose, usually, but not exclusively, in conjunction with acetaminophen-induced *hepatotoxicity*.

Those indicating need for medical attention only if they continue or are bothersome
Incidence more frequent
Drowsiness

Incidence less frequent or rare—dose-related
Dizziness; fast or irregular heartbeat

Patient Consultation

In providing consultation, consider emphasizing the following selected information (» = major clinical significance):

Before using this medication
» Conditions affecting use, especially:
Allergic reaction to acetaminophen or to this combination medication, history of
Pregnancy—Acetaminophen crosses the placenta
Breast-feeding—Acetaminophen is excreted in breast milk
Use by athletes—Isometheptene is banned and tested for in athletes by the International Olympic Committee (IOC), the U.S. Olympic Committee (USOC), and the National Collegiate Athletic Association (NCAA); dichloralphenazone is banned in competitors in biathlon and modern pentathlon events by the USOC
Other medications, especially monoamine oxidase inhibitors
Other medical problems, especially alcoholism (active), glaucoma, hypertension, heart disease, hepatic disease or viral hepatitis, and severe renal function impairment

Proper use of this medication

» Importance of not taking more medication than the amount prescribed; risk of tolerance and dependence with too frequent use; also, acetaminophen may cause liver damage with long-term use or greater than recommended doses
» Most effective when taken as soon as headache appears or at first sign of migraine attack (prodromal stage)
» Lying down in a quiet, dark room after taking initial dose
» Compliance with prophylactic therapy, if prescribed Proper dosing
» Proper storage

Precautions while using this medication

» Checking with physician if usual dose fails to relieve headaches, or if frequency and/or severity of headaches increases; possibility that tolerance to the medication has developed and/or withdrawal (rebound) or chronic, daily headaches are occurring
» Caution if other medications containing acetaminophen are used
» Caution when driving or doing jobs requiring alertness because of possible drowsiness or dizziness, especially if also taking a CNS depressant.
» Avoiding use of alcohol, which increases the risk of liver toxicity with high doses of acetaminophen, especially in alcoholics; also, alcohol may aggravate or induce headache

Side/adverse effects

Signs of potential side effects, especially allergic dermatitis, blood dyscrasias, hepatotoxicity, and methemoglobinemia

General Dosing Information

Therapy is most effective when initiated at the first symptoms of a headache (during the prodrome, for migraine with aura).

After the first dose has been administered, it is recommended that the patient lie down and relax in a quiet, darkened room, because this contributes to relief of headaches.

In headache-prone individuals, frequent use of headache relievers may cause tolerance, leading to an increased dosage requirement, and to physical dependence, leading to both medication abuse and chronic (daily or near-daily) headaches. Patients who experience frequent headaches may also be dependent on a variety of other medications, including opioid analgesics, barbiturate-containing analgesic combinations, simple analgesics such as acetaminophen or aspirin, ergotamine, and antianxiety agents or sedatives.

Chronic headaches resulting from overmedication may be difficult to relieve, especially if the patient continues to take headache suppressants and/or analgesics. It is recommended that all such medications be discontinued. In-patient treatment may be necessary during detoxification. Naproxen, alone or together with amitriptyline, may reduce the severity of the headaches. Repetitive intravenous administration of dihydroergotamine (in conjunction with metoclopramide [to control dihydroergotamine-induced nausea and vomiting]) is recommended by some headache specialists to relieve chronic, intractable headaches associated with dependency on headache-aborting medications. Appropriate treatment for symptoms of withdrawal from other substances frequently used or abused by chronic headache patients may also be needed. In addition, appropriate prophylactic treatment should be initiated or adjusted to reduce the frequency and/or severity of future headaches.

Oral Dosage Forms

ISOMETHEPTENE MUCATE, DICHLORALPHENAZONE, AND ACETAMINOPHEN CAPSULES

Usual adult dose:

Tension-type headache—Oral, 1 or 2 capsules every four hours as needed, up to 8 capsules a day.
Vascular headache suppressant (migraine)—Oral, 2 capsules at the start of the attack (during the prodrome, for migraine with aura), followed by 1 capsule every hour as needed, up to 5 capsules in twelve hours.

ISOPROTERENOL AND PHENYLEPHRINE   Systemic

Some commonly used *brand names* are:
    In the U.S.—*Duo-Medihaler*
    In Canada—*Duo-Medihaler; Isuprel-Neo Mistometer*

INHALATION

Isoproterenol Hydrochloride and Phenylephrine Bitartrate Inhalation Aerosol USP
    In the U.S. and Canada—*Duo-Medihaler*
Isoproterenol Hydrochloride and Phenylephrine Hydrochloride Inhalation Aerosol*
    In Canada—*Isuprel-Neo Mistometer*

---

*Not commercially available in the U.S.

Category: Bronchodilator-decongestant.

Indications

Accepted

Asthma, bronchial (treatment);
Bronchiectasis (treatment);
Bronchitis (treatment);
Emphysema, pulmonary (treatment); or

Pulmonary disease, chronic obstructive, other (treatment)—Isoproterenol and phenylephrine combination is indicated for the treatment of bronchospasm associated with acute and chronic bronchial asthma, pulmonary emphysema, bronchitis, bronchiectasis, and other chronic obstructive pulmonary disease.

Pharmacology

Mechanism of action/Effect:

Isoproterenol—Isoproterenol is a direct-acting sympathomimetic amine that acts predominantly on beta-adrenergic receptors. It relaxes bronchial smooth muscle by acting on beta-2-adrenergic receptors, thereby relieving bronchospasm, increasing vital capacity, reducing residual volume in the lungs, and facilitating passage of pulmonary secretions. It may also inhibit antigen-induced release of histamine.

Phenylephrine—Phenylephrine is both a direct-acting and an indirect-acting sympathomimetic amine. It acts on alpha-adrenergic receptors of the bronchiolar vascular beds to produce vasoconstriction, thereby reducing bronchiolar blood flow, shrinking swollen membranes, relieving congestion and edema, and prolonging the duration of action of the isoproterenol by slowing systemic absorption of the medication.

Onset of action: Within a few minutes.

Duration of action: Up to 3 hours.

Precautions to Consider

Cross-sensitivity and/or related problems
Patients sensitive to other sympathomimetics may be sensitive to this medication also.

Geriatrics
No published geriatrics-specific information is available.

Drug interactions and/or related problems
The following drug interactions and/or related problems have been selected on the basis of their potential clinical significance (possible mechanism in parentheses where appropriate)—not necessarily inclusive (» = major clinical significance):

Note: Combinations containing any of the following medications, depending on the amount present, may also interact with this medication.

Anesthetics, hydrocarbon inhalation, such as:
Chloroform
Cyclopropane
Enflurane
Halothane
Isoflurane
Methoxyflurane
Trichloroethylene
(administration of high doses of isoproterenol and phenylephrine combination prior to or shortly after anesthesia with chloroform, cyclopropane, halothane, or trichloroethylene may increase the risk of severe ventricular arrhythmias, especially in patients with pre-existing heart disease, because these anesthetics greatly sensitize the myocardium to the effects of sympathomimetics)

(enflurane, isoflurane, or methoxyflurane may also cause some sensitization of the myocardium to the effects of sympathomimetics; caution is recommended during concurrent use with the sympathomimetic)

» Antidepressants, tricyclic, or
» Maprotiline
(concurrent use may potentiate cardiovascular effects of isoproterenol and phenylephrine, possibly resulting in arrhythmias, tachycardia, or severe hypertension or hyperpyrexia)

Antihypertensives or
Diuretics used as antihypertensives
(antihypertensive effects may be reduced when these medications are used concurrently with isoproterenol and phenylephrine; the patient should be carefully monitored to confirm that the desired effect is being obtained)

» Beta-adrenergic blocking agents
(concurrent use with isoproterenol may result in mutual inhibition of therapeutic effects; beta-blockade may antagonize beta-2-adrenergic bronchodilating effects of isoproterenol; use of a cardioselective beta-2-adrenergic blocker, such as acebutolol, atenolol, or metoprolol, at low doses may reduce antagonism of the bronchodilating effect)

Central nervous system (CNS) stimulation-producing medications, other
(concurrent use with isoproterenol may result in additive CNS stimulation to excessive levels, which may cause unwanted effects such as nervousness, irritability, insomnia, or possibly convulsions or cardiac arrhythmias; close observation is recommended)

» Cocaine, mucosal-local
(in addition to increasing CNS stimulation, concurrent use with phenylephrine may increase the cardiovascular effects of either or both medications and the risk of adverse effects)

» Digitalis glycosides
(concurrent use with isoproterenol and phenylephrine may increase the risk of cardiac arrhythmias; caution and electrocardiographic monitoring are very important if concurrent use is necessary)

Dihydroergotamine or
» Ergoloid mesylates or
Ergonovine or
» Ergotamine or
Methylergonovine or
Methysergide or
Oxytocin
(concurrent use of dihydroergotamine, ergonovine, methylergonovine, or methysergide with phenylephrine may result in enhanced vasoconstriction; dosage adjustments may be necessary)

(concurrent use of ergoloid mesylates or ergotamine with phenylephrine may produce peripheral vascular ischemia and gangrene and is not recommended)

(concurrent use of ergonovine, ergotamine, methylergonovine, or oxytocin with phenylephrine may potentiate the pressor effect of phenylephrine with possible severe hypertension and rupture of cerebral blood vessels)

Guanadrel or
Guanethidine
(in addition to possibly decreasing the hypotensive effect of guanadrel or guanethidine, concurrent use may potentiate the pressor effect of phenylephrine; these actions are a result of inhibition of sympathomimetic uptake by adrenergic neurons and may lead to hypertension and cardiac arrhythmias)

Levodopa
(concurrent use with isoproterenol and phenylephrine may increase the possibility of cardiac arrhythmias; dosage reduction of the sympathomimetic is recommended)

Mazindol or
Methylphenidate
(concurrent use may potentiate the pressor effect of phenylephrine)

Mecamylamine or
» Methyldopa or
Trimethaphan
(in addition to possibly decreasing the hypotensive effects of these medications, concurrent use may enhance the pressor response to phenylephrine)

» Monoamine oxidase (MAO) inhibitors, including furazolidone, pargyline, and procarbazine
(concurrent use may prolong and intensify cardiac stimulant and vasopressor effects of phenylephrine because of release of catecholamines that accumulate in intraneuronal storage sites during MAO inhibitor therapy, resulting in headache, cardiac arrhythmias, vomiting, or sudden and severe hypertensive and/or hyperpyretic crises; phenylephrine should not be administered during or within 14 days following administration of MAO inhibitors)

Nitrates
(concurrent use with isoproterenol and phenylephrine may reduce the antianginal effects of these medications)

Rauwolfia alkaloids
(in addition to possibly decreasing the hypotensive effects of rauwolfia alkaloids, concurrent use may theoretically prolong the action of direct-acting sympathomimetics, such as phenylephrine, by preventing uptake into storage granules; a "denervation supersensitivity" response is also possible; although concurrent use with systemic phenylephrine is not known to produce severe adverse effects, a significant increase in blood pressure has been documented when phenylephrine ophthalmic drops have been administered to patients taking reserpine, and caution and close observation are recommended)

Sympathomimetics, other
(concurrent use may increase the cardiovascular effects of either the other sympathomimetics or isoproterenol and phenylephrine and the potential for side effects)

Thyroid hormones
(concurrent use may increase the effects of either these medications or isoproterenol and phenylephrine; thyroid hormones enhance risk of coronary insufficiency when sympathomimetic agents are administered to patients with coronary artery disease; dosage adjustment is recommended, although problem is reduced in euthyroid patients)

Xanthines, such as:
Aminophylline
Caffeine
Dyphylline
Oxtriphylline
Theophylline
(in addition to possibly increasing CNS stimulation, concurrent use with isoproterenol may result in other additive toxic effects)

Contraindications/Medical problems

The contraindications/medical problems included have been selected on the basis of their potential clinical significance (reasons given in parentheses where appropriate)—not necessarily inclusive (» = major clinical significance).

Risk-benefit should be considered when the following medical problems exist:

» Cardiac arrhythmias associated with tachycardia, pre-existing, or Cardiovascular disorders, including coronary insufficiency, or Hypertension
(condition may be exacerbated due to drug-induced cardiovascular effects)

Diabetes mellitus
Hyperthyroidism
(adverse reactions more likely to occur)

Sensitivity to isoproterenol, phenylephrine, or other sympathomimetics

Side/Adverse Effects

The following side/adverse effects have been selected on the basis of their potential clinical significance (possible signs and symptoms in parentheses where appropriate)—not necessarily inclusive:

Those indicating need for medical attention
Incidence rare
Angina (chest pain); *cardiac arrhythmias* (irregular heartbeat)

Symptoms of overdose
Angina (chest pain), *continuing or severe; bradycardia* (slow heartbeat), *continuing; cardiac arrhythmias* (irregular heartbeat), *continuing or severe; dizziness or lightheadedness, continuing or severe; headache, continuing or severe; increase in blood pressure; nausea or vomiting, continuing or severe; palpitations* (pounding heartbeat), *continuing; sensation of fullness in head; tachycardia* (fast heartbeat), *continuing; tingling in hands or feet; trembling, severe; unusual anxiety, nervousness, or restlessness; weakness, severe*

Those indicating need for medical attention only if they continue or are bothersome
Incidence more frequent
Insomnia (trouble in sleeping); *nervousness or restlessness*

Incidence less frequent
Dizziness or lightheadedness; flushing or redness of face or skin; headache; increased sweating; nausea or vomiting; palpitations (pounding heartbeat); *tachycardia* (fast heartbeat); *trembling; weakness*

Those not indicating need for medical attention
Pinkish to red coloration of saliva

Patient Consultation

In providing consultation, consider emphasizing the following selected information (» = major clinical significance):

Before using this medication
» Conditions affecting use, especially:
Sensitivity to isoproterenol, phenylephrine, or other sympathomimetics
Pregnancy—Use of phenylephrine during late pregnancy or during labor may cause fetal anoxia and bradycardia by increasing contractility of the uterus and decreasing uterine blood flow
Other medications, especially antidepressants, beta-adrenergic blocking agents, cocaine (mucosal-local), digitalis glycosides, ergoloid mesylates, ergotamine, or methyldopa
Other medical problems, especially pre-existing cardiac arrhythmias associated with tachycardia

Proper use of this medication
Proper administration: Reading patient instructions carefully before using
Avoiding contact with the eyes
» Taking no more than 2 inhalations at one time with interval of 1 to 5 minutes between inhalations
Saving applicator; refill units may be available
» Importance of not using more medication than the amount prescribed
» Proper storage

Precautions while using this medication
» Checking with physician immediately if difficulty in breathing persists after using this medication or if condition becomes worse

For patients also using an adrenocorticoid or ipratropium inhalation aerosol
» Using isoproterenol and phenylephrine inhalation aerosol 5 minutes prior to the adrenocorticoid or ipratropium inhalation aerosol, unless otherwise directed by physician

Side/adverse effects
Signs of potential side effects, especially chest pain and irregular heartbeat
Pinkish to red coloration of saliva caused by oxidation of isoproterenol in mouth may be alarming to patient although medically insignificant

General Dosing Information

Excessive use may result in loss of effectiveness. If this occurs, discontinuation of the medication and use of alternative therapy are recommended.

Repeated excessive use may result in severe paradoxical airway resistance.

Isoproterenol and epinephrine may be used alternately, but not concurrently, provided that enough time has elapsed for the effects of one medication to subside before the alternate medication is administered.

When used in conjunction with an adrenocorticoid or ipratropium oral inhalation aerosol, isoproterenol and phenylephrine inhalation aerosol should be administered 5 minutes prior to the adrenocorticoid or ipratropium inhalation aerosol. This interval allows for bronchodilation to occur and increased deposition of the adrenocorticoid or ipratropium within the bronchi.

Inhalation Dosage Forms

ISOPROTERENOL HYDROCHLORIDE AND PHENYLEPHRINE BITARTRATE INHALATION AEROSOL USP

Usual adult and adolescent dose: Asthma, bronchial; bronchiectasis; bronchitis; emphysema, pulmonary; or other chronic obstructive pulmonary disease—Oral inhalation, 1 inhalation, repeated after two to five minutes if necessary, four to six times a day.

Auxiliary labeling:
- For oral inhalation only.
- Shake well.
- Store away from heat and direct sunlight.

ISOPROTERENOL HYDROCHLORIDE AND PHENYLEPHRINE HYDROCHLORIDE INHALATION AEROSOL

Note: Isoproterenol hydrochloride and phenylephrine hydrochloride inhalation aerosol is not commercially available in the U.S.

Usual adult and adolescent dose: Asthma, bronchial; bronchitis, chronic; or emphysema, pulmonary—Oral inhalation, 1 inhalation, repeated after one minute if necessary, not to exceed eight treatments in twenty-four hours.

Auxiliary labeling:
- For oral inhalation only.
- Shake well.
- Store away from heat and direct sunlight.

KAOLIN AND PECTIN   Oral-Local

Some commonly used *brand names* are:

In the U.S.—

Kao-tin	*K-P*
Kapectolin	*K-Pek*
K-C	

In Canada—

Donnagel-MB	*Kao-Con*

ORAL-LOCAL
Kaolin and Pectin Oral Suspension
In the U.S.—*Kao-tin; Kapectolin; K-C; K-P; K-Pek;* GENERIC
In Canada—*Donnagel-MB; Kao-Con*

Category: Antidiarrheal (adsorbent).

Indications

Accepted
Diarrhea (treatment)—Kaolin and pectin may be indicated as an adjunct to rest, fluids, and an appropriate diet in the symptomatic treatment of mild to moderately acute diarrhea. Use is recommended in chronic diarrhea only as temporary symptomatic treatment until the etiology is determined.

Pharmacology

Mechanism of action/Effect: Adsorbent and protectant. Kaolin is a natural hydrated aluminum silicate that supposedly adsorbs large numbers of bacteria and toxins and reduces water loss. Pectin is a polyuronic polymer whose mechanism of action is unknown and which consists of purified carbohydrate extracted from citrus fruit or apple pomace. However, one study showed no decrease in stool frequency or fecal weight and water content with this combination even though stools appeared more formed.

Precautions to Consider

Geriatrics
In geriatric patients with diarrhea, caution is recommended because of the risk of fluid and electrolyte loss; these patients should be referred to a physician.

Drug interactions and/or related problems
The following drug interactions and/or related problems have been selected on the basis of their potential clinical significance (possible mechanism in parentheses where appropriate)—not necessarily inclusive (» = major clinical significance):

Note: Combinations containing any of the following medications, depending on the amount present, may also interact with this medication.

Anticholinergics or other medications with anticholinergic activity, or
Antidyskinetics or
Digitalis glycosides or
Lincomycins or
Loxapine or
Phenothiazines or
Thioxanthenes or
Xanthines, such as:
  Aminophylline
  Caffeine
  Dyphylline
  Oxtriphylline

Theophylline
  (concurrent use with kaolin and pectin may impair absorption of these medications when administered orally, resulting in decreased therapeutic effectiveness; it is recommended that kaolin and pectin be administered not less than 2 hours before or 3 to 4 hours after oral lincomycins; patients on digitalis should be monitored closely for evidence of altered effect)
Oral medications, other
  (prolonged use of adsorbents may interfere with absorption of other oral agents administered concurrently; it is recommended that kaolin and pectin be administered at least 2 to 3 hours before or after other oral medications)

Contraindications/Medical problems
The contraindications/medical problems included have been selected on the basis of their potential clinical significance (reasons given in parentheses where appropriate)—not necessarily inclusive (» = major clinical significance).

Risk-benefit should be considered when the following medical problems exist:

»   Dehydration
  (although adsorbent antidiarrheals may increase the consistency of feces and decrease the frequency of evacuation, they do not reduce the amount of fluid loss, but only mask its extent; rehydration therapy is essential if signs of dehydration, such as dry mouth, excessive thirst, wrinkled skin, decreased urination, and dizziness or lightheadedness are present; fluid loss may have serious consequences, such as circulatory collapse and renal failure, especially in young children)
Diarrhea, parasite-associated, suspected
  (use of adsorbent antidiarrheals may make recognition of parasitic causes of diarrhea more difficult; if parasitic agents are suspected pathogens, appropriate stool analyses should be performed prior to therapy with adsorbents)

»   Dysentery, acute, characterized by bloody stools and elevated temperature
  (sole treatment with adsorbent antidiarrheals may be inadequate; antibiotic therapy may be required)

Side/Adverse Effects

The following side/adverse effects have been selected on the basis of their potential clinical significance (possible signs and symptoms in parentheses where appropriate)—not necessarily inclusive:

Those indicating need for medical attention only if they continue or are bothersome
Incidence dose-related
  Constipation—usually mild and transient, but may rarely lead to fecal impaction

Patient Consultation

In providing consultation, consider emphasizing the following selected information (» = major clinical significance):

Before using this medication
»   Conditions affecting use, especially:
    Use in children—Risk of dehydration associated with diarrhea
    Use in the elderly—Risk of dehydration associated with diarrhea
    Other medical problems, especially dehydration and acute dysentery

Proper use of this medication
    Taking after each loose bowel movement until diarrhea is controlled

» Importance of maintaining adequate hydration and proper diet
» Proper storage

Precautions while using this medication
» Checking with physician if diarrhea is not controlled within 48
     hours and/or fever develops
     Taking doses of other oral medications 2 to 3 hours before or after
     doses of kaolin and pectin

Oral Dosage Forms

KAOLIN AND PECTIN ORAL SUSPENSION

Usual adult and adolescent dose: Oral, 45 to 90 mL of the concentrate or 60 to 120 mL of the regular-strength suspension after each
loose bowel movement.

Auxiliary labeling: • Shake well.

KAOLIN, PECTIN, BELLADONNA ALKALOIDS, AND OPIUM   Systemic

Category: Antidiarrheal (adsorbent).

Note: The Food and Drug Administration (FDA) has banned the inclusion of belladonna alkaloids and opium in antidiarrheal preparations because of lack of proof of their effectiveness. FDA has
requested manufacturers wishing to obtain the agency's approval to include these ingredients in their product to provide
FDA with evidence that the ingredients are safe and effective
for their intended use.

Indications

Accepted

Diarrhea (treatment)—This medication may be indicated as an adjunct
to rest, fluids, and an appropriate diet in the symptomatic treatment
of mild to moderately acute diarrhea. Use is recommended in
chronic diarrhea only as temporary symptomatic treatment until
the etiology is determined.

Patient Consultation

In providing consultation, consider emphasizing the following selected information (» = major clinical significance):

Before using this medication
» Conditions affecting use, especially:
     Sensitivity to any of the opium or belladonna alkaloids
     Pregnancy—Belladonna alkaloids and opium cross the placenta;
        maternal dependence may result in fetal dependence
     Breast-feeding—Belladonna alkaloids and opium are excreted
        in breast milk
     Use in children—Risk of dehydration associated with diarrhea;
        increased susceptibility to toxic effects of belladonna alka-
        loids and opium
     Use in the elderly—Risk of dehydration associated with diar-
        rhea; increased sensitivity to effects of opium and bella-
        donna alkaloids
     Use by athletes—Opium is banned and tested for in athletes by
        the U.S. Olympic Committee (USOC)
     Dental—Possible development of dental problems because of
        decreased salivary flow
     Other medications, especially CNS depressants, ketoconazole,
        MAO inhibitors, naltrexone, or potassium chloride
     Other medical problems, especially asthma or respiratory dis-
        ease, severe colitis, dehydration, diarrhea caused by poi-
        soning, acute dysentery, glaucoma, hepatic and/or renal func-
        tion impairment, or urinary retention

Proper use of this medication
     Taking with food or meals if gastric irritation occurs
» Importance of not taking more medication than the amount pre-
     scribed because of habit-forming potential

» Importance of maintaining adequate hydration and proper diet
» Proper storage

Precautions while using this medication
» Consulting physician if diarrhea is not controlled within 48 hours
     and/or fever develops
» Avoiding use of alcohol or other CNS depressants
» Caution if drowsiness occurs
     Possible increased sensitivity of eyes to light
» Caution during exercise and hot weather; overheating may result
     in heat stroke
     Possible dryness of mouth, nose, and throat; using sugarless candy
        or gum, ice, or saliva substitute for relief; checking with physi-
        cian or dentist if dry mouth continues for more than 2 weeks

Side/adverse effects
     Signs of potential side effects, especially allergic reaction, CNS
        depression, hallucinations, increased intraocular pressure, para-
        lytic ileus or toxic megacolon, or slow heartbeat

Oral Dosage Forms

KAOLIN, PECTIN, HYOSCYAMINE SULFATE, ATROPINE SULFATE, SCOPOLAMINE HYDROBROMIDE, AND OPIUM ORAL SUSPENSION

Note: Kaolin, pectin, hyoscyamine sulfate, atropine sulfate, scopolamine hydrobromide, and opium oral suspension is not available
in Canada.

Usual adult and adolescent dose: Antidiarrheal (adsorbent)—Oral,
30 mL initially, followed by 15 mL every three hours as needed to
control diarrhea.

Usual adult prescribing limits: Up to four doses in twenty-four
hours.

Usual geriatric dose: See *Usual adult and adolescent dose.*

Note: Geriatric patients may be more sensitive to the effects of the
usual adult dose.

Auxiliary labeling:
• May cause drowsiness.
• Avoid alcoholic beverages.
• Do not take other medicines without your doctor's advice.
• Keep out of reach of children.
• May be habit-forming.
• Shake well before using.

KAOLIN, PECTIN, AND PAREGORIC   Systemic

Category: Antidiarrheal (adsorbent).

Note: The Food and Drug Administration (FDA) has banned the inclusion of paregoric in antidiarrheal preparations because of lack of proof of its effectiveness. FDA has requested manufacturers wishing to obtain the agency's approval to include this ingredient in their product to provide FDA with evidence that the ingredient is safe and effective for its intended use.

Indications

Accepted

Diarrhea (treatment)—This medication may be indicated as an adjunct to rest, fluids, and an appropriate diet in the symptomatic treatment of mild to moderately acute diarrhea. Use is recommended in chronic diarrhea only as temporary symptomatic treatment until the etiology is determined.

Patient Consultation

In providing consultation, consider emphasizing the following selected information (» = major clinical significance):

Before using this medication
» Conditions affecting use, especially:

Sensitivity to paregoric or other opiates

Pregnancy—Opium alkaloids cross placenta; possible fetal dependence with regular use

Breast-feeding—Opium alkaloids excreted in breast milk

Use in children—Risk of dehydration associated with diarrhea; increased sensitivity to opiate effects

Use in the elderly—Risk of dehydration associated with diarrhea; increased sensitivity to opiate effects

Use by athletes—Paregoric is banned and tested for by the U.S. Olympic Committee (USOC)

Other medications, especially antiperistaltic antidiarrheals and CNS depressants; spacing doses of other oral medications 2 to 3 hours before or after doses of kaolin- and pectin-containing medication is recommended

Other medical problems, especially dehydration, acute dysentery, asthma or respiratory disease, and severe inflammatory bowel disease

Proper use of this medication
Taking with food or meals if gastric irritation occurs
» Importance of not taking more medication than the amount prescribed because of habit-forming potential
» Importance of maintaining adequate hydration and proper diet
» Proper storage

Precautions while using this medication
» Consulting physician if diarrhea is not controlled within 48 hours and/or fever develops
» Caution if taking alcohol or other central nervous system (CNS) depressants
» Caution if drowsiness occurs

Side/adverse effects
Signs of potential side effects, especially allergic reaction, histamine-release related effects, mental depression, and toxic megacolon

Oral Dosage Forms

KAOLIN, PECTIN, AND PAREGORIC ORAL SUSPENSION

Usual adult and adolescent dose: Oral, 15 to 30 mL after each loose bowel movement, up to four doses in twelve hours.

Usual geriatric dose: See *Usual adult and adolescent dose.*

Note: Geriatric patients may be more sensitive to the effects of the usual adult dose.

Auxiliary labeling:
• May cause drowsiness.
• Avoid alcoholic beverages.
• Do not take other medicines without your doctor's advice.
• Keep out of reach of children.
• May be habit-forming.
• Shake well before using.

KETOCONAZOLE   Systemic

A commonly used *brand name* in the U.S. and Canada is *Nizoral.*

ORAL
Ketoconazole Oral Suspension*
In Canada—*Nizoral*
Ketoconazole Tablets USP
In the U.S. and Canada—*Nizoral*

*Not commercially available in the U.S.

Category: Antifungal (systemic); antiadrenal; antineoplastic.

Indications

Note: Bracketed information in the *Indications* section refers to uses not included in U.S. product labeling.

Accepted
Blastomycosis (treatment)—Ketoconazole is indicated in the treatment of pulmonary and disseminated blastomycosis.

Candidiasis, disseminated (treatment); or

Candidiasis, mucocutaneous, chronic (treatment)—Ketoconazole is indicated in the treatment of disseminated candidiasis and chronic extensive mucocutaneous candidiasis caused by *Candida* species.

Candidiasis, oropharyngeal (treatment)—Ketoconazole is indicated in the treatment of oropharyngeal candidiasis (thrush) caused by *Candida* species.

Candiduria (treatment)—Ketoconazole is indicated in the treatment of candiduria caused by *Candida* species. However, in the treatment of renal and urinary tract infections, urinary concentrations of ketoconazole may be borderline or inadequate.

Chromomycosis (treatment)—Ketoconazole is indicated as a secondary agent in the treatment of chromomycosis caused by *Cladosporium carrioni, Exophiala dermatitidis, Fonsecaea pedrosi, F. compactum, Phialophora verrucosa, Rhinocladiella aquaspersa,* and *R. cerophilum.*

Coccidioidomycosis (treatment)—Ketoconazole is indicated in the treatment of pulmonary and disseminated coccidioidomycosis caused by *Coccidioides immitis.*

Histoplasmosis (treatment)—Ketoconazole is indicated in the treatment of pulmonary and disseminated histoplasmosis caused by *Histoplasma capsulatum*.

Paracoccidioidomycosis (treatment)—Ketoconazole is indicated in the treatment of paracoccidioidomycosis caused by *Paracoccidioides brasiliensis*.

Pityriasis versicolor (treatment);

Tinea corporis (treatment);

Tinea cruris (treatment); or

Tinea pedis (treatment)—Ketoconazole is indicated in the treatment of recalcitrant or very severe disfiguring or disabling pityriasis versicolor, tinea corporis, tinea cruris, and tinea pedis infections unresponsive to griseofulvin, or in patients allergic to or unable to tolerate griseofulvin.

[Candidiasis, vulvovaginal (treatment)][1]—Ketoconazole is used in the treatment of vulvovaginal candidiasis.

[Carcinoma, prostatic (treatment)][1]—Ketoconazole is used in the treatment of prostatic carcinoma.

[Cushing's syndrome (treatment)][1]—Ketoconazole is used as a secondary agent in the treatment of Cushing's syndrome.

[Paronychia (treatment)][1];

[Pneumonia, fungal (treatment)][1];

[Septicemia, fungal (treatment)][1];

[Sporotrichosis, disseminated (treatment)][1];

[Urinary bladder infections, fungal (treatment)][1]; or

[Urinary tract infections, fungal (treatment)][1]—Ketoconazole is used in the treatment of paronychia, fungal pneumonia, fungal septicemia, disseminated sporotrichosis, fungal urinary bladder infections, and other fungal urinary tract infections.

[Tinea barbae (treatment)][1]; or

[Tinea capitis (treatment)][1]—Systemic ketoconazole is used in combination with topical imidazoles in the treatment of griseofulvin-resistant tinea barbae and tinea capitis.

[Tinea unguium (treatment)][1]—Ketoconazole is used in the treatment of tinea unguium (onychomycosis) caused by *Trichophyton* unresponsive to griseofulvin, and *Candida* species.

Not all species or strains of a particular organism may be susceptible to ketoconazole.

Unaccepted

Ketoconazole is not effective in the treatment of fungal meningitis since it penetrates poorly into the cerebrospinal fluid (CSF). Also, it is not effective against *Aspergillus* or *Zygomycetes* (agents of mucormycosis) or in mycetoma.

---

[1]Not included in Canadian product labeling.

Pharmacology

Mechanism of action/Effect: Antifungal (systemic)—Fungistatic; may be fungicidal, depending on concentration; inhibits biosynthesis of ergosterol or other sterols, damaging the fungal cell membrane and altering its permeability; as a result, loss of essential intracellular elements may occur; also inhibits biosynthesis of triglycerides and phospholipids by fungi; in addition, inhibits oxidative and peroxidative enzyme activity, resulting in intracellular buildup of toxic concentrations of hydrogen peroxide, which may contribute to deterioration of subcellular organelles and cellular necrosis. In *Candida albicans*, inhibits transformation of blastospores into invasive mycelial form.

Precautions to Consider

Cross-sensitivity and/or related problems

Patients allergic to other azole antifungals (itraconazole, fluconazole, miconazole) may also be allergic to ketoconazole.

Geriatrics

No information is available on the relationship of age to the effects of ketoconazole in geriatric patients.

Drug interactions and/or related problems

The following drug interactions and/or related problems have been selected on the basis of their potential clinical significance (possible mechanism in parentheses where appropriate)—not necessarily inclusive (» = major clinical significance):

Note: Combinations containing any of the following medications, depending on the amount present, may also interact with this medication.

» Alcohol or

» Hepatotoxic medications, other

(concurrent use with ketoconazole may result in an increased incidence of hepatotoxicity; patients, especially those on prolonged administration or those with a history of liver disease, should be carefully monitored and should be advised to avoid alcoholic beverages and other hepatotoxins; with concurrent use of dantrolene, females over 35 years of age may be especially at risk)

(concurrent ingestion of alcohol with ketoconazole has been reported to result in a disulfiram-like reaction, characterized by facial flushing; other symptoms may include difficult breathing, slight fever, and tightness of the chest; these effects usually subside spontaneously within 24 hours with no lasting ill effects)

» Antacids or

» Anticholinergics/antispasmodics or

» Histamine H_2-receptor antagonists or

» Omeprazole

(may cause increased gastrointestinal pH; concurrent use with ketoconazole may result in a marked reduction in absorption of ketoconazole; patients should be advised to take these medications at least 2 hours after ketoconazole)

Anticoagulants, coumarin- or indandione-derivative

(anticoagulant effects may be increased when these agents are used concurrently with ketoconazole; patients should be closely monitored, and dosage adjustments may be necessary during and after ketoconazole therapy)

» Cyclosporine

(ketoconazole has been reported to increase plasma concentrations of cyclosporine by inhibiting its metabolism; this may increase the risk of nephrotoxicity; concurrent use is recommended only with great caution; serum concentrations of cyclosporine should be monitored and the dose of cyclosporine may need to be reduced)

» Dideoxyinosine (ddI)

(concurrent administration of ketoconazole with ddI may decrease the absorption of ketoconazole; ddI must be given with a buffer to neutralize stomach acidity in order to increase its absorption, and ketoconazole requires an acidic environment for optimal absorption; ketoconazole should be administered at least 2 hours before or 2 hours after ddI is given)

» Isoniazid or

» Rifampin

(concurrent use of isoniazid or rifampin either separately or together with ketoconazole may result in significantly decreased serum concentrations of ketoconazole; therefore, isoniazid or rifampin, alone or in combination, should be used with caution when given concurrently with ketoconazole)

Phenytoin

(concurrent use with ketoconazole may result in altered metabolism of either or both medications; serum concentrations of phenytoin have been reported to be increased by miconazole, another imidazole derivative; in addition, time to peak ketoconazole serum concentrations may be delayed; response to both medications should be closely monitored)

» Terfenadine
(concurrent use has been reported to increase plasma levels of terfenadine because of inhibition of the P-450 metabolic pathways by ketoconazole; the increased plasma level of terfenadine has resulted in cardiotoxicity [torsades de pointes])

Contraindications/Medical problems

The contraindications/medical problems included have been selected on the basis of their potential clinical significance (reasons given in parentheses where appropriate)—not necessarily inclusive (» = major clinical significance).

Risk-benefit should be considered when the following medical problems exist:

» Achlorhydria or hypochlorhydria
(may cause marked reduction in absorption of ketoconazole; patients with acquired immune deficiency syndrome [AIDS] may have reduced ketoconazole absorption due to hypochlorhydria)

» Alcoholism, active or in remission, or

» Hepatic function impairment
(ketoconazole is metabolized in the liver and may be hepatotoxic)

Hypersensitivity to ketoconazole

Side/Adverse Effects

Note: Hepatotoxicity, consisting primarily of hepatocellular damage or mixed hepatocellular and cholestatic changes, has been reported in approximately 1 in 10,000 exposed patients. It is usually, but not always, reversible upon discontinuation of ketoconazole, and fatalities have been reported rarely. It is considered to be an idiosyncratic reaction and can occur at any time during therapy. Females and patients over the age of 40 may be predisposed to hepatotoxicity. Several cases of hepatitis have also been reported in children.

High-dose ketoconazole therapy has also been shown to suppress corticosteroid secretion. In addition, ketoconazole has been shown to lower serum testosterone concentrations, which return to baseline values when ketoconazole is discontinued.

The following side/adverse effects have been selected on the basis of their potential clinical significance (possible signs and symptoms in parentheses where appropriate)—not necessarily inclusive:

Those indicating need for medical attention

Incidence rare
Hepatitis (dark or amber urine, loss of appetite, pale stools, stomach pain, unusual tiredness or weakness, yellow eyes or skin); *hypersensitivity* (skin rash or itching)

Those indicating need for medical attention only if they continue or are bothersome

Incidence less frequent
Gastrointestinal disturbances (diarrhea, nausea or vomiting)
Incidence rare
CNS effects (dizziness, drowsiness, headache); *gynecomastia* (enlargement of the breasts in males)—inhibition of testosterone and adrenal steroid synthesis; *impotence* (decreased sexual ability in males)—inhibition of testosterone and adrenal steroid synthesis; *menstrual irregularities; photophobia* (increased sensitivity of the eyes to light)

Patient Consultation

In providing consultation, consider emphasizing the following selected information (» = major clinical significance):

Before using this medication

» Conditions affecting use, especially:
Hypersensitivity to ketoconazole
Pregnancy—Ketoconazole crosses the placenta

Breast-feeding—Ketoconazole is excreted in breast milk and may cause kernicterus in the nursing infant

Use in children—Appropriate studies have not been performed in children up to 2 years of age; hepatitis has been reported in children

Other medications, especially alcohol or other hepatotoxic medications, cyclosporine, antacids, anticholinergics/antispasmodics, dideoxyinosine, histamine H_2-receptor antagonists, isoniazid, omeprazole, rifampin, or terfenadine

Other medical problems, especially achlorhydria or hypochlorhydria; alcoholism, active or in remission; or hepatic function impairment

Proper use of this medication

Taking with a meal or snack
Proper administration technique for oral liquids
Proper administration technique in achlorhydria

» Compliance with full course of therapy, which may take months or years

» Importance of not missing doses and taking at same time every day
Missed dose: Taking as soon as possible; not taking if almost time for next dose; not doubling doses

» Proper storage

Precautions while using this medication

Regular visits to physician to check progress
Checking with physician if no improvement within a few weeks (or months for some infections)

» Taking histamine H_2-receptor antagonists at least 2 hours after ketoconazole

» Avoiding alcoholic beverages while taking ketoconazole
Possible photophobic reactions; wearing sunglasses and avoiding bright light to minimize potential eye discomfort

» Caution if dizziness or drowsiness occurs

Side/adverse effects

Signs of potential side effects, especially hepatitis and hypersensitivity reactions

General Dosing Information

Ketoconazole may be taken with a meal or snack to minimize nausea or vomiting and to promote absorption.

In patients with achlorhydria or hypochlorhydria, higher serum concentrations may be achieved by dissolving each tablet in 4 mL of 0.2 *N* hydrochloric acid. Patients may further dilute the resulting mixture in a small amount of water and should be instructed to drink it through a plastic or glass straw to avoid contact with the teeth. This should be followed by $^1/_2$ glass (120 mL) of water, which is swished around in the mouth and swallowed.

Therapy should be continued for at least 1 to 2 weeks in candidiasis (3 to 5 days in vaginal candidiasis); for 1 to 8 weeks in dermatomycoses caused by yeasts or dermatophytes, and mycoses of hair and scalp; for 3 months to 1 year in paracoccidioidomycosis; and for 6 months or longer in other systemic mycoses. Chronic mucocutaneous candidiasis usually requires indefinite maintenance treatment to prevent relapse.

Oral Dosage Forms

Note: Bracketed uses in the *Dosage Forms* section refer to categories of use and/or indications that are not included in U.S. product labeling.

KETOCONAZOLE ORAL SUSPENSION

Usual adult and adolescent dose:
Antifungal (systemic)—
[Candidiasis, vulvovaginal][1]: Oral, 200 to 400 mg once a day for five days.
[Paronychia][1]; or
[Urinary bladder infections, fungal][1]; or

[Urinary tract infections, fungal][1]: Oral, 200 to 400 mg once a day.

Pityriasis versicolor: Oral, 200 mg once a day for five to ten days.

[Pneumonia, fungal][1]; or

[Septicemia, fungal][1]: Oral, 400 mg to 1 gram once a day.

Other infections: Oral, 200 to 400 mg once a day.

[Antiadrenal—Cushing's syndrome][1]: Oral, 600 mg to 1.2 grams once a day.

[Antineoplastic—Carcinoma, prostatic][1]: Oral, 400 mg three times a day.

Usual adult prescribing limits:

Antifungal (systemic)—Up to 1 gram daily.

[Antiadrenal; antineoplastic][1]—Up to 1.2 grams daily.

Auxiliary labeling:

- Shake well.
- Avoid alcoholic beverages.
- May cause dizziness or drowsiness.
- Continue medicine for full time of treatment (antifungal only).

KETOCONAZOLE TABLETS USP

Usual adult and adolescent dose: See *Ketoconazole Oral Suspension.*

Usual adult prescribing limits: See *Ketoconazole Oral Suspension.*

Auxiliary labeling:

- Avoid alcoholic beverages.
- May cause dizziness or drowsiness.
- Continue medicine for full time of treatment (antifungal only).

[1]Not included in Canadian product labeling.

KETOCONAZOLE   Topical

Some commonly used *brand names* in the U.S. and Canada are *Nizoral Cream* and *Nizoral Shampoo.*

TOPICAL

Ketoconazole Cream

In the U.S. and Canada—*Nizoral Cream*

Ketoconazole Shampoo

In the U.S. and Canada—*Nizoral Shampoo*

Category: Antifungal (topical).

Indications

Note: Bracketed information in the *Indications* section refers to uses not included in U.S. product labeling.

Accepted

Tinea corporis (treatment); or

Tinea cruris (treatment)—Ketoconazole cream is indicated as a primary agent in the topical treatment of tinea corporis (ringworm of the body) and tinea cruris (ringworm of the groin; jock itch) caused by *Trichophyton rubrum, T. mentagrophytes,* and *Epidermophyton floccosum (Acrothesium floccosum).*

Tinea versicolor (treatment)—Ketoconazole cream is indicated as a primary agent in the topical treatment of tinea versicolor (pityriasis versicolor; "sun fungus") caused by *Malassezia furfur (Pityrosporon orbiculare).*

Candidiasis, cutaneous (treatment)[1]—Ketoconazole cream is indicated as a primary agent in the topical treatment of cutaneous candidiasis caused by *Candida* species.

Seborrheic dermatitis (treatment)—Ketoconazole cream is indicated in the treatment of seborrheic dermatitis.

Dandruff (treatment)—Ketoconazole shampoo is indicated for the reduction of scaling due to dandruff.

[Paronychia (treatment)][1];

[Tinea barbae (treatment)][1];

[Tinea capitis (treatment)][1]; or

[Tinea pedis (treatment)]—Ketoconazole cream is used as a primary agent in the topical treatment of paronychia and tinea pedis (ringworm of the foot; athlete's foot). Ketoconazole cream is used as a secondary agent in the topical treatment of tinea barbae and tinea capitis.

Not all species or strains of a particular organism may be susceptible to ketoconazole.

[1]Not included in Canadian product labeling.

Pharmacology

Mechanism of action/Effect: Fungistatic; may be fungicidal, depending on concentration; inhibits biosynthesis of ergosterol or other sterols, damaging the fungal cell membrane and altering its permeability; as a result, loss of essential intracellular elements may occur; also inhibits biosynthesis of triglycerides and phospholipids by fungi; in addition, inhibits oxidative and peroxidative enzyme activity, resulting in intracellular buildup of toxic concentrations of hydrogen peroxide, which may contribute to deterioration of subcellular organelles and cellular necrosis. In the treatment of *Candida albicans,* inhibits transformation of blastospores into invasive mycelial form.

Precautions to Consider

Cross-sensitivity and/or related problems

Persons sensitive to miconazole or other imidazoles may be sensitive to ketoconazole also.

Geriatrics

No information is available on the relationship of age to the effects of this medicine in geriatric patients.

Contraindications/Medical problems

The contraindications/medical problems included have been selected on the basis of their potential clinical significance (reasons given in parentheses where appropriate)—not necessarily inclusive (» = major clinical significance).

Risk-benefit should be considered when the following medical problem exists:

Sensitivity to topical ketoconazole

Side/Adverse Effects

The following side/adverse effects have been selected on the basis of their potential clinical significance (possible signs and symptoms in parentheses where appropriate)—not necessarily inclusive:

Those indicating need for medical attention
Incidence more frequent
Itching, stinging, or irritation not present before therapy

Patient Consultation

In providing consultation, consider emphasizing the following selected information (» = major clinical significance):

Before using this medication
» Conditions affecting use, especially:
  Sensitivity to topical ketoconazole
  Pregnancy—Ketoconazole crosses the placenta; studies in animals found ketoconazole to be teratogenic

Proper use of this medication
» Avoiding contact with the eyes
  Missed dose: Applying as soon as possible; not applying if almost time for next dose
» Proper storage
For the cream form
  Applying sufficient medication to cover affected and surrounding areas, and rubbing in gently
» Compliance with full course of therapy; fungal infections may require prolonged therapy
For the shampoo form
  Wetting hair and scalp with water
  Applying adequate shampoo for lather and massaging in for approximately 1 minute
  Rinsing and repeating application
  Leaving shampoo on an additional 3 minutes
  Rinsing throughly and drying hair

Precautions while using this medication
For the cream form
  Checking with physician if no improvement within 2 to 4 weeks
» Using hygienic measures to cure infection and prevent reinfection
For tinea cruris
  Not wearing underwear that is tight-fitting or made from synthetic materials; wearing loose-fitting cotton underwear instead
  Using a bland, absorbent powder or an antifungal powder on the skin; using the powder between administration times for .the cream
For tinea pedis
  Carefully drying feet, especially between toes, after bathing
  Not wearing socks made from wool or synthetic materials; wearing clean, cotton socks and changing them daily or more often if feet perspire excessively

Wearing sandals or well-ventilated shoes
Using a bland, absorbent powder or an antifungal powder between toes, on feet, and in socks and shoes liberally once or twice daily; using the powder between administration times for the cream

Side/adverse effects
  Signs of potential side effects, especially itching, stinging, or irritation

General Dosing Information

Prolonged use of topical ketoconazole may rarely lead to skin sensitization, resulting in hypersensitivity reactions with subsequent topical or systemic use of the medication.

For cream dosage form
To reduce the possibility of recurrence of infection, candida, tinea corporis, tinea cruris, and tinea versicolor should be treated for at least 2 weeks. Seborrheic dermatitis should be treated for at least 4 weeks or until clinical clearing.

Topical Dosage Forms

Note: Bracketed uses in the *Dosage Forms* section refer to categories of use and/or indications that are not included in U.S. product labeling.

KETOCONAZOLE CREAM

Usual adult and adolescent dose:
  Tinea corporis; or
  Tinea cruris; or
  Tinea versicolor—Topical, to the affected skin and surrounding areas, once a day.
  Candidiasis, cutaneous—Topical, to the affected skin and surrounding areas, once a day.
  Seborrheic dermatitis—Topical, to the affected skin and surrounding areas, two times a day.
  [Paronychia][1]; or
  [Tinea barbae][1]; or
  [Tinea capitis][1]; or
  [Tinea pedis]—Topical, to the affected skin and surrounding areas, two or three times a day.

Auxiliary labeling:
  • For external use only.
  • Continue medicine for full time of treatment.

KETOCONAZOLE SHAMPOO

Usual adult and adolescent dose: Dandruff—Topical, as a shampoo, every four days for 4 weeks, then once every one or two weeks.

KETOROLAC   Systemic†

A commonly used *brand name* in the U.S. is *Toradol*.

PARENTERAL
Ketorolac Tromethamine Injection†
    In the U.S.—*Toradol*

---

†Not commercially available in Canada.

Category: Analgesic.

Indications

Accepted

Pain (treatment)—Ketorolac is indicated for the short-term management of pain.

Unaccepted

Ketorolac is not recommended for obstetrical analgesia because its safety has not been adequately studied. Inhibition of prostaglandin synthesis by nonsteroidal anti-inflammatory drugs such as ketorolac may decrease uterine contractility and/or cause premature constriction of the fetal ductus arteriosus.

Pharmacology

Mechanism of action/Effect: Ketorolac is a nonsteroidal anti-inflammatory drug (NSAID) chemically related to indomethacin and tolmetin. Currently available NSAIDs inhibit the activity of the enzyme cyclo-oxygenase, leading to decreased formation of precursors of prostaglandins and thromboxanes from arachidonic acid. The resultant reduction in prostaglandin synthesis and activity may be at least partially responsible for many of the adverse, as well as the therapeutic, effects of these medications. Analgesia is probably produced via a peripheral action in which blockade of pain impulse generation results from decreased prostaglandin activity. However, inhibition of the synthesis or actions of other substances that sensitize pain receptors to mechanical or chemical stimulation may also contribute to the analgesic effect.

Other actions/effects:

Ketorolac has anti-inflammatory and antipyretic actions that, together with its analgesic effects, may mask the onset and/or progression of an infection.

Ketorolac inhibits platelet aggregation. This effect is reversible (unlike aspirin-induced platelet inhibition, which persists for the life of the exposed platelets). Recovery of platelet function usually occurs within 24 to 48 hours following discontinuation of ketorolac.

Like other NSAIDs, ketorolac may cause gastrointestinal toxicity, probably by reducing the synthesis and activity of prostaglandins that exert a protective effect on the gastrointestinal mucosa.

Like other NSAIDs, ketorolac may cause renal toxicity (i.e., decreased renal perfusion, sodium and fluid retention, and decreased renal function), probably by inhibiting the synthesis and activity of renal prostaglandins, which are directly involved in the maintenance of renal hemodynamics and sodium and fluid balance. Renal prostaglandins are especially important in maintaining renal function in the presence of generalized vasoconstriction or volume depletion.

Onset of action: About 10 minutes.

Time to peak effect: 75 to 150 minutes.

Precautions to Consider

Cross-sensitivity and/or related problems

Patients sensitive to aspirin or other nonsteroidal anti-inflammatory drugs (NSAIDs) may be sensitive to ketorolac also.

Geriatrics

Studies have shown that clearance of ketorolac is reduced in healthy individuals 65 years of age or older, leading to significant prolongation of the elimination half-life. Also, geriatric patients are more likely to have age-related renal function impairment, which may further reduce ketorolac clearance and increase the risk of NSAID-induced renal or hepatic toxicity. In addition, although an increased risk of serious gastrointestinal toxicity during NSAID therapy in geriatric patients has not been established, NSAID-induced gastrointestinal ulceration and/or bleeding may be more likely to cause serious consequences, including fatalities, in geriatric patients than in younger adults. It is recommended that ketorolac be used with caution, in the lower of the recommended dosage regimens, and with careful monitoring of the patient.

Drug interactions and/or related problems

The following drug interactions and/or related problems have been selected on the basis of their potential clinical significance (possible mechanism in parentheses where appropriate)—not necessarily inclusive (» = major clinical significance):

Note: Combinations containing any of the following medications, depending on the amount present, may also interact with this medication.

All of the interactions listed below have not been documented with ketorolac. However, they have been reported with other NSAIDs and should be considered potential precautions to the use of ketorolac also, especially if the analgesic will be given for longer than a few days.

In addition to the interactions listed below, the possibility should be considered that additive or multiple effects leading to impaired blood clotting and/or increased risk of bleeding may occur if any NSAID is used concurrently with any medication having a significant potential for causing hypoprothrombinemia, thrombocytopenia, or gastrointestinal ulceration or hemorrhage.

Acetaminophen
    (prolonged concurrent use of acetaminophen with an NSAID may increase the risk of adverse renal effects; it is recommended that patients be under close medical supervision while receiving such combined therapy)

Adrenocorticoids, glucocorticoid, or
Alcohol or
Corticotropin (chronic therapeutic use) or
Potassium supplements
    (concurrent use with an NSAID may increase the risk of gastrointestinal side effects, including ulceration or hemorrhage)

» Anticoagulants, coumarin- or indandione-derivative, or
» Heparin or
» Thrombolytic agents, such as:
    Alteplase
    Anistreplase
    Streptokinase
    Urokinase
        (ketorolac has not been shown to alter the pharmacokinetic or pharmacodynamic properties of warfarin or heparin; however, inhibition of platelet aggregation by ketorolac, and the potential occurrence of gastrointestinal ulceration or bleeding with prolonged ketorolac administration, may be hazardous to patients receiving anticoagulant or thrombolytic therapy)

Antidiabetic agents, oral, or
Insulin
　　(NSAIDs may increase the hypoglycemic effect of these medications because prostaglandins are directly involved in regulatory mechanisms of glucose metabolism and possibly because of displacement of the oral antidiabetics from serum proteins; dosage adjustments of the antidiabetic agent may be necessary; glipizide and glyburide, due to their nonionic binding characteristics, may not be affected as much as the other oral antidiabetic agents; however, caution with concurrent use is recommended)

Antihypertensives or
Diuretics
　　(increased monitoring of the response to any antihypertensive agent may be advisable when ketorolac is used concurrently because several other NSAIDs have been shown to reduce or reverse the effects of many antihypertensives, possibly by inhibiting renal prostaglandin synthesis and/or by causing sodium and fluid retention)

　　(NSAIDs may decrease the diuretic and natriuretic, as well as the antihypertensive, effects of diuretics, probably by inhibiting renal prostaglandin synthesis)

　　(concurrent use of an NSAID and a diuretic may also increase the risk of renal failure secondary to a decrease in renal blood flow caused by inhibition of renal prostaglandin synthesis)

» Aspirin or other salicylates or
» Other NSAIDs
　　(concurrent use of aspirin or other NSAIDs with ketorolac is not recommended because of the potential for additive toxicity)

　　(concurrent use of ketorolac with antirheumatic doses of salicylates other than aspirin should be undertaken with caution and in reduced doses because therapeutic plasma concentrations of salicylate [30 mg per 100 mL (2.17 mmol per L)] decrease the protein binding of ketorolac sufficiently to potentially double the plasma concentration of free [unbound] ketorolac)

» Cefamandole or
» Cefoperazone or
» Cefotetan or
» Moxalactam or
» Plicamycin or
» Valproic acid
　　(these medications may cause hypoprothrombinemia; in addition, plicamycin or valproic acid may inhibit platelet aggregation, and moxalactam may cause irreversible platelet damage; concurrent use with an NSAID may increase the risk of bleeding because of additive interferences with blood clotting and/or the potential occurrence of gastrointestinal ulceration or hemorrhage during NSAID therapy)

Gold compounds
　　(although other NSAIDs are commonly used concurrently with gold compounds in the treatment of arthritis, the possibility should be considered that concurrent use of a gold compound with any NSAID, including ketorolac, may increase the risk of adverse renal effects)

» Lithium
　　(although the effect of ketorolac on lithium plasma concentration has not been studied, several other NSAIDs have been reported to increase steady-state plasma lithium concentrations; increased monitoring of lithium plasma concentrations is recommended during and following concurrent use so that lithium dosage can be adjusted if necessary)

» Methotrexate
　　(the effect of ketorolac on methotrexate concentrations and/or toxicity has not been studied; however, administration of moderate- or high-dose methotrexate infusions to patients receiving other NSAIDs has resulted in severe, sometimes fatal, methotrexate toxicity, possibly because NSAIDs may reduce renal function, thereby decreasing methotrexate excretion; it is recommended that ketorolac not be administered for 24 hours prior to, and for at least 12 hours [or until the methotrexate plasma concentration has decreased to a nontoxic level] following, a high-dose methotrexate infusion)

　　(severe, sometimes fatal, methotrexate toxicity has also been reported with the relatively low to moderate doses of methotrexate used in the treatment of rheumatoid arthritis or psoriasis when an NSAID was given concurrently; it is recommended that concurrent use of ketorolac with low to moderate doses of methotrexate also be undertaken with caution, with methotrexate dosage being adjusted as determined by monitoring plasma methotrexate concentration and/or adequacy of the patient's renal function)

Nephrotoxic medications, other
　　(concurrent use with an NSAID may increase the risk and/or severity of adverse renal effects)

Nifedipine or
Verapamil
　　(caution in concurrent use with any NSAID is recommended because of possible displacement of either or both medications from protein-binding sites, leading to increased plasma concentrations of the free [unbound] medications and increased risk of toxicity)

Platelet aggregation inhibitors, other
　　(concurrent use of any of these medications with an NSAID, including ketorolac, may increase the risk of bleeding because of additive inhibition of platelet aggregation as well as the potential occurrence of gastrointestinal ulceration or hemorrhage during NSAID therapy)

» Probenecid
　　(although the effect of probenecid on the pharmacokinetics of ketorolac has not been studied, concurrent use of the 2 medications should be undertaken with caution, because probenecid decreases the renal clearance of many other NSAIDs, resulting in increased plasma concentrations and risk of toxicity)

Contraindications/Medical problems
The contraindications/medical problems included have been selected on the basis of their potential clinical significance (reasons given in parentheses where appropriate)—not necessarily inclusive (» = major clinical significance).

Except under special circumstances, this medication should not be used when the following medical problems exist:
» Nasal polyps associated with bronchospasm, aspirin-induced, or angioedema, anaphylaxis, or other severe allergic reaction induced by aspirin, ketorolac, or other NSAIDs, history of

Risk-benefit should be considered when the following medical problems exist:
» Allergic reaction, mild, such as allergic rhinitis, urticaria, or skin rash, induced by aspirin, ketorolac, or other NSAIDs, history of

Asthma
　　(may be exacerbated)

Cholestasis or
Hepatitis, active
　　(although other forms of hepatic function impairment apparently do not alter the clearance of ketorolac, studies to assess the possible effect of cholestasis or active hepatitis on the pharmacokinetics of the medication have not been done)

Conditions predisposing to gastrointestinal toxicity, such as:
Alcoholism, active
» Peptic ulcer, ulcerative colitis, or upper gastrointestinal disease, active or history of
Tobacco use, or recent history of
(NSAIDs should preferably not be given to patients with active peptic ulcer disease or gastrointestinal bleeding; if ketorolac administration is considered essential, an antiulcer regimen should be administered concurrently)

(caution and close supervision are also recommended for other patients in whom there is a significant risk of gastrointestinal toxicity; misoprostol or sucralfate should be considered as prophylaxis for those at high risk)

Conditions predisposing to fluid retention, such as:
Compromised cardiac function
Hypertension
(ketorolac may cause fluid retention and edema; hypertension may be exacerbated)
Congestive heart failure or
Diabetes mellitus or
Edema, pre-existing, or
Extracellular volume depletion or
Hepatic function impairment or
Sepsis
(increased risk of renal failure)

» Hemophilia or other bleeding problems including coagulation or platelet function disorders
(increased risk of bleeding because ketorolac inhibits platelet aggregation and may cause gastrointestinal ulceration or hemorrhage)

» Renal function impairment
(ketorolac and its metabolites are excreted primarily via the kidney, which may also be a site of ketorolac metabolism; a substantial reduction in ketorolac clearance, leading to significant prolongation of its half-life, has been demonstrated in patients with renal function impairment, but studies have not been done in patients with severe impairment [patients requiring dialysis or having creatinine concentrations higher than 5 mg per 100 mL]; a reduction in dosage may be required to prevent accumulation)

(caution and careful monitoring of the patient are also recommended because of possible patient predisposition toward development of NSAID-induced adverse renal effects, including acute renal failure)

Systemic lupus erythematosus (SLE)
(increased risk of renal function impairment)

Side/Adverse Effects

Note: Ketorolac, especially with chronic use, shares the risks associated with other NSAIDs, including gastrointestinal and/or renal toxicity.

The side effects listed below were reported in studies in which the medication was administered for a maximum of 5 days (20 doses). During more prolonged therapy, the frequency of adverse effects may be increased by 10 to 50%. Also, side effects are more frequent when plasma concentrations of ketorolac exceed 5 mcg per mL.

The following side/adverse effects have been selected on the basis of their potential clinical significance (possible signs and symptoms in parentheses where appropriate)—not necessarily inclusive:

Those indicating need for medical attention
Incidence less frequent (1 to 3%)
Edema (swelling of face, fingers, lower legs, ankles, and/or feet; unusual weight gain)

Incidence rare (<1%)
Any change in vision; asthma or dyspnea (shortness of breath, troubled breathing, tightness in chest, and/or wheezing); *bloody stools; increased urinary frequency; mental depression; oliguria* (decrease in amount of urine); *peptic ulceration* (abdominal pain, cramping, or burning, severe; bloody or black, tarry stools; vomiting of blood or material that looks like coffee grounds; nausea, heartburn, and/or indigestion, severe and continuing); *purpura* (small, red spots on skin; bruising); *rectal bleeding; stomatitis, aphthous* (sores, ulcers, or white spots on lips or in mouth)

Those indicating need for medical attention only if they continue or are bothersome
Incidence more frequent (>3%)
Abdominal pain; bruising at injection site; drowsiness; indigestion
Incidence less frequent (1 to 3%)
Burning or pain at injection site; diarrhea; dizziness; headache; increased sweating

Patient Consultation

In providing consultation, consider emphasizing the following selected information (» = major clinical significance):

Before using this medication
» Conditions affecting use, especially:
Sensitivity to ketorolac, aspirin, or any other nonsteroidal anti-inflammatory drug (NSAID)
Pregnancy—Crosses the placenta; use during second half of pregnancy may cause adverse effects on fetal or neonatal blood flow
Breast-feeding—Small quantities excreted in breast milk
Use in children—Not studied in children; no information available
Use in the elderly—Higher risk of toxicity because of increased sensitivity to adverse renal effects and reduced clearance
Other medications, especially anticoagulants, aspirin or other salicylates, other NSAIDs, those cephalosporins that may adversely affect blood clotting, lithium, methotrexate, plicamycin, and probenecid
Other medical problems, especially clotting defects, peptic ulcer or other gastrointestinal tract disease, and renal function impairment

Proper use of this medication
Proper injection technique (if self-medicating at home)
» Not using more medication than prescribed
Missed dose (scheduled dosing): Using as soon as possible; not using if almost time for next dose; not doubling doses
» Proper storage

Precautions while using this medication
» Not using acetaminophen concurrently for more than a few days, and not using aspirin, other salicylates, or other NSAIDs concurrently, unless combination therapy prescribed and monitored by physician or dentist
Caution if dizziness or drowsiness occurs; not driving, using machines, or doing anything else that requires alertness

Side/adverse effects
Signs of potential side effects, especially gastrointestinal ulceration or bleeding, edema, allergic dermatitis, purpura, asthma, dyspnea, vision disturbances, and increased or decreased urination

General Dosing Information

Ketorolac may be administered on a scheduled or on an as-needed basis, depending on the type and severity of pain.

Administration of an initial 30- or 60-mg loading dose is recommended to achieve therapeutic plasma concentrations more rapidly and to provide a faster onset of analgesic action.

Concurrent use of ketorolac with an opioid analgesic provides additive analgesia and may permit lower doses of the opioid analgesic to be utilized.

Parenteral Dosage Forms

KETOROLAC TROMETHAMINE INJECTION

Usual adult and adolescent dose: Analgesic—Intramuscular, 60 mg as an initial loading dose, followed by 30 mg every six hours.

Note: A lower dose of 30 mg initially, followed by 15 mg every six hours, is recommended for patients weighing less than 50 kg and for patients with reduced renal function. This reduced dose may also be sufficient for some other adult patients.

After the patient's response to the recommended dosage regimen has been established, dosage may be adjusted as needed. Individual doses may be increased or decreased by up to 50%, if necessary, to maintain an every-six-hour dosing regimen, provided that the maximum recommended daily dose is not exceeded. Alternatively, if the recommended dose provides pain relief lasting significantly longer than six hours, that dose may be administered at longer intervals.

Usual adult prescribing limits: Intramuscular, 150 mg on the first day (including the initial loading dose of 60 mg), then 120 mg per day thereafter.

Usual geriatric dose: Patients 65 years of age and older—Intramuscular, 30 mg as an initial loading dose, followed by 15 mg every six hours. Dosage may then be adjusted according to patient tolerance and response, provided that the maximum recommended adult doses are not exceeded.

LAXATIVES   Local

INN: Included in brackets after individual generic listings, if different from the U.S. generic names.

BISACODYL
Oral
Bisacodyl Tablets USP
In the U.S.—*Bisac-Evac; Carter's Little Pills; Dacodyl; Deficol; Dulcolax; Fleet Bisacodyl;* GENERIC
In Canada—*Bisacolax; Dulcolax; Laxit*
Rectal
Bisacodyl Rectal Solution
In the U.S.—*Fleet Bisacodyl; Fleet Bisacodyl Prep*
In Canada—*Dulcolax*
Bisacodyl Suppositories USP
In the U.S.—*Bisco-Lax; Dacodyl; Deficol; Dulcolax; Fleet Bisacodyl; Theralax;* GENERIC
In Canada—*Bisacolax; Dulcolax; Laxit;* GENERIC
Bisacodyl Tannex Powder for Rectal Solution†
In the U.S.—*Clysodrast*
BISACODYL AND DOCUSATE*
Oral
Bisacodyl and Docusate Sodium Tablets*
In Canada—*Dulcodos*
CARBOXYMETHYLCELLULOSE, CASANTHRANOL, AND DOCUSATE†
Oral
Carboxymethylcellulose Sodium, Casanthranol, and Docusate Sodium Capsules†
In the U.S.—*Disolan Forte*
CARBOXYMETHYLCELLULOSE AND DOCUSATE†
Oral
Carboxymethylcellulose Sodium and Docusate Sodium Capsules†
In the U.S.—*Disoplex*
CASANTHRANOL†
Oral
Casanthranol Syrup†
In the U.S.—*Black-Draught*
CASANTHRANOL AND DOCUSATE
Oral
Casanthranol and Docusate Potassium Capsules†
In the U.S.—*Dialose Plus; Diocto-K Plus; Docu-K Plus; DSMC Plus*
Casanthranol and Docusate Sodium Capsules
In the U.S.—*Afko-Lube Lax; Diothron; Disanthrol; D-S-S plus; Peri-Colace; Pro-Sof Plus; Regulace;* GENERIC
In Canada—*Peri-Colace*
Casanthranol and Docusate Sodium Syrup†
In the U.S.—*Diocto-C; Peri-Colace;* GENERIC
Casanthranol and Docusate Sodium Tablets†
In the U.S.—*Di-Sosul Forte; Molatoc-CST*
CASCARA SAGRADA†
Oral
Aromatic Cascara Fluidextract USP†
In the U.S.—GENERIC
Cascara Tablets USP†
In the U.S.—GENERIC
CASCARA SAGRADA AND ALOE†
Oral
Cascara Sagrada and Aloe Tablets†
In the U.S.—*Nature's Remedy*
CASCARA SAGRADA AND PHENOLPHTHALEIN†
Oral
Cascara Sagrada Extract and Phenolphthalein Tablets†
In the U.S.—*Caroid Laxative*

CASTOR OIL
Oral
Castor Oil USP
In the U.S.—*Kellogg's Castor Oil; Purge;* GENERIC
In Canada—GENERIC
Castor Oil Emulsion USP†
In the U.S.—*Alphamul; Emulsoil; Fleet Flavored Castor Oil; Neoloid*
DANTHRON AND DOCUSATE*
Oral
Danthron and Docusate Sodium Capsules*
In Canada—*Regulex-D*
Danthron and Docusate Sodium Tablets*
In Canada—*Doss*
DEHYDROCHOLIC ACID†
Oral
Dehydrocholic Acid Tablets USP†
In the U.S.—*Cholan-HMB; Decholin; Hepahydrin;* GENERIC
DEHYDROCHOLIC ACID AND DOCUSATE†
Oral
Dehydrocholic Acid and Docusate Sodium Capsules†
In the U.S.—*Bilax*
Dehydrocholic Acid and Docusate Sodium Tablets†
In the U.S.—*Neolax*
DEHYDROCHOLIC ACID, DOCUSATE, AND PHENOLPHTHALEIN†
Oral
Dehydrocholic Acid, Docusate Sodium, and Phenolphthalein Capsules†
In the U.S.—*Trilax*
DOCUSATE
Oral
Docusate Calcium Capsules USP
In the U.S.—*Pro-Cal-Sof; Surfak;* GENERIC
In Canada—GENERIC
Docusate Potassium Capsules USP†
In the U.S.—*Dialose; Diocto-K; Kasof*
Docusate Sodium Capsules USP
In the U.S.—*Afko-Lube; Colace; Dioeze; Diosuccin; Dio-Sul; Disonate; Doss; Doxinate; D-S-S; Duosol; Laxinate 100; Modane Soft; Pro-Sof; Regulax SS;* GENERIC
In Canada—*Colace; Regulex*
Docusate Sodium Solution USP (Oral)
In the U.S.—*Colace; Diocto; Disonate; Doxinate; Pro-Sof Liquid Concentrate*
In Canada—*Colace*
Docusate Sodium Syrup USP
In the U.S.—*Colace; Diocto; Disonate; Doss; Pro-Sof;* GENERIC
In Canada—*Colace*
Docusate Sodium Tablets USP†
In the U.S.—*Di-Sosul; Molatoc; Regutol; Stulex;* GENERIC
Rectal
Docusate Sodium Rectal Solution†
In the U.S.—*Therevac Plus; Therevac-SB*
DOCUSATE AND PHENOLPHTHALEIN
Oral
Docusate Calcium and Phenolphthalein Capsules
In the U.S.—*Docucal-P; Doxidan*
In Canada—*Doxidan*
Docusate Sodium and Phenolphthalein Capsules†
In the U.S.—*Disolan; Phillips' LaxCaps*
Docusate Sodium and Phenolphthalein Tablets
In the U.S.—*Colax; Correctol; Extra Gentle Ex-Lax; Feen-a-Mint Pills*
In Canada—*Extra Gentle Ex-Lax*

Docusate Sodium and Phenolphthalein Chewable Tablets†
  In the U.S.—*Feen-a-Mint*
GLYCERIN
Rectal
  Glycerin Rectal Solution†
    In the U.S.—*Fleet Babylax*
  Glycerin Suppositories USP
    In the U.S.—*Sani-Supp;* GENERIC
    In Canada—GENERIC
LACTULOSE
Oral
  Lactulose Syrup USP
    In the U.S.—*Cholac; Chronulac; Constilac; Constulose; Du-phalac; Enulose; Generlac; Portalac*
    In Canada—*Chronulac; Lactulax*
MAGNESIUM CITRATE
Oral
  Magnesium Citrate Oral Solution USP
    In the U.S.—*Citroma; Citro-Nesia;* GENERIC
    In Canada—*Citro-Mag*
MAGNESIUM HYDROXIDE§
Oral
  Milk of Magnesia USP
    In the U.S.—*Phillips' Milk of Magnesia;* GENERIC
    In Canada—*Phillips' Milk of Magnesia*
  Magnesia Tablets USP
    In the U.S.—GENERIC
    In Canada—*Phillips' Magnesia Tablets*
MAGNESIUM HYDROXIDE AND MINERAL OIL†
Oral
  Milk of Magnesia and Mineral Oil Emulsion†
    In the U.S.—*Haley's M-O*
MAGNESIUM HYDROXIDE, MINERAL OIL, AND GLYCERIN*
Oral
  Milk of Magnesia, Mineral Oil, and Glycerin Emulsion*
    In Canada—*Magnolax*
MAGNESIUM OXIDE§†
Oral
  Magnesium Oxide Tablets USP†
    In the U.S.—*Mag-Ox 400; Maox*
MAGNESIUM SULFATE†
Oral
  Magnesium Sulfate Crystals†
    In the U.S.—GENERIC
  Magnesium Sulfate Tablets†
    In the U.S.—*Bilagog‡*
MALT SOUP EXTRACT†
Oral
  Malt Soup Extract Powder†
    In the U.S.—*Maltsupex*
  Malt Soup Extract Oral Solution†
    In the U.S.—*Maltsupex*
  Malt Soup Extract Tablets†
    In the U.S.—*Maltsupex*
MALT SOUP EXTRACT AND PSYLLIUM†
Oral
  Malt Soup Extract and Psyllium Powder†
    In the U.S.—*Syllamalt*
METHYLCELLULOSE†
Oral
  Methylcellulose Capsules†
    In the U.S.—GENERIC
  Methylcellulose Granules†
    In the U.S.—*Citrucel*
  Methylcellulose Powder†
    In the U.S.—GENERIC
  Methylcellulose Oral Solution USP†
    In the U.S.—*Cologel*

Methylcellulose Tablets USP†
  In the U.S.—GENERIC
MINERAL OIL
Oral
  Mineral Oil USP
    In the U.S.—*Nujol;* GENERIC
    In Canada—GENERIC
  Mineral Oil Emulsion USP
    In the U.S.—*Agoral Plain; Kondremul Plain; Liqui-Doss; Milkinol; Zymenol*
    In Canada—*Kondremul*
  Mineral Oil Gel
    In the U.S.—*Neo-Cultol*
    In Canada—*Lansoÿl*
  Mineral Oil Oral Suspension†
    In the U.S.—*Petrogalar Plain*
Rectal
  Mineral Oil Enema USP
    In the U.S.—*Fleet Enema Mineral Oil*
    In Canada—*Fleet Enema Mineral Oil*
MINERAL OIL AND CASCARA SAGRADA†
Oral
  Mineral Oil and Cascara Sagrada Extract Emulsion†
    In the U.S.—*Kondremul with Cascara*
MINERAL OIL, GLYCERIN, AND PHENOLPHTHALEIN*
Oral
  Mineral Oil, Glycerin, and Phenolphthalein Emulsion*
    In Canada—*Agarol*
MINERAL OIL AND PHENOLPHTHALEIN†
Oral
  Mineral Oil and Phenolphthalein Emulsion†
    In the U.S.—*Agoral; Agoral Marshmallow; Agoral Raspberry; Kondremul with Phenolphthalein*
  Mineral Oil and Phenolphthalein Oral Suspension†
    In the U.S.—*Phenolphthalein Petrogalar*
PHENOLPHTHALEIN (White or Yellow)
Oral
  Phenolphthalein Chewing Gum†
    In the U.S.—*Feen-a-Mint Gum*
  Phenolphthalein Tablets USP
    In the U.S.—*Alophen; Ex-Lax Pills; Medilax; Modane*
    In Canada—*Ex-Lax Pills*
  Phenolphthalein Tablets USP (Chewable)
    In the U.S.—*Espotabs; Evac-U-Gen; Evac-U-Lax; Ex-Lax*
    In Canada—*Ex-Lax*
  Phenolphthalein Wafers†
    In the U.S.—*Phenolax*
POLOXAMER 188†
Oral
  Poloxamer 188 Capsules†
    In the U.S.—*Alaxin*
POLYCARBOPHIL
Oral
  Calcium Polycarbophil Tablets†
    In the U.S.—*Fibercon*
  Calcium Polycarbophil Chewable Tablets
    In the U.S.—*Equalactin; Mitrolan*
    In Canada—*Mitrolan*
POTASSIUM BITARTRATE AND SODIUM BICARBONATE†
Rectal
  Potassium Bitartrate and Sodium Bicarbonate Suppositories†
    In the U.S.—*Ceo-Two*
PSYLLIUM
Oral
  Psyllium Caramels†
    In the U.S.—*Naturacil*

Psyllium Granules
  In the U.S.—*Perdiem Plain; Siblin*
  In Canada—*Siblin*
Psyllium Powder†
  In the U.S.—*Cillium; Konsyl; Syllact*
PSYLLIUM HYDROPHILIC MUCILLOID
Oral
  Psyllium Hydrophilic Mucilloid Granules*
    In Canada—*Prodiem Plain*
  Psyllium Hydrophilic Mucilloid Powder
    In the U.S.—*Fiberall; Hydrocil Instant; Konsyl-D; Metamucil;*
    Metamucil Orange Flavor; Metamucil Strawberry Flavor;
    Metamucil Sugar Free; Modane Bulk; Pro-Lax; Reguloid
    Natural; Reguloid Orange; Serutan; Versabran; V-Lax
    In Canada—*Karacil; Metamucil; Metamucil Orange Flavor;*
    Metamucil Sugar Free
  Psyllium Hydrophilic Mucilloid Effervescent Powder
    In the U.S.—*Effer-syllium; Metamucil Instant Mix; Metamucil*
    Instant Mix, Orange Flavor
    In Canada—*Metamucil Instant Mix, Orange Flavor*
  Psyllium Hydrophilic Mucilloid Wafers†
    In the U.S.—*Fiberall*
PSYLLIUM HYDROPHILIC MUCILLOID AND CARBOXY-
METHYLCELLULOSE†
Oral
  Psyllium Hydrophilic Mucilloid and Carboxymethylcellulose So-
  dium Granules†
    In the U.S.—*Serutan Toasted Granules*
PSYLLIUM HYDROPHILIC MUCILLOID AND SENNA*
Oral
  Psyllium Hydrophilic Mucilloid and Senna Granules*
    In Canada—*Prodiem*
PSYLLIUM HYDROPHILIC MUCILLOID AND SENNOSIDES†
Oral
  Psyllium Hydrophilic Mucilloid and Sennosides Powder†
    In the U.S.—*Prompt*
PSYLLIUM AND SENNA†
Oral
  Psyllium and Senna Granules†
    In the U.S.—*Perdiem*
SENNA
Oral
  Senna Granules
    In the U.S.—*Black-Draught Lax-Senna; Senokot*
    In Canada—*Senokot*
  Senna Oral Solution†
    In the U.S.—*Fletcher's Castoria; X-Prep Liquid*
  Senna Syrup USP
    In the U.S. and Canada—*Senokot*
  Senna Tablets
    In the U.S.—*Black-Draught Lax-Senna; Senexon; Senokot;*
    Senolax
    In Canada—*Senokot*
Rectal
  Senna Suppositories
    In the U.S. and Canada—*Senokot*
SENNA AND DOCUSATE
Oral
  Senna and Docusate Sodium Tablets
    In the U.S.—*Gentlax S; Senokot-S*
    In Canada—*Senokot-S*
SENNOSIDES
Oral
  Sennosides Tablets USP
    In the U.S.—*Gentle Nature; Nytilax*
    In Canada—*Glysennid*

SODIUM PHOSPHATE
Oral
  Effervescent Sodium Phosphate†
    In the U.S.—GENERIC
  Sodium Phosphates Oral Solution USP†
    In the U.S.—*Fleet Phospho-Soda;* GENERIC
Rectal
  Sodium Phosphates Enema
    In the U.S. and Canada—*Fleet Enema*

---

*Not commercially available in the U.S.
† Not commercially available in Canada.
‡Contains other active ingredients that have no laxative properties.
§See *Antacids (Oral-Local)* for antacid use of magnesium hydrox-
ide and magnesium oxide.

Category

Note: The term "laxative" includes the historically used terms "cathartic," "drastic," and "purgative."

Laxative—
  Bulk-forming: Malt Soup Extract; Malt Soup Extract and Psyl-
    lium; Methylcellulose; Polycarbophil; Psyllium; Psyllium Hy-
    drophilic Mucilloid; Psyllium Hydrophilic Mucilloid and Car-
    boxymethylcellulose.
  Bulk-forming and stool softener: Carboxymethylcellulose and
    Docusate.
  Bulk-forming, stimulant, and stool softener: Carboxymethylcellu-
    lose, Casanthranol, and Docusate.
  Bulk-forming and stimulant: Psyllium Hydrophilic Mucilloid and
    Senna; Psyllium Hydrophilic Mucilloid and Sennosides; Psyl-
    lium and Senna.
  Carbon dioxide-releasing: Potassium Bitartrate and Sodium Bicar-
    bonate.
  Hyperosmotic: Glycerin; Lactulose.
  Hyperosmotic, saline: Magnesium Citrate; Magnesium Hydrox-
    ide; Magnesium Oxide; Magnesium Sulfate; Sodium Phosphate.
  Hyperosmotic and lubricant: Magnesium Hydroxide and Mineral
    Oil; Magnesium Hydroxide, Mineral Oil, and Glycerin.
  Hyperosmotic, lubricant, and stimulant: Mineral Oil, Glycerin, and
    Phenolphthalein.
  Lubricant: Mineral Oil.
  Lubricant and stimulant: Mineral Oil and Cascara Sagrada; Min-
    eral Oil and Phenolphthalein.
  Stimulant or contact: Bisacodyl; Casanthranol; Cascara Sagrada;
    Cascara Sagrada and Aloe; Cascara Sagrada and Phenolphtha-
    lein; Castor Oil; Dehydrocholic Acid; Phenolphthalein (White
    or Yellow); Senna; Sennosides.
  Stimulant and stool softener: Bisacodyl and Docusate; Casanthranol
    and Docusate; Danthron and Docusate; Dehydrocholic Acid
    and Docusate; Dehydrocholic Acid, Docusate, and Phenolphtha-
    lein; Docusate and Phenolphthalein; Senna and Docusate.
  Stool softener or emollient: Docusate; Poloxamer 188 (poloxalkol).
Antacid—Magnesium Hydroxide; Magnesium Oxide.
Antihyperammonemic—Lactulose.
Hydrocholeretic—Dehydrocholic Acid.
Antidiarrheal—Polycarbophil; Psyllium Hydrophilic Mucilloid.
Antihyperlipidemic—Psyllium Hydrophilic Mucilloid.

Indications

Note: Bracketed information in the *Indications* section refers to uses
  not included in U.S. product labeling.

In the treatment of constipation or in the evacuation of the bowel, or in
  any other conditions in which a laxative is indicated, the advantage of using certain laxative combinations rather than a single
  laxative preparation has not been established. In some instances,
  just as with the selection of a single entity laxative, the improper selection of a laxative combination may turn constipa-

tion into a more serious condition. FDA's tentative final monograph for laxative drug products for OTC use has listed specific active laxative ingredients to be included in bulk-forming, bulk-forming and lubricant, bulk-forming and stimulant, lubricant and stimulant, lubricant and saline, saline and stimulant, and stimulant combinations.

Some of the laxative combinations contain other active ingredients that have no laxative properties. For example, atropine has been added for its antispasmodic properties probably as an adjunct to relieve constipation-induced cramping. However, a fixed combination of a laxative with any other medication is generally considered irrational and may be unsafe in some combinations.

Accepted

Constipation (prophylaxis)—Oral bulk-forming, lubricant, and stool softener laxatives are indicated prophylactically in patients who should not strain during defecation, such as those with an episiotomy wound, painful thrombosed hemorrhoids, fissures or perianal abscesses, body wall and diaphragmatic hernias, anorectal stenosis, or postmyocardial infarction.

Constipation (treatment)—Oral laxatives are indicated for the short-term relief of constipation. Oral bulk-forming laxatives, stimulant laxatives, and carbon dioxide-releasing suppositories are indicated to facilitate defecation in geriatric patients with diminished colonic motor response. Oral bulk-forming laxatives and stool softener laxatives are preferred to treat constipation that may occur during pregnancy and postpartum to help re-establish normal bowel function or to avoid straining if hemorrhoids are present.

In severe cases of constipation, such as with fecal impaction, mineral oil and stool softener laxatives administered orally or rectally are indicated to soften the impacted feces. To help complete the evacuation of the impacted colon, a rectal stimulant or saline laxative may follow.

Bowel evacuation—

Pre- and postpartum: Carbon dioxide-releasing suppositories are indicated to evacuate the colon in preparation for delivery and for a few days after to help re-establish normal bowel function.

Preoperative and

Pre-radiography: Oral or rectal stimulant and oral saline laxatives, rectal preparations of glycerin, and carbon dioxide-releasing suppositories are also indicated to evacuate the colon in preparation for rectal and bowel examinations, and elective colon surgery.

Parasites, intestinal (treatment adjunct): Oral saline laxatives are indicated to accelerate excretion of various parasites including nematodes, after anthelmintic therapy.

Toxicity, nonspecific (treatment adjunct): Oral saline laxatives are also indicated to hasten excretion of poisonous substances (except acids or alkalies) from the gastrointestinal tract.

Laxative dependency (treatment)—Glycerin suppositories are indicated temporarily to re-establish normal bowel function in laxative-dependent patients.

Hyperacidity (treatment)—See *Magnesium Hydroxide* and *Magnesium Oxide, Antacids (Oral-Local).*

Hyperammonemia (prophylaxis and treatment)—Lactulose is indicated for the prevention and treatment of portal-systemic encephalopathy, including the stages of hepatic pre-coma and coma.

Biliary tract disorders (treatment)—Dehydrocholic acid is indicated as an adjunct in conditions involving the biliary tract.

Diarrhea (treatment)—Polycarbophil is indicated in the treatment of diarrhea associated with irritable bowel syndrome and diverticulosis, and actue nonspecific diarrhea. [Psyllium hydrophilic mucilloid is used in the treatment of choleretic diarrhea and diarrhea caused by vagotomy, small bowel resection, or disease of the terminal ileum.]

Bowel syndrome, irritable (treatment adjunct)—Polycarbophil is indicated [and other bulk-forming laxatives are used] to relieve constipation associated with irritable or spastic bowel.

[Hyperlipidemia (treatment)]—Psyllium hydrophilic mucilloid is used as an adjunct to diet in the treatment of mild to moderate hypercholesterolemia.

Pharmacology

Mechanism of action/Effect:

Bulk-forming—Absorb water and expand to provide increased bulk and moisture content to the stool. The increased bulk encourages normal peristalsis and bowel motility.

Carbon dioxide-releasing—Carbon dioxide released from combined potassium bitartrate and sodium bicarbonate induces gentle pressure in the rectum, thus promoting bowel movement.

Hyperosmotic—

Glycerin: Attracts water into the stool thereby stimulating rectal contraction; also, lubricates and softens inspissated fecal mass.

Lactulose: Produces osmotic effect in colon resulting from biodegradation by colonic bacterial flora into lactic, formic, and acetic acids. Fluid accumulation produces distention which in turn promotes increased peristalsis and bowel evacuation.

Saline: Produce osmotic effect primarily in small intestine by drawing water into the intestinal lumen. Fluid accumulation produces distention, which in turn promotes increased peristalsis and bowel evacuation. During the use of saline laxatives, the release of cholecystokinin from the intestinal mucosa may enhance the laxative effect.

Lubricant—Increase water retention in the stool by coating surfaces of stool and intestines with a water-immiscible film. Lubricant effect eases passage of contents through intestines. Emulsification of lubricant tends to enhance its ability to soften stool mass.

Stool softener—Reduce surface film tension of interfacing liquid contents of the bowel, promoting permeation of additional liquid into the stool to form a softer mass.

Stimulant—Precise mechanism of action is unknown. Thought to increase peristalsis by a direct effect on the smooth intestinal musculature by stimulation of intramural nerve plexi. Also have been shown to promote fluid and ion accumulation in the colon (castor oil and phenolphthalein act on the small intestine) to increase the laxative effect.

Antihyperammonemic—Lactulose decreases blood ammonia concentrations probably as a result of its bacterial degradation, in the colon, into low molecular weight organic acids which decrease the pH of the colonic contents. Acidification of colonic contents results in the retention of ammonia in the colon as the ammonium ion. The osmotic laxative action of the metabolites of lactulose expels the trapped ammonium from the colon.

Hydrocholeretic—Dehydrocholic acid has no effect on the production of bile salts; however, it increases bile volume and flow by increasing water output, thus producing bile of relatively low specific gravity, viscosity, and total solid content.

Antidiarrheal—Psyllium hydrophilic mucilloid and polycarbophil's water and bile salt binding capacity may result in fewer and bulkier stools.

Antihyperlipidemic—Psyllium hydrophilic mucilloid has an antihyperlipidemic effect. It decreases serum total cholesterol, low-density lipoprotein (LDL) cholesterol, and the ratio of LDL cholesterol to high-density lipoprotein (HDL) cholesterol. Although exact mechanism of psyllium's antihyperlipidemic effect is not known, it is believed that psyllium increases bile acid secretion, thus draining cholesterol products from the body.

Note: Knowledge of many specifics of the mechanisms of action is limited. The determination of influence of factors such as cyclic-AMP, electrolyte transportation, hormones, and enzymes may change such currently accepted mechanisms.

Precautions to Consider

Geriatrics

For lubricant

Oral mineral oil is not recommended for bedridden elderly patients since they are more prone to aspiration of oil droplets, which may produce lipid pneumonia.

For stimulant

Weakness, incoordination, and orthostatic hypotension may be exacerbated in elderly patients as a result of significant electrolyte loss when stimulant laxatives are used repeatedly to evacuate the colon.

For rectal solutions

Weakness, excessive perspiration, shock, seizures, and/or coma may occur in elderly patients with the use of rectal solutions due to water intoxication or dilutional hyponatremia.

Drug interactions and/or related problems

The following drug interactions and/or related problems have been selected on the basis of their potential clinical significance (possible mechanism in parentheses where appropriate)—not necessarily inclusive (» = major clinical significance):

Note: Combinations containing any of the following medications, depending on the amount present, may also interact with this medication.

For all classes

Diuretics, potassium-sparing, or

Potassium supplements

(chronic use or overuse of laxatives may reduce serum potassium concentrations by promoting excessive potassium loss from the intestinal tract; may interfere with potassium-retaining effects of potassium-sparing diuretics)

For bulk-forming

Anticoagulants, oral, or

Digitalis glycosides or

Salicylates

(concurrent use with cellulose bulk-forming laxatives may reduce the desired effect because of physical binding or other absorptive hindrance; a 2-hour interval between dosage with such medication and laxative dosage is recommended)

» Tetracyclines, oral

(concurrent use with calcium polycarbophil may decrease absorption because of possible formation of nonabsorbable complexes with free calcium released after ingestion; patients should be advised not to take calcium polycarbophil laxative within 1 to 2 hours of tetracyclines)

For hyperosmotic-saline, magnesium-containing

» Anticoagulants, coumarin- or indandione-derivative, oral, or

» Digitalis glycosides or

Phenothiazines, especially chlorpromazine

(these medications have been shown to have reduced effectiveness in the presence of aluminum- and magnesium-containing antacids; pending further studies, their concurrent administration with magnesium-containing saline hyperosmotic laxatives is best avoided)

» Sodium polystyrene sulfonate

(sodium polystyrene sulfonate may bind with magnesium, preventing neutralization of bicarbonate ions and leading to systemic alkalosis, which may be severe; concurrent use is not recommended, although the risk may be less with rectal administration of the resin)

» Tetracyclines, oral

(concurrent use with magnesium-containing laxatives may result in formation of nonabsorbable complexes; patients should be advised not to take these laxatives within 1 to 2 hours of tetracyclines)

For lubricant

Anticoagulants, coumarin- or indandione-derivative, oral, or

Contraceptives, oral, or

Digitalis glycosides or

Vitamins, fat-soluble, such as A, D, E, and K

(concurrent use with mineral oil may interfere with the proper absorption of these or other medications and reduce their effectiveness)

(in addition to interfering with absorption of oral anticoagulants, mineral oil also decreases absorption of vitamin K, which may lead to increased anticoagulant effects)

Stool softener laxatives

(concurrent use may cause increased absorption of mineral oil and result in the formation of tumor-like deposits in tissues)

For stimulant

Antacids or

Histamine H_2-receptor antagonists, such as:

Cimetidine

Famotidine

Nizatidine

Ranitidine or

Milk

(administration within one hour of bisacodyl tablets may cause the enteric coating to dissolve too rapidly, resulting in gastric or duodenal irritation)

For stool softener

Danthron or

Mineral oil or

Phenolphthalein

(concurrent use with a stool softener laxative may enhance the systemic absorption of these agents. Although such combinations are intentionally used in some "fixed-dose" laxative preparations, the propensity for toxic effects is greatly increased. Liver injury has been reported with the danthron combination following repeated dosage)

Contraindications/Medical problems

The contraindications/medical problems included have been selected on the basis of their potential clinical significance (reasons given in parentheses where appropriate)—not necessarily inclusive (» = major clinical significance).

Except under special circumstances, this medication should not be used when the following medical problems exist:

For all classes

» Appendicitis, or symptoms of

» Bleeding, rectal, undiagnosed

» Congestive heart failure or

» Hypertension

Note: Applies to those preparations containing sodium; an alternative sodium-free laxative may usually be used. Preparations containing less than 5 mg of sodium per dose unit are utilized in many cases.

» Diabetes mellitus

Note: Applies to those preparations containing substantial amounts of dextrose, galactose, and/or sucrose; bulk-forming and liquid dosage forms of laxatives cause most concern.

» Intestinal obstruction

» Sensitivity to the class of laxative being used

For bulk-forming

» Dysphagia

(esophageal obstruction may occur)

For hyperosmotic—saline
»   Dehydration
       (may be aggravated by repeated use of saline laxatives)
»   Renal function impairment
       (hyperkalemia and hypermagnesemia may result, especially with
       preparations containing magnesium and potassium salts; tetany
       with hypocalcemia and hyperphosphatemia may occur with the
       use of phosphate salts)

For hyperosmotic—saline and lubricant
»   Colostomy or
»   Ileostomy
       (increased risk of electrolyte or fluid imbalance)

For lubricant
»   Dysphagia
       (oral mineral oil may be aspirated and cause lipid pneumonitis)
»   Caution is also recommended with bedridden patients, who may
       develop lipid pneumonia from aspiration of mineral oil.

Side/Adverse Effects

Note: Steatorrhea, proteinuria, hematuria and anuria, and a systemic
       lupus-like syndrome have been reported rarely with phenol-
       phthalein.

The following side/adverse effects have been selected on the basis of
       their potential clinical significance (possible signs and symptoms
       in parentheses where appropriate)—not necessarily inclusive:

Those indicating need for medical attention
Incidence less frequent
  For rectal solutions—more frequent with sodium phosphates
     Rectal irritation (rectal bleeding, blistering, burning, itching,
     or pain)
Incidence rare
  For bulk-forming
     Allergies to some vegetable components (difficulty breathing,
     skin rash or itching); **esophageal blockage or intestinal impac-
     tion**
       Note: Usually *esophageal blockage* or *intestinal impaction* oc-
       curs because of insufficient fluid intake
  For hyperosmotic—saline
     Electrolyte imbalance—due to acute overdosage or chronic
     misuse (confusion, irregular heartbeat, muscle cramps, unusual
     tiredness or weakness); **magnesium accumulation in presence
     of renal function impairment** (dizziness or lightheadedness)
  For stimulant
     Allergic reaction to dehydrocholic acid or phenolphthalein
     (skin rash); **electrolyte imbalance**—due to acute overdosage or
     chronic misuse (confusion, irregular heartbeat, muscle cramps,
     unusual tiredness or weakness); **pink to red discoloration of
     alkaline urine and feces**—with phenolphthalein only; **pink to
     red, red to violet, or red to brown discoloration of alkaline
     urine**—with cascara, danthron, and/or senna only; **yellow to
     brown discoloration of acid urine**—with cascara, phenolphtha-
     lein, and/or senna only
  For stool softeners
     Allergies, undetermined (skin rash)

Those indicating need for medical attention only if they continue
or are bothersome
Incidence less frequent
  For hyperosmotic—glycerin
     Skin irritation—surrounding rectal area
  For hyperosmotic—lactulose or saline
     Cramping; diarrhea; gas formation; increased thirst
  For lubricant
     Skin irritation—surrounding rectal area

  For stimulant
     Belching; cramping—more frequent with aloe and certain senna
     preparations; **diarrhea; nausea; rectal irritation**—with sup-
     pository dosage form (skin irritation surrounding rectal area)
  For stool softeners
     Stomach and/or intestinal cramping; throat irritation—with
     liquid forms

Patient Consultation

In providing consultation, consider emphasizing the following selected information:

Before using this medication
  Importance of diet, fluids, and exercise
»   Conditions affecting use, especially:
       Sensitivity to a particular class of laxative
       Pregnancy—
          For saline: May promote sodium retention resulting in edema
          For lubricant: Mineral oil may decrease absorption of foods,
             fat-soluble vitamins, and medications; possibility of hy-
             poprothrombinemia and hemorrhage in neonate
          For stimulant: Castor oil not recommended; pelvic engorge-
             ment may stimulate uterus
       Breast-feeding—For stimulant: May be excreted in breast milk
          and may produce loose stools in nursing infant
       Use in children—Proper diagnosis recommended before using
          laxatives
          For lubricant: Risk of pneumonia due to aspiration of min-
             eral oil droplets
          For stimulant: Bisacodyl enteric-coated tablets not recom-
             mended because of risk of gastric irritation if chewed
          For rectal solutions: Risk of water intoxication or dilutional
             hyponatremia; risk of seizures if large amounts of phos-
             phate absorbed (for sodium phosphates)
       Use in the elderly—
          For lubricant: Risk of pneumonia in bedridden patients due
             to aspiration of mineral oil droplets
          For stimulant: Possible exacerbation of weakness, incoordi-
             nation, and hypotension due to electrolyte loss with re-
             peated use
          For rectal solutions: Risk of water intoxication or dilutional
             hyponatremia
       Other medications, especially anticoagulants, digitalis glyco-
          sides, sodium polystyrene sulfonate (with magnesium-con-
          taining), or tetracyclines (with bulk-forming and magne-
          sium-containing)
       Other medical problems, especially appendicitis, intestinal ob-
          struction, or rectal bleeding; congestive heart failure or hy-
          pertension (with sodium-containing); diabetes (with dex-
          trose-, galactose-, or sucrose-containing); dysphagia (with
          bulk-forming or lubricant); dehydration or renal function
          impairment (with hyperosmotic, saline); colostomy or il-
          eostomy (with hyperosmotic [saline] or lubricant)

Proper use of this medication
For all classes
  Following physician's directions on prescribed laxative
  Following manufacturer's package directions on nonprescription
     (OTC) laxative
»   Proper storage
For oral dosage forms
  Drinking at least 6 to 8 full glasses (240 mL each) of liquids each
     day when using any laxative, to aid stool softening
For rectal dosage forms
  Proper administration technique; reading patient directions care-
     fully
  Lubrication of anus with petroleum jelly before insertion of enema
     applicator and careful insertion to prevent damage to rectal
     wall

Moistening suppository with water by placing either under water tap for 30 seconds or in a cup of water for at least 10 seconds, before rectal insertion

For bulk-forming

Not swallowing in dry form; taking with liquid

Drinking a full glass (240 mL) or more of liquid with each dose plus additional liquid during the day

Results obtained in 12 hours to 3 days

For carbon dioxide-releasing

Results usually obtained in 5 to 30 minutes

For hyperosmotic—glycerin

Results usually obtained in 15 minutes to 1 hour

For hyperosmotic—lactulose

Drinking a full glass (240 mL) of liquid or more with each dose for best results

Flavor improved by following dose with fruit juice or citrus-flavored carbonated beverage

May require 24 to 48 hours for results

For hyperosmotic—saline

Oral dosage forms only:

Drinking a full glass (240 mL) of liquid or more with each dose to prevent dehydration

Flavor improved by following dose with fruit juice or citrus-flavored carbonated beverage

Results obtained within $1/2$ to 3 hours; not taking late in day unless at bedtime with food

Faster effect when taken on empty stomach, with a full glass (240 mL) of liquid or more

Rectal dosage forms only:

Results usually obtained in 2 to 5 minutes with sodium phosphates enema

For lubricant

Oral dosage forms only:

Not taking within 2 hours of meals; may interfere with absorption of food nutrients and vitamins

Usually taken at bedtime, but not while reclining; results obtained in about 6 to 8 hours

Rectal dosage forms only:

Results usually obtained in 2 to 15 minutes

For stimulant

Oral dosage forms only:

Taking on empty stomach for faster results

Preparations of this group (except castor oil) are sometimes taken at bedtime for morning results (some require up to 24 hours)

Bisacodyl only:

—not chewing or crushing tablets; swallowing whole because of enteric coating; not taking with milk or antacids

Castor oil only:

—not taking late in day; results within 2 to 6 hours

—chilling and mixing in cold orange juice to improve taste; emulsion available

Phenolphthalein only:

—may cause laxative effect for up to 3 days in some individuals

Rectal dosage forms only:

Results usually obtained in 15 minutes to 1 hour with bisacodyl; or in 30 minutes to 2 hours with senna

For stool softeners

Oral dosage forms only:

Flavor of liquid forms improved in milk or fruit juice

Results usually obtained in 1 to 2 days after first dose; may require 3 to 5 days

Rectal dosage forms only:

Results usually obtained in 2 to 15 minutes

Precautions while using this medication

For all classes

» Not using laxatives:

—if symptoms of appendicitis are present

—more often than recommended

—unnecessarily (for example, for cold, as tonic, to clean system)

—because bowel movement is missed 1 or 2 days

» Checking with physician if sudden change in bowel habit persists beyond 2 weeks

Avoiding laxative habit; overuse or extended use may cause dependence for bowel function

For oral laxatives

» Not taking:

—longer than 1 week unless by physician's order

—within 2 hours of other medicine

» Checking with physician if skin rash develops while taking

For rectal laxatives

» Checking with physician if signs of rectal irritation or infection occur with the use of rectal solutions

Not lubricating suppository with mineral oil or petroleum jelly

For bulk-forming

Diabetics and patients on sodium-restricted diet—Some products are high in sugar and/or sodium content

For hyperosmotic (oral dosage forms only)

Diabetics and patients on sodium-restricted diet—Some products contain sugar and/or sodium

For lubricant (oral dosage forms only)

Not to be taken repeatedly for prolonged time—Some absorption may cause problems; may interfere with absorption of food nutrients and vitamins A, D, E, and K

Need for protection of clothing, since large doses may cause oil leakage from rectum

Inhalation of oil droplets may cause a form of pneumonia, especially in children and bedridden elderly

Not taking mineral oil within 2 hours of a stool softener; absorption of mineral oil may be increased

For stimulant (oral dosage forms only)

Often associated with:

—laxative habit

—skin rash

—cramping, especially on empty stomach

—potassium loss

Diabetics and patients on sodium-restricted diet—Some products contain sugar and/or sodium

Side/adverse effects

Signs of potential side effects, especially rectal irritation (with rectal solutions); allergic reactions; esophageal blockage or intestinal impaction (with bulk-forming); electrolyte imbalance (with hyperosmotic [saline] or stimulant); discoloration of urine and feces (with cascara, danthron, phenolphthalein, senna)

General Dosing Information

For bulk-forming

Bulk-forming laxatives are suitable for long-term therapy, if necessary.

For polycarbophil when used as antidiarrheal

Polycarbophil is available as chewable tablets that absorb up to 60 times their weight in water. They are sometimes utilized to control diarrheal conditions by administering less fluid with each dose.

The usual oral adult dose of calcium polycarbophil when used as antidiarrheal is 1 gram one to four times a day.

The usual oral pediatric dose for children 3 to 6 years of age is 500 mg two times a day; for children 6 to 12 years of age the dose may be given three times a day, but not to exceed 3 grams a day.

For psyllium hydrophilic mucilloid when used as antihyperlipidemic
Reduced values for serum total cholesterol, low density lipoprotein (LDL), and for the ratio of LDL cholesterol to high density lipoprotein (HDL) cholesterol have been achieved with three 3.4-gram doses of psyllium per day.

For hyperosmotic—lactulose and saline
For lactulose
Has no effect on small intestine; lowers pH of colon.

Use with caution in diabetics—Contains up to 1.2 grams of lactose and up to 2.2 grams of galactose per 15 mL.

Dose may be mixed with milk or fruit juice to improve flavor.

For lactulose when used as an antihyperammonemic
The usual oral adult dose of lactulose when used as antihyper-ammonemic is 20 to 30 grams (30 to 45 mL) three or four times a day. This dose may be adjusted every day or two to produce two to three soft stools daily. In the initial phase of therapy 20 to 30 grams (30 to 45 mL) may be given every hour to induce rapid laxation.

Concurrent use of other laxatives during initial phase of therapy for portal-systemic encephalopathy may result in loose stools and falsely suggest adequate lactulose dosage has been obtained.

For saline
Solid forms must be completely dissolved before swallowing.

Because of relatively short response time, saline laxatives are not usually given at bedtime or late in the day unless the dose is relatively small and given with food.

This type of laxative may contain large amounts of sodium (up to 1 gram or more per dose in some preparations).

For lubricant
Commonly administered at bedtime, when slower peristalsis allows longer transit time to improve laxative effect. If administered at bedtime, patient should not be reclining to avoid aspiration of oil droplets.

Because mineral oil may interfere with absorption of oil-soluble nutrients and/or medications, this type of laxative is not administered within 2 hours of meals or other medications.

To avoid oil leakage through the anal sphincter, the dose of mineral oil may be reduced or divided, or a stable emulsion may be used instead.

For stimulant
Many preparations of this group are administered at bedtime with a snack to produce results in the morning—*except* castor oil. Because of its shorter response time, castor oil is not usually taken at bedtime or late in the day.

Bisacodyl tannex (bisacodyl and tannic acid complex) should not be used if multiple enemas are required. If absorbed in sufficient amounts, tannic acid is hepatotoxic.

Phenolphthalein discolors alkaline feces and urine pink to red and acid urine yellow to brown.

Cascara, danthron, and/or senna preparations may discolor alkaline urine pink to red, red to violet, or red to brown. Acid urine may be discolored yellow to brown with cascara and/or senna preparations.

For dehydrocholic acid when used as hydrocholeretic
The usual oral adult dose of dehydrocholic acid when used as hydrocholeretic is 244 to 500 mg three times a day after meals.

For stool softeners
Because stool softener laxatives may increase absorption of other laxatives, including mineral oil, they are not given within 2 hours of such preparations. Patients should be informed.

The bitter taste of some liquid preparations of this type of laxative may be improved by diluting each dose in milk or fruit juice.

For oral dosage forms
With the possible exception of bulk-forming laxatives, more rapid results are obtained when laxatives are taken on an empty stomach. When taken with food and/or at bedtime, results tend to be delayed.

Intake of at least 6 to 8 full glasses (240 mL each) of fluid per day is necessary to aid in producing a soft stool and to protect the patient against dehydration when large volumes of water are lost with passage of the stool.

For rectal dosage forms
Lubrication of anus with petroleum jelly is recommended to prevent rectal abrasion and/or laceration produced by the insertion of a hard enema tip.

Lubrication of suppositories with mineral oil or petrolatum is not recommended since it may interfere with the action of the suppository. Instead, the suppository should be moistened with water by placing under a water tap for 30 seconds or in a cup of water for at least 10 seconds, before rectal insertion.

LEUCOVORIN   Systemic

A commonly used *brand name* in the U.S. is *Wellcovorin*.
Other commonly used names are citrovorum factor and folinic acid.

ORAL
Leucovorin Calcium Tablets
    In the U.S.—*Wellcovorin*; GENERIC
    In Canada—GENERIC

PARENTERAL
Leucovorin Calcium Injection USP
    In the U.S.—*Wellcovorin*; GENERIC
    In Canada—GENERIC
Leucovorin Calcium for Injection†
    In the U.S.—*Wellcovorin*; GENERIC

---

†Not commercially available in Canada.

Category: Antidote (to folic acid antagonists); antianemic; antineoplastic adjunct.

Indications

Note: Bracketed information in the *Indications* section refers to uses not included in U.S. product labeling.

Accepted
Methotrexate toxicity (prophylaxis and treatment);
Pyrimethamine toxicity (prophylaxis and treatment); or
Trimethoprim toxicity (prophylaxis and treatment)—Leucovorin is indicated as an antidote to the toxic effects of folic acid antagonists such as methotrexate, pyrimethamine, or trimethoprim.

Leucovorin is indicated as a rescue after high-dose methotrexate therapy in osteosarcoma[1].

Leucovorin is indicated to prevent severe toxicity due to overdose of methotrexate or high-dose[1] methotrexate therapy, to treat severe reactions to low or moderate doses of methotrexate, and [as a part of chemotherapeutic treatment programs in the management of several forms of cancer][1].

Anemia, megaloblastic (treatment)—Leucovorin is indicated to treat megaloblastic anemias associated with sprue, nutritional deficiency, pregnancy, and infancy when oral folic acid therapy is not feasible.

Leucovorin is not recommended for use in the treatment of pernicious anemia or other megaloblastic anemias secondary to lack of vitamin B_{12}, since it may produce a hematologic remission while neurologic manifestations continue to progress.

Carcinoma, colorectal (treatment adjunct)[1]—Leucovorin is indicated for use in combination with fluorouracil to prolong survival in the palliative treatment of patients with advanced colorectal cancer.

---

[1]Not included in Canadian product labeling.

Pharmacology

Mechanism of action/Effect: Antidote (to folic acid antagonists)—Leucovorin is a reduced form of folic acid, which is readily converted to other reduced folic acid derivatives (e.g., tetrahydrofolate). Because it does not require reduction by dihydrofolate reductase as does folic acid, leucovorin is not affected by blockage of this enzyme by folic acid antagonists (dihydrofolate reductase inhibitors). This allows purine and thymidine synthesis, and thus DNA, RNA, and protein synthesis, to occur. Leucovorin may limit methotrexate action on normal cells by competing with methotrexate for the same transport processes into the cell. Leucovorin given at the appropriate time rescues bone marrow and gastrointestinal cells from methotrexate but has no apparent effect on pre-existing methotrexate nephrotoxicity.

Onset of action:
Oral—20 to 30 minutes.
Intramuscular—10 to 20 minutes.
Intravenous—Less than 5 minutes.

Duration of action: All routes—3 to 6 hours.

Precautions to Consider

Geriatrics
No information is available on the relationship of age to the effects of leucovorin in geriatric patients. However, elderly patients are more likely to have age-related renal function impairment, which may require adjustment of dosage in patients receiving leucovorin as a rescue from the effects of high-dose methotrexate.

Drug interactions and/or related problems
The following drug interactions and/or related problems have been selected on the basis of their potential clinical significance (possible mechanism in parentheses where appropriate)—not necessarily inclusive (» = major clinical significance):

Note: Combinations containing any of the following medications, depending on the amount present, may also interact with this medication.

Anticonvulsants, barbiturate or
Anticonvulsants, hydantoin or
Primidone
(large doses of leucovorin may counteract the anticonvulsant effects of these medications)

Central nervous system (CNS) depression-producing medications (should be used with caution in patients receiving leucovorin calcium oral solution, because of its high alcohol content)

Fluorouracil
(concurrent use of leucovorin may increase the therapeutic and toxic effects of fluorouracil; although the two medications may be used together for therapeutic advantage, caution is necessary)

Contraindications/Medical problems
The contraindications/medical problems included have been selected on the basis of their potential clinical significance (reasons given in parentheses where appropriate)—not necessarily inclusive (» = major clinical significance).

This medication should not be used as the sole antianemic agent when the following medical problems exist:
» Pernicious anemia or
» Vitamin B_{12} deficiency
(may produce a partial hematologic response while neurologic manifestations continue to progress)

This medication should be used with caution when the following medical problem exists:
Sensitivity to leucovorin

This medication should be used with caution as a rescue from the effects of high-dose methotrexate when the following medical problems exist:
Aciduria (urine pH less than 7) or
Ascites or
Dehydration or
Gastrointestinal obstruction or
Pleural or peritoneal effusions or
» Renal function impairment
(risk of methotrexate toxicity is increased because elimination of methotrexate may be impaired and accumulation may occur; even small doses of methotrexate may lead to severe myelosuppression and mucositis; larger doses and/or increased duration of leucovorin treatment may be necessary, along with careful monitoring of methotrexate concentrations)

Nausea and vomiting
(absorption of leucovorin may be impaired; parenteral administration recommended; inadequate hydration secondary to severe nausea and vomiting may also result in increased methotrexate toxicity)

Side/Adverse Effects

The following side/adverse effects have been selected on the basis of their potential clinical significance (possible signs and symptoms in parentheses where appropriate)—not necessarily inclusive:

Those indicating need for medical attention
Incidence rare
Allergic reaction (skin rash, hives, or itching; wheezing)

Patient Consultation

In providing consultation, consider emphasizing the following selected information (» = major clinical significance):

Before using this medication
» Conditions affecting use, especially:
Sensitivity to leucovorin
Use in children—May increase frequency of seizures in susceptible children
Other medical problems, especially renal function impairment

Proper use of this medication
» Importance of taking as directed and not missing doses; taking at evenly spaced times
» Checking with physician before discontinuing medication or if vomiting occurs shortly after dose is taken

» Missed dose: Checking with physician right away; possible need for additional leucovorin; importance of not increasing dose unless directed by physician
» Proper storage

Side/adverse effects
Signs of potential side effects, especially allergic reaction

General Dosing Information

A 15-mg dose produces a serum reduced folate concentration of approximately 1 micromolar (1×10^{-6} M).

For use as an antidote to folic acid antagonists
Patients receiving leucovorin as a "rescue" from the toxic effects of methotrexate should be under supervision of a physician experienced in high-dose methotrexate therapy.

Parenteral administration of leucovorin is recommended if it appears that absorption may be impaired as a result of nausea and vomiting.

Methotrexate administration should not be initiated unless creatinine clearance and serum creatinine concentrations are normal. If renal function impairment develops during therapy, methotrexate should be withdrawn until renal function becomes acceptable.

High-dose methotrexate administration should not be initiated unless leucovorin is physically present and ready to be administered, since rescue is critical.

A variety of dosage schedules of leucovorin in combination with high-dose methotrexate have been used. Since this regimen is still largely investigational, the prescriber should consult the medical literature in choosing a specific dosage. Alkalinization of urine (with bicarbonate and/or acetazolamide) and intravenous hydration (1000 mL per square meter of body surface over six hours prior to beginning the methotrexate infusion and 3000 mL per square meter of body surface per day during the methotrexate infusion and for two days after the infusion is completed) are also important to prevent renal toxicity caused by methotrexate and/or its metabolites.

Administration of leucovorin should be consecutive to rather than simultaneous with methotrexate administration so as not to interfere with methotrexate's antineoplastic effects. However, leucovorin has been administered simultaneously with pyrimethamine and trimethoprim in oral or intramuscular doses ranging from 400 mcg (0.4 mg) to 5 mg to prevent megaloblastic anemia due to high doses of these medications.

In general, it is recommended that the first dose of leucovorin be administered within the first 24 to 42 hours of starting a high-dose methotrexate infusion (within 1 hour of an overdose), in a dosage to produce blood concentrations equal to or greater than methotrexate blood concentrations (leucovorin in a dose of 15 mg produces peak plasma concentrations of approximately 1 micromolar [1×10^{-6} M]). Duration of leucovorin administration varies with the dosage of methotrexate and plasma concentrations achieved (including rate of elimination); in general, leucovorin administration is continued until methotrexate concentrations fall to less than 5×10^{-8} M.

A larger dose and/or longer duration of leucovorin treatment may be required in patients with aciduria, ascites, dehydration, gastrointestinal obstruction, renal function impairment, or pleural or peritoneal effusions because excretion of methotrexate is slowed and the length of time for plasma methotrexate concentrations to decrease to nontoxic levels ($<5 \times 10^{-8}$ M) is increased. It is recommended that duration of leucovorin administration in these patients be based on determination of plasma methotrexate concentrations.

For use as an adjunct to fluorouracil for colorectal carcinoma
Patients receiving leucovorin in combination with fluorouracil should be under supervision of a physician experienced in cancer chemotherapy.

Oral Dosage Forms

LEUCOVORIN CALCIUM TABLETS
Usual adult and adolescent dose:
Antidote (to folic acid antagonists)—
To methotrexate: Oral, 10 mg (base) per square meter of body surface every six hours until methotrexate blood concentrations fall to less than 5×10^{-8} M.
To pyrimethamine or trimethoprim:
Prevention—Oral, 400 mcg (0.4 mg) to 5 mg (base) with each dose of the folic acid antagonist.
Treatment—Oral, 5 to 15 mg (base) per day.
Antianemic—Megaloblastic anemia, secondary to folate deficiency: Oral, up to 1 mg (base) per day.
Note: Doses higher than 25 mg should be given parenterally because oral absorption is saturable at doses above 25 mg.

Parenteral Dosage Forms

LEUCOVORIN CALCIUM INJECTION USP
Usual adult and adolescent dose:
Antidote (to folic acid antagonists)—
To methotrexate (inadvertent overdose): Intramuscular or intravenous, 10 mg (base) per square meter of body surface every six hours until methotrexate blood concentrations fall to less than 5×10^{-8} M.
Note: If, at 24 hours following methotrexate administration, the serum creatinine is increased by 50% or greater over baseline or serum methotrexate is greater than 5×10^{-6} M, the dose of leucovorin should be 100 mg (base) per square meter of body surface every three hours intravenously until methotrexate concentrations are reduced to appropriate levels. *Leucovorin calcium injection containing benzyl alcohol should not be used for doses greater than 10 mg per square meter of body surface.*
To pyrimethamine or trimethoprim:
Prevention—Intramuscular, 400 mcg (0.4 mg) to 5 mg (base) with each dose of the folic acid antagonist.
Treatment—Intramuscular, 5 to 15 mg (base) per day.
Antianemic—Megaloblastic anemia, secondary to folate deficiency: Intramuscular, up to 1 mg (base) per day.

Note: This product should *not* be used for doses greater than 10 mg per square meter of body surface.

LEUCOVORIN CALCIUM FOR INJECTION
Usual adult and adolescent dose:
Antidote (to folic acid antagonists)—
To methotrexate (inadvertent overdose): Intramuscular or intravenous, 10 mg (base) per square meter of body surface every six hours until methotrexate blood concentrations fall to less than 5×10^{-8} M.
Note: If, at 24 hours following methotrexate administration, the serum creatinine is increased 50% over baseline or serum methotrexate is greater than 5×10^{-6} M, the dose of leucovorin should be 100 mg (base) per square meter of body surface every three hours intravenously until methotrexate concentrations are reduced to appropriate levels. *Only solutions prepared with sterile water for injection (i.e., without benzyl alcohol) should be used for doses greater than 10 mg per square meter of body surface.*

To pyrimethamine or trimethoprim:
  Prevention—Intramuscular, 400 mcg (0.4 mg) to 5 mg (base)
    with each dose of the folic acid antagonist.
  Treatment—Intramuscular, 5 to 15 mg (base) per day.
Antianemic—Megaloblastic anemia, secondary to folate deficiency:
  Intramuscular, up to 1 mg (base) per day.
Carcinoma, colorectal (treatment adjunct)—
  Intravenous, 200 mg per square meter of body surface over a
    minimum of three minutes, followed by fluorouracil 370
    mg per square meter of body surface intravenously, or

Intravenous, 20 mg per square meter of body surface, followed
  by fluorouracil 425 mg per square meter of body surface
  intravenously.
Either regimen is given daily for five days, and the course may
  be repeated at four-week intervals for two courses and then
  at four-to five-week intervals, as determined by toxicity to
  the previous course.
Note: Only solutions prepared with sterile water for injection
  (i.e., without benzyl alcohol) should be used, since the
  dose is greater than 10 mg per square meter of body
  surface.

LEVOBUNOLOL   Ophthalmic

Some commonly used *brand names* are:
  In the U.S.—*Betagan C Cap B.I.D.; Betagan C Cap Q.D.; Betagan
    Standard Cap*
  In Canada—*Betagan C Cap B.I.D.; Betagan Standard Cap*

OPHTHALMIC
Levobunolol Hydrochloride Ophthalmic Solution USP
  In the U.S.—*Betagan C Cap B.I.D.; Betagan C Cap Q.D.; Betagan
    Standard Cap*
  In Canada—*Betagan C Cap B.I.D.; Betagan Standard Cap*

Category: Antiglaucoma agent (ophthalmic).

Indications

Note: Bracketed information in the *Indications* section refers to uses
  not included in U.S. product labeling.

Accepted
Glaucoma, open-angle (treatment);
[Glaucoma, in aphakic eyes (treatment)][1];
[Glaucoma, secondary (treatment)][1]; or
Hypertension, ocular (treatment)—Levobunolol lowers intraocular pressure and is indicated in the treatment of ocular hypertension and
  chronic open-angle glaucoma. It may be used alone or in conjunction with other antiglaucoma agents. In addition, levobunolol may
  be used in patients with glaucoma in aphakic eyes and in some
  patients with secondary glaucoma.
[Glaucoma, angle-closure (treatment adjunct)][1]—Levobunolol may be
  used in conjunction with a miotic to reduce elevated intraocular
  pressure in acute and chronic angle-closure glaucoma. However,
  levobunolol's action alone is unlikely to terminate an acute attack
  of angle-closure glaucoma, because levobunolol produces little or
  no constriction of the pupil, which is necessary to pull the iris
  away from the trabeculum to relieve blockage of the trabecular
  meshwork.
[Glaucoma, angle-closure, *during* or *after* iridectomy (treatment)][1]; or
[Glaucoma, malignant (treatment)][1]—Levobunolol is used to lower
  intraocular pressure in the treatment of angle-closure glaucoma
  during or *after* iridectomy and in the treatment of malignant glaucoma.

[1]Not included in Canadian product labeling.

Pharmacology

Mechanism of action/Effect Levobunolol is a nonselective beta-adrenergic blocking agent, equipotent at both beta-1 and beta-2 receptors. The exact mechanism of the ocular hypotensive action of

levobunolol in reducing intraocular pressure has not been established. However, its mechanism of action may be similar to that of
  timolol, which appears to lower intraocular pressure by reducing
  aqueous humor production.

Other actions/effects:
Reduces cardiac output in both healthy individuals and patients
  with heart disease.
Decreases heart rate and blood pressure in some patients.
Produces beta-adrenergic receptor blockade in the bronchi and
  bronchioles.
Has little or no effect on pupil size or accommodation compared to
  miosis produced by cholinergic agents.

Onset of action: Within 1 hour following a single dose.

Time to peak effect: Between 2 and 6 hours following a single dose.

Duration of action: A significant lowering of intraocular pressure
  may be maintained for up to 24 hours following a single dose.

Precautions to Consider

Cross-sensitivity and/or related problems
Patients intolerant of other beta-adrenergic blockers, either systemic
  or ophthalmic, (such as acebutolol, atenolol, betaxolol, carteolol,
  labetalol, metipranolol, metoprolol, nadolol, oxprenolol, penbutolol,
  pindolol, propranolol, sotalol, or timolol) may be intolerant of
  levobunolol also.

Geriatrics
Although appropriate studies on the relationship of age to the effects
  of this medicine have not been performed in the geriatric population, no geriatrics-specific problems have been documented to date.
  However, if significant systemic absorption of ophthalmic beta-
  blockers occurs, the same geriatrics-related problems may occur
  that are possible with the systemic beta-blockers. These include
  increased myocardial depression because of reduced metabolic
  and excretory capabilities in many elderly patients and the increased risk of beta-blocker-induced hypothermia in elderly patients.
In addition, elderly patients are more likely to have age-related peripheral vascular disease, which may require caution in patients receiving beta-blockers.

Drug interactions and/or related problems
The following drug interactions and/or related problems have been
  selected on the basis of their potential clinical significance (possible mechanism in parentheses where appropriate)—not necessarily inclusive (» = major clinical significance):

Note: Combinations containing any of the following medications, depending on the amount present, may also interact with this medication.

Information concerning interactions between ophthalmic levobunolol and other medications is still limited. Some of the following potential interactions apply to beta-adrenergic blocking agents in general and are stated for cautionary reference until additional information specific for levobunolol is available.

Amphetamines

(if significant systemic absorption of the ophthalmic beta-adrenergic blocking agents, betaxolol, levobunolol, and timolol, occurs, concurrent use of amphetamines may result in unopposed alpha-adrenergic activity with a risk of hypertension and excessive bradycardia and possible heart block)

Anesthetics, hydrocarbon inhalation, such as:
  Chloroform
  Cyclopropane
  Enflurane
  Halothane
  Isoflurane
  Methoxyflurane
  Trichloroethylene

(if significant systemic absorption of the ophthalmic beta-adrenergic blocking agents, betaxolol, levobunolol, and timolol, occurs, concurrent use of hydrocarbon inhalation anesthetics may result in prolonged severe hypotension because the beta-adrenergic blockade reduces the ability of the heart to respond to beta-adrenergically mediated sympathetic reflex stimuli; if necessary to reverse the effects of beta-adrenergic blocking agents during surgery, agonists, such as dobutamine, dopamine, isoproterenol, or norepinephrine, may be used but should be administered with caution, especially in patients receiving halothane. Some clinicians recommend gradual withdrawal of beta-adrenergic blocking agents 48 hours prior to elective surgery; however, this recommendation is controversial)

Antidiabetic agents, oral, or
Insulin

(systemic beta-adrenergic blocking agents may affect diabetes mellitus therapy. This may also occur with the ophthalmic beta-adrenergic blocking agents, betaxolol, levobunolol, and timolol, if there is significant systemic absorption. Nonselective beta-adrenergic blocking agents impair glycogenolysis and the hyperglycemic response to endogenous epinephrine, leading to persistence of hypoglycemia. Also, beta-adrenergic blocking agents, especially nonselective agents, decrease the release of insulin in response to hyperglycemia. Dosage adjustment of the antidiabetic agent may be required to avoid severe hypoglycemic reaction. In addition, beta-adrenergic blocking agents may complicate patient monitoring by masking symptoms of hypoglycemia caused by epinephrine, such as increased heart rate and increased blood pressure, but not dizziness and sweating. Although selective or relatively selective beta-adrenergic blocking agents usually cause fewer problems with blood glucose levels, they may still mask symptoms of hypoglycemia)

Beta-adrenergic blocking agents, systemic

(if significant systemic absorption of the ophthalmic beta-adrenergic blocking agents, betaxolol, levobunolol, and timolol, occurs, concurrent use may result in an additive effect either on intraocular pressure or on systemic effects of beta-blockade)

Calcium channel blocking agents

(if significant systemic absorption of the ophthalmic beta-adrenergic blocking agents, betaxolol, levobunolol, and timolol, occurs, concurrent use of calcium channel blocking agents, such as diltiazem, nicardipine, nifedipine, nimodipine, and verapamil, may result in atrioventricular conduction disturbances, left ventricular failure, and hypotension; in some patients, if a calcium antagonist is necessary, nicardipine or nifedipine may be preferred because it has less effect on heart rate and conduction, although it may also cause greater hypotension; concurrent use of calcium channel blockers and ophthalmic beta-adrenergic blocking agents should be used with care in patients with impaired cardiac function)

Catecholamine-depleting medications, such as the rauwolfia alkaloids:
  Alseroxylon
  Deserpidine
  Rauwolfia serpentina
  Reserpine

(if significant systemic absorption of the ophthalmic beta-adrenergic blocking agents, betaxolol, levobunolol, and timolol, occurs, concurrent use of catecholamine-depleting medications may result in additive and possibly excessive beta-adrenergic blockade; although this effect is largely theoretical, close observation is recommended, since bradycardia and marked hypotension may occur)

Cocaine

(cocaine may inhibit the therapeutic effects of systemic beta-adrenergic blocking agents, and may also have this effect on ophthalmic betaxolol, levobunolol, or timolol)

(concurrent use of a systemic beta-adrenergic blocking agent with cocaine may increase the risk of hypertension, excessive bradycardia, and possibly heart block because beta-blockade may leave cocaine's alpha-adrenergic activity unopposed. This may also occur with the ophthalmic beta-adrenergic blocking agents, betaxolol, levobunolol, or timolol, if significant systemic absorption of the ophthalmic beta-blocker occurs)

Diazoxide

(if significant systemic absorption of the ophthalmic beta-adrenergic blocking agents, levobunolol, timolol, and possibly betaxolol, occurs, concurrent use may prevent the diazoxide-induced tachycardia; however, the risk of hypotension may be increased)

Dipivefrin or
Epinephrine, ophthalmic

(concurrent use of dipivefrin or ophthalmic epinephrine with the ophthalmic beta-adrenergic blocking agents, betaxolol, levobunolol, and timolol, may provide a beneficial additive effect in lowering intraocular pressure in some patients)

Fentanyl derivatives

(chronic preoperative use of ophthalmic beta-adrenergic blocking agents [especially levobunolol, timolol, and possibly betaxolol] may increase the risk of initial bradycardia following induction doses of a fentanyl derivative)

Flecainide

(if significant systemic absorption of the ophthalmic beta-adrenergic blocking agents, betaxolol, levobunolol, and timolol, occurs, concurrent use may result in additive negative cardiac inotropic effects)

Hypotension-producing medications, other

(if significant systemic absorption of the ophthalmic beta-adrenergic blocking agents, levobunolol, timolol, and possibly betaxolol, occurs, concurrent use may potentiate the hypotensive effects of these medications)

Phenothiazines

(if significant systemic absorption of the ophthalmic beta-adrenergic blocking agents, betaxolol, levobunolol, and timolol, occurs, concurrent use may result in an increased plasma concentration of either the phenothiazines or the beta-adrenergic blocking agents because of inhibition of metabolism. This may result in additive hypotensive effects, irreversible retinopathy, cardiac arrhythmias, or tardive dyskinesia)

Sympathomimetics, systemic
(if significant systemic absorption of ophthalmic levobunolol occurs, concurrent use may result in inhibition of therapeutic effects of sympathomimetics with beta-adrenergic stimulant activity; in addition, beta-adrenergic blockade may result in unopposed alpha-adrenergic activity with a risk of hypertension and excessive bradycardia with possible heart block)

(for sympathomimetics with both alpha- and beta-adrenergic effects used as bronchodilators [ephedrine, epinephrine], beta-adrenergic blockade may antagonize the bronchodilating effect of ephedrine and epinephrine)

(for sympathomimetics with beta-adrenergic effects only, beta-adrenergic blockade may antagonize beta-1-adrenergic cardiac effects [dobutamine, dopamine, metaraminol, norepinephrine] or the beta-2-adrenergic bronchodilating effect [albuterol, bitolterol, ethylnorepinephrine, fenoterol, isoetharine, metaproterenol, pirbuterol, terbutaline] or both [isoproterenol])

Xanthines, such as:
Aminophylline
Caffeine
Dyphylline
Oxtriphylline
Theophylline
(if significant systemic absorption of the ophthalmic beta-adrenergic blocking agents, levobunolol, timolol, and possibly betaxolol, occurs, concurrent use may result in inhibition of therapeutic effects of xanthines; in addition, concurrent use of xanthines [except dyphylline] with the ophthalmic beta-adrenergic blocking agents, levobunolol, timolol, and possibly betaxolol, may decrease theophylline clearance, especially in patients with increased theophylline clearance induced by smoking; concurrent use requires careful monitoring)

(in addition, concurrent use with caffeine may enhance the cardiac inotropic effects of the ophthalmic beta-adrenergic blocking agents, levobunolol, timolol, and possibly betaxolol, if significant systemic absorption occurs)

Contraindications/Medical problems
The contraindications/medical problems included have been selected on the basis of their potential clinical significance (reasons given in parentheses where appropriate)—not necessarily inclusive (» = major clinical significance).

Except under special circumstances, this medication should not be used when the following medical problems exist:

Asthma, bronchial, or history of, or
» Pulmonary disease, obstructive, severe chronic
(severe respiratory reactions, including death due to bronchospasm, have been reported in patients with asthma following administration of ophthalmic beta-adrenergic blocking agents)

» Cardiac failure, overt, or
» Heart block, 2nd- or 3rd-degree atrioventricular (AV), or
» Shock, cardiogenic, or
» Sinus bradycardia
(risk of further myocardial depression)

» Previous allergic reaction to levobunolol

Risk-benefit should be considered when the following medical problems exist:

» Bronchitis, nonallergenic or chronic, or
» Emphysema or
» Pulmonary function impairment, other
(ophthalmic levobunolol may promote bronchospasm and block bronchodilation produced by endogenous and exogenous catecholamine stimulation of beta-2 receptors)

» Congestive heart failure
(risk of further depression of myocardial contractility)

» Diabetes mellitus, especially labile diabetes
(levobunolol may mask some signs and symptoms of hypoglycemia, such as tachycardia and tremor, but not dizziness and sweating)

» Hyperthyroidism
(levobunolol may mask certain signs and symptoms of hyperthyroidism; abrupt withdrawal may precipitate a thyroid storm)

Myasthenia gravis
(beta-adrenergic blockade may potentiate muscle weakness related to certain myasthenic symptoms, such as diplopia, ptosis, and generalized weakness)

Side/Adverse Effects

Note: Although levobunolol has a minimal membrane-stabilizing action, decreased corneal sensitivity may occur following prolonged use. Decreased corneal sensitivity has been reported in a few patients.

Even in patients *without* a history of cardiac failure, continued depression of the myocardium with beta-blockers, including ophthalmic levobunolol if significant systemic absorption occurs, over a period of time can lead to cardiac failure. At the first sign or symptom of cardiac failure, levobunolol should be discontinued.

The following side/adverse effects have been selected on the basis of their potential clinical significance (possible signs and symptoms in parentheses where appropriate)—not necessarily inclusive:

Those indicating need for medical attention
Incidence less frequent
Blepharoconjunctivitis—frequency 5% (severe irritation or inflammation of eye)

Incidence rare
Allergic reaction (skin rash, hives, or itching); *iridocyclitis or keratitis* (severe irritation or inflammation of eye or eyelid); *vision disturbances*

Symptoms of systemic absorption
Chest pain; clumsiness or unsteadiness; confusion or mental depression; congestive heart failure (swelling of feet, ankles, or lower legs); *dizziness or feeling faint; headache; irregular, slow, or pounding heartbeat; nausea or vomiting; unusual tiredness or weakness; wheezing or troubled breathing, especially in patients with predisposition to bronchoconstriction*

Those indicating need for medical attention only if they continue or are bothersome
Incidence more frequent
Burning or stinging of eye—frequency 30%
Incidence less frequent or rare
Hair loss

Patient Consultation

In providing consultation, consider emphasizing the following selected information (» = major clinical significance):

Before using this medication
» Conditions affecting use, especially:
Allergy to sulfites or to levobunolol or other beta-blockers (such as acebutolol, atenolol, betaxolol, carteolol, labetalol, metipranolol, metoprolol, nadolol, oxprenolol, penbutolol, pindolol, propranolol, sotalol, or timolol)

Pregnancy—Medication may be absorbed into the body. Some studies in animals have shown that levobunolol causes harm to the animal fetus

Use in children—Infants may be especially sensitive to the effects of levobunolol, thus increasing the risk of side effects

Use in the elderly—If significant systemic absorption of ophthalmic beta-blockers occurs, the chance of side effects during treatment may be increased, since elderly people are especially sensitive to the effects of these medications

Use by athletes—Beta-blockers are banned and tested for in athletes; because ophthalmic levobunolol may be absorbed into the body, the medication may appear in the urine; if the agent is found in the urine, the athlete will be disqualified

Other medical problems, especially bronchial asthma, or history of, severe chronic obstructive pulmonary disease, overt cardiac failure, 2nd- or 3rd-degree atrioventricular (AV) heart block, cardiogenic shock, sinus bradycardia, nonallergenic or chronic bronchitis, emphysema or other pulmonary function impairment, congestive heart failure, diabetes mellitus, or hyperthyroidism

Proper use of this medication

» Proper administration technique; using nasolacrimal occlusion is especially important in infants and children

Preventing contamination: Not touching applicator tip to any surface; keeping container tightly closed

Proper use of medication having compliance cap

» Importance of not using more medication than the amount prescribed

Missed dose: If dosing schedule is—

Once a day: Applying as soon as possible; not applying if not remembered until next day; applying regularly scheduled dose

More than once a day: Applying as soon as possible; not applying if almost time for next dose; applying next dose at regularly scheduled time

» Proper storage

Precautions while using this medication

Regular visits to physician to check eye pressure during therapy

» Caution if any kind of surgery (including dental surgery) or emergency treatment is required

» Diabetics: May mask some signs of hypoglycemia, such as increased pulse rate and trembling, but not dizziness and sweating; also may cause decreased or sometimes increased blood glucose concentrations

Side/adverse effects

Signs of potential side effects, especially blepharoconjunctivitis, allergic reaction, iridocyclitis, keratitis, vision disturbances, or symptoms of systemic absorption

General Dosing Information

Although some manufacturers recommend a dose of 2 drops of an ophthalmic solution at appropriate intervals, the conjunctival sac will usually hold only 1 drop.

When levobunolol is used to replace another ophthalmic beta-adrenergic blocking agent, the other beta-blocker should be discontinued simultaneously to initiating therapy with levobunolol.

When levobunolol is used to replace a single antiglaucoma agent other than another ophthalmic beta-blocker, the other antiglaucoma agent may be continued on the first day that levobunolol is used but should be discontinued on the second day.

When levobunolol is used to replace several concomitantly administered antiglaucoma agents, the patient's dosage should be individualized as required. If any of the other antiglaucoma agents used is a beta-blocker, it should be discontinued before levobunolol is added to the regimen. The other antiglaucoma agents being used may be continued on the first day that levobunolol is used but one of the agents should be discontinued on the second day. Then the remaining antiglaucoma agents may be decreased or discontinued according to patient's response. Additional adjustments usually should involve only one agent at a time and should be made at intervals of not less than one week.

Levobunolol may be used concurrently with direct and indirect muscarinic agonists (e.g., pilocarpine, echothiophate, carbachol), beta-agonists (e.g., ophthalmic epinephrine or dipivefrin), and/or systemic carbonic anhydrase inhibitors (e.g., acetazolamide), if necessary to control intraocular pressure.

In patients scheduled for major surgery, some practitioners recommend that beta-adrenergic blocking agents be gradually withdrawn 48 hours prior to surgery because beta-adrenergic receptor blockade impairs the ability of the heart to respond to beta-adrenergically mediated reflex stimuli. This recommendation is controversial. However, since ophthalmic levobunolol may be absorbed systemically, gradual withdrawal of the medication should be considered for patients undergoing elective surgery because prolonged severe hypotension during anesthesia has occurred in some patients receiving systemic beta-adrenergic blocking agents. If necessary during surgery, the effects of beta-adrenergic blocking agents may be reversed by sufficient doses of agonists, such as isoproterenol, dopamine, dobutamine, or norepinephrine.

Ophthalmic Dosage Forms

LEVOBUNOLOL HYDROCHLORIDE OPHTHALMIC SOLUTION USP

Usual adult and adolescent dose: Topical, to the conjunctiva, 1 drop of a 0.25% solution one or two times a day or 1 drop of a 0.5% solution once a day.

Usual adult prescribing limits: Dosages above 1 drop of a 0.5% solution two times a day are generally not more effective.

Auxiliary labeling:
• For the eye.
• Keep container tightly closed.

LEVODOPA   Systemic

Some commonly used *brand names* are:
    In the U.S.—*Dopar; Larodopa*
    In Canada—*Larodopa*

ORAL
Levodopa Capsules USP†
    In the U.S.—*Dopar; Larodopa*
Levodopa Tablets USP
    In the U.S. and Canada—*Larodopa*

---

†Not commercially available in Canada.

Category: Antidyskinetic.

Indications

Accepted
Parkinsonism (treatment)—Levodopa is indicated to alleviate symptoms and allow more normal body movements with improved muscular control in the treatment of idiopathic Parkinson's disease (paralysis agitans), postencephalitic parkinsonism, or symptomatic parkinsonism that may follow injury to the nervous system by carbon monoxide intoxication or manganese intoxication. It is also indicated in parkinsonism associated with cerebral arteriosclerosis.

Pharmacology

Mechanism of action/Effect: The precise mechanism of action has not been established. It is believed that the small percentage of each dose crossing the blood-brain barrier is decarboxylated to dopamine. The dopamine then stimulates dopaminergic receptors in the basal ganglia to improve the balance between cholinergic and dopaminergic activity, resulting in the improved modulation of voluntary nerve impulses transmitted to the motor cortex.

Other actions/effects: Levodopa's metabolite, dopamine, stimulates beta-adrenergic cardiac receptors, interacts with chemoreceptors in the medullary emetic center, and promotes release of pituitary growth hormone.

Onset of action: Significant improvement may occur in 2 to 3 weeks. Some patients may require up to 6 months of continuous levodopa therapy to obtain optimal therapeutic benefit.

Duration of action: Up to 5 hours per dose.

Precautions to Consider

Geriatrics
Smaller doses may be required in geriatric patients since they may have a reduced tolerance to the effects of levodopa. Also, peripheral dopa decarboxylase, the enzyme responsible for decarboxylation, decreases with age, thus making large doses unnecessary.
Geriatric patients, especially those with osteoporosis, responsive to antiparkinsonian therapy should resume normal activity gradually and with caution because increased mobility may increase risk of fractures.
Psychic side effects, such as anxiety, confusion, or nervousness, occur more frequently in geriatric patients receiving other antiparkinsonian medications, especially anticholinergics.
Geriatric patients, especially those with pre-existing coronary disease, are more susceptible to levodopa's cardiac effects, such as arrhythmias. These cardiac effects are minimized or eliminated when levodopa is combined with carbidopa.

Dental
Involuntary movements of jaws may result in poor retention of full dentures; dosage reduction may be required.

Drug interactions and/or related problems
The following drug interactions and/or related problems have been selected on the basis of their potential clinical significance (possible mechanism in parentheses where appropriate)—not necessarily inclusive (» = major clinical significance):

Note: Combinations containing any of the following medications, depending on the amount present, may also interact with this medication.

Amantadine or
Benztropine or
Procyclidine or
Trihexyphenidyl
    (concurrent use may result in increased efficacy of levodopa; however, concurrent use is not recommended if there is a history of psychosis)
» Anesthetics, hydrocarbon inhalation
    (concurrent administration may result in cardiac arrhythmias because of increased endogenous dopamine concentration; levodopa should be discontinued 6 to 8 hours before administration of anesthetics, especially halothane)
» Anticonvulsants, hydantoin, or
Benzodiazepines or
Droperidol or
» Haloperidol or
Loxapine or
Metyrosine or
Papaverine or
» Phenothiazines or
Rauwolfia alkaloids or
Thioxanthenes
    (concurrent use may decrease the therapeutic effects of levodopa; hydantoin anticonvulsants increase the metabolism of levodopa when used concurrently, thus decreasing its effect; since droperidol, haloperidol, loxapine, papaverine, phenothiazines, and the thioxanthenes block the dopamine receptors in the brain, they may induce extrapyramidal symptoms, thus aggravating parkinsonism and antagonizing the effects of levodopa; the rauwolfia alkaloids cause dopamine depletion in the brain, thus opposing the effects of levodopa)
Bromocriptine
    (may produce additive effects, allowing reduction in levodopa dosage)
» Cocaine
    (concurrent use with levodopa may increase the risk of cardiac arrhythmias; if use of cocaine is necessary in patients receiving levodopa, it is recommended that cocaine be administered with caution, in reduced dosage, and in conjunction with electrocardiographic monitoring)
Foods, especially high-protein
    (concurrent or previous ingestion of food may decrease the absorption of levodopa from the gastrointestinal tract, consequently delaying its effect; in addition, proteins in food may be degraded into the amino acids that compete with levodopa for transport to the brain, thus decreasing and/or making erratic the response to levodopa; however, rather than cutting down on daily protein intake to avoid this effect on levodopa, it is recommended that the intake of proteins be distributed equally throughout the day)
Hypotension-producing medications, other
    (concurrent use with levodopa may result in an increased hypotensive effect)

Methyldopa
(concurrent use with levodopa may alter the antiparkinsonian effects of levodopa and may also produce additive toxic CNS effects such as psychosis)

Metoclopramide
(gastric emptying of levodopa may be accelerated with concurrent use of metoclopramide, thus possibly increasing levodopa's rate and extent of absorption from the small intestine; the clinical significance of this interaction has not been determined)

Molindone
(concurrent use may inhibit antiparkinsonian effects of levodopa by blocking dopamine receptor in the brain; also, levodopa may counteract the antipsychotic effects of molindone)

» Monoamine oxidase (MAO) inhibitors, including furazolidone and procarbazine
(concurrent use with levodopa is not recommended as the combination may result in a hypertensive crisis; it is recommended that MAO inhibitors be discontinued for 2 to 4 weeks prior to initiation of levodopa therapy)

» Pyridoxine
(concurrent use with levodopa is not recommended since levodopa's antiparkinsonian effects are reversed by as little as 10 mg of orally administered pyridoxine)

» Selegiline
(although sometimes used in conjunction with levodopa or with carbidopa and levodopa combination, selegiline may enhance levodopa-induced dyskinesias, nausea, orthostatic hypotension, confusion, and hallucinations; levodopa dosage should be reduced within 2 to 3 days after the initiation of selegiline therapy)

Sympathomimetics
(concurrent use with levodopa may increase the possibility of cardiac arrhythmias; dosage reduction of the sympathomimetic is recommended; the administration of carbidopa with levodopa reduces the tendency of sympathomimetics to cause dopamine-induced cardiac arrhythmias)

Contraindications/Medical problems
The contraindications/medical problems included have been selected on the basis of their potential clinical significance (reasons given in parentheses where appropriate)—not necessarily inclusive (» = major clinical significance).

Risk-benefit should be considered when the following medical problems exist:

» Bronchial asthma, emphysema, and other severe pulmonary diseases
(respiratory effects of levodopa may aggravate condition)

» Cardiovascular disease, severe
(increased risk of cardiac arrhythmias)

Convulsive disorders, history of
(use of levodopa may precipitate seizures)

Diabetes mellitus
(use of levodopa may adversely affect control of glucose in blood)

Endocrine diseases
(use of levodopa may adversely affect hypothalamus or pituitary function)

» Glaucoma, angle-closure, or predisposition to
(mydriatic effect resulting in increased intraocular pressure may precipitate an acute attack of angle-closure glaucoma)

Glaucoma, open-angle, chronic
(mydriatic effect may cause a slight increase in intraocular pressure; glaucoma therapy may need to be adjusted)

Hepatic function impairment

» Melanoma, history of or suspected
(use of levodopa may activate a malignant melanoma)

» Myocardial infarction, history of, with residual arrhythmias
(use of levodopa may precipitate or aggravate condition)

» Peptic ulcer, history of
(increased risk of upper gastrointestinal hemorrhage)

» Psychotic states
(increased risk of developing depression and suicidal tendencies)

» Renal function impairment
(use of levodopa may lead to urinary retention)

Sensitivity to levodopa

» Urinary retention
(use of levodopa may precipitate or aggravate condition)

Side/Adverse Effects

Note: Patients receiving this medication for one to several years may experience sudden, unexpected akinesia, tremor, and rigidity, such as the "on-off" phenomenon. Emotional stress may precipitate akinesia paradoxica or "start hesitation" in these patients.

A syndrome resembling neuroleptic malignant syndrome, which includes intermittent dystonia alternating with substantial agitation, hyperthermia, and mental changes, has been reported after the abrupt discontinuation of levodopa therapy.

Convulsions have been reported but a causal relationship to the use of levodopa has not been established.

The following side/adverse effects have been selected on the basis of their potential clinical significance (possible signs and symptoms in parentheses where appropriate)—not necessarily inclusive:

Those indicating need for medical attention
Incidence more frequent
Difficult urination; dizziness or lightheadedness when getting up from a lying or sitting position (orthostatic hypotension); *irregular heartbeat; mental depression; mood or mental changes, such as aggressive behavior; nausea or vomiting, severe or continuing; unusual and uncontrolled movements of the body, including the face, tongue, arms, hands, head, and upper body* (may indicate excessive concentration of dopamine in the striatum)

Note: *Orthostatic hypotension* occurs in about 30% of patients at the initiation of levodopa therapy.

Nausea and vomiting occur in nearly 80% of patients in early levodopa therapy with tolerance being gradually achieved during continued use.

Difficult urination, dizziness or lightheadedness, irregular heartbeat, and *nausea and vomiting* may become less frequent when levodopa is combined with carbidopa because of the reduced dose requirements and unavailability of peripheral dopamine.

Choreiform and other involuntary movements occur in 50 to 80% of patients and are usually dose-related.

Incidence less frequent
Spasm or closing of eyelids (possible early sign of overdose)

Incidence rare
Duodenal ulcer (stomach pain); *hemolytic anemia* (unusual tiredness or weakness); *hypertension* (high blood pressure)

Those indicating need for medical attention only if they continue or are bothersome
Incidence more frequent
Anxiety, confusion, or nervousness—especially in elderly patients receiving other antiparkinsonian medication; *constipation; nightmares*

Note: *Constipation* and *nightmares* may become less frequent when levodopa is combined with carbidopa because of the reduced dose requirements and unavailability of peripheral dopamine.

Incidence less frequent
> *Anorexia* (loss of appetite); *diarrhea; dryness of mouth; flushing of skin; headache; insomnia* (trouble in sleeping); *muscle twitching; unusual tiredness or weakness*

Those not indicating need for medical attention
Incidence less frequent
> *Darkening in color of urine or sweat*

Patient Consultation

In providing consultation, consider emphasizing the following selected information (» = major clinical significance):

Before using this medication
» Conditions affecting use, especially:
  Sensitivity to levodopa
  Pregnancy—No studies in humans; depressed growth and malformations in animal studies
  Breast-feeding—Excreted in breast milk; may inhibit lactation
  Use in the elderly—Reduced tolerance to effects of levodopa; caution in resuming normal activity, especially in patients with osteoporosis
  Dental—Possible difficulty in retention of full dentures
  Other medications, especially haloperidol, hydantoin anticonvulsants, hydrocarbon inhalation anesthetics. phenothiazines, cocaine, MAO inhibitors, pyridoxine, and selegiline
  Other medical problems, especially severe cardiovascular disease, severe pulmonary diseases, glaucoma, melanoma (history of or suspected), peptic ulcer (history of), psychosis, renal function impairment, or urinary retention

Proper use of this medication
» Taking food shortly after taking medication to relieve gastric irritation; taking food before or concurrently may retard levodopa's effect
» Compliance with therapy; taking medication only as directed; not stopping medication unless ordered by physician
» Maximum effectiveness of medication may not occur for several weeks or months after therapy is initiated
  Missed dose: Taking as soon as possible; skipping dose if next scheduled dose is within 2 hours; not doubling doses
» Proper storage

Precautions while using this medication
  Caution if any kind of surgery (including dental surgery) or emergency treatment is required
  Diabetics: May interfere with urine tests for sugar and ketones
» Caution if drowsiness occurs
» Caution when getting up suddenly from lying or sitting position; dizziness and fainting may occur
» Avoiding foods or vitamin products containing pyridoxine (vitamin B_6); diminished levodopa effect when used with pyridoxine
» Caution in resuming normal physical activities when condition has improved, especially for geriatric patients
  Possibility of "on-off" phenomenon

Side/adverse effects
  Signs of potential side effects, especially difficult urination, duodenal ulcer, hemolytic anemia, hypertension, irregular heartbeat, mental depression, mood or mental changes, severe nausea or vomiting, orthostatic hypotension, spasm or closing of eyelids, uncontrolled movements of body
  Occasional darkening of urine or sweat may be alarming to patient although medically insignificant

General Dosing Information

Titrated dosage is necessary to achieve the individual therapeutic blood concentration requirements and to minimize side effects. This is especially important for geriatric patients and patients receiving other medications.

Postencephalitic and geriatric patients often require and tolerate lower dosage levels than other parkinsonism patients.

The concurrent administration of carbidopa may permit the dose of levodopa to be reduced by up to 75% and yet achieve equal therapeutic results. Carbidopa also reduces the adverse effect of pyridoxine on levodopa.

Amantadine or anticholinergic medications are often used concurrently with levodopa in the more advanced cases of parkinsonism or when response to levodopa decreases. Gradual dosage reduction of these medications is recommended during initiation of therapy with levodopa and after optimum dosage is reached to maintain proper control of the patient's condition.

When levodopa is to be discontinued, dosage should be reduced gradually to prevent the occurrence of a syndrome that resembles the neuroleptic malignant syndrome. Careful patient monitoring after withdrawal of levodopa will allow early diagnosis and treatment of neuroleptic malignant-like syndrome.

Diet/Nutrition
Food should be eaten shortly after levodopa is taken to relieve gastric irritation; taking food before or concurrently may retard levodopa's effects.

High protein diets should be avoided, because amino acid degradation products compete with levodopa for transport to the brain, resulting in a decreased or erratic response to levodopa. It is recommended that intake of normal amounts of protein be distributed equally throughout the day.

In addition, pyridoxine (vitamin B_6) reverses the effects of levodopa. Vitamin products containing pyridoxine should be avoided; intake of foods containing large amounts of pyridoxine (such as avocado, bacon, beans, beef liver, dry skim milk, oatmeal, peas, pork, sweet potato, tuna, and certain health foods) may need to be limited.

Oral Dosage Forms

LEVODOPA CAPSULES USP

Usual adult and adolescent dose: Antidyskinetic—Oral, 250 mg two to four times a day initially, the dosage per day being increased by an additional 100 to 750 mg at three- to seven-day intervals as tolerated until the desired response is obtained.

Note: Postencephalitic patients may be more sensitive to the effects of the usual adult dose.

Usual adult prescribing limits: Up to 8 grams daily.

Usual geriatric dose: See *Usual adult and adolescent dose.*

Note: Geriatric patients may be more sensitive to the effects of the usual adult dose.

Auxiliary labeling: • May darken urine or sweat.

LEVODOPA TABLETS USP

Usual adult and adolescent dose: See *Levodopa Capsules USP.*

Usual adult prescribing limits: See *Levodopa Capsules USP.*

Usual geriatric dose: See *Levodopa Capsules USP.*

Auxiliary labeling: • May darken urine or sweat.

LITHIUM   Systemic

Some commonly used *brand names* are:

In the U.S.—

Cibalith-S	Lithobid
Eskalith	Lithonate
Eskalith CR	Lithotabs
Lithane	

In Canada—

Carbolith	Lithane
Duralith	Lithizine

ORAL

Lithium Carbonate Capsules USP
  In the U.S.—*Eskalith; Lithonate;* GENERIC
  In Canada—*Carbolith; Lithane*
Lithium Carbonate Slow-release Capsules*
  In Canada—*Lithizine*
Lithium Carbonate Tablets USP
  In the U.S.—*Eskalith; Lithane; Lithotabs;* GENERIC
  In Canada—*Lithane*
Lithium Carbonate Extended-release Tablets
  In the U.S.—*Eskalith CR; Lithobid*
  In Canada—*Duralith*
Lithium Citrate Syrup USP†
  In the U.S.—*Cibalith-S;* GENERIC

---

*Not commercially available in the U.S.
†Not commercially available in Canada.

Category: Antimanic; antidepressant therapy adjunct; granulopoietic; vascular headache prophylactic.

Indications

Note: Bracketed information in the *Indications* section refers to uses not included in U.S. product labeling.

Accepted

Bipolar disorder (treatment)—Lithium is indicated as the primary agent in the treatment of acute manic and hypomanic episodes in bipolar disorder, and for maintenance therapy to help diminish the intensity and frequency of subsequent manic episodes in patients with a history of mania.

Lithium is used in some patients as the agent of choice in the prevention of bipolar depression. Clinicians have observed a diminished intensity and frequency of severe depressive episodes.

[Depression, mental (treatment)][1]—Lithium is used alone for maintenance therapy in unipolar depression, and for acute and maintenance therapy in schizoaffective disorder. It is also used to augment the antidepressant effect of tricyclic or monoamine oxidase (MAO) inhibitor antidepressants in the treatment of major unipolar depression in patients not responsive to antidepressants alone.

[Headache, vascular (prophylaxis)][1]—Lithium is used to reduce the frequency of the occurrence of episodic and chronic cluster headaches.

[Neutropenia (treatment)][1]—Lithium is used to reduce the incidence of infection in patients with chemotherapy-induced neutropenia and in patients with chronic or acquired neutropenia.

---

[1]Not included in Canadian product labeling.

Pharmacology

Mechanism of action/Effect:
  Antimanic—Has not been established. The mood-stabilizing effect has been postulated to relate to a reduction of catecholamine neurotransmitter concentration, possibly mediated by lithium ion (Li^1) effect on Na^1K^1 adenosine triphosphatase ($Na^1K^1ATPase$) to produce improved transneuronal membrane transport of sodium ion. An alternate postulate is that lithium may decrease cyclic adenosine monophosphate (cyclic AMP) concentrations, which would result in decreased sensitivity of hormonal-sensitive adenylcyclase receptors. Another hypothesis is the "second messenger" theory of lithium's interference with lipid inositol metabolism. This theory postulates that a group of improperly regulated neurons may be the underlying cause of manic symptoms. A phospholipase C-type enzyme hydrolyzes the plasma membrane-located lipid, phosphatidylinositol biphosphate, to diacyglycerol and inositol triphosphate, postsynaptic second messengers that contribute to chronic cell stimulation by altering electrical activity in the neuron. Inositol formed during this process is recycled by the inositol phospholipid-synthesizing enzymes in the CNS. There is evidence that cells in the CNS do not have access to plasma sources of inositol but, instead, depend on the synthesis of inositol for the transduction of neuronal signals. Lithium, in therapeutic concentrations, blocks the activity of the enzyme, inositol-1-phosphatase, resulting in a depletion of neuronal inositol and ultimately a decrease in the levels of phosphatidylinositol biphosphate. The lipid will no longer be able to stimulate the formation of adequate quantities of the second messengers or alter electrical activity. Subsequent cells in the CNS become relatively insensitive to the agonist stimulation, and clinical improvement results.

Granulopoietic—The exact mechanism of action has not been established; however, studies have shown that lithium stimulates granulopoiesis, enhances marrow proliferation, elevates neutrophil production, and increases the granulocyte pool.

Vascular headache prophylactic—Specific mechanism has not been established. It has been postulated that the action of lithium in cluster headaches may be directly related to changes in platelet serotonin and histamine concentrations.

Antidepressant—Has not been established. However, the mechanism may involve enhancement of serotonergic activity and downregulation of beta-receptors.

Onset of therapeutic action: Clinical improvement—1 to 3 weeks.

Precautions to Consider

Geriatrics

Geriatric patients and patients with organic brain disease usually require lower lithium dosage, lower serum concentration, and more frequent monitoring than younger adults because renal clearance rate and distribution volume are reduced. Lithium is more toxic to the central nervous system (CNS) in the elderly, even when serum lithium concentrations are within the therapeutic range for younger adults. Also, the elderly are possibly more prone to develop lithium-induced goiter and clinical hypothyroidism. Excessive thirst and larger volume of urine as early side effects of lithium therapy may be more frequent in the elderly.

Drug interactions and/or related problems

The following drug interactions and/or related problems have been selected on the basis of their potential clinical significance (possible mechanism in parentheses where appropriate)—not necessarily inclusive (» = major clinical significance):

Note: Combinations containing any of the following medications, depending on the amount present, may also interact with this medication.

Amphetamines
  (concurrent use with lithium may antagonize the CNS stimulating effects of amphetamines)

Antidepressants, tricyclic
(since tricyclics may cause a swing into mania and a rapid recycling between mania and depression, lithium plasma concentrations at or greater than 0.8 mEq per liter may be needed to prevent the tricyclic switch process)

» Antithyroid agents or
» Calcium iodide or
» Iodinated glycerol or
» Potassium iodide
(concurrent use with lithium may potentiate the hypothyroid and goitrogenic effects of either these medications or lithium)

» Anti-inflammatory drugs, nonsteroidal (NSAIDs)
(concurrent use may increase the toxic effects of lithium by decreasing its renal excretion, thereby increasing the steady-state plasma lithium concentration by 39 to 50%; patient should be observed for symptoms of lithium toxicity, and increased monitoring of lithium plasma concentrations is recommended during concurrent use)

Atracurium or
Pancuronium or
Succinylcholine
(neuromuscular blocking effects may be potentiated or prolonged when these medications are used concurrently with chronic lithium therapy)

Carbamazepine or
Desmopressin or
Lypressin or
Posterior pituitary or
Vasopressin
(lithium may decrease the antidiuretic effect of these medications when used concurrently)

(lithium may prevent or decrease carbamazepine-induced leukopenia with a possible increase in therapeutic effect when carbamazepine is used to treat psychotic disorders or bipolar conditions)

Calcium channel blocking agents
(concurrent use with lithium may increase the risk of neurotoxicity in the form of ataxia, tremors, nausea, vomiting, diarrhea, and/or tinnitus; caution is recommended)

» Chlorpromazine and possibly other phenothiazines
(concurrent use with lithium may reduce gastrointestinal absorption of the phenothiazine, thereby decreasing its serum concentrations by as much as 40%; phenothiazines, especially chlorpromazine, increase intracellular lithium concentration; concurrent use may increase rate of renal excretion of lithium; extrapyramidal symptoms, delirium, and cerebellar function impairment may be increased, especially in elderly patients; also, nausea and vomiting, early indications of lithium toxicity, may be masked by the antiemetic effect of some phenothiazines; admixture of lithium citrate syrup with any liquid forms of phenothiazines may form a precipitate of the free phenothiazine)

» Diuretics
(concurrent use with lithium may provoke severe lithium toxicity by delaying renal excretion of lithium and consequently increasing serum and red blood cell lithium concentrations; close monitoring of lithium plasma concentrations is essential since sodium and lithium reabsorption in the proximal tubule is increased, due to the body sodium deficit; a reduction in lithium dosage may be necessary)

Fluoxetine
(lithium concentrations may be altered, leading to toxicity; close monitoring of lithium concentrations is recommended)

» Haloperidol
(lithium is frequently used concurrently with haloperidol during the first one or two weeks of treatment for acute manic episodes, but lithium alone may be adequate thereafter. However, concurrent use with lithium has been reported, in a few cases, to be associated with irreversible neurological toxicity and brain damage, especially in patients with organic brain syndrome or other CNS impairment, although this interaction is controversial; extrapyramidal symptoms may be increased by enhancement of dopamine blockade by haloperidol; patients should be monitored closely during concurrent use; dosage adjustments may be necessary)

(admixture of the liquid forms of lithium and haloperidol may precipitate free haloperidol)

Methyldopa
(concurrent use may increase the risk of lithium toxicity even though serum lithium concentrations remain within the recommended therapeutic range)

Metronidazole
(concurrent use may promote renal retention of lithium, leading to lithium toxicity; reducing the dose or discontinuing the use of lithium may be necessary during metronidazole therapy; if not feasible to discontinue, frequent monitoring of serum creatinine, electrolyte and lithium concentrations, and urine osmolality to detect possible nephrogenic diabetes insipidus are recommended)

» Molindone
(concurrent use with lithium may produce neurotoxic symptoms such as confusion, delirium, seizures, somnambulism, or abnormal electroencephalogram [EEG] changes)

Norepinephrine
(concurrent use with lithium may decrease the pressor response to norepinephrine; a higher dose of norepinephrine may be required to achieve the desired effect)

Sodium-containing medications or foods, especially sodium bicarbonate or sodium chloride
(high sodium intake enhances lithium excretion, possibly resulting in decreased efficacy)

Urea
(may increase the renal excretion of lithium, thereby decreasing its effects)

Xanthines such as:
Aminophylline
Caffeine
Dyphylline
Oxtriphylline
Theophylline
(concurrent use of these medications with lithium increases urinary excretion of lithium, thereby possibly reducing its therapeutic effect)

Contraindications/Medical problems
The contraindications/medical problems included have been selected on the basis of their potential clinical significance (reasons given in parentheses where appropriate)—not necessarily inclusive (» = major clinical significance).

Except under special circumstances, this medication should not be used when the following medical problem exists:

» Leukemia, history of
(leukemia may be reactivated by lithium)

Risk-benefit should be considered when the following medical problems exist:

» Cardiovascular disease
(may be exacerbated; possible interference with lithium excretion)

» CNS disorders, such as epilepsy and parkinsonism
(may be exacerbated; lithium-induced neurotoxicity may be masked)

» Dehydration, severe
(risk of toxicity is increased; the loss of large volumes of body fluid as in prolonged vomiting, diarrhea, or profuse perspiration due to fever, exercise, saunas, or hot baths may result in increased serum lithium concentration; such loss of body fluid may necessitate dosage adjustment of lithium and/or the supplemental intake of sodium and fluids until hydration status and electrolytes are stable)

Diabetes mellitus
(serum insulin concentration may be increased)

Goiter or
Hypothyroidism
(latent hypothyroidism may be induced in predisposed or elderly patients)

Hyperparathyroidism
(calcium metabolism may be altered after long-term use)

» Infections, severe
(fever with prolonged sweating, diarrhea, or vomiting may necessitate a decrease in lithium dosage to prevent lithium toxicity)

Organic brain disease or
Schizophrenia
(patients may be hypersensitive to lithium and exhibit increased confusion, seizures, or electroencephalogram [EEG] changes at normal serum lithium concentrations)

Psoriasis
(may be aggravated by lithium; dosage adjustments of lithium and/or other medications may be necessary)

» Renal insufficiency or
» Urinary retention
(lithium excretion may be delayed, leading to toxicity)

Sensitivity to lithium

Caution should be used also in severely debilitated patients or in patients on a sodium-restricted diet because these conditions may increase the risk of toxicity by delaying renal excretion of lithium.

Side/Adverse Effects

The following side/adverse effects have been selected on the basis of their potential clinical significance (possible signs and symptoms in parentheses where appropriate)—not necessarily inclusive:

Those indicating need for medical attention
Incidence less frequent
Cardiovascular problems (fainting, fast or slow heartbeat, irregular pulse, troubled breathing [dyspnea] on exertion); *leukocytosis* (unusual tiredness or weakness); *weight gain*

Note: *Sinus node function impairment, sinoatrial block,* or *ventricular irritability* may occur at therapeutic serum lithium concentrations; possibly reversible when lithium is discontinued.

Leukocytosis is usually reversible upon discontinuation of lithium, but may be possible rare leukemia that develops during lithium therapy.

Incidence rare
Blue color and pain in fingers and toes; coldness of arms and legs; pseudotumor cerebri (dizziness, eye pain, headache, nausea or vomiting, noises in ears, vision problems)

Note: If undetected, *pseudotumor cerebri* may result in enlargement of blind spot, constriction of visual fields, and eventual blindness, due to optic atrophy.

Early symptoms of toxicity
Diarrhea; drowsiness; loss of appetite; muscle weakness; nausea or vomiting; slurred speech; trembling

Late symptoms of toxicity
Blurred vision; clumsiness or unsteadiness; confusion; convulsions; dizziness; increase in amount of urine; trembling, severe
Symptoms of hypothyroidism
Dry, rough skin; hair loss; hoarseness; mania (unusual excitement); *mental depression; sensitivity to cold; swelling of feet or lower legs; swelling of neck*

Those indicating need for medical attention only if they continue or are bothersome
Incidence more frequent
Diarrhea; stress incontinence or urinary urgency (increased frequency of urination; loss of bladder control); *increased thirst; nausea, mild; trembling of hands, slight*

Note: *Stress incontinence* or *urinary urgency* is dose-related; more common in women; usually begins two to seven years after start of treatment with lithium.

Incidence less frequent
Acne or skin rash; bloated feeling or pressure in the stomach; muscle twitching, slight

Patient Consultation

In providing consultation, consider emphasizing the following selected information (» = major clinical significance):

Before using this medication
» Conditions affecting use, especially:
Sensitivity to lithium
Pregnancy—Lithium crosses placenta; contraindicated in first trimester because of possible neonatal goiter and cardiovascular malformations; at delivery, hypotonia, lethargy, cyanosis, in newborns of mothers taking lithium at term
Breast-feeding—Excreted in breast milk; may cause hypotonia, hypothermia, cyanosis, and ECG changes in some babies
Use in children—May decrease bone formation or density
Use in the elderly—Elderly more prone to develop CNS toxicity, hypothyroidism and goiter; lower doses and more frequent monitoring required
Other medications, especially antithyroid agents, iodine-containing preparations, nonsteroidal anti-inflammatory drugs, chlorpromazine (and possibly other phenothiazines), diuretics, haloperidol, or molindone
Other medical problems, especially history of leukemia, cardiovascular disease, epilepsy, parkinsonism, severe dehydration, renal insufficiency, urinary retention, or severe infections with prolonged sweating, vomiting, or diarrhea

Proper use of this medication
Taking after a meal or snack to prevent laxative action and to decrease the severity of stomach upset, tremors, or weakness by slowing absorption rate
» Importance of adequate fluid (2.5 to 3 liters each day) and sodium intake
» Importance of not taking more medication than the amount prescribed
» Compliance with therapy; improvement in condition may require 1 to 3 weeks; importance of maintaining adequate blood levels even though symptoms improved
Missed dose: Taking as soon as possible, unless within 4 hours (6 hours for extended-release tablets or slow-release capsules) of next scheduled dose; not doubling doses
» Proper storage
For extended-release or slow-release dosage form
Swallowing tablet or capsule whole
Not breaking, crushing, or chewing
For syrup dosage form
Diluting dose with fruit juice or other flavored beverage before taking

Precautions while using this medication

» Regular visits to physician to check progress during therapy; importance of serum lithium monitoring

Caution in drinking large amounts of coffee, tea, or colas because of diuretic effect

» Possible drowsiness or dizziness; caution if driving or doing jobs requiring alertness

» Caution during exercise, saunas, and hot weather

» Caution during illnesses that cause high fevers with profuse sweating, vomiting, or diarrhea

» Caution on self-imposed dieting

» Importance of patient and family knowing early symptoms of overdose or toxicity

For slow-release dosage form

» Not using interchangeably with any other dosage form

Side/adverse effects

» Early symptoms of lithium overdose or toxicity:

Diarrhea

Drowsiness

Loss of appetite

Muscle weakness

Nausea or vomiting

Slurred speech

Trembling

Side effects are more likely to occur in the elderly

Signs of potential side effects, especially cardiovascular problems, leukocytosis, weight gain, blue color of fingers and toes, coldness of arms and legs, pseudotumor cerebri, symptoms of hypothyroidism

General Dosing Information

Warning—Lithium toxicity can occur with doses at or near therapeutic serum concentrations. Facilities for prompt and accurate serum lithium determinations must be available during therapy. Accurate patient evaluation requires both clinical and laboratory analysis.

During the acute manic phase, the patient may have a greater ability to tolerate lithium. This tolerance decreases as the manic symptoms subside and often necessitates a corresponding dosage adjustment.

During the acute manic phase, lithium administration of 300 (8 mEq) to 600 mg three times a day should usually produce effective serum concentrations ranging from 0.8 to 1.2 mEq per liter, with weekly adjustments based on plasma lithium concentrations. An increase of 8 mEq a day will increase plasma concentrations by 0.3±0.1 mEq per liter. The maintenance dose of 300 mg three or four times a day usually produces effective serum concentrations ranging from 0.5 to 1.0 mEq per liter.

If a satisfactory therapeutic response to lithium at the highest tolerated serum concentrations within the therapeutic range is not achieved within 3 weeks, lithium therapy should be discontinued.

Slow-release lithium carbonate capsules and tablets are not bioequivalent to other lithium dosage forms and should not be used interchangeably with them.

Diet/Nutrition

Since lithium decreases sodium reabsorption by the renal tubules, a normal diet with an average consumption of salt and adequate fluid intake, 2.5 to 3 liters of fluid per day, is essential to prevent sodium depletion leading to lithium toxicity.

This medication may be taken with food, juice, or milk, if necessary, to lessen laxative action, stomach irritation, tremors, or weakness, by slowing absorption of lithium. The syrup must be diluted in juice or other flavored beverage before administration.

Oral Dosage Forms

LITHIUM CARBONATE CAPSULES USP

Usual adult and adolescent dose: Antimanic—

Acute mania: Oral, initially 300 to 600 mg (8 to 16 mEq) three times a day, the dosage being adjusted as needed and tolerated at weekly intervals.

Maintenance: Oral, 300 mg three or four times a day, the dosage being adjusted as needed and tolerated.

Note: Geriatric or debilitated patients usually require a lower dosage.

Usual adult prescribing limits: Up to 2.4 grams a day.

Auxiliary labeling:

• May cause drowsiness.

• Take after a meal or snack.

LITHIUM CARBONATE SLOW-RELEASE CAPSULES

Note: Lithium carbonate slow-release capsules are not commercially available in the U.S.

Usual adult and adolescent dose: Antimanic—

Acute mania: Oral, initially 600 to 900 mg a day on the first day, the dosage being increased, thereafter, to 1200 to 1800 mg a day in three divided doses, as needed and tolerated.

Maintenance: Oral, 900 to 1200 mg a day in three divided doses, the dosage being adjusted as needed and tolerated.

Usual adult prescribing limits: Up to 2.4 grams a day.

Usual geriatric dose: Antimanic—Oral, 600 to 1200 mg a day in three divided doses.

Note: Not bioequivalent to other lithium dosage forms and should not be used interchangeably with them.

Auxiliary labeling:

• Swallow whole.

• May cause drowsiness.

LITHIUM CARBONATE TABLETS USP

Usual adult and adolescent dose: Antimanic—

Acute mania: Oral, initially 300 to 600 mg (8 to 16 mEq) three times a day, the dosage being adjusted as needed and tolerated at weekly intervals.

Maintenance: Oral, 300 mg three or four times a day, the dosage being adjusted as needed and tolerated.

Note: Geriatric or debilitated patients usually require a lower dosage.

Usual adult prescribing limits: Up to 2.4 grams a day.

Auxiliary labeling:

• May cause drowsiness.

• Take after a meal or snack.

LITHIUM CARBONATE EXTENDED-RELEASE TABLETS

Usual adult and adolescent dose: Antimanic—

Acute mania: Oral, 450 to 900 mg two times a day or 300 to 600 mg three times a day, the dosage being adjusted as needed and tolerated.

Maintenance: Oral, 450 mg two times a day or 300 mg three times a day, the dosage being adjusted as needed and tolerated.

Note: Geriatric or debilitated patients usually require a lower dosage.

Usual adult prescribing limits: Up to 2.4 grams a day.

Auxiliary labeling:

• Swallow whole.

• May cause drowsiness.

• Take after a meal or snack.

LITHIUM CITRATE SYRUP USP

Note: Lithium citrate syrup is not commercially available in Canada.

Usual adult and adolescent dose: Antimanic—
Acute mania: Oral, the equivalent of 300 to 600 mg (8 to 16 mEq) of lithium carbonate three times a day, the dosage being adjusted as needed and tolerated.
Maintenance: Oral, the equivalent of 300 mg of lithium carbonate three or four times a day, the dosage being adjusted as needed and tolerated.

Note: Geriatric or debilitated patients usually require a lower dosage.

Usual adult prescribing limits: Up to the equivalent of 2.4 grams of lithium carbonate a day.

Auxiliary labeling:
- May cause drowsiness.
- Take after a meal or snack.
- Dilute with juice or other beverage before taking.

LOMUSTINE   Systemic

A commonly used *brand name* in the U.S. and Canada is *CeeNU*.
Another commonly used name is CCNU.

ORAL
Lomustine Capsules
    In the U.S. and Canada—*CeeNU*

Category: Antineoplastic.

Indications

Note: Bracketed information in the *Indications* section refers to uses not included in U.S. product labeling.

Accepted
Tumors, brain, primary (treatment);
[Carcinoma, gastrointestinal (treatment)][1];
[Carcinoma, lung (treatment)];
[Carcinoma, renal (treatment)]; or
[Carcinoma, breast (treatment)]—Lomustine is indicated for treatment of both primary and metastatic brain tumors, in patients who have already received appropriate surgical and/or radiotherapeutic procedures. It is also used for treatment of gastrointestinal carcinoma, lung carcinoma (squamous cell, anaplastic large cell, and adenocarcinoma), renal carcinoma, and advanced breast carcinoma after conventional therapy has failed.

Lymphomas, Hodgkin's (treatment)—Lomustine is indicated for treatment of Hodgkin's disease, as secondary therapy in combination with other drugs in patients who relapse while being treated with primary therapy or in patients who fail to respond to primary therapy.

[Multiple myeloma (treatment)][1]—Lomustine is also used for treatment of multiple myeloma.

[Melanoma, malignant (treament)]—Lomustine is used for treatment of malignant melanoma, alone or in combination with other drugs.

[1]Not included in Canadian product labeling.

Pharmacology

Mechanism of action/Effect: Lomustine is an alkylating agent of the nitrosourea type. Lomustine (and/or its metabolites) interferes with the function of DNA and RNA. It is cell cycle-phase nonspecific. Lomustine also acts to inhibit DNA synthesis by inhibiting key enzymatic processes.

Precautions to Consider

Geriatrics
No information is available on the relationship of age to the effects of lomustine in geriatric patients. However, elderly patients are more likely to have age-related renal function impairment, which may require caution in patients receiving lomustine.

Dental
The bone marrow depressant effects of lomustine may result in an increased incidence of microbial infection, delayed healing, and gingival bleeding. Dental work, whenever possible, should be completed prior to initiation of therapy or deferred until blood counts have returned to normal. Patients should be instructed in proper oral hygiene during treatment, including caution in use of regular toothbrushes, dental floss, and toothpicks.
Lomustine may also cause stomatitis associated with considerable discomfort.

Drug interactions and/or related problems
The following drug interactions and/or related problems have been selected on the basis of their potential clinical significance (possible mechanism in parentheses where appropriate)—not necessarily inclusive (» = major clinical significance):

Blood dyscrasia-causing medications
    (leukopenic and/or thrombocytopenic effects of lomustine may be increased with concurrent or recent therapy if these medications cause the same effects; dosage adjustment of lomustine, if necessary, should be based on blood counts)

» Bone marrow depressants, other or
Radiation therapy
    (additive bone marrow depression may occur; dosage reduction may be required when two or more bone marrow depressants, including radiation, are used concurrently or consecutively)

Vaccines, killed virus
    (because normal defense mechanisms may be suppressed by lomustine therapy, the patient's antibody response to the vaccine may be decreased. The interval between discontinuation of medications that cause immunosuppression and restoration of the patient's ability to respond to the vaccine depends on the intensity and type of immunosuppression-causing medication used, the underlying disease, and other factors; estimates vary from 3 months to 1 year)

» Vaccines, live virus
    (because normal defense mechanisms may be suppressed by lomustine therapy, concurrent use with a live virus vaccine may potentiate the replication of the vaccine virus, may increase the side/adverse effects of the vaccine virus, and/or may

decrease the patient's antibody response to the vaccine; immunization of these patients should be undertaken only with extreme caution after careful review of the patient's hematologic status and only with the knowledge and consent of the physician managing the lomustine therapy. The interval between discontinuation of medications that cause immunosuppression and restoration of the patient's ability to respond to the vaccine depends on the intensity and type of immunosuppression-causing medication used, the underlying disease, and other factors; estimates vary from 3 months to 1 year. Patients with leukemia in remission should not receive live virus vaccine until at least 3 months after their last chemotherapy. Immunization with oral poliovirus vaccine should also be postponed in persons in close contact with the patient, especially family members)

Contraindications/Medical problems
The contraindications/medical problems included have been selected on the basis of their potential clinical significance (reasons given in parentheses where appropriate)—not necessarily inclusive (» = major clinical significance).

Risk-benefit should be considered when the following medical problems exist:

» Bone marrow depression
» Chickenpox, existing or recent (including recent exposure), or
» Herpes zoster
   (risk of severe generalized disease)
» Infection
» Pulmonary function impairment, especially with a baseline below 70% of the forced vital capacity (FVC) or carbon monoxide diffusion capacity (DLCO)
   (increased risk of pulmonary toxicity)
» Renal function impairment
» Sensitivity to lomustine
» Caution should be used also in patients who have had previous cytotoxic drug therapy and radiation therapy.

Side/Adverse Effects

Note: Many "side effects" of antineoplastic therapy are unavoidable and represent the medication's pharmacologic action. Some of these (for example, leukopenia and thrombocytopenia) are actually used as parameters to aid in individual dosage titration.

The following side/adverse effects have been selected on the basis of their potential clinical significance (possible signs and symptoms in parentheses where appropriate)—not necessarily inclusive:

Those indicating need for medical attention
Incidence more frequent
   Immunosuppression or leukopenia or infection (usually asymptomatic; less frequently, fever or chills, cough or hoarseness, lower back or side pain, painful or difficult urination); *thrombocytopenia* (usually asymptomatic; less frequently, unusual bleeding or bruising; black, tarry stools; blood in urine or stools; pinpoint red spots on skin)
   Note: Maximum *thrombocytopenia* occurs about 4 weeks after a dose and persists for 1 to 2 weeks. Maximum *leukopenia* occurs about 4 to 6 weeks after a dose and persists for 1 to 2 weeks. Recovery usually occurs within 6 to 7 weeks after administration. Severity of bone marrow depression varies and determines subsequent dosage of lomustine.
Incidence less frequent
   Anemia (unusual tiredness or weakness); *neurotoxicity* (awkwardness, confusion, slurred speech, unusual tiredness)—not definitely attributed to medication; *renal toxicity and failure* (decrease in urination, swelling of feet or lower legs)—especially with long-term therapy; *stomatitis* (sores in mouth and on lips)

Incidence rare
   Hepatotoxicity (usually not symptomatic); *pulmonary infiltrates and/or fibrosis* (cough, shortness of breath)
   Note: *Pulmonary toxicity* has occurred after cumulative doses ranging from 600 to 1240 mg or therapy of 6 months or more.

Those indicating need for medical attention only if they continue or are bothersome
Incidence more frequent
   Loss of appetite; nausea and vomiting
   Note: *Loss of appetite* may persist for 2 to 3 days after a dose.
      Nausea and vomiting occur 3 to 6 hours after a dose and usually persist less than 24 hours.
Incidence less frequent
   Darkening of skin; diarrhea; skin rash and itching

Those not indicating need for medical attention
Incidence less frequent
   Loss of hair

Those indicating the need for medical attention if they occur after medication is discontinued
   Bone marrow depression (black, tarry stools; blood in urine or stools; cough or hoarseness; fever or chills; lower back or side pain; painful or difficult urination; pinpoint red spots on skin; unusual bleeding or bruising)
   Note: Cumulative *myelosuppression* may occur with repeated doses.

Patient Consultation

In providing consultation, consider emphasizing the following selected information (» = major clinical significance):

Before using this medication
» Conditions affecting use, especially:
      Sensitivity to lomustine
      Pregnancy—Use not recommended because of mutagenic, teratogenic, and carcinogenic potential; advisability of using contraception; telling physician immediately if pregnancy is suspected
      Breast-feeding—Not recommended because of risk of serious side effects
      Other medications, especially other bone marrow depressants or previous cytotoxic drug or radiation therapy
      Other medical problems, especially chickenpox, herpes zoster, infection, pulmonary function impairment, or renal function impairment

Proper use of this medication
» Importance of not taking more or less medication than the amount prescribed
   Explanation of different kinds of capsules included in one container
   Caution in taking combination therapy; taking each medication at the right time
   Frequency of nausea and vomiting, which usually lasts less than 24 hours; taking on an empty stomach to reduce nausea
   Checking with physician if vomiting occurs shortly after dose is taken

Precautions while using this medication
» Importance of close monitoring by the physician
» Avoiding immunizations unless approved by physician; other persons in patient's household should avoid immunizations with oral poliovirus vaccine; avoiding other persons who have taken oral poliovirus vaccine or wearing a protective mask that covers nose and mouth
   Caution if bone marrow depression occurs:
»   Avoiding exposure to persons with bacterial infections, especially during periods of low blood counts; checking with physician immediately if fever or chills, cough or hoarse-

ness, lower back or side pain, or painful or difficult urination occur

» Checking with physician immediately if unusual bleeding or bruising; black, tarry stools; blood in urine or stools; or pinpoint red spots on skin occur

Caution in use of regular toothbrush, dental floss, or toothpick; physician, dentist, or nurse may suggest alternatives; checking with physician before having dental work done

Not touching eyes or inside of nose unless hands washed immediately before

Using caution to avoid accidental cuts with use of sharp objects such as safety razor or fingernail or toenail cutters

Avoiding contact sports or other situations where bruising or injury could occur

Side/adverse effects

May cause adverse effects such as blood problems, loss of hair, and cancer; importance of discussing possible effects with physician

Signs of potential side effects, especially immunosuppression, leukopenia, infection, thrombocytopenia, anemia, neurotoxicity, renal toxicity, stomatitis, hepatotoxicity, and pulmonary infiltrates and/or fibrosis

Physician or nurse can help in dealing with side effects

General Dosing Information

Patients receiving lomustine should be under supervision of a physician experienced in cancer chemotherapy.

A variety of dosage schedules and regimens of lomustine, alone or in combination with other antitumor agents, are used. The prescriber may consult the medical literature as well as the manufacturer's literature in choosing a specific dosage.

Treatment with lomustine is continued as long as the medication is effective. If no response occurs after 1 or 2 courses, a response is unlikely.

Some cross-resistance has been reported between lomustine and carmustine.

Frequency and duration of nausea and vomiting may be reduced in some patients by administration of antiemetics prior to dosing and by administration of lomustine to fasting patients.

Dosage subsequent to the initial dose should be adjusted to meet the individual requirements of each patient based on the hematological response of the patient to the previous dose. An additional course of lomustine should be given only after circulating blood elements have returned to acceptable levels (leukocytes above 4000 per cubic millimeter and platelets above 100,000 per cubic millimeter).

Because of the delayed and cumulative bone marrow suppression caused by lomustine, the medication should be given no more frequently than every 6 weeks.

Special precautions are recommended in patients who develop thrombocytopenia as a result of administration of lomustine. These may include extreme care in performing invasive procedures; regular inspection of intravenous sites, skin (including perirectal area), and mucous membrane surfaces for signs of bleeding or bruising; limiting frequency of venipuncture and avoiding intramuscular injections; testing urine, emesis, stool, and secretions for occult blood; care in use of regular toothbrushes, dental floss, toothpicks, safety razors, and fingernail and toenail cutters; avoiding constipation; and using caution to prevent falls and other injuries. Such patients should avoid alcohol and any aspirin intake because of the risk of gastrointestinal bleeding. Platelet transfusions may be required.

Patients who develop leukopenia should be observed carefully for signs of infection. Antibiotic support may be required. In neutropenic patients who develop fever, broad-spectrum antibiotic coverage should be initiated empirically, pending bacterial cultures and appropriate diagnostic tests.

Combination chemotherapy

Lomustine may be used in combination with other agents in various regimens. As a result, incidence and/or severity of side effects may be altered and different dosages (usually reduced) may be used. For example, lomustine is part of the following chemotherapeutic combinations (some commonly used acronyms are in parentheses):

—lomustine, doxorubicin, and vinblastine (CAVe).

—cyclophosphamide, methotrexate, and lomustine (CMC-High dose).

—methotrexate, doxorubicin, cyclophosphamide, and lomustine (MACC).

—procarbazine, vincristine, cyclophosphamide, and lomustine (POCC).

For specific dosages and schedules, consult the literature. For information regarding each agent, consult the individual monographs.

Oral Dosage Forms

Note: Bracketed uses in the *Dosage Forms* section refer to categories of use and/or indications that are not included in U.S. product labeling.

LOMUSTINE CAPSULES

Usual adult and adolescent dose:

Tumors, brain, primary; or
[Carcinoma, gastrointestinal][1]; or
[Carcinoma, lung]; or
[Carcinoma, renal]; or
[Carcinoma, breast]; or
Lymphomas, Hodgkin's; or
[Multiple myeloma]; or
[Melanoma, malignant]—Initial: As a single agent—Oral, 100 to 130 mg per square meter of body surface as a single dose, repeated every six weeks. A lower dose is used when lomustine is combined with other agents.

Note: In patients with suppressed bone marrow function, dosage is reduced to 100 mg per square meter of body surface as a single dose, repeated every six weeks.

A suggested dosage adjustment schedule for subsequent doses is:

Nadir after Prior Dose (cells per cubic millimeter)		Prior Dose To Be Given (%)
Leukocytes	Platelets	
>4000	>100,000	100
3000–3999	75,000–99,999	75
2000–2999	25,000–74,999	50
<2000	<25,000	0

Auxiliary labeling:

• There may be two or more different types of capsules in this container. This is not an error. It is important that you take all of the capsules so that you receive the right dose of the medicine.

• Take on an empty stomach.

[1]Not included in Canadian product labeling.

LOPERAMIDE   Oral-Local

Some commonly used *brand names* are:
In the U.S.—*Imodium; Imodium A-D; Imodium A-D Caplets*
In Canada—*Imodium*

ORAL
Loperamide Hydrochloride Capsules USP
In the U.S. and Canada—*Imodium*
Loperamide Hydrochloride Oral Solution
In the U.S.—*Imodium A-D*
In Canada—*Imodium*
Loperamide Hydrochloride Tablets
In the U.S.—*Imodium A-D Caplets*
In Canada—*Imodium*

Category: Antidiarrheal (antiperistaltic).

Indications

Accepted
Diarrhea (treatment)—Loperamide is indicated for the control and symptomatic relief of acute nonspecific diarrhea and of chronic diarrhea associated with inflammatory bowel disease. Also indicated to reduce the volume of discharge from ileostomies.

Pharmacology

Mechanism of action/Effect: Reduction of intestinal motility by direct effect on the nerve endings and/or intramural ganglia of the intestinal wall. Loperamide exerts its antidiarrheal action not only by slowing intestinal transit and increasing contact time but also by directly inhibiting fluid and electrolyte secretion and/or stimulating salt and water absorption.

Other actions/effects: High doses may inhibit gastric acid secretion.

Duration of action: Up to 24 hours.

Precautions to Consider

Geriatrics
In geriatric patients with diarrhea, caution is recommended because of the risk of fluid and electrolyte loss. Dehydration may further influence the variability of response to loperamide.

Drug interactions and/or related problems
The following drug interactions and/or related problems have been selected on the basis of their potential clinical significance (possible mechanism in parentheses where appropriate)—not necessarily inclusive (» = major clinical significance):

Opioid (narcotic) analgesics
(concurrent use of loperamide with an opioid analgesic may increase the risk of severe constipation)

Contraindications/Medical problems
The contraindications/medical problems included have been selected on the basis of their potential clinical significance (reasons given in parentheses where appropriate)—not necessarily inclusive (» = major clinical significance).

Except under special circumstances, this medication should not be used when the following medical problems exist:
» Colitis, severe
(patient may develop toxic megacolon)
» Diarrhea associated with pseudomembranous colitis resulting from treatment with broad-spectrum antibiotics
(inhibition of peristalsis may delay the removal of toxins from the colon, thereby prolonging and/or worsening the diarrhea)

Risk-benefit should be considered when the following medical problems exist:
» Dehydration
(rehydration therapy is essential if signs of dehydration, such as dry mouth, excessive thirst, wrinkled skin, decreased urination, and dizziness or lightheadedness, are present; fluid loss may have serious consequences, such as circulatory collapse and renal failure, especially in young children)
Diarrhea caused by infectious organisms
(bacterial diarrhea may, on rare occasions, worsen due to the increased contact time between the mucosa and the penetrating microorganism; however, evidence of this occurring in actual practice is lacking)
» Dysentery, acute, characterized by bloody stools and elevated temperature
(sole treatment with antiperistaltic antidiarrheals may be inadequate; antibiotic therapy may be required)
Hepatic function impairment
(increased risk of CNS toxicity because of extensive first pass metabolism of loperamide in liver)
» Sensitivity to loperamide

Side/Adverse Effects

Note: Adverse effects may be difficult to distinguish from the diarrheal syndrome itself and are usually self-limited.

Although human data are inconclusive, animal pharmacological and toxicological data indicate that overdosage may result in CNS depression, constipation, and gastrointestinal irritation.

The following side/adverse effects have been selected on the basis of their potential clinical significance (possible signs and symptoms in parentheses where appropriate)—not necessarily inclusive:

Those indicating need for medical attention
Incidence rare
Allergic reaction (skin rash); *toxic megacolon* (bloating, constipation, loss of appetite, severe stomach pain with nausea and vomiting)

Those indicating need for medical attention only if they continue or are bothersome
Incidence rare
Drowsiness or dizziness; dryness of mouth

Patient Consultation

In providing consultation, consider emphasizing the following selected information (» = major clinical significance):

Before using this medication
» Conditions affecting use, especially:
Sensitivity to loperamide
Use in children—Risk of dehydration; variability in response to loperamide; increased susceptibility to CNS effects
Use in the elderly—Risk of dehydration; variability in response to loperamide
Other medical problems, especially diarrhea caused by antibiotics, severe colitis, or acute dysentery

Proper use of this medication
» Importance of not taking more medication than the amount prescribed
» Importance of maintaining adequate hydration and proper diet
Missed dose: Not taking missed dose; not doubling doses
» Proper storage

Precautions while using this medication

Regular visits to physician to check progress during prolonged therapy

» Consulting physician if diarrhea is not controlled within 48 hours and/or fever develops

Side/adverse effects

Signs of potential side effects, especially allergic reaction or toxic megacolon

General Dosing Information

Reduction of intestinal motility in patients with travelers' diarrhea may result in prolonged fever by slowing expulsion of infectious organisms that penetrate intestinal mucosa (for example, *Shigella*, *Salmonella*, and certain strains of *Escherichia coli*).

Inhibition of peristalsis may produce fluid retention in the bowel which may aggravate and mask dehydration and depletion of electrolytes, especially in young children, and may also increase variability of response to the medication. If dehydration or electrolyte imbalance occurs, loperamide therapy should be withheld until appropriate corrective therapy has begun.

In patients with acute ulcerative colitis, treatment with loperamide should be discontinued promptly in the event of abdominal distention or other symptoms that may indicate impending toxic megacolon.

Neither tolerance to the antidiarrheal effects nor physical dependence on loperamide has been reported in humans, although a morphine-like dependence has occurred in monkeys receiving high doses.

In acute diarrhea, treatment with loperamide should be discontinued after 48 hours if improvement does not occur. In chronic diarrhea, if no improvement has occurred after at least 10 days of treatment with the maximum dose, loperamide is unlikely to be effective, although further administration may be the only alternative when diet and specific treatment are inadequate.

Oral Dosage Forms

LOPERAMIDE HYDROCHLORIDE CAPSULES USP

Usual adult and adolescent dose:

Acute diarrhea—Oral, 4 mg after first loose bowel movement, followed by 2 mg after each subsequent loose bowel movement.

Chronic diarrhea—

Initial: Oral, 4 mg, followed by 2 mg after each subsequent loose bowel movement until diarrhea is controlled.

Maintenance: Oral, 4 to 8 mg a day in divided daily doses as needed.

Usual adult prescribing limits: 16 mg per day.

LOPERAMIDE HYDROCHLORIDE ORAL SOLUTION

Usual adult and adolescent dose:

Acute diarrhea—Oral, 4 mg after first loose bowel movement, followed by 2 mg after each subsequent loose bowel movement.

Chronic diarrhea—

Initial: Oral, 4 mg, followed by 2 mg after each subsequent loose bowel movement until diarrhea is controlled.

Maintenance: Oral, 4 to 8 mg a day in divided daily doses as needed.

Usual adult prescribing limits: Up to 16 mg per day.

Note: Maximum daily dosage for self-medication using the over-the-counter product of loperamide is 8 mg.

LOPERAMIDE HYDROCHLORIDE TABLETS

Usual adult and adolescent dose:

Acute diarrhea—Oral, 4 mg after first loose bowel movement, followed by 2 mg after each subsequent loose bowel movement.

Chronic diarrhea—

Initial: Oral, 4 mg, followed by 2 mg after each subsequent loose bowel movement until diarrhea is controlled.

Maintenance: Oral, 4 to 8 mg a day in divided daily doses as needed.

Usual adult prescribing limits: 16 mg per day.

Note: Maximum daily dosage for self-medication using the over-the-counter product of loperamide is 8 mg.

LOXAPINE   Systemic

Some commonly used *brand names* are:

In the U.S.—*Loxitane; Loxitane C; Loxitane IM*
In Canada—*Loxapac*

ORAL

Loxapine Hydrochloride Oral Solution
In the U.S.—*Loxitane C*
In Canada—*Loxapac*
Loxapine Succinate Capsules†
In the U.S.—*Loxitane;* GENERIC
Loxapine Succinate Tablets*
In Canada—*Loxapac*

PARENTERAL

Loxapine Hydrochloride Injection
In the U.S.—*Loxitane IM*
In Canada—*Loxapac*

*Not commercially available in the U.S.
†Not commercially available in Canada.

Category: Antipsychotic; antianxiety agent-antidepressant.

Indications

Note: Bracketed information in the *Indications* section refers to uses not included in U.S. product labeling.

Accepted

Psychotic disorders (treatment)—Loxapine is indicated for the management of symptoms and characteristics of psychotic conditions.

[Anxiety associated with mental depression (treatment)][1]—Loxapine has been used to treat anxiety neurosis with depression.

---

[1]Not included in Canadian product labeling.

Pharmacology

Note: The pharmacological effects of loxapine are similar to those of phenothiazines.

Mechanism of action/Effect: Although the exact mechanism of action has not been completely established, loxapine is thought to improve psychotic conditions by blocking dopamine at postsynaptic receptor sites in the brain.

Other actions/effects:
Antiemetic—Inhibits the medullary chemoreceptor trigger zone.
Sedative—May cause indirect reduction of stimuli to the brain reticular activating system.

Onset of action: 30 minutes.

Time to peak effect: $1^1/_2$ to 3 hours.

Duration of action: Up to 12 hours.

Precautions to Consider

Cross-sensitivity and/or related problems

Patients sensitive to amoxapine (a dibenzoxazepine derivative) may be sensitive to loxapine also.

Geriatrics

Geriatric patients tend to develop higher plasma concentrations of loxapine because of changes in distribution due to decreases in lean body mass, total body water, and albumin, and often an increase in total body fat composition. These patients usually require lower initial dosage and a more gradual titration of dose.

Elderly patients also appear to be more prone to orthostatic hypotension and exhibit an increased sensitivity to the anticholinergic and sedative effects of loxapine. In addition, they are more prone to develop extrapyramidal side effects, such as tardive dyskinesia and parkinsonism. The signs of tardive dyskinesia are persistent, difficult to control, and, in some patients, appear to be irreversible. There is no known effective treatment. The symptoms may be masked during long treatment but may appear if loxapine is discontinued. Careful observation during treatment for early signs of tardive dyskinesia and reduction of dosage or discontinuation of medication may prevent a more severe manifestation of the syndrome.

Dental

The peripheral anticholinergic effects of loxapine may decrease or inhibit salivary flow, especially in middle-aged or elderly patients, thus contributing to the development of caries, periodontal disease, oral candidiasis, and discomfort.

Extrapyramidal reactions induced by loxapine will result in increased motor activity of the head, face, and neck. Occlusal adjustments, bite registrations, and treatment for bruxism may be made less reliable.

The leukopenic and thrombocytopenic effects of loxapine may result in an increased incidence of microbial infection, delayed healing, and gingival bleeding. Although the occurrence is rare with loxapine, if leukopenia or thrombocytopenia occurs, dental work should be deferred until blood counts have returned to normal. Patients should be instructed in proper oral hygiene, including caution in use of regular toothbrushes, dental floss, and toothpicks.

Drug interactions and/or related problems

The following drug interactions and/or related problems have been selected on the basis of their potential clinical significance (possible mechanism in parentheses where appropriate)—not necessarily inclusive (» = major clinical significance):

Note: Combinations containing any of the following medications, depending on the amount present, may also interact with this medication.

Although not all of the following interactions have been documented specifically for loxapine, a potential exists for their occurrence because of loxapine's close pharmacological similarity to phenothiazine medications.

» Alcohol or
» Central nervous system (CNS) depression-producing medications, other, especially anesthetics, barbiturates, and opioid (narcotic) analgesics
(concurrent use may potentiate and prolong the CNS depressant effects of either these medications or loxapine; dosage adjustments to approximately $^1/_2$ to $^1/_4$ of the usual dose may be necessary)

Amphetamines
(concurrent use may decrease the effects of amphetamines since loxapine produces alpha-adrenergic blockade)

Antacids or
Antidiarrheals, adsorbent
(concurrent use may inhibit the absorption of orally administered loxapine)

Anticholinergics or other medications with anticholinergic activity or
Antidyskinetic agents
(concurrent use with loxapine may intensify anticholinergic effects of both medications; patients should be advised to report gastrointestinal problems since paralytic ileus may occur; antidyskinetic agents should not be used for prophylaxis of pseudoparkinsonism during therapy with loxapine)

Anticonvulsants
(loxapine may lower the seizure threshold; dosage adjustment of anticonvulsant medications may be necessary; potentiation of anticonvulsant effects does not occur)

Antidepressants, tricyclic, or
Monoamine oxidase (MAO) inhibitors, including furazolidone, procarbazine, and more than 10 mg of selegiline a day
(concurrent use may prolong and intensify the sedative and anticholinergic effects of either these medications or loxapine; serum concentrations of the antidepressant may be increased when it is administered concomitantly with loxapine; dosage reduction of antidepressant may be necessary)

Bromocriptine
(concurrent use with loxapine may antagonize effects of bromocriptine on serum prolactin activity; dosage adjustment of bromocriptine may be necessary)

Carbamazepine
(in addition to enhancement of CNS depressant effects and lowering of seizure threshold, the concurrent use of carbamazepine with loxapine, and possibly other neuroleptics, may decrease plasma concentrations of the neuroleptic; patient should be observed for clinical signs of ineffectiveness of loxapine and dosage adjusted accordingly)

Dopamine
(when dopamine is used concurrently with loxapine, alpha-adrenergic blocking action of loxapine may antagonize peripheral vasoconstriction produced by high doses of dopamine)

Ephedrine
(when used concurrently with loxapine, alpha-adrenergic blocking action of loxapine may decrease the pressor response to ephedrine)

Epinephrine
(alpha-adrenergic effects of epinephrine may be blocked when epinephrine is used concurrently with loxapine, possibly resulting in severe hypotension and tachycardia)

» Extrapyramidal reaction-causing medications, other
(concurrent use with loxapine may increase the severity and frequency of extrapyramidal effects)

» Guanadrel or
» Guanethidine
(concurrent use with loxapine may decrease the hypotensive effects of these agents because of their displacement from and inhibition of uptake by adrenergic neurons)

Levodopa
(concurrent use may inhibit the antiparkinsonian effects of levodopa by blocking dopamine receptors in the brain)

Metaraminol
(concurrent use usually decreases, but does not reverse or completely block, the pressor effect of metaraminol)

Methoxamine
(prior administration of alpha-adrenergic blocking agents such as loxapine may block the pressor effect and decrease the duration of action of methoxamine)

Ototoxic medications, especially ototoxic antibiotics
(concurrent use with loxapine may mask the symptoms of ototoxicity such as tinnitus, dizziness, or vertigo)

Phenylephrine or
Norepinephrine
(prior administration of loxapine may decrease the pressor response to phenylephrine or norepinephrine because of the alpha-adrenergic blocking action of loxapine, but severe hypotension associated with overdosage of loxapine would be expected to respond to either agent)

Contraindications/Medical problems
The contraindications/medical problems included have been selected on the basis of their potential clinical significance (reasons given in parentheses where appropriate)—not necessarily inclusive (» = major clinical significance).

Except under special circumstances, this medication should not be used when the following medical problems exist:

» CNS depression, drug-induced, severe, or
» Comatose states
(may be exacerbated)

Risk-benefit should be considered when the following medical problems exist:

» Alcoholism, active
(CNS depression may be potentiated)

Cardiovascular disease
(increased risk of arrhythmias and hypotension)

Glaucoma, or predisposition to, or
Parkinson's disease or
Urinary retention
(may be exacerbated)

» Hepatic function impairment
(metabolism may be altered)

Prostatic hypertrophy, symptomatic
(risk of urinary retention)

Seizure disorders
(seizure threshold may be lowered)

Sensitivity to amoxapine or loxapine

Side/Adverse Effects
The following side/adverse effects have been selected on the basis of their potential clinical significance (possible signs and symptoms in parentheses where appropriate)—not necessarily inclusive:

Those indicating need for medical attention
Incidence more frequent
Akathisia (restlessness or need to keep moving); *extrapyramidal effects, parkinsonian* (difficulty in speaking or swallowing, loss of balance control, mask-like face, shuffling walk, slowed movements, stiffness of arms and legs, trembling and shaking of fingers and hands); *tardive dyskinesia, persistent* (lip smacking or puckering; puffing of cheeks; rapid or worm-like movements of tongue; uncontrolled movements of the arms and legs; uncontrolled chewing movements)

Note: *Parkinsonian extrapyramidal effects* are more common during first few days of treatment or following dosage increases.

Tardive dyskinesia is initially dose related, but may increase with long-term treatment and total cumulative dose; may persist after discontinuation of loxapine.

Incidence less frequent
Allergic reaction (skin rash); *anticholinergic effect* (difficult urination); *constipation, severe* (may lead to paralytic ileus); *extrapyramidal effects, dystonic* (difficulty in swallowing; inability to move eyes; muscle spasms, especially of the neck and back; twisting movements of body)—may be severe

Incidence rare
Agranulocytosis (sore throat and fever, unusual bleeding or bruising); *jaundice, obstructive* (yellow eyes or skin); *neuroleptic malignant syndrome [NMS]* (convulsions, difficult or unusually fast breathing, fast heartbeat or irregular pulse, high fever, high or low [irregular] blood pressure, increased sweating, loss of bladder control, severe muscle stiffness or rigidity, unusual tiredness or weakness, unusually pale skin); *tardive dystonia* (increased blinking or spasms of eyelid; unusual facial expressions or body positions; uncontrolled twisting movements of neck, trunk, arms, or legs)

Note: *NMS* may occur at any time during neuroleptic therapy, but is more commonly seen soon after start of therapy, or after patient has switched from one neuroleptic to another, during combined therapy with another psychotropic medication, or after a dosage increase. Along with the overt signs of skeletal muscle rigidity, hyperthermia, autonomic dysfunction, and altered consciousness, differential diagnosis may reveal leukocytosis (9500 to 26,000 cells per cubic millimeter), elevated liver function tests, and elevated creatine phosphokinase (CPK).

Symptoms of overdose
Dizziness; drowsiness, severe, or comatose state; muscle trembling, jerking, stiffness, or uncontrolled movements, severe; troubled breathing, severe; unusual tiredness or weakness, severe

Those indicating need for medical attention only if they continue or are bothersome
Incidence more frequent
Blurred vision; confusion; drowsiness; dryness of mouth; hypotension, orthostatic (dizziness, lightheadedness, or fainting)

Incidence less frequent
Constipation, mild; decreased sexual ability; enlargement of breasts, in males and females; headache; increased sensitivity of skin to sun; missing menstrual periods; nausea or vomiting; trouble in sleeping; unusual secretion of milk; weight gain

Those indicating the need for medical attention if they occur after the medication is discontinued

Dizziness; dyskinesia, withdrawal emergent (uncontrolled, repetitive movements of mouth, tongue, and jaw); *nausea and vomiting; stomach upset or pain; trembling of fingers and hands*

Patient Consultation

In providing consultation, consider emphasizing the following selected information (» = major clinical significance):

Before using this medication

» Conditions affecting use, especially:

Sensitivity to loxapine or amoxapine

Pregnancy—Studies in rats showed an increased number of fetal resorptions and decreased fetal weight

Use in elderly—Elderly patients are more likely to develop extrapyramidal, anticholinergic, hypotensive, and sedative effects; reduced dosage recommended

Use by athletes—Loxapine is banned and, in some cases, tested for in competitors in biathlon and modern pentathlon events by the USOC

Dental—Loxapine-induced blood dyscrasias may result in infections, delayed healing, and bleeding; dry mouth may cause caries and candidiasis; increased motor activity of face, head, and neck may interfere with some dental procedures

Other medications, especially alcohol, other CNS depression-producing medications, other extrapyramidal reaction-producing medications, guanadrel, or guanethidine

Other medical problems, especially severe CNS depression, active alcoholism, or hepatic function impairment

Proper use of this medication

Taking with food, milk, or water to reduce stomach irritation

Measuring oral solution only with dropper provided by manufacturer

Mixing oral solution with orange or grapefruit juice just before each dose

» Compliance with therapy; not taking more or less medicine, nor taking more often, than directed

» Proper dosing

Missed dose: Taking as soon as possible; not taking if within 1 hour of next dose; return to regular dosing schedule; not doubling doses

» Proper storage

Precautions while using this medication

Regular visits to physician to check progress of therapy

» Checking with physician before discontinuing medication; gradual dosage reduction may be needed

» Avoiding use of alcoholic beverages or other CNS depressants during therapy

Avoiding use with antacids or antidiarrheal medication within 2 hours of taking loxapine

» Possible drowsiness; caution when driving, using machines, or doing other things requiring alertness while taking loxapine

Possible dizziness or lightheadedness; caution when getting up suddenly from a lying or sitting position

Possible skin photosensitivity; avoiding unprotected exposure to sun; using protective clothing; using a sun block product that includes protection against both UVA-caused photosensitivity reactions and UVB-caused sunburn reactions; avoiding use of sunlamp, tanning bed, or tanning booth

Possible dryness of the mouth: using sugarless gum or candy, ice, or saliva substitute for relief; checking with physician or dentist if dry mouth continues for more than 2 weeks

» Caution if any kind of surgery, dental treatment, or emergency treatment is required

Side/adverse effects

Side effects are more likely to occur in the elderly

Signs of potential side effects, especially tardive dyskinesia, akathisia, dystonias, parkinsonian effects, anticholinergic effects, allergic skin reactions, agranulocytosis, obstructive jaundice, neuroleptic malignant syndrome (NMS), constipation (severe)

» Stopping medication and notifying physician immediately if symptoms of NMS appear, especially muscle rigidity, fever, difficult or fast breathing, seizures, fast heartbeat, increased sweating, loss of bladder control, unusually pale skin, unusual tiredness or weakness

» Notifying physician immediately if early symptoms of tardive dyskinesia appear, such as fine worm-like movements of the tongue or other uncontrolled movements of the mouth, tongue, jaw, or arms and legs; dosage adjustment or discontinuation may be needed to prevent irreversibility

Possibility of withdrawal symptoms

General Dosing Information

Dosage must be individualized by titration from the lower dose range over the first 7 to 10 days of therapy until effective control of psychotic symptoms is obtained. After such control is established, the dosage is gradually decreased to the lowest level that will maintain an adequate clinical response.

Loxapine has an antiemetic effect that may mask signs of overdose of other medication or may obscure diagnosis of conditions whose main symptoms include nausea. However, since the antiemetic effect of loxapine is central, nausea is not affected when it results from vestibular stimulation or local gastrointestinal irritation.

Upon cessation of extended maintenance therapy, a gradual reduction in loxapine dosage is recommended since abrupt withdrawal may cause some patients to experience transient dyskinetic signs, nausea, vomiting, gastritis, trembling, and dizziness.

For oral dosage forms only

The oral solution should be measured only with the dropper provided by the manufacturer and diluted with orange or grapefruit juice just before each dose.

For parenteral dosage form only

Because hypotension is a possible side effect of loxapine, intramuscular administration is used for bedfast patients or for appropriate acute ambulatory patients who can be closely monitored. Patients should remain lying down for at least 1/2 hour after the injection to avoid possible acute orthostatic hypotensive effects.

Diet/Nutrition

This medication may be taken with food or a full glass (240 mL) of water or milk if necessary to lessen stomach irritation.

Oral Dosage Forms

Note: The dosing and strengths of the dosage forms available are expressed in terms of loxapine base.

LOXAPINE HYDROCHLORIDE ORAL SOLUTION

Usual adult dose: Antipsychotic—

Initial: Oral, 10 mg (base) two times a day, the dosage being increased gradually during the first seven to ten days as needed for symptomatic control and as tolerated.

Maintenance: Oral, 15 to 25 mg (base) two to four times a day.

Note: This dosage form is intended primarily for institutional use.

Dose to be measured only with calibrated dropper provided by manufacturer.

Severely disturbed patients—Initial: Oral, 10 to 25 mg (base) two times a day.

Usual adult prescribing limits: Up to 250 mg (base) a day.

Usual geriatric dose: Initial, oral, 3 to 5 mg (base) two times a day.

Auxiliary labeling:
- Take by mouth.
- May cause drowsiness.
- Avoid alcoholic beverages.
- Must be diluted before use.

LOXAPINE SUCCINATE CAPSULES

Usual adult dose: See *Loxapine Hydrochloride Oral Solution.*

Auxiliary labeling:
- May cause drowsiness.
- Avoid alcoholic beverages.

LOXAPINE SUCCINATE TABLETS

Usual adult dose: See *Loxapine Hydrochloride Oral Solution.*

Auxiliary labeling:
- May cause drowsiness.
- Avoid alcoholic beverages.

Parenteral Dosage Forms

Note: The dosing and strengths of the dosage forms available are expressed in terms of loxapine base.

LOXAPINE HYDROCHLORIDE INJECTION

Usual adult dose: Intramuscular, 12.5 to 50 mg (base) every four to six hours as needed and tolerated.

Note: For intramuscular administration only. Not for intravenous use.

Usual adult prescribing limits: Up to 250 mg (base) a day.

Note: Advise patient to remain lying down for $1/2$ hour following administration to avoid severe orthostatic hypotension.

MAPROTILINE   Systemic

A commonly used *brand name* in the U.S. and Canada is *Ludiomil*.

ORAL
Maprotiline Hydrochloride Tablets USP
  In the U.S.—*Ludiomil;* GENERIC
  In Canada—*Ludiomil*

Category: Antidepressant; antineuralgic.

Indications

Note: Bracketed information in the *Indications* section refers to uses not included in U.S. product labeling.

Accepted

Depression, mental (treatment)—Maprotiline is indicated in the treatment of patients with major depressive disorder (unipolar depression); dysthymia (depressive neurosis); and bipolar disorder, depressed type.

Anxiety associated with mental depression (treatment)—Maprotiline is also indicated for the management of anxiety associated with mental depression.

[Pain, neurogenic (treatment)][1]—Maprotiline is used to treat some types of chronic pain.

[1]Not included in Canadian product labeling.

Pharmacology

Mechanism of action/Effect: A tetracyclic antidepressant, maprotiline is thought to increase the synaptic concentration of norepinephrine in the central nervous system (CNS) by blocking its re-uptake by the presynaptic neuronal membrane. No effect on serotonin re-uptake has been observed. Recent research has suggested that after long-term treatment with antidepressants, changes in postsynaptic beta-adrenergic receptor sensitivity and enhancement of response to alpha-adrenergic and serotonergic stimulation may contribute to the mechanism of antidepressant action. Antidepressants may produce a downregulation (desensitization) of presynaptic alpha2 receptors, equilibrating the noradrenergic system, and thus correcting the dysregulated output of depressed patients.

Onset of action: For desired therapeutic effect, up to 2 or 3 weeks, but sometimes within 7 days.

Precautions to Consider

Note: The similarity of pharmacological effects of maprotiline and tricyclic antidepressants suggests that the same considerations and precautions be observed in the use of both medications. Therefore, until additional specific clinical information on maprotiline is available, certain precautionary guidelines for tricyclic antidepressants are included for consideration.

Geriatrics

Elderly patients are more likely to exhibit increased dose sensitivity to the anticholinergic, sedative, and hypotensive effects of maprotiline; therefore, a lower initial dose should usually be used and the dosage maintained at the lowest effective level. Careful monitoring is necessary to maintain optimum therapeutic serum concentrations in the elderly. Orthostatic hypotension, although rare, may occur in elderly patients and caution must be observed to prevent falls.

Dental

The peripheral anticholinergic effects of maprotiline may decrease or inhibit salivary flow, especially in middle-aged or elderly patients, thus contributing to the development of caries, periodontal disease, oral candidiasis, and discomfort.

Although rarely reported, the blood dyscrasia-causing effects of maprotiline may result in an increased incidence of microbial infection, delayed healing, and gingival bleeding. If agranulocytosis, eosinophilia, purpura, or thrombocytopenia occurs, dental work should be deferred until blood counts have returned to normal. Patient instruction in proper oral hygiene should include caution in use of regular toothbrushes, dental floss, and toothpicks.

Drug interactions and/or related problems

The following drug interactions and/or related problems have been selected on the basis of their potential clinical significance (possible mechanism in parentheses where appropriate)—not necessarily inclusive (» = major clinical significance):

Note: Combinations containing any of the following medications, depending on the amount present, may also interact with this medication.

Although not all of the following interactions have been documented to pertain specifically to maprotiline, a potential exists for their occurrence because of the close similarity of maprotiline's pharmacological effects to those of tricyclic antidepressants.

» Alcohol or
» CNS depression-producing medications, other
      (concurrent use with maprotiline may result in serious potentiation of CNS depressant effects)

Anticholinergics or other medications with anticholinergic activity or
Antihistamines
      (concurrent use may potentiate the anticholinergic effects of either these medications or maprotiline; dosage adjustments may be necessary)

Anticonvulsants
      (maprotiline may enhance CNS depression, lower the seizure threshold, and decrease the effects of the anticonvulsant medication)

Antidepressants, tricyclic, or
Bupropion or
Clozapine or
Haloperidol or
Loxapine or
Molindone or
Phenothiazines or
Pimozide or
Thioxanthenes or
Trazodone
      (concurrent use may prolong and intensify the anticholinergic and sedative effects of either these medications or maprotiline; in addition, these medications may increase the risk of seizures by lowering the seizure threshold, and should be added or withdrawn with caution)

Cimetidine
      (concurrent use may increase plasma concentrations of maprotiline; dosage adjustment of maprotiline may be necessary when cimetidine therapy is initiated or discontinued)

Clonidine or
Guanadrel or

Guanethidine
(antihypertensive effects may be decreased when these medications are used concurrently with maprotiline)
(concurrent use of clonidine with maprotiline may result in serious potentiation of CNS depressant effects)

Contraceptives, oral, estrogen-containing, or

Estrogens
(concurrent use of large doses of estrogens with tricyclic antidepressants may potentiate antidepressant side effects and reduce the therapeutic effects of the tricyclic antidepressants; although not documented, similar effects may occur with maprotiline, a tetracyclic antidepressant)

Fluoxetine
(plasma concentrations of tricyclic antidepressants may be increased twofold or more when fluoxetine is used concurrently; although not documented, similar increases may occur with maprotiline, a tetracyclic antidepressant; some clinicians recommend dosage reductions of maprotiline of 50% or greater if used concomitantly with fluoxetine)

» Monoamine oxidase (MAO) inhibitors, including furazolidone, procarbazine, and selegiline
(concurrent use with maprotiline is generally not recommended, especially on an outpatient basis, as hyperpyretic episodes, severe convulsions, hypertensive crises, and death have resulted in a small number of patients from concurrent use with tricyclic antidepressants; a minimum of 14 days should elapse between discontinuing MAO inhibitors and initiating maprotiline therapy)

Naphazoline, ophthalmic, or
Oxymetazoline, nasal, or
Phenylephrine, nasal or ophthalmic, or
Xylometazoline, nasal
(if significant systemic absorption occurs, concurrent use with maprotiline may potentiate pressor effects of these medications)

» Sympathomimetics
(concurrent use with maprotiline may potentiate cardiovascular effects, possibly resulting in arrhythmias, tachycardia, or severe hypertension or hyperpyrexia; phentolamine can control the adverse reaction)
(significant systemic absorption of ophthalmic epinephrine may also potentiate cardiovascular effects; also, local anesthetics with vasoconstrictors should be avoided or a minimal amount of the vasoconstrictor should be used with the local anesthetic)
(concurrent use with maprotiline may decrease the pressor effects of ephedrine and mephentermine)

Thyroid hormones
(concurrent use with maprotiline may enhance the possibility of cardiac arrhythmias; dosage adjustments may be necessary)

Contraindications/Medical problems

The contraindications/medical problems included have been selected on the basis of their potential clinical significance (reasons given in parentheses where appropriate)—not necessarily inclusive (» = major clinical significance):

Except under special circumstances, this medication should not be used when the following medical problems exist:

» Myocardial infarction, during the acute recovery period
» Seizure disorders, including epilepsy, or history of seizures
   (risk of seizures is increased)

Risk-benefit should be considered when the following medical problems exist:

» Alcoholism, active
   (increased risk of seizures and CNS depression)

» Asthma or
» Blood disorders or
» Glaucoma, angle-closure, or
» Increased intraocular pressure or
» Urinary retention, or history of
   (may be exacerbated)
» Bipolar disorder
   (swing to hypomanic or manic phase may be accelerated and rapid cycling between mania and depression may be induced by maprotiline)
» Cardiovascular disorders
   (increased risk of conduction defects, arrhythmias, myocardial infarction, strokes, and tachycardia)
   Gastrointestinal disorders
   (risk of paralytic ileus)
» Hepatic function impairment
   (metabolism may be altered)
» Hyperthyroidism
   (increased risk of cardiovascular toxicity)
» Myocardial infarction, history of
   (increased risk of recurrence)
   Prostatic hypertrophy
   (risk of urinary retention)
» Schizophrenia
   (psychosis may be aggravated)
   Sensitivity to maprotiline or tricyclic antidepressants

Side/Adverse Effects

Note: Although not all of the following side effects have been attributed specifically to maprotiline, a potential exists for their occurrence as with the tricyclic antidepressants.

The following side/adverse effects have been selected on the basis of their potential clinical significance (possible signs and symptoms in parentheses where appropriate)—not necessarily inclusive:

Those indicating need for medical attention

Incidence more frequent
   Skin rash, redness, swelling, or itching

Incidence less frequent
   Constipation, severe—may lead to paralytic ileus; *convulsions; nausea or vomiting; shakiness or trembling; unusual excitement; weight loss*

   Note: *Seizures* may occur in patients with or without a history of seizures, usually with doses above 200 mg a day. The lowest effective maintenance dose is recommended to reduce further risk. Drugs that alter seizure threshold should be added to or withdrawn from maprotiline regimen with caution.

Incidence rare
   Agranulocytosis (sore throat and fever)—rarely reported for maprotiline, but has occurred with tricyclic antidepressants; *anticholinergic effect* (difficulty in urinating); *breast enlargement*—in males and females; *confusion*—especially in elderly; *hallucinations; hypotension* (fainting); *inappropriate secretion of milk*—in females; *irregular heartbeat; jaundice, cholestatic* (yellow eyes or skin); *swelling of testicles*

Symptoms of overdose
   Coma; convulsions; dizziness, severe; drowsiness, severe; fast or irregular heartbeat; fever; muscle stiffness or weakness, severe; restlessness or agitation; trouble in breathing; vomiting

   Note: Risk of *seizures, respiratory complications,* and *cardiotoxicity* is greater with maprotiline than with tricyclic antidepressants, and duration of comatose state and QRS complex is longer.

Those indicating need for medical attention only if they continue or are bothersome
Incidence more frequent
Blurred vision; dizziness or lightheadedness—especially in the elderly; *drowsiness; dryness of mouth; headache; impotence* (decreased sexual ability); *increased or decreased sexual drive; tiredness or weakness*
Incidence less frequent
Constipation (mild); *diarrhea; heartburn; increased appetite and weight gain*—related to carbohydrate craving; *increased sensitivity of skin to sunlight; increased sweating; insomnia* (trouble in sleeping); *weight loss*

Patient Consultation

In providing consultation, consider emphasizing the following selected information (» = major clinical significance):

Before using this medication
» Conditions affecting use, especially:
    Sensitivity to maprotiline or tricyclic antidepressants
    Use in the elderly—Elderly patients may be more prone to develop anticholinergic, sedative, and hypotensive effects
    Use by athletes—Maprotiline is banned and, in some cases, tested for in competitors in biathlon and modern pentathlon events by the U.S. Olympic Committee (USOC)
    Dental—Dry mouth may cause caries, oral candidiasis, periodontal disease, and discomfort; rare blood dyscrasias may result in increased incidence of microbial infection, delayed healing, and gingival bleeding
    Other medications, especially alcohol or other CNS depression-producing medications, MAO inhibitors, or sympathomimetics
    Other medical problems, especially cardiovascular disorders, active alcoholism, seizure disorders, asthma, blood disorders, glaucoma, increased intraocular pressure, urinary retention, bipolar disorder, hepatic function impairment, hyperthyroidism, or schizophrenia

Proper use of this medication
» Compliance with therapy
» May require up to 2 to 3 weeks of therapy to obtain optimal antidepressant effects
    Missed dose: If dosing schedule is:
        More than one dose a day—Taking as soon as possible; if almost time for next dose, skipping missed dose; going back to regular dosing schedule; not doubling doses
        One dose a day at bedtime—Not taking missed dose following morning; checking with doctor
» Proper storage

Precautions while using this medication
    Regular visits to physician to check progress during therapy
» Avoiding the use of alcohol or other CNS depressants during maprotiline therapy
» Possible drowsiness; caution when driving, using machines, or doing other things requiring alertness
» Possible dizziness or lightheadedness; caution when getting up suddenly from a lying or sitting position
» Possible dryness of mouth; using sugarless gum or candy, ice, or saliva substitute for relief; checking with physician or dentist if dry mouth continues for more than 2 weeks
» Caution if any kind of surgery, dental treatment, or emergency treatment is required
» Checking with physician before discontinuing medication; gradual dosage reduction may be needed

Side/adverse effects
    Anticholinergic, sedative, and hypotensive effects more likely to occur in the elderly
    Precautions followed for 3 to 7 days after discontinuing medication
    Signs of potential side effects, especially skin rash, redness, swelling, or itching; severe constipation; convulsions; nausea or vomiting; shakiness or trembling; unusual excitement; weight loss; agranulocytosis; anticholinergic effect; confusion; hallucinations; breast enlargement in males and females; inappropriate secretion of milk; irregular heartbeat; swelling of testicles; or jaundice

General Dosing Information

Dosage of maprotiline must be individualized for each patient by titration.

Correlations between plasma concentration, clinical response, side effects, and toxicity have not been established.

Some clinicians recommend that for maintenance therapy, the optimal daily dose may be reduced somewhat, sometimes given as a single dose at bedtime, and often continued for 6 months to 1 year. (A divided dose may be preferred for geriatric, adolescent, or cardiovascular patients.) In patients with recurrent depression, however, continuation of the full treatment dose during maintenance therapy may be optimal.

The single daily dose at bedtime is useful when side effects such as excessive drowsiness or dizziness might be bothersome or dangerous during working hours.

A gradual reduction in dosage is recommended when this medication is to be discontinued.

Potentially suicidal patients should not have access to large quantities of this medication since depressed patients, particularly those who may use alcohol excessively, may continue to exhibit suicidal tendencies until significant improvement occurs. Some clinicians recommend that the patient be supplied with the least amount of medication necessary for satisfactory patient management.

Oral Dosage Forms

MAPROTILINE HYDROCHLORIDE TABLETS USP

Usual adult and adolescent dose: Depression—Oral, initially 25 to 75 mg a day, in divided doses, for at least two weeks, the dosage being adjusted gradually by 25 mg a day as needed and tolerated.

Note: The effective maintenance dose is usually about 150 mg a day, often given once a day at bedtime.

Usual adult prescribing limits:
Outpatients—Up to 150 mg a day.
Hospitalized patients—Up to 225 mg a day.

Usual geriatric dose:
Initial—Oral, 25 mg a day.
Maintenance—Oral, 50 to 75 mg a day.

Auxiliary labeling:
• May cause drowsiness.
• Avoid alcoholic beverages.

MECAMYLAMINE   Systemic†

A commonly used *brand name* in the U.S. is *Inversine*.

ORAL
Mecamylamine Hydrochloride Tablets USP
   In the U.S.—*Inversine*

---

†Not commercially available in Canada.

Category: Antihypertensive.

Indications

Accepted
Hypertension (treatment)—Mecamylamine is indicated in the treatment of moderately severe to severe hypertension and uncomplicated malignant hypertension. It is not considered to be a primary agent in the treatment of hypertension. Use has declined because of the numerous side effects.

Nonpharmacologic management (especially sodium restriction, weight reduction and exercise, and moderation of alcohol consumption) is recommended first for some patients, including those with mild hypertension, and is recommended as an adjunct to all pharmacologic hypertensive therapy.

Pharmacology

Mechanism of action/Effect: Ganglionic blocker; prevents stimulation of postsynaptic receptors by acetylcholine released from presynaptic nerve endings; hypotensive effect is due to reduction in sympathetic tone, vasodilation, and reduced cardiac output, and is primarily postural.

Onset of action: 30 minutes to 2 hours.

Duration of action: 6 to 12 hours or more.

Precautions to Consider

Geriatrics
Although appropriate studies on the relationship of age to the effects of mecamylamine have not been performed in the geriatric population, the elderly may be more sensitive to the hypotensive effects. In addition, elderly patients are more likely to have age-related renal function impairment, which may require caution in patients receiving mecamylamine.

Dental
Use of mecamylamine may decrease or inhibit salivary flow, thus contributing to the development of caries, periodontal disease, oral candidiasis, and discomfort.

Drug interactions and/or related problems
The following drug interactions and/or related problems have been selected on the basis of their potential clinical significance (possible mechanism in parentheses where appropriate)—not necessarily inclusive (» = major clinical significance):

Note: Combinations containing any of the following medications, depending on the amount present, may also interact with this medication.

» Alkalizers, urinary, especially carbonic anhydrase inhibitors, antacids, or sodium bicarbonate
   (alkalinization of urine by these agents slows excretion and prolongs the effects of mecamylamine; concurrent use is not recommended)

   Allopurinol or
   Colchicine or

Probenecid or
Sulfinpyrazone
   (mecamylamine may raise the concentration of blood uric acid; dosage adjustment of antigout medications may be necessary to control hyperuricemia and gout)

» Ambenonium or
» Neostigmine or
» Pyridostigmine
   (concurrent use may interfere with the antimyasthenic effect of ambenonium, neostigmine, or pyridostigmine, leading to weakness and sudden inability to swallow)

» Antibiotics or
» Sulfonamides
   (patients with chronic pyelonephritis being treated with these medications should not be treated with ganglionic blockers)

Anti-inflammatory drugs, nonsteroidal (NSAIDs), especially indomethacin
   (antihypertensive effects of mecamylamine may be reduced when it is used concurrently with these agents; indomethacin, and possibly other NSAIDs, may antagonize the antihypertensive effect by inhibiting renal prostaglandin synthesis and/or by causing sodium and fluid retention; the patient should be carefully monitored to confirm that the desired effect is being obtained)

Estrogens
   (estrogen-induced fluid retention may lead to increased blood pressure)

Hypotension-producing medications, other
   (antihypertensive effects may be potentiated when these medications are used concurrently with mecamylamine; although some combinations are frequently used for therapeutic advantage, dosage adjustments may be necessary during concurrent use; if mecamylamine is given with a thiazide diuretic, the dose of mecamylamine, not the diuretic, should be reduced)

Preanesthetic and anesthetic agents used in surgery, especially spinal anesthetics
   (may potentiate the hypotensive response, with increased risk of severe hypotension, shock, and cardiovascular collapse during surgery)

Sympathomimetics
   (mecamylamine may enhance the pressor response to sympathomimetic pressor amines, and the hypotensive effect of mecamylamine may be decreased or reversed by all sympathomimetics)

Contraindications/Medical problems
The contraindications/medical problems included have been selected on the basis of their potential clinical significance (reasons given in parentheses where appropriate)—not necessarily inclusive (» = major clinical significance).

Risk-benefit should be considered when the following medical problems exist:
   Bladder neck obstruction or
   Prostatic hypertrophy or
   Urethral stricture
      (because of possible urinary retention)
» Cardiovascular insufficiency, including coronary insufficiency, or
   Cerebrovascular insufficiency or
» Myocardial infarction, recent
      (ischemia may be aggravated by hypotension)
   Fever or infection or
   Hemorrhage or

Salt depletion as a result of diminished intake or nausea and vomiting, diarrhea, excessive sweating, or use of diuretics
(hypotensive effects may be potentiated)
» Glaucoma, predisposition to
(high doses may increase intraocular pressure)
» Organic pyloric stenosis
(may increase risk of ileus)
Renal function impairment or
» Uremia
(increased effects due to reduced excretion)
Sensitivity to mecamylamine

Side/Adverse Effects

Note: Most side effects are dose-related.

The following side/adverse effects have been selected on the basis of
their potential clinical significance (possible signs and symptoms
in parentheses where appropriate)—not necessarily inclusive:

Those indicating need for medical attention
Incidence more frequent—dose-related
Hypotension, postural (dizziness or lightheadedness, especially
when getting up from a lying or sitting position)
Incidence less frequent—dose-related
Parasympathetic blockade (difficult urination)
Incidence rare
*Central nervous system (CNS) stimulation, specifically chorei-
form movements* (uncontrolled movements of face, hands, arms,
or legs); *convulsions; mental changes* (confusion or excitement,
mental depression); *tremors* (trembling); *interstitial pulmonary
edema and fibrosis* (shortness of breath); *paralytic ileus* (bloating,
frequent loose stools; followed by severe constipation)

**Those indicating need for medical attention only if they continue
or are bothersome**
Incidence more frequent—dose-related
Drowsiness; parasympathetic blockade (constipation; less frequently or rarely, blurred vision, decreased sexual ability, dryness
of mouth, enlarged pupils, weakness); *unusual tiredness*
Note: *Constipation* may be preceded by small, frequent liquid
stools and may rarely lead to paralytic ileus.
Incidence less frequent or rare—dose-related
*Decreased sexual ability or interest in sex; loss of appetite; nau-
sea and vomiting*

Patient Consultation

In providing patient consultation, consider emphasizing the following
selected information (» = major clinical significance):

Before using this medication
» Conditions affecting use, especially:
Sensitivity to mecamylamine
Pregnancy—Use not recommended because of risk of decreased
gastrointestinal motility in fetus and increased maternal sen-
sitivity to hypotensive effects
Breast-feeding—May be excreted in breast milk
Use in the elderly—Increased sensitivity to hypotensive effects
Other medications, especially urinary alkalizers, antimyas-
thenics, antibiotics, or sulfonamides
Other medical problems, especially cardiovascular insufficiency,
recent myocardial infarction, glaucoma, organic pyloric stenosis, or uremia

Proper use of this medication
Possible need for control of weight and diet, especially sodium
intake
» Patient may not experience symptoms of hypertension; importance
of taking medication even if feeling well

» Does not cure, but helps control hypertension; possible need for
lifelong therapy; checking with physician before discontinuing
medication; serious consequences of untreated hypertension
Getting into habit of taking at same time each day to help increase
compliance
» Proper dosing
» Missed dose: Taking as soon as possible; checking with physician
if two or more doses in a row are missed; possible severe
reaction if stopped abruptly
» Proper storage

Precautions while using this medication
Regular visits to physician to check progress
» Checking with physician before discontinuing medication; gradual
dosage reduction may be necessary to avoid serious rebound
hypertension
» Having enough medication on hand to get through weekends, holidays, and vacations; possibly carrying second prescription for
emergency use
» Not taking other medications, especially nonprescription sympathomimetics, unless discussed with physician
» Caution when getting up suddenly from a lying or sitting position,
especially in the morning
» Caution in using alcohol, while standing for long periods or exercising, and during hot weather because of enhanced orthostatic
hypotensive effects
Caution in taking antacids, especially those containing sodium
bicarbonate
Reporting fever or infection to physician; dosage adjustment may
be required
Possible dryness of mouth; using sugarless candy or gum, ice, or
saliva substitute for relief; checking with physician or dentist if
dry mouth continues for more than 2 weeks
Caution if any kind of surgery (including dental surgery) or emergency treatment is required

Side/adverse effects
Signs of potential side effects, especially convulsions, mental
changes, tremors, postural hypotension, parasympathetic blockade, CNS stimulation, interstitial pulmonary edema and fibrosis, and paralytic ileus

General Dosing Information

Because of wide individual variation in response to mecamylamine,
dosage must be adjusted to meet the individual requirements of
each patient on the basis of clinical response.

The optimal dosage of mecamylamine is at or just under that which
produces dizziness or faintness in the standing position.

The hypotensive effect of mecamylamine is especially pronounced
when the patient is standing. If feasible, blood pressure readings
should be taken in the supine position, after standing for 10 minutes, and immediately after exercise. Dosage increases should be
made only if there has been no decrease in the standing blood
pressure from previous levels.

Hospitalized patients should not be discharged until the effect of
mecamylamine on their standing blood pressure has been determined.

Incidence and severity of side effects may be reduced by initiating
therapy at a low dose and increasing gradually to the minimum
effective dose.

It is recommended that dosage increments be made no more frequently than every 2 days.

It is recommended that a morning dose, if given at all, be the smallest
dose of the day since an increased hypotensive response may occur
in the morning.

More frequent daily doses may be given to patients in whom smooth
control is difficult to obtain.

Recent evidence suggests that withdrawal of antihypertensive therapy prior to surgery is not necessary but that the anesthesiologist must be aware of such therapy.

With continuing use, limited tolerance to the antihypertensive effects of mecamylamine may develop as a result of fluid retention and expanded plasma volume.

The abrupt interruption of mecamylamine therapy, including several consecutive missed doses, may result in severe rebound hypertension, especially in patients being treated for malignant hypertension. This may lead to cerebrovascular accidents or acute congestive heart failure. Gradual withdrawal is recommended when mecamylamine is discontinued, and substitution of other antihypertensive therapy may be necessary.

Diet/Nutrition

It is recommended that mecamylamine be administered at consistent times in relationship to meals, since hypotension may occur after a meal because of dilation of splanchnic blood vessels. Administration after meals may be preferable to administration on an empty stomach, resulting in more gradual absorption and smoother control of high blood pressure.

Oral Dosage Forms

MECAMYLAMINE HYDROCHLORIDE TABLETS USP

Usual adult dose: Antihypertensive—
Initial: Oral, 2.5 mg two times a day, the dosage being increased in increments of 2.5 mg every two or more days until the optimal response is achieved.
Maintenance: Oral, 25 mg a day in three divided doses.

Note: Geriatric patients may be more sensitive to the effects of the usual adult dose.

Auxiliary labeling: • Do not take other medicines without your doctor's advice.

MELPHALAN   Systemic

A commonly used *brand name* in the U.S. and Canada is *Alkeran*.

Other commonly used names are L-PAM and phenylalanine mustard.

ORAL
Melphalan Tablets USP
In the U.S. and Canada—*Alkeran*

Category: Antineoplastic.

Indications

Note: Bracketed information in the *Indications* section refers to uses not included in U.S. product labeling.

Accepted
Carcinoma, ovarian (treatment);
[Carcinoma, breast (treatment)][1]; or
[Carcinoma, testicular (treatment)][1]—Melphalan is indicated for the palliative treatment of nonresectable epithelial carcinoma of the ovary. It is also used for treatment of breast carcinoma and testicular carcinoma.

Multiple myeloma (treatment)—Melphalan is indicated for the palliative treatment of multiple myeloma.

---

[1]Not included in Canadian product labeling.

Pharmacology

Mechanism of action/Effect: Melphalan is an alkylating agent of the nitrogen mustard type. Melphalan is a bifunctional alkylating agent and is cell cycle-phase nonspecific. Activity occurs as a result of formation of an unstable ethylenimmonium ion, which alkylates or binds with many intracellular molecular structures including nucleic acids. Its cytotoxic action is primarily due to cross-linking of strands of DNA and RNA, as well as inhibition of protein synthesis.

Other actions/effects: Has some immunosuppressant activity.

Precautions to Consider

Cross-sensitivity and/or related problems
Patients sensitive to chlorambucil may also be sensitive (in form of skin rash) to melphalan.

Geriatrics
No geriatrics-specific information is available on the use of melphalan in geriatric patients. However, elderly patients are more likely to have age-related renal function impairment, which may require caution in patients receiving melphalan.

Dental
The bone marrow depressant effects of melphalan may result in an increased incidence of microbial infection, delayed healing, and gingival bleeding. Dental work, whenever possible, should be completed prior to initiation of therapy or deferred until blood counts have returned to normal. Patients should be instructed in proper oral hygiene during treatment, including caution in use of regular toothbrushes, dental floss, and toothpicks.

Melphalan may also rarely cause stomatitis associated with considerable discomfort.

Drug interactions and/or related problems
The following drug interactions and/or related problems have been selected on the basis of their potential clinical significance (possible mechanism in parentheses where appropriate)—not necessarily inclusive (» = major clinical significance):

Note: Combinations containing any of the following medications, depending on the amount present, may also interact with this medication.

Allopurinol or
Colchicine or
» Probenecid or
» Sulfinpyrazone
(melphalan may raise the concentration of blood uric acid; dosage adjustment of antigout agents may be necessary to control hyperuricemia and gout; allopurinol may be preferred to prevent or reverse melphalan-induced hyperuricemia because of risk of uric acid nephropathy with uricosuric antigout agents)

Blood dyscrasia-causing medications
(leukopenic and/or thrombocytopenic effects of melphalan may be increased with concurrent or recent therapy if these medications cause the same effects; dosage adjustment of melphalan, if necessary, should be based on blood counts)

» Bone marrow depressants, other or
Radiation therapy
(additive bone marrow depression may occur; dosage reduction may be required when two or more bone marrow depressants, including radiation, are used concurrently or consecutively)

Vaccines, killed virus
(because normal defense mechanisms may be suppressed by melphalan therapy, the patient's antibody response to the vaccine may be decreased. The interval between discontinuation of medications that cause immunosuppression and restoration of the patient's ability to respond to the vaccine depends on the intensity and type of immunosuppression-causing medication used, the underlying disease, and other factors; estimates vary from 3 months to 1 year)

» Vaccines, live virus
(because normal defense mechanisms may be suppressed by melphalan therapy, concurrent use with a live virus vaccine may potentiate the replication of the vaccine virus, may increase the side/adverse effects of the vaccine virus, and/or may decrease the patient's antibody response to the vaccine; immunization of these patients should be undertaken only with extreme caution after careful review of the patient's hematologic status and only with the knowledge and consent of the physician managing the melphalan therapy. The interval between discontinuation of medications that cause immunosuppression and restoration of the patient's ability to respond to the vaccine depends on the intensity and type of immunosuppression-causing medication used, the underlying disease, and other factors; estimates vary from 3 months to 1 year. Patients with leukemia in remission should not receive live virus vaccine until at least 3 months after their last chemotherapy. Immunization with oral poliovirus vaccine should also be postponed in persons in close contact with the patient, especially family members)

Contraindications/Medical problems

The contraindications/medical problems included have been selected on the basis of their potential clinical significance (reasons given in parentheses where appropriate)—not necessarily inclusive (» = major clinical significance).

Risk-benefit should be considered when the following medical problems exist:

» Bone marrow depression
» Chickenpox, existing or recent (including recent exposure), or
» Herpes zoster
(risk of severe generalized disease)
Gout, history of, or
Urate renal stones, history of
(risk of hyperuricemia)
» Infection
» Renal function impairment
(effect on toxicity difficult to predict)
Sensitivity to melphalan
» Tumor cell infiltration of bone marrow
» Caution should be used also in patients who have had previous cytotoxic drug therapy and radiation therapy within 3 to 4 weeks.

Side/Adverse Effects

Note: Many "side effects" of antineoplastic therapy are unavoidable and represent the medication's pharmacologic action. Some of these (for example, leukopenia and thrombocytopenia) are actually used as parameters to aid in individual dosage titration.

A severe recurrent vasculitis and pulmonary fibrosis occurring with prolonged melphalan therapy have been reported.

The following side/adverse effects have been selected on the basis of their potential clinical significance (possible cause in parentheses where appropriate)—not necessarily inclusive:

Those indicating need for medical attention

Incidence more frequent—dose-related
Neutropenia or infection (usually asymptomatic; less frequently, fever or chills, cough or hoarseness, lower back or side pain,

painful or difficult urination); *thrombocytopenia* (usually asymptomatic; less frequently, unusual bleeding or bruising; black, tarry stools; blood in urine or stools; pinpoint red spots on skin)

Note: *Myelosuppression* usually occurs within 2 to 3 weeks of initiation of therapy, although leukopenia may occur within 5 days in a few patients. The nadir of leukocyte and platelet counts usually occurs within 3 to 5 weeks, and leukocyte and platelet counts usually return to normal within 4 to 8 weeks.

Incidence less frequent or rare
Allergic reaction (sudden skin rash or itching); *hyperuricemia or uric acid nephropathy* (joint pain, lower back or side pain, swelling of feet or lower legs); *stomatitis* (sores in mouth and on lips)

Note: *Hyperuricemia or uric acid nephropathy* occurs most commonly during initial treatment of patients with leukemia or lymphoma, as a result of rapid cell breakdown which leads to elevated serum uric acid concentrations.

Those indicating need for medical attention only if they continue or are bothersome

Incidence less frequent
Nausea and vomiting—dose-related

Those indicating the need for medical attention if they occur after medication is discontinued

Bone marrow depression (black, tarry stools; blood in urine or stools; cough or hoarseness; fever or chills; lower back or side pain; painful or difficult urination; pinpoint red spots on skin; unusual bleeding or bruising)

Note: Cumulative *myelosuppression* may occur with repeated dosing.

Patient Consultation

Consider advising the patient on the following (» = major clinical significance):

Before using this medication

Advisability of using nonhormonal contraception; telling physician immediately if pregnancy is suspected
See also *Precautions to Consider.*

Proper use of this medication

» Importance of not taking more or less medication than the amount prescribed
Caution in taking combination therapy; taking each medication at the right time
Importance of ample fluid intake and subsequent increase in urine output to aid in excretion of uric acid
» Frequency of nausea and vomiting; importance of continuing medication despite stomach upset
Checking with physician if vomiting occurs shortly after dose is taken
Missed dose: Not taking at all; not doubling doses
» Proper storage

Precautions while using this medication

» Importance of close monitoring by the physician
» Avoiding immunizations unless approved by physician; other persons in patient's household should avoid immunizations with oral poliovirus vaccine; avoiding other persons who have taken oral poliovirus vaccine or wearing a protective mask that covers nose and mouth
Caution if bone marrow depression occurs:
» Avoiding exposure to persons with bacterial infections, especially during periods of low blood counts; checking with physician immediately if fever or chills, cough or hoarseness, lower back or side pain, or painful or difficult urination occur
» Checking with physician immediately if unusual bleeding or bruising; black, tarry stools; blood in urine or stools; or pinpoint red spots on skin occur

Caution in use of regular toothbrush, dental floss, or toothpick; physician, dentist, or nurse may suggest alternatives; checking with physician before having dental work done

Not touching eyes or inside of nose unless hands washed immediately before

Using caution to avoid accidental cuts with use of sharp objects such as safety razor or fingernail or toenail cutters

Avoiding contact sports or other situations where bruising or injury could occur

Side/adverse effects

May cause adverse effects such as blood problems and cancer; importance of discussing possible effects with physician

Physician or nurse can help in dealing with side effects

General Dosing Information

Patients receiving melphalan should be under supervision of a physician experienced in cancer chemotherapy.

A variety of dosage schedules and regimens of melphalan, alone or in combination with other antitumor agents, are used. The prescriber may consult the medical literature as well as the manufacturer's literature in choosing a specific dosage.

Dosage must be adjusted to meet the individual requirements of each patient, based on clinical response and degree of bone marrow depression. This is especially important because of unreliable absorption of orally administered melphalan.

Development of uric acid nephropathy in patients with leukemia or lymphoma may be prevented by adequate oral hydration and, in some cases, administration of allopurinol. Alkalinization of urine may be necessary if serum uric acid concentrations are elevated.

It is recommended that melphalan therapy be discontinued if marked leukopenia (particularly granulocytopenia) or thrombocytopenia occurs. Therapy may be resumed at a lower dosage when the clinical and laboratory examinations are satisfactory.

Special precautions are recommended in patients who develop thrombocytopenia as a result of administration of melphalan. These may include extreme care in performing invasive procedures; regular inspection of intravenous sites, skin (including perirectal area), and mucous membrane surfaces for signs of bleeding or bruising; limiting frequency of venipuncture and avoiding intramuscular injections; testing urine, emesis, stool, and secretions for occult blood; care in use of regular toothbrushes, dental floss, toothpicks, safety razors, and fingernail and toenail cutters; avoiding constipation; and using caution to prevent falls and other injuries; Such patients should avoid alcohol and any aspirin intake because of the risk of gastrointestinal bleeding. Platelet transfusions may be required.

Patients who develop leukopenia should be observed carefully for signs of infection. Antibiotic support may be required. In neutropenic patients who develop fever, broad-spectrum antibiotic coverage should be initiated empirically, pending bacterial cultures and appropriate diagnostic tests.

Combination chemotherapy

Melphalan may be used in combination with other agents in various regimens. As a result, incidence and/or severity of side effects may be altered and different dosages (usually reduced) may be used. For example, melphalan is part of the following chemotherapeutic combinations (some commonly used acronyms are in parentheses):

—vincristine, carmustine, cyclophosphamide, melphalan, and prednisone (M-2 Protocol).

—melphalan and prednisone (MPL + PRED, MP).

For specific dosages and schedules, consult the literature. For information regarding each agent, consult the individual monographs.

Oral Dosage Forms

MELPHALAN TABLETS USP

Usual adult dose:

Multiple myeloma—

Oral, 150 mcg (0.15 mg) per kg of body weight per day for seven days, followed by a rest period of at least three weeks, during which time the leukocyte count will fall. When white cell and platelet counts are rising, a maintenance dose of 50 mcg (0.05 mg) per kg of body weight per day may be instituted, or

Oral, 100 to 150 mcg (0.1 to 0.15 mg) per kg of body weight per day for two to three weeks, or 250 mcg (0.25 mg) per kg of body weight per day for four days, followed by a rest period of two to four weeks. When leukocyte counts rise above 3000 to 4000 per cubic millimeter and platelet counts above 100,000 per cubic millimeter, a maintenance dose of 2 to 4 mg per day may be instituted, or

Oral, 7 mg per square meter of body surface or 250 mcg (0.25 mg) per kg of body weight per day for five days every five to six weeks, adjusted to produce mild leukopenia and thrombocytopenia.

Ovarian carcinoma—Oral, 200 mcg (0.2 mg) per kg of body weight per day for five days, repeated every four to five weeks if blood counts return to normal.

Note: Dispense in a glass container.

MEPROBAMATE   Systemic

Some commonly used *brand names* are:

In the U.S.—
Equanil
Meprospan 200
Meprospan 400
'Miltown'-200

'Miltown'-400
'Miltown'-600
Probate
Trancot

In Canada—
Apo-Meprobamate
Equanil

Meprospan-400
Miltown

ORAL

Meprobamate Extended-release Capsules
In the U.S. —*Meprospan 200; Meprospan 400*
In Canada—*Meprospan-400*

Meprobamate Tablets USP
In the U.S.—*Equanil; 'Miltown'-200; 'Miltown'-400; 'Miltown'-600; Probate; Trancot;* GENERIC
In Canada—*Apo-Meprobamate; Equanil; Miltown*

Category: Antianxiety agent.

Indications

Accepted

Anxiety (treatment)—Meprobamate is indicated for the management of anxiety disorders or for the short-term relief of the symptoms of anxiety. Meprobamate is usually not indicated for the treatment of anxiety or tension associated with everyday life. Effectiveness of this medication for long-term (more than 4 months) management of anxiety has not been assessed by systematic clinical studies. The medication's efficacy should be reassessed at periodic intervals.

Pharmacology

Mechanism of action/Effect: The mechanism of action of meprobamate is not known. It appears to act at multiple sites in the central nervous system (CNS), including the thalamus and limbic system.

Precautions to Consider

Cross-sensitivity and/or related problems

Patients sensitive to other carbamate derivatives (for example, carbromal, carisoprodol, mebutamate, or tybamate) may be sensitive to this medication also.

Geriatrics

Elderly patients may be more sensitive to the effects of meprobamate. The lowest effective dose should be administered to these patients to avoid oversedation. In addition, elderly patients are more likely to have age-related renal function impairment, which may require reduction of dosage in patients receiving meprobamate.

Dental

Prolonged use of meprobamate may decrease or inhibit salivary flow, thus contributing to the development of caries, periodontal disease, oral candidiasis, and discomfort.

Drug interactions and/or related problems

The following drug interactions and/or related problems have been selected on the basis of their potential clinical significance (possible mechanism in parentheses where appropriate)—not necessarily inclusive (» = major clinical significance):

Note: Combinations containing any of the following medications, depending on the amount present, may also interact with this medication.

Addictive medications, other, especially central nervous system (CNS) depressants with habituating potential
(prolonged concurrent use may increase the risk of habituation; caution is recommended)

» Alcohol or
» CNS depression-producing medications, other
(concurrent use may increase the CNS depressant effects of either these medications or meprobamate; caution is recommended and dosage of one or both agents should be reduced)

Contraindications/Medical problems

The contraindications/medical problems included have been selected on the basis of their potential clinical significance (reasons given in parentheses where appropriate)—not necessarily inclusive (» = major clinical significance).

Risk-benefit should be considered when the following medical problems exist:

» Alcoholism, active or in remission, or
» Drug abuse or dependence, history of
(predisposition of patients to habituation and dependence)
Epilepsy
(seizures may be precipitated)
Hepatic function impairment
(meprobamate metabolized in liver)
» Porphyria, acute intermittent
(condition may be exacerbated)
Renal function impairment
(meprobamate excreted via kidneys)
Sensitivity to meprobamate or other carbamate derivatives, such as carbromal, carisoprodol, mebutamate, or tybamate

Side/Adverse Effects

The following side/adverse effects have been selected on the basis of their potential clinical significance (possible signs and symptoms in parentheses where appropriate)—not necessarily inclusive:

Those indicating need for medical attention
Incidence less frequent
Allergic reaction (skin rash, hives, or itching; wheezing, shortness of breath, or troubled breathing [rare])
Incidence rare
Fast, pounding, or irregular heartbeat; intolerance to meprobamate (confusion); *leukopenia* (sore throat and fever); *paradoxical reaction* (unusual excitement); *thrombocytopenia* (unusual bleeding or bruising)
Symptoms of acute toxicity
Confusion, severe; drowsiness, severe; shortness of breath or slow or troubled breathing; slow heartbeat; weakness, severe
Symptoms of chronic toxicity
Dizziness or lightheadedness, continuing; slurred speech; staggering

Those indicating need for medical attention only if they continue or are bothersome
Incidence more frequent
Clumsiness or unsteadiness; drowsiness
Incidence less frequent
Blurred vision or change in near or distant vision; diarrhea; dizziness or lightheadedness; false sense of well-being; headache; nausea or vomiting; unusual tiredness or weakness

Those indicating possible withdrawal and the need for medical attention if they occur (usually within 2 days) after medication is discontinued
Clumsiness or unsteadiness; confusion; convulsions; hallucinations; increased dreaming; insomnia (trouble in sleeping); *muscle twitching; nausea or vomiting; nervousness or restlessness; nightmares; trembling*

Patient Consultation

In providing consultation, consider emphasizing the following selected information (» = major clinical significance):

Before using this medication
» Conditions affecting use, especially:
Sensitivity to meprobamate or other carbamate derivatives, such as carbromal, carisoprodol, mebutamate, or tybamate
Pregnancy—Meprobamate crosses placenta; risk of congenital malformations may be increased when medication used during first trimester of pregnancy
Breast-feeding—Excreted in breast milk in concentration of 2 to 4 times maternal plasma concentrations; use by nursing mothers may cause sedation in infant
Use in the elderly—Elderly patients may be more sensitive to effects of meprobamate; lowest effective dose should be administered to avoid oversedation
Use by athletes—Meprobamate is banned and, in some cases, tested for in competitors in biathlon and modern pentathlon events by the U.S. Olympic Committee (USOC)
Dental—Prolonged use of meprobamate may decrease or inhibit salivary flow, which may contribute to development of caries, periodontal disease, oral candidiasis, and discomfort
Other medications, especially alcohol or other CNS depression-producing medications
Other medical problems, especially alcohol or drug abuse or dependence, or acute intermittent porphyria

Proper use of this medication
» Importance of not using more medication than the amount prescribed because of habit-forming potential

» Proper dosing
   Missed dose: Taking right away if remembered within an hour or so; not taking if remembered later; not doubling doses
» Proper storage

Precautions while using this medication

Regular visits to physician to check progress during prolonged therapy

Checking with physician before discontinuing medication after prolonged use; gradual dosage reduction may be necessary to avoid possibility of withdrawal symptoms

» Avoiding use of alcohol or other CNS depressants

Caution if any laboratory tests required; possible interference with results of metyrapone or phentolamine tests

» Suspected overdose: Getting emergency help at once
» Caution if dizziness, lightheadedness, or drowsiness occurs

Possible dryness of mouth; using sugarless gum or candy, ice, or saliva substitute for relief; checking with dentist if dry mouth continues for more than 2 weeks

Side/adverse effects

Signs of potential side effects, especially allergic reaction; fast, pounding, or irregular heatbeat; intolerance to meprobamate; leukopenia; paradoxical reaction; and thrombocytopenia

General Dosing Information

Prolonged use in larger than usual therapeutic doses may result in psychological or physical dependence.

Following prolonged administration, meprobamate should be withdrawn gradually in order to avoid the possibility of precipitating withdrawal symptoms.

For treatment of dependence

Dosage of meprobamate should be reduced gradually over a period of 1 to 2 weeks. Alternatively, a barbiturate such as phenobarbital may be substituted, then gradually reduced.

Oral Dosage Forms

MEPROBAMATE EXTENDED-RELEASE CAPSULES

Usual adult dose: Antianxiety agent—Oral, 400 to 800 mg two times a day, in the morning and at bedtime.

Note: Geriatric or debilitated patients may be more sensitive to the effects of the usual adult dose.

Usual adult prescribing limits: Up to 2.4 grams daily.

Auxiliary labeling:
• Avoid alcoholic beverages.
• May cause drowsiness.

MEPROBAMATE TABLETS USP

Usual adult dose: Antianxiety agent—Oral, 400 mg three or four times a day; or 600 mg two times a day.

Note: Geriatric or debilitated patients may be more sensitive to the effects of the usual adult dose.

Usual adult prescribing limits: Up to 2.4 grams daily.

Auxiliary labeling:
• Avoid alcoholic beverages.
• May cause drowsiness.

MEPROBAMATE AND ASPIRIN   Systemic

Category: Analgesic.

Indications

Accepted

Pain, with anxiety and tension (treatment); or

Headache, tension (treatment)—Meprobamate and aspirin combination is indicated as an adjunct in the short-term treatment of pain accompanied by tension and/or anxiety in patients with musculoskeletal disease or tension headache. It appears to provide greater relief of pain in these conditions than when aspirin is used alone. Effectiveness of this medication for long-term (more than 4 months) management of anxiety has not been assessed by systematic clinical studies. The medication's efficacy should be reassessed at periodic intervals.

Patient Consultation

In providing consultation, consider emphasizing the following selected information (» = major clinical significance):

Before using this medication

» Conditions affecting use, especially:
   Sensitivity to meprobamate or other carbamate derivatives, such as carbromal, carisoprodol, mebutamate, or tybamate, or to aspirin or other salicylates including methyl salicylate (oil of wintergreen) or other nonsteroidal anti-inflammatory drugs or related analgesics
   Pregnancy—
      Meprobamate crosses placenta; risk of congenital malformations may be increased when meprobamate is used during first trimester

Aspirin and its salicylate metabolite readily cross placenta; studies in animals have shown that aspirin increases fetal resorptions and birth defects; use of aspirin during pregnancy reported to increase risk of birth defects in humans, but controlled studies using usual therapeutic doses have not shown proof of teratogenicity; chronic, high-dose aspirin therapy may prolong gestation, increase risk of postmaturity syndrome, and increase risk of maternal antenatal hemorrhage; ingestion of aspirin during last 2 weeks of pregnancy may increase risk of fetal or neonatal hemorrhage; regular use of aspirin during late pregnancy may result in constriction or premature closure of fetal ductus arteriosus, possibly leading to persistent pulmonary hypertension and heart failure in the neonate; overuse or abuse of aspirin late in pregnancy reported to reduce birthweight and to increase risk of stillbirth or neonatal death, possibly because of hemorrhage or premature ductus arteriosus closure

Labor and delivery—Chronic, high-dose aspirin therapy late in pregnancy may result in prolonged labor, complicated deliveries, and increased risk of maternal or fetal hemorrhage

Breast-feeding-
   Meprobamate excreted in breast milk in concentration of 2 to 4 times maternal plasma concentrations; use by nursing mothers may cause sedation in infant
   Salicylate excreted in breast milk

Use in children and teenagers—Checking with physician before giving medication to children or teenagers with symptoms of acute febrile illness, especially influenza or varicella, because of the risk of Reye's syndrome; also, pediatric patients, especially those with fever and dehydration, may be more susceptible to toxic effects of aspirin

Use in the elderly—Elderly patients may be more sensitive to effects of meprobamate; also, they may be more susceptible to toxic effects of aspirin

Use by athletes—Meprobamate is banned and, in some cases, tested for in competitors in biathlon and modern pentathlon events by the U.S. Olympic Committee (USOC)

Dental—Prolonged use of meprobamate may decrease or inhibit salivary flow, which may contribute to development of caries, periodontal disease, oral candidiasis, and discomfort

Other medications, especially alcohol or other CNS depression-producing medications, anticoagulants, antidiabetic agents (oral), cefamandole, cefoperazone, cefotetan, heparin, methotrexate, moxalactam, nonsteroidal anti-inflammatory drugs (other), platelet aggregation inhibitors, plicamycin, probenecid, sulfinpyrazone, thrombolytic agents, urinary alkalizers, valproic acid, or vancomycin

Other medical problems, especially asthma, allergies, and nasal polyps; bleeding ulcers or other hemorrhagic states; erosive gastritis; peptic ulcer; coagulation or platelet function disorders; history of alcohol or drug abuse or dependence; or acute intermittent porphyria

Proper use of this medication

» Taking with food or a full glass (240 mL) of water to minimize gastrointestinal irritation

» Not taking medication if it has a strong vinegar-like odor

» Not giving to children or teenagers with symptoms of influenza or varicella without first checking with physician because of risk of Reye's syndrome

» Importance of not taking more medication than the amount prescribed; meprobamate is potentially habit-forming and too much aspirin may cause stomach problems or result in overdose

» Proper dosing

» Proper storage

Precautions while using this medication

Regular visits to physician to check progress during prolonged therapy

Checking with physician before discontinuing medication after prolonged use; gradual dosage reduction may be necessary to avoid possibility of meprobamate withdrawal symptoms

» Caution if other medications containing aspirin or other salicylates (including bismuth subsalicylate) are used

» Avoiding use of alcohol or other CNS depressants

Alcohol consumption may increase risk of salicylate-induced gastrointestinal toxicity

Not using a nonsteroidal anti-inflammatory drug together with this medication on a regular basis, unless otherwise directed by physician or dentist

Not taking a cellulose-containing laxative within 2 hours of this combination containing aspirin

Diabetics: Aspirin present in combination may cause false urine sugar test results with prolonged use of 8 or more 325-mg (5-grain) doses per day

Caution if any laboratory tests required; possible interference with results of metyrapone and phentolamine tests

Caution if any kind of surgery is required; aspirin should be discontinued 5 days prior to surgery unless otherwise directed by physician

» Suspected overdose: Getting emergency help at once

» Caution if dizziness, lightheadedness, or drowsiness occurs

Possible dryness of mouth; using sugarless gum or candy, ice, or saliva substitute for relief; checking with dentist if dry mouth continues for more than 2 weeks

Side/adverse effects

Signs of potential side effects, especially aspirin-induced gastrointestinal bleeding or ulceration, intolerance to meprobamate, allergic reactions, blood dyscrasias due to meprobamate

Oral Dosage Forms

MEPROBAMATE AND ASPIRIN TABLETS

Usual adult dose: Analgesic—Oral, 1 or 2 tablets three or four times a day as needed.

Note: Geriatric or debilitated patients may be more sensitive to the effects of the usual adult dose.

Auxiliary labeling:
• Avoid alcoholic beverages.
• May cause drowsiness.

MERCAPTOPURINE   Systemic

A commonly used *brand name* in the U.S. and Canada is *Purinethol*.

Another commonly used name is 6-MP.

ORAL
Mercaptopurine Tablets USP
  In the U.S. and Canada—*Purinethol*

Category: Antineoplastic; immunosuppressant.

Indications

Note: Bracketed information in the *Indications* section refers to uses not included in U.S. product labeling.

Accepted
Leukemia, acute lymphocytic (treatment);
Leukemia, acute myelocytic (treatment); or
Leukemia, acute myelomonocytic (treatment)—Mercaptopurine is indicated for remission induction and maintenance therapy of acute lymphocytic, acute myelocytic, and acute myelomonocytic leukemia.

[Leukemia, chronic myelocytic (treatment)]—Mercaptopurine is used for treatment of chronic myelocytic leukemia.

[Lymphomas, non-Hodgkin's (treatment)][1]—Mercaptopurine is used for treatment of some pediatric non-Hodgkin's lymphomas.

[Polycythemia vera (treatment)][1]—Mercaptopurine is used for treatment of polycythemia vera.

[Bowel disease, inflammatory (treatment)][1]—Mercaptopurine is also being used in the treatment of regional enteritis (Crohn's disease) and ulcerative colitis.

[Arthritis, psoriatic (treatment)][1]—Mercaptopurine is being used in the treatment of selected cases of severe psoriatic arthritis.

Extreme caution is recommended in use of mercaptopurine for nonneoplastic conditions because of potential carcinogenicity with long-term use of this agent.

---

[1]Not included in Canadian product labeling.

Pharmacology

Mechanism of action/Effect: Mercaptopurine is an antimetabolite of the purine analog type. Mercaptopurine is cell cycle-specific for the S phase of cell division. Activity occurs as the result of activation in the tissues and may include inhibition of DNA synthesis with a lesser effect on RNA synthesis.

Precautions to Consider

Geriatrics

No geriatrics-specific information is available on the use of mercaptopurine in geriatric patients. However, elderly patients are more likely to have age-related renal function impairment, which may require dosage reduction in patients receiving mercaptopurine.

Dental

The bone marrow depressant effects of mercaptopurine may result in an increased incidence of microbial infection, delayed healing, and gingival bleeding. Dental work, whenever possible, should be completed prior to initiation of therapy or deferred until blood counts have returned to normal. Patients should be instructed in proper oral hygiene during treatment, including caution in use of regular toothbrushes, dental floss, and toothpicks.

Mercaptopurine may also cause stomatitis associated with considerable discomfort.

Drug interactions and/or related problems

The following drug interactions and/or related problems have been selected on the basis of their potential clinical significance (possible mechanism in parentheses where appropriate)—not necessarily inclusive (» = major clinical significance):

Note: Combinations containing any of the following medications, depending on the amount present, may also interact with this medication.

» Allopurinol or
   Colchicine or
» Probenecid or
» Sulfinpyrazone
   (concurrent use with allopurinol may result in greatly increased mercaptopurine activity and toxicity because of inhibition of metabolism; careful monitoring is recommended. It is recommended that mercaptopurine dosage be reduced to one-third to one-fourth of the usual dosage in patients receiving 300 to 600 mg of allopurinol a day concurrently to reduce or prevent hyperuricemia or to slow the metabolism of mercaptopurine. In addition, mercaptopurine may raise the concentration of blood uric acid; dosage adjustment of antigout agents may be necessary to control hyperuricemia and gout; concurrent use of uricosuric antigout agents should be avoided because of the risk of uric acid nephropathy)

Anticoagulants, coumarin- or indandione-derivative
   (mercaptopurine may increase anticoagulant activity and/or increase the risk of hemorrhage as a result of decreased hepatic synthesis of procoagulant factors and interference with platelet formation or may reduce anticoagulant activity by means of increased prothrombin synthesis or activation)

Blood dyscrasia-causing medications
   (leukopenic and/or thrombocytopenic effects of mercaptopurine may be increased with concurrent or recent therapy if these medications cause the same effects; dosage adjustment of mercaptopurine, if necessary, should be based on blood counts)

» Bone marrow depressants, other or
   Radiation therapy
   (additive bone marrow depression may occur; dosage reduction may be required when two or more bone marrow depressants, including radiation, are used concurrently or consecutively)

» Hepatotoxic medications, other
   (concurrent use may increase the risk of hepatotoxicity and should be avoided)

» Immunosuppressants, other, such as:
   Adrenocorticoids, glucocorticoid
   Azathioprine
   Chlorambucil
   Corticotropin (ACTH)
   Cyclophosphamide
   Cyclosporine
   Muromonab-CD3
   (concurrent use with mercaptopurine may increase the risk of infection and development of neoplasms)

Vaccines, killed virus
   (because normal defense mechanisms may be suppressed by mercaptopurine therapy, the patient's antibody response to the vaccine may be decreased. The interval between discontinuation of medications that cause immunosuppression and restoration of the patient's ability to respond to the vaccine depends on the intensity and type of immunosuppression-causing medication used, the underlying disease, and other factors; estimates vary from 3 months to 1 year)

» Vaccines, live virus
   (because normal defense mechanisms may be suppressed by mercaptopurine therapy, concurrent use with a live virus vaccine may potentiate the replication of the vaccine virus, may increase the side/adverse effects of the vaccine virus, and/or may decrease the patient's antibody response to the vaccine; immunization of these patients should be undertaken only with extreme caution after careful review of the patient's hematologic status and only with the knowledge and consent of the physician managing the mercaptopurine therapy. The interval between discontinuation of medications that cause immunosuppression and restoration of the patient's ability to respond to the vaccine depends on the intensity and type of immunosuppression-causing medication used, the underlying disease, and other factors; estimates vary from 3 months to 1 year. Patients with leukemia in remission should not receive live virus vaccine until at least 3 months after their last chemotherapy. Immunization with oral poliovirus vaccine should also be postponed in persons in close contact with the patient, especially family members)

Contraindications/Medical problems

The contraindications/medical problems included have been selected on the basis of their potential clinical significance (reasons given in parentheses where appropriate)—not necessarily inclusive (» = major clinical significance).

Risk-benefit should be considered when the following medical problems exist:

» Bone marrow depression
» Chickenpox, existing or recent (including recent exposure), or
» Herpes zoster
   (risk of severe generalized disease)

Gout, history of, or
Urate renal stones, history of
   (risk of hyperuricemia)

» Hepatic function impairment
   (lower dosage recommended)

» Infection

» Renal function impairment
   (lower dosage recommended)

Sensitivity to mercaptopurine

» Caution should be used also in patients who have had previous cytotoxic drug therapy and radiation therapy.

Side/Adverse Effects

Note: Many "side effects" of antineoplastic therapy are unavoidable and represent the medication's pharmacologic action. Some of these (for example, leukopenia and thrombocytopenia) are actually used as parameters to aid in individual dosage titration.

The following side/adverse effects have been selected on the basis of their potential clinical significance (possible signs and symptoms in parentheses where appropriate)—not necessarily inclusive:

Those indicating need for medical attention
Incidence more frequent
> *Anemia* (unusual tiredness or weakness); *hepatotoxicity or biliary stasis* (yellow eyes or skin); *immunosuppression, leukopenia, or infection* (usually asymptomatic; less frequently, fever or chills, cough or hoarseness, lower back or side pain, painful or difficult urination); *thrombocytopenia* (usually asymptomatic; less frequently, unusual bleeding or bruising; black, tarry stools; blood in urine or stools; pinpoint red spots on skin)
>
> Note: *Anemia* occurs with high doses.
>
>> *Leukopenia* and *thrombocytopenia* (usually mild) may begin 5 to 6 days after initiation of therapy and persist about 7 days after withdrawal.

Incidence less frequent
> *Hyperuricemia or uric acid nephropathy* (joint pain, lower back or side pain, swelling of feet or lower legs); *loss of appetite or nausea and vomiting*
>
> Note: *Hyperuricemia* and *uric acid nephropathy* occur most commonly during initial treatment of patients with leukemia or lymphoma, as a result of rapid cell breakdown which leads to elevated serum uric acid concentrations.
>
>> Crystals of mercaptopurine have been found in urine of children receiving high dosage (1000 mg per square meter of body surface daily).
>>
>> *Loss of appetite* or *nausea and vomiting* may be symptoms of overdosage.

Incidence rare
> *Gastrointestinal ulceration* (black, tarry stools; stomach pain); *stomatitis* (sores in mouth and on lips)
>
> Note: *Stomatitis* is common with large doses.

Those indicating need for medical attention only if they continue or are bothersome
Incidence less frequent
> *Darkening of skin; diarrhea; headache; skin rash and itching; weakness*

Those indicating need for medical attention if they occur after medication is discontinued
> *Bone marrow depression* (black, tarry stools; blood in urine or stools; cough or hoarseness; fever or chills; lower back or side pain; painful or difficult urination; pinpoint red spots on skin; unusual bleeding or bruising); *hepatotoxicity* (yellow eyes or skin)

Patient Consultation

Consider advising the patient on the following:

Before using this medication
> Advisability of using nonhormonal contraception; telling physician immediately if pregnancy is suspected
>
> See also *Precautions to Consider*.

Proper use of this medication
» Importance of not taking more or less medication than the amount prescribed
> Caution in taking combination therapy; taking each medication at the right time
> Importance of ample fluid intake and subsequent increase in urine output to aid in excretion of uric acid
> Checking with physician if vomiting occurs shortly after dose is taken
> Missed dose: Not taking at all; not doubling doses
» Proper storage

Precautions while using this medication
» Importance of close monitoring by the physician
» Possibility of increased toxicity if alcohol is ingested
» Avoiding immunizations unless approved by physician; other persons in patient's household should avoid immunizations with oral poliovirus vaccine; avoiding other persons who have taken oral poliovirus vaccine or wearing a protective mask that covers nose and mouth
> Caution if bone marrow depression occurs:
» Avoiding exposure to persons with bacterial infections, especially during periods of low blood counts; checking with physician immediately if fever or chills, cough or hoarseness, lower back or side pain, or painful or difficult urination occur
» Checking with physician immediately if unusual bleeding or bruising; black, tarry stools; blood in urine or stools; or pinpoint red spots on skin occur
> Caution in use of regular toothbrush, dental floss, or toothpick; physician, dentist, or nurse may suggest alternatives; checking with physician before having dental work done
> Not touching eyes or inside of nose unless hands washed immediately before
> Using caution to avoid accidental cuts with use of sharp objects such as safety razor or fingernail or toenail cutters
> Avoiding contact sports or other situations where bruising or injury could occur
> Caution if any laboratory tests required; possible interference with serum glucose and uric acid values measured by sequential multiple analyzer (SMA)

Side/adverse effects
> May cause adverse effects such as blood problems, liver problems, and cancer; importance of discussing possible effects with physician
> Signs of potential side effects, especially anemia, hepatotoxicity, biliary stasis, immunosuppression, leukopenia, infection, thrombocytopenia, hyperuricemia, uric acid nephropathy, gastrointestinal ulceration, and stomatitis
> Physician or nurse can help in dealing with side effects

General Dosing Information

Patients receiving mercaptopurine should be under supervision of a physician experienced in immunosuppressive and antimetabolite chemotherapy.

A variety of dosage schedules and regimens of mercaptopurine, alone or in combination with other antitumor agents, are used. The prescriber may consult the medical literature as well as the manufacturer's literature in choosing a specific dosage.

Dosage must be adjusted to meet the individual requirements of each patient, based on clinical response and appearance or severity of toxicity.

Development of uric acid nephropathy in patients with leukemia or lymphoma may be prevented by adequate oral hydration. Alkalinization of urine may be necessary if serum uric acid concentrations are elevated. Allopurinol should be administered with caution and only if uric acid concentrations are unacceptably high.

It is recommended that mercaptopurine dosage be reduced to one-third to one-fourth of the usual dosage in patients receiving 300 to 600 mg of allopurinol a day concurrently to reduce or prevent hyperuricemia or to slow the metabolism of mercaptopurine.

Because the actions of mercaptopurine may be delayed, it is recommended that mercaptopurine therapy be discontinued promptly at the first sign of marked leukopenia (particularly granulocytopenia) or thrombocytopenia, hemorrhage or bleeding tendencies, or jaundice. Therapy may be resumed at one-half the previous dosage when the leukocyte count remains constant for 2 or 3 days, or rises.

In acute leukemia, mercaptopurine may be administered despite the presence of thrombocytopenia and bleeding; stoppage of bleeding and increase in platelet count have occurred during treatment in some cases and platelet transfusions may be useful in others.

Special precautions are recommended in patients who develop thrombocytopenia as a result of administration of mercaptopurine. These may include extreme care in performing invasive procedures; regular inspection of intravenous sites, skin (including perirectal area), and mucous membrane surfaces for signs of bleeding or bruising; limiting frequency of venipuncture and avoiding intramuscular injections; testing urine, emesis, stool, and secretions for occult blood; care in use of regular toothbrushes, dental floss, toothpicks, safety razors, and fingernail and toenail cutters; avoiding constipation; and using caution to prevent falls and other injuries. Such patients should avoid alcohol and any aspirin intake because of the risk of gastrointestinal bleeding. Platelet transfusions may be required.

Patients who develop leukopenia should be observed carefully for signs of infection. Antibiotic support may be required. In neutropenic patients who develop fever, broad-spectrum antibiotic coverage should be initiated empirically, pending bacterial cultures and appropriate diagnostic tests.

Combination chemotherapy

Mercaptopurine may be used in combination with other agents in various regimens. As a result, incidence and/or severity of side effects may be altered and different dosages (usually reduced) may be used. For example, mercaptopurine is part of the following chemotherapeutic combinations (some commonly used acronyms are in parentheses):

—daunorubicin, cytarabine, prednisolone, and mercaptopurine (Ara-C + DNR + PRED + MP).

—methotrexate and mercaptopurine (MTX + MP).

—methotrexate, mercaptopurine, and cyclophosphamide (MTX + MP + CTX).

For specific dosages and schedules, consult the literature. For information regarding each agent, consult the individual monographs.

Oral Dosage Forms

Note: Bracketed uses in the *Dosage Forms* section refer to categories of use and/or indications that are not included in U.S. product labeling.

MERCAPTOPURINE TABLETS USP

Usual adult dose:

Leukemia, acute lymphocytic; or

Leukemia, acute myelocytic; or

Leukemia, acute myelomonocytic—

Initial: Oral, 2.5 mg per kg of body weight or 80 to 100 mg per square meter of body surface (to the nearest 25 mg) a day in single or divided doses. If there is no clinical improvement and no leukocyte depression after four weeks at this dosage, an increase in dosage to 5 mg per kg of body weight a day may be attempted.

Maintenance: Oral, 1.5 to 2.5 mg per kg of body weight or 50 to 100 mg per square meter of body surface a day.

[Inflammatory bowel disease][1]—Oral, 1.5 mg per kg of body weight per day, the dosage being adjusted as necessary. If there is no clinical improvement and no leukocyte depression after two to three months at this dosage, a gradual increase in dosage to 2.5 mg per kg of body weight per day may be attempted.

MESALAMINE   Rectal-Local

INN: Mesalazine

Some commonly used *brand names* are:

In the U.S.—*Rowasa*

In Canada—*Salofalk*

Other commonly used names are 5-aminosalicylic acid and 5-ASA.

RECTAL

Mesalamine Rectal Suspension

In the U.S.—*Rowasa*

In Canada—*Salofalk*

Mesalamine Suppositories

In the U.S.—*Rowasa*

In Canada—*Salofalk*

Category: Bowel disease (inflammatory) suppressant.

Indications

Accepted

Bowel disease, inflammatory (treatment)—Mesalamine is indicated for the treatment of mild to moderate distal ulcerative colitis, proctosigmoiditis, and proctitis.

Pharmacology

Mechanism of action/Effect: Uncertain. Mesalamine, by blocking cyclooxygenase and inhibiting prostaglandin production in the colon, appears to produce a local inhibitory effect on the mucosal production of arachidonic acid metabolites, which are increased in patients with chronic inflammatory bowel disease.

Precautions to Consider

Cross-sensitivity and/or related problems

Patients sensitive to olsalazine, sulfasalazine, or salicylates may be sensitive to mesalamine also.

Geriatrics

No information is available on the relationship of age to the effects of mesalamine in geriatric patients.

Drug interactions and/or related problems

The following drug interactions and/or related problems have been selected on the basis of their potential clinical significance (possible mechanism in parentheses where appropriate)—not necessarily inclusive (» = major clinical significance):

Note: Combinations containing any of the following medications, depending on the amount present, may also interact with this medication.

Sulfasalazine, oral
(concurrent use may increase the risk of renal toxicity)

Contraindications/Medical problems

The contraindications/medical problems included have been selected on the basis of their potential clinical significance (reasons given in parentheses where appropriate)—not necessarily inclusive (» = major clinical significance).

Risk-benefit should be considered when the following medical problems exist:

Renal function impairment
(although absorption of mesalamine is limited, the possibility of increased risk of renal damage should be considered)
Sensitivity to mesalamine

Side/Adverse Effects

The following side/adverse effects have been selected on the basis of their potential clinical significance (possible signs and symptoms in parentheses where appropriate)—not necessarily inclusive:

Those indicating need for medical attention

Incidence rare
Anal irritation; intolerance syndrome, acute (severe abdominal or stomach cramps or pain, bloody diarrhea, fever, severe headache, skin rash)
Note: Prompt withdrawal of mesalamine is recommended at the first signs of the *intolerance syndrome,* particularly in patients with a known allergy to sulfasalazine.

Those indicating need for medical attention only if they continue or are bothersome

Incidence more frequent
Abdominal or stomach cramps or pain, mild; gas or flatulence; headache, mild; nausea

Incidence less frequent or rare
Loss of hair

Patient Consultation

In providing consultation, consider emphasizing the following selected information (» = major clinical significance):

Before using this medication

» Conditions affecting use, especially:
Sensitivity to mesalamine, olsalazine, sulfasalazine, or salicylates
Other medical problems, especially renal function impairment

Proper use of this medication

Reading patient directions carefully before using
Emptying bowel immediately prior to enema, for best results

» Compliance with full course of therapy
Missed dose: Using as soon as possible if remembered same night; using next dose at regularly scheduled time; not doubling doses
» Proper storage

Precautions while using this medication

Regular visits to physician to check progress
Checking with physician if signs of rectal irritation occur

Side/adverse effects

Signs of potential side effects, especially anal irritation and intolerance syndrome

General Dosing Information

Mesalamine rectal suspension should be used at bedtime with the objective of retaining it all night.

For best results, bowel should be emptied immediately prior to the rectal administration of mesalamine.

Response to therapy with mesalamine may occur within 3 to 21 days; however, the usual course of therapy is from 3 to 6 weeks depending on symptoms and sigmoidoscopic examinations.

After remission, some patients may be maintained on a less than nightly schedule; however, the possibility of relapse increases as the frequency of mesalamine enema administration is decreased.

Rectal Dosage Forms

MESALAMINE RECTAL SUSPENSION

Usual adult and adolescent dose: Bowel disease (inflammatory) suppressant—Rectal, 4 grams as a retention enema each night for three to six weeks.
Note: For maintenance therapy—Alternate days or every third day intervals, or lower doses (1 or 2 grams) have been used; however, optimal maintenance regimen has not been determined.

Usual geriatric dose: See *Usual adult and adolescent dose.*

Auxiliary labeling:
• For rectal use.
• Shake well.

MESALAMINE SUPPOSITORIES

Usual adult and adolescent dose: Bowel disease (inflammatory) suppressant—Rectal, 500 mg two or three times a day.

Usual geriatric dose: See *Usual adult and adolescent dose.*

Auxiliary labeling: • For rectal use.

METHENAMINE   Systemic

Some commonly used *brand names* are:
In the U.S.—*Hiprex; Mandelamine; Urex*
In Canada—*Hip-Rex; Mandelamine*

ORAL

Methenamine Hippurate Tablets USP
In the U.S.—*Hiprex; Urex*
In Canada—*Hip-Rex*
Methenamine Mandelate for Oral Solution USP (Granules)†
In the U.S.—*Mandelamine*

Methenamine Mandelate Oral Suspension USP†
In the U.S.—*Mandelamine;* GENERIC
Methenamine Mandelate Tablets USP (Enteric-coated)†
In the U.S.—GENERIC
Methenamine Mandelate Tablets USP
In the U.S.—*Mandelamine;* GENERIC
In Canada—*Mandelamine*

---

†Not commercially available in Canada.

Category: Antibacterial (systemic).

Indications

Accepted

Urinary tract infections, bacterial (prophylaxis); or

Urinary tract infections, bacterial (treatment)—Methenamine is indicated in the prophylaxis of urinary tract infections in patients with sterile urine after the eradication of urinary tract infections by other antibacterials.

Methenamine is indicated in the treatment of uncomplicated lower urinary tract infections and in the suppressive treatment of urinary tract infections in patients with neurogenic bladder or in patients being catheterized intermittently.

Virtually all bacteria and fungi are susceptible to the nonspecific action of free formaldehyde produced by the hydrolysis of methenamine.

Unaccepted

Methenamine is not recommended when urine acidification to a pH of 5.5 or below is contraindicated or unattainable.

Methenamine is not effective in patients with indwelling urinary catheters.

Pharmacology

Mechanism of action/Effect: Methenamine, an inactive weak base, slowly hydrolyzes in acidic urine to ammonia and the nonspecific antibacterial, formaldehyde. Formaldehyde is thought to act by denaturation of protein. Urinary formaldehyde concentrations may be bactericidal or bacteriostatic, depending on urine pH (which controls the amount of formaldehyde released), volume, and flow rate. Most organisms are susceptible and resistance does not develop. Acids that dissociate from the hippurate or mandelate salt may contribute to maintenance of acidic urinary pH and liberation of formaldehyde.

Precautions to Consider

Geriatrics

No information is available on the relationship of age to the effects of methenamine in geriatric patients.

Drug interactions and/or related problems

The following drug interactions and/or related problems have been selected on the basis of their potential clinical significance (possible mechanism in parentheses where appropriate)—not necessarily inclusive (» = major clinical significance):

Note: Combinations containing any of the following medications, depending on the amount present, may also interact with this medication.

» Alkalizers, urinary, such as:
  Antacids, calcium- and/or magnesium-containing
  Carbonic anhydrase inhibitors
  Citrates
  Sodium bicarbonate or
» Diuretics, thiazide
  (may cause the urine to become alkaline, thereby reducing the effectiveness of methenamine by inhibiting its conversion to formaldehyde; concurrent use is not recommended)

  Sulfamethizole
  (in acid urine methenamine breaks down into formaldehyde, which may form an insoluble precipitate with sulfamethizole, and may also increase the danger of crystalluria; concurrent use is not recommended)

Contraindications/Medical problems

The contraindications/medical problems included have been selected on the basis of their potential clinical significance (reasons given in parentheses where appropriate)—not necessarily inclusive (» = major clinical significance).

Risk-benefit should be considered when the following medical problems exist:

  Dehydration, severe, or
» Renal function impairment, severe
  (salts of methenamine may precipitate, causing crystalluria, in patients with a low urine output)
» Hepatic function impairment, severe
  (because methenamine is hydrolyzed to ammonia, it should not be given to patients with severe hepatic impairment)
  Hypersensitivity to methenamine

Side/Adverse Effects

Note: Large doses of methenamine (8 grams daily for 3 to 4 weeks) have been reported to cause bladder irritation, painful and frequent urination, and gross hematuria.

The following side/adverse effects have been selected on the basis of their potential clinical significance (possible signs and symptoms in parentheses where appropriate)—not necessarily inclusive:

Those indicating need for medical attention
Incidence less frequent
  Skin rash
Incidence rare
  Crystalluria or hematuria (blood in urine, lower back pain, pain or burning while urinating)

Those indicating need for medical attention only if they continue or are bothersome
Incidence less frequent
  Gastrointestinal disturbance (nausea and vomiting)

Patient Consultation

In providing consultation, consider emphasizing the following selected information (» = major clinical significance):

Before using this medication
» Conditions affecting use, especially:
  Hypersensitivity to methenamine
  Pregnancy—Methenamine crosses the placenta
  Breast-feeding—Methenamine is excreted in breast milk
  Other medications, especially urinary alkalinizers or thiazide diuretics
  Other medical problems, especially severe hepatic function impairment or severe renal function impairment

Proper use of this medication
» Using phenaphthazine paper or other test and dietary measures to measure and appropriately adjust urine pH; importance of maintaining acidic urine (pH 5.5 or below)
  Taking after meals and at bedtime if nausea or gastrointestinal irritation occurs
  Proper administration technique for dry granules, oral liquids, and enteric-coated tablets
» Compliance with full course of therapy
  Missed dose: Taking as soon as possible; if almost time for next dose and dosing schedule is—
    2 doses a day: Spacing missed dose and next dose 5 to 6 hours apart
    3 or more doses a day: Spacing missed dose and next dose 2 to 4 hours apart
» Proper storage

Precautions while using this medication
  Checking with physician if no improvement within a few days

Side/adverse effects
  Signs of potential side effects, especially crystalluria, hematuria, and skin rash

General Dosing Information

Urine pH should be monitored before starting and throughout therapy since the effectiveness of methenamine is increased if a pH of 5.5 or below is maintained. To check urine pH, phenaphthazine paper, which has a pH range of 4.5 to 7.5, may be used.

To maintain a urine pH of 5.5 or below, most fruits (especially citrus fruits and juices), milk and other dairy products, and other alkalinizing foods should be avoided. A protein-rich diet with liberal amounts of cranberries (especially ascorbic acid-enriched cranberry juice), plums, or prunes may be helpful. If these measures do not produce a sufficiently acid urine, they may be supplemented with large doses of ascorbic acid (4 grams or more per day), arginine hydrochloride, or methionine. However, some brands of ascorbic acid may contain varying amounts of ascorbate sodium and may actually alkalinize the urine. Alternatively, ammonium chloride or sodium biphosphate may be given (caution—large doses of ammonium chloride may cause metabolic acidosis in patients with impaired renal function and may be contraindicated in patients with hepatic insufficiency).

Methenamine may be taken after meals and at bedtime to help minimize nausea or gastrointestinal irritation.

Urea-splitting organisms (e.g., *Proteus mirabilis* and some strains of *Pseudomonas* and *Enterobacter*) may cause an increase in urine pH and thereby decrease the effectiveness of methenamine. Care should be taken to ensure urine acidification.

If recurrent urinary tract infections are prevented by 4 grams of methenamine mandelate daily, the dose may be reduced to a maintenance level of 1 gram of the mandelate two times a day. However, close observation of the patient is recommended to ensure the continued effectiveness of the lower dose of medication.

Methenamine may cause dysuria, which may be controlled by reducing the dose and the urinary acidification.

Oral Dosage Forms

METHENAMINE HIPPURATE TABLETS USP

Usual adult and adolescent dose: Oral, 1 gram two times a day, morning and evening.

Usual adult prescribing limits: Up to 4 grams daily.

Auxiliary labeling:
- Maintain acid urine.
- Continue medicine for full time of treatment.

METHENAMINE MANDELATE FOR ORAL SOLUTION USP (GRANULES)

Usual adult and adolescent dose: Oral, 1 gram four times a day, after meals and at bedtime.

Usual adult prescribing limits: Up to 12 grams daily.

Auxiliary labeling:
- Maintain acid urine.
- Dissolve in water before taking.
- Continue medicine for full time of treatment.

METHENAMINE MANDELATE ORAL SUSPENSION USP

Usual adult and adolescent dose: See *Methenamine Mandelate for Oral Solution USP (Granules)*.

Usual adult prescribing limits: See *Methenamine Mandelate for Oral Solution USP (Granules)*.

Auxiliary labeling:
- Maintain acid urine.
- Shake well.
- Continue medicine for full time of treatment.

METHENAMINE MANDELATE TABLETS USP (ENTERIC-COATED)

Usual adult and adolescent dose: See *Methenamine Mandelate for Oral Solution USP (Granules)*.

Usual adult prescribing limits: See *Methenamine Mandelate for Oral Solution USP (Granules)*.

Auxiliary labeling:
- Maintain acid urine.
- Swallow tablets whole.
- Continue medicine for full time of treatment.

METHENAMINE MANDELATE TABLETS USP

Usual adult and adolescent dose: See *Methenamine Mandelate for Oral Solution USP (Granules)*.

Usual adult prescribing limits: See *Methenamine Mandelate for Oral Solution USP (Granules)*.

Auxiliary labeling:
- Maintain acid urine.
- Swallow tablets whole.
- Continue medicine for full time of treatment.

METHOTREXATE—For Cancer   Systemic

Some commonly used *brand names* in the U.S. are:

Folex	*Mexate*
Folex PFS	*Mexate-AQ*

Another commonly used name is amethopterin.

ORAL
Methotrexate Tablets USP
  In the U.S. and Canada—GENERIC

PARENTERAL
Methotrexate Sodium Injection USP
  In the U.S.—*Folex PFS; Mexate-AQ;* GENERIC
  In Canada—GENERIC

Methotrexate Sodium for Injection USP
  In the U.S.—*Folex; Mexate;* GENERIC
  In Canada—GENERIC

Category: Antineoplastic.

Indications

Note: Bracketed information in the *Indications* section refers to uses that are not included in U.S. product labeling.

Accepted
Carcinoma, breast (treatment);[1]
Carcinoma, head and neck (treatment);[1]
Carcinoma, lung (treatment);[1]

Tumors, trophoblastic (treatment);
[Carcinoma, cervical (treatment)][1];
[Carcinoma, ovarian (treatment)][1];
[Carcinoma, bladder (treatment)][1];
[Carcinoma, renal (treatment)][1];
[Carcinoma, prostatic (treatment)][1]; or
[Carcinoma, testicular (treatment)][1]—Methotrexate is indicated for treatment of breast carcinoma, head and neck cancers (epidermoid), lung carcinoma (especially squamous cell and small cell types), trophoblastic tumors (gestational choriocarcinoma, chorioadenoma destruens, hydatidiform mole), cervical carcinoma, ovarian carcinoma, bladder carcinoma, renal carcinoma, prostatic carcinoma, and testicular carcinoma.

Leukemia, acute lymphocytic (treatment);
Leukemia, meningeal (prophylaxis and treatment); or
[Leukemia, acute myelocytic (treatment)][1]—Methotrexate is indicated for treatment of acute lymphocytic leukemia, prophylaxis and treatment of meningeal leukemia, and treatment of acute myelocytic leukemia.

Lymphomas, non-Hodgkin's (treatment)—Methotrexate is indicated for treatment of non-Hodgkin's lymphomas, including advanced cases of lymphosarcoma (particularly in children).

Mycosis fungoides (treatment)—Methotrexate is indicated for treatment of advanced cases of mycosis fungoides.

Osteosarcoma (treatment)[1]—Methotrexate is indicated in high doses along with leucovorin rescue, in combination with other agents, for treatment of nonmetastatic osteosarcoma in patients who have undergone primary surgical treatment.

[Multiple myeloma (treatment)][1]—Methotrexate is used for treatment of multiple myeloma.

---

[1]Not included in Canadian product labeling.

Pharmacology

Mechanism of action/Effect: Methotrexate is an antimetabolite of the folic acid analog type. Methotrexate is cell cycle-specific for the S phase of cell division. Activity is due to inhibition of DNA, RNA, thymidylate, and protein synthesis as a result of relatively irreversible binding with dihydrofolate reductase, which prevents reduction of dihydrofolate to the active tetrahydrofolate. Growth of rapidly proliferating cells (malignant cells, bone marrow, fetal cells, buccal and intestinal mucosa, cells of the urinary bladder, spermatogonia) is affected more than growth of most normal tissues and skin.

Other actions/effects: Also has mild immunosuppressant activity.

Precautions to Consider

Geriatrics

Although appropriate studies with methotrexate have not been performed in the geriatric population, caution should be used in the elderly because of possible reduced renal and hepatic function and reduced folate stores. Dosage adjustment, especially on the basis of renal function, may be necessary.

Dental

The bone marrow depressant effects of methotrexate may result in an increased incidence of microbial infection, delayed healing, and gingival bleeding. Dental work, whenever possible, should be completed prior to initiation of therapy or deferred until blood counts have returned to normal. Patients should be instructed in proper oral hygiene during treatment, including caution in use of regular toothbrushes, dental floss, and toothpicks.

Methotrexate also commonly causes ulcerative stomatitits, gingivitis, and pharyngitis associated with considerable discomfort.

Drug interactions and/or related problems

The following drug interactions and/or related problems have been selected on the basis of their potential clinical significance (possible mechanism in parentheses where appropriate)—not necessarily inclusive (» = major clinical significance):

　Note: Combinations containing any of the following medications, depending on the amount present, may also interact with this medication.

» Acyclovir, parenteral
　(concurrent administration of intrathecal methotrexate with acyclovir may result in neurological abnormalities; use with caution)

» Alcohol or
» Hepatotoxic medications, other
　(concurrent use may increase the risk of hepatotoxicity)

　Allopurinol or
　Colchicine or
» Probenecid or
» Sulfinpyrazone
　(methotrexate may raise the concentration of blood uric acid; dosage adjustment of antigout agents may be necessary to control hyperuricemia and gout; allopurinol may be preferred to prevent or reverse methotrexate-induced hyperuricemia because of risk of uric acid nephropathy with uricosuric antigout agents)

　Anticoagulants, coumarin- or indandione-derivative
　(methotrexate may increase anticoagulant activity and/or increase the risk of hemorrhage as a result of decreased hepatic synthesis of procoagulant factors and interference with platelet formation)

» Anti-inflammatory analgesics, nonsteroidal (NSAIAs)
　(concurrent use of phenylbutazone with methotrexate may increase the risk of agranulocytosis or bone marrow depression and is not recommended; also, phenylbutazone may displace methotrexate from its protein-binding sites and decrease its renal clearance, leading to increased methotrexate plasma concentration and risk of toxicity, especially during high-dose methotrexate infusion therapy. If concurrent use with phenylbutazone cannot be avoided, especially careful monitoring of the patient for plasma methotrexate concentrations or signs of methotrexate toxicity and/or adequacy of renal function is recommended; also, phenylbutazone therapy should be discontinued for 7 to 12 days prior to, and for at least 12 hours [depending on plasma methotrexate concentrations] following, administration of a high-dose methotrexate infusion)

　(administration of high-dose methotrexate infusions to patients receiving diflunisal or ketoprofen has resulted in severe and [with ketoprofen] sometimes fatal methotrexate toxicity; a few fatalities have also occurred in patients receiving intermediate-dose methotrexate infusions concurrently with indomethacin, possibly because of decreased methotrexate excretion leading to increased and prolonged methotrexate plasma concentration; however, severe methotrexate toxicity did not occur when ketoprofen was administered 12 hours following completion of the methotrexate infusion. It is recommended that NSAIA therapy be discontinued for 24 to 48 hours [for diflunisal] or 12 to 24 hours [for ketoprofen] prior to, and for at least 12 hours [depending on plasma methotrexate concentrations] following, a high-dose methotrexate infusion and that indomethacin be discontinued for 24 to 48 hours prior to, and for at least 12 hours [depending on plasma methotrexate concentrations] following, administration of an intermediate- or high-dose methotrexate infusion)

　(although not well documented, the possibility exists that other NSAIAs may also decrease methotrexate excretion and increase its plasma concentration to potentially toxic levels; it is recommended that NSAIA therapy be discontinued for 12 to 24 hours [for NSAIAs with a short elimination half-life] up to 10 days [for piroxicam] prior to, and for at least 12 hours [depending on plasma methotrexate concentrations] following, administration of a high-dose methotrexate infusion)

(severe, sometimes fatal, methotrexate toxicity has also been reported with low to moderate doses in patients receiving diclofenac, indomethacin, naproxen, or phenylbutazone]; it is recommended that use of NSAIAs with low to moderate doses of methotrexate be undertaken with caution, with methotrexate dosage being adjusted by monitoring plasma methotrexate concentrations and/or adequacy of renal function)

» Asparaginase

(concurrent use may block the effects of methotrexate by inhibiting cell replication; this inhibition of methotrexate's action appears to correlate with suppression of asparagine concentrations. Some studies indicate that administration of asparaginase 9 to 10 days before or within 24 hours after methotrexate does not produce this inhibition of antineoplastic effect and may reduce the gastrointestinal and hematological effects of methotrexate)

Blood dyscrasia-causing medications

(leukopenic and/or thrombocytopenic effects of methotrexate may be increased with concurrent or recent therapy if these medications cause the same effects; dosage adjustment of methotrexate, if necessary, should be based on blood counts)

» Bone marrow depressants, other or
  Radiation therapy

(additive bone marrow depression may occur; dosage reduction may be required when two or more bone marrow depressants, including radiation, are used concurrently or consecutively)

(leukoencephalopathy has been reported following intravenous methotrexate administration to patients who have received craniospinal irradiation)

Cytarabine

(administration of cytarabine 48 hours before or 10 minutes after initiation of methotrexate therapy may result in a synergistic cytotoxic effect; however, evidence is inconclusive and dosage adjustment based on routine hematologic monitoring is recommended)

Folic acid

(may interfere with the antifolate effects of methotrexate)

Neomycin, oral

(may decrease absorption of oral methotrexate)

» Probenecid

(concurrent use may inhibit renal excretion of methotrexate and result in toxic plasma concentrations; if used concurrently with probenecid, methotrexate dosage should be decreased, the patient observed for signs of toxicity, and/or plasma methotrexate concentrations monitored)

Pyrimethamine or
Triamterene or
Trimethoprim

(concurrent use may rarely increase the toxic effects of methotrexate because of similar folic acid antagonist actions)

» Salicylates and other weak organic acids

(concurrent use may inhibit renal tubular secretion of methotrexate and result in toxic plasma concentrations; salicylates may also increase plasma concentrations by displacing methotrexate from binding sites; if methotrexate is used concurrently with these medications, the patient should be observed for signs of toxicity and/or methotrexate plasma concentration monitored. In addition, it is recommended that salicylate therapy be discontinued for 24 to 48 hours prior to, and for at least 12 hours [depending on plasma methotrexate concentrations] following, administration of a high-dose methotrexate infusion)

Sulfonamides

(in addition to increased risk of hepatotoxicity that may occur when sulfonamides are used concurrently with other hepatotoxic medications, medications that cause displacement from plasma protein binding may theoretically produce toxic plasma concentrations of methotrexate when used concurrently, although clinical significance has not been established)

Vaccines, killed virus

(because normal defense mechanisms may be suppressed by methotrexate therapy, the patient's antibody response to the vaccine may be decreased. The interval between discontinuation of medications that cause immunosuppression and restoration of the patient's ability to respond to the vaccine depends on the intensity and type of immunosuppression-causing medication used, the underlying disease, and other factors; estimates vary from 3 months to 1 year)

» Vaccines, live virus

(because normal defense mechanisms may be suppressed by methotrexate therapy, concurrent use with a live virus vaccine may potentiate the replication of the vaccine virus, may increase the side/adverse effects of the vaccine virus, and/or may decrease the patient's antibody response to the vaccine; immunization of these patients should be undertaken only with extreme caution after careful review of the patient's hematologic status and only with the knowledge and consent of the physician managing the methotrexate therapy. The interval between discontinuation of medications that cause immunosuppression and restoration of the patient's ability to respond to the vaccine depends on the intensity and type of immunosuppression-causing medication used, the underlying disease, and other factors; estimates vary from 3 months to 1 year. Patients with leukemia in remission should not receive live virus vaccine until at least 3 months after their last chemotherapy. Immunization with oral poliovirus vaccine should also be postponed in persons in close contact with the patient, especially family members)

Contraindications/Medical problems

The contraindications/medical problems included have been selected on the basis of their potential clinical significance (reasons given in parentheses where appropriate)—not necessarily inclusive (» = major clinical significance).

Except under special circumstances, this medication should not be used when the following medical problem exists:

» Immunodeficiency

Risk-benefit should be considered when the following medical problems exist:

Aciduria (urine pH less than 7) or
» Ascites or
Dehydration or
Gastrointestinal obstruction or
» Pleural or peritoneal effusions or
» Renal function impairment

(risk of methotrexate toxicity is increased because elimination of methotrexate may be impaired and accumulation may occur; even small doses may lead to severe myelosuppression and mucositis; larger doses and/or increased duration of leucovorin treatment, if used, may be necessary, along with careful monitoring of methotrexate concentrations)

(a lower dosage of methotrexate and careful monitoring of plasma or serum methotrexate concentrations are recommended for patients with impaired renal function)

» Bone marrow depression

» Chickenpox, existing or recent (including recent exposure), or
» Herpes zoster

(risk of severe generalized disease)

Gout, history of, or
Urate renal stones, history of

(risk of hyperuricemia)

» Hepatic function impairment
» Infection
» Mucositis, oral
   Nausea and vomiting
      (inadequate hydration secondary to severe nausea and vomiting may result in increased methotrexate toxicity)
» Peptic ulcer
   Sensitivity to methotrexate
» Ulcerative colitis
» Caution should be used also in patients who have had previous cytotoxic drug therapy and radiation therapy, and in cases of general debility.

Side/Adverse Effects

Note: Many "side effects" of antineoplastic therapy are unavoidable and represent the medication's pharmacologic action. Some of these (for example, leukopenia and thrombocytopenia) are actually used as parameters to aid in individual dosage titration.

Incidence and severity of side effects, particularly hepatotoxicity, appear to be related to dosage frequency and duration of methotrexate therapy. Toxicity tends to occur less frequently and be less severe with a total dose administered as intermittent weekly dosage than with prolonged daily dosage.

The following side/adverse effects have been selected on the basis of their potential clinical significance (possible signs and symptoms in parentheses where appropriate)—not necessarily inclusive:

Those indicating need for medical attention
Incidence more frequent
   Gastrointestinal ulceration and bleeding, enteritis, or intestinal perforation, which may be fatal (black, tarry stools; bloody vomit; diarrhea; stomach pain); *leukopenia, bacterial infection, or septicemia* (usually asymptomatic; less frequently, fever or chills, cough or hoarseness, lower back or side pain, painful or difficult urination); *thrombocytopenia* (usually asymptomatic; less frequently, unusual bleeding or bruising; black, tarry stools; blood in urine or stools; pinpoint red spots on skin); *stomatitis, ulcerative, gingivitis, or pharyngitis* (sores in mouth and on lips)
   Note: With *leukopenia* and *thrombocytopenia* the nadir of the leukocyte and platelet counts occurs after 7 to 10 days, with recovery 7 days later.
Incidence more frequent (with high-dose therapy)
   Renal failure, azotemia, hyperuricemia, or servere nephropathy (blood in urine, joint pain, swelling of feet or lower legs); *severe acute methotrexate toxicity, cutaneous vasculitis, or reactivation of sunburn or increased erythematous response to ultraviolet therapy* (reddening of skin)
   Note: *Hyperuricemia* and *uric acid nephropathy* occur most commonly during initial treatment of patients with leukemia or lymphoma, as a result of rapid cell breakdown which leads to elevated serum uric acid concentrations. With high-dose methotrexate therapy, symptoms resembling uric acid nephropathy may also be due to renal tubular damage resulting from precipitation of methotrexate or metabolites in the urine.
Incidence less frequent, more frequent with prolonged daily therapy
   Hepatotoxicity, including liver atrophy, necrosis, cirrhosis, fatty changes, periportal fibrosis (dark urine, yellow eyes or skin); *pneumonitis, potentially fatal, or pulmonary fibrosis* (cough, shortness of breath)
Incidence less frequent, more frequent with intrathecal or prolonged high-dose administration
   Central nervous system (CNS) effects, increased cerebrospinal fluid pressure, leukoencephalopathy, demyelination, or chemical arachnoiditis (back pain, blurred vision, confusion, convulsions, dizziness, drowsiness, fever, headache, unusual tiredness or weakness)

Those indicating need for medical attention only if they continue or are bothersome
Incidence more frequent
   Loss of appetite; nausea or vomiting
Incidence less frequent
   Acne; boils; pale skin; skin rash or itching

Those not indicating need for medical attention
Incidence less frequent
   Loss of hair

Those indicating need for medical attention if they occur after medication is discontinued
   CNS toxicity (encephalopathy, especially after intrathecal administration, or CNS leukemia) (back pain; blurred vision; confusion; convulsions; dizziness; drowsiness; fever; headache; unusual tiredness or weakness)

Patient Consultation

Consider advising the patient on the following (» = major clinical significance):

Before using this medication
   Advisability of using nonhormonal contraception; telling physician immediately if pregnancy is suspected
   See also *Precautions to Consider.*

Proper use of this medication
» Importance of not taking more or less medication than the amount prescribed
   Caution in taking combination therapy; taking each medication at the right time
   Importance of ample fluid intake and subsequent increase in urine output to prevent nephrotoxicity and aid in excretion of uric acid in some patients
» Frequency of nausea and vomiting; importance of continuing medication despite stomach upset
   Checking with physician if vomiting occurs shortly after dose is taken
   Missed dose: Not taking at all; not doubling doses
» Proper storage

Precautions while using this medication
» Importance of close monitoring by physician
» Avoiding alcoholic beverages, which may increase hepatotoxicity
   Possible photosensitivity reactions; avoiding too much unprotected exposure to sun or overuse of sunlamp
» Avoiding salicylate-containing products and nonsteroidal anti-inflammatories, which may increase toxicity
» Avoiding immunizations unless approved by physician; other persons in patient's household should avoid immunizations with oral poliovirus vaccine; avoiding other persons who have taken oral poliovirus vaccine or wearing a protective mask that covers nose and mouth
   Caution if bone marrow depression occurs:
» Avoiding exposure to persons with bacterial infections, especially during periods of low blood counts; checking with physician immediately if fever or chills, cough or hoarseness, lower back or side pain, or painful or difficult urination occur
» Checking with physician immediately if unusual bleeding or bruising; black, tarry stools; blood in urine or stools; or pinpoint red spots on skin occur
   Caution in use of regular toothbrush, dental floss, or toothpick; physician, dentist, or nurse may suggest alternatives; checking with physician before having dental work done
   Not touching eyes or inside of nose unless hands washed immediately before
   Using caution to avoid accidental cuts with use of sharp objects such as safety razor or fingernail or toenail cutters

> Avoiding contact sports or other situations where bruising or injury could occur

Side/adverse effects

> May cause adverse effects such as blood problems, stomach, kidney, or liver problems, loss of hair, or cancer; importance of discussing possible effects with physician
>
> Signs of potential side effects, especially gastrointestinal ulceration and bleeding, enteritis, intestinal perforation, leukopenia, bacterial infection, septicemia, thrombocytopenia, ulcerative stomatitis, gingivitis, pharyngitis, renal failure, azotemia, hyperuricemia, severe nephropathy, severe acute methotrexate toxicity, cutaneous vasculitis, reactivation of sunburn or reaction to ultraviolet light, hepatotoxicity, pneumonitis, pulmonary fibrosis, and CNS effects
>
> Physician or nurse can help in dealing with side effects
>
> Possibility of hair loss; should return after treatment has ended

General Dosing Information

Patients receiving methotrexate should be under supervision of a physician experienced in antineoplastic chemotherapy.

A variety of dosage schedules and regimens of methotrexate, alone or in combination with other antitumor agents, are used. The prescriber may consult the medical literature as well as the manufacturer's literature in choosing a specific dosage.

Dosage must be adjusted to meet the individual requirements of each patient, based on clinical response and appearance or severity of toxicity.

In general, use of intermittent courses of methotrexate is associated with less risk of serious toxicity than prolonged daily dosage.

A significant amount of methotrexate passes into systemic circulation after intrathecal administration and may produce toxic levels in patients also receiving systemic methotrexate therapy; an adjustment in systemic dosage may be necessary.

Development of uric acid nephropathy in patients with leukemia or lymphoma may be prevented by adequate oral hydration and, in some cases, administration of allopurinol. Alkalinization of urine may be necessary if serum uric acid concentrations are elevated.

If severe bone marrow depression occurs, withdrawal of methotrexate may be necessary. However, in some patients with acute leukemia, methotrexate may be administered despite the presence of thrombocytopenia and bleeding; stoppage of bleeding and increase in platelet count have occurred during treatment in some cases and platelet transfusions may be useful in others.

Special precautions are recommended in patients who develop thrombocytopenia as a result of administration of methotrexate. These may include extreme care in performing invasive procedures; regular inspection of intravenous sites, skin (including perirectal area), and mucous membrane surfaces for signs of bleeding or bruising; limiting frequency of venipuncture and avoiding intramuscular injections; testing urine, emesis, stool, and secretions for occult blood; care in use of regular toothbrushes, dental floss, toothpicks, safety razors, and fingernail and toenail cutters; avoiding constipation; and using caution to prevent falls and other injuries. Such patients should avoid alcohol and any aspirin intake because of the risk of gastrointestinal bleeding. Platelet transfusions may be required.

Patients who develop leukopenia should be observed carefully for signs of infection. Antibiotic support may be required. In neutropenic patients who develop fever, broad-spectrum antibiotic coverage should be initiated empirically, pending bacterial cultures and appropriate diagnostic tests.

It is recommended that methotrexate therapy be interrupted if diarrhea or ulcerative stomatitis occurs, because of the risk of hemorrhagic enteritis and fatal intestinal perforation.

It is recommended that methotrexate therapy be interrupted if pulmonary symptoms (especially a dry, unproductive cough) occur, because of the risk of potentially irreversible pulmonary toxicity.

For use in high-dose methotrexate therapy

Because of its ability to bypass the effects of methotrexate, leucovorin calcium (folinic acid, citrovorum factor) is administered as a "rescue" from the hematologic and gastrointestinal effects of high-dosage methotrexate.

High-dose methotrexate administration should not be initiated unless leucovorin is physically present and ready to be administered, since rescue is critical.

Methotrexate administration should not be initiated unless creatinine clearance and serum creatinine concentrations are normal. If renal function impairment develops during therapy, methotrexate should be withdrawn until renal function becomes acceptable.

A variety of dosage schedules of leucovorin in combination with high-dose methotrexate have been used. The prescriber should consult the medical literature in choosing a specific dosage. Alkalinization of urine (with bicarbonate and/or acetazolamide) and intravenous hydration (1000 mL per square meter of body surface over six hours prior to beginning the methotrexate infusion and 3000 mL per square meter of body surface per day during the methotrexate infusion and for two days after the infusion is completed) are also important to prevent renal toxicity caused by methotrexate and/or its metabolites.

Administration of leucovorin should be consecutive to rather than simultaneous with methotrexate administration so as not to interfere with methotrexate's antineoplastic effects.

In general, it is recommended that the first dose of leucovorin be administered within the first 24 to 42 hours of starting a high-dose methotrexate infusion (within 1 hour of an overdose), in a dosage to produce blood concentrations equal to or greater than methotrexate blood concentrations (leucovorin in a dose of 15 to 25 mg per square meter of body surface produces peak plasma concentrations of approximately 1 micromolar or 1×10^{-6} M). Duration of leucovorin administration varies with the dosage of methotrexate and plasma concentrations achieved (including rate of elimination); in general, leucovorin administration is continued until methotrexate concentrations fall to less than 5×10^{-8} M.

A larger dose and/or longer duration of leucovorin treatment may be required in patients with aciduria, ascites, dehydration, gastrointestinal obstruction, pleural or peritoneal effusions, renal function impairment, or pleural or peritoneal effusions because excretion of methotrexate is slowed and the length of time for plasma methotrexate concentrations to decrease to nontoxic levels ($<5 \times 10^{-8}$ M) is increased. It is recommended that duration of leucovorin administration in these patients be based on determination of plasma methotrexate concentrations.

For parenteral use

Methotrexate may be administered intramuscularly, intravenously (rapid or continuous infusion), intrathecally, intra-arterially, or intraventricularly.

Caution is recommended in making sure that the appropriate diluent for the intended route of administration is used when preparing methotrexate for administration.

Combination chemotherapy

Methotrexate may be used in combination with other agents in various regimens. As a result, incidence and/or severity of side effects may be altered and different dosages (usually reduced) may be used. For example, methotrexate is part of the following chemotherapeutic combinations (some commonly used acronyms are in parentheses):

> —cyclophosphamide, doxorubicin, methotrexate, and procarbazine (CAMP).
>
> —cyclophosphamide, methotrexate, and lomustine (CMC-High dose).

—cyclophosphamide, methotrexate, and fluorouracil (CMF).

—cyclophosphamide, methotrexate, fluorouracil, and prednisone (CMFP).

—cyclophosphamide, methotrexate, fluorouracil, vincristine, and prednisone (CMFVP, Cooper's Regimen).

—methotrexate, doxorubicin, cyclophosphamide, and lomustine (MACC).

—methotrexate and mercaptopurine (MTX + MP).

—methotrexate, mercaptopurine, and cyclophosphamide (MTX + MP + CTX).

—methotrexate and fluorouracil.

For specific dosages and schedules, consult the literature. For information regarding each agent, consult the individual monographs.

Oral Dosage Forms

METHOTREXATE TABLETS USP

Usual adult dose:

Antineoplastic—

Choriocarcinoma; or

Chorioadenoma destruens; or

Hydatidiform mole: Oral, 15 to 30 mg per day for five days, the course being repeated three to five times with one to two weeks between courses. Usually, one or two courses are given after normalization of urinary human chorionic gonadotropin (HCG) concentrations.

Acute lymphocytic leukemia:

Induction—Oral, 3.3 mg per square meter of body surface per day in combination with prednisone or other agents.

Maintenance—Oral, 30 mg per square meter of body surface per week.

Burkitt's lymphoma:

Stages I-II—Oral, 10 to 25 mg per day for four to eight days, the course being repeated several times with seven to ten days between courses.

Stage III—Oral, as for Stage I-II, in combination with other agents.

Lymphosarcoma (Stage III): Oral, 625 mcg (0.625 mg) to 2.5 mg per kg of body weight per day.

Mycosis fungoides—Oral, 2.5 to 10 mg a day for weeks or months.

Auxiliary labeling:

• Avoid alcoholic beverages.

• Do not take other medicines without advice from your doctor.

• Avoid overexposure to sun.

Parenteral Dosage Forms

METHOTREXATE SODIUM INJECTION USP

Usual adult dose:

Antineoplastic—

Choriocarcinoma; or

Chorioadenoma destruens; or

Hydatidiform mole: Intramuscular, 15 to 30 mg (base) per day for five days, the course being repeated three to five times with one to two weeks between courses. Usually, one or two courses are given after normalization of urinary human chorionic gonadotropin (HCG) concentrations.

Acute lymphocytic leukemia:

Induction—Intramuscular, 3.3 mg (base) per square meter of body surface per day in combination with prednisone or other agents.

Maintenance—

Intramuscular, 30 mg (base) per square meter of body surface per week; or

Intravenous, 2.5 mg (base) per kg of body weight every fourteen days.

Osteosarcoma: Intravenous infusion (over four hours), 12 grams (base) per square meter of body surface, followed by leucovorin rescue (usually 15 mg orally every six hours for ten doses starting at twenty-four hours after the methotrexate infusion is started), on weeks 4, 5, 6, 7, 11, 12, 15, 16, 29, 30, 44, and 45 after surgery on a combination chemotherapy schedule that also includes doxorubicin, cisplatin, bleomycin, cyclophosphamide, and dactinomycin. The dose may be increased, if necessary, to 15 grams (base) per square meter of body surface to achieve a peak serum methotrexate concentration of 13×10^{-3} M per liter.

Note: *High-dose methotrexate administration should not be initiated unless leucovorin is physically present and ready to be administered, since rescue is critical.*

If the patient is vomiting or cannot take oral medication, leucovorin may be administered intravenously or intramuscularly in the same dose as the oral dose.

Mycosis fungoides—Intramuscular, 50 mg (base) once a week or 25 mg (base) two times a week.

METHOTREXATE SODIUM FOR INJECTION USP

Usual adult dose:

Meningeal leukemia—

Induction: Intrathecal, 12 mg (base) per square meter of body surface to a maximum of 15 mg every two to five days until the cell count of the cerebrospinal fluid (CSF) returns to normal.

Prophylaxis: Intrathecal, 12 mg (base) per square meter of body surface to a maximum of 15 mg at an interval determined by consultation of the medical literature.

Choriocarcinoma; or

Chorioadenoma destruens; or

Hydatidiform mole—Intramuscular, 15 to 30 mg (base) per day for five days, the course being repeated three to five times with one to two weeks between courses. Usually, one or two courses are given after normalization of urinary human chorionic gonadotropin (HCG) concentrations.

Acute lymphocytic leukemia—

Induction: Intramuscular, 3.3 mg (base) per square meter of body surface per day in combination with prednisone or other agents.

Maintenance:

Intramuscular, 30 mg (base) per square meter of body surface per week; or

Intravenous, 2.5 mg (base) per kg of body weight every fourteen days.

Osteosarcoma—Intravenous infusion (over four hours), 12 grams (base) per square meter of body surface, followed by leucovorin rescue (usually 15 mg orally every six hours for ten doses starting at twenty-four hours after the methotrexate infusion is started), on weeks 4, 5, 6, 7, 11, 12, 15, 16, 29, 30, 44, and 45 after surgery on a combination chemotherapy schedule that also includes doxorubicin, cisplatin, bleomycin, cyclophosphamide, and dactinomycin. The dose may be increased, if necessary, to 15 grams (base) per square meter of body surface to achieve a peak serum methotrexate concentration of 13×10^{-3} M per liter.

Note: *High-dose methotrexate administration should not be initiated unless leucovorin is physically present and ready to be administered, since rescue is critical.*

If the patient is vomiting or cannot take oral medication, leucovorin may be administered intravenously or intramuscularly in the same dose as the oral dose.

Mycosis fungoides—Intramuscular, 50 mg (base) once a week or 25 mg (base) two times a week.

METHOTREXATE—For Noncancerous Conditions   Systemic

Some commonly used *brand names* in the U.S. are:

Folex	*Mexate-AQ*
Folex PFS	*Rheumatrex*
Mexate	

Another commonly used name is amethopterin.

ORAL
Methotrexate Tablets USP
  In the U.S. —*Rheumatrex;* GENERIC
  In Canada—GENERIC

PARENTERAL
Methotrexate Sodium Injection USP
  In the U.S.—*Folex PFS; Mexate-AQ;* GENERIC
  In Canada—GENERIC
Methotrexate Sodium for Injection USP
  In the U.S.—*Folex; Mexate;* GENERIC
  In Canada—GENERIC

Category: Antipsoriatic (systemic); antirheumatic (disease-modifying).

Indications

Note: Bracketed information in the *Indications* section refers to uses not included in U.S. product labeling.

Accepted

Psoriasis (treatment)—Methotrexate is indicated only for treatment of severe, recalcitrant, disabling psoriasis not adequately responsive to other forms of therapy, as confirmed by biopsy and/or dermatologic consultation. Methotrexate is contraindicated in pregnant psoriatic patients and those with existing severe renal or hepatic disease or pre-existing blood dyscrasias.

Arthritis, rheumatoid (treatment)[1]—Methotrexate is also used in the treatment of selected cases of severe rheumatoid arthritis not adequately responsive to other forms of therapy, as confirmed by rheumatologic consultation. Methotrexate is contraindicated in pregnant rheumatoid arthritis patients and those with existing renal or hepatic disease or pre-existing blood dyscrasias.

[Arthritis, psoriatic (treatment)][1]—Methotrexate is being used in the treatment of selected cases of active severe psoriatic arthritis.

[Dermatomyositis, systemic (treatment)][1]—Methotrexate is used for treatment of systemic dermatomyositis (polymyositis).

Caution is recommended in use of methotrexate for non-neoplastic conditions because of potential toxicity with long-term use of this agent.

---

[1]Not included in Canadian product labeling.

Pharmacology

Mechanism of action/Effect: Methotrexate is an antimetabolite of the folic acid analog type. Methotrexate is cell cycle-specific for the S phase of cell division. Activity is due to inhibition of DNA, RNA, thymidylate, and protein synthesis as a result of relatively irreversible binding with dihydrofolate reductase, which prevents reduction of dihydrofolate to the active tetrahydrofolate. Growth of rapidly proliferating cells (epithelial cells in psoriasis, bone marrow, fetal cells, buccal and intestinal mucosa, cells of the urinary bladder, spermatogonia) is affected more than growth of most normal tissues and skin.

Other actions/effects: Also has mild immunosuppressant activity.

Precautions to Consider

Geriatrics

Although appropriate studies with methotrexate have not been performed in the geriatric population, caution should be used in the elderly because of possible reduced renal and hepatic function and reduced folate stores. Dosage adjustment, especially on the basis of renal function, may be necessary.

Dental

The bone marrow depressant effects of methotrexate may result in an increased incidence of microbial infection, delayed healing, and gingival bleeding. Dental work, whenever possible, should be completed prior to initiation of therapy or deferred until blood counts have returned to normal. Patients should be instructed in proper oral hygiene during treatment, including caution in use of regular toothbrushes, dental floss, and toothpicks.

Methotrexate also commonly causes ulcerative stomatitits, gingivitis, and pharyngitis associated with considerable discomfort.

Drug interactions and/or related problems

The following drug interactions and/or related problems have been selected on the basis of their potential clinical significance (possible mechanism in parentheses where appropriate)—not necessarily inclusive (» = major clinical significance):

Note: Combinations containing any of the following medications, depending on the amount present, may also interact with this medication.

» Alcohol or
» Hepatotoxic medications, other
  (concurrent use may increase the risk of hepatotoxicity)

Anticoagulants, coumarin- or indandione-derivative
  (methotrexate may increase anticoagulant activity and/or increase the risk of hemorrhage as a result of decreased hepatic synthesis of procoagulant factors and interference with platelet formation)

» Anti-inflammatory analgesics, nonsteroidal (NSAIAs)
  (concurrent use of phenylbutazone with methotrexate may increase the risk of agranulocytosis or bone marrow depression and is not recommended; also, phenylbutazone may displace methotrexate from its protein-binding sites and decrease its renal clearance, leading to increased methotrexate plasma concentration and risk of toxicity. If concurrent use with phenylbutazone cannot be avoided, especially careful monitoring of the patient for plasma methotrexate concentrations or signs of methotrexate toxicity and/or adequacy of renal function is recommended)

  (although not well documented, the possibility exists that other NSAIAs may also decrease methotrexate excretion and increase its plasma concentration to potentially toxic levels)

  (severe, sometimes fatal, methotrexate toxicity has also been reported with low to moderate doses in patients receiving diclofenac, indomethacin, naproxen, or phenylbutazone; it is recommended that use of NSAIAs with low to moderate doses of methotrexate be undertaken with caution, with methotrexate dosage being adjusted by monitoring plasma methotrexate concentrations and/or adequacy of renal function)

Blood dyscrasia-causing medications
  (leukopenic and/or thrombocytopenic effects of methotrexate may be increased with concurrent or recent therapy if these medications cause the same effects; dosage adjustment of methotrexate, if necessary, should be based on blood counts)

» Bone marrow depressants, other or
Radiation therapy
  (additive bone marrow depression may occur; dosage reduction may be required when two or more bone marrow depres-

sants, including radiation, are used concurrently or consecutively)

Folic acid
(may interfere with the antifolate effects of methotrexate)

Neomycin, oral
(may decrease absorption of oral methotrexate)

» Probenecid
(concurrent use may inhibit renal excretion of methotrexate and result in toxic plasma concentrations; if used concurrently with probenecid, methotrexate dosage should be decreased, the patient observed for signs of toxicity, and/or plasma methotrexate concentrations monitored)

Pyrimethamine or
Triamterene or
Trimethoprim
(concurrent use may rarely increase the toxic effects of methotrexate because of similar folic acid antagonist actions)

» Salicylates and other weak organic acids
(concurrent use may inhibit renal tubular secretion of methotrexate and result in toxic plasma concentrations; salicylates may also increase plasma concentrations by displacing methotrexate from binding sites; if methotrexate is used concurrently with these medications, the patient should be observed for signs of toxicity and/or methotrexate plasma concentration monitored)

Sulfonamides
(in addition to increased risk of hepatotoxicity that may occur when sulfonamides are used concurrently with other hepatotoxic medications, medications that cause displacement from plasma protein binding may theoretically produce toxic plasma concentrations of methotrexate when used concurrently, although clinical significance has not been established)

Vaccines, killed virus
(because normal defense mechanisms may be suppressed by methotrexate therapy, the patient's antibody response to the vaccine may be decreased. The interval between discontinuation of medications that cause immunosuppression and restoration of the patient's ability to respond to the vaccine depends on the intensity and type of immunosuppression-causing medication used, the underlying disease, and other factors; estimates vary from 3 months to 1 year)

» Vaccines, live virus
(because normal defense mechanisms may be suppressed by methotrexate therapy, concurrent use with a live virus vaccine may potentiate the replication of the vaccine virus, may increase the side/adverse effects of the vaccine virus, and/or may decrease the patient's antibody response to the vaccine; immunization of these patients should be undertaken only with extreme caution after careful review of the patient's hematologic status and only with the knowledge and consent of the physician managing the methotrexate therapy. The interval between discontinuation of medications that cause immunosuppression and restoration of the patient's ability to respond to the vaccine depends on the intensity and type of immunosuppression-causing medication used, the underlying disease, and other factors; estimates vary from 3 months to 1 year. Immunization with oral poliovirus vaccine should also be postponed in persons in close contact with the patient, especially family members)

Contraindications/Medical problems
The contraindications/medical problems included have been selected on the basis of their potential clinical significance (reasons given in parentheses where appropriate)—not necessarily inclusive (» = major clinical significance).

Except under special circumstances, this medication should not be used when the following medical problems exist:

» Bone marrow depression

» Hepatic function impairment, severe
» Immunodeficiency
» Renal function impairment, severe

Risk-benefit should be considered when the following medical problems exist:

» Ascites or
Gastrointestinal obstruction or
» Pleural or peritoneal effusions or
» Renal function impairment
(risk of methotrexate toxicity is increased because elimination of methotrexate may be impaired and accumulation may occur; even small doses may lead to severe myelosuppression and mucositis)
(a lower dosage of methotrexate and careful monitoring of plasma or serum methotrexate concentrations are recommended for patients with impaired renal function)

» Chickenpox, existing or recent (including recent exposure), or
» Herpes zoster
(risk of severe generalized disease)

» Hepatic function impairment
» Infection
» Mucositis, oral
Nausea and vomiting
(inadequate hydration secondary to severe nausea and vomiting may result in increased methotrexate toxicity)

» Peptic ulcer
Sensitivity to methotrexate
» Ulcerative colitis
» Caution should be used also in patients who have had previous cytotoxic drug therapy and radiation therapy, and in cases of general debility.

Side/Adverse Effects

Note: Incidence and severity of side effects, particularly hepatotoxicity, appear to be related to dosage frequency and duration of methotrexate therapy. Toxicity tends to occur less frequently and be less severe with a total dose administered as intermittent weekly dosage than with prolonged daily dosage.

The following side/adverse effects have been selected on the basis of their potential clinical significance (possible signs and symptoms in parentheses where appropriate)—not necessarily inclusive:

Those indicating need for medical attention
Incidence less frequent
Gastrointestinal ulceration and bleeding, enteritis, or intestinal perforation, which may be fatal (diarrhea, stomach pain); *leukopenia, bacterial infection, or septicemia* (usually asymptomatic; rarely, fever or chills, cough or hoarseness, lower back or side pain, painful or difficult urination); *thrombocytopenia* (usually asymptomatic; rarely, unusual bleeding or bruising; black, tarry stools; blood in urine or stools; pinpoint red spots on skin); *severe acute methotrexate toxicity, cutaneous vasculitis, or reactivation of sunburn or increased erythematous response to ultraviolet therapy* (reddening of skin); *ulcerative stomatitis, gingivitis, or pharyngitis* (sores in mouth and on lips)

Note: With *leukopenia* and *thrombocytopenia,* the nadir of the leukocyte and platelet counts occurs after 7 to 10 days, with recovery 7 days later.

Incidence rare—dose-related
Central nervous system (CNS) effects, increased cerebrospinal fluid pressure, leukoencephalopathy, demyelination, or chemical arachnoiditis (back pain, blurred vision, convulsions, dizziness, drowsiness, fever, headache, unusual tiredness or weakness); *hepatotoxicity, including liver atrophy, necrosis, cirrhosis, fatty*

changes, periportal fibrosis (yellow eyes or skin); *pneumonitis, potentially fatal, or pulmonary fibrosis* (cough, shortness of breath)

Those indicating need for medical attention only if they continue or are bothersome
Incidence less frequent or rare
Acne; boils; loss of appetite; nausea; pale skin; skin rash or itching; vomiting

Those not indicating need for medical attention
Incidence less frequent or rare
Loss of hair

Patient Consultation

In providing consultation, consider emphasizing the following selected information (» = major clinical significance):

Before using this medication
Advisability of using contraception; telling physician immediately if pregnancy is suspected
See also *Precautions to Consider.*

Proper use of this medication
» Importance of not taking more or less medication than the amount prescribed
» Frequency of nausea; importance of continuing medication despite stomach upset; checking with physician if vomiting occurs
Checking with physician if vomiting occurs shortly after dose is taken
Missed dose: Not taking at all; not doubling doses
» Proper storage

Precautions while using this medication
» Importance of close monitoring by physician
» Avoiding alcoholic beverages, which may increase hepatotoxicity
Possible photosensitivity reactions, particularly for patients with psoriasis; avoiding unprotected exposure to sun or overuse of sunlamp
» Avoiding salicylate-containing products and nonsteroidal anti-inflammatories, which may increase toxicity
» Avoiding immunizations unless approved by physician; other persons in patient's household should avoid immunizations with oral poliovirus vaccine; avoiding other persons who have taken oral poliovirus vaccine or wearing a protective mask that covers nose and mouth
Caution if bone marrow depression occurs:
» Avoiding exposure to persons with bacterial infections, especially during periods of low blood counts; checking with physician immediately if fever or chills, cough or hoarseness, lower back or side pain, or painful or difficult urination occur
» Checking with physician immediately if unusual bleeding or bruising; black, tarry stools; blood in urine or stools; or pinpoint red spots on skin occur
Caution in use of regular toothbrush, dental floss, or toothpick; physician, dentist, or nurse may suggest alternatives; checking with physician before having dental work done
Not touching eyes or inside of nose unless hands washed immediately before
Using caution to avoid accidental cuts with use of sharp objects such as safety razor or fingernail or toenail cutters
Avoiding contact sports or other situations where bruising or injury could occur

Side/adverse effects
May cause adverse effects such as blood problems, stomach, kidney, or liver problems, loss of hair, or cancer; importance of discussing possible effects with physician
Signs of potential side effects, especially gastrointestinal ulceration and bleeding, enteritis, intestinal perforation, leukopenia, bacterial infection, septicemia, thrombocytopenia, severe acute methoxtrexate toxicity, cutaneous vasculitis, reactivation of sun-

burn or reaction to ultraviolet light, ulcerative stomatitis, gingivitis, pharyngitis, CNS effects, hepatotoxicity, pneumonitis, and pulmonary fibrosis
Physician or nurse can help in dealing with side effects
Possibility of hair loss; should return after treatment has ended

General Dosing Information

Patients receiving methotrexate should be under supervision of a physician experienced in antimetabolite chemotherapy.

In general, use of intermittent courses of methotrexate is associated with less risk of serious toxicity than prolonged daily dosage.

It is recommended that methotrexate therapy be interrupted if diarrhea or ulcerative stomatitis occurs, because of the risk of hemorrhagic enteritis and fatal intestinal perforation.

It is recommended that methotrexate therapy be interrupted if pulmonary symptoms (especially a dry, unproductive cough) occur, because of the risk of potentially irreversible pulmonary toxicity.

If bone marrow depression occurs, withdrawal of methotrexate is recommended. The following precautions may also be useful:

• Special precautions are recommended in patients who develop thrombocytopenia as a result of administration of methotrexate. These may include extreme care in performing invasive procedures; regular inspection of intravenous sites, skin (including perirectal area), and mucous membrane surfaces for signs of bleeding or bruising; limiting frequency of venipuncture and avoiding intramuscular injections; testing urine, emesis, stool, and secretions for occult blood; care in use of regular toothbrushes, dental floss, toothpicks, safety razors, and fingernail and toenail cutters; avoiding constipation; and using caution to prevent falls and other injuries. Such patients should avoid alcohol and any aspirin intake because of the risk of gastrointestinal bleeding. Platelet transfusions may be required.

• Patients who develop leukopenia should be observed carefully for signs of infection. Antibiotic support may be required. In neutropenic patients who develop fever, broad-spectrum antibiotic coverage should be initiated empirically, pending bacterial cultures and appropriate diagnostic tests.

For use as an antipsoriatic
After a favorable response is obtained, it is recommended that the dosage be decreased gradually to the lowest dosage and longest rest period that will maintain an adequate clinical response. To reduce the methotrexate requirement, it is recommended that an attempt be made to return to conventional therapy or to concomitant topical conventional therapy as soon as possible.

For use as an antirheumatic
Methotrexate appears to be effective by the oral, intramuscular, or intravenous route; however, oral administration is associated with less toxicity.

For parenteral use
Methotrexate may be administered intramuscularly or intravenously (rapid or continuous infusion).

Oral Dosage Forms

Note: Bracketed uses in the *Dosage Forms* section refer to categories of use and/or indications that are not included in U.S. product labeling.

METHOTREXATE TABLETS USP

Usual adult dose:
Psoriasis; or
Rheumatoid arthritis[1]; or
[Psoriatic arthritis][1]—
Oral, initially 2.5 to 5 mg every twelve hours for three doses once a week, the dosage being increased as necessary in increments of 2.5 mg per week up to a maximum of 20 mg per week; or

Oral, initially 10 mg once a week, the dosage being increased as necessary up to 25 mg once a week.

Note: Some clinicians recommend an initial test dose at the lowest dosage level because of interindividual variation in sensitivity to methotrexate.

Auxiliary labeling:
- Avoid alcoholic beverages.
- Do not take other medicines without advice from your doctor.
- Avoid overexposure to sun.

Parenteral Dosage Forms

Note: Bracketed uses in the *Dosage Forms* section refer to categories of use and/or indications that are not included in U.S. product labeling.

METHOTREXATE SODIUM INJECTION USP
Usual adult dose:
Psoriasis; or
[Rheumatoid arthritis][1]—Intramuscular or intravenous, initially 10 mg (base) once a week, the dosage being increased as necessary up to 25 mg (base) once a week.

Note: Some clinicians recommend an initial test dose of 10 mg because of interindividual variation in sensitivity to methotrexate.

METHOTREXATE SODIUM FOR INJECTION USP
Usual adult dose:
Psoriasis; or
[Rheumatoid arthritis][1]—Intramuscular or intravenous, initially 10 mg (base) once a week, the dosage being increased as necessary up to 25 mg (base) once a week.

Note: Some clinicians recommend an initial test dose of 10 mg because of interindividual variation in sensitivity to methotrexate.

METHYLDOPA   Systemic

Some commonly used *brand names* are:
In the U.S.—
Aldomet
In Canada—
Aldomet   *Dopamet*
Apo-Methyldopa   *Novomedopa*

ORAL
Methyldopa Oral Suspension USP†
In the U.S.—*Aldomet*
Methyldopa Tablets USP
In the U.S.—*Aldomet;* GENERIC
In Canada—*Aldomet; Apo-Methyldopa; Dopamet; Novomedopa;* GENERIC

PARENTERAL
Methyldopate Hydrochloride Injection USP
In the U.S.—*Aldomet;* GENERIC
In Canada—*Aldomet*

†Not commercially available in Canada.

Category: Antihypertensive.

Indications

Accepted
Hypertension (treatment)—Methyldopa is indicated in the treatment of moderate to severe hypertension, including that complicated by renal disease.

In the 1988 Report of the Joint National Committee on Detection, Evaluation, and Treatment of High Blood Pressure, a progression in choice of treatments for essential hypertension is recommended:

Nonpharmacologic management (especially sodium restriction, weight reduction and exercise, and moderation of alcohol consumption) is recommended first for some patients, including those with mild hypertension, and is recommended as an adjunct to all pharmacologic hypertensive therapy.

Initial drug therapy usually consists of a diuretic, beta-adrenergic blocking agent, calcium channel blocking agent, or angiotensin-converting enzyme (ACE) inhibitor. If adequate blood pressure control is not achieved and the patient is adherent to the treatment program and not experiencing significant side effects, dosage of the drug may be increased, a drug from another one of these initial classes may be added or substituted, or a second drug from a different class—centrally acting alpha-adrenergic blockers (e.g., clonidine, guanabenz, guanfacine, methyldopa), peripheral-acting adrenergic antagonists (e.g., guanadrel, guanethidine, rauwolfia alkaloids), post-synaptic alpha-1 peripheral adrenergic blocking agents (e.g., prazosin, terazosin), or vasodilators (e.g., hydralazine, minoxidil)—may be added or substituted.

If necessary, a drug from another class in the second group may be substituted or added as a third drug. If blood pressure control is still not achieved, a drug from still another class may be substituted or added as a fourth drug, or the patient may need further evaluation and/or referral.

Methyldopate may be used intravenously in the treatment of hypertensive crises. However, because of its slow onset of action, methyldopate is generally not recommended as sole initial therapy in hypertensive crises.

Pharmacology

Mechanism of action/Effect: The exact mechanism of antihypertensive action is unknown. It is thought to involve stimulation of central alpha-adrenergic receptors by a metabolite, alpha-methylnorepinephrine, thus inhibiting sympathetic outflow to the heart, kidneys, and peripheral vasculature. Reduced peripheral resistance and plasma renin activity levels may also contribute to its effect.

Time to peak effect:
Single dose—4 to 6 hours.
Multiple doses—2 to 3 days.

Duration of action: Variable—
Oral:
Single dose—12 to 24 hours.
Multiple doses—24 to 48 hours.
Intravenous: 10 to 16 hours.

Precautions to Consider

Cross-sensitivity and/or related problems
Patients sensitive to sulfites may be sensitive to some methyldopa products because of the sulfite preservatives present.

Geriatrics

Although appropriate studies on the relationship of age to the effects of methyldopa have not been performed in the geriatric population, the elderly may be more sensitive to the hypotensive and sedative effects. In addition, elderly patients are more likely to have age-related renal function impairment, which may require lower doses in patients receiving methyldopa.

Dental

Use of methyldopa may decrease or inhibit salivary flow, thus contributing to the development of caries, periodontal disease, oral candidiasis, and discomfort.

Drug interactions and/or related problems

The following drug interactions and/or related problems have been selected on the basis of their potential clinical significance (possible mechanism in parentheses where appropriate)—not necessarily inclusive (» = major clinical significance):

Note: Combinations containing any of the following medications, depending on the amount present, may also interact with this medication.

Alcohol or

Central nervous system (CNS) depression-producing medications
(concurrent use may enhance the CNS depressant effects of either these medications or methyldopa)

Anticoagulants, coumarin- or indandione-derivative
(concurrent use with methyldopa may increase the anticoagulant effect of these medications; adjustment of anticoagulant dosage based on prothrombin-time determinations is recommended)

Antidepressants, tricyclic
(may reduce antihypertensive effects of methyldopa; the patient should be carefully monitored to confirm that the desired effect is being obtained)

Anti-inflammatory drugs, nonsteroidal (NSAIDs), especially indomethacin
(antihypertensive effects of methyldopa may be reduced when it is used concurrently with these medications; indomethacin, and possibly other NSAIDs, may antagonize the antihypertensive effect by inhibiting renal prostaglandin synthesis and/or by causing sodium and fluid retention; the patient should be carefully monitored to confirm that the desired effect is being obtained)

Appetite suppressants, with the exception of fenfluramine
(concurrent use may decrease the hypotensive effects of methyldopa)

Bromocriptine
(methyldopa may increase serum prolactin concentrations and interfere with effects of bromocriptine; dosage adjustment of bromocriptine may be necessary)

Estrogens
(estrogen-induced fluid retention tends to increase blood pressure)

Fenfluramine
(concurrent use may increase the hypotensive effects of methyldopa)

Haloperidol
(concurrent use of haloperidol with methyldopa may cause unwanted mental effects such as disorientation and slowed or difficult thought process)

Hypotension-producing medications, other
(hypotensive effects may be potentiated when these medications are used concurrently with methyldopa; although some antihypertensive and/or diuretic combinations are frequently used for therapeutic advantage, dosage adjustments may be necessary during concurrent use)

Levodopa
(concurrent use with methyldopa may alter the antiparkinsonian effects of levodopa and may also produce additive toxic CNS effects such as psychosis)

Lithium
(concurrent use with methyldopa may increase the risk of lithium toxicity, even though serum lithium concentrations remain within the recommended therapeutic range)

» Monoamine oxidase (MAO) inhibitors, including furazolidone, pargyline, procarbazine, and selegiline
(methyldopa may cause hyperexcitability in patients receiving MAO inhibitors; headache, severe hypertension, and hallucinations have been reported)

Sympathomimetics, such as:

» Cocaine
Dobutamine
Dopamine
Ephedrine
Epinephrine
Mephentermine
Metaraminol
Methoxamine
» Norepinephrine
» Phenylephrine, or
Phenylpropanolamine
(concurrent use with sympathomimetic pressor amines may decrease the hypotensive effect of methyldopa and potentiate the pressor effect of these medications; if concurrent use of cocaine, norepinephrine, or phenylephrine is indicated, caution is required, and only very small initial doses should be administered)

Contraindications/Medical problems

The contraindications/medical problems included have been selected on the basis of their potential clinical significance (reasons given in parentheses where appropriate)—not necessarily inclusive (» = major clinical significance).

Except under special circumstances, this medication should not be used when the following medical problem exists:

» Hepatic disease, active, such as acute hepatitis and active cirrhosis

Risk-benefit should be considered when the following medical problems exist:

Cerebrovascular disease, severe bilateral
(rarely, involuntary choreoathetotic movements have been observed during methyldopa therapy)

Coronary insufficiency, including angina pectoris
(may be aggravated)

» Hemolytic anemia, autoimmune, history of

» Hepatic disease, history of, in conjunction with past use of methyldopa

Hepatic function impairment
(reduced biotransformation; lower doses may be required)

Mental depression, history of

Parkinson's disease
(may be exacerbated)

» Pheochromocytoma
(interference with tests for catecholamines; in addition, pressor responses have been reported)

Renal function impairment
(increased sensitivity to effects of methyldopa, possibly due to accumulation of the sulfate conjugate; lower doses may be required)

Sensitivity to methyldopa

Side/Adverse Effects

The following side/adverse effects have been selected on the basis of their potential clinical significance (possible signs and symptoms in parentheses where appropriate)—not necessarily inclusive:

Those indicating need for medical attention

Incidence more frequent

Edema, peripheral (swelling of feet or lower legs)

Incidence less frequent
> *Drug fever* (fever, shortly after onset of therapy); *mental status changes* (mental depression or anxiety, nightmares or unusually vivid dreams)
>
> Note: *Drug fever* usually occurs within the first 3 months of therapy and is sometimes accompanied by eosinophilia or hepatic function test changes. The hepatic reaction to methyldopa appears to be immunologic or hypersensitive in nature.

Incidence rare
> *Colitis* (severe or continuing diarrhea or stomach cramps); *hemolytic anemia, autoimmune* (continuing tiredness or weakness after having taken this medication for several weeks); *cholestasis or hepatitis and hepatocellular injury* (dark or amber urine, pale stools, yellow eyes or skin); *leukopenia, reversible, or granulocytopenia, reversible; myocarditis* (fever, chills, troubled breathing, and fast heartbeat); *pancreatitis* (severe stomach pain with nausea and vomiting); *systemic lupus erythematosus (SLE)-like syndrome* (general feeling of discomfort or illness or weakness, joint pain, skin rash or itching); *thrombocytopenia*
>
> Note: *Hemolytic anemia* occurs in less than 5% of patients showing a positive Coombs' test.
>
> Rarely, fatal *hepatic necrosis* has been reported. Darkening of urine on exposure to air, caused by breakdown of methyldopa or its metabolites, may occur rarely.

Those indicating need for medical attention only if they continue or are bothersome
Incidence more frequent—more than 5%
> Drowsiness; dryness of mouth; headache
>
> Note: *Drowsiness* is especially likely to occur at initiation of therapy and after dosage increases.

Incidence less frequent or rare
> *Decreased sexual ability or interest in sex, more common in men than in women; diarrhea; hyperprolactinemia* (swelling of breasts or unusual milk production); *nausea or vomiting; orthostatic hypotension* (dizziness or lightheadedness when getting up from a lying or sitting postion); *paresthesias* (numbness, tingling, pain, or weakness in hands or feet); *sinus bradycardia* (slow heartbeat); *stuffy nose*

Patient Consultation
In providing consultation, consider emphasizing the following selected information (» = major clinical significance):

Before using this medication
» Conditions affecting use, especially:
>> Sensitivity to methyldopa
>> Breast-feeding—Excreted in breast milk
>> Use in the elderly—Increased sensitivity to hypotensive and sedative effects
>> Other medications, especially MAO inhibitors
>> Other medical problems, especially active hepatic disease, history of hepatic disease associated with methyldopa, history of autoimmune hemolytic anemia, or pheochromocytoma

Proper use of this medication
> Possible need for control of weight and diet, especially sodium intake
» Patient may not experience symptoms of hypertension; importance of taking medication even if feeling well
» Does not cure, but helps control hypertension; possible need for lifelong therapy; checking with physician before discontinuing medication; serious consequences of untreated hypertension
> Getting into habit of taking at same time each day to help increase compliance
> Missed dose: Taking as soon as possible; not taking if almost time for next dose; not doubling doses
» Proper storage

Precautions while using this medication
> Regular visits to physician to check progress

» Not using other medications, especially nonprescription sympathomimetics, unless ordered by physician
» Reporting fever to physician
> Caution if any kind of surgery (including dental surgery) or emergency treatment is required
» Caution when driving or doing things requiring alertness, because of possible drowsiness
> Caution when getting up suddenly from a lying or sitting position
> Possible dryness of mouth; using sugarless candy or gum, ice, or saliva substitute for relief; checking with physician or dentist if dry mouth continues for more than 2 weeks
> Caution if any laboratory tests required; possible interference with test results

Side/adverse effects
> Signs of potential side effects, especially edema, drug fever, mental status changes, colitis, hemolytic anemia, cholestasis, hepatitis, leukopenia, granulocytopenia, myocarditis, pancreatitis, SLE-like syndrome, and thrombocytopenia

General Dosing Information
If methyldopa is added to a thiazide diuretic regimen, the dosage of the thiazide need not be changed. If methyldopa is to be given with other antihypertensives, the initial dosage of methyldopa for an adult should be limited to 500 mg daily.

Any increase in dosage should be initiated with the evening dose of methyldopa to minimize the effects of sedation.

Tolerance to methyldopa may develop within 2 or 3 months after initiation of therapy as a result of fluid retention and expanded plasma volume. Adding a diuretic or increasing the dosage of methyldopa may restore control. Addition of thiazide diuretics to the regimen is recommended if therapy has not been started with a thiazide or if a daily dose of 2 grams of methyldopa does not maintain control.

If orthostatic hypotension occurs, dosage reduction is recommended.

Recent evidence suggests that withdrawal of antihypertensive therapy prior to surgery is not necessary, but that the anesthesiologist must be aware of such therapy.

It is recommended that methyldopa be discontinued if Coombs' positive hemolytic anemia occurs. Although the anemia usually remits promptly, adrenocorticoids may be administered if necessary. If this effect is shown to be due to methyldopa, therapy with the drug should not be reinstituted.

If a blood transfusion is needed in a patient receiving methyldopa, both a direct and indirect Coombs' test are recommended. If hemolytic anemia is not present, usually only the direct Coombs' test will be positive, which will not interfere with typing or positive cross-matching. However, a positive indirect Coombs' test may interfere with the major crossmatch, and a hematologist or transfusion expert will be needed.

It is recommended that methyldopa be withdrawn if fever, abnormal liver function tests, or jaundice occurs. If these effects are shown to be due to methyldopa, therapy with the drug should not be reinstituted.

For parenteral dosage forms only
Intramuscular or subcutaneous administration is not recommended because of unreliable absorption.

Following stabilization of blood pressure using intravenous methyldopate, the patient should be transferred to methyldopa tablets at the same dosage as was used parenterally.

Oral Dosage Forms

METHYLDOPA ORAL SUSPENSION USP

Usual adult dose: Antihypertensive—
> Initial: Oral, 250 mg two or three times a day for two days, the dosage then being adjusted, preferably at intervals of not less than two days, until the desired response is obtained.

Maintenance: Oral, 500 mg to 2 grams a day, divided into two to four doses.

Note: Geriatric patients may be more sensitive to the effects of the usual adult dose and may require a lower dose to prevent syncope.

Usual adult prescribing limits: Up to 3 grams a day.

Auxiliary labeling:
- Shake well.
- May cause drowsiness.
- Do not take other medicines without your doctor's advice.

METHYLDOPA TABLETS USP

Usual adult dose: Antihypertensive—

Initial: Oral, 250 mg two or three times a day for two days, the dosage then being adjusted, preferably at intervals of not less than two days, until the desired response is obtained.

Maintenance: Oral, 500 mg to 2 grams a day, divided into two to four doses.

Note: Geriatric patients may be more sensitive to the effects of the usual adult dose and may require a lower dose to prevent syncope.

Usual adult prescribing limits: Up to 3 grams a day.

Auxiliary labeling:
- May cause drowsiness.
- Do not take other medicines without your doctor's advice.

Parenteral Dosage Forms

METHYLDOPATE HYDROCHLORIDE INJECTION USP

Usual adult dose: Antihypertensive—Intravenous infusion, 250 to 500 mg in 100 mL of 5% dextrose injection, administered slowly over a thirty- to sixty-minute period, every six hours if necessary.

Note: Geriatric patients may be more sensitive to the effects of the usual adult dose and may require a lower dose to prevent syncope.

Usual adult prescribing limits: Up to 1 gram every 6 to 12 hours.

METHYLDOPA AND THIAZIDE DIURETICS   Systemic

Category: Antihypertensive.

Indications

Accepted

Hypertension (treatment)—This combination is indicated for treatment of hypertension.

Fixed-dosage combinations are generally not recommended for initial therapy and are useful for subsequent therapy only when the proportion of the component agents corresponds to the dose of the individual agents, as determined by titration.

Nonpharmacologic management (especially sodium restriction, weight reduction and exercise, and moderation of alcohol consumption) is recommended first for some patients, including those with mild hypertension, and is recommended as an adjunct to all pharmacologic hypertensive therapy.

Patient Consultation

In providing consultation, consider emphasizing the following selected information (» = major clinical significance):

Before using this medication
» Conditions affecting use, especially:
  Sensitivity to methyldopa, thiazide diuretics, other sulfonamide-type medications, bumetanide, furosemide, or carbonic anhydrase inhibitors
  Pregnancy—Thiazide diuretics may cause jaundice, thrombocytopenia, hypokalemia in infant
  Breast-feeding—Excreted in breast milk
  Use in the elderly—Increased sensitivity to hypotensive, sedative, and electrolyte effects
  Other medications, especially MAO inhibitors, adrenocorticoids, digitalis glycosides, lithium, or methenamine
  Other medical problems, especially active hepatic disease, history of hemolytic anemia, history of hepatic disease associated with methyldopa, pheochromocytoma, or anuria or severe renal function impairment

Proper use of this medication
  Importance of diet; possible need for sodium restriction and/or weight reduction

» Patient may not experience symptoms of hypertension; importance of taking medication even if feeling well
» Does not cure, but helps control hypertension; possible need for lifelong therapy; checking with physician before discontinuing medication; serious consequences of untreated hypertension
  Diuretic effects of the medication and timing of doses to minimize inconvenience of diuresis
  Getting into habit of taking at same time each day to help increase compliance
  Missed dose: Taking as soon as possible; not taking if almost time for next dose; not doubling doses
» Proper storage

Precautions while using this medication
  Regular visits to physician to check progress
» Not using other medications, especially nonprescription sympathomimetics, unless ordered by physician
» Possibility of hypokalemia; possible need for additional potassium in diet; not changing diet without first checking with physician
  To prevent dehydration, checking with physician if severe nausea, vomiting, or diarrhea occurs and continues
  Caution if any kind of surgery (including dental surgery) or emergency treatment is required
» Reporting fever to physician
» Caution when driving or doing things requiring alertness because of possible drowsiness
  Caution when getting up suddenly from a lying or sitting position
» Caution in using alcohol, while standing for long periods or exercising, and during hot weather because of enhanced orthostatic hypotensive effects
  Diabetics: May increase blood sugar levels
  Possible dryness of mouth; using sugarless candy or gum, ice, or saliva substitute for relief; checking with physician or dentist if dry mouth continues for more than 2 weeks
» Possible photosensitivity; avoiding unprotected exposure to sun; using protective clothing and sun block product; avoiding use of sunlamp, tanning bed, or tanning booth
  Caution if any laboratory tests required; possible interference with test results

Side/adverse effects
  Signs of potential side effects, especially drug fever, hypokalemia, mental changes, allergic reaction, colitis, hemolytic anemia,

cholestasis, hepatitis, hyperuricemia, gout, leukopenia, granulocytopenia, myocarditis, pancreatitis, SLE-like syndrome, and thrombocytopenia

Oral Dosage Forms

METHYLDOPA AND CHLOROTHIAZIDE TABLETS USP

Usual adult dose: Antihypertensive—Oral, 2 to 4 tablets a day in single or divided daily doses, as determined by individual titration with the component agents.

Note: Geriatric patients may be more sensitive to the effects of the usual adult dose and may require a lower dose to prevent syncope.

Auxiliary labeling:
- May cause drowsiness.
- Do not take other medicines without your doctor's advice.

METHYLDOPA AND HYDROCHLOROTHIAZIDE TABLETS USP

Usual adult dose: Antihypertensive—Oral, 2 to 4 tablets a day in single or divided daily doses, as determined by individual titration with the component agents.

Note: Geriatric patients may be more sensitive to the effects of the usual adult dose and may require a lower dose to prevent syncope.

Auxiliary labeling:
- May cause drowsiness.
- Do not take other medicines without your doctor's advice.

METHYSERGIDE   Systemic

A commonly used *brand name* in the U.S. and Canada is *Sansert*.

ORAL
Methysergide Maleate Tablets USP
In the U.S. and Canada—*Sansert*

Category: Vascular headache prophylactic.

Indications

Accepted
Headache vascular (prophylaxis)—Methysergide is indicated for prevention of vascular headaches such as migraine and cluster headaches in patients with frequent and/or disabling headaches not responsive to other treatment.

Unaccepted
Methysergide is not recommended for treatment of acute attacks or tension headaches.

Pharmacology

Mechanism of action/Effect: Antiserotonin; actions on central nervous system (CNS); direct stimulation of smooth muscle leading to vasoconstriction. Little alpha-adrenergic blocking activity. The exact mechanism of action in preventing migraine is unknown, although it may be related to the antiserotonin effect.

Onset of action: 1 to 2 days.

Duration of action: 1 to 2 days.

Precautions to Consider

Cross-sensitivity and/or related problems
Patients sensitive to other ergot derivatives may be sensitive to this medication also.

Geriatrics
Caution is recommended in the elderly, who are more likely to have occlusive peripheral vascular disease, and are therefore more likely to be adversely affected by peripheral vasoconstriction, than are younger adults. This increases the risk of hypothermia and other ischemic complications. Elderly patients are also more likely to have age-related renal function impairment, which requires caution in patients receiving methysergide.

Drug interactions and/or related problems
The following drug interactions and/or related problems have been selected on the basis of their potential clinical significance (possible mechanism in parentheses where appropriate)—not necessarily inclusive (» = major clinical significance):

Note: Combinations containing any of the following medications, depending on the amount present, may also interact with this medication.

Ergot alkaloids, other, or
Vasoconstrictors, systemic, other, such as:
Cocaine
Epinephrine, parenteral
Metaraminol
Methoxamine
Norepinephrine
Phenylephrine, parenteral, or
Vasoconstrictor-containing local anesthetic solutions
(concurrent use with methysergide may result in enhanced vasoconstriction; a reduced dosage of ergot alkaloids may be necessary when they are used to treat an acute attack)

Smoking, tobacco
(administration of methysergide to patients who smoke heavily may increase the risk of peripheral vascular ischemia because nicotine also constricts blood vessels)

Contraindications/Medical problems
The contraindications/medical problems included have been selected on the basis of their potential clinical significance (reasons given in parentheses where appropriate)—not necessarily inclusive (» = major clinical significance).

Risk-benefit should be considered when the following medical problems exist:

» Coronary artery disease, especially:
» Angina, unstable or vasospastic
(vasospasm may aggravate existing angina, or cause angina or myocardial infarction)

» Hepatic function impairment
(impaired metabolism may result in ergot poisoning)

» Hypertension, severe
(may be aggravated)

Peptic ulcer
(methysergide may elevate gastric hydrochloric acid concentrations)

» Peripheral vascular disease, occlusive, or
» Pruritus, severe, especially when associated with hepatic disease, or
» Sepsis or other severe infection
    (sensitivity to vascular effects may be increased)
» Pulmonary disease or
» Rheumatoid arthritis or other collagen diseases or
» Valvular heart disease
    (risk of retroperitoneal, pleuropulmonary, or cardiac fibrosis)
» Renal function impairment
    Sensitivity to methysergide or other ergot alkaloids, history of

Side/Adverse Effects

Note: Most side effects are dose-related and are usually relieved by a reduction in dosage or withdrawal of the medication.

The following side/adverse effects have been selected on the basis of their potential clinical significance (possible signs and symptoms in parentheses where appropriate)—not necessarily inclusive:

Those indicating need for medical attention
Incidence more frequent
Ischemia, peripheral vasospasm-induced (abdominal pain; chest pain; itching of skin; numbness and tingling of fingers, toes, or face; pain in arms, legs, or lower back; pale or cold hands or feet; weakness in legs)—specific symptoms are dependent on the blood vessel(s) involved, and may also rarely be caused by vascular insufficiency
Incidence less frequent or rare—dose-related
Changes in vision; clumsiness or unsteadiness; CNS stimulation, mild (excitement or difficulty in thinking, feeling of being outside the body, hallucinations, nightmares); *edema, peripheral* (swelling of hands, ankles, feet, or lower legs); *fast or slow heartbeat; leukopenia* (usually asymptomatic; rarely, fever or chills, cough or hoarseness, lower back or side pain, painful or difficult urination); *mental depression; redness or flushing of face; skin rash; telangiectasia* (raised red spots on skin)
Note: Although methysergide is chemically related to the hallucinogen lysergic acid diethylamide (LSD), some of the listed CNS symptoms may be associated with vascular headaches rather than an effect of the medication.
Incidence rare—dependent on duration of therapy
Fibrosis (chest pain; difficult or painful urination; fever; large increase or decrease in amount of urine; leg cramps; loss of appetite; lower back, side, or groin pain; shortness of breath or difficult breathing; swelling of hands, ankles, feet, or lower legs; tightness in chest; weight loss)—fibrosis may occur in cardiac, penile, pleuropulmonary, and/or retroperitoneal tissues; specific symptoms depend on the site involved and the occurrence of associated complications, such as ureteral obstruction and vascular insufficiency
Signs and symptoms of overdose
Cold and pale hands or feet; dizziness, severe; excitement

Those indicating need for medical attention only if they continue or are bothersome
Incidence more frequent
CNS effect or hypotension, orthostatic (dizziness or lightheadedness, especially when getting up from a lying or sitting position); *diarrhea; drowsiness; nausea, vomiting, or stomach pain*
Incidence less frequent or rare
Constipation; heartburn; trouble in sleeping

Those indicating possible withdrawal and the need for medical attention if they occur after medication is discontinued
Headache

Patient Consultation

In providing consultation, consider emphasizing the following selected information (» = major clinical significance):

Before using this medication
» Conditions affecting use, especially:
    Sensitivity to ergot derivatives
    Breast-feeding—Ergot alkaloids inhibit lactation; also, they are excreted in breast milk and may cause ergotism in the infant
    Use in children—Use is not recommended, because of the hazards associated with long-term use of methysergide
    Use in the elderly—Increased risk of hypothermia and other adverse effects associated with peripheral vasoconstriction
    Other medical problems, especially cardiovascular disease, hepatic function impairment, hypertension, peripheral vascular disease, severe pruritus (especially when associated with hepatic disease), severe infection, pulmonary disease, rheumatoid arthritis, valvular heart disease, and renal function impairment

Proper use of this medication
» Importance of not using more medication than the amount prescribed; risk of ergotism and gangrene with overdosage
» Taking with meals or milk to reduce gastrointestinal irritation
    Missed dose: Not taking at all; not doubling doses
» Proper storage

Precautions while using this medication
» Checking with physician before discontinuing medication; withdrawal headache may occur
» Not taking for longer than 6 months at a time
» Caution in driving or doing jobs requiring alertness because of possible dizziness, lightheadedness, or drowsiness
    Caution when getting up suddenly from a lying or sitting position
    Avoiding alcohol, which aggravates headache
    Avoiding smoking since nicotine constricts blood vessels
    Avoiding exposure to excessive cold, which may aggravate peripheral vasoconstriction
    Notifying physician if infection develops, since infection may cause increased sensitivity to medication

Side/adverse effects
    Signs of potential side effects, especially CNS stimulation, fibrosis, ischemia, peripheral edema, and leukopenia

General Dosing Information

Methysergide is not as potent a vasoconstrictor as ergotamine.

Because of the risk of fibrosis, methysergide should be administered for no longer than 6 months, with a drug-free interval of 3 to 4 weeks between each course.

Incidence and severity of some of the side effects may be minimized if the dosage is increased slowly to its therapeutic concentration and methysergide is given with meals.

If a response has not occurred after 3 weeks of treatment, further treatment is unlikely to produce an effect.

Gradual withdrawal of methysergide over 2 to 3 weeks is recommended to prevent rebound headache.

It is recommended that methysergide be withdrawn immediately and diagnostic tests performed if signs of retroperitoneal, pleuropulmonary, or cardiac fibrosis occur. Partial to complete regression may occur after the medication is discontinued, although surgery may be necessary in some patients.

Methysergide should be withdrawn at the first sign of vascular insufficiency.

Oral Dosage Forms

METHYSERGIDE MALEATE TABLETS USP

Usual adult dose: Oral, 4 to 6 mg a day in divided doses.

Auxiliary labeling: • Take with meals or milk.

METIPRANOLOL   Ophthalmic

A commonly used *brand name* in the U.S. is *OptiPranolol*.

OPHTHALMIC
Metipranolol Hydrochloride Ophthalmic Solution
  In the U.S.—*OptiPranolol*

Category: Antiglaucoma agent (ophthalmic).

Indications

Note: Bracketed information in the *Indications* section refers to uses not included in U.S. product labeling.

Accepted
Glaucoma, open-angle (treatment);
[Glaucoma, in aphakic eyes (treatment)];
[Glaucoma, secondary (treatment)]; or
Hypertension, ocular (treatment)—Metipranolol is indicated in the treatment of ocular hypertension and chronic open-angle glaucoma. It may be used alone or in conjunction with other antiglaucoma agents. In addition, metipranolol may be used in patients with glaucoma in aphakic eyes and in some patients with secondary glaucoma.

[Glaucoma, angle-closure (treatment adjunct)]—Metipranolol may be used in conjunction with a miotic to reduce elevated intraocular pressure in acute and chronic angle-closure glaucoma; however, metipranolol's action alone is unlikely to terminate an acute attack of angle-closure glaucoma, because metipranolol produces little or no constriction of the pupil, which is necessary to pull the iris away from the trabeculum to relieve blockage of the trabecular meshwork.

[Glaucoma, angle-closure, *during* or *after* iridectomy (treatment)]; or
[Glaucoma, malignant (treatment)]—Metipranolol is used to lower intraocular pressure in the treatment of angle-closure glaucoma *during* or *after* iridectomy and in the treatment of malignant glaucoma.

Pharmacology

Mechanism of action/Effect: Metipranolol is a beta-1 and beta-2 (nonselective) adrenergic blocking agent. The exact mechanism of the ocular hypotensive action of metipranolol has not been established; however, it appears to lower intraocular pressure by reducing aqueous humor production. A slight increase in outflow may be an additional mechanism.

Other actions/effects:
  Reduces cardiac output in both healthy individuals and patients with heart disease.
  Produces beta-adrenergic receptor blockade in the bronchi and bronchioles.
  Has little or no effect on pupil size or accommodation.

Onset of action: Within 30 minutes following a single dose.

Time to peak effect: Approximately 2 hours following a single dose.

Duration of action: More than 24 hours following a single dose.

Precautions to Consider

Cross-sensitivity and/or related problems
Patients sensitive to other beta-adrenergic blockers, either systemic or ophthalmic (such as acebutolol, atenolol, betaxolol, carteolol, labetalol, levobunolol, metoprolol, nadolol, oxprenolol, penbutolol, pindolol, propranolol, sotalol, or timolol), may be sensitive to metipranolol also.

Geriatrics
No information is available on the relationship of age to the effects of metipranolol in geriatric patients. However, if significant systemic absorption of ophthalmic beta-blockers occurs, the same geriatrics-related problems may occur that are possible with the systemic beta-blockers. These include increased myocardial depression because of reduced metabolic and excretory capabilities in many elderly patients and the increased risk of beta-blocker-induced hypothermia in elderly patients.
In addition, elderly patients are more likely to have age-related peripheral vascular disease, which may require caution in patients receiving beta-blockers.

Drug interactions and/or related problems
The following drug interactions and/or related problems have been selected on the basis of their potential clinical significance (possible mechanism in parentheses where appropriate)—not necessarily inclusive (» = major clinical significance):

Note: Combinations containing any of the following medications, depending on the amount present, may also interact with this medication.

  Information concerning interactions between ophthalmic metipranolol and other medications is limited. Some of the following potential interactions apply to beta-adrenergic blocking agents in general and are stated for cautionary reference until additional information specific for metipranonol is available.

Amphetamines
  (if significant systemic absorption of the ophthalmic beta-adrenergic blocking agents occurs, concurrent use of amphetamines may result in unopposed alpha-adrenergic activity with a risk of hypertension and excessive bradycardia and possible heart block)

Anesthetics, hydrocarbon inhalation, such as:
  Chloroform
  Cyclopropane
  Enflurane
  Halothane
  Isoflurane
  Methoxyflurane
  Trichloroethylene
    (if significant systemic absorption of the ophthalmic beta-adrenergic blocking agents occurs, concurrent use of hydrocarbon inhalation anesthetics may result in prolonged severe hypotension because the beta-adrenergic blockade reduces the ability of the heart to respond to beta-adrenergically mediated sympathetic reflex stimuli; if necessary to reverse the effects of beta-adrenergic blocking agents during surgery, agonists, such as dobutamine, dopamine, isoproterenol, or norepinephrine, may be used but should be administered with caution, especially in patients receiving halothane. Some clinicians recommend gradual withdrawal of beta-adrenergic blocking agents 48 hours prior to elective surgery; however, this recommendation is controversial)

Antidiabetic agents, oral, or
Insulin
    (systemic beta-adrenergic blocking agents may affect diabetes mellitus therapy. This may also occur with ophthalmic beta-adrenergic blocking agents if there is significant systemic absorption. Nonselective beta-adrenergic blocking agents impair glycogenolysis and the hyperglycemic response to endogenous epinephrine, leading to persistence of hypoglycemia. Also, beta-adrenergic blocking agents, especially nonselective agents, decrease the release of insulin in response to hyperglycemia. Dosage adjustment of the antidiabetic agent may be required to avoid severe hypoglycemic reaction. In addition, beta-adrener-

gic blocking agents may complicate patient monitoring by masking symptoms of hypoglycemia caused by epinephrine, such as increased heart rate and increased blood pressure, but not dizziness and sweating. Although selective or relatively selective beta-adrenergic blocking agents usually cause fewer problems with blood glucose levels, they may still mask symptoms of hypoglycemia)

Beta-adrenergic blocking agents, systemic
(if significant systemic absorption of ophthalmic beta-adrenergic blocking agents occurs, concurrent use may result in an additive effect either on intraocular pressure or on systemic effects of beta-blockade)

Calcium channel blocking agents
(if significant systemic absorption of ophthalmic beta-adrenergic blocking agents occurs, concurrent use of calcium channel blocking agents, such as diltiazem, nicardipine, nifedipine, nimodipine, and verapamil, may result in atrioventricular conduction disturbances, left ventricular failure, and hypotension; in some patients, if a calcium antagonist is necessary, nicardipine or nifedipine may be preferred because it has less effect on heart rate and conduction, although it may also cause greater hypotension; concurrent use of calcium channel blockers and metipranolol should be used with care in patients with impaired cardiac function)

Catecholamine-depleting medications, such as the rauwolfia alkaloids:
Alseroxylon
Deserpidine
Rauwolfia serpentina
Reserpine
(if significant systemic absorption of the ophthalmic beta-adrenergic blocking agents occurs, concurrent use of catecholamine-depleting medications may result in additive and possible excessive beta-adrenergic blockade; although this effect is largely theoretical, close observation is recommended, since bradycardia and marked hypotension may occur)

Cocaine
(cocaine may inhibit the therapeutic effects of systemic beta-adrenergic blocking agents, and may also have this effect on ophthalmic beta-adrenergic blocking agents)

(concurrent use of a systemic beta-adrenergic blocking agent with cocaine may increase the risk of hypertension, excessive bradycardia, and possibly heart block because beta-blockade may leave cocaine's alpha-adrenergic activity unopposed. This may also occur with ophthalmic beta-adrenergic blocking agents if significant systemic absorption of the ophthalmic beta-blocker occurs)

Diazoxide
(if significant systemic absorption of the ophthalmic beta-adrenergic blocking agents occurs, concurrent use may prevent the diazoxide-induced tachycardia; however, the risk of hypotension may be increased)

Dipivefrin or
Epinephrine, ophthalmic
(concurrent use of dipivefrin or ophthalmic epinephrine with the ophthalmic beta-adrenergic blocking agents may provide a beneficial additive effect in lowering intraocular pressure in some patients)

Fentanyl derivatives
(chronic preoperative use of ophthalmic beta-adrenergic blocking agents may increase the risk of initial bradycardia following induction doses of a fentanyl derivative)

Flecainide
(if significant systemic absorption of the ophthalmic beta-adrenergic blocking agents occurs, concurrent use may result in additive negative cardiac inotropic effects)

Hypotension-producing medications, other
(if significant systemic absorption of the ophthalmic beta-adrenergic blocking agents occurs, concurrent use may potentiate the hypotensive effects of these medications)

Phenothiazines
(if significant systemic absorption of the ophthalmic beta-adrenergic blocking agents occurs, concurrent use may result in an increased plasma concentration of either the phenothiazines or the beta-adrenergic blocking agents because of inhibition of metabolism. This may result in additive hypotensive effects, irreversible retinopathy, cardiac arrhythmias, or tardive dyskinesia)

Sympathomimetics, systemic
(if significant systemic absorption of ophthalmic metipranolol occurs, concurrent use may result in inhibition of therapeutic effects of sympathomimetics with beta-adrenergic stimulant activity; in addition, beta-adrenergic blockade may result in unopposed alpha-adrenergic activity with a risk of hypertension and excessive bradycardia with possible heart block)

(for sympathomimetics with both alpha- and beta-adrenergic effects used as bronchodilators [ephedrine, epinephrine], beta-adrenergic blockade may antagonize the bronchodilating effect of ephedrine and epinephrine)

(for sympathomimetics with beta-adrenergic effects only, beta-adrenergic blockade may antagonize beta-1-adrenergic cardiac effects [dobutamine, dopamine, metaraminol, norepinephrine] or the beta-2-adrenergic bronchodilating effect [albuterol, bitolterol, ethylnorepinephrine, fenoterol, isoetharine, metaproterenol, pirbuterol, terbutaline] or both [isoproterenol])

Xanthines, such as:
Aminophylline
Caffeine
Dyphylline
Oxtriphylline
Theophylline
(if significant systemic absorption of the ophthalmic beta-adrenergic blocking agents occurs, concurrent use may result in inhibition of therapeutic effects of xanthines; in addition, concurrent use of xanthines [except dyphylline] with the ophthalmic beta-adrenergic blocking agents may decrease theophylline clearance, especially in patients with increased theophylline clearance induced by smoking; concurrent use requires careful monitoring)

(in addition, concurrent use with caffeine may enhance the cardiac inotropic effects of the ophthalmic beta-adrenergic blocking agents if significant systemic absorption occurs)

Contraindications/Medical problems
The contraindications/medical problems included have been selected on the basis of their potential clinical significance (reasons given in parentheses where appropriate)—not necessarily inclusive (» = major clinical significance).

Except under special circumstances, this medication should not be used when the following medical problems exist:

» Asthma, bronchial, or history of, or
» Pulmonary disease, obstructive, severe chronic
(severe respiratory reactions, including death due to bronchospasm, have been reported in patients with asthma following administration of ophthalmic beta-adrenergic blocking agents)

» Cardiac failure, overt, or
» Heart block, 2nd- or 3rd-degree atrioventricular (AV), or
» Shock, cardiogenic, or
» Sinus bradycardia
(risk of further myocardial depression)

» Previous allergic reaction to metipranolol

Risk-benefit should be considered when the following medical problems exist:

» Bronchitis, nonallergenic or chronic, or
» Emphysema or
» Pulmonary function impairment, other
   (ophthalmic metipranolol may promote bronchospasm and block bronchodilation produced by endogenous and exogenous catecholamine stimulation of beta-2 receptors)

   Cerebrovascular insufficiency
   (potential effects on blood pressure and pulse; if signs of reduced cerebral blood flow occur following initiation of therapy, alternative therapy should be considered)

» Diabetes mellitus, especially labile diabetes
   (metipranolol may mask some signs and symptoms of hypoglycemia, such as tachycardia and tremor, but not dizziness and sweating)

» Hyperthyroidism
   (metipranolol may mask certain signs and symptoms of hyperthyroidism; abrupt withdrawal may precipitate a thyroid storm)

   Myasthenia gravis
   (beta-adrenergic blockade may potentiate muscle weakness related to certain myasthenic symptoms, such as diplopia, ptosis, and generalized weakness)

Side/Adverse Effects

Note: Even in patients *without* a history of cardiac failure, continued depression of the myocardium with beta-blockers, including ophthalmic metipranolol if significant systemic absorption occurs, over a period of time can lead to cardiac failure. At the first sign or symptom of cardiac failure, metipranolol should be discontinued.

The following side/adverse effects have been selected on the basis of their potential clinical significance (possible signs and symptoms in parentheses where appropriate)—not necessarily inclusive:

Those indicating need for medical attention
Incidence rare
   Allergic reaction (skin rash, hives, or itching); *blepharitis, conjunctivitis, dermatitis of eyelid, or edema* (swelling, irritation, or inflammation of eye or eyelid)

Symptoms of systemic absorption
   Anxiety or nervousness; chest pain; coughing, wheezing, or troubled breathing; dizziness; headache; hypertension; irregular, slow, or pounding heartbeat; mental depression; muscle or joint aches or pain; nausea; runny or bleeding nose; sleepiness; unusual tiredness or weakness

Those indicating need for medical attention only if they continue or are bothersome
Incidence more frequent
   Stinging of eye or other eye irritation—transient upon administration of medication

Incidence less frequent
   Blurred vision or other vision problems; browache; increased sensitivity of eye to light; redness or watering of eye

Patient Consultation

In providing consultation, consider emphasizing the following selected information (» = major clinical significance):

Before using this medication
» Conditions affecting use, especially:
   Allergy to metipranolol or other beta-blockers (such as acebutolol, atenolol, betaxolol, carteolol, labetalol, levobunolol, metoprolol, nadolol, oxprenolol, penbutolol, pindolol, propranolol, sotalol, or timolol)

Pregnancy—Ophthalmic metipranolol may be absorbed into the body. Some studies in animals have shown that metipranolol increases the incidence of death in the animal fetus

Use in children—Infants may be especially sensitive to the effects of metipranolol, thus increasing the risk of side effects

Use in the elderly—If significant systemic absorption of ophthalmic beta-blockers occurs, the chance of side effects during treatment may be increased, since elderly people are especially sensitive to the effects of these medications

Use by athletes—Beta-blockers are banned and tested for in athletes; because ophthalmic metipranolol may be absorbed into the body, the medication may appear in the urine; if the agent is found in the urine, the athlete will be disqualified

Other medical problems, especially bronchial asthma, or history of; severe chronic obstructive pulmonary disease; overt cardiac failure; 2nd- or 3rd-degree atrioventricular (AV) heart block; cardiogenic shock; sinus bradycardia; nonallergenic or chronic bronchitis; emphysema or other pulmonary function impairment; diabetes mellitus; or hyperthyroidism

Proper use of this medication
» Proper administration technique; using nasolacrimal occlusion is especially important in infants and children
   Preventing contamination: Not touching applicator tip to any surface; keeping container tightly closed
» Importance of not using more medication than the amount prescribed
   Missed dose: If dosing schedule is—
      Once a day: Applying as soon as possible; not applying if not remembered until next day; applying regularly scheduled dose
      More than once a day: Applying as soon as possible; not applying if almost time for next dose; applying next dose at regularly scheduled time
» Proper storage

Precautions while using this medication
   Regular visits to physician to check eye pressure during therapy
» Caution if any kind of surgery (including dental surgery) or emergency treatment is required
» Diabetics: May mask some signs of hypoglycemia, such as increased pulse rate and trembling, but not dizziness and sweating; also, may cause decreased or sometimes increased blood glucose concentrations
   Possible photophobia: Wearing sunglasses and avoiding too much exposure to bright light

Side/adverse effects
   Signs of potential side effects, especially allergic reaction, symptoms of systemic absorption, or blepharitis, conjunctivitis, dermatitis, or edema of eyelid or eye

General Dosing Information

Although some manufacturers recommend a dose of 2 drops of an ophthalmic solution at appropriate intervals, the conjunctival sac will usually hold only 1 drop.

When metipranolol is used to replace another ophthalmic beta-adrenergic blocking agent, the other beta-blocker should be discontinued simultaneously with initiation of therapy with metipranolol.

When metipranolol is used to replace a single antiglaucoma agent other than another ophthalmic beta-adrenergic agent, the other antiglaucoma agent may be continued on the first day that metipranolol is used but should be discontinued on the second day.

When metipranolol is used to replace several concomitantly administered antiglaucoma agents, the patient's dosage should be individualized as required. If any of the other antiglaucoma agents used is a beta-blocker, it should be discontinued before metipranolol is added to the regimen. The other antiglaucoma agents being used may be continued on the first day that metipranolol is used but one of the agents should be discontinued on the second day. Then the remaining antiglaucoma agents may be decreased or discontinued according to patient's response. Additional adjustments usually should involve only one agent at a time and should be made at intervals of not less than one week.

Metipranolol may be used concurrently with direct and indirect muscarinic agonists (e.g., pilocarpine, echothiophate, carbachol), beta-agonists (e.g., ophthalmic epinephrine or dipivefrin), and/or systemic carbonic anhydrase inhibitors (e.g., acetazolamide), if necessary to control intraocular pressure.

In patients scheduled for major surgery, some practitioners recommend that beta-adrenergic blocking agents be gradually withdrawn 48 hours prior to surgery because beta-adrenergic receptor blockade impairs the ability of the heart to respond to beta-adrenergically mediated reflex stimuli. This recommendation remains controversial. However, since ophthalmic metipranolol may be absorbed systemically, gradual withdrawal of the medication should be considered for patients undergoing elective surgery because prolonged severe hypotension during anesthesia has occurred in some patients receiving systemic beta-adrenergic blocking agents. If necessary during surgery, the effects of beta-adrenergic blocking agents may be reversed by sufficient doses of agonists, such as isoproterenol, dopamine, dobutamine, or norepinephrine.

Ophthalmic Dosage Forms

METIPRANOLOL HYDROCHLORIDE OPHTHALMIC SOLUTION

Usual adult and adolescent dose: Topical, to the conjunctiva, 1 drop of a 0.3% solution of metipranolol (base) two times a day.

Usual adult prescribing limits: Dosages above 1 drop of a 0.3% solution two times a day is not known to be of benefit.

Auxiliary labeling:
- For the eye.
- Keep container tightly closed.

METOCLOPRAMIDE   Systemic

Some commonly used *brand names* are:

In the U.S.—

Clopra	Reclomide
Octamide	Reglan
Octamide PFS	

In Canada—

Apo-Metoclop	Maxeran
Emex	Reglan

ORAL

Metoclopramide Tablets USP
In the U.S.—*Clopra; Octamide; Reclomide; Reglan;* GENERIC
In Canada—*Apo-Metoclop; Emex; Maxeran; Reglan*
Metoclopramide Hydrochloride Syrup
In the U.S.—*Reglan;* GENERIC
In Canada—*Maxeran; Reglan*

PARENTERAL

Metoclopramide Injection USP
In the U.S.—*Octamide PFS; Reglan;* GENERIC
In Canada—*Maxeran; Reglan*

Category: Dopaminergic blocking agent; gastrointestinal emptying (delayed) adjunct; peristaltic stimulant; antiemetic.

Indications

Note: Bracketed information in the *Indications* section refers to uses not included in U.S. product labeling.

Accepted
Radiography, gastrointestinal, adjunct; and
Intubation, intestinal—Metoclopramide injection is indicated to facilitate intestinal intubation in adults and children, and to stimulate gastric emptying and intestinal transit of barium in cases where delayed emptying interferes with radiological examinations of stomach or small intestine.
Gastroparesis (treatment)[1]—Metoclopramide is indicated for the relief of symptoms of acute and recurrent diabetic gastroparesis.
Nausea and vomiting, cancer chemotherapy-induced (prophylaxis)—Metoclopramide injection is indicated in high doses for the prevention of nausea and vomiting associated with emetogenic cancer chemotherapy.

Some clinicians may prefer ondansetron to high-dose metoclopramide for prophylaxis of cancer chemotherapy-induced nausea and vomiting because ondansetron is less toxic, and in some studies, has been proven more effective than high-dose metoclopramide.

Nausea and vomiting, postoperative (prophylaxis)—Metoclopramide is indicated for the prophylaxis of postoperative nausea and vomiting in cases where nasogastric suction is undesirable.

Reflux, gastroesophageal (treatment)[1]—Oral metoclopramide is indicated in adults for the symptomatic short-term treatment of heartburn and reflux esophagitis due to delayed gastric emptying. [In infants, it is used in the treatment of chronic vomiting and recurrent bronchopulmonary manifestations associated with gastroesophageal reflux.]

[Nausea and vomiting, postoperative, drug-related (treatment)]—Metoclopramide is used in the treatment of drug-related postoperative nausea and vomiting.

[Gastric emptying, slow (treatment)]; or
[Gastric stasis, in preterm infants (treatment)]—Metoclopramide is used for correcting the slow gastric emptying in postvagotomy stasis, in idiopathic stasis, and in various collagen diseases such as scleroderma. In addition, it is used for persistent functional feeding intolerance and gastric stasis in preterm infants.

[Pneumonitis, aspiration (prophylaxis)][1]—Metoclopramide is used prior to general anesthesia to promote gastric emptying and reduce the risk of aspiration, especially in emergency surgery, cesarean sections, or delivery.

[Headache, vascular (treatment adjunct)][1]—Metoclopramide is used to counteract the gastric stasis and nausea associated with migraine, and to promote the absorption of orally administered analgesics given in the treatment of migraine.

[Hiccups, persistent (treatment)][1]—Metoclopramide is used in the control of persistent hiccups.

[Metoclopramide has been used in the treatment of lactation deficiency; however, it has generally been replaced by more effective medications.]

---

[1]Not included in Canadian product labeling.

Pharmacology

Mechanism of action/Effect:

Dopaminergic blocking agents—Gastrointestinal emptying (delayed) adjunct; peristaltic stimulant: Exact mechanism of action is unknown; however, it is believed that metoclopramide inhibits gastric smooth muscle relaxation produced by dopamine thus enhancing cholinergic responses of the gastrointestinal smooth muscle. Accelerates intestinal transit and gastric emptying by preventing relaxation of gastric body and increasing the phasic activity of antrum. At the same time, this action is accompanied by relaxation of the upper small intestine, resulting in an improved coordination between the body and antrum of the stomach and the upper small intestine. Decreases reflux into the esophagus by increasing the resting pressure of the lower esophageal sphincter and improves acid clearance from the esophagus by increasing amplitude of esophageal peristaltic contractions.

Antiemetic—Dopamine antagonist action raises the threshold of activity in the chemoreceptor trigger zone and decreases the input from afferent visceral nerves. High doses of metoclopramide have been found to antagonize 5-hydroxytryptamine (5-HT) receptors in the peripheral nervous system in animals.

Other actions/effects:
Metoclopramide stimulates prolactin secretion and causes a transient increase in circulating aldosterone levels, which may be associated with transient fluid retention.

Onset of action:
Intramuscular—10 to 15 minutes.
Intravenous—1 to 3 minutes.
Oral—30 to 60 minutes.

Duration of action: 1 to 2 hours.

Precautions to Consider

Cross-sensitivity and/or related problems
Patients sensitive to procaine and procainamide may be sensitive to this medication also.

Geriatrics
Extrapyramidal effects, especially parkinsonism and tardive dyskinesia, of metoclopramide are more likely to occur in elderly patients following usual or high doses over a long period of time.

Drug interactions and/or related problems
The following drug interactions and/or related problems have been selected on the basis of their potential clinical significance (possible mechanism in parentheses where appropriate)—not necessarily inclusive (» = major clinical significance):

Note: Combinations containing any of the following medications, depending on the amount present, may also interact with this medication.

Only specific interactions between metoclopramide and other oral medications have been identified in this monograph. However, because of increased gastrointestinal motility and decreased gastric emptying time caused by metoclopramide, absorption of oral medications from the stomach may be decreased, while absorption from the small intestine may be enhanced.

» Alcohol
(concurrent use may increase the central nervous system [CNS] depressant effects of either alcohol or metoclopramide; concurrent use also may accelerate gastric emptying of alcohol, thus possibly increasing its rate and extent of absorption from the small intestine)

Anticholinergics or other medications with anticholinergic activity
or
Opioid-containing medications
(concurrent use may antagonize the effects of metoclopramide on gastrointestinal motility)

Apomorphine
(prior administration of metoclopramide may decrease the emetic response to apomorphine; also, concurrent use may potentiate the CNS depressant effects of either apomorphine or metoclopramide)

Bromocriptine
(metoclopramide may increase serum prolactin concentrations and interfere with effects of bromocriptine; dosage adjustment of bromocriptine may be necessary)

Cimetidine
(concurrent use may decrease the effect of cimetidine due to decreased absorption)

» CNS depression-producing medications, other
(concurrent use may increase the sedative effects of either these medications or metoclopramide)

Cyclosporine
(the decrease in gastric emptying time caused by metoclopramide may increase the bioavailability of cyclosporine; monitoring of cyclosporine concentrations may be necessary)

Digoxin
(concurrent use may decrease absorption of digoxin from stomach; dosage adjustment of digoxin may be necessary)

Extrapyramidal reaction-causing medications
(concurrent use with metoclopramide may increase the frequency and severity of extrapyramidal effects)

Hepatotoxic medications
(concurrent use with metoclopramide may increase the risk of hepatotoxicity)

Levodopa
(metoclopramide has been reported to decrease the effectiveness of levodopa with concurrent use)

Mexiletine
(concurrent use with metoclopramide may accelerate absorption of mexiletine)

Monoamine oxidase (MAO) inhibitors, including furazolidine and procarbazine
(metoclopramide releases catecholamines in patients with essential hypertension and should be used cautiously in patients receiving MAO inhibitors)

Pergolide
(dopamine antagonists such as metoclopramide may decrease the effectiveness of pergolide)

Succinylcholine
(metoclopramide has been reported to prolong succinylcholine block; dosage reduction of succinylcholine may be necessary with concurrent use)

Contraindications/Medical problems
The contraindications/medical problems included have been selected on the basis of their potential clinical significance (reasons given in parentheses where appropriate)—not necessarily inclusive (» = major clinical significance).

Except under special circumstances, this medication should not be used when the following medical problems exist:

» Epilepsy
(severity and frequency of seizures may be increased)

» Gastrointestinal hemorrhage, mechanical obstruction, or perforation
(stimulation of gastrointestinal motility may aggravate condition)

» Pheochromocytoma
(may cause hypertensive crisis)

Risk-benefit should be considered when the following medical problems exist:

Asthma
(administration of metoclopramide may increase risk of bronchospasm)

Hypertension
(administration of intravenous metoclopramide may worsen condition due to release of catecholamines)

Liver failure
(risk of increased adverse effects because of increased accumulation of the drug due to impaired clearance; reduced dosage is recommended)

Parkinson's disease
(symptoms may be exacerbated)

» Renal failure, severe, chronic
(risk of extrapyramidal effects may be increased; reduced dosage is recommended)

Sensitivity to metoclopramide, procaine, or procainamide

Side/Adverse Effects

Note: Methemoglobinemia has been reported in premature and full-term neonates receiving metoclopramide intramuscularly at a dose of 1 to 2 mg per kg of body weight (mg/kg) a day for 3 days or more.

The following side/adverse effects have been selected on the basis of their potential clinical significance (possible signs and symptoms in parentheses where appropriate)—not necessarily inclusive:

Those indicating need for medical attention
Incidence rare
Agranulocytosis (chills, fever, sore throat, general feeling of tiredness or weakness); *cardiovascular effects, specifically hypotension* (dizziness or fainting), *hypertension* (dizziness, severe or continuing headaches, or increase in blood pressure), or *tachycardia* (fast or irregular heartbeat); *extrapyramidal effects, parkinsonian* (difficulty in speaking or swallowing, loss of balance control, mask-like face, shuffling walk, stiffness of arms or legs, trembling and shaking of hands and fingers); *tardive dyskinesia* (lip smacking or puckering, puffing of cheeks, rapid or worm-like movements of tongue, uncontrolled chewing movements, uncontrolled movements of arms and legs)—usually occurs after at least one year of continuous treatment and may persist after discontinuation of metoclopramide

Note: *Extrapyramidal effects* may occur at therapeutic doses in any age group. However, they occur more frequently in children and young adults, and at the higher doses used in prophylaxis of vomiting due to cancer chemotherapy. Dystonic reactions may start within minutes after start of intravenous therapy, and disappear within 24 hours after discontinuation of metoclopramide. Onset of *parkinsonian* symptoms may vary from a few weeks to several months after initiation of therapy and are reversible upon discontinuation of metoclopramide.

With high doses
Agitation (unusual nervousness, restlessness, or irritability); *panic-like sensation; restless legs syndrome* (aching or discomfort in lower legs or sensation of crawling in legs)

Note: The onset may occur within minutes of receiving high doses of metoclopramide and may last for 2 to 24 hours.

Symptoms of overdose
Confusion; drowsiness, severe

Those indicating need for medical attention only if they continue or are bothersome
Incidence more frequent
Diarrhea—with high doses; *drowsiness*—about 10%; *restlessness*—about 10%; *unusual tiredness or weakness*—about 10%
Incidence less frequent or rare
Breast tenderness and swelling; changes in menstruation; constipation; depression; dizziness; headache; prolactin stimulation (increased flow of breast milk); *nausea; skin rash; trouble in sleeping; unusual dryness of mouth; unusual irritability*

Patient Consultation

In providing consultation, consider emphasizing the following selected information (» = major clinical significance):

Before using this medication
» Conditions affecting use, especially:
Sensitivity to metoclopramide, procaine, or procainamide
Breast-feeding—Excreted in breast milk
Use in children—Extrapyramidal effects more likely; increased risk of methemoglobinemia in premature and full-term infants
Use in the elderly—Extrapyramidal effects more likely
Use by athletes—Antiemetics are banned and, in some cases, tested for in competitors in biathlon and modern pentathlon events by the U.S. Olympic Committee (USOC)
Other medications, especially alcohol and CNS depressants
Other medical problems, especially epilepsy; gastrointestinal bleeding, mechanical obstruction, or perforation; or severe renal function impairment

Proper use of this medication
» Taking 30 minutes before meals and at bedtime (for oral dosage forms)
» Not taking more medication than the amount prescribed
Missed dose: Using as soon as possible; not using if almost time for next dose
» Proper storage

Precautions while using this medication
» Avoiding use of alcohol or other CNS depressants
» Caution if drowsiness occurs

Side/adverse effects
Signs of potential side effects, especially agranulocytosis, extrapyramidal effects, and tardive dyskinesia

General Dosing Information

In patients with hepatic or severe renal function impairment, the normally prescribed dose should be reduced by 50%, since adverse effects are more likely to be exacerbated.

For parenteral dosage forms only
Intravenous injections of metoclopramide should be made *slowly* over a 1- to 2-minute period, since a transient but intense feeling of anxiety and restlessness followed by drowsiness may occur with rapid administration.

Intravenous infusion should be made *slowly* over a period of not less than 15 minutes. Metoclopramide injection may be diluted for intravenous infusion with 50 mL of 5% dextrose in water, sodium chloride injection, 5% dextrose in 0.45% sodium chloride, Ringer's injection, or lactated Ringer's injection.

Oral Dosage Forms

Note: Bracketed uses in the *Dosage Forms* section refer to categories of use and/or indications that are not included in U.S. product labeling.

The dosing and strengths of the dosage forms available are expressed in terms of metoclopramide base.

METOCLOPRAMIDE TABLETS USP

Usual adult and adolescent dose:
Treatment of diabetic gastroparesis[1]—Oral, 10 mg thirty minutes before symptoms are likely to occur or before each meal and at bedtime, up to four times a day.

Note: In the initial treatment of diabetic gastroparesis, the parenteral route of administration is recommended if severe symptoms are present. Therapy may begin at 10 mg administered intramuscularly or intravenously three or four times a day, the dose adjusted as needed.

Treatment of gastroesophageal reflux[1]—Oral, 10 to 15 mg thirty minutes before symptoms are likely to occur or before each meal and at bedtime, up to four times a day.

Note: Intermittent symptoms may be treated by taking 20 mg of metoclopramide prior to the provoking situation.

[Treatment of hiccups][1]—Oral, 10 to 20 mg four times a day for seven days.

Note: An initial dose of 10 mg intramuscularly may be given if necessary.

Usual adult and adolescent prescribing limits: Up to 500 mcg (0.5 mg) per kg of body weight per day.

Usual geriatric dose: See *Usual adult and adolescent dose.*

Note: Geriatric patients may be more sensitive to the usual adult dose.

Auxiliary labeling:
- May cause drowsiness.
- Avoid alcoholic beverages.

METOCLOPRAMIDE HYDROCHLORIDE SYRUP

Usual adult and adolescent dose:

Treatment of diabetic gastroparesis[1]—Oral, 10 mg (base) thirty minutes before symptoms are likely to occur or before each meal and at bedtime, up to four times a day.

Note: In the initial treatment of diabetic gastroparesis, the parenteral route of administration is recommended if severe symptoms are present. Therapy may begin at 10 mg (base) administered intramuscularly or intravenously three or four times a day, the dose adjusted as needed.

Treatment of gastroesophageal reflux[1]—Oral, 10 to 15 mg (base) thirty minutes before symptoms are likely to occur or before each meal and at bedtime, up to four times a day.

Note: Intermittent symptoms may be treated by taking 20 mg of metoclopramide prior to the provoking situation.

[Treatment of hiccups][1]—Oral, 10 to 20 mg (base) four times a day for seven days.

Note: An initial dose of 10 mg intramuscularly may be given if necessary.

Usual adult and adolescent prescribing limits: Up to 500 mcg (0.5 mg) per kg of body weight per day.

Auxiliary labeling:
- May cause drowsiness.
- Avoid alcoholic beverages.

Parenteral Dosage Forms

Note: Bracketed uses in the *Dosage Forms* section refer to categories of use and/or indications that are not included in U.S. product labeling.

METOCLOPRAMIDE INJECTION USP

Usual adult and adolescent dose:

Gastrointestinal emptying (delayed) adjunct or

Peristaltic stimulant—Intravenous, 10 mg as a single dose.

[Treatment of hiccups][1]: Intramuscular, 10 mg initially, followed by oral metoclopramide at a dose of 10 to 20 mg four times a day for seven days.

Antiemetic—

For prevention of cancer chemotherapy-induced emesis:

Intravenous infusion, 2 mg per kg of body weight, administered thirty minutes before cisplatin or other highly emetogenic chemotherapeutic agent; may be repeated as needed every two or three hours.

Note: For prevention of emesis induced by chemotherapeutic agents with low emetic potential—Intravenous infusion, 1 mg per kg of body weight.

Continuous intravenous infusion, 3 mg per kg of body weight before chemotherapy, followed by 0.5 mg per kg of body weight per hour for eight hours.

For prevention of postoperative emesis: Intramuscular, 10 to 20 mg near the end of surgery.

METRONIDAZOLE   Systemic

Some commonly used *brand names* are:

In the U.S.—

Flagyl	*Metric 21*
Flagyl I.V.	*Metro I.V.*
Flagyl I.V. RTU	*Protostat*

In Canada—

Apo-Metronidazole	*Novonidazol*
Flagyl	*Trikacide*

ORAL

Metronidazole Capsules*
In Canada—*Flagyl; Trikacide*
Metronidazole Tablets USP
In the U.S.—*Flagyl; Metric 21; Protostat;* GENERIC
In Canada—*Apo-Metronidazole; Flagyl; Novonidazol; Trikacide*

PARENTERAL

Metronidazole Injection USP
In the U.S.—*Flagyl I.V. RTU; Metro I.V.;* GENERIC
In Canada—*Flagyl;* GENERIC
Metronidazole Hydrochloride for Injection
In the U.S.—*Flagyl I.V.*

*Not commercially available in the U.S.

Category: Antibacterial (systemic); antiprotozoal; bowel disease (inflammatory) suppressant; anthelmintic (systemic).

Indications

Note: Bracketed information in the *Indications* section refers to uses not included in U.S. product labeling.

Accepted

Amebiasis, extraintestinal (treatment)—Metronidazole is indicated in the treatment of extraintestinal amebiasis, including amebic liver abscess, caused by *Entamoeba histolytica.* When used in the treatment of invasive amebiasis, metronidazole should be administered concurrently or sequentially with a luminal amebicide (e.g., iodoquinol, paromomycin, tetracycline, diloxanide furoate).

Amebiasis, intestinal (treatment)—Oral metronidazole is indicated in the treatment of acute intestinal amebiasis caused by *Entamoeba histolytica.* Metronidazole may not eradicate intestinal amebic infections, requiring treatment with a luminal amebicide.

Bone and joint infections (treatment)—Metronidazole is indicated in the treatment of bone and joint infections caused by *Bacteroides* species, including the *B. fragilis* group (*B. fragilis, B. distasonis, B. ovatus, B. thetaiotaomicron, B. vulgatus*).

Brain abscess (treatment)—Metronidazole is indicated in the treatment of brain abscess caused by *Bacteroides* species, including the *B. fragilis* group.

Central nervous system (CNS) infections (treatment)—Metronidazole is indicated in the treatment of CNS infections, including meningitis, caused by *Bacteroides* species, including the *B. fragilis* group.

Endocarditis, bacterial (treatment)—Metronidazole is indicated in the treatment of endocarditis caused by *Bacteroides* species, including the *B. fragilis* group.

Intra-abdominal infections (treatment)—Metronidazole is indicated in the treatment of intra-abdominal infections, including peritonitis, intra-abdominal abscess, and liver abscess, caused by *Bacteroides* species, including the *B. fragilis* group, *Clostridium* species, *Eubacterium* species, *Peptococcus* species, and *Peptostreptococcus* species.

Pelvic infections, female (treatment)—Metronidazole is indicated in the treatment of female pelvic infections, including endometritis, endomyometritis, tubo-ovarian abscess, and postsurgical vaginal cuff infections, caused by *Bacteroides* species, including the *B. fragilis* group, *Clostridium* species, *Peptococcus* species, and *Peptostreptococcus* species.

Perioperative infections, colorectal (prophylaxis)—Intravenous metronidazole is indicated for the prophylaxis of perioperative infections during colorectal surgery.

Pneumonia, *Bacteroides* species (treatment)—Metronidazole is indicated in the treatment of lower respiratory tract infections, including pneumonia, empyema, and lung abscess, caused by *Bacteroides* species, including the *B. fragilis* group.

Septicemia, bacterial (treatment)—Metronidazole is indicated in the treatment of bacterial septicemia caused by *Bacteroides* species, including the *B. fragilis* group, and *Clostridium* species.

Skin and soft tissue infections (treatment)—Metronidazole is indicated in the treatment of skin and soft tissue infections caused by *Bacteroides* species, including the *B. fragilis* group, *Clostridium* species, *Fusobacterium* species, *Peptococcus* species, and *Peptostreptococcus* species.

Trichomoniasis (treatment)—Oral metronidazole is indicated in the treatment of symptomatic and asymptomatic trichomoniasis, in males and females, caused by *Trichomonas vaginalis*.

[Balantidiasis (treatment)][1]—Metronidazole is used in the treatment of *Balantidium coli* infection.

[Bowel disease, inflammatory (treatment)][1]—Metronidazole is used in the treatment of inflammatory bowel disease.

[Colitis, antibiotic-associated (treatment)][1]—Metronidazole is used in the treatment of antibiotic-associated diarrhea and colitis caused by *C. difficile*.

[Dracunculiasis (treatment)][1]—Metronidazole is used in the treatment of dracunculiasis (guinea worm infection) caused by *Dracunculus medinensis*. It decreases the inflammation around the ulcer, increasing the ease of removing the worm.

[Gastritis, *Helicobacter pylori*-associated (treatment adjunct)][1]; or [Ulcer, duodenal, *Helicobacter pylori*-associated (treatment adjunct)][1]—Some studies indicate that metronidazole may be effective, in combination with bismuth subsalicylate or colloidal bismuth subcitrate, and other oral antibiotic therapy, such as ampicillin or amoxicillin, in the treatment of *Helicobacter pylori*-associated gastritis and duodenal ulcer. However, metronidazole resistance may occur, especially in patients who have been previously exposed to metronidazole.

[Giardiasis (treatment)][1]—Oral metronidazole is used in the treatment of giardiasis caused by *Giardia lamblia*.

[Periodontal infections (treatment)][1]—Metronidazole is used in the treatment of periodontal infections caused by *Bacteroides* species.

[Vaginosis, bacterial (treatment)][1]—Oral metronidazole is used in the treatment of bacterial vaginosis caused by *Gardnerella vaginalis*.

Not all species or strains of a particular organism may be equally susceptible to metronidazole.

Unaccepted

Metronidazole is not effective against facultative anaerobes, obligate aerobes, *Propionibacterium acnes*, *Actinomyces* species, or *Candida albicans*.

---

[1]Not included in Canadian product labeling.

Pharmacology

Mechanism of action/Effect: Antibacterial (systemic); antiprotozoal—Microbicidal; active against most obligate anaerobic bacteria and protozoa by undergoing intracellular chemical reduction via mechanisms unique to anaerobic metabolism. Reduced metronidazole, which is cytotoxic but short-lived, interacts with DNA to cause a loss of helical structure, strand breakage, and resultant inhibition of nucleic acid synthesis and cell death.

Precautions to Consider

Geriatrics

No information is available on the relationship of age to the effects of metronidazole in geriatric patients. However, elderly patients are more likely to have an age-related decrease in hepatic function, which may require an adjustment in dosage in patients receiving metronidazole.

Dental

Metronidazole may cause dry mouth, an unpleasant or sharp metallic taste, and alteration of taste sensation. Dry mouth may contribute to the development of caries, periodontal disease, oral candidiasis, and discomfort.

Drug interactions and/or related problems

The following drug interactions and/or related problems have been selected on the basis of their potential clinical significance (possible mechanism in parentheses where appropriate)—not necessarily inclusive (» = major clinical significance):

Note: Combinations containing any of the following medications, depending on the amount present, may also interact with this medication.

» Alcohol
(it is recommended that metronidazole not be used concurrently with, or for at least 1 day following, ingestion of alcohol; accumulation of acetaldehyde by interference with the oxidation of alcohol may occur, resulting in disulfiram-like effects such as abdominal cramps, nausea, vomiting, headache, or flushing; in addition, modifications in the taste of alcoholic beverages have been reported during concurrent use)

» Anticoagulants, coumarin- or indandione-derivative
(effects may be potentiated when these agents are used concurrently with metronidazole, because of inhibition of enzymatic metabolism of anticoagulants; periodic prothrombin time determinations may be required during therapy to determine if dosage adjustments of anticoagulants are necessary)

Cimetidine
(hepatic metabolism of metronidazole may be decreased when metronidazole and cimetidine are used concurrently, possibly resulting in delayed elimination and increased serum metronidazole concentrations; monitoring of serum concentrations as a guide to dosage is recommended since dosage adjustments of metronidazole may be necessary during and after cimetidine therapy)

» Disulfiram
   (it is recommended that metronidazole not be used concurrently with, or for 2 weeks following, disulfiram in alcoholic patients; such use may result in confusion and psychotic reactions because of combined toxicity)

Neurotoxic medications, other
   (concurrent use of metronidazole with other neurotoxic medications may increase the potential for neurotoxicity)

Phenobarbital
   (phenobarbital may induce microsomal liver enzymes, increasing metronidazole's metabolism and resulting in a decrease in half-life and plasma concentration)

Phenytoin
   (metronidazole may impair the clearance of phenytoin, increasing phenytoin's plasma concentration)

Contraindications/Medical problems

The contraindications/medical problems included have been selected on the basis of their potential clinical significance (reasons given in parentheses where appropriate)—not necessarily inclusive (» = major clinical significance).

Risk-benefit should be considered when the following medical problems exist:

» Active organic disease of the CNS, including epilepsy
   (metronidazole may cause CNS toxicity, including seizures with high doses, and peripheral neuropathy)

» Blood dyscrasias, or history of
   (metronidazole may cause leukopenia)

Cardiac function impairment
   (parenteral dosage forms—because of sodium content)

» Hepatic function impairment, severe
   (metabolized in the liver; hepatic dysfunction may lead to decreased plasma clearance and accumulation of metronidazole and its metabolites; dosage may need to be reduced with severe hepatic function impairment)

Hypersensitivity to metronidazole

Side/Adverse Effects

The following side/adverse effects have been selected on the basis of their potential clinical significance (possible signs and symptoms in parentheses where appropriate)—not necessarily inclusive:

Those indicating need for medical attention

Incidence less frequent
   Peripheral neuropathy (numbness, tingling, pain, or weakness in hands or feet)—usually with high doses or prolonged use; *seizures*—usually with high doses

Incidence rare
   CNS toxicity (ataxia—clumsiness or unsteadiness; encephalopathy—mood or other mental changes); *hypersensitivity* (skin rash, hives, redness, or itching); *leukopenia* (sore throat and fever); *pancreatitis* (severe abdominal and back pain, anorexia, nausea and vomiting); *thrombophlebitis* (pain, tenderness, redness, or swelling at site of injection); *vaginal candidiasis* (any vaginal irritation, discharge, or dryness not present before therapy)

Those indicating need for medical attention only if they continue or are bothersome

Incidence more frequent
   CNS effects (dizziness or lightheadedness, headache); *gastrointestinal disturbance* (diarrhea, loss of appetite, nausea or vomiting, stomach pain or cramps)

Incidence less frequent or rare
   Change in taste sensation; dryness of mouth; unpleasant or sharp metallic taste

Those not indicating need for medical attention
Incidence less frequent or rare
   Dark urine

Patient Consultation

In providing consultation, consider emphasizing the following selected information (» = major clinical significance):

Before using this medication
» Conditions affecting use, especially:
   Hypersensitivity to metronidazole
   Pregnancy—Metronidazole crosses the placenta; use is not recommended during the first trimester of pregnancy
   Breast-feeding—Metronidazole is excreted in breast milk; metronidazole is not recommended during breast-feeding
   Dental—Metronidazole may cause dry mouth, an unpleasant or sharp metallic taste, and alteration of taste sensation
   Other medications, especially alcohol, coumarin- or indandione-derivative anticoagulants, or disulfiram
   Other medical problems, especially active organic disease of the CNS, a history of blood dyscrasias, or severe hepatic function impairment

Proper use of this medication
   Taking with meals or a snack to minimize gastrointestinal irritation
» Compliance with full course of therapy
» Importance of not missing doses and taking at evenly spaced times
   Missed dose: Taking as soon as possible; not taking if almost time for next dose; not doubling doses
» Proper storage

Precautions while using this medication
   Follow-up visit to physician after treatment for giardiasis to ensure that infection has been eradicated.
   Checking with physician if no improvement within a few days
» Avoiding use of alcoholic beverages or other alcohol-containing preparations while taking and for at least 1 day after discontinuing this medication
   Possible dryness of mouth; using sugarless candy or gum, ice, or saliva substitute for relief; checking with dentist if dry mouth continues for more than 2 weeks
» Caution if dizziness or lightheadedness occurs
   Prevention of reinfection in trichomoniasis; possible need for concurrent treatment of male sexual partner and use of a condom

Side/adverse effects
   Signs of potential side effects, especially CNS toxicity, hypersensitivity, leukopenia, pancreatitis, seizures, peripheral neuropathy, vaginal candidiasis, and thrombophlebitis
   Dark urine may be alarming to patient although medically insignificant

General Dosing Information

Patients with severely impaired hepatic function metabolize metronidazole slowly. Close monitoring for toxicity, as well as reduction in dose, may be required.

Anuric patients do not generally require a reduction in dose since metabolites of metronidazole may be rapidly removed by hemodialysis. Also, reduced renal function does not significantly affect single-dose pharmacokinetics of metronidazole.

For oral dosage forms only
Metronidazole may be taken with meals or a snack to lessen gastrointestinal irritation.

When metronidazole is used in the treatment of trichomoniasis, sexual partners should receive concurrent therapy since asymptomatic trichomoniasis in the male partner is a frequent source of reinfection in the female. The male partner should be advised to use a condom for the duration of treatment.

For parenteral dosage forms only

Parenteral metronidazole should be administered by slow intravenous infusion only, either continuously or intermittently over a 1-hour period.

If metronidazole is administered concurrently with a primary intravenous solution, the primary solution should be discontinued while metronidazole is being infused.

Oral Dosage Forms

Note: Bracketed uses in the *Dosage Forms* section refer to categories of use and/or indications that are not included in U.S. product labeling.

METRONIDAZOLE CAPSULES

Usual adult and adolescent dose:
Antibacterial (systemic)—
   Anaerobic infections: Oral, 7.5 mg (base) per kg of body weight, up to a maximum of 1 gram, every six hours for seven days or longer.
   [Bowel disease, inflammatory][1]: Oral, 500 mg (base) four times a day.
   [Colitis, antibiotic-associated][1]: Oral, 500 mg (base) three or four times a day.
   [Gastritis, *Helicobacter pylori*-associated (treatment adjunct)][1]; or
   [Ulcer, duodenal, *Helicobacter pylori*-associated (treatment adjunct)][1]—Oral, 500 mg (base) three times a day, in conjunction with bismuth subsalicylate or colloidal bismuth subcitrate and other oral antibiotic therapy, such as ampicillin or amoxicillin, for one to two weeks.
   [Vaginosis, bacterial][1]: Oral, 500 mg (base) two times a day for seven days.
Antiprotozoal—
   Amebiasis: Oral, 500 to 750 mg (base) three times a day for five to ten days.
   [Balantidiasis][1]: Oral, 750 mg (base) three times a day for five or six days.
   [Giardiasis][1]: Oral, 2 grams (base) once a day for three days; or 250 mg three times a day for five to seven days.
   Trichomoniasis: Oral, 2 grams (base) as a single dose; 1 gram two times a day for one day; or 250 mg three times a day for seven days.
   Anthelmintic (systemic)—[Dracunculiasis][1]: Oral, 250 mg (base) three times a day for ten days.

Usual adult prescribing limits: Antibacterial (systemic)—Up to a maximum of 4 grams (base) daily.

Auxiliary labeling:
• Avoid alcoholic beverages.
• May cause dizziness.
• Continue medicine for full time of treatment.

METRONIDAZOLE TABLETS USP

Usual adult and adolescent dose: See *Metronidazole Capsules.*

Usual adult prescribing limits: See *Metronidazole Capsules.*

Auxiliary labeling:
• Avoid alcoholic beverages.
• May cause dizziness.
• Continue medicine for full time of treatment.

Parenteral Dosage Forms

Note: Bracketed uses in the *Dosage Forms* section refer to categories of use and/or indications that are not included in U.S. product labeling.

      The dosing and dosage forms available are expressed in terms of metronidazole base.

METRONIDAZOLE INJECTION USP

Usual adult dose:
Antibacterial (systemic)—
   Anaerobic infections: Intravenous infusion, 15 mg (base) per kg of body weight initially, then 7.5 mg per kg of body weight, up to a maximum of 1 gram, every six hours for seven days or longer.
   Perioperative infections, colonic (prophylaxis): Intravenous infusion, 15 mg (base) per kg of body weight one hour prior to the start of surgery; and 7.5 mg per kg of body weight six and twelve hours after the initial dose.
   [Antiprotozoal—Amebiasis][1]: Intravenous infusion, 500 to 750 mg (base) every eight hours for five to ten days.

Usual adult prescribing limits: Antibacterial (systemic)—Up to a maximum of 4 grams (base) daily.

Additional information:
   Metronidazole Injection USP is an isotonic (297 to 310 mOsm per liter), ready-to-use solution, requiring no dilution or buffering prior to administration.
   Metronidazole Injection USP in prefilled plastic minibags should not be used in series connections. This may result in air embolism because of residual air (approximately 15 mL), which may be drawn from the primary plastic bag before administration of the infusion from the secondary plastic bag is completed.

METRONIDAZOLE HYDROCHLORIDE FOR INJECTION

Usual adult dose: See *Metronidazole Injection USP.*

Usual adult prescribing limits: See *Metronidazole Injection USP.*

MEXILETINE   Systemic

A commonly used *brand name* in the U.S. and Canada is *Mexitil*.

ORAL
Mexiletine Hydrochloride Capsules USP
   In the U.S. and Canada—*Mexitil*

Category: Antiarrhythmic.

Indications

Accepted
Arrhythmias, ventricular (treatment)—Mexiletine is indicated for the treatment of documented, life-threatening ventricular arrhythmias, such as ventricular tachycardia.

Unaccepted
Mexiletine is not recommended for use in the treatment of lesser arrhythmias, such as asymptomatic premature ventricular contractions following an acute myocardial infarction. Although the Cardiac Arrhythmias Suppression Trial (CAST) showed that treatment of asymptomatic, non-life-threatening arrhythmias following an acute myocardial infarction with encainide or flecainide was deleterious, the extrapolation of these results to other patient populations or antiarrhythmic agents remains uncertain.

Pharmacology

Mechanism of action/Effect: Blocks the fast sodium channel in cardiac tissues, especially the Purkinje network, without involvement of the autonomic system. Reduces the rate of rise and amplitude of the action potential and decreases automaticity (increases the threshold of excitability) in the Purkinje fibers. Shortens the action potential duration and, to a lesser extent, decreases the effective refractory period in the Purkinje fibers. Does not usually alter conduction velocity, although it may slow conduction in patients with pre-existing conduction abnormalities. Does not significantly affect resting membrane potential or sinus node automaticity, left ventricular function, systolic arterial blood pressure, atrioventricular (AV) conduction velocity, or QRS or QT intervals. In the Vaughan Williams classification of antiarrhythmics, mexiletine is considered to be a class IB agent.

Other actions/effects: Also has local anesthetic and anticonvulsant properties.

Onset of action: 30 minutes to 2 hours.

Precautions to Consider

Cross-sensitivity and/or related problems
Patients sensitive to other amide-type anesthetics (e.g., lidocaine) may be sensitive to mexiletine also.

Geriatrics
No information is available on the relationship of age to the effects of mexiletine in geriatric patients.

Drug interactions and/or related problems
The following drug interactions and/or related problems have been selected on the basis of their potential clinical significance (possible mechanism in parentheses where appropriate)—not necessarily inclusive (» = major clinical significance):

Note: Combinations containing any of the following medications, depending on the amount present, may also interact with this medication.

Acidifiers, urinary, such as:
   Ammonium chloride
   Ascorbic acid

Potassium or sodium phosphates
   (marked acidification of urine may accelerate renal excretion of mexiletine)
Alkalizers, urinary, such as:
   Antacids, calcium- and/or magnesium-containing
   Carbonic anhydrase inhibitors
   Citrates
   Sodium bicarbonate
      (marked alkalinization of urine may retard renal excretion of mexiletine)
Antiarrhythmics, other
   (concurrent use with mexiletine may produce additive cardiac effects; although some combinations are used for therapeutic advantage, when used concurrently dosage adjustments may be necessary)
Hepatic enzyme inducers
   (may accelerate metabolism and result in decreased plasma concentrations of mexiletine; plasma concentrations of mexiletine should be monitored during concurrent use to ensure that efficacy is maintained)
Metoclopramide
   (may accelerate absorption of mexiletine)
Smoking, tobacco
   (may induce hepatic metabolism and reduce the half-life of mexiletine)
Theophylline
   (concurrent use may decrease theophylline clearance, resulting in prolonged elimination half-life, increased serum theophylline concentrations, and increased risk of theophylline-related CNS toxicity; serum theophylline concentrations should be monitored and dosage adjustments may be required)

Contraindications/Medical problems
The contraindications/medical problems included have been selected on the basis of their potential clinical significance (reasons given in parentheses where appropriate)—not necessarily inclusive (» = major clinical significance).

Risk-benefit should be considered when the following medical problems exist:
» Atrioventricular (AV) block, pre-existing 2nd or 3rd degree, without pacemaker
      (risk of complete heart block)
» Cardiogenic shock
      (risk of further reduction of blood pressure)
Congestive heart failure, severe, or
Myocardial infarction, acute
      (may reduce hepatic metabolism and result in prolongation of effect)
      (congestive heart failure may be aggravated by mexiletine)
Hepatic function impairment
      (possible prolongation of effect)
Hypotension
      (may be exacerbated)
Intraventricular conduction abnormalities or
Sinus node function impairment
      (use of mexiletine has been reported to result in depression of sinus rate, prolongation of sinus node recovery time, decreased conduction velocity, and increased effective refractory period of the intraventricular conduction system)
Seizure disorders
      (mexiletine may precipitate seizures)
Sensitivity to mexiletine

Side/Adverse Effects

Note: In the National Heart, Lung and Blood Institute's Cardiac Arrhythmias Suppression Trial (CAST), treatment with encainide or flecainide was found to be associated with excessive mortality or increased nonfatal cardiac arrest rate, as compared with placebo, in patients with asymptomatic, non-life-threatening arrhythmias who had a recent myocardial infarction. The implications of these results for other patient populations or other antiarrhythmic agents are uncertain.

Incidence of side effects, especially some central nervous system (CNS) side effects, is related to plasma mexiletine concentrations and is greatest at concentrations exceeding 2 mcg per mL.

Exacerbation of ventricular arrhythmias, including torsade de pointes, may occur.

Hepatic necrosis has occurred rarely.

A fatal overdose caused gastrointestinal disturbances, respiratory failure, and asystole.

Pulmonary changes, including pulmonary fibrosis, have been reported in patients receiving other medications or having other conditions known to result in pulmonary toxicity; therefore, the relationship to mexiletine is unknown.

The following side/adverse effects have been selected on the basis of their potential clinical significance (possible signs and symptoms in parentheses where appropriate)—not necessarily inclusive:

Those indicating need for medical attention
Incidence less frequent
Chest pain; premature ventricular contractions (fast or irregular heartbeat); *shortness of breath*
Incidence rare
Leukopenia or agranulocytosis (fever or chills) *or thrombocytopenia* (unusual bleeding or bruising); *seizures*
Note: *Thrombocytopenia* occurs within a few days after initiation of therapy, and blood counts usually return to normal within 1 month after withdrawal of mexiletine.

Those indicating need for medical attention only if they continue or are bothersome
Incidence more frequent
CNS effects (dizziness or lightheadedness, nervousness, trembling or shaking of hands, unsteadiness or trouble in walking); *heartburn; nausea and vomiting*
Note: *Nausea* and *vomiting* usually occur within 2 hours after a dose and tend to lessen with continued treatment.
Incidence less frequent
Blurred vision; confusion; constipation or diarrhea; headache; numbness or tingling of fingers and toes; ringing in the ears; skin rash; slurred speech; trouble in sleeping; unusual tiredness or weakness

Patient Consultation

In providing consultation, consider emphasizing the following selected information (» = major clinical significance):

Before using this medication
» Conditions affecting use, especially:
   Sensitivity to amide-type anesthetics
   Pregnancy—Increased incidence of fetal resorptions in animals
   Breast-feeding—Excreted in breast milk
   Medical problems, especially atrioventricular (AV) block, preexisting 2nd or 3rd degree, without pacemaker or cardiogenic shock

Proper use of this medication
» Compliance with therapy; taking as directed even if feeling well Taking with food, milk, or an antacid to reduce stomach upset
» Importance of not missing doses and taking at evenly spaced intervals
   Missed dose: Taking as soon as possible if remembered within 4 hours; not taking if remembered later; not doubling doses
» Proper storage

Precautions while using the medication
   Regular visits to physician to check progress
   Carrying medical identification card or bracelet
» Caution if any kind of surgery (including dental surgery) or emergency treatment is required
» Caution when driving or doing things requiring alertness, because of possible dizziness

Side/adverse effects
   Signs of adverse effects, especially chest pain, premature ventricular contractions, shortness of breath, leukopenia, agranulocytosis, thrombocytopenia, and seizures

General Dosing Information

When mexiletine is replacing other antiarrhythmic therapy, the first dose may be given 6 to 12 hours after the last dose of quinidine sulfate or disopyramide, 3 to 6 hours after the last dose of procainamide, or 8 to 12 hours after the last dose of tocainide. In patients being transferred from parenteral lidocaine to oral mexiletine, substantial reduction of dose or withdrawal of lidocaine is recommended 1 to 2 hours after initiation of mexiletine therapy; lower initial doses of mexiletine (e.g., 100 to 200 mg every eight hours) may also be appropriate. In patients at risk of life-threatening arrhythmias, transfer to mexiletine therapy should take place in the hospital.

Mexiletine should be taken with food, milk, or antacid to reduce gastrointestinal irritation.

Patients with impaired hepatic function or severe congestive heart failure may require lower or less frequent doses of mexiletine.

It is recommended that dosage adjustments be made no more frequently than every 2 to 3 days.

It is recommended that the patient be evaluated carefully and mexiletine therapy may need to be withdrawn if significant leukopenia or thrombocytopenia occurs.

Oral Dosage Forms

MEXILETINE HYDROCHLORIDE CAPSULES USP

Usual adult dose: Arrhythmias, ventricular (treatment)—Oral, initially 200 mg every eight hours, the dosage being increased or decreased in increments or decrements of 50 to 100 mg per dose every two to three days as needed and tolerated.

Note: For rapid control of ventricular arrhythmias, a loading dose of 400 mg may be administered, followed by a 200-mg dose eight hours later.

Some patients may tolerate twice-a-day dosing. For patients adequately maintained on a dose of 300 mg or less every eight hours, the total daily dose may be given in divided doses every twelve hours.

Patients not adequately controlled by dosing every eight hours (i.e., those experiencing breakthrough ectopy two hours before the next dose) may respond to dosing four times a day.

Usual adult prescribing limits: Up to 1200 mg per day when given every eight hours (i.e., 400 mg per dose) or 900 mg per day when given every twelve hours (i.e., 450 mg per dose).

Auxiliary labeling: • Take with food, milk, or antacid.

MINOXIDIL   Systemic

A commonly used *brand name* in the U.S. and Canada is *Loniten.*

ORAL
Minoxidil Tablets USP
In the U.S.—*Loniten;* GENERIC
In Canada—*Loniten*

Category: Antihypertensive.

Indications

Accepted
Hypertension (treatment)—Minoxidil is indicated for treatment of hypertension.

> Because of its serious side effects, minoxidil is not considered to be a primary agent in the treatment of essential hypertension. It is recommended for use only in patients with symptomatic or organ-damaging hypertension not responsive to other treatment.

> In the 1988 Report of the Joint National Committee on Detection, Evaluation, and Treatment of High Blood Pressure, a step-like progression in choice of treatments for essential hypertension is recommended:

>> Nonpharmacologic management (especially sodium restriction, weight reduction and exercise, and moderation of alcohol consumption) is recommended first for some patients, including those with mild hypertension, and is recommended as an adjunct to all pharmacologic hypertensive therapy.

>> Initial drug therapy usually consists of a diuretic, beta-adrenergic blocking agent, calcium channel blocker, or angiotensin-converting enzyme (ACE) inhibitor. If adequate blood pressure control is not achieved and the patient is adherent to the treatment program and not experiencing significant side effects, dosage of the drug may be increased, a drug from another one of these initial classes may be added or substituted, or a second drug from a different class—centrally acting alpha-adrenergic blockers (e.g., clonidine, guanabenz, guanfacine, methyldopa), peripheral-acting adrenergic antagonists (e.g., guanadrel, guanethidine, rauwolfia alkaloids), post-synaptic alpha-1 peripheral adrenergic inhibitors (e.g., prazosin, terazosin), or vasodilators (e.g., hydralazine, minoxidil)—may be added or substituted.

>> If necessary, a drug from another class in the second group may be substituted or added as a third drug. If blood pressure control is still not achieved, a drug from still another class may be substituted or added as a fourth drug, or the patient may need further evaluation and/or referral.

Unaccepted
Because of lack of data on the best formulation and the risks associated with possible systemic absorption, use of extemporaneous topical preparations from minoxidil oral tablets is not recommended for treatment of male pattern baldness. (However, a topical product is commercially available.)

Pharmacology

Mechanism of action/Effect: Exact cellular mechanism of antihypertensive action unknown. The predominant effect of minoxidil is direct vasodilation of arterioles with little effect on veins. It reduces peripheral resistance and causes a reflex increase in heart rate and cardiac output.

Onset of action: 30 minutes.

Time to peak effect:
Single dose—2 to 3 hours.

Multiple doses—Maximum blood pressure response with continued use usually occurs within 3 to 7 days (patients receiving the largest doses respond in the shortest period of time and vice versa).

Duration of action: Usually 24 to 48 hours; up to 75 hours in some patients.

Precautions to Consider

Geriatrics
Although appropriate studies with minoxidil have not been performed in the geriatric population, the elderly may be more sensitive to the hypotensive effects. In addition, the risk of minoxidil-induced hypothermia may be increased in elderly patients. Elderly patients are also more likely to have age-related renal function impairment, which may require reduction of dosage in patients receiving minoxidil.

Drug interactions and/or related problems
The following drug interactions and/or related problems have been selected on the basis of their potential clinical significance (possible mechanism in parentheses where appropriate)—not necessarily inclusive (» = major clinical significance)

Note: Combinations containing any of the following medications, depending on the amount present, may also interact with this medication.

» Antihypertensives, potent parenteral, such as diazoxide or nitroprusside, or
» Guanethidine or
» Nitrates
(concurrent use with minoxidil may result in a severe, additive hypotensive effect; patients should be continuously observed for excessive fall in blood pressure for several hours after concurrent administration of potent peripheral antihypertensives or nitrates; concurrent use with guanethidine is not recommended)

Anti-inflammatory analgesics, nonsteroidal (NSAIAs), especially indomethacin
(may reduce antihypertensive effects of minoxidil; indomethacin, and possibly other NSAIAs, may antagonize the antihypertensive effect by inhibiting renal prostaglandin synthesis and/or by causing sodium and fluid retention; the patient should be carefully monitored to confirm that the desired effect is being obtained)

Estrogens
(estrogen-induced fluid retention may increase blood pressure)

Hypotension-producing medications, other
(hypotensive effects may be potentiated when these medications are used concurrently with minoxidil)

(although some antihypertensive and/or diuretic combinations are used for therapeutic advantage, dosage adjustments may be necessary during concurrent use)

Sympathomimetics
(may reduce antihypertensive effects of minoxidil; the patient should be carefully monitored to confirm that the desired effect is being obtained)

Contraindications/Medical problems
The contraindications/medical problems included have been selected on the basis of their potential clinical significance (reasons given in parentheses where appropriate)—not necessarily inclusive (» = major clinical significance).

Risk-benefit should be considered when the following medical problems exist:

Cerebrovascular disease or accident

» Congestive heart failure not due to hypertension

» Coronary insufficiency, including angina pectoris
   (may be exacerbated)

Myocardial infarction

» Pericardial effusion

» Pheochromocytoma
   (use may stimulate release of catecholamines from the tumor)

» Renal function impairment
   (reduced elimination; lower doses may be required)

Sensitivity to minoxidil

Side/Adverse Effects

Note: Minoxidil has been shown to cause severe myocardial toxicity in dogs. However, this effect has not been observed in other animals or in humans at this time, although nonspecific electrocardiogram (ECG) changes are commonly seen, pericardial effusion (sometimes progressing to cardiac tamponade) occurs in about 3% of patients, and pericarditis has been reported.

The following side/adverse effects have been selected on the basis of their potential clinical significance (possible signs and symptoms in parentheses where appropriate)—not necessarily inclusive:

Those indicating need for medical attention
Incidence more frequent
   Reflex sympathetic activation (fast or irregular heartbeat, flushing or redness of skin); *sodium and water retention* (bloating, swelling of feet or lower legs, rapid weight gain of more than 5 pounds [2 kg] in adults or 2 pounds [1 kg] in children)
Incidence less frequent
   Angina, new or exacerbated, or pericarditis (chest pain)
Incidence rare
   Allergic reaction or Stevens-Johnson syndrome (skin rash and itching)
With long-term use
   Paresthesia (numbness or tingling of hands, feet, or face); *pericardial effusion or pulmonary hypertension* (shortness of breath)

Those indicating need for medical attention only if they continue or are bothersome
Incidence more frequent—occurs in most patients
   Hypertrichosis (excessive hair growth, usually on face, arms, and back)
   Note: *Hypertrichosis* usually develops within 3 to 6 weeks after initiation of minoxidil therapy, and return to pretreatment appearance occurs approximately 1 to 6 months after the medication is withdrawn. The increased hair growth may be extensive and may be especially disturbing to women and children; various depilatory methods may help.
Incidence less frequent or rare
   Vasodilation (headache)

Patient Consultation

In providing consultation, consider emphasizing the following selected information (» = major clinical significance):

Before using this medication
» Conditions affecting use, especially:
   Sensitivity to minoxidil
   Pregnancy—Decreased conception and increased resorption in animals; hypertrichosis reported in newborns
   Breast-feeding—Passes into breast milk
   Other medications, especially guanethidine or nitrates

Other medical problems, especially congestive heart failure, coronary insufficiency, pericardial effusion, pheochromocytoma, or renal function impairment

Proper use of this medication
Importance of diet; possible need for sodium restriction and/or weight reduction
» Patient may not experience symptoms of hypertension; importance of taking medication even if feeling well
» Does not cure, but helps control hypertension; possible need for lifelong therapy; serious consequences of untreated hypertension
Getting into the habit of taking at same time each day to help increase compliance
Caution in taking combination therapy; taking each drug at the right time
Missed dose: Taking as soon as remembered if within a few hours; not taking if forgotten until next day; not doubling doses
» Proper storage

Precautions while using this medication
Regular visits to physician to check progress
» Checking resting pulse as directed; checking with physician if an increase of 20 or more beats per minute above normal occurs
» Checking weight daily; weight gain of 2–3 lb (approximately 1 kg) in adults is normal and is usually lost with continued treatment; checking with physician if rapid weight gain of more than 5 lb (2 lb in children) or signs of fluid retention occur
» Not taking other medications, especially nonprescription sympathomimetics, unless discussed with physician

Side/adverse effects
Probability of hypertrichosis, which is reversible when medication is withdrawn
Signs of potential side effects, especially sodium and water retention, reflex sympathetic activation, angina, pericarditis, allergic reaction, Stevens-Johnson syndrome, paresthesia, and pulmonary hypertension

General Dosing Information

Sodium and water retention occurs rapidly in almost all patients receiving minoxidil and is difficult to control. Concomitant use of a diuretic (usually a loop diuretic) is recommended to prevent serious fluid accumulation and possible development of tolerance due to expansion of plasma volume.

Reflex tachycardia also occurs very commonly and may be less pronounced if a beta-adrenergic blocking agent or other sympathetic nervous system suppressant is used concurrently. The usual dose of beta-adrenergic blocker recommended is the equivalent of 80 to 160 mg of propranolol a day in divided doses. If beta-blockers cannot be used, methyldopa in a dose of 250 to 750 mg twice a day may be substituted. Some investigators have used clonidine in a dose of 100 to 200 mcg (0.1 to 0.2 mg) twice a day.

If pericardial effusion occurs and does not respond to therapeutic measures, it is recommended that minoxidil therapy be withdrawn.

Because a few cases of rebound hypertension have been reported following abrupt withdrawal of minoxidil, caution is recommended when discontinuing the medication.

Oral Dosage Forms

MINOXIDIL TABLETS USP

Usual adult and adolescent dose:
Initial—Oral, 5 mg a day as a single dose or as two divided doses, the dosage being adjusted in 100% increments as required (i.e., up to 10, 20, 40 mg, etc.).
Maintenance—Oral, 10 to 40 mg a day, as a single dose or in divided daily doses.

Note: It is recommended that an interval of at least three days be allowed between each dosage adjustment, in order for the full effect of each dose to be obtained. In some patients, dosage adjustment may be made every six hours with careful monitoring.

Geriatric patients may be more sensitive to effects of the usual adult dose.

Usual adult prescribing limits: Up to 100 mg a day.

Auxiliary labeling: • Do not take other medicines without your doctor's advice.

MISOPROSTOL   Systemic

A commonly used *brand name* in the U.S. and Canada is *Cytotec*.

ORAL
Misoprostol Tablets
  In the U.S. and Canada—*Cytotec*

Category: Gastric mucosa protectant; antiulcer agent.

Indications

Note: Bracketed information in the *Indications* section refers to uses not included in U.S. product labeling.

Accepted
Ulcer, gastric, nonsteroidal anti-inflammatory drug-induced (prophylaxis)—Misoprostol is indicated for the prevention of gastric ulcer associated with the use of nonsteroidal anti-inflammatory drugs (NSAIDs), including aspirin, in patients at high risk of complications from gastric ulcer, such as the elderly, and in patients with concomitant disease or patients at high risk of developing gastric ulceration, such as those with a history of ulcer.

[Ulcer, duodenal (treatment)]—Misoprostol is indicated in the short-term treatment of duodenal ulcer.

Pharmacology

Mechanism of action/Effect:
  Cytoprotective—Misoprostol enhances natural gastromucosal defense mechanisms and healing in acid-related disorders, probably by increasing production of gastric mucus and mucosal secretion of bicarbonate.
  Antisecretory—Misoprostol inhibits basal and nocturnal gastric acid secretion by direct action on the parietal cells; also inhibits gastric acid secretion stimulated by food, histamine, and pentagastrin. It decreases pepsin secretion under basal, but not histamine stimulation. Misoprostol has no significant effect on fasting or postprandial gastrin or intrinsic factor output.

Duration of action: 3–6 hours.

Precautions to Consider

Cross-sensitivity and/or related problems
Patients sensitive to other prostaglandins or prostaglandin analogs may be sensitive to misoprostol also.

Geriatrics
Studies performed in approximately 500 ulcer patients 65 years of age or older have not demonstrated geriatrics-specific problems that would limit the usefulness of misoprostol in the elderly.

Drug interactions and/or related problems
The following drug interactions and/or related problems have been selected on the basis of their potential clinical significance (pos-

sible mechanism in parentheses where appropriate)—not necessarily inclusive (» = major clinical significance):
Note: Combinations containing any of the following medications, depending on the amount present, may also interact with this medication.
  Magnesium-containing antacids
    (concurrent use with misoprostol may aggravate misoprostol-induced diarrhea)

Contraindications/Medical problems
The contraindications/medical problems included have been selected on the basis of their potential clinical significance (reasons given in parentheses where appropriate)—not necessarily inclusive (» = major clinical significance).

Risk-benefit should be considered when the following medical problems exist:
  Cerebral vascular disease or
  Coronary artery disease
    (although the effect has not been reported with misoprostol, prostaglandins and prostaglandin analogs have been reported to cause hypotension, thus increasing the risk of severe complications in these conditions)
  Epilepsy
    (although the effect has not been reported with misoprostol, prostaglandins and prostaglandin analogs have been reported to cause epileptic seizures when given by routes other than oral; it is recommended that misoprostol be used in epileptics only when their condition is adequately controlled)
  Sensitivity to prostaglandins or prostaglandin analogs

Side/Adverse Effects

The following side/adverse effects have been selected on the basis of their potential clinical significance (possible signs and symptoms in parentheses where appropriate)—not necessarily inclusive:

Those indicating need for medical attention only if they continue or are bothersome
Incidence more frequent
  Abdominal or stomach pain, mild; diarrhea—13 to 40%
    Note: *Diarrhea is* dose-related; usually developing early in the course of therapy. Self-limiting, often resolving after 8 days. However, some patients (<2%) have required discontinuation of misoprostol because of continuing severe diarrhea.
Incidence less frequent or rare
  Constipation—1.1%; *flatulence*—2.9%; *headache*—2.4%; *nausea and/or vomiting; uterine stimulation* (cramps in lower abdomen or stomach area); *vaginal bleeding*

Patient Consultation

In providing consultation, consider emphasizing the following selected information (» = major clinical significance):

Before using this medication
» Conditions affecting use, especially:
    Sensitivity to prostaglandins or prostaglandin analogs

Pregnancy—Contraindicated during pregnancy because of risk of miscarriage; patients of childbearing potential must take measures to assure they are not pregnant prior to therapy and to prevent pregnancy during therapy

Breast-feeding—Not recommended because of possibility of causing diarrhea in nursing infant

Proper use of this medication

Taking with or after meals and at bedtime

Missed dose: Taking as soon as possible; not taking if almost time for next dose; not doubling doses

» Proper storage

For use in the treatment of duodenal ulcer

Taking antacids for relief of ulcer pain; not taking magnesium-containing antacids

Compliance with full course of therapy and keeping appointments for check-ups

» Not taking for more than 4 weeks unless otherwise directed by physician

Precautions while using this medication

Stopping medication and checking with physician immediately if pregnancy is suspected

Consulting physician if diarrhea develops and continues for more than a week

Side/adverse effects

Signs of potential side effects, especially continuing and severe diarrhea

General Dosing Information

Misoprostol therapy should be started at the onset of treatment with nonsteroidal anti-inflammatory drugs (NSAIDs).

Misoprostol should be taken with or after meals and at bedtime, for maximum effectiveness.

For treatment of duodenal ulcer

If required, antacids may be administered before or after misoprostol for the relief of pain. However, magnesium-containing antacids are not recommended since they may aggravate the misoprostol-induced diarrhea.

Therapy with misoprostol should continue for a total of 4 weeks unless healing has been documented by endoscopic examination. If necessary, treatment may continue for an additional 4 weeks if ulcers have not fully healed after the initial 4 weeks.

Oral Dosage Forms

Note: Bracketed uses in the *Dosage forms* section refer to categories of use and/or indications that are not included in U.S. product labeling.

MISOPROSTOL TABLETS

Usual adult dose:

Prevention of nonsteroidal anti-inflammatory drug-induced gastric ulcer; or

[Treatment of duodenal ulcer]—Oral, 200 mcg (0.2 mg) four times a day with or after meals and at bedtime; or 400 mcg (0.4 mg) two times a day with the last dose taken at bedtime.

Note: Dose may be reduced to 100 mcg (0.1 mg) in those patients sensitive to higher doses.

Usual geriatric dose: See *Usual adult dose.*

Auxiliary labeling:
- Continue medicine for full time of treatment.
- Do not give medication to any other persons.

MOLINDONE   Systemic†

Some commonly used *brand names* in the U.S. are *Moban* and *Moban Concentrate.*

ORAL

Molindone Hydrochloride Oral Solution†
In the U.S.—*Moban Concentrate*
Molindone Hydrochloride Tablets†
In the U.S.—*Moban*

†Not commercially available in Canada.

Category: Antipsychotic.

Indications

Accepted

Psychotic disorders (treatment)—Molindone is indicated for the management of the manifestations of psychotic conditions, especially in patients with chronic schizophrenia, brief reactive psychosis, or schizophreniform disorders.

Unaccepted

Molindone is *not* recommended for management of behavioral complications in mentally retarded patients.

Pharmacology

Mechanism of action/Effect: The exact mechanism has not been established; however, based on electroencephalogram (EEG) stud-

ies, molindone is thought to act by occupying dopamine (D_2) receptor sites in the reticular activating and limbic systems in the brain, thus decreasing dopamine activity.

Other actions/effects:

Causes changes in resting and sleeping EEG readings.
May decrease the duration of sleep.
May have an antiemetic effect.

Duration of action: 24 to 36 hours.

Precautions to Consider

Cross-sensitivity and/or related problems

Patients sensitive to other antipsychotic agents, such as phenothiazines, thioxanthenes, haloperidol, and loxapine, may be sensitive to this medication also.

Geriatrics

Geriatric patients tend to develop higher plasma concentrations of molindone because of changes in distribution due to decreases in lean body mass, total body water, and albumin, and often an increase in total body fat composition. Therefore, these patients usually require lower initial dosage and a more gradual titration of dose.

Elderly patients appear to be more prone to orthostatic hypotension and exhibit an increased sensitivity to the anticholinergic and sedative effects of molindone. In addition, they are more prone to develop extrapyramidal side effects, such as tardive dyskinesia and parkinsonism. The symptoms of tardive dyskinesia are persistent, difficult to control, and, in some patients, appear to be irreversible. There is no known effective treatment. Careful observation during treatment for early signs of tardive dyskinesia and reduction of dosage or discontinuation of medication may prevent a more severe manifestation of the syndrome.

It has been suggested that elderly patients should receive half the usual adult dose. A periodic attempt should be made to discontinue medication as soon as the patient improves.

Dental

The peripheral anticholinergic effects of molindone may decrease or inhibit salivary flow, especially in middle-aged or elderly patients, thus contributing to the development of caries, periodontal disease, candidiasis, or discomfort.

Extrapyramidal reactions induced by molindone will result in increased motor activity of the head, face, and neck. Occlusal adjustments, bite registrations, and treatment for bruxism may be made less reliable.

Drug interactions and/or related problems

The following drug interactions and/or related problems have been selected on the basis of their potential clinical significance (possible mechanism in parentheses where appropriate)—not necessarily inclusive (» = major clinical significance):

Note: Combinations containing any of the following medications, depending on the amount present, may also interact with this medication.

Although not all of the following interactions have been documented specifically for molindone, a potential exists for their occurrence because of the close similarity of molindone's pharmacological effects to those of phenothiazines and other antipsychotic medications.

» Alcohol or
» Central nervous system (CNS) depression-producing medications, other, especially anesthetics, barbiturates, benzodiazepines, and opioid (narcotic) analgesics
(concurrent use may potentiate and prolong the CNS depressant effects of either these medications or molindone)

Amphetamines
(concurrent use with molindone may antagonize the stimulant effects of amphetamines and counteract the antipsychotic effects of molindone)

Antacids or
Antidiarrheals, adsorbent
(concurrent use may inhibit the absorption of molindone; these medications should not be taken within 1 to 2 hours of molindone)

Anticholinergics or other medications with anticholinergic activity or
Antidyskinetic agents or
Antihistamines
(concurrent use with molindone may potentiate anticholinergic effects, such as urinary retention, blurred vision, dry mouth, and constipation)

Antidepressants, tricyclic, or
Maprotiline or
Monoamine oxidase (MAO) inhibitors, including furazolidone, pargyline, and procarbazine, or
Trazodone
(concurrent use may prolong and intensify the sedative or anticholinergic effects of these medications or molindone)

Antidiabetic agents, oral, or
Insulin
(high doses of molindone, when added to an existing antidiabetic regimen, may increase plasma glucose concentrations, leading to loss of control of diabetes)

Beta-adrenergic blocking agents, especially metoprolol or propranolol
(concurrent use may increase the effects of beta-blockers by decreasing first-pass metabolism; reduction in dosage of beta-blocking agent may be required)

Bromocriptine
(molindone may increase serum prolactin concentrations and interfere with therapeutic effects of bromocriptine; dosage increase of bromocriptine may be necessary)

» Extrapyramidal reaction-causing medications, other
(concurrent use with molindone may increase the severity and frequency of extrapyramidal effects)

Levodopa
(concurrent use may inhibit antiparkinsonian effects of levodopa by blocking dopamine receptors in the brain and may counteract the antipsychotic effects of molindone)

» Lithium
(concurrent use with molindone may produce neurotoxic symptoms, such as confusion, delirium, seizures, somnambulism, or abnormal EEG changes; extrapyramidal symptoms may be increased; also, antiemetic effect of molindone may mask nausea and vomiting, which are early signs of lithium toxicity)

Phenytoin or
Tetracycline
(calcium ions from the excipient in molindone may interfere with the absorption of these medications)

Contraindications/Medical problems

The contraindications/medical problems included have been selected on the basis of their potential clinical significance (reasons given in parentheses where appropriate)—not necessarily inclusive (» = major clinical significance).

Except under special circumstances, this medication should not be used when the following medical problems exist:

» CNS depression, severe, drug-induced

» Comatose states

Risk-benefit should be considered when the following medical problems exist:

Brain tumor or
Intestinal obstruction
(antiemetic effect of molindone may mask early signs of brain tumor or intestinal obstruction and interfere with diagnosis)

Glaucoma or
Hepatic function impairment or
Prostatic hypertrophy or
Urinary retention
(may be aggravated)

Parkinson's disease
(potentiation of extrapyramidal effects)

Sensitivity to molindone or other antipsychotic medications

Side/Adverse Effects

The following side/adverse effects have been selected on the basis of their potential clinical significance (possible signs and symptoms in parentheses where appropriate)—not necessarily inclusive:

Those indicating need for medical attention

Incidence more frequent
Akathisia (severe restlessness or need to keep moving)—may be more frequent in elderly patients; *extrapyramidal effects, dystonic* (muscle spasms of face, neck, and back; tic-like or twitching movements; twisting movements of body; inability to move eyes; weakness of arms and legs); *extrapyramidal effects, parkinsonian* (difficulty in talking; loss of balance control; mask-like face; shuffling walk; stiffness of arms and legs; trembling and shaking of hands);

tardive dyskinesia, persistent (lip smacking or puckering; puffing of cheeks; rapid or worm-like movements of tongue; uncontrolled movements of arms and legs; uncontrolled chewing movements)

Note: *Akathisia* or *dystonic extrapyramidal effects* may occur within 24 to 48 hours of first dose; more frequent in young and male patients.

Parkinsonian extrapyramidal effects may appear in the first few days of treatment; frequency usually increases with increase of dosage; may be more frequent in elderly patients.

Tardive dyskinesia occurs more frequently in elderly females; initially dose-related, but may appear when doses are small and treatment periods are brief; may increase with long-term treatment and total cumulative dose; may be masked when dosage is increased or treatment reinitiated, or may persist after molindone is discontinued.

Incidence less frequent
Mental depression

Incidence rare
Allergic reaction (skin rash); **heat stroke** (hot, dry skin; inability to sweat; muscle weakness; confusion); **hepatitis or jaundice, cholestatic** (yellow eyes or skin); **neuroleptic malignant syndrome (NMS)** (convulsions; fast heartbeat; fever; high or low (irregular) blood pressure; increased sweating; loss of bladder control; severe muscle stiffness; troubled breathing; unusually pale skin; unusual tiredness)

Note: *Heat stroke* may occur in environmental conditions of high heat and high humidity; caused by molindone-induced suppression of central and peripheral temperature regulation in the hypothalamus. The effectiveness of sweating as a cooling mechanism may be reduced by humid conditions and by the anticholinergic effects of molindone or its combination with other anticholinergic medications such as nonprescription cold medications or antihistamines. Adequate interior temperature control (air conditioning) must be maintained for institutionalized patients during hot weather because of the increased risk of heat stroke and NMS. Patients should be advised to avoid exertion, stay in cool areas, and avoid dehydration and other anticholinergic medications.

NMS may occur at any time during neuroleptic therapy, but is more commonly seen soon after start of therapy, or after patient has switched from one neuroleptic to another, during combined therapy with another psychotropic medication, or after a dosage increase. Along with the overt signs of skeletal muscle rigidity, hyperthermia, autonomic dysfunction, and altered consciousness, differential diagnosis may reveal leukocytosis (9,500 to 26,000 cells per cubic millimeter), elevated liver function tests, and elevated creatine phosphokinase (CPK).

Those indicating need for medical attention only if they continue or are bothersome
Incidence more frequent
Blurred vision; constipation; decreased sweating; difficult urination; drowsiness; dryness of mouth; headache; hypotension, orthostatic (dizziness or lightheadedness, especially when getting up suddenly from a lying or sitting position); **nausea; stuffy nose**

Incidence less frequent
Changes in menstrual periods; decreased sexual ability; false sense of well-being; swelling of breasts; unusual secretion of milk

Those indicating the need for medical attention if they occur after medication is discontinued
Tardive dyskinesia, withdrawal emergent (lip smacking or puckering; puffing of cheeks; rapid or worm-like movements of tongue; uncontrolled chewing movements; uncontrolled movements of arms and legs)

Patient Consultation

In providing consultation, consider emphasizing the following selected information (» = major clinical significance):

Before using this medication
» Conditions affecting use, especially:
   Sensitivity to molindone or other antipsychotic medications
   Pregnancy—Studies in mice have shown a slight increase in resorptions
   Use in the elderly—Elderly patients are more likely to develop extrapyramidal, anticholinergic, hypotensive, and sedative effects; reduced dosage recommended
   Use by athletes—Molindone is banned and, in some cases, tested for in competitors in certain events by the U.S. Olympic Committee (USOC) and the National Collegiate Athletic Association (NCAA)
   Dental—Dry mouth may cause caries, candidiasis, periodontal disease, and discomfort; increased motor activity of face, head, and neck may interfere with some dental procedures
   Other medications, especially alcohol, other CNS depression-producing medications, other extrapyramidal reaction-producing medications, or lithium
   Other medical problems, especially severe drug-induced CNS depression

Proper use of this medication
   Taking with food or a full glass (8 ounces) of water or milk to reduce gastric irritation
   Taking liquid form of medicine undiluted or mixed with water, milk, fruit juice, or carbonated beverage
» Compliance with therapy: importance of not taking more or less medication than the amount prescribed
» May require several weeks of therapy to obtain optimal effects
   Missed dose: Taking as soon as possible; not taking if within 2 hours of next scheduled dose; resuming regular schedule; not doubling doses
» Proper storage

Precautions while using this medication
   Regular visits to physician to check progress of therapy
» Checking with physician before discontinuing medication; gradual dosage reduction may be needed
» Avoiding use of antacids or antidiarrheal medication within 2 hours of taking molindone
» Avoiding use of alcoholic beverages or other CNS depressants during therapy
   Avoiding the use of over-the-counter medications for colds or allergies, to prevent increased anticholinergic effects and risk of heat stroke
» Possible drowsiness; caution when driving, using machinery, or doing other things that require alertness
» Possible dizziness or lightheadedness; caution when getting up suddenly from a lying or sitting position
» Possible heat stroke: caution during exercise, hot weather, or hot baths or saunas
   Possible dryness of mouth; using sugarless gum or candy, ice, or saliva substitute for relief; checking with physician or dentist if dry mouth continues for more than 2 weeks

Side/adverse effects
» Stopping medication and notifying physician immediately if symptoms of neuroleptic malignant syndrome (NMS) appear
» Notifying physician as soon as possible if early signs of tardive dyskinesia appear
   Possibility of withdrawal emergent dyskinesia
   Signs of potential side effects, especially akathisia, dystonias, parkinsonism, tardive dyskinesia, allergic reaction, mental depression, symptoms of dehydration, neuroleptic malignant syndrome (NMS), cholestatic jaundice, or heat stroke

General Dosing Information

Diet/Nutrition

Molindone should be taken with food or a full glass (8 ounces) of water or milk to reduce gastric irritation.

Oral Dosage Forms

MOLINDONE HYDROCHLORIDE ORAL SOLUTION

Note: Molindone hydrochloride oral solution is not commercially available in Canada.

Usual adult dose: Antipsychotic—
Initial: Oral, 50 to 75 mg a day, in three or four divided doses, the dose being increased to 100 mg a day in three to four days as needed and tolerated.
Maintenance:
Mild psychosis—Oral, 5 to 15 mg three or four times a day.
Moderate psychosis—Oral, 10 to 25 mg three or four times a day.
Severe psychosis—Oral, 225 mg a day in divided doses.

Note: Elderly or debilitated patients usually require a lower initial dose, the dose being adjusted gradually as needed and tolerated.

Usual adult prescribing limits: 225 mg a day.

Auxiliary labeling:
- May cause drowsiness.
- Avoid alcoholic beverages.

Additional information: Studies have shown that oral doses of the tablet and solution are equivalent in bioavailability.

MOLINDONE HYDROCHLORIDE TABLETS

Note: Molindone hydrochloride tablets are not commercially available in Canada.

Usual adult dose: Antipsychotic—
Initial: Oral, 50 to 75 mg a day, in three or four divided doses, the dose being increased to 100 mg per day in three to four days as needed and tolerated.
Maintenance:
Mild psychosis—Oral, 5 to 15 mg three or four times a day.
Moderate psychosis—Oral, 10 to 25 mg three or four times a day.
Severe psychosis—Oral, 225 mg a day in divided doses.

Note: Elderly or debilitated patients usually require a lower initial dose, the dose being adjusted gradually as needed and tolerated.

Usual adult prescribing limits: 225 mg a day.

Auxiliary labeling:
- May cause drowsiness.
- Avoid alcoholic beverages.

Additional information: Studies have shown that oral doses of the tablet and solution are equivalent in bioavailability.

MORICIZINE Systemic†

INN: Moracizine

A commonly used *brand name* in the U.S. is *Ethmozine*.

ORAL

Moricizine Hydrochloride Tablets†
In the U.S.—*Ethmozine*

---

†Not commercially available in Canada.

Category: Antiarrhythmic.

Indications

Accepted

Arrhythmias, ventricular (treatment)—Moricizine is indicated for suppression of documented life-threatening ventricular arrhythmias, including sustained ventricular tachycardia.

Unaccepted

Use of moricizine is not accepted for treatment of less severe arrhythmias such as nonsustained ventricular tachycardias or frequent premature ventricular contractions, even if patients are symptomatic. In these cases, there is a possibility that proarrhythmic potential may outweigh any beneficial effect. In the National Heart, Lung and Blood Institute's Cardiac Arrhythmia Suppression Trial (CAST), encainide or flecainide treatment was associated with excessive mortality or increased nonfatal cardiac arrest rate as compared with placebo in patients with asymptomatic, non-life-threatening arrhythmias who had a recent myocardial infarction; and, therefore, the encainide and flecainide arms of CAST were prematurely terminated. The CAST protocol was modified and continued as CAST-II with the moricizine arm compared to pla-cebo. However, CAST-II was subsequently terminated prematurely because of excessive cardiac mortality during the first 2 weeks of moricizine exposure as compared to placebo. Furthermore, it appeared unlikely that moricizine would improve long-term survival.

Pharmacology

Mechanism of action/Effect: Inhibits the rapid inward sodium current across myocardial cell membranes. Has potent local anesthetic activity and membrane stabilizing effect. Decreases excitability, conduction velocity, and automaticity as a result of slowed atrioventricular (AV) nodal and His-Purkinje conduction. Decreases the action potential duration (APD) in Purkinje fibers; also decreases the effective refractory period (ERP) but to a lesser extent than the APD, so the ERP/APD ratio is increased. Decreases the maximum rate of Phase 0 depolarization (Vmax), but does not affect action potential amplitude or maximum diastolic potential. Does not affect atrial, AV nodal, or left ventricular refractory periods and has minimal effect on ventricular repolarization (evidenced by the overall decrease in JT interval). Has no effect on sinoatrial (SA) nodal or intra-atrial conduction and only minimal effect on sinus cycle length and sinus node recovery time. In the Vaughan Williams classification of antiarrhythmics, moricizine is considered to be a class I agent. It has properties of class IA, IB, and IC agents but does not clearly belong to any of the three subclasses. It has less effect on the slope of phase 0 and a greater effect on action potential duration and effective refractory period than class IC agents).

Other actions/effects: Causes a small but consistent increase in resting blood pressure and heart rate. May inhibit platelet aggregation. May have anticholinergic effects.

Onset of action:
Prolongation of PR interval—Occurs promptly but normalization occurs within 2 hours.
Effect on ventricular premature depolarization (VPD) rates—Within 2 hours.

Time to peak effect:
Shortening of JT interval—6 hours.
Effect on VPD rates—10 to 14 hours.

Duration of action:
Shortening of JT interval—At least 10 hours.
Effect on VPD rates—In full for more than 10 hours and continues to be significant at 24 hours.

Precautions to Consider

Geriatrics

One study found a decreased incidence of neurological side/adverse effects in patients over 65 years of age; there were no other age-related differences in incidence of side/adverse effects. In addition, elderly patients are more likely to have age-related renal function impairment, which, when significant, may require dosage reduction in patients receiving moricizine.

Drug interactions and/or related problems

The following drug interactions and/or related problems have been selected on the basis of their potential clinical significance (possible mechanism in parentheses where appropriate)—not necessarily inclusive (» = major clinical significance):

Antiarrhythmics, other
(although some antiarrhythmic agents may be used in combination for therapeutic advantage, combined use may potentiate risk of adverse cardiac effects)

Cimetidine
(concurrent use of cimetidine has been reported to decrease clearance of moricizine by about 49% and increase plasma concentrations 1.4 fold; although clinical effects of moricizine do not appear to be changed, caution is recommended if concurrent use with cimetidine is necessary)

Theophylline
(concurrent use with moricizine significantly increases clearance and decreases half-life of theophylline, with a resultant decrease in plasma theophylline concentrations, possibly as a result of hepatic microsomal enzyme induction; monitoring of plasma theophylline concentrations is recommended when moricizine therapy is initiated or discontinued)

Contraindications/Medical problems

The contraindications/medical problems included have been selected on the basis of their potential clinical significance (reasons given in parentheses where appropriate)—not necessarily inclusive (» = major clinical significance).

Except under special circumstances, this medication should not be used when the following medical problems exist:

» Atrioventricular (AV) block, pre-existing second or third degree without pacemaker, or
» Right bundle branch block associated with a left hemiblock (bifascicular block) without pacemaker
(risk of complete heart block)

Risk-benefit should be considered when the following medical problems exist:

» Cardiogenic shock
Cardiomegaly
(incidence of moricizine-induced arrhythmias is increased; the possibility of proarrhythmic effects should be kept in mind during moricizine therapy)

Congestive heart failure, severe
(worsening has been reported; incidence of moricizine-induced arrhythmias is increased; absorption, half-life, and clearance of moricizine are not affected)

Coronary artery disease
(incidence of moricizine-induced arrhythmias is increased; the possibility of proarrhythmic effects should be kept in mind during moricizine therapy)

Hepatic function impairment
(reduced clearance and increased half-life of moricizine; lower doses of moricizine and close monitoring are recommended)

Hypokalemia or hyperkalemia or
Hypomagnesemia
(effects of moricizine may be altered; any electrolyte imbalance should be corrected prior to beginning therapy with moricizine)

Myocardial infarction, history of
(incidence of moricizine-induced arrhythmias is increased; the possibility of proarrhythmic effects should be kept in mind during moricizine therapy)

Renal function impairment
(reduced elimination; if significant, dosage reduction and close monitoring are recommended)

» Sensitivity to moricizine
» Sick sinus syndrome
(sinus node recovery time prolonged; sinus bradycardia, sinus pause, or sinus arrest may occur)

Caution is also recommended in patients with existing pacemakers because the risk of moricizine-induced arrhythmias may be increased; the effect of moricizine on endocardial pacing thresholds has not been studied.

Side/Adverse Effects

Note: In the National Heart, Lung and Blood Institute's Cardiac Arrhythmia Suppression Trial (CAST), encainide or flecainide treatment was found to be associated with excessive mortality or increased nonfatal cardiac arrest rate as compared with placebo in patients with asymptomatic, non-life-threatening arrhythmias who had a recent myocardial infarction. CAST-II comparing moricizine to placebo was discontinued because of excessive cardiac mortality during the first 2 weeks of moricizine exposure as compared to placebo. Furthermore, it appeared unlikely that moricizine would improve long-term survival.

Adverse cardiac effects reported with moricizine administration include new or exacerbated ventricular arrhythmias in about 3.7% of patients and, in 1% or less of patients, new or exacerbated congestive heart failure, second or third degree atrioventricular (AV) block, sinus bradycardia, sinus pause, or sinus arrest.

Side/adverse effects are usually mild and transient. However, deaths have been reported from overdosage of moricizine.

The following side/adverse effects have been selected on the basis of their potential clinical significance (possible signs and symptoms in parentheses where appropriate)—not necessarily inclusive:

Those indicating need for medical attention
Incidence less frequent
Chest pain; congestive heart failure (shortness of breath, swelling of feet or lower legs); *ventricular tachyarrhythmias* (fast or irregular heartbeat)
Note: *Ventricular tachyarrhythmias* are potentially fatal; incidence is increased in patients with coronary artery disease, sustained ventricular tachycardia, cardiomegaly, congestive heart failure, or history of myocardial infarction. Proarrhythmic effects usually occur during the first week of therapy and are not dose-related.

Incidence rare
  Drug fever (sudden high fever); *hepatotoxicity* (not symptomatic)
Signs and symptoms of overdose
  Conduction disturbances; hypotension; exacerbation of congestive heart failure; myocardial infarction; sinus arrest; arrhythmias (including junctional bradycardia, ventricular tachycardia, ventricular fibrillation, and asystole); *emesis; lethargy; coma; syncope; and respiratory failure*

Those indicating need for medical attention only if they continue or are bothersome
Incidence more frequent
  Dizziness—dose-related
Incidence less frequent
  Blurred vision; diarrhea; dryness of mouth; headache; hypesthesias or paresthesias (numbness or tingling in arms or legs or around mouth); *nausea or vomiting; nervousness; pain in arms or legs; stomach pain; trouble in sleeping; unusual tiredness or weakness*

Patient Consultation

In providing consultation, consider emphasizing the following selected information (» = major clinical significance):

Before using this medication
» Conditions affecting use, especially:
    Sensitivity to moricizine
    Other medical problems, especially second or third degree atrioventricular (AV) block, right bundle branch block associated with a left hemiblock, cardiogenic shock, or sick sinus syndrome

Proper use of this medication
» Compliance with therapy; taking as directed even if feeling well
» Importance of not missing doses and taking at evenly spaced intervals
    Missed dose: Taking as soon as possible if remembered within 4 hours; not taking if remembered later; not doubling doses
» Proper storage

Precautions while using this medication
    Regular visits to physician to check progress
    Carrying medical identification card or bracelet
» Caution if any kind of surgery (including dental surgery) or emergency treatment is required
    Caution when driving or doing things requiring alertness because of possible dizziness

Side/adverse effects
    Signs of potential side effects, especially chest pain, congestive heart failure, ventricular tachyarrhythmias, and drug fever

General Dosing Information

It is recommended that treatment be initiated in the hospital because of the risk of proarrhythmic effects associated with moricizine administration.

In general, it is recommended that previous antiarrhythmic therapy be withdrawn 1 to 2 plasma half-lives before initiation of moricizine therapy. However, individual circumstances must be taken into consideration.

If second- or third-degree AV block occurs, moricizine therapy should be withdrawn unless a ventricular pacemaker is in place.

Oral Dosage Forms

MORICIZINE HYDROCHLORIDE TABLETS

Usual adult dose: Antiarrhythmic—Oral, 600 to 900 mg per day in three divided doses given every eight hours, the dosage being increased, if necessary, in increments of 150 mg per day at three-day intervals up to a total dose of 900 mg per day.

Note: In patients with hepatic function impairment or significant renal function impairment, an initial dose of 600 mg per day or less is recommended with close monitoring, including ECG intervals, before dosage adjustment.

Some patients whose arrhythmias are well-controlled may be changed to every-twelve-hour dosing if necessary to aid in compliance. Incidence of dizziness and nausea may be increased with higher doses.

NALIDIXIC ACID   Systemic

A commonly used *brand name* in the U.S. and Canada is *NegGram*.

ORAL
Nalidixic Acid Oral Suspension USP†
    In the U.S.—*NegGram*
Nalidixic Acid Tablets USP
    In the U.S.—*NegGram;* GENERIC
    In Canada—*NegGram*

---

†Not commercially available in Canada.

Category: Antibacterial (systemic).
Note: Nalidixic acid is a synthetic narrow-spectrum antibacterial. It is
    bacteriostatic or bactericidal depending on the concentration.
    At urine concentrations normally found clinically, it is bacteri-
    cidal against most gram-negative bacilli (except *Pseudomonas*
    species) that commonly cause urinary tract infections.

Indications

Accepted
Urinary tract infections, bacterial (treatment)—Nalidixic acid is indi-
    cated in the treatment of urinary tract infections caused by suscep-
    tible strains of gram-negative organisms, including *Proteus* spe-
    cies, *Klebsiella* species, *Enterobacter* species, and *Escherichia coli.*

Since nalidixic acid achieves only low concentrations in the serum
    and is concentrated in the urine, it is indicated only in the treat-
    ment of urinary tract infections.

Not all species or strains of a particular organism may be susceptible
    to nalidixic acid.

Pharmacology

Mechanism of action/Effect: Nalidixic acid appears to act by inhibit-
    ing bacterial DNA synthesis, probably by interfering with DNA
    polymerization. Resistance may develop rapidly during treatment.

Precautions to Consider

Cross-sensitivity and/or related problems
Since nalidixic acid is closely related chemically to other quinolone
    derivatives (e.g., cinoxacin, ciprofloxacin, lomefloxacin, norflox-
    acin, ofloxacin), patients hypersensitive to other quinolones may
    also be hypersensitive to this medication.

Geriatrics
Studies performed to date have not demonstrated geriatrics-specific
    problems that would limit the usefulness of nalidixic acid in the
    elderly. However, elderly patients are more likely to have age-
    related decrease in renal function, resulting in a prolonged half-life
    and decreased drug clearance.

Drug interactions and/or related problems
The following drug interactions and/or related problems have been
    selected on the basis of their potential clinical significance (pos-
    sible mechanism in parentheses where appropriate)—not necessar-
    ily inclusive (» = major clinical significance):
Note: Combinations containing any of the following medications, de-
    pending on the amount present, may also interact with this
    medication.
» Anticoagulants, coumarin- or indandione-derivative
    (coumarin- or indandione-derivative anticoagulants, especially
    warfarin and dicumarol, may be displaced from protein-bind-
    ing sites by nalidixic acid, resulting in increased anticoagulant
    effect; dosage adjustments may be necessary during and after
    nalidixic acid therapy)

Nitrofurantoin
    (nitrofurantoin interferes with the therapeutic effects of nalid-
    ixic acid)

Contraindications/Medical problems
The contraindications/medical problems included have been selected
    on the basis of their potential clinical significance (reasons given
    in parentheses where appropriate)—not necessarily inclusive (» =
    major clinical significance).

Risk-benefit should be considered when the following medical prob-
    lems exist:
Cerebral arteriosclerosis, severe, or
» Seizure disorders, history of
    (patients with severe cerebral arteriosclerosis or a history of
    seizure disorders may be at increased risk of toxicity)
Glucose-6-phosphate dehydrogenase (G6PD) deficiency
    (hemolytic anemia may occur)
» Hepatic function impairment
    (patients with hepatic function impairment may be at increased
    risk of toxicity)
Hypersensitivity to nalidixic acid or other quinolone derivatives
    (cinoxacin, ciprofloxacin, lomefloxacin, norfloxacin, ofloxacin)
Renal function impairment, severe
    (patients with severe renal function impairment [creatinine clear-
    ance of <10 mL/min] may be at increased risk of toxicity)

Side/Adverse Effects

The following side/adverse effects have been selected on the basis of
    their potential clinical significance (possible signs and symptoms
    in parentheses where appropriate)—not necessarily inclusive:

Those indicating need for medical attention
Incidence less frequent
    Visual disturbances (blurred or decreased vision, change in color
    vision, double vision, halos around lights, overbright appearance
    of lights)
Incidence rare
    Blood dyscrasias (pale skin, sore throat and fever, unusual bleed-
    ing or bruising, unusual tiredness or weakness); *cholestatic jaun-*
    dice (dark or amber urine; pale stools; stomach pain, severe; yel-
    low eyes or skin); *CNS toxicity, specifically hallucinations, mood*
    or other mental changes, seizures—usually with excessive doses,
    increased intracranial pressure (bulging anterior fontanel, papill-
    edema, headache); *hypersensitivity* (skin rash, redness, itching)

Those indicating need for medical attention only if they continue
or are bothersome
Incidence more frequent
    CNS toxicity (dizziness, drowsiness, headache); *gastrointestinal*
    disturbance (abdominal pain, diarrhea, nausea, vomiting)
Incidence less frequent
    Photosensitivity (increased sensitivity of skin to sunlight)

Patient Consultation

In providing consultation, consider emphasizing the following se-
    lected information (» = major clinical significance):

Before using this medication
» Conditions affecting use, especially:
    Hypersensitivity to nalidixic acid or other quinolones (cinoxacin,
    ciprofloxacin, lomefloxacin, norfloxacin, ofloxacin)
    Pregnancy—Nalidixic acid crosses the placenta and is not rec-
    ommended during pregnancy
    Breast-feeding—Nalidixic acid is excreted in breast milk

Use in children—Nalidixic acid is not recommended in infants up to 3 months of age since it has been found to cause arthropathy in young animals

Other medications, especially coumarin- and indandione-derivative anticoagulants

Other medical problems, especially a history of seizure disorders or severe hepatic impairment

Proper use of this medication

» Not giving to infants up to 3 months of age; has caused arthropathy in immature animals

Taking on an empty stomach, or with food or milk if gastrointestinal irritation occurs

Proper administration technique for oral liquids

» Compliance with full course of therapy

Missed dose: Taking as soon as possible; not taking if almost time for next dose; not doubling doses

» Proper storage

Precautions while using this medication

Regular visits to physician to check progress if therapy lasts longer than 2 weeks

Checking with physician if no improvement within 2 days

» Caution if blurred vision or other vision problems, dizziness, or drowsiness occurs

» Possible skin photosensitivity; avoiding unprotected exposure to sun; using protective clothing; using a sun block product that includes protection against both UVA-caused photosensitivity reactions and UVB-caused sunburn reactions; avoiding use of sunlamp, tanning bed, or tanning booth

» Diabetics: False-positive reactions with copper sulfate urine glucose tests may occur

Side/adverse effects

Signs of potential side effects, especially blood dyscrasias, cholestatic jaundice, CNS toxicity, hypersensitivity, and visual disturbances

General Dosing Information

Nalidixic acid should preferably be taken with a full glass (240 mL) of water on an empty stomach (either 1 hour before or 2 hours after meals) to obtain optimum urine concentrations. However, if gastrointestinal irritation occurs, this medication may be taken with food or milk.

Oral Dosage Forms

NALIDIXIC ACID ORAL SUSPENSION USP

Usual adult and adolescent dose: Antibacterial—
Initial: Oral, 1 gram every six hours for one to two weeks.
Maintenance: Oral, 500 mg every six hours.

Usual adult prescribing limits: Up to 4 grams daily.

Note: Doses up to 6 grams daily have been used in severe urinary tract infections, although side effects may be increased at high dosage.

Auxiliary labeling:
- Shake well.
- May cause blurred vision, dizziness, or drowsiness.
- Avoid too much sun or use of sunlamp.
- Continue medicine for full time of treatment.

NALIDIXIC ACID TABLETS USP

Usual adult and adolescent dose: See *Nalidixic Acid Oral Suspension USP*.

Usual adult prescribing limits: See *Nalidixic Acid Oral Suspension USP*.

Auxiliary labeling:
- May cause blurred vision, dizziness, or drowsiness.
- Avoid too much sun or use of sunlamp.
- Continue medicine for full time of treatment.

NIACIN   Systemic

INN: Nicotinic acid

Some commonly used *brand names* are:

In the U.S.—

Endur-Acin	*Nicobid*
Nia-Bid	*Nicolar*
Niac	*Nicotinex Elixir*
Niacels	*Slo-Niacin*
Niacor	*Tega-Span*
Nico-400	

In Canada—
Tri-B3

Other commonly used names are niacinamide, nicotinamide, nicotinic acid, and vitamin B_3.

NIACIN
Oral
Niacin Extended-release Capsules
In the U.S.—*Nia-Bid; Niac; Niacels; Nico-400; Nicobid; Tega-Span;* GENERIC
In Canada—*Tri-B3*
Niacin Oral Solution
In the U.S.—*Nicotinex Elixir*
Niacin Tablets USP
In the U.S.—*Niacor; Nicolar;* GENERIC
In Canada—GENERIC

Niacin Extended-release Tablets
In the U.S.—*Endur-Acin; Slo-Niacin;* GENERIC
Parenteral
Niacin Injection USP
In the U.S.—GENERIC
NIACINAMIDE
Oral
Niacinamide Capsules
In the U.S.—GENERIC
Niacinamide Tablets USP
In the U.S. and Canada—GENERIC
Parenteral
Niacinamide Injection USP
In the U.S.—GENERIC

Category

Note: Niacin and niacinamide (vitamin B_3) are water-soluble vitamins.

Nutritional supplement (vitamin)—Niacin; Niacinamide.
Antihyperlipidemic—Niacin.

Indications

Accepted

Vitamin deficiency (prophylaxis and treatment)—

Niacin and niacinamide are indicated for prevention and treatment of vitamin B_3 deficiency states. Vitamin B_3 deficiency may occur as a result of inadequate nutrition or intestinal malabsorption but does not occur in healthy individuals receiving an adequate balanced diet. Simple nutritional deficiency of individual B vitamins is rare since dietary inadequacy usually results in multiple deficiencies. Dietary improvement is preferred over supplementation whenever possible.

Deficiency of niacin may lead to pellagra.

Requirements may be increased and/or supplementation may be necessary in the following persons or conditions (although clinical deficiencies are usually rare):

Diabetes mellitus
Fever, chronic
Gastrectomy
Hartnup disease
Hepatic-biliary tract disease—cirrhosis
Hyperthyroidism
Infection, chronic
Intestinal diseases—celiac disease, persistent diarrhea, tropical sprue, regional enteritis
Malabsorption syndromes associated with pancreatic insufficiency
Malignancy
Oropharyngeal lesions
Stress, continuing

Some unusual diets (e.g., reducing diets that drastically restrict food selection) may not supply minimum daily requirements of niacin. Supplementation is necessary in patients receiving total parenteral nutrition (TPN) or undergoing rapid weight loss or in those with malnutrition, because of inadequate dietary intake.

Requirements for all vitamins and most minerals are increased during pregnancy; however, they should be provided by an adequate diet. Many physicians recommend that pregnant women receive multivitamin and mineral supplements, especially those pregnant women who do not consume an adequate diet and those in high-risk categories (i.e., women carrying more than one fetus, heavy cigarette smokers, and alcohol and drug abusers). However, taking excessive amounts of a multivitamin and mineral supplement may be harmful to the mother and/or fetus and should be avoided.

Requirements for all vitamins and most minerals are increased during breast-feeding.

Hyperlipidemia (treatment)—Niacin (but not niacinamide) is also indicated in the treatment of hyperlipidemia. Niacin is recommended for use only in patients with primary hyperlipidemia (type IIa, IIb, III, IV, or V hyperlipoproteinemia) and a significant risk of coronary artery disease who have not responded to other measures alone. It is one of the drugs of first choice for initiating therapy to reduce low density lipoprotein (LDL)-cholesterol concentrations and triglycerides, and to increase high density lipoprotein (HDL)-cholesterol concentrations.

In the 1988 Report of the National Cholesterol Education Program Expert Panel on Detection, Evaluation, and Treatment of High Blood Cholesterol in Adults, the following guidelines for the treatment of high blood cholesterol are recommended:

Nonpharmacologic management (especially reduction in dietary intake of saturated fatty acids and cholesterol, weight reduction and exercise, and quitting smoking) is recommended first for all patients and as an adjunct to all pharmacologic cholesterol therapy.

If, after six months of diet therapy, adequate LDL-cholesterol reduction is not achieved, then medication therapy is recommended to be added to diet therapy.

Initial medication therapy usually consists of a bile acid sequestrant (e.g., cholestyramine, colestipol) or niacin. A 3-hydroxy-3-methylglutanyl coenzyme A (HMG-CoA) reductase inhibitor (e.g., lovastatin) should be considered after the bile acid sequestrants and niacin. Other lipid-lowering agents, including fibric acid derivatives (e.g., gemfibrozil and clofibrate) and probucol, are not as effective in lowering LDL cholesterol as the above mentioned medications. Two other agents, neomycin (not approved by FDA as a lipid-lowering agent) and dextrothyroxine are not recommended for general use because other medications are available that have a more favorable benefit/risk ratio.

If adequate LDL-cholesterol control is not achieved with initial medication therapy, it is recommended that the patient be switched to another medication or a combination of two medications with synergistic mechanisms of action. Although experience with such drug combinations is somewhat limited, preliminary studies indicate that the bile acid sequestrants given with either niacin, lovastatin, probucol, or gemfibrozil are useful in controlling LDL cholesterol. Lovastatin in combination with either niacin or gemfibrozil needs further study because of the potential increased risk of side effects.

If effective control of LDL cholesterol is not obtained after use of primary medications and medication combinations, then referral to a lipid specialist may be necessary.

Studies have suggested that control of elevated cholesterol and triglycerides may not lessen the danger of cardiovascular disease and mortality, although incidence of nonfatal myocardial infarctions may be decreased.

Unaccepted

Niacin is not useful for treatment of schizophrenia and other mental disorders not related to niacin deficiency. Niacin also has not been proven effective for treatment of acne, alcohol dependence, drug-induced hallucinations, hyperkinesis, leprosy, livedoid vasculitis, peripheral vascular disease, motion sickness, or for prevention of heart attacks.

Pharmacology

Mechanism of action/Effect:

Vitamin—Niacin, after conversion to niacinamide, is a component of two coenzymes, nicotinamide adenine dinucleotide (NAD) and nicotinamide adenine dinucleotide phosphate (NADP), which are necessary for tissue respiration; glycogenolysis; and lipid, amino acid, protein, and purine metabolism.

Antihyperlipidemic—Niacin lowers serum cholesterol and triglyceride concentrations by inhibiting the synthesis of very low density lipoproteins (VLDL), which are precursors to the formation of low-density lipoproteins, the principal carrier of blood cholesterol.

Other actions/effects: Niacin (but not niacinamide) causes direct peripheral vasodilation.

Onset of action:

Reduced cholesterol concentrations—Oral: Several days.
Reduced triglyceride concentrations—Oral: Several hours.

Precautions to Consider

Geriatrics

Appropriate studies on the relationship of age to the effects of niacin have not been performed in the geriatric population. However, no geriatrics-specific problems have been documented to date.

Drug interactions and/or related problems

The following drug interactions and/or related problems have been selected on the basis of their potential clinical significance (possible mechanism in parentheses where appropriate)—not necessarily inclusive (» = major clinical significance):

Chenodiol or
Ursodiol
    (effect may be decreased when chenodiol or ursodiol is used concurrently with antihyperlipidemics, which tend to increase cholesterol saturation of bile)

Lovastatin or
Pravastatin or
Simvastatin
    (concurrent use with niacin may be associated with an increased risk of rhabdomyolysis and acute renal failure; combined therapy with lovastatin, pravastatin, or simvastatin should include careful monitoring for symptoms of myopathy or rhabdomyolysis)

Contraindications/Medical problems

The contraindications/medical problems included have been selected on the basis of their potential clinical significance (reasons given in parentheses where appropriate)—not necessarily inclusive (» = major clinical significance).

Risk-benefit should be considered when the following medical problems exist:

» Arterial bleeding or hemorrhage or
Glaucoma
    (these conditions may be exacerbated)

» Diabetes mellitus
    (large doses of niacin may cause impaired glucose tolerance)
Gout
    (large doses may cause hyperuricemia)

» Hepatic disease
    (large doses may cause hepatic damage)
Hypotension
    (may worsen due to vasodilating effects of niacin)

» Peptic ulcer
    (large doses may activate peptic ulcer)
Sensitivity to niacin or niacinamide

Side/Adverse Effects

Note: Flushing and pruritus may be reduced with the extended-release dosage form of niacin.

The following side/adverse effects have been selected on the basis of their potential clinical significance (possible signs and symptoms in parentheses where appropriate)—not necessarily inclusive:

Those indicating need for medical attention

Incidence rare
Allergic reaction, anaphylactic (skin rash or itching; wheezing)—after intravenous administration; *hepatotoxicity or cholestasis* (darkening of urine, light gray-colored stools, loss of appetite, severe stomach pain, or yellow eyes or skin)—with long-term use of extended-release niacin

Those indicating need for medical attention only if they continue or are bothersome

Incidence less frequent—with niacin only
Feeling of warmth; flushing or redness of skin, especially on face and neck; headache
With high oral doses
Cardiac arrhythmias (unusually fast, slow, or irregular heartbeat); *diarrhea; dizziness or faintness; dryness of skin or eyes; hyperglycemia* (frequent urination or unusual thirst)—may occasionally be fatal; *hyperuricemia* (joint pain; side, lower back, or stomach

pain; or swelling of feet or lower legs); *myalgia* (fever, muscle aching or cramping, unusual tiredness or weakness); *nausea or vomiting; peptic ulcer, aggravation of* (stomach pain); *pruritus* (itching of skin)—may be severe

Note: Rarely, along with markedly elevated creatine kinase (CK) concentrations, fever, muscle aching or cramping, or unusual tiredness or weakness may be symptoms of myositis or rhabdomyolysis; incidence may be increased in patients treated concurrently with lovastatin, pravastatin, or simvastatin.

Patient Consultation

In providing consultation, consider emphasizing the following selected information (» = major clinical significance):

Description of use

Description should include function in the body, signs of deficiency, and unproven uses

Importance of diet

For use as a dietary supplement
Diet as treatment of choice; importance of eating properly
Food sources of niacin; effects of processing
Not using vitamins as substitute for balanced diet
Supplement may be needed because of inadequate intake or increased requirements
Importance of not exceeding RDA if self-medicating with vitamin supplements

Before using this medication

» Conditions affecting use, especially:
    Sensitivity to niacin or niacinamide
    Use in children—Not recommended as antihyperlipidemic in children under 2 years of age since cholesterol is required for normal development
    Other medical problems, especially arterial bleeding or hemorrhage, diabetes mellitus, hepatic disease, or peptic ulcer

For use as a dietary supplement
See *Indications* for conditions and medications affecting requirements.

For use as an antihyperlipidemic (niacin only)
Diet as preferred therapy

Proper use of this medication

Possibility of stomach upset; taking with meals or milk; checking with physician if stomach upset continues
Proper administration of extended-release dosage forms: Swallowing whole without crushing, breaking, or chewing; contents of capsule may be mixed with jam or jelly and swallowed without chewing

» Proper storage

For use as a dietary supplement
Megadoses not recommended without physician's advice
Missed dose: No cause for concern because of length of time necessary for depletion; remembering to take as directed

For use as an antihyperlipidemic (niacin only)
» Importance of not taking more or less medication than prescribed
Niacin does not cure the condition but instead helps control it
» Importance of following prescribed diet
Missed dose: Taking as soon as possible; not taking if almost time for next dose; not doubling doses

Precautions while using this medication

Caution if dizziness or faintness occurs

For use as an antihyperlipidemic (niacin only)
» Importance of close monitoring by physician to check progress
» Checking with physician before discontinuing medication; blood lipid concentrations may increase significantly

Side/adverse effects

Signs of potential side effects, especially anaphylactic reaction with injection only; hepatotoxicity or cholestasis with high doses of extended-release niacin

General Dosing Information

Dosages of niacin and niacinamide as vitamin supplements are equal; some clinicians prefer niacinamide because of its lack of vaso-dilating effect.

Because of the infrequency of single B vitamin deficiencies, combinations are commonly administered. Many commercial combinations of B vitamins are available.

When used for treatment of pellagra, niacin or niacinamide is usually given in combination with 5 mg each of thiamine, riboflavin, and pyridoxine.

The effectiveness of megadoses (10 times the RDA or more) for treatment of various conditions is unproven and their use should be discouraged until benefit has been proven.

For parenteral dosage forms only

In most cases, parenteral administration is indicated only when oral administration is not acceptable (for example, in nausea, vomiting, and preoperative and postoperative conditions) or possible (for example, in malabsorption syndromes or following gastric resection).

When administered intravenously, niacin or niacinamide should be given at a rate not exceeding 2 mg per minute.

Diet/Nutrition

Niacin or niacinamide may be taken with meals or milk if nausea, vomiting, or diarrhea occurs. A physician should be consulted if stomach upset continues.

Recommended dietary allowances (RDA) for vitamins are values determined by the Food and Nutrition Board of the National Research Council. Intake of the RDA provides adequate nutrition in most healthy persons under usual environmental stresses; they are not minimum requirements. RDA are not the same as USRDA (United States Recommended Daily Allowances), which are values established by the FDA for labeling purposes.

RDA of niacin per day:

Infants and children—
  Birth to 6 months: 5 mg.
  6 months to 1 year: 6 mg.
  1 to 3 years: 9 mg.
  4 to 6 years: 12 mg.
  7 to 10 years: 13 mg.
Adolescent and adult males—
  11 to 14 years: 17 mg.
  15 to 18 years: 20 mg.
  19 to 50 years: 19 mg.
  50 years and over: 15 mg.
Adolescent and adult females—
  11 to 50 years: 15 mg.
  50 years and over: 13 mg.
Pregnant females—17 mg.
Lactating females—20 mg.

These are usually provided by adequate diets.

Best dietary sources of niacin include meats, eggs, and milk and dairy products; dietary tryptophan (from protein) is converted to niacin. There is little loss of niacin from foods with ordinary cooking.

NIACIN

Oral Dosage Forms

NIACIN EXTENDED-RELEASE CAPSULES

Note: Dose-related hepatotoxicity may be more prevalent with high doses of the extended-release dosage form of niacin.

Flushing and pruritus may be reduced with the extended-release dosage form of niacin.

Usual adult and adolescent dose:

Vitamin—Oral, up to 500 mg a day.
Antihyperlipidemic—
  Initial: Oral, 1 gram three times a day, the dosage being increased in increments of 500 mg a day every two to four weeks as needed.
  Note: Some clinicians may begin with 500 mg per day and gradually increase the dosage to 4 grams a day.
  Maintenance: Oral, 1 to 2 grams three times a day.

Usual adult prescribing limits: Oral, 6 grams a day.

Auxiliary labeling:
• Swallow capsules whole.
• Take with meals or milk.

Note: Contents of capsule may be mixed with jelly or jam and swallowed without chewing.

NIACIN ORAL SOLUTION

Usual adult and adolescent dose:

Vitamin—Oral, up to 500 mg a day.
Antihyperlipidemic—
  Initial: Oral, 1 gram three times a day, the dosage being increased in increments of 500 mg a day every two to four weeks as needed.
  Maintenance: Oral, 1 to 2 grams three times a day.

Usual adult prescribing limits: Oral, 6 grams a day.

Auxiliary labeling: • Take with meals or milk.

NIACIN TABLETS USP

Usual adult and adolescent dose:

Vitamin—Oral, up to 500 mg a day.
Antihyperlipidemic—
  Initial: Oral, 1 gram three times a day, the dosage being increased in increments of 500 mg a day every two to four weeks as needed.
  Note: Some clinicians may begin with 100 mg per day and gradually increase the dosage to 4 grams per day.
  Maintenance: Oral, 1 to 2 grams three times a day.

Usual adult prescribing limits: Oral, 6 grams a day.

Auxiliary labeling: • Take with meals or milk.

NIACIN EXTENDED-RELEASE TABLETS

Note: Dose-related hepatotoxicity may be more prevalent with high doses of the extended-release dosage form.

Flushing and pruritus may be reduced with the extended-release dosage form of niacin.

Usual adult and adolescent dose:

Vitamin—Oral, up to 500 mg a day.
Antihyperlipidemic—
  Initial: Oral, 1 gram three times a day, the dosage being increased in increments of 500 mg a day every two to four weeks as needed and tolerated.

Note: Some clinicians may begin with 500 mg per day and gradually increase the dosage to 3 grams a day.

Maintenance: Oral, 1 to 2 grams three times a day.

Note: Some clinicians may use a maintenance dose of 500 mg to 1 gram two to three times a day.

Usual adult prescribing limits: Oral, 6 grams a day.

Auxiliary labeling:
- Swallow tablets whole.
- Take with meals or milk.

Note: If tablets are scored, they may be broken, but not crushed or chewed, before swallowing.

Parenteral Dosage Forms

NIACIN INJECTION USP

Usual adult and adolescent dose: Vitamin—Pellagra:
Intramuscular, 50 to 100 mg five or more times a day.
Intravenous (slow), 25 to 100 mg two or more times a day.

NIACINAMIDE

Oral Dosage Forms

NIACINAMIDE CAPSULES

Usual adult and adolescent dose: Vitamin—Oral, up to 500 mg a day.

NIACINAMIDE TABLETS USP

Usual adult and adolescent dose: Vitamin—Up to 500 mg a day.

Parenteral Dosage Forms

NIACINAMIDE INJECTION USP

Usual adult and adolescent dose: Vitamin—Pellagra:
Intramuscular, 50 to 100 mg five or more times a day.
Intravenous (slow), 25 to 100 mg two or more times a day.

NICOTINYL ALCOHOL   Systemic*

A commonly used *brand name* in Canada is *Roniacol*.

ORAL
Nicotinyl Alcohol Tartrate Extended-release Tablets*
In Canada—*Roniacol*

*Not commercially available in the U.S.

Category: Vasospastic therapy adjunct.

Indications

Accepted
Vascular disease, peripheral (treatment);
Vascular spasm (treatment);
Ulcer, varicose (treatment);
Ulcer, decubital (treatment);
Frostbite (treatment);
Ear, inner, circulatory disturbances of (Menière's syndrome) (treatment); or
Vertigo (treatment)—Nicotinyl alcohol may be effective for its labeled indications, which include peripheral vascular disease, vascular spasm, varicose ulcers, decubital ulcers, chilblains (frostbite), Menière's syndrome, and vertigo.

Pharmacology

Mechanism of action/Effect: Nicotinyl alcohol's action occurs as a result of its *in vivo* conversion to niacin (nicotinic acid). Nicotinic acid produces weak peripheral vasodilation by a direct effect on vascular smooth muscle; however, in usual doses it is probable that only cutaneous vessels are affected.

Onset of action: Vasodilator effect—
Extended-release tablets: 30 minutes.

Time to peak effect: Clinical improvement may occur gradually over several weeks.

Duration of action: Vasodilator effect—
Extended-release tablets: 6–12 hours.

Precautions to Consider

Geriatrics
The risk of nicotinyl alcohol-induced hypothermia may be increased in elderly patients.

Drug interactions and/or related problems
The following drug interactions and/or related problems have been selected on the basis of their potential clinical significance (possible mechanism in parentheses where appropriate)—not necessarily inclusive (» = major clinical significance):

Smoking, tobacco
(heavy smoking may interfere with the therapeutic effect of nicotinyl alcohol because nicotine constricts blood vessels)

Contraindications/Medical problems
The contraindications/medical problems included have been selected on the basis of their potential clinical significance (reasons given in parentheses where appropriate)—not necessarily inclusive (» = major clinical significance).

Risk-benefit should be considered when the following medical problems exist:

» Active peptic ulcer or gastritis
» Cerebrovascular disease, severe, or
» Myocardial infarction, recent, or
» Obliterative coronary artery disease, severe
(a "steal effect" may occur, since nicotinyl alcohol has a greater effect on peripheral vessels than on cerebral and coronary vessels, leading to a further decrease in flow to ischemic areas)

Diabetes mellitus
(nicotinyl alcohol may increase fasting blood sugar concentrations)

Glaucoma, predisposition to

Hyperlipidemia
(large doses necessary to treat this condition may cause impaired glucose tolerance)

Sensitivity to nicotinyl alcohol

Side/Adverse Effects

The following side/adverse effects have been selected on the basis of their potential clinical significance (possible signs and symptoms in parentheses where appropriate)—not necessarily inclusive:

Those indicating need for medical attention
Incidence rare—dose-related
Hepatotoxicity (swelling of feet or lower legs, yellow eyes or skin)
Note: *Hepatotoxicity* occurs only with very high doses.

Those indicating need for medical attention only if they continue or are bothersome
Incidence more frequent
Vasodilation, especially on face and neck (flushing, warmth or tingling)

Incidence less frequent or rare
Allergic reaction (skin rash); *diarrhea; hypotension* (dizziness or faintness); *increased hair loss; nausea and vomiting*

Patient Consultation

In providing consultation, consider emphasizing the following selected information (» = major clinical significance):

Before using this medication
» Conditions affecting use, especially:
Sensitivity to nicotinyl alcohol
Use in the elderly—Increased risk of hypothermia

Other medical problems, especially peptic ulcer or gastritis (active), cerebrovascular disease, recent myocardial infarction, or obliterative coronary artery disease (severe)

Proper use of this medication
Swallowing tablets whole; not breaking, crushing, or chewing prior to swallowing
Missed dose: Taking as soon as possible; not taking if almost time for next dose; not doubling doses
» Proper storage

Precautions while using this medication
Checking with physician before discontinuing medication
Avoiding smoking (nicotine constricts blood vessels)

Side/adverse effects
Signs of potential side effects, especially hepatotoxicity

Oral Dosage Forms

Note: The dosage and strengths of the dosage form available are expressed in terms of nicotinyl alcohol.

NICOTINYL ALCOHOL TARTRATE EXTENDED-RELEASE TABLETS

Usual adult dose: Vasospastic therapy adjunct—Oral, 150 to 300 mg (nicotinyl alcohol) two times a day, in the morning and evening.

Auxiliary labeling: • Swallow tablets whole.

NITRATES   Systemic

INN: Included in brackets after individual generic listings.

Some commonly used *brand names* are:

In the U.S.—
Cardilate [Erythrityl Tetranitrate]
Deponit [Nitroglycerin]
Dilatrate-SR [Isosorbide Dinitrate]
Duotrate [Pentaerythritol Tetranitrate]
Iso-Bid [Isosorbide Dinitrate]
Isonate [Isosorbide Dinitrate]
Isorbid [Isosorbide Dinitrate]
Isordil [Isosorbide Dinitrate]
Isotrate [Isosorbide Dinitrate]
Klavikordal [Nitroglycerin]
Naptrate [Pentaerythritol Tetranitrate]
Niong [Nitroglycerin]
Nitro-Bid [Nitroglycerin]
Nitrocap [Nitroglycerin]
Nitrocap T.D. [Nitroglycerin]
Nitrocine [Nitroglycerin]
Nitrodisc [Nitroglycerin]
Nitro-Dur [Nitroglycerin]
Nitro-Dur II [Nitroglycerin]

Nitrogard [Nitroglycerin]
Nitroglyn [Nitroglycerin]
Nitroject [Nitroglycerin]
Nitrol [Nitroglycerin]
Nitrolin [Nitroglycerin]
Nitrolingual [Nitroglycerin]
Nitronet [Nitroglycerin]
Nitrong [Nitroglycerin]
Nitrospan [Nitroglycerin]
Nitrostat [Nitroglycerin]
NTS [Nitroglycerin]
Pentritol [Pentaerythritol Tetranitrate]
Pentylan [Pentaerythritol Tetranitrate]
Peritrate [Pentaerythritol Tetranitrate]
Peritrate SA [Pentaerythritol Tetranitrate]
Sorbitrate [Isosorbide Dinitrate]
Sorbitrate SA [Isosorbide Dinitrate]
Transderm-Nitro [Nitroglycerin]
Tridil [Nitroglycerin]

In Canada—
Apo-ISDN [Isosorbide Dinitrate]
Cardilate [Erythrityl Tetranitrate]
Cedocard-SR [Isosorbide Dinitrate]
Coronex [Isosorbide Dinitrate]
Isordil [Isosorbide Dinitrate]
Nitro-Bid [Nitroglycerin]
Nitrogard SR [Nitroglycerin]
Nitroject [Nitroglycerin]
Nitrol [Nitroglycerin]
Nitrolingual [Nitroglycerin]

Nitrong [Nitroglycerin]
Nitrong SR [Nitroglycerin]
Nitrostat [Nitroglycerin]
Novosorbide [Isosorbide Dinitrate]
Peritrate [Pentaerythritol Tetranitrate]
Peritrate Forte [Pentaerythritol Tetranitrate]
Peritrate SA [Pentaerythritol Tetranitrate]
Transderm-Nitro [Nitroglycerin]
Tridil [Nitroglycerin]

Other commonly used names are:
Eritrityl tetranitrate [Erythrityl Tetranitrate]
Erythritol tetranitrate [Erythrityl Tetranitrate]
Glyceryl trinitrate [Nitroglycerin]

Pentaerithrityl tetranitrate [Pentaerythritol Tetranitrate]
P.E.T.N. [Pentaerythritol Tetranitrate]

AMYL NITRITE—See Amyl Nitrite (Systemic).
ERYTHRITYL TETRANITRATE [INN: Eritrityl Tetranitrate]
Oral/Sublingual
Erythrityl Tetranitrate Tablets USP
In the U.S. and Canada—*Cardilate*
ISOSORBIDE DINITRATE
Oral
Isosorbide Dinitrate Capsules†
In the U.S.—GENERIC

Isosorbide Dinitrate Extended-release Capsules USP†
  In the U.S.—*Dilatrate-SR; Iso-Bid; Isorbid; Isordil; Isotrate;* GENERIC
Isosorbide Dinitrate Tablets USP
  In the U.S.—*Isonate; Isorbid; Isordil; Sorbitrate;* GENERIC
  In Canada—*Apo-ISDN; Coronex; Isordil; Novosorbide*
Isosorbide Dinitrate Chewable Tablets USP†
  In the U.S.—*Sorbitrate*
Isosorbide Dinitrate Extended-release Tablets USP
  In the U.S.—*Isonate; Isorbid; Isordil; Sorbitrate SA;* GENERIC
  In Canada—*Cedocard-SR*
Sublingual
  Isosorbide Dinitrate Sublingual Tablets USP
    In the U.S.—*Isonate; Isorbid; Isordil; Sorbitrate;* GENERIC
    In Canada—*Apo-ISDN; Coronex; Isordil*
NITROGLYCERIN
Buccal
  Nitroglycerin Extended-release Buccal Tablets
    In the U.S.—*Nitrogard*
    In Canada—*Nitrogard SR*
Lingual
  Nitroglycerin Lingual Aerosol
    In the U.S. and Canada—*Nitrolingual*
Oral
  Nitroglycerin Extended-release Capsules†
    In the U.S.—*Nitro-Bid; Nitrocap; Nitrocap T.D.; Nitrocine; Nitroglyn; Nitrolin; Nitrospan;* GENERIC
  Nitroglycerin Extended-release Tablets
    In the U.S.—*Klavikordal; Niong; Nitronet; Nitrong*
    In Canada—*Nitrong SR*
Parenteral
  Nitroglycerin Injection USP
    In the U.S.—*Nitro-Bid; Nitroject; Nitrol; Nitrostat; Tridil;* GENERIC
    In Canada—*Nitro-Bid; Nitroject; Nitrostat; Tridil;* GENERIC
Sublingual
  Nitroglycerin Tablets USP (Sublingual)
    In the U.S. and Canada—*Nitrostat;* GENERIC
Topical
  Nitroglycerin Ointment USP
    In the U.S.—*Nitro-Bid; Nitrol; Nitrong; Nitrostat;* GENERIC
    In Canada—*Nitro-Bid; Nitrol; Nitrong*
  Nitroglycerin Transdermal Systems
    In the U.S.—*Deponit; Nitrocine; Nitrodisc; Nitro-Dur; Nitro-Dur II; NTS; Transderm-Nitro;* GENERIC
    In Canada—*Transderm-Nitro*
PENTAERYTHRITOL TETRANITRATE [INN: Pentaerithrityl Tetranitrate]
Oral
  Pentaerythritol Tetranitrate Extended-release Capsules†
    In the U.S.—*Duotrate; Pentritol;* GENERIC
  Pentaerythritol Tetranitrate Tablets USP
    In the U.S.—*Naptrate; Pentylan; Peritrate;* GENERIC
    In Canada—*Peritrate; Peritrate Forte*
  Pentaerythritol Tetranitrate Extended-release Tablets
    In the U.S.—*Peritrate SA;* GENERIC
    In Canada—*Peritrate SA*

---

†Not commercially available in Canada.

Category

Note: All of the nitrates have similar pharmacologic actions; however, clinical uses among specific agents may vary because of actual pharmacokinetic differences, availability of specific testing, and/or availability of clinical-use data.

Antianginal—Erythrityl Tetranitrate; Isosorbide Dinitrate; Nitroglycerin; Pentaerythritol Tetranitrate.
Antihypertensive—Nitroglycerin Injection.

Vasodilator, congestive heart failure—Nitroglycerin; Erythrityl Tetranitrate; Isosorbide Dinitrate; Pentaerythritol Tetranitrate.

Indications

Note: Bracketed information in the *Indications* section refers to uses not included in U.S. product labeling.
See also *Table 1*, page 777.

Accepted
Angina pectoris, acute (treatment)—The sublingual, lingual, and extended-release buccal[1] dosage forms of nitroglycerin and the sublingual[1] and chewable dosage forms of isosorbide dinitrate are indicated for the relief of pain of an acute episode of angina pectoris due to coronary artery disease. Sublingual or lingual nitroglycerin is preferred; isosorbide dinitrate should be used in patients intolerant of or unresponsive to nitroglycerin. Sublingual isosorbide dinitrate[1] or sublingual or lingual nitroglycerin may be administered to relieve acute anginal attacks that may occur while the patient is on oral prophylactic therapy.

Angina pectoris, acute (prophylaxis)—The sublingual, lingual[1], and extended-release buccal dosage forms of nitroglycerin; the sublingual dosage form of erythrityl tetranitrate; and the sublingual or chewable dosage forms of isosorbide dinitrate are indicated for prophylaxis of acute angina attacks in situations (such as stress or exertion) likely to provoke such attacks.

Angina pectoris, chronic (treatment)—The oral/sublingual dosage form of erythrityl tetranitrate; the regular, chewable, sublingual, and extended-release oral dosage forms of isosorbide dinitrate; and the extended-release oral and buccal dosage forms of nitroglycerin are indicated for the prophylaxis and long-term treatment of angina pectoris due to coronary artery disease, but not in the treatment of acute anginal attacks (except for chewable isosorbide dinitrate and buccal nitroglycerin). Rapid first-pass hepatic destruction of nitroglycerin may increase the dosage requirements of the oral extended-release capsules and tablets in the prophylaxis and treatment of angina.

FDA has classified the oral dosage forms of pentaerythritol tetranitrate as *possibly effective* in the prophylaxis of angina pectoris, but not in the treatment of acute attacks. This classification requires the submission of adequate and well-controlled studies in order to provide substantial evidence of effectiveness.

Nitroglycerin injection is indicated in the treatment of unstable angina pectoris in patients who have not responded to recommended doses of other organic nitrates and/or a beta-blocker.

Nitroglycerin ointment and nitroglycerin transdermal systems are indicated for the prophylaxis and long-term treatment of angina pectoris but are not indicated for the relief of an acute angina episode.

Hypertension (treatment); or
Hypotension, controlled—Nitroglycerin injection is indicated for blood pressure control during certain surgical procedures and for controlled hypotension during surgery to reduce bleeding into the surgical field.

Myocardial infarction (treatment adjunct); or
Congestive heart failure (treatment)—Nitroglycerin injection is indicated in the adjunctive therapy for congestive heart failure associated or not associated with acute myocardial infarction. (Treatment of congestive heart failure not associated with acute myocardial infarction is not included in Canadian product labeling.) [Sublingual][1], [lingual][1], and [topical][1] nitroglycerin; [regular oral and sublingual erythrityl tetranitrate][1]; [regular oral], [chewable], and [sublingual][1] isosorbide dinitrate; and [regular oral pentaerythritol tetranitrate][1] are also being used for treatment of congestive heart failure, whether or not it is associated with acute myocardial infarction. In general, the oral extended-release dosage forms are not recommended because the effects are difficult to terminate if excessive hypotension or tachycardia develops, al-

though these dosage forms may be acceptable once the patient is stabilized.

---

[1]Not included in Canadian product labeling.

Pharmacology

Mechanism of action/Effect:

Antianginal or

Cardiac load-reducing agent—Not specifically known but thought to cause a reduction of myocardial oxygen demand. This is attributed to a reduction in left ventricular preload and afterload because of venous (predominantly) and arterial dilation with a more efficient redistribution of blood flow within the myocardium.

Antihypertensive—Peripheral vasodilation.

Onset of action:

Note: Although information is limited, pharmacokinetics of sublingual tablets administered buccally are probably similar to those after sublingual administration.

Erythrityl tetranitrate—
    Oral tablets: 15 to 30 minutes.
    Sublingual tablets: 5 minutes.
Isosorbide dinitrate—
    Oral capsules and tablets: 15 to 40 minutes.
    Chewable tablets: 2 to 5 minutes.
    Extended-release capsules and tablets: 30 minutes.
    Sublingual tablets: 2 to 5 minutes.
Nitroglycerin—
    Buccal tablets: 3 minutes.
    Lingual aerosol: 2 to 4 minutes.
    Intravenous infusion: Immediate.
    Sublingual tablets: 1 to 3 minutes.
    Ointment: Within 30 minutes.
    Transdermal systems: Within 30 minutes.
Pentaerythritol tetranitrate—
    Oral tablets: 30 minutes.
    Extended-release capsules and tablets: Slow.

Duration of action:

Note: Although information is limited, pharmacokinetics of sublingual tablets administered buccally are probably similar to those after sublingual administration.

Erythrityl tetranitrate—
    Oral tablets: Up to 6 hours.
    Sublingual tablets: 2 to 3 hours.
Isosorbide dinitrate—
    Oral capsules and tablets: 4 to 6 hours.
    Chewable tablets: 1 to 2 hours.
    Extended-release capsules and tablets: 12 hours.
    Sublingual tablets: 1 to 2 hours.
Nitroglycerin—
    Buccal extended-release tablets: Approximately 5 hours.
    Extended-release capsules and tablets: 8 to 12 hours.
    Intravenous infusion: Several minutes (dose-dependent).
    Sublingual tablets: 30 to 60 minutes.
    Ointment: 4 to 8 hours.
    Transdermal systems: 8 to 24 hours.
Pentaerythritol tetranitrate—
    Oral tablets: 4 to 5 hours.
    Extended-release capsules and tablets: 12 hours.

Precautions to Consider

Cross-sensitivity and/or related problems

Patients sensitive to one nitrate may be sensitive to other nitrates also, although the reaction is rare.

Patients sensitive to nitrites may be sensitive to nitrates also, although the reaction is rare.

Geriatrics

Although appropriate studies with nitrates have not been performed in the geriatric population, elderly patients may be more sensitive to the hypotensive effects. In addition, elderly patients are more likely to have age-related renal function impairment, which may require caution in patients receiving nitrates.

Drug interactions and/or related problems

The following drug interactions and/or related problems have been selected on the basis of their potential clinical significance (possible mechanism in parentheses where appropriate)—not necessarily inclusive (» = major clinical significance)

Note: Combinations containing any of the following medications, depending on the amount present, may also interact with this medication.

Acetylcholine or
Histamine or
Norepinephrine (levarterenol)
    (effects of these medications may be decreased when they are used concurrently with nitrates)
»   Alcohol, moderate or excessive amounts, or
»   Antihypertensives or
Hypotension-producing medications, other or
Opioid (narcotic) analgesics or
»   Vasodilators, other
    (concurrent use may intensify the orthostatic hypotensive effects of nitrates; dosage adjustments may be necessary)
Heparin
    (the anticoagulant effect of heparin may be decreased in patients receiving nitroglycerin via intravenous infusion; adjustment of heparin dosage may be required to maintain the desired degree of anticoagulation during and following administration of a nitroglycerin infusion)
Sympathomimetics
    (concurrent use may reduce the antianginal effects of nitrates)
    (nitrates may counteract the pressor effect of sympathomimetics, possibly resulting in hypotension)

Contraindications/Medical problems

The contraindications/medical problems included have been selected on the basis of their potential clinical significance (reasons given in parentheses where appropriate)—not necessarily inclusive (» = major clinical significance).

Except under special circumstances, this medication should not be used when the following medical problems exists:

For nitroglycerin injection only
»   Cerebral hemorrhage or
»   Head trauma, recent
    (nitroglycerin may increase cerebrospinal fluid pressure)
»   Pericardial tamponade
»   Pericarditis, constrictive

Risk-benefit should be considered when the following medical problems exist:

For all nitrates
»   Anemia, severe
»   Cerebral hemorrhage or
»   Head trauma, recent
    (nitrates may increase cerebrospinal fluid pressure)
»   Glaucoma
    (nitrates may increase intraocular pressure)
Hepatic function impairment, severe
    (increased risk of methemoglobinemia)
»   Hyperthyroidism
Hypertrophic cardiomyopathy
    (angina may be aggravated)

Hypotension, with low systolic pressure
(may be aggravated, accompanied by paradoxical bradycardia and increased angina pectoris)
» Myocardial infarction, recent
(risk of hypotension and tachycardia, which may aggravate ischemia)
Renal function impairment, severe
Sensitivity to the nitrate prescribed
For oral dosage forms only (in addition to the above)
Gastrointestinal hypermotility or
Malabsorption syndrome
(use of extended-release dosage forms should be avoided because they may not dissolve and may be excreted intact)
For nitroglycerin injection only (in addition to the above)
» Hypovolemia
(risk of producing severe hypotension and shock; should be corrected prior to use of nitroglycerin)
» Normal or low pulmonary capillary wedge pressure
(patients may be unusually sensitive to hypotensive effects)

Side/Adverse Effects

The following side/adverse effects have been selected on the basis of their potential clinical significance (possible signs and symptoms in parentheses where appropriate)—not necessarily inclusive:

Those indicating need for medical attention
Incidence rare
Blurred vision; dry mouth; headache, severe or prolonged; skin rash
Signs and symptoms of overdose (in order of occurrence)
Bluish-colored lips, fingernails, or palms of hands; dizziness, extreme, or fainting; feeling of extreme pressure in head; shortness of breath; unusual tiredness or weakness; weak and fast heartbeat; fever; convulsions
Note: Cyanosis may occur at blood methemoglobin concentrations of 1.5 grams per 100 mL. More pronounced signs of methemoglobinemia (pressure in head, tiredness or weakness, shortness of breath) occur at concentrations of 20 to 50 grams per 100 mL.

Those indicating need for medical attention only if they continue or are bothersome
Incidence more frequent—dose-related
Fast pulse; flushing of face and neck; headache; nausea or vomiting; orthostatic hypotension (dizziness or lightheadedness, especially when getting up from a lying or sitting position); *restlessness*
Incidence less frequent
Sore, reddened skin—topical nitroglycerin dosage forms

Patient Consultation

See *Table 2*, page 778.

General Dosing Information

Dosage must be adjusted to the needs and tolerance of the individual patient. Dosage requirements may be increased by a worsening of the patient's condition or a loss of medication potency.

Tolerance to nitrate medications has been reported and may result in an increase of patient medication requirements. Careful monitoring is recommended to make sure that the desired effect is being maintained. If tolerance occurs, there is some evidence that withdrawal of the particular nitrate for several hours (12 to 36 hours in most of the current literature), and subsequent reinstitution of the same product, will restore patient responsiveness.

Nitrate therapy should be discontinued if blurred vision or dry mouth continues or is severe.

When this medication is to be discontinued following high-dose or long-term administration, dosage should be reduced gradually to prevent possible withdrawal rebound angina.

For oral dosage forms only
There have been reports of patients finding intact or partially dissolved extended-release isosorbide dinitrate or pentaerythritol tetranitrate tablets in the stool. Some patients may benefit by a change from the extended-release tablet to the extended-release capsule or the regular oral tablet and an increase in dosage to an effective level for each individual patient.

For buccal extended-release nitroglycerin tablets or sublingual tablets administered buccally only
The tablet should be placed between upper lip and gum (above the incisors) or between cheek and upper gum, and allowed to dissolve in place. Tablet placement sites may be alternated as patient desires.

The dissolution time of the buccal extended-release tablet may vary from 3 to 5 hours in most patients. The dissolution rate is increased when the tablet is touched with the tongue or the patient drinks hot liquids. The buccal extended-release tablet utilizes an inert polymer vehicle which enables a metered nitroglycerin release not affected by pH, food, or drink (placement is suggested behind the upper lip if food and drink are to be taken during dosing).

Use at bedtime is not recommended because of the risk of aspiration.

Sublingual erythrityl tetranitrate, isosorbide dinitrate, and nitroglycerin tablets may also be administered buccally. Although information is limited, onset and duration of action are probably similar to sublingual dosing.

Diet/Nutrition
The regular oral dosage forms of this medication should preferably be taken with a glass of water on an empty stomach (either 1 hour before or 2 hours after meals) for faster absorption.

ERYTHRITYL TETRANITRATE

Summary of Differences

Indications: Although available in sublingual dosage form, is not useful for treatment of acute angina attacks.
Pharmacology: Onset and duration of action—See *Pharmacology*.

Oral Dosage Forms

ERYTHRITYL TETRANITRATE TABLETS USP

Usual adult dose: Antianginal—Oral, sublingual, or buccal, 5 to 10 mg three or four times a day, the dosage being adjusted as needed and tolerated.

Note: The regular tablet of erythrityl tetranitrate currently marketed may be utilized for oral, sublingual, or buccal dosage.

Usual adult prescribing limits: Up to 100 mg daily.

Auxiliary labeling:
• Caution with alcoholic beverages.
• Keep container tightly closed.
• Store in a cool, dry place.

ISOSORBIDE DINITRATE

Summary of Differences

Pharmacology: Onset and duration of action—See *Pharmacology*.

Oral Dosage Forms

ISOSORBIDE DINITRATE CAPSULES

Note: Isosorbide dinitrate capsules are not commercially available in Canada.

Usual adult dose: Antianginal—Oral, 5 to 20 mg every six hours, the dosage being adjusted as needed and tolerated. The dosage range is 5 to 40 mg four times a day, with the usual dosage range being 20 to 40 mg four times a day.

Auxiliary labeling:
*   Caution with alcoholic beverages.
*   Store in a cool, dry place.

ISOSORBIDE DINITRATE EXTENDED-RELEASE CAPSULES USP

Note: Isosorbide dinitrate extended-release capsules are not commercially available in Canada.

Usual adult dose: Antianginal—Oral, 40 to 80 mg every eight to twelve hours.

Auxiliary labeling:
*   Caution with alcoholic beverages.
*   Swallow capsules whole.
*   Store in a cool, dry place.

ISOSORBIDE DINITRATE TABLETS USP

Usual adult dose: Antianginal—Oral, 5 to 20 mg every six hours, the dosage being adjusted as needed and tolerated. The dosage range is 5 to 40 mg four times a day, with the usual dosage range being 20 to 40 mg four times a day.

Auxiliary labeling:
*   Caution with alcoholic beverages.
*   Store in a cool, dry place.

ISOSORBIDE DINITRATE CHEWABLE TABLETS USP

Note: Isosorbide dinitrate chewable tablets are not commercially available in Canada.

Usual adult dose: Antianginal—Oral, 5 mg chewed well every two to three hours, the dosage being adjusted as needed and tolerated.

Note: Chewed tablet is to be held in mouth for one or two minutes to allow time for absorption through buccal tissues.

Auxiliary labeling:
*   Caution with alcoholic beverages.
*   Chew well before swallowing.
*   Store in a cool, dry place.

ISOSORBIDE DINITRATE EXTENDED-RELEASE TABLETS USP

Usual adult dose: Antianginal—Oral, 20 to 80 mg every eight to twelve hours.

Auxiliary labeling:
*   Caution with alcoholic beverages.
*   Swallow tablets whole.
*   Store in a cool, dry place.

Sublingual Dosage Forms

ISOSORBIDE DINITRATE SUBLINGUAL TABLETS USP

Usual adult dose: Antianginal—Sublingual or buccal, 2.5 to 5 mg every two to three hours as needed.

Auxiliary labeling:
*   Caution with alcoholic beverages.
*   Dissolve tablets under tongue.
*   Store in a cool, dry place.

NITROGLYCERIN

Summary of Differences

Category: Antihypertensive; cardiac load-reducing agent.
Indications: Hypertension (parenteral dosage form); hypotension, controlled (parenteral dosage form); acute myocardial infarction; congestive heart failure.
Pharmacology:
  Half-life—1 to 4 minutes.
  Onset and duration of action—See *Pharmacology*.
Precautions: Contraindications/medical problems—Contraindicated in increased intracranial pressure, constrictive pericarditis (parenteral dosage form); caution needed in hypovolemia or severe hepatic or renal function impairment (parenteral dosage form).

Additional Dosing Information

See also *General Dosing Information*.

For sublingual tablets only
Judging the ability of a sublingual tablet to relieve angina by the presence of a tingling or burning sensation after a tablet has been dissolved under the tongue, is not completely reliable since some patients may be unable to detect these effects. Newer, stabilized sublingual nitroglycerin tablets are making such potency testing less useful, since the stabilized tablets may be less likely to produce these detectable effects.

Repeated opening of container may shorten the period of potency. Many patients replace tablet stock every 6 months during frequent use to ensure results. Stabilized tablets are designed to provide potency for longer periods, but must still receive proper storage.

A supplementary stainless steel container has been developed and approved for temporary storage of small quantities of nitroglycerin tablets. The pendant-type container on a chain, which can be worn around the patient's neck, is intended to provide a convenient source of nitroglycerin for emergency use.

For intravenous infusion form only
Special nitroglycerin infusion sets made of non-PVC plastic cause minimal absorption; therefore, nearly all the calculated dose will be delivered to the patient. When these sets are used, *dosage instructions should be followed with care,* as changing from a standard set (PVC) to a special set (non-PVC) may result in excessive nitroglycerin dosage unless allowances are made for the difference in the amount of nitroglycerin actually delivered to the patient.

For ointment dosage form only
The dose should be individualized starting with $1/2$ to 1 inch of ointment as squeezed from the tube and then increasing the dose by $1/2$ inch at each application until the desired clinical effect and the greatest asymptomatic decrease in resting blood pressure occur. The largest dose that does not cause symptomatic hypotension is used as the patient's individualized dose.

The ointment is applied with the dose-measuring application papers supplied with the medicine. The ointment is squeezed onto the measuring scale printed on the paper. The paper is then used to spread the ointment onto the skin in a thin, even layer, covering an area (at least 2 by 3 inches) of the same size at each dose without rubbing or massage.

The site of ointment application may be the non-hairy skin of the chest, stomach, front of the thighs, or any other accessible area of clean, dry skin. Application to the chest is commonly preferred since the patient also benefits psychologically from applying medication to the area where the pain is experienced.

For transdermal dosage forms only

Application should preferably be made at the same time each day (after removal of the previous system) to areas of clean, dry, hairless skin on the chest, inner side of the upper arm, or shoulders; application to extremities below the knee or elbow should be avoided. Skin areas with extensive scarring, calluses, or irritation should also be avoided. Application sites should be varied to avoid causing skin irritation.

All available transdermal systems provide therapeutic effects within 30 minutes and sustain the required plasma concentration of nitroglycerin for 8 to 24 hours.

The transdermal units *should not* be cut or trimmed in an attempt to adjust dosage.

A new dosage unit should be applied if the first becomes loosened or falls off.

Removal of the transdermal unit before defibrillation or cardioversion is recommended because of the potential for altered electrical conductivity and enhanced risk of arcing associated with use of defibrillators.

Buccal Dosage Forms

NITROGLYCERIN EXTENDED-RELEASE BUCCAL TABLETS

Usual adult dose: Antianginal—Buccal, 1 mg dissolved in place on the oral mucosa every five hours during waking hours, the dosage being increased by frequency and/or strength as required.

Auxiliary labeling:
- Caution with alcoholic beverages.
- Dissolve tablet between lip or cheek and upper gum.
- Do not chew or swallow.
- Keep in original container, tightly closed.
- Store in a cool, dry place.

Lingual Dosage Forms

NITROGLYCERIN LINGUAL AEROSOL

Usual adult dose: Antianginal—On or under the tongue, 1 or 2 metered doses (400 or 800 mcg [0.4 or 0.8 mg]) repeated at five-minute intervals as needed for relief of angina attack.

Note: If relief is not obtained after a total of 3 metered doses in a fifteen-minute period, the physician should be contacted or the patient taken to a hospital.

Usual adult prescribing limits: Up to 1.2 mg per day.

Auxiliary labeling:
- Do not shake.
- Caution with alcoholic beverages.
- Store in a cool place.

Oral Dosage Forms

NITROGLYCERIN EXTENDED-RELEASE CAPSULES

Note: Nitroglycerin extended-release capsules are not commercially available in Canada.

Usual adult dose: Antianginal—Oral, 2.5, 6.5, or 9.0 mg every twelve hours, the dosage being increased to every eight hours if needed and tolerated.

Auxiliary labeling:
- Caution with alcoholic beverages.
- Swallow capsules whole.
- Keep container tightly closed.
- Store in a cool, dry place.

NITROGLYCERIN EXTENDED-RELEASE TABLETS

Usual adult dose: Antianginal—Oral, 1.3, 2.6, or 6.5 mg every twelve hours, the dosage being increased to every eight hours as needed and tolerated.

Auxiliary labeling:
- Caution with alcoholic beverages.
- Swallow tablets whole.
- Keep container tightly closed.
- Store in a cool, dry place.

Parenteral Dosage Forms

NITROGLYCERIN INJECTION USP

Usual adult dose:

Antianginal; or

Antihypertensive; or

Cardiac load-reducing agent—Intravenous infusion, initially administered at a rate of 5 mcg (0.005 mg) per minute, the dosage being increased by increments of 5 mcg per minute at three- to five-minute intervals until an effect is obtained or until the rate is 20 mcg (0.02 mg) per minute. If no effect is obtained at 20 mcg per minute, the dosage may be increased further by increments of 10 mcg (0.01 mg) per minute at the same time intervals, and later increased by increments of 20 mcg (0.02 mg) per minute if necessary to obtain an effect. The dosage increments should be reduced and the time interval between dosage increases lengthened when a partial effect is observed, to attain the desired response cautiously.

Note: Close attention must be given to manufacturers' instructions for dilution, dosage, and administration because concentrations and/or volume per vial of nitroglycerin may differ among the several products available from different manufacturers.

Stated dosage is based on use of special, non-polyvinylchloride (non-PVC) intravenous infusion sets. Dosage requirements may vary when standard infusion sets of PVC are used. Continuous concurrent monitoring of blood pressure and heart rate in *all patients* must be performed to establish the correct effective dose.

To achieve optimal control of dosage and effects, it is recommended that nitroglycerin be administered intravenously by means of an infusion pump, a micro-drip regulator, or a similar device to allow precise adjustment of the flow rate.

Standard intravenous infusion sets made of polyvinyl chloride (PVC) plastic may unpredictably absorb 40 to 80% of the nitroglycerin from a diluted solution for infusion.

Some intravenous filters may also absorb nitroglycerin, but the effect is variable; since nitroglycerin dosage is titrated according to response, no precaution is necessary.

Extra caution should be observed when non-PVC infusion sets are used to administer intravenous nitroglycerin. Some infusion pumps—
- When turned off may not completely stop the flow of infusion solution with these non-PVC sets.
- May not accurately deliver the infusion solution at low rates of flow.
- Require extension sets and other connecting equipment made of PVC, thus partially negating the advantage of the non-PVC infusion set.

Close monitoring of patient hemodynamic response is required. All infusion pumps should be tested with the infusion set being used to ensure accurate delivery of nitroglycerin at low flow rates and complete interruption of flow when the set is turned off.

Usual adult prescribing limits: No fixed maximum dose established. Dosage is titrated to individual patient response beginning with small doses (to which hypersensitive patients may respond).

Note:
Manufacturer's package information must be checked for dilution, administration, and dosage because of product differences.
Some products contain substantial amounts of propylene glycol or ethanol.

Sublingual Dosage Forms

NITROGLYCERIN TABLETS USP (SUBLINGUAL)

Usual adult dose: Antianginal—Sublingual or buccal, 150 to 600 mcg (0.15 to 0.6 mg) repeated at five-minute intervals as needed for relief of angina attack.

Note: If relief is not obtained after a total of 3 tablets used over a fifteen-minute period, the physician should be contacted or the patient taken to a hospital.

Usual adult prescribing limits: Up to 10 mg per day.

Auxiliary labeling:
• Caution with alcoholic beverages.
• Dissolve tablets under tongue.
• Keep in original container, tightly closed.
• Store in a cool, dry place.

Topical Dosage Forms

NITROGLYCERIN OINTMENT USP

Usual adult dose: Antianginal—Topical, to the skin, 15 to 30 mg of nitroglycerin (contained in 2.5 to 5 cm [1 to 2 inches] of ointment as squeezed from the tube) every eight hours during the day and at bedtime. If angina occurs between doses, frequency of application may be increased to every six hours.

Note: Ointment is applied in a thin, even layer covering an area of the same size (measuring at least 2 by 3 inches) at each use, but is not to be rubbed or massaged into the skin.

Usual adult prescribing limits: Up to 75 mg of nitroglycerin (contained in 12.5 cm [5 inches] of ointment as squeezed from the tube) per application. Rarely, application as frequently as every four hours may be necessary.

Auxiliary labeling:
• Caution with alcoholic beverages.
• For external use only.
• Store in a cool place.
• Keep tightly closed.

NITROGLYCERIN TRANSDERMAL SYSTEMS

Usual adult dose: Antianginal—Topical, to the intact skin, 1 transdermal dosage system, delivering the smallest available dose of nitroglycerin in its dosage series, every twenty-four hours. Dosage adjustments may be made by changing to the next larger dosage system in the series or to a combination of systems.

Note: To prevent tolerance, it is recommended that the patch be left on only 12 to 14 hours a day, with a patch-off period of 10 to 12 hours before the next daily patch is applied.

Auxiliary labeling:
• Caution with alcoholic beverages.
• For external use only.
• Store in a cool place.

PENTAERYTHRITOL TETRANITRATE

Summary of Differences

Pharmacology: Onset and duration of action—See *Pharmacology*.

Oral Dosage Forms

PENTAERYTHRITOL TETRANITRATE EXTENDED-RELEASE CAPSULES

Note: Pentaerythritol tetranitrate extended-release capsules are not commercially available in Canada.

Usual adult dose: Antianginal—Oral, 30 to 80 mg two times a day.

Usual adult prescribing limits: Up to 160 mg daily.

Auxiliary labeling:
• Caution with alcoholic beverages.
• Swallow capsules whole.
• Keep container tightly closed.
• Store in a cool, dry place.

PENTAERYTHRITOL TETRANITRATE TABLETS USP

Usual adult dose: Antianginal—Oral, 10 to 20 mg four times a day, the dosage being adjusted as needed and tolerated.

Usual adult prescribing limits: Up to 160 mg daily.

Auxiliary labeling:
• Caution with alcoholic beverages.
• Keep container tightly closed.
• Store in a cool, dry place.

PENTAERYTHRITOL TETRANITRATE EXTENDED-RELEASE TABLETS

Usual adult dose: Antianginal—Oral, up to 80 mg two times a day.

Usual adult prescribing limits: Oral, up to 160 mg daily.

Auxiliary labeling:
• Caution with alcoholic beverages.
• Swallow tablets whole.
• Keep container tightly closed.
• Store in a cool, dry place.

Table 1. Indications

Note: Bracketed information in the *Indications* section refers to uses that are not included in U.S. product labeling.

Legend:
I = Angina pectoris, acute (treatment)
II = Angina pectoris, acute (prophylaxis)
III = Angina pectoris, chronic (treatment)
IV = Hypertension (treatment); or Hypotension, controlled
V = Myocardial infarction (treatment adjunct)
VI = Congestive heart failure (treatment)

	I	II	III	IV	V	VI
Erythrityl tetranitrate						
Oral/Sublingual		✓	✓		[✓]¹	[✓]¹
Isosorbide dinitrate						
Oral						
Capsules and tablets, regular			✓		[✓]¹	[✓]¹
Extended-release capsules or tablets			✓			
Chewable tablets	✓	✓	✓		[✓]	[✓]
Sublingual	✓¹	✓	✓		[✓]¹	[✓]¹
Nitroglycerin						
Buccal, extended-release	✓¹	✓	✓			
Lingual, aerosol	✓	✓¹			[✓]¹	[✓]¹
Oral, extended-release			✓			
Parenteral			✓	✓	✓	✓
Sublingual	✓	✓			[✓]¹	[✓]¹
Topical						
Ointment			✓		[✓]¹	[✓]¹
Transdermal systems			✓		[✓]	[✓]
Pentaerythritol tetranitrate						
Oral						
Tablets, regular			✓		[✓]¹	[✓]¹
Extended-release capsules and tablets			✓			

¹Not included in Canadian product labeling.

Table 2. Patient Consultation

	Buccal	Lingual	Oral			Sublingual			Topical	
	Legend: **I** = Extended-release nitroglycerin	**II** = Aerosol nitroglycerin	**III** = Regular **IV** = Chewable **V** = Extended-release			**VI** = Erythrityl-tetranitrate **VII** = Isosorbide dinitrate **VIII** = Nitroglycerin			**IX** = Nitroglycerin ointment **X** = Transdermal nitroglycerin	
Consider advising the patient on the following:	**I**	**II**	**III**	**IV**	**V**	**VI**	**VII**	**VIII**	**IX**	**X**
Before using this medication See *Precautions to Consider*.	✓	✓	✓	✓	✓	✓	✓	✓	✓	✓
Proper use of this medication » Compliance with therapy	✓	✓	✓	✓	✓	✓	✓	✓	✓	✓
» Reading patient instructions carefully		✓							✓	✓
Proper administration: » Regular or extended-release capsule or tablet—Taking with full glass of water on empty stomach			✓		✓					
» Buccal— Under upper lip (above incisors) against gum or between cheek and upper gum; placing between upper lip (above incisors) and gum if food or drink to be taken within 3 to 5 hours; patients with dentures may place anywhere between cheek and gum	✓					✓	✓	✓		
Touching with tongue or drinking hot liquids may increase rate of dissolution	✓					✓	✓	✓		
Bedtime use not recommended because of risk of aspiration	✓					✓	✓	✓		
Replacing tablet if inadvertently swallowed	✓					✓	✓	✓		
Not using chewing tobacco while tablet in place	✓									
» Chewable tablet—Chewing well and holding in mouth for approximately 2 minutes				✓						
» Lingual aerosol— Removing plastic cover; not shaking container		✓								
Holding container vertically and spraying onto or under tongue; not inhaling spray		✓								
Closing mouth after each spray; not swallowing immediately		✓								
» Sublingual tablet—Under the tongue; avoiding eating, drinking, smoking, or using chewing tobacco while tablet is dissolving						✓	✓	✓		
» Ointment—Cleansing skin before applying; measuring; using applicator; spreading evenly over same size of skin area in each application; not rubbing into skin; applying to skin free of hair, in different areas; proper application of occlusive dressing, if ordered									✓	

Table 2. Patient Consultation *(continued)*

	Buccal	Lingual	Oral			Sublingual			Topical	
Legend:	I = Extended-release nitroglycerin	II = Aerosol nitroglycerin	III = Regular IV = Chewable V = Extended-release			VI = Erythrityl-tetranitrate VII = Isosorbide dinitrate VIII = Nitroglycerin			IX = Nitroglycerin ointment X = Transdermal nitroglycerin	
	I	**II**	**III**	**IV**	**V**	**VI**	**VII**	**VIII**	**IX**	**X**
Transdermal—Not trimming or cutting patch; applying to clean, dry skin free of hair, scars, cuts, or irritation (after removal of previous system); replacing systems that have loosened or fallen off; alternating application sites										✔
» Not chewing, crushing, or swallowing	✔					✔	✔	✔		
» Not breaking, crushing, or chewing before swallowing					✔					
For use in treating acute angina attacks										
» Sitting down and using medication at first sign of angina attack; caution if dizziness or faintness occurs	✔	✔		✔			✔	✔		
Remaining calm until medicine has opportunity to work	✔	✔		✔						
» Relief usually occurs within 5 minutes—	✔	✔		✔			✔	✔		
Dose may be repeated if pain not relieved in 5 to 10 minutes; calling physician or going to emergency room if angina pain not relieved by 3 doses in 15 minutes		✔		✔			✔	✔		
Not repeating dose; using sublingual nitroglycerin and calling physician or going to emergency room if angina pain not relieved in 15 minutes	✔									
For use in preventing angina										
» This dosage form does not relieve angina attacks but rather prevents them (exceptions are chewable and sublingual isosorbide dinitrate)			✔	✔	✔	✔			✔	✔
Using 5 to 10 minutes prior to anticipated stress to prevent attack	✔	✔		✔		✔	✔	✔		
Missed dose:										
Taking/using as soon as possible unless next scheduled dose is within:										✔
—2 hours (exception is oral extended-release);	✔		✔	✔		✔	✔		✔	
—6 hours (for oral extended-release);					✔					
Returning to regular dosing schedule; not doubling doses	✔		✔	✔	✔	✔	✔	✔	✔	✔
» Proper storage	✔	✔	✔	✔	✔	✔	✔	✔	✔	
Protecting from freezing		✔								
Not puncturing, breaking, or burning aerosol container		✔								
Storing in cool place, tightly closed									✔	
Tablets may retain adequate potency for only 3 to 6 months (longer if stabilized)								✔		
Lack of reliability of flushing or headache as test of potency								✔		

Table 2. Patient Consultation *(continued)*

	Buccal	Lingual	Oral			Sublingual			Topical	
	Legend: **I** = Extended-release nitroglycerin	**II** = Aerosol nitroglycerin	**III** = Regular **IV** = Chewable **V** = Extended-release			**VI** = Erythrityl-tetranitrate **VII** = Isosorbide dinitrate **VIII** = Nitroglycerin			**IX** = Nitroglycerin ointment **X** = Transdermal nitroglycerin	
	I	**II**	**III**	**IV**	**V**	**VI**	**VII**	**VIII**	**IX**	**X**
» Keeping sublingual nitroglycerin in original glass, screw-cap bottle (unless using special nitroglycerin container) with cotton plug removed; avoiding handling tablets; capping quickly and tightly after each use; not storing in same container as other medications; not carrying close to body or in auto glove compartment; not storing in refrigerator or bathroom medicine cabinet								✔		
Precautions while using this medication » Checking with physician before discontinuing medication; gradual dosage reduction may be needed	✔	✔	✔	✔	✔	✔	✔	✔	✔	✔
» Caution when getting up suddenly from a lying or sitting position	✔	✔	✔	✔	✔	✔	✔	✔	✔	✔
» Caution in using alcohol, while standing for long periods or exercising, and during hot weather because of enhanced orthostatic hypotensive effects	✔	✔	✔	✔	✔	✔	✔	✔	✔	✔
» Headache as a common effect; should decrease with continuing therapy; checking with physician if continuing or severe	✔	✔	✔	✔	✔	✔	✔	✔	✔	✔
Notifying physician if undigested extended-release tablets are found in stools (for isosorbide dinitrate and pentaerythritol tetranitrate only)					✔					
Side/adverse effects Signs of potential side effects, especially blurred vision, dry mouth, severe or prolonged headache, and skin rash	✔	✔	✔	✔	✔	✔	✔	✔	✔	✔

NITROFURANTOIN   Systemic

Some commonly used *brand names* are:

In the U.S.—
    Furadantin   *Macrobid*
    Furalan   *Macrodantin*
    Furatoin   *Nitrofuracot*

In Canada—
    Apo-Nitrofurantoin   *Macrodantin*

ORAL

Nitrofurantoin Capsules USP
    In the U.S.—*Macrodantin;* GENERIC
    In Canada—*Macrodantin*
Nitrofurantoin Extended-release Capsules†
    In the U.S.—*Macrobid*
Nitrofurantoin Oral Suspension USP†
    In the U.S.—*Furadantin*
Nitrofurantoin Tablets USP
    In the U.S.—*Furalan; Furatoin; Nitrofuracot;* GENERIC
    In Canada—*Apo-Nitrofurantoin*

†Not commercially available in Canada.

Category: Antibacterial (systemic).

Indications

Note: Bracketed information in the *Indications* section refers to uses not included in U.S. product labeling.

Accepted

Urinary tract infections, bacterial (treatment)—Nitrofurantoin is indicated in the treatment of urinary tract infections caused by susceptible strains of *Escherichia coli*, enterococci, *Staphylococcus aureus, S. saprophyticus, Klebsiella* species, *Enterobacter* species, and *Proteus* species.

[Urinary tract infections, bacterial (prophylaxis)][1]—Nitrofurantoin is used in the prophylaxis of urinary tract infections.

Not all species or strains of a particular organism may be susceptible to nitrofurantoin.

[1]Not included in Canadian product labeling.

Pharmacology

Mechanism of action/Effect: Nitrofurantoin, a synthetic, broad-spectrum, weakly acidic antibacterial, is generally bactericidal at therapeutic concentrations. Therapeutic concentrations are achieved only in the urine. The mechanism of antimicrobial action is unique among antibacterials. Nitrofurantoin is reduced by bacterial flavoproteins to reactive intermediates, which inactivate or alter bacterial ribosomal proteins and other macromolecules.

Precautions to Consider

Cross-sensitivity and/or related problems

Patients hypersensitive to one nitrofuran may be hypersensitive to other nitrofurans also.

Geriatrics

No information is available on the relationship of age to the effects of nitrofurantoin in geriatric patients. However, elderly patients are more likely to have an age-related decrease in renal function, which may require a decrease in dosage or change in medication. Side effects, such as acute pneumonitis and peripheral polyneuropathy, may also occur more frequently in elderly patients.

Drug interactions and/or related problems

The following drug interactions and/or related problems have been selected on the basis of their potential clinical significance (possible mechanism in parentheses where appropriate)—not necessarily inclusive (» = major clinical significance):

Note: Combinations containing any of the following medications, depending on the amount present, may also interact with this medication.

» Hemolytics, other
    (concurrent use with nitrofurantoin may increase the potential for toxic side effects)

Hepatotoxic medications, other
    (concurrent use of nitrofurantoin with other hepatotoxic medications may increase the potential for hepatotoxicity)

Magnesium trisilicate
    (magnesium trisilicate reduces both the rate and extent of absorption of nitrofurantoin, probably by adsorption of nitrofurantoin to its surface)

Nalidixic acid
    (nitrofurantoin interferes with the therapeutic effects of nalidixic acid)

» Neurotoxic medications, other
    (concurrent use of nitrofurantoin with other neurotoxic medications may increase the potential for neurotoxicity)

» Probenecid or
» Sulfinpyrazone
    (these medications may inhibit renal tubular secretion of nitrofurantoin, resulting in increased serum concentrations and/or toxicity, prolonged elimination half-life, and reduced urinary concentrations and effectiveness; dosage adjustment of probenecid may be necessary)

Contraindications/Medical problems

The contraindications/medical problems included have been selected on the basis of their potential clinical significance (reasons given in parentheses where appropriate)—not necessarily inclusive (» = major clinical significance).

Risk-benefit should be considered when the following medical problems exist:

» Glucose-6-phosphate dehydrogenase (G6PD) deficiency
    (hemolysis may occur in patients with G6PD deficiency who take nitrofurantoin)

Hypersensitivity to nitrofurans

» Neuropathy, peripheral
    (nitrofurantoin may cause peripheral neuropathy)

» Pulmonary disease
    (nitrofurantoin may cause acute, subacute, and chronic pulmonary reactions, including pneumonitis)

» Renal function impairment
    (because nitrofurantoin is excreted through the kidneys, it is recommended that nitrofurantoin not be given to patients with a creatinine clearance of less than 40 to 60 mL per minute [0.67 to 1.00 mL per second]; nitrofurantoin loses its effectiveness in patients with renal function impairment, and toxic effects are increased)

Side/Adverse Effects

Note: Acute pneumonitis is more common in the elderly; symptoms usually occur within the first week of therapy. The pneumonitis is often reversible with discontinuation of the drug; corticosteroids may be beneficial in severe cases. Chronic pulmonary reactions, including diffuse interstitial pneumonitis and fibrosis, are insidious in onset and are more likely to occur in patients who have been on nitrofurantoin therapy for at least 6 months. Pulmonary function may be permanently impaired even after the drug has been stopped, especially if pulmonary reactions are not recognized early.

Peripheral polyneuropathy is an ascending sensorimotor neuropathy, which may be progressive if the drug is not discontinued immediately. Polyneuropathy occurs more frequently in patients with renal dysfunction and in the elderly; however, it also occurs in patients with normal renal function who have received nitrofurantoin for prolonged periods of time. Demyelination and degeneration of both sensory and motor nerves occur. Nitrofurantoin should be stopped at the first signs of neuritis.

The following side/adverse effects have been selected on the basis of their potential clinical significance (possible signs and symptoms in parentheses where appropriate)—not necessarily inclusive:

Those indicating need for medical attention
Incidence more frequent
  Pneumonitis (chest pain, chills, cough, fever, troubled breathing)
Incidence less frequent
  Hematologic reactions, specifically granulocytopenia (sore throat and fever), *leukopenia* (sore throat and fever), *or megaloblastic anemia* (unusual tiredness or weakness); *neurotoxicity* (dizziness, drowsiness, headache, unusual tiredness or weakness); *polyneuropathy* (numbness, tingling, or burning of face or mouth; unusual muscle weakness)
Incidence rare
  Hemolytic anemia (pale skin, unusual tiredness or weakness); *hepatitis* (yellow eyes or skin); *hypersensitivity* (skin rash, itching, arthralgia, fever, chills)

Those indicating need for medical attention only if they continue or are bothersome
Incidence more frequent
  Gastrointestinal disturbances (abdominal or stomach pain or upset, diarrhea, loss of appetite, nausea or vomiting)

Those not indicating need for medical attention
  Rust-yellow to brown discoloration of urine

Patient Consultation

In providing consultation, consider emphasizing the following selected information (» = major clinical significance):

Before using this medication
» Conditions affecting use, especially:
    Hypersensitivity to nitrofurans
    Pregnancy—Nitrofurantoin is contraindicated at term and during labor and delivery because of the possibility of hemolytic anemia in the fetus
    Breast-feeding—Not recommended since hemolytic anemia may occur in G6PD-deficient infants
    Use in children—Nitrofurantoin is contraindicated in infants up to 1 month of age because of the possibility of hemolytic anemia
    Use in the elderly—Side effects, such as acute pneumonitis and peripheral polyneuropathy, may occur more frequently in elderly patients
    Other medications, especially other hemolytics, other neurotoxic medications, probenecid, or sulfinpyrazone
    Other medical problems, especially G6PD deficiency, peripheral neuropathy, pulmonary disease, or renal function impairment

Proper use of this medication
» Not giving to infants up to 1 month of age
    Taking with food or milk
    Proper administration technique for oral liquid:
      Shaking well before each dose
      Using a specially marked measuring spoon or other device
      May be mixed with water, milk, fruit juices, or infants' formulas
    Proper administration technique for extended-release tablets: Swallowing tablet whole; not breaking, crushing, or chewing before swallowing
» Compliance with full course of therapy
» Proper dosage
    Missed dose: Taking as soon as possible; not taking if almost time for next dose; not doubling doses
» Proper storage

Precautions while using this medication
    Regular visits to physician to check progress if on long-term therapy
    Checking with physician if no improvement within a few days
» Diabetics: False-positive reactions with copper sulfate urine glucose tests may occur

Side/adverse effects
    Rust-yellow to brown discoloration of urine may be alarming to patient although medically insignificant
    Signs of potential side effects, especially hemolytic anemia, jaundice, neurotoxicity, pneumonitis, and polyneuropathy

General Dosing Information

Nitrofurantoin should preferably be taken with food or milk. This minimizes gastrointestinal irritation, delays and increases absorption of both the macrocrystalline and microcrystalline forms, increases the peak concentration of the macrocrystalline form, and prolongs the duration of therapeutic concentrations in the urine.

Patients on long-term suppressive therapy require a reduction in dose.

Patients with impaired renal function (creatinine clearance less than 40 to 60 mL per minute [0.67 to 1.00 mL per second]) should not receive nitrofurantoin since increased toxicity due to possible accumulation of toxic metabolites may occur. Also, nitrofurantoin is ineffective in patients whose creatinine clearance is less than 40 mL per minute.

Oral Dosage Forms

Note: Bracketed uses in the *Dosage Forms* section refer to categories of use and/or indications that are not included in U.S. product labeling.

NITROFURANTOIN CAPSULES USP

Usual adult and adolescent dose: Antibacterial—Oral, 50 to 100 mg every six hours.

Note: [Urinary tract infections, bacterial (prophylaxis)][1]—Oral, 50 to 100 mg once a day at bedtime.

  Most uncomplicated infections caused by susceptible bacteria are adequately treated with 50 mg three times a day.

Usual adult prescribing limits: Up to 600 mg daily; or up to 10 mg per kg of body weight daily.

Auxiliary labeling:
• Continue medicine for full time of treatment.
• Take with food or milk.
• May discolor urine.

NITROFURANTOIN EXTENDED-RELEASE CAPSULES

Usual adult and adolescent dose: Antibacterial—Oral, 100 mg every twelve hours for seven days.

Auxiliary labeling:
- Continue medicine for full time of treatment.
- Take with food or milk.
- May discolor urine.

NITROFURANTOIN ORAL SUSPENSION USP

Usual adult and adolescent dose: See *Nitrofurantoin Capsules USP*.

Usual adult prescribing limits: See *Nitrofurantoin Capsules USP*.

Auxiliary labeling:
- Shake well.
- Continue medicine for full time of treatment.
- Take with food or milk.
- May discolor urine.

Additional information: The oral suspension dosage form is readily miscible with water, milk, fruit juices, or infants' formulas.

NITROFURANTOIN TABLETS USP

Usual adult and adolescent dose: See *Nitrofurantoin Capsules USP*.

Usual adult prescribing limits: See *Nitrofurantoin Capsules USP*.

Auxiliary labeling:
- Continue medicine for full time of treatment.
- Take with food or milk.
- May discolor urine.

---

[1]Not included in Canadian product labeling.

NORFLOXACIN   Systemic

A commonly used *brand name* in the U.S. and Canada is *Noroxin*.

ORAL
Norfloxacin Tablets USP
   In the U.S. and Canada—*Noroxin*

Category: Antibacterial (systemic).
Note: Norfloxacin is a broad-spectrum anti-infective, active against a wide range of aerobic gram-positive and gram-negative organisms.

Indications

Note: Bracketed information in the *Indications* section refers to uses not included in U.S. product labeling.

Accepted
Gonorrhea (treatment); or
Urethritis, gonococcal (treatment)—Norfloxacin is indicated in the treatment of uncomplicated gonorrhea and gonococcal urethritis caused by penicillinase-producing *Neisseria gonorrhoeae*.

Urinary tract infections, bacterial (treatment)—Norfloxacin is indicated in adults in the treatment of complicated and uncomplicated urinary tract infections caused by *Citrobacter freundii, Enterobacter cloacae, Escherichia coli, Klebsiella pneumoniae, Proteus mirabilis,* indole-positive *Proteus* species (including *P. vulgaris, Providencia rettgerii,* and *Morganella morganii*), *Pseudomonas aeruginosa, Staphylococcus epidermidis,* and group D streptococci.

[Gastroenteritis, bacterial (treatment)][1]—Norfloxacin is used as a primary agent in the treatment of bacterial gastroenteritis caused by *Aeromonas hydrophilia,* enterotoxigenic *E. coli, Salmonella* species, *Shigella flexneri, S. sonnei,* and *Vibrio parahaemolyticus.*

Not all species or strains of a particular organism may be susceptible to norfloxacin.

Unaccepted
Norfloxacin is not generally effective against obligate anaerobes or *Chlamydia trachomatis.*

---

[1]Not included in Canadian product labeling.

Pharmacology

Physicochemical properties: Molecular weight—319.34.

Mechanism of action/Effect: Bacteriostatic at low concentrations; at higher concentrations, bactericidal, even following phagocytosis; exact mechanism unknown; norfloxacin acts intracellularly by inhibiting the A subunit of DNA gyrase, a type II topoisomerase essential for ATP-dependent coiling and supercoiling of bacterial DNA, enabling it to be replicated and repacked in both daughter cells; inhibits relaxation of supercoiled DNA; and promotes double-stranded DNA breakage.

Precautions to Consider

Cross-sensitivity and/or related problems
Since norfloxacin is closely related chemically to other quinolone derivatives (e.g., cinoxacin, ciprofloxacin, lomefloxacin, nalidixic acid, ofloxacin), patients hypersensitive to other quinolones may be hypersensitive to this medication also.

Geriatrics
When norfloxacin was administered to six patients, 67 to 74 years old, with normal renal function (creatinine clearance 91 mL/min/1.73 m^2 [1.50 mL/sec]), the plasma half-life was slightly prolonged (3.9 vs 3.2 hours) and there was a small increase in the plasma concentration (2.0 vs 1.5 hours). Alterations in dosage are not recommended unless the patient has severe renal function impairment (creatinine clearance 30 mL/min/1.73 m^2 [0.50 mL/sec]).

Drug interactions and/or related problems
The following drug interactions and/or related problems have been selected on the basis of their potential clinical significance (possible mechanism in parentheses where appropriate)—not necessarily inclusive (» = major clinical significance):

Note: Combinations containing any of the following medications, depending on the amount present, may also interact with this medication.

Alkalizers, urinary, such as:
   Carbonic anhydrase inhibitors
   Citrates
   Sodium bicarbonate
      (urinary alkalizers may reduce the solubility of norfloxacin in the urine; patients should be observed for signs of crystalluria and nephrotoxicity, although the incidence is rare)

» Antacids, aluminum-, calcium-, and magnesium-containing, or Ferrous sulfate or
» Sucralfate

   (antacids and sucralfate may significantly reduce the absorption of norfloxacin by chelation, resulting in lower serum and urine concentrations of norfloxacin; therefore, concurrent use is not recommended; patients should be advised to take antacids, ferrous sulfate, or sucralfate *at least* 2 to 3 hours after norfloxacin)

   Caffeine

   (hepatic metabolism and clearance of caffeine may be reduced, increasing the risk of caffeine-related CNS stimulation)

   Cyclosporine

   (concurrent use with norfloxacin has been reported to elevate serum levels of cyclosporine; cyclosporine levels should be monitored, and dosage adjustments may be required)

   Probenecid

   (decreases renal tubular secretion of norfloxacin when used concurrently, resulting in decreased urinary excretion of norfloxacin, increased and more prolonged norfloxacin serum concentrations, prolonged elimination half-life, and increased risk of toxicity)

» Theophylline

   (concurrent use with norfloxacin reduces the clearance of theophylline, probably by competitive inhibition at the cytochrome P-450 binding sites, resulting in prolonged elimination half-life, increased theophylline serum concentrations, and increased risk of theophylline-related toxicity; serum theophylline concentrations should be monitored and dosage adjustments may be required)

» Warfarin

   (concurrent use with norfloxacin has been reported to increase the anticoagulant effect of warfarin, increasing the chance of bleeding; the prothrombin time [PT] of patients receiving warfarin should be carefully monitored)

Contraindications/Medical problems

The contraindications/medical problems included have been selected on the basis of their potential clinical significance (reasons given in parentheses where appropriate)—not necessarily inclusive (» = major clinical significance).

Risk-benefit should be considered when the following medical problems exist:

Hypersensitivity to norfloxacin or other quinolones
» Renal function impairment

   (because norfloxacin is primarily eliminated through the kidneys, it is recommended that patients with a creatinine clearance of less than 30 mL per minute receive half the standard dosage of norfloxacin)

   Seizures, or history of

   (norfloxacin may cause central nervous system [CNS] toxicity, including seizures)

Side/Adverse Effects

Note: Norfloxacin is relatively insoluble at an alkaline pH and has caused crystalluria in a small number of volunteers who took large doses (1200 to 1600 mg per day) and whose urinary pH exceeded 7.0. Because normal urinary pH is acidic, approximately 5–6, crystalluria is very unlikely to occur with usual doses unless the patient's urine has become alkalinized.

The following side/adverse effects have been selected on the basis of their potential clinical significance (possible signs and symptoms in parentheses where appropriate)—not necessarily inclusive:

Those indicating need for medical attention
Incidence rare

   CNS toxicity (confusion, mental depression, muscle tremors, seizures); *hypersensitivity* (skin rash, itching, or redness; swelling of face or neck; swollen or inflamed joints or tendons)

Those indicating need for medical attention only if they continue or are bothersome
Incidence more frequent

   CNS effects (dizziness, drowsiness, headache, insomnia, lightheadedness); *gastrointestinal disturbance* (abdominal or stomach pain or upset, constipation, diarrhea, loss of appetite, nausea or vomiting)

Incidence less frequent or rare

   Photosensitivity (increased sensitivity to sunlight)

Patient Consultation

In providing consultation, consider emphasizing the following selected information (» = major clinical significance):

Before using this medication
» Conditions affecting use, especially:

   Hypersensitivity to norfloxacin or other quinolone derivatives
   Pregnancy—Norfloxacin is not recommended during pregnancy, because it has been shown to cause arthropathy in immature animals
   Breast-feeding—Not recommended since norfloxacin has been shown to cause arthropathy in immature animals
   Use in children—Norfloxacin is not recommended in infants, children, and adolescents since it has been shown to cause arthropathy in immature animals
   Other medications, especially antacids, sucralfate, theophylline, or warfarin
   Other medical problems, especially renal function impairment

Proper use of this medication
» Not giving to infants or children; may cause arthropathy in immature animals
» Taking with full glass (240 mL) of water on empty stomach; maintaining adequate fluid intake
» Compliance with full course of therapy
» Importance of not missing doses and taking at evenly spaced times
   Missed dose: Taking as soon as possible; not taking if almost time for next dose; not doubling doses
» Proper storage

Precautions while using this medication
   Checking with physician if no improvement within a few days
» Avoiding concurrent use of antacids or sucralfate and norfloxacin; taking antacids or sucralfate *at least* 2 to 3 hours after taking norfloxacin
   Possible photophobic reactions; wearing sunglasses and avoiding prolonged exposure to bright light
» Caution if dizziness, lightheadedness, or drowsiness occurs

Side/adverse effects
   Signs of potential side effects, especially CNS effects and toxicity and hypersensitivity

General Dosing Information

The presence of food in the stomach may slightly decrease or delay absorption of norfloxacin. Therefore, norfloxacin should preferably be taken with a full glass (240 mL) of water on an empty stomach (either 1 hour before or 2 hours after meals).

In studies with human volunteers, crystalluria has been reported, especially with high doses (1200 or 1600 mg) and alkaline urine (pH 7 or above). Although crystalluria has not been reported with usual adult doses (400 mg twice a day), fluid intake should be sufficient to maintain urine output of at least 1200 to 1500 mL per day in adults.

Oral Dosage Forms

Note: Bracketed uses in the *Dosage Forms* section refer to categories of use and/or indications that are not included in U.S. product labeling.

NORFLOXACIN TABLETS USP

Usual adult dose:
Urinary tract infections (uncomplicated)—Oral, 400 mg every twelve hours for three days.
Urinary tract infections (complicated)—Oral, 400 mg every twelve hours for ten to twenty-one days.
Gonorrhea; or
Urethritis, gonococcal—Oral, 800 mg as a single dose.
[Gastroenteritis, bacterial][1]—Oral, 400 mg every eight to twelve hours for five days.

Note: Adults with impaired renal function (creatinine clearance 30 mL per minute per 1.73 M^2 [0.50 mL per second]) require a reduction in dose as follows:
Urinary tract infections—Oral, 400 mg once a day for seven to ten days (uncomplicated) or ten to twenty-one days (complicated).

Usual adult prescribing limits:
Urinary tract infections—Up to a maximum of 800 mg daily.
[Gastroenteritis]—Up to 1.2 grams daily.

Auxiliary labeling:
• Take with a full glass of water.
• Take on empty stomach.
• May cause dizziness, lightheadedness, or drowsiness.
• Continue medicine for full time of treatment.

---

[1]Not included in Canadian product labeling.

NYLIDRIN   Systemic

Some commonly used *brand names* are:
In the U.S.—*Arlidin*
In Canada—*Arlidin; Arlidin Forte; PMS Nylidrin*

ORAL
Nylidrin Hydrochloride Tablets USP
In the U.S.—*Arlidin;* GENERIC
In Canada—*Arlidin; Arlidin Forte; PMS Nylidrin*

Category: Vasospastic therapy adjunct.

Indications

Accepted
Vascular disease, peripheral (treatment); or
Ear, inner, circulatory disturbances of (treatment)—FDA has classified nylidrin as being "possibly" effective for its labeled indications, which include peripheral vasospastic disorders such as arteriosclerosis obliterans; thromboangiitis obliterans; diabetic vascular disease; night leg cramps; Raynaud's phenomenon and disease; frostbite; acrocyanosis; acroparesthesia; thrombophlebitis; and cold feet, legs, and hands; as well as circulatory disturbances of the inner ear such as primary cochlear cell ischemia, cochlear stria vascular ischemia, macular or ampullar ischemia, and other disturbances due to labyrinthine artery spasm or obstruction. This classification requires the submission of adequate and well-controlled studies in order to provide substantial evidence of effectiveness.

Unaccepted
FDA has classified nylidrin as "lacking substantial evidence of effectiveness" in cerebral ischemia, cerebral arteriosclerosis, and other circulatory insufficiencies of the brain.

Pharmacology

Mechanism of action/Effect: Vasodilation of skeletal arteries and arterioles via beta-adrenergic receptor stimulation and possibly also a direct effect.

Onset of action: 10 minutes.

Time to peak effect: 30 minutes.

Duration of action: 2 hours.

Precautions to Consider

Geriatrics
The risk of nylidrin-induced hypothermia may be increased in elderly patients.

Drug interactions and/or related problems
The following drug interactions and/or related problems have been selected on the basis of their potential clinical significance (possible mechanism in parentheses where appropriate)—not necessarily inclusive (» = major clinical significance):

Smoking, tobacco
(heavy smoking may interfere with the therapeutic effect of nylidrin because nicotine constricts blood vessels)

Contraindications/Medical problems
The contraindications/medical problems included have been selected on the basis of their potential clinical significance (reasons given in parentheses where appropriate)—not necessarily inclusive (» = major clinical significance).

» Angina pectoris, progressive, or
» Myocardial infarction, recent
(a "steal effect" may occur, since nylidrin has a greater effect on peripheral than on coronary vessels, leading to a further decrease in flow to ischemic areas)

Cardiac disease
Congestive heart failure, uncompensated
Peptic ulcer
(nylidrin increases gastric acid secretion)
Sensitivity to nylidrin
» Tachycardia, paroxysmal
» Thyrotoxicosis

Side/Adverse Effects

The following side/adverse effects have been selected on the basis of their potential clinical significance (possible signs and symptoms in parentheses where appropriate)—not necessarily inclusive:

Those indicating need for medical attention
Incidence less frequent
Anemia (continuing tiredness or weakness); *dizziness, not associated with labyrinthine artery insufficiency; fast or irregular heartbeat*

Signs and symptoms of overdose
  Blurred vision; chest pain; decrease in urination or inability to urinate; fever; metallic taste

Those indicating need for medical attention only if they continue or are bothersome
Incidence less frequent
  Chilliness; flushing or redness of face; headache; nausea and vomiting; nervousness; trembling

Patient Consultation

In providing consultation, consider emphasizing the following selected information (» = major clinical significance):

Before using this medication
» Conditions affecting use, especially:
    Sensitivity to nylidrin
    Use in the elderly—Increased risk of hypothermia
    Other medical problems, especially angina pectoris, recent myocardial infarction, paroxysmal tachycardia, and thyrotoxicosis

Proper use of this medication
    Timing of doses to minimize interference with sleep due to palpitations; avoiding taking last dose at bedtime
    Missed dose: Taking as soon as possible; not taking if almost time for next dose; not doubling doses
» Proper storage

Precautions while using this medication
    Checking with physician before discontinuing medication
    Avoiding smoking (nicotine constricts blood vessels)

Side/adverse effects
    Signs of potential side effects, especially anemia, dizziness, and fast or irregular heartbeat

Oral Dosage Forms

NYLIDRIN HYDROCHLORIDE TABLETS USP

Usual adult dose: Oral, 3 to 12 mg three or four times a day.

NYSTATIN   Vaginal

Some commonly used *brand names* are:
    In the U.S.—
      Mycostatin   *Nilstat*
    In Canada—
      Mycostatin   *Nilstat*
      Nadostine   *Nyaderm*

VAGINAL
Nystatin Vaginal Cream*
    In Canada—*Mycostatin; Nadostine; Nilstat; Nyaderm*
Nystatin Vaginal Tablets USP
    In the U.S.—*Mycostatin; Nilstat;* GENERIC
    In Canada—*Mycostatin; Nadostine; Nilstat*

*Not commercially available in the U.S.

Category: Antifungal (vaginal).

Indications

Note: Bracketed information in the *Indications* section refers to uses not included in U.S. product labeling.

Accepted
Candidiasis, vulvovaginal (treatment)—Vaginal nystatin is indicated in the local treatment of vulvovaginal candidiasis caused by *Candida (Monilia) albicans* and other *Candida* species.

[Candidiasis, oropharyngeal (treatment)]—Nystatin vaginal tablets are used as lozenges to treat oropharyngeal candidiasis since their slow dissolution rate provides prolonged oral contact.

Not all species or strains of a particular organism may be susceptible to nystatin.

Unaccepted
Nystatin is not effective against *Trichomonas vaginalis* or *Gardnerella vaginalis (Haemophilus vaginalis)*.

Pharmacology

Mechanism of action/Effect: Binds to sterols in the fungal cell membrane, resulting in the cell membrane's inability to function as a selective barrier, which allows loss of essential cellular constituents.

Precautions to Consider

Geriatrics
No information is available on the relationship of age to the effects of vaginal nystatin in geriatric patients.

Contraindications/Medical problems
The contraindications/medical problems included have been selected on the basis of their potential clinical significance (reasons given in parentheses where appropriate)—not necessarily inclusive (» = major clinical significance).

Risk-benefit should be considered when the following medical problem exists:
    Sensitivity to nystatin

Side/Adverse Effects

The following side/adverse effects have been selected on the basis of their potential clinical significance (possible signs and symptoms in parentheses where appropriate)—not necessarily inclusive:

Those indicating need for medical attention
Incidence rare
    Vaginal irritation not present before therapy

Patient Consultation

In providing consultation, consider emphasizing the following selected information (» = major clinical significance):

Before using this medication
» Conditions affecting use, especially:
    Sensitivity to nystatin

Proper use of this medication

Reading patient instructions before using medication

Proper administration technique

» Compliance with full course of therapy

Missed dose: Inserting as soon as possible; not inserting if almost time for next dose

» Proper storage

Precautions while using this medication

» Using hygienic measures to control sources of infection or reinfection

Checking with physician about douching or intercourse during therapy

Protection of clothing because of possible vaginal drainage

Side/adverse effects

Signs of potential side effects, especially vaginal irritation not present before therapy

General Dosing Information

Therapy for a period of 2 weeks is usually sufficient, but more prolonged treatment may be necessary.

To prevent thrush in the newborn, it is suggested that nystatin vaginal tablets be administered to pregnant patients with candidal vaginitis in a dosage of 100,000 to 200,000 Units daily for 3 to 6 weeks prior to delivery.

Vaginal Dosage Forms

NYSTATIN VAGINAL CREAM

Usual adult and adolescent dose: Antifungal—Intravaginal, 1 100,000-Unit applicatorful one or two times a day for two weeks; or 1 500,000-Unit applicatorful once daily.

Note: For severe infections, *Nilstat* vaginal cream may be repeated every 12 hours.

Auxiliary labeling:
• Continue medicine for full time of treatment.
• For vaginal use only

NYSTATIN VAGINAL TABLETS USP

Usual adult and adolescent dose: Antifungal—Intravaginal, 100,000 Units one or two times a day for two weeks.

Auxiliary labeling:
• Continue medicine for full time of treatment.
• For vaginal use only

OFLOXACIN   Systemic

Some commonly used *brand names* are:
  In the U.S.—*Floxin; Floxin IV*
  In Canada—*Floxin*

ORAL
Ofloxacin Tablets
  In the U.S. and Canada—*Floxin*

PARENTERAL
Ofloxacin in Dextrose Injection†
  In the U.S.—*Floxin IV*
Ofloxacin Injection†
  In the U.S.—*Floxin IV*

---

†Not commercially available in Canada.

Category: Antibacterial (systemic).

Indications

Accepted
Ofloxacin is a broad spectrum fluorinated quinolone that has been shown *in vitro* to be active against many gram-negative and gram-positive organisms. Most Enterobacteriaceae, such as *Citrobacter* species (including *C. diversus* and *C. freundii*), *Enterobacter* species (including *E. cloacae* and *E. aerogenes*), *Escherichia coli*, *Klebsiella* species, *Morganella morganii*, *Proteus* species (including *P. mirabilis* and *P. vulgaris*), *Salmonella* species, *Shigella* species, and *Yersinia enterocolitica*, are susceptible to ofloxacin. The potency of ofloxacin against these organisms is equivalent to that of norfloxacin, greater than that of nalidixic acid, and slightly less than that of ciprofloxacin. Because ofloxacin is more bioavailable than ciprofloxacin and provides higher serum concentrations, the effective activities of ciprofloxacin and ofloxacin are considered to be comparable against these organisms. Compared to norfloxacin, ofloxacin is more potent against *Serratia* species, and equipotent against *Providencia* species. Ofloxacin's potency against *Pseudomonas aeruginosa* is similar to that of norfloxacin, and lower than that of ciprofloxacin. However, *Xanthomonas maltophilia* is more susceptible to ofloxacin than to ciprofloxacin. Other gram-negative organisms, including beta-lactamase negative and positive strains of *Neisseria gonorrhoeae*, *N. meningitidis*, *Haemophilus ducreyi*, *Legionella pneumophila*, *Vibrio cholerae*, and beta-lactamase negative and positive strains of *H. influenzae*, are highly susceptible *in vitro* to ofloxacin, although ciprofloxacin is more potent against *H. influenzae*. *Gardnerella vaginalis* is moderately susceptible to ofloxacin.

Ofloxacin is a potent inhibitor *in vitro* of *Staphylococcus aureus*, including methicillin-resistant (MRSA) strains. However, MRSA resistance has developed rapidly to other fluoroquinolone agents; if MRSA is found to be resistant to another fluoroquinolone, such strains may also be resistant to ofloxacin. Streptococci, including *S. pneumoniae*, *S. pyogenes*, and *Enterococcus faecalis*, are all moderately susceptible. Ofloxacin's potency against all of these organisms is equal to that of ciprofloxacin.

Ofloxacin is less active against anaerobic bacteria than it is against most gram-negative or gram-positive organisms and has not been shown to be effective in anaerobic infections. *Bacteroides fragilis* is considered to have intermediate susceptibility or to be resistant. *Clostridium difficile* is also resistant to ofloxacin. *Peptostreptococcus* species are moderately susceptible, and *Fusobacterium* species range from moderately susceptible to resistant.

Ofloxacin has been found to have good *in vitro* activity against *Chlamydia trachomatis* and *Mycoplasma pneumoniae*. It is also bactericidal against *Mycobacterium tuberculosis* and a more potent in-

hibitor than standard antituberculars. *M. intracellulare*, however, is less susceptible and requires significantly higher levels of ofloxacin for inhibition.

Ofloxacin is used for the treatment of the following infections caused by susceptible organisms:

  Bronchitis, bacterial exacerbations
  Cervicitis, nongonococcal
  Chlamydial infections, endocervical and urethral
  Gonorrhea, endocervical and urethral
  Pneumonia, bacterial, gram-negative and streptococcal
  Prostatitis, bacterial
  Skin and soft tissue infections
  Urethritis, nongonococcal
  Urinary tract infections, bacterial

Note: Caution should be used in treating streptococcal and pneumococcal pneumonia with quinolones. Although they have been effective in limited trials, treatment failures have been reported; quinolones should not be considered the drug of first choice in the treatment of presumed or confirmed pneumococcal pneumonia.

Not all species or strains of a particular organism may be susceptible to ofloxacin.

Unaccepted
Ofloxacin has not been shown to be active against *Treponema pallidum*.

Pharmacology

Mechanism of action/Effect: Bactericidal; ofloxacin acts by inhibiting the resealing of DNA double-strands by the A subunits, and possibly the B subunits, of DNA gyrase following supercoiling. DNA gyrase is an essential bacterial enzyme, which is a critical catalyst in the duplication, transcription, and repair of bacterial DNA.

Precautions to Consider

Cross-sensitivity and/or related problems
Since ofloxacin is closely related chemically to other quinolone derivatives (e.g., ciprofloxacin, cinoxacin, nalidixic acid, norfloxacin), patients allergic to other quinolones may be allergic to this medication also.

Geriatrics
Studies performed to date have not demonstrated geriatrics-specific problems that would limit the usefulness of ofloxacin in the elderly. However, elderly patients are more likely to have an age-related decrease in renal function, which may require an adjustment of dosage in patients receiving ofloxacin.

Drug interactions and/or related problems
The following drug interactions and/or related problems have been selected on the basis of their potential clinical significance (possible mechanism in parentheses where appropriate)—not necessarily inclusive (» = major clinical significance):

Note: Combinations containing any of the following medications, depending on the amount present, may also interact with this medication.

» Antacids, aluminum- and magnesium-containing, or
Ferrous sulfate or
Sucralfate or
Zinc
    (antacids, ferrous sulfate, sucralfate, and zinc may reduce ofloxacin absorption by chelation, resulting in lower serum and urine concentrations of ofloxacin; therefore, concurrent use is

not recommended; ofloxacin should be taken at least 2 hours before or 2 hours after any of these products)

Theophylline

(concurrent use with ofloxacin may reduce the hepatic metabolism and clearance of theophylline; one study found an increase of approximately 10% in the theophylline serum concentration and area under the curve; however, other studies have found that ofloxacin has a negligible effect on theophylline metabolism)

Contraindications/Medical problems

The contraindications/medical problems included have been selected on the basis of their potential clinical significance (reasons given in parentheses where appropriate)—not necessarily inclusive (» = major clinical significance).

Except under special circumstances, this medication should not be used when the following medical problem exists:

» Allergy to ofloxacin or other quinolones

Risk-benefit should be considered when the following medical problems exist:

Hepatic function impairment, severe

(patients with severe hepatic function impairment, such as cirrhosis with ascites, may have decreased clearance of ofloxacin, and an increase in peak serum concentration and elimination half-life)

» Renal function impairment

(ofloxacin elimination is primarily through the kidneys; it is recommended that ofloxacin dosage be reduced in patients with impaired renal function)

Side/Adverse Effects

The following side/adverse effects have been selected on the basis of their potential clinical significance (possible signs and symptoms in parentheses where appropriate)—not necessarily inclusive:

Those indicating need for medical attention

Incidence rare

Hypersensitivity reactions (skin rash, itching, shortness of breath, vasculitis); *neuropsychiatric toxicity* (acute psychosis, hallucinations, agitation, confusion); *phlebitis* (pain or redness at site of injection)

Symptoms of overdose

Central nervous system (CNS) toxicity (dizziness, drowsiness, mild to moderate disorientation, slurred speech, nausea)

Note: There is a single case report of a 26-year-old woman who received 3 grams of ofloxacin intravenously over a 45 minute period. She experienced the above *CNS side effects;* however, all the symptoms, except for dizziness and nausea, resolved within one hour of discontinuation of the infusion. Within 9 hours, the patient was asymptomatic.

Those indicating need for medical attention only if they continue or are bothersome

Incidence more frequent

CNS toxicity (dizziness, headache, insomnia); *gastrointestinal reactions* (abdominal discomfort, diarrhea, nausea or vomiting)

Patient Consultation

In providing consultation, consider emphasizing the following selected information (» = major clinical significance):

Before using this medication

» Conditions affecting use, especially:

Allergies to ofloxacin or other quinolone derivatives

Pregnancy—Ofloxacin is not recommended for use during pregnancy because it has been shown to cause arthropathy in immature animals

Breast-feeding—Ofloxacin is not recommended since ofloxacin has been shown to cause arthropathy in immature animals

Use in children—Use of ofloxacin is not recommended for use in infants, children, and adolescents since it has been shown to cause arthropathy in immature animals

Other medications, especially aluminum- and magnesium-containing antacids

Other medical problems, especially allergy to quinolones and renal function impairment

Proper use of this medication

» Not giving to infants, children, adolescents, or pregnant women; has been shown to cause arthropathy in immature animals

» Taking with full glass (240 mL) of water; maintaining adequate fluid intake

» Taking on an empty stomach

» Compliance with full course of therapy

» Importance of not missing doses and taking at evenly spaced times

Missed dose: Taking as soon as possible; not taking if almost time for next dose; not doubling doses

» Proper storage

Precautions while using this medication

Checking with physician if no improvement within a few days

» Avoiding concurrent use of aluminum- or magnesium-containing antacids and ofloxacin; taking antacids at least 2 hours before or 2 hours after administration of ofloxacin

Caution if dizziness or drowsiness occurs

Side/adverse effects

Signs of potential side effects, especially hypersensitivity reactions and neuropsychiatric toxicity

General Dosing Information

Ofloxacin injection should only be administered by slow intravenous infusion over 60 minutes. Rapid or bolus injection may result in hypotension.

Patients with renal function impairment may need an adjustment in dosage, based on creatinine clearance. Creatinine clearance (in mL per minute) may be calculated as follows:

Adult males: Creatinine clearance

$$= \frac{(140 - \text{age}) \times (\text{ideal body weight in kg})}{72 \times \text{serum creatinine (mg per dL)}}$$

Adult females: Creatinine clearance

$$= \frac{(140 - \text{age}) \times (\text{ideal body weight in kg})}{72 \times \text{serum creatinine (mg per dL)}} \times 0.85$$

Creatinine clearance may also be calculated in SI units (as mL per second) as follows:

Adult males: Creatinine clearance

$$= \frac{(140 - \text{age}) \times (\text{ideal body weight in kg})}{50 \times \text{serum creatinine (micromoles per L)}}$$

Adult females: Creatinine clearance

$$= \frac{(140 - \text{age}) \times (\text{ideal body weight in kg})}{50 \times \text{serum creatinine (micromoles per L)}} \times 0.85$$

Oral Dosage Forms

OFLOXACIN TABLETS

Usual adult dose:

Bronchitis, bacterial exacerbations, or Pneumonia—Oral, 400 mg every twelve hours for ten days.

Chlamydial infections, endocervical and urethral, with or without concurrent gonorrhea—Oral, 300 mg every twelve hours for seven days.

Gonorrhea, uncomplicated—Oral, 400 mg as a single dose.

Prostatitis—Oral, 300 mg every twelve hours for six weeks.

Skin and soft tissue infections—Oral, 400 mg every twelve hours for ten days.

Urinary tract infections—

Cystitis due to *E. coli* or *K. pneumoniae*: Oral, 200 mg every twelve hours for three days.

Cystitis due to other organisms: Oral, 200 mg every twelve hours for seven days.

Complicated urinary tract infections: Oral, 200 mg every twelve hours for ten days.

Adults with impaired renal function may require a reduction in dose as follows:

Creatinine Clearance (mL/min)/(mL/sec)	Dose %	Dosing Interval (hr)
>50/(0.83)	100	12
10–50/(0.17–0.83)	100	24
<10/(0.17)	50	24

Auxiliary labeling:
- Take with a full glass of water.
- Continue medicine for full time of treatment.
- Do not take antacids, or zinc or iron preparations within 2 hours of this medicine.

Parenteral Dosage Forms

OFLOXACIN IN DEXTROSE INJECTION

Usual adult dose:

Bronchitis, bacterial exacerbations, or Pneumonia—Intravenous infusion, 400 mg, administered over 60 minutes, every twelve hours for ten days.

Chlamydial infections, endocervical and urethral, with or without concurrent gonorrhea—Intravenous infusion, 300 mg, administered over 60 minutes, every twelve hours for seven days.

Gonorrhea, uncomplicated—Intravenous infusion, 400 mg, administered over 60 minutes, as a single dose.

Prostatitis—Intravenous infusion, 300 mg, administered over 60 minutes, every twelve hours for six weeks.

Skin and soft tissue infections—Intravenous infusion, 400 mg, administered over 60 minutes, every twelve hours for ten days.

Urinary tract infections—

Cystitis due to *E. coli* or *K. pneumoniae*: Intravenous infusion, 200 mg, administered over 60 minutes, every twelve hours for three days.

Cystitis due to other organisms: Intravenous infusion, 200 mg, administered over 60 minutes, every twelve hours for seven days.

Complicated urinary tract infections: Intravenous infusion, 200 mg, administered over 60 minutes, every twelve hours for ten days.

Adults with impaired renal function may require a reduction in dose as follows:

Creatinine Clearance (mL/min)/(mL/sec)	Dose %	Dosing Interval (hr)
>50/(0.83)	100	12
10–50/(0.17–0.83)	100	24
<10/(0.17)	50	24

OFLOXACIN INJECTION

Usual adult dose: See *Ofloxacin in Dextrose Injection.*

OLSALAZINE   Oral-Local

A commonly used *brand name* in the U.S. and Canada is *Dipentum.*

Other commonly used names are sodium azodisalicylate and azodisal sodium.

ORAL

Olsalazine Sodium Capsules
In the U.S. and Canada—*Dipentum*

Category: Bowel disease (inflammatory) suppressant.

Indications

Accepted

Bowel disease, inflammatory (prophylaxis)—Olsalazine is indicated to maintain remission of ulcerative colitis in patients who are intolerant of sulfasalazine.

Pharmacology

Mechanism of action/Effect: Uncertain. Mesalamine (which is released from olsalazine by colonic bacterial action), by blocking cyclooxygenase and inhibiting prostaglandin production in the colon, appears to produce a local inhibitory effect on the mucosal production of arachidonic acid metabolites, which are increased in patients with chronic inflammatory bowel disease.

Precautions to Consider

Cross-sensitivity and/or related problems

Since olsalazine is a sodium salt of a salicylate, patients sensitive to salicylates may be sensitive to olsalazine also. In addition, patients sensitive to mesalamine may be sensitive to this medication.

Geriatrics

Appropriate studies on the relationship of age to the effects of olsalazine have not been performed in the geriatric population. However, geriatrics-specific problems that would limit the usefulness of this medication in the elderly are not expected.

Contraindications/Medical problems

The contraindications/medical problems included have been selected on the basis of their potential clinical significance (reasons given in parentheses where appropriate)—not necessarily inclusive (» = major clinical significance).

Risk-benefit should be considered when the following medical problems exist:

Renal function impairment
(increased risk of renal [tubular] damage)

Sensitivity to olsalazine

Side/Adverse Effects

The following side/adverse effects have been selected on the basis of their potential clinical significance (possible signs and symptoms in parentheses where appropriate)—not necessarily inclusive:

Those indicating need for medical attention
Incidence rare
Blood dyscrasias (fever, pale skin, sore throat, unusual bleeding, bruising, unusual tiredness or weakness); *exacerbation of ulcerative colitis* (bloody diarrhea, fever, skin rash); *hepatitis* (yellow eyes or skin)

Those indicating need for medical attention only if they continue or are bothersome
Incidence more frequent
Gastrointestinal disturbances (abdominal or stomach pain or upset, diarrhea, loss of appetite, nausea or vomiting)

Note: In controlled studies, *diarrhea* has been reported in approximately 11% of the patients, resulting in treatment withdrawal in approximately 6% of patients.

Incidence less frequent
Aching joints and muscles; acne; anxiety or depression; drowsiness or dizziness; headache; insomnia

Patient Consultation

In providing consultation, consider emphasizing the following selected information (» = major clinical significance):

Before using this medication
» Conditions affecting use, especially:
    Sensitivity to olsalazine, mesalamine, or salicylates
    Other medical problems, especially renal function impairment

Proper use of this medication
Taking with food to lessen gastrointestinal irritation
» Compliance with full course of therapy
    Missed dose: Taking as soon as possible; not taking if almost time for next dose; not doubling doses
» Proper storage

Precautions while using this medication
» Regular visits to physician to check blood counts in patients on long-term therapy

Side/adverse effects
Signs of potential side effects, especially blood dyscrasias, exacerbation of ulcerative colitis, and hepatitis

General Dosing Information

Olsalazine should be taken with food to decrease gastrointestinal irritation.

The total daily dose should be taken in evenly divided doses.

Oral Dosage Forms

OLSALAZINE SODIUM CAPSULES

Usual adult and adolescent dose: Oral, 1 gram a day, in two evenly divided doses.

Usual geriatric dose: See *Usual adult and adolescent dose.*

Auxiliary labeling:
- Continue medicine for full time of treatment.
- Take with food.

OMEPRAZOLE   Systemic

Some commonly used *brand names* are:
    In the U.S.—*Prilosec*
    In Canada—*Losec*

ORAL
Omeprazole Delayed-release Capsules
    In the U.S.—*Prilosec*
    In Canada—*Losec*

Category: Gastric acid pump inhibitor; antiulcer agent.

Indications

Note: Bracketed information in the *Indications* section refers to uses not included in U.S. product labeling.

Accepted
Reflux, gastroesophageal (treatment)—Omeprazole is indicated for the short-term treatment of severe erosive esophagitis associated with gastroesophageal reflux disease and for symptomatic gastroesophageal reflux disease poorly responsive to customary medical treatment, including H_2-receptor antagonist therapy.

Hypersecretory conditions, gastric (treatment);
Zollinger-Ellison syndrome (treatment);
Mastocytosis, systemic (treatment); or
Adenoma, multiple endocrine (treatment)—Omeprazole is indicated for the long-term treatment of pathologic gastric hypersecretion associated with Zollinger-Ellison syndrome (alone or as part of multiple endocrine neoplasia Type-1), systemic mastocytosis, and multiple endocrine adenoma.

Ulcer, duodenal (treatment)—Omeprazole is indicated in the short-term treatment of active duodenal ulcer.

[Ulcer, gastric (treatment)]—Omeprazole is indicated in the short-term treatment of active benign gastric ulcer.

Pharmacology

Mechanism of action/Effect: Omeprazole is activated at an acidic pH to a sulphenamide derivative that binds irreversibly to H^1/K^1 ATPase, an enzyme system found at the secretory surface of parietal cells. It thereby inhibits the final transport of hydrogen ions (via exchange with potassium ions) into the gastric lumen. Since the H^1/K^1 ATPase enzyme system is regarded as the acid (proton) pump of the gastric mucosa, omeprazole is known as a gastric acid pump inhibitor. Omeprazole inhibits both basal and stimulated acid secretion irrespective of the stimulus.

Other actions/effects: Inhibits hepatic cytochrome P-450 mixed function oxidase system.

Onset of action: Within one hour.

Time to peak effect: Within 2 hours.

Duration of action: Up to 72 hours or more (96 hours required for full restoration of acid production).

Precautions to Consider

Geriatrics
No information is available on the relationship of age to the effects of omeprazole in geriatric patients. However, a somewhat decreased rate of elimination and an increased bioavailability are more likely to occur in geriatric patients taking omeprazole.

Drug interactions and/or related problems
The following drug interactions and/or related problems have been selected on the basis of their potential clinical significance (possible mechanism in parentheses where appropriate)—not necessarily inclusive (» = major clinical significance):

Note: Only specific interactions between omeprazole and other medications have been identified in this monograph. However, omeprazole, by increasing gastric pH, has the potential to affect the bioavailability of any medication whose absorption is pH-dependent. Also, omeprazole may prevent the degradation of acid-labile drugs.

In addition, because of omeprazole's ability to inhibit hepatic microsomal drug metabolism, elimination of other medications that require hepatic metabolism via the cytochrome P-450 system or that are highly extracted by the liver may be decreased during concurrent use with omeprazole.

Combinations containing any of the following medications, depending on the amount present, may also interact with this medication.

Ampicillin esters
Iron salts or
Ketoconazole
  (omeprazole may increase gastrointestinal pH; concurrent use with omeprazole may result in a reduction in absorption of ampicillin esters, iron salts, or ketoconazole)
» Anticoagulants, coumarin- or indandione-derivative, or
» Diazepam or
» Phenytoin
  (inhibition of the cytochrome P-450 enzyme system by omeprazole, especially in high doses, may cause a decrease in the hepatic metabolism of these medications, which may result in delayed elimination and increased blood concentrations, when these medications are used concurrently with omeprazole)
  (monitoring of blood concentrations, or prothrombin time for anticoagulants, is recommended as a guide to dosage since dosage adjustment of these medications may be necessary during and after omeprazole therapy to prevent bleeding due to anticoagulant potentiation)
Bone marrow depressants
  (concurrent use of omeprazole with these medications may increase the leukopenic and/or thrombocytopenic effects of both these medications; if concurrent use is required, close observation for toxic effects should be considered)

Contraindications/Medical problems
The contraindications/medical problems included have been selected on the basis of their potential clinical significance (reasons given in parentheses where appropriate)—not necessarily inclusive (» = major clinical significance).

Risk-benefit should be considered when the following medical problems exist:
» Hepatic disease, chronic, current or history of
  (dosage reduction may be required due to increased half-life in chronic hepatic disease)
Sensitivity to omeprazole

Side/Adverse Effects

Note: There is no experience to date with deliberate overdose. In animals, toxic doses of omeprazole have caused sedation, ptosis, and convulsions; decreased activity, body temperature, and respiratory rate; and increased depth of respiration.

The following side/adverse effects have been selected on the basis of their potential clinical significance (possible signs and symptoms in parentheses where appropriate)—not necessarily inclusive:

Those indicating need for medical attention
Incidence rare
  Hematologic abnormalities, specifically anemia (unusual tiredness or weakness); *eosinopenia; leukocytosis* (sore throat and fever); *neutropenia* (continuing ulcers or sores in mouth); *pancytopenia or thrombocytopenia* (unusual bleeding or bruising); *hematuria* (bloody urine); *proteinuria* (cloudy urine); *urinary tract infection* (difficult, burning, or painful urination; frequent urge to urinate; or bloody or cloudy urine)

Those indicating need for medical attention only if they continue or are bothersome
Incidence more frequent
  Abdominal pain or colic
Incidence less frequent
  Asthenia (unusual tiredness, muscle pain); *central nervous system (CNS) disturbances, specifically dizziness, headache, somnolence* (unusual drowsiness), *or unusual tiredness; chest pain; gastrointestinal disturbances, specifically acid regurgitation* (heartburn), *constipation, diarrhea or loose stools, flatulence* (gas), *or nausea and vomiting; skin rash or itching*

Patient Consultation

In providing consultation, consider emphasizing the following selected information (» = major clinical significance):

Before using this medication
» Conditions affecting use, especially:
    Sensitivity to omeprazole
    Breast feeding—May be excreted in breast milk; may cause potentially serious adverse effects in nursing infants
    Other medical problems, especially chronic hepatic disease or history of
    Other medications, especially anticoagulants, diazepam, or phenytoin

Proper use of this medication
    Taking medication immediately before a meal, preferably the morning meal
    May take antacids for relief of pain, unless otherwise instructed by physician
    Swallowing capsule whole; not crushing, breaking, chewing, or opening the capsule
» Compliance with full course of therapy
    Missed dose: Taking as soon as possible; not taking if almost time for next dose; not doubling doses
» Proper storage

Precautions while using this medication
    Checking with physician if condition does not improve or worsens

Side/adverse effects
    Signs of potential side effects, especially hematologic abnormalities, hematuria, proteinuria, and urinary tract infection

General Dosing Information

Use of omeprazole in the treatment of gastrointestinal reflux disease rarely continues beyond 8 weeks, because of the potential for carcinoid tumors associated with long-term therapy. If there is recurrence of severe or symptomatic gastroesophageal reflux poorly responsive to customary medical treatment, additional 4 to 8 week courses of omeprazole may be considered.

Although the symptoms of duodenal ulcers may subside within 1 or 2 weeks after initiation of therapy, unless healing has been documented by endoscopic examination or x-rays, therapy should be continued for at least 4 to 6 weeks.

Omeprazole may be taken with antacids, especially for the first few doses, to aid in the relief of pain.

Initial titration of doses and subsequent dosage adjustment of omeprazole is recommended in the long-term treatment of pathological hypersecretory conditions (e.g., Zollinger-Ellison syndrome, systemic mastocytosis, multiple endocrine adenomas). Total daily doses of up to 120 mg, in divided doses, have been administered. Patients may require at least one increase in dose per year. Zollinger-Ellison syndrome has been treated continuously with omeprazole for more than 5 years.

Diet/Nutrition

Omeprazole should be taken immediately before meals, preferably in the morning.

Oral Dosage Forms

Note: Bracketed uses in the *Dosage Forms* section refer to categories of use and/or indications that are not included in U.S. product labeling.

OMEPRAZOLE DELAYED-RELEASE CAPSULES

Usual adult dose:

Gastroesophageal reflux—Oral, 20 mg once a day for four to eight weeks.

Note: A dosage of 40 mg once a day has been used for esophagitis associated with gastroesophageal reflux disease refractory to other treatment regimens.

Gastric hypersecretory conditions (e.g., Zollinger-Ellison syndrome, systemic mastocytosis, multiple endocrine adenomas)—Oral, 60 mg once a day, the dosage being adjusted as needed, and therapy continued for as long as clinically indicated.

Duodenal ulcer—Oral, 20 mg once a day.

Note: The dosage can be increased to 40 mg once a day for duodenal ulcer refractory to other treatment regimens.

[Gastric ulcer, active]—Oral, 20 mg once a day.

Note: The dosage can be increased to 40 mg once a day for gastric ulcer refractory to other treatment regimens.

If healing of gastric ulcer has not occurred within 4 weeks, an additional 4 weeks of treatment is recommended.

Geriatric prescribing limits: In geriatric patients, the daily doses usually should not exceed 20 mg.

Auxiliary labeling:
• Take before meals.
• Swallow capsules whole.

OPIOID (NARCOTIC) ANALGESICS Systemic

INN: Included in brackets after individual generic listings, if different from U.S. generic names.

Some commonly used *brand names* are:

In the U.S.—

Astramorph [Morphine]
Astramorph PF [Morphine]
Darvon [Propoxyphene]
Darvon-N [Propoxyphene]
Demerol [Meperidine]
Dilaudid [Hydromorphone]
Dilaudid-HP [Hydromorphone]
Dolene [Propoxyphene]
Dolophine [Methadone]
Doraphen [Propoxyphene]
Doxaphene [Propoxyphene]
Duramorph [Morphine]
Levo-Dromoran [Levorphanol]
Methadose [Methadone]
M S Contin [Morphine]
MSIR [Morphine]

Nubain [Nalbuphine]
Numorphan [Oxymorphone]
Pantopon [Opium]
Profene [Propoxyphene]
Pro Pox [Propoxyphene]
Propoxycon [Propoxyphene]
RMS Uniserts [Morphine]
Roxanol [Morphine]
Roxanol 100 [Morphine]
Roxanol SR [Morphine]
Roxicodone [Oxycodone]
Stadol [Butorphanol]
Talwin [Pentazocine]
Talwin-Nx [Pentazocine and Naloxone]

In Canada—

Darvon-N [Propoxyphene]
Demerol [Meperidine]
Dilaudid [Hydromorphone]
Dilaudid-HP [Hydromorphone]
Dolophine [Methadone]

Epimorph [Morphine]
Hycodan [Hydrocodone]
Levo-Dromoran [Levorphanol]
Morphine H.P. [Morphine]
Morphitec [Morphine]

M.O.S. [Morphine]
M.O.S.-S.R. [Morphine]
M S Contin [Morphine]
Novopropoxyn [Propoxyphene]
Nubain [Nalbuphine]
Numorphan [Oxymorphone]
Pantopon [Opium]

Paveral [Codeine]
Robidone [Hydrocodone]
Roxanol [Morphine]
642 [Propoxyphene]
Stadol [Butorphanol]
Statex [Morphine]
Supeudol [Oxycodone]
Talwin [Pentazocine]

Other commonly used names are:

Dextropropoxyphene [Propoxyphene]
Dihydromorphinone [Hydromorphone]
Laudanum [Opium Tincture]

Levorphan [Levorphanol]
Pethidine [Meperidine]
Papaveretum [Opium (Parenteral)]

ALFENTANIL—See Fentanyl Derivatives (Systemic).
BUPRENORPHINE—See Buprenorphine (Systemic).
BUTORPHANOL
Parenteral
    Butorphanol Tartrate Injection USP
        In the U.S. and Canada—*Stadol*
CODEINE
Oral
    Codeine Phosphate Oral Solution
        In the U.S.—GENERIC
        In Canada—*Paveral*
    Codeine Phosphate Tablets USP
        In the U.S. and Canada—GENERIC

Codeine Sulfate Tablets USP†
    In the U.S.—GENERIC
Parenteral
    Codeine Phosphate Injection USP
        In the U.S. and Canada—GENERIC
    Codeine Phosphate Soluble Tablets†
        In the U.S.—GENERIC
    Codeine Sulfate Soluble Tablets†
        In the U.S.—GENERIC
DEZOCINE—See Dezocine (Systemic).
FENTANYL—See Fentanyl Derivatives (Systemic).
HYDROCODONE*
Oral
    Hydrocodone Bitartrate Syrup*
        In Canada—*Hycodan; Robidone*
    Hydrocodone Bitartrate Tablets USP*
        In Canada—*Hycodan*
HYDROMORPHONE
Oral
    Hydromorphone Hydrochloride Tablets USP
        In the U.S.—*Dilaudid;* GENERIC
        In Canada—*Dilaudid*
Parenteral
    Hydromorphone Hydrochloride Injection USP
        In the U.S.—*Dilaudid; Dilaudid-HP;* GENERIC
        In Canada—*Dilaudid; Dilaudid-HP*
Rectal
    Hydromorphone Hydrochloride Suppositories
        In the U.S. and Canada—*Dilaudid*
LEVORPHANOL
Oral
    Levorphanol Tartrate Tablets USP
        In the U.S.—*Levo-Dromoran;* GENERIC
        In Canada—*Levo-Dromoran*
Parenteral
    Levorphanol Tartrate Injection USP
        In the U.S. and Canada—*Levo-Dromoran*
MEPERIDINE [INN: Pethidine]
Oral
    Meperidine Hydrochloride Syrup USP†
        In the U.S.—*Demerol;* GENERIC
    Meperidine Hydrochloride Tablets USP
        In the U.S. and Canada—*Demerol;* GENERIC
Parenteral
    Meperidine Hydrochloride Injection USP
        In the U.S. and Canada—*Demerol;* GENERIC
METHADONE
Oral
    Methadone Hydrochloride Oral Concentrate USP
        In the U.S.—*Methadose;* GENERIC
    Methadone Hydrochloride Oral Solution USP
        In the U.S.—GENERIC
    Methadone Hydrochloride Tablets USP‡
        In the U.S.—*Dolophine;* GENERIC
    Methadone Hydrochloride Tablets USP (Dispersible)‡
        In the U.S.—GENERIC
Parenteral
    Methadone Hydrochloride Injection USP‡
        In the U.S.—*Dolophine*
MORPHINE
Oral
    Morphine Hydrochloride Syrup*
        In Canada—*Morphitec; M.O.S.*
    Morphine Hydrochloride Tablets*
        In Canada—*M.O.S.*
    Morphine Hydrochloride Extended-release Tablets*
        In Canada—*M.O.S.-S.R.*
    Morphine Sulfate Oral Solution
        In the U.S.—*MSIR; Roxanol; Roxanol 100;* GENERIC
        In Canada—*Roxanol; Statex*

Morphine Sulfate Syrup*
    In Canada—*Statex*
Morphine Sulfate Tablets
    In the U.S.—*MSIR;* GENERIC
    In Canada—*Statex*
Morphine Sulfate Extended-release Tablets
    In the U.S.—*M S Contin; Roxanol SR*
    In Canada—*M S Contin*
Parenteral
    Morphine Sulfate Injection USP
        In the U.S.—*Astramorph; Astramorph PF; Duramorph;* GENERIC
        In Canada—*Epimorph; Morphine H.P.;* GENERIC
    Morphine Sulfate Soluble Tablets†
        In the U.S.—GENERIC
Rectal
    Morphine Hydrochloride Suppositories*
        In Canada—*M.O.S.*
    Morphine Sulfate Suppositories
        In the U.S.—*RMS Uniserts;* GENERIC
        In Canada—*Statex*
NALBUPHINE
Parenteral
    Nalbuphine Hydrochloride Injection
        In the U.S.—*Nubain;* GENERIC
        In Canada—*Nubain*
OPIUM
Oral
    Opium Tincture USP (Laudanum)
        In the U.S. and Canada—GENERIC
Parenteral
    Opium Alkaloids Hydrochlorides Injection (Papaveretum)
        In the U.S. and Canada—*Pantopon*
OXYCODONE
Oral
    Oxycodone Hydrochloride Oral Solution USP†
        In the U.S.—*Roxicodone*
    Oxycodone Tablets USP
        In the U.S—*Roxicodone*
        In Canada—*Supeudol*
Rectal
    Oxycodone Hydrochloride Suppositories*
        In Canada—*Supeudol*
OXYMORPHONE
Parenteral
    Oxymorphone Hydrochloride Injection USP
        In the U.S. and Canada—*Numorphan*
Rectal
    Oxymorphone Hydrochloride Suppositories USP
        In the U.S. and Canada—*Numorphan*
PENTAZOCINE
Oral
    Pentazocine Hydrochloride Tablets USP*
        In Canada—*Talwin*
    Pentazocine and Naloxone Hydrochlorides Tablets USP†
        In the U.S.—*Talwin-Nx*
Parenteral
    Pentazocine Lactate Injection USP
        In the U.S. and Canada—*Talwin*
PROPOXYPHENE [INN: Dextropropoxyphene]
Oral
    Propoxyphene Hydrochloride Capsules USP
        In the U.S.—*Darvon; Dolene; Doraphen; Doxaphene; Profene; Pro Pox; Propoxycon;* GENERIC
        In Canada—*Novopropoxyn*
    Propoxyphene Hydrochloride Tablets*
        In Canada—*642*
    Propoxyphene Napsylate Capsules*
        In Canada—*Darvon-N*

Propoxyphene Napsylate Oral Suspension USP†
   In the U.S.—*Darvon-N*
Propoxyphene Napsylate Tablets USP†
   In the U.S.—*Darvon-N;* GENERIC
SUFENTANIL—See Fentanyl Derivatives (Systemic).

---

*Not commercially available in the U.S.
†Not commercially available in Canada.
‡In Canada, may be available through authorized practitioners only.

Category

Note: All of the opioid analgesics have similar pharmacologic actions; however, clinical uses among specific agents may vary because of actual pharmacokinetic differences, differences in potential for causing adverse effects, lack of specific testing, and/or lack of clinical-use data.

Analgesic—Butorphanol; Codeine; Hydrocodone; Hydromorphone; Levorphanol; Meperidine; Methadone; Morphine; Nalbuphine; Opium; Oxycodone; Oxymorphone; Pentazocine; Propoxyphene.

   Note: Butorphanol, nalbuphine, and pentazocine are opioid agonist/antagonist analgesics; the other agents in this group are opioid agonist analgesics.

Anesthesia adjunct (opioid analgesic)—Parenteral dosage forms only: Butorphanol; [Hydromorphone][1]; Levorphanol; Meperidine; Morphine; Nalbuphine; Oxymorphone; Pentazocine.

   Note: For other opioids used primarily as anesthesia adjuncts, see *Fentanyl Derivatives (Systemic)*.

Antidiarrheal—[Codeine][1]; [Morphine]; Opium Tincture.

   Note: For other opioids used only as antidiarrheals, see individual monograph listings for *Difenoxin and Atropine, Diphenoxylate and Atropine, Loperamide,* and *Paregoric*.

Antitussive—Codeine (oral dosage forms only); Hydrocodone; Hydromorphone[1]; [Methadone][1]; [Morphine][1].

   Note: For use of hydromorphone as an antitussive, see *Cough-Cold Combinations (Systemic)—Hydromorphone and Guaifenesin*.

Suppressant (narcotic abstinence syndrome)—Methadone; [Opium Tincture][1].

Pulmonary edema therapy adjunct—Morphine.

Indications

Note: Bracketed information in the *Indications* section refers to uses not included in U.S. product labeling.

Accepted
Pain (treatment)—Morphine, methadone, and parenteral opium are indicated for relief of severe pain; codeine and propoxyphene are indicated for relief of mild to moderate pain; and the other opioid analgesics are indicated for relief of moderate to severe pain.

   Epidural or intrathecal administration of small doses of opioid analgesics may provide prolonged pain relief. Although administration via these routes may decrease the risk of some side/adverse effects, respiratory depression may occur. Solutions containing a preservative must *not* be used. Only morphine sulfate is currently commercially available in a dosage form that is FDA-approved for administration via these routes.

   For relief of pain due to acute myocardial infarction, morphine is usually considered the drug of choice. Butorphanol and pentazocine are less desirable than other opioid analgesics for this purpose because they have cardiovascular effects that tend to increase cardiac work. Although nalbuphine has not been reported to adversely affect cardiovascular function in patients with acute myocardial infarction (and may be less likely than morphine to cause hypotension), its effects in patients with severely compromised cardiac

function caused by acute myocardial infarction have not been fully determined. Therefore, these agents should be used with caution in such patients.

   Parenterally administered opioid analgesics (except for methadone) are indicated to provide obstetrical analgesia.

   Controlled clinical studies have shown that intrathecal, but not epidural, administration of opioid analgesics provides adequate relief of labor pain. Only a preservative-free solution should be used. Morphine sulfate is the only opioid analgesic currently commercially available in a dosage form that is FDA-approved for administration via these routes.

Anesthesia, general or local, adjunct—Parenteral dosage forms of butorphanol, [hydromorphone], levorphanol, meperidine, morphine, nalbuphine, oxymorphone, and pentazocine are indicated to supplement general, regional, or local anesthesia. During surgery, they are often used in conjunction with other agents, such as a combination of an ultrashort-acting barbiturate, a neuromuscular blocking agent, and an inhalation anesthetic (usually nitrous oxide), for the maintenance of "balanced" anesthesia.

   Parenteral dosage forms of most opioid analgesics are indicated to provide analgesic, antianxiety, and sedative effects as presurgical medication. However, other medications, such as benzodiazepines, are more commonly used if the patient is not in pain.

Diarrhea (treatment)—[Codeine][1], [morphine], and opium tincture are indicated for treatment of diarrhea. In diarrhea caused by poisoning, these agents should not be used until the toxic material has been eliminated from the gastrointestinal tract.

Cough (treatment)—Although only codeine (oral dosage forms), hydrocodone, and hydromorphone are indicated as antitussives, all opioid analgesics depress the cough reflex. Meperidine, oxymorphone, and propoxyphene have relatively less antitussive activity than other opioid analgesics, especially in low or moderate doses.

   [Methadone and morphine are sometimes used as antitussives when severe pain is present and coughing cannot be relieved by other means.]

Opioid (narcotic) abstinence syndrome (prophylaxis and treatment); or

Opioid (narcotic) drug use, illicit (treatment)—Methadone is indicated as a suppressant to permit detoxification. Oral methadone is also indicated as maintenance therapy to discourage addicts from returning to illicit use of other opioid drugs.

Edema, pulmonary, acute (treatment adjunct)—Morphine is indicated as adjunctive therapy in the treatment of acute pulmonary edema secondary to left ventricular failure.

   Oxymorphone is also FDA-approved as an adjunct in the treatment of acute pulmonary edema. However, oxymorphone is rarely if ever used for this indication; morphine is the preferred medication.

[Opioid (narcotic) dependence, neonatal (treatment)]—Opium tincture is used in diluted form in the treatment of neonatal opioid dependence.

Unaccepted
Methadone is not recommended for obstetrical analgesia because its long duration of action increases the risk of neonatal respiratory depression.

---

[1]Not included in Canadian product labeling.

Pharmacology

See also *Table 1*, page 810.

Mechanism of action/Effect:
   Opioid analgesics bind with stereospecific receptors at many sites within the central nervous system (CNS) to alter processes affecting both the perception of pain and the emotional response to pain. Although the precise sites and mechanisms of action have not been fully determined, alterations in release of

various neurotransmitters from afferent nerves sensitive to painful stimuli may be partially responsible for the analgesic effects. When these medications are used as adjuncts to anesthesia, analgesic actions may provide dose-related protection against hemodynamic responses to surgical stress.

It has been proposed that there are multiple subtypes of opioid receptors, each mediating various therapeutic and/or side effects of opioid drugs. The actions of an opioid analgesic may therefore depend upon its binding affinity for each type of receptor and on whether it acts as a full agonist or a partial agonist or is inactive at each type of receptor.

At least two types of opioid receptors (mu and kappa) mediate analgesia. A third type of receptor (sigma) may not mediate analgesia; actions at this receptor may produce the subjective and psychotomimetic effects characteristic of pentazocine and, to a lesser extent, butorphanol and nalbuphine. Morphine and other opioid agonists exert their agonist activity primarily at the mu receptor, whereas buprenorphine, nalbuphine, and pentazocine exert agonist activity at the kappa and sigma receptors. Mu receptors are widely distributed throughout the CNS, especially in the limbic system (frontal cortex, temporal cortex, amygdala, and hippocampus), thalamus, striatum, hypothalamus, and midbrain as well as laminae I, II, IV, and V of the dorsal horn in the spinal cord. Kappa receptors are localized primarily in the spinal cord and in the cerebral cortex.

Nalbuphine and pentazocine may displace opioids having only agonist activity from their receptor binding sites and competitively inhibit their actions. The medications may therefore precipitate withdrawal symptoms in patients who are physically dependent on such agonists. Butorphanol appears to have no significant antagonist activity at the mu receptor; in some studies, it failed to produce withdrawal symptoms in patients physically dependent on morphine. However, butorphanol does not substitute for mu-receptor agonists sufficiently to prevent or attenuate withdrawal symptoms caused by abrupt discontinuation of these agonists in physically dependent patients. Also, opioid agonist/antagonist drugs share several pharmacologic actions that differ from those of opioids having only agonist activity; i.e., different respiratory depressant, subjective, psychotomimetic, and hemodynamic effects; lower dependence liability; and reduced severity of withdrawal symptoms produced when they are discontinued after prolonged use.

Antidiarrheal—Act locally and possibly centrally to alter intestinal motility.

Antitussive—Suppress the cough reflex by a direct central action, probably in the medulla or pons.

Suppressant (narcotic abstinence syndrome)—Substitute for other opioid drugs when administered orally and prevent or attenuate withdrawal symptoms during detoxification. Withdrawal symptoms that may occur when the substituted opioid is discontinued are usually greatly reduced in severity. With continued administration, methadone may produce cross-tolerance to the euphoric effects of other opioid drugs, thereby reducing the patient's desire for such drugs.

Precautions to Consider

Geriatrics

Geriatric patients may be more susceptible to the effects, especially the respiratory depressant effects, of these medications. Also, geriatric patients are more likely to have prostatic hypertrophy or obstruction and age-related renal function impairment, and are therefore more likely to be adversely affected by opioid-induced urinary retention. In addition, geriatric patients may metabolize or eliminate these medications more slowly than younger adults. Lower doses or longer dosing intervals than those usually recommended for adults may be required, and are usually therapeutically effective, for these patients.

Dental

Opioid analgesics may decrease or inhibit salivary flow, thus contributing to the development of caries, periodontal disease, oral candidiasis, and discomfort.

Drug interactions and/or related problems

See *Table 2*, page 812.

Contraindications/Medical problems

The contraindications/medical problems included have been selected on the basis of their potential clinical significance (reasons given in parentheses where appropriate)—not necessarily inclusive (» = major clinical significance).

Except under special circumstances, this medication should not be used when the following medical problems exist:

For all opioid analgesic usage

» Diarrhea associated with pseudomembranous colitis caused by cephalosporins, lincomycins (possibly including topical clindamycin), or penicillins or

» Diarrhea caused by poisoning, until toxic material has been eliminated from gastrointestinal tract
(opioid analgesics may slow elimination of toxic material, thereby worsening and/or prolonging the diarrhea)

» Respiratory depression, acute
(may be exacerbated)

For epidural or intrathecal administration

» Any condition that precludes epidural or intrathecal administration, such as:

» Coagulation defects caused by anticoagulant therapy or hematologic disorders
(trauma to a blood vessel during administration may result in uncontrollable CNS or soft tissue hemorrhage)

» Infection at or near site of administration
(risk of spreading the infection into the CNS)

Risk-benefit should be considered when the following medical problems exist:

For all opioid analgesics

Abdominal conditions, acute
(diagnosis or clinical course may be obscured)

Allergic reaction to the opioid analgesic considered for use, history of

» Asthma, acute attack, or

» Respiratory impairment or disease, chronic
(opioids may decrease respiratory drive and increase airway resistance in patients with these conditions)

Cardiac arrhythmias or

Convulsions, history of
(may be induced or exacerbated by opioids; meperidine and propoxyphene may be especially likely to induce or exacerbate convulsions; with meperidine, the proconvulsant activity of its metabolite normeperidine may be responsible)

Drug abuse or dependence, current or history of, including alcoholism, or

Emotional instability or

Suicidal ideation or attempts
(patient predisposition to drug abuse)

Gallbladder disease or gallstones
(opioids [except butorphanol] may cause biliary contraction)

Gastrointestinal tract surgery, recent
(opioids may alter gastrointestinal motility)

Head injury or

Increased intracranial pressure, pre-existing, or

Intracranial lesions
(risk of respiratory depression and further elevation of cerebrospinal fluid pressure is increased; also, opioids may cause sedation and pupillary changes that may obscure clinical course of head injury)

Hepatic function impairment
  (opioids metabolized in liver)

Hypothyroidism
  (risk of respiratory depression and prolonged CNS depression is greatly increased)

» Inflammatory bowel disease, severe
  (risk of toxic megacolon may be increased, especially with repeated dosing)

Prostatic hypertrophy or obstruction or
Urethral stricture or
Urinary tract surgery, recent
  (opioids may cause urinary retention)

Renal function impairment
  (increased risk of convulsions [with meperidine] or other adverse effects because opioids and/or their metabolites excreted primarily via kidneys; also, opioids may cause urinary retention)

Caution is also advised in administration to very young, elderly, or very ill or debilitated patients, who may be more sensitive to the effects, especially the respiratory depressant effects, of these medications.

For butorphanol, nalbuphine, or pentazocine only (in addition to those medical problems listed above)

Dependence on opioid agonist analgesics, current
  (nalbuphine and pentazocine may precipitate, and butorphanol does not prevent occurrence of, withdrawal symptoms)

Hypertension
  (butorphanol may increase blood pressure in these patients when used as presurgical medication)

» Myocardial infarction, acute
  (pentazocine and butorphanol may increase cardiac work; effects of nalbuphine in patients with severely compromised cardiac function have not been fully evaluated)

For epidural or intrathecal administration (in addition to those medical problems listed above as applying to all opioid analgesics)

Dependence on opioid analgesics, current
  (low doses of opioids administered via epidural or intrathecal injection will not prevent withdrawal symptoms from occurring in a physically dependent patient)

Side/Adverse Effects

See also *Table 3*, page 817.

Note: Physical dependence, with or without psychological dependence, may occur with chronic administration of opioid analgesics; an abstinence syndrome may occur when these drugs are discontinued. Specific withdrawal symptoms that may occur, and their severity, depend upon the specific drug used, the abruptness of withdrawal, and the degree to which dependence has developed. Butorphanol, nalbuphine, and pentazocine have lower dependence liability and potential for abuse than opioid agonists; codeine and propoxyphene have lower dependence liability and potential for abuse than other agonists because of their comparatively lower potency with usual doses.

Epidural or intrathecal administration does not eliminate the risk of severe side effects common to systemic opioid analgesics. Respiratory depression may occur shortly after administration because of direct venous redistribution to the respiratory centers in the CNS. Also, delayed respiratory depression may occur up to 24 hours after administration, possibly as the result of rostral spread of the medication. Intrathecal administration and/or injection into thoracic sites are more likely to cause respiratory depression than epidural administration and/or injection into lumbar sites.

Following epidural or intrathecal administration of morphine, urinary retention occurs very frequently (incidence about 90% in males and somewhat lower in females) and may persist for 10 to 20 hours following injection. Catheterization may be required. Also, dose-related generalized pruritus occurs frequently. Excessive sedation is uncommon, and loss of motor, sensory, or sympathetic function does not occur.

The following side/adverse effects have been selected on the basis of their potential clinical significance (possible signs and symptoms in parentheses where appropriate)—not necessarily inclusive:

Signs and symptoms of overdose indicating need for medical attention
  Cold, clammy skin; confusion; convulsions; dizziness, severe; drowsiness, severe; low blood pressure; nervousness or restlessness, severe; pinpoint pupils of eyes; slow heartbeat; slow or troubled breathing; unconsciousness; weakness, severe

Note: *Convulsions* are more likely to occur with meperidine or propoxyphene than with other opioids.

Those indicating possible withdrawal and the need for medical attention if they occur after medication is discontinued
  Body aches; diarrhea; fast heartbeat; fever; runny nose, or sneezing; gooseflesh; increased sweating; increased yawning; loss of appetite; nausea or vomiting; nervousness, restlessness, or irritability; shivering or trembling; stomach cramps; trouble in sleeping; unusually large pupils; weakness

Note: *The signs and symptoms of withdrawal* listed above are characteristic of the abstinence syndrome produced by abrupt discontinuation of mu-receptor agonists such as morphine. The milder abstinence syndrome produced by abrupt discontinuation of opioids having mixed agonist/antagonist activity may also include some of these signs and symptoms.

It has been proposed that adverse effects (such as tachycardia, hypertension, hyperpnea, hyperalgesia, nausea, and vomiting) occurring (rarely) after naloxone is administered for postoperative reversal of opioid effects following a lengthy surgical procedure may be manifestations of an induced abstinence syndrome in acutely dependent individuals. However, other symptoms more commonly associated with an opioid withdrawal syndrome have not been reported.

Patient Consultation

In providing consultation, consider emphasizing the following selected information (» = major clinical significance):

Before using this medication
» Conditions affecting use, especially:
  Sensitivity to the opioid considered for use, history of
  Pregnancy—Opioids cross the placenta; regular use by pregnant women may cause physical dependence in the fetus and withdrawal symptoms in the neonate
  Breast-feeding—Butorphanol, codeine, meperidine, methadone, morphine, and propoxyphene are known to be excreted in breast milk; high-dose methadone may cause dependence in nursing infants
  Use in children—Children up to 2 years of age are more susceptible to the effects of opioids, especially respiratory depression; also, children may be more likely to experience paradoxical CNS excitation during therapy
  Use in the elderly—Geriatric patients are more susceptible to the effects of opioids, especially respiratory depression
  Dental—May cause dryness of mouth, which can lead to caries, periodontal disease, oral candidiasis, and discomfort
  Use by athletes—Opioid analgesics are banned and tested for in athletes by the U.S. Olympic Committee (USOC)
  Other medical problems, especially diarrhea caused by antibiotics or poisoning, asthma or other respiratory problems, and severe inflammatory bowel disease
  Other medications, especially alcohol or other CNS depressants, monoamine oxidase inhibitors, naltrexone, rifampin, and zidovudine

Proper use of this medication

Proper administration of:
- » Injections (if dispensed to the patient for home use)
- » Meperidine syrup—Mixing with $1/2$ glass (4 ounces) of water to lessen numbing effect in mouth and throat
- » Methadone oral concentrate—Diluting with water to at least 1 ounce before taking, unless premixed at a methadone treatment center
- » Methadone dispersible tablets—Must be dissolved in water or fruit juice before taking

  Morphine oral liquid—May be mixed with fruit juice to improve taste
- » Morphine extended-release tablets—Swallowing tablets whole; not breaking, crushing, or chewing

  Suppository dosage forms—proper administration technique

  Proper administration of opium tincture:

  Medication may be diluted in water, which will cause it to turn milky

  Taking with food or meals if gastrointestinal irritation occurs
- » Importance of not taking more medication than the amount prescribed because of danger of overdose and habit-forming potential
- » Not increasing dose if medication is less effective after a few weeks; checking with physician
- » Missed dose (if on scheduled dosing): Taking as soon as possible; not taking if almost time for next dose; not doubling doses
- » Proper storage

Precautions while using this medication

Regular visits to physician to check progress during long-term therapy
- » Avoiding use of alcoholic beverages or other CNS depressants during therapy, unless prescribed or otherwise approved by physician
- » Caution if dizziness, drowsiness, lightheadedness, or false sense of well-being occurs
- » Caution when getting up suddenly from a lying or sitting position

  Lying down if nausea or vomiting, or dizziness or lightheadedness occurs

  Need to inform physician or dentist of use of medication if any kind of surgery (including dental surgery) or emergency treatment is required

  Possible dryness of mouth; using sugarless gum or candy, ice, or saliva substitute for relief; checking with dentist if dry mouth continues for more than 2 weeks
- » Checking with physician before discontinuing medication after prolonged use of high doses; gradual dosage reduction may be necessary to avoid withdrawal symptoms
- » Suspected overdose: Getting emergency help at once

For opium tincture when used as antidiarrheal only
- » Consulting physician if diarrhea continues and/or fever develops

Side/adverse effects

Signs of potential side effects, especially respiratory depression or impairment; allergic reactions; confusion, convulsions, hallucinations, mental depression, or other signs of CNS toxicity; hepatotoxicity; hypertension; and paradoxical CNS excitation, especially in children

General Dosing Information

These medications may suppress respiration, especially in very young, elderly, very ill, or debilitated patients and those with respiratory problems. Lower doses may be required for these patients. However, elderly patients may also be more sensitive to the analgesic effects of these medications so that lower doses or an increased dosing interval may be sufficient to provide effective analgesia.

Dosage and dosing intervals should be individualized on the basis of the potency and duration of action of the specific drug used, the severity of pain, the condition of the patient, other medications given concurrently, and patient response.

Concurrent administration of a nonopioid analgesic (such as aspirin or other salicylates, other nonsteroidal anti-inflammatory analgesics, or acetaminophen) with opioid analgesics provides additive analgesia and may permit lower doses of the opioid analgesic to be utilized.

Some clinicians recommend that patients in severe chronic pain receive opioid analgesics on a fixed dosage schedule so that they remain free of pain rather than on an as needed basis after pain recurs. The medication should be given orally if possible.

Tolerance to many of the effects of these medications may develop with repeated administration. The first sign of tolerance is usually a decrease in the duration of adequate analgesia. Tolerance to the respiratory depressant effects of opioid analgesics develops concurrently with tolerance to their analgesic effects. Careful adjustment of dosage as required to provide adequate analgesia is not likely to increase the risk of respiratory depression. Patients who become tolerant to one of these agents may be partially cross-tolerant to the others. However, when an alternate opioid analgesic is substituted for one to which tolerance has developed, it is recommended that one-half of the equianalgesic dose of the new medication be used initially. Dosage of the new medication may then be adjusted as necessary.

Psychological and physical dependence may occur with chronic administration of opioid analgesics, including epidurally or intrathecally administered opioid analgesics; an abstinence syndrome may occur when these drugs are discontinued. Physical dependence in patients receiving prolonged therapy for severe chronic pain rarely leads to true addiction, i.e., a desire to continue taking the drug (for its euphoric effect) after it is no longer required for treatment. Fear of causing addiction should not result in failure to provide adequate pain relief, although caution is advised if patient predisposition toward drug abuse is known or strongly suspected. Gradual withdrawal may minimize the development of withdrawal symptoms following prolonged use.

For parenteral dosage forms only

Rapid intravenous injection of most opioid analgesics has caused anaphylactoid reactions, severe respiratory depression, hypotension, peripheral circulatory collapse, and cardiac arrest. It is recommended that when an opioid analgesic must be given intravenously, dosage should be reduced and a dilute solution should be injected slowly over a period of several minutes. An opioid antagonist and equipment for artificial ventilation should be available.

When an opioid analgesic is administered parenterally, the patient usually should be lying down and should remain recumbent for a period of time to minimize side effects such as hypotension, dizziness, lightheadedness, nausea, and vomiting. If these side effects occur in an ambulatory patient, they may be relieved if the patient lies down.

In patients with shock, impaired perfusion may prevent complete absorption following intramuscular or subcutaneous injection. Repeated administration may result in overdose due to an excessive amount suddenly being absorbed when circulation is restored.

Opioid analgesics may not provide sufficient analgesia to prevent or overcome hemodynamic responses to surgical stress when used as the sole intravenous supplement to nitrous oxide for the maintenance of balanced anesthesia. Concurrent use of other medications, such as a benzodiazepine, an ultrashort-acting barbiturate, or a potent hydrocarbon inhalation anesthetic, may be required.

Epidural or intrathecal administration of opioid analgesics should be performed only by physicians experienced in these techniques. Solutions containing a preservative must *not* be injected via these routes. *Resuscitative equipment and medications should be immediately available for management of respiratory depression or other complications that may arise from inadvertent intrathecal or intravascular administration.* Also, facilities for adequate monitoring of the patient's respiratory status must be available.

For epidural or intrathecal administration, injection into the lumbar area may be preferred because of the increased risk of respiratory depression with injection into the thoracic area. Also, the epidural route is preferred, whenever possible, because of the increased risk of respiratory depression with intrathecal administration.

Prior to epidural administration, proper placement of the needle or catheter in the epidural space must be verified. Aspiration to check for blood in the cerebrospinal fluid may be performed; however, the fact that intravascular administration is possible even when aspiration for blood is negative must be kept in mind. Alternatively, administration of 5 mL (3 mL for obstetrical patients) of preservative-free 1.5% lidocaine hydrochloride with epinephrine 1:200,000 injection may be used to verify placement in the epidural space. Tachycardia occurring after injection of the test medication indicates that the medication has entered the circulation; sudden onset of segmental anesthesia indicates that the medication has been administered intrathecally.

Following epidural or intrathecal injection of an opioid analgesic, administration of low doses of naloxone via continuous intravenous infusion for 24 hours may decrease the incidence of potential side effects without interfering with the analgesic effectiveness of the medication.

BUTORPHANOL

Summary of Differences

Indications: Caution required when used as analgesic to relieve pain due to acute myocardial infarction because of cardiovascular effects that tend to increase cardiac work.

Pharmacology:

Mechanism of action/effect—An opioid agonist/antagonist analgesic.

Agonist: Has agonist activity at the kappa and sigma receptors.

Antagonist: Probably has no direct antagonist activity at the mu receptor; antagonist effects may result from failure to substitute for mu-receptor agonists sufficiently to prevent or attenuate withdrawal symptoms in physically dependent patients.

Equivalence—2 mg via intramuscular injection therapeutically equivalent to 10 mg of intramuscular morphine.

Protein binding—High.

Half-life—2.5–4 hours.

Onset of action—

Intramuscular: 10–30 minutes.

Intravenous: 2–3 minutes.

Time to peak concentration—0.5–1 hour.

Peak plasma concentration—2.2 nanograms/mL.

Time to peak effect—

Intramuscular: 30–60 minutes.

Intravenous: 30 minutes.

Duration of action (nontolerant patients only; decreases as tolerance develops during chronic therapy)—

Intramuscular: 3–4 hours.

Intravenous: 2–4 hours.

Elimination—72% Renal, <5% as unchanged buprenorphine; 15% biliary.

Precautions:

Laboratory value alterations—

Does not intefere with hepatobiliary imaging.

Does not increase plasma amylase or lipase activity.

Contraindications/medical problems—

Caution not required in gallbladder disease or gallstones.

Also, should be used with caution in patients physically dependent on opioid agonists, in hypertensive patients (when used preoperatively), and in patients with acute myocardial infarction.

Side/adverse effects:

Less likely to cause constipation than most other opioids.

Biliary spasm has not been reported.

Rarely, may cause subjective and psychotomimetic effects characteristic of sigma receptor agonists.

Has lower dependence liability than opioid agonists.

Withdrawal symptoms less severe than those produced by opioid agonist analgesics.

Parenteral Dosage Forms

BUTORPHANOL TARTRATE INJECTION USP

Usual adult dose:

Analgesic—

Intramuscular, 1 to 4 mg (usually 2 mg) every three to four hours as needed.

Intravenous, 500 mcg (0.5 mg) to 2 mg (usually 1 mg) every three to four hours as needed.

Anesthesia adjunct—

Preoperative: Intravenous, usually 2 mg sixty to ninety minutes prior to surgery, although dosage must be individualized.

Balanced anesthesia: Intravenous, initially 1 to 4 mg, followed by supplemental doses of 500 mcg (0.5 mg) to 1 mg as needed.

Note: Dosage must be individualized. Supplemental doses of up to 60 mcg (0.06 mg) per kg of body weight may be necessary in some patients.

The total quantity of butorphanol required during surgery usually ranges between 60 and 180 mcg (0.06 and 0.18 mg) per kg of body weight.

Auxiliary labeling:

• May cause drowsiness.

• Avoid alcoholic beverages.

CODEINE

Summary of Differences

Indications:

Oral dosage forms also indicated as antitussive.

Also, used as antidiarrheal.

Pharmacology:

Mechanism of action/effect—An opioid agonist analgesic; exerts agonist activity primarily at the mu receptor, but with usual doses is relatively weak.

Equivalence—120 mg via intramuscular injection or 200 mg via oral administration therapeutically equivalent to 10 mg of intramuscular morphine.

Protein binding—Very low.

Half-life—2.5–4 hours.

Biotransformation—Hepatic; about 10% demethylated to morphine.

Onset of action—Analgesic:

Intramuscular—10–30 minutes.

Subcutaneous—10–30 minutes.

Oral—30–45 minutes.

Time to peak effect—Analgesic:

Intramuscular—30–60 minutes.

Oral—1–2 hours.

Duration of action—

Analgesic (in nontolerant patients only; decreases as tolerance develops during chronic therapy): Intramuscular, subcutaneous, or oral—4 hours.

Antitussive: Oral—4–6 hours.

Elimination—Renal, 5–15% as unchanged codeine and 10% as unchanged or conjugated morphine.

Side/adverse effects:
>   More likely than most other opioids to cause constipation, especially during chronic therapy.
>   Has lower dependence liability than most other opioid agonists.
>   Withdrawal symptoms less severe than those produced by stronger opioid agonist analgesics.

Additional Dosing Information

See also *General Dosing Information.*

For parenteral dosage forms only
Local tissue irritation, pain, and induration may occur with repeated subcutaneous injection.

Oral Dosage Forms

Note: Bracketed uses in the *Dosage Forms* section refer to categories of use and/or indications that are not included in U.S. product labeling.

CODEINE PHOSPHATE ORAL SOLUTION

Usual adult dose:
>   Analgesic—Oral, 15 to 60 mg (usually 30 mg) every three to six hours as needed.
>   [Antidiarrheal][1]—Oral, 30 mg up to four times a day.
>   Antitussive—Oral, 10 to 20 mg every four to six hours.

Usual adult prescribing limits: Antitussive—Up to 120 mg in twenty-four hours.

Auxiliary labeling:
- May cause drowsiness.
- Avoid alcoholic beverages.
- May be habit-forming.

CODEINE PHOSPHATE TABLETS USP

Usual adult dose:
>   Analgesic—Oral, 15 to 60 mg (usually 30 mg) every three to six hours as needed.
>   [Antidiarrheal][1]—Oral, 30 mg up to four times a day.
>   Antitussive—Oral, 10 to 20 mg every four to six hours.

Usual adult prescribing limits: Antitussive—Up to 120 mg in twenty-four hours.

Auxiliary labeling:
- May cause drowsiness.
- Avoid alcoholic beverages.
- May be habit-forming.

CODEINE SULFATE TABLETS USP

Note: Codeine sulfate tablets are not commercially available in Canada.

Usual adult dose:
>   Analgesic—Oral, 15 to 60 mg (usually 30 mg) every three to six hours as needed.
>   [Antidiarrheal]—Oral, 30 mg up to four times a day.
>   Antitussive—Oral, 10 to 20 mg every four to six hours.

Auxiliary labeling:
- May cause drowsiness.
- Avoid alcoholic beverages.
- May be habit-forming.

Parenteral Dosage Forms

CODEINE PHOSPHATE INJECTION USP

Usual adult dose: Analgesic—Intramuscular, intravenous, or subcutaneous, 15 to 60 mg (usually 30 mg) every four to six hours as needed.

Auxiliary labeling:
- May cause drowsiness.
- Avoid alcoholic beverages.
- May be habit-forming.

CODEINE PHOSPHATE SOLUBLE TABLETS

Note: Codeine phosphate soluble tablets are not commercially available in Canada.

Usual adult dose: Analgesic—Intramuscular or subcutaneous, 15 to 60 mg (usually 30 mg) every four to six hours as needed.

Auxiliary labeling:
- May cause drowsiness.
- Avoid alcoholic beverages.
- May be habit-forming.

CODEINE SULFATE SOLUBLE TABLETS

Note: Codeine sulfate soluble tablets are not commercially available in Canada.

Usual adult dose: Analgesic—Intramuscular or subcutaneous, 15 to 60 mg (usually 30 mg) every four to six hours as needed.

Auxiliary labeling:
- May cause drowsiness.
- Avoid alcoholic beverages.
- May be habit-forming.

---

[1]Not included in Canadian product labeling.

HYDROCODONE

Summary of Differences

Indications: Also, indicated as an antitussive.
Pharmacology:
>   Mechanism of action/effect—An opioid agonist analgesic; exerts agonist activity primarily at the mu receptor.
>   Half-life—3.8 hours.
>   Onset of action—Analgesic: Oral—10–30 minutes.
>   Time to peak effect—Analgesic: Oral—30–60 minutes.
>   Duration of action—
>>   Analgesic (nontolerant patients only; decreases as tolerance develops during chronic therapy): Oral—4–6 hours.
>>   Antitussive: Oral—4–6 hours.
>   Elimination—Renal.
Side/adverse effects: More likely than most other opioids to cause side effects associated with histamine release.

Oral Dosage Forms

HYDROCODONE BITARTRATE SYRUP

Note: Hydrocodone bitartrate syrup is not commercially available in the U.S.

>   In Canada, *Hycodan* contains only hydrocodone bitartrate; in the U.S., *Hycodan* contains homatropine in addition to hydrocodone bitartrate.

Usual adult dose: Antitussive—Oral, 5 mg every four to six hours as needed.

Auxiliary labeling:
- May cause drowsiness.
- Avoid alcoholic beverages.
- May be habit-forming.

HYDROCODONE BITARTRATE TABLETS USP

Note: Hydrocodone bitartrate tablets are not commercially available in the U.S.

In Canada, *Hycodan* contains only hydrocodone bitartrate; in the U.S., *Hycodan* contains homatropine in addition to hydrocodone bitartrate.

Usual adult dose:

Analgesic—Oral, 5 to 10 mg every four to six hours as needed.
Antitussive—Oral, 5 mg every four to six hours as needed.

Auxiliary labeling:

- May cause drowsiness.
- Avoid alcoholic beverages.
- May be habit-forming.

HYDROMORPHONE

Summary of Differences

Indications: Also, indicated as an antitussive; see also *Cough/Cold Combinations (Systemic)—Hydromorphone and Guaifenesin.*
Pharmacology:
   Mechanism of action/effect—An opioid agonist analgesic; exerts agonist activity primarily at the mu receptor.
   Equivalence—1.5 mg via intramuscular injection, 7.5 mg via oral administration, or 3 mg via rectal administration therapeutically equivalent to 10 mg of intramuscular morphine.
   Half-life—2.6–4 hours.
   Onset of action—
      Intramuscular: 15 minutes.
      Intravenous: 10–15 minutes.
      Oral: 30 minutes.
      Subcutaneous: 15 minutes.
   Time to peak effect—
      Intramuscular: 30–60 minutes.
      Intravenous: 15–30 minutes.
      Oral: 90–120 minutes.
      Subcutaneous: 30–90 minutes.
   Duration of action (nontolerant patients only; decreases as tolerance develops during chronic therapy)—
      Intramuscular: 4–5 hours.
      Intravenous: 2–3 hours.
      Oral: 4 hours.
      Subcutaneous: 4 hours.
   Elimination—Renal.

Oral Dosage Forms

HYDROMORPHONE HYDROCHLORIDE TABLETS USP

Usual adult dose: Analgesic—Oral, 2 mg every three to six hours as needed.

Note: Dosage may be increased to 4 mg or more every four to six hours, depending on the severity of pain; however, patients receiving these high doses must be carefully monitored.

Auxiliary labeling:

- May cause drowsiness.
- Avoid alcoholic beverages.
- May be habit-forming.

Parenteral Dosage Forms

HYDROMORPHONE HYDROCHLORIDE INJECTION USP

Usual adult dose: Analgesic—
   Intramuscular or subcutaneous, 1 to 2 mg every three to six hours as needed; may be increased to 3 or 4 mg every four to six hours if pain is severe.

   Note: For opioid-tolerant patients requiring high-dose therapy, the 10-mg-per-mL concentration may be substituted for lower strengths of hydromorphone hydrochloride injection or for other opioid analgesics. Dosage must be individualized, depending on the severity of pain, opioid requirements at the time therapy with the high-potency injection is initiated, and patient response. Although patients who have become tolerant to another opioid may be at least partially cross-tolerant to hydromorphone also, it is recommended that one-half of the equianalgesic dose of hydromorphone be used initially, then adjusted as necessary.

   Intravenous, 500 mcg (0.5 mg) to 1 mg every three hours as needed; administered slowly.

Auxiliary labeling:

- May cause drowsiness.
- Avoid alcoholic beverages.
- May be habit-forming.

Rectal Dosage Forms

HYDROMORPHONE HYDROCHLORIDE SUPPOSITORIES

Usual adult dose: Analgesic—Rectal, 3 mg every four to eight hours as needed.

Auxiliary labeling:

- May cause drowsiness.
- Avoid alcoholic beverages.
- May be habit-forming.
- Store in refrigerator.

LEVORPHANOL

Summary of Differences

Pharmacology:
   Mechanism of action/effect—An opioid agonist analgesic; exerts agonist activity primarily at the mu receptor.
   Equivalence—2 mg via intramuscular injection or 4 mg via oral administration therapeutically equivalent to 10 mg of intramuscular morphine.
   Protein binding—Moderate.
   Onset of action—Oral: 10–60 minutes.
   Time to peak effect—
      Intramuscular: 60 minutes.
      Intravenous: Within 20 minutes.
      Oral: 90–120 minutes.
      Subcutaneous: 60–90 minutes.
   Duration of action (nontolerant patients only; duration decreases as tolerance develops during chronic therapy)—Intramuscular, intravenous, oral, or subcutaneous: 4–5 hours.
   Elimination—Renal.

Oral Dosage Forms

LEVORPHANOL TARTRATE TABLETS USP

Usual adult dose: Analgesic—Oral, 2 mg; may be increased to 3 or 4 mg if pain is severe.

Auxiliary labeling:
• May cause drowsiness.
• Avoid alcoholic beverages.
• May be habit-forming.

Parenteral Dosage Forms

LEVORPHANOL TARTRATE INJECTION USP

Usual adult dose: Analgesic—Subcutaneous, 2 mg; may be increased to 3 mg if pain is severe.

Note: The medication may also be given intravenously.

For preoperative analgesia—Subcutaneous, 1 to 2 mg ninety minutes prior to surgery.

Auxiliary labeling:
• May cause drowsiness.
• Avoid alcoholic beverages.
• May be habit-forming.

MEPERIDINE

Summary of Differences

Pharmacology:
Mechanism of action/effect—An opioid agonist analgesic; exerts agonist activity primarily at the mu receptor.
Equivalence—75 mg via intramuscular injection or 300 mg via oral administration therapeutically equivalent to 10 mg of intramuscular morphine.
Protein binding—High.
Half-life—2.4–4 hours.
Biotransformation—Metabolized to normeperidine, which is active and toxic.
Onset of action—
Intramuscular: 10–15 minutes.
Intravenous: 1 minute.
Oral: 15 minutes.
Subcutaneous: 10–15 minutes.
Time to peak effect—
Intramuscular: 30–50 minutes.
Intravenous: 5–7 minutes.
Oral: 60–90 minutes.
Subcutaneous: 30–50 minutes.
Duration of action (nontolerant patients only; decreases as tolerance develops during chronic therapy)—Intramuscular, intravenous, oral, or subcutaneous: 2–4 hours.
Elimination—Renal, 5% as unchanged meperidine.
Precautions: Drug interactions and/or related problems—
May increase effects of coumarin- or indandione-derivative anticoagulants.
Contraindicated in patients who have received a monoamine oxidase (MAO) inhibitor within past 14–21 days; concurrent use has produced serious, sometimes fatal, reactions.
Concurrent use with amphetamines, which have some MAO inhibiting activity, not recommended because of risk of serious reactions similar to those reported with other MAO inhibitors.
Side/adverse effects: More likely than most other opioids to cause side effects associated with histamine release, convulsions, or constipation.

Additional Dosing Information

See also *General Dosing Information.*

For oral dosage forms only
The syrup may be diluted with ¹/₂ glass (120 mL) of water to prevent a slight topical anesthetic effect on the mucous membranes.

For parenteral dosage forms only
Intramuscular administration is preferred when repeated doses are required. Repeated subcutaneous administration causes local tissue irritation and induration.

Inadvertent injection around a nerve trunk may cause sensory-motor paralysis, which is usually, but not always, transitory.

Oral Dosage Forms

MEPERIDINE HYDROCHLORIDE SYRUP USP

Note: Meperidine hydrochloride syrup is not commercially available in Canada.

Usual adult dose: Analgesic—Oral, 50 to 150 mg (usually 100 mg) every three to four hours as needed.

Auxiliary labeling:
• May cause drowsiness.
• Avoid alcoholic beverages.
• May be habit-forming.

MEPERIDINE HYDROCHLORIDE TABLETS USP

Usual adult dose: Analgesic—Oral, 50 to 150 mg (usually 100 mg) every three to four hours as needed.

Auxiliary labeling:
• May cause drowsiness.
• Avoid alcoholic beverages.
• May be habit-forming.

Parenteral Dosage Forms

MEPERIDINE HYDROCHLORIDE INJECTION USP

Usual adult dose:
Analgesic—
Intramuscular (preferred) or subcutaneous, 50 to 150 mg (usually 100 mg) every three to four hours as needed.
Intravenous infusion, 15 to 35 mg per hour as required, administered using an infusion pump.
Note: Dosage must be adjusted according to the severity of pain and patient response.

Obstetrical analgesia: Intramuscular (preferred) or subcutaneous, 50 to 100 mg administered when pains become regular. May be repeated at one- to three-hour intervals as needed.
Anesthesia adjunct—
Preoperative: Intramuscular (preferred) or subcutaneous, 50 to 100 mg thirty to ninety minutes prior to anesthesia.
Intravenous, by repeated slow injection of fractional doses of a solution diluted to 10 mg per mL.
Intravenous infusion, as a solution diluted to 1 mg per mL.
Note: Dosage must be titrated to the needs of the patient, depending on the premedication given, the type of anesthesia, and the nature and duration of the surgical procedure.

Auxiliary labeling:
• May cause drowsiness.
• Avoid alcoholic beverages.
• May be habit-forming.

METHADONE

Note: In the U.S., hospital and community pharmacies must have approval from FDA and appropriate state authorities to engage in methadone detoxification or maintenance programs. Approved maintenance programs are authorized to dispense methadone in the oral form only and must comply with treatment requirements as set forth in the Federal Methadone Regulations. Consult the manufacturer's labeling for federal laws that apply when dispensing methadone as a narcotic abstinence syndrome suppressant.

In Canada, methadone is a controlled substance (Classification N). It is available only through physicians who have received special authorization to prescribe the medication.

Summary of Differences

Indications:
Also, indicated as narcotic abstinence syndrome suppressant.
Also, used as antitussive.
Not recommended for obstetrical analgesia.
Pharmacology:
Mechanism of action/effect—An opioid agonist analgesic; exerts agonist activity primarily at the mu receptor.
Equivalence—10 mg via intramuscular injection or 20 mg via oral administration therapeutically equivalent to 10 mg of intramuscular morphine.
Protein binding—High.
Half-life—15–25 hours; increases with repeated administration.
Onset of action—
Intramuscular: 10–20 minutes.
Oral: 30–60 minutes.
Time to peak effect—
Intramuscular: 1–2 hours.
Intravenous: 15–30 minutes.
Oral: 1.5–2 hours.
Duration of action (in nontolerant patients, may increase considerably with chronic use because of accumulation of methadone or active metabolites; may then decrease as tolerance develops during chronic therapy)—
Intramuscular: 4–5 hours.
Intravenous: 3–4 hours.
Oral: 4–6 hours.
Elimination—Primarily renal (rate increased in acidic urine); also some biliary elimination.
Precautions: Drug interactions and/or related problems—
Urinary acidifiers may increase methadone elimination, thereby reducing the plasma concentration; withdrawal symptoms may occur in some physically dependent patients.
Phenytoin or rifampin may increase methadone metabolism and precipitate withdrawal symptoms in physically dependent patients.
Side/adverse effects: May be more likely than most other opioids to cause constipation.

Additional Dosing Information

See also *General Dosing Information.*

In the U.S., use of methadone in a detoxification regimen (to suppress withdrawal symptoms following discontinuation of an opioid drug in dependent patients) consists of administering gradually decreasing doses of methadone for up to 3 weeks. After 3 weeks, treatment is considered to be maintenance therapy (to discourage the patient from returning to illicit opioid drug use) and must be undertaken only in approved methadone maintenance programs. Dosage in maintenance programs may be gradually increased to meet the needs of the individual patient. Oral administration is preferred for detoxification and mandatory for maintenance.

For parenteral dosage forms only
Intramuscular administration is recommended when repeated doses are required. Repeated subcutaneous administration causes local tissue irritation and induration.

Oral Dosage Forms

METHADONE HYDROCHLORIDE ORAL CONCENTRATE USP

Usual adult dose:
Analgesic—Oral, 5 to 20 mg every four to eight hours. Dosage may be increased or the interval between doses decreased if pain is very severe or if the patient becomes tolerant to the medication.
Suppressant (narcotic abstinence syndrome)—
Detoxification: Oral, 15 to 40 mg once a day or as needed to control observed withdrawal symptoms; dosage to be reduced at one- or two-day intervals according to patient response.
Maintenance: Dosage must be individualized.

Usual adult prescribing limits: Up to 120 mg per day.

Auxiliary labeling:
• May cause drowsiness.
• Avoid alcoholic beverages.
• May be habit-forming.

METHADONE HYDROCHLORIDE ORAL SOLUTION USP

Usual adult dose: Analgesic—Oral, 5 to 20 mg every four to eight hours. Dosage may be increased or the interval between doses decreased if pain is very severe or if the patient becomes tolerant to the medication.

Auxiliary labeling:
• May cause drowsiness.
• Avoid alcoholic beverages.
• May be habit-forming.

METHADONE HYDROCHLORIDE TABLETS USP

Usual adult dose: Analgesic—Oral, 2.5 to 10 mg every three to four hours as needed initially. For chronic use, dose and dosing interval to be adjusted according to patient response.

Auxiliary labeling:
• May cause drowsiness.
• Avoid alcoholic beverages.
• May be habit-forming.

METHADONE HYDROCHLORIDE TABLETS USP (DISPERSIBLE)

Usual adult dose: Suppressant (narcotic abstinence syndrome)—
Detoxification: Oral, 15 to 40 mg once a day or as needed to control observed withdrawal symptoms; dosage to be reduced at one- or two-day intervals according to patient response.
Maintenance: Dosage must be individualized.

Usual adult prescribing limits: Up to 120 mg per day.

Auxiliary labeling:
• May cause drowsiness.
• Avoid alcoholic beverages.
• May be habit-forming.

Parenteral Dosage Forms

METHADONE HYDROCHLORIDE INJECTION USP

Usual adult dose:
Analgesic—Intramuscular or subcutaneous, 2.5 to 10 mg every three to four hours as needed.

Suppressant (narcotic abstinence syndrome)—For detoxification only: Intramuscular or subcutaneous, 15 to 40 mg once a day or as needed to control observed withdrawal symptoms; dosage to be reduced at one- or two-day intervals according to patient response.

Note: Parenteral administration in a detoxification regimen is recommended only for patients unable to take medication orally.

Auxiliary labeling:
- May cause drowsiness.
- Avoid alcoholic beverages.
- May be habit-forming.

MORPHINE

Summary of Differences

Indications:

Drug of choice to relieve pain due to acute myocardial infarction.

Also, indicated as adjunctive therapy in the treatment of acute pulmonary edema secondary to left ventricular failure.

Also, used as antitussive.

Pharmacology:

Mechanism of action/effect—An opioid agonist analgesic; exerts agonist activity primarily at the mu receptor.

Equivalence—60 mg via oral administration therapeutically equivalent to 10 mg intramuscularly; however, with chronic use on a fixed schedule may decrease to 20–30 mg.

Protein binding—Low.

Half-life—2–3 hours.

Onset of action—

Epidural: 15–60 minutes.

Intramuscular: 10–30 minutes.

Intrathecal: 15–60 minutes.

Rectal: 20–60 minutes.

Subcutaneous: 10–30 minutes.

Time to peak effect—

Intramuscular: 30–60 minutes.

Intravenous: 20 minutes.

Oral (immediate-release dosage forms): 1–2 hours.

Subcutaneous: 50–90 minutes.

Duration of action (nontolerant patients only; may decrease as tolerance develops during chronic therapy)—

Epidural: Up to 24 hours.

Intramuscular: 4–5 hours.

Intrathecal: Up to 24 hours.

Intravenous: 4–5 hours.

Oral: 4–5 hours with immediate-release dosage forms; 8 or 12 hours (depending on specific product) with extended-release dosage forms.

Subcutaneous: 4–5 hours.

Elimination—85% Renal, 9–12% as unchanged morphine; 7–10% biliary.

Precautions: Drug interactions and/or related problems—Also may decrease clearance of zidovudine; toxicity of either or both medications may be potentiated.

Side/adverse effects: More likely than most other opioids to cause constipation and to produce symptoms associated with histamine release.

Additional Dosing Information

See also *General Dosing Information.*

For oral dosage forms only

The oral dosage forms are recommended for administration via a fixed dosage schedule to patients with severe, chronic pain.

Periodic attempts should be made to reduce the dosage after an initial response has been achieved and maintained for at least 3 days.

The oral liquid may be diluted in a glass of fruit juice just prior to ingestion, if desired, to improve the taste.

The extended-release tablets are to be swallowed whole. They should not be broken, crushed, or chewed.

For parenteral dosage forms only

Intramuscular administration is recommended when repeated doses are required. Repeated subcutaneous administration causes local tissue irritation, pain, and induration.

The 25- or 50-mg per mL concentration of morphine sulfate injection available in Canada may be administered undiluted to opioid-tolerant patients requiring high-dose therapy. The 25-mg-per-mL concentration of morphine sulfate injection available in the U.S. is intended only for the preparation of intravenous infusion solutions and is not to be administered via other parenteral routes.

Oral Dosage Forms

MORPHINE HYDROCHLORIDE SYRUP

Note: Morphine hydrochloride syrup is not commercially available in the U.S.

Usual adult dose: Analgesic—Chronic pain: Dosage and dosing interval must be individualized by the physician according to the severity of pain and patient response. Initial oral doses of 10 to 30 mg every four hours are recommended by most manufacturers of oral morphine products. However, some patients receiving the medication via the recommended fixed dosing schedule may respond to lower doses, while others have required 75 mg or more.

Auxiliary labeling:
- May cause drowsiness.
- Avoid alcoholic beverages.
- May be habit-forming.

MORPHINE HYDROCHLORIDE TABLETS

Note: Morphine hydrochloride tablets are not commercially available in the U.S.

Usual adult dose: Analgesic—Chronic pain: Dosage and dosing interval must be individualized by the physician according to the severity of pain and patient response. Initial oral doses of 10 to 30 mg every four hours are recommended by most manufacturers of oral morphine products. However, some patients receiving the medication via the recommended fixed dosing schedule may respond to lower doses, while others have required 75 mg or more.

Auxiliary labeling:
- May cause drowsiness.
- Avoid alcoholic beverages.
- May be habit-forming.

MORPHINE HYDROCHLORIDE EXTENDED-RELEASE TABLETS

Note: Morphine hydrochloride extended-release tablets are not commercially available in the U.S.

Usual adult dose: Analgesic—Chronic pain: Dosage must be individualized by the physician according to the severity of pain and patient response.

Auxiliary labeling:
- Swallow tablets whole.
- May cause drowsiness.
- Avoid alcoholic beverages.
- May be habit-forming.

MORPHINE SULFATE ORAL SOLUTION

Usual adult dose: Analgesic—Chronic pain: Dosage and dosing interval must be individualized by the physician according to the severity of pain and patient response. Initial oral doses of 10 to 30 mg every four hours are recommended by most manufacturers of oral morphine products. However, some patients receiving the medication via the recommended fixed dosing schedule may respond to lower doses, while others have required 75 mg or more.

Auxiliary labeling:
- May cause drowsiness.
- Avoid alcoholic beverages.
- May be habit-forming.

MORPHINE SULFATE SYRUP

Note: Morphine sulfate syrup is not commercially available in the U.S.

Usual adult dose: Analgesic—Chronic pain: Dosage and dosing interval must be individualized by the physician according to the severity of pain and patient response. Initial oral doses of 10 to 30 mg every four hours are recommended by most manufacturers of oral morphine products. However, some patients receiving the medication via the recommended fixed dosing schedule may respond to lower doses, while others have required 75 mg or more.

Auxiliary labeling:
- May cause drowsiness.
- Avoid alcoholic beverages.
- May be habit-forming.

MORPHINE SULFATE TABLETS

Usual adult dose: Analgesic—Chronic pain: Dosage and dosing interval must be individualized by the physician according to the severity of pain and patient response. Initial oral doses of 10 to 30 mg every four hours are recommended by most manufacturers of oral morphine products. However, some patients receiving the medication via the recommended fixed dosing schedule may respond to lower doses, while others have required 75 mg or more.

Auxiliary labeling:
- May cause drowsiness.
- Avoid alcoholic beverages.
- May be habit-forming.

MORPHINE SULFATE EXTENDED-RELEASE TABLETS

Usual adult dose: Analgesic—Chronic pain: Oral, 30 mg every eight or every twelve hours, depending on specific product, initially, with dosage and dosing interval then being adjusted according to the requirements of the individual patient.

Note: Patients being transferred from other opioid analgesics or other morphine dosage forms to the morphine sulfate extended-release tablets should receive a total daily dose of oral morphine sulfate equivalent to the established total daily dose of previously administered medication, administered in divided doses at eight-hour intervals (for *Roxanol SR*) or twelve-hour intervals (for *M S Contin*). Consult manufacturers' prescribing information for recommendations for calculating equivalent dosage.

Auxiliary labeling:
- Swallow tablets whole.
- May cause drowsiness.
- Avoid alcoholic beverages.
- May be habit-forming.

Parenteral Dosage Forms

MORPHINE SULFATE INJECTION USP

Usual adult dose: Analgesic—

Intramuscular or subcutaneous, 5 to 20 mg (usually 10 mg, initially) every four hours as needed.

Note: The recommendation of an initial 10-mg dose is based on a 70-kg person.

In Canada, the 25- or 50-mg-per-mL concentration may be substituted for lower strengths of morphine sulfate injection or for other opioid analgesics in opioid-tolerant patients requiring high-dose therapy. Dosage must be individualized, depending on the severity of pain, opioid requirements at the time therapy with the high-potency injection is initiated, and patient response. Although patients who have become tolerant to another opioid may be at least partially cross-tolerant to morphine also, it is recommended that one-half of the equianalgesic dose of morphine be used initially, then adjusted as necessary.

Intravenous, 4 to 10 mg diluted in 4 to 5 mL of sterile water for injection, administered slowly.

Epidural (in the lumbar region), 5 mg.

Note: If adequate pain relief is not achieved within one hour, incremental doses of 1 to 2 mg may be administered at intervals sufficient to assess effectiveness, up to a maximum of 10 mg per twenty-four hours.

Intrathecal, 200 mcg (0.2 mg) to 1 mg as a single dose.

Note: Clinical experience with repeated intrathecal injections is limited. Therefore, repeated administration via this route is not recommended. Alternate routes of administration should be considered for treating recurrent or chronic pain.

Auxiliary labeling:
- May cause drowsiness.
- Avoid alcoholic beverages.
- May be habit-forming.

MORPHINE SULFATE SOLUBLE TABLETS

Note: Morphine sulfate soluble tablets are not commercially available in Canada.

Usual adult dose: Analgesic—Intramuscular or subcutaneous, 5 to 20 mg (usually 10 mg, initially) every four hours as needed.

Note: The recommendation of an initial 10-mg dose is based on a 70-kg person.

Auxiliary labeling:
- May cause drowsiness.
- Avoid alcoholic beverages.
- May be habit-forming.

Rectal Dosage Forms

MORPHINE HYDROCHLORIDE SUPPOSITORIES

Note: Morphine hydrochloride suppositories are not commercially available in the U.S.

Usual adult dose: Analgesic—Rectal, 20 to 30 mg every four to six hours.

Auxiliary labeling:
- May cause drowsiness.
- Avoid alcoholic beverages.
- May be habit-forming.

MORPHINE SULFATE SUPPOSITORIES

Usual adult dose: Analgesic—Rectal, 10 to 30 mg every four hours or as required.

Note: Dosage must be individualized according to the severity of pain and the response of the patient.

Auxiliary labeling:
- May cause drowsiness.
- Avoid alcoholic beverages.
- May be habit-forming.

NALBUPHINE

Summary of Differences

Indications: Caution required when used as analgesic to relieve pain in patients with severely compromised cardiac function; cardiovascular effects in these patients have not been fully evaluated.

Pharmacology:
  Mechanism of action/effect—An opioid agonist/antagonist analgesic.
    Agonist: Has agonist activity at the kappa and sigma receptors.
    Antagonist: Has antagonist activity at the mu receptor; may precipitate withdrawal symptoms in patients who are physically dependent on mu-receptor agonists.
  Equivalence—10 mg via intramuscular injection therapeutically equivalent to 10 mg of intramuscular morphine.
  Half-life—5 hours.
  Onset of action—
    Intramuscular: Within 15 minutes.
    Intravenous: 2–3 minutes.
    Subcutaneous: Within 15 minutes.
  Time to peak concentration—Intramuscular: 0.5 hour.
  Peak plasma concentration—48 nanograms per mL.
  Time to peak effect—
    Intramuscular: 60 minutes.
    Intravenous: 30 minutes.
  Duration of action (nontolerant patients only; decreases as tolerance develops during chronic therapy)—
    Intramuscular: 3–6 hours.
    Intravenous: 3–4 hours.
    Subcutaneous: 3–6 hours.
  Elimination—Renal.

Precautions:
  Drug interactions and/or related problems—May antagonize effects of mu-receptor agonists.
  Contraindications/medical problems—Also should be used with caution in patients who are physically dependent on opioid agonists.

Side/adverse effects:
  Rarely, may cause subjective and psychotomimetic effects characteristic of sigma receptor agonists.
  Respiratory depression subject to a "ceiling effect," after which the depth of respiratory depression does not increase with dose.
  More likely than most other opioid analgesics to produce symptoms associated with histamine release.
  Has lower dependence liability than opioid agonists.
  Withdrawal symptoms less severe than those produced by opioid agonist analgesics.

Parenteral Dosage Forms

NALBUPHINE HYDROCHLORIDE INJECTION

Usual adult dose:
  Analgesic—Intramuscular, intravenous, or subcutaneous, 10 mg every three to six hours as needed.

  Note: The usual adult dose is based on a 70-kg person.

Anesthesia adjunct (balanced anesthesia)—
  Initial: Intravenous, 300 mcg (0.3 mg) to 3 mg per kg of body weight, administered over a ten- to fifteen-minute period.
  Supplemental: Intravenous, 250 to 500 mcg (0.25 to 0.5 mg) per kg of body weight, as required.

Usual adult prescribing limits: For nontolerant patients—Up to 20 mg as a single dose and up to 160 mg as a total daily dose.

Auxiliary labeling:
- May cause drowsiness.
- Avoid alcoholic beverages.

OPIUM

Summary of Differences

Indications: Oral dosage form—
  Indicated as antidiarrheal.
  Also, used as narcotic abstinence syndrome suppressant in neonates.

Pharmacology:
  Mechanism of action/effect—An opioid agonist analgesic; has agonist activity primarily at the mu receptor.
  Equivalence—13.3 mg parenterally is therapeutically equivalent to 10 mg of intramuscular morphine.
  Elimination—Renal and biliary.

Additional Dosing Information

See also *General Dosing Information.*

The effects of opium preparations are due primarily to the morphine component.

For oral dosage form only

Alteration of intestinal motility in patients with traveler's diarrhea may result in prolonged fever by slowing expulsion of infectious organisms that penetrate intestinal mucosa (for example, *Shigella, Salmonella,* and certain strains of *Escherichia coli*).

Opium may produce fluid retention in the bowel, which may mask dehydration and electrolyte depletion caused by severe diarrhea, especially in young children. Patients with severe or prolonged diarrhea should be monitored for signs of dehydration or electrolyte imbalance, and corrective therapy administered as required.

To reduce the risk of toxic megacolon in patients with acute inflammatory bowel disease, treatment with opium tincture should be discontinued promptly if abdominal distention or other gastrointestinal symptoms occur.

Tolerance to the antidiarrheal effects of opium tincture may develop with prolonged use.

Following prolonged administration of high doses, opium tincture should be withdrawn gradually in order to reduce the possibility of withdrawal symptoms.

Many clinicians have recommended use of diluted opium tincture instead of paregoric in the treatment of neonatal narcotic dependence, because of the risks associated with two of the components of the paregoric formulation. Opium tincture is diluted to produce the same concentration of morphine as paregoric and may be administered every 3 hours, with gradual withdrawal over 2 to 4 weeks when symptoms are controlled.

For parenteral dosage form only

This formulation contains all of the alkaloids of opium as the hydrochlorides.

Oral Dosage Forms

OPIUM TINCTURE USP (LAUDANUM)

Usual adult dose: Antidiarrheal—Oral, 0.3 to 1.0 mL (usually 0.6 mL) (the equivalent of morphine—3 to 10 mg) four times a day.

Usual adult prescribing limits: A single dose of 1 mL, or a total of 6 mL within twenty-four hours.

Auxiliary labeling:
- May cause drowsiness.
- Avoid alcoholic beverages.
- Do not take other medicines without your doctor's advice.
- Keep out of reach of children.
- May be habit-forming.

Parenteral Dosage Forms

OPIUM ALKALOIDS HYDROCHLORIDES INJECTION (PAPAVERETUM)

Usual adult dose: Analgesic—Intramuscular or subcutaneous, 5 to 20 mg every four to five hours as needed.

Auxiliary labeling:
- May cause drowsiness.
- Avoid alcoholic beverages.
- May be habit-forming.

OXYCODONE

Summary of Differences

Pharmacology:
> Mechanism of action/effect—An opioid agonist analgesic; has agonist activity primarily at the mu receptor.
> Equivalence—30 mg via oral administration therapeutically equivalent to 10 mg of intramuscular morphine.
> Half-life—2–3 hours.
> Time to peak effect—Oral: 1 hour.
> Duration of action (nontolerant patients only; duration decreases as tolerance develops during chronic therapy)—Oral: 3–4 hours.
> Elimination—Renal.

Oral Dosage Forms

OXYCODONE HYDROCHLORIDE ORAL SOLUTION USP

Note: Oxycodone hydrochloride oral solution is not commercially available in Canada.

Usual adult dose: Analgesic—Oral, 5 mg every three to six hours as needed; may be increased if severe pain is present.

Auxiliary labeling:
- May cause drowsiness.
- Avoid alcoholic beverages.
- May be habit-forming.

OXYCODONE TABLETS USP

Usual adult dose: Analgesic—Oral, 5 mg every three to six hours or 10 mg three or four times a day as needed; may be increased if severe pain is present.

Auxiliary labeling:
- May cause drowsiness.
- Avoid alcoholic beverages.
- May be habit-forming.

Rectal Dosage Forms

OXYCODONE HYDROCHLORIDE SUPPOSITORIES

Note: Oxycodone hydrochloride suppositories are not commercially available in the U.S.

Usual adult dose: Analgesic—Rectal, 10 to 40 mg three or four times a day.

Auxiliary labeling:
- May cause drowsiness.
- Avoid alcoholic beverages.
- May be habit-forming.
- Store in refrigerator. Protect from freezing.

OXYMORPHONE

Summary of Differences

Indications: Also, FDA-approved, but rarely if ever used, as adjunctive therapy in the treatment of acute pulmonary edema secondary to left ventricular failure.

Pharmacology:
> Mechanism of action/effect—An opioid agonist analgesic; has agonist activity primarily at the mu receptor.
> Equivalence—1 mg via intramuscular injection or 10 mg rectally therapeutically equivalent to 10 mg of intramuscular morphine.
> Onset of action—
>> Intramuscular: 10–15 minutes.
>> Intravenous: 5–10 minutes.
>> Subcutaneous: 10–20 minutes.
>> Rectal: 15–30 minutes.
> Time to peak effect—
>> Intramuscular: 30–90 minutes.
>> Intravenous: 15–30 minutes.
>> Rectal: 2 hours.
> Duration of action (nontolerant patients only; duration decreases as tolerance develops during chronic therapy)—
>> Intramuscular: 3–6 hours.
>> Intravenous: 3–4 hours.
>> Subcutaneous: 3–6 hours.
>> Rectal: 3–6 hours.
> Elimination—Renal.

Parenteral Dosage Forms

OXYMORPHONE HYDROCHLORIDE INJECTION USP

Usual adult dose: Analgesic—
> Intramuscular or subcutaneous, 1 to 1.5 mg every three to six hours as needed.
> Intravenous, 500 mcg (0.5 mg).

Note: Doses may be cautiously increased, if necessary, if pain is severe.
> For obstetrical analgesia—Intramuscular, 500 mcg (0.5 mg) to 1 mg.

Auxiliary labeling:
- May cause drowsiness.
- Avoid alcoholic beverages.
- May be habit-forming.

Rectal Dosage Forms

OXYMORPHONE HYDROCHLORIDE SUPPOSITORIES USP

Usual adult dose: Analgesic—Rectal, 5 mg every four to six hours as needed.

Auxiliary labeling:
- May cause drowsiness.
- Avoid alcoholic beverages.
- May be habit-forming.
- Store in refrigerator. Protect from freezing.

PENTAZOCINE

Summary of Differences

Indications: Less desirable than morphine or other opioid agonist analgesics for relief of pain due to acute myocardial infarction because of cardiovascular effects that tend to increase cardiac work.

Pharmacology:
  Mechanism of action/effect—An opioid agonist/antagonist analgesic.
    Agonist: Has agonist activity at the kappa and sigma receptors.
    Antagonist: Has antagonist activity at the mu receptor; may precipitate withdrawal symptoms in patients who are physically dependent on mu-receptor agonists.
  Equivalence—60 mg via intramuscular injection or 180 mg via oral administration therapeutically equivalent to 10 mg of intramuscular morphine.
  Protein binding—Moderate.
  Half-life—2–3 hours.
  Onset of action—
    Intramuscular: 15–20 minutes.
    Intravenous: 2–3 minutes.
    Oral: 15–30 minutes.
    Subcutaneous: 15–20 minutes.
  Time to peak effect—
    Intramuscular: 30–60 minutes.
    Intravenous: 15–30 minutes.
    Oral: 60–90 minutes.
    Subcutaneous: 30–60 minutes.
  Duration of action (nontolerant patients only; decreases as tolerance develops during chronic therapy)—
    Intramuscular: 2–3 hours.
    Intravenous: 2–3 hours.
    Oral: 3 hours.
    Subcutaneous: 2–3 hours.
  Elimination—Renal, 5–23% as unchanged pentazocine, and biliary.
Precautions:
  Drug interactions and/or related problems—May antagonize the effects of mu-receptor agonists.
  Contraindications/medical problems—Also must be used with caution in patients physically dependent on opioid agonists and in patients with acute myocardial infarction.
Side/adverse effects:
  Although occurs rarely, more likely than butorphanol or nalbuphine to cause subjective and psychotomimetic effects characteristic of sigma receptor agonists.
  Respiratory depression subject to a "ceiling effect," after which the depth of respiratory depression does not increase with dose.
  Has lower dependence liability than opioid agonists.
  Withdrawal symptoms less severe than those produced by opioid agonist analgesics.

Additional Dosing Information

See also *General Dosing Information.*

The naloxone present in the pentazocine and naloxone dosage formulation has no pharmacologic activity when administered orally. If the product is misused by injection, the naloxone antagonizes the effects of pentazocine. Also, injection of the medication will precipitate withdrawal symptoms if the patient is physically dependent on an opioid agonist.

For long-term administration, the oral form of the medication is preferred. If the parenteral form is used instead, dosage should be reduced gradually when the medication is to be discontinued to reduce the risk of withdrawal symptoms.

The extent to which pentazocine may produce withdrawal symptoms in patients who are physically dependent on opioid analgesics depends upon the dose of pentazocine, the specific opioid drug involved, and the degree to which physical dependence has developed.

For parenteral dosage forms only

Intravenous or intramuscular administration is recommended, especially when repeated doses are required. Subcutaneous administration may lead to severe tissue damage at the injection site. When the intramuscular route is used, rotation of injection sites is essential to prevent tissue damage.

Oral Dosage Forms

PENTAZOCINE HYDROCHLORIDE TABLETS USP

Note: Pentazocine hydrochloride tablets are not commercially available in the U.S.

Usual adult dose: Analgesic—Oral, 50 mg of pentazocine (base) every three to four hours as needed. The dose may be increased to 100 mg (base) if necessary, but total daily dosage should not exceed 600 mg (base).

Usual adult prescribing limits: Analgesic—Up to 600 mg of pentazocine (base) per day.

Auxiliary labeling:
- May cause drowsiness.
- Avoid alcoholic beverages.
- May be habit-forming.

PENTAZOCINE AND NALOXONE HYDROCHLORIDES TABLETS USP

Note: Pentazocine and naloxone hydrochlorides tablets are not commercially available in Canada.

Usual adult dose: Analgesic—Oral, 50 mg of pentazocine (base) every three to four hours as needed. The dose may be increased to 100 mg (base) if necessary, but total daily dosage should not exceed 600 mg (base).

Usual adult prescribing limits: Analgesic—Up to 600 mg of pentazocine (base) per day.

Auxiliary labeling:
- May cause drowsiness.
- Avoid alcoholic beverages.
- May be habit-forming.

Parenteral Dosage Forms

PENTAZOCINE LACTATE INJECTION USP

Usual adult dose:
  Analgesic—Intramuscular, intravenous, or subcutaneous, 30 mg (base) every three to four hours as needed.

Obstetrical analgesia—

    Intramuscular, 30 mg (base) as a single dose; or

    Intravenous, 20 mg (base) administered when contractions become regular and repeated two or three times at two- to three-hour intervals as needed.

Usual adult prescribing limits:

Up to 360 mg (base) daily.

As a single dose, up to 30 mg (base) intravenously or 60 mg (base) intramuscularly.

Auxiliary labeling:
- May cause drowsiness.
- Avoid alcoholic beverages.
- May be habit-forming.

PROPOXYPHENE

Summary of Differences

Pharmacology:

    Mechanism of action/effect—An opioid agonist analgesic; has agonist activity at the mu receptor.

    Equivalence—Dose therapeutically equivalent to 10 mg of intramuscular morphine too toxic to administer.

    Protein binding—High.

    Biotransformation—Metabolite norpropoxyphene is toxic.

    Half-life—

        Propoxyphene: 6–12 hours.

        Norpropoxyphene: 30–36 hours.

    Onset of action—Oral: 15–60 minutes.

    Time to peak concentration—Oral: 2–2.5 hours.

    Peak plasma concentration—0.05–0.1 mcg per mL.

    Time to peak effect—Oral: 2 hours.

    Duration of action (nontolerant patients only; decreases as tolerance develops during chronic therapy)—Oral: 4–6 hours.

    Elimination—Renal, <10% as unchanged propoxyphene; biliary.

Precautions:

    Drug interactions and/or related problems—

        Risk of convulsions if overdose of propoxyphene administered to amphetamine-treated patients.

        May increase effects of coumarin- or indandione-derivative anticoagulants.

        Concurrent use with carbamazepine not recommended because may decrease carbamazepine metabolism, leading to increased risk of toxicity.

        Effects may be decreased in patients who smoke because tobacco smoking increases propoxyphene metabolism.

    Laboratory value alterations—May elevate levels of enzymes in liver function tests.

Side/adverse effects:

    May be more likely than most opioid analgesics to cause convulsions.

    Hepatotoxicity has been reported.

    Has lower dependence liability than other opioid agonists.

    Withdrawal symptoms less severe than those produced by stronger opioid agonist analgesics.

Additional Dosing Information

See also *General Dosing Information.*

100 mg of propoxyphene napsylate are equivalent to 65 mg of propoxyphene hydrochloride.

Oral Dosage Forms

PROPOXYPHENE HYDROCHLORIDE CAPSULES USP

Usual adult dose: Analgesic—Oral, 65 mg every four hours as needed.

Usual adult prescribing limits: Up to 390 mg daily.

Auxiliary labeling:
- May cause drowsiness.
- Avoid alcoholic beverages.
- May be habit-forming.

PROPOXYPHENE HYDROCHLORIDE TABLETS

Note: Propoxyphene hydrochloride tablets are not commercially available in the U.S.

Usual adult dose: Analgesic—Oral, 65 mg every four hours as needed.

Usual adult prescribing limits: Analgesic—Oral, up to 390 mg daily.

Auxiliary labeling:
- May cause drowsiness.
- Avoid alcoholic beverages.
- May be habit-forming.

PROPOXYPHENE NAPSYLATE CAPSULES

Note: Propoxyphene napsylate capsules are not commercially available in the U.S.

Usual adult dose: Analgesic—Oral, 100 mg every four hours as needed.

Usual adult prescribing limits: Analgesic—Up to 600 mg daily.

Auxiliary labeling:
- May cause drowsiness.
- Avoid alcoholic beverages.
- May be habit-forming.

PROPOXYPHENE NAPSYLATE ORAL SUSPENSION USP

Note: Propoxyphene napsylate oral suspension is not commercially available in Canada.

Usual adult dose: Analgesic—Oral, 100 mg every four hours as needed.

Usual adult prescribing limits: Analgesic—Up to 600 mg daily.

Auxiliary labeling:
- Shake well.
- May cause drowsiness.
- Avoid alcoholic beverages.
- May be habit-forming.

PROPOXYPHENE NAPSYLATE TABLETS USP

Note: Propoxyphene napsylate tablets are not commercially available in Canada.

Usual adult dose: Analgesic—Oral, 100 mg every four hours as needed.

Usual adult prescribing limits: Analgesic—Up to 600 mg daily.

Auxiliary labeling:
- May cause drowsiness.
- Avoid alcoholic beverages.
- May be habit-forming.

Table 1. Pharmacology

Drug and Route*	Therapeutic Effects		
	Onset of Analgesic Action (min)	Peak Analgesic Effect (min)	Duration of Action Analgesic (hr)‡/ Antitussive (hr)
Butorphanol			
IM	10–30	30–60	3–4
IV	2–3	30	2–4
Codeine			
Oral	30–45	60–120	4/4–6
IM	10–30	30–60	4
SC	10–30		4
Hydrocodone			
Oral	10–30	30–60	4–6/4–6
Hydromorphone			
Oral	30	90–120	4
IM	15	30–60	4–5
IV	10–15	15–30	2–3
SC	15	30–90	4
Rectal			
Levorphanol			
Oral	10–60	90–120	4–5
IM		60	4–5
IV		Within 20	4–5
SC		60–90	4–5
Meperidine			
Oral	15	60–90	2–4
IM	10–15	30–50	2–4
IV	1	5–7	2–4
SC	10–15	30–50	2–4
Methadone			
Oral	30–60	90–120	4–6#
IM	10–20	60–120	4–5#
IV		15–30	3–4#
Morphine			
Oral			
Extended-release tablets			8–12
Other oral dosage forms	Slower than IM	60–120	4–5
IM	10–30	30–60	4–5
IV		20	4–5
SC	10–30	50–90	4–5
Epidural	15–60		Up to 24
Intrathecal	15–60		Up to 24
Rectal	20–60		
Nalbuphine			
IM	Within 15	60	3–6
IV	2–3	30	3–4
SC	Within 15		3–6

Table 1. Pharmacology *(continued)*

Drug and Route*	Therapeutic Effects		
	Onset of Analgesic Action (min)	Peak Analgesic Effect (min)	Duration of Action Analgesic (hr)‡/ Antitussive (hr)
Oxycodone			
Oral		60	3–4
Oxymorphone			
IM	10–15	30–90	3–6
IV	5–10	15–30	3–4
SC	10–20		3–6
Rectal	15–30	120	3–6
Pentazocine			
Oral	15–30	60–90	3
IM	15–20	30–60	2–3
IV	2–3	15–30	2–3
SC	15–20	30–60	2–3
Propoxyphene			
Oral	15–60	120	4–6

*IM=Intramuscular; IV=Intravenous; SC=Subcutaneous.

‡In nontolerant patients only. The first sign of tolerance is usually a decrease in the duration of adequate analgesia. Also, may be increased in geriatric patients because of decreased clearance rate.

#Increases with repeated dosing because of accumulation of drug and/or active metabolites.

Table 2. Drug Interactions and/or Related Problems

The following drug interactions and/or related problems have been selected on the basis of their potential clinical significance (possible mechanism in parentheses where appropriate)—not necessarily inclusive (» = major clinical significance):

Note: Combinations containing any of the following medications, depending on the amount present, may also interact with this medication.

Legend:
I = Codeine
II = Hydrocodone
III = Hydromorphone
IV = Levorphanol
V = Meperidine
VI = Methadone
VII = Morphine
VIII = Opium
IX = Oxycodone
X = Oxymorphone
XI = Propoxyphene
XII = Butorphanol
XIII = Nalbuphine
XIV = Pentazocine

Drug Interaction and/or Related Problem	Agonist											Agonist/Antagonist		
	I	II	III	IV	V	VI	VII	VIII	IX	X	XI	XII	XIII	XIV
Acidifiers, urinary, such as: Ammonium chloride; Ascorbic acid; Potassium or sodium phosphate (acidification of the urine by these medications increases methadone excretion, resulting in decreased methadone plasma concentrations; high doses of urinary acidifiers, such as several grams daily of ammonium chloride, may cause withdrawal symptoms in patients who are dependent on methadone)						✓								
» Alcohol or » CNS depression-producing medications, other (concurrent use with opioid analgesics may result in increased CNS depressant, respiratory depressant, and hypotensive effects; caution is recommended and dosage of one or both agents should be reduced. In addition, some phenothiazines increase, while others decrease, the effects of opioid analgesics used as adjuncts to anesthesia) (concurrent use with other CNS depressants having habituation potential may increase the risk of habituation)	✓	✓	✓	✓	✓		✓	✓	✓	✓		✓	✓	✓
Amphetamines (amphetamines may potentiate the analgesic effects of meperidine; however, concurrent use of the 2 medications is not recommended because the monoamine oxidase inhibiting effect of amphetamines may increase the risk of hypotension, severe respiratory depression, coma, convulsions, hyperpyrexia, vascular collapse, and death) (an overdose of propoxyphene may potentiate the CNS stimulating effects of amphetamines; fatal convulsions can result)					✓									
Anticholinergics or other medications with anticholinergic activity (concurrent use with opioid analgesics may result in increased risk of severe constipation, which may lead to paralytic ileus, and/or urinary retention)	✓	✓	✓	✓	✓	✓	✓					✓	✓	✓
Anticoagulants, coumarin- or indandione-derivative (meperidine and propoxyphene have been reported to increase the effects of these anticoagulants; although clinical significance has not been established, the possibility should be considered that adjustment of anticoagulant dosage based on prothrombin time determinations may be necessary during and following concurrent use)					✓						✓			

Table 2. Drug Interactions and/or Related Problems *(continued)*

Legend:
I = Codeine
II = Hydrocodone
III = Hydromorphone
IV = Levorphanol

Agonist
V = Meperidine
VI = Methadone
VII = Morphine

VIII = Opium
IX = Oxycodone
X = Oxymorphone
XI = Propoxyphene

Agonist/Antagonist
XII = Butorphanol
XIII = Nalbuphine
XIV = Pentazocine

Drug Interactions and/or Related Problems	I	II	III	IV	V	VI	VII	VIII	IX	X	XI	XII	XIII	XIV
Antidiarrheals, antiperistaltic, such as: Difenoxin and atropine; Diphenoxylate and atropine; Kaolin, pectin, belladonna alkaloids, and opium; Loperamide; Opium tincture; Paregoric (concurrent use with an opioid analgesic may increase the risk of severe constipation as well as central nervous system [CNS] depression)	✓	✓	✓	✓	✓	✓	✓	✓	✓	✓	✓	✓	✓	✓
Antihypertensives, especially ganglionic blockers such as guanadrel, guanethidine, and mecamylamine, or Diuretics or Hypotension-producing medications, other (hypotensive effects of these medications may be potentiated when used concurrently with opioid analgesics, leading to increased risk of orthostatic hypotension; patients should be monitored during concurrent use)	✓	✓	✓	✓	✓	✓	✓	✓	✓	✓	✓	✓	✓	✓
» **Buprenorphine** (buprenorphine is a partial mu-receptor agonist with high affinity for, and a slow rate of dissociation from, the mu receptor; if administered prior to another opioid agonist, it may reduce the therapeutic effects of the other opioid; in one study in opioid addicts receiving chronic administration of 8 mg of buprenorphine per day, the effects of large doses [up to 120 mg] of morphine were blocked during buprenorphine therapy and for at least 30 hours following the last dose of buprenorphine)	✓	✓	✓	✓	✓	✓	✓	✓	✓	✓	✓			
(buprenorphine may also have some antagonist activity at the kappa receptor; the possibility should be considered that it may also reduce the therapeutic effects of subsequently administered butorphanol, nalbuphine, or pentazocine)										✓		✓	✓	✓
(buprenorphine antagonizes the respiratory depressant effects of large doses of previously administered mu-receptor agonists; however, additive respiratory depression may occur if buprenorphine is administered in conjunction with low doses of other mu-receptor agonists or with kappa-receptor agonists)					✓	✓	✓	✓	✓	✓	✓	✓		✓
(buprenorphine may precipitate withdrawal symptoms in physically dependent patients who are chronically receiving potent mu-receptor agonists; however, because of its partial agonist activity, buprenorphine may partially suppress spontaneous withdrawal symptoms caused by abrupt discontinuation of these agonists)	✓			✓	✓	✓		✓	✓	✓				✓

Table 2. Drug Interactions and/or Related Problems *(continued)*

Legend:

	Agonist											Agonist/Antagonist		
	I = Codeine II = Hydrocodone III = Hydromorphone IV = Levorphanol				V = Meperidine VI = Methadone VII = Morphine			VIII = Opium IX = Oxycodone X = Oxymorphone XI = Propoxyphene				XII = Butorphanol XIII = Nalbuphine XIV = Pentazocine		
	I	II	III	IV	V	VI	VII	VIII	IX	X	XI	XII	XIII	XIV
Carbamazepine											✓			
Hydroxyzine		✓	✓	✓	✓	✓	✓	✓	✓	✓	✓		✓	✓
Metoclopramide		✓	✓	✓	✓	✓	✓	✓	✓	✓	✓		✓	✓
Monoamine oxidase (MAO) inhibitors	✓	✓	✓	✓	✓	✓	✓	✓	✓	✓	✓	✓	✓	✓
Naloxone	✓	✓	✓	✓	✓	✓	✓	✓	✓	✓	✓	✓	✓	✓
Naltrexone	✓	✓	✓	✓	✓	✓	✓	✓	✓	✓	✓	✓	✓	✓

» Carbamazepine
(concurrent use with propoxyphene may result in decreased carbamazepine metabolism and lead to increased carbamazepine blood concentration and toxicity; concurrent use is not recommended)

Hydroxyzine
(concurrent use with opioid analgesics may result in increased analgesia as well as increased CNS depressant and hypotensive effects)

Metoclopramide
(opioid analgesics may antagonize the effects of metoclopramide on gastrointestinal motility)

» Monoamine oxidase (MAO) inhibitors, including furazolidone, pargyline, and procarbazine
(concurrent use with meperidine has resulted in unpredictable, severe, and sometimes fatal reactions, including immediate excitation, sweating, rigidity, and severe hypertension, or, in some patients, hypotension, severe respiratory depression, coma, seizures, hyperpyrexia, and cardiovascular collapse; meperidine is contraindicated in patients who have received an MAO inhibitor within 14 to 21 days)

(other opioid analgesics may be used cautiously and in reduced dosage in patients receiving MAO inhibitors; however, it is recommended that a small test dose [1/4 of the usual dose] or several small incremental test doses over a period of several hours first be administered to permit observation of any interaction)

Naloxone
(antagonizes the analgesic, CNS, and respiratory depressant effects of opioid analgesics; however, larger doses may be required to reverse the effects of butorphanol, nalbuphine, pentazocine, or propoxyphene than are needed to reverse the effects of other opioids; also, because naloxone may precipitate withdrawal symptoms in physically dependent patients, dosage of naloxone should be carefully titrated when used to treat opioid overdosage in dependent patients)

» Naltrexone
(administration of naltrexone to a patient physically dependent on opioid drugs will precipitate withdrawal symptoms; symptoms may appear within 5 minutes of naltrexone administration, persist for up to 48 hours, and be difficult to reverse)

Table 2. Drug Interactions and/or Related Problems *(continued)*

Legend:

Agonist	Agonist/Antagonist
I = Codeine II = Hydrocodone III = Hydromorphone IV = Levorphanol V = Meperidine VI = Methadone VII = Morphine VIII = Opium IX = Oxycodone X = Oxymorphone XI = Propoxyphene	XII = Butorphanol XIII = Nalbuphine XIV = Pentazocine

Interaction	I	II	III	IV	V	VI	VII	VIII	IX	X	XI	XII	XIII	XIV
» **Naltrexone** *(continued)*														
(naltrexone blocks the therapeutic effects of opioids [i.e., analgesic, antidiarrheal, and antitussive]; naltrexone therapy should not be initiated in patients receiving these agents for therapeutic purposes; also, patients receiving naltrexone should be advised to use alternative medications when necessary)	✓	✓	✓	✓	✓	✓	✓	✓	✓	✓	✓	✓	✓	✓
(administration of increased doses of opioids to override naltrexone blockade of opioid receptors may result in increased and prolonged respiratory depression and/or circulatory collapse)	✓	✓	✓	✓	✓	✓	✓	✓	✓	✓	✓	✓	✓	✓
(naltrexone should be discontinued several days prior to elective surgery if administration of an opioid prior to, during, or following surgery is unavoidable)	✓	✓	✓	✓	✓	✓	✓	✓	✓	✓	✓	✓	✓	✓
(the efficacy of naltrexone in antagonizing opioid effects not mediated via opioid receptors [i.e., those that may be caused by histamine release, such as facial swelling, itching, generalized erythema, hives, and, to some extent, hypotension] has not been fully determined; naltrexone may not antagonize these effects completely)	✓	✓	✓	✓	✓	✓	✓	✓	✓	✓	✓	✓	✓	✓
Neuromuscular blocking agents and possibly other medications having some neuromuscular blocking activity														
(respiratory depressant effects of neuromuscular blockade may be additive to central respiratory depressant effects of opioid analgesics; increased or prolonged respiratory depression [apnea] or paralysis may occur but is of minor clinical significance if the patient is being mechanically ventilated; however, caution and careful monitoring of the patient are recommended during and following concurrent or sequential use, especially if there is a possibility of incomplete reversal of neuromuscular blockade postoperatively)	✓	✓	✓	✓	✓	✓	✓	✓	✓	✓	✓	✓	✓	✓
Nicotine chewing gum or Other smoking deterrents or Smoking, tobacco, or cessation of														
(tobacco smoking may increase the metabolism of propoxyphene leading to decreased therapeutic effects; also, smoking cessation by a patient receiving propoxyphene chronically may increase its effects)											✓			

Table 2. Drug Interactions and/or Related Problems (continued)

Legend:
I = Codeine
II = Hydrocodone
III = Hydromorphone
IV = Levorphanol
V = Meperidine
VI = Methadone
VII = Morphine
VIII = Opium
IX = Oxycodone
X = Oxymorphone
XI = Propoxyphene
XII = Butorphanol
XIII = Nalbuphine
XIV = Pentazocine

	Agonist											Agonist/Antagonist		
	I	II	III	IV	V	VI	VII	VIII	IX	X	XI	XII	XIII	XIV
Opioid agonist analgesics, including alfentanil, fentanyl, and sufentanil (additive CNS depressant, respiratory depressant, and hypotensive effects may occur if two or more opioid agonist analgesics are used concurrently)	✓	✓	✓	✓	✓	✓	✓	✓	✓	✓	✓			
(pentazocine and nalbuphine may partially antagonize the analgesic and CNS depressant effects of opioid agonists)													✓	✓
(in patients who are not physically dependent on opioid agonists, concurrent use of butorphanol, nalbuphine, or pentazocine may result in additive side effects)												✓	✓	✓
(in patients who are physically dependent on opioid agonists, nalbuphine and pentazocine may precipitate, and butorphanol will not prevent or attenuate, withdrawal symptoms)												✓	✓	✓
» Phenytoin, chronic use of, or Rifampin (these medications may increase methadone metabolism, probably via induction of hepatic microsomal enzyme activity, and may precipitate withdrawal symptoms in patients being treated for opioid dependence; methadone dosage adjustments may be necessary when phenytoin or rifampin therapy is initiated or discontinued)						✓								
» Zidovudine (morphine may competitively inhibit the hepatic glucuronidation and decrease the clearance of zidovudine; concurrent use should be avoided because the toxicity of either or both of these medications may be potentiated)							✓							

Table 3. Side/Adverse Effects*

The following side/adverse effects have been selected on the basis of their potential clinical significance (possible signs and symptoms in parentheses where appropriate)—not necessarily inclusive:

Legend:
I = Butorphanol
II = Codeine
III = Hydrocodone
IV = Hydromorphone
V = Levorphanol
VI = Meperidine
VII = Methadone
VIII = Morphine
IX = Nalbuphine
X = Opium
XI = Oxycodone
XII = Oxymorphone
XIII = Pentazocine
XIV = Propoxyphene

	I	II	III	IV	V	VI	VII	VIII	IX	X	XI	XII	XIII	XIV
Medical attention needed														
Allergic reaction (skin rash, hives, and/or itching†; swelling of face)	R (<1%)	L	R	R	R	R	R	L	L	R	R	R	L	L
Atelectasis; bronchospastic allergic reaction; laryngeal edema, allergic; laryngospasm, allergic; or respiratory depression‡ (shortness of breath, slow or irregular breathing, troubled breathing)	R (<1%)	L	L	L	L	L	L	L	R (<1%)	R	R	L	L	U
CNS stimulation, paradoxical (unusual excitement or restlessness)—especially in children	R	L	R	R	R	R	R	R	R	R	R	R	R	R
Confusion§—may include delusions and feelings of depersonalization or unreality	R (<1%)	L	L	L	L	L	L	L	R (<1%)	L	R	L	R	R
Convulsions	U	R	R	U	U	L	U	U	U	U	U	U	R	L
Fast, slow, or pounding heartbeat	R (<1%)	L	L	L	L	L	L	L	R (<1%)	R	U	L	L	U
Hallucinations§	R (<1%)	R	R	R	R	R	R	R	R (<1%)	R	R	R	U	R
Hepatotoxicity (dark urine, pale stools, yellow eyes or skin)	U	U	U	U	U	U	U	U	U	U	U	U	U	R
Histamine release (decreased blood pressure, fast heartbeat, increased sweating, redness or flushing of face, wheezing or troubled breathing)	L	L	M	L	R	M	M	M	M	L	L	L	L	L
Increased blood pressure	R (<1%)	U	R	U	U	U	U	U	R (<1%)	U	U	U	L	R
Mental depression	R (<1%)	R	R	R	R	R	R	R	R (<1%)	R	R	R	R	R
Muscle rigidity, especially in muscles of respiration—with large doses	U	R	R	U	U	U	U	R	U	U	U	U	U	R

*Differences in frequency of occurrence may reflect either lack of clinical-use data or actual pharmacologic distinctions among agents (although their pharmacologic similarity suggests that side effects occurring with one may occur with the others). M = more frequent; L = less frequent; R = rare; U =unknown.

†*Generalized or facial pruritus* may represent an opioid-induced dysesthesia rather than an allergic reaction, especially following epidural or intrathecal administration, and requires medical attention only if bothersome to the patient.

‡*Respiratory depression* induced by butorphanol, nalbuphine, and pentazocine differs from that due to other opioid analgesics in that the depth of respiratory depression is not increased with higher doses (ceiling effect); however, with butorphanol the duration of respiratory depression is increased with higher doses.

§Although these effects may occur with large doses of any opioid analgesic, with butorphanol, nalbuphine, and pentazocine they may be part of a group of subjective and psychotomimetic effects characteristic of opioids having sigma-receptor activity. These effects include *confusion, delusions, feelings of depersonalization or unreality, hallucinations* (usually visual), *dysphoria, nightmares, and nervousness or anxiety*. These effects generally occur with large doses of these drugs; although they occur rarely with any of them, they may be most likely to occur with pentazocine.

Table 3. Side/Adverse Effects* *(continued)*

Legend:
I = Butorphanol   V = Levorphanol   VIII = Morphine   XI = Oxycodone
II = Codeine   VI = Meperidine   IX = Nalbuphine   XII = Oxymorphone
III = Hydrocodone   VII = Methadone   X = Opium   XIII = Pentazocine
IV = Hydromorphone   XIV = Propoxyphene

	I	II	III	IV	V	VI	VII	VIII	IX	X	XI	XII	XIII	XIV
Paralytic ileus or toxic megacolon (severe constipation, bloating, nausea, stomach cramps or pain, vomiting)—in patients with inflammatory bowel disease	R	R	R	R	R	R	R	R	R	R	R	R	R	R
Ringing or buzzing in the ears	R	U	R	U	U	U	U	U	U	U	U	U	R	L
Trembling or uncontrolled muscle movements	U	R	R	L	U	L	U	L	U	L	U	U	R	L
Medical attention needed only if continuing or bothersome *Antidiuretic effect* (decreased urination)	L	L	L	L	L	L	L	L	R (<1%)	L	L	L	L	L
Biliary spasm (stomach cramps or pain)	U	R	R	L	L	L	L (<1%)	L	R (<1%)	R	U	L	R	R
Blurred or double vision or other changes in vision	R (<1%)	L	L	L	L	L	L	L	R (<1%)	L	U	L	L	L
Constipation	R	M	L	L	L	M	M	M	U	R	L	L	L	L
Dizziness, feeling faint, or lightheadedness—especially in ambulatory patients.	L	L	M	M	M	M	M	M	L	M	M	M	L	M
Drowsiness	M (40%)	M	M	M	M	M	M	M	M (36%)	M	M	M	M	M
Dry mouth	R (<1%)	L	L	L	L	L	L	L	L (4%)	L	L	L	L	L
False sense of well-being	R (<1%)	L	L	L	U	L	L	L	R (<1%)	L	U	L	M	L
Gastrointestinal irritation (stomach cramps or pain)	R	R	R	L	L	L	L	L	R	R	U	L	R	R
General feeling of discomfort or illness§	L	L	L	L	L	L	L	L	R (<1%)	L	L	L	L	L
Headache	L (3%)	L	L	L	L	L	L	L	L (3%)	L	L	L	L	L
Hypotension (dizziness, feeling faint, lightheadedness, unusual tiredness or weakness)—although hypotension may occur in recumbent patients, orthostatic hypotension commonly occurs in ambulatory patients	L	L	M	M	M	M	M	M	L	M	M	M	L	M

Table 3. Side/Adverse Effects* *(continued)*

	Legend: **I** = Butorphanol **II** = Codeine **III** = Hydrocodone **IV** = Hydromorphone				**V** = Levorphanol **VI** = Meperidine **VII** = Methadone			**VIII** = Morphine **IX** = Nalbuphine **X** = Opium			**XI** = Oxycodone **XII** = Oxymorphone **XIII** = Pentazocine **XIV** = Propoxyphene			
	I	**II**	**III**	**IV**	**V**	**VI**	**VII**	**VIII**	**IX**	**X**	**XI**	**XII**	**XIII**	**XIV**
Loss of appetite	L	L	L	M	L	L	L	L	L	R	U	R	R	R
Nausea or vomiting—occurs more frequently in ambulatory patients; are more frequent with initial doses, and are less likely to occur with subsequent doses	L (6%)	L	L	L	M	M	M	M	L (6%)	R	M	M	M	M
Nervousness or restlessness§	R (<1%)	L	L	L	L	L	L	L	R (<1%)	L	L	L	L	L
Nightmares or unusual dreams§	R (<1%)	R	R	U	U	L	U	U	R (<1%)	U	U	U	L	L
Redness, swelling, pain, or burning at site of injection	R	L	—	L	L	L	R	L	L	L	—	L	L	—
Unusual tiredness or weakness	L	L	M	M	M	M	M	M	L	M	M	M	L	M
Ureteral spasm (difficult or painful urination, frequent urge to urinate)	L	L	L	L	L	L	L	L	R (<1%)	L	L	L	L	L
Trouble in sleeping	R	R	R	R	R	R	L	R	R	R	R	R	R	R

*Differences in frequency of occurrence may reflect either lack of clinical-use data or actual pharmacologic distinctions among agents (although their pharmacologic similarity suggests that side effects occurring with one may occur with the others). M = more frequent; L = less frequent; R = rare; U =unknown.

†*Generalized or facial pruritus* may represent an opioid-induced dysesthesia rather than an allergic reaction, especially following epidural or intrathecal administration, and requires medical attention only if bothersome to the patient.

‡*Respiratory depression* induced by butorphanol, nalbuphine, and pentazocine differs from that due to other opioid analgesics in that the depth of respiratory depression is not increased with higher doses (ceiling effect); however, with butorphanol the duration of respiratory depression is increased with higher doses.

§Although these effects may occur with large doses of any opioid analgesic, with butorphanol, nalbuphine, and pentazocine they may be part of a group of subjective and psychotomimetic effects characteristic of opioids having sigma-receptor activity. These effects include *confusion, delusions, feelings of depersonalization or unreality, hallucinations* (usually visual), *dysphoria, nightmares, and nervousness or anxiety.* These effects generally occur with large doses of these drugs; although they occur rarely with any of them, they may be most likely to occur with

OPIOID (NARCOTIC) ANALGESICS AND ACETAMINOPHEN   Systemic

INN:
  Acetaminophen—Paracetamol
  Meperidine—Pethidine
  Propoxyphene—Dextropropoxyphene

Category: Analgesic.

Note: Opioid agonist analgesics—Codeine, Dihydrocodeine, Hydrocodone, Meperidine, Oxycodone, and Propoxyphene.
  Opioid agonist/antagonist analgesic—Pentazocine.

Indications

Accepted
Pain (treatment)—Indicated for the symptomatic relief of:
  Mild to moderate pain—Pentazocine and acetaminophen; propoxy-
    phene and acetaminophen.
  Mild to severe pain (depending on the dose of codeine)—Acetami-
    nophen and codeine.
  Moderate to moderately severe pain—Dihydrocodeine and acetami-
    nophen; hydrocodone and acetaminophen; oxycodone and ac-
    etaminophen.
  Moderate to severe pain—Meperidine and acetaminophen.

Patient Consultation

In providing consultation, consider emphasizing the following selected information (» = major clinical significance):

Before using this medication
» Conditions affecting use, especially:
    Sensitivity to acetaminophen or to opioid analgesic considered
      for use, history of
    Pregnancy—Acetaminophen and opioid analgesics cross the
      placenta; regular use of opioids by pregnant women may
      cause physical dependence in the fetus and withdrawal symp-
      toms in the neonate
    Breast-feeding—Acetaminophen, codeine, meperidine, and
      propoxyphene are excreted in breast milk
    Use in children—Children up to 2 years of age are more sus-
      ceptible to the effects of opioids, especially respiratory de-
      pression; also, children may be more likely to experience
      paradoxical CNS excitation during therapy
    Use in the elderly—Geriatric patients are more susceptible to
      the effects of opioids, especially respiratory depression
    Use by athletes—Opioids are banned and tested for in athletes
      by the U.S. Olympic Committee (USOC); caffeine (present
      in some formulations) is tested for in athletes by the USOC
      and the National Collegiate Athletic Association (NCAA);
      urine concentrations of caffeine above 12 mcg per mL
      (USOC) and 15 mcg per mL (NCAA) are considered unac-
      ceptable
    Other medications, especially alcohol or other CNS depres-
      sants, monoamine oxidase inhibitors, tricyclic antidepres-
      sants, zidovudine, and naltrexone
    Other medical problems, especially alcoholism (active or in
      remission), diarrhea caused by antibiotics or poisoning,
      asthma or other respiratory problems, hepatic disease, viral
      hepatitis, and severe inflammatory bowel disease

Proper use of this medication
» Importance of not taking more medication than the amount pre-
    scribed because of danger of overdose and habit-forming po-
    tential of opioid analgesics; also, acetaminophen may cause
    liver damage with long-term or high-dose use

» Not increasing dose if medication is less effective after a few
    weeks; checking with physician
» Missed dose (if on scheduled dosing): Taking as soon as possible;
    not taking if almost time for next dose; not doubling doses
» Proper storage

Precautions while using this medication
    Regular visits to physician to check progress during long-term or
      high-dose therapy
» Caution if other medications containing opioid analgesics or ac-
    etaminophen are used
» Avoiding use of alcohol or other central nervous system (CNS)
    depressants during therapy unless prescribed or otherwise ap-
    proved by physician
    Possibility that drinking large amounts of alcohol may increase
      risk of liver damage with acetaminophen
    Not regularly taking aspirin or other salicylates or other nonsteroi-
      dal anti-inflammatory analgesics concurrently, unless directed
      by physician or dentist
» Caution if dizziness, drowsiness, lightheadedness, or false sense of
    well-being occurs
    Caution when getting up suddenly from a lying or sitting position
    Lying down if nausea or vomiting, or dizziness or lightheadedness
      occurs
    Caution if any kind of surgery (including dental surgery) or emer-
      gency treatment is required
    Possible dryness of mouth; using sugarless gum or candy, ice, or
      saliva substitute for relief; checking with dentist if dry mouth
      continues for more than 2 weeks
» Checking with physician before discontinuing medication after
    prolonged use of high doses; gradual dosage reduction may be
    necessary to avoid withdrawal symptoms
» Suspected overdose: Getting emergency help at once

Side/adverse effects
    Signs of potential side effects, especially respiratory depression or
      impairment; allergic reactions; confusion, convulsions, halluci-
      nations, mental depression, or other signs of CNS toxicity;
      agranulocytosis; hepatotoxicity; hypertension; paradoxical CNS
      excitation, especially in children; renal function impairment;
      and thrombocytopenia

Oral Dosage Forms

ACETAMINOPHEN AND CODEINE PHOSPHATE CAPSULES USP

Note: Acetaminophen and codeine phosphate capsules are not commercially available in Canada.

  In Canada, *Phenaphen with Codeine* contains phenobarbital,
  aspirin, and codeine.

Usual adult dose: Analgesic—
  Oral, 1 or 2 capsules containing 325 mg of acetaminophen and 15
    or 30 mg of codeine phosphate every four hours as needed; or
  Oral, 1 capsule containing 325 mg of acetaminophen and 60 mg of
    codeine phosphate every four hours as needed.

Auxiliary labeling:
• May cause drowsiness.
• Avoid alcoholic beverages.
• May be habit-forming.

ACETAMINOPHEN AND CODEINE PHOSPHATE ELIXIR USP

Usual adult dose: Oral, 15 mL every four hours, as needed.

Auxiliary labeling:
- May cause drowsiness.
- Avoid alcoholic beverages.
- May be habit-forming.

ACETAMINOPHEN AND CODEINE PHOSPHATE ORAL SUSPENSION

Note: Acetaminophen and codeine phosphate oral suspension is not commercially available in Canada.

Usual adult dose: Analgesic—Oral, 15 mL every four hours, as needed.

Auxiliary labeling:
- May cause drowsiness.
- Avoid alcoholic beverages.
- Shake well.
- May be habit-forming.

ACETAMINOPHEN AND CODEINE PHOSPHATE TABLETS USP

Usual adult dose:

Oral, 1 or 2 tablets containing 300 mg of acetaminophen and 7.5, 15, or 30 mg of codeine phosphate every four hours as needed; or

Oral, 1 or 2 tablets containing 325 mg of acetaminophen and 15 or 30 mg of codeine phosphate every four hours as needed; or

Oral, 1 tablet containing 300 or 325 mg of acetaminophen and 60 mg of codeine phosphate every four hours as needed; or

Oral, 1 tablet containing 650 mg of acetaminophen and 30 mg of codeine phosphate every four hours as needed.

Auxiliary labeling:
- May cause drowsiness.
- Avoid alcoholic beverages.
- May be habit-forming.

ACETAMINOPHEN, CODEINE PHOSPHATE, AND CAFFEINE CAPSULES

Note: Acetaminophen, codeine phosphate, and caffeine capsules are not commercially available in the U.S.

Usual adult dose: Analgesic—Oral, one or two capsules every four hours as needed.

Auxiliary labeling:
- May cause drowsiness.
- Avoid alcoholic beverages.
- May be habit-forming.

ACETAMINOPHEN, CODEINE PHOSPHATE, AND CAFFEINE TABLETS

Usual adult dose: Oral, 1 or 2 tablets every four hours as needed.

Auxiliary labeling:
- May cause drowsiness.
- Avoid alcoholic beverages.
- May be habit-forming.

Oral Dosage Forms

DIHYDROCODEINE BITARTRATE, ACETAMINOPHEN, AND CAFFEINE CAPSULES

Note: Dihydrocodeine bitartrate, acetaminophen, and caffeine capsules are not commercially available in Canada.

Usual adult dose: Analgesic—Oral, 2 capsules every four hours.

Auxiliary labeling:
- May cause drowsiness.
- Avoid alcoholic beverages.
- May be habit-forming.

Oral Dosage Forms

HYDROCODONE BITARTRATE AND ACETAMINOPHEN CAPSULES

Note: Hydrocodone bitartrate and acetaminophen capsules are not commercially available in Canada.

Usual adult dose: Analgesic—Oral, one capsule every four to six hours, as needed. Dosage may be increased to two capsules every six hours if necessary.

Usual adult prescribing limits: Analgesic—Up to eight capsules per 24 hours.

Auxiliary labeling:
- May cause drowsiness.
- Avoid alcoholic beverages.
- May be habit-forming.

HYDROCODONE BITARTRATE AND ACETAMINOPHEN ORAL SOLUTION

Note: Hydrocodone bitartrate and acetaminophen oral solution is not commercially available in Canada.

Usual adult dose: Analgesic—Oral, 5 to 15 mL every four to six hours as needed.

Auxiliary labeling:
- May cause drowsiness.
- Avoid alcoholic beverages.
- May be habit-forming.

HYDROCODONE BITARTRATE AND ACETAMINOPHEN TABLETS

Note: Hydrocodone bitartrate and acetaminophen tablets are not commercially available in Canada.

Usual adult dose: Analgesic—

Oral, 1 or 2 tablets containing 2.5 mg of hydrocodone bitartrate and 500 mg of acetaminophen every four to six hours; or

Oral, 1 tablet containing 5 mg of hydrocodone bitartrate and 500 mg of acetaminophen every four to six hours as needed, with dosage being increased to 2 tablets every six hours if necessary; or

Oral, 1 tablet containing 7.5 mg of hydrocodone bitartrate and 650 mg of acetaminophen every four to six hours as needed, with dosage being increased to 2 tablets every six hours if necessary; or

Oral, 1 tablet containing 7.5 mg of hydrocodone bitartrate and 750 mg of acetaminophen every four to six hours as needed.

Usual adult prescribing limits: Up to 40 mg of hydrocodone bitartrate and 4 grams of acetaminophen in twenty-four hours.

Auxiliary labeling:
- May cause drowsiness.
- Avoid alcoholic beverages.
- May be habit-forming.

Oral Dosage Forms

MEPERIDINE HYDROCHLORIDE AND ACETAMINOPHEN TABLETS

Note: Meperidine hydrochloride and acetaminophen tablets are not commercially available in Canada.

Usual adult dose: Analgesic—Oral, one or two tablets every three to four hours as needed.

Auxiliary labeling:
- May cause drowsiness.
- Avoid alcoholic beverages.
- May be habit-forming.

Oral Dosage Forms

OXYCODONE AND ACETAMINOPHEN CAPSULES USP

Note: Oxycodone and acetaminophen capsules are not commercially available in Canada.

Usual adult dose: Analgesic—Oral, one capsule every four to six hours as needed.

Auxiliary labeling:
- May cause drowsiness.
- Avoid alcoholic beverages.
- May be habit-forming.

OXYCODONE AND ACETAMINOPHEN ORAL SOLUTION

Note: Oxycodone and acetaminophen oral solution is not commercially available in Canada.

Usual adult dose: Analgesic—Oral, 5 mL every four to six hours as needed.

Auxiliary labeling:
- May cause drowsiness.
- Avoid alcoholic beverages.
- May be habit-forming.

OXYCODONE AND ACETAMINOPHEN TABLETS USP

Usual adult dose: Oral, one tablet every four to six hours as needed.

Auxiliary labeling:
- May cause drowsiness.
- Avoid alcoholic beverages.
- May be habit-forming.

Oral Dosage Forms

PENTAZOCINE HYDROCHLORIDE AND ACETAMINOPHEN TABLETS

Note: Pentazocine hydrochloride and acetaminophen tablets are not commercially available in Canada.

Usual adult dose: Analgesic—Oral, 1 tablet every four hours.

Usual adult prescribing limits: Up to 6 tablets daily.

Auxiliary labeling:
- May cause drowsiness.
- Avoid alcoholic beverages.
- May be habit-forming.

Oral Dosage Forms

PROPOXYPHENE HYDROCHLORIDE AND ACETAMINOPHEN CAPSULES

Note: Propoxyphene hydrochloride and acetaminophen capsules are not commercially available in Canada.

Usual adult dose: Analgesic—Oral, 65 mg of propoxyphene with 650 mg of acetaminophen every four hours, as needed.

Auxiliary labeling:
- May cause drowsiness.
- Avoid alcoholic beverages.
- May be habit-forming.

PROPOXYPHENE HYDROCHLORIDE AND ACETAMINOPHEN TABLETS USP

Note: Propoxyphene hydrochloride and acetaminophen tablets are not commercially available in Canada.

Usual adult dose: Analgesic—Oral, 65 mg of propoxyphene with 650 mg of acetaminophen every four hours, as needed.

Auxiliary labeling:
- May cause drowsiness.
- Avoid alcoholic beverages.
- May be habit-forming.

PROPOXYPHENE NAPSYLATE AND ACETAMINOPHEN TABLETS USP

Note: Propoxyphene napsylate and acetaminophen tablets are not commercially available in Canada.

Usual adult dose: Analgesic—Oral, 100 mg of propoxyphene napsylate and 650 mg of acetaminophen every four hours, as needed.

Auxiliary labeling:
- May cause drowsiness.
- Avoid alcoholic beverages.
- May be habit-forming.

OPIOID (NARCOTIC) ANALGESICS AND ASPIRIN   Systemic

INN: Propoxyphene—Dextropropoxyphene

Category: Analgesic.

Note: Opioid agonist analgesics—Codeine, dihydrocodeine, hydrocodone, oxycodone, and propoxyphene.
Opioid agonist/antagonist analgesic—Pentazocine.

Indications

Accepted

Pain (treatment)—Indicated for symptomatic relief of:
Mild to severe pain (depending on the dose of codeine)—Aspirin and codeine; buffered aspirin and codeine.
Mild to moderate pain—Propoxyphene and aspirin.
Moderate pain—Pentazocine and aspirin.
Moderate to moderately severe pain—Aspirin and dihydrocodeine; oxycodone and aspirin.
Moderate to severe pain—Hydrocodone and aspirin.

Patient Consultation

In providing consultation, consider emphasizing the following selected information (» = major clinical significance):

Before using this medication
» Conditions affecting use, especially:
Sensitivity to the opioid considered for use, to aspirin, or to nonsteroidal anti-inflammatory drugs (NSAIDs), history of
Pregnancy—Aspirin and opioid analgesics cross the placenta; high-dose chronic use or abuse of aspirin in the third trimester may be hazardous to the mother as well as the fetus and/or neonate, causing heart problems in fetus or neonate and/or bleeding in mother, fetus, or neonate; high-dose chronic use or abuse may also prolong and complicate labor and delivery; also, regular use of opioids by pregnant women may cause physical dependence in the fetus and withdrawal symptoms in the neonate; not taking aspirin during the third trimester unless prescribed by physician

Breast-feeding—Aspirin, codeine, and propoxyphene are excreted in breast milk

Use in children and teenagers—Checking with physician before giving to children or teenagers with symptoms of acute febrile illness, especially influenza or varicella, because of the risk of Reye's syndrome; also, increased susceptibility to aspirin toxicity in children, especially with fever and dehydration; also, children up to 2 years of age are more susceptible to the effects of opioids, especially respiratory depression; in addition, children may be more likely to experience opioid-induced paradoxical CNS excitation during therapy

Use in the elderly—Increased risk of aspirin toxicity and of opioid-induced adverse effects, especially respiratory depression

Use by athletes—Opioid analgesics are banned and tested for in athletes by the U.S. Olympic Committee (USOC). Also, the caffeine in some of these formulations is tested for in athletes by the USOC and the National Collegiate Athletic Association (NCAA); urine concentrations of caffeine above 12 mcg per mL (USOC) and 15 mcg per mL (NCAA) are considered unacceptable

Other medications, especially alcohol or other CNS depressants, anticoagulants, antidiabetic agents (oral), those cephalosporins that may cause hypoprothrombinemia, methotrexate, monoamine oxidase inhibitors, moxalactam, naltrexone, NSAIDs, platelet aggregation inhibitors, plicamycin, probenecid, sulfinpyrazone, urinary alkalizers, valproic acid, vancomycin, and zidovudine

Other medical problems, especially coagulation or platelet function disorders, diarrhea caused by antibiotics or poisoning, asthma or other respiratory problems, and gastrointestinal problems such as ulceration or erosive gastritis (especially a bleeding ulcer) or other severe inflammatory bowel disease

Proper use of this medication

» Taking with food or a full glass (240 mL) of water to minimize stomach irritation

» Not taking medication if it has a strong vinegar-like odor

» Importance of not taking more medication than the amount prescribed because of danger of overdose of aspirin or opioid analgesics and habit-forming potential of opioid analgesics

» Not increasing dose if medication seems less effective after a few weeks; checking with physician instead

» Missed dose (if on scheduled dosing): Taking as soon as possible; not taking if almost time for next dose; not doubling doses

» Proper storage

Precautions while using this medication

Regular visits to physician to check progress during long-term therapy

» Caution if other medications containing aspirin or other salicylates or opioid analgesics are used

» Avoiding use of alcohol or other central nervous system (CNS) depressants during therapy unless prescribed or otherwise approved by physician; also, alcohol consumption may increase risk of aspirin-induced stomach problems

Not taking acetaminophen or ibuprofen or other nonsteroidal antiinflammatory analgesics concurrently for more than a few days unless directed by physician or dentist

» Caution if dizziness, drowsiness, lightheadedness, or false sense of well-being occurs

Caution when getting up suddenly from a lying or sitting position

Lying down if nausea or vomiting, or dizziness or lightheadedness occurs

Need to inform physician or dentist of use of medication if any kind of surgery (including dental surgery) or emergency treatment is required

Caution if any kind of surgery is required; aspirin should be discontinued 5 days prior to surgery unless otherwise directed by physician or dentist

Not taking a tetracycline antibiotic within 1 to 2 hours of buffered formulations

Diabetics: Aspirin may cause false urine sugar test results with prolonged use of 8 or more 325-mg (5-grain), or 4 or more 650-mg (10-grain), doses per day

Possible dryness of mouth; using sugarless gum or candy, ice, or saliva substitute for relief; checking with dentist if dry mouth continues for more than 2 weeks

» Checking with physician before discontinuing medication after prolonged use of high doses; gradual dosage reduction may be necessary to avoid withdrawal symptoms

» Suspected overdose: Getting emergency help at once

Side/adverse effects

Signs of potential side effects, especially respiratory depression or impairment; allergic reactions; confusion, convulsions, hallucinations, mental depression, or other signs of CNS toxicity; gastrointestinal toxicity; hepatotoxicity; hypertension, and paradoxical CNS excitation, especially in children

Oral Dosage Forms

ASPIRIN AND CODEINE PHOSPHATE TABLETS USP

Usual adult dose: Oral, 1 or 2 tablets every four hours as needed.

Auxiliary labeling:
• May cause drowsiness.
• Avoid alcoholic beverages.
• Take with food or with a full glass of water.
• May be habit-forming.

ASPIRIN, CODEINE PHOSPHATE, AND CAFFEINE TABLETS USP

Note: Aspirin, codeine phosphate, and caffeine tablets are not commercially available in the U.S.

Usual adult dose: Analgesic—Oral, one or two tablets every four hours as needed.

Auxiliary labeling:
• May cause drowsiness.
• Avoid alcoholic beverages.
• Take with food or with a full glass of water.
• May be habit-forming.

Oral Dosage Forms

ASPIRIN, CODEINE PHOSPHATE, CAFFEINE, ALUMINA, AND MAGNESIA TABLETS

Note: Aspirin, codeine phosphate, caffeine, alumina, and magnesia tablets are not commercially available in the U.S.

Usual adult dose: Analgesic—Oral, one or two tablets every four hours as needed.

Auxiliary labeling:
• May cause drowsiness.
• Avoid alcoholic beverages.
• Take with food or with a full glass of water.
• May be habit-forming.

Oral Dosage Forms

ASPIRIN, CAFFEINE, AND DIHYDROCODEINE CAPSULES USP

Note: Dihydrocodeine, aspirin, and caffeine capsules are not commercially available in Canada.

Usual adult dose: Analgesic—Oral, 2 capsules every four hours as needed.

Auxiliary labeling:
- May cause drowsiness.
- Avoid alcoholic beverages.
- Take with food or with a full glass of water.
- May be habit-forming.

Oral Dosage Forms

HYDROCODONE BITARTRATE AND ASPIRIN TABLETS

Note: Hydrocodone bitartrate and aspirin tablets are not commercially available in Canada.

Usual adult dose: Analgesic—Oral, 1 or 2 tablets every four to six hours as needed.

Auxiliary labeling:
- May cause drowsiness.
- Avoid alcoholic beverages.
- Take with food or with a full glass of water.
- May be habit-forming.

HYDROCODONE BITARTRATE, ASPIRIN, AND CAFFEINE TABLETS

Note: Hydrocodone bitartrate, aspirin, and caffeine tablets are not commercially available in Canada.

Usual adult dose: Analgesic—Oral, 1 or 2 tablets every four to six hours as needed.

Auxiliary labeling:
- May cause drowsiness.
- Avoid alcoholic beverages.
- Take with food or with a full glass of water.
- May be habit-forming.

Oral Dosage Forms

OXYCODONE AND ASPIRIN TABLETS USP

Usual adult dose: Analgesic—Oral, 1 or 2 half-strength tablets or 1 full-strength tablet, every four to six hours as needed. Dosage may be increased if necessary for severe pain.

Auxiliary labeling:
- May cause drowsiness.
- Avoid alcoholic beverages.
- Take with food or with a full glass of water.
- May be habit-forming.

Oral Dosage Forms

PENTAZOCINE HYDROCHLORIDE AND ASPIRIN TABLETS USP

Note: Pentazocine hydrochloride and aspirin tablets are not commercially available in Canada.

Usual adult dose: Analgesic—Oral, 2 tablets three or four times a day as needed.

Auxiliary labeling:
- May cause drowsiness.
- Avoid alcoholic beverages.
- Take with food or with a full glass of water.
- May be habit-forming.

Oral Dosage Forms

PROPOXYPHENE HYDROCHLORIDE AND ASPIRIN CAPSULES

Note: Propoxyphene hydrochloride and aspirin capsules are not commercially available in Canada.

Usual adult dose: Analgesic—Oral, 1 capsule every four hours, as needed.

Usual adult prescribing limits: Up to 6 capsules a day.

Auxiliary labeling:
- May cause drowsiness.
- Avoid alcoholic beverages.
- Take with food or with a full glass of water.
- May be habit-forming.

PROPOXYPHENE HYDROCHLORIDE, ASPIRIN, AND CAFFEINE CAPSULES USP

Usual adult dose: Oral, 1 capsule every four hours, as needed.

Usual adult prescribing limits: Up to 390 mg of propoxyphene hydrochloride a day.

Auxiliary labeling:
- May cause drowsiness.
- Avoid alcoholic beverages.
- Take with food or with a full glass of water.
- May be habit-forming.

PROPOXYPHENE HYDROCHLORIDE, ASPIRIN, AND CAFFEINE TABLETS

Note: Propoxyphene hydrochloride, aspirin, and caffeine tablets are not commercially available in the U.S.

Usual adult dose: Analgesic—Oral, 1 tablet every four hours, as needed.

Usual adult prescribing limits: Up to 390 mg of propoxyphene hydrochloride a day.

Auxiliary labeling:
- May cause drowsiness.
- Avoid alcoholic beverages.
- Take with food or with a full glass of water.
- May be habit-forming.

PROPOXYPHENE NAPSYLATE AND ASPIRIN CAPSULES

Note: Propoxyphene napsylate and aspirin capsules are not commercially available in the U.S.

Usual adult dose: Analgesic—Oral, 1 capsule every four hours, as needed.

Usual adult prescribing limits: Up to 600 mg of propoxyphene napsylate a day.

Auxiliary labeling:
- May cause drowsiness.
- Avoid alcoholic beverages.
- Take with food or with a full glass of water.
- May be habit-forming.

PROPOXYPHENE NAPSYLATE AND ASPIRIN TABLETS USP

Note: Propoxyphene napsylate and aspirin tablets are not commercially available in Canada.

Usual adult dose: Analgesic—Oral, 1 tablet every four hours, as needed.

Usual adult prescribing limits: Up to 600 mg of propoxyphene napsylate a day.

Auxiliary labeling:
- May cause drowsiness.
- Avoid alcoholic beverages.
- Take with food or with a full glass of water.
- May be habit-forming.

PROPOXYPHENE NAPSYLATE, ASPIRIN, AND CAFFEINE CAPSULES

Note: Propoxyphene napsylate, aspirin, and caffeine capusles are not commercially available in the U.S.

Usual adult dose: Analgesic—Oral, 1 tablet every four hours, as needed.

Usual adult prescribing limits: Up to 600 mg of propoxyphene napsylate a day.

Auxiliary labeling:
- May cause drowsiness.
- Avoid alcoholic beverages.
- Take with food or with a full glass of water.
- May be habit-forming.

OXTRIPHYLLINE AND GUAIFENESIN   Systemic

Category: Bronchodilator.

Indications

Accepted
Asthma, bronchial (treatment);

Bronchitis (treatment);

Emphysema, pulmonary (treatment); or

Pulmonary disease, chronic obstructive, other (treatment)—Oxtriphylline and guaifenesin combination is indicated as an adjunct in the management of bronchitis, pulmonary emphysema, and similar chronic obstructive lung diseases.

Patient Consultation

In providing consultation, consider emphasizing the following selected information (» = major clinical significance):

Before using this medication
» Conditions affecting use, especially:

Sensitivity to oxtriphylline or other xanthines

Mutagenicity—Theophylline reported to cause chromosomal breakage in human cells in culture at concentrations up to 50 times maximum therapeutic serum concentration

Pregnancy—Studies in mice have shown theophylline to cause teratogenic effects when given in doses 30 times the human dose (FDA Pregnancy Category C); use during pregnancy may result in potentially dangerous serum theophylline and caffeine concentrations in neonates; tachycardia, jitteriness, irritability, gagging, and vomiting reported in some neonates; neonates of mothers taking theophylline during pregnancy should be monitored for signs of theophylline toxicity

Breast-feeding—Theophylline excreted in breast milk; use of oxtriphylline by nursing mothers may cause irritability, fretfulness, or insomnia in infants

Use in children—Possible decreased plasma clearance and increased serum concentrations and/or toxicity in neonates, especially premature neonates; repeated doses should not be given if heart rate greater than 80 beats per minute

Use in the elderly—Possible decreased plasma clearance and increased potential for toxicity in patients over 55 years of age

Other medications, especially beta-adrenergic blocking agents, cimetidine, ciprofloxacin, erythromycin, nicotine chewing gum, norfloxacin, phenytoin, ranitidine, troleandomycin, or smoking tobacco or marijuana

Other medical problems, especially active gastritis or active or history of peptic ulcer

Proper use of this medication
» Taking on empty stomach with a glass of water for faster absorption or, if necessary, taking with meals or immediately after meals to lessen gastrointestinal irritation

» Importance of not taking more medication than the amount prescribed

» Compliance with therapy; not missing any doses

Missed dose: Taking as soon as possible; not taking if almost time for next dose; not doubling doses

» Proper storage

Precautions while using this medication

Regular visits to physician to check progress during initial period of therapy

» Caution in eating or drinking large amounts of xanthine-containing foods or beverages during therapy with this medication

Not eating charcoal-broiled foods daily because of possible decrease in effects of medication

» Notifying physician immediately if symptoms of influenza, a fever, or diarrhea occur because of possible need to alter dosage

Side/adverse effects
Signs of potential side effects, especially gastroesophageal reflux

Oral Dosage Forms

Note: The dose of oxtriphylline and guaifenesin combination should be determined on the basis of the anhydrous theophylline content of the oxtriphylline component.

OXTRIPHYLLINE AND GUAIFENESIN ELIXIR

Usual adult dose:

Acute attack—

Loading dose:

For patients *not* currently receiving theophylline preparations—Oral, the equivalent of 5 to 6 mg of anhydrous theophylline per kg of body weight.

For patients currently receiving theophylline preparations—A serum theophylline measurement should be obtained immediately if possible. The loading dose for theophylline is based on the principle that each 0.5 mg of theophylline per kg of lean (ideal) body weight will result in a 1 (range, 0.5 to 1.6) mcg per mL increase in serum theophylline concentration. If a serum theophylline measurement cannot be obtained rapidly and the patient's condition requires immediate therapy, a single dose of the equivalent of 2.5 mg of anhydrous theophylline per kg of body weight may be administered if there are no symptoms of theophylline toxicity.

Maintenance (in acute attack):
Young adult smokers—Oral, the equivalent of anhydrous theophylline: 4 mg per kg of body weight every six hours.
Otherwise healthy nonsmoking adults—Oral, the equivalent of anhydrous theophylline: 3 mg per kg of body weight every eight hours.
Older patients and patients with cor pulmonale—Oral, the equivalent of anhydrous theophylline: 2 mg per kg of body weight every eight hours.
Patients with congestive heart failure or liver failure—Oral, the equivalent of anhydrous theophylline: 2 mg per kg of body weight every twelve hours.

Note: **To achieve optimal therapeutic theophylline dosage, and minimize the risk of toxicity, monitoring of serum theophylline concentration and patient response is recommended.**

In patients with cor pulmonale, congestive heart failure, or liver failure, dosage should not exceed the equivalent of 400 mg of anhydrous theophylline per day unless serum theophylline concentrations can be monitored at twenty-four-hour intervals.

Chronic therapy—Oral, the equivalent of anhydrous theophylline: Initially, 6 to 8 mg per kg of body weight, up to a maximum of 400 mg, per day in three or four divided doses at six- to eight-hour intervals. The dosage may be increased, if tolerated, in approximately 25% increments at two- to three-day intervals, up to a maximum dose of 13 mg per kg of body weight or 900 mg per day, whichever is less, without measurement of serum concentration.

Note: If the above maximum dose in chronic therapy is to be maintained or exceeded, serum theophylline measurement is recommended. Final dosage adjustment is based on subsequent serum theophylline measurements and patient response.

Auxiliary labeling: • Keep container tightly closed.

OXTRIPHYLLINE AND GUAIFENESIN TABLETS

Usual adult dose:
Acute attack—
Loading dose:
For patients *not* currently receiving theophylline preparations—Oral, the equivalent of 5 to 6 mg of anhydrous theophylline per kg of body weight.
For patients currently receiving theophylline preparations—A serum theophylline measurement should be obtained immediately if possible. The loading dose for theophylline is based on the principle that each 0.5 mg of theophylline per kg of lean (ideal) body weight will result in

a 1 (range, 0.5 to 1.6) mcg per mL increase in serum theophylline concentration. If a serum theophylline measurement cannot be obtained rapidly and the patient's condition requires immediate therapy, a single dose of the equivalent of 2.5 mg of anhydrous theophylline per kg of body weight may be administered if there are no symptoms of theophylline toxicity.

Maintenance (in acute attack):
Young adult smokers—Oral, the equivalent of anhydrous theophylline: 4 mg per kg of body weight every six hours.
Otherwise healthy nonsmoking adults—Oral, the equivalent of anhydrous theophylline: 3 mg per kg of body weight every eight hours.
Older patients and patients with cor pulmonale—Oral, the equivalent of anhydrous theophylline: 2 mg per kg of body weight every eight hours.
Patients with congestive heart failure or liver failure—Oral, the equivalent of anhydrous theophylline: 2 mg per kg of body weight every twelve hours.

Note: **To achieve optimal therapeutic theophylline dosage, and minimize the risk of toxicity, monitoring of serum theophylline concentration and patient response is recommended.**

In patients with cor pulmonale, congestive heart failure, or liver failure, dosage should not exceed the equivalent of 400 mg of anhydrous theophylline per day unless serum theophylline concentrations can be monitored at twenty-four-hour intervals.

Chronic therapy—Oral, the equivalent of anhydrous theophylline: Initially, 6 to 8 mg per kg of body weight, up to a maximum of 400 mg, per day in three or four divided doses at six- to eight-hour intervals. The dosage may be increased, if tolerated, in approximately 25% increments at two- to three-day intervals, up to a maximum dose of 13 mg per kg of body weight or 900 mg per day, whichever is less, without measurement of serum concentration.

Note: If the above maximum dose in chronic therapy is to be maintained or exceeded, serum theophylline measurement is recommended. Final dosage adjustment is based on subsequent serum theophylline measurements and patient response.

OXYMETAZOLINE　Nasal

Some commonly used *brand names* are:

In the U.S.—

Afrin Children's Strength 12 Hour Nose Drops	*Neo-Synephrine 12 Hour Nasal Spray Pump*
Afrin Children's Strength Nose Drops	*Neo-Synephrine 12 Hour Nose Drops*
Afrin 12 Hour Nasal Spray	*Neo-Synephrine 12 Hour Vapor Nasal Spray*
Afrin 12 Hour Nose Drops	*Nostrilla 12 Hour Nasal Decongestant*
Afrin Menthol Nasal Spray	
Afrin Nasal Spray	*Nostril Nasal Decongestant Mild*
Afrin Nasal Spray Pump	
Afrin Nose Drops	*Nostril Nasal Decongestant Regular*
Allerest 12 Hour Nasal Spray	*NTZ Long Acting Decongestant Nasal Spray*
Coricidin Nasal Mist	
Dristan Long Lasting Menthol Nasal Spray	*NTZ Long Acting Decongestant Nose Drops*
Dristan Long Lasting Nasal Pump Spray	*Sinarest 12 Hour Nasal Spray*
Dristan Long Lasting Nasal Spray	*Vicks Sinex 12-Hour Formula Decongestant Nasal Spray*
Dristan Long Lasting Nasal Spray 12 Hour Metered Dose Pump	*Vicks Sinex 12-Hour Formula Decongestant Ultra Fine Mist*
Duramist Plus Up To 12 Hours Decongestant Nasal Spray	*Vicks Sinex Long-Acting 12 Hour Nasal Spray*
Duration 12 Hour Nasal Spray Pump	*4-Way Long Acting Nasal Spray*
Neo-Synephrine 12 Hour Nasal Spray	

In Canada—

Nafrine Decongestant Nasal Drops	*Nafrine Decongestant Pediatric Nasal Spray/Drops*
Nafrine Decongestant Nasal Spray	

NASAL
Oxymetazoline Hydrochloride Nasal Solution USP

In the U.S.—*Afrin Children's Strength 12 Hour Nose Drops; Afrin Children's Strength Nose Drops; Afrin 12 Hour Nasal Spray; Afrin 12 Hour Nose Drops; Afrin Menthol Nasal Spray; Afrin Nasal Spray; Afrin Nasal Spray Pump; Afrin Nose Drops; Allerest 12 Hour Nasal Spray; Coricidin Nasal Mist; Dristan Long Lasting Menthol Nasal Spray; Dristan Long Lasting Nasal Pump Spray; Dristan Long Lasting Nasal Spray; Dristan Long Lasting Nasal Spray 12 Hour Metered Dose Pump; Duramist Plus Up To 12 Hours Decongestant Nasal Spray; Duration 12 Hour Nasal Spray Pump; Neo-Synephrine 12 Hour Nasal Spray; Neo-Synephrine 12 Hour Nasal Spray Pump; Neo-Synephrine 12 Hour Nose Drops; Neo-Synephrine 12 Hour Vapor Nasal Spray; Nostrilla 12 Hour Nasal Decongestant; Nostril Nasal Decongestant Mild; Nostril Nasal Decongestant Regular; NTZ Long Acting Decongestant Nose Drops; NTZ Long Acting Decongestant Nasal Spray; Sinarest 12 Hour Nasal Spray; Vicks Sinex 12-Hour Formula Decongestant Nasal Spray; Vicks Sinex 12-Hour Formula Decongestant Ultra Fine Mist; Vicks Sinex Long-Acting 12 Hour Nasal Spray; 4-Way Long Acting Nasal Spray*

In Canada—*Nafrine Decongestant Nasal Drops; Nafrine Decongestant Nasal Spray; Nafrine Decongestant Pediatric Nasal Spray/Drops*

Category: Decongestant (topical).

Indications

Note: Bracketed information in the *Indications* section refers to uses not included in U.S. product labeling.

Accepted

Congestion, nasal (treatment)—Oxymetazoline is indicated for temporary relief of nasal congestion due to the common cold, sinusitis, hay fever, or other upper respiratory allergies.

[Congestion, sinus (treatment)]—Nasal oxymetazoline is also used for the relief of sinus congestion.

Pharmacology

Mechanism of action/Effect: Oxymetazoline is a direct-acting sympathomimetic amine. It acts on alpha-adrenergic receptors in the arterioles of the nasal mucosa to produce constriction, resulting in decreased blood flow and decreased nasal congestion.

Precautions to Consider

Cross-sensitivity and/or related problems

Patients sensitive to other nasal decongestants may be sensitive to this medication also.

Geriatrics

Although appropriate studies with oxymetazoline have not been performed in the geriatric population, no geriatrics-specific problems have been documented to date.

Drug interactions and/or related problems

The following drug interactions and/or related problems have been selected on the basis of their potential clinical significance (possible mechanism in parentheses where appropriate)—not necessarily inclusive (» = major clinical significance):

Note: Combinations containing any of the following medications, depending on the amount present, may also interact with this medication.

Antidepressants, tricyclic, or
Maprotiline
　(if significant systemic absorption of nasal oxymetazoline occurs, concurrent use of maprotiline or tricyclic antidepressants may potentiate the pressor effect of oxymetazoline)

Contraindications/Medical problems

The contraindications/medical problems included have been selected on the basis of their potential clinical significance (reasons given in parentheses where appropriate)—not necessarily inclusive (» = major clinical significance).

Risk-benefit should be considered when the following medical problems exist:

Coronary artery disease or
Heart disease, including angina, or
Hypertension
　(condition may be exacerbated due to drug-induced cardiovascular effects)

Diabetes mellitus

Hyperthyroidism

Sensitivity to oxymetazoline or other nasal decongestants

Side/Adverse Effects

The following side/adverse effects have been selected on the basis of their potential clinical significance (possible signs and symptoms in parentheses where appropriate)—not necessarily inclusive:

Those indicating need for medical attention
> *Rebound congestion* (increase in runny or stuffy nose)

Symptoms of systemic absorption
> *Fast, irregular, or pounding heartbeat; headache or lightheadedness; nervousness; trembling; trouble in sleeping*

Those indicating need for medical attention only if they continue or are bothersome
> *Burning, dryness, or stinging of nasal mucosa; sneezing*

Patient Consultation

In providing consultation, consider emphasizing the following selected information (» = major clinical significance):

Before using this medication
> » Conditions affecting use, especially:
>> Sensitivity to oxymetazoline or other nasal decongestants
>> Use in children—Children may be especially sensitive to the effects of oxymetazoline

Proper use of this medication
> Proper administration technique
> Preventing contamination: Wiping tip of applicator with clean, damp tissue; replacing cap right after use
> Preventing spread of infection: Not using bottle for more than 1 person

> » Importance of not using more medication than the amount recommended
> Missed dose: If on scheduled dosing regimen—Using right away if remembered within an hour or so; if not remembered until later, skipping missed dose and returning to regular dosing schedule; not doubling doses
> » Proper storage

Side/adverse effects
> Signs of potential side effects, especially rebound congestion or systemic sympathomimetic effects

General Dosing Information

Prolonged or excessive use of this medication will cause rebound congestion with chronic swelling of nasal mucosa.

Nasal Dosage Forms

OXYMETAZOLINE HYDROCHLORIDE NASAL SOLUTION USP

Usual adult and adolescent dose: Intranasal, 2 or 3 drops or sprays of a 0.05% solution into each nostril two times a day, morning and evening.

Note: The nasal spray form of the medication is more effective and less likely to cause systemic absorption.

Auxiliary labeling: • For the nose.

PANCREATIN, PEPSIN, BILE SALTS, HYOSCYAMINE, ATROPINE, SCOPOLAMINE, AND PHENOBARBITAL　Systemic

A commonly used *brand name* in the U.S. and Canada is *Donnazyme*.

ORAL
Pancreatin, Pepsin, Bile Salts, Hyoscyamine Sulfate, Atropine Sulfate,
　Scopolamine Hydrobromide, and Phenobarbital Tablets
　In the U.S. and Canada—*Donnazyme*

Category: Digestant-anticholinergic-sedative.

Indications

Accepted
Digestive disorders (treatment)—This combination may be indicated
　for the symptomatic treatment of digestive disorders and as a
　supplement in conditions where natural digestive enzymes are de-
　ficient. However, specific enzyme deficiencies are better treated
　with the deficient substance rather than a combination of miscella-
　neous components.

Pharmacology

Mechanism of action/Effect:
　Pancreatin—Enzymatic components of pancreatin (trypsin, amy-
　　lase, and lipase) enhance the digestion of proteins, starches,
　　and fats in the gastrointestinal tract, primarily in the alkaline
　　medium of the duodenum and upper jejunum. Trypsin breaks
　　down larger protein fractions into peptides; amylase converts
　　starch into maltose; and lipase splits fat into fatty acids and
　　glycerin.
　Pepsin—Aids in the digestion of proteins.
　Bile salts—Enhance fat-splitting action of lipase and aid in the
　　emulsification of fats and the absorption of fatty acids.
　Atropine, hyoscyamine, and scopolamine—The principal bella-
　　donna alkaloids produce an anticholinergic effect by the com-
　　petitive inhibition of acetylcholine at the parasympathetic neuro-
　　effector junction.
　Phenobarbital—Although the mechanism of action has not been
　　completely established, the barbiturates produce a sedative ef-
　　fect probably as a result of their inhibition of synaptic neu-
　　rotransmitters in the central nervous system (CNS).

Duration of action:
　Atropine—4 to 6 hours.
　Hyoscyamine—4 to 6 hours.
　Phenobarbital—10 to 12 hours.
　Scopolamine—4 to 6 hours.

Precautions to Consider

Cross-sensitivity and/or related problems
Patients sensitive to beef or pork proteins, other belladonna alkaloids,
　or other barbiturates may be sensitive to this medication also.

Geriatrics
Geriatric patients may respond to usual doses of the belladonna alka-
　loids and barbiturates with excitement, agitation, drowsiness, or
　confusion.
Memory may become severely impaired in geriatric patients, espe-
　cially those who already have memory problems, with the contin-
　ued use of belladonna alkaloids since these drugs block the actions
　of acetylcholine, which is responsible for many functions of the
　brain, including memory functions.

Dental
Prolonged use of belladonna alkaloids may decrease or inhibit sali-
　vary flow, thus contributing to the development of caries, peri-
　odontal disease, oral candidiasis, and discomfort.

Drug interactions and/or related problems
The following drug interactions and/or related problems have been
　selected on the basis of their potential clinical significance (pos-
　sible mechanism in parentheses where appropriate)—not necessar-
　ily inclusive (» = major clinical significance):

Note: Only specific interactions between belladonna alkaloids and
　　other oral medications have been identified in this monograph.
　　However, because of decreased gastrointestinal motility and
　　delayed gastric emptying, absorption of other oral medications
　　may be decreased during concurrent use with belladonna alka-
　　loids.

　　Combinations containing any of the following medications, de-
　　pending on the amount present, may also interact with this
　　medication.

» Alcohol or
» Anesthetics, general, or
» Central nervous system (CNS) depressants, other, or
　Magnesium sulfate, parenteral, or
　Monoamine oxidase (MAO) inhibitors, including furazolidone, pro-
　　carbazine, and selegiline
　　(concurrent use may increase the CNS depressant effects of
　　either these medications or phenobarbital)

　Alkalizers, urinary, such as:
　　Antacids, calcium- and/or magnesium-containing
　　Carbonic anhydrase inhibitors
　　Citrates
　　Sodium bicarbonate
　　　(urinary excretion of belladonna alkaloids may be delayed by
　　　alkalinization of urine, thus potentiating side effects)
» Antacids or
» Antidiarrheals, adsorbent
　　(simultaneous use may reduce absorption of the belladonna
　　alkaloids, resulting in decreased therapeutic effectiveness; doses
　　of these medications should be spaced 1 hour apart from doses
　　of this combination)

　Anticholinergics or other medications with anticholinergic activity
　　(concurrent use may intensify the side effects of the belladonna
　　alkaloids)
» Anticoagulants, coumarin- or indandione-derivative
　　(effects may be decreased when used concurrently with pheno-
　　barbital because of increased metabolism resulting from induc-
　　tion of hepatic microsomal enzymes; periodic prothrombin-
　　time determinations may be required to determine if dosage
　　adjustments of anticoagulants are necessary)

　Antidepressants, tricyclic
　　(concurrent use with belladonna alkaloids may intensify anti-
　　cholinergic effects; concurrent use with phenobarbital may de-
　　crease the effect of the antidepressant as a result of hepatic
　　microsomal enzyme induction; dosage adjustments of tricyclic
　　antidepressant may be necessary during and after concurrent
　　therapy with this medication)
» Digitalis glycosides
　　(effects of digitalis glycosides may be decreased when they are
　　used concurrently with phenobarbital because of enhanced me-
　　tabolism resulting from induction of hepatic microsomal en-
　　zymes)

Griseofulvin
(absorption may be decreased when griseofulvin is used concurrently with barbiturates, especially phenobarbital, resulting in decreased blood concentrations; although the effect of decreased blood concentrations on therapeutic response has not been established, concurrent use should be avoided)

Iron supplements or preparations
(iron absorption may be decreased when used concurrently with pancreatin)

» Ketoconazole
(belladonna alkaloids may increase gastrointestinal pH; concurrent administration with belladonna alkaloids may result in a marked reduction in absorption of ketoconazole; patients should be advised to take these medications at least 2 hours after ketoconazole)

Opioid analgesics
(concurrent use with belladonna alkaloids may result in increased risk of severe constipation, which may lead to paralytic ileus, and/or urinary retention)

Phenytoin and possibly other hydantoin anticonvulsants
(concurrent use with barbiturates may produce variable and unpredictable effects on phenytoin; serum phenytoin concentrations should be monitored)

» Potassium chloride, especially wax-matrix preparations
(concurrent use with belladonna alkaloids may increase severity of potassium chloride-induced gastrointestinal lesions)

Valproic acid
(concurrent use with barbiturates may cause higher serum concentrations of barbiturates, leading to increased CNS depression and neurological toxicity, because of protein binding displacement of the barbiturate and reduced barbiturate metabolism; half-life of valproic acid is decreased; dosage adjustment of barbiturates may be necessary)

Contraindications/Medical problems

The contraindications/medical problems included have been selected on the basis of their potential clinical significance (reasons given in parentheses where appropriate)—not necessarily inclusive (» = major clinical significance).

Risk-benefit should be considered when the following medical problems exist:

Biliary obstruction, complete, or
Jaundice, severe
(use of bile salts may aggravate condition)

» Cardiac disease, especially mitral stenosis, cardiac arrhythmias, congestive heart failure, coronary heart disease
(increase in heart rate that may be caused by the belladonna alkaloids would be undesirable)

» Drug abuse or dependence, history of
(use of phenobarbital is not recommended because of predisposition of patient to habituation and dependence)

» Esophagitis, reflux
(decrease in esophageal and gastric motility and relaxation of lower esophageal sphincter caused by the belladonna alkaloids may promote gastric retention by delaying gastric emptying)

» Gastrointestinal tract obstructive disease, as in achalasia and pyloroduodenal stenosis
(decrease in motility and tone caused by belladonna alkaloids may occur, resulting in obstruction and gastric retention)

» Glaucoma, angle-closure, or predisposition to
(mydriatic effect of belladonna alkaloids may increase intraocular pressure and may precipitate an acute attack of angle-closure glaucoma)

» Hemorrhage, acute, with unstable cardiovascular status
(belladonna alkaloids may increase heart rate, which would be undesirable)

Hepatic function impairment
(decreased metabolism of belladonna alkaloids, bile salts, and phenobarbital)

» Hiatal hernia associated with reflux esophagitis
(belladonna alkaloids may aggravate condition)

Hypertension
(may be aggravated by the belladonna alkaloids)

Hyperthyroidism
(characterized by tachycardia, which is increased by belladonna alkaloids)

» Intestinal atony in the elderly or debilitated patient
(use of belladonna alkaloids may result in obstruction)

» Myasthenia gravis
(use of belladonna alkaloids may aggravate condition because of inhibition of acetylcholine action)

Neuropathy, autonomic
(urinary retention and cycloplegia may be aggravated by the use of belladonna alkaloids)

» Paralytic ileus
(use of belladonna alkaloids may lead to obstruction)

Porphyria, acute, intermittent or variegata, or history of
(phenobarbital may aggravate symptoms by inducing enzymes responsible for porphyrin synthesis)

» Prostatic hypertrophy, nonobstructive
(reduction in tone of urinary bladder caused by the belladonna alkaloids may lead to complete urinary retention)

Renal function impairment
(decreased excretion of belladonna alkaloids and phenobarbital may increase risk of side effects)

Sensitivity to any of the ingredients of this combination, beef or pork proteins, other belladonna alkaloids, or other barbiturates

» Tachycardia
(may be increased by the use of belladonna alkaloids)

» Ulcerative colitis, severe
(large doses of belladonna alkaloids may suppress intestinal motility and may cause paralytic ileus; also, use of belladonna alkaloids may precipitate or aggravate the serious complication of toxic megacolon)

» Urinary retention or
» Uropathy, obstructive, such as bladder neck obstruction due to prostatic hypertrophy
(urinary retention may be precipitated or aggravated)

Xerostomia
(prolonged use of belladonna alkaloids may further reduce limited salivary flow)

Caution in use is also recommended in patients over 40 years of age because of danger of precipitating undiagnosed glaucoma.

Side/Adverse Effects

Note: When the belladonna alkaloids are given to patients where the environmental temperature is high, there is risk of a rapid increase in body temperature because of suppression of sweat gland activity.

Geriatric or debilitated patients may respond to usual doses of the belladonna alkaloids and phenobarbital with excitement, agitation, drowsiness, or confusion.

Memory may become severely impaired in geriatric patients, especially those who already have memory problems, with the continued use of belladonna alkaloids.

The following side/adverse effects have been selected on the basis of their potential clinical significance (possible signs and symptoms in parentheses where appropriate)—not necessarily inclusive:

Those indicating need for medical attention
Incidence rare
  Agranulocytosis (sore throat and fever); *allergic reaction* (skin rash or hives); *hepatitis; jaundice* (yellow eyes or skin); *intraocular pressure* (eye pain); *thrombocytopenia* (unusual bleeding or bruising); *gastrointestinal effects, specifically, diarrhea, nausea or vomiting, stomach cramps or pain*—with large doses of pancreatin; *hyperuricemia or hyperuricosuria* (blood in urine, joint pain, swelling of feet or lower legs)—with large doses of pancreatin

Symptoms of overdose
  Clumsiness, unsteadiness, or staggering; confusion, especially in the elderly; dizziness; fever; flushing or redness of face; hallucinations; respiratory depression (shortness of breath or troubled breathing); *slow or fast heartbeat; unusual excitement, nervousness, restlessness, or irritability*

Those indicating need for medical attention only if they continue or are bothersome
Incidence more frequent
  Constipation; decreased sweating; drowsiness; dryness of mouth, nose, and throat
Incidence less frequent or rare
  Decreased flow of breast milk; decreased saliva secretion (difficulty in swallowing); *decreased sexual ability; difficult urination, especially in older men; difficulty in accommodation* (blurred vision); *headache; mydriatic effect* (increased sensitivity of eyes to sunlight); *trouble in sleeping; unusual tiredness or weakness*

Patient Consultation

In providing consultation, consider emphasizing the following selected information (» = major clinical significance):

Before using this medication
» Conditions affecting use, especially:
  Sensitivity to beef or pork proteins, any of the belladonna alkaloids, or barbiturates
  Breast-feeding—Excreted in breast milk; possible inhibition of lactation
  Use in children—Increased susceptibility to toxic effects of belladonna alkaloids and barbiturates
  Use in the elderly—Increased susceptibility to mental and other toxic effects of belladonna alkaloids and barbiturates; possible impairment of memory
  Dental—Possible development of dental problems because of decreased salivary flow
  Other medications, especially antacids, anticoagulants, antidiarrheals, digitalis glycosides, ketoconazole, CNS depressants, and potassium chloride
  Other medical problems, especially cardiac disease, gastrointestinal obstructive disease, glaucoma, hemorrhage, reflux esophagitis, ulcerative colitis, or urinary retention

Proper use of this medication
  Taking dose with or after meals unless otherwise directed by physician
» Importance of not taking more medication than the amount prescribed
  Importance of following diet ordered by physician

» Not chewing tablets; otherwise mouth irritation may occur
  Missed dose: Not taking missed dose at all; not doubling doses
» Proper storage

Precautions while using this medication
» Avoiding use of alcohol or other CNS depressants
  Possible eye photosensitivity; wearing sunglasses that block ultraviolet light
» Caution if drowsiness or blurred vision occurs
» Caution during exercise and hot weather; overheating may result in heat stroke
  Possible dryness of mouth, nose, and throat; using sugarless gum or candy, ice, or saliva substitute for relief; checking with dentist if dry mouth continues for more than 2 weeks

Side/adverse effects
  Signs of potential side effects, especially agranulocytosis, allergic reaction, hepatitis, increased intraocular pressure, and thrombocytopenia

General Dosing Information

Prolonged uninterrupted use of barbiturates has the potential of producing psychic or physical dependence, especially in the higher dose range.

To avoid irritation of the mouth, lips, and tongue, the tablets should not be chewed. Pancreatic enzymes, such as pancreatin, when in contact with the mouth will begin to digest the mucous membranes and cause ulcerations.

Diet/Nutrition
This medication should preferably be taken with or after meals for maximum effectiveness.

Dosage should be individualized and determined by the degree of maldigestion and malabsorption, the fat content of the diet, and the enzyme activity of the preparation.

To avoid temporary indigestion when pancreatin is taken, a proper balance of fat, protein, and starch intake should be maintained.

Oral Dosage Forms

PANCREATIN, PEPSIN, BILE SALTS, HYOSCYAMINE SULFATE, ATROPINE SULFATE, SCOPOLAMINE HYDROBROMIDE, AND PHENOBARBITAL TABLETS

Usual adult and adolescent dose: Oral, 2 tablets after meals, the dosage being adjusted as needed and tolerated.

Usual geriatric dose: See *Usual adult and adolescent dose.*

Note: Geriatric patients may be more sensitive to the effects of the usual adult dose; lower doses may be required.

Auxiliary labeling:
• Avoid alcoholic beverages.
• May cause drowsiness.
• Do not chew.

PANCRELIPASE   Systemic

Some commonly used *brand names* are:

In the U.S.—

Cotazym	*Pancrease MT 10*
Cotazym-S	*Pancrease MT 16*
Enzymase-16	*Protilase*
Ilozyme	*Ultrase MT 12*
Ku-Zyme HP	*Ultrase MT 20*
Pancoate	*Ultrase MT 24*
Pancrease	*Viokase*
Pancrease MT 4	*Zymase*

In Canada—

Cotazym	*Pancrease*
Cotazym-65 B	*Pancrease MT 4*
Cotazym E.C.S. 8	*Pancrease MT 10*
Cotazym E.C.S. 20	*Pancrease MT 16*

Another commonly used name is lipancreatin.

ORAL
Pancrelipase Capsules USP
In the U.S.—*Cotazym; Ku-Zyme HP*
In Canada—*Cotazym; Cotazym-65 B*
Pancrelipase Delayed-release Capsules
In the U.S.—*Cotazym-S; Enzymase-16; Pancoate; Pancrease; Pancrease MT 4; Pancrease MT 10; Pancrease MT 16; Protilase; Ultrase MT 12; Ultrase MT 20; Ultrase MT 24; Zymase;* GENERIC
In Canada—*Cotazym E.C.S. 8; Cotazym E.C.S. 20; Pancrease; Pancrease MT 4; Pancrease MT 10; Pancrease MT 16*
Pancrelipase Powder†
In the U.S.—*Viokase*
Pancrelipase Tablets USP†
In the U.S.—*Ilozyme; Viokase*

---

†Not commercially available in Canada.

Category: Enzyme (pancreatic) replenisher; digestant; diagnostic aid (pancreatic function).

Indications

Note: Bracketed information in the *Indications* section refers to uses not included in U.S. product labeling.

Accepted
Pancreatic insufficiency (treatment)—Pancrelipase is indicated as a pancreatic enzyme supplement and replacement therapy in conditions where pancreatic enzymes are either absent or deficient, resulting in inadequate fat and carbohydrate digestion. Such conditions are usually due to chronic pancreatitis, pancreatectomy, cystic fibrosis, gastrointestinal bypass surgery (Billroth II and total), and ductal obstruction from neoplasm (of the pancreas or common bile duct).

Steatorrhea (treatment)—Indicated for treating steatorrhea associated with the postgastrectomy syndrome and bowel resection, and for decreasing malabsorption in these patients.

[Pancreatic insufficiency (diagnosis)][1]—Pancrelipase is used as a presumptive test for pancreatic function, especially in pancreatic insufficiency due to chronic pancreatitis.

Unaccepted
Pancrelipase is not effective in the treatment of gastrointestinal disorders unrelated to pancreatic enzyme insufficiency.

---

[1]Not included in Canadian product labeling.

Pharmacology

Mechanism of action/Effect: Proteolytic, amylolytic, and lipolytic enzymes in pancrelipase enhance the digestion of proteins, starches, and fats in the gastrointestinal tract, primarily in the duodenum and upper jejunum. The activity of pancrelipase is greater in neutral or faintly alkaline media. Pancrelipase has about 12 times the lipolytic activity, 4 times the proteolytic activity, and 4 times the amylolytic activity of pancreatin.

The efficacy of pancrelipase activity is dependent on how much of the enzyme reaches the small intestine. This can be influenced by the enzyme dose, the prevention of release of pancrelipase in the stomach, the microsphere size of the delayed-release product, and the pH at which the microsphere dissolves and releases the enzyme, with activity being greater at a neutral or alkaline pH.

Precautions to Consider

Cross-sensitivity and/or related problems
Patients sensitive to pancreatin or pork protein may be sensitive to this medication also.

Geriatrics
Appropriate studies on the relationship of age to the effects of pancrelipase have not been performed in the geriatric population. However, geriatrics-specific problems that would limit the usefulness of this medication in the elderly are not expected.

Drug interactions and/or related problems
The following drug interactions and/or related problems have been selected on the basis of their potential clinical significance (possible mechanism in parentheses where appropriate)—not necessarily inclusive (» = major clinical significance):

Note: Combinations containing any of the following medications, depending on the amount present, may also interact with this medication.

Antacids, calcium carbonate- and/or magnesium hydroxide-containing
(concurrent administration of antacids may be required to prevent inactivation of pancrelipase [except the enteric-coated dosage forms] by gastric pepsin and acid pH; however, calcium carbonate- and/or magnesium hydroxide-containing antacids are not recommended since they may decrease the effectiveness of pancrelipase)

Iron, supplements or preparations
(iron absorption may be decreased when used concurrently with pancrelipase)

Contraindications/Medical problems
The contraindications/medical problems included have been selected on the basis of their potential clinical significance (reasons given in parentheses where appropriate)—not necessarily inclusive (» = major clinical significance).

Except under special circumstances, this medication should not be used if the following medical problems exist:
» Pancreatitis, acute
» Sensitivity to pork protein, pancrelipase, or pancreatin

Side/Adverse Effects

The following side/adverse effects have been selected on the basis of their potential clinical significance (possible signs and symptoms in parentheses where appropriate)—not necessarily inclusive:

Those indicating need for medical attention

Incidence rare

Allergic reaction (skin rash or hives); *irritation of the mouth*—induced by enzymatic digestion of mucous membranes when tablet dosage form is retained in mouth; *sensitization* (shortness of breath, stuffy nose, troubled breathing, wheezing, or tightness in chest)—induced by repeated inadvertent inhalation of powder dosage form or the powder from opened capsules

With high doses

Gastrointestinal effects, specifically diarrhea, intestinal obstruction, nausea, or stomach cramps or pain; hyperuricemia or hyperuricosuria (blood in urine, joint pain, swelling of feet or lower legs)—more frequent with extremely high doses of the purine-rich older formulations of pancrelipase)

Patient Consultation

In providing consultation, consider emphasizing the following selected information (» = major clinical significance):

Before using this medication

»   Conditions affecting use of pancrelipase, especially:
     Sensitivity to pork protein, pancrelipase, or pancreatin
     Other medical problems, especially acute pancreatitis

Proper use of this medication

     Taking dose before or with meals for maximum effectiveness
»   Importance of following diet ordered by physician
»   Not chewing tablets; swallowing them quickly with liquid to lessen potential for mouth irritation
     Not chewing or crushing capsules containing enteric-coated spheres
     Missed dose: Not taking missed dose at all; not doubling doses
»   Proper storage

Precautions while using this medication

     Possible concurrent use with antacids that contain calcium carbonate and/or magnesium hydroxide
     Not changing brands or dosage forms of pancrelipase without checking with physician
     Possible sensitization resulting from repeated inhalation of powder, either from opened capsules or from powder dosage form

Side/adverse effects

     Signs of potential side effects, especially allergic reaction, hyperuricemia or hyperuricosuria (with extremely high doses); gastrointestinal effects; irritation of mucous membranes; and respiratory problems (with inhalation of powder)

General Dosing Information

The destruction of pancrelipase's enzymes by gastric pepsin or their inactivation by acid pH may be prevented by the use of enteric-coated dosage forms, particularly the enteric-coated spheres. Or, if dosage forms of pancrelipase which are not enteric-coated are used, the gastric and duodenal pH may be raised instead by the concurrent administration of sodium bicarbonate, aluminum hydroxide, histamine H_2-receptor antagonists, misoprostol, or omeprazole (also, antacid, H_2-receptor antagonist, misoprostol, or omeprazole administration may be necessary in patients with deficient pancreatic bicarbonate secretion for the control of steatorrhea). An H_2-receptor antagonist administered with meals may be preferred instead of antacids, especially in patients with high rates of acid secretion.

Dosage should be individualized and determined by the degree of maldigestion and malabsorption, the fat content of the diet, and the enzyme activity of each preparation rather than by the weight of the extract. Ideally, a starting dose of 8,000 to 10,000 Units of lipase should be given with each meal.

To avoid irritation of the mouth, lips, and tongue, the tablets should not be chewed. Instead, the tablets should be swallowed quickly, preferably with some liquid, since proteolytic enzymes (trypsin and chymotrypsin) present in pancrelipase, when retained in the mouth may begin to digest the mucous membranes and cause ulcerations.

Retention of the tablet dosage form in the esophagus may occur in some patients with esophageal abnormalities or in patients taking the tablet in a recumbent position. To decrease the likelihood of mucous membrane digestion, 1 or 2 mouthfuls of solid food should be swallowed after each dose.

Diet/Nutrition

Pancrelipase should preferably be taken before or with meals for maximum effectiveness.

In pancreatic insufficiency, a high-calorie diet which is high in protein and low in fat is recommended. In severe cases, higher doses of pancrelipase and dietary adjustment may be necessary. Some clinicians recommend that cystic fibrosis patients consume a liberal fat diet along with an increase in pancelipase dosage to ensure adequate energy intake.

Capsule dosage forms may be opened and sprinkled on food for administration to young children. However, capsules containing the enteric-coated spheres should be taken with liquids or small amounts of soft foods (e.g., applesauce, gelatin) that do not require chewing.

Bioequivalence information

The microsphere size of the delayed-release product, among other factors, determines how much of the enzyme reaches the small intestine. It has been found that some delayed-release pancrelipase products provide higher levels of enzyme activity than labeled. Since substitution of one manufacturer's delayed-release product for another may sometimes be accompanied by therapeutic failure, caution should be exercised in substituting.

Oral Dosage Forms

PANCRELIPASE CAPSULES USP

Usual adult and adolescent dose:
Enzyme (pancreatic) replenisher; and
Digestant—Oral, 1 to 3 capsules before or with meals and snacks, the dosage being adjusted as needed and tolerated.

Usual geriatric dose: See *Usual adult and adolescent dose.*

Auxiliary labeling:
- Take before or with meals.
- If capsules are opened, do not inhale powder.

PANCRELIPASE DELAYED-RELEASE CAPSULES

Note: Substitution of one manufacturer's delayed-release product for another has resulted in therapeutic failure.

Usual adult and adolescent dose:
Enzyme (pancreatic) replenisher; and
Digestant—Oral, 1 or 2 capsules before or with meals and snacks, the dosage being adjusted as needed and tolerated.

Usual geriatric dose: See *Usual adult and adolescent dose.*

Auxiliary labeling:
- Take before or with meals.
- Do not chew or crush (for capsules containing the enteric-coated spheres only).

PANCRELIPASE POWDER

Usual adult and adolescent dose:
Enzyme (pancreatic) replenisher; and
Digestant—Oral, 0.7 gram with meals and snacks, the dosage being adjusted as needed and tolerated.

Usual geriatric dose: See *Usual adult and adolescent dose.*

Auxiliary labeling:
- Take with meals.
- Do not inhale.

PANCRELIPASE TABLETS USP

Usual adult and adolescent dose:
Enzyme (pancreatic) replenisher; and

Digestant—Oral, 1 to 3 tablets before or with meals and snacks, the dosage being adjusted as needed and tolerated.

Usual geriatric dose: See *Usual adult and adolescent dose.*

Auxiliary labeling:
- Take before or with meals.
- Do not chew.

PAPAVERINE   Intracavernosal

PARENTERAL
Papaverine Hydrochloride Injection USP
   In the U.S. and Canada—GENERIC

Category: Impotence therapy.

Indications

Note: Bracketed information in the *Indications* section refers to uses
      not included in U.S. product labeling.

Accepted
[Impotence (treatment)][1]—Papaverine is used, sometimes in combination with an alpha-adrenergic blocking agent such as phentolamine,
by intracavernosal injection to facilitate erections in men with
impotence. In general, it is most useful in patients with organic
impotence (neurogenic and, to a lesser extent, vascular). It is less
useful in patients with impotence due to endocrine problems (hypogonadism, hyper- or hypothyroidism) or medications.

[Impotence (diagnosis)][1]—Papaverine is used, sometimes in combination with phentolamine, by intracavernosal injection as an aid in
the evaluation of penile vasculature, alone or prior to angiography,
corpus cavernosography, or cavernosometry.

Unaccepted
Use of papaverine to enhance erections in men who are not impotent
is not recommended because of the risk of priapism and permanent
damage to penile tissues.

[1]Not included in Canadian product labeling.

Pharmacology

Mechanism of action/Effect: Papaverine has a direct, nonspecific
relaxant effect on smooth muscle. When administered by intracavernous injection, it is thought to cause relaxation of the trabecular cavernous smooth muscles and vasodilation of the penile
arteries. This results in increased arterial blood flow into the corpus cavernosa, and swelling and elongation of the penis; the glans
and corpus spongiosum swell very little, if at all. Venous outflow
is also reduced, possibly as a result of increased venous resistance.

Time to peak effect: Variable, but usually within 10 minutes.

Duration of action: 1 to 6 hours; dose-related; prolonged by concurrent administration with phentolamine.

Precautions to Consider

Geriatrics
No information is available on the relationship of age to the use of
papaverine intracavernosally in geriatric patients. However, geriatrics-specific problems that would limit the usefulness of this medication in the elderly are not expected.

Drug interactions and/or related problems
The following drug interactions and/or related problems have been
selected on the basis of their potential clinical significance (possible mechanism in parentheses where appropriate)—not necessarily inclusive (» = major clinical significance):

Sympathomimetics, alpha-adrenergic, especially metaraminol, epinephrine, and phenylephrine
   (reverse the vasodilating effect of papaverine; may be used to
   treat priapism or overdose)

Contraindications/Medical problems
The contraindications/medical problems included have been selected
on the basis of their potential clinical significance (reasons given
in parentheses where appropriate)—not necessarily inclusive (» =
major clinical significance).

*Risk-benefit should be considered when the following medical prob-
lems exist:*

Allergy to papaverine
» Coagulation defects, severe
   (risk of bleeding at injection site)
Hepatic function impairment
   (papaverine may cause hepatotoxicity when used systemically,
   but is only slowly absorbed systemically after intracavernosal
   administration)
» Priapism, history of, or
» Sickle cell disease
   (increased risk of priapism)

Side/Adverse Effects
The following side/adverse effects have been selected on the basis of
their potential clinical significance (possible signs and symptoms
in parentheses where appropriate)—not necessarily inclusive:

Those indicating need for medical attention
Incidence rare
   Dizziness; fibrosis (lumps in penis); *priapism* (erection, continu-
   ing for more than 4 hours, or painful erection)
Note: *Fibrosis* of the corpus cavernosum, resulting in blockage
      and inability to insert a penile prosthesis, has been reported.
      Priapism is usually due to excessive dosage. Prolonged erec-
      tion may resolve spontaneously, but in most cases will re-
      quire treatment.

**Those indicating need for medical attention only if they continue
or are bothersome**
Incidence less frequent or rare
   *Burning, mild, along penis; difficulty in ejaculating; inadvertent
   subcutaneous administration* (bruising or bleeding at site of injection, swelling at site of injection); *superficial hematoma* (bruising
   or bleeding at site of injection)
Note: *Burning* may be more severe with inadvertent subcutaneous
      administration.

Those not indicating need for medical attention
Incidence more frequent
Tingling at tip of penis

Patient Consultation

In providing consultation, consider emphasizing the following selected information (» = major clinical significance):

Before using this medication
» Conditions affecting use, especially:
   Allergy to papaverine
   Other medical problems, especially severe coagulation defects, history of priapism, or sickle cell disease

Proper use of this medication
   Proper administration:
» Cleansing injection site with alcohol; injecting slowly and directly into corpus cavernosum at base of penis; avoiding subcutaneous administration; if inadvertently injected subcutaneously (as evidenced by pain at injection site), stopping, withdrawing, and repositioning needle
   Putting pressure on injection site for 1 to 2 minutes to prevent bruising; massaging penis, as directed by physician, to distribute medication
   Effect begins in about 10 minutes; attempting intercourse within 2 hours after administration
» Proper storage

Precautions while using this medication
» Compliance with therapy; importance of not exceeding prescribed dosage and frequency of use; risk of priapism, tissue ischemia, and permanent damage with overdose
» Telling physician immediately if erection persists longer than 4 hours or becomes painful
   If bleeding occurs at injection site, applying pressure; checking with physician if bleeding persists
   Examining penis regularly for signs of fibrosis at injection site or for curvature; checking with physician if either of these occurs

Side/adverse effects
   Signs of potential side effects, especially dizziness, priapism, and fibrosis
   Injection may cause tingling at tip of penis; no cause for concern

General Dosing Information

Patients receiving intracavernosal papaverine should be under supervision of a physician experienced in its use and familiar with proper management of sustained erection and priapism.

Dosage adjustment should be made carefully, based on the degree and duration of tumescence achieved with the previous dose. In general, patients with neurogenic impotence may be more sensitive to the effects of intracavernosal vasodilators and may require lower doses.

Intracavernosal papaverine may be self-administered by the patient, but only after careful training in the technique to reduce the incidence of inadvertent subcutaneous administration, ecchymosis, and urethral injury.

For treatment of impotence, papaverine is injected slowly (over 1 to 2 minutes), directly into the corpus cavernosum at the base of the penis. A characteristic give should be noticed as the needle penetrates the tunica albuginea and enters the corpus cavernosum. Proper injection technique is necessary to avoid injury or injection of the urethra or vessels on the dorsal aspect of the penis.

After completion of the injection, pressure is applied to the injection site to prevent bleeding. Then the entire length of the corpus cavernosum should be squeezed firmly to distribute medication to the other side, followed by the same procedure on the other side. The penis should then be pinched transversely in several places to distribute medication to both ends of the corpus cavernosa.

If a sustained erection occurs, the next dose of papaverine should be reduced.

Intercourse should be attempted within 2 hours after administration.

If fibrosis occurs, discontinuation of papaverine therapy may be necessary, especially if a penile implant is planned in the future.

For treatment of prolonged erection or priapism
A sustained erection should be treated if it persists for longer than 4 hours; priapism should be treated promptly. If tumescence is not reversed, interruption of blood flow may result in penile tissue ischemia and permanent damage.

Depending on the severity, treatment may include:
• Aspiration of intracavernous blood.
• Irrigation of the corpus cavernosa with saline to remove clotted blood.
• Intracavernous administration of an alpha-adrenergic agonist, such as metaraminol, epinephrine, or phenylephrine.
• Surgery.

Parenteral Dosage Forms

Note: Bracketed uses in the *Dosage Forms* section refer to categories of use and/or indications that are not included in U.S. product labeling.

PAPAVERINE HYDROCHLORIDE INJECTION USP

Usual adult dose: [Impotence therapy][1]—
   Intracavernosal, a mixture of 30 mg Papaverine Hydrochloride Injection USP and 0.5 to 1.0 mg of reconstituted Phentolamine Mesylate for Injection USP (5 mg per mL), the dosage being adjusted according to response, or
   Intracavernosal, initially 30 mg of Papaverine Hydrochloride Injection USP alone, the dosage being adjusted, up to 60 mg, according to response.

Note: Patients with neurogenic impotence may require lower doses or use of papaverine alone.

Usual adult prescribing limits: Impotence therapy—Up to 60 mg of papaverine hydrochloride per dose. The injection should not be given more than three times weekly or two days in succession.

PARALDEHYDE   Systemic

A commonly used *brand name* in the U.S. is *Paral.*

ORAL/RECTAL
Paraldehyde USP†
  In the U.S.—*Paral;* GENERIC

Note: In Canada, the sterile paraldehyde dosage form can be used whenever oral or rectal paraldehyde is prescribed.

PARENTERAL
Sterile Paraldehyde USP*
  In Canada—GENERIC

---

  *Not commercially available in the U.S.
  †Not commercially available in Canada.

Category: Anticonvulsant.

Indications

Accepted
Convulsions (treatment);
Status epilepticus (treatment); or
Toxicity, convulsant drug (treatment)—Parenteral paraldehyde may be indicated in the emergency treatment of status epilepticus and of convulsions induced by tetanus, eclampsia, and poisoning by convulsant drugs, when other agents are not effective. Oral paraldehyde may be used in the management of convulsions induced by tetanus and convulsant drug poisoning, when other agents are not effective.

Unaccepted
Paraldehyde has been used as a sedative-hypnotic; however, it generally has been replaced by safer and/or more effective agents for the following indications:
Insomnia
Sedation
Delirium tremens and other psychiatric states characterized by excitement, to quiet the patient and produce sleep (generally replaced by benzodiazepines such as chlordiazepoxide and diazepam)
Parenterally for intractable pain not responsive to other types of therapy (e.g., in an occasional patient with acute coronary thrombosis who fails to obtain relief from repeated injections of morphine sulfate)
Intramuscularly to induce artificial sleep and thereby to facilitate electroencephalographic study, especially in children

Pharmacology

Mechanism of action/Effect: The precise mechanism of action of paraldehyde is unknown. It may depress many levels of the central nervous system (CNS) including the ascending reticular activating system to produce imbalances between facilitatory and inhibitory mechanisms.

Onset of action: Hypnotic—Within 15 minutes.

Time to peak serum concentration:
  Oral—30 to 60 minutes.
  Rectal—About 2.5 hours.

Duration of action: Hypnotic—About 8 to 12 hours.

Precautions to Consider

Geriatrics
No information is available on the relationship of age to the effects of paraldehyde in geriatric patients.

Drug interactions and/or related problems
The following drug interactions and/or related problems have been selected on the basis of their potential clinical significance (possible mechanism in parentheses where appropriate)—not necessarily inclusive (» = major clinical significance):

Note: Combinations containing any of the following medications, depending on the amount present, may also interact with this medication.

  Addictive medications, other, especially central nervous system (CNS) depressants with habituating potential
    (prolonged concurrent use may increase the risk of habituation; caution is recommended)
» Alcohol or
» CNS depression-producing medications, other
    (concurrent use may increase the CNS depressant effects of either these medications or paraldehyde; caution is recommended and dosage of one or both agents should be reduced)
» Disulfiram
    (concurrent use with paraldehyde is not recommended because disulfiram may decrease the metabolism of paraldehyde by inhibition of acetaldehyde dehydrogenase, resulting in increased blood concentrations of paraldehyde and acetaldehyde)

Contraindications/Medical problems
The contraindications/medical problems included have been selected on the basis of their potential clinical significance (reasons given in parentheses where appropriate)—not necessarily inclusive (» = major clinical significance).

Risk-benefit should be considered when the following medical problems exist:

  Alcoholism, active or in remission, or
  Drug abuse or dependence, history of
    (predisposition of patient to habituation and dependence)
» Bronchopulmonary disease
    (paraldehyde excreted via lungs)
» Hepatic function impairment
    (paraldehyde metabolized in liver; patients may be more susceptible to effects of paraldehyde)
  Sensitivity to paraldehyde
With oral use
  Gastroenteritis or
» Peptic ulcer
    (condition may be exacerbated)
With rectal use
  Colitis
    (condition may be exacerbated)

Side/Adverse Effects

The following side/adverse effects have been selected on the basis of their potential clinical significance (possible signs and symptoms in parentheses where appropriate)—not necessarily inclusive:

Those indicating need for medical attention
Incidence more frequent
  Effects on pulmonary capillaries (coughing)—with intravenous administration only; *skin rash*
Incidence less frequent
  Thrombophlebitis (redness, swelling, or pain at injection site)
With prolonged use
  Hepatitis (yellow eyes or skin)
Symptoms of overdose
  Cloudy urine; decreased urination; fast and deep breathing; metabolic acidosis (confusion, muscle tremors, continuing or severe

nausea or vomiting, nervousness, restlessness, irritability, severe stomach cramps); *shortness of breath or slow or troubled breathing; slow heartbeat; weakness, severe*

Those indicating need for medical attention only if they continue or are bothersome
Incidence more frequent
   Drowsiness; unpleasant breath odor
With oral use
   Nausea or vomiting; stomach pain
Incidence less frequent
   Clumsiness or unsteadiness; dizziness; "hangover" effect

Those indicating possible withdrawal and the need for medical attention if they occur after medication is discontinued
   Convulsions; hallucinations; increased sweating; muscle cramps; nausea or vomiting; stomach cramps; trembling

Patient Consultation

In providing consultation, consider emphasizing the following selected information (» = major clinical significance):

Before using this medication
» Conditions affecting use, especially:
   Sensitivity to paraldehyde
   Pregnancy—Paraldehyde crosses placenta
   Labor—Use of paraldehyde during labor may cause respiratory depression in neonate
   Other medications, especially alcohol or other CNS depression-producing medications or disulfiram
   Other medical problems, especially bronchopulmonary disease, hepatic function impairment, or peptic ulcer (with oral use only)

Proper use of this medication
» Not using medication if it is brownish in color or has a strong vinegar-like odor
   Avoiding contact with eyes, skin, and clothing
   Keeping away from heat, open flame, and sparks
» Not using plastic containers for administration of this medication
» Importance of not using more medication than the amount prescribed because of habit-forming potential
   Missed dose: If on scheduled dosing regimen—Taking right away if remembered within an hour or so; not taking if remembered later; not doubling doses
» Proper storage
For oral use
» Taking liquid diluted in milk or iced fruit juice to mask odor and taste and to minimize gastric irritation
For rectal use
   Proper administration: Paraldehyde may need diluting before using

Precautions while using this medication
   Regular visits to physician to check progress during prolonged therapy
   Checking with physician before discontinuing medication after prolonged use; gradual dosage reduction may be necessary to avoid possibility of withdrawal symptoms
» Avoiding use of alcohol or other CNS depressants
   Caution if any laboratory tests required; possible interference with metyrapone or phentolamine test results
» Suspected overdose: Getting emergency help at once
» Caution if drowsiness occurs

Side/adverse effects
   Signs of potential side effects, especially effects on pulmonary capillaries (with intravenous use only), skin rash, thrombophlebitis (with injection only), and, with prolonged use, hepatitis

Strong unpleasant breath odor may be alarming to patient although medically insignificant

General Dosing Information

Do not use plastic containers or plastic syringes or tubing for administration since paraldehyde is incompatible with many plastics.

Prolonged use of larger than usual therapeutic doses may result in tolerance and psychic or physical dependence.

Following prolonged administration, paraldehyde should be withdrawn gradually in order to avoid the possibility of precipitating withdrawal symptoms.

For oral use only
When paraldehyde is administered orally, it should be well diluted in milk or iced fruit juice to mask the odor and taste and to minimize gastric irritation.

For parenteral use only
Intramuscular injection is the preferred route of administration. The paraldehyde injection should be administered deeply into the gluteus maximus muscle, care being taken to avoid nerve trunks because paraldehyde may cause nerve injury and paralysis. No more than 5 mL should be administered at each injection site.

Paraldehyde should not be administered subcutaneously because it is irritating to tissue.

Intravenous administration is not recommended except in emergencies, since it may produce circulatory collapse or pulmonary edema.

If administered intravenously, paraldehyde should be diluted with several volumes of 0.9% sodium chloride injection and injected slowly at a rate not to exceed 1 mL per minute.

For rectal use only
For rectal administration, paraldehyde should be diluted with 1 or 2 parts of olive oil, cottonseed oil, or 0.9% sodium chloride solution to prevent rectal irritation.

Oral/Rectal Dosage Forms

PARALDEHYDE USP

Usual adult dose: Anticonvulsant—
   Oral, up to 12 mL (diluted to a 10% solution) via gastric tube every four hours as needed.
   Rectal, 10 to 20 mL.

Auxiliary labeling:
• Avoid alcoholic beverages.
• May cause drowsiness.
• Discard any unused liquid if container has been opened for more than 24 hours.

Parenteral Dosage Forms

STERILE PARALDEHYDE USP

Usual adult dose: Anticonvulsant—
   Intramuscular, 5 to 10 mL.
   Intravenous infusion, 5 mL diluted with at least 100 mL of 0.9% sodium chloride injection and administered slowly at a rate not exceeding 1 mL per minute.

Auxiliary labeling: • For single dose only. Discard unused portion.

PAREGORIC   Systemic

A commonly used name is Camphorated opium tincture.

ORAL
Paregoric USP
In the U.S. and Canada—GENERIC

Category: Antidiarrheal.

Indications

Note: Bracketed information in the *Indications* section refers to uses
not included in U.S. product labeling.

Accepted
Diarrhea (treatment)—Paregoric is indicated in the treatment of diarrhea. However, the medication should not be used in treating diarrhea caused by poisoning until after the toxic material has been
eliminated from the gastrointestinal tract because it may slow the
elimination of the toxic material.

[Opioid (narcotic) dependence, neonatal (treatment)][1]—Use of paregoric in the treatment of neonatal opioid dependence is controversial and many clinicians recommend use of diluted opium tincture
instead. Paregoric contains benzoic acid, which may theoretically
displace bilirubin from albumin binding. It may also contain camphor, which may cause serious toxicity, including convulsions and
respiratory depression, in infants. These ingredients may cause
further problems in opioid-dependent neonates, who are predisposed to convulsions and hyperbilirubinemia.

Unaccepted
Paregoric should not be used to treat diarrhea associated with
pseudomembranous colitis caused by cephalosporins, lincomycins
(possibly including topical clindamycin), or penicillins, because
paregoric-induced alteration of intestinal motility may delay removal of toxins from the gastrointestinal tract, thereby prolonging
and/or worsening the diarrhea.

Applying paregoric to the gums of a teething child (to provide local
anesthesia and permit sleep) is no longer recommended.

[1]Not included in Canadian product labeling.

Pharmacology

Mechanism of action/Effect: Most of the effects of paregoric are due
to the morphine component. Usefulness in the treatment of diarrhea is due to alteration of intestinal motility.

Duration of action: 4 to 5 hours.

Precautions to Consider

Cross-sensitivity and/or related problems
Patients hypersensitive to other opium alkaloids may be hypersensitive to this medication also.

Geriatrics
Geriatric patients may be more susceptible to the effects, especially
the respiratory depressant effects, of opiates. Also, geriatric patients are more likely to have prostatic hypertrophy or obstruction
and age-related renal function impairment; opiate-induced urinary
retention may be detrimental to these patients.

Drug interactions and/or related problems
The following drug interactions and/or related problems have been
selected on the basis of their potential clinical significance (pos-

sible mechanism in parentheses where appropriate)—not necessarily inclusive (» = major clinical significance):
Note: Combinations containing any of the following medications, depending on the amount present, may also interact with this
medication.

Addictive medications, other, especially central nervous system
(CNS) depressants with habituating potential
(prolonged concurrent use may increase the risk of habituation;
caution is recommended)
» Alcohol or
» Antidiarrheals, antiperistaltic, such as:
»   Difenoxin and atropine
»   Diphenoxylate and atropine
»   Kaolin, pectin, belladonna alkaloids, and opium
»   Loperamide
»   Opium tincture, or
» CNS depression-producing medications, other
(concurrent use of these medications with paregoric may result
in increased CNS depressant, respiratory depressant, and hypotensive effects; concurrent use should be undertaken with caution, and dosage of one or both agents should be reduced)
(concurrent use of any opioid-containing analgesic or antidiarrheal with paregoric may also increase the risk of severe constipation)
Anticholinergics or other medications with anticholinergic activity
(concurrent use with paregoric may result in increased risk of
severe constipation, which may lead to paralytic ileus, and/or
urinary retention)
Metoclopramide
(paregoric may antagonize the effects of metoclopramide on
gastrointestinal motility)
Monoamine oxidase (MAO) inhibitors, including furazolidone,
pargyline and procarbazine
(caution is recommended when using any opioid in patients
who have received an MAO inhibitor within 14 days because
concurrent use of MAO inhibitors with meperidine has resulted
in unpredictable, severe, and sometimes fatal reactions, including immediate excitation, sweating, rigidity, and severe hypertension, or, in some patients, hypotension, severe respiratory
depression, coma, convulsions, hyperpyrexia, and vascular collapse)
» Naltrexone
(naltrexone blocks the therapeutic effects of paregoric; naltrexone therapy should not be initiated in a patient receiving
paregoric; patients receiving naltrexone should be treated with
nonopioid medications when antidiarrheal treatment is required)

Contraindications/Medical problems
The contraindications/medical problems included have been selected
on the basis of their potential clinical significance (reasons given
in parentheses where appropriate)—not necessarily inclusive (» =
major clinical significance).

***Except under special circumstances, this medication should not be
used when the following medical problems exist:***
» Diarrhea associated with pseudomembranous colitis caused by
cephalosporins; lincomycins, possibly including topical clindamycin; or penicillins, or
» Diarrhea caused by poisoning until the toxic material is eliminated
from the gastrointestinal tract
(paregoric may delay removal of toxins from the colon, thereby
prolonging and/or worsening the diarrhea)
» Respiratory depression, acute
(may be exacerbated)

Risk-benefit should be considered (if paregoric is to be used over prolonged periods) when the following medical problems exist:

Alcoholism, active or in remission, or
Drug abuse or dependence, history of
(patient predisposition to drug abuse)
» Asthma, acute attack, or
» Respiratory disease or impairment
(paregoric may decrease respiratory drive and increase airway resistance in these patients)
Cardiac arrhythmias or
Convulsions, history of
(may be exacerbated)
Gallbladder disease or gallstones
(paregoric may cause biliary contraction)
Head injury or
Increased intracranial pressure, pre-existing, or
Intracranial lesions
(increased risk of respiratory depression and further increase in cerebrospinal fluid pressure)
Hepatic function impairment
Hypersensitivity to paregoric or other opiates, history of
Hypothyroidism
(increased risk of respiratory depression and CNS depression)
» Inflammatory bowel disease, severe
(risk of toxic megacolon may be increased, especially with repeated dosing)
Prostatic hypertrophy or obstruction or
Urethral stricture
(paregoric may cause urinary retention)
Renal function impairment
(components of this formulation excreted primarily via kidneys; also, paregoric may cause urinary retention)
Caution is also advised in administration to very young, elderly, or very ill or debilitated patients, who may be more sensitive to the effects, especially the respiratory depressant effects, of opiates.

Side/Adverse Effects

Note: At high doses, paregoric exhibits effects of opiates.

Physical dependence with or without psychological dependence may occur with chronic administration of high doses of paregoric; an abstinence syndrome may occur when the medication is discontinued.

Dizziness, feeling faint, or lightheadedness occurs more frequently in ambulatory patients receiving opiates and may be a sign of orthostatic hypotension; however, these effects may also reflect the CNS depressant effects of opiates and may occur independently of hypotension.

The following side/adverse effects have been selected on the basis of their potential clinical significance (possible signs and symptoms in parentheses where appropriate)—not necessarily inclusive:

Those indicating need for medical attention
Incidence rare
Allergic reaction (skin rash, hives, itching); *histamine release* (decreased blood pressure; fast heartbeat; increased sweating; redness or flushing of face; shortness of breath, wheezing, or troubled breathing); *mental depression; toxic megacolon* (bloating, constipation, loss of appetite, nausea or vomiting, stomach pain)
Symptoms of overdose of opiates
Cold, clammy skin; confusion; convulsions; dizziness, severe; drowsiness, severe; low blood pressure; nervousness or restlessness, severe; pinpoint pupils; respiratory depression (slow or irregular breathing); *slow heartbeat; unconsciousness; weakness, severe*

Those indicating need for medical attention only if they continue or are bothersome
Incidence more frequent with large doses
Antidiuretic effect (decreased urination); *CNS effects or hypotension, including orthostatic hypotension* (dizziness, feeling faint, lightheadedness, unusual tiredness or weakness); *drowsiness; nervousness or restlessness; ureteral spasm* (difficult or painful urination, frequent urge to urinate)

Those indicating possible withdrawal and the need for medical attention if they occur after medication is discontinued
Body aches; diarrhea; fast heartbeat; fever, runny nose, or sneezing; gooseflesh; increased sweating; increased yawning; loss of appetite; nausea or vomiting; nervousness, restlessness, or irritability; shivering or trembling; stomach cramps; trouble in sleeping; unusually large pupils; weakness, severe

Patient Consultation

In providing consultation, consider emphasizing the following selected information (» = major clinical significance):

Before using this medication
» Conditions affecting use, especially:
Hypersensitivity to paregoric or other opiates, history of
Pregnancy—Opiates and camphor cross the placenta; regular use of opiates may cause physical dependence in the fetus, leading to withdrawal symptoms in the neonate; camphor may cause respiratory depression and other serious adverse effects in the neonate
Breast-feeding—Opium alkaloids excreted in breast milk
Use in children—Increased sensitivity to respiratory depressant effects in children up to 2 years of age
Use in the elderly—Increased sensitivity to respiratory depressant effects in geriatric patients
Use by athletes—Opiates are banned and tested for in athletes by the U.S. Olympic Committee (USOC)
Other medications, especially alcohol or other CNS depressants, other antiperistaltic antidiarrheals, and naltrexone
Other medical problems, especially diarrhea caused by antibiotics or poisoning, asthma or other respiratory disease or impairment, and severe inflammatory bowel disease

Proper use of this medication
Proper administration
Taking with food or meals if gastrointestinal irritation occurs
» Importance of not taking more medication than the amount prescribed because of danger of overdose and habit-forming potential
» Missed dose: Taking as soon as possible; not taking if almost time for next dose; not doubling doses
» Proper storage

Precautions while using this medication
» Consulting physician if diarrhea continues and/or fever develops
» Avoiding use of alcoholic beverages or other CNS depressants during therapy unless prescribed or otherwise approved by physician
» Caution if drowsiness, dizziness, or lightheadedness occurs
Caution when getting up suddenly from a lying or sitting position
» Checking with physician before discontinuing medication after prolonged use of high doses; gradual dosage reduction may be necessary to avoid possible withdrawal symptoms
» Suspected overdose: Getting emergency help at once

Side/adverse effects
Signs of potential side effects, especially allergic reaction, histamine release, mental depression, and toxic megacolon

General Dosing Information

Alteration of intestinal motility in patients with traveler's diarrhea may result in prolonged fever by slowing expulsion of infectious organisms that penetrate the intestinal mucosa (for example, *Shigella, Salmonella,* and certain strains of *Escherichia coli*).

Paregoric may produce fluid retention in the bowel, which may mask dehydration and electrolyte depletion caused by severe diarrhea, especially in young children. Patients with severe or prolonged diarrhea should be monitored for signs of dehydration or electrolyte imbalances, and corrective therapy administered as required.

To reduce the risk of toxic megacolon in patients with acute inflammatory bowel disease, treatment with paregoric should be discontinued promptly if abdominal distention or other gastrointestinal symptoms occur.

Prolonged use of larger than usual therapeutic doses may result in physical and psychological dependence.

Tolerance to the antidiarrheal effects of paregoric may develop with prolonged use.

Following prolonged administration of high doses, paregoric should be withdrawn gradually in order to reduce the possibility of precipitating withdrawal symptoms.

This medication may suppress respiration, especially in very young, elderly, very ill, or debilitated patients, and those patients with respiratory problems. Lower doses may be required for these patients.

In patients with impaired hepatic function, if this medication is administered at all over prolonged periods, it should be in reduced dosage.

The effect of 4 mL of paregoric is similar to that of 2.5 mg of diphenoxylate.

Oral Dosage Forms

PAREGORIC USP

Usual adult dose: Oral, 5 to 10 mL (the equivalent of morphine—2 to 4 mg) one to four times a day until diarrhea is controlled.

Usual adult prescribing limits: 10 mL four times a day.

Auxiliary labeling:
- May cause drowsiness.
- Avoid alcoholic beverages.
- Do not take other medicines without your doctor's advice.
- Keep out of reach of children.
- May be habit-forming.
- Shake well before using.

PARGYLINE   Systemic†‡

A commonly used *brand name* in the U.S. is *Eutonyl.*

ORAL
Pargyline Hydrochloride Tablets USP†‡
    In the U.S.—*Eutonyl*

---

†Not commercially available in Canada.
‡Product is no longer being manufactured in the U.S. but may still be in circulation.

Category: Antihypertensive.

Indications

Accepted
Hypertension (treatment)—Pargyline is indicated in the treatment of moderate to severe hypertension, although its use has generally been replaced by that of safer and more effective agents.

Nonpharmacologic management (especially sodium restriction, weight reduction and exercise, and moderation of alcohol consumption) is recommended first for some patients, including those with mild hypertension, and is recommended as an adjunct to all pharmacologic hypertensive therapy.

Pharmacology

Mechanism of action/Effect: Exact mechanism of antihypertensive action is unknown, although the hypotensive effect is primarily postural, indicating possible interference with sympathetic vasoconstriction. Pargyline produces inactivation of monoamine oxidase (MAO), an enzyme involved in the metabolism of catecholamines (norepinephrine, dopamine) and 5-hydroxytryptamine (5-HT) or serotonin. This results in accumulation of norepinephrine in nerve endings and increased intracellular catecholamines.

Other actions/effects:
Pargyline has antidepressant and mood-elevating properties but is not specifically used for those indications.

MAO inhibitors prevent the inactivation of tyramine by hepatic and gastrointestinal monoamine oxidase. Tyramine in the bloodstream releases norepinephrine from the sympathetic nerve terminals and produces a sudden increase in blood pressure.

Time to peak effect: The full therapeutic effects may not occur until 4 days to 3 weeks after initiation of therapy.

Duration of action: The therapeutic effect persists for up to 3 weeks after withdrawal (time required for regeneration of enzyme).

Precautions to Consider

Geriatrics
Although appropriate studies with pargyline have not been performed in the geriatric population, the potential for increased vascular accidents (especially in the event of sudden hypertensive episodes), increased sensitivity to hypotensive effects, and reduced metabolic capacity discourages the first-time use of MAO inhibitors in patients over 60 years of age. When an MAO inhibitor is prescribed for an elderly patient, the patient's history of depression, ability to comply with prescribing instructions, and any potential drug interactions must also be considered. In addition, elderly patients are more likely to have age-related renal function impairment, which may require caution in patients receiving pargyline.

Dental
Use of pargyline may decrease or inhibit salivary flow, thus contributing to the development of caries, periodontal disease, oral candidiasis, and discomfort.

Drug interactions and/or related problems
The following drug interactions and/or related problems have been selected on the basis of their potential clinical significance (pos-

sible mechanism in parentheses where appropriate)—not necessarily inclusive (» = major clinical significance):

Note: Combinations containing any of the following medications, depending on the amount present, may also interact with this medication.

» Alcohol or
» Central nervous system (CNS) depression-producing medications, other
  (concurrent use with pargyline may increase CNS depression and aggravate postural hypotension; concurrent use with antihistamines is not recommended; also, possible tyramine content in alcoholic beverages, especially beer, wine, or ale, may induce hypertensive reactions)

» Anesthetics, local, with epinephrine or levonordefrin, or
» Cocaine
  (concurrent use with pargyline may cause severe hypertension as a result of sympathomimetic effects)
  (cocaine should not be administered during or within 14 days following administration of an MAO inhibitor)

» Anesthetics, spinal
  (hypotensive effects may be potentiated when spinal anesthetics are used concurrently with pargyline; discontinuation of pargyline at least 10 days before elective surgery if spinal anesthesia is planned may be advisable)

» Anticholinergics or other medications with anticholinergic activity or
Antidyskinetic agents or
» Antihistamines
  (concurrent use with pargyline may intensify anticholinergic effects because of the secondary anticholinergic activities of MAO inhibitors; also, concurrent use with MAO inhibitors may block detoxification of anticholinergics, thus potentiating their action; patients should be advised to report occurrence of gastrointestinal problems promptly since paralytic ileus may occur with concurrent therapy)
  (concurrent use with MAO inhibitors may also prolong and intensify CNS depressant and anticholinergic effects of antihistamines; concurrent use is not recommended)

Anticoagulants, coumarin- and indandione-derivative
  (concurrent use may increase anticoagulant activity; although the mechanism of action and clinical significance are unknown, caution is recommended)

Anticonvulsants
  (in addition to the increased CNS depressant effects, concurrent use of anticonvulsants with pargyline may cause a change in the pattern of epileptiform seizures; dosage adjustment of anticonvulsant may be necessary)

» Antidepressants, tricyclic
  (in addition to increased anticholinergic effects, concurrent use may result in hyperpyretic episodes, hypertensive crises, severe convulsions, and death; however, recent studies have shown that some tricyclic antidepressants can be used concurrently with MAO inhibitors with no adverse effects if both medications are initiated simultaneously at lower than usual doses and the doses raised gradually, or if the MAO inhibitor is gradually added to the tricyclic also at low doses; tricyclics should not be added to an established MAO inhibitor regimen; careful monitoring for side effects of either medication is necessary)

» Antidiabetic agents, oral, or
» Insulin
  (pargyline may enhance hypoglycemic effects; dosage reduction of hypoglycemic medication may be necessary during and after such combined therapy)

Antihypertensives, other, or
Diuretics or

Hypotension-producing medications, other
  (concurrent use may result in an enhanced hypotensive effect; dosage adjustment may be necessary)
  (antihypertensives with CNS depressant effects, such as clonidine, guanabenz, methyldopa, or metyrosine, may increase CNS depression)

Anti-inflammatory analgesics, nonsteroidal (NSAIAs), especially indomethacin
  (antihypertensive effects of pargyline may be reduced when it is used concurrently with these agents; indomethacin, and possibly other NSAIAs, may antagonize the antihypertensive effect by inhibiting renal prostaglandin synthesis and/or by causing sodium and fluid retention; the patient should be carefully monitored to confirm that the desired effect is being obtained)

Beta-adrenergic blocking agents, including ophthalmic beta-blockers absorbed systemically
  (possible significant hypertension may theoretically occur up to 14 days following discontinuation of the MAO inhibitor; however, sufficient clinical reports are lacking)

Bromocriptine
  (concurrent use may increase serum prolactin concentrations and interfere with effects of bromocriptine; dosage adjustment of bromocriptine may be necessary)

» Buspirone
  (concurrent use with MAO inhibitors is not recommended because elevation of blood pressure may occur)

» Caffeine-containing preparations
  (concurrent use of excessive amounts of caffeine, consumed in chocolate, coffee, cola, tea, or "stay awake" products, with pargyline may produce dangerous cardiac arrhythmias or severe hypertension because of sympathomimetic effects of caffeine)

» Carbamazepine or
» Cyclobenzaprine or
» Maprotiline or
» Monoamine oxidase (MAO) inhibitors, other, including furazolidone and procarbazine
  (concurrent use with pargyline is not recommended on an outpatient basis, as hyperpyretic crises, severe seizures, and death could result; prior to initiation of pargyline therapy, 14 days should elapse after discontinuance of one of these medications)

» Dextromethorphan
  (concurrent use with pargyline may cause excitation, hypertension, and hyperpyrexia)

» Doxapram
  (concurrent use may increase the pressor effects of either doxapram or pargyline)

» Estrogens
  (estrogen-induced fluid retention may lead to increased blood pressure)

» Fluoxetine
  (concurrent use may result in confusion, agitation, restlessness, and gastrointestinal symptoms, or possibly hyperpyretic episodes, severe convulsions, and hypertensive crises. Based on experience with tricyclic antidepressants, at least 14 days should elapse between discontinuation of an MAO inhibitor and initiation of fluoxetine. However, because of the long half-lives of fluoxetine and its active metabolite, at least 5 weeks [approximately 5 half-lives of norfluoxetine] should elapse between discontinuation of fluoxetine and initiation of therapy with an MAO inhibitor. Administration of an MAO inhibitor within 5 weeks of discontinuation of fluoxetine may increase the risk of serious events. While a causal relationship to fluoxetine has not been established, death has been reported following the initiation of an MAO inhibitor shortly after fluoxetine administration was stopped)

» Guanadrel or
» Guanethidine or
» Rauwolfia alkaloids
(administration to patients receiving pargyline may result in sudden release of accumulated catecholamines and a hypertensive reaction; parenteral administration is not recommended during and for 1 week following pargyline therapy)

(when an MAO inhibitor is added to existing therapy with a rauwolfia alkaloid, serious potentiation of CNS depressant effects may result; however, if a rauwolfia alkaloid is added to an MAO inhibitor regimen, CNS excitation and hypertension may result from release of excessive amounts of accumulated norepinephrine and serotonin)

Haloperidol or
Loxapine or
Molindone or
Phenothiazines or
Pimozide or
Thioxanthenes
(concurrent use may prolong and intensify the sedative, hypotensive, and anticholinergic effects of either these medications or pargyline)

» Levodopa
(concurrent use with MAO inhibitors is not recommended, as the combination may result in sudden moderate to severe hypertensive crisis; a period of 2 to 4 weeks is recommended after withdrawal of MAO inhibitors before levodopa is administered)

» Meperidine and possibly other opioid (narcotic) analgesics
(concurrent use with pargyline may produce immediate excitation, sweating, rigidity, and severe hypertension; in some patients, hypotension, severe respiratory depression, coma, convulsions, hyperpyrexia, vascular collapse, and death may occur; reactions may be due to accumulation of serotonin resulting from MAO inhibition; avoidance of meperidine use within 2 to 3 weeks following pargyline is recommended; other opioid analgesics such as morphine are not likely to cause such severe reactions and may be used cautiously in reduced dosage in patients receiving MAO inhibitors; however, it is recommended that a small test dose [one-quarter of the usual dose] or several small incremental test doses over a period of several hours should first be administered to permit observation of any adverse effects)

(caution is also recommended in the use of alfentanil, fentanyl, or sufentanil as an adjunct to anesthesia if the patient has received pargyline within 14 days; although the risk of a significant interaction has been questioned, the use of a small test dose is advised to detect any possible interaction)

» Methyldopa
(may cause hyperexcitability in patients receiving pargyline; also headache, severe hypertension, and hallucinations have been reported with concurrent use)

» Methylphenidate
(concurrent use with pargyline may potentiate the CNS stimulant effects of methylphenidate, possibly resulting in a hypertensive crisis; methylphenidate should not be administered during or within 14 days following the administration of pargyline)

Metrizamide
(concurrent use with pargyline may lower the seizure threshold; pargyline should be discontinued at least 48 hours before myelography and should not be resumed for at least 24 hours after procedure)

Phenylephrine, nasal or ophthalmic
(if significant systemic absorption of nasal or ophthalmic phenylephrine occurs, concurrent use with pargyline may potentiate pressor effects; these medications should not be adminis-

tered during or within 14 days following the administration of pargyline)

» Sympathomimetics
(concurrent use with pargyline may prolong and intensify cardiac stimulant and vasopressor effects [including headache, cardiac arrhythmias, vomiting, sudden and severe hypertensive and hyperpyretic crises] of these medications because of release of catecholamines that accumulate in intraneuronal storage sites during MAO inhibitor therapy; these medications should not be administered during or within 14 days following the administration of pargyline)

» Tryptophan
(concurrent use with MAO inhibitors may cause hyperreflexia, shivering, hyperventilation, hyperthermia, mania or hypomania, and disorientation or confusion; when tryptophan is added to an MAO inhibitor regimen, it should be started in low dosages and the dose titrated upwards gradually with close monitoring of mental status and blood pressure)

» Tyramine- or other high pressor amine-containing foods and beverages, such as aged cheese; beer; reduced-alcohol and alcohol-free beer and wine; red and white wines; sherry; liqueurs; yeast/protein extracts; fava or broad bean pods; smoked or pickled meats, poultry, or fish; fermented sausage (bologna, pepperoni, salami, summer sausage) or other fermented meat; and any overripe fruit
(concurrent use with pargyline may cause sudden and severe hypertensive reactions; reactions are usually limited to a few hours and easily treated with phentolamine; severity depends on amount of tyramine ingested, rate of gastric emptying, and length of interval between dose of pargyline and ingestion of tyramine; when pargyline is discontinued, dietary restrictions must continue for at least 2 weeks; other tyramine- or high pressor amine-containing foods, such as yogurt, sour cream, cream cheese, cottage cheese, chocolate, and soy sauce, if eaten when fresh and in moderation, are considered unlikely to cause serious problems)

Contraindications/Medical problems
The contraindications/medical problems included have been selected on the basis of their potential clinical significance (reasons given in parentheses where appropriate)—not necessarily inclusive (» = major clinical significance).

Except under special circumstances, this medication should not be used when the following medical problems exist:
» Alcoholism, active
» Congestive heart failure
» Hepatic function impairment, severe
(hepatic precoma may be precipitated in patients with cirrhosis, who are extremely sensitive to effects of MAO inhibitors)
» Pheochromocytoma
(pressor substances secreted by such tumors may alter blood pressure during therapy with MAO inhibitors)
» Renal function impairment, severe
(cumulative effects of MAO inhibitors may occur because of reduced renal excretion)

Risk-benefit should be considered when the following medical problems exist:
Asthma or bronchitis
» Cardiac arrhythmias
» Cardiovascular disease or coronary insufficiency, including angina pectoris, or
Cerebrovascular disease
(ischemia may be aggravated as a result of reduced blood pressure)
Diabetes mellitus
(pargyline may alter insulin or oral hypoglycemic requirements)

Epilepsy
(pargyline may cause change in pattern of epileptiform seizures)

Fever
(dosage requirements may be reduced)

Glaucoma
(may be aggravated)

» Headaches, severe or frequent
(headache as a first sign of hypertensive reaction during therapy may be masked)

» Hepatic function impairment
(pargyline may precipitate hepatic precoma in patients with cirrhosis, who are extremely sensitive to effects)

Hyperthyroidism
(sensitivity to pressor amines may be increased)

» Paranoid schizophrenia or other hyperexcitable personality states
(MAO inhibitors may cause excessive stimulation in schizophrenic patients; in manic-depressive states, may effect a swing from depressive to manic phase)

Parkinsonism
(may be aggravated)

» Renal function impairment
(cumulative effects may occur)

Sensitivity to pargyline

» Caution is required also in patients who have undergone sympathectomy, who may be more sensitive to the hypotensive effects of pargyline.

Side/Adverse Effects

The following side/adverse effects have been selected on the basis of their potential clinical significance (possible signs and symptoms in parentheses where appropriate)—not necessarily inclusive:

Those indicating need for medical attention
Incidence less frequent
Fluid retention (swelling of feet or lower legs); *orthostatic hypotension, severe* (fainting); *sympathomimetic stimulation* (diarrhea, fast or pounding heartbeat)

Note: *Swelling of feet or lower legs* may subside spontaneously within a week; however, if persistent, electrolytes should be monitored to rule out syndrome of inappropriate antidiuretic hormone (SIADH) secretion.

Incidence rare
CNS stimulation, severe (hallucinations); *hepatitis* (dark urine, yellow eyes or skin); *hypertensive crisis, possible* (severe chest pain; enlarged pupils; fast or slow heartbeat; severe headache; increased sensitivity of eyes to light; increased sweating, possibly with fever or cold, clammy skin; nausea or vomiting; stiff or sore neck)

Those indicating need for medical attention only if they continue or are bothersome
Incidence more frequent
Constipation; difficult urination; drowsiness; dryness of mouth; orthostatic hypotension (dizziness or lightheadedness, especially when getting up from a lying or sitting position; unusual tiredness or weakness)

Incidence less frequent or rare
CNS stimulation (muscle twitching during sleep, nightmares, restlessness or agitation, trouble in sleeping); *increase in appetite and weight gain; increased sensitivity of skin to sunlight; shakiness*

Note: *Increase in appetite and weight gain* are related to carbohydrate craving.

Patient Consultation

Consider advising the patient on the following:

Before using this medication
See *Precautions to Consider.*

Proper use of this medication
Importance of diet; possible need for sodium restriction and/or weight reduction

» Patient may not experience symptoms of hypertension; importance of taking medication even if feeling well

» Does not cure, but helps control hypertension; possible need for lifelong therapy; checking with physician before discontinuing medication; serious consequences of untreated hypertension
Getting into the habit of taking at same time each day to help increase compliance
Missed dose: Taking as soon as possible if remembered within 2 hours; not taking if more than 2 hours late; not doubling doses

» Proper storage

Precautions while using this medication
Regular visits to physician to check progress

» Checking with hospital emergency room or physician if symptoms of hypertensive crisis develop

» Avoiding tyramine-containing foods, alcoholic beverages and large quantities of caffeine-containing beverages, nonprescription cough and cold medicines, and other medication unless prescribed; having list of such for reference

» Obeying rules of caution during 14 days after discontinuing medication

» Caution in taking alcohol and other CNS depressants

» Caution when driving or doing things requiring alertness because of possible drowsiness

» Caution when getting up suddenly from a lying or sitting position
Diabetics: Checking urine or blood sugar levels; results may be lowered by medication

» Caution if any kind of surgery (including dental surgery) or emergency treatment is required
Carrying medical identification card
Reporting fever to physician; dosage adjustment may be required

» Patients with angina: Not increasing physical activities without consulting physician; medication may cause increased sense of well-being

Side/adverse effects
Signs of potential side effects, especially fluid retention, severe orthostatic hypotension, sympathomimetic stimulation, severe CNS stimulation, hepatitis, and hypertensive crisis

General Dosing Information

There is no known advantage to prescribing pargyline more frequently than once a day. Initial doses should be small with gradual increases being made if necessary. Unless the patient is hospitalized, dosage increases should not be made more often than every 7 days.

The hypotensive effect of pargyline is especially pronounced when the patient is standing. If feasible, blood pressure readings should be taken in the supine position, after standing for 10 minutes, and immediately after exercise. Dosage increases should be made only if there has been no decrease in the standing blood pressure from previous levels.

Hospitalized patients should not be discharged until the effect of pargyline on their standing blood pressure has been determined.

The frequency of side effects becomes greater as the dose is increased.

It is recommended that pargyline be taken in the morning to minimize interference with nighttime sleep.

It is recommended that pargyline therapy be withdrawn gradually at least 2 weeks prior to surgery. If emergency surgery is required, reduction of opioid (narcotic) analgesic or other premedication dosage to one-quarter the usual amount is recommended, along with careful adjustment of anesthetic dosage.

Diet/Nutrition

Foods and beverages containing tyramine or other high pressor amines, such as aged cheese; beer; reduced-alcohol and alcohol-free beer and wine; red and white wines; sherry; liqueurs; yeast/protein extracts; fava or broad bean pods; smoked or pickled meats, poultry, or fish; fermented sausage (bologna, pepperoni, salami, summer sausage) or other fermented meat; and any overripe fruit, when used concurrently with MAO inhibitors, may cause sudden and severe hypertensive reactions. The reactions are usually limited to a few hours and are easily treated with phentolamine. The severity depends on the amount of tyramine ingested, rate of gastric emptying, and length of the interval between the dose of MAO inhibitor and ingestion of tyramine. When MAO inhibitors are discontinued, dietary restrictions must continue for at least 2 weeks. Other foods, such as yogurt, sour cream, cream cheese, cottage cheese, chocolate, and soy sauce, if eaten when fresh and in moderation, are considered unlikely to cause serious problems.

Oral Dosage Forms

PARGYLINE HYDROCHLORIDE TABLETS USP

Note: Pargyline hydrochloride tablets are not commercially available in Canada.

Usual adult and adolescent dose:
Initial—Oral, 25 mg once a day, the dosage being increased by 10-mg increments at weekly intervals until the desired response is obtained.
Maintenance—Oral, 25 to 50 mg once a day.
Note: Geriatric patients—Extreme caution and close supervision are required; reduced dosage is often necessary.

Usual adult prescribing limits: 200 mg.

Auxiliary labeling:
- Avoid alcoholic beverages.
- May cause drowsiness.
- Do not take other medicines without your doctor's advice.
- Avoid certain foods.

PARGYLINE AND METHYCLOTHIAZIDE   Systemic‡

Category: Antihypertensive.

Indications

Accepted
Hypertension (treatment)—This combination is indicated for treatment of moderate to severe hypertension, although its use has generally been replaced by that of safer and more effective agents.

Fixed-dosage combinations are generally not recommended for initial therapy and are useful for subsequent therapy only when the proportion of the component agents corresponds to the dose of the individual agents, as determined by titration.

Nonpharmacologic management (especially sodium restriction, weight reduction and exercise, and moderation of alcohol consumption) is recommended first for some patients, including those with mild hypertension, and is recommended as an adjunct to all pharmacologic hypertensive therapy.

Patient Consultation

Consider advising the patient on the following (» = major clinical significance):

Before using this medication
See *Precautions to Consider.*

Proper use of this medication
Importance of diet; possible need for sodium restriction and/or weight reduction
» Patient may not experience symptoms of hypertension; importance of taking medication even if feeling well
» Does not cure, but helps control hypertension; possible need for lifelong therapy; checking with physician before discontinuing medication; serious consequences of untreated hypertension
Diuretic effects of the medication and timing of doses to minimize inconvenience of diuresis
Getting into the habit of taking at same time each day to help increase compliance
Missed dose: Taking as soon as possible if remembered within 2 hours; not taking if almost time for next dose; not doubling doses
» Proper storage

Precautions while using this medication
Regular visits to physician to check progress
» Avoiding use of tyramine-containing foods, alcoholic beverages and large quantities of caffeine-containing beverages, nonprescription cough and cold medicines, and other medication unless prescribed; having list of such for reference
» Obeying rules of caution during 14 days after discontinuing medication
» Caution in taking alcohol or other central nervous system (CNS) depressants
» Caution if any kind of surgery (including dental surgery) or emergency treatment is required
Possibility of hypokalemia; possible need for additional potassium in diet; not changing diet without first checking with physician
» Patients with angina: Not increasing physical activities without consulting physician; medication may cause increased sense of well-being
Diabetics: Checking urine or blood sugar levels; results may be affected by medication
Carrying medical identification card
» Checking with hospital emergency room or physician if symptoms of hypertensive crisis develop
» Caution when driving or doing other things requiring alertness because of possible drowsiness
» Caution when getting up suddenly from a lying or sitting position
Reporting fever to physician; dosage adjustment may be required
To prevent dehydration, checking with physician if severe nausea, vomiting, or diarrhea occurs and continues
» Possible photosensitivity; avoiding unprotected exposure to sun or overuse of sunlamp

Side/adverse effects
Signs and symptoms of hypokalemia
See also *Side/Adverse Effects.*

Oral Dosage Forms

PARGYLINE HYDROCHLORIDE AND METHYCLOTHIAZIDE TABLETS

Note: Pargyline hydrochloride and methyclothiazide tablets are not commercially available in Canada.

Usual adult and adolescent dose: Oral, 1 tablet per day, as determined by individual titration with the component agents.

Note: Geriatric patients—Extreme caution and close supervision are required; reduced dosage is often necessary.

Auxiliary labeling:
- Avoid alcoholic beverages.
- May cause drowsiness.
- Do not take other medicines without your doctor's advice.
- Avoid certain foods.

PENICILLAMINE   Systemic

Some commonly used *brand names* in the U.S. and Canada are *Cuprimine* and *Depen*.

ORAL
Penicillamine Capsules USP
  In the U.S. and Canada—*Cuprimine*
Penicillamine Tablets USP
  In the U.S. and Canada—*Depen*

Category: Chelating agent; antirheumatic (disease-modifying); antiurolithic (cystine calculi); antidote (to heavy metals).

Indications

Note: Bracketed information in the *Indications* section refers to uses not included in U.S. product labeling.

Accepted
Wilson's disease (treatment)—Penicillamine is indicated in the treatment of symptomatic patients (those with tissue damage due to deposition of excessive copper in various tissues) and as prophylaxis against the development of tissue damage in asymptomatic patients.

Arthritis, rheumatoid (treatment);
[Felty's syndrome (treatment)][1]; or
[Vasculitis, rheumatoid (treatment)][1]—Penicillamine is indicated in the treatment of patients with severe, active rheumatoid arthritis [including Felty's syndrome or rheumatoid vasculitis] who have not responded to other therapy.

Cystinuria (treatment) or
Renal calculi, cystine, recurrence (prophylaxis)—Penicillamine is indicated in the treatment of patients with excessive urinary cystine concentration and/or recurrent cystine stone formation who have not responded to or will not comply with other prophylactic measures.

[Toxicity, heavy metal (treatment)]—Penicillamine is less effective than other chelating agents (edetate calcium disodium or dimercaprol) for the treatment of severe lead poisoning. It is used as adjunctive treatment following initial therapy with another chelating agent. It may also be used as sole therapy in the treatment of asymptomatic patients with moderately elevated blood concentrations of lead. Penicillamine is also used in the treatment of poisoning due to other heavy metals, including mercury.

Unaccepted
Penicillamine is not effective in treating ankylosing spondylitis or psoriatic arthritis.

---

[1]Not included in Canadian product labeling.

Pharmacology

Mechanism of action/Effect:
  Chelating agent—Penicillamine chelates mercury, lead, copper, iron, and probably other heavy metals to form stable, soluble complexes that are readily excreted in the urine.

  Antirheumatic—The mechanism of action of penicillamine in rheumatoid arthritis is not known, but may involve improvement of lymphocyte function. It markedly reduces IgM rheumatoid factor and immune complexes in serum and synovial fluid, but does not significantly lower absolute concentrations of serum immunoglobulins. *In vitro,* penicillamine depresses T-cell but not B-cell activity. However, the relationship of these effects to the activity of penicillamine in rheumatoid arthritis is not known.

  Antiurolithic (cystine calculi)—Penicillamine combines chemically with cystine (cysteine-cysteine disulfide) to form penicillamine-cysteine disulfide, which is more soluble than cystine and is readily excreted. As a result, urinary cystine concentrations are lowered and the formation of cystine calculi is prevented. With prolonged treatment, existing cystine calculi may be gradually dissolved.

  Antidote (to heavy metals)—See *Chelating agent* above.

Onset of action:
  Wilson's disease—1 to 3 months.
  Rheumatoid arthritis—2 to 3 months.

Precautions to Consider

Cross-sensitivity and/or related problems
Patients sensitive to penicillin may be sensitive to this medication also.

Geriatrics
Patients 65 years of age or older may be more likely to develop hematologic toxicity with penicillamine. Also, elderly patients are more likely to have age-related renal function impairment, which increases the risk of adverse renal effects in patients receiving penicillamine for the treatment of rheumatoid arthritis.

Dental
The leukopenic and thrombocytopenic effects of penicillamine may result in an increased incidence of microbial infection, delayed healing, and gingival bleeding. If leukopenia or thrombocytopenia occurs, dental work should be delayed until blood counts have returned to normal, and patients should be instructed in proper oral hygiene, including caution in use of regular toothbrushes, dental floss, and toothpicks.

Penicillamine may cause oral ulcerations, which in some cases have the appearance of aphthous stomatitis, and, rarely, cheilosis, glossitis, or gingivostomatitis.

Drug interactions and/or related problems
The following drug interactions and/or related problems have been selected on the basis of their potential clinical significance (possible mechanism in parentheses where appropriate)—not necessarily inclusive (» = major clinical significance):

Note: Combinations containing any of the following medications, depending on the amount present, may also interact with this medication.

4-Aminoquinolines or
Bone marrow depressants or
» Gold compounds or

Immunosuppressants, excepting glucocorticoids
(concurrent use with penicillamine may increase the potential for serious hematologic and/or renal adverse reactions; concurrent use with gold compounds is not recommended)

(concurrent use with 4-aminoquinolines may also increase the risk of severe dermatologic reactions)

Iron supplements
(concurrent use may decrease the effects of penicillamine; if necessary, iron may be administered in short courses, but a period of 2 hours should elapse between administration of penicillamine and iron)

Pyridoxine
(penicillamine may cause anemia or peripheral neuritis by acting as a pyridoxine antagonist or increasing renal excretion of pyridoxine; requirements for pyridoxine may be increased during penicillamine therapy)

Contraindications/Medical problems

The contraindications/medical problems included have been selected on the basis of their potential clinical significance (reasons given in parentheses where appropriate)—not necessarily inclusive (» = major clinical significance).

Risk-benefit should be considered when the following medical problems exist:

» Agranulocytosis or aplastic anemia, penicillamine-related, history of
(risk of recurrence)

Sensitivity to penicillamine, history of

In rheumatoid arthritis patients
Renal function impairment, current or history of
(increased risk of adverse renal effects)

Side/Adverse Effects

The following side/adverse effects have been selected on the basis of their potential clinical significance (possible signs and symptoms in parentheses where appropriate)—not necessarily inclusive:

Those indicating need for medical attention
Incidence more frequent
Allergic reaction (fever; joint pain; skin rash, hives, and/or itching; swelling of lymph glands); *ulcers, sores, or white spots in mouth*

Incidence less frequent
Agranulocytosis (sore throat and fever with or without chills; sores, ulcers, or white spots on lips or in mouth); *aplastic anemia* (shortness of breath, troubled breathing, tightness in chest, and/or wheezing; sores, ulcers, or white spots on lips or in mouth; swollen and/or painful glands; unusual bleeding or bruising; unusual tiredness or weakness); *glomerulopathy, possible impending* (bloody or cloudy urine; swelling of face, feet, or lower legs; weight gain)—glomerulopathy may progress to nephrotic syndrome; *hemolytic anemia* (troubled breathing, exertional; unusual tiredness or weakness); *leukopenia* (usually asymptomatic; rarely, fever or chills, cough or hoarseness, lower back or side pain, painful or difficult urination); *thrombocytopenia* (usually asymptomatic; rarely, unusual bleeding or bruising; black, tarry stools; blood in urine or stools; pinpoint red spots on skin)

Incidence rare
Bronchiolitis, obstructive (coughing, wheezing, or shortness of breath); *dermatitis, exfoliative* (fever with or without chills; red, thickened, or scaly skin; swollen and/or painful glands; unusual bruising); *Goodpasture's syndrome* (difficulty in breathing, spitting blood, unusual tiredness or weakness); *jaundice, cholestatic* (dark urine, itching, pale stools, yellow eyes or skin); *myasthenia gravis syndrome* (difficulty in breathing, chewing, talking, or swallowing; double vision; muscle weakness); *necrolysis, toxic epidermal* (redness, tenderness, itching, burning, or peeling of skin; sore throat; fever with or without chills; red or irritated eyes); *neuritis, optic* (eye pain, blurred vision, or any change in vision)—may be caused by pyridoxine deficiency; *pancreatitis or peptic ulcer reactivation* (abdominal or stomach pain, severe); *ringing or buzzing in ears; systemic lupus erythematosus* (SLE)-like syndrome (skin rash, hives, and/or itching; blisters on skin; chest pain; general feeling of discomfort or illness; joint pain)

Those indicating need for medical attention only if continuing or bothersome
Incidence more frequent
Diarrhea; lessening or loss of taste sense; loss of appetite; nausea or vomiting; stomach pain, mild

Patient Consultation

In providing consultation, consider emphasizing the following selected information (» = major clinical significance):

Before using this medication
» Conditions affecting use, especially:
Sensitivity to penicillamine or penicillin, history of
Pregnancy—Has been reported to cause birth defects in humans
Use in the elderly—Increased risk of hematologic toxicity
Other medications, especially gold compounds
Other medical problems, especially a history of penicillamine-induced agranulocytosis or aplastic anemia

Proper use of this medication
For patients with cystinuria
Importance of high fluid intake, especially at night
Possible need for low-methionine diet

For patients with rheumatoid arthritis
Taking medication on an empty stomach
Improvement in condition may require 2 to 3 months of therapy

For patients with Wilson's disease
Taking medication on an empty stomach
Possible need for low-copper diet
Improvement in condition may require 1 to 3 months of therapy

For patients with lead poisoning
Taking medication on an empty stomach

For all patients
» Compliance with therapy; checking with physician before discontinuing medication since interruption of therapy may cause sensitivity reactions when therapy is reinstituted
Missed dose: If dosing schedule is—
Once a day: Taking as soon as possible; not taking if not remembered until next day; not doubling doses
Two times a day: Taking as soon as possible; not taking if almost time for next dose; not doubling doses
More than two times a day: Taking if remembered within an hour; not taking if not remembered until later; not doubling doses
» Proper storage

Precautions while using this medication
Regular visits to physician to check progress during therapy
Caution if any kind of surgery (including dental surgery) is required because of the effects of penicillamine on collagen and elastin
Avoiding concurrent use of iron-containing medications

Side/adverse effects
Signs of potential side effects, especially allergic reactions, blood dyscrasias, exfoliative dermatitis, glomerulopathy, Goodpasture's syndrome, jaundice, myasthenia gravis syndrome, obstructive bronchiolitis, optic neuritis, pancreatitis, peptic ulcer reactivation, SLE-like syndrome, and toxic epidermal necrolysis

General Dosing Information

Penicillamine therapy should be continued on a daily basis because interruptions for even a few days may cause sensitivity reactions following reinstitution of therapy.

If surgery is necessary during penicillamine therapy, the dosage should be reduced to 250 mg daily because of the effects on collagen and elastin. Reinstitution of full therapy should be delayed until wound healing is complete.

In the treatment of cystinuria or Wilson's disease, a daily dose of 250 mg may be administered with the dosage being increased gradually to the optimum dosage if the patient cannot tolerate the usual initial dose of penicillamine. This may also help to reduce the incidence of adverse reactions.

Patients with rheumatoid arthritis (whose nutrition is impaired), cystinuria, or Wilson's disease should be given 25 mg of pyridoxine daily during therapy because penicillamine increases the intake requirement for this vitamin.

Impairment of taste may occur with penicillamine therapy. Except for patients with Wilson's disease, normal taste acuity may be restored while therapy with penicillamine is continued by administering 5 to 10 mg of copper daily (5 to 10 drops of a 4% cupric sulfate solution may be administered in fruit juice 2 times a day).

If therapy is interrupted for any reason, it should be reinstituted with a small dosage, which is gradually increased until full dosage is achieved.

In cystinuria

The daily dosage of penicillamine may range from 1 to 4 grams.

The dosage of penicillamine should be based on measurements of urinary cystine excretion. Urinary cystine excretion should be maintained at less than 100 mg daily in patients with a history of renal calculi and/or pain, or at 100 to 200 mg daily in patients without a history of renal calculi.

If administration in 4 equally divided doses is not possible, the larger dose should be given at bedtime; or, if the occurrence of side effects requires dosage reduction, the bedtime dose should be one of the doses retained.

To help prevent the formation of cystine stones, a high fluid intake is recommended. The patient should drink 500 mL of water at bedtime and another 500 mL once during the night when the urine is more concentrated and more acidic than during the day. Usually the greater the fluid intake, the lower the required dose of penicillamine.

A diet low in methionine may be necessary to minimize cystine production. This diet is not recommended in growing children or during pregnancy because of its low protein content.

In lead poisoning

Penicillamine should be administered on an empty stomach, 2 hours before meals or at least 3 hours after meals.

In rheumatoid arthritis

Penicillamine should be given on an empty stomach (at least 1 hour before meals or 2 hours after meals) and at least 1 hour apart from any other medication, food, or milk in order to achieve maximum absorption and to reduce the possibility of inactivation by metal binding.

Dosage up to 500 mg per day may be given as a single dose. Dosage above 500 mg per day should be administered in divided doses.

During initial therapy, if the dosage has been increased up to 1 to 1.5 grams of penicillamine per day and after 3 to 4 months there is still no improvement in the patient's condition, the medication should be discontinued.

The maintenance dosage of penicillamine may need adjustment during the course of treatment. Changes in maintenance dosage levels may not be noticed clinically or in the erythrocytic sedimentation rate for 2 or 3 months after each dosage adjustment.

For those patients who require an increase in the maintenance dosage to achieve maximal disease suppression after the first 6 to 9 months of therapy, the daily dosage may be increased by 125 or 250 mg per day at 3-month intervals up to 1.5 grams per day.

In Wilson's disease

Dosage of penicillamine should be determined by measurements of urinary copper excretion to achieve and maintain a negative copper balance.

Penicillamine should be administered on an empty stomach (30 minutes to 1 hour before meals and at least 2 hours after the evening meal).

The dosage may be increased as indicated by urinary copper analyses, but dosage greater than 2 grams daily is usually not necessary.

In conjunction with penicillamine therapy, a low-copper diet of less than 2 mg daily should be maintained. Such a diet should exclude, most importantly, chocolate, nuts, shellfish, mushrooms, liver, molasses, broccoli, and cereals enriched with copper. Distilled or demineralized water should be used if the patient's drinking water contains more than 100 mcg (0.1 mg) of copper per liter.

Sulfurated potash (10 to 40 mg) may be administered with meals to minimize absorption of copper (capsules of sulfurated potash may be prepared by using light magnesium oxide as a diluent).

Oral Dosage Forms

Note: Bracketed uses in the *Dosage Forms* section refer to categories of use and/or indications that are not included in U.S. product labeling.

PENICILLAMINE CAPSULES USP

Usual adult and adolescent dose:

Chelating agent—Oral, 250 mg four times a day.

Antirheumatic—Oral, initially 125 or 250 mg once a day as a single dose, the dosage being increased, if necessary and tolerated, by adding 125 or 250 mg per day at two- to three-month intervals up to a maximum of 1.5 grams per day.

Note: Some clinicians recommend a maximum dose of 1 gram per day in rheumatoid arthritis.

Antiurolithic—Oral, 500 mg four times a day.

[Antidote (to heavy metals)]—Oral, 500 mg to 1.5 grams per day for one to two months.

Usual geriatric dose: Oral, initially 125 mg per day. Dosage may be increased, if necessary and tolerated, by adding 125 mg per day at two- to three-month intervals, up to a maximum of 750 mg per day.

Auxiliary labeling: • Take on an empty stomach.

PENICILLAMINE TABLETS USP

Usual adult and adolescent dose:

Chelating agent—Oral, 250 mg four times a day.

Antirheumatic—Oral, initially 125 or 250 mg once a day as a single dose, the dosage being increased, if necessary and tolerated, by adding 125 or 250 mg per day at two- to three-month intervals up to a maximum of 1.5 grams per day.

Note: Some clinicians recommend a maximum dose of 1 gram per day in rheumatoid arthritis.

Antiurolithic—Oral, 500 mg four times a day.

[Antidote (to heavy metals)]—Oral, 500 mg to 1.5 grams per day for one to two months.

Usual geriatric dose: Oral, initially 125 mg per day. Dosage may be increased, if necessary and tolerated, by adding 125 mg per day at two- to three-month intervals, up to a maximum of 750 mg per day.

Auxiliary labeling: • Take on an empty stomach.

PENICILLINS   Systemic

INN: Included in brackets after individual generic listings, if different from U.S. generic names.

Some commonly used *brand names* are:

In the U.S.—

Amoxil [Amoxicillin]	*Pen Vee K* [Penicillin V]
Augmentin [Amoxicillin and Clavulanate]	*Pfizerpen* [Penicillin G]
Azlin [Azlocillin]	*Pfizerpen-AS* [Penicillin G]
Bactocill [Oxacillin]	*Pipracil* [Piperacillin]
Beepen-VK [Penicillin V]	*Polycillin* [Ampicillin]
Betapen-VK [Penicillin V]	*Polycillin-N* [Ampicillin]
Bicillin L-A [Penicillin G]	*Polymox* [Amoxicillin]
Cloxapen [Cloxacillin]	*Principen* [Ampicillin]
Crysticillin 300 AS [Penicillin G]	*Prostaphlin* [Oxacillin]
Dycill [Dicloxacillin]	*Robicillin VK* [Penicillin V]
Dynapen [Dicloxacillin]	*Spectrobid* [Bacampicillin]
Geocillin [Carbenicillin]	*Staphcillin* [Methicillin]
Geopen [Carbenicillin]	*Tegopen* [Cloxacillin]
Larotid [Amoxicillin]	*Ticar* [Ticarcillin]
Ledercillin VK [Penicillin V]	*Timentin* [Ticarcillin and Clavulanate]
Mezlin [Mezlocillin]	*Trimox* [Amoxicillin]
Nafcil [Nafcillin]	*Unasyn* [Ampicillin and Sulbactam]
Nallpen [Nafcillin]	*Unipen* [Nafcillin]
Omnipen [Ampicillin]	*V-Cillin K* [Penicillin V]
Omnipen-N [Ampicillin]	*Veetids* [Penicillin V]
Pathocil [Dicloxacillin]	*Wycillin* [Penicillin G]
Pentids [Penicillin G]	*Wymox* [Amoxicillin]

In Canada—

Amoxil [Amoxicillin]	*Novopen-VK* [Penicillin V]
Ampicin [Ampicillin]	*Nu-Amoxi* [Amoxicillin]
Apo-Amoxi [Amoxicillin]	*Nu-Ampi* [Ampicillin]
Apo-Ampi [Ampicillin]	*Nu-Cloxi* [Cloxacillin]
Apo-Cloxi [Cloxacillin]	*Nu-Pen-VK* [Penicillin V]
Apo-Pen-VK [Penicillin V]	*Orbenin* [Cloxacillin]
Ayercillin [Penicillin G]	*Penbritin* [Ampicillin]
Bicillin L-A [Penicillin G]	*Penglobe* [Bacampicillin]
Clavulin [Amoxicillin and Clavulanate]	*Pen-Vee* [Penicillin V]
Crystapen [Penicillin G]	*Pipracil* [Piperacillin]
Geopen Oral [Carbenicillin]	*PVF* [Penicillin V]
Ledercillin [Penicillin V]	*PVF K* [Penicillin V]
Megacillin [Penicillin G]	*Pyopen* [Carbenicillin]
Nadopen-V 200 [Penicillin V]	*Tegopen* [Cloxacillin]
Nadopen-V 400 [Penicillin V]	*Ticar* [Ticarcillin]
Nadopen-VK [Penicillin V]	*Timentin* [Ticarcillin and Clavulanate]
Novamoxin [Amoxicillin]	*Unipen* [Nafcillin]
Novo Ampicillin [Ampicillin]	*V-Cillin K* [Penicillin V]
	VC-K [Penicillin V]
Novocloxin [Cloxacillin]	*Wycillin* [Penicillin G]

AMOXICILLIN [INN: Amoxicilline]
Oral
    Amoxicillin Capsules USP
        In the U.S.—*Amoxil; Larotid; Polymox; Trimox; Wymox;* GENERIC
        In Canada—*Amoxil; Apo-Amoxi; Novamoxin; Nu-Amoxi*
    Amoxicillin for Oral Suspension USP
        In the U.S.—*Amoxil; Larotid; Polymox; Trimox; Wymox;* GENERIC
        In Canada—*Amoxil; Apo-Amoxi; Novamoxin; Nu-Amoxi*
    Amoxicillin Tablets USP (Chewable)
        In the U.S. and Canada—*Amoxil*

AMOXICILLIN AND CLAVULANATE
Oral
    Amoxicillin and Clavulanate Potassium for Oral Suspension USP
        In the U.S.—*Augmentin*
        In Canada—*Clavulin*
    Amoxicillin and Clavulanate Potassium Tablets USP
        In the U.S.—*Augmentin*
        In Canada—*Clavulin*
    Amoxicillin and Clavulanate Potassium Tablets USP (Chewable)†
        In the U.S.—*Augmentin*
AMPICILLIN
Oral
    Ampicillin Capsules USP
        In the U.S.—*Omnipen; Polycillin; Principen;* GENERIC
        In Canada—*Apo-Ampi; Novo Ampicillin; Nu-Ampi; Penbritin*
    Ampicillin for Oral Suspension USP
        In the U.S.—*Omnipen; Polycillin; Principen;* GENERIC
        In Canada—*Apo-Ampi; Novo Ampicillin; Nu-Ampi; Penbritin*
Parenteral
    Sterile Ampicillin Sodium USP
        In the U.S.—*Omnipen-N; Polycillin-N;* GENERIC
        In Canada—*Ampicin; Penbritin*
AMPICILLIN AND SULBACTAM†
Parenteral
    Sterile Ampicillin Sodium and Sulbactam Sodium USP†
        In the U.S.—*Unasyn*
AZLOCILLIN†
Parenteral
    Sterile Azlocillin Sodium USP†
        In the U.S.—*Azlin*
BACAMPICILLIN
Oral
    Bacampicillin Hydrochloride for Oral Suspension USP†
        In the U.S.—*Spectrobid*
    Bacampicillin Hydrochloride Tablets USP
        In the U.S.—*Spectrobid*
        In Canada—*Penglobe*
CARBENICILLIN [INN (Carbenicillin Indanyl Sodium): Carindacillin]
Oral
    Carbenicillin Indanyl Sodium Tablets USP
        In the U.S.—*Geocillin*
        In Canada—*Geopen Oral*
Parenteral
    Sterile Carbenicillin Disodium USP
        In the U.S.—*Geopen*
        In Canada—*Pyopen*
CLOXACILLIN
Oral
    Cloxacillin Sodium Capsules USP
        In the U.S.—*Cloxapen; Tegopen;* GENERIC
        In Canada—*Apo-Cloxi; Novocloxin; Nu-Cloxi; Orbenin*
    Cloxacillin Sodium for Oral Solution USP
        In the U.S.—*Tegopen;* GENERIC
        In Canada—*Apo-Cloxi; Novocloxin; Nu-Cloxi; Orbenin*
Parenteral
    Cloxacillin Sodium Injection*
        In Canada—*Orbenin; Tegopen*
CYCLACILLIN [INN: Ciclacillin]†
Oral
    Cyclacillin Tablets USP†
        In the U.S.—GENERIC
DICLOXACILLIN†
Oral
    Dicloxacillin Sodium Capsules USP†
        In the U.S.—*Dycill; Dynapen; Pathocil;* GENERIC

Dicloxacillin Sodium for Oral Suspension USP†
    In the U.S.—*Dynapen; Pathocil*
METHICILLIN [INN: Meticillin]†
Parenteral
    Methicillin Sodium for Injection USP†
        In the U.S.—*Staphcillin*
MEZLOCILLIN†
Parenteral
    Sterile Mezlocillin Sodium USP†
        In the U.S.—*Mezlin*
NAFCILLIN
Oral
    Nafcillin Sodium Capsules USP†
        In the U.S.—*Unipen*
    Nafcillin Sodium for Oral Solution USP†
        In the U.S.—*Unipen*
    Nafcillin Sodium Tablets USP†
        In the U.S.—*Unipen*
Parenteral
    Nafcillin Sodium for Injection USP
        In the U.S.—*Nafcil; Nallpen; Unipen;* GENERIC
        In Canada—*Unipen*
OXACILLIN†
Oral
    Oxacillin Sodium Capsules USP†
        In the U.S.—*Bactocill; Prostaphlin;* GENERIC
    Oxacillin Sodium for Oral Solution USP†
        In the U.S.—*Prostaphlin;* GENERIC
Parenteral
    Oxacillin Sodium for Injection USP†
        In the U.S.—*Bactocill; Prostaphlin;* GENERIC
PENICILLIN G [INN (Penicillin G Benzathine): Benzathine Benzyl-
    penicillin]
Oral
    Penicillin G Benzathine Suspension*
        In Canada—*Megacillin*
    Penicillin G Potassium for Oral Solution USP†
        In the U.S.—*Pentids;* GENERIC
    Penicillin G Potassium Tablets USP
        In the U.S.—*Pentids;* GENERIC
        In Canada—*Megacillin*
Parenteral
    Sterile Penicillin G Benzathine Suspension USP
        In the U.S. and Canada—*Bicillin L-A*
    Penicillin G Potassium for Injection USP
        In the U.S.—*Pfizerpen;* GENERIC
        In Canada—GENERIC
    Sterile Penicillin G Procaine Suspension USP
        In the U.S.—*Crysticillin 300 AS; Pfizerpen-AS; Wycillin*
        In Canada—*Ayercillin; Wycillin*
    Penicillin G Sodium for Injection USP
        In the U.S.—GENERIC
        In Canada—*Crystapen;* GENERIC
PENICILLIN V [INN: Phenoxymethylpenicillin]
Oral
    Penicillin V Benzathine Suspension*
        In Canada—*Pen-Vee; PVF*
    Penicillin V Potassium for Oral Solution USP
        In the U.S.—*Beepen-VK; Betapen-VK; Ledercillin VK; Pen
            Vee K; V-Cillin K; Veetids;* GENERIC
        In Canada—*Apo-Pen-VK; Nadopen-V 200; Nadopen-V 400;
            Novopen-VK; V-Cillin K; VC-K*
    Penicillin V Potassium Tablets USP
        In the U.S.—*Beepen-VK; Betapen-VK; Ledercillin VK; Pen
            Vee K; Robicillin VK; V-Cillin K; Veetids;* GENERIC
        In Canada—*Apo-Pen-VK; Ledercillin; Nadopen-VK; Novopen-
            VK; Nu-Pen-VK; Pen Vee; PVF K; V-Cillin K*

PIPERACILLIN
Parenteral
    Sterile Piperacillin Sodium USP
        In the U.S. and Canada—*Pipracil*
TICARCILLIN
Parenteral
    Sterile Ticarcillin Disodium USP
        In the U.S. and Canada—*Ticar*
TICARCILLIN AND CLAVULANATE
Parenteral
    Sterile Ticarcillin Disodium and Clavulanate Potassium USP
        In the U.S. and Canada—*Timentin*

---

*Not commercially available in the U.S.
†Not commercially available in Canada.

Category: Antibacterial (systemic).

Indications

Note: Bracketed information in the *Indications* section refers to uses
    not included in U.S. product labeling.

Accepted
Not all species or strains of a particular organism may be susceptible
    to a specific penicillin.
Clavulanic acid, a beta-lactam structurally related to the penicillins,
    inhibits some beta-lactamases, enzymes that inactivate beta-lactam
    antibacterials (e.g., penicillins and cephalosporins).
Cloxacillin, dicloxacillin, methicillin, nafcillin, and oxacillin are peni-
    cillinase-resistant penicillins and are effective only in the treat-
    ment of infections caused by pneumococci, Group A beta-hemolytic
    streptococci [and other nonenterococcal streptococci], and penicil-
    lin G-resistant and penicillin G-sensitive staphylococci.
Sulbactam, a derivative of the basic penicillin nucleus, inhibits some
    beta-lactamases, enzymes that inactivate beta-lactam antibacterials
    (e.g., penicillins and cephalosporins).

For amoxicillin
    Genitourinary tract infections (treatment)—Genitourinary tract in-
        fections caused by *Escherichia coli, Proteus mirabilis,* and
        Enterococcus faecalis.
    Gonorrhea (treatment)—Acute uncomplicated anogenital and ure-
        thral gonorrhea in males and females caused by *Neisseria
        gonorrhoeae.*

    Otitis media, acute (treatment);
    Pharyngitis, bacterial (treatment); or
    Sinusitis (treatment)—Acute otitis media, pharyngitis, and sinus-
        itis caused by streptococci, pneumococci, nonpenicillinase-pro-
        ducing staphylococci, and *Haemophilus influenzae.*

    Skin and soft tissue infections (treatment)—Skin and soft tissue
        infections, including burn wound infections, caused by strepto-
        cocci, nonpenicillinase-producing staphylococci, *E. coli,* [and
        Proteus mirabilis].
    [Biliary tract infections (treatment).]
    [Bronchitis (treatment).]
    [Lyme disease (treatment)]—Amoxicillin is used in the treatment
        of early infection, mild neurologic and cardiac symptoms, and
        arthritis associated with Lyme disease.

    [Typhoid fever (treatment).]
    [Urethritis, gonococcal (treatment).]

For amoxicillin and clavulanate combination
    Otitis media, acute (treatment); or
    Sinusitis (treatment)—Acute otitis media and sinusitis caused by
        beta-lactamase-producing strains of *Branhamella catarrhalis*
        and *Haemophilus influenzae.*

    Pneumonia, *Haemophilus influenzae* (treatment); or

Pneumonia, *Branhamella catarrhalis* (treatment)—Pneumonia caused by beta-lactamase-producing strains of *H. influenzae* and *B. catarrhalis*.

Skin and soft tissue infections (treatment)—Skin and soft tissue infections, including burn wound infections, caused by beta-lactamase-producing strains of *Staphylococcus aureus, Escherichia coli,* and *Klebsiella* species.

Urinary tract infections, bacterial (treatment)—Urinary tract infections caused by beta-lactamase-producing strains of *E. coli, Klebsiella* species, and *Enterobacter* species.

[Biliary tract infections (treatment).]

[Bronchitis (treatment).]

[Chancroid (treatment).]

Infections caused by ampicillin-susceptible organisms are also susceptible to amoxicillin and clavulanate combination because of its amoxicillin content. Mixed infections caused by ampicillin-susceptible and beta-lactamase-producing organisms are susceptible to amoxicillin and clavulanate combination as well.

For ampicillin

Genitourinary tract infections (treatment);

Gonorrhea (treatment);

Meningitis, meningococcal (treatment);

Otitis media, acute (treatment);

Paratyphoid fever (treatment);

Pharyngitis, bacterial (treatment);

Pneumonia, *Haemophilus influenzae* (treatment);

Pneumonia, *Proteus mirabilis* (treatment);

Septicemia, bacterial (treatment);

Sinusitis (treatment); or

Skin and soft tissue infections (treatment)—Genitourinary tract infections (including gonorrhea in females and urethritis in males and females), meningococcal meningitis, acute otitis media, paratyphoid fever, pharyngitis, pneumonia, bacterial septicemia (intravenous only), sinusitis, and skin and soft tissue infections, including burn wound infections, caused by streptococci, pneumococci, penicillin G-sensitive staphylococci, enterococci, *Haemophilus influenzae, Escherichia coli, Proteus mirabilis, Neisseria gonorrhoeae, N. meningitidis, Shigella* species, *Salmonella typhi,* and other *Salmonella* species.

Ampicillin is also indicated in the treatment of gastrointestinal tract infections caused by susceptible organisms.

[Arthritis, gonococcal (treatment).]

[Biliary tract infections (treatment).]

[Brain abscess (treatment).]

[Bronchitis (treatment).]

[Endocarditis, bacterial (prophylaxis).]

[Enterocolitis, *Shigella* species (treatment).]

[Listeriosis (treatment).]

[Meningitis, *Escherichia coli* (treatment).]

[Meningitis, *Haemophilus influenzae* (treatment).]

[Typhoid fever (treatment)—Parenteral ampicillin is used in the treatment of typhoid fever.]

[Urethritis, gonococcal (treatment).]

For ampicillin and sulbactam combination

Genitourinary tract infections (treatment)—Secondary agent in the treatment of genitourinary tract infections caused by beta-lactamase-producing strains of *E. coli* and *Bacteroides* species (including *B. fragilis*).

Intra-abdominal infections (treatment)—Intra-abdominal infections caused by beta-lactamase-producing strains of *Escherichia coli, Klebsiella* species [including *K. pneumoniae*], and *Bacteroides* species (including *B. fragilis*).

Skin and soft tissue infections (treatment)—Secondary agent in the treatment of skin and soft tissue infections, including burn wound infections, caused by beta-lactamase-producing strains of *Acinetobacter calcoaceticus, B. fragilis, E. coli, Klebsiella* species (including *K. pneumoniae*), *Proteus mirabilis,* and *Staphylococcus aureus.*

Infections caused by ampicillin-susceptible organisms are also susceptible to ampicillin and sulbactam combination because of its ampicillin content. Mixed infections caused by ampicillin-susceptible and certain beta-lactamase-producing organisms may be susceptible to ampicillin and sulbactam combination as well.

[Biliary tract infections (treatment).]

For azlocillin

Bone and joint infections (treatment)—Bone and joint infections (including osteomyelitis) caused by *Pseudomonas aeruginosa.*

Pneumonia, anaerobic (treatment);

Pneumonia, *Bacteroides* species (treatment);

Pneumonia, *Enterobacter* species (treatment);

Pneumonia, *Escherichia coli* (treatment);

Pneumonia, *Haemophilus influenzae* (treatment);

Pneumonia, *Klebsiella* species (treatment);

Pneumonia, *Pseudomonas aeruginosa* (treatment); or

Pneumonia, *Serratia* species (treatment)—Pneumonia caused by anaerobic cocci, *Bacteroides* species, *Enterobacter* species, *Escherichia coli, Haemophilus influenzae, Klebsiella* species, *P. aeruginosa,* and *Serratia* species.

Septicemia, bacterial (treatment)—Bacterial septicemia caused by *P. aeruginosa, E. coli,* and *Enterobacter aerogenes.*

Skin and soft tissue infections (treatment)—Skin and soft tissue infections (including ulcers, abscesses, burns, and severe external otitis) caused by *P. aeruginosa, E. coli, Proteus mirabilis,* and *Enterococcus faecalis.*

Urinary tract infections, bacterial (treatment)—Complicated and uncomplicated upper and lower urinary tract infections caused by *P. aeruginosa, E. coli, P. mirabilis,* and *E. faecalis.*

[Biliary tract infections (treatment).]

[Brain abscess (treatment).]

[Intra-abdominal infections (treatment).]

[Meningitis, *Pseudomonas aeruginosa* (treatment).]

Azlocillin may also be indicated concurrently with an aminoglycoside or a cephalosporin for various infections, as well as the treatment of febrile episodes in immunosuppressed patients with granulocytopenia. Azlocillin and aminoglycosides (amikacin, gentamicin, or tobramycin) are also synergistic against many strains of *P. aeruginosa,* including life-threatening infections such as acute pulmonary exacerbation in patients with cystic fibrosis, and certain susceptible strains of Enterobacteriaceae.

Azlocillin, an acylureidopenicillin, is a broad-spectrum penicillin similar to mezlocillin and piperacillin.

For bacampicillin

Gonorrhea (treatment)—Acute, uncomplicated urogenital infections (gonorrhea) caused by *Neisseria gonorrhoeae.*

Otitis media, acute (treatment);

Pharyngitis, bacterial (treatment);

Pneumonia, *Haemophilus influenzae* (treatment); or

Sinusitis (treatment)—Acute otitis media, pharyngitis, pneumonia, and sinusitis caused by streptococci (beta-hemolytic streptococci, *S. pyogenes*), pneumococci (*S. pneumoniae*), nonpenicillinase-producing staphylococci, and *Haemophilus influenzae.*

Skin and soft tissue infections (treatment)—Skin and soft tissue infections, including burn wound infections, caused by streptococci and staphylococci.

Urinary tract infections, bacterial (treatment)—Urinary tract infections caused by *Escherichia coli, Proteus mirabilis,* and *E. faecalis.*

[Biliary tract infections (treatment).]

Bacampicillin, which has no *in vitro* antibacterial activity itself, is rapidly and completely hydrolyzed *in vivo* to ampicillin.

For carbenicillin (oral)

Prostatitis (treatment)—Prostatitis caused by *Escherichia coli, Enterococcus faecalis, Proteus mirabilis,* and *Enterobacter* species.

Urinary tract infections, bacterial (treatment)—Acute and chronic upper and lower and asymptomatic bacteriuria (urinary tract infections) caused by *E. coli, P. mirabilis, Morganella morganii, Providencia rettgerii, P. vulgaris, Pseudomonas* species, *Enterobacter* species, and enterococci.

For carbenicillin (parenteral)

Genitourinary tract infections (treatment)—Genitourinary tract infections (such as endometritis, pelvic inflammatory disease, pelvic abscess, and salpingitis) caused by *Neisseria gonorrhoeae, Enterobacter* species, *Enterococcus faecalis,* and anaerobes.

Intra-abdominal infections (treatment)—Intra-abdominal infections (such as peritonitis and abscess) caused by anaerobes.

Pneumonia, anaerobic (treatment);

Pneumonia, *Bacteroides* species (treatment);

Pneumonia, *Enterobacter* species (treatment);

Pneumonia, *Escherichia coli* (treatment);

Pneumonia, *Haemophilus influenzae* (treatment);

Pneumonia, *Klebsiella* species (treatment);

Pneumonia, *Pseudomonas aeruginosa* (treatment); or

Pneumonia, *Serratia* species (treatment)—Pneumonia caused by anaerobic cocci, *Bacteroides* species, *Enterobacter* species, *Escherichia coli, Haemophilus influenzae, Klebsiella* species, *P. aeruginosa,* and *Serratia* species.

Septicemia, bacterial (treatment)—Intravenous carbenicillin is indicated in the treatment of bacterial septicemia caused by *Haemophilus influenzae, S. pneumoniae,* and anaerobes.

Skin and soft tissue infections (treatment)—Skin and soft tissue infections, including burn wound infections, caused by anaerobes and other susceptible organisms.

Urinary tract infections, bacterial (treatment)—Urinary tract infections caused by *Pseudomonas aeruginosa, Proteus* species (especially indole-positive strains), and *Escherichia coli.*

[Biliary tract infections (treatment).]

[Brain abscess (treatment).]

[Meningitis, *Pseudomonas aeruginosa* (treatment).]

[Otitis media, chronic suppurative (treatment).]

Carbenicillin disodium and gentamicin or tobramycin are synergistic against certain susceptible strains of *Pseudomonas aeruginosa* when given concurrently (but not mixed together in the same intravenous bag or bottle) in full therapeutic doses.

For cloxacillin

Pneumonia, staphylococcal (treatment);

Sinusitis (treatment); or

Skin and soft tissue infections (treatment)—Pneumonia, sinusitis, and skin and soft tissue infections, including burn wound infections, caused by pneumococci, Group A beta-hemolytic streptococci [and other nonenterococcal streptococci], and penicillin G-resistant and penicillin G-sensitive staphylococci.

[Biliary tract infections (treatment).]

[Endocarditis, bacterial (prophylaxis).]

For cyclacillin

Bronchitis (treatment)—Acute exacerbation of chronic bronchitis caused by *Haemophilus influenzae* and bronchitis caused by *Streptococcus pneumoniae.*

Otitis media, acute (treatment)—Acute otitis media caused by *S. pneumoniae* and *H. influenzae.*

Pharyngitis, bacterial (treatment)—Pharyngitis (including tonsillitis) caused by Group A beta-hemolytic streptococci.

Skin and soft tissue infections (treatment)—Skin and soft tissue infections, including burn wound infections, caused by Group A beta-hemolytic streptococci and nonpenicillinase-producing staphylococci.

Urinary tract infections, bacterial (treatment)—Urinary tract infections caused by *Escherichia coli* and *Proteus mirabilis.*

[Biliary tract infections (treatment).]

[Sinusitis (treatment).]

Cyclacillin produces serum concentrations at least three times higher than those produced by ampicillin. However, it has less *in vitro* activity than ampicillin and other antibiotics in the ampicillin class.

For dicloxacillin—See *cloxacillin.*

For methicillin

Pneumonia, staphylococcal (treatment);

Septicemia, bacterial (treatment);

Sinusitis (treatment); or

Skin and soft tissue infections (treatment)—Pneumonia, bacterial septicemia, sinusitis, and skin and soft tissue infections, including burn wound infections, caused by pneumococci, Group A beta-hemolytic streptococci [and other nonenterococcal streptococci], and penicillin G-resistant and penicillin G-sensitive staphylococci.

[Biliary tract infections (treatment).]

[Endocarditis, bacterial (prophylaxis).]

[Meningitis, staphylococcal (treatment).]

For mezlocillin

Genitourinary tract infections (treatment)—Genitourinary tract infections (including endometritis, pelvic cellulitis, pelvic inflammatory disease) caused by *Neisseria gonorrhoeae, Peptococcus* species, *Peptostreptococcus* species, *Bacteroides* species, *Escherichia coli, Proteus mirabilis, Klebsiella* species, and *Enterobacter* species.

Intra-abdominal infections (treatment)—Intra-abdominal infections (including acute cholecystitis, cholangitis, peritonitis, hepatic abscess, intra-abdominal abscess) caused by *E. coli, P. mirabilis, Klebsiella* species, *Pseudomonas* species, *Enterococcus faecalis, Bacteroides* species, *Peptococcus* species, and *Peptostreptococcus* species.

Pneumonia, anaerobic (treatment);

Pneumonia, *Bacteroides* species (treatment);

Pneumonia, *Enterobacter* species (treatment);

Pneumonia, *Escherichia coli* (treatment);

Pneumonia, *Haemophilus influenzae* (treatment);

Pneumonia, *Klebsiella* species (treatment);

Pneumonia, *Pseudomonas aeruginosa* (treatment); or

Pneumonia, *Serratia* species (treatment)—Pneumonia caused by anaerobic cocci, *Bacteroides* species, *Enterobacter* species, *E. coli, Haemophilus influenzae, Klebsiella* species, *P. aeruginosa,* and *Serratia* species.

Septicemia, bacterial (treatment)—Bacterial septicemia caused by *E. coli, Klebsiella* species, *Enterobacter* species, *Pseudomonas* species, *Bacteroides* species, and *Peptococcus* species.

Skin and soft tissue infections (treatment)—Skin and soft tissue infections, including burn wound infections, caused by *E. faecalis, E. coli, P. mirabilis, Proteus* species (indole-positive), *P. vulgaris, Providencia rettgerii, Klebsiella* species, *Enterobacter* species, *Pseudomonas* species, *Peptococcus* species, and *Bacteroides* species.

Urinary tract infections, bacterial (treatment)—Urinary tract infections caused by *E. coli, P. mirabilis, Proteus* species (indole-positive), *Morganella morganii (Proteus morganii), Klebsiella* species, *Enterobacter* species, *Serratia* species, *Pseudomonas* species, *E. faecalis* (enterococci).

[Biliary tract infections (treatment).]

[Bone and joint infections (treatment).]

[Brain abscess (treatment).]

[Meningitis, *Escherichia coli* (treatment).]

[Meningitis, *Pseudomonas aeruginosa* (treatment).]

Mezlocillin may also be indicated concurrently with an aminoglycoside for various infections, as well as the treatment of febrile episodes in immunosuppressed patients with granulocytopenia. Mezlocillin and aminoglycosides (amikacin, gentamicin, or tobramycin) are synergistic against certain susceptible strains of *E. faecalis, P. aeruginosa,* and Enterobacteriaceae. They may also be synergistic against *Serratia* species, *Klebsiella* species, *Acinetobacter* species, *Citrobacter* species, indole-positive *Proteus* species, and *E. coli.*

Mezlocillin is an acylureidopenicillin chemically related to ampicillin, but is similar to carbenicillin and ticarcillin in antibacterial spectrum.

For nafcillin

Pneumonia, staphylococcal (treatment);

Septicemia, bacterial (treatment);

Sinusitis (treatment); or

Skin and soft tissue infections (treatment)—Pneumonia, septicemia (intravenous only), sinusitis, and skin and soft tissue infections, including burn wound infections, caused by pneumococci, Group A beta-hemolytic streptococci [and other nonenterococcal streptococci], and penicillin G-resistant and penicillin G-sensitive staphylococci.

[Biliary tract infections (treatment).]

[Endocarditis, bacterial (prophylaxis).]

[Meningitis, staphylococcal (treatment).]

For oxacillin—See *nafcillin.*

For penicillin G benzathine (oral)

Otitis media, acute (treatment)—Acute otitis media caused by pneumococci.

Pharyngitis, bacterial (treatment)—Pharyngitis (including scarlet fever) caused by Group A streptococci.

Rheumatic fever (prophylaxis)—Long-term prophylaxis of rheumatic fever.

Skin and soft tissue infections (treatment)—Skin and soft tissue infections caused by nonpenicillinase-producing staphylococci.

[Erysipeloid (treatment).]

[Sinusitis (treatment).]

For penicillin G benzathine (parenteral)

Bejel (treatment)—Bejel caused by *Treponema* species.

Erysipelas (treatment)—Erysipelas caused by Group A streptococci.

Pharyngitis, bacterial (treatment)—Pharyngitis, without bacteremia, caused by Group A streptococci.

Pinta (treatment)—Pinta caused by *T. carateum.*

Rheumatic fever (prophylaxis)—Long-term prophylaxis of rheumatic fever.

Syphilis (treatment)—Primary, secondary, latent, tertiary, and congenital syphilis caused by *T. pallidum.*

Yaws (treatment)—Yaws caused by *T. pertenue.*

[Erysipeloid (treatment).]

For penicillin G (oral)

Endocarditis, bacterial (prophylaxis)—Since oral penicillin G is not reliably absorbed from the gastrointestinal tract, the American Heart Association (AHA) and the American Dental Association (ADA) no longer recommend it in the short-term prophylaxis of bacterial endocarditis in patients with valvular heart disease who undergo dental or surgical procedures.

Erysipelas (treatment)—Erysipelas caused by Group A streptococci.

Gingivostomatitis, necrotizing ulcerative (treatment).

Pharyngitis, bacterial (treatment); or

Pneumonia, pneumococcal (treatment)—Pharyngitis (including scarlet fever) and pneumonia caused by pneumococci, staphylococci, and Group A streptococci.

Rheumatic fever (prophylaxis)—Long-term prophylaxis of streptococcal infections in patients with a history of rheumatic fever.

Skin and soft tissue infections (treatment)—Skin and soft tissue infections, including burn wound infections, caused by Group A streptococci and penicillin G-sensitive staphylococci.

[Relapsing fever (treatment).]

For penicillin G (parenteral)

Actinomycosis (treatment)—Actinomycosis caused by *Actinomyces israelii.*

Anthrax (treatment)—Anthrax caused by *Bacillus anthracis.*

Arthritis, gonococcal (treatment); or

Endocarditis, gonococcal (treatment)—Gonococcal arthritis and endocarditis caused by *Neisseria gonorrhoeae.*

Diphtheria (prophylaxis)—Diphtheria caused by *Corynebacterium diphtheriae* (prophylaxis of the carrier state).

Endocarditis, bacterial (prophylaxis).

Endocarditis, bacterial (treatment)—Endocarditis caused by streptococci, *Erysipelothrix insidiosa,* and other susceptible organisms.

Genitourinary tract infections (treatment)—Genitourinary tract infections caused by *Fusobacterium fusiformisans.*

Gingivostomatitis, necrotizing ulcerative (treatment)—Necrotizing ulcerative gingivostomatitis caused by *F. fusiformisans.*

Listeriosis (treatment)—Listeriosis caused by *Listeria monocytogenes.*

Meningitis, meningococcal (treatment);

Meningitis, *Pasteurella multocida* (treatment); or

Meningitis, streptococcal (treatment)—Meningitis caused by streptococci, *P. multocida, N. meningitidis,* and other susceptible organisms.

Pericarditis, bacterial (treatment)—Pericarditis caused by streptococci and pneumococci.

Pneumonia, anaerobic (treatment);

Pneumonia, pneumococcal (treatment);

Pneumonia, staphylococcal (treatment); or

Pneumonia, streptococcal (treatment)—Pneumonia caused by pneumococci, streptococci, penicillin G-sensitive staphylococci, *Clostridia,* and *Fusobacterium fusiformisans.*

Rat-bite fever (treatment)—Rat-bite fever caused by *Spirillum minus* and *Streptobacillus moniliformis.*

Septicemia, bacterial (treatment)—Intravenous penicillin G is indicated in the treatment of bacterial septicemia caused by *Proteus mirabilis,* streptococci, and *Pasteurella multocida.*

Syphilis (treatment)—Syphilis (including congenital) caused by *Treponema pallidum.*

[Brain abscess (treatment).]

[Lyme disease (treatment)]—Intravenous penicillin G is used in the treatment of more serious neurologic and cardiac symptoms, and arthritis associated with Lyme disease.

[Meningitis, staphylococcal (treatment).]

[Pneumonia, meningococcal (treatment).]

[Pneumonia, *Proteus mirabilis* (treatment).]

[Relapsing fever (treatment).]

For penicillin G procaine

Anthrax (treatment)—Anthrax caused by *Bacillus anthracis.*

Bejel (treatment)—Bejel caused *Treponema* species.

Diphtheria (treatment)—Diphtheria caused by *Corynebacterium diphtheriae* (as an adjunct to antitoxin).

Endocarditis, bacterial (prophylaxis).

Endocarditis, bacterial (treatment)—Subacute bacterial endocarditis caused by Group A streptococci [and other streptococci].

Erysipelas (treatment)—Erysipelas caused by Group A streptococci.

Erysipeloid (treatment).

Gingivostomatitis, necrotizing ulcerative (treatment)—Necrotizing ulcerative gingivostomatitis caused by *F. fusiformisans.*

Gonorrhea (treatment)—Acute and chronic gonorrhea (without bacteremia) caused by *Neisseria gonorrhoeae.*

Pharyngitis, bacterial (treatment);

Pneumonia, pneumococcal (treatment); or

Pneumonia, streptococcal (treatment)—Pharyngitis (including scarlet fever) and pneumonia caused by pneumococci and Group A streptococci.

Pinta (treatment)—Pinta caused by *T. carateum*.

Rat-bite fever (treatment)—Rat-bite fever caused by *Spirillum minus* and *Streptobacillus moniliformis*.

Skin and soft tissue infections (treatment)—Skin and soft tissue infections caused by Group A streptococci and penicillin G-sensitive staphylococci.

Syphilis (treatment)—Syphilis (all types) caused by *T. pallidum*.

Yaws (treatment)—Yaws caused by *T. pertenue*.

[Pneumonia, meningococcal (treatment).]

[Relapsing fever (treatment).]

For penicillin V

Endocarditis, bacterial (prophylaxis).

Erysipelas (treatment)—Erysipelas caused by streptococci.

Gingivostomatitis, necrotizing ulcerative (treatment)—Necrotizing ulcerative gingivostomatitis caused by *Fusobacterium fusiformisans*.

Pharyngitis, bacterial (treatment)—Pharyngitis (including scarlet fever) caused by pneumococci and streptococci.

Rheumatic fever (prophylaxis)—Long-term prophylaxis of streptococcal infections in patients with a history of rheumatic fever.

Skin and soft tissue infections (treatment)—Skin and soft tissue infections caused by penicillin G-sensitive staphylococci.

[Actinomycosis (treatment).]

[Anthrax (treatment).]

[Lyme disease (treatment)]—Penicillin V is used in the treatment of early infection, mild neurologic and cardiac symptoms, and arthritis associated with Lyme disease.

For piperacillin

Bone and joint infections (treatment)—Bone and joint infections caused by *Pseudomonas aeruginosa*, enterococci, *Bacteroides* species, and anaerobic cocci.

Genitourinary tract infections (treatment)—Genitourinary tract infections (including endometritis, pelvic inflammatory disease, pelvic cellulitis) caused by *Bacteroides* species (including *B. fragilis*), anaerobic cocci, *N. gonorrhoeae*, and *Enterococcus faecalis*.

Intra-abdominal infections (treatment)—Intra-abdominal infections (including hepatobiliary and surgical infections) caused by *Escherichia coli*, *P. aeruginosa*, enterococci, *Clostridium* species, anaerobic cocci, and *Bacteroides* species (including *B. fragilis*).

Perioperative infections (prophylaxis)—Prophylaxis of perioperative infections, including those associated with intra-abdominal (gastrointestinal and biliary tract) procedures, vaginal or abdominal hysterectomy, and cesarean section.

Pneumonia, anaerobic (treatment);

Pneumonia, *Bacteroides* species (treatment);

Pneumonia, *Enterobacter* species (treatment);

Pneumonia, *Escherichia coli* (treatment);

Pneumonia, *Haemophilus influenzae* (treatment);

Pneumonia, *Klebsiella* species (treatment);

Pneumonia, *Pseudomonas aeruginosa* (treatment); or

Pneumonia, *Serratia* species (treatment)—Pneumonia caused by *E. coli*, *Klebsiella* species, *Enterobacter* species, *P. aeruginosa*, *Serratia* species, *Haemophilus influenzae*, *Bacteroides* species, and anaerobic cocci.

Septicemia, bacterial (treatment)—Bacterial septicemia caused by *E. coli*, *Klebsiella* species, *Enterobacter* species, *Serratia* species, *Proteus mirabilis*, *S. pneumoniae*, enterococci, *P. aeruginosa*, *Bacteroides* species, and anaerobic cocci.

Skin and soft tissue infections (treatment)—Skin and soft tissue infections, including burn wound infections, caused by *E. coli*, *Klebsiella* species, *Serratia* species, *Acinetobacter* species, *Enterobacter* species, *P. aeruginosa*, *Proteus* species (indole-positive), *P. mirabilis*, *Bacteroides* species (including *B. fragilis*), anaerobic cocci, and enterococci.

Urethritis, gonococcal (treatment)—Uncomplicated gonococcal urethritis caused by *Neisseria gonorrhoeae*.

Urinary tract infections, bacterial (treatment)—Urinary tract infections caused by *E. coli*, *Klebsiella* species, *P. aeruginosa*, *Proteus* species (including *P. mirabilis*), and enterococci.

[Biliary tract infections (treatment).]

[Brain abscess (treatment).]

[Meningitis, *Escherichia coli* (treatment).]

[Meningitis, *Pseudomonas aeruginosa* (treatment).]

Piperacillin may also be indicated concurrently with an aminoglycoside for various infections, as well as the treatment of febrile episodes in immunosuppressed patients with granulocytopenia. Piperacillin and aminoglycosides (amikacin, gentamicin, or tobramycin) are also synergistic against certain susceptible strains of *P. aeruginosa*, *Serratia* species, *Klebsiella* species, *Proteus* (indole-positive) species, *Providencia* species, Enterobacteriaceae, and staphylococci. Piperacillin and some cephalosporins may be synergistic against certain susceptible bacteria, including *E. coli*, *Pseudomonas* species, *Klebsiella* species, and *Proteus* species. However, piperacillin and cefoxitin may be antagonistic against *Pseudomonas*, *Serratia*, *Proteus*, and *Enterobacter* species.

Piperacillin, the piperazine derivative of ampicillin, is a broad-spectrum penicillin similar in antibacterial spectrum to mezlocillin.

For ticarcillin

Genitourinary tract infections (treatment)—Complicated and uncomplicated genitourinary tract infections (including endometritis, pelvic inflammatory disease, pelvic abscess, and salpingitis) caused by *Pseudomonas aeruginosa*, *Proteus* (indole-positive and indole-negative), *Escherichia coli*, *Enterobacter* species, anaerobes, and *Enterococcus faecalis*.

Intra-abdominal infections (treatment)—Intra-abdominal infections (such as peritonitis and abscess) caused by anaerobes.

Pneumonia, anaerobic (treatment);

Pneumonia, *Bacteroides* species (treatment);

Pneumonia, *Enterobacter* species (treatment);

Pneumonia, *Escherichia coli* (treatment);

Pneumonia, *Haemophilus influenzae* (treatment);

Pneumonia, *Klebsiella* species (treatment);

Pneumonia, *Pseudomonas aeruginosa* (treatment); or

Pneumonia, *Serratia* species (treatment)—Pneumonia caused by anaerobic cocci, *Bacteroides* species, *Enterobacter* species, *E. coli*, *Haemophilus influenzae*, *Klebsiella* species, *P. aeruginosa*, and *Serratia* species.

Septicemia, bacterial (treatment)—Bacterial septicemia caused by *P. aeruginosa*, *Proteus* species (indole-positive and indole-negative), *E. coli*, and anaerobes.

Skin and soft tissue infections (treatment)—Skin and soft tissue infections, including burn wound infections, caused by *P. aeruginosa*, *Proteus* species (indole-positive and indole-negative), *E. coli*, and anaerobes.

Urinary tract infections, bacterial (treatment).

Ticarcillin and gentamicin or tobramycin are synergistic against certain susceptible strains of *Pseudomonas aeruginosa* when given concurrently (but not mixed together in the same intravenous bag or bottle) in full therapeutic doses.

[Biliary tract infections (treatment).]

[Bone and joint infections (treatment).]

[Brain abscess (treatment).]

[Meningitis, *Escherichia coli* (treatment).]

[Meningitis, *Pseudomonas aeruginosa* (treatment).]

[Otitis media, chronic suppurative (treatment).]

For ticarcillin and clavulanate combination

Bone and joint infections (treatment)—Bone and joint infections caused by beta-lactamase-producing strains of *Staphylococcus aureus*.

Pneumonia, *Haemophilus influenzae* (treatment);
Pneumonia, *Klebsiella* species (treatment);
Pneumonia, *Pseudomonas aeruginosa* (treatment); or
Pneumonia, staphylococcal (treatment)—Pneumonia caused by beta-lactamase-producing strains of *S. aureus, Haemophilus influenzae, Pseudomonas aeruginosa,* and *Klebsiella* species.
Septicemia, bacterial (treatment)—Bacterial septicemia caused by beta-lactamase-producing strains of *Klebsiella* species, *Escherichia coli, S. aureus, Pseudomonas aeruginosa,* and other *Pseudomonas* species.
Skin and soft tissue infections (treatment)—Skin and soft tissue infections, including burn wound infections, caused by beta-lactamase-producing strains of *S. aureus, Klebsiella* species, and *E. coli.*
Urinary tract infections, bacterial (treatment)—Complicated and uncomplicated urinary tract infections caused by beta-lactamase-producing strains of *E. coli, Klebsiella* species, *Pseudomonas aeruginosa,* other *Pseudomonas* species, *Citrobacter* species, *Enterobacter cloacae, Serratia marcescens,* and *S. aureus.*
[Biliary tract infections (treatment).]
Infections caused by ticarcillin-susceptible organisms are also susceptible to ticarcillin and clavulanate combination because of its ticarcillin content. Mixed infections caused by ticarcillin-susceptible and beta-lactamase-producing organisms are susceptible to ticarcillin and clavulanate combination as well.
Ticarcillin and clavulanate combination and aminoglycosides are synergistic against certain susceptible strains of *Pseudomonas aeruginosa* when given concurrently (but not mixed together in the same intravenous bag or bottle) in full therapeutic doses.

Unaccepted

Amoxicillin (an analog of ampicillin), ampicillin, azlocillin, bacampicillin, carbenicillin, cyclacillin (closely related to ampicillin), mezlocillin, penicillin G, penicillin V, piperacillin, and ticarcillin are penicillinase-sensitive penicillins and therefore are not effective against penicillinase-producing bacteria, especially staphylococci.
Cloxacillin and dicloxacillin are not indicated in the treatment of meningitis since they penetrate poorly into cerebrospinal fluid.

For azlocillin
Azlocillin is not effective against penicillinase-producing *Staphylococcus aureus* or beta-lactamase-producing Enterobacteriaceae.

For bacampicillin
Bacampicillin is not effective against beta-lactamase-producing bacteria (e.g., certain strains of *Enterobacter* species, *Citrobacter* species, *Haemophilus influenzae,* or *Escherichia coli*), most strains of staphylococci, and indole-positive *Proteus* species. In addition, bacampicillin is not effective against *Pseudomonas, Klebsiella,* or *Serratia* species.

For carbenicillin (oral)
Since effective serum concentrations are not achieved with oral carbenicillin, it is indicated only for urinary tract infections and prostatitis.

For mezlocillin
Mezlocillin is not effective against penicillinase-producing *Staphylococcus aureus* or beta-lactamase-producing *Haemophilus influenzae.* In addition, some USP medical experts doubt its efficacy in infections caused by *Klebsiella* species.

For penicillin G benzathine (parenteral)
Parenteral penicillin G benzathine is not indicated for the treatment of meningitis.

For penicillin G (oral)
Because of low serum concentrations, oral penicillin G is not indicated for the treatment of severe infections.

For penicillin G procaine
Parenteral penicillin G procaine is not indicated for the treatment of meningitis.

For penicillin V
Penicillin V is not indicated for the treatment of severe infections because of low serum concentrations.

For piperacillin
Piperacillin is not effective against beta-lactamase-producing staphylococci, *Haemophilus influenzae,* and other gram-negative organisms. However, piperacillin is effective against beta-lactamase-producing gonococci.

Pharmacology

Mechanism of action/Effect:

Clavulanic acid—Penetrates bacterial cell wall; acts as a "suicidal" inhibitor of a wide variety of plasmid-mediated and some chromosomally mediated bacterial beta-lactamases (Richmond classes II through V); initially acts as a competitive inhibitor, but ultimately becomes noncompetitive and irreversible; because of the resulting beta-lactamase inhibition, beta-lactam antibacterials (e.g., penicillins and cephalosporins) are protected from enzymatic degradation; since clavulanic acid binds to penicillin-binding protein-2 (PBP-2), synergy with other beta-lactams is possible; to be effective, clavulanic acid must be present at the same sites as the beta-lactam in effective concentrations at the same time.

Sulbactam sodium—Irreversible inhibitor of bacterial beta-lactamases; because of the resulting beta-lactamase inhibition, beta-lactam antibacterials (e.g., penicillins and cephalosporins) are protected from enzymatic degradation; has little useful antibacterial activity alone.

Penicillins—Bactericidal; action depends on ability to reach and bind penicillin-binding proteins (PBP-1 and PBP-3) located in bacterial cytoplasmic membranes; other penicillins inhibit bacterial septum and cell wall synthesis, probably by acylation of membrane-bound transpeptidase enzymes; this prevents cross-linkage of peptidoglycan chains, which is necessary for bacterial cell wall strength and rigidity; also, cell division and growth are inhibited and lysis and elongation of susceptible bacteria frequently occur; rapidly dividing bacteria are the most susceptible to the action of penicillins.

Precautions to Consider

Cross-sensitivity and/or related problems

Patients allergic to one penicillin may be allergic to other penicillins also.

Patients allergic to cephalosporins, cephamycins, griseofulvin, or penicillamine may be allergic to penicillins also. Although cephalosporins or cephamycins have been administered without incident to some patients with rash-type penicillin allergy, caution is recommended when cephalosporins or cephamycins are administered to patients with a history of penicillin anaphylaxis.

Patients allergic to procaine or other ester-type local anesthetics may also be allergic to sterile penicillin G procaine suspension, which is an equimolar compound of procaine and penicillin G and may contain, in addition, up to 2% of procaine hydrochloride.

Geriatrics

Penicillins have been used in geriatric patients and no geriatrics-specific problems have been documented to date. However, elderly patients are more likely to have an age-related decrease in renal function, which may require an adjustment in dosage in patients receiving penicillins.

Dental
Prolonged use of penicillins may lead to the development of oral candidiasis.

Drug interactions and/or related problems
The following drug interactions and/or related problems have been selected on the basis of their potential clinical significance (possible mechanism in parentheses where appropriate)—not necessarily inclusive (» = major clinical significance):

Note: Combinations containing any of the following medications, depending on the amount present, may also interact with this medication.

In addition to the interactions listed below, the possibility should be considered that additive or multiple effects leading to impaired blood clotting and increased risk of bleeding may occur if carbenicillin or ticarcillin is used concurrently with any other medication having a significant potential for causing hypoprothrombinemia, thrombocytopenia, or gastrointestinal ulceration or hemorrhage.

Allopurinol
(concurrent use with ampicillin or bacampicillin may significantly increase the possibility of skin rash, especially in hyperuricemic patients; however, it has not been established that allopurinol, rather than the presence of hyperuricemia, is responsible for this effect)

» Anticoagulants, coumarin- or indandione-derivative, or
» Heparin or
» Thrombolytic agents
(concurrent use of these medications with high-dose parenteral carbenicillin or ticarcillin may increase the risk of hemorrhage because these penicillins inhibit platelet aggregation; patients should be monitored carefully for signs of bleeding; concurrent use of these penicillins with thrombolytic agents may increase the risk of severe hemorrhage and is not recommended)

» Anti-inflammatory drugs, nonsteroidal (NSAIDs), especially aspirin, or
Diflunisal, very high doses, or
Other salicylates or
» Platelet aggregation inhibitors, other or
» Sulfinpyrazone
(concurrent use of these medications with high-dose parenteral carbenicillin or ticarcillin may increase the risk of hemorrhage because of additive inhibition of platelet function; in addition, hypoprothrombinemia induced by large doses of salicylates and the gastrointestinal ulcerative or hemorrhagic potential of NSAIDs, salicylates, or sulfinpyrazone may also increase the risk of hemorrhage when these medications are used concurrently with these penicillins)

» Captopril or
» Diuretics, potassium-sparing, or
» Enalapril or
» Lisinopril or
» Potassium-containing medications, other, or
» Potassium supplements
(concurrent administration of these medications with parenteral penicillin G potassium tends to promote serum potassium accumulation with possible resultant hyperkalemia, especially in patients with renal insufficiency)
(concurrent administration of captopril, enalapril, or lisinopril with parenteral penicillin G potassium may result in hyperkalemia since reduction of aldosterone production induced by ACE inhibitors may lead to elevation of serum potassium)

Chloramphenicol or
Erythromycins or
Sulfonamides or

Tetracyclines
(since bacteriostatic drugs may interfere with the bactericidal effect of penicillins in the treatment of meningitis or in other situations where a rapid bactericidal effect is necessary, it is best to avoid concurrent therapy; however, chloramphenicol and ampicillin are sometimes administered concurrently in pediatric patients)

» Cholestyramine or
» Colestipol
(may impair absorption of oral penicillin G when used concurrently; patients should be advised to take oral penicillin G and these medications several hours apart)

» Contraceptives, estrogen-containing, oral
(concurrent use with ampicillin, bacampicillin, or penicillin V may decrease the effectiveness of oral contraceptives because of stimulation of estrogen metabolism or reduction in enterohepatic circulation of estrogens, resulting in menstrual irregularities, intermenstrual bleeding, and unplanned pregnancies; interaction may be of greater clinical significance with long-term use of these penicillins; patients should be advised to use an alternate or additional method of contraception while taking any of these penicillins)

Disulfiram
(metabolism of the ester moiety of bacampicillin yields acetaldehyde and ethanol, which is later converted to acetaldehyde, also; since disulfiram blocks the hepatic conversion of acetaldehyde to nontoxic compounds, concurrent use with bacampicillin may result in nausea, vomiting, confusion, and cardiovascular abnormalities; however, metabolism of a 400-mg dose of bacampicillin yields only approximately 37 mg of alcohol and 35 mg of acetaldehyde; therefore, the risk of serious side effects following concurrent administration of disulfiram and bacampicillin is quite low)

Hepatotoxic medications, other
(concurrent use of other hepatotoxic medications with azlocillin, mezlocillin, or piperacillin may increase the potential for hepatotoxicity)

Neomycin, oral
(concurrent use with penicillin V should be avoided since malabsorption of penicillin V may occur)

» Probenecid
(decreases renal tubular secretion of penicillins and sulbactam when used concurrently, resulting in increased and more prolonged penicillin and sulbactam serum concentrations, prolonged elimination half-life, and increased risk of toxicity; however, penicillins and probenecid may be used concurrently in the treatment of infections, such as sexually transmitted diseases [STD's] or other infections, in which high and/or prolonged antibiotic serum and tissue concentrations are required)
(probenecid has no effect on the renal tubular secretion of clavulanic acid, in spite of the chemical similarity of clavulanic acid and the beta-lactams)

Contraindications/Medical problems
The contraindications/medical problems included have been selected on the basis of their potential clinical significance (reasons given in parentheses where appropriate)—not necessarily inclusive (» = major clinical significance).

Except under special circumstances, this medication should not be used when the following medical problem exists:

» Allergy to penicillins, cephalosporins, cephamycins, or penicillamine

Risk-benefit should be considered when the following medical problems exist:

Allergy, general, history of, such as asthma, eczema, hay fever, hives

» Bleeding disorders, history of
(some penicillins, especially carbenicillin and ticarcillin, may cause platelet dysfunction and hemorrhage)

» Gastrointestinal disease, history of, especially ulcerative colitis, regional enteritis, or antibiotic-associated colitis
(penicillins may cause pseudomembranous colitis)

» Mononucleosis, infectious
(skin rash may occur in a high percentage of patients who are taking penicillins)

» Renal function impairment
(because most penicillins are excreted through the kidneys, a reduction in dosage, or increase in dosing interval, is recommended in patients with renal function impairment)

For carbenicillin (parenteral), ticarcillin, and ticarcillin and clavulanate combination

» Bleeding time determinations
(may be required prior to and during prolonged therapy in patients with renal function impairment receiving high doses since hemorrhagic manifestations may occur, although rarely)

Serum potassium and sodium concentrations
(may be required periodically during therapy in patients receiving high doses since alterations in serum potassium and sodium concentrations may occur)

For azlocillin and mezlocillin

Serum potassium concentrations
(may be required periodically during prolonged therapy in patients receiving high doses since hypokalemia may occur)

For methicillin

» Renal function determinations
(may be required during prolonged therapy since methicillin may cause interstitial nephritis in up to 12% of patients)

For penicillin G (parenteral)

Serum potassium or sodium concentrations
(may be required periodically during therapy in patients receiving high doses of penicillin G potassium or penicillin G sodium since hyperkalemia or hypernatremia may occur; very high doses of penicillin G potassium may cause severe or fatal hyperkalemia; very high doses of penicillin G sodium may cause congestive heart failure)

For piperacillin

Serum potassium concentrations
(may be required periodically during therapy in patients with low potassium reserves or in patients receiving cytotoxic medications or diuretics since hypokalemia may occur)

For all penicillins (if antibiotic-associated pseudomembranous colitis occurs)

» Stool examinations
(cytotoxin assays of stool samples for the presence of *Clostridium difficile* and its cytotoxins, neutralizable by *C. sordellii* antitoxin, may be required prior to treatment in patients with AAPMC to document the presence of *C. difficile* and/or its cytotoxin; however, *C. difficile* and its cytotoxins may persist following treatment with oral vancomycin, cholestyramine, bacitracin, or metronidazole despite clinical improvement; follow-up cultures and cytotoxin assays are generally not recommended with complete clinical improvement)

Side/Adverse Effects

The following side/adverse effects have been selected on the basis of their potential clinical significance (possible signs and symptoms in parentheses where appropriate)—not necessarily inclusive:

Those indicating need for medical attention
Incidence rare

Allergic reactions, specifically anaphylaxis (bronchospasm, hypotension), *serum sickness-like reactions* (skin rash, joint pain, fever), *skin rash, hives, or itching; hematologic reactions, specifically neutropenia* (sore throat and fever)—especially with high doses; *platelet dysfunction* (unusual bleeding or bruising)—especially with carbenicillin and ticarcillin; *interstitial nephritis* (fever, rash, possibly decreased urine output, proteinuria, hematuria)—seen primarily with methicillin, but may occur with any penicillin; *pseudomembranous colitis* (severe abdominal or stomach cramps and pain; abdominal tenderness; watery and severe diarrhea, which may also be bloody; fever); *seizures*—with high parenteral doses, especially in uremic patients

Those indicating need for medical attention only if they continue or are bothersome
Incidence more common

Gastrointestinal reactions (mild diarrhea, nausea or vomiting); *oral candidiasis* (sore mouth or tongue)

Those indicating possible pseudomembranous colitis and the need for medical attention if they occur after medication is discontinued
Severe abdominal or stomach cramps and pain; abdominal tenderness; diarrhea, watery and severe, which may also be bloody; fever

Patient Consultation

In providing consultation, consider emphasizing the following selected information (» = major clinical significance):

Before using this medication

» Conditions affecting use, especially:
Allergy to penicillins, cephalosporins, cephamycins, griseofulvin, or penicillamine
Pregnancy—Penicillins cross the placenta
Breast-feeding—Penicillins are excreted in breast milk
Use in children—Neonates and young infants may have reduced elimination of renally eliminated penicillins due to incompletely developed renal function
Other medications, especially coumarin- or indandione-derivative anticoagulants; heparin; thrombolytic agents; nonsteroidal anti-inflammatory drugs, (NSAIDs), especially aspirin; other platelet aggregation inhibitors; sulfinpyrazone; captopril; diuretics, potassium-sparing; enalapril; lisinopril; other potassium-containing medications; potassium supplements; cholestyramine; colestipol; estrogen-containing oral contraceptives; or probenecid
Other medical problems, especially a history of bleeding disorders; a history of gastrointestinal disease, especially ulcerative colitis, regional enteritis, or antibiotic-associated colitis; infectious mononucleosis; or renal function impairment

Proper use of this medication

Taking on an empty stomach (for ampicillin, bacampicillin oral suspension, cloxacillin, cyclacillin, dicloxacillin, nafcillin, oxacillin, penicillin G)

Taking on a full or empty stomach (for amoxicillin, amoxicillin and clavulanate, bacampicillin tablets, penicillin V); absorption of carbenicillin may be enhanced when administered with food

Taking amoxicillin suspension straight or mixed with formulas, milk, fruit juice, water, ginger ale, or other cold drinks; taking immediately after mixing; drinking full dose

Avoiding acidic juices and beverages concurrently with penicillin G

Proper administration technique for oral liquids and/or pediatric drops; not using after expiration date

» Compliance with full course of therapy, especially in streptococcal infections
» Importance of not missing doses and taking at evenly spaced times
  Missed dose: Taking as soon as possible; not taking if almost time for next dose; not doubling doses
» Proper storage

Precautions while using this medication

Checking with physician if no improvement within a few days
Carrying medical identification card or wearing medical identification bracelet if previous anaphylactic reaction to penicillins
» For severe diarrhea, checking with physician before taking any antidiarrheals; for mild diarrhea, kaolin- or attapulgite-containing, but not other, antidiarrheals may be tried; checking with physician or pharmacist if mild diarrhea continues or worsens
» Use of an alternate or additional method of contraception if taking estrogen-containing oral contraceptives concurrently, especially with ampicillin, bacampicillin, or penicillin V
» Diabetics: False-positive reactions with copper sulfate urine glucose tests may occur, especially with amoxicillin, amoxicillin and clavulanate, ampicillin, ampicillin and sulbactam, bacampicillin, and penicillin G
  Caution if diagnostic tests are required

Side/adverse effects

Signs of potential side effects, especially pseudomembranous colitis, allergic reactions, neutropenia, platelet dysfunction, interstitial nephritis, oral candidiasis, seizures, and gastrointestinal reactions

General Dosing Information

Therapy should be continued for at least 10 days in Group A beta-hemolytic streptococcal infections to help prevent the occurrence of acute rheumatic fever.

For oral dosage forms only

Penicillins, except bacampicillin hydrochloride tablets, amoxicillin, amoxicillin and clavulanate combination, and penicillin V, should preferably be taken with a full glass (240 mL) of water on an empty stomach (either 1 hour before or 2 hours after meals) to obtain optimum serum and/or urine concentrations. Bacampicillin hydrochloride tablets, amoxicillin, amoxicillin and clavulanate combination, and penicillin V may be taken on a full or empty stomach.

AMOXICILLIN

Summary of Differences

Category: Penicillinase-sensitive penicillin.
Precautions:
  Laboratory value alterations—False-positive results with copper sulfate urine glucose determinations.
  Contraindications/medical problems—Caution also needed in infectious mononucleosis.

Additional Dosing Information

Patients with impaired renal function do not generally require a reduction in dose unless the impairment is severe.

For oral dosage forms only:
• Amoxicillin may be taken on a full or empty stomach.
• Amoxicillin may be taken with formulas, milk, fruit juice, water, ginger ale, or other cold drinks.

Oral Dosage Forms

Note: Bracketed uses in the *Dosage Forms* section refer to categories of use and/or indications that are not included in U.S. product labeling.

AMOXICILLIN CAPSULES USP

Usual adult and adolescent dose: Oral, 250 to 500 mg (base) every eight hours.
Note: Gonorrhea—Oral, 3 grams (base) and 1 gram of probenecid simultaneously as a single dose.
  [Lyme disease]—Oral, 250 to 500 mg (base) three or four times a day for ten to thirty days. Duration of therapy is based on clinical response. Current recommendations are based on limited data; treatment failures have occurred and retreatment may be necessary.

Usual adult prescribing limits: Up to 4.5 grams (base) daily.

Auxiliary labeling: • Continue medicine for full time of treatment.

AMOXICILLIN FOR ORAL SUSPENSION USP

Usual adult and adolescent dose: See *Amoxicillin Capsules.*

Usual adult prescribing limits: See *Amoxicillin Capsules.*

Auxiliary labeling:
• Refrigerate.
• Shake well.
• Continue medicine for full time of treatment.
• Beyond-use date.
• Take by mouth only (pediatric drops).

AMOXICILLIN TABLETS USP (CHEWABLE)

Usual adult and adolescent dose: See *Amoxicillin Capsules.*

Usual adult prescribing limits: See *Amoxicillin Capsules.*

Auxiliary labeling:
• Should be chewed or crushed.
• Continue medicine for full time of treatment.

AMOXICILLIN AND CLAVULANATE

Summary of Differences

Category: Penicillinase-sensitive penicillin in combination with a beta-lactamase inhibitor.
Pharmacology:
  Clavulanic acid acts as a "suicidal" molecule and irreversibly binds to bacterial beta-lactamases.
Precautions:
  Drug interactions and/or related problems—Clavulanic acid does not interact with disulfiram or probenecid.
  Laboratory value alterations—False-positive results with copper sulfate urine glucose determinations.
  Contraindications/medical problems—Caution also needed in infectious mononucleosis.

Additional Dosing Information

Patients with impaired renal function do not generally require a reduction in dose unless the impairment is severe.

Amoxicillin and clavulanate combination may be taken on a full or empty stomach.

Oral Dosage Forms

AMOXICILLIN AND CLAVULANATE POTASSIUM FOR ORAL SUSPENSION USP

Usual adult and adolescent dose:
Pneumonia and other severe infections—Oral, 500 mg (anhydrous amoxicillin) and 125 mg (clavulanic acid) every eight hours.
Other infections—Oral, 250 mg (anhydrous amoxicillin) and 62.5 mg (clavulanic acid) every eight hours.

Auxiliary labeling:
- Refrigerate.
- Shake well.
- Continue medicine for full time of treatment.
- Beyond-use date.

AMOXICILLIN AND CLAVULANATE POTASSIUM TABLETS USP

Usual adult and adolescent dose:
Pneumonia and other severe infections—Oral, 500 mg (anhydrous amoxicillin) and 125 mg (clavulanic acid) every eight hours.
Other infections—Oral, 250 mg (anhydrous amoxicillin) and 125 mg (clavulanic acid) every eight hours.

Note: Two 250-mg tablets are not equivalent to one 500-mg tablet since both contain equal amounts of clavulanate potassium.

Auxiliary labeling: • Continue medicine for full time of treatment.

AMOXICILLIN AND CLAVULANATE POTASSIUM TABLETS USP (CHEWABLE)

Usual adult and adolescent dose: See *Amoxicillin and Clavulanate Potassium for Oral Suspension.*

Auxiliary labeling:
- Should be chewed or crushed.
- Continue medicine for full time of treatment.

AMPICILLIN

Summary of Differences

Category: Penicillinase-sensitive penicillin.
Precautions:
Drug interactions and/or related problems—Also interacts with allopurinol and oral contraceptives.
Laboratory value alterations—False-positive results with copper sulfate urine glucose determinations.
Contraindications/medical problems—Caution also needed in infectious mononucleosis.

Additional Dosing Information

Patients with impaired renal function do not generally require a reduction in dose unless the impairment is severe.

Oral Dosage Forms

AMPICILLIN CAPSULES USP

Usual adult and adolescent dose: Oral, 250 to 500 mg (base) every six hours.

Note: Gonorrhea—Oral, 3.5 grams (base) and 1 gram of probenecid simultaneously as a single dose.

Usual adult prescribing limits: Up to 6 grams (base) daily.

Auxiliary labeling:
- Continue medicine for full time of treatment.
- Take on empty stomach.

AMPICILLIN FOR ORAL SUSPENSION USP

Usual adult and adolescent dose: See *Ampicillin Capsules.*

Usual adult prescribing limits: See *Ampicillin Capsules.*

Auxiliary labeling:
- Refrigerate.
- Shake well.
- Continue medicine for full time of treatment.
- Beyond-use date.
- Take by mouth only (pediatric drops).
- Take on empty stomach.

Parenteral Dosage Forms

STERILE AMPICILLIN SODIUM USP

Usual adult and adolescent dose: Intramuscular or intravenous, 250 to 500 mg (base) every six hours.

Note: Bacterial meningitis; septicemia—Intramuscular or intravenous, 1 to 2 grams (base) every three to four hours; 18.75 to 25 mg per kg of body weight every three hours; or 25 to 33.3 mg per kg of body weight every four hours.

Gonorrhea—Intramuscular or intravenous, 500 mg (base) every eight to twelve hours for two doses. Treatment may be repeated if necessary.

Usual adult prescribing limits: Up to 300 mg (base) per kg of body weight or 16 grams daily.

Additional information: The sodium content is approximately 2.7 to 3.4 mEq (62 to 78 mg) per gram of ampicillin, depending on the manufacturer. This must be considered in patients on a restricted sodium intake when calculating total daily sodium intake.

AMPICILLIN AND SULBACTAM

Summary of Differences

Category: Penicillinase-sensitive penicillin in combination with a beta-lactamase inhibitor.
Pharmacology:
Sulbactam acts as an irreversible inhibitor of bacterial beta-lactamases, protecting ampicillin from enzymatic degradation.
Precautions:
Laboratory value alterations—False-positive results with copper sulfate urine glucose determinations.
Contraindications/medical problems—Caution also needed in infectious mononucleosis.

Additional Dosing Information

Ampicillin and sulbactam combination should be administered by deep intramuscular injection or by direct, slow intravenous injection over at least a 10- to 15-minute period. It may also be administered by intravenous infusion in 50 to 100 mL of a suitable diluent over a 15- to 30-minute period.

Patients with impaired renal function may require a reduction in dose.

Parenteral Dosage Forms

STERILE AMPICILLIN SODIUM AND SULBACTAM SODIUM USP

Usual adult and adolescent dose: Intramuscular or intravenous, 1.5 to 3 grams (1 to 2 grams [ampicillin] and 500 mg to 1 gram [sulbactam]) every six hours.

Note: Adults with impaired renal function may require a reduction in dose as follows:

Creatinine Clearance (mL/min)/(mL/sec)	Dose (ampicillin and sulbactam)
30/(0.50)	1.5 to 3 grams every 6 to 8 hours
15–29/(0.25–0.48)	1.5 to 3 grams every 12 hours
5–14/(0.08–0.23)	1.5 to 3 grams every 24 hours

Usual adult prescribing limits: Up to a maximum of 4 grams (sulbactam) daily.

Additional information: The sodium content (derived from ampicillin sodium and sulbactam sodium) is approximately 5 mEq (115 mg) per 1.5 grams (1 gram of ampicillin and 500 mg of sulbactam). This must be considered in patients on a restricted sodium intake when calculating total daily sodium intake.

AZLOCILLIN

Summary of Differences

Category: Penicillinase-sensitive penicillin.
Precautions:
  Drug interactions and/or related problems—Also interacts with other hepatotoxic medications.
  Laboratory value alterations—False-positive results with various urine protein tests.
  Patient monitoring—Serum potassium determinations may be required.

Additional Dosing Information

Azlocillin should be administered by direct, slow intravenous injection over a period of 5 minutes or more (in adults) or by intravenous infusion over a 30-minute period (in adults and children). Rapid intravenous administration may result in transient chest discomfort and is not recommended.

Serum determinations are recommended in patients with impaired renal and hepatic function.

Parenteral Dosage Forms

STERILE AZLOCILLIN SODIUM USP

Usual adult and adolescent dose: Intravenous, 33.3 to 50 mg (base) per kg of body weight every four hours; 50 to 75 mg per kg of body weight every six hours; 3 grams every four hours; or 4 grams every six hours.

Note: Urinary tract infections (complicated)—Intravenous, 37.5 to 50 mg (base) per kg of body weight every six hours; or 3 grams every six hours.

  Urinary tract infections (uncomplicated)—Intravenous, 25 to 31.25 mg (base) per kg of body weight every six hours; or 2 grams every six hours.

Adults with impaired renal function may require a reduction in dose as follows:

Creatinine Clearance (mL/min)/(mL/sec)	Dose	
	Urinary Tract Infections	Serious Systemic Infections
>30/(0.50)	See *Usual adult and adolescent dose*	See *Usual adult and adolescent dose*
10–30/(0.17–0.50)	1.5 grams every 8 to 12 hours	2 grams every 8 hours
<10/(0.17)	1.5 to 2 grams every 12 hours	3 grams every 12 hours
Hemodialysis patients	—	3 grams after each dialysis, then every 12 hours

Usual adult prescribing limits: Up to 350 mg (base) per kg of body weight or 24 grams daily in life-threatening infections.

Additional information: The sodium content is approximately 2.2 mEq (50 mg) per gram of azlocillin. This must be considered in patients on a restricted sodium intake when calculating total daily sodium intake.

BACAMPICILLIN

Summary of Differences

Category: Beta-lactamase-sensitive penicillin.
Precautions:
  Drug interactions and/or related problems—Also interacts with allopurinol, disulfiram, and oral contraceptives.
  Contraindications/medical problems—Caution also needed in infectious mononucleosis.

Additional Dosing Information

Bacampicillin is stable in the presence of gastric acid. Also, food does not delay or reduce absorption of bacampicillin hydrochloride tablets. Therefore, the tablets may be taken on a full or empty stomach. However, bacampicillin hydrochloride oral suspension should preferably be taken with a full glass (240 mL) of water on an empty stomach (either 1 hour before or 2 hours after meals) to obtain optimum serum and/or urine concentrations.

Patients with impaired renal function do not generally require a reduction in dose unless the impairment is severe. However, renal clearance of penicillins is decreased in neonates and may necessitate a decrease in dose.

Oral Dosage Forms

BACAMPICILLIN HYDROCHLORIDE FOR ORAL SUSPENSION USP

Usual adult and adolescent dose:
  Pneumonia—Oral, 800 mg every twelve hours.
  Skin and soft tissue infections, acute otitis media, pharyngitis, sinusitis, and urinary tract infections—400 to 800 mg every twelve hours.

Note: Gonorrhea (acute, uncomplicated urogenital infections in males and females)—Oral, 1.6 grams and 1 gram of probenecid simultaneously as a single dose.

Urinary tract infections (chronic)—Doses less than the usual adult dose are not recommended.

Usual adult prescribing limits: Up to 3.2 grams daily.

Auxiliary labeling:
- Refrigerate.
- Shake well.
- Continue medicine for full time of treatment.
- Beyond-use date.
- Take on empty stomach.

BACAMPICILLIN HYDROCHLORIDE TABLETS USP

Usual adult and adolescent dose: See *Bacampicillin Hydrochloride for Oral Suspension.*

Usual adult prescribing limits: See *Bacampicillin Hydrochloride for Oral Suspension.*

Auxiliary labeling: • Continue medicine for full time of treatment.

CARBENICILLIN

Summary of Differences

Category: Penicillinase-sensitive penicillin.
Precautions:
  Drug interactions and/or related problems—Parenteral carbenicillin also interacts with anticoagulants and other medications that affect blood clotting.
  Laboratory value alterations—May increase bleeding time.
  Patient monitoring—Bleeding time and serum potassium and sodium determinations may be required (parenteral only).

Additional Dosing Information

For oral dosage forms only:
- Patients with severely impaired renal function (creatinine clearance less than 10 mL per minute) will not achieve therapeutic urine concentrations of carbenicillin.

For parenteral dosage forms only:
- Since carbenicillin disodium is not absorbed orally, it must be administered by intramuscular or intravenous injection only. Intramuscular injections should not exceed 2 grams in each site.
- Intermittent infusions may be administered over a 30-minute to 2-hour period.
- Patients with impaired renal function may require a reduction in dose and should be observed for hemorrhagic complications.

Oral Dosage Forms

CARBENICILLIN INDANYL SODIUM TABLETS USP

Usual adult dose: Oral, 382 to 764 mg (base) every six hours.

Auxiliary labeling: • Continue medicine for full time of treatment.

Parenteral Dosage Forms

STERILE CARBENICILLIN DISODIUM USP

Usual adult and adolescent dose:
  Septicemia, meningitis, pneumonia, or skin and soft-tissue infections—Intramuscular or intravenous, 50 to 83.3 mg (base) per kg of body weight every four hours.

Urinary tract infections—Intramuscular or intravenous, 1 to 2 grams (base) every six hours; or up to 50 mg per kg of body weight every six hours.

Note: Gonorrhea—Intramuscular, 4 grams (base), divided between two sites, and 1 gram of probenecid orally, administered approximately thirty minutes prior to carbenicillin.
  Patients with impaired renal function (creatinine clearance less than 5 mL per minute)—Intravenous, 2 grams (base) every eight to twelve hours.

Usual adult prescribing limits: Up to 40 grams (base) daily.

Additional information: The sodium content is approximately 4.7 to 5.3 mEq (108 to 122 mg), but may be as high as 6.5 mEq (150 mg), per gram of carbenicillin. This must be considered in patients on a restricted sodium intake when calculating total daily sodium intake.

CLOXACILLIN

Summary of Differences

Category: Penicillinase-resistant penicillin.

Additional Dosing Information

Patients with impaired renal function do not generally require a reduction in dose unless the impairment is severe.

Oral Dosage Forms

CLOXACILLIN SODIUM CAPSULES USP

Usual adult and adolescent dose: Oral, 250 to 500 mg (base) every six hours.

Usual adult prescribing limits: Up to 6 grams (base) daily.

Auxiliary labeling:
- Continue medicine for full time of treatment.
- Take on empty stomach.

CLOXACILLIN SODIUM FOR ORAL SOLUTION USP

Usual adult and adolescent dose: See *Cloxacillin Sodium Capsules.*

Usual adult prescribing limits: See *Cloxacillin Sodium Capsules.*

Auxiliary labeling:
- Refrigerate.
- Continue medicine for full time of treatment.
- Beyond-use date.
- Take on empty stomach.

Parenteral Dosage Forms

Note: The dosing and dosage forms available are expressed in terms of cloxacillin base.

CLOXACILLIN SODIUM INJECTION

Usual adult and adolescent dose: Intravenous, 250 to 500 mg (base) every six hours.

Note: Larger and more frequent doses may be required for more severe infections.

Usual adult prescribing limits: Up to 6 grams (base) daily.

CYCLACILLIN

Summary of Differences

Category: Penicillinase-sensitive penicillin.

Additional Dosing Information

Patients with impaired renal function may require a reduction in dose.

Oral Dosage Forms

CYCLACILLIN TABLETS USP

Usual adult and adolescent dose: Oral, 250 to 500 mg every six hours.

Note: Patients with impaired renal function may require a reduction in dose as follows:

Creatinine Clearance (mL/min)/(mL/sec)	Dose
>50/(0.83)	Up to 500 mg every 6 hours
30–50/(0.50–0.83)	Up to 500 mg every 12 hours
15–30/(0.25–0.50)	Up to 500 mg every 18 hours
10–15/(0.17–0.25)	Up to 500 mg every 24 hours
10/(0.17)	Serum determinations are recommended to determine dose and frequency

Usual adult prescribing limits: Up to 8 grams daily have been used.

Auxiliary labeling:
- Continue medicine for full time of treatment.
- Take on empty stomach.

DICLOXACILLIN

Summary of Differences

Category: Penicillinase-resistant penicillin.

Additional Dosing Information

Patients with impaired renal function do not generally require a reduction in dose unless the impairment is severe.

Oral Dosage Forms

DICLOXACILLIN SODIUM CAPSULES USP

Usual adult and adolescent dose: Oral, 125 to 250 mg (base) every six hours.

Usual adult prescribing limits: Up to 6 grams (base) daily.

Auxiliary labeling:
- Continue medicine for full time of treatment.
- Take on empty stomach.

DICLOXACILLIN SODIUM FOR ORAL SUSPENSION USP

Usual adult and adolescent dose: See *Dicloxacillin Sodium Capsules*.

Usual adult prescribing limits: See *Dicloxacillin Sodium Capsules*.

Auxiliary labeling:
- Refrigerate.
- Shake well.
- Continue medicine for full time of treatment.
- Beyond-use date.
- Take on empty stomach.

METHICILLIN

Summary of Differences

Category: Penicillinase-resistant penicillin.
Precautions:
    Drug interactions and/or related problems—May also interact with other nephrotoxic medications.
    Patient monitoring—Renal function determinations may be required because of interstitial nephritis.

Additional Dosing Information

Methicillin sodium for injection should be administered by deep intragluteal injection or by intravenous injection only.

Patients with impaired renal function require a reduction in dose.

Parenteral Dosage Forms

METHICILLIN SODIUM FOR INJECTION USP

Usual adult and adolescent dose:
    Intramuscular, 1 gram (base) every four to six hours.
    Intravenous, 1 to 2 grams (base) every four hours.

Usual adult prescribing limits: Up to 24 grams (base) daily.

Additional information: The total sodium content (derived from sodium citrate buffer and methicillin sodium) is approximately 2.9 to 3.1 mEq (67 to 71 mg) per gram of methicillin sodium. This must be considered in patients on a restricted sodium intake when calculating total daily sodium intake.

MEZLOCILLIN

Summary of Differences

Category: Beta-lactamase-sensitive penicillin.
Precautions:
    Drug interactions and/or related problems—Also interacts with other hepatotoxic medications.
    Laboratory value alterations—May produce false-positive protein reactions with various urine protein tests.
    Contraindications/medical problems—Caution also needed in hepatic function impairment.
    Patient monitoring—Serum potassium determinations may be required.

Additional Dosing Information

Intramuscular injections should not exceed 2 grams in each site.

Serum determinations are recommended in patients with impaired renal and hepatic function.

Parenteral Dosage Forms

STERILE MEZLOCILLIN SODIUM USP

Usual adult and adolescent dose: Intramuscular or intravenous, 33.3 to 58.3 mg (base) per kg of body weight every four hours; 50 to 87.5 mg per kg of body weight every six hours; or 3 to 4 grams every four to six hours.

Note: Acute, uncomplicated gonococcal urethritis—Intramuscular or intravenous, 1 to 2 grams (base) as a single dose and 1 gram of probenecid orally, administered up to approximately thirty minutes prior to mezlocillin or simultaneously.

Urinary tract infections (complicated)—Intravenous, 37.5 to 50 mg (base) per kg of body weight every six hours; or 3 grams every six hours.

Urinary tract infections (uncomplicated)—Intramuscular or intravenous, 25 to 31.25 mg (base) per kg of body weight every six hours; or 1.5 to 2 grams every six hours.

Adults with impaired renal function may require a reduction in dose as follows:

Creatinine Clearance (mL/min)/(mL/sec)	Dose (base)
>30/(0.50)	See *Usual adult and adolescent dose*
10–30/(0.17–0.50)	1.5 to 3 grams every 6 to 8 hours
<10/(0.17)	1.5 to 2 grams every 6 to 8 hours
Hemodialysis patients	3 to 4 grams after each dialysis, then every 12 hours
Peritoneal dialysis patients	3 grams every 12 hours

Usual adult prescribing limits: Up to 24 grams (base) daily. Doses up to 500 mg per kg of body weight daily have also been used.

Additional information: The sodium content is approximately 1.9 mEq (43 mg) per gram of mezlocillin. This must be considered in patients on a restricted sodium intake when calculating total daily sodium intake.

NAFCILLIN

Summary of Differences

Category: Penicillinase-resistant penicillin.
Precautions: Drug interactions and/or related problems—May also interact with other nephrotoxic medications.

Additional Dosing Information

Nafcillin sodium for injection should be administered by deep intragluteal injection or by intravenous injection only.

Patients with impaired renal or hepatic function do not generally require a reduction in usual doses. However, high doses may not be tolerated.

Oral Dosage Forms

NAFCILLIN SODIUM CAPSULES USP

Usual adult and adolescent dose: Oral, 250 mg to 1 gram (base) every four to six hours.

Usual adult prescribing limits: Up to 6 grams (base) daily.

Auxiliary labeling:
• Continue medicine for full time of treatment.
• Take on empty stomach.

Note: Capsules are buffered with calcium carbonate, which may interact with other medications.

NAFCILLIN SODIUM FOR ORAL SOLUTION USP

Usual adult and adolescent dose: See *Nafcillin Sodium Capsules.*

Usual adult prescribing limits: See *Nafcillin Sodium Capsules.*

Auxiliary labeling:
• Refrigerate.
• Continue medicine for full time of treatment.
• Beyond-use date.
• Take on empty stomach.

NAFCILLIN SODIUM TABLETS USP

Usual adult and adolescent dose: See *Nafcillin Sodium Capsules.*

Usual adult prescribing limits: See *Nafcillin Sodium Capsules.*

Auxiliary labeling:
• Continue medicine for full time of treatment.
• Take on empty stomach.

Note: Tablets are buffered with calcium carbonate, which may interact with other medications.

Parenteral Dosage Forms

NAFCILLIN SODIUM FOR INJECTION USP

Usual adult and adolescent dose:
Intramuscular, 500 mg (base) every four to six hours.
Intravenous, 500 mg to 1.5 grams (base) every four hours.

Usual adult prescribing limits:
Intramuscular—Up to 12 grams (base) daily.
Intravenous—Up to 20 grams (base) daily.

Additional information: The total sodium content (derived from sodium citrate buffer and nafcillin sodium) is approximately 2.9 mEq (67 mg) per gram of nafcillin. This must be considered in patients on a restricted sodium intake when calculating total daily sodium intake.

OXACILLIN

Summary of Differences

Category: Penicillinase-resistant penicillin.
Precautions: Drug interactions and/or related problems—May also interact with other nephrotoxic medications.

Additional Dosing Information

Patients with impaired renal function do not generally require a reduction in dose.

Neonates and other infants may develop transient hematuria, albuminuria, and azotemia when given large doses (150 to 175 mg per kg of body weight [mg/kg] daily).

Oral Dosage Forms

OXACILLIN SODIUM CAPSULES USP

Usual adult and adolescent dose: Oral, 500 mg to 1 gram (base) every four to six hours.

Usual adult prescribing limits: Up to 6 grams (base) daily.

Auxiliary labeling:
- Continue medicine for full time of treatment.
- Take on empty stomach.

OXACILLIN SODIUM FOR ORAL SOLUTION USP

Usual adult and adolescent dose: See *Oxacillin Sodium Capsules*.

Usual adult prescribing limits: See *Oxacillin Sodium Capsules*.

Auxiliary labeling:
- Refrigerate.
- Continue medicine for full time of treatment.
- Beyond-use date.
- Take on empty stomach.

Parenteral Dosage Forms

OXACILLIN SODIUM FOR INJECTION USP

Usual adult and adolescent dose: Intramuscular or intravenous, 1 to 2 grams (base) every four hours.

Usual adult prescribing limits: Up to 20 grams (base) daily in severe septicemia and meningitis.

Additional information: The total sodium content (derived from dibasic sodium phosphate buffer and oxacillin sodium) is approximately 2.8 to 3.1 mEq (64 to 71 mg) per gram of oxacillin. This must be considered in patients on a restricted sodium intake when calculating total daily sodium intake.

PENICILLIN G

Summary of Differences

Category: Penicillinase-sensitive penicillin.
Precautions:
Cross-sensitivity and/or related problems—Cross-sensitivity with other ester-type local anesthetics may also occur (penicillin G procaine).
Drug interactions and/or related problems—May also interact with other nephrotoxic medications.
Laboratory value alterations—False-positive results with copper sulfate urine glucose determinations.
Patient monitoring—Serum potassium or sodium determinations may be required (parenteral only).

Additional Dosing Information

Patients with impaired renal function do not generally require a reduction in dose unless the impairment is severe.

For oral dosage forms only:
- Oral administration of penicillin G commonly results in low serum concentrations. Therefore, severe infections should not be treated with oral penicillin during the acute stage.
- Penicillin G is an acid-labile penicillin; therefore, concurrent administration with acidic fruit juices and other acidic beverages should be avoided.

Oral Dosage Forms

PENICILLIN G BENZATHINE SUSPENSION

Usual adult and adolescent dose: Oral, 250,000 to 500,000 Units (base) every four to six hours.

Note: Continuous prophylaxis of streptococcal infections in patients with a history of rheumatic heart disease—Oral, 200,000 to 250,000 Units (base) every twelve hours.

Auxiliary labeling:
- Continue medicine for full time of treatment.
- Take on empty stomach.

PENICILLIN G POTASSIUM FOR ORAL SOLUTION USP

Usual adult and adolescent dose: Oral, 200,000 to 500,000 Units (125 to 312 mg) (base) every six to eight hours.

Note: Continuous prophylaxis of streptococcal infections in patients with a history of rheumatic heart disease—Oral, 200,000 to 250,000 Units (125 to 156 mg) (base) every twelve hours.

Usual adult prescribing limits: Up to 12,000,000 Units (7.5 grams) (base) daily.

Auxiliary labeling:
- Refrigerate.
- Continue medicine for full time of treatment.
- Beyond-use date.
- Take on empty stomach.

PENICILLIN G POTASSIUM TABLETS USP

Usual adult and adolescent dose: See *Penicillin G Potassium for Oral Solution*.

Usual adult prescribing limits: See *Penicillin G Potassium for Oral Solution*.

Auxiliary labeling:
- Continue medicine for full time of treatment.
- Take on empty stomach.

Note: Tablets are buffered with calcium carbonate, which may interact with other medications.

Parenteral Dosage Forms

Note: Bracketed uses in the *Dosage Forms* section refer to categories of use and/or indications that are not included in U.S. product labeling.

STERILE PENICILLIN G BENZATHINE SUSPENSION USP

Usual adult and adolescent dose: Group A streptococcal pharyngitis—Intramuscular, 1,200,000 Units (base) as a single dose.

Note: Continuous prophylaxis of streptococcal infections in patients with a history of rheumatic heart disease—Intramuscular, 1,200,000 Units (base) once a month; or 600,000 Units every two weeks.

Syphilis (primary, secondary, and latent)—Intramuscular, 2,400,000 Units (base) as a single dose.

Syphilis (tertiary and neurosyphilis)—Intramuscular, 2,400,000 Units (base) once a week for three weeks; or 3,000,000 Units once a week for two to three weeks.

Usual adult prescribing limits: Up to 2,400,000 Units (base) daily.

Additional information:

For deep intramuscular use only. Do not administer intravenously, intra-arterially, subcutaneously, or by fat-layer injection. Intravenous injection may cause embolic or toxic reactions. Intra-arterial injection may cause extensive necrosis of the extremity or organ, especially in children. Subcutaneous and fat-layer injection may cause pain and induration.

Injection of penicillin G benzathine should be made at a slow, steady rate to prevent blockage of the needle because of the high concentration of suspended material.

Intramuscular administration of penicillin G benzathine results in much lower and more prolonged serum concentrations than those attained with other parenteral penicillins.

PENICILLIN G POTASSIUM FOR INJECTION USP

Usual adult and adolescent dose: Intramuscular or intravenous, 1,000,000 to 5,000,000 Units (base) every four to six hours.

Note: Actinomycosis—Intravenous infusion, 10,000,000 to 20,000,000 Units (base) daily.

Clostridial infections—20,000,000 Units (base) daily.

Erysipeloid endocarditis—10,000,000 to 20,000,000 Units (base) daily.

Gingivostomatitis, necrotizing ulcerative—10,000,000 to 20,000,000 Units (base) daily.

Gonococcal endocarditis and arthritis—10,000,000 to 20,000,000 Units (base) daily.

Listeria endocarditis and meningitis—15,000,000 to 20,000,000 Units (base) daily.

Meningococcal meningitis—1,000,000 to 2,000,000 Units (base) every two hours; or intravenous infusion, 20,000,000 to 30,000,000 Units (base) daily.

Pasteurella multocida septicemia and meningitis—10,000,000 to 20,000,000 Units (base) daily.

Rat-bite fever—10,000,000 to 20,000,000 Units (base) daily.

[Lyme disease]—Intravenous, 3,300,000 to 4,000,000 Units (base) every four hours for ten to twenty-one days. Duration of therapy is based on clinical response. Current recommendations are based on limited data; treatment failures have occurred and retreatment may be necessary.

Usual adult prescribing limits: Up to 100,000,000 Units (base) daily.

Additional information:

Daily doses of 10,000,000 Units or more should be administered by slow intravenous infusion or by intermittent piggyback infusion because of possible electrolyte imbalance.

The potassium content and sodium content (derived from sodium citrate buffer) of penicillin G potassium for injection are approximately 1.7 mEq (66.3 mg) and 0.3 mEq (6.9 mg) per 1,000,000 Units of penicillin G, respectively. The sodium content must be considered in patients on a restricted sodium intake when calculating total daily sodium intake.

STERILE PENICILLIN G PROCAINE SUSPENSION USP

Usual adult and adolescent dose: Intramuscular, 600,000 to 1,200,000 Units (base) daily.

Note: Diphtheria—Intramuscular, 300,000 to 600,000 Units (base) daily as adjunctive therapy to diphtheria antitoxin.

Gonorrhea—Intramuscular, 4,800,000 Units (base), divided between two sites, and 1 gram of probenecid orally, administered approximately thirty minutes prior to penicillin or simultaneously as a single dose.

Syphilis—Intramuscular, 600,000 Units (base) daily for eight days (primary, secondary, and latent), or for ten to fifteen days (tertiary, neurosyphilis).

Usual adult prescribing limits: Up to 4,800,000 Units (base) daily.

Additional information:

For deep intramuscular use only. Do not administer intravenously or intra-arterially. Intravenous injection may cause embolic or toxic reactions. Intra-arterial injection may cause extensive necrosis of the extremity or organ, especially in children.

Intramuscular administration of penicillin G procaine results in lower and more prolonged serum concentrations than those produced by other parenteral penicillins (except penicillin G benzathine).

Some patients may experience immediate toxic reactions to procaine, especially when administered in large single doses. These reactions, usually transient, may be characterized by anxiety, confusion, agitation or combativeness, depression, seizures, hallucinations, or expressed fear of impending death.

PENICILLIN G SODIUM FOR INJECTION USP

Usual adult and adolescent dose: See *Penicillin G Potassium for Injection.*

Usual adult prescribing limits: See *Penicillin G Potassium for Injection.*

Additional information:

Daily doses of 10,000,000 Units or more should be administered by slow intravenous infusion because of possible electrolyte imbalance.

Sterile penicillin G sodium may also be administered subcutaneously.

Note: It contains 2.0 mEq of sodium per million Penicillin G Units.

PENICILLIN V

Summary of Differences

Category: Penicillinase-sensitive penicillin.

Precautions: Drug interactions and/or related problems—Also interacts with oral contraceptives and oral neomycin.

Additional Dosing Information

Penicillin V may be taken on a full or empty stomach.

Oral administration of penicillin V commonly results in low serum concentrations. Therefore, severe infections should not be treated with oral penicillin V during the acute stage.

Patients with impaired renal function do not generally require a reduction in dose unless the impairment is severe.

Oral Dosage Forms

Note: Bracketed uses in the *Dosage Forms* section refer to categories of use and/or indications that are not included in U.S. product labeling.

PENICILLIN V BENZATHINE SUSPENSION

Usual adult and adolescent dose: Oral, 200,000 to 500,000 Units (base) every six to eight hours.

Note: Continuous prophylaxis of streptococcal infections in patients with a history of rheumatic heart disease—Oral, 200,000 Units (base) every twelve hours.

Auxiliary labeling:
- Continue medicine for full time of treatment.
- Beyond-use date.

PENICILLIN V POTASSIUM FOR ORAL SOLUTION USP

Usual adult and adolescent dose: Oral, 125 to 500 mg (200,000 to 800,000 Units) (base) every six to eight hours.

Note: Continuous prophylaxis of streptococcal infections in patients with a history of rheumatic heart disease—Oral, 125 to 250 mg (200,000 to 400,000 Units) (base) every twelve hours.

   [Lyme disease]—Oral, 250 to 500 mg (base) three or four times a day for ten to twenty-one days. Duration of therapy is based on clinical response. Current recommendations are based on limited data; treatment failures have occurred and retreatment may be necessary.

Usual adult prescribing limits: Up to 7.2 grams (11,520,000 Units) (base) daily.

Auxiliary labeling:
- Refrigerate.
- Continue medicine for full time of treatment.
- Beyond-use date.

PENICILLIN V POTASSIUM TABLETS USP

Usual adult and adolescent dose: See *Penicillin V Potassium for Oral Solution.*

Usual adult prescribing limits: See *Penicillin V Potassium for Oral Solution.*

Auxiliary labeling: • Continue medicine for full time of treatment.

PIPERACILLIN

Summary of Differences

Category: Beta-lactamase-sensitive penicillin.
Precautions:
   Drug interactions and/or related problems—Also interacts with other hepatotoxic medications.
   Contraindications/medical problems—Caution also needed in hepatic function impairment.
   Patient monitoring—Serum potassium determinations may be required.

Additional Dosing Information

Intramuscular injections should not exceed 2 grams in each site.

Serum determinations are recommended in patients with impaired renal and hepatic function.

Parenteral Dosage Forms

STERILE PIPERACILLIN SODIUM USP

Usual adult and adolescent dose: Intramuscular or intravenous, 3 to 4 grams (base) every four to six hours.

Note: Gonorrhea (uncomplicated)—Intramuscular, 2 grams (base) as a single dose and 1 gram of probenecid orally, administered thirty minutes prior to injection.

   Perioperative prophylaxis—Abdominal hysterectomy patients: 2 grams (base) intravenously one-half to one hour prior to the start of surgery, 2 grams upon return to the recovery room, and 2 grams given six hours later.

   Perioperative prophylaxis—Cesarean-section patients: 2 grams (base) intravenously as soon as the umbilical cord is clamped and 2 grams intravenously four and eight hours after the first dose.

   Perioperative prophylaxis—Intra-abdominal procedures: 2 grams (base) intravenously one-half to one hour prior to the start of surgery 2 grams during surgery; and 2 grams every six hours following surgery for up to twenty-four hours.

   Perioperative prophylaxis—Vaginal hysterectomy patients: 2 grams (base) intravenously one-half to one hour prior to the start of surgery and 2 grams intravenously six and twelve hours after the first dose.

   Septicemia, nosocomial pneumonia, intra-abdominal infections, genitourinary tract infections, skin and soft tissue infections—Intravenous, 2 to 3 grams (base) every four hours or 3 to 4 grams every six hours; or 33.3 to 50 mg per kg of body weight every four hours or 50 to 75 mg per kg of body weight every six hours.

   Urinary tract infections (complicated)—Intravenous, 3 to 4 grams (base) every six to eight hours; or 31.25 to 50 mg per kg of body weight every six hours or 41.7 to 66.7 mg per kg of body weight every eight hours.

   Urinary tract infections (uncomplicated) and community-acquired pneumonia—Intramuscular or intravenous, 1.5 to 2 grams (base) every six hours or 3 to 4 grams every twelve hours; or 25 to 31.25 mg per kg of body weight every six hours or 50 to 62.5 mg per kg of body weight every twelve hours.

   Adults with impaired renal function may require a reduction in dose as follows:

Creatinine Clearance (mL/min)/(mL/sec)	Dose (base)
>40/(0.67)	See *Usual adult and adolescent dose*
20–40/(0.33–0.67)	3 to 4 grams every 8 hours
<20/(0.33)	3 to 4 grams every 12 hours
Hemodialysis patients	1 gram after each dialysis, then 2 grams every 8 hours

Usual adult prescribing limits: Up to 24 grams (base) daily. Doses up to 500 mg per kg of body weight daily have also been used.

Additional information: The sodium content is approximately 1.98 mEq (45.5 mg) per gram of piperacillin. This must be considered in patients on a restricted sodium intake when calculating total daily sodium intake.

TICARCILLIN

Summary of Differences

Category: Penicillinase-sensitive penicillin.
Precautions:
   Drug interactions and/or related problems—Also interacts with anticoagulants and other medications that affect blood clotting.

Laboratory value alterations—May increase bleeding time and may cause false-positive protein reaction for various urine protein tests.

Patient monitoring—Bleeding time and serum potassium and sodium determinations may be required.

Additional Dosing Information

Since ticarcillin disodium is not absorbed orally, it must be administered by intramuscular or intravenous injection only. Intramuscular injections should not exceed 2 grams in each site.

Patients with impaired renal function may require a reduction in dose and should be observed for hemorrhagic complications.

Parenteral Dosage Forms

STERILE TICARCILLIN DISODIUM USP

Usual adult and adolescent dose:

Septicemia, pneumonia, skin and soft tissue, intra-abdominal, and genitourinary tract infections—Intravenous infusion, 3 grams (base) every three to six hours; 25 to 37.5 mg per kg of body weight every three hours; 33.3 to 50 mg per kg of body weight every four hours; or 50 to 75 mg per kg of body weight every six hours.

Urinary tract infections, bacterial (complicated)—Intravenous infusion, 3 grams (base) every four to six hours; 25 to 33.3 mg per kg of body weight every four hours; or 37.5 to 50 mg per kg of body weight every six hours.

Urinary tract infections, bacterial (uncomplicated)—Intramuscular or intravenous, 1 gram (base) every four to six hours.

Note: After an initial intravenous loading dose of 3 grams (base), adults with impaired renal function may require a reduction in dose as follows—

Creatinine Clearance (mL/min)/(mL/sec)	Dose (base)
>60/(1.00)	3 grams every 4 hours
30–60/(0.50–1.00)	2 grams every 4 hours
10–30/(0.17–0.50)	2 grams every 8 hours
<10/(0.17)	2 grams every 12 hours
<10 with impaired hepatic function	2 grams every 24 hours

Usual adult prescribing limits: Up to 500 mg (base) per kg of body weight daily.

Additional information: The sodium content is approximately 5.2 mEq (120 mg), but may be as high as 6.5 mEq (150 mg), per gram of ticarcillin. This must be considered in patients on a restricted sodium intake when calculating total daily sodium intake.

TICARCILLIN AND CLAVULANATE

Summary of Differences

Category: Penicillinase-sensitive penicillin in combination with a beta-lactamase inhibitor.

Pharmacology:

Clavulanic acid acts as a "suicidal" molecule and irreversibly binds to bacterial beta-lactamases.

Precautions:

Drug interactions and/or related problems—Ticarcillin also interacts with anticoagulants and other medications that affect blood clotting; clavulanic acid does not interact with disulfiram or probenecid.

Laboratory value alterations—May increase bleeding time and may cause false-positive protein reaction for various urine protein tests.

Contraindications/medical problems—Caution also required in patients with history of bleeding problems.

Patient monitoring—Bleeding time and serum potassium and sodium determinations may be required.

Additional Dosing Information

Since ticarcillin disodium is not absorbed orally, ticarcillin disodium and clavulanate potassium combination must be administered by intravenous infusion only.

Patients with impaired renal function may require a reduction in dose and should be observed for hemorrhagic complications.

Sterile ticarcillin disodium and clavulanate potassium should be administered by intravenous infusion over a 30-minute period.

Parenteral Dosage Forms

STERILE TICARCILLIN DISODIUM AND CLAVULANATE POTASSIUM USP

Usual adult dose: Systemic and urinary tract infections—

Adults under 60 kg of body weight: Intravenous infusion, 33.3 to 50 mg (ticarcillin) per kg of body weight every four hours; or 50 to 75 mg per kg of body weight every six hours.

Adults 60 kg of body weight: Intravenous infusion, 3 grams (ticarcillin) and 100 mg (clavulanic acid) every four to six hours.

Note: After an initial loading dose of 3 grams (ticarcillin) and 100 mg (clavulanic acid), adults with impaired renal function may require a reduction in dose as follows—

Creatinine Clearance (mL/min)/(mL/sec)	Dose
>60/(1.00)	3.1 grams every 4 hours
30–60/(0.50–1.00)	2 grams every 4 hours
10–30/(0.17–0.50)	2 grams every 8 hours
<10/(0.17)	2 grams every 12 hours
<10 with hepatic dysfunction	2 grams every 24 hours
Peritoneal dialysis patients	3.1 grams every 12 hours
Hemodialysis patients	2 grams every 12 hours; and 3.1 grams after each dialysis

Additional information:

The sodium content (theoretical) is approximately 4.75 mEq (109 mg) per gram of ticarcillin. This must be considered in patients on a restricted sodium intake when calculating total daily sodium intake.

The potassium content is approximately 0.15 mEq (6 mg) per 100 mg of clavulanic acid.

PENTAMIDINE　Inhalation

Some commonly used *brand names* are:
　In the U.S.—*NebuPent*
　In Canada—*Pentacarinat; Pneumopent*

INHALATION
Pentamidine Isethionate for Inhalation Solution
　In the U.S.—*NebuPent*
　In Canada—*Pentacarinat; Pneumopent*

Category: Antiprotozoal.

Indications

Note:　Bracketed information in the *Indications* section refers to uses not included in U.S. product labeling.

Accepted

Pneumonia, *Pneumocystis carinii* (PCP) (prophylaxis)—Aerosolized pentamidine is indicated in both secondary prophylaxis (patients who have already had at least one episode of *Pneumocystis carinii* pneumonia), and primary prophylaxis (HIV-infected patients with a CD4 lymphocyte count less than or equal to 200 cells per cubic millimeter) of *Pneumocystis carinii* pneumonia.

[Pneumonia, *Pneumocystis carinii* (PCP) (treatment)][1]—Aerosolized pentamidine is used in the treatment of mild (A-a gradient <30 mm Hg) *Pneumocystis carinii* pneumonia. However, preliminary studies have suggested that aerosolized pentamidine may be less effective than conventional systemic therapies; patients receiving this regimen should be followed closely for evidence of progressive disease.

[1]Not included in Canadian product labeling.

Pharmacology

Mechanism of action/Effect: Not clearly defined; pentamidine may interfere with incorporation of nucleotides into RNA and DNA and may inhibit oxidative phosphorylation, resulting in inhibition of DNA, RNA, phospholipid, and protein biosynthesis; may also interfere with folate transformation.

Precautions to Consider

Geriatrics
No information is available on the relationship of age to the effects of pentamidine in geriatric patients.

Dental
Pentamidine may cause a bitter or metallic taste, gingivitis, hypersalivation, or dry mouth.

Drug interactions and/or related problems
At this time, no clinically significant drug interactions and/or related problems have been documented in patients receiving prophylactic aerosolized pentamidine.

Contraindications/Medical problems
The contraindications/medical problems included have been selected on the basis of their potential clinical significance (reasons given in parentheses where appropriate)—not necessarily inclusive (» = major clinical significance).

Except under special circumstances, this medication should not be used when the following medical problem exists:
»　Allergy to pentamidine
　　(aerosolized pentamidine is contraindicated in patients with a

history of an anaphylactic reaction to inhaled or systemic pentamidine)

Risk-benefit should be considered when the following medical problem exists:
　Asthma
　　(aerosolized pentamidine may induce acute bronchospasm, usually in patients with a history of asthma; this may be reduced by pretreatment with a bronchodilator)

Side/Adverse Effects

Note:　The prophylactic use of aerosolized pentamidine has a very low incidence of severe side effects. Many adverse reactions will be due to other medications, other concurrent infections, or the HIV disease itself, and may be difficult to differentiate.

Coughing and bronchospasm occur primarily in patients who are cigarette smokers and continue to smoke, or have an underlying pulmonary disease, such as asthma.

A number of cases of extrapulmonary pneumocystosis and pneumothorax have been reported in patients receiving aerosolized pentamidine. These are thought to be infectious complications due to subclinical, peripheral infection and poor systemic distribution of aerosolized pentamidine. Although the incidence is not known at this time, one study found that extrapulmonary pneumocystosis appears to occur more frequently in, but is not limited to, patients who have been diagnosed with AIDS for longer than 12 months. These patients usually have had prior episodes of PCP, often do not have concurrent pneumonia, are receiving concurrent zidovudine, and have had prolonged treatment with aerosolized pentamidine. It is suggested that use of zidovudine and prophylactic aerosolized pentamidine may allow for the emergence of extrapulmonary pneumocystosis.

The following side/adverse effects have been selected on the basis of their potential clinical significance (possible signs and symptoms in parentheses where appropriate)—not necessarily inclusive:

Those indicating need for medical attention
Incidence more frequent
　Chest pain or congestion; coughing; dyspnea (difficulty in breathing); *pharyngitis* (burning pain, dryness, or sensation of lump in throat; difficulty in swallowing); *skin rash; wheezing*

Incidence rare
　Extrapulmonary pneumocystosis—most frequent sites include the spleen, liver, lymph nodes, and eyes; *pancreatitis* (pain in upper abdomen, possibly radiating to the back; nausea; vomiting)—may occur more frequently with prolonged use; *pneumothorax* (sudden onset of severe breathing difficulty, severe pain in chest)

Incidence rare—with daily treatment doses only
　Hypoglycemia, mild (anxiety; chills; cold sweats; cool, pale skin; headache; increased hunger; nausea; nervousness; shakiness); *renal insufficiency* (decreased urination, unusual tiredness, loss of appetite, nausea)

Those not indicating need for medical attention
Incidence less frequent
　Bitter or metallic taste

Patient Consultation

In providing consultation, consider emphasizing the following selected information (» = major clinical significance):

Before using this medication
»　Conditions affecting use, especially:
　　Allergy to pentamidine

Proper use of this medication

Importance of receiving medication for full course of therapy and on regular schedule

Missed dose: Receiving therapy as soon as possible

Precautions while using this medication

If also using a bronchodilator inhaler, using about 5 to 10 minutes prior to aerosolized pentamidine

Possible bitter or metallic taste; dissolving a hard candy in mouth after administration of medication

Cigarette smokers who continue to smoke are more likely to experience coughing and bronchospasm during aerosolized pentamidine therapy

Side/adverse effects

Signs of potential side effects, especially chest pain or congestion, coughing, dyspnea, hypoglycemia, pancreatitis, pharyngitis, pneumothorax, renal insufficiency, skin rash, extrapulmonary pneumocystosis, and wheezing

A bitter or metallic taste may occur; however, it is medically insignificant

General Dosing Information

Coughing and bronchospasm occur primarily in cigarette smokers who continue to smoke, or patients with an underlying pulmonary disease, such as asthma. A higher incidence of coughing and bronchospasm may be related to larger particle sizes; however, these symptoms appears to occur most frequently due to an increased particle load with larger doses. Pretreatment with a bronchodilator, like albuterol, metaproterenol, or terbutaline, helps to alleviate this problem and may improve pentamidine distribution in the lung.

It is important that as much medication as possible reach the upper lobes of the lungs, since upper lobe *P. carinii* pneumonia relapses have occurred in patients while they were receiving aerosolized pentamidine. There appears to be a more uniform distribution of aerosolized pentamidine in the lungs when it is administered to patients in a supine or recumbent position.

Before aerosolized pentamidine treatment is started, a tuberculin skin test, chest x-ray, and sputum culture, if possible, should be performed to rule out tuberculosis due to *Mycobacterium tuberculosis*. A tuberculin skin test alone may not be useful because false negative readings often occur in AIDS patients. The risk of active disease or reactivation of latent tuberculosis infection is more prevalent in HIV-infected people. Also, the risk of transmission of tuberculosis to health care workers or others in the vicinity may exist.

Health care workers are advised to administer aerosolized pentamidine in a well-ventilated room if possible. Although one study found the environmental levels of pentamidine in a treatment room to be low, long-term occupational studies have not been done and the risk has not been established. Of primary concern are the previously mentioned risk of transmission of tuberculosis or other respiratory pathogens via aerosols, as well as anecdotal reports of a reversible decrease in pulmonary function testing parameters and chemical conjunctivitis due to ocular exposure to aerosolized pentamidine.

Two types of nebulizers have been shown to be effective in decreasing the incidence of *P. carinii* pneumonia. Respirgard II is a jet nebulizer and is used with NebuPent and Pentacarinat; Fisoneb is an ultrasonic nebulizer and is used with Pneumopent. Jet nebulizers use a high-flow gas to shear liquid strands from a thin layer of solution. The liquid strands hit a baffle, creating a wide variety of particle sizes. Larger particles generally fall by gravity and get reincorporated into the solution. Ultrasonic nebulizers generate an ultrahigh frequency sound, creating a geyser from which particles are expelled. When the flow through the nebulizer is interrupted, as with tidal breathing, the smaller particles coalesce into larger particles. Because of this, measurements of output and particle size will vary with different operating conditions.

Particle size produced by the nebulizer is an important factor in the location of aerosol deposition. The optimal size for deposition in the alveoli, where *Pneumocystis carinii* pneumonia (PCP) causes damage, is 1 to 2 microns; the optimal size for tracheobronchial deposition is 4 to 7 microns. Many factors can affect and limit aerosol deposition into the alveoli, including inspiratory flowrates, frequency of respiration, breath-holding, tidal volumes, and airway narrowing from bronchospasm, emphysema, mucus, and PCP.

Because of the differences in nebulizers and the efficacy with which they deliver aerosolized pentamidine, the nebulizers should not be utilized interchangeably with the different dosing regimens. The two regimens shown to be effective are described below.

Inhalation Dosage Forms

Note: Bracketed uses in the *Dosage Forms* section refer to categories of use and/or indications that are not included in U.S. product labeling.

PENTAMIDINE ISETHIONATE FOR INHALATION SOLUTION

Usual adult and adolescent dose: Pneumonia, *Pneumocystis carinii*—For *NebuPent* and *Pentacarinat* using the Respirgard II jet nebulizer:

Prophylaxis—Oral inhalation, 300 mg every four weeks, administered via the Respirgard II nebulizer. The aerosol treatment should be continued over a period of approximately thirty to forty-five minutes, until the nebulizer chamber is empty.

Note: A prophylactic dose of 150 mg every two weeks, administered via the Respirgard II nebulizer, has also been used if the patient cannot tolerate a single monthly dose. One study found that although patients who received 300 mg monthly had a lower rate of PCP than those receiving 150 mg every two weeks, the difference was not significant.

[Treatment][1]—Oral inhalation, 600 mg a day, administered via the Respirgard II nebulizer for twenty-one days. Continue the aerosol treatment over a period of approximately twenty-five to thirty minutes.

Note: The flow rate for the nebulizer should be 5 to 7 liters per minute from a 40- to 50-pounds-per-square-inch (PSI) air or oxygen source.

Low pressure compressors (<20 PSI) should not be used.

For *Pneumopent* using the Fisoneb ultrasonic nebulizer:

Loading dose (prophylaxis)—Oral inhalation, 60 mg, administered via the Fisoneb ultrasonic nebulizer, every twenty-four to seventy-two hours for a total of 5 doses over a two week period. The aerosol treatment should be continued over a period of approximately fifteen minutes, until the nebulizer chamber is empty.

Maintenance dose (prophylaxis)—Oral inhalation, 60 mg, administered via the Fisoneb ultrasonic nebulizer, every two weeks.

Note: The flow rate of the nebulizer should be set at the mid-flow mark.

Additional information:

Pentamidine inhalation solution should not be mixed with any other medications.

Do not use the Respirgard II nebulizer to administer a bronchodilator.

---

[1]Not included in Canadian product labeling.

PERGOLIDE   Systemic

A commonly used *brand name* in the U.S. and Canada is *Permax*.

ORAL
Pergolide Mesylate Tablets
   In the U.S. and Canada—*Permax*

Category: Antidyskinetic (dopamine agonist).

Indications

Accepted
Parkinsonism (treatment adjunct)—Pergolide is indicated, as an adjunct to levodopa or levodopa/carbidopa therapy, for treatment of the signs and symptoms of idiopathic or postencephalitic Parkinson's disease to allow achievement of symptomatic relief with lower doses of levodopa or levodopa/carbidopa.

Pharmacology

Mechanism of action/Effect: Stimulation of post-synaptic dopamine receptors (at both D_1 and D_2 receptor sites) in the nigrostriatal system. Unlike bromocriptine, but similar to apomorphine and lysuride, postsynaptic dopamine agonist properties are independent of presynaptic dopamine synthesis or stores.

Other actions/effects: Inhibits secretion of prolactin; causes transient rise in serum concentration of growth hormone in normal patients while in patients with acromegaly it causes a decrease; causes decrease in serum concentrations of luteinizing hormone (LH).

Precautions to Consider

Cross-sensitivity and/or related problems
Patients sensitive to other ergot derivatives may be sensitive to this medication also.

Geriatrics
Studies performed to date have not demonstrated geriatrics-specific problems that would limit the usefulness of pergolide in the elderly.

Dental
Pergolide may decrease or inhibit salivary flow, thus contributing to the development of caries, periodontal disease, oral candidiasis, and discomfort.

Drug interactions and/or related problems
The following drug interactions and/or related problems have been selected on the basis of their potential clinical significance (possible mechanism in parentheses where appropriate)—not necessarily inclusive (» = major clinical significance):

Note: Combinations containing any of the following medications, depending on the amount present, may also interact with this medication.

   Droperidol or
   Haloperidol or
   Loxapine or
   Methyldopa or
   Metoclopramide or
   Molindone or
   Papaverine or
   Phenothiazines or
   Reserpine or
   Thioxanthenes or
      (dopamine antagonists may decrease the effectiveness of pergolide)
   Hypotension-producing medications, other
      (concurrent use may result in additive hypotensive effects)

Contraindications/Medical problems
The contraindications/medical problems included have been selected on the basis of their potential clinical significance (reasons given in parentheses where appropriate)—not necessarily inclusive (» = major clinical significance).

Except under special circumstances, this medication should not be used when the following medical problem exists:
» Sensitivity to pergolide or other ergot alkaloids

Risk-benefit should be considered when the following medical problems exist:
   Cardiac dysrhythmias
      (increased risk of atrial premature contractions and sinus tachycardia)
   Psychiatric disorders
      (pre-existing states of confusion and hallucinations may be exacerbated)

Side/Adverse Effects
The following side/adverse effects have been selected on the basis of their potential clinical significance (possible signs and symptoms in parentheses where appropriate)—not necessarily inclusive:

Those indicating need for medical attention
Incidence more frequent
   CNS effects (confusion, dyskinesias [uncontrolled movements of the body, such as the face, tongue, arms, hands, head, and upper body], hallucinations); *urinary tract infections* (pain or burning while urinating)
Incidence less frequent
   Hypertension
Incidence rare
   Cerebrovascular hemorrhage (severe or continuing headache; seizures; vision changes, such as blurred vision or temporary blindness; sudden weakness); *myocardial infarction* (severe chest pain, fainting, fast heartbeat, increased sweating, continuing or severe nausea and vomiting, nervousness, unexplained shortness of breath, weakness)

Those indicating need for medical attention only if they continue or are bothersome
Incidence more frequent
   Abdominal or stomach pain; constipation; dizziness or drowsiness; flu-like symptoms; hypotension (dizziness or lightheadedness, especially when getting up from a lying or sitting position); *lower back pain; nausea; rhinitis* (runny nose); *weakness*
Note: Approximately 10% of patients experience *orthostatic hypotension* during initial treatment. Tolerance usually develops with gradual dosage titration.
Incidence less frequent
   Chills; diarrhea; dryness of mouth; facial edema (swelling of the face); *loss of appetite; vomiting*

Patient Consultation

In providing consultation, consider emphasizing the following selected information (» = major clinical significance):

Before using this medication
» Conditions affecting use, especially:
      Sensitivity to pergolide or other ergot alkaloids
      Breast-feeding—May prevent lactation in mothers who intend to breast-feed
      Dental—Reduced salivary flow may contribute to dental problems

Proper use of this medication
  Taking with meals to reduce gastric effects
  Missed dose: Taking as soon as possible; not taking if almost time for next dose; not doubling doses
» Proper storage

Precautions while using this medication
  Regular visits to physician to check progress
» Caution when driving or doing jobs requiring alertness, because of possible drowsiness or dizziness
  Dizziness may be more likely to occur after initial doses; taking first dose at bedtime or while lying down; getting up slowly from sitting or lying position
  Possible dryness of mouth; using sugarless gum or candy, ice, or saliva substitute for relief; checking with physician or dentist if dry mouth continues for more than 2 weeks
  Checking with physician before reducing dosage or discontinuing medication

Side/adverse effects
  Signs of potential side effects, especially cerebrovascular hemorrhage, CNS effects, hypertension, myocardial infarction, urinary tract infection

General Dosing Information

Titrated dosage is necessary to achieve the individual therapeutic blood concentration requirements and to minimize the risk of side effects.

Nausea and dizziness associated with initiation of pergolide therapy usually resolve with continued therapy; however, incidence and severity of these side effects may be reduced with a decrease in pergolide dose. Dizziness and nausea may be better tolerated by administering the initial dose at bedtime or while lying down. Also, administration of pergolide with food may alleviate the nausea.

Oral Dosage Forms

PERGOLIDE MESYLATE TABLETS

Usual adult and adolescent dose: Oral, 50 mcg (0.05 mg) (base) a day for the first two days; the dosage being increased gradually by 100 or 150 mcg (0.1 or 0.15 mg) (base) every third day over the next twelve days of therapy. Afterwards, the dose may be increased by 250 mcg (0.25 mg) (base) every third day until optimum therapeutic effect is achieved.

Note: Usually administered in divided doses three times a day.
   During dosage titration of pergolide the concurrent dose of levodopa or levodopa/carbidopa may be decreased with caution according to clinical response.

Usual adult prescribing limits: Up to 5 mg daily.

Usual geriatric dose: See *Usual adult and adolescent dose.*

Auxiliary labeling: • May cause drowsiness.

PHENACEMIDE   Systemic†

Some commonly used *brand names* are:
  In the U.S.—*Phenurone*
  Other—*Epiclase; Phetylureum*
Another commonly used name is phenacetylcarbamide.

ORAL
Phenacemide Tablets USP†
  In the U.S.—*Phenurone*

†Not commercially available in Canada.

Category: Anticonvulsant.

Indications

Accepted
Epilepsy, complex partial seizure pattern (treatment)—Phenacemide is indicated for control of severe epilepsy, particularly mixed forms of complex partial (psychomotor or temporal lobe) seizures, refractory to other anticonvulsants. Phenacemide should not be used unless other less toxic anticonvulsants have been ineffective in controlling seizures.

Pharmacology

Mechanism of action/Effect: The mechanism of action in humans has not been established. However, in animals, at doses well below those causing neurological signs, phenacemide elevates the threshold for minimal electroshock convulsions and abolishes the tonic phase of maximal electroshock seizures. It also prevents or modifies seizures induced by pentylenetetrazol or other convulsants.

Precautions to Consider

Geriatrics
No geriatrics-specific information is available.

Drug interactions and/or related problems
The following drug interactions and/or related problems have been selected on the basis of their potential clinical significance (possible mechanism in parentheses where appropriate)—not necessarily inclusive (» = major clinical significance):

Note: Combinations containing any of the following medications, depending on the amount present, may also interact with this medication.
  Alcohol and
  Central nervous system (CNS) depression-producing medications, other
   (CNS depression may be enhanced)
» Anticonvulsants, other, especially ethotoin
   (risk of additive toxicity when these medications are used concurrently with phenacemide; concurrent use of ethotoin with phenacemide has been reported to cause paranoid symptoms; extreme caution is recommended during concurrent use of phenacemide with other anticonvulsants

Contraindications/Medical problems
The contraindications/medical problems included have been selected on the basis of their potential clinical significance (reasons given in parentheses where appropriate)—not necessarily inclusive (» = major clinical significance).

Risk-benefit should be considered when the following medical problems exist:
» Blood dyscrasias, history of
   (deaths due to phenacemide-induced aplastic anemia have occurred)

» Hepatic function impairment, history of
    (deaths due to phenacemide-induced liver damage have occurred)
» Personality disorders, history of
    (personality changes including attempts at suicide and psychoses requiring hospitalization have occurred; patient hospitalization during the first week of treatment may be advisable)
» Renal function impairment, history of
    (condition may be aggravated)
» Sensitivity to phenacemide or history of allergy to other anticonvulsants

Side/Adverse Effects

The following side/adverse effects have been selected on the basis of their potential clinical significance (possible signs and symptoms in parentheses where appropriate)—not necessarily inclusive:

Those indicating need for medical attention
Incidence more frequent
    Behavior or mood changes
Incidence rare
    Allergic reactions (skin rash);*blood dyscrasias, such as aplastic anemia* (shortness of breath; troubled breathing, wheezing, or tightness in chest; sores, ulcers, or white spots on lips or in mouth; swollen or painful glands; unusual bleeding or bruising), *leukopenia* (fever, chills, or sore throat), *or neutropenia* (fever, chills, or continuing ulcers or sores in mouth or throat); *hepatitis* (dark-colored urine, flu-like symptoms, fever with or without chills, headache, body ache, yellow eyes or skin); *nephritis* (difficulty in breathing, drowsiness or unusual tiredness or weakness, nausea or vomiting, blood in urine, unusual weight gain, or swelling of face, feet, or lower legs)
    Note: If *hepatitis* or jaundice occurs, the medication should be discontinued.
Symptoms of overdose (in order of occurrence)
    Excitement or mania (unusual nervousness or irritability); *ataxia* (clumsiness or unsteadiness); *drowsiness, severe*

Those indicating need for medical attention only if they continue or are bothersome
Incidence more frequent
    Anorexia (loss of appetite); *drowsiness; headache*
Incidence less frequent or rare
    Dizziness; fever; insomnia (trouble in sleeping); *muscle pain; palpitation* (pounding heartbeat); *paresthesias* (tingling, burning, or prickly sensations); *unusual tiredness or weakness; weight loss, unusual*

Patient Consultation

In providing consultation, consider emphasizing the following selected information (» = major clinical significance):

Before using this medication
» Conditions affecting use, especially:
    Sensitivity to phenacemide or history of allergy to other anticonvulsants
    Pregnancy—Increased risk of fetal damage

    Delivery—Possibility of life-threatening hemorrhage in the neonate
    Use by athletes—Phenacemide is banned and, in some cases, tested for in shooters by the U.S. Olympic Committee (USOC) and the National Collegiate Athletic Association (NCAA)
    Other medications, especially other anticonvulsants
    Other medical problems, especially a history of personality disorders, blood dyscrasias, or hepatic or renal function impairment

Proper use of this medication
» Compliance with therapy; taking every day as directed by physician
    Missed dose: Taking as soon as possible; not taking if almost time for next scheduled dose; not doubling doses
» Proper storage

Precautions while using this medication
» Regular visits to physician to check progress of therapy
» Checking with physician before discontinuing this medication; gradual dosage reduction may be necessary
» Reporting sore throat, fever, and any unusual bleeding or bruising to physician as soon as possible
» Reporting behavioral changes such as decreased interest in surroundings, depression, or aggressiveness to physician as soon as possible
» Avoiding the use of alcoholic beverages; not taking other medication unless prescribed by physician
    Possibility of drowsiness; caution if driving or doing things requiring alertness

Side/adverse effects
» Potential side effects, especially behavior changes, allergic reaction, or symptoms of blood dyscrasias, hepatitis, and nephritis

General Dosing Information

Because of the potential for serious toxic effects, the dosage of phenacemide should be maintained at the minimum amount necessary to achieve seizure control.

Withdrawal of phenacemide or transition to or from other anticonvulsants should be made gradually to maintain seizure control.

Oral Dosage Forms

PHENACEMIDE TABLETS USP

Note: Phenacemide tablets are not commercially available in Canada.

Usual adult and adolescent dose: Anticonvulsant—Oral, initially 500 mg three times a day; after 1 week, an additional 500 mg may be taken upon arising; in the third week, if necessary, the dose may be increased by adding 500 mg at bedtime.

Usual adult prescribing limits: Up to 5 grams daily

PHENOTHIAZINES   Systemic

INN: Included in brackets after individual generic listings, if different from the U.S. or Canadian generic name.

Some commonly used *brand names* are:

In the U.S.—

Compa-Z
  [Prochlorperazine]
Compazine
  [Prochlorperazine]
Compazine Spansule
  [Prochlorperazine]
Cotranzine
  [Prochlorperazine]
Levoprome
  [Methotrimeprazine]
Mellaril [Thioridazine]
Mellaril Concentrate
  [Thioridazine]
Mellaril-S [Thioridazine]
Ormazine [Chlorpromazine]
Permitil [Fluphenazine]
Permitil Concentrate
  [Fluphenazine]
Primazine [Promazine]
Prolixin [Fluphenazine]
Prolixin Concentrate
  [Fluphenazine]
Prolixin Decanoate
  [Fluphenazine]

Prolixin Enanthate
  [Fluphenazine]
Prozine-50 [Promazine]
Serentil [Mesoridazine]
Serentil Concentrate
  [Mesoridazine]
Sparine [Promazine]
Stelazine [Trifluoperazine]
Stelazine Concentrate
  [Trifluoperazine]
Thorazine
  [Chlorpromazine]
Thorazine Concentrate
  [Chlorpromazine]
Thorazine Spansule
  [Chlorpromazine]
Thor-Prom
  [Chlorpromazine]
Tindal [Acetophenazine]
Trilafon [Perphenazine]
Trilafon Concentrate
  [Perphenazine]
Ultrazine-10
  [Prochlorperazine]
Vesprin [Triflupromazine]

In Canada—

Apo-Fluphenazine
  [Fluphenazine]
Apo-Perphenazine
  [Perphenazine]
Apo-Thioridazine
  [Thioridazine]
Apo-Trifluoperazine
  [Trifluoperazine]
Chlorpromanyl-5
  [Chlorpromazine]
Chlorpromanyl-20
  [Chlorpromazine]
Chlorpromanyl-40
  [Chlorpromazine]
Dartal [Thiopropazate]
Largactil [Chlorpromazine]
Largactil Liquid
  [Chlorpromazine]
Largactil Oral Drops
  [Chlorpromazine]
Majeptil [Thioproperazine]
Mellaril [Thioridazine]
Modecate [Fluphenazine]
Modecate Concentrate
  [Fluphenazine]
Moditen Enanthate
  [Fluphenazine]
Moditen HCl
  [Fluphenazine]
Moditen HCl-H.P.
  [Fluphenazine]
Neuleptil [Pericyazine]
Novo-Chlorpromazine
  [Chlorpromazine]
Novo-Flurazine
  [Trifluoperazine]

Novo-Ridazine
  [Thioridazine]
Nozinan
  [Methotrimeprazine]
Nozinan Liquid
  [Methotrimeprazine]
Nozinan Oral Drops
  [Methotrimeprazine]
Permitil [Fluphenazine]
Piportil L₄ [Pipotiazine]
PMS Perphenazine
  [Perphenazine]
PMS Prochlorperazine
  [Prochlorperazine]
PMS Thioridazine
  [Thioridazine]
PMS Trifluoperazine
  [Trifluoperazine]
Prorazin
  [Prochlorperazine]
Serentil [Mesoridazine]
Solazine [Trifluoperazine]
Sparine [Promazine]
Stelazine [Trifluoperazine]
Stelazine Concentrate
  [Trifluoperazine]
Stemetil [Prochlorperazine]
Stemetil Liquid
  [Prochlorperazine]
Terfluzine
  [Trifluoperazine]
Terfluzine Concentrate
  [Trifluoperazine]
Trilafon [Perphenazine]
Trilafon Concentrate
  [Perphenazine]

ACETOPHENAZINE†
Oral
  Acetophenazine Maleate Tablets USP†
    In the U.S.—*Tindal*
CHLORPROMAZINE
Oral
  Chlorpromazine Hydrochloride Extended-release Capsules†
    In the U.S.—*Thorazine Spansule*
  Chlorpromazine Hydrochloride Oral Concentrate USP
    In the U.S.—*Thorazine Concentrate; Thor-Prom;* GENERIC
    In Canada—*Chlorpromanyl-40; Largactil Oral Drops*
  Chlorpromazine Hydrochloride Syrup USP
    In the U.S.—*Thorazine;* GENERIC
    In Canada—*Chlorpromanyl-5; Chlorpromanyl-20; Largactil Liquid*
  Chlorpromazine Hydrochloride Tablets USP
    In the U.S.—*Thorazine; Thor-Prom;* GENERIC
    In Canada—*Largactil; Novo-Chlorpromazine;* GENERIC
Parenteral
  Chlorpromazine Hydrochloride Injection USP
    In the U.S.—*Ormazine; Thorazine;* GENERIC
    In Canada—*Largactil;* GENERIC
Rectal
  Chlorpromazine Suppositories USP
    In the U.S.—*Thorazine*
    In Canada—*Largactil*
ETHOPROPAZINE—See Antidyskinetics (Systemic).
FLUPHENAZINE
Oral
  Fluphenazine Hydrochloride Elixir USP
    In the U.S.—*Prolixin*
    In Canada—*Moditen HCl*
  Fluphenazine Hydrochloride Oral Solution USP†
    In the U.S.—*Permitil Concentrate; Prolixin Concentrate;* GENERIC
  Fluphenazine Hydrochloride Tablets USP
    In the U.S.—*Permitil; Prolixin;* GENERIC
    In Canada—*Apo-Fluphenazine; Moditen HCl; Permitil*
Parenteral
  Fluphenazine Decanoate Injection
    In the U.S.—*Prolixin Decanoate;* GENERIC
    In Canada—*Modecate; Modecate Concentrate*
  Fluphenazine Enanthate Injection USP
    In the U.S.—*Prolixin Enanthate*
    In Canada—*Moditen Enanthate*
  Fluphenazine Hydrochloride Injection USP
    In the U.S.—*Prolixin;* GENERIC
    In Canada—*Moditen HCl-H.P.*
MESORIDAZINE
Oral
  Mesoridazine Besylate Oral Solution USP†
    In the U.S.—*Serentil Concentrate*
  Mesoridazine Besylate Tablets USP
    In the U.S. and Canada—*Serentil*
Parenteral
  Mesoridazine Besylate Injection USP†
    In the U.S.—*Serentil*
METHOTRIMEPRAZINE [INN: Levomepromazine]
Oral
  Methotrimeprazine Hydrochloride Oral Solution*
    In Canada—*Nozinan Oral Drops*
  Methotrimeprazine Hydrochloride Syrup*
    In Canada—*Nozinan Liquid*
  Methotrimeprazine Maleate Tablets*
    In Canada—*Nozinan*

Parenteral
    Methotrimeprazine Injection USP
        In the U.S.—*Levoprome*
        In Canada—*Nozinan*
PERICYAZINE* [INN: Periciazine]
Oral
    Pericyazine Capsules*
        In Canada—*Neuleptil*
    Pericyazine Oral Solution*
        In Canada—*Neuleptil*
PERPHENAZINE
Oral
    Perphenazine Oral Solution USP
        In the U.S.—*Trilafon Concentrate*
        In Canada—*PMS Perphenazine; Trilafon Concentrate*
    Perphenazine Syrup USP*
        In Canada—*Trilafon*
    Perphenazine Tablets USP
        In the U.S.—*Trilafon;* GENERIC
        In Canada—*Apo-Perphenazine; PMS Perphenazine; Trilafon;* GENERIC
Parenteral
    Perphenazine Injection USP
        In the U.S. and Canada—*Trilafon*
PIPOTIAZINE*
Parenteral
    Pipotiazine Palmitate Injection*
        In Canada—*Piportil L₄*
PROCHLORPERAZINE
Oral
    Prochlorperazine Edisylate Syrup USP†
        In the U.S.—*Compazine*
    Prochlorperazine Maleate Extended-release Capsules†
        In the U.S.—*Compazine Spansule*
    Prochlorperazine Maleate Tablets USP
        In the U.S.—*Compazine;* GENERIC
        In Canada—*PMS Prochlorperazine; Prorazin; Stemetil*
    Prochlorperazine Mesylate Syrup*
        In Canada—*Stemetil Liquid*
Parenteral
    Prochlorperazine Edisylate Injection USP†
        In the U.S.—*Compa-Z; Compazine; Cotranzine; Ultrazine-10;* GENERIC
    Prochlorperazine Mesylate Injection*
        In Canada—*PMS Prochlorperazine; Stemetil;* GENERIC
Rectal
    Prochlorperazine Suppositories USP
        In the U.S.—*Compazine*
        In Canada—*PMS Prochlorperazine; Prorazin; Stemetil;* GENERIC
PROMAZINE
Oral
    Promazine Hydrochloride Tablets USP†
        In the U.S.—*Sparine*
Parenteral
    Promazine Hydrochloride Injection USP
        In the U.S.—*Primazine; Prozine-50; Sparine;* GENERIC
        In Canada—GENERIC
PROMETHAZINE—See Promethazine (Systemic).
PROPIOMAZINE—See Propiomazine (Systemic).
THIOPROPAZATE*
Oral
    Thiopropazate Hydrochloride Tablets*
        In Canada—*Dartal*
THIOPROPERAZINE*
Oral
    Thioproperazine Mesylate Tablets*
        In Canada—*Majeptil*

THIORIDAZINE
Oral
    Thioridazine Oral Suspension USP
        In the U.S.—*Mellaril-S*
        In Canada—*Mellaril*
    Thioridazine Hydrochloride Oral Solution USP
        In the U.S.—*Mellaril Concentrate;* GENERIC
        In Canada—*Mellaril*
    Thioridazine Hydrochloride Tablets USP
        In the U.S.—*Mellaril;* GENERIC
        In Canada—*Apo-Thioridazine; Mellaril; Novo-Ridazine; PMS Thioridazine*
TRIFLUOPERAZINE
Oral
    Trifluoperazine Hydrochloride Oral Solution
        In the U.S.—*Stelazine Concentrate;* GENERIC
        In Canada—*Stelazine Concentrate; Terfluzine Concentrate*
    Trifluoperazine Hydrochloride Syrup USP*
        In Canada—*PMS Trifluoperazine; Terfluzine*
    Trifluoperazine Hydrochloride Tablets USP
        In the U.S.—*Stelazine;* GENERIC
        In Canada—*Apo-Trifluoperazine; Novo-Flurazine; PMS Trifluoperazine; Solazine; Stelazine; Terfluzine*
Parenteral
    Trifluoperazine Hydrochloride Injection USP
        In the U.S.—*Stelazine;* GENERIC
        In Canada—*Stelazine*
TRIFLUPROMAZINE†
Parenteral
    Triflupromazine Hydrochloride Injection USP†
        In the U.S.—*Vesprin*
TRIMEPRAZINE—See Trimeprazine (Systemic).

---

*Not commercially available in the U.S.
†Not commercially available in Canada.

Category

Antipsychotic—Acetophenazine; Chlorpromazine; Fluphenazine; Mesoridazine; Methotrimeprazine; Pericyazine; Perphenazine; Pipotiazine; Prochlorperazine; Promazine; Thiopropazate; Thioproperazine; Thioridazine; Trifluoperazine; Triflupromazine.

Antiemetic—Chlorpromazine; Perphenazine; Prochlorperazine; Triflupromazine.

Analgesic—Methotrimeprazine.

Sedative (preoperative)—Methotrimeprazine.

Antidyskinetic (Huntington's disease)—Chlorpromazine; Thioridazine.

Antineuralgia adjunct—Fluphenazine.

Indications

Note: Bracketed information in the *Indications* section refers to uses not included in U.S. product labeling.

Accepted

Psychotic disorders (treatment)—Acetophenazine, chlorpromazine, fluphenazine, mesoridazine, [methotrimeprazine], pericyazine, perphenazine, pipotiazine, prochlorperazine, promazine, thiopropazate, thioproperazine, thioridazine, trifluoperazine, and triflupromazine are indicated in the management of psychotic conditions. They are clearly effective in schizophrenia, and for production of a quieting effect in hyperactive or excited psychotic patients.

Chlorpromazine, mesoridazine, and thioridazine are used for the treatment of children or adults with severe behavior problems associated with psychotic disorders or neurologic disease, who show combativeness and/or explosive, hyperexcitable behavior that is out of proportion to the immediate provocation. These agents are also used in the short-term treatment of hyperactive children who show excessive motor activity with accompanying conduct disorders such as impulsivity, mood lability, aggressiveness, short attention span, and poor frustration tolerance. Pericyazine is a more sedative phenothiazine with weak antipsychotic properties. It is indicated as an adjunctive medication in some psychotic patients for the control of residual prevailing hostility, impulsiveness, and aggressiveness.

Long-acting parenteral forms, fluphenazine decanoate and enanthate and pipotiazine palmitate, are indicated for the maintenance treatment of chronic, non-agitated schizophrenic patients stabilized with shorter-acting neuroleptics, who may benefit from a transfer to the longer-acting drug.

Thioridazine is indicated for the short-term treatment of adult patients with moderate to severe mental depression with varying degrees of anxiety and geriatric patients with multiple symptoms such as anxiety, agitation, depressed mood, tension, sleep disturbances, and fears. Chlorpromazine is used for anxiety, apprehension, and restlessness before surgery.

Nausea and vomiting (treatment)—Prochlorperazine, chlorpromazine, perphenazine, and triflupromazine are indicated in the control of severe nausea and vomiting in selected patients, with prochlorperazine being superior to other phenothiazines.

Pain (treatment)—Methotrimeprazine is indicated for the relief of moderate to severe pain in nonambulatory patients, and to produce obstetrical analgesia when respiratory depression should be avoided.

Sedation—Methotrimeprazine is indicated as a presurgical or obstetrical medication to produce sedation and somnolence.

[Anesthesia, general, adjunct]—Intravenous administration of methotrimeprazine is indicated as an adjunct to anesthesia, to increase the effects of anesthetics. The dose of a barbiturate or narcotic should be reduced by half when used with methotrimeprazine during surgery or labor.

Tetanus (treatment adjunct)—Chlorpromazine is indicated, usually in conjunction with a barbiturate, for the treatment of tetanus.

Porphyria, acute, intermittent (treatment)—Chlorpromazine is indicated in the treatment of acute intermittent porphyria.

Hiccups, intractable (treatment)—Chlorpromazine is indicated in the control of intractable hiccups.

[Pain, neurogenic (treatment adjunct)][1]—Fluphenazine has been used as an adjunct to tricyclic antidepressant therapy for some chronic pain states, as in patients trying to withdraw from narcotics, and in treatment of symptoms of diabetic neuropathy.

[Huntington's disease, choreiform movement of (treatment)][1]—Chlorpromazine and thioridazine are effective in reducing choreiform movement in Huntington's disease, and have been used as alternatives to haloperidol.

[1]Not included in Canadian product labeling.

Pharmacology

Mechanism of action/Effect:

Antipsychotic—Thought to improve psychotic conditions by blocking postsynaptic mesolimbic dopaminergic receptors in the brain. Phenothiazines also produce an alpha-adrenergic blocking effect and depress the release of hypothalamic and hypophyseal hormones. However, blockade of dopamine receptors increases prolactin release by the pituitary.

Antiemetic—Phenothiazines act centrally to inhibit or block the dopamine (D_2) receptors in the medullary chemoreceptor trigger zone (CTZ) and peripherally by blocking the vagus nerve in the gastrointestinal tract. The antiemetic effects of phenothiazines may be augmented by their anticholinergic, sedative, and antihistaminic effects.

Antianxiety—Thought to cause indirect reduction in arousal and increased filtering of internal stimuli to the brainstem reticular system.

Analgesic; sedative—Methotrimeprazine raises pain threshold and produces amnesia by suppression of sensory impulses. The

alpha-adrenergic blocking effects of phenothiazines may produce sedation and tranquilization.

Drug	Action*				
	Legend: **I** = Antiemetic **II** = Anticholinergic **III** = Extrapyramidal **IV** = Hypotensive **V** = Sedative				
	I	**II**	**III**	**IV**	**V**
Aliphatic					
Chlorpromazine	S	M–S	W–M	S	S
Methotrimeprazine	W	M	W–M	S	S
Promazine	M	S	W	S	S
Triflupromazine	S	S	M–S	M	M–S
Piperazine					
Acetophenazine	W	W	M	W	M
Fluphenazine	W	W	S	W	W
Perphenazine	S	W–M	S	W	W–M
Prochlorperazine	S	W	S	W	M
Thiopropazate	W	W	S	W	W
Thioproperazine	W	W	S	W	W
Trifluoperazine	S	W	S	W	W
Piperidine					
Mesoridazine	W	M	W	M–S	S
Pericyazine	S	S	M	M	S
Pipotiazine	W	W	S	W	W
Thioridazine	W	M	W	M–S	M

*S=strong; M=moderate; W=weak.

Onset of action:

Antipsychotic effect—Gradual (up to several weeks) and variable between patients.

Long-acting parenteral dosage forms:

Fluphenazine decanoate injection—Antipsychotic effects usually begin between 24 and 72 hours after administration and become significant within 48 to 96 hours.

Pipotiazine palmitate injection—Antipsychotic effects usually begin within the first 48 to 72 hours after administration and become significant within 1 week.

Time to peak effect:

Antipsychotic effect—Approximately 4 to 7 days to achieve steady-state plasma concentrations; peak therapeutic effects may take from 6 weeks to 6 months.

Analgesic effect (methotrimeprazine)—Within 20 to 40 minutes after intramuscular injection, maintained for about 4 hours.

Precautions to Consider

Cross-sensitivity and/or related problems

Patients sensitive to one phenothiazine may be sensitive to other phenothiazines also.

Geriatrics

Geriatric patients tend to develop higher plasma concentrations of phenothiazines because of changes in distribution due to decreases in lean body mass, total body water, and albumin, and often an increase in total body fat composition. Therefore, these patients usually require lower initial dosage and a more gradual titration of dose.

Elderly patients appear to be more prone to orthostatic hypotension and exhibit an increased sensitivity to the anticholinergic and sedative effects of phenothiazines. In addition, they are more prone to develop extrapyramidal side effects, such as tardive dyskinesia and parkinsonism. The symptoms of tardive dyskinesia are persistent, difficult to control, and, in some patients, appear to be irreversible. There is no known effective treatment. Careful observation during treatment for early signs of tardive dyskinesia and reduction of dosage or discontinuation of medication may prevent a more severe manifestation of the syndrome.

It has been suggested that elderly patients receive half the usual adult dose. Patients with organic brain syndrome or acute confusional states, should initially receive one-third to one-half the usual adult dose, with the dose being increased no more frequently than every 2 or 3 days, preferably at intervals of 7 to 10 days, if possible. After clinical improvement occurs, periodic attempts should be made to discontinue medication.

Dental

The peripheral anticholinergic effects of phenothiazines may decrease or inhibit salivary flow, especially in middle-aged or elderly patients, thus contributing to the development of caries, periodontal disease, oral candidiasis, and discomfort.

Extrapyramidal reactions induced by phenothiazines will result in increased motor activity of the head, face, and neck. Occlusal adjustments, bite registrations, and treatment for bruxism may be made less reliable.

The leukopenic and thrombocytopenic effects of phenothiazines may result in an increased incidence of microbial infection, delayed healing, and gingival bleeding. If leukopenia or thrombocytopenia occurs, dental work should be deferred until blood counts have returned to normal, and patients should be instructed in proper oral hygiene, including caution in use of regular toothbrushes, dental floss, and toothpicks.

Drug interactions and/or related problems

The following drug interactions and/or related problems have been selected on the basis of their potential clinical significance (possible mechanism in parentheses where appropriate)—not necessarily inclusive (» = major clinical significance):

Note: Combinations containing any of the following medications, depending on the amount present, may also interact with this medication.

» Alcohol or
» CNS depression-producing medications, other
  (concurrent use with phenothiazines may result in increased CNS and respiratory depression and increased hypotensive effects; dosage reductions of either drug may be necessary during concurrent use or when sequence of use enhances CNS effects)

  (alcohol may increase the risk of heat stroke when taken concurrently with phenothiazines)

  (in addition, barbiturates increase the metabolism of chlorpromazine by induction of hepatic microsomal enzymes, thus decreasing plasma concentrations, and possibly the therapeutic effect, of chlorpromazine; conversely, thioridazine may reduce serum phenobarbital concentrations)

Amantadine or
Antidyskinetics or
Antihistamines or
Anticholinergics or other medications with anticholinergic action
  (concurrent use with phenothiazines may intensify anticholinergic side effects, especially confusion, hallucinations, and nightmares, because of the phenothiazines' secondary anticholinergic effects; medications with anticholinergic effects may potentiate the hyperpyretic effect of phenothiazines, especially when environmental temperatures are high, by preventing sweating as a cooling mechanism; this effect could lead to heat stroke; also, patients should be advised to report occurrence of gastrointestinal problems since paralytic ileus may occur with concurrent therapy)

  (trihexyphenidyl may decrease plasma phenothiazine concentrations by decreasing gastrointestinal motility and increasing metabolism of the phenothiazine; since the antipsychotic effectiveness may be reduced, dosage adjustment of the phenothiazine may be required)

(parenteral methotrimeprazine, used as preanesthetic medication, may be administered concurrently, but with caution, with lowered doses of atropine or scopolamine; tachycardia and a fall in blood pressure may occur, and CNS reactions, such as stimulation, delirium, and extrapyramidal reactions, may be aggravated)

Amphetamines
  (stimulant effects may be decreased when amphetamines are used concurrently with phenothiazines since phenothiazines produce alpha-adrenergic blockade; also, the antipsychotic effectiveness of phenothiazines may be reduced)

Antacids, aluminum- or magnesium-containing, or
Antidiarrheals, adsorbent
  (concurrent use of these medications with phenothiazines may inhibit the absorption of orally administered phenothiazines, especially chlorpromazine; simultaneous use should be avoided)

Anticonvulsants, including barbiturates
  (phenothiazines may lower the seizure threshold; dosage adjustment of anticonvulsant medications may be necessary)

  (phenothiazines may inhibit phenytoin metabolism, leading to phenytoin toxicity)

» Antidepressants, tricyclic, or
Maprotiline or
Monoamine oxidase (MAO) inhibitors, including furazolidone, procarbazine, and selegiline
  (concurrent use may prolong and intensify the sedative and anticholinergic effects of either these medications or phenothiazines; phenothiazines may increase plasma concentrations of cyclic antidepressants by inhibiting metabolism; conversely, cyclic antidepressants may inhibit phenothiazine metabolism; also, the risk of neuroleptic malignant syndrome [NMS] may be increased)

» Antithyroid agents
  (concurrent use with phenothiazines may increase the risk of agranulocytosis)

Apomorphine
  (prior ingestion of phenothiazine antiemetics may decrease the emetic response to apomorphine; also, the CNS depressant effects of phenothiazine antiemetics are additive to those of apomorphine and may induce dangerous respiratory depression, circulatory system effects, or prolonged sleep)

Appetite suppressants
  (concurrent use with phenothiazines may antagonize the anorectic effect of appetite suppressants, with the exception of fenfluramine and phenmetrazine)

Beta-adrenergic blocking agents
  (concurrent use of beta-blockers, possibly including ophthalmics, with phenothiazines may result in an increased plasma concentration of each medication because of inhibition of metabolism; this may result in additive hypotensive effects, irreversible retinopathy, cardiac arrhythmias, and tardive dyskinesia)

Bromocriptine
  (concurrent use may increase serum prolactin concentrations and interfere with effects of bromocriptine; dosage adjustments may be necessary)

Cimetidine
  (concurrent use may decrease steady-state chlorpromazine concentrations by impairing its gastrointestinal absorption)

Diuretics, thiazide
  (concurrent use may potentiate hyponatremia and water intoxication; alternate methods of hypertension control should be considered)

Dopamine
  (concurrent use may antagonize the peripheral vasoconstriction produced by high doses of dopamine, because of the alpha-adrenergic blocking action of phenothiazines)

Ephedrine
(concurrent use with phenothiazines may decrease the pressor response to ephedrine)

» Epinephrine
(the use of epinephrine to treat phenothiazine-induced hypotension should be avoided because the alpha-adrenergic effects of epinephrine may be blocked, resulting in beta stimulation only and causing severe hypotension and tachycardia)

» Extrapyramidal reaction-causing medications, other
(concurrent use with phenothiazines may increase the severity and frequency of extrapyramidal effects)

Hepatotoxic medications, other
(concurrent use of phenothiazines with medications known to alter hepatic microsomal enzyme activity may result in an increased incidence of hepatotoxicity; patients, especially those on prolonged administration or with a history of liver disease, should be carefully monitored)

» Hypotension-producing medications, other
(concurrent use with phenothiazines may produce severe hypotension with postural syncope)

» Levodopa
(antiparkinsonian effects of levodopa may be inhibited when it is used concurrently with phenothiazines, because of blockade of dopamine receptors in brain; levodopa has not been shown to be effective in the treatment of phenothiazine-induced parkinsonism)

» Lithium
(concurrent use with chlorpromazine and possibly other phenothiazines may reduce gastrointestinal absorption of the phenothiazine, thereby decreasing its serum concentrations by as much as 40%; concurrent use may increase rate of renal excretion of lithium; extrapyramidal symptoms may be increased; also, nausea and vomiting, early indications of lithium toxicity, may be masked by the antiemetic effect of some phenothiazines)

Metaraminol
(concurrent use with phenothiazines usually decreases, but does not reverse or completely block, the pressor effect of metaraminol because of the alpha-adrenergic blocking action of phenothiazines)

Mephentermine
(concurrent use with phenothiazines, especially chlorpromazine, may antagonize the antipsychotic effect of the phenothiazine or the pressor effect of mephentermine by exerting opposing effects on monoaminergic functions in the central and peripheral nervous systems)

Methoxamine
(prior administration of phenothiazines may decrease the pressor effect and shorten the duration of action of methoxamine, because of the alpha-adrenergic blocking action of phenothiazines)

» Metrizamide
(concurrent use with phenothiazines may lower the seizure threshold; phenothiazines should be discontinued at least 48 hours before, and not resumed for at least 24 hours following, myelography)

Ototoxic medications, especially ototoxic antibiotics
(concurrent use with phenothiazines may mask some symptoms of ototoxicity such as tinnitus, dizziness, or vertigo)

Opioid (narcotic) analgesics
(in addition to increased CNS and respiratory depression, concurrent use with phenothiazines increases orthostatic hypotension and increases the risk of severe constipation, which may lead to paralytic ileus, and/or urinary retention)

Phenylephrine
(prior administration of phenothiazines may decrease the pressor effect and shorten the duration of action of phenylephrine)

Photosensitizing medications, other
(concurrent use with phenothiazines may cause additive photosensitizing effects)

(in addition, concurrent use of systemic methoxsalen, trioxsalen, or tetracyclines with phenothiazines may potentiate intraocular photochemical damage to the choroid, retina, or lens)

Probucol
(additive QT interval prolongation may increase the risk of ventricular tachycardia)

Succinylcholine
(concurrent use with methotrimeprazine may cause tachycardia and a fall in blood pressure, CNS stimulation and delirium, and an aggravation of extrapyramidal effects)

Contraindications/Medical problems
The contraindications/medical problems included have been selected on the basis of their potential clinical significance (reasons given in parentheses where appropriate)—not necessarily inclusive (» = major clinical significance).

Except under special circumstances, this medicine should not be used when the following medical problems exist:

» Cardiovascular disease, severe, or
» CNS depression, severe, or
» Comatose states
(may be exacerbated)

Risk-benefit should be considered when the following medical problems exist:

» Alcoholism, active
(CNS depression may be potentiated; risk of heat stroke may be increased; chronic alcohol abusers may be predisposed to hepatotoxic reactions during phenothiazine therapy)

Angina pectoris
(pain may be increased with use of trifluoperazine)

» Blood dyscrasias
(may be exacerbated; treatment may have to be discontinued)

Breast cancer
(potentially higher risk of disease progression and possible increased resistance to endocrine and cytotoxic treatment, due to phenothiazine-induced prolactin secretion)

Cardiovascular disease
(increased risk of hypotension; myocardial depression, cardiomegaly, congestive heart failure [CHF], and arrhythmias may be induced)

Glaucoma, or predisposition to
(may be potentiated)

» Hepatic function impairment
(metabolism may be decreased; higher serum phenothiazine concentrations may increase sensitivity to CNS effects)

Parkinson's disease
(potentiation of extrapyramidal effects)

Peptic ulcer or
Urinary retention
(may be exacerbated)

Prostatic hypertrophy, symptomatic
(increased risk of urinary retention)

Respiratory disorders, chronic, especially in children
(may be potentiated)

» Reye's syndrome
(increased risk of hepatotoxicity in children and adolescents whose signs and symptoms suggest Reye's syndrome)

Seizure disorders
(seizures may be precipitated)

Sensitivity to any phenothiazine
(may be potentiated upon re-exposure to any phenothiazine in patients with a history of phenothiazine-induced blood dyscrasias, jaundice, or skin reactions)

Vomiting

(antiemetic action of phenothiazines may mask vomiting caused by overdose of other medications)

Caution should also be used in geriatric, emaciated, and debilitated patients, who usually require a lower initial dose.

Side/Adverse Effects

The following side/adverse effects have been selected on the basis of their potential clinical significance (possible signs and symptoms in parentheses where appropriate)—not necessarily inclusive:

Those indicating need for medical attention
Incidence more frequent

Akathisia (restlessness or need to keep moving); *blurred vision associated with anticholinergic effect; deposition of opaque material in lens, cornea, and retina* (blurred vision); *dystonic extrapyramidal effects* (muscle spasms of face, neck, and back, tic-like or twitching movements, twisting movements of body, inability to move eyes, weakness of arms and legs); *parkinsonian extrapyramidal effects* (difficulty in speaking or swallowing, loss of balance control, mask-like face, shuffling walk, stiffness of arms or legs, trembling and shaking of hands and fingers); *hypotension* (fainting)—less common with the piperazine phenothiazines; *pigmentary retinopathy* (blurred vision, defective color vision, difficulty seeing at night)—more frequent with high doses of thioridazine; *tardive dyskinesia* (lip smacking or puckering, puffing of cheeks, rapid or worm-like movements of tongue, uncontrolled chewing movements, uncontrolled movements of arms and legs)—more frequent in elderly patients, women, and patients with brain damage

Note: *Parkinsonian* effects are more frequent in the elderly, whereas *dystonias* occur more often in younger patients. Symptoms may be seen in the first few days of treatment or after prolonged treatment, and can recur after even a single dose. The effects are more common with the piperazine phenothiazines.

Incidence less frequent

Difficulty in urinating; increased sensitivity of skin to sun (rash, severe sunburn); *skin rash associated with contact dermatitis* (with liquid products) or other allergic reaction, or cholestatic jaundice

Incidence rare

Agranulocytosis (sore throat, fever, unusual bleeding or bruising, unusual tiredness or weakness)—more frequent with aliphatic phenothiazines; *cholestatic jaundice* (abdominal or stomach pains, aching muscles and joints, fever and chills, severe skin itching, yellow eyes or skin, fatigue, nausea, vomiting, or diarrhea); *heat stroke* (hot dry skin, inability to sweat, muscle weakness, confusion); *neuroleptic malignant syndrome (NMS)* (convulsions, difficult or fast breathing, fast heartbeat or irregular pulse, fever, high or low [irregular] blood pressure, increased sweating, loss of bladder control, severe muscle stiffness, unusually pale skin, unusual tiredness or weakness); *priapism* (prolonged, painful, inappropriate penile erection); *melanosis* (tanning or blue-gray discoloration of skin)—more common with long-term, high-dose, low-potency chlorpromazine and thioridazine

Note: *Agranulocytosis* can develop within the first 3 months of treatment, with recovery within 1 to 2 weeks after medication is discontinued; may recur upon rechallenge in recovered patients.

Liver function tests may be abnormal without overt jaundice. *Jaundice* may appear about 2 weeks after severe pruritus and may progress to chronic active hepatitis. Discontinuing medication may be necessary.

Heat stroke, caused by phenothiazine-induced suppression of central and peripheral temperature regulation in the hypothalamus, may occur in environmental conditions of high heat and high humidity. The effectiveness of sweating as a cooling mechanism may be reduced by humid conditions

and by the *anticholinergic effects* of phenothiazines or their combination with other anticholinergic medications such as nonprescription cold medications or antihistamines. Adequate interior temperature control (air-conditioning) must be maintained for institutionalized patients during hot weather because of the increased risk of *heat stroke* and *neuroleptic malignant syndrome (NMS)*. Patients should be advised to avoid exertion, stay in cool areas, and avoid dehydration and other anticholinergic medications. Phenothiazines may also cause hypothermia in cold weather, since the disruption of the thermoregulatory mechanisms results in a poikilothermic state.

NMS may occur at any time during neuroleptic therapy and is potentially fatal. It is more commonly seen soon after start of therapy or after patient has switched from one neuroleptic to another, during combined therapy with another psychotropic medication, or after a dosage increase. Along with the overt signs of skeletal muscle rigidity, hyperthermia, autonomic dysfunction, and altered consciousness, differential diagnosis may reveal leukocytosis (9500 to 26,000 cells per cubic millimeter), elevated liver enzyme tests, and elevated creatine phosphokinase (CPK).

Those indicating need for medical attention only if they continue or are bothersome
Incidence more frequent

Anticholinergic effects (constipation, decreased sweating, dizziness [orthostatic hypotension], drowsiness, dry mouth)—less frequent with piperazine phenothiazines; *nasal congestion*

Incidence less frequent

Changes in menstrual period; decreased sexual ability; secretion of milk, unusual; swelling or pain in breasts; weight gain, unusual

Those indicating need for medical attention if they occur after the medication is discontinued
Incidence more frequent

Tardive dyskinesia, persistent (lip smacking or puckering, puffing of cheeks, rapid or worm-like movements of tongue, uncontrolled chewing movements, uncontrolled movements of arms and legs)—more frequent in elderly patients, women, and patients with brain damage

Incidence less frequent

Dizziness; nausea and vomiting; stomach pain; trembling of fingers and hands

Patient Consultation

In providing consultation, consider emphasizing the following selected information (» = major clinical significance):

Before using this medication
» Conditions affecting use, especially:

Sensitivity to any phenothiazine

Pregnancy—Not recommended for use during pregnancy because of reports of jaundice, hypo- or hyperreflexia, and extrapyramidal symptoms in neonates

Breast-feeding—Excreted in breast milk; may cause drowsiness, dystonias, and tardive dyskinesia in the baby

Use in children—Children, especially those with acute illnesses, are more prone to extrapyramidal symptoms

Use in the elderly—Elderly patients are more likely to develop extrapyramidal, anticholinergic, hypotensive, and sedative effects; reduced dosage recommended

Use by athletes—Phenothiazines are banned and, in some cases, tested for in competitors in biathlon and modern pentathlon events by the U.S. Olympic Committee (USOC)

Dental—Phenothiazine-induced blood dyscrasias may result in infections, delayed healing, and bleeding; dry mouth may cause caries and candidiasis; increased motor activity of face, head, and neck may interfere with some dental procedures

Other medications, especially alcohol, other CNS depression-producing medications, tricyclic antidepressants, antithyroid agents, epinephrine, other hypotension-producing medications, other extrapyramidal-producing medications, levodopa, lithium, or metrizamide

Other medical problems, especially cardiovascular disease, severe CNS depression, active alcoholism, blood dyscrasias, liver disease, or Reye's syndrome

Proper use of this medication

Proper administration of this medication:

For oral dosage forms

Taking with food, milk, or water to reduce stomach irritation

» Diluting medication that comes in dropper bottle with recommended beverages prior to use

Swallowing the extended-release dosage form whole

For rectal dosage forms

Chilling suppository if too soft to insert

How to insert suppository

» Compliance with therapy; not taking more or less medication than prescribed

» Several weeks of therapy may be required to produce desired effects in treatment of nervous, mental, or emotional conditions

Missed dose: When dosing schedule is—

One dose a day: Taking as soon as possible unless almost time for next dose, then going back to regular dosing schedule; not doubling doses

More than one dose a day: Taking as soon as possible if within an hour or so of missed dose; skipping missed dose if not remembered until later; going back to regular dosing schedule; not doubling doses

» Proper storage

Precautions while using this medication

Regular visits to physician to check progress of therapy

» Checking with physician before discontinuing medication; gradual dosage reduction may be needed

Avoiding use of antacids or antidiarrheal medication within 2 hours of taking phenothiazine

» Avoiding use of alcoholic beverages or other CNS depressants during therapy

Avoiding the use of over-the-counter medications for colds or allergies, to prevent increased anticholinergic effects and risk of heat stroke

Caution if any laboratory tests required; possible interference with ECG readings, and with gonadorelin, immunologic urine pregnancy, metyrapone, and urine bilirubin test results

» Caution if any kind of surgery, dental treatment, or emergency treatment is required; telling physician or dentist in charge about phenothiazine because of possible drug interactions or blood dyscrasias

» Possible drowsiness or blurred vision; caution when driving, using machines, or doing other things requiring alertness or accurate vision

» Possible dizziness or lightheadedness (orthostatic hypotension); caution when getting up suddenly from a lying or sitting position

» Possible heat stroke: Caution during exercise, hot weather, or when taking hot baths

Possible hypothermia: Caution during prolonged exposure to cold

» Possible dryness of mouth; using sugarless gum or candy, ice, or saliva substitute for relief; checking with physician or dentist if dry mouth continues for more than 2 weeks

» Possible skin photosensitivity; avoiding unprotected exposure to sun; using protective clothing; using a sun block product that includes protection against both UVA-caused photosensitivity reactions and UVB-caused sunburn reactions; avoiding use of sunlamp, tanning bed, or tanning booth

» Possible eye photosensitivity; wearing sunglasses that block ultraviolet light

» Avoiding spilling liquid dosage form on skin or clothing; may cause skin irritation

» Observing precautions for up to 12 weeks with long-acting parenteral forms

Side/adverse effects

Side effects more likely to occur in the elderly

Signs of potential side effects, especially tardive dyskinesia, dystonias, parkinsonian effects, anticholinergic effects, blurred vision, possible pigmentary retinopathy, allergic skin reactions, photosensitivity, agranulocytosis, cholestatic jaundice, heat stroke, neuroleptic malignant syndrome, priapism, melanosis, dryness of mouth, orthostatic hypotension, or akathisia

» Stopping medication and notifying physician immediately if symptoms of neuroleptic malignant syndrome (NMS) appear, especially muscle rigidity, fever, difficult or fast breathing, seizures, fast heartbeat, increased sweating, loss of bladder control, unusually pale skin, unusual tiredness or weakness

» Notifying physician immediately if early symptoms of tardive dyskinesia appear, such as fine worm-like movements of the tongue or other uncontrolled movements of the mouth, tongue, jaw, or arms and legs; dosage adjustment or discontinuation may be needed to prevent irreversibility

Possibility of withdrawal symptoms

General Dosing Information

Dosage must be individualized by titration from the lower dose range. After a favorable psychiatric response is noted (within several days to several months), that dosage should be continued for about 2 weeks, then gradually decreased to the lowest level that will maintain an adequate clinical response.

When extended therapy is discontinued, a gradual reduction in phenothiazine dosage over several weeks is recommended, since abrupt withdrawal may cause some patients on high or long-term dosage to experience transient dyskinetic signs, nausea, vomiting, gastritis, trembling, and dizziness.

The antiemetic effect of some phenothiazines may mask signs of drug toxicity or obscure diagnosis of conditions whose primary symptom is nausea. Phenothiazines have no antiemetic effect when nausea is a result of vestibular stimulation or local gastrointestinal irritation.

Antidyskinetic agents such as trihexyphenidyl or benztropine may be used concurrently to control phenothiazine-induced extrapyramidal symptoms. They should be used only when required (not prophylactically), and, generally, are only needed for a few weeks to two or three months.

Avoid skin contact with liquid forms of phenothiazine medication; contact dermatitis has resulted.

For parenteral dosage forms only

Because hypotension is a possible side effect of phenothiazines, parenteral administration should be used only in patients who are bedfast or for appropriate acute therapy in ambulatory patients who can be closely monitored. A possible exception may be those patients who are dose-stabilized on the extended-action injectable forms.

Intramuscular injections should be administered slowly and deeply into the upper outer quadrant of the buttock. Patient should remain lying down for at least $1/2$ hour after injection to avoid possible hypotensive effects.

To prevent irritation or sterile abscesses at the site of intramuscular injection, rotation of the injection sites, dilution of the phenothiazine injection with sodium chloride injection, and/or addition of 2% procaine are recommended.

Effects of the extended-action injectable forms may last for up to 12 weeks in some patients. The side effects information and precautions apply during this period of time.

The dose of the extended-action injectable forms should *not* be increased to prolong the dosing interval. Each patient must be carefully supervised to determine the optimal dosing interval and lowest effective dose, depending on patient's response, age, physical condition, symptoms, severity of illness, and drug history.

Geriatric and pediatric patients, especially those acutely ill or dehydrated, should be monitored very carefully during parenteral therapy because of a higher incidence of hypotensive and extrapyramidal reactions in these age groups.

Diet/Nutrition

The oral dosage forms of this medication may be taken with food or a full glass (240 mL) of water or milk, if necessary, to lessen stomach irritation.

Requirements for riboflavin may be increased in patients receiving phenothiazines.

ACETOPHENAZINE

Summary of Differences

Pharmacology:
    Chemical Group—Piperazine
    Actions—
        Antiemetic: Weak
        Anticholinergic: Weak
        Extrapyramidal: Moderate
        Hypotensive: Weak
        Sedative: Moderate

Oral Dosage Forms

ACETOPHENAZINE MALEATE TABLETS USP

Usual adult and adolescent dose: Psychotic disorders—Oral, 20 mg three times a day, the dosage being adjusted as needed and tolerated.

Note: Geriatric, emaciated, or debilitated patients usually require a lower initial dose, the dosage being gradually increased as needed and tolerated.

Usual adult prescribing limits: Up to 120 mg a day.

Auxiliary labeling:
- May cause drowsiness.
- Avoid alcoholic beverages.

CHLORPROMAZINE

Summary of Differences

Category: Includes antiemetic and antidyskinetic (Huntington's disease) uses.
Pharmacology:
    Chemical group—Aliphatic
    Actions—
        Antiemetic: Strong
        Anticholinergic: Moderate to strong
        Extrapyramidal: Weak to moderate
        Hypotensive: Strong
        Sedative: Strong

Additional Dosing Information

See also *General Dosing Information.*

For intractable hiccups, chlorpromazine is initially administered orally. If symptoms persist for 2 or 3 days, intramuscular administration is indicated, followed by slow intravenous infusion if hiccups continue.

For parenteral use

Chlorpromazine injection must not be administered subcutaneously, because it causes severe tissue necrosis.

For intramuscular injection, diluting chlorpromazine injection with sodium chloride injection and/or adding 2% procaine may prevent irritation at the injection site.

The intravenous route of administration is used only for severe hiccups, surgery, and tetanus.

Before intravenous injection, chlorpromazine hydrochloride injection should be diluted with sodium chloride injection.

Close monitoring of blood pressure for hypotension is necessary during parenteral administration.

Oral Dosage Forms

Note: The dosing and strengths of the dosage forms available are expressed in terms of chlorpromazine base (not the hydrochloride salt).

CHLORPROMAZINE HYDROCHLORIDE EXTENDED-RELEASE CAPSULES

Usual adult and adolescent dose: Psychotic disorders—Oral, 30 to 300 mg (base) one to three times a day, the dosage being adjusted as needed and tolerated.

Note: Geriatric, emaciated, or debilitated patients usually require a lower initial dose, the dosage being gradually increased as needed and tolerated.

    The 300-mg extended-release capsules are used only in severe neuropsychiatric conditions.

Usual adult prescribing limits: Up to 1 gram (base) a day.

Note: Although doses are sometimes gradually increased to 2 grams a day or more for short periods, 1 gram or less is usually sufficient for extended therapy.

Auxiliary labeling:
- May cause drowsiness.
- Avoid alcoholic beverages.

CHLORPROMAZINE HYDROCHLORIDE ORAL CONCENTRATE USP

Usual adult and adolescent dose:
    Psychotic disorders—Oral, 10 to 25 mg (base) two to four times a day, the dosage being increased by 20 to 50 mg a day every three or four days as needed and tolerated.
    Nausea and vomiting—Oral, 10 to 25 mg (base) every four hours, the dosage being increased as needed and tolerated.
    Anxiety, presurgical—Oral, 25 to 50 mg (base) two to three hours before surgery.
    Hiccups; or
    Porphyria—Oral, 25 to 50 mg (base) three or four times a day.

Note: Geriatric, emaciated, or debilitated patients usually require a lower initial dose, the dosage being gradually increased as needed and tolerated.

Usual adult prescribing limits: Up to 1 gram (base) a day.

Note: Although doses are sometimes gradually increased to 2 grams a day or more for short periods, 1 gram or less is usually sufficient for extended therapy.

Auxiliary labeling:
- May cause drowsiness.
- Avoid alcoholic beverages.
- Do not spill on skin or clothing.
- Must be diluted before use.

Note:

Avoid skin contact with liquid forms of this medication; contact dermatitis has resulted.

Each dose must be diluted just before administration in a half glass (120 mL) of coffee, tea, milk, tomato or fruit juice, water, soup, or carbonated beverage.

Explain dilution and dosage measurement to patient if self-administered.

CHLORPROMAZINE HYDROCHLORIDE SYRUP USP

Usual adult and adolescent dose:

Psychotic disorders—Oral, 10 to 25 mg (base) two to four times a day, the dosage being increased by 20 to 50 mg a day every three or four days as needed and tolerated.

Nausea and vomiting—Oral, 10 to 25 mg (base) every four hours, the dosage being increased as needed and tolerated.

Anxiety, presurgical—Oral, 25 to 50 mg (base) two to three hours before surgery.

Hiccups; or

Porphyria—Oral, 25 to 50 mg (base) three or four times a day.

Note: Geriatric, emaciated, or debilitated patients usually require a lower initial dose, the dosage being gradually increased as needed and tolerated.

Usual adult prescribing limits: Up to 1 gram (base) a day.

Note: Although doses are sometimes gradually increased to 2 grams a day or more for short periods, 1 gram or less is usually sufficient for extended therapy.

Auxiliary labeling:
- May cause drowsiness.
- Avoid alcoholic beverages.
- Do not spill on skin or clothing.

Note: Avoid skin contact with liquid forms of this medication; contact dermatitis has resulted.

CHLORPROMAZINE HYDROCHLORIDE TABLETS USP

Usual adult and adolescent dose:

Psychotic disorders—Oral, 10 to 25 mg (base) two to four times a day, the dosage being increased by 20 to 50 mg a day every three to four days as needed and tolerated.

Nausea and vomiting—Oral, 10 to 25 mg (base) every four hours, the dosage being increased as needed and tolerated.

Anxiety, presurgical—Oral, 25 to 50 mg (base) two to three hours before surgery.

Hiccups; or

Porphyria—Oral, 25 to 50 mg (base) three or four times a day.

Note: Geriatric, emaciated, or debilitated patients usually require a lower initial dose, the dosage being gradually increased as needed and tolerated.

The 100- and 200-mg tablets are for use in severe neuropsychiatric conditions.

Usual adult prescribing limits: Up to 1 gram (base) a day.

Note: Although doses are sometimes gradually increased to 2 grams a day or more for short periods, 1 gram or less is usually sufficient for extended therapy.

Auxiliary labeling:
- May cause drowsiness.
- Avoid alcoholic beverages.

Parenteral Dosage Forms

Note: The dosing and strengths of the dosage forms available are expressed in terms of chlorpromazine base (not the hydrochloride salt).

CHLORPROMAZINE HYDROCHLORIDE INJECTION USP

Usual adult dose:

Psychotic disorders (severe)—Intramuscular, 25 to 50 mg (base), the dose being repeated in one hour if needed, and every three to twelve hours thereafter as needed and tolerated. The dosage may be gradually increased over several days as needed and tolerated.

Nausea and vomiting—Intramuscular, 25 mg (base) in a single dose, the dosage being increased to 25 to 50 mg every three to four hours as needed and tolerated until vomiting stops.

Nausea and vomiting during surgery—

Intramuscular: 12.5 mg (base) in a single dose, the dose being repeated in thirty minutes as needed and tolerated.

Intravenous infusion: Up to 25 mg (base), diluted to a concentration of at least 1 mg per mL of 0.9% sodium chloride injection, administered at a rate of no more than 2 mg every 2 minutes.

Anxiety, presurgical—Intramuscular, 12.5 to 25 mg (base) one or two hours before surgery.

Hiccups—

Intramuscular: 25 to 50 mg (base) three or four times a day.

Intravenous infusion: 25 to 50 mg (base), diluted in 500 to 1000 mL sodium chloride injection, administered slowly at a rate of 1 mg per minute.

Porphyria—Intramuscular, 25 mg every (base) six or eight hours until patient can take oral therapy.

Tetanus—

Intramuscular: 25 to 50 mg (base) three or four times a day, the dosage being increased gradually as needed and tolerated.

Intravenous infusion: 25 to 50 mg (base), diluted to a concentration of at least 1 mg per mL with sodium chloride injection, administered at a rate of 1 mg per minute.

Note: Geriatric, emaciated, or debilitated patients usually require a lower initial dose, the dosage being gradually increased as needed and tolerated.

Usual adult prescribing limits: Up to 1 gram (base) a day.

Note: Although antipsychotic doses are sometimes gradually increased to 2 grams a day or more for short periods, 1 gram or less is usually sufficient for extended therapy.

Note: Avoid skin contact with liquid forms of this medication; contact dermatitis has resulted.

Rectal Dosage Forms

CHLORPROMAZINE SUPPOSITORIES USP

Usual adult and adolescent dose: Nausea and vomiting—Rectal, 50 to 100 mg every six to eight hours as needed.

Note: Geriatric, emaciated, or debilitated patients usually require a lower initial dose, the dosage being gradually increased as needed and tolerated.

Usual adult prescribing limits: Up to 400 mg a day.

Auxiliary labeling:
- May cause drowsiness.
- Avoid alcoholic beverages.
- For rectal use only.

FLUPHENAZINE

Summary of Differences

Category: Includes use as antineuralgia adjunct in patients with chronic pain.

Pharmacology:

Chemical group—Piperazine

Actions—

Antiemetic: Weak

Anticholinergic: Weak

Extrapyramidal: Strong

Hypotensive: Weak

Sedative: Weak

Additional Dosing Information

See also *General Dosing Information*.

For long-acting parenteral dosage forms

A dry syringe and needle (at least 21 gauge) should be used, since use of a wet needle may cause the solution to become cloudy.

After the initial dose of the decanoate or enanthate extended-action injection, dosages and dosing intervals are determined by the patient's response.

Oral Dosage Forms

FLUPHENAZINE HYDROCHLORIDE ELIXIR USP

Usual adult and adolescent dose: Psychotic disorders—

Initial: Oral, 2.5 to 10 mg a day in divided doses every six to eight hours, the dosage being increased gradually as needed and tolerated.

Maintenance: Oral, 1 to 5 mg a day as a single dose or in divided doses.

Note: Emaciated or debilitated patients usually require a lower initial dosage (1 to 2.5 mg daily), the dosage being gradually increased as needed and tolerated.

Usual adult prescribing limits: Up to 20 mg a day.

Usual geriatric dose: Psychotic disorders—Oral, 1 to 2.5 mg a day, the dosage being gradually increased as needed and tolerated.

Auxiliary labeling:

- May cause drowsiness.
- Avoid alcoholic beverages.
- Do not spill on skin or clothing.
- Keep container tightly closed.

Note: Avoid skin contact with liquid forms of this medication; contact dermatitis has resulted.

FLUPHENAZINE HYDROCHLORIDE ORAL SOLUTION USP

Usual adult and adolescent dose: Psychotic disorders—

Initial: Oral, 2.5 to 10 mg a day in divided doses every six to eight hours, the dosage being increased gradually as needed and tolerated.

Maintenance: Oral, 1 to 5 mg a day as a single dose or in divided doses.

Note: Emaciated or debilitated patients usually require a lower initial dosage (1 to 2.5 mg daily), the dosage being gradually increased as needed and tolerated.

Usual adult prescribing limits: Up to 20 mg a day.

Usual geriatric dose: Psychotic disorders—Oral, 1 to 2.5 mg a day, the dosage being gradually increased as needed and tolerated.

Auxiliary labeling:

- May cause drowsiness.
- Avoid alcoholic beverages.
- Do not spill on skin or clothing.
- Must be diluted before use.

Note:

Avoid skin contact with liquid forms of this medication; contact dermatitis has resulted.

Each dose must be diluted just before administration in a half (120 mL) to a full (240 mL) glass of milk, tomato or fruit juice, water, soup, or carbonated beverage.

Explain dilution and dosage measurement to patient if self-administered.

FLUPHENAZINE HYDROCHLORIDE TABLETS USP

Usual adult and adolescent dose: Psychotic disorders—

Initial: Oral, 2.5 to 10 mg a day in divided doses every six to eight hours, the dosage being increased gradually as needed and tolerated.

Maintenance: Oral, 1 to 5 mg a day as a single dose or in divided doses.

Note: Emaciated or debilitated patients usually require a lower initial dosage (1 to 2.5 mg daily), the dosage being gradually increased as needed and tolerated.

Usual adult prescribing limits: Up to 20 mg a day.

Usual geriatric dose: Psychotic disorders—Oral, 1 to 2.5 mg a day, the dosage being gradually increased as needed and tolerated.

Auxiliary labeling:

- May cause drowsiness.
- Avoid alcoholic beverages.

Parenteral Dosage Forms

FLUPHENAZINE DECANOATE INJECTION

Usual adult dose: Psychotic disorders—

Initial: Intramuscular or subcutaneous, 12.5 to 25 mg, the dose being repeated or increased every one to three weeks as needed and tolerated.

Maintenance: Intramuscular or subcutaneous, usually up to 50 mg every one to four weeks, as needed and tolerated.

Note: For doses greater than 50 mg, increases should be made cautiously in increments of 12.5 mg.

Usual adult prescribing limits: Up to 100 mg per dose.

Note: Avoid skin contact with liquid forms of this medication; contact dermatitis has resulted.

Additional information:

The onset of action of the initial dose is generally between 24 and 72 hours after administration, and antipsychotic effects become significant within 48 to 96 hours.

The effects of a single injection of the extended-action injectable forms may last for up to 6 weeks in some patients. The side effects information and precautions apply during this period of time.

The time to steady-state from a dosage change requires 6 to 12 weeks or longer.

FLUPHENAZINE ENANTHATE INJECTION USP

Usual adult and adolescent dose: Psychotic disorders—Intramuscular or subcutaneous, 25 mg, the dosage being repeated or increased every one to three weeks as needed and tolerated.

Note: For doses greater than 50 mg, increases should be made cautiously in increments of 12.5 mg.

Usual adult prescribing limits: Up to 100 mg per dose.

Note: Avoid skin contact with liquid forms of this medication; contact dermatitis has resulted.

Additional information: The effects of a single dose of the extended-action injectable forms may last for up to 6 weeks in some patients. The side effects information and precautions apply during this period of time.

FLUPHENAZINE HYDROCHLORIDE INJECTION USP

Usual adult and adolescent dose: Psychotic disorders—Intramuscular, 1.25 to 2.5 mg every six to eight hours as needed and tolerated.

Note: Emaciated or debilitated patients usually require a lower initial dose (1 to 2.5 mg daily), the dosage being increased gradually as needed and tolerated.

Usual adult prescribing limits: Up to 10 mg a day.

Usual geriatric dose: Psychotic disorders—Intramuscular, 1 to 2.5 mg a day, the dosage being increased gradually as needed and tolerated.

Note: Avoid skin contact with liquid forms of this medication; contact dermatitis has resulted.

MESORIDAZINE

Summary of Differences

Pharmacology:
    Chemical group—Piperidine
    Actions—
        Antiemetic: Weak
        Anticholinergic: Moderate
        Extrapyramidal: Weak
        Hypotensive: Strong
        Sedative: Strong

Oral Dosage Forms

Note: The dosing and strengths of the dosage forms available are expressed in terms of mesoridazine base (not the besylate salt).

MESORIDAZINE BESYLATE ORAL SOLUTION USP

Usual adult and adolescent dose: Psychotic disorders—Oral, 30 to 150 mg (base) a day in two or three divided doses, the dosage being adjusted as needed and tolerated.

Note: Geriatric, emaciated, or debilitated patients usually require a lower initial dose, the dosage being increased gradually as needed and tolerated.

Auxiliary labeling:
- May cause drowsiness.
- Avoid alcoholic beverages.
- Do not spill on skin or clothing.
- Must be diluted before use.

Note:
    Avoid skin contact with liquid forms of this medication; contact dermatitis has resulted.
    Each dose must be diluted just before administration in distilled water, acidified tap water, orange juice, or grapefruit juice. The recommended dilution is 25 mg in 2 teaspoonsful of diluent. Higher doses require more diluent. Preparation and storage of bulk dilution is not recommended.
    Explain dilution and dosage measurement to patient if self-administered.

MESORIDAZINE BESYLATE TABLETS USP

Usual adult and adolescent dose: Psychotic disorders—Oral, 30 to 150 mg (base) a day in two or three divided doses, the dosage being adjusted as needed and tolerated.

Note: Geriatric, emaciated, or debilitated patients usually require a lower initial dose, the dosage being increased gradually as needed and tolerated.

Auxiliary labeling:
- May cause drowsiness.
- Avoid alcoholic beverages.

Parenteral Dosage Forms

Note: The dosing and strengths of the dosage forms available are expressed in terms of mesoridazine base (not the besylate salt).

MESORIDAZINE BESYLATE INJECTION USP

Usual adult and adolescent dose: Psychotic disorders—Intramuscular, 25 mg (base), the dose being repeated in one-half to one hour as needed and tolerated.

Note: Geriatric, emaciated, or debilitated patients usually require a lower initial dose, the dosage being gradually increased as needed and tolerated.

Note: Avoid skin contact with liquid forms of this medication; contact dermatitis has resulted.

METHOTRIMEPRAZINE

Summary of Differences

Category: In addition to being used as an antipsychotic, methotrimeprazine is used as an analgesic, antianxiety agent, and sedative.
Indications: Also indicated for relief of moderate to severe pain in nonambulatory patients, and for obstetrical pain and sedation when respiratory depression should be avoided; anxiety, apprehension, restlessness, and sedation before surgery; adjunctive therapy in general anesthesia to increase effects of anesthetics.
Pharmacology:
    Chemical group—Aliphatic
    Actions—
        Antiemetic: Weak
        Anticholinergic: Moderate
        Extrapyramidal: Weak to moderate
        Hypotensive: Strong
        Sedative: Strong

Oral Dosage Forms

Note: The dosing and strengths of the dosage forms available are expressed in terms of methotrimeprazine base (not the hydrochloride or maleate salts).

METHOTRIMEPRAZINE HYDROCHLORIDE ORAL SOLUTION

Usual adult and adolescent dose:
    Psychotic disorders or
    Pain—Oral, initially, 6 to 25 mg (base) a day in three divided doses with meals (mild to moderate pain or psychosis), or 50 to 75 mg a day in two or three divided doses with meals (severe pain or psychosis), the dosage being gradually increased as needed and tolerated.

    Note: If doses of 100 to 200 mg a day are required, the patient should be confined to bed for the first few days to prevent orthostatic hypotension.

Sedation, presurgical—Oral, initially, 6 to 25 mg (base) a day in three divided doses with meals, the dosage being increased gradually as needed and tolerated.

Auxiliary labeling:
- May cause drowsiness.
- Avoid alcoholic beverages.
- Do not spill on skin or clothing.

Additional information: Only enclosed calibrated dropper should be used for measuring dose.

Note: Avoid skin contact with liquid forms of this medication; contact dermatitis may result.

METHOTRIMEPRAZINE HYDROCHLORIDE SYRUP

Usual adult and adolescent dose:
Psychotic disorders or
Pain—Oral, initially, 6 to 25 mg (base) a day in three divided doses with meals (mild to moderate pain or psychosis), or 50 to 75 mg a day in two or three divided doses with meals (severe pain or psychosis), the dosage being increased gradually as needed and tolerated.
  Note: If doses of 100 to 200 mg a day are required, the patient should be confined to bed for the first few days to prevent orthostatic hypotension.
Sedation, presurgical—Oral, initially, 6 to 25 mg (base) a day in three divided doses with meals, the dosage being increased gradually as needed and tolerated.

Auxiliary labeling:
- May cause drowsiness.
- Avoid alcoholic beverages.
- Do not spill on skin or clothing.

Note: Avoid skin contact with liquid forms of this medication; contact dermatitis may result.

METHOTRIMEPRAZINE MALEATE TABLETS

Usual adult and adolescent dose:
Psychotic disorders or
Pain—Oral, initially, 6 to 25 mg (base) a day in three divided doses with meals (mild to moderate pain or psychosis), or 50 to 75 mg a day in two or three divided doses with meals (severe pain or psychosis), the dosage being increased gradually as needed and tolerated.
  Note: If doses of 100 to 200 mg a day are required, the patient should be confined to bed for the first few days to prevent orthostatic hypotension.
Sedation, presurgical—Oral, initially, 6 to 25 mg (base) a day in three divided doses with meals, the dosage being gradually increased as needed and tolerated.

Auxiliary labeling:
- May cause drowsiness.
- Avoid alcoholic beverages.

Parenteral Dosage Forms

Note: Bracketed uses in the *Dosage Forms* section refer to categories of use and/or indications that are not included in U.S. product labeling.

METHOTRIMEPRAZINE INJECTION USP

Usual adult and adolescent dose:
[Psychotic disorders, severe] or
Pain, acute or intractable—Intramuscular, initially, 10 to 20 mg at four- to six-hour intervals, the dosage being increased as needed for pain and sedation.
Pain, obstetrical—Intramuscular, initially 15 to 20 mg, the dose being adjusted and repeated as needed.

Pain, postoperative—Intramuscular, 2.5 to 7.5 mg immediately after surgery, the dosage being adjusted and repeated every three to four hours as needed.
  Note: After initial dose, the patient should be confined to bed or carefully supervised for at least 6 hours following administration, to prevent orthostatic hypotension, dizziness, or fainting.
       Residual effects of anesthetic agents may be additive to the effects of methotrimeprazine.
Sedation, preanesthetic—Intramuscular, 2 to 20 mg administered forty-five minutes to three hours before surgery.
[Anesthesia adjunct during surgery or labor]—Intravenous infusion, 10 to 25 mg in 500 mL of 5% dextrose injection administered at a rate of 20 to 40 drops a minute.

Usual geriatric dose: Pain—Intramuscular, initially, 5 to 10 mg every four to six hours, the dosage being increased gradually as needed and tolerated.

Note: Avoid skin contact with liquid forms of this medication; contact dermatitis may result.

PERICYAZINE

Summary of Differences

Indications: Indicated in some psychotic patients for the control of residual prevailing hostility, impulsivity, and aggressiveness.
Pharmacology:
  Chemical group—Piperidine
  Actions—
    Antiemetic: Strong
    Anticholinergic: Strong
    Extrapyramidal: Moderate
    Hypotensive: Moderate
    Sedative: Strong

Oral Dosage Forms

PERICYAZINE CAPSULES

Usual adult dose: Psychotic disorders—
Initial: Oral, 5 to 20 mg in the morning and 10 to 40 mg in the evening as needed and tolerated.
Maintenance: Oral, 2.5 to 15 mg in the morning and 5 to 30 mg in the evening.

Usual geriatric dose: Psychotic disorders—Oral, initially, 5 mg a day, the dosage being increased gradually as needed and tolerated, up to about 30 mg a day.

Auxiliary labeling:
- May cause drowsiness.
- Avoid alcoholic beverages.

PERICYAZINE ORAL SOLUTION

Usual adult dose: Psychotic disorders—
Initial: Oral, 5 to 20 mg in the morning and 10 to 40 mg in the evening as needed and tolerated.
Maintenance: Oral, 2.5 to 15 mg in the morning and 5 to 30 mg in the evening.

Usual geriatric dose: Psychotic disorders—Oral, initially, 5 mg a day, the dosage being increased gradually as needed and tolerated up to about 30 mg a day.

Auxiliary labeling:
- May cause drowsiness.
- Avoid alcoholic beverages.
- Do not spill on skin or clothing.

Additional information: Only enclosed calibrated dropper should be used for measuring dose.

Note: Avoid skin contact with liquid forms of this medication; contact dermatitis may result.

PERPHENAZINE

Summary of Differences

Category: Includes antiemetic use.
Pharmacology:
    Chemical group—Piperazine
    Actions—
        Antiemetic: Strong
        Anticholinergic: Weak to moderate
        Extrapyramidal: Strong
        Hypotensive: Weak
        Sedative: Weak to moderate

Oral Dosage Forms

Note: Bracketed uses in the *Dosage Forms* section refer to categories of use and/or indications that are not included in U.S. product labeling.

PERPHENAZINE ORAL SOLUTION USP

Usual adult and adolescent dose: Psychotic disorders (hospitalized patients)—Oral, 8 to 16 mg two to four times a day, up to 64 mg a day, the dosage being adjusted as needed and tolerated.

Note: Geriatric, emaciated, or debilitated patients usually require a lower initial dose, the dosage being gradually increased as needed and tolerated.

    Adolescents usually require the lowest limit of the adult dose range.

Auxiliary labeling:
- May cause drowsiness.
- Avoid alcoholic beverages.
- Do not spill on skin or clothing.
- Must be diluted before use.

Note:
The oral solution is intended primarily for institutional usage.

Avoid skin contact with liquid forms of this medication; contact dermatitis has resulted.

Each dose must be measured with accompanying dropper and diluted before administration in water, salt solution, milk, tomato or fruit juice (except apple juice), soup, or carbonated beverage. The oral solution should not be mixed with beverages containing caffeine or tannins (colas, coffee, or tea). The recommended dilution is 2 fluid ounces (60 mL) of diluent for each teaspoonful (5 mL) of perphenazine oral solution.

Explain dilution and dosage measurement to patient if self-administered.

PERPHENAZINE SYRUP USP

Usual adult and adolescent dose:
Psychotic disorders—Oral, 2 to 16 mg two to four times a day, the dosage being adjusted gradually as needed and tolerated.
Nausea and vomiting—Oral, 2 to 4 mg two to four times a day, the dosage being adjusted gradually as needed and tolerated.

Note: Geriatric, emaciated, or debilitated patients usually require a lower initial dose, the dosage being gradually increased as needed and tolerated.

    Adolescents usually require the lowest limit of the adult dose range.

Auxiliary labeling:
- May cause drowsiness.
- Avoid alcoholic beverages.
- Do not spill on skin or clothing.

Note: Avoid skin contact with liquid forms of this medication; contact dermatitis has resulted.

PERPHENAZINE TABLETS USP

Usual adult and adolescent dose:
Psychotic disorders—Oral, 4 to 16 mg two to four times a day, the dosage being adjusted gradually as needed and tolerated.
Nausea and vomiting—Oral, 8 to 16 mg a day in divided doses, the dosage being decreased as early as possible.

Note: Geriatric, emaciated, or debilitated patients usually require a lower initial dose, the dosage being increased gradually as needed and tolerated.

    Adolescents usually require the lowest limit of the adult dose range.

Usual adult prescribing limits:
Psychotic disorders—Up to 64 mg a day.
Nausea and vomiting—Up to 24 mg a day.

Auxiliary labeling:
- May cause drowsiness.
- Avoid alcoholic beverages.

Parenteral Dosage Forms

PERPHENAZINE INJECTION USP

Usual adult and adolescent dose:
Psychotic disorders—Intramuscular, 5 to 10 mg every six hours, the dosage being adjusted as needed and tolerated.
Nausea and vomiting—
    Intramuscular, 5 mg, the dose being increased to 10 mg as needed and tolerated for rapid control of severe vomiting.
    Intravenous, up to 5 mg diluted to 0.5 mg per mL with 0.9% sodium chloride injection, in divided doses, not more than 1 mg administered not less than every one to two minutes; or administered as an infusion at a rate not to exceed 1 mg per minute.

Note: Geriatric, emaciated, or debilitated patients usually require a lower initial dose, the dosage being gradually increased as needed and tolerated.

    Adolescents usually require the lowest limit of the adult dose range.

    In psychotic conditions, most patients are controlled and amenable to oral therapy within a maximum of 24 to 48 hours.

Usual adult prescribing limits:
    Ambulatory patients—Up to 15 mg daily.
Institutionalized patients—Up to 30 mg daily.
Intravenous administration—Up to 5 mg.

Note: Avoid skin contact with liquid forms of this medication; contact dermatitis has resulted.

PIPOTIAZINE

Summary of Differences

Indications: For the maintenance treatment of chronic, non-agitated schizophrenic patients stabilized on shorter-acting neuroleptics.
Pharmacology:
    Chemical group—Piperidine

Actions—
Antiemetic: Weak
Anticholinergic: Weak
Extrapyramidal: Strong
Hypotensive: Weak
Sedative: Weak

Additional Dosing Information

See also *General Dosing Information.*

A dry syringe and needle (at least 21 gauge) should be used, since use of a wet needle or syringe may cause the solution to become cloudy.

After the initial dose of pipotiazine palmitate extended-action injection, dosages and dosing intervals are determined by the patient's response.

Parenteral Dosage Forms

PIPOTIAZINE PALMITATE INJECTION

Usual adult and adolescent dose: Psychotic disorders—Intramuscular, initially, 50 to 100 mg, the dosage being increased in increments of 25 mg every two to three weeks, as needed and tolerated, usually up to a maintenance dose of 75 to 150 mg every four weeks.

Note: Geriatric patients usually require lower initial doses and, after initial titration, dosage should be reduced to the lowest effective maintenance dosages as soon as possible.

Additional information: The onset of action is usually within the first 2 or 3 days after injection, and antipsychotic effects become significant within 1 week.

The effects of a single injection may last from 3 to 6 weeks, but adequate symptom control may be maintained with one injection every 4 weeks.

Note: Avoid skin contact with liquid forms of this medication; contact dermatitis may result.

PROCHLORPERAZINE

Summary of Differences

Category: Includes antiemetic use.
Pharmacology:
Chemical group—Piperazine
Actions—
Antiemetic: Strong
Anticholinergic: Weak
Extrapyramidal: Strong
Hypotensive: Weak
Sedative: Moderate

Additional Dosing Information

See also *General Dosing Information.*

For parenteral dosage forms only:

• Must be injected deep into upper outer quadrant of the buttock.
  • Subcutaneous administration is not recommended because of irritation at injection site and a potential for sterile abscesses.

Oral Dosage Forms

Note: The dosing and strengths of the dosage forms available are expressed in terms of prochlorperazine base (not the edisylate, maleate, or mesylate salts).

PROCHLORPERAZINE EDISYLATE SYRUP USP

Usual adult and adolescent dose:
Psychotic disorders—Oral, 5 to 10 mg (base) three or four times a day, the dosage being gradually increased every two to three days as needed and tolerated.
Anxiety—Oral, 5 mg (base) three or four times a day, up to 20 mg a day, for no longer than twelve weeks.
Nausea and vomiting—Oral, 5 to 10 mg (base) three or four times a day, up to 40 mg a day.
Note: Geriatric, emaciated, or debilitated patients usually require a lower initial dose, the dosage being gradually increased as needed and tolerated.

Usual adult prescribing limits: Up to 150 mg (base) a day.

Auxiliary labeling:
• May cause drowsiness.
• Avoid alcoholic beverages.
• Do not spill on skin or clothing.

Note: Avoid skin contact with liquid forms of this medication; contact dermatitis has resulted.

PROCHLORPERAZINE MALEATE EXTENDED-RELEASE CAPSULES

Usual adult and adolescent dose:
Psychotic disorders—Oral, 5 to 10 mg (base) every three or four hours, the dosage being increased gradually every two or three days as needed and tolerated, up to 100 to 150 mg a day.
Anxiety—Oral, 15 mg (base) in the morning; or 10 mg every twelve hours, up to 20 mg a day for no longer than 12 weeks.
Nausea and vomiting—Oral, 15 to 30 mg (base) once a day in the morning; or 10 mg every twelve hours, up to 40 mg a day as needed and tolerated.
Note: Daily dosages above 40 mg should be used only in resistant cases.
Note: Geriatric, emaciated, or debilitated patients usually require a lower initial dose, the dosage being gradually increased as needed and tolerated.

Usual adult prescribing limits: Psychotic disorders—Up to 150 mg (base) daily.

Auxiliary labeling:
• May cause drowsiness.
• Avoid alcoholic beverages.
• Swallow capsule whole.

PROCHLORPERAZINE MALEATE TABLETS USP

Usual adult and adolescent dose:
Psychotic disorders—Oral, 5 to 10 mg (base) three or four times a day, the dosage being gradually increased every two or three days as needed and tolerated.
Anxiety—Oral, 5 mg (base) three or four times a day, up to 20 mg a day, for no longer than twelve weeks.
Nausea and vomiting—Oral, 5 to 10 mg (base) three or four times a day, up to 40 mg a day.
Note: Daily dosages above 40 mg should be used only in resistant cases.
Note: Geriatric, emaciated, or debilitated patients usually require a lower initial dose, the dosage being gradually increased as needed and tolerated.

Usual adult prescribing limits: Psychotic disorders—Up to 150 mg (base) a day.

Auxiliary labeling:
• May cause drowsiness.
• Avoid alcoholic beverages.

PROCHLORPERAZINE MESYLATE SYRUP

Usual adult and adolescent dose:

Psychotic disorders—Oral, 5 to 10 mg (base) three or four times a day, the dosage being gradually increased every two to three days as needed and tolerated.

Anxiety—Oral, 5 mg (base) three or four times a day, up to 20 mg a day, for no longer than twelve weeks.

Nausea and vomiting—Oral, 5 to 10 mg (base) three or four times a day, up to 40 mg a day.

Note: Geriatric, emaciated, or debilitated patients usually require a lower initial dose, the dosage being gradually increased as needed and tolerated.

Auxiliary labeling:

- May cause drowsiness.
- Avoid alcoholic beverages.
- Do not spill on skin or clothing.

Note: Avoid skin contact with liquid forms of this medication; contact dermatitis has resulted.

Parenteral Dosage Forms

Note: The dosing and strengths of the dosage forms available are expressed in terms of prochlorperazine base (not the edisylate or mesylate salts).

PROCHLORPERAZINE EDISYLATE INJECTION USP

Usual adult and adolescent dose:

Nausea and vomiting—

Intramuscular, 5 to 10 mg (base), the dosage to be repeated every three to four hours as needed.

Intravenous, 2.5 to 10 mg as a slow injection or infusion, at a rate not exceeding 5 mg per minute, up to 40 mg a day.

Note: May be administered undiluted or diluted in isotonic solution.

Single dose should not exceed 10 mg.

Nausea and vomiting in surgery—

Intramuscular, 5 to 10 mg (base) one to two hours before induction of anesthesia, or to control acute symptoms during or after surgery, the dose being repeated once in thirty minutes if needed.

Intravenous, 5 to 10 mg (base), administered as a slow injection or infusion fifteen to thirty minutes before induction of anesthesia, or to control acute symptoms during or after surgery, at a rate not exceeding 5 mg per mL per minute, the dose being repeated once if needed.

Note: May be administered undiluted or diluted in isotonic solution.

Single dose should not exceed 10 mg.

Psychotic disorders—

Initial (for immediate control of severely disturbed patients): Intramuscular, 10 to 20 mg (base), the dose being repeated every two to four hours as needed, usually up to three or four doses.

Maintenance: Intramuscular, 10 to 20 mg (base) every four to six hours.

Anxiety:

Intramuscular, 5 to 10 mg (base), the dosage to be repeated every three to four hours as needed.

Intravenous, 2.5 to 10 mg as a slow injection or infusion, at a rate not exceeding 5 mg per minute, up to 40 mg a day.

Note: May be administered undiluted or diluted in isotonic solution.

Single dose should not exceed 10 mg.

Note: Geriatric, emaciated, or debilitated patients usually require a lower dose, the dosage being increased gradually as needed and tolerated.

Usual adult prescribing limits:

Nausea and vomiting or anxiety—Up to 40 mg (base) a day.

Psychotic disorders—Up to 200 mg (base) a day.

Note: Avoid skin contact with liquid forms of this medication; contact dermatitis has resulted.

PROCHLORPERAZINE MESYLATE INJECTION

Usual adult and adolescent dose:

Nausea and vomiting—Intramuscular, 5 to 10 mg (base), the dose being repeated every three to four hours if needed.

Nausea and vomiting in surgery—

Intramuscular, 5 to 10 mg (base) one to two hours before induction of anesthesia, or to control acute symptoms during or after surgery, the dose being repeated once in thirty minutes if needed.

Intravenous, 5 to 10 mg (base), administered fifteen to thirty minutes before induction of anesthesia, or to control acute symptoms during or after surgery, at a rate not to exceed 5 mg per mL per minute, the dose being repeated once if needed.

Intravenous infusion, 20 mg (base) in no less than 1 liter of isotonic solution, administered fifteen to thirty minutes before induction of anesthesia.

Psychotic disorders—

Initial (for immediate control of severely disturbed patients): Intramuscular, 10 to 20 mg (base), the dose being repeated every two to four hours as needed, usually up to three or four doses.

Maintenance: Intramuscular, 10 to 20 mg (base) every four to six hours.

Anxiety—Intramuscular, 5 to 10 mg (base), the dose being repeated every three to four hours if needed.

Note: Geriatric, emaciated, or debilitated patients usually require a lower dose, the dosage being increased gradually as needed and tolerated.

Usual adult prescribing limits:

Nausea and vomiting—Up to 40 mg (base) a day.

Psychotic disorders—Up to 200 mg (base) a day.

Note: Avoid skin contact with liquid forms of this medication; contact dermatitis has resulted.

Rectal Dosage Forms

PROCHLORPERAZINE SUPPOSITORIES USP

Usual adult and adolescent dose:

Nausea and vomiting—Rectal, 5 to 10 mg two times a day.

Psychotic disorders—Rectal, 10 mg three or four times a day, the dosage being increased gradually by 5 to 10 mg every two to three days as needed and tolerated.

Note: Geriatric, emaciated, or debilitated patients usually require a lower initial dose, the dosage being gradually increased as needed and tolerated.

Auxiliary labeling:

- May cause drowsiness.
- Avoid alcoholic beverages.
- For rectal use only.

PROMAZINE

Summary of Differences

Pharmacology:
　　Chemical group—Aliphatic
　　Actions—
　　　　Antiemetic: Moderate
　　　　Anticholinergic: Strong
　　　　Extrapyramidal: Weak
　　　　Hypotensive: Strong
　　　　Sedative: Strong

Oral Dosage Forms

PROMAZINE HYDROCHLORIDE TABLETS USP

Usual adult dose: Psychotic disorders—Oral, 10 to 200 mg every four to six hours, the dosage being adjusted gradually as needed and tolerated.

Note: Geriatric, emaciated, or debilitated patients usually require a lower initial dose, the dosage being gradually increased as needed and tolerated.

Usual adult prescribing limits: Up to 1 gram a day.

Auxiliary labeling:
- May cause drowsiness.
- Avoid alcoholic beverages.

Parenteral Dosage Forms

PROMAZINE HYDROCHLORIDE INJECTION USP

Usual adult dose: Psychotic disorders—
　　Intramuscular:
　　　　Initial—50 to 150 mg, the dosage being increased, if necessary, after thirty minutes.
　　　　Maintenance—10 to 200 mg, the dose being repeated at four- to six-hour intervals as needed and tolerated.
　　Intravenous: Administered slowly after being diluted to 25 mg or less per mL with 0.9% sodium chloride injection.

Note: Geriatric, emaciated, or debilitated patients usually require a lower initial dose, the dosage being gradually increased as needed and tolerated.

　　Intravenous injection should be reserved for severely agitated hospitalized patients.

　　In acutely inebriated patients, the initial dose should not exceed 50 mg.

Usual adult prescribing limits: Up to 1 gram a day.

Note: Although doses are sometimes gradually increased to 2 grams a day or more for short periods, extended therapy with 1 gram or less is usually sufficient.

Note: Avoid skin contact with liquid forms of this medication; contact dermatitis has resulted.

THIOPROPAZATE

Summary of Differences

Pharmacology:
　　Chemical group—Piperazine
　　Actions—
　　　　Antiemetic: Weak
　　　　Anticholinergic: Weak
　　　　Extrapyramidal: Strong
　　　　Hypotensive: Weak
　　　　Sedative: Weak

Oral Dosage Forms

THIOPROPAZATE HYDROCHLORIDE TABLETS

Usual adult and adolescent dose: Psychotic disorders—
　　Initial: Oral, 10 mg three times a day, the dosage being adjusted gradually by 10 mg every three or four days as needed and tolerated.
　　Maintenance: Oral, 10 to 20 mg two to four times a day.

Note: Geriatric, emaciated, or debilitated patients usually require a lower initial dose, the dosage being increased gradually as needed and tolerated, and decreased to the lowest effective dose as soon as possible.

Usual adult prescribing limits: Up to 100 mg a day.

Auxiliary labeling:
- May cause drowsiness.
- Avoid alcoholic beverages.

THIOPROPERAZINE

Summary of Differences

Pharmacology:
　　Chemical group—Piperazine
　　Actions—
　　　　Antiemetic: Weak
　　　　Anticholinergic: Weak
　　　　Extrapyramidal: Strong
　　　　Hypotensive: Weak
　　　　Sedative: Weak

Oral Dosage Forms

Note: The dosing and strengths of the dosage forms available are expressed in terms of thioproperazine base (not the mesylate salt).

THIOPROPERAZINE MESYLATE TABLETS

Usual adult and adolescent dose: Psychotic disorders—Oral, initially, 5 mg (base) a day, the dosage being adjusted gradually by 5 mg every two or three days as needed and tolerated.

Note: The usual effective dose is about 30 to 40 mg a day. In some patients, 90 mg or more a day may be necessary to control symptoms. Once symptoms are controlled, dosage should be reduced gradually to the lowest effective maintenance dose.

Auxiliary labeling:
- May cause drowsiness.
- Avoid alcoholic beverages.

THIORIDAZINE

Summary of Differences

Pharmacology:
　　Chemical group—Piperidine
　　Actions—
　　　　Antiemetic: Weak
　　　　Anticholinergic: Moderate

Extrapyramidal: Weak
Hypotensive: Moderate to strong
Sedative: Moderate
Side/adverse effects: In high doses, more likely to cause pigmentary retinopathy than other phenothiazines.

Oral Dosage Forms

THIORIDAZINE ORAL SUSPENSION USP

Usual adult and adolescent dose: Psychotic disorders—
Initial: Oral, 25 to 100 mg (hydrochloride) three times a day, the dosage being adjusted gradually as needed and tolerated.
Maintenance: Oral, 10 to 200 mg (hydrochloride) two to four times a day.
Note: Geriatric, emaciated, or debilitated patients usually require a lower initial dose, the dosage being gradually increased as needed and tolerated.

Usual adult prescribing limits: Up to 800 mg (hydrochloride) a day.

Auxiliary labeling:
• Shake well before using.
• May cause drowsiness.
• Avoid alcoholic beverages.
• Do not spill on skin or clothing.

Note: Avoid skin contact with liquid forms of this medication; contact dermatitis has resulted.

THIORIDAZINE HYDROCHLORIDE ORAL SOLUTION USP

Usual adult and adolescent dose: Psychotic disorders—
Initial: Oral, 25 to 100 mg three times a day, the dosage being adjusted gradually as needed and tolerated.
Maintenance: Oral, 10 to 200 mg two to four times a day.
Note: Geriatric, emaciated, or debilitated patients usually require a lower initial dose, the dosage being gradually increased as needed and tolerated.

Usual adult prescribing limits: Up to 800 mg a day.

Auxiliary labeling:
• May cause drowsiness.
• Avoid alcoholic beverages.
• Do not spill on skin or clothing.
• Must be diluted before use.

Note:
Avoid skin contact with liquid forms of this medication; contact dermatitis has resulted.
Each dose must be diluted just before administration in a half glass (120 mL) of distilled water, acidified tap water, orange juice, or grapefruit juice.
Explain dilution and dosage measurement to patient if self-administered.

THIORIDAZINE HYDROCHLORIDE TABLETS USP

Usual adult and adolescent dose: Psychotic disorders—
Initial: Oral, 25 to 100 mg three times a day, the dosage being adjusted gradually as needed and tolerated.
Maintenance: Oral, 10 to 200 mg two to four times a day.
Note: Geriatric, emaciated, or debilitated patients usually require a lower initial dose, the dosage being gradually increased as needed and tolerated.

Usual adult prescribing limits: Up to 800 mg a day.

Auxiliary labeling:
• May cause drowsiness.
• Avoid alcoholic beverages.

TRIFLUOPERAZINE

Summary of Differences

Pharmacology:
Chemical group—Piperazine
Actions—
Antiemetic: Strong
Anticholinergic: Weak
Extrapyramidal: Strong
Hypotensive: Weak
Sedative: Weak

Oral Dosage Forms

Note: The dosing and strengths of the dosage forms available are expressed in terms of trifluoperazine base (not the hydrochloride salt).

TRIFLUOPERAZINE HYDROCHLORIDE ORAL SOLUTION

Usual adult and adolescent dose:
Psychotic disorders—Oral, 2 to 5 mg (base) two times a day initially, the dosage being gradually increased as needed and tolerated.
Anxiety—1 to 2 mg (base) a day, up to a total of 6 mg a day, for no longer than twelve weeks.
Note: Geriatric, emaciated, or debilitated patients usually require a lower initial dose, the dosage being gradually increased as needed and tolerated.

Usual adult prescribing limits: Up to 40 mg (base) a day.

Auxiliary labeling:
• May cause drowsiness.
• Avoid alcoholic beverages.
• Do not spill on skin or clothing.
• Must be diluted before use.

Note:
The oral solution is intended primarily for institutional usage.
Avoid skin contact with liquid forms of this medication; contact dermatitis has resulted.
Each dose must be diluted just before administration in a half glass (120 mL) of milk, tomato or fruit juice, water, or soup.
Explain dilution and dosage measurement to patient if self-administered.

TRIFLUOPERAZINE HYDROCHLORIDE SYRUP USP

Usual adult and adolescent dose:
Psychotic disorders—Oral, 2 to 5 mg (base) two times a day initially, the dosage being gradually increased as needed and tolerated.
Anxiety—1 to 2 mg (base) a day, up to a total of 6 mg a day, for no longer than twelve weeks.
Note: Geriatric, emaciated, or debilitated patients usually require a lower initial dose, the dosage being gradually increased as needed and tolerated.

Usual adult prescribing limits: Up to 40 mg (base) a day.

Auxiliary labeling:
• May cause drowsiness.
• Avoid alcoholic beverages.

TRIFLUOPERAZINE HYDROCHLORIDE TABLETS USP

Usual adult and adolescent dose:

Psychotic disorders—Oral, 2 to 5 mg (base) two times a day initially, the dosage being gradually increased as needed and tolerated.

Anxiety—1 to 2 mg (base) a day, up to a total of 6 mg a day, for not longer than twelve weeks.

Note: Geriatric, emaciated, or debilitated patients usually require a lower initial dose, the dosage being gradually increased as needed and tolerated.

Usual adult prescribing limits: Up to 40 mg (base) a day.

Auxiliary labeling:

• May cause drowsiness.
• Avoid alcoholic beverages.

Parenteral Dosage Forms

Note: The dosing and strengths of the dosage forms available are expressed in terms of trifluoperazine base (not the hydrochloride salt).

TRIFLUOPERAZINE HYDROCHLORIDE INJECTION USP

Usual adult and adolescent dose: Psychotic disorders—Intramuscular, 1 to 2 mg (base) every four to six hours as needed.

Note: Geriatric, emaciated, or debilitated patients usually require a lower initial dose, the dosage being increased gradually as needed and tolerated.

Usual adult prescribing limits: Up to 10 mg (base) a day.

Note: Avoid skin contact with liquid forms of this medication; contact dermatitis has resulted.

TRIFLUPROMAZINE

Summary of Differences

Category: Includes antiemetic use.
Pharmacology:
  Chemical group—Aliphatic
  Actions—
    Antiemetic: Strong
    Anticholinergic: Strong
    Extrapyramidal: Moderate to strong
    Hypotensive: Moderate
    Sedative: Moderate to strong

Parenteral Dosage Forms

TRIFLUPROMAZINE HYDROCHLORIDE INJECTION USP

Usual adult and adolescent dose:

Psychotic disorders—Intramuscular, 60 mg as needed.
Nausea and vomiting—
  Intramuscular, 5 to 15 mg every four hours.
  Intravenous, 1 mg as needed.

Note: Geriatric, emaciated, or debilitated patients usually require a lower initial dose, the dosage being increased as needed and tolerated.

Usual adult prescribing limits:

Psychotic disorders—Intramuscular, up to 150 mg a day.
Nausea and vomiting—
  Intramuscular, up to 60 mg a day.
  Intravenous, up to 3 mg a day.

Note: Avoid skin contact with liquid forms of this medication; contact dermatitis has resulted.

PHENOXYBENZAMINE   Systemic

A commonly used *brand name* in the U.S. is *Dibenzyline*.

ORAL
Phenoxybenzamine Hydrochloride Capsules USP
  In the U.S.—*Dibenzyline*

Category: Antihypertensive (pheochromocytoma); benign prostatic hypertrophy therapy.

Indications

Note: Bracketed information in the *Indications* section refers to uses not included in U.S. product labeling.

Accepted
Pheochromocytoma (treatment)—Phenoxybenzamine is indicated to control episodes of hypertension and sweating in the treatment of pheochromocytoma as preoperative preparation for surgery, in management of patients when surgery is contraindicated, and in chronic management of patients with malignant pheochromocytoma.

[Benign prostatic hypertrophy (treatment)]—Phenoxybenzamine is used for the treatment of urinary symptoms associated with benign prostatic hypertrophy (BPH).

Unaccepted
Phenoxybenzamine is not useful in the treatment of essential hypertension because of its side effects, particularly reflex tachycardia.

Pharmacology

Mechanism of action/Effect: Nonselective alpha-adrenergic blockade; phenoxybenzamine combines irreversibly with postganglionic alpha-adrenergic receptor sites, preventing or reversing effects of endogenous or exogenous catecholamines; no effect on beta-adrenergic receptors.

Onset of action: Alpha-adrenergic blockade—Several hours.

Note: Alpha-adrenergic blocking effects are cumulative over approximately 7 days with daily dosing.

Duration of action: Alpha-adrenergic blockade—3 to 4 days after a single dose.

Precautions to Consider

Geriatrics
Although appropriate studies on the relationship of age to the effects of phenoxybenzamine have not been performed in the geriatric population, no geriatrics-specific problems have been documented to date. However, the elderly may be more sensitive to the hypo-

tensive effects and the risk of phenoxybenzamine-induced hypothermia may be increased in elderly patients. Furthermore, elderly patients are also more likely to have age-related renal function impairment, which may require caution in patients receiving phenoxybenzamine.

Dental

Use of phenoxybenzamine may decrease or inhibit salivary flow, thus contributing to the development of caries, periodontal disease, oral candidiasis, and discomfort.

Drug interactions and/or related problems

The following drug interactions and/or related problems have been selected on the basis of their potential clinical significance (possible mechanism in parentheses where appropriate)—not necessarily inclusive (» = major clinical significance):

Note: Combinations containing any of the following medications, depending on the amount present, may also interact with this medication.

Diazoxide
(concurrent use with phenoxybenzamine antagonizes the inhibition of insulin release by diazoxide)

Guanadrel or
Guanethidine
(concurrent use with phenoxybenzamine may cause an increased incidence of orthostatic hypotension or bradycardia)

Sympathomimetics, such as:
Dopamine
Ephedrine
» Epinephrine
» Metaraminol
» Methoxamine
» Phenylephrine
(concurrent use of dopamine with phenoxybenzamine antagonizes the peripheral vasoconstriction produced by high doses of dopamine)

(concurrent use of ephedrine with phenoxybenzamine may decrease the pressor response to ephedrine)

(concurrent use of epinephrine with phenoxybenzamine may block the alpha-adrenergic effects of epinephrine, possibly resulting in severe hypotension and tachycardia)

(alpha-adrenergic blocking agents such as phenoxybenzamine usually decrease, but do not reverse, pressor response to metaraminol)

(prior administration of phenoxybenzamine may block the pressor response to methoxamine, possibly resulting in severe hypotension)

(prior administration of phenoxybenzamine may decrease the pressor response to phenylephrine)

Contraindications/Medical problems

The contraindications/medical problems included have been selected on the basis of their potential clinical significance (reasons given in parentheses where appropriate)—not necessarily inclusive (» = major clinical significance).

Risk-benefit should be considered when the following medical problems exist:

Cerebrovascular insufficiency
(reduced blood pressure may aggravate ischemia)

Congestive heart failure, compensated, or
Coronary artery disease
(reflex tachycardia may precipitate frank congestive heart failure and angina)

Renal function impairment

Respiratory infection
(symptoms such as nasal congestion may be aggravated)

Sensitivity to phenoxybenzamine

Side/Adverse Effects

The following side/adverse effects have been selected on the basis of their potential clinical significance (possible signs and symptoms in parentheses where appropriate)—not necessarily inclusive:

Those indicating need for medical attention only if they continue or are bothersome

Incidence more frequent—resulting from alpha-adrenergic blockade
Miosis (pinpoint pupils); *nasal congestion* (stuffy nose); *postural hypotension* (dizziness or lightheadedness, especially when getting up from a lying or sitting position); *tachycardia, reflex* (fast heartbeat)

Incidence less frequent
Confusion; drowsiness; dryness of mouth; headache; inability to ejaculate; lack of energy; unusual tiredness or weakness

Note: *Inability to ejaculate* is caused by alpha-adrenergic blockade.

Patient Consultation

In providing consultation, consider emphasizing the following selected information (» = major clinical significance):

Before using this medication
» Conditions affecting use, especially:
Sensitivity to phenoxybenzamine
Use in the elderly—Elderly patients may be more sensitive to the hypotensive effects; risk of phenoxybenzamine-induced hypothermia may be increased
Dental—May decrease or inhibit salivary flow

Proper use of this medication
Getting into the habit of taking at same times each day to help increase compliance
Missed dose: Taking as soon as possible; not taking if almost time for next dose; not doubling doses
» Proper storage

Precautions while using this medication
Regular visits to physician to check progress during therapy
» Not taking other medications, especially nonprescription sympathomimetics, unless discussed with physician
» Caution when driving or doing things requiring alertness because of possible dizziness or drowsiness
» Caution when getting up suddenly from a lying or sitting position
» Caution in using alcohol, while standing for long periods or exercising, and during hot weather because of enhanced orthostatic hypotensive effects
» Caution if any kind of surgery (including dental surgery) or emergency treatment is required
Possible dryness of mouth; using sugarless candy or gum, ice, or saliva substitute for relief; checking with physician or dentist if dry mouth continues for more than 2 weeks

General Dosing Information

Dosage must be adjusted to meet the individual requirements of each patient, on the basis of clinical response and urinary catecholamine determinations.

Incidence and severity of side effects may be reduced by initiating therapy at a low dose and increasing gradually to the minimum effective dose.

It is recommended that dosage increments be made no more frequently than every 4 days.

Concurrent administration of a beta-adrenergic blocker may be necessary if reflex tachycardia is severe.

If gastrointestinal irritation occurs, phenoxybenzamine may be administered with meals or milk; dosage reduction may be necessary.

Oral Dosage Forms

Note: Bracketed uses in the *Dosage Forms* section refer to categories of use and/or indications that are not included in U.S. product labeling.

PHENOXYBENZAMINE HYDROCHLORIDE CAPSULES USP

Usual adult dose:
Antihypertensive (pheochromocytoma)—
Initial: Oral, 10 mg twice a day, increased by increments of 10 mg every other day until an adequate response is achieved.

Maintenance: Oral, 20 to 40 mg two or three times a day.
[Benign prostatic hypertrophy therapy]—10 to 20 mg per day.

Note: Geriatric patients may be more sensitive to the effects of the usual adult dose.

PHENTOLAMINE   Intracavernosal

Some commonly used *brand names* are:
In the U.S.—*Regitine*
In Canada—*Rogitine*

PARENTERAL
Phentolamine Mesylate for Injection USP
In the U.S.—*Regitine*
In Canada—*Rogitine*

Category: Impotence therapy adjunct.

Indications

Note: Bracketed information in the *Indications* section refers to uses not included in U.S. product labeling.

Accepted
[Impotence (treatment adjunct)][1]—Phentolamine is used in combination with papaverine, by intracavernosal injection, to facilitate erections in men with impotence. In general, the combination is most useful in patients with organic impotence (neurogenic and, to a lesser extent, vascular). It is less useful in patients with impotence due to endocrine problems (hypogonadism, hyper- or hypothyroidism) or medications.

[Impotence (diagnosis)][1]—Phentolamine is used with papaverine, by intracavernosal injection, as an aid in the evaluation of penile vasculature, alone or prior to angiography, corpus cavernosography, or cavernosometry.

Unaccepted
Use of phentolamine and papaverine to enhance erections in men who are not impotent is not recommended because of the risk of priapism and permanent damage to penile tissues.

[1]Not included in Canadian product labeling.

Pharmacology

Mechanism of action/Effect: Alpha-adrenergic blockade (alpha$_1$ and alpha$_2$ receptors) and antagonism of effects of circulating epinephrine and norepinephrine to cause vasodilation and reduction in peripheral resistance. When administered by intracavernous injection, it is thought to cause relaxation of the trabecular cavernous smooth muscles and vasodilation of the penile arteries. This results in increased arterial blood flow into the corpus cavernosa, and swelling and elongation of the penis; the glans and corpus spongiosum swell very little, if at all. Venous outflow is also reduced by papaverine, possibly as a result of increased venous resistance.

Time to peak effect: In combination with papaverine—Variable, but usually within 10 minutes.

Duration of action: In combination with papaverine—1 to 6 hours; dose-related.

Precautions to Consider

Geriatrics
No information is available on the relationship of age to the effects of phentolamine for impotence in geriatric patients. However, geriatrics-specific problems that would limit the usefulness of this medication in the elderly are not expected.

Drug interactions and/or related problems
The following drug interactions and/or related problems have been selected on the basis of their potential clinical significance (possible mechanism in parentheses where appropriate)—not necessarily inclusive (» = major clinical significance):

Sympathomimetics, alpha-adrenergic, especially metaraminol, epinephrine, and phenylephrine
(reverse the vasodilating effect of phentolamine; may be used to treat priapism or overdose)

Contraindications/Medical problems
The contraindications/medical problems included have been selected on the basis of their potential clinical significance (reasons given in parentheses where appropriate)—not necessarily inclusive (» = major clinical significance).

Risk-benefit should be considered when the following medical problems exist:
Allergy to phentolamine
» Coagulation defects, severe
(risk of bleeding at injection site)
» Priapism, history of
» Sickle cell disease
(increased risk of priapism)

Side/Adverse Effects

The following side/adverse effects have been selected on the basis of their potential clinical significance (possible signs and symptoms in parentheses where appropriate)—not necessarily inclusive:

Those indicating need for medical attention
Incidence rare
Dizziness; fibrosis (lumps in penis); *priapism* (erection, continuing for more than 4 hours, or painful erection)

Note: *Fibrosis* of the corpus cavernosum, resulting in blockage and inability to insert a penile prosthesis, has been reported in a patient using papaverine injection.

Priapism is usually due to excessive dosage. Prolonged erection may resolve spontaneously, but in most cases will require treatment.

Those indicating need for medical attention only if they continue or are bothersome
Incidence less frequent or rare
Burning, mild, along penis; difficulty in ejaculating; inadvertent subcutaneous administration (bruising or bleeding at site of injection, swelling at site of injection); *superficial hematoma* (bruising or bleeding at site of injection)

Note: *Burning* may be more severe with inadvertent subcutaneous administration.

Those not indicating need for medical attention
Incidence more frequent
Tingling at tip of penis

Patient Consultation

In providing consultation, consider emphasizing the following selected information (» = major clinical significance):

Before using this medication
» Conditions affecting use, especially:
   Allergy to phentolamine
   Other medical problems, especially severe coagulation defects, history of priapism, or sickle cell disease

Proper use of this medication
   Proper administration:
» Cleansing injection site with alcohol; injecting slowly and directly into corpus cavernosum at base of penis; avoiding subcutaneous administration; if inadvertently injected subcutaneously (as evidenced by pain at injection site), stopping, withdrawing, and repositioning needle
   Putting pressure on injection site for 1 to 2 minutes to prevent bruising; massaging penis, as directed by physician, to distribute medication
   Effect begins in about 10 minutes; attempting intercourse within 2 hours after administration
» Proper storage

Precautions while using this medication
» Compliance with therapy; importance of not exceeding prescribed dosage and frequency of use; risk of priapism, tissue ischemia, and permanent damage with overdose
» Telling physician immediately if erection persists longer than 4 hours or becomes painful
   If bleeding occurs at injection site, applying pressure; checking with physician if bleeding persists
   Examining penis regularly for signs of fibrosis at injection site or for curvature; checking with physician if either of these occurs

Side/adverse effects
   Signs of potential side effects, especially dizziness, fibrosis, priapism
   Injection may cause tingling at tip of penis; no cause for concern

General Dosing Information

Patients receiving intracavernosal phentolamine and papaverine should be under supervision of a physician experienced in their use and familiar with proper management of sustained erection and priapism.

Dosage adjustment should be made carefully, based on the degree and duration of tumescence achieved with the previous dose. In general, patients with neurogenic impotence may be more sensitive to the effects of intracavernosal vasodilators and may require lower doses.

Intracavernosal phentolamine and papaverine may be self-administered by the patient, but only after careful training in the technique to reduce the incidence of inadvertent subcutaneous administration, ecchymosis, and urethral injury.

For treatment of impotence, phentolamine and papaverine are injected slowly (over 1 to 2 minutes), directly into the corpus cavernosum at the base of the penis. A characteristic give should be noticed as the needle penetrates the tunica albuginea and enters the corpus cavernosum. Proper injection technique is necessary to avoid injury or injection of the urethra or vessels on the dorsal aspect of the penis.

After completion of the injection, pressure is applied to the injection site to prevent bleeding. Then the entire length of the corpus cavernosum should be squeezed firmly to distribute medication to the other side, followed by the same procedure on the other side. The penis should then be pinched transversely in several places to distribute medication to both ends of the corpus cavernosa.

If a sustained erection occurs, the next dose of phentolamine and papaverine should be reduced.

Intercourse should be attempted within 2 hours after administration.

If fibrosis occurs, discontinuation of phentolamine and papaverine therapy may be necessary, especially if a penile implant is planned in the future.

For treatment of prolonged erection or priapism
A sustained erection should be treated if it persists for longer than 4 hours; priapism should be treated promptly. If tumescence is not reversed, interruption of blood flow may result in penile tissue ischemia and permanent damage.

Depending on the severity, treatment may include:
   • Aspiration of intracavernous blood.
   • Irrigation of the corpus cavernosa with saline to remove clotted blood.
   • Intracavernous administration of an alpha-adrenergic agonist, such as metaraminol, epinephrine, or phenylephrine.
   • Surgery.

Parenteral Dosage Forms

Note: Bracketed uses in the *Dosage Forms* section refer to categories of use and/or indications that are not included in U.S. product labeling.

PHENTOLAMINE MESYLATE FOR INJECTION USP

Usual adult dose: [Impotence therapy][1]—Intracavernosal, a mixture of 30 mg Papaverine Hydrochloride Injection USP and 0.5 to 1.0 mg of reconstituted Phentolamine Mesylate for Injection USP, the dosage being adjusted according to response.

Note: Patients with neurogenic impotence may require lower doses or use of papaverine alone.

Usual adult prescribing limits: Impotence therapy—Up to 60 mg of papaverine hydrochloride per dose. The injection should not be given more than three times weekly or two days in succession.

PHENYLEPHRINE   Nasal

Some commonly used *brand names* are:

In the U.S.—

Alconefrin 12	Nostril
Alconefrin 25	Rhinall
Alconefrin 50	Rhinall-10 Children's
Doktors	Flavored Nose Drops
Duration	St. Joseph
Neo-Synephrine	Vicks Sinex

In Canada—
    Neo-Synephrine

NASAL

Phenylephrine Hydrochloride Nasal Jelly USP
    In the U.S.—*Neo-Synephrine*
Phenylephrine Hydrochloride Nasal Solution USP
    In the U.S.—*Alconefrin 12; Alconefrin 25; Alconefrin 50; Doktors; Duration; Neo-Synephrine; Nostril; Rhinall; Rhinall-10 Children's Flavored Nose Drops; St. Joseph; Vicks Sinex;* GE-NERIC
    In Canada—*Neo-Synephrine*

Category: Decongestant (topical).

Indications

Note: Bracketed information in the *Indications* section refers to uses not included in U.S. product labeling.

Accepted

Congestion, nasal (treatment)—Nasal phenylephrine is indicated for the symptomatic relief of nasal congestion due to the common cold or hay fever, sinusitis, or other upper respiratory allergies.

[Congestion, sinus (treatment)]—Nasal phenylephrine is also used for relief of sinus congestion.

Congestion, eustachian tube (treatment)—Nasal phenylephrine may be useful in the adjunctive therapy of middle ear infections by decreasing congestion around the eustachian ostia.

Pharmacology

Mechanism of action/Effect: Phenylephrine is primarily a direct-acting sympathomimetic amine. It acts on alpha-adrenergic receptors in the arterioles of the nasal mucosa to produce constriction, resulting in decreased nasal congestion.

Duration of action: 30 minutes to 4 hours.

Precautions to Consider

Cross-sensitivity and/or related problems

Patients sensitive to other nasal decongestants may be sensitive to this medication also.

Geriatrics

Although appropriate studies with phenylephrine have not been performed in the geriatric population, no geriatrics-specific problems have been documented to date.

Drug interactions and/or related problems

The following drug interactions and/or related problems have been selected on the basis of their potential clinical significance (possible mechanism in parentheses where appropriate)—not necessarily inclusive (» = major clinical significance):

Note: Combinations containing any of the following medications, depending on the amount present, may also interact with this medication.

Antidepressants, tricyclic, or
Maprotiline or
Monoamine oxidase (MAO) inhibitors, including furazolidone, pargyline, and procarbazine
    (if significant systemic absorption of nasal phenylephrine occurs, concurrent use of these medications may potentiate the pressor effect of phenylephrine; nasal phenylephrine should not be administered within 14 days following the administration of MAO inhibitors)

Guanadrel or
Guanethidine
    (if significant systemic absorption of nasal phenylephrine occurs, concurrent use of guanadrel or guanethidine may potentiate the pressor effect of phenylephrine, possibly resulting in hypertension and/or cardiac arrhythmias)

Contraindications/Medical problems

The contraindications/medical problems included have been selected on the basis of their potential clinical significance (reasons given in parentheses where appropriate)—not necessarily inclusive (» = major clinical significance).

Risk-benefit should be considered when the following medical problems exist:

Coronary artery disease or
Heart disease, including angina, or
Hypertension
    (condition may be exacerbated because of drug-induced cardiovascular effects)

Diabetes mellitus
Hyperthyroidism
Sensitivity to phenylephrine or other nasal decongestants

Side/Adverse Effects

The following side/adverse effects have been selected on the basis of their potential clinical significance (possible signs and symptoms in parentheses where appropriate)—not necessarily inclusive:

Those indicating need for medical attention
    Rebound congestion (increase in runny or stuffy nose)
Symptoms of systemic absorption
    Fast, irregular, or pounding heartbeat; headache or dizziness; increased sweating; nervousness; paleness; trembling; trouble in sleeping

Those indicating need for medical attention only if they continue or are bothersome
    Burning, dryness, or stinging of nasal mucosa

Patient Consultation

In providing consultation, consider emphasizing the following selected information (» = major clinical significance):

Before using this medication
» Conditions affecting use, especially:
        Sensitivity to phenylephrine or other nasal decongestants
        Use in children—Children may be especially prone to systemic absorption of nasal phenylephrine and resulting side/adverse effects
        Use by athletes—Phenylephrine is banned and tested for in athletes by the U.S. Olympic Committee (USOC)

Proper use of this medication
    Proper administration technique
    Preventing contamination:
        Replacing cap right after use

For nasal drops
   After using—Rinsing dropper with hot water and drying with clean tissue
For nasal spray
   After using—Rinsing tip of spray bottle with hot water, taking care not to suck water into bottle, and drying with clean tissue
For nasal jelly
   After using—Wiping tip of tube with clean, damp tissue
   Preventing spread of infection: Not using container for more than one person
» Importance of not using more medication than the amount recommended
   Missed dose: If on scheduled dosing regimen—Using right away if remembered within an hour or so; not using if remembered later; not doubling doses
» Proper storage

Side/adverse effects
   Signs of potential side effects, especially rebound congestion and sympathomimetic systemic effects

General Dosing Information

Prolonged or excessive use of this medication will cause rebound congestion with chronic swelling of nasal mucosa.

To reduce the chance of rebound congestion and systemic side effects, the weakest strength that is effective should be used.

Nasal Dosage Forms

PHENYLEPHRINE HYDROCHLORIDE NASAL JELLY USP

Usual adult and adolescent dose: Intranasal, a small quantity of a 0.5% jelly placed into each nostril and sniffed well back into the nasal passages every three or four hours as needed.

Auxiliary labeling: • For the nose.

PHENYLEPHRINE HYDROCHLORIDE NASAL SOLUTION USP

Usual adult and adolescent dose:
   Drops—Intranasal, 2 or 3 drops of a 0.25 to 0.5% solution into each nostril every three to four hours as needed.
   Spray—Intranasal, 1 or 2 sprays of a 0.25 to 0.5% solution into each nostril. After three to five minutes, blow nose, and then repeat dose. Subsequent doses may be administered every three to four hours as needed.
Note: The nasal spray form of this medication is more effective and less likely to cause systemic absorption.
   In cases of extreme nasal congestion, the 1% solution may be used initially.

Auxiliary labeling: • For the nose.

PHENYLPROPANOLAMINE   Systemic†

Some commonly used *brand names* are:
   In the U.S.—

Acutrim 16 Hour	*Dexatrim Maximum*
Acutrim Late Day	*Strength Pre-Meal*
Acutrim II Maximum	*Caplets*
Strength	*Diet-Aid Maximum*
Control	*Strength*
Dex-A-Diet Maximum	*Efed II Yellow*
Strength	*Phenyldrine*
Dex-A-Diet Maximum	*Prolamine*
Strength Caplets	*Propagest*
Dexatrim	*Rhindecon*
Dexatrim Maximum	*Stay Trim Diet Gum*
Strength	*Unitrol*
Dexatrim Maximum	
Strength Caplets	

Another commonly used name is PPA.

ORAL
Phenylpropanolamine Hydrochloride Capsules†
   In the U.S.—*Efed II Yellow; Prolamine*
Phenylpropanolamine Hydrochloride Extended-release Capsules USP†
   In the U.S.—*Control; Dex-A-Diet Maximum Strength; Dexatrim; Dexatrim Maximum Strength; Diet-Aid Maximum Strength; Rhindecon; Unitrol;* GENERIC
Phenylpropanolamine Hydrochloride Tablets†
   In the U.S.—*Dexatrim Maximum Strength Pre-Meal Caplets; Propagest;* GENERIC
Phenylpropanolamine Hydrochloride Chewing Gum Tablets†
   In the U.S.—*Stay Trim Diet Gum*

Phenylpropanolamine Hydrochloride Extended-release Tablets†
   In the U.S.—*Acutrim 16 Hour; Acutrim Late Day; Acutrim II Maximum Strength; Dex-A-Diet Maximum Strength Caplets; Dexatrim Maximum Strength Caplets; Phenyldrine*

†Not commercially available in Canada.

Category: Sympathomimetic (adrenergic) agent; appetite suppressant; decongestant, nasal (systemic).

Indications

Note: Bracketed information in the *Indications* section refers to uses not included in U.S. product labeling.

Accepted
Obesity, exogenous (treatment)—Phenylpropanolamine (PPA) is indicated in the management of exogenous obesity for short-term use (6 to 12 weeks) in conjunction with a regimen of weight reduction based on caloric restriction, exercise, and behavior modification.

Nasal congestion (treatment)—Administered orally, phenylpropanolamine is indicated in the temporary, symptomatic relief of local swelling and congestion of nasal mucous membranes.

[Urinary incontinence (treatment)]—Phenylpropanolamine is used in the treatment of mild to moderate stress incontinence; it may be effective in up to 75% of patients with mild to moderate conditions. In females, phenylpropanolamine may be used in combination with estrogen therapy for a synergistic clinical effect.

Pharmacology

Mechanism of action/Effect:

Appetite suppression—A mixed-acting sympathomimetic amine with predominantly alpha-adrenergic activity, phenylpropanolamine is believed to suppress the appetite control center in the hypothalamus. Other CNS actions and/or metabolic effects may also be involved. PPA acts as an agonist at central norepinephrine receptors and may also have dopamine agonist properties.

Decongestion, nasal—Phenylpropanolamine acts on alpha-adrenergic receptors in the mucosa of the respiratory tract to produce vasoconstriction, which temporarily reduces the swelling associated with inflammation of the mucous membranes lining the nasal passages.

Urinary incontinence—Phenylpropanolamine produces contraction of the bladder neck and of the smooth muscle of the urethra, possibly due to stimulation of alpha-adrenergic receptors.

Other actions/effects:

Increases heart rate, force of contraction, and cardiac output and excitability, possibly by stimulating beta-adrenergic receptors in the heart.

Causes CNS stimulation by releasing norepinephrine from storage sites.

Produces mydriasis.

Onset of action: Nasal decongestion—15 to 30 minutes.

Duration of action:

Capsules and tablets—3 hours.

Extended-release—12 to 16 hours.

Precautions to Consider

Cross-sensitivity and/or related problems

Patients sensitive to other sympathomimetics (for example, amphetamines, ephedrine, epinephrine, isoproterenol, metaproterenol, norepinephrine, phenylephrine, pseudoephedrine, terbutaline) may be sensitive to this medication also.

Geriatrics

No information is available on the relationship of age to the effects of phenylpropanolamine in geriatric patients.

Drug interactions and/or related problems

The following drug interactions and/or related problems have been selected on the basis of their potential clinical significance (possible mechanism in parentheses where appropriate)—not necessarily inclusive (» = major clinical significance):

Note: Combinations containing any of the following medications, depending on the amount present, may also interact with this medication.

» Anesthetics, hydrocarbon inhalation
(chronic use of phenylpropanolamine prior to anesthesia with these agents may increase the risk of cardiac arrhythmias, since these medications may sensitize the myocardium to the effects of phenylpropanolamine; arrhythmias may respond to a beta-adrenergic blocking agent such as propranolol)

Antidepressants, tricyclic
(tricyclic antidepressants may potentiate the response to sympathomimetic amines such as PPA by blocking the reuptake of biogenic amines by nerve terminals)

Antihypertensives or
Diuretics used as antihypertensives
(hypotensive effects of these medications may be reduced during concurrent use with phenylpropanolamine; the patient should be carefully monitored to confirm that the desired effect is being obtained)

» Beta-adrenergic blocking agents
(concurrent use with phenylpropanolamine may result in significant hypertension and excessive bradycardia with possible heart block; concurrent use requires careful monitoring)

» CNS stimulation-producing medications or
» Sympathomimetics, other
(concurrent use with phenylpropanolamine may result in additive CNS stimulation to excessive levels, causing nervousness, irritability, insomnia, or possibly seizures or cardiac arrhythmias; close monitoring is recommended)
(also, concurrent use of other sympathomimetics with phenylpropanolamine may increase pressor or cardiovascular effects of either medication)

» Digitalis glycosides
(concurrent use may result in cardiac arrhythmias)

» Monoamine oxidase (MAO) inhibitors
(concurrent use may potentiate the pressor effect of phenylpropanolamine with resultant hypertensive crisis by releasing catecholamines, which accumulate during therapy with MAO inhibitors, from intraneuronal storage sites; phenylpropanolamine should not be administered during or within 14 days following administration of MAO inhibitors)

» Rauwolfia alkaloids
(concurrent use may inhibit the indirect-acting sympathomimetic action of phenylpropanolamine by depleting catecholamine stores)

Contraindications/Medical problems

The contraindications/medical problems included have been selected on the basis of their potential clinical significance (reasons given in parentheses where appropriate)—not necessarily inclusive (» = major clinical significance).

Except under special circumstances, this medication should not be used when the following medical problems exist:

» Coronary artery disease, severe
(phenylpropanolamine may increase heart rate and force of contraction, with resultant decreased cardiac efficiency)

» Hypertension, severe
(pressor effect of phenylpropanolamine may result in hypertensive crisis)

Risk-benefit should be considered when the following medical problems exist:

» Cardiovascular disorders
(phenylpropanolamine may cause cardiac excitation leading to arrhythmias)

Diabetes mellitus
(adrenergic properties of phenylpropanolamine may lead to increased blood glucose concentrations)

Glaucoma, angle-closure
(condition may be aggravated)

» Hypertension, mild
(vasoconstrictive properties of phenylpropanolamine may exacerbate condition)

Hyperthyroidism
(symptoms may be exacerbated by cardiac stimulant properties of phenylpropanolamine)

Prostatic hypertrophy
(urinary retention may be precipitated)

Sensitivity to phenylpropanolamine or other sympathomimetics

Side/Adverse Effects

Note: The safety profile of phenylpropanolamine is controversial. Most controlled studies have demonstrated minimal side effects from PPA. Serious adverse reactions including hypertensive crises, stroke, arrhythmias, acute renal failure, rhabdomyolysis, psychotic disturbances, hallucinations, and seizures have been reported following consumption of PPA; however, case studies in many of these patients have revealed confounding factors such as pre-existing conditions and/or consumption of medications in addition to PPA.

Some investigators have suggested that serious cardiovascular side effects may be more likely to occur in patients prone to hypertension (as in obese patients, patients under stress, elderly patients, or female patients receiving oral contraceptives); in patients with eating disorders such as anorexia nervosa or bulimia (who may tend to abuse such drugs); and in females and children who receive a greater dose per unit of body weight.

Similarly, serious CNS side effects may occur more frequently in patients with a history of pre-existing neurological or psychiatric conditions. In addition, one study noted that organic symptoms (such as dizziness, loss of motor coordination, confusion, and photophobia) that have occurred in many patients are comparable to CNS dysfunction due to increased blood pressure.

Increases in blood pressure and CNS toxicity may represent idiosyncratic reactions in some patients.

The following side/adverse effects have been selected on the basis of their potential clinical significance (possible signs and symptoms in parentheses where appropriate)—not necessarily inclusive:

Those indicating need for medical attention
Incidence rare
  Headache, severe—may be prodromal of severe side effects related to elevated blood pressure; *increased blood pressure; painful or difficult urination; tightness in chest*
Early symptoms of overdose
  Abdominal or stomach pain; fast, pounding, or irregular heartbeat; headache, severe; increased sweating not associated with exercise; nausea and vomiting, severe; nervousness or restlessness, severe
Late symptoms of overdose
  Confusion; convulsions; fast breathing; fast and irregular pulse; hallucinations; hostile behavior; muscle trembling

Those indicating need for medical attention only if they continue or are bothersome
Incidence less frequent—more frequent with high doses
  Dizziness; dryness of nose or mouth; false sense of well-being; headache, mild; insomnia (trouble in sleeping); *nausea, mild; nervousness, mild; restlessness, mild*

Patient Consultation

In providing consultation, consider emphasizing the following selected information (» = major clinical significance):

Before using this medication
» Conditions affecting use, especially:
    Sensitivity to phenylpropanolamine or other sympathomimetics
    Pregnancy—Psychiatric side effects more likely in postpartum women
    Use in children—Psychiatric side effects more likely in children up to 6 years of age; not recommended for use as appetite suppressant in children up to 12 years of age; in adolescents between 12 and 18 years of age, use for appetite suppression recommended only with doctor's supervision
    Use by athletes—Phenylpropanolamine is banned, and in some cases, tested for by the U.S. Olympic Committee (USOC)
    Other medications, especially beta-adrenergic blocking agents, CNS stimulation-producing medications, other sympathomimetics, digitalis glycosides, monoamine oxidase (MAO) inhibitors, or rauwolfia alkaloids
    Other medical problems, especially severe coronary artery disease, other cardiovascular disorders, or hypertension

Proper use of this medication
    Proper administration of extended-release dosage forms:
      Swallowing whole; not breaking, crushing, or chewing
      Taking once a day in morning after breakfast
» Importance of not taking more medication than the amount recommended or for a longer period of time than directed
    Taking the medication a few hours before bedtime to minimize the possibility of insomnia
For decongestant use only
    Missed dose: Taking as soon as possible; not taking within 2 hours (12 hours for extended-release dosage forms) of next scheduled dose; not doubling doses
» Proper storage

Precautions while using this medication
    Not drinking large amounts of caffeine-containing coffee, tea, or colas
For decongestant use only
» Checking with physician if cold symptoms do not improve within 7 days or if fever is present

Side/adverse effects
    Signs of potential side effects, especially severe headache, increased blood pressure, painful or difficult urination, or tightness in chest

General Dosing Information

To minimize the possibility of insomnia, the last dose of phenylpropanolamine for each day should be administered a few hours before bedtime (for extended-release dosage forms, 12 hours before bedtime).

With prolonged use or too frequent administration, tolerance to the therapeutic effects of phenylpropanolamine may develop. Phenylpropanolamine is effective as an appetite suppressant only for a few weeks.

Oral Dosage Forms

Note: Bracketed uses in the *Dosage Forms* section refer to categories of use and/or indications that are not included in U.S. product labeling.

PHENYLPROPANOLAMINE HYDROCHLORIDE CAPSULES

Usual adult dose:
    Appetite suppressant—Oral, 25 mg three times a day, not to exceed 75 mg in twenty-four hours.
    Decongestant—Oral, 25 mg every four hours as needed, not to exceed 150 mg in twenty-four hours.
    [Urinary incontinence]—Oral, 50 to 150 mg a day, in divided doses.

PHENYLPROPANOLAMINE HYDROCHLORIDE EXTENDED-RELEASE CAPSULES USP

Usual adult dose:
    Appetite suppressant—Oral, 75 mg once a day in the morning.
    Decongestant—Oral, 75 mg every twelve hours.
    [Urinary incontinence]—Oral, 50 to 150 mg a day, in divided doses.

Auxiliary labeling: • Swallow capsules whole.

PHENYLPROPANOLAMINE HYDROCHLORIDE TABLETS

Usual adult dose: See *Phenylpropanolamine Hydrochloride Capsules.*

PHENYLPROPANOLAMINE HYDROCHLORIDE CHEWING GUM TABLETS

Usual adult dose: Appetite suppressant—25 mg, as 3 pieces of chewing gum, three times a day, before meals.

Auxiliary labeling:
* Chew slowly.
* Do not chew more than 9 pieces in one day.

PHENYLPROPANOLAMINE HYDROCHLORIDE EXTENDED-RELEASE TABLETS

Usual adult dose:
  Appetite suppressant—Oral, 75 mg once a day after breakfast.
  [Urinary incontinence]—Oral, 50 to 150 mg a day, in divided doses.

Auxiliary labeling: • Swallow tablets whole.

PHOSPHATES   Systemic

Some commonly used *brand names* are:

In the U.S.—
  K-Phos M. F. [Potassium and Sodium Phosphates]
  K-Phos Neutral [Potassium and Sodium Phosphates]
  K-Phos No. 2 [Potassium and Sodium Phosphates]
  K-Phos Original [Potassium Phosphate, Monobasic]
  Neutra-Phos [Potassium and Sodium Phosphates]
  Neutra-Phos-K [Potassium Phosphates]
  Uro-KP-Neutral [Potassium and Sodium Phosphates]

In Canada—
  Uro-KP-Neutral [Potassium and Sodium Phosphates]

POTASSIUM PHOSPHATES
Oral
  Monobasic Potassium Phosphate Tablets for Oral Solution†
    In the U.S.—*K-Phos Original*
  Potassium Phosphates Capsules for Oral Solution†
    In the U.S.—*Neutra-Phos-K*
  Potassium Phosphates for Oral Solution†
    In the U.S.—*Neutra-Phos-K*
Parenteral
  Potassium Phosphates Injection USP
    In the U.S. and Canada—GENERIC
POTASSIUM AND SODIUM PHOSPHATES
Oral
  Monobasic Potassium and Sodium Phosphates Tablets for Oral Solution†
    In the U.S.—*K-Phos M. F.; K-Phos Neutral; K-Phos No. 2*
  Potassium and Sodium Phosphates Capsules for Oral Solution†
    In the U.S.—*Neutra-Phos*
  Potassium and Sodium Phosphates for Oral Solution†
    In the U.S.—*Neutra-Phos*
  Potassium and Sodium Phosphates Tablets for Oral Solution
    In the U.S. and Canada—*Uro-KP-Neutral*
SODIUM PHOSPHATES†
Parenteral
  Sodium Phosphates Injection USP†
    In the U.S.—GENERIC

---

†Not commercially available in Canada.

Category

Acidifier (urinary)—Monobasic Potassium Phosphate; Potassium and Sodium Phosphates.

Antiurolithic (calcium calculi)—Monobasic Potassium Phosphate; Potassium and Sodium Phosphates.

Electrolyte replenisher—Potassium Phosphates; Potassium and Sodium Phosphates; Sodium Phosphates.

Indications

Accepted

Hypophosphatemia (prophylaxis and treatment)—
  Phosphates, both oral and parenteral, provide supplemental ionic phosphorus for correction of hypophosphatemia in patients with low or restricted oral intake or conditions with increased requirements for phosphorus, such as premature infants fed human milk, or patients who have inadequately controlled diabetes mellitus, hyperparathyroidism, hyperthyroidism, chronic alcoholism, renal tubular defects leading to increased urinary phosphate loss, respiratory alkalosis, gastrectomy, vitamin D deficiency, total parenteral nutrition (TPN) therapy, or patients who use thiazide diuretics, intravenous dextrose solutions, or those who chronically use aluminum- or magnesium-containing antacids.

  Requirements for all vitamins and most minerals are increased during pregnancy; however, they should be provided by an adequate diet. Many physicians recommend that pregnant women receive multivitamin and mineral supplements, especially those pregnant women who do not consume an adequate diet and those in high-risk categories (i.e., women carrying more than one fetus, heavy cigarette smokers, and alcohol and drug abusers). Taking excessive amounts of a multivitamin and mineral supplement may be harmful to the mother and/or fetus and should be avoided.

  Requirements for all vitamins and minerals are increased during breast-feeding.

Urinary tract infections (treatment adjunct)—Urinary acidification by potassium and sodium phosphates combination and monobasic potassium phosphate augments the efficacy of methenamine mandelate and methenamine hippurate, which are dependent upon an acid medium for antibacterial activity. Phosphates eliminate the odor, rash, and turbidity present with ammoniacal urine associated with urinary tract infections. However, use of phosphates for urea splitting urinary tract infections may predispose to struvite stones that form in alkaline urine.

Renal calculi, calcium (prophylaxis)—Potassium and sodium phosphates combination and monobasic potassium phosphate have been used to reduce urinary calcium concentration and help prevent precipitation of calcium deposits in the urinary tract.

Unaccepted

Although sodium and/or potassium phosphates have been used in the treatment of hypercalcemia, USP medical advisory panels do not recommend this use since these medications have been replaced by safer and more effective agents.

Pharmacology

Mechanism of action/Effect:
  Urinary acidification—At the renal distal tubule, the secretion of hydrogen by the tubular cell in exchange for sodium in the tubular urine converts dibasic phosphate salts to monobasic

phosphate salts. Therefore, large amounts of acid can be excreted without lowering the pH of the urine to a degree that would block hydrogen transport by a high concentration gradient between the tubular cell and luminal fluid.

Antiurolithic—Phosphates inhibit spontaneous nucleation of calcium oxalate, thus reducing the possibility of calcium urolithiasis.

Electrolyte replenisher—Phosphorus modifies the steady state of calcium concentrations, has a buffering effect on acid-base equilibrium, and influences the renal excretion of hydrogen ion.

Precautions to Consider

Geriatrics
No information is available on the relationship of age to the effects of phosphates in geriatric patients.

Drug interactions and/or related problems
The following drug interactions and/or related problems have been selected on the basis of their potential clinical significance (possible mechanism in parentheses where appropriate)—not necessarily inclusive (» = major clinical significance):

Note: Combinations containing any of the following medications, depending on the amount present, may also interact with this medication.

» Adrenocorticoids, glucocorticoid, especially with significant mineralocorticoid activity, or
» Adrenocorticoids, mineralocorticoid, or
» Corticotropin (ACTH)
   (concurrent use with sodium phosphates may result in edema, due to the sodium content)

   Anabolic steroids or
   Androgens or
   Estrogens
   (concurrent use with sodium phosphates may increase the risk of edema, due to the sodium content)

» Antacids, aluminum- or magnesium-containing, or
   Oxalates, found in large quantities in rhubarb and spinach, or
   Phytates, in bran and whole-grain cereals,
   (concurrent use with phosphates may bind the phosphate and prevent its absorption)

» Calcium-containing medications, including dietary supplements and antacids
   (concurrent use with phosphates may increase risk of deposition of calcium in soft tissues, if serum ionized calcium is high; also, phosphate absorption may be reduced because of formation of large amounts of insoluble phosphate)

» Anti-inflammatory drugs, nonsteroidal (NSAIDs), or
» Captopril or
» Cyclosporine or
» Diuretics, potassium-sparing, or
» Enalapril or
» Heparin, chronic use of, or
» Lisinopril or
» Low-salt milk or
» Potassium-containing medications, other, or
» Salt substitutes
   (concurrent use with potassium phosphate may result in hyperkalemia, especially in patients with renal impairment; patient should have serum potassium concentration determinations at periodic intervals)

» Digitalis glycosides
   (use of potassium phosphates injection in digitalized patients with severe or complete heart block is not recommended because of possible hyperkalemia)

Iron supplements
   (concurrent use with foods or medicines containing phosphates will decrease iron absorption because of the formation of less soluble or insoluble complexes; iron supplements should not be taken within 1 hour before or 2 hours after ingestion of phosphates)

» Phosphate-containing medication, other
   (concurrent use with other phosphate containing medications may increase the risk of hyperphosphatemia, especially in patients with renal disease)

Salicylates
   (concurrent use with potassium and sodium phosphates combination or monobasic potassium phosphate may increase plasma concentrations of salicylates since salicylate excretion is decreased in acidified urine; addition of these phosphates to patients stabilized on a salicylate may lead to toxic salicylate concentrations)

» Sodium-containing medications
   (concurrent use with sodium phosphates may increase the risk of edema, especially in patients with renal disease)

Vitamin D, including calcifediol and calcitriol
   (concurrent use with phosphorus-containing medications in high doses may increase the potential for hyperphosphatemia because of vitamin D enhancement of phosphate absorption)

Zinc supplements
   (concurrent use of phosphorus-containing medications with zinc supplements may reduce zinc absorption by formation of nonabsorbable complexes; phosphorus-containing medications should be taken 2 hours after zinc supplements)

Contraindications/Medical problems
The contraindications/medical problems included have been selected on the basis of their potential clinical significance (reasons given in parentheses where appropriate)—not necessarily inclusive (» = major clinical significance).

Except under special circumstances, this medication should not be used when the following medical problems exist:

» Hyperphosphatemia
   (phosphates may further increase serum phosphate concentrations, especially in patients with renal disease)

» Renal function impairment, severe—less than 30% of normal
   (use may result in increased serum phosphate concentrations)

   Urinary tract infections caused by urea splitting organisms
   (use of phosphates may predispose to struvite stone formation)

» Urolithiasis, magnesium ammonium phosphate, infected
   (condition may be exacerbated)

Risk-benefit should be considered when the following medical problems exist:

For all phosphates
» Conditions in which high phosphate concentrations may be encountered, such as:
   Hypoparathyroidism
   Renal disease, chronic
   Rhabdomyolysis
   (administration of phosphates may further increase serum phosphate concentrations)

» Conditions in which low calcium concentrations may be encountered, such as:
   Hypoparathyroidism
   Osteomalacia
   Pancreatitis, acute
   Renal disease, chronic
   Rhabdomyolysis
   Rickets
   (administration of phosphates may further decrease serum calcium concentrations)

   Sensitivity to potassium, sodium, or phosphates

For potassium-containing phosphates only
Cardiac disease, particularly in digitalized patients
  (condition may be exacerbated)
» Conditions in which high potassium concentrations may be encountered, such as:
  Adrenal insufficiency, severe—Addison's disease
  Dehydration, acute
  Pancreatitis
  Physicial exercise, strenous, in unconditioned persons
  Renal insufficiency, severe
  Rhabdomyolysis
  Tissue breakdown, extensive, such as severe burns
    (increased serum potassium concentrations leading to cardiac arrest may occur; exercise-induced hyperkalemia is transient and is a problem only in patients with renal insufficiency or those taking medications that increase serum potassium)
  Myotonia congenita
    (condition may be exacerbated)
For sodium-containing phosphates only
Cardiac failure or
Cirrhosis of liver or severe hepatic disease or
Edema, peripheral and pulmonary or
» Hypernatremia or
Hypertension or
Renal function impairment or
Toxemia of pregnancy
    (sodium salts should be used cautiously in patients with these conditions to prevent exacerbation; also, patients on sodium restricted diets should not use sodium phosphates)

Side/Adverse Effects

The following side/adverse effects have been selected on the basis of their potential clinical significance (possible signs and symptoms in parentheses where appropriate)—not necessarily inclusive:

Those indicating need for medical attention
Incidence less frequent or rare
  Fluid retention (swelling of feet or lower legs; weight gain); *hyperkalemia* (confusion; tiredness or weakness; irregular or slow heartbeat; numbness or tingling around lips, hands, or feet; unexplained anxiety; weakness or heaviness of legs; shortness of breath or troubled breathing); *hypernatremia* (confusion; tiredness or weakness; convulsions; decrease in amount of urine or in frequency of urination; fast heartbeat; headache or dizziness; increased thirst); *hyperphosphatemia or; hypocalcemic tetany* (convulsions, muscle cramps, numbness, tingling, pain, or weakness in hands or feet; shortness of breath, tremor or troubled breathing); *metastatic calcification*

Those indicating need for medical attention only if they continue or are bothersome
Incidence less frequent—for oral dosage forms only
  Laxative effect or diarrhea; nausea or vomiting; stomach pain

Patient Consultation

In providing consultation, consider emphasizing the following selected information (» = major clinical significance):

Importance of Diet
  Diet as treatment of choice; supplement under physician's care may be needed because of inadequate dietary intake or increased requirements; importance of eating properly
  Food sources of phosphorus
  List of RDA for various age groups
  Not exceeding recommended amounts of phosphorus

Before using this medication
» Conditions affecting use, especially:
  Sensitivity to potassium, sodium, or phosphates

Other medications, especially adrenocorticoids, antacids, calcium-containing medications, captopril, corticotropin (ACTH), cyclosporine, digitalis glycosides, enalapril, chronic use of heparin, lisinopril, low-salt milk, nonsteroidal anti-inflammatory drugs, other potassium-containing medications, potassium-sparing diuretics, salt substitutes, or sodium-containing medicines
Other medical problems, especially severe kidney disease, infected urolithiasis, hypoparathyroidism, osteomalacia, acute pancreatitis, rickets, Addison's disease, hypernatremia, edema, severe dehydration, hyperphosphatemia, or acute dehydration

Proper use of this medication
  Taking dissolved in water
» Taking after meals or with food to minimize possible stomach upset or laxative action
» Importance of high fluid intake (8-ounce glass of water every hour) to prevent kidney stones
» Importance of not taking more medication than the amount recommended
» For patients taking sodium-containing phosphates: Importance of low-sodium diet
  Missed dose: Taking as soon as possible; not taking if within 1 or 2 hours of next dose; not doubling doses
» Proper storage

Precautions while using this medication
  Regular visits to physician to check progress during therapy
  Not taking iron supplements within 1 to 2 hours of phosphates
  Checking with physician before beginning exercise program if on potassium-containing phosphate
  Possible need for potassium or sodium restriction

Side/adverse effects
  Signs of potential side effects, especially hyperkalemia, hypernatremia, hyperphosphatemia, hypocalcemic tetany, or fluid retention

General Dosing Information

The normal concentration of serum inorganic phosphate is 3 to 4.5 mg (0.1 to 0.15 mmol) per 100 mL in adults and 4 to 7 mg (0.13 to 0.2 mmol) per 100 mL in children.

For oral dosage forms
Before this medication is taken, it must be thoroughly dissolved in water.

For parenteral dosage forms
Before administration, the concentrated phosphates injection (3 mmol of phosphorus per mL) must be diluted and thoroughly mixed with a larger volume of fluid.

The dose and rate of administration must be individualized.

When used as an electrolyte replenisher, a dose of the equivalent of 10 to 15 mmol (310 mg to 465 mg) of phosphorus a day is usually sufficient to maintain normal serum phosphate, although larger amounts may be required in hypermetabolic states.

The solution should be infused slowly to avoid phosphate intoxication.

Intravenous infusion of phosphates in high concentrations may cause hypocalcemia.

Diet/Nutrition
This medication should be taken immediately after a meal or with food to minimize possible stomach upset or laxative action.

Recommended dietary allowances (RDA) for vitamins and minerals are values determined by the Food and Nutrition Board of the National Research Council. Intake of the RDA provides adequate nutrition in most healthy persons under usual environmental stresses; they are not minimum requirements. RDA are not the same as USRDA (United States Recommended Daily Allowances), which are values established by the FDA for labeling purposes.

The RDA for phosphorus per day:
Infants and children—
Birth to 6 months: 400 mg.
6 months to 1 year: 500 mg.
1 to 10 years: 800 mg.
Adolescent and adult males—
11 to 24 years: 1200 mg.
25 years and over: 800 mg.
Adolescent and adult females—
11 to 24 years: 1200 mg.
25 years and over: 800 mg.
Pregnant females—1200 mg.
Lactating females—1200 mg.
The best dietary sources of phosphorus include dairy products, meat, poultry, fish, and cereal products.

POTASSIUM PHOSPHATES

Oral Dosage Forms

MONOBASIC POTASSIUM PHOSPHATE TABLETS FOR ORAL SOLUTION

Usual adult and adolescent dose:
Acidifier (urinary) or
Antiurolithic or
Electrolyte replenisher—Oral, 1 gram (228 mg or 7.4 mmol of phosphorus) in 180 to 240 mL of water four times a day, with meals and at bedtime.

Auxiliary labeling:
• Do not swallow tablet.
• Dissolve tablet in a full glass (8 ounces) of water.

Additional information: Each 500-mg tablet supplies 114 mg (3.7 mmol) of phosphorus and 3.7 mEq (144 mg) of potassium.

POTASSIUM PHOSPHATES CAPSULES FOR ORAL SOLUTION

Usual adult and adolescent dose: Electrolyte replenisher—Oral, 1.45 grams (250 mg or 8 mmol of phosphorus) in 75 mL of water or juice four times a day, after meals and at bedtime.

Auxiliary labeling:
• Do not swallow filled capsule.
• Mix contents of each capsule with one-third glass of water or juice.

Additional information: Each 1.45-gram capsule supplies 250 mg (8 mmol) of phosphorus and 14.25 mEq (556 mg) of potassium, as monobasic and dibasic potassium phosphates per 75 mL of water or juice, or 200 mg (6.4 mmol) per 60 mL of water or juice, when reconstituted according to manufacturer's instructions.

POTASSIUM PHOSPHATES FOR ORAL SOLUTION

Usual adult and adolescent dose: Electrolyte replenisher—Oral, the equivalent of 250 mg (8 mmol) of phosphorus four times a day, after meals and at bedtime.

Additional information: Each 75 mL of solution or the solution prepared from one packet, when constituted according to manufacturer's instructions, supplies 250 mg (8 mmol) of phosphorus and 14.25 mEq (556 mg) of potassium, as monobasic and dibasic potassium phosphates.

Parenteral Dosage Forms

POTASSIUM PHOSPHATES INJECTION USP

Note: Potassium phosphates injection must be diluted prior to intravenous administration.

Usual adult and adolescent dose: Electrolyte replenisher—Intravenous infusion, the equivalent of 10 mmol (310 mg) of phosphorus a day.

Additional information: Each mL of potassium phosphates injection supplies 283.5 mg of phosphate (approximately 3 mmol [93 mg] of phosphorus) and 4.4 mEq (170.2 mg) of potassium.

POTASSIUM AND SODIUM PHOSPHATES

Oral Dosage Forms

MONOBASIC POTASSIUM AND SODIUM PHOSPHATES TABLETS FOR ORAL SOLUTION

Usual adult and adolescent dose:
Acidifier (urinary) or
Antiurolithic or
Electrolyte replenisher—Oral, 250 mg (8 mmol) of phosphorus with a full glass (240 mL) of water four times a day, after meals and at bedtime.
Note: When the urine is difficult to acidify, a dose of the equivalent of 250 mg (8 mmol) of phosphorus may be administered every two hours, not to exceed 2 grams of phosphorus in a twenty-four-hour period.

Auxiliary labeling:
• Do not swallow tablet.
• Dissolve tablet in a full glass (8 ounces) of water.

Additional information:
A dose of 155 mg of monobasic potassium phosphate and 350 mg of anhydrous monobasic sodium phosphate supplies 125.6 mg (4 mmol) of phosphorus, 1.14 mEq (44.5 mg) of potassium, and 2.9 mEq (67 mg) of sodium.
A dose of 305 mg of monobasic potassium phosphate and 700 mg of anhydrous monobasic sodium phosphate supplies 250 mg (8 mmol) of phosphorus, 2.3 mEq (88 mg) of potassium, and 5.8 mEq (134 mg) of sodium.
A dose of 155 mg of monobasic potassium phosphate, 130 mg of hydrous monobasic sodium phosphate, and 852 mg of anhydrous dibasic sodium phosphate supplies 250 mg (8 mmol) of phosphorus, 1.15 mEq (45 mg) of potassium, and 12.9 mEq (298 mg) of sodium.

POTASSIUM AND SODIUM PHOSPHATES CAPSULES FOR ORAL SOLUTION

Usual adult and adolescent dose: Electrolyte replenisher—Oral, 1.25 grams (250 mg or 8 mmol of phosphorus) in 75 mL of water or juice four times a day, after meals and at bedtime.

Auxiliary labeling:
• Do not swallow filled capsule.
• Mix contents of each capsule with one-third glass of water or juice.

Additional information: Each 1.25-gram capsule supplies 250 mg (8 mmol) of phosphorus, 278 mg (7.125 mEq) of potassium, and 164 mg (7.125 mEq) of sodium.

POTASSIUM AND SODIUM PHOSPHATES FOR ORAL SOLUTION

Usual adult and adolescent dose: Electrolyte replenisher—Oral, 250 mg (8 mmol) of phosphorus four times a day, after meals and at bedtime.

Additional information: Each 75 mL of solution or solution prepared from one packet supplies 250 mg (8 mmol) of phosphorus, 7.125 mEq (278 mg) of potassium, and 7.125 mEq (164 mg) of sodium.

POTASSIUM AND SODIUM PHOSPHATES TABLETS FOR ORAL SOLUTION

Usual adult and adolescent dose: Electrolyte replenisher—Oral, the equivalent of 250 mg (8 mmol) of phosphorus with a full glass (240 mL) of water four times a day.

Auxiliary labeling:
- Do not swallow tablet.
- Dissolve tablet in a full glass (8 ounces) of water.

Additional information: Each tablet supplies 250 mg (8 mmol) of phosphorus, 1.28 mEq (50 mg) of potassium, and 10.8 mEq (250 mg) of sodium, as anhydrous dibasic sodium phosphate, anhydrous dibasic potassium phosphate, and anhydrous monobasic sodium phosphate.

SODIUM PHOSPHATES

Parenteral Dosage Forms

Note: Sodium phosphates injection must be diluted prior to intravenous administration.

SODIUM PHOSPHATES INJECTION USP

Usual adult and adolescent dose: Electrolyte replenisher—Intravenous infusion, 10 to 15 mmol (310 to 465 mg) of phosphorus a day.

Additional information: Each mL of sodium phosphates injection supplies 285 mg of phosphate (approximately 3 mmol [93 mg] of phosphorus) and 4 mEq (92 mg) of sodium.

PHYSOSTIGMINE   Ophthalmic

Some commonly used *brand names* in the U.S. are *Eserine Salicylate, Eserine Sulfate,* and *Isopto Eserine.*

OPHTHALMIC
Physostigmine Salicylate Ophthalmic Solution USP
   In the U.S.—*Eserine Salicylate and Isopto Eserine*
Physostigmine Sulfate Ophthalmic Ointment USP
   In the U.S.—*Eserine Sulfate*

Category: Antiglaucoma agent (ophthalmic); miotic.

Indications

Note: Bracketed information in the *Indications* section refers to uses not included in U.S. product labeling.

Accepted
Glaucoma, open-angle (treatment)—Indicated for reduction of intraocular pressure in open-angle glaucoma. Physostigmine may be used in conjunction with beta-adrenergic blockers, carbonic anhydrase inhibitors, or hyperosmotic agents.

[Glaucoma, angle-closure, *during* or *after* iridectomy (treatment)]— Physostigmine is used in the treatment of angle-closure glaucoma during or after iridectomy.

[Glaucoma, secondary (treatment)]—Physostigmine is used in the treatment of secondary glaucoma if there is no active intraocular inflammation present.

Pharmacology

Mechanism of action/Effect:
   Physostigmine is an indirect-acting parasympathomimetic drug that promotes accumulation and potentiation of the actions of endogenous acetylcholine via a temporary inactivation of cholinesterase. It produces contraction of the iris sphincter muscle, resulting in pupillary constriction (miosis); constriction of the ciliary muscle, resulting in increased accommodation; and a reduction in intraocular pressure associated with decreased resistance to aqueous humor outflow.

In chronic open-angle glaucoma, the exact mechanism by which miotics lower intraocular pressure is not precisely known; however, contraction of the ciliary muscle apparently opens the intertrabecular spaces and facilitates aqueous humor outflow.

Onset of action: Miosis—Within 10 to 30 minutes.

Duration of action: Miosis—12 to 48 hours.

Precautions to Consider

Geriatrics
Appropriate studies with physostigmine have not been performed in the geriatric population. However, no geriatrics-specific problems have been documented to date.

Drug interactions and/or related problems
The following drug interactions and/or related problems have been selected on the basis of their potential clinical significance (possible mechanism in parentheses where appropriate)—not necessarily inclusive (» = major clinical significance):

Note: Combinations containing any of the following medications, depending on the amount present, may also interact with this medication.

   Belladonna alkaloids, ophthalmic
      (concurrent use may antagonize the antiglaucoma and miotic actions of physostigmine)

   Echothiophate or
   Isoflurophate
      (duration of action may be shortened by prior use of physostigmine)

Contraindications/Medical problems
The contraindications/medical problems included have been selected on the basis of their potential clinical significance (reasons given in parentheses where appropriate)—not necessarily inclusive (» = major clinical significance).

Risk-benefit should be considered when the following medical problems exist:

Corneal injury

Sensitivity to physostigmine

» Uveitis, active

Side/Adverse Effects

The following side/adverse effects have been selected on the basis of their potential clinical significance (possible signs and symptoms in parentheses where appropriate)—not necessarily inclusive:

Those indicating need for medical attention

Symptoms of systemic absorption

Increased sweating; loss of bladder control; muscle weakness; nausea, vomiting, diarrhea, or stomach cramps or pain; shortness of breath, tightness in chest, or wheezing; slow or irregular heartbeat; unusual tiredness or weakness; watering of mouth

Those indicating need for medical attention only if they continue or are bothersome

Incidence more frequent

Blurred vision or change in near or distant vision; eye pain

Incidence less frequent

Burning, redness, stinging, or other eye irritation; headache or browache; twitching of eyelids; watering of eyes

Patient Consultation

In providing consultation, consider emphasizing the following selected information (» = major clinical significance):

Before using this medication

» Conditions affecting use, especially:

Sensitivity to phenylephrine

Other medical problems, especially active uveitis

Proper use of this medication

Not using solution if it becomes discolored

Proper administration technique

Washing hands immediately after application to remove any medication that may be on them

» Importance of not using more medication than the amount prescribed

Missed dose: If dosing schedule is—

Once a day: Applying as soon as possible; not applying if not remembered until next day; applying next regularly scheduled dose

More than once a day: Applying as soon as possible; not applying if almost time for next dose; applying next dose at regularly scheduled time

Preventing contamination:

For solution dosage form

Not touching applicator tip to any surface; keeping container tightly closed

For ointment dosage form

Not touching applicator tip to any surface; wiping tip of ointment tube with clean tissue; keeping tube tightly closed

» Proper storage

Precautions while using this medication

Regular visits to physician to check eye pressure during therapy

» Caution if blurred vision or change in near or distant vision occurs, especially at night

Side/adverse effects

Signs of potential side effects, especially systemic absorption

General Dosing Information

Although some manufacturers recommend a dose of 2 drops of an ophthalmic solution at appropriate intervals, the conjunctival sac will usually hold only 1 drop.

More frequent instillation·or use of a stronger concentration may be required to produce adequate miosis and reduction in intraocular pressure in eyes with brown or hazel irides than in eyes with blue or light-colored irides.

Tolerance to physostigmine may develop with prolonged use. Effectiveness may be restored by changing to another miotic for a short time and then resuming the original medication.

For the ointment dosage form only

At night, the ophthalmic ointment may be used to provide prolonged contact with the medication.

For the solution dosage form only

To avoid excessive systemic absorption, patient should press finger to the lacrimal sac during and for 1 or 2 minutes following instillation of the ophthalmic solution.

Ophthalmic Dosage Forms

PHYSOSTIGMINE SALICYLATE OPHTHALMIC SOLUTION USP

Usual adult and adolescent dose: Topical, to the conjunctiva, 1 drop of a 0.25 or 0.5% solution up to four times a day.

Usual geriatric dose: See *Usual adult and adolescent dose.*

Auxiliary labeling:
- For the eye.
- Keep container tightly closed.

PHYSOSTIGMINE SULFATE OPHTHALMIC OINTMENT USP

Usual adult and adolescent dose: Topical, to the conjunctiva, 1 cm of a 0.25% ointment one to three times a day.

Usual geriatric dose: See *Usual adult and adolescent dose.*

Auxiliary labeling:
- For the eye.
- Keep container tightly closed.

PILOCARPINE　Ophthalmic

Some commonly used *brand names* are:

In the U.S.—

Adsorbocarpine	*Pilocar*
Akarpine	*Pilokair*
I-Pilocarpine	*Pilopine HS*
Isopto Carpine	*Piloptic-1*
Ocu-Carpine	*Piloptic-2*
Ocusert Pilo-20	*Piloptic-4*
Ocusert Pilo-40	*Pilostat*
Pilagan	*Spectro-Pilo*

In Canada—

Isopto Carpine	*Pilopine HS*
Minims Pilocarpine	*Pilostat*
Miocarpine	*P.V. Carpine Liquifilm*
Ocusert Pilo-20	*Spersacarpine*
Ocusert Pilo-40	

OPHTHALMIC

Pilocarpine Ocular System USP
In the U.S. and Canada—*Ocusert Pilo-20; Ocusert Pilo-40*
Pilocarpine Hydrochloride Ophthalmic Gel
In the U.S. and Canada—*Pilopine HS*
Pilocarpine Hydrochloride Ophthalmic Solution USP
In the U.S.—*Adsorbocarpine; Akarpine; I-Pilocarpine; Isopto Carpine; Ocu-Carpine; Pilocar; Pilokair; Piloptic-1; Piloptic-2; Piloptic-4; Pilostat;* GENERIC
In Canada—*Isopto Carpine; Miocarpine; Pilostat; Spersacarpine*
Pilocarpine Nitrate Ophthalmic Solution USP
In the U.S.—*Pilagan; Spectro-Pilo*
In Canada—*Minims Pilocarpine; P.V. Carpine Liquifilm*

Category: Antiglaucoma agent (ophthalmic); miotic.

Indications

Accepted

Glaucoma, open-angle (treatment)—Indicated primarily for the treatment of open-angle (chronic simple) glaucoma. Pilocarpine may be used in conjunction with a carbonic anhydrase inhibitor, epinephrine, timolol, fluorescein, or anesthetic, antibiotic, or anti-inflammatory steroid ophthalmic solutions.

Glaucoma, angle-closure (treatment)—Pilocarpine (hydrochloride or nitrate) ophthalmic solution is indicated for use alone or in combination with carbonic anhydrase inhibitors or hyperosmotic agents to lower intraocular pressure in the emergency treatment of acute angle-closure glaucoma prior to surgery or laser iridotomy. In addition, pilocarpine may be indicated for the treatment of chronic angle-closure glaucoma.

Glaucoma, angle-closure, *during* or *after* iridectomy (treatment)—Pilocarpine may be indicated for the treatment of angle-closure glaucoma *during* or *after* iridectomy.

Glaucoma, secondary (treatment)—May be indicated for the treatment of nonuveitic secondary glaucoma.

Miosis induction, postoperative; or
Miosis induction, following ophthalmoscopy—Pilocarpine (hydrochloride or nitrate) ophthalmic solution is indicated to produce miosis in order to counteract the effects of cycloplegics and mydriatics following surgery or ophthalmoscopic examination.

Pharmacology

Mechanism of action/Effect:

Pilocarpine is a parasympathomimetic that directly stimulates cholinergic receptors. It produces contraction of the iris sphincter muscle, resulting in pupillary constriction (miosis); constriction of the ciliary muscle, resulting in increased accommodation; and a reduction in intraocular pressure associated with decreased resistance to aqueous humor outflow. Pilocarpine may also inhibit aqueous humor secretion.

In chronic open-angle glaucoma, the exact mechanism by which miotics lower intraocular pressure is not precisely known; however, contraction of the ciliary muscle apparently opens the intertrabecular spaces and facilitates aqueous humor outflow.

In angle-closure glaucoma, constriction of the pupil apparently pulls the iris away from the trabeculum, thereby relieving blockage of the trabecular meshwork.

Onset of action: Miosis—Solution (1%): Within 10 to 30 minutes.

Time to peak effect: Reduction in intraocular pressure—
Ocular system: 1.5 to 2 hours.
Solution: Within 75 minutes, depending on strength used.

Duration of action:
Miosis—
Solution: About 4 to 8 hours.
Reduction in intraocular pressure—
Ocular system: 7 days.
Solution: 4 to 14 hours, depending on strength used.

Precautions to Consider

Geriatrics

Appropriate studies with pilocarpine have not been performed in the geriatric population. However, no geriatrics-specific problems have been documented to date.

Drug interactions and/or related problems

The following drug interactions and/or related problems have been selected on the basis of their potential clinical significance (possible mechanism in parentheses where appropriate)—not necessarily inclusive (» = major clinical significance):

Belladonna alkaloids, ophthalmic, or
Cyclopentolate
(concurrent use may interfere with the antiglaucoma action of pilocarpine; also, concurrent use with pilocarpine counteracts the mydriatic effects of these medications, which may be used to therapeutic advantage)

Contraindications/Medical problems

The contraindications/medical problems included have been selected on the basis of their potential clinical significance (reasons given in parentheses where appropriate)—not necessarily inclusive (» = major clinical significance).

Risk-benefit should be considered when the following medical problems exist:

Asthma, bronchial

Infectious conjunctivitis or keratitis, acute—for ocular system dosage form only

» Iritis, acute, or other conditions in which pupillary constriction is undesirable

Retinal detachment, history of or predisposition to

Sensitivity to pilocarpine

Side/Adverse Effects

The following side/adverse effects have been selected on the basis of their potential clinical significance (possible signs and symptoms in parentheses where appropriate)—not necessarily inclusive:

Those indicating need for medical attention
Symptoms of systemic absorption
  Increased sweating; muscle tremors; nausea, vomiting, or diarrhea; troubled breathing or wheezing; watering of mouth

Those indicating need for medical attention only if they continue or are bothersome
Incidence more frequent
  Blurred vision or change in near or distant vision; eye pain
Incidence less frequent
  Eye irritation; headache or browache

Patient Consultation

In providing consultation, consider emphasizing the following selected information (» = major clinical significance):

Before using this medication
» Conditions affecting use, especially:
    Sensitivity to pilocarpine
    Other medical problems, especially acute iritis or other conditions in which pupillary constriction is undesirable

Proper use of this medication
  Proper administration technique
  Washing hands immediately after application to remove any medication that may be on them
» Importance of not using more medication than the amount prescribed
» Proper storage
For gel or solution dosage forms
  Preventing contamination: Not touching applicator tip to any surface; keeping container tightly closed
  Missed dose:
    For gel dosage form—Applying as soon as possible; not applying if not remembered until next day; applying next dose at regularly scheduled time
    For solution dosage form—Applying as soon as possible; not applying if almost time for next dose; applying next dose at regularly scheduled time
For ocular system dosage form
  Reading patient instructions carefully before using
  Not using if damaged
  Removing and replacing with new unit if too much medicine is being released

Precautions while using this medication
  Regular visits to physician to check eye pressure during therapy
» Caution if blurred vision or change in near or distant vision occurs, especially at night

Side/adverse effects
  Signs of potential side effects, especially symptoms of systemic absorption

General Dosing Information

Tolerance to pilocarpine may develop with prolonged use. Effectiveness may be restored by changing to another miotic for a short time and then resuming the original medication.

For the ocular system dosage form
The system should be placed in the eye at bedtime so that the pilocarpine-induced myopia may reach a stable level by morning.

Damaged or deformed systems should not be placed or retained in the eye. If a system is believed to be associated with an unexpected increase in action of the medication, it should be removed and replaced with a new system.

For the solution dosage forms
Although some manufacturers recommend a dose of 2 drops of an ophthalmic solution at appropriate intervals, the conjunctival sac will usually hold only 1 drop.

To avoid excessive systemic absorption, patient should press finger to the lacrimal sac during and for 1 or 2 minutes following instillation of the solution.

Although some manufacturers recommend that patients not wear soft contact lenses during treatment with pilocarpine ophthalmic solution, USP medical experts do not believe this precaution is necessary unless the patient has corneal epithelial problems and the medication is to be used more often than once every 1 to 2 hours. No significant problems have been documented with opththalmic solutions containing 0.03% or less of benzalkonium chloride as a preservative that are used in patients with no significant corneal surface problems.

Ophthalmic Dosage Forms

PILOCARPINE OCULAR SYSTEM USP

Usual adult and adolescent dose: Antiglaucoma agent (ophthalmic)— Topical, to the conjunctiva, 1 ocular system delivering 20 or 40 mcg (0.02 or 0.04 mg) per hour, once every seven days.

Usual geriatric dose: See *Usual adult and adolescent dose.*

Auxiliary labeling:
 • For the eye.
 • Refrigerate.

PILOCARPINE HYDROCHLORIDE OPHTHALMIC GEL

Usual adult and adolescent dose: Antiglaucoma agent (ophthalmic)— Topical, to the conjunctiva, approximately 1.5 cm (1/2-inch strip) of a 4% gel once a day at bedtime.

Usual geriatric dose: See *Usual adult and adolescent dose.*

Auxiliary labeling:
 • For the eye.
 • Keep container tightly closed.

PILOCARPINE HYDROCHLORIDE OPHTHALMIC SOLUTION USP

Usual adult and adolescent dose:
  Antiglaucoma agent (ophthalmic)—
    Chronic glaucoma: Topical, to the conjunctiva, 1 drop of a 0.5 to 4% solution up to four times a day.
    Acute angle-closure glaucoma: Topical, to the conjunctiva, 1 drop of a 1 or 2% solution every five to ten minutes for three to six doses, then 1 drop every one to three hours until intraocular pressure is reduced.
    Note: To possibly avoid a bilateral attack of angle-closure glaucoma, 1 drop of a 1 or 2% solution may be instilled in the unaffected eye every six to eight hours. However, more intensive treatment may precipitate an attack in the unaffected eye and should be avoided.
  Miotic—
    To counteract mydriatic effects of sympathomimetics: Topical, to the conjunctiva, 1 drop of a 1% solution.
    Prior to surgery for congenital glaucoma (goniotomy): Topical, to the conjunctiva, 1 drop of a 2% solution every four to six hours (usually for one or two doses) before surgery.
    Prior to iridectomy: Topical, to the conjunctiva, 1 drop of a 2% solution for four doses immediately before surgery.

Usual geriatric dose: See *Usual adult and adolescent dose.*

Auxiliary labeling:
- For the eye.
- Keep container tightly closed.

PILOCARPINE NITRATE OPHTHALMIC SOLUTION USP

Usual adult and adolescent dose:
Antiglaucoma agent (ophthalmic)—
Chronic glaucoma: Topical, to the conjunctiva, 1 drop of a 1 to 4% solution two to four times a day.
Acute angle-closure glaucoma: Topical, to the conjunctiva, 1 drop of a 1 or 2% solution every five to ten minutes for three to six doses, then 1 drop every one to three hours until intraocular pressure is reduced.
Note: To possibly avoid a bilateral attack of angle-closure glaucoma, 1 drop of a 1 or 2% solution may be instilled in the unaffected eye every six to eight hours. However, more intensive treatment may precipitate an attack in the unaffected eye and should be avoided.

Miotic—
To counteract mydriatic effects of sympathomimetics: Topical, to the conjunctiva, 1 drop of a 1% solution.
Prior to surgery for congenital glaucoma (goniotomy): Topical, to the conjunctiva, 1 drop of a 2% solution every four to six hours (usually for one or two doses) before surgery.
Prior to iridectomy: Topical, to the conjunctiva, 1 drop of a 2% solution for four doses immediately before surgery.

Usual geriatric dose: See *Usual adult and adolescent dose.*

Auxiliary labeling:
- For the eye.
- Keep container tightly closed.

PIMOZIDE   Systemic

A commonly used *brand name* in the U.S. and Canada is *Orap*.

ORAL
Pimozide Tablets USP
In the U.S. and Canada—*Orap*

Category: Antidyskinetic (Gilles de la Tourette's syndrome); antipsychotic.

Indications

Note: Bracketed information in the *Indications* section refers to uses not included in U.S. product labeling.

Accepted
Gilles de la Tourette's syndrome (treatment)[1]—Pimozide is indicated for the suppression of motor and vocal tics in patients with Tourette's disorder whose symptoms are severe and who cannot tolerate or have failed to respond satisfactorily to haloperidol.

[Psychotic disorders (treatment)]—Pimozide is used for maintenance therapy in the management of *chronic* schizophrenic patients *without* symptoms of excitement, agitation, or hyperactivity.

Unaccepted
Pimozide must not be used for simple tics or tics that are not associated with Tourette's disorder because of the high risk of cardiovascular and extrapyramidal effects.

Pimozide is ineffective and should not be used for the management of patients with mania or acute schizophrenia.

---

[1]Not included in Canadian product labeling.

Pharmacology

Mechanism of action/Effect: Pimozide's exact mechanism of action in Tourette's disorder has not been established; however, pimozide is thought to block dopamine nonselectively at both the pre- and postsynaptic receptors on neurons in the central nervous system (CNS).

Secondary changes in central dopamine function and metabolism, such as altered dopamine release and increased brain turnover of dopamine (but not of norepinephrine), may also contribute to both therapeutic and adverse effects. There are also various effects, not fully characterized, on other CNS receptor systems.

In psychotic disorders, pimozide is thought to have more specific dopamine receptor blocking activity, less potential for inducing sedation, and fewer autonomic effects than other neuroleptic agents.

Precautions to Consider

Cross-sensitivity and/or related problems
Patients sensitive to neuroleptic agents such as haloperidol, loxapine, molindone, phenothiazines, or thioxanthenes may also be sensitive to pimozide.

Geriatrics
Geriatric patients tend to develop higher plasma concentrations because of changes in distribution due to decreases in lean body mass, total body water, and albumin, and often an increase in total body fat composition. These patients usually require lower initial dosage and a more gradual titration of dose. Also, elderly patients are more prone to develop transient hypotension and exhibit an increased sensitivity to the anticholinergic and sedative effects of pimozide.

In addition, older patients tend to develop extrapyramidal side effects more frequently, especially persistent tardive dyskinesia and parkinsonism. Tardive dyskinesia may be difficult to control and, in some patients, appears to be irreversible. The symptoms of tardive dyskinesia may be masked during therapy but may appear after reduction of dose or withdrawal of pimozide. There is no known effective treatment. Careful observation during pimozide therapy for early signs of tardive dyskinesia and reduction of dosage or discontinuation of medication may prevent a more severe manifestation of the syndrome.

Dental

The peripheral anticholinergic effects of pimozide may decrease or inhibit salivary flow, especially in middle-aged or elderly patients, thus contributing to the development of caries, periodontal disease, oral candidiasis, and discomfort.

Extrapyramidal reactions induced by pimozide will result in increased motor activity of the head, face, and neck. Occlusal adjustments, bite registrations, and treatment for bruxism may be made less reliable.

The blood dyscrasia-causing effects of pimozide may result in an increased incidence of microbial infection, delayed healing, and gingival bleeding. If leukopenia or thrombocytopenia occurs, dental work should be deferred until blood counts have returned to normal. Patients should be instructed in proper oral hygiene, including caution in use of regular toothbrushes, dental floss, and toothpicks.

Drug interactions and/or related problems

The following drug interactions and/or related problems have been selected on the basis of their potential clinical significance (possible mechanism in parentheses where appropriate)—not necessarily inclusive (» = major clinical significance):

Note: Combinations containing any of the following medications, depending on the amount present, may also interact with this medication.

» Alcohol or
» CNS depression-producing medications, other
    (concurrent use with pimozide may potentiate the CNS depressant effects of these medications)

» Amphetamines or
» Methylphenidate or
» Pemoline
    (concurrent use with pimozide may mask the cause of tics since these medications themselves may provoke tics; before therapy with pimozide is initiated, these medications should be withdrawn)

» Anticholinergics or other medications with anticholinergic activity
    (concurrent use with pimozide may intensify anticholinergic effects, especially those of dry mouth, constipation, and unusual excitability, because of secondary anticholinergic effects of pimozide)

Anticonvulsants
    (although there has been no primary documentation for a drug interaction with pimozide and anticonvulsants, the potential exists for a lowering of the convulsive threshold with concurrent use; dosage adjustment of anticonvulsant may be necessary when pimozide treatment is initiated or discontinued or when the dose is reduced)

» Antidepressants, tricyclic, or
» Disopyramide or
» Maprotiline or
» Phenothiazines or
» Procainamide or
» Quinidine
    (concurrent use of these agents with pimozide may potentiate cardiac arrhythmias, which are seen on electrocardiogram [ECG] as prolongation of the QT interval)
    (in addition, concurrent use of phenothiazines with pimozide may potentiate the anticholinergic, CNS depressant, and extrapyramidal effects of both medications)

» Extrapyramidal reaction-causing medications, other
    (concurrent use of these agents with pimozide may increase the anticholinergic, CNS depressant, and extrapyramidal effects of both medications)

Contraindications/Medical problems

The contraindications/medical problems included have been selected on the basis of their potential clinical significance (reasons given in parentheses where appropriate)—not necessarily inclusive (» = major clinical significance).

Except under special circumstances, this medication should not be used when the following medical problems exist:

» Cardiac arrhythmias, history of, or
» Long QT syndrome, congenital
    (may be aggravated by use of pimozide, predisposing patients to ventricular arrhythmias)

» CNS depression, severe, or
» Comatose states
    (may be potentiated)

» Tics, motor or vocal, other than those caused by Tourette's disorder
    (risk of cardiovascular and extrapyramidal effects)

Risk-benefit should be considered when the following medical problems exist:

» Breast cancer, history of
    (may be aggravated by increased serum prolactin concentrations)

Hepatic function impairment or
Renal function impairment
    (metabolism and excretion of pimozide may be altered)

» Hypokalemia
    (potassium deficiency, especially from diarrhea or use of diuretics, should be corrected before initiation of pimozide therapy because of risk of ventricular arrhythmias)

Sensitivity to pimozide or other neuroleptics, such as haloperidol, loxapine, molindone, phenothiazines, or thioxanthenes

Side/Adverse Effects

The following side/adverse effects have been selected on the basis of their potential clinical significance (possible signs and symptoms in parentheses where appropriate)—not necessarily inclusive:

Those indicating need for medical attention

Incidence more frequent
    Akathisia (restlessness or need to keep moving); *arrhythmias, ventricular* (fast or irregular heartbeat)—seen on ECG as prolonged QT interval; *extrapyramidal effects, parkinsonian* (difficulty in speaking; loss of balance control; mask-like face; shuffling walk; slowed movements; stiffness of arms and legs; trembling and shaking of fingers and hands); *mood or behavior changes*

Note: *Parkinsonian extrapyramidal effects* often occur during first few days of treatment, even at relatively low doses, and are usually mild to moderately severe.

Incidence less frequent
    Extrapyramidal reactions, dystonic (difficulty in swallowing; inability to move eyes; muscle spasms, especially of the face, neck, or back; twisting movements of the body); *tardive dyskinesia, persistent* (lip smacking or puckering; puffing of cheeks; rapid or worm-like movements of tongue; uncontrolled chewing movements; uncontrolled movements of arms and legs)

Note: *Tardive dyskinesia* is initially dose related, but may increase with long-term treatment and total cumulative dose; may persist after discontinuation of pimozide.

Incidence rare
    Blood dyscrasias (sore throat and fever; unusual bleeding or bruising); *jaundice, obstructive* (yellow eyes or skin); *neuroleptic malignant syndrome* (NMS) (convulsions; difficult or unusually fast breathing; high fever; high or low [irregular] blood pressure; in-

creased sweating; loss of bladder control; severe muscle stiffness; tiredness or weakness; unusually pale skin)

Note: Additional signs of *NMS* may include fast heartbeat, elevated creatine phosphokinase (CPK), myoglobinuria [rhabdomyolysis], and acute renal failure. NMS may occur at any time during neuroleptic therapy, but is more commonly seen soon after start of therapy, or after patient has switched from one neuroleptic to another, during combined therapy with another psychotropic medication, or after a dosage increase.

Symptoms of overdose

Drowsiness or dizziness, severe, or comatose state; muscle trembling, jerking, stiffness, or uncontrolled movements, severe; troubled breathing, severe; unusual tiredness or weakness, severe

Those indicating need for medical attention only if they continue or are bothersome

Incidence more frequent

Blurred vision or other vision problems; constipation; drowsiness; dryness of mouth; hypotension, orthostatic (dizziness, lightheadedness, or fainting, especially when getting up from a lying or sitting position); *skin rash, itching, or discoloration; swelling or soreness of breasts; unusual secretion of milk*

Incidence less frequent

Decreased sexual ability; diarrhea; headache; loss of appetite and weight; mental depression; nausea and vomiting; swelling of the face

Those indicating the need for medical attention if they occur after the medication is discontinued

Dyskinesia, withdrawal emergent (lip smacking or puckering; puffing of cheeks; rapid or worm-like movements of tongue; uncontrolled chewing movements; uncontrolled movements of arms and legs)

Patient Consultation

In providing consultation, consider emphasizing the following selected information (» = major clinical significance):

Before using this medication

» Conditions affecting use, especially:

Sensitivity to pimozide or other neuroleptic agents

Pregnancy—Animal studies have shown fewer pregnancies; retarded fetal development; maternal toxicity; mortality; decreased weight gain; embryotoxicity; increased resorptions

Use in children—Not recommended for any condition other than Tourette's syndrome; therapy should be initiated gradually in patients up to 12 years of age; children are more sensitive to effects of pimozide

Use in the elderly—Elderly patients are more likely to develop extrapyramidal, anticholinergic, hypotensive, and sedative effects; reduced dosage recommended

Dental—Pimozide-induced blood dyscrasias may result in infections, delayed healing, and bleeding; dry mouth may cause caries, candidiasis, periodontal disease, and discomfort; increased motor activity of face, head, and neck may interfere with some dental procedures

Other medications, especially alcohol, other CNS depression-producing medications, amphetamines, methylphenidate, pemoline, tricyclic antidepressants, disopyramide, maprotiline, other extrapyramidal reaction-producing medications, procainamide, quinidine, or anticholinergics

Other medical problems, especially cardiac arrhythmias, tics other than those caused by Tourette's disorder, severe CNS depression, history of breast cancer, or hypokalemia

Proper use of this medication

» Importance of not taking more medication than the amount prescribed

Missed dose: Taking as soon as possible; taking any remaining doses for that day at regularly spaced intervals; not doubling doses

» Proper storage

Precautions while using this medication

Regular visits to physician to check progress of therapy

» Checking with physician before discontinuing medication; gradual dosage reduction may be needed

» Avoiding use of alcoholic beverages or other CNS depressants during therapy

» Possible drowsiness, blurred vision, or muscle stiffness; caution when driving, using machinery, or doing other things requiring alertness, clear vision, and good muscle control

Possible dizziness or lightheadedness; avoiding getting up suddenly from a sitting or lying position

» Caution if any kind of surgery, dental treatment, or emergency surgery is required

Possible dryness of mouth; using sugarless gum or candy, ice, or saliva substitute for relief; checking with physician or dentist if dry mouth continues for more than 2 weeks

Side/adverse effects

Side effects more likely in children and elderly or debilitated patients

» Stopping medication and notifying physician immediately if symptoms of neuroleptic malignant syndrome (NMS) appear

» Notifying physician as soon as possible if early symptoms of tardive dyskinesia appear

Possibility of withdrawal symptoms

Signs of potential side effects, especially parkinsonism, ventricular arrhythmias, mood or behavior changes, akathisia, tardive dyskinesia, dystonic reactions, NMS, blood dyscrasias, or obstructive jaundice

General Dosing Information

Periodic attempts should be made to reduce the dosage of pimozide gradually to see whether tics persist at the level and extent first identified. In doing so, consideration should be given to the possibility that any increases in tic intensity and frequency may represent a transient withdrawal-related phenomenon rather than a return of disease symptoms. Two to three weeks should elapse before a final conclusion is reached that an increase in tic manifestations is a function of the underlying disease syndrome rather than a response to pimozide withdrawal. Also, spontaneous remission and fluctuating symptoms may occur in many patients, since pimozide's poor absorption and presystemic metabolism profile may result in a highly variable absorption from day to day.

Oral Dosage Forms

Note: Bracketed uses in the *Dosage Forms* section refer to categories of use and/or indications that are not included in U.S. product labeling.

PIMOZIDE TABLETS USP

Usual adult and adolescent dose:

Tourette's disorder[1]—Oral, initially, 1 to 2 mg a day in divided doses, the dosage being increased gradually every other day as needed and tolerated.

Note: Most patients are maintained at daily doses of up to 200 mcg (0.2 mg) per kg of body weight, or 10 mg a day, whichever is less.

[Psychotic disorders]—Oral, 2 to 4 mg once a day, the dosage being increased at weekly intervals by 2 to 4 mg a day.

Note: The average maintenance dose is 6 mg a day, with a usual range of 2 to 12 mg a day. Daily doses above 30 mg are seldom required.

Usual adult prescribing limits: Up to 300 mcg (0.3 mg) per kg of body weight a day or 20 mg a day in divided doses.

Auxiliary labeling:
- May cause drowsiness.
- Avoid alcoholic beverages.

[1]Not included in Canadian product labeling.

POTASSIUM IODIDE   Systemic

Some commonly used *brand names* are:

In the U.S.—*Pima*
In Canada—*Thyro-Block*

Other commonly used names are KI and SSKI.

ORAL
Potassium Iodide Oral Solution USP
In the U.S.—GENERIC
Potassium Iodide Syrup
In the U.S.—*Pima*
Potassium Iodide Tablets USP*
In Canada—*Thyro-Block*
Potassium Iodide Tablets USP (Enteric-coated)
In the U.S.—GENERIC

Note: Enteric-coated potassium iodide tablets are not recommended since the administration of this dosage form has been associated with small bowel lesions, which can cause obstruction, hemorrhage, perforation, and possibly death.

---

*Not commercially available in the U.S.; however, potassium iodide tablets are available to government and public health organizations for use in radiation emergencies.

Category: Antihyperthyroid agent; radiation protectant (thyroid gland); thyroid inhibitor; antifungal (systemic); iodine replenisher.

Indications

Note: Bracketed information in the *Indications* section refers to uses not included in U.S. product labeling.

Accepted
Hyperthyroidism (treatment)[1]—Potassium iodide is indicated in the treatment of hyperthyroidism.

Radiation protection, thyroid gland—Potassium iodide is indicated as a radiation protectant (thyroid gland) prior to and following oral administration or inhalation of radioactive isotopes of iodine or in radiation emergencies.

[Erythema nodosum (treatment)][1]—Potassium iodide is used in the treatment of erythema nodosum.

[Iodine deficiency (treatment)][1]—Potassium iodide is used in the treatment of iodine deficiency.

[Sporotrichosis, cutaneous lymphatic (treatment)][1]—Potassium iodide is used in the treatment of cutaneous lymphatic sporotrichosis.

[Thyroid involution, preoperative][1]—Potassium iodide is used concurrently with an antithyroid agent to induce thyroid involution prior to thyroidectomy.

Unaccepted
Potassium iodide has not been shown to have a clinically significant expectorant action.

---

[1]Not included in Canadian product labeling.

Pharmacology

Mechanism of action/Effect:
Antihyperthyroid agent—In hyperthyroid patients, potassium iodide produces rapid remission of symptoms by inhibiting the release of thyroid hormone into the circulation. The effects of potassium iodide on the thyroid gland include reduction of vascularity, a firming of the glandular tissue, shrinkage of the size of individual cells, reaccumulation of colloid in the follicles, and increases in bound iodine. These actions may facilitate thyroidectomy when the medication is given prior to surgery.

Radiation protectant—When administered prior to and following administration of radioactive isotopes and in radiation emergencies involving the release of radioactive iodine, potassium iodide protects the thyroid gland by blocking the thyroidal uptake of radioactive isotopes of iodine.

When potassium iodide is administered simultaneously with radiation exposure, the protectant effect is approximately 97%. Potassium iodide given 12 and 24 hours before exposure yields a 90% and 70% protectant effect, respectively. However, potassium iodide administered 1 and 3 hours after exposure results in an 85% and 50% protectant effect, respectively. Potassium iodide administered more than 6 hours after exposure is thought to have a negligible protectant effect.

Precautions to Consider

Geriatrics
Appropriate studies on the relationship of age to the effects of potassium iodide have not been performed in the geriatric population. However, geriatrics-specific problems that would limit the usefulness of this medication in the elderly are not expected.

Dental
Potassium iodide may cause salivary gland swelling or tenderness, burning of mouth or throat, metallic taste, soreness of teeth and gums, and unusual increase in salivation.

Drug interactions and/or related problems
The following drug interactions and/or related problems have been selected on the basis of their potential clinical significance (pos-

sible mechanism in parentheses where appropriate)—not necessarily inclusive (» = major clinical significance):

Note: Combinations containing any of the following medications, depending on the amount present, may also interact with this medication.

»   Antithyroid agents
(concurrent use of these medications with potassium iodide may potentiate the hypothyroid and goitrogenic effects of antithyroid agents or potassium iodide; baseline thyroid status should be determined at periodic intervals to detect changes in the thyroid-pituitary response)

Captopril or
Enalapril or
Lisinopril
(concurrent use of captopril, enalapril, or lisinopril with potassium iodide may result in hyperkalemia; serum potassium concentrations should be monitored)

»   Diuretics, potassium-sparing
(concurrent use with potassium iodide may increase the effects of potassium, possibly resulting in hyperkalemia and cardiac arrhythmias or cardiac arrest; serum potassium concentrations should be monitored)

»   Lithium
(concurrent use with potassium iodide may potentiate the hypothyroid and goitrogenic effects of either medication; baseline thyroid status should be determined at periodic intervals to detect changes in the thyroid-pituitary response)

Sodium iodide I 131, therapeutic
(potassium iodide may decrease thyroidal uptake of I 131)

Contraindications/Medical problems
The contraindications/medical problems included have been selected on the basis of their potential clinical significance (reasons given in parentheses where appropriate)—not necessarily inclusive (» = major clinical significance).

Risk-benefit should be considered when the following medical problems exist:

»   Hyperkalemia
(condition may be exacerbated)

Hyperthyroidism (for use other than thyroid inhibitor)
(prolonged use of iodine may cause thyroid gland hyperplasia, thyroid adenoma, goiter, or hypothyroidism)

Myotonia congenita
(condition may be exacerbated by potassium)

»   Renal function impairment
(may cause excessive serum potassium concentrations)

Sensitivity to potassium iodide

Tuberculosis
(may cause irritation and increase secretions)

Side/Adverse Effects
The following side/adverse effects have been selected on the basis of their potential clinical significance (possible signs and symptoms in parentheses where appropriate)—not necessarily inclusive:

Those indicating need for medical attention
Incidence less frequent
Allergic reactions, specifically angioedema (swelling of the arms, face, legs, lips, tongue, and/or throat); *arthralgia* (joint pain); *eosinophilia; swelling of lymph nodes; urticaria* (hives)

With prolonged use
Iodism (burning of mouth or throat, gastric irritation, increased watering of mouth, metallic taste, severe headache, skin lesions, soreness of teeth and gums, symptoms of head cold); *potassium*

toxicity (confusion; irregular heartbeat; numbness, tingling, pain, or weakness in hands or feet; unusual tiredness; weakness or heaviness of legs)

Those indicating need for medical attention only if they continue or are bothersome
Incidence less frequent
Diarrhea; nausea or vomiting; stomach pain

Patient Consultation
In providing consultation, consider emphasizing the following selected information (» = major clinical significance):

Before using this medication
»   Conditions affecting use, especially:
Sensitivity to iodine or potassium iodide
Pregnancy—May cause thyroid problems or goiter in the newborn infant
Breast-feeding—May cause skin rash and thyroid problems in nursing babies
Use in children—May cause skin rash and thyroid problems in nursing infants
Dental—May cause swelling of salivary glands, burning of mouth or throat, metallic taste, soreness of teeth and gums, or increase in salivation
Other medications, especially antithyroid agents, diuretics (potassium sparing), or lithium
Other medical problems, especially hyperkalemia or renal function impairment

Proper use of this medication
»   Taking after meals or with food or milk to minimize gastrointestinal irritation
Proper administration technique for oral liquids:
Taking medication by mouth even if dispensed in a dropper bottle
Not using if solution turns brownish yellow
Taking medication in a full glass (240 mL) of water or in fruit juice, milk, or broth to improve taste and lessen gastric upset; drinking full dose
If crystals form in solution, warming closed container in warm water and gently shaking container
Proper administration technique for uncoated tablets:
Dissolving each tablet in $1/2$ glass (120 mL) of water or milk before taking; drinking full dose
»   Compliance with full course of therapy (fungal infections)
Missed dose: Taking as soon as possible; not taking if almost time for next dose; not doubling doses
»   Proper storage
For use as a radiation protectant (thyroid gland)
Taking medication only upon instructions from state or local health authorities
»   Taking medication daily for 10 days, unless otherwise instructed; not taking more medication or more often than instructed

Precautions while using this medication
Regular visits to physician to check progress during therapy
»   Caution in patients on potassium-restricted diet

Side/adverse effects
Signs of potential side effects, especially allergic reactions, iodism, or potassium toxicity

General Dosing Information
The potassium content is 6 mEq (234 mg) per gram of potassium iodide.

To minimize stomach upset, the medication may be administered after meals and at bedtime with food or milk.

To protect against possible gastrointestinal injury, which has been associated with the oral ingestion of concentrated potassium salt preparations, it is recommended that the oral solution be administered in a full glass (240 mL) of water, or in fruit juice, milk, or broth. It is also recommended that each regular tablet be dissolved in ¹/₂ glass (120 mL) of water or milk before ingestion.

Prolonged use may result in hypothyroidism, parotitis, iodism, and, particularly in postpubescent patients, acneiform skin lesions.

Oral Dosage Forms

Note: Bracketed uses in the *Dosage Forms* section refer to categories of use and/or indications that are not included in U.S. product labeling.

POTASSIUM IODIDE ORAL SOLUTION USP

Usual adult and adolescent dose:
Antihyperthyroid agent[1]—Oral, 250 mg three times a day.
   Radiation protectant (thyroid gland)—Oral, 100 to 150 mg twenty-four hours prior to and once a day for three to ten days following administration of, or exposure to, radioactive isotopes of iodine.
   [Antifungal (systemic)][1]—Oral, 600 mg three times a day, the dosage being increased by 60 mg at each dose until the maximum tolerated dose is reached.
   [Iodine replenisher][1]—Oral, 5 to 10 mg per day.
   [Thyroid involution, preoperative][1]—Prior to thyroidectomy: Oral, 5 drops of a 1-gram-per-mL solution (approximately 250 mg) three times a day for ten days before surgery, usually administered concurrently with an antithyroid agent.

Usual adult prescribing limits: Up to 12 grams daily.

Auxiliary labeling:
• For oral use only.
• Do not refrigerate.
• Continue medicine for full time of treatment (antifungal).

POTASSIUM IODIDE SYRUP

Usual adult and adolescent dose:
Radiation protectant (thyroid gland)—Oral, 100 to 150 mg twenty-four hours prior to and once a day for three to ten days following administration of, or exposure to, radioactive isotopes of iodine.

[Antifungal (systemic)][1]—Oral, 600 mg three times a day, the dosage being increased by 60 mg at each dose until the maximum tolerated dose is reached.
[Iodine replenisher][1]—Oral, 5 to 10 mg per day.
[Thyroid involution, preoperative][1]—Prior to thyroidectomy: Oral, 4 mL (approximately 260 mg) three times a day for ten days before surgery, usually administered concurrently with an antithyroid agent.

Usual adult prescribing limits: Up to 12 grams daily.

Auxiliary labeling:
• For oral use only.
• Continue medicine for full time of treatment (for 3-day uncinariasis treatment).

POTASSIUM IODIDE TABLETS USP

Usual adult and adolescent dose:
Radiation protectant (thyroid gland)—Oral, 100 to 150 mg twenty-four hours prior to and once a day for three to ten days following administration of, or exposure to, radioactive isotopes of iodine.
   [Antifungal (systemic)][1]—Oral, 600 mg three times a day, the dosage being increased by 60 mg at each dose until the maximum tolerated dose is reached.
   [Iodine replenisher][1]—Oral, 5 to 10 mg per day.
   [Thyroid involution, preoperative][1]—Prior to thyroidectomy: Oral, Dissolve 2 tablets (approximately 260 mg) in 1 glassful of water, three times a day for ten days before surgery, usually administered concurrently with an antithyroid agent.

Usual adult prescribing limits: Up to 12 grams daily.

Auxiliary labeling:
• Dissolve in liquid before taking.
• Continue medicine for full time of treatment (for 3-day uncinariasis treatment).

POTASSIUM IODIDE TABLETS USP (ENTERIC-COATED)

Note: Enteric-coated potassium iodide tablets are not recommended since the administration of this dosage form has been associated with small bowel lesions, which can cause obstruction, hemorrhage, perforation, and possibly death.

[1]Not included in Canadian product labeling.

PRAZOSIN   Systemic

A commonly used *brand name* in the U.S. and Canada is *Minipress*.

ORAL
Prazosin Hydrochloride Capsules USP†
   In the U.S.—*Minipress;* GENERIC
Prazosin Hydrochloride Tablets*
   In Canada—*Minipress*

*Not commercially available in the U.S.
†Not commercially available in Canada.

Category: Antihypertensive; vasodilator, congestive heart failure; antidote (to ergot alkaloid poisoning); vasospastic therapy adjunct.

Indications

Note: Bracketed information in the *Indications* section refers to uses not included in U.S. product labeling.

Accepted
Hypertension (treatment)—Prazosin is indicated in the treatment of hypertension.

In the 1988 Report of the Joint National Committee on Detection, Evaluation, and Treatment of High Blood Pressure, a progression in choice of treatments for essential hypertension is recommended:

Nonpharmacologic management (especially sodium restriction, weight reduction and exercise, and moderation of alcohol consumption) is recommended first for some patients, including those with mild hypertension, and is recommended as an adjunct to all pharmacologic hypertensive therapy.

Initial drug therapy usually consists of a diuretic, beta-adrenergic blocking agent, calcium channel blocking agent, or angiotensin-converting enzyme (ACE) inhibitor. If adequate blood pressure control is not achieved and the patient is adherent to the treatment program and not experiencing significant side effects, dosage of the drug may be increased, a drug from another one of these initial classes may be added or substituted, or a second drug from a different class—centrally acting alpha-adrenergic blocking agent (e.g., clonidine, guanabenz, guanfacine, methyldopa), peripheral-acting adrenergic antagonists (e.g., guanadrel, guanethidine, rauwolfia alkaloids), post-synaptic alpha-1 peripheral adrenergic inhibitors (e.g., prazosin, terazosin), or vasodilators (e.g., hydralazine, minoxidil)—may be added or substituted.

If necessary, a drug from another class in the second group may be substituted or added as a third drug. If blood pressure control is still not achieved, a drug from still another class may be substituted or added as a fourth drug, or the patient may need further evaluation and/or referral.

[Congestive heart failure (treatment)][1]—Prazosin may be used as an adjunct to digoxin and diuretics for the treatment of congestive heart failure. However, prazosin has not been shown to improve survival in these patients.

[Toxicity, ergot alkaloid (treatment)][1]—Prazosin is used for treatment of peripheral vasospasm caused by ergot alkaloid overdose.

[Pheochromocytoma (treatment)][1]—Prazosin is used for the management of hypertension associated with pheochromocytoma.

[Raynaud's phenomenon (treatment)][1]—Prazosin is used for treatment of Raynaud's phenomenon.

[Benign prostatic hypertrophy (treatment)][1]—Prazosin is used for the treatment of urinary symptoms associated with benign prostatic hypertrophy.

---

[1]Not included in Canadian product labeling.

Pharmacology

Mechanism of action/Effect: Prazosin is a selective post-synaptic alpha$_1$-adrenergic blocking agent. The alpha$_1$-adrenergic blocking action is thought to account primarily for its effects.
  Hypertension—Prazosin produces vasodilation and reduces peripheral resistance but generally has little effect on cardiac output. Antihypertensive effect is usually not accompanied by reflex tachycardia. There is little or no effect on renal blood flow or glomerular filtration rate.
  Congestive heart failure—Beneficial vasodilator effects are due to decreased systemic resistance, preload and afterload reduction, and resulting improved cardiac output.
  Raynaud's phenomenon—Therapeutic effect for vasospasm is due to inhibition of vasoconstriction by blocking of postsynaptic alpha$_1$ receptors.

Other actions/effects: Prazosin may effect serum lipids. The most consistent changes observed are a decrease in levels of serum total cholesterol and low density lipoprotein (LDL) cholesterol. However, the implications of these changes are unclear.

Onset of action:
  Hypertension—Within 30 to 90 minutes after a single dose.
  Congestive heart failure—Rapid.

Time to peak effect:
  Hypertension—
    Single dose: 2 to 4 hours.
    Multiple doses: Up to 3 to 4 weeks of therapy may be required for maximal therapeutic effect.
  Congestive heart failure—1 hour.

Duration of action:
  Hypertension—Single dose: 7 to 10 hours.
  Congestive heart failure—6 hours.

Precautions to Consider

Cross-sensitivity and/or related problems
Patients sensitive to other quinazolines (doxazosin, terazosin) may also be sensitive to prazosin.

Geriatrics
Although appropriate studies on the relationship of age to the effects of prazosin have not been performed in the geriatric population, geriatrics-specific problems are not expected to limit the usefulness of prazosin in the elderly. However, elderly patients may be more sensitive to the hypotensive effects and are more likely to have age-related renal function impairment, which may require lower prazosin doses. In addition, the risk of prazosin-induced hypothermia may be increased in elderly patients.

Drug interactions and/or related problems
The following drug interactions and/or related problems have been selected on the basis of their potential clinical significance (possible mechanism in parentheses where appropriate)—not necessarily inclusive (» = major clinical significance):

Note: Combinations containing any of the following medications, depending on the amount present, may also interact with this medication.

Anti-inflammatory drugs, nonsteroidal (NSAIDs), especially indomethacin
  (antihypertensive effects of prazosin may be reduced when it is used concurrently with these agents; indomethacin, and possibly other NSAIDs, may antagonize the antihypertensive effect by inhibiting renal prostaglandin synthesis and/or by causing sodium and fluid retention; the patient should be carefully monitored to confirm that the desired effect is being obtained)

Estrogens
  (estrogen-induced fluid retention tends to increase blood pressure)

Hypotension-producing medications, other
  (antihypertensive effects may be potentiated when these medications are used concurrently with prazosin; although some antihypertensive and/or diuretic combinations are frequently used to therapeutic advantage, dosage adjustments are necessary when these medications are used concurrently)

Sympathomimetics
  (antihypertensive effects of prazosin may be reduced when it is used concurrently with these agents; the patient should be carefully monitored to confirm that the desired effect is being obtained)
  (concurrent use of prazosin antagonizes the peripheral vasoconstriction produced by high doses of dopamine)
  (concurrent use of prazosin may decrease the pressor response to ephedrine)
  (concurrent use of prazosin may block the alpha-adrenergic effects of epinephrine, possibly resulting in severe hypotension and tachycardia)
  (concurrent use of prazosin usually decreases, but does not reverse or completely block, the pressor effect of metaraminol)
  (prior administration of prazosin may decrease the pressor effect and shorten the duration of action of methoxamine and phenylephrine)

Contraindications/Medical problems
The contraindications/medical problems included have been selected on the basis of their potential clinical significance (reasons given in parentheses where appropriate)—not necessarily inclusive (» = major clinical significance).

Risk-benefit should be considered when the following medical problems exist:

Angina pectoris
  (may induce angina or aggravate pre-existing angina)

» Cardiac disease, severe
  (prazosin is usually not used alone, although it may improve cardiac performance in some patients with severe refractory congestive heart failure)

Narcolepsy
  (may exacerbate cataplexy; however, a clear cause-effect relationship has not been established)
Renal function impairment
  (increased sensitivity to prazosin's effects; lower doses may be
  required)
Sensitivity to prazosin

Side/Adverse Effects

Note: A "first-dose orthostatic hypotensive reaction" sometimes occurs, most frequently 30 to 90 minutes after the initial dose of
  prazosin, and may be severe. Syncope or other postural symptoms, such as dizziness, may occur. Subsequent occurrence
  with dosage increases is also possible. Incidence appears to be
  dose-related; thus, it is important that therapy be initiated with
  the lowest possible dose. Patients who are volume-depleted or
  sodium-restricted may be more sensitive to the orthostatic hypotensive effects of prazosin, and the effect may be exaggerated after exercise.

  Hypotensive side effects may be more likely to occur in geriatric patients.

The following side/adverse effects have been selected on the basis of
  their potential clinical significance (possible signs and symptoms
  in parentheses where appropriate)—not necessarily inclusive:

Those indicating need for medical attention
Incidence more frequent
  Dizziness; orthostatic hypotension (dizziness or lightheadedness
  when getting up from a lying or sitting position; sudden fainting)
Incidence less frequent
  Edema (swelling of feet or lower legs); *palpitations* (pounding
  heartbeat); *urinary incontinence* (loss of bladder control)
Incidence rare
  Angina (chest pain); *dyspnea* (shortness of breath); *priapism* (pain-
  ful, inappropriate erection of the penis, continuing)

**Those indicating need for medical attention only if they continue
or are bothersome**
Incidence more frequent
  Drowsiness; headache; malaise (lack of energy)
Incidence less frequent
  Dryness of mouth; fatigue (unusual tiredness or weakness); *ner-
  vousness*
Incidence rare
  Nausea; urinary frequency (frequent urge to urinate)

Patient Consultation

In providing consultation, consider emphasizing the following selected information (» = major clinical significance):

Before using this medication
» Conditions affecting use, especially:
    Sensitivity to quinazolines
    Breast-feeding—Excreted in breast milk in small amounts
    Use in the elderly—Increased sensitivity to hypotensive effects
      and increased risk of prazosin-induced hypothermia
    Other medical problems, especially severe cardiac disease

Proper use of this medication
  Getting into the habit of taking at same times each day to help
    increase compliance
  Missed dose: Taking as soon as possible; not taking if almost time
    for next dose; not doubling doses
» Proper storage
For use as an antihypertensive
  Possible need for control of weight and diet, especially sodium
    intake

» Patient may not experience symptoms of hypertension; importance
  of taking medication even if feeling well
» Does not cure, but helps control hypertension; possible need for
  lifelong therapy; serious consequences of untreated hypertension

Precautions while using this medication
  Regular visits to physician to check progress
» Caution if dizziness, lightheadedness, or sudden fainting occurs,
  especially after initial dose; taking first dose at bedtime
» Caution when getting up suddenly from a lying or sitting position
» Caution in using alcohol, while standing for long periods or exer-
  cising, and during hot weather because of enhanced orthostatic
  hypotensive effects
» Possibility of drowsiness
» Caution when driving or doing anything else requiring alertness
  because of possible drowsiness, dizziness, or lightheadedness
» Not taking other medications, especially nonprescription sympatho-
  mimetics, unless discussed with physician

Side/adverse effects
  Signs of potential side effects, especially angina, dizziness, dyspnea, edema, orthostatic hypotension, palpitations, priapism,
  and urinary incontinence

General Dosing Information

Dosage of prazosin should be adjusted to meet the individual requirements of each patient, on the basis of blood pressure response.

Prazosin may be used alone or in combination with a thiazide diuretic
  or beta-adrenergic blocker, both of which reduce the tendency for
  sodium and water retention, although they also produce additive
  hypotension. If combination therapy is indicated, individual titration is required to ensure the lowest possible therapeutic dose of
  each drug.

In order to minimize the "first-dose orthostatic hypotensive reaction,"
  an initial dose of 1 mg is recommended, with gradual increments
  as needed. Administration of the initial dose at bedtime is recommended, as well as the initial dose of each increment.

When a diuretic or other antihypertensive agent is added to prazosin
  therapy, the dose of prazosin should be reduced to 1 or 2 mg three
  times a day, followed by titration of dosage of the combination.
  When prazosin is added to existing diuretic or antihypertensive
  therapy, the dose of the other agent should be reduced and prazosin
  started at a dose of 0.5 or 1 mg two or three times a day.

Tolerance to the effects of prazosin may occur during treatment of
  congestive heart failure but usually not during treatment of hypertension. An early, transient (usually within the first few doses)
  blunting of hemodynamic effect may occur due to reflex activation
  of the sympathetic nervous system. The hemodynamic effect may
  spontaneously restore with uninterrupted therapy or the blunted
  effect may be overcome by temporarily interrupting prazosin
  therapy. A later apparent tolerance may result from fluid retention,
  requiring increased doses of diuretics; this effect may be minimized by increasing the dose of prazosin, temporarily interrupting
  prazosin therapy, or substituting another vasodilator.

Oral Dosage Forms

Note: Bracketed uses in the *Dosage Forms* section refer to categories
  of use and/or indications that are not included in U.S. product
  labeling.

PRAZOSIN HYDROCHLORIDE CAPSULES USP

Note: The dosing and strengths of the dosage forms available are
  expressed in terms of prazosin base (not the hydrochloride
  salt).

Usual adult dose:
  Antihypertensive—
    Initial: Oral, 1 mg (base) two or three times a day.

Maintenance: Oral, adjusted gradually to meet individual requirements, most commonly 6 to 15 mg (base) a day in two or three divided daily doses.

[Toxicity, ergot alkaloid]—Oral, 1 mg three times a day.

[Vasospastic therapy adjunct—Raynaud's phenomenon]: Oral, 1 mg three times a day.

[Benign prostatic hypertrophy]—

Initial: Oral, 1 mg (base) two times a day.

Maintenance: Oral, 1 to 5 mg (base) two times a day.

Note: Geriatric patients may be more sensitive to the effects of the usual adult dose.

Usual adult prescribing limits: Daily doses higher than 20 mg (base) usually do not have increased efficacy, although some patients respond to up to 40 mg a day.

Auxiliary labeling:
- Do not take other medicines without your doctor's advice.
- May cause dizziness.

PRAZOSIN HYDROCHLORIDE TABLETS

Note: The dosing and strengths of the dosage forms available are expressed in terms of prazosin base (not the hydrochloride salt).

Usual adult dose: Antihypertensive—

Initial: Oral, 500 mcg (0.5 mg) two or three times a day for at least 3 days. If tolerated, increase to 1 mg (base) two or three times a day for a further 3 days.

Maintenance: Oral, adjusted gradually to meet individual requirements, most commonly 6 to 15 mg (base) a day in two or three divided doses.

Toxicity, ergot alkaloid[1]—Oral, 1 mg three times a day.

Vasospastic therapy adjunct—Raynaud's phenomenon[1]: Oral, 1 mg three times a day.

Benign prostatic hypertrophy[1]—

Initial: Oral, 1 mg (base) two times a day.

Maintenance: Oral, 1 to 5 mg (base) two times a day.

Note: Geriatric patients may be more sensitive to the effects of the usual adult dose.

Usual adult prescribing limits: Daily doses higher than 20 mg (base) usually do not have increased efficacy, although some patients respond to up to 40 mg a day.

Auxiliary labeling:
- Do not take other medicines without your doctor's advice.
- May cause dizziness.

---

[1]Not included in Canadian product labeling.

PRAZOSIN AND POLYTHIAZIDE Systemic

Category: Antihypertensive.

Indications

Accepted

Hypertension (treatment)—Prazosin and polythiazide combination is indicated in the treatment of hypertension.

Fixed-dosage combinations are generally not recommended for initial therapy and are useful for subsequent therapy only when the proportion of the component agents corresponds to the dose of the individual agents, as determined by titration.

Nonpharmacologic management (especially sodium restriction, weight reduction and exercise, and moderation of alcohol consumption) is recommended first for some patients, including those with mild hypertension, and is recommended as an adjunct to all pharmacologic hypertensive therapy.

Patient Consultation

In providing consultation, consider emphasizing the following selected information (» = major clinical significance):

Before using this medication
» Conditions affecting use, especially:

Sensitivity to quinazolines, thiazide diuretics, other sulfonamide-type medications, bumetanide, furosemide, or carbonic anhydrase inhibitors

Pregnancy—Not recommended for routine use; thiazide diuretics may cause jaundice, thrombocytopenia, hypokalemia in infant

Breast-feeding—Excreted in breast milk; recommended that nursing mothers avoid thiazides diuretics during first month of breast-feeding because of reports of suppression of lactation

Use in children—Caution if giving to infants with jaundice

Use in the elderly—Elderly patients may be more sensitive to hypotensive effects; potential for increased risk of prazosin-induced hypothermia and electrolyte effects of polythiazide

Use by athletes—Diuretics are banned and tested for by the U.S. Olympic Committee (USOC), the International Olympic Committee (IOC), and the National Collegiate Athletic Association (NCAA)

Other medications, especially cholestyramine, colestipol, digitalis glycosides, or lithium

Other medical problems, especially anuria, severe cardiac disease, severe renal function impairment, or infants with jaundice

Proper use of this medication

Possible need for control of weight and diet, especially sodium intake

» Patient may not experience symptoms of hypertension; importance of taking medication even if feeling well

» Does not cure, but helps control hypertension; possible need for lifelong therapy; serious consequences of untreated hypertension

Diuretic effects of the medication and timing of doses to minimize inconvenience of diuresis

Getting into the habit of taking at same time each day to help increase compliance

Missed dose: Taking as soon as possible; not taking if almost time for next dose; not doubling doses

» Proper storage

Precautions while using this medication

Regular visits to physician to check progress

» Not taking other medications, especially nonprescription sympathomimetics, unless discussed with physician

Possibility of hypokalemia; possible need for additional potassium in diet; not changing diet without first checking with physician

To prevent dehydration, checking with physician if severe nausea, vomiting, or diarrhea occurs and continues

May increase blood sugar levels in diabetics

Possible photosensitivity; avoiding unprotected exposure to sun; using protective clothing and sun block product; avoiding use of sunlamp, tanning bed, or tanning booth

» Caution if dizziness, lightheadedness, or sudden fainting occurs, especially after initial dose; taking first dose at bedtime
» Caution when getting up suddenly from a lying or sitting position
» Caution in using alcohol, while standing for long periods or exercising, and during hot weather because of enhanced orthostatic hypotensive effects
» Possibility of drowsiness
» Caution when driving or doing anything else requiring alertness because of possible drowsiness, dizziness, or lightheadedness

Side/adverse effects

Signs of potential side effects, especially dizziness, edema, urinary incontinence, priapism, electrolyte imbalance, orthostatic hypotension, agranulocytosis, allergic reaction, angina, cholecystitis, pancreatitis, hepatic function impairment, palpitations, shortness of breath, hyperuricemia, gout, and thrombocytopenia

Oral Dosage Forms

PRAZOSIN HYDROCHLORIDE AND POLYTHIAZIDE CAPSULES

Usual adult dose: Antihypertensive—Oral, 1 capsule two or three times a day, as determined by individual titration with the component agents.

Note: Geriatric patients may be more sensitive to the effects of the usual adult dose and may require a lower dose in order to prevent syncope.

Auxiliary labeling: • Do not take other medicines without your doctor's advice.

PRIMAQUINE   Systemic

ORAL
Primaquine Phosphate Tablets USP
In the U.S. and Canada—GENERIC

Category: Antiprotozoal.

Indications

Note: Bracketed information in the *Indications* section refers to uses not included in U.S. product labeling.

Accepted
Malaria (treatment)—Primaquine is indicated for the prevention of relapses (radical cure) of malaria caused by *Plasmodium vivax* [and *P. ovale*]. Primaquine is also effective against the gametocytes of *P. falciparum*.

[Pneumonia, *Pneumocystis carinii* (treatment)][1]—Primaquine is used in combination with clindamycin in the treatment of *Pneumocystis carinii* pneumonia (PCP) in patients unresponsive or intolerant to standard therapy.

---

[1]Not included in Canadian product labeling.

Pharmacology

Mechanism of action/Effect: The precise mechanism of action has not been determined, but may be based on primaquine's ability to bind to and alter the properties of DNA. Primaquine is highly active against the exoerythrocytic stages of *P. vivax* and *P. ovale* and against the primary exoerythrocytic stages of *P. falciparum*. It is also highly active against the sexual forms (gametocytes) of plasmodia, especially *P. falciparum*, disrupting transmission of the disease by eliminating the reservoir from which the mosquito carrier is infected.

Precautions to Consider

Cross-sensitivity and/or related problems
Patients hypersensitive to iodoquinol, a chemically related 8-aminoquinoline, may be hypersensitive to this medication also.

Geriatrics
No information is available on the relationship of age to the effects of primaquine in geriatric patients.

Drug interactions and/or related problems
The following drug interactions and/or related problems have been selected on the basis of their potential clinical significance (possible mechanism in parentheses where appropriate)—not necessarily inclusive (» = major clinical significance):

Note: Combinations containing any of the following medications, depending on the amount present, may also interact with this medication.

Bone marrow depressants or
» Hemolytics, other
    (concurrent use of primaquine with bone marrow depressants may increase the leukopenic effects; if concurrent use is required, close observation for myelotoxic effects should be considered)
    (concurrent use of primaquine with other hemolytics may increase the potential for toxic side effects)
» Quinacrine
    (concurrent use is not recommended since it may increase the toxic effects of primaquine)

Contraindications/Medical problems
The contraindications/medical problems included have been selected on the basis of their potential clinical significance (reasons given in parentheses where appropriate)—not necessarily inclusive (» = major clinical significance).

Risk-benefit should be considered when the following medical problems exist:
Favism or acute hemolytic anemia, history of (family or personal) or
» Glucose-6-phosphate dehydrogenase (G6PD) deficiency
    (primaquine may cause hemolytic anemia, especially in G6PD-deficient patients)
Hypersensitivity to primaquine
Nicotinamide adenine dinucleotide (NADH) methemoglobin reductase deficiency
    (primaquine may cause methemoglobinemia, especially in patients with NADH methemoglobin reductase deficiency)

Side/Adverse Effects

The following side/adverse effects have been selected on the basis of their potential clinical significance (possible signs and symptoms in parentheses where appropriate)—not necessarily inclusive:

Those indicating need for medical attention
Incidence more frequent
Hemolytic anemia (dark urine; back, leg, or stomach pains; loss of appetite; pale skin; unusual tiredness or weakness; fever)—severity of hemolysis in patients with G6PD deficiency is directly related to the degree of deficiency and the dose of primaquine administered
Incidence less frequent
Methemoglobinemia (cyanosis—bluish fingernails, lips, or skin; dizziness or lightheadedness; difficulty breathing; unusual tiredness or weakness)—especially with high doses or in patients with NADH methemoglobin reductase deficiency
Incidence rare
Leukopenia (sore throat and fever)

Those indicating need for medical attention only if they continue or are bothersome
Incidence more frequent
Gastrointestinal effects (abdominal pain or cramps, nausea or vomiting)

Patient Consultation

In providing consultation, consider emphasizing the following selected information (» = major clinical significance):

Before using this medication
» Conditions affecting use, especially:
　Hypersensitivity to primaquine
　Pregnancy—Use is not recommended
　Other medications, especially other hemolytics and quinacrine
　Other medical problems, especially G6PD deficiency

Proper use of this medication
» Taking with meals or antacids to minimize gastric irritation
» Compliance with full course of therapy

» Proper dosing
　Missed dose: Taking as soon as possible; not taking if almost time for next dose; not doubling doses
» Proper storage

Precautions while using this medication
　Regular visits to physician to check progress during therapy

Side/adverse effects
　Signs of potential side effects, especially hemolytic anemia, leukopenia, and methemoglobinemia.

General Dosing Information

Primaquine may be taken with meals or antacids to minimize gastric irritation.

When used to prevent relapses, primaquine may be administered concurrently or consecutively with chloroquine or hydroxychloroquine.

Oral Dosage Forms

PRIMAQUINE PHOSPHATE TABLETS USP

Note: Bracketed uses in the *Dosage Forms* section refer to categories of use and/or indications that are not included in U.S. product labeling.

Usual adult and adolescent dose:
　Malaria—Oral, 26.3 mg (15 mg base) once a day for fourteen days.
　Note: For some strains of *Plasmodium vivax* (particularly those from Southeast Asia), a dose of 39.4 to 52.6 mg (22.5 to 30 mg base) daily for fourteen days may be required for radical cure of malaria.
　　To eliminate gametocytes of *P. falciparum*, a single dose of 78.9 mg (45 mg base) may be administered.
　[*Pneumocystis carinii* pneumonia][1]—Oral, 26.3 mg to 52.6 mg (15 to 30 mg base) once a day for twenty-one days.

Auxiliary labeling: • Continue medicine for full time of treatment.

---

[1]Not included in Canadian product labeling.

PRIMIDONE　Systemic

Some commonly used *brand names* are:
　In the U.S.—*Myidone; Mysoline*
　In Canada—*Apo-Primidone; Mysoline; PMS Primidone; Sertan*

ORAL
Primidone Oral Suspension USP†
　In the U.S.—*Mysoline*
Primidone Tablets USP
　In the U.S.—*Myidone; Mysoline;* GENERIC
　In Canada—*Apo-Primidone; Mysoline; PMS Primidone; Sertan;* GENERIC
Primidone Chewable Tablets*
　In Canada—*Mysoline*

---

*Not commercially available in the U.S.
†Not commercially available in Canada.

Category: Anticonvulsant.

Indications

Note: Bracketed information in the *Indications* section refers to uses not included in U.S. product labeling.

Accepted
Epilepsy (treatment)—Primidone, either alone or used concomitantly with other anticonvulsants, is indicated in the control of generalized tonic-clonic (grand mal), nocturnal myoclonic, complex partial (psychomotor), and simple partial (cortical focal) epileptic seizures.
[Essential tremor (treatment)][1]—Primidone is used in the treatment of essential (familial) tremor. Although propranolol is considered to be the treatment of choice for essential tremor, primidone provides effective treatment for some patients.

---

[1]Not included in Canadian product labeling.

Pharmacology

Mechanism of action/Effect: Unknown, but anticonvulsant effects are thought to be due to the parent compound, primidone, as well as its two active metabolites, phenobarbital and phenylethylmalonamide (PEMA), whose actions may be synergistic.

Precautions to Consider

Cross-sensitivity and/or related problems
Patients sensitive to barbiturates may be sensitive to this medication also.

Geriatrics
Unusual restlessness and excitement may sometimes occur as a paradoxical reaction in the elderly.

Drug interactions and/or related problems
The following drug interactions and/or related problems have been selected on the basis of their potential clinical significance (possible mechanism in parentheses where appropriate)—not necessarily inclusive (» = major clinical significance):

Note: Combinations containing any of the following medications, depending on the amount present, may also interact with this medication.

Although not all of the following interactions have been documented to pertain specifically to primidone, a potential exists for their occurrence because of the barbiturate metabolite of primidone.

Acetaminophen
(when acetaminophen in therapeutic doses is used concurrently in patients receiving chronic primidone therapy, its effects may be decreased because of increased metabolism resulting from induction of hepatic microsomal enzymes by the phenobarbital metabolite; also, risk of hepatotoxicity with single toxic doses or prolonged use of acetaminophen may be increased in chronic alcoholics or in patients regularly using hepatic-enzyme inducing agents)

» Adrenocorticoids, glucocorticoid and mineralocorticoid, or
» Anticoagulants, coumarin- or indandione-derivative, or
Antidepressants, tricyclic, or
Chloramphenicol or
» Contraceptives, oral, estrogen-containing, or
» Corticotropin (ACTH) or
Cyclosporine or
Dacarbazine or
Digitalis glycosides, with possible exception of digoxin, or
Disopyramide or
Doxycycline or
Levothyroxine or
Metronidazole or
Mexiletine or
Quinidine
(concurrent use with primidone may decrease the effects of these medications because of increased metabolism resulting from induction of hepatic microsomal enzymes by the barbiturate metabolite; dosage increases may be necessary during and after primidone therapy)

(use of a nonhormonal method of birth control or a progestin-only oral contraceptive may be necessary during primidone therapy)

(also, concurrent use of tricyclic antidepressants with primidone may enhance central nervous system [CNS] depression, lower convulsive threshold, and decrease the effects of primidone; dosage adjustments may be necessary to control seizures)

» Alcohol or
» CNS depression-producing medications, other
(concurrent use may potentiate the CNS and respiratory depressant effects of either these medications or primidone; dosage adjustment of primidone may be necessary)

Amphetamines
(concurrent use may cause a delay in the intestinal absorption of the phenobarbital metabolite)

» Anticonvulsants, other
(concurrent use may cause a change in the pattern of epileptiform seizures because of altered medication metabolism; monitoring of plasma concentrations of both medications is recommended; dosage adjustments may be necessary)

(carbamazepine induces metabolism and decreases effects of primidone; monitoring of plasma concentrations is recommended as a guide to dosage if either medication is added or withdrawn from an existing regimen)

(concurrent use of valproic acid with primidone may cause higher serum concentrations of primidone leading to increased CNS depression and neurological toxicity because of protein binding displacement and reduced metabolism; half-life of valproic acid may be decreased; in addition, primidone may enhance valproic acid hepatotoxicity, presumably through the formation of hepatotoxic valproate metabolites; dosage adjustment of primidone may be necessary)

Carbonic anhydrase inhibitors
(osteopenia induced by primidone may be enhanced; it is recommended that patients receiving concurrent therapy be monitored for early signs of osteopenia and that the carbonic acid anhydrase inhibitor be discontinued and appropriate treatment initiated if necessary)

Cyclophosphamide
(concurrent use with primidone may induce microsomal metabolism to increase the formation of alkylating metabolites of cyclophosphamide, thereby reducing the half-life and increasing the leukopenic activity of cyclophosphamide)

Enflurane or
Halothane or
Methoxyflurane
(chronic use of primidone prior to anesthesia may increase anesthetic metabolism, leading to increased risk of hepatotoxicity)

(also, chronic use of primidone prior to anesthesia with methoxyflurane may increase formation of nephrotoxic metabolites, leading to increased risk of nephrotoxicity)

Guanadrel or
Guanethidine
(concurrent use with primidone may aggravate orthostatic hypotension)

Fenoprofen
(concurrent use with primidone may decrease the elimination half-life of fenoprofen, possibly because of increased metabolism resulting from induction of hepatic microsomal enzyme activity; fenoprofen dosage adjustment may be required)

Folic acid
(requirements for folic acid may be increased in patients receiving anticonvulsant therapy)

Griseofulvin
(antifungal effects may be decreased when griseofulvin is used concurrently with primidone because of impaired absorption resulting in decreased serum concentrations; although the ef-

fect of decreased serum concentrations on therapeutic response has not been established, concurrent use preferably should be avoided)

Haloperidol or
Loxapine or
Maprotiline or
Molindone or
Phenothiazines or
Thioxanthenes
> (concurrent use may lower the seizure threshold because of altered metabolism; CNS depression may be increased; decreases in primidone dosage may be necessary)
>
> (serum concentrations of neuroleptics may be significantly reduced when these medications are used concurrently with primidone because of increased metabolism)

Leucovorin
> (large doses may counteract the anticonvulsant effects of primidone)

Methylphenidate
> (concurrent use may increase serum concentrations of primidone because of metabolism inhibition, possibly resulting in toxicity; dosage adjustments may be necessary)

» Monoamine oxidase (MAO) inhibitors, including furazolidone, procarbazine, or selegiline
> (concurrent use may prolong the effects of primidone because metabolism of the barbiturate metabolite may be inhibited; changes in the pattern of epileptiform seizures may occur; dosage adjustments of primidone may be necessary)

Phenobarbital
> (although concurrent use with primidone is rarely indicated, since primidone is metabolized to phenobarbital, it may cause a change in the pattern of epileptiform seizures because of altered medication metabolism and also increase the sedative effect of either primidone or the barbiturate anticonvulsant; decreases in primidone dosage may be necessary)

Phenylbutazone
> (concurrent use may decrease the efficacy of the phenobarbital metabolite of primidone by inducing hepatic microsomal enzymes and increasing its metabolism; also, hepatic enzyme inducers such as barbiturates may increase phenylbutazone metabolism and decrease its half-life)

Posterior pituitary
> (concurrent use with primidone may increase the risk of cardiac arrhythmias and coronary insufficiency)

Rifampin
> (concurrent use of rifampin with barbiturates may enhance the metabolism of hexobarbital by induction of hepatic microsomal enzymes, resulting in lower serum concentrations; there is conflicting data on rifampin's effect on phenobarbital blood levels; dosage adjustment may be required)

Vitamin D
> (effects may be reduced by primidone, because of accelerated metabolism by hepatic microsomal enzyme induction; vitamin D supplementation may be required in patients on long-term primidone therapy to prevent osteomalacia, although rickets is rare)

Xanthines, such as:
Aminophylline
Caffeine
Oxtriphylline
Theophylline
> (concurrent use with primidone, because of the barbiturate metabolite, may increase metabolism of the xanthines [except dyphylline] by induction of hepatic microsomal enzymes, resulting in increased theophylline clearance)

Contraindications/Medical problems
The contraindications/medical problems included have been selected on the basis of their potential clinical significance (reasons given in parentheses where appropriate)—not necessarily inclusive (» = major clinical significance).

This medication should not be used when the following medical problem exists:

» Porphyria, acute intermittent or variegate, or history of
> (barbiturate metabolite of primidone may aggravate symptoms of porphyria by inducing enzymes responsible for porphyria synthesis)

Risk-benefit should be considered when the following medical problems exist:

Hepatic function impairment
> (possible systemic accumulation of barbiturate metabolite)

Hyperkinesia
> (may be precipitated or aggravated by primidone)

Renal function impairment
> (possible systemic accumulation of barbiturate metabolite)

» Respiratory diseases such as asthma, emphysema, or those involving dyspnea or obstruction
> (serious ventilatory depression may occur)

Sensitivity to primidone or barbiturates

Side/Adverse Effects

The following side/adverse effects have been selected on the basis of their potential clinical significance (possible signs and symptoms in parentheses where appropriate)—not necessarily inclusive:

Those indicating need for medical attention
Incidence less frequent
> *Paradoxical reaction* (unusual excitement or restlessness)—especially in children and the elderly

Incidence rare
> *Anemia, megaloblastic* (unusual tiredness or weakness); *skin rash*
>
> Note: *Megaloblastic anemia* may respond to folic acid without discontinuation of anticonvulsant therapy.

Signs of intolerance or overdose
> *Confusion; diplopia* (double vision); *nystagmus* (continuous, uncontrolled back-and-forth and/or rolling eye movements); *shortness of breath or troubled breathing*

Those indicating need for medical attention only if they continue or are bothersome
Incidence more frequent
> *Ataxia* (clumsiness or unsteadiness); *dizziness*

Incidence less frequent
> *Anorexia* (loss of appetite); *drowsiness; impotence* (decreased sexual ability); *mood or mental changes; nausea or vomiting*—usually decreases or disappears with continued use of medication

Patient Consultation

In providing consultation, consider emphasizing the following selected information (» = major clinical significance):

Before using this medication
» Conditions affecting use, especially:
> Sensitivity to primidone or barbiturates
> Pregnancy—Abnormalities similar to fetal hydantoin syndrome may occur; neonatal hemorrhaging may occur at delivery

Breast-feeding—Excreted in breast milk, causing drowsiness in the baby

Use in children—Paradoxical excitement and restlessness may occur

Use in the elderly—Paradoxical excitement and restlessness may occur

Use by athletes—Primidone is banned and, in some cases, tested for in competitors in biathlon and modern pentathlon events by the U.S. Olympic Committee (USOC)

Other medications, especially adrenocorticoids, anticoagulants, estrogens, estrogen-containing contraceptives, CNS depression-producing medications, other anticonvulsants, or monoamine oxidase inhibitors

Other medical problems, especially acute intermittent porphyria, or respiratory diseases

Proper use of this medication

» Compliance with therapy; taking every day in doses spaced as directed

Missed dose: Taking as soon as possible, unless within an hour of next scheduled dose; not doubling doses

» Proper storage

Precautions while using this medication

Regular visits to physician to check progress of therapy

Checking with physician before discontinuing medication; gradual dosage reduction may be needed

Caution if any kind of surgery, dental treatment, or emergency treatment is required

» Avoiding use of alcoholic beverages; not taking other CNS depressants unless prescribed by physician

» Possible drowsiness; caution when driving or doing other things requiring alertness

» Possible dizziness or lightheadedness; caution when getting up suddenly from a lying or sitting position

Caution if any laboratory tests required; possible interference with results of cyanocobalamin Co 57, metyrapone, or phentolamine tests.

Side/adverse effects

Signs of potential side effects, especially excitement or restlessness, allergic reaction, or megaloblastic anemia

General Dosing Information

Because primidone serum concentrations vary greatly among patients after oral administration, it is very important that the dosage be individualized. One of primidone's metabolites, phenobarbital, greatly influences its serum concentration, side effects, and interactions, as well as its therapeutic effect.

When primidone is to be discontinued, dosage should be reduced gradually. Abrupt withdrawal may precipitate status epilepticus.

When used with or to replace other anticonvulsant therapy, the dosage of primidone should be increased gradually while that of the other medication is maintained or decreased gradually in order to maintain seizure control. When therapy with primidone alone is the objective, the transition should not be completed in less than 2 weeks.

Many of the common side effects such as nausea, dizziness, and drowsiness diminish in frequency and intensity with continued use of the medication or reduction of dosage.

Diet/Nutrition

Patients on long-term anticonvulsant therapy have increased folate requirements. In addition, patients on long-term therapy may require vitamin D supplementation to prevent osteomalacia.

Oral Dosage Forms

PRIMIDONE ORAL SUSPENSION USP

Usual adult and adolescent dose:

Anticonvulsant—

Initial: Oral, 100 or 125 mg once a day at bedtime for the first three days, the daily dose being increased to 100 or 125 mg two times a day for the fourth, fifth, and sixth days, and then increased to 100 or 125 mg three times a day for the seventh, eighth, and ninth days. On the tenth day a maintenance dosage of 250 mg three times a day may be established and then adjusted according to patient needs and tolerance but not to exceed 2 grams a day.

Note: Initial doses as low as 25 mg twice a day have been used in patients experiencing troublesome nausea and vomiting.

Maintenance: Oral, 250 mg three or four times a day.

[Tremorlytic][1]—Oral, initially 50 to 62.5 mg a day, the dosage being increased as needed and tolerated up to a maximum of 750 mg a day.

Auxiliary labeling:
* Shake well.
* May cause drowsiness.
* Avoid alcoholic beverages.
* Do not freeze.

PRIMIDONE TABLETS USP

Usual adult and adolescent dose: Anticonvulsant—See *Primidone Oral Suspension USP.*

Auxiliary labeling:
* May cause drowsiness.
* Avoid alcoholic beverages.

PRIMIDONE CHEWABLE TABLETS

Usual adult and adolescent dose: Anticonvulsant—See *Primidone Oral Suspension USP.*

Auxiliary labeling:
* Chew tablets before swallowing
* May cause drowsiness.
* Avoid alcoholic beverages.

---

[1]Not included in Canadian product labeling.

PROBUCOL   Systemic

Some commonly used *brand names* are:
In the U.S.—
  Lorelco
In Canada—
  Lorelco
Other—
  Bifenabid   *Panesclerina*
  Lesterol   *Superlipid*
  Lurselle

ORAL
Probucol Tablets
  In the U.S. and Canada—*Lorelco*
  Other—*Bifenabid; Lesterol; Lurselle; Panesclerina; Superlipid*

Category: Antihyperlipidemic.

Indications

Accepted
Hyperlipidemia (treatment)—Probucol is recommended for use as an adjunct mainly in patients with primary hypercholesterolemia (type IIa hyperlipoproteinemia) and a significant risk of coronary artery disease, who have not responded to diet or other measures alone. Probucol reduces plasma cholesterol concentrations, but has a variable effect on serum triglyceride concentrations, and so is not useful in patients with elevated triglyceride concentrations alone. Its use is limited in other types of hyperlipidemia (including type IIb) because it may cause further elevation of triglycerides. Its main advantage over the anion exchange resins is its ease of administration and better acceptance and tolerance by the patient.

In the 1988 Report of the National Cholesterol Education Program Expert Panel on Detection, Evaluation, and Treatment of High Blood Cholesterol in Adults, the following guidelines for the treatment of high blood cholesterol are recommended:

Nonpharmacologic management (especially reduction in dietary intake of saturated fatty acids and cholesterol, weight reduction and exercise, and quitting smoking) is recommended first for all patients and as an adjunct to all pharmacologic cholesterol therapy.

If, after six months of diet therapy, adequate low-density lipoprotein (LDL)-cholesterol reduction is not achieved, then medication therapy is recommended to be added to diet therapy.

Initial medication therapy usually consists of a bile acid sequestrant (e.g., cholestyramine, colestipol) or niacin. A 3-hydroxy-3-methylglutanyl coenzyme A (HMG CoA) reductase inhibitor (e.g., lovastatin) should be considered after the bile acid sequestrants and niacin. Other lipid-lowering agents, including fibric acid derivatives (e.g., gemfibrozil and clofibrate) and probucol, are not as effective in lowering LDL cholesterol as the above mentioned medications. Two other agents, neomycin (not approved by FDA as a lipid-lowering agent) and dextrothyroxine are not recommended for general use because other medications are available that have a more favorable benefit/risk ratio.

If adequate LDL-cholesterol control is not achieved with initial medication therapy, it is recommended that the patient be switched to another medication or a combination of two medications with synergistic mechanisms of action. Although experience with such drug combinations is somewhat limited, pre-liminary studies indicate that the bile acid sequestrants given with either niacin, lovastatin, probucol, or gemfibrozil are useful in controlling LDL cholesterol. Lovastatin in combination with either niacin or gemfibrozil needs further study because of the potential increased risk of side effects.

If effective control of LDL cholesterol is not obtained after use of primary medications and medication combinations, then referral to a lipid specialist may be necessary.

Studies have suggested that control of elevated cholesterol and triglycerides may not lessen the danger of cardiovascular disease and mortality, although incidence of nonfatal myocardial infarctions may be decreased.

Pharmacology

Mechanism of action/Effect: Exact mechanism of action in reducing serum cholesterol concentrations is unknown, although it is thought to affect the early rather than the late stages of cholesterol biosynthesis. There may also be a slight inhibition of dietary absorption. Studies also indicate that probucol increases the rate of low-density lipoprotein (LDL) catabolism and clearance, which may account for the increased excretion of fecal bile acids. Recent information suggests that probucol may inhibit the oxidation and tissue deposition of LDL cholesterol, thereby inhibiting atherogenesis.

Time to peak effect: Maximal reduction in plasma cholesterol concentrations usually occurs within 20 to 50 days after initiation of probucol therapy, although a further decrease may occur gradually over several months. A clinical response usually occurs within 1 to 3 months.

Precautions to Consider

Geriatrics
No information is available on the relationship of age to the effects of probucol in geriatric patients.

Drug interactions and/or related problems
The following drug interactions and/or related problems have been selected on the basis of their potential clinical significance (possible mechanism in parentheses where appropriate)—not necessarily inclusive:

Antiarrhythmics with QT interval prolongation, such as:
  Amiodarone
  Bretylium
  Disopyramide
  Encainide
  Flecainide
  Indecainide
  Lidocaine
  Lorcainide
  Mexiletine
  Moricizine
  Procainamide
  Propafenone
  Quinidine
  Sotalol
  Tocainide, or
Antidepressants, tricyclic, or
Phenothiazines
    (additive QT interval prolongation may increase risk of ventricular tachycardia)

Beta-adrenergic blocking agents or
Digoxin
(the effect of beta-adrenergic blocking agents on the atrial rate
and the effect of digoxin on AV block can cause bradycardia;
when these medications are given in conjunction with a medication that prolongs the QT interval [i.e. probucol], the risk of
ventricular tachycardia may be increased)

Chenodiol or
Ursodiol
(effect may be decreased when chenodiol or ursodiol is used
concurrently with antihyperlipidemics since they tend to increase cholesterol saturation of bile)

Contraindications/Medical problems

The contraindications/medical problems included have been selected
on the basis of their potential clinical significance (reasons given
in parentheses where appropriate)—not necessarily inclusive (» =
major clinical significance).

*Except under special circumstances, this medication should not be
used when the following medical problems exist:*

» Primary biliary cirrhosis
(may further raise the cholesterol concentration)

» QT interval prolongation
(probucol may prolong QT interval)

*Risk-benefit should be considered when the following medical prob-
lems exist:*

Bradycardia, intrinsic, severe, or
Hypokalemia or
Hypomagnesemia
(the risk of ventricular tachycardia may be increased because
probucol prolongs the QT interval)

» Cardiac arrhythmias or evidence of recent or progressive myocardial damage
(condition may be exacerbated; probucol should be used only
with periodic electrocardiogram [ECG] monitoring)

» Congestive heart failure, unresponsive, or
Gallstones
(conditions may be exacerbated)

Hepatic function impairment
(higher blood levels of probucol may result)

Sensitivity to probucol

Side/Adverse Effects

Note: Prolongation of QT interval associated with serious arrhythmias
has been reported in patients treated with probucol.

The following side/adverse effects have been selected on the basis of
their potential clinical significance (possible signs and symptoms
in parentheses where appropriate)—not necessarily inclusive:

Those indicating need for medical attention
Incidence more frequent
Eosinophilia; QT interval prolongation (dizziness or fainting)
Incidence rare
Anemia (unusual tiredness or weakness); *angioneurotic edema*
(swellings on face, hands, or feet, or in mouth); *tachycardia* (fast
or irregular heartbeat)—a result of QT interval prolongation; *throm-
bocytopenia* (unusual bleeding or bruising)

**Those indicating need for medical attention only if they continue
or are bothersome**
Incidence more frequent
Gastrointestinal irritation (bloating, diarrhea, nausea and vomit-
ing, stomach pain)
Note: *Gastrointestinal irritation* is usually transient and mild.

Incidence less frequent
*Dizziness; headache; numbness or tingling of fingers, toes, or
face*

Patient Consultation

In providing consultation, consider emphasizing the following selected information (» = major clinical significance):

Before using this medication
Diet as preferred therapy; importance of following prescribed diet
» Conditions affecting use, especially:
Sensitivity to probucol
Breast-feeding—Use not recommended because of potentially
serious adverse effects on nursing infants
Use in children—Not recommended in children under 2 years
of age since cholesterol is required for normal development
Other medical problems, especially primary biliary cirrhosis,
and cardiac abnormalities including congestive heart failure
and QT interval prolongation

Proper use of this medication
» Importance of not taking more or less medication than the amount
prescribed
This medication does not cure the condition but rather helps con-
trol it
» Compliance with prescribed diet
Taking with meals, since medication is more effective with food
Missed dose: Taking as soon as possible; not taking if almost time
for next dose; not doubling doses
» Proper storage

Precautions while using this medication
» Importance of close monitoring by the physician
» Checking with physician before discontinuing medication; blood
lipid concentrations may increase significantly

Side/adverse effects
Signs of potential side effects, especially angioneurotic edema,
blood dyscrasias, QT interval prolongation, and tachycardia

General Dosing Information

If unexplained or cardiovascular-related syncope occurs, probucol
therapy should be withdrawn and ECG monitored.

If response is inadequate after 4 months of treatment, probucol therapy
should be re-evaluated and possibly withdrawn, except in the case
of xanthoma tuberosum, which may require up to 1 year of treatment as long as reduction in size and/or number of xanthomata
occurs.

When probucol is discontinued, an appropriate hypolipidemic diet and
monitoring of serum lipids are recommended until the patient stabilizes, since a rise in serum cholesterol concentrations to or above
the original base may occur.

Diet/Nutrition
It is recommended that probucol be taken with food to maximize
absorption.

Oral Dosage Forms

PROBUCOL TABLETS

Usual adult dose: Oral, 500 mg two times a day with the morning and
evening meals.

Auxiliary labeling: • Take with meals.

PROCAINAMIDE   Systemic

Some commonly used *brand names* are:

In the U.S.—
   Procan SR   *Pronestyl*
   Promine   *Pronestyl-SR*
In Canada—
   Procan SR   *Pronestyl-SR*
   Pronestyl

ORAL

Procainamide Hydrochloride Capsules USP
   In the U.S.—*Promine; Pronestyl;* GENERIC
   In Canada—*Pronestyl;* GENERIC
Procainamide Hydrochloride Tablets USP†
   In the U.S.—*Pronestyl;* GENERIC
Procainamide Hydrochloride Extended-release Tablets USP
   In the U.S.—*Procan SR; Pronestyl-SR;* GENERIC
   In Canada—*Procan SR; Pronestyl-SR*

PARENTERAL

Procainamide Hydrochloride Injection USP
   In the U.S.—*Pronestyl;* GENERIC
   In Canada—*Pronestyl*

   †Not commercially available in Canada.

Category: Antiarrhythmic.

Indications

Accepted
Cardiac arrhythmias (prophylaxis and treatment)—Procainamide is indicated in the treatment and control of atrial fibrillation, paroxysmal atrial tachycardia, premature ventricular contractions, and ventricular tachycardia. Parenteral procainamide is also indicated for treatment of ventricular extrasystoles and cardiac arrhythmias associated with anesthesia and surgery.

Pharmacology

Mechanism of action/Effect: Direct cardiac effect—Decreases excitability, conduction velocity, automaticity, and membrane responsiveness with prolonged refractory period. No effect on contractility or cardiac output unless myocardial damage present. Larger doses may induce atrioventricular (AV) block. In the Vaughan Williams classification of antiarrhythmics, procainamide is considered to be a Class I antiarrhythmic.

Other actions/effects: Relatively weak anticholinergic action diminishes vagal transmission, resulting in increased heart rate, usually with higher dosages. Alpha-adrenergic blockade does not occur. Also causes peripheral vasodilation.

Time to peak effect:
   Oral—60 to 90 minutes.
   Intravenous—Immediately.
   Intramuscular—15 to 60 minutes.

Precautions to Consider

Cross-sensitivity and/or related problems
Patients sensitive to procaine or other related agents may be sensitive to procainamide also.

Geriatrics
Although appropriate studies with procainamide have not been performed in the geriatric population, elderly patients may be more prone to hypotension, especially with parenteral use or when very high doses are taken. In addition, elderly patients are more likely to have age-related renal function impairment, which may require lower doses in patients receiving procainamide.

Dental
The leukopenic and thrombocytopenic effects of procainamide may result in an increased incidence of microbial infection, delayed healing, and gingival bleeding. If leukopenia or thrombocytopenia occurs, dental work should be deferred until blood counts have returned to normal, and patients should be instructed in proper oral hygiene, including caution in use of regular toothbrushes, dental floss, and toothpicks.

The secondary anticholinergic effects of procainamide may decrease or inhibit salivary flow, especially in middle-aged or elderly patients, thus contributing to the development of caries, periodontal disease, oral candidiasis, and discomfort.

Drug interactions and/or related problems
The following drug interactions and/or related problems have been selected on the basis of their potential clinical significance (possible mechanism in parentheses where appropriate)—not necessarily inclusive (» = major clinical significance):

Note: Combinations containing any of the following medications, depending on the amount present, may also interact with this medication.

» Antiarrhythmics, other
      (concurrent use with procainamide may produce additive cardiac effects)

Anticholinergics, especially atropine or related compounds, or
Antidyskinetics or
Antihistamines
      (concurrent use with procainamide may intensify atropine-like side effects because of the secondary anticholinergic activities of procainamide; patients should be advised to report occurrence of gastrointestinal problems promptly since paralytic ileus may occur with concurrent therapy)

» Antihypertensives
      (concurrent use with procainamide, especially intravenous procainamide, may produce additive hypotensive effects)

» Antimyasthenics
      (neuromuscular blocking action and/or secondary anticholinergic activity of procainamide may antagonize the effect of antimyasthenics on skeletal muscle; dosage adjustments of antimyasthenics may be necessary to control symptoms of myasthenia gravis)

Bethanechol
      (concurrent use with procainamide may antagonize the cholinergic effects of bethanechol)

Bone marrow depressants
      (concurrent use of procainamide with these medications may increase the leukopenic and/or thrombocytopenic effects; if concurrent use is required, close observation for toxic effects should be considered)

Bretylium
      (concurrent administration may counteract inotropic effect of bretylium and potentiate hypotension)

» Neuromuscular blocking agents
      (effects of these medications may be prolonged or enhanced when they are used concurrently with procainamide; careful postoperative monitoring of the patient may be necessary following concurrent or sequential use, especially if there is a possibility of incomplete reversal of neuromuscular blockade)

» Pimozide
(concurrent use with procainamide may potentiate cardiac arrhythmias, which are seen on electrocardiogram [ECG] as prolongation of QT interval)

Contraindications/Medical problems
The contraindications/medical problems included have been selected on the basis of their potential clinical significance (reasons given in parentheses where appropriate)—not necessarily inclusive (» = major clinical significance).

Except under special circumstances, this medication should not be used when the following medical problems exist:
» Atrioventricular (AV) block, complete, and also 2nd and 3rd degree AV block unless controlled by electrical pacemaker (risk of additive cardiac depression)

Risk-benefit should be considered when the following medical problems exist:
» AV block or
» Bundle branch block or
» Digitalis intoxication, severe
(risk of additive cardiac depression and ventricular asystole or fibrillation)
Bronchial asthma
(possible hypersensitivity)
» Congestive heart failure or
Hepatic function impairment or
» Renal function impairment
(possible accumulation leading to toxicity; lower doses may be required in patients with congestive heart failure or renal function impairment)
» Lupus erythematosus, history of
(procainamide may precipitate active lupus)
» Myasthenia gravis
(procainamide may increase muscle weakness)
Sensitivity to procainamide
» Ventricular tachycardia during an occlusive coronary episode

Side/Adverse Effects

Note: Tachycardia may occur at high plasma procainamide concentrations as a reflex sympathetic response to the hypotensive effect, due to the anticholinergic effect on the atrioventricular (AV) node, or in response to slowing of the atrial rate in treatment of atrial fibrillation. Tachycardia is especially hazardous in patients with myocardial damage, because of the risk of emboli. Adequate digitalization reduces, but does not abolish, the risk.

Intravenous administration may cause a transient but sometimes severe reduction in blood pressure, especially in conscious patients. Hypotension is less frequent with intramuscular administration and rare with oral use (except with excessive doses).

Ventricular asystole or fibrillation may occur, especially with too-rapid intravenous administration or excessive doses; death has occurred rarely.

The following side/adverse effects have been selected on the basis of their potential clinical significance (possible signs and symptoms in parentheses where appropriate)—not necessarily inclusive:

Those indicating need for medical attention
Incidence less frequent
Allergic reaction or systemic lupus erythematosus (SLE)-like syndrome (fever and chills, joint pain or swelling, pains with breathing, skin rash or itching)
Note: After extended maintenance therapy nearly 80% of patients treated show an increased titer of antinuclear antibodies (an early sign of developing SLE), often within 1 to 12 months

of commencing therapy. Nearly 30% of these patients develop clinical symptoms that resemble SLE. This *SLE-like condition* is usually reversible with discontinuation of procainamide therapy.

Incidence rare
Central nervous system (CNS) effects (confusion, hallucinations, mental depression); *Coombs' positive hemolytic anemia* (unusual tiredness or weakness); *leukopenia (neutropenia) and possible agranulocytosis, which may be fatal* (fever or sore mouth, gums, or throat); *thrombocytopenia* (unusual bleeding or bruising)
Note: *Coombs' positive hemolytic anemia* may be related to the SLE-like syndrome.
Leukopenia may be more likely to occur with use of the extended-release dosage form, especially after cardiovascular surgery. Leukopenia usually occurs within the first 3 months of therapy, and counts recover within a few weeks after procainamide is withdrawn. Leukopenia also may occur in association with the SLE-like syndrome.
Thrombocytopenia may be related to the SLE-like syndrome.

Signs and symptoms of overdose
Confusion; decrease in urination; dizziness, severe, or fainting; drowsiness; fast or irregular heartbeat; nausea and vomiting

Those indicating need for medical attention only if they continue or are bothersome
Incidence more frequent, especially with daily doses > 4 grams
Diarrhea; loss of appetite
Incidence less frequent
Dizziness or lightheadedness

Patient Consultation

Consider advising the patient on the following:

Before using this medication
See *Precautions to Consider.*

Proper use of this medication
» Taking exactly as directed even if feeling well
Taking on empty stomach for faster absorption, or with food or milk to reduce stomach irritation
Proper administration of extended-release tablets: Swallowing tablets whole, without breaking, crushing, or chewing
» Importance of not missing doses and of taking at evenly spaced intervals
Missed dose: Taking as soon as possible if remembered within 2 hours (4 hours for extended-release tablets); not taking if remembered later; not doubling doses
» Proper storage

Precautions while using this medication
Regular visits to physician to check progress
» Checking with physician before discontinuing medication; gradual dosage reduction may be necessary to avoid worsening of condition
» Caution if any kind of surgery (including dental surgery) or emergency treatment is required
Carrying medical identification card or bracelet
» Possibility of dizziness with high dosage, especially in elderly; caution when driving or doing things requiring alertness
Caution if any laboratory tests required; possible interference with test results

Side/adverse effects
Signs of potential side effects, especially allergic reaction, SLE-like syndrome, CNS effects, Coombs' positive hemolytic anemia, leukopenia, and thrombocytopenia
Extended-release tablet matrix may be seen in stool and is to be expected

General Dosing Information

Dosage must be adjusted to meet the individual requirements of each patient, on the basis of clinical response.

Procainamide therapy should be withdrawn if signs or symptoms of systemic lupus erythematosus (SLE)-like syndrome, leukopenia, or hemolytic anemia occur.

For oral dosage forms only

A period of 3 to 4 hours should elapse after the last intravenous dose before administration of the first oral dose.

For parenteral dosage forms only

Procainamide Hydrochloride Injection USP is always diluted before intravenous administration.

Intravenous administration should be limited to hospitals where monitoring facilities are available.

Intramuscular injection is usually used only when the oral or intravenous routes are not feasible.

Procainamide intravenous injection should be administered at a rate not exceeding 50 mg per minute.

Because hypotension may develop rapidly during intravenous administration, it is highly recommended that blood pressure be monitored continuously, with the patient in a supine position. Phenylephrine and norepinephrine injections should be available to counteract severe hypotension.

Diet/Nutrition

Oral procainamide should preferably be taken with a glass of water on an empty stomach (either 1 hour before or 2 hours after meals) for faster absorption; however, it may be taken with meals or immediately after meals to lessen gastrointestinal irritation.

Oral Dosage Forms

PROCAINAMIDE HYDROCHLORIDE CAPSULES USP

Usual adult dose:
Atrial arrhythmias—
Initial: Oral, 1.25 grams, followed in one hour by 750 mg if necessary; then 500 mg to 1 gram every two or three hours as needed and tolerated.
Maintenance: Oral, 500 mg to 1 gram every four to six hours, the dosage being adjusted as needed and tolerated.
Ventricular arrhythmias—Oral, 1 gram initially; then 50 mg per kg of body weight per day in eight divided doses (every three hours), the dosage being adjusted as needed and tolerated according to patient weight:

As a general guide, patients of different body size might require the following doses every three hours in order to receive 50 mg of procainamide per kg of body weight per day—

Weight (kg)	Dose (mg)
<55	250
55–91	375
>91	500

Note: The initial loading doses as stated above are not used often. Oral procainamide is used more often at maintenance dosage following conversion of arrhythmias.

Geriatric patients may be more sensitive to the hypotensive effects of the usual adult dose.

Usual adult prescribing limits: Maintenance—Up to 6 grams daily.

Auxiliary labeling:
• Keep container tightly closed.
• Do not take other medicines without your doctor's advice.

PROCAINAMIDE HYDROCHLORIDE TABLETS USP

Note: Procainamide hydrochloride tablets are not commercially available in Canada.

Usual adult dose:
Atrial arrhythmias—
Initial: Oral, 1.25 grams, followed in one hour by 750 mg if necessary; then 500 mg to 1 gram every two or three hours as needed and tolerated.
Maintenance: Oral, 500 mg to 1 gram every four to six hours, the dosage being adjusted as needed and tolerated.
Ventricular arrhythmias—Oral, 1 gram initially; then 50 mg per kg of body weight per day in eight divided doses (every three hours), the dosage being adjusted as needed and tolerated according to patient weight:

As a general guide, patients of different body size might require the following doses every three hours in order to receive 50 mg of procainamide per kg of body weight per day—

Weight (kg)	Dose (mg)
<55	250
55–91	375
>91	500

Note: The initial loading doses as stated above are not used often. Oral procainamide is used more often at maintenance dosage following conversion of arrhythmias.

Geriatric patients may be more sensitive to the hypotensive effects of the usual adult dose.

Auxiliary labeling:
• Keep container tightly closed.
• Do not take other medicines without your doctor's advice.

PROCAINAMIDE HYDROCHLORIDE EXTENDED-RELEASE TABLETS USP

Usual adult dose:
Atrial arrhythmias—Maintenance: Oral, 1 gram every six hours, the dosage being adjusted as needed and tolerated.
Ventricular arrhythmias—Maintenance: Oral, 50 mg per kg of body weight per day in four divided doses (every six hours), the dosage being adjusted as needed and tolerated according to patient weight:

As a general guide, patients of different body sizes might require the following doses every six hours in order to receive 50 mg of procainamide per kg of body weight per day—

Weight (kg)	Dose (mg)
< 55	500
55–91	750
>91	1000

Note: The extended-release dosage form is intended for maintenance dosage, and not for initial dosage.

Geriatric patients may be more sensitive to the hypotensive effects of the usual adult dose.

Usual adult prescribing limits: Maintenance—Up to 6 grams daily.

Auxiliary labeling:
• Keep container tightly closed.
• Do not take other medicines without your doctor's advice.
• Swallow tablets whole.

Parenteral Dosage Forms

PROCAINAMIDE HYDROCHLORIDE INJECTION USP

Usual adult dose:
Intramuscular—500 mg to 1 gram every four to eight hours.
Intravenous—
Initial:
Intravenous (direct), 100 mg (diluted in an appropriate volume of 5% dextrose injection to facilitate control of dosage rate) administered slowly (not exceeding 50 mg per minute) and repeated every five minutes until arrhythmia is controlled or up to a maximum total dose of 1 gram, or
Intravenous infusion, 500 to 600 mg diluted and administered at a constant rate over a period of twenty-five to thirty minutes.
Maintenance: Intravenous infusion, diluted and administered at a rate of 2 to 6 mg per minute to maintain control of arrhythmia.

PROCARBAZINE   Systemic

Some commonly used *brand names* are:
In the U.S.—*Matulane*
In Canada—*Natulan*

ORAL
Procarbazine Hydrochloride Capsules USP
In the U.S.—*Matulane*
In Canada—*Natulan*

Category: Antineoplastic.

Indications

Note: Bracketed information in the *Indications* section refers to uses not included in U.S. product labeling.

Accepted
Lymphomas, Hodgkin's (treatment); or
[Lymphomas, non-Hodgkin's (treatment)][1]—Procarbazine is indicated, in combination with other agents, for treatment of Hodgkin's disease (Stage III and IV) and some non-Hodgkin's lymphomas.
[Tumors, brain, primary (treatment)][1]; or
[Carcinoma, lung (treatment)][1]—Procarbazine is used for treatment of brain tumors and bronchogenic carcinoma.
[Malignant melanoma (treatment)][1]—Procarbazine is used for treatment of malignant melanoma.
[Multiple myeloma (treatment)][1]—Procarbazine is used for treatment of multiple myeloma.
[Polycythemia vera (treatment)][1]—Procarbazine is used for treatment of polycythemia vera.

[1]Not included in Canadian product labeling.

Pharmacology

Mechanism of action/Effect: Procarbazine is an alkylating agent and a monoamine oxidase (MAO) inhibitor. Procarbazine causes weak inhibition of monoamine oxidase (MAO). The exact mechanism of antineoplastic action is unknown but is thought to resemble that of the alkylating agents; procarbazine is cell cycle-specific for the S phase of cell division. Procarbazine is thought to inhibit DNA, RNA, and protein synthesis.

Other actions/effects: MAO inhibitors prevent the inactivation of tyramine by hepatic and gastrointestinal monoamine oxidase. Tyramine in the bloodstream releases norepinephrine from the sympathetic nerve terminals and produces a sudden increase in blood pressure.

Precautions to Consider

Geriatrics
Although appropriate studies with procarbazine have not been performed in the geriatric population, the potential for increased vascular accidents (especially in the event of sudden hypertensive episodes), increased sensitivity to hypotensive effects, and reduced metabolic capacity discourages the first-time use of MAO inhibitors in patients over 60 years of age. When an MAO inhibitor is prescribed for an elderly patient, the patient's history of depression, ability to comply with prescribing instructions, and any potential drug interactions must also be considered. In addition, elderly patients are more likely to have age-related renal function impairment, which may require a lower dosage or, in severe cases, avoidance of use of procarbazine.

Dental
The bone marrow depressant effects of procarbazine may result in an increased incidence of microbial infection, delayed healing, and gingival bleeding. Dental work, whenever possible, should be completed prior to initiation of therapy or deferred until blood counts have returned to normal. Patients should be instructed in proper oral hygiene during treatment, including caution in use of regular toothbrushes, dental floss, and toothpicks.
Procarbazine may also cause stomatitis associated with considerable discomfort.
The secondary anticholinergic effects of procarbazine may decrease or inhibit salivary flow, especially in middle-aged or elderly patients, thus contributing to the development of caries, periodontal disease, oral candidiasis, and discomfort.

Drug interactions and/or related problems
The following drug interactions and/or related problems have been selected on the basis of their potential clinical significance (possible mechanism in parentheses where appropriate)—not necessarily inclusive (» = major clinical significance):
Note: Combinations containing any of the following medications, depending on the amount present, may also interact with this medication.

Most drug interactions are due to procarbazine's monoamine oxidase-inhibiting activity.

» Alcohol
(concurrent use with procarbazine may result in a disulfiram-like reaction and additive central nervous system (CNS) depression and postural hypotension; also, possible tyramine content in alcoholic beverages, especially beer, wine, or ale, may induce hypertensive reactions)

» Anesthetics, local, with epinephrine or levonordefrin, or
» Cocaine
(concurrent use with procarbazine may cause severe hypertension due to sympathomimetic effects)

(cocaine should not be administered during or within 14 days following administration of an MAO inhibitor)

» Anesthetics, spinal

(hypotensive effects may be potentiated when spinal anesthetics are used concurrently with procarbazine; discontinuation of procarbazine at least 10 days before elective surgery if spinal anesthesia is planned may be advisable)

» Anticholinergics or other medications with anticholinergic activity or

Antidyskinetic agents or

» Antihistamines

(concurrent use with procarbazine may intensify anticholinergic effects because of the secondary anticholinergic activities of MAO inhibitors; also, MAO inhibitors may block detoxification of anticholinergics, thus potentiating their action; patients should be advised to report occurrence of gastrointestinal problems promptly since paralytic ileus may occur with concurrent therapy)

(concurrent use with MAO inhibitors may also prolong and intensify CNS depressant and anticholinergic effects of antihistamines; concurrent use is not recommended)

Anticoagulants, coumarin- and indandione-derivative

(concurrent use may increase anticoagulant activity; although the mechanism of action and clinical significance are unknown, caution is recommended)

Anticonvulsants

(concurrent use of anticonvulsants with procarbazine may lead to increased CNS depressant effects as well as a change in the pattern of epileptiform seizures; dosage adjustment of anticonvulsant may be necessary)

» Antidepressants, tricyclic

(in addition to increased anticholinergic effects, concurrent use with procarbazine may result in hyperpyretic crises, severe convulsions, and death; however, recent studies have shown that some tricyclic antidepressants can be used concurrently with MAO inhibitors with no adverse effects if both medications are initiated simultaneously at lower than usual doses and the doses raised gradually, or if the MAO inhibitor is gradually added to the tricyclic also at low doses; tricyclics should not be added to an established MAO inhibitor regimen; careful monitoring for side effects of either medication is necessary)

» Antidiabetic agents, oral, or

» Insulin

(procarbazine may enhance hypoglycemic effects; dosage reduction of hypoglycemic medication may be necessary during and after such combined therapy)

Antihypertensives or
Diuretics or
Hypotension-producing medications, other

(concurrent use with procarbazine may result in an enhanced hypotensive effect; dosage adjustment may be necessary)

(antihypertensives with CNS depressant effects, such as clonidine, guanabenz, methyldopa, or metyrosine, may increase CNS depression)

Beta-adrenergic blocking agents, including ophthalmic beta-blockers absorbed systemically

(possible significant hypertension may theoretically occur up to 14 days following discontinuation of procarbazine; however, sufficient clinical reports are lacking)

Blood dyscrasia-causing medications

(leukopenic and/or thrombocytopenic effects of procarbazine may be increased with concurrent or recent therapy if these medications cause the same effects; dosage adjustment of procarbazine, if necessary, should be based on blood counts)

» Bone marrow depressants, other or
Radiation therapy

(additive bone marrow depression may occur; dosage reduction may be required when two or more bone marrow depressants, including radiation, are used concurrently or consecutively)

Bromocriptine

(concurrent use may increase serum prolactin concentrations and interfere with effects of bromocriptine; dosage adjustment of bromocriptine may be necessary)

» Buspirone

(concurrent use with MAO inhibitors is not recommended because elevation of blood pressure may occur)

» Caffeine-containing preparations

(concurrent use of excessive amounts of caffeine, consumed in chocolate, coffee, cola, tea, or "stay awake" products, with procarbazine may produce dangerous cardiac arrhythmias or severe hypertension because of sympathomimetic effects of caffeine)

» Carbamazepine or
» Cyclobenzaprine or
» Maprotiline or
» Monoamine oxidase (MAO) inhibitors, other, including furazolidone and pargyline

(concurrent use with procarbazine is not recommended on an outpatient basis, as hyperpyretic crises, severe seizures, and death could result; prior to initiation of procarbazine therapy, 14 days should elapse after discontinuance of one of these medications)

» CNS depression-producing medications, other

(CNS depression and postural hypotension may be enhanced; concurrent use with antihistamines is not recommended)

» Dextromethorphan

(concurrent use with procarbazine may cause excitation, hypertension, and hyperpyrexia)

» Doxapram

(concurrent use may increase the pressor effects of either doxapram or procarbazine)

» Fluoxetine

(concurrent use may result in confusion, agitation, restlessness, and gastrointestinal symptoms, or possibly hyperpyretic episodes, severe convulsions, and hypertensive crises. Based on experience with tricyclic antidepressants, at least 14 days should elapse between discontinuation of an MAO inhibitor and initiation of fluoxetine. However, because of the long half-lives of fluoxetine and its active metabolite, at least 5 weeks [approximately 5 half-lives of norfluoxetine] should elapse between discontinuation of fluoxetine and initiation of therapy with an MAO inhibitor. Administration of an MAO inhibitor within 5 weeks of discontinuation of fluoxetine may increase the risk of serious events. While a causal relationship to fluoxetine has not been established, death has been reported following the initiation of an MAO inhibitor shortly after fluoxetine administration was stopped)

» Guanadrel or
» Guanethidine or
» Rauwolfia alkaloids

(administration to patients receiving procarbazine may result in sudden release of accumulated catecholamines and a hypertensive reaction; parenteral administration is not recommended during and for 1 week following procarbazine therapy)

(when an MAO inhibitor is added to existing therapy with a rauwolfia alkaloid, serious potentiation of CNS depressant effects may result; however, if a rauwolfia alkaloid is added to an MAO inhibitor regimen, CNS excitation and hypertension may result from release of excessive amounts of accumulated norepinephrine and serotonin)

Haloperidol or
Loxapine or
Molindone or
Phenothiazines or
Pimozide or
Thioxanthenes
    (concurrent use may prolong and intensify the sedative, hypo-
    tensive, and anticholinergic effects of either these medications
    or procarbazine)

» Levodopa
    (concurrent use with MAO inhibitors is not recommended, as
    the combination may result in sudden moderate to severe hy-
    pertensive crisis; a period of 2 to 4 weeks is recommended
    after withdrawal of MAO inhibitors before levodopa is admin-
    istered)

» Meperidine and possibly other opioid (narcotic) analgesics
    (concurrent use with procarbazine may produce immediate ex-
    citation, sweating, rigidity, and severe hypertension; in some
    patients, hypotension, severe respiratory depression, coma, con-
    vulsions, hyperpyrexia, vascular collapse, and death may oc-
    cur; reactions may be due to accumulation of serotonin result-
    ing from MAO inhibition; avoidance of meperidine use within
    2 to 3 weeks following procarbazine is recommended; other
    opioid analgesics, such as morphine, are not likely to cause
    such severe reactions and may be used cautiously in reduced
    dosage in patients receiving MAO inhibitors; however, it is
    recommended that a small test dose [one-quarter of the usual
    dose] or several small incremental test doses over a period of
    several hours should first be administered to permit observa-
    tion of any adverse effects)

    (caution is also recommended in the use of alfentanil, fentanyl,
    or sufentanil as an adjunct to anesthesia if the patient has
    received procarbazine within 14 days; although the risk of a
    significant interaction has been questioned, the use of a small
    test dose is advised to detect any possible interaction)

» Methyldopa
    (concurrent use with procarbazine may cause hyperexcitability;
    also headache, severe hypertension, and hallucinations have
    been reported)

» Methylphenidate
    (concurrent use with procarbazine may potentiate the CNS
    stimulant effects of methylphenidate, possibly resulting in a
    hypertensive crisis; should not be administered during or within
    14 days following the administration of procarbazine)

Metrizamide
    (concurrent use with procarbazine may lower the seizure thresh-
    old; procarbazine should be discontinued at least 48 hours be-
    fore myelography and should not be resumed for at least 24
    hours after procedure)

Phenylephrine, nasal or ophthalmic
    (if significant systemic absorption of nasal or ophthalmic phe-
    nylephrine occurs, concurrent use with procarbazine may po-
    tentiate pressor effects; these medications should not be admin-
    istered during or within 14 days following the administration
    of procarbazine)

» Sympathomimetics
    (concurrent use with procarbazine may prolong and intensify
    cardiac stimulant and vasopressor effects [including headache,
    cardiac arrhythmias, vomiting, sudden and severe hypertension
    and hyperpyretic crises] of these medications because of re-
    lease of catecholamines which accumulate in intraneuronal stor-
    age sites during MAO inhibitor therapy; these medications
    should not be administered during or within 14 days following
    the administration of procarbazine)

» Tryptophan
    (concurrent use with MAO inhibitors may cause hyperreflexia,
    shivering, hyperventilation, hyperthermia, mania or hypoma-
    nia, and disorientation or confusion; when tryptophan is added

to an MAOI regimen, it should be started in low dosages and
the dose titrated upwards gradually with close monitoring of
mental status and blood pressure)

» Tyramine- or other high pressor amine-containing foods and bev-
    erages, such as aged cheese; beer; reduced-alcohol and alco-
    hol-free beer and wine; red and white wines; sherry; liqueurs;
    yeast/protein extracts; fava or broad bean pods; smoked or
    pickled meats, poultry, or fish; fermented sausage (bologna,
    pepperoni, salami, summer sausage) or other fermented meat;
    and any overripe fruit
    (concurrent use with procarbazine may cause sudden and se-
    vere hypertensive reactions; reactions are usually limited to a
    few hours and easily treated with phentolamine; severity de-
    pends on amount of tyramine ingested, rate of gastric empty-
    ing, and length of interval between dose of procarbazine and
    ingestion of tyramine; when procarbazine is discontinued, di-
    etary restrictions must continue for at least 2 weeks; other
    tyramine- or high pressor amine-containing foods, such as yo-
    gurt, sour cream, cream cheese, cottage cheese, chocolate, and
    soy sauce, if eaten when fresh and in moderation, are consid-
    ered unlikely to cause serious problems)

Vaccines, killed virus
    (because normal defense mechanisms may be suppressed by
    procarbazine therapy, the patient's antibody response to the
    vaccine may be decreased. The interval between discontinua-
    tion of medications that cause immunosuppression and restora-
    tion of the patient's ability to respond to the vaccine depends
    on the intensity and type of immunosuppression-causing medi-
    cation used, the underlying disease, and other factors; esti-
    mates vary from 3 months to 1 year)

» Vaccines, live virus
    (because normal defense mechanisms may be suppressed by
    procarbazine therapy, concurrent use with a live virus vaccine
    may potentiate the replication of the vaccine virus, may in-
    crease the side/adverse effects of the vaccine virus, and/or may
    decrease the patient's antibody response to the vaccine; immu-
    nization of these patients should be undertaken only with ex-
    treme caution after careful review of the patient's hematologic
    status and only with the knowledge and consent of the physi-
    cian managing the procarbazine therapy. The interval between
    discontinuation of medications that cause immunosuppression
    and restoration of the patient's ability to respond to the vaccine
    depends on the intensity and type of immunosuppression-caus-
    ing medication used, the underlying disease, and other factors;
    estimates vary from 3 months to 1 year. Patients with leukemia
    in remission should not receive live virus vaccine until at least
    3 months after their last chemotherapy. Immunization with oral
    poliovirus vaccine should also be postponed in persons in close
    contact with the patient, especially family members)

Contraindications/Medical problems
The contraindications/medical problems included have been selected
    on the basis of their potential clinical significance (reasons given
    in parentheses where appropriate)—not necessarily inclusive (» =
    major clinical significance).

*Except under special circumstances, this medication should not be
used when the following medical problems exist:*

» Alcoholism, active

» Congestive heart failure

» Hepatic function impairment, severe
    (procarbazine may precipitate hepatic precoma in patients with
    cirrhosis, who are extremely sensitive to effects)

» Pheochromocytoma
    (pressor substances secreted by such tumors may alter blood
    pressure during therapy with MAO inhibitors)

» Renal function impairment, severe
    (cumulative effects of procarbazine may occur because of re-
    duced renal excretion)

Risk-benefit should be considered when the following medical problems exist:

- » Bone marrow depression
- » Cardiac arrhythmias
- » Cardiovascular disease or coronary insufficiency
      (ischemia may be aggravated as a result of reduced blood pressure)
    Cerebrovascular disease
      (cerebral ischemia may be aggravated as a result of reduced blood pressure)
- » Chickenpox, existing or recent (including recent exposure), or
- » Herpes zoster
      (risk of severe generalized disease)
    Diabetes mellitus
      (procarbazine may alter insulin or oral hypoglycemic requirements)
    Epilepsy
      (pattern of epileptiform seizures may be changed)
- » Headaches, severe or frequent
      (headache as a first sign of hypertensive reaction during therapy may be masked)
- » Hepatic function impairment
      (procarbazine may precipitate hepatic precoma in patients with cirrhosis, who are extremely sensitive to effects; lower dosage is recommended; use not recommended in severe function impairment)
    Hyperthyroidism
      (sensitivity to pressor amines may be increased)
- » Infection
- » Paranoid schizophrenia or other hyperexcitable personality states
      (MAO inhibitors may cause excessive stimulation in schizophrenic patients; in manic-depressive states, may effect a swing from depressive to manic phase)
    Parkinsonism
      (may be aggravated)
- » Renal function impairment
      (cumulative effects may occur; lower dosage is recommended; use not recommended in severe function impairment)
    Sensitivity to procarbazine
- » Caution should be used also in patients who have had previous cytotoxic drug therapy or radiation therapy.
- » In addition, caution should be used in patients who have undergone sympathectomy, who may be more sensitive to the hypotensive effects of MAO inhibitors.

Side/Adverse Effects

Note: Many "side effects" of antineoplastic therapy are unavoidable and represent the medication's pharmacologic action. Some of these (for example, leukopenia and thrombocytopenia) are actually used as parameters to aid in individual dosage titration.

Except for hematologic, pulmonary, and gastrointestinal toxicity, adverse effects of procarbazine resemble those of the MAO inhibitors used in treating psychiatric disorders.

Toxicity is increased in patients with renal or hepatic function impairment or bone marrow depression.

The following side/adverse effects have been selected on the basis of their potential clinical significance (possible signs and symptoms in parentheses where appropriate)—not necessarily inclusive:

Those indicating need for medical attention
Incidence more frequent
   Anemia; CNS stimulation, excessive (confusion, convulsions, hallucinations); *immunosuppression, infection, or leukopenia* (usually asymptomatic; less frequently, fever or chills, cough or hoarseness, lower back or side pain, painful or difficult urination); *thrombocytopenia* (usually asymptomatic; less frequently, unusual bleeding or bruising; black, tarry stools; blood in urine or stools; pinpoint red spots on skin); *hemolytic anemia* (continuing tiredness or weakness); *missing menstrual periods; pneumonitis* (cough, shortness of breath, thickening of bronchial secretions)
   Note: With *leukopenia* and *thrombocytopenia,* the nadir of the platelet count occurs after about 4 weeks, followed by the leukocyte count, with recovery complete in about 6 weeks.
      Missing menstrual periods occur with high doses.
Incidence less frequent
   Gastrointestinal toxicity (diarrhea); *hepatotoxicity* (yellow eyes or skin); *peripheral neuropathy* (tingling or numbness of fingers or toes, unsteadiness or awkwardness); *stomatitis* (sores in mouth and on lips)
Incidence rare
   Allergic reaction (skin rash, hives or itching; wheezing); *hypertensive crisis* (severe chest pain; enlarged pupils; fast or slow heartbeat; severe headache; increased sensitivity of eyes to light; increased sweating, possibly with fever or cold, clammy skin; stiff or sore neck); *orthostatic hypotension* (fainting)

Those indicating need for medical attention only if they continue or are bothersome
Incidence more frequent
   CNS stimulation, excessive (drowsiness, muscle or joint pain, muscle twitching, nervousness, nightmares, trouble in sleeping); *nausea and vomiting; unusual tiredness or weakness*
Incidence less frequent
   Constipation; darkening of skin; difficulty in swallowing; dry mouth; feeling of warmth and redness in face; headache; loss of appetite; mental depression; orthostatic hypotension (dizziness or lightheadedness when getting up from a lying or sitting position)

Those not indicating need for medical attention
Incidence less frequent
   Loss of hair

Patient Consultation

Consider advising the patient on the following (» = major clinical significance):

Before using this medication
   Advisability of using nonhormonal contraception; telling physician immediately if pregnancy is suspected
   See also *Precautions to Consider.*

Proper use of this medication
- » Importance of not taking more or less medication than the amount prescribed
    Caution in taking combination chemotherapy; taking each medication at the right time
- » Frequency of nausea and vomiting; importance of continuing medication despite stomach upset
    Checking with physician if vomiting occurs shortly after dose is taken
    Missed dose: Taking as soon as remembered if within a few hours; not taking if several hours have passed or if almost time for next dose; not doubling doses
- » Proper storage

Precautions while using this medication
- » Importance of close monitoring by the physician
- » Checking with hospital emergency room or physician if symptoms of hypertensive crisis develop
- » Avoiding use of tyramine-containing foods, alcoholic beverages and large quantities of caffeine-containing beverages, over-the-counter cold and cough medicines, and other medication unless prescribed; having list of such for reference
- » Obeying rules of caution during 14 days after discontinuing medication

» Caution in taking alcohol or other CNS depressants
» Caution if drowsiness occurs, especially when driving or doing things requiring alertness
» Avoiding immunizations unless approved by physician; other persons in patient's household should avoid immunizations with oral poliovirus vaccine; avoiding other persons who have taken oral poliovirus vaccine or wearing a protective mask that covers nose and mouth

Caution if bone marrow depression occurs:

» Avoiding exposure to persons with bacterial infections, especially during periods of low blood counts; checking with physician immediately if fever or chills, cough or hoarseness, lower back or side pain, or painful or difficult urination occur
» Checking with physician immediately if unusual bleeding or bruising; black, tarry stools; blood in urine or stools; or pinpoint red spots on skin occur

Caution in use of regular toothbrush, dental floss, or toothpick; physician, dentist, or nurse may suggest alternatives; checking with physician before having dental work done

Not touching eyes or inside of nose unless hands washed immediately before

Using caution to avoid accidental cuts with use of sharp objects such as safety razor or fingernail or toenail cutters

Avoiding contact sports or other situations where bruising or injury could occur

Diabetics: Checking urine or blood sugar levels

» Caution if any kind of surgery (including dental surgery) or emergency treatment is required

Carrying medical identification card

Side/adverse effects

May cause adverse effects such as blood problems, loss of hair, hypertensive crisis, and cancer; importance of discussing possible effects with physician

Signs of potential side effects, especially anemia, excessive CNS stimulation, immunosuppression, infection, leukopenia, thrombocytopenia, hemolytic anemia, missing menstrual periods, pneumonitis, gastrointestinal toxicity, hepatotoxicity, peripheral neuropathy, stomatitis, allergic reaction, hypertensive crisis, and orthostatic hypotension

Physician or nurse can help in dealing with side effects

General Dosing Information

Patients receiving procarbazine should be under supervision of a physician experienced in cancer chemotherapy.

A variety of dosage schedules and regimens of procarbazine, alone or in combination with other antitumor agents, are used. The prescriber may consult medical literature as well as the manufacturer's literature in choosing a specific dosage.

Dosage must be adjusted to meet the individual requirements of each patient, based on clinical response and appearance or severity of toxicity.

Although dosages are based on the patient's actual weight, use of estimated lean body mass (dry weight) is recommended in obese patients or those with weight gain due to edema, ascites, or other abnormal fluid retention.

It is recommended that procarbazine therapy be discontinued promptly if any of the following occur:

Allergic reaction
Diarrhea
Hemorrhage or bleeding tendencies
Leukopenia (particularly granulocytopenia), marked
Stomatitis
Thrombocytopenia, marked

Therapy may be resumed at a lower dosage when the clinical and laboratory examinations are satisfactory.

Because of the risk of enhanced bone marrow toxicity, an interval of at least 1 month (based on bone marrow studies) is recommended before starting procarbazine therapy after a patient has received radiation or chemotherapy with medications that depress bone marrow function.

After dosage is stopped, monoamine oxidase (MAO) inhibitor effects of this medication may persist for up to 2 weeks after withdrawal (time required for regeneration of enzyme). During this period, food and drug contraindications must be observed.

Special precautions are recommended in patients who develop thrombocytopenia as a result of administration of procarbazine. These may include extreme care in performing invasive procedures; regular inspection of intravenous sites, skin (including perirectal area), and mucous membrane surfaces for signs of bleeding or bruising; limiting frequency of venipuncture and avoiding intramuscular injections; testing urine, emesis, stool, and secretions for occult blood; care in use of regular toothbrushes, dental floss, toothpicks, safety razors, and fingernail and toenail cutters; avoiding constipation; and using caution to prevent falls and other injuries. Such patients should avoid alcohol and any aspirin intake because of the risk of gastrointestinal bleeding. Platelet transfusions may be required.

Patients who develop leukopenia should be observed carefully for signs of infection. Antibiotic support may be required. In neutropenic patients who develop fever, broad-spectrum antibiotic coverage should be initiated empirically, pending bacterial cultures and appropriate diagnostic tests.

Diet/Nutrition

Foods and beverages containing tyramine or other high pressor amines, such as aged cheese; beer; reduced-alcohol and alcohol-free beer and wine; red and white wines; sherry; liqueurs; yeast/protein extracts; fava or broad bean pods; smoked or pickled meats, poultry, or fish; fermented sausage (bologna, pepperoni, salami, summer sausage) or other fermented meat; and any overripe fruit, when used concurrently with MAO inhibitors, may cause sudden and severe hypertensive reactions. The reactions are usually limited to a few hours and are easily treated with phentolamine. The severity depends on the amount of tyramine ingested, rate of gastric emptying, and length of the interval between the dose of MAO inhibitor and ingestion of tyramine. When MAO inhibitors are discontinued, dietary restrictions must continue for at least 2 weeks. Other foods, such as yogurt, sour cream, cream cheese, cottage cheese, chocolate, and soy sauce, if eaten when fresh and in moderation, are considered unlikely to cause serious problems.

Combination chemotherapy

Procarbazine may be used in combination with other agents in various regimens. As a result, incidence and/or severity of side effects may be altered and different dosages (usually reduced) may be used. For example, procarbazine is part of the following chemotherapeutic combinations (some commonly used acronyms are in parentheses):

—doxorubicin, cyclophosphamide, vincristine, procarbazine, and prednisone (A-COPP).
—carmustine, cyclophosphamide, vinblastine, procarbazine, and prednisone (BCVPP).
—cyclophosphamide, doxorubicin, methotrexate, and procarbazine (CAMP).
—cyclophosphamide, vincristine, procarbazine, and prednisone (COPP or "C"MOPP).
—mechlorethamine, vincristine, procarbazine, and prednisone (MOPP).
—mechlorethamine, vincristine, procarbazine, prednisone, and bleomycin (MOPP-LO BLEO).
—procarbazine, vincristine, cyclophosphamide, and lomustine (POCC).

For specific dosages and schedules, consult the literature. For information regarding each agent, consult the individual monographs.

Oral Dosage Forms

PROCARBAZINE HYDROCHLORIDE CAPSULES USP

Usual adult dose: Lymphomas, Hodgkin's—

Initial: Oral, 2 to 4 mg (base) per kg of body weight (to the nearest 50 mg) a day in single or divided doses for the first week, followed by 4 to 6 mg per kg of body weight a day until leukopenia, thrombocytopenia, or maximum response occurs.

Note: If hematologic toxicity occurs, the medication is withdrawn until the toxicity is resolved, then treatment may be resumed with 1 to 2 mg (base) per kg of body weight a day.

Maintenance: Oral, 1 to 2 mg (base) per kg of body weight a day.

Auxiliary labeling:
- Avoid alcoholic beverages.
- May cause drowsiness.
- Do not take other medicines without your doctor's advice.
- Avoid certain foods as directed.

PROGESTINS   Systemic

INN: Included in brackets after individual generic listings, if different from U.S. generic names.

Some commonly used *brand names* are:

Amen
  [Medroxyprogesterone]
Aygestin [Norethindrone]
Curretab
  [Medroxyprogesterone]
Cycrin
  [Medroxyprogesterone]
Delalutin
  [Hydroxyprogesterone]
Depo-Provera
  [Medroxyprogesterone]
Duralutin
  [Hydroxyprogesterone]
Femotrone
  [Progesterone]
Gesterol [Progesterone]
Gesterol L.A.
  [Hydroxyprogesterone]
Hylutin
  [Hydroxyprogesterone]

Hyprogest
  [Hydroxyprogesterone]
Hyproval P.A.
  [Hydroxyprogesterone]
Megace [Megestrol]
Micronor [Norethindrone]
Norlutate [Norethindrone]
Norlutin [Norethindrone]
Nor-Q.D. [Norethindrone]
Ovrette [Norgestrel]
Pro-Depo
  [Hydroxyprogesterone]
Prodrox
  [Hydroxyprogesterone]
Progestaject
  [Progesterone]
Progestilin [Progesterone]
Provera
  [Medroxyprogesterone]

HYDROXYPROGESTERONE
Parenteral
  Hydroxyprogesterone Caproate Injection USP [*Delalutin; Duralutin; Gesterol L.A.; Hylutin; Hyprogest; Hyproval P.A.; Pro-Depo; Prodrox*]†

MEDROXYPROGESTERONE
Oral
  Medroxyprogesterone Acetate Tablets USP [*Amen; Curretab; Cycrin; Provera*]†
Parenteral
  Sterile Medroxyprogesterone Acetate Suspension USP [*Depo-Provera*]

MEGESTROL
Oral
  Megestrol Acetate Tablets USP [*Megace*]

NORETHINDRONE [INN: Norethisterone]
Oral
  Norethindrone Tablets USP [*Micronor; Norlutin; Nor-Q.D.*]
  Norethindrone Acetate Tablets USP [*Aygestin; Norlutate*]

NORGESTREL
Oral
  Norgestrel Tablets USP [*Ovrette*]

PROGESTERONE
Parenteral
  Progesterone Injection USP [*Femotrone; Gesterol; Progestaject; Progestilin*]†
  Sterile Progesterone Suspension USP†
Rectal
  Progesterone Suppositories*
Vaginal
  Progesterone Suppositories*

---

  *Not commercially available in the U.S. or Canada.
  †Generic name product available in the U.S.

Category

Progestin—Hydroxyprogesterone; Medroxyprogesterone, Oral; Norethindrone; Norgestrel; Progesterone.

Antineoplastic—Hydroxyprogesterone; Medroxyprogesterone, Parenteral; Megestrol.

Contraceptive (systemic)—Medroxyprogesterone, Parenteral; Norethindrone (base); Norgestrel.

Indications

Note: Bracketed information in the *Indications* section refers to uses not included in U.S. product labeling.

Accepted

Hormonal imbalance, female (treatment)—Hydroxyprogesterone, oral medroxyprogesterone, norethindrone (base and acetate), and progesterone are indicated in the treatment of amenorrhea and functional uterine bleeding due to hormonal imbalance. Hydroxyprogesterone is indicated for the production of secretory endometrium and desquamation.

[Oral progestins are also used in conjunction with long-term estrogen replacement therapy; oral medroxyprogesterone is also used in conjunction with estrogens in the treatment of menopausal symptoms and hypermenorrhea. Studies have shown that administration of a progestin for 10 to 13 days of an estrogen cycle is associated with a lower incidence of endometrial hyperplasia and endometrial carcinoma than an estrogen-only cycle.]

Endometriosis (treatment)—Norethindrone (base and acetate) is indicated in the treatment of endometriosis.

Estrogen production, endogenous (diagnosis)—Hydroxyprogesterone is indicated as a test for endogenous estrogen production; [oral medroxyprogesterone is also used].

Carcinoma (treatment)—
  Hydroxyprogesterone is indicated for the treatment of carcinoma of the uterine corpus.

Parenteral medroxyprogesterone and megestrol are indicated in the treatment of metastatic endometrial carcinoma.

Parenteral medroxyprogesterone is indicated also in the treatment of metastatic renal carcinoma.

Megestrol is indicated also in the treatment of metastatic breast carcinoma.

Note: Progestins are recommended only for adjunctive and palliative therapy when used in the treatment of advanced (inoperable, recurrent, or metastatic) carcinoma.

Pregnancy (prophylaxis)—Norethindrone (base) and norgestrel are indicated for the prevention of pregnancy. [Parenteral medroxyprogesterone is also used to prevent pregnancy.]

[Corpus luteum insufficiency (treatment)]—Progesterone is used to treat corpus luteum dysfunction.

[Polycystic ovary syndrome (treatment)]—Medroxyprogesterone is used in the treatment of polycystic ovary syndrome.

[Puberty, precocious (treatment)]—Parenteral medroxyprogesterone is used in the treatment of precocious puberty.

Unaccepted
There is no acceptable evidence that progesterone is effective in the treatment of premenstrual syndrome.

Progestins are no longer recommended for use in pregnancy tests because of possible teratogenic effects. Newer test methods are safer and more efficient.

With the exception of progesterone, progestins have no proven value in the treatment of threatened abortion and are no longer recommended for such use.

Pharmacology

Mechanism of action/Effect: Progestins increase the synthesis of RNA by means of interaction with chromatin (DNA). Larger doses inhibit the release of luteinizing hormone (LH) from the anterior pituitary. Relatively small doses cause an increase in cervical mucus viscosity.

Precautions to Consider

Note: The possibility should be considered that other precautions for oral contraceptives containing both estrogens and progestins may apply to progestin-only oral contraceptives also. See *Estrogens and Progestins (Oral Contraceptives), (Systemic)*.

Geriatrics
Studies performed to date have not demonstrated geriatrics-specific problems that would limit the usefulness of progestins in the elderly.

Dental
Progestins may predispose the patient to bleeding of the gingival tissues. In addition, gingival hyperplasia may occur during progestin therapy, usually starting as gingivitis or gum inflammation. A strictly enforced program of teeth cleaning by a professional, combined with plaque control by the patient, will minimize growth rate and severity of gingival enlargement.

Drug interactions and/or related problems
The following drug interactions and/or related problems have been selected on the basis of their potential clinical significance (possible mechanism in parentheses where appropriate)—not necessarily inclusive (» = major clinical significance):

Note: The possibility should be considered that other drug interactions and/or related problems reported for oral contraceptives containing both estrogens and progestins may apply to progestin-only oral contraceptives also.

» Bromocriptine
    (progestins may cause amenorrhea and/or galactorrhea, interfering with effects of bromocriptine; concurrent use is not recommended)

Contraindications/Medical problems
The contraindications/medical problems included have been selected on the basis of their potential clinical significance (reasons given in parentheses where appropriate)—not necessarily inclusive (» = major clinical significance).

Except under special circumstances, this medication should not be used when the following medical problems exist:
» Carcinoma of breast or reproductive organs, except in selected patients for palliative therapy
» Hepatic disease or dysfunction
» Incomplete abortion
» Suspected pregnancy—should not be used in diagnostic test
» Vaginal bleeding, abnormal and undiagnosed

Risk-benefit should be considered when the following medical problems exist:

Asthma or
Cardiac insufficiency or
Epilepsy or
Migraine headaches or
Renal dysfunction
    (fluid retention may be caused by some progestins and may aggravate the above conditions)

Diabetes mellitus
    (possible decrease in glucose tolerance when progestins are used in combination with estrogen; caution advised with use of progestin-only products)

Ectopic pregnancy, history of

Hyperlipidemia
    (some progestins may elevate LDL concentration; condition may be aggravated, particularly with long-term use)

Intolerance to progestins

Mental depression, or history of
    (condition may be aggravated)

» Thrombophlebitis, thromboembolic disorders, or cerebral apoplexy, or history of

Side/Adverse Effects

Note: Progestins may be associated with the occurrence of thrombophlebitis, pulmonary embolism, cerebrovascular disorders, and retinal thrombosis. This effect has been documented with the use of progestins in combination with estrogens. Although this association is still controversial because of minimal clinical information concerning progestin-only preparations, it is recommended that during therapy with progestin-only preparations, consideration be given to the possibility of clot formation.

The possibility should be considered that other side/adverse effects reported for oral contraceptives containing both estrogens and progestins may apply to progestin-only oral contraceptives also. See *Estrogens and Progestins (Oral Contraceptives), (Systemic)*.

Continuous administration of progestins may alter the menstrual pattern of the patient and result in unpredictable bleeding during the time of therapy.

The following side/adverse effects have been selected on the basis of their potential clinical significance (possible cause in parentheses where appropriate)—not necessarily inclusive:

Those indicating need for medical attention
Incidence more frequent
    Changes in vaginal bleeding pattern, including irregular cycle time, spotting, breakthrough bleeding, complete lack of bleeding
Incidence less frequent or rare
    Blood clots (headache, severe or sudden; loss of coordination, sudden; pains in chest, groin, or leg, especially in calf of leg; shortness of breath, sudden, unexplained; slurred speech, sudden;

vision changes, sudden; weakness, numbness, or pain in arm or leg)—increased risk occurs with use of progestins in combination with estrogens; caution with use of progestin-only products; *galactorrhea* (secretion from breasts); *hepatitis or gallbladder obstruction* (pains in stomach, side, or abdomen; yellow eyes or skin); *hypersensitivity* (skin rash or itching); *mental depression; neuroocular lesions* (bulging eyes; double vision; loss of vision, gradual, partial, or complete)—associated with the use of progestins in combination with estrogens; caution with use of progestin-only products

Those indicating need for medical attention only if they continue or are bothersome

Incidence more frequent

Changes in appetite; changes in weight; edema (swelling of ankles and feet); *pain or irritation at injection site*—with progesterone, especially with the aqueous vehicle; *unusual tiredness or weakness*

Incidence less frequent or rare

Acne; fever; increased body and facial hair; increased breast tenderness; melasma or chloasma (brown, blotchy spots on exposed skin); *nausea; some loss of scalp hair; trouble in sleeping*

Patient Consultation

Consider advising the patient on the following (» = major clinical significance):

Before using this medication

Reading patient package insert

See also *Precautions to Consider.*

Proper use of this medication

» Compliance with therapy; taking medication at the same time each day, every day of the year if used for contraception

Missed dose:

When used other than as contraceptive—Taking missed dose as soon as possible; not taking at all if almost time for next dose; not doubling doses

When used as contraceptive—Discontinuing medication when a dose is missed and using alternative birth control method until menstrual period begins or pregnancy is ruled out

Proper storage

» Keeping out of reach of children

Storing away from heat and direct light

Not storing in bathroom medicine cabinet

Protecting injection dosage form from freezing

Not keeping outdated medication or medication no longer needed; ensuring that discarded medication is out of reach of children

Precautions while using this medication

» Importance of close monitoring by physician

Checking with physician as soon as possible if menstrual period is missed or unusual bleeding occurs, especially if using progestin as a contraceptive

» Stopping medication immediately and checking with physician if pregnancy is suspected

If scheduled for laboratory tests, telling physician if taking progestins; certain blood tests may be affected by progestins

Possibility of dental problems, such as tenderness, swelling, or bleeding of gums; brushing and flossing teeth, massaging gums, and having dentist clean teeth regularly; checking with dentist if there are questions about care of teeth or gums or if tenderness, swelling, or bleeding of gums is noticed

Keeping an extra 1-month supply available when using as oral contraceptive

Keeping tablets in original container especially when using as oral contraceptive

Importance of not giving medication to anyone else

Side/adverse effects

Progestins may be associated with the occurrence of thrombophlebitis, pulmonary embolism, cerebrovascular disorders, and retinal thrombosis

See also *Side/Adverse Effects.*

General Dosing Information

When used as an oral contraceptive, progestins are administered daily without interruption, regardless of menstrual cycle.

The cyclical administration of progestins is based on an assumed menstrual cycle of 28 days.

Regulations do not require that a patient package insert (PPI) be dispensed when a progestin is prescribed as an antineoplastic adjunct. However, when a progestin is dispensed to the patient for any other use, a PPI is mandatory.

Progesterone is not effective when administered orally, because of rapid metabolism; therefore, synthetic progestins are utilized for oral administration.

HYDROXYPROGESTERONE

Summary of Differences

Category: Indicated only as a progestin and an antineoplastic.

Parenteral Dosage Forms

HYDROXYPROGESTERONE CAPROATE INJECTION

USP *[Delalutin; Duralutin; Gesterol L.A.; Hylutin; Hyprogest; Hyproval P.A.; Pro-Depo; Prodrox]*

Usual adult dose:

Hormonal imbalance, female—

Amenorrhea, primary and secondary; or

Functional uterine bleeding: Intramuscular, 375 mg, started any time during cycle. After 4 days of desquamation, or 21 days after the injection if there is no bleeding, start cyclic therapy schedule (see note below). Repeat cyclic therapy schedule every 28 days for 4 cycles. The patient should be observed for 2 or 3 cycles after cessation of therapy to determine onset of normal cyclic function.

Production of secretory endometrium and desquamation:

For patients not on estrogen therapy—Start cyclic therapy schedule (see note below). Repeat cyclic therapy schedule every 28 days until no longer required. Menstruation may not occur until estrogen has been given for several months if estrogen deficiency has been prolonged.

For patients currently on estrogen therapy—Intramuscular, 375 mg, started any time during cycle. After 4 days of desquamation, or 21 days after the injection if there is no bleeding, start cyclic therapy schedule (see note below). Repeat cyclic therapy schedule every 28 days until no longer required. Menstruation may not occur until estrogen has been given for several months if estrogen deficiency has been prolonged.

Note: Cyclic therapy schedule—Intramuscular, 20 mg estradiol valerate injection on Day 1 of cycle, followed by 250 mg hydroxyprogesterone caproate injection and 5 mg estradiol valerate injection on Day 15 of cycle.

Adenocarcinoma of uterine corpus, advanced (Stage III or IV)—Intramuscular, 1 gram, one to seven times a week until relapse occurs or, if no desirable results are obtained, until a total of twelve weeks of therapy.

Test for endogenous estrogen production—Intramuscular, 250 mg, the dosage being repeated four weeks after the first injection for confirmation. In the nonpregnant patient with responsive endometrium, bleeding will occur 7 to 14 days following injection.

MEDROXYPROGESTERONE

Summary of Differences

Category: Oral medroxyprogesterone indicated only as a progestin. Parenteral medroxyprogesterone indicated only as an antineoplastic; also used as a systemic contraceptive.

Indications: Parenteral medroxyprogesterone indicated only for endometrial or renal carcinoma.

Oral Dosage Forms

MEDROXYPROGESTERONE ACETATE TABLETS USP
[Amen; Curretab; Cycrin; Provera]

Usual adult dose: Hormonal imbalance, female—
Amenorrhea, secondary: Oral, 5 to 10 mg a day for five to ten days, started any time during cycle.
Functional uterine bleeding: Oral, 5 to 10 mg a day for five to ten days, commencing on the calculated Day 16 or Day 21 of the menstrual cycle.

Note: Withdrawal bleeding usually occurs within 3 to 7 days after discontinuing therapy.
For inducing an optimum secretory transformation of an endometrium that has been adequately primed with either endogenous or exogenous estrogens—10 mg daily for ten to thirteen days (starting on Day 16 to Day 13, respectively, for functional uterine bleeding).

Parenteral Dosage Forms

Note: Bracketed uses in the *Dosage Forms* section refer to categories of use or indications that are not included in U.S. product labeling.

STERILE MEDROXYPROGESTERONE ACETATE SUSPENSION USP *[Depo-Provera]*

Usual adult dose:
Carcinoma, endometrial or renal—Intramuscular:
Initially—400 mg to 1 gram, the dose being repeated at one-week intervals.
Maintenance—When improvement occurs and the disease appears stabilized, it may be possible to maintain improvement with as little as 400 mg a month.
[Contraceptive]—Intramuscular, 150 mg, the dose being repeated at three-month intervals.

Auxiliary labeling: • Shake well.

MEGESTROL

Summary of Differences

Category: Indicated only as an antineoplastic; this is the only oral progestin indicated as an antineoplastic.

Indications: Indicated only for endometrial or breast carcinoma.

Oral Dosage Forms

MEGESTROL ACETATE TABLETS USP *[Megace]*

Usual adult dose:
Breast carcinoma—Oral, 40 mg four times a day.
Endometrial carcinoma—Oral, 10 to 80 mg four times a day.

Note: At least two months of continuous treatment is considered an adequate period for determining the efficacy of megestrol acetate.

NORETHINDRONE

Summary of Differences

Category: Indicated as a progestin (both forms) and systemic contraceptive (norethindrone base).

Indication: This is the only progestin indicated for endometriosis. In addition, norethindrone tablets are indicated as a systemic contraceptive.

Oral Dosage Forms

NORETHINDRONE TABLETS USP *[Micronor; Norlutin; Nor-Q.D.]*

Usual adult dose:
Hormonal imbalance, female—
Amenorrhea; or
Functional uterine bleeding: Oral, 5 to 20 mg a day on Day 5 through Day 25 of the menstrual cycle.
Endometriosis—Oral, initially 10 mg a day for two weeks, the daily dosage then being increased by 5 mg at two-week intervals to a total of 30 mg a day, which is then continued for six to nine months unless temporarily discontinued because of breakthrough bleeding.
Contraceptive—Oral, 350 mcg (0.35 mg) a day, starting on Day 1 of menstrual cycle and continuing uninterrupted thereafter.

NORETHINDRONE ACETATE TABLETS USP *[Aygestin; Norlutate]*

Usual adult dose:
Hormonal imbalance, female—
Amenorrhea; or
Functional uterine bleeding: Oral, 2.5 to 10 mg a day on Day 5 through Day 25 of the menstrual cycle.
Endometriosis—Oral, initially 5 mg a day for two weeks, the daily dosage then being increased by 2.5 mg at two-week intervals to a total of 15 mg a day, which is then continued for six to nine months unless temporarily discontinued because of breakthrough bleeding.

NORGESTREL

Summary of Differences

Category: Indicated only as a progestin and systemic contraceptive.

Oral Dosage Forms

NORGESTREL TABLETS USP [Ovrette]

Usual adult dose: Contraceptive—Oral, 75 mcg (0.075 mg) a day, starting on Day 1 of menstrual cycle and continuing uninterrupted thereafter.

PROGESTERONE

Summary of Differences

Category: Indicated only as a progestin.
Side/adverse effects: Pain or irritation at site of injection, especially with aqueous vehicle.

Parenteral Dosage Forms

PROGESTERONE INJECTION USP *[Femotrone; Gesterol; Progestaject; Progestilin]*

Usual adult dose:
Hormonal imbalance, female—
Amenorrhea: Intramuscular, a single dose of 50 to 100 mg; or 5 to 10 mg a day for six to eight days, usually commencing eight to ten days before anticipated menstruation.
Note: If there has been sufficient ovarian activity to produce a proliferative endometrium, withdrawal bleeding will occur 48 to 72 hours after the last injection. This may be followed by spontaneous normal cycles. Progesterone should be discontinued if menses occurs during the series of injections.
Functional uterine bleeding: Intramuscular, a single dose of 50 to 100 mg; or 5 to 10 mg a day for six days.
Note: Bleeding should cease within 6 days. When estrogen is being given, the administration of progesterone should begin after 2 weeks of estrogen therapy. Progesterone should be discontinued if menses occurs during the series of injections.

Corpus luteum insufficiency—Intramuscular, 12.5 mg a day at onset of ovulation. Treatment duration is usually two weeks, but it may be continued, if necessary, up to eleventh week of gestation.

Usual adult prescribing limits: Up to 50 mg daily.

STERILE PROGESTERONE SUSPENSION USP

Usual adult dose: See *Progesterone Injection.*

Rectal Dosage Forms

PROGESTERONE SUPPOSITORIES

Note: Progesterone suppositories are not commercially available in the U.S. or Canada.

Usual adult dose: Corpus luteum insufficiency—Rectal, 25 mg two times a day at onset of ovulation. Treatment duration is usually two weeks, but it may be continued, if necessary, up to eleventh week of gestation.

Auxiliary labeling: • For rectal use only.

Vaginal Dosage Forms

PROGESTERONE SUPPOSITORIES

Note: Progesterone suppositories are not commercially available in the U.S. or Canada.

Usual adult dose: Corpus luteum insufficiency—Vaginal, 25 mg two times a day at onset of ovulation. Treatment duration is usually two weeks, but it may be continued, if necessary, up to eleventh week of gestation.

Note: Vaginal suppositories are better tolerated than other dosage forms of progesterone and are therefore more frequently prescribed for this indication.

Auxiliary labeling: • For vaginal use only.

PROPAFENONE Systemic

A commonly used *brand name* in the U.S. and Canada is *Rythmol.*

ORAL
Propafenone Hydrochloride Tablets
In the U.S. and Canada—*Rythmol*

Category: Antiarrhythmic.

Indications

Accepted
Arrhythmias, ventricular (treatment)—Propafenone is indicated for suppression of documented life-threatening ventricular arrhythmias, including sustained ventricular tachycardia.

[Arrhythmias, supraventricular (treatment)][1]—Propafenone may be used for the treatment of supraventricular arrhythmias such as, intranodal and extranodal (e.g., Wolff-Parkinson-White Syndrome)

reentrant tachycardias. Data for use of propafenone in the treatment of atrial fibrillation/flutter are less convincing, although it may help some patients. Caution is warranted when administering propafenone to patients in atrial fibrillation/flutter and structural heart disease because of the possibility of serious proarrhythmia, including ventricular tachycardia.

Unaccepted
Use of propafenone is not recommended in the U.S. for treatment of less severe arrhythmias such as nonsustained ventricular tachycardias or frequent premature ventricular contractions, even if patients are symptomatic, because of results of a study in patients following a myocardial infarction that found increased mortality in patients with non-life-threatening ventricular arrhythmias who were treated with encainide and flecainide.

---

[1]Not included in Canadian product labeling.

Pharmacology

Mechanism of action/Effect: Reduces the inward sodium current in Purkinje and myocardial cells. Decreases excitability, conduction velocity, and automaticity in atrioventricular (AV) nodal, His-Purkinje, and intraventricular tissue, and causes a slight but significant prolongation of refractory periods in AV nodal tissue. The greatest effect is on the His-Purkinje system. Decreases the rate of rise of the action potential without markedly affecting its duration. Also, prolongs conduction velocity and effective refractory periods in accessory pathways in both directions. Electrophysiologic effects are greater in ischemic than in normal myocardial tissue. In the Vaughan Williams classification of antiarrhythmics, propafenone is considered to be a class IC agent.

Other actions/effects: Negative inotropic effect. Has approximately one-fortieth the beta-adrenergic blocking activity of propranolol, which may become clinically significant in some patients. Has weak calcium channel blocking properties. Has local anesthetic activity approximately equal to that of procaine.

Precautions to Consider

Geriatrics

Although appropriate studies on the relationship of age to the effects of propafenone have not been performed in the geriatric population, no geriatrics-specific problems have been documented to date. However, elderly patients are more likely to have age-related hepatic and renal function impairment, which may require dosage reduction in patients receiving propafenone.

Drug interactions and/or related problems

The following drug interactions and/or related problems have been selected on the basis of their potential clinical significance (possible mechanism in parentheses where appropriate)—not necessarily inclusive (» = major clinical significance):

Anesthetics, local
(concurrent use with propafenone may increase the risk of central nervous system [CNS] side effects)

Antiarrhythmics, other
(although some antiarrhythmic agents may be used in combination for therapeutic advantage, combined use may sometimes potentiate risk of adverse cardiac effects)

Beta-adrenergic blocking agents
(concurrent use with propafenone results in significant increases in plasma concentrations and half-life of propranolol and metoprolol, without affecting plasma propafenone concentrations; dosage reduction of the beta-blocker may be necessary)

Cimetidine
(concurrent use of cimetidine produces a 20% [approximate] increase in plasma concentrations of propafenone; however, because of wide interindividual variability in plasma concentrations and, therefore, lack of direct correlation with clinical effect, effects of propafenone on electrocardiogram parameters are unchanged)

» Digoxin
(concurrent use with propafenone results in an increase in serum digoxin concentrations ranging from 35 to 85%, which appears to be unrelated to digoxin renal clearance but which may be related to a decrease in volume of distribution and nonrenal clearance; careful monitoring of digoxin concentrations and dosage reduction of digoxin are recommended when propafenone is initiated; subsequent dosage adjustments should be based on plasma digoxin concentrations)

Quinidine
(small doses completely inhibit hydroxylation of propafenone, effectively making patients poor metabolizers of propafenone; however, dosage adjustment of propafenone is usually not necessary)

» Warfarin
(concurrent use with propafenone results in a significant increase [approximately 40%] in mean steady-state warfarin plasma concentrations, with a corresponding increase in prothrombin time of approximately 25%; monitoring of prothrombin time and appropriate adjustment of warfarin dosage are recommended during concurrent use)

Contraindications/Medical problems

The contraindications/medical problems included have been selected on the basis of their potential clinical significance (reasons given in parentheses where appropriate)—not necessarily inclusive (» = major clinical significance).

Except under special circumstances, this medication should not be used when the following medical problems exist:

» Atrioventricular (AV) block, pre-existing second or third degree without pacemaker, or

» Right bundle branch block associated with a left hemiblock (bifascicular block) without pacemaker
(risk of complete heart block)

Risk-benefit should be considered when the following medical problems exist:

Asthma or
Bronchospasm, nonallergenic (e.g., chronic bronchitis, emphysema)
(because of its beta-adrenergic blocking effect, propafenone may promote bronchospasm)

» Cardiogenic shock or

» Sinus bradycardia
(risk of further myocardial depression)

Cardiomyopathy

» Congestive heart failure
(negative inotropic effect of propafenone; also, risk of further depression of myocardial contractility because of beta-adrenergic blocking activity of propafenone)

Hepatic function impairment
(reduced first-pass effect results in increased bioavailability, to approximately 70%; increased half-life; dosage of propafenone should be reduced to approximately 20 to 30% of the usual dose, with careful monitoring)

Hypokalemia or hyperkalemia
(effects of propafenone may be altered; any electrolyte imbalance should be corrected prior to beginning therapy with propafenone)

Hypotension, marked
(may be aggravated)

Myocardial infarction, history of, especially with associated left ventricular function impairment

Renal function impairment
(reduced elimination; dosage reduction may be necessary)

Sensitivity to propafenone

» Sick sinus syndrome
(sinus node recovery time prolonged; sinus bradycardia, sinus pause, or sinus arrest may occur)

Caution is recommended in patients with permanent pacemakers or temporary pacing electrodes; propafenone may increase endocardial pacing thresholds and may suppress ventricular escape rhythms; use is not recommended in patients with existing poor thresholds or nonprogrammable pacemakers unless suitable pacing rescue is available.

Side/Adverse Effects

Note: In the National Heart, Lung and Blood Institute's Cardiac Arrhythmia Suppression Trial (CAST), encainide and flecainide treatment were found to be associated with excessive mortality or increased nonfatal cardiac arrest rate as compared with placebo in patients with asymptomatic, non-life-threatening arrhythmias who had a recent myocardial infarction. The implications of these results for other patient populations or other antiarrhythmic agents are uncertain.

Adverse cardiac effects reported with propafenone administration include new or exacerbated ventricular arrhythmias in about 4.7% of patients; new or exacerbated congestive heart failure in 1% or less of patients; first, second, or third degree atrioventricular (AV) block in 2.5%, 0.6%, and 0.2% of patients, respectively; sinus bradycardia in 1.5% of patients; and rarely, sinus pause or sinus arrest.

Incidence of cardiac and other effects is at least partially dose-related.

Signs of overdose, usually most severe within 3 hours of ingestion, include hypotension, somnolence, bradycardia, AV dissociation, and intra-arterial and intraventricular conduction disturbances; asystole may develop. Convulsions and high grade ventricular arrhythmias have been reported rarely.

The following side/adverse effects have been selected on the basis of their potential clinical significance (possible signs and symptoms in parentheses where appropriate)—not necessarily inclusive:

Those indicating need for medical attention
Incidence more frequent
Ventricular tachyarrhythmias (fast or irregular heartbeat)
Note: Like other antiarrhythmic agents, propafenone may induce new arrhythmias and/or worsen an existing arrhythmia. *Ventricular tachyarrhythmias* are dose-related and potentially fatal; incidence increased in patients with sustained ventricular tachycardia, coronary artery disease, or history of myocardial infarction. Proarrhythmic effects usually occur during the first week of therapy, although effects are also seen later.
Incidence less frequent
Angina (chest pain); *bradycardia* (slow heartbeat); *congestive heart failure* (shortness of breath, swelling of feet or lower legs)
Incidence rare
Agranulocytosis (fever or chills); *conduction abnormalities, including atrioventricular block, bundle branch block; hypotension* (low blood pressure); *joint pain; supraventricular tachyarrhythmias, including atrial flutter, atrial fibrillation; trembling or shaking*

Those indicating need for medical attention only if they continue or are bothersome
Incidence more frequent
Dizziness; taste disturbance (change in taste; bitter or metallic taste)
Incidence less frequent
Blurred vision; constipation or diarrhea; dryness of mouth; headache; nausea and/or vomiting; skin rash; unusual tiredness or weakness

Patient Consultation

In providing consultation, consider emphasizing the following selected information (» = major clinical significance):

Before using this medication
» Conditions affecting use, especially:
    Sensitivity to propafenone

Pregnancy—Reduces fertility in monkeys, dogs, and rabbits; in rats, causes increased maternal and neonatal mortality, decreased maternal and infant weight gain, and reduced neonatal development
Other medical problems, especially second or third degree atrioventricular (AV) block, right bundle branch block associated with a left hemiblock, cardiogenic shock, congestive heart failure, sick sinus syndrome, or sinus bradycardia,
Other medications, especially digoxin or warfarin

Proper use of this medication
» Compliance with therapy; taking as directed even if feeling well
» Importance of not missing doses and taking at evenly spaced intervals
    Missed dose: Taking as soon as possible if remembered within 4 hours; not taking if remembered later; not doubling doses
» Proper storage

Precautions while using this medication
    Regular visits to physician to check progress
    Carrying medical identification card or bracelet
» Caution if any kind of surgery (including dental surgery) or emergency treatment is required
    Caution when driving or doing things requiring alertness because of possible dizziness

Side/adverse effects
    Signs of potential side effects, especially ventricular tachyarrhythmias, angina, congestive heart failure, agranulocytosis, bradycardia, conduction abnormalities, hypotension, joint pain, and trembling or shaking

General Dosing Information

Because of wide interindividual variability in plasma concentrations, careful titration of dosage is recommended. However, because steady-state concentrations are achieved after the same amount of time in both extensive and poor metabolizers, and because the difference in peak plasma concentrations decreases at high doses and the active 5-hydroxy metabolite is absent in poor metabolizers, the recommended dosage regimen is the same for both groups of patients.

Dosage increments should be made no more frequently than every 3 to 4 days.

It is recommended that treatment be initiated in the hospital because of the increased risk of proarrhythmic effects associated with propafenone administration.

In general, it is recommended that previous antiarrhythmic therapy be withdrawn 2 to 5 half-lives before initiation of propafenone therapy.

In patients with pacemakers, pacing threshold should be monitored and programmed at periodic intervals during propafenone therapy.

Oral Dosage Forms

PROPAFENONE HYDROCHLORIDE TABLETS

Usual adult dose:
    Antiarrhythmic—Ventricular; or
    [Antiarrhythmic—Supraventricular]: Oral, initially 150 mg every eight hours, increased, if necessary, after three to four days to 225 mg every eight hours (U.S. labeling) or 300 mg every twelve hours (Canadian labeling); may be further increased after an additional three to four days, if necessary, to 300 mg every eight hours.

PSEUDOEPHEDRINE   Systemic

Some commonly used *brand names* are:

In the U.S.—

Afrinol Repetabs	Halofed Adult Strength
AlleRid	Myfedrine
Cenafed	NeoFed
Children's Sudafed Liquid	Novafed
Chlor-Trimeton Non-	PediaCare Infants' Oral
Drowsy Formula	Decongestant Drops
Decofed	Pseudo
DeFed-60	Pseudogest
Dorcol Children's	SinuStat
Decongestant Liquid	Sudafed
Drixoral Non-Drowsy	Sudafed 60
Formula	Sudafed 12 Hour
Genaphed	Sudrin
Halofed	Sufedrin

In Canada—

Congestac N.D. Caplets	Otrivin
Eltor 120	Pseudofrin
Maxenal	Robidrine
Ornex Cold	Sudafed

ORAL

Pseudoephedrine Hydrochloride Capsules
  In the U.S.—*AlleRid; SinuStat*
  In Canada—*Ornex Cold*
Pseudoephedrine Hydrochloride Extended-release Capsules
  In the U.S.—*Novafed*
  In Canada—*Eltor 120; Maxenal; Otrivin*
Pseudoephedrine Hydrochloride Oral Solution
  In the U.S.—*Children's Sudafed Liquid; Dorcol Children's Decongestant Liquid; Myfedrine; PediaCare Infants' Oral Decongestant Drops;* GENERIC
  In Canada—*Ornex Cold*
Pseudoephedrine Hydrochloride Syrup USP
  In the U.S.—*Cenafed; Decofed; Halofed; Pseudo; Pseudogest; Sufedrin;* GENERIC
  In Canada—*Pseudofrin; Robidrine; Sudafed*
Pseudoephedrine Hydrochloride Tablets USP
  In the U.S.—*Cenafed; Decofed; DeFed-60; Genaphed; Halofed; Halofed Adult Strength; NeoFed; Pseudogest; Sudafed; Sudafed 60; Sudrin; Sufedrin;* GENERIC
  In Canada—*Congestac N.D. Caplets; Pseudofrin; Robidrine; Sudafed*
Pseudoephedrine Sulfate Tablets
  In the U.S.—*Chlor-Trimeton Non-Drowsy Formula*
Pseudoephedrine Sulfate Extended-release Tablets
  In the U.S.—*Afrinol Repetabs; Drixoral Non-Drowsy Formula; Sudafed 12 Hour*

Category: Decongestant, nasal (systemic).

Indications

Accepted
Congestion, nasal (treatment);
Congestion, sinus (treatment); or
Congestion, eustachian tube (treatment)—Pseudoephedrine is indicated for temporary relief of congestion associated with acute coryza, acute eustachian salpingitis, serous otitis media with eustachian tube congestion, vasomotor rhinitis, and aerotitis (barotitis) media. Pseudoephedrine also may be indicated as an adjunct to analgesics, antihistamines, antibiotics, antitussives, or expectorants for optimum results in allergic rhinitis, croup, acute and subacute sinusitis, acute otitis media, and acute tracheobronchitis.

Pharmacology

Mechanism of action/Effect: Pseudoephedrine acts on alpha-adrenergic receptors in the mucosa of the respiratory tract, producing vasoconstriction. The medication shrinks swollen nasal mucous membranes; reduces tissue hyperemia, edema, and nasal congestion; and increases nasal airway patency. Also, drainage of sinus secretions may be increased and obstructed eustachian ostia may be opened.

Onset of action: 15 to 30 minutes.

Time to peak effect: Within 30 to 60 minutes.

Duration of action:
Tablets, oral solution, and syrup—3 to 4 hours.
Extended-release capsules and tablets—8 to 12 hours.

Precautions to Consider

Cross-sensitivity and/or related problems
Patients sensitive to other sympathomimetics (for example, albuterol, amphetamines, ephedrine, epinephrine, isoproterenol, metaproterenol, norepinephrine, phenylephrine, phenylpropanolamine, terbutaline) may be sensitive to this medication also.

Geriatrics
No published geriatrics-specific information is available. However, elderly patients are more likely to have age-related prostatic hypertrophy, which may require adjustment of dosage in patients receiving pseudoephedrine.

Drug interactions and/or related problems
The following drug interactions and/or related problems have been selected on the basis of their potential clinical significance (possible mechanism in parentheses where appropriate)—not necessarily inclusive (» = major clinical significance):

Note: Combinations containing any of the following medications, depending on the amount present, may also interact with this medication.

Anesthetics, hydrocarbon inhalation, such as:
  Chloroform
  Cyclopropane
  Enflurane
  Halothane
  Isoflurane
  Methoxyflurane
  Trichloroethylene
  (administration of pseudoephedrine prior to or shortly after anesthesia with chloroform, cyclopropane, halothane, or trichloroethylene may increase the risk of severe ventricular arrhythmias, especially in patients with pre-existing heart disease, because these anesthetics greatly sensitize the myocardium to the effects of sympathomimetics)
  (enflurane, isoflurane, or methoxyflurane may also cause some sensitization of the myocardium to the effects of sympathomimetics; caution is recommended in patients taking pseudoephedrine)

Antihypertensives or
Diuretics used as antihypertensives
  (antihypertensive effects may be reduced when these medications are used concurrently with pseudoephedrine; the patient should be carefully monitored to confirm that the desired effect is being obtained)

» Beta-adrenergic blocking agents
  (concurrent use with pseudoephedrine may inhibit the therapeutic effect of these medications; beta-blockade may result in unopposed alpha-adrenergic activity of pseudoephedrine with

a risk of hypertension and excessive bradycardia and possible heart block)

Central nervous system (CNS) stimulation-producing medications, other

(concurrent use with pseudoephedrine may result in additive CNS stimulation to excessive levels, which may cause unwanted effects such as nervousness, irritability, insomnia, or possibly convulsions or cardiac arrhythmias; close observation is recommended)

Citrates

(concurrent use may inhibit urinary excretion and prolong the duration of action of pseudoephedrine)

» Cocaine, mucosal-local

(in addition to increasing CNS stimulation, concurrent use with pseudoephedrine may increase the cardiovascular effects of either or both medications and the risk of adverse effects)

Digitalis glycosides

(concurrent use with pseudoephedrine may increase the risk of cardiac arrhythmias; caution and electrocardiographic monitoring are very important if concurrent use is necessary)

Levodopa

(concurrent use with pseudoephedrine may increase the possibility of cardiac arrhythmias; dosage reduction of the sympathomimetic is recommended)

» Monoamine oxidase (MAO) inhibitors, including furazolidone, pargyline, and procarbazine

(concurrent use may prolong and intensify the cardiac stimulant and vasopressor effects of pseudoephedrine because of release of catecholamines which accumulate in intraneuronal storage sites during MAO inhibitor therapy, resulting in headache, cardiac arrhythmias, vomiting, or sudden and severe hypertensive and/or hyperpyretic crises; pseudoephedrine should not be administered during or within 14 days following administration of MAO inhibitors)

Nitrates

(concurrent use with pseudoephedrine may reduce the antianginal effects of these medications)

Rauwolfia alkaloids

(concurrent use may inhibit the action of pseudoephedrine by depleting catecholamine stores)

Sympathomimetics, other

(in addition to possibly increasing CNS stimulation, concurrent use may increase the cardiovascular effects of either the other sympathomimetics or pseudoephedrine and the potential for side effects)

Thyroid hormones

(concurrent use may increase the effects of either these medications or pseudoephedrine; thyroid hormones enhance risk of coronary insufficiency when sympathomimetic agents are administered to patients with coronary artery disease; dosage adjustment is recommended, although problem is reduced in euthyroid patients)

Contraindications/Medical problems

The contraindications/medical problems included have been selected on the basis of their potential clinical significance (reasons given in parentheses where appropriate)—not necessarily inclusive (» = major clinical significance).

Risk-benefit should be considered when the following medical problems exist:

Cardiovascular disease, including ischemic heart disease, or

» Coronary artery disease, severe, or

Hypertension, mild to moderate, or

» Hypertension, severe

(condition may be exacerbated due to drug-induced cardiovascular effects)

Diabetes mellitus

Glaucoma, predisposition to

Hyperthyroidism

Prostatic hypertrophy

Sensitivity to pseudoephedrine or other sympathomimetics

Side/Adverse Effects

The following side/adverse effects have been selected on the basis of their potential clinical significance (possible signs and symptoms in parentheses where appropriate)—not necessarily inclusive:

Those indicating need for medical attention

Incidence rare—more frequent with high doses

Convulsions; hallucinations; irregular or slow heartbeat; shortness of breath or troubled breathing

Symptoms of overdose

Convulsions; fast breathing; hallucinations; increase in blood pressure; irregular heartbeat, continuing; shortness of breath or troubled breathing, severe or continuing; slow or fast heartbeat, severe or continuing; unusual nervousness, restlessness, or excitement

Those indicating need for medical attention only if they continue or are bothersome

Incidence more frequent

Nervousness; restlessness; trouble in sleeping

Incidence less frequent

Difficult or painful urination; dizziness or lightheadedness; fast or pounding heartbeat; headache; increased sweating; nausea or vomiting; trembling; troubled breathing; unusual paleness; weakness

Patient Consultation

In providing consultation, consider emphasizing the following selected information (» = major clinical significance):

Before using this medication

» Conditions affecting use, especially:

Sensitivity to pseudoephedrine or other sympathomimetics

Pregnancy—In animal studies, pseudoephedrine caused reduced average weight, length, and rate of skeletal ossification in animal fetus

Breast-feeding—Pseudoephedrine excreted in breast milk; use by nursing mothers not recommended because of higher than usual risk of side effects for infants, especially newborn and premature infants

Use in children—Caution should be used in infants, especially newborn and premature infants, because of higher than usual risk of side/adverse effects

Use by athletes—Pseudoephedrine is banned and tested for in athletes by the U.S. Olympic Committee (USOC)

Other medications, especially beta-adrenergic blocking agents, mucosal-local cocaine, or monoamine oxidase (MAO) inhibitors

Other medical problems, especially severe coronary artery disease or severe hypertension

Proper use of this medication

Proper administration of extended-release dosage forms:

Swallowing capsules or tablets whole; if capsule too large to swallow, mixing contents with jam or jelly and swallowing without chewing

Not crushing, breaking, or chewing

» Taking the medication a few hours before bedtime to minimize the possibility of insomnia

» Importance of not taking more medication than the amount recommended

Missed dose: Taking right away if remembered within an hour or so; not taking if remembered later; not doubling doses

» Proper storage

Precautions while using this medication
» Checking with physician if symptoms do not improve within 5 days or if fever is present

Side/adverse effects
Signs of potential side effects, especially convulsions, hallucinations, irregular or slow heartbeat, and shortness of breath or troubled breathing

General Dosing Information

To minimize the possibility of insomnia, the last dose of pseudoephedrine for each day should be administered a few hours before bedtime.

For patients who have difficulty in swallowing the extended-release capsule, the contents of the capsule may be mixed with jam or jelly and taken without chewing.

Oral Dosage Forms

PSEUDOEPHEDRINE HYDROCHLORIDE CAPSULES

Usual adult and adolescent dose: Decongestant, nasal—Oral, 60 mg every four to six hours.

Usual adult prescribing limits: 240 mg in twenty-four hours.

PSEUDOEPHEDRINE HYDROCHLORIDE EXTENDED-RELEASE CAPSULES

Usual adult and adolescent dose: Decongestant, nasal—Oral, 120 mg every twelve hours; or 240 mg every twenty-four hours.

Usual adult prescribing limits: 240 mg in twenty-four hours.

Auxiliary labeling: • Swallow capsules whole.

PSEUDOEPHEDRINE HYDROCHLORIDE ORAL SOLUTION

Usual adult and adolescent dose: Decongestant, nasal—Oral, 60 mg every four to six hours, not to exceed 240 mg in twenty-four hours.

PSEUDOEPHEDRINE HYDROCHLORIDE SYRUP USP

Usual adult and adolescent dose: Decongestant, nasal—Oral, 60 mg every four to six hours, not to exceed 240 mg in twenty-four hours.

PSEUDOEPHEDRINE HYDROCHLORIDE TABLETS USP

Usual adult and adolescent dose: Decongestant, nasal—Oral, 60 mg every four to six hours, not to exceed 240 mg in twenty-four hours.

PSEUDOEPHEDRINE SULFATE TABLETS

Usual adult and adolescent dose: Decongestant, nasal—Oral, 60 mg every four to six hours.

Usual adult prescribing limits: 240 mg in twenty-four hours.

PSEUDOEPHEDRINE SULFATE EXTENDED-RELEASE TABLETS

Usual adult and adolescent dose: Decongestant, nasal—Oral, 120 mg every twelve hours.

Usual adult prescribing limits: 240 mg in twenty-four hours.

Auxiliary labeling: • Swallow tablets whole.

PYRIMETHAMINE   Systemic

A commonly used *brand name* in the U.S. and Canada is *Daraprim.*

ORAL
Pyrimethamine Tablets USP
In the U.S. and Canada—*Daraprim*

Category: Antiprotozoal.

Indications

Note: Bracketed information in the *Indications* section refers to uses not included in U.S. product labeling.

Accepted
Malaria (treatment)—Pyrimethamine is indicated in combination with sulfadoxine and quinine in the treatment of chloroquine-resistant *Plasmodium falciparum* malaria. It is also indicated in combination with mefloquine and sulfadoxine, or quinine and sulfadoxine in the treatment of chloroquine-resistant *P. falciparum* malaria acquired in Southeast Asia, Bangladesh, East Africa, or the Amazon basin. Pyrimethamine is indicated in combination with sulfadoxine in the presumptive treatment of chloroquine-resistant *P. falciparum* malaria for self-treatment of febrile illness when medical care is not immediately available.

Toxoplasmosis (treatment)—Pyrimethamine is indicated in combination with a sulfapyrimidine-type sulfonamide in the treatment of toxoplasmosis caused by *Toxoplasma gondii.* [Pyrimethamine is also used with clindamycin in the treatment of toxoplasmosis in patients who are unresponsive to or intolerant of standard therapy.][1]

[Isosporiasis (prophylaxis and treatment)][1]—Pyrimethamine is used with sulfadoxine in the prophylaxis and treatment of isosporiasis caused by *Isospora belli.* It has also been used alone in a limited number of patients in the prophylaxis and treatment of isosporiasis.

[Pneumonia, *Pneumocystis carinii* (treatment)][1]—Pyrimethamine is used in combination with sulfadiazine, sulfadoxine, or dapsone, in the treatment of mild to moderate pneumonia caused by *Pneumocystis carinii* in patients who are unresponsive to or intolerant of standard therapy.

Not all species or strains of a particular organism may be susceptible to pyrimethamine. Resistance to pyrimethamine has been reported in *P. falciparum* and *P. vivax* malaria and may be widespread in certain areas.

Unaccepted
Pyrimethamine is not indicated alone in the treatment of acute attacks of malaria in nonimmune patients. Fast-acting schizonticides (e.g., 4-aminoquinolines, quinine) are preferred for these patients.

[1]Not included in Canadian product labeling.

Pharmacology

Mechanism of action/Effect: Binds to and reversibly inhibits the protozoal enzyme dihydrofolate reductase, selectively blocking conversion of dihydrofolic acid to its functional form, tetrahydrofolic acid. This depletes folate, an essential cofactor in the biosynthesis of nucleic acids, resulting in interference with protozoal nucleic acid and protein production. Protozoal dihydrofolate reductase is many times more tightly bound by pyrimethamine than the corresponding mammalian enzyme.

Exerts its effect in the folate biosynthesis at a step immediately subsequent to the one at which sulfonamides exert their effect. When administered concurrently with sulfonamides, synergism occurs, which is attributed to inhibition of tetrahydrofolate production at 2 sequential steps in its biosynthesis.

Active against asexual erythrocytic forms and, to a lesser degree, tissue forms of *P. falciparum* malaria. Does not destroy gametocytes, but arrests sporogony in the mosquito. Used alone, pyrimethamine does not produce radical cure in vivax or ovale malaria since it does not kill the latent hepatic stages of these parasites.

Precautions to Consider

Geriatrics
No information is available on the relationship of age to the effects of pyrimethamine in geriatric patients.

Dental
High doses of pyrimethamine not supplemented by leucovorin (folinic acid) may cause a folic acid deficiency, which may be characterized by a change in or loss of taste, or pain, burning, or inflammation of the tongue.

The leukopenic and thrombocytopenic effects of high doses of pyrimethamine may result in an increased incidence of certain microbial infections, delayed healing, and gingival bleeding. If leukopenia or thrombocytopenia occurs, dental work should be deferred until blood counts have returned to normal. Patients should be instructed in proper oral hygiene, including caution in use of regular toothbrushes, dental floss, and toothpicks.

Drug interactions and/or related problems
The following drug interactions and/or related problems have been selected on the basis of their potential clinical significance (possible mechanism in parentheses where appropriate)—not necessarily inclusive (» = major clinical significance):

Note: Combinations containing any of the following medications, depending on the amount present, may also interact with this medication.

» Bone marrow depressants
(concurrent use of pyrimethamine with bone marrow depressants may increase the leukopenic and/or thrombocytopenic effects; if concurrent use is required, the possibility of increased myelotoxic effects should be considered, especially when pyrimethamine is used in large doses such as those required in the treatment of toxoplasmosis)

Folate antagonists, other
(concurrent use of other folate antagonists with pyrimethamine or use of pyrimethamine between courses of other folate antagonists is not recommended because of the possible development of megaloblastic anemia)

Contraindications/Medical problems
The contraindications/medical problems included have been selected on the basis of their potential clinical significance (reasons given in parentheses where appropriate)—not necessarily inclusive (» = major clinical significance).

Risk-benefit should be considered when the following medical problems exist:

» Anemia or
» Bone marrow depression
(pyrimethamine may cause folic acid deficiency, resulting in megaloblastic anemia, and blood dyscrasias, including agranulocytosis and thrombocytopenia)

Hepatic function impairment
(pyrimethamine is metabolized in the liver)

Hypersensitivity to pyrimethamine

» Seizure disorders, history of
(pyrimethamine may cause central nervous system [CNS] toxicity when used in high doses, as in the treatment of toxoplasmosis)

Side/Adverse Effects

Note: When pyrimethamine is used for malaria in usual recommended dosage, side/adverse effects usually are rare; however, with large doses, as for toxoplasmosis, side effects may occur more frequently unless pyrimethamine is given concurrently with folinic acid.

The following side/adverse effects have been selected on the basis of their potential clinical significance (possible signs and symptoms in parentheses where appropriate)—not necessarily inclusive:

Those indicating need for medical attention
Incidence more frequent with high doses
Atrophic glossitis (pain, burning, or inflammation of the tongue; change in or loss of taste)—due to folic acid deficiency; *blood dyscrasias, specifically agranulocytosis* (fever and sore throat), *megaloblastic anemia* (unusual tiredness or weakness), *or thrombocytopenia* (unusual bleeding or bruising)
Incidence rare
Hypersensitivity (skin rash)
Symptoms of overdose—in order of occurrence
Gastrointestinal toxicity (abdominal pain, severe and repeated vomiting); *neurotoxicity* (hyperexcitability, seizures)—usually occurs within 30 minutes to 2 hours of ingestion; *respiratory depression; circulatory collapse*

Those indicating need for medical attention only if they continue or are bothersome
Incidence more frequent with high doses
Gastrointestinal disturbances (anorexia, diarrhea, nausea and vomiting)

Patient Consultation

In providing consultation, consider emphasizing the following selected information (» = major clinical significance):

Before using this medication
» Conditions affecting use, especially:
Hypersensitivity to pyrimethamine
Pregnancy—Pyrimethamine crosses the placenta
Breast-feeding—Pyrimethamine is excreted in breast milk
Dental—High doses may cause atrophic glossitis, leukopenia, or thrombocytopenia
Other medications, especially bone marrow depressants
Other medical problems, especially anemia, bone marrow depression, or a history of seizure disorders

Proper use of this medication
» Keeping medication out of reach of children; overdose is very dangerous
Taking with meals or a snack if gastric irritation occurs
» Compliance with full course of therapy
» Importance of not missing doses and taking medication on a regular schedule
» Proper dosing
Missed dose: Taking as soon as possible; not taking if almost time for next dose; not doubling doses
» Proper storage

Precautions while using this medication
» Regular visits to physician to check blood counts, especially during high-dose therapy for toxoplasmosis
Checking with physician if no improvement within a few days
Importance of taking leucovorin concurrently if anemia occurs

Using caution in use of regular toothbrushes, dental floss, and toothpicks; deferring dental work until blood counts have returned to normal; checking with physician or dentist concerning proper oral hygiene

Side/adverse effects

Signs of potential side effects, especially blood dyscrasias, hypersensitivity, and symptoms of folic acid deficiency

General Dosing Information

Pyrimethamine may cause gastric irritation, sometimes resulting in vomiting, when given in high doses. To minimize this, pyrimethamine may be taken with meals or a snack or the dosage may be reduced.

Therapy should be discontinued if symptoms of folic acid deficiency occur. However, to prevent folic acid deficiency, leucovorin (folinic acid) may be administered concurrently to restore normal hematopoiesis. Leucovorin does not interfere with the antiprotozoal activity of pyrimethamine. Since malarial parasites are unable to utilize preformed folic acid, the antimalarial effect of pyrimethamine should not be affected. However, folic acid may interfere with the action of pyrimethamine on *T. gondii*, and concurrent use in toxoplasmosis is not recommended. In adults, 5 to 15 mg of leucovorin may be given orally, intramuscularly, or intravenously once a day for 3 days or as required. Alternatively, adults may be given 9 mg of leucovorin 2 or 3 times a week. Doses of up to 50 mg per day of leucovorin have been used with pyrimethamine in AIDS patients. Infants may be given 1 mg of leucovorin once a day.

Patients with impaired renal function receiving pyrimethamine prophylactically do not generally require a reduction in dose. However, patients receiving pyrimethamine more frequently should be monitored closely for signs of toxicity.

For toxoplasmosis

The dose of pyrimethamine that is required in the treatment of toxoplasmosis is 10 to 20 times greater than the antimalarial dose. Concurrent prophylactic administration of leucovorin in doses up to 50 mg daily with pyrimethamine is recommended to avoid folic acid deficiency.

In patients with seizure disorders, small initial doses of pyrimethamine are recommended in the treatment of toxoplasmosis to avoid potential CNS toxicity.

In patients who also have AIDS, treatment with pyrimethamine and sulfonamides may be required indefinitely. Clindamycin has been used with pyrimethamine in doses of 900 mg to 2.4 grams daily in patients who experienced adverse reactions to sulfonamides.

Oral Dosage Forms

Note: Bracketed uses in the *Dosage Forms* section refer to categories of use and/or indications that are not included in U.S. product labeling.

PYRIMETHAMINE TABLETS USP

Usual adult and adolescent dose:

Malaria—

Treatment:

Chloroquine-resistant *P. falciparum* malaria—Oral, 75 mg of pyrimethamine in combination with 1.5 grams of sulfadoxine as a single dose on day three of quinine therapy.

Chloroquine-resistant *P. falciparum* malaria acquired in Southeast Asia, Bangladesh, East Africa, or the Amazon basin—Oral, 75 mg of pyrimethamine in combination with 750 mg of mefloquine and 1.5 grams of sulfadoxine as a single dose.

Presumptive treatment: Oral, 75 mg of pyrimethamine in combination with 1.5 grams of sulfadoxine as a single dose for self-treatment of febrile illness when medical care is not immediately available.

Toxoplasmosis—

AIDS patients:

Loading dose—Oral, 100 to 200 mg of pyrimethamine per day in combination with 500 mg to 1.5 grams of a sulfadiazine every six hours, or 600 mg of clindamycin every six hours, for one to two days.

Treatment—Oral, 50 to 100 mg of pyrimethamine per day in combination with 500 mg to 1.5 grams of a sulfadiazine every six hours, or 600 mg of clindamycin every six hours, for three to six weeks.

Maintenance—Oral, 25 to 50 mg of pyrimethamine per day in combination with 250 mg to 1 gram of a sulfadiazine every six hours, or 600 mg of clindamycin every six hours, as life-long therapy.

Other patients:

Loading dose—Oral, 50 to 200 mg per day in combination with 250 mg to 1 gram of a sulfapyrimidine-type sulfonamide every six hours, for one to two days.

Treatment—Oral, 25 to 50 mg per day in combination with 125 to 500 mg of a sulfapyrimidine-type sulfonamide every six hours, for two to four weeks if patient is immunocompetent, and four to six weeks if patient is immunocompromised.

[Isosporiasis][1]—

Treatment: Oral, 50 to 75 mg of pyrimethamine per day for three to four weeks.

Prophylaxis: Oral, 25 mg of pyrimethamine in combination with 500 mg of sulfadoxine once a week; or 25 mg of pyrimethamine alone once a day.

Note: These doses are based on very limited data.

Auxiliary labeling:

• Continue medicine for full time of treatment.
• Keep out of reach of children.

---

[1]Not included in Canadian product labeling.

PYRITHIONE   Topical

Some commonly used *brand names* are:

In the U.S.—

Danex

DHS Zinc Dandruff
  Shampoo

Head & Shoulders
  Antidandruff Cream
  Shampoo Normal to Dry
  Formula

Head & Shoulders
  Antidandruff Cream
  Shampoo Normal to Oily
  Formula

Head & Shoulders Dry Scalp
  Conditioning Formula
  Lotion Shampoo

Head & Shoulders Dry
  Scalp Regular Formula
  Lotion Shampoo

Head & Shoulders Dry
  Scalp 2 in 1 (Dry Scalp
  Shampoo Plus
  Conditioner in One)
  Formula Lotion Shampoo

Head & Shoulders
  Antidandruff Lotion
  Shampoo Normal to Dry
  Formula

Head & Shoulders
  Antidandruff Lotion
  Shampoo Normal to
  Oily Formula

Head & Shoulders
 Antidandruff Lotion
 Shampoo 2 in 1
 (Complete Dandruff
 Shampoo plus
 Conditioner in One)
 Formula
In Canada—
 Dan-Gard
 Sebulon

Sebex
Sebulon
Zincon Dandruff Lotion
 Shampoo
ZNP Bar Shampoo
ZNP Shampoo

TOPICAL

Pyrithione Zinc Bar Shampoo
 In the U.S.—*ZNP Bar Shampoo*
Pyrithione Zinc Cream Shampoo
 In the U.S.—*Head & Shoulders Antidandruff Cream Shampoo Normal to Dry Formula; Head & Shoulders Antidandruff Cream Shampoo Normal to Oily Formula*
Pyrithione Zinc Lotion Shampoo
 In the U.S.—*Danex; DHS Zinc Dandruff Shampoo; Head & Shoulders Dry Scalp Conditioning Formula Lotion Shampoo; Head & Shoulders Dry Scalp Regular Formula Lotion Shampoo; Head & Shoulders Dry Scalp 2 in 1 (Dry Scalp Shampoo Plus Conditioner in One) Formula Lotion Shampoo; Head & Shoulders Antidandruff Lotion Shampoo Normal to Dry Formula; Head & Shoulders Antidandruff Lotion Shampoo Normal to Oily Formula; Head & Shoulders Antidandruff Lotion Shampoo 2 in 1 (Complete Dandruff Shampoo plus Conditioner in One) Formula; Sebex; Sebulon; Zincon Dandruff Lotion Shampoo; ZNP Shampoo*
 In Canada—*Dan-Gard; Sebulon*

Category: Antiseborrheic.

Indications

Accepted
Dandruff (treatment); or
Dermatitis, seborrheic (treatment)—Indicated to help control dandruff and seborrheic dermatitis of the scalp.

Pharmacology

Mechanism of action/Effect: Pyrithione may act by an antimitotic action, resulting in a reduction in the turnover of epidermal cells. It also has bacteriostatic and fungistatic activity, but it is not known if this action contributes to the antiseborrheic effects of the drug.

Precautions to Consider

Geriatrics
Appropriate studies on the relationship of age to the effects of pyrithione have not been performed in the geriatric population. However, no geriatrics-specific problems have been documented to date.

Contraindications/Medical problems
The contraindications/medical problems included have been selected on the basis of their potential clinical significance (reasons given in parentheses where appropriate)—not necessarily inclusive (» = major clinical significance).

Risk-benefit should be considered when the following medical problem exists:
 Sensitivity to pyrithione

Side/Adverse Effects

The following side/adverse effects have been selected on the basis of their potential clinical significance (possible signs and symptoms in parentheses where appropriate)—not necessarily inclusive:

Those indicating need for medical attention
Irritation of skin

Patient Consultation

In providing consultation, consider emphasizing the following selected information (» = major clinical significance):

Before using this medication
» Conditions affecting use, especially:
 Sensitivity to pyrithione

Proper use of this medication
 For best results, using medication at least 2 times a week or as directed by physician
 Proper administration:
  Before applying—Wetting hair and scalp with lukewarm water
  Applying enough shampoo to work up lather; rubbing in well; rinsing
  Applying shampoo again and rinsing thoroughly
» Avoiding contact with the eyes; flushing thoroughly with water if medication accidentally gets in eyes
» Proper dosage
 Missed dose: Using as soon as possible; not using if almost time for next dose
» Proper storage

Precautions while using this medication
 Checking with physician if condition does not get better after regular use, or if it gets worse

Side/adverse effects
 Signs of potential side effects, especially skin irritation

General Dosing Information

The scalp and hair should be wet with lukewarm water and enough shampoo massaged into the scalp to work up a lather; then the scalp and hair should be rinsed. Application should be repeated, then the scalp and hair rinsed thoroughly.

Topical Dosage Forms

PYRITHIONE ZINC BAR SHAMPOO

Usual adult and adolescent dose: Topical, to the scalp, two times a week.

Auxiliary labeling: • For external use only.

PYRITHIONE ZINC CREAM SHAMPOO

Usual adult and adolescent dose: Topical, to the scalp, two times a week.

Auxiliary labeling: • For external use only.

PYRITHIONE ZINC LOTION SHAMPOO

Usual adult and adolescent dose: Topical, to the scalp, two times a week.

Auxiliary labeling:
• Shake well.
• For external use only.

QUINIDINE   Systemic

Some commonly used *brand names* are:

In the U.S.—

Cardioquin [Quinidine Polygalacturonate]	*Quinaglute Dura-tabs* [Quinidine Gluconate]
Cin-Quin [Quinidine Sulfate]	*Quinalan* [Quinidine Gluconate]
Duraquin [Quinidine Gluconate]	*Quinidex Extentabs* [Quinidine Sulfate]
	Quinora [Quinidine Sulfate]

In Canada—

Apo-Quinidine [Quinidine Sulfate]	*Quinaglute Dura-tabs* [Quinidine Gluconate]
Cardioquin [Quinidine Polygalacturonate]	*Quinate* [Quinidine Gluconate]
Novoquinidin [Quinidine Sulfate]	*Quinidex Extentabs* [Quinidine Sulfate]

ORAL

Quinidine Gluconate Tablets*
   In Canada—*Quinate*
Quinidine Gluconate Extended-release Tablets
   In the U.S.—*Duraquin; Quinaglute Dura-tabs; Quinalan;* GENERIC
   In Canada—*Quinaglute Dura-tabs*
Quinidine Polygalacturonate Tablets
   In the U.S. and Canada—*Cardioquin*
Quinidine Sulfate Capsules USP†
   In the U.S.—*Cin-Quin;* GENERIC
Quinidine Sulfate Tablets USP
   In the U.S.—*Cin-Quin; Quinora;* GENERIC
   In Canada—*Apo-Quinidine; Novoquinidin;* GENERIC
Quinidine Sulfate Extended-release Tablets USP
   In the U.S. and Canada—*Quinidex Extentabs*

PARENTERAL

Quinidine Gluconate Injection USP†
   In the U.S.—GENERIC
Quinidine Sulfate Injection
   In the U.S. and Canada—GENERIC

---

*Not commercially available in the U.S.
†Not commercially available in Canada.

Category: Antiarrhythmic.

Indications

Note: Bracketed information in the *Indications* section refers to uses not included in U.S. product labeling.

Accepted
Cardiac arrhythmias (prophylaxis and treatment)—Treatment and control of:
   Atrial fibrillation, established
   Atrial flutter
   Paroxysmal atrial fibrillation
   Paroxysmal atrial tachycardia
   Paroxysmal atrioventricular (AV) junctional rhythm
   Paroxysmal ventricular tachycardia not associated with complete heart block
   Premature contractions, atrial and ventricular
[Malaria (treatment)][1]—Quinidine may also be used in the treatment of malaria, although quinine is preferred.

---

[1]Not included in Canadian product labeling.

Pharmacology

Mechanism of action/Effect: Quinidine has both direct and indirect (anticholinergic) effects on cardiac tissue. Automaticity, conduction velocity, and membrane responsiveness are decreased, possibly because quinidine inhibits movement of potassium ions across membranes. The effective refractory period is prolonged. The anticholinergic action reduces vagal tone. An alpha-adrenergic blocking action often produces increased beta-adrenergic effects such as peripheral vasodilation. In the Vaughan Williams classification of antiarrhythmics, quinidine is considered to be a Class I antiarrhythmic.

Duration of action: Oral—
   Regular tablets or capsules: 6 to 8 hours.
   Extended-release tablets: About 12 hours.

Precautions to Consider

Cross-sensitivity and/or related problems
Patients sensitive to quinine may be sensitive to this medication also.

Geriatrics
Although appropriate studies with quinidine have not been performed in the geriatric population, geriatrics-specific problems that would limit the usefulness of this medication in the elderly are not expected. However, elderly patients are more likely to have age-related renal function impairment, which may require dosage adjustment in patients receiving quinidine.

Dental
The secondary anticholinergic effects of quinidine may decrease or inhibit salivary flow, especially in middle-aged or elderly patients, thus contributing to the development of caries, periodontal disease, oral candidiasis, and discomfort.

Drug interactions and/or related problems
The following drug interactions and/or related problems have been selected on the basis of their potential clinical significance (possible mechanism in parentheses where appropriate)—not necessarily inclusive (» = major clinical significance):

Note: Combinations containing any of the following medications, depending on the amount present, may also interact with this medication.

» Alkalizers, urinary, such as:
   Antacids, calcium- and/or magnesium-containing
   Carbonic anhydrase inhibitors
   Citrates
   Sodium bicarbonate
      (concurrent use may increase the potential for toxic effects of quinidine; serum quinidine concentration is increased by enhanced renal absorption, which is promoted by the higher urinary pH; dosage adjustments may be needed when urinary alkalizer therapy is initiated or discontinued or if the dosage is changed)

» Antiarrhythmics, other, or
   Phenothiazines or
   Rauwolfia alkaloids
      (concurrent use with quinidine may result in additive cardiac effects)
   Anticholinergics
      (concurrent use with quinidine may intensify atropine-like side effects because of the secondary anticholinergic activities of quinidine)

» Anticoagulants, coumarin- or indandione-derivative
      (concurrent use with quinidine may cause additive hypoprothrombinemia as a result of alteration of procoagulant factor

synthesis or catabolism and increased receptor affinity for the anticoagulant; dosage adjustments of anticoagulant may be necessary during and after quinidine therapy)

Antimyasthenics
(neuromuscular blocking and/or secondary anticholinergic actions of quinidine may antagonize the effect of antimyasthenics on skeletal muscle; dosage adjustments of antimyasthenics may be necessary to control symptoms of myasthenia gravis)

Bethanechol
(concurrent use with quinidine may antagonize the cholinergic effects of bethanechol)

Bretylium
(concurrent administration with quinidine may counteract inotropic effect of bretylium and potentiate hypotension)

Cimetidine
(as a result of inhibition of hepatic microsomal enzymes, cimetidine reduces total body clearance and prolongs the half-life of quinidine; dosage adjustment may be necessary)

Digitalis glycosides
(concurrent use is reported to have increased serum concentrations of digoxin; studies also indicate possible increased serum concentrations of digitoxin when used concurrently with quinidine. Serum concentrations of the glycoside should be monitored and dosage adjusted as indicated)

Hepatic enzyme inducers
(concurrent use with quinidine may decrease serum quinidine concentrations because of enhanced hepatic metabolism; adjustments of quinidine dosage may be necessary)

» Neuromuscular blocking agents
(effects may be potentiated when these medications are used concurrently with quinidine; careful postoperative monitoring of the patient may be necessary following concurrent or sequential use, especially if there is a possibility of incomplete reversal of neuromuscular blockade)

» Pimozide
(concurrent use with quinidine may potentiate cardiac arrhythmias, which are seen on electrocardiogram [ECG] as prolongation of QT interval)

Potassium-containing medications
(concurrent use usually enhances quinidine's effects)

Quinine
(concurrent use with quinidine may increase the possibility of cinchonism)

Contraindications/Medical problems
The contraindications/medical problems included have been selected on the basis of their potential clinical significance (reasons given in parentheses where appropriate)—not necessarily inclusive (» = major clinical significance).

Except under special circumstances, this medication should not be used when the following medical problems exist:

» Atrioventricular (AV) block, complete, or
» Digitalis toxicity with AV conduction disorder or
» Intraventricular conduction defects, severe
(additive cardiac depression)

Risk-benefit should be considered when the following medical problems exist:

Asthma or emphysema
(possible hypersensitivity)
» AV block, incomplete
(quinidine may produce complete block)
» Digitalis intoxication
(additive cardiac depression and intracardial conduction inhibition)
» Hepatic function impairment or

» Renal function impairment
(possible accumulation; dosage adjustment may be required)
Hyperthyroidism
Hypokalemia
(reduced effect)
Infections, acute
» Myasthenia gravis
(quinidine may increase muscle weakness)
Psoriasis
Sensitivity to quinidine
» Thrombocytopenia, or history of

Side/Adverse Effects

Note: Quinidine is potentially cardiotoxic, especially at dosages exceeding 2.4 grams per day. Possible cardiovascular effects include QRS widening, cardiac asystole, ventricular ectopic beats, idioventricular rhythms (including ventricular tachycardia and fibrillation), paradoxical tachycardia, and arterial embolism.

The following side/adverse effects have been selected on the basis of their potential clinical significance (possible signs and symptoms in parentheses where appropriate)—not necessarily inclusive:

Those indicating need for medical attention
Incidence less frequent
Allergic reaction (fever; skin rash, hives, or itching; wheezing, shortness of breath, or troubled breathing); *cinchonism* (blurred vision or any change in vision, dizziness or lightheadedness, severe headache, ringing or buzzing in ears or any loss of hearing); *hypotension or extreme CNS effects* (fainting)
Note: In sensitive patients, *cinchonism* may occur after a single dose.
Incidence rare
Anemia (unusual tiredness or weakness); *tachycardia, paradoxical* (fast heartbeat); *thrombocytopenia* (unusual bleeding or bruising)

Those indicating need for medical attention only if they continue or are bothersome
Incidence more frequent
Bitter taste; diarrhea; flushing of skin with itching; loss of appetite; nausea or vomiting; stomach pain or cramping
Incidence less frequent
Confusion

Patient Consultation

Consider advising the patient on the following:

Before using this medication
See *Precautions to Consider.*

Proper use of this medication
Taking medication with water at least 1 hour before or 2 hours after meals for better absorption; may be taken with food or milk to lessen gastrointestinal irritation
Proper administration of extended-release tablets: Swallowing tablet whole; not breaking, crushing, or chewing before swallowing
» Compliance with therapy; taking as directed even if feeling well
Missed dose: Taking as soon as possible if remembered within 2 hours; if remembered later, not taking at all; not doubling doses
» Proper storage

Precautions while using this medication
Regular visits to physician to check progress
» Checking with physician before discontinuing medication
» Caution if any kind of surgery (including dental surgery) or emergency treatment is required
Carrying medical identification card

» Checking with physician if symptoms of quinidine intolerance occur

Side/adverse effects

Signs of potential side effects, especially allergic reaction, cinchonism, hypotension or extreme CNS effects, anemia, paradoxical tachycardia, and thrombocytopenia

General Dosing Information

Dosage must be adjusted to meet the individual requirements of each patient, on the basis of clinical response.

A test dose of one regular oral tablet may be administered prior to quinidine therapy to check for intolerance.

Higher serum quinidine concentrations are usually required to correct atrial arrhythmias than for ventricular arrhythmias.

Diet/Nutrition

This medication is preferably taken with a full glass (240 mL) of water on an empty stomach 1 hour before or 2 hours after meals for better absorption; however, it may be taken with food or milk when necessary to lessen gastrointestinal irritation.

Oral Dosage Forms

QUINIDINE GLUCONATE TABLETS

Note: Quinidine gluconate tablets are not commercially available in the U.S.

Usual adult dose: Antiarrhythmic—Maintenance: Oral, 325 to 650 mg every six hours as needed and tolerated.

Auxiliary labeling: • Do not take other medicines without advice from your doctor.

QUINIDINE GLUCONATE EXTENDED-RELEASE TABLETS

Usual adult dose: Maintenance—Oral, 324 to 660 mg every six to twelve hours as needed and tolerated.

Auxiliary labeling:
• Swallow tablet whole. Do not break or chew.
• Do not take other medicines without advice from your doctor.

QUINIDINE POLYGALACTURONATE TABLETS

Usual adult dose:

Initial—Oral, 275 to 825 mg every three to four hours for three or four doses with subsequent doses being increased by 137.5 to 275 mg every third or fourth dose until rhythm is restored or toxic effects occur.

Maintenance—Oral, 275 mg two or three times a day as needed and tolerated.

Auxiliary labeling: • Do not take other medicines without advice from your doctor.

QUINIDINE SULFATE CAPSULES USP

Note: Quinidine sulfate capsules are not commercially available in Canada.

Usual adult dose: Antiarrhythmic—

Initial:

Premature atrial and ventricular contractions—Oral, 200 to 300 mg three or four times per day.

Paroxysmal supraventricular tachycardias—Oral, 400 to 600 mg every two or three hours until the paroxysm is terminated.

Atrial flutter—Oral, by individual titration following digitalization.

Conversion of atrial fibrillation—Oral, 200 mg every two or three hours for five to eight doses, with subsequent daily increases as needed and tolerated.

Maintenance: Oral, 200 to 300 mg three or four times a day as needed and tolerated.

Usual adult prescribing limits: Up to 4 grams daily.

Auxiliary labeling: • Do not take other medicines without advice from your doctor.

QUINIDINE SULFATE TABLETS USP

Usual adult dose: Antiarrhythmic—

Initial:

Premature atrial and ventricular contractions—Oral, 200 to 300 mg three or four times per day.

Paroxysmal supraventricular tachycardias—Oral, 400 to 600 mg every two or three hours until the paroxysm is terminated.

Atrial flutter—Oral, by individual titration following digitalization.

Conversion of atrial fibrillation—Oral, 200 mg every two or three hours for five to eight doses, with subsequent daily increases as needed and tolerated.

Maintenance: Oral, 200 to 300 mg three or four times a day as needed and tolerated.

Usual adult prescribing limits: Up to 4 grams daily.

Auxiliary labeling: • Do not take other medicines without advice from your doctor.

QUINIDINE SULFATE EXTENDED-RELEASE TABLETS USP

Usual adult dose: Oral, 300 or 600 mg every eight to twelve hours as needed and tolerated.

Auxiliary labeling:
• Swallow tablets whole. Do not break or chew.
• Do not take other medicines without advice from your doctor.

Parenteral Dosage Forms

QUINIDINE GLUCONATE INJECTION USP

Note: Quinidine gluconate injection is not commercially available in Canada.

Usual adult dose:

Intramuscular, 600 mg initially; then 400 mg repeated as often as every two hours if necessary.

Intravenous infusion, 800 mg in 40 mL of 5% Dextrose Injection USP administered at a rate of 1 mL per minute with electrocardiogram (ECG) and blood pressure monitoring.

Usual adult prescribing limits: Up to 5 grams daily.

QUINIDINE SULFATE INJECTION

Usual adult dose: Intravenous infusion, 600 mg in 40 mL of 5% Dextrose Injection USP administered at a rate of 1 mL per minute with ECG and blood pressure monitoring.

Usual adult prescribing limits: Up to 3.75 grams daily.

RAUWOLFIA ALKALOIDS   Systemic

Some commonly used *brand names* are:

In the U.S.—
Harmonyl [Deserpidine]
Raudixin [Rauwolfia
   Serpentina]
Rauval [Rauwolfia
   Serpentina]

Rauverid [Rauwolfia
   Serpentina]
Serpalan [Reserpine]
Wolfina [Rauwolfia
   Serpentina]

In Canada—
Novoreserpine [Reserpine]
Reserfia [Reserpine]

Serpasil [Reserpine]

ORAL
DESERPIDINE†
Deserpidine Tablets†
   In the U.S.—*Harmonyl*
RAUWOLFIA SERPENTINA†
Rauwolfia Serpentina Tablets USP†
   In the U.S.—*Raudixin; Rauval; Rauverid; Wolfina;* GENERIC
RESERPINE
Reserpine Tablets USP
   In the U.S.—*Serpalan;* GENERIC
   In Canada—*Novoreserpine; Reserfia; Serpasil;* GENERIC

†Not commercially available in Canada.

Category: Antihypertensive; vasospastic therapy adjunct.

Indications

Note: Bracketed information in the *Indications* section refers to uses not included in U.S. product labeling.

Accepted
Hypertension (treatment)—Rauwolfia alkaloids are indicated in the treatment of hypertension.

In the 1988 Report of the Joint National Committee on Detection, Evaluation, and Treatment of High Blood Pressure, a progression in choice of treatments for essential hypertension is recommended:

Nonpharmacologic management (especially sodium restriction, weight reduction and exercise, and moderation of alcohol consumption) is recommended first for some patients, including those with mild hypertension, and is recommended as an adjunct to all pharmacologic hypertensive therapy.

Initial drug therapy usually consists of a diuretic, beta-adrenergic blocking agent, calcium channel blocker, or angiotensin-converting enzyme (ACE) inhibitor. If adequate blood pressure control is not achieved and the patient is adherent to the treatment program and not experiencing significant side effects, dosage of the drug may be increased, a drug from another one of these initial classes may be added or substituted, or a second drug from a different class—centrally acting alpha-adrenergic blockers (e.g., clonidine, guanabenz, guanfacine, methyldopa), peripheral-acting adrenergic antagonists (e.g., guanadrel, guanethidine, rauwolfia alkaloids), post-synaptic alpha-1 peripheral adrenergic blocking agents (e.g., doxazosin, prazosin, terazosin), or vasodilators (e.g., hydralazine, minoxidil)—may be added or substituted.

If necessary, a drug from another class in the second group may be substituted or added as a third drug. If blood pressure control is still not achieved, a drug from still another class may be substituted or added as a fourth drug, or the patient may need further evaluation and/or referral.

[Raynaud's phenomenon (treatment)][1]—Reserpine has also been used to treat Raynaud's phenomenon.

Unaccepted
Rauwolfia alkaloids have been used for relief of symptoms in agitated psychotic states such as schizophrenia; however, use as antipsychotics and sedatives has been superseded by use of more effective, safer agents.

[1]Not included in Canadian product labeling.

Pharmacology

Note: Information (except physicochemical characteristics) available only for reserpine.

Mechanism of action/Effect: Acts at postganglionic sympathetic nerve endings; depletes tissue and central nervous system (CNS) stores of catecholamines and serotonin; antihypertensive activity thought to be due to reduced cardiac output and possibly some decrease in peripheral resistance.

Onset of action:
Antihypertensive—Oral: Several days to 3 weeks (multiple doses).
Catecholamine depletion—Within 1 hour (single dose).

Time to peak effect:
Antihypertensive—Oral: 3 to 6 weeks (multiple doses).
Catecholamine depletion—Within 24 hours (single dose).

Duration of action: Antihypertensive—Oral: 1 to 6 weeks.

Precautions to Consider

Cross-sensitivity and/or related problems
Patients sensitive to one rauwolfia alkaloid may be sensitive to other rauwolfia alkaloids also.

Geriatrics
Although appropriate studies on the relationship of age to the effects of the rauwolfia alkaloids have not been performed in the geriatric population, the elderly may be more sensitive to the CNS depressant and hypotensive effects. In addition, elderly patients are more likely to have age-related renal function impairment, which may require caution in patients receiving rauwolfia alkaloids. A lower dose is recommended in the elderly.

Dental
Use of rauwolfia alkaloids may decrease or inhibit salivary flow, thus contributing to the development of caries, periodontal disease, oral candidiasis, and discomfort.

Drug interactions and/or related problems
The following drug interactions and/or related problems have been selected on the basis of their potential clinical significance (possible mechanism in parentheses where appropriate)—not necessarily inclusive (» = major clinical significance):

Note: Combinations containing any of the following medications, depending on the amount present, may also interact with this medication.

Alcohol or
CNS depression-producing medications
   (concurrent use may enhance the CNS depressant effects of either these medications or rauwolfia alkaloids)

Anti-inflammatory drugs, nonsteroidal (NSAIDs), especially indomethacin
   (antihypertensive effects of rauwolfia alkaloids may be reduced when used concurrently with these agents; indomethacin, and possibly other NSAIDs, may antagonize the antihypertensive effect by inhibiting renal prostaglandin synthesis and/or by causing sodium and fluid retention; the patient should be carefully monitored to confirm that the desired effect is being obtained)

Anticholinergics or other medications with anticholinergic action
(concurrent use of rauwolfia alkaloids may antagonize the inhibitory action of these medications on gastric acid secretion)

Beta-adrenergic blocking agents, including ophthalmic beta-blockers absorbed systemically
(concurrent administration with beta-blockers may result in additive and possibly excessive beta-adrenergic blockade; although this effect is largely theoretical, close observation is recommended since bradycardia and hypotension may occur)

Bromocriptine
(reserpine may increase serum prolactin concentrations, and interfere with effects of bromocriptine; dosage adjustment of bromocriptine may be necessary)

Digitalis glycosides or
Quinidine
(concurrent use may result in cardiac arrhythmias; although this interaction is controversial and does not appear to be significant with usual doses, caution is recommended, especially when large doses of rauwolfia alkaloids are used in digitalized patients)

Estrogens
(concurrent use may decrease the antihypertensive effect of rauwolfia alkaloids because estrogen-induced fluid retention may lead to increased blood pressure)

Extrapyramidal reaction-causing medications, other
(concurrent use with rauwolfia alkaloids may potentiate the extrapyramidal effects)

Hypotension-producing medications, other, except MAO inhibitors
(antihypertensive effects may be potentiated when these medications are used concurrently with rauwolfia alkaloids; although some combinations are frequently used for therapeutic advantage, when used concurrently dosage adjustments may be necessary)

(concurrent use of guanadrel or guanethidine with rauwolfia alkaloids may cause an increased incidence of orthostatic hypotension or bradycardia)

Levodopa
(rauwolfia alkaloids may cause dopamine depletion and parkinsonian effects, decreasing the therapeutic effects of levodopa; dosage adjustments of either or both medications may be necessary)

» Monoamine oxidase (MAO) inhibitors, including furazolidone, procarbazine, and selegiline
(when an MAO inhibitor is added to existing therapy with rauwolfia alkaloids, serious potentiation of CNS depressant effect may result; however, if a rauwolfia alkaloid is added to an MAO inhibitor regimen, excessive stimulation of receptors caused by the sudden release of accumulated norepinephrine and serotonin may result in moderate to sudden and severe hypertension and hyperpyrexia, which can reach crisis levels; administration of rauwolfia alkaloids is not recommended during and for 1 week following MAO inhibitor therapy)

Sympathomimetics
(antihypertensive effects of rauwolfia alkaloids may be reduced when used concurrently with these agents; the patient should be carefully monitored to confirm that the desired effect is being obtained)

Indirect-acting amines, such as amphetamines, phenylpropanolamine, pseudoephedrine, and tyramine, or

Direct- and indirect-acting (primarily indirect-acting) amines, such as ephedrine and mephentermine
(rauwolfia alkaloids inhibit the action of indirect-acting sympathomimetics by depleting catecholamine stores)

Direct-acting amines such as epinephrine or norepinephrine (levarterenol) or

Direct- and indirect-acting (primarily direct-acting) amines such as appetite suppressants (except fenfluramine), dobutamine,

dopamine, metaraminol, methoxamine, and phenylephrine
(rauwolfia alkaloids may theoretically prolong the action of direct-acting sympathomimetics by preventing uptake into storage granules; a "denervation supersensitivity" response is also possible; although concurrent use with rauwolfia alkaloids is not known to produce severe adverse effects, a significant increase in blood pressure has been documented when phenylephrine ophthalmic drops have been administered to patients taking reserpine, and caution and close observation are recommended; on the other hand, concurrent use with fenfluramine may increase the hypotensive effects of rauwolfia alkaloids)

Contraindications/Medical problems
The contraindications/medical problems included have been selected on the basis of their potential clinical significance (reasons given in parentheses where appropriate)—not necessarily inclusive (» = major clinical significance).

Risk-benefit should be considered when the following medical problems exist:

Cardiac arrhythmias

Cardiac depression

Epilepsy

» Gallstones or

» Peptic ulcer or

» Ulcerative colitis
(rauwolfia alkaloids increase gastrointestinal motility and secretion; may precipitate biliary colic)

» Mental depression, or history of

Parkinsonism

Pheochromocytoma

Renal function impairment
(patients with renal insufficiency may adjust poorly to reduced blood pressure levels. However, dosage reduction is not necessary in these patients)

Respiratory problems

Sensitivity to the rauwolfia alkaloid prescribed

» Caution is required also in patients receiving electroconvulsive therapy, as well as in the severely debilitated.

Side/Adverse Effects

Note: Side effects occur more frequently with high-dose administration.

The following side/adverse effects have been selected on the basis of their potential clinical significance (possible cause in parentheses where appropriate)—not necessarily inclusive:

Those indicating need for medical attention
Incidence more frequent
Dizziness
Incidence less frequent
Arrhythmias (irregular heartbeat); *black, tarry stools; bloody vomit, stomach cramps or pain; bradycardia* (slow heartbeat); *chest pain; drowsiness or faintness; headache; impotence or decreased sexual interest; lack of energy or weakness; mental depression or inability to concentrate; nervousness or anxiety; shortness of breath; vivid dreams or nightmares or early-morning sleeplessness*

Note: *CNS* effects are dose-related, occurring more frequently with doses exceeding 500 mcg (0.5 mg) per day.

Incidence rare
Painful or difficult urination; skin rash or itching; stiffness or trembling and shaking of hands and fingers; thrombocytopenia (unusual bleeding or bruising)

Signs and symptoms of overdose
Dizziness or drowsiness, severe; flushing of skin; pinpoint pupils of eyes; slow pulse

Those indicating need for medical attention only if they continue or are bothersome

Incidence more frequent

Anorexia (loss of appetite); *diarrhea; dryness of mouth; nasal congestion* (stuffy nose); *nausea and vomiting*

Incidence less frequent

Edema, peripheral (swelling of feet and lower legs)

Those indicating the need for medical attention if they occur after medication is discontinued

Arrhythmias (irregular heartbeat); *bradycardia* (slow heartbeat); *drowsiness or faintness; impotence or decreased sexual interest; lack of energy or weakness; mental depression or inability to concentrate; nervousness or anxiety; vivid dreams or nightmares or early-morning sleeplessness*

Note: *Mental depression* may have an insidious onset, may be severe enough to cause suicide, and may persist for several months following withdrawal of this medication.

Patient Consultation

In providing consultation, consider emphasizing the following selected information (» = major clinical significance):

Before using this medication

» Conditions affecting use, especially:

Sensitivity to any of the rauwolfia alkaloids

Pregnancy—Teratogenic in animals

Breast-feeding—Excreted in breast milk

Use in the elderly—May be more sensitive to the CNS depressant and hypotensive effects

Dental—May decrease or inhibit salivary flow

Other medications, especially monoamine oxidase (MAO) inhibitors

Other medical problems, especially gallstones, peptic ulcer, ulcerative colitis, or mental depression

Proper use of this medication

Possible need for control of weight and diet, especially sodium intake

» Patient may not experience symptoms of hypertension; importance of taking medication even if feeling well

» Does not cure but helps control hypertension; possible need for lifelong therapy; serious consequences of untreated hypertension

Getting into the habit of taking at same time each day to help increase compliance

Caution in taking combination therapy; taking each medication at the right time

Taking with meals or milk to reduce gastrointestinal irritation

Missed dose: Not taking missed dose at all and not doubling doses

» Proper storage

Precautions while using this medication

Regular visits to physician to check progress

» Not taking other medications, especially nonprescription sympathomimetics, unless discussed with physician

» Caution if any kind of surgery (including dental surgery) or emergency treatment is required

» Caution if depression or changes in sleep pattern occur

» Caution in taking alcohol or other CNS depressants

» Caution when driving or doing things requiring alertness because of possible drowsiness or dizziness

Possible dryness of mouth; using sugarless candy or gum, ice, or saliva substitute for relief; checking with physician or dentist if dry mouth continues for more than 2 weeks

Nasal stuffiness may occur; nasal decongestants or other OTC preparations containing sympathomimetics should not be used without first consulting physician or pharmacist

Side/adverse effects

Dizziness, arrhythmias, bradycardia, black, tarry stools, bloody vomit, chest pain, drowsiness or faintness, headache, impotence or decreased sexual interest, lack of energy or weakness, mental depression or inability to concentrate, nervousness or anxiety, vivid dreams or nightmares or early-morning sleeplessness, shortness of breath

General Dosing Information

Dosage must be adjusted to meet the individual requirements of each patient, on the basis of clinical response, with the lowest effective dosage being utilized in order to minimize problems with mental depression, orthostatic hypotension, and other side effects.

Rauwolfia alkaloids are usually used in combination with a diuretic to prevent sodium and water retention.

A lower dose is recommended in the elderly or severely debilitated.

Doses higher than the recommended dose should be used with caution because of the risk of severe mental depression.

Antihypertensive effects of rauwolfia alkaloids may not be observed for a few days to several weeks after oral administration and may persist for 1 to 6 weeks after withdrawal of the medication. It is recommended that adjustments in dosage be made every 7 to 14 days to allow the full effects of the preceding dose to occur.

It is recommended that this medication be withdrawn at the first sign of despondency, early-morning insomnia, loss of appetite, impotence, or self-deprecation.

It is recommended that rauwolfia alkaloids be withdrawn 2 weeks before electroconvulsive therapy is employed.

Recent evidence suggests that withdrawal of catecholamine-depleting antihypertensive therapy prior to surgery is not necessary, but that the anesthesiologist must be aware of such therapy. Administration of atropine prior to induction may prevent excessive bradycardia. If a hypotensive episode occurs, use of a weak direct-acting sympathomimetic agent is recommended.

Diet/Nutrition

It is recommended that these medications be taken with food or milk to minimize gastrointestinal upset.

DESERPIDINE

Oral Dosage Forms

DESERPIDINE TABLETS

Usual adult dose: Antihypertensive—Oral, 250 to 500 mcg (0.25 to 0.5 mg) a day as a single dose or in two divided daily doses.

Note: Geriatric patients may be more sensitive to the effects of the usual adult dose.

Auxiliary labeling:

• Take with meals or milk.

• Do not take other medicines without your doctor's advice.

RAUWOLFIA SERPENTINA

Oral Dosage Forms

RAUWOLFIA SERPENTINA TABLETS USP

Usual adult dose: Antihypertensive—Oral, 50 to 200 mg a day as a single dose or in two divided daily doses.

Note: Geriatric patients may be more sensitive to the effects of the usual adult dose.

Auxiliary labeling:
- Take with meals or milk.
- Do not take other medicines without your doctor's advice.

RESERPINE

Oral Dosage Forms

Note: Bracketed uses in the *Dosage Forms* section refer to categories of use and/or indications that are not included in U.S. product labeling.

RESERPINE TABLETS USP

Usual adult dose:
Antihypertensive or
[Vasospastic therapy adjunct—Raynaud's phenomenon][1]: Oral, 100 to 250 mcg (0.1 to 0.25 mg) a day.

Note: Geriatric patients may be more sensitive to the effects of the usual adult dose.

Auxiliary labeling:
- Take with meals or milk.
- Do not take other medicines without your doctor's advice.

---

[1]Not included in Canadian product labeling.

RAUWOLFIA ALKALOIDS AND THIAZIDE DIURETICS   Systemic

Category: Antihypertensive.

Indications

Accepted

Hypertension (treatment)—This combination is indicated for treatment of hypertension.

Fixed-dosage combinations are generally not recommended for initial therapy and are useful for subsequent therapy only when the proportion of the component agents corresponds to the dose of the individual agents, as determined by titration.

Nonpharmacologic management (especially sodium restriction, weight reduction and exercise, and moderation of alcohol consumption) is recommended first for some patients, including those with mild hypertension, and is recommended as an adjunct to all pharmacologic hypertensive therapy.

Patient Consultation

In providing consultation, consider emphasizing the following selected information (» = major clinical significance):

Before using this medication
» Conditions affecting use, especially:
  Sensitivity to rauwolfia alkaloids, thiazide diuretics, other sulfonamide-type medications, bumetanide, furosemide, or carbonic anhydrase inhibitors
  Pregnancy—Reserpine is teratogenic in animals; thiazide diuretics are not recommended for routine use and may cause jaundice, thrombocytopenia, hypokalemia in infant
  Breast-feeding—Reserpine and thiazide diuretics are excreted in breast milk; recommended that nursing mothers avoid thiazide diuretics during first month of breast-feeding because of reports of suppression of lactation
  Use in the elderly—May be more sensitive to the hypotensive and electrolyte effects
  Use by athletes—Diuretics are banned and tested for by the U.S. Olympic Committee (USOC), the International Olympic Committee (IOC), and the National Collegiate Athletic Association (NCAA)
  Other medications, especially monoamine oxidase (MAO) inhibitors, cholestyramine, colestipol, digitalis glycosides, or lithium
  Other medical problems, especially gallstones, peptic ulcer, ulcerative colitis, mental depression, or anuria or severe renal function impairment

Proper use of this medication
  Possible need for control of weight and diet, especially sodium intake
» Patient may not experience symptoms of hypertension; importance of taking medication even if feeling well
» Does not cure, but helps control hypertension; possible need for lifelong therapy; serious consequences of untreated hypertension
  Diuretic effects of medications and timing of doses to minimize inconvenience of diuresis
  Getting into habit of taking at same time each day to help increase compliance
  Taking with meals or milk to reduce gastrointestinal irritation
  Missed dose: Taking as soon as possible; not taking if almost time for next dose; not doubling doses
» Proper storage

Precautions while using this medication
  Regular visits to physician to check progress
» Not taking other medications, especially nonprescription sympathomimetics, unless discussed with physician
» Caution if any kind of surgery (including dental surgery) or emergency treatment is required
  Possibility of hypokalemia; possible need for additional potassium in diet; not changing diet without first checking with physician
  To prevent dehydration, checking with physician if severe nausea, vomiting, or diarrhea occurs and continues
» Caution when driving or doing things requiring alertness because of possible drowsiness or dizziness
» Caution if orthostatic hypotension occurs
» Caution if depression or changes in sleep pattern occur
» Caution in taking alcohol or other central nervous system (CNS) depressants
  Diabetics: May increase blood sugar levels
  Possible photosensitivity; avoiding unprotected exposure to sun; using protective clothing and sun block product; avoiding use of sunlamp, tanning bed, or tanning booth
  Nasal stuffiness may occur; nasal decongestants or other OTC preparations containing sympathomimetics should not be used without first consulting physician or pharmacist
  Possible dryness of mouth; using sugarless candy or gum, ice, or saliva substitute for relief; checking with physician or dentist if dry mouth continues for more than 2 weeks

Side/adverse effects
  Signs and symptoms of potential side effects, especially electrolyte imbalance, agranulocytosis, allergic reaction, cholecysti-

tis, pancreatitis, hepatic function impairment, hyperuricemia, gout, thrombocytopenia, dizziness, arrhythmias, bradycardia, black tarry stools, bloody vomit, chest pain, drowsiness or faintness, headache, impotence or decreased sexual interest, lack of energy or weakness, mental depression or inability to concentrate, nervousness or anxiety, vivid dreams or night-mares or early-morning sleeplessness, and shortness of breath

Oral Dosage Forms

DESERPIDINE AND HYDROCHLOROTHIAZIDE TABLETS

Usual adult dose: Antihypertensive—Oral, 1 tablet two times a day as determined by individual titration with the component agents.

Note: Geriatric patients may be more sensitive to the effects of the usual adult dose.

Auxiliary labeling:
• Take with meals or milk.
• Do not take other medicines without your doctor's advice.

Oral Dosage Forms

DESERPIDINE AND METHYCLOTHIAZIDE TABLETS

Usual adult dose: Antihypertensive—Oral, $1/2$ to 1 tablet a day as determined by individual titration with the component agents.

Note: Geriatric patients may be more sensitive to the effects of the usual adult dose.

Auxiliary labeling:
• Take with meals or milk.
• Do not take other medicines without your doctor's advice.

Oral Dosage Forms

RAUWOLFIA SERPENTINA AND BENDROFLUMETHIAZIDE TABLETS

Usual adult dose: Antihypertensive—Oral, 1 to 4 tablets a day as determined by individual titration with the component agents.

Note: Geriatric patients may be more sensitive to the effects of the usual adult dose.

Auxiliary labeling:
• Take with meals or milk.
• Do not take other medicines without your doctor's advice.

Oral Dosage Forms

RESERPINE AND CHLOROTHIAZIDE TABLETS USP

Usual adult dose: Antihypertensive—Oral, 1 or 2 tablets one or two times a day as determined by individual titration with the compo-nent agents.

Note: Geriatric patients may be more sensitive to the effects of the usual adult dose.

Auxiliary labeling:
• Take with meals or milk.
• Do not take other medicines without your doctor's advice.

Oral Dosage Forms

RESERPINE AND CHLORTHALIDONE TABLETS

Usual adult dose: Antihypertensive—Oral, 1 or 2 tablets once a day as determined by individual titration with the component agents.

Note: Geriatric patients may be more sensitive to the effects of the usual adult dose.

Auxiliary labeling:
• Take with meals or milk.
• Do not take other medicines without your doctor's advice.

Oral Dosage Forms

RESERPINE AND HYDROCHLOROTHIAZIDE TABLETS USP

Usual adult dose: Antihypertensive—Oral, 1 tablet one to four times a day as determined by individual titration with the component agents.

Note: Geriatric patients may be more sensitive to the effects of the usual adult dose.

Auxiliary labeling:
• Take with meals or milk.
• Do not take other medicines without your doctor's advice.

Oral Dosage Forms

RESERPINE AND HYDROFLUMETHIAZIDE TABLETS

Note: In Canada, *Salutensin* also contains 200 mcg (0.2 mg) of pro-toveratrine A.

Usual adult dose: Antihypertensive—Oral, 1 tablet one or two times a day as determined by individual titration with the component agents.

Note: Geriatric patients may be more sensitive to the effects of the usual adult dose.

Auxiliary labeling:
• Take with meals or milk.
• Do not take other medicines without your doctor's advice.

Oral Dosage Forms

RESERPINE AND METHYCLOTHIAZIDE TABLETS

Usual adult dose: Antihypertensive—Oral, 1 to 4 tablets a day as determined by individual titration with the component agents.

Note: Geriatric patients may be more sensitive to the effects of the usual adult dose.

Auxiliary labeling:
• Take with meals or milk.
• Do not take other medicines without your doctor's advice.

Oral Dosage Forms

RESERPINE AND POLYTHIAZIDE TABLETS

Usual adult dose: Antihypertensive—Oral, $1/2$ to 2 tablets a day as determined by individual titration with the component agents.

Note: Geriatric patients may be more sensitive to the effects of the usual adult dose.

Auxiliary labeling:
• Take with meals or milk.
• Do not take other medicines without your doctor's advice.

Oral Dosage Forms

RESERPINE AND TRICHLORMETHIAZIDE TABLETS

Usual adult dose: Antihypertensive—Oral, 1 or 2 tablets a day as a single dose or in divided daily doses as determined by individual titration with the component agents.

Note: Geriatric patients may be more sensitive to the effects of the usual adult dose.

Auxiliary labeling:
• Take with meals or milk.
• Do not take other medicines without your doctor's advice.

RESERPINE AND HYDRALAZINE   Systemic

Category: Antihypertensive.

Indications

Accepted

Hypertension (treatment)—Reserpine and hydralazine combination is indicated for treatment of hypertension.

Fixed-dosage combinations are generally not recommended for initial therapy and are useful for subsequent therapy only when the proportion of the component agents corresponds to the dose of the individual agents, as determined by titration.

Nonpharmacologic management (especially sodium restriction, weight reduction and exercise, and moderation of alcohol consumption) is recommended first for some patients, including those with mild hypertension, and is recommended as an adjunct to all pharmacologic hypertensive therapy.

Patient Consultation

In providing consultation, consider emphasizing the following selected information (» = major clinical significance):

Before using this medication

» Conditions affecting use, especially:

    Sensitivity to rauwolfia alkaloids or hydralazine

    Pregnancy—Reserpine is teratogenic in animals; hydralazine is reported to cause blood problems in infants of mothers who took hydralazine and causes birth defects in animals

    Breast-feeding—Reserpine excreted in breast milk

    Use in the elderly—May be more sensitive to the CNS depressant and hypotensive effects

    Dental—May decrease or inhibit salivary flow

    Other medications, especially monoamine oxidase (MAO) inhibitors and diazoxide

    Other medical problems, especially coronary artery disease, rheumatic heart disease, gallstones, peptic ulcer, ulcerative colitis, or mental depression

Proper use of this medication

    Possible need for control of weight and diet, especially sodium intake

» Patient may not experience symptoms of hypertension; importance of taking medication even if feeling well

» Does not cure, but helps control hypertension; possible need for lifelong therapy; serious consequences of untreated hypertension

    Getting into habit of taking at same time each day to help increase compliance

    Taking with meals or milk to reduce gastrointestinal irritation

    Missed dose: Taking as soon as possible; not taking if almost time for next dose; not doubling doses

» Proper storage

Precautions while using this medication

    Regular visits to physician to check progress

» Not taking other medications, especially nonprescription sympathomimetics, unless discussed with physician

» Caution if any kind of surgery (including dental surgery) or emergency treatment is required

» Caution when driving or doing things requiring alertness because of possible headache, drowsiness, or dizziness

» Caution if depression or changes in sleep pattern occur

» Caution in taking alcohol or other central nervous system (CNS) depressants

    Nasal stuffiness may occur; nasal decongestants or other OTC preparations containing sympathomimetics should not be used without first consulting physician or pharmacist

    Possible dryness of mouth; using sugarless candy or gum, ice, or saliva substitute for relief; checking with physician or dentist if dry mouth continues for more than 2 weeks

Side/adverse effects

Signs and symptoms of potential side effects, especially dizziness; arrhythmias; bradycardia; black, tarry stools; bloody vomit; chest pain; drowsiness or faintness; headache; impotence or decreased sexual interest; lack of energy or weakness; mental depression or inability to concentrate; nervousness or anxiety; vivid dreams or nightmares or early-morning sleeplessness; shortness of breath; allergic reaction; cutaneous vasculitis; lymphadenopathy; peripheral neuritis; sodium and water retention; edema; and SLE-like syndrome

Oral Dosage Forms

RESERPINE AND HYDRALAZINE HYDROCHLORIDE TABLETS

Usual adult dose: Antihypertensive—Oral, 1 tablet four times a day as determined by individual titration with the component agents.

Note: Geriatric patients may be more sensitive to the effects of the usual adult dose.

Auxiliary labeling:

• Avoid alcoholic beverages.

• Take with meals or milk.

• Do not take other medicines without your doctor's advice.

RESERPINE, HYDRALAZINE, AND HYDROCHLOROTHIAZIDE   Systemic

Category: Antihypertensive.

Indications

Accepted

Hypertension (treatment)—This combination is indicated for treatment of hypertension.

Fixed-dosage combinations are generally not recommended for initial therapy and are useful for subsequent therapy only when the proportion of the component agents corresponds to the dose of the individual agents, as determined by titration.

Nonpharmacologic management (especially sodium restriction, weight reduction and exercise, and moderation of alcohol consumption) is recommended first for some patients, including those with mild hypertension, and is recommended as an adjunct to all pharmacologic hypertensive therapy.

Patient Consultation

In providing consultation, consider emphasizing the following selected information (» = major clinical significance):

Before using this medication
» Conditions affecting use, especially:
  Sensitivity to any of the rauwolfia alkaloids, hydralazine, thiazide diuretics, other sulfonamide-type medications, bumetanide, furosemide, or carbonic anhydrase inhibitors
  Pregnancy—Reserpine teratogenic in animals; hydralazine reported to cause blood problems in infants of mothers who took hydralazine and causes birth defects in animals; hydrochlorothiazide not recommended for routine use and may cause jaundice, thrombocytopenia, hypokalemia in infant
  Breast-feeding—Reserpine and hydrochlorothiazide excreted in breast milk; recommended that nursing mothers avoid hydrochlorothiazide during first month of breast-feeding because of reports of suppression of lactation
  Use in the elderly—May be more sensitive to the CNS depressant, hypotensive, and electrolyte effects
  Dental—May decrease or inhibit salivary flow
  Use by athletes—Diuretics are banned and tested for by the U.S. Olympic Committee (USOC), the International Olympic Committee (IOC), and the National Collegiate Athletic Association (NCAA)
  Other medications, especially monoamine oxidase (MAO) inhibitors, diazoxide, cholestyramine, colestipol, digitalis glycosides, or lithium
  Other medical problems, especially gallstones, peptic ulcer, ulcerative colitis, mental depression, coronary artery disease, rheumatic heart disease, or anuria or severe renal function impairment

Proper use of this medication
  Possible need for control of weight and diet, especially sodium intake
» Patient may not experience symptoms of hypertension; importance of taking medication even if feeling well
» Does not cure, but helps control hypertension; possible need for lifelong therapy; serious consequences of untreated hypertension
  Diuretic effects of medication and timing of doses to minimize inconvenience of diuresis
  Getting into habit of taking at same time each day to help increase compliance
  Taking with meals or milk to reduce gastrointestinal irritation
  Missed dose: Taking as soon as possible; not taking if almost time for next dose; not doubling doses
» Proper storage

Precautions while using this medication
  Regular visits to physician to check progress
» Not taking other medications, especially nonprescription sympathomimetics, unless discussed with physician

» Caution if any kind of surgery (including dental surgery) or emergency treatment is required
» Caution when driving or doing things requiring alertness because of possible headache, drowsiness, or dizziness
  Caution if orthostatic hypotension occurs
» Caution if depression or changes in sleep pattern occur
» Caution in taking alcohol or other central nervous system (CNS) depressants
  Possibility of hypokalemia; possible need for additional potassium in diet; not changing diet without first checking with physician
  To prevent dehydration, checking with physician if severe nausea, vomiting, or diarrhea occurs and continues
  Diabetics: May increase blood sugar levels
  Possible photosensitivity; avoiding unprotected exposure to sun; using protective clothing and sun block product; avoiding use of sunlamp, tanning bed, or tanning booth
  Nasal stuffiness may occur; nasal decongestants or other OTC preparations containing sympathomimetics should not be used without first consulting physician or pharmacist
  Possible dryness of mouth; using sugarless candy or gum, ice, or saliva substitute for relief; checking with physician or dentist if dry mouth continues for more than 2 weeks

Side/adverse effects
  Signs and symptoms of potential side effects, especially electrolyte imbalance, agranulocytosis, allergic reaction, angina pectoris, cutaneous vasculitis, lymphadenopathy, peripheral neuritis, SLE-like syndrome, cholecystitis, pancreatitis, hepatic function impairment, hyperuricemia, gout, thrombocytopenia, dizziness, arrhythmias, bradycardia, black tarry stools, bloody vomit, drowsiness or faintness, headache, impotence or decreased sexual interest, lack of energy or weakness, mental depression or inability to concentrate, nervousness or anxiety, vivid dreams or nightmares or early-morning sleeplessness, and shortness of breath

Oral Dosage Forms

RESERPINE, HYDRALAZINE HYDROCHLORIDE, AND HYDROCHLOROTHIAZIDE TABLETS USP

Usual adult dose: Antihypertensive—Oral, 1 or 2 tablets three times a day as determined by individual titration with the component agents.

Note: Geriatric patients may be more sensitive to the effects of the usual adult dose.

Auxiliary labeling:
• Avoid alcoholic beverages.
• Take with meals or milk.
• Do not take other medicines without your doctor's advice.

RESORCINOL   Topical

A commonly used *brand name* in the U.S. is *RA*.

TOPICAL
Resorcinol Lotion
  In the U.S.—*RA*
Resorcinol Ointment*

*Not commercially available in the U.S.

Category: Keratolytic (topical).

Indications

Accepted
Acne vulgaris (treatment);
Dermatitis, seborrheic (treatment);
Eczema (treatment);
Psoriasis (treatment);
Urticaria (treatment); or
Skin disorders, inflammatory (treatment)—Resorcinol may be used in the treatment of acne vulgaris, seborrheic dermatitis, eczema, psoriasis, urticaria, and other inflammatory disorders of the skin.

Calluses (treatment);

Corns (treatment); or

Verruca vulgaris (treatment)—Resorcinol may also be used in preparations for the removal of corns, warts, or calluses.

Pharmacology

Mechanism of action/Effect: The effectiveness of resorcinol in treating various dermatological conditions is probably related to its antibacterial, antifungal, local irritant, and keratolytic actions. Its antibacterial and antifungal actions may be the result of protein precipitation; however, its keratolytic action may contribute to the antifungal effect because removal of the stratum corneum suppresses fungal growth.

Precautions to Consider

Geriatrics

Appropriate studies on the relationship of age to the effects of resorcinol have not been performed in the geriatric population. However, no geriatrics-specific problems have been documented to date.

Drug interactions and/or related problems

The following drug interactions and/or related problems have been selected on the basis of their potential clinical significance (possible mechanism in parentheses where appropriate)—not necessarily inclusive (» = major clinical significance):

Note: Combinations containing any of the following medications, depending on the amount present, may also interact with this medication.

  Abrasive or medicated soaps or cleansers or

  Acne preparations or preparations containing a peeling agent, such as:

    Benzoyl peroxide

    Salicylic acid

    Sulfur

    Tretinoin, or

  Acne preparations, topical, other, or

  Alcohol-containing preparations, topical, such as:

    After-shave lotions

    Astringents

    Perfumed toiletries

    Shaving creams or lotions, or

  Cosmetics or soaps with a strong drying effect or

  Isotretinoin or

  Medicated cosmetics or "cover-ups"

    (concurrent use with resorcinol may cause a cumulative irritant or drying effect, especially with the application of peeling, desquamating, or abrasive agents, resulting in excessive irritation of the skin)

Contraindications/Medical problems

The contraindications/medical problems included have been selected on the basis of their potential clinical significance (reasons given in parentheses where appropriate)—not necessarily inclusive (» = major clinical significance).

Risk-benefit should be considered when the following medical problem exists:

  Sensitivity to resorcinol

Side/Adverse Effects

The following side/adverse effects have been selected on the basis of their potential clinical significance (possible signs and symptoms in parentheses where appropriate)—not necessarily inclusive:

Those indicating need for medical attention

  Skin irritation not present before therapy

Symptoms of systemic toxicity

  Diarrhea, nausea, stomach pain, or vomiting; drowsiness; met-

hemoglobinemia (dizziness, severe or continuing headache, troubled breathing, unusual tiredness or weakness)—especially in children; *nervousness or restlessness; slow heartbeat, shortness of breath, or troubled breathing; sweating*

Those indicating need for medical attention only if they continue or are bothersome

Incidence more frequent

  Redness and peeling of skin—may occur after a few days

Patient Consultation

In providing consultation, consider emphasizing the following selected information (» = major clinical significance):

Before using this medication

» Conditions affecting use, especially:

    Sensitivity to resorcinol

    Use in children—Resorcinol may be absorbed through the skin and should not be used on large areas of the bodies of infants and children; resorcinol should not be used on wounds, since it may cause methemoglobinemia

Proper use of this medication

» Importance of not using more medication than the amount prescribed

    Proper administration: Applying enough to cover affected areas; rubbing in gently

    Washing hands immediately after application to remove any medication that may be on them

» Avoiding contact with the eyes

    Missed dose: Applying as soon as possible; not applying if almost time for next dose

» Proper storage

Precautions while using this medication

» Avoiding simultaneous use with other topical acne preparations or preparations containing peeling agents, alcohol-containing preparations, abrasive soaps or cleansers, cosmetics or soaps with drying effect, medicated cosmetics, or other topical skin medication, unless otherwise directed by physician

» Medication may darken light-colored hair

Side/adverse effects

  Signs of potential side effects, especially skin irritation not present before therapy or symptoms of resorcinol poisoning

General Dosing Information

This medication is not recommended for application over large areas of the body, especially when used in high concentrations or in infants and children.

Prolonged use may lead to myxedema because of the antithyroid action of resorcinol, particularly when used on ulcerated surfaces.

Resorcinol is not recommended for use in blacks, since it may cause hyperpigmentation.

This medication may darken light-colored hair.

Topical Dosage Forms

RESORCINOL LOTION

Usual adult and adolescent dose: Topical, to the skin.

Auxiliary labeling:

• Shake well.

• For external use only.

RESORCINOL OINTMENT

Usual adult and adolescent dose: Topical, to the skin, as a 2 to 20% ointment.

Auxiliary labeling: • For external use only.

SALICYLATES   Systemic

Some commonly used *brand names* are:

In the U.S.—

Amigesic [Salsalate]

Anacin [Aspirin and Caffeine]

APAC Improved [Aspirin and Caffeine]

Arthritis Pain Formula [Aspirin, Alumina, and Magnesia]

Arthropan [Choline Salicylate]

Ascriptin [Aspirin, Buffered]

Ascriptin A/D [Aspirin, Buffered]

Aspergum [Aspirin]

Bayer Aspirin [Aspirin]

Buffaprin [Aspirin, Buffered]

Bufferin [Aspirin, Buffered]

Buffinol [Aspirin, Buffered]

Cama Arthritis Pain Reliever [Aspirin, Alumina, and Magnesium Oxide]

Diagen [Salsalate]

Disalcid [Salsalate]

Doan's [Magnesium Salicylate]

Easprin [Aspirin]

Ecotrin [Aspirin]

Empirin [Aspirin]

8-Hour Bayer Timed-Release [Aspirin]

Halfprin [Aspirin]

Magan [Magnesium Salicylate]

Magnaprin [Aspirin, Alumina, and Magnesia]

Magnaprin Arthritis Strength [Aspirin, Alumina, and Magnesia]

Maprin [Aspirin, Alumina, and Magnesia]

Maprin I-B [Aspirin, Alumina, and Magnesia]

Measurin [Aspirin]

Mobidin [Magnesium Salicylate]

Mono-Gesic [Salsalate]

Norwich Aspirin [Aspirin]

P-A-C Revised Formula [Aspirin and Caffeine]

Salcylic Acid [Salsalate]

Salflex [Salsalate]

Salgesic [Salsalate]

Salsitab [Salsalate]

St. Joseph Adult Chewable Aspirin [Aspirin]

Therapy Bayer [Aspirin]

Tricosal [Choline and Magnesium Salicylates]

Trilisate [Choline and Magnesium Salicylates]

Uracel [Sodium Salicylate]

ZORprin [Aspirin]

In Canada‡—

Anacin [ASA and Caffeine]

APF Arthritic Pain Formula [ASA, Alumina, and Magnesia]

Apo-Asa [ASA]

Apo-Asen [ASA]

Arthrinol [ASA]

Arthrisin [ASA]

Artria S.R. [ASA]

Aspergum [ASA]

Aspirin [ASA]

Astrin [ASA]

Back-Ese [Magnesium Salicylate]

Bayer Timed-Release Arthritic Pain Formula [ASA]

Bufferin [ASA, Buffered]

C2 [ASA and Caffeine]

C2 Buffered [ASA and Caffeine, Buffered]

Coryphen [ASA]

Doan's [Magnesium Salicylate]

Dodd's Pills [Sodium Salicylate]

Ecotrin [ASA]

Entrophen [ASA]

Headstart [ASA]

Instantine [ASA and Caffeine]

Nervine [ASA and Caffeine]

Novasen [ASA]

Riphen [ASA]

Sal-Adult [ASA]

Sal-Infant [ASA]

Supasa [ASA]

217 [ASA and Caffeine]

217 Strong [ASA and Caffeine]

Triaphen [ASA]

Trilisate [Choline and Magnesium Salicylates]

Other commonly used names are:

Acetylsalicylic Acid [Aspirin]‡

ASA [Aspirin]‡

Choline Magnesium Trisalicylate [Choline and Magnesium Salicylates]

Salicylsalicylic Acid [Salsalate]

ASPIRIN‡

Oral

Aspirin Delayed-release Capsules USP*

In Canada‡—*Arthrinol*

Note: Aspirin delayed-release capsules contain enteric-coated granules.

Aspirin Tablets USP

In the U.S.—*Bayer Aspirin; Empirin; Norwich Aspirin;* GENERIC

In Canada‡—*Apo-Asa; Apo-Asen; Aspirin‡; Riphen*

Aspirin Tablets USP (Chewable)

In the U.S.—*Bayer Aspirin; St. Joseph Adult Chewable Aspirin;* GENERIC

In Canada‡—*Aspirin‡*

Aspirin Chewing Gum Tablets

In the U.S. and Canada‡—*Aspergum*

Aspirin Delayed-release Tablets USP

In the U.S.—*Easprin; Ecotrin; Halfprin; Therapy Bayer;* GENERIC

In Canada‡—*Astrin; Coryphen; Ecotrin; Entrophen; Novasen; Triaphen*

Note: Aspirin delayed-release tablets are enteric-coated.

Aspirin Dispersible Tablets*

In Canada—*Headstart*

Aspirin Extended-release Tablets USP

In the U.S.—*8-Hour Bayer Timed-Release; Measurin; ZORprin;* GENERIC

In Canada‡—*Arthrisin; Artria S.R.; Bayer Timed-Release Arthritic Pain Formula*

Aspirin and Caffeine Capsules*

In Canada—*Anacin*

Aspirin and Caffeine Tablets

In the U.S.—*Anacin; APAC Improved; P-A-C Revised Formula*

In Canada‡—*Anacin; C2; Instantine; Nervine; 217; 217 Strong*

Rectal

Aspirin Suppositories USP

In the U.S.—GENERIC

In Canada‡—*Sal-Adult; Sal-Infant; Supasa*

ASPIRIN, BUFFERED

Oral

Aspirin, Alumina, and Magnesia Tablets USP

In the U.S.—*Arthritis Pain Formula; Magnaprin; Magnaprin Arthritis Strength; Maprin; Maprin I-B*

In Canada‡—*APF Arthritic Pain Formula*

Aspirin, Alumina, and Magnesium Oxide Tablets USP

In the U.S.—*Cama Arthritis Pain Reliever*

Buffered Aspirin Tablets USP

In the U.S.—*Ascriptin; Ascriptin A/D; Buffaprin; Bufferin; Buffinol;* GENERIC

In Canada—*Bufferin*

Buffered Aspirin and Caffeine Tablets*

In Canada—*C2 Buffered*

CHOLINE SALICYLATE

Oral

Choline Salicylate Oral Solution

In the U.S.—*Arthropan*

CHOLINE AND MAGNESIUM SALICYLATES

Oral

Choline and Magnesium Salicylates Oral Solution

In the U.S.—*Trilisate*

Choline and Magnesium Salicylates Tablets

In the U.S.—*Tricosal; Trilisate*

In Canada—*Trilisate*

DIFLUNISAL—See Anti-inflammatory Analgesics, Nonsteroidal (Systemic).

MAGNESIUM SALICYLATE

Oral

Magnesium Salicylate Tablets USP

In the U.S.—*Doan's; Magan; Mobidin*

In Canada—*Back-Ese; Doan's*

SALSALATE

Oral

Salsalate Capsules USP

In the U.S.—*Amigesic; Disalcid*

Salsalate Tablets

In the U.S.—*Amigesic; Diagen; Disalcid; Mono-Gesic; Salcylic Acid; Salflex; Salgesic; Salsitab;* GENERIC

SODIUM SALICYLATE

Oral

Sodium Salicylate Tablets USP

In the U.S.—GENERIC

In Canada—*Dodd's Pills*

Sodium Salicylate Delayed-release Tablets

In the U.S.—*Uracel;* GENERIC

Note: Sodium salicylate delayed-release tablets are enteric-coated.

---

*Not commercially available in the U.S.

‡*Aspirin* is a brand name in Canada; acetylsalicylic acid is the generic name. ASA, a commonly used designation for aspirin (or acetylsalicylic acid) in both the U.S. and Canada, is the term used in Canadian product labeling.

Category

Note: All of the salicylates have analgesic, anti-inflammatory, and antipyretic actions; however, clinical uses among specific agents or dosage formulations may vary because of actual pharmacokinetic differences, lack of specific testing, and/or lack of clinical-use data.

Analgesic—Aspirin; Aspirin, Buffered; Choline Salicylate; Choline and Magnesium Salicylates; Magnesium Salicylate; [Salsalate]; Sodium Salicylate.

Anti-inflammatory (nonsteroidal)—Aspirin; Aspirin, Buffered; Choline Salicylate; Choline and Magnesium Salicylates; Magnesium Salicylate; [Salsalate]; Sodium Salicylate.

Antipyretic—Aspirin; Aspirin, Buffered; Choline Salicylate; Choline and Magnesium Salicylates; [Magnesium Salicylate]; [Salsalate]; Sodium Salicylate.

Antirheumatic (nonsteroidal anti-inflammatory)—Aspirin; Aspirin, Buffered; Choline Salicylate; Choline and Magnesium Salicylates; Magnesium Salicylate; Salsalate; Sodium Salicylate.

Platelet aggregation inhibitor—Aspirin Capsules; Aspirin Tablets; Aspirin Tablets (Chewable); Aspirin Delayed-release Tablets; Aspirin, Buffered.

Antithrombotic—Aspirin Capsules; Aspirin Tablets; Aspirin Tablets (Chewable); Aspirin Delayed-release Tablets; Aspirin, Buffered.

Myocardial infarction prophylactic—Aspirin Capsules; Aspirin Tablets; Aspirin Tablets (Chewable); Aspirin Delayed-release Tablets; Aspirin, Buffered.

Myocardial reinfarction prophylactic—Aspirin Capsules; Aspirin Tablets; Aspirin Tablets (Chewable); Aspirin Delayed-release Tablets; Aspirin, Buffered.

Indications

Note: Bracketed information in the *Indications* section refers to uses not included in U.S. product labeling.

Accepted

Pain (treatment); or

Fever (treatment)—Salicylates are indicated to relieve mild to moderate pain such as headache, toothache, and menstrual cramps and to reduce fever. These medications provide only symptomatic relief; additional therapy to treat the cause of the pain or fever should be instituted when necessary. However, the presence of an illness that may predispose toward Reye's syndrome (i.e., an acute febrile illness, especially influenza or varicella) should be ruled out before salicylate therapy is initiated in a pediatric or adolescent patient.

Salicylates are recommended for relief of mild to moderate bone pain caused by metastatic neoplastic disease. However, careful patient selection is necessary, especially in patients receiving chemotherapy, because of the platelet aggregation-inhibiting effect of aspirin and because salicylates may cause hypoprothrombinemia or gastrointestinal or renal toxicity.

Delayed-release formulations containing aspirin or sodium salicylate may not be as useful as immediate-release formulations for single-dose administration for analgesia or antipyresis because the delayed absorption prolongs the onset of action.

Note: The FDA has proposed that caffeine (present as an analgesic adjuvant in some aspirin products) be classified as a Category III ingredient (i.e., lacking documentation of efficacy) in OTC analgesic/antipyretic medications.

Inflammation, nonrheumatic (treatment)—Salicylates are indicated to relieve myalgia, musculoskeletal pain, and other symptoms of nonrheumatic inflammatory conditions such as athletic injuries, bursitis, capsulitis, tendinitis, and nonspecific acute tenosynovitis.

Arthritis, rheumatoid (treatment);

Arthritis, juvenile (treatment); or

Osteoarthritis (treatment)—Salicylates are indicated for the symptomatic relief of acute and chronic rheumatoid arthritis, juvenile arthritis, osteoarthritis, and related rheumatic diseases. Aspirin is usually the first agent to be used and may be the drug of choice in patients able to tolerate prolonged therapy with high doses. These agents do not affect the progressive course of rheumatoid arthritis.

Concurrent treatment with a glucocorticoid or a disease-modifying antirheumatic agent may be needed, depending on the condition being treated and patient response.

[Salicylates are also used to reduce arthritic complications associated with systemic lupus erythematosus.]

Rheumatic fever (treatment)—Salicylates are indicated to reduce fever and inflammation in rheumatic fever. However, they do not prevent cardiac or other complications associated with this condition. Sodium salicylate should be avoided in rheumatic fever if congestive cardiac complications are present because of its sodium content. Also, large doses of any salicylate should be avoided in rheumatic fever if severe carditis is present because of possible adverse cardiovascular effects.

Platelet aggregation (prophylaxis)—Aspirin (capsules, tablets, chewable tablets, delayed-release capsules or tablets, and buffered formulations) is indicated as a platelet aggregation inhibitor in the following:

Ischemic attacks, transient, in males (prophylaxis);

Thromboembolism, cerebral (prophylaxis); or

[Thromboembolism, cerebral, recurrence (prophylaxis)][1]—

Aspirin is indicated in the treatment of men who have had transient brain ischemia due to fibrin platelet emboli to reduce the recurrence of transient ischemic attacks (TIAs) and the risk of stroke and death.

[Aspirin is also used in the treatment of women with transient brain ischemia due to fibrin platelet emboli. However, its efficacy in preventing stroke and death in female patients has not been established.][1]

[Aspirin is also indicated in the treatment of patients with documented, unexplained TIAs associated with mitral valve prolapse. However, if TIAs continue to occur after an adequate trial of aspirin therapy, aspirin should be discontinued and an oral anticoagulant administered instead.][1]

[Aspirin is also indicated to prevent initial or recurrent cerebrovascular embolism, TIAs, and stroke following carotid endarterectomy.]

[Aspirin is indicated in the treatment of patients who have had a completed thrombotic stroke, to prevent a recurrence.][1]

Myocardial infarction (prophylaxis); or

Myocardial reinfarction (prophylaxis)—Aspirin is indicated to prevent myocardial infarction in patients with unstable angina pectoris and to prevent recurrence of myocardial infarction in patients with a history of myocardial infarction.

In one study, aspirin significantly reduced the rate of reocclusion, reinfarction, stroke, and death when a single dose was administered within a few hours after the onset of symptoms of acute myocardial infarction and daily thereafter. The benefit of early treatment with aspirin was additive to that of streptokinase. Therefore, it is recommended that aspirin therapy be initiated as soon as possible after the onset of symptoms, even if the patient is receiving thrombolytic therapy.

[One study has shown that aspirin may also prevent myocardial infarction in individuals 50 years of age and older who have no history of unstable angina pectoris or myocardial infarction. However, the incidence of hemorrhagic stroke (but not the total number of hemorrhagic plus thrombotic strokes) was slightly increased in subjects receiving aspirin. Also, the incidence of myocardial infarction, although higher in the placebo group than in the aspirin group, was low in both groups. Therefore, aspirin's benefit in apparently healthy individuals has not been established. However, aspirin may be indicated for prevention of an initial myocardial infarction in selected patients, especially those who may be at risk because of the presence of chronic stable coronary artery disease (as shown by exertional or episodic angina pectoris, abnormal coronary arteriogram, or positive stress test) and/or other risk factors.][1]

[Thromboembolism (prophylaxis)]—

Aspirin is used in low doses to decrease the risk of thromboembolism following orthopedic (hip) surgery (especially total hip replacement) and in patients with arteriovenous shunts.

Platelet aggregation inhibitors, although not as consistently effective as an anticoagulant or an anticoagulant plus dipyridamole, may provide some protection against the development of thromboembolic complications in patients with mechanical prosthetic heart valves. Therefore, administration of aspirin, alone or in combination with dipyridamole, may be considered if anticoagulant therapy is contraindicated for these patients. Patients with bioprosthetic cardiac valves who are in normal sinus rhythm generally do not require prolonged antithrombotic therapy, but long-term aspirin administration may be considered on an individual basis.[1]

Aspirin is also indicated, alone[1] or in combination with dipyridamole, to reduce the risk of thrombosis and/or reocclusion of saphenous vein aortocoronary bypass grafts following coronary bypass surgery.

Aspirin is also indicated, alone or in combination with dipyridamole, to reduce the risk of thrombosis and/or reocclusion of prosthetic or saphenous vein femoral popliteal bypass grafts.[1]

Because the patient may be at risk for thromboembolic complications, including myocardial infarction and stroke, long-term aspirin therapy may also be indicated for maintaining patency following coronary or peripheral vascular angioplasty and for treating patients with peripheral vascular insufficiency caused by arteriosclerosis.[1]

Prolonged antithrombotic therapy is generally not needed to maintain vessel patency following vascular reconstruction procedures in high-flow, low-resistance arteries larger than 6 mm in diameter. However, long-term aspirin therapy may be indicated, because patients requiring such procedures may be at risk for other thrombotic complications.[1]

[Kawasaki disease (treatment)][1]—Aspirin is indicated for its anti-inflammatory, antipyretic, and antithrombotic effects in the treatment of Kawasaki disease (Kawasaki syndrome, mucocutaneous lymph node syndrome) in children. It reduces fever, relieves inflammation (e.g., lymphadenitis, mucositis, conjunctivitis, serositis), and may reduce the occurrence of cardiovascular complications. However, the combination of high-dose intravenous gamma globulin and aspirin has been shown to be more effective than aspirin alone in reducing the formation of coronary artery abnormalities.

---

[1]Not included in Canadian product labeling.

Pharmacology

Mechanism of action/Effect: The analgesic, antipyretic, and anti-inflammatory effects of aspirin are due to actions by both the acetyl and the salicylate portions of the intact molecule as well as by the active salicylate metabolite. The actions of other salicylates are due only to the salicylate portion of the molecule. Aspirin directly inhibits the activity of the enzyme cyclo-oxygenase to decrease the formation of precursors of prostaglandins and thromboxanes from arachidonic acid. Salicylate may competitively inhibit prostaglandin formation. Although many of the therapeutic and adverse effects of these medications may result from inhibition of prostaglandin synthesis (and consequent reduction of prostaglandin activity) in various tissues, other actions may also contribute significantly to the therapeutic effects.

Analgesic—

Salicylates: Produce analgesia through a peripheral action by blocking pain impulse generation and via a central action, possibly in the hypothalamus. The peripheral action may predominate and probably involves inhibition of the synthesis of prostaglandins, and possibly inhibition of the synthesis and/or actions of other substances, which sensitize pain receptors to mechanical or chemical stimulation.

Caffeine: A mild central nervous system (CNS) stimulant. Caffeine-induced constriction of cerebral blood vessels, which leads to a decrease in cerebral blood flow and in the oxygen tension of the brain, may contribute to relief of some types of headache. It has been suggested that the addition of caffeine to aspirin may provide a more rapid onset of action and/or enhanced pain relief with lower doses of analgesic. However, the FDA has determined that studies performed to date have not demonstrated that caffeine is an effective analgesic adjuvant or that it does not interfere with aspirin's efficacy as an antipyretic.

Anti-inflammatory (nonsteroidal)—Exact mechanisms have not been determined. Salicylates may act peripherally in inflamed tissue, probably by inhibiting the synthesis of prostaglandins and possibly by inhibiting the synthesis and/or actions of other mediators of the inflammatory response. Inhibition of leukocyte migration, inhibition of the release and/or actions of lysosomal enzymes, and actions on other cellular and immunological processes in mesenchymal and connective tissues may be involved.

Antipyretic—May produce antipyresis by acting centrally on the hypothalamic heat-regulating center to produce peripheral vasodilation resulting in increased cutaneous blood flow, sweating, and heat loss. The central action may involve inhibition of prostaglandin synthesis in the hypothalamus; however, there is some evidence that fevers caused by endogenous pyrogens that do not act via a prostaglandin mechanism may also respond to salicylate therapy.

Antirheumatic (nonsteroidal anti-inflammatory)—Act via analgesic and anti-inflammatory mechanisms; the therapeutic effects are not due to pituitary-adrenal stimulation.

Platelet aggregation inhibitor—The platelet aggregation-inhibiting effect of aspirin specifically involves the compound's ability to act as an acetyl donor to the platelet membrane; the nonacetylated salicylates have no clinically significant effect on platelet aggregation. Aspirin affects platelet function by inhibiting the enzyme prostaglandin cyclooxygenase in platelets, thereby preventing the formation of the aggregating agent thromboxane A_2. This action is irreversible; the effects persist for the life of the platelets exposed. Aspirin may also inhibit formation of the platelet aggregation inhibitor prostacyclin (prostaglandin I_2) in blood vessels; however, this action is reversible. These actions may be dose-dependent. Although there is some evidence that doses lower than 100 mg per day may not inhibit prostacyclin synthesis, optimum dosage that will suppress thromboxane A_2 formation without suppressing prostacyclin generation has not been determined.

Other actions/effects: It is proposed that the gastrointestinal toxicity of salicylates, especially aspirin, may be caused primarily by reduction of the activity of prostaglandins (which exert a protective effect on the gastrointestinal mucosa) because upper gastrointestinal toxicity has been reported following rectal or parenteral administration of nonsteroidal anti-inflammatory drugs. However, when administered orally, these acidic medications (unless administered in an enteric-coated formulation) probably also exert a direct irritant or erosive effect on the mucosa.

Time to peak effect: Antirheumatic—May require 2 to 3 weeks or more of continuous therapy.

Precautions to Consider

Cross-sensitivity and/or related problems
Patients sensitive to one salicylate, including methyl salicylate (oil of wintergreen), or to other nonsteroidal anti-inflammatory drugs (NSAIDs) may be sensitive to other salicylates also.

Patients sensitive to aspirin may not necessarily be sensitive to nonacetylated salicylates.

Patients sensitive to tartrazine dye may be sensitive to aspirin also, and vice versa.

Cross-sensitivity between aspirin and other NSAIDs that results in bronchospastic or cutaneous reactions may be eliminated if the patient undergoes a desensitization procedure (See *General Dosing Information*).

Patients sensitive to other xanthines (aminophylline, dyphylline, oxtriphylline, theobromine, theophylline) may be sensitive to caffeine also.

Geriatrics
Geriatric patients may be more susceptible to the toxic effects of salicylates, possibly because of decreased renal function. Lower doses than those usually recommended for adults, especially for long-term use or for use of long-acting salicylates (such as choline and magnesium salicylates and salsalate), may be required.

Drug interactions and/or related problems
The following drug interactions and/or related problems have been selected on the basis of their potential clinical significance (possible mechanism in parentheses where appropriate)—not necessarily inclusive (» = major clinical significance):

Note: Combinations containing any of the following medications, depending on the amount present, may also interact with this medication.

In addition to the interactions listed below, the possibility should be considered that additive or multiple effects leading to impaired blood clotting and/or increased risk of bleeding may occur if a salicylate, especially aspirin, is used concurrently with any medication having a significant potential for causing hypoprothrombinemia, thrombocytopenia, or gastrointestinal ulceration or hemorrhage.

For all salicylates
Acetaminophen
(prolonged concurrent use of acetaminophen with a salicylate is not recommended because chronic, high-dose administration of the combined analgesics [1.35 grams daily, or cumulative ingestion of 1 kg annually, for 3 years or longer] significantly increases the risk of analgesic nephropathy, renal papillary necrosis, end-stage renal disease, and cancer of the kidney or urinary bladder; also, it is recommended that for short-term use the combined dose of acetaminophen plus a salicylate not exceed that recommended for acetaminophen or a salicylate given individually)

Acidifiers, urinary, such as:
  Ammonium chloride
  Ascorbic acid (Vitamin C)
  Potassium or sodium phosphates
  (acidification of the urine by these medications decreases salicylate excretion, leading to increased salicylate plasma concentrations; initiation of therapy with these medications in patients stabilized on a salicylate may lead to toxic salicylate concentrations)

  (aspirin may increase urinary excretion of ascorbic acid; clinical significance is unclear, but some clinicians recommend ascorbic acid supplementation in patients receiving prolonged high-dose aspirin therapy)

Adrenocorticoids, glucocorticoid, or
Corticotropin (ACTH), chronic therapeutic use of
  (glucocorticoids or corticotropin may increase salicylate excretion, resulting in lower plasma concentrations and increased salicylate dosage requirements; salicylism may result when glucocorticoid or corticotropin dosage is subsequently decreased or discontinued, especially in patients receiving large [antirheumatic] doses of salicylate; also, the risk of gastrointestinal side effects, including ulceration and gastrointestinal blood loss, may be increased; however, concurrent use in the treatment of arthritis may provide additive therapeutic benefit and permit reduction of glucocorticoid or corticotropin dosage)

  (because adrenocorticoids and corticotropin may cause sodium and fluid retention, caution in concurrent use with large doses of sodium salicylate is recommended)

Alcohol or
» Nonsteroidal anti-inflammatory drugs (NSAIDs), other
  (concurrent use of these medications with a salicylate may increase the risk of gastrointestinal side effects, including ulceration and gastrointestinal blood loss; also, concurrent use of a salicylate with an NSAID may increase the risk of severe gastrointestinal side effects without providing additional symptomatic relief and is therefore not recommended)

  (aspirin may decrease the bioavailability of many NSAIDs, including diflunisal, fenoprofen, indomethacin, meclofenamate, piroxicam [to 80% of the usual plasma concentration], and the active sulfide metabolite of sulindac; aspirin has also been shown to decrease the protein binding and increase the plasma clearance of ketoprofen, and to decrease the formation and excretion of ketoprofen conjugates)

(concurrent use of other NSAIDs with aspirin may also increase the risk of bleeding at sites other than the gastrointestinal tract because of additive inhibition of platelet aggregation)

» Alkalizers, urinary, such as:
  Carbonic anhydrase inhibitors
  Citrates
  Sodium bicarbonate, or
  Antacids, chronic high-dose use, especially calcium- and/or magnesium-containing
    (alkalinization of the urine by these medications increases salicylate excretion, leading to decreased salicylate plasma concentrations, reduced effectiveness, and shortened duration of action; also, withdrawal of a urinary alkalizer from a patient stabilized on a salicylate may increase the plasma salicylate concentration to a toxic level; however, the antacids present in buffered aspirin formulations may not be present in sufficient quantity to alkalinize the urine)

    (metabolic acidosis induced by carbonic anhydrase inhibitors may increase penetration of salicylate into the brain and increase the risk of salicylate toxicity in patients taking large [antirheumatic] doses of salicylate; if acetazolamide is used to produce forced alkaline diuresis in the treatment of salicylate poisoning, the increased risk of severe metabolic acidosis and increased salicylate toxicity must be considered and an alkaline intravenous solution given concurrently)

» Anticoagulants, coumarin- or indandione-derivative, or
» Heparin or
» Thrombolytic agents, such as:
  Alteplase
  Anistreplase
  Streptokinase
  Urokinase
    (salicylates may displace a coumarin- or indandione-derivative anticoagulant from its protein-binding sites, and, in high doses, may cause hypoprothrombinemia, leading to increased anticoagulation and risk of bleeding)

    (the potential occurrence of gastrointestinal ulceration or hemorrhage during salicylate, especially aspirin, therapy may cause increased risk to patients receiving anticoagulant or thrombolytic therapy)

    (because aspirin-induced inhibition of platelet function may lead to prolonged bleeding time and increased risk of hemorrhage, concurrent use of aspirin with an anticoagulant or a thrombolytic agent is recommended only within a carefully monitored antithrombotic regimen; although a recent study has shown that initiation of therapy with 160 mg of aspirin a day concurrently with short-term [1-hour] intravenous infusion of streptokinase in patients with acute coronary arterial occlusion significantly decreases the risk of reocclusion, reinfarction, stroke, and death without increasing the risk of adverse effects [as compared with streptokinase alone], other studies using higher doses of aspirin and/or more prolonged administration of a thrombolytic agent have demonstrated an increased risk of bleeding)

Anticonvulsants, hydantoin
    (salicylates may decrease hydantoin metabolism, leading to increases in hydantoin plasma concentrations, efficacy, and/or toxicity; adjustment of hydantoin dosage may be required when chronic salicylate therapy is initiated or discontinued)

» Antidiabetic agents, oral, or
  Insulin
    (effects of these medications may be increased by large doses of salicylates; dosage adjustments may be necessary; potentiation of oral antidiabetic agents may be caused partially by displacement from serum proteins; glipizide and glyburide, because of their nonionic binding characteristics, may not be affected as much as the other oral agents; however, caution in concurrent use is recommended)

Antiemetics, including antihistamines and phenothiazines
    (antiemetics may mask the symptoms of salicylate-induced ototoxicity, such as dizziness, vertigo, and tinnitus)

Bismuth subsalicylate
    (ingestion of large repeated doses as for traveler's diarrhea may produce substantial plasma salicylate concentrations; concurrent use with large doses of analgesic salicylates may increase the risk of salicylate toxicity)

» Cefamandole or
» Cefoperazone or
» Cefotetan or
» Moxalactam or
» Plicamycin or
» Valproic acid
    (these medications may cause hypoprothrombinemia; in addition, plicamycin or valproic acid may inhibit platelet aggregation, and moxalactam may cause irreversible platelet damage; concurrent use with aspirin may increase the risk of bleeding because of additive interferences with blood clotting)

    (hypoprothrombinemia induced by large doses of salicylates, and the potential occurrence of gastrointestinal ulceration or hemorrhage during salicylate, especially aspirin, therapy, may increase the risk of bleeding complications in patients receiving these medications)

    (concurrent use of aspirin with valproic acid has also been reported to increase the plasma concentration of valproic acid and induce valproic acid toxicity)

Furosemide
    (in addition to increasing the risk of ototoxicity, concurrent use of furosemide with high doses of salicylate may lead to salicylate toxicity because of competition for renal excretory sites)

Laxatives, cellulose-containing
    (concurrent use may reduce the salicylate effect because of physical binding or other absorptive hindrance; medications should be administered 2 hours apart)

» Methotrexate
    (salicylates may displace methotrexate from its binding sites and decrease its renal clearance, leading to toxic methotrexate plasma concentrations; if they are used concurrently, methotrexate dosage should be decreased, the patient observed for signs of toxicity, and/or methotrexate plasma concentration monitored; also, it is recommended that salicylate therapy be discontinued 24 to 48 hours prior to administration of a high-dose methotrexate infusion, and not resumed until the plasma methotrexate concentration has decreased to a nontoxic level [usually at least 12 hours postinfusion])

Nifedipine or
Verapamil
    (concurrent use with a salicylate may result in displacement of either or both medications from protein-binding sites, leading to increased plasma concentrations of the free [unbound] medications and increased risk of toxicity)

Ototoxic medications, other, especially
» Vancomycin
    (concurrent or sequential administration of these medications with a salicylate should be avoided may the potential for ototoxicity may be increased; hearing loss may occur and may progress to deafness even after discontinuation of the medication; these effects may be reversible, but usually are permanent)

» Platelet aggregation inhibitors
    (concurrent use with aspirin is not recommended, except in a monitored antithrombotic regimen, because the risk of bleeding may be increased)

(the potential occurrence of gastrointestinal ulceration or hemorrhage during salicylate therapy, and the hypoprothrombinemic effect of large doses of salicylate, may cause increased risk to patients receiving a platelet aggregation inhibitor)

» Probenecid or
» Sulfinpyrazone

(concurrent use of a salicylate is not recommended when these medications are used to treat hyperuricemia or gout, because the uricosuric effect of these medications may be decreased by doses of salicylates that produce serum salicylate concentrations above 5 mg per 100 mL; also, these medications may inhibit the uricosuric effect achieved when serum salicylate concentrations are above 10 to 15 mg per 100 mL)

(probenecid may decrease renal clearance and increase plasma concentrations and toxicity of salicylates)

(sulfinpyrazone may decrease salicylate excretion and/or displace salicylate from its protein binding sites, possibly leading to increased salicylate concentrations and toxicity)

(although low doses of sulfinpyrazone and aspirin have been used concurrently to provide additive inhibition of platelet aggregation, the efficacy of the combination has not been established and the increased risk of bleeding must be considered; also, concurrent use of sulfinpyrazone with aspirin may increase the risk of gastrointestinal ulceration or hemorrhage)

Salicylic acid or other salicylates, topical

(concurrent use with systemic salicylates may increase the risk of salicylate toxicity if significant quantities are absorbed)

Vitamin K

(requirements for this vitamin may be increased in patients receiving high doses of salicylate)

» Zidovudine

(aspirin may competitively inhibit the hepatic glucuronidation and decrease the clearance of zidovudine, leading to potentiation of zidovudine toxicity; the possibility must be considered that aspirin toxicity may also be increased; concurrent use of the 2 medications should be avoided)

For buffered aspirin formulations, choline and magnesium salicylates, and magnesium salicylate (in addition to those interactions listed above as applying to all salicylates)

» Ketoconazole or
» Tetracyclines, oral

(antacids present in buffered aspirin formulations, and the magnesium in choline and magnesium salicylates or magnesium salicylate, may form nonabsorbable complexes with oral tetracyclines; the medications should be taken at least 3 to 4 hours apart)

(antacids present in buffered aspirin formulations may increase intragastric pH, which may result in a marked reduction of ketoconazole absorption; it is recommended that buffered aspirin formulations be taken at least 3 hours before or after ketoconazole)

For enteric-coated formulations (in addition to those interactions listed above as applying to all salicylates)

Antacids or
Histamine H_2-receptor antagonists

(concurrent administration of these medications, which increase intragastric pH, with an enteric-coated medication may cause premature dissolution, and loss of the protective effect, of the enteric coating)

For formulations containing caffeine (in addition to those interactions listed above as applying to all salicylates)

CNS stimulation-producing medications, other

(concurrent use with caffeine may result in excessive CNS stimulation, which may cause unwanted effects such as ner-

vousness, irritability, insomnia, or possibly convulsions or cardiac arrhythmias; close observation is recommended)

Lithium

(caffeine increases urinary excretion of lithium, thereby possibly reducing its therapeutic effect)

Monoamine oxidase (MAO) inhibitors, including furazolidone, pargyline, and procarbazine

(concurrent use of large amounts of caffeine with MAO inhibitors may produce dangerous cardiac arrhythmias or severe hypertension because of the sympathomimetic side effects of caffeine)

The contraindications/medical problems included have been selected on the basis of their potential clinical significance (reasons given in parentheses where appropriate)—not necessarily inclusive (» = major clinical significance).

Except under special circumstances. this medication should not be used when the following medical problems exist:

For all salicylates

» Bleeding ulcers or
» Hemorrhagic states, other active

(may be exacerbated, especially by aspirin)

» Hemophilia or other bleeding problems, including coagulation or platelet function disorders

(increased risk of hemorrhage, especially with aspirin)

For aspirin only (in addition to the contraindications listed above for all salicylates)

» Angioedema, anaphylaxis, or other severe sensitivity reaction induced by aspirin or other NSAIDs, history of, or
» Nasal polyps associated with asthma, induced or exacerbated by aspirin

(high risk of severe sensitivity reaction to aspirin)

» Thrombocytopenia

(increased risk of bleeding because aspirin inhibits platelet aggregation)

For choline and magnesium salicylates and for magnesium salicylate only (in addition to the contraindications listed above for all salicylates)

» Renal insufficiency, chronic advanced

(risk of hypermagnesemic toxicity)

Risk-benefit should be considered when the following medical problems exist:

For all salicylates

Anemia

(may be exacerbated by gastrointestinal blood loss during salicylate, especially aspirin, therapy; also, salicylate-induced peripheral vasodilation may lead to pseudoanaemia)

Conditions predisposing to fluid retention, such as:
Compromised cardiac function or
Hypertension

(in patients with carditis, high doses of salicylates may precipitate congestive heart failure or pulmonary edema)

(patients with congestive heart disease may be more susceptible to adverse renal effects)

(sodium content of sodium salicylate may be detrimental to these patients when large doses are administered chronically)

» Gastritis, erosive, or
» Peptic ulcer

(may be exacerbated because of ulcerogenic effects, especially with aspirin; risk of gastrointestinal bleeding is increased)

Gout

(salicylates may increase serum uric acid concentrations and may interfere with efficacy of uricosuric agents)

Hepatic function impairment
　　(salicylates metabolized hepatically; also, patients with decompensated hepatic cirrhosis may be more susceptible to adverse renal effects)
　　(in severe hepatic impairment, inhibition of platelet function by aspirin may increase the risk of hemorrhage)
Hypoprothrombinemia or
Vitamin K deficiency
　　(increased risk of bleeding because of antiplatelet action of aspirin and the hypoprothrombinemic effect of high doses of salicylates)
Renal function impairment
　　(salicylate elimination may be reduced; also, the risk of renal adverse effects may be increased)
　　(choline and magnesium salicylates or magnesium salicylate should be used with caution in patients with mild or moderate renal impairment because of the risk of hypermagnesemic toxicity; however, as stated above, these medications should *not* be used if chronic advanced renal insufficiency is present)
Sensitivity reaction, mild, to aspirin or other NSAIDs, history of
　　(risk of sensitivity reaction, especially with aspirin)
Symptoms of nasal polyps associated with bronchospasm, or angioedema, anaphylaxis, or other severe allergic reactions induced by aspirin or other NSAIDs
　　(although cross-sensitivity leading to severe reactions occurs very rarely with the nonacetylated salicylates, caution is recommended; however, as indicated above, aspirin should *not* be used)
Thyrotoxicosis
　　(may be exacerbated by large doses)
For aspirin only (in addition to those listed above for all salicylates)
» Asthma
　　(increased risk of bronchospastic sensitivity reaction)
Glucose-6-phosphate dehydrogenase (G6PD) deficiency
　　(rarely, aspirin has caused hemolytic anemia in these patients)
For formulations containing caffeine
Cardiac disease, severe
　　(high doses of caffeine may increase risk of tachycardia or extrasystoles, which may lead to heart failure)
Sensitivity to caffeine, history of
　　(risk of allergic reaction)

Side/Adverse Effects

Note: Salicylates may decrease renal function, especially when serum salicylate concentrations reach 250 mcg per mL (25 mg per 100 mL). However, the risk of complications due to this action appears minimal in patients with normal renal function.

Aspirin-induced bronchospasm is most likely to occur in patients with the triad of asthma, allergies, and nasal polyps induced by aspirin. Nonacetylated salicylates may rarely cause bronchospastic reactions in susceptible people when very large doses are given.

Angioedema or urticaria may be more likely to occur in patients with a history of recurrent idiopathic angioedema or urticaria.

Gastrointestinal side effects are more likely to occur with aspirin than with other salicylates; also, they may be more likely to occur with chronic, high-dose administration than with occasional use. Use of enteric-coated formulations may reduce the potential for gastrointestinal side effects.

Adverse effects are more likely to occur at serum salicylate concentrations of 300 mcg per mL (30 mg per 100 mL) or above; however, they may also occur at lower serum concentrations, especially in patients 60 years of age or older. Serum

concentrations at which adverse or toxic effects have been reported during chronic therapy include:

Salicylate Concentration (mcg per mL/ mg per 100 mL)	Effect
195–210/19.5–21	Mild toxicity (tinnitus, decreased hearing)
250/25	Hepatotoxicity (abnormal liver function tests)
250/25	Decreased renal function
300/30	Decreased prothrombin time
310/31	Deafness
350/35	Hyperventilation
> 400/40	Metabolic acidosis, other signs of severe toxicity

The following side/adverse effects have been selected on the basis of their potential clinical significance (possible signs and symptoms in parentheses where appropriate)—not necessarily inclusive:

Those indicating need for medical attention
Incidence less frequent or rare
　　Anaphylactoid reaction (bluish discoloration or flushing or redness of skin; coughing; difficulty in swallowing; dizziness or feeling faint, severe; skin rash, hives [may include giant urticaria], and/or itching; stuffy nose; swelling of eyelids, face, or lips; tightness in chest, troubled breathing, and/or wheezing, especially in asthmatic patients); *anemia* (unusual tiredness or weakness)—for aspirin or buffered aspirin only; may occur secondary to gastrointestinal microbleeding; *anemia, hemolytic* (troubled breathing, exertional; unusual tiredness or weakness)—reported with aspirin only, almost always in patients with glucose-6-phosphate (G6PD) deficiency; *bronchospastic allergic reaction* (shortness of breath, troubled breathing, tightness in chest, and/or wheezing); *dermatitis, allergic* (skin rash, hives, or itching); *gastrointestinal ulceration, possibly with bleeding* (bloody or black, tarry stools; stomach pain, severe; vomiting of blood or material that looks like coffee grounds)
Incidence unknown
　　Rectal irritation—for aspirin suppository dosage form
Signs and symptoms of overdose
　　Mild overdose [salicylism] (continuing ringing or buzzing in ears or hearing loss; confusion; severe or continuing diarrhea, stomach pain, and/or headache; dizziness or lightheadedness; severe drowsiness; fast or deep breathing; continuing nausea and/or vomiting; uncontrollable flapping movements of the hands, especially in elderly patients; increased thirst; vision problems)—tinnitus and/or headache may be the earliest symptoms of salicylism
　　Severe overdose (bloody urine; convulsions; hallucinations; severe nervousness, excitement, or confusion; shortness of breath or troubled breathing; unexplained fever)
Note: In young children, the only signs of an overdose may be changes in behavior, severe drowsiness or tiredness, and/or fast or deep breathing.
　　Laboratory findings in overdose may indicate encephalographic abnormalities, alterations in acid-base balance (especially respiratory alkalosis and metabolic acidosis), hyperglycemia or hypoglycemia (especially in children), ketonuria, hyponatremia, hypokalemia, and proteinuria.

Those indicating need for medical attention only if they continue or are bothersome

Incidence more frequent with aspirin; less frequent with enteric-coated or buffered formulations and with other salicylates

Gastrointestinal irritation (mild stomach pain, heartburn or indigestion, nausea with or without vomiting)

Incidence less frequent

For caffeine-containing formulations

CNS stimulation (trouble in sleeping, nervousness, or jitters)

Patient Consultation

In providing consultation, consider emphasizing the following selected information (» = major clinical significance):

Before using this medication

» Conditions affecting use, especially:

Sensitivity to any of the salicylates, including methyl salicylate, or nonsteroidal anti-inflammatory drugs (NSAIDs), history of

Diet—Sodium content of sodium salicylate must be considered for patients on a sodium-restricted diet, especially with chronic use of antirheumatic doses

Pregnancy—Salicylates and caffeine (present in some formulations) cross the placenta; high-dose chronic use or abuse of aspirin in the third trimester may be hazardous to the mother as well as the fetus and/or neonate, causing heart problems in fetus or neonate and/or bleeding in mother, fetus, or neonate; high-dose chronic use or abuse of any salicylate late in pregnancy may also prolong and complicate labor and delivery; not taking aspirin during the third trimester unless prescribed by physician

Breast-feeding—Salicylates and caffeine (present in some formulations) are excreted in breast milk

Use in children and teenagers—Checking with physician before giving to children or teenagers with symptoms of acute febrile illness, especially influenza or varicella, because of the risk of Reye's syndrome; determining ahead of time what physician wants done if a child receiving chronic therapy develops fever or other symptoms of acute illness that may predispose to Reye's syndrome; also, increased susceptibility to salicylate toxicity in children, especially with fever and dehydration

Use in the elderly—Increased susceptibility to salicylate toxicity

Use by athletes—Caffeine (present in some formulations) is tested for in athletes by the U.S. Olympic Committee (USOC) and the National Collegiate Athletic Association (NCAA); urine concentrations above 12 mcg per mL (USOC) and 15 mcg per mL (NCAA) are considered unacceptable

Other medications, especially anticoagulants, antidiabetic agents (oral), those cephalosporins that may cause hypoprothrombinemia, moxalactam, plicamycin, valproic acid, methotrexate, NSAIDs, platelet aggregation inhibitors, probenecid, sulfinpyrazone, urinary alkalizers, vancomycin, zidovudine (for aspirin only), ketoconazole (for buffered formulations only), and oral tetracyclines (for buffered formulations, choline and magnesium salicylates, and magnesium salicylate only)

Other medical problems, especially coagulation or platelet function disorders, gastrointestinal problems such as ulceration or erosive gastritis (especially a bleeding ulcer), thyrotoxicosis, and (for choline and magnesium salicylates and for magnesium salicylate) chronic advanced renal insufficiency

Proper use of this medication

» Taking nonenteric-coated oral dosage forms after meals or with food to minimize stomach irritation

» Taking all tablet or capsule dosage forms with a full glass of water and not lying down for 15 to 30 minutes after taking

» Not taking aspirin or buffered aspirin if it has a strong vinegar-like odor

Not chewing aspirin or buffered aspirin dosage forms within 7 days after tonsillectomy, tooth extraction, or other oral surgery

Not placing aspirin or buffered aspirin tablet directly on tooth or gum surface, to prevent tissue damage

Proper administration of:

Aspirin

Chewable tablets—May be chewed, dissolved in liquid, crushed, or swallowed whole

Delayed-release tablets—Must be swallowed whole

Dispersible tablets—To be dissolved in mouth before swallowing; if necessary, a little water may be sipped to facilitate dissolution

Extended-release tablets—May be broken or crumbled (but not ground up) if necessary, unless specified by manufacturer to be swallowed whole; see manufacturer's prescribing information

Suppository—Proper administration technique

Choline and magnesium salicylates oral solution

Liquid may be mixed with fruit juice just prior to taking, if desired

Sodium salicylate delayed-release tablets

Tablets must be swallowed whole

Importance of not taking more medication than prescribed by physician or dentist or recommended on package label

Unless otherwise directed by physician, children not taking more often than 5 times daily

Compliance with therapy (for arthritis); may take 2 to 3 weeks or longer for maximum effectiveness

Missed dose: If on scheduled dosing regimen—taking as soon as possible; not taking if almost time for next dose; not doubling doses

» Proper storage

Precautions while using this medication

» Possibility of overdose if other medications containing aspirin or other salicylates (possibly including topical products) are used

» Regular visits to physician to check progress if long-term or high-dose therapy is prescribed

Checking with physician if—

Taking for pain or fever, and pain persists for longer than 10 days for adults or 5 days for children, fever persists for longer than 3 days, condition becomes worse, new symptoms occur, or redness or swelling is present

Taking for sore throat, and sore throat is severe, persists for longer than 2 days, or occurs together with or is followed by fever, headache, rash, nausea, or vomiting

Symptoms of ringing or buzzing in ears or headache occur during long-term therapy

Patients taking aspirin as a platelet aggregation inhibitor:

» Taking only the amount of aspirin prescribed; checking with prescribing physician about proper medication to use for relief of pain, fever, or arthritis

» Not discontinuing treatment for any reason without first consulting prescribing physician

» Not taking acetaminophen, ibuprofen, or other NSAIDs concurrently with salicylates for longer than a few days, unless specifically prescribed by physician or dentist, especially if using salicylates on a long-term and/or high-dose basis

Diabetics:

Possibility of false urine sugar test results with prolonged use (per day) of—

8 or more 325-mg (5-grain), 4 or more 500-mg or 650-mg (10-grain), 3 or more 800-mg or 975-mg (15-grain) doses of aspirin

8 or more 325-mg (5-grain) or 4 or more 500-mg or 650-mg (10-grain) doses of buffered aspirin or sodium salicylate

4 or more 870-mg doses of choline salicylate

5 or more 500-mg, 4 or more 750-mg, or 2 or more 1000-mg, doses of choline and magnesium salicylates

7 or more 325-mg, or 4 or more 500-mg or higher, doses of magnesium salicylate

4 or more 500-mg, or 3 or more 750-mg, doses of salsalate

Checking with physician, nurse, or pharmacist if unsure of daily dose being taken, if changes in urine sugar test results occur, or if any other questions, especially if diabetes not well-controlled

Caution if any kind of surgery is required; not taking aspirin for 5 days prior to surgery unless otherwise directed by physician or dentist because of risk of bleeding

Not taking a tetracycline antibiotic within 1 to 2 hours of buffered aspirin, choline and magnesium salicylates, or magnesium salicylate

Not taking a cellulose-containing laxative within 2 hours of a salicylate

Alcohol consumption may increase probability of stomach problems (for oral dosage forms only)

Checking with physician if rectal irritation occurs with aspirin suppositories

Caution if any laboratory tests required; possible interference with some test results by salicylates; possible interference with dipyridamole-assisted myocardial imaging by formulations containing caffeine

» Suspected overdose: Getting emergency help immediately

Side/adverse effects

Signs of potential side effects, especially allergic reactions, anemia, and gastrointestinal toxicity and, with aspirin suppositories, rectal irritation

General Dosing Information

A reduction in initial dosage is recommended for geriatric patients, especially those receiving long-acting salicylates (e.g., choline and magnesium salicylates, salsalate) or prolonged therapy. These patients may be more susceptible to salicylate toxicity, especially if accumulation occurs because of impaired renal function. If the reduced dosage is not effective, dosage may gradually be increased as tolerated.

For treatment of arthritis, dosage is usually increased gradually until symptoms are relieved, therapeutic plasma concentrations are achieved, or signs of toxicity, such as tinnitus or headache, occur. If these signs should appear, dosage should be reduced. However, tinnitus is not a reliable index of maximum salicylate tolerance, especially in very young or geriatric patients or those with impaired hearing.

For treatment of arthritis, dosage adjustments should not be made more frequently than once weekly, unless a reduction in dosage is required because of side effects, because up to 7 days may be required to achieve steady-state plasma concentrations.

The risk of Reye's syndrome must be considered when salicylates are administered to children and teenagers. It is recommended that salicylates be withheld from pediatric and adolescent patients with a fever or other symptoms of an illness that may predispose to Reye's syndrome until it has been determined that such an illness is not present or has run its course.

Dosage should be reduced if fever or illness causes fluid depletion, especially in children.

In general, it is recommended that aspirin therapy be discontinued 5 days before surgery to prevent possible occurrence of bleeding problems.

Patients who experience bronchospastic or cutaneous allergic reactions to aspirin may be desensitized to these effects by administration of initially small and gradually increasing doses of aspirin. *Desensitization must be carried out only by clinicians who are familiar with the technique, and only in a facility having trained personnel, medications, and equipment immediately available for treating any adverse reaction to the medication (especially anaphylaxis or severe bronchospasm).* This procedure also desensitizes the patient to other nonsteroidal anti-inflammatory drugs (NSAIDs). However, unless aspirin or another NSAID is then administered on a daily basis, sensitivity to these medications redevelops within a few days.

For oral dosage forms only

These medications (except enteric-coated formulations) should be administered after meals or with food to lessen gastric irritation.

It is recommended that tablet and capsule dosage forms of these medications always be administered with a full glass (240 mL) of water and that the patient remain in an upright position for 15 to 30 minutes after administration. These measures may reduce the risk of the medication becoming lodged in the esophagus, which has been reported to cause prolonged esophageal irritation and difficulty in swallowing in some patients receiving NSAIDs.

It is recommended that aspirin or buffered aspirin products not be chewed before swallowing for at least 7 days following tonsillectomy or oral surgery because of possible injury to oral tissues from prolonged contact with aspirin.

Aspirin or buffered aspirin tablets should not be placed directly on a tooth or gum surface because of possible injury to tissues.

Concurrent use of an antacid and/or a histamine (H_2)-receptor antagonist (cimetidine, famotidine, or ranitidine) may protect against salicylate-induced gastric irritation or ulceration. However, the fact that chronic, high-dose antacid use may alkalinize the urine and increase salicylate excretion must be considered. Also, because these medications may cause premature dissolution, and loss of the protective effect, of enteric coatings, they will not provide additive protection against gastric irritation when administered concurrently with enteric-coated dosage forms.

ASPIRIN

Summary of Differences

Category/indications: Aspirin (capsules, tablets, chewable tablets, and delayed-release tablets) also indicated as a platelet aggregation inhibitor.

Pharmacology: Aspirin irreversibly inhibits platelet aggregation.

Precautions:

Cross-sensitivity and/or related problems—Risk of cross-sensitivity with other nonsteroidal anti-inflammatory drugs (NSAIDs) significantly greater than with other salicylates.

Drug interactions and/or related problems—

May increase ascorbic acid requirement (prolonged high-dose use).

May decrease zidovudine clearance.

Higher risk of bleeding (compared with other salicylates) when used concurrently with other medications that may inhibit blood clotting or cause gastrointestinal ulceration or bleeding.

Laboratory value alterations—

Interferes with urine 5-hydroxyindoleacetic acid determinations.

Interferes with protirelin-induced thyroid-stimulating hormone release determinations.

Prolongs bleeding time.

Contraindications/medical problems—
>Should not be used in patients with a history of severe sensitivity reactions to aspirin, other NSAIDs, nasal polyps and asthma, or thrombocytopenia
>Should be used with caution in patients with asthma or glucose-6-phosphate dehydrogenase (G6PD) deficiency.

Side/adverse effects:
>More ulcerogenic than other salicylates.
>Rarely, causes hemolytic anemia (in patients with G6PD deficiency).
>Suppository dosage form may cause rectal bleeding.

Additional Dosing Information

See also *General Dosing Information.*

Salicylate toxicity requiring treatment generally occurs with doses of 200 mg per kg of body weight (mg/kg), especially in children.

The general doses for aspirin products other than aspirin chewing gum tablets are based on the FDA's dosing recommendations for aspirin. The dosage unit of 80 mg (1.23 grains) is used for pediatric doses; the dosage unit of 325 mg (5 grains) is used for adult doses. The conversion factor of 1 grain equal to 65 mg is used. Strengths of specific products may vary, depending on the manufacturer.

The extended-release tablet, the suppository, and the chewing gum tablet dosage forms may give incomplete or unreliable absorption.

Chewable aspirin tablets may be chewed, dissolved in liquid, or swallowed whole.

The delayed-release tablets must be swallowed whole.

The dispersible tablets are to be dissolved in the mouth prior to swallowing. A little water may be used, if necessary, to facilitate dissolution.

Some extended-release tablets may be broken or crumbled but must not be ground up before swallowing. Others must be swallowed whole. Consult manufacturers' prescribing information for individual products.

Oral Dosage Forms

Note: Bracketed uses in the *Dosage Forms* section refer to categories of use and/or indications that are not included in U.S. product labeling.

ASPIRIN DELAYED-RELEASE CAPSULES USP

Note: Aspirin delayed-release capsules are not commercially available in the U.S.

Usual adult and adolescent dose:
Analgesic/antipyretic—Oral, 325 to 500 mg every three hours, 325 to 650 mg every four hours, or 650 to 1000 mg every six hours as needed, while symptoms persist.
>Note: For patient self-medication, it is recommended that the total daily dose not exceed 4 grams, and that a physician be consulted if pain is not relieved within ten days, fever within three days, or sore throat within two days.

Antirheumatic (nonsteroidal anti-inflammatory)—Oral, 3.6 to 5.4 grams a day in divided doses.
>Note: In acute rheumatic fever, up to 7.8 grams a day in divided doses may be given.

Platelet aggregation inhibitor—Oral, 325 mg a day, with the following exceptions:
Ischemic attacks, transient, in males; or
Thromboembolism, cerebral, recurrence[1]—Oral, 1 gram a day. Dosage may be reduced to 325 mg a day if the patient is unable to tolerate the higher dose.
Ischemic attacks, transient, occurring in association with mitral valve prolapse[1]—Oral, 325 mg to 1 gram a day.

Prevention of thrombosis or occlusion of coronary bypass graft—Oral, 325 mg seven hours postoperatively (via a nasogastric tube), then 325 mg three times daily, concurrently with 75 mg of dipyridamole. Dipyridamole may be discontinued one week postoperatively, but aspirin should be continued indefinitely.

Platelet aggregation inhibitor therapy is most effective when it is initiated two days prior to scheduled surgery. However, preoperative administration of aspirin has been shown to increase perisurgical bleeding and is not recommended. Therapy is therefore initiated with dipyridamole (recommended dosage 100 mg four times a day for two days prior to surgery and 100 mg one hour postoperatively [via a nasogastric tube]). Dipyridamole therapy is continued postoperatively (recommended dosage 75 mg seven hours postoperatively, via a nasogastric tube, then 75 mg three times a day, concurrently with aspirin) for at least one week.

Note: Although the doses recommended above for use of aspirin as a platelet aggregation inhibitor have been found effective in clinical studies, optimum dosage has not been established. For indications other than prevention of transient ischemic attacks or recurrence of cerebral thromboembolism, lower doses are often used. A few studies have shown that 160 mg of aspirin every twenty-four hours, or 325 mg every forty-eight hours, may effectively inhibit platelet aggregation while minimizing the risk of aspirin-induced side effects.

Auxiliary labeling: • Take with a full glass of water.

ASPIRIN TABLETS USP

Usual adult and adolescent dose:
Analgesic/antipyretic—Oral, 325 to 500 mg every three hours, 325 to 650 mg every four hours, or 650 mg to 1000 mg every six hours as needed, while symptoms persist.
>Note: For patient self-medication, it is recommended that the total daily dose not exceed 4 grams, and that a physician be consulted if pain is not relieved within ten days, fever within three days, or sore throat within two days.

Antirheumatic (nonsteroidal anti-inflammatory)—Oral, 3.6 to 5.4 grams a day in divided doses.
>Note: In acute rheumatic fever, up to 7.8 grams a day in divided doses may be given.

Platelet aggregation inhibitor—Oral, 325 mg a day, with the following exceptions:
Ischemic attacks, transient, in males; or
[Thromboembolism, cerebral, recurrence][1]—Oral, 1 gram a day. Dosage may be reduced to 325 mg a day if the patient is unable to tolerate the higher dose.
[Ischemic attacks, transient, occurring in association with mitral valve prolapse][1]—Oral, 325 mg to 1 gram a day.
[Prevention of thrombosis or occlusion of coronary bypass graft]—Oral, 325 mg seven hours postoperatively (via a nasogastric tube), then 325 mg three times daily, concurrently with 75 mg of dipyridamole. Dipyridamole may be discontinued one week postoperatively, but aspirin should be continued indefinitely.

Platelet aggregation inhibitor therapy is most effective when it is initiated two days prior to scheduled surgery. However, preoperative administration of aspirin has been shown to increase perisurgical bleeding and is not recommended. Therapy is therefore initiated with dipyridamole (recommended dosage 100 mg four times a day for two days prior to surgery and 100 mg one hour postoperatively [via a nasogastric tube]). Dipyridamole therapy is continued postoperatively (recommended dosage 75 mg seven hours postoperatively, via a nasogastric tube, then 75 mg three times a day, concurrently with aspirin) for at least one week.

Note: Although the doses recommended above for use of aspirin as a platelet aggregation inhibitor have been found effective in clinical studies, optimum dosage has not been established. For indications other than prevention of transient ischemic attacks or recurrence of cerebral thromboembolism, lower doses are often used. A few studies have shown that 160 mg of aspirin every twenty-four hours, or 325 mg every forty-eight hours, may effectively inhibit platelet aggregation while minimizing the risk of aspirin-induced side effects.

Auxiliary labeling: • Take with food and a full glass of water.

ASPIRIN TABLETS USP (CHEWABLE)

Usual adult and adolescent dose:

Analgesic/antipyretic—Adult-strength product not available.

Antirheumatic—Adult-strength product not available.

Platelet aggregation inhibitor—Oral, 80 to 160 mg a day, usually in combination with dipyridamole.

Note: Optimum dosage has not been established. One clinical study has shown that 160 mg of aspirin a day inhibits platelet aggregation and prevents recurrences of myocardial infarction, and other studies have shown that single doses of 40 to 80 mg also inhibit platelet aggregation. However, higher doses have been used in most clinical studies; therefore, doses ranging from 325 mg to 1 gram a day are usually recommended, depending on the specific condition being treated.

Auxiliary labeling:
• May be chewed.
• Take with food and a full glass of water.

ASPIRIN CHEWING GUM TABLETS

Usual adult and adolescent dose: Analgesic—Oral, 454 mg. May be repeated every four hours as needed.

Note: For patient self-medication, it is recommended that a physician be consulted if pain is not relieved within ten days or sore throat within two days.

Auxiliary labeling:
• To be chewed.
• Take with food.
• Drink a full glass of water after chewing.

ASPIRIN DELAYED-RELEASE TABLETS USP

Usual adult and adolescent dose:

Analgesic/antipyretic—Oral, 325 to 500 mg every three hours, 325 to 650 mg every four hours, or 650 mg to 1000 mg every six hours as needed, while symptoms persist.

Note: For patient self-medication, it is recommended that the total daily dose not exceed 4 grams, and that a physician be consulted if pain is not relieved within ten days, fever within three days, or sore throat within two days.

Antirheumatic (nonsteroidal anti-inflammatory)—Oral, 3.6 to 5.4 grams a day in divided doses.

Note: In acute rheumatic fever, up to 7.8 grams a day in divided doses may be given.

Platelet aggregation inhibitor—Oral, 325 mg a day, with the following exceptions:

Ischemic attacks, transient, in males; or

[Thromboembolism, cerebral, recurrence][1]—Oral, 1 gram a day. Dosage may be reduced to 325 mg a day if the patient is unable to tolerate the higher dose.

[Ischemic attacks, transient, occurring in association with mitral valve prolapse][1]—Oral, 325 mg to 1 gram a day.

[Prevention of thrombosis or occlusion of coronary bypass graft]—Oral, 325 mg seven hours postoperatively (via a nasogastric tube), then 325 mg three times daily, concurrently with 75 mg of dipyridamole. Dipyridamole may be discontinued one week postoperatively, but aspirin should be continued indefinitely.

Platelet aggregation inhibitor therapy is most effective when it is initiated two days prior to scheduled surgery. However, preoperative administration of aspirin has been shown to increase perisurgical bleeding and is not recommended. Therapy is therefore initiated with dipyridamole (recommended dosage 100 mg four times a day for two days prior to surgery and 100 mg one hour postoperatively [via a nasogastric tube]). Dipyridamole therapy is continued postoperatively (recommended dosage 75 mg seven hours postoperatively, via a nasogastric tube, then 75 mg three times a day, concurrently with aspirin) for at least one week.

Note: Although the doses recommended above for use of aspirin as a platelet aggregation inhibitor have been found effective in clinical studies, optimum dosage has not been established. For indications other than prevention of transient ischemic attacks or recurrence of cerebral thromboembolism, lower doses are often used. A few studies have shown that 160 mg of aspirin every twenty-four hours, or 325 mg every forty-eight hours, may effectively inhibit platelet aggregation while minimizing the risk of aspirin-induced side effects.

Auxiliary labeling:
• Swallow tablets whole.
• Take with a full glass of water.

ASPIRIN DISPERSIBLE TABLETS

Note: Aspirin dispersible tablets are not commercially available in the U.S.

Usual adult and adolescent dose:

Analgesic/antipyretic—Oral, 325 to 500 mg every three hours, 325 to 650 mg every four hours, or 650 to 1000 mg every six hours as needed, while symptoms persist.

Note: For patient self-medication, it is recommended that the total daily dose not exceed 4 grams, and that a physician be consulted if pain is not relieved within ten days, fever within three days, or sore throat within two days.

Antirheumatic (nonsteroidal anti-inflammatory)—Oral, 3.6 to 5.4 grams a day in divided doses.

Note: In acute rheumatic fever, up to 7.8 grams a day in divided doses may be given.

Auxiliary labeling:
• Take after food.
• Dissolve in the mouth before swallowing.

Additional information: These rapidly dispersible tablets are intended to be dissolved in the mouth before swallowing. If the mouth is dry, a small quantity of water may be used to moisten the mouth and the tablets may then be swallowed with a little water.

ASPIRIN EXTENDED-RELEASE TABLETS USP

Usual adult and adolescent dose: Oral, 650 mg to 1.3 grams as 650-mg tablets every eight hours, or 1.6 grams as 800-mg tablets twice a day.

Note: The extended-release tablets have not been recommended by FDA for use as a platelet aggregation inhibitor.

For treatment of arthritis, the recommended initial dosage may be adjusted according to patient requirements and response.

Auxiliary labeling:
- Take with food and a full glass of water.
- Swallow tablets whole (if specified by manufacturer).

ASPIRIN AND CAFFEINE CAPSULES

Note: Aspirin and caffeine capsules are not commercially available in the U.S.

Usual adult and adolescent dose:

Analgesic/antipyretic—Oral, 325 to 500 mg every three hours, 325 to 650 mg every four hours, or 650 mg to 1000 mg every six hours as needed, while symptoms persist.

Note: For patient self-medication, it is recommended that the total daily dose not exceed 4 grams, and that a physician be consulted if pain is not relieved within ten days, fever within three days, or sore throat within two days.

Antirheumatic (nonsteroidal anti-inflammatory)—Oral, 3.6 to 5.4 grams a day in divided doses.

Platelet aggregation inhibitor—Oral, 325 mg a day, with the following exceptions:

Ischemic attacks, transient, in males; or

Thromboembolism, cerebral, recurrence[1]—Oral, 1 gram a day. Dosage may be reduced to 325 mg a day if the patient is unable to tolerate the higher dose.

Ischemic attacks, transient, occurring in association with mitral valve prolapse[1]—Oral, 325 mg to 1 gram a day.

Prevention of thrombosis or occlusion of coronary bypass graft—Oral, 325 mg seven hours postoperatively (via a nasogastric tube), then 325 mg three times daily, concurrently with 75 mg of dipyridamole. Dipyridamole may be discontinued one week postoperatively, but aspirin should be continued indefinitely.

Platelet aggregation inhibitor therapy is most effective when it is initiated two days prior to scheduled surgery. However, preoperative administration of aspirin has been shown to increase perisurgical bleeding and is not recommended. Therapy is therefore initiated with dipyridamole (recommended dosage 100 mg four times a day for two days prior to surgery and 100 mg one hour postoperatively [via a nasogastric tube]). Dipyridamole therapy is continued postoperatively (recommended dosage 75 mg seven hours postoperatively, via a nasogastric tube, then 75 mg three times a day, concurrently with aspirin) for at least one week.

Note: Although the doses recommended above for use of aspirin as a platelet aggregation inhibitor have been found effective in clinical studies, optimum dosage has not been established. For indications other than prevention of transient ischemic attacks or recurrence of cerebral thromboembolism, lower doses are often used. A few studies have shown that 160 mg of aspirin every twenty-four hours, or 325 mg every forty-eight hours, may effectively inhibit platelet aggregation while minimizing the risk of aspirin-induced side effects.

Auxiliary labeling: • Take with food and a full glass of water.

ASPIRIN AND CAFFEINE TABLETS

Usual adult and adolescent dose:

Analgesic/antipyretic—Oral, 325 to 500 mg every three hours, 325 to 650 mg every four hours, or 650 mg to 1000 mg every six hours as needed, while symptoms persist.

Note: For patient self-medication, it is recommended that the total daily dose not exceed 4 grams, and that a physician be consulted if pain is not relieved within ten days, fever within three days, or sore throat within two days.

Antirheumatic (nonsteroidal anti-inflammatory)—Oral, 3.6 to 5.4 grams a day in divided doses.

Platelet aggregation inhibitor—Oral, 325 mg a day, with the following exceptions:

Ischemic attacks, transient, in males; or

[Thromboembolism, cerebral, recurrence][1]—Oral, 1 gram a day. Dosage may be reduced to 325 mg a day if the patient is unable to tolerate the higher dose.

[Ischemic attacks, transient, occurring in association with mitral valve prolapse][1]—Oral, 325 mg to 1 gram a day.

[Prevention of thrombosis or occlusion of coronary bypass graft]—Oral, 325 mg seven hours postoperatively (via a nasogastric tube), then 325 mg three times daily, concurrently with 75 mg of dipyridamole. Dipyridamole may be discontinued one week postoperatively, but aspirin should be continued indefinitely.

Platelet aggregation inhibitor therapy is most effective when it is initiated two days prior to scheduled surgery. However, preoperative administration of aspirin has been shown to increase perisurgical bleeding and is not recommended. Therapy is therefore initiated with dipyridamole (recommended dosage 100 mg four times a day for two days prior to surgery and 100 mg one hour postoperatively [via a nasogastric tube]). Dipyridamole therapy is continued postoperatively (recommended dosage 75 mg seven hours postoperatively, via a nasogastric tube, then 75 mg three times a day, concurrently with aspirin) for at least one week.

Note: Although the doses recommended above for use of aspirin as a platelet aggregation inhibitor have been found effective in clinical studies, optimum dosage has not been established. For indications other than prevention of transient ischemic attacks or recurrence of cerebral thromboembolism, lower doses are often used. A few studies have shown that 160 mg of aspirin every twenty-four hours, or 325 mg every forty-eight hours, may effectively inhibit platelet aggregation while minimizing the risk of aspirin-induced side effects.

Auxiliary labeling: • Take with food and a full glass of water.

Rectal Dosage Forms

Note: Bracketed uses in the *Dosage Forms* section refer to categories of use and/or indications that are not included in U.S. product labeling.

ASPIRIN SUPPOSITORIES USP

Usual adult and adolescent dose:

Analgesic/antipyretic—Rectal, 325 to 650 mg every four hours as needed, while symptoms persist.

Note: For patient self-medication, it is recommended that the total daily dose not exceed 4 grams, and that a physician be consulted if pain is not relieved within ten days, fever within three days, or sore throat within two days.

Antirheumatic (nonsteroidal anti-inflammatory)—Rectal, 3.6 to 5.4 grams a day in divided doses.

Note: In acute rheumatic fever, up to 7.8 grams a day in divided doses may be given.

Platelet aggregation inhibitor—The suppositories have not been recommended by FDA for use as a platelet aggregation inhibitor.

Auxiliary labeling:
- Store in a cool place. May be refrigerated.
- For rectal use only.

---

[1]Not included in Canadian product labeling.

ASPIRIN, BUFFERED

Summary of Differences

Category/indications: Aspirin, buffered, also indicated as a platelet aggregation inhibitor.

Pharmacology: Aspirin irreversibly inhibits platelet aggregation.

Precautions:

Cross-sensitivity and/or related problems—Risk of cross-sensitivity with other nonsteroidal anti-inflammatory drugs (NSAIDs) significantly greater with aspirin than with other salicylates.

Drug interactions and/or related problems—

Aspirin may increase ascorbic acid requirement (prolonged high-dose use).

Aspirin may decrease zidovudine clearance.

Higher risk of bleeding (compared with other salicylates) when aspirin is used concurrently with other medications that may inhibit blood clotting or cause gastrointestinal ulceration or bleeding.

Antacids present as buffering agents decrease absorption of ketoconazole and oral tetracyclines.

Laboratory value alterations—

Aspirin interferes with urine 5-hydroxyindoleacetic acid determinations.

Aspirin interferes with protirelin-induced thyroid stimulating hormone release determinations.

Aspirin prolongs bleeding time.

Contraindications/medical problems—

Aspirin should not be used in patients with a history of severe sensitivity reactions to aspirin, other NSAIDs, nasal polyps and asthma, or thrombocytopenia.

Aspirin should be used with caution in patients with asthma or glucose-6-phosphate dehydrogenase (G6PD) deficiency.

Side/adverse effects:

Aspirin is more ulcerogenic than other salicylates.

Rarely, aspirin causes hemolytic anemia (in patients with G6PD deficiency).

Additional Dosing Information

See also *General Dosing Information.*

The doses for buffered aspirin formulations are based on the FDA's dosing recommendations for aspirin. The dosage unit of 325 mg (5 grains) is used. The conversion factor of 1 grain equal to 65 mg is used. Strengths of specific products may vary, depending on the manufacturer.

The amount and type of buffering may vary among products.

Oral Dosage Forms

Note: Bracketed uses in the *Dosage Forms* section refer to categories of use and/or indications that are not included in U.S. product labeling.

ASPIRIN, ALUMINA, AND MAGNESIA TABLETS USP

Usual adult and adolescent dose:

Analgesic/antipyretic—Oral, 325 to 500 mg every three hours, 325 to 650 mg every four hours, or 650 mg to 1000 mg every six hours as needed, while symptoms persist.

Note: For patient self-medication, it is recommended that the total daily dose not exceed 4 grams, and that a physician be consulted if pain is not relieved within ten days, fever within three days, or sore throat within two days.

Antirheumatic (nonsteroidal anti-inflammatory)—Oral, 3.6 to 5.4 grams a day in divided doses.

Note: In acute rheumatic fever, up to 7.8 grams a day in divided doses may be given.

Platelet aggregation inhibitor—Oral, 325 mg a day, with the following exceptions:

Ischemic attacks, transient, in males; or

[Thromboembolism, cerebral, recurrence][1]—Oral, 1 gram a day. Dosage may be reduced to 325 mg a day if the patient is unable to tolerate the higher dose.

[Ischemic attacks, transient, occurring in association with mitral valve prolapse][1]—Oral, 325 mg to 1 gram a day.

[Prevention of thrombosis or occlusion of coronary bypass graft]—Oral, 325 mg seven hours postoperatively (via a nasogastric tube), then 325 mg three times daily, concurrently with 75 mg of dipyridamole. Dipyridamole may be discontinued one week postoperatively, but aspirin should be continued indefinitely.

Platelet aggregation inhibitor therapy is most effective when it is initiated two days prior to scheduled surgery. However, preoperative administration of aspirin has been shown to increase perisurgical bleeding and is not recommended. Therapy is therefore initiated with dipyridamole (recommended dosage 100 mg four times a day for two days prior to surgery and 100 mg one hour postoperatively [via a nasogastric tube]). Dipyridamole therapy is continued postoperatively (recommended dosage 75 mg seven hours postoperatively, via a nasogastric tube, then 75 mg three times a day, concurrently with aspirin) for at least one week.

Note: Although the doses recommended above for use of aspirin as a platelet aggregation inhibitor have been found effective in clinical studies, optimum dosage has not been established. For indications other than prevention of transient ischemic attacks or recurrence of cerebral thromboembolism, lower doses are often used. A few studies have shown that 160 mg of aspirin every twenty-four hours, or 325 mg every forty-eight hours, may effectively inhibit platelet aggregation while minimizing the risk of aspirin-induced side effects.

Auxiliary labeling: • Take with food and a full glass of water.

ASPIRIN, ALUMINA, AND MAGNESIUM OXIDE TABLETS USP

Usual adult and adolescent dose:

Analgesic/antipyretic—Oral, 500 mg every three or four hours or 1000 mg every six hours as needed, while symptoms persist.

Note: For patient self-medication, it is recommended that the total daily dose not exceed 4 grams, and that a physician be consulted if pain is not relieved within ten days, fever within three days, or sore throat within two days.

Antirheumatic (nonsteroidal anti-inflammatory)—Oral, 3.6 to 5.4 grams a day in divided doses.

Note: In acute rheumatic fever, up to 7.8 grams a day in divided doses may be given.

Platelet aggregation inhibitor—

Ischemic attacks, transient, in males; or

[Thromboembolism, cerebral, recurrence][1]: Oral, 1 gram a day. Dosage may be reduced to 325 mg a day if the patient is unable to tolerate the higher dose.

[Ischemic attacks, transient, occurring in association with mitral valve prolapse][1]: Oral, 325 mg to 1 gram a day.

Note: Although the doses recommended above for use of aspirin as a platelet aggregation inhibitor have been found effective in clinical studies, optimum dosage has not been established. For other indications responsive to platelet aggregation inhibitor therapy, aspirin is usually administered in doses of 325 mg a day or lower (using another product).

Auxiliary labeling: • Take with food and a full glass of water.

BUFFERED ASPIRIN TABLETS USP

Usual adult and adolescent dose:

Analgesic/antipyretic—Oral, 325 to 500 mg every three hours, 325 to 650 mg every four hours, or 650 mg to 1000 mg every six hours as needed, while symptoms persist.

> Note: For patient self-medication, it is recommended that the total daily dose not exceed 4 grams, and that a physician be consulted if pain is not relieved within ten days, fever within three days, or sore throat within two days.

Platelet aggregation inhibitor—Oral, 325 mg a day, with the following exceptions:

Ischemic attacks, transient, in males; or

[Thromboembolism, cerebral, recurrence][1]—Oral, 1 gram a day. Dosage may be reduced to 325 mg a day if the patient is unable to tolerate the higher dose.

[Ischemic attacks, transient, occurring in association with mitral valve prolapse][1]—Oral, 325 mg to 1 gram a day.

[Prevention of thrombosis or occlusion of coronary bypass graft]—Oral, 325 mg seven hours postoperatively (via a nasogastric tube), then 325 mg three times daily, concurrently with 75 mg of dipyridamole. Dipyridamole may be discontinued one week postoperatively, but aspirin should be continued indefinitely.

Platelet aggregation inhibitor therapy is most effective when it is initiated two days prior to scheduled surgery. However, preoperative administration of aspirin has been shown to increase perisurgical bleeding and is not recommended. Therapy is therefore initiated with dipyridamole (recommended dosage 100 mg four times a day for two days prior to surgery and 100 mg one hour postoperatively [via a nasogastric tube]). Dipyridamole therapy is continued postoperatively (recommended dosage 75 mg seven hours postoperatively, via a nasogastric tube, then 75 mg three times a day, concurrently with aspirin) for at least one week.

> Note: Although the doses recommended above for use of aspirin as a platelet aggregation inhibitor have been found effective in clinical studies, optimum dosage has not been established. For indications other than prevention of transient ischemic attacks or recurrence of cerebral thromboembolism, lower doses are often used. A few studies have shown that 160 mg of aspirin every twenty-four hours, or 325 mg every forty-eight hours, may effectively inhibit platelet aggregation while minimizing the risk of aspirin-induced side effects.

Auxiliary labeling: • Take with food and a full glass of water.

BUFFERED ASPIRIN AND CAFFEINE TABLETS

Note: Buffered aspirin and caffeine tablets are not commercially available in the U.S.

Usual adult and adolescent dose:

Analgesic/antipyretic—Oral, 325 to 500 mg every three hours, 325 to 650 mg every four hours, or 650 mg to 1000 mg every six hours as needed, while symptoms persist.

> Note: For patient self-medication, it is recommended that the total daily dose not exceed 4 grams, and that a physician be consulted if pain is not relieved within ten days, fever within three days, or sore throat within two days.

Platelet aggregation inhibitor—Oral, 325 mg a day, with the following exceptions:

Ischemic attacks, transient, in males; or

Thromboembolism, cerebral, recurrence[1]—Oral, 1 gram a day. Dosage may be reduced to 325 mg a day if the patient is unable to tolerate the higher dose.

Ischemic attacks, transient, occurring in association with mitral valve prolapse[1]—Oral, 325 mg to 1 gram a day.

Prevention of thrombosis or occlusion of coronary bypass graft—Oral, 325 mg seven hours postoperatively (via a nasogastric tube), then 325 mg three times daily, concurrently with 75 mg of dipyridamole. Dipyridamole may be discontinued one week postoperatively, but aspirin should be continued indefinitely.

Platelet aggregation inhibitor therapy is most effective when it is initiated two days prior to scheduled surgery. However, preoperative administration of aspirin has been shown to increase perisurgical bleeding and is not recommended. Therapy is therefore initiated with dipyridamole (recommended dosage 100 mg four times a day for two days prior to surgery and 100 mg one hour postoperatively [via a nasogastric tube]). Dipyridamole therapy is continued postoperatively (recommended dosage 75 mg seven hours postoperatively, via a nasogastric tube, then 75 mg three times a day, concurrently with aspirin) for at least one week.

> Note: Although the doses recommended above for use of aspirin as a platelet aggregation inhibitor have been found effective in clinical studies, optimum dosage has not been established. For indications other than prevention of transient ischemic attacks or recurrence of cerebral thromboembolism, lower doses are often used. A few studies have shown that 160 mg of aspirin every twenty-four hours, or 325 mg every forty-eight hours, may effectively inhibit platelet aggregation while minimizing the risk of aspirin-induced side effects.

Auxiliary labeling: • Take with food and a full glass of water.

---

[1]Not included in Canadian product labeling.

CHOLINE SALICYLATE

Summary of Differences

Pharmacology: Choline salicylate does not have a clinically significant effect on platelet aggregation.

Precautions:

Cross-sensitivity and/or related problems—Lower risk than with aspirin of cross-sensitivity to nonsteroidal anti-inflammatory drugs (NSAIDs).

Drug interactions and/or related problems—Lower risk of bleeding (compared with aspirin) when used concurrently with other medications that may inhibit blood clotting or cause gastrointestinal ulceration or bleeding.

Contraindications/medical problems—May be used in patients with a history of severe sensitivity reactions to aspirin or other NSAIDs, although caution is advised.

Side/adverse effects: Less ulcerogenic than aspirin.

Additional Dosing Information

See also *General Dosing Information.*

The nonarthritic doses are based on the FDA's dosing recommendations for aspirin.

A 435-mg dose of choline salicylate is equivalent in salicylate content to 325 mg of aspirin.

Oral Dosage Forms

CHOLINE SALICYLATE ORAL SOLUTION

Usual adult and adolescent dose:

Analgesic/antipyretic—Oral, 435 to 669 mg (equivalent in salicylate content to 325 to 500 mg of aspirin) every three hours, 435 to 870 mg (equivalent in salicylate content to 325 to 650 mg of aspirin) every four hours, or 870 to 1338 mg (equivalent in salicylate content to 650 to 1000 mg of aspirin) every six hours as needed, while symptoms persist.

Note: For patient self-medication, it is recommended that the total daily dose not exceed 5352 mg, and that a physician be consulted if pain is not relieved within ten days, fever within three days, or sore throat within two days.

Antirheumatic (nonsteroidal anti-inflammatory)—Oral, 4.8 to 7.2 grams (equivalent in salicylate content to 3.6 to 5.4 grams of aspirin) a day in divided doses.

Auxiliary labeling: • Take with food or a full glass of water.

CHOLINE AND MAGNESIUM SALICYLATES

Summary of Differences

Pharmacology: This medication does not have a clinically significant effect on platelet aggregation.

Precautions:

Cross-sensitivity and/or related problems—Lower risk than with aspirin of cross-sensitivity to nonsteroidal anti-inflammatory drugs (NSAIDs).

Drug interactions and/or related problems—Lower risk of bleeding (compared with aspirin) when used concurrently with other medications that may inhibit blood clotting or cause gastrointestinal ulceration or bleeding.

Contraindications/medical problems—

Should not be used in patients with chronic advanced renal impairment because of risk of hypermagnesemic toxicity.

May be used in patients with a history of severe sensitivity reactions to aspirin or other NSAIDs, although caution is advised.

Patient monitoring—Monitoring of serum magnesium concentration recommended if large doses administered to patients with renal insufficiency.

Side/adverse effects: Less ulcerogenic than aspirin.

Additional Dosing Information

See also *General Dosing Information.*

Choline and magnesium salicylates oral solution may be mixed with fruit juices just prior to administration.

Oral Dosage Forms

CHOLINE AND MAGNESIUM SALICYLATES ORAL SOLUTION

Usual adult and adolescent dose:

Analgesic; or

Antipyretic—Oral, 2 to 3 grams of salicylate a day in two or three divided doses.

Anti-inflammatory (nonsteroidal); or

Antirheumatic—Oral, 3 grams of salicylate a day in a single dose at bedtime, or in two or three divided doses, initially. Dosage must then be adjusted according to the requirements and response of the individual patient.

Auxiliary labeling: • Take with food or a full glass of water.

CHOLINE AND MAGNESIUM SALICYLATES TABLETS

Usual adult and adolescent dose:

Analgesic; or

Antipyretic—Oral, 2 to 3 grams of salicylate a day in two or three divided doses.

Anti-inflammatory (nonsteroidal); or

Antirheumatic—Oral, 3 grams of salicylate a day in a single dose at bedtime, or in two or three divided doses, initially. Dosage must then be adjusted according to the requirements and response of the individual patient.

Auxiliary labeling: • Take with food and a full glass of water.

MAGNESIUM SALICYLATE

Summary of Differences

Pharmacology: Magnesium salicylate does not have a clinically significant effect on platelet aggregation.

Precautions:

Cross-sensitivity and/or related problems—Lower risk than with aspirin of cross-sensitivity to nonsteroidal anti-inflammatory drugs (NSAIDs).

Drug interactions and/or related problems—Lower risk of bleeding (compared with aspirin) when used concurrently with other medications that may inhibit blood clotting or cause gastrointestinal ulceration or bleeding.

Contraindications/medical problems—

Should not be used in patients with chronic advanced renal impairment.

May be used in patients with a history of severe sensitivity reactions to aspirin or other NSAIDs, although caution is advised.

Patient monitoring—Monitoring of serum magnesium concentration recommended if large doses are administered to patients with renal insufficiency.

Side/adverse effects: Less ulcerogenic than aspirin.

Additional Dosing Information

See also *General Dosing Information.*

A 545-mg dose of magnesium salicylate is equivalent in salicylate content to 650 mg of aspirin.

Oral Dosage Forms

MAGNESIUM SALICYLATE TABLETS USP

Usual adult and adolescent dose: Oral, 325 mg to 1.3 grams three or four times a day, initially. Dosage may be increased if necessary to achieve the desired effect.

Note: For patient self-medication, it is recommended that the total daily dose not exceed 4 grams, and that a physician be consulted if pain is not relieved within ten days, fever within three days, or sore throat within two days.

Auxiliary labeling: • Take with food and a full glass of water.

SALSALATE

Summary of Differences

Pharmacology: Salsalate does not have a clinically significant effect on platelet aggregation.

Precautions:
  Cross-sensitivity and/or related problems—Lower risk than with aspirin of cross-sensitivity to nonsteroidal anti-inflammatory drugs (NSAIDs).
  Drug interactions and/or related problems—Lower risk of bleeding (compared with aspirin) when used concurrently with other medications that may inhibit blood clotting or cause gastrointestinal ulceration or bleeding.
  Contraindications/medical problems—May be used in patients with a history of severe sensitivity reactions to aspirin or other NSAIDs, although caution is advised.
Side/adverse effects: Less ulcerogenic than aspirin.

Oral Dosage Forms

SALSALATE CAPSULES USP

Usual adult and adolescent dose: Oral, 1 gram three times a day initially. Dosage may then be titrated according to patient response.

Auxiliary labeling: • Take with food and a full glass of water.

SALSALATE TABLETS

Usual adult and adolescent dose: Oral, 500 mg to 1 gram two or three times a day initially. Dosage may then be titrated according to patient response.

Auxiliary labeling: • Take with food and a full glass of water.

SODIUM SALICYLATE

Summary of Differences

Pharmacology: Sodium salicylate does not have a clinically significant effect on platelet aggregation.
Precautions:
  Cross-sensitivity and/or related problems—Lower risk than with aspirin of cross-sensitivity to nonsteroidal anti-inflammatory drugs (NSAIDs).
  Drug interactions and/or related problems—
    Caution required when large doses administered concurrently with sodium-retaining medications.
    Lower risk of bleeding (compared with aspirin) when used concurrently with other medications that may inhibit blood clotting or cause gastrointestinal ulceration or bleeding.
  Contraindications/medical problems—
    Caution required in hypertensive patients or those on a sodium-restricted diet because of sodium content.

May be used in patients with a history of severe sensitivity reactions to aspirin or other NSAIDs, although caution is advised.
Side/adverse effects: Less ulcerogenic than aspirin.

Additional Dosing Information

See also *General Dosing Information.*

The nonarthritic doses are based on the FDA's dosing recommendations for sodium salicylate. The dosage unit of 325 mg (5 grains) is used for adult doses. The conversion factor of 65 mg equal to 1 grain is used. Strengths of specific products may vary, depending on the manufacturer.

The uncoated tablet form of sodium salicylate should be administered with food or a full glass (240 mL) of water to lessen gastric irritation.

Each 325-mg tablet of sodium salicylate contains 2 mEq (46 mg) of sodium.

Oral Dosage Forms

SODIUM SALICYLATE TABLETS USP

Usual adult and adolescent dose:
  Analgesic/antipyretic—Oral, 325 to 650 mg every four hours as needed, while symptoms persist.
    Note: For patient self-medication, it is recommended that the total daily dose not exceed 4 grams, and that a physician be consulted if pain is not relieved within ten days, fever within three days, or sore throat within two days.
  Antirheumatic (nonsteroidal anti-inflammatory)—Oral, 3.6 to 5.4 grams a day in divided doses.

Auxiliary labeling: • Take with food and a full glass of water.

SODIUM SALICYLATE DELAYED-RELEASE TABLETS

Usual adult and adolescent dose:
  Analgesic/antipyretic—Oral, 325 to 650 mg every four hours as needed, while symptoms persist.
    Note: For patient self-medication, it is recommended that the total daily dose not exceed 4 grams, and that a physician be consulted if pain is not relieved within ten days, fever within three days, or sore throat within two days.
  Antirheumatic (nonsteroidal anti-inflammatory)—Oral, 3.6 to 5.4 grams a day in divided doses.

Auxiliary labeling:
  • Swallow tablets whole.
  • Take with a full glass of water.

SALICYLIC ACID   Topical

Some commonly used *brand names* are:
  In the U.S.—

Antinea	*Clearasil Double Textured*
Buf-Puf Acne Cleansing	*Pads Maximum Strength*
Bar with Vitamin E	*Clearasil Double Textured*
Calicylic Creme	*Pads Regular Strength*
Clearasil Clearstick	*Clearasil Medicated Deep*
Maximum Strength	*Cleanser Topical*
Topical Solution	*Solution*
Clearasil Clearstick	*Clear Away*
Regular Strength Topical	*Clear by Design Medicated*
Solution	*Cleansing Pads*

Compound W Gel	*Keralyt*
Compound W Liquid	*Keratex Gel*
Duofilm	*Lactisol*
Duoplant Topical Solution	*Listerex Golden Scrub*
Freezone	*Lotion*
Gordofilm	*Listerex Herbal Scrub*
Hydrisalic	*Lotion*
Ionax Astringent Skin	*Mediplast*
Cleanser Topical	*Noxzema Anti-Acne Gel*
Solution	*Noxzema Anti-Acne Pads*
Ionil Plus Shampoo	*Maximum Strength*
Ionil Shampoo	*Noxzema Anti-Acne Pads*
	Regular Strength

Occlusal-HP Topical Solution
Occlusal Topical Solution
Off-Ezy Topical Solution Corn & Callus Remover Kit
Off-Ezy Topical Solution Wart Removal Kit
Oxy Clean Medicated Cleanser
Oxy Clean Medicated Pads Maximum Strength
Oxy Clean Medicated Pads Regular Strength
Oxy Clean Medicated Pads Sensitive Skin
Oxy Night Watch Maximum Strength Lotion
Oxy Night Watch Sensitive Skin Lotion
Paplex
Paplex Ultra
Propa pH Medicated Acne Cream Maximum Strength
Propa pH Medicated Cleansing Pads Maximum Strength
Propa pH Medicated Cleansing Pads Sensitive Skin
Propa pH Perfectly Clear Skin Cleanser Topical Solution Normal/ Combination Skin
Propa pH Perfectly Clear Skin Cleanser Topical Solution Oily Skin

Propa pH Perfectly Clear Skin Cleanser Topical Solution Sensitive Skin Formula
P&S
Salac
Salacid
Sal-Acid Plaster
Salactic Film Topical Solution
Sal-Clens Plus Shampoo
Sal-Clens Shampoo
Saligel
Salonil
Sal-Plant Gel Topical Solution
Sebucare
Stri-Dex Dual Textured Pads Maximum Strength
Stri-Dex Dual Textured Pads Regular Strength
Stri-Dex Dual Textured Pads Sensitive Skin
Stri-Dex Maximum Strength Pads
Stri-Dex Regular Strength Pads
Stri-Dex Super Scrub Pads
Trans-Plantar
Trans-Ver-Sal
Verukan-HP Topical Solution
Verukan Topical Solution
Viranol
Wart-Off Topical Solution
X-Seb

In Canada—
Compound W Gel
Compound W Liquid
Cuplex Gel
Occlusal-HP Topical Solution
Occlusal Topical Solution
Oxy Clean Extra Strength Medicated Pads
Oxy Clean Extra Strength Skin Cleanser Topical Solution
Oxy Clean Medicated Soap
Oxy Clean Regular Strength Medicated Cleanser Topical Solution
Oxy Clean Regular Strength Medicated Pads

Oxy Clean Sensitive Skin Cleanser Topical Solution
Oxy Clean Sensitive Skin Pads
Oxy Night Watch Night Time Acne Medication Extra Strength Lotion
Oxy Night Watch Night Time Acne Medication Regular Strength Lotion
Oxy Sensitive Skin Vanishing Formula Lotion
Salac
Tersac Cleansing Gel
Trans-Ver-Sal

In Canada—*Oxy Night Watch Night Time Acne Medication Extra Strength Lotion; Oxy Night Watch Night Time Acne Medication Regular Strength Lotion; Oxy Sensitive Skin Vanishing Formula Lotion*

Salicylic Acid Ointment
In the U.S.—*Salacid; Salonil*

Salicylic Acid Pads
In the U.S.—*Clearasil Double Textured Pads Maximum Strength; Clearasil Double Textured Pads Regular Strength; Clear by Design Medicated Cleansing Pads; Noxzema Anti-Acne Pads Maximum Strength; Noxzema Anti-Acne Pads Regular Strength; Oxy Clean Medicated Pads Maximum Strength; Oxy Clean Medicated Pads Regular Strength; Oxy Clean Medicated Pads Sensitive Skin; Propa pH Medicated Cleansing Pads Maximum Strength; Propa pH Medicated Cleansing Pads Sensitive Skin; Stri-Dex Dual Textured Pads Maximum Strength; Stri-Dex Dual Textured Pads Regular Strength; Stri-Dex Dual Textured Pads Sensitive Skin; Stri-Dex Maximum Strength Pads; Stri-Dex Regular Strength Pads; Stri-Dex Super Scrub Pads*
In Canada—*Oxy Clean Extra Strength Medicated Pads; Oxy Clean Regular Strength Medicated Pads; Oxy Clean Sensitive Skin Pads*

Salicylic Acid Plaster USP
In the U.S.—*Clear Away; Mediplast; Sal-Acid Plaster; Trans-Plantar; Trans-Ver-Sal*
In Canada—*Trans-Ver-Sal*

Salicylic Acid Shampoo
In the U.S.—*Ionil Plus Shampoo; Ionil Shampoo; P&S; Sal-Clens Plus Shampoo; Sal-Clens Shampoo; X-Seb*

Salicylic Acid Soap
In the U.S.—*Buf-Puf Acne Cleansing Bar with Vitamin E; Salac;* GENERIC
In Canada—*Oxy Clean Medicated Soap; Salac; Tersac Cleansing Gel*

Salicylic Acid Topical Solution
In the U.S.—*Clearasil Clearstick Maximum Strength Topical Solution; Clearasil Clearstick Regular Strength Topical Solution; Clearasil Medicated Deep Cleanser Topical Solution; Compound W Liquid; Duofilm; Duoplant Topical Solution; Freezone; Gordofilm; Ionax Astringent Skin Cleanser Topical Solution; Lactisol; Occlusal-HP Topical Solution; Occlusal Topical Solution; Off-Ezy Topical Solution Corn & Callus Remover Kit; Off-Ezy Topical Solution Wart Removal Kit; Oxy Clean Medicated Cleanser; Paplex; Paplex Ultra; Propa pH Perfectly Clear Skin Cleanser Topical Solution Normal/Combination Skin; Propa pH Perfectly Clear Skin Cleanser Topical Solution Oily Skin; Propa pH Perfectly Clear Skin Cleanser Topical Solution Sensitive Skin Formula; Salactic Film Topical Solution; Sal-Plant Gel Topical Solution; Verukan-HP Topical Solution; Verukan Topical Solution; Viranol; Wart-Off Topical Solution*
In Canada—*Compound W Liquid; Occlusal-HP Topical Solution; Occlusal Topical Solution; Oxy Clean Extra Strength Skin Cleanser Topical Solution; Oxy Clean Regular Strength Medicated Cleanser Topical Solution; Oxy Clean Sensitive Skin Cleanser Topical Solution*

TOPICAL

Salicylic Acid Cream
In the U.S.—*Antinea; Calicylic Creme; Propa pH Medicated Acne Cream Maximum Strength;* GENERIC

Salicylic Acid Gel USP
In the U.S.—*Compound W Gel; Hydrisalic; Keralyt; Keratex Gel; Noxzema Anti-Acne Gel; Saligel; Viranol*
In Canada—*Compound W Gel; Cuplex Gel*

Salicylic Acid Lotion
In the U.S.—*Listerex Golden Scrub Lotion; Listerex Herbal Scrub Lotion; Oxy Night Watch Maximum Strength Lotion; Oxy Night Watch Sensitive Skin Lotion; Sebucare*

Category

Keratolytic (topical)—Salicylic Acid Cream; Salicylic Acid Gel USP; Salicylic Acid Lotion; Salicylic Acid Ointment; Salicylic Acid Pads; Salicylic Acid Plaster USP; Salicylic Acid Shampoo; Salicylic Acid Soap; Salicylic Acid Topical Solution.

Antiacne agent (topical)—Salicylic Acid Gel USP; Salicylic Acid Lotion; Salicylic Acid Ointment; Salicylic Acid Pads; Salicylic Acid Soap; Salicylic Acid Topical Solution.

Antiseborrheic—Salicylic Acid Lotion; Salicylic Acid Ointment; Salicylic Acid Shampoo.

Antipsoriatic (topical)—Salicylic Acid Gel USP; Salicylic Acid Ointment.

Caustic—Salicylic Acid Cream; Salicylic Acid Ointment; Salicylic Acid Plaster USP; Salicylic Acid Topical Solution.

Indications

Accepted

Acne vulgaris (treatment)—Salicylic acid gel, lotion, ointment, pads, soap, and topical solution are indicated as peeling and drying agents in the treatment of acne vulgaris.

Dandruff (treatment);

Dermatitis, seborrheic (treatment); or

Dermatitis, seborrheic, of scalp (treatment)—Salicylic acid lotion and shampoo are indicated to help control scaling of the scalp associated with dandruff and seborrheic dermatitis. Salicylic acid ointment is indicated in the treatment of seborrheic dermatitis.

Psoriasis (treatment)—Salicylic acid gel and ointment are indicated as adjuncts in the treatment of psoriasis.

Hyperkeratotic skin disorders (treatment)—Salicylic acid is indicated as a topical aid in the removal of excessive keratin in hyperkeratotic skin disorders, including verrucae and the various ichthyoses (vulgaris, sex-linked, and lamellar); keratosis palmaris and plantaris; keratosis pilaris; and pityriasis rubra pilaris. It is also indicated as a topical aid in the removal of excessive keratin on dorsal and plantar hyperkeratotic lesions. Salicylic acid cream, plaster, and topical solution are indicated to treat corns and calluses. Salicylic acid gel, ointment, plaster, and topical solution are indicated to treat common warts; the plaster and topical solution are indicated to treat plantar warts.

Pharmacology

Mechanism of action/Effect: Salicylic acid facilitates desquamation by solubilizing the intercellular cement that binds scales in the stratum corneum, thereby loosening the keratin. This keratolytic effect may provide an antifungal action because removal of the stratum corneum suppresses fungal growth; it also aids in the penetration of other antifungal agents. Salicylic acid also has a mild antiseptic action.

Precautions to Consider

Geriatrics

Appropriate studies on the relationship of age to the effects of salicylic acid have not been performed in the geriatric population. However, elderly patients are more likely to have age-related peripheral vascular disease and therefore may be more prone to acute inflammation or ulceration of the extremities when they are treated with the 25 or 60% cream, 12 to 17% gel, 25 to 60% ointment, 12 to 50% plaster, and 5 to 27% topical solution.

Drug interactions and/or related problems

The following drug interactions and/or related problems have been selected on the basis of their potential clinical significance (possible mechanism in parentheses where appropriate)—not necessarily inclusive (» = major clinical significance):

Note: Combinations containing any of the following medications, depending on the amount present, may also interact with this medication.

Abrasive or medicated soaps or cleansers or

Acne preparations or preparations containing a peeling agent, such as:

  Benzoyl peroxide

  Resorcinol

  Sulfur

  Tretinoin, or

Acne preparations, topical, other, or

Alcohol-containing preparations, topical, such as:

  After-shave lotions

  Astringents

  Perfumed toiletries

  Shaving creams or lotions, or

Cosmetics or soaps with a strong drying effect or

Isotretinoin or

Medicated cosmetics or "cover-ups"

  (concurrent use with salicylic acid may cause a cumulative irritant or drying effect, especially with the application of peeling, desquamating, or abrasive agents, resulting in excessive irritation of the skin)

Contraindications/Medical problems

The contraindications/medical problems included have been selected on the basis of their potential clinical significance (reasons given in parentheses where appropriate)—not necessarily inclusive (» = major clinical significance).

Risk-benefit should be considered when the following medical problems exist:

  Sensitivity to salicylic acid

For 25 and 60% cream, 25 to 60% ointment, 12 to 50% plaster, 12 to 17% gel, and 5 to 27% topical solution

  Diabetes mellitus or

  Peripheral vascular disease

    (acute inflammation or ulceration may occur, especially on the extremities)

  Inflammation, irritation, or infection of skin

Side/Adverse Effects

Note: The treatment of warts using high concentrations of salicylic acid may cause skin erosion. This erosion may facilitate the spread of the warts.

The following side/adverse effects have been selected on the basis of their potential clinical significance (possible signs and symptoms in parentheses where appropriate)—not necessarily inclusive:

Those indicating need for medical attention

Skin irritation, moderate to severe, not present before therapy; skin ulceration or erosion—especially when using medication with a high percentage of salicylic acid

Symptoms of salicylism

Confusion; dizziness; headache, severe or continuing; rapid breathing; ringing or buzzing in ears, continuing

Those indicating need for medical attention only if they continue or are bothersome

Incidence more frequent

Skin irritation, mild, not present before therapy; stinging

Patient Consultation

In providing consultation, consider emphasizing the following selected information (» = major clinical significance):

Before using this medication

» Conditions affecting use, especially:

  Sensitivity to salicylic acid

  Pregnancy—Medication may be absorbed through the skin; studies in animals have shown that salicylic acid causes birth defects when given orally in doses about 6 times the maximum daily human dose applied topically over a large body surface

Use in children—Young children may be at increased risk of toxicity because of increased absorption of salicylic acid through the skin. Salicylic acid should not be applied to large areas of the body or for long periods of time

Proper use of this medication

» Importance of using medication only as directed

Proper use of occlusive dressing, if prescribed: Understanding exactly how to apply; using only as directed

» Avoiding contact with the eyes and other mucous membranes; if contact occurs, immediately flushing with water for 15 minutes

Washing hands immediately after applying medication, unless hands are being treated

Missed dose: Applying as soon as possible; not applying if almost time for next dose

Proper administration:

For cream, lotion, or ointment dosage form

Applying enough to cover affected area; rubbing in gently

For gel dosage form

Before using—Applying wet packs to affected area for at least 5 minutes

Applying enough to cover affected area; rubbing in gently

For pad dosage form

Wiping pad over affected area; not rinsing off medication after treatment

For plaster dosage form

Reading patient instructions carefully before using medication

» Not using on irritated, inflamed, or infected skin, or if diabetic or have impaired blood circulation

» Not using on facial, genital, nasal, or oral warts; warts with hair growing from them; moles; or birthmarks

Washing affected area and drying thoroughly; if treating warts, soaking warts in warm water for 5 minutes before drying

Cutting plaster to fit wart, corn, or callus

If treating corns or calluses, repeating application every 48 hours for up to 14 days; soaking corns or calluses in warm water for 5 minutes to assist in removal

If treating warts, depending on product, either applying plaster and repeating every 48 hours or applying plaster at bedtime, leaving in place for at least 8 hours, removing in the morning, and repeating application every 24 hours; repeating application for up to 12 weeks

Checking with doctor if discomfort increases during treatment or persists after treatment

For shampoo dosage form

Before applying—Wetting hair and scalp with lukewarm water

Applying enough to work up lather; rubbing well into scalp for 2 or 3 minutes; rinsing

Applying again; rinsing thoroughly

For soap dosage form

Working up lather with soap, using hot water

Scrubbing entire affected area with a washcloth or facial sponge or mitt

Using in a foot bath—Working up rich suds in hot water; soaking feet for 10 to 15 minutes; patting dry without rinsing

For topical solution dosage form used for acne

Applying medication to cotton ball or pad; wiping over affected area; not rinsing off medication after treatment

For topical solution dosage form used for corns, calluses, or warts

Reading patient instructions carefully before using medication

» Not using near heat or open flame or while smoking

» Not using on irritated, inflamed, or infected skin, or if diabetic or have impaired blood circulation

» Not using on facial, genital, nasal, or oral warts; warts with hair growing from them; moles; or birthmarks

Avoiding inhalation of vapors

Washing affected area and drying thoroughly; if treating warts, warts may be soaked in warm water for 5 minutes before drying

Applying medication one drop at a time to sufficiently cover each wart, corn, or callus; letting dry

If treating warts, repeating procedure once or twice daily for up to 12 weeks

If treating corns or calluses, repeating procedure once or twice daily for up to 14 days

Soaking corns and calluses in warm water for 5 minutes to assist in removal

Checking with doctor if discomfort increases during treatment or persists after treatment

» Proper storage

Precautions while using this medication

» Avoiding simultaneous use (at same site) with other topical acne preparations or preparations containing peeling agents, alcohol-containing preparations, abrasive soaps or cleansers, cosmetics or soaps with drying effect, medicated cosmetics, or other topical skin medication, unless otherwise directed by physician

Side/adverse effects

Signs of potential side effects, especially skin irritation not present before therapy or symptoms of salicylism

General Dosing Information

In young children, use is not recommended on large areas of the body, for prolonged periods of time, or under occlusion to sizable areas of the body.

For the stronger strengths of salicylic acid, such as the 25 and 60% cream, 25 and 60% ointment, 12 to 50% plaster, 12 to 17% gel, and 5 to 27% topical solution

These products are not recommended for use on irritated, inflamed, or infected skin; facial, genital, nasal, or oral warts; warts with hair growing from them; moles; or birthmarks. In addition, these products are not recommended for use on patients with diabetes mellitus or impaired blood circulation.

For the gel dosage form

Before application of the gel, wet packs should be applied to the affected areas for at least 5 minutes in order to enhance its effect.

The method of use usually preferred is application of the gel to the affected area with an occlusive dressing at night.

For the 25 to 60% creams and ointments

Application of these creams or ointments should be made only by a physician.

Caution should be used to avoid getting these creams or ointments on skin surrounding the area being treated.

Following application of these creams or ointments, an occlusive dressing is applied.

For the 12 to 50% plaster dosage form

The affected area should be washed and dried. Warts may be soaked in warm water for 5 minutes before drying.

The plaster should be cut to fit the wart, corn, or callus.

For corns and calluses: Application should be repeated every 48 hours as needed for up to 14 days until corn or callus is removed. The corn or callus may be soaked in warm water for 5 minutes to aid in removal.

For warts: Depending on the product, the plaster should either be applied every 48 hours or applied at bedtime, left in place for at least 8 hours, removed in the morning, and the application repeated every 24 hours. In either case, application should be repeated for up to 12 weeks until wart is removed.

For the 5 to 27% topical solution dosage form for treatment of warts, corns, or calluses

The affected areas should be washed and dried. Warts may be soaked in warm water for 5 minutes before drying.

Medication should be applied one drop at a time to completely cover wart, corn, or callus.

Procedure should be repeated once or twice daily for up to 14 days for corns or calluses or up to 12 weeks for warts, until wart, corn, or callus is removed.

Corns and calluses may be soaked in water for 5 minutes to aid in removal.

Topical Dosage Forms

SALICYLIC ACID CREAM

Usual adult and adolescent dose:
Keratolytic (topical)—Topical, to the skin, as a 2 to 10% cream.
Caustic—Topical, to the skin, as a 25 to 60% cream once every three to five days, under occlusion.

Auxiliary labeling: • For external use only.

SALICYLIC ACID GEL USP

Usual adult and adolescent dose:
Antiacne agent (topical)—Topical, to the skin, as a 0.5% to 5% gel once a day.
Antipsoriatic (topical)—Topical, to the skin, as a 5% gel once a day.
Keratolytic (topical)—Topical, to the skin, as a 5 to 17% gel once a day, preferably under occlusion.

Auxiliary labeling: • For external use only.

SALICYLIC ACID LOTION

Usual adult and adolescent dose:
Antiacne agent (topical)—Topical to the skin, as a 1 to 2% lotion one to three times a day.
Antiseborrheic or
Keratolytic (topical)—Topical, to the scalp, as a 1.8 to 2% lotion one or two times a day.

Auxiliary labeling:
• For external use only.
• Keep container tightly closed.

SALICYLIC ACID OINTMENT

Usual adult and adolescent dose:
Antiacne agent (topical)—Topical, to the skin, as a 3 to 6% ointment.

Antipsoriatic (topical) or
Antiseborrheic or
Keratolytic (topical)—Topical, to the skin, as a 3 to 10% ointment.
Caustic—Topical, to the skin, as a 25 to 60% ointment once every three to five days, under occlusion.

Auxiliary labeling: • For external use only.

SALICYLIC ACID PADS

Usual adult and adolescent dose: Antiacne agent (topical)—Topical, to the skin, as a 0.5 to 2% pad one to three times a day.

Auxiliary labeling: • For external use only.

SALICYLIC ACID PLASTER USP

Usual adult and adolescent dose:
Caustic or
Keratolytic (topical)—Topical, to the skin, as a 12 to 50% plaster every other day or every day.

Auxiliary labeling: • For external use only.

SALICYLIC ACID SHAMPOO

Usual adult and adolescent dose:
Antiseborrheic or
Keratolytic (topical)—Topical, to the scalp, as a 2 to 4% shampoo one or two times a week.

Auxiliary labeling:
• Shake well.
• For external use only.

SALICYLIC ACID SOAP

Usual adult and adolescent dose:
Antiacne agent (topical) or
Keratolytic (topical)—Topical, to the skin, as a 2 to 3.5% soap.

Auxiliary labeling: • For external use only.

SALICYLIC ACID TOPICAL SOLUTION

Usual adult and adolescent dose:
Antiacne agent (topical)—Topical to the skin, as a 0.5 to 2% solution up to three times a day.
Keratolytic (topical)—Topical, to the skin:
For warts—As a 5 to 27% solution one or two times a day.
For corns and calluses—As a 12 to 27% solution one or two times a day.

Auxiliary labeling:
• Flammable.
• For external use only.

SALICYLIC ACID AND SULFUR   Topical

Category

Keratolytic (topical)—Salicylic Acid and Sulfur.

Antiacne agent (topical)—Salicylic Acid and Sulfur Cleansing Cream; Salicylic Acid and Sulfur Lotion; Salicylic Acid and Sulfur Cleansing Lotion; Salicylic Acid and Sulfur Bar Soap; Salicylic Acid and Sulfur Cleansing Suspension; Salicylic Acid and Sulfur Topical Suspension.

Antiseborrheic—Salicylic Acid and Sulfur Cream Shampoo; Salicylic Acid and Sulfur Lotion Shampoo; Salicylic Acid and Sulfur Suspension Shampoo.

Indications

Accepted

Acne vulgaris (treatment); or

Oily skin (treatment)—Salicylic acid and sulfur combination (cleansing cream, lotion, cleansing lotion, bar soap, cleansing suspension, and topical suspension) is indicated for the treatment of acne and oily skin.

Dandruff (treatment); or

Dermatitis, seborrheic, of scalp (treatment)—Salicylic acid and sulfur shampoo is indicated for the temporary control of scaling and itching associated with dandruff and seborrheic dermatitis of the scalp.

Patient Consultation

In providing consultation, consider emphasizing the following selected information (» = major clinical significance):

Before using this medication

» Conditions affecting use, especially:

Sensitivity to salicylic acid or sulfur

Use in children—Young children may be at increased risk of toxicity because of increased absorption of salicylic acid through the skin

Proper use of this medication

» Importance of not using more medication than the amount recommended

Washing hands immediately after application to remove any medication that may be on them

» Avoiding contact with the eyes

Missed dose: Using as soon as possible; not using if almost time for next dose

Proper administration:

For cleanser dosage forms

After wetting skin—Applying medication with fingertips or a wet sponge; rubbing in gently to work up lather; rinsing thoroughly and patting dry

For lotion and topical suspension dosage form

Applying small amount to affected area; rubbing in gently

For shampoo dosage form

Wetting hair and scalp with lukewarm water

Applying enough to work up lather; rubbing into scalp

Continuing to rub lather into scalp for several minutes or allowing to remain on scalp for about 5 minutes, depending on product

Applying medication again; rinsing thoroughly

For bar soap dosage form

After wetting skin—Using to wash face and other affected areas; rinsing thoroughly; patting dry

» Proper storage

Precautions while using this medication

» Avoiding simultaneous use with other topical acne preparations or preparations containing peeling agents, alcohol-containing preparations, abrasive soaps or cleansers, cosmetics or soaps with drying effect, medicated cosmetics, or other topical skin medication, unless otherwise directed by physician

» Avoiding concurrent use with topical mercury-containing preparations

Caution if medications containing aspirin or other salicylates are used

Side/adverse effects

Signs of potential side effects, especially skin irritation not present before therapy

Topical Dosage Forms

SALICYLIC ACID AND SULFUR CLEANSING CREAM

Usual adult and adolescent dose: Antiacne agent (topical)—Topical, to the skin two or three times a day.

Auxiliary labeling: • For external use only.

SALICYLIC ACID AND SULFUR LOTION

Usual adult and adolescent dose: Antiacne agent (topical)—Topical, to the skin, one or two times a day.

Auxiliary labeling:
• Shake well.
• For external use only.

SALICYLIC ACID AND SULFUR CLEANSING LOTION

Usual adult and adolescent dose: Antiacne agent (topical)—Topical, to the skin, one to three times a day.

Auxiliary labeling:
• Shake well.
• For external use only.

SALICYLIC ACID AND SULFUR CREAM SHAMPOO

Usual adult and adolescent dose: Antiseborrheic—Topical, to the scalp, one or two times a week or as needed.

Auxiliary labeling: • For external use only.

SALICYLIC ACID AND SULFUR LOTION SHAMPOO

Usual adult and adolescent dose: Antiseborrheic—Topical, to the scalp, one or two times a week or as needed.

Auxiliary labeling:
• Shake well.
• For external use only.

SALICYLIC ACID AND SULFUR SUSPENSION SHAMPOO

Usual adult and adolescent dose: Antiseborrheic—Topical, to the scalp, one or two times a week or as needed.

Auxiliary labeling:
• Shake well.
• For external use only.

SALICYLIC ACID AND SULFUR BAR SOAP

Usual adult and adolescent dose: Antiacne agent (topical)—Topical, to the skin, two or three times a day.

Auxiliary labeling: • For external use only.

SALICYLIC ACID AND SULFUR CLEANSING SUSPENSION

Usual adult and adolescent dose: Antiacne agent (topical)—Topical, to the skin, one or two times a day.

Auxiliary labeling:
- Shake well.
- For external use only.

SALICYLIC ACID AND SULFUR TOPICAL SUSPENSION

Usual adult and adolescent dose: Antiacne agent (topical)—Topical, to the skin, one or two times a day.

Auxiliary labeling:
- Shake well.
- For external use only.

SALICYLIC ACID, SULFUR, AND COAL TAR   Topical

Category: Keratolytic (topical); antiseborrheic; antipsoriatic (topical).

Indications

Accepted
Dandruff (treatment); or

Dermatitis, seborrheic, of scalp (treatment)—Salicylic acid, sulfur, and coal tar cream shampoo and lotion shampoo are indicated as adjuncts in the treatment of dandruff and seborrheic dermatitis to relieve itching and scaling of the scalp.

Psoriasis, of scalp (treatment)—Salicylic acid, sulfur, and coal tar cream shampoo and lotion shampoo are indicated in the treatment of psoriasis to relieve itching and scaling of the scalp.

Patient Consultation

In providing consultation, consider emphasizing the following selected information (» = major clinical significance):

Before using this medication
» Conditions affecting use, especially:
   Sensitivity to salicylic acid, sulfur, or coal tar
   Use in children—Children may be at increased risk of toxicity because of increased absorption of salicylic acid through the skin

Proper use of this medication
» Importance of not using more medication than the amount recommended
» Avoiding contact with the eyes
   Washing hands immediately after application to remove any medication that may be on them
   Proper administration:
   Before using—Wetting hair and scalp with lukewarm water

Applying a generous amount to scalp; working up a rich lather
Rubbing lather into scalp for 5 minutes; rinsing
Applying medication again; rinsing thoroughly
Missed dose: Using as soon as possible; not using if almost time for next dose
» Proper storage

Precautions while using this medication
» Avoiding concurrent use with topical mercury-containing preparations
   Medication may temporarily discolor blond, bleached, or tinted hair

Side/adverse effects
Signs of potential side effects, especially skin irritation not present before therapy

Topical Dosage Forms

SALICYLIC ACID, SULFUR, AND COAL TAR CREAM SHAMPOO

Usual adult and adolescent dose: Topical, to the scalp, one or two times a week or as needed.

Auxiliary labeling: • For external use only.

SALICYLIC ACID, SULFUR, AND COAL TAR LOTION SHAMPOO

Usual adult and adolescent dose: Topical, to the scalp, one or two times a week or as needed.

Auxiliary labeling:
- Shake well.
- For external use only.

SELEGILINE   Systemic

Some commonly used *brand names* are:
   In the U.S.—*Eldepryl*
   In Canada—*Eldepryl; SD Deprenyl*
   Other—*Jumex; Jumexal; Juprenil; Movergan; Procythol*
Other commonly used names are deprenil and deprenyl.

ORAL
Selegiline Hydrochloride Tablets
   In the U.S.—*Eldepryl*
   In Canada—*Eldepryl; SD Deprenyl*
   Other—*Jumex; Jumexal; Juprenil; Movergan; Procythol*

Category: Antidyskinetic.

Indications

Note: Bracketed information in the *Indications* section refers to uses not included in U.S. product labeling.

Accepted
Parkinsonism (treatment adjunct)—Selegiline is indicated for use with levodopa or levodopa and carbidopa combination in the treatment of idiopathic Parkinson's disease (paralysis agitans).

[Some studies have suggested that the initial use of selegiline may delay the need for addition of levodopa to the treatment regimen; in addition, these studies have shown that selegiline alone or in combination with levodopa may slow the progression of Parkinson's disease, possibly by preventing selective destruction of dopaminergic neurons in the substantia nigra. One retrospective study showed selegiline to possibly prolong the lifespan of patients with idiopathic Parkinson's disease.]

[The addition of selegiline to levodopa in patients experiencing fluctuating responses ("wearing off" effect or "on-off" phenomenon) may be of moderate benefit. However, the initial response to selegiline may not be sustained, with the degree of improvement declining over 6 months to 4 years. Selegiline is ineffective in advanced disease with extreme fluctuations. Motor control fluctuations may be due to factors other than the central pharmacokinetics of dopamine; hence prolongation of dopamine effects may fail in some cases to improve this problem.]

Note: Preliminary studies have demonstrated that selegiline may be useful as an antidepressant, usually when given in doses greater than those used for its antidyskinetic effect. However, there are *insufficient data* to definitively establish effectiveness of selegiline and criteria for its use in mental depression.

Pharmacology

Mechanism of action/Effect: The action of selegiline is thought to be related to its irreversible inhibition of monoamine oxidase type B (MAO B), the major form of the enzyme in the human brain. MAO B, which is involved in the oxidative deamination of dopamine in the brain, is inhibited when selegiline binds covalently and stoichiometrically to the isoalloxazine flavin adenine dinucleotide (FAD) at its active center. Administration of 10 mg of selegiline a day produces almost complete inhibition of MAO B in the brain. Selegiline becomes a non-selective inhibitor of all monoamine oxidase (MAO) at higher doses, possibly at 20 to 40 mg a day. At these doses, tyramine-mediated hypertensive reactions from MAO A blockade ("cheese reactions") may occur.

Selegiline (or its metabolites) may also act through other mechanisms to increase dopaminergic activity, including interfering with dopamine re-uptake at the synapse.

Duration of action: Duration of clinical action depends on the regeneration time of MAO B.

Precautions to Consider

Geriatrics
No geriatrics-related problems have been documented in studies done to date that included elderly patients.

Dental
Selegiline may decrease or inhibit salivary flow, thus contributing to the development of caries, periodontal disease, oral candidiasis, and discomfort.

Drug interactions and/or related problems
The following drug interactions and/or related problems have been selected on the basis of their potential clinical significance (possible mechanism in parentheses where appropriate)—not necessarily inclusive (» = major clinical significance):

Note: Combinations containing any of the following medications, depending on the amount present, may also interact with this medication.

For all doses of selegiline
» Fluoxetine
   (mania, as well as a reaction resembling the serotonin syndrome, has been reported rarely following concurrent use of selegiline with fluoxetine. [The serotonin syndrome may occur

as the result of combining a serotonergic agent such as fluoxetine with an MAO inhibitor. The syndrome may be manifest by mental status changes (confusion, hypomania), restlessness, myoclonus, hyperreflexia, diaphoresis, shivering, tremor, diarrhea, incoordination, and/or fever. If recognized early, the syndrome usually resolves quickly upon withdrawal of the offending agents.] Based on experience with nonselective MAO inhibitors, concurrent use of selegiline with fluoxetine is not recommended because of the potential for confusion, agitation, restlessness, gastrointestinal symptoms, hyperpyretic episodes, severe convulsions, and hypertensive crises. At least 14 days should elapse between discontinuation of an MAO inhibitor and initiation of fluoxetine. However, because of the long half-lives of fluoxetine and its active metabolite, at least 5 weeks [approximately 5 half-lives] should elapse between discontinuation of fluoxetine and initiation of therapy with an MAO inhibitor)

Levodopa
(although selegiline is used in conjunction with levodopa, it may enhance levodopa-induced dyskinesias, nausea, orthostatic hypotension, confusion, and hallucinations; reduction of levodopa dosage may be necessary within 2 to 3 days after the initiation of selegiline therapy)

» Meperidine, and possibly other opioid (narcotic) analgesics
(at least one interaction of meperidine with selegiline has been reported; concurrent use of meperidine with non-selective monoamine oxidase inhibitors [MAOIs] may produce immediate excitation, sweating, rigidity, and severe hypertension; in some patients, hypotension, severe respiratory depression, coma, convulsions, hyperpyrexia, vascular collapse, and death may occur; avoidance of meperidine use within 2 to 3 weeks following MAO inhibition is recommended; other opioid analgesics such as morphine are not likely to cause such severe reactions and may be used cautiously in reduced dosage in patients receiving MAOIs; however, it is recommended that a small test dose [$^{1}/_{4}$ of the usual dose] or several small incremental test doses over a period of several hours should first be administered to permit observation of any adverse effects; caution is also recommended in the use of alfentanil, fentanyl, or sufentanil as an adjunct to anesthesia if the patient has received an MAOI within 14 days; because the risk of a significant interaction has been questioned, the use of a small test dose is advised to detect any possible interaction)

For doses of 20 mg or more of selegiline per day
» Tyramine- or other high pressor amine-containing foods and beverages, such as aged cheese; fava or broad bean pods; yeast/protein extracts; smoked or pickled meats, poultry, or fish; fermented sausage (bologna, pepperoni, salami, summer sausage) or other fermented meat; sauerkraut; any overripe fruit; beer; reduced-alcohol and alcohol-free beer and wine; red and white wines; sherry; and liqueurs
(concurrent use with MAOIs, including selegiline in doses of 20 mg a day or greater, may cause sudden and severe hypertensive reactions; reactions are usually limited to a few hours and are easily treated with rapidly acting hypotensive agents [such as labetalol, nifedipine, or, if necessary in severe cases refractory to other agents, phentolamine]; severity of reaction depends on amount of tyramine ingested, rate of gastric emptying, and length of interval between dose of MAOI and ingestion of tyramine; when MAOIs are discontinued, dietary restrictions must continue for at least 2 weeks; other tyramine- or high pressor amine-containing foods, such as yogurt, sour cream, cream cheese, cottage cheese, chocolate, and soy sauce, if eaten when fresh and in moderation, are considered unlikely to cause serious problems)

Contraindications/Medical problems

The contraindications/medical problems included have been selected on the basis of their potential clinical significance (reasons given in parentheses where appropriate)—not necessarily inclusive (» = major clinical significance).

Risk-benefit should be considered when the following medical problems exist:

Dementia, profound, or
Psychosis, severe, or
Tardive dyskinesia or
Tremor, excessive
    (condition may be exacerbated)
» Peptic ulcer disease, history of
    (activation of pre-existing ulcers may occur, probably due to stimulation of the H_2 receptors in the stomach or inhibition of MAO-mediated gastric histamine catabolism)

Sensitivity to selegiline

Side/Adverse Effects

Note: Selegiline enhances the dose-related side effects of levodopa, but few side effects are attributable to selegiline itself. When selegiline is used as an adjunct to levodopa or levodopa and carbidopa combination, adverse effects can usually be ameliorated by reducing the dose of levodopa or levodopa and carbidopa.

In addition, selegiline may cause elevation of liver enzymes.

The following side/adverse effects have been selected on the basis of their potential clinical significance (possible signs and symptoms in parentheses where appropriate)—not necessarily inclusive:

Those indicating need for medical attention

Incidence more frequent
    Dyskinesias (increase in unusual movements of body); *mood or other mental changes*

Incidence less frequent or rare
    Angina pectoris, new or increased (chest pain); *arrhythmias* (irregular heartbeat); *asthma* (wheezing, difficulty in breathing, or tightness in chest); *bradycardia, sinus* (slow heartbeat); *edema, peripheral* (swelling of feet or lower legs); *motor/coordination/extrapyramidal effects* (difficulty in speaking; loss of balance control; uncontrolled movements, especially of face, neck, and back; restlessness or desire to keep moving; or twisting movements of body); *gastrointestinal bleeding* (bloody or black, tarry stools; severe stomach pain; or vomiting of blood or material that looks like coffee grounds); *hallucinations; headache, severe; hypertension, severe; orthostatic hypotension* (dizziness or lightheadedness, especially when getting up from a lying or sitting position); *prostatic hypertrophy* (difficult or frequent urination); *tardive dyskinesia* (lip smacking or puckering, puffing of cheeks, rapid or wormlike movements of tongue, uncontrolled chewing movements, uncontrolled movements of arms and legs)

Symptoms of hypertensive crisis
    Chest pain, severe; enlarged pupils; fast or slow heartbeat; headache, severe; increased sensitivity of eyes to light; increased sweating, possibly with fever or cold, clammy skin; nausea or vomiting, severe; stiff or sore neck

Symptoms of MAOI overdose
    Agitation or irritability; chest pain; convulsions; cool, clammy skin; diaphoresis (increased sweating); *dizziness, severe, or fainting; fast or irregular pulse, continuing; high or low blood pressure; hyperpyrexia* (high fever); *opisthotonus* (severe spasm where the head and heels are bent backward and the body arched forward); *respiratory depression* (troubled breathing); *trismus* (difficulty opening the mouth; lockjaw)

Note: The above symptoms of *overdose* occur with the non-selective monoamine oxidase inhibitors. However, at high doses, selegiline loses its selectivity for MAO B, and the potential exists for these symptoms to occur with selegiline.

Symptoms of overdose may not be evident until about 12 hours following ingestion and may not reach maximum effect for 24 to 48 hours. Death has resulted.

Those indicating need for medical attention only if they continue or are bothersome

Incidence more frequent
    Abdominal or stomach pain; dizziness or feeling faint; dryness of mouth; insomnia (trouble in sleeping); *nausea or vomiting*

Incidence less frequent or rare
    Anxiety, nervousness, or restlessness; apraxia, increased (inability to move); *blepharospasm* (sudden closing of eyelids); *blurred or double vision; body ache or back or leg pain; bradykinesia, increased* (slowed movements); *chills; constipation or diarrhea; diaphoresis* (increased sweating); *drowsiness; headache; heartburn; hypertension or hypotension* (high or low blood pressure); *impaired memory*—more frequent with doses greater than 10 mg a day; *slow or difficult urination; frequent urge to urinate; irritability, temporary; loss of appetite or weight loss; muscle cramps or numbness of fingers or toes; palpitations or tachycardia* (pounding or fast heartbeat); *paresthesias, circumoral* (burning of lips or mouth) *or burning of throat; photosensitivity* (increased sensitivity of skin and eyes to sunlight); *skin rash; tinnitus* (ringing or buzzing in ears); *taste changes; unusual feeling of well-being; unusual tiredness or weakness*

With doses greater than 10 mg a day
    Bruxism (clenching, gnashing, or grinding teeth); *muscle twitches or myoclonic jerks* (sudden jerky movements of body)

Note: *Bruxism* and *myoclonic jerks* may be considered to be adverse effects only if not previously present and beginning shortly after the start of therapy with selegiline.

Patient Consultation

In providing consultation, consider emphasizing the following selected information (» = major clinical significance):

Before using this medication

» Conditions affecting use, especially:
    Sensitivity to selegiline
    Other medications, especially fluoxetine or meperidine and possibly other narcotic (opioid) analgesics
    Other medical problems, especially a history of peptic ulcer disease

Proper use of this medication

» Importance of not taking more medication than the amount prescribed; to do so may increase the risk of side effects
    Missed dose: Taking as soon as possible; not taking in the late afternoon or evening; not taking if almost time for next dose; not doubling doses.
» Proper storage

Precautions while using this medication

» If taking 20 mg or more of selegiline a day, avoiding tyramine-containing foods, alcoholic beverages, and large quantities of caffeine-containing beverages, over-the-counter cold and cough medicines, and other medications, unless prescribed
» Checking with hospital emergency room or physician if symptoms of hypertensive crisis develop
» Possibility of orthostatic hypotension; caution when getting up suddenly from a lying or sitting position
    Possible dryness of mouth; using sugarless candy or gum, ice, or saliva substitute for relief; checking with physician or dentist if dryness of mouth continues for more than 2 weeks

Side/adverse effects

Signs of potential side effects, especially dyskinesias, mood or mental changes, angina pectoris, arrhythmias, asthma, bradycardia, peripheral edema, extrapyramidal effects, hallucinations, severe headache, severe hypertension, gastrointestinal bleeding, orthostatic hypotension, prostatic hypertrophy, and tardive dyskinesia

General Dosing Information

Selegiline should not be used in the treatment of Parkinson's disease at doses exceeding 10 mg a day because of the risks associated with non-selective inhibition of monoamine oxidase (MAO). A tyramine-mediated hypertensive reaction has been reported when selegiline was administered at a dose of 20 mg a day. In addition, selegiline in doses greater than 10 mg a day has not demonstrated increased effectiveness in the treatment of Parkinson's disease.

When selegiline is used as an adjunct to levodopa or levodopa and carbidopa combination, adverse effects such as involuntary movements or hallucinations may result, and doses of levodopa may need to be reduced. If necessary, doses of levodopa should be reduced after 2 to 3 days by 10 to 30%, and possibly by as much as 50% with continued therapy.

Because selegiline may produce insomnia, it should not be administered in the late afternoon or evening.

Diet/Nutrition

Selegiline should be administered with breakfast and lunch to minimize possible nausea and insomnia.

When monoamine oxidase inhibitors, including selegiline at doses of 20 mg a day or greater, are used concurrently with foods and beverages containing tyramine or other high pressor amines, sudden and severe hypertensive reactions may result. These reactions are usually limited to a few hours and are easily treated with rapidly acting hypotensive agents (such as labetalol, nifedipine, or, if necessary in severe cases refractory to other agents, phentolamine). The severity of the reaction depends on the amount of tyramine ingested, the rate of gastric emptying, and the length of the interval between the dose of MAO inhibitor and ingestion of tyramine. When MAO inhibitors are discontinued, dietary restrictions must continue for at least 2 weeks. Foods and beverages containing tyramine or other high pressor amines include aged cheese; fava or broad bean pods; yeast/protein extracts; smoked or pickled meats, poultry, or fish; fermented sausage (bologna, pepperoni, salami, summer sausage) or other fermented meat; sauerkraut; any overripe fruit; beer; reduced-alcohol and alcohol-free beer and wine; red and white wines; sherry; and liqueurs. Other foods, such as yogurt, sour cream, cream cheese, cottage cheese, chocolate, and soy sauce, if eaten when fresh and in moderation, are considered unlikely to cause serious problems.

Oral Dosage Forms

SELEGILINE HYDROCHLORIDE TABLETS

Usual adult dose: Parkinsonism—Oral, 5 mg two times a day, at breakfast and lunch.

Note: In some cases, some clinicians recommend that the total daily dose be divided (2.5 mg four times a day) to decrease the side effects induced by concomitant administration of levodopa.

Usual geriatric dose: See *Usual adult dose.*

SELENIUM SULFIDE　Topical

Some commonly used *brand names* are:

In the U.S.—

Exsel Lotion Shampoo
Glo-Sel
Head & Shoulders Intensive Treatment Conditioning Formula Dandruff Lotion Shampoo
Head & Shoulders Intensive Treatment Regular Formula Dandruff Lotion Shampoo
Head & Shoulders Intensive Treatment 2 in 1 (Persistent Dandruff Shampoo plus Conditioner in One) Formula Dandruff Lotion Shampoo

Selsun
Selsun Blue Dry Formula
Selsun Blue Extra Conditioning Formula
Selsun Blue Extra Medicated Formula
Selsun Blue Oily Formula
Selsun Blue Regular Formula

In Canada—
Selsun
Selsun Blue

Selsun Blue Extra Conditioning Formula
Versel Lotion

mula Dandruff Lotion Shampoo; Head & Shoulders Intensive Treatment 2 in 1 (Persistent Dandruff Shampoo plus Conditioner in One) Formula Dandruff Lotion Shampoo; Selsun; Selsun Blue Dry Formula; Selsun Blue Extra Conditioning Formula; Selsun Blue Extra Medicated Formula; Selsun Blue Oily Formula; Selsun Blue Regular Formula; GENERIC

In Canada—*Selsun; Selsun Blue; Selsun Blue Extra Conditioning Formula; Versel Lotion*

Category: Antiseborrheic.

Indications

Accepted

Dandruff (treatment); or

Dermatitis, seborrheic, of scalp (treatment)—Indicated for the treatment of dandruff or seborrheic dermatitis of the scalp.

Tinea versicolor (treatment)—Indicated for the treatment of tinea versicolor.

Pharmacology

Mechanism of action/Effect: Selenium sulfide may act by an antimitotic action, resulting in a reduction in the turnover of epidermal cells. It also has local irritant, antibacterial, and mild antifungal activity, which may contribute to its effectiveness.

TOPICAL

Selenium Sulfide Lotion USP

In the U.S.—*Exsel Lotion Shampoo; Glo-Sel; Head & Shoulders Intensive Treatment Conditioning Formula Dandruff Lotion Shampoo; Head & Shoulders Intensive Treatment Regular For-*

Precautions to Consider

Geriatrics

Appropriate studies on the relationship of age to the effects of selenium sulfide have not been performed in the geriatric population. However, geriatrics-specific problems that would limit the usefulness of this medication in the elderly are not expected.

Contraindications/Medical problems

The contraindications/medical problems included have been selected on the basis of their potential clinical significance (reasons given in parentheses where appropriate)—not necessarily inclusive (» = major clinical significance).

Risk-benefit should be considered when the following medical problems exist:

Inflammation or exudation of skin, acute (an increase in absorption may occur)

Sensitivity to selenium sulfide

Side/Adverse Effects

The following side/adverse effects have been selected on the basis of their potential clinical significance (possible signs and symptoms in parentheses where appropriate)—not necessarily inclusive:

Those indicating need for medical attention
Skin irritation

Those indicating need for medical attention only if they continue or are bothersome
Incidence more frequent
Unusual dryness or oiliness of hair or scalp

Incidence less frequent
Increase in normal hair loss

Patient Consultation

In providing consultation, consider emphasizing the following selected information (» = major clinical significance):

Before using this medication
» Conditions affecting use, especially:
   Sensitivity to selenium sulfide
   Pregnancy—Not using medication for the treatment of tinea versicolor

Proper use of this medication
» Importance of not using more of the 2.5% strength medication than the amount recommended
   For best results, using the 1% strength medication at least 2 times a week or as directed by your doctor
   Proper administration of the medication for dandruff or seborrheic dermatitis:
   Before using—Wetting hair and scalp with lukewarm water
   Applying enough to scalp (approximately 1 or 2 teaspoonsful) to work up lather
   Allowing lather to remain on scalp for 2 to 3 minutes, then rinsing
   Applying medication again and rinsing thoroughly
   If using on light or blond, gray, or chemically treated (bleached, tinted, permanent-waved) hair, rinsing hair well for at least 5 minutes after using medication to lessen chance of hair discoloration

After treatment, washing your hands thoroughly
Proper administration of the medication for tinea versicolor:
   Applying medication to affected areas of body, except face and genitals
   Working up lather using a small amount of water
   Allowing medication to remain on skin for 10 minutes
   Rinsing body well to remove all medication
» Not using medication if blistered, raw, or oozing areas are present on scalp or body
» Avoiding contact with the eyes; flushing thoroughly with water if medication accidentally gets in eyes
» Proper dosage
   Missed dose: Using as soon as possible; not using if almost time for next dose
» Proper storage

Precautions while using this medication
Checking with physician if condition does not get better after regular use, or if it gets worse

Side/adverse effects
Signs of potential side effects, especially skin irritation

General Dosing Information

Selenium sulfide should not be used when acute inflammation or exudate is present, because an increase in absorption may occur.

Discoloration of the hair may occur following use of selenium sulfide, especially if used on hair that is light, blond, or gray or on hair that has been chemically treated (i.e., bleached, tinted, or permanent-waved). The discoloration may be minimized or avoided by thoroughly rinsing the hair for at least 5 minutes after treatment.

Topical Dosage Forms

SELENIUM SULFIDE LOTION USP

Usual adult and adolescent dose:
Dandruff or seborrheic dermatitis—Topical, to the scalp as a 1% lotion, two times a week; or topical, to the scalp as a 2.5% lotion, two times a week for two weeks and then at less frequent intervals of once a week or once every two or more weeks.

Note: The medication should not be used more frequently than required to maintain control.

Tinea versicolor—Topical, to the body as a 2.5% lotion, once a day for seven days.

Note: The lotion should be applied to all affected areas, except for the face and genitals, and left on for 10 minutes. Then the medication should be thoroughly rinsed off.

Auxiliary labeling:
• Shake well.
• For external use only.

SKELETAL MUSCLE RELAXANTS Systemic

Some commonly used *brand names* are:

In the U.S.—

Banflex [Orphenadrine]	*O-Flex* [Orphenadrine]
Blanex [Orphenadrine]	*Orflagen* [Orphenadrine]
Carbacot [Methocarbamol]	*Orfro* [Orphenadrine]
Delaxin [Methocarbamol]	*Orphenate* [Orphenadrine]
Disipal [Orphenadrine]	*Paraflex* [Chlorzoxazone]
Flexagin [Orphenadrine]	*Parafon Forte DSC*
Flexain [Orphenadrine]	[Chlorzoxazone]
Flexoject [Orphenadrine]	*Rela* [Carisoprodol]
Flexon [Orphenadrine]	*Robamol* [Methocarbamol]
K-Flex [Orphenadrine]	*Robaxin* [Methocarbamol]
Maolate [Chlorphenesin]	*Robomol* [Methocarbamol]
Marbaxin [Methocarbamol]	*Skelaxin* [Metaxalone]
Marflex [Orphenadrine]	*Sodol* [Carisoprodol]
Myolin [Orphenadrine]	*Soma* [Carisoprodol]
Myotrol [Orphenadrine]	*Soprodol* [Carisoprodol]
Neocyten [Orphenadrine]	*Soridol* [Carisoprodol]
Noradex [Orphenadrine]	*Tega-Flex* [Orphenadrine]
Norflex [Orphenadrine]	

In Canada—

Disipal [Orphenadrine]	*Robaxin* [Methocarbamol]
Norflex [Orphenadrine]	*Soma* [Carisoprodol]

BACLOFEN—See Baclofen (Systemic).
CARISOPRODOL
Oral
  Carisoprodol Tablets USP
    In the U.S—*Rela; Sodol; Soma; Soprodol; Soridol;* GENERIC
    In Canada—*Soma*
CHLORPHENESIN
Oral
  Chlorphenesin Carbamate Tablets
    In the U.S.—*Maolate*
CHLORZOXAZONE
Oral
  Chlorzoxazone Tablets USP
    In the U.S.—*Paraflex; Parafon Forte DSC;* GENERIC
CYCLOBENZAPRINE—See Cyclobenzaprine (Systemic).
DANTROLENE—See Dantrolene (Systemic).
DIAZEPAM—See Benzodiazepines (Systemic).
METAXALONE
Oral
  Metaxalone Tablets
    In the U.S.—*Skelaxin*
METHOCARBAMOL
Oral
  Methocarbamol Tablets USP
    In the U.S.—*Delaxin; Marbaxin; Robamol; Robaxin; Robomol;* GENERIC
    In Canada—*Robaxin*
Parenteral
  Methocarbamol Injection USP
    In the U.S.—*Carbacot; Robaxin;* GENERIC
    In Canada—*Robaxin*
ORPHENADRINE
Oral
  Orphenadrine Citrate Extended-release Tablets
    In the U.S.—*Marflex; Noradex; Norflex; Orflagen;* GENERIC
    In Canada—*Norflex*
  Orphenadrine Hydrochloride Tablets
    In the U.S. and Canada—*Disipal*

Parenteral
  Orphenadrine Citrate Injection USP
    In the U.S.—*Banflex; Blanex; Flexagin; Flexain; Flexoject; Flexon; K-Flex; Marflex; Myolin; Myotrol; Neocyten; Norflex; O-Flex; Orfro; Orphenate; Tega-Flex;* GENERIC
    In Canada—*Norflex*

Category

Skeletal muscle relaxant—Carisoprodol; Chlorphenesin; Chlorzoxazone; Metaxalone; Methocarbamol; Orphenadrine Citrate.
Parkinsonism therapy adjunct—Orphenadrine Hydrochloride.

Indications

Accepted

Spasm, skeletal muscle (treatment)—Skeletal muscle relaxants are indicated as adjuncts to other measures, such as rest and physical therapy, for the relief of muscle spasm associated with acute, painful musculoskeletal conditions.

Parkinsonism (treatment adjunct)—Orphenadrine hydrochloride is indicated (but is rarely used) as an adjunct to physical therapy and other medications in the treatment of postencephalic, arteriosclerotic, or idiopathic parkinsonism. It produces symptomatic relief of tremor. The medication may be used concurrently with reduced dosages of more potent medications in treating patients who cannot tolerate effective doses of the other medications.

Unaccepted

Methocarbamol is also FDA-approved for control of the neuromuscular manifestations of tetanus. However, it has largely been replaced in the treatment of tetanus by diazepam, or, in severe cases, a neuromuscular blocking agent such as pancuronium. Such therapy is used as an adjunct to other measures, such as debridement, tetanus antitoxin, penicillin, tracheotomy, fluid and electrolyte replacement, and supportive treatment.

Pharmacology

See also *Table 1*, page 983.

Mechanism of action/Effect:

Skeletal muscle relaxant—Precise mechanism of action has not been determined. These agents act in the central nervous system (CNS) rather than directly on skeletal muscle. Several of these medications have been shown to preferentially depress polysynaptic reflexes. The muscle relaxant effects of most of these agents may be related to their CNS depressant (sedative) effects. Carisoprodol blocks interneuronal activity in the descending reticular formation and in the spinal cord. Chlorzoxazone acts primarily at the spinal cord level and at subcortical areas of the brain. Orphenadrine has analgesic activity, which may contribute to its skeletal muscle relaxant properties.

Parkinsonism therapy adjunct—Orphenadrine has mild anticholinergic actions, which produce its beneficial effect in parkinsonism.

Precautions to Consider

Cross-sensitivity and/or related problems

Patients sensitive to other carbamate derivatives (for example, carbromal, meprobamate, mebutamate, or tybamate) may be sensitive to carisoprodol also.

Geriatrics

No published geriatrics-specific information is available. However, elderly males are more likely to have age-related prostatic hypertrophy and may therefore be adversely affected by orphenadrine's anticholinergic activity. Also, elderly patients are more likely to have age-related renal function impairment, which may require that parenteral methocarbamol not be used at all and that other skeletal muscle relaxants be used with caution.

Dental

The peripheral anticholinergic effects of orphenadrine may decrease or inhibit salivary flow, thus contributing to the development of caries, periodontal disease, oral candidiasis, and discomfort.

Drug interactions and/or related problems

The following drug interactions and/or related problems have been selected on the basis of their potential clinical significance (possible mechanism in parentheses where appropriate)—not necessarily inclusive (» = major clinical significance):

Note: Combinations containing any of the following medications, depending on the amount present, may also interact with this medication.

» CNS depression-producing medications, other
(concurrent use with a skeletal muscle relaxant may result in additive CNS depressant effects; caution is recommended and dosage of one or both agents should be reduced)

For orphenadrine only (in addition to the interaction listed above)
Anticholinergics or other medications with anticholinergic action
(anticholinergic effects may be intensified when these medications are used concurrently with orphenadrine because of orphenadrine's secondary anticholinergic activity)

Contraindications/Medical problems

The contraindications/medical problems included have been selected on the basis of their potential clinical significance (reasons given in parentheses where appropriate)—not necessarily inclusive (» = major clinical significance).

See *Table 2*, page 984.

Side/Adverse Effects

See also *Table 3*, page 985.

Note: Rarely, an idiosyncratic reaction to carisoprodol may occur within minutes or hours following the first dose of the medication. Reported symptoms include agitation, ataxia, confusion, disorientation, euphoria, extreme weakness, speech disturbances, temporary loss of vision or other vision disturbances, and transient quadriplegia. Symptoms usually subside within several hours, but in some cases, supportive and symptomatic therapy, including hospitalization, may be necessary.

Psychological dependence and abuse have occurred very rarely with carisoprodol. Signs of abstinence have not been reported with clinical usage; however, in one study abrupt withdrawal of 100 mg per kg of body weight (mg/kg) per day of carisoprodol (5 times the recommended daily dose) produced withdrawal symptoms including abdominal cramps, insomnia, chills, headache, and nausea.

Patient Consultation

See *Table 4*, page 987.

CARISOPRODOL

Summary of Differences

Pharmacology:
Physicochemical characteristics—Molecular weight: 260.33.
Biotransformation—Hepatic; one metabolite is meprobamate.
Half-life—8 hours.
Onset of action—0.5 hours.
Time to peak concentration—4 hours (350-mg single dose).
Peak serum concentration—4–7 mcg per mL.
Duration of action—4–6 hours.
Elimination—Renal, <1% as unchanged carisoprodol. Carisoprodol is dialyzable.
Precautions:
Cross-sensitivity and/or related problems—May occur with other carbamate derivatives.
Breast-feeding—Excreted in breast milk in significant quantities; may cause sedation and gastrointestinal upset in the nursing infant.
Contraindications/medical problems—
Should not be used in patients with known or suspected acute intermittent porphyria.
Caution also recommended in patients with a history of drug abuse or dependence.
Side/adverse effects:
Idiosyncratic reactions may occur shortly after first dose.
Psychological dependence and abuse reported very rarely.
Also may cause orthostatic hypotension, fast heartbeat, mental depression, clumsiness or unsteadiness, fever (allergic), stinging or burning of eyes, angioedema, bronchospastic allergic reaction, blurred vision, and flushing.

Oral Dosage Forms

CARISOPRODOL TABLETS USP

Usual adult and adolescent dose: Oral, 350 mg four times a day.

Auxiliary labeling:
• May cause drowsiness.
• Avoid alcoholic beverages.

CHLORPHENESIN

Summary of Differences

Pharmacology:
Physicochemical characteristics—Molecular weight: 245.66.
Absorption—Rapid; complete.
Biotransformation—Hepatic; at least partially metabolized.
Half-life—2.5–5 hours.
Time to peak concentration—1–3 hours.
Peak serum concentration—3.8–17 mcg per mL (800-mg single dose).
Elimination—Renal; 85% of a dose excreted within 24 hours as the glucuronide metabolite.
Side/adverse effects:
Gastrointestinal bleeding reported, but causal relationship not established.

Also may cause fever (allergic), agranulocytosis, leukopenia, or thrombocytopenia.

Additional Dosing Information

The safety of administering chlorphenesin for longer than 8 weeks has not been established.

Oral Dosage Forms

CHLORPHENESIN CARBAMATE TABLETS

Usual adult and adolescent dose: Oral, 800 mg three times a day initially; may be decreased to 400 mg four times a day or less, as required to maintain the desired response.

Auxiliary labeling:
- May cause drowsiness.
- Avoid alcoholic beverages.

CHLORZOXAZONE

Summary of Differences

Pharmacology:
　　Physicochemical characteristics—Molecular weight: 169.57.
　　Absorption—Rapid; complete.
　　Biotransformation—Hepatic.
　　Half-life—1–2 hours.
　　Onset of action—Within 1 hour.
　　Time to peak concentration—1–2 hours.
　　Peak serum concentration—10–30 mcg per mL (750-mg single dose).
　　Duration of action—3–4 hours.
　　Elimination—Renal; <1% as unchanged chlorzoxazone.
Precautions: Contraindications/medical problems—Also should be used with caution in patients with allergies (or history of).
Side/adverse effects:
　　Also may cause agranulocytosis, gastrointesinal bleeding, angioedema, anemia, diarrhea, heartburn, and constipation.
　　Hepatotoxicity reported, but causal association not established.

Additional Dosing Information

Discontinuation of chlorzoxazone therapy is recommended if symptoms of hepatotoxicity occur.

Oral Dosage Forms

CHLORZOXAZONE TABLETS USP

Usual adult and adolescent dose: Oral, 250 to 750 mg three or four times a day; usually 500 mg three or four times a day initially and increased or decreased as determined by patient response.

Auxiliary labeling:
- May cause drowsiness.
- Avoid alcoholic beverages.

METAXALONE

Summary of Differences

Pharmacology:
　　Physicochemical characteristics—Molecular weight: 221.26.
　　Biotransformation—Hepatic.
　　Half-life—2–3 hours.
　　Onset of action—1 hour.
　　Time to peak concentration—2 hours (800-mg single dose).
　　Peak serum concentration—295 mcg per mL (800-mg single dose).
　　Elimination—Renal.
Precautions:
　　Laboratory value alterations—
　　　　May interfere with copper sulfate urine sugar test results.
　　　　May cause liver function test abnormalities.
　　Contraindications/medical problems—Also should not be used in patients with hemolytic anemia or a history of hemolytic anemia, especially if drug-induced.
　　Patient monitoring—Liver function tests recommended during prolonged therapy.
Side/adverse effects: Also may cause hemolytic anemia and hepatotoxicity.

Additional Dosing Information

Discontinuation of metaxalone therapy is recommended if signs of hepatotoxicity occur.

Oral Dosage Forms

METAXALONE TABLETS

Usual adult and adolescent dose: Oral, 800 mg three or four times a day.

Auxiliary labeling:
- May cause drowsiness.
- Avoid alcoholic beverages.

METHOCARBAMOL

Summary of Differences

Pharmacology:
　　Physicochemical characteristics—Molecular weight: 241.24.
　　Absorption—Rapid.
　　Biotransformation—Probably hepatic.
　　Half-life (elimination)—0.9–2.2 hours.
　　Onset of action—
　　　　Oral: Within 0.5 hour.
　　　　Intravenous: Immediate.
　　Time to peak concentration—
　　　　Oral: 2 hours (2-gram single dose).
　　　　Intravenous: Almost immediate.
　　Peak serum concentration—
　　　　Oral: 16 mcg per mL (2-gram single dose).
　　　　Intravenous: 19 mcg per mL (1-gram single dose).
　　Elimination—Renal and fecal.

Precautions:
Breast-feeding—Excreted in breast milk in small quantities.
Laboratory value alterations—
Urinary 5-hydroxyindoleacetic acid (5-HIAA) may be falsely increased (with nitrosonaphthol reagent).
Urinary vanillylmandelic acid (VMA) may be falsely increased (with the Gitlow screening method).
Contraindications/medical problems—
Parenteral dosage form should not be used in patients with renal function impairment or disease because the polyethylene glycol 300 vehicle is nephrotoxic.
Parenteral dosage form also should be used with caution in patients with epilepsy.
Patient monitoring—Renal function determinations recommended if parenteral therapy lasts 3 days or more.
Side/adverse effects:
Parenteral dosage form also reported to cause convulsions, fainting, slow heartbeat, muscle weakness, nystagmus, and facial flushing, especially when given too rapidly.
Parenteral dosage form may also cause pain or peeling of skin at injection site and thrombophlebitis.
Also may cause fever (allergic), conjunctivitis and nasal congestion, and leukopenia.
May be more likely than other muscle relaxants to cause blurred or double vision.

Additional Dosing Information

For parenteral dosage forms only

Do not administer the injections subcutaneously.

The polyethylene glycol 300 vehicle in the parenteral dosage form may be nephrotoxic.

The medication may be administered intravenously undiluted at a rate not to exceed 3 mL (300 mg) per minute. It may also be given as an intravenous infusion in sodium chloride injection or 5% dextrose injection.

The patient should lie down during and for at least 10 to 15 minutes following intravenous administration.

Extravasation should be avoided, since the injection is hypertonic and may cause thrombophlebitis.

For special directions for use in tetanus, see manufacturer's labeling.

Not more than 5 mL (500 mg) should be given intramuscularly into each gluteal region at one time. The injections may be repeated at 8-hour intervals, if necessary.

Oral Dosage Forms

METHOCARBAMOL TABLETS USP

Usual adult and adolescent dose: Skeletal muscle relaxant—
Initial: Oral, 1.5 grams four times a day for the first 48 to 72 hours of therapy. For severe conditions, 8 grams a day may be administered initially.
Maintenance: Oral, 750 mg every four hours; 1 gram four times a day; or 1.5 grams three times a day.
Note: If used as adjunctive therapy in the treatment of tetanus—Via nasogastric tube, up to 24 grams a day depending on patient response.

Auxiliary labeling:
- May cause drowsiness.
- Avoid alcoholic beverages.

Parenteral Dosage Forms

METHOCARBAMOL INJECTION USP

Usual adult and adolescent dose: Skeletal muscle relaxant—Intramuscular or intravenous, 1 to 3 grams a day for three days. Following a drug-free interval of 48 hours, the course may be repeated if necessary.

Note: If used as adjunctive therapy in the treatment of tetanus—Intravenous, 1 or 2 grams by direct intravenous injection. An additional 1 or 2 grams may be administered by intravenous infusion, so that a total initial dose of up to 3 grams is administered. Repeat this regimen every six hours until therapy via a nasogastric tube can be instituted.

Usual adult prescribing limits: Total adult dosage should not exceed 3 grams per day for more than three consecutive days except in the treatment of tetanus.

ORPHENADRINE

Summary of Differences

Category: Hydrochloride salt indicated to relieve tremor in parkinsonism.
Pharmacology:
Physicochemical characteristics—Molecular weight:
Orphenadrine citrate—461.51.
Orphenadrine hydrochloride—305.85.
Mechanism of action (parkinsonism therapy adjunct)—Has anticholinergic activity.
Protein binding—Low.
Biotransformation—Hepatic.
Half-life—14 hours (parent compound; half-life of metabolites may range from 2 to 25 hours).
Onset of action—
Orphenadrine citrate:
Oral (extended-release tablets)—Within 1 hour.
Intramuscular—5 minutes.
Intravenous—Immediate.
Orphenadrine hydrochloride: Oral—Within 1 hour.
Time to peak concentration—
Orphenadrine citrate:
Oral (extended-release tablets)—6–8 hours (100-mg single dose).
Intramuscular—0.5 hour (60-mg single dose).
Intravenous—Immediate.
Orphenadrine hydrochloride: Oral—3 hours (50-mg single dose).
Peak serum concentration—
Orphenadrine citrate: Oral (extended-release tablets)—60-120 nanograms per mL (100-mg single dose).
Orphenadrine hydrochloride: Oral—110–210 nanograms per mL (100-mg single dose).
Elimination: Renal and fecal.
Precautions:
Dental—May cause dryness of mouth.
Contraindications/medical problems—
Also should not be used in patients with medical conditions in which anticholinergic actions are detrimental.
Also should be used with caution in patients with cardiac disease or arrhythmias, especially tachycardia.
Patient monitoring—Blood count and hepatic and renal function tests recommended during prolonged therapy.

Side/adverse effects:
   Also may cause side effects typical of anticholinergics and aplastic anemia.
   Also may cause hallucinations, syncope, confusion (especially in the elderly), and blurred or double vision; anticholinergic as well as CNS actions may contribute to these effects.

Additional Dosing Information

The safety of continuous long-term administration of orphenadrine has not been established.

Oral Dosage Forms

ORPHENADRINE CITRATE EXTENDED-RELEASE TABLETS

Usual adult and adolescent dose: Oral, 100 mg twice a day.

Auxiliary labeling:
• May cause drowsiness.
• Avoid alcoholic beverages.

ORPHENADRINE HYDROCHLORIDE TABLETS

Usual adult and adolescent dose: Oral, 50 mg three times a day.

Note: Smaller doses may suffice if other antiparkinson medications are being administered concurrently.

Usual adult prescribing limits: Up to 250 mg a day.

Auxiliary labeling:
• May cause drowsiness.
• Avoid alcoholic beverages.

Parenteral Dosage Forms

ORPHENADRINE CITRATE INJECTION USP

Usual adult and adolescent dose: Intramuscular or intravenous, 60 mg every twelve hours as needed.

Table 1. Pharmacology

Drug	Onset of Action	Duration of Action (hr)
Carisoprodol	0.5 hr	4–6
Chlorphenesin		
Chlorzoxazone	Within 1hr	3–4
Metaxalone	1 hr	

Methocarbamol
   Oral
   IV (300 mg/min)
	Within 0.5 hr
	Immediate	

Orphenadrine citrate*
   Oral (extended-release tablets)
   IM
   IV
	Within 1 hr
	5 min
	Immediate
		12

Orphenadrine hydrochloride†	Within 1 hr	8

*Relief of muscle spasm.
†In parkinsonism.

Table 2. Contraindications/Medical Problems

The contraindications/medical problems included have been selected on the basis of their potential clinical significance (reasons given in parentheses where appropriate)—not necessarily inclusive (» = major clinical significance).	Legend: **I** = Carisoprodol **II** = Chlorphenesin **III** = Chlorzoxazone			**IV** = Metaxalone **V** = Methocarbamol **VI** = Orphenadrine		
	I	**II**	**III**	**IV**	**V**	**VI**
Except under special circumstances, these medications should not be used when the following medical problems exist:						
» Achalasia or						✔
» Bladder neck obstruction or						✔
» Glaucoma, or predisposition to, or						✔
» Myasthenia gravis or						✔
» Peptic ulcer, stenosing, or						✔
» Prostatic hypertrophy or						✔
» Pyloric or duodenal obstruction (anticholinergic actions detrimental in these conditions)						✔
» Hemolytic anemia, or history of, especially if drug-induced (may be induced by metaxalone)				✔		
» Porphyria, acute intermittent, known or suspected	✔					
» Renal function impairment or disease (for parenteral dosage form only—polyethylene glycol 300 vehicle is nephrotoxic and may cause increased urea retention and acidosis in these patients)					✔	
Risk-benefit should be considered when the following medical problems exist: Allergic reaction to the medication considered for use, history of	✔	✔	✔	✔	✔	✔
Allergies or history of			✔			
Cardiac disease or arrhythmias or Tachycardia (orphenadrine may cause tachycardia)						✔ ✔
CNS depression (may be exacerbated)	✔	✔	✔	✔	✔	✔
Drug abuse or dependence, history of (psychological dependence and abuse reported rarely)	✔					
Epilepsy (for parenteral dosage form only—may increase risk of seizures)					✔	
Hepatic function impairment (metabolized in liver)	✔	✔			✔	✔
» Hepatic function impairment or disease (metabolized in liver; also, potentially hepatotoxic)			✔	✔		
Renal function impairment (excreted via kidneys)	✔	✔	✔	✔	✔	✔
» Renal function impairment, severe (excreted via kidneys)				✔		

Table 3. Side/Adverse Effects*

The following side/adverse effects have been selected on the basis of their potential clinical significance (possible signs and symptoms in parentheses where appropriate)—not necessarily inclusive:	Legend: **I** = Carisoprodol **II** = Chlorphenesin **III** = Chlorzoxazone			**IV** = Metaxalone **V** = Methocarbamol **VI** = Orphenadrine		
	I	**II**	**III**	**IV**	**V**	**VI**
Medical attention needed *Anticholinergic effects, specifically:* **Decreased urination**	—	—	—	—	—	L
Increased intraocular pressure (eye pain)	—	—	—	—	—	L
Cardiovascular effects, specifically: **Fast heartbeat**—with orphenadrine, anticholinergic activity may contribute to this effect	L	U	U	U	U	L
Pounding heartbeat	U	U	U	U	U	L
Slow heartbeat—with parenteral dosage form only	—	—	—	—	L‡	U
Thrombophlebitis (local pain, tenderness, heat, redness, swelling at site of affected vein)—with parenteral administration only	—	—	—	—	R	U
Central nervous system effects, specifically: **Convulsions**	U	U	U	U	R‡	U
Fainting—with carisoprodol, may also be caused by orthostatic hypotension	L	U	U	U	R‡	L
Hallucinations—orphenadrine's anticholinergic activity may contribute to this effect	U	U	U	U	U	R
Mental depression	L	U	U	U	U	U
Gastrointestinal bleeding (bloody or black, tarry stools; vomiting of blood or material that looks like coffee grounds)	U	R†	R	U	U	U
Hematologic effects, specifically: **Agranulocytosis** (fever with or without chills; sores, ulcers, or white spots on lips or in mouth; sore throat)	U	R	R	U	U	U
Anemia (unusual tiredness or weakness)	U	U	R	U	U	U
Anemia, aplastic [pancytopenia] (shortness of breath, troubled breathing, tightness in chest, and/or wheezing; sores, ulcers, or white spots on lips or in mouth; swollen and/or painful glands; unusual bleeding or bruising; unusual tiredness or weakness)	R†	U	U	U	U	R
Anemia, hemolytic (troubled breathing, exertional; unusual tiredness or weakness)	U	U	U	R	U	U
Leukopenia (usually asymptomatic; rarely, fever or chills, cough or hoarseness, lower back or side pain, painful or difficult urination)	R†	R	U	R	R	U
Thrombocytopenia (usually asymptomatic; rarely, unusual bleeding or bruising; black, tarry stools; blood in urine or stools; pinpoint red spots on skin)	U	R	U	U	U	U
Hepatotoxicity (yellow eyes or skin)	U	U	R†	R	U	U
Hypersensitivity reactions, specifically: **Anaphylactic or anaphylactoid reaction** (changes in facial skin color; skin rash, hives, and/or itching; fast or irregular breathing; puffiness or swelling of the eyelids or around the eyes; shortness of breath, troubled breathing, tightness in chest, and/or wheezing)—with carisoprodol, anaphylactic shock with sudden, severe decrease in blood pressure and collapse has also occurred	R	R	R	R	U	U
Angioedema (hive-like swellings, large, on face, eyelids, mouth, lips, and/or tongue)	L	U	R	U	U	U
Bronchospastic allergic reaction (shortness of breath, troubled breathing, tightness in chest, and/or wheezing)	L	U	U	U	U	U

*Differences in frequency of occurrence may reflect either lack of clinical-use data or actual pharmacologic distinctions among agents (although their pharmacologic similarity suggests that side effects occurring with one may occur with the others, except for those caused by anticholinergic activity, which is specific for orphenadrine). M = more frequent; L = less frequent; R = rare; U = unknown.

†A causal association has not been established.

‡Usually reported with too-rapid intravenous administration.

Table 3. Side/Adverse Effects* *(continued)*

	Legend: **I** = Carisoprodol **II** = Chlorphenesin **III** = Chlorzoxazone			**IV** = Metaxalone **V** = Methocarbamol **VI** = Orphenadrine		
	I	**II**	**III**	**IV**	**V**	**VI**
Conjunctivitis and nasal congestion (stuffy nose and red or bloodshot eyes)	U	U	U	U	L	U
Dermatitis, allergic (skin rash, hives, itching, and/or redness)—with carisoprodol, fixed drug eruptions with cross-sensitivity to meprobamate have also been reported; with chlorzoxazone, petechial rashes and ecchymoses have also been reported	L	R	R	R	L	U
Eosinophilia	R	U	U	U	U	U
Erythema multiforme (fever with or without chills; muscle cramps or pain; skin rash; sores, ulcers, or white spots on lips or in mouth)	R	U	U	U	U	U
Fever, allergic	L	R	U	U	L	U
Stinging or burning of eyes	L	U	U	U	U	U
Medical attention needed only if continuing or bothersome *Anticholinergic effects* (dryness of mouth [more frequent], confusion, difficult urination, constipation, unusually large pupils, blurred or double vision, weakness)	—	—	—	—	—	L
Central nervous system effects, specifically: *Blurred or double vision or any change in vision*—with orphenadrine, anticholinergic activity may also contribute to this effect	R	U	U	U	M	L
Clumsiness or unsteadiness	R	U	U	U	U	U
Confusion—with orphenadrine, anticholinergic activity may also contribute to this effect, especially in elderly patients	U	L	U	U	U	L
Dizziness or lightheadedness—with carisoprodol, orthostatic hypotension may also contribute to this effect	L	L	M	M	M	L
Drowsiness	M	L	M	M	M	L
Headache	L	R	L	M	L	L
Muscle weakness	U	R	U	U	L‡	R
Nystagmus (uncontrolled movements of eyes)	U	U	U	U	L‡	U
Stimulation, paradoxical (excitement, nervousness, restlessness, irritability, trouble in sleeping)	L	R	L	M	U	L
Trembling	L	U	U	U	U	L
Flushing or redness of face	L	U	U	U	L‡	U
Gastrointestinal irritation, specifically: *Abdominal or stomach cramps or pain*	L	R	L	M	U	L
Constipation—with orphenadrine, anticholinergic activity may contribute to this effect	U	U	L	U	U	L
Diarrhea	U	U	L	U	U	U
Heartburn	U	U	L	U	U	U
Hiccups	L	U	U	U	U	U
Nausea or vomiting	L	R	L	M	L	L
Pain or peeling at place of injection	—	—	—	—	L‡	U

*Differences in frequency of occurrence may reflect either lack of clinical-use data or actual pharmacologic distinctions among agents (although their pharmacologic similarity suggests that side effects occurring with one may occur with the others, except for those caused by anticholinergic activity, which is specific for orphenadrine). M = more frequent; L = less frequent; R = rare; U = unknown.

†A causal association has not been established.

‡Usually reported with too-rapid intravenous administration.

Table 4. Patient Consultation

In providing consultation, consider emphasizing the following selected information (» = major clinical significance):	Legend: **I** = Carisoprodol **II** = Chlorphenesin **III** = Chlorzoxazone			**IV** = Metaxalone **V** = Methocarbamol **VI** = Orphenadrine		
	I	**II**	**III**	**IV**	**V**	**VI**
Before using this medication						
» Conditions affecting use, especially:						
Sensitivity to the muscle relaxant considered for use, history of, and, for carisoprodol, sensitivity to other carbamate derivatives	✔	✔	✔	✔	✔	✔
Breast-feeding—Carisoprodol excreted in breast milk and may cause sedation and gastrointestinal upset in the infant; problems in nursing infants have not been reported with other skeletal muscle relaxants	✔					
Use by athletes—Skeletal muscle relaxants are banned and tested for in shooters by the U.S. Olympic Committee (USOC) and the National Collegiate Athletic Association (NCAA)	✔	✔	✔	✔	✔	✔
Other medical problems, especially:						
Acute intermittent porphyria (known or suspected)	✔					
Conditions that may be adversely affected by anticholinergic activity						✔
Hemolytic anemia, or history of				✔		
Hepatic function impairment or disease	✔	✔	✔	✔	✔	✔
Renal function impairment or disease	✔	✔	✔	✔	✔	✔
Other medications, especially other CNS depression-producing medications	✔	✔	✔	✔	✔	✔
Proper use of this medication						
Tablets may be crushed and mixed with food or liquid for ease of administration				✔	✔	✔
Missed dose: Taking if remembered within an hour or so; not taking if remembered later; not doubling doses	✔	✔	✔	✔	✔	✔
» Proper storage	✔	✔	✔	✔	✔	✔
Precautions while using this medication						
Regular visits to physician to check progress during prolonged therapy	✔	✔	✔	✔	✔	✔
» Avoiding use of alcohol or other CNS depressants during therapy unless prescribed or otherwise approved by physician	✔	✔	✔	✔	✔	✔
» Caution if any of the following occur:						
Blurred vision or other vision problems	✔				✔	✔
Clumsiness or unsteadiness	✔				✔	
Dizziness or lightheadedness	✔	✔	✔	✔	✔	✔
Drowsiness	✔	✔	✔	✔	✔	✔
Faintness	✔				✔	✔
Muscle weakness						✔
Possible dryness of mouth; using sugarless gum or candy, ice, or saliva substitute for relief; checking with dentist if dry mouth continues for more than 2 weeks						✔
Diabetics: May cause false-positive urine sugar tests				✔		
Side/adverse effects						
Signs and symptoms of potential side effects, especially:						
Allergic reactions	✔	✔	✔	✔	✔	✔
Anticholinergic effects						✔
Blood dyscrasias		✔	✔	✔	✔	✔
Convulsions					✔*	
Fainting	✔				✔*	✔
Fast heartbeat	✔					✔
Gastrointestinal bleeding			✔			
Hallucinations						
Hepatotoxicity				✔		
Mental depression	✔					
Pounding heartbeat						✔
Slow heartbeat					✔*	
Medication may color urine orange or reddish purple			✔			
Medication may color urine black, brown, or green, especially if allowed to stand					✔	

*For parenteral administration only.

SODIUM BICARBONATE   Systemic

Some commonly used *brand names* are:
In the U.S.—
  Arm and Hammer   *Citrocarbonate*
    Pure Baking Soda   *Soda Mint*
  Bell/ans
In Canada—
  Citrocarbonate

ORAL
Effervescent Sodium Bicarbonate
  In the U.S. and Canada—*Citrocarbonate*
Sodium Bicarbonate Oral Powder USP
  In the U.S.—*Arm and Hammer Pure Baking Soda;* GENERIC
  In Canada—GENERIC
Sodium Bicarbonate Tablets USP
  In the U.S.—*Bell/ans; Soda Mint;* GENERIC
  In Canada—GENERIC

PARENTERAL
Sodium Bicarbonate Injection USP
  In the U.S. and Canada—GENERIC

Category

Alkalizer (systemic; urinary)—Sodium Bicarbonate Injection USP; Sodium Bicarbonate Oral Powder USP; Sodium Bicarbonate Tablets USP.
Antacid—Effervescent Sodium Bicarbonate; Sodium Bicarbonate Oral Powder USP; Sodium Bicarbonate Tablets USP.
Electrolyte replenisher—Sodium Bicarbonate Injection USP.

Indications

Note: Bracketed information in the *Indications* section refers to uses not included in U.S. product labeling.

Accepted
Metabolic acidosis (treatment)—
  Acute mild to moderate;
  In renal tubular disorders;
  In severe renal disease (renal tubular acidosis);
  In circulatory insufficiency, due to shock or severe dehydration;
  In cardiac arrest;
  In extracorporeal circulation of blood; and
  In primary lactic acidosis, severe—Oral sodium bicarbonate is indicated in the treatment of metabolic acidosis. It is preferred over parenteral therapy in acute mild to moderate acidosis. Oral sodium bicarbonate is also indicated to correct acidosis in renal tubular disorders. Parenteral sodium bicarbonate is indicated to minimize risks of metabolic acidosis in severe renal disease, circulatory insufficiency due to shock or severe dehydration, extracorporeal circulation of blood, cardiac arrest, and severe primary lactic acidosis.

    Intravenous sodium bicarbonate has been used to minimize the risks of metabolic acidosis in uncontrolled diabetes; however, it generally has been replaced by low-dose insulin therapy and saline, potassium, and fluid replacement. With low-dose insulin therapy there is less risk of developing serious hypoglycemia and/or hypokalemia.

Renal calculi, uric acid (prophylaxis)—Oral sodium bicarbonate is indicated to reduce uric acid crystallization as an adjuvant to uricosuric medication in gout.
Hyperacidity (treatment)—Also indicated orally to provide symptomatic relief of upset stomach associated with hyperacidity. It may also be used in the treatment of the symptoms of peptic ulcer disease.
Diarrhea (treatment adjunct)—Parenteral sodium bicarbonate is indicated in severe diarrhea in which the loss of bicarbonate is significant.
Toxicity, nonspecific (treatment)—Parenteral sodium bicarbonate is indicated in the treatment of certain drug intoxications, including barbiturates, and in poisoning by salicylates or methyl alcohol.

Sodium bicarbonate is not recommended for use as an antidote following the ingestion of strong mineral acids, since the formation of carbon dioxide may distend the weakened stomach and lead to gastric rupture.

Sodium bicarbonate has been used as a urinary alkalizer to increase sulfonamide solubility and prevent crystallization that may lead to renal calculi or nephrotoxicity; however, poorly soluble sulfonamides are rarely used now.

[Sodium bicarbonate has been used in the treatment of sickle cell anemia; however, it generally has been replaced by more effective agents.]

Pharmacology

Mechanism of action/Effect:
  Alkalizer, systemic—Increases the plasma bicarbonate, buffers excess hydrogen ion concentration, and raises blood pH, thereby reversing the clinical manifestations of acidosis.
  Alkalizer, urinary—Increases the excretion of free bicarbonate ions in the urine, thus effectively raising the urinary pH. By maintaining an alkaline urine, the actual dissolution of uric acid stones may be accomplished.
  Antacid—Reacts chemically to neutralize or buffer existing quantities of stomach acid but has no direct effect on its output. This action results in increased pH value of stomach contents, thus providing relief of hyperacidity symptoms.

Precautions to Consider

Geriatrics
No information is available on the relationship of age to the effects of sodium bicarbonate in geriatric patients. However, elderly patients are more likely to have age-related renal function impairment, which may require caution in patients receiving sodium bicarbonate.

Drug interactions and/or related problems
The following drug interactions and/or related problems have been selected on the basis of their potential clinical significance (possible mechanism in parentheses where appropriate)—not necessarily inclusive (» = major clinical significance):

Note: Not all interactions between sodium bicarbonate and other oral medications have been identified in this monograph. Because concurrent use may increase or reduce the rate and/or extent of absorption of other oral medications, patients should be advised not to take any other oral medications within 1 to 2 hours of sodium bicarbonate.

    Combinations containing any of the following medications, depending on the amount present, may also interact with this medication.

Acidifiers, urinary, such as:
  Ammonium chloride
  Ascorbic acid
  Potassium or sodium phosphates
    (antacids may alkalinize the urine and counteract the effect of urinary acidifiers; frequent use of antacids, especially in high doses, is best avoided by patients receiving therapy to acidify the urine)

Amphetamines or
Quinidine
(urinary excretion may be inhibited when these medications
are used concurrently with sodium bicarbonate, possibly resulting in toxicity; dosage adjustment may be needed when sodium
bicarbonate therapy is initiated or discontinued or if dosage is
changed)

Anticholinergics or other medications with anticholinergic action
(concurrent use with sodium bicarbonate may decrease absorption, reducing the effectiveness of the anticholinergic; doses of
these medications should be spaced 1 hour apart from doses of
sodium bicarbonate; also, urinary excretion may be delayed by
alkalinization of the urine, thus potentiating the side effects of
the anticholinergic)

Calcium-containing preparations or
Milk or milk products
(concurrent and prolonged use with sodium bicarbonate may
result in the milk-alkali syndrome)

Ciprofloxacin or
Norfloxacin or
Ofloxacin
(alkalinization of the urine may reduce the solubility of ciprofloxacin, norfloxacin, or ofloxacin in the urine; patients should
be observed for signs of crystalluria and nephrotoxicity)

Citrates
(concurrent use with antacids containing sodium bicarbonate
may result in systemic alkalosis)
(concurrent use with sodium bicarbonate may promote the development of calcium stones in patients with uric acid stones,
due to sodium ion opposition to the hypocalciuric effect of the
alkaline load; may also cause hypernatremia)

Enteric-coated medications, such as bisacodyl
(concurrent administration of antacids with enteric-coated tablets may cause the enteric coating to dissolve too rapidly, resulting in gastric or duodenal irritation)

Ephedrine
(urine alkalinization induced by sodium bicarbonate may increase the half-life of ephedrine and prolong its duration of
action, especially if the urine remains alkaline for several days
or longer; dosage adjustment of ephedrine may be necessary)

Histamine H_2-receptor antagonists, such as:
Cimetidine
Famotidine
Nizatidine
Ranitidine
(concurrent use with sodium bicarbonate may be indicated in
the treatment of peptic ulcer to relieve pain; however, simultaneous administration of antacids of medium to high potency
[80 mmol to 150 mmol HCl] is not recommended since absorption of these medications may be decreased; patients should
be advised not to take any antacids within one-half to 1 hour of
histamine H_2-receptor antagonists)

Iron supplements or preparations, oral
(absorption may be decreased when these preparations are used
concurrently with antacids containing carbonate; because of
the formation of less soluble complexes, iron supplements should
not be taken within 1 hour before or 2 hours after sodium
bicarbonate)

» Ketoconazole
(sodium bicarbonate may cause increased gastrointestinal pH;
concurrent administration with sodium bicarbonate may result
in a marked reduction in absorption of ketoconazole; patients
should take sodium bicarbonate at least 2 hours after ketoconazole)

Lithium
(sodium bicarbonate enhances lithium excretion, possibly resulting in decreased efficacy; this may be partly due to the
sodium content)

» Mecamylamine
(alkalinization of the urine caused by sodium bicarbonate slows
excretion and prolongs the effects of mecamylamine; concurrent use is not recommended)

» Methenamine
(alkalinization of the urine caused by sodium bicarbonate may
reduce the effectiveness of methenamine by inhibiting its conversion to formaldehyde; concurrent use is not recommended)

Mexiletine
(marked alkalinization of the urine caused by sodium bicarbonate may retard renal excretion of mexiletine)

Potassium supplements
(concurrent use of sodium bicarbonate infusion decreases serum potassium concentration by promoting a shift of potassium
ion into the cells)

Salicylates
(alkalinization of the urine may increase renal salicylate excretion and lower serum salicylate concentrations; dosage adjustments of salicylates may be necessary when chronic high-dose
antacid therapy with sodium bicarbonate is started or stopped,
especially in patients receiving large doses of the salicylate,
such as those with rheumatoid arthritis and rheumatic fever)

Sucralfate
(concurrent use with sodium bicarbonate may be indicated in
the treatment of duodenal ulcer to relieve pain; however, simultaneous administration is not recommended since antacids,
such as sodium bicarbonate, may interfere with binding of
sucralfate to the mucosa; patients should be advised not to take
sodium bicarbonate within one-half hour before or 1 hour after
sucralfate)

» Tetracyclines, oral
(absorption may be decreased when oral tetracyclines are used
concurrently with sodium bicarbonate because of increase in
intragastric pH; patients should be advised not to take sodium
bicarbonate within 1 to 2 hours of tetracyclines)

Contraindications/Medical problems
The contraindications/medical problems included have been selected
on the basis of their potential clinical significance (reasons given
in parentheses where appropriate)—not necessarily inclusive (» =
major clinical significance).

*Except under special circumstances, this medication should not be
used when the following medical problems exist:*

For parenteral dosage form
» Alkalosis, metabolic or respiratory
(may be exacerbated)

» Chloride loss due to vomiting or continuous gastrointestinal suction
(increased risk of severe alkalosis)

» Hypocalcemia
(increased risk of alkalosis producing tetany)

*Risk-benefit should be considered when the following medical prob-
lems exist:*

» Anuria or oliguria
(increased risk of excessive sodium retention)

» Edematous sodium-retaining conditions such as:
Cirrhosis of liver
Congestive heart failure
Renal function impairment
Toxemia of pregnancy

» Hypertension
(may be exacerbated)

For antacid use
» Appendicitis, or symptoms of
(sodium bicarbonate may complicate existing condition)

» Bleeding, gastrointestinal or rectal, undiagnosed

Side/Adverse Effects

The following side/adverse effects have been selected on the basis of their potential clinical significance (possible signs and symptoms in parentheses where appropriate)—not necessarily inclusive:

Those indicating need for medical attention

With excessive parenteral administration

Hypokalemia (dryness of mouth, increased thirst, irregular heartbeat, mood or mental changes, muscle cramps or pain, weak pulse)

With large doses

Swelling of feet or lower legs

With large doses or in renal insufficiency

Metabolic alkalosis (mood or mental changes, muscle pain or twitching, nervousness or restlessness, slow breathing, unpleasant taste, unusual tiredness or weakness)

With long-term use

Hypercalcemia associated with milk-alkali syndrome (frequent urge to urinate, continuing headache, continuing loss of appetite, nausea or vomiting, unusual tiredness or weakness)

Those indicating need for medical attention only if they continue or are bothersome

Incidence less frequent

Increased thirst; stomach cramps

Patient Consultation

In providing consultation, consider emphasizing the following selected information:

Before using this medication

» Conditions affecting use, especially:

Pregnancy—Chronic use may lead to systemic alkalosis; sodium may cause edema and weight gain

Use in children—Not recommended, because serious side effects may result

Other medications, especially ketoconazole, mecamylamine, methenamine, or oral tetracyclines

Other medical problems, especially anuria or oliguria, appendicitis, bleeding of gastrointestinal tract or rectum, chloride loss, edema, hypertension, hypocalcemia, or metabolic or respiratory alkalosis

Proper use of this medication

Following physician's or manufacturer's instructions

Missed dose: If on regular dosing schedule—Taking as soon as possible; not taking if almost time for next dose; not doubling doses

» Proper storage

For antacid use

» Compliance with therapy, especially for ulcer patients

Taking 1 and 3 hours after meals and at bedtime for maximum effectiveness (for ulcer patients)

Precautions while using this medication

Regular visits to physician to check progress during long-term therapy

» Not taking:

—within 1 to 2 hours of other oral medication

—for a prolonged period of time because of increased possibility of side effects

Caution for sodium restriction

For antacid use

» Not taking:

—if symptoms of appendicitis are present; checking with physician for proper diagnosis

—concurrently with large amounts of milk or milk products

—for more than 2 weeks or if problem is recurring, unless otherwise directed by physician

Side/adverse effects

Signs of potential side effects, especially hypokalemia, hypercalcemia, or metabolic alkalosis

General Dosing Information

Prolonged sodium bicarbonate therapy is not recommended because of the high risk of causing metabolic alkalosis or sodium overload.

In acute mild to moderate acidosis, oral treatment is preferred to intravenous therapy. In severe acute acidosis, sodium bicarbonate may be given intravenously.

For oral dosage forms only

Sodium bicarbonate is a fast-acting antacid, but has a short duration of effect. It has a high neutralizing capacity.

The maximum daily dosage of sodium is 200 mEq (16.6 grams of sodium bicarbonate) in patients younger than 60 years of age and 100 mEq (8.3 grams of sodium bicarbonate) in patients 60 years of age or older.

When sodium bicarbonate is used as an antacid, the maximum dosage allowed should not be taken for more than 2 weeks except with the advice or under the supervision of a physician.

In the treatment of peptic ulcer disease, sodium bicarbonate may be administered 1 and 3 hours after meals and at bedtime. Additional doses of antacids may be administered to relieve the pain that may occur between the regularly scheduled doses.

For parenteral dosage forms only

Commercially available parenteral solutions are generally hypertonic and require dilution.

Sodium bicarbonate solution may be administered intravenously or, following dilution to isotonicity (1.5%), subcutaneously.

For intravenous administration, suitable concentrations range from 1.5% (isotonic) to 8.4% (undiluted), depending on the clinical condition and requirements of the patient.

For subcutaneous administration, an isotonic solution (1.5%) of sodium bicarbonate may be prepared by diluting 1 mL of 8.4% sodium bicarbonate solution with 4.6 mL of sterile water for injection. However, it should be noted that absorption from subcutaneous administration is unpredictable. This route of administration is not generally recommended except in those cases where the intravenous route is not available.

Bicarbonate therapy should always be planned in a careful, controlled way, since the degree of response to a given dose is not precisely predictable. Ideally, sodium bicarbonate should always be given according to the results of measurement of arterial blood pH, carbon dioxide content of the plasma, and calculation of base deficit.

Excessive administration may induce hypokalemia and may predispose the patient to cardiac arrhythmias.

Too rapid administration of sodium bicarbonate may produce severe alkalosis, which may be accompanied by hyperirritability or tetany.

Overdosage and alkalosis may be avoided by giving repeated small doses. Periodic monitoring is recommended.

Rapid injection (10 mL per minute) of hypertonic sodium bicarbonate solutions may produce hypernatremia, a decrease in cerebrospinal fluid pressure, and possible intracranial hemorrhage, especially in neonates and children under 2 years of age. No more than 8 mEq per kg of body weight per day of a 4.2% solution should be administered.

In cardiac arrest emergencies, the risk of rapid infusion may be necessary because of the fatality risk due to acidosis.

Adequate alveolar ventilation must be ensured following sodium bicarbonate administration during cardiac arrest, to allow for the continued excretion of the carbon dioxide released. This is important for the control of arterial pH.

Oral Dosage Forms

EFFERVESCENT SODIUM BICARBONATE

Usual adult and adolescent dose: Antacid—Oral, 3.9 to 10 grams in a glass of cold water after meals.

Note: Patients 60 years of age and over—Oral, 1.9 to 3.9 grams after meals.

Usual adult and adolescent prescribing limits: Oral, 19.5 grams per day.

Note: Alert patients on sodium-restricted diet. Product contains 30.46 mEq (700.6 mg) of sodium per 3.9 grams.

SODIUM BICARBONATE ORAL POWDER USP

Usual adult and adolescent dose:

Antacid—Oral, 1/2 teaspoonful in a glass of water every two hours, the dose being adjusted as needed.

Urinary alkalizer—Oral, 1 teaspoonful in a glass of water every four hours, the dose being adjusted as needed.

Usual adult prescribing limits: Up to 60 years of age—Up to 4 teaspoonsful daily.

Note: Each 1/2 teaspoonful contains 20.9 mEq (476 mg) of sodium.

Note: Alert patients on sodium-restricted diet. Products contain 41.8 mEq (952 mg) of sodium per teaspoonful.

SODIUM BICARBONATE TABLETS USP

Usual adult and adolescent dose:

Antacid—Oral, 325 mg to 2 grams one to four times a day.
Urinary alkalizer—Oral, 4 grams initially, then 1 to 2 grams every four hours.

Usual adult prescribing limits: Up to 16 grams daily.

Note: Alert patients on sodium-restricted diet. Products contain sodium as follows: 325 mg tablets (3.9 mEq), 520 mg tablets (6.2 mEq), and 650 mg tablets (7.7 mEq).

Parenteral Dosage Forms

SODIUM BICARBONATE INJECTION USP

Usual adult and adolescent dose:

Systemic alkalizer—

In cardiac arrest: Intravenous, initially 1 mEq per kg of body weight; 0.5 mEq per kg of body weight may be repeated every ten minutes of continued arrest.

In less urgent forms of metabolic acidosis: Intravenous infusion, 2 to 5 mEq per kg of body weight, administered over a period of four to eight hours.

Note: Frequency of administration and the size of the dose may be reduced after severe symptoms have abated.

Urinary alkalizer—Intravenous, 2 to 5 mEq per kg of body weight, administered over a period of four to eight hours.

SPERMICIDES   Vaginal

INN: Included in brackets after individual generic listings, if different from the U.S. generic name.

Some commonly used *brand names* are:

In the U.S.—

Because [Nonoxynol 9]
Conceptrol Contraceptive Inserts [Nonoxynol 9]
Conceptrol Gel [Nonoxynol 9]
Delfen [Nonoxynol 9]
Emko [Nonoxynol 9]
Encare [Nonoxynol 9]
Gynol II Extra Strength Contraceptive Jelly [Nonoxynol 9]
Gynol II Original Formula Contraceptive Jelly [Nonoxynol 9]
Koromex Cream [Octoxynol 9]

Koromex Crystal Clear Gel [Nonoxynol 9]
Koromex Foam [Nonoxynol 9]
Koromex Jelly [Nonoxynol 9]
Ortho-Creme [Nonoxynol 9]
Ortho-Gynol [Octoxynol 9]
Pre-Fil [Nonoxynol 9]
Ramses Crystal Clear Gel [Nonoxynol 9]
Semicid [Nonoxynol 9]
Shur-Seal [Nonoxynol 9]
Today [Nonoxynol 9]
VCF [Nonoxynol 9]

In Canada—

Delfen [Nonoxynol 9]
Emko [Nonoxynol 9]
Ortho-Gynol [Octoxynol 9]
Pharmatex [Benzalkonium Chloride]

Ramses Contraceptive Foam [Nonoxynol 9]
Ramses Contraceptive Vaginal Jelly [Nonoxynol 9]
Today [Nonoxynol 9]

NONOXYNOL 9 [Nonoxinol 9]
Nonoxynol 9 Vaginal Cream
In the U.S.—*Ortho-Creme*
In Canada—*Delfen*
Nonoxynol 9 Vaginal Film
In the U.S.—*VCF*
Nonoxynol 9 Vaginal Foam
In the U.S.—*Because; Delfen; Emko; Koromex Foam; Pre-Fil*
In Canada—*Delfen; Emko; Ramses Contraceptive Foam*
Nonoxynol 9 Vaginal Gel
In the U.S.—*Conceptrol Gel; Koromex Crystal Clear Gel; Ramses Crystal Clear Gel; Shur-Seal*
Nonoxynol 9 Vaginal Jelly
In the U.S.—*Gynol II Extra Strength Contraceptive Jelly; Gynol II Original Formula Contraceptive Jelly; Koromex Jelly*
In Canada—*Ramses Contraceptive Vaginal Jelly*
Nonoxynol 9 Vaginal Sponge
In the U.S. and Canada—*Today*
Nonoxynol 9 Vaginal Suppositories
In the U.S.—*Conceptrol Contraceptive Inserts; Encare; Semicid*
OCTOXYNOL 9 [Octoxinol]
Octoxynol 9 Vaginal Cream
In the U.S.—*Koromex Cream*
Octoxynol 9 Vaginal Jelly
In the U.S. and Canada—*Ortho-Gynol*

---

*Not commercially available in the U.S.

VAGINAL
BENZALKONIUM CHLORIDE*
Benzalkonium Chloride Vaginal Suppositories*
In Canada—*Pharmatex*

Category: Contraceptive, vaginal.

Indications

Note: Bracketed information in the *Indications* section refers to uses not included in U.S. product labeling.

Accepted

Pregnancy (prophylaxis)—Vaginal spermicides are used in the prevention of pregnancy. Because of the high failure rate associated with these products when used alone, suppositories, soluble films, creams, foams, gels, and jellies are generally recommended for use in combination with mechanical barrier methods of contraception (condom, cervical cap, or diaphragm) or for patients with a low level of fertility or suspected infertility, or patients who have intercourse infrequently.

These preparations are also used in combination with mechanical barrier contraceptives to prevent pregnancy at times when oral contraceptives or intrauterine devices may not be effective or are contraindicated, or as an adjuvant to the periodic abstinence (rhythm) method of contraception.

Vaginal spermicides provide a back-up to the condom in case of leaking or spilling of ejaculate or rupture of the condom during coitus. The contraceptive sponge may also be used in combination with the condom. Cervical caps and diaphragms are designed to hold the spermicide near the cervical os, which is particularly important in the event that the cap or diaphragm is dislodged or does not form a complete seal around the cervix. Jellies and gels also provide a high level of lubrication, which may ease insertion of a cervical cap or diaphragm, may decrease the risk of condom rupture during intercourse, or may decrease frictional trauma to the vaginal mucosa during intercourse.

[Sexually transmitted diseases (prophylaxis)][1]—The use of vaginal spermicides in combination with latex condoms may be partially effective in reducing the risk of acquiring many sexually transmitted diseases (STDs). However, the extent of this additional protection against acquiring STDs (especially viral) has not yet been determined.

Vaginal spermicides provide a backup to the condom in case of leaking or spilling of ejaculate or rupture of the condom during coitus. They may be recommended for use by patients using non-barrier contraceptives such as the intrauterine device or oral contraceptives, ideally in combination with latex condoms, to reduce the risk of acquiring STDs. The use of spermicides in combination with latex condoms may also be considered for those patients at high risk of acquiring STDs (especially HIV infection) during pregnancy.

Nonoxynol-9 has been shown to inhibit the *in vitro* growth of the following STD pathogens:

> *Chlamydia trachomatis*
> *Gardnerella vaginalis*
> *Mycoplasma hominis*
> *Neisseria gonorrhoeae*
> *Trichomonas vaginalis*
> *Ureaplasma urealyticum*

In vitro, nonoxynol 9 also decreases the infectivity of *Treponema pallidum*, the pathogenic agent of syphilis.

Clinical studies have shown a reduction in the rate of occurrence of chlamydia, gonorrhea, trichomoniasis, and bacterial vaginosis with the use of nonoxynol 9-containing preparations, especially in combination with mechanical barrier contraceptives.

In vitro, nonoxynol 9 has been shown to inactivate herpes simplex viruses (HSV) I and II and human immunodeficiency virus (HIV or the AIDS virus). Benzalkonium chloride has also been shown to inactivate HIV *in vitro*.

The use of vaginal spermicides in combination with latex condoms may afford some degree of protection against viral STDs. However, this recommendation is based on *in vitro* data and no appropriate clinical studies have been completed that document a reduction in the vaginal, rectal, or oropharyngeal transmission of these diseases by the use of spermicides alone or a further reduction when used in combination with mechanical barrier contraceptives. Because clinical studies have not been performed that document the safety and efficacy of spermicides in reducing STD transmission, the following points should be considered: it is not known whether subinhibitory concentrations of spermicides would result from application or use within the rectum; or whether spermicides may cause epithelial damage to the mucosa, damage to cells of the immune system, or Y-lymphocyte activation, resulting in an increased risk of transmission. Also, because protection from pregnancy is frequently incomplete, the same possibility must be considered for the use of spermicides for STD prevention.

[Pelvic inflammatory disease (prophylaxis)][1]—Use of vaginal spermicides, especially in combination with mechanical barrier contraceptives, decreases the risk of development of pelvic inflammatory disease and subsequent tubal damage and infertility. One study showed a reduction in the incidence of tubal infertility among users of mechanical barrier contraceptives combined with a spermicide, which was greater than the reduction with either method alone. The use of spermicides in combination with latex condoms may also be considered for those patients at high risk of development of PID during pregnancy.

A reduced incidence of cervical neoplasia has been observed in epidemiologic studies among users of vaginal spermicides, especially when used in combination with a mechanical barrier method of contraception. However, the nature and extent of this reduction in incidence has not yet been clearly documented. It has been proposed that spermicides may provide protection against cervical cancer by virtue of their antiviral actions, since there is some evidence that cervical neoplasia may be associated with sexual transmission of human papillomavirus.

Unaccepted

One study has shown nonoxynol 9 cream to be ineffective in the treatment of genital herpes (HSV II) infections.

---

[1]Not included in Canadian product labeling.

Pharmacology

Mechanism of action/Effect:

For the prevention of pregnancy—

All products: Vaginal spermicides are considered chemical forms of barrier contraceptives because they form a chemical barrier between the mucous membranes and ejaculate. Mechanical barrier contraceptives include the condom, diaphragm, cervical cap, and vaginal sponge (which also contains nonoxynol 9). The active chemicals in vaginal spermicides interact with the lipoproteins of the cell membrane to permanently disrupt the cell membranes of spermatozoa, resulting in severe damage to the acrosome (head), neck, midpiece, and tail of the sperm and rapid, irreversible loss of function and motility within the vagina and viability. Cell permeability increases and the leaking of cellular components occurs. Studies also indicate that carbohydrate-metabolizing enzymes and the mitochondriae are disturbed. Additionally, the inactive vehicle itself may form a mechanical barrier to the cervical os, inhibiting the passage of sperm.

Benzalkonium chloride may make the cervical mucus hostile to sperm by disrupting the electrolyte balance of the aqueous phase. It also coagulates ovulatory cervical mucus, resulting in a mesh of less than 5 microns, which may inhibit sperm passage.

Contraceptive sponge: Nonoxynol 9 is released from the sponge matrix at a rate of 125 mg per 24 hours. Also, the polyurethane foam sponge serves as a mechanical barrier to the cervical os, inhibiting the passage of sperm, and absorbs ejaculate.

The following are the results of studies examining failure rates reported during the use of various contraceptive methods, as the percentage of women experiencing accidental pregnancy.

In the second column, interstudy variations in failure rates may be due to differences in study design or patient population characteristics, such as motivation, fecundity, or socioeconomic factors (including level of education). Studies reported also include failure rates beyond the first year, which generally decline with continued use of a specific method.

In the third column are failure rates expected among *typical* adult couples who start using the method listed (not necessarily for the first time) and do not stop use of this method in the first year for any reason other than accidental pregnancy. Failure rates among adolescents may be higher, due to poor compliance.

Method used	Ranges seen in clinical studies (%)	Typical first year failure rates (%)
None	78–94	89
Spermicides*	0.3–37	21
Periodic abstinence	13–35	20
Withdrawal	7–22	18
Cervical cap with spermicide	6–27	18
Sponge	5->28	18
Diaphragm with spermicide		2–23
Condom without spermicide	2–14	12
IUD	0.5–6	6
Oral contraceptive		
Combination	0–6	3
Progestin only	1–10	5
Progestin injection	0–4	
Medroxyprogesterone		0.3
Norethisterone		2
Implants		
Capsules	0.3–0.4	0.3
Rods	0–0.2	0.2
Sterilization		
Female	0–8	0.4
Male	0–0.5	0.15

*Spermicides studied include creams, foams, gels, jellies, and suppositories.

For prevention of sexually transmitted diseases—

All products: The majority of studies conducted have concerned the most commonly used spermicide, nonoxynol 9. *In vitro,* nonoxynol 9 has been shown to produce bactericidal and virucidal effects by disrupting the cell membrane and the viral envelope. The active chemicals in vaginal spermicides interact with the lipoproteins of the cell membrane to permanently disrupt the cell membranes. Nonoxynol 9 may also exert antimicrobial activity against *Chlamydia trachomatis* receptors on target cells. Low concentrations *in vitro* have been shown to block cellular attachment and/or penetration by *C. trachomatis* organisms. In one study, nonoxynol 9 caused significant chemorepulsion of *Trichomonas vaginalis in vitro.*

Any method covering the cervix may protect against gonorrhea and chlamydia because the causative organisms primarily infect cervical tissues. Therefore, spermicides alone or in combination with a mechanical barrier contraceptive may protect against transmission of these infections. Spermicidal preparations that are well-distributed within the vagina, such as foams or sponges, may be best for those organisms that reside mostly in the vagina, such as *T. vaginalis.*

Other—Sperm acrosin is inactivated by nonoxynol 9.

Onset of action:

Foams, creams, gels, and jellies—Immediately effective.

Sponge—Immediately effective, upon activation of the spermicide with water.

Film and suppositories—5 to 15 minutes, depending upon individual product, to allow for melting or effervescence and dispersion within the vagina.

Precautions to Consider

Cross-sensitivity and/or related problems

Because of close similarities in composition, activity, and structure, patients allergic to nonoxynol 9 are likely to be allergic to octoxynol 9 also and should avoid further use of either product if sensitization occurs.

Drug interactions and/or related problems

The following drug interactions and/or related problems have been selected on the basis of their potential clinical significance (possible mechanism in parentheses where appropriate)—not necessarily inclusive (» = major clinical significance):

Note: Combinations containing any of the following medications, depending on the amount present, may also interact with this medication.

» Vaginal or topical medications, especially those containing:

Aluminum or
Citrate or
Cotton dressings or
Hydrogen peroxide or
Iodides or
Lanolin, hydrous, or
Nitrates or
Permanganates or
Salicylates or
Silver salts or
Soaps, surfactants, or detergents, ionic, or
Sulfonamides or
Tartrates

(benzalkonium chloride may be chemically inactivated by the above agents; contact between benzalkonium chloride spermicides and any product containing the above ingredients should be avoided)

» Vaginal douche products or other vaginal or local cleansing

(vaginal douching is not recommended or necessary after use of these products, but, if performed, at least 8 hours [cervical cap and *Ramses Contraceptive Vaginal Jelly*] or 6 hours [most products] should pass following the last act of intercourse to allow for adequate contact of the spermicide with ejaculate, which ensures maximal contraceptive effect)

Contraindications/Medical problems

The contraindications/medical problems included have been selected on the basis of their potential clinical significance (reasons given in parentheses where appropriate)—not necessarily inclusive (» = major clinical significance).

Except under special circumstances, this medication should not be used when the following medical problems exist:

For all products

» Allergy to benzalkonium chloride, octoxynol, or nonoxynol

For cervical cap, contraceptive sponge, and diaphragm only

» Menstruation

(the cervical cap, contraceptive sponge, or diaphragm should not be used during menstruation, as the risk of toxic shock syndrome may be increased; it may be recommended that condoms and a spermicide be used instead during menses)

»   Toxic-shock syndrome, history of, especially with prior use of cervical cap, contraceptive sponge, diaphragm or tampons
(the cervical cap, contraceptive sponge, or diaphragm should not be used, since these patients may be at increased risk of recurrence)

Risk-benefit should be considered when the following medical problems exist:

For all products
Allergy, chronic, local, or
Contact dermatitis, genital
(moderate to severe irritation may occur with the use of spermicides)

»   Medical or psychosocial conditions where a critical need exists for highly effective contraception
(when spermicides are used alone, a high rate of failure occurs)

For benzalkonium chloride only
Vaginal infection
(efficacy of benzalkonium chloride may be affected)

For cervical cap, contraceptive sponge, or diaphragm only
Parturition or abortion, recent
(a physician should be consulted prior to use or resumption of use of these products, as use in the postpartum or postabortal period is not recommended and may increase the risk of development of toxic-shock syndrome)

For prevention of sexually transmitted diseases only
»   Genital ulcers or
»   Vaginal epithelial irritation
(it is not known whether vaginal spermicides may cause further epithelial damage, resulting in an increased risk of transmission of STDs)

Side/Adverse Effects

The following side/adverse effects have been selected on the basis of their potential clinical significance (possible signs and symptoms in parentheses)—not necessarily inclusive:

Note: The safety of the use of spermicides on the rectal mucosa is unknown. However, no serious adverse effects have been reported.

In one study in rats and rabbits given high doses of nonoxynol 9 peritoneally or vaginally, some evidence of hepatotoxicity and nephrotoxicity was seen. However, these effects or other serious systemic side effects have not been seen in humans.

Those indicating need for medical attention
Incidence rare
For all products
Allergic vaginitis (persistent vaginal redness, irritation, rash, dryness, or whitish discharge); ***contact dermatitis*** (persistent skin rash, redness, irritation, or itching); ***urinary tract infection, female*** (increased frequency of urination, pain on urination, bladder pain, cloudy or bloody urine)
Note: An increased risk of *urinary tract infection* may occur in females, independent of diaphragm use, possibly due to changes in vaginal flora.

For cervical cap, contraceptive sponge, or diaphragm only
Candidiasis, vulvovaginal (thick, white, or curd-like vaginal discharge); ***toxic-shock syndrome*** (dizziness; fever; lightheadedness; chills; sunburn-like rash that is followed by peeling of the skin; muscle aches; hypotension; unusual redness of the mucous membranes inside of the mouth, nose, throat, vagina, or conjunctivae; confusion)
Note: An increased *relative risk* of acquiring nonmenstrual toxic-shock syndrome has been reported with the use of a cervical cap, contraceptive sponge, and diaphragm. However, its occurrence is rare and the *absolute risk* of

nonmenstrual toxic-shock is still very low with the correct use of any of these contraceptive methods.

Those indicating need for medical attention only if they continue or are bothersome
Incidence less frequent
Burning, stinging, warmth, itching, or other irritation of the skin, penis, rectum, or vagina; vaginal discharge, transient—with suppositories, creams, or foams; ***vaginal dryness or odor***
Note: *Local irritation* of the skin, penis, rectum, or vagina may require use of a product with a lower concentration of spermicide or different ingredients or wetting of benzalkonium chloride suppository prior to insertion.

Patient Consultation

In providing consultation, consider emphasizing the following selected information (» = major clinical significance):

Before using this medication
»   Conditions affecting use:
Allergies to spermicides
Other medications, especially:
For all products—Vaginal douches or cleansing
For benzalkonium chloride only—Vaginal or topical medications, especially those containing aluminum, citrate, cotton dressings, hydrogen peroxide, lanolin, iodides, nitrates, permanganates, salicylates, silver salts, soaps, detergents, surfactants, sulfonamides, or tartrates
Medical problems, especially:
For all products—Conditions where a critical need exists for contraception, local allergy, or genital contact dermatitis
For benzalkonium chloride only—Vaginal infection
For cervical cap, contraceptive sponge, and diaphragm only—Postpartum or postabortal status, history of toxic-shock syndrome, or menstruation
For prevention of STDs—Genital ulcers or vaginal epithelial irritation

Proper use of this medication
Reading package insert carefully and following manufacturer instructions for use
»   Using correctly and consistently with every act of intercourse
Proper use of sponge
Proper use of spermicide with condom, cervical cap, or diaphragm
»   Not douching until 6 or 8 hours (product-dependent) have passed after last act of intercourse
»   Proper storage
For contraceptive sponge and diaphragm only
»   Not removing sponge or diaphragm until 6 or 8 (product-dependent) hours have passed after last act of intercourse
For cervical cap only
»   Not removing cervical cap until 8 hours have passed after last act of intercourse

Precautions while using this medication
For cervical cap, contraceptive sponge, or diaphragm only
»   Contacting physician if difficulty in removing
»   Contacting physician immediately if any symptoms of toxic-shock syndrome occur after use

Side/adverse effects
Signs of potential side effects, especially vaginitis, dermatitis, and urinary tract infection; in addition, for cervical cap, sponge, and diaphragm only—toxic-shock syndrome

General Dosing Information

Vaginal spermicides should be placed deep within the vagina, on the cervix, to allow for maximal contact and efficacy.

The use of spermicides, especially gels and jellies, provides additional lubrication during intercourse or insertion of a diaphragm. If additional lubrication is desired, only the appropriate water-based lubricants should be used, such as sterile surgical lubricant or a personal lubricant formulated for use with a diaphragm. Oil-based products such as hand, body, or face cream; petroleum jelly; cooking oils or shortenings; or baby oil will weaken latex and increase the risk of condom rupture during intercourse. These oil-based products will also weaken latex diaphragms and cervical caps, requiring early replacement.

For use of spermicides with a cervical cap

Prior to insertion, the cervical cap should be filled one-third full with spermicidal cream, foam, gel, or jelly. The spermicide should not be applied to the rim of the cervical cap, because it may interfere with the suction seal against the cervix. The patient should check the cap for proper placement on the cervix before and after each act of intercourse. Additional spermicide may be applied vaginally prior to each repeat act of intercourse. The cervical cap must remain in the proper place for at least 8 hours after the last act of intercourse. The cervical cap may be worn up to 48 hours.

For use of spermicides with a condom

Spermicide should be put on the outside of the condom after it is unrolled onto the penis. It is especially important that a female partner also use spermicide in the vagina. Such use is more likely to afford greater efficacy.

For use of spermicides with a diaphragm

Prior to insertion of the diaphragm, a generous amount of cream, foam, gel, or jelly should be spread along the rim of the diaphragm that will be in contact with the cervix. Then, manufacturer's instructions should be followed in placing spermicide in the cup of the diaphragm. Some physicians also recommend that a generous amount of spermicide be spread on the outer surface of the diaphragm.

The diaphragm and spermicide should not be removed until at least 6 (most products) or 8 (*Ramses Contraceptive Vaginal Jelly*) hours have passed after the last last act of intercourse. The diaphragm should not be removed when additional spermicide is applied during this time. After 6 or 8 hours, the diaphragm may be removed. A diaphragm should not be left in place for longer than 24 hours, since doing so may increase the risk of developing toxic-shock syndrome.

To be maximally effective, diaphragms must be used in combination with a spermicide each time that intercourse occurs. Some women choose nightly insertion of the diaphragm to minimize the occurrence of unprotected intercourse. Additional spermicide should be applied each time that intercourse is repeated.

For use of contraceptive sponge only

Before insertion, the sponge must be saturated with clean water and compressed, until the sponge is thoroughly wet and foams easily upon compression.

The sponge should be folded in half and then inserted so that the concave side fits directly onto the cervix. It should remain in the vagina for at least 6 hours after the last act of intercourse and not longer than 30 hours after insertion. It is not necessary to apply additional spermicide during the time the sponge is in proper position, regardless of the number of acts of intercourse that occur during the 24-hour period of effectiveness. The sponge activity is not affected by bathing or swimming.

A polyester loop is imbedded at two edges of the sponge to facilitate removal. A physician should be contacted if there is difficulty in removing the sponge after use or if the sponge is torn during removal. Wearing the sponge for longer than recommended periods, use during the menstrual period, injury to the vagina during removal, use during the postpartum or postabortal period, or leaving fragments of the sponge in the vagina may increase the risk of toxic-shock syndrome.

The sponge may be displaced or expelled during urination or a bowel movement. If the sponge is displaced from the cervix but not expelled from the vagina, the user should use one finger to gently push the sponge back into place. If expulsion of the sponge occurs within 6 hours of the last intercourse, a new sponge should be immediately wetted and inserted.

BENZALKONIUM CHLORIDE

Vaginal Dosage Forms

BENZALKONIUM CHLORIDE VAGINAL SUPPOSITORIES

Usual adult and adolescent dose:

For use alone—*Pharmatex:* Intravaginal, 1 suppository inserted at least ten minutes, and not longer than four hours, prior to intercourse. An additional suppository should be inserted into vagina at least ten minutes, and not longer than four hours, prior to each repeat act of intercourse.

For use with a diaphragm—*Pharmatex:* Intravaginal, one suppository inserted at least ten minutes, and not longer than four hours, prior to each act of intercourse after initial placement of diaphragm with spermicide or if intercourse takes place later than six hours after diaphragm placement.

Auxiliary labeling: • Not to be taken by mouth.

NONOXYNOL 9

Vaginal Dosage Forms

NONOXYNOL 9 VAGINAL CREAM

Usual adult and adolescent dose:

For use alone—*Delfen:* Intravaginal, 1 applicatorful of a 5% cream inserted just prior to intercourse. An additional applicatorful should be inserted into vagina just prior to each repeat act of intercourse.

For use with a diaphragm—

Delfen: Intravaginal, initially 1 applicatorful (approximately one teaspoonful) of a 5% cream placed into cup and additional spermicide spread along the rim of diaphragm just before insertion of diaphragm and not longer than six hours prior to intercourse. An additional applicatorful should be inserted into the vagina just prior to each repeat act of intercourse or if intercourse occurs later than six hours after initial diaphragm placement; or

Ortho-Creme: Intravaginal, initially 1 applicatorful (approximately one teaspoonful) of a 2% cream placed into cup and additional spermicide spread along the rim of diaphragm just before insertion of diaphragm and not longer than six hours prior to intercourse. An additional applicatorful should be inserted into the vagina just prior to each repeat act of intercourse or if intercourse occurs later than six hours after initial diaphragm placement.

Auxiliary labeling: • Not to be taken by mouth.

NONOXYNOL 9 VAGINAL FILM

Usual adult and adolescent dose: For use alone—*VCF:* Intravaginal, 1 film inserted at least five (preferably fifteen) minutes, and not longer than one and one-half hours, prior to each act of intercourse.

Auxiliary labeling: • Not to be taken by mouth.

NONOXYNOL 9 VAGINAL FOAM

Usual adult and adolescent dose:

For use alone—*Because; Delfen; Emko; Koromex Foam; Pre-Fil; Ramses Contraceptive Foam:* Intravaginal, 1 applicatorful inserted just prior to and not longer than one hour prior to each act of intercourse.

For use with a diaphragm—

Because; Emko; Pre-Fil; Ramses Contraceptive Foam: Intravaginal, initially 1 applicatorful placed into vagina and additional spermicide spread along the rim of diaphragm just before insertion of diaphragm and not longer than one hour prior to intercourse. An additional applicatorful should be inserted into vagina just prior to, and not longer than one hour before, each repeat act of intercourse; or

Koromex Foam: Intravaginal, initially 1 applicatorful placed into cup and additional spermicide spread along the rim of diaphragm just before insertion of diaphragm and not longer than one hour prior to intercourse. An additional applicatorful should be inserted into vagina just prior to, and not longer than one hour before, each repeat act of intercourse.

Auxiliary labeling:
- Not to be taken by mouth.
- Shake well before using.

NONOXYNOL 9 VAGINAL GEL

Usual adult and adolescent dose:

For use alone—

Conceptrol Gel: Intravaginal, 1 applicatorful of a 4% gel inserted just prior to and not longer than one hour prior to intercourse; or

Ramses Crystal Clear Gel: Intravaginal, 1 applicatorful of a 5% gel inserted just prior to each act of intercourse.

For use with diaphragm—

Koromex Crystal Clear Gel: Intravaginal, initially 2 teaspoonsful of a 2% gel placed into cup and additional spermicide spread along the rim of diaphragm just before insertion of diaphragm and not longer than six hours prior to intercourse. An additional applicatorful should be inserted into vagina just prior to each repeat act of intercourse or if intercourse takes place later than six hours after initial diaphragm placement; or

Ramses Crystal Clear Gel: Intravaginal, initially 1 teaspoonful of a 5% gel placed into cup and additional spermicide spread along the rim of diaphragm just before insertion of diaphragm and not longer than six hours prior to intercourse. An additional applicatorful should be inserted into vagina just prior to each repeat act of intercourse or if intercourse takes place later than six hours after initial diaphragm placement; or

Shur-Seal: Intravaginal, initially contents of 1 packet of 2% gel placed into cup and spread along the rim of diaphragm just before insertion of diaphragm and intercourse. The contents of an additional packet should be inserted into vagina just prior to each repeat act of intercourse. Applicator not provided for vaginal application; contents of packet are to be inserted vaginally by placing contents on 1 or 2 fingers and deposited on the outer surface of diaphragm.

Auxiliary labeling: • Not to be taken by mouth.

NONOXYNOL 9 VAGINAL JELLY

Usual adult and adolescent dose:

For use alone—

Gynol II Extra Strength Contraceptive Jelly; Koromex Jelly: Intravaginal, 1 applicatorful of a 3% jelly inserted just prior to, and not longer than one hour prior to, each act of intercourse; or

Ramses Contraceptive Vaginal Jelly: Intravaginal, 1 applicatorful of a 5% jelly inserted just prior to each act of intercourse.

For use with diaphragm—

Gynol II Extra Strength Contraceptive Jelly: Intravaginal, initially 1 applicatorful (one teaspoonful) of a 3% jelly placed into cup and additional spermicide spread along the rim of diaphragm just before insertion of diaphragm and not longer than six hours prior to intercourse. An additional applicatorful should be inserted into vagina just prior to each repeat act of intercourse or if intercourse occurs later than six hours after initial diaphragm placement; or

Gynol II Original Formula Contraceptive Jelly: Intravaginal, initially 1 applicatorful (approximately 1 teaspoonful) of a 2% jelly placed into cup and additional spermicide spread along the rim of diaphragm just before insertion of diaphragm and not longer than six hours prior to intercourse. An additional applicatorful should be inserted into vagina just prior to each repeat act of intercourse or if intercourse occurs later than six hours after initial diaphragm placement; or

Koromex Jelly: Intravaginal, initially 2 teaspoonsful of a 3% jelly placed into cup and additional spermicide spread along the rim of diaphragm just before insertion of diaphragm and not longer than six hours prior to intercourse. An additional applicatorful should be inserted into vagina just prior to each repeat act of intercourse or if intercourse occurs later than six hours after initial diaphragm placement.

Auxiliary labeling: • Not to be taken by mouth.

NONOXYNOL 9 VAGINAL SPONGE

Usual adult and adolescent dose: For use alone—*Today:* Intravaginal, 1 sponge inserted not longer than twenty-four hours prior to intercourse.

NONOXYNOL 9 VAGINAL SUPPOSITORIES

Usual adult and adolescent dose:

For use alone—

Conceptrol Contraceptive Inserts; Encare: Intravaginal, 1 suppository inserted at least ten minutes, and not longer than one hour, prior to each act of intercourse; or

Semicid: Intravaginal, 1 suppository inserted at least fifteen minutes, and not longer than one hour, prior to each act of intercourse.

For use with diaphragm—

Encare: Intravaginal, one suppository inserted at least ten minutes, and not longer than one hour, prior to each act of intercourse after initial insertion of diaphragm with spermicide or if intercourse takes place later than six hours after diaphragm placement; or

Semicid: Intravaginal, one suppository inserted at least fifteen minutes, and not longer than one hour, prior to each act of intercourse after initial insertion of diaphragm with spermicide or if intercourse takes place later than six hours after diaphragm placement.

Auxiliary labeling: • Not to be taken by mouth.

OCTOXYNOL 9

Vaginal Dosage Forms

OCTOXYNOL 9 VAGINAL CREAM

Usual adult and adolescent dose: For use with a diaphragm—*Koromex Cream:* Intravaginal, initially 2 teaspoonsful placed into cup and additional spermicide spread along the rim of diaphragm just before insertion of diaphragm and not longer than six hours prior to intercourse. An additional applicatorful should be inserted into vagina just prior to each repeat act of intercourse or if intercourse occurs later than six hours after initial diaphragm placement.

Auxiliary labeling: • Not to be taken by mouth.

OCTOXYNOL 9 VAGINAL JELLY

Usual adult and adolescent dose: For use with a diaphragm—*Ortho-Gynol:* Intravaginal, initially 1 applicatorful (approximately 1 teaspoonful) placed into cup and additional spermicide spread along the rim of diaphragm just before insertion of diaphragm and not longer than six hours prior to intercourse. An additional applicatorful should be inserted into vagina just prior to each repeat act of intercourse or if intercourse occurs later than six hours after initial diaphragm placement.

Auxiliary labeling: • Not to be taken by mouth.

SUCRALFATE   Oral-Local

Some commonly used *brand names* are:

In the U.S.—*Carafate*
In Canada—*Sulcrate*

ORAL
Sucralfate Oral Suspension*
In Canada—*Sulcrate*
Sucralfate Tablets
In the U.S.—*Carafate*
In Canada—*Sulcrate*

---

*Not commercially available in the U.S.

Category: Antiulcer agent; gastric mucosa protectant.

Indications

Note: Bracketed information in the *Indications* section refers to uses not included in U.S. product labeling.

Accepted
Ulcer, duodenal (treatment)—Sucralfate is indicated in the short-term (up to 8 weeks) treatment of duodenal ulcer.

Ulcer, duodenal (prophylaxis)—Sucralfate is used in the prevention of duodenal ulcer recurrence.

[Ulcer, gastric (treatment)]—Sucralfate is used for the short-term treatment of benign gastric ulcer.

[Arthritis, rheumatoid (treatment adjunct)][1]—Sucralfate is used for the relief of gastrointestinal symptoms associated with the use of nonsteroidal anti-inflammatory drugs in the treatment of rheumatoid arthritis.

[Stress-related mucosal damage (prophylaxis and treatment)][1]—Sucralfate is used to prevent and treat gastrointestinal, stress-induced ulceration and bleeding, especially in intensive care patients.

[Reflux, gastroesophageal (treatment)]—Sucralfate is used in the treatment of gastroesophageal reflux disease.

---

[1]Not included in Canadian product labeling.

Pharmacology

Mechanism of action/Effect: Exact mechanism of action is not known; however, sucralfate is thought to form an ulcer-adherent complex with proteinaceous exudate, such as albumin and fibrinogen, at the ulcer site, protecting it against further acid attack. To a lesser extent, sucralfate forms a viscous, adhesive barrier on the surface of intact mucosa of the stomach and duodenum. Sucralfate also inhibits pepsin activity and has been found to bind bile salts *in vitro*. Recent information suggests that sucralfate may increase the production of prostaglandin E_2 and gastric mucus.

Precautions to Consider

Geriatrics
Although adequate and well-controlled studies on the relationship of age to the effects of sucralfate have not been performed in the geriatric population, no geriatrics-specific problems have been documented to date.

Drug interactions and/or related problems
The following drug interactions and/or related problems have been selected on the basis of their potential clinical significance (possible mechanism in parentheses where appropriate)—not necessarily inclusive (» = major clinical significance):

Note: Combinations containing any of the following medications, depending on the amount present, may also interact with this medication.

Aluminum-containing medications, such as:
Antacids
Antidiarrheals
Aspirin, buffered with aluminum
Vaginal douches
(concurrent use with sucralfate in patients with renal failure may cause aluminum toxicity)

Antacids
(concurrent use with antacids in the treatment of duodenal ulcer may be indicated for the relief of pain; however, simultaneous administration is not recommended since antacids may interfere with binding of sucralfate to the mucosa; patient should be advised not to take antacids within $^1/_2$ hour before or after sucralfate)

Cimetidine or
Ranitidine
(concurrent use with sucralfate may decrease the absorption of cimetidine or ranitidine; patients should be advised to take cimetidine or ranitidine 2 hours before sucralfate)

» Ciprofloxacin or
» Norfloxacin or
» Ofloxacin
(concurrent use with sucralfate may decrease the absorption of ciprofloxacin, norfloxacin, or ofloxacin by chelation, resulting in lower serum and urine concentrations of these 3 medicines; patients should be advised to take ciprofloxacin, norfloxacin, or ofloxacin 2 to 3 hours before sucralfate)

» Digoxin or
» Theophylline
(concurrent use with sucralfate may decrease the absorption of digoxin or theophylline; patients should be advised not to take sucralfate within 2 hours of digoxin or theophylline)
» Phenytoin
(concurrent use with sucralfate may decrease the absorption of phenytoin enough to reduce the steady-state blood concentrations of phenytoin with a resultant loss of seizure control; patients should be advised not to take sucralfate within 2 hours of phenytoin)
Tetracyclines, oral
(absorption may be decreased when oral tetracyclines are used concurrently with sucralfate, since sucralfate is an aluminum salt and may form nonabsorbable complexes with tetracycline; patients should be advised not to take sucralfate within 2 hours of tetracyclines)

Contraindications/Medical problems

The contraindications/medical problems included have been selected on the basis of their potential clinical significance (reasons given in parentheses where appropriate)—not necessarily inclusive (» = major clinical significance).

Risk-benefits should be considered when the following medical problems exists:

Dysphagia or
Gastrointestinal tract obstruction disease
(patients with these conditions may be at risk of bezoar formation because of the protein-binding properties of sucralfate)
Renal failure
(absorption of the aluminum in sucralfate in patients with renal failure may cause aluminum toxicity, especially with long-term use)
Sensitivity to sucralfate

Side/Adverse Effects

Note: Occurrence of drowsiness progressing to seizures in patients with renal failure may indicate aluminum toxicity.

The following side/adverse effects have been selected on the basis of their potential clinical significance (possible signs and symptoms in parentheses where appropriate)—not necessarily inclusive:

Those indicating need for medical attention only if they continue or are bothersome
Incidence more frequent
   Constipation
Incidence less frequent or rare
   Backache; diarrhea; dizziness or lightheadedness; drowsiness; dryness of mouth; indigestion; nausea; skin rash, hives, or itching; stomach cramps or pain

Patient Consultation

In providing consultation, consider emphasizing the following selected information (» = major clinical significance):

Before using this medication
» Conditions affecting use, especially:
   Sensitivity to sucralfate
   Other medications, especially ciprofloxacin, digoxin, norfloxacin, ofloxacin, phenytoin, and theophylline

Proper use of this medication
   Taking on empty stomach 1 hour before meals and at bedtime
   Compliance with full course of therapy and keeping appointments for check-ups
   Missed dose: Taking as soon as possible; not taking if almost time for next dose; not doubling doses
» Proper storage

Precautions while using this medication
» Not taking antacids within ½ hour before or after sucralfate

Side/adverse effects
   Signs of potential side effects, especially aluminum toxicity

General Dosing Information

Sucralfate should be taken with water on an empty stomach, 1 hour before each meal and at bedtime, for maximum effectiveness.

Short-term treatment with sucralfate may result in complete healing of the ulcer but it may not alter the posthealing frequency or severity of duodenal ulceration.

If required, antacids may be administered ½ hour before or after sucralfate for the relief of pain.

Even though the symptoms of duodenal ulcers may subside, unless healing has been documented by x-ray or endoscopic examination, therapy should continue for at least 4 to 8 weeks.

Use of sucralfate in a nasogastric feeding tube has resulted in bezoar formation with other medications or enteral feedings, due to the protein-binding properties of sucralfate.

Oral Dosage Forms

Note: Bracketed uses in the *Dosage Forms* section refer to categories of use and/or indications that are not included in U.S. product labeling.

SUCRALFATE ORAL SUSPENSION

Usual adult and adolescent dose:
   Duodenal ulcer (treatment)—Oral, 1 gram four times a day one hour before each meal and at bedtime; or 2 grams two times a day on waking and at bedtime on an empty stomach.
   [Gastroesophageal reflux]—Oral, 1 gram four times a day one hour before each meal and at bedtime.

Auxiliary labeling: • Shake well.

SUCRALFATE TABLETS

Usual adult and adolescent dose:
   Duodenal ulcer (treatment)—Oral, 1 gram four times a day one hour before each meal and at bedtime.
   Duodenal ulcer (prophylaxis)—Oral, 1 gram two times a day on an empty stomach.
   [Gastric ulcer (treatment)] or
   [Gastroesophageal reflux]—Oral, 1 gram four times a day one hour before each meal and at bedtime.

Auxiliary labeling: • Continue medicine for full time of treatment.

SULFAMETHOXAZOLE AND TRIMETHOPRIM   Systemic

Some commonly used *brand names* are:

In the U.S.—

Bactrim	*Sulfatrim*
Bactrim DS	*Sulfatrim DS*
Cotrim	*Sulfoxaprim*
Cotrim DS	*Sulfoxaprim DS*
Septra	*Triazole*
Septra DS	*Triazole DS*
Sulfamethoprim	*Trimeth-Sulfa*
Sulfamethoprim DS	*Trisulfam*
Sulfaprim	*Uroplus DS*
Sulfaprim DS	*Uroplus SS*

In Canada—

Apo-Sulfatrim	*Nu-Cotrimox*
Apo-Sulfatrim DS	*Nu-Cotrimox DS*
Bactrim	*Roubac*
Bactrim DS	*Septra*
Novotrimel	*Septra DS*
Novotrimel DS	

Other commonly used names are cotrimoxazole and SMZ-TMP.

ORAL

Sulfamethoxazole and Trimethoprim Oral Suspension USP
    In the U.S.—*Bactrim; Cotrim; Septra; Sulfaprim; Sulfatrim; Trimeth-Sulfa; Trisulfam;* GENERIC
    In Canada—*Apo-Sulfatrim; Bactrim; Novotrimel; Nu-Cotrimox; Septra*

Sulfamethoxazole and Trimethoprim Tablets USP
    In the U.S.—*Bactrim; Bactrim DS; Cotrim; Cotrim DS; Septra; Septra DS; Sulfamethoprim; Sulfamethoprim DS; Sulfaprim DS; Sulfatrim; Sulfatrim DS; Sulfoxaprim; Sulfoxaprim DS; Triazole; Triazole DS; Uroplus DS; Uroplus SS;* GENERIC
    In Canada—*Apo-Sulfatrim; Apo-Sulfatrim DS; Bactrim; Bactrim DS; Novotrimel; Novotrimel DS; Nu-Cotrimox; Nu-Cotrimox DS; Roubac; Septra; Septra DS*

PARENTERAL

Sulfamethoxazole and Trimethoprim Concentrate for Injection USP
    In the U.S.—*Bactrim; Septra; Sulfamethoprim;* GENERIC
    In Canada—*Bactrim; Septra*

Category: Antibacterial (systemic); antiprotozoal.

Indications

Note: Bracketed information in the *Indications* section refers to uses not included in U.S. product labeling.

Accepted

Bronchitis (treatment)—Sulfamethoxazole and trimethoprim combination is indicated in adults in the treatment of acute exacerbations of chronic bronchitis caused by *Haemophilus influenzae* or *Streptococcus pneumoniae*.

Enterocolitis, *Shigella* species (treatment)—Sulfamethoxazole and trimethoprim combination is indicated in the treatment of enterocolitis caused by *Shigella flexneri* and *S. sonnei*.

Otitis media, acute (treatment)—Sulfamethoxazole and trimethoprim combination is indicated in children in the treatment of acute otitis media caused by *H. influenzae* or *S. pneumoniae*.

Pneumonia, *Pneumocystis carinii* (treatment)—Sulfamethoxazole and trimethoprim combination is indicated as a primary agent in the treatment of *Pneumocystis carinii* pneumonia (PCP) in immunocompromised patients, including patients with acquired immunodeficiency syndrome (AIDS). Pentamidine is considered an alternative agent for PCP.

Traveler's diarrhea (treatment)—Sulfamethoxazole and trimethoprim combination is indicated in the treatment of traveler's diarrhea caused by enterotoxigenic *Escherichia coli* and *Shigella* species.

Urinary tract infections, bacterial (treatment)—Sulfamethoxazole and trimethoprim combination is indicated in the treatment of urinary tract infections caused by *E. coli, Klebsiella* species, *Enterobacter* species, *P. mirabilis, P. vulgaris,* and *Morganella morganii*.

[Biliary tract infections (treatment)]—Sulfamethoxazole and trimethoprim combination is used in the treatment of biliary tract infections.

[Bone and joint infections (treatment)][1]—Sulfamethoxazole and trimethoprim combination is used in the treatment of bone and joint infections caused by sensitive organisms.

[Chancroid (treatment)][1]—Sulfamethoxazole and trimethoprim combination is used in the treatment of chancroid.

[Chlamydial infections (treatment)][1]—Sulfamethoxazole and trimethoprim combination is used in the treatment of chlamydial infections.

[Endocarditis, bacterial (treatment)][1]—Sulfamethoxazole and trimethoprim combination is used in the treatment of bacterial endocarditis.

[Gonorrhea (treatment)]—Sulfamethoxazole and trimethoprim combination is used in the treatment of gonorrhea.

[Granuloma inguinale (treatment)][1]—Sulfamethoxazole and trimethoprim combination is used in the treatment of granuloma inguinale.

[Intra-abdominal infections (treatment)]—Sulfamethoxazole and trimethoprim combination is used in the treatment of intra-abdominal infections.

[Isosporiasis (prophylaxis and treatment)][1]—Sulfamethoxazole and trimethoprim combination is used in the prophylaxis and treatment of isosporiasis caused by *Isospora belli*.

[Lymphogranuloma venereum (treatment)][1]—Sulfamethoxazole and trimethoprim combination is used in the treatment of lymphogranuloma venereum.

[Meningitis (treatment)]—Sulfamethoxazole and trimethoprim combination is used in the treatment of meningitis caused by susceptible organisms.

[Meningococcal carriers (treatment)][1]—Sulfamethoxazole and trimethoprim combination is used in the treatment of meningococcal carriers.

[Nocardiosis (treatment)][1]—Sulfamethoxazole and trimethoprim combination is used in the treatment of nocardiosis.

[Paracoccidioidomycosis (treatment)][1]—Sulfamethoxazole and trimethoprim combination is used in the treatment of paracoccidioidomycosis.

[Paratyphoid fever (treatment)][1]; or
[Typhoid fever (treatment)][1]—Sulfamethoxazole and trimethoprim combination is used in the treatment of paratyphoid and typhoid fever when chloramphenicol or ampicillin is contraindicated.

[Pneumonia, *Pneumocystis carinii* (PCP) (prophylaxis)][1]—Sulfamethoxazole and trimethoprim combination is used in both secondary prophylaxis (patients who have already had at least one episode of PCP), and primary prophylaxis (HIV-infected adults with a CD4 lymphocyte count less than or equal to 200 cells per cubic millimeter and/or less than 20% of total lymphocytes) of PCP.

Sulfamethoxazole and trimethoprim combination is used in the prophylaxis of PCP in children with cancer who are receiving chemotherapy and in HIV-infected children. Prophylaxis in HIV-infected children 1 month of age or older should be initiated if the patient has had at least one episode of PCP or if the CD4 lymphocyte count is less than 20% of total lymphocytes. However, the indications for prophylaxis in other HIV-infected children is complex, depending on the age of the child, the CD4 cell count, and their infection status. Please refer to contemporary guidelines (See *Selected Bibliography*).

[Sinusitis (treatment)][1]—Sulfamethoxazole and trimethoprim combination is used in the treatment of sinusitis.

[Septicemia, bacterial (treatment)]—Sulfamethoxazole and trimethoprim combination is used in the treatment of bacterial septicemia.

[Skin and soft tissue infections (treatment)]—Sulfamethoxazole and trimethoprim combination is used in the treatment of skin and soft tissue infections, including burn wound infections.

[Urinary tract infections, bacterial (prophylaxis)][1]—Sulfamethoxazole and trimethoprim combination is used in the prophylaxis of bacterial urinary tract infections.

Not all species or strains of a particular organism may be susceptible to sulfamethoxazole and trimethoprim combination.

Unaccepted

Sulfamethoxazole and trimethoprim combination is not indicated for prophylaxis or prolonged therapy in otitis media.

Sulfamethoxazole and trimethoprim combination should not be used in the treatment of group A beta-hemolytic streptococcal tonsillopharyngitis since it may not eradicate streptococci and therefore may not prevent sequelae such as rheumatic fever.

---

[1]Not included in Canadian product labeling.

Pharmacology

Mechanism of action/Effect:

Sulfamethoxazole—Sulfamethoxazole is a broad-spectrum, bacteriostatic anti-infective. It is a structural analog of para-aminobenzoic acid (PABA) and competitively inhibits a bacterial enzyme, dihydropteroate synthetase, that is responsible for incorporation of PABA into dihydrofolic acid. This blocks the synthesis of dihydrofolic acid and decreases the amount of metabolically active tetrahydrofolic acid, a cofactor for the synthesis of purines, thymidine, and DNA.

Susceptible bacteria are those which must synthesize folic acid. The action of sulfamethoxazole is antagonized by PABA and its derivatives (e.g., procaine and tetracaine) and by the presence of pus or tissue breakdown products, which provide the necessary components for bacterial growth.

Trimethoprim—Trimethoprim is a bacteriostatic lipophilic weak base structurally related to pyrimethamine. It binds to and reversibly inhibits the bacterial enzyme dihydrofolate reductase, selectively blocking conversion of dihydrofolic acid to its functional form, tetrahydrofolic acid. This depletes folate, an essential cofactor in the biosynthesis of nucleic acids, resulting in interference with bacterial nucleic acid and protein production. Bacterial dihydrofolate reductase is approximately 50,000 to 60,000 times more tightly bound by trimethoprim than is the corresponding mammalian enzyme.

Trimethoprim exerts its effect at a step in the folate biosynthesis immediately subsequent to the one at which sulfonamides exert their effect. When trimethoprim is administered concurrently with sulfonamides, synergism occurs, which is attributed to inhibition of tetrahydrofolate production at 2 sequential steps in its biosynthesis.

Precautions to Consider

Cross-sensitivity and/or related problems

Patients allergic to one sulfonamide may be allergic to other sulfonamides also.

Patients allergic to furosemide, thiazide diuretics, sulfonylureas, or carbonic anhydrase inhibitors may be allergic to sulfonamides also.

Geriatrics

Elderly patients may be at increased risk of severe side/adverse effects. Severe skin reactions, generalized bone marrow depression, and decreased platelet count (with or without purpura) are the most frequently reported severe side/adverse effects in the elderly. An increased incidence of thrombocytopenia with purpura has been reported in elderly patients who are receiving diuretics, primarily thiazides, concurrently with sulfamethoxazole and trimethoprim combination.

Dental

The leukopenic and thrombocytopenic effects of sulfonamides may result in an increased incidence of certain microbial infections, delayed healing, and gingival bleeding. If leukopenia or thrombocytopenia occurs, dental work should be deferred until blood counts have returned to normal. Patients should be instructed in proper oral hygiene, including caution in use of regular toothbrushes, dental floss, and toothpicks.

Drug interactions and/or related problems

The following drug interactions and/or related problems have been selected on the basis of their potential clinical significance (possible mechanism in parentheses where appropriate)—not necessarily inclusive (» = major clinical significance):

Note: Combinations containing any of the following medications, depending on the amount present, may also interact with this medication.

» Anticoagulants, coumarin- or indandione-derivative, or
» Anticonvulsants, hydantoin, or
» Antidiabetic agents, oral
    (these medications may be displaced from protein binding sites and/or their metabolism may be inhibited by some sulfonamides, resulting in increased or prolonged effects and/or toxicity; dosage adjustments may be necessary during and after sulfonamide therapy)

Bone marrow depressants
    (concurrent use of bone marrow depressants with sulfonamides may increase the leukopenic and/or thrombocytopenic effects; if concurrent use is required, close observation for myelotoxic effects should be considered)

Contraceptives, estrogen-containing, oral
    (concurrent long-term use of sulfonamides may result in reduced contraceptive reliability and increased incidence of breakthrough bleeding)

Cyclosporine
    (concurrent use with sulfonamides may increase the metabolism of cyclosporine, resulting in decreased plasma concentrations and potential transplant rejection; there may also be additive nephrotoxicity; plasma cyclosporine concentrations and renal function should be monitored)

Dapsone
    (concurrent use with trimethoprim will usually increase the plasma concentrations of both dapsone and trimethoprim, possibly due to an inhibition in dapsone metabolism, and/or competition for renal secretion between the 2 medications; increased serum dapsone concentrations may increase the number and severity of side effects, especially methemoglobinemia)

Folate antagonists, other
    (concurrent use with trimethoprim or use of trimethoprim between courses of other folic acid antagonists is not recommended because of the possibility of megaloblastic anemia)

» Hemolytics, other
    (concurrent use with sulfonamides may increase the potential for toxic side effects)

» Hepatotoxic medications, other
    (concurrent use with sulfonamides may result in an increased incidence of hepatotoxicity; patients, especially those on prolonged administration or those with a history of liver disease, should be carefully monitored)

» Methenamine
(in acid urine, methenamine breaks down into formaldehyde, which may form an insoluble precipitate with certain sulfonamides and may also increase the danger of crystalluria; concurrent use is not recommended)

» Methotrexate or
Phenylbutazone or
Sulfinpyrazone
(the effects of these medications may be potentiated during concurrent use with sulfonamides because of displacement from plasma protein binding sites)

Rifampin
(concurrent use may significantly increase the elimination and shorten the elimination half-life of trimethoprim)

Contraindications/Medical problems

The contraindications/medical problems included have been selected on the basis of their potential clinical significance (reasons given in parentheses where appropriate)—not necessarily inclusive (» = major clinical significance).

Except under special circumstances, this medication should not be used when the following medical problem exists:

» Allergy to sulfonamides, furosemide, thiazide diuretics, sulfonylureas, carbonic anhydrase inhibitors, or trimethoprim

Risk-benefit should be considered when the following medical problems exist:

» Blood dyscrasias or
» Megaloblastic anemia due to folate deficiency
(trimethoprim may cause folic acid deficiency; sulfonamides and trimethoprim may cause blood dyscrasias)
» Glucose-6-phosphate dehydrogenase (G6PD) deficiency
(hemolysis may occur)
» Hepatic function impairment
(sulfonamides and trimethoprim are metabolized in the liver; may cause fulminant hepatic necrosis)
» Porphyria
(sulfonamides may precipitate an acute attack of porphyria)
» Renal function impairment
(sulfonamides and trimethoprim are renally excreted)

Side/Adverse Effects

Note: Fatalities have occurred, although rarely, due to severe reactions such as Stevens-Johnson syndrome, toxic epidermal necrolysis, fulminant hepatic necrosis, agranulocytosis, aplastic anemia, and other blood dyscrasias. Therapy should be discontinued at the first appearance of skin rash or any serious side/adverse effects or if signs of folic acid deficiency occur.

Patients with acquired immunodeficiency syndrome (AIDS) may have a greater incidence of side/adverse effects, especially rash, fever, and leukopenia, than do non-AIDS patients.

The following side/adverse effects have been selected on the basis of their potential clinical significance (possible signs and symptoms in parentheses where appropriate)—not necessarily inclusive:

Those indicating need for medical attention
Incidence more frequent
Hypersensitivity (fever, itching, skin rash); *photosensitivity* (increased sensitivity of skin to sunlight)
Incidence less frequent
Blood dyscrasias (fever and sore throat, pale skin, unusual bleeding or bruising, unusual tiredness or weakness); *hepatitis* (yellow eyes or skin); *Stevens-Johnson syndrome* (aching joints and muscles; redness, blistering, peeling, or loosening of skin; unusual tiredness or weakness); *toxic epidermal necrolysis* (difficulty in swallowing; redness, blistering, peeling, or loosening of skin)

Incidence rare
Crystalluria or hematuria (blood in urine, lower back pain, pain or burning while urinating); *goiter or thyroid function disturbance* (swelling of front part of neck); *interstitial nephritis or tubular necrosis* (greatly increased or decreased frequency of urination or amount of urine, increased thirst, loss of appetite, nausea, vomiting); *methemoglobinemia* (bluish fingernails, lips, or skin; difficult breathing; pale skin; sore throat and fever; unusual bleeding or bruising; unusual tiredness or weakness)

Those indicating need for medical attention only if they continue or are bothersome
Incidence more frequent
Dizziness; headache; gastrointestinal disturbances (diarrhea, loss of appetite, nausea or vomiting)

Patient Consultation

In providing consultation, consider emphasizing the following selected information (» = major clinical significance):

Before using this medication
» Conditions affecting use, especially:
Allergy to sulfonamides, furosemide, thiazide diuretics, sulfonylureas, carbonic anhydrase inhibitors, or trimethoprim
Pregnancy—Sulfamethoxazole and trimethoprim cross the placenta; trimethoprim may interfere with folic acid metabolism
Breast-feeding—Sulfamethoxazole and trimethoprim are excreted in breast milk; sulfamethoxazole may cause kernicterus in nursing infants; trimethoprim may interfere with folic acid metabolism
Use in children—Sulfamethoxazole and trimethoprim combination is contraindicated in infants up to 2 months of age for most indications since sulfonamides may cause kernicterus in neonates; the fixed ratio (1:5) combination of sulfamethoxazole and trimethoprim is inappropriate in neonates and older infants because of the altered disposition of sulfamethoxazole and trimethoprim in these patients
Use in the elderly—Elderly patients may be at increased risk of severe side/adverse effects
Other medications, especially coumarin- or indandione-derivative anticoagulants, hydantoin anticonvulsants, oral antidiabetic agents, other hemolytics, other hepatotoxic medications, or methotrexate
Other medical problems, especially blood dyscrasias, G6PD deficiency, hepatic function impairment, megaloblastic anemia due to folic acid deficiency, porphyria, and renal function impairment

Proper use of this medication
» Maintaining adequate fluid intake
Proper administration technique for oral liquids
» Compliance with full course of therapy
» Importance of not missing doses and taking at evenly spaced times
Missed dose: Taking as soon as possible; not taking if almost time for next dose; not doubling doses
» Proper storage

Precautions while using this medication
» Regular visits to physician to check blood counts
Checking with physician if no improvement within a few days
Using caution in use of regular toothbrushes, dental floss, and toothpicks; deferring dental work until blood counts have returned to normal; checking with physician or dentist concerning proper oral hygiene
» Possible skin photosensitivity; avoiding unprotected exposure to sun; using protective clothing; using a sun block product that includes protection against both UVA-caused photosensitivity reactions and UVB-caused sunburn reactions; avoiding use of sunlamp, tanning bed, or tanning booth
» Caution if dizziness occurs

Side/adverse effects

Severe skin problems and blood problems may be more likely to occur in elderly patients who are taking sulfamethoxazole and trimethoprim combination, especially if diuretics are being taken concurrently

Signs of potential side effects, especially blood dyscrasias, crystalluria, goiter, hematuria, hepatitis, hypersensitivity, interstitial nephritis, methemoglobinemia, photosensitivity, Stevens-Johnson syndrome, thyroid function disturbance, toxic epidermal necrolysis, and tubular necrosis

General Dosing Information

Fluid intake should be sufficient to maintain urine output of at least 1200 to 1500 mL per day in adults.

Therapy should be continued for at least 10 to 14 days in acute exacerbations of chronic bronchitis; as single dose therapy or for 3 days in urinary tract infections; for 5 days in shigellosis; for 10 days in acute otitis media in children; and for 21 days in *Pneumocystis carinii* pneumonia. Sulfamethoxazole and trimethoprim combination may also be given for 1 or 2 days or as single-dose therapy for lower urinary tract infections. Therapy should be continued for 14 days or more in upper urinary tract infections.

Adults and children with impaired renal function require a reduction in dose, based on creatinine clearance. Creatinine clearance (in mL per minute) may be calculated as follows:

Adult males: Creatinine clearance

$$= \frac{(140 - age) \times (body\ weight\ in\ kg)}{72 \times patient's\ serum\ creatinine\ concentration}$$

Adult females: Creatinine clearance

$$= \frac{(140 - age) \times (body\ weight\ in\ kg)}{72 \times patient's\ serum\ creatinine\ concentration} \times 0.85$$

Creatinine clearance may also be calculated in SI units (as mL per second) as follows:

Adult males: Creatinine clearance

$$= \frac{(140 - age) \times (ideal\ body\ weight\ in\ kg)}{50 \times serum\ creatinine\ (micromoles\ per\ L)}$$

Adult females: Creatinine clearance

$$= \frac{(140 - age) \times (ideal\ body\ weight\ in\ kg)}{50 \times serum\ creatinine\ (micromoles\ per\ L)} \times 0.85$$

Adults and children with renal function impairment require a reduction in dose as follows:

Creatinine Clearance (mL/min)/(mL/sec)	Dose
>30/(0.50)	See *Usual adult and adolescent dose*
15–30/(0.25–0.50)	¹/₂ the *Usual adult and adolescent dose*
<15/(0.25)	Use is not recommended

Oral Dosage Forms

SULFAMETHOXAZOLE AND TRIMETHOPRIM ORAL SUSPENSION USP

Usual adult and adolescent dose:

Antibacterial (systemic)—Oral, 160 mg of trimethoprim and 800 mg of sulfamethoxazole every twelve hours.

Pneumocystis carinii pneumonia:

Treatment—Oral, 3.75 to 5 mg of trimethoprim and 18.75 to 25 mg of sulfamethoxazole per kg of body weight every six hours.

[Prophylaxis][1]—Oral, 160 mg of trimethoprim and 800 mg of sulfamethoxazole once daily.

Note: Studies have found that less frequent dosing with sulfamethoxazole and trimethoprim combination was also effective and well tolerated in HIV-infected patients. The dose used was 160 mg of trimethoprim and 800 mg of sulfamethoxazole three times a week (e.g., Monday, Wednesday, Friday), without leucovorin.

Usual adult prescribing limits: Up to 640 mg of trimethoprim and 3.2 grams of sulfamethoxazole daily.

Auxiliary labeling:

- Shake well.
- Take with a full glass of water.
- May cause dizziness.
- Avoid too much sun or use of sunlamp.
- Continue medicine for full time of treatment.

SULFAMETHOXAZOLE AND TRIMETHOPRIM TABLETS USP

Usual adult and adolescent dose: See *Sulfamethoxazole and Trimethoprim Oral Suspension.*

Usual adult prescribing limits: See *Sulfamethoxazole and Trimethoprim Oral Suspension.*

Auxiliary labeling:

- Take with a full glass of water.
- May cause dizziness.
- Avoid too much sun or use of sunlamp.
- Continue medicine for full time of treatment.

Parenteral Dosage Forms

SULFAMETHOXAZOLE AND TRIMETHOPRIM CONCENTRATE FOR INJECTION USP

Usual adult and adolescent dose:

Antibacterial (systemic)—Intravenous infusion, 2 to 2.5 mg of trimethoprim and 10 to 12.5 mg of sulfamethoxazole per kg of body weight every six hours; 2.7 to 3.3 mg of trimethoprim and 13.3 to 16.7 mg of sulfamethoxazole per kg of body weight every eight hours; or 4 to 5 mg of trimethoprim and 20 to 25 mg of sulfamethoxazole per kg of body weight every twelve hours.

Pneumocystis carinii pneumonia: Intravenous infusion, 3.75 to 5 mg of trimethoprim and 18.75 to 25 mg of sulfamethoxazole per kg of body weight every six hours; or 5.0 to 6.7 mg of trimethoprim and 25 to 33.3 mg of sulfamethoxazole per kg of body weight every eight hours.

Additional information:

Do not administer rapidly or by bolus injection.

Do not administer intramuscularly.

SULFASALAZINE   Systemic

Some commonly used *brand names* are:
In the U.S.—
Azulfidine   Azulfidine EN-Tabs
In Canada—
PMS Sulfasalazine   Salazopyrin EN-Tabs
PMS Sulfasalazine E.C.   S.A.S.-500
Salazopyrin   S.A.S. Enteric-500

Other commonly used names are salazosulfapyridine and salicylazosulfapyridine.

ORAL

Sulfasalazine Oral Suspension†
    In the U.S.—*Azulfidine*
Sulfasalazine Tablets USP
    In the U.S.—*Azulfidine*; GENERIC
    In Canada—*PMS Sulfasalazine; Salazopyrin; S.A.S.-500*
Sulfasalazine Tablets USP (Enteric-coated)
    In the U.S.—*Azulfidine EN-Tabs*; GENERIC
    In Canada—*PMS Sulfasalazine E.C.; Salazopyrin EN-Tabs; S.A.S. Enteric-500*

---

†Not commercially available in Canada.

Category: Bowel disease (inflammatory) suppressant; antirheumatic (disease-modifying).

Indications

Note: Bracketed information in the *Indications* section refers to uses not included in U.S. product labeling.

Accepted
Bowel disease, inflammatory (prophylaxis and treatment)—Sulfasalazine is indicated to treat and to maintain remission of inflammatory bowel disease (e.g., ulcerative colitis or Crohn's disease affecting the colon). It is indicated in the treatment of mild to moderate ulcerative colitis and as adjunctive treatment of severe ulcerative colitis.
[Ankylosing spondylitis (treatment)][1]; or
[Arthritis, rheumatoid (treatment)][1]—Sulfasalazine is used in the treatment of ankylosing spondylitis and rheumatoid arthritis.

---

[1]Not included in Canadian product labeling.

Pharmacology

Mechanism of action/Effect: Bowel disease (inflammatory) suppressant—Uncertain; may be related to sulfasalazine's immunosuppressant effects, which have been observed in animals, its affinity for connective tissue, and/or its relatively high concentrations in serous fluids, the liver, and intestinal wall. Sulfasalazine is considered a vehicle for carrying its principal metabolites to the colon. Unabsorbed sulfasalazine is cleaved in the colon by intestinal bacteria to form sulfapyridine and mesalamine (5-aminosalicylic acid; 5-ASA), both of which may act locally within the gut. Mesalamine (5-ASA), which is different from aminosalicylates used to treat tuberculosis, is thought to be the major active moiety.

Precautions to Consider

Cross-sensitivity and/or related problems
Patients allergic to one sulfonamide may be allergic to other sulfonamides also.

Patients allergic to furosemide, thiazide diuretics, sulfonylureas, carbonic anhydrase inhibitors, or salicylates may be allergic to this medication also.

Geriatrics
No information is available on the relationship of age to the effects of sulfasalazine in geriatric patients.

Dental
The leukopenic and thrombocytopenic effects of sulfasalazine may result in an increased incidence of certain microbial infections, delayed healing, and gingival bleeding. If leukopenia or thrombocytopenia occurs, dental work should be deferred until blood counts have returned to normal. Patients should be instructed in proper oral hygiene, including caution in use of regular toothbrushes, dental floss, and toothpicks.

Drug interactions and/or related problems
The following drug interactions and/or related problems have been selected on the basis of their potential clinical significance (possible mechanism in parentheses where appropriate)—not necessarily inclusive (» = major clinical significance):

Note: Combinations containing any of the following medications, depending on the amount present, may also interact with this medication.

» Anticoagulants, coumarin- or indandione-derivative, or
» Anticonvulsants, hydantoin, or
» Antidiabetic agents, oral
        (may be displaced from protein binding sites and/or metabolism may be inhibited by sulfonamides, resulting in increased or prolonged effects and/or toxicity; dosage adjustments may be necessary during and after sulfonamide therapy)

Bone marrow depressants
        (concurrent use of sulfasalazine with bone marrow depressants may increase the leukopenic and/or thrombocytopenic effects; if concurrent use is required, close observation for myelotoxic effects should be considered)

Digitalis glycosides or
Folic acid
        (sulfasalazine may inhibit absorption and lower the serum concentrations of these medications; folic acid requirements may be increased in patients receiving sulfasalazine; patients taking digitalis glycosides should be monitored closely for evidence of altered digitalis effect)

» Hemolytics, other
        (concurrent use with sulfasalazine may increase the potential for toxic side effects)

» Hepatotoxic medications, other
        (concurrent use with sulfonamides may result in an increased incidence of hepatotoxicity; patients, especially those on prolonged administration or those with a history of liver disease, should be carefully monitored)

» Methotrexate or
Phenylbutazone or
Sulfinpyrazone
        (the effects of these medications may be potentiated during concurrent use with sulfonamides because of displacement from plasma protein binding sites; phenylbutazone and sulfinpyrazone have also been reported to potentiate the effects of sulfonamides)

Contraindications/Medical problems
The contraindications/medical problems included have been selected on the basis of their potential clinical significance (reasons given in parentheses where appropriate)—not necessarily inclusive (» = major clinical significance).

Except under special circumstances, this medication should not be used when the following medical problem exists:

» Allergy to sulfonamides, salicylates, furosemide, thiazide diuretics, sulfonylureas, or carbonic anhydrase inhibitors

Risk-benefit should be considered when the following medical problems exist:

» Blood dyscrasias
  (sulfasalazine may cause agranulocytosis, aplastic anemia, or other blood dyscrasias)
» Glucose-6-phosphate dehydrogenase (G6PD) deficiency
  (sulfasalazine may cause hemolytic anemia in G6PD-deficient patients)
» Hepatic function impairment
  (sulfonamides are metabolized in the liver and may cause hepatitis)
» Porphyria
  (sulfonamides may precipitate an acute attack of porphyria)
» Renal function impairment
  (the metabolite, sulfapyridine, is excreted primarily through the kidneys)

Side/Adverse Effects

Note: Deaths have been reported from hypersensitivity reactions, agranulocytosis, aplastic anemia, other blood dyscrasias, renal and hepatic damage, irreversible neuromuscular and central nervous system (CNS) changes, and fibrosing alveolitis in patients taking sulfasalazine. If toxic or hypersensitivity reactions occur, sulfasalazine should be discontinued immediately.

Oligospermia and infertility, reported to be reversible upon discontinuation of sulfasalazine, have been reported in males taking this medication.

Daily doses of 4 grams or more and total sulfapyridine serum concentrations >50 mcg per mL may be associated with an increased incidence of side/adverse effects.

The following side/adverse effects have been selected on the basis of their potential clinical significance (possible signs and symptoms in parentheses where appropriate)—not necessarily inclusive:

Those indicating need for medical attention
Incidence more frequent
  Headache, continuing; hypersensitivity (fever, itching, skin rash, arthralgia); *photosensitivity* (increased sensitivity of skin to sunlight)
Incidence less frequent
  Blood dyscrasias, specifically agranulocytosis or neutropenia (fever and sore throat), *hemolytic anemia* (back, leg, or stomach pains; loss of appetite; pale skin; unusual tiredness or weakness; fever), *or thrombocytopenia* (unusual bleeding or bruising); *exacerbation of ulcerative colitis* (bloody diarrhea, fever, rash); *hepatitis* (yellow eyes or skin); *Lyell's syndrome* (difficulty in swallowing; redness, blistering, peeling, or loosening of skin)
Incidence rare
  Exacerbation of ulcerative colitis (bloody diarrhea, fever, rash); *interstitial pneumonitis* (cough, difficult breathing, fever); *Stevens-Johnson syndrome* (aching joints and muscles; redness, blistering, peeling, or loosening of skin; unusual tiredness or weakness)

Those indicating need for medical attention only if they continue or are bothersome
Incidence more frequent
  Dizziness; gastrointestinal disturbances (abdominal or stomach pain or upset, diarrhea, loss of appetite, nausea or vomiting)

Those not indicating need for medical attention
Incidence more frequent
  Orange-yellow discoloration of urine or skin

Patient Consultation

In providing consultation, consider emphasizing the following selected information (» = major clinical significance):

Before using this medication
» Conditions affecting use, especially:
    Allergies to sulfonamides, salicylates, furosemide, thiazide diuretics, sulfonylureas, carbonic anhydrase inhibitors
    Pregnancy—Sulfasalazine and sulfapyridine cross the placenta
    Breast-feeding—Sulfasalazine and sulfapyridine are excreted in breast milk
    Use in children—Use is contraindicated in infants and children up to 2 years of age since sulfonamides may cause kernicterus
    Other medications, especially coumarin- or indandione-derivative anticoagulants, hydantoin anticonvulsants, oral antidiabetic agents, hemolytics, hepatotoxic medications, and methotrexate
    Other medical problems, especially blood dyscrasias, G6PD deficiency, hepatic function impairment, porphyria, and renal function impairment

Proper use of this medication
» Not giving to infants up to 2 years of age; sulfasalazine may cause kernicterus
    Taking after meals or with food to lessen gastrointestinal irritation
» Maintaining adequate fluid intake
    Proper administration technique for enteric-coated tablets
» Compliance with full course of therapy
    Missed dose: Taking as soon as possible; not taking if almost time for next dose; not doubling doses
» Proper storage

Precautions while using this medication
» Regular visits to physician to check blood counts in patients on long-term therapy
    Checking with physician if no improvement within a month or 2
    Using caution in use of regular toothbrushes, dental floss, and toothpicks; deferring dental work until blood counts have returned to normal; checking with physician or dentist concerning proper oral hygiene
» Possible photosensitivity reactions
» Caution if dizziness occurs
    Possible interference with bentiromide diagnostic test for pancreatic function

Side/adverse effects
    Signs of potential side effects, especially blood dyscrasias, headache (continuing), hepatitis, interstitial pneumonitis, hypersensitivity, Lyell's syndrome, photosensitivity, Stevens-Johnson syndrome, and exacerbation of ulcerative colitis
    Orange-yellow discoloration of alkaline urine or skin may be alarming to patient although medically insignificant

General Dosing Information

Fluid intake should be sufficient to maintain urine output of at least 1200 to 1500 mL per day in adults.

Sulfasalazine should preferably be taken after meals or with food. Also, when sulfasalazine is being taken for inflammatory bowel disease, spreading out the total daily dose more evenly (e.g., up to hourly doses) may help. In some patients it may be necessary to initiate therapy with smaller doses (e.g., 1 to 2 grams daily) to lessen gastrointestinal irritation.

When endoscopic examination confirms satisfactory improvement, dosage may be reduced to maintenance level.

If diarrhea recurs, dosage should be increased to previously effective level.

Intervals between the bedtime dose and the morning dose should not exceed 8 hours.

Patients with impaired renal function may require a reduction in dose.

Adverse reactions tend to increase with total daily doses of 4 grams or more or serum concentrations greater than the equivalent of 50 mcg of sulfapyridine per mL.

Oral Dosage Forms

Note: Bracketed uses in the *Dosage Forms* section refer to categories of use and/or indications that are not included in U.S. product labeling.

SULFASALAZINE ORAL SUSPENSION

Usual adult and adolescent dose:
Bowel disease (inflammatory) suppressant—
Initial: Oral, 1 gram every six to eight hours. An initial dose of 500 mg every six to twelve hours may be recommended to lessen gastrointestinal side effects.
Maintenance: Oral, 500 mg every six hours, adjusted according to patient response and tolerance.
[Antirheumatic]—Oral, 500 mg to 1 gram daily for the first week; increase the daily dose by 500 mg each week, up to a maintenance dose of 2 grams daily. The dose may be administered two times a day.

Usual adult prescribing limits: Total daily doses of greater than 4 grams may increase the risk of side effects and toxicity.

Auxiliary labeling:
- Shake well.
- Take with a full glass of water.
- Avoid too much sun or use of sunlamp.
- Continue medicine for full time of treatment.
- May discolor urine.
- May cause dizziness.

SULFASALAZINE TABLETS USP

Usual adult and adolescent dose:
Bowel disease (inflammatory) suppressant—See *Sulfasalazine Oral Suspension.*
[Antirheumatic][1]—Oral, 500 mg to 1 gram daily for the first week; increase the daily dose by 500 mg each week, up to a maintenance dose of 2 grams daily. The dose may be administered two times a day.

Usual adult prescribing limits: See *Sulfasalazine Oral Suspension.*

Auxiliary labeling:
- Take with a full glass of water.
- Avoid too much sun or use of sunlamp.
- Continue medicine for full time of treatment.
- May discolor urine.
- May cause dizziness.

SULFASALAZINE TABLETS USP (ENTERIC-COATED)

Usual adult and adolescent dose:
Bowel disease (inflammatory) suppressant—See *Sulfasalazine Oral Suspension.*
Initial: Oral, 1 to 2 grams every six to eight hours.
[Antirheumatic][1]—See *Sulfasalazine Tablets.*

Usual adult prescribing limits: See *Sulfasalazine Oral Suspension.*

Auxiliary labeling:
- Take with a full glass of water.
- Avoid too much sun or use of sunlamp.
- Continue medicine for full time of treatment.
- May discolor urine.
- Swallow tablets whole.
- May cause dizziness.

Note: Dissolution of enteric-coated tablets is much more variable and unreliable than that of nonenteric-coated tablets.

---

[1]Not included in Canadian product labeling.

SULFINPYRAZONE   Systemic

Some commonly used *brand names* are:
In the U.S.—*Anturane*
In Canada—*Anturan; Apo-Sulfinpyrazone; Novopyrazone*

ORAL
Sulfinpyrazone Capsules USP
In the U.S.—*Anturane;* GENERIC
Sulfinpyrazone Tablets USP
In the U.S.—*Anturane;* GENERIC
In Canada—*Anturan; Apo-Sulfinpyrazone; Novopyrazone*

Category: Antigout agent; antihyperuricemic.

Indications

Note: Bracketed information in the *Indications* section refers to uses not included in U.S. product labeling.

Accepted
Gouty arthritis, chronic (treatment); or
Hyperuricemia (treatment)—Sulfinpyrazone is indicated for the long-term management of hyperuricemia associated with chronic gout. It is recommended only for patients whose 24-hour renal excretion of urate is 800 mg (4.8 mmol) or lower (i.e., patients who are hyperuricemic as a result of underexcretion, rather than overpro-

duction, of urate). The aim of sulfinpyrazone therapy is to reduce the number of acute gout attacks.

Sulfinpyrazone is not effective in the treatment of acute gout attacks and does not eliminate the need to use colchicine or a nonsteroidal anti-inflammatory drug (NSAID) to relieve an attack. Also, sulfinpyrazone therapy should not be initiated during an attack, because it may induce fluctuations in urate concentration that may result in prolongation of the attack or initiation of a new attack.

[Sulfinpyrazone is sometimes used in the treatment of hyperuricemia not associated with gout. However, treatment of asymptomatic hyperuricemia is often unnecessary; the need for such therapy should be determined on an individual basis.][1]

Although a few studies have shown that sulfinpyrazone may reduce the risk of reinfarction and/or sudden cardiac death during the first 7 months after an initial myocardial infarction, the results of these studies have been questioned on methodological grounds. Aspirin is the drug of choice for preventing reinfarction, because its efficacy is more clearly established. However, sulfinpyrazone may be a suitable alternative for patients unable to take aspirin for this indication.

Unaccepted
Sulfinpyrazone is not recommended in circumstances in which there is an especially high risk of adverse effects associated with crystallization and deposition of urate in renal tissues, such as formation

of renal calculi and uric acid nephropathy. It therefore should not be used for treatment of gout in patients whose 24-hour urate excretion exceeds 800 mg (4.8 mmol) or who have extensive tophi, or for treatment of hyperuricemia associated with neoplastic disease or its treatment (chemotherapy with rapidly cytolytic antineoplastic agents or radiation therapy). Allopurinol, which decreases the quantity of urate that reaches the kidneys in addition to decreasing the concentration of urate in the blood, is recommended in these circumstances.

Sulfinpyrazone has also been used to prevent the occurrence or reoccurrence of venous thrombosis or embolism and thrombotic complications associated with rheumatic mitral stenosis, unstable angina pectoris, and transient cerebral ischemic attacks. Also, sulfinpyrazone has been used to prevent occlusion (by clotted blood) of aortocoronary bypass grafts, arteriovenous shunts, and prosthetic mitral valves. However, sulfinpyrazone's efficacy has not been established and further study has been recommended. Aspirin is the agent of choice for these indications. Dipyridamole is also effective in protecting against thrombotic complications associated with prosthetic valves or other foreign surfaces.

---

[1]Not included in Canadian product labeling.

Pharmacology

Mechanism of action/Effect:
Antigout agent; antihyperuricemic—Sulfinpyrazone is a uricosuric agent. By competitively inhibiting the active reabsorption of urate at the proximal renal tubule, it increases the urinary excretion of uric acid and lowers serum urate concentrations. By lowering serum concentrations of uric acid below its solubility limits, sulfinpyrazone may decrease or prevent urate deposition, tophi formation, and chronic joint changes; promote resolution of existing urate deposits; and, after several months of therapy, reduce the frequency of acute attacks of gout. Sulfinpyrazone does not have clinically useful anti-inflammatory or analgesic activity.

Antithrombotic; myocardial infarction prophylactic—Sulfinpyrazone restores toward normal the shortened platelet survival time often associated with thromboembolic disorders. It decreases platelet adhesiveness to subendothelial cells and possibly to prosthetic surfaces. Although sulfinpyrazone also inhibits the activity of the enzyme cyclo-oxygenase, resulting in decreased synthesis of thromboxane A2 (a prostaglandin in platelets that promotes aggregation) and the platelet release reaction (an essential step in platelet aggregation and subsequent thrombus formation), it is a relatively weak inhibitor of platelet aggregation. Whether inhibition of platelet aggregation contributes significantly to the medication's antithrombotic activity has therefore been questioned. Sulfinpyrazone's effects on platelets are due primarily to an active sulfide metabolite.

Other actions/effects:
Although sulfinpyrazone lacks clinically useful anti-inflammatory or analgesic activity, it inhibits prostaglandin synthesis and shares some of the risks associated with phenylbutazone (to which it is chemically related) and other nonsteroidal anti-inflammatory drugs (NSAIDs), including the potential for causing gastrointestinal, renal, or hematologic toxicity.

There is some evidence that sulfinpyrazone induces the activity of hepatic microsomal enzymes and, with chronic use, enhances its own metabolism. Although sulfinpyrazone has been shown to increase antipyrine clearance, the possibility that it may induce the metabolism of other medications has not been fully investigated. However, sulfinpyrazone has been shown to inhibit (rather than increase) metabolism of several medications, including warfarin, tolbutamide, and phenytoin, that are metabolized via the hepatic P-450 microsomal enzyme system.

Onset of action: Antithrombotic effect—Approximately 4 days.

Time to peak effect: Antithrombotic effect—Approximately 1 to 2 weeks after initiation of treatment with 200 mg 4 times a day.

Duration of action: Single dose—The uricosuric action usually lasts for 4 to 6 hours, but may persist for up to 10 hours in some patients.

Precautions to Consider

Cross-sensitivity and/or related problems
Patients sensitive to aspirin, oxyphenbutazone, or phenylbutazone may be sensitive to this medication also. In challenge tests, sulfinpyrazone caused dyspnea, wheezing, and/or a fall in peak expiratory flow rate in 4 of 11 patients with aspirin-induced asthma but no reaction in individuals with documented sensitivity (history of anaphylaxis and positive skin tests) to dipyrone.

The possibility of cross-sensitivity between sulfinpyrazone and other nonsteroidal anti-inflammatory drugs (NSAIDs) should be considered, especially for patients in whom cross-sensitivity between aspirin and other NSAIDs has been reported.

Geriatrics
No published information is available on the relationship of age to the effects of sulfinpyrazone in geriatric patients. However, elderly patients are more likely to have age-related renal function impairment, which may decrease the efficacy of uricosuric agents and/or increase the risk of adverse effects in patients receiving sulfinpyrazone.

Drug interactions and/or related problems
The following drug interactions and/or related problems have been selected on the basis of their potential clinical significance (possible mechanism in parentheses where appropriate)—not necessarily inclusive (» = major clinical significance):

Note: Combinations containing any of the following medications, depending on the amount present, may also interact with this medication.

In addition to the interactions listed below, the possibility should be considered that additive or multiple effects leading to impaired blood clotting and/or increased risk of bleeding may occur if sulfinpyrazone is administered concurrently with any medication having a significant potential for causing hypoprothrombinemia, thrombocytopenia, or gastrointestinal ulceration or hemorrhage.

Alcohol or
Diazoxide or
Mecamylamine or
Pyrazinamide
(these medications may increase serum uric acid concentrations; dosage adjustment of sulfinpyrazone may be necessary to control hyperuricemia)

Aminosalicylate sodium
(sulfinpyrazone may decrease renal tubular secretion of aminosalicylate sodium, resulting in increased and more prolonged serum concentrations and/or toxicity; patient should be monitored and dosage adjusted as necessary)

» Anticoagulants, coumarin- or indandione-derivative, or
» Heparin or
» Thrombolytic agents, such as:
Alteplase (tissue-type plasminogen activator, recombinant)
Anistreplase (anisoylated plasminogen-streptokinase activator complex, APSAC)
Streptokinase
Urokinase
(prolongation of the prothrombin time and severe gastrointestinal or renal bleeding have resulted from concurrent use of sulfinpyrazone with acenocoumarol [nicoumalone] or warfarin; studies have demonstrated that sulfinpyrazone has stereoselective effects on warfarin kinetics, i.e., it displaces from protein-binding sites and increases clearance of the (R)-enantiomer of

warfarin, but inhibits metabolism of the substantially more potent (S)-enantiomer by the hepatic P-450 enzyme system, resulting in a net increase in warfarin activity; careful monitoring of the prothrombin time is recommended when sulfinpyrazone therapy is initiated or discontinued so that anticoagulant dosage can be adjusted as needed)

(although sulfinpyrazone has also been shown to inhibit enzymatic metabolism of phenprocoumon, concurrent use of the 2 medications does not lead to a significant increase in the prothrombin time, possibly because a comparatively small quantity of phenprocoumon is eliminated via this mechanism; however, inhibition of platelet function by sulfinpyrazone, and its potential for causing gastrointestinal ulceration or hemorrhage, may increase the risk of hemorrhage in patients receiving any anticoagulant or thrombolytic agent)

Antidiabetic agents, oral
(sulfinpyrazone may decrease the metabolism of an oral antidiabetic agent, leading to prolonged half-life and increased hypoglycemic effect; dosage adjustments may be necessary during and following sulfinpyrazone therapy)

Anti-inflammatory drugs, nonsteroidal (NSAIDs), or
» Platelet aggregation-inhibiting medications
(concurrent use with sulfinpyrazone may increase the risk of bleeding because of additive inhibition of platelet function and sulfinpyrazone's potential for causing gastrointestinal ulceration or hemorrhage; concurrent use with NSAIDs may also increase the risk of gastrointestinal ulceration or hemorrhage)

Antimicrobial agents
(antimicrobial therapy may suppress formation by intestinal microflora of the active sulfide metabolite of sulfinpyrazone, which is responsible for sulfinpyrazone's antithrombotic activity)

» Antineoplastic agents, rapidly cytolytic
(concurrent use with sulfinpyrazone is not recommended because of the risk of uric acid nephropathy; allopurinol is the antihyperuricemic agent of choice for reducing risks [gout and/or urate nephropathy] associated with chemotherapy-induced hyperuricemia; also, rapidly cytolytic antineoplastic agents may increase serum uric acid concentrations and interfere with control of pre-existing hyperuricemia and gout)

» Aspirin or other salicylates, including bismuth subsalicylate
(salicylates inhibit sulfinpyrazone's uricosuric action; although occasional use of a salicylate in low to moderate analgesic doses, or chronic administration of 80 mg per day of aspirin as an antithrombotic, is not likely to interfere with sulfinpyrazone's uricosuric effect, chronic use of analgesic or antirheumatic doses of a salicylate together with sulfinpyrazone is not recommended; sulfinpyrazone also inhibits the uricosuria induced by high doses of salicylates; in addition, sulfinpyrazone may decrease excretion of salicylate and/or displace salicylate from its plasma protein-binding sites, possibly leading to increased salicylate concentrations and toxicity)

(low doses of sulfinpyrazone and aspirin have been used together as an antithrombotic regimen in a few studies; however, whether the combination is more effective than aspirin alone has not been established, and the increased risk of bleeding must be considered)

» Cefamandole or
» Cefoperazone or
» Cefotetan or
» Moxalactam or
» Plicamycin or
» Valproic acid
(these medications may cause hypoprothrombinemia; in addition, plicamycin or valproic acid may inhibit platelet aggregation, and moxalactam may also cause irreversible platelet damage; inhibition of platelet function by sulfinpyrazone, as well as its potential for causing gastrointestinal ulceration or hemor-

rhage, may increase the risk of severe hemorrhage when these medications are used concurrently)

» Nitrofurantoin
(sulfinpyrazone may increase serum concentrations of nitrofurantoin by decreasing its renal clearance, possibly increasing the potential for toxic reactions and reducing nitrofurantoin's effectiveness as a urinary tract anti-infective; concurrent use should be avoided)

Phenytoin and possibly other hydantoin anticonvulsants
(sulfinpyrazone may displace these medications from plasma protein-binding sites and decrease their metabolism, possibly leading to increased plasma concentration and elimination half-life; although hydantoin plasma concentration is not consistently increased, it is recommended that patients be monitored for signs of hydantoin toxicity during concurrent use)

Probenecid
(probenecid inhibits the renal tubular secretion of sulfinpyrazone and its active para-hydroxy metabolite; however, the uricosuric effects of the medications are additive, and increased therapeutic benefit has been reported during concurrent use)

Contraindications/Medical problems
The contraindications/medical problems included have been selected on the basis of their potential clinical significance (reasons given in parentheses where appropriate)—not necessarily inclusive (» = major clinical significance).

Except under special circumstances, this medication should not be used when the following medical conditions exist:
» Any condition in which there is an increased risk of uric acid renal calculus formation or urate nephropathy, such as:
» Cancer chemotherapy with rapidly cytolytic antineoplastic agents
» Radiation therapy for malignancy
» Renal calculi or history of, especially uric acid calculi
» Urate excretion higher than 800 mg (4.8 mmol) in 24 hours
» Urate nephropathy or history of
(sulfinpyrazone is likely to induce, or exacerbate pre-existing, renal calculi and/or urate nephropathy; allopurinol is the antihyperuricemic agent recommended in these circumstances)

» Blood dyscrasias
(may be exacerbated)
» Peptic ulcer, active
(may be exacerbated)
» Renal function impairment, moderate to severe
(may be exacerbated; also, sulfinpyrazone's efficacy as a uricosuric agent decreases with increasing degrees of renal function impairment, and the medication may be completely ineffective when the patient's creatinine clearance is lower than 30 mL per minute [0.5 mL per second])

Risk-benefit should be considered when the following medical problems exist:
Bronchospastic reaction to aspirin, history of, or
Sensitivity to sulfinpyrazone or to NSAIDs, especially oxyphenbutazone or phenylbutazone, history of
(risk of cross-sensitivity)

Blood dyscrasias, history of
(increased risk of sulfinpyrazone-induced blood dyscrasias)
» Gastrointestinal inflammation or ulceration, active or history of, or
» Peptic ulcer, history of
(may be exacerbated or reactivated; if sulfinpyrazone is used for patients with these conditions, concurrent use of an appropriate treatment or prophylactic regimen for gastrointestinal ulceration should be considered)

» Renal function impairment, mild
(may be exacerbated; also, sulfinpyrazone's efficacy as a uricosuric agent begins to decrease when the creatinine clearance is 80 mL per minute [1.33 mL per second])

Side/Adverse Effects

The following side/adverse effects have been selected on the basis of their potential clinical significance (possible signs and symptoms in parentheses where appropriate)—not necessarily inclusive:

Those indicating need for medical attention
Incidence more frequent
   Renal calculi, urate (lower back and/or side pain, painful urination, with or without blood in urine)—may occur in up to 10% of patients early in sulfinpyrazone treatment
Incidence less frequent
   Dermatitis, allergic (skin rash)
Incidence rare
   Agranulocytosis (fever with or without chills; sores, ulcers, or white spots on lips or in mouth; sore throat); *anemia* (unusual tiredness or weakness); *aplastic anemia [pancytopenia]* (shortness of breath, troubled breathing, tightness in chest, and/or wheezing; sores, ulcers, or white spots on lips or in mouth; swollen and/or painful glands; unusual bleeding or bruising; unusual tiredness or weakness); *fever, allergic; gastrointestinal bleeding* (bloody or black, tarry stools; vomiting of blood or material that looks like coffee grounds); *leukopenia* (fever with or without chills, sore throat, unusual tiredness or weakness); *renal failure, possibly associated with urate nephropathy* (increased blood pressure; shortness of breath, troubled breathing, tightness in chest, and/or wheezing; sudden decrease in amount of urine; swelling of face, fingers, feet, and/or lower legs; unusual tiredness or weakness; weight gain); *thrombocytopenia* (usually asymptomatic; rarely, unusual bleeding or bruising; black, tarry stools; blood in urine or stools; pinpoint red spots on skin)
   Note: *Renal failure not associated with urate nephropathy* has been reported, rarely, during sulfinpyrazone therapy, but a direct causal relationship has not always been clearly established. Sulfinpyrazone has caused *acute interstitial nephritis* (including cases documented as being hypersensitivity-mediated) and *acute renal tubular necrosis* in a few patients. Also, *transient renal function impairment* (which improved despite continued administration) has occurred in postmyocardial infarction patients and postaortocoronary bypass patients receiving sulfinpyrazone. It has been proposed that sulfinpyrazone may cause transient renal ischemia by temporarily inhibiting the synthesis of renal vasodilator prostaglandins and/or kinins, and that the presence of congestive heart failure may be a predisposing factor in the development of sulfinpyrazone-induced renal complications.
Symptoms of overdose
   Clumsiness or unsteadiness; convulsions; diarrhea; nausea or vomiting, severe or continuing; stomach pain, severe or continuing; difficulty in breathing

Those indicating need for medical attention only if they continue or are bothersome
Incidence more frequent
   Gouty arthritis, acute attack (joint pain, redness, swelling); *nausea or vomiting; stomach pain*
   Note: An increase in the frequency of *acute attacks of gout* during the first few months of therapy may be anticipated, unless adequate prophylaxis with colchicine (or, if the patient is unable to take colchicine, a nonsteroidal anti-inflammatory drug [NSAID]) is given concurrently with the sulfinpyrazone. Up to 20% of patients started on treatment with a uricosuric agent alone may experience acute attacks within the first few days of treatment.

Patient Consultation

In providing consultation, consider emphasizing the following selected information (» = major clinical significance):

Before using this medication
» Conditions affecting use, especially:
      Sensitivity to sulfinpyrazone or NSAIDs, especially aspirin, oxyphenbutazone, or phenylbutazone, history of
      Other medications, especially anticoagulants, rapidly cytolytic antineoplastic agents, aspirin or other salicylates, hypoprothrombinemia-inducing cephalosporins, moxalactam, nitrofurantoin, platelet aggregation inhibitors, plicamycin, and valproic acid
      Other medical problems, especially cancer treated with rapidly cytolytic antineoplastic agents or radiation therapy, renal calculi or history of (especially uric acid calculi), renal function impairment, blood dyscrasias, gastrointestinal inflammation or ulceration, and active peptic ulcer

Proper use of this medication
» Taking with food or an antacid to minimize gastrointestinal irritation
» Compliance with therapy
      Importance of high fluid intake and compliance with therapy for alkalinization of urine, if prescribed, to minimize kidney stone formation
» Proper dosing
      Missed dose: Taking as soon as possible; not taking if almost time for next dose; not doubling doses
» Proper storage
For use as antigout agent
      Several months of continuous therapy may be required for maximum effectiveness
» Medication does not relieve acute gout attacks but rather helps to prevent them; need to continue taking sulfinpyrazone with medication prescribed for gout attacks

Precautions while using this medication
      Regular visits to physician to check progress during therapy
      Caution if any laboratory tests required; possible interference with test results
For use as antihyperuricemic (including gout therapy)
» Aspirin or other salicylates may decrease the uricosuric effects of sulfinpyrazone; checking with physician regarding concurrent use, since effect is dependent on salicylate dose and duration of use
» Possibility that alcohol taken in large amounts may increase blood uric acid concentration and reduce effectiveness of medication

Side/adverse effects
      Signs and symptoms of potential side effects, especially renal calculi, dermatitis, blood dyscrasias, fever, gastrointestinal bleeding, and renal failure

General Dosing Information

Sulfinpyrazone therapy for gouty arthritis should not be initiated until 2 to 3 weeks after an acute attack has subsided. However, if an acute attack occurs in a patient already receiving sulfinpyrazone, the medication should be continued at the same dose while therapeutic doses of colchicine or a nonsteroidal anti-inflammatory drug (NSAID) are given to relieve the attack.

Sulfinpyrazone may be administered with food or an antacid to reduce gastrointestinal irritation.

Because sulfinpyrazone may increase the frequency of acute attacks of gout during the early months of therapy, prophylactic doses of colchicine (or, if the patient is unable to take colchicine, an NSAID) should be administered concurrently during the first 3 to 6 months of sulfinpyrazone therapy. However, even with prophylactic therapy, acute attacks of gout requiring treatment with full therapeutic doses of colchicine or an NSAID may occur.

To reduce the risk of urate stone formation, especially in patients with hyperuricemia, it is recommended that sulfinpyrazone therapy be initiated with a low dose, followed by a gradual increase in dosage. Also, a high fluid intake (no less than 2.5 to 3 liters daily) and maintenance of an alkaline urine by administration of sodium bicarbonate (3 to 7.5 grams daily), potassium citrate (7.5 grams daily), or acetazolamide (250 mg daily) are recommended. The risk of urate stone formation is highest during the first few weeks of therapy, when urate excretion is high; after hyperuricemia has been controlled and urinary excretion of uric acid decreases, the need for these measures is reduced.

Sulfinpyrazone may be given concurrently with allopurinol for treatment of gout; the antihyperuricemic effects of the 2 medications are additive.

Determination of serum or urine (24-hour) uric acid concentrations may be necessary for proper dosing in uricosuric therapy.

Oral Dosage Forms

Note: Bracketed uses in the *Dosage Forms* section refer to categories of use and/or indications that are not included in U.S. product labeling.

SULFINPYRAZONE CAPSULES USP

Usual adult dose: Antigout agent—
Initial: Oral, 100 to 200 mg two times a day, the dose being increased by 200 mg a day at two-day intervals, if necessary, up to a maximum of 800 mg per day.

Note: Some clinicians recommend initiating treatment with a lower dose of 50 mg two times a day and increasing the dose more gradually (e.g., at three- to four-day intervals).
Patients who were previously controlled with other uricosuric therapy may be transferred to sulfinpyrazone at full maintenance dosage.

Maintenance: Oral, dosage to be adjusted to the lowest dose that maintains the serum uric acid concentration at the desired level, usually 200 to 400 mg per day. However, some patients may require maintenance doses of up to 800 mg a day.

Note: The initial dose recommended for treatment of gout is also appropriate if sulfinpyrazone is used as an antithrombotic. However, it is recommended that myocardial reinfarction prophylaxis with sulfinpyrazone not be initiated until at least fourteen days after the acute event. Delaying treatment may decrease the risk of renal function impairment in patients receiving sulfinpyrazone for this purpose.

For preventing myocardial reinfarction, the usual maintenance dose is 800 mg per day, in four divided doses. For other antithrombotic indications, the usual maintenance dose is 600 to 800 mg per day, in three or four divided doses.

SULFINPYRAZONE TABLETS USP

Usual adult dose: See *Sulfinpyrazone Capsules USP.*

SULFONAMIDES   Ophthalmic

Some commonly used *brand names* are:

In the U.S.—
Ak-Sulf [Sulfacetamide]
Bleph-10 [Sulfacetamide]
Cetamide [Sulfacetamide]
Gantrisin [Sulfisoxazole]
Isopto-Cetamide
  [Sulfacetamide]
I-Sulfacet [Sulfacetamide]
Ocu-Sul-10 [Sulfacetamide]
Ocu-Sul-15 [Sulfacetamide]
Ocu-Sul-30 [Sulfacetamide]
Ocusulf-10 [Sulfacetamide]
Ophthacet [Sulfacetamide]
Sodium Sulamyd
  [Sulfacetamide]

Spectro-Sulf
  [Sulfacetamide]
Steri-Units Sulfacetamide
  [Sulfacetamide]
Sulf-10 [Sulfacetamide]
Sulfair [Sulfacetamide]
Sulfair 10 [Sulfacetamide]
Sulfair 15 [Sulfacetamide]
Sulfair Forte
  [Sulfacetamide]
Sulfamide [Sulfacetamide]
Sulten-10 [Sulfacetamide]

In Canada—
Ak-Sulf [Sulfacetamide]
Bleph-10 [Sulfacetamide]
Cetamide [Sulfacetamide]
Isopto-Cetamide
  [Sulfacetamide]

Sodium Sulamyd
  [Sulfacetamide]
Sulfex [Sulfacetamide]

Another commonly used name for sulfisoxazole is sulfafurazole.

OPHTHALMIC
SULFACETAMIDE
Sulfacetamide Sodium Ophthalmic Ointment USP
  In the U.S.—*Ak-Sulf; Bleph-10; Cetamide; Ocu-Sul-10; Sodium Sulamyd; Sulfair 10;* GENERIC
  In Canada—*Ak-Sulf; Cetamide; Sodium Sulamyd*
Sulfacetamide Sodium Ophthalmic Solution USP
  In the U.S.—*Ak-Sulf; Bleph-10; Isopto-Cetamide; I-Sulfacet; Ocu-Sul-10; Ocu-Sul-15; Ocu-Sul-30; Ocusulf-10; Ophthacet; Sodium Sulamyd; Spectro-Sulf; Steri-Units Sulfac-*

etamide; Sulf-10; Sulfair; Sulfair 10; Sulfair 15; Sulfair Forte; Sulfamide; Sulten-10; GENERIC
  In Canada—*Ak-Sulf; Bleph-10; Isopto-Cetamide; Sodium Sulamyd; Sulfex*
SULFISOXAZOLE
Sulfisoxazole Diolamine Ophthalmic Ointment USP
  In the U.S.—*Gantrisin*
Sulfisoxazole Diolamine Ophthalmic Solution USP
  In the U.S.—*Gantrisin*

Category: Antibacterial (ophthalmic).

Indications

Note: Bracketed information in the *Indications* section refers to uses not included in U.S. product labeling.

Accepted
Conjunctivitis, bacterial (treatment); or
Ocular infections, other (treatment)—Ophthalmic sulfonamides are indicated in the treatment of conjunctivitis and other superficial ocular infections caused by susceptible organisms.

Trachoma (treatment); or
Chlamydial infections, other (treatment)—Ophthalmic sulfonamides are indicated concurrently with systemic sulfonamides in the treatment of trachoma and other chlamydial infections.

[Blepharitis, bacterial (treatment)]—Ophthalmic sulfonamides are used in the treatment of bacterial blepharitis.

[Blepharoconjunctivitis (treatment)]—Ophthalmic sulfonamides are used in the treatment of blepharoconjunctivitis.

[Keratitis, bacterial (treatment)]—Ophthalmic sulfonamides are used in the treatment of bacterial keratitis.

[Keratoconjunctivitis, bacterial (treatment)]—Ophthalmic sulfonamides are used in the treatment of bacterial keratoconjunctivitis.

Not all species or strains of a particular organism may be susceptible to a specific sulfonamide.

Pharmacology

Mechanism of action/Effect: Sulfonamides are broad-spectrum, bacteriostatic anti-infectives. They are structural analogs of aminobenzoic acid (PABA) and competitively inhibit a bacterial enzyme, dihydropteroate synthetase, that is responsible for incorporation of PABA into dihydrofolic acid. This blocks the synthesis of dihydrofolic acid and decreases the amount of metabolically active tetrahydrofolic acid, a cofactor for the synthesis of purines, thymidine, and DNA.

Susceptible bacteria are those which must synthesize folic acid. The action of sulfonamides is antagonized by PABA and its derivatives (e.g., procaine and tetracaine) and by the presence of pus or tissue breakdown products which provide the necessary components for bacterial growth.

Precautions to Consider

Cross-sensitivity and/or related problems
Patients sensitive to one sulfonamide may be sensitive to other sulfonamides also.

Patients sensitive to furosemide, thiazide diuretics, sulfonylureas, or carbonic anhydrase inhibitors may be sensitive to sulfonamides also.

Geriatrics
Appropriate studies with sulfonamides have not been performed in the geriatric population. However, no geriatrics-specific problems have been documented to date.

Drug interactions and/or related problems
The following drug interactions and/or related problems have been selected on the basis of their potential clinical significance (possible mechanism in parentheses where appropriate)—not necessarily inclusive (» = major clinical significance):

Note: Combinations containing any of the following medications, depending on the amount present, may also interact with this medication.

» Silver preparations, such as silver nitrate, mild silver protein (topical sulfonamides are incompatible with silver salts; concurrent use is not recommended)

Contraindications/Medical problems
The contraindications/medical problems included have been selected on the basis of their potential clinical significance (reasons given in parentheses where appropriate)—not necessarily inclusive (» = major clinical significance).

Risk-benefit should be considered when the following medical problem exists:
Sensitivity to sulfonamides

Side/Adverse Effects

The following side/adverse effects have been selected on the basis of their potential clinical significance (possible signs and symptoms in parentheses where appropriate)—not necessarily inclusive:

Those indicating need for medical attention
Incidence more frequent
Hypersensitivity (itching, redness, swelling, or other sign of irritation not present before therapy)

Patient Consultation

In providing consultation, consider emphasizing the following selected information (» = major clinical significance):

Before using this medication
» Conditions affecting use, especially:
Sensitivity to sulfonamides, furosemide, thiazide diuretics, sulfonylureas, or carbonic anhydrase inhibitors
Other medications, especially silver preparations, such as silver nitrate or mild silver protein

Proper use of this medication
Proper administration technique for ophthalmic solution and ophthalmic ointment
» Compliance with full course of therapy
Missed dose: Applying as soon as possible; not applying if almost time for next dose
» Proper storage

Precautions while using this medication
Blurred vision after application of ophthalmic ointments
Possibility of stinging or burning after application
Checking with physician if no improvement within a few days

Side/adverse effects
Signs of potential side effects, especially hypersensitivity

General Dosing Information

At night the ophthalmic ointment may be used as an adjunct to the ophthalmic solution to provide prolonged contact with the medication.

Although some manufacturers recommend a dose of 2 drops of an ophthalmic solution at appropriate intervals, the conjunctival sac will usually hold only 1 drop.

SULFACETAMIDE

Ophthalmic Dosage Forms

SULFACETAMIDE SODIUM OPHTHALMIC OINTMENT USP

Usual adult and adolescent dose: Topical, to the conjunctiva, a thin strip (approximately 1.25 to 2.5 cm) of ointment every six hours and at bedtime.

Auxiliary labeling:
• For the eye.
• Continue medicine for full time of treatment.

SULFACETAMIDE SODIUM OPHTHALMIC SOLUTION USP

Usual adult and adolescent dose: Topical, to the conjunctiva, 1 drop every one to three hours during the day and less frequently during the night.

Auxiliary labeling:
• For the eye.
• Keep in a cool place.
• Continue medicine for full time of treatment.
• Discard if dark brown.

SULFISOXAZOLE

Ophthalmic Dosage Forms

SULFISOXAZOLE DIOLAMINE OPHTHALMIC OINTMENT USP

Usual adult and adolescent dose: Topical, to the conjunctiva, a thin strip (approximately 1.25 to 2.5 cm) of ointment every eight to twenty-four hours and at bedtime.

Auxiliary labeling:
- For the eye.
- Continue medicine for full time of treatment.

SULFISOXAZOLE DIOLAMINE OPHTHALMIC SOLUTION USP

Usual adult and adolescent dose: Topical, to the conjunctiva, 1 drop every eight hours or more frequently.

Auxiliary labeling:
- For the eye.
- Continue medicine for full time of treatment.

SULFONAMIDES Systemic

Some commonly used *brand names* are:

In the U.S.—
Gantanol [Sulfamethoxazole]
Gantrisin [Sulfisoxazole]
Renoquid [Sulfacytine]
Thiosulfil Forte [Sulfamethizole]

In Canada—
Apo-Sulfamethoxazole [Sulfamethoxazole]
Gantanol [Sulfamethoxazole]
Novosoxazole [Sulfisoxazole]

Another commonly used name for sulfisoxazole is sulfafurazole.

SULFACYTINE†
Oral
Sulfacytine Tablets†
In the U.S.—*Renoquid*
SULFADIAZINE†
Oral
Sulfadiazine Tablets†
In the U.S.—GENERIC
SULFAMETHIZOLE†
Oral
Sulfamethizole Tablets USP†
In the U.S.—*Thiosulfil Forte*
SULFAMETHOXAZOLE
Oral
Sulfamethoxazole Oral Suspension USP†
In the U.S.—*Gantanol*
Sulfamethoxazole Tablets USP
In the U.S.—*Gantanol;* GENERIC
In Canada—*Apo-Sulfamethoxazole; Gantanol*
SULFISOXAZOLE
Oral
Sulfisoxazole Tablets USP
In the U.S.—*Gantrisin;* GENERIC
In Canada—*Novosoxazole*
Sulfisoxazole Acetyl Oral Suspension USP†
In the U.S.—*Gantrisin*
Sulfisoxazole Acetyl Oral Syrup†
In the U.S.—*Gantrisin*

---

†Not commercially available in Canada.

Category

Antibacterial (urinary)—Sulfamethizole.
Antibacterial (systemic)—Sulfacytine; Sulfadiazine; Sulfamethoxazole; Sulfisoxazole.
Antiprotozoal—Sulfamethoxazole; Sulfisoxazole.

Indications

Accepted

Sulfonamides are active *in vitro* against a broad spectrum of gram-positive and gram-negative bacteria. They also have activity *in vitro* against *Actinomyces, Chlamydia trachomatis, Nocardia asteroides, Plasmodium falciparum,* and *Toxoplasma gondii.* Susceptibility of an organism to sulfonamides is variable; many bacteria have become resistant to sulfonamides, with resistance occurring in more than 20% of community and nosocomial bacterial isolates. Resistance has developed in strains of staphylococci, *Neisseria gonorrhoeae, N. meningitidis,* Enterbacteriaceae, and *Pseudomonas* species.

Sulfonamides are commonly used in the treatment of acute, uncomplicated urinary tract infections caused by susceptible bacteria. Because sulfacytine and sulfamethizole produce low plasma levels and are rapidly eliminated, they are recommended only for use in urinary tract infections, not systemic infections. Sulfadiazine is not recommended for the treatment of urinary tract infections because of its relatively lower urine solubility and the increased chance of crystalluria; other, more soluble agents, such as sulfisoxazole, are generally preferred.

Sulfonamides are also used to treat infections caused by *C. trachomatis,* although they are not considered to be the drug of choice. These infections include chlamydial urethritis and cervicitis, lymphogranuloma venereum, inclusion conjunctivitis, and trachoma. Sulfonamides may also be used in the treatment of melioidosis, caused by *Pseudomonas pseudomallei,* the prophylaxis of rheumatic fever associated with Group A beta-hemolytic streptococci infections, and the treatment of paracoccidioidomycosis, caused by *Paracoccidioides brasiliensis.*

Combinations of a sulfonamide and another antibacterial are common for several infections. These include the use of sulfadiazine with pyrimethamine for the treatment of both toxoplasmosis, caused by *T. gondii,* and malaria caused by chloroquine-resistant *P. falciparum.* Sulfonamides may be used with other antibacterials for the treatment of nocardiosis, caused by *N. asteroides,* and the treatment of otitis media and sinusitis caused by susceptible strains of *Haemophilus influenza,* streptococci, and pneumococci.

Not all species or strains of a particular organism may be susceptible to a specific sulfonamide.

Unaccepted

Sulfonamides should not be used in the treatment of Group A beta-hemolytic streptococcal tonsillopharyngitis since they may not eradicate streptococci and therefore may not prevent sequelae such as rheumatic fever.

Pharmacology

Mechanism of action/Effect:

Sulfonamides are broad-spectrum, bacteriostatic anti-infectives. They are structural analogs of para-aminobenzoic acid (PABA) and competitively inhibit a bacterial enzyme, dihydropteroate synthetase, that is responsible for incorporation of PABA into dihydrofolic acid. This blocks the synthesis of dihydrofolic acid and decreases the amount of metabolically active tetrahydrofolic acid, a cofactor for the synthesis of purines, thymidine, and DNA.

Susceptible bacteria are those which must synthesize folic acid. The action of sulfonamides is antagonized by PABA and its derivatives (e.g., procaine and tetracaine) and by the presence of pus or tissue breakdown products, which provide the necessary components for bacterial growth.

Duration of action:

Sulfacytine—Short-acting sulfonamide.
Sulfadiazine—Short-acting sulfonamide.
Sulfamethizole—Short-acting sulfonamide.
Sulfamethoxazole—Intermediate-acting sulfonamide.
Sulfisoxazole—Short-acting sulfonamide.

Precautions to Consider

Cross-sensitivity and/or related problems

Patients allergic to one sulfonamide may be allergic to other sulfonamides also.

Patients allergic to furosemide, thiazide diuretics, sulfonylureas, or carbonic anhydrase inhibitors may be allergic to sulfonamides also.

Geriatrics

Elderly patients may be at increased risk of severe side/adverse effects. Severe skin reactions, generalized bone marrow depression, and decreased platelet count (with or without purpura) are the most frequently reported severe side/adverse effects in the elderly. An increased incidence of thrombocytopenia with purpura has been reported in elderly patients who are receiving diuretics, primarily thiazides, concurrently with sulfamethoxazole and trimethoprim combination. The potential for these problems should also be considered for elderly patients taking other sulfonamide medications.

Dental

The leukopenic and thrombocytopenic effects of sulfonamides may result in an increased incidence of certain microbial infections, delayed healing, and gingival bleeding. If leukopenia or thrombocytopenia occurs, dental work should be deferred until blood counts have returned to normal. Patients should be instructed in proper oral hygiene, including caution in use of regular toothbrushes, dental floss, and toothpicks.

Drug interactions and/or related problems

The following drug interactions and/or related problems have been selected on the basis of their potential clinical significance (possible mechanism in parentheses where appropriate)—not necessarily inclusive (» = major clinical significance):

Note: Combinations containing any of the following medications, depending on the amount present, may also interact with this medication.

» Anticoagulants, coumarin- or indandione-derivative, or
» Anticonvulsants, hydantoin, or

» Antidiabetic agents, oral
(these medications may be displaced from protein binding sites and/or their metabolism may be inhibited by some sulfonamides, resulting in increased or prolonged effects and/or toxicity; dosage adjustments may be necessary during and after sulfonamide therapy)

Bone marrow depressants
(concurrent use of bone marrow depressants with sulfonamides may increase the leukopenic and/or thrombocytopenic effects; if concurrent use is required, close observation for myelotoxic effects should be considered)

Contraceptives, estrogen-containing, oral
(concurrent long-term use of sulfonamides may result in increased incidence of breakthrough bleeding and pregnancy)

Cyclosporine
(concurrent use with sulfonamides may increase the metabolism of cyclosporine, resulting in decreased plasma concentrations and potential transplant rejection, and additive nephrotoxicity; plasma cyclosporine concentrations and renal function should be monitored)

» Hemolytics, other
(concurrent use with sulfonamides may increase the potential for toxic side effects)

» Hepatotoxic medications, other
(concurrent use with sulfonamides may result in an increased incidence of hepatotoxicity; patients, especially those on prolonged administration or those with a history of liver disease, should be carefully monitored)

» Methenamine
(in acid urine, methenamine breaks down into formaldehyde, which may form an insoluble precipitate with certain sulfonamides, especially those that are less soluble in urine, and may also increase the danger of crystalluria; concurrent use is not recommended)

» Methotrexate or
Phenylbutazone or
Sulfinpyrazone
(the effects of these medications may be potentiated during concurrent use with sulfonamides because of displacement from plasma protein binding sites)

Penicillins
(since bacteriostatic drugs may interfere with the bactericidal effect of penicillins in the treatment of meningitis or in other situations where a rapid bactericidal effect is necessary, it is best to avoid concurrent therapy)

Contraindications/Medical problems

The contraindications/medical problems included have been selected on the basis of their potential clinical significance (reasons given in parentheses where appropriate)—not necessarily inclusive (» = major clinical significance).

Except under special circumstances, this medication should not be used when the following medical problems exist:

Allergy to sulfonamides, furosemide, thiazide diuretics, sulfonylureas, or carbonic anhydrase inhibitors

Risk-benefit should be considered when the following medical problems exist:

» Blood dyscrasias or
» Megaloblastic anemia due to folate deficiency
(sulfonamides may cause blood dyscrasias)

» Glucose-6-phosphate dehydrogenase (G6PD) deficiency
(hemolysis may occur)

» Hepatic function impairment
(sulfonamides are metabolized in the liver; may cause fulminant hepatic necrosis)

» Porphyria
(sulfonamides may precipitate an acute attack of porphyria)
» Renal function impairment
(sulfonamides are renally excreted; may cause tubular necrosis or interstitial nephritis)

Side/Adverse Effects

Note: Fatalities have occurred, although rarely, due to severe reactions such as Stevens-Johnson syndrome, toxic epidermal necrolysis, fulminant hepatic necrosis, agranulocytosis, aplastic anemia, and other blood dyscrasias. Therapy should be discontinued at the first appearance of skin rash or any serious side/adverse effects.

Patients with acquired immunodeficiency syndrome (AIDS) may have a greater incidence of side/adverse effects, especially rash, fever, and leukopenia, than do non-AIDS patients.

The following side/adverse effects have been selected on the basis of their potential clinical significance (possible signs and symptoms in parentheses where appropriate)—not necessarily inclusive:

Those indicating need for medical attention
Incidence more frequent
Hypersensitivity (fever, itching, skin rash); *photosensitivity* (increased sensitivity of skin to sunlight)

Incidence less frequent
Blood dyscrasias (fever and sore throat, pale skin, unusual bleeding or bruising, unusual tiredness or weakness); *hepatitis* (yellow eyes or skin); *Lyell's syndrome* (difficulty in swallowing; redness, blistering, peeling, or loosening of skin); *Stevens-Johnson syndrome* (aching joints and muscles; redness, blistering, peeling, or loosening of skin; unusual tiredness or weakness)

Incidence rare
Crystalluria or hematuria (blood in urine, lower back pain, pain or burning while urinating); *goiter or thyroid function disturbance* (swelling of front part of neck); *interstitial nephritis or tubular necrosis* (greatly increased or decreased frequency of urination or amount of urine, increased thirst, loss of appetite, nausea, vomiting)

Those indicating need for medical attention only if they continue or are bothersome
Incidence more frequent
Central nervous system effects (dizziness, headache, lethargy); *gastrointestinal disturbances* (diarrhea, loss of appetite, nausea or vomiting)

Patient Consultation

In providing consultation, consider emphasizing the following selected information (» = major clinical significance):

Before using this medication
» Conditions affecting use, especially:
Allergy to sulfonamides, furosemide, thiazide diuretics, sulfonylureas, carbonic anhydrase inhibitors
Pregnancy—Sulfonamides cross the placenta
Breast-feeding—Sulfonamides are excreted in breast milk; may cause kernicterus in nursing infants
Use in children—Sulfamethoxazole and sulfisoxazole are contraindicated in infants up to 2 months of age since sulfonamides may cause kernicterus in neonates; sulfacytine is not recommended in children up to 14 years of age
Other medications, especially coumarin- or indandione-derivative anticoagulants, hydantoin anticonvulsants, oral antidiabetic agents, other hemolytics, other hepatotoxic medications, methenamine, or methotrexate

Other medical problems, especially blood dyscrasias, G6PD deficiency, hepatic function impairment, megaloblastic anemia, porphyria, and renal function impairment

Proper use of this medication
» Not giving to children under 14 years of age (sulfacytine) or to infants under 2 months of age (other sulfonamides)
» Maintaining adequate fluid intake
Proper administration technique for oral liquids
» Compliance with full course of therapy
» Importance of not missing doses and taking at evenly spaced times
Missed dose: Taking as soon as possible; not taking if almost time for next dose; not doubling doses
» Proper storage

Precautions while using this medication
» Regular visits to physician to check blood counts
Checking with physician if no improvement within a few days
Using caution in use of regular toothbrushes, dental floss, and toothpicks; deferring dental work until blood counts have returned to normal; checking with physician or dentist concerning proper oral hygiene
» Possible photosensitivity reactions
» Caution if dizziness occurs

Side/adverse effects
Severe skin problems and blood problems may be more likely to occur in the elderly who are taking sulfamethoxazole and trimethoprim combination, especially if taking diuretics concurrently
Signs of potential side effects, especially blood dyscrasias, crystalluria, goiter, hematuria, hepatitis, hypersensitivity, interstitial nephritis, Lyell's syndrome, photosensitivity, Stevens-Johnson syndrome, thyroid function disturbance, and tubular necrosis

General Dosing Information

Fluid intake should be sufficient to maintain urine output of at least 1200 to 1500 mL per day in adults.

SULFACYTINE

Summary of Differences

Indications: Sulfacytine is recommended for use only in the treatment of urinary tract infections, not systemic infections.
Precautions: Pediatrics—Not recommended for children up to 14 years of age.

Additional Dosing Information

Fluid intake should be sufficient to maintain urine output of at least 1200 to 1500 mL per day in adults.

Patients with impaired renal function may require a reduction in dose.

Oral Dosage Forms

SULFACYTINE TABLETS

Usual adult dose: Antibacterial (systemic)—Oral, 500 mg initially, then 250 mg every six hours.

Usual adult prescribing limits: Up to 2 grams daily have been used.

Auxiliary labeling:
• Take with a full glass of water.
• Avoid too much sun or use of sunlamp.
• May cause dizziness.
• Continue medicine for full time of treatment.

SULFADIAZINE

Summary of Differences

Indications: Because of its relatively low urine solubility and the increased chance of crystalluria, sulfadiazine is not recommended for the treatment of urinary tract infections. Sulfadiazine, used in combination with pyrimethamine, is used for the treatment of toxoplasmosis and malaria caused by chloroquine-resistant *P. falciparum*.

Additional Dosing Information

Fluid intake should be sufficient to maintain urine output of at least 1200 to 1500 mL per day in adults.

Patients with impaired renal function may require a reduction in dose.

Oral Dosage Forms

SULFADIAZINE TABLETS

Usual adult dose: Antibacterial (systemic)—Oral, 2 to 4 grams initially, then 1 gram every four to six hours.

Usual adult prescribing limits: Up to 6 grams daily.

Auxiliary labeling:
- Take with a full glass of water.
- Avoid too much sun or use of sunlamp.
- May cause dizziness.
- Continue medicine for full time of treatment.

SULFAMETHIZOLE

Summary of Differences

Indications: Sulfamethizole is recommended for use only in the treatment of urinary tract infections, not systemic infections.

Additional Dosing Information

Fluid intake should be sufficient to maintain urine output of at least 1200 to 1500 mL per day in adults.

Patients with impaired renal function may require a reduction in dose.

Oral Dosage Forms

SULFAMETHIZOLE TABLETS USP

Usual adult and adolescent dose: Antibacterial—Oral, 500 mg to 1 gram every six to eight hours.

Auxiliary labeling:
- Take with a full glass of water.
- Avoid too much sun or use of sunlamp.
- May cause dizziness.
- Continue medicine for full time of treatment.

SULFAMETHOXAZOLE

Additional Dosing Information

Fluid intake should be sufficient to maintain urine output of at least 1200 to 1500 mL per day in adults.

Although sulfamethoxazole has a greater tendency to cause crystalluria than sulfisoxazole because of slower absorption and excretion, alkalinization of the urine is usually unnecessary.

Therapy should be continued for at least 7 to 10 days in urinary tract infections.

Patients with impaired renal function may require a reduction in dose.

Oral Dosage Forms

SULFAMETHOXAZOLE ORAL SUSPENSION USP

Usual adult and adolescent dose: Antibacterial (systemic); antiprotozoal—Oral, 2 grams initially, then 1 gram every eight to twelve hours.

Auxiliary labeling:
- Shake well.
- Take with a full glass of water.
- May cause dizziness.
- Avoid too much sun or use of sunlamp.
- Continue medicine for full time of treatment.

SULFAMETHOXAZOLE TABLETS USP

Usual adult and adolescent dose: See *Sulfamethoxazole Oral Suspension USP*.

Auxiliary labeling:
- Take with a full glass of water.
- May cause dizziness.
- Avoid too much sun or use of sunlamp.
- Continue medicine for full time of treatment.

SULFISOXAZOLE

Additional Dosing Information

Fluid intake should be sufficient to maintain urine output of at least 1200 to 1500 mL per day in adults.

Because of its relatively high solubility even in acid urine, the risk of crystalluria with sulfisoxazole is low and alkalinization of the urine is usually unnecessary.

Therapy should be continued for at least 7 to 10 days in urinary tract infections.

Patients with impaired renal function may require a reduction in dose.

Oral Dosage Forms

SULFISOXAZOLE TABLETS USP

Usual adult and adolescent dose: Antibacterial (systemic); antiprotozoal—Oral, 2 to 4 grams initially, then 750 mg to 1.5 grams every four hours; or 1 to 2 grams every six hours.

Usual adult prescribing limits: Up to 12 grams daily.

Auxiliary labeling:
- Take with a full glass of water.
- May cause dizziness.
- Avoid too much sun or use of sunlamp.
- Continue medicine for full time of treatment.

SULFISOXAZOLE ACETYL ORAL SUSPENSION USP

Usual adult and adolescent dose: See *Sulfisoxazole Tablets USP*.

Usual adult prescribing limits: See *Sulfisoxazole Tablets USP*.

Auxiliary labeling:
- Shake well.
- Take with a full glass of water.
- May cause dizziness.
- Avoid too much sun or use of sunlamp.
- Continue medicine for full time of treatment.

SULFISOXAZOLE ACETYL ORAL SYRUP

Usual adult and adolescent dose: See *Sulfisoxazole Tablets USP.*

Usual adult prescribing limits: See *Sulfisoxazole Tablets USP.*

Auxiliary labeling:
- Take with a full glass of water.
- May cause dizziness.
- Avoid too much sun or use of sunlamp.
- Continue medicine for full time of treatment.

SULFONAMIDES AND PHENAZOPYRIDINE   Systemic

Category: Antibacterial-analgesic (urinary tract).

Indications

Accepted

Urinary tract infections, bacterial (treatment)—Sulfonamide and phenazopyridine combinations are indicated in the treatment of the acute, painful phase of uncomplicated urinary tract infections caused by *Escherichia coli, Klebsiella* species, *Enterobacter* species, *Proteus mirabilis, P. vulgaris,* and *Staphylococcus aureus.* After relief of pain has been obtained, treatment should be continued with either sulfamethoxazole or sulfisoxazole alone.

Not all species or strains of a particular organism may be susceptible to a specific sulfonamide.

Patient Consultation

In providing consultation, consider emphasizing the following selected information (» = major clinical significance):

Before using this medication
» Conditions affecting use, especially:
   Allergies to sulfonamides, furosemide, thiazide diuretics, sulfonylureas, carbonic anhydrase inhibitors, or phenazopyridine
   Pregnancy—Sulfonamides cross the placenta; use is contraindicated at term since sulfonamides may cause kernicterus
   Breast-feeding—Sulfonamides are excreted in breast milk; may cause kernicterus in the nursing infant
   Use in children—Use is contraindicated in children up to 12 years of age
   Other medications, especially coumarin- or indandione-derivative anticoagulants, hydantoin anticonvulsants, oral antidiabetic agents, hemolytics, hepatotoxic medications, methenamine, and methotrexate
   Other medical problems, especially blood dyscrasias, G6PD deficiency, hepatic function impairment, hepatitis, megaloblastic anemia due to folate deficiency, porphyria, and renal function impairment

Proper use of this medication
» Maintaining adequate fluid intake; taking with or following meals if gastrointestinal irritation occurs
» Compliance with full course of therapy
» Importance of not missing doses and taking at evenly spaced times
» Proper dosing; not giving to infants and children up to 12 years of age
   Missed dose: Taking as soon as possible; not taking if almost time for next dose; not doubling doses
» Proper storage

Precautions while using this medication
   Checking with physician if no improvement within a few days or if symptoms become worse

   Using caution with regular toothbrushes, dental floss, and toothpicks; deferring dental work until blood counts have returned to normal; checking with physician or dentist concerning proper oral hygiene
» Possible photosensitivity reactions
» Caution if dizziness occurs
» Medication causes urine to turn reddish orange and may stain clothing
» Diabetics: May cause false urine sugar and urine ketone test results

Side/adverse effects
   Reddish orange discoloration of urine may be alarming to patient although medically insignificant
   Signs of potential side effects, especially blood dyscrasias, crystalluria, goiter, headache, hematuria, hemolytic anemia, hepatitis, hypersensitivity, interstitial nephritis, Lyell's syndrome, methemoglobinemia, photosensitivity, Stevens-Johnson syndrome, thyroid function disturbance, and tubular necrosis

Oral Dosage Forms

SULFAMETHOXAZOLE AND PHENAZOPYRIDINE HYDROCHLORIDE TABLETS

Usual adult and adolescent dose: Urinary tract infections, bacterial—Oral, 2 grams of sulfamethoxazole and 400 mg of phenazopyridine hydrochloride initially, then 1 gram of sulfamethoxazole and 200 mg of phenazopyridine hydrochloride every twelve hours for up to two days.

Auxiliary labeling:
- Take with a full glass of water.
- Avoid too much sun or use of sunlamp.
- May cause dizziness.
- Continue medicine for full time of treatment.
- May discolor urine.

Oral Dosage Forms

SULFISOXAZOLE AND PHENAZOPYRIDINE HYDROCHLORIDE TABLETS

Usual adult and adolescent dose: Urinary tract infections, bacterial—Oral, 2 to 3 grams of sulfisoxazole and 200 to 300 mg of phenazopyridine hydrochloride initially, then 1 gram of sulfisoxazole and 100 mg of phenazopyridine hydrochloride every six hours for up to two days.

Auxiliary labeling:
- Take with a full glass of water.
- Avoid too much sun or use of sunlamp.
- May cause dizziness.
- Continue medicine for full time of treatment.
- May discolor urine.

SULFUR   Topical

Some commonly used *brand names* are:

In the U.S.—

Cuticura Ointment	*Fostril Lotion*
Finac	*Lotio Alsulfa*
Fostex Regular Strength	*Sulpho-Lac*
Medicated Cover-Up	

In Canada—

Fostex CM	*Fostril Cream*

TOPICAL

Sulfur Cream
In the U.S.—*Fostex Regular Strength Medicated Cover-Up*
In Canada—*Fostex CM; Fostril Cream*
Sulfur Lotion
In the U.S.—*Finac; Fostril Lotion; Lotio Alsulfa*
Sulfur Ointment USP
In the U.S.—*Cuticura Ointment;* GENERIC
Sulfur Bar Soap
In the U.S.—*Sulpho-Lac;* GENERIC
In Canada—GENERIC

Category

Keratolytic (topical)—Sulfur Cream; Sulfur Lotion; Sulfur Ointment USP; Sulfur Bar Soap.
Antiacne agent (topical)—Sulfur Cream; Sulfur Lotion; Sulfur Ointment USP; Sulfur Bar Soap.
Antiseborrheic—Sulfur Ointment USP.
Scabicide—Sulfur Ointment USP.
Antirosacea agent (topical)—Sulfur Cream; Sulfur Lotion; Sulfur Ointment USP; Sulfur Bar Soap.

Indications

Note: Bracketed information in the *Indications* section refers to uses not included in U.S. product labeling.

Accepted

Acne vulgaris (treatment)—Sulfur (cream, lotion, ointment, and bar soap) is indicated as an aid in the treatment of acne vulgaris.

Dermatitis, seborrheic (treatment)—Sulfur ointment is indicated for the treatment of seborrheic dermatitis.

Scabies (treatment)—Sulfur ointment is indicated for the treatment of scabies, especially in infants under 2 months of age and in pregnant and nursing women.

[Rosacea (treatment)]—Sulfur (cream, lotion, ointment, and bar soap) is used in strengths of up to 15% to treat rosacea.

Pharmacology

Mechanism of action/Effect: Sulfur has germicidal, fungicidal, parasiticidal, and keratolytic actions. Its germicidal activity may be the result of its conversion to pentathionic acid by epidermal cells or by certain microorganisms.

Precautions to Consider

Geriatrics

Appropriate studies on the relationship of age to the effects of sulfur have not been performed in the geriatric population. However, no geriatrics-specific problems have been documented to date.

Drug interactions and/or related problems

The following drug interactions and/or related problems have been selected on the basis of their potential clinical significance (possible mechanism in parentheses where appropriate)—not necessarily inclusive (» = major clinical significance):

Note: Combinations containing any of the following medications, depending on the amount present, may also interact with this medication.

Abrasive or medicated soaps or cleansers or
Acne preparations or preparations containing a peeling agent, such as:
  Benzoyl peroxide
  Resorcinol
  Salicylic acid
  Tretinoin, or
Acne preparations, topical, other, or
Alcohol-containing preparations, topical, such as:
  After-shave lotions
  Astringents
  Perfumed toiletries
  Shaving creams or lotions, or
Cosmetics or soaps with a strong drying effect or
Isotretinoin or
Medicated cosmetics or "cover-ups"
  (concurrent use with sulfur may cause a cumulative irritant or drying effect, especially with the application of peeling, desquamating, or abrasive agents, resulting in excessive irritation of the skin)

Mercury compounds, topical
  (concurrent use with sulfur may result in a chemical reaction releasing hydrogen sulfide, which has a foul odor, may be irritating, and may stain the skin black)

Contraindications/Medical problems

The contraindications/medical problems included have been selected on the basis of their potential clinical significance (reasons given in parentheses where appropriate)—not necessarily inclusive (» = major clinical significance).

Risk-benefit should be considered when the following medical problem exists:

Sensitivity to sulfur

Side/Adverse Effects

The following side/adverse effects have been selected on the basis of their potential clinical significance (possible signs and symptoms in parentheses where appropriate)—not necessarily inclusive:

Those indicating need for medical attention
Skin irritation not present before therapy

Those indicating need for medical attention only if they continue or are bothersome
Redness and peeling of skin—may occur after a few days

Patient Consultation

In providing consultation, consider emphasizing the following selected information (» = major clinical significance):

Before using this medication
» Conditions affecting use, especially:
    Sensitivity to sulfur

Proper use of this medication
» Importance of not using more medication than the amount recommended
» Avoiding contact with the eyes
    Missed dose: Using as soon as possible; not using if almost time for next dose

Proper administration:
For cream, and lotion dosage forms
   Before applying—Washing affected areas with soap and water; drying thoroughly
   Applying enough to cover affected areas; rubbing in gently
For ointment dosage form used for seborrheic dermatitis
   Before applying—Washing affected areas with soap and water; drying thoroughly
   Applying enough to cover affected areas; rubbing in gently
For ointment dosage form used for scabies
   Before applying—Washing entire body with soap and water; drying thoroughly.
   Applying enough at bedtime to cover entire body from neck down; rubbing in gently; leaving on body for 24 hours; washing entire body before applying again
   Importance of washing entire body thoroughly 24 hours after the last treatment
For soap dosage form
   Working up rich lather with soap, using warm water
   Washing affected areas and rinsing thoroughly
   Applying lather again; rubbing in gently for a few minutes
   Removing excess lather with a towel or tissue without rinsing
»   Proper storage

Precautions while using this medication
»   Avoiding simultaneous use with other topical acne preparations or preparations containing peeling agents, alcohol-containing preparations, abrasive soaps or cleansers, cosmetics or soaps with drying effect, medicated cosmetics, or other topical skin medication, unless otherwise directed by physician
»   Avoiding concurrent use with topical mercury-containing preparations

Side/adverse effects
   Signs of potential side effects, especially skin irritation not present before therapy

General Dosing Information

Before the ointment is applied, the affected areas should be washed with soap and water and then dried thoroughly.

Topical Dosage Forms

SULFUR CREAM

Usual adult and adolescent dose: Antiacne agent (topical)—Topical, to the skin.

Auxiliary labeling: • For external use only.

SULFUR LOTION

Usual adult and adolescent dose: Antiacne agent (topical)—Topical, to the skin, two or three times a day.

Auxiliary labeling: • For external use only.

SULFUR OINTMENT USP

Usual adult and adolescent dose:
   Antiacne agent (topical)—Topical, to the skin, as a 0.5% ointment as needed.
   Antiseborrheic or
   Keratolytic (topical)—Topical, to the skin, as a 5 to 10% ointment one or two times a day.
   Scabicide—Topical, to the entire body from the neck down, as 6% sulfur in petrolatum at bedtime for 3 nights; patients may bathe before each application and should bathe 24 hours following the last application.
   Note: Treatment may be repeated after 1 week if there is no clinical improvement; additional weekly treatments should be administered only if there are live mites.

Auxiliary labeling: • For external use only.

SULFUR BAR SOAP

Usual adult and adolescent dose:
   Antiacne agent (topical) or
   Keratolytic (topical)—Topical, to the skin.

Auxiliary labeling: • For external use only.

SULFURATED LIME   Topical

Some commonly used *brand names* are:
   In the U.S.—*Vlemasque*
   In Canada—*Vlemasque*
Another commonly used name is Vleminckx's solution.

TOPICAL
Sulfurated Lime Mask
   In the U.S. and Canada—*Vlemasque*
Sulfurated Lime Topical Solution
   In the U.S.—GENERIC

Category

Antiacne agent (topical)—Sulfurated Lime Mask; Sulfurated Lime Topical Solution.
Keratolytic (topical)—Sulfurated Lime Mask; Sulfurated Lime Topical Solution.
Scabicide—Sulfurated Lime Topical Solution.

Indications

Accepted
Acne vulgaris (treatment)—Sulfurated lime mask and solution are indicated for the treatment of cystic and papular types of acne vulgaris.
Dermatitis, seborrheic (treatment); or
Pustular infections (treatment)—Sulfurated lime solution is indicated for the treatment of seborrheic dermatitis, pustular infections, and other dermatoses.
Scabies (treatment)—Sulfurated lime solution is indicated for the control and treatment of scabies.

Pharmacology

Mechanism of action/Effect: Sulfurated lime has a mild desquamative action.

Precautions to Consider

Geriatrics
Appropriate studies on the relationship of age to the effects of sulfurated lime have not been performed in the geriatric population. However, no geriatrics-specific problems have been documented to date.

Drug interactions and/or related problems
The following drug interactions and/or related problems have been selected on the basis of their potential clinical significance (possible mechanism in parentheses where appropriate)—not necessarily inclusive (» = major clinical significance):

Note: Combinations containing any of the following medications, depending on the amount present, may also interact with this medication.

Abrasive or medicated soaps or cleansers or
Acne preparations or preparations containing a peeling agent, such as:
  Benzoyl peroxide
  Resorcinol
  Salicylic acid
  Sulfur
  Tretinoin, or
Acne preparations, topical, other, or
Alcohol-containing preparations, topical, such as:
  After-shave lotions
  Astringents
  Perfumed toiletries
  Shaving creams or lotions, or
Cosmetics or soaps with a strong drying effect or
Isotretinoin or
Medicated cosmetics or "cover-ups"
  (concurrent use with sulfurated lime may cause a cumulative irritant or drying effect, especially with the application of peeling, desquamating, or abrasive agents, resulting in excessive irritation of the skin)
Mercury compounds, topical
  (concurrent use with sulfurated lime may result in a chemical reaction releasing hydrogen sulfide, which has a foul odor, may be irritating, and may stain the skin black)

Contraindications/Medical problems
The contraindications/medical problems included have been selected on the basis of their potential clinical significance (reasons given in parentheses where appropriate)—not necessarily inclusive (» = major clinical significance).

Risk-benefit should be considered when the following medical problem exists:
  Sensitivity to sulfurated lime

Side/Adverse Effects

The following side/adverse effects have been selected on the basis of their potential clinical significance (possible signs and symptoms in parentheses where appropriate)—not necessarily inclusive:

Those indicating need for medical attention
  Skin irritation not present before therapy

Those indicating need for medical attention only if they continue or are bothersome
  Redness and peeling of skin—may occur after a few days; *unusual dryness of skin*

Patient Consultation

In providing consultation, consider emphasizing the following selected information (» = major clinical significance):

Before using this medication
» Conditions affecting use, especially:
    Sensitivity to sulfurated lime

Proper use of this medication
» Importance of not using more medication than the amount recommended
» Avoiding contact with the eyes
  Proper administration:
  For mask dosage form
    Applying generous amount over entire face and neck
    Allowing to remain on affected areas for 20 to 25 minutes
    Removing with lukewarm water, using gentle circular motion; patting skin dry
  For topical solution dosage form
    Diluting before using; knowing correct administration technique
    Avoiding contact with jewelry and other metals
  Missed dose: Applying as soon as possible; not applying if almost time for next dose
» Proper storage

Precautions while using this medication
» Avoiding simultaneous use with other topical acne preparations or preparations containing peeling agents, alcohol-containing preparations, abrasive soaps or cleansers, cosmetics or soaps with drying effect, medicated cosmetics, or other topical skin medication, unless otherwise directed by physician
» Avoiding concurrent use with topical mercury-containing preparations

Side/adverse effects
  Signs of potential side effects, especially skin irritation not present before therapy

General Dosing Information

For mask dosage form
Sulfurated lime solution 6% in a drying clay mask should be applied in a generous layer over the entire face and neck or other affected areas. It should be allowed to remain on the affected areas for 20 to 25 minutes and then removed with lukewarm water. Skin should be patted dry.

For topical solution dosage form
After dilution, the topical solution may be used for wet dressings, as a soak, or in a bath.

Solutions having a concentration of 1:10,000 are used initially, with the concentration being increased at frequent intervals up to a concentration of 1:10 as tolerated.

When Sulfurated Lime Topical Solution USP XXI is used, the solution should be diluted with at least 9 volumes of water before use.

For use as a wet dressing, compresses should be soaked in the hot solution and applied for 10 to 20 minutes.

Topical Dosage Forms

SULFURATED LIME MASK

Usual adult and adolescent dose: Antiacne agent (topical)—Topical, to the skin, once a day.

Auxiliary labeling: • For external use only.

SULFURATED LIME TOPICAL SOLUTION

Usual adult and adolescent dose:
  Antiacne agent (topical); or
  Keratolytic (topical)—Topical, to the skin, as a diluted solution (1:32 to 1:9) one or two times a day.
  Scabicide—Topical, to the skin, as a diluted solution (1:9) one or two times a day for three days or as directed.

Auxiliary labeling:
  • For external use only.
  • Must be diluted before using.

TAMOXIFEN   Systemic

Some commonly used *brand names* are:
   In the U.S.—*Nolvadex*
   In Canada—*Nolvadex; Nolvadex-D; Novo-Tamoxifen; Tamofen;
   Tamone*

ORAL
Tamoxifen Citrate Tablets USP
   In the U.S.—*Nolvadex*
   In Canada—*Nolvadex; Novo-Tamoxifen; Tamofen; Tamone*
Tamoxifen Citrate Enteric-coated Tablets*
   In Canada—*Nolvadex-D*

---

*Not commercially available in the U.S.

Category: Antineoplastic.

Indications

Accepted
Carcinoma, breast (treatment)—
   Adjuvant therapy: Tamoxifen is effective in delaying recurrence
      following total mastectomy and axillary dissection or segmen-
      tal mastectomy, axillary dissection, and breast irradiation in
      women with axillary node-negative breast cancer. Data are
      insufficient to predict which women are most likely to benefit
      and to determine if tamoxifen provides any benefit in women
      with tumors of less than 1 cm.
   Tamoxifen is effective in delaying recurrence following total
      mastectomy and axillary dissection in postmenopausal women
      with breast cancer (T_{1-3}, N_1, M_0). In some tamoxifen adjuvant
      studies, most of the benefit to date has been in the subgroup
      with 4 or more positive axillary nodes.
   The estrogen and progesterone receptor values may help to
      predict whether adjuvant tamoxifen therapy is likely to be ben-
      eficial.
   Therapy for advanced disease: Tamoxifen is indicated in the treat-
      ment of metastatic breast cancer in women. It is effective in
      premenopausal women as an alternative to oophorectomy or
      ovarian irradiation. Available evidence indicates that patients
      whose tumors are estrogen receptor positive are more likely to
      benefit from tamoxifen therapy.

Pharmacology

Mechanism of action/Effect: Tamoxifen is a nonsteroidal antiestrogen
   agent that also has weak estrogenic effects. The exact mechanism
   of antineoplastic action is unknown, but may be related to its
   antiestrogen effects; tamoxifen blocks uptake of estradiol.

Other actions/effects: Tamoxifen may induce ovulation in anovula-
   tory women, stimulating release of gonadotropin-releasing hormone from the hypothalamus, which in turn stimulates release of
   pituitary gonadotropins.

Onset of action: An objective response usually occurs within 4 to 10
   weeks of therapy, but may take several months in patients with
   bone metastases.

Duration of action: Estrogen antagonism may persist for several
   weeks following a single dose.

Precautions to Consider

Geriatrics
Appropriate studies on the relationship of age to the effects of tamoxifen
   have not been performed in the geriatric population. However, this
medication is commonly used in elderly patients and geriatrics-
specific problems that would limit the usefulness of this medication in the elderly are not expected.

Drug interactions and/or related problems
The following drug interactions and/or related problems have been
   selected on the basis of their potential clinical significance (possible mechanism in parentheses where appropriate)—not necessarily inclusive (» = major clinical significance):
Note: Combinations containing any of the following medications, de-
      pending on the amount present, may also interact with this
      medication.

   Antacids or
   Cimetidine or
   Famotidine or
   Ranitidine
      (these medications increase intragastric pH and may therefore
      cause premature dissolution, and loss of the protective effect,
      of enteric coatings; a 1- to 2-hour interval should elapse be-
      tween administration of an antacid and enteric-coated tamoxifen;
      also, the probability should be considered that concurrent use
      of an enteric-coated formulation with cimetidine, famotidine,
      or ranitidine will not provide greater protection against gastric
      irritation or ulceration than is provided by the histamine H_2-
      receptor antagonist alone)

   Estrogens
      (concurrent use may interfere with tamoxifen's therapeutic ef-
      fect)

Contraindications/Medical problems
The contraindications/medical problems included have been selected
   on the basis of their potential clinical significance (reasons given
   in parentheses where appropriate)—not necessarily inclusive (» =
   major clinical significance).

***Risk-benefit should be considered when the following medical prob-
lems exist:***
   Cataracts or vision disturbances
      (visual disturbances, including corneal changes, cataracts, and
      retinopathy, have been reported in patients receiving tamoxifen)
   Hyperlipidemia
      (increased serum lipid concentrations have been reported infre-
      quently)
   Leukopenia
      (leukopenia has been reported occasionally in patients receiv-
      ing tamoxifen)
   » Sensitivity to tamoxifen
   Thrombocytopenia
      (thrombocytopenia has been reported occasionally in patients
      receiving tamoxifen, although platelet counts recovered even
      with continued therapy)

Side/Adverse Effects

Note: A transient, sometimes severe, increase in bone or tumor pain
      may occur shortly after initiation of therapy but usually sub-
      sides with continued tamoxifen treatment. Analgesics may be
      required during this time.

      Tamoxifen induces ovulation, which puts patients at risk for
      becoming pregnant.

      Ovarian cysts have been reported in a small number of pre-
      menopausal patients treated with tamoxifen for advanced breast
      carcinoma.

The following side/adverse effects have been selected on the basis of their potential clinical significance (possible signs and symptoms in parentheses where appropriate)—not necessarily inclusive:

Those indicating need for medical attention
Incidence less frequent or rare
Confusion; pulmonary embolus (shortness of breath); *thrombosis* (pain or swelling in legs); *weakness or sleepiness; endometrial hyperplasia, endometrial polyps, or endometrial carcinoma* (vaginal bleeding)

Incidence related to high (240 to 320 mg per day), prolonged (17 months or more) dosage
Retinopathy or corneal opacities (blurred vision)

Those indicating need for medical attention only if they continue or are bothersome
Incidence more frequent—10 to 20%
Hot flashes; nausea and/or vomiting; weight gain

Note: *Weight gain* is an estrogen effect.

Incidence less frequent
Changes in menstrual period; headache; itching in genital area; transient local disease flare (bone pain); *skin rash or dryness; vaginal discharge*

Note: *Transient local disease flare* may also consist of a sudden increase in the size of pre-existing lesions in patients with soft tissue disease, sometimes associated with marked erythema within and surrounding the lesions and/or the development of new lesions. Bone pain or other disease flare usually occurs shortly after initiation of therapy and subsides rapidly.

Patient Consultation

In providing consultation, consider emphasizing the following selected information (» = major clinical significance):

Before using this medication
» Conditions affecting use, especially:
    Sensitivity to tamoxifen
    Pregnancy—Use not recommended because of risk of miscarriage, death of the fetus, birth defects, and vaginal bleeding; advisability of using nonhormonal contraception; telling physician immediately if pregnancy is suspected
    Breast-feeding—Not recommended because of risk of serious side effects

Proper use of this medication
» Importance of not taking more or less medication than the amount prescribed
    Proper administration of enteric-coated tablets: Swallowing whole without crushing or breaking
» Frequency of nausea and vomiting; importance of continuing medication despite stomach upset
    Checking with physician if vomiting occurs shortly after dose is taken
    Missed dose: Not taking at all; not doubling doses
» Proper storage

Precautions while using this medication
» Importance of close monitoring by the physician
    Advisability of using nonhormonal contraception during therapy; telling physician immediately if pregnancy is suspected
    Not taking an antacid within 1 or 2 hours of taking enteric-coated dosage form of tamoxifen

Side/adverse effects
    Signs of potential side effects, especially confusion, pulmonary embolus, thrombosis, weakness or sleepiness, retinopathy, and corneal opacities
    Physician or nurse can help in dealing with side effects

General Dosing Information

Patients receiving tamoxifen should be under supervision of a physician experienced in cancer chemotherapy.

If side effects are severe, dosage may sometimes be reduced without loss of control of the disease.

If severe hypercalcemia occurs, tamoxifen should be discontinued.

Oral Dosage Forms

TAMOXIFEN CITRATE TABLETS USP

Note: The dosing and strengths available are expressed in terms of tamoxifen base.

Usual adult dose: Breast carcinoma—Oral, 10 to 20 mg (base) two times a day (in the morning and evening).

TAMOXIFEN CITRATE ENTERIC-COATED TABLETS

Usual adult dose: Breast carcinoma—Oral, 10 or 20 mg once a day.

Auxiliary labeling:
  • Swallow tablets whole.
  • Do not take antacids within 1 to 2 hours of taking this medicine.

TERAZOSIN   Systemic

A commonly used *brand name* in the U.S. and Canada is *Hytrin*.

ORAL
Terazosin Hydrochloride Tablets
    In the U.S. and Canada—*Hytrin*

Category: Antihypertensive.

Indications

Note: Bracketed information in the *Indications* section refers to uses not included in U.S. product labeling.

Accepted
Hypertension (treatment)—Terazosin is indicated in the treatment of hypertension.

In the 1988 Report of the Joint National Committee on Detection, Evaluation, and Treatment of High Blood Pressure, a progression in choice of treatments for essential hypertension is recommended:

Nonpharmacologic management (especially sodium restriction, weight reduction and exercise, and moderation of alcohol consumption) is recommended first for some patients, including those with mild hypertension, and is recommended as an adjunct to all pharmacologic hypertensive therapy.

Initial drug therapy usually consists of a diuretic, beta-adrenergic blocking agent, calcium channel blocking agent, or angiotensin-converting enzyme (ACE) inhibitor. If adequate blood pressure control is not achieved and the patient is adherent to the treatment program and not experiencing significant side effects, dosage of the drug may be increased, a drug from another one of these initial classes may be added or substituted, or a second drug from a different class—centrally acting alpha-adrenergic blocking agents (e.g., clonidine, guanabenz, guanfacine, methyldopa), peripheral-acting adrenergic antagonists (e.g., guanadrel, guanethidine, rauwolfia alkaloids), post-synaptic alpha-1 peripheral adrenergic inhibitors (e.g., doxazosin, prazosin, terazosin), or vasodilators (e.g., hydralazine, minoxidil)—may be added or substituted.

If necessary, a drug from another class in the second group may be substituted or added as a third drug. If blood pressure control is still not achieved, a drug from still another class may be substituted or added as a fourth drug, or the patient may need further evaluation and/or referral.

[Benign prostatic hypertrophy (treatment)][1]—Terazosin may be used for the treatment of urinary symptoms associated with benign prostatic hypertrophy. Although studies with terazosin for this indication are limited, controlled trials with prazosin have shown beneficial results.

---

[1]Not included in Canadian product labeling.

Pharmacology

Mechanism of action/Effect: Terazosin has a peripheral post-synaptic alpha1-adrenergic blocking action, which is thought to account primarily for its effects.
　Hypertension—Terazosin produces vasodilation and reduces peripheral resistance but generally has little effect on cardiac output. Antihypertensive effect with chronic dosing is usually not accompanied by reflex tachycardia. There is little or no effect on renal blood flow or glomerular filtration rate.

Other actions/effects: Terazosin may effect serum lipids. The most consistent changes observed are a decrease in levels of serum total cholesterol and low density lipoprotein (LDL) cholesterol plus very low density lipoprotein (VLDL) cholesterol fraction. However, the implications of these changes are unclear.

Onset of action: Single dose—15 minutes.

Time to peak effect:
　Single dose—2 to 3 hours.
　Multiple doses—Up to 6 to 8 weeks.

Duration of action: Single dose—24 hours.

Precautions to Consider

Geriatrics
Although appropriate studies on the relationship of age to the effects of terazosin have not been performed in the geriatric population, clinical trials have included patients over 65 years of age and have not demonstrated geriatrics-specific problems that would limit the usefulness of terazosin in the elderly. However, the elderly may be more sensitive to the hypotensive effects of terazosin.

Drug interactions and/or related problems
The following drug interactions and/or related problems have been selected on the basis of their potential clinical significance (possible mechanism in parentheses where appropriate)—not necessarily inclusive (» = major clinical significance):
Note: Combinations containing any of the following medications, depending on the amount present, may also interact with this medication.
　Anti-inflammatory drugs, nonsteroidal (NSAIDs), especially indomethacin
　　(indomethacin, and probably other NSAIDs, may antagonize the antihypertensive effect of terazosin by inhibiting renal pros-

taglandin synthesis and/or by causing sodium and fluid retention; the patient should be carefully monitored to confirm that the desired effect is being obtained)
　Estrogens
　　(antihypertensive effects of terazosin may be reduced when it is used concurrently with these agents; estrogen-induced fluid retention tends to increase blood pressure; the patient should be carefully monitored to confirm that the desired effect is being obtained)
　Hypotension-producing medications, other
　　(antihypertensive effects may be potentiated when these medications are used concurrently with terazosin; although some antihypertensive and/or diuretic combinations are frequently used to therapeutic advantage, when used concurrently dosage adjustments are necessary)
　Sympathomimetics
　　(antihypertensive effects of terazosin may be reduced when it is used concurrently with these agents; the patient should be carefully monitored to confirm that the desired effect is being obtained)
　　(concurrent use of terazosin antagonizes the peripheral vasoconstriction produced by high doses of dopamine)
　　(concurrent use of terazosin may decrease the pressor response to ephedrine)
　　(concurrent use of terazosin may block the alpha-adrenergic effects of epinephrine, possibly resulting in severe hypotension and tachycardia)
　　(concurrent use of terazosin usually decreases, but does not reverse or completely block, the pressor effect of metaraminol)
　　(prior administration of terazosin may decrease the pressor effect and shorten the duration of action of methoxamine and phenylephrine)

Contraindications/Medical problems
The contraindications/medical problems included have been selected on the basis of their potential clinical significance (reasons given in parentheses where appropriate)—not necessarily inclusive (» = major clinical significance).

Risk-benefit should be considered when the following medical problems exist:
　Angina or
　Cardiac disease, severe
　　(may induce angina or aggravate pre-existing angina)
　Hepatic function impairment
　　(although studies in patients with impaired hepatic function have not been done, terazosin undergoes hepatic metabolism, and, therefore, increased sensitivity or prolonged terazosin effect may occur)
　Renal function impairment
　　(approximately 40% of terazosin dose is eliminated by the kidneys as parent drug or metabolites; therefore, prolonged hypotensive effects may occur)
　Sensitivity to terazosin

Side/Adverse Effects

Note: A "first-dose orthostatic hypotensive reaction" sometimes occurs, most frequently 30 minutes to 2 hours after the initial dose of terazosin, and may be severe. Syncope or other postural symptoms, such as dizziness, may occur. Subsequent occurrence with dosage increases is also possible. Incidence appears to be dose-related; thus, it is important that therapy be initiated with a 1-mg dose given at bedtime. Patients who are volume-depleted or sodium-restricted may be more sensitive to the orthostatic hypotensive effects of terazosin, and the effect may be exaggerated after exercise.

The following side/adverse effects have been selected on the basis of their potential clinical significance (possible signs and symptoms in parentheses where appropriate)—not necessarily inclusive:

Those indicating need for medical attention
Incidence more frequent
 Dizziness
Incidence less frequent
 Angina (chest pain); *dyspnea* (shortness of breath); *edema, peripheral* (swelling of feet or lower legs); *orthostatic hypotension* (dizziness or lightheadedness, when getting up from a lying or sitting position; sudden fainting); *palpitations* (pounding heartbeat); *tachycardia* (fast or irregular heartbeat)
  Note: Rarely, weight gain (usually 1 kg [2 lb] or less) may occur with *peripheral edema.*

Those indicating need for medical attention only if they continue or are bothersome
Incidence more frequent
 Asthenia (unusual tiredness or weakness); *headache*
Incidence less frequent
 Back or joint pain; blurred vision; nasal congestion (stuffy nose); *nausea or vomiting; somnolence* (drowsiness)

Patient Consultation

In providing consultation, consider emphasizing the following selected information (» = major clinical significance):

Before using this medication
» Conditions affecting use, especially:
  Sensitivity to quinazolines
  Use in the elderly—Increased sensitivity to hypotensive effects
  Other medical problems, especially angina, severe cardiac disease, hepatic function impairment, or renal function impairment

Proper use of this medication
  Getting into the habit of taking at same time each day to help increase compliance
  Missed dose: Taking as soon as possible the same day; not taking if not remembered until next day; not doubling doses
» Proper storage
For use as an antihypertensive
  Possible need for control of weight and diet, especially sodium intake
» Patient may not experience symptoms of hypertension; importance of taking medication even if feeling well
» Does not cure, but helps control hypertension; possible need for lifelong therapy; serious consequences of untreated hypertension

Precautions while using this medication
  Regular visits to physician to check progress
» Caution if dizziness, lightheadedness, or sudden fainting occurs, especially after initial dose; taking first dose at bedtime
» Caution when getting up suddenly from a lying or sitting position
» Caution in using alcohol, while standing for long periods or exercising, and during hot weather because of enhanced orthostatic hypotensive effects
» Possibility of drowsiness
» Caution when driving or doing anything else requiring alertness because of possible drowsiness, dizziness, or lightheadedness
» Not taking other medication, especially nonprescription sympathomimetics, unless discussed with physician

Side/adverse effects
  Signs of potential side effects, especially angina, dizziness, dyspnea, orthostatic hypotension, palpitations, peripheral edema, and tachycardia

General Dosing Information

Dosage of terazosin should be adjusted to meet the individual requirements of each patient, on the basis of blood pressure response.

Terazosin may be used alone or in combination with a thiazide diuretic or beta-adrenergic blocker, both of which reduce the tendency for sodium and water retention, although they also produce additive hypotension. If combination therapy is indicated, individual titration is required to ensure the lowest possible therapeutic dose of each drug.

In order to minimize the "first-dose orthostatic hypotensive reaction," an initial dose of 1 mg is recommended, with gradual increments as needed. Administration of the initial dose at bedtime is recommended, as well as for the initial dose at each increment.

When a diuretic or other antihypertensive agent is added to terazosin therapy, the dose of terazosin should be reduced, followed by titration of dosage of the combination. When terazosin is added to existing diuretic or antihypertensive therapy, the dose of the other agent should be reduced and terazosin started at a dose of 1 mg once a day.

Oral Dosage Forms

Note: Bracketed uses in the *Dosage Forms* section refer to categories of use and/or indications that are not included in U.S. product labeling.

TERAZOSIN HYDROCHLORIDE TABLETS

Note: The dosing and strengths of the dosage forms available are expressed in terms of terazosin base (not the hydrochloride salt).

Usual adult dose:
  Antihypertensive—
   Initial: Oral, 1 mg (base) once a day, at bedtime.
   Maintenance: Oral, adjusted gradually to meet individual requirements, usually 1 to 5 mg (base) once a day.
   Note: If the antihypertensive effect is not maintained for a full 24 hours, twice daily dosing may be more effective.
  [Benign prostatic hypertrophy][1]—
   Initial: Oral, 1 mg (base), at bedtime.
   Maintenance: Oral, adjusted gradually up to 5 to 10 mg (base) once a day.

Note: Geriatric patients may be more sensitive to the effects of the usual adult dose.

Usual adult prescribing limits: Daily doses higher than 20 mg (base) usually do not have increased efficacy.

Auxiliary labeling:
 • Do not take other medicines without your doctor's advice.
 • May cause dizziness.

---

[1]Not included in Canadian product labeling.

TESTOLACTONE   Systemic†

A commonly used *brand name* in the U.S. is *Teslac*.

ORAL
Testolactone Tablets USP†
   In the U.S.—*Teslac*

---

†Not commercially available in Canada.

Category: Antineoplastic.

Indications

Accepted
Carcinoma, breast (treatment)—Testolactone is indicated as adjunctive therapy in the palliative treatment of advanced or disseminated breast cancer in postmenopausal women when hormone therapy is indicated. It may also be used in women who were diagnosed with disseminated breast carcinoma when premenopausal, in whom ovarian function has subsequently been terminated.

Testolactone is not recommended for treatment of breast cancer in males.

Pharmacology

Mechanism of action/Effect: Testolactone is structurally similar to androgens but is not known to cause virilization. The mechanism of its antineoplastic activity is unknown, although it is reported to inhibit steroid aromatase activity (the effect may be noncompetitive and irreversible) and reduce estrone synthesis from adrenal androstenedione (the major source of estrogen in postmenopausal women).

Onset of action: Clinical effects may not be apparent for 6 to 12 weeks.

Precautions to Consider

Geriatrics
No information is available on the relationship of age to the effects of testolactone in geriatric patients.

Drug interactions and/or related problems
The following drug interactions and/or related problems have been selected on the basis of their potential clinical significance (possible mechanism in parentheses where appropriate)—not necessarily inclusive (» = major clinical significance):

Anticoagulants, coumarin- or indandione-type
   (effects may be increased by concurrent use of testolactone; dosage adjustment of oral anticoagulants may be necessary)

Contraindications/Medical problems
The contraindications/medical problems included have been selected on the basis of their potential clinical significance (reasons given in parentheses where appropriate)—not necessarily inclusive (» = major clinical significance).

Risk-benefit should be considered when the following medical problems exist:
» Cardiorenal disease
» Hypercalcemia
» Sensitivity to testolactone

Side/Adverse Effects
The following side/adverse effects have been selected on the basis of their potential clinical significance (possible signs and symptoms in parentheses where appropriate)—not necessarily inclusive:

Those indicating need for medical attention
Incidence less frequent
   Peripheral neuropathies (numbness or tingling of fingers, toes, or face)

Those indicating need for medical attention only if they continue or are bothersome
Incidence less frequent
   Diarrhea; loss of appetite; nausea or vomiting; pain or swelling in feet or lower legs; swelling or redness of tongue

Patient Consultation
Consider advising the patient on the following (» = major clinical significance):

Before using this medication
» Conditions affecting use, especially:
   Sensitivity to testolactone
   Pregnancy—Causes increased fetal and pup mortality and abnormal fetal development in rats
   Other medical problems, especially cardiorenal disease

Proper use of this medication
» Importance of not taking more or less medication than the amount prescribed
» Possible nausea and vomiting; importance of continuing medication despite stomach upset
   Checking with physician if vomiting occurs shortly after dose is taken
   Missed dose: Taking as soon as possible, not taking if almost time for next dose; not doubling doses; checking with physician if two or more doses in a row are missed
» Proper storage

Precautions while using this medication
» Importance of close monitoring by the physician

Side/adverse effects
   Signs of potential side effects, especially peripheral neuropathies
   Physician or nurse can help in dealing with side effects

General Dosing Information
Patients receiving testolactone should be under supervision of a physician experienced in cancer chemotherapy.

If hypercalcemia occurs, therapy with testolactone should be withdrawn and the patient treated with large volumes of fluid.

Testolactone should be given for at least 3 months before it is considered ineffective, unless active progression of the disease occurs.

Oral Dosage Forms

TESTOLACTONE TABLETS USP

Usual adult dose: Breast carcinoma—Oral, 250 mg four times a day.

TETRACYCLINES   Ophthalmic

Some commonly used *brand names* are:
In the U.S. and Canada—
Achromycin [Tetracycline]
Aureomycin [Chlortetracycline]

OPHTHALMIC
CHLORTETRACYCLINE
Chlortetracycline Hydrochloride Ophthalmic Ointment USP
In the U.S. and Canada—*Aureomycin*
TETRACYCLINE
Tetracycline Hydrochloride Ophthalmic Ointment USP
In the U.S. and Canada—*Achromycin*
Tetracycline Hydrochloride Ophthalmic Suspension USP
In the U.S.—*Achromycin*

Category: Antibacterial (ophthalmic).

Indications

Note: Bracketed information in the *Indications* section refers to uses
not included in U.S. product labeling.

Accepted
Ocular infections (treatment)—Ophthalmic chlortetracycline is indicated in the treatment of superficial ocular infections caused by
*Staphylococcus aureus, Streptococcus epidemicus (Streptococcus
pyogenes), Neisseria gonorrhoeae, S. pneumoniae (Diplococcus
pneumoniae), Haemophilus influenzae, H. ducreyi, Klebsiella
pneumoniae, Francisella tularensis (Pasteurella tularensis), Yersinia pestis (Pasteurella pestis), Escherichia coli, Bacillus anthracis,*
and *Lymphogranuloma venereum.*

Ophthalmic tetracycline is indicated in the treatment of superficial
ocular infections caused by *Staphylococcus aureus,* streptococci
including *Streptococcus epidemicus (Streptococcus pyogenes)* and
S. pneumoniae (Diplococcus pneumoniae), Neisseria gonorrhoeae,
and *Escherichia coli.*

Ophthalmia neonatorum (prophylaxis)—Ophthalmic [chlortetracycline]
and tetracycline are indicated in the prophylaxis of ophthalmia
neonatorum caused by *N. gonorrhoeae* and *Chlamydia trachomatis.*

Trachoma (treatment)—Ophthalmic chlortetracycline and tetracycline
are indicated in the treatment of trachoma caused by *Chlamydia
trachomatis.* They should be used concurrently with oral tetracyclines.

[Blepharitis, bacterial (treatment)];
[Blepharoconjunctivitis (treatment)];
[Conjunctivitis, bacterial (treatment)];
[Keratitis, bacterial (treatment)];
[Keratoconjunctivitis, bacterial (treatment)]; or
[Meibomianitis (treatment)]—Ophthalmic chlortetracycline and tetra-
cycline are used in the treatment of bacterial blepharitis, blepharo-
conjunctivitis, bacterial conjunctivitis, bacterial keratitis, bacterial
keratoconjunctivitis, and meibomianitis.

[Chlamydial infections (treatment)]; or
[Rosacea, ocular (treatment)]—Ophthalmic tetracycline is used in the
treatment of chlamydial infections and ocular rosacea.

Not all species or strains of a particular organism may be susceptible
to a specific tetracycline.

Unaccepted
Tetracycline is not effective against *Haemophilus influenzae, Klebsiella* species, *Enterobacter (Aerobacter)* species, *Pseudomonas
aeruginosa,* or *Serratia marcescens.*

Pharmacology

Mechanism of action/Effect: Tetracyclines are broad-spectrum bacteriostatic agents and act by inhibiting protein synthesis by blocking the binding of aminoacyl tRNA (transfer RNA) to the mRNA
(messenger RNA) ribosome complex. Reversible binding occurs
primarily at the 30 S ribosomal subunit of susceptible organisms.
Bacterial cell wall synthesis is not inhibited.

Precautions to Consider

Cross-sensitivity and/or related problems
Patients sensitive to one tetracycline, tetracycline combination, or
tetracycline derivative may be sensitive to other tetracyclines also.

Geriatrics
Appropriate studies with tetracyclines have not been performed in the
geriatric population. However, no geriatrics-specific problems have
been documented to date.

Contraindications/Medical problems
The contraindications/medical problems included have been selected
on the basis of their potential clinical significance (reasons given
in parentheses where appropriate)—not necessarily inclusive (» =
major clinical significance).

*Risk-benefit should be considered when the following medical prob-
lem exists:*
Sensitivity to tetracyclines

Patient Consultation

In providing consultation, consider emphasizing the following selected information (» = major clinical significance):

Before using this medication
» Conditions affecting use, especially:
Sensitivity to tetracycline, chlortetracycline, or any related antibiotic, such as demeclocycline, doxycycline, methacycline,
minocycline, or oxytetracycline

Proper use of this medication
Proper administration technique for ophthalmic suspension and
ophthalmic ointment
» Compliance with full course of therapy
Missed dose: Applying as soon as possible; not applying if almost
time for next dose
» Proper storage

Precautions while using this medication
Blurred vision after application of ophthalmic ointments and oph-
thalmic suspensions in oil (tetracycline)
Checking with physician if no improvement within a few days

General Dosing Information

Blurred vision after application of ophthalmic suspensions in oil or
ophthalmic ointments is to be expected.

Therapy should be continued for 1 to 2 months or longer in acute and
chronic trachoma. Severe infections may also require concurrent
oral therapy for trachoma.

In term infants born to mothers with clinically apparent gonorrhea, a
single intramuscular or intravenous dose of 50,000 Units of penicillin G potassium is administered concurrently with ophthalmic
tetracycline. In low-birth-weight infants, the dose is 20,000 Units.

At night, the ophthalmic ointment may be used as an adjunct to the ophthalmic suspension to provide prolonged contact with the medication.

Although some manufacturers recommend a dose of 2 drops of an ophthalmic solution at appropriate intervals, the conjunctival sac will usually hold only 1 drop.

CHLORTETRACYCLINE

Ophthalmic Dosage Forms

CHLORTETRACYCLINE HYDROCHLORIDE OPHTHALMIC OINTMENT USP

Usual adult and adolescent dose: Ocular infections—Topical, to the conjunctiva, a thin strip (approximately 1 cm) of ointment every two to four hours or more frequently.

Auxiliary labeling:
- For the eye.
- Continue medicine for full time of treatment.

TETRACYCLINE

Ophthalmic Dosage Forms

TETRACYCLINE HYDROCHLORIDE OPHTHALMIC OINTMENT USP

Usual adult and adolescent dose:
Ocular infections—Topical, to the conjunctiva, a thin strip (approximately 1 cm) of ointment every two to four hours or more frequently.
Ophthalmia neonatorum—Topical, to the conjunctiva, a thin strip (approximately 1 cm) of ointment as a single dose.

Auxiliary labeling:
- For the eye.
- Continue medicine for full time of treatment.

TETRACYCLINE HYDROCHLORIDE OPHTHALMIC SUSPENSION USP

Usual adult and adolescent dose:
Ocular infections—Topical, to the conjunctiva, 1 drop every six to twelve hours or more frequently.
Ophthalmia neonatorum—Topical, to the conjunctiva, 1 drop as a single dose.

Auxiliary labeling:
- Shake well.
- For the eye.
- Continue medicine for full time of treatment.

TETRACYCLINES   Systemic

Some commonly used *brand names* are:

In the U.S.—

Achromycin [Tetracycline]	*Panmycin* [Tetracycline]
Achromycin V [Tetracycline]	*Robitet* [Tetracycline]
Declomycin [Demeclocycline]	*Sumycin* [Tetracycline]
	Terramycin [Oxytetracycline]
Doryx [Doxycycline]	*Tetracyn* [Tetracycline]
Doxy [Doxycycline]	*Tija* [Oxytetracycline]
Doxy-Caps [Doxycycline]	*Vibramycin* [Doxycycline]
Minocin [Minocycline]	*Vibra-Tabs* [Doxycycline]
Monodox [Doxycycline]	

In Canada—

Achromycin [Tetracycline]	*Doxycin* [Doxycycline]
Achromycin V [Tetracycline]	*Minocin* [Minocycline]
Apo-Doxy [Doxycycline]	*Novodoxylin* [Doxycycline]
Apo-Tetra [Tetracycline]	*Novotetra* [Tetracycline]
Declomycin [Demeclocycline]	*Nu-Tetra* [Tetracycline]
Doryx [Doxycycline]	*Tetracyn* [Tetracycline]
	Vibramycin [Doxycycline]
	Vibra-Tabs [Doxycycline]

DEMECLOCYCLINE
Oral
Demeclocycline Hydrochloride Capsules USP
In the U.S.—*Declomycin*
Demeclocycline Hydrochloride Tablets USP
In the U.S. and Canada—*Declomycin*

DOXYCYCLINE
Oral
Doxycycline for Oral Suspension USP
In the U.S.—*Vibramycin*
Doxycycline Calcium Oral Suspension USP
In the U.S.—*Vibramycin*
Doxycycline Hyclate Capsules USP
In the U.S.—*Doxy-Caps; Monodox; Vibramycin;* GENERIC
In Canada—*Apo-Doxy; Doxycin; Novodoxylin; Vibramycin*
Doxycycline Hyclate Delayed-release Capsules USP
In the U.S. and Canada—*Doryx*
Doxycycline Hyclate Tablets USP
In the U.S.—*Vibra-Tabs;* GENERIC
In Canada—*Doxycin; Vibra-Tabs*
Parenteral
Doxycycline Hyclate for Injection USP
In the U.S.—*Doxy; Vibramycin;* GENERIC
In Canada—*Vibramycin*
MINOCYCLINE
Oral
Minocycline Hydrochloride Capsules USP
In the U.S.—*Minocin;* GENERIC
In Canada—*Minocin*
Minocycline Hydrochloride Oral Suspension USP
In the U.S.—*Minocin*
Minocycline Hydrochloride Tablets
In the U.S.—GENERIC
Parenteral
Sterile Minocycline Hydrochloride USP
In the U.S.—*Minocin*

OXYTETRACYCLINE†
Oral
Oxytetracycline Hydrochloride Capsules USP
In the U.S.—*Terramycin; Tija;* GENERIC
Parenteral
Oxytetracycline Injection USP
In the U.S.—*Terramycin*
Oxytetracycline Hydrochloride for Injection USP
In the U.S.—*Terramycin*
TETRACYCLINE
Oral
Tetracycline Oral Suspension USP
In the U.S.—*Achromycin V; Sumycin;* GENERIC
In Canada—*Novotetra*
Tetracycline Hydrochloride Capsules USP
In the U.S.—*Achromycin V; Panmycin; Robitet; Sumycin; Tetracyn;* GENERIC
In Canada—*Achromycin V; Apo-Tetra; Novotetra; Nu-Tetra; Tetracyn*
Tetracycline Hydrochloride Tablets USP
In the U.S.—*Sumycin*
In Canada—*Novotetra*
Parenteral
Tetracycline Hydrochloride for Injection USP (Intramuscular)
In the U.S. and Canada—*Achromycin*

†Not commercially available in Canada.

Category

Antibacterial (systemic); antiprotozoal—Demeclocycline; Doxycycline; Minocycline; Oxytetracycline; Tetracycline.
Antiacne agent (systemic)—Minocycline (oral); tetracycline (oral).
Diuretic (syndrome of inappropriate antidiuretic hormone)—Demeclocycline.

Indications

Note: Bracketed information in the *Indications* section refers to uses not included in U.S. product labeling.

Accepted
Acne vulgaris (treatment)—Although all tetracyclines may be indicated as adjunctive treatment, they are generally no more effective in the initial treatment of acne and are more expensive than tetracycline. However, oral minocycline may be more effective in severe or resistant acne and may be effective in acne unresponsive to oral tetracycline.

Actinomycosis (treatment)—Systemic tetracyclines are indicated in the treatment of actinomycosis caused by *Actinomyces israelii.*

Anthrax (treatment)—Systemic tetracyclines are indicated in the treatment of anthrax caused by *Bacillus anthracis.*

Bronchitis (treatment)—Systemic tetracyclines are indicated in the treatment of bronchitis.

Brucellosis (treatment)—Systemic tetracyclines are indicated in the treatment of brucellosis.

Conjunctivitis, inclusion (treatment)—Systemic tetracyclines are indicated in the treatment of inclusion conjunctivitis.

Genitourinary tract infections (treatment)—Systemic tetracyclines are indicated in the treatment of genitourinary tract infections (including acute epididymo-orchitis) caused by *N. gonorrhoeae.*

Doxycycline is indicated in the treatment of genitourinary tract infections (including acute epididymo-orchitis) caused by *Chlamydia trachomatis.*

Doxycycline, minocycline, oxytetracycline, and tetracycline are indicated in the treatment of uncomplicated genitourinary tract infections (including endocervical infections) caused by *Chlamydia trachomatis.*

Minocycline is indicated in the treatment of uncomplicated genitourinary tract infections (including endocervical infections) caused by *Ureaplasma urealyticum.*

Gingivostomatitis, necrotizing ulcerative (treatment)—Systemic tetracyclines are indicated in the treatment of necrotizing ulcerative gingivostomatitis (Vincent's infection) caused by *Fusobacterium fusiformisans (Fusiformis fusiformisans).*

Granuloma inguinale (treatment)—Systemic tetracyclines are indicated in the treatment of granuloma inguinale caused by *Calymmatobacterium granulomatis.*

Lymphogranuloma venereum (treatment)—Systemic tetracyclines are indicated in the treatment of lymphogranuloma venereum caused by *Chlamydia* species.

Meningococcal carriers (treatment)—Oral minocycline is indicated in the treatment of asymptomatic meningococcal carriers to eliminate *Neisseria meningitidis* from the nasopharynx.

Otitis media, acute (treatment);
Pharyngitis, bacterial (treatment);
Pneumonia, *Haemophilus influenzae* (treatment);
Pneumonia, *Klebsiella* species (treatment); or
Sinusitis (treatment)—Systemic tetracyclines are indicated in the treatment of acute otitis media, pharyngitis, pneumonia, and sinusitis caused by *H. influenzae* and *Klebsiella* species.

Doxycycline is indicated in the treatment of the above-listed infections caused by *Staphylococcus aureus.* However, some USP medical experts do not recommend the use of tetracyclines for infections caused by *S. aureus.*

Psittacosis (treatment)—Systemic tetracyclines are indicated in the treatment of psittacosis caused by *Chlamydia psittaci.*

Q fever (treatment);
Rickettsial pox (treatment);
Rocky Mountain spotted fever (treatment); or
Typhus infections (treatment)—Systemic tetracyclines are indicated in the treatment of Q fever, rickettsial pox, Rocky Mountain spotted fever (including tick fevers), and typhus infections caused by Rickettsiae.

Relapsing fever (treatment)—Systemic tetracyclines are indicated in the treatment of relapsing fever caused by *Borrelia recurrentis.*

Skin and soft tissue infections (treatment)—Systemic tetracyclines are indicated in the treatment of skin and soft tissue infections, including burn wound infections, caused by *Staphylococcus aureus.* However, some USP medical experts do not recommend the use of tetracyclines for infections caused by *S. aureus.*

Syphilis (treatment)—Systemic tetracyclines are indicated in the treatment of syphilis caused by *Treponema pallidum.*

Trachoma (treatment)—Systemic tetracyclines are indicated in the treatment of trachoma.

Urethritis, nongonococcal (treatment)—Doxycycline is indicated in the treatment of nongonococcal urethritis caused by *Chlamydia trachomatis* and *Ureaplasma urealyticum.*

Urinary tract infections, bacterial (treatment)—Systemic tetracyclines are indicated in the treatment of urinary tract infections caused by [susceptible organisms, including *Escherichia coli* and] *Klebsiella* species.

Yaws (treatment)—Systemic tetracyclines are indicated in the treatment of yaws caused by *T. pertenue.*

Doxycycline, minocycline, oxytetracycline, and tetracycline are indicated in the treatment of uncomplicated rectal infections caused by *Chlamydia trachomatis.* Minocycline is indicated in the treatment of uncomplicated rectal infections caused by *Ureaplasma urealyticum.*

[Amebiasis, extraintestinal (treatment)]—Tetracycline, a lumenal amebicide, is used concurrently or sequentially with metronidazole in the treatment of extraintestinal amebiasis caused by *Entamoeba histolytica.*

[Arthritis, gonococcal (treatment)];

[Bejel (treatment)];

[Biliary tract infections (treatment)];

[Enterocolitis, *Shigella* species (treatment)];

[Intra-abdominal infections (treatment)];

[Pinta (treatment)];

[Plague (treatment)];

[Pneumonia, mycoplasmal (treatment)];

[Septicemia, bacterial (treatment)];

[Tularemia (treatment)]; or

[Urethritis, gonococcal (treatment)]—Systemic tetracyclines are used in the treatment of the above-listed infections.

[Chlamydial infections (treatment)]; or

[Rosacea, ocular (treatment)]—Systemic tetracycline is used in the treatment of chlamydial infections and ocular rosacea.

[Gonorrhea (treatment)]; or

[Malaria (treatment)]—Systemic doxycycline and tetracycline are used in the treatment of gonorrhea and malaria.

[Mycobacterial infections, atypical (treatment)]—Systemic doxycycline and minocycline are used in the treatment of atypical mycobacterial infections.

[Nocardiosis (treatment)]—Systemic minocycline is used in the treatment of nocardiosis.

[Syndrome of inappropriate antidiuretic hormone (SIADH) (treatment)]—Demeclocycline is used in the treatment of syndrome of inappropriate (excess) antidiuretic hormone (SIADH).

[Traveler's diarrhea (prophylaxis and treatment)]—Doxycycline is used in the prophylaxis and treatment of traveler's diarrhea caused by enterotoxigenic *Escherichia coli*, *Salmonella* species, and *Shigella* species in high-risk patients in whom diarrhea and dehydration may result in serious consequences because of chronic underlying health problems.

Tetracyclines are also indicated in the treatment of infections caused by *Mycobacterium marinum* (oral minocycline), *Mycoplasma pneumoniae*, *Yersinia pestis*, *Francisella tularensis*, *Bartonella bacilliformis*, *Bacteroides* species, *Vibrio cholerae*, *Campylobacter fetus*, *Brucella* species (concurrently with streptomycin), *Escherichia coli*, *Enterobacter aerogenes*, *Shigella* species, *Acinetobacter* species, streptococci, *Streptococcus pneumoniae*, *Neisseria gonorrhoeae*, *N. meningitidis* (parenteral doxycycline, minocycline, and tetracycline), *Listeria monocytogenes*, *Clostridium* species, and *Actinomyces* species.

Not all species or strains of a particular organism may be susceptible to a specific tetracycline.

Unaccepted

Oral minocycline is no longer recommended by the Centers for Disease Control (CDC) for the treatment of meningococcal carriers because of vestibular toxicity. Oral minocycline is not indicated in the treatment of meningococcal infections.

Pharmacology

Mechanism of action/Effect:

Antibacterial (systemic); antiprotozoal—Tetracyclines are broad-spectrum bacteriostatic agents and act by inhibiting protein synthesis by blocking the binding of aminoacyl tRNA (transfer RNA) to the mRNA (messenger RNA) ribosome complex. Reversible binding occurs primarily at the 30 S ribosomal subunit of susceptible organisms. Bacterial cell wall synthesis is not inhibited.

Diuretic (Syndrome of inappropriate diuretic hormone [SIADH])—In the treatment of the SIADH, demeclocycline acts by inhibiting ADH-induced water reabsorption in the distal portion of the convoluted tubules and collecting ducts of the kidneys, thereby causing water diuresis.

Onset of action: SIADH syndrome (demeclocycline)—24 to 48 hours.

Precautions to Consider

Cross-sensitivity and/or related problems

Patients hypersensitive to one tetracycline may be hypersensitive to other tetracyclines also.

Patients hypersensitive to lidocaine, procaine, or other "caine-type" local anesthetics may also be hypersensitive to the lidocaine component of oxytetracycline injection or to the procaine component of tetracycline hydrochloride for intramuscular injection.

Geriatrics

No information is available on the relationship of age to the effects of tetracyclines in geriatric patients.

Dental

Use of systemic tetracyclines during pregnancy or in infants and children up to 8 years of age may cause permanent discoloration of teeth and enamel hypoplasia. Therefore, use is not recommended unless other antibacterials are unlikely to be effective or are contraindicated. Vital bleaching or esthetic restoration may be required if staining is objectionable.

Systemic tetracyclines may also contribute to the development of oral candidiasis.

Drug interactions and/or related problems

The following drug interactions and/or related problems have been selected on the basis of their potential clinical significance (possible mechanism in parentheses where appropriate)—not necessarily inclusive (» = major clinical significance):

Note: Combinations containing any of the following medications, depending on the amount present, may also interact with this medication.

» Antacids or

» Calcium supplements such as calcium carbonate or

» Choline and magnesium salicylates or

» Iron supplements or

» Magnesium salicylate or

» Magnesium-containing laxatives

Sodium bicarbonate

(concurrent use may result in formation of nonabsorbable complexes; also, concurrent use with antacids or sodium bicarbonate may result in decreased absorption of oral tetracyclines because of increased intragastric pH; patients should be advised not to take these medications within 1 to 3 hours of oral tetracyclines)

Barbiturates or

Carbamazepine or

Phenytoin

(concurrent use with doxycycline may result in decreased doxycycline serum concentrations due to induction of microsomal enzyme activity; adjustment of doxycycline dosage or substitution of another tetracycline may be necessary)

» Cholestyramine or

» Colestipol

(concurrent use with cholestyramine or colestipol may result in binding of oral tetracyclines, thus impairing their absorption; an interval of several hours between administration of cholestyramine or colestipol and oral tetracyclines is recommended)

» Contraceptives, estrogen-containing, oral

(concurrent long-term use with tetracyclines may result in reduced contraceptive reliability and increased incidence of breakthrough bleeding)

Methoxyflurane

(concurrent use with tetracyclines may increase the potential for nephrotoxicity)

Penicillins

(since bacteriostatic drugs may interfere with the bactericidal effect of penicillins in the treatment of meningitis or in other situations where a rapid bactericidal effect is necessary, it is best to avoid concurrent therapy)

Vitamin A
(concurrent use with tetracycline has been reported to cause benign intracranial hypertension)

Contraindications/Medical problems

The contraindications/medical problems included have been selected on the basis of their potential clinical significance (reasons given in parentheses where appropriate)—not necessarily inclusive (» = major clinical significance).

Risk-benefit should be considered when the following medical problems exist:

» Diabetes insipidus, nephrogenic
(demeclocycline induces a reversible nephrogenic diabetes insipidus)

Hepatic function impairment
(doxycycline and minocycline are partially metabolized in the liver; hepatic function impairment may prolong the elimination half-life)

Hypersensitivity to tetracyclines, or "caine-type" local anesthetics (e.g., lidocaine, procaine)

» Renal function impairment
(the half-life of tetracyclines, except doxycycline or minocycline, is prolonged in patients with renal function impairment)

Side/Adverse Effects

Note: Tetracycline-induced hepatotoxicity is usually seen as a fatty degeneration of the liver. It is more likely to occur in pregnant women, in patients receiving high-dose intravenous therapy, and in patients with renal function impairment. However, hepatotoxicity has also occurred in patients without these predisposing conditions. Tetracycline-induced pancreatitis has also been described in associated with hepatotoxicity, and without associated liver disease.

The following side/adverse effects have been selected on the basis of their potential clinical significance (possible signs and symptoms in parentheses where appropriate)—not necessarily inclusive:

Those indicating need for medical attention
Incidence more frequent
Discoloration of infants' or children's teeth; photosensitivity (increased sensitivity of skin to sunlight)

Incidence less frequent
Nephrogenic diabetes insipidus (greatly increased frequency of urination or amount of urine; increased thirst; unusual tiredness or weakness)—with demeclocycline; *pigmentation of skin and mucous membranes*—primarily with minocycline

Incidence rare
Benign intracranial hypertension (anorexia, headache, vomiting, papilledema, visual changes, bulging fontanel in infants); *hepatotoxicity* (abdominal pain, nausea and vomiting, yellowing skin); *pancreatitis* (abdominal pain, nausea and vomiting)

Those indicating need for medical attention only if they continue or are bothersome
Incidence more frequent
CNS toxicity (dizziness, lightheadedness, or unsteadiness); *gastrointestinal disturbances* (cramps or burning of the stomach, diarrhea, nausea or vomiting); *photosensitivity* (increased sensitivity of skin to sunlight)

Incidence less frequent
Fungal overgrowth (itching of the rectal or genital areas, sore mouth or tongue); *hypertrophy of the papilla* (darkened or discolored tongue)

Patient Consultation

In providing consultation, consider emphasizing the following selected information (» = major clinical significance):

Before using this medication
» Conditions affecting use, especially:
Sensitivity to tetracyclines
Pregnancy—Tetracyclines cross the placenta; use is not recommended during the last half of pregnancy since tetracyclines may cause permanent discoloration of teeth, enamel hypoplasia, and inhibition of skeletal growth in the fetus; also, fatty infiltration of the liver may occur in pregnant women, especially with high intravenous doses
Breast-feeding—Tetracyclines are excreted in breast milk; although tetracyclines may form nonabsorbable complexes with breast-milk calcium, use is not recommended because of the possibility of their causing permanent discoloration of teeth, enamel hypoplasia, inhibition of linear skeletal growth, photosensitivity reactions, and oral and vaginal thrush in infants
Use in children—In infants and children up to 8 years of age, tetracyclines may cause permanent discoloration of teeth, enamel hypoplasia, and a decrease in linear skeletal growth rate
Other medications, especially antacids, calcium supplements, cholestyramine, choline and magnesium salicylates, colestipol, estrogen-containing oral contraceptives, iron supplements, magnesium salicylate, or magnesium-containing laxatives
Other medical problems, especially nephrogenic diabetes insipidus or renal function impairment

Proper use of this medication
» Not giving to children up to 8 years of age
Taking with at least a full glass of water while in an upright position to avoid esophageal ulceration or to decrease gastrointestinal irritation
» Avoiding concurrent use of milk or other dairy products when taking oral demeclocycline, oxytetracycline, and tetracycline; if gastrointestinal irritation still occurs, these medicines may be taken with food
Oral doxycycline and minocycline may be taken with food or milk if gastric irritation occurs
» Discarding outdated or decomposed tetracyclines (decomposed products may be toxic)
» Compliance with full course of therapy
» Importance of not missing doses and taking at evenly spaced times
Missed dose: Taking as soon as possible; not taking if almost time for next dose; not doubling doses
» Proper storage

Precautions while using this medication
Checking with physician if no improvement within a few days (or a few weeks or months for acne patients)
» Avoiding antacids, calcium supplements, choline and magnesium salicylates, iron supplements, magnesium salicylate, magnesium-containing laxatives, sodium bicarbonate within 1 to 3 hours of oral tetracyclines
» Use of an alternate or additional method of contraception if concurrently taking estrogen-containing oral contraceptives
Caution if surgery with general anesthesia is required
» Possible photosensitivity reactions
» Caution if dizziness, lightheadedness, or unsteadiness occurs

Side/adverse effects
Signs of potential side effects such as discoloration of infant's or children's teeth, nephrogenic diabetes insipidus—with demeclocycline, pigmentation of skin and mucous membranes—with minocycline, benign intracranial hypertension, hepatotoxicity, pancreatitis, and photosensitivity

General Dosing Information

Use of tetracyclines (except doxycycline and minocycline) in patients with impaired renal function is not recommended.

For oral dosage forms only
All tetracyclines should be taken with a full glass (240 mL) of water to avoid esophageal ulceration and to decrease gastrointestinal irritation. In addition, most tetracyclines (except doxycycline and minocycline) should preferably be taken on an empty stomach (either 1 hour before or 2 hours after meals) to obtain optimum serum concentrations.

DEMECLOCYCLINE

Summary of Differences

Indications: Also used as a diuretic (syndrome of inappropriate diuretic hormone [SIADH]).
Pharmacology: Different mechanism of action in SIADH.
Precautions:
   Drug interactions and/or related problems—Also interacts with desmopressin.
   Contraindications/medical problems—Caution also needed in nephrogenic diabetes insipidus.
Side/adverse effects: May also cause greatly increased frequency of urination or amount of urine, increased thirst, or unusual tiredness or weakness (nephrogenic diabetes insipidus).

Oral Dosage Forms

Note: Bracketed uses in the *Dosage Forms* section refer to categories of use and/or indications that are not included in U.S. product labeling.

   The dosing and dosage forms available are expressed in terms of demeclocycline hydrochloride.

DEMECLOCYCLINE HYDROCHLORIDE CAPSULES USP

Usual adult and adolescent dose:
   Antibacterial (systemic); antiprotozoal—Oral, 150 mg every six hours; or 300 mg every twelve hours.
      Note: Gonorrhea—Oral, 300 mg every twelve hours for four days, up to a total dose of 3 grams.
   [Diuretic (SIADH)]—Oral, 3.25 to 3.75 mg per kg of body weight every six hours.

Usual adult prescribing limits:
   Antibacterial (systemic); antiprotozoal—Up to 2.4 grams daily.
   [Diuretic (SIADH)]—300 mg to 1.2 grams daily.

Auxiliary labeling:
 • Continue medicine for full time of treatment.
 • Do not take within 1 to 3 hours of other medicines, milk, or other dairy products.
 • Avoid too much sun or use of sunlamp.
 • Keep container tightly closed in a dry place.

DEMECLOCYCLINE HYDROCHLORIDE TABLETS USP

Usual adult and adolescent dose: See *Demeclocycline Hydrochloride Capsules USP*.

Usual adult prescribing limits: See *Demeclocycline Hydrochloride Capsules USP*.

Auxiliary labeling:
 • Continue medicine for full time of treatment.
 • Do not take within 1 to 3 hours of other medicines, milk, or other dairy products.

 • Avoid too much sun or use of sunlamp.
 • Keep container tightly closed in a dry place.

DOXYCYCLINE

Summary of Differences

Precautions:
   Drug interactions and/or related problems—
      Also interacts with barbiturates, carbamazepine, and phenytoin. No interaction with methoxyflurane.
   Laboratory value alterations—No increase in BUN concentrations.
   Contraindications/medical problems—Caution not needed in renal impairment.
General dosing information:
   No dosage reduction in renal impairment.
   May be taken with food, milk, or carbonated beverages.

Additional Dosing Information

Even though approximately 40% of a dose of doxycycline may be eliminated through the kidneys in patients with normal renal function, patients with impaired renal function do not generally require a reduction in dose since doxycycline alternatively may be eliminated through the liver, biliary tract, and gastrointestinal tract and does not have the antianabolic effect of other tetracyclines.

For oral dosage forms only:
 • Doxycycline may be taken with food or milk if gastrointestinal irritation occurs.

Oral Dosage Forms

Note: Bracketed uses in the *Dosage Forms* section refer to categories of use and/or indications that are not included in U.S. product labeling.

DOXYCYCLINE FOR ORAL SUSPENSION USP

Usual adult and adolescent dose: Antibacterial (systemic); antiprotozoal—Oral, 100 mg (base) every twelve hours the first day, then 100 to 200 mg once a day; or 50 to 100 mg every twelve hours.

Note: Gonococcal infections, uncomplicated (except anorectal infections in men)—Oral, 100 mg (base) every twelve hours for seven days; or 300 mg initially, then 300 mg one hour later.

   Nongonococcal urethritis caused by *Chlamydia trachomatis* or *Ureaplasma urealyticum*, and
   Uncomplicated urethral, endocervical, or rectal infection caused by *Chlamydia trachomatis*—Oral, 100 mg (base) two times a day for at least seven days.

   Syphilis (primary and secondary)—Oral, 150 mg (base) every twelve hours for at least ten days.

   [Traveler's diarrhea (prophylaxis)]—Oral, 100 mg (base) once a day for three weeks.

Usual adult prescribing limits: Up to 300 mg (base) daily; or up to 600 mg daily for five days in acute gonococcal infections.

Auxiliary labeling:
 • Shake well.
 • Continue medicine for full time of treatment.
 • Do not take within 1 to 3 hours of other medicines.
 • Avoid too much sun or use of sunlamp.
 • Beyond-use date.

DOXYCYCLINE CALCIUM ORAL SUSPENSION USP

Usual adult and adolescent dose: See *Doxycycline for Oral Suspension USP*.

Usual adult prescribing limits: See *Doxycycline for Oral Suspension USP.*

Auxiliary labeling:
- Shake well.
- Continue medicine for full time of treatment.
- Do not take within 1 to 3 hours of other medicines.
- Avoid too much sun or use of sunlamp.

DOXYCYCLINE HYCLATE CAPSULES USP

Usual adult and adolescent dose: See *Doxycycline for Oral Suspension USP.*

Usual adult prescribing limits: See *Doxycycline for Oral Suspension USP.*

Auxiliary labeling:
- Continue medicine for full time of treatment.
- Do not take within 1 to 3 hours of other medicines.
- Avoid too much sun or use of sunlamp.
- Keep container tightly closed in a dry place.

DOXYCYCLINE HYCLATE DELAYED-RELEASE CAPSULES USP

Usual adult and adolescent dose: See *Doxycycline for Oral Suspension USP.*

Usual adult prescribing limits: See *Doxycycline for Oral Suspension USP.*

Auxiliary labeling:
- Continue medicine for full time of treatment.
- Do not take within 1 to 3 hours of other medicines.
- Avoid too much sun or use of sunlamp.
- Keep container tightly closed in a dry place.
- Swallow capsules whole.

DOXYCYCLINE HYCLATE TABLETS USP

Usual adult and adolescent dose: See *Doxycycline for Oral Suspension USP.*

Usual adult prescribing limits: See *Doxycycline for Oral Suspension USP.*

Auxiliary labeling:
- Continue medicine for full time of treatment.
- Do not take within 1 to 3 hours of other medicines.
- Avoid too much sun or use of sunlamp.
- Keep container tightly closed in a dry place.

Parenteral Dosage Forms

DOXYCYCLINE HYCLATE FOR INJECTION USP

Usual adult and adolescent dose: Antibacterial (systemic); antiprotozoal—Intravenous infusion, 200 mg (base) once a day or 100 mg every twelve hours the first day, then 100 to 200 mg once a day; or 50 to 100 mg every twelve hours.

Note: Syphilis (primary and secondary)—Intravenous infusion, 150 mg (base) every twelve hours for at least ten days.

Usual adult prescribing limits: Up to 300 mg (base) daily.

Additional information:
Concentrations less than 100 mcg (0.1 mg) per mL or greater than 1 mg per mL are not recommended.
Infusions may be administered over a 1- to 4-hour period. Avoid rapid administration.
Do not administer intramuscularly or subcutaneously.

MINOCYCLINE

Summary of Differences

Precautions:
Laboratory value alterations—No increase in BUN concentrations.
Contraindications/medical problems—Caution not needed in renal impairment.
Side/adverse effects: May also cause dizziness, lightheadedness, or unsteadiness (central nervous system [CNS] toxicity); and pigmentation of skin and mucous membranes.
General dosing information:
No dosage reduction in renal impairment.
May be taken with food or milk.

Additional Dosing Information

For oral dosage forms only:
- Minocycline may be taken with food or milk if gastrointestinal irritation occurs.

Oral Dosage Forms

MINOCYCLINE HYDROCHLORIDE CAPSULES USP

Usual adult and adolescent dose: Antibacterial (systemic); antiprotozoal—Oral, 200 mg (base) initially, then 100 mg every twelve hours; or 100 to 200 mg initially, then 50 mg every six hours.

Note: Gonorrhea—Oral, 100 mg (base) every twelve hours for at least four days.

Mycobacterium marinum infections—Oral, 100 mg (base) every twelve hours for six to eight weeks.

Neisseria meningitidis carriers (asymptomatic)—Oral, 100 mg (base) every twelve hours for five days.

Uncomplicated urethral, endocervical, or rectal infection caused by *Chlamydia trachomatis*—Oral, 100 mg (base) two times a day for at least seven days.

Usual adult prescribing limits: Up to 350 mg (base) the first day; then up to 200 mg a day.

Auxiliary labeling:
- Continue medicine for full time of treatment.
- Do not take within 1 to 3 hours of other medicines.
- Avoid too much sun or use of sunlamp.
- Keep container tightly closed in a dry place.
- May cause dizziness.

MINOCYCLINE HYDROCHLORIDE ORAL SUSPENSION USP

Usual adult and adolescent dose: See *Minocycline Hydrochloride Capsules.*

Usual adult prescribing limits: See *Minocycline Hydrochloride Capsules USP.*

Auxiliary labeling:
- Shake well.
- Continue medicine for full time of treatment.
- Do not take within 1 to 3 hours of other medicines.
- Avoid too much sun or use of sunlamp.
- May cause dizziness.

MINOCYCLINE HYDROCHLORIDE TABLETS

Usual adult and adolescent dose: See *Minocycline Hydrochloride Capsules USP.*

Usual adult prescribing limits: See *Minocycline Hydrochloride Capsules USP.*

Auxiliary labeling:
- Continue medicine for full time of treatment.
- Do not take within 1 to 3 hours of other medicines.
- Avoid too much sun or use of sunlamp.
- May cause dizziness.
- Keep container tightly closed and in a dry place.

Parenteral Dosage Forms

STERILE MINOCYCLINE HYDROCHLORIDE USP

Usual adult and adolescent dose: Intravenous infusion, 200 mg (base) initially, then 100 mg every twelve hours.

Usual adult prescribing limits: Up to 400 mg (base) daily.

OXYTETRACYCLINE

Additional Dosing Information

For parenteral dosage forms only:
- Serum concentrations should not exceed 15 mcg per mL, especially in pregnant or postpartum patients with pyelonephritis.

Oral Dosage Forms

OXYTETRACYCLINE HYDROCHLORIDE CAPSULES USP

Usual adult and adolescent dose: Antibacterial (systemic); antiprotozoal—Oral, 250 to 500 mg (base) every six hours.

Note: Brucellosis—Oral, 500 mg (base) every six hours for three weeks, given concurrently with 1 gram of streptomycin intramuscularly every twelve hours the first week and once a day the second week.

Gonorrhea, uncomplicated—Oral, 500 mg (base) every six hours, up to a total dose of 9 grams.

Syphilis—Oral, 500 mg (base) every six hours for fifteen days (early syphilis) or for thirty days (late syphilis).

Usual adult prescribing limits: Up to 4 grams (base) daily.

Auxiliary labeling:
- Continue medicine for full time of treatment.
- Do not take within 1 to 3 hours of other medicines, milk, or other dairy products.
- Avoid too much sun or use of sunlamp.
- Keep container tightly closed in a dry place.

Parenteral Dosage Forms

OXYTETRACYCLINE INJECTION USP

Usual adult and adolescent dose: Antibacterial (systemic); antiprotozoal—Intramuscular, 100 mg (base) every eight hours; 150 mg every twelve hours; or 250 mg once a day.

Usual adult prescribing limits: Up to 500 mg (base) daily.

Additional information:
Cross-sensitivity with other "caine-type" local anesthetics may also occur.

For deep intramuscular use only. Do not administer intravenously. May cause intense pain and local irritation at the site of intramuscular injections.

Since intramuscular administration of oxytetracycline produces lower serum concentrations than oral administration in recommended doses, patients should be changed to an oral dosage form as soon as feasible.

When rapid, high serum concentrations are required, an intravenous form (oxytetracycline hydrochloride) should be used.

OXYTETRACYCLINE HYDROCHLORIDE FOR INJECTION USP

Usual adult and adolescent dose: Antibacterial (systemic); antiprotozoal—Intravenous infusion, 250 to 500 mg (base) every twelve hours.

Usual adult prescribing limits: Up to 2 grams (base) daily.

Additional information:
Avoid rapid administration. If patient complains of vein irritation, decrease the rate of administration or increase the volume of diluent.

Do not administer intramuscularly or subcutaneously.

TETRACYCLINE

Additional Dosing Information

For parenteral dosage forms only:
- Serum concentrations should not exceed 15 mcg per mL, especially in pregnant or postpartum patients with pyelonephritis.

Oral Dosage Forms

Note: The dosing and dosage forms available are expressed in terms of tetracycline hydrochloride.

TETRACYCLINE ORAL SUSPENSION USP

Usual adult and adolescent dose:
Antibacterial (systemic); antiprotozoal—Oral, 250 to 500 mg every six hours; or 500 mg to 1 gram every twelve hours.

Antiacne agent (systemic)—Oral, 500 mg to 2 grams daily in divided doses initially in moderate to severe cases as adjunctive therapy. When improvement is noted (usually after 3 weeks), dosage should be reduced gradually to a maintenance dose of 125 to 1000 mg daily. Adequate remission of lesions may also be possible with alternate-day or intermittent therapy.

Note: Brucellosis—Oral, 500 mg every six hours for three weeks, given concurrently with 1 gram of streptomycin intramuscularly every twelve hours the first week and once a day the second week.

Gonorrhea—Oral, 500 mg every six hours for five days.

Syphilis—Oral, 500 mg every six hours for fifteen days (early syphilis) or for thirty days (late syphilis).

Uncomplicated urethral, endocervical, or rectal infection caused by *Chlamydia trachomatis*—Oral, 500 mg four times a day for at least seven days.

Usual adult prescribing limits: Up to 4 grams daily.

Auxiliary labeling:
- Shake well.
- Continue medicine for full time of treatment.
- Do not take within 1 to 3 hours of other medicines, milk, or other dairy products.
- Avoid too much sun or use of sunlamp.

TETRACYCLINE HYDROCHLORIDE CAPSULES USP

Usual adult and adolescent dose: See *Tetracycline Oral Suspension USP.*

Usual adult prescribing limits: See *Tetracycline Oral Suspension USP.*

Auxiliary labeling:
- Continue medicine for full time of treatment.
- Do not take within 1 to 3 hours of other medicines, milk or other dairy products.
- Avoid too much sun or use of sunlamp.
- Keep container tightly closed in a dry place.

TETRACYCLINE HYDROCHLORIDE TABLETS USP

Usual adult and adolescent dose: See *Tetracycline Oral Suspension USP*.

Usual adult prescribing limits: See *Tetracycline Oral Suspension USP*.

Auxiliary labeling:
- Continue medicine for full time of treatment.
- Do not take within 1 to 3 hours of other medicines, milk, or other dairy products.
- Avoid too much sun or use of sunlamp.
- Keep container tightly closed in a dry place.

Parenteral Dosage Forms

Note: The dosing and dosage forms available are expressed in terms of tetracycline hydrochloride.

TETRACYCLINE HYDROCHLORIDE FOR INJECTION USP (INTRAMUSCULAR)

Usual adult and adolescent dose: Antibacterial (systemic); antiprotozoal—Intramuscular, 100 mg every eight hours; 150 mg every twelve hours; or 250 mg once daily.

Usual adult prescribing limits: Up to 1 gram daily.

Additional information:

Cross-sensitivity with other "caine-type" local anesthetics may also occur.

For deep intramuscular use only. Do not administer intravenously, subcutaneously, or into fat layers of the skin.

May cause intense pain and local irritation at the site of injection.

Intramuscular injections should not exceed 2 mL in each site. Injection sites should be alternated.

Since intramuscular administration of tetracycline hydrochloride produces lower serum concentrations than oral administration in recommended doses, patients should be changed to an oral dosage form as soon as feasible.

When rapid, high serum concentrations are required, an intravenous form of tetracycline hydrochloride should be used.

THEOPHYLLINE AND GUAIFENESIN   Systemic

Category: Bronchodilator.

Indications

Accepted

Asthma, bronchial (treatment);
Bronchitis (treatment);
Emphysema, pulmonary (treatment); or
Pulmonary disease, chronic obstructive, other (treatment)—Theophylline and guaifenesin combination is indicated for relief and/or prevention of symptoms of bronchial asthma and reversible bronchospasm associated with chronic bronchitis and pulmonary emphysema.

Patient Consultation

In providing consultation, consider emphasizing the following selected information (» = major clinical significance):

Before using this medication
» Conditions affecting use, especially:
  Sensitivity to theophylline or other xanthines
  Mutagenicity—Theophylline reported to cause chromosomal breakage in human cells in culture at concentrations up to 50 times maximum therapeutic serum concentration
  Pregnancy—Studies in mice have shown theophylline to cause teratogenic effects when given in doses 30 times the human dose (FDA Pregnancy Category C); use during pregnancy may result in potentially dangerous serum theophylline and caffeine concentrations in neonates; tachycardia, jitteriness, irritability, gagging, and vomiting reported in some neonates; neonates of mothers taking theophylline during pregnancy should be monitored for signs of theophylline toxicity
  Breast-feeding—Theophylline excreted in breast milk; use by nursing mothers may cause irritability, fretfulness, or insomnia in infants
  Use in children—Possible decreased plasma clearance and increased serum concentrations of theophylline and/or toxic-

ity in neonates, especially premature neonates; repeated doses should not be given if heart rate greater than 80 beats per minute
  Use in the elderly—Possible decreased plasma clearance of theophylline and increased potential for toxicity in patients over 55 years of age
  Other medications, especially beta-adrenergic blocking agents, cimetidine, ciprofloxacin, erythromycin, nicotine chewing gum, norfloxacin, phenytoin, ranitidine, troleandomycin, or smoking tobacco or marijuana
  Other medical problems, especially active gastritis or active or history of peptic ulcer

Proper use of this medication
» Taking on empty stomach with a glass of water for faster absorption or, if necessary, taking with meals or immediately after meals to lessen gastrointestinal irritation
» Importance of not taking more medication than the amount prescribed
» Compliance with therapy; not missing any doses
  Missed dose: Taking as soon as possible; not taking if almost time for next dose; not doubling doses
» Proper storage

Precautions while using this medication
  Regular visits to physician to check progress during initial period of therapy
» Caution in eating or drinking large amounts of xanthine-containing foods or beverages during therapy with this medication
  Not eating charcoal-broiled foods daily because of possible decrease in effects of medication
» Notifying physician immediately if symptoms of influenza, a fever, or diarrhea occur because of possible need to alter dosage

Side/adverse effects
  Signs of potential side effects, especially gastroesophageal reflux

Oral Dosage Forms

THEOPHYLLINE AND GUAIFENESIN CAPSULES USP

Usual adult dose:
　Acute attack—
　　Loading dose:
　　　For patients *not* currently receiving theophylline prepara-
　　　tions—Oral, the equivalent of 5 to 6 mg of anhydrous
　　　theophylline per kg of body weight.
　　　For patients currently receiving theophylline preparations—
　　　A serum theophylline measurement should be obtained
　　　immediately, if possible. The loading dose for theophyl-
　　　line is based on the principle that each 0.5 mg of theo-
　　　phylline per kg of lean (ideal) body weight will result in
　　　a 1 (range, 0.5 to 1.6) mcg per mL increase in serum
　　　theophylline concentration. If a serum theophylline mea-
　　　surement cannot be obtained rapidly and the patient's
　　　condition requires immediate therapy, a single dose of
　　　the equivalent of 2.5 mg of anhydrous theophylline per
　　　kg of body weight may be administered if there are no
　　　symptoms of theophylline toxicity.
　　Maintenance (in acute attack):
　　　Young adult smokers—Oral, the equivalent of anhydrous
　　　theophylline: 4 mg per kg of body weight every six
　　　hours.
　　　Otherwise healthy nonsmoking adults—Oral, the equiva-
　　　lent of anhydrous theophylline: 3 mg per kg of body
　　　weight every eight hours.
　　　Older patients and patients with cor pulmonale—Oral, the
　　　equivalent of anhydrous theophylline: 2 mg per kg of
　　　body weight every eight hours.
　　　Patients with congestive heart failure or liver failure—Oral,
　　　the equivalent of anhydrous theophylline: 2 mg per kg
　　　of body weight every twelve hours.
　　Note: **To achieve optimal therapeutic theophylline dosage,
　　　and minimize the risk of toxicity, monitoring of se-
　　　rum theophylline concentration and patient response
　　　is recommended.**
　　　In patients with cor pulmonale, congestive heart failure,
　　　or liver failure, dosage should not exceed the equivalent
　　　of 400 mg of anhydrous theophylline per day unless
　　　serum theophylline concentrations can be monitored at
　　　twenty-four-hour intervals.
　Chronic therapy—Oral, the equivalent of anhydrous theophylline:
　　Initially, 6 to 8 mg per kg of body weight, up to a maximum of
　　400 mg, per day in three or four divided doses at six- to eight-
　　hour intervals. The dosage may be increased, if tolerated, in
　　approximately 25% increments at two- to three-day intervals,
　　up to a maximum dose of 13 mg per kg of body weight or 900
　　mg per day, whichever is less, without measurement of serum
　　concentration.
　Note: If the above maximum dose in chronic therapy is to be
　　maintained or exceeded, serum theophylline measure-
　　ment is recommended. Final dosage adjustment is based
　　on subsequent serum theophylline measurements and
　　patient response.

THEOPHYLLINE AND GUAIFENESIN ELIXIR

Usual adult dose:
　Acute attack—
　　Loading dose:
　　　For patients *not* currently receiving theophylline prepara-
　　　tions—Oral, the equivalent of 5 to 6 mg of anhydrous
　　　theophylline per kg of body weight.
　　　For patients currently receiving theophylline preparations—
　　　A serum theophylline measurement should be obtained
　　　immediately, if possible. The loading dose for theophyl-

line is based on the principle that each 0.5 mg of theophylline per kg of lean (ideal) body weight will result in
a 1 (range, 0.5 to 1.6) mcg per mL increase in serum
theophylline concentration. If a serum theophylline measurement cannot be obtained rapidly and the patient's
condition requires immediate therapy, a single dose of
the equivalent of 2.5 mg of anhydrous theophylline per
kg of body weight may be administered if there are no
symptoms of theophylline toxicity.
　Maintenance (in acute attack):
　　Young adult smokers—Oral, the equivalent of anhydrous
　　theophylline: 4 mg per kg of body weight every six
　　hours.
　　Otherwise healthy nonsmoking adults—Oral, the equiva-
　　lent of anhydrous theophylline: 3 mg per kg of body
　　weight every eight hours.
　　Older patients and patients with cor pulmonale—Oral, the
　　equivalent of anhydrous theophylline: 2 mg per kg of
　　body weight every eight hours.
　　Patients with congestive heart failure or liver failure—Oral,
　　the equivalent of anhydrous theophylline: 2 mg per kg
　　of body weight every twelve hours.
　Note: **To achieve optimal therapeutic theophylline dosage,
　　and minimize the risk of toxicity, monitoring of se-
　　rum theophylline concentration and patient response
　　is recommended.**
　　In patients with cor pulmonale, congestive heart failure,
　　or liver failure, dosage should not exceed the equivalent
　　of 400 mg of anhydrous theophylline per day unless
　　serum theophylline concentrations can be monitored at
　　twenty-four-hour intervals.
　Chronic therapy—Oral, the equivalent of anhydrous theophylline:
　　Initially, 6 to 8 mg per kg of body weight, up to a maximum of
　　400 mg, per day in three or four divided doses at six- to eight-
　　hour intervals. The dosage may be increased, if tolerated, in
　　approximately 25% increments at two- to three-day intervals,
　　up to a maximum dose of 13 mg per kg of body weight or 900
　　mg per day, whichever is less, without measurement of serum
　　concentration.
　Note: If the above maximum dose in chronic therapy is to be
　　maintained or exceeded, serum theophylline measure-
　　ment is recommended. Final dosage adjustment is based
　　on subsequent serum theophylline measurements and
　　patient response.

Auxiliary labeling: • Keep container tightly closed.

THEOPHYLLINE AND GUAIFENESIN ORAL SOLUTION
USP

Usual adult dose:
　Acute attack—
　　Loading dose:
　　　For patients *not* currently receiving theophylline prepara-
　　　tions—Oral, the equivalent of 5 to 6 mg of anhydrous
　　　theophylline per kg of body weight.
　　　For patients currently receiving theophylline preparations—
　　　A serum theophylline measurement should be obtained
　　　immediately, if possible. The loading dose for theophyl-
　　　line is based on the principle that each 0.5 mg of theo-
　　　phylline per kg of lean (ideal) body weight will result in
　　　a 1 (range, 0.5 to 1.6) mcg per mL increase in serum
　　　theophylline concentration. If a serum theophylline mea-
　　　surement cannot be obtained rapidly and the patient's
　　　condition requires immediate therapy, a single dose of
　　　the equivalent of 2.5 mg of anhydrous theophylline per
　　　kg of body weight may be administered if there are no
　　　symptoms of theophylline toxicity.

Maintenance (in acute attack):

Young adult smokers—Oral, the equivalent of anhydrous theophylline: 4 mg per kg of body weight every six hours.

Otherwise healthy nonsmoking adults—Oral, the equivalent of anhydrous theophylline: 3 mg per kg of body weight every eight hours.

Older patients and patients with cor pulmonale—Oral, the equivalent of anhydrous theophylline: 2 mg per kg of body weight every eight hours.

Patients with congestive heart failure or liver failure—Oral, the equivalent of anhydrous theophylline: 2 mg per kg of body weight every twelve hours.

Note: **To achieve optimal therapeutic theophylline dosage, and minimize the risk of toxicity, monitoring of serum theophylline concentration and patient response is recommended.**

In patients with cor pulmonale, congestive heart failure, or liver failure, dosage should not exceed the equivalent of 400 mg of anhydrous theophylline per day unless serum theophylline concentrations can be monitored at twenty-four-hour intervals.

Chronic therapy—Oral, the equivalent of anhydrous theophylline: Initially, 6 to 8 mg per kg of body weight, up to a maximum of 400 mg, per day in three or four divided doses at six- to eight-hour intervals. The dosage may be increased, if tolerated, in approximately 25% increments at two- to three-day intervals, up to a maximum dose of 13 mg per kg of body weight or 900 mg per day, whichever is less, without measurement of serum concentration.

Note: If the above maximum dose in chronic therapy is to be maintained or exceeded, serum theophylline measurement is recommended. Final dosage adjustment is based on subsequent serum theophylline measurements and patient response.

THEOPHYLLINE AND GUAIFENESIN SYRUP

Usual adult dose:

Acute attack—

Loading dose:

For patients *not* currently receiving theophylline preparations—Oral, the equivalent of 5 to 6 mg of anhydrous theophylline per kg of body weight.

For patients currently receiving theophylline preparations— A serum theophylline measurement should be obtained immediately, if possible. The loading dose for theophylline is based on the principle that each 0.5 mg of theophylline per kg of lean (ideal) body weight will result in a 1 (range, 0.5 to 1.6) mcg per mL increase in serum theophylline concentration. If a serum theophylline measurement cannot be obtained rapidly and the patient's condition requires immediate therapy, a single dose of the equivalent of 2.5 mg of anhydrous theophylline per kg of body weight may be administered if there are no symptoms of theophylline toxicity.

Maintenance (in acute attack):

Young adult smokers—Oral, the equivalent of anhydrous theophylline: 4 mg per kg of body weight every six hours.

Otherwise healthy nonsmoking adults—Oral, the equivalent of anhydrous theophylline: 3 mg per kg of body weight every eight hours.

Older patients and patients with cor pulmonale—Oral, the equivalent of anhydrous theophylline: 2 mg per kg of body weight every eight hours.

Patients with congestive heart failure or liver failure—Oral, the equivalent of anhydrous theophylline: 2 mg per kg of body weight every twelve hours.

Note: **To achieve optimal therapeutic theophylline dosage, and minimize the risk of toxicity, monitoring of serum theophylline concentration and patient response is recommended.**

In patients with cor pulmonale, congestive heart failure, or liver failure, dosage should not exceed the equivalent of 400 mg of anhydrous theophylline per day unless serum theophylline concentrations can be monitored at twenty-four-hour intervals.

Chronic therapy—Oral, the equivalent of anhydrous theophylline: Initially, 6 to 8 mg per kg of body weight, up to a maximum of 400 mg, per day in three or four divided doses at six- to eight-hour intervals. The dosage may be increased, if tolerated, in approximately 25% increments at two- to three-day intervals, up to a maximum dose of 13 mg per kg of body weight or 900 mg per day, whichever is less, without measurement of serum concentration.

Note: If the above maximum dose in chronic therapy is to be maintained or exceeded, serum theophylline measurement is recommended. Final dosage adjustment is based on subsequent serum theophylline measurements and patient response.

THEOPHYLLINE AND GUAIFENESIN TABLETS

Usual adult dose:

Acute attack—

Loading dose:

For patients *not* currently receiving theophylline preparations—Oral, the equivalent of 5 to 6 mg of anhydrous theophylline per kg of body weight.

For patients currently receiving theophylline preparations— A serum theophylline measurement should be obtained immediately, if possible. The loading dose for theophylline is based on the principle that each 0.5 mg of theophylline per kg of lean (ideal) body weight will result in a 1 (range, 0.5 to 1.6) mcg per mL increase in serum theophylline concentration. If a serum theophylline measurement cannot be obtained rapidly and the patient's condition requires immediate therapy, a single dose of the equivalent of 2.5 mg of anhydrous theophylline per kg of body weight may be administered if there are no symptoms of theophylline toxicity.

Maintenance (in acute attack):

Young adult smokers—Oral, the equivalent of anhydrous theophylline: 4 mg per kg of body weight every six hours.

Otherwise healthy nonsmoking adults—Oral, the equivalent of anhydrous theophylline: 3 mg per kg of body weight every eight hours.

Older patients and patients with cor pulmonale—Oral, the equivalent of anhydrous theophylline: 2 mg per kg of body weight every eight hours.

Patients with congestive heart failure or liver failure—Oral, the equivalent of anhydrous theophylline: 2 mg per kg of body weight every twelve hours.

Note: **To achieve optimal therapeutic theophylline dosage, and minimize the risk of toxicity, monitoring of serum theophylline concentration and patient response is recommended.**

In patients with cor pulmonale, congestive heart failure, or liver failure, dosage should not exceed the equivalent of 400 mg of anhydrous theophylline per day unless serum theophylline concentrations can be monitored at twenty-four-hour intervals.

Chronic therapy—Oral, the equivalent of anhydrous theophylline: Initially, 6 to 8 mg per kg of body weight, up to a maximum of 400 mg, per day in three or four divided doses at six- to eight-hour intervals. The dosage may be increased, if tolerated, in approximately 25% increments at two- to three-day intervals, up to a maximum dose of 13 mg per kg of body weight or 900 mg per day, whichever is less, without measurement of serum concentration.

Note: If the above maximum dose in chronic therapy is to be maintained or exceeded, serum theophylline measurement is recommended. Final dosage adjustment is based on subsequent serum theophylline measurements and patient response.

THEOPHYLLINE SODIUM GLYCINATE AND GUAIFENESIN ELIXIR

Usual adult dose:

Acute attack—

Loading dose:

For patients *not* currently receiving theophylline preparations—Oral, the equivalent of 5 to 6 mg of anhydrous theophylline per kg of body weight.

For patients currently receiving theophylline preparations—A serum theophylline measurement should be obtained immediately, if possible. The loading dose for theophylline is based on the principle that each 0.5 mg of theophylline per kg of lean (ideal) body weight will result in a 1 (range, 0.5 to 1.6) mcg per mL increase in serum theophylline concentration. If a serum theophylline measurement cannot be obtained rapidly and the patient's condition requires immediate therapy, a single dose of the equivalent of 2.5 mg of anhydrous theophylline per kg of body weight may be administered if there are no symptoms of theophylline toxicity.

Maintenance (in acute attack):

Young adult smokers—Oral, the equivalent of anhydrous theophylline: 4 mg per kg of body weight every six hours.

Otherwise healthy nonsmoking adults—Oral, the equivalent of anhydrous theophylline: 3 mg per kg of body weight every eight hours.

Older patients and patients with cor pulmonale—Oral, the equivalent of anhydrous theophylline: 2 mg per kg of body weight every eight hours.

Patients with congestive heart failure or liver failure—Oral, the equivalent of anhydrous theophylline: 2 mg per kg of body weight every twelve hours.

Note: **To achieve optimal therapeutic theophylline dosage, and minimize the risk of toxicity, monitoring of serum theophylline concentration and patient response is recommended.**

In patients with cor pulmonale, congestive heart failure, or liver failure, dosage should not exceed the equivalent of 400 mg of anhydrous theophylline per day unless serum theophylline concentrations can be monitored at twenty-four-hour intervals.

Chronic therapy—Oral, the equivalent of anhydrous theophylline: Initially, 6 to 8 mg per kg of body weight, up to a maximum of 400 mg, per day in three or four divided doses at six- to eight-hour intervals. The dosage may be increased, if tolerated, in approximately 25% increments at two- to three-day intervals, up to a maximum dose of 13 mg per kg of body weight or 900 mg per day, whichever is less, without measurement of serum concentration.

Note: If the above maximum dose in chronic therapy is to be maintained or exceeded, serum theophylline measurement is recommended. Final dosage adjustment is based on subsequent serum theophylline measurements and patient response.

Auxiliary labeling: • Keep container tightly closed.

THEOPHYLLINE SODIUM GLYCINATE AND GUAIFENESIN SYRUP

Usual adult dose:

Acute attack—

Loading dose:

For patients *not* currently receiving theophylline preparations—Oral, the equivalent of 5 to 6 mg of anhydrous theophylline per kg of body weight.

For patients currently receiving theophylline preparations—A serum theophylline measurement should be obtained immediately, if possible. The loading dose for theophylline is based on the principle that each 0.5 mg of theophylline per kg of lean (ideal) body weight will result in a 1 (range, 0.5 to 1.6) mcg per mL increase in serum theophylline concentration. If a serum theophylline measurement cannot be obtained rapidly and the patient's condition requires immediate therapy, a single dose of the equivalent of 2.5 mg of anhydrous theophylline per kg of body weight may be administered if there are no symptoms of theophylline toxicity.

Maintenance (in acute attack):

Young adult smokers—Oral, the equivalent of anhydrous theophylline: 4 mg per kg of body weight every six hours.

Otherwise healthy nonsmoking adults—Oral, the equivalent of anhydrous theophylline: 3 mg per kg of body weight every eight hours.

Older patients and patients with cor pulmonale—Oral, the equivalent of anhydrous theophylline: 2 mg per kg of body weight every eight hours.

Patients with congestive heart failure or liver failure—Oral, the equivalent of anhydrous theophylline: 2 mg per kg of body weight every twelve hours.

Note: **To achieve optimal therapeutic theophylline dosage, and minimize the risk of toxicity, monitoring of serum theophylline concentration and patient response is recommended.**

In patients with cor pulmonale, congestive heart failure, or liver failure, dosage should not exceed the equivalent of 400 mg of anhydrous theophylline per day unless serum theophylline concentrations can be monitored at twenty-four-hour intervals.

Chronic therapy—Oral, the equivalent of anhydrous theophylline: Initially, 6 to 8 mg per kg of body weight, up to a maximum of 400 mg, per day in three or four divided doses at six- to eight-hour intervals. The dosage may be increased, if tolerated, in approximately 25% increments at two- to three-day intervals, up to a maximum dose of 13 mg per kg of body weight or 900 mg per day, whichever is less, without measurement of serum concentration.

Note: If the above maximum dose in chronic therapy is to be maintained or exceeded, serum theophylline measurement is recommended. Final dosage adjustment is based on subsequent serum theophylline measurements and patient response.

THEOPHYLLINE SODIUM GLYCINATE AND GUAIFENESIN TABLETS

Usual adult dose:

Acute attack—

Loading dose:

For patients *not* currently receiving theophylline preparations—Oral, the equivalent of 5 to 6 mg of anhydrous theophylline per kg of body weight.

For patients currently receiving theophylline preparations—A serum theophylline measurement should be obtained immediately, if possible. The loading dose for theophylline is based on the principle that each 0.5 mg of theophylline per kg of lean (ideal) body weight will result in a 1 (range, 0.5 to 1.6) mcg per mL increase in serum theophylline concentration. If a serum theophylline measurement cannot be obtained rapidly and the patient's condition requires immediate therapy, a single dose of the equivalent of 2.5 mg of anhydrous theophylline per kg of body weight may be administered if there are no symptoms of theophylline toxicity.

Maintenance (in acute attack):

Young adult smokers—Oral, the equivalent of anhydrous theophylline: 4 mg per kg of body weight every six hours.

Otherwise healthy nonsmoking adults—Oral, the equivalent of anhydrous theophylline: 3 mg per kg of body weight every eight hours.

Older patients and patients with cor pulmonale—Oral, the equivalent of anhydrous theophylline: 2 mg per kg of body weight every eight hours.

Patients with congestive heart failure or liver failure—Oral, the equivalent of anhydrous theophylline: 2 mg per kg of body weight every twelve hours.

Note: **To achieve optimal therapeutic theophylline dosage, and minimize the risk of toxicity, monitoring of serum theophylline concentration and patient response is recommended.**

In patients with cor pulmonale, congestive heart failure, or liver failure, dosage should not exceed the equivalent of 400 mg of anhydrous theophylline per day unless serum theophylline concentrations can be monitored at twenty-four-hour intervals.

Chronic therapy—Oral, the equivalent of anhydrous theophylline: Initially, 6 to 8 mg per kg of body weight, up to a maximum of 400 mg, per day in three or four divided doses at six- to eight-hour intervals. The dosage may be increased, if tolerated, in approximately 25% increments at two- to three-day intervals, up to a maximum dose of 13 mg per kg of body weight or 900 mg per day, whichever is less, without measurement of serum concentration.

Note: If the above maximum dose in chronic therapy is to be maintained or exceeded, serum theophylline measurement is recommended. Final dosage adjustment is based on subsequent serum theophylline measurements and patient response.

THIOGUANINE   Systemic

A commonly used *brand name* in Canada is *Lanvis*.

ORAL
Thioguanine Tablets USP
   In the U.S.—GENERIC
   In Canada—*Lanvis*

Category: Antineoplastic.

Indications

Note: Bracketed information in the *Indications* section refers to uses not included in U.S. product labeling.

Accepted
Leukemia, acute myelocytic (treatment); or

[Leukemia, acute lymphocytic (treatment)]—Thioguanine is indicated for treatment of acute nonlymphocytic leukemia and is also used for treatment of acute lymphocytic leukemia.

Leukemia, chronic myelocytic (treatment)—Thioguanine is used for treatment of chronic myelocytic leukemia, although busulfan is usually preferred.

Pharmacology

Mechanism of action/Effect: Thioguanine is an antimetabolite of the purine analog type. Thioguanine is cell cycle-specific for the S phase of cell division. Activity occurs as the result of activation in the tissues and may include inhibition of DNA synthesis with a lesser effect on RNA synthesis.

Precautions to Consider

Geriatrics
No geriatrics-specific information is available on the use of thioguanine in geriatric patients. However, elderly patients are more likely to have age-related renal function impairment, which may require lower dosage in patients receiving thioguanine.

Dental
The bone marrow depressant effects of thioguanine may result in an increased incidence of microbial infection, delayed healing, and gingival bleeding. Dental work, whenever possible, should be completed prior to initiation of therapy or deferred until blood counts have returned to normal. Patients should be instructed in proper oral hygiene during treatment, including caution in use of regular toothbrushes, dental floss, and toothpicks.

Thioguanine may also rarely cause stomatitis associated with considerable discomfort.

Drug interactions and/or related problems
The following drug interactions and/or related problems have been selected on the basis of their potential clinical significance (possible mechanism in parentheses where appropriate)—not necessarily inclusive (» = major clinical significance):

Note: Combinations containing any of the following medications, depending on the amount present, may also interact with this medication.

Allopurinol or
Colchicine or
» Probenecid or
» Sulfinpyrazone
      (thioguanine may raise the concentration of blood uric acid; dosage adjustment of antigout agents may be necessary to control hyperuricemia and gout; allopurinol may be preferred to prevent or reverse thioguanine-induced hyperuricemia because of risk of uric acid nephropathy with uricosuric antigout agents)

Blood dyscrasia-causing medications
      (leukopenic and/or thrombocytopenic effects of thioguanine may be increased with concurrent or recent therapy if these medications cause the same effects; dosage adjustment of thioguanine, if necessary, should be based on blood counts)

» Bone marrow depressants, other or
Radiation therapy
      (additive bone marrow depression may occur; dosage reduction may be required when two or more bone marrow depres-

sants, including radiation, are used concurrently or consecutively)

Vaccines, killed virus

(because normal defense mechanisms may be suppressed by thioguanine therapy, the patient's antibody response to the vaccine may be decreased. The interval between discontinuation of medications that cause immunosuppression and restoration of the patient's ability to respond to the vaccine depends on the intensity and type of immunosuppression-causing medication used, the underlying disease, and other factors; estimates vary from 3 months to 1 year)

» Vaccines, live virus

(because normal defense mechanisms may be suppressed by thioguanine therapy, concurrent use with a live virus vaccine may potentiate the replication of the vaccine virus, may increase the side/adverse effects of the vaccine virus, and/or may decrease the patient's antibody response to the vaccine; immunization of these patients should be undertaken only with extreme caution after careful review of the patient's hematologic status and only with the knowledge and consent of the physician managing the thioguanine therapy. The interval between discontinuation of medications that cause immunosuppression and restoration of the patient's ability to respond to the vaccine depends on the intensity and type of immunosuppression-causing medication used, the underlying disease, and other factors; estimates vary from 3 months to 1 year. Patients with leukemia in remission should not receive live virus vaccine until at least 3 months after their last chemotherapy. Immunization with oral poliovirus vaccine should also be postponed in persons in close contact with the patient, especially family members)

Contraindications/Medical problems

The contraindications/medical problems included have been selected on the basis of their potential clinical significance (reasons given in parentheses where appropriate)—not necessarily inclusive (» = major clinical significance).

Risk-benefit should be considered when the following medical problems exist:

» Bone marrow depression
» Chickenpox, existing or recent (including recent exposure), or
» Herpes zoster

(risk of severe generalized disease)

Gout, history of, or
Urate renal stones, history of

(risk of hyperuricemia)

» Hepatic function impairment

(reduced biotransformation; lower dosage is recommended)

» Infection
» Renal function impairment

(reduced elimination; lower dosage is recommended)

Sensitivity to thioguanine

» Caution should be used also in patients who have had cytotoxic drug therapy and radiation therapy within 4 to 6 weeks.

Side/Adverse Effects

Note: Many "side effects" of antineoplastic therapy are unavoidable and represent the medication's pharmacologic action. Some of these (for example, leukopenia and thrombocytopenia) are actually used as parameters to aid in individual dosage titration.

The following side/adverse effects have been selected on the basis of their potential clinical significance (possible signs and symptoms in parentheses where appropriate)—not necessarily inclusive:

Those indicating need for medical attention
Incidence more frequent

Immunosuppression, leukopenia, or infection (usually asymptomatic; less frequently, fever or chills, cough or hoarseness, lower back or side pain, painful or difficult urination); *thrombocytopenia* (usually asymptomatic; less frequently, unusual bleeding or bruising; black, tarry stools; blood in urine or stools)

Note: *Bone marrow depression* usually occurs over 2 to 4 weeks, although a rapid fall in leukocyte count may occur within 1 to 2 weeks.

Incidence less frequent

Hyperuricemia or uric acid nephropathy (joint pain, lower back or side pain, swelling of feet or lower legs); *unsteadiness when walking*

Note: *Hyperuricemia or uric acid nephropathy* occurs most commonly during initial treatment of patients with leukemia or lymphoma, as a result of rapid cell breakdown, which leads to elevated serum uric acid concentrations.

Incidence rare

Gastrointestinal ulceration (black, tarry stools); *hepatotoxicity, hepatic fibrosis, or toxic hepatitis* (yellow eyes or skin); *stomatitis, dose-related* (sores in mouth and on lips)

Those indicating need for medical attention only if they continue or are bothersome
Incidence less frequent

Diarrhea; loss of appetite; nausea and vomiting; skin rash or itching

Note: *Loss of appetite* or *nausea and vomiting* occur especially with overdosage.

Those indicating the need for medical attention if they occur after medication is discontinued

Bone marrow depression (black, tarry stools; blood in urine or stools; cough or hoarseness; fever or chills; lower back or side pain; painful or difficult urination; pinpoint red spots on skin; unusual bleeding or bruising)

Patient Consultation

Consider advising the patient on the following (» = major clinical significance):

Before using this medication

Advisability of using nonhormonal contraception; telling physician immediately if pregnancy is suspected

See also *Precautions to Consider.*

Proper use of this medication

» Importance of not taking more or less medication than the amount prescribed

Caution in taking combination chemotherapy; taking each medication at the right time

Importance of ample fluid intake and subsequent increase in urine output to aid in excretion of uric acid

» Possible nausea and vomiting; importance of continuing medication despite stomach upset

Checking with physician if vomiting occurs shortly after dose is taken

Missed dose: Not taking at all; not doubling doses

» Proper storage

Precautions while using this medication

» Importance of close monitoring by the physician
» Avoiding immunizations unless approved by physician; other persons in patient's household should avoid immunizations with oral poliovirus vaccine; avoiding other persons who have taken oral poliovirus vaccine or wearing a protective mask that covers nose and mouth

Caution if bone marrow depression occurs:
» Avoiding exposure to persons with bacterial infections, especially during periods of low blood counts; checking with physician immediately if fever or chills, cough or hoarseness, lower back or side pain, or painful or difficult urination occur
» Checking with physician immediately if unusual bleeding or bruising; black, tarry stools; blood in urine or stools; or pinpoint red spots on skin occur

Caution in use of regular toothbrush, dental floss, or toothpick; physician, dentist, or nurse may suggest alternatives; checking with physician before having dental work done

Not touching eyes or inside of nose unless hands washed immediately before

Using caution to avoid accidental cuts with use of sharp objects such as safety razor or fingernail or toenail cutters

Avoiding contact sports or other situations where bruising or injury could occur

Side/adverse effects

May cause adverse effects such as blood problem and cancer; importance of discussing possible effects with physician

Signs of potential side effects, especially immunosuppression, leukopenia, infection, thrombocytopenia, hyperuricemia, uric acid nephropathy, gastrointestinal ulceration, hepatotoxicity, and stomatitis

Physician or nurse can help in dealing with side effects

General Dosing Information

Patients receiving thioguanine should be under supervision of a physician experienced in antimetabolite chemotherapy.

Dosage must be adjusted to meet the individual requirements of each patient, based on clinical response and appearance or severity of toxicity.

Development of uric acid nephropathy in patients with leukemia or lymphoma may be prevented by adequate oral hydration and, in some cases, administration of allopurinol. Alkalinization of urine may be necessary if serum uric acid concentrations are elevated.

Unlike mercaptopurine and azathioprine, thioguanine may be continued in the usual dosage when the patient is receiving allopurinol concurrently to inhibit uric acid formation, because xanthine oxidase is not involved in metabolism of thioguanine.

Patients who have failed to respond to mercaptopurine are unlikely to respond to thioguanine.

Because the actions of thioguanine may be delayed, it is recommended that thioguanine therapy be discontinued promptly at the first sign of leukopenia (particularly granulocytopenia), thrombocytopenia, jaundice, or hemorrhage or bleeding tendencies. Therapy may be resumed at a lower dosage when laboratory values return to satisfactory levels.

In acute leukemia, thioguanine may sometimes be administered despite the presence of thrombocytopenia and bleeding; stoppage of bleeding and increase in platelet count have occurred during treatment in some cases and platelet transfusions may be useful in others.

Special precautions are recommended in patients who develop thrombocytopenia as a result of administration of thioguanine. These may include extreme care in performing invasive procedures; regular inspection of intravenous sites, skin (including perirectal area), and mucous membrane surfaces for signs of bleeding or bruising; limiting frequency of venipuncture and avoiding intramuscular injections; testing urine, emesis, stool, and secretions for occult blood; care in use of regular toothbrushes, dental floss, toothpicks, safety razors, and fingernail and toenail cutters; avoiding constipation; and using caution to prevent falls and other injuries. Such patients should avoid alcohol and any aspirin intake because of the risk of gastrointestinal bleeding. Platelet transfusions may be required.

Patients who develop leukopenia should be observed carefully for signs of infection. Antibiotic support may be required. In neutropenic patients who develop fever, broad-spectrum antibiotic coverage should be initiated empirically, pending bacterial cultures and appropriate diagnostic tests.

Combination chemotherapy

Thioguanine may be used in combination with other agents in various regimens. As a result, incidence and/or severity of side effects may be altered and different dosages (usually reduced) may be used. For example, thioguanine is part of the following chemotherapeutic combination (a commonly used acronym is in parentheses):

—cytarabine and thioguanine (Ara-C + 6-TG).

For specific dosages and schedules, consult the literature. For information regarding each agent, consult the individual monographs.

Oral Dosage Forms

Note: Bracketed uses in the *Dosage Forms* section refer to categories of use and/or indications that are not included in U.S. product labeling.

THIOGUANINE TABLETS USP

Usual adult and adolescent dose:
[Leukemia, acute lymphocytic]; or
Leukemia, acute myelocytic; or
Leukemia, chronic myelocytic—
Induction: Oral, 2 mg per kg of body weight or 75 to 100 mg per square meter of body surface (to the closest 20 mg) a day in a single dose. If there is no clinical improvement and no leukocyte depression after 4 weeks at this dosage, a cautious increase in dosage to 3 mg per kg of body weight a day may be attempted.
Maintenance: Oral, 2 to 3 mg per kg of body weight or 100 mg per square meter of body surface a day.

THIOXANTHENES Systemic

Some commonly used *brand names* are:

In the U.S.—
  Navane [Thiothixene]
  Taractan [Chlorprothixene]

In Canada—
  Fluanxol [Flupenthixol]   *Navane* [Thiothixene]
  Fluanxol Depot   *Tarasan* [Chlorprothixene]
    [Flupenthixol]

CHLORPROTHIXENE
Oral
  Chlorprothixene Oral Suspension USP†
    In the U.S.—*Taractan*
  Chlorprothixene Tablets USP
    In the U.S.—*Taractan*
    In Canada—*Tarasan*
Parenteral
  Chlorprothixene Injection USP†
    In the U.S.—*Taractan*

FLUPENTHIXOL*
Oral
  Flupenthixol Dihydrochloride Tablets*
    In Canada—*Fluanxol*
Parenteral
  Flupenthixol Decanoate Injection*
    In Canada—*Fluanxol Depot*

THIOTHIXENE
Oral
  Thiothixene Capsules USP
    In the U.S.—*Navane;* GENERIC
    In Canada—*Navane*
  Thiothixene Hydrochloride Oral Solution USP†
    In the U.S.—*Navane;* GENERIC
Parenteral
  Thiothixene Hydrochloride Injection USP†
    In the U.S.—*Navane*
  Thiothixene Hydrochloride for Injection USP†
    In the U.S.—*Navane*

---

*Not commercially available in the U.S.
†Not commercially available in Canada.

Category: Antipsychotic.

Indications

Accepted
Psychotic disorders (treatment)—Indicated for management of primary and secondary symptoms of psychotic disorders.

The long-acting flupenthixol decanoate injection may be used in the management of nonagitated, chronic, schizophrenic patients who have been stabilized with short-acting neuroleptics.

Unaccepted
Flupenthixol is *not* indicated for the management of severely agitated psychotic patients, psychoneurotic patients, or geriatric patients with confusion and/or agitation.

Pharmacology

Mechanism of action/Effect: Antipsychotic—Thioxanthenes are thought to benefit psychotic conditions by blocking postsynaptic dopamine receptors in the brain. They also produce an alpha-adrenergic blocking effect and depress the release of most hypothalamic and hypophyseal hormones. However, the concentration of prolactin is increased due to blockade of prolactin inhibitory factor (PIF), which inhibits the release of prolactin from the pituitary gland.

Other actions/effects:
Antiemetic—Chlorprothixene also inhibits the medullary chemoreceptor trigger zone to produce an antiemetic effect.
Sedative—Chlorprothixene is also thought to cause an indirect reduction of stimuli to the brainstem reticular system to produce a sedative effect.

Duration of action:
Chlorprothixene—Intramuscular, up to 12 hours.
Flupenthixol decanoate—3 weeks.

Precautions to Consider

Cross-sensitivity and/or related problems
Patients sensitive to one thioxanthene may be sensitive to the other also, and possibly to the phenothiazines.

Geriatrics
Geriatric patients tend to develop higher plasma concentrations of neuroleptics because of changes in distribution due to decreases in lean body mass, total body water, and albumin, and often an increase in total body fat composition. These patients usually require a lower initial dosage and a more gradual titration of dose.
Elderly patients appear to be more prone to orthostatic hypotension, and exhibit an increased sensitivity to the anticholinergic and sedative effects of neuroleptics. They are also more prone to develop extrapyramidal side effects, such as tardive dyskinesia and parkinsonism. The signs of tardive dyskinesia are persistent, difficult to control, and, in some patients, appear to be irreversible. There is no known effective treatment. Careful observation during treatment for early signs of tardive dyskinesia and dosage adjustment of the thioxanthene may prevent a more severe manifestation of the syndrome.

Dental
The peripheral anticholinergic effects of thioxanthenes may decrease or inhibit salivary flow, especially in middle-aged or elderly patients, thus contributing to the development of caries, periodontal disease, oral candidiasis, and discomfort.
Extrapyramidal reactions induced by thioxanthenes will result in increased motor activity of the head, face, and neck. Occlusal adjustments, bite registrations, and treatment for bruxism may be made less reliable.
The leukopenic and thrombocytopenic effects of thioxanthenes may result in an increased incidence of microbial infection, delayed healing, and gingival bleeding. If leukopenia or thrombocytopenia occurs, dental work should be deferred until blood counts have returned to normal, and patients should be instructed in proper oral hygiene, including caution in use of regular toothbrushes, dental floss, and toothpicks.

Drug interactions and/or related problems
The following drug interactions and/or related problems have been selected on the basis of their potential clinical significance (possible mechanism in parentheses where appropriate)—not necessarily inclusive (» = major clinical significance):
Note: Combinations containing any of the following medications, depending on the amount present, may also interact with this medication.

Although not all of the following interactions have been documented specifically for thioxanthenes, a potential exists for their occurrence because of the close similarity of the pharmacological effects of thioxanthenes with those of phenothiazine medications.

» Alcohol or
» Central nervous system (CNS) depression-producing medications, other, especially anesthetics, barbiturates, and opioid (narcotic) analgesics
   (concurrent use may potentiate and prolong the CNS depressant effects of either these medications or the thioxanthenes; dosage adjustments may be necessary)

Amphetamines
   (concurrent use with thioxanthenes may inhibit the CNS-stimulating effects of amphetamines due to alpha-adrenergic blockade by the thioxanthenes; also, the antipsychotic effects of thioxanthenes may be reduced when they are used concurrently with amphetamines)

Antacids or
Antidiarrheals, adsorbent
   (concurrent use may inhibit the absorption of an orally administered thioxanthene)

Anticholinergics or other medications with anticholinergic action or
Antidyskinetic agents or
Antihistamines
   (anticholinergic effects, especially confusion, hallucinations, nightmares, and increased intraocular pressure, may be potentiated when these medications are used concurrently with thioxanthenes, because of secondary anticholinergic action of thioxanthenes)

Anticonvulsants
   (thioxanthenes may lower the seizure threshold; dosage adjustment of anticonvulsant medications may be necessary; potentiation of anticonvulsant effects does not occur)

Antidepressants, tricyclic, or
Maprotiline or
Monoamine oxidase (MAO) inhibitors, including furazolidone, pargyline, or procarbazine, or
Trazodone
   (concurrent use with thioxanthenes may prolong and intensify the sedative and anticholinergic effects of either these medications or the thioxanthenes)

Bromocriptine
   (concurrent use with thioxanthenes may increase serum prolactin concentrations and interfere with effects of bromocriptine; dosage adjustment of bromocriptine may be necessary)

Dopamine
   (concurrent use may antagonize peripheral vasoconstriction produced by high doses of dopamine, because of the alpha-adrenergic blocking action of thioxanthenes)

Ephedrine
   (alpha-adrenergic blocking action of thioxanthenes may decrease the pressor response to these medications when they are used concurrently with thioxanthenes)

» Epinephrine
   (alpha-adrenergic effects of epinephrine may be blocked when it is used concurrently with thioxanthenes, possibly resulting in severe hypotension and tachycardia)

» Extrapyramidal reaction-causing medications, other
   (concurrent use with thioxanthenes may increase the severity and frequency of extrapyramidal effects)

Guanadrel or
Guanethidine
   (concurrent use with thioxanthenes may decrease the hypotensive effects of these medications because of their displacement from and inhibition of uptake by adrenergic neurons)

» Levodopa
   (concurrent use with thioxanthenes may inhibit the antiparkinsonian effects of levodopa because thioxanthenes block dopamine receptors in the brain; however, levodopa is not indicated for prophylaxis or treatment of the extrapyramidal effects of thioxanthenes)

Metaraminol
   (concurrent use usually decreases, but does not reverse or completely block, the pressor response to metaraminol, because of the alpha-adrenergic blocking action of thioxanthenes)

Methoxamine
   (prior administration of thioxanthenes may decrease the pressor effect and duration of action of methoxamine because of the alpha-adrenergic blocking action of thioxanthenes)

Ototoxic medications, especially ototoxic antibiotics
   (concurrent use with thioxanthenes may mask the symptoms of ototoxicity such as tinnitus, dizziness, or vertigo)

Phenylephrine
   (prior administration of thioxanthenes may decrease the pressor response to phenylephrine because of the alpha-adrenergic blocking action of thioxanthenes)

Photosensitizing medications, other
   (concurrent use with thioxanthenes may cause additive photosensitizing effects)

» Quinidine
   (concurrent use with thioxanthenes may result in additive cardiac effects)

Contraindications/Medical problems
The contraindications/medical problems included have been selected on the basis of their potential clinical significance (reasons given in parentheses where appropriate)—not necessarily inclusive (» = major clinical significance).

Except under special circumstances, this medication should not be used when the following medical problems exist:
» Blood dyscrasias or
» Bone marrow depression
   (may be exacerbated)
» Circulatory collapse
» CNS depression
» Comatose states, drug-induced

Risk-benefit should be considered when the following medical problems exist:
» Alcoholism
   (CNS depression may be potentiated)
» Cardiovascular disease
   (increased risk of transient hypotension)
Glaucoma, or predisposition to, or
Peptic ulcer or
Respiratory disorders due to acute infections, asthma, or emphysema, or
Urinary retention
   (may be exacerbated)
» Hepatic function impairment
   (metabolism may be altered)
Parkinson's disease
   (potentiation of extrapyramidal effects)
Prostatic hypertrophy, symptomatic
   (increased risk of urinary retention)
» Reye's syndrome
Seizure disorders
   (seizures may be precipitated because of lowered seizure threshold)
Sensitivity to thioxanthenes or phenothiazines

Side/Adverse Effects

Note: A few cases of sudden death have been reported in patients who were receiving phenothiazine derivatives. Although the possibility exists, there is no definite evidence that the phenothiazines are causative agents.

Although not all of these side effects have been attributed specifically to each thioxanthene or its phenothiazine analog, a potential exists for their occurrence during the use of any thioxanthene or its analog.

The following side/adverse effects have been selected on the basis of their potential clinical significance (possible signs and symptoms in parentheses where appropriate)—not necessarily inclusive:

Those indicating need for medical attention
Incidence more frequent
> *Akathisia* (severe restlessness or need to keep moving)—may appear within first 6 hours after dose; *dystonic reactions* (difficulty in swallowing; inability to move eyes; muscle spasms, especially of neck and back; unusual twisting movements of body); *extrapyramidal effects, parkinsonian* (difficulty in talking; loss of balance control; mask-like face; shuffling walk; stiffness of arms and legs; trembling and shaking of fingers and hands); *tardive dyskinesia, persistent* (lip smacking or puckering; puffing of cheeks; rapid or worm-like movements of tongue; uncontrolled chewing movements; uncontrolled movements of arms and legs)

> Note: *Dystonic reactions* appear most often in children and young adults and early in treatment; may subside within 24 to 48 hours after medication has been discontinued.
>
> *Parkinsonian extrapyramidal effects* may be seen in the first few days of treatment, but frequency usually increase with increase of dosage; may be more frequent in elderly patients and older children.
>
> *Tardive dyskinesia* is initially dose related, but may increase with long-term treatment and total cumulative dose; may persist after discontinuation of thioxanthenes.

Incidence less frequent
> *Allergic reaction* (skin rash); *anticholinergic effect* (difficult urination); *deposition of opaque substances in lens and cornea* or; *retinopathy* (blurred vision or other eye problems); *hypotension* (fainting); *skin discoloration*—more frequent in females on high-dose and prolonged therapy

Incidence rare
> *Agranulocytosis or other blood dyscrasias* (sore throat and fever; unusual bleeding or bruising); *heat stroke* (hot, dry skin or lack of sweating; muscle weakness); *jaundice, obstructive* (yellow eyes or skin); *neuroleptic malignant syndrome* (NMS) (convulsions; difficulty in breathing; fast heartbeat; high fever; high or low blood pressure; increased sweating; loss of bladder control; severe muscle stiffness; unusually pale skin; tiredness)

> Note: *Heat stroke* may occur in environmental conditions of high heat and high humidity. Adequate interior temperature control (air-conditioning) must be maintained for institutionalized patients during hot weather because of the increased risk of heat stroke and neuroleptic malignant syndrome (NMS).
>
> *NMS* may occur at any time during neuroleptic therapy, but is more commonly seen soon after start of therapy, or after patient has switched from one neuroleptic to another, during combined therapy with another psychotropic medication, or after a dosage increase. Along with the overt signs of skeletal muscle rigidity, hyperthermia, autonomic dysfunction, and altered consciousness, differential diagnosis may reveal leukocytosis (9500 to 26,000 cells per cubic millimeter), elevated liver enzymes, and elevated creatine phosphokinase (CPK).

Symptoms of overdose
> *Convulsions; difficulty in breathing, severe; dizziness, severe* (hypotension); *drowsiness, severe, or coma; fast heartbeat; fever; muscle trembling, jerking, stiffness, or uncontrolled movements, severe; small pupils; unusual excitement; unusual tiredness or weakness, severe*

Those indicating need for medical attention only if they continue or are bothersome
Incidence more frequent
> *Constipation; decreased sweating; dizziness, lightheadedness, or fainting* (orthostatic hypotension); *drowsiness, mild; dryness of mouth; increased appetite and weight; increased sensitivity of skin to sunlight; nasal congestion* (stuffy nose)

Incidence less frequent
> *Changes in menstrual period; decreased sexual ability; swelling of breasts*—in males and females; *unusual secretion of milk*

Those indicating need for medical attention if they occur after medication is discontinued
> *Dyskinesia, withdrawal emergent* (dizziness; nausea and vomiting; stomach pain; trembling of fingers and hands; uncontrolled, continuing movements of mouth, tongue, or jaw)

Patient Consultation

In providing consultation, consider emphasizing the following selected information (» = major clinical significance):

Before using this medication
» Conditions affecting use, especially:
> Sensitivity to thioxanthenes or phenothiazines
>
> Pregnancy—Reports of hyperreflexia in neonates when pharmacologically-related phenothiazines were used during pregnancy; animal studies have shown an increase in resorption rates and decreased fertility with phenothiazines
>
> Breast-feeding—Pharmacologically-related phenothiazines are excreted in breast milk causing tardive dyskinesia and possible drowsiness in nursing baby
>
> Use in children—Children are more prone to extrapyramidal symptoms
>
> Use in the elderly—Elderly patients are more likely to develop extrapyramidal, anticholinergic, hypotensive, and sedative effects; reduced dosage recommended
>
> Use by athletes—Thioxanthenes are banned and, in some cases, tested for in shooters by the U.S. Olympic Committee (USOC) and the National Collegiate Athletic Association (NCAA)
>
> Dental—Thioxanthene-induced blood dyscrasias may result in infections, delayed healing, and bleeding; dry mouth may cause caries and candidiasis; increased motor activity of face, head, and neck may interfere with some dental procedures
>
> Other medications, especially alcohol or other CNS depression-producing medications, epinephrine, other extrapyramidal reaction-causing medications, levodopa, or quinidine
>
> Other medical problems, especially blood dyscrasias, bone marrow depression, circulatory collapse, CNS depression, alcoholism, cardiovascular disease, hepatic function impairment, Reye's syndrome

Proper use of this medication
> Taking with food or milk to reduce gastrointestinal irritation
» Compliance with therapy; not taking more medication or more often than directed
» May require several weeks of therapy to obtain desired effects
> Missed dose: Taking as soon as possible; not taking if within 2 hours of next scheduled dose; continuing on regular schedule; not doubling doses
» Proper storage

Precautions while using this medication
> Regular visits to physician to check progress of therapy
> Checking with physician before discontinuing medication; gradual dosage reduction may be needed
» Avoiding use of alcoholic beverages or other CNS depressants during therapy
> Avoiding use of antacids or medicine for diarrhea within 2 hours of taking thioxanthenes

» Caution if any kind of surgery, dental treatment, or emergency treatment is required
» Possible drowsiness; caution when driving, using machines, or doing other things requiring alertness
» Possible dizziness or lightheadedness; caution when getting up suddenly from a lying or sitting position
» Checking with physician if restlessness or excitement occurs
» Possible heatstroke: caution during exercise, hot weather, or when taking hot baths
» Possible skin photosensitivity; avoiding unprotected exposure to sun; using protective clothing; using a sun block product that includes protection against both UVA-caused photosensitivity reactions and UVB-caused sunburn reactions; avoiding use of sunlamp, tanning bed, or tanning booth
  Possible dryness of mouth; using sugarless gum or candy, ice, or saliva substitute for relief; checking with physician or dentist if dry mouth continues for more than 2 weeks
» Avoiding spilling liquid medication on skin or clothing; may cause possible contact dermatitis
  Observing precautions for long-acting parenteral form for up to 3 weeks

Side/adverse effects

» Stopping medication and notifying physician immediately if symptoms of neuroleptic malignant syndrome (NMS) appear
» Notifying physician as soon as possible if early signs of tardive dyskinesia appear
  Possibility of withdrawal symptoms
  Signs of potential side effects, especially tardive dyskinesia, dystonias, parkinsonian effects, anticholinergic effects, skin discoloration, blood dyscrasias, allergic skin reactions, photosensitivity, obstructive jaundice, heat stroke, NMS, or akathisia

General Dosing Information

Dosage must be individualized by titration from the lower dose range. After a favorable psychiatric response is noted (within several days to several months), that dosage should be continued for about 2 weeks, then gradually decreased to the lowest level that will maintain an adequate clinical response.

When extended therapy is discontinued, a gradual reduction in thioxanthene dosage over several weeks is recommended. Abrupt withdrawal may cause some patients on high or long-term dosage to experience transient dyskinetic signs, nausea, vomiting, gastritis, trembling, and dizziness.

The antiemetic effect of thioxanthenes may mask signs of drug toxicity or may obscure diagnosis of conditions whose primary symptom is nausea.

Avoid skin contact with liquid forms of this medication; contact dermatitis has resulted with use of similar medications.

For parenteral dosage forms only

Because hypotension is a common side effect of thioxanthenes, parenteral administration should be used only for those patients who are bedfast or for appropriate acute, ambulatory patients who can be closely monitored. A possible exception may be those patients who are dose-stabilized on the extended-action injectable form.

Intramuscular injections should be administered slowly and deeply into the upper outer quadrant of the buttock. Patient should remain lying down for at least half an hour after injection to avoid possible hypotensive effects.

Effects of the extended-action injectable form may last for up to 3 weeks. The precautions and side effects information applies during this period of time.

Geriatric patients and children should be monitored very carefully during parenteral therapy because of a higher incidence of hypotensive and extrapyramidal reactions.

The changeover from other neuroleptic medication to long-acting flupenthixol should be done gradually and under close supervision to prevent overdosage or insufficient suppression of psychotic symptoms before the next injection.

Diet/Nutrition

This medication may be taken with food or a full glass (240 mL) of water or milk, if necessary, to lessen stomach irritation.

CHLORPROTHIXENE

Summary of Differences

Pharmacology:
  Other actions/effects—Antiemetic and sedative effects are more prominent than those of thiothixene.
  Duration of action—Intramuscular dosage may produce effects lasting up to 12 hours.
Precautions: Laboratory value alterations—
  More likely to cause Q-T wave changes on ECG readings than is thiothixene.
  May produce false-positive results on immunologic urine pregnancy test.

Oral Dosage Forms

CHLORPROTHIXENE ORAL SUSPENSION USP

Note: Chlorprothixene oral suspension is not commercially available in Canada.

Usual adult and adolescent dose: Antipsychotic—Oral, 25 to 50 mg three or four times a day.

Note: Geriatric or debilitated patients usually require a lower initial dose, the dosage being increased gradually as needed and tolerated.

Usual adult prescribing limits: Up to 600 mg a day.

Auxiliary labeling:
• Shake well.
• May cause drowsiness.
• Avoid alcoholic beverages.
• Do not spill on skin or clothing.

Note: Avoid skin contact with liquid forms of this medication; contact dermatitis has resulted.

CHLORPROTHIXENE TABLETS USP

Usual adult and adolescent dose: Antipsychotic—Oral, 25 to 50 mg three or four times a day.

Note: Geriatric or debilitated patients usually require a lower initial dose, the dosage being increased gradually as needed and tolerated.

Usual adult prescribing limits: Up to 600 mg a day.

Auxiliary labeling:
• May cause drowsiness.
• Avoid alcoholic beverages.

Parenteral Dosage Forms

CHLORPROTHIXENE INJECTION USP

Note: Chlorprothixene injection is not commercially available in Canada.

Usual adult and adolescent dose: Antipsychotic—Intramuscular, 25 to 50 mg three or four times a day.

Note: Geriatric or debilitated patients and adolescents usually require a lower initial dose, the dosage being increased gradually as needed and tolerated.

Note: Avoid skin contact with liquid forms of this medication; contact dermatitis has resulted with similar medications.

FLUPENTHIXOL

Additional Dosing Information

See also *General Dosing Information.*

For parenteral dosage form only

Flupenthixol is for intramuscular injection only. It is *not* for intravenous use.

As with all oily injections, aspiration before injection ensures that inadvertent intravascular injection has not occurred.

Administration is by deep intramuscular injection into the gluteal region.

Patients not previously treated with a long-acting depot neuroleptic should be given a test dose of 5 to 20 mg of flupenthixol decanoate. The 5-mg test dose is usually recommended for elderly or debilitated patients, or for patients who may have a predisposition to extrapyramidal effects.

During the 5 to 10 days following the test dose, the patient should be carefully monitored for therapeutic response and appearance of extrapyramidal side effects. Any oral neuroleptic dosage should be reduced in this period.

A single injection may last for two to three weeks. However, when higher doses are used, a single injection may last for four weeks or more. Since higher doses also increase the incidence of adverse effects, dose increases should be made in increments not to exceed 20-mg.

Oral Dosage Forms

FLUPENTHIXOL DIHYDROCHLORIDE TABLETS

Note: Flupenthixol dihydrochloride tablets are not commercially available in the U.S.

Usual adult dose: Antipsychotic—
Initial: Oral, 1 mg three times a day, the dosage being increased by 1 mg every two to three days as needed and tolerated.
Maintenance: Oral, 3 to 6 mg a day in divided doses, up to 12 mg a day or more.

Note: Geriatric or debilitated patients usually require a lower initial dose, the dosage being increased gradually as needed and tolerated.

Auxiliary labeling:
• May cause drowsiness.
• Avoid alcoholic beverages.

Parenteral Dosage Forms

FLUPENTHIXOL DECANOATE INJECTION

Note: Flupenthixol decanoate injection is not commercially available in the U.S.

Usual adult dose: Antipsychotic—Intramuscular, initially 20 to 40 mg, the dose being repeated in four to ten days. Dosage may be increased in increments of not more than 20 mg.

Note:
Most patients require 20 to 40 mg every two to three weeks. Doses greater than 80 mg are rarely necessary, although higher doses may be used in some patients.

Additional information: Vehicle is a thin vegetable oil.

THIOTHIXENE

Summary of Differences

Precautions: Laboratory value alterations—With physiology/laboratory test values: Serum uric acid may be decreased.

Oral Dosage Forms

THIOTHIXENE CAPSULES USP

Usual adult and adolescent dose: Antipsychotic—Oral, initially 2 mg three times a day for milder conditions, or 5 mg two times a day for more severe conditions, the dosage being adjusted gradually as needed and tolerated, usually up to 60 mg a day.

Note: Dosages over 60 mg a day rarely increase the beneficial effect. Geriatric or debilitated patients usually require a lower initial dose, the dosage being increased gradually as needed and tolerated.

Auxiliary labeling:
• May cause drowsiness.
• Avoid alcoholic beverages.

THIOTHIXENE HYDROCHLORIDE ORAL SOLUTION USP

Note: Thiothixene hydrochloride oral solution is not commercially available in Canada.

Usual adult and adolescent dose: Antipsychotic—Oral, initially, 2 mg (base) three times a day for milder conditions, or 5 mg two times a day for severe conditions, the dosage being adjusted gradually as needed and tolerated, up to 60 mg a day.

Note: Dosages over 60 mg a day rarely increase the beneficial effect. Geriatric or debilitated patients usually require a lower initial dose, the dosage being increased gradually as needed and tolerated.

Auxiliary labeling:
• May cause drowsiness.
• Avoid alcoholic beverages.
• Do not spill on skin or clothing.
• Must be diluted before use.

Parenteral Dosage Forms

THIOTHIXENE HYDROCHLORIDE INJECTION USP

Note: Thiothixene hydrochloride injection is not commercially available in Canada.

Usual adult and adolescent dose: Antipsychotic—Intramuscular, 4 mg (base) two to four times a day, the dosage being adjusted gradually as needed and tolerated, but not to exceed a total of 30 mg a day.

Note: Geriatric or debilitated patients usually require a lower initial dose, the dosage being increased gradually as needed and tolerated.

Note: Avoid skin contact with liquid forms of this medication; contact dermatitis has resulted from use of similar medications.

THIOTHIXENE HYDROCHLORIDE FOR INJECTION USP

Note: Thiothixene hydrochloride for injection is not commercially available in Canada.

Usual adult and adolescent dose: Antipsychotic—Intramuscular, 4 mg (base) two to four times a day, the dosage being adjusted gradually as needed and tolerated, but not to exceed a total of 30 mg a day.

Note: Geriatric or debilitated patients usually require a lower initial dose, the dosage being increased gradually as needed and tolerated.

Note: Avoid skin contact with liquid forms of this medication; contact dermatitis has resulted with similar medications.

THYROID HORMONES   Systemic

Some commonly used *brand names* are:

In the U.S.—
    Cytomel [Liothyronine]   *Levoxine* [Levothyroxine]
    Euthroid [Liotrix]   *Synthroid* [Levothyroxine]
    Levoid [Levothyroxine]   *Thyrolar* [Liotrix]
    Levothroid [Levothyroxine]

In Canada—
    Cytomel [Liothyronine]   *Synthroid* [Levothyroxine]
    Eltroxin [Levothyroxine]   *Thyrolar* [Liotrix]
    Proloid [Thyroglobulin]

Another commonly used name is:
    L-Thyroxine [Levothyroxine]

LEVOTHYROXINE
Oral
    Levothyroxine Sodium Tablets USP
        In the U.S.—*Levothroid; Levoxine; Synthroid;* GENERIC
        In Canada—*Eltroxin; Synthroid*
Parenteral
    Levothyroxine Sodium for Injection
        In the U.S.—*Levothroid; Levoxine; Synthroid;* GENERIC
        In Canada—*Synthroid*
    Levothyroxine Sodium Injection†
        In the U.S.—*Levoid;* GENERIC
LIOTHYRONINE
Oral
    Liothyronine Sodium Tablets USP
        In the U.S.—*Cytomel;* GENERIC
        In Canada—*Cytomel*
LIOTRIX
Oral
    Liotrix Tablets USP
        In the U.S.—*Euthroid; Thyrolar*
        In Canada—*Thyrolar*
THYROGLOBULIN*
Oral
    Thyroglobulin Tablets USP*
        In Canada—*Proloid*
THYROID
Oral
    Thyroid Tablets USP
        In the U.S. and Canada—GENERIC
    Thyroid Enteric-coated Tablets†
        In the U.S.—GENERIC

*Not commercially available in the U.S.
†Not commercially available in Canada.

Category

Thyroid hormone—Levothyroxine; Liothyronine; Liotrix; Thyroglobulin; Thyroid.

Antineoplastic—Levothyroxine; Liothyronine; Liotrix; Thyroglobulin; Thyroid.
Diagnostic aid (thyroid function)—Levothyroxine; Liothyronine.

Indications

Accepted

Hypothyroidism (diagnosis and treatment)—Thyroid hormones are indicated as replacement therapy in the treatment of thyroid hormone deficiency (hypothyroidism) of any etiology (except transient hypothyroidism during the recovery phase of subacute thyroiditis), as well as for simple (nonendemic) goiter and chronic lymphocytic (Hashimoto's) thyroiditis[1].

In general, levothyroxine is the preferred thyroid hormone for use in the treatment of hypothyroidism because of the absence of variability and the ease of monitoring of plasma concentrations; it is the drug of choice in the treatment of congenital hypothyroidism. Liothyronine is recommended by some clinicians because of its short half-life and readily reversible effects for initial therapy in myxedema and myxedema coma, as well as for hypothyroid patients who also have heart disease, although there are significant risks associated with the latter use. Liothyronine may also be preferred during preparation for radioisotope scanning procedures or when gastrointestinal absorption processes are impaired. Disadvantages of thyroid extract and thyroglobulin tablets are their variable potencies and the fact that triiodothyronine (T_3) and thyroxine (T_4) concentrations fluctuate and cannot be used to regulate dosage. Liotrix is no longer considered advantageous because of the natural conversion of T_4 to T_3 in the tissues.

Goiter (prophylaxis[1] and treatment)—Thyroid hormones are indicated to suppress the growth of some adenomatous goiters, and to prevent the goitrogenic effects of other medications such as lithium, aminosalicylic acid, and some sulfonamide compounds.

Carcinoma, thyroid (prophylaxis and treatment)[1]—Thyroid hormones are indicated in the treatment of thyrotropin-dependent thyroid gland carcinoma. Some clinicians believe that prophylactic administration of thyroid hormones after neck irradiation will prevent development of thyroid gland carcinoma.

Thyroid function studies—Levothyroxine[1] and liothyronine are indicated as diagnostic aids (for example, the T_3 suppression test), although this use has generally been replaced by other tests.

Unaccepted

Use of thyroid hormones to treat vague symptoms such as dry skin, fatigue, constipation, abnormalities of reproductive function, growth retardation, or obesity without laboratory confirmation of contributing hypothyroidism is inappropriate and may cause hyperthyroidism in euthyroid individuals.

[1]Not included in Canadian product labeling.

Pharmacology

Mechanism of action/Effect: The action of thyroid hormones is not completely understood, but they have both catabolic (calorigenic) and anabolic effects and are therefore involved in normal metabolism, growth, and development, especially the development of the central nervous system (CNS) of infants. A feedback system involving the hypothalamus, anterior pituitary, and thyroid normally regulates circulating thyroid hormone concentrations.

Time to peak therapeutic effect: With chronic stable oral dosing—
Levothyroxine, thyroglobulin, thyroid: 3 to 4 weeks.
Liothyronine: 48 to 72 hours.

Duration of therapeutic action: After withdrawal of chronic therapy—
Levothyroxine, thyroglobulin, thyroid: 1 to 3 weeks.
Liothyronine: Up to 72 hours.

Precautions to Consider

Note: The following precautions apply to patients with *abnormal thyroid status* (hypothyroidism or, in some cases, hyperthyroidism). Patients in stable euthyroid condition as a result of continuing thyroid hormone therapy may be expected to respond in the same way as individuals with normal thyroid function and, therefore, the following precautions (except for *Patient monitoring*) do not usually apply in those circumstances.

Geriatrics
The elderly may be more sensitive to the effects of thyroid hormones. Thyroid hormone replacement requirements are about 25% lower in some patients over the age of 60 years than in younger adults, although individualization of dose is recommended.

Drug interactions and/or related problems
The following drug interactions and/or related problems have been selected on the basis of their potential clinical significance (possible mechanism in parentheses where appropriate)—not necessarily inclusive (» = major clinical significance):

Note: Combinations containing any of the following medications, depending on the amount present, may also interact with this medication.

In most cases, relative need for thyroid hormone dosage adjustment will depend on the thyroid state of the patient and the dosages of all medications involved. Dosage adjustment should be based on results of thyroid function tests and clinical status.

Adrenocorticoids, glucocorticoid with mineralocorticoid activity, or
Adrenocorticoids, mineralocorticoid, or
Corticotropin (ACTH)
 (changes in the thyroid status of the patient that may occur as a result of administration, changes in dosage, or discontinuation of thyroid hormones may necessitate adjustment of adrenocorticoid dosage because metabolic clearance of adrenocorticoids is decreased in hypothyroid patients and increased in hyperthyroid patients)

» Anticoagulants, coumarin- or indandione-derivative
 (the effects of the oral anticoagulant may be altered, depending on the thyroid status of the patient; an increase in dosage of thyroid hormone may necessitate a decrease in oral anticoagulant dosage; adjustment of oral anticoagulant dosage on the basis of prothrombin time is recommended)

Antidepressants, tricyclic
 (concurrent use with thyroid hormones may increase the therapeutic and toxic effects of both drugs, possibly due to increased receptor sensitivity to catecholamines; toxic effects include cardiac arrhythmias and CNS stimulation; also the onset of action of tricyclics may be accelerated)

Antidiabetic agents, oral, or
Insulin
 (thyroid hormones may increase insulin or antidiabetic agent requirements; careful monitoring of diabetic control is recommended, especially when thyroid therapy is started, changed, or discontinued)

Beta-adrenergic blocking agents
 (may decrease peripheral conversion of T_4 [thyroxine] to T_3 [triiodothyronine])

» Cholestyramine or
» Colestipol
 (concurrent use may decrease the effects of thyroid hormones by binding and delaying or preventing absorption; an interval of 4 to 5 hours between administration of the two medications and regular monitoring of thyroid function tests are recommended)

Estrogens
 (increase serum thyroxine-binding globulin; in patients with a nonfunctioning thyroid gland, thyroid hormone requirements may be increased)

Hepatic enzyme inducers
 (increase hepatic degradation of levothyroxine, which may result in increased requirements; dosage adjustment may be necessary)
 (phenytoin also reduces serum protein binding of levothyroxine, and reduces total and free serum T_4 by 15 to 25%; despite this, most patients remain euthyroid and dosage of thyroid hormone does not need to be adjusted)

Ketamine
 (concurrent use may produce marked hypertension and tachycardia; cautious administration to patients receiving thyroid hormone therapy is recommended)

Maprotiline
 (concurrent use with thyroid hormones may enhance the possibility of cardiac arrhythmias; dosage adjustment may be necessary)

Sodium iodide I 123 or
Sodium iodide I 131 or
Sodium pertechnetate Tc 99m
 (thyroid hormones may decrease the normal thyroidal uptake of I 123, I 131, or pertechnetate ion)

Somatrem or
Somatropin
 (concurrent excessive use of thyroid hormones with somatrem or somatropin may accelerate epiphyseal closure. However, untreated hypothyroidism may interfere with growth response to somatrem or somatropin; prior and/or concurrent thyroid hormone replacement is recommended)

» Sympathomimetics
 (concurrent use may increase the effects of these medications or thyroid hormone; thyroid hormones enhance risk of coronary insufficiency when sympathomimetic agents are administered to patients with coronary artery disease)

Contraindications/Medical problems
The contraindications/medical problems included have been selected on the basis of their potential clinical significance (reasons given in parentheses where appropriate)—not necessarily inclusive (» = major clinical significance).

Risk-benefit should be considered when the following medical problems exist:

» Adrenocortical insufficiency
 (must be corrected while thyroid replacement therapy is being given, to prevent precipitation of acute adrenocortical insufficiency)

» Cardiovascular disease, including angina pectoris, arteriosclerosis, coronary artery disease, hypertension, myocardial infarction (because of the risks associated with overly rapid thyroid hormone replacement and increased metabolic demands; mobilization of myxedema fluid may produce pitting edema 1 to 3 or more weeks after a change in dosage)

Diabetes mellitus
(possible reduced glucose tolerance and increased insulin or oral antidiabetic agent requirements)

» Hyperthyroidism, history of
(residual autonomous thyroid function may be present after therapy for hyperthyroidism, necessitating lower than typical doses)

Malabsorption states, such as celiac disease
(absorption, especially of levothyroxine, is reduced; dosage adjustment may be necessary)

» Pituitary insufficiency
(associated adrenocortical insufficiency must be corrected before thyroid replacement therapy is initiated, to prevent precipitation of acute adrenocortical insufficiency)

Sensitivity to thyroid hormone

» Thyrotoxicosis being treated with antithyroid medication

» Caution is required also in patients with long-standing hypothyroidism or myxedema, who may be more sensitive to effects of thyroid hormones.

Side/Adverse Effects

Note: Side/adverse effects are dose-related and the dose at which they occur varies with each patient; incidence may be reduced by slowly increasing the initial dose to the minimum effective dose.

Side/adverse effects may occur more rapidly with liothyronine than with levothyroxine or thyroid because of its rapid onset of action.

In infants, excessive doses may result in craniosynostosis.

Partial loss of hair may occur in children during the first few months of treatment; normal hair growth usually returns, even with continued treatment.

The following side/adverse effects have been selected on the basis of their potential clinical significance (possible signs and symptoms in parentheses where appropriate)—not necessarily inclusive:

Those indicating need for medical attention
Incidence rare
Allergic reaction (skin rash or hives); *pseudotumor cerebri, in children* (severe headache); *hyperthyroidism or overdosage* (changes in appetite; changes in menstrual periods; chest pain; diarrhea; fast or irregular heartbeat; fever; hand tremors; headache; irritability; leg cramps; nervousness; sensitivity to heat; shortness of breath; sweating; trouble in sleeping; vomiting; weight loss)

Those indicating need for medical attention only if they continue or are bothersome
Hypothyroidism or underdosage (changes in menstrual periods; clumsiness; coldness; constipation; dry, puffy skin; headache; listlessness; muscle aches; sleepiness; tiredness; weakness; weight gain)

Patient Consultation

Consider advising the patient on the following:

Before using this medication
See *Precautions to Consider.*

Proper use of this medication
» Importance of not taking more or less medication than the amount prescribed; taking medication at the same time every day for consistent effect

» Possible need for lifelong therapy; checking with physician before discontinuing medication
Missed dose: Taking as soon as possible; not taking if almost time for next dose and not doubling doses; notifying physician if two or more doses in a row are missed
» Proper storage

Precautions while using this medication
» Importance of close monitoring by the physician
Caution with angina or coronary artery disease; heavy exercise or exertion may precipitate angina
» Caution if any kind of surgery (including dental surgery) or emergency treatment is required
Avoiding other medications unless prescribed by physician because of possible interference with effects of thyroid hormone

Side/adverse effects
Signs of potential side effects, especially allergic reaction and pseudotumor cerebri

General Dosing Information

Dosage must be adjusted to meet the individual requirements of each patient, on the basis of clinical response and results of thyroid function tests.

Levothyroxine is the preferred form of thyroid replacement therapy.

Patients who are more than mildly hypothyroid initially should be treated with less than a full replacement dose, with doses then being increased gradually over a period of weeks. Otherwise, nervousness and rapid heart rate may occur.

Thyroid hormone replacement therapy for congenital hypothyroidism should be initiated as soon as possible after birth to minimize impaired mental and physical development. Treatment after about 3 months of age may reverse many of the physical effects but not all of the mental effects of hypothyroidism. Treatment should be continued for life, unless transient hypothyroidism is suspected, in which case therapy may be withdrawn for 2 to 8 weeks after 3 years of age; if thyroid-stimulating hormone (TSH) and thyroxine (T_4) concentrations remain normal throughout the withdrawal period, treatment is no longer necessary.

Suppression of TSH to normal levels must not be used as the sole criterion of adequacy of dose in congenital hypothyroidism, since TSH concentrations may remain elevated despite adequate or even excessive doses of thyroid hormone. Maintenance of appropriate T_4 concentrations for age is a more accurate guideline during infancy and childhood.

In general, thyroid hormone therapy is begun at a low dose, which is increased gradually to obtain a euthyroid state, followed by the dose required to maintain the response. However, this is not necessary in neonates, in whom rapid replacement is important, and who may be started at the full replacement dose. Adverse effects such as hyperactivity in the older child may be lessened by utilizing a starting dose of one-fourth the full replacement dose, and increasing the dose by one-fourth weekly until the full replacement dose is reached.

Rapid replacement of thyroid hormone is associated with less risk in younger adults than in older ones.

In hypothyroid patients with adrenocortical insufficiency or panhypopituitarism, replacement therapy with thyroid hormones must be preceded by adequate amounts of corticosteroids to prevent precipitation of acute adrenocortical insufficiency by the increase in metabolism. Supplemental adrenocortical steroids may also be necessary for patients with prolonged or severe hypothyroidism, including myxedema.

In hypothyroid patients with myxedema or cardiovascular disease, the initial dosage of thyroid hormones should be very small and must be increased very gradually to prevent precipitation of angina, coronary occlusion, or stroke. If cardiovascular reactions occur, a reduction in thyroid hormone dosage may be required. Although some clinicians prefer to use liothyronine in these patients because its effects disappear more rapidly after withdrawal, regulation of dosage is more difficult and its rapid onset of action may also produce adverse cardiac effects as a result of abrupt changes in metabolic demands.

If, after prolonged therapy (2 to 6 months), no response occurs with physiologic doses or a response occurs only with large doses of thyroid hormone, it is recommended that the diagnosis be reevaluated.

LEVOTHYROXINE

Summary of Differences

Indications: Usual drug of choice. Advantage over thyroid and thyroglobulin is predictable effect because of standard hormonal content.

Pharmacology: Absorption after oral administration is incomplete and variable, especially when taken with food.

Precautions: Medical problems/contraindications—Absorption may be significantly reduced in patients with malabsorption states.

Oral Dosage Forms

LEVOTHYROXINE SODIUM TABLETS USP

Usual adult dose:
Initial—
Mild hypothyroidism: Oral, 50 mcg (0.05 mg) as a single daily dose, with increments of 25 to 50 mcg (0.025 to 0.05 mg) at two- to three-week intervals until the desired result is obtained.
Severe hypothyroidism: Oral, 12.5 to 25 mcg (0.0125 to 0.025 mg) as a single daily dose, with increments of 25 mcg (0.025 mg) at two- to three-week intervals until the desired result is obtained.
Maintenance—Oral, 75 to 125 mcg (0.075 to 0.125 mg) per day (or 1.5 mcg per kg of body weight per day) as a single daily dose. A higher maintenance dose (up to 200 mcg per day) may be necessary in some patients (e.g., those with malabsorption).

Note: In the elderly and in patients with long-standing hypothyroidism, myxedematous infiltration, or cardiovascular dysfunction, the initial dose is usually 12.5 to 25 mcg (0.0125 to 0.025 mg) a day, and dosage is incremented at three- to four-week intervals. In the elderly, the maintenance dose is usually about 75 mcg (0.075 mg) per day.

Usual adult prescribing limits: Failure to respond to a daily dose of 150 mcg (0.15 mg) or more may indicate erroneous diagnosis of hypothyroidism, malabsorption, or poor compliance.

Auxiliary labeling:
• Take on empty stomach.
• Do not take other medicines without your doctor's advice.

Parenteral Dosage Forms

LEVOTHYROXINE SODIUM FOR INJECTION

Usual adult dose:
Hypothyroidism—Intravenous or intramuscular, 50 to 100 mcg (0.05 to 0.1 mg) as a single daily dose.
Myxedema coma or stupor—Initial: Intravenous, 200 to 500 mcg (0.2 to 0.5 mg, even in the elderly; an additional 100 to 300 mcg (0.1 to 0.3 mg) may be given on the second day if improvement has not occurred, followed by continuous daily administration of smaller doses, until the patient can tolerate oral administration.

Note: Smaller doses may be required in patients with concomitant cardiovascular disease.

LEVOTHYROXINE SODIUM INJECTION

Note: Levothyroxine sodium injection is not commercially available in Canada.

Usual adult dose:
Hypothyroidism—Intravenous or intramuscular, 50 to 100 mcg (0.05 to 0.1 mg) as a single daily dose.
Myxedema coma or stupor—Initial: Intravenous, 200 to 500 mcg (0.2 to 0.5 mg), even in the elderly; an additional 100 to 300 mcg (0.1 to 0.3 mg) may be given on the second day if improvement has not occurred, followed by continuous daily administration of smaller doses, until the patient can tolerate oral administration.
Note: Smaller doses may be required in patients with concomitant cardiovascular disease.

LIOTHYRONINE

Summary of Differences

Indications: Advantage over thyroid and thyroglobulin is predictable effect because of standard hormonal content. May be preferred over levothyroxine when a rapid effect or rapidly reversible effect is desired, or when gastrointestinal absorption processes or peripheral conversion of T_4 (thyroxine) to T_3 (triiodothyronine) is impaired; however, regulation of dosage is more difficult and rapid onset of action may also produce adverse cardiac effects as a result of abrupt changes in metabolic demands.

Pharmacology: Maximal effects with continued use occur within 48 to 72 hours and persist for up to 72 hours after withdrawal.

Side/adverse effects: May occur more rapidly with liothyronine than with levothyroxine or thyroid.

General dosing information:
Rapid action and abrupt increase in metabolic demands may produce adverse cardiac effects.
If symptoms of hyperthyroidism occur, withdrawal for 2 to 3 days is recommended before resumption at a lower dose.

Additional Dosing Information

See also *General Dosing Information.*

When a patient is transferred to liothyronine from other thyroid therapy, the other therapy is discontinued and liothyronine is initiated at a low dosage, increased gradually on the basis of patient response. Keep in mind that the effects of liothyronine occur rapidly, while the effects of other thyroid hormones may persist for several weeks.

Liothyronine may be given in divided daily doses to minimize fluctuations in T_3 concentrations.

Oral Dosage Forms

LIOTHYRONINE SODIUM TABLETS USP

Usual adult dose:
Mild hypothyroidism—
Initial: Oral, 25 mcg (0.025 mg) a day, with increments of 12.5 or 25 mcg (0.0125 or 0.025 mg) every one or two weeks until the desired result is obtained.
Maintenance: Oral, 25 to 50 mcg (0.025 to 0.05 mg) a day.
Myxedema—
Initial: Oral, 2.5 to 5 mcg (0.0025 to 0.005 mg) a day, with increments of 5 to 10 mcg (0.005 to 0.01 mg) every one or two weeks. When 25 mcg (0.025 mg) a day is reached, increments may sometimes be by 12.5 to 25 mcg (0.0125 to 0.025 mg) every one or two weeks.

Maintenance: Oral, 25 to 50 mcg (0.025 to 0.05 mg) a day.
Simple (nontoxic) goiter—
    Initial: Oral, 5 mcg (0.005 mg) a day, with increments of 5 to 10 mcg (0.005 to 0.01 mg) every one or two weeks. When 25 mcg (0.025 mg) a day is reached, increments may be by 12.5 or 25 mcg (0.0125 or 0.025 mg) every week.
    Maintenance: Oral, 50 to 100 mcg (0.05 to 0.1 mg) a day.

Note: In patients with cardiovascular disease, the initial dose is 5 mcg (0.005 mg) a day, with increments of no more than 5 mcg every two weeks. In the elderly also, the initial dose is 5 mcg a day, with increments of no more than 5 mcg at the recommended intervals.

Auxiliary labeling: • Do not take other medicines without your doctor's advice.

LIOTRIX

Summary of Differences

Indications: Advantage over thyroid and thyroglobulin is predictable effect because of standard hormonal content; provision of a product containing T_3 (triiodothyronine) no longer considered an advantage because of natural conversion of T_4 (thyroxine) to T_3 in the tissues.

Oral Dosage Forms

LIOTRIX TABLETS USP

Usual adult and adolescent dose:
    Initial—
        Hypothyroidism without myxedema: Oral, 50 mcg (0.05 mg) of levothyroxine and 12.5 mcg (0.0125 mg) of liothyronine or 60 mcg (0.06 mg) of levothyroxine and 15 mcg (0.015 mg) of liothyronine a day, with increments of a like amount at monthly intervals until the desired result is obtained.
        Myxedema or hypothyroidism with cardiovascular disease: Oral, 12.5 mcg (0.0125 mg) of levothyroxine and 3.1 mcg (0.0031 mg) of liothyronine a day, with increments of a like amount at two- to three-week intervals until the desired result is obtained.
    Maintenance—Oral, 50 to 100 mcg (0.05 to 0.1 mg) of levothyroxine and 12.5 to 25 mcg (0.0125 to 0.025 mg) of liothyronine a day.

Note: In the elderly, the initial dose is one-fourth to one-half the usual adult dose, doubled at six- to eight-week intervals until the desired result is obtained.

Auxiliary labeling: • Do not take other medicines without your doctor's advice.

THYROGLOBULIN

Summary of Differences

Indications: Disadvantages include variable hormonal content of commercial preparations and fluctuation of T_3 (triiodothyronine) and T_4 (thyroxine) concentrations produced.

Oral Dosage Forms

THYROGLOBULIN TABLETS USP

Usual adult and adolescent dose:
    Hypothyroidism without myxedema—
        Initial: Oral, 32 mg a day, with increments every one or two weeks until the desired result is obtained.
        Maintenance: Oral, 65 to 160 mg a day.
    Myxedema or hypothyroidism with cardiovascular disease—
        Initial: Oral, 16 to 32 mg a day, with increments of a like amount every two weeks until the desired result is obtained.
        Maintenance: 65 to 160 mg a day.

Auxiliary labeling: • Do not take other medicines without your doctor's advice.

THYROID

Summary of Differences

Indications: Disadvantages include variable hormonal content of commercial preparations and fluctuation of T_3 (triiodothyronine) and T_4 (thyroxine) concentrations produced.

Oral Dosage Forms

THYROID TABLETS USP

Usual adult and adolescent dose:
    Hypothyroidism without myxedema—
        Initial: Oral, 60 mg a day, with increments of 30 mg at monthly intervals until the desired result is obtained.
        Maintenance: Oral, 60 to 120 mg a day.
    Myxedema or hypothyroidism with cardiovascular disease—
        Initial: Oral, 15 mg a day, increased to 30 mg a day after two weeks, and to 60 mg a day after a further two weeks. Careful clinical assessment is recommended after one month and two months of treatment at 60 mg a day. If necessary, dosage may then be increased to 120 mg a day. If necessary, further increases of 30 or 60 mg may be made.
        Maintenance: Oral, 60 to 120 mg a day.

Note: An initial dose of 7.5 to 15 mg a day is recommended in the elderly; this dose may be doubled every six to eight weeks until the desired result is obtained.

Auxiliary labeling: • Do not take other medicines without your doctor's advice.

THYROID ENTERIC-COATED TABLETS

Note: Enteric-coated tablets of thyroid hormone may give unreliable absorption. USP Advisory Panels are not aware of any specific indication for enteric-coated preparations.

TIMOLOL Ophthalmic

Some commonly used *brand names* are:

In the U.S.—*Timoptic; Timoptic in Ocudose*
In Canada—*Apo-Timop; Timoptic*

OPHTHALMIC
Timolol Maleate Ophthalmic Solution USP
In the U.S.—*Timoptic; Timoptic in Ocudose*
In Canada—*Apo-Timop; Timoptic*

Category: Antiglaucoma agent (ophthalmic).

Indications

Note: Bracketed information in the *Indications* section refers to uses
not included in U.S. product labeling.

Accepted
Glaucoma, open-angle (treatment);
Glaucoma, in aphakic eyes (treatment);
Glaucoma, secondary (treatment); or
Hypertension, ocular (treatment)—Timolol has been shown to be effective in lowering intraocular pressure and may be indicated in
patients with chronic open-angle glaucoma or glaucoma in aphakic
eyes; some patients with secondary glaucoma; and other patients
with elevated intraocular pressure who are at sufficient risk to
require lowering of the ocular pressure.

In patients who respond inadequately to multiple antiglaucoma
drug therapy, addition of timolol may produce a further reduction
of intraocular pressure.

[Glaucoma, angle-closure (treatment adjunct)]—Timolol may be used
in conjunction with a miotic to reduce elevated intraocular pressure in acute and chronic angle-closure glaucoma; however,
timolol's action alone is unlikely to terminate an acute attack of
angle-closure glaucoma, because timolol produces little or no constriction of the pupil, which is necessary to pull the iris away from
the trabeculum to relieve blockage of the trabecular meshwork.

[Glaucoma, angle-closure, *during* or *after* iridectomy (treatment)][1]; or
[Glaucoma, malignant (treatment)][1]—Timolol is used to lower intraocular pressure in the treatment of angle-closure glaucoma *during* or *after* iridectomy and in the treatment of malignant glaucoma.

---

[1]Not included in Canadian product labeling.

Pharmacology

Mechanism of action/Effect: Timolol is a beta-1 and beta-2 (nonselective) adrenergic blocking agent. The exact mechanism of the
ocular hypotensive action of timolol has not been established.
Tonography and fluorophotometry studies in humans suggest that
timolol lowers intraocular pressure by reducing aqueous humor
production.

Other actions/effects:
Reduces cardiac output in both healthy individuals and patients
with heart disease.
Decreases heart rate and blood pressure in some patients.
Produces beta-adrenergic receptor blockade in the bronchi and
bronchioles.
Has little or no effect on pupil size or accommodation compared to
miosis produced by cholinergic agents.

Onset of action: Within 30 minutes following a single dose.

Time to peak effect: Within 1 to 2 hours following a single dose.

Duration of action: A significant lowering of intraocular pressure
may be maintained for up to 24 hours following a single dose.

Precautions to Consider

Cross-sensitivity and/or related problems
Patients intolerant of other beta-adrenergic blockers, either systemic
or ophthalmic (such as acebutolol, atenolol, betaxolol, carteolol,
labetalol, levobunolol, metipranolol, metoprolol, nadolol, oxprenolol, penbutolol, pindolol, propranolol, or sotalol), may be intolerant of timolol also.

Geriatrics
Although appropriate studies on the relationship of age to the effects
of this medicine have not been performed in the geriatric population, no geriatrics-specific problems have been documented to date.
However, if significant systemic absorption of ophthalmic betablockers occurs, the same geriatrics-related problems may occur
that are possible with the systemic beta-blockers. These include
increased myocardial depression because of reduced metabolic
and excretory capabilities in many elderly patients and the increased risk of beta-blocker-induced hypothermia in elderly patients.
In addition, elderly patients are more likely to have age-related peripheral vascular disease, which may require caution in patients receiving beta-blockers.

Drug interactions and/or related problems
The following drug interactions and/or related problems have been
selected on the basis of their potential clinical significance (possible mechanism in parentheses where appropriate)—not necessarily inclusive (» = major clinical significance):

Note: Combinations containing any of the following medications, depending on the amount present, may also interact with this
medication.

Information concerning interactions between ophthalmic timolol
and other medications is still limited. Some of the following
potential interactions apply to beta-adrenergic blocking agents
in general and are stated for cautionary reference until additional information specific for timolol is available.

Amphetamines
(if significant systemic absorption of the ophthalmic beta-adrenergic blocking agents, betaxolol, levobunolol, and timolol,
occurs, concurrent use of amphetamines may result in unopposed alpha-adrenergic activity with a risk of hypertension and
excessive bradycardia and possible heart block)

Anesthetics, hydrocarbon inhalation, such as:
Chloroform
Cyclopropane
Enflurane
Halothane
Isoflurane
Methoxyflurane
Trichloroethylene
(if significant systemic absorption of the ophthalmic beta-adrenergic blocking agents, betaxolol, levobunolol, and timolol,
occurs, concurrent use of hydrocarbon inhalation anesthetics
may result in prolonged severe hypotension because the betaadrenergic blockade reduces the ability of the heart to respond
to beta-adrenergically mediated sympathetic reflex stimuli; if
necessary to reverse the effects of beta-adrenergic blocking
agents during surgery, agonists, such as dobutamine, dopamine, isoproterenol, or norepinephrine, may be used but should
be administered with caution, especially in patients receiving
halothane. Some clinicians recommend gradual withdrawal of
beta-adrenergic blocking agents 48 hours prior to elective surgery; however, this recommendation is controversial)

Antidiabetic agents, oral, or
Insulin

(systemic beta-adrenergic blocking agents may affect diabetes mellitus therapy. This may also occur with the ophthalmic beta-adrenergic blocking agents, betaxolol, levobunolol, and timolol, if there is significant systemic absorption. Nonselective beta-adrenergic blocking agents impair glycogenolysis and the hyperglycemic response to endogenous epinephrine, leading to persistence of hypoglycemia. Also, beta-adrenergic blocking agents, especially nonselective agents, decrease the release of insulin in response to hyperglycemia. Dosage adjustment of the antidiabetic agent may be required to avoid severe hypoglycemic reaction. In addition, beta-adrenergic blocking agents may complicate patient monitoring by masking symptoms of hypoglycemia caused by epinephrine, such as increased heart rate and increased blood pressure, but not dizziness and sweating. Although selective or relatively selective beta-adrenergic blocking agents usually cause fewer problems with blood glucose levels, they may still mask symptoms of hypoglycemia)

Beta-adrenergic blocking agents, systemic

(if significant systemic absorption of the ophthalmic beta-adrenergic blocking agents, betaxolol, levobunolol, and timolol, occurs, concurrent use may result in an additive effect either on intraocular pressure or on systemic effects of beta-blockade)

Calcium channel blocking agents

(if significant systemic absorption of the ophthalmic beta-adrenergic blocking agents, betaxolol, levobunolol, and timolol, occurs, concurrent use of calcium channel blocking agents, such as diltiazem, nicardipine, nifedipine, nimodipine, and verapamil, may result in atrioventricular conduction disturbances, left ventricular failure, and hypotension; in some patients, if a calcium antagonist is necessary, nicardipine or nifedipine may be preferred because it has less effect on heart rate and conduction, although it may also cause greater hypotension; concurrent use of calcium channel blockers and ophthalmic beta-adrenergic blocking agents should be used with care in patients with impaired cardiac function)

Catecholamine-depleting medications, such as the rauwolfia alkaloids:
Alseroxylon
Deserpidine
Rauwolfia serpentina
Reserpine

(if significant systemic absorption of the ophthalmic beta-adrenergic blocking agents, betaxolol, levobunolol, and timolol, occurs, concurrent use of catecholamine-depleting medications may result in additive and possible excessive beta-adrenergic blockade; although this effect is largely theoretical, close observation is recommended, since bradycardia and marked hypotension may occur)

Cocaine

(cocaine may inhibit the therapeutic effects of systemic beta-adrenergic blocking agents, and may also have this effect on ophthalmic betaxolol, levobunolol, or timolol)

(concurrent use of a systemic beta-adrenergic blocking agent with cocaine may increase the risk of hypertension, excessive bradycardia, and possibly heart block because beta-blockade may leave cocaine's alpha-adrenergic activity unopposed. This may also occur with the ophthalmic beta-adrenergic blocking agents, betaxolol, levobunolol, or timolol, if significant systemic absorption of the ophthalmic beta-blocker occurs)

Diazoxide

(if significant systemic absorption of the ophthalmic beta-adrenergic blocking agents, levobunolol, timolol, and possibly betaxolol, occurs, concurrent use may prevent the diazoxide-induced tachycardia; however, the risk of hypotension may be increased)

Dipivefrin or
Epinephrine, ophthalmic

(concurrent use of dipivefrin or ophthalmic epinephrine with the ophthalmic beta-adrenergic blocking agents, betaxolol, levobunolol, and timolol, may provide a beneficial additive effect in lowering intraocular pressure in some patients)

Fentanyl derivatives

(chronic preoperative use of ophthalmic beta-adrenergic blocking agents [especially levobunolol, timolol, and possibly betaxolol] may increase the risk of initial bradycardia following induction doses of a fentanyl derivative)

Flecainide

(if significant systemic absorption of the ophthalmic beta-adrenergic blocking agents, betaxolol, levobunolol, and timolol, occurs, concurrent use may result in additive negative cardiac inotropic effects)

Hypotension-producing medications, other

(if significant systemic absorption of the ophthalmic beta-adrenergic blocking agents, levobunolol, timolol, and possibly betaxolol, occurs, concurrent use may potentiate the hypotensive effects of these medications)

Phenothiazines

(if significant systemic absorption of the ophthalmic beta-adrenergic blocking agents, betaxolol, levobunolol, and timolol, occurs, concurrent use may result in an increased plasma concentration of either the phenothiazines or the beta-adrenergic blocking agents because of inhibition of metabolism. This may result in additive hypotensive effects, irreversible retinopathy, cardiac arrhythmias, or tardive dyskinesia)

Sympathomimetics, systemic

(if significant systemic absorption of ophthalmic timolol occurs, concurrent use may result in inhibition of therapeutic effects of sympathomimetics with beta-adrenergic stimulant activity; in addition, beta-adrenergic blockade may result in unopposed alpha-adrenergic activity with a risk of hypertension and excessive bradycardia with possible heart block)

(for sympathomimetics with both alpha- and beta-adrenergic effects used as bronchodilators [ephedrine, epinephrine], beta-adrenergic blockade may antagonize the bronchodilating effect of ephedrine and epinephrine)

(for sympathomimetics with beta-adrenergic effects only, beta-adrenergic blockade may antagonize beta-1-adrenergic cardiac effects [dobutamine, dopamine, metaraminol, norepinephrine] or the beta-2-adrenergic bronchodilating effect [albuterol, bitolterol, ethylnorepinephrine, fenoterol, isoetharine, metaproterenol, pirbuterol, terbutaline] or both [isoproterenol])

Xanthines, such as:
Aminophylline
Caffeine
Dyphylline
Oxtriphylline
Theophylline

(if significant systemic absorption of the ophthalmic beta-adrenergic blocking agents, levobunolol, timolol, and possibly betaxolol, occurs, concurrent use may result in inhibition of therapeutic effects of xanthines; in addition, concurrent use of xanthines [except dyphylline] with the ophthalmic beta-adrenergic blocking agents, levobunolol, timolol, and possibly betaxolol, may decrease theophylline clearance, especially in patients with increased theophylline clearance induced by smoking; concurrent use requires careful monitoring)

(in addition, concurrent use with caffeine may enhance the cardiac inotropic effects of the ophthalmic beta-adrenergic blocking agents, levobunolol, timolol, and possibly betaxolol, if significant systemic absorption occurs)

Contraindications/Medical problems

The contraindications/medical problems included have been selected on the basis of their potential clinical significance (reasons given in parentheses where appropriate)—not necessarily inclusive (» = major clinical significance).

Except under special circumstances, this medication should not be used when the following medical problems exist:

» Asthma, bronchial (or history of), or
» Pulmonary disease, obstructive, severe chronic
   (severe respiratory reactions, including death due to bronchospasm, have been reported in patients with asthma, following administration of ophthalmic timolol)
» Cardiac failure, overt, or
» Cardiogenic shock or
» Heart block, 2nd- or 3rd-degree atrioventricular (AV), or
» Sinus bradycardia
   (risk of further myocardial depression)
» Previous allergic reaction to timolol

Risk-benefit should be considered when the following medical problems exist:

» Bronchitis, nonallergenic or chronic, or
» Emphysema or
» Pulmonary function impairment, other
   (use may promote bronchospasm and block bronchodilation produced by endogenous and exogenous catecholamine stimulation of beta-2-receptors)
   Cardiac disease, severe
   (monitoring of pulse rates and for signs of cardiac failure is suggested)
   Cerebrovascular insufficiency
   (potential effects on blood pressure and pulse; if signs of reduced cerebral blood flow occur following initiation of therapy, alternative therapy should be considered)
» Congestive heart failure
   (risk of further depression of myocardial contractility)
» Diabetes mellitus, especially labile diabetes
   (timolol may mask some signs and symptoms of hypoglycemia, such as tachycardia and tremor, but not dizziness and sweating)
» Hyperthyroidism
   (timolol may mask certain signs and symptoms of hyperthyroidism; abrupt withdrawal may precipitate a thyroid storm)
   Myasthenia gravis
   (use of ophthalmic timolol has been reported rarely to potentiate muscle weakness in some patients with myasthenia gravis or myasthenic symptoms)

Side/Adverse Effects

Note: Even in patients *without* a history of cardiac failure, continued depression of the myocardium with beta-blockers, including ophthalmic timolol if significant systemic absorption occurs, over a period of time can lead to cardiac failure. At the first sign or symptom of cardiac failure, timolol should be discontinued.

The following side/adverse effects have been selected on the basis of their potential clinical significance (possible signs and symptoms in parentheses where appropriate)—not necessarily inclusive:

Those indicating need for medical attention
Incidence rare
   Allergic reaction (skin rash, hives, or itching); *blepharitis, conjunctivitis, or keratitis* (severe irritation or inflammation of eye or eyelid); *vision disturbances*

Symptoms of systemic absorption
   Anxiety; chest pain; confusion or mental depression; congestive heart failure (swelling of feet, ankles, or lower legs); *decreased sexual ability; diarrhea; dizziness or feeling faint; hallucinations; headache; irregular, slow, or pounding heartbeat; nausea or vomiting; stomach cramps or pain; unusual tiredness or weakness; wheezing or troubled breathing, especially in patients with predisposition to bronchoconstriction*

Those indicating need for medical attention only if they continue or are bothersome
Incidence less frequent or rare
   Burning or stinging of eye; hair loss

Patient Consultation

In providing consultation, consider emphasizing the following selected information (» = major clinical significance):

Before using this medication
» Conditions affecting use, especially:
   Allergy to timolol or other beta-blockers (such as acebutolol, atenolol, betaxolol, carteolol, labetalol, levobunolol, metipranolol, metoprolol, nadolol, oxprenolol, penbutolol, pindolol, propranolol, or sotalol)
   Pregnancy—Medication may be absorbed into the body. Studies in animals have shown that timolol delays the formation of bone and increases the chance of death in the animal fetus
   Use in children—Infants may be especially sensitive to the effects of timolol, thus increasing the risk of side effects
   Use in the elderly—If significant systemic absorption of ophthalmic beta-blockers occurs, the chance of side effects during treatment may be increased, since elderly people are especially sensitive to the effects of these medications
   Use by athletes—Beta-blockers are banned and tested for in athletes; because ophthalmic timolol may be absorbed into the body, the medication may appear in the urine; if the agent is found in the urine, the athlete will be disqualified
   Other medical problems, especially bronchial asthma, or history of, severe chronic obstructive pulmonary disease, overt cardiac failure, 2nd- or 3rd-degree atrioventricular (AV) heart block, cardiogenic shock, sinus bradycardia, nonallergenic or chronic bronchitis, emphysema or other pulmonary function impairment, congestive heart failure, diabetes mellitus, or hyperthyroidism

Proper use of this medication
» Proper administration technique; using nasolacrimal occlusion is especially important in infants and children
   Preventing contamination: Not touching applicator tip to any surface; keeping container tightly closed
» Importance of not using more medication than the amount prescribed
   Missed dose: If dosing schedule is—
      Once a day: Applying as soon as possible; not applying if not remembered until next day; applying regularly scheduled dose
      More than once a day: Applying as soon as possible; not applying if almost time for next dose; applying next dose at regularly scheduled time
» Proper storage

Precautions while using this medication
   Regular visits to physician to check eye pressure during therapy
» Caution if any kind of surgery (including dental surgery) or emergency treatment is required
» Diabetics: May mask some signs of hypoglycemia, such as increased pulse rate and trembling, but not dizziness and sweating; also, may cause decreased or sometimes increased blood glucose concentrations

Side/adverse effects

Signs of potential side effects, especially allergic reaction, blepharitis, conjunctivitis, keratitis, vision disturbances, or symptoms of systemic absorption

General Dosing Information

Although some manufacturers recommend a dose of 2 drops of an ophthalmic solution at appropriate intervals, the conjunctival sac will usually hold only 1 drop.

When timolol is used to replace another ophthalmic beta-adrenergic blocking agent, the other beta-blocker should be discontinued simultaneously with initiation of therapy with timolol.

When timolol is used to replace a single antiglaucoma agent other than another ophthalmic beta-blocker, the other antiglaucoma agent may be continued on the first day that timolol is used but should be discontinued on the second day.

When timolol is used to replace several concomitantly administered antiglaucoma agents, the patient's dosage should be individualized as required. If any of the other antiglaucoma agents used is a beta-blocker, it should be discontinued before timolol is added to the regimen. The other antiglaucoma agents being used may be continued on the first day that timolol is used but one of the agents should be discontinued on the second day. Then the remaining antiglaucoma agents may be decreased or discontinued according to patient's response. Additional adjustments usually should involve only one agent at a time and should be made at intervals of not less than one week.

Timolol may be used concurrently with direct and indirect muscarinic agonists (e.g., pilocarpine, echothiophate, carbachol), beta agonists (e.g., ophthalmic epinephrine or dipivefrin), and/or systemic carbonic anhydrase inhibitors (e.g., acetazolamide), if necessary to control intraocular pressure.

In patients scheduled for major surgery, some practitioners recommend that beta-adrenergic blocking agents be gradually withdrawn 48 hours prior to surgery because beta-adrenergic receptor blockade impairs the ability of the heart to respond to beta-adrenergically mediated reflex stimuli. This recommendation remains controversial. However, since ophthalmic timolol may be absorbed systemically, gradual withdrawal of the medication should be considered for patients undergoing elective surgery because prolonged severe hypotension during anesthesia has occurred in some patients receiving systemic beta-adrenergic blocking agents.If necessary during surgery, the effects of beta-adrenergic blocking agents may be reversed by sufficient doses of agonists, such as isoproterenol, dopamine, dobutamine, or norepinephrine.

Ophthalmic Dosage Forms

TIMOLOL MALEATE OPHTHALMIC SOLUTION USP

Usual adult and adolescent dose: Topical, to the conjunctiva, 1 drop of a 0.25 or 0.5% solution of timolol (base) one or two times a day.

Auxiliary labeling:
- For the eye.
- Keep container tightly closed.

TIOPRONIN   Systemic†

Some commonly used *brand names* are:

In the U.S.—
   Thiola
Other—

Capen	*Sutilan*
Captimer	*Thiosol*
Epatiol	*Tioglis*
Mucolysin	*Vincol*

ORAL
Tiopronin Tablets†
   In the U.S.—*Thiola*
   Other—*Capen; Captimer; Epatiol; Mucolysin; Sutilan; Thiosol; Tioglis; Vincol*

---

†Not commercially available in Canada.

Category: Antiurolithic (cystine calculi).

Indications

Accepted
Cystinuria (treatment); or
Renal calculi, cystine (prophylaxis)—Tiopronin is indicated for the prevention of cystine kidney stones in patients with severe homozygous cystinuria who have a urinary cystine concentration greater than 500 mg a day; are resistant to treatment with high fluid intake, alkali, and diet modification; or have had adverse reactions to penicillamine.

Pharmacology

Mechanism of action/Effect: Tiopronin is an active reducing agent that undergoes thiol-disulfide exchange with cystine (cysteine-cysteine disulfide) to form tiopronin-cystine disulfide, which is more water soluble than cystine and is readily excreted. As a result, urinary cystine calculi are prevented.

Onset of action: Rapid.

Duration of action: Very short; effect of tiopronin shown to disappear within 8 to 10 hours after administration.

Precautions to Consider

Cross-sensitivity and/or related problems
Patients sensitive to penicillamine may be sensitive to this medication also.

Geriatrics
Although appropriate studies on the relationship of age to the effects of tiopronin have not been performed in the geriatric population, no geriatrics-specific problems have been documented to date. However, elderly patients are more likely to have age-related renal function impairment, which may require adjustment of dosage or dosing interval in patients receiving tiopronin.

Drug interactions and/or related problems
The following drug interactions and/or related problems have been selected on the basis of their potential clinical significance (possible mechanism in parentheses where appropriate)—not necessarily inclusive (» = major clinical significance):

Note: Combinations containing any of the following medications, depending on the amount present, may also interact with this medication.

Bone marrow depressants
(concurrent use of these medications with tiopronin may increase the leukopenic and/or thrombocytopenic effects; if concurrent use is required, close observation for toxic effects should be considered)

Hepatotoxic medications
(concurrent use of these medications with tiopronin may increase the hepatotoxic effects of either medication)

Nephrotoxic medications
(concurrent use of these medications with tiopronin may increase the nephrotoxic effects of either medication)

Contraindications/Medical problems

The contraindications/medical problems included have been selected on the basis of their potential clinical significance (reasons given in parentheses where appropriate)—not necessarily inclusive (» = major clinical significance).

Risk-benefit should be considered when the following medical problems exist:

» Agranulocytosis, aplastic anemia, or thrombocytopenia, history of (risk of recurrence)

Hepatic function impairment
(condition may be exacerbated)

Renal function impairment, current or history of
(cumulative effects of tiopronin may occur)

Sensitivity to tiopronin or penicillamine

Side/Adverse Effects

The following side/adverse effects have been selected on the basis of their potential clinical significance (possible signs and symptoms in parentheses where appropriate)—not necessarily inclusive:

Those indicating need for medical attention
Incidence more frequent
Dermatologic effects specifically ecchymosis (pain, swelling, tenderness of subcutaneous tissue in affected area); *elastosis perforans serpiginosa or pemphigus* (itching of skin); *skin rash or itching; ulcers or sores in mouth; urticaria* (hives); *jaundice* (yellow skin or eyes)

Note: If *pemphigus-type reaction* develops, tiopronin therapy should be stopped. Steroid treatment may be necessary.

Skin rash may appear during the first few months of treatment, but may be controlled with antihistamine therapy. Less commonly, rash may appear late in the course of treatment (after more than 6 months); this rash is usually located on the trunk and is associated with intense pruritus. The early rash recedes when tiopronin therapy is discontinued and seldom recurs when treatment is restarted at a lower dosage. The later rash recedes slowly after discontinuation of tiopronin and usually recurs when treatment is restarted.

Incidence less frequent
Allergic reactions, specifically adenopathy (tenderness of glands*), arthralgia* (pain in joints), *or chills; dyspnea or respiratory distress* (difficulty in breathing); *fever; increased bleeding; laryngeal edema* (difficulty in breathing, difficulty in swallowing, also hoarseness)*; myalgia* (muscle pain); *weakness; hematologic abnormalities, specifically anemia* (unusual tiredness or weakness), *eosinophilia, leukopenia* (sore throat and fever), *or thrombocytopenia* (unusual bleeding or bruising); *renal effects, specifically edema* (swelling of feet or lower legs), *hematuria* (bloody urine*), nephrotic syndrome* (cloudy or bloody urine, high blood pressure, swelling of feet or lower legs), *or proteinuria* (cloudy urine)

Note: Drug-induced *fever* may develop during the first month of therapy. This will recede when tiopronin is discontinued; therapy can then be reinstated at smaller doses and increased until desired levels are achieved.

Leukopenia of granulocytic series may develop without eosinophilia. *Thrombocytopenia* may be immunologic in origin or occur on an idiosyncratic basis. The reduction in peripheral white blood cell count to less than 3500 per cubic mm or in platelet count to below 100,000 per cubic mm mandates cessation of therapy.

Incidence rare
Goodpasture's syndrome (difficulty in breathing, spitting up blood, or unusual tiredness or weakness); *myasthenia gravis syndrome* (difficulty in breathing, chewing, talking, or swallowing; double vision; muscle weakness); *pulmonary effects, specifically bronchiolitis* (cough, difficulty in breathing, fever), *dyspnea* (difficulty in breathing), *hemoptysis* (coughing up blood), *pharyngitis* (hoarseness, sore throat), *or pulmonary infiltrates* (cough, chest pain, unusual tiredness or weakness); *systemic lupus erythematosus (SLE)-like syndrome* (fever, general feeling of discomfort, illness, or weakness, joint pain, skin rash, blisters, hives or itching, swelling of lymph glands)

Note: With abnormal urinary findings of *hemoptysis* and *pulmonary infiltrates,* tiopronin treatment should be stopped.

Appearance of *myasthenia gravis syndrome* requires cessation of tiopronin therapy.

SLE-like syndrome may be associated with a positive antinuclear antibody test, but not necessarily nephropathy. It may require discontinuance of tiopronin treatment.

Those indicating need for medical attention only if they continue or are bothersome
Incidence more frequent
Gastrointestinal disturbances, specifically abdominal pain, anorexia (loss of appetite), *bloating or gas, diarrhea or soft stools, or nausea and vomiting; warts; wrinkling, peeling, or unusually dry skin*

Incidence less frequent
Changes in taste or smell

Patient Consultation

In providing consultation, consider emphasizing the following selected information (» = major clinical significance):

Before using this medication
» Conditions affecting use, especially:
Sensitivity to tiopronin or penicillamine
Breast-feeding—May be excreted in breast milk; may cause potentially serious adverse effects in nursing infants
Other medical problems, especially agranulocytosis, aplastic anemia, or thrombocytopenia (history of)

Proper use of this medication
Taking medication on empty stomach
Importance of high fluid intake, especially at night
Possible need for low-methionine diet
Compliance with therapy; checking with physician before discontinuing medication since interruption of therapy may cause sensitivity reactions when therapy is reinstituted
Missed dose: Taking as soon as possible; not taking if almost time for next dose; not doubling doses
» Proper storage

Precautions while using this medication
Regular visits to physician to check progress during therapy

Side/adverse effects
Signs of potential side effects, especially dermatologic effects, allergic reactions, hematologic abnormalities, jaundice, renal effects, Goodpasture's syndrome, myasthenia gravis syndrome, pulmonary effects, and systemic lupus erythematosus (SLE)-like syndrome

General Dosing Information

Tiopronin therapy should be added to a treatment regimen only when the patient continues to form cystine stones on a high fluid intake (3 liters per day) and alkali therapy to maintain a urinary pH at a high normal range (6.5 to 7.0). Calcium phosphate nephrolithiasis may result if urinary alkalinization (pH is increased above 7.0) is continued without aggressively maintaining a high fluid intake.

To help prevent the formation of cystine stones, a high fluid intake is recommended. The patient should drink 2 full glasses (8 ounces each) of water with each meal and at bedtime. The patient should drink another 2 glasses (8 ounces each) during the night when the urine is more concentrated and more acidic than during the day.

For patients who have developed toxicity to penicillamine, tiopronin therapy may be initiated at lower doses.

Dosage of tiopronin should be based on the amount required to keep the urinary cystine concentration below the solubility limit (generally < 250 mg per L). The extent of cystine excretion is generally dependent on tiopronin dosage.

Diet/Nutrition

A diet low in methionine may be necessary to minimize cystine production (methionine is a precursor to cystine and is found in animal proteins such as milk, eggs, cheese, and fish). This diet is not recommended in growing children or during pregnancy because of its low protein content.

Tiopronin should be taken on an empty stomach (either 30 minutes before meals or 2 hours after meals) for faster absorption.

Oral Dosage Forms

TIOPRONIN TABLETS

Usual adult dose: Oral, initially, 800 mg a day in three divided doses, adjusted according to urinary cystine concentrations.

Auxiliary labeling: • Take on an empty stomach.

TOCAINIDE   Systemic

A commonly used *brand name* in the U.S. and Canada is *Tonocard.*

ORAL
Tocainide Hydrochloride Tablets USP
In the U.S. and Canada—*Tonocard*

Category: Antiarrhythmic.

Indications

Accepted

Arrhythmias, ventricular (prophylaxis and treatment)—Tocainide is indicated for suppression of life-threatening ventricular arrhythmias.

Pharmacology

Mechanism of action/Effect: Blocks the fast sodium channel in cardiac tissues, especially the Purkinje network, without involvement of the autonomic system. Reduces the rate of rise and amplitude of the action potential and decreases automaticity (increases the threshold of excitability) in the Purkinje fibers. Shortens the action potential duration and, to a lesser extent, decreases the effective refractory period in the Purkinje fibers. Does not usually alter conduction velocity, although it may slow conduction in patients with pre-existing conduction abnormalities. Does not significantly affect resting membrane potential or sinus node automaticity, left ventricular function, systolic arterial blood pressure, atrioventricular (AV) conduction velocity, or QRS or QT intervals. In the Vaughan Williams classification of antiarrhythmics, tocainide is considered to be a class IB agent.

Duration of action: 8 hours.

Precautions to Consider

Cross-sensitivity and/or related problems

Patients sensitive to other amide-type anesthetics may be sensitive to tocainide also. Cross-sensitivity with procainamide or quinidine has not been reported.

Geriatrics

Although appropriate studies on the relationship of age to the effects of tocainide have not been performed in geriatric patients, elderly patients are more likely to have age-related renal function impairment, which may require lower or less frequent doses in patients receiving tocainide. In addition, elderly patients may be more to prone to dizziness and hypotension.

Dental

The leukopenic and thrombocytopenic effects of tocainide may result in an increased incidence of microbial infection, delayed healing, and gingival bleeding. If leukopenia or thrombocytopenia occurs, dental work should be deferred until blood counts have returned to normal and patients should be instructed in proper oral hygiene during treatment, including caution in use of regular toothbrushes, dental floss, and toothpicks.

Drug interactions and/or related problems

The following drug interactions and/or related problems have been selected on the basis of their potential clinical significance (possible mechanism in parentheses where appropriate)—not necessarily inclusive (» = major clinical significance):

Note: Combinations containing any of the following medications, depending on the amount present, may also interact with this medication.

Antiarrhythmics, other
(although some antiarrhythmic agents may be used in combination for therapeutic advantage, combined use may potentiate risk of adverse cardiac effects)

Beta-adrenergic blocking agents
(concurrent use with tocainide may result in an additive increase in pulmonary wedge pressure and reduction in cardiac index; caution is recommended, especially in patients with heart failure)

Bone marrow depressants
(although problems have not been reported, concurrent use with tocainide may increase the risk of leukopenia and thrombocytopenia)

Contraindications/Medical problems

The contraindications/medical problems included have been selected on the basis of their potential clinical significance (reasons given in parentheses where appropriate)—not necessarily inclusive (» = major clinical significance).

Except under special circumstances, this medication should not be used when the following medical problem exists:

» Atrioventricular (AV) block pre-existing second or third degree without pacemaker

Risk-benefit should be considered when the following medical problems exist:

Atrial flutter or fibrillation
    (acceleration of ventricular rate occurs infrequently)

Congestive heart failure
    (may be aggravated as a result of a small negative inotropic effect and slight increase in peripheral resistance caused by tocainide)

Hepatic function impairment
    (reduced biotransformation; lower or less frequent doses may be required)

Renal function impairment
    (reduced elimination; lower or less frequent doses may be required)

Sensitivity to tocainide

Side/Adverse Effects

The following side/adverse effects have been selected on the basis of their potential clinical significance (possible signs and symptoms in parentheses where appropriate)—not necessarily inclusive:

Those indicating need for medical attention

Incidence less frequent
    Trembling or shaking
    Note: *Trembling or shaking* may indicate that maximum dose is being reached.

Incidence rare
    Leukopenia or agranulocytosis (fever or chills), *thrombocytopenia* (unusual bleeding or bruising); *pneumonitis, pulmonary fibrosis, alveolitis, pulmonary edema, or pneumonia* (cough or shortness of breath); *skin reactions, severe, including Stevens-Johnson syndrome and exfoliative dermatitis* (blisters on skin, peeling or scaling of skin, severe skin rash, sores in mouth; fever may also be associated with Stevens-Johnson syndrome); *ventricular arrhythmias* (irregular heartbeat)
    Note: *Leukopenia, agranulocytosis,* or *thrombocytopenia* usually occur after 2 to 12 weeks of therapy; blood counts usually return to normal within 1 month after withdrawal of therapy.
    Pulmonary adverse effects usually occur after 3 to 18 weeks of therapy; fatalities reported.
    Fatalities have been reported with *severe skin reactions.*

Those indicating need for medical attention only if they continue or are bothersome

Incidence more frequent
    Anorexia (loss of appetite); *dizziness or lightheadedness; nausea*
Incidence less frequent
    Blurred vision; confusion; headache; nervousness; numbness or tingling of fingers and toes; skin rash; sweating; vomiting

Patient Consultation

In providing consultation, consider emphasizing the following selected information (» = major clinical significance):

Before using this medication

» Conditions affecting use, especially:
    Sensitivity to tocainide or amide-type anesthetics
    Pregnancy—Increased possibility of death in animal fetuses
    Use in elderly—Elderly may be more prone to dizziness and hypotension
    Other medical problems, especially second or third degree atrioventricular (AV) block

Proper use of this medication

» Compliance with therapy; taking as directed even if feeling well
    May be taken with food or milk to reduce stomach upset

» Importance of not missing doses and taking at evenly spaced intervals
    Missed dose: Taking as soon as possible if remembered within 4 hours; not taking if remembered later; not doubling doses

» Proper storage

Precautions while using this medication

Regular visits to physician to check progress
Carrying medical identification card or bracelet
» Caution when driving or doing things requiring alertness because of possible dizziness
» Caution if any kind of surgery (including dental surgery) or emergency treatment is required

Side/adverse effects

Signs of potential side effects, especially trembling or shaking, leukopenia or agranulocytosis, thrombocytopenia, pulmonary problems, severe skin reactions, and ventricular arrhythmias

General Dosing Information

Patients who experience adverse effects shortly after dosing with tocainide may require a shorter dosing interval (i.e., further division of the daily dose). Patients who experience worsening of arrhythmias shortly before the next scheduled dose may require an increased dose and/or a shorter dosing interval.

The appearance of tremor may be used as an indication that the maximum dose is being reached.

It is recommended that tocainide therapy be withdrawn if bone marrow depression, pulmonary fibrosis, or a severe skin reaction occurs.

Diet/Nutrition

Tocainide may be taken with food or milk to reduce gastrointestinal irritation.

Oral Dosage Forms

TOCAINIDE HYDROCHLORIDE TABLETS USP

Usual adult dose: Antiarrhythmic—
    Initial: Oral, 400 mg every eight hours, the dose being adjusted as needed and tolerated.
    Maintenance: Oral, 1200 to 1800 mg per day in three divided doses.
    Note: Some patients may tolerate twice daily dosing.
        Geriatric patients may be more sensitive to the effects of the usual adult dose.

TRAZODONE   Systemic

Some commonly used *brand names* are:
   In the U.S.—*Desyrel; Trazon; Trialodine*
   In Canada—*Desyrel*

ORAL
Trazodone Tablets USP
   In the U.S.—*Desyrel; Trazon; Trialodine;* GENERIC
   In Canada—*Desyrel*

Category: Antidepressant; antineuralgic.

Indications

Note: Bracketed information in the *Indications* section refers to uses not included in U.S. product labeling.

Accepted
Depression, mental (treatment)—Trazodone is indicated in the treatment of major depressive episodes with or without prominent anxiety.

[Pain, neurogenic (treatment)][1]—Trazodone has been used to treat painful diabetic neuropathy and other types of chronic pain.

---

[1]Not included in Canadian product labeling.

Pharmacology

Mechanism of action/Effect: Not completely established in humans. Animal studies indicate that trazodone selectively inhibits serotonin re-uptake in the brain, causes beta-receptor subsensitivity, and induces significant changes in serotonin-receptor binding with only a slight effect on alpha-adrenergic receptors. Also, trazodone potentiates the behavioral changes in animals induced by 5-hydroxytryptophan, a serotonin precursor.

Onset of therapeutic action: In clinical trials, significant therapeutic results occurred after 2 weeks of therapy in 75% of the patients responsive to the medication, with some patients showing definite improvement after 1 week of therapy; 25% of the responding patients required 2 to 4 weeks of therapy before noticeable improvement occurred.

Precautions to Consider

Geriatrics
Elderly patients are more likely than younger adults to experience the sedative or hypotensive effects of trazodone; therefore, initial doses as low as half the recommended adult dose should be used in elderly patients, with adjustments made as needed and tolerated.

Dental
Peripheral anticholinergic effects, although they occur much less frequently with trazodone than with tricyclic antidepressants, may decrease or inhibit salivary flow, especially in middle-aged or elderly patients, thus contributing to the development of caries, periodontal disease, oral candidiasis, and discomfort.

Drug interactions and/or related problems
The following drug interactions and/or related problems have been selected on the basis of their potential clinical significance (possible mechanism in parentheses where appropriate)—not necessarily inclusive (» = major clinical significance):

Note: Combinations containing any of the following medications, depending on the amount present, may also interact with this medication.

» Alcohol or
» Central nervous system (CNS) depression-producing medications, other
   (concurrent use with trazodone may result in potentiation of CNS depressant effects)

Anticholinergics or other medications with anticholinergic activity or
Antidyskinetics or
Antihistamines
   (concurrent use with trazodone may intensify anticholinergic effects because of secondary anticholinergic activities of trazodone)
   (also, concurrent use of trazodone with antihistamines may potentiate the CNS depressant effects of either medication)

Antidepressants, tricyclic, or
Haloperidol or
Loxapine or
Maprotiline or
Molindone or
Phenothiazines or
Pimozide or
Thioxanthenes
   (concurrent use may prolong and intensify the sedative and anticholinergic effects of either these medications or trazodone)

» Antihypertensives
   (concurrent use with trazodone may increase the likelihood of hypotension; dosage reduction of the antihypertensive medication may be necessary; also, antihypertensives with CNS depressant effects, such as clonidine, guanabenz, methyldopa, metyrosine, and rauwolfia alkaloids, may potentiate CNS depression when used concurrently with trazodone)

Digoxin
   (concurrent use with trazodone may increase serum concentration of digoxin and may result in digoxin toxicity)

Phenytoin and possibly other hydantoin anticonvulsants
   (increased plasma phenytoin concentrations have been reported when phenytoin was used concurrently with trazodone; caution and close monitoring are suggested)

Contraindications/Medical problems
The contraindications/medical problems included have been selected on the basis of their potential clinical significance (reasons given in parentheses where appropriate)—not necessarily inclusive (» = major clinical significance).

Except under special circumstances, this medication should not be used when the following medical problem exists:

» Myocardial infarction, during the acute recovery period

Risk-benefit should be considered when the following medical problems exist:

Alcoholism, active
   (possible excessive CNS depression)

» Cardiac disease, especially arrhythmias
   (ventricular arrhythmias, premature ventricular contractions, and ventricular tachycardia may be potentiated)

» Hepatic function impairment
   (possible serum trazodone accumulation resulting in potentiation of side effects)

» Renal function impairment
   (may result in prolonged trazodone effects)

Sensitivity to trazodone

Side/Adverse Effects

The following side/adverse effects have been selected on the basis of their potential clinical significance (possible signs and symptoms in parentheses where appropriate)—not necessarily inclusive:

Those indicating need for medical attention
Incidence less frequent
   CNS effects (confusion; muscle tremors)
Incidence rare
   Allergic reaction (skin rash); *fast or slow heartbeat; hypotension* (fainting); *priapism* (prolonged, painful, inappropriate penile erection); *unusual excitement*
   Note: When *abnormal erectile activity* occurs, the patient should be advised to discontinue medication immediately and consult with physician.
Symptoms of overdose
   Drowsiness; loss of muscle coordination; nausea and vomiting

Those indicating need for medical attention only if they continue or are bothersome
Incidence more frequent
   Dizziness or lightheadedness; drowsiness; dryness of mouth, usually mild; headache; nausea and vomiting; unpleasant taste
Incidence less frequent or rare
   Blurred vision; constipation; diarrhea; muscle aches or pains; unusual tiredness or weakness

Patient Consultation

In providing consultation, consider emphasizing the following selected information (» = major clinical significance):

Before using this medication
» Conditions affecting use, especially:
   Sensitivity to trazodone
   Pregnancy—Animal studies have shown congenital anomalies and increased fetal resorptions with large doses
   Breast-feeding—Excreted in breast milk
   Use in the elderly—Elderly are more prone to develop sedative and hypotensive effects
   Dental—Dry mouth may result in caries, periodontal disease, oral candidiasis, and discomfort
   Other medications, especially alcohol or other CNS depression-producing medications, or antihypertensives
   Other medical problems, especially myocardial infarction, arrhythmias or other cardiac disease, hepatic function impairment, or renal function impairment

Proper use of this medication
   Taking with or soon after a meal or light snack to minimize stomach upset and dizziness or lightheadedness
» Compliance with therapy
» May require up to 4 weeks to produce significant therapeutic results, although 75% of responding patients benefit within 2 weeks
» Proper dosing
   Missed dose: Taking as soon as possible; not taking if within 4 hours of next scheduled dose; not doubling doses
» Proper storage

Precautions while using this medication
   Regular visits to physician to check progress during therapy
» Checking with physician before discontinuing medication; gradual dosage reduction may be needed
» Caution if any kind of surgery, dental treatment, or emergency treatment is required
» Avoiding use of alcohol or other CNS depressants during therapy
» Possible drowsiness; caution when driving or doing other things requiring alertness
» Possible dizziness; caution when getting up suddenly from a lying or sitting position

   Possible dryness of mouth; using sugarless gum or candy, ice, or saliva substitute for relief; checking with physician or dentist if dry mouth continues for more than 2 weeks
Side/adverse effects
   Sedative and hypotensive side effects more likely to occur in the elderly
   Priapism may occur; discontinuing medication and checking with physician immediately
   Signs of potential side effects, especially CNS effects, fast or slow heartbeat, hypotension, priapism, unusual excitement, or allergic reaction

General Dosing Information

Dosage of trazodone must be individualized for each patient by titration.

Potentially suicidal patients should not have access to large quantities of this medication since depressed patients, particularly those who may use alcohol excessively, may continue to exhibit suicidal tendencies until significant improvement occurs. Some clinicians recommend that the patient be supplied with the least amount of medication necessary for satisfactory patient management.

Daily dosage should be divided into at least two doses, because of trazodone's short elimination half-life. Trazodone should not be given as a single daily dose.

When side effects such as excessive drowsiness or dizziness might be bothersome or dangerous during waking hours, a larger portion (about two-thirds) of the total daily dose may be given at bedtime, with the balance being administered in the morning or during the day in divided doses.

To avoid a possible increase in side effects or aggravation of the patient's condition, any change or discontinuation of dosage should be accomplished gradually.

Diet/Nutrition
Each dose is best taken with or shortly after a meal or light snack. Food reduces the incidence and severity of side effects such as nausea or dizziness, by slowing trazodone's rate of absorption, decreasing the maximum concentration, and lengthening the time to maximum concentration.

Oral Dosage Forms

TRAZODONE TABLETS USP

Note: The dosing and strengths of the dosage forms available are expressed in terms of trazodone hydrochloride.

Usual adult and adolescent dose: Antidepressant—Oral, initially 150 mg a day in divided doses, the dosage being increased by 50 mg per day at three- or four-day intervals, as needed and tolerated.

Usual adult prescribing limits:
   Outpatients—Up to 400 mg a day.
   Inpatients—Up to 600 mg a day.

Usual geriatric dose: Antidepressant—Oral, initially 75 mg a day in divided doses, the dosage being increased gradually at three- or four-day intervals, as needed and tolerated.

Auxiliary labeling:
• May cause drowsiness.
• Avoid alcoholic beverages.
• Take with or immediately after food.

Additional information:
   The 150-mg tablet may be broken to yield doses of 50, 75, or 100 mg.
   The 300-mg tablet may be broken to yield three 100-mg doses, two 150-mg doses, or one 200-mg dose.

TRIMETHOPRIM   Systemic

Some commonly used *brand names* are:
      In the U.S.—*Proloprim; Trimpex*
      In Canada—*Proloprim*

ORAL
Trimethoprim Tablets USP
      In the U.S.—*Proloprim; Trimpex;* GENERIC
      In Canada—*Proloprim*

Category: Antibacterial (systemic).

Indications

Note: Bracketed information in the *Indications* section refers to uses
      not included in U.S. product labeling.

Accepted
Urinary tract infections, bacterial (treatment)—Trimethoprim is indicated in the treatment of initial, uncomplicated urinary tract infections caused by susceptible strains of *Escherichia coli, Proteus
mirabilis, Klebsiella pneumoniae, Enterobacter* species, and co-
agulase-negative *Staphylococcus* species, including *S. saprophyticus.*

[Urinary tract infections, bacterial (prophylaxis)][1]—Trimethoprim is
used in the prophylaxis of bacterial urinary tract infections.

[Pneumonia, *Pneumocystis carinii* (treatment)][1]—Trimethoprim is used
in combination with dapsone in the treatment of mild to moderate
pneumonia caused by *Pneumocystis carinii* (PCP).

Not all species or strains of a particular organism may be susceptible
to trimethoprim.

Unaccepted
Trimethoprim is not effective against *Pseudomonas aeruginosa* or
Bacteroides fragilis.

[1]Not included in Canadian product labeling.

Pharmacology

Mechanism of action/Effect:
Bacteriostatic lipophilic weak base structurally related to pyrimethamine, binds to and reversibly inhibits the bacterial enzyme dihydrofolate reductase, selectively blocking conversion
of dihydrofolic acid to its functional form, tetrahydrofolic acid.
This depletes folate, an essential cofactor in the biosynthesis of
nucleic acids, resulting in interference with bacterial nucleic
acid and protein production. Bacterial dihydrofolate reductase
is approximately 50,000 to 60,000 times more tightly bound by
trimethoprim than the corresponding mammalian enzyme.

Exerts its effect at a step in the folate biosynthesis immediately
subsequent to the one in which sulfonamides exert their effect.
When administered concurrently with sulfonamides, synergism
occurs and is attributed to inhibition of tetrahydrofolate production at two sequential steps in its biosynthesis.

Precautions to Consider

Geriatrics
An increased incidence of thrombocytopenia with purpura has been
reported in elderly patients who are receiving diuretics, primarily
thiazides, concurrently with trimethoprim.

Dental
The leukopenic and thrombocytopenic effects of trimethoprim may
result in an increased incidence of certain microbial infections,
delayed healing, and gingival bleeding. If leukopenia or thrombocytopenia occurs, dental work should be deferred until blood counts
have returned to normal. Patients should be instructed in proper
oral hygiene, including caution in use of regular toothbrushes,
dental floss, and toothpicks.

Drug interactions and/or related problems
The following drug interactions and/or related problems have been
selected on the basis of their potential clinical significance (possible mechanism in parentheses where appropriate)—not necessarily inclusive (» = major clinical significance):

Note: Combinations containing any of the following medications, de-
      pending on the amount present, may also interact with this
      medication.

Bone marrow depressants
      (concurrent use of bone marrow depressants with trimethoprim
      may increase the leukopenic and/or thrombocytopenic effects;
      if concurrent use is required, close observation for myelotoxic
      effects should be considered)

Cyclosporine
      (concurrent use of cyclosporine with trimethoprim may in-
      crease the incidence of nephrotoxicity)

Dapsone
      (concurrent use with trimethoprim will usually increase the
      plasma concentrations of both dapsone and trimethoprim, pos-
      sibly due to an inhibition in dapsone metabolism, and/or com-
      petition for renal secretion between the 2 medications; increased
      serum dapsone concentrations may increase the number and
      severity of side effects, especially methemoglobinemia)

» Folate antagonists, other
      (concurrent use with trimethoprim or use of trimethoprim be-
      tween courses of other folic acid antagonists, such as metho-
      trexate or pyrimethamine, is not recommended because of the
      possibility of an increased incidence of megaloblastic anemia)

Phenytoin
      (trimethoprim may inhibit the hepatic metabolism of pheny-
      toin, increasing the half-life of phenytoin by up to 50% and
      decreasing its clearance by 30%)

Procainamide
      (concurrent use with trimethoprim may increase the plasma
      concentration of both procainamide and its metabolite NAPA
      by decreasing their renal clearance)

Rifampin
      (concurrent use may significantly increase the elimination and
      shorten the elimination half-life of trimethoprim)

Warfarin
      (trimethoprim may potentiate the anticoagulant activity of war-
      farin by inhibiting its metabolism)

Contraindications/Medical problems
The contraindications/medical problems included have been selected
on the basis of their potential clinical significance (reasons given
in parentheses where appropriate)—not necessarily inclusive (» =
major clinical significance).

*Risk-benefit should be considered when the following medical prob-
lems exist:*
Hypersensitivity to trimethoprim

» Megaloblastic anemia due to folic acid deficiency

» Renal function impairment
    (trimethoprim is primarily renally excreted)

Side/Adverse Effects

The following side/adverse effects have been selected on the basis of their potential clinical significance (possible signs and symptoms in parentheses where appropriate)—not necessarily inclusive:

Those indicating need for medical attention
Incidence rare
Aseptic meningitis (headache, neck stiffness, malaise, nausea); *blood dyscrasias* (pale skin, sore throat and fever, unusual bleeding or bruising, unusual tiredness or weakness); *hypersensitivity* (skin rash or itching); *methemoglobinemia* (bluish fingernails, lips, or skin; difficult breathing; pale skin; sore throat and fever; unusual bleeding or bruising; unusual tiredness or weakness); *Stevens-Johnson syndrome* (aching joints and muscles; redness, blistering, peeling, or loosening of skin; unusual tiredness or weakness)

Those indicating need for medical attention only if they continue or are bothersome
Incidence less frequent
Gastrointestinal disturbances (diarrhea, loss of appetite, nausea or vomiting, stomach cramps or pain); *headache*

Patient Consultation

In providing consultation, consider emphasizing the following selected information (» = major clinical significance):

Before using this medication
» Conditions affecting use, especially:
    Hypersensitivity to trimethoprim
    Pregnancy—Trimethoprim crosses the placenta; may interfere with folic acid metabolism
    Breast-feeding—Trimethoprim is excreted in breast milk; may interfere with folic acid metabolism in the newborn
    Other medications, especially folic acid antagonists
    Other medical problems, especially megaloblastic anemia due to folic acid deficiency and renal function impairment

Proper use of this medication
» Not giving this medication to infants or children unless directed by physician
    Taking on an empty stomach or, if gastrointestinal irritation occurs, with food
» Compliance with full course of therapy
» Importance of not missing doses and taking at evenly spaced times
    Missed dose: Taking as soon as possible; if almost time for next dose and dosing schedule is—
        1 dose a day: Spacing missed dose and next dose 10 to 12 hours apart
        2 doses a day: Spacing missed dose and next dose 5 to 6 hours apart
» Proper storage

Precautions while using this medication
    Importance of regular visits to physician to check progress if on prolonged therapy
    Checking with physician if no improvement within a few days
    Importance of taking folic acid concurrently if anemia occurs

Using caution in use of regular toothbrushes, dental floss, and toothpicks; deferring dental work until blood counts have returned to normal; checking with physician or dentist concerning proper oral hygiene

Side/adverse effects
    Signs of potential side effects, especially blood dyscrasias, aseptic meningitis, hypersensitivity, Stevens-Johnson syndrome, and methemoglobinemia

General Dosing Information

Trimethoprim may be taken on an empty stomach or, if gastrointestinal irritation occurs, it may be taken with food.

If trimethoprim causes folic acid deficiency, folates may be administered concurrently without interfering with the antibacterial activity of trimethoprim since bacteria are unable to utilize preformed folates. If signs of bone marrow depression occur, trimethoprim should be discontinued. Leucovorin (folinic acid) 3 to 6 mg may be given intramuscularly once a day for 3 days or as required to restore normal hematopoiesis. In chronic overdose of trimethoprim, leucovorin may be given in high doses and/or for an extended period of time.

Oral Dosage Forms

Note: Bracketed uses in the *Dosage Forms* section refer to categories of use and/or indications that are not included in U.S. product labeling.

TRIMETHOPRIM TABLETS USP

Usual adult and adolescent dose: Oral, 100 mg every twelve hours for ten days; or 200 mg once a day for ten days.
    [Pneumonia, *Pneumocystis carinii* (treatment)][1]—Oral, 20 mg per kg of body weight per day of trimethoprim in combination with 100 mg of dapsone once a day for 21 days.
    [Prophylaxis of urinary tract infections][1]—Oral, 100 mg once a day.

Note: Adults with impaired renal function may require a reduction in dose as follows:

Creatinine Clearance (mL/min)	Dose
>30	See *Usual adult and adolescent dose*
15–30	50% of usual dose
<15	Use is not recommended

Usual adult prescribing limits: Doses greater than 600 mg are often used when treating *Pneumocystis carinii* pneumonia.

Auxiliary labeling: • Continue medicine for full time of treatment.

[1]Not included in Canadian product labeling.

URSODIOL   Systemic†

INN: Ursodeoxycholic acid

A commonly used *brand name* in the U.S. is *Actigall*.

ORAL
Ursodiol Capsules†
    In the U.S.—*Actigall*

───────────────────────────

†Not commercially available in Canada.

Category: Anticholelithic.

Indications

Note: Bracketed information in the *Indications* section refers to uses not included in U.S. product labeling.

Accepted
Gallstone disease (treatment)—Indicated by oral administration for dissolution of cholesterol gallstones in selected patients with uncomplicated radiolucent gallstone disease. However, alternative therapies should be considered since gallstone dissolution with ursodiol may require many months of treatment; complete dissolution does not occur in all patients; and recurrence of stones occurs within 5 years in about 50% of patients who have had stones dissolved by use of bile acid therapy.

Ursodiol therapy is more likely to be effective if the stones are small (<20 mm) and of the floatable type.

Body weight and dietary factors may influence gallstone formation and/or dissolution rate.

[Atresia, biliary (treatment)];
[Cholangitis, sclerosing (treatment)];
[Cirrhosis, alcoholic (treatment)];
[Cirrhosis, biliary (treatment)];
[Hepatic disease, cholestatic, chronic (treatment)];
[Hepatic disease, cystic fibrosis-associated (treatment)]; and
[Hepatitis, chronic (treatment)]—Ursodiol is used for the treatment of some chronic liver diseases, including primary biliary cirrhosis, primary sclerosing cholangitis, cystic fibrosis-associated liver disease, biliary atresia, chronic hepatitis, and alcoholic cirrhosis.

[Transplant rejection, liver (prophylaxis)]—Ursodiol is used as adjuvant therapy following orthotopic liver transplantation to prevent early graft rejection.

[Gallstone formation (prophylaxis)]—Ursodiol is used in the prevention of gallstone formation in obese patients during rapid weight loss.

Unaccepted
Ursodiol is *not* indicated when there are calcified cholesterol stones, radiopaque stones (calcium-containing), radiolucent bile pigment stones, or when surgery is clearly indicated.

Pharmacology

Mechanism of action/Effect: Anticholelithic—Although the exact mechanism of ursodiol's anticholelithic action is not completely understood, it is known that when administered orally ursodiol is concentrated in bile and decreases biliary cholesterol saturation by suppressing hepatic synthesis and secretion of cholesterol, and by inhibiting its intestinal absorption. The reduced cholesterol saturation permits the gradual solubilization of cholesterol from gallstones, resulting in their eventual dissolution.

Other actions/effects: Ursodiol increases bile flow. In chronic liver disease, ursodiol appears to reduce the detergent properties of the bile salts, thus reducing their cytotoxicity. Also, ursodiol may protect liver cells from the damaging activity of toxic bile acids (e.g., lithocholate, deoxycholate, and chenodeoxycholate), which increase in concentration in patients with chronic liver disease.

Precautions to Consider

Cross-sensitivity and/or related problems
Patients sensitive to other bile acids products may be sensitive to ursodiol also.

Geriatrics
Appropriate studies on the relationship of age to the effects of ursodiol have not been performed in the geriatric population. However, geriatrics-specific problems that would limit the usefulness of this medication in the elderly are not expected.

Drug interactions and/or related problems
The following drug interactions and/or related problems have been selected on the basis of their potential clinical significance (possible mechanism in parentheses where appropriate)—not necessarily inclusive (» = major clinical significance):

Note: Combinations containing any of the following medications, depending on the amount present, may also interact with this medication.

Antacids, aluminum-containing, or
Cholestyramine or
Colestipol
    (concurrent use may result in binding of ursodiol, thus decreasing its absorption)

Antihyperlipidemics, especially clofibrate, or
Estrogens or
Neomycin or
Progestins
    (concurrent use of these medications with ursodiol may decrease ursodiol's ability to dissolve cholesterol gallstones, since they tend to increase cholesterol saturation of bile)

Contraindications/Medical problems
The contraindications/medical problems included have been selected on the basis of their potential clinical significance (reasons given in parentheses where appropriate)—not necessarily inclusive (» = major clinical significance).

Risk-benefit should be considered when the following medical problems exist:
» Gallstone complications, such as:
    Biliary gastrointestinal fistula
    Biliary obstruction
    Cholangitis
    Cholecystitis
    Pancreatitis
        (medical treatment with ursodiol would be too lengthy; surgery may be indicated)
Hepatic function impairment, chronic
        (bile acid metabolism may be further impaired; however, in some studies ursodiol caused a return of abnormal liver tests toward normal. Data, at present, seem to indicate a possible therapeutic role for ursodiol in chronic cholestatic liver disease, wherein cholestasis [bile toxicity] appears to play an important role)
Sensitivity to ursodiol or to bile acids

Side/Adverse Effects

Note: Hepatotoxicity has not been associated with ursodiol therapy. However, in some individuals with a congenital or acquired reduction in ability to sulfate lithocholic acid, which is hepatotoxic, the risk of lithocholate-induced liver damage may be increased.

The following side/adverse effects have been selected on the basis of their potential clinical significance (possible signs and symptoms in parentheses where appropriate)—not necessarily inclusive:

Those indicating need for medical attention only if they continue or are bothersome
Incidence less frequent or rare
Diarrhea

Patient Consultation

In providing consultation, consider emphasizing the following selected information (» = major clinical significance):

Before using this medication
See *Precautions to Consider.*
» Conditions affecting use, especially:
   Sensitivity to bile acids
   Other medical problems, especially gallstone complications

Proper use of this medication
Taking with meals for optimal therapeutic effect
» Compliance with full course of therapy
   Missed dose: Taking as soon as possible or doubling the next dose
» Proper storage

Precautions while using this medication
» Regular visits to physician to check progress; laboratory tests may be required during therapy
   Avoiding aluminum-containing antacids; may interfere with absorption of ursodiol
» Notifying physician immediately if symptoms of acute cholecystitis develop

General Dosing Information

Ursodiol should preferably be taken with meals or a snack since it dissolves more rapidly when bile and pancreatic juice are present in the intestinal chyme.

Gallstone dissolution may require 6 months to 2 years of continuous dosing depending on the size and composition of the stone(s). Response should be monitored by ultrasonograms performed at 6-month intervals during the first year of therapy. After complete dissolution, it is recommended that ursodiol be continued for at least 3 months to promote dissolution of residue when particle size is too small to image.

Ursodiol therapy is unlikely to be effective if partial dissolution has not occurred after 12 months of treatment.

Although a nonfunctioning (nonvisualized) gallbladder prior to the initiation of therapy is not a contraindication to the use of ursodiol, gallbladder nonvisualization developing during therapy is an indication that complete stone dissolution will not occur and therapy should be discontinued.

Oral Dosage Forms

URSODIOL CAPSULES

Usual adult and adolescent dose:
   Anticholelithic—Oral, 8 to 10 mg per kg of body weight a day, divided into two or three doses, usually taken with meals.
   [Hepatic disease, cholestatic, chronic]—Oral, 8 to 10 mg per kg of body weight a day, divided into one or two doses. Larger doses have been used.
   [Gallstone prophylaxis]—Oral, 2 to 10 mg per kg of body weight a day.

Usual geriatric dose: See *Usual adult and adolescent dose.*

Auxiliary labeling:
   • Continue medicine for full time of treatment.
   • Take with food.

VALPROIC ACID   Systemic

Some commonly used *brand names* are:

In the U.S.—
   Dalpro
   Depakene   *Depakote Sprinkle*
   Depakote   *Myproic Acid*

In Canada—
   Epival
   Depakene

ORAL
Divalproex Sodium Delayed-release Capsules†
   In the U.S.—*Depakote Sprinkle*
Divalproex Sodium Delayed-release Tablets
   In the U.S.—*Depakote*
   In Canada—*Epival*
Valproic Acid Capsules USP
   In the U.S.—*Dalpro; Depakene;* GENERIC
   In Canada—*Depakene*
Valproic Acid Syrup USP
   In the U.S.—*Depakene; Myproic Acid;* GENERIC
   In Canada—*Depakene*

†Not commercially available in Canada.

Category: Anticonvulsant.

Indications

Note: Bracketed information in the *Indications* section refers to uses not included in U.S. product labeling.

Accepted
Epilepsy, absence seizure pattern (treatment)—Valproic acid is indicated in the treatment of simple and complex absence (petit mal) seizures. Although valproic acid may be used alone or with other anticonvulsant medication, monotherapy with valproic acid, whenever possible, is preferred because of unpredictable interactions with hepatic enzyme-inducing anticonvulsants and because of the increased risk of hepatotoxicity.

Epilepsy, mixed seizure pattern (treatment adjunct)—Valproic acid is indicated as an adjunct in conditions of multiple seizures that include absence seizures.

[Epilepsy, myoclonic seizure pattern (treatment)]—Valproic acid is used as a primary agent for myoclonic seizures.

[Epilepsy, simple partial seizure pattern (treatment)]; or
[Epilepsy, complex partial seizure pattern (treatment)]—Valproic acid may be useful in patients with partial seizures that are refractory to other anticonvulsants.

[Epilepsy, tonic-clonic seizure pattern (treatment)]—Valproic acid is used as a primary agent in the treatment of tonic-clonic (grand mal) seizures.

[Bipolar disorder (prophylaxis and treatment)]—Valproic acid may be useful in the prophylaxis and treatment of manic-depressive illness refractory to treatment with lithium or other agents.

Pharmacology

Mechanism of action/Effect: The mechanism of action has not been established; however, it is thought to be related to a direct or secondary increase in concentrations of the inhibitory neurotransmitter, gamma aminobutyric acid (GABA), possibly caused by its decreased metabolism or decreased re-uptake in brain tissues. Another hypothesis is that valproate acts on postsynaptic receptor sites to mimic or enhance the inhibitory action of GABA. The effect on the neuronal membrane is not completely understood. Some studies suggest a possible direct effect on membrane activity related to changes in potassium conductance. Also, valproate has been shown in animal studies to block sustained neuronal bursting responses by reducing the amplitude of sodium-dependent action potentials in a voltage- and use-dependent manner.

Divalproex sodium is a stable coordination compound composed of equal parts of valproic acid and sodium valproate. In the gastrointestinal tract, divalproex sodium dissociates into valproate and then produces the bioequivalent pharmacologic activity of valproic acid.

Precautions to Consider

Geriatrics
Geriatric patients tend to have increased free, unbound valproic acid concentrations and lowered intrinsic clearances, indicating a reduction of valproate metabolizing capacity and a fall in serum albumin. Therefore, these patients should receive a lower daily dosage, and the serum concentrations should be kept in the lower therapeutic range, because of the higher free valproic acid serum concentrations.

Dental
Valproic acid inhibits the secondary phase of platelet aggregation, which may be reflected in prolonged bleeding time and/or frank hemorrhaging.

In addition, the leukopenic and thrombocytopenic effects of valproic acid may result in an increased incidence of microbial infection, delayed healing, and gingival bleeding. If leukopenia or thrombocytopenia occurs, dental work, whenever possible, should be deferred until blood counts have returned to normal. Patients should be instructed in proper oral hygiene, including caution in use of regular toothbrushes, dental floss, and toothpicks.

Drug interactions and/or related problems
The following drug interactions and/or related problems have been selected on the basis of their potential clinical significance (possible mechanism in parentheses where appropriate)—not necessarily inclusive (» = major clinical significance):

Note: Combinations containing any of the following medications, depending on the amount present, may also interact with this medication.

In addition to the interactions listed below, the possibility should be considered that additive or multiple effects leading to impaired blood clotting and/or increased risk of bleeding may occur if valproic acid is used concurrently with any other medication having a significant potential for inhibiting platelet aggregation or for causing hypoprothrombinemia, thrombocytopenia, or gastrointestinal ulceration or hemorrhage.

» Alcohol or
» CNS depression-producing medications, other
    (concurrent use with valproic acid may potentiate CNS depressant effects)

    Anticoagulants, coumarin- or indandione-derivative, or
» Heparin or
» Thrombolytic agents
    (valproic acid-induced hypoprothrombinemia may increase the activity of coumarin- and indandione-derivatives and may increase the risk of bleeding in patients receiving heparin or thrombolytic agents)

    (also, inhibition of platelet aggregation, and reduction of platelet numbers or thrombocytopenia, may increase the risk of hemorrhage in patients receiving anticoagulant or thrombolytic therapy)

Antidepressants, tricyclic, or
Haloperidol or
Loxapine or
Maprotiline or
Molindone or
Monoamine oxidase (MAO) inhibitors or
Phenothiazines or
Thioxanthenes
  (in addition to enhancing central nervous system (CNS) depression when used concurrently with valproic acid, these medications may lower the seizure threshold; dosage adjustments may be necessary to control seizures)

» Barbiturates or
» Primidone
  (concurrent use with valproic acid causes higher serum concentrations of barbiturates or primidone, leading to increased CNS depression and neurological toxicity because of protein binding displacement of the barbiturate and reduced barbiturate metabolism; half-life of valproic acid is decreased; dosage adjustment of barbiturates or primidone may be necessary)

» Carbamazepine
  (concurrent use may result in decreased serum concentrations and half-life of valproic acid due to increased metabolism induced by hepatic microsomal enzyme activity; valproic acid causes an increase in the active 10,11-epoxide metabolite of carbamazepine by inhibition of its breakdown; monitoring of serum concentrations as a guide to dosage is recommended, especially when either medication is added to or withdrawn from an existing regimen)

Clonazepam
  (concurrent use with valproic acid may produce absence status)

Ethosuximide, and possibly other succinimide anticonvulsants
  (concurrent use with valproic acid has been reported to both increase and decrease ethosuximide concentrations; monitoring of serum concentrations as a guide to dosage is recommended)

» Hepatotoxic medications, other
  (concurrent use with valproic acid may increase the risk of hepatotoxicity; patients on prolonged administration or with a history of liver disease should be carefully monitored)

Levocarnitine
  (requirements for carnitine may be increased in patients receiving valproic acid)

» Mefloquine
  (concurrent use with valproic acid may result in low valproic acid serum concentrations and loss of seizure control; monitoring of valproic acid serum concentrations is recommended and dosage adjustments may be necessary during and after therapy with mefloquine)

» Phenytoin, and possibly other hydantoin anticonvulsants
  (concurrent use with valproic acid has resulted in breakthrough seizures or phenytoin toxicity because valproic acid may interfere with phenytoin protein binding, and phenytoin, through enzyme induction, will lower valproate levels; concurrent use requires close monitoring of the patient since variable serum phenytoin concentrations have resulted because valproate increases unbound phenytoin concentrations and decreases intrinsic clearance by inhibiting metabolism of phenytoin; total phenytoin serum concentrations may not reflect unbound phenytoin activity, and unbound phenytoin concentrations may be more reliable; dosage of phenytoin should be adjusted as required by clinical situation)

» Platelet aggregation inhibitors, other
  (concurrent use with valproic acid may increase the risk of hemorrhage because of additive or multiple actions that may decrease blood-clotting ability)

(the gastrointestinal ulcerative or hemorrhagic potential of aspirin, anti-inflammatory analgesics, or sulfinpyrazone may increase the risk of hemorrhage in patients receiving valproic acid)

(in addition, salicylates may displace valproic acid from protein binding sites, as well as altering valproic acid metabolism and excretion, resulting in increased levels of free [unbound] valproic acid, which may cause toxic effects)

Contraindications/Medical problems
The contraindications/medical problems included have been selected on the basis of their potential clinical significance (reasons given in parentheses where appropriate)—not necessarily inclusive (» = major clinical significance).

Except under special circumstances, this medication should not be used when the following medical problems exist:
» Hepatic disease or
» Hepatic function impairment, significant

Risk-benefit should be considered when the following medical problems exist:
  Blood dyscrasias
  Brain disease, organic
  Hepatic disease, history of
  Hypoalbuminemia
  Intolerance to valproic acid
  Renal function impairment
    (metabolites may accumulate; valproate binding to serum albumin is decreased and volume of distribution is increased)

Side/Adverse Effects

Note: Hepatic failure resulting in death has occurred in patients receiving valproic acid and its derivatives. These incidents usually have occurred during the first six months of treatment. Patients at greatest risk are children receiving other anticonvulsants with valproic acid. Serious or fatal hepatotoxicity may be preceded by nonspecific symptoms such as loss of seizure control, malaise, weakness, lethargy, Reye's-like syndrome, anorexia, vomiting, jaundice, and edema. In some cases, hepatic function impairment has progressed in spite of discontinuation of medication.

The following side/adverse effects have been selected on the basis of their potential clinical significance (possible signs and symptoms in parentheses where appropriate)—not necessarily inclusive:

Those indicating need for medical attention
Incidence less frequent or rare
  Behaviorial, mood, or mental changes; hepatotoxicity or hyperammonemia (increase in frequency of seizures, loss of appetite, continuing nausea or vomiting, swelling of face, tiredness and weakness, yellow eyes or skin); ***ophthalmological effects, specifically diplopia*** (double vision), ***nystagmus*** (continuous, uncontrolled back-and-forth and/or rolling eye movements), ***or spots before eyes; pancreatitis*** (severe abdominal or stomach cramps; continuing nausea and vomiting); ***platelet aggregation inhibition or thrombocytopenia*** (unusual bleeding or bruising)

  Note: Evidence of hemorrhage, bruising, or a disorder of coagulation or hemostasis is an indication for reduction of dosage or discontinuation of therapy.

Those indicating need for medical attention only if they continue or are bothersome
Incidence more frequent
  Abdominal or stomach cramps, mild—may also indicate a risk of pancreatitis; less frequent with divalproex; ***anorexia*** (loss of appetite); ***change in menstrual periods; diarrhea; hair loss; indigestion; nausea and vomiting; trembling of hands and arms; unusual weight loss or gain***

Incidence less frequent or rare
Clumsiness or unsteadiness; constipation; dizziness; drowsiness; headache; skin rash; unusual excitement, restlessness, or irritability

Patient Consultation

In providing consultation, consider emphasizing the following selected information (» = major clinical significance):

Before using this medication
» Conditions affecting use, especially:
  Sensitivity to valproic acid
  Fertility—Fertility studies in animals given large doses have shown reduced spermatogenesis and testicular atrophy
  Pregnancy—Pregnancy studies in animals have shown skeletal abnormalities involving ribs and vertebrae in offspring of mothers given large doses; in humans, crosses placenta in first trimester and may cause neural tube defects in fetus
  Breast-feeding—Excreted in breast milk
  Use in children—Children are at an increased risk of serious hepatotoxicity
  Use in the elderly—Elderly patients tend to have higher serum concentrations of free valproic acid; lower daily dosages recommended
  Use by athletes—Valproic acid is banned and, in some cases, tested for in shooters by the U.S. Olympic Committee (USOC) and the National Collegiate Athletic Association (NCAA)
  Dental—Prolonged bleeding time and/or hemorrhaging; leukopenia and thrombocytopenia may result in increased incidence of microbial infection, delayed healing, and gingival bleeding
  Other medications, especially alcohol or other CNS depression-producing medications, heparin or thrombolytic agents, barbiturates, primidone, carbamazepine, other hepatotoxic medications, phenytoin, or other platelet aggregation inhibitors
  Other medical problems, especially significant hepatic disease or hepatic function impairment

Proper use of this medication
  Proper administration:
  For valproic acid capsules
    Swallowing capsules whole with water only; not breaking, chewing, or crushing
  For divalproex sodium delayed-release tablets
    Swallowing tablets whole with water only; not breaking, chewing, or crushing; not taking tablets with milk, to prevent destruction of coating and premature dissolution
  For divalproex sodium delayed-release capsules
    Swallowing capsules whole, or sprinkling the contents on a small amount of cool, soft food (such as applesauce or pudding) and swallowing, not chewing, immediately after preparation
  For valproic acid syrup
    Mixing with any liquid or adding to a small amount of food to enhance palatability
  Taking with food if necessary to reduce gastrointestinal side effects
» Compliance with therapy; taking exactly as directed by physician
  Missed dose: If dosing schedule is—
  One dose a day: Taking as soon as possible; not taking if not remembered until next day; not doubling doses
  Two or more doses a day: Taking if remembered within 6 hours; taking remaining doses for that day at equally spaced intervals; not doubling doses
» Proper storage

Precautions while using this medication
» Regular visits to physician to check progress of therapy
» Checking with physician before discontinuing medication; gradual dosage reduction may be necessary
» Possible prolonged bleeding or hemorrhage: caution if any kind of surgery, dental treatment, or emergency treatment is required
» Avoiding use of alcoholic beverages or other CNS depressants during therapy
  Diabetic patients: When testing for urine ketones, possible false-positive test results
  Caution if any laboratory tests required; possible interference with results of metyrapone or thyroid function tests
  Possible need for carrying medical identification card or bracelet
» Possible drowsiness; caution when driving or doing other things requiring alertness

Side/adverse effects
  Signs of potential side effects, especially behavioral, mood, or mental changes; hepatotoxicity; hyperammonemia; ophthalmological effects; pancreatitis; platelet aggregation inhibition; or thrombocytopenia

General Dosing Information

Patients at primary risk for fatal liver failure with valproic acid treatment include:
  • Children up to 2 years old who are receiving multiple anticonvulsants and also have significant medical problems in addition to severe epilepsy (e.g., mental retardation, developmental delay, congenital abnormalities, and metabolic disorders).
  • All patients receiving concomitant anticonvulsants, especially phenytoin and phenobarbital, which induce P450 enzymes and enhance the production of a toxic metabolite.
  • Patients with familial liver disease.

Recommendations for reducing the risk of serious hepatotoxicity with valproate include:
  • Avoiding the administration of valproate with other anticonvulsants whenever possible, especially in children up to 3 years old, unless monotherapy has failed or the benefits of polytherapy outweigh the risks.
  • Avoiding valproate therapy in patients with pre-existing liver disease or a family history of childhood hepatic disease.
  • Administering valproate in as low a dose as possible to achieve seizure control.
  • Avoiding concurrent administration with other hepatotoxic medications, especially salicylates.
  • Monitoring for prodromal symptoms (e.g., nausea or vomiting, headache, edema, jaundice, or seizure breakthrough, especially after a febrile illness).
  • Avoiding administration to patients with congenital metabolic disorders, or severe seizure disorders accompanied by mental retardation or organic brain disease.

When valproic acid is to be discontinued, dosage should be reduced gradually since abrupt withdrawal may precipitate seizures or status epilepticus.

The serum concentration of valproic acid (valproate) does not always correspond with therapeutic effect; therefore, the evaluation of the patient's progress must be based on total clinical assessment.

When valproic acid is used to replace or supplement other anticonvulsant therapy, the dosage should be increased gradually to achieve therapeutic serum concentrations, while that of the replaced medication is decreased gradually in order to maintain seizure control. The addition of valproic acid may cause increases in the serum concentrations of enzyme-inducing anticonvulsants (phenytoin, phenobarbital, primidone, and carbamazepine). Conversely, discontinuation of these will cause an increase in valproic acid serum concentrations by about 60 to 100%.

The possible prolongation of bleeding time, in addition to potentiation of depressant effect by CNS depressants, should be considered when surgery, dental treatment, or emergency treatment is required.

Diet/Nutrition

Valproic acid may be taken with food to reduce gastrointestinal side effects.

The divalproex sodium delayed-release tablets should not be taken with milk, to prevent destruction of the enteric coating and premature dissolution.

The contents of divalproex sodium delayed-release capsules may be sprinkled on a small amount of cool, soft food (such as applesauce or pudding) and swallowed, not chewed, immediately after preparation.

The syrup may be mixed with a small amount of food to enhance the palatability.

Oral Dosage Forms

DIVALPROEX SODIUM DELAYED-RELEASE CAPSULES

Note: Divalproex sodium delayed-release capsules are not commercially available in Canada.

Usual adult and adolescent dose:

Monotherapy—Oral, the equivalent of valproic acid: Initially, 5 to 15 mg per kg of body weight a day, the dosage being increased at one-week intervals by 5 to 10 mg per kg of body weight a day as needed and tolerated.

Polytherapy—Oral, the equivalent of valproic acid: Initially, 10 to 30 mg per kg of body weight a day, the dosage being increased at one-week intervals by 5 to 10 mg per kg of body weight a day as needed and tolerated.

Note: If the total daily dose exceeds 250 mg, it should be divided into two or more doses (usually every 12 hours) to lessen the possibility of gastrointestinal irritation.

Geriatric patients may need lower doses.

Patients also taking an enzyme-inducing medication may need higher dosages depending on predose serum concentrations.

Usual adult prescribing limits: Up to 60 mg per kg of body weight a day.

Auxiliary labeling:
- May cause drowsiness.
- Avoid alcoholic beverages.
- Do not chew contents of capsule.

DIVALPROEX SODIUM DELAYED-RELEASE TABLETS

Usual adult and adolescent dose:

Monotherapy—Oral, the equivalent of valproic acid: Initially, 5 to 15 mg per kg of body weight a day, the dosage being increased at one-week intervals by 5 to 10 mg per kg of body weight a day as needed and tolerated.

Polytherapy—Oral, the equivalent of valproic acid: Initially, 10 to 30 mg per kg of body weight a day, the dosage being increased at one-week intervals by 5 to 10 mg per kg of body weight a day as needed and tolerated.

Note: If the total daily dose exceeds 250 mg, it should be divided into two or more doses (usually every 12 hours) to lessen the possibility of gastrointestinal irritation.

Geriatric patients may need lower doses.

Patients also taking an enzyme-inducing medication may need higher dosages depending on predose serum concentrations.

Usual adult prescribing limits: Up to 60 mg per kg of body weight a day.

Auxiliary labeling:
- May cause drowsiness.
- Avoid alcoholic beverages.
- Swallow tablets whole. Do not break or chew.

VALPROIC ACID CAPSULES USP

Usual adult and adolescent dose:

Monotherapy—Oral, initially, 5 to 15 mg per kg of body weight a day, the dosage being increased at one-week intervals by 5 to 10 mg per kg of body weight a day as needed and tolerated.

Polytherapy—Oral, initially, 10 to 30 mg per kg of body weight a day, the dosage being increased at one-week intervals by 5 to 10 mg per kg of body weight a day as needed and tolerated.

Note: If the total daily dose exceeds 250 mg, it should be divided into two or more doses (usually every 12 hours) to lessen the possibility of gastrointestinal irritation.

Geriatric patients may need lower doses.

Patients also taking an enzyme-inducing medication may need higher dosages depending on predose serum concentrations.

Usual adult prescribing limits: Up to 60 mg per kg of body weight a day.

Auxiliary labeling:
- May cause drowsiness.
- Avoid alcoholic beverages.
- Swallow capsules whole. Do not break or chew.

VALPROIC ACID SYRUP USP

Usual adult and adolescent dose:

Monotherapy—Oral, initially, 5 to 15 mg per kg of body weight a day, the dosage being increased at one-week intervals by 5 to 10 mg per kg of body weight a day as needed and tolerated.

Polytherapy—Oral, initially, 10 to 30 mg per kg of body weight a day, the dosage being increased at one-week intervals by 5 to 10 mg per kg of body weight a day as needed and tolerated.

Note: If the total daily dose exceeds 250 mg, it should be divided into two or more doses (usually every 12 hours) to lessen the possibility of gastrointestinal irritation.

Geriatric patients may need lower doses.

Patients also taking an enzyme-inducing medication may need higher dosages depending on predose serum concentrations.

Usual adult prescribing limits: Up to 60 mg per kg of body weight a day.

Auxiliary labeling:
- May cause drowsiness.
- Avoid alcoholic beverages.

VASCULAR HEADACHE SUPPRESSANTS, ERGOT DERIVATIVE-CONTAINING   Systemic

Some commonly used *brand names* are:

In the U.S.—

Cafergot [Ergotamine and Caffeine]

Cafertine [Ergotamine and Caffeine]

Cafetrate [Ergotamine and Caffeine]

D.H.E. 45 [Dihydroergotamine]

Ercaf [Ergotamine and Caffeine]

Ergo-Caff [Ergotamine and Caffeine]

Ergostat [Ergotamine]

Gotamine [Ergotamine and Caffeine]

Migergot [Ergotamine and Caffeine]

Wigraine [Ergotamine and Caffeine]

In Canada—

Cafergot [Ergotamine and Caffeine]

Cafergot-PB [Ergotamine, Caffeine, Belladonna Alkaloids, and Pentobarbital]

Dihydroergotamine-Sandoz [Dihydroergotamine]

Ergodryl [Ergotamine, Caffeine, and Diphenhydramine]

Ergomar [Ergotamine]

Gravergol [Ergotamine, Caffeine, and Dimenhydrinate]

Gynergen [Ergotamine]

Medihaler Ergotamine [Ergotamine]

Megral [Ergotamine, Caffeine, and Cyclizine]

Wigraine [Ergotamine, Caffeine, and Belladonna Alkaloids]

DIHYDROERGOTAMINE

Parenteral

Dihydroergotamine Mesylate Injection USP

In the U.S.—*D.H.E. 45*

In Canada—*Dihydroergotamine-Sandoz*

ERGOTAMINE

Inhalation

Ergotamine Tartrate Inhalation Aerosol USP*

In Canada—*Medihaler Ergotamine*

Oral

Ergotamine Tartrate Tablets USP*

In Canada—*Gynergen*

Ergotamine Tartrate Tablets USP (Sublingual)

In the U.S.—*Ergostat*

In Canada—*Ergomar*

ERGOTAMINE AND CAFFEINE

Oral

Ergotamine Tartrate and Caffeine Tablets USP

In the U.S.—*Cafergot; Ercaf; Ergo-Caff; Gotamine; Wigraine;* GENERIC

In Canada—*Cafergot*

Rectal

Ergotamine Tartrate and Caffeine Suppositories USP

In the U.S.—*Cafergot; Cafertine; Cafetrate; Migergot; Wigraine;* GENERIC

In Canada—*Cafergot*

ERGOTAMINE, CAFFEINE, AND BELLADONNA ALKALOIDS*

Oral

Ergotamine Tartrate, Caffeine, and Belladonna Alkaloids Tablets*

In Canada—*Wigraine*

Rectal

Ergotamine Tartrate, Caffeine, and Belladonna Alkaloids Suppositories*

In Canada—*Wigraine*

ERGOTAMINE, CAFFEINE, BELLADONNA ALKALOIDS, AND PENTOBARBITAL*

Oral

Ergotamine Tartrate, Caffeine, Belladonna Alkaloids, and Pentobarbital Sodium Tablets*

In Canada—*Cafergot-PB*

Rectal

Ergotamine Tartrate, Caffeine, Belladonna Alkaloids, and Pentobarbital Suppositories*

In Canada—*Cafergot-PB*

ERGOTAMINE, CAFFEINE, AND CYCLIZINE*

Oral

Ergotamine Tartrate, Caffeine, and Cyclizine Hydrochloride Tablets*

In Canada—*Megral*

ERGOTAMINE, CAFFEINE, AND DIMENHYDRINATE*

Oral

Ergotamine Tartrate, Caffeine, and Dimenhydrinate Capsules*

In Canada—*Gravergol*

ERGOTAMINE, CAFFEINE, AND DIPHENHYDRAMINE*

Oral

Ergotamine Tartrate, Caffeine, and Diphenhydramine Hydrochloride Capsules*

In Canada—*Ergodryl*

---

*Not commercially available in the U.S.

Category

Vascular headache suppressant—Dihydroergotamine; Ergotamine; Ergotamine and Caffeine; Ergotamine, Caffeine, and Belladonna Alkaloids; Ergotamine, Caffeine, Belladonna Alkaloids, and Pentobarbital; Ergotamine, Caffeine, and Cyclizine; Ergotamine, Caffeine, and Dimenhydrinate; Ergotamine, Caffeine, and Diphenhydramine.

Thrombosis prophylaxis adjunct—Dihydroergotamine.

Antihypotensive—Dihydroergotamine.

Note: Some headache specialists question the validity of the term "vascular headache" because a correlation between dilatation of cerebral blood vessels and symptoms of migraine or cluster headaches has not been demonstrated conclusively. A clinical distinction between vascular, tension-type, and coexisting migraine and tension-type ("mixed") headaches may be difficult to ascertain in some patients.

Indications

Note: Bracketed information in the *Indications* section refers to uses not included in U.S. product labeling.

Accepted

Headache, vascular (treatment)—Ergot derivative-containing headache suppressants are indicated in the treatment of vascular headaches, such as migraine (with or without aura), cluster headache (histaminic cephalalgia, migrainous neuralgia, ciliary neuralgia, Horton's headache), and migraine variants.

For migraine: Ergot derivative-containing headache suppressants are used to relieve (abort) acute migraine headaches in patients who report that sufficient relief is not obtained with analgesics (e.g., acetaminophen, aspirin, other nonsteroidal anti-inflammatory drugs [NSAIDs]). When incapacitating migraines occur more frequently than twice a month, additional prophylactic treatment is recommended to reduce the severity and duration, as well as the number, of headaches. However, too frequent use of an ergotamine-containing headache suppressant may cause tolerance, leading to decreased efficacy, and physical dependence, leading to more frequent headaches (including withdrawal [rebound] headaches and chronic, intractable headaches) and medication abuse. Chronic use of ergot derivatives may also cause peripheral vasospasm, which may lead to arterial insufficiency, ischemia, and even gangrene. Therefore, these agents are not recommended for long-term migraine prophylaxis. Beta-adrenergic blocking agents, calcium channel blocking agents, tricyclic antidepressants, monoamine oxidase inhibitors, methysergide, pizotyline (pizotifen [not commercially available in the U.S.]), and sometimes cyproheptadine (especially in children) are used for prophylaxis.

Parenteral dihydroergotamine is used for rapid relief of severe, refractory migraine, including status migrainosus and chronic, intractable headaches resulting from overuse of ergotamine or analgesics. Some physicians consider it the treatment of choice in status migrainosus. Prophylactic treatment may also be needed to reduce recurrences.

For cluster headache: Ergot derivative-containing headache suppressants are indicated to abort headaches in patients who experience episodic or chronic cluster headaches. These headaches may occur daily, often more than once a day, for several months (a cluster period), followed by a headache-free interval. Cluster headaches often are unresponsive to simple analgesics. Prophylactic therapy is advisable during cluster periods, but many of the agents commonly used for migraine prophylaxis are ineffective in reducing the frequency or severity of cluster headaches (especially chronic cluster headaches), or lose efficacy after 1 or 2 cluster periods. [Ergotamine is therefore used prophylactically during cluster periods][1], alone or concurrently with a calcium channel blocking agent, usually verapamil, and/ or lithium. Prophylactic administration of ergotamine during cluster periods is not likely to cause dependence of the type associated with its chronic use by migraine patients.

Ergot derivative-containing headache suppressants are generally not used in the treatment of chronic paroxysmal hemicrania, a cluster headache variant. Indomethacin is highly effective in relieving and preventing these headaches, and is considered the agent of choice for management of this condition.

Note: Other measures that may reduce the need for medication in headache patients include identification and avoidance of headache precipitants (for migraine or cluster headaches) and relaxation and/or biofeedback techniques (for migraine).

[Thrombosis, deep venous (prophylaxis adjunct)][1]; and
[Thromboembolism, pulmonary (prophylaxis adjunct)][1]—Dihydroergotamine is used in combination with low-dose heparin for the prevention of postoperative deep-vein thrombosis and pulmonary embolism following elective orthopedic procedures, such as total hip replacement, or major abdominal, thoracic, or pelvic surgery. Prophylactic therapy with heparin is generally reserved for high-risk patients, such as patients with a history of thromboembolism or patients requiring prolonged immobilization following surgery, especially if they are 40 years of age or older. The combination of dihydroergotamine and heparin may be more effective than low-dose heparin alone in some cases, e.g., in hip replacement surgery. However, this combination of medications has been reported to cause serious complications, including severe peripheral ischemia, probably resulting from dihydroergotamine-induced vasospasm. Especially careful patient selection and careful monitoring throughout therapy are required to reduce the risk of such complications.

[Hypotension, orthostatic (prophylaxis and treatment)][1]—Dihydroergotamine is used to prevent or treat orthostatic hypotension that may occur in conjunction with spinal or epidural anesthesia. It is also used to treat orthostatic hypotension due to autonomic insufficiency or other causes.

Unaccepted

Dihydroergotamine, ergotamine, and ergotamine-containing combinations are not recommended for long-term migraine prophylaxis.

Although ergotamine has oxytocic effects, it is not used clinically to produce these effects because other ergot alkaloids are more effective and less toxic.

---

[1]Not included in Canadian product labeling.

Pharmacology

Note: Pharmacology information for the adjuvants present in headache suppressant formulations (caffeine, belladonna alkaloids, cyclizine, dimenhydrinate, diphenhydramine, and pentobarbital) is limited to brief descriptions of the effects that may be pertinent to treatment of patients with vascular headaches. Gastric stasis that accompanies migraine headaches tends to inhibit absorption of orally administered medications and may therefore alter their pharmacokinetic profiles. For additional information on the actions of these agents, see—

Caffeine: *Caffeine (Systemic)*.
Belladonna alkaloids: *Anticholinergics/Antispasmodics (Systemic)*.
Cyclizine: *Cyclizine (Systemic)*.
Dimenhydrinate: *Antihistamines (Systemic)*.
Diphenhydramine: *Antihistamines (Systemic)*.
Pentobarbital: *Barbiturates (Systemic)*.

Mechanism of action/Effect:
Dihydroergotamine and

Ergotamine—These ergot derivatives interact with several neurotransmitter receptors, including alpha-adrenergic, serotonergic (tryptaminergic), and dopaminergic receptors. Both agonistic (or partial agonistic) and antagonistic actions have been reported at different receptor types or subtypes. These medications directly stimulate vascular smooth muscle, causing constriction of both arteries and veins, and depress vasomotor centers in the brain. Dihydroergotamine's adrenergic blocking actions are somewhat more pronounced, and its vasoconstrictive actions (especially in arteries) are less pronounced, than those of ergotamine.

Vascular headache suppressant: Ergot derivative-induced decreases in the firing of serotonergic (5-hydroxytryptaminergic, 5-HT) neurons may be responsible for headache suppression. Specifically, it is thought that agonist activity at the 5-HT_{1D} receptor subtype provides relief of acute headache, whereas antagonist activity at the 5-HT_2 receptor subtype provides headache prophylaxis. It has been proposed that constriction of cerebral blood vessels by the ergot derivative (resulting from alpha-adrenergic stimulation as well as from activity at 5-HT receptors) reduces the pulsation in cerebral arteries that may be responsible for the pain of vascular headaches. However, studies have not consistently shown a significant correlation between dilatation of cerebral blood vessels and pain or other symptoms of migraine or cluster headaches, or between the vasoconstrictive effect of an ergot derivative and relief of these headaches.

Dihydroergotamine and ergotamine may decrease hyperperfusion in the area of the basilar artery, but they do not reduce cerebral hemispheric blood flow.

Thrombosis prophylaxis adjunct and

Antihypotensive: Dihydroergotamine's constrictive effect on capacitance (venous) vasculature is significantly greater than its constrictive effect on resistance (arterial) vasculature. As a result, the velocity of venous blood flow in the legs is increased, venous return to the heart is enhanced, venous pooling (which may increase the risk of thrombus formation) is reduced, and arterial blood pressure is maintained or increased. It has also been proposed that dihydroergotamine may enhance the effects of heparin in preventing thrombosis.

Caffeine—Caffeine constricts the cerebral vasculature and decreases both cerebral blood flow and the oxygen tension of the brain. However, it is believed that the caffeine in many ergotamine-containing formulations acts primarily by increasing both the rate and extent of absorption of orally or rectally administered ergotamine, thereby hastening the onset of action and increasing the effect of ergotamine.

Belladonna alkaloids—Belladonna alkaloids are used in headache suppressant formulations for their antiemetic effects, because nausea and vomiting may occur in association with the migraine headache and/or as a result of ergotamine administration.

Cyclizine and
Dimenhydrinate and
Diphenhydramine—These antihistamines are used in headache suppressant formulations for their antiemetic and sedative effects.

Pentobarbital—This barbiturate is used in headache suppressant formulations for its sedative effects.

Other actions/Effects:

Dihydroergotamine and
Ergotamine—These medications may cause nausea and vomiting via direct stimulation of the chemoreceptor trigger zone.

Like other ergot derivatives, dihydroergotamine and ergotamine stimulate uterine smooth muscle via an action on alpha-adrenergic receptors and/or 5-HT receptors. Ergotamine is much more potent than dihydroergotamine as a uterine stimulant.

Peripheral vasoconstriction induced by dihydroergotamine and ergotamine may lead to decreased blood flow in various organs, increased peripheral vascular resistance, and increased blood pressure. However, with the doses usually used in the treatment of migraine or cluster headaches, increases in blood pressure are usually slight.

Large doses of dihydroergotamine and ergotamine may cause constriction of the coronary vasculature and bradycardia. These effects may result from increased vagal activity as well as direct actions on the myocardium and the vasculature.

Caffeine—Caffeine has central nervous system (CNS) stimulant activity and may therefore inhibit sleep. Because sleep contributes to relief of migraine headaches, this action may be detrimental to the patient.

Belladonna alkaloids—Belladonna alkaloids have anticholinergic activity.

Cyclizine and
Dimenhydrinate and
Diphenhydramine—These medications have antihistaminic, anticholinergic, and CNS depressant activities.

Pentobarbital—Barbiturates have CNS depressant activity.

Onset of action: Acute headaches—

Note: For relief of acute migraine or cluster headaches, the onset of action is highly dependent on the duration of the headache prior to initiation of therapy as well as on the route of administration. The most rapid onset of action is achieved when the medication is administered as soon as the first symptoms appear (during the prodrome, for migraine with aura).

Dihydroergotamine:
Intramuscular—15 to 30 minutes.
Intravenous—Variable; usually less than 5 minutes.

Time to peak effect: Relief of acute headache—

Dihydroergotamine: Parenteral—15 minutes to 2 hours.
Ergotamine: Oral—Variable; usually within 1 to 2 hours, but up to 5 hours in some patients.

Duration of action: Dihydroergotamine—Vasoconstrictive and antihypotensive effects—About 8 hours, following intravenous or subcutaneous administration.

Precautions to Consider

Note: Information in this section concerning the adjuvants present in ergotamine-containing headache suppressant formulations (caffeine, belladonna alkaloids, cyclizine, dimenhydrinate, diphenhydramine, and pentobarbital) is limited to brief summaries of the major precautions that may apply to their use in doses recommended for treatment of vascular headaches. For more complete information that may apply, especially if these agents are ingested frequently or in higher-than-recommended doses, see—

Caffeine: *Caffeine (Systemic).*
Belladonna alkaloids: *Anticholinergics/Antispasmodics (Systemic).*
Cyclizine: *Cyclizine (Systemic).*
Dimenhydrinate: *Antihistamines (Systemic).*
Diphenhydramine: *Antihistamines (Systemic).*
Pentobarbital: *Barbiturates (Systemic).*

Geriatrics

Dihydroergotamine and
Ergotamine—Caution is recommended in the elderly, who are more likely to have occlusive peripheral vascular disease, and are therefore more likely to be adversely affected by peripheral vasoconstriction, than are younger adults. This increases the risk of hypothermia and other ischemic complications. The risk of cardiac ischemia is also increased in geriatric patients. Elderly patients are also more likely to have age-related renal function impairment, which requires caution in patients receiving these medications.

Belladonna alkaloids—Geriatric patients may respond to usual doses of these medications with excitement, agitation, drowsiness, or confusion.

Belladonna alkaloids and
Cyclizine and
Dimenhydrinate and
Diphenhydramine—Caution is recommended when these medications are used in the elderly, who are especially sensitive to anticholinergic side effects. Also, the risk of precipitating undiagnosed glaucoma in the elderly must be considered. Dizziness, sedation, and hypotension are also more likely to occur in elderly patients receiving antihistamines such as cyclizine, dimenhydrinate, and diphenhydramine.

Pentobarbital—Excitement, depression, and confusion may be more likely to occur in elderly patients, who are generally more susceptible than younger adults to the effects of barbiturates.

Drug interactions and/or related problems

The following drug interactions and/or related problems have been selected on the basis of their potential clinical significance (possible mechanism in parentheses where appropriate)—not necessarily inclusive (» = major clinical significance):

Note: Combinations containing any of the following medications, depending on the amount present, may also interact with this medication.

Barbiturates such as pentobarbital induce hepatic chromosomal enzymes and may thereby increase the metabolism and decrease the efficacy of many medications that are metabolized by these enzymes. The most clinically significant interactions have been reported with adrenocorticoids, corticotropin, coumarin- or indandione-derivative anticoagulants, anticonvulsants (carbamazepine, divalproex sodium, valproic acid), and estrogen-containing oral contraceptives (see *Barbiturates [Systemic]*). Although occasional use of a pentobarbital-containing headache suppressant may not cause significant interference with the effects of most of these agents, selection of a formulation that does not contain pentobarbital may be advisable in some cases.

For dihydroergotamine and ergotamine
    Antibiotics, macrolide, especially:
      Erythromycin
      Troleandomycin
        (these antibiotics may inhibit the metabolism of the ergot derivative and increase the risk of vasospasm)
    Beta-adrenergic blocking agents
      (peripheral vasoconstriction and vasospastic reactions have occurred in a few patients receiving a beta-adrenergic blocking agent for migraine prophylaxis after administration of usual doses of dihydroergotamine or ergotamine; although most patients are able to tolerate the combination of medications without ill effects, closer monitoring of patients receiving both types of medication may be warranted)
» Ergot alkaloids, other, or
» Vasoconstrictors, systemic, other, such as:
    Cocaine
    Epinephrine, parenteral
    Metaraminol
    Methoxamine
    Norepinephrine
    Phenylephrine, parenteral, or
» Vasoconstrictor-containing local anesthetic solutions
    (concurrent use with dihydroergotamine or ergotamine may produce peripheral vascular ischemia and gangrene and is not recommended)
    (the pressor effect of sympathomimetic pressor amines may be potentiated, resulting in possible severe hypertension and rupture of cerebral blood vessels)
    Nitroglycerin
      (the vasoconstrictive effect of dihydroergotamine or ergotamine may oppose the vasodilating effect of nitroglycerin, thereby reducing nitroglycerin's efficacy as an antianginal agent)
      (nitroglycerin may also reduce hepatic metabolism of dihydroergotamine)
    Smoking, tobacco
      (administration of ergotamine to a patient who smokes heavily may increase the risk of peripheral vascular ischemia because nicotine also constricts blood vessels)

For formulations containing caffeine
    Caffeine from any other dietary or medicinal source, or
    CNS stimulation-producing medications, other
      (excessive CNS stimulation, which may lead to nervousness, irritability, insomnia, or possibly convulsions or cardiac arrhythmias, may occur; close observation is recommended)
    Monoamine oxidase (MAO) inhibitors, including furazolidone, procarbazine, and selegiline
      (the sympathomimetic side effects of caffeine may lead to cardiac arrhythmias or severe hypertension when large doses are used concurrently with MAO inhibitors; even small doses may cause tachycardia and a slight increase in blood pressure)

For formulations containing belladonna alkaloids, cyclizine, dimenhydrinate, diphenhydramine, or pentobarbital
    Anticholinergics or other medications with anticholinergic activity, other, or
    CNS depression-producing medications, other, including alcohol
      (the risk of additive anticholinergic effects must be considered when any medication having anticholinergic activity is used concurrently with belladonna alkaloids, cyclizine, dimenhydrinate, or diphenhydramine)
      (the risk of additive CNS depression must be considered when any medication having CNS depressant activity is used concurrently with cyclizine, dimenhydrinate, diphenhydramine, or pentobarbital)

Contraindications/Medical problems
The contraindications/medical problems included have been selected on the basis of their potential clinical significance (reasons given

in parentheses where appropriate)—not necessarily inclusive (» = major clinical significance).

Except under special circumstances, this medication should not be used when the following medical problems exist:
For dihydroergotamine and ergotamine
» Angioplasty, recent or contemplated, or
» Vascular surgery, especially arterial, recent or contemplated
    (increased risk of ischemia)
» Hypertension, severe, uncontrolled
    (may be aggravated)

Risk-benefit should be considered when the following medical problems exist:
For dihydroergotamine and ergotamine
    Allergic reaction to dihydroergotamine or ergotamine, history of
» Coronary artery disease, especially:
»   Angina pectoris, unstable or vasospastic, or other indication of coronary ischemia
      (vasospasm may aggravate existing angina pectoris, or cause angina pectoris or myocardial infarction)
    Diarrhea—for suppository dosage forms
      (impaired absorption of medications)
» Hepatic function impairment
    (impaired metabolism may result in ergot poisoning)
» Hypertension, not optimally controlled
    (may be aggravated)
    Hyperthyroidism
    (possible increased risk of ergotism)
    Malnutrition
    (risk of ergotism may be increased because malnutrition-associated metabolic disturbances may lead to increased concentrations of the ergot derivative and/or to hyperreactivity to the medication)
» Peripheral vascular disease, occlusive, or
» Pruritus, severe, especially when associated with hepatic disease, or
» Sepsis or other severe infection
    (increased risk of complications associated with vasospasm)
» Renal function impairment
    Caution is also recommended in geriatric patients, who may be especially susceptible to complications associated with vasospasm and to hypothermia.

For dihydroergotamine only, when used concurrently with low-dose heparin for prophylaxis against perioperative thrombotic complications (in addition to the medical problems listed above)
» Trauma
    (increased risk of vasospastic reactions, especially in an injured extremity of patients with multiple fractures)

For formulations containing caffeine
» Anxiety disorders, including
    Agoraphobia
    Panic attacks
      (increased risk of anxiety, nervousness, fear, nausea, palpitation, rapid heartbeat, restlessness, and trembling)
» Cardiac disease, severe
    (high doses of caffeine are not recommended because of an increased risk of tachycardia or extrasystoles, which may lead to heart failure)
» Insomnia
    (may be potentiated; this effect may be particularly detrimental to patients with a vascular headache, because sleep also helps relieve headache)
» Peptic ulcer
    (may be aggravated)
    Sensitivity to caffeine

For formulations containing belladonna alkaloids, cyclizine, dimen-hydrinate, or diphenhydramine

Any condition in which the anticholinergic effects of these medications may be detrimental, such as:
Bladder neck obstruction
Gastrointestinal tract obstructive disease
Glaucoma, not optimally controlled, or predisposition to
Prostatic hypertrophy
Urinary retention
Sensitivity to the agent considered for use

Side/Adverse Effects

Note: Most side/adverse effects are dose-related and are usually relieved by a reduction in dose or withdrawal of the medication.

Although acute ergot poisoning is rare, patient sensitivity to the effects of ergotamine varies widely and symptoms of ergot toxicity (peripheral ischemia, paresthesia, headache, nausea and vomiting) may occur even with usual doses.

Nausea and vomiting may be caused by migraine headaches as well as by an ergot derivative.

The risk of side effects being induced by recommended doses of the adjuvants in ergotamine-containing combination formulations has not been determined. In general, it is expected that such effects, even in overdose situations, would be overshadowed by those of ergotamine. However, with acute overdose of formulations containing belladonna alkaloids, cyclizine, dimenhydrinate, or diphenhydramine, the possibility of severe symptoms associated with their anticholinergic activity should be considered. Also, with acute overdose of formulations containing pentobarbital, the possibility of severe CNS depression should be considered.

The following side/adverse effects have been selected on the basis of their potential clinical significance (possible signs and symptoms in parentheses where appropriate)—not necessarily inclusive:

Those indicating need for medical attention
Incidence more frequent
Edema, localized (swelling of face, fingers, feet, and/or lower legs)
Incidence less frequent or rare
Cardiovascular effects, specifically angina pectoris, coronary vasospasm-induced (chest pain); *fast or slow heartbeat; increase or decrease in blood pressure; rapid, weak pulse; ischemia, cerebral* (anxiety, confusion); *ischemia, peripheral vasospasm-induced* (itching of skin; numbness and tingling of fingers, toes, or face; pain in arms, legs, or lower back, especially pain in calves and/or heels upon exertion; pale, bluish-colored, or cold hands or feet; weak or absent pulses; weakness in legs); and *vasospasm, ocular* (changes in vision, miosis)

Note: *Myocardial infarction* and *cerebral infarction* have also been reported.

Cerebral ischemia and/or *peripheral ischemia* may be signs of acute or chronic overdose. Continued chronic use of an ergot derivative after early signs and symptoms of peripheral ischemia appear may lead to *gangrene* (red or violet blisters on skin of hands or feet may be first signs) or to *thrombotic complications.*

In addition to vision changes associated with *ocular vasospasm* listed above, one case of reversible *bilateral papillitis with ring scotomata* has been reported in chronic overdose.

Symptoms of acute overdose (in addition to vascular effects listed above)
CNS toxicity (convulsions; severe confusion, dizziness, or drowsiness; weakness; one-sided paralysis; loss of consciousness); *diarrhea, vomiting, stomach pain or bloating; respiratory depression* (shortness of breath)

Note: After an acute overdose has been ingested, *CNS and gastrointestinal manifestations, hypotension,* and *tachycardia* may occur within a few hours, but signs and symptoms of *peripheral ischemia* may not appear until the next day.

Hypotension and sometimes *shock* may occur following initial *hypertension.*

Symptoms of chronic overdose (in addition to vascular effects listed above)
Fibrosis, pleural or retroperitoneal (shortness of breath, chest pain)—reported in isolated patients; *loss of appetite; nausea or vomiting, severe or continuing; headache; rectal ulceration* (abdominal pain, irregular bowel movements, rectal discomfort, difficulty in moving bowels).

Note: Increased frequency and/or severity of *migraine headaches* may indicate tolerance to ergotamine. Frequent use of ergotamine by migraineurs may also lead to the development of *chronic, intractable headaches* with both migrainous and nonmigrainous manifestations. These *chronic headaches* will not subside as long as ergotamine and/or analgesics continue to be taken. If specific treatment (e.g., intravenous dihydroergotamine) is not given after other headache-aborting medications are discontinued, the headaches usually become worse (being most severe on the third or fourth day) and may persist for 2 weeks or longer.

Rectal ulceration has been reported with chronic overuse of the rectal suppository dosage form of ergotamine and caffeine.

Those indicating need for medical attention only if they continue or are bothersome
Incidence more frequent
CNS effects (dizziness or drowsiness occurring without other signs and symptoms of overdose [especially with formulations containing cyclizine, dimenhydrinate, diphenhydramine, or pentobarbital]; rarely, nervousness, racing thoughts, and restlessness)—these dysphoric effects may be especially severe with repetitive administration of intravenous dihydroergotamine and metoclopramide for intractable headaches; *dryness of mouth*—especially likely with formulations containing belladonna alkaloids; may also occur with formulations containing cyclizine, dimenhydrinate, or diphenhydramine; *diarrhea, nausea, or vomiting* occurring without other signs and symptoms of overdose; *peripheral vascular effects, mild and lasting 1 hour or less* (cold fingers or toes, itching of skin, numbness or tingling of fingers or toes, weakness in the legs occurring without other signs and symptoms of ischemia)

Those indicating possible withdrawal and the need for medical attention if they occur after medication is discontinued
Headache—severe withdrawal (rebound) headaches may occur in migraineurs who overuse ergotamine; they are generally most severe for the first 24 to 48 hours, and usually last about 72 hours, after the last dose of ergotamine, and may lead to increased use of ergotamine and/or analgesics, dependence, and chronic, intractable headaches

Patient Consultation

In providing consultation, consider emphasizing the following selected information (» = major clinical significance):

Before using this medication
» Conditions affecting use, especially:
Sensitivity to any ingredient in the product considered for use
Pregnancy—Use is not recommended because ergot derivatives have oxytocic activity, which may lead to miscarriage, and vasoconstrictive activity, which may result in fetotoxicity
Breast-feeding—Ergot alkaloids are distributed into breast milk and may cause adverse effects in the infant; ergot alkaloids and medications having anticholinergic activity (belladonna alkaloids, cyclizine, dimenhydrinate, diphenhydramine) may also inhibit lactation; caffeine and pentobarbital are also

distributed into breast milk and may cause CNS stimulation or CNS depression, respectively

Use in children—Pediatrics-specific problems have not been reported in children 6 years of age or older, but dihydro-ergotamine and ergotamine are recommended only for patients unresponsive to less toxic medications; young children, especially those with spastic paralysis or brain damage, may be especially susceptible to the effects of belladonna alkaloids; also, risk of paradoxical hyperexcitability in children receiving cyclizine, dimenhydrinate, diphenhydramine, or pentobarbital

Use in the elderly—Increased risk of hypothermia and other adverse effects associated with ergot derivative-induced peripheral and coronary vasoconstriction; increased susceptibility to effects of medications with anticholinergic activity and to barbiturates

Use by athletes—Caffeine (present in some formulations) is tested for in athletes by the International Olympic Committee (IOC), the U.S. Olympic Committee (USOC), and the National Collegiate Athletic Association (NCAA); an athlete can be disqualified if urine concentrations are higher than the acceptable limits set by these organizations; medications with sedative effects present in specific formulations (pentobarbital, cyclizine, dimenhydrinate, diphenhydramine) are banned in competitors in biathlon and modern pentathlon events by the USOC

Other medications, especially other vasoconstrictors (including other ergot alkaloids and vasoconstrictors present in local anesthetic solutions)

Other medical problems, especially angina pectoris or other coronary artery disease, hepatic function impairment, hypertension, severe infection, peripheral vascular disease, pruritus, renal function impairment, and recent or contemplated angioplasty or vascular surgery (for dihydroergotamine and ergotamine); anxiety disorders (e.g., agoraphobia, panic attacks), severe cardiac disease, insomnia, or peptic ulcer (for caffeine-containing formulations)

Proper use of this medication

» Importance of not using more medication than the amount prescribed; risk of habituation with too frequent use and of peripheral vasoconstriction or other signs and symptoms of ergotism with acute or chronic overdosage

» Taking at first sign of headache (prodromal stage, for migraine with aura)

» Lying down in a quiet, dark room after taking initial dose

» Compliance with prophylactic therapy, if prescribed

Proper administration techniques for—
Dihydroergotamine injection
Ergotamine inhalation: Reading patient directions; shaking container after removing cap; exhaling, placing mouthpiece in mouth aimed at back of throat, simultaneously inhaling and pressing vial down into the adapter; holding breath as long as possible after inhaling medication
Ergotamine sublingual tablets: Allowing to dissolve under tongue; not chewing or swallowing whole; not eating, drinking, or smoking while tablet is dissolving
Ergotamine-containing rectal suppositories
If dividing suppository dosage form: Dividing lengthwise into pieces of equal size; easier to accomplish if suppositories have been refrigerated

» Proper dosing
» Proper storage

Precautions while using this medication

» Checking with physician if usual dose fails to relieve headaches, or if frequency and/or severity of headaches increases; possibility that tolerance to or dependence on the medication has developed, leading to withdrawal (rebound) or chronic headaches

Avoiding alcohol, which aggravates headache

Avoiding smoking because nicotine constricts blood vessels

Avoiding exposure to excessive cold, which may intensify peripheral vasoconstriction

Notifying physician if infection develops; severe infection may cause increased sensitivity to medication

For ergotamine inhalation—Possible hoarseness or throat irritation, which may be prevented by gargling and rinsing mouth after use; checking with physician if continuing or bothersome

Possible interferences with laboratory tests; not taking caffeine for 12 hours prior to dipyridamole-assisted myocardial perfusion study, belladonna alkaloids for 24 hours prior to gastric acid secretion test, and cyclizine, dimenhydrinate, or diphenhydramine for 72 hours prior to skin tests using allergen extracts

» *For formulations containing cyclizine, dimenhydrinate, diphenhydramine, or pentobarbital*

Caution when driving or doing jobs requiring alertness because of possible dizziness, lightheadedness, or drowsiness, especially if taking other CNS depressants concurrently

For formulations containing belladonna alkaloids, cyclizine, dimenhydrinate, or diphenhydramine

Possible dryness of mouth, nose, and throat; using sugarless candy or gum, ice, or saliva substitute for relief

Side/adverse effects

Signs and symptoms of potential side effects, especially edema, fast or slow heartbeat, cerebral or peripheral ischemia, gangrene, and coronary or ocular vasospasm

General Dosing Information

Abortive therapy is most effective when initiated at the first symptoms of a migraine attack (during the prodrome, for migraine with aura). Delay in starting treatment increases the required dose and prolongs the onset of action of the ergot derivative.

After the first dose has been administered, it is recommended that the patient lie down and relax in a quiet, darkened room, because this contributes to relief of migraines.

To reduce the risk of adverse effects, the ergot derivative should be used in the lowest dose that provides adequate relief of headache. However, individual sensitivity to the effects of ergot derivatives varies, and signs and symptoms of toxicity may occur in some patients even with usual doses. Therapy should be withdrawn at the first sign of vasospasm.

Analgesics, antiemetics, antianxiety agents, and/or sedatives may be used concurrently with the ergot derivative, if needed, for relief of an acute migraine attack. Regimens used for relief of severe, refractory migraine utilize metoclopramide or prochlorperazine together with intravenous dihydroergotamine. However, medications having the potential to cause habituation (e.g., opioid analgesics, barbiturates, benzodiazepines) should be used with caution and as infrequently as possible.

Atropine, metoclopramide, or a phenothiazine antiemetic may be administered to prevent or relieve nausea and vomiting induced by an ergot derivative or by the migraine itself.

Tolerance to the effects of ergotamine may develop in migraineurs, leading to an increased dosage requirement, dependence, withdrawal (rebound) or chronic, intractable headaches, and abuse of the medication. The caffeine in many ergotamine-containing formulations may contribute to the development of dependence and withdrawal or chronic, intractable headaches, and the pentobarbital in some formulations may also be habit-forming. However, repetitive administration of intravenous dihydroergotamine over a 2- to 3-day period for treatment of chronic, intractable headaches associated with dependence on ergotamine or analgesics has not been reported to increase or prolong dependence.

To reduce the risk of dependence, it is recommended that ergotamine not be administered to migraine patients more frequently than every fifth day.

For rectal dosage forms only

Ergotamine-containing rectal suppositories are torpedo-shaped and are not scored. To assure proper dosage when a portion of a suppository is to be administered, the suppository should be cut lengthwise into pieces of equal size. This is easier to accomplish when the suppository has been refrigerated.

DIHYDROERGOTAMINE

Summary of Differences

Category/indications:

May be agent of choice for treatment of status migrainosus or other severe, refractory headaches, including chronic headaches associated with dependence on ergotamine or analgesics.

Also, indicated as a thrombosis prophylaxis adjunct, being used concurrently with low-dose heparin to prevent postoperative thrombotic complications.

Also, indicated as an antihypotensive, to prevent or treat orthostatic hypotension.

Pharmacology:

Mechanism of action/effects—Adrenergic blocking actions are somewhat more pronounced, and vasoconstrictive actions less pronounced, than those of ergotamine.

Other actions/effects—Much less potent as a uterine stimulant than ergotamine.

Time to peak effect—Relieves acute headache in 15 minutes to 2 hours.

Duration of action—Subcutaneous or intravenous: About 8 hours.

Precautions:

Contraindications/medical problems—When used concurrently with heparin to prevent postoperative thrombotic complications, caution also needed if trauma of an extremity is present because of the increased risk of vasospastic reactions.

Patient monitoring—

Blood pressure monitoring needed when medication is administered repetitively for treatment of severe, intractable headache.

Examination of extremities and palpation of peripheral pulses recommended when medication is administered daily for prophylaxis against postoperative thrombotic complications (concurrently with heparin) or for treatment of orthostatic hypotension.

Additional Dosing Information

See also *General Dosing Information.*

Dihydroergotamine is administered via intramuscular, intravenous, or subcutaneous injection. Intra-arterial injection must be avoided.

When dihydroergotamine is used in conjunction with heparin for prophylaxis against postoperative thrombotic complications, all of the precautions pertinent to use of heparin must also be kept in mind.

Parenteral Dosage Forms

Note: Bracketed uses in the *Dosage Forms* section refer to categories of use and/or indications that are not included in U.S. product labeling.

DIHYDROERGOTAMINE MESYLATE INJECTION USP

Usual adult dose:

Vascular headache suppressant—

Acute migraine or cluster headache (outpatient treatment): Intramuscular (preferred) or subcutaneous, 1 mg at the start of the attack. May be repeated in one hour, if needed. The maximum recommended daily dose is 3 mg.

Intravenous, 500 mcg (0.5 mg) at the start of the attack, administered in conjunction with an antiemetic. May be repeated in one hour, if necessary. The maximum recommended daily dose is 2 mg.

Chronic, intractable headache (inpatient treatment): Intravenous, initially 500 mcg (0.5 mg), administered over one minute, three to five minutes after intravenous administration of an antiemetic (10 mg of metoclopramide is most commonly used). The dosage of dihydroergotamine and/or the antiemetic should be adjusted as needed to reduce the occurrence of side effects (especially to prevent nausea and vomiting) while providing adequate control of the headache; up to 1 mg of dihydroergotamine may be given for subsequent doses if needed and tolerated. This regimen may be repeated every eight hours until relief is obtained, although an antiemetic is usually no longer needed after six doses of dihydroergotamine have been administered. One specialist recommends an additional two or three doses of dihydroergotamine, administered at twelve-hour intervals after the headache is relieved, to reduce the likelihood of headache recurrence.

[Thrombosis prophylaxis adjunct][1]—To be administered concurrently with 5000 USP Units of subcutaneously administered heparin:

Abdominal, thoracic, or pelvic surgery—Subcutaneous, 500 mcg (0.5 mg) two hours prior to surgery, then every twelve hours for five to seven days.

Total hip replacement surgery—Subcutaneous, 500 mcg (0.5 mg) two hours prior to surgery, then every eight hours for seven to fourteen days.

[Antihypotensive][1]—

Prevention of orthostatic hypotension associated with spinal or epidural anesthesia: Intravenous, 500 mcg (0.5 mg), administered a few minutes prior to the anesthetic.

Treatment of orthostatic hypotension:

Intramuscular, 1 mg once a day.

Subcutaneous, 6.5 to 13 mcg (0.0065 to 0.013 mg) per kg of body weight once a day, in the morning. Breakthrough episodes of hypotension may occur after meals when this dose is used, but can be prevented by oral administration of 250 mg of caffeine one-half hour before meals.

Usual adult prescribing limits: Vascular headache suppressant (migraine or cluster [acute])—6 mg per week.

ERGOTAMINE

Summary of Differences

Pharmacology:

Mechanism of action/effects—Adrenergic blocking actions somewhat less pronounced, and vasoconstrictive actions more pronounced, than those of dihydroergotamine.

Other actions/effects—Much more potent as a uterine stimulant than dihydroergotamine.

Time to peak effect—Oral: Usually within 1 to 2 hours, but up to 5 hours in some patients..

Inhalation Dosage Forms

ERGOTAMINE TARTRATE INHALATION AEROSOL USP

Usual adult dose: Vascular headache suppressant (migraine or cluster [acute])—Oral inhalation, 360 mcg (0.36 mg—1 metered spray) at the start of the attack, repeated at intervals of at least five minutes as needed for full relief, up to a total of 2.16 mg (6 metered sprays) per day.

Usual adult prescribing limits: To reduce the risk of dependence on ergotamine, it is recommended that the medication be used no more often than two times a week, preferably at least five days apart.

Auxiliary labeling: • Shake well.

Oral Dosage Forms

ERGOTAMINE TARTRATE TABLETS USP

Usual adult dose: Vascular headache suppressant (migraine or cluster [acute])—Oral, 1 or 2 tablets (1 or 2 mg of ergotamine) at the start of the attack, followed by an additional 1 or 2 tablets at intervals of at least thirty minutes, up to a total of 6 tablets (6 mg of ergotamine) per day. If an additional dose was needed, and the initial dose was well tolerated, a higher initial dose may be administered at the start of subsequent attacks. The maximum recommended initial dose is 3 tablets (3 mg of ergotamine).

Usual adult prescribing limits: To reduce the risk of dependence on ergotamine, it is recommended that the medication be used no more often than two times a week, preferably at least five days apart.

ERGOTAMINE TARTRATE TABLETS USP (SUBLINGUAL)

Usual adult dose: Vascular headache suppressant (migraine or cluster [acute])—Sublingual, 2 mg at the start of the attack, repeated at intervals of at least thirty minutes, if necessary, up to a total of 6 mg per day.

Usual adult prescribing limits: To reduce the risk of dependence on ergotamine, it is recommended that the medication be used no more often than two times a week, preferably at least five days apart.

ERGOTAMINE AND CAFFEINE

Summary of Differences

Pharmacology:
  Mechanism of action/effects—
    Ergotamine: Adrenergic blocking actions somewhat less pronounced, and vasoconstrictive actions more pronounced, than those of dihydroergotamine.
    Caffeine: Probably contributes to efficacy of the combination by enhancing ergotamine absorption.
  Other actions/effects—
    Ergotamine: Much more potent as a uterine stimulant than dihydroergotamine.
    Caffeine: Has CNS stimulating effects; may inhibit sleep.
  Time to peak effect—Ergotamine: Oral—Usually within 1 to 2 hours, but up to 5 hours in some patients.
Precautions:
  Breast-feeding—Caffeine: Total daily intake by breast-feeding women should be limited, because accumulation and stimulant effects in the infant have been reported.
  Drug interactions and/or related problems—Caffeine: Potential excessive stimulation if used concurrently with other CNS stimulants; potential hypertension and arrhythmias if used concurrently with MAO inhibitors.
  Laboratory value alterations—Caffeine: May interfere with dipyridamole-assisted myocardial perfusion studies and serum urate determinations (Bittner method).

Contraindications/medical problems—Caffeine: Caution also recommended in patients with anxiety disorders, insomnia, peptic ulceration, and severe cardiac disease.

Oral Dosage Forms

Note: Bracketed uses in the *Dosage Forms* section refer to categories of use and/or indications that are not included in U.S. product labeling.

ERGOTAMINE TARTRATE AND CAFFEINE TABLETS USP

Usual adult dose: Vascular headache suppressant (migraine or cluster)—
  Acute headache: Oral, 1 or 2 tablets (1 or 2 mg of ergotamine) at the start of the attack, followed by an additional 1 or 2 tablets (1 or 2 mg of ergotamine) at intervals of at least thirty minutes, up to a total of 6 tablets (6 mg of ergotamine) per day. If an additional dose was needed, and the initial dose was well tolerated, a higher initial dose may be administered at the start of subsequent attacks. The maximum recommended initial dose is 3 tablets (3 mg of ergotamine).
  [Cluster headache prophylaxis][1]: Oral, 1 or 2 tablets (1 or 2 mg of ergotamine) one to three times a day, one or two hours prior to the time that attacks usually occur. Cluster headaches that occur only during the night may be prevented by a single dose, administered one or two hours before bedtime.

Usual adult prescribing limits: Acute migraine—To reduce the risk of dependence on ergotamine, it is recommended that the medication be used no more often than two times a week, preferably at least five days apart.

Rectal Dosage Forms

ERGOTAMINE TARTRATE AND CAFFEINE SUPPOSITORIES USP

Usual adult dose: Vascular headache suppressant (migraine or cluster [acute])—Rectal, one-fourth to 1 suppository (500 mcg [0.5 mg] to 2 mg of ergotamine) initially, repeated at intervals of at least thirty minutes, if needed and tolerated, up to a total dose of 2 suppositories (4 mg of ergotamine) per day. Most patients respond well to an initial dose of one-half suppository (1 mg of ergotamine). However, if a repeat dose was necessary, and the first dose did not cause undue nausea, the initial dose for subsequent attacks may be increased. Up to 1½ suppositories (3 mg of ergotamine) may be administered as a single initial dose, if tolerated.

Note: One headache specialist recommends that the patient determine a dose that does not cause nausea (during a headache-free period) by inserting one-fourth of a suppository every 60 minutes, until nausea occurs or a maximum of 1 suppository has been used. The highest cumulative dose that does not cause nausea may then be used as the initial dose during an acute attack. For example, if nausea occurs after the third dose (a total of three-fourths of a suppository), the initial dose for that patient should be one-half suppository.

Usual adult prescribing limits: To reduce the risk of dependence on ergotamine, it is recommended that the medication be used no more often than two times a week, preferably at least five days apart.

Auxiliary labeling:
  • For rectal use only.
  • Store in a cool place.

ERGOTAMINE, CAFFEINE, AND BELLADONNA ALKALOIDS

Summary of Differences

Pharmacology:
    Mechanism of action/effects—
        Ergotamine: Adrenergic blocking actions somewhat less pronounced, and vasoconstrictive actions more pronounced, than those of dihydroergotamine.
        Caffeine: Probably contributes to efficacy of the combination by enhancing ergotamine absorption.
        Belladonna alkaloids: Provide an antiemetic effect.
    Other actions/effects—
        Ergotamine: Much more potent as a uterine stimulant than dihydroergotamine.
        Caffeine: Has CNS stimulating effects; may inhibit sleep.
        Belladonna alkaloids: Have anticholinergic activity.
    Time to peak effect—Ergotamine: Oral—Usually within 1 to 2 hours, but up to 5 hours in some patients.
Precautions:
    Breast-feeding—
        Caffeine: Total daily intake by breast-feeding women should be limited, because accumulation and stimulant effects in the infant have been reported.
        Belladonna alkaloids: May inhibit lactation.
    Pediatrics—Belladonna alkaloids: Young children, especially with spastic paralysis or brain damage, are especially susceptible to toxic effects of anticholinergics.
    Geriatrics—Belladonna alkaloids: Increased risk of excitement, agitation, drowsiness, or confusion; also, risk of precipitating undiagnosed glaucoma.
    Drug interactions and/or related problems—
        Caffeine: Potential excessive stimulation if used concurrently with other CNS stimulants; potential hypertension and arrhythmias if used concurrently with MAO inhibitors.
        Belladonna alkaloids: Potential additive anticholinergic effects if administered concurrently with other medications having similar activity.
    Laboratory value alterations—
        Caffeine: May interfere with dipyridamole-assisted myocardial perfusion studies and serum urate determinations (Bittner method).
        Belladonna alkaloids: Interfere with gastric acid secretion tests.
    Contraindications/medical problems—
        Caffeine: Caution also recommended in patients with anxiety disorders, insomnia, peptic ulceration, and severe cardiac disease.
        Belladonna alkaloids: Caution also required in patients with conditions that may be adversely affected by anticholinergic effects.

Oral Dosage Forms

ERGOTAMINE TARTRATE, CAFFEINE, AND BELLADONNA ALKALOIDS TABLETS

Usual adult dose: Vascular headache suppressant (migraine or cluster [acute])—Oral, 1 or 2 tablets (1 or 2 mg of ergotamine) at the start of the attack, followed by an additional 1 or 2 tablets (1 or 2 mg of ergotamine) at intervals of at least thirty minutes, up to a total of 6 tablets (6 mg of ergotamine) per day. If an additional dose was needed, and the initial dose was well tolerated, a higher initial dose may be administered at the start of subsequent attacks. The maximum recommended initial dose is 3 tablets (3 mg of ergotamine).

Usual adult prescribing limits: To reduce the risk of dependence on ergotamine, it is recommended that the medication be used no more often than two times a week, preferably at least five days apart.

Rectal Dosage Forms

ERGOTAMINE TARTRATE, CAFFEINE, AND BELLADONNA ALKALOIDS SUPPOSITORIES

Usual adult dose: Vascular headache suppressant (migraine or cluster [acute]): Rectal, one-half to 2 suppositories (500 mcg [0.5 mg] to 2 mg of ergotamine) initially, repeated at intervals of at least thirty minutes, if needed and tolerated, up to a total dose of 4 suppositories (4 mg of ergotamine) per day. Most patients respond well to an initial dose of one suppository (1 mg of ergotamine). However, if a repeat dose was necessary, and the first dose did not cause undue nausea, the initial dose for subsequent attacks may be increased. Up to 3 suppositories (3 mg of ergotamine) may be administered as a single initial dose, if tolerated.

Note: One headache specialist recommends that the patient determine a dose that does not cause nausea (during a headache-free period) by inserting one-half of a suppository every 60 minutes, until nausea occurs or a maximum of 2 suppositories has been used. The highest cumulative dose that does not cause nausea may then be used as the initial dose during an acute attack. For example, if nausea occurs after the third dose (a total of $1^{1}/_{2}$ suppositories), the initial dose for that patient should be 1 suppository.

Usual adult prescribing limits: To reduce the risk of dependence on ergotamine, it is recommended that the medication be used no more often than two times a week, preferably at least five days apart.

Auxiliary labeling:
- For rectal use only.
- Store in a cool place.

ERGOTAMINE, CAFFEINE, BELLADONNA ALKALOIDS, AND PENTOBARBITAL

Summary of Differences

Pharmacology:
    Mechanism of action/effects—
        Ergotamine: Adrenergic blocking actions somewhat less pronounced, and vasoconstrictive actions more pronounced, than those of dihydroergotamine.
        Caffeine: Probably contributes to efficacy of the combination by enhancing ergotamine absorption.
        Belladonna alkaloids: Provide an antiemetic effect.
        Pentobarbital: Provides a sedative effect.
    Other actions/effects—
        Ergotamine: Much more potent as a uterine stimulant than dihydroergotamine.
        Caffeine: Has CNS stimulating effects; may inhibit sleep.
        Belladonna alkaloids: Have anticholinergic activity.
        Pentobarbital: Has CNS depressant effects.
    Time to peak effect—Ergotamine: Oral—Usually within 1 to 2 hours, but up to 5 hours in some patients.
Precautions:
    Breast-feeding—
        Caffeine: Total daily intake by breast-feeding women should be limited, because accumulation and stimulant effects in the infant have been reported.
        Belladonna alkaloids: May inhibit lactation.
        Pentobarbital: May be distributed into breast milk.

Pediatrics—
Belladonna alkaloids: Young children, especially with spastic paralysis or brain damage, are especially susceptible to toxic effects of anticholinergics.
Pentobarbital: May cause paradoxical excitement.
Geriatrics—
Belladonna alkaloids: Increased risk of excitement, agitation, drowsiness, or confusion; also, risk of precipitating undiagnosed glaucoma.
Pentobarbital: Risk of excitement, depression, and/or confusion.
Drug interactions and/or related problems—
Caffeine: Potential excessive stimulation if used concurrently with other CNS stimulants; potential hypertension and arrhythmias if used concurrently with MAO inhibitors.
Belladonna alkaloids: Potential additive anticholinergic effects if administered concurrently with other medications having similar activity.
Pentobarbital: Potential additive effects with other CNS depressants.
Laboratory value alterations—
Caffeine: Interference with dipyridamole-assisted myocardial perfusion studies and serum urate determinations (Bittner method).
Belladonna alkaloids: Interfere with gastric acid secretion tests.
Contraindications/medical problems—
Caffeine: Caution also recommended in patients with anxiety disorders, insomnia, peptic ulceration, and severe cardiac disease.
Belladonna alkaloids: Caution also required in patients with conditions that may be adversely affected by anticholinergic effects.

Oral Dosage Forms

ERGOTAMINE TARTRATE, CAFFEINE, BELLADONNA ALKALOIDS, AND PENTOBARBITAL SODIUM TABLETS

Usual adult dose: Vascular headache suppressant (migraine or cluster [acute])—Oral, 1 or 2 tablets (1 or 2 mg of ergotamine) at the start of the attack, followed by an additional 1 or 2 tablets (1 or 2 mg of ergotamine) at intervals of at least thirty minutes, up to a total of 6 tablets (6 mg of ergotamine) per day. If an additional dose was needed, and the initial dose was well tolerated, a higher initial dose may be administered at the start of subsequent attacks. The maximum recommended initial dose is 3 tablets (3 mg of ergotamine).

Note: Geriatric and debilitated patients may react to usual doses of barbiturates with excitement, confusion, or mental depression. A reduction in dosage may be required in these patients.

Usual adult prescribing limits: To reduce the risk of dependence on ergotamine, it is recommended that the medication be used no more often than two times a week, preferably at least five days apart.

Auxiliary labeling:
• May cause drowsiness.
• Avoid alcoholic beverages.

Rectal Dosage Forms

ERGOTAMINE TARTRATE, CAFFEINE, BELLADONNA ALKALOIDS, AND PENTOBARBITAL SUPPOSITORIES

Usual adult dose: Vascular headache suppressant (migraine or cluster [acute])—Rectal, one-fourth to 1 suppository (500 mcg [0.5 mg] to 2 mg of ergotamine) initially, repeated at intervals of at least thirty minutes, if needed and tolerated, up to a total dose of 2 suppositories (4 mg of ergotamine) per day. Most patients respond

well to an initial dose of one-half suppository (1 mg of ergotamine). However, if a repeat dose was necessary, and the first dose did not cause undue nausea, the initial dose for subsequent attacks may be increased. Up to 1¹/₂ suppositories (3 mg of ergotamine) may be administered as a single initial dose, if tolerated.

Note: One headache specialist recommends that the patient determine a dose that does not cause nausea (during a headache-free period) by inserting one-fourth of a suppository every 60 minutes, until nausea occurs or a maximum of 1 suppository has been used. The highest cumulative dose that does not cause nausea may then be used as the initial dose during an acute attack. For example, if nausea occurs after the third dose (a total of three-fourths of a suppository), the initial dose for that patient should be one-half suppository.

Geriatric and debilitated patients may react to usual doses of barbiturates with excitement, confusion, or mental depression. A reduction in dosage may be required in these patients.

Usual adult prescribing limits: To reduce the risk of dependence on ergotamine, it is recommended that the medication be used no more often than two times a week, preferably at least five days apart.

Auxiliary labeling:
• For rectal use only.
• Store in a cool place.
• Avoid alcoholic beverages.
• May cause drowsiness.

ERGOTAMINE, CAFFEINE, AND CYCLIZINE

Summary of Differences

Pharmacology:
Mechanism of action/effects—
Ergotamine: Adrenergic blocking actions somewhat less pronounced, and vasoconstrictive actions more pronounced, than those of dihydroergotamine.
Caffeine: Probably contributes to efficacy of the combination by enhancing ergotamine absorption.
Cyclizine: Provides antiemetic and sedative effects.
Other actions/effects—
Ergotamine: Much more potent as a uterine stimulant than dihydroergotamine.
Caffeine: Has CNS stimulating effects; may inhibit sleep.
Cyclizine: Has antihistaminic, anticholinergic, and CNS depressant activities.
Time to peak effect—Ergotamine: Usually within 1 to 2 hours, but up to 5 hours in some patients[xu.
Precautions:
Breast-feeding—
Caffeine: Total daily intake by breast-feeding women should be limited, because accumulation and stimulant effects in the infant have been reported.
Cyclizine: May inhibit lactation and may be distributed into breast milk.
Pediatrics—Cyclizine: May cause paradoxical excitement.
Geriatrics—Cyclizine: Increased sensitivity to anticholinergic side effects; increased risk of dizziness, sedation, and hypotension.
Drug interactions and/or related problems—
Caffeine: Potential excessive stimulation if used concurrently with other CNS stimulants; potential hypertension and arrhythmias if used concurrently with MAO inhibitors.
Cyclizine: Risk of additive anticholinergic and/or CNS effects if used concurrently with other medications having similar actions.

Laboratory value alterations—
Caffeine: May interfere with dipyridamole-assisted myocardial perfusion studies and serum urate determinations (Bittner method).
Cyclizine: Interferes with skin tests using allergen extracts.
Contraindications/medical problems—
Caffeine: Caution also recommended in patients with anxiety disorders, insomnia, peptic ulceration, and severe cardiac disease.
Cyclizine: Caution also recommended in patients who may be adversely affected by anticholinergic effects.

Oral Dosage Forms

ERGOTAMINE TARTRATE, CAFFEINE, AND CYCLIZINE TABLETS

Usual adult dose: Vascular headache suppressant (migraine or cluster [acute])—Oral, one-half or 1 tablet (1 or 2 mg of ergotamine) at the start of the attack, followed by an additional one-half or 1 tablet (1 or 2 mg of ergotamine) at intervals of at least thirty minutes, up to a total of 3 tablets (6 mg of ergotamine) per day. If an additional dose was needed, and the initial dose was well tolerated, a higher initial dose may be administered at the start of subsequent attacks. The maximum recommended initial dose is $1^1/_2$ tablets (3 mg of ergotamine).

Usual adult prescribing limits: To reduce the risk of dependence on ergotamine, it is recommended that the medication be used no more often than two times a week, preferably at least five days apart.

Auxiliary labeling:
• May cause drowsiness.
• Avoid alcoholic beverages.

ERGOTAMINE, CAFFEINE, AND DIMENHYDRINATE

Summary of Differences

Pharmacology:
Mechanism of action/effects—
Ergotamine: Adrenergic blocking actions somewhat less pronounced, and vasoconstrictive actions more pronounced, than those of dihydroergotamine.
Caffeine: Probably contributes to efficacy of the combination by enhancing ergotamine absorption.
Dimenhydrinate: Provides antiemetic and sedative effects.
Other actions/effects—
Ergotamine: Much more potent as a uterine stimulant than dihydroergotamine.
Caffeine: Has CNS stimulating effects; may inhibit sleep.
Dimenhydrinate: Has antihistaminic, anticholinergic, and CNS depressant activities.
Time to peak effect—Ergotamine: Usually 1 to 2 hours, but up to 5 hours in some patients.
Precautions:
Breast-feeding—
Caffeine: Total daily intake by breast-feeding women should be limited, because accumulation and stimulant effects in the infant have been reported.
Dimenhydrinate: May inhibit lactation and is distributed into breast milk.
Pediatrics—Dimenhydrinate: May cause paradoxical excitement.
Geriatrics—Dimenhydrinate: Increased sensitivity to anticholinergic side effects; increased risk of dizziness, sedation, and hypotension.

Drug interactions and/or related problems—
Caffeine: Potential excessive stimulation if used concurrently with other CNS stimulants; potential hypertension and arrhythmias if used concurrently with MAO inhibitors.
Dimenhydrinate: Risk of additive anticholinergic and/or CNS effects if used concurrently with other medications having similar actions.
Laboratory value alterations—
Caffeine: May interfere with dipyridamole-assisted myocardial perfusion studies and serum urate determinations (Bittner method).
Dimenhydrinate: Interferes with skin tests using allergen extracts.
Contraindications/medical problems—
Caffeine: Caution also recommended in patients with anxiety disorders, insomnia, peptic ulceration, and severe cardiac disease.
Dimenhydrinate: Caution also recommended in patients who may be adversely affected by anticholinergic effects.

Oral Dosage Forms

ERGOTAMINE TARTRATE, CAFFEINE, AND DIMENHYDRINATE CAPSULES

Usual adult dose: Vascular headache suppressant (migraine or cluster [acute])—Oral, 1 or 2 capsules (1 or 2 mg of ergotamine) at the start of the attack, followed by an additional 1 or 2 capsules (1 or 2 mg of ergotamine) at intervals of at least thirty minutes, up to a total of 6 capsules (6 mg of ergotamine) per day. If an additional dose was needed, and the initial dose was well tolerated, a higher initial dose may be administered at the start of subsequent attacks. The maximum recommended initial dose is 3 capsules (3 mg of ergotamine).

Usual adult prescribing limits: To reduce the risk of dependence on ergotamine, it is recommended that the medication be used no more often than two times a week, preferably at least five days apart.

Auxiliary labeling:
• May cause drowsiness.
• Avoid alcoholic beverages.

ERGOTAMINE, CAFFEINE, AND DIPHENHYDRAMINE

Summary of Differences

Pharmacology:
Mechanism of action/effects—
Ergotamine: Adrenergic blocking actions somewhat less pronounced, and vasoconstrictive actions more pronounced, than those of dihydroergotamine.
Caffeine: Probably contributes to efficacy of the combination by enhancing ergotamine absorption.
Diphenhydramine: Provides antiemetic and sedative effects.
Other actions/effects—
Ergotamine: Much more potent as a uterine stimulant than dihydroergotamine.
Caffeine: Has CNS stimulating effects; may inhibit sleep.
Diphenhydramine: Has antihistaminic, anticholinergic, and CNS depressant activities.
Time to peak effect—Ergotamine: Usually within 1 to 2 hours, but up to 5 hours in some patients.

Precautions:

Breast-feeding—

Caffeine: Total daily intake by breast-feeding women should be limited, because accumulation and stimulant effects in the infant have been reported.

Diphenhydramine: May inhibit lactation.

Pediatrics—Diphenhydramine: May cause paradoxical excitement.

Geriatrics—Diphenhydramine: Increased susceptibility to anticholinergic side effects; increased risk of dizziness, sedation, and hypotension.

Drug interactions and/or related problems—

Caffeine: Potential excessive stimulation if used concurrently with other CNS stimulants; potential hypertension and arrhythmias if used concurrently with MAO inhibitors.

Diphenhydramine: Risk of additive anticholinergic and/or CNS effects if used concurrently with other medications having similar actions.

Laboratory value alterations—

Caffeine: May interfere with dipyridamole-assisted myocardial perfusion studies and serum urate determinations (Bittner method).

Diphenhydramine: Interferes with skin tests using allergen extracts.

Contraindications/medical problems—

Caffeine: Caution also recommended in patients with anxiety disorders, insomnia, peptic ulceration, and severe cardiac disease.

Diphenhydramine: Caution also recommended in patients who may be adversely affected by anticholinergic effects.

Oral Dosage Forms

ERGOTAMINE TARTRATE, CAFFEINE, AND DIPHENHYDRAMINE CAPSULES

Usual adult dose: Vascular headache suppressant (migraine or cluster [acute])—Oral, 1 or 2 capsules (1 or 2 mg of ergotamine) at the start of the attack, followed by an additional 1 or 2 capsules (1 or 2 mg of ergotamine) at intervals of at least thirty minutes, up to a total of 6 capsules (6 mg of ergotamine) per day. If an additional dose was needed, and the initial dose was well tolerated, a higher initial dose may be administered at the start of subsequent attacks. The maximum recommended initial dose is 3 capsules (3 mg of ergotamine).

Usual adult prescribing limits: To reduce the risk of dependence on ergotamine, it is recommended that the medication be used no more often than two times a week, preferably at least five days apart.

Auxiliary labeling:

- May cause drowsiness.
- Avoid alcoholic beverages.

VITAMIN B$_{12}$ Systemic

Some commonly used *brand names* are:

In the U.S.—

Alphamine
[Hydroxocobalamin]

Cobex [Cyanocobalamin]

Crystamine
[Cyanocobalamin]

Crysti-12
[Cyanocobalamin]

Cyanoject
[Cyanocobalamin]

Cyomin [Cyanocobalamin]

Hydrobexan
[Hydroxocobalamin]

Hydro-Cobex
[Hydroxocobalamin]

Hydro-Crysti-12
[Hydroxocobalamin]

LA-12
[Hydroxocobalamin]

Rubesol-1000
[Cyanocobalamin]

Rubramin PC
[Cyanocobalamin]

In Canada—

Anacobin
[Cyanocobalamin]

Bedoz [Cyanocobalamin]

Rubion [Cyanocobalamin]

Rubramin
[Cyanocobalamin]

CYANOCOBALAMIN

Oral

Cyanocobalamin Tablets

In the U.S. and Canada—GENERIC

Parenteral

Cyanocobalamin Injection USP

In the U.S.—*Cobex; Crystamine; Crysti-12; Cyanoject; Cyomin; Rubesol-1000; Rubramin PC;* GENERIC

In Canada—*Anacobin; Bedoz; Rubion; Rubramin;* GENERIC

HYDROXOCOBALAMIN†

Parenteral

Hydroxocobalamin Injection USP†

In the U.S.—*Alphamine; Hydrobexan; Hydro-Cobex; Hydro-Crysti-12; LA-12;* GENERIC

---

†Not commercially available in Canada.

Category: Nutritional supplement (vitamin); antianemic; diagnostic aid (vitamin B$_{12}$ deficiency).

Note: Vitamin B$_{12}$ (also known as the cobalamins) is a water-soluble vitamin.

Indications

Note: Bracketed information in the *Indications* section refers to uses not included in U.S. product labeling.

Indications for cyanocobalamin and hydroxocobalamin are the same, although hydroxocobalamin may be preferred for treatment of vitamin B$_{12}$ deficiency since optic neuropathies may degenerate with administration of cyanocobalamin. However, some patients develop antibodies to the hydroxocobalamin-transcobalamin II complex.

Accepted

Anemia, pernicious (treatment)—Vitamin B$_{12}$ is indicated for treatment of pernicious anemia (due to lack of or inhibition of intrinsic factor).

Vitamin deficiency (prophylaxis and treatment)—

Vitamin B$_{12}$ is indicated for prevention and treatment of vitamin B$_{12}$ deficiency.

Deficiency of vitamin B$_{12}$ may lead to macrocytic, megaloblastic anemia and possible irreversible neurologic damage.

Vitamin B$_{12}$ deficiency may occur as a result of inadequate nutrition or intestinal malabsorption but does not occur in healthy individuals receiving an adequate balanced diet. However, simple vitamin B$_{12}$ deficiency may occur in strict vegetarians (vegan-vegetarians) and their breast-fed infants since vitamin B$_{12}$ is found in animal protein and not in vegetables. Dietary sources are preferred over supplementation whenever possible.

Requirements may be increased and/or supplementation may be necessary in the following conditions (although clinical deficiencies are usually rare):

Alcoholism
Anemia, hemolytic
Fever, chronic
Fish tapeworm infestation
Gastrectomy
Gastritis, atropic with achlorhydria
Genetic disorders—homocystinuria and/or methylmalonic aciduria
Hepatic-biliary tract disease—hepatic function impairment, alcoholism with cirrhosis
Hyperthyroidism
Intestinal diseases—celiac, tropical sprue, regional enteritis, bacterial overgrowth of small intestine, persistent diarrhea, ileal resection
Infection, prolonged
Malabsorption syndromes associated with pancreatic insufficiency
Malignancy of pancreas or bowel
Renal disease
Stress, prolonged

Some unusual diets (e.g., vegan-vegetarian, macrobiotic, or reducing diets that drastically restrict food selection) may not supply minimum daily requirements of vitamin B$_{12}$. Supplementation is necessary in patients receiving total parenteral nutrition (TPN) or undergoing rapid weight loss or in those with malnutrition, because of inadequate dietary intake.

Requirements for all vitamins and most minerals are increased during pregnancy; however, they should be provided by an adequate diet. Many physicians recommend that pregnant women receive multivitamin and mineral supplements, especially those pregnant women who do not consume an adequate diet and those in high-risk categories (i.e., women carrying more than one fetus, heavy cigarette smokers, and alcohol and drug abusers). Taking excessive amounts of a multivitamin and mineral supplement may be harmful to the mother and/or fetus and should be avoided.

Pregnant women who are strict vegetarians (vegan-vegetarians) may need vitamin B$_{12}$ supplementation.

Requirements for all vitamins and most minerals are increased during breast-feeding.

Requirements may be increased by the following medications: Aminosalicylates, colchicine, and epoetin.

Vitamin B$_{12}$ should not be administered as a dietary supplement before pernicious anemia or folic acid deficiency has been ruled out.

[Vitamin B$_{12}$ deficiency (diagnosis)]—Cyanocobalamin or hydroxocobalamin may be used as the flushing dose in the Schilling test for vitamin B$_{12}$ malabsorption.

Unaccepted

Cyanocobalamin has not been proven effective for treatment of acute viral hepatitis; aging; allergies; amblyopia; delayed growth, poor appetite, or malnutrition; dermatologic disorders; fatigue; mental disorders; multiple sclerosis; sterility; thyrotoxicosis; and trigeminal neuralgia and other neuropathies.

Pharmacology

Mechanism of action/Effect: Vitamin B$_{12}$ acts as a coenzyme for various metabolic functions, including fat and carbohydrate metabolism and protein synthesis. It is necessary for growth, cell replication, hematopoiesis, and nucleoprotein and myelin synthesis, largely due to its effects on metabolism of methionine, folic acid, and malonic acid.

Precautions to Consider

Cross-sensitivity and/or related problems
Patients sensitive to other cobalamins (found naturally in foods) may be sensitive to vitamin B$_{12}$ also.

Geriatrics
Appropriate studies performed to date have not demonstrated geriatrics-specific problems that would limit the usefulness of vitamin B$_{12}$ in the elderly.

Drug interactions and/or related problems
The following drug interactions and/or related problems have been selected on the basis of their potential clinical significance (possible mechanism in parentheses where appropriate)—not necessarily inclusive (» = major clinical significance):

Note: Combinations containing any of the following medications, depending on the amount present, may also interact with this medication.

Alcohol, excessive intake for longer than 2 weeks, or
Aminosalicylates or
Colchicine, especially in combination with aminoglycosides
(may act to reduce absorption of vitamin B$_{12}$ from the gastrointestinal tract; requirements for vitamin B$_{12}$ may be increased in patients receiving these medications)

Antibiotics
(may interfere with the microbiologic method of assay for serum and erythrocyte vitamin B$_{12}$ concentrations and cause falsely low results)

Ascorbic acid
(may destroy vitamin B$_{12}$; patients should be advised to avoid ingestion of large doses within 1 hour of oral vitamin B$_{12}$)

Folic acid
(large and continuous doses may reduce vitamin B$_{12}$ concentrations in blood)

Contraindications/Medical problems
The contraindications/medical problems included have been selected on the basis of their potential clinical significance (reasons given in parentheses where appropriate)—not necessarily inclusive (» = major clinical significance).

Except under special circumstances, this medication should not be used when the following medical problem exists:

For cyanocobalamin
» Leber's disease
(optic nerve atrophy has occurred rapidly after administration; cyanocobalamin concentrations are already elevated)

Risk-benefit should be considered when the following medical problem exists:

Sensitivity to cyanocobalamin or hydroxocobalamin

Side/Adverse Effects

Note: Water-soluble vitamins seldom cause toxicity in persons with normal renal function.

Treatment with vitamin B$_{12}$ may unmask the signs of polycythemia vera.

The following side/adverse effects have been selected on the basis of their potential clinical significance (possible signs and symptoms in parentheses where appropriate)—not necessarily inclusive:

Those indicating need for medical attention
Incidence rare
Anaphylactic reaction (skin rash, itching, wheezing)—after parenteral administration

Those indicating need for medical attention only if they continue or are bothersome
Incidence less frequent
Diarrhea; itching of skin

Patient Consultation

In providing consultation, consider emphasizing the following selected information (» = major clinical significance):

Description of use
Description should include function in the body, signs of deficiency, and unproven uses

Importance of diet
Diet as treatment of choice; importance of diet; lack of vitamin B$_{12}$ in strict vegetarian diets
Food sources of vitamin B$_{12}$; effects of processing
Not using vitamins as substitute for balanced diet
Supplement may be needed because of inadequate dietary intake or increased requirements
Importance of not exceeding recommended dietary allowances (RDA) if self-medicating with vitamin supplements

Before using this dietary supplement
» Conditions affecting use, especially:
Sensitivity to cobalamins
Other medical problems, especially Leber's disease

Proper use of this dietary supplement
Megadoses not recommended without physician's advice
» Need for lifelong therapy for pernicious anemia or following gastrectomy or ileal resection
Missed dose: No cause for concern because of length of time necessary for depletion; remembering to take as directed
» Proper storage

Side/adverse effects
Signs of potential side effects, especially anaphylactic reaction

General Dosing Information

Because of the infrequency of single B vitamin deficiencies, combinations are commonly administered. Many commercial combinations of B vitamins are available.

Vitamin B$_{12}$ is also synthesized by bacteria in the gastrointestinal tract but is not absorbed and is excreted in the feces.

A diagnosis of vitamin B$_{12}$ deficiency should be confirmed by laboratory investigations before institution of vitamin B$_{12}$ therapy; vitamin B$_{12}$ administration may mask folic acid deficiency.

The effectiveness of megadoses (10 times the RDA or more) for treatment of various conditions is unproven and their use should be discouraged until benefit has been proven.

For oral dosage forms only
The oral route is useful only for treating nutritional vitamin B$_{12}$ deficiency (when gastrointestinal absorption is normal or in vegan-vegetarians); it is not useful in small bowel disease, malabsorption syndromes, or following gastric or ileal resection. Oral preparations containing intrinsic factor have little reliable continuous efficacy in pernicious anemia.

For parenteral dosage forms only
Cyanocobalamin or hydroxocobalamin injection should not be administered intravenously, although small amounts of cyanocobalamin are sometimes included in total parenteral nutrition (TPN) solutions.

Diet/Nutrition
Recommended dietary allowances (RDA) for vitamins are values determined by the Food and Nutrition Board of the National Research Council. Intake of the RDA provides adequate nutrition in most healthy persons under usual environmental stresses; they are not minimum requirements. RDA are not the same as USRDA

(United States Recommended Daily Allowances), which are values established by the FDA for labeling purposes.
RDA of vitamin B$_{12}$ per day:
Infants and children—
Birth to 6 months: 0.3 mcg.
6 months to 1 year: 0.5 mcg.
1 to 3 years: 0.7 mcg.
4 to 6 years: 1 mcg.
7 to 10 years: 1.4 mcg.
Adolescent and adult males—11 years and over: 2 mcg.
Adolescent and adult females—11 years and over: 2 mcg.
Pregnant females—2.2 mcg.
Lactating females—2.6 mcg.
These are usually provided by adequate diets.

Best dietary sources of vitamin B$_{12}$ are fish, seafood, egg yolk, milk, and fermented cheeses. Vitamin B$_{12}$ is not found in vegetables; however, bacteria found on vegetables may be a source of vitamin B$_{12}$ for vegan-vegetarians. There is little loss of vitamin B$_{12}$ from foods with ordinary cooking; however, severe heating may cause degeneration.

CYANOCOBALAMIN

Summary of Differences

Indications for cyanocobalamin and hydroxocobalamin are the same, although hydroxocobalamin may be preferred for treatment of vitamin B$_{12}$ deficiency since optic neuropathies may degenerate with administration of cyanocobalamin. However, some patients develop antibodies to the hydroxocobalamin-transcobalamin II complex.

Oral Dosage Forms

CYANOCOBALAMIN TABLETS

Usual adult and adolescent dose: Nutritional supplement (vitamin)—Dietary supplement: Oral, 1 mcg (0.001 mg) per day (or up to 25 mcg [0.025 mg] per day when conditions causing increased requirements are present).

Parenteral Dosage Forms

Note: Bracketed uses in the *Dosage Forms* section refer to categories of use and/or indications that are not included in U.S. product labeling.

CYANOCOBALAMIN INJECTION USP

Usual and adolescent adult dose:
Nutritional supplement (vitamin)—Treatment of deficiency:
Initial—Intramuscular or deep subcutaneous, 100 mcg (0.1 mg) per day for six or seven days, followed by 100 mcg (0.1 mg) every other day for seven doses if clinical improvement and a reticulocyte response occur, then 100 mcg (0.1 mg) every three or four days for another two to three weeks.
Maintenance—Intramuscular, 100 to 200 mcg (0.1 to 0.2 mg) once a month (in pernicious anemia and following total gastrectomy and extensive ileal resection, parenteral maintenance supplementation is continued for life).
[Diagnostic aid (vitamin B$_{12}$ deficiency)]—Intramuscular, 1 mcg (0.001 mg) per day for ten days plus low dietary folic acid and vitamin B$_{12}$. The flushing dose for the Schilling test is 1000 mcg (1 mg) intramuscularly.

HYDROXOCOBALAMIN

Summary of Differences

Indications for cyanocobalamin and hydroxocobalamin are the same, although hydroxocobalamin may be preferred for treatment of vitamin B_{12} deficiency since optic neuropathies may degenerate with administration of cyanocobalamin. However, some patients develop antibodies to the hydroxocobalamin-transcobalamin II complex.

Parenteral Dosage Forms

Note: Bracketed uses in the *Dosage Forms* section refer to categories of use and/or indications that are not included in U.S. product labeling.

HYDROXOCOBALAMIN INJECTION USP

Usual adult and adolescent dose:
  Nutritional supplement (vitamin)—Treatment of deficiency:
    Initial—Intramuscular or deep subcutaneous, 30 to 50 mcg (0.03 to 0.05 mg) per day (100 mcg [0.1 mg] if megaloblastic anemia is severe) for five to ten days.
    Maintenance—Intramuscular, 100 to 200 mcg (0.1 to 0.2 mg) once a month (in pernicious anemia and following total gastrectomy and extensive ileal resection, parenteral maintenance supplementation is continued for life).
  [Diagnostic aid (vitamin B_{12} deficiency)]—Intramuscular, 1 mcg (0.001 mg) per day for ten days plus low dietary folic acid and vitamin B_{12}. The flushing dose for the Schilling test is 1000 mcg (1 mg) intramuscularly.

XYLOMETAZOLINE   Nasal

Some commonly used *brand names* are:
  In the U.S.—

Chlorohist-LA	*Otrivin Nasal Drops*
Neo-Synephrine II Long	*Otrivin Nasal Spray*
Acting Nasal Spray Adult	*Otrivin Pediatric Nasal*
Strength	*Drops*
Neo-Synephrine II Long	
Acting Nose Drops Adult	
Strength	

  In Canada—

Otrivin Decongestant Nose	*Otrivin Pediatric Nasal*
Drops	*Spray*
Otrivin Nasal Spray	*Otrivin With M-D Pump*
Otrivin Pediatric	
Decongestant Nose	
Drops	

NASAL
Xylometazoline Hydrochloride Nasal Solution USP
  In the U.S.—*Chlorohist-LA; Neo-Synephrine II Long Acting Nasal Spray Adult Strength; Neo-Synephrine II Long Acting Nose Drops Adult Strength; Otrivin Nasal Drops; Otrivin Nasal Spray; Otrivin Pediatric Nasal Drops;* GENERIC
  In Canada—*Otrivin Decongestant Nose Drops; Otrivin Nasal Spray; Otrivin Pediatric Decongestant Nose Drops; Otrivin Pediatric Nasal Spray; Otrivin With M-D Pump*

Category: Decongestant (topical).

Indications

Note: Bracketed information in the *Indications* section refers to uses not included in U.S. product labeling.

Accepted
Congestion, nasal (treatment)—Xylometazoline is indicated for the temporary relief of nasal congestion due to colds, sinusitis, hay fever, or other upper respiratory allergies.

[Congestion, sinus (treatment)]—Nasal xylometazoline is also used for the relief of sinus congestion.

Pharmacology

Mechanism of action/Effect: A direct-acting sympathomimetic amine. Xylometazoline acts on alpha-adrenergic receptors in the nasal mucosa to produce constriction, resulting in decreased blood flow and decreased nasal congestion.

Duration of action: Up to 10 hours.

Precautions to Consider

Cross-sensitivity and/or related problems
Patients sensitive to other nasal decongestants may be sensitive to this medication also.

Geriatrics
Appropriate studies with xylometazoline have not been performed in the geriatric population. However, no geriatrics-specific problems have been documented to date.

Drug interactions and/or related problems
The following drug interactions and/or related problems have been selected on the basis of their potential clinical significance (possible mechanism in parentheses where appropriate)—not necessarily inclusive (» = major clinical significance):

Note: Combinations containing any of the following medications, depending on the amount present, may also interact with this medication.

Antidepressants, tricyclic, or
Maprotiline
    (if significant systemic absorption of nasal xylometazoline occurs, concurrent use of maprotiline or tricyclic antidepressants may potentiate the pressor effect of xylometazoline)

Contraindications/Medical problems
The contraindications/medical problems included have been selected on the basis of their potential clinical significance (reasons given in parentheses where appropriate)—not necessarily inclusive (» = major clinical significance).

Risk-benefit should be considered when the following medical problems exist:

Coronary artery disease or
Heart disease, including angina, or

Hypertension
  (condition may be exacerbated due to drug-induced cardiovascular effects)
Diabetes mellitus
» Glaucoma, narrow-angle, predisposition to
Hyperthyroidism
Sensitivity to xylometazoline or other nasal decongestants

Side/Adverse Effects

The following side/adverse effects have been selected on the basis of their potential clinical significance (possible signs and symptoms in parentheses where appropriate)—not necessarily inclusive:

Those indicating need for medical attention
  Rebound congestion (increase in runny or stuffy nose)

Symptoms of systemic absorption
  Blurred vision; headache or lightheadedness; nervousness; pounding, irregular, or fast heartbeat; trouble in sleeping

Those indicating need for medical attention only if they continue or are bothersome
  Burning, dryness, or stinging of nasal mucosa; sneezing

Patient Consultation

In providing consultation, consider emphasizing the following selected information (» = major clinical significance):

Before using this medication
» Conditions affecting use, especially:
    Sensitivity to xylometazoline or other nasal decongestants
    Use in children—Children may be especially prone to systemic absorption of nasal xylometazoline and resulting side/adverse effects
    Use by athletes—Xylometazoline is banned in athletes by the U.S. Olympic Committee (USOC)
    Other medical problems, especially predisposition to narrow-angle glaucoma

Proper use of this medication
  Proper administration technique
  Preventing contamination:
    Replacing cap right after use
  For nose drops
    Rinsing dropper with hot water; drying with a clean tissue
  For nose spray
    Rinsing tip of spray bottle with hot water, taking care not to suck water into bottle; drying with a clean tissue
  Preventing spread of infection: Not using container for more than one person
» Importance of not using more medication than the amount recommended
  Missed dose: Using right away if remembered within an hour or so; not using if remembered later; not doubling doses
» Proper storage

Side/adverse effects
  Signs of potential side effects, especially rebound congestion and sympathomimetic systemic effects

General Dosing Information

Prolonged or excessive use of this medication will cause rebound congestion with chronic swelling of nasal mucosa.

Medication is more effective if 3 to 5 minutes are allowed to elapse between each spray per nostril, and nose is blown thoroughly before next spray is administered. Continue until complete dose is used.

Nasal Dosage Forms

XYLOMETAZOLINE HYDROCHLORIDE NASAL SOLUTION USP

Usual adult and adolescent dose: Intranasal, 2 or 3 drops or 1 or 2 sprays into each nostril every eight to ten hours as needed.

Note: The nasal spray form of the medication is more effective and less likely to cause systemic absorption.

Auxiliary labeling: • For the nose.

YOHIMBINE   Systemic

Some commonly used *brand names* are:
  In the U.S.—*Actibine; Aphrodyne; Yocon; Yohimex*
  In Canada—*Yocon; Yohimide*

ORAL
Yohimbine Hydrochloride Tablets
  In the U.S.—*Actibine; Aphrodyne; Yocon; Yohimex;* GENERIC
  In Canada—*Yocon; Yohimide;* GENERIC

Category: Impotence therapy agent.

Indications

Note: Bracketed information in the *Indications* section refers to uses not included in U.S. product labeling.

Accepted
[Impotence (treatment)][1]—Yohimbine is used in the treatment of erectile impotence.

---
[1]Not included in Canadian product labeling.

Pharmacology

Mechanism of action/Effect: Yohimbine is a pre-synaptic alpha2-adrenergic blocking agent. The exact mechanism for its use in impotence has not been fully elucidated. However, yohimbine may exert its beneficial effect on erectile ability through blockade of central alpha$_2$-adrenergic receptors producing an increase in sympathetic drive secondary to an increase in norepinephrine release and in firing rate of cells in the brain noradrenergic nuclei. Yohimbine-mediated norepinephrine release at the level of the corporeal tissues may also be involved. In addition, beneficial effects may involve other neurotransmitters such as dopamine and serotonin and cholinergic receptors.

Other actions/effects: Yohimbine exerts a stimulant effect on mood and may increase blood pressure at higher doses. Yohimbine may also have mild antidiuretic action, possibly due to release of antidiuretic hormone.

Onset of action: Approximately 2 to 3 weeks for onset of therapeutic effect.

Precautions to Consider

Cross-sensitivity and/or related problems
Patients sensitive to rauwolfia alkaloids such as deserpidine, rauwolfia serpentina, or reserpine may also be sensitive to yohimbine.

Geriatrics
Although appropriate studies on the relationship of age to the effects of yohimbine have not been performed in the geriatric population, some studies have included a small number of patients 65 years of age and older and have not demonstrated geriatrics-specific problems that would limit the usefulness of yohimbine in the elderly.

Drug interactions and/or related problems
The following drug interactions and/or related problems have been selected on the basis of their potential clinical significance (possible mechanism in parentheses where appropriate)—not necessarily inclusive (» = major clinical significance):

Note: Combinations containing any of the following medications, depending on the amount present, may also interact with this medication.

Antidepressants or
Mood-modifying medications, other
(yohimbine may antagonize the effects of these agents when used concurrently)

Antihypertensive agents
(yohimbine may antagonize the antihypertensive effects of these agents when used concurrently)

Contraindications/Medical problems
The contraindications/medical problems included have been selected on the basis of their potential clinical significance (reasons given in parentheses where appropriate)—not necessarily inclusive (» = major clinical significance).

Except under special circumstances, this medication should not be used when the following medical problems exist:

» Angina pectoris or
» Cardiac disease or
» Hypertension
     (may be aggravated)
» Renal function impairment
     (yohimbine may worsen this condition)

Risk-benefit should be considered when the following medical problems exist:

Depression or
Psychiatric illness, other
     (yohimbine may enhance anxiety or other CNS symptoms)
Hepatic function impairment
     (although not fully determined, may interfere with biotransformation of yohimbine)
Sensitivity to yohimbine

Side/Adverse Effects

The following side/adverse effects have been selected on the basis of their potential clinical significance (possible signs and symptoms in parentheses where appropriate)—not necessarily inclusive:

Those indicating need for medical attention
Incidence less frequent
     Increased blood pressure; increased heart rate

Those indicating need for medical attention only if they continue or are bothersome
Incidence less frequent
     Dizziness; headache; irritability; nervousness or restlessness
Incidence rare
     Nausea or vomiting; skin flushing; sweating; tremor

Patient Consultation

In providing consultation, consider emphasizing the following selected information (» = major clinical significance):

Before using this medication
» Conditions affecting use, especially:
     Sensitivity to yohimbine or rauwolfia alkaloids such as deserpidine, rauwolfia serpentina, or reserpine
     Other medical problems, especially angina pectoris, cardiac disease, hypertension, or renal function impairment

Proper use of this medication
May require 2 to 3 weeks before beneficial effects are evident
» Proper dosing
     Missed dose: Taking as soon as possible if remembered within 4 hours; not taking if remembered later; not doubling doses
» Proper storage

Precautions while using this medication
Regular visits to physician to check progress
Compliance with therapy; importance of not exceeding prescribed dosage

Side/adverse effects
Signs of potential side effects, especially increased blood pressure and increased heart rate

General Dosing Information

Patients receiving yohimbine should be under the supervision of a physician experienced in its use.

Oral Dosage Forms

Note: Bracketed uses in the *Dosage Forms* section refer to categories of use and/or indications that are not included in U.S. product labeling.

YOHIMBINE HYDROCHLORIDE TABLETS

Usual adult dose: [Impotence][1]—Oral, 5.4 to 6 mg three times a day.
Note: If side effects occur, dosage may be reduced in half, followed by gradual increases.

A dose of 10 mg three times a day may be appropriate in some patients; however, the incidence of side effects may be increased.

---

[1]Not included in Canadian product labeling.

General Index

A selected number of brand names *(italicized)* and manufacturers have been included in this index. The inclusion of a brand name does not mean that the United States Pharmacopeial Convention or Johns Hopkins Medical Institutions has any particular knowledge that the brand listed has properties different from other brands of the same drug, nor should it be interpreted as an endorsement of the brand by either of these organizations. Similarly, any exclusion of a particular brand in no way indicates that the product has been judged to be unsatisfactory or unacceptable.

Acetaminophen and Codeine Phosphate (*continued*)
  Codeine No.2 (U.S.)*; Tylenol with Codeine No.3 (U.S.); Tylenol with Codeine No.4 (U.S. and Canada); Ty-Pap with Codeine; Ty-Tab with Codeine No.2; Ty-Tab with Codeine No.3; Ty-Tab with Codeine No.4]*
  See Opioid (Narcotic) Analgesics and Acetaminophen (Systemic), 820

Acetaminophen, Codeine Phosphate, and Caffeine [*Atasol-8; Atasol-15; Atasol-30; Codalan No.1; Codalan No.2; Codalan No.3; Codamin #2; Codamin #3; Codaminophen; Exdol-8; Exdol-15; Exdol-30; Lenoltec with Codeine No.1; Lenoltec with Codeine No.2; Lenoltec with Codeine No.3; Novogesic C8; Novogesic C15; Novogesic C30; Tylenol No.1; Tylenol No.1 Forte; Tylenol with Codeine No.2 (Canada); Tylenol with Codeine No.3 (Canada); Veganin]*
  See Opioid (Narcotic) Analgesics and Acetaminophen (Systemic), 820

Acetaminophen and Salicylamide [*Duoprin*]
  See Acetaminophen and Salicylates (Systemic), 5

Acetaminophen, Salicylamide, and Caffeine [*Rid-A-Pain Compound; S-A-C*]
  See Acetaminophen and Salicylates (Systemic), 5

Acetaminophen and Salicylates **(Systemic), 5**

Acetaminophen, Salicylates, and Codeine **(Systemic), 12**

Acetaminophen Uniserts—Upsher-Smith (U.S.) brand of Acetaminophen (Systemic), 1

Aceta Tablets—Century (U.S.) brand of Acetaminophen (Systemic), 1

Acetazolam—ICN (Canada) brand of Acetazolamide—**See Carbonic Anhydrase Inhibitors (Systemic), 382**

Acetazolamide [*Acetazolam; Ak-Zol; Apo-Acetazolamide; Dazamide; Diamox; Diamox Sequels*]
  See Carbonic Anhydrase Inhibitors (Systemic), 382

Acetazolamide Sodium [*Diamox*]
  See Carbonic Anhydrase Inhibitors (Systemic), 382

Acetohexamide [*Dimelor; Dymelor*]
  See Antidiabetic Agents, Oral (Systemic), 129

Acetohydroxamic Acid [*Lithostat*] **(Systemic), 13**

Acetophenazine Maleate [*Tindal*]
  See Phenothiazines (Systemic), 872

Acetylcysteine [*Airbron; Mucomyst; Mucosil*]
  (Inhalation-Local), 14

Acetylsalicylic acid—Aspirin—**See Salicylates (Systemic), 953**

Aches-N-Pain—Lederle Standard (U.S.) brand of Ibuprofen—**See Anti-inflammatory Analgesics, Nonsteroidal (Systemic), 168**

Achromycin—Lederle (U.S. and Canada) brand of Tetracycline—**See Tetracyclines (Ophthalmic), 1024; Tetracyclines (Systemic), 1025**

Achromycin V—Lederle (U.S. and Canada) brand of Tetracycline—**See Tetracyclines (Systemic), 1025**

Aciclovir—*See* Acyclovir (Systemic), 16

Aclophen—Nutripharm (U.S.) brand of Chlorpheniramine, Phenylephrine, and Acetaminophen—**See Antihistamines, Decongestants, and Analgesics (Systemic), 162**

Aclovate—Glaxo (U.S.) brand of Alclometasone—**See Corticosteroids (Topical), 458**

Acno—Baker/Cummins (U.S.) brand of Salicylic Acid and Sulfur (Topical), 973

Acnotex—C&M (U.S.) brand of Salicylic Acid and Sulfur (Topical), 973

Actacin—Vangard (U.S.) brand of Triprolidine and Pseudoephedrine—**See Antihistamines and Decongestants (Systemic), 161**

Actagen—Generix (U.S.) brand of Triprolidine and Pseudoephedrine—**See Antihistamines and Decongestants (Systemic), 161**

Actagen-C Cough—Goldline (U.S.) brand of Triprolidine, Pseudoephedrine, and Codeine—**See Cough/Cold Combinations (Systemic), 488**

Actamin—Buffington (U.S.) brand of Acetaminophen (Systemic), 1

Actamin Extra—Buffington (U.S.) brand of Acetaminophen (Systemic), 1

Actamin Super—Buffington (U.S.) brand of Acetaminophen and Caffeine—**See Acetaminophen (Systemic), 1**

ACTH—Corticotropin—**See Corticosteroids/Corticotropin—Glucocorticoid Effects (Systemic), 472**

Acthar—Armour (U.S.) and Rorer (Canada) brand of Corticotropin—**See Corticosteroids/Corticotropin—Glucocorticoid Effects (Systemic), 472**

Acthar Gel (H.P.)—Rorer (Canada) brand of Corticotropin—**See Corticosteroids/Corticotropin—Glucocorticoid Effects (Systemic), 472**

Actibine—CMC (U.S.) brand of Yohimbine (Systemic), 1081

Acticort 100—Baker/Cummins (U.S.) brand of Hydrocortisone—**See Corticosteroids (Topical), 458**

Actidil—BW (U.S.) brand of Triprolidine—**See Antihistamines (Systemic), 147**

Actidose-Aqua—Paddock (U.S.) brand of Charcoal, Activated (Oral-Local), 404

Actidose with Sorbitol—Paddock (U.S.) brand of Charcoal, Activated, and Sorbitol—**See Charcoal, Activated (Oral-Local), 404**

Actifed—BW (U.S. and Canada) brand of Triprolidine and Pseudoephedrine—**See Antihistamines and Decongestants (Systemic), 161**

Actifed-A—BW (Canada) brand of Triprolidine, Pseudoephedrine, and Acetaminophen—**See Antihistamines, Decongestants, and Analgesics (Systemic), 162**

Actifed with Codeine Cough—BW (U.S.) brand of Triprolidine, Pseudoephedrine, and Codeine—**See Cough/Cold Combinations (Systemic), 488**

Actifed DM—BW (Canada) brand of Triprolidine, Pseudoephedrine, and Dextromethorphan—**See Cough/Cold Combinations (Systemic), 488**

Actifed 12-Hour—BW (U.S.) brand of Triprolidine and Pseudoephedrine—**See Antihistamines and Decongestants (Systemic), 161**

Actifed Plus—BW (U.S.) brand of Triprolidine, Pseudoephedrine, and Acetaminophen—**See Antihistamines, Decongestants, and Analgesics (Systemic), 162**

Actifed Plus Caplets—BW (U.S.) brand of Triprolidine, Pseudoephedrine, and Acetaminophen—**See Antihistamines, Decongestants, and Analgesics (Systemic), 162**

Actigall—Summit (U.S.) brand of Ursodiol (Systemic), 1060

Actiprofen Caplets—Sterling Winthrop (Canada) brand of Ibuprofen—**See Anti-inflammatory Analgesics, Nonsteroidal (Systemic), 168**

Acutrim 16 Hour—CIBA Consumer (U.S.) brand of Phenylpropanolamine (Systemic), 894

Acutrim Late Day—CIBA Consumer (U.S.) brand of Phenylpropanolamine (Systemic), 894

Acutrim II Maximum Strength—CIBA Consumer (U.S.) brand of Phenylpropanolamine (Systemic), 894

Acycloguanosine—*See* Acyclovir (Systemic), 16

Acyclovir [*aciclovir; acycloguanosine; Zovirax*] **(Systemic), 16**

Acyclovir Sodium [*aciclovir; acycloguanosine; Zovirax*] **(Systemic), 16**

Adalat—Miles (U.S. and Canada) brand of Nifedipine—**See Calcium Channel Blocking Agents (Systemic), 343**

Adalat FT—Miles (Canada) brand of Nifedipine—**See Calcium Channel Blocking Agents (Systemic), 343**

Alferon N—Purdue Frederick (U.S.) brand of Interferon Alfa-n3—**See Interferons, Alpha (Systemic)**, 648

Algenic Alka—Rugby (U.S.) brand of Alumina and Magnesia—**See Antacids (Oral-Local)**, 61

Algicon—Rorer (U.S. and Canada) brand of Alumina and Magnesium Carbonate—**See Antacids (Oral-Local)**, 61

Alimemazine—Trimeprazine—**See Antihistamines, Phenothiazine-derivative (Systemic)**, 163

Alka-Butazolidin—Geigy (Canada) brand of Phenylbutazone, Buffered—**See Anti-inflammatory Analgesics, Nonsteroidal (Systemic)**, 168

Alkabutazone—ICN (Canada) brand of Phenylbutazone, Buffered—**See Anti-inflammatory Analgesics, Nonsteroidal (Systemic)**, 168

Alka-Mints—Miles (U.S.) brand of Calcium Carbonate—**See Antacids (Oral-Local)**, 61

Alka-Phenylbutazone—ProDoc (Canada) brand of Phenylbutazone, Buffered—**See Anti-inflammatory Analgesics, Nonsteroidal (Systemic)**, 168

Alka-Seltzer Effervescent Pain Reliever and Antacid—Miles (U.S. and Canada) brand of Aspirin, Sodium Bicarbonate, and Citric Acid (Systemic), 215

Alka-Seltzer Plus Cold—Miles (U.S.) brand of Chlorpheniramine, Phenylpropanolamine, and Aspirin—**See Antihistamines, Decongestants, and Analgesics (Systemic)**, 162

Alka-Seltzer Plus Maximum Strength Sinus Allergy Medicine—Miles (U.S.) brand of Brompheniramine, Phenylpropanolamine, and Aspirin—**See Antihistamines, Decongestants, and Analgesics (Systemic)**, 162

Alka-Seltzer Plus Nighttime Cold—Miles (U.S.) brand of Diphenhydramine, Phenylpropanolamine, and Aspirin—**See Antihistamines, Decongestants, and Analgesics (Systemic)**, 162

Alkeran—BW (U.S. and Canada) brand of Melphalan (Systemic), 717

Alkets—Upjohn (U.S.) brand of Calcium and Magnesium Carbonates and Magnesium Oxide—**See Antacids (Oral-Local)**, 61

Allay—LuChem (U.S.) brand of Hydrocodone and Acetaminophen—**See Opioid (Narcotic) Analgesics and Acetaminophen (Systemic)**, 820

Allent—Ascher (U.S.) brand of Brompheniramine and Pseudoephedrine—**See Antihistamines and Decongestants (Systemic)**, 161

Alleract—BW (U.S.) brand of Triprolidine—**See Antihistamines (Systemic)**, 147

Aller-Chlor—Rugby (U.S.) brand of Chlorpheniramine—**See Antihistamines (Systemic)**, 147

Allercort—LaSalle (U.S.) brand of Hydrocortisone—**See Corticosteroids (Topical)**, 458

Allerdryl—ICN (Canada) brand of Diphenhydramine—**See Antihistamines (Systemic)**, 147

Allerest—Pharmacraft (U.S.) brand of Chlorpheniramine and Phenylpropanolamine—**See Antihistamines and Decongestants (Systemic)**, 161

Allerest Headache Strength—Pharmacraft (U.S.) brand of Chlorpheniramine, Phenylpropanolamine, and Acetaminophen—**See Antihistamines, Decongestants, and Analgesics (Systemic)**, 162

Allerest 12 Hour—Pharmacraft (U.S.) brand of Chlorpheniramine and Phenylpropanolamine—**See Antihistamines and Decongestants (Systemic)**, 161

Allerest 12 Hour Caplets—Fisons (U.S.) brand of Chlorpheniramine and Phenylpropanolamine—**See Antihistamines and Decongestants (Systemic)**, 161

Allerest 12 Hour Nasal Spray—Pennwalt (U.S.) brand of Oxymetazoline (Nasal), 827

Allerest No-Drowsiness—Fisons (U.S.) brand of Pseudoephedrine and Acetaminophen—**See Decongestants and Analgesics (Systemic)**, 497

Allerest Sinus Pain Formula—Pharmacraft (U.S.) brand of Chlorpheniramine, Phenylpropanolamine, and Acetaminophen—**See Antihistamines, Decongestants, and Analgesics (Systemic)**, 162

Allerfrin—Rugby (U.S.) brand of Triprolidine and Pseudoephedrine—**See Antihistamines and Decongestants (Systemic)**, 161

Allerfrin with Codeine—Rugby (U.S.) brand of Triprolidine, Pseudoephedrine, and Codeine—**See Cough/Cold Combinations (Systemic)**, 488

Allergy Formula Sinutab—Warner Lambert (U.S.) brand of Dexbrompheniramine and Pseudoephedrine—**See Antihistamines and Decongestants (Systemic)**, 161

Allergy Relief Medicine—Rugby (U.S.) brand of Chlorpheniramine and Phenylpropanolamine—**See Antihistamines and Decongestants (Systemic)**, 161

AlleRid—Murdock (U.S.) brand of Pseudoephedrine (Systemic), 936

AllerMax Caplets—Pfeiffer (U.S.) brand of Diphenhydramine—**See Antihistamines (Systemic)**, 147

Aller-med—Republic (U.S.) brand of Diphenhydramine—**See Antihistamines (Systemic)**, 147

Allerphed—Great Southern (U.S.) brand of Triprolidine and Pseudoephedrine—**See Antihistamines and Decongestants (Systemic)**, 161

Alloprin—ICN (Canada) brand of Allopurinol (Systemic), 22

Allopurinol [*Alloprin; Apo-Allopurinol; Lopurin; Novopurol; Purinol; Zyloprim*] **(Systemic)**, 22

Almacone—Rugby (U.S.) brand of Alumina, Magnesia, and Simethicone—**See Antacids (Oral-Local)**, 61

Almacone II—Rugby (U.S.) brand of Alumina, Magnesia, and Simethicone—**See Antacids (Oral-Local)**, 61

Alma-Mag Improved—Rugby (U.S.) brand of Alumina, Magnesia, and Simethicone—**See Antacids (Oral-Local)**, 61

Alma-Mag #4 Improved—Rugby (U.S.) brand of Alumina, Magnesia, and Simethicone—**See Antacids (Oral-Local)**, 61

Alophen—PD (U.S.) brand of Phenolphthalein—**See Laxatives (Local)**, 682

Alphaderm—Lemmon (U.S.) brand of Hydrocortisone—**See Corticosteroids (Topical)**, 458

Alphamine—Vortech (U.S.) brand of Hydroxocobalamin—**See Vitamin B$_{12}$ (Systemic)**, 1077

Alphamul—Lannett (U.S.) brand of Castor Oil—**See Laxatives (Local)**, 682

Alpha-Phed—Metro Med (U.S.) brand of Pseudoephedrine, Aspirin, and Caffeine—**See Decongestants and Analgesics (Systemic)**, 497

Alphatrex—Savage (U.S.) brand of Betamethasone—**See Corticosteroids (Topical)**, 458

Alphosyl—Reed & Carnrick (U.S. and Canada) brand of Coal Tar (Topical), 443

Alprazolam [*Apo-Alpraz; Novo-Alprazol; Nu-Alpraz; Xanax*] **See Benzodiazepines (Systemic)**, 251

Alprostadil [*PGE$_1$; prostaglandin E$_1$; Prostin VR; Prostin VR Pediatric*] **(Intracavernosal)**, 26

Altace—Hoechst (U.S.) brand of Ramipril—**See Angiotensin-converting Enzyme (ACE) Inhibitors (Systemic)**, 49

AlternaGEL—Johnson and Johnson-Merck (U.S.) brand of Aluminum Hydroxide—**See Antacids (Oral-Local)**, 61

Altretamine [*Hexalen; hexamethylmelamine; Hexastat*] **(Systemic)**, 27

Alu-Cap—Riker (U.S.) brand of Aluminum Hydroxide—**See Antacids (Oral-Local)**, 61

Aludrox—Wyeth-Ayerst (U.S.) brand of Alumina, Magnesia, and Simethicone—**See Antacids (Oral-Local)**, 61

Bayhistine Expectorant—Bay Labs (U.S.) brand of Pseudoephedrine, Codeine, and Guaifenesin—**See Cough/Cold Combinations (Systemic)**, 488

Baytussin AC—Bay Labs (U.S.) brand of Codeine and Guaifenesin—**See Cough/Cold Combinations (Systemic)**, 488

Baytussin DM—Bay Labs (U.S.) brand of Dextromethorphan and Guaifenesin—**See Cough/Cold Combinations (Systemic)**, 488

BC Cold Powder Non-Drowsy Formula—Block (U.S.) brand of Phenylpropanolamine and Aspirin—**See Decongestants and Analgesics (Systemic)**, 497

Beben—PD (Canada) brand of Betamethasone—**See Corticosteroids (Topical)**, 458

Because—Schering (U.S.) brand of Nonoxynol 9—**See Spermicides (Vaginal)**, 991

Beclomethasone—Beclomethasone—**See Corticosteroids (Inhalation-Local)**, 448; **Corticosteroids (Nasal)**, 455; **Corticosteroids (Topical)**, 458

Beclomethasone Dipropionate [beclometasone; *Beclovent; Beclovent Rotacaps; Vanceril*] **See Corticosteroids (Inhalation-Local)**, 448

Beclomethasone Dipropionate [beclometasone; *Beconase; Vancenase*] **See Corticosteroids (Nasal)**, 455

Beclomethasone Dipropionate [beclometasone; *Propaderm*] **See Corticosteroids (Topical)**, 458

Beclomethasone Dipropionate Monohydrate [beclometasone; *Beconase AQ; Vancenase AQ*] **See Corticosteroids (Nasal)**, 455

Beclovent—Glaxo (U.S. and Canada) brand of Beclomethasone—**See Corticosteroids (Inhalation-Local)**, 448

Beclovent Rotacaps—Glaxo (Canada) brand of Beclomethasone—**See Corticosteroids (Inhalation-Local)**, 448

Beconase—Glaxo (U.S. and Canada) and Allen & Hanburys (U.K.) brand of Beclomethasone—**See Corticosteroids (Nasal)**, 455

Beconase AQ—Glaxo (U.S. and Canada) brand of Beclomethasone—**See Corticosteroids (Nasal)**, 455

Bedoz—Nadeau (Canada) brand of Cyanocobalamin—**See Vitamin B$_{12}$ (Systemic)**, 1077

Beepen-VK—Beecham (U.S.) brand of Penicillin V—**See Penicillins (Systemic)**, 848

Beldin—Halsey (U.S.) brand of Diphenhydramine—**See Antihistamines (Systemic)**, 147

Belix—Halsey (U.S.) brand of Diphenhydramine—**See Antihistamines (Systemic)**, 147

Belladonna **See Anticholinergics/Antispasmodics (Systemic)**, 73

Belladonna Alkaloids and Barbiturates (Systemic), 246

Belladonna Extract and Butabarbital Sodium [*Butibel*] **See Belladonna Alkaloids and Barbiturates (Systemic)**, 246

Belladonna Extract and Phenobarbital [*Chardonna-2*] **See Belladonna Alkaloids and Barbiturates (Systemic)**, 246

Bellalphen—CMC-CONS (U.S.) brand of Atropine, Hyoscyamine, Scopolamine, and Phenobarbital—**See Belladonna Alkaloids and Barbiturates (Systemic)**, 246

Bell/ans—C.S. Dent (U.S.) brand of Sodium Bicarbonate (Systemic), 988

Bellergal—Sandoz (Canada) brand of Ergotamine, Belladonna Alkaloids, and Phenobarbital (Systemic), 555

Bellergal-S—Sandoz (U.S.) brand of Ergotamine, Belladonna Alkaloids, and Phenobarbital (Systemic), 555

Bellergal Spacetabs—Sandoz (Canada) brand of Ergotamine, Belladonna Alkaloids, and Phenobarbital (Systemic), 555

Bena-D 10—Seatrace (U.S.) brand of Diphenhydramine—**See Antihistamines (Systemic)**, 147

Bena-D 50—Seatrace (U.S.) brand of Diphenhydramine—**See Antihistamines (Systemic)**, 147

Benadryl—PD (U.S. and Canada) brand of Diphenhydramine—**See Antihistamines (Systemic)**, 147

Benadryl 25—PD (U.S.) brand of Diphenhydramine—**See Antihistamines (Systemic)**, 147

Benadryl Decongestant—PD (U.S.) brand of Diphenhydramine and Pseudoephedrine—**See Antihistamines and Decongestants (Systemic)**, 161

Benadryl Kapseals—PD (U.S.) brand of Diphenhydramine—**See Antihistamines (Systemic)**, 147

Benadryl Plus—PD (U.S.) brand of Diphenhydramine, Pseudoephedrine, and Acetaminophen—**See Antihistamines, Decongestants, and Analgesics (Systemic)**, 162

Benadryl Plus Nighttime Liquid—PD (U.S.) brand of Diphenhydramine, Pseudoephedrine, and Acetaminophen—**See Antihistamines, Decongestants, and Analgesics (Systemic)**, 162

Benahist 10—Keene (U.S.) brand of Diphenhydramine—**See Antihistamines (Systemic)**, 147

Benahist 50—Keene (U.S.) brand of Diphenhydramine—**See Antihistamines (Systemic)**, 147

Ben-Allergin-50—Dunhall (U.S.) brand of Diphenhydramine—**See Antihistamines (Systemic)**, 147

Benazepril Hydrochloride [*Lotensin*] **See Angiotensin-converting Enzyme (ACE) Inhibitors (Systemic)**, 49

Bendroflumethiazide [*Naturetin*] **See Diuretics, Thiazide (Systemic)**, 541

Benoject-10—Mayrand (U.S.) brand of Diphenhydramine—**See Antihistamines (Systemic)**, 147

Benoject-50—Mayrand (U.S.) brand of Diphenhydramine—**See Antihistamines (Systemic)**, 147

Bensylate—ICN (Canada) brand of Benztropine—**See Antidyskinetics (Systemic)**, 135

Bentyl—Lakeside/Merrell Dow (U.S.) brand of Dicyclomine—**See Anticholinergics/Antispasmodics (Systemic)**, 73

Bentylol—Marion Merrell Dow (Canada) brand of Dicyclomine—**See Anticholinergics/Antispasmodics (Systemic)**, 73

Benylin with Codeine—PD (Canada) brand of Diphenhydramine, Codeine, and Ammonium Chloride—**See Cough/Cold Combinations (Systemic)**, 488

Benylin Cold—PD (Canada) brand of Chlorpheniramine and Pseudoephedrine—**See Antihistamines and Decongestants (Systemic)**, 161

Benylin Cough—PD (U.S.) brand of Diphenhydramine—**See Antihistamines (Systemic)**, 147

Benylin Decongestant—PD (U.S.) brand of Diphenhydramine and Pseudoephedrine—**See Antihistamines and Decongestants (Systemic)**, 161

Benylin-DM—PD (Canada) brand of Diphenhydramine, Dextromethorphan, and Ammonium Chloride—**See Cough/Cold Combinations (Systemic)**, 488

Benylin DM—PD (U.S.) brand of Dextromethorphan (Systemic), 502

Benylin Expectorant Cough Formula—PD (U.S.) brand of Dextromethorphan and Guaifenesin—**See Cough/Cold Combinations (Systemic)**, 488

Benzalkonium Chloride [*Pharmatex*] **See Spermicides (Vaginal)**, 991

Benzathine benzylpenicillin—Penicillin G—**See Penicillins (Systemic)**, 848

Benzatropine—Benztropine—**See Antidyskinetics (Systemic)**, 135

Benzodiazepines (Systemic), 251

Benzonatate [*Tessalon*]
(**Systemic**), 266
Benzthiazide [*Exna; Hydrex*]
See **Diuretics, Thiazide (Systemic)**, 541
Benztropine Mesylate [*Apo-Benztropine; Bensylate;* benzatropine; *Cogentin; PMS Benztropine*]
See **Antidyskinetics (Systemic)**, 135
Bepadin—Wallace (U.S.) brand of Bepridil—See **Calcium Channel Blocking Agents (Systemic)**, 343
Bepridil Hydrochloride [*Bepadin; Vascor*]
See **Calcium Channel Blocking Agents (Systemic)**, 343
Berotec—Boehringer Ingelheim (Canada) brand of Fenoterol—See **Bronchodilators, Adrenergic (Systemic)**, 294
Beta-adrenergic Blocking Agents (**Systemic**), 267
Beta-adrenergic Blocking Agents and Thiazide Diuretics (**Systemic**), 283
Betacort Scalp Lotion—ICN (Canada) brand of Betamethasone—See **Corticosteroids (Topical)**, 458
Betaderm—K-Line (Canada) brand of Betamethasone—See **Corticosteroids (Topical)**, 458
Betaderm Scalp Lotion—K-Line (Canada) brand of Betamethasone—See **Corticosteroids (Topical)**, 458
Betagan C Cap B.I.D.—Allergan (U.S. and Canada) brand of Levobunolol (Ophthalmic), 692
Betagan C Cap Q.D.—Allergan (U.S.) brand of Levobunolol (Ophthalmic), 692
Betagan Standard Cap—Allergan (U.S. and Canada) brand of Levobunolol (Ophthalmic), 692
Beta-HC—Beta Dermaceuticals (U.S.) brand of Hydrocortisone—See **Corticosteroids (Topical)**, 458
Betaloc—Astra (Canada) brand of Metoprolol—See **Beta-adrenergic Blocking Agents (Systemic)**, 267
Betaloc Durules—Astra (Canada) brand of Metoprolol—See **Beta-adrenergic Blocking Agents (Systemic)**, 267
Betamethasone [*Betnelan; Betnesol; Celestone*]
See **Corticosteroids/Corticotropin— Glucocorticoid Effects (Systemic)**, 472
Betamethasone Benzoate [*Beben; Uticort*]
See **Corticosteroids (Topical)**, 458
Betamethasone Dipropionate [*Alphatrex; Diprolene; Diprosone; Maxivate; Teladar; Topilene; Topisone*]
See **Corticosteroids (Topical)**, 458
Betamethasone Dipropionate, Augmented [*Diprolene; Diprolene AF*]
See **Corticosteroids (Topical)**, 458

Betamethasone Disodium Phosphate [*Betnesol*]
See **Corticosteroids/Corticotropin— Glucocorticoid Effects (Systemic)**, 472
Betamethasone Sodium Phosphate [*Celestone; Celestone Phosphate; Selestoject*]
See **Corticosteroids/Corticotropin— Glucocorticoid Effects (Systemic)**, 472
Betamethasone Sodium Phosphate and Betamethasone Acetate [*Celestone Soluspan*]
See **Corticosteroids/Corticotropin— Glucocorticoid Effects (Systemic)**, 472
Betamethasone Valerate [*Betacort Scalp Lotion; Betaderm; Betaderm Scalp Lotion; Betatrex; Beta-Val; Betnovate; Betnovate-1/2; Celestoderm-V; Celestoderm-V/2; Dermabet; Ectosone Mild; Ectosone Regular; Ectosone Scalp Lotion; Metaderm Mild; Metaderm Regular; Novobetamet; Prevex B; Valisone; Valisone Reduced Strength; Valisone Scalp Lotion; Valnac*]
See **Corticosteroids (Topical)**, 458
Betapen-VK—Bristol (U.S.) brand of Penicillin V—See **Penicillins (Systemic)**, 848
Beta-Phed—Metro Med (U.S.) brand of Pseudoephedrine, Acetaminophen, and Caffeine—See **Decongestants and Analgesics (Systemic)**, 497
Betatrex—Savage (U.S.) brand of Betamethasone—See **Corticosteroids (Topical)**, 458
Beta-Val—Lemmon (U.S.) brand of Betamethasone—See **Corticosteroids (Topical)**, 458
Betaxolol Hydrochloride [*Betoptic; Betoptic S*]
(**Ophthalmic**), 285
Betaxolol Hydrochloride [*Kerlone*]
See **Beta-adrenergic Blocking Agents (Systemic)**, 267
Betnelan—Glaxo (Canada) brand of Betamethasone—See **Corticosteroids/ Corticotropin—Glucocorticoid Effects (Systemic)**, 472
Betnesol—Glaxo (Canada) brand of Betamethasone—See **Corticosteroids/ Corticotropin—Glucocorticoid Effects (Systemic)**, 472
Betnovate—Glaxo (Canada and U.K.) brand of Betamethasone—See **Corticosteroids (Topical)**, 458
Betnovate-1/2—Glaxo (Canada) brand of Betamethasone—See **Corticosteroids (Topical)**, 458
Betoptic—Alcon (U.S. and Canada) brand of Betaxolol (Ophthalmic), 285
Betoptic S—Alcon (U.S.) brand of Betaxolol (Ophthalmic), 285

Bexophene—Mallard (U.S.) brand of Propoxyphene and Aspirin—See **Opioid (Narcotic) Analgesics and Aspirin (Systemic)**, 822
Biaxin—Abbott (U.S.) brand of Clarithromycin (Systemic), 431
Bicillin L-A—Wyeth-Ayerst (U.S.) and Wyeth (Canada) brand of Penicillin G— See **Penicillins (Systemic)**, 848
Bicitra—Willen (U.S.) brand of Sodium Citrate and Citric Acid—See **Citrates (Systemic)**, 426
Bifenabid—Merrell Dow (Spain and Argentina) brand of Probucol (Systemic), 919
Bilagog—Wesley (U.S.) brand of Magnesium Sulfate—See **Laxatives (Local)**, 682
Bilax—Drug Industries (U.S.) brand of Dehydrocholic Acid and Docusate—See **Laxatives (Local)**, 682
BioCal—Miles (U.S.) brand of Calcium Carbonate—See **Calcium Supplements (Systemic)**, 357
Bio-Syn—Clay-Park (U.S.) brand of Fluocinolone—See **Corticosteroids (Topical)**, 458
Biotirmone—See Dextrothyroxine (Systemic), 503
Biperiden Hydrochloride [*Akineton*]
See **Antidyskinetics (Systemic)**, 135
Biperiden Lactate [*Akineton*]
See **Antidyskinetics (Systemic)**, 135
Biphetamine 12½—Fisons (U.S.) brand of Amphetamine and Dextroamphetamine Resin Complex—See **Amphetamines (Systemic)**, 35
Biphetamine 20—Fisons (U.S.) brand of Amphetamine and Dextroamphetamine Resin Complex—See **Amphetamines (Systemic)**, 35
Biphetane DC Cough—Bay Labs (U.S.) brand of Brompheniramine, Phenylpropanolamine, and Codeine—See **Cough/ Cold Combinations (Systemic)**, 488
Bisac-Evac—G&W (U.S.) brand of Bisacodyl—See **Laxatives (Local)**, 682
Bisacodyl [*Bisac-Evac; Bisacolax; Bisco-Lax; Carter's Little Pills; Dacodyl; Deficol; Dulcolax; Fleet Bisacodyl; Fleet Bisacodyl Prep; Laxit; Theralax*]
See **Laxatives (Local)**, 682
Bisacodyl and Docusate Sodium [*Dulcodos*]
See **Laxatives (Local)**, 682
Bisacodyl Tannex [*Clysodrast*]
See **Laxatives (Local)**, 682
Bisacolax—ICN (Canada) brand of Bisacodyl—See **Laxatives (Local)**, 682
Bisco-Lax—Raway (U.S.) brand of Bisacodyl—See **Laxatives (Local)**, 682
Bismuth Subsalicylate [*Pepto-Bismol*]
(**Oral-Local**), 288

Bisodol—Whitehall (U.S.) brand of Calcium Carbonate and Magnesia—**See Antacids (Oral-Local)**; Magnesium Carbonate and Sodium Bicarbonate—**See Antacids (Oral-Local)**, 61

Bitolterol Mesylate [*Tornalate*]
   See Bronchodilators, Adrenergic (Systemic), 294

Black-Draught—Chattem (U.S.) brand of Casanthranol—**See Laxatives (Local)**, 682

Black-Draught Lax-Senna—Chattem (U.S.) brand of Senna—**See Laxatives (Local)**, 682

Blanex—Edwards (U.S.) brand of Orphenadrine—**See Skeletal Muscle Relaxants (Systemic)**, 979

Bleph-10—Allergan (U.S. and Canada) brand of Sulfacetamide—**See Sulfonamides (Ophthalmic)**, 1009

Blocadren—MSD (U.S.) and Frosst (Canada) brand of Timolol—**See Beta-adrenergic Blocking Agents (Systemic)**, 267

BQ Cold—Bristol-Myers (U.S.) brand of Chlorpheniramine, Phenylpropanolamine, and Acetaminophen—**See Antihistamines, Decongestants, and Analgesics (Systemic)**, 162

Breonesin—Sterling Winthrop (U.S.) brand of Guaifenesin (Systemic), 606

Brethaire—Geigy (U.S.) brand of Terbutaline—**See Bronchodilators, Adrenergic (Systemic)**, 294

Brethine—Geigy (U.S.) brand of Terbutaline—**See Bronchodilators, Adrenergic (Systemic)**, 294

Brexin—Savage (U.S.) brand of Carbinoxamine, Pseudoephedrine, and Guaifenesin—**See Cough/Cold Combinations (Systemic)**, 488

Brexin L.A.—Savage (U.S.) brand of Chlorpheniramine and Pseudoephedrine—**See Antihistamines and Decongestants (Systemic)**, 161

Bricanyl—Lakeside/Merrell Dow (U.S.) and Astra (Canada) brand of Terbutaline—**See Bronchodilators, Adrenergic (Systemic)**, 294

Bromanate DC Cough—Barre (U.S.); Bioline (U.S.); Dixon-Shane (U.S.); Gen-King (U.S.); Harber (U.S.); Parmed (U.S.); Perrigo (U.S.); United Research (U.S.); and Williams (U.S.) brand of Brompheniramine, Phenylpropanolamine, and Codeine—**See Cough/Cold Combinations (Systemic)**, 488

Bromatap—Goldline (U.S.) brand of Brompheniramine and Phenylpropanolamine—**See Antihistamines and Decongestants (Systemic)**, 161

Bromatapp—Copley (U.S.) brand of Brompheniramine and Phenylpropanolamine—**See Antihistamines and Decongestants (Systemic)**, 161

Bromazepam [*Lectopam*]
   See Benzodiazepines (Systemic), 251

Bromazine—Bromodiphenhydramine—**See Antihistamines (Systemic)**, 147

Bromfed—Muro (U.S.) brand of Brompheniramine and Pseudoephedrine—**See Antihistamines and Decongestants (Systemic)**, 161

Bromfed-AT—Muro (U.S.) brand of Brompheniramine, Pseudoephedrine, and Dextromethorphan—**See Cough/Cold Combinations (Systemic)**, 488

Bromfed-DM—Muro (U.S.) brand of Brompheniramine, Pseudoephedrine, and Dextromethorphan—**See Cough/Cold Combinations (Systemic)**, 488

Bromfed-PD—Muro (U.S.) brand of Brompheniramine and Pseudoephedrine—**See Antihistamines and Decongestants (Systemic)**, 161

Bromocriptine Mesylate [*Parlodel*] (Systemic), 290

Bromodiphenhydramine [bromazine] (Systemic), 147

Bromodiphenhydramine Hydrochloride and Codeine Phosphate [*Ambay Cough; Ambenyl Cough*]
   See Cough/Cold Combinations (Systemic), 488

Bromodiphenhydramine Hydrochloride, Diphenhydramine Hydrochloride, Codeine Phosphate, Ammonium Chloride, and Potassium Guaiacolsulfonate [*Ambophen Expectorant*]
   See Cough/Cold Combinations (Systemic), 488

Bromophen T.D.—Rugby (U.S.) brand of Brompheniramine, Phenylephrine, and Phenylpropanolamine—**See Antihistamines and Decongestants (Systemic)**, 161

Bromphen—Schein (U.S.) brand of Brompheniramine—**See Antihistamines (Systemic)**, 147

Bromphen DC with Codeine Cough—Rugby (U.S.) brand of Brompheniramine, Phenylpropanolamine, and Codeine—**See Cough/Cold Combinations (Systemic)**, 488

Brompheniramine Maleate [*Bromphen; Chlorphed; Codimal-A; Conjec-B; Cophene-B; Dehist; Diamine T.D.; Dimetane; Dimetane Extentabs; Histaject Modified; Nasahist B; ND-Stat Revised; Oraminic II; Veltane*]
   See Antihistamines (Systemic), 147

Brompheniramine Maleate and Phenylephrine Hydrochloride [*Dimetane Decongestant; Dimetane Decongestant Caplets*]
   See Antihistamines and Decongestants (Systemic), 161

Brompheniramine Maleate, Phenylephrine Hydrochloride, and Phenylpropanolamine Hydrochloride [*Bromophen T.D.; Dimaphen S.A.; Dimetapp; Dimetapp Extentabs; Dimetapp Oral Infant Drops; Normatane; Tamine S.R.; Veltap*]
   See Antihistamines and Decongestants (Systemic), 161

Brompheniramine Maleate, Phenylephrine Hydrochloride, Phenylpropanolamine Hydrochloride, and Acetaminophen [*Dimetapp-A; Dimetapp-A Pediatric*]
   See Antihistamines, Decongestants, and Analgesics (Systemic), 162

Brompheniramine Maleate, Phenylephrine Hydrochloride, Phenylpropanolamine Hydrochloride, and Codeine Phosphate [*Dimetapp with Codeine*]
   See Cough/Cold Combinations (Systemic), 488

Brompheniramine Maleate, Phenylephrine Hydrochloride, Phenylpropanolamine Hydrochloride, Codeine Phosphate, and Guaifenesin [*Dimetane Expectorant-C*]
   See Cough/Cold Combinations (Systemic), 488

Brompheniramine Maleate, Phenylephrine Hydrochloride, Phenylpropanolamine Hydrochloride, and Dextromethorphan Hydrobromide [*Dimetapp-DM*]
   See Cough/Cold Combinations (Systemic), 488

Brompheniramine Maleate, Phenylephrine Hydrochloride, Phenylpropanolamine Hydrochloride, and Guaifenesin [*Dimetane Expectorant*]
   See Cough/Cold Combinations (Systemic), 488

Brompheniramine Maleate, Phenylephrine Hydrochloride, Phenylpropanolamine Hydrochloride, Hydrocodone Bitartrate, and Guaifenesin [*Dimetane Expectorant-DC*]
   See Cough/Cold Combinations (Systemic), 488

Brompheniramine Maleate, Phenylpropanolamine Bitartrate, and Aspirin [*Alka-Seltzer Plus Maximum Strength Sinus Allergy Medicine*]
   See Antihistamines, Decongestants, and Analgesics (Systemic), 162

Brompheniramine Maleate and Phenylpropanolamine Hydrochloride [*Bromatap; Bromatapp; Dimetapp; Dimetapp Extentabs; Genatap; Myphetapp*]
   See Antihistamines and Decongestants (Systemic), 161

Brompheniramine Maleate, Phenylpropano-
lamine Hydrochloride, and Acetamino-
phen [*Dimetapp Plus Caplets*]
　　See Antihistamines, Decongestants, and
　　Analgesics (Systemic), 162
Brompheniramine Maleate, Phenylpropano-
lamine Hydrochloride, and Codeine
Phosphate [*Biphetane DC Cough;*
Bromanate DC Cough; Bromphen DC
with Codeine Cough; Dimetane-DC
Cough; Myphetane DC Cough;
Normatane DC; Poly-Histine-CS]
　　See Cough/Cold Combinations (Sys-
　　temic), 488
Brompheniramine Maleate, Phenylpropano-
lamine Hydrochloride, and
Dextromethorphan Hydrobromide
[*Dimetapp DM Cough and Cold; Poly-*
Histine-DM]
　　See Cough/Cold Combinations (Sys-
　　temic), 488
Brompheniramine Maleate,
Phenyltoloxamine Citrate, and
Phenylephrine Hydrochloride [*Atrohist*
Sprinkle]
　　See Antihistamines and Decongestants
　　(Systemic), 161
Brompheniramine Maleate and Pseudoephed-
rine Hydrochloride [*Allent; Bromfed;*
Bromfed-PD; Dallergy Jr.; Endafed]
　　See Antihistamines and Decongestants
　　(Systemic), 161
Brompheniramine Maleate, Pseudoephedrine
Hydrochloride, and Dextromethorphan
Hydrobromide [*Bromfed-AT; Bromfed-*
DM; Brotane DX Cough; Dimetane-DX
Cough]
　　See Cough/Cold Combinations (Sys-
　　temic), 488
Brompheniramine Maleate and Pseudoephed-
rine Sulfate [*Drixoral*]
　　See Antihistamines and Decongestants
　　(Systemic), 161
Brompheril—Copley (U.S.) brand of
Dexbrompheniramine and Pseudoephed-
rine—**See Antihistamines and**
Decongestants (Systemic), 161
Bronalide—Syntex (Canada) brand of
Flunisolide—**See Corticosteroids**
(Inhalation-Local), 448
Bronchial—Geneva Generics (U.S.) and H.
L. Moore (U.S.) brand of Theophylline
and Guaifenesin (Systemic), 1032
Bronchodilators, Adrenergic
(Systemic), 294
Bronchodilators, Xanthine-derivative
(Systemic), 315
Broncho-Grippol-DM—Charton (Canada)
brand of Dextromethorphan (Systemic),
502

Broncholate—Bock (U.S.) brand of
Ephedrine and Guaifenesin—**See**
Cough/Cold Combinations (Systemic),
488
Brondecon—PD (U.S.) brand of
Oxtriphylline and Guaifenesin (Sys-
temic), 825
Brondelate—Balan (U.S.); Barre (U.S.);
CMC-CONS (U.S.); Dixon-Shane
(U.S.); Gen-King (U.S.); Harber (U.S.);
Major (U.S.); Schein (U.S.); and Texas
Drug (U.S.) brand of Oxtriphylline and
Guaifenesin (Systemic), 825
Bronitin Mist—Whitehall (U.S.) brand of
Epinephrine—**See Bronchodilators,**
Adrenergic (Systemic), 294
Bronkaid Mist—Sterling Winthrop (U.S.)
brand of Epinephrine—**See**
Bronchodilators, Adrenergic
(Systemic), 294
Bronkaid Mistometer—Sterling Winthrop
(Canada) brand of Epinephrine—**See**
Bronchodilators, Adrenergic
(Systemic), 294
Bronkaid Mist Suspension—Sterling
Winthrop (U.S.) brand of Epinephrine—
See Bronchodilators, Adrenergic
(Systemic), 294
Bronkephrine—Sterling Winthrop (U.S.)
brand of Ethylnorepinephrine—**See**
Bronchodilators, Adrenergic
(Systemic), 294
Bronkodyl—Sterling Winthrop (U.S.) brand
of Theophylline—**See Bronchodilators,**
Xanthine-derivative (Systemic), 315
Bronkometer—Sterling Winthrop (U.S.)
brand of Isoetharine—**See**
Bronchodilators, Adrenergic
(Systemic), 294
Bronkosol—Sterling Winthrop (U.S.) brand
of Isoetharine—**See Bronchodilators,**
Adrenergic (Systemic), 294
Bronkotuss Expectorant—Hyrex (U.S.) brand
of Chlorpheniramine, Ephedrine, and
Guaifenesin—**See Cough/Cold**
Combinations (Systemic), 488
Brotane DX Cough—Bioline (U.S.) brand of
Brompheniramine, Pseudoephedrine,
and Dextromethorphan—**See Cough/**
Cold Combinations (Systemic), 488
Bucet—UAD (U.S.) brand of Butalbital and
Acetaminophen—**See Barbiturates and**
Analgesics (Systemic), 233
Buffaprin—Buffington (U.S.) brand of
Aspirin, Buffered—**See Salicylates**
(Systemic), 953
Bufferin—Bristol-Myers (U.S. and Canada)
brand of Aspirin, Buffered—**See**
Salicylates (Systemic), 953
Buffets II—Jones (U.S.) brand of Acetamino-
phen, Aspirin, and Caffeine, Buffered—
See Acetaminophen and Salicylates
(Systemic), 5

Buffinol—Otis Clapp (U.S.) brand of Aspirin,
Buffered—**See Salicylates (Systemic),**
953
Buf-Puf Acne Cleansing Bar with Vitamin
E—Personal Care Products/3M (U.S.)
brand of Salicylic Acid (Topical), 968
Bumetanide [*Bumex*]
　　See Diuretics, Loop (Systemic), 524
Bumex—Roche (U.S.) brand of
Bumetanide—**See Diuretics, Loop**
(Systemic), 524
Buprenex—Reckitt and Colman (U.S.) brand
of Buprenorphine (Systemic), 330
Buprenorphine Hydrochloride [*Buprenex*]
(Systemic), 330
Bupropion Hydrochloride [amfebutamone;
Wellbutrin]
(Systemic), 334
Buscopan—Boehringer Ingelheim (Canada)
brand of Scopolamine—**See Anticholin-**
ergics/Antispasmodics (Systemic), 73
Busodium—Truxton (U.S.) brand of
Butabarbital—**See Barbiturates**
(Systemic), 223
BuSpar—Mead Johnson (U.S.) and Bristol
(Canada) brand of Buspirone (Sys-
temic), 336
Buspirone Hydrochloride [*BuSpar*]
(Systemic), 336
Busulfan [*Myleran*]
(Systemic), 337
Butabarbital Sodium [*Busodium; Butalan;*
Butisol; Sarisol No. 2]
　　See Barbiturates (Systemic), 223
Butace—American Urologicals (U.S.) brand
of Butalbital, Acetaminophen, and
Caffeine—**See Barbiturates and**
Analgesics (Systemic), 233
Butalan—Lannett (U.S.) brand of
Butabarbital—**See Barbiturates**
(Systemic), 223
Butalbital-AC—Butalbital, Aspirin, and
Caffeine—**See Barbiturates and**
Analgesics (Systemic), 233
Butalbital and Acetaminophen [*Bancap;*
Bucet; Conten; Phrenilin; Phrenilin
Forte; Sedapap; Tencon; Triaprin]
　　See Barbiturates and Analgesics
　　(Systemic), 233
Butalbital, Acetaminophen, and Caffeine
[*Amaphen; Anolor-300; Anoquan;*
Arcet; Butace; Dolmar; Endolor; Esgic;
Esgic-Plus; Ezol; Femcet; Fioricet;
Isocet; Isopap; Medigesic; Pacaps;
Pharmagesic; Repan; Tencet; Triad;
Two-Dyne]
　　See Barbiturates and Analgesics
　　(Systemic), 233
Butalbital and Aspirin [*Axotal*]
　　See Barbiturates and Analgesics
　　(Systemic), 233

Butalbital, Aspirin, and Caffeine [butalbital-AC; butalbital compound; *Butalgen; Fiorgen; Fiorinal; Fiormor; Fortabs; Isobutal; Isobutyl; Isolin; Isollyl; Laniroif; Lanorinal; Marnal; Tecnal; Vibutal*]
See Barbiturates and Analgesics (Systemic), 233

Butalbital, Aspirin, Codeine Phosphate, and Caffeine [*Ascomp with Codeine No.3; Butalbital Compound with Codeine; Butinal with Codeine No.3; Fiorinal-C 1/4; Fiorinal-C 1/2; Fiorinal with Codeine No.3; Idenal with Codeine; Isollyl with Codeine; Tecnal-C 1/4; Tecnal-C 1/2*]
See Barbiturates and Analgesics (Systemic), 233

Butalbital compound—Butalbital, Aspirin, and Caffeine—**See Barbiturates and Analgesics (Systemic)**, 233

Butalbital Compound with Codeine—Best Generics (U.S.); Dixon-Shane (U.S.); Parmed (U.S.); and Qualitest (U.S.) brand of Butalbital, Aspirin, Codeine, and Caffeine—**See Barbiturates and Analgesics (Systemic)**, 233

Butalgen—Genetco (U.S.) brand of Butalbital, Aspirin, and Caffeine—**See Barbiturates and Analgesics (Systemic)**, 233

Butatab—Hauck (U.S.) brand of Phenylbutazone—**See Anti-inflammatory Analgesics, Nonsteroidal (Systemic)**, 168

Butazolidin—Geigy (U.S. and Canada) brand of Phenylbutazone—**See Anti-inflammatory Analgesics, Nonsteroidal (Systemic)**, 168

Butazone—Major (U.S.) brand of Phenylbutazone—**See Anti-inflammatory Analgesics, Nonsteroidal (Systemic)**, 168

Butibel—Wallace (U.S.) brand of Belladonna and Butabarbital—**See Belladonna Alkaloids and Barbiturates (Systemic)**, 246

Butinal with Codeine No.3—Breckenridge (U.S.) brand of Butalbital, Aspirin, Codeine, and Caffeine—**See Barbiturates and Analgesics (Systemic)**, 233

Butisol—Wallace (U.S.) and Horner (Canada) brand of Butabarbital—**See Barbiturates (Systemic)**, 223

Butoconazole Nitrate [*Femstat*]
See Antifungals, Azole (Vaginal), 140

Butorphanol Tartrate [*Stadol*]
See Opioid (Narcotic) Analgesics (Systemic), 793

Bydramine Cough—Major (U.S.) brand of Diphenhydramine—**See Antihistamines (Systemic)**, 147

C

C2—Wampole (Canada) brand of Aspirin and Caffeine—**See Salicylates (Systemic)**, 953

Cafergot—Sandoz (U.S. and Canada) brand of Ergotamine and Caffeine—**See Vascular Headache Suppressants, Ergot Derivative-containing (Systemic)**, 1066

Cafergot-PB—Sandoz (Canada) brand of Ergotamine, Caffeine, Belladonna Alkaloids, and Pentobarbital—**See Vascular Headache Suppressants, Ergot Derivative-containing (Systemic)**, 1066

Cafertine—Balan (U.S.) brand of Ergotamine and Caffeine—**See Vascular Headache Suppressants, Ergot Derivative-containing (Systemic)**, 1066

Cafetrate—Qualitest (U.S.) brand of Ergotamine and Caffeine—**See Vascular Headache Suppressants, Ergot Derivative-containing (Systemic)**, 1066

Calan—Searle (U.S.) brand of Verapamil—**See Calcium Channel Blocking Agents (Systemic)**, 343

Calan SR—Searle (U.S.) brand of Verapamil—**See Calcium Channel Blocking Agents (Systemic)**, 343

Calcarb 600—Goldline (U.S.) brand of Calcium Carbonate—**See Calcium Supplements (Systemic)**, 357

Calcibind—Mission (U.S.) brand of Cellulose Sodium Phosphate (Systemic), 387

Calci-Chew—R & D (U.S.) brand of Calcium Carbonate—**See Calcium Supplements (Systemic)**, 357

Calciday 667—Nature's Bounty (U.S.) brand of Calcium Carbonate—**See Calcium Supplements (Systemic)**, 357

Calcidrine—Abbott (U.S.) brand of Codeine and Calcium Iodide—**See Cough/Cold Combinations (Systemic)**, 488

Calciject—Omega (Canada) brand of Calcium Chloride—**See Calcium Supplements (Systemic)**, 357

Calcilac—Schein (U.S.) brand of Calcium Carbonate—**See Antacids (Oral-Local)**, 61; **Calcium Supplements (Systemic)**, 357

Calcimar—Rorer (U.S. and Canada) brand of Calcitonin-Salmon—**See Calcitonin (Systemic)**, 341

Calcite 500—Riva (Canada) brand of Calcium Carbonate—**See Calcium Supplements (Systemic)**, 357

Calcitonin (Systemic), 341

Calcitonin-Human [*Cibacalcin*]
See Calcitonin (Systemic), 341

Calcitonin-Salmon [*Calcimar; Miacalcin*]
See Calcitonin (Systemic), 341

Calcium 500—Trianon (Canada) brand of Calcium Carbonate—**See Calcium Supplements (Systemic)**, 357

Calcium 600—Schein (U.S.) brand of Calcium Carbonate—**See Calcium Supplements (Systemic)**, 357

Calcium Carbonate [*Alka-Mints; Amitone; Calcilac; Calglycine; Chooz; Dicarbosil; Equilet; Genalac; Glycate; Mallamint; Rolaids Calcium Rich; Titracid; Titralac; Titralac Extra Strength; Tums; Tums E-X; Tums Liquid Extra Strength*]
See Antacids (Oral-Local), 61

Calcium Carbonate [*Apo-Cal; BioCal; Calcarb 600; Calci-Chew; Calciday 667; Calcilac; Calcite 500; Calcium 500; Calcium 600; Calglycine; Calsan; Caltrate 300; Caltrate 600; Caltrate Chewable; Chooz; Dicarbosil; Gencalc; Mallamint; Mega-Cal; Nephro-Calci; Nu-Cal; Os-Cal; Os-Cal 500; Os-Cal Chewable; Oysco; Oysco 500 Chewable; Oyst-Cal 500; Oyst-Cal 500 Chewable; Oystercal 500; Rolaids Calcium Rich; Super Calcium 1200; Titralac; Tums; Tums E-X*]
See Calcium Supplements (Systemic), 357

Calcium Carbonate and Magnesia [*Bisodol; Rolaids Sodium Free*]
See Antacids (Oral-Local), 61

Calcium Carbonate, Magnesia, and Simethicone [*Advanced Formula Di-Gel*]
See Antacids (Oral-Local), 61

Calcium and Magnesium Carbonates [*Marblen; Noralac; Spastosed*]
See Antacids (Oral-Local), 61

Calcium and Magnesium Carbonates and Magnesium Oxide [*Alkets*]
See Antacids (Oral-Local), 61

Calcium Carbonate and Simethicone [*Titralac Plus; Tums Liquid Extra Strength with Simethicone*]
See Antacids (Oral-Local), 61

Calcium Channel Blocking Agents (Systemic), 343

Calcium Chloride [*Calciject*]
See Calcium Supplements (Systemic), 357

Calcium Citrate [*Citracal; Citracal Liquitabs*]
See Calcium Supplements (Systemic), 357

Calcium Glubionate [*Calcium-Sandoz; Neo-Calglucon*]
See Calcium Supplements (Systemic), 357

Calcium Gluceptate [calcium glucoheptonate]
See Calcium Supplements (Systemic), 357

Calcium Gluceptate and Calcium Gluconate [*Calcium Stanley*]
See Calcium Supplements (Systemic), 357

Calcium glucoheptonate—Calcium Gluceptate—**See Calcium Supplements (Systemic)**, 357

Calcium Gluconate [*Kalcinate*]
See Calcium Supplements (Systemic), 357

Calcium Glycerophosphate and Calcium Lactate [*Calphosan*]
See Calcium Supplements (Systemic), 357

Calcium Lactate
See Calcium Supplements (Systemic), 357

Calcium Lactate-Gluconate and Calcium Carbonate [*Calcium-Sandoz Forte; Gramcal*]
See Calcium Supplements (Systemic), 357

Calcium Phosphate, Dibasic
See Calcium Supplements (Systemic), 357

Calcium Phosphate, Tribasic [*Posture*]
See Calcium Supplements (Systemic), 357

Calcium Polycarbophil [*Equalactin; Fibercon; Mitrolan*]
See Laxatives (Local), 682

Calcium-Sandoz—Sandoz (Canada) brand of Calcium Glubionate—**See Calcium Supplements (Systemic)**, 357

Calcium-Sandoz Forte—Sandoz (Canada) brand of Calcium Lactate-Gluconate and Calcium Carbonate—**See Calcium Supplements (Systemic)**, 357

Calcium Stanley—Stanley (Canada) brand of Calcium Gluceptate and Calcium Gluconate—**See Calcium Supplements (Systemic)**, 357

Calcium Supplements **(Systemic)**, 357

CaldeCORT Anti-Itch—Pharmacraft (U.S.) brand of Hydrocortisone—**See Corticosteroids (Topical)**, 458

CaldeCORT Light—Pharmacraft (U.S.) brand of Hydrocortisone—**See Corticosteroids (Topical)**, 458

Caldomine-DH Forte—Technilab (Canada) brand of Pheniramine, Pyrilamine, Phenylpropanolamine, and Hydrocodone—**See Cough/Cold Combinations (Systemic)**, 488

Caldomine-DH Pediatric—Technilab (Canada) brand of Pheniramine, Pyrilamine, Phenylpropanolamine, and Hydrocodone—**See Cough/Cold Combinations (Systemic)**, 488

Calglycine—Rugby (U.S.) brand of Calcium Carbonate—**See Antacids (Oral-Local)**, 61; **Calcium Supplements (Systemic)**, 357

Calicylic Creme—Gordon (U.S.) brand of Salicylic Acid (Topical), 968

Calm X—Republic (U.S.) brand of Dimenhydrinate—**See Antihistamines (Systemic)**, 147

Calmylin with Codeine—Technilab (Canada) brand of Diphenhydramine, Codeine, and Ammonium Chloride—**See Cough/Cold Combinations (Systemic)**, 488

Calphosan—Glenwood (U.S.) brand of Calcium Glycerophosphate and Calcium Lactate—**See Calcium Supplements (Systemic)**, 357

Calsan—Sandoz (Canada) brand of Calcium Carbonate—**See Calcium Supplements (Systemic)**, 357

Caltrate 300—Lederle (Canada) brand of Calcium Carbonate—**See Calcium Supplements (Systemic)**, 357

Caltrate 600—Lederle (U.S. and Canada) brand of Calcium Carbonate—**See Calcium Supplements (Systemic)**, 357

Caltrate Chewable—Lederle (Canada) brand of Calcium Carbonate—**See Calcium Supplements (Systemic)**, 357

Cama Arthritis Pain Reliever—Sandoz Consumer (U.S.) brand of Aspirin, Alumina, and Magnesium Oxide—**See Salicylates (Systemic)**, 953

Camalox—Rorer (U.S.) brand of Alumina, Magnesia, and Calcium Carbonate—**See Antacids (Oral-Local)**, 61

Cam-Ap-Es—Camall (U.S.) brand of Reserpine, Hydralazine, and Hydrochlorothiazide (Systemic), 950

Camphorated opium tincture—*See* Paregoric (Systemic), 838

Canesten—Miles (Canada) brand of Clotrimazole—**See Antifungals, Azole (Vaginal)**, 140

Canesten 1—Miles (Canada) brand of Clotrimazole—**See Antifungals, Azole (Vaginal)**, 140

Canesten 3—Miles (Canada) brand of Clotrimazole—**See Antifungals, Azole (Vaginal)**, 140

Canesten 10%—Miles (Canada) brand of Clotrimazole—**See Antifungals, Azole (Vaginal)**, 140

Cantil—Merrell Dow (U.S.) brand of Mepenzolate—**See Anticholinergics/Antispasmodics (Systemic)**, 73

Capen—Phoenix (Argentina) brand of Tiopronin (Systemic), 1052

Capital with Codeine—Carnrick (U.S.) brand of Acetaminophen and Codeine—**See Opioid (Narcotic) Analgesics and Acetaminophen (Systemic)**, 820

Capitrol—Westwood (U.S.) brand of Chloroxine (Topical), 418

Capoten—Squibb (U.S. and Canada) brand of Captopril—**See Angiotensin-converting Enzyme (ACE) Inhibitors (Systemic)**, 49

Capozide—Squibb (U.S.) brand of Captopril and Hydrochlorothiazide—**See Angiotensin-converting Enzyme (ACE) Inhibitors and Hydrochlorothiazide (Systemic)**, 56

Capsaicin [*Axsain; Zostrix; Zostrix-HP*] **(Topical)**, 366

Captimer—Fresenius (Germany) brand of Tiopronin (Systemic), 1052

Captopril [*Capoten*]
See Angiotensin-converting Enzyme (ACE) Inhibitors (Systemic), 49

Captopril and Hydrochlorothiazide [*Capozide*]
See Angiotensin-converting Enzyme (ACE) Inhibitors and Hydrochlorothiazide (Systemic), 56

Carafate—Marion (U.S.) brand of Sucralfate (Oral-Local), 997

Carbachol [carbamylcholine; *Isopto Carbachol; Miostat*] **(Ophthalmic)**, 368

Carbacot—Truxton (U.S.) brand of Methocarbamol—**See Skeletal Muscle Relaxants (Systemic)**, 979

Carbamazepine [*Apo-Carbamazepine; Epitol; Mazepine; Novocarbamaz; PMS Carbamazepine; Tegretol; Tegretol Chewtabs; Tegretol CR*] **(Systemic)**, 369

Carbamylcholine—*See* Carbachol (Ophthalmic), 368

Carbenicillin Disodium [*Geopen; Pyopen*]
See Penicillins (Systemic), 848

Carbenicillin Indanyl Sodium [carindacillin; *Geocillin; Geopen Oral*]
See Penicillins (Systemic), 848

Carbidopa and Levodopa [*Sinemet; Sinemet CR*] **(Systemic)**, 375

Carbinoxamine
See Antihistamines (Systemic), 147

Carbinoxamine Compound—PBI (U.S.) brand of Carbinoxamine, Pseudoephedrine, and Dextromethorphan—**See Cough/Cold Combinations (Systemic)**, 488

Carbinoxamine Maleate and Pseudoephedrine Hydrochloride [*Carbiset; Carbodec; Carbodec TR; Cardec-S; Rondec; Rondec Drops; Rondec-TR*]
See Antihistamines and Decongestants (Systemic), 161

Carbinoxamine Maleate, Pseudoephedrine Hydrochloride, and Dextromethorphan Hydrobromide [*Baydec DM Drops; Carbinoxamine Compound; Carbodec DM Drops; Pseudo-Car DM; Rondec-DM; Rondec-DM Drops; Tussafed*]
See Cough/Cold Combinations (Systemic), 488

Carbinoxamine Maleate, Pseudoephedrine Hydrochloride, and Guaifenesin [*Brexin*]
See Cough/Cold Combinations (Systemic), 488

Carbiset—Nutripharm (U.S.) brand of Carbinoxamine and Pseudoephedrine— **See Antihistamines and Decongestants (Systemic),** 161

Carbodec—Rugby (U.S.) brand of Carbinoxamine and Pseudoephedrine— **See Antihistamines and Decongestants (Systemic),** 161

Carbodec DM Drops—Rugby (U.S.) brand of Carbinoxamine, Pseudoephedrine, and Dextromethorphan—**See Cough/ Cold Combinations (Systemic),** 488

Carbodec TR—Rugby (U.S.) brand of Carbinoxamine and Pseudoephedrine— **See Antihistamines and Decongestants (Systemic),** 161

Carbohydrates and Electrolytes **(Systemic),** 379

Carbolith—ICN (Canada) brand of Lithium (Systemic), 699

Carbonic Anhydrase Inhibitors **(Systemic),** 382

Carboxymethylcellulose Sodium, Casanthranol, and Docusate Sodium [*Disolan Forte*]
See Laxatives (Local), 682

Carboxymethylcellulose Sodium and Docusate Sodium [*Disoplex*]
See Laxatives (Local), 682

Cardec-S—Balan (U.S.); Barre (U.S.); Goldline (U.S.); Murray (U.S.); Parmed (U.S.); and Williams (U.S.) brand of Carbinoxamine and Pseudoephedrine— **See Antihistamines and Decongestants (Systemic),** 161

Cardene—Syntex (U.S.) and Syntex/Ayerst (Canada) brand of Nicardipine—**See Calcium Channel Blocking Agents (Systemic),** 343

Cardilate—BW (U.S. and Canada) brand of Erythrityl Tetranitrate—**See Nitrates (Systemic),** 770

Cardioquin—Purdue Frederick (U.S. and Canada) brand of Quinidine (Systemic), 942

Cardizem—Marion (U.S.) and Marion Merrell Dow (Canada) brand of Diltiazem—**See Calcium Channel Blocking Agents (Systemic),** 343

Cardizem CD—Marion (U.S.) brand of Diltiazem—**See Calcium Channel Blocking Agents (Systemic),** 343

Cardizem SR—Marion (U.S.) and Marion Merrell Dow (Canada) brand of Diltiazem—**See Calcium Channel Blocking Agents (Systemic),** 343

Cardura—Pfizer-Roerig (U.S.) and Astra (Canada) brand of Doxazosin (Systemic), 548

Carindacillin—Carbenicillin—**See Penicillins (Systemic),** 848

Carisoprodol [*Rela; Sodol; Soma; Soprodol; Soridol*]
See Skeletal Muscle Relaxants (Systemic), 979

Carmol-HC—Syntex (U.S.) brand of Hydrocortisone—**See Corticosteroids (Topical),** 458

Caroid Laxative—Sterling Winthrop (U.S.) brand of Cascara Sagrada and Phenolphthalein—**See Laxatives (Local),** 682

Carteolol Hydrochloride [*Cartrol*]
See Beta-adrenergic Blocking Agents (Systemic), 267

Carter's Little Pills—Carter (U.S.) brand of Bisacodyl—**See Laxatives (Local),** 682

Cartrol—Abbott (U.S.) brand of Carteolol— **See Beta-adrenergic Blocking Agents (Systemic),** 267

Casanthranol [*Black-Draught*]
See Laxatives (Local), 682

Casanthranol and Docusate Potassium [*Dialose Plus; Diocto-K Plus; Docu-K Plus; DSMC Plus*]
See Laxatives (Local), 682

Casanthranol and Docusate Sodium [*Afko-Lube Lax; Diocto-C; Diothron; Disanthrol; Di-Sosul Forte; D-S-S plus; Molatoc-CST; Peri-Colace; Pro-Sof Plus; Regulace*]
See Laxatives (Local), 682

Cascara Sagrada
See Laxatives (Local), 682

Cascara Sagrada and Aloe [*Nature's Remedy*]
See Laxatives (Local), 682

Cascara Sagrada Extract and Phenolphthalein [*Caroid Laxative*]
See Laxatives (Local), 682

Castor Oil [*Alphamul; Emulsoil; Fleet Flavored Castor Oil; Kellogg's Castor Oil; Neoloid; Purge*]
See Laxatives (Local), 682

Catapres—Boehringer Ingelheim (U.S. and Canada) brand of Clonidine (Systemic), 438

Catapres-TTS—Boehringer Ingelheim (U.S.) brand of Clonidine (Systemic), 438

C2 Buffered—Wampole (Canada) brand of Aspirin, Buffered, and Caffeine—**See Salicylates (Systemic),** 953

C2 Buffered with Codeine—Wampole (Canada) brand of Aspirin, Codeine, Alumina, and Magnesia—**See Opioid (Narcotic) Analgesics and Aspirin (Systemic),** 822

CCNU—*See* Lomustine (Systemic), 703

C2 with Codeine—Wampole (Canada) brand of Aspirin and Codeine—**See Opioid (Narcotic) Analgesics and Aspirin (Systemic),** 822

Ceclor—Lilly (U.S. and Canada) brand of Cefaclor—**See Cephalosporins (Systemic),** 389

Cedilanid—Sandoz (Canada) brand of Deslanoside—**See Digitalis Glycosides (Systemic),** 510

Cedilanid-D—Sandoz (U.S.) brand of Deslanoside—**See Digitalis Glycosides (Systemic),** 510

Cedocard-SR—Pharmascience (Canada) brand of Isosorbide Dinitrate—**See Nitrates (Systemic),** 770

CeeNU—Bristol (U.S. and Canada) brand of Lomustine (Systemic), 703

Cefaclor [*Ceclor*]
See Cephalosporins (Systemic), 389

Cefadroxil [*Duricef; Ultracef*]
See Cephalosporins (Systemic), 389

Cefadyl—Bristol (U.S. and Canada) brand of Cephapirin—**See Cephalosporins (Systemic),** 389

Cefamandole Nafate [*Mandol*]
See Cephalosporins (Systemic), 389

Cefanex—Bristol Myers (U.S.) brand of Cephalexin—**See Cephalosporins (Systemic),** 389

Cefazolin Sodium [*Ancef; Kefzol; Zolicef*]
See Cephalosporins (Systemic), 389

Cefixime [*Suprax*]
See Cephalosporins (Systemic), 389

Cefizox—SKF (U.S. and Canada) brand of Ceftizoxime—**See Cephalosporins (Systemic),** 389

Cefmetazole Sodium [*Zefazone*]
See Cephalosporins (Systemic), 389

Cefobid—Roerig (U.S.) and Pfizer (Canada) brand of Cefoperazone—**See Cephalosporins (Systemic),** 389

Cefonicid Sodium [*Monocid*]
See Cephalosporins (Systemic), 389

Cefoperazone Sodium [*Cefobid*]
See Cephalosporins (Systemic), 389

Ceforanide [*Precef*]
See Cephalosporins (Systemic), 389

Cefotan—Stuart (U.S. and Canada) brand of Cefotetan—**See Cephalosporins (Systemic),** 389

Cefotaxime Sodium [*Claforan*]
See Cephalosporins (Systemic), 389

Cefotetan Disodium [*Cefotan*]
See Cephalosporins (Systemic), 389

Cefoxitin Sodium [*Mefoxin*]
See Cephalosporins (Systemic), 389

Cefprozil [*Cefzil*]
See Cephalosporins (Systemic), 389

Ceftazidime [*Ceptaz; Fortaz; Tazicef; Tazidime*]
See Cephalosporins (Systemic), 389

Ceftin—Glaxo (U.S.) brand of Cefuroxime— **See Cephalosporins (Systemic),** 389

Ceftizoxime Sodium [*Cefizox*]
See Cephalosporins (Systemic), 389

Ceftriaxone Sodium [*Rocephin*]
See Cephalosporins (Systemic), 389
Cefuroxime Axetil [*Ceftin*]
See Cephalosporins (Systemic), 389
Cefuroxime Sodium [*Kefurox; Zinacef*]
See Cephalosporins (Systemic), 389
Cefzil—Bristol Myers Squibb (U.S.) brand of
Cefprozil—**See Cephalosporins
(Systemic)**, 389
Celestoderm-V—Schering (Canada) brand of
Betamethasone—**See Corticosteroids
(Topical)**, 458
Celestoderm-V/2—Schering (Canada) brand
of Betamethasone—**See Corticoste-
roids (Topical)**, 458
Celestone—Schering (U.S. and Canada)
brand of Betamethasone—**See Cortico-
steroids/Corticotropin—Glucocorti-
coid Effects (Systemic)**, 472
Celestone Phosphate—Schering (U.S.) brand
of Betamethasone—**See Corticoste-
roids/Corticotropin—Glucocorticoid
Effects (Systemic)**, 472
Celestone Soluspan—Schering (U.S. and
Canada) brand of Betamethasone—**See
Corticosteroids/Corticotropin—
Glucocorticoid Effects (Systemic)**, 472
Cellulose Sodium Phosphate [*Calcibind*]
(Systemic), 387
Celontin—PD (U.S. and Canada) brand of
Methsuximide—**See Anticonvulsants,
Succinimide (Systemic)**, 110
Cenafed—Century (U.S.) brand of Pseudo-
ephedrine (Systemic), 936
Cenafed Plus—Century (U.S.) brand of
Triprolidine and Pseudoephedrine—**See
Antihistamines and Decongestants
(Systemic)**, 161
Cenocort A-40—Central (U.S.) brand of
Triamcinolone—**See Corticosteroids/
Corticotropin—Glucocorticoid Effects
(Systemic)**, 472
Cenocort Forte—Central (U.S.) brand of
Triamcinolone—**See Corticosteroids/
Corticotropin—Glucocorticoid Effects
(Systemic)**, 472
Centrax—PD (U.S.) brand of Prazepam—
See Benzodiazepines (Systemic), 251
Ceo-Two—Beutlich (U.S.) brand of
Potassium Bitartrate and Sodium
Bicarbonate—**See Laxatives (Local)**,
682
Cephalexin [*Apo-Cephalex; Cefanex;
Ceporex; C-Lexin; Keflet; Keflex;
Novolexin; Nu-Cephalex*]
See Cephalosporins (Systemic), 389
Cephalexin Hydrochloride [*Keftab*]
See Cephalosporins (Systemic), 389
Cephalosporins
(Systemic), 389
Cephalothin Sodium [*Ceporacin; Keflin*]
See Cephalosporins (Systemic), 389

Cephapirin Sodium [*Cefadyl*]
See Cephalosporins (Systemic), 389
Cephradine [*Anspor; Velosef*]
See Cephalosporins (Systemic), 389
Ceporacin—Glaxo (Canada) brand of
Cephalothin—**See Cephalosporins
(Systemic)**, 389
Ceporex—Glaxo (Canada) brand of
Cephalexin—**See Cephalosporins
(Systemic)**, 389
Ceptaz—Glaxo (U.S. and Canada) brand of
Ceftazidime—**See Cephalosporins
(Systemic)**, 389
Cerose-DM—Wyeth-Ayerst (U.S.) brand of
Chlorpheniramine, Phenylephrine, and
Dextromethorphan—**See Cough/Cold
Combinations (Systemic)**, 488
C.E.S.—ICN (Canada) brand of Estrogens,
Conjugated—**See Estrogens (Sys-
temic)**, 566
Cetacort—Owen/Allercreme (U.S.) brand of
Hydrocortisone—**See Corticosteroids
(Topical)**, 458
Cetamide—Alcon (U.S. and Canada) brand
of Sulfacetamide—**See Sulfonamides
(Ophthalmic)**, 1009
Cetirizine [*Reactine*]
See Antihistamines (Systemic), 147
Charac-50—Omega (Canada) brand of
Charcoal, Activated (Oral-Local), 404
Charac-tol 50—Omega (Canada) brand of
Charcoal, Activated, and Sorbitol—**See
Charcoal, Activated (Oral-Local)**, 404
Charcoaid—Requa (U.S.) brand of Charcoal,
Activated, and Sorbitol—**See Charcoal,
Activated (Oral-Local)**, 404
Charcoal, Activated [*Actidose-Aqua;
Aqueous Charcodote; Charac-50;
Charcocaps; Insta-Char; Insta-Char
Aqueous Suspension; Liqui-Char;
Pediatric Aqueous Charcodote*]
(Oral-Local), 404
Charcoal, Activated, and Sorbitol [*Actidose
with Sorbitol; Charac-tol 50;
Charcoaid; Charcodote; Charcodote
TFS; Pediatric Charcodote*]
See Charcoal, Activated (Oral-Local),
404
Charcocaps—Requa (U.S.) brand of
Charcoal, Activated (Oral-Local), 404
Charcodote—Pharmascience (Canada) brand
of Charcoal, Activated, and Sorbitol—
See Charcoal, Activated (Oral-Local),
404
Charcodote TFS—Pharmascience (Canada)
brand of Charcoal, Activated, and
Sorbitol—**See Charcoal, Activated
(Oral-Local)**, 404
Chardonna-2—Rorer (U.S.) brand of
Belladonna and Phenobarbital—**See
Belladonna Alkaloids and Barbitu-
rates (Systemic)**, 246

Chenix—Reid-Rowell (U.S.) brand of
Chenodiol (Systemic), 407
Chenodeoxycholic acid—*See* Chenodiol
(Systemic), 407
Chenodiol [*Chenix;* chenodeoxycholic acid]
(Systemic), 407
Cheracol—Upjohn (U.S.) brand of Codeine
and Guaifenesin—**See Cough/Cold
Combinations (Systemic)**, 488
Cheracol D Cough—Upjohn (U.S.) brand of
Dextromethorphan and Guaifenesin—
**See Cough/Cold Combinations
(Systemic)**, 488
Cheracol Plus—Upjohn (U.S.) brand of
Chlorpheniramine, Phenylpropano-
lamine, and Dextromethorphan—**See
Cough/Cold Combinations (Systemic)**,
488
Cherapas—Kay Pharm (U.S.) brand of
Reserpine, Hydralazine, and Hydrochlo-
rothiazide (Systemic), 950
Children's Advil—Whitehall (U.S.) brand of
Ibuprofen—**See Anti-inflammatory
Analgesics, Nonsteroidal (Systemic)**,
168
Children's Hold—Beecham (U.S.) brand of
Dextromethorphan (Systemic), 502
*Children's NyQuil Nighttime Cold Medi-
cine*—Richardson-Vicks (U.S.) brand of
Chlorpheniramine, Pseudoephedrine,
and Dextromethorphan—**See Cough/
Cold Combinations (Systemic)**, 488
Children's Sudafed Liquid—BW (U.S.)
brand of Pseudoephedrine (Systemic),
936
Children's Tylenol Cold—McNeil (U.S.)
brand of Chlorpheniramine, Pseudo-
ephedrine, and Acetaminophen—**See
Antihistamines, Decongestants, and
Analgesics (Systemic)**, 162
Chlo-Amine—Hollister-Stier (U.S.) brand of
Chlorpheniramine—**See Antihistamines
(Systemic)**, 147
Chlophedianol Hydrochloride [*Ulone*]
(Systemic), 408
Chlor-100—Vortech (U.S.) brand of
Chlorpheniramine—**See Antihistamines
(Systemic)**, 147
Chlorafed—Hauck (U.S.) brand of
Chlorpheniramine and Pseudoephed-
rine—**See Antihistamines and
Decongestants (Systemic)**, 161
Chlorafed H.S. Timecelles—Hauck (U.S.)
brand of Chlorpheniramine and
Pseudoephedrine—**See Antihistamines
and Decongestants (Systemic)**, 161
Chlorafed Timecelles—Hauck (U.S.) brand
of Chlorpheniramine and Pseudoephed-
rine—**See Antihistamines and
Decongestants (Systemic)**, 161
Chlorambucil [*Leukeran*]
(Systemic), 409

Clavulin—Beecham (Canada) brand of Amoxicillin and Clavulanate—**See Penicillins (Systemic)**, 848

Clearasil Clearstick Maximum Strength Topical Solution—Richardson-Vicks (U.S.) brand of Salicylic Acid (Topical), 968

Clearasil Clearstick Regular Strength Topical Solution—Richardson-Vicks (U.S.) brand of Salicylic Acid (Topical), 968

Clearasil Double Textured Pads Maximum Strength —Richardson-Vicks (U.S.) brand of Salicylic Acid (Topical), 968

Clearasil Double Textured Pads Regular Strength —Richardson-Vicks (U.S.) brand of Salicylic Acid (Topical), 968

Clearasil Medicated Deep Cleanser Topical Solution—Richardson-Vicks (U.S.) brand of Salicylic Acid (Topical), 968

Clear Away—Scholl (U.S.) brand of Salicylic Acid (Topical), 968

Clear by Design Medicated Cleansing Pads—SmithKline Beecham (U.S.) brand of Salicylic Acid (Topical), 968

Clemastine Fumarate [*Tavist; Tavist-1*] **See Antihistamines (Systemic)**, 147

Clemastine Fumarate and Phenylpropanolamine Hydrochloride [*Tavist-D*] **See Antihistamines and Decongestants (Systemic)**, 161

Cleocin—Upjohn (U.S.) brand of Clindamycin (Systemic), 433

Cleocin Pediatric—Upjohn (U.S.) brand of Clindamycin (Systemic), 433

C-Lexin—Hauck (U.S.) brand of Cephalexin—**See Cephalosporins (Systemic)**, 389

Clidinium Bromide [*Quarzan*] **See Anticholinergics/Antispasmodics (Systemic)**, 73

Clindamycin Hydrochloride [*Cleocin; Dalacin C*] **(Systemic)**, 433

Clindamycin Palmitate Hydrochloride [*Cleocin Pediatric; Dalacin C Palmitate*] **(Systemic)**, 433

Clindamycin Phosphate [*Cleocin; Dalacin C Phosphate*] **(Systemic)**, 433

Clindex—Rugby (U.S.) brand of Chlordiazepoxide and Clidinium (Systemic), 413

Clinoril—MSD (U.S.) and Frosst (Canada) brand of Sulindac—**See Anti-inflammatory Analgesics, Nonsteroidal (Systemic)**, 168

Clinoxide—Geneva Generics (U.S.) brand of Chlordiazepoxide and Clidinium (Systemic), 413

Clipoxide—Schein (U.S.) brand of Chlordiazepoxide and Clidinium (Systemic), 413

Clobetasol Propionate [*Dermovate; Dermovate Scalp Lotion; Temovate; Temovate Scalp Application*] **See Corticosteroids (Topical)**, 458

Clobetasone Butyrate [*Eumovate*] **See Corticosteroids (Topical)**, 458

Clocortolone Pivalate [*Cloderm*] **See Corticosteroids (Topical)**, 458

Cloderm—Hermal (U.S.) brand of Clocortolone—**See Corticosteroids (Topical)**, 458

Clofibrate [*Abitrate; Atromid-S; Claripex; Novofibrate*] **(Systemic)**, 435

Clomipramine Hydrochloride [*Anafranil*] **See Antidepressants, Tricyclic (Systemic)**, 119

Clonazepam [*Klonopin: Rivotril*] **See Benzodiazepines (Systemic)**, 251

Clonidine [*Catapres-TTS*] **(Systemic)**, 438

Clonidine Hydrochloride [*Catapres; Dixarit*] **(Systemic)**, 438

Clonidine Hydrochloride and Chlorthalidone [*Combipres*] **(Systemic)**, 442

Clopra—Quantum Pharmics (U.S.) brand of Metoclopramide (Systemic), 746

Clorazepate Dipotassium [*Apo-Clorazepate; Gen-XENE; Novoclopate; Tranxene; Tranxene-SD; Tranxene T-Tab*] **See Benzodiazepines (Systemic)**, 251

Clotrimazole [*Canesten; Canesten 1; Canesten 3; Canesten 10%; Gyne-Lotrimin; Mycelex-G; Myclo*] **See Antifungals, Azole (Vaginal)**, 140

Cloxacillin Sodium [*Apo-Cloxi; Cloxapen; Novocloxin; Nu-Cloxi; Orbenin; Tegopen*] **See Penicillins (Systemic)**, 848

Cloxapen—Beecham (U.S.) brand of Cloxacillin—**See Penicillins (Systemic)**, 848

Clysodrast—Armour (U.S.) brand of Bisacodyl—**See Laxatives (Local)**, 682

CoActifed—BW (Canada) brand of Triprolidine, Pseudoephedrine, and Codeine—**See Cough/Cold Combinations (Systemic)**, 488

CoActifed Expectorant—BW (Canada) brand of Triprolidine, Pseudoephedrine, Codeine, and Guaifenesin—**See Cough/Cold Combinations (Systemic)**, 488

CoAdvil Caplets—Whitehall (U.S.) brand of Pseudoephedrine and Ibuprofen—**See Decongestants and Analgesics (Systemic)**, 497

Coal Tar [*Alphosyl; Aquatar; Balnetar; Balnetar Therapeutic Tar Bath; Cutar Water Dispersible Emollient Tar; Denorex; Denorex Extra Strength Medicated Shampoo; Denorex Extra Strength Medicated Shampoo with Conditioners; Denorex Medicated Shampoo; Denorex Medicated Shampoo*

Coal Tar *(continued)*
and Conditioner; Denorex Mountain Fresh Herbal Scent Medicated Shampoo; DHS Tar Gel Shampoo; DHS Tar Shampoo; Doak Oil; Doak Oil Forte; Doak Oil Forte Therapeutic Bath Treatment; Doak Oil Therapeutic Bath Treatment For All-Over Body Care; Doak Tar Lotion; Doak Tar Shampoo; Doctar Hair & Scalp Shampoo and Conditioner; Doctar Shampoo; Estar; Fototar; Ionil T Plus; Lavatar; Liquor Carbonis Detergens; Medotar; Pentrax Anti-Dandruff Tar Shampoo; Pentrax Extra-Strength Therapeutic Tar Shampoo; Psorigel; PsoriNail Topical Solution; Taraphilic; Tarbonis; Tar Doak; Tarpaste; Tarpaste 'Doak'; T/Derm Tar Emollient; Tegrin Lotion for Psoriasis; Tegrin Medicated Cream Shampoo; Tegrin Medicated Shampoo Concentrated Gel; Tegrin Medicated Shampoo Extra Conditioning Formula; Tegrin Medicated Shampoo Herbal Formula; Tegrin Medicated Shampoo Original Formula; Tegrin Medicated Soap for Psoriasis; Tegrin Skin Cream for Psoriasis; Tersa-Tar Mild Therapeutic Shampoo with Protein and Conditioner; Tersa-Tar Soapless Tar Shampoo; Tersa-Tar Therapeutic Shampoo; T-Gel; T/Gel Therapeutic Conditioner; T/Gel Therapeutic Shampoo; Theraplex T Shampoo; Zetar Emulsion; Zetar Medicated Antiseborrheic Shampoo; Zetar Shampoo]
(Topical), 443

Co-Apap—Rugby (U.S.) brand of Chlorpheniramine, Pseudoephedrine, Dextromethorphan, and Acetaminophen—**See Cough/Cold Combinations (Systemic)**, 488

Cobex—Pasadena (U.S.) brand of Cyanocobalamin—**See Vitamin B$_{12}$ (Systemic)**, 1077

Codalan No.1—Lannett (U.S.) brand of Acetaminophen and Codeine—**See Opioid (Narcotic) Analgesics and Acetaminophen (Systemic)**, 820

Codalan No.2—Lannett (U.S.) brand of Acetaminophen and Codeine—**See Opioid (Narcotic) Analgesics and Acetaminophen (Systemic)**, 820

Codalan No.3—Lannett (U.S.) brand of Acetaminophen and Codeine—**See Opioid (Narcotic) Analgesics and Acetaminophen (Systemic)**, 820

Codamin #2—Clark (Canada) brand of Acetaminophen and Codeine—**See Opioid (Narcotic) Analgesics and Acetaminophen (Systemic)**, 820

Codamin #3—Clark (Canada) brand of Acetaminophen and Codeine—**See Opioid (Narcotic) Analgesics and Acetaminophen (Systemic)**, 820

Codamine—Barre (U.S.); Bioline (U.S.);
CMC-CONS (U.S.); Cooper (U.S.);
Dixon-Shane (U.S.); Generix (U.S.);
Interstate (U.S.); Murray (U.S.);
Spencer-Mead (U.S.); and Vita-Rx
(U.S.) brand of Phenylpropanolamine
and Hydrocodone—**See Cough/Cold
Combinations (Systemic)**, 488
Codamine Pediatric—Barre-National (U.S.)
brand of Phenylpropanolamine and
Hydrocodone—**See Cough/Cold
Combinations (Systemic)**, 488
Codaminophen—Clark (Canada) brand of
Acetaminophen and Codeine—**See
Opioid (Narcotic) Analgesics and
Acetaminophen (Systemic)**, 820
Codan—WC (U.S.) brand of Hydrocodone
and Homatropine—**See Cough/Cold
Combinations (Systemic)**, 488
Codegest Expectorant—Great Southern
(U.S.) brand of Phenylpropanolamine,
Codeine, and Guaifenesin—**See Cough/
Cold Combinations (Systemic)**, 488
Codehist DH—Geneva Generics (U.S.) brand
of Chlorpheniramine, Pseudoephedrine,
and Codeine—**See Cough/Cold
Combinations (Systemic)**, 488
Codeine and Calcium Iodide [*Calcidrine*]
**See Cough/Cold Combinations (Sys-
temic)**, 488
Codeine Phosphate [*Paveral*]
**See Opioid (Narcotic) Analgesics
(Systemic)**, 793
Codeine Phosphate and Guaifenesin
[*Baytussin AC; Cheracol; Glydeine
Cough; Guiatuss A.C.; Guiatussin with
Codeine Liquid; Mytussin AC;
Nortussin with Codeine; Robitussin A-
C; Tolu-Sed Cough*]
**See Cough/Cold Combinations (Sys-
temic)**, 488
Codeine Phosphate and Iodinated Glycerol
[*Iophen-C Liquid; Iotuss; Par Glycerol
C; Tussi-Organidin Liquid*]
**See Cough/Cold Combinations (Sys-
temic)**, 488
Codeine Sulfate
**See Opioid (Narcotic) Analgesics
(Systemic)**, 793
Codiclear DH—Central (U.S.) brand of
Hydrocodone and Guaifenesin—**See
Cough/Cold Combinations (Systemic)**,
488
Codimal—Central (U.S.) brand of
Chlorpheniramine, Pseudoephedrine,
and Acetaminophen—**See Antihista-
mines, Decongestants, and Analgesics
(Systemic)**, 162
Codimal-A—Central (U.S.) brand of
Brompheniramine—**See Antihistamines
(Systemic)**, 147
Codimal DH—Central (U.S.) brand of
Pyrilamine, Phenylephrine, and
Hydrocodone—**See Cough/Cold
Combinations (Systemic)**, 488

Codimal DM—Central (U.S.) brand of
Pyrilamine, Phenylephrine, and
Dextromethorphan—**See Cough/Cold
Combinations (Systemic)**, 488
Codimal Expectorant—Central (U.S.) brand
of Phenylpropanolamine and
Guaifenesin—**See Cough/Cold
Combinations (Systemic)**, 488
Codimal-L.A.—Central (U.S.) brand of
Chlorpheniramine and Pseudoephed-
rine—**See Antihistamines and
Decongestants (Systemic)**, 161
Codimal PH—Central (U.S.) brand of
Pyrilamine, Phenylephrine, and
Codeine—**See Cough/Cold Combina-
tions (Systemic)**, 488
Codistan No. 1—Vortech (U.S.) brand of
Dextromethorphan and Guaifenesin—
**See Cough/Cold Combinations
(Systemic)**, 488
Cogentin—MSD (U.S. and Canada) brand of
Benztropine—**See Antidyskinetics
(Systemic)**, 135
Co-Gesic—Central (U.S.) brand of
Hydrocodone and Acetaminophen—**See
Opioid (Narcotic) Analgesics and
Acetaminophen (Systemic)**, 820
Colace—Mead Johnson (U.S. and Canada)
brand of Docusate—**See Laxatives
(Local)**, 682
Colax—Rugby (U.S.) brand of Docusate and
Phenolphthalein—**See Laxatives
(Local)**, 682
Coldrine—Hauck (U.S.) brand of Pseudo-
ephedrine and Acetaminophen—**See
Decongestants and Analgesics
(Systemic)**, 497
Colestid—Upjohn (U.S. and Canada) brand
of Colestipol (Oral-Local), 445
Colestipol Hydrochloride [*Colestid*]
(Oral-Local), 445
Cologel—Lilly (U.S.) brand of Methylcellu-
lose—**See Laxatives (Local)**, 682
Coltab Children's—Hauck (U.S.) brand of
Chlorpheniramine and Phenylephrine—
**See Antihistamines and Decongestants
(Systemic)**, 161
Combipres—Boehringer Ingelheim (U.S. and
Canada) brand of Clonidine and
Chlorthalidone (Systemic), 442
Comhist—Procter & Gamble (U.S.) brand of
Chlorpheniramine, Phenyltoloxamine,
and Phenylephrine—**See Antihista-
mines and Decongestants (Systemic)**,
161
Comhist LA—Procter & Gamble (U.S.) brand
of Chlorpheniramine, Phenyltoloxamine,
and Phenylephrine—**See Antihista-
mines and Decongestants (Systemic)**,
161
Compal—Reid-Rowell (U.S.) brand of
Dihydrocodeine and Acetaminophen—
**See Opioid (Narcotic) Analgesics and
Acetaminophen (Systemic)**, 820

Compa-Z—Hauck (U.S.) brand of
Prochlorperazine—**See Phenothiazines
(Systemic)**, 872
Compazine—SKF (U.S.) brand of
Prochlorperazine—**See Phenothiazines
(Systemic)**, 872
Compazine Spansule—SKF (U.S.) brand of
Prochlorperazine—**See Phenothiazines
(Systemic)**, 872
Compound W Gel—Whitehall (U.S. and
Canada) brand of Salicylic Acid
(Topical), 968
Compound W Liquid—Whitehall (U.S. and
Canada) brand of Salicylic Acid
(Topical), 968
Compoz—Med-Tech (U.S.) brand of
Diphenhydramine—**See Antihistamines
(Systemic)**, 147
Comtrex A/S—Bristol-Myers (U.S.) brand of
Chlorpheniramine, Pseudoephedrine,
and Acetaminophen—**See Antihista-
mines, Decongestants, and Analgesics
(Systemic)**, 162
Comtrex A/S Caplets—Bristol-Myers (U.S.)
brand of Chlorpheniramine, Pseudo-
ephedrine, and Acetaminophen—**See
Antihistamines, Decongestants, and
Analgesics (Systemic)**, 162
Comtrex Daytime Caplets—Bristol-Myers
(U.S.) brand of Pseudoephedrine,
Dextromethorphan, and Acetamino-
phen—**See Cough/Cold Combinations
(Systemic)**, 488
Comtrex Multi-Symptom Cold Reliever—
Bristol-Myers (U.S.) brand of
Chlorpheniramine, Phenylpropano-
lamine, Dextromethorphan, and
Acetaminophen—**See Cough/Cold
Combinations (Systemic)**, 488
*Comtrex Multi-Symptom Non-Drowsy
Caplets*—Bristol-Myers (U.S.) brand of
Pseudoephedrine, Dextromethorphan,
and Acetaminophen—**See Cough/Cold
Combinations (Systemic)**, 488
Comtrex Nighttime—Bristol-Myers (U.S.)
brand of Chlorpheniramine, Pseudo-
ephedrine, Dextromethorphan, and
Acetaminophen—**See Cough/Cold
Combinations (Systemic)**, 488
Conar—Beecham (U.S.) brand of Phe-
nylephrine and Dextromethorphan—**See
Cough/Cold Combinations (Systemic)**,
488
Conar-A—Beecham (U.S.) brand of
Phenylephrine, Dextromethorphan,
Guaifenesin, and Acetaminophen—**See
Cough/Cold Combinations (Systemic)**,
488
Conar Expectorant—Beecham (U.S.) brand
of Phenylephrine, Dextromethorphan,
and Guaifenesin—**See Cough/Cold
Combinations (Systemic)**, 488
Concentrin—PD (U.S.) brand of Pseudo-
ephedrine, Dextromethorphan, and
Guaifenesin—**See Cough/Cold
Combinations (Systemic)**, 488

Dilaudid Cough—Knoll (U.S.) brand of Hydromorphone and Guaifenesin—**See Cough/Cold Combinations (Systemic)**, 488

Dilaudid-HP—Knoll (U.S. and Canada) brand of Hydromorphone—**See Opioid (Narcotic) Analgesics (Systemic)**, 793

Dilor—Savage (U.S.) brand of Dyphylline—**See Bronchodilators, Xanthine-derivative (Systemic)**, 315

Dilor-400—Savage (U.S.) brand of Dyphylline—**See Bronchodilators, Xanthine-derivative (Systemic)**, 315

Dilotab—Zee (U.S.) brand of Phenylpropanolamine and Acetaminophen—**See Decongestants and Analgesics (Systemic)**, 497

Diltiazem [*Apo-Diltiaz; Cardizem; Novo-Diltiazem; Nu-Diltiaz; Syn-Diltiazem*] **See Calcium Channel Blocking Agents (Systemic)**, 343

Diltiazem Hydrochloride [*Cardizem; Cardizem CD; Cardizem SR*] **See Calcium Channel Blocking Agents (Systemic)**, 343

Dimacol—Robins (U.S.) brand of Pseudoephedrine, Dextromethorphan, and Guaifenesin—**See Cough/Cold Combinations (Systemic)**, 488

Dimaphen S.A.—Major (U.S.) brand of Brompheniramine, Phenylephrine, and Phenylpropanolamine—**See Antihistamines and Decongestants (Systemic)**, 161

Dimelor—Lilly (Canada) brand of Acetohexamide—**See Antidiabetic Agents, Oral (Systemic)**, 129

Dimenhydrinate [*Apo-Dimenhydrinate; Calm X; Dimetabs; Dinate; Dommanate; Dramamine; Dramamine Chewable; Dramamine Liquid; Dramanate; Dramocen; Dramoject; Dymenate; Gravol; Gravol L/A; Hydrate; Marmine; Nauseatol; Nico-Vert; Novodimenate; PMS-Dimenhydrinate; Tega-Vert; Travamine; Triptone Caplets; Vertab*] **See Antihistamines (Systemic)**, 147

Dimetabs—Jones Medical (U.S.) brand of Dimenhydrinate—**See Antihistamines (Systemic)**, 147

Dimetane—Robins (U.S. and Canada) brand of Brompheniramine—**See Antihistamines (Systemic)**, 147

Dimetane-DC Cough—Robins (U.S.) brand of Brompheniramine, Phenylpropanolamine, and Codeine—**See Cough/Cold Combinations (Systemic)**, 488

Dimetane Decongestant—Robins (U.S.) brand of Brompheniramine and Phenylephrine—**See Antihistamines and Decongestants (Systemic)**, 161

Dimetane Decongestant Caplets—Robins (U.S.) brand of Brompheniramine and Phenylephrine—**See Antihistamines and Decongestants (Systemic)**, 161

Dimetane-DX Cough—Robins (U.S.) brand of Brompheniramine, Pseudoephedrine, and Dextromethorphan—**See Cough/Cold Combinations (Systemic)**, 488

Dimetane Expectorant—Robins (Canada) brand of Brompheniramine, Phenylephrine, Phenylpropanolamine, and Guaifenesin—**See Cough/Cold Combinations (Systemic)**, 488

Dimetane Expectorant-C—Robins (Canada) brand of Brompheniramine, Phenylephrine, Phenylpropanolamine, Codeine, and Guaifenesin—**See Cough/Cold Combinations (Systemic)**, 488

Dimetane Expectorant-DC—Robins (Canada) brand of Brompheniramine, Phenylephrine, Phenylpropanolamine, Hydrocodone, and Guaifenesin—**See Cough/Cold Combinations (Systemic)**, 488

Dimetane Extentabs—Robins (U.S. and Canada) brand of Brompheniramine—**See Antihistamines (Systemic)**, 147

Dimetapp—Robins (Canada) brand of Brompheniramine, Phenylephrine, and Phenylpropanolamine—**See Antihistamines and Decongestants (Systemic)**, 161; Robins (U.S.) brand of Brompheniramine and Phenylpropanolamine—**See Antihistamines and Decongestants (Systemic)**, 161

Dimetapp-A—Robins (Canada) brand of Brompheniramine, Phenylephrine, Phenylpropanolamine, and Acetaminophen—**See Antihistamines, Decongestants, and Analgesics (Systemic)**, 162

Dimetapp-A Pediatric—Robins (Canada) brand of Brompheniramine, Phenylephrine, Phenylpropanolamine, and Acetaminophen—**See Antihistamines, Decongestants, and Analgesics (Systemic)**, 162

Dimetapp with Codeine—Robins (Canada) brand of Brompheniramine, Phenylephrine, Phenylpropanolamine, and Codeine—**See Cough/Cold Combinations (Systemic)**, 488

Dimetapp-DM—Robins (Canada) brand of Brompheniramine, Phenylephrine, Phenylpropanolamine, and Dextromethorphan—**See Cough/Cold Combinations (Systemic)**, 488

Dimetapp DM Cough and Cold—Robins (U.S.) brand of Brompheniramine, Phenylpropanolamine, and Dextromethorphan—**See Cough/Cold Combinations (Systemic)**, 488

Dimetapp Extentabs—Robins (Canada) brand of Brompheniramine, Phenylephrine, and Phenylpropanolamine—**See Antihistamines and Decongestants (Systemic)**, 161; Robins (U.S.) brand of Brompheniramine and Phenylpropanolamine—**See Antihistamines and Decongestants (Systemic)**, 161

Dimetapp Oral Infant Drops—Robins (Canada) brand of Brompheniramine, Phenylephrine, and Phenylpropanolamine—**See Antihistamines and Decongestants (Systemic)**, 161

Dimetapp Plus Caplets—Robins Consumers (U.S.) brand of Brompheniramine, Phenylpropanolamine, and Acetaminophen—**See Antihistamines, Decongestants, and Analgesics (Systemic)**, 162

Dinate—Seatrace (U.S.) brand of Dimenhydrinate—**See Antihistamines (Systemic)**, 147

Diocto—Barre-National (U.S.); Bioline (U.S.); Cooper (U.S.); Dixon-Shane (U.S.); Goldline (U.S.); Moore (U.S.); Rugby (U.S.); Schein (U.S.); Unit Dose (U.S.); and United Research (U.S.) brand of Docusate—**See Laxatives (Local)**, 682

Diocto-C—Rugby (U.S.) brand of Casanthranol and Docusate—**See Laxatives (Local)**, 682

Diocto-K—Rugby (U.S.) brand of Docusate—**See Laxatives (Local)**, 682

Diocto-K Plus—Rugby (U.S.) brand of Casanthranol and Docusate—**See Laxatives (Local)**, 682

Dioeze—Century (U.S.) brand of Docusate—**See Laxatives (Local)**, 682

Diosuccin—CMC-CONS (U.S.) brand of Docusate—**See Laxatives (Local)**, 682

Dio-Sul—Vortech (U.S.) brand of Docusate—**See Laxatives (Local)**, 682

Diothron—Vortech (U.S.) brand of Casanthranol and Docusate—**See Laxatives (Local)**, 682

Dioval—Keene (U.S.) brand of Estradiol—**See Estrogens (Systemic)**, 566

Dioval 40—Keene (U.S.) brand of Estradiol—**See Estrogens (Systemic)**, 566

Dioval XX—Keene (U.S.) brand of Estradiol—**See Estrogens (Systemic)**, 566

Diovol—Horner (Canada) brand of Alumina and Magnesia—**See Antacids (Oral-Local)**, 61

Diovol Ex—Horner (Canada) brand of Alumina and Magnesia—**See Antacids (Oral-Local)**, 61

Diovol Plus—Horner (Canada) brand of Alumina, Magnesia, and Simethicone—**See Antacids (Oral-Local)**, 61; Horner (Canada) brand of Simethicone, Alumina, Magnesium Carbonate, and Magnesia—**See Antacids (Oral-Local)**, 61

Dipentum—Pharmacia (U.S. and Canada) brand of Olsalazine (Oral-Local), 790

Diphenacen-50—Central (U.S.) brand of Diphenhydramine—**See Antihistamines (Systemic)**, 147

Diphenadryl—Schein (U.S.) brand of Diphenhydramine—**See Antihistamines (Systemic)**, 147

Diurese-R—American Urologicals (U.S.) brand of Reserpine and Trichlormethiazide—**See Rauwolfia Alkaloids and Thiazide Diuretics (Systemic)**, 948

Diuretics, Loop **(Systemic)**, 524

Diuretics, Potassium-sparing **(Systemic)**, 531

Diuretics, Potassium-sparing, and Hydrochlorothiazide **(Systemic)**, 536

Diuretics, Thiazide **(Systemic)**, 541

Diurigen with Reserpine—Goldline (U.S.) brand of Reserpine and Chlorothiazide—**See Rauwolfia Alkaloids and Thiazide Diuretics (Systemic)**, 948

Diuril—MSD (U.S.) brand of Chlorothiazide—**See Diuretics, Thiazide (Systemic)**, 541

Diutensen-R—Wallace (U.S.) brand of Reserpine and Methyclothiazide—**See Rauwolfia Alkaloids and Thiazide Diuretics (Systemic)**, 948

Divalproex Sodium [*Depakote; Depakote Sprinkle; Epival*] **See Valproic Acid (Systemic)**, 1062

Dixarit—Boehringer Ingelheim (Canada) brand of Clonidine (Systemic), 438

DM Syrup—PD (Canada) brand of Dextromethorphan (Systemic), 502

Doak Oil—T.C.D. (Canada) brand of Coal Tar (Topical), 443

Doak Oil Forte—T.C.D. (Canada) brand of Coal Tar (Topical), 443

Doak Oil Forte Therapeutic Bath Treatment—Doak (U.S.) brand of Coal Tar (Topical), 443

Doak Oil Therapeutic Bath Treatment For All-Over Body Care—Doak (U.S.) brand of Coal Tar (Topical), 443

Doak Tar Lotion—Doak (U.S.) brand of Coal Tar (Topical), 443

Doak Tar Shampoo—Doak (U.S.) brand of Coal Tar (Topical), 443

Doan's—Sandoz Consumer (U.S.) and CIBA-GEIGY (Canada) brand of Magnesium Salicylate—**See Salicylates (Systemic)**, 953

Doctar Hair & Scalp Shampoo and Conditioner—Savage (U.S.) brand of Coal Tar (Topical), 443

Doctar Shampoo—Savage (U.S.) brand of Coal Tar (Topical), 443

Docucal-P—Parmed (U.S.) brand of Docusate and Phenolphthalein—**See Laxatives (Local)**, 682

Docu-K Plus—Newtron (U.S.) brand of Casanthranol and Docusate—**See Laxatives (Local)**, 682

Docusate Calcium [*Pro-Cal-Sof; Surfak*] **See Laxatives (Local)**, 682

Docusate Calcium and Phenolphthalein [*Docucal-P; Doxidan*] **See Laxatives (Local)**, 682

Docusate Potassium [*Dialose; Diocto-K; Kasof*] **See Laxatives (Local)**, 682

Docusate Sodium [*Afko-Lube; Colace; Diocto; Dioeze; Diosuccin; Dio-Sul; Disonate; Di-Sosul; Doss; Doxinate; D-S-S; Duosol; Laxinate 100; Modane Soft; Molatoc; Pro-Sof; Pro-Sof Liquid Concentrate; Regulax SS; Regulex; Regutol; sodium dioctyl sulfosuccinate; Stulex; Therevac Plus; Therevac-SB*] **See Laxatives (Local)**, 682

Docusate Sodium and Phenolphthalein [*Colax; Correctol; Disolan; Extra Gentle Ex-Lax; Feen-a-Mint; Feen-a-Mint Pills; Phillips' LaxCaps*] **See Laxatives (Local)**, 682

Dodd's Pills—Fulford (Canada) brand of Sodium Salicylate—**See Salicylates (Systemic)**, 953

Doktors—Scherer (U.S.) brand of Phenylephrine (Nasal), 893

Dolacet—Hauck (U.S.) brand of Hydrocodone and Acetaminophen—**See Opioid (Narcotic) Analgesics and Acetaminophen (Systemic)**, 820

Dolanex—Lannett (U.S.) brand of Acetaminophen (Systemic), 1

Dolene—Lederle (U.S.) brand of Propoxyphene—**See Opioid (Narcotic) Analgesics (Systemic)**, 793

Dolene-AP-65—Lederle (U.S.) brand of Propoxyphene and Acetaminophen—**See Opioid (Narcotic) Analgesics and Acetaminophen (Systemic)**, 820

Dolgesic—Marlop (U.S.) brand of Ibuprofen—**See Anti-inflammatory Analgesics, Nonsteroidal (Systemic)**, 168

Dolmar—Marlop (U.S.) brand of Butalbital, Acetaminophen, and Caffeine—**See Barbiturates and Analgesics (Systemic)**, 233

Dolobid—MSD (U.S.) and Frosst (Canada) brand of Diflunisal—**See Anti-inflammatory Analgesics, Nonsteroidal (Systemic)**, 168

Dolophine—Lilly (U.S. and Canada) brand of Methadone—**See Opioid (Narcotic) Analgesics (Systemic)**, 793

Dommanate—Forest (U.S.) brand of Dimenhydrinate—**See Antihistamines (Systemic)**, 147

Donatussin—Laser (U.S.) brand of Chlorpheniramine, Phenylephrine, Dextromethorphan, and Guaifenesin—**See Cough/Cold Combinations (Systemic)**, 488

Donatussin DC—Laser (U.S.) brand of Phenylephrine, Hydrocodone, and Guaifenesin—**See Cough/Cold Combinations (Systemic)**, 488

Donatussin Drops—Laser (U.S.) brand of Chlorpheniramine, Phenylephrine, and Guaifenesin—**See Cough/Cold Combinations (Systemic)**, 488

Dondril—Whitehall (U.S.) brand of Chlorpheniramine, Phenylephrine, and Dextromethorphan—**See Cough/Cold Combinations (Systemic)**, 488

Donnagel-MB—Robins (Canada) brand of Kaolin and Pectin (Oral-Local), 671

Donnagel-PG—Robins (U.S.) brand of Kaolin, Pectin, Belladonna Alkaloids, and Opium (Systemic), 672; Robins (Canada) brand of Kaolin, Pectin, and Paregoric (Systemic), 673

Donnamor—H.L. Moore (U.S.) brand of Atropine, Hyoscyamine, Scopolamine, and Phenobarbital—**See Belladonna Alkaloids and Barbiturates (Systemic)**, 246

Donnapectolin-PG—Major (U.S.) brand of Kaolin, Pectin, Belladonna Alkaloids, and Opium (Systemic), 672

Donnapine—Major (U.S.) brand of Atropine, Hyoscyamine, Scopolamine, and Phenobarbital—**See Belladonna Alkaloids and Barbiturates (Systemic)**, 246

Donnatal—Robins (U.S. and Canada) brand of Atropine, Hyoscyamine, Scopolamine, and Phenobarbital—**See Belladonna Alkaloids and Barbiturates (Systemic)**, 246

Donnatal Extentabs—Robins (U.S. and Canada) brand of Atropine, Hyoscyamine, Scopolamine, and Phenobarbital—**See Belladonna Alkaloids and Barbiturates (Systemic)**, 246

Donnatal No. 2—Robins (U.S.) brand of Atropine, Hyoscyamine, Scopolamine, and Phenobarbital—**See Belladonna Alkaloids and Barbiturates (Systemic)**, 246

Donnazyme—Robins (U.S. and Canada) brand of Pancreatin, Pepsin, Bile Salts, Hyoscyamine, Atropine, Scopolamine, and Phenobarbital (Systemic), 829

Donphen—Lemmon (U.S.) brand of Atropine, Hyoscyamine, Scopolamine, and Phenobarbital—**See Belladonna Alkaloids and Barbiturates (Systemic)**, 246

Dopamet—ICN (Canada) brand of Methyldopa (Systemic), 737

Dopar—Roberts (U.S.) brand of Levodopa (Systemic), 696

Doral—Wallace (U.S.) brand of Quazepam—**See Benzodiazepines (Systemic)**, 251

Doraphen—Cenci (U.S.) brand of Propoxyphene—**See Opioid (Narcotic) Analgesics (Systemic)**, 793

Doraphen Compound-65—Cenci (U.S.) brand of Propoxyphene and Aspirin—**See Opioid (Narcotic) Analgesics and Aspirin (Systemic)**, 822

Ergotamine Tartrate, Caffeine, Belladonna Alkaloids, and Pentobarbital [*Cafergot-PB*]
See Vascular Headache Suppressants, Ergot Derivative-containing (Systemic), 1066

Ergotamine Tartrate, Caffeine, Belladonna Alkaloids, and Pentobarbital Sodium [*Cafergot-PB*]
See Vascular Headache Suppressants, Ergot Derivative-containing (Systemic), 1066

Ergotamine Tartrate, Caffeine Citrate, and Diphenhydramine Hydrochloride [*Ergodryl*]
See Vascular Headache Suppressants, Ergot Derivative-containing (Systemic), 1066

Ergotamine Tartrate, Caffeine, and Cyclizine Hydrochloride [*Megral*]
See Vascular Headache Suppressants, Ergot Derivative-containing (Systemic), 1066

Ergotamine Tartrate, Caffeine, and Dimenhydrinate [*Gravergol*]
See Vascular Headache Suppressants, Ergot Derivative-containing (Systemic), 1066

Eritrityl tetranitrate—Erythrityl Tetranitrate—**See Nitrates (Systemic)**, 770

Erybid—Abbott (Canada) brand of Erythromycin Base—**See Erythromycins (Systemic)**, 557

ERYC—PD (U.S.) brand of Erythromycin Base—**See Erythromycins (Systemic)**, 557

ERYC-125—PD (Canada) brand of Erythromycin Base—**See Erythromycins (Systemic)**, 557

ERYC-250—PD (Canada) brand of Erythromycin Base—**See Erythromycins (Systemic)**, 557

EryPed—Abbott (U.S.) brand of Erythromycin Ethylsuccinate—**See Erythromycins (Systemic)**, 557

Ery-Tab—Abbott (U.S.) brand of Erythromycin Base—**See Erythromycins (Systemic)**, 557

Erythritol tetranitrate—Erythrityl Tetranitrate—**See Nitrates (Systemic)**, 770

Erythrityl Tetranitrate [*Cardilate*; eritrityl tetranitrate; erythritol tetranitrate]
See Nitrates (Systemic), 770

Erythro—Balan (U.S.) brand of Erythromycin Ethylsuccinate—**See Erythromycins (Systemic)**, 557

Erythrocin—Abbott (U.S. and Canada) brand of Erythromycin Lactobionate—**See Erythromycins (Systemic)**, 557; Abbott (U.S. and Canada) brand of Erythromycin Stearate—**See Erythromycins (Systemic)**, 557

Erythrocot—Truxton (U.S.) brand of Erythromycin Stearate—**See Erythromycins (Systemic)**, 557

Erythromid—Abbott (Canada) brand of Erythromycin Base—**See Erythromycins (Systemic)**, 557

Erythromycin [*Ilotycin*] **(Ophthalmic)**, 556

Erythromycin Base [*Apo-Erythro; Apo-Erythro-EC; E-Mycin; Erybid; ERYC; ERYC-125; ERYC-250; Ery-Tab; Erythromid; Novorythro; PCE Dispertab; Robimycin*]
See Erythromycins (Systemic), 557

Erythromycin Estolate [*Erythrozone; Ilosone; Novorythro*]
See Erythromycins (Systemic), 557

Erythromycin Ethylsuccinate [*Apo-Erythro-ES; E.E.S.; EryPed; Erythro*]
See Erythromycins (Systemic), 557

Erythromycin Ethylsuccinate and Sulfisoxazole Acetyl [*Eryzole; Pediazole; Sulfimycin*]
(Systemic), 562

Erythromycin Gluceptate [*Ilotycin*]
See Erythromycins (Systemic), 557

Erythromycin Lactobionate [*Erythrocin*]
See Erythromycins (Systemic), 557

Erythromycins **(Systemic)**, 557

Erythromycin Stearate [*Apo-Erythro-S; Erythrocin; Erythrocot; My-E; Novorythro; Wintrocin; Wyamycin-S*]
See Erythromycins (Systemic), 557

Erythrozone—Balan (U.S.) brand of Erythromycin Estolate—**See Erythromycins (Systemic)**, 557

Eryzole—Alra (U.S.) brand of Erythromycin and Sulfisoxazole (Systemic), 562

Eserine Salicylate—Alcon (U.S.) brand of Physostigmine (Ophthalmic), 901

Eserine Sulfate—CMC-CONS (U.S.); Harber (U.S.); Iolab (U.S.); Pharmaderm (U.S.); Pharmafair (U.S.); Pharmex (U.S.); Schein (U.S.); and Scrip (U.S.) brand of Physostigmine (Ophthalmic), 901

Esgic—Forest (U.S.) brand of Butalbital, Acetaminophen, and Caffeine—**See Barbiturates and Analgesics (Systemic)**, 233

Esgic-Plus—Forest (U.S.) brand of Butalbital, Acetaminophen, and Caffeine—**See Barbiturates and Analgesics (Systemic)**, 233

Esidrix—CIBA (U.S.) brand of Hydrochlorothiazide—**See Diuretics, Thiazide (Systemic)**, 541

Esimil—CIBA (U.S.) brand of Guanethidine and Hydrochlorothiazide (Systemic), 614

Eskalith—SKF (U.S.) brand of Lithium (Systemic), 699

Eskalith CR—SKF (U.S.) brand of Lithium (Systemic), 699

Espotabs—Combe (U.S.) brand of Phenolphthalein—**See Laxatives (Local)**, 682

Estar—Westwood (U.S.) and Westwood-Squibb (Canada) brand of Coal Tar (Topical), 443

Estazolam [*ProSom*]
See Benzodiazepines (Systemic), 251

Esterified estrogens—Estrogens, Esterified—**See Estrogens (Systemic)**, 566

Estinyl—Schering (U.S. and Canada) brand of Ethinyl Estradiol—**See Estrogens (Systemic)**, 566

Estrace—Mead Johnson (U.S.) and Bristol (Canada) brand of Estradiol—**See Estrogens (Systemic)**, 566; Mead Johnson (U.S.) brand of Estradiol—**See Estrogens (Vaginal)**, 572

Estracyt—See Estramustine (Systemic), 563

Estra-D—Seatrace (U.S.) brand of Estradiol—**See Estrogens (Systemic)**, 566

Estraderm—CIBA (U.S. and Canada) brand of Estradiol—**See Estrogens (Systemic)**, 566

Estradiol [*Estrace; Estraderm*]
See Estrogens (Systemic), 566

Estradiol [*Estrace*]
See Estrogens (Vaginal), 572

Estradiol Cypionate [*depGynogen; Depo-Estradiol; Depogen; Dura-Estrin; E-Cypionate; Estra-D; Estro-Cyp; Estrofem; Estroject-LA; Estronol-LA; Hormogen Depot*]
See Estrogens (Systemic), 566

Estradiol L.A.—Vortech (U.S.) brand of Estradiol—**See Estrogens (Systemic)**, 566

Estradiol L.A. 20—Vortech (U.S.) brand of Estradiol—**See Estrogens (Systemic)**, 566

Estradiol L.A. 40—Vortech (U.S.) brand of Estradiol—**See Estrogens (Systemic)**, 566

Estradiol Valerate [*Deladiol-40; Delestrogen; Dioval; Dioval 40; Dioval XX; Duragen-10; Duragen-20; Duragen-40; Estradiol L.A.; Estradiol L.A. 20; Estradiol L.A. 40; Estra-L 20; Estra-L 40; Estraval; Femogex; Gynogen L.A. 10; Gynogen L.A. 20; Gynogen L.A. 40; L.A.E. 20; Valergen-10; Valergen-20*]
See Estrogens (Systemic), 566

Estra-L 20—Pasadena (U.S.) brand of Estradiol—**See Estrogens (Systemic)**, 566

Estra-L 40—Pasadena (U.S.) brand of Estradiol—**See Estrogens (Systemic)**, 566

Estramustine Phosphate Sodium [*Emcyt; Estracyt*]
(Systemic), 563

Estratab—Reid-Rowell (U.S.) brand of Estrogens, Esterified—**See Estrogens (Systemic)**, 566

Estraval—Kay (U.S.) brand of Estradiol—
   See Estrogens (Systemic), 566
Estro-Cyp—Keene (U.S.) brand of Estra-
   diol—**See Estrogens (Systemic),** 566
Estrofem—Pasadena (U.S.) brand of
   Estradiol—**See Estrogens (Systemic),**
   566
Estrogens
   (Systemic), 566
Estrogens
   (Vaginal), 572
Estrogens, Conjugated [*C.E.S.; Conjugated
   Estrogens C.S.D.; Premarin; Premarin
   Intravenous*]
   See Estrogens (Systemic), 566
Estrogens, Conjugated [*Premarin*]
   See Estrogens (Vaginal), 572
Estrogens, Esterified [*Estratab; Menest; Neo-
   Estrone*]
   See Estrogens (Systemic), 566
Estroject-2—Mayrand (U.S.) brand of
   Estrone—**See Estrogens (Systemic),**
   566
Estroject-LA—Mayrand (U.S.) brand of
   Estradiol—**See Estrogens (Systemic),**
   566
Estrone [*Estroject-2; Estrone '5'; Estrone-A;
   Estronol; Femogen Forte; Foygen
   Aqueous; Gynogen; Kestrin Aqueous;
   Kestrone-5; Theelin Aqueous; Unigen;
   Wehgen*]
   See Estrogens (Systemic), 566
Estrone [*Oestrilin*]
   See Estrogens (Vaginal), 572
Estrone '5'—Kay (U.S.) brand of Estrone—
   See Estrogens (Systemic), 566
Estrone-A—Kay (U.S.) brand of Estrone—
   See Estrogens (Systemic), 566
Estronol—Central (U.S.) brand of Estrone—
   See Estrogens (Systemic), 566
Estronol-LA—Central (U.S.) brand of
   Estradiol—**See Estrogens (Systemic),**
   566
Estropipate [*Ogen; Ogen .625; Ogen 1.25;
   Ogen 2.5; Ogen 5; piperazine estrone
   sulfate*]
   See Estrogens (Systemic), 566
Estropipate [*Ogen; piperazine estrone
   sulfate*]
   See Estrogens (Vaginal), 572
Estrovis—PD (U.S.) brand of Quinestrol—
   See Estrogens (Systemic), 566
Etacrynic acid—Ethacrynic Acid—**See
   Diuretics, Loop (Systemic),** 524
Ethacrynate Sodium [*Edecrin*]
   See Diuretics, Loop (Systemic), 524
Ethacrynic Acid [*Edecrin;* etacrynic acid]
   See Diuretics, Loop (Systemic), 524
Ethinyl Estradiol [*Estinyl; Feminone*]
   See Estrogens (Systemic), 566
Ethmozine—Du Pont (U.S.) brand of
   Moricizine (Systemic), 761
Ethopropazine Hydrochloride [*Parsidol;
   Parsitan;* profenamine]
   See Antidyskinetics (Systemic), 135

Ethosuximide [*Zarontin*]
   **See Anticonvulsants, Succinimide
   (Systemic),** 110
Ethotoin [*Peganone*]
   **See Anticonvulsants, Hydantoin
   (Systemic),** 102
Ethylnorepinephrine Hydrochloride
   [*Bronkephrine*]
   **See Bronchodilators, Adrenergic
   (Systemic),** 294
Etodolac [etodolic acid; *Lodine*]
   (Systemic), 575
Etodolic acid—*See* Etodolac (Systemic), 575
Euflex—Schering (Canada) brand of
   Flutamide (Systemic), 589
Euglucon—Rorer (Canada) brand of
   Glyburide—**See Antidiabetic Agents,
   Oral (Systemic),** 129
Eulexin—Schering (U.S.) brand of Flutamide
   (Systemic), 589
Eulipos—Boehringer Mannheim (Germany)
   brand of Dextrothyroxine (Systemic),
   503
Eumovate—Glaxo (Canada) brand of
   Clobetasone—**See Corticosteroids
   (Topical),** 458
Euthroid—PD (U.S.) brand of Liotrix—**See
   Thyroid Hormones (Systemic),** 1044
Eutonyl—Abbott (U.S.) brand of Pargyline
   (Systemic), 840
Eutron—Abbott (U.S.) brand of Pargyline
   and Methyclothiazide (Systemic), 844
Evac-U-Gen—Walker (U.S.) brand of
   Phenolphthalein—**See Laxatives
   (Local),** 682
Evac-U-Lax—Mallard (U.S.) brand of
   Phenolphthalein—**See Laxatives
   (Local),** 682
Everone—Hyrex (U.S.) brand of Testoster-
   one—**See Androgens (Systemic),** 44
E-Vista—Seatrace (U.S.) brand of Hy-
   droxyzine—**See Antihistamines
   (Systemic),** 147
Excedrin Caplets—Bristol-Myers (Canada)
   brand of Acetaminophen and Caffeine—
   See Acetaminophen (Systemic), 1
Excedrin Extra-Strength Caplets—Bristol-
   Myers (U.S.) brand of Acetaminophen,
   Aspirin, and Caffeine—**See Acetamino-
   phen and Salicylates (Systemic),** 5
Excedrin Extra Strength Caplets—Bristol-
   Myers (Canada) brand of Acetamino-
   phen and Caffeine—**See Acetamino-
   phen (Systemic),** 1
Excedrin Extra-Strength Tablets—Bristol-
   Myers (U.S.) brand of Acetaminophen,
   Aspirin, and Caffeine—**See Acetamino-
   phen and Salicylates (Systemic),** 5
Exdol—Frosst (Canada) brand of Acetamino-
   phen (Systemic), 1
Exdol-8—Frosst (Canada) brand of Acet-
   aminophen and Codeine—**See Opioid
   (Narcotic) Analgesics and Acetamino-
   phen (Systemic),** 820

Exdol-15—Frosst (Canada) brand of
   Acetaminophen and Codeine—**See
   Opioid (Narcotic) Analgesics and
   Acetaminophen (Systemic),** 820
Exdol-30—Frosst (Canada) brand of
   Acetaminophen and Codeine—**See
   Opioid (Narcotic) Analgesics and
   Acetaminophen (Systemic),** 820
Exdol Strong—Frosst (Canada) brand of
   Acetaminophen (Systemic), 1
Ex-Lax—Ex-Lax (U.S.) and Ancalab
   (Canada) brand of Phenolphthalein—
   See Laxatives (Local), 682
Ex-Lax Pills—Ex-Lax (U.S.) and Ancalab
   (Canada) brand of Phenolphthalein—
   See Laxatives (Local), 682
Exna—Robins (U.S.) brand of
   Benzthiazide—**See Diuretics, Thiazide
   (Systemic),** 541
Exsel Lotion Shampoo—Allergan Herbert
   (U.S.) brand of Selenium Sulfide
   (Topical), 977
Extra Action Cough—Rugby (U.S.) brand of
   Dextromethorphan and Guaifenesin—
   **See Cough/Cold Combinations
   (Systemic),** 488
Extra Gentle Ex-Lax—Ex-Lax (U.S.) and
   Ancalab (Canada) brand of Docusate
   and Phenolphthalein—**See Laxatives
   (Local),** 682
Extreme Cold Formula Caplets—Major
   (U.S.) brand of Chlorpheniramine,
   Phenylpropanolamine, and Acetamino-
   phen—**See Antihistamines, Deconges-
   tants, and Analgesics (Systemic),** 162
Ezol—Stewart Jackson (U.S.) brand of
   Butalbital, Acetaminophen, and
   Caffeine—**See Barbiturates and
   Analgesics (Systemic),** 233

F

Famotidine [*Pepcid; Pepcid I.V.*]
   **See Histamine H_2-receptor Antagonists
   (Systemic),** 622
Father John's Medicine Plus—Medtech
   (U.S.) brand of Chlorpheniramine,
   Phenylephrine, Dextromethorphan,
   Guaifenesin, and Ammonium Chlo-
   ride—**See Cough/Cold Combinations
   (Systemic),** 488
5-FC—*See* Flucytosine (Systemic), 583
Fedahist—Kremers-Urban (U.S.) brand of
   Chlorpheniramine and Pseudoephed-
   rine—**See Antihistamines and
   Decongestants (Systemic),** 161
Fedahist Decongestant—Kremers Urban
   (U.S.) brand of Chlorpheniramine and
   Pseudoephedrine—**See Antihistamines
   and Decongestants (Systemic),** 161
Fedahist Expectorant—Kremers-Urban
   (U.S.) brand of Pseudoephedrine and
   Guaifenesin—**See Cough/Cold
   Combinations (Systemic),** 488

Fostex Medicated Cleansing Bar—Westwood-Squibb (Canada) brand of Salicylic Acid and Sulfur (Topical), 973

Fostex Medicated Cleansing Cream (for face and scalp)—Westwood-Squibb (Canada) brand of Salicylic Acid and Sulfur (Topical), 973

Fostex Medicated Cleansing Liquid—Westwood-Squibb (Canada) brand of Salicylic Acid and Sulfur (Topical), 973

Fostex Regular Strength Medicated Cleansing Bar—Westwood (U.S.) brand of Salicylic Acid and Sulfur (Topical), 973

Fostex Regular Strength Medicated Cleansing Cream (for face and scalp)—Westwood (U.S.) brand of Salicylic Acid and Sulfur (Topical), 973

Fostex Regular Strength Medicated Cover-Up—Westwood (U.S.) brand of Sulfur (Topical), 1016

Fostril Cream—Westwood-Squibb (Canada) brand of Sulfur (Topical), 1016

Fostril Lotion—Westwood (U.S.) brand of Sulfur (Topical), 1016

Fototar—Elder (U.S.) brand of Coal Tar (Topical), 443

Fowler's Diarrhea Tablets—Ancalab (Canada) brand of Attapulgite (Oral-Local), 217

Foygen Aqueous—Foy (U.S.) brand of Estrone—**See Estrogens (Systemic)**, 566

Freezone—Whitehall (U.S.) brand of Salicylic Acid (Topical), 968

Froben—Organon (Canada) brand of Flurbiprofen—**See Anti-inflammatory Analgesics, Nonsteroidal (Systemic)**, 168

5-FU—*See* Fluorouracil (Topical), 585

Fumasorb—MiLance (U.S.) brand of Ferrous Fumarate—**See Iron Supplements (Systemic)**, 657

Fumerin—Laser (U.S.) brand of Ferrous Fumarate—**See Iron Supplements (Systemic)**, 657

Furadantin—Procter & Gamble (U.S.) brand of Nitrofurantoin (Systemic), 781

Furalan—Lannett (U.S.) brand of Nitrofurantoin (Systemic), 781

Furatoin—Vortech (U.S.) brand of Nitrofurantoin (Systemic), 781

Furosemide [*Apo-Furosemide; Furoside; Lasix; Lasix Special; Myrosemide; Novosemide; Uritol*]
See Diuretics, Loop (Systemic), 524

Furoside—ICN (Canada) brand of Furosemide—**See Diuretics, Loop (Systemic)**, 524

Fynex—Mallard (U.S.) brand of Diphenhydramine—**See Antihistamines (Systemic)**, 147

G

Gantanol—Roche (U.S. and Canada) brand of Sulfamethoxazole—**See Sulfonamides (Systemic)**, 1011

Gantrisin—Roche (U.S.) brand of Sulfisoxazole—**See Sulfonamides (Ophthalmic)**, 1009; **Sulfonamides (Systemic)**, 1011

Gas-is-gon—Major (U.S.) brand of Alumina, Magnesium Trisilicate, and Sodium Bicarbonate—**See Antacids (Oral-Local)**, 61

Gastrolyte—Rorer (Canada) brand of Oral Rehydration Salts—**See Carbohydrates and Electrolytes (Systemic)**, 379

Gastrosed—Hauck (U.S.) brand of Hyoscyamine—**See Anticholinergics/Antispasmodics (Systemic)**, 73

Gastrozepin—Boehringer Ingelheim (Canada) brand of Pirenzepine—**See Anticholinergics/Antispasmodics (Systemic)**, 73

Gaviscon—Marion (U.S.) brand of Alumina and Magnesium Carbonate—**See Antacids (Oral-Local)**, 61; Marion (U.S.) and Sterling Winthrop (Canada) brand of Alumina and Magnesium Trisilicate—**See Antacids (Oral-Local)**, 61; Sterling Winthrop (Canada) brand of Aluminum Hydroxide—**See Antacids (Oral-Local)**, 61

Gaviscon-2—Marion (U.S.) brand of Alumina and Magnesium Trisilicate—**See Antacids (Oral-Local)**, 61

Gaviscon Extra Strength Relief Formula—Marion (U.S.) brand of Alumina and Magnesium Carbonate—**See Antacids (Oral-Local)**, 61

2/G-DM Cough—Merrell Dow (U.S.) brand of Dextromethorphan and Guaifenesin—**See Cough/Cold Combinations (Systemic)**, 488

Gee-Gee—Bowman (U.S.) brand of Guaifenesin (Systemic), 606

Gelamal—Halsey (U.S.) brand of Alumina and Magnesia—**See Antacids (Oral-Local)**, 61

Gelpirin—Alra (U.S.) brand of Acetaminophen, Aspirin, and Caffeine, Buffered—**See Acetaminophen and Salicylates (Systemic)**, 5

Gelusil—PD (Canada) brand of Alumina and Magnesia—**See Antacids (Oral-Local)**, 61; PD (U.S.) brand of Alumina, Magnesia, and Simethicone—**See Antacids (Oral-Local)**, 61

Gelusil-II—PD (U.S.) brand of Alumina, Magnesia, and Simethicone—**See Antacids (Oral-Local)**, 61

Gelusil Extra Strength—PD (Canada) brand of Alumina and Magnesia—**See Antacids (Oral-Local)**, 61

Gemfibrozil [*Lopid*]
(Systemic), 593

Gemnisyn—Schwarz Pharma (U.S.) brand of Acetaminophen and Aspirin—**See Acetaminophen and Salicylates (Systemic)**, 5

Gemonil—Metharbital—**See Barbiturates (Systemic)**, 223

Genac—Goldline (U.S.) brand of Triprolidine and Pseudoephedrine—**See Antihistamines and Decongestants (Systemic)**, 161

Genagesic—Goldline (U.S.) brand of Propoxyphene and Acetaminophen—**See Opioid (Narcotic) Analgesics and Acetaminophen (Systemic)**, 820

Genahist—Goldline (U.S.) brand of Diphenhydramine—**See Antihistamines (Systemic)**, 147

Genalac—Goldline (U.S.) brand of Calcium Carbonate—**See Antacids (Oral-Local)**, 61

Genallerate—Goldline (U.S.) brand of Chlorpheniramine—**See Antihistamines (Systemic)**, 147

Genamin—Goldline (U.S.) brand of Chlorpheniramine and Phenylpropanolamine—**See Antihistamines and Decongestants (Systemic)**, 161

Genapap Children's Elixir—Goldline (U.S.) brand of Acetaminophen (Systemic), 1

Genapap Children's Tablets—Goldline (U.S.) brand of Acetaminophen (Systemic), 1

Genapap Extra Strength Caplets—Goldline (U.S.) brand of Acetaminophen (Systemic), 1

Genapap Extra Strength Tablets—Goldline (U.S.) brand of Acetaminophen (Systemic), 1

Genapap, Infants'—Goldline (U.S.) brand of Acetaminophen (Systemic), 1

Genapap Regular Strength Tablets—Goldline (U.S.) brand of Acetaminophen (Systemic), 1

Genapax—Key (U.S.) brand of Gentian Violet (Vaginal), 595

Genaphed—Goldline (U.S.) brand of Pseudoephedrine (Systemic), 936

Genatap—Goldline (U.S.) brand of Brompheniramine and Phenylpropanolamine—**See Antihistamines and Decongestants (Systemic)**, 161

Genaton—Goldline (U.S.) brand of Alumina and Magnesium Trisilicate—**See Antacids (Oral-Local)**, 61

Genatuss—Goldline (U.S.) brand of Guaifenesin (Systemic), 606

Gencalc—Goldline (U.S.) brand of Calcium Carbonate—**See Calcium Supplements (Systemic)**, 357

Gencold—Goldline (U.S.) brand of Chlorpheniramine and Phenylpropanolamine—**See Antihistamines and Decongestants (Systemic)**, 161

Guanethidine Monosulfate [*Apo-Guanethi-dine; Ismelin*] **(Systemic)**, 612

Guanethidine Monosulfate and Hydrochlorothiazide [*Esimil; Ismelin-Esidrix*] **(Systemic)**, 614

Guanfacine Hydrochloride [*Tenex*] **(Systemic)**, 615

Guiamid D.M. Liquid—Vangard (U.S.) brand of Dextromethorphan and Guaifenesin—**See Cough/Cold Combinations (Systemic)**, 488

Guiatuss—Bell (U.S.); Generix (U.S); Moore (U.S.); Schein (U.S.); and United Research (U.S.) brand of Guaifenesin (Systemic), 606

Guiatuss A.C.—Schein (U.S.) brand of Codeine and Guaifenesin—**See Cough/Cold Combinations (Systemic)**, 488

Guiatuss-DM—Vangard (U.S.) brand of Dextromethorphan and Guaifenesin—**See Cough/Cold Combinations (Systemic)**, 488

Guiatussin with Codeine Liquid—Rugby (U.S.) brand of Codeine and Guaifenesin—**See Cough/Cold Combinations (Systemic)**, 488

Gynecort—Combe (U.S.) brand of Hydrocortisone—**See Corticosteroids (Topical)**, 458

Gynecort 10—Combe (U.S.) brand of Hydrocortisone—**See Corticosteroids (Topical)**, 458

Gyne-Lotrimin—Schering (U.S.) brand of Clotrimazole—**See Antifungals, Azole (Vaginal)**, 140

Gynergen—Sandoz (Canada) brand of Ergotamine—**See Vascular Headache Suppressants, Ergot Derivative-containing (Systemic)**, 1066

Gynogen—Forest (U.S.) brand of Estrone—**See Estrogens (Systemic)**, 566

Gynogen L.A. 10—Forest (U.S.) brand of Estradiol—**See Estrogens (Systemic)**, 566

Gynogen L.A. 20—Forest (U.S.) brand of Estradiol—**See Estrogens (Systemic)**, 566

Gynogen L.A. 40—Forest (U.S.) brand of Estradiol—**See Estrogens (Systemic)**, 566

Gynol II Extra Strength Contraceptive Jelly—Ortho (U.S.) brand of Nonoxynol 9—**See Spermicides (Vaginal)**, 991

Gynol II Original Formula Contraceptive Jelly—Ortho (U.S.) brand of Nonoxynol 9—**See Spermicides (Vaginal)**, 991

Gyno-Trosyd—Pfizer (Canada) brand of Tioconazole—**See Antifungals, Azole (Vaginal)**, 140

H

Halazepam [*Paxipam*] **See Benzodiazepines (Systemic)**, 251

Halcinonide [*Halog; Halog-E*] **See Corticosteroids (Topical)**, 458

Halcion—Upjohn (U.S. and Canada) brand of Triazolam—**See Benzodiazepines (Systemic)**, 251

Haldol—McNeil (U.S. and Canada) brand of Haloperidol (Systemic), 618

Haldol Decanoate—McNeil (U.S.) brand of Haloperidol (Systemic), 618

Haldol LA—McNeil (Canada) brand of Haloperidol (Systemic), 618

Haldrone—Lilly (U.S.) brand of Paramethasone—**See Corticosteroids/Corticotropin—Glucocorticoid Effects (Systemic)**, 472

Halenol Elixir—Gen-King (U.S.) and Halsey (U.S.) brand of Acetaminophen (Systemic), 1

Halenol Extra Strength Caplets—Halsey (U.S.) brand of Acetaminophen (Systemic), 1

Halenol Extra Strength Tablets—Halsey (U.S.) brand of Acetaminophen (Systemic), 1

Halenol Regular Strength Tablets—Halsey (U.S.) brand of Acetaminophen (Systemic), 1

Haley's M-O—Sterling Winthrop (U.S.) brand of Magnesium Hydroxide and Mineral Oil—**See Laxatives (Local)**, 682

Halfprin—Kramer (U.S.) brand of Aspirin—**See Salicylates (Systemic)**, 953

Halobetasol Propionate [*ulobetasol; Ultravate*] **See Corticosteroids (Topical)**, 458

Halofed—Halsey (U.S.) brand of Pseudoephedrine (Systemic), 936

Halofed Adult Strength—Halsey (U.S.) brand of Pseudoephedrine (Systemic), 936

Halog—Squibb (U.S. and Canada) brand of Halcinonide—**See Corticosteroids (Topical)**, 458

Halog-E—Squibb (U.S.) brand of Halcinonide—**See Corticosteroids (Topical)**, 458

Haloperidol [*Apo-Haloperidol; Haldol; Novo-Peridol; Peridol; PMS Haloperidol*] **(Systemic)**, 618

Haloperidol Decanoate [*Haldol Decanoate; Haldol LA*] **(Systemic)**, 618

Halotestin—Upjohn (U.S. and Canada) brand of Fluoxymesterone—**See Androgens (Systemic)**, 44

Halotussin—Halsey (U.S.) brand of Guaifenesin (Systemic), 606

Halotussin-DM Expectorant—Halsey (U.S.) brand of Dextromethorphan and Guaifenesin—**See Cough/Cold Combinations (Systemic)**, 488

Haltran—Roberts (U.S.) brand of Ibuprofen—**See Anti-inflammatory Analgesics, Nonsteroidal (Systemic)**, 168

Harmonyl—Abbott (U.S.) brand of Deserpidine—**See Rauwolfia Alkaloids (Systemic)**, 945

Head & Shoulders Antidandruff Cream Shampoo Normal to Dry Formula—Procter & Gamble (U.S.) brand of Pyrithione (Topical), 940

Head & Shoulders Antidandruff Cream Shampoo Normal to Oily Formula—Procter & Gamble (U.S.) brand of Pyrithione (Topical), 940

Head & Shoulders Antidandruff Lotion Shampoo 2 in 1 (Complete Dandruff Shampoo plus Conditioner in One) Formula—Procter & Gamble (U.S.) brand of Pyrithione (Topical), 940

Head & Shoulders Antidandruff Lotion Shampoo Normal to Dry Formula—Procter & Gamble (U.S.) brand of Pyrithione (Topical), 940

Head & Shoulders Antidandruff Lotion Shampoo Normal to Oily Formula—Procter & Gamble (U.S.) brand of Pyrithione (Topical), 940

Head & Shoulders Dry Scalp Conditioning Formula Lotion Shampoo—Procter & Gamble (U.S.) brand of Pyrithione (Topical), 940

Head & Shoulders Dry Scalp 2 in 1 (Dry Scalp Shampoo Plus Conditioner in One) Formula Lotion Shampoo—Procter & Gamble (U.S.) brand of Pyrithione (Topical), 940

Head & Shoulders Dry Scalp Regular Formula Lotion Shampoo—Procter & Gamble (U.S.) brand of Pyrithione (Topical), 940

Head & Shoulders Intensive Treatment Conditioning Formula Dandruff Lotion Shampoo—Procter & Gamble (U.S.) brand of Selenium Sulfide (Topical), 977

Head & Shoulders Intensive Treatment 2 in 1 (Persistent Dandruff Shampoo plus Conditioner in One) Formula Dandruff Lotion Shampoo—Procter & Gamble (U.S.) brand of Selenium Sulfide (Topical), 977

Head & Shoulders Intensive Treatment Regular Formula Dandruff Lotion Shampoo—Procter & Gamble (U.S.) brand of Selenium Sulfide (Topical), 977

Headstart—CIBA-GEIGY (Canada) brand of Aspirin—**See Salicylates (Systemic)**, 953

Hemocyte—U.S. Pharmaceutical (U.S.) brand of Ferrous Fumarate—**See Iron Supplements (Systemic)**, 657

Hemril-HC—Upsher-Smith (U.S.) brand of Hydrocortisone—**See Corticosteroids (Topical)**, 458

Hydrocortone Phosphate—MSD (U.S.) brand of Hydrocortisone—**See Corticosteroids/Corticotropin—Glucocorticoid Effects (Systemic)**, 472

Hydro-Crysti-12—Hauck (U.S.) brand of Hydroxocobalamin—**See Vitamin B$_{12}$ (Systemic)**, 1077

Hydro-D—Halsey (U.S.) brand of Hydrochlorothiazide—**See Diuretics, Thiazide (Systemic)**, 541

HydroDIURIL—MSD (U.S. and Canada) brand of Hydrochlorothiazide—**See Diuretics, Thiazide (Systemic)**, 541

Hydroflumethiazide [*Diucardin; Saluron*] **See Diuretics, Thiazide (Systemic)**, 541

Hydrogesic—Edwards (U.S.) brand of Hydrocodone and Acetaminophen—**See Opioid (Narcotic) Analgesics and Acetaminophen (Systemic)**, 820

Hydromine—WC (U.S.) brand of Phenylpropanolamine and Hydrocodone—**See Cough/Cold Combinations (Systemic)**, 488

Hydromine Pediatric—WC (U.S.) brand of Phenylpropanolamine and Hydrocodone—**See Cough/Cold Combinations (Systemic)**, 488

Hydromorphone Hydrochloride [dihydromorphinone; *Dilaudid; Dilaudid-HP*] **See Opioid (Narcotic) Analgesics (Systemic)**, 793

Hydromorphone Hydrochloride and Guaifenesin [*Dilaudid Cough*] **See Cough/Cold Combinations (Systemic)**, 488

Hydromox—Lederle (U.S.) brand of Quinethazone—**See Diuretics, Thiazide (Systemic)**, 541

Hydropane—Halsey (U.S.) brand of Hydrocodone and Homatropine—**See Cough/Cold Combinations (Systemic)**, 488

Hydrophen—Rugby (U.S.) brand of Phenylpropanolamine and Hydrocodone—**See Cough/Cold Combinations (Systemic)**, 488

Hydropine—Rugby (U.S.) brand of Reserpine and Hydroflumethiazide—**See Rauwolfia Alkaloids and Thiazide Diuretics (Systemic)**, 948

Hydropine H.P.—Rugby (U.S.) brand of Reserpine and Hydroflumethiazide—**See Rauwolfia Alkaloids and Thiazide Diuretics (Systemic)**, 948

Hydropres—MSD (U.S. and Canada) brand of Reserpine and Hydrochlorothiazide—**See Rauwolfia Alkaloids and Thiazide Diuretics (Systemic)**, 948

Hydrosine—Major (U.S.) brand of Reserpine and Hydrochlorothiazide—**See Rauwolfia Alkaloids and Thiazide Diuretics (Systemic)**, 948

Hydrotensin—Mayrand (U.S.) brand of Reserpine and Hydrochlorothiazide— **See Rauwolfia Alkaloids and Thiazide Diuretics (Systemic)**, 948

Hydro-Tex—Syosset (U.S.) brand of Hydrocortisone—**See Corticosteroids (Topical)**, 458

Hydroxacen—Central (U.S.) brand of Hydroxyzine—**See Antihistamines (Systemic)**, 147

Hydroxocobalamin [*Alphamine; Hydrobexan; Hydro-Cobex; Hydro-Crysti-12; LA-12;* vitamin B$_{12}$] **See Vitamin B$_{12}$ (Systemic)**, 1077

Hydroxychloroquine Sulfate [*Plaquenil*] **(Systemic)**, 636

Hydroxyprogesterone Caproate [*Delalutin; Duralutin; Gesterol L.A.; Hylutin; Hyprogest; Hyproval P.A.; Pro-Depo; Prodrox*] **See Progestins (Systemic)**, 929

Hydroxyurea [*Hydrea*] **(Systemic)**, 639

Hydroxyzine Hydrochloride [*Anxanil; Apo-Hydroxyzine; Atarax; E-Vista; Hydroxacen; Hyzine-50; Multipax; Novohydroxyzin; Quiess; Vistaject-25; Vistaject-50; Vistaril; Vistazine 50*] **See Antihistamines (Systemic)**, 147

Hydroxyzine Pamoate [*Vistaril*] **See Antihistamines (Systemic)**, 147

Hygroton—Rorer (U.S.) and Geigy (Canada) brand of Chlorthalidone—**See Diuretics, Thiazide (Systemic)**, 541

Hylorel—Pennwalt (U.S.) brand of Guanadrel (Systemic), 609

Hylutin—Hyrex (U.S.) brand of Hydroxyprogesterone—**See Progestins (Systemic)**, 929

Hyoscine hydrobromide—Scopolamine—**See Anticholinergics/Antispasmodics (Systemic)**, 73

Hyoscine methobromide— Methscopolamine—**See Anticholinergics/Antispasmodics (Systemic)**, 73

Hyoscyamine [*Cystospaz*] **See Anticholinergics/Antispasmodics (Systemic)**, 73

Hyoscyamine and Scopolamine [*Bellafoline*] **See Anticholinergics/Antispasmodics (Systemic)**, 73

Hyoscyamine Sulfate [*Anaspaz; Cystospaz-M; Gastrosed; Levsin; Levsinex Timecaps; Levsin S/L; Neoquess*] **See Anticholinergics/Antispasmodics (Systemic)**, 73

Hyoscyamine Sulfate and Phenobarbital [*Levsin-PB; Levsin with Phenobarbital*] **See Belladonna Alkaloids and Barbiturates (Systemic)**, 246

Hyosophen—Rugby (U.S.) brand of Atropine, Hyoscyamine, Scopolamine, and Phenobarbital—**See Belladonna Alkaloids and Barbiturates (Systemic)**, 246

HY-PHEN—Ascher (U.S.) brand of Hydrocodone and Acetaminophen—**See Opioid (Narcotic) Analgesics and Acetaminophen (Systemic)**, 820

Hyprogest—Keene (U.S.) brand of Hydroxyprogesterone—**See Progestins (Systemic)**, 929

Hyproval P.A.—Reid-Rowell (U.S.) brand of Hydroxyprogesterone—**See Progestins (Systemic)**, 929

Hyrexin-50—Hyrex (U.S.) brand of Diphenhydramine—**See Antihistamines (Systemic)**, 147

Hytinic—Hyrex (U.S.) brand of Iron-Polysaccharide—**See Iron Supplements (Systemic)**, 657

Hytone—Dermik (U.S.) brand of Hydrocortisone—**See Corticosteroids (Topical)**, 458

Hytrin—Abbott (U.S. and Canada) brand of Terazosin (Systemic), 1020

Hytuss—Hyrex (U.S.) brand of Guaifenesin (Systemic), 606

Hytuss-2X—Hyrex (U.S.) brand of Guaifenesin (Systemic), 606

Hyzine-50—Hyrex (U.S.) brand of Hydroxyzine—**See Antihistamines (Systemic)**, 147

I

Ibren—Econo-Med (U.S.) brand of Ibuprofen—**See Anti-inflammatory Analgesics, Nonsteroidal (Systemic)**, 168

Ibumed—Med-Tek (U.S.) brand of Ibuprofen—**See Anti-inflammatory Analgesics, Nonsteroidal (Systemic)**, 168

Ibuprin—Thompson (U.S.) brand of Ibuprofen—**See Anti-inflammatory Analgesics, Nonsteroidal (Systemic)**, 168

Ibupro-600—Econo-Med (U.S.) brand of Ibuprofen—**See Anti-inflammatory Analgesics, Nonsteroidal (Systemic)**, 168

Ibuprofen [*Aches-N-Pain; Actiprofen Caplets; Advil; Advil Caplets; Amersol; Apo-Ibuprofen; Children's Advil; Dolgesic; Genpril; Genpril Caplets; Haltran; Ibren; Ibumed; Ibuprin; Ibrupro-600; Ibuprohm; Ibuprohm Caplets; Ibu-Tab; Ibutex; Ifen; Medipren; Medipren Caplets; Midol 200 Caplets; Motrin; Motrin-IB; Motrin-IB Caplets; Novoprofen; Nuprin; Nuprin Caplets; Pamprin-IB; PediaProfen; Profen; Ro-Profen; Rufen; Trendar*] **See Anti-inflammatory Analgesics, Nonsteroidal (Systemic)**, 168

Ibuprohm—Ohm (U.S.) brand of Ibuprofen—**See Anti-inflammatory Analgesics, Nonsteroidal (Systemic)**, 168

Inversine—MSD (U.S.) brand of Mecamylamine (Systemic), 715

*Ionax Astringent Skin Cleanser Topical
Solution*—Owen/Galderma (U.S.) brand
of Salicylic Acid (Topical), 968

Ionil Plus Shampoo—Owen/Galderma (U.S.)
brand of Salicylic Acid (Topical), 968

Ionil Shampoo—Owen/Galderma (U.S.)
brand of Salicylic Acid (Topical), 968

Ionil T plus—Owen (U.S.) brand of Coal Tar
(Topical), 443

Iophen-C Liquid—Barre (U.S.); Murray
(U.S.); Rugby (U.S.); Schein (U.S.); and
Vita-Rx (U.S.) brand of Codeine and
Iodinated Glycerol—**See Cough/Cold
Combinations (Systemic)**, 488

Iopidine—Alcon (U.S.) brand of
Apraclonidine (Ophthalmic), 214

Iotuss—Muro (U.S.) brand of Codeine and
Iodinated Glycerol—**See Cough/Cold
Combinations (Systemic)**, 488

Iotuss-DM—Muro (U.S.) brand of
Dextromethorphan and Iodinated
Glycerol—**See Cough/Cold Combina-
tions (Systemic)**, 488

I-Pilocarpine—Americal (U.S.) brand of
Pilocarpine (Ophthalmic), 903

Ipratropium Bromide [*Atrovent*]
(Inhalation-Local), 655

Ipsatol Cough Formula for Children—
Kenwood (U.S.) brand of Phenylpro-
panolamine, Dextromethorphan, and
Guaifenesin—**See Cough/Cold
Combinations (Systemic)**, 488

Ircon—Key (U.S.) brand of Ferrous
Fumarate—**See Iron Supplements
(Systemic)**, 657

Iron Dextran [*Imferon; InFeD*]
See Iron Supplements (Systemic), 657

Iron-Polysaccharide [*Hytinic; Niferex;
Niferex-150; Nu-Iron; Nu-Iron 150*]
See Iron Supplements (Systemic), 657

Iron Sorbitol [*Jectofer*]
See Iron Supplements (Systemic), 657

Iron Supplements
(Systemic), 657

Ismelin—CIBA (U.S. and Canada) brand of
Guanethidine (Systemic), 612

Ismelin-Esidrix—CIBA (Canada) brand of
Guanethidine and Hydrochlorothiazide
(Systemic), 614

Iso-Acetazone—Rugby (U.S.) brand of
Isometheptene, Dichloralphenazone, and
Acetaminophen (Systemic), 665

Iso-Bid—Geriatric (U.S.) brand of Isosorbide
Dinitrate—**See Nitrates (Systemic)**, 770

Isobutal—Balan (U.S.) brand of Butalbital,
Aspirin, and Caffeine—**See Barbiturates and Analgesics (Systemic)**, 233

Isobutyl—Bioline (U.S.) brand of Butalbital,
Aspirin, and Caffeine—**See Barbiturates and Analgesics (Systemic)**, 233

Isocarboxazid [*Marplan*]
**See Antidepressants, Monoamine
Oxidase (MAO) Inhibitor (Systemic)**,
113

Isocet—Rugby (U.S.) brand of Butalbital,
Acetaminophen, and Caffeine—**See
Barbiturates and Analgesics (Sys-
temic)**, 233

Isoclor—Du Pont Critical Care (U.S.) brand
of Chlorpheniramine and Pseudoephedrine—**See Antihistamines and
Decongestants (Systemic)**, 161

Isoclor Expectorant—Fisons (U.S.) brand of
Pseudoephedrine, Codeine, and
Guaifenesin—**See Cough/Cold
Combinations (Systemic)**, 488

Isoclor Timesules—Du Pont Critical Care
(U.S.) brand of Chlorpheniramine and
Pseudoephedrine—**See Antihistamines
and Decongestants (Systemic)**, 161

Isocom—Nutripharm (U.S.) brand of
Isometheptene, Dichloralphenazone, and
Acetaminophen (Systemic), 665

Isoetharine [*Arm-a-Med Isoetharine;
Bronkosol; Dey-Dose Isoetharine; Dey-
Dose Isoetharine S/F; Dey-Lute
Isoetharine; Dey-Lute Isoetharine S/F;
Dispos-a-Med Isoetharine*]
**See Bronchodilators, Adrenergic
(Systemic)**, 294

Isoetharine Mesylate [*Bronkometer*]
**See Bronchodilators, Adrenergic
(Systemic)**, 294

Isoflurophate [DFP; difluorophate; dyflos;
Floropryl]
**See Antiglaucoma Agents, Cholinergic,
Long-acting (Ophthalmic)**, 143

Isolin—Glenlawn (U.S.) brand of Butalbital,
Aspirin, and Caffeine—**See Barbiturates and Analgesics (Systemic)**, 233

Isollyl—Rugby (U.S.) and Spencer-Mead
(U.S.) brand of Butalbital, Aspirin, and
Caffeine—**See Barbiturates and
Analgesics (Systemic)**, 233

Isollyl with Codeine—Rugby (U.S.) brand of
Butalbital, Aspirin, Codeine, and
Caffeine—**See Barbiturates and
Analgesics (Systemic)**, 233

Isometheptene, dichloralphenazone, and
paracetamol—*See* Isometheptene,
Dichloralphenazone, and Acetaminophen (Systemic), 665

Isometheptene Mucate, Dichloralphenazone,
and Acetaminophen [*Amidrine; I.D.A.;
Iso-Acetazone; Isocom;* isometheptene,
dichloralphenazone, and paracetamol;
*Midchlor; Midrin; Migquin; Migrapap;
Migratine; Migrazone; Migrend;
Migrex; Mitride*]
(Systemic), 665

Isonate—Major (U.S.) brand of Isosorbide
Dinitrate—**See Nitrates (Systemic)**, 770

Isopap—Columbia Drug (U.S.) brand of
Butalbital, Acetaminophen, and
Caffeine—**See Barbiturates and
Analgesics (Systemic)**, 233

Isopropamide Iodide [*Darbid*]
**See Anticholinergics/Antispasmodics
(Systemic)**, 73

Isoproterenol [*Aerolone; Dey-Dose Isoprot-
erenol; Dispos-a-Med Isoproterenol;
Isuprel; Vapo-Iso*]
**See Bronchodilators, Adrenergic
(Systemic)**, 294

Isoproterenol Hydrochloride [*Isuprel; Isuprel
Glossets; Isuprel Mistometer;
Norisodrine Aerotrol*]
**See Bronchodilators, Adrenergic
(Systemic)**, 294

Isoproterenol Hydrochloride and Phenylephrine Bitartrate [*Duo-Medihaler*]
(Systemic), 667

Isoproterenol Hydrochloride and Phenyleph-
rine Hydrochloride [*Isuprel-Neo
Mistometer*]
(Systemic), 667

Isoproterenol Sulfate [*Medihaler-Iso*]
**See Bronchodilators, Adrenergic
(Systemic)**, 294

Isoptin—Knoll (U.S. and Canada) and Searle
(Canada) brand of Verapamil—**See
Calcium Channel Blocking Agents
(Systemic)**, 343

Isoptin SR—Knoll (U.S.) and Searle
(Canada) brand of Verapamil—**See
Calcium Channel Blocking Agents
(Systemic)**, 343

Isopto Carbachol—Alcon (U.S. and Canada)
brand of Carbachol (Ophthalmic), 368

Isopto Carpine—Alcon (U.S. and Canada)
brand of Pilocarpine (Ophthalmic), 903

Isopto-Cetamide—Alcon (U.S. and Canada)
brand of Sulfacetamide—**See Sulfonamides (Ophthalmic)**, 1009

Isopto Eserine—Alcon (U.S.) brand of
Physostigmine (Ophthalmic), 901

Isorbid—Bioline (U.S.) brand of Isosorbide
Dinitrate—**See Nitrates (Systemic)**, 770

Isordil—Ives (U.S.) and Wyeth (Canada)
brand of Isosorbide Dinitrate—**See
Nitrates (Systemic)**, 770

Isosorbide Dinitrate [*Apo-ISDN; Cedocard-
SR; Coronex; Dilatrate-SR; Iso-Bid;
Isonate; Isorbid; Isordil; Isotrate;
Novosorbide; Sorbitrate; Sorbitrate SA*]
See Nitrates (Systemic), 770

Isotrate—Hauck (U.S.) brand of Isosorbide
Dinitrate—**See Nitrates (Systemic)**, 770

Isradipine [*DynaCirc*]
**See Calcium Channel Blocking Agents
(Systemic)**, 343

I-Sulfacet—Americal (U.S.) brand of
Sulfacetamide—**See Sulfonamides
(Ophthalmic)**, 1009

Isuprel—Sterling Winthrop (U.S. and
Canada) brand of Isoproterenol—**See
Bronchodilators, Adrenergic
(Systemic)**, 294

Isuprel Glossets—Sterling Winthrop (U.S.)
brand of Isoproterenol—**See
Bronchodilators, Adrenergic
(Systemic)**, 294

Klavikordal—U.S. Ethicals (U.S.) brand of Nitroglycerin—**See Nitrates (Systemic)**, 770

Klerist-D—Nutripharm (U.S.) brand of Chlorpheniramine and Pseudoephedrine—**See Antihistamines and Decongestants (Systemic)**, 161

Klonopin—Roche (U.S.) brand of Clonazepam—**See Benzodiazepines (Systemic)**, 251

Koffex—Rougier (Canada) brand of Dextromethorphan (Systemic), 502

Kolephrin—Pfeiffer (U.S.) brand of Chlorpheniramine, Phenylephrine, Acetaminophen, Salicylamide, and Caffeine—**See Antihistamines, Decongestants, and Analgesics (Systemic)**, 162

Kolephrin/DM—Pfeiffer (U.S.) brand of Chlorpheniramine, Phenylpropanolamine, Dextromethorphan, Acetaminophen, and Caffeine—**See Cough/Cold Combinations (Systemic)**, 488

Kolephrin GG/DM—Pfeiffer (U.S.) brand of Dextromethorphan and Guaifenesin—**See Cough/Cold Combinations (Systemic)**, 488

Kolephrin NN Liquid—Pfeiffer (U.S.) brand of Pyrilamine, Phenylpropanolamine, Dextromethorphan, and Sodium Salicylate—**See Cough/Cold Combinations (Systemic)**, 488

Kondremul—Cowling & Braithwaite (Canada) brand of Mineral Oil—**See Laxatives (Local)**, 682

Kondremul with Cascara—Fisons (U.S.) brand of Mineral Oil and Cascara Sagrada—**See Laxatives (Local)**, 682

Kondremul with Phenolphthalein—Fisons (U.S.) brand of Mineral Oil and Phenolphthalein—**See Laxatives (Local)**, 682

Kondremul Plain—Fisons (U.S.) brand of Mineral Oil—**See Laxatives (Local)**, 682

Konsyl—Lafayette (U.S.) brand of Psyllium—**See Laxatives (Local)**, 682

Konsyl-D—Lafayette (U.S.) brand of Psyllium Hydrophilic Mucilloid—**See Laxatives (Local)**, 682

Kophane—Pfeiffer (U.S.) brand of Chlorpheniramine, Phenylpropanolamine, Dextromethorphan, and Ammonium Chloride—**See Cough/Cold Combinations (Systemic)**, 488

Kophane Cough and Cold Formula—Pfeiffer (U.S.) brand of Chlorpheniramine, Phenylpropanolamine, and Dextromethorphan—**See Cough/Cold Combinations (Systemic)**, 488

Korigesic—Trimen (U.S.) brand of Chlorpheniramine, Phenylephrine, Acetaminophen, and Caffeine—**See Antihistamines, Decongestants, and Analgesics (Systemic)**, 162

Koromex Cream—Schmid (U.S.) brand of Octoxynol 9—**See Spermicides (Vaginal)**, 991

Koromex Crystal Clear Gel—Schmid (U.S.) brand of Nonoxynol 9—**See Spermicides (Vaginal)**, 991

Koromex Foam—Schmid (U.S.) brand of Nonoxynol 9—**See Spermicides (Vaginal)**, 991

Koromex Jelly—Schmid (U.S.) brand of Nonoxynol 9—**See Spermicides (Vaginal)**, 991

K-P—Century (U.S.) brand of Kaolin and Pectin (Oral-Local), 671

K-Pek—Rugby (U.S.) brand of Kaolin and Pectin (Oral-Local), 671

K-Phos M. F.—Beach (U.S.) brand of Potassium and Sodium Phosphates—**See Phosphates (Systemic)**, 897

K-Phos Neutral—Beach (U.S.) brand of Potassium and Sodium Phosphates—**See Phosphates (Systemic)**, 897

K-Phos No. 2—Beach (U.S.) brand of Potassium and Sodium Phosphates—**See Phosphates (Systemic)**, 897

K-Phos Original—Beach (U.S.) brand of Potassium Phosphate, Monobasic—**See Phosphates (Systemic)**, 897

Kronofed-A Jr. Kronocaps—Ferndale (U.S.) brand of Chlorpheniramine and Pseudoephedrine—**See Antihistamines and Decongestants (Systemic)**, 161

Kronofed-A Kronocaps—Ferndale (U.S.) brand of Chlorpheniramine and Pseudoephedrine—**See Antihistamines and Decongestants (Systemic)**, 161

Kudrox Double Strength—Kremers-Urban (U.S.) brand of Alumina, Magnesia, and Simethicone—**See Antacids (Oral-Local)**, 61

Ku-Zyme HP—Kremers-Urban (U.S.) brand of Pancrelipase (Systemic), 832

Kwelcof Liquid—Ascher (U.S.) brand of Hydrocodone and Guaifenesin—**See Cough/Cold Combinations (Systemic)**, 488

L

LA-12—Hyrex (U.S.) brand of Hydroxocobalamin—**See Vitamin B_{12} (Systemic)**, 1077

Labetalol Hydrochloride [*Normodyne; Trandate*]
See Beta-adrenergic Blocking Agents (Systemic), 267

Labetalol Hydrochloride and Hydrochlorothiazide [*Normozide; Trandate HCT*]
See Beta-adrenergic Blocking Agents and Thiazide Diuretics (Systemic), 283

LactiCare-HC—Stiefel (U.S.) brand of Hydrocortisone—**See Corticosteroids (Topical)**, 458

Lactisol—C&M (U.S.) brand of Salicylic Acid (Topical), 968

Lactulax—Rougier (Canada) brand of Lactulose—**See Laxatives (Local)**, 682

Lactulose [*Cholac; Chronulac; Constilac; Constulose; Duphalac; Enulose; Generlac; Lactulax; Portalac*]
See Laxatives (Local), 682

L.A.E. 20—Seatrace (U.S.) brand of Estradiol—**See Estrogens (Systemic)**, 566

Lanacort—Combe (U.S.) brand of Hydrocortisone—**See Corticosteroids (Topical)**, 458

Lanacort 10—Combe (U.S.) brand of Hydrocortisone—**See Corticosteroids (Topical)**, 458

Lanatuss Expectorant—Lannett (U.S.) brand of Chlorpheniramine, Phenylpropanolamine, Guaifenesin, Sodium Citrate, and Citric Acid—**See Cough/Cold Combinations (Systemic)**, 488

Laniroif—Truxton (U.S.) brand of Butalbital, Aspirin, and Caffeine—**See Barbiturates and Analgesics (Systemic)**, 233

Lanophyllin—Lannett (U.S.) brand of Theophylline—**See Bronchodilators, Xanthine-derivative (Systemic)**, 315

Lanophyllin-GG—Lannett (U.S.) brand of Theophylline and Guaifenesin (Systemic), 1032

Lanorinal—Lannett (U.S.) and Texas Drug Reps (U.S.) brand of Butalbital, Aspirin, and Caffeine—**See Barbiturates and Analgesics (Systemic)**, 233

Lanoxicaps—BW (U.S.) brand of Digoxin—**See Digitalis Glycosides (Systemic)**, 510

Lanoxin—BW (U.S. and Canada) brand of Digoxin—**See Digitalis Glycosides (Systemic)**, 510

Lansoÿl—Jouveinal (Canada) brand of Mineral Oil—**See Laxatives (Local)**, 682

Lanvis—BW (Canada) brand of Thioguanine (Systemic), 1036

Largactil—Rhone-Poulenc (Canada) brand of Chlorpromazine—**See Phenothiazines (Systemic)**, 872

Largactil Liquid—Rhone-Poulenc (Canada) brand of Chlorpromazine—**See Phenothiazines (Systemic)**, 872

Largactil Oral Drops—Rhone-Poulenc (Canada) brand of Chlorpromazine—**See Phenothiazines (Systemic)**, 872

Larodopa—Roche (U.S. and Canada) brand of Levodopa (Systemic), 696

Larotid—Beecham (U.S.) brand of Amoxicillin—**See Penicillins (Systemic)**, 848

Lasix—Hoechst-Roussel (U.S.) and Hoechst (Canada) brand of Furosemide—**See Diuretics, Loop (Systemic)**, 524

Lasix Special—Hoechst (Canada) brand of Furosemide—**See Diuretics, Loop (Systemic)**, 524

M

Maalox—Rorer (U.S. and Canada) brand of Alumina and Magnesia—**See Antacids (Oral-Local)**, 61

Maalox Extra Strength—Rorer (U.S.) brand of Alumina and Magnesia—**See Antacids (Oral-Local)**, 61

Maalox Plus—Rorer (U.S. and Canada) brand of Alumina, Magnesia, and Simethicone—**See Antacids (Oral-Local)**, 61

Maalox Plus, Extra Strength—Rorer (U.S.) brand of Alumina, Magnesia, and Simethicone—**See Antacids (Oral-Local)**, 61

Maalox TC—Rorer (U.S. and Canada) brand of Alumina and Magnesia—**See Antacids (Oral-Local)**, 61

Maalox Whip—Rorer (U.S.) brand of Alumina and Magnesia—**See Antacids (Oral-Local)**, 61

Macrobid—Procter & Gamble (U.S.) brand of Nitrofurantoin (Systemic), 781

Macrodantin—Procter & Gamble (U.S. and Canada) brand of Nitrofurantoin (Systemic), 781

Magaldrate [*Antiflux; Lowsium; Riopan; Riopan Extra Strength*] **See Antacids (Oral-Local)**, 61

Magaldrate and Simethicone [*Losotron Plus; Lowsium Plus; Riopan Plus; Riopan Plus 2; Riopan Plus Extra Strength*] **See Antacids (Oral-Local)**, 61

Magan—Adria (U.S.) brand of Magnesium Salicylate—**See Salicylates (Systemic)**, 953

Magnagel—Hauck (U.S.) brand of Alumina and Magnesium Carbonate—**See Antacids (Oral-Local)**, 61

Magnaprin—Rugby (U.S.) brand of Aspirin, Alumina, and Magnesia—**See Salicylates (Systemic)**, 953

Magnaprin Arthritis Strength—Rugby (U.S.) brand of Aspirin, Alumina, and Magnesia—**See Salicylates (Systemic)**, 953

Magnatril—Lannett (U.S.) brand of Magnesium Trisilicate, Alumina, and Magnesia—**See Antacids (Oral-Local)**, 61

Magnesium Carbonate and Sodium Bicarbonate [*Bisodol*] **See Antacids (Oral-Local)**, 61

Magnesium Citrate [citrate of magnesia; *Citroma; Citro-Mag; Citro-Nesia*] **See Laxatives (Local)**, 682

Magnesium Hydroxide [*Phillips' Magnesia Tablets; Phillips' Milk of Magnesia*] **See Laxatives (Local)**, 682

Magnesium Hydroxide [*Phillips' Milk of Magnesia*] **See Antacids (Oral-Local)**, 61

Magnesium Hydroxide and Mineral Oil [*Haley's M-O*] **See Laxatives (Local)**, 682

Magnesium Hydroxide, Mineral Oil, and Glycerin [*Magnolax*] **See Laxatives (Local)**, 682

Magnesium Oxide [*Mag-Ox 400; Maox*] **See Laxatives (Local)**, 682

Magnesium Oxide [*Mag-Ox 400; Maox; Uro-Mag*] **See Antacids (Oral-Local)**, 61

Magnesium Salicylate [*Back-Ese; Doan's; Magan; Mobidin*] **See Salicylates (Systemic)**, 953

Magnesium Sulfate [*Bilagog*; epsom salts] **See Laxatives (Local)**, 682

Magnesium Trisilicate, Alumina, and Magnesia [*Magnatril*] **See Antacids (Oral-Local)**, 61

Magnolax—Wampole (Canada) brand of Magnesium Hydroxide, Mineral Oil, and Glycerin—**See Laxatives (Local)**, 682

Mag-Ox 400—Blaine (U.S.) brand of Magnesium Oxide—**See Antacids (Oral-Local)**, 61; **Laxatives (Local)**, 682

Majeptil—Rhone-Poulenc (Canada) brand of Thioproperazine—**See Phenothiazines (Systemic)**, 872

Malatal—Mallard (U.S.) brand of Atropine, Hyoscyamine, Scopolamine, and Phenobarbital—**See Belladonna Alkaloids and Barbiturates (Systemic)**, 246

Mallamint—Hauck (U.S.) brand of Calcium Carbonate—**See Antacids (Oral-Local)**, 61; Mallard (U.S.) brand of Calcium Carbonate—**See Calcium Supplements (Systemic)**, 357

Mallergan-VC with Codeine—Mallard (U.S.) brand of Promethazine, Phenylephrine, and Codeine—**See Cough/Cold Combinations (Systemic)**, 488

Mallopres—Mallard (U.S.) brand of Reserpine and Hydrochlorothiazide—**See Rauwolfia Alkaloids and Thiazide Diuretics (Systemic)**, 948

Malogen—Stickley (Canada) brand of Testosterone—**See Androgens (Systemic)**, 44

Malogex—Stickley (Canada) brand of Testosterone—**See Androgens (Systemic)**, 44

Malotuss—Hauck (U.S.) brand of Guaifenesin (Systemic), 606

Malt Soup Extract [*Maltsupex*] **See Laxatives (Local)**, 682

Malt Soup Extract and Psyllium [*Syllamalt*] **See Laxatives (Local)**, 682

Maltsupex—Wallace (U.S.) brand of Malt Soup Extract—**See Laxatives (Local)**, 682

Mandelamine—PD (U.S. and Canada) brand of Methenamine (Systemic), 726

Mandol—Lilly (U.S. and Canada) brand of Cefamandole—**See Cephalosporins (Systemic)**, 389

Maolate—Upjohn (U.S.) brand of Chlorphenesin—**See Skeletal Muscle Relaxants (Systemic)**, 979

Maox—Kenneth A. Manne (U.S.) brand of Magnesium Oxide—**See Antacids (Oral-Local)**, 61; **Laxatives (Local)**, 682

Maprin—Quantum (U.S.) brand of Aspirin, Alumina, and Magnesia—**See Salicylates (Systemic)**, 953

Maprin I-B—Quantum (U.S.) brand of Aspirin, Alumina, and Magnesia—**See Salicylates (Systemic)**, 953

Maprotiline Hydrochloride [*Ludiomil*] (Systemic), 712

Marbaxin—Vortech (U.S.) brand of Methocarbamol—**See Skeletal Muscle Relaxants (Systemic)**, 979

Marblen—Fleming (U.S.) brand of Calcium and Magnesium Carbonates—**See Antacids (Oral-Local)**, 61

Marflex—Vortech (U.S.) brand of Orphenadrine—**See Skeletal Muscle Relaxants (Systemic)**, 979

Margesic A-C—Vortech (U.S.) brand of Propoxyphene and Aspirin—**See Opioid (Narcotic) Analgesics and Aspirin (Systemic)**, 822

Marmine—Vortech (U.S.) brand of Dimenhydrinate—**See Antihistamines (Systemic)**, 147

Marnal—Vortech (U.S.) brand of Butalbital, Aspirin, and Caffeine—**See Barbiturates and Analgesics (Systemic)**, 233

Marplan—Roche (U.S. and Canada) brand of Isocarboxazid—**See Antidepressants, Monoamine Oxidase (MAO) Inhibitor (Systemic)**, 113

Matulane—Roche (U.S.) brand of Procarbazine (Systemic), 924

Maxair—Riker (U.S.) brand of Pirbuterol—**See Bronchodilators, Adrenergic (Systemic)**, 294

Maxenal—Janssen (Canada) brand of Pseudoephedrine (Systemic), 936

Maxeran—Marion Merrell Dow (Canada) brand of Metoclopramide (Systemic), 746

Maxiflor—Allergan Herbert (U.S.) brand of Diflorasone—**See Corticosteroids (Topical)**, 458

Maximum Strength Cortaid—Upjohn (U.S.) brand of Hydrocortisone—**See Corticosteroids (Topical)**, 458

Maximum Strength Tylenol Allergy Sinus Caplets—McNeil-CPC (U.S.) brand of Chlorpheniramine, Pseudoephedrine, and Acetaminophen—**See Antihistamines, Decongestants, and Analgesics (Systemic)**, 162

Maxivate—Westwood (U.S.) brand of Betamethasone—**See Corticosteroids (Topical), 458**

Maxzide—Lederle (U.S.) brand of Triamterene and Hydrochlorothiazide—**See Diuretics, Potassium-sparing, and Hydrochlorothiazide (Systemic), 536**

Mazepine—ICN (Canada) brand of Carbamazepine (Systemic), 369

Measurin—Sterling Winthrop (U.S.) brand of Aspirin—**See Salicylates (Systemic), 953**

Mebaral—Sterling Winthrop (U.S. and Canada) brand of Mephobarbital—**See Barbiturates (Systemic), 223**

Mecamylamine Hydrochloride [*Inversine*] **(Systemic), 715**

Meclofen—Major (U.S.) brand of Meclofenamate—**See Anti-inflammatory Analgesics, Nonsteroidal (Systemic), 168**

Meclofenamate Sodium [*Meclofen; Meclomen*] **See Anti-inflammatory Analgesics, Nonsteroidal (Systemic), 168**

Meclomen—PD (U.S.) brand of Meclofenamate—**See Anti-inflammatory Analgesics, Nonsteroidal (Systemic), 168**

Meda-Cap—Circle (U.S.) brand of Acetaminophen (Systemic), 1

Meda Syrup Forte—Dal-Med (U.S.) brand of Chlorpheniramine, Phenylephrine, Dextromethorphan, and Guaifenesin—**See Cough/Cold Combinations (Systemic), 488**

Medatussin—Dal-Med (U.S.) brand of Dextromethorphan, Guaifenesin, Potassium Citrate, and Citric Acid—**See Cough/Cold Combinations (Systemic), 488**

Medatussin Plus—Dal-Med (U.S.) brand of Chlorpheniramine, Phenyltoloxamine, Phenylpropanolamine, Dextromethorphan, and Guaifenesin—**See Cough/Cold Combinations (Systemic), 488**

Medi-Flu—PD (U.S.) brand of Chlorpheniramine, Pseudoephedrine, Dextromethorphan, and Acetaminophen—**See Cough/Cold Combinations (Systemic), 488**

Medi-Flu Caplets—PD (U.S.) brand of Chlorpheniramine, Pseudoephedrine, Dextromethorphan, and Acetaminophen—**See Cough/Cold Combinations (Systemic), 488**

Medigesic—U.S. Chemical (U.S.) brand of Butalbital, Acetaminophen, and Caffeine—**See Barbiturates and Analgesics (Systemic), 233**

Medihaler-Epi—Riker (U.S. and Canada) brand of Epinephrine—**See Bronchodilators, Adrenergic (Systemic), 294**

Medihaler Ergotamine—Riker (Canada) brand of Ergotamine—**See Vascular Headache Suppressants, Ergot Derivative-containing (Systemic), 1066**

Medihaler-Iso—Riker (U.S. and Canada) brand of Isoproterenol—**See Bronchodilators, Adrenergic (Systemic), 294**

Medilax—Mission (U.S.) brand of Phenolphthalein—**See Laxatives (Local), 682**

Mediplast—Beiersdorf (U.S.) brand of Salicylic Acid (Topical), 968

Medipren—McNeil Consumer (U.S. and Canada) brand of Ibuprofen—**See Anti-inflammatory Analgesics, Nonsteroidal (Systemic), 168**

Medipren Caplets—McNeil Consumer (U.S. and Canada) brand of Ibuprofen—**See Anti-inflammatory Analgesics, Nonsteroidal (Systemic), 168**

Mediquell—Warner-Lambert (U.S.) brand of Dextromethorphan (Systemic), 502

Mediquell Decongestant Formula—Warner-Lambert (U.S.) brand of Pseudoephedrine and Dextromethorphan—**See Cough/Cold Combinations (Systemic), 488**

Medotar—Medco (U.S.) brand of Coal Tar (Topical), 443

Medralone-40—Keene (U.S.) brand of Methylprednisolone—**See Corticosteroids/Corticotropin—Glucocorticoid Effects (Systemic), 472**

Medralone-80—Keene (U.S.) brand of Methylprednisolone—**See Corticosteroids/Corticotropin—Glucocorticoid Effects (Systemic), 472**

Medrol—Upjohn (U.S. and Canada) brand of Methylprednisolone—**See Corticosteroids/Corticotropin—Glucocorticoid Effects (Systemic), 472**

Medrol Enpak—Upjohn (U.S.) brand of Methylprednisolone—**See Corticosteroids/Corticotropin—Glucocorticoid Effects (Systemic), 472**

Medroxyprogesterone Acetate [*Amen; Curretab; Cycrin; Depo-Provera; Provera*] **See Progestins (Systemic), 929**

Mefenamic Acid [*Ponstan; Ponstel*] **See Anti-inflammatory Analgesics, Nonsteroidal (Systemic), 168**

Mefoxin—MSD (U.S.) and Frosst (Canada) brand of Cefoxitin—**See Cephalosporins (Systemic), 389**

Mega-Cal—Jamieson (Canada) brand of Calcium Carbonate—**See Calcium Supplements (Systemic), 357**

Megace—Bristol-Myers (U.S.) and Bristol (Canada) brand of Megestrol—**See Progestins (Systemic), 929**

Megacillin—Frosst (Canada) brand of Penicillin G—**See Penicillins (Systemic), 848**

Megagesic—Shoals (U.S.) brand of Hydrocodone and Acetaminophen—**See Opioid (Narcotic) Analgesics and Acetaminophen (Systemic), 820**

Megestrol Acetate [*Megace*] **See Progestins (Systemic), 929**

Megral—BW (Canada) brand of Ergotamine, Caffeine, and Cyclizine—**See Vascular Headache Suppressants, Ergot Derivative-containing (Systemic), 1066**

Mellaril—Sandoz (U.S. and Canada) brand of Thioridazine—**See Phenothiazines (Systemic), 872**

Mellaril Concentrate—Sandoz (U.S.) brand of Thioridazine—**See Phenothiazines (Systemic), 872**

Mellaril-S—Sandoz (U.S.) brand of Thioridazine—**See Phenothiazines (Systemic), 872**

Melphalan [*Alkeran*; L-PAM; phenylalanine mustard] **(Systemic), 717**

Menest—Beecham (U.S.) brand of Estrogens, Esterified—**See Estrogens (Systemic), 566**

Mepenzolate Bromide [*Cantil*] **See Anticholinergics/Antispasmodics (Systemic), 73**

Meperidine Hydrochloride [*Demerol*; pethidine] **See Opioid (Narcotic) Analgesics (Systemic), 793**

Meperidine Hydrochloride and Acetaminophen [*Demerol-APAP*] **See Opioid (Narcotic) Analgesics and Acetaminophen (Systemic), 820**

Mephenytoin [*Mesantoin*] **See Anticonvulsants, Hydantoin (Systemic), 102**

Mephobarbital [*Mebaral*] **See Barbiturates (Systemic), 223**

Meprobamate [*Apo-Meprobamate; Equanil; Meprospan 200; Meprospan 400; Meprospan-400; Miltown; 'Miltown'-200; 'Miltown'-400; 'Miltown'-600; Probate; Trancot*] **(Systemic), 719**

Meprobamate and Aspirin [*Epromate-M; Equagesic; Heptogesic; Meprogesic; Meprogesic Q; Micrainin*] **(Systemic), 721**

Meprogesic—Balan (U.S.) and Dixon-Shane (U.S.) brand of Meprobamate and Aspirin (Systemic), 721

Meprogesic Q—Best (U.S.); Harber (U.S.); and Texas Drug (U.S.) brand of Meprobamate and Aspirin (Systemic), 721

Meprolone—Major (U.S.) brand of Methylprednisolone—**See Corticosteroids/Corticotropin—Glucocorticoid Effects (Systemic), 472**

Meprospan 200—Wallace (U.S.) brand of Meprobamate (Systemic), 719

Mygel—Geneva Generics (U.S.) brand of Alumina, Magnesia, and Simethicone—**See Antacids (Oral-Local), 61**

Mygel II—Geneva Generics (U.S.) brand of Alumina, Magnesia, and Simethicone—**See Antacids (Oral-Local), 61**

Myhistine—My-K Labs (U.S.) brand of Chlorpheniramine and Phenylephrine—**See Antihistamines and Decongestants (Systemic), 161**

Myhistine DH—My-K Labs (U.S.) brand of Chlorpheniramine, Pseudoephedrine, and Codeine—**See Cough/Cold Combinations (Systemic), 488**

Myhistine Expectorant—My-K Labs (U.S.) brand of Pseudoephedrine, Codeine, and Guaifenesin—**See Cough/Cold Combinations (Systemic), 488**

Myhydromine—My-K Labs (U.S.) brand of Phenylpropanolamine and Hydrocodone—**See Cough/Cold Combinations (Systemic), 488**

Myhydromine Pediatric—My-K Labs (U.S.) brand of Phenylpropanolamine and Hydrocodone—**See Cough/Cold Combinations (Systemic), 488**

Myidil—My-K Labs (U.S.) brand of Triprolidine—**See Antihistamines (Systemic), 147**

Myidone—Major (U.S.) brand of Primidone (Systemic), 915

Mykrox—Pennwalt (U.S.) brand of Metolazone—**See Diuretics, Thiazide (Systemic), 541**

Mylanta—Johnson and Johnson-Merck (U.S.) brand of Alumina, Magnesia, and Simethicone—**See Antacids (Oral-Local), 61**

Mylanta-2—PD (Canada) brand of Alumina, Magnesia, and Simethicone—**See Antacids (Oral-Local), 61**

Mylanta-II—Johnson and Johnson-Merck (U.S.) brand of Alumina, Magnesia, and Simethicone—**See Antacids (Oral-Local), 61**

Mylanta-2 Extra Strength—PD (Canada) brand of Alumina, Magnesia, and Simethicone—**See Antacids (Oral-Local), 61**

Mylanta-2 Plain—PD (Canada) brand of Alumina and Magnesia—**See Antacids (Oral-Local), 61**

Myleran—BW (U.S. and Canada) brand of Busulfan (Systemic), 337

Mymethasone—My-K Labs (U.S.) brand of Dexamethasone—**See Corticosteroids/Corticotropin—Glucocorticoid Effects (Systemic), 472**

Myminic—My-K Labs (U.S.) brand of Chlorpheniramine and Phenylpropanolamine—**See Antihistamines and Decongestants (Systemic), 161**

Myochrysine—MSD (U.S.) and Rhone-Poulenc (Canada) brand of Gold Sodium Thiomalate—**See Gold Compounds (Systemic), 599**

Myolin—Hauck (U.S.) brand of Orphenadrine—**See Skeletal Muscle Relaxants (Systemic), 979**

Myotrol—Legere (U.S.) brand of Orphenadrine—**See Skeletal Muscle Relaxants (Systemic), 979**

Myphetane DC Cough—My-K Labs (U.S.) brand of Brompheniramine, Phenylpropanolamine, and Codeine—**See Cough/Cold Combinations (Systemic), 488**

Myphetapp—Bay (U.S.) brand of Brompheniramine and Phenylpropanolamine—**See Antihistamines and Decongestants (Systemic), 161**

Myproic Acid—My-K Labs (U.S.) brand of Valproic Acid (Systemic), 1062

Myrosemide—My-K Labs (U.S.) brand of Furosemide—**See Diuretics, Loop (Systemic), 524**

Mysoline—Wyeth-Ayerst (U.S.) and Ayerst (Canada) brand of Primidone (Systemic), 915

Mytussin—PBI (U.S.) brand of Guaifenesin (Systemic), 606

Mytussin AC—My-K Labs (U.S.) brand of Codeine and Guaifenesin—**See Cough/Cold Combinations (Systemic), 488**

Mytussin DAC—My-K Labs (U.S.) brand of Pseudoephedrine, Codeine, and Guaifenesin—**See Cough/Cold Combinations (Systemic), 488**

Mytussin DM—My-K Labs (U.S.) brand of Dextromethorphan and Guaifenesin—**See Cough/Cold Combinations (Systemic), 488**

9-1-1—Rydelle (U.S.) brand of Hydrocortisone—**See Corticosteroids (Topical), 458**

N

Nadolol [*Corgard; Syn-Nadolol*]
See Beta-adrenergic Blocking Agents (Systemic), 267

Nadolol and Bendroflumethiazide [*Corzide*]
See Beta-adrenergic Blocking Agents and Thiazide Diuretics (Systemic), 283

Nadopen-V 200—Nadeau (Canada) brand of Penicillin V—**See Penicillins (Systemic), 848**

Nadopen-V 400—Nadeau (Canada) brand of Penicillin V—**See Penicillins (Systemic), 848**

Nadopen-VK—Nadeau (Canada) brand of Penicillin V—**See Penicillins (Systemic), 848**

Nadostine—Nadeau (Canada) brand of Nystatin (Vaginal), 786

Nadrothyron-D—*See* Dextrothyroxine (Systemic), 503

Nafcil—Bristol (U.S.) brand of Nafcillin—**See Penicillins (Systemic), 848**

Nafcillin Sodium [*Nafcil; Nallpen; Unipen*]
See Penicillins (Systemic), 848

Nafrine Decongestant Nasal Drops—Schering (Canada) brand of Oxymetazoline (Nasal), 827

Nafrine Decongestant Nasal Spray—Schering (Canada) brand of Oxymetazoline (Nasal), 827

Nafrine Decongestant Pediatric Nasal Spray/Drops—Schering (Canada) brand of Oxymetazoline (Nasal), 827

Nalbuphine Hydrochloride [*Nubain*]
See Opioid (Narcotic) Analgesics (Systemic), 793

Naldecon—Bristol (U.S.) brand of Chlorpheniramine, Phenyltoloxamine, Phenylephrine, and Phenylpropanolamine—**See Antihistamines and Decongestants (Systemic), 161**

Naldecon-CX Adult Liquid—Bristol (U.S.) brand of Phenylpropanolamine, Codeine, and Guaifenesin—**See Cough/Cold Combinations (Systemic), 488**

Naldecon-DX Adult Liquid—Bristol (U.S.) brand of Phenylpropanolamine, Dextromethorphan, and Guaifenesin—**See Cough/Cold Combinations (Systemic), 488**

Naldecon-DX Children's Syrup—Bristol (U.S.) brand of Phenylpropanolamine, Dextromethorphan, and Guaifenesin—**See Cough/Cold Combinations (Systemic), 488**

Naldecon-DX Pediatric Drops—Bristol (U.S.) brand of Phenylpropanolamine, Dextromethorphan, and Guaifenesin—**See Cough/Cold Combinations (Systemic), 488**

Naldecon-EX—Bristol (U.S.) brand of Phenylpropanolamine and Guaifenesin—**See Cough/Cold Combinations (Systemic), 488**

Naldecon Pediatric Drops—Bristol (U.S.) brand of Chlorpheniramine, Phenyltoloxamine, Phenylephrine, and Phenylpropanolamine—**See Antihistamines and Decongestants (Systemic), 161**

Naldecon Pediatric Syrup—Bristol (U.S.) brand of Chlorpheniramine, Phenyltoloxamine, Phenylephrine, and Phenylpropanolamine—**See Antihistamines and Decongestants (Systemic), 161**

Naldecon Senior DX—Bristol (U.S.) brand of Dextromethorphan and Guaifenesin—**See Cough/Cold Combinations (Systemic), 488**

Naldecon Senior EX—Bristol (U.S.) brand of Guaifenesin (Systemic), 606

Naldegesic—Bristol (U.S.) brand of Pseudoephedrine and Acetaminophen—**See Decongestants and Analgesics (Systemic)**, 497

Naldelate—Columbia Medical (U.S.); CMC-CONS (U.S.); Dixon-Shane (U.S.); Moore (U.S.); Parmed (U.S.); and United Research (U.S.) brand of Chlorpheniramine, Phenyltoloxamine, Phenylephrine, and Phenylpropanolamine—**See Antihistamines and Decongestants (Systemic)**, 161

Naldelate Pediatric Syrup—Balan (U.S.); Barre (U.S.); CMC-CONS (U.S.); Dixon-Shane (U.S.); Gen-King (U.S.); Glenlawn (U.S.); Harber (U.S.); Moore (U.S.); Qualitest (U.S.); Redi-Med (U.S.); Texas Drug (U.S.); and United Research (U.S.) brand of Chlorpheniramine, Phenyltoloxamine, Phenylephrine, and Phenylpropanolamine—**See Antihistamines and Decongestants (Systemic)**, 161

Nalfon—Dista (U.S.) and Lilly (Canada) brand of Fenoprofen—**See Anti-inflammatory Analgesics, Nonsteroidal (Systemic)**, 168

Nalfon 200—Dista (U.S.) brand of Fenoprofen—**See Anti-inflammatory Analgesics, Nonsteroidal (Systemic)**, 168

Nalgest—Major (U.S.) brand of Chlorpheniramine, Phenyltoloxamine, Phenylephrine, and Phenylpropanolamine—**See Antihistamines and Decongestants (Systemic)**, 161

Nalidixic Acid [*NegGram*] **(Systemic)**, 764

Nallpen—Beecham (U.S.) brand of Nafcillin—**See Penicillins (Systemic)**, 848

Nandrobolic—Forest (U.S.) brand of Nandrolone—**See Anabolic Steroids (Systemic)**, 40

Nandrobolic L.A.—Forest (U.S.) brand of Nandrolone—**See Anabolic Steroids (Systemic)**, 40

Nandrolone Decanoate [*Anabolin LA-100; Androlone 50; Androlone D; Deca-Durabolin; Hybolin Decanoate; Kabolin; Nandrobolic L.A.; Neo-Durabolic*] **See Anabolic Steroids (Systemic)**, 40

Nandrolone Phenpropionate [*Anabolin; Androlone; Durabolin; Hybolin-Improved; Nandrobolic*] **See Anabolic Steroids (Systemic)**, 40

Napril—Milance (U.S.) brand of Chlorpheniramine and Pseudoephedrine—**See Antihistamines and Decongestants (Systemic)**, 161

Naprosyn—Syntex (U.S. and Canada) brand of Naproxen—**See Anti-inflammatory Analgesics, Nonsteroidal (Systemic)**, 168

Naprosyn-SR—Syntex (Canada) brand of Naproxen—**See Anti-inflammatory Analgesics, Nonsteroidal (Systemic)**, 168

Naproxen [*Apo-Naproxen; Naprosyn; Naprosyn-SR; Naxen; Novonaprox*] **See Anti-inflammatory Analgesics, Nonsteroidal (Systemic)**, 168

Naproxen Sodium [*Anaprox; Anaprox DS; Apo-Napro-Na; Novonaprox Sodium; Synflex*] **See Anti-inflammatory Analgesics, Nonsteroidal (Systemic)**, 168

Naptrate—Vortech (U.S.) brand of Pentaerythritol Tetranitrate—**See Nitrates (Systemic)**, 770

Naqua—Schering (U.S.) brand of Trichlormethiazide—**See Diuretics, Thiazide (Systemic)**, 541

Naquival—Schering (U.S.) brand of Reserpine and Trichlormethiazide—**See Rauwolfia Alkaloids and Thiazide Diuretics (Systemic)**, 948

Nardil—PD (U.S. and Canada) brand of Phenelzine—**See Antidepressants, Monoamine Oxidase (MAO) Inhibitor (Systemic)**, 113

Nasahist—Keene (U.S.) brand of Chlorpheniramine, Phenylephrine, and Phenylpropanolamine—**See Antihistamines and Decongestants (Systemic)**, 161

Nasahist B—Keene (U.S.) brand of Brompheniramine—**See Antihistamines (Systemic)**, 147

Nasalcrom—Fisons (U.S.) brand of Cromolyn (Nasal), 493

Nasalide—Syntex (U.S.) brand of Flunisolide—**See Corticosteroids (Nasal)**, 455

Natulan—Roche (Canada) brand of Procarbazine (Systemic), 924

Naturacil—Mead Johnson (U.S.) brand of Psyllium—**See Laxatives (Local)**, 682

Naturalyte—United Beverages (U.S.) brand of Dextrose and Electrolytes—**See Carbohydrates and Electrolytes (Systemic)**, 379

Nature's Remedy—Norcliff Thayer (U.S.) brand of Cascara Sagrada and Aloe—**See Laxatives (Local)**, 682

Naturetin—Princeton (U.S.) and Squibb (Canada) brand of Bendroflumethiazide—**See Diuretics, Thiazide (Systemic)**, 541

Nauseatol—Sabex (Canada) brand of Dimenhydrinate—**See Antihistamines (Systemic)**, 147

Navane—Roerig (U.S.) and Pfizer (Canada) brand of Thiothixene—**See Thioxanthenes (Systemic)**, 1039

Naxen—SynCare (Canada) brand of Naproxen—**See Anti-inflammatory Analgesics, Nonsteroidal (Systemic)**, 168

ND Clear T.D.—Seatrace (U.S.) brand of Chlorpheniramine and Pseudoephedrine—**See Antihistamines and Decongestants (Systemic)**, 161

ND-Gesic—Hyrex (U.S.) brand of Chlorpheniramine, Pyrilamine, Phenylephrine, and Acetaminophen—**See Antihistamines, Decongestants, and Analgesics (Systemic)**, 162

ND-Stat Revised—Hyrex (U.S.) brand of Brompheniramine—**See Antihistamines (Systemic)**, 147

NebuPent—LyphoMed (U.S.) brand of Pentamidine (Inhalation), 867

NegGram—Sterling Winthrop (U.S. and Canada) brand of Nalidixic Acid (Systemic), 764

Nembutal—Abbott (U.S. and Canada) brand of Pentobarbital—**See Barbiturates (Systemic)**, 223

Neo-Calglucon—Sandoz (U.S.) brand of Calcium Glubionate—**See Calcium Supplements (Systemic)**, 357

Neo Citran Sinus Medicine—Sandoz (Canada) brand of Phenylephrine and Acetaminophen—**See Decongestants and Analgesics (Systemic)**, 497

Neo-Codema—Neolab (Canada) brand of Hydrochlorothiazide—**See Diuretics, Thiazide (Systemic)**, 541

Neo-Cultol—Fisons (U.S.) brand of Mineral Oil—**See Laxatives (Local)**, 682

Neocyten—Central (U.S.) brand of Orphenadrine—**See Skeletal Muscle Relaxants (Systemic)**, 979

Neo-DM—Neolab (Canada) brand of Dextromethorphan (Systemic), 502

Neo-Durabolic—Hauck (U.S.) brand of Nandrolone—**See Anabolic Steroids (Systemic)**, 40

Neo-Estrone—Neolab (Canada) brand of Estrogens, Esterified—**See Estrogens (Systemic)**, 566

NeoFed—Vale (U.S.) brand of Pseudoephedrine (Systemic), 936

Neo-Fer—Neolab (Canada) brand of Ferrous Fumarate—**See Iron Supplements (Systemic)**, 657

Neolax—Central (U.S.) brand of Dehydrocholic Acid and Docusate—**See Laxatives (Local)**, 682

Neoloid—Lederle (U.S.) brand of Castor Oil—**See Laxatives (Local)**, 682

Neopap—Alcon (U.S.) brand of Acetaminophen (Systemic), 1

Neoquess—Forest (U.S.) brand of Dicyclomine—**See Anticholinergics/Antispasmodics (Systemic)**, 73; Forest (U.S.) brand of Hyoscyamine—**See Anticholinergics/Antispasmodics (Systemic)**, 73

Neo-Synephrine—Sterling Winthrop (U.S. and Canada) brand of Phenylephrine (Nasal), 893

Novahistex—Marion Merrell Dow (Canada) brand of Chlorpheniramine and Pseudoephedrine—**See Antihistamines and Decongestants (Systemic)**, 161

Novahistex C—Marion Merrell Dow (Canada) brand of Diphenylpyraline, Phenylephrine, and Codeine—**See Cough/Cold Combinations (Systemic)**, 488

Novahistex DH—Marion Merrell Dow (Canada) brand of Diphenylpyraline, Phenylephrine, and Hydrocodone—**See Cough/Cold Combinations (Systemic)**, 488

Novahistex DH Expectorant—Marion Merrell Dow (Canada) brand of Diphenylpyraline, Phenylephrine, Hydrocodone, and Guaifenesin—**See Cough/Cold Combinations (Systemic)**, 488

Novahistex DM—Marion Merrell Dow (Canada) brand of Diphenylpyraline, Phenylephrine, and Dextromethorphan—**See Cough/Cold Combinations (Systemic)**, 488

Novahistine—Merrell Dow (U.S.) brand of Chlorpheniramine and Phenylephrine—**See Antihistamines and Decongestants (Systemic)**, 161

Novahistine DH—Marion Merrell Dow (Canada) brand of Diphenylpyraline, Phenylephrine, and Hydrocodone—**See Cough/Cold Combinations (Systemic)**, 488

Novahistine DH Expectorant—Marion Merrell Dow (Canada) brand of Diphenylpyraline, Phenylephrine, Hydrocodone, and Guaifenesin—**See Cough/Cold Combinations (Systemic)**, 488

Novahistine DH Liquid—Lakeside/Merrell Dow (U.S.) brand of Chlorpheniramine, Pseudoephedrine, and Codeine—**See Cough/Cold Combinations (Systemic)**, 488

Novahistine DMX Liquid—Lakeside/Merrell Dow (U.S.) brand of Pseudoephedrine, Dextromethorphan, and Guaifenesin—**See Cough/Cold Combinations (Systemic)**, 488

Novahistine Expectorant—Lakeside/Merrell Dow (U.S.) brand of Pseudoephedrine, Codeine, and Guaifenesin—**See Cough/Cold Combinations (Systemic)**, 488

Novamoxin—Novopharm (Canada) brand of Amoxicillin—**See Penicillins (Systemic)**, 848

Nova Rectal—Sabex (Canada) brand of Pentobarbital—**See Barbiturates (Systemic)**, 223

Novasen—Novopharm (Canada) brand of Aspirin—**See Salicylates (Systemic)**, 953

Novo-Alprazol—Novopharm (Canada) brand of Alprazolam—**See Benzodiazepines (Systemic)**, 251

Novo Ampicillin—Novopharm (Canada) brand of Ampicillin—**See Penicillins (Systemic)**, 848

Novobetamet—Novopharm (Canada) brand of Betamethasone—**See Corticosteroids (Topical)**, 458

Novobutamide—Novopharm (Canada) brand of Tolbutamide—**See Antidiabetic Agents, Oral (Systemic)**, 129

Novobutazone—Novopharm (Canada) brand of Phenylbutazone—**See Anti-inflammatory Analgesics, Nonsteroidal (Systemic)**, 168

Novocarbamaz—Novopharm (Canada) brand of Carbamazepine (Systemic), 369

Novo-Chlorpromazine—Novopharm (Canada) brand of Chlorpromazine—**See Phenothiazines (Systemic)**, 872

Novocimetine—Novopharm (Canada) brand of Cimetidine—**See Histamine H_2-receptor Antagonists (Systemic)**, 622

Novoclopate—Novopharm (Canada) brand of Clorazepate—**See Benzodiazepines (Systemic)**, 251

Novocloxin—Novopharm (Canada) brand of Cloxacillin—**See Penicillins (Systemic)**, 848

Novodigoxin—Novopharm (Canada) brand of Digoxin—**See Digitalis Glycosides (Systemic)**, 510

Novo-Diltazem—Novopharm (Canada) brand of Diltiazem—**See Calcium Channel Blocking Agents (Systemic)**, 343

Novodimenate—Novopharm (Canada) brand of Dimenhydrinate—**See Antihistamines (Systemic)**, 147

Novodipam—Novopharm (Canada) brand of Diazepam—**See Benzodiazepines (Systemic)**, 251

Novodoparil—Novopharm (Canada) brand of Methyldopa and Hydrochlorothiazide—**See Methyldopa and Thiazide Diuretics (Systemic)**, 740

Novo-Doxepin—Novopharm (Canada) brand of Doxepin—**See Antidepressants, Tricyclic (Systemic)**, 119

Novodoxylin—Novopharm (Canada) brand of Doxycycline—**See Tetracyclines (Systemic)**, 1025

Novoferrogluc—Novopharm (Canada) brand of Ferrous Gluconate—**See Iron Supplements (Systemic)**, 657

Novoferrosulfa—Novopharm (Canada) brand of Ferrous Sulfate—**See Iron Supplements (Systemic)**, 657

Novofibrate—Novopharm (Canada) brand of Clofibrate (Systemic), 435

Novoflupam—Novopharm (Canada) brand of Flurazepam—**See Benzodiazepines (Systemic)**, 251

Novo-Flurazine—Novopharm (Canada) brand of Trifluoperazine—**See Phenothiazines (Systemic)**, 872

Novo-Folacid—Novopharm (Canada) brand of Folic Acid (Systemic), 590

Novofumar—Novopharm (Canada) brand of Ferrous Fumarate—**See Iron Supplements (Systemic)**, 657

Novogesic C8—Novopharm (Canada) brand of Acetaminophen and Codeine—**See Opioid (Narcotic) Analgesics and Acetaminophen (Systemic)**, 820

Novogesic C15—Novopharm (Canada) brand of Acetaminophen and Codeine—**See Opioid (Narcotic) Analgesics and Acetaminophen (Systemic)**, 820

Novogesic C30—Novopharm (Canada) brand of Acetaminophen and Codeine—**See Opioid (Narcotic) Analgesics and Acetaminophen (Systemic)**, 820

Novohexidyl—Novopharm (Canada) brand of Trihexyphenidyl—**See Antidyskinetics (Systemic)**, 135

Novo-Hydrazide—Novopharm (Canada) brand of Hydrochlorothiazide—**See Diuretics, Thiazide (Systemic)**, 541

Novohydrocort—Novopharm (Canada) brand of Hydrocortisone—**See Corticosteroids (Topical)**, 458

Novohydroxyzin—Novopharm (Canada) brand of Hydroxyzine—**See Antihistamines (Systemic)**, 147

Novo-Hylazin—Novapharm (Canada) brand of Hydralazine (Systemic), 632

Novolexin—Novopharm (Canada) brand of Cephalexin—**See Cephalosporins (Systemic)**, 389

Novolin 70/30—Squibb-Novo (U.S.) brand of Insulin, Isophane, Human, and Insulin Human (Systemic), 644

Novolin L—Squibb-Novo (U.S.) brand of Insulin Zinc, Human (Systemic), 644

Novolin N—Squibb-Novo (U.S.) brand of Insulin, Isophane, Human (Systemic), 644

Novolin R—Squibb-Novo (U.S.) brand of Insulin Human (Systemic), 644

Novolorazem—Novopharm (Canada) brand of Lorazepam—**See Benzodiazepines (Systemic)**, 251

Novomedopa—Novopharm (Canada) brand of Methyldopa (Systemic), 737

Novomethacin—Novopharm (Canada) brand of Indomethacin—**See Anti-inflammatory Analgesics, Nonsteroidal (Systemic)**, 168

Novometoprol—Novopharm (Canada) brand of Metoprolol—**See Beta-adrenergic Blocking Agents (Systemic)**, 267

Novonaprox—Novopharm (Canada) brand of Naproxen—**See Anti-inflammatory Analgesics, Nonsteroidal (Systemic)**, 168

Nucochem Expectorant—LuChem (U.S.) brand of Pseudoephedrine, Codeine, and Guaifenesin—**See Cough/Cold Combinations (Systemic)**, 488

Nucochem Pediatric Expectorant—LuChem (U.S.) brand of Pseudoephedrine, Codeine, and Guaifenesin—**See Cough/ Cold Combinations (Systemic)**, 488

Nucofed—Beecham (U.S.) brand of Pseudoephedrine and Codeine—**See Cough/Cold Combinations (Systemic)**, 488

Nucofed Expectorant—Beecham (U.S.) brand of Pseudoephedrine, Codeine, and Guaifenesin—**See Cough/Cold Combinations (Systemic)**, 488

Nucofed Pediatric Expectorant—Beecham (U.S.) brand of Pseudoephedrine, Codeine, and Guaifenesin—**See Cough/ Cold Combinations (Systemic)**, 488

Nu-Cotrimox—Nu-Pharm (Canada) brand of Sulfamethoxazole and Trimethoprim (Systemic), 999

Nu-Cotrimox DS—Nu-Pharm (Canada) brand of Sulfamethoxazole and Trimethoprim (Systemic), 999

Nu-Diltiaz—Nu-Pharm (Canada) brand of Diltiazem—**See Calcium Channel Blocking Agents (Systemic)**, 343

Nu-Iron—Mayrand (U.S.) brand of Iron-Polysaccharide—**See Iron Supplements (Systemic)**, 657

Nu-Iron 150—Mayrand (U.S.) brand of Iron-Polysaccharide—**See Iron Supplements (Systemic)**, 657

Nujol—Plough (U.S.) brand of Mineral Oil—**See Laxatives (Local)**, 682

Nu-Loraz—Nu-Pharm (Canada) brand of Lorazepam—**See Benzodiazepines (Systemic)**, 251

Numorphan—Du Pont (U.S. and Canada) brand of Oxymorphone—**See Opioid (Narcotic) Analgesics (Systemic)**, 793

Nu-Nifed—Nu-Pharm (Canada) brand of Nifedipine—**See Calcium Channel Blocking Agents (Systemic)**, 343

Nu-Pen-VK—Nu-Pharm (Canada) brand of Penicillin V—**See Penicillins (Systemic)**, 848

Nuprin—Bristol-Myers (U.S. and Canada) brand of Ibuprofen—**See Anti-inflammatory Analgesics, Nonsteroidal (Systemic)**, 168

Nuprin Caplets—Bristol-Myers (U.S.) brand of Ibuprofen—**See Anti-inflammatory Analgesics, Nonsteroidal (Systemic)**, 168

Nu-Tetra—Nu-Pharm (Canada) brand of Tetracycline—**See Tetracyclines (Systemic)**, 1025

Nutracort—Owen/Allercreme (U.S.) brand of Hydrocortisone—**See Corticosteroids (Topical)**, 458

Nu-Triazo—Nu-Pharm (Canada) brand of Triazolam—**See Benzodiazepines (Systemic)**, 251

Nu-Verap—Nu-Pharm (Canada) brand of Verapamil—**See Calcium Channel Blocking Agents (Systemic)**, 343

Nyaderm—Taro (Canada) brand of Nystatin (Vaginal), 786

Nylidrin Hydrochloride [*Arlidin; Arlidin Forte; PMS Nylidrin*] (Systemic), 785

NyQuil Liquicaps—Richardson-Vicks (U.S.) brand of Diphenhydramine, Pseudoephedrine, Dextromethorphan, and Acetaminophen—**See Cough/Cold Combinations (Systemic)**, 488

NyQuil Nighttime Colds Medicine—Richardson-Vicks (U.S.) brand of Doxylamine, Pseudoephedrine, Dextromethorphan, and Acetaminophen—**See Cough/Cold Combinations (Systemic)**, 488

Nystatin [*Mycostatin; Nadostine; Nilstat; Nyaderm*] (Vaginal), 786

Nytilax—Mentholatum (U.S.) brand of Sennosides—**See Laxatives (Local)**, 682

Nytime Cold Medicine Liquid—Rugby (U.S.) brand of Doxylamine, Pseudoephedrine, Dextromethorphan, and Acetaminophen—**See Cough/Cold Combinations (Systemic)**, 488

Nytol with DPH—Block (U.S.) brand of Diphenhydramine—**See Antihistamines (Systemic)**, 147

Nytol Maximum Strength—Block (U.S.) brand of Diphenhydramine—**See Antihistamines (Systemic)**, 147

O

Occlusal-HP Topical Solution—GenDerm (U.S. and Canada) brand of Salicylic Acid (Topical), 968

Occlusal Topical Solution—GenDerm (U.S. and Canada) brand of Salicylic Acid (Topical), 968

Octamide—Adria (U.S.) brand of Metoclopramide (Systemic), 746

Octamide PFS—Adria (U.S.) brand of Metoclopramide (Systemic), 746

Octatropine—Anisotropine—**See Anticholinergics/Antispasmodics (Systemic)**, 73

Octoxinol—Octoxynol 9—**See Spermicides (Vaginal)**, 991

Octoxynol 9 [*Koromex Cream;* octoxinol; *Ortho-Gynol*] **See Spermicides (Vaginal)**, 991

Ocu-Carpine—Ocumed (U.S.) brand of Pilocarpine (Ophthalmic), 903

Ocusert Pilo-20—Alza (U.S. and Canada) brand of Pilocarpine (Ophthalmic), 903

Ocusert Pilo-40—Alza (U.S. and Canada) brand of Pilocarpine (Ophthalmic), 903

Ocu-Sul-10—Ocumed (U.S.) brand of Sulfacetamide—**See Sulfonamides (Ophthalmic)**, 1009

Ocu-Sul-15—Ocumed (U.S.) brand of Sulfacetamide—**See Sulfonamides (Ophthalmic)**, 1009

Ocu-Sul-30—Ocumed (U.S.) brand of Sulfacetamide—**See Sulfonamides (Ophthalmic)**, 1009

Ocusulf-10—Optopics (U.S.) brand of Sulfacetamide—**See Sulfonamides (Ophthalmic)**, 1009

Oestrilin—Desbergers (Canada) brand of Estrone—**See Estrogens (Vaginal)**, 572

Off-Ezy Topical Solution Corn & Callus Remover Kit—Commerce (U.S.) brand of Salicylic Acid (Topical), 968

Off-Ezy Topical Solution Wart Removal Kit—Commerce (U.S.) brand of Salicylic Acid (Topical), 968

O-Flex—Seatrace (U.S.) brand of Orphenadrine—**See Skeletal Muscle Relaxants (Systemic)**, 979

Ofloxacin [*Floxin; Floxin IV*] (Systemic), 788

Ofloxacin in Dextrose [*Floxin IV*] (Systemic), 788

Ogen—Abbott (Canada) brand of Estropipate—**See Estrogens (Systemic)**, 566; Abbott (U.S.) brand of Estropipate—**See Estrogens (Vaginal)**, 572

Ogen .625—Abbott (U.S.) brand of Estropipate—**See Estrogens (Systemic)**, 566

Ogen 1.25—Abbott (U.S.) brand of Estropipate—**See Estrogens (Systemic)**, 566

Ogen 2.5—Abbott (U.S.) brand of Estropipate—**See Estrogens (Systemic)**, 566

Ogen 5—Abbott (U.S.) brand of Estropipate—**See Estrogens (Systemic)**, 566

Olsalazine Sodium [azodisal sodium; *Dipentum;* sodium azodisalicylate] (Oral-Local), 790

Omeprazole [*Losec; Prilosec*] (Systemic), 791

Omnicol—Delta (U.S.) brand of Chlorpheniramine, Phenindamine, Phenylephrine, Dextromethorphan, Acetaminophen, Salicylamide, Caffeine, and Ascorbic Acid—**See Cough/Cold Combinations (Systemic)**, 488

Omnipen—Wyeth-Ayerst (U.S.) brand of Ampicillin—**See Penicillins (Systemic)**, 848

Omnipen-N—Wyeth-Ayerst (U.S.) brand of Ampicillin—**See Penicillins (Systemic)**, 848

Oxy Night Watch Night Time Acne Medication Regular Strength Lotion—SmithKline Beecham (Canada) brand of Salicylic Acid (Topical), 968

Oxy Night Watch Sensitive Skin Lotion—SmithKline Beecham (U.S.) brand of Salicylic Acid (Topical), 968

Oxyphencyclimine Hydrochloride [*Daricon*] **See Anticholinergics/Antispasmodics (Systemic)**, 73

Oxy Sensitive Skin Vanishing Formula Lotion—SmithKline Beecham (Canada) brand of Salicylic Acid (Topical), 968

Oxytetracycline [*Terramycin*] **See Tetracyclines (Systemic)**, 1025

Oxytetracycline Hydrochloride [*Terramycin; Tija*] **See Tetracyclines (Systemic)**, 1025

Oysco—Ruglex (U.S.) brand of Calcium Carbonate—**See Calcium Supplements (Systemic)**, 357

Oysco 500 Chewable—Ruglex (U.S.) brand of Calcium Carbonate—**See Calcium Supplements (Systemic)**, 357

Oyst-Cal 500—Goldline (U.S.) brand of Calcium Carbonate—**See Calcium Supplements (Systemic)**, 357

Oyst-Cal 500 Chewable—Goldline (U.S.) brand of Calcium Carbonate—**See Calcium Supplements (Systemic)**, 357

Oystercal 500—Nature's Bounty (U.S.) brand of Calcium Carbonate—**See Calcium Supplements (Systemic)**, 357

P

Pacaps—Lunsco (U.S.) brand of Butalbital, Acetaminophen, and Caffeine—**See Barbiturates and Analgesics (Systemic)**, 233

P-A-C Revised Formula—Upjohn (U.S.) brand of Aspirin and Caffeine—**See Salicylates (Systemic)**, 953

Palafer—Beecham (Canada) brand of Ferrous Fumarate—**See Iron Supplements (Systemic)**, 657

Palafer Pediatric Drops—Beecham (Canada) brand of Ferrous Fumarate—**See Iron Supplements (Systemic)**, 657

Palaron—Fisons (Canada) brand of Aminophylline—**See Bronchodilators, Xanthine-derivative (Systemic)**, 315

Palmiron—Hauck (U.S.) brand of Ferrous Fumarate—**See Iron Supplements (Systemic)**, 657

Pamelor—Sandoz (U.S.) brand of Nortriptyline—**See Antidepressants, Tricyclic (Systemic)**, 119

Pamine—Upjohn (U.S.) brand of Methscopolamine—**See Anticholinergics/Antispasmodics (Systemic)**, 73

P-aminoclonidine—*See* Apraclonidine (Ophthalmic), 214

Pamprin-IB—Chattem (U.S.) brand of Ibuprofen—**See Anti-inflammatory Analgesics, Nonsteroidal (Systemic)**, 168

Panadol—Sterling Winthrop (Canada) brand of Acetaminophen (Systemic), 1

Panadol, Children's—Glenbrook (U.S.) brand of Acetaminophen (Systemic), 1

Panadol Extra Strength—Sterling Winthrop (Canada) brand of Acetaminophen (Systemic), 1

Panadol, Infants'—Glenbrook (U.S.) brand of Acetaminophen (Systemic), 1

Panadol Junior Strength Caplets—Glenbrook (U.S.) brand of Acetaminophen (Systemic), 1

Panadol Maximum Strength Caplets—Glenbrook (U.S.) brand of Acetaminophen (Systemic), 1

Panadol Maximum Strength Tablets—Glenbrook (U.S.) brand of Acetaminophen (Systemic), 1

Panadyl—Misemer (U.S.) brand of Pheniramine, Pyrilamine, and Phenylpropanolamine—**See Antihistamines and Decongestants (Systemic)**, 161

Pancoate—Parmed (U.S.) brand of Pancrelipase (Systemic), 832

Pancrease—McNeil (U.S. and Canada) brand of Pancrelipase (Systemic), 832

Pancrease MT 4—McNeil (U.S. and Canada) brand of Pancrelipase (Systemic), 832

Pancrease MT 10—McNeil (U.S. and Canada) brand of Pancrelipase (Systemic), 832

Pancrease MT 16—McNeil (U.S. and Canada) brand of Pancrelipase (Systemic), 832

Pancreatin, Pepsin, Bile Salts, Hyoscyamine Sulfate, Atropine Sulfate, Scopolamine Hydrobromide, and Phenobarbital [*Donnazyme*] (Systemic), 829

Pancrelipase [*Cotazym; Cotazym-65 B; Cotazym E.C.S. 8; Cotazym E.C.S. 20; Cotazym-S; Enzymase-16; Ilozyme; Ku-Zyme HP;* lipancreatin; *Pancoate; Pancrease; Pancrease MT 4; Pancrease MT 10; Pancrease MT 16; Protilase; Ultrase MT 12; Ultrase MT 20; Ultrase MT 24; Viokase; Zymase*] (Systemic), 832

Panectyl—May & Baker (Canada) brand of Trimeprazine—**See Antihistamines, Phenothiazine-derivative (Systemic)**, 163

Panesclerina—Infale (Spain) brand of Probucol (Systemic), 919

Panex—Mallard (U.S.) brand of Acetaminophen (Systemic), 1

Panex-500—Mallard (U.S.) brand of Acetaminophen (Systemic), 1

Panmycin—Upjohn (U.S.) brand of Tetracycline—**See Tetracyclines (Systemic)**, 1025

Pantopon—Roche (U.S. and Canada) brand of Opium—**See Opioid (Narcotic) Analgesics (Systemic)**, 793

Panwarfin—Abbott (U.S.) brand of Warfarin—**See Anticoagulants (Systemic)**, 88

Papaveretum—Opium Alkaloids Hydrochlorides—**See Opioid (Narcotic) Analgesics (Systemic)**, 793

Papaverine Hydrochloride **(Intracavernosal)**, 834

Paplex—Medicis (U.S.) brand of Salicylic Acid (Topical), 968

Paplex Ultra—Medicis (U.S.) brand of Salicylic Acid (Topical), 968

Paracetamol—*See* Acetaminophen (Systemic), 1

Paradione—Abbott (U.S.) brand of Paramethadione—**See Anticonvulsants, Dione (Systemic)**, 100

Paraflex—McNeil (U.S.) brand of Chlorzoxazone—**See Skeletal Muscle Relaxants (Systemic)**, 979

Parafon Forte DSC—McNeil (U.S.) brand of Chlorzoxazone—**See Skeletal Muscle Relaxants (Systemic)**, 979

Paral—Forest (U.S.) brand of Paraldehyde (Systemic), 836

Paraldehyde [*Paral*] **(Systemic)**, 836

Paramethadione [*Paradione*] **See Anticonvulsants, Dione (Systemic)**, 100

Paramethasone Acetate [*Haldrone*] **See Corticosteroids/Corticotropin—Glucocorticoid Effects (Systemic)**, 472

Paregoric [camphorated opium tincture] **(Systemic)**, 838

Parepectolin—Rorer (U.S.) brand of Kaolin, Pectin, and Paregoric (Systemic), 673

Par Glycerol C—Par (U.S.) brand of Codeine and Iodinated Glycerol—**See Cough/Cold Combinations (Systemic)**, 488

Par Glycerol DM—Par (U.S.) brand of Dextromethorphan and Iodinated Glycerol—**See Cough/Cold Combinations (Systemic)**, 488

Pargyline Hydrochloride [*Eutonyl*] **(Systemic)**, 840

Pargyline Hydrochloride and Methyclothiazide [*Eutron*] **(Systemic)**, 844

Parlodel—Sandoz (U.S. and Canada) brand of Bromocriptine (Systemic), 290

Parnate—SKF (U.S. and Canada) brand of Tranylcypromine—**See Antidepressants, Monoamine Oxidase (MAO) Inhibitor (Systemic)**, 113

Parsidol—PD (U.S.) brand of Ethopropazine—**See Antidyskinetics (Systemic)**, 135

Parsitan—Rhone-Poulenc (Canada) brand of Ethopropazine—**See Antidyskinetics (Systemic)**, 135

Phenolphthalein Petrogalar—Wyeth-Ayerst (U.S.) brand of Mineral Oil and Phenolphthalein—**See Laxatives (Local)**, 682

Phenothiazines **(Systemic)**, 872

Phenoxybenzamine Hydrochloride [*Dibenzyline*] **(Systemic)**, 889

Phenoxymethylpenicillin—Penicillin V—**See Penicillins (Systemic)**, 848

Phensuximide [*Milontin*] **See Anticonvulsants, Succinimide (Systemic)**, 110

Phentolamine Mesylate [*Regitine; Rogitine*] **(Intracavernosal)**, 891

Phentox Compound—My-K Labs (U.S.) brand of Chlorpheniramine, Phenyltoloxamine, Phenylephrine, and Phenylpropanolamine—**See Antihistamines and Decongestants (Systemic)**, 161

Phenurone—Abbott (U.S.) brand of Phenacemide (Systemic), 870

Phenylalanine mustard—*See* Melphalan (Systemic), 717

Phenylbutazone [*Apo-Phenylbutazone; Butatab; Butazolidin; Butazone; Intrabutazone; Novobutazone*] **See Anti-inflammatory Analgesics, Nonsteroidal (Systemic)**, 168

Phenylbutazone, Buffered [*Alka-Butazolidin; Alkabutazone; Alka-Phenylbutazone; Phenylone Plus*] **See Anti-inflammatory Analgesics, Nonsteroidal (Systemic)**, 168

Phenyldrine—Rugby (U.S.) brand of Phenylpropanolamine (Systemic), 894

Phenylephrine Hydrochloride [*Alconefrin 12; Alconefrin 25; Alconefrin 50; Doktors; Duration; Neo-Synephrine; Nostril; Rhinall; Rhinall-10 Children's Flavored Nose Drops; St. Joseph; Vicks Sinex*] **(Nasal)**, 893

Phenylephrine Hydrochloride and Acetaminophen [*Congespirin for Children Cold Tablets; Neo Citran Sinus Medicine*] **See Decongestants and Analgesics (Systemic)**, 497

Phenylephrine Hydrochloride and Dextromethorphan Hydrobromide [*Conar*] **See Cough/Cold Combinations (Systemic)**, 488

Phenylephrine Hydrochloride, Dextromethorphan Hydrobromide, and Guaifenesin [*Conar Expectorant*] **See Cough/Cold Combinations (Systemic)**, 488

Phenylephrine Hydrochloride, Dextromethorphan Hydrobromide, Guaifenesin, and Acetaminophen [*Conar-A*] **See Cough/Cold Combinations (Systemic)**, 488

Phenylephrine Hydrochloride, Guaifenesin, Acetaminophen, Salicylamide, and Caffeine [*Fendol*] **See Cough/Cold Combinations (Systemic)**, 488

Phenylephrine Hydrochloride, Hydrocodone Bitartrate, and Guaifenesin [*Donatussin DC*] **See Cough/Cold Combinations (Systemic)**, 488

Phenylephrine Hydrochloride, Phenylpropanolamine Hydrochloride, and Guaifenesin [*Banex; Banex Liquid; Entex; Entex Liquid; Respinol-G; Rymed; Rymed Liquid*] **See Cough/Cold Combinations (Systemic)**, 488

Phenylfenesin L.A.—Goldline (U.S.) brand of Phenylpropanolamine and Guaifenesin—**See Cough/Cold Combinations (Systemic)**, 488

Phenylone Plus—Medic (Canada) brand of Phenylbutazone, Buffered—**See Anti-inflammatory Analgesics, Nonsteroidal (Systemic)**, 168

Phenylpropanolamine Hydrochloride [*Acutrim 16 Hour; Acutrim Late Day; Acutrim II Maximum Strength; Control; Dex-A-Diet Maximum Strength; Dex-A-Diet Maximum Strength Caplets; Dexatrim; Dexatrim Maximum Strength; Dexatrim Maximum Strength Caplets; Dexatrim Maximum Strength Pre-Meal Caplets; Diet-Aid Maximum Strength; Efed II Yellow*; *PPA; Phenyldrine; Prolamine; Propagest; Rhindecon; Stay Trim Diet Gum; Unitrol*] **(Systemic)**, 894

Phenylpropanolamine Hydrochloride and Acetaminophen [*Congespirin for Children Liquid Cold Medicine; Dilotab; Genex; PhenAPAP No. 2; St. Joseph Cold Tablets for Children*] **See Decongestants and Analgesics (Systemic)**, 497

Phenylpropanolamine Hydrochloride, Acetaminophen, and Aspirin [*Rhinocaps*] **See Decongestants and Analgesics (Systemic)**, 497

Phenylpropanolamine Hydrochloride, Acetaminophen, Aspirin, and Caffeine [*Drinophen*] **See Decongestants and Analgesics (Systemic)**, 497

Phenylpropanolamine Hydrochloride, Acetaminophen, Salicylamide, and Caffeine [*Saleto D*] **See Decongestants and Analgesics (Systemic)**, 497

Phenylpropanolamine Hydrochloride and Aspirin [*BC Cold Powder Non-Drowsy Formula*] **See Decongestants and Analgesics (Systemic)**, 497

Phenylpropanolamine Hydrochloride and Caramiphen Edisylate [*Rescaps-D S.R.; Tuss-Ade; Tuss Allergine Modified T.D.; Tussogest; Tuss-Ornade Liquid; Tuss-Ornade Spansules*] **See Cough/Cold Combinations (Systemic)**, 488

Phenylpropanolamine Hydrochloride, Codeine Phosphate, and Guaifenesin [*Codegest Expectorant; Conex with Codeine Liquid; Naldecon-CX Adult Liquid; Triaminic Expectorant with Codeine*] **See Cough/Cold Combinations (Systemic)**, 488

Phenylpropanolamine Hydrochloride and Dextromethorphan Hydrobromide [*Efficol Cough Whip (Cough Suppressant/Decongestant); Hold (Children's Formula); Snaplets-DM; Syracol Liquid; Triaminic-DM Cough Formula; Tricodene Pediatric*] **See Cough/Cold Combinations (Systemic)**, 488

Phenylpropanolamine Hydrochloride, Dextromethorphan Hydrobromide, and Acetaminophen [*Contac Jr. Children's Cold Medicine; Saleto-CF*] **See Cough/Cold Combinations (Systemic)**, 488

Phenylpropanolamine Hydrochloride, Dextromethorphan Hydrobromide, and Guaifenesin [*Coricidin Cough; Dorcol DM; Ipsatol Cough Formula for Children; Kiddy Koff; Naldecon-DX Adult Liquid; Naldecon-DX Children's Syrup; Naldecon-DX Pediatric Drops; Robitussin-CF*] **See Cough/Cold Combinations (Systemic)**, 488

Phenylpropanolamine Hydrochloride and Guaifenesin [*Ami-Tex LA; Banex-LA; Bayaminic Expectorant; Codimal Expectorant; Conex; Dura-Vent; Entex LA; Gentab-LA; Guaipax; Naldecon-EX; Nolex LA; Phenylfenesin L.A.; Prominic Expectorant; Snaplets-EX; Triaminic Expectorant; Triphenyl Expectorant; Utex-S.R.*] **See Cough/Cold Combinations (Systemic)**, 488

Phenylpropanolamine Hydrochloride and Hydrocodone Bitartrate [*Baycomine; Baycomine Pediatric; Codamine; Codamine Pediatric; Hycomine; Hycomine Pediatric; Hydromine; Hydromine Pediatric; Hydrophen; Myhydromine; Myhydromine Pediatric*] **See Cough/Cold Combinations (Systemic)**, 488

Phenyltoloxamine Citrate, Phenylpropanolamine Hydrochloride, and Acetaminophen [*Sinubid; Sinutab SA*] **See Antihistamines, Decongestants, and Analgesics (Systemic)**, 162

Phenyltoloxamine and Hydrocodone Polistirexes [*Tussionex*]
See Cough/Cold Combinations (Systemic), 488

Phenytex—Bolar (U.S.) brand of Phenytoin—**See Anticonvulsants, Hydantoin (Systemic), 102**

Phenytoin [*Dilantin-30; Dilantin-125; Dilantin Infatabs; Dilantin-30 Pediatric;* diphenylhydantoin]
See Anticonvulsants, Hydantoin (Systemic), 102

Phenytoin Sodium [*Dilantin; Dilantin Kapseals; Diphenylan;* diphenylhydantoin; *Phenytex*]
See Anticonvulsants, Hydantoin (Systemic), 102

Pherazine VC—Halsey (U.S.) brand of Promethazine and Phenylephrine—**See Antihistamines and Decongestants (Systemic), 161**

Pherazine VC with Codeine—Halsey (U.S.) brand of Promethazine, Phenylephrine, and Codeine—**See Cough/Cold Combinations (Systemic), 488**

Phetylureum—See Phenacemide (Systemic), 870

Phillips' LaxCaps—Glenbrook (U.S.) brand of Docusate and Phenolphthalein—**See Laxatives (Local), 682**

Phillips' Magnesia Tablets—Sterling Winthrop (Canada) brand of Magnesium Hydroxide—**See Laxatives (Local), 682**

Phillips' Milk of Magnesia—Glenbrook (U.S.) and Sterling Winthrop (Canada) brand of Magnesium Hydroxide—**See Antacids (Oral-Local), 61; Laxatives (Local), 682**

Phosphates (Systemic), 897

Phospholine Iodide—Wyeth-Ayerst (U.S.) and Ayerst (Canada) brand of Echothiophate—**See Antiglaucoma Agents, Cholinergic, Long-acting (Ophthalmic), 143**

Phrenilin—Carnrick (U.S.) brand of Butalbital and Acetaminophen—**See Barbiturates and Analgesics (Systemic), 233**

Phrenilin Forte—Carnrick (U.S.) brand of Butalbital and Acetaminophen—**See Barbiturates and Analgesics (Systemic), 233**

Phyllocontin—Purdue Frederick (U.S. and Canada) brand of Aminophylline—**See Bronchodilators, Xanthine-derivative (Systemic), 315**

Phyllocontin-350—Purdue Frederick (Canada) brand of Aminophylline—**See Bronchodilators, Xanthine-derivative (Systemic), 315**

Physostigmine Salicylate [*Eserine Salicylate; Isopto Eserine*] (Ophthalmic), 901

Physostigmine Sulfate [*Eserine Sulfate*] (Ophthalmic), 901

Pilagan—Allergan (U.S.) brand of Pilocarpine (Ophthalmic), 903

Pilocar—Iolab (U.S.) brand of Pilocarpine (Ophthalmic), 903

Pilocarpine [*Ocusert Pilo-20; Ocusert Pilo-40*] (Ophthalmic), 903

Pilocarpine Hydrochloride [*Adsorbocarpine; Akarpine; I-Pilocarpine; Isopto Carpine; Miocarpine; Ocu-Carpine; Pilocar; Pilokair; Pilopine HS; Piloptic-1; Piloptic-2; Piloptic-4; Pilostat; Spersacarpine*] (Ophthalmic), 903

Pilocarpine Nitrate [*Minims Pilocarpine; Pilagan; P.V. Carpine Liquifilm; Spectro-Pilo*] (Ophthalmic), 903

Pilokair—Pharmafair (U.S.) and Texas Drugs (U.S.) brand of Pilocarpine (Ophthalmic), 903

Pilopine HS—Alcon (U.S. and Canada) brand of Pilocarpine (Ophthalmic), 903

Piloptic-1—Optopics (U.S.) brand of Pilocarpine (Ophthalmic), 903

Piloptic-2—Optopics (U.S.) brand of Pilocarpine (Ophthalmic), 903

Piloptic-4—Optopics (U.S.) brand of Pilocarpine (Ophthalmic), 903

Pilostat—B & L (U.S. and Canada) brand of Pilocarpine (Ophthalmic), 903

Pima—Fleming (U.S.) brand of Potassium Iodide (Systemic), 908

Pimozide [*Orap*] (Systemic), 905

Pindolol [*Syn-Pindolol; Visken*]
See Beta-adrenergic Blocking Agents (Systemic), 267

Pindolol and Hydrochlorothiazide [*Viskazide*]
See Beta-adrenergic Blocking Agents and Thiazide Diuretics (Systemic), 283

Piperacillin Sodium [*Pipracil*]
See Penicillins (Systemic), 848

Piperazine estrone sulfate—Estropipate—**See Estrogens (Systemic), 566; Estrogens (Vaginal), 572**

Piportil L₄—Rhone-Poulenc (Canada) brand of Pipotiazine—**See Phenothiazines (Systemic), 872**

Pipotiazine Palmitate [*Piportil L₄*]
See Phenothiazines (Systemic), 872

Pipracil—Lederle (U.S. and Canada) brand of Piperacillin—**See Penicillins (Systemic), 848**

Pirbuterol Acetate [*Maxair*]
See Bronchodilators, Adrenergic (Systemic), 294

Pirenzepine Hydrochloride [*Gastrozepin*]
See Anticholinergics/Antispasmodics (Systemic), 73

Piroxicam [*Apo-Piroxicam; Feldene; Novopirocam*]
See Anti-inflammatory Analgesics, Nonsteroidal (Systemic), 168

Plaquenil—Sterling Winthrop (U.S. and Canada) brand of Hydroxychloroquine (Systemic), 636

Plendil—MSD (U.S.) and Astra (Canada) brand of Felodipine—**See Calcium Channel Blocking Agents (Systemic), 343**

PMS Amitriptyline—Pharmascience (Canada) brand of Amitriptyline—**See Antidepressants, Tricyclic (Systemic), 119**

PMS Benztropine—Pharmascience (Canada) brand of Benztropine—**See Antidyskinetics (Systemic), 135**

PMS Carbamazepine—Pharmascience (Canada) brand of Carbamazepine (Systemic), 369

PMS Diazepam—Pharmascience (Canada) brand of Diazepam—**See Benzodiazepines (Systemic), 251**

PMS-Dimenhydrinate—Pharmascience (Canada) brand of Dimenhydrinate—**See Antihistamines (Systemic), 147**

PMS Dopazide—Pharmascience (Canada) brand of Methyldopa and Hydrochlorothiazide—**See Methyldopa and Thiazide Diuretics (Systemic), 740**

PMS Ferrous Sulfate—Pharmascience (Canada) brand of Ferrous Sulfate—**See Iron Supplements (Systemic), 657**

PMS Haloperidol—Pharmascience (Canada) brand of Haloperidol (Systemic), 618

PMS Imipramine—Pharmascience (Canada) brand of Imipramine—**See Antidepressants, Tricyclic (Systemic), 119**

PMS Nylidrin—Pharmascience (Canada) brand of Nylidrin (Systemic), 785

PMS Perphenazine—Pharmascience (Canada) brand of Perphenazine—**See Phenothiazines (Systemic), 872**

PMS Primidone—Pharmascience (Canada) brand of Primidone (Systemic), 915

PMS Prochlorperazine—Pharmascience (Canada) brand of Prochlorperazine—**See Phenothiazines (Systemic), 872**

PMS Procyclidine—Pharmascience (Canada) brand of Procyclidine—**See Antidyskinetics (Systemic), 135**

PMS Promethazine—Pharmascience (Canada) brand of Promethazine—**See Antihistamines, Phenothiazine-derivative (Systemic), 163**

pms Propranolol—Pharmascience (Canada) brand of Propranolol—**See Beta-adrenergic Blocking Agents (Systemic), 267**

Propoxyphene Hydrochloride and Aspirin [*Darvon with A.S.A.*]
  See Opioid (Narcotic) Analgesics and Aspirin (Systemic), 822
Propoxyphene Hydrochloride, Aspirin, and Caffeine [*Bexophene; Cotanal-65; Darvon Compound; Darvon Compound-65; Doraphen Compound-65; Doxaphene Compound; Margesic A-C; Novopropoxyn Compound; Pro Pox Plus;* propoxyphene hydrochloride compound; 692]
  See Opioid (Narcotic) Analgesics and Aspirin (Systemic), 822
Propoxyphene hydrochloride compound— Propoxyphene, Aspirin, and Caffeine— **See Opioid (Narcotic) Analgesics and Aspirin (Systemic)**, 822
Propoxyphene Napsylate [*Darvon-N; dextropropoxyphene*]
  See Opioid (Narcotic) Analgesics (Systemic), 793
Propoxyphene Napsylate and Acetaminophen [*Darvocet-N 50; Darvocet-N 100; Doxapap-N; Propacet 100;* propoxyphene with APAP]
  See Opioid (Narcotic) Analgesics and Acetaminophen (Systemic), 820
Propoxyphene Napsylate and Aspirin [*Darvon-N with A.S.A.*]
  See Opioid (Narcotic) Analgesics and Aspirin (Systemic), 822
Propoxyphene Napsylate, Aspirin, and Caffeine [*Darvon-N Compound*]
  See Opioid (Narcotic) Analgesics and Aspirin (Systemic), 822
Propranolol Hydrochloride [*Apo-Propranolol; Detensol; Inderal; Inderal LA; Novopranol; pms Propranolol*]
  See Beta-adrenergic Blocking Agents (Systemic), 267
Propranolol Hydrochloride and Hydrochlorothiazide [*Inderide; Inderide LA*]
  See Beta-adrenergic Blocking Agents and Thiazide Diuretics (Systemic), 283
Propylthiouracil [*Propyl-Thyracil*]
  See Antithyroid Agents (Systemic), 211
Propyl-Thyracil—Frosst (Canada) brand of Propylthiouracil—**See Antithyroid Agents (Systemic)**, 211
Prorazin—Technilab (Canada) brand of Prochlorperazine—**See Phenothiazines (Systemic)**, 872
Prorex-25—Hyrex (U.S.) brand of Promethazine—**See Antihistamines, Phenothiazine-derivative (Systemic)**, 163
Prorex-50—Hyrex (U.S.) brand of Promethazine—**See Antihistamines, Phenothiazine-derivative (Systemic)**, 163
Proscar—MSD (U.S. and Canada) brand of Finasteride (Systemic), 581
Pro-Sof—Vangard (U.S.) brand of Docusate—**See Laxatives (Local)**, 682

Pro-Sof Liquid Concentrate—Vangard (U.S.) brand of Docusate—**See Laxatives (Local)**, 682
Pro-Sof Plus—Vangard (U.S.) brand of Casanthranol and Docusate—**See Laxatives (Local)**, 682
ProSom—Abbott (U.S.) brand of Estazolam—**See Benzodiazepines (Systemic)**, 251
Prostaglandin E$_1$—*See* Alprostadil (Intracavernosal), 26
Prostaphlin—Bristol (U.S.) brand of Oxacillin—**See Penicillins (Systemic)**, 848
Prostin VR—Upjohn (Canada) brand of Alprostadil (Intracavernosal), 26
Prostin VR Pediatric—Upjohn (U.S.) brand of Alprostadil (Intracavernosal), 26
Protamine Zinc & Iletin I—Lilly (U.S.) brand of Insulin, Protamine Zinc (Systemic), 644
Protamine Zinc & Iletin II—Lilly (U.S.) brand of Insulin, Protamine Zinc (Systemic), 644
Prothazine—Vortech (U.S.) brand of Promethazine—**See Antihistamines, Phenothiazine-derivative (Systemic)**, 163
Prothazine Plain—Vortech (U.S.) brand of Promethazine—**See Antihistamines, Phenothiazine-derivative (Systemic)**, 163
Protilase—Rugby (U.S.) brand of Pancrelipase (Systemic), 832
Protophylline—Rougier (Canada) brand of Dyphylline—**See Bronchodilators, Xanthine-derivative (Systemic)**, 315
Protostat—Ortho (U.S.) brand of Metronidazole (Systemic), 749
Protriptyline Hydrochloride [*Triptil; Vivactil*]
  See Antidepressants, Tricyclic (Systemic), 119
Proval—Reid-Rowell (U.S.) brand of Acetaminophen and Codeine—**See Opioid (Narcotic) Analgesics and Acetaminophen (Systemic)**, 820
Proventil—Schering (U.S.) brand of Albuterol—**See Bronchodilators, Adrenergic (Systemic)**, 294
Proventil Repetabs—Schering (U.S.) brand of Albuterol—**See Bronchodilators, Adrenergic (Systemic)**, 294
Provera—Upjohn (U.S. and Canada) brand of Medroxyprogesterone—**See Progestins (Systemic)**, 929
Prozac—Lilly (U.S. and Canada) brand of Fluoxetine (Systemic), 587
Prozine-50—Hauck (U.S.) brand of Promazine—**See Phenothiazines (Systemic)**, 872
P&S—Baker/Cummins (U.S.) brand of Salicylic Acid (Topical), 968
Pseudo—Major (U.S.) brand of Pseudoephedrine (Systemic), 936

Pseudo-Car DM—Geneva Generics (U.S.) brand of Carbinoxamine, Pseudoephedrine, and Dextromethorphan—**See Cough/Cold Combinations (Systemic)**, 488
Pseudo-Chlor—Major (U.S.) brand of Chlorpheniramine and Pseudoephedrine—**See Antihistamines and Decongestants (Systemic)**, 161
Pseudodine C Cough—Bay Labs (U.S.) brand of Triprolidine, Pseudoephedrine, and Codeine—**See Cough/Cold Combinations (Systemic)**, 488
Pseudoephedrine Hydrochloride [*AlleRid; Cenafed; Children's Sudafed Liquid; Congestac N.D. Caplets; Decofed; DeFed-60; Dorcol Children's Decongestant Liquid; Eltor 120; Genaphed; Halofed; Halofed Adult Strength; Maxenal; Myfedrine; NeoFed; Novafed; Ornex Cold; Otrivin; PediaCare Infants' Oral Decongestant Drops; Pseudo; Pseudofrin; Pseudogest; Robidrine; SinuStat; Sudafed; Sudafed 60; Sudrin; Sufedrin*]
  (Systemic), 936
Pseudoephedrine Hydrochloride and Acetaminophen [*Allerest No-Drowsiness; Coldrine; Contac Maximum Strength Sinus Caplets; Dristan Maximum Strength Caplets; Naldegesic; Ornex No Drowsiness Caplets; Sinarest No-Drowsiness; Sine-Aid; Sine-Aid Maximum Strength; Sine-Aid Maximum Strength Caplets; Sine-Off Maximum Strength No Drowsiness Formula Caplets; Sinus Excedrin No Drowsiness; Sinus Excedrin No Drowsiness Caplets; Sinutab II Maximum Strength; Sinutab Maximum Strength Without Drowsiness; Sinutab Maximum Strength Without Drowsiness Caplets; Sinutab No Drowsiness; Sinutab No Drowsiness Extra Strength; Sudafed Sinus Maximum Strength; Sudafed Sinus Maximum Strength Caplets; Super-Anahist; Tylenol Sinus Maximum Strength; Tylenol Sinus Maximum Strength Caplets; Tylenol Sinus Medication; Tylenol Sinus Medication Extra Strength*]
  See Decongestants and Analgesics (Systemic), 497
Pseudoephedrine Hydrochloride, Acetaminophen, and Caffeine [*Beta-Phed*]
  See Decongestants and Analgesics (Systemic), 497
Pseudoephedrine Hydrochloride and Aspirin [*Ursinus Inlay*]
  See Decongestants and Analgesics (Systemic), 497
Pseudoephedrine Hydrochloride, Aspirin, and Caffeine [*Alpha-Phed*]
  See Decongestants and Analgesics (Systemic), 497

Pyrilamine Maleate, Phenylephrine Hydrochloride, Hydrocodone Bitartrate, and Ammonium Chloride [*Hycomine; Hycomine-S Pediatric*]
   See Cough/Cold Combinations (Systemic), 488

Pyrilamine Maleate, Phenylpropanolamine Hydrochloride, Acetaminophen, and Caffeine [*Histosal*]
   See Antihistamines, Decongestants, and Analgesics (Systemic), 162

Pyrilamine Maleate, Phenylpropanolamine Hydrochloride, Dextromethorphan Hydrobromide, Guaifenesin, Potassium Citrate, and Citric Acid [*Phanadex*]
   See Cough/Cold Combinations (Systemic), 488

Pyrilamine Maleate, Phenylpropanolamine Hydrochloride, Dextromethorphan Hydrobromide, and Sodium Salicylate [*Kolephrin NN Liquid*]
   See Cough/Cold Combinations (Systemic), 488

Pyrimethamine [*Daraprim*]
   (Systemic), 938

Pyrithione Zinc [*Danex; Dan-Gard; DHS Zinc Dandruff Shampoo; Head & Shoulders Antidandruff Cream Shampoo Normal to Dry Formula; Head & Shoulders Antidandruff Cream Shampoo Normal to Oily Formula; Head & Shoulders Antidandruff Lotion Shampoo Normal to Dry Formula; Head & Shoulders Antidandruff Lotion Shampoo Normal to Oily Formula; Head & Shoulders Antidandruff Lotion Shampoo 2 in 1 (Complete Dandruff Shampoo plus Conditioner in One) Formula; Head & Shoulders Dry Scalp Conditioning Formula Lotion Shampoo; Head & Shoulders Dry Scalp 2 in 1 (Dry Scalp Shampoo plus Conditioner in One) Formula Lotion Shampoo; Head & Shoulders Dry Scalp Regular Formula Lotion Shampoo; Sebex; Sebulon; Zincon Dandruff Lotion Shampoo; ZNP Bar Shampoo; ZNP Shampoo*]
   (Topical), 940

Pyrroxate—Upjohn (U.S.) brand of Chlorpheniramine, Phenylpropanolamine, and Acetaminophen—**See Antihistamines, Decongestants, and Analgesics (Systemic)**, 162

PZI insulin—*See* Insulin, Protamine Zinc (Systemic), 644

Q

Q-B—Major (U.S.) brand of Theophylline and Guaifenesin (Systemic), 1032

Quarzan—Roche (U.S.) brand of Clidinium—**See Anticholinergics/Antispasmodics (Systemic)**, 73

Quazepam [*Doral*]
   See Benzodiazepines (Systemic), 251

Quelidrine Cough—Abbott (U.S.) brand of Chlorpheniramine, Ephedrine, Phenylephrine, Dextromethorphan, Ammonium Chloride, and Ipecac—**See Cough/Cold Combinations (Systemic)**, 488

Queltuss—Forest (U.S.) brand of Dextromethorphan and Guaifenesin—**See Cough/Cold Combinations (Systemic)**, 488

Questran—Mead Johnson (U.S.) and Bristol (Canada) brand of Cholestyramine (Oral-Local), 419

Questran Light—Mead Johnson (U.S.) and Bristol (Canada) brand of Cholestyramine (Oral-Local), 419

Quiagel PG—Rugby (U.S.) brand of Kaolin, Pectin, Belladonna Alkaloids, and Opium (Systemic), 672

Quiagen—Goldline (U.S.) brand of Theophylline and Guaifenesin (Systemic), 1032

Quibron—Bristol (U.S.) brand of Theophylline and Guaifenesin (Systemic), 1032

Quibron-300—Bristol (U.S.) brand of Theophylline and Guaifenesin (Systemic), 1032

Quibron-T—Bristol (Canada) brand of Theophylline—**See Bronchodilators, Xanthine-derivative (Systemic)**, 315

Quibron-T Dividose—Mead Johnson (U.S.) brand of Theophylline—**See Bronchodilators, Xanthine-derivative (Systemic)**, 315

Quibron-T/SR—Bristol (Canada) brand of Theophylline—**See Bronchodilators, Xanthine-derivative (Systemic)**, 315

Quibron-T/SR Dividose—Mead Johnson (U.S.) brand of Theophylline—**See Bronchodilators, Xanthine-derivative (Systemic)**, 315

Quiess—Forest (U.S.) brand of Hydroxyzine—**See Antihistamines (Systemic)**, 147

Quinaglute Dura-tabs—Berlex (U.S. and Canada) brand of Quinidine (Systemic), 942

Quinalan—Lannett (U.S.) brand of Quinidine (Systemic), 942

Quinapril Hydrochloride [*Accupril*]
   See Angiotensin-converting Enzyme (ACE) Inhibitors (Systemic), 49

Quinate—Rougier (Canada) brand of Quinidine (Systemic), 942

Quinestrol [*Estrovis*]
   See Estrogens (Systemic), 566

Quinethazone [*Hydromox*]
   See Diuretics, Thiazide (Systemic), 541

Quinidex Extentabs—Robins (U.S. and Canada) brand of Quinidine (Systemic), 942

Quinidine Gluconate [*Duraquin; Quinaglute Dura-tabs; Quinalan; Quinate*]
   (Systemic), 942

Quinidine Polygalacturonate [*Cardioquin*]
   (Systemic), 942

Quinidine Sulfate [*Apo-Quinidine; Cin-Quin; Novoquinidin; Quinidex Extentabs; Quinora*]
   (Systemic), 942

Quinora—Key (U.S.) brand of Quinidine (Systemic), 942

R

RA—Medco Lab (U.S.) brand of Resorcinol (Topical), 951

Racepinephrine [*AsthmaNefrin; Dey-Dose Racepinephrine; Vaponefrin*]
   See Bronchodilators, Adrenergic (Systemic), 294

Ramipril [*Altace*]
   See Angiotensin-converting Enzyme (ACE) Inhibitors (Systemic), 49

Ramses Contraceptive Foam—Schmid (Canada) brand of Nonoxynol 9—**See Spermicides (Vaginal)**, 991

Ramses Contraceptive Vaginal Jelly—Schmid (Canada) brand of Nonoxynol 9—**See Spermicides (Vaginal)**, 991

Ramses Crystal Clear Gel—Schmid (U.S.) brand of Nonoxynol 9—**See Spermicides (Vaginal)**, 991

Ranitidine [*Apo-Ranitidine; Zantac; Zantac-C*]
   See Histamine H$_2$-receptor Antagonists (Systemic), 622

Ranitidine Hydrochloride [*Zantac*]
   See Histamine H$_2$-receptor Antagonists (Systemic), 622

Rapolyte—Richmond (Canada) brand of Oral Rehydration Salts—**See Carbohydrates and Electrolytes (Systemic)**, 379

Raudixin—Princeton (U.S.) brand of Rauwolfia Serpentina—**See Rauwolfia Alkaloids (Systemic)**, 945

Rauval—Vale (U.S.) brand of Rauwolfia Serpentina—**See Rauwolfia Alkaloids (Systemic)**, 945

Rauverid—Forest (U.S.) brand of Rauwolfia Serpentina—**See Rauwolfia Alkaloids (Systemic)**, 945

Rauwolfia Alkaloids (Systemic), 945

Rauwolfia Alkaloids and Thiazide Diuretics (Systemic), 948

Rauwolfia Serpentina [*Raudixin; Rauval; Rauverid; Wolfina*]
   See Rauwolfia Alkaloids (Systemic), 945

Rauwolfia Serpentina and Bendroflumethiazide [*Rauzide*]
   See Rauwolfia Alkaloids and Thiazide Diuretics (Systemic), 948

Rauzide—Princeton (U.S.) brand of Rauwolfia Serpentina and Bendroflumethiazide—**See Rauwolfia Alkaloids and Thiazide Diuretics (Systemic)**, 948

Razepam—Major (U.S.) brand of Temazepam—**See Benzodiazepines (Systemic)**, 251

Reactine—Pfizer (Canada) brand of Cetirizine—**See Antihistamines (Systemic)**, 147

Reclomide—Ultra (U.S.) brand of Metoclopramide (Systemic), 746

Rectocort—Welcker-Lyster (Canada) brand of Hydrocortisone—**See Corticosteroids (Topical)**, 458

Rederm—Med-Derm (U.S.) brand of Hydrocortisone—**See Corticosteroids (Topical)**, 458

Redutemp—International Ethical (U.S.) brand of Acetaminophen (Systemic), 1

Regitine—CIBA (U.S.) brand of Phentolamine (Intracavernosal), 891

Reglan—Robins (U.S. and Canada) brand of Metoclopramide (Systemic), 746

Regroton—Rorer (U.S.) brand of Reserpine and Chlorthalidone—**See Rauwolfia Alkaloids and Thiazide Diuretics (Systemic)**, 948

Regulace—Republic (U.S.) brand of Casanthranol and Docusate—**See Laxatives (Local)**, 682

Regular Iletin I—Lilly (U.S.) brand of Insulin (Systemic), 644

Regular Iletin II—Lilly (U.S.) brand of Insulin (Systemic), 644

Regular (Concentrated) Iletin II, U-500—Lilly (U.S.) brand of Insulin (Systemic), 644

Regular Insulin—Squibb-Novo (U.S.) brand of Insulin (Systemic), 644

Regular insulin—*See* Insulin (Systemic), 644

Regulax SS—Republic (U.S.) brand of Docusate—**See Laxatives (Local)**, 682

Regulex—Ayerst (Canada) brand of Docusate—**See Laxatives (Local)**, 682

Regulex-D—Ayerst (Canada) brand of Danthron and Docusate—**See Laxatives (Local)**, 682

Reguloid Natural—Rugby (U.S.) brand of Psyllium Hydrophilic Mucilloid—**See Laxatives (Local)**, 682

Reguloid Orange—Rugby (U.S.) brand of Psyllium Hydrophilic Mucilloid—**See Laxatives (Local)**, 682

Regutol—Plough (U.S.) brand of Docusate—**See Laxatives (Local)**, 682

Rehydralyte—Ross (U.S.) brand of Dextrose and Electrolytes—**See Carbohydrates and Electrolytes (Systemic)**, 379

Rela—Schering (U.S.) brand of Carisoprodol—**See Skeletal Muscle Relaxants (Systemic)**, 979

Relaxadon—Geneva Generics (U.S.) brand of Atropine, Hyoscyamine, Scopolamine, and Phenobarbital—**See Belladonna Alkaloids and Barbiturates (Systemic)**, 246

Remcol-C—Shionogi (U.S.) brand of Chlorpheniramine, Dextromethorphan, and Acetaminophen—**See Cough/Cold Combinations (Systemic)**, 488

Remcol Cold—Shionogi (U.S.) brand of Chlorpheniramine, Phenylpropanolamine, and Acetaminophen—**See Antihistamines, Decongestants, and Analgesics (Systemic)**, 162

Renedil—Hoechst (Canada) brand of Felodipine—**See Calcium Channel Blocking Agents (Systemic)**, 343

Renese—Pfizer (U.S.) brand of Polythiazide—**See Diuretics, Thiazide (Systemic)**, 541

Renese-R—Pfizer (U.S.) brand of Reserpine and Polythiazide—**See Rauwolfia Alkaloids and Thiazide Diuretics (Systemic)**, 948

Renoquid—Glenwood (U.S.) brand of Sulfacytine—**See Sulfonamides (Systemic)**, 1011

Rentamine Pediatric—Major (U.S.) brand of Chlorpheniramine, Ephedrine, Phenylephrine, and Carbetapentane—**See Cough/Cold Combinations (Systemic)**, 488

Repan—Everett (U.S.) brand of Butalbital, Acetaminophen, and Caffeine—**See Barbiturates and Analgesics (Systemic)**, 233

Rep-Pred 40—Central (U.S.) brand of Methylprednisolone—**See Corticosteroids/Corticotropin—Glucocorticoid Effects (Systemic)**, 472

Rep-Pred 80—Central (U.S.) brand of Methylprednisolone—**See Corticosteroids/Corticotropin—Glucocorticoid Effects (Systemic)**, 472

Resaid S.R.—Geneva Generics (U.S.) brand of Chlorpheniramine and Phenylpropanolamine—**See Antihistamines and Decongestants (Systemic)**, 161

Rescaps-D S.R.—Geneva Generics (U.S.) brand of Phenylpropanolamine and Caramiphen—**See Cough/Cold Combinations (Systemic)**, 488

Reserfia—Medic (Canada) brand of Reserpine—**See Rauwolfia Alkaloids (Systemic)**, 945

Reserpine [*Novoreserpine; Reserfia; Serpalan; Serpasil*]
See Rauwolfia Alkaloids (Systemic), 945

Reserpine and Chlorothiazide [*Diupres; Diurigen with Reserpine*]
See Rauwolfia Alkaloids and Thiazide Diuretics (Systemic), 948

Reserpine and Chlorthalidone [*Demi-Regroton; Regroton*]
See Rauwolfia Alkaloids and Thiazide Diuretics (Systemic), 948

Reserpine and Hydralazine Hydrochloride [*Serpasil-Apresoline*]
(Systemic), 950

Reserpine, Hydralazine Hydrochloride, and Hydrochlorothiazide [*Cam-Ap-Es; Cherapas; Ser-A-Gen; Seralazide; Ser-Ap-Es; Serpazide; Tri-Hydroserpine; Unipres*]
(Systemic), 950

Reserpine and Hydrochlorothiazide [*Hydropres; Hydrosine; Hydrotensin; Mallopres*]
See Rauwolfia Alkaloids and Thiazide Diuretics (Systemic), 948

Reserpine and Hydroflumethiazide [*Hydropine; Hydropine H.P.; Salazide; Salutensin; Salutensin-Demi*]
See Rauwolfia Alkaloids and Thiazide Diuretics (Systemic), 948

Reserpine and Methyclothiazide [*Diutensen-R*]
See Rauwolfia Alkaloids and Thiazide Diuretics (Systemic), 948

Reserpine and Polythiazide [*Renese-R*]
See Rauwolfia Alkaloids and Thiazide Diuretics (Systemic), 948

Reserpine and Trichlormethiazide [*Diurese-R; Metatensin; Naquival*]
See Rauwolfia Alkaloids and Thiazide Diuretics (Systemic), 948

Resol—Wyeth-Ayerst (U.S.) brand of Dextrose and Electrolytes—**See Carbohydrates and Electrolytes (Systemic)**, 379

Resorcinol [*RA*]
(Topical), 951

Respaire-60 SR—Laser (U.S.) brand of Pseudoephedrine and Guaifenesin—**See Cough/Cold Combinations (Systemic)**, 488

Respaire-120 SR—Laser (U.S.) brand of Pseudoephedrine and Guaifenesin—**See Cough/Cold Combinations (Systemic)**, 488

Respbid—Boehringer Ingelheim (U.S.) brand of Theophylline—**See Bronchodilators, Xanthine-derivative (Systemic)**, 315

Respinol-G—Misemer (U.S.) brand of Phenylephrine, Phenylpropanolamine, and Guaifenesin—**See Cough/Cold Combinations (Systemic)**, 488

Resporal TR—Pioneer (U.S.) brand of Dexbrompheniramine and Pseudoephedrine—**See Antihistamines and Decongestants (Systemic)**, 161

Restoril—Sandoz (U.S. and Canada) brand of Temazepam—**See Benzodiazepines (Systemic)**, 251

Resyl—CIBA-GEIGY (Canada) brand of Guaifenesin (Systemic), 606

Rheaban—Lemming (U.S.) brand of Attapulgite (Oral-Local), 217

Rheumatrex—Lederle (U.S.) brand of Methotrexate—For Noncancerous Conditions (Systemic), 734

Rhinalar—SynCare (Canada) brand of Flunisolide—**See Corticosteroids (Nasal)**, 455

Salac—GenDerm (U.S. and Canada) brand of Salicylic Acid (Topical), 968

Salacid—Gordon (U.S.) brand of Salicylic Acid (Topical), 968

Sal-Acid Plaster—Pedinol (U.S.) brand of Salicylic Acid (Topical), 968

Salactic Film Topical Solution—Pedinol (U.S.) brand of Salicylic Acid (Topical), 968

Sal-Adult—Beecham (Canada) brand of Aspirin—**See Salicylates (Systemic),** 953

Salazide—Major (U.S.) brand of Reserpine and Hydroflumethiazide—**See Rauwolfia Alkaloids and Thiazide Diuretics (Systemic),** 948

Salazopyrin—Pharmacia (Canada) brand of Sulfasalazine (Systemic), 1003

Salazopyrin EN-Tabs—Pharmacia (Canada) brand of Sulfasalazine (Systemic), 1003

Salazosulfapyridine—*See* Sulfasalazine (Systemic), 1003

Salbutamol—Albuterol—**See Bronchodilators, Adrenergic (Systemic),** 294

Sal-Clens Plus Shampoo—C&M (U.S.) brand of Salicylic Acid (Topical), 968

Sal-Clens Shampoo—C&M (U.S.) brand of Salicylic Acid (Topical), 968

Salcylic Acid—Rugby (U.S.) brand of Salsalate—**See Salicylates (Systemic),** 953

Saleto—Hauck (U.S.) brand of Acetaminophen, Aspirin, Salicylamide, and Caffeine—**See Acetaminophen and Salicylates (Systemic),** 5

Saleto-CF—Mallard (U.S.) brand of Phenylpropanolamine, Dextromethorphan, and Acetaminophen—**See Cough/Cold Combinations (Systemic),** 488

Saleto D—Hauck (U.S.) brand of Phenylpropanolamine, Acetaminophen, Salicylamide, and Caffeine—**See Decongestants and Analgesics (Systemic),** 497

Salflex—Carnrick (U.S.) brand of Salsalate—**See Salicylates (Systemic),** 953

Salgesic—Balan (U.S.); Best Generics (U.S.); Dixon-Shane (U.S.); Gen-King (U.S.); and Sidmak (U.S.) brand of Salsalate—**See Salicylates (Systemic),** 953

Salicylates **(Systemic),** 953

Salicylazosulfapyridine—*See* Sulfasalazine (Systemic), 1003

Salicylic Acid [*Antinea; Buf-Puf Acne Cleansing Bar with Vitamin E; Calicylic Creme; Clearasil Clearstick Maximum Strength Topical Solution; Clearasil Clearstick Regular Strength Topical Solution; Clearasil Double Textured Pads Maximum Strength; Clearasil Double Textured Pads Regular Strength; Clearasil Medicated Deep*

Salicylic Acid (*continued*)

Cleanser Topical Solution; Clear Away; Clear by Design Medicated Cleansing Pads; Compound W Gel; Compound W Liquid; Cuplex Gel; Duofilm; Duoplant Topical Solution; Freezone; Gordofilm; Hydrisalic; Ionax Astringent Skin Cleanser Topical Solution; Ionil Plus Shampoo; Ionil Shampoo; Keralyt; Keratex Gel; Lactisol; Listerex Golden Scrub Lotion; Listerex Herbal Scrub Lotion; Mediplast; Noxzema Anti-Acne Gel; Noxzema Anti-Acne Pads Maximum Strength; Noxzema Anti-Acne Pads Regular Strength; Occlusal-HP Topical Solution; Occlusal Topical Solution; Off-Ezy Topical Solution Corn and Callus Remover Kit; Off-Ezy Topical Solution Wart Removal Kit; Oxy Clean Extra Strength Medicated Pads; Oxy Clean Extra Strength Skin Cleanser Topical Solution; Oxy Clean Medicated Cleanser; Oxy Clean Medicated Pads Maximum Strength; Oxy Clean Medicated Pads Regular Strength; Oxy Clean Medicated Pads Sensitive Skin; Oxy Clean Medicated Soap; Oxy Clean Regular Strength Medicated Cleanser Topical Solution; Oxy Clean Regular Strength Medicated Pads; Oxy Clean Sensitive Skin Cleanser Topical Solution; Oxy Clean Sensitive Skin Pads; Oxy Night Watch Maximum Strength Lotion; Oxy Night Watch Night Time Acne Medication Extra Strength Lotion; Oxy Night Watch Night Time Acne Medication Regular Strength Lotion; Oxy Night Watch Sensitive Skin Lotion; Oxy Sensitive Skin Vanishing Formula Lotion; Paplex; Paplex Ultra; Propa pH Medicated Acne Cream Maximum Strength; Propa pH Medicated Cleansing Pads Sensitive Skin; Propa pH Perfectly Clear Skin Cleanser Topical Solution Normal/ Combination Skin; Propa pH Perfectly Clear Skin Cleanser Topical Solution Oily Skin; Propa pH Perfectly Clear Skin Cleanser Topical Solution Sensitive Skin Formula; P&S; Salac; Salacid; Sal-Acid Plaster; Salactic Film Topical Solution; Sal-Clens Plus Shampoo; Sal-Clens Shampoo; Saligel; Salonil; Sal-Plant Gel Topical Solution; Sebucare; Stri-Dex Dual Textured Pads Maximum Strength; Stri-Dex Dual Textured Pads Regular Strength; Stri-Dex Dual Textured Pads Sensitive Skin; Stri-Dex Maximum Strength Pads; Stri-Dex Regular Strength Pads; Stri-Dex Super Scrub Pads; Tersac Cleansing Gel; Trans-Plantar; Trans-Ver-Sal; Verukan-HP Topical Solution; Verukan Topical Solution; Viranol; Wart-Off Topical Solution; X-Seb]
(Topical), 968

Salicylic Acid and Sulfur [*Acno; Acnotex; Aveeno Acne Bar; Aveeno Cleansing Bar; Creamy SS Shampoo; Fostex Medicated Cleansing Bar; Fostex Medicated Cleansing Cream (for face and scalp); Fostex Medicated Cleansing Liquid; Fostex Regular Strength Medicated Cleansing Bar; Fostex Regular Strength Medicated Cleansing Cream (for face and scalp); Meted Maximum Strength Anti-Dandruff Shampoo with Conditioners; Night Cast R; Night Cast Regular Formula Masklotion; Pernox Lemon Medicated Scrub Cleanser; Pernox Lotion Lathering Abradant Scrub Cleanser; Pernox Lotion Lathering Scrub Cleanser; Pernox Regular Medicated Scrub Cleanser; Sastid (AL) Scrub; Sastid Plain Shampoo and Acne Wash; Sastid Soap; Sebasorb Liquid; Sebex; Sebulex Antiseborrheic Treatment and Conditioning Shampoo; Sebulex Antiseborrheic Treatment Shampoo; Sebulex Conditioning Suspension Shampoo; Sebulex Cream Medicated Shampoo; Sebulex Lotion Shampoo; Sebulex Medicated Dandruff Shampoo with Conditioners; Sebulex Medicated Shampoo; Sebulex Regular Medicated Dandruff Shampoo; Sulsal Soap; Therac Lotion; Vanseb Cream Dandruff Shampoo; Vanseb Lotion Dandruff Shampoo*]
(Topical), 973

Salicylic Acid, Sulfur, and Coal Tar [*Sebex-T Tar Shampoo; Sebutone; Vanseb-T*]
(Topical), 974

Salicylsalicylic acid—Salsalate—**See Salicylates (Systemic),** 953

Saligel—Stiefel (U.S.) brand of Salicylic Acid (Topical), 968

Sal-Infant—Beecham (Canada) brand of Aspirin—**See Salicylates (Systemic),** 953

Salofalk—Interfalk (Canada) brand of Mesalamine (Rectal-Local), 725

Salonil—Torch (U.S.) brand of Salicylic Acid (Topical), 968

Salphenyl—Hauck (U.S.) brand of Chlorpheniramine, Phenylephrine, Acetaminophen, and Salicylamide—**See Antihistamines, Decongestants, and Analgesics (Systemic),** 162

Sal-Plant Gel Topical Solution—Pedinol (U.S.) brand of Salicylic Acid (Topical), 968

Salsalate [*Amigesic; Diagen; Disalcid; Mono-Gesic; Salcylic Acid; Salflex; Salgesic; salicylsalicylic acid; Salsitab*]
See Salicylates (Systemic), 953

Salsitab—Upsher-Smith (U.S.) brand of Salsalate—**See Salicylates (Systemic),** 953

Sudafed Severe Cold Formula Caplets—BW (U.S.) brand of Pseudoephedrine, Dextromethorphan, and Acetaminophen—**See Cough/Cold Combinations (Systemic)**, 488

Sudafed Sinus Maximum Strength—BW (U.S.) brand of Pseudoephedrine and Acetaminophen—**See Decongestants and Analgesics (Systemic)**, 497

Sudafed Sinus Maximum Strength Caplets—BW (U.S.) brand of Pseudoephedrine and Acetaminophen—**See Decongestants and Analgesics (Systemic)**, 497

Sudrin—Bowman (U.S.) brand of Pseudoephedrine (Systemic), 936

Sufedrin—Lannett (U.S.) brand of Pseudoephedrine (Systemic), 936

Sul-Azo—Lunsco (U.S.) brand of Sulfisoxazole and Phenazopyridine—**See Sulfonamides and Phenazopyridine (Systemic)**, 1015

Sulcrate—Marion Merrell Dow (Canada) brand of Sucralfate (Oral-Local), 997

Sulf-10—Iolab (U.S.) brand of Sulfacetamide—**See Sulfonamides (Ophthalmic)**, 1009

Sulfacetamide Sodium [*Ak-Sulf; Bleph-10; Cetamide; Isopto-Cetamide; I-Sulfacet; Ocu-Sul-10; Ocu-Sul-15; Ocu-Sul-30; Ocusulf-10; Ophthacet; Sodium Sulamyd; Spectro-Sulf; Steri-Units Sulfacetamide; Sulf-10; Sulfair; Sulfair 10; Sulfair 15; Sulfair Forte; Sulfamide; Sulfex; Sulten-10*]
See Sulfonamides (Ophthalmic), 1009

Sulfacytine [*Renoquid*]
See Sulfonamides (Systemic), 1011

Sulfadiazine
See Sulfonamides (Systemic), 1011

Sulfafurazole—Sulfisoxazole—**See Sulfonamides (Ophthalmic)**, 1009; **Sulfonamides (Systemic)**, 1011

Sulfair—Best Generics (U.S.); Dixon-Shane (U.S.); Gen-King (U.S.); and Texas Drugs (U.S.) brand of Sulfacetamide—**See Sulfonamides (Ophthalmic)**, 1009

Sulfair 10—Pharmafair (U.S.) brand of Sulfacetamide—**See Sulfonamides (Ophthalmic)**, 1009

Sulfair 15—Pharmafair (U.S.) brand of Sulfacetamide—**See Sulfonamides (Ophthalmic)**, 1009

Sulfair Forte—Pharmafair (U.S.) brand of Sulfacetamide—**See Sulfonamides (Ophthalmic)**, 1009

Sulfamethizole [*Thiosulfil Forte*]
(Systemic), 1011

Sulfamethoprim—Par (U.S.) and Quad (U.S.) brand of Sulfamethoxazole and Trimethoprim (Systemic), 999

Sulfamethoprim DS—Par (U.S.) brand of Sulfamethoxazole and Trimethoprim (Systemic), 999

Sulfamethoxazole [*Apo-Sulfamethoxazole; Gantanol*]
See Sulfonamides (Systemic), 1011

Sulfamethoxazole and Phenazopyridine Hydrochloride [*Azo Gantanol; Azo-Sulfamethoxazole*]
See Sulfonamides and Phenazopyridine (Systemic), 1015

Sulfamethoxazole and Trimethoprim [*Apo-Sulfatrim; Apo-Sulfatrim DS; Bactrim; Bactrim DS; Cotrim; Cotrim DS;* cotrimoxazole; *Novotrimel; Novotrimel DS; Nu-Cotrimox; Nu-Cotrimox DS; Roubac; Septra; Septra DS;* SMZ-TMP; *Sulfamethoprim; Sulfamethoprim DS; Sulfaprim; Sulfaprim DS; Sulfatrim; Sulfatrim DS; Sulfoxaprim; Sulfoxaprim DS; Triazole; Triazole DS; Trimeth-Sulfa; Trisulfam; Uroplus DS; Uroplus SS*]
(Systemic), 999

Sulfamide—Horizon (U.S.); Rugby (U.S.); and Texas Drugs (U.S.) brand of Sulfacetamide—**See Sulfonamides (Ophthalmic)**, 1009

Sulfaprim—Balan (U.S.) brand of Sulfamethoxazole and Trimethoprim (Systemic), 999

Sulfaprim DS—Balan (U.S.) brand of Sulfamethoxazole and Trimethoprim (Systemic), 999

Sulfasalazine [*Azulfidine; Azulfidine EN-Tabs; PMS Sulfasalazine; PMS Sulfasalazine E.C.; Salazopyrin; Salazopyrin EN-Tabs;* salazosulfapyridine; salicylazosulfapyridine; *S.A.S.-500; S.A.S. Enteric-500*]
(Systemic), 1003

Sulfatrim—Barre (U.S.) brand of Sulfamethoxazole and Trimethoprim (Systemic), 999

Sulfatrim DS—Barre (U.S.) brand of Sulfamethoxazole and Trimethoprim (Systemic), 999

Sulfex—Charton (Canada) brand of Sulfacetamide—**See Sulfonamides (Ophthalmic)**, 1009

Sulfimycin—Rugby (U.S.) brand of Erythromycin and Sulfisoxazole (Systemic), 562

Sulfinpyrazone [*Anturan; Anturane; Apo-Sulfinpyrazone; Novopyrazone*]
(Systemic), 1005

Sulfisoxazole [*Gantrisin; Novosoxazole;* sulfafurazole]
See Sulfonamides (Systemic), 1011

Sulfisoxazole Acetyl [*Gantrisin*]
See Sulfonamides (Systemic), 1011

Sulfisoxazole Diolamine [*Gantrisin;* sulfafurazole]
See Sulfonamides (Ophthalmic), 1009

Sulfisoxazole and Phenazopyridine Hydrochloride [*Azo Gantrisin; Azo-Sulfisoxazole; Azo-Truxazole; Sul-Azo*]
See Sulfonamides and Phenazopyridine (Systemic), 1015

Sulfonamides
(Ophthalmic), 1009

Sulfonamides
(Systemic), 1011

Sulfonamides and Phenazopyridine
(Systemic), 1015

Sulfoxaprim—Bioline (U.S.) brand of Sulfamethoxazole and Trimethoprim (Systemic), 999

Sulfoxaprim DS—Bioline (U.S.) brand of Sulfamethoxazole and Trimethoprim (Systemic), 999

Sulfur [*Cuticura Ointment; Finac; Fostex CM; Fostex Regular Strength Medicated Cover-Up; Fostril Cream; Fostril Lotion; Lotio-Alsulfa; Sulpho-Lac*]
(Topical), 1016

Sulfurated Lime [*Vlemasque* Vleminckx's solution]
(Topical), 1017

Sulindac [*Apo-Sulin; Clinoril; Novo-Sundac*]
See Anti-inflammatory Analgesics, Nonsteroidal (Systemic), 168

Sulpho-Lac—Bradley (U.S.) brand of Sulfur (Topical), 1016

Sulsal Soap—T.C.D. (Canada) brand of Salicylic Acid and Sulfur (Topical), 973

Sulten-10—Bausch & Lomb (U.S.) brand of Sulfacetamide—**See Sulfonamides (Ophthalmic)**, 1009

Summit—Pfeiffer (U.S.) brand of Acetaminophen and Caffeine—**See Acetaminophen (Systemic)**, 1

Sumycin—Squibb (U.S.) brand of Tetracycline—**See Tetracyclines (Systemic)**, 1025

Supac—Mission (U.S.) brand of Acetaminophen, Aspirin, and Caffeine, Buffered—**See Acetaminophen and Salicylates (Systemic)**, 5

Supasa—Marion Merrell Dow (Canada) brand of Aspirin—**See Salicylates (Systemic)**, 953

Super-Anahist—Warner-Lambert (U.S.) brand of Pseudoephedrine and Acetaminophen—**See Decongestants and Analgesics (Systemic)**, 497

Super Calcium 1200—Schiff (U.S.) brand of Calcium Carbonate—**See Calcium Supplements (Systemic)**, 357

Superlipid—Berenguer-Beneyto (Spain) brand of Probucol (Systemic), 919

Supeudol—Sabex (Canada) brand of Oxycodone—**See Opioid (Narcotic) Analgesics (Systemic)**, 793

Suppap-120—Raway (U.S.) brand of Acetaminophen (Systemic), 1

Suppap-325—Raway (U.S.) brand of Acetaminophen (Systemic), 1

Tolmetin Sodium [*Tolectin 200; Tolectin 400; Tolectin 600; Tolectin DS*] **See Anti-inflammatory Analgesics, Nonsteroidal (Systemic)**, 168

Tolu-Sed Cough—Scherer (U.S.) brand of Codeine and Guaifenesin—**See Cough/ Cold Combinations (Systemic)**, 488

Tolu-Sed DM Cough—Scherer (U.S.) brand of Dextromethorphan and Guaifenesin—**See Cough/Cold Combinations (Systemic)**, 488

Tonocard—MSD (U.S.) and Astra (Canada) brand of Tocainide (Systemic), 1054

Topicort—Hoechst-Roussel (U.S.) and Hoechst (Canada) brand of Desoximetasone—**See Corticosteroids (Topical)**, 458

Topicort LP—Hoechst-Roussel (U.S.) brand of Desoximetasone—**See Corticosteroids (Topical)**, 458

Topicort Mild—Hoechst (Canada) brand of Desoximetasone—**See Corticosteroids (Topical)**, 458

Topilene—Technilab (Canada) brand of Betamethasone—**See Corticosteroids (Topical)**, 458

Topisone—Technilab (Canada) brand of Betamethasone—**See Corticosteroids (Topical)**, 458

Topsyn—Syntex (Canada) brand of Fluocinonide—**See Corticosteroids (Topical)**, 458

Toradol—Roche (U.S.) and Syntex (U.S.) brand of Ketorolac (Systemic), 678

Tornalate—Sterling Winthrop (U.S.) brand of Bitolterol—**See Bronchodilators, Adrenergic (Systemic)**, 294

T-Phyl—Purdue Frederick (U.S.) brand of Theophylline—**See Bronchodilators, Xanthine-derivative (Systemic)**, 315

T-Quil—Lederle (U.S.) brand of Diazepam—**See Benzodiazepines (Systemic)**, 251

Trancopal—Sterling (Canada) brand of Chlormezanone (Systemic), 414

Trancopal Caplets—Sterling Winthrop (U.S.) brand of Chlormezanone (Systemic), 414

Trancot—Truxton (U.S.) brand of Meprobamate (Systemic), 719

Trandate—Allen & Hanburys (U.S.) and Glaxo (Canada) brand of Labetalol—**See Beta-adrenergic Blocking Agents (Systemic)**, 267

Trandate HCT—Allen & Hanburys (U.S.) brand of Labetalol and Hydrochlorothiazide—**See Beta-adrenergic Blocking Agents and Thiazide Diuretics (Systemic)**, 283

Transact—Westwood (U.S.) brand of Alcohol and Sulfur (Topical), 21

Transderm-Nitro—Summit (U.S. and Canada) brand of Nitroglycerin—**See Nitrates (Systemic)**, 770

Transderm-Sc;amop—CIBA (U.S.) brand of Scopolamine—**See Anticholinergics/ Antispasmodics (Systemic)**, 73

Transderm-V—CIBA-GEIGY (Canada) brand of Scopolamine—**See Anticholinergics/Antispasmodics (Systemic)**, 73

Trans-Plantar—Tsumura (U.S.) brand of Salicylic Acid (Topical), 968

Trans-Ver-Sal—Tsumura (U.S.) and Westwood-Squibb (Canada) brand of Salicylic Acid (Topical), 968

Tranxene—Abbott (Canada) brand of Clorazepate—**See Benzodiazepines (Systemic)**, 251

Tranxene-SD—Abbott (U.S.) brand of Clorazepate—**See Benzodiazepines (Systemic)**, 251

Tranxene T-Tab—Abbott (U.S.) brand of Clorazepate—**See Benzodiazepines (Systemic)**, 251

Tranylcypromine Sulfate [*Parnate*] **See Antidepressants, Monoamine Oxidase (MAO) Inhibitor (Systemic)**, 113

Trasicor—CIBA (Canada) brand of Oxprenolol—**See Beta-adrenergic Blocking Agents (Systemic)**, 267

Travamine—ICN (Canada) brand of Dimenhydrinate—**See Antihistamines (Systemic)**, 147

Trazodone [*Desyrel; Trazon; Trialodine*] **(Systemic)**, 1056

Trazon—Sidmak (U.S.) brand of Trazodone (Systemic), 1056

Trendar—Whitehall (U.S.) brand of Ibuprofen—**See Anti-inflammatory Analgesics, Nonsteroidal (Systemic)**, 168

Triacet—Lemmon (U.S.) brand of Triamcinolone—**See Corticosteroids (Topical)**, 458

Triacin C Cough—Balan (U.S.); Barre (U.S.); Bioline (U.S.); CMC-CONS (U.S.); Dixon-Shane (U.S.); Gen-King (U.S.); Harber (U.S.); Moore (U.S.); Parmed (U.S.); Richie (U.S.); United Research (U.S.); and Williams (U.S.) brand of Triprolidine, Pseudoephedrine, and Codeine—**See Cough/Cold Combinations (Systemic)**, 488

Triad—UAD (U.S.) brand of Butalbital, Acetaminophen, and Caffeine—**See Barbiturates and Analgesics (Systemic)**, 233

Triadapin—Fisons (Canada) brand of Doxepin—**See Antidepressants, Tricyclic (Systemic)**, 119

Triaderm—Taro (Canada) brand of Triamcinolone—**See Corticosteroids (Topical)**, 458

Trialodine—Quantum (U.S.) brand of Trazodone (Systemic), 1056

Triam-A—Hyrex (U.S.) brand of Triamcinolone—**See Corticosteroids/Corticotropin—Glucocorticoid Effects (Systemic)**, 472

Triamcinolone [*Aristocort; Kenacort*] **See Corticosteroids/Corticotropin—Glucocorticoid Effects (Systemic)**, 472

Triamcinolone Acetonide [*Azmacort*] **See Corticosteroids (Inhalation-Local)**, 448

Triamcinolone Acetonide [*Cenocort A-40; Cinonide 40; Kenaject-40; Kenalog-10; Kenalog-40; Tac-3; Triam-A; Triamonide 40; Tri-Kort; Trilog*] **See Corticosteroids/Corticotropin—Glucocorticoid Effects (Systemic)**, 472

Triamcinolone Acetonide [*Aristocort; Aristocort A; Aristocort C; Aristocort D; Aristocort R; Delta-Tritex; Flutex; Kenac; Kenalog; Kenalog-H; Kenalog in Orabase; Kenonel; Oracort; Oralone; Triacet; Triaderm; Trianide Mild; Trianide Regular; Triderm*] **See Corticosteroids (Topical)**, 458

Triamcinolone Diacetate [*Amcort; Aristocort; Aristocort Forte; Aristocort Intralesional; Articulose-L.A.; Cenocort Forte; Cinalone 40; Kenacort Diacetate; Triam-Forte; Triamolone 40; Trilone; Tristoject*] **See Corticosteroids/Corticotropin—Glucocorticoid Effects (Systemic)**, 472

Triamcinolone Hexacetonide [*Aristospan Intra-articular; Aristospan Intralesional*] **See Corticosteroids/Corticotropin—Glucocorticoid Effects (Systemic)**, 472

Triam-Forte—Hyrex (U.S.) brand of Triamcinolone—**See Corticosteroids/ Corticotropin—Glucocorticoid Effects (Systemic)**, 472

Triaminic—Ancalab (Canada) brand of Chlorpheniramine and Phenylpropanolamine—**See Antihistamines and Decongestants (Systemic)**, 161; Ancalab (Canada) brand of Pheniramine, Pyrilamine, and Phenylpropanolamine—**See Antihistamines and Decongestants (Systemic)**, 161

Triaminic-12—Dorsey (U.S.) brand of Chlorpheniramine and Phenylpropanolamine—**See Antihistamines and Decongestants (Systemic)**, 161

Triaminic Allergy—Sandoz (U.S.) brand of Chlorpheniramine and Phenylpropanolamine—**See Antihistamines and Decongestants (Systemic)**, 161

Triaminic Chewables—Dorsey (U.S.) brand of Chlorpheniramine and Phenylpropanolamine—**See Antihistamines and Decongestants (Systemic)**, 161

Triaminic Cold—Dorsey (U.S.) brand of Chlorpheniramine and Phenylpropanolamine—**See Antihistamines and Decongestants (Systemic)**, 161

Triaminic-DM Cough Formula—Dorsey (U.S.) brand of Phenylpropanolamine and Dextromethorphan—**See Cough/ Cold Combinations (Systemic)**, 488